KV-623-053

DOD'S
PARLIAMENTARY
COMPANION
2004

Dod's Scotland, Wales and Northern Ireland Companion 2003

FIRST EDITION

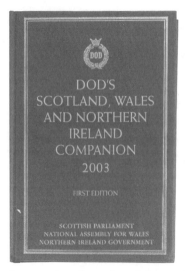

Dod's Scotland, Wales and Northern Ireland Companion 2003 provides unrivalled biographical information on all individuals within the Scottish Parliament, National Assembly for Wales and the Northern Ireland Government.

With in-depth biographies, latest election results and detailed information about each parliament or assembly and the role they play within the UK political scene, this companion will quickly become indispensable.

Dod's Scotland, Wales and Northern Ireland Companion 2003 includes the results from the May 2003 elections held in Wales and Scotland.

A comprehensive review of the results includes details of how the results affect each party structure, the share of the vote, seats by percentage majority, share of the vote by region and the geographical whereabouts of the constituencies.

To order call our Hotline now on 020 7630 7619

Vacher Dod Publishing
1 Douglas Street, London SW1P 4PA
Tel: 020 7630 7619   Fax: 020 7233 7266
Email: subscriptions@vacherdod.co.uk
Website: www.DodonLine.co.uk

Dod's Parliamentary Companion 2004

172nd year

1832

Dod's Parliamentary Companion published since 1832

©185th edition Vacher Dod Publishing 2003

Published by
Vacher Dod Publishing
1 Douglas Street
London SW1P 4PA

Tel: 020 7828 7256
Fax: 020 7828 7269
E-mail: politics@vacherdod.co.uk
Website: www.DodOnline.co.uk

Vacher Dod Publishing is a trading division of Huveaux plc

Acknowledgements

The Editor would like to thank the following for their help:

House of Commons and House of Lords, Scottish Parliament, National Assembly for Wales and Northern Ireland Assembly; MPs and Peers for providing biographical information; Donald Shell, Department of Politics, Bristol University; Colin Mellors and Darren Darcy, Bradford University; Labour Party; Conservative Party; Liberal Democrat Party; Plaid Cymru; Scottish National Party; Ulster Unionist Party; Democrat Unionist Party; Sinn Fein; Social Democratic and Labour Party; Alliance Party of Northern Ireland; Green Party; Socialist Alliance; Socialist Labour Party; United Kingdom Independence Party

ISBN 0 905702 43 3   ISSN 0070-7007

All rights reserved. No part of this publication may be reproduced or used in any form or by any means – graphic; electronic or mechanical, including photocopying, recording, taping or information storage and retrieval systems – without written permission from the publishers.

Database typesetting by Vacher Dod Publishing

Printed in Great Britain by The Cromwell Press, Trowbridge, Wiltshire

The Parliamentary Bookshop
Parliament page by page

At the Parliamentary Bookshop we specialise in publications relating to current Parliamentary and Government business. Our staff are informed House of Commons employees and our range of services is designed to help you to access the information you need quickly and easily.

We offer:

- the fastest possible access to all Parliamentary documents
- pre-ordering of future publications
- daily e-mail bulletins listing new publications
- early opening for clients collecting daily papers
- client collection points
- legislation tracking service
- standing order and account facilities
- easy ordering by phone, fax, e-mail or online at www.bookshop.parliament.uk
- same day order processing
- free post and packing on UK deliveries.

The Parliamentary Bookshop
12 Bridge Street
Parliament Square
London SW1A 2JX

T 020 7219 3890
F 020 7219 3866
E bookshop@parliament.uk
www.bookshop.parliament.uk

Strategic
Public
Policy Advice

Expert (handwritten)

PUT EXPERIENCE IN PLACE FROM THE BEGINNING

With offices in the UK, Europe, North America and Asia-Pacific, Citigate
Public Affairs offers global reach, as well as hands-on experience in local
and national governments, political parties and institutions.

For more information contact Warwick Smith or
Simon Nayyar on Tel: +44(0)20 7838 4800
Email: warwick.smith@citigatepa.co.uk or simon.nayyar@citigatepa.co.uk

www.citigatepa.com   *Member of the APPC and PRCA*

| Citigate
Public Affairs

CONTENTS

Visit the Vacher Dod Website . . .

- House of Commons
- House of Lords
- Stop Press News
- Today's Business
- This Week's Business
- Progress of Bills
- Select Committees
- Government and Opposition
- The Queen's Speech
- Terms and Procedures

- Government Departments
- Key Political Sites
- Scottish Parliament
- National Assembly for Wales
- Northern Ireland Assembly
- Greater London Authority
- European Union
- Archive

Political information updated daily

Vacher Dod Publishing
1 Douglas Street, London SW1P 4PA
Tel: 020 7630 7619   Fax: 020 7233 7266
E-mail: subscriptions@vacherdod.co.uk
Website: www.DodOnline.co.uk

FOREWORD

Since the Great Reform Act of 1832, the same year in which Dod's Parliamentary Companion was first published, Parliament has been constantly changing and adapting to circumstances. This continues: recently and currently there have been major changes in membership of the House of Lords and in the working practices of the House of Commons as well as devolution of some powers to bodies in Scotland, Wales and Northern Ireland.

Dod's Parliamentary Companion has chronicled all these changes and their effects year by year and has established itself as an indispensbale guide to the people and procedures of Westminster. It remains the standard work of reference for everyone with an interest in the personalities and processes of the British Parliament.

The Rt Hon the Lord Falconer of Thoroton QC
Secretary of State for Constitutuional Affairs and Lord Chancellor

FLYING COLOURS
P H O T O G R A P H Y

Political Photo Library

Flying Colours is a unique photo library. We have created over 2000 studio
photographs of British Politicians. These are a matching set of exclusive
portraits of Members of Parliament and Prospective Parliamentary Candidates.
We have high resolution press-ready scans of all our images, enabling us
to instantly send them to you via our fast ISDN or ADSL connections.

For more information, prices and to preview our photographs,
visit our web site

www.flycols.com

Flying Colours Ltd, 3 Wyfold Studios, 11 Wyfold Road, London SW6 6SE
Tel : 0207 386 8041 Email : mail@flycols.com

Parliamentary Notes

The State Opening of the 2002-03 Session of Parliament was on 13 November 2002. The entire session has been dominated by the mounting crisis over Iraq, the decision to go to war, and the aftermath of war. The Prime Minister has struggled to keep some semblance of unity in his own party.

Legislative programme

The Queen's Speech contained no great surprises, being dominated as usual by Bills from the Home Office, including the Criminal Justice Bill, which sought among other things to restrict the right to trial by jury, end the absolute application of the principle of double jeopardy so that a second trial may be possible where new evidence emerges relating to serious crimes, and to make a number of other changes which tend to tilt the law in favour of the prosecution and away from the defence. An Anti-social Behaviour Bill, introducing a range of new measures to tackle what might be described as sub-criminal behaviour, was also introduced, as was a bill to modernise the law on sexual offences (which caused some alarm in the naturist community). Yet another paves the way to new arrangements for international co-operation against crime.

The provisions of the Criminal Justice Bill restricting the right to trial by jury were rejected by the Lords in July, the fourth occasion on which this has happened to the various forms in which they have been put forward. This promised another end of session confrontation between the two Houses which threatened to delay the implementation of the other measures in the bill as well.

A bill was also introduced by the then Lord Chancellor's Department to reform the administration of the courts: in July the government also announced its intention to take the law lords out of the House of Lords and establish a United Kingdom supreme court.

The most controversial bills among the others were the Health and Social Care Bill proposing further reform of the NHS, including the establishment of so-called "foundation hospitals"; the Licensing Bill, introducing wholesale reform of the licensing laws (with proposals to control the performance of live music); and the Communications Bill, reforming the entire system of regulation of the broadcast media. The Health and Social Care Bill narrowly escaped a back-bench rebellion at its report stage, when an amendment rejecting the foundation hospitals provisions was defeated by only 35 votes, the government's smallest majority since 1997 on a major vote.

Less controversial measures related to reform of local government financing; preparations for referendums to be held on the establishment of regional government in England; streamlining of the planning system; and railway safety.

Yet another Bill was introduced to control hunting with dogs – the third since 1997. It came in a multiple choice form; initially the Commons seemed likely to agree on the "middle way" option of extensive regulation and licensing of hunting. However, it was altered at report stage by a back-bench amendment agreed by an overwhelming majority of Labour MPs to replace the "middle way" option with what amounted to something near a total ban on hunting with dogs. After being recommitted to tidy up the loose ends this left, the Bill went up to the House of Lords in July, where it is confidently predicted that the total ban will once again be rejected. If it is, and no compromise can be reached, there is the possibility of the Parliament Acts being once again invoked to get it on the statute book.

The Budget

Military action in Iraq forced a delay in the presentation of the Budget, which the Chancellor of the Exchequer announced to the House only on 9 April. It was largely uncontroversial, containing no great tax or spending surprises, though his relatively upbeat assessment of the state of the economy was widely disputed.

The Euro

On 9 June Gordon Brown made his long-awaited announcement on whether the government had decided that the famous "five tests" for UK membership of the euro had been passed. The short summary of the 18 volumes of Treasury analysis which accompanied his statement was that they had not been – yet. However, legislation to pave the way to a referendum was promised so it remains a possibility (though most analysts agreed a distant one) that there could be a referendum on the question in this Parliament.

Iraq

Following mounting pressure throughout the 2002 summer recess, the Government finally asked the Speaker to recall Parliament for a debate on the Iraq "crisis" on 24 September. The Prime Minister published a dossier of evidence (later to be subject to much close scrutiny) on Saddam Hussein's weapons programmes on the morning of the recall. Sixty-eight Members (including the four tellers) voted against the adjournment motion in the Commons at the end of the debate, almost all from the government side. The government and the official opposition abstained, with only the Ulster Unionists supporting the motion.

In the event, nothing of significance occurred between the recall and the return of the House some three weeks later, on 15 October. In November the Security Council agreed a new resolution on the return of the UN weapons inspectors, which seemed to point to a possible resolution of international disagreement. For a period the controversy receded, while at the same time there was a steady build-up of US forces in the region.

However, domestic opposition to war was growing, and on Saturday 15 February, in what most commentators agree was the largest ever demonstration in the UK, upwards of half a million people marched through the streets of London to protest against a possible war. The government produced a further dossier of evidence on the case for war which was to come back to haunt them – the so-called "dodgy dossier" which included an apparent claim that Iraq had the ability to mobilise chemical and biological weapons within 45 minutes. On 26 February, in what was at that point the largest ever rebellion against the government line in the House of Commons, 122 Labour back-benchers voted for an amendment to the government's motion arguing that the case for war was not proved. After this, attention began to focus on diplomatic attempts to secure a further resolution from the UN Security Council explicitly backing the use of military intervention to enforce the terms of previous resolutions, particularly that of November. Over the weekend of 16/17 March these efforts finally ran into the sand in the face of unremitting resistance from France and Germany.

As military action seemed increasingly inevitable, without UN sanction, the Prime Minister assured the Commons of his intention to give the House the opportunity to vote on a substantive motion in advance of hostilities commencing – a historic concession. Robin Cook, then Leader of the House of Commons, announced his resignation from the Cabinet on the eve of the debate, and made a statement to the House explaining his reasons for being unable to support the government motion. Over the course of the next 24 hours, two further Ministers (John Denham and Lord Hunt of Kings Heath) resigned from the government, and seven Parliamentary Private Secretaries also resigned their honorary posts in protest at the government's policy.

The debate took place on Tuesday 18 March. The government's motion authorised it to take all reasonable steps, including military action. An amendment was proposed by Chris Smith which essentially demanded explicit UN authorisation for military action. Following the debate the amendment was supported by 139 Labour rebels, but defeated overall by 396 votes to 217. However, with the support of the Conservative Party, and some other opposition Members, plus abstentions by some rebels who had voted for the amendment, the Government easily secured support for its motion by 412 votes to 149.

The first US missiles hit Baghdad on 20 March. Over the next few days US and UK ground forces gradually began to infiltrate Iraq from different directions. The UK forces concentrated on the southern part of the country, dominated by the city of Basra. The US forces drove relentlessly towards the capital. On 9 April US forces entered central Baghdad virtually unopposed. By the end of the month, despite the levels of anarchy still persisting throughout the country, it was apparent that the main military work was over.

There continued to be controversy in the weeks and months following the invasion. Clare Short, the Secretary of State for International Development, whose continued presence in the Cabinet after her attack on the PM in a radio broadcast on 10 March astonished almost everyone, resigned from the government on 12 May, citing her unhappiness with the plans for post-war reconstruction in Iraq as the cause. However, she was soon attacking the Prime Minister in more fundamental ways, and the debate over the justification for war intensified as weeks and then months passed without the occupying forces uncovering evidence of weapons of mass destruction in Iraq.

The Commons Foreign Affairs Committee launched an inquiry into the decision to go to war in Iraq shortly after hostilities had ended. The Committee's inquiry focused on the nature of the intelligence which the government had suggested indicated that Saddam Hussein's regime was a real and present threat – the principal justification given for going to war. The inquiry got caught up in a fierce debate between No.10 and the BBC over a report by the Today programme's defence correspondent, Andrew Gilligan, that the Downing Street press officers had interfered in the content of the dossier presented to Parliament in February, and had over-ruled the cautious advice of the intelligence services. Both Gilligan and Alastair Campbell appeared before the committee. Gilligan refused to reveal his source for the allegation on the content and wording of the "dodgy dossier". The report of the Committee was published on 7 July, and concluded that Mr Campbell had had no intention to deceive Parliament.

However, the controversy was almost immediately reignited when a government scientific adviser, Dr David Kelly, was named in the press as the source of Gilligan's story. He was summoned before a hastily reconvened Committee, and subjected to some fairly harsh questioning during a public cross-examination in which he appeared to claim that he was not Gilligan's source. Gilligan was also re-examined by the Committee, this time in private, after which the Chairman of the Committee, Donald Anderson, described him as an unsatisfactory witness. The BBC top brass, however, continued to support the reporter, and declined to confirm or deny that Kelly was his source.

The Conservative Party used their last opposition day before the summer recess to hold a debate on the Committee's report, and to call for a wider judicial inquiry. The Foreign Affairs Committee indicated for their part that they believed Dr Kelly had not been the source. On Friday 18 July, the day after Parliament had risen for the summer, Dr Kelly's body was found near his home in Oxfordshire – he had apparently committed suicide. This precipitated a further crisis within both the government and the BBC. The government announced an inquiry into the events surrounding Dr Kelly's death, to be conducted by Lord Hutton, the former Chief Justice of Northern Ireland, and the BBC confirmed eventually that Dr Kelly had been Gilligan's source, and that he had also spoken to two other BBC reporters.

It looks as if the debate on the decision to go to war in Iraq is going to continue for some time.

Arrivals and departures

Having been precipitated into an early reshuffle in May 2002 with the resignation of Stephen Byers, the Prime Minister's hand was forced once again by the unheralded resignation of Estelle Morris as Secretary of State for Education and Skills on 23 October. Like Mr Byers, Ms Morris had been under sustained media attack for some months, especially over the A-level debacle in the summer. However, no-one had predicted that she would go when she did. Her disarming comments, following her resignation, on what she perceived as her own shortcomings in the role of Secretary of State, produced from many quarters a most untypical outpouring of regrets at her going, and she returned to government in July 2003 as Minister for the Arts in the Department for Culture, Media and Sport.

Her place at Education and Skills was taken by Charles Clarke, who moved from being party chairman and Minister without Portfolio. That role was taken (briefly) by John Reid, whose position as Secretary of State for Northern Ireland was taken by Paul Murphy. Mr Murphy's place as Secretary of State for Wales was taken by Peter Hain.

Some considerable time after Robin Cook's resignation, the Prime Minister appointed Dr Reid to succeed him as Leader of the House of Commons, and Ian McCartney to take Dr Reid's place as Party Chairman and Minister without Portfolio.

It was announced on the morning of 12 May that Clare Short had resigned from the Government. By the time she was making her personal statement to the Commons that afternoon, Baroness Amos had been appointed to replace her as Secretary of State for International Development.

Clare Short's resignation was widely interpreted as a pre-emptive strike against the Prime Minister before he had the opportunity to sack her in his summer reshuffle. That followed exactly a month later on 12 June. The biggest shock, which seemed to have come as a genuine surprise to his colleagues, was the resignation of Alan Milburn as Secretary of State for Health – he cited the impossibility of combining a family life with the duties of a cabinet minister as his reason for going. He was replaced in the reshuffle by John Reid, making Dr Reid something of a record-holder for moving round government. Dr Reid was succeeded as Leader of the House by Peter Hain, who retained his post as Secretary of State for Wales as well.

The other most notable disappearance in the July reshuffle was that of Derry Irvine as Lord Chancellor. He was replaced by Lord (Charlie) Falconer, but it was announced at the same time that the role of Lord Chancellor was to be abolished in its present form. The House of Lords will have to find a way of appointing its own Speaker, or presiding officer, and a select committee has been appointed to look at the matter. The Lord Chancellor's Department was rechristened the Department for Constitutional Affairs, and Lord Falconer became the Secretary of State for Constitutional Affairs and (pro tem) Lord Chancellor.

In a linked change to the machinery of government, the Scotland Office and the Wales Office were absorbed into the new Department, although the titles of the two Secretaries of State were retained by Cabinet Ministers outside that Department – Peter Hain for Wales and Alistair Darling for Scotland, the former combining the job with that of Leader of the House and the latter with that of Secretary of State for Transport. There was considerable criticism of the rather sudden nature of these announcements (though all the proposals had been widely canvassed by reformers before) and of the somewhat incoherent-seeming arrangements which follow them, at least in the short term.

The other Cabinet member to go in the reshuffle was Helen Liddell, who had been Secretary of State for Scotland. Michael Meacher left the post of Environment Minister which he had held since 1997, to be replaced by Elliot Morley. Other departures from the ranks of junior Ministers were Barbara Roche, Brian Wilson, Nick Brown, Lord (Gus) MacDonald, Baroness Blackstone, Sally Keeble, Lewis Moonie and Dan Norris. The new arrivals included Caroline Flint, Stephen Ladyman, Fiona Mactaggart, Chris Pond and Lord Warner. Chris Mullin, who had indicated in 2001 that he did not wish to be appointed a Minister, preferring to return to the chairmanship of the Home Affairs Committee, made a surprise comeback as a Minister in the Foreign and Commonwealth Office with special responsibility for Africa. His place as chair of the Home Affairs Committee was taken by John Denham, who had resigned as a Home Office Minister over the decision to go to war in Iraq.

Iain Duncan Smith was also forced to reshuffle his front bench team in November 2002 when his shadow work and pensions spokesman, John Bercow, resigned in protest at the imposition of a three-line whip on amendments made by the Lords to the Adoption and Children Bill, restricting the rights of unmarried couples to adopt. On the morning of Gunpowder Plot day, following the previous evening's debate on adoption, in which there had been an extensive rebellion on the Conservative benches, Central Office announced an emergency press conference was to be held at noon, at which Mr Duncan Smith was to make "a brief personal statement". This produced a frenzy of speculation. In the event the statement was not about the leader's own future, but an attack on unnamed members of his own party who he said were in danger of destroying it through disunity. He ended with the resounding injunction to his colleagues to "unite or die". This met with mixed reactions from his fellow MPs – in May, an attempt was made by a former front bencher, Crispin Blunt, to precipitate a leadership election to unseat him. However, following the better than feared results in the local government elections, he failed to gather the necessary 25 signatures to require a vote of no confidence.

Iain Duncan-Smith also experienced opposition to his unequivocal support for government policy towards Iraq: John Baron, Humfrey Malins, Jonathan Sayeed and John Randall all resigned from his front bench in protest before the debate in February. In July three of these rebels, John Baron, John Randall and Humfrey Malins, were re-appointed. At the same time Patrick Mercer was appointed as spokesman for "Homeland Security", although there is no equivalent in the government, and Julian Brazier moved from the whips' office to support Oliver Letwin on Home Affairs. Bill Wiggin and Michael Fabricant also moved to the front bench.

The Conservative party leader had also come in for criticism in February, when he replaced Mark MacGregor as the chief executive of Central Office with Barry Legg, a former MP and a fellow Maastrich rebel. Michael Portillo was provoked into a very direct public attack on his former leadership rival by the controversy over this move. However, the controversial appointee, Barry Legg, resigned in May when his post at Central Office was "abolished following a strategic review".

Charles Kennedy did not get an altogether smooth ride either, having to face critics within his own party of his leadership style. However, he was the only party leader allowed to reshuffle his front bench at a time of his own choosing, though it was also in response to changes in the government machinery. He divided responsibility for shadowing Margaret Beckett's environment, food and rural affairs portfolio between Norman Baker (environment) and Andrew George (food and rural affairs). Don Foster retained the transport portfolio, and Edward Davey took the job of shadowing John Prescott's new Office of the Deputy Prime Minister, covering local government and regional affairs. Menzies Campbell continued as foreign affairs and defence spokesman throughout his treatment for cancer, maintaining a strongly critical line on the government's policy on Iraq.

House of Lords Reform

In November 2001 the Government's White Paper responding to the recommendations of the Wakeham Commission had received such a comprehensive drubbing from every quarter, having failed apparently to please any of the entrenched and opposing parties, that the government eventually abandoned its proposals. In May 2002 Robin Cook had announced that the problem was to be handed over to a joint committee of the two Houses to try and come up with a solution, and the committee was established shortly before the 2002 summer recess with the former Labour Cabinet Minister Jack Cunningham as its Chairman. It published a report in November, proposing that the two Houses should vote on a number of options for the composition of the upper House, ranging from wholly elected to wholly appointed, with a range of different proportions of each in between.

When both Houses came to vote on the range of options put forward by the Joint Committee on 4 February the Commons agreed to none of them, though the nearest result was a majority of three against an 80 per cent elected House, and there was a majority of only 17 against a wholly elected House. The option of a fully-appointed House was decisively rejected by the Commons, although an amendment calling for abolition attracted 172 supporters. The Lords, on the other hand, decisively supported a wholly appointed House, and decisively rejected a wholly elected House and any of the compromise options, with the vast majority of Conservative peers continuing to repudiate their official party line.

In May 2003 the Joint Committee published a further report inviting the government to indicate a way forward. Their report indicated areas of potential reform (apart from composition) on which they believed some consensus could be achieved. The government's response, published in July, suggested that any proposals for introducing an elected element into the House were now put off to the crack of doom, and that it would concentrate on making the best of the present House by improving the transparency in the method of appointment of life peers. It also reaffirmed its commitment to removing the remaining hereditaries. As the government noted, it had already pre-empted some aspects of reform by its decision to establish a separate supreme court and abolish the function of the Lord Chancellor as Speaker of the House. No-one is quite sure where this leaves the debate, though the Joint Committee does not seem to have received the unequivocally clear signal it might have been hoping for.

The continuing presence of the hereditaries produced an unexpected diversion. When "Phase 1" of Lords reform was initiated, including the deal in which 92 of the hereditary peers were allowed to remain in the House, it was widely supposed that the complex arrangements for replenishing their number would never be used, as they would have disappeared by the end of the first session following the next general election. However, they have held on, and following the death of the Viscount of Oxfuird in January 2003, a by-election had to be held to replace him. As Viscount Oxfuird was one of those elected by the whole House, the electoral college for his successor was likewise the whole House. The election took place on 25/26 March. There were 81 candidates, of whom 44 received first preference votes. After 42 transfers, Viscount Ullswater ultimately defeated Viscount Montgomery of Alamein by 151 votes to 116.

Modernisation

The Commons Modernisation Committee, then chaired by Robin Cook, in a report published in September 2002 made some radical recommendations for modernisation of the House's practices and procedures. These were debated on and voted on by the House on 29 October. The Committee, chaired by Robin Cook, the Leader of the House, had proposed that the "parallel Chamber" in Westminster Hall should be made permanent and that the earlier (11.30 am) meeting of the House should be extended from Thursdays to Tuesdays and Wednesdays as well.

The first of these proposals proved uncontroversial, but the second was debated fiercely. However, on a free vote (though largely opposed by the Conservatives) the House narrowly agreed to the proposals for earlier sittings on Tuesdays and Wednesdays. From 1 January 2003 to the end of this Parliament, the House will normally meet from 2.30 to 10.30 pm on Mondays, from 11.30 am to 7.30 pm on Tuesdays and Wednesdays, and from 11.30 am to 6.30 pm on Thursdays. The House also agreed to the Committee's proposal that Friday sittings should disappear except for the 13 Fridays each session set aside for private Members' bills. There have been predictable grumblings from the small "c" conservatives in every party about the new hours – it is too early to predict whether the reforms will hold, but the evenings in Westminster now often seem eerily quiet.

The House also agreed, in the teeth of the official opposition, to endorse the proposals to allow Bills to be rolled over from one session to the one following, and to continue the experimental arrangements for "deferred divisions", which enable votes which would otherwise be held late at night to be taken in a sort of "postal vote" form on Wednesday afternoons. It also agreed to continue and develop the arrangements for the "programming" of the passage of Bills through the Commons, and to endorse cross-party consultation on the "shape" of the annual legislative programme (including over which Bills to roll over, and which Bills to introduce in draft form) more widely.

The House also endorsed the proposal to move to a fixed parliamentary timetable, with recess dates announced at the beginning of the year, and with holidays more aligned with school holidays, with the House rising earlier in July, and sitting in mid-September, before breaking for a "Conference Recess". Following this, Robin Cook announced on 31 October, at business questions, the sitting pattern of the House up to the end of the new session, including the first new term from 8 to 17 September 2003.

On the same evening the House also endorsed the proposals of the Procedure Committee, made in its report published in July, to reduce the period of notice required for oral questions, to make them more topical. The Procedure Committee had also proposed the introduction of some form of oral question time in Westminster Hall, including occasions when Ministers from more than one department would be available to answer questions on "cross-cutting" issues, and this idea was also approved in principle. The first few such sessions have already taken place, and have been generally judged a success.

The new sitting hours now mean that the Prime Minister makes his regular weekly appearances at noon on Wednesdays, and many have detected a more subdued atmosphere in the House at this pre-prandial event. The Prime Minister made his second and third appearances before the Liaison Committee (the committee of chairmen of select committees) in January and July.

Standing order changes to create a new proceeding of "written statements" from Ministers, to replace "planted" questions were also agreed, as were provisions for time limits on back-bench speeches in all debates (to be determined by the Speaker case by case but to be no shorter than eight minutes).

The House also established an additional departmental select committee to oversee the work of the Lord Chancellor's Department (previously a rather neglected element of the remit of the Home Affairs Committee). It elected the Liberal Democrat Alan Beith as its Chairman. The Committee's name, but not its responsibilities, will have to be changed following the creation of the Department for Constitutional Affairs. For the time being at least, it seems the Scottish and Welsh affairs committees will retain an independent existence.

Shortly before the summer break the Commons passed some minor reforms to its system for policing and investigating issues relating to the conduct of Members, in response to the recommendations of the Wicks Committee following the Elizabeth Filkin controversies of a year ago. It is hoped that these will help further cool the tit-for-tat "sleaze wars" that marred the last Parliament.

The Lords too will be experimenting with more modest reforms of their own procedures. The principal changes are aimed at ending the sittings by 10 pm on Mondays to Wednesdays and earlier on Thursdays. Greater use is also being made of "Grand Committees" (committees of the whole House sitting separately from the main chamber) to consider bills.

Suspension of the Northern Ireland Assembly

On 14 October 2002 the then Northern Ireland Secretary, John Reid, was forced to respond to the growing crisis in the peace process (precipitated by a police raid on Sinn Fein's offices in Stormont) by once again suspending the devolved institutions and re-imposing direct rule. As a result of the re-imposition of direct rule, two temporary additional Ministers were added to the complement of the Northern Ireland Office.

In an effort to give time for the peace process to advance, emergency legislation was passed to delay the elections to the Northern Ireland Assembly from the due day of 1 May to 29 May. But at the end of April the Prime Minister stated that the IRA had so far failed to make a sufficiently unequivocal statement that the armed struggle was over to allow devolution to be restarted. After further fruitless talks and declarations, the government announced that the Assembly elections were to be further postponed – probably till the autumn, and yet another Act was passed which gave discretion to the Secretary of State to fix the date by order. The Act incidentally reduced the salaries of the suspended MLAs.

David Trimble had to face down yet more attempts in the early summer to unseat him by members of his own party. Following an unsuccessful attempt to secure a vote of no confidence, three UUP MPs, Jeffrey Donaldson, the Rev Martin Smyth and David Burnside, resigned the party whip. They were subsequently suspended from the party, a decision they are contesting in the courts.

On 2 October 2002 the Conservative MP for Basingstoke, Andrew Hunter, had announced he was resigning the Conservative whip in order to stand in the Northern Ireland Assembly elections as a DUP candidate. Meanwhile, he has stated his intention of continuing to support his former party in the Commons.

Scotland

The second general election to the Scottish Parliament took place on 1 May. The result was somewhat inconclusive. The Labour Party lost ground, with six fewer seats overall, but the official opposition, the SNP, did worse, losing eight seats. The Conservatives made a modest advance by increasing the number of their "first-past-the-post" seats from one to three, but the effect of the PR system was to leave their total number of seats unchanged at 18. The Liberal Democrats (Labour's coalition partners on the Executive) also remained unchanged. The big winners were the minor parties, doing particularly well out of the proportional "top-up" arrangements of the regional list system, with the Greens increasing their representation from one to seven and the Scottish Socialist Party from one to six. The number of independents increased to four, with Margo MacDonald (formerly of the SNP), Dr Jean Turner (campaigning against a local hospital closure in Strathkelvin and Bearsden) and John Swinburne (of the Senior Citizens Unity Party) joining former Labour MP Dennis Canavan at Holyrood.

Turnout, at 49 per cent, was disappointing to all supporters of devolution. The final result was Labour 50, SNP 27, Conservatives 18, Liberal Democrats 17, Greens 7, SSP 6 and 4 independents. A Labour and Liberal Democrat coalition executive was again formed, following a prolonged period of negotiations. Jack McConnell was re-elected as First Minister and he re-appointed Jim Wallace as his deputy, though Mr Wallace swapped his justice portfolio for enterprise. George Reid of the SNP was elected as the new presiding officer of the Parliament, following the decision of Sir David Steel not to seek re-election. The Queen addressed the new Parliament on 3 June. In July it was announced that the SNP leader, John Swinney, was to face a leadership battle, following the party's disappointing performance in the May elections. The still-unfinished parliament building at Holyrood continued to be an embarrassment to all involved.

Wales

The elections to the National Assembly for Wales also took place on 1 May. The result was better than in Scotland for the Labour Party, which increased its overall tally of seats by two, regaining its heartland seats in the valleys lost to Plaid Cymru in 1999. The Conservatives also gained two more seats, bringing their total to 11, just one behind Plaid Cymru, the official opposition, which did badly, losing five seats overall. The Liberal Democrats remained unchanged. In Wrexham, the former Labour MP and AM, Dr John Marek, who had been deselected by his local party, retained his seat standing as an independent.

Turnout, which fell from 46 per cent in 1999 to 38 per cent, was again very disappointing to supporters of devolution, even in a nation which had supported the establishment of the National Assembly only by a majority of some 6,000 in 1998. The final result was Labour 30, Plaid Cymru 12, Conservatives 11, Liberal Democrats 6, and one independent. The National Assembly became the first UK legislature, and probably the first in the world, to have a 50 per cent female membership.

Rhodri Morgan is seeking to govern without a coalition, despite having no overall majority. His ability to do so was strengthened by the decision of the Assembly to re-elect as Presiding Officer and his deputy Lord Elis-Thomas and Dr John Marek, both from the opposition. The leader of the official Plaid Cymru opposition, Ieuan Wyn Jones, resigned following his party's poor showing in the elections. His successor will be elected in the autumn. The Queen addressed the new Assembly on 5 June.

Local government and the regions

On the same day that Scotland and Wales were electing their new legislators, local elections were held in most parts of England. The results were generally assessed as reasonable for the Conservative Party, which gained 565 seats compared to 1999, and won control of a number of councils. Labour lost 839 seats, and control of a number of flagship local authorities, including Birmingham and Bristol. The Liberal Democrats had a successful, if not spectacular night, equalling Labour's share of the national vote at 30 per cent, just 4 per cent behind the Conservatives.

Trevor Phillips resigned from the London Assembly, with effect from 1 March, on taking up his post as Chair of the Commission for Racial Equality. His seat was taken without a by-election by Diana Johnson, the next eligible candidate on the Labour regional list. Sally Hamwee (Liberal Democrat) was elected to replace him as Chair of the Assembly (for a second term), and Samantha Heath (Labour) was elected as her deputy. The government announced that it intends to move the date for the GLA and local government elections, due to fall on 6 May next year, to 10 June, to coincide with the elections to the European Parliament. There are those who speculated that this would be a good day to hold a referendum on the euro as well, but ministers quickly squashed such speculation.

The Regional Assemblies (Preparations) Bill, paving the way to possible future referendums and elections for regional assemblies in England, received the royal assent on 8 May. A draft bill on the powers and functions of the assemblies is promised for next session. Meanwhile the Office of the Deputy Prime Minister published the results of its preliminary consultations testing the strength of support for the proposed assemblies, indicating that the three northern regions of the North East, the North West and Yorkshire and the Humber would get the first chance to vote on elected assemblies.

On 2 August the government passed a landmark by becoming the longest surviving Labour administration ever, overtaking the Attlee administration's previous record. It also broke the Attlee administration's record for the longest period in which a government had not suffered a by-election defeat. However, Paul Daisley, the Labour Member for Brent East since 2001, died on 18 June. He had been ill since his election. The by-election in the autumn will be closely watched for signs of the current state of the political weather.

PARLIAMENTARY SUMMARY AND LEGISLATION SEPTEMBER 2002 – JULY 2003

END OF 2001–02 SESSION

RECALL OF PARLIAMENT 24 SEPTEMBER 2002

Both Houses were recalled for the day on Tuesday, *24 September*, to debate Iraq. Tony Blair made a Statement introducing a 22,000-word 50-page dossier made available by the Government at 8 am that morning. He said this showed that Saddam Hussein's "weapons of mass destruction programme is active, detailed and growing", and that these weapons could be "activated within 45 minutes". The Leader of the Opposition, Iain Duncan Smith, said Saddam had the "means, the mentality and the motive to pose a threat to Britain's national security and the wider international order". The Liberal Democrat leader, Charles Kennedy, said there were two important issues of principle. The first concerned the role of the House of Commons and the second the role of the United Nations, both of which had to be involved. In response the Prime Minister said a new UN resolution was needed, but if it was not forthcoming we still "have to find a way of dealing with this". He added that while regime change in Iraq would be "a wonderful thing" that is "not the purpose of our action".

The Foreign Secretary, Jack Straw, then introduced a debate in which 50 back-bench speeches were made over the following eight hours. He set out the case for action against Iraq, arguing that it was justifiable to use force. For the Conservative Opposition Michael Ancram said: "We support the Prime Minister's stance today. We share his analysis of the threat", but he went on to say that too much hope should not be invested in the UN. Donald Anderson called the dossier "a very British document, low-key and with no hyperbole, but sober and chilling". Menzies Campbell for the Liberal Democrats said that even though from a strictly legal point of view no new UN resolution may be necessary, from a political and diplomatic point of view a new resolution was essential. He also wondered if the costs of containment and deterrence would not be significantly less than the costs of war.

In the ensuing debate many back-bench speakers expressed views at variance to those of their respective front benches. Concluding for the Conservatives Bernard Jenkin said that it was right not to rule out military action even if it was not possible to secure unanimity on a UN resolution. For the Government Adam Ingram, Minister of State for Defence, said that those who insisted on prior UN approval should ask themselves whether if it was given, they would find some other excuse to oppose international resolve. At the end of the debate Government Whips declined to appoint tellers, but Labour back benchers forced a token division.

In the House of Lords Baroness Symons of Vernham Dean, Deputy Leader (and Minister for Trade), emphasised that the dossier did not show any link between the events of 11 September or Al'Quaeda and the issue of Iraq "which stands by itself". David Howell from the Conservative front bench pointed out that this was not how American rhetoric portrayed the situation. Baroness Williams of Crosby, Leader of the Liberal Democrats in the House, said there was an element of hypocrisy in the debate in that the USA had in the past opposed a UN resolution condemning earlier use of chemical weapons by Iraq. Furthermore, the UK had been among countries selling "conventional arms to Iraq for years after it was clear she was using unacceptable weapons". Lord Craig of Radley, Convenor of the Cross-bench peers and the first of five former Chiefs of Defence Staff who took part in the debate, stressed the need for planning the post-war situation, and asked what had happened to the "once fashionable and effective policy of deterrence". The Bishop of London spoke of the danger of hyper-moralism which lacks practical wisdom. The Bishop of Oxford outlined the classic just war arguments and said a policy of containment and deterrence had worked for more than ten years and the criteria for military action against Iraq were in his judgment not met "on present evidence". Lord Jenkins of Hillhead said that the Prime Minister possibly had too much conviction, "particularly when dealing with the world beyond Britain". Concluding the $10^{1}/_{2}$-hour debate, in which 63 peers made speeches, Lord Wallace of Saltaire for the Liberal Democrats said if war came, as a last resort, it had to be "the collective intervention of the international community". Lord Bach, junior Defence Minister, said "of course we shall go down the UN inspection route, but we shall do so with our eyes open, never letting up the pressure on Iraq. That pressure must include the possible use of force". The House rose without a division at 11.10 pm.

7 – 11 OCTOBER

When the House of Lords returned on Monday *7 October*, Lord Filkin, junior Home Office Minister, made a Statement explaining why the Government had tabled significant new amendments to the **Nationality, Immigration and Asylum Bill**. Lord Whitty also made a Statement on amendments to be made to the **Animal Health Bill** following consideration given to reports published earlier in the Summer. Peers then spent that day and *8 October* on the committee stage of this latter Bill. On *9 October* the House began the report stage of the **Nationality, Immigration and Asylum Bill**. An amendment dealing with the size and siting of Accommodation Centres, moved from the Conservative front bench, and was carried against the Government by 171 votes to 107. A further Government defeat, by 83 votes to 82, occurred on an amendment moved by the Bishop of Portsmouth designed to allow asylum seekers children to be educated in local state schools rather than specialist education units within the proposed accommodation centres. On *10 October* the Government suffered a further defeat on the same Bill when the House voted by 77 to 71 in support of an amendment moved by Lord Kingsland seeking to redefine a "serious criminal" as someone sentenced for an offence in the UK or abroad for which the maximum term of imprisonment is ten years rather than two years. On Friday *11 October* the House dealt with private members' legislation, givng a third reading to the **Copyright (Visually Impaired Persons) Bill**, then debating at second reading the **Sexual Offences (Amendment) Bill**, which sought to give better protection to people with learning disabilities. The **Private Hire Vehicles Bill** and the **Commonwealth Bill** were also debated and approved at second reading.

14 – 17 OCTOBER

On *14 October* peers debated the **Adoption and Children Bill** at report stage, with the Government defeating amendments concerned with adoption procedures. A debate also took place on European Scrutiny, with a number of peers expressing concern over the apparent erosion of the parliamentary reserve.

On Tuesday *15 October* the House of Commons re-assembled, to hear first a Statement from the Prime Minister on the weekend bombing in Bali, in which he said up to 30 Britons were among the 180 plus people feared dead. Dr John Reid, Secretary of State for Northern Ireland, made a Statement on the suspension of devolved government in the province. A third Statement followed from Estelle Morris, Secretary of State for Education and Skills, on A-level grading. In this she said that as a result of the Tomlinson inquiry 1,945 candidates had had overall grades raised, of whom 168 appeared to be eligible for a change of university on the basis of these increased grades. MPs then debated and approved by 271 votes to 170 the Urban Post Office Reinvention Programme authorising expenditure of a further £210 million on post offices. The House also approved the **Public Trustee (Liability and Fees) Bill** at third reading without a division, and then debated local government finance. The House of Lords debated the **Enterprise Bill** at report stage with the Government being defeated by 134 votes to 123 on an amendment moved by Lord Hunt of Wirral separating the roles of chairman and chief executive of such regulatory bodies as the Office of Fair Trading (OFT).

The *16 October* was the 18th Opposition Day with a Conservative motion attacking the Secretary of State for Education for various alleged policy failures and blunders in her Department being rejected by 191 votes to 293. A second motion on the rural economy was debated and rejected by 192 votes to 283. Peers further considered the **Adoption and Children Bill** at report stage. A Conservative front-bench amendment disallowing adoption by unmarried or same sex couples was carried on what was technically a free vote by 196 votes to 162, thus reversing amendments made earlier by MPs on a free vote in the Commons.

On *17 October* the Secretary of State for Defence, Geoffrey Hoon, introduced a debate on Defence in the World, the fourth of five themed defence debates planned to take place in the House during the session. In Westminster Hall Gwyneth Dunwoody introduced a debate on the speed of road traffic based on a report from the Transport Select Committee. The House of Lords that day considered the **Nationality, Immigration and Asylum Bill** on re-commitment, with Government amendments being made to end what Lord Filkin described as "the presumption of support for those who apply for asylum in-country, unless they give a truthful and creditable account of their circumstances and how they arrived here at the earliest opportunity". Neither House sat on Friday *18 October.*

21 – 24 OCTOBER

The Foreign Secretary, Jack Straw, made a Statement on the terrorist bomb attack in Bali at the commencement of business on *21 October*. In this he said that 11 British citizens had definitely died in the attack and a further 22 were missing out of a death total of more than 180. Among responses was one from Douglas Hogg who suggested that military action against Iraq "would increase support for terrorist activity in Islamic counties", which Mr Straw said was a "curious assertion". MPs then completed work on the **Tobacco Advertising and Promotion Bill**, with Hazel Blears for the Government saying smoking eventually kills one in two of all smokers – 120,000 people a year in the UK. Main business in the House of Lords that day was further consideration on report of the **Enterprise Bill**. Lord Graham of Edmonton then introduced the second reading of a private Bill, the **London Local Authorities and Transport for London Bill**, saying this would give new powers to help London local authorities respond to the challenges they face in regard to traffic management.

On *22 October* the Deputy Prime Minister, John Prescott, made a Statement on the firefighters' dispute in which he criticised the Fire Brigades Union for refusing to suspend the dispute while Professor Sir George Bain conducted a review into their pay. The day was then taken as an unallotted Opposition Day, with two Liberal Democrat motions being debated. The first, moved by Don Foster, was critical of the Government for its inadequate response to the need for affordable housing, and was defeated by 50 votes to 447. The second moved by Dr Vincent Cable criticised the Government for putting "at risk over £600 million of public funds in order to prevent the bankruptcy of the privatised nuclear power Company British Energy". This was defeated by 54 votes to 313. Peers began report stage consideration of the **Animal Health Bill** that day with the Countess of Mar moving an amendment requiring higher priority to be given to vaccination rather than slaughter. This was carried against the Government by 171 votes to 123. Earl Peel then moved an amendment to give greater prominence to disease detection, which was also carried against the Government, by 186 votes to 127.

24 October was the 19th Opposition Day with a Conservative motion saying money raised through the National Lottery should not be used to fund projects which are the responsibility of Government being defeated by 138 votes to 391. Following this Claire Curtis-Thomas moved a motion to allow for the **Mersey Tunnels Bill**, a private Bill, to be carried over to the following session, which gave rise to some sharp debate, but was carried by 164 votes to 64. Peers had a third report stage day on the **Adoption and Children Bill**. An amendment concerned with ensuring the availability of independent representation for children in regard to proceedings about residence or contact with their birth parents was carried against the Government by 136 votes to 129 despite ministerial assurances that it was unnecessary. During the evening Lord Astor of Hever initiated a short debate on the state of the motorsport industry which he said employed 40,000 people in 4,000 businesses but was drifting into crisis.

Oral questions in the Commons on *24 October* were on education. Several MPs prefaced their questions with tributes to Estelle Morris whose resignation as Secretary of State had been announced the previous evening. Debate on local government finance followed, with some back-bench Labour MPs joining with Conservatives and Liberal Democrats in criticising the Government's proposals for formula grant review. Ministerial assurances were given not only to boost local authority spending but also to listen carefully to all arguments about the fairness of the distribution. A two-hour debate was then held in government time at the request of the Opposition on various Orders relating to asbestos. During this Nicholas Brown, Minister for Work, said that between 1968 and 1998 some 50,000 people died in the UK from asbestos-related diseases, and that something like 500,000 buildings in the UK still have materials in them containing asbestos. In Westminster Hall the Minister for Policing, Crime Reduction and Community Safety, John Denham, made a wide-ranging speech when introducing a three-hour debate on the UN Convention on the Rights of the Child. The Conservative front-bench spokesman Dominic Grieve was critical of proposals to outlaw the smacking of children. Other MPs expressed disappointment that no back-bench speeches were made by any non-Labour MPs. Peers debated the **Nationality, Immigration and Asylum Bill** at report stage for almost nine hours that day, with the Government successfully resisting in the division lobby Liberal Democrat amendments concerned with the circumstances in which asylum seekers may be deprived of support. Neither House sat on Friday *25 October*.

28 OCTOBER – 1 NOVEMBER

The Prime Minister made a Statement on *28 October* on the meeting of the European Council held in Brussels the previous week, which, he said, had "set the framework for the final stage of the enlargement negotiations". Later on this the 20th Opposition Day MPs debated a Conservative motion calling for the resolution of the House granting facilities and other support to Sinn Féin members who had not taken their seats to be rescinded. Replying to the debate Robin Cook said that in 18 years in Opposition the Labour Party had never opposed the previous Government's policy on Northern Ireland on an Opposition Day. The motion was defeated by 336 votes to 140. Following this a motion noting with concern the impact of the European Convention on Human Rights on the sentencing powers of Home Secretary, and calling for a review of the Human Rights Act 1998, was debated and defeated by 133 votes to 350. Peers debated the **Enterprise Bill** at third reading with a Conservative amendment to allow the courts to transfer some cases to the new Competition Appeal Tribunal being carried against the Government by 92 votes to 86. Later the Government were again narrowly defeated when peers voted 119 to 112 in support of an amendment to raise from £45 million to £100 million the turnover threshold below which companies would be exempt from the monopolies and merger regime.

On *29 October* MPs debated proposals contained in the Second Report from the Select Committee on Modernisation, including "routine publication of bills in draft for pre-legislative scrutiny"; "sittings in September balanced by an earlier recess in July"; more flexibility in programming business, and more effective use of the Chamber. Introducing this Robin Cook, Leader of the House, said the antiquity of Parliament strengthened legitimacy but could also be a trap if desirable change was resisted. The shadow Leader, Eric Forth, argued that the proposal to meet at 11.30 am was "the worst of all worlds", and that if morning sittings were to take place, 9.30 am would be better. Several senior Labour back benchers spoke against the proposed 11.30 am start on the grounds that it would interfere too much with select committee work and Westminster Hall debates, and that rising by 7 pm was unnecessarily early. In divisions all the main proposals made by the Modernisation Committee were accepted, though some quite narrowly. MPs agreed to sit from 11.30 am to 7 pm on Tuesdays and Wednesdays and from 11.30 to 6 pm on Thursdays, and to regular September sittings. The House approved the carry-over of Bills from one session to the next, and agreed to make permanent the provision for debates in Westminster Hall. Peers spent the day debating the **Animal Health Bill** at report stage with the Government suffering two further defeats in the division lobby. First an Opposition amendment designed to strengthen the control regime on meat imports was carried against the Government by 182 votes to 129. Second, an amendment to extend the national contingency plan to include other dangerous contagious animal diseases besides foot-and-mouth was approved by 179 votes to 133.

On *30 October* the House of Commons considered Lords' amendments to the **Enterprise Bill**, voting to delete those providing for a statutory post of chief executive at the Office of Fair Trading separate from that of chairman, and those allowing the courts to transfer cases to the Competition Appeal Tribunal. But on the Lords amendment raising the threshold of turnover below which companies would escape monopolies and merger investigations the Government compromised by agreeing a threshold of £70 million rather than its original £40 million. The House of Lords debated the **Adoption and Children Bill** at third reading that day.

MPs held the last of their five themed debates on defence on a Government motion for the adjournment on *31 October* focusing on defence within the UK. Peers debated the **Nationality, Immigration and Asylum Bill** with the Government suffering four further defeats, first on the power of the Home Secretary to amend the Bill using "Henry VIII" powers (171 to 116); second to restrict the maximum time anyone spent in an accommodation centre to four months (144 to 121); third to strengthen the obligation on Government to ensure appropriate legal advice is available in accommodation centres (147 to 103); and fourth to clarify the position with regard to the deportation of asylum seekers who have criminal records (96 to 93). Finally just after midnight the Bill passed the House.

On Friday *1 November* the Commons did not sit, but the Lords did and debated two reports from the European Union Committee on asylum and on refugee status. A Prayer moved by Lord Howell of Guildford calling for the annulment of regulations relating to Zimbabwean financial assets was withdrawn after debate.

4 – 7 NOVEMBER
On *4 November* MPs debated Lords' amendments to the **Adoption and Children Bill** on the rights of unmarried couples of different or the same sex to adopt. In a passionate five-hour debate all agreed that the welfare of the child was paramount, but there were sharp differences of view about whether this would best be served by allowing unmarried couples to adopt. The Conservative Opposition

imposed a three-line whip which resulted in John Bercow resigning his front-bench post to speak and vote against his party line, as did other senior Conservatives, including Kenneth Clarke and Michael Portillo. By 344 votes to 145 the House reversed the position taken by the Lords. The Government was defeated six times in the Lords division lobbies that day. Four of these defeats were during the final stages of the **Animal Health Bill;** by 165 votes to 128 the House voted to clarify the 20-day livestock movement restriction rule. Then by 174 to 132 peers amended rules relating to warrants for entry and slaughter. Finally by 167 to 139 and 169 to 130 the House supported amendments to extend the list of those that must be consulted and informed on mandatory bio-security measures. Peers then considered MPs' amendments to the **Enterprise Bill** with the Government suffering a further defeat by 148 votes to 136 on whether corporate bodies such as OFT ought to have separate chairmen and chief executives. Then by 147 votes to 129 the Government was defeated on the extent of OFT's obligation to keep to the generally accepted principles of good corporate governance.

On 5 *November* Lords amendments to the **Nationality, Immigration and Asylum Bill** were considered in the Commons. On the location of accommodation centres the Government pointed to adjustments made to the Bill, but the Opposition still expressed disquiet at ministerial intentions. Lords amendments on the schooling of the children of detained asylum seekers were also defeated. MPs then turned to the **Enterprise Bill**, with a Government compromise amendment providing that the posts of chief executive and chairman of OFT would be combined only for a transitional period of two years up to 2005 being agreed. Peers spent over three hours debating the Commons change to the **Adoption and Children Bill** which allowed adoption by unmarried couples, with the Conservative Opposition moving that the House insist on its amendments on this point. Some peers wanted to allow heterosexual couples to adopt, whether married or not, but reject adoption by couples of the same sex, but by 184 to 215 peers voted to accept the Commons version of the Bill. Later a debate on the select committee report on the crash of the Chinook helicopter on the Mull of Kintyre in 1994 took place, with Lord Chalfont moving that the Government "set aside the finding of gross negligence", a view rejected on a government whip by 34 votes to 65.

On 6 *November* Margaret Beckett, Secretary of State for Environment, Food and Rural Affairs, made a Statement indicating the Government's acceptance of recommendations made in official reports on the foot-and-mouth crisis. Slaughter would remain the basic strategy but "emergency vaccination could form part of the control strategy from the start". MPs then turned to consider Lords' amendments to the **Animal Health Bill**, with a compromise amendment on vaccination resisted by Conservative and Liberal Democrat spokesmen being carried on division by 314 votes to 190. Other Lords' amendments on the so-called 20-day rule and on powers of entry were overturned. Peers considered the decisions of the Commons in relation to their amendments to the **Nationality, Immigration and Asylum Bill**. On the location of proposed accommodation centres the Lords (in debating the deletion of their earlier amendment) considered an Opposition alternative stating that regard must be given to the needs of the persons to be accommodated. This was resisted by the Government on the grounds that it would "open up scope for unreasonable challenges to the location of accommodation centres", but was carried against the Government by 171 votes to 120. On the question of schooling for children held in accommodation centres, the Bishop of Portsmouth moved for the rejection of the Commons compromise, but his motion was lost by 52 votes to 84. Soon after 11 pm the House turned again to the **Enterprise Bill**, with peers quickly agreeing the compromise already endorsed by the Commons on the separation of the appointments of chairman and chief executive of OFT.

On the final day of the session, 7 *November*, peers began the day by debating the Commons response to their changes to the **Animal Health Bill**. On the issue of giving priority to vaccination, Lord Greaves for the Liberal Democrats said that the Government amendment represented a "substantial victory" for the House of Lords. Without a division the House agreed to this, as it did also to the removal of its amendment concerning the 20-day rule. However, on powers of entry Lord Greaves moved a motion rejecting the Commons version and this was carried by 144 votes to 108. The Bill was immediately returned to the Commons. Meanwhile in the lower House MPs debated the message received from the Lords on the **Nationality, Immigration and Asylum Bill**, with David Blunkett, Home Secretary, moving to reject the Lords amendment concerned with the location of asylum centres, but proposing instead a compromise involving monitoring accommodation centres to ensure their location did not prevent residents' needs being met. This was carried by 248 votes to 38 with Liberal Democrats sustaining opposition. Then the House returned again to the **Animal Health**

Bill with the Government moving that the House insist on its disagreement with the Lords on amendments concerned with powers of entry, but again offering a compromise whereby information and representations made by a farmer to a district veterinary officer would be included in the information set before a magistrate. This was agreed without a division. After an adjournment peers returned to consider the **Nationality, Immigration and Asylum Bill**, with the Conservative front bench saying the Government amendment agreed in the Commons earlier that day represented a substantial concession, a view endorsed from the Liberal Democrat benches. After a further adjournment peers returned to consider again the **Animal Health Bill**, with a welcome being given by the Liberal Democrats to the last-minute changes made to the Bill. These and other Bills were given Royal Assent, following which the Lord Chancellor read the prorogation speech bringing the session to an end.

2002-03 SESSION

13 – 15 NOVEMBER
The Queen's Speech opening the new session of Parliament was delivered on Wednesday *13 November.* In the Commons George Foulkes moved the Loyal Address in reply, which was seconded by Oona King. Both followed tradition in speaking humorously of their parliamentary experiences. Oona King spoke about race, making a plea "as one of only two black or ethnic minority women ever elected to the British Parliament" for a more representative democracy, and also spoke movingly of the evidence of genocide she had witnessed during a recent visit to Rwanda. The Leader of the Opposition, Iain Duncan Smith, said parts of the Government programme were welcome, such as promised legislation on licensing reform and the introduction of a single media regulator. But he criticised the Government for failing "to reform public services, which is why they are having to spend so much money". Responding, the Prime Minister was very critical of Conservative party proposals and emphasised the fundamental differences between the two main parties on a wide range of issues. The Liberal Democrat leader, Charles Kennedy, said there was a basic issue of philosophical principle and policy distinction between his party and the Government over proposals to reduce the rights of defendants in criminal cases. In later speeches Andrew Mackinlay said he was concerned that the reference in the Speech to giving further consideration to reform of the House of Lords "was parliamentary speak for kicking into touch", but Clive Soley intervened to say that the Joint Select Committee on reform, of which he was a member, would not allow this to happen. Peter Bottomley criticised the slow governmental and parliamentary response to the implementation of reports from the Law Commission, while David Amess asked: "What is the point of any legislation, given that laws are not enforced?"

On *14 November* John Prescott as Deputy Prime Minister made a Statement on the firemen's strike saying Sir George Bain's interim report recommended "an increase in the pay bill of up to 11 per cent over two years, subject to necessary and long overdue modernisation", and he appealed to the firemen to "talk not walk". The Queen's Speech debate then dealt with health and pensions. Alan Milburn, Secretary of State for Health, explained the Government's thinking in relation to so-called foundation hospitals. Liam Fox for the Opposition promised support for some of the Government proposals. Stephen Byers in his first Commons speech since moving to the back benches said the country was increasingly divided between the "asset-poor and the asset-rich". For the Liberal Democrats Evan Harris described the Government's plans as a "re-re-re-reform Bill" because it was their fourth attempt to reform the health service. Frank Dobson said he disliked the proposals for foundation hospitals.

Debate continued on *15 November* on education, culture, media and sport. Charles Clarke, Secretary of State for Education, opened by saying that setting standards of achievement was at the core of the Government programme. He also thanked leaders of the university world, who he said had been very understanding of his wish to delay publication of the White Paper on higher education funding so that as the new minister he would have "a chance to read the material and understand the issues fully".

In the House of Lords the Loyal Address in reply was moved on *13 November* by Baroness Turner of Camden and seconded by Lord Alli. Lord Strathclyde, Leader of the Conservative peers, reckoned the promised Criminal Justice Bill was the eleventh or twelfth since 1997, and said that since Labour came to power it "has been a case of tax and spend, and churn so much, and achieve so little". Baroness Williams of Crosby referred to the Civil Service Bill and the Mental Health Bill as the dogs that did not bark. Lord Williams of Mostyn, Leader of the House, said the House had sat for 200 days in the previous session, and that the Government had been defeated 56 times in divisions, "more than any Government since 1977". He said the House needed to "work carefully in continuing recognition of the undisputed primacy of the Commons", and that the "Government remain committed to further reform" of the House. On Thursday *14 November* the House met at its new Thursday time of 11 am, and adjourned from 1.30 to 3 pm. In debate on foreign affairs, international development and defence, Lord Howell of Guildford said: "The concern to create a European superpower is an elitist's dream. It is utterly remote from the people of Europe, and will not bring a single benefit to Europe's citizens". Lord Maclennan of Rogart said the citizens of Europe would "appear to favour greater coherence in the delivery of a common foreign policy". Many peers spoke about the Iraqi situation. Lord Howe of Aberavon said that in the coming months "restraint will be as necessary as resolution, wisdom as necessary as determination". The House of Lords did not sit on Friday *15 November*.

18 – 21 NOVEMBER

On *18 November* MPs continued debate on the Queen's Speech, focusing on the economy, trade and industry. The Chancellor Gordon Brown said that continent by continent we faced "the first simultaneous world slowdown for almost 30 years", but that in the UK there were 1.5 million more jobs than in 1997. Kenneth Clarke said the Chancellor was skating on very thin ice, and that present growth was dependent on a housing boom and an associated boom in consumer spending which had lifted household debt to 109 per cent of gross domestic product.

On *19 November* the Queen's Speech debate focused on the regions, transport and Defra, with an Opposition amendment critical of the burden of regulation on business and of the centralising nature of the Government's plans for regional and local government. Much of the debate focused on the proposed regional assemblies. On *20 November*, the sixth and final day of the debate, Oliver Letwin moved the Opposition amendment that expressed regret at the "failure of the Government to address the central issues of crime today". Chris Mullin, Chairman of the Home Affairs Select Committee said: "We live in a society where an increased sense of rights has been matched by a diminishing sense of responsibility". Sir Brian Mawhinney said the Government had created expectations they were incapable of fulfilling, and as an example he cited the Crime and Disorder Act 1998. Many MPs spoke with feeling of the effect of anti-social behaviour in their constituencies. The Opposition amendment was defeated by 152 votes to 372, and the Liberal Democrat amendment by 55 votes to 319. During the six-day debate on the Queen's Speech 149 MPs made speeches.

In the upper House the debate on Monday *18 November* dealt with regional and local government, education, environment and rural affairs, with peers especially focusing on proposals for regional assemblies and for reform of university finances. On *19 November* debate was on health and social affairs, and on *20 November* on economic and industrial affairs, culture and media. On the final day, *21 November*, peers concentrated on home affairs and criminal justice, with a number of peers speaking out strongly against the proposed reforms to the criminal justice system. The Lord Chancellor concluded with a robust reply saying: "those who trumpet a liberal position must always be on guard against falling into the conservative error that no change is ever possible". Debate on the Queen's Speech concluded with 141 peers having made speeches spread over the six days.

Back in the Commons on *21 November* MPs debated the Common Fisheries Policy and then the representation of smaller parties on select committees. MPs also heard a Statement from the Deputy Prime Minister, John Prescott, on the impending eight-day firemen's strike.

25 – 28 NOVEMBER

The Prime Minister answered an urgent question from the Leader of the Opposition on *25 November* on the firemen's dispute, saying that he deeply regretted the continuation of the dispute and believed it was not justified. Following this Tony Blair made a Statement on the Prague NATO summit which had decided to issue to seven East European countries invitations to join NATO. MPs then debated a Government motion expressing support for UN Security Council resolution 1441 on Iraq. Jack Straw, Foreign Secretary, made clear that this did not stipulate there had to be a second resolution to authorise military action in the event of a material breach by Iraq, but went on to say the preference of the Government would in those circumstances be for a second resolution. He also said that any decision to take military action would "be put before the House as soon as possible after it has been taken", but that the safety of our forces may require an element of surprise in the taking of action. The Conservative spokesman, Michael Ancram, supported the Government, but the Liberal Democrats moved an amendment stipulating that both a further UN resolution and a substantive motion in the House should be passed before military action took place. The Liberal Democrat amendment was defeated by 85 votes to 452. Peers debated a motion stating that "subject to the requirements of business, in 2003 the summer recess should begin not later than the middle of July and the House should sit for two weeks in September". While the Conservative Leader, Lord Strathclyde, supported the proposal, a number of other senior peers opposed it, but on a division it was carried by 160 votes to 76. Baroness Symons of Vernham Dean then introduced the second reading of the **Arms Control and Disarmament (Inspections) Bill**, saying this would deal with amendments made in 1999 to the 1990 Treaty on Conventional Armed Forces in Europe.

On *26 November* John Prescott, Deputy Prime Minister, made a further Statement on the fire dispute calling for negotiations to take place. He then introduced the second reading of the **Regional Assemblies (Preparations) Bill**, which he said was "at the heart of our programme to modernise our constitution, to decentralise power and to deliver better public services". For the Conservatives David Davis moved an amendment saying the Bill was a centralising measure that would undermine local democracy. For the Liberal Democrats Edward Davey said his party supported the Bill as far as it went but wanted greater devolution. Several MPs argued that creating assemblies where members represented some 250,000 voters each, and abolishing county councils would take government further away from the people rather than bring it closer to them. The Opposition motion was defeated by 141 votes to 389, and the Bill then approved at second reading by 386 to 134, with a programme motion being carried by 318 votes to 178. The House of Lords debated the **Licensing Bill** at second reading, with Baroness Blackstone, Minister of State at the Department of Culture, Media and Sport, saying this would "provide greater choice tempered with the provision of strengthened protection". For the Opposition Baroness Buscombe said she feared the Bill would lead to "higher costs and more regulation".

On *27 November* the Chancellor, Gordon Brown, gave his pre-budget report, saying that last year the British economy was the fastest growing of the world's major economies. From the Opposition front bench Michael Howard said this was "a moment of humiliation" for the Chancellor because his forecasts on growth, revenue, borrowing and the deficit had all been proved wrong. The House then debated the **Health (Wales) Bill** which the Secretary of State for Wales, Peter Hain, said had been subject to pre-legislative scrutiny both by the House through its select committee, and by the National Assembly for Wales. The Bill was not opposed but the programme motion for its consideration was, though carried by 240 votes to 72. In Westminster Hall Graham Allen introduced a debate on the European Constitution, making a range of unfavourable comparisons between the American Founding Fathers and the Convention on the Future of Europe. One of these concerned the language used; the draft prepared by Giscard d'Estaing had "all the inspiration of the EU sheep meat directive". Lord Baker of Dorking introduced a debate on university finance in the upper House in which 30 peers made speeches, most of which were highly critical of government handling of the universities.

On *28 November* Alistair Darling, Secretary of State for Transport, made a Statement on consultation on airport capacity, saying the Government now accepted that Gatwick must be included in the consultation exercise. This was followed by a Statement from Patricia Hewitt, Secretary of State for Trade and Industry, on British Energy, in which she explained why the Government were making a credit facility of £650 million available to the company. MPs debated the **Community Care (Delayed Discharges etc.) Bill** at second reading, with Alan Milburn, Secretary of State for Health, saying it was about tackling problems that arose when partnership between hospitals and social services did not work effectively. For the Opposition Liam Fox said it would undermine successful working partnerships and impose a negative fining system rather than promote positive policies to tackle the problem. Among Labour members who criticised the Bill was David Hinchliffe, chairman of the Health Select Committee. After the Opposition amendment had been defeated by 136 votes to 238, the Bill was approved at second reading, then a programme motion was agreed by 228 votes to 119. In Westminster Hall Gwyneth Dunwoody, chairman of the Transport Select Committee, introduced a debate on a report from that Committee on the Government's 10-year transport plan.

The House of Lords debated the UN resolution on Iraq. Lord Howell of Guildford said Saddam Hussein was a "uniquely dangerous threat to Europe and the United States" because he combined weapons of mass destruction with support for several terrorist groups. Some peers questioned the linking of Iraq with the US war on terrorism, but others said Iraq had a long history of supporting terrorism and the minister replying to the debate, Lord Bach, said that the Government kept "an open mind on links with Al'Quaeda".

2 – 5 DECEMBER

David Blunkett, Home Secretary, made a Statement on *2 December* on the agreement to close the Sangatte Centre in northern France and the UK's acceptance of up to 1000 Iraqis on work visas. Ian Paisley then introduced a debate on policing in Northern Ireland on this unallotted Opposition half-day with a motion declaring that IRA representatives were "not fit to participate in the government of part of the United Kingdom", and expressing opposition to "offering non-elected convicted terrorists places in district policing partnerships". His motion was defeated by 6 votes to 298. Following this Peter Hain, Secretary of State for Wales, but speaking as the Government's representative on the Convention on the Future of Europe, introduced a debate on that Convention. He said that radical reform was needed as the EU expanded to 25 members, and in his view this had to begin with the Council of Ministers where "first and foremost democratic accountability lies". For the Opposition Michael Ancram said everything the Government was doing was moving in an integrationist direction, the opposite to the "partnership of sovereign states" which he espoused. Peers debated the **Crime (International Co-operation) Bill** at second reading that day, with Lord Filkin, Under-Secretary at the Home Office, presenting the Bill as mainly implementing Schengen measures. Baroness Anelay of St Johns for the Opposition said her party wholeheartedly supported that part of the Bill dealing with terrorism, but that the rest looked as if "the Government are leading us gently by the nose into Schengen by the back door".

Alan Michael, Minister for Rural Affairs, made a Statement on hunting with dogs on *3 December* in which he argued that cruelty and utility were two principles that "ran like a golden thread through the Bill" he was publishing. Charles Clarke, Secretary of State for Education and Skills, then made a Statement on the Tomlinson Inquiry into A-level results, the recommendations of which – mainly for greater transparency and professionalism – the Government accepted. MPs debated at second reading the **Communications Bill** with Tessa Jowell, Secretary of State for Culture, Media and Sport, paying tribute to the pre-legislative scrutiny given to the Bill by a joint committee chaired by Lord Puttnam during the previous session; she said the Government had accepted "more than 120 of its 148 recommendations". But the Bill was the first that could not receive ministerial endorsement for compatibility with the Human Rights Act 1998. A hostile amendment moved by Simon Thomas on behalf of the Nationalist parties emphasised the failure to secure representation for Scotland and Wales on the proposed regulatory body, but was defeated by 14 votes to 329, following which a programme motion was accepted by 287 votes to 102. In the Lords the second reading debate on the **Waste and Emissions Trading Bill** took place with a number of speakers, including the spokesmen for both Opposition parties, expressing disappointment with the Bill.

On *4 December* David Blunkett, Home Secretary, introduced the second reading debate on this session's **Criminal Justice Bill**, saying this was a further step in the process of pulling "together a range of issues that are relevant to the reform and modernisation of the criminal justice system". Chris Mullin, chairman of the Home Affairs Select Committee, drew attention to a report on the Bill from his Committee published that day, but said how difficult it was to give proper scrutiny when the Bill that had only been published 13 days earlier. Robert Marshall-Andrews said parts of the Bill were "conspicuously and dreadfully bad", including the "assault on jury trial". Other speakers expressed concern at the provisions on "double jeopardy" and those on disclosure of previous convictions. The Conservative Opposition did not divide against the Bill, which was, however, opposed by the Liberal Democrats, but approved by 303 votes to 67. A programme motion was opposed by the Conservatives, but carried by 345 votes to 58. Peers debated crime prevention on the initiative of Lord Dholakia who said the links between social exclusion and crime were very clear, and that "we spend over £10 billion on the criminal process but less than £500 million on crime prevention".

On *5 December* Nick Raynsford, Minister for Local Government and the Regions, made a Statement on the local government financial settlement for 2003-04, indicating an 8 per cent increase in support from government grant and business rates. MPs then debated Government drugs policy on this the first Estimates Day of the session, based on a report from the Home Affairs Select Committee. Introducing this Chris Mullin, committee chairman, argued that cannabis and ecstasy though harmful should be re-categorised because they did so much less damage than crack cocaine and heroin. But the Conservative spokesman, Nick Hawkins, argued that any such reclassification would send out the wrong signals. Peter Lilley disagreed with his front-bench spokesman, saying the "attempt to demonise cannabis had done immense harm". Concluding the debate Chris Mullin said it had been excellent and that it illustrated a great strength of select committees, which allowed a mature debate to take place on issues that could not be so discussed otherwise within the political system. In Westminster Hall another select committee report was debated, that from the International Development Committee on global climate change and sustainable development. Peers debated the report from the Select Committee on Stem Cell Research introduced by the committee chairman the Bishop of Oxford. Most broadly supported the conclusions of the committee, namely that stem cell research on embryonic stem cells should be allowed as currently provided for and regulated by legislation.

9 – 12 DECEMBER

On Monday *9 December* Charles Clarke, Secretary of State for Education and Skills, made a Statement on his departmental spending plans announcing extra funding to "enable local authorities to provide universal nursery education for three-year-olds", and an increase in funding per school pupil of "at least 3.2 per cent". John Denham, Minister for Policing, Crime Reduction and Community Service, then introduced the second reading debate on the **Extradition Bill** which would he said "bring 19th century extradition arrangements into the very different world of the 21st century". Much of the debate focused on part one of the Bill dealing with the European Arrest warrant. Second reading was agreed by 325 votes to 146, and a programme motion was accepted by 321 votes to 149. The House of Lords debated the **Courts Bill** at second reading. The Lord Chancellor, Lord Irvine of Lairg, said this built on the Auld Report and would create a single executive agency responsible for the administration of all courts in England and Wales. For the Opposition Baroness Seccombe said that like so many government Bills this was described by ministers as decentralising, yet "study reveals that it is completely the opposite". Other speakers took up this criticism, including Lord Goodhart, who said the Liberal Democrats wanted to see much more devolution and local management. The Lord Chief Justice, Lord Woolf, opened his speech by commenting on the unique privilege he had among chief justices around the world in being able directly to address the legislature, adding: "I value that privilege, but I am conscious that it should be used sparingly".

On *10 December* Alistair Darling, Secretary of State for Transport, made a Statement on transport investment, saying the Government was simultaneously trying to cope with the challenges of economic success while also "dealing with the problems resulting from decades of under-investment in our transport infrastructure". MPs then debated the **European Parliamentary (Representation) Bill** at second reading which Yvette Cooper, Parliamentary Secretary in the Lord Chancellor's Department, said would allow for the reduction of UK MEPs from 87 to 72 to provide space in a 732-member European Parliament for representation from new members states. The Bill would also allow the people of Gibraltar to be represented in the parliament for the first time. Angus Robertson said the existing disparity by which Scotland had half the representation of Denmark, though similar sized populations would get worse. The Bill was unopposed in the division lobby, nor was the programme motion opposed. Lord McIntosh of Haringey opened a debate that day on the Government's pre-budget report; Lord Howe of Aberavon said the Chancellor had been "carried away by euphoric insights into his own performance".

On *11 December* Jack Straw, Home Secretary, made a Statement on the report of the Intelligence and Security Committee on the October Bali bombing, saying that since September 2001 the volume of material available to intelligence agencies had increased by a factor of at least ten. Later Jack Straw introduced a debate on European affairs with particular reference to the Copenhagen Summit about to take place. He especially emphasised the significance of the creation of a "new Europe – a unified political and economic entity that is larger than the United States of America and Japan combined". Michael Ancram from the Opposition front bench said there should be a referendum on the outcome of the Convention on the Future of Europe. Two former cabinet ministers introduced debates in Westminster Hall that day, first Kenneth Clarke on policing in Nottinghamshire, then Stephen Byers on the Common Agricultural Policy in relation to the Copenhagen Summit. In the Lords a debate took place on "the growth of government and its attendant regulations and the case for action to reduce them".

On *12 December* MPs debated Government responses to the reports on foot-and-mouth disease and reports from the Agriculture Select Committee on that subject and on the future of agriculture. Margaret Beckett, Secretary of State for Environment, Food and Rural Affairs, introduced the Government's self-congratulatory motion, which was opposed in an amendment moved by the Opposition spokesman, David Lidington. The amendment was defeated by 145 votes to 238, and the government motion accepted by 232 votes to 141. In the Lords that day peers debated the **Licensing Bill** in committee. Among amendments considered was one from the Bishop of London seeking exemption for places of worship in regard to licensing for plays and concerts, which was withdrawn when Baroness Blackstone said the Government would give further consideration to this point.

16 – 19 DECEMBER

The Prime Minister in a Statement on *16 December* said the European Council meeting in Copenhagen had successfully concluded negotiations to admit ten new countries, bringing the total size of the EU to 450 million people. Later the House debated the **Hunting Bill** at second reading with the Minster for Rural Affairs, Alan Michael, setting out the regulation option embodied in the Bill, but saying this could be amended to provide for a total ban. From the Opposition front-bench David Lidington moved an amendment saying the Bill would "impose unjustifiable restrictions on individual freedom", and "increase the suffering of foxes", as well as "rob British citizens of their livelihood". While the Minister had argued that the Bill was based on clear ethical principles, this was strongly contested by other speakers. At the close of a lively debate the House voted five times, approving second reading by 368 votes (including 6 Conservatives) to 155 (including 3 Labour), and a programme motion by 331 to 165. Peers debated the **Police (Northern Ireland) Bill** at second reading, with Lord Williams of Mostyn saying the Bill would amend legislation enacted in 2000 to give greater flexibility to arrangements.

On *December 17* Andrew Smith, Secretary of State for Work and Pensions, made a Statement introducing a Green Paper on pensions. Alistair Darling, Secretary of State for Transport, then made a Statement on transport investment, saying the Government was committed to spending £180 billion over ten years on public and private transport investment. Following this Barbara Roche, Minister for Social Exclusion, introduced the second reading of the **Planning and Compulsory Purchase Bill**, which she said introduced a reformed planning system which would be faster and fairer. The Bill was approved at second reading by 320 votes to 182, and a programme motion was passed by 353 votes to 142. Peers debated the **Licensing Bill** in committee with many probing amendments being moved and withdrawn on promises of further ministerial thinking. Lord Phillips of Sudbury said that if passed in its present form the Bill would be a "catastrophe for national amenity".

Helen Liddell, Secretary of State for Scotland, made a Statement on *18 December* saying there was strong support for keeping the Scottish Parliament at its present size of 129, rather than reducing it to around 104 when the number of Westminster seats in Scotland was reduced. The House then debated the **Regional Assemblies Bill** in committee. Peers debated the British Constitution on a motion moved by Lord Norton of Louth, chairman of the House Constitution Committee, who argued that the changes enacted under the present Government had no coherence and had resulted in a new constitutional "unsettlement". Lord Sheldon said there had been a diminution in the House of Commons, election to which was now "largely obtained by means of persevering in party politics". Lord Holme of Cheltenham said that the constitution had something of the characteristic of a mirage, while the former Speaker of the Commons, Lord Weatherill, said he was "increasingly alarmed by the way in which our constitution is overridden by a flood of European directives and regulations". The Lord Chancellor, Lord Irvine, in reply argued that the Government's approach had been "pragmatism based on principle, without the need for an all-embracing theory". A debate on the possibility of the 2012 Olympic Games being sited in London then took place with all 13 peers who spoke strongly supporting such a bid.

Thursday *19 December* was the last day before the Christmas recess, with main business in the Commons being adjournment debates. All told 27 MPs made speeches on diverse issues many of them constituency related. Ben Bradshaw, Parliamentary Secretary at the Privy Council Office then replied, saying that the subjects raised, in order of frequency were: the NHS, transport, crime, pensions, "bad councils", and the international situation. Peers spent most of the day considering further the **Licensing Bill** in committee with once again no divisions but lots of probing amendments and Government promises to think further about the provisions in the Bill. Among five statutory instruments approved after brief debates at the end of the day was the Regulatory Reform (Special Occasions Licensing) Order 2002. This made permanent the relaxation in licensing first introduced for the Millennium New Year's eve, allowing pubs to stay open throughout the night until the start of licensing hours on New Year's day, thus providing for continuous serving of alcohol for 36 hours.

7 – 9 JANUARY

Both Houses returned from the Christmas recess on *7 January*. Geoffrey Hoon, Secretary of State for Defence, made a Statement on Iraq saying call-out notices were being sent to 1,500 reservists, who were only called up when "absolutely necessary". Tam Dalyell made an application for an emergency debate but this was refused by the Speaker (who also declined another request for such a debate from Tam Dalyell the following day). The House then considered at second reading the **Local Government Bill**. The Minister for Local Government and the Regions, Nick Raynsford, said this was "an ambitious and far-reaching Bill, which extends substantial new freedoms and benefits to local government". For the Opposition Eric Pickles moved an amendment describing the Bill as "a centralising measure that will have the effect of undermining local democracy"; this was defeated by 141 votes to 370, and the Bill then approved by 368 to 142, with a programme motion being accepted by 318 votes to 183. In Westminster Hall that day Julia Drown initiated a debate on foundation hospitals arguing that the Government had done much that was good for the NHS but that these proposed reforms could be divisive and constitute a dangerous distraction. Peers began business with tributes to Lord Jenkins of Hillhead who died at the week-end. Baroness Scotland of Asthal, Parliamentary Secretary, Lord Chancellor's Department, then initiated a debate on the Convention on the Future of Europe, arguing among other things that taxation and social security, as well as foreign and defence policy, "must remain matters for national governments and parliaments". Lord Maclennan of Rogart said the EU was already a "living constitutional polity, with executive, legislative and judicial arms . . . polity unlike a state only in the limitation of its powers". The Bishop of St Albans said that in the new European institutions "God is simply discounted and denied". Lord Wallace of Saltaire said that in the ten months since the Convention opened no Green Paper had appeared and it was now "time for the Government to be more active". But Baroness Symons of Vernham Dean replying for the Government said "we have from June 2003 probably until May 2004 to develop the national debate".

The first Opposition Day of the session was taken on *8 January*, with a Conservative motion welcoming the principle of foundation hospitals and urging the Government to allow all hospitals to bid for foundation status. In moving this Liam Fox referred to an early day motion expressing concern at the introduction of such status for some hospitals signed by 109 Labour back benchers. The former Labour Secretary of State for Health, Frank Dobson, said most of his concern about foundation hospitals was practical, but he also had ideological objections. The Opposition motion was defeated by 144 votes to 381. In the upper House Lord Toombs initiated a debate on the electricity supply industry, and Lord Russell-Johnston one on the Balkans.

On *9 January* MPs considered the **Health (Wales) Bill** on report, and then approved the Bill (which had passed all its Commons stages without amendment) at third reading. Peers debated and approved at second reading the **Voting Age (Reduction to 16) Bill** introduced by Lord Lucas, upon which the Government front-bench spokesman, Lord Bassam, declared Government neutrality. Baroness Gardner of Parkes then took her **High Hedges Bill** through its committee stage without amendment, and Lord Campbell of Alloway re-introduced his **Public Services (Disruption) Bill** for second reading debate following its lapse at the end of the previous session. Later Baroness Finlay of Llandaff introduced a short debate on the Public Health Laboratory Service, explaining her concern about the reorganisation of the service and the vulnerability this represented at a time of bio-terrorist threat.

13 – 16 JANUARY

Following question time on *13 January* Tam Dalyell again raised as a point of order the fact that while press conferences and discussion about possible war with Iraq could proliferate, it remained impossible for the House of Commons to discuss these "very important issues". This was reinforced by five further interventions from different MPs, before the Speaker said that he hoped "Ministers would come to make statements at appropriate times". This was taken as the second Opposition Day, with Oliver Letwin from the Conservative front bench moving two different motions. The first concerned gun crime and burglary and spoke of the "apparent inability of the Government to provide a coherent long-term strategy" to deal with these problems; this was defeated by 152 votes to 365. The second called for mandatory intensive treatment and rehabilitation for young heroin and cocaine addicts, and was defeated by 143 votes to 375. Peers spent a fourth committee day on the **Licensing Bill** with the Government suffering its first defeat of the session by a single vote. This occurred when the House supported by 112 votes to 111 an amendment designed to give Members of Parliament an "interested party" status for licence applications for premises in their constituencies, with parallel status for MEPs, and for local councillors within their wards.

The Speaker allowed an urgent question on *14 January* on the subject of security at Sizewell nuclear power station, following entry the previous evening by Greenpeace activists. The Government said no penetration of secure areas had taken place. Roy Beggs moved a motion on Northern Ireland education, this being taken as an unallotted Opposition half Day. This was followed by a debate on a bid for the 2012 Olympics opened by Tessa Jowell, Secretary of State for Culture, Media and Sport, on a government motion for the adjournment. Among some sharply contested views were those expressed by the Chairman of the Departmental Select Committee, Gerald Kaufman, who said any public sector project would cost far more than estimated. Peers briefly debated a report establishing that from autumn 2004 expense claims made by individual peers for the sessions 2001–02 onwards would be published in accordance with provisions of the Freedom of Information Act 2000. Baroness Harris of Richmond then introduced a debate on an EU Committee report on flexibility in European labour markets, and this was followed by a debate on a special report from the Delegated Powers and Regulatory Reform Committee on Henry VIII powers. Initiating this the Committee chairman, Lord Dahrendorf, drew attention to the desirability of wording such clauses so that they were restricted in their application.

On *15 January* David Blunkett, Home Secretary, made a Statement on the murder of Detective Constable Stephen Oake during police operations in Manchester the previous day. The Secretary of State for Defence, Geoffrey Hoon, then made a Statement saying the Government would agree to an American request for the upgrade of Fylingdales because of the "increase to the threat to our security from weapons of mass destruction and their means of delivery". MPs then completed work on the **Community Care Bill**. Simon Burns for the Conservatives described this as a "nasty and flawed measure" which in "no shape or form recognises the crisis in long-term care in Britain". The Labour Chairman of the Health Select Committee, David Hinchliffe, said he could not support the Bill because "it is a bad measure that has not been thought through". Sir George Young said it would receive "very serious consideration" when it reached the House of Lords, and Paul Burstow said his party, the Liberal Democrats, would do all they could to ensure that it did "not have a safe passage" through the Lords. Third reading was approved by 323 votes to 188. In the upper House peers debated sentencing policy, with many references to the reported conflict of view between the Lord Chief Justice and the Lord Chancellor, especially on the appropriate sentence for burglary. Baroness Cumberledge then introduced a debate on maternity services, making a powerful call for fewer births by caesarian section.

On *16 January* Elliot Morley, Under-Secretary of State for Environment, Food and Rural Affairs, introduced a debate to take note of the outcome of the EU Fisheries Council saying that he had "no illusions about the severe impact that the recovery proposals finally agreed will have on sections of our white fish fleet". Austin Mitchell offered congratulations to the Minister, but said that it was the foolishness of the Conservative Government of 1972 in accepting a programme of equal access to a common resource that was the root of the present disaster. Peers debated the **Licensing Bill** in committee, with Lord Faulkner of Worcester introducing as an amendment the private member's bill he had taken through the House the previous session outlawing sex discrimination in private members' clubs. The amendments were withdrawn on the offer by the Minister in charge to discuss changes to be brought forward later during the Bill's passage.

20 – 23 JANUARY

20 January was then taken as the third Opposition Day, with first a debate on occupational pensions taking place on a Conservative motion expressing "deep concern at current arrangements for winding-up" such pensions. For the Liberal Democrats Steve Webb criticised the narrow scope of the motion saying it "was about carving up an inadequate pot more fairly", when the real problem was the inaction of the Government on the larger question of pension provision. The motion was defeated by 191 votes to 315. Liam Fox then moved a second motion concerned with the Food Supplements Directive, which he said would result in some 270 safe and popular nutrient sources being lost to consumers in the UK. The Opposition motion was defeated by 196 votes to 309. Peers continued with the committee stage of the **Licensing Bill**, and then began committee consideration of the **Courts Bill**.

On *21 January* both Houses debated reform of the House of Lords on a motion taking note from the report of the Joint Select Committee chaired by Jack Cunningham. The Leader of the House, Robin Cook, confirmed that no collective view would be expressed by the Government. In the Commons the former Conservative leader William Hague said: "The powers and ability of this House and of Parliament as a whole are inadequate to bring proper balance to our constitution. It is possible to govern with authority without being able to legislate with impunity. Today, however, the Government expects to be able to do both. That is why Parliament as a whole needs to be strengthened". Kenneth Clarke said the real concern was to strengthen Parliament's control over the Executive and that he preferred a 100 per cent elected House, but that he was prepared to compromise and have some appointed members. Tony Wright, chairman of the Public Administration Select Committee, said the second chamber needed a membership that would make it legitimate, otherwise its decisions could be "routinely rolled over" by Government whips. Sir Patrick Cormack said that for over seven months a group called the campaign for an effective second chamber had been meeting and advocated a wholly appointed House. George Howarth said 90 members supported an early day motion he had put down calling for the abolition of the second chamber and that this ought to be an option on which the House could vote. In the upper House Lord Howe of Aberavon, as deputy chairman of the joint committee, introduced the debate. He suggested a "hybrid" or mixed House would probably prove essential, and argued that representativeness, independence, expertise and legitimacy were four essential qualities in the reformed House. Lord Carter supported an all-appointed House. Baroness Williams of Crosby said the Parliament Acts already underpinned the primacy of the Commons, and that the public was "deeply distrustful of a House composed entirely or largely of political appointments". Lord Wakeham said he stood by the "carefully crafted compromise" put forward in the Royal Commission report. Lord Richard, former Leader of the House, said that a mixed House would work and that it would be possible "to have a largely democratic second chamber without challenging the supremacy of the House of Commons". The debate continued on *22 January,* with all told 94 peers making speeches. Summing up for the Liberal Democrats Lord Goodhart said he thought the debate had been "deeply depressing" and "riddled with complacency and self-congratulation". Lord Strathclyde for the Conservatives disagreed, saying it had been notable for the number of peers who had changed their minds. The Lord Chancellor spoke of the "parliamentary disaster of hybridity" and said that plainly the dominant view expressed in the debate had been in favour of an all-appointed House.

On *22 January* Charles Clarke, Secretary of State for Education and Skills, made a Statement on the future of higher education. He began by saying the universities were a great success story, and that over the next three years they would receive an average 6 per cent a year increase in real term funding. He reaffirmed the Government's commitment to a 50 per cent participation rate by the end of the decade. He went on to say "the social class gap among those entering higher education is a national disgrace", and that the Government would establish an access regulator. Responding from the Opposition front bench Damien Green said 135 Labour members had signed an early day motion opposing top-up fees. The House then debated Defence in the World on a Government motion for the adjournment. Geoffrey Hoon, Secretary of State for Defence, in opening this debate outlined the threats to British interests, emphasising international terrorism. Robert Marshall-Andrews spoke of the American paradox, a country with a greater breadth of internal freedoms than any other on the globe, but a country reviled because it is perceived as denying those freedoms to others. Tam Dalyell forced a procedural vote in which 53 MPs registered their protest at the absence of a substantive vote on Iraq.

MPs completed work on the **Regional Assemblies (Preparations) Bill** on *23 January.* First a programme motion was carried by 292 votes to 153. The House then debated seven groups of new clauses and amendments concluding with a series of divisions, before according the Bill a third reading by 331 votes to 123. For the first time oral questions that day took place in Westminster Hall. Unlike question time in the Chamber questions related to an overall cross-cutting theme (on this first occasion, youth policy) and junior ministers from four different departments were present to answer (the Home Office, Department for Health, the Department for Education and Skills, and the Minister for Sport from the Department of Culture, Media and Sport). Peers debated the **Police (Northern Ireland) Bill** on report.

27 – 31 JANUARY

Andrew Smith, Secretary of State for work and Pensions, made a Statement on *27 January* on plans to introduce greater transparency into the child support system. The House then debated the **Electricity (Miscellaneous Provisions) Bill** at second reading. Brian Wilson, Minister for Energy and Conservation, defined the purpose of the Bill as being to allow for the successful restructuring or administration of British Energy, saying this was "an essential, pragmatic, good Bill to deal with a situation that is not of our making". For the Opposition Crispin Blunt said the Government were asking for a blank cheque so that they could "spend and do whatever they like to get themselves out of the mess" that was "much of their own creation". Second reading was carried by 314 votes to 167, and a programme motion by 311 votes to 167. Later Ben Bradshaw, Parliamentary Secretary, Privy Council Office, moved a motion to establish a select committee on the Lord Chancellor's Department. At question time in the upper House Lord Barnett asked about the "Barnett Formula", which he said was "grossly unfair and should not have been continued", but Lord McIntosh of Haringey for the Government said there were no plans to discontinue using it as the basis for funding devolved administrations. Lord Hunt of Kings Heath, Under-Secretary at the Department of Health, then introduced the second reading of the **Community Care (Delayed Discharges Etc) Bill**. From the Liberal Democrat front bench Lord Clement-Jones moved a motion expressing regret at the Bill and received support from almost all peers who spoke including the Conservative spokesman, Lord Howe, but he withdrew the motion at the end of the debate. Baroness Blatch then moved to annul nine sets of regulations concerned with admission forums for schools, which she said had been laid without proper consultation and were far too complex, but this was defeated by 70 votes to 130.

On *28 January* Alistair Darling, Secretary of State for Transport, moved the second reading of the **Railways and Transport Safety Bill** which he said would create a new accident investigation safety branch, introduce new alcohol offences, and create an independent police authority for British Transport Police. The Bill was unopposed, but a programme motion was divided on, though carried by 346 votes to 95. MPs then debated a motion on the composition of the new Select Committee on the Lord Chancellor's Department which was carried by 233 votes to 62, with minor party MPs protesting at the basis on which entitlement to seats were calculated. Peers' main business was a second committee day on the **Courts Bill**. An amendment moved from the Opposition front bench to impose a duty on the Lord Chancellor to make proper provision of the physical resources needed to support the judicial system (rather than leaving him discretion in the matter) was carried against the Government by 100 votes to 92. In reply to a written question from Lord Oakeshott of Seagrove Bay, the Leader of the House said the cost of purchasing the Lord Chancellor's pension package would be around £2 million.

At Prime Minister's question time on *29 January* Tony Blair said that he thought a "hybrid" House of Lords would not work. The Secretary of State for Trade and Industry, Patricia Hewitt, then made a Statement on auditing and accounting, giving the outcome of a review she had established following the collapse in the USA of Enron, Worldcom and Andersens. Edward Leigh, chairman of the Public Accounts Committee, introduced the annual debate on reports from the Committee, which he said had produced almost 70 reports in the previous 12 months, "probably more than in any one year in our 140-year history". Of the 12 members who made speeches, 11 were members of the 16-strong Public Accounts Committee, the sole exception being the Conservative front-bench spokesman Howard Flight.

On *30 January* at business questions Sir Patrick Cormack asked if there could be an early opportunity to vote again on the "ridiculous new hours which are undermining the work of Parliament", but in reply Robin Cook said three weeks was too short a time to reach a mature judgment on the matter. Geoffrey Hoon, Secretary of State for Defence, then made a Statement on the future aircraft carrier programme announcing that two British companies, BAE Systems and Thales UK, would be contracted to work together on two new aircraft carriers. This was the fourth Opposition Day with a debate on contingency planning to meet humanitarian needs in Iraq taking place on a Conservative motion, which unusually was accepted without a division. In Westminster Hall Jimmy Hood, chairman of the European Scrutiny Committee, introduced a debate on democracy and accountability in the EU, with particular reference to the role of national parliaments. Peers that day quickly completed work on the **National Minimum Wage (Enforcement Notices) Bill**, before turning to the third reading of the **Police (Northern Ireland) Bill**.

On Friday *31 January* Mark Todd's **Company and Community Societies Bill** received an unopposed second reading. Next, as Archie Norman was about to introduce the second reading debate of his **Company Directors' Performance and Compensation Bill**, Gareth Thomas from the Labour back benches moved that the House sit in private. This was defeated 0 votes to 23, but with fewer than 40 members voting the House moved immediately to next business, the second reading of Lawrie Quinn's **Health and Safety at Work (Offences) Bill**. For the next two hours a number of Conservative MPs proceeded to demonstrate great interest in this Bill, ensuring that it failed to complete its second reading.

3 – 7 FEBRUARY

When the Prime Minister made a Statement on *3 February* reporting on his recent visit to Washington to discuss Iraq, Iain Duncan Smith gave his party's support to the Prime Minister, but Charles Kennedy said "The Government have still to make a credible case". Some back-bench MPs expressed disquiet; Gordon Prentice said he and many other people believed "we are being led by the nose into war". MPs then debated the **European Parliament (Representation) Bill** at report stage. Various amendments, including one moved by William Cash designed to curtail the ability of Government by an order-making power to anticipate further changes in EU law, were defeated on division before the Bill was approved without a vote at third reading. Peers that day debated the **Waste and Emissions Trading Bill** at report stage.

Both Houses voted on the various options put forward by the Joint Select Committee on Lords reform on *4 February.* In the Commons votes were preceded by debate. Opening this the leader of the House, Robin Cook, said it was crucial that the House "come to one clear, single and commanding view on the way forward". Later he said: "My personal view is that if we are serious about reform we should have a largely or wholly elected second chamber. In the modern world legitimacy is conferred by democracy". Eric Forth, Shadow Leader, spoke of his preference for either a 100 per cent or 80 per cent elected House, but along with Robin Cook he emphasised that this was a free vote. George Howarth moved an amendment calling for a unicameral parliament. MPs voted 390 to 172 against abolition, then 323 to 245 against 100 per cent appointed and 289 to 272 against 100 per cent elected. The 80 per cent appointed and 20 per cent elected option was then negatived without a division. The 80 per cent elected and 20 per cent appointed option was defeated by 284 votes to 281, the narrowest vote of the day. The 60 per cent elected and 40 per cent appointed option was defeated by 316 votes to 253, while the seventh option of 50 per cent elected and 50 per cent appointed was negatived without a division. At the conclusion of the votes Robin Cook said the best thing to do was to "go home and sleep on this interesting position". Peers refrained from further debate, but voted 335 to 110 in favour of a 100 per cent appointed House, and then by substantial margins rejected all other options. In Westminster Hall that day MPs debated deaths in army barracks on a motion moved by Kevin McNamara with several MPs making speeches calling for further inquiry into the deaths of members of their constituents' families. Peers spent the rest of the day further debating in committee the **Courts Bill.**

On *5 February* John Prescott, Deputy Prime Minister, made a Statement on sustainable communities. Later MPs debated the Police Grant Report for 2003–04, approving this by 345 votes to 197, and then the Local Government Finance (England) Report for 2003–04, which was approved by 316 votes to 190. Peers held two main debates that day. The first on local government was introduced by Lord Hanningfield, leader of Essex County Council, who said nine of the nineteen Bills announced in the Queen's Speech had direct relevance to local authorities, and that the future vitality and health of local government was under threat. Lord Lamont of Lerwick then introduced a debate on university teachers' pay, saying over the previous 20 years academic pay had increased by only 4 per cent in real terms, compared with an increase in average earnings of 45 per cent.

At business questions on *6 February* the Leader of the House, Robin Cook, when asked about Lords reform, said "all options were defeated on Tuesday; there were no winners", and that "there will be no reform of the House of Lords until there is a majority vote in the House of Commons". Geoffrey Hoon, Secretary of State for Defence, then made a Statement on further contingency preparations in relation to Iraq, concentrating on the Royal Air Force. The **Electricity (Miscellaneous) Provisions Bill** was then debated in committee, before being approved at third reading by 274 to 157. When peers gave a second reading to the **Health (Wales) Bill**, Lord Thomas of Gresford from the Liberal Democrat benches said his "party would think it entirely wrong to attempt to move amendments altering the policy behind the Bill, which is essentially to be determined in Cardiff". Later Lord Brabazon of Tara, Chairman of Committees, said the House Procedure Committee had recommended that there should be a Northern Ireland Orders Grand Committee to provide a forum for debate while the Northern Ireland Assembly remained suspended. Six Northern Ireland Orders were then moved and agreed to without debate. Lord Plant of Highfield introduced a debate on the role of the voluntary and community sector in service delivery in the light of the report from the Strategy Unit, "Private Action, Public Benefit". Lord Dahrendorf said that the state, the market and civil society are all needed in their own right, but in his view "trying to bring them too close may rob them of their innate strengths".

On Friday *7 February* David Cairns introduced his **Sunday Trading (Scotland) Bill** which after debate was given an unopposed second reading, as was Frank Roy's **Aviation (Offences) Bill**.

10 – 13 FEBRUARY

On *10 February* the Father of the House, Tam Dalyell, raised as a point of order the Speaker's refusal to allow an emergency debate on what he described as the "misleading of Parliament and the people" by the Government through the inclusion of a plagiarised out-of-date PhD thesis in the recently released official dossier on Iraq. The confrontation between him and the Speaker ended with the Speaker saying that with great reluctance he had to ask Mr Dalyell to withdraw. The House then debated at second reading the **Police (Northern Ireland) Bill** which had already passed the Lords. Introducing this Paul Murphy, Secretary of State for Northern Ireland, said that the 22 Bills that would have passed the suspended Northern Ireland Assembly in the remaining months of its session would be introduced as Orders at Westminster. From the Opposition front bench Quentin Davies said the Bill was part of a bargain between the Government and the SDLP, but Jane Kennedy, Minister of State at the Northern Ireland Office, said the Bill was not about deals and bartering. Second reading was approved by 334 votes to 11. Peers continued the committee stage of the **Courts Bill**, and then debated the Northern Ireland Arms Decommissioning Act 1997 (Amnesty Period) Order 2003, with two further Northern Ireland Orders being considered in the Northern Ireland Orders Grand Committee which met for the first time that day.

On *11 February* the Minister of State at Defence, Adam Ingram, answered an urgent question from Bernard Jenkin about the NATO meeting of the previous day which had undertaken contingency planning in relation to possible threats to Turkey. Later MPs debated the **National Minimum Wage (Enforcement Notices) Bill**, which was given an unopposed second reading. The House also debated the Northern Ireland Arms Decommissioning Order. David Burnside said, "we do not understand how the Prime Minister's strong stand against international terrorism – the good from the evil of 11 September – is translated into Northern Ireland". The Order was approved by 404 votes to 8. Lord Weatherill introduced his House of Lords (Amendment) Bill that day, the purpose of which was to "repeal the provision for by-elections of hereditary peers". Peers further considered the **Courts Bill**.

February 12 was taken as the fourth Opposition Day. Michael Howard moved a motion on the economy saying the "British people's love affair with new Labour" was coming to an end, and the "unthinking loyalty of Labour back benchers" was reaching breaking point. Responding, the Chancellor, Gordon Brown, said Britain had the lowest inflation rate for 40 years, the lowest interest rates for 48 years, and that the economy had generated a record number of new jobs in the past five years. The Opposition motion was defeated by 141 votes to 363; the Government amendment accepted by 310 votes to 186. Dawn Primarolo, Paymaster General, then introduced the third reading of the **Income Tax (Earnings and Pensions) Bill** which she said was the second measure to emerge from the tax law rewrite project set up in 1996 to rewrite 7,000 pages of tax legislation enacted over the past 200 years. Later the House debated the Common Agricultural Policy with a report from the Environment, Food and Rural Affairs Committee assisting the debate. In the Lords a debate on the Arts was introduced by Lord Harrison who gave particular emphasis to the contribution made through free access to museums and art galleries to the cultural life of the country. Following this Baroness Massey of Darwen initiated a debate calling attention to the need for co-ordination of health and social services to improve the life chances of children and young people.

On *13 February* Jack Straw, Foreign Secretary, made a Statement on the report to be made to the UN Security Council the following day by Dr Hans Blix on Iraqi weapons, saying armed intervention was not inevitable, and that a peaceful resolution of the crisis remained in Saddam Hussein's hands. David Miliband, Minister for School Standards, introduced a debate on the Government response to the consultation exercise on educating 14 to19 year olds. Peers debated the **Sexual Offences Bill** at second reading. Lord Lloyd of Berwick said he had been a member of the Criminal Law Revision Committee, which had been asked in 1975 to examine the law on sexual offences. The Committee had reported in 1983, but it had taken almost 20 years for the Government to act on this report. After this, Lord Howe moved a motion resolving that the Commission for Patient and Public Involvement in Health (Functions) Regulations 2002 should be revoked. He said that Ministers had abandoned undertakings given in connection with the removal of Community Health Councils, now to take place on 1 September. After debate Lord Howe withdrew his motion but said the House would return to these matters.

17 – 20 FEBRUARY

The House of Commons did not meet during the week beginning the *17 February*, but the House of Lords did. The committee stage of the **Community Care (Delayed Discharges) Bill** began on *17 February*, and was completed the following day. The Government suffered a defeat when peers voted by 152 votes to 123 to accept an amendment moved by Lord Howe seeking to delay the commencement of the new system of penalties from 1 April 2003 to 1 April 2004. On *18 February* Baroness Noakes moved an amendment to ensure external scrutiny of the impact of the Bill on patients and carers, and this too was carried against the Government by 110 votes to 109. Later that day the **Courts Bill** received further committee consideration, with the Government being defeated by 37 votes to 36 on an amendment moved by Lord Hunt of the Wirral designed to ensure that in prescribing fees the Lord Chancellor should have regard to the need to facilitate access to justice.

On *19 February* Lord Strabolgi introduced a debate on the Report of the Reviewing Committee on the Export of Works of Art, and this was followed by a debate introduced by the Earl of Sandwich on Southern Africa. The House then debated Child Support Regulations and four Orders arising from the Proceeds of Crime Act 2002. On *20 February* peers debated the **European Parliament (Representation) Bill** with a number of peers reflecting concern expressed by the Delegated Powers and Regulatory Reform Committee on the degree of parliamentary scrutiny proposed for Orders. Following this the **Regional Assemblies (Preparations) Bill** also received a second reading debate with sharply differing views being expressed about the merits of this Bill.

24 – 28 FEBRUARY

Patricia Hewitt, Secretary of State for Trade and Industry, made a Statement on *24 February* on the Government's Energy White Paper published that day, saying this set out a new policy designed to meet the changing challenges we faced. Alan Johnson, Minister for Employment Relations, Industry and the Regions, then introduced the second reading of the **Industrial Development (Financial Assistance) Bill**, which altered limits on financial assistance, but which the Conservatives opposed on the grounds of inadequate parliamentary accountability. Peers began work on the report stage of the **Licensing Bill**, with the Government suffering four defeats in the division lobby: first by 151 to 115 votes on an amendment to treat live music equally with recorded music for exemption purposes; second by 169 votes to 107 to exclude educational establishments from the "burdens imposed by the Bill"; third to make a central licensing authority or register mandatory by 143 votes to 111; and finally by 135 votes to 99 to ensure that "amenity" was given due consideration in the licensing process.

On *25 February* the Prime Minister made a Statement saying that a new resolution was to be tabled at the UN declaring that "Iraq has failed to take the final opportunity afforded to it in Resolution 1441", but voting would be delayed to give Saddam a final opportunity to disarm voluntarily. The House then dealt with the **Communications Bill** at report stage, and approved without debate by 293 votes to 184 a further programme motion in respect of the **Local Government Bill**. The House of Lords debated the **Crime (International Co-operation) Bill** at report stage. A number of amendments were rejected on division, including two requiring annual reports to be made to Parliament. Peers also gave a second reading to the **Income Tax (Earnings and Pensions) Bill**, with several speakers paying tribute to the work of Lord Howe of Aberavon on the tax re-write project.

At Prime Minster's question time on *26 February* Iain Duncan Smith asked if it was now the Prime Minister's position that he would support military action against Iraq even if there was no majority for a second UN resolution. Tony Blair replied that he believed there would be support for a second resolution. Jack Straw, Foreign Secretary, opened a debate on Iraq saying that country presented a uniquely dangerous threat. For the Opposition Michael Ancram gave support to the Government. Chris Smith moved an amendment saying that the case for military action was as yet unproven. From the Opposition benches Douglas Hogg and Kenneth Clarke supported the amendment, the latter saying that "middle England and those of moderate political opinions have many doubts" about the wisdom of going to war. The amendment was lost by 199 votes to 393, (the minority consisting of 121 Labour, 13 Conservative, all 52 Liberal Democrats and 13 from other parties). The Government motion was then approved by 434 votes to 124. Peers also debated Iraq that day with a similar mix of supporting and opposing speeches. Baroness Symons of Vernham Dean, Minister for Trade, said that it was wrong to talk of a rush to war but there was no peace either, and that non-compliance with resolution 1441 was the heart of the issue.

On *27 February* Sir George Young as chairman of the Committee on Standards and Privileges moved that the House accept the Third Report from the Committee and agree to suspend Michael Trend from the service of the House for two weeks because of his mistake in falsely claiming additional costs allowance. The House then dealt with the Social Security Benefits Uprating Order 2003 and the draft Guaranteed Minimum Pensions Order 2003, both being accepted without divisions. In the Lords that day the Government suffered two further defeats on the **Licensing Bill**, first by 99 votes to 92 on an amendment requiring owners of licensed premises as well as licensees to be registered by the local authority, and second by 98 votes to 97 on one to strengthen the position of local authorities in the licensing regime.

On *28 February* Bill Tynan introduced his **Fireworks Bill**, which he said was as consensual as possible, and Keith Simpson his **National Lottery (Funding of Endowments) Bill**, both of which received unopposed second readings. Peers that day completed the report stage of the **High Hedges Bill**, and then debated and approved at second reading Lord Beaumont of Whitley's **Road Traffic (Amendment) Bill**, which sought to regulate more carefully the use on public roads of vehicles containing horses or other animals. Lord Lester of Herne Hill then introduced his **Equality Bill**, which sought to update law on discrimination, and bring legislation on equality into a single Act, a principle approved widely in the second reading debate, though this also revealed varied views on proposed detailed changes in the law.

3 – 7 MARCH

On *3 March* Jack Straw, Foreign Secretary, initiated a debate on the Intelligence and Security Committee report on the Bali bombings and the Government response to this. One result had been the urgent re-examination of Foreign Office travel advice – its purpose, its target audience and its presentation. Peers debated the **Electricity (Miscellaneous Provisions) Bill** at second reading, and then spent further time on the report stage of the **Crime (International Co-operation) Bill**.

On *4 March* MPs debated the **Communications Bill** at report stage. The Opposition argued for a new clause to impose a duty on Ofcom to promote competition, reduce regulation and encourage the rapid deployment of broadband, but the Government said this was unnecessary. At third reading Patricia Hewitt, Secretary of State for Trade and Industry, said she was greatly encouraged by the consensus that existed on so much of the Bill, and by all the extensive consultation and scrutiny which underlay the Bill. The third reading was unopposed. Peers spent a third day on report stage of the **Licensing Bill**. An amendment to ensure that an adult should accompany children under 14 in pubs was carried against the Government by 184 votes to 111.

On *5 March* the report stage of the **Local Government Bill** commenced, with much of the debate centring on whether the Bill increased freedom and flexibility or conversely increased restrictions for local authorities. An amendment moved from the Opposition front bench by Philip Hammond and supported by the Liberal Democrats, sought to give greater flexibility to "prudent, debt-free local authorities". This was defeated by 183 votes to 312. A further amendment with similar support designed to prevent council tax ever being used to fund regional bodies was defeated by 178 votes to 298. In the upper House Lord Fowler introduced a debate on pensions in which he described as "breathtaking" the decision by MPs to improve their own already generous pension scheme. Seventeen further speeches were made before the Minister replied, with all reflecting a sombre mood and the feeling that the Government's response was simply inadequate. Baroness Park of Monmouth than introduced a debate on Zimbabwe, following which an Order raising the maximum number of High Court judges from 106 to 108 was accepted.

On *6 March* the Minister for Women, Patricia Hewitt, introduced a debate on International Women's Day in which 12 of the 15 speeches made came from women; she said only 252 women had ever been elected to the House of Commons and only 18 had served in the cabinet. In Westminster Hall the Parliamentary Secretary in the Lord Chancellor's Department, Yvette Cooper, introduced a debate on electoral turnout, focusing especially on practical ways that might increase voter turnout, such as weekend voting and e-voting. Peers dealt with the **Waste and Emissions Trading Bill** at third reading with the Government suffering two defeats. The first carried by 115 votes to 99 was on an amendment moved by Lord Hanningfield requiring councils in areas where two-tier authorities operate to have a joint municipal waste strategy. The second, moved by Lord Dixon-Smith, concerned the temperature at which composting of waste should take place, and was carried by 125 votes to 107. Later Baroness Farrington of Ribbleton, a Government Whip, introduced the second reading of the **Water Bill**, which she said was firmly grounded in the principles of sustainable development. The Bill was given a general welcome in debate. Following this Baroness Gould of Potternewton initiated a debate on barriers to full participation by women in the political, economic and social life of the country. Responding to the debate Baroness Scotland of Asthal of the Lord Chancellor's Department said currently 16 per cent of the House of Lords was made up of women, and that six of the seventeen on the Government front bench were women.

On Friday *7 March* Edward Garnier's **Retirement Income Reform Bill** was debated and approved the second reading by 127 votes to 26. In the Lords Baroness Harris of Richmond introduced a debate on a report from the EU Committee entitled "A Common Policy for Immigration". Lord Donoughue then introduced the second reading of his **Wild Mammals (Protection)(Amendment)(No 2) Bill**, supported by the NFU, the Country Land and Business Association, and the Countryside Alliance. Lord Whitty responding for the Government said the Bill did not avoid ambiguity, conflict and argument. Lord Goodhart then introduced his **Ministerial and other Salaries (Amendment) Bill**, the purpose of which was to link the salary of the Lord Chancellor to that of a Secretary of State, thus approximately halving his pay.

10 – 14 MARCH

On *10 March* Jack Straw, Foreign Secretary, in a Statement on Iraq and Israel/Palestine emphasised the need "to stand firm in pursuing our objective of disarmament" on Iraq, and outlined steps being taken to promote a peace settlement in relation to Israel and the occupied territories. The House then debated the **Local Government Bill** at report stage, with an amendment to make the repeal of Section 28 subject to various safeguards in relation to sex education being lost on a free vote by 127 to 356. An amendment to keep Section 28 was lost by 77 votes to 368, while Government amendments concerned with the Fire Services Act 1947 were agreed. The Bill was approved at third reading by 349 to 136. Peers that day debated the **Community Care (Delayed Discharges etc) Bill** on report with the Government suffering two defeats, one exempting patients receiving mental health treatment from the Bill carried by 124 votes to 113, and the other ensuring patients gave consent to their own discharge by 142 votes to 131.

At question time on *11 March* the Leader of the House, Robin Cook, resisted suggestions for an early review of the new sitting hours of the House. Donald Anderson, chairman of the Foreign Affairs Select Committee, introduced an Estimates Day debate on a report from his Committee on the war against terrorism. He particularly spoke of difficulties in establishing a doctrine of pre-emptive self-defence. Many speeches in this debate returned to the issue of Iraq. Andrew Tyrie described the committee report as "outstanding", and remarked that "in the past few weeks the House of Commons has played a crucial role in international affairs", something that "had not happened often in the past 50 years". Replying to the debate Donald Anderson said select committees provided a "monitoring device to place a check on the Executive", and that in a "professional world the legislative body must itself be expert". Peers completed work on the **Licensing Bill** with the Government suffering a further defeat when the House voted 150 to 120 in support of an amendment to exempt small premises providing entertainment for fewer than 250 people. At the end of the debate Baroness Buscombe said that as well as the nine defeats on important issues, the Government had made a "considerable number of important concessions as a result of our debates".

At Prime Minister's questions on *12 March* Charles Kennedy asked if the Attorney-General had advised that "war on Iraq in the absence of a second UN resolution authorising force would be legal". Tony Blair replied "We would not do anything as a country that did not have a proper legal basis to it". David Blunkett, Home Secretary, then made a Statement on Government policies to correct anti-social behaviour. Replying, Oliver Letwin said the Opposition and the Government did not disagree on diagnosis but on cure, with legislation "seeping out of every pore of the Home Office". The House then held its delayed St David's day debate on Welsh Affairs which was characterised by sharp pre Assembly election exchanges. For the Liberal Democrats Lembit Öpik said his party had produced "a campaign charter to try and improve the style of politics that we practise in Wales and, in the longer term, elsewhere". In the upper House Lord Brennan introduced a debate on corporate governance, and Lord Redesdale one on the implications of the decision to upgrade Fylingdales. Baroness Knight of Collingtree introduced for second reading her **Patients' Protection Bill**. This resulted in an interesting two-hour debate on the rights and wrongs of allowing doctors to withdraw tube-delivered food and fluid.

On *13 March* a debate on flood and coastal defence policy took place in government time, with many members speaking of the extensive improvements that had taken place in the last two years or so. Peers commenced the committee stage of the **Regional Assemblies (Preparations) Bill** with a lengthy discussion of the problem of defining acceptable regional boundaries.

On *14 March* private members bills introduced by two Labour back benchers were debated and approved without divisions at second reading. First was Joan Ruddock's **Municipal Waste Recycling Bill** which sought to increase the recycling of waste, and then Chris Mole's **Legal Deposit Libraries Bill**, which sought to ensure the safe collection and storage of non-print material in the same way as print material in legal deposit libraries. John Bercow then introduced his **Government Powers (Limitation) Bill**, but after ten minutes the debate was adjourned when a division was called in which fewer than 40 voted. Peers debated two Select Committee reports, first on microchips, and second on environmental regulation and agriculture. During the committee stage of Lord Lester of Herne Hill's **Equality Bill** Baroness Scotland of Asthal for the Government made clear she could not support the Bill generally, though she believed it would make a valuable contribution to an ongoing debate.

17 – 21 MARCH

On *17 March* MPs took all stages of the **Northern Ireland (Assembly Elections) Bill**, with Jane Kennedy, Minister of State, explaining that the Bill's simple purpose was to allow for a 28-day postponement of the Assembly elections currently due on 1 May. Jack Straw, Foreign Secretary, then made a Statement on Iraq saying that Britain had reluctantly concluded no Security Council consensus on a new resolution would be possible, and no further effort would be made to propose a resolution. Robin Cook, Leader of the House, then made a personal statement explaining that he had resigned from the Government because Britain was "embarking on a war without agreement in any of the international bodies of which we are a leading partner". He went on to say: "Iraq probably has no weapons of mass destruction in the commonly understood sense of the term – namely a credible device capable of being delivered against a strategic city target". He then asked: "Why is it now so urgent that we should take military action to disarm a military capacity that has been there for 20 years and which we helped to create?" His Statement was greeted with a standing ovation in the House. Peers debated the **Community Care (Delayed Discharges etc.) Bill** at third reading with the Government suffering three further defeats; by 134 votes to 119 on the definition of notice periods; by 145 votes to 112 on the time scale for imposing financial penalties; and by 145 votes to 115 on the introduction of a five-year life on the Bill. A further Government defeat took place when on the third reading of the **Crime (International Co-operation) Bill** an Opposition amendment limiting the rights of officers of foreign governments was carried by 122 votes to 117. Later Lord Goodhart introduced a three-hour debate on the legality of the use of armed force in Iraq. He argued that military action was not legal under international law, as did most other speakers in the debate including Lord Lloyd of Berwick, former Lord Justice of Appeal, Lord Archer of Sandwell, former Labour Solicitor-General, Lord Brennan, a Labour QC, as well as two other Liberal Democrat lawyers, Lord Lester of Herne Hill and Lord Thomas of Gresford. Those arguing the contrary view included Lord Mayhew of Twysden, a former Conservative Solicitor-General, Lord Grabiner, a Labour lawyer, and among non-lawyers, Baroness Ramsay of Cartvale, former diplomat, and from the cross-benches Lord Owen, former Labour Foreign Secretary. Part of the background to the debate was the advice to the Government disclosed in a written answer that day by the Attorney-General, Lord Goldsmith, to the effect that the use of armed force against Iraq was legal. Some peers criticised Lord Goldsmith for failing to speak in the debate.

In both Houses on the following day a Government motion expressing support for the decision to use "all means necessary to ensure the disarmament of Iraq's weapons of mass destruction" was debated. In the Commons 57 MPs spoke in this historic nine and a half-hour debate, which was opened by the Prime Minister who made a 48-minute speech, described by many as passionate and powerful. In this he argued that the choice before the House was tough and stark, either "to stand British troops down now and turn back, or to hold firm to the course we have set". He then argued that two "begetters of chaos" were tyrannical regimes armed with weapons of mass destruction, and extreme terrorist groups. Iain Duncan Smith offered firm support to the Government. But an amendment saying that "the case for war against Iraq has not yet been established, especially given the absence of specific UN authorisation" was moved by Peter Kilfoyle, who argued that the war was "illegal, immoral and illogical". Charles Kennedy spoke in support of the amendment. At the end of the debate 217 MPs (139 of them Labour) voted for the amendment and 396 against, following which the main motion was carried by 412 votes to 149. In the House of Lords during a six-hour debate (not followed by any divisions) 43 peers made speeches. Summing up Lord Howell of Guildford said a majority of speakers had expressed doubts and scepticism about going to war. Baroness Symons of Vernham Dean said Saddam did have the means to deliver strategically his weapons of mass destruction, and that removal of these – not regime change – was the motivation for this war.

On *19 March* MPs debated Lords amendments to the **Community Care (Delayed Discharges etc.) Bill**. On the crucial amendment (which was deleted) to delay for a year implementation of the Bill, supporters of the Lords view included David Hinchliffe, Labour chairman of the Health Select Committee. Peers completed all stages of the **Northern Ireland Assembly Elections Bill**. Two further debates also took place, the first introduced by Baroness Rendell of Babaregh on racism in the performing arts, and the second introduced by Baroness Howe of Idlicote on university funding.

On *20 March* Geoffrey Hoon, Secretary of State for Defence, made a Statement on events in Iraq saying that at 3.15 am President Bush had announced the commencement of coalition operations, during which every possible care would be taken to minimise civilian casualties. Later in answer to a question he said: "There are clear links between the Iraqi regime and al-Quaeda". In a further Statement on the firemen's dispute John Prescott, Deputy Prime Minister, announced that legislation would be introduced giving Government power to impose terms and conditions on the fire service. MPs then debated at second reading the **Waste and Emissions Trading Bill** which was not divided against and upon which a programme motion was accepted, also without a division. In Westminster Hall a debate on the Convention on the Future of Europe was introduced by Peter Hain in his capacity as the Government representative on the Convention. He described the plans for Europe as based on the principle of "a partnership, a union of sovereign member states", and resisted suggestions that a unitary European state was emerging. Peers spent a second committee day on the **Regional Assemblies (Preparations) Bill** with an Opposition amendment supported by the Liberal Democrats designed to specify more precisely the necessary level of interest before a referendum could be ordered being carried by 110 votes to 86.

On *21 March* the Commons gave unopposed second readings to Ann Clwyd's **Female Genital Mutilation Bill**, and John Greenway's **Equine Welfare (Ragwort Control) Bill**. Next Hugh Robertson introduced the **Endangered Species (Illegal Trade) Bill**, which would increase the maximum sentence for those caught trading in endangered species. The Government spokesman said a better way would be to tackle the issue through an amendment to the Criminal Justice Bill, and Hugh Robertson withdrew his Bill.

24 – 28 MARCH

The Prime Minister made a Statement on *24 March* saying the war in Iraq was "not of conquest but of liberation", and that although there were deep divisions at the recent European Council meeting, nevertheless there had been "understanding and support for the British position from many nations represented" there, especially the 10 accession countries. The House then considered the **Licensing Bill** at second reading, with Tessa Jowell, Secretary of State for Culture, Media and Sport, welcoming the scrutiny the Bill had already received in the Lords and saying many Lords amendments would be accepted. The Bill was not opposed in the division lobby, but the programme motion was, though carried by 304 votes to 84. In a written statement that day the Parliamentary Secretary at the Privy Council Office, Ben Bradshaw, explained that due to a deficit in the Parliamentary Pension Fund, the level of Exchequer contributions would increase from 1 April from 7.9 per cent of pay to 24 per cent, while Members' contributions would remain unchanged. Peers continued with the committee stage of the **Regional Assemblies (Preparations) Bill**, in a sitting that lasted until 2.23 am. As well as many probing amendments the Government successfully resisted in the division lobby two amendments forced to a vote, one of which would have required that a referendum majority would be valid only if a majority of the electorate had voted.

On *25 March* the Commons dealt with remaining stages of the **Extradition Bill**, with third reading being carried by 303 votes to 142. The House of Lords debated the **Communications Bill** at second reading, with 49 speeches being made. Lord Puttnam, who chaired the joint select committee, which had given pre-legislative scrutiny to the Bill, expressed appreciation for the way the Government had listened, amended and improved the Bill. But he also stressed the need to resource Ofcom adequately, and to support "plurality and diversity with intelligent and sensitive regulation". This latter point led him to oppose any provision that would allow channel five or any terrestrial television channel to be owned "wholly or partially by a large newspaper group".

On *26 March* Charles Kennedy asked the Prime Minster to persuade the American President that any post-military conflict administration in Iraq should be UN-led rather then US-led. Tony Blair would only promise endorsement by the UN. Geoffrey Hoon, Secretary of State for Defence, than made a Statement on Iraq in which he said Saddam Hussein had miscalculated the resolve of western democracies. Tam Dalyell called for troops to be pulled out of Iraq before "they are cooked in the sands of the desert". The House then turned to the **Police (Northern Ireland) Bill**, first accepting a programme motion by 277 votes to 152, which required proceedings on the Bill to be completed the following day. Quentin Davies from the Opposition front bench said the Government's new clauses and schedules meant the Bill now bore little relation to the one considered in Committee, and accused the Government of by-passing the whole Committee stage with impunity. Concern especially focused on the way the Government had altered the Bill allegedly in order to facilitate negotiations with Sinn Féin-IRA. On *27 March* third reading was approved by 216 votes to 98.

In the House of Lords two debates took place on *26 March*. The first was introduced by Lord Chalfont and dealt with the need for a balance between national security and individual liberty in a democratic society. Lord Wilson of Dinton, former cabinet secretary, made a maiden speech in which he spoke of the "great respect" he had developed over the years for the House, which was a "great national institution", and concluded by describing the role of the House in oversight of the Executive as "crucial". Lord Northbourne introduced a debate on children and parents, during which both the new Archbishop of Canterbury, and his predecessor, Lord Carey of Clifton, made their maiden speeches. In the House of Lords on *27 March* the Clerk of the Parliaments announced that in the first hereditary peers by-election Viscount Ullswater had been the winner. That day the House also turned its attention again to the **Courts Bill** with an amendment moved by Lord Hunt of the Wirral seeking to exclude the recovery of judicial salaries from consideration in the setting of court fees being carried against the Government by 90 votes to 87. The House then completed work on the committee stage of the **European Parliament (Representation) Bill**, and also considered Commons changes to the **Community Care (Delayed Discharges etc.) Bill**. Several Lords amendments had been reversed in the Commons, but on others compromises had been reached, and Opposition peers in general expressed satisfaction at the adjustments made to the Bill, with no further divisions taking place. In Westminster Hall on *27 March* Roger Berry introduced a debate on the report on strategic export controls produced by the Quadripartite Committee (made up from the Select Committees on Defence, Foreign Affairs, International Development and Trade and Industry).

On *28 March* the Lords did not sit, but in the Commons three private members' bills were debated and given unopposed second readings. These were Brian White's **Sustainable Energy Bill**, Stephen McCabe's **Human Fertilisation and Embryology (Deceased Fathers) Bill**, and the **High Hedges (No 2) Bill** introduced by Stephen Pound, an identical Bill to one already piloted through the Lords by Baroness Gardner of Parkes.

31 MARCH – 4 APRIL

MPs turned to the report stage of the **Railways and Transport Safety Bill** on *31 March*. Opposition spokesmen said some changes made to the Bill were very worthwhile, including the imposition of a duty on the Chief Inspector of Rail Accidents to produce an annual report, and the imposition of a legal requirement on highway authorities to remove snow and ice from roads. Further amendments to reduce the permitted alcohol limits for drivers; to ensure more freight went by rail rather than road;

and to require an annual report on road safety statistics were all rejected in divisions before the Bill received an unopposed third reading. The House of Lords that day began committee consideration of the **Sexual Offences Bill**, with debate centring on the redefinition of rape proposed in the Bill. Later the House debated the Special Immigration Appeals Commission (Procedure) Rules 2003, which had earlier been withdrawn and amended following scrutiny by the legal adviser to the Joint Committee on Statutory Instruments. Lord Dholakia then moved a motion of regret (later withdrawn) on the Asylum (Designated States) Order 2003 at the failure yet to establish an advisory panel under the Nationality Immigration and Asylum Act 2002.

On *1 April* MPs debated the **Crime (International Co-operation) Bill**, which had already received what the Minister Beverley Hughes described as "careful and helpful scrutiny" in the House of Lords. Second reading was unopposed though plenty of concerns were raised. A programme motion was approved by 320 votes to 170. MPs then returned to the **Community Care Bill** agreeing further amendments embodying compromises on the treatment of patients receiving mental health care. In Westminster Hall Alan Whitehead introduced what he said was the first debate on Parliament and the Executive Agencies since 1997. He drew attention to recent reports from the Cabinet Office and the National Audit Office, but said very few inquiries had been conducted into Agencies by select committees. Peers spent a second committee day on the **Sexual Offences Bill**, with debate focused on the protection of young people. Baroness Blatch, Conservative deputy leader, opposed amendments moved by her fellow front-bencher, Baroness Noakes, which she said would "abolish the age of consent". Later the two Baronesses disagreed over amendments relating to "sexual grooming".

On *2 April* MPs accepted without a division a programme motion giving three days for report stage consideration of the **Criminal Justice Bill**, though Opposition MPs expressed fears over inadequate consideration of the Bill. An Opposition amendment seeking to remove the provision giving police a general right to hold arrested persons for 36 rather than 24 hours without charge was rejected by 163 votes to 285. A further amendment from the Liberal Democrats sought to reverse a proposal to remove the duty of the police to list the property of a detained person but was also rejected by a similar margin. An amendment moved from the Labour back benches by Vera Baird seeking to alter the proposals in the Bill concerning the disclosure to courts of defendants' records was defeated by 201 votes to 266. Lord Blackwell introduced a debate in the Lords on the Convention on the Future of Europe, arguing that the proposals emerging "constituted a major constitutional shift" and that if any such proposals were finalised they should be subject to a referendum. Lord Grenfell, chairman of the European Scrutiny Committee, spoke of the various reports made by his Committee. Lord Norton of Louth said the Convention was the wrong size and did not have an appropriate membership. It also failed to "consult adequately with civil society", and was "proceeding almost in a vacuum". Following this debate Lord Thomas of Gresford introduced a debate on public interest immunity to which the Attorney-General Lord Goldsmith replied.

On *3 April* Geoffrey Hoon, Secretary of State for Defence, made a further Statement on Iraq, saying that the campaign continued to make remarkable progress. The House then debated the Easter adjournment, with MPs raising various issues, some constituency and some national. Adverse comment was made on the new sitting times of the House, and a few offered views about the role and reform of the House of Lords. In Westminster Hall Ian Gibson introduced a three-hour debate on science education based on a report from the Science and Technology Committee. Peers debated the **Electricity (Miscellaneous Provisions) Bill** at report stage, then considered Commons amendments to the **Police (Northern Ireland) Bill**. In a rather unhappy debate various peers argued that this Bill should not have been extensively changed late in its parliamentary passage to meet Sinn Féin demands, and that such changes should not be made until Sinn Féin had delivered on earlier commitments. The House then debated at second reading the **Local Government Bill**, which had already passed the Commons, and finally the Bishop of Winchester initiated a debate on the Congo.

On *4 April* MPs completed report and remaining stages on Mark Todd's **Co-operatives and Community Benefit Societies Bill**, and then gave a second reading to Richard Allan's **Dealing in Cultural Objects (Offences) Bill**, which also had Government support. Peers debated various draft codes, and then the **Prevention of Driving under the Influence of Drugs Bill**, before Lord Lester of Herne Hill led report stage consideration of his **Equality Bill.**

7 – 14 APRIL

On *7 April* MPs debated further amendments made in the Lords to the **Police (Northern Ireland) Bill**, before considering at report stage the **Industrial Development (Financial Assistance) Bill** which was approved at third reading without a division and without any amendments having been made during its passage through the House. Peers that day commenced report stage of the **Regional Assemblies (Preparations) Bill**. Baroness Hamwee speaking for the Liberal Democrats explained that her party had reached a compromise agreement with the Government under which they would not press for the retention of two-tier local government where regional assemblies were introduced, but in return the Government had agreed to allow that referendums in such areas would also test opinion about local government structure. Lord Greaves explained that he had withdrawn from the Liberal Democrat team on the Bill because he disagreed with the compromise. The Conservative spokesman, Baroness Hanham, described it as the "nail in the coffin of county councils".

On *8 April* during second reading of the **Anti-social Behaviour Bill** many MPs were critical of the short period allowed for consultation on the Bill and of the lack of pre-legislative scrutiny. David Blunkett, Home Secretary, acknowledged this with regret, and promised that "over the next two years, my Department will work to ensure that, wherever possible, all Bills appearing in our legislative programme will appear in draft form". Many MPs recounted matters from their constituency mail and surgeries illustrating the need for action against anti-social behaviour, but many also expressed doubts about the likelihood of the Bill altering the situation much. The Bill was given an unopposed second reading, with a programme motion being carried by 338 votes to 147, though the Liberal Democrats in particular voted against this in order to try and force the referral of the Bill to a Special Standing Committee. Peers spent a second report stage day on the **Regional Assemblies (Preparations) Bill**. Opposition amendments to ensure more information about the powers, responsibilities and costs of assemblies would be available, and to define more precisely the meaning of public backing for an assembly, were withdrawn or defeated.

The Chancellor, Gordon Brown, presented his budget on *9 April*, the first while Britain was "engaged in a large scale military conflict" for 50 years. The Chancellor's watchwords were "flexibility" and "enterprise", but he also emphasised that over the economic cycle "we will not only achieve a balance but achieve an estimated surplus of £32 billion". The Leader of the Opposition said the Chancellor had once more got his forecasts wrong, and had now imposed 53 tax rises since 1997. Charles Kennedy for the Liberal Democrats said it was "not only a buck-passing budget, but a cross your fingers and hope for the best budget". In the upper House the Bishop of Oxford introduced a debate "calling attention to the religious element in global terrorism and appropriate interfaith responses". Lord Desai said that in his view "every religion preaches peace, and it is used as a cause for war". The Bishop of Portsmouth talked of the shift "from ideology to identity" in the contemporary world and "the re-emergence of religion as a serious player on the world stage, including Europe".

On *10 April* during business questions Robin Cook asked his successor as Leader of the House, Dr John Reid, to take special note of the agreement he would find in his in-tray providing that most Government Bills would be published in draft form. Jack Straw, Foreign Secretary, made a Statement on Iraq speaking of the "extraordinary events" and the "understandable euphoria" of the past few days, and declaring that "as soon as possible Iraq should be governed by Iraqi people themselves". Clare Short, Secretary of State for International Development, made a Statement on humanitarian aid to Iraq. Following this the budget debate continued with the former Tory Chancellor, Kenneth Clarke, saying that the Chancellor now hardly delivers a budget speech at all; instead he goes "into long, tedious details of changes in various departmental policies". Peers that day returned to the committee stage of the **Sexual Offences Bill** with debate focusing on the varied forms of family relationship in relation to sexual abuse. The House of Lords then rose for the Easter recess.

On Friday *11 April* MPs continued to debate the budget, focusing on the skills agenda, with the final day's debate taking place on Monday *14 April*, culminating in eight divisions taking some 90 minutes, all of which of course the Government won with a wide margin. The Prime Minister also made a Statement that day on Iraq saying that some disorder and some looting had been inevitable, but affirming that the process of Iraq's reconstruction would now formally begin. He emphasised that Saddam had had six months to "put in place a systematic campaign of concealment of weapons of mass destruction" which may well take some time to uncover. The House of Commons then rose for the Easter recess.

28 APRIL – 1 MAY

Jack Straw, Foreign Secretary, made a Statement on *28 April* saying that looting and civil disorder in Iraq had now declined, and that a second meeting of national Iraqi representatives was taking place that day in Baghdad. Alan Milburn, Secretary of State for Health, then made a Statement in which he outlined steps being taken to combat SARS, which he said had now spread to 26 countries. A third Statement came from Dawn Primarolo, Paymaster General, apologising for the difficulties experienced by the public in relation to the new tax credit scheme. She said the Treasury helpline was receiving nearly 2 million calls a day at its peak, but Michael Howard wanted to know why a helpline that had cost £53 million to set up had effectively collapsed. MPs then considered Lords amendments to the **European Parliament (Representation) Bill**, agreeing after debate to these, in some cases after divisions forced by Conservatives. Next the **National Minimum Wage (Enforcement Notices) Bill** was given an unopposed third reading. Peers dealt with the **Regional Assemblies (Preparations) Bill** at third reading, and then continued with the committee stage of the **Sexual Offences Bill** dealing especially with amendments relating to the position of people with learning disabilities or mental disorders.

29 April was taken as the fifth Opposition Day with a Conservative motion expressing deep concern at the "collapse of community services in Britain". Conservative MPs attacked the Government on a broad front over crime, education, and health care. Responding, Nick Raynsford, Minister for Local Government and the Regions, said that he had listened to a "litany of misinformed rhetoric, remorselessly negative in tone, which undermines public services and demoralises the many dedicated people who deliver our public services". The Opposition motion was defeated by 139 votes to 327. Peers continued with the committee stage of the **Communications Bill** with several different amendments concerned with the public interest and public service broadcasting being debated then withdrawn.

On *30 April* Lords amendments to the **Regional Assemblies (Preparations) Bill** were considered by MPs and agreed after debate without further division. When a motion replacing Robin Cook with John Reid on the Modernisation select committee was debated, the shadow Leader of the House, Eric Forth, gave vent to his feelings, saying: "The so-called modernisation process has been a wicked and evil development that has systematically diminished the power of the House of Commons effectively to hold the Government to account . . . All the proposals emanating from the Modernistaion Committee have been to the detriment of the House of Commons as a legislature". Sir Patrick Cormack also argued that the Modernisation Committee had done "untold harm" to the House. In Westminster Hall that day Denis Murphy introduced a debate calling for a new offence of aggravated dangerous driving to be introduced. Peers held three debates, on the European Year of Disabled People, on tourism and finally on methicillin resistant staphylococcus aureus (MRSA) in hospitals,

On *1 May* Paul Murphy, Secretary of State for Northern Ireland, made a Statement saying continued lack of clarity on the part of the IRA had led the Government to postpone elections, and that legislation to this effect would be introduced the following week. For the Conservative Opposition Quentin Davies said the Government was suspending democracy for all parries and citizens in Northern Ireland because one party had misbehaved. MPs then debated what the Minister for E-Commerce and Competitiveness, Stephen Timms, described as the "slow start" made by the UK with broadband communication, with particular emphasis being given to the lack of availability of broadband in many rural areas. Peers gave second reading debates to three Bills which had already been through the Commons, the **Railways and Transport Safety Bill**, the **Industrial Development (Financial Assistance) Bill**, and the **Extradition Bill**. On the latter Bill it was clear that many peers had strong misgivings about part one.

6 – 9 MAY

MPs debated the **Finance Bill** at second reading on *6 May.* An Opposition amendment declared the Bill increased the burden of taxation, failed to take account of the effects of inflation and would lead to a further decline in the competitiveness and relative attractiveness of the UK as a location for investment. John Redwood said the debate was about the biggest tax bill in history – an extra £26 billion this year, but Dawn Primarolo concluding the debate said the Government was determined to "build a tax system that supports families". The amendment was lost by 149 votes to 379, and the second reading then approved by 331 to 198. The House heard a Statement from Paul Murphy, Secretary of State, on the further postponement of elections for the Northern Ireland Assembly, in which he said the "draft statement by the IRA and subsequent comments by Gerry Adams, President of Sinn Féin, were neither clear nor unambiguous". In Westminster Hall Archie Norman introduced a debate on non-executive directors with special attention being given to the Higgs Report. When Lord Filkin moved that the **Extradition Bill** be committed to a Grand Committee, Lord Bledisloe moved an amendment seeking to ensure Part one dealing with the "European arrest warrant" should be dealt with on the floor of the House. Support came from various parts of the House with Baroness Turner of Camden and Lord Wedderburn of Charlton both speaking of the "unhappy experience" of taking the Employment Bill in Grand Committee. But from the Opposition front bench Lord Cope of Berkeley said the House should abide by its agreement to experiment for two years with Grand Committees, and on division the amendment was lost by 94 votes to 172. The House then debated the **Communications Bill** in committee giving particular attention to the regulatory regime proposed, but with no amendments being pressed to division.

MPs debated the **Health and Social Care Bill** at second reading on *7 May*, with the Secretary of State, Alan Milburn, arguing that the principles of the NHS were right, but that the way the NHS worked in practice did now need to be altered. NHS foundation trusts would strengthen, not weaken public ownership. For the Opposition Liam Fox said the Bill was a timid imitation of what his party had hoped for. The Chairman of the Health Select Committee, David Hinchliffe, moved an amendment declining to give the Bill a second reading because it would introduce "further layers of bureaucracy" and would "increase disparities between hospitals". He was supported from the Labour benches by Frank Dobson who said foundation hospitals would be a "cuckoo in the local health nest", and Angela Eagle who said "foundation hospitals are a cul-de-sac on the road to reform". Others, however, expressed support for the Government, including Robin Cook and Jim Dowd, the latter also a member of the Health select committee. The amendment was lost by 117 votes to 297, with 65 Labour MPs and the Liberal Democrats voting against the Bill. The second reading was then carried by 304 votes to 230, and a programme motion by 326 votes to 204. In Westminster Hall Tim Boswell introduced a debate on mental health saying that in his 15 years in the House he had never seen any Government legislation so completely excoriated by professionals as the draft Mental Health Bill. Baroness Hogg initiated a debate on the burdens on business. Lord Haskel said no one would be happy to live in a minimalist state. Lord Hanningfield then introduced a debate on school funding saying that far from partnership there was now confrontation between local and central government on this matter.

At business questions on *8 May* Eric Forth, shadow leader of the House, said postal ballots in local elections were a threat to democracy as the secrecy of the ballot was effectively disappearing "before our very eyes". Later John Prescott, the Deputy Prime Minister, introduced the second reading of the **Fire Services Bill**, saying this would allow him to secure an arbitrated settlement of both pay and conditions. Almost every Labour MP who spoke expressed opposition to the Bill, but on division it was carried by 284 votes to 59, with 27 Labour MPs voting against the Government alongside the Liberal Democrats. In Westminster Hall Tony Wright, chairman of the Public Administration Committee said he felt the delay in bringing forward a Civil Service Bill was because no cabinet minister was prepared to champion such a Bill, though opposition to it was actually not great. Peers debated the **Courts Bill** at report stage, with the Government suffering three defeats. First by 98 votes to 83 the House supported an amendment requiring the Lord Chancellor to give written reasons if he rejected certain categories of recommendation about a business plan made by a Courts Board; second by 95 votes to 85 one requiring Courts Boards to have two magistrates rather than one in their membership; and third by 90 to 89 to ensure the local accessibility of magistrates courts.

The Commons did not sit on Friday *9 May*, but in the Lords a debate took place on the scrutiny of European legislation introduced by Lord Grenfell, chairman of the EU Committee. Baroness Park of Monmouth said around 70 per cent of EU legislation was ultimately implemented by local authorities who should therefore have a say in scrutiny. Baroness Billingham said there should be closer links with MEPs, while Lord Scott of Foscote said that if the Government chose to override persistent objections made by the scrutiny committee, they should be required to seek a positive resolution of the House. Lord Williamson of Horton said more attention had to be given to second and third pillar matters. Lord Howell of Guildford said that in 2002 in 71 cases Ministers "simply overrode scrutiny and carried on regardless", and that under proposals now being made by the Convention on the Future of Europe the "powers of the Commission to make laws, which are to be called non-legislative acts, will increase". For the Government Baroness Symons of Vernham Dean made a full response, rejecting a number of the proposals and suggesting others were for the House as whole to decide about.

12 – 16 MAY

On *12 May* Jack Straw, Foreign Secretary, made a Statement on reconstruction in Iraq. This drew some hostile responses, including one from Gerald Kaufman, who asked: "how giving Iraq back to the people of Iraq is accomplished by transferring the governance of Iraq to a crony of Donald Rumsfeld?" Clare Short then made a personal Statement explaining her resignation from the Government. She said she was ashamed of the UK Government's agreement to the resolution tabled at the UN concerning the future of Iraq, and "shocked by the secrecy and lack of consultation with Departments with direct responsibility". Later she broadened her critique, saying that in the first term of office the Labour Government's problem had been spin, "endless announcements, exaggerations and manipulation of the media that undermined people's respect for the Government and trust in what we said". In the second term the problem had become one of centralisation of power around the Prime Minister, with the cabinet marginalised, and a failure to consult Departments where the real expertise in Government lay, with the result that there were "increasingly badly thought through policy initiatives". MPs then took the **Northern Ireland Assembly (Elections and Period of Suspension) Bill** through all its stages that day, first approving an allocation of time order by 274 votes to 175. David Trimble argued that the Bill was unnecessary, while the Conservative Opposition said it resulted from the muddle and confusion in the Government's policy towards Northern Ireland. Peers continued with the report stage of the **Courts Bill**.

MPs spent the next two days, *13 and 14 May* on the committee stage of the **Finance Bill**, beginning with a programme motion approved by 244 votes to 137, and then debating selected items, including tobacco duty, hydrocarbon oil duties, bingo duty, vehicle excise duty and other matters. Peers debated the **Northern Ireland Assembly (Elections and Period of Suspension) Bill** at second reading for two hours, then continued with the committee stage of the **Sexual Offences Bill**.

At Prime Minister's question time on *14 May* Iain Duncan Smith pressed the Prime Minister to agree to a referendum on the new European Union constitution, saying 34 referendums had been held since 1997, some on matters much less momentous. The House then continued debating the **Finance Bill**, examining various tax changes including income tax, corporation tax, landfill tax and duty on spirits. Both Houses also that day debated amendments to the **Northern Ireland Assembly (Elections and Period of Suspension) Bill**. In Westminster Hall MPs debated the Stevens Inquiry at the instigation of Kevin McNamara, who said that the stark message of the report was that "successive British Government's have sanctioned murder". In the Lords Baroness Williams of Crosby introduced a debate on "the case for reconstructing the international order and transforming international political institutions". She argued that military power alone would never eradicate the roots of terrorism, which among other things required a recognition of the resentment felt towards global injustice. Lord Howell of Guildford said it was no good trying to replicate "the old protective inward-looking centralised nation state"; rather there had to be recognition of a new network world, a new emerging society of nations, working in agile and adaptable relationships. Lord Wallace of Saltaire suggested that the House establish a sessional committee to examine this theme.

On *15 May* Tessa Jowell, Secretary of State for Culture Media and Sport, in a Statement said the Government had decided to give its wholehearted backing to a bid to host the 2012 Olympic games in London. For the Opposition John Whittingdale expressed support for the bid, but then asked a range of sceptical sounding questions. A debate on school funding was also held, this being the topic chosen by the Opposition for the first part of the sixth Opposition day; their motion was defeated by 128 votes to 296. In Westminster Hall Jean Corston, chairman of the Joint Select Committee on Human Rights introduced a debate on the report made by her Committee on the Human Rights Commission. Peers spent the day debating in committee the **Communications Bill**.

On Friday *16 May* MPs debated and approved at third reading three private members' bills, first David Cairns **Sunday Working (Scotland) Bill**, second Frank Roy's **Aviation (Offences) Bill**, and third Brian Iddon's **Marine Safety Bill**. Peers that day debated a report from their European Union Committee on EU Russia Relations.

19 – 22 MAY

At the end of oral questions on *19 May* the Speaker said the House was not getting through questions fast enough because ministerial replies "are far too long-winded". The House then began two days report stage on the **Criminal Justice Bill**, first approving a programme motion by 283 votes to 160, during debate on which David Heath from the Liberal Democrat front bench said the Bill could not receive the scrutiny it deserved given that almost 500 amendments including 28 Government new clauses, which were not lightweight matters of detail, were now before the House. Among changes made were those permitting the police to keep fingerprints taken without consent from persons arrested and limitations to the right to jury trial in complex fraud cases. This latter change was carried by 299 votes to 277, but with 33 Labour MPs voting against the Government. Amendments allowing retrial where new evidence came to light were agreed by 330 votes to 189. Peers debated the **Courts Bill** at third reading with the Government suffering two defeats. The first was on a proposal to use police areas as the "building blocks of the new courts board system", and was approved by 136 votes to 115; the second carried by 141 votes to 122 sought to make more strict the rules regarding local councillors who are also magistrates. The House then continued and completed the committee stage of the **Sexual Offences Bill**, sitting until after 2 am, though not without protests. Among many issues discussed were the definition of genitals, sexual intercourse with animals, intercourse with the dead, and sexual activity in public places, but no divisions took place.

At question time on *20 May* the treatment of the **Criminal Justice Bill** was raised, with Graham Allen expressing dismay as a member of the Bill's standing committee that about half the Bill now before the House was new because of the large number of Government amendments. The Bill was later given a third reading by 296 votes to 183. Peers had a fourth committee day on the **Communications Bill**, with debate especially focusing on the mobile phone industry and then the role of Ofcom, but without any amendments being pressed to divisions.

On *21 May* Jack Straw, Foreign Secretary, introduced the second reading debate on the **European Union (Accessions) Bill**, which made provision in UK law for the accession of new members of the EU. Much of the debate however focused on the EU Constitutional Convention, and in particular whether a referendum ought to be held. Michael Ancram, from the Opposition front bench, explained why he had voted against a referendum on Maastricht, but supported one now because "since 1997 we have lived in an age of referendums". The Bill was approved at second reading by 491 votes to 0, the Opposition forcing a division in order to demonstrate their support for the Bill. The House of Lords debated development in African countries and then Lord Rodgers of Quarry Bank introduced a debate on the relationship between the judiciary, the legislature and the executive and judicial participation in public controversy. In his speech he said the "antagonism of the Home Secretary towards the judiciary is a matter of serious concern". The Lord Chief Justice, Lord Woolf, said there were times "when the judiciary is left with the impression that its efforts [to co-operate with the Home Office] are neither appreciated nor welcomed". Lord Morris of Aberavon said the time had come to review the position of the Lord Chancellor, primarily because the head of "a great spending department" should be in the House of Commons. Lord Lloyd of Berwick, said it was helpful for senior judges such as him to sit in the House of Lords "provided they exercise all proper self restraint", just as some recorders sat in the Commons. Lord Plant of Highfield said he thought we were "on the move from a strongly majoritarian Parliament-based view of British democracy towards a more constitutionalised and judicialised one", with ministers answerable politically to Parliament and legally to the courts. Lord Smith of Clifton said the "most serious problem is the lack of any radical reform of the House of Commons", and that "unbridled presidentialism is now the operational basis of British government". A further debate then took place on the Clergy Discipline Measure, introduced by the Bishop of Winchester, during which some criticism from various parts of the House was made of the appropriateness of Parliament's Ecclesiastical Committee.

On *22 May* Gordon Prentice questioned the Leader of the House about the continued existence of the House of Lords Appointments Commission at an estimated cost of £120,000 a year, though no appointments had been made through this body for over two years. The day was then taken with debate on the Whitsun adjournment, with a miscellany of topics (including Cyprus, the future of the UN, devolution arrangements in Wales and positive parenting) being raised in what Tony Banks described as "this traditional and amiably pointless debate". Paul Tyler took the opportunity to expound the document recently drawn up by a number of MPs (including himself) constituting the Parliament First Group, entitled *Parliament's Last Chance*, which called among other things for a business committee to be set up to manage the business of the House rather than leaving this task to the Government. Peers continued work on the **Communications Bill** with amendments dealing with Ofcom's role in relation to programming competition, the role of the Comptroller and Auditor General in relation to the BBC, Gaelic broadcasting, and the regulation of independent radio. The House, like the Commons, then adjourned for the Whitsun recess.

2 – 6 JUNE

The House of Lords returned from the Whitsun recess on *2 June* for the first report stage day on the **Sexual Offences Bill**. The Government was defeated by 109 votes to 105 on an amendment to confer the same anonymity on defendants as that accorded to complainants in rape cases.

MPs debated a further programme motion on the **Fire Services Bill** on Tuesday *3 June*, with Richard Shepherd saying that 23 Bills had been subject to "the guillotine" already this session. The motion was carried by 284 votes to 184, and the Bill given a third reading by 263 votes to 198. Peers spent a further day on the committee stage of the **Communications Bill**, with debates focusing especially on programme quality, including debate on an amendment moved by Lord Holme of Cheltenham on the coverage of Parliament.

Iraq dominated business of *4 June*, being the first topic for morning debate in Westminster Hall, replied to by Hilary Benn, Minister of State, Department for International Development, who emphasised the scale of the task of reconstruction in that country. At Prime Minister's question time Iain Duncan Smith used all his allocation of questions to challenge Tony Blair about the reliability of the Security Services' information. The Prime Minister then made a Statement on the G8 Summit during which he was again subjected to questions on Iraq. Kenneth Clarke asked if he still believed that the weapons of mass destruction possessed by Iraq had posed such a serious and imminent threat as to justify immediate military invasion. Sir Peter Tapsell asked if the Prime Minister had deliberately sought to mislead the House or was his "blunder based on unsound intelligence reaching him?" Tony Blair disagreed with his questioners but refused to set up the independent inquiry which many of them sought. Menzies Campbell then initiated debate on Iraq on this the seventh Opposition Day, with a motion calling for an independent inquiry into information on weapons of mass destruction, to which Jack Straw responded with an amendment stating that an inquiry by Parliament's Intelligence and Security Committee would be appropriate. Among those intervening in a hostile way on Jack Straw's speech was his predecessor as Foreign Secretary, Robin Cook, who asked why the UK Government did not simply say "we were wrong" on weapons of mass destruction as the Americans had said. Clare Short said the conclusions she had reached about the "way in which the Prime Minister misled us in order to rush to war in Iraq are serious indeed". On division the Liberal Democrat motion was defeated by 203 votes to 301. Steve Webb, again from the Liberal Democrat benches, then opened a debate on pensions, saying the Government had shown remarkable complacency in the face of the crisis in pensions. This motion was defeated by 202 votes to 313. The House of Lords debated a report from their select committee on Economic Affairs on globalisation, and then a report from the EU Committee on the stability and growth pact.

On *5 June* MPs debated the **European Union Accessions Bill** in committee of the whole House, and then gave the Bill an unopposed third reading. In Westminster Hall Donald Anderson, chairman of the Foreign Affairs Select Committee, introduced a debate on a Committee report on human rights. Peers further debated the **Communications Bill** in committee with many probing amendments being discussed.

The Commons did not sit on Friday *6 June*, but the Lords that day spent almost seven hours debating at second reading the **Patient (Assisted Dying) Bill** introduced by Lord Joffe. The 48 speeches made on the Bill were almost exactly evenly divided between supporters and opponents. Lord Joffe defined the Bill as enabling "a competent adult who is suffering unbearably as a result of a terminal or serious, incurable and progressive physical illness to receive medical help to die at his own considered and persistent request". Baroness Finlay of Llandaff said the Bill would not increase "true patient choice", but would increase the "vulnerability of patients and the power of others over them". This theme of increased vulnerability ran through many speeches against the Bill, while supporters emphasised freedom of choice for patients. Baroness Andrews said the Government "do not oppose the Bill", which was approved at second reading without a division.

9 – 13 JUNE

Gordon Brown, Chancellor of the Exchequer, made his long awaited Statement on Economic and Monetary Union on *9 June*. In this he said that only one of the five tests for UK entry to the Euro had been met, that on the effect on the financial services industry. But he said his Statement strengthened "our commitment to and support for the principle of joining the Euro" because he was also setting out a "clear path". This involved changes to the mortgage market and the planning system, as well as setting a new inflation target aligned with that of the European Central Bank. A draft Referendum Bill would be published in the autumn, as would other paving legislation. Responding, Michael Howard for the Opposition said of the Prime Minister and the Chancellor: "there they sit, united in rivalry, each determined to frustrate the other… so there is no clarity of policy and no consistency of purpose". MPs then debated the **Courts Bill**, which was given an unopposed second reading, with a programme motion being passed by 291 votes to 82. Peers spent a second report stage day on the **Sexual Offences Bill**, with an amendment to create an offence of sexual activity in a public lavatory being carried against the Government by 133 votes to 95.

On *10 June* MPs debated three motions providing for the carry-over and re-committal of the **Planning and Compulsory Purchase Bill**. The Opposition spokesman, Geoffrey Clifton-Brown, said this was a "deeply flawed Bill", while Eric Forth, Shadow Leader of the House, said the debate justified his worst fears about "carry over". For the Government Tony McNulty said the Bill would be better after further committee scrutiny and Government amendments, and it was this that justified its carry-over to the next session. The motion was agreed by 279 to 162, with a second motion to provide for a six month extension in the period allowed for consideration of the Bill being approved by 287 votes to 181. MPs then debated a private Bill, the **Mersey Tunnels Bill**, at report stage. Main business in the Lords that day was a debate on the Common Agricultural Policy based on an EU Committee report introduced by Lord Selborne, who explained why this recommended that payments to farmers should be capped, a proposal welcomed by Lord Plumb and others.

The Secretary of State for Work and Pensions, Andrew Smith, made a Statement on *11 June* outlining Government plans for introducing better regulation of occupational pensions. David Willetts responding for the Conservatives was critical of the fact that no debate on pensions had taken place in Government time for three years despite a flurry of activity and numerous consultations. This was then taken as the eighth Opposition Day with Michael Ancram moving a motion calling for a referendum to be held on the proposed constitution for the EU. For the Government Jack Straw argued that earlier EU treaties, such as the Single European Act and the Treaty of European Union had involved more fundamental change than that now contemplated. For the Liberal Democrats Michael Moore said the changes would not necessarily have constitutional implications for this country, so his party could not support the motion, but nor could they support the Government amendment because it was wrong to prejudge the Intergovernmental Conference and declare "there is no case for a referendum". The Conservative motion was defeated by 155 votes to 293. A second motion called on the Government to allow for the continuation of benefit and pension payments through Post Office card accounts. In moving this Oliver Heald noted that the terms of the motion exactly matched an Early Day Motion signed by almost 400 Members including over 170 Labour Members. The Opposition motion was defeated by 314 votes to 187. The House of Lords debated the countryside expressing very varied concerns. Among those who spoke was the Duke of Norfolk making his maiden speech having just inherited his seat as Earl Marshal following his father's death. Peers also debated Amendment Regulations to the Race Relations Act 1976, which Baroness Anelay of St Johns opposed because she argued they effectively reversed the burden of proof in race relations tribunal cases. Lord Lester of Herne Hill and Lord Ouseley were critical of the Regulations because they represented a lost opportunity.

On *12 June* at business questions Eric Forth referred to an Early Day Motion identifying some 80 Labour MPs who had voted with the Government the previous day on Post Office accounts despite having signed a motion identical to that which the Conservatives had advanced. Paul Tyler for the Liberal Democrats asked John Reid to reflect on the fact that in his position as Leader of the House his responsibility was not to the Government, the Cabinet or the Prime Minister, but to the House. Adam Ingram, Minister of State at Defence, then made a Statement on the deployment of British forces as part of a French-led EU force in the Congo, with several MPs drawing attention to the unprecedented nature of this as an EU rather than a NATO force. The House then debated reports from the Defence Select Committee on armed forces personnel, while in Westminster Hall a debate took place on three separate select committee reports on energy issues. The House of Lords began report stage of the **Water Bill**. An Opposition amendment inserting a new clause stipulating a duty to conserve water was carried against the Government by 89 votes to 76, then another moved from the Liberal Democrat benches seeking to introduce the Water Framework Directive principles on the face of the Bill was carried by 94 votes to 89. A third amendment was carried against the Government when peers voted 91 to 89 in support of an Opposition change dealing with trickle irrigation and abstraction licences. Later Lord Onslow interrupted proceedings with a motion calling for the adjournment of the House because as he put it "it had been announced on the television that the office of Lord Chancellor should be abolished", but his motion was defeated by 23 votes to 81.

On Friday *13 June* MPs completed debate on the **Fireworks Bill** and the **Human Fertilisation and Embryology Bill**. In the House of Lords peers welcomed Lord Falconer of Thoroton to the Woolsack, and heard the Leader of the House say he would make a Statement on the Government's proposals concerning the Speakership of the House on Monday. The House then dealt briefly with four private members' bills brought up from the Commons, and a number of Government introduced Orders.

16 – 20 JUNE

The Deputy Prime Minister, John Prescott, made a Statement on *16 June* announcing plans to hold referendums in autumn 2004 on regional assemblies in three regions, the North-East, the North-West, and Yorkshire and the Humber. While the Conservative spokesman expressed profound scepticism, the Liberal Democrats welcomed the announcement, though expressing preference for "a far richer devolution". Sir Patrick Cormack raised as a point of order the "extraordinary behaviour" of the Government in abolishing the office of Lord Chancellor to which the Speaker responded by saying that he had "been in touch with Downing Street to ask that a statement be made", and that the Prime Minister had agreed to do this on Wednesday. Main business of the day was report stage debate on the **Licensing Bill** for which the Government had put down a programme motion allowing five and a half hours, but before this a motion to approve the absence of the Speaker on Wednesday 18 of June had to be taken. The shadow leader of the House, Eric Forth, made a 35-minute speech on this, and was followed by other Conservatives, with the result that after some two hours the House divided and agreed the Speaker's absence by 324 votes to 105. Debate then took place on the 115 amendments and new clauses put down on the Bill, concluding with a third reading division soon after 1 am, when it was approved by 227 votes to 121. Peers heard a Statement that day from the Leader of their House, Lord Williams of Mostyn, on the Speakership of the House in which he said the Government believed it right both to reform the office of the Lord Chancellor, and to allow the House to choose its own presiding officer. Lord Strathclyde for the Conservatives said the Leader should uphold the right of the House to be "informed and heard" in the sweeping changes being proposed. The House then debated the **Criminal Justice Bill** at second reading, introduced by the Lord Chancellor, Lord Falconer of Thoroton. Baroness Anelay of St Johns said the Conservatives supported "most of the measures in the Bill", but would "resist any erosion of liberty that is not backed by overwhelming arguments in its favour". Lord Woolf, Lord Chief Justice, said he had consulted the senior judiciary, who collectively shared his concerns on "changes to the right to trial by jury, the rules of evidence and the retrial of serious offences". All told 30 peers spoke in a debate lasting over six hours.

On *17 June*, the ninth Opposition Day, Eric Forth moved a motion critical of the manner in which the recent ministerial reshuffle had been carried out and the confusion which had resulted, especially over the office of Lord Chancellor, the changes made to the Scotland and Wales Offices, and the appointment as Secretary of State for Health of someone who "has no control over health policies in his own constituency". Peter Hain, the new Leader of the House (and still also Secretary of State for Wales), opened his speech by describing Eric Forth's as "an exercise in Tory self-inflated cant, bombast and hypocrisy". Sir Patrick Cormack said that if the Leader of the House was to make a success of his job he should "try to be a little less partisan than he was this afternoon". The Opposition motion was defeated by 183 votes to 327. Tim Yeo than moved a second Opposition motion on community pharmacies, which was defeated by 197 votes to 338. Peers debated the **Sexual Offences Bill** at third reading. Government amendments offering a compromise on the test of reasonableness in relation to consent were accepted, though not without reluctance in some quarters. Baroness Blatch continued to protest against amendments relating to offences arising out of consensual sexual activity by children, saying these almost completely invalidated the notion of an age of consent. She later divided the House against amendments seeking to protect those giving sex education to children, describing these as a "paedophile's charter", but lost by 72 votes to 192. The Bill was passed and sent to the Commons. Lord Lester of Herne Hill then moved a motion "inviting the Government to withdraw the draft Employment Equality (Sexual Orientation) regulations 2003" and to lay new Regulations to conform with the relevant EC Framework Directive. In support of his motion he cited the report from the Joint Select Committee on Statutory Instruments which had found the Regulations in some respects *intra vires*. The Bishop of Blackburn spoke in defence of the Regulations, which were designed to allow Churches and Faith Communities to preserve a "measure of freedom to determine their own requirements in relation to the sexual conduct – not orientation – of those who wish to serve or represent them". Lord Pilkington of Oxenford said faith communities should not be "dictated to by the State" on this matter. But the Bishop of Worcester spoke in support of Lord Lestor, as did Baroness Turner of Camden and others. On division Lord Lestor's motion was defeated by 50 votes to 85.

At Prime Minister's question time on *18 June* Michael Meacher (until the previous week Minister of State for the Environment) challenged Tony Blair on the absence of human feeding trials on GM foods. Tony Blair made a Statement defending his changes to Government departments, which Iain Duncan Smith described as "the most botched, bungled and damaged reshuffle of modern times", and referred to the Prime Minister as having "ripped up the constitution in a matter of hours". The Home Secretary, David Blunkett, made a Statement on domestic violence, following which Jack Straw, Foreign Secretary, introduced a debate on European affairs focusing especially on the proposed constitution for Europe. Gisela Stuart said the draft document was good, but not perfect, and ought to receive further amendment, while David Heathcoat-Amory explained why he as the other Parliamentary delegate to the convention had refused to sign the draft. Conservatives in general argued for a referendum, while Labour portrayed Conservatives as actually wanting withdrawal from the EU. In the Lords a debate on defence policy was initiated by Lord King of Bridgwater, with much emphasis being placed on the possible inadequacy of the armed forces to meet all pressures that exist on them.

On *19 June* Alistair Darling, Secretary of State for Transport, made a Statement on rail fare increases. This was the third Estimates Day, with first a report from the Home Affairs Select Committee on investigations into children's homes being debated, during which Claire Curtis-Thomas, founder of the all-party group on abuse investigation, made a passionate 30-minute speech arguing that the integrity of the process of investigation of alleged abusers was badly flawed, and that the Government's response to the Committee's report was hugely disappointing. This was followed by a debate on waste management arising out of a report from the Food and Rural Affairs Select Committee. In Westminster Hall a third select committee report was debated, on affordable housing. Peers considered Commons amendments to the **Licensing Bill** with a number of matters being contested. First the Liberal Democrat Lord Redesdale sought further change to a compromise amendment on the new central licensing authority, but this was defeated narrowly – by 113 votes to 117. On exemption for small premises Baroness Buscombe for the Conservatives argued that the Commons amendments did not provide a workable solution to safeguard the playing of live music in pubs, and her motion to reject the Commons version of the Bill was carried by 128 votes to 113. The House then considered the **Railways and Transport Safety Bill** at report stage, before Lord Rooker introduced the second reading of the **Fire Services Bill** warning in his speech that the House should not reject a Bill sent to it from the elected House, and that to do so would "sign the death knell to the current arrangements". But Lord McCarthy said it was a "botch-up", and because the Bill could not be satisfactorily amended the only way to make the Government think again was to reject the Bill. Every other speaker in the debate opposed the Bill. Lord McCarthy said no one defended the Bill, "not even the Minister other than to say the matter was decided in the Commons", but his motion to defeat it was lost by 4 votes to 61.

On Friday *20 June* MPs completed work on the **National Lottery (Funding of Endowments) Bill**, but then ran out of time on the **High Hedges Bill**, which was opposed by a number of Conservatives. Peers debated the Select Committee on the Constitution report on Inter-Institutional Relations within the UK introduced by the Committee chairman, Lord Norton of Louth, who argued that devolution had bedded in with remarkably few problems. Lord Holme of Cheltenham said that recent ministerial and departmental changes were not so much the product of joined up thinking as "dismembered improvisation". Lord Scott of Foscote then introduced a debate on an EU Committee report on the incorporation of the European Charter of Fundamental Rights in the proposed new EU constitution.

23 – 27 JUNE

On *23 June* the Prime Minister made a Statement on the European Council Meeting held in Greece on 19 and 20 June saying the draft European constitution was "a good basis for starting the intergovernmental conference in October", and that it "would provide a greater role for national Parliaments". Responding Iain Duncan Smith said it "would change the way every country in Europe is governed", and he again challenged the Prime Minister to hold a referendum. Replying to a later question, Tony Blair said the minority report made by David Heathcoat-Amory "would mean that Britain would become a different type of member of the European Union" which was a "perfectly honourable position", but it would completely change our relationship with Europe. Two Liberal Democrat motions were then debated on this the tenth Opposition Day. The first stated simply, "This House calls on the Government not to allow universities to introduce top-up fees". It was moved by Phil Willis who said 139 back-bench Labour Members had signed an early day motion to this effect. The motion was lost by 193 votes to 267 with ten Labour MPs voting against the Government but up to 100 others abstaining. The second motion called for a full time Secretary of State for Transport "for the duration of the crisis in transport". Alistair Darling, the Secretary of State, who had also taken responsibility for the Scotland Office, responded to a wide-ranging debate, with the Government winning the division by 300 to 174. Peers debated the **Communications Bill** at report stage with Lord Puttnam moving amendments to re-define the "principal duty" of Ofcom to further the interests of consumers and citizens. With the help of 33 Labour peers this was carried against the Government by 179 votes to 74. Later the Government were defeated narrowly, by 113 votes to 111, on an amendment moved by Lord Northesk to give Ofcom a specific remit to encourage broadband.

At question time on *24 June* the Leader of the House, Peter Hain, said the Government believed the "arrangements for programming Bills are broadly satisfactory", and that as well as the five Bills published in draft form already in the current session, four more would follow. A programme motion for the **Anti-social Behaviour Bill** was carried by 282 votes to 175 despite Opposition complaints that with 105 government new clauses and amendments put down, the six hours being made available was insufficient. Tony Paice for the Opposition said the Government had in at least eight separate areas come forward with changes that addressed issues his party had raised in committee. The Bill was approved at third reading by 419 votes to 43. A further programme motion was then agreed by 274 votes to 158 allowing for one hour to debate Lords amendments to the **Licensing Bill**, which were then rejected by 268 votes to 159. The House of Lords debated the **Water Bill** on report with the Government being defeated by 123 votes to 120 on an amendment creating a right of appeal on enforcement decisions not related to competition.

On *25 June* Damien Green moved a motion declaring that tuition fees "would act as a severe deterrent to many students from hard-working but less well-off families" on this the 11th Opposition Day. Charles Clarke, Secretary of State for Education, argued that with a current graduate paying on average about £850,000 in tax and National Insurance over a 40-year period, repayments would not be so obvious and onerous an extra burden. The Conservative motion was defeated by 191 votes to 293. A later Opposition motion focused on fair trade, and was defeated by 177 votes to 295. Peers debated the steel industry, then took the committee stage of the **Patients' Protection Bill**.

At business questions in the Commons on *26 June* Gerald Kaufman asked if there was any possibility of the Hunting Bill being recommitted after report stage the following week. Peter Hain, Leader of the House, said that if the Bill was amended to contain provisions banning hunting outright, he had been advised re-commitment would be necessary, in which case the Bill was unlikely to reach the Lords before the recess. This brought strong protests from some Labour back benchers. Margaret Beckett than made a Statement on the reform of the Common Agricultural Policy, saying that an agreement reached early that morning had "delivered what we wanted, as well as real change". For the Opposition David Lidington said it was "a botched compromise that falls far short of the radical changes that are needed". Later the House debated a report from the Committee on Standards and Privileges, which responded to the Eighth Report from the Committee on Standards in Public Life. Peers further debated the **Communications Bill** on report.

On Friday *27 June* the House of Commons did not sit, but the House of Lords debated Lord Pearson of Rannoch's **European Unity (Implications of Withdrawal) Bill**, which would require the Government to set up an independent inquiry into the implications of withdrawal from the EU. Lord Griffiths of Fforesfach argued that the Bill would provide for a properly informed debate. Lord Weatherill said he supported the Bill because "we have a sacred duty to explain the pros and cons of ever-closer union", not because he was anti-European. Replying for the Government, Baroness Symons of Vernham Dean opposed a committee of inquiry saying it would only "tell us what we know already", and that the benefits of EU membership were self-evident.

30 JUNE – 4 JULY

On *30 June* John Prescott, Deputy Prime Minister, made a Statement about the White Paper "Our Fire and Rescue Service" published that day, which he said gave greater emphasis to fire prevention, and an enhanced role to Chief Fire Officers in policy development. The House then turned its attention to the **Hunting Bill**. A programme motion to ensure debate ended after five and a half hours was approved by 292 votes to 161. Some Opposition MPs wondered why the Bill had languished for so long given that its committee stage had been completed in February. During debate the Minister for Rural Affairs, Alun Michael, came under mounting pressure to drop his new clause on regulation, which in the closing moments he withdrew, leaving a free vote on the total ban clause. This was carried by 362 votes to 154, with only six Conservatives voting for the ban, while Government ministers overwhelmingly did so. Peers began the committee stage of the **Criminal Justice Bill** with the Government suffering defeat by 117 votes to 115 on a vote to remove Clause 4 concerned with police detention. Later a motion calling on the Government to revoke a statutory instrument dealing with the implementation of an EU directive on food supplements was carried against the Government by 132 votes to 79.

On *1 July* the Commons approved a programme motion by 273 votes to 155 allowing one day's debate for remaining stages of the **Finance Bill**. Government rules on tax credits for ISAs and PEPs were approved by 301 votes to 189, while Opposition amendments on bingo tax were defeated by 185 votes to 304 and those dealing with stamp duty land tax were rejected by 173 votes to 291. The Bill was then approved at third reading by 285 votes to 175, with Paul Boateng saying its examination had been an "example of Parliament working at its best". The House of Lords further debated the **Communications Bill** on report, focusing on various topics including the rules for approving new services, the definition of religion and other matters.

The 12th Opposition Day was taken on *2 July*, with two motions being debated. The first (lost by 151 votes to 382) was critical of the Government's record on road and rail transport. The second deplored the "impact of Government policy on small and medium-sized enterprises" and was defeated by 190 votes to 343. The House of Lords continued with report stage of the **Communications Bill**, with the Government being defeated by 158 votes to 117 on an amendment seeking to give greater clarity to Ofcom's powers to ban advertisements by replacing the word "unsuitable" with the words "misleading, harmful or offensive". Lord Puttnam then moved an amendment tightening the public interest test in relation to the plurality of media ownership, explaining that in so doing he was speaking "for all the members of the Joint Scrutiny Committee" in both Houses. Replying for the Government Lord McIntosh of Haringey promised amendments on the subject at third reading, and after debate Lord Puttnam withdrew his amendment saying: "this has been a good day for the House". The Government lost a further division by 115 votes to 99 when Baroness Buscombe sought to remove what she saw as limitations on religious broadcasting.

On *3 July* the Minister for Europe, Denis MacShane, introduced an adjournment debate on the annual report from the Intelligence and Security Committee. Andrew Mackinlay from the Labour back benches described the whole report as "dotty and barmy", and said people should not pretend that it represented "a satisfactory oversight of our security and intelligence services". Ann Taylor, Chairman of the Committee, said that the briefings they received were not minimalist in any way and that the Committee held the services it scrutinised in high regard. Many of those who spoke in the debate focused their attention on the so-called "dodgy dossier" on Iraq's alleged weapons of mass destruction. Business began in the Lords with Lord Williams of Mostyn, Leader of the House, moving that a "Select Committee of 11 Lords be appointed to consider the future arrangements for the Speakership of the House". Peers completed work on the **Railways and Transport Safety Bill**, with the Government being defeated by 132 votes to 110 on an amendment moved by Baroness Scott of Needham Market seeking to ensure national trails were protected from unnecessary vehicular traffic. Commons amendments to the **Licensing Bill** were considered with a new compromise Government amendment being moved on the vexed issue of the conditions being attached to the playing of live music. This did not however satisfy Baroness Buscombe speaking for the Opposition who forced a division, but this she lost by 75 votes to 145. Baroness Symons of Vernham Dean moved the second reading of the **European Union (Accessions) Bill**, which was followed by Lord McIntosh moving the second reading of the **Finance Bill**. During the latter debate Lord Peston as chairman of the Economic Affairs Committee of the House spoke of the report made on the Bill by his Committee. Lord Higgins spoke of the deteriorating position in regard to scrutiny of complex legislation in the Commons. The House then took all remaining stages of the Bill formally.

On Friday *4 July* MPs considered and agreed Lords amendments to the **Co-operatives and Community Benefits Societies Bill**, and then dealt with the report stages of the **Dealing in Cultural Objects (Offences) Bill**, the **Legal Deposits Libraries Bill**, and the **Sustainable Energy Bill**, all of which also received unopposed third readings. Peers also debated a variety of private members' bills that day, along with a number of Orders. Lord Lucas protested that the **Fireworks Bill** would involve a total ban on the individual use of fireworks, but Lord Carter warned that any amendment to the Bill would kill it, given the timetabling problems in the Commons.

7 – 11 JULY

On *7 July* the Speaker allowed an urgent question from Douglas Hogg on the detention of British nationals in Guantanamo Bay. Chris Mullin, Under-Secretary at the Foreign Office in answering said the British Government had "strong reservations" about the procedure being adopted. This was the 13th Opposition Day with debate on a motion noting "the abject failure of the Government to meet its targets for delivery on public services", which was defeated by 178 votes to 366. A second motion condemning the Government for its failure to pay new tax credits on time was defeated by 186 votes to 329. Peers debated the **Criminal Justice Bill** in committee. Lord Dholakia moved an amendment on the retention by the police of samples taken from suspects. After a Government reply promising further consultations the amendment was withdrawn. Later the Government was defeated by 114 votes to 97 on an amendment preventing the reduction of the minimum age for drug testing children.

On *8 July* David Winnick introduced a ten-minute rule Bill (approved by 171 votes to 73) calling for the removal of remaining hereditary peers from the House of Lords. Douglas Hogg opposed this on the grounds that merely to remove the "anomaly" of hereditary peers would leave the Prime Minister with exactly what he wanted – a wholly appointed House lacking legitimacy. A programme motion relating to the report stage of the **Health and Social Care (Community Health and Standards) Bill** was then approved by 314 votes to 164, with Opposition spokesman Liam Fox arguing that the proposed time limits were ridiculous given the large number of Government amendments. David Hinchliffe, Chairman of the Health Select Committee, moved amendments to delete proposals for foundation trust hospitals which were narrowly lost, by 251 votes to 286 (press reports indicated 62 Labour MPs voted against the Government, and over 70 more abstained). Later at third reading Liam Fox said it was bizarre that the Secretary of State in charge of health care in England "does not have to take responsibility for any of his actions in respect of his own constituents in Scotland". Evan Harris from the Liberal Democrat front bench said it was "unfortunate when every question about the Government's policies draws as a response an attack on the policies of Opposition parties". Third reading was approved by 306 votes to 57. The House then considered and approved without division Lords' amendments to the **Railways and Transport Safety Bill** concerned with the powers of transport police, which the Minister described as being the result of "productive and substantive debate". Next MPs considered and agreed Lords' amendments to the **Licensing Bill** regarding licences for live entertainment which represented a compromise on earlier positions. In Westminster Hall during a debate on genetic modification, former environment minister, Michael Meacher, raised many questions about the adequacy of the trials of GM crops. When the House of Lords debated the **Communications Bill** at third reading an amendment resisted by the Government to " put specific restrictions on the ownership of Channel 5 in terms of cross-media" and defeated by 137 to 167. A Government amendment introducing a plurality test for ownership was welcomed by Lord Puttnam and accepted without a division. The Government was, however, defeated by 158 votes to 141on an amendment restricting the role of the consumer panel so as to avoid potential confusion with the content board.

On *9 July* a Statement from Charles Clarke, Secretary of State for Education and Skills, marked the publication of a White Paper setting out the Government's strategy for meeting the skills shortage. Another from Alistair Darling, Secretary of State for Transport, dealt with transport investment. Responding to the latter Tim Collins for the Opposition said the announcements on motorway widening were "hugely welcome but also hugely belated". Jack Straw, Foreign Secretary, then introduced a debate on the Convention on the Future of Europe on a Government motion for the adjournment. The Opposition focused on their demand for a referendum, but their amendment was defeated by 205 votes to 315. Next the House considered the **Hunting Bill** on report (following its re-committal) with an Opposition amendment concerned with compensation being debated for two hours and defeated by 145 votes to 282, following which an hour-long third reading debate culminated in a 317 to 145 vote for the Bill. In the Lords a motion naming 11 Members to sit on the select committee on the Speakership of the House, under the chairmanship of Lord Lloyd of Berwick was approved. The House then turned its attention to the **Water Bill** which was recommitted in respect of fluoridation, with an amendment allowing the fluoridation of water supplies on the initiative of health authorities and after consultation with local communities being approved by 153 votes to 31. Lord Saatchi introduced his **Tax (Information) Bill** which provided for a bank holiday each year on the day when people stop "working for the Government", which he said would be 2 June in 2003 and 5 June in 2004, but 40 years ago it would have come in April. The House then completed consideration of the **Water Bill**, passing it just after midnight.

On *10 July* Gordon Brown introduced a debate on economic and monetary union, which drew particularly on the sixth report from the Treasury Committee on the UK and the Euro. Peers approved a Commons amendment to the **Railways and Transport Safety Bill** in lieu of one their House had earlier made on the use of national trails by vehicles. Later during report stage of the **Local Government Bill** Baroness Blatch moved an amendment seeking to delay repeal of the law banning the promotion of homosexuality ("Section 28"), but on a free vote her amendment was rejected by 180 to 130.

On Friday *11 July* MPs completed report and third reading stages on three Bills, John Greenway's **Ragwort Control Bill**, Joan Ruddock's **Household Waste Recyling Bill**, and then Ann Clwyd's **Female Genital Mutilation Bill**, all of which had Government support. Peers also sat that day and considered Lord Walpole's **National Lottery (Funding of Endowments) Bill**.

14 – 18 JULY

The Lord Chancellor in a Statement on constitutional reform on *14 July* announced the publication of three consultation papers, the first on a supreme court, the second on an independent judicial appointments commission, and the third on the future of QCs. In reply to a question from Lord Lloyd of Berwick, Lord Falconer confirmed that there had been no consultation of any kind with the law lords. The House of Lords then gave further committee consideration to the **Criminal Justice Bill**. MPs accepted by 306 votes to 165 a programme motion for consideration of Lords amendments to the **Communications Bill**, following which Tessa Jowell, Secretary of State for Culture, Media and Sport, introduced a number of compromise amendments which were agreed without divisions. These dealt with the duty of Ofcom to citizens as opposed to consumers, the commitment to broadband, and other matters, while the Government agreed other Lords amendments concerned with the plurality test and the treatment of disability and equal opportunities. But on the question of removing restrictions on religious bodies holding broadcast licences MPs voted 314 to 175 to overturn changes made in the Lords.

On *15 July* Jack Straw, Foreign Secretary, made a Statement reporting that a sovereign Iraqi government had been established the previous Sunday. MPs then debated at second reading the **Sexual Offences Bill**, with a large measure of agreement being expressed both about the Bill and the benefit gained through the consideration it had already been given in the House of Lords. The second reading was unopposed, but a division was forced on the programme motion, which was, however, carried by 320 votes to 140. During questions in the House of Lords Lord Rooker, Minister for Regeneration and the Regions, said that his two years' experience in the House of Lords had convinced him that the level of scrutiny by the House was superior to that of the Commons. The House then debated the **Criminal Justice Bill**, with an amendment to remove clause 41, concerned with limitations on the right to trial by jury, being carried against the Government by 210 votes to 136.

On *16 July* at Prime Minister's question time Tony Blair described the behaviour of the House of Lords in rejecting Government plans to limit jury trials as "absolutely shameful". Michael Ancram then introduced a motion calling for an independent judicial inquiry in relation to the use of intelligence material on Iraq. He argued that the House had been asked to vote on the decision to go to war, and it was therefore essential that the House had total confidence in intelligence information vouchsafed to it by the Prime Minister. The Government amendment moved by Jack Straw cited the report already made by the Foreign Affairs Select Committee, and drew attention to the inquiry being conducted by the Intelligence and Security Committee. But Donald Anderson, chairman of the Foreign Affairs Select Committee said the Government had "hampered our inquiry by not allowing us full access to the relevant information", while others argued that the Intelligence and Security Committee was a Governmental rather than a Parliamentary Committee. The Opposition motion was, however, defeated by 200 votes to 299. Debate on a second Conservative motion, on vulnerable children, on this the 14th Opposition Day, included very sharp exchanges on the suitability of Margaret Hodge as the recently appointed Minister for Children, with the Opposition motion being defeated by 179 votes to 316. Peers debated Commons amendments to the **Communication Bill** with Baroness Wilcox seeking to insist on Lords amendments relating to religious bodies and broadcast licences, but her motion to this effect was lost by 111 votes to 165. The House then considered the **Local Government Bill** at report stage. An Opposition amendment to remove the power for the Secretary of State to set a minimum level of reserve for a local authority, was defeated by 111 votes to 117.

On *17 July* at business questions Paul Tyler described the Government response to the report of the Joint Select Committee on House of Lords Reform as a "miserable little" document, "deliberately misleading in several respects", while Robin Cook warned that the Government would have difficulty getting such a "pusillanimous, pathetic, mean measure through Parliament". Charles Clarke, Secretary of State for Education and Skills, made a Statement on school funding emphasising increases since 1997, but acknowledging "many schools have experienced real difficulties this year with their budget allocations". On this the last day of the session among the 45 ministerial written statements published was one reporting the Review Body on Senior Salaries report recommending that select committee chairmen should receive an extra payment of £12,500 a year. The House of Lords dealt further at report stage with the **Local Government Bill**, followed by a continuation of the committee stage of the **Criminal Justice Bill** with debate especially focusing on the double jeopardy rule. The Leader of the House, Lord Williams of Mostyn, announced the publication of the first report of the House of Lords Appointments Commission covering the period 2000 to 2003, and said the Prime Minister would be inviting the Commission to recommend a small number of new non-party-political peers.

On Friday *18 July* the Commons did not meet, while the Lords debated the **Anti-social Behaviour Bill** at second reading. The Earl of Shrewsbury said he would be bringing forward amendments relating to young people and air rifles, though in replying to the debate Baroness Scotland indicated the Government was unlikely to accept these. Like the Commons the House then rose until Monday 8 September.

PUBLIC LEGISLATION 2002–03

* legislation introduced by a private member whose name is given immediately after the title of the Act.

HL: legislation introduced into the House of Lords.

Dates are of Royal Assent.

(Attaining Royal Assent between 1 August 2002 and 31 July 2003)

Adoption and Children Act 2002 (7 November 2002)

Repeals and replaces most existing legislation relating to adoption, including the Adoption Act 1976; includes provisions relating to step-parent adoption and inter-country adoption (replacing most of the Adoption (Intercountry Aspects) Act 1999), in particular making procedures more stringent and penalties for breaches of procedures more severe; allows for adoption jointly by unmarried couples including couples of the same gender; introduces a new Special Guardianship Order to provide more settled responsibility for guardians; imposes new duties on local authorities regarding adoption support; establishes a new review mechanism for rejected applicants; introduces new procedures for adopted persons seeking to identify natural parents.

Animal Health Act 2002 (7 November 2002)

Provides extra powers for the Minister of Agriculture to cull farm animals for reasons of disease, especially foot and mouth; makes provision to accelerate the eradication of scrapie and other TSEs from the national sheep flock; provides new powers of entry and surveillance; applies to England and Wales.

*Commonwealth Act 2002 *David Willetts* (7 November 2002)

Gives recognition to the establishment as an independent charitable company of the Commonwealth Institute; provides for recognition of Cameroon and Mozambique as members of the Commonwealth.

*Copyright (Visually Impaired Persons) Act 2002 *Rachel Squire* (7 November 2002)

Allows exceptions to copyright enabling a wide range of copyright material to be copied for visually impaired people.

*Employee Share Scheme Act 2002 *Mark Lazarowicz* (7 November 2002)

Provides for changes in the rules regarding Share Incentive Plans to allow elected employees to act as trustees of employee shareholders' interests; to allow for corporation tax relief on transfer of shares beyond a certain value into a trust on behalf of employees; and to allow companies owned by employee trusts to set up a share incentive plan.

Enterprise Act 2002 (7 November 2002)

Reforms the merger regime and removes decision-making power from Ministers; provides for a new competition-based test to be used by the Office of Fair Trading and the Competition Commission, with ability to take into account consumer benefits; provides that breaches in competition law can become a ground for director disqualification; allows the Office of Fair Trading to prioritise as "super-complaints" certain cases presented by consumer organisations and provides for representative actions to be brought on behalf of groups of consumers; reforms corporate insolvency law to curtail the use of administrative receiverships; introduces a new Bankruptcy Restriction Order regime lasting up to 15 years for culpable or reckless bankrupts, while reducing the bankruptcy discharge period to one year for non-culpable ("honest") bankrupts; applies to UK except that provisions on bankruptcy do not apply to Scotland and Northern Ireland.

Nationality, Immigration and Asylum Act 2002 (7 November 2002)

Introduces new requirements for those who seek British citizenship through naturalisation, including knowledge about life in the UK; introduces citizenship ceremonies; alters procedures for depriving a person of citizenship; amends nationality law to enable the UK to ratify the European Convention on Nationality; provides for the introduction of Accommodation Centres for asylum seekers and alters support system for asylum seekers; makes new provision for the detention and removal of asylum seekers and for immigration and asylum appeals; introduces charges for immigrants work permits and other changes in relation to immigration procedure.

*Private Hire Vehicles (Carriage of Guide Dogs Etc) Act 2002 *Neil Gerrard* (7 November 2002)
Amends the Disability Discrimination Act 1995 to impose a requirement on private hire vehicles to carry assistance dogs in line with a similar requirement already made of licensed taxi drivers.

Public Trustee (Liability and Fees) Act 20002 *HL* (7 November 2002)
Amends the Public Trustee Act 1906 to removes the requirement for full-cost recovery for trust work now carried out by the Official Solicitor or the Public Guardianship Office.

Tobacco Advertising and Promotion Act 2002 *HL* (7 November 2002)
Provides for a ban on advertising and promotion of tobacco products with specified exceptions; applies to the UK, and will come into force on dates to be decided by Ministers.

(Attaining Royal Assent between Queen's Speech 2002 and 31 July 2003)

*Aviation (Offences) Act 2003 *Frank Roy* (10 July 2003)
Provides for police powers of arrest of drunk and disorderly passengers on aircraft; amends Civil Aviation Act 1982 to provide for increased penalties for endangering aircraft or persons on an aircraft.

Communications Act 2003 (17 July 2003)
Prescribes functions to be transferred or assigned to Ofcom; sets out rules and general duties for Ofcom in regard to the regulation of broadcasting and telecommunications; provides for the establishment of a consumer panel and a content board; amends the law relating to media ownership; removes the ban on non-European Economic Area nationals holding broadcast licences; lifts restrictions on the number of Channel 3 licences a company may own and on the ownership of Channel 5 by newspaper groups; amends the law relating to newspaper mergers to conform with merger controls in the Enterprise Act 2002, but with exceptions for particularly significant proposed mergers; allows for continuation of a ban on political advertising on television and radio; sets a new framework for the regulation of electronic communication networks and services and for spectrum.

Community Care (Delayed Discharges Etc) Act 2003 (8 April 2003)
Creates new duties for local authorities and the NHS in relation to the assessment of needs before the discharge from hospital of patients requiring community care; requires local authorities to make payments to NHS bodies where the discharge of patients is delayed because assessments are incomplete or community care services not in place; provides for the creation of a panel to resolve disputes between NHS bodies and social service authorities.

Consolidated Fund (No 2) Act 2002 (17 December 2002)
Gives Parliamentary authority for sums to be issued out of the consolidated fund to meet the Government's expenditure requirements.

Consolidated Fund Act 2003 (20 March 2003)
Gives Parliamentary authority for sums to be issued out of the consolidated fund to meet the Government's expenditure requirements.

Appropriation (No 2) Act 2002 (17 December 2002)
[Introduced as Consolidated Fund Appropriation Bill]
Prescribes how expenditure is appropriated in order to finance specific public services.

Appropriation Act 2003 (10 July 2003)
[Introduced as Consolidated Fund Appropriation (No 2) Bill]
Prescribes how expenditure is appropriated in order to finance specific public services.

*Co-operatives and Community Benefit Societies Act 2003 *Mark Todd* (10 July 2003)
Provides an "asset lock" for Community Benefit Societies to allow for the prevention of asset distribution except for defined community purposes; amends industrial and provident law in certain respects in line with developments in company law.

Electricity (Miscellaneous Provisions) Act 2003 (8 May 2003)
Provides parliamentary authority for expenditure on British Energy plc or its subsidiaries; amends the Electricity Act 1989 to remove the barrier to Government acquiring shares in 'successor companies' and to remove the ceiling on financial assistance in relation to nuclear liabilities, and changes the tax status of such assistance.

European Parliament (Representation) Act 2003 (8 May 2003)
Provides for reduction in the number of UK seats in the European Parliament consequent on the Treaty of Nice; provides for representation of the people of Gibraltar by becoming part of a UK region for electoral purposes.

Finance Act 2003 (10 July 2003)
Provides for measures to counter tax avoidance by individuals and companies in various ways; extends Inland Revenue and Customs and Excuse powers relating to tax avoidance; amends law relating to research and development tax credits; removes stamp duty for non-residential property transactions in disadvantaged areas; adjusts employee share schemes; establishes duty differentials for sulphur-free fuels; provides for increases in landfill tax and amends the landfill tax credit scheme; introduces income tax exemptions for foster carers; includes other provisions.

Health (Wales) Act 2003 (8 April 2003)
Extends powers of Community Health Councils in Wales; establishes the Wales Centre for Health to oversee and provide research and training on public health issues; establishes the Health Professions Wales to assume responsibilities in relation to the education and training of health care professionals and support workers.

Income Tax (Earnings and Pensions) Act 2003 (6 March 2003)
The second Bill to be brought forward through the Tax Law Rewrite Project which seeks to preserve the policy effects of existing legislation while making clarifications, corrections and minor changes; rewrites tax law in relation to employment and pension income; systematises share related remuneration; introduces a "benefits code" for the taxation of all benefits in kind.

Industrial Development (Financial Assistance) Act 2003 (8 May 2003)
Amends the Industrial Development Act 1982 so as to raise the financial limits for assistance given to industry outside areas granted Assisted Area status.

Licensing Act 2003 *HL* (10 July 2003)
Establishes a single system of licensing under local authority control for the licensing of alcohol sales and the provision of public entertainment; abolishes fixed closing times for licensed premises; introduces a personal licence for the supply of alcohol; provides for a system of authorisation for qualifying clubs and temporary events; confers powers on certain police officers to close licensed premises for specified periods of time to prevent or limit disturbance; increases police powers to confiscate alcohol; provides for a new regime in respect of the admission of children to licensed premises; amends the law relating to entertainment licences, with exceptions for churches, schools and other bodies.

*Marine Safety Act 2003 *Brian Iddon* (10 July 2003)
Confers powers to ensure land and certain facilities can be made available to prevent or minimise pollution resulting from a marine accident; provides for compensation to be paid where such facilities have been used; amends the Fire Services Act 1947 to allow for Fire Authorities to recover costs incurred in fire-fighting and related actions undertaken outside their areas.

National Minimum Wage (Enforcement Notices) Act 2003 *HL* (8 May 2003)
Amends the National Minimum Wages Act 1998 to provide for enforcement notices to be made applicable to former employees.

Northern Ireland Assembly Elections Act 2003 (20 March 2003)
Provides for the postponement of elections to the Northern Ireland Assembly for a period of 28 days from 1 May; provides for the dissolution of the suspended Assembly on 28 April.

Northern Ireland Assembly (Elections and Periods of Suspension) Act 2003 (15 May 2003)
Provides for the postponement of the elections for the Northern Ireland Assembly due on 29 May; gives the Secretary of State power to specify a new date for elections; makes provision for payments to registered parties and candidates in respect of expenditure already incurred relating to elections now postponed; makes provision for continued payment of salaries and allowances to former members of the dissolved Assembly.

Police (Northern Ireland) Act 2003 *HL* (8 April 2003)
Strengthens the role of the Policing Board and adjusts the relationship between the Secretary of State, the Chief Constable and the Policing Board in relation to the setting of police objectives and the construction of policing plans; provides for special treatment of sensitive information given to the Policing Board and amends procedures in relation to inquiries conducted by the Policing Board; extends the powers of the Police Ombudsman to investigate the police; places new obligations on the Policing Board in relation to the appointment of members of District Police Partnerships; allows for the deployment of more police support officers.

Railways and Transport Safety Act 2003 (10 July 2003)
Establishes a new Railways Accident Investigation Branch to inquire into the causes of railway accidents; establishes an Office of Rail Regulation to replace the rail regulator; creates an independent police authority for the British Transport Police; introduces new alcohol offences in relation to marine and aviation with exceptions for non-professional mariners in certain kinds of craft; confers powers to create a levy on the rail industry to meet costs of the Health and Safety Executive in respect of railways; and other miscellaneous provisions.

Regional Assemblies (Preparations) Act 2003 (8 May 2003)
A paving measure providing for referendums to be held on the establishment of elected assemblies for English regions (excluding London), such referendums to take place on the Secretary of State's recommendation following his assessment of the level of popular support; provides for the Electoral Commission to conduct a review of local government boundaries in areas where referendums are to be held with a view to recommending a unitary structure of local government in the region concerned; confers new powers on the Secretary of State to make grants in respect of the activities of existing voluntary regional chambers (assemblies).

*Sunday Working Scotland Act 2003 *David Cairns* (10 July 2003)
Extends existing protection for shop workers in England and Wales against being obliged to work on Sundays to shop workers in Scotland.

Departmental Select Committee Reports 2002–03

excluding special reports

HEALTH

1st	The Work of the Health Committee 2002, *HC 261*
2nd	Foundation Trusts, *HC 395*
3rd	Sexual Health, *HC 69*
4th	The Provision of Maternity Services, *HC 464*
5th	The Control of Entry Regulation and Retail Pharmacy Services in the UK, *HC 571*
6th	The Victoria Climbie Inquiry Report, *HC 570*
7th	Patient and Public Involvement in the NHS, *HC 697*
8th	Inequality in Access to Maternity Services, *HC 696*
9th	Choice in Maternity Services, *HC 796*

HOME AFFAIRS

1st	Extradition Bill, *HC 138*
2nd	Criminal Justice Bill, *HC 83*
3rd	The Work of the Home Affairs Committee in 2002, *HC 336*
4th	Asylum Removals, *HC 654*
5th	Sexual Offences Bill, *HC 639*

HOUSING, PLANNING, LOCAL GOVERNMENT AND THE REGIONS (OFFICE OF THE DEPUTY PRIME MINISTER)

1st	Local Government Finance: Formula Grant Distribution, *HC 164*
2nd	Annual Report to the Liaison Committee, *HC 288*
3rd	Affordable Housing, *HC 75*
4th	Planning Competitiveness and Productivity, *HC 114*
5th	Departmental Annual Report and Estimates 2002, *HC 78*
6th	The Licensing Bill (Lords) and the Evening Economy, *HC 541*
7th	The Effectiveness of Government Regeneration Initiatives, *HC 76*
8th	Planning for Sustainable Housing and Communities: Sustainable Communities in the South East, *HC 77*
9th	Reducing Regional Disparities in Prosperity, *HC 492*
10th	The Draft Housing Bill, *HC 751*
11th	Living Places: Cleaner, Safer, Greener, *HC 673*
12th	The Evening Economy and the Urban Renaissance, *HC 396*

INTERNATIONAL DEVELOPMENT

1st	Afghanistan: The Transition from Humanitarian Relief to Reconstruction and Development Assistance, *HC 84*
2nd	Annual Report 2002, *HC 331*
3rd	The Humanitarian Crisis in Southern Africa, *HC 116*
4th	Preparing for the Humanitarian Consequences of Possible Military Action against Iraq, *HC 444*
*5th	The Government's Proposals for Secondary legislation under the Export Control Act, *HC 620*
*6th	Strategic Export Control Annual Report for 2001: Licensing Policy and Parliamentary Scrutiny *HC 474*
7th	Trade and Development at the WTO: Issues for Cancun, *HC 400*

THE LORD CHANCELLOR'S DEPARTMENT

1st	Courts Bill, *HC 526*
2nd	Judicial Appointments: Lessons from the Scottish Experience, *HC 902*
3rd	Children and Family Courts Advisory and Support Services (CAFCASS), *HC 614*

NORTHERN IRELAND AFFAIRS

1st	The Impact in Northern Ireland of Cross-Border Road Fuel Price Differentials: Three Years On, *HC 105*
2nd	Annual Report 2002, *HC 271*
3rd	The Police (Northern Ireland) Bill, *HC 233*
4th	The Control of Firearms in Northern Ireland and the Draft Firearms (Northern Ireland) Order 2002, *HC 67*
5th	Forensic Science in Northern Ireland, *HC 204*

6th   The UK and the Euro, *HC 187*
7th   2003 Budget, *HC 652*
8th   Appointment to the Monetary Committee of the Bank of England of Mr Richard Lambert, *HC 811*
9th   Appointment of Ms Rachel Lomax as a Deputy Governor of the Bank of England and member of the Monetary Policy Committee, *HC 1011*
10th   Inland Revenue Matters, *HC 834*

WELSH AFFAIRS
1st   Broadband in Wales, *HC 95*
2nd   Transport in Wales, *HC 205*
3rd   Work of the Committee in 2002, *HC 263*
4th   The Primary Legislative Process as it affects Wales, *HC 79*
5th   Draft Public Audit (Wales) Bill, *HC 763*

WORK AND PENSIONS
1st   The Social Security Advisory Committee, *HC 296*
2nd   The Committee's Work in 2002, *HC 297*
3rd   The Future of Pensions, *HC 92*
4th   Employment for All: Interim Report, *HC 401*
5th   Childcare for Working Parents, *HC 564*

*Joint Reports of the Defence, Foreign Affairs, International Development and Trade and Industry Committees

Selected List of other Select Committee Reports

HOUSE OF COMMONS

Environmental Audit Committee
1st   Pesticides – The Voluntary Initiative *HC 100*
2nd   Johannesburg and Back – The World Summit on Sustainable Development *HC 169*
3rd   Environmental Audit Committee Annual Report 2002 *HC 262*
4th   The Pre-Budget Report 2002 *HC 167*
5th   Waste – An Audit *HC 99*
6th   Buying Time for Forests: Timber Trade and Public Procurement - Government Response to the Committee's Sixth Report, Session 2001-02. *HC 909*
7th   Export Credits Guarantee Department and Sustainable Development *HC 689*
8th   Energy White Paper - Empowering Change? *HC 618*
9th   Budget 2003 and Aviation *HC 672*
10th   Learning the Sustainability Lesson. *HC 472*

European Scrutiny Committee
24th   The Convention on the Future of Europe and the Role of National Parliaments, *HC 63-xxiv*
26th   The Convention's Proposals on Criminal Justice *HC 64-xxvi*
30th   European Scrutiny in the Commons, *HC 64-xxx*

Liaison
1st   Annual Report 2002 *HL 558*

Procedure
1st   Delegated Legislation: Proposals for a Sifting Committee, *HC 501*

HOUSE OF LORDS

Constitution
2nd   Devolution: Inter-institutional Relations in the UK *HL 28*

Economic Affairs
1st   Globalisation *HL 5*
3rd   Finance Bill 2003 *HL 121*

Religious Offences
1st   Religious Offences in England and Wales *HL95*

Science and Technology
2nd   Chips for Everything: Britain's Opportunity in the Global Market *HL 13*
4th   Fighting Infection *HL 138*
5th   Science and the RDAs: Setting the Agenda *HL 140*

dodonline.co.uk

The UK's leading political website from Vacher Dod Publishing . . .

- Full biographies with photographs
- Fully printable and searchable
- Comprehensive contact database
- Export names and addresses for mail merge

- Personal notepad and search facility
- Constituency profiles
- General election and by-election results
- Events as they happen

DodOnline is the premier service designed for those at the forefront of their fields with a need for accurate and updated political knowledge. Simple to use, with thousands of contacts at your fingertips, as well as a mass of supporting information – and the ability to interactively tailor the service to your needs.

Extensive coverage of: Westminster, Scotland, Wales, Northern Ireland, European Union and the GLA.

Call Yasmin Mirza, Aby Farsoun or Michael Mand now on 020 7630 7643 for a instant free trial

Vacher Dod Publishing
1 Douglas Street, London, SW1P 4PA
Tel: 020 7630 7619
Fax: 020 7233 7266
E-mail: subscriptions@vacherdod.co.uk
Website: www.DodOnline.co.uk

PARLIAMENT

Government and Opposition

Vacher's Parliamentary Companion

Published continuously since 1832 and updated quarterly

Published quarterly, *Vacher's Parliamentary Companion* covers the UK and European political scene, with constantly updated information on:

- House of Commons
- House of Lords
- Government Departments
- Scottish Parliament
- National Assembly for Wales
- Northern Ireland Assembly
- European Union – 200-page coverage will keep you abreast of moves and appointments in the EU

To order call our Hotline now on 020 7630 7619

Vacher Dod Publishing
1 Douglas Street, London, SW1P 4PA
Tel: 020 7630 7619   Fax: 020 7233 7266
Email: subscriptions@vacherdod.co.uk
Website: www.DodOnline.co.uk

The Government

The Cabinet

Prime Minister, First Lord of the Treasury and Minister for the Civil Service	Rt Hon **Tony Blair** MP
Deputy Prime Minister and First Secretary of State	Rt Hon **John Prescott** MP
Chancellor of the Exchequer	Rt Hon **Gordon Brown** MP
Secretary of State for Foreign and Commonwealth Affairs	Rt Hon **Jack Straw** MP
Secretary of State for the Home Department	Rt Hon **David Blunkett** MP
Secretary of State for Environment, Food and Rural Affairs	Rt Hon **Margaret Beckett** MP
Secretary of State for Transport and Secretary of State for Scotland	Rt Hon **Alistair Darling** MP
Secretary of State for Health	Rt Hon Dr **John Reid** MP
Secretary of State for Northern Ireland	Rt Hon **Paul Murphy** MP
Secretary of State for Defence	Rt Hon **Geoffrey Hoon** MP
Secretary of State for Work and Pensions	Rt Hon **Andrew Smith** MP
Leader of the House of Lords and Lord President of the Council	Rt Hon **Lord Williams of Mostyn** QC
Secretary of State for Trade and Industry, Minister for Women and e-Minister in Cabinet	Rt Hon **Patricia Hewitt** MP
Secretary of State for Culture, Media and Sport	Rt Hon **Tessa Jowell** MP
Parliamentary Secretary to the Treasury and Chief Whip	Rt Hon **Hilary Armstrong** MP
Secretary of State for Education and Skills	Rt Hon **Charles Clarke** MP
Chief Secretary to the Treasury	Rt Hon **Paul Boateng** MP
Leader of the House of Commons, Lord Privy Seal and Secretary of State for Wales	Rt Hon **Peter Hain** MP
Minister without Portfolio and Labour Party Chair	Rt Hon **Ian McCartney** MP
Secretary of State for International Development	Rt Hon **Baroness Amos**
Secretary of State for Constitutional Affairs	Rt Hon **Lord Falconer of Thoroton** QC
Also attending Cabinet Lords Chief Whip	Rt Hon **Lord Grocott**

Visit the Vacher Dod Website . . .
www.DodOnline.co.uk

Departmental Ministers

OFFICE OF THE DEPUTY PRIME MINISTER

Deputy Prime Minister and
   First Secretary of State   Rt Hon **John Prescott** MP
Ministers of State   Rt Hon **Nick Raynsford** MP
                                 Rt Hon **Lord Rooker**
                                 Rt Hon **Keith Hill** MP
Parliamentary Under-Secretaries of State   **Yvette Cooper** MP
                                 Phil Hope MP*

*Unpaid

CABINET OFFICE

Minister for the Cabinet Office and
   Chancellor of the Duchy of Lancaster   **Douglas Alexander** MP

DEPARTMENT FOR CONSTITUTIONAL AFFAIRS

Secretary of State for Constitutional Affairs
   and Lord Chancellor   Rt Hon **Lord Falconer of Thoroton** QC†
Parliamentary Under-Secretaries of State   **Christopher Leslie** MP
                                 David Lammy MP
                                 Lord Filkin CBE

†During the transitional period, Lord Falconer will carry out all the functions of Lord Chancellor as necessary. He will not sit as a judge in the House of Lords before the new Supreme Court is established.

DEPARTMENT FOR CULTURE, MEDIA AND SPORT

Secretary of State for Culture,
   Media and Sport   Rt Hon **Tessa Jowell** MP
Ministers of State   Rt Hon **Richard Caborn** MP
                                 Rt Hon **Estelle Morris** MP
Parliamentary Under-Secretary of State   Rt Hon **Lord McIntosh of Haringey**

MINISTRY OF DEFENCE

Secretary of State for Defence   Rt Hon **Geoffrey Hoon** MP
Minister of State   Rt Hon **Adam Ingram** MP
Parliamentary Under-Secretaries of State   **Ivor Caplin** MP
                                 Lord Bach

DEPARTMENT FOR EDUCATION AND SKILLS

Secretary of State for Education and Skills   Rt Hon **Charles Clarke** MP
Ministers of State   Rt Hon **Margaret Hodge** MBE MP
                                 David Miliband MP
                                 Rt Hon **Alan Johnson** MP
Parliamentary Under-Secretary of State
   (also DWP)   **Baroness Ashton of Upholland**
Parliamentary Under-Secretaries of State   **Ivan Lewis** MP
                                 Stephen Twigg MP

DEPARTMENT FOR ENVIRONMENT, FOOD AND RURAL AFFAIRS

Secretary of State for Environment,
   Food and Rural Affairs   Rt Hon **Margaret Beckett** MP
Ministers of State   **Elliot Morley** MP
                                 Rt Hon **Alun Michael** MP
Parliamentary Under-Secretaries of State   **Lord Whitty**
                                   Ben Bradshaw MP

FOREIGN AND COMMONWEALTH OFFICE

Secretary of State for Foreign and Commonwealth Affairs	Rt Hon **Jack Straw** MP
Ministers of State	Rt Hon Dr **Denis MacShane** MP
	Rt Hon **Baroness Symons of Vernham Dean**
also DTI	**Mike O'Brien** MP
Parliamentary Under-Secretaries of State	**Bill Rammell** MP
	Chris Mullin MP

DEPARTMENT OF HEALTH

Secretary of State for Health	Rt Hon Dr **John Reid** MP
Ministers of State	Rt Hon **John Hutton** MP
	Rosie Winterton MP
Parliamentary Under-Secretaries of State	**Melanie Johnson** MP
	Dr **Stephen Ladyman** MP
	Lord Warner

HOME OFFICE

Secretary of State for the Home Department	Rt Hon **David Blunkett** MP
Ministers of State	**Hazel Blears** MP
	Rt Hon **Baroness Scotland of Asthal** QC
	Beverley Hughes MP
Parliamentary Under-Secretaries of State	**Caroline Flint** MP
	Fiona Mactaggart MP
	Paul Goggins MP

DEPARTMENT FOR INTERNATIONAL DEVELOPMENT

Secretary of State for International Development	Rt Hon **Baroness Amos**
Minister of State	**Hilary Benn** MP
Parliamentary Under-Secretary of State	**Gareth Richard Thomas** MP

LAW OFFICERS' DEPARTMENT

Attorney General	Rt Hon **Lord Goldsmith** QC
Solicitor General	Rt Hon **Harriet Harman** QC MP

LEADER OF THE HOUSE OF COMMONS

Leader of the House of Commons and Lord Privy Seal	Rt Hon **Peter Hain** MP
Deputy Leader of the House of Commons	**Phil Woolas** MP

LEADER OF THE HOUSE OF LORDS AND LORD PRESIDENT OF THE COUNCIL

Leader of the House of Lords and Lord President of the Council	Rt Hon **Lord Williams of Mostyn** QC
Deputy Leader of the House of Lords	Rt Hon **Baroness Symons of Vernham Dean**

LORD CHANCELLOR – SEE DEPARTMENT FOR CONSTITUTIONAL AFFAIRS

MINISTER WITHOUT PORTFOLIO AND LABOUR PARTY CHAIR

	Rt Hon **Ian McCartney** MP

NORTHERN IRELAND OFFICE

Secretary of State for Northern Ireland	Rt Hon **Paul Murphy** MP
Ministers of State	Rt Hon **John Spellar** MP
	Rt Hon **Jane Kennedy** MP
Parliamentary Under-Secretaries of State	**Ian Pearson** MP
	Angela Smith MP

PRIVY COUNCIL OFFICE
Lord President of the Council and
    Leader of the House of Lords   Rt Hon **Lord Williams of Mostyn** QC

SCOTLAND OFFICE
Secretary of State for Scotland   Rt Hon **Alistair Darling** MP
Parliamentary Under-Secretary of State   **Anne McGuire** MP
Advocate General for Scotland   Dr **Lynda Clark** QC MP

DEPARTMENT OF TRADE AND INDUSTRY
Secretary of State for Trade and Industry,
    Minister for Women and e-Minister
    in Cabinet   Rt Hon **Patricia Hewitt** MP
Ministers of State   **Stephen Timms** MP
    (also FCO)   **Mike O'Brien** MP
                     Rt Hon **Jacqui Smith** MP
Parliamentary Under-Secretaries of State   **Nigel Griffiths** MP
                     Gerry Sutcliffe MP
                     Lord Sainsbury of Turville*

*Unpaid

DEPARTMENT FOR TRANSPORT
Secretary of State for Transport and
    Secretary of State for Scotland   Rt Hon **Alistair Darling** MP
Minister of State   Dr **Kim Howells** MP
Parliamentary Under-Secretaries of State   **David Jamieson** MP
                     Tony McNulty MP

HM TREASURY
Chancellor of the Exchequer   Rt Hon **Gordon Brown** MP
Chief Secretary to the Treasury   Rt Hon **Paul Boateng** MP
Paymaster General   Rt Hon **Dawn Primarolo** MP
Financial Secretary   **Ruth Kelly** MP
Economic Secretary   **John Healey** MP

WALES OFFICE
Secretary of State for Wales   Rt Hon **Peter Hain** MP
Parliamentary Under-Secretary of State   **Don Touhig** MP

DEPARTMENT FOR WORK AND PENSIONS
Secretary of State for Work and Pensions   Rt Hon **Andrew Smith** MP
Ministers of State   **Des Browne** MP
                     Malcolm Wicks MP
Parliamentary Under-Secretaries of State   Rt Hon **Baroness Hollis of Heigham** DL
                     Maria Eagle MP
                     Chris Pond MP
    (also DfES)   **Baroness Ashton of Upholland**

Visit the Vacher Dod Website . . .
www.DodOnline.co.uk

Government Whips

House of Commons

Chief Whip
Parliamentary Secretary to the Treasury   Rt Hon **Hilary Armstrong** MP

Deputy Chief Whip
Treasurer of HM Household   **Bob Ainsworth** MP

Whips
Comptroller of HM Household
Pairing Whip   **Thomas McAvoy** MP
Vice-Chamberlain of HM Household   **Jim Fitzpatrick** MP
Lord Commissioners   **John Heppell** MP
                                                 Nick Ainger MP
                                                 Jim Murphy MP
                                                 Joan Ryan MP
                                                 Derek Twigg MP

Assistant Whips
                                                 Fraser Kemp MP
                                                 Charlotte Atkins MP
                                                 Gillian Merron MP
                                                 Vernon Coaker MP
                                                 Paul Clark MP
                                                 Margaret Moran MP
                                                 Bridget Prentice MP

House of Lords

Chief Whip
Captain of the Honourable Corps of the
Gentlemen-at-Arms   Rt Hon **Lord Grocott**

Deputy Chief Whip
Captain of The Queen's Bodyguard of
the Yeomen of the Guard   **Lord Davies of Oldham**

Whips
Lords in Waiting   **Lord Bassam of Brighton**
                                                 Lord Evans of Temple Guiting CBE

Baronesses in Waiting   **Baroness Farrington of Ribbleton**
                                                 Baroness Andrews OBE
                                                 Baroness Crawley

---

DodOnline
An Electronic Directory without rival . . .

MPs' biographies and photographs available with daily updates *via* the internet

For a *free* trial, call Yasmin Mirza, Aby Farsoun or Michael Mand on 020 7630 7643

Alphabetical list of Ministers and Whips

AINGER Nick	Whip
AINSWORTH Bob	Deputy Chief Whip
ALEXANDER Douglas	Minister for the Cabinet Office and Chancellor of the Duchy of Lancaster
AMOS Rt Hon Baroness	Secretary of State for International Development
ANDREWS Baroness	Lords Whip
ARMSTRONG Rt Hon Hilary	Chief Whip
ASHTON of UPHOLLAND Baroness	Parliamentary Under-Secretary of State, Department for Education and Skills and Department for Work and Pensions
ATKINS Charlotte	Assistant Whip
BACH Lord	Parliamentary Under-Secretary of State, Ministry of Defence
BASSAM of BRIGHTON Lord	Lords Whip
BECKETT Rt Hon Margaret	Secretary of State for Environment, Food and Rural Affairs
BENN Hilary	Minister of State, Department for International Development
BLAIR Rt Hon Tony	Prime Minister
BLEARS Hazel	Minister of State, Home Office
BLUNKETT Rt Hon David	Home Secretary
BOATENG Rt Hon Paul	Chief Secretary to the Treasury
BRADSHAW Ben	Parliamentary Under-Secretary of State, Department for Environment, Food and Rural Affairs
BROWN Rt Hon Gordon	Chancellor of the Exchequer
BROWNE Des	Minister of State, Department for Work and Pensions
CABORN Rt Hon Richard	Minister of State, Department for Culture, Media and Sport
CAPLIN Ivor	Parliamentary Under-Secretary of State, Ministry of Defence
CLARK Dr Lynda	Advocate General
CLARK Paul	Assitant Whip
CLARKE Rt Hon Charles	Secretary of State for Education and Skills
COAKER Vernon	Assistant Whip
COOPER Yvette	Parliamentary Under-Secretary of State, Office of the Deputy Prime Minister
CRAWLEY Baroness	Lords Whip
DARLING Rt Hon Alistair	Secretary of State for Transport and for Scotland
DAVIES of OLDHAM Lord	Lords Whip
EAGLE Maria	Parliamentary Under-Secretary of State, Department for Work and Pensions
EVANS OF TEMPLE GUITING Lord	Lords Whip
FALCONER of THOROTON Rt Hon Lord	Secretary of State for Constitutional Affairs
FARRINGTON of RIBBLETON	Lords Whip
FILKIN Lord	Parliamentary Under-Secretary of State, Department for Constitutional Affairs
FITZPATRICK Jim	Whip
FLINT Caroline	Parliamentary Under-Secretary of State, Home Office
GOGGINS Paul	Parliamentary Under-Secretary of State, Home Office
GOLDSMITH Rt Hon Lord	Attorney General
GRIFFITHS Nigel	Parliamentary Under-Secretary of State, Department of Trade and Industry
GROCOTT Lord	Lords Chief Whip

HAIN Rt Hon Peter	Leader of the House of Commons, Lord Privy Seal and Secretary of State for Wales
HARMAN Rt Hon Harriet	Solicitor General
HEALEY John	Economic Secretary, HM Treasury
HEPPELL John	Whip
HEWITT Rt Hon Patricia	Secretary of State for Trade and Industry and Minister for Women
HILL Rt Hon Keith	Minister of State, Office of the Deputy Prime Minister
HODGE Rt Hon Margaret	Minister of State, Department for Education and Skills
HOLLIS of HEIGHAM Rt Hon Baroness	Parliamentary Under-Secretary of State, Department for Work and Pensions
HOON Rt Hon Geoffrey	Secretary of State for Defence
HOPE Phil	Parliamentary Under-Secretary of State, Office of the Deputy Prime Minister
HOWELLS Dr Kim	Minister of State, Department for Transport
HUGHES Beverley	Minister of State, Home Office
HUTTON Rt Hon John	Minister of State, Department of Health
INGRAM Rt Hon Adam	Minister of State, Ministry of Defence
JAMIESON David	Parliamentary Under-Secretary of State, Department for Transport
JOHNSON Rt Hon Alan	Minister of State, Department for Education and Skills
JOHNSON Melanie	Parliamentary Under-Secretary of State, Department of Health
JOWELL Rt Hon Tessa	Secretary of State for Culture, Media and Sport
KELLY Ruth	Financial Secretary, HM Treasury
KEMP Fraser	Assistant Whip
KENNEDY Rt Hon Jane	Minister of State, Northern Ireland Office
LADYMAN Dr Stephen	Parliamentary Under-Secretary of State, Department of Health
LAMMY David	Parliamentary Under-Secretary of State, Department for Constitutional Affairs
LESLIE Christopher	Parliamentary Under-Secretary of State, Department for Constitutional Affairs
LEWIS Ivan	Parliamentary Under-Secretary of State, Department for Education and Skills
McAVOY Thomas	Whip
McCARTNEY Rt Hon Ian	Minister without Portfolio and Labour Party Chair
McINTOSH of HARINGEY Rt Hon Lord	Parliamentary Under-Secretary of State, Department for Culture, Media and Sport
McGUIRE Anne	Parliamentary Under-Secretary of State, Scotland Office
McNULTY Tony	Parliamentary Under-Secretary of State, Department for Transport
MacSHANE Rt Hon Dr Denis	Minister of State, Foreign and Commonwealth Office
MACTAGGART Fiona	Parliamentary Under-Secretary of State, Home Office
MERRON Gillian	Assistant Whip
MICHAEL Rt Hon Alun	Minister of State, Department for Environment, Food and Rural Affairs
MILIBAND David	Minister of State, Department for Education and Skills
MORAN Margaret	Assistant Whip
MORLEY Elliot	Minister of State, Department for Environment, Food and Rural Affairs
MORRIS Rt Hon Estelle	Minister of State, Department for Culture, Media and Sport
MULLIN Chris	Parliamentary Under-Secretary of State, Foreign and Commonwealth Office

MURPHY Jim	Whip
MURPHY Rt Hon Paul	Secretary of State for Northern Ireland
O'BRIEN Mike	Minister of State, Foreign and Commonwealth Office and Department of Trade and Industry
PEARSON Ian	Parliamentary Under-Secretary of State, Northern Ireland Office
POND Chris	Parliamentary Under-Secretary of State, Department for Work and Pensions
PRENTICE Bridget	Assistant Whip
PRESCOTT Rt Hon John	Deputy Prime Minister and First Secretary of State
PRIMAROLO Rt Hon Dawn	Paymaster General, HM Treasury
RAMMELL Bill	Parliamentary Under-Secretary of State, Foreign and Commonwealth Office
RAYNSFORD Rt Hon Nick	Minister of State, Office of the Deputy Prime Minister
REID Rt Hon Dr John	Secretary of State for Health
ROOKER Rt Hon Lord	Minister of State, Office of the Deputy Prime Minister
RYAN Joan	Whip
SAINSBURY of TURVILLE Lord	Parliamentary Under-Secretary of State, Department of Trade and Industry
SCOTLAND of ASTHAL Rt Hon Baroness	Minister of State, Home Office
SMITH Rt Hon Andrew	Secretary of State for Work and Pensions
SMITH Angela	Parliamentary Under-Secretary of State, Northern Ireland Office
SMITH Rt Hon Jacqui	Minister of State, Department of Trade and Industry
SPELLAR Rt Hon John	Minister of State, Northern Ireland Office
STRAW Rt Hon Jack	Foreign Secretary
SUTCLIFFE Gerry	Parliamentary Under-Secretary of State, Department for Trade and Industry
SYMONS of VERNHAM DEAN Rt Hon Baroness	Minister of State, Foreign and Commonwealth Office; Deputy Leader of the House of Lords
THOMAS Gareth Richard	Parliamentary Under-Secretary of State, Department for International Development
TIMMS Stephen	Minister of State, Department of Trade and Industry
TOUHIG Don	Parliamentary Under-Secretary of State, Wales Office
TWIGG Derek	Whip
TWIGG Stephen	Parliamentary Under-Secretary of State, Department for Education and Skills
WARNER Lord	Parliamentary Under-Secretary of State, Department of Health
WHITTY Lord	Parliamentary Under-Secretary of State, Department for Environment, Food and Rural Affairs
WICKS Malcolm	Minister of State, Department for Work and Pensions
WILLIAMS of MOSTYN Rt Hon Lord	Leader of the House of Lords
WINTERTON Rosie	Minister of State, Department of Health
WOOLAS Philip	Deputy Leader of the House of Commons

Visit the Vacher Dod Website . . .
www.DodOnline.co.uk

Ministerial Responsibilities

Prime Minister

Prime Minister, First Lord of the Treasury and Minister for the Civil Service
Rt Hon **Tony Blair** MP

Office of the Deputy Prime Minister – ODPM

Deputy Prime Minister and First Secretary of State   Rt Hon **John Prescott** MP

Overall ministerial responsibility for the Office; deputising for the Prime Minister across Government; chairing British-Irish Council and Joint Ministerial Committee

Minister of State for Local and Regional Government   Rt Hon **Nick Raynsford** MP

Local government, including: local government performance and practice, local government finance, Audit Commission, Local Government Ombudsman, local elections; Regional governance; Fire Service; Civil resilience

Minister of State for Regeneration and Regional Development   Rt Hon **Lord Rooker**

Other growth areas; Market Renewal Pathfinders; Neighbourhood renewal; Social exclusion; Homlessness; Regional Co-ordination Unit (RCU) and Government Offices; Regional economic growth. Lords spokesperson

Minister of State for Housing and Planning   Rt Hon **Keith Hill** MP

Housing; Planning, including Planning Inspectorate; Thames Gateway; Minister for the Dome; Minister for London; Urban policy and liveability

Parliamentary Under-Secretary of State   **Phil Hope** MP

Building regulations; Regulatory reform and public sector reform; E-champion; E-local government; Green Minister; Fire safety and Fire Service College. Supports Nick Raynsford

Parliamentary Under-Secretary of State   **Yvette Cooper** MP

Ordnance Survey; Queen Elizabeth II Conference Centre; The Rent Service; Corporate issues; Equality, diversity and public appointments. Planning Minister for the Dome and for London. Supports Keith Hill and Lord Rooker

Cabinet Office

Minister for the Cabinet Office and Chancellor of the Duchy of Lancaster
Douglas Alexander MP

Delivery and reform of public services; Strategy Unit; Better regulation agenda across government; E-transformation in government; Aspects of Civil Contingencies Secretariat's work on UK resilience; Government Information and Communication Service; Civil Service issues; Public appointments and public bodies. General administration of the Duchy of Lancaster. Lords spokesperson for transport

Department for Constitutional Affairs

Secretry of State for Constitutional Affairs   Rt Hon **Lord Falconer of Thoroton** QC

Resourcing of his Departments; Constitutional issues including House of Lords reform; All appointments judicial or otherwise; Royal, church and hereditary issues, and Lord Lieutenants; Making or approving rules of court; Lords spokesperson for devolution and Scottish and Welsh business

Parliamentary Under-Secretary of State   **David Lammy** MP

Legal aid, Legal Services Commission and Community Legal Service; Civil justice policy; Civil law development; Domestic and international legal services; Legal Services Ombudsman; Law Commission; Land law; Immigration and asylum policy; Human rights; Channel Islands and the Isle of Man; Land Registry

Parliamentary Under-Secretary of State   **Christopher Leslie** MP

Criminal justice policy; Court Service, Magistrates' Court and the creation of the unified courts administration; Judicial Group other than individual appointments and casework; Support to the Secretary of State on policy for Judicial Appointments Commission and creation of a Supreme Court; IT and e-government policy; The Electoral Commission; Policy on electoral law; Referendum; Party funding

Parliamentary Under-Secretary of State   **Lord Filkin** CBE

Customer strategy; Change Programme; Operation of the Family Justice System (including implementation of Adoption Act); Mental incapacity; Gender recognition; Divorce reform, marriage law and civil partnerships; Freedom of information; Data protection, data sharing and privacy project; Tribunals policy and strategy and the creation of unified tribunal service; Devolution issues and regional policy; Social exclusion; International policy and the European Union; Public Guardianship Office; Official Solicitor's Office; Council on Tribunals; National Archives; Statutory Publications Office; Northern Ireland Court Service

Department for Culture, Media and Sport – DCMS

Secretary of State for Culture, Media and Sport   Rt Hon **Tessa Jowell** MP

Departmental strategy, expenditure and organisation; National Lottery policy; Public appointments; Chair Millennium Commission; Olympics Bid; Lead on international responsibilities, overall responsibility for arts, sport and historic environment, museums and galleries, tourism, film broadcasting and gambling

Minister of State (Minister for Sport)   Rt Hon **Richard Caborn** MP

Sport; Regional and local authority policy issues; Horse racing; The Tote; Gambling licensing; Olympics, Lottery, Bills in the Commons, Tourism, alcohol and entertainment licensing; DCMS interest in IT, e-government; Supports the Secretary of State on the National Lottery

Minister of State (Minister for the Arts)   Rt Hon **Estelle Morris** MP

Arts, crafts, music, Government Art Collection; Museums, galleries and libraries; Cultural property; Women's issues; Green issues; Training and education; European and international matters. Creative industries and film; National Lottery, including volunteering and community aspects

Parliamentary Under-Secretary of State (Minister for Media and Heritage)
Rt Hon **Lord McIntosh of Haringey**

Broadcasting, film and press censorship, Social policy, access and equal opportunities. Gambling, libraries; historic environment, architecture and design; Royal Estate (including Royal Parks); Lords spokesperson for Culture, Media and Sport and for Treasury

Ministry of Defence – MoD

Secretary of State for Defence   Rt Hon **Geoffrey Hoon** MP

Overall responsibility for the Department; Major current and potential operational commitments; Modernisation; NATO/ESDP; Chairman of Defence Council and its three Boards (the Admiralty Board, the Army Board and the Air Force Board)

Minister of State for the Armed Forces   Rt Hon **Adam Ingram** MP

Military capability; Continuing operational commitments; Defence Logistics Organisation; Intelligence and security; Domestic policy agenda (MoD input) Defence diplomacy and conflict prevention; Arms control issues; Defence exports control issues

Parliamentary Under-Secretary of State (Minister for Defence Procurement)   **Lord Bach**

Forward equipment programme; Acquisition policy; Science and technology strategy and research; Defence exports and disposal; Lords spokesperson for Defence

Parliamentary Under-Secretary of State (Minister for Veterans)   **Ivor Caplin** MP

Veterans' issues; Defence estate, works and disposals; Service personnel policy and casework; MoD policy operations; Defence Medical Services; Reserves and cadets; Claims policy and casework; Defence policy presentation and communication; Nuclear procurement; Visits by Peers and MPs/Armed Forces Parliamentary Scheme

Department for Education and Skills – DfES

Secretary of State for Education   Rt Hon **Charles Clarke** MP

Overall responsibility for the Department; Finance and public expenditure including local authority finance; Economic issues; Major appointments; Green and environment issues; Reducing bureaucracy; ICT, RE and maths

Minister of State for Children   Rt Hon **Margaret Hodge** MBE MP

Children and family policy: Children's social services; Child protection; Children in care; Family Policy Unit; Family and parenting law; Parental responsibility; Extended schools. Young People: Connexions service/Connexions card; Careers Service; Youth Service; Neighbourhood support fund; Children and Young People's Unit and Children's Fund; Young people at risk; Homelessness policy; Social inclusion

Minister of State for School Standards   **David Miliband** MP

Transforming secondary education: Key Stage 3 Strategy; OFSTED; Excellence in Cities; Education Action Zones and excellence clusters; Diversity in schools; Specialist schools; Beacon schools; Academies; Independent schools; schools plus. Transforming the school workforce: Support staff in schools; teacher workload; Teachers' pay, performance management and conditions; Teacher recruitment and retention; Teacher training; National College for School Leadership; Teacher Training Agency; General Teaching Council; Teachers' pensions; Teacher misconduct. Raising Attainment at 14-19: Relations with the Qualifications Curriculum Authority (including the Tomlinson review) and the organisation and funding of sixth form study. Curriculum and testing: Overall policy on the National Curriculum testing and assessment; Performance tables; Music and art. School organisation and funding: School recurrent funding; Local authority funding; Capital and PPP/PFI

Minister of State for Lifelong Learning, Further and Higher Education
Rt Hon **Alan Johnson** MP

Higher education (HE): Standards in post-19 learning; Widening participation in HE; Review of student support; Quality assurance in HE; Research and innovation in HE; Relations with DTI; HEFCE. Raising standards in further education (FE): FE and training for adults; FE corporations and governance; Area reviews of 16-19 provision; Lifelong learning. Learning and Skills Council: Pay in HE and FE sectors; Student support post-16 including Student Loans Company; Inspection post-16. European Union and overview of international relations: Non-EU business; Regional and regeneration and urban policy

Parliamentary Under-Secretary of State for Sure Start (also DWP)
Baroness Ashton of Upholland

Sure Start; Early Years Education; Childcare; foundation stage of curriculum. Special education needs. Lords spokesperson

Parliamentary Under-Secretary of State for Skills and Vocational Education
Ivan Lewis MP

Works with Alan Johnson on lifelong learning issues; Raising attainment at 14 to 19 (supporting David Miliband): Chair of 14-19 Steering Group; Strategy Unit report on soft skills; Education maintenance allowances. Adult Skills and Vocational Education: Adult skills strategy; Adult basic skills; Adult community education; Employment and competitiveness; Skills agenda and delivery of White Paper adult information, advice and guidance; Sector Skills Council and National Training organisations; Foundation apprenticeships and modern apprenticeships; Workforce development; Relationships with employers; Union Learning Fund; Union Learning Representatives; Regional

Development Agencies; Individual Learning Accounts; Funding of adult learning; Prison education; Investors in People; Universities for Industry; Learn Direct and links with the Department for Work and Pensions (DWP); UK Online Centres; Work related learning, enterprise and education business links across sectors; Gap years; Volunteering. Learning and Skills Council; International Strategy post-16 (other than European business); Behaviour and discipline (working with Margaret Hodge), Street Crime Minister; Behaviour and discipline, truancy, education welfare service

Parliamentary Under-Secretary of State for Schools　**Stephen Twigg** MP

London: Raising standards in London schools: Area reviews of 16-19 provision in London (working with Alan Johnson); School admissions and organisation casework for primary and secondary schools in London. Raising Standards in primary schools: Literacy and numeracy strategies; Class sizes; Primary school curriculum. The school curriculum: History, geography, citizenship, English, MFL, sport, PE and playing fields. Drug and alcohol education; Teenage Pregnancy Unit; sex education in schools; and PSHE (working with Margaret Hodge). Equality issues including race and ethnic minorities in education; Rural schools. Regulatory reform, raising standards of customer service, departmental efficiency and effectiveness and public service reform; Analytical service and research. International issues (excluding EU business) in schools (with Alan Johnson)

Department for Environment, Food and Rural Affairs – Defra

Secretary of State for Environment, Food and Rural Affairs
Rt Hon **Margaret Beckett** MP

Overall responsibility for all Departmental issues. Represents the UK at the EU Agriculture and Fisheries Council and at the EU Environment Council. Leads for the UK in international negotiations on sustainable development and climate change

Minister of State (Minister for Environment and Agri-Environment)　**Elliot Morley** MP

Climate change; Global and marine biodiversity (including OSPAR); GMOs; Policy on agri-environment, including relevant aspects of ERDP; Waste (including incineration issues); Radioactive substances; Chair of Green Ministers; Environment Agency; Water; Floods and coastal defence. Business continuity and resilience; Horizontal environmental issues

Minister of State (Minister for Rural Affairs and Local Environmental Quality)
Rt Hon **Alun Michael** MP

Rural policy; Hunting with dogs; Inland waterways, Countryside Agency and Rural Payments Agency; Access, Rights of way and Commons, National parks; Horse issues; General oversight of ERDP; Local environment issues; Lead Defra Minister on planning, regional and local government issues; Environmental liability, Pesticides policy (including Pesticides Safety Directorate); Chemicals. Response to Rural Delivery Review, in liaison with other ministers. Also responsible for e-government issues, and Departmental administration issues, including freedom of information and preparation for the euro

Parliamentary Under-Secretary of State (Minister for Nature Conservation and Fisheries)　**Ben Bradshaw** MP

Biodiversity (including whales and Centre for Environment, Fisheries and Aquaculture Science); Nature conservation, SSSIs and English Nature; Areas of outstanding natural beauty; Forestry; Fisheries; Plant health, plant variety rights and seeds; Organic food and farming; Animal health and welfare (including the Veterinary Laboratory Agency and Veterinary Medicines Directorate)

Parliamentary Under-Secretary of State (Minister for Farming, Food and Sustainable Energy)　**Lord Whitty**

Sustainable farming (including horticulture); CAP; Trade issues; Food industry; Science issues (including the Central Science Laboratory); Transport and the environment; Air quality and noise; Business and the environment; Energy issues (including energy efficiency); Non-food crops; Kew Gardens, Horticulture Research International and Covent Garden Market Authority; Smart regulation; Departmental Green Minister. Cross-cutting EU issues and general oversight of laboratory agencies

Foreign and Commonwealth Office – FCO

Secretary of State for Foreign and Commonwealth Affairs (Foreign Secretary)
Rt Hon **Jack Straw** MP

Overall responsibility for the work of the Office; Press; Parliamentary relations; Directorate for Strategy and Innovation; Legal advisers; Records and Historical Department; Research analysts; Honours; Whitehall Liaison Department

Minister of State for Europe   Dr **Denis MacShane** MP

Europe; Economic policy; Balkans; Ukraine, Belarus, Moldova; Commons cover: international security

Minister of State for the Middle East   Rt Hon **Baroness Symons of Vernham Dean**

Middle East; International security; Consular; Personnel; Deputy Leader of the House of Lords; Lords spokesperson

Minister of State for Trade and Foreign Affairs (also DSTI)   **Mike O'Brien** MP

Trade and trade policy; South East Asia; South Asia and Afghanistan; North America; Outreach. At DTI: trade policy and ECGD. Commons cover: personnel

Parliamentary Under-Secretary of State   **Bill Rammell** MP

Latin America and Caribbean; Overseas Trritories; East Asia and the Pacific; Global isues; Administration (except personnel); Immigration/asylum policy; Dugs issues; Russia, Central Asia and South Caucasus; Commons cover: Middle East

Parliamentary Under-Secretary of State   **Chris Mullin** MP

Africa Command; Commonwealth Co-ordination Department; Caribbean; Consular Division; Personnel Command; Overseas Territories; Lords spokesperson

Department of Health – DH

Secretary of State for Health   Rt Hon Dr **John Reid** MP

Overall responsibility for the work of the Department. Finance and resources, capital and PFI and strategic communications

Minister of State for Health   Rt Hon **John Hutton** MP

2002-03 Session NHS Bill; Access and performance; Bio-terrorism /emergency preparedness; Commissioning policy at local, regional and national level; Configuring hospitals project/Independent Reconfiguration Panel; General hospital services; International business; London regional works; NHSIT programme; NHS pay; NHS workforce; Nursing issues; Allied health professions; Diversity; PCT Policy; Primary care; Private sector projects/capacity/capital; treatment of patients abroad; NHS LIFT); Regulation of healthcare profession including UKCHR

Minister of State   **Rosie Winterton** MP

Accident and emergency services; Ambulance services; Clinical negligence; Critical care services; Defence Medical Services; Dental services; Diabetes; Informed Consent and Organ Retention; Injury cost recovery; Mental health service (including high security hospitals); National Survey of National Health Service Patients; NHS appointments; NHS chaplaincy services; NHS Complaints and Independent Advocacy Services; NHS Direct; NHS Plus; Occupational health; Optical services; Overview and Scrutiny Committees; Patient advocacy liaison services; Patient and public involvement; Patient experience issues; Patient forums; Pharmacy services; Rehabilitation and retention pilots; Renal services; South of England regional work; Transplants policy

Parliamentary Under-Secretary of State (Lords)   **Lord Warner**

Better regulation policy; Clinical governance and quality issues; Commission for Health Improvement (CHI) and new Commission for Healthcare Audit and Inspection; Controls assurance; Counter fraud; Departmental management; Euro issues; Freedom of information; Generics; Genetics and biotechnology; Infection control (including antibiotic resistance); Medicines and Healthcare Products Regulatory Agency; Modernisation Agency; National Institute for Clinical Excellence (NICE); NHS Estates; NHS Pensions; NHS Purchasing and Supply Agency; Pharmaceutical policy and relationship with industry; Research and development policy; Statistics

Parliamentary Under-Secretary of State for Public Health   **Melanie Johnson** MP

Abortion; Alcohol; Blood policy; Bovine Spongiform Encephalopathy (BSE) and Creutzfeldt-Jakob Disease (CJD); Cancer services; Communicable and infectious diseases; Complementary medicines; Coronary heart disease and stroke services; Dangerous pathogens; Diet and nutrition; Drug Misuse and National Treatment Agengy (and DH lead on street crime); Electro-magnetic radiation; Environment and health; Ethnic health issues; Fluoridation policy; Food Standards Agency; Fuel poverty; Genetically modified foods; Health Development Agency; Health inequalities; Health Protection Agency; HIV and AIDS policy; Human Fertilisation and Embryology Authority; Infertility; Men's health; National Radiation Protection Board; NHS treatment for asylum seekers; Northern regional work; Pesticides; Physical activity; Women's health issues

Parliamentary Under-Secretary of State for Health   Dr **Stephen Ladyman** MP

Care trusts, carers' issues; Child and adolescent mental health services; Children's health; National Service framework; Children's trusts – main point of contact with DfES; Community equipment services; CSCI; Delayed discharges; Disability services; Domiciliary care; General Social Care Council; Health visiting; Intermediate care; Learning disabilities services; Local government issues (as they relate to adult Social Services); Long term conditions (including National Service framework); Maternity services; Midlands and East Regional work; National Care Standards Commission; Nursing homes; Older people's services (including National Service framework); Prison healthcare policy; PSS finance; Residential care homes; School nursing; Social Care Institute of Excellence; Social Services for asylum seekers; Social Services performance; Social Services training and development; Voluntary sector policy

Home Office

Secretary of State for the Home Department (Home Secretary)
Rt Hon **David Blunkett** MP

Overall responsibility for the work of the Department, civil emergencies, security, terrorism and expenditure

Minister of State (Crime Reduction, Policing, and Community Safety)
Hazel Blears MP

Police policy; Crime reduction and community safety; Domestic violence; Minister for Children and Young People; Football disorder

Minister of State (Criminal Justice System and Law Reform)
Rt Hon **Baroness Scotland of Asthal** QC

Reform and modernisation of criminal justice system and oversight of all criminal justice issues – particular responsibility for sentencing policy, disclosure, rules of evidence, and bringing more offences to justice; Support for victims and witnesses. Criminal Justice White Paper. Strategic issues on the correctional services strategy; Wrongful convictions; Bribery and corruption; Criminal records, Criminal Injuries Compensation and Criminal Cases Review

Minister of State (Citizenship, Immigration and Counter-Terrorism)
Beverley Hughes MP

Nationality, immigration and asylum including work permits; Nationality including coherent citizenship and inward migration policies; UK Passport Agency; Identity cards; Counter-terrorism and resilience; Strategic oversight of policy on civil renewal; Women's issues

Parliamentary Under-Secretary of State (Tackling Drugs, Reducing Organised and International Crime)   **Caroline Flint** MP

Support to Minister of State for crime reduction, policing and community safety, with particular responsibility for Action Against Drugs including development of a coherent drugs and alcohol abuse strategy and programme for delivery; Organised and international crime including European law enforcement and judicial co-operation; Animal procedures

Parliamentary Under-Secretary of State (Correctional Services and Reducing Re-offending)   **Paul Goggins** MP

Support to Minister of State for Criminal Justice, Sentencing and Law Reform, with particular responsibility for correctional services (prisons, probation and the Youth Justice Board) and reducing re-offending; managing restricted patients. Rehabilitation policy; Sex offenders and sex offences; Public protection and dangerous offenders policy. Drugs in prison; coroners. Obscenity and child protection internet task force. Criminal Justice System business in the House of Commons

Parliamentary Under-Secretary of State (Race Equality, Community Policy and Civil Renewal)   **Fiona Mactaggart** MP

European and international business; Race equality; Voluntary and community policy; Green minister; Design Champion. Support to Minister of State for Citizenship and Immigration

Department for International Development – DFID

Secretary of State for International Development   **Baroness Amos**

Overall responsibility for the work of the Department; Certain overseas pensions

Minister of State   **Hilary Benn** MP

Africa; Middle East; Finance and corporate performance; International financial institutions (including Regional Development Banks); United Nations; Commonwealth; Conflict and Humanitarian Affairs Department; International Trade Departments; Policy Evaluation Department; Commonwealth Development Corporation/Private sector infrastructure

Parliamentary Under-Secretary of State   **Gareth Richard Thomas** MP

Asia; Eastern Europe; Latin America and Caribbean; Overseas territories; Human resources; European Union; Information (NGOs, Development awareness)

Law Officers' Department

Attorney General   Rt Hon **Lord Goldsmith** QC

Overall responsibility for the work of Treasury Solicitor's Department, Crown Prosecution Service, Serious Fraud Office and Legal Secretariat to the Law Officers; Oversees the functions of the Director of Public Prosecutions for Northern Ireland; Government's principal legal adviser; Questions of law arising on Bills, and with issues of legal policy; All major international and domestic litigation involving the Government; Enforcement of the criminal law. Also Attorney General for Northern Ireland

Solicitor General   Rt Hon **Harriet Harman** QC MP

All the powers of the Attorney General and of the Attorney General for Northern Ireland and can act in any matter as the Attorney General requires

Office of the Leader of the House of Commons

Leader of the House of Commons and Lord Privy Seal
Rt Hon **Peter Hain** MP

Arrangement of Government business in the Commons and planning and supervising the Government's legislative programme. Chairs the Ministerial Committees on the Legislative Programme; Electoral policy and the Government's response to parliamentary modernisation

Deputy Leader of the House of Commons   **Phil Woolas** MP

Deputises for the Leader of the House of Commons in supervising and arranging the Government's business in the Commons

Leader of the House of Lords and President of the Council

Leader of the House of Lords and Lord President of the Council
Rt Hon **Lord Williams of Mostyn** QC

As Leader of the House of Lords supports the Lord Chancellor in his responsibility for Lords reform; leading the Government front bench in the Lords; conduct of Government business in the Lords (joint responsibility with the Lords Chief Whip); giving guidance to the House on matters of order and procedure; taking part in formal ceremonies in the House, such as the State Opening of Parliament; Lords spokesperson on Northern Ireland and Cabinet Office; Chairman of the Special Adviser Remuneration Committee; and Chairman of the Board of Trustees for the Government Houses

Deputy Leader of the House of Lords   Rt Hon **Baroness Symons of Vernham Dean**

Minister without Portfolio

Minister without Portfolio and Labour Party Chair
Rt Hon **Ian McCartney** MP

Government's decision-making processes as a member of the Cabinet and a number of Cabinet Committees; Link between the Goverment and the Labour Party; Provides the Prime Minister with strategic thinking on the general direction of Govervnment's policy and on the values underpinning it

Northern Ireland Office – NIO

Secretary of State for Northern Ireland   Rt Hon **Paul Murphy** MP

Northern Ireland Office matters not devolved to the Northern Ireland Assembly: Policing, security policy, prisons, criminal justice, victims, rights and equality and political development; Jointly responsible with Irish Government for the British Irish Intergovernmental Conference. Represents Northern Ireland's interest in the UK Cabinet.

Following the suspension of devolution on 14 October 2002, the eleven departments previously led by the Northern Ireland Executive are now the responsibility of the Secretary of State for Northern Ireland

Minister of State   Rt Hon **John Spellar** MP

Political development, criminal justice, human rights and equality, Department for Social Development; Department for Regional Development

Minister of State   Rt Hon **Jane Kennedy** MP

Security; Policing and prisons, Department of Education, Department of Employment and Learning, Assets Recovery Agency and Organised Crime Task Force

*Parliamentary Under-Secretary of State   **Ian Pearson** MP

Department of Finance and Personnel; Department of Enterprise, Trade and Investment; Department of Agriculture and Rural Development; Europe; review of Public Administration

*Parliamentary Under-Secretary of State   **Angela Smith** MP

Department of the Environment; Department of Culture, Arts and Leisure; Department of Health, Social Services and Public Safety, Victims and Reconciliation

Privy Council Office

Lord President of the Council and Leader of the House of Lords
Rt Hon **Lord Williams of Mostyn** QC

Work of the Privy Council Office; meetings of the Privy Council, signs draft orders of Council, exercises jurisdiction of Visitor in respect of 17 Universities. Lords Spokesperson

Scotland Office

Secretary of State for Scotland   Rt Hon **Alastair Darling** MP

Representing Scottish interests in matters reserved to the United Kingdom Parliament and promoting the devolution settlement for Scotland. Paying grant to the Scottish Consolidated Fund and managing other financial transactions. Reserved matters include: the Constitution; foreign affairs; defence; international development, the Civil Service; financial and economic matters; national security; immigration and nationality, misuse of drugs, trade and industry, various aspects of energy regulation (eg. electricity, coal, oil and gas; nuclear energy); various aspects of transport (eg. regulation of air service, rail and international shipping); Social Security, employment, abortion, genetics, surrogacy, medicines, broadcasting, equal opportunities

Parliamentary Under-Secretary of State, Scotland   **Anne McGuire** MP

Assists the Secretary of State for Scotland in representing Scottish interests within the UK government in matters reserved to the UK Parliament

Advocate General for Scotland   **Lynda Clark** QC MP

Chief legal adviser to UK Government on matters of Scottish law. Overall responsibility for the work for her legal secretariat and of the office of the Solicitor to the Advocate General, which provides legal services relating to Scotland to UK departments and agencies

Department of Trade and Industry – DTI

Secretary of State for Trade and Industry, Minister for Women and e-Minister in Cabinet
Rt Hon **Patricia Hewitt** MP

Overall responsibility for the Department, the Office of Science and Technology and Export Credits Guarantee Department

Minister of State (Energy, e-Commerce and Postal Services)   **Stephen Timms** MP

Energy and sustainable development; E-Commerce, Communications and Information Industries, Postal services; Corporate social responsibility and social enterprise

Minister of State for International Trade and Investment (also FCO)   **Mike O'Brien** MP

British Trade International; Trade policy; Export Credits Guarantee Department; South East Asia, Afghanistan; North America (part of FCO post)

Minister of State (Industry and the Regions and Deputy Minister for Women and Equality)   Rt Hon **Jacqui Smith** MP

Industry, unless otherwise stated, Regions; Women and equality; Corporate governance; European policy

Parliamentary Under-Secretary of State (Science and Innovation)
Lord Sainsbury of Turville

Office of Science and Technology; Innovation, design, chemical industry, bioscience industry, space policy (British National Space Centre), regional clusters, engineering profession, National Measurement System, standards and technical regulations

Parliamentary Under-Secretary of State (Employment Relations; Competition and Consumers)   **Gerry Sutcliffe** MP

Employment relations including Employment Tribunal Service, ACAS; Low Pay Commission; Competition policy; Consumer policy; Insolvency Service; Companies House. Supports Jacqui Smith on European policy and on corporate governance

Parliamentary Under-Secretary of State (Small Business and Enterprise)
Nigel Griffiths MP

Small Business Service; Export Control and Non-proliferation, and the Trawlermen's compensation scheme. Supports Mike O'Brien on trade promotion, investment and policy, and Jacqui Smith on regional policy

Department for Transport – DfT

Secretary of State for Transport   Rt Hon **Alistair Darling** MP

Overall responsibility for the Department for Transport. Secretary of State for Scotland

Minister of State for Transport   Dr **Kim Howells** MP

Ten Year Plan; Buses and taxis; Rail, aviation; British Transport Police; Roads, including the transport agencies; Walking and cycling; Maritime

Parliamentary Under-Secretary of State for Transport   **David Jamieson** MP

Roads: road safety; Cleaner vehicles and fuels; Licensing; Roadworthiness and insurance; Haulage; Logistics and maritime; Highways Agency; DVO Group Agencies

Parliamentary Under-Secretary of State for Transport   **Tony McNulty** MP

Aviation; London including Tube and Crossrail; Regional and sub-regional issues; Local authority public transport; Buses and taxis; Mobility and inclusion issues; Corporate issues; Green Minister

HM Treasury – HMT

Prime Minister, First Lord of the Treasury   Rt Hon **Tony Blair** MP

Chancellor of the Exchequer   Rt Hon **Gordon Brown** MP

Overall responsibility for the work of the Treasury

Chief Secretary to the Treasury   Rt Hon **Paul Boateng** MP

Public expenditure planning and control (including local authorities and nationalised industries finance); Value for money in the public services, including Public Service Agreements; Departmental investment strategies including Capital Modernisation Fund and Invest to Save budget; Public private partnerships including Private Finance Initiative; Procurement policy; Public sector pay; Presentation of economic policy and economic briefing; Welfare reform; Devolution; Strategic oversight of banking, financial services and insurance; Resource accounting and budgeting

Paymaster General   Rt Hon **Dawn Primarolo** MP

Strategic oversight of taxation; Departmental Minister for Inland Revenue and the Valuation Office; Personal income tax (except company car tax, savings and pensions), national insurance contributions and tax credits; Direct business taxation and tax aspects of the enterprise agenda; Capital gains tax; Inheritance tax; Treasury interest in childcare issues and Treasury interest in women's issues; Regulatory Reform Minister for the Chancellor's departments; Welfare Reform Group (welfare fraud)

Financial Secretary   **Ruth Kelly** MP

Banking, financial services and insurance, and the Financial Services Authority; Support to the Chief Secretary in his strategic oversight of banking, financial services and insurance; Financial services tax issues, including ISAs, taxation of savings, Stamp Duty, Insurance Premium Tax and pensions; Foreign exchange reserves and debt management policy; Support to the Chancellor on EU issues; EMU business preparations; Economic reform in Europe; National Savings, Debt Management Office, Office for National Statistics, Royal Mint and the Government Actuary's Department; Personal savings policy; Support to the Chief Secretary on public spending issues; Support to the Paymaster General on the Finance Bill; Departmental Minister for HM Treasury

Economic Secretary   **John Healey** MP

Departmental Minister for Customs and Excise; VAT; Alcohol and tobacco duties; Betting and gaming taxation; Environmental issues; Environmental taxes; Transport taxes; Urban regeneration; Productivity and enterprise; Competition and deregulation policy; Science, research and development; Welfare to Work and social exclusion issues; Charities and charity taxation; Support to the Chancellor on international issues

Wales Office

Secretary of State for Wales   Rt Hon **Peter Hain** MP

Represents Wales in the Cabinet and is responsible for defence and foreign affairs, justice, police and prison systems, taxation and social security benefits and macro-economic policy

Parliamentary Under-Secretary of State   **Don Touhig** MP

Responsibility for education; health; local government; environment

Department for Work and Pensions – DWP

Secretary of State for Work and Pensions   Rt Hon **Andrew Smith** MP

Overall responsibility for all work and pension matters; Public expenditure issues

Minister of State for Work   Rt Hon **Des Browne** MP

Welfare to Work; Adult disadvantage; Jobcentre Plus; New Deals; Employers; Employment zones; Incapacity benefit; Industrial injuries disablement benefit; Action Teams for Jobs; Health and safety; Rapid Response Service; labour market and the economy; Skills and links within the DfES

Minister of State for Pensions   **Malcolm Wicks** MP

Pensions; The Pension Service; Minimum income guarantee; Pension credit; Winter fuel payments; Older people issues; E-government

Parliamentary Under-Secretary of State (Minister for Children and the Family)
Rt Hon **Baroness Hollis of Heigham**

Child Support Agency; Poverty and social exclusion; Asylum; Green issues; Maternity and paternity pay; Appeals Service and adjudication issues; Civil partnerships; Devolution issues; Freedom of information and data protection issues; Human rights; New Deal for Communities; Research; Diversity issues

Parliamentary Under-Secretary of State (Minister for Disabled People)   **Maria Eagle** MP

Deputy to the Minister for Pensions on all pensions issues; Disability policy and the Disability Rights Commission; Disability benefits; Carer benefits, Long-term care; Sure Start and Early Years child care (Commons)

Parliamentary Under-Secretary of State (Work)   **Chris Pond** MP

Deputy to the Minister for Work on all work issues; Housing benefit; Bereavement benefits; Social Fund; Fraud; Income support; Jobseeker's allowance; International and European relations; Debt management policy; Child Support Agency (Commons); Direct payments, Council tax benefit

Parliamentary Under-Secretary of State (DfES/DWP)   **Baroness Ashton of Upholland**

Sure Start; Early years education; Childcare; Daycare services; Schools Plus: extended schools and study support pre-14; Sport; Sport and PE in the curriculum; Sports co-ordinators; School playing fields. Special education needs; English and modern foreign languages; Deputises for Secretary of State on RE and ICT

DodOnline

An Electronic Directory without rival . . .

MPs' biographies and photographs available with daily updates *via* the internet

For a *free* trial, call Yasmin Mirza, Aby Farsoun or Michael Mand on 020 7630 7643

Ministerial salaries 2003–04

Figures are as set on 1 April 2003
* including MP's salary of £56,358

	Ministerial £	Total salary* £
House of Commons		
Prime Minister	119,056	175,414
Cabinet Minister	71,433	127,791
Government Chief Whip	71,433	127,791
Minister of State	37,055	93,413
Parliamentary Under Secretary of State	28,125	84,483
Solicitor General	62,241	118,599
Advocate General	62,241	118,599
Government Deputy Chief Whip	37,055	93,413
Government Whip	23,847	80,205
Assistant Government Whip	23,847	80,205
Leader of the Opposition	65,482	121,840
Opposition Chief Whip	37,055	93,413
Deputy Opposition Chief Whip	23,847	80,205
Speaker	71,433	127,791
Chairman of Ways and Means (Deputy Speaker)	37,055	93,413
First Deputy Chairman of Ways and Means (Deputy Speaker)	32,567	88,925
Second Deputy Chairman of Ways and Means (Deputy Speaker)	32,567	88,925
House of Lords		
Cabinet Minister	96,960	
Minister of State	75,706	
Parliamentary Under Secretary of State	65,936	
Lord Chancellor	202,736	
Attorney General	101,432	
Government Chief Whip	75,706	
Government Deputy Chief Whip	65,936	
Government Whip	60,972	
Leader of the Opposition	65,936	
Opposition Chief Whip	60,972	
Chairman of Committees	75,706	
Principal Deputy Chairman of Committees	70,826	

DodOnline

An Electronic Directory without rival . . .

MPs' biographies and photographs available with daily updates *via* the internet

For a *free* trial, call Yasmin Mirza, Aby Farsoun or Michael Mand on 020 7630 7643

Government Spokespeople in the Lords

Lord Privy Seal and Leader of the House of Lords	Rt Hon **Lord Williams of Mostyn** QC
Deputy Leader	Rt Hon **Baroness Symons of Vernham Dean**
Attorney General's Office	Rt Hon **Lord Goldsmith** QC
Cabinet Office	**Lord Williams of Mostyn** **Lord Bassam of Brighton**
Culture, Media and Sport	Rt Hon **Lord McIntosh of Haringey** **Lord Davies of Oldham**
Defence	**Lord Bach** **Baroness Crawley**
Office of the Deputy Prime Minister	Rt Hon **Lord Rooker** **Lord Evans of Temple Guiting** CBE
Education and Skills	**Baroness Ashton of Upholland** **Baroness Andrews** OBE
Environment, Food and Rural Affairs	**Lord Whitty** **Baroness Farrington of Ribbleton**
Foreign and Commonwealth Office	Rt Hon **Baroness Symons of Vernham Dean** **Baroness Crawley**
Health	**Lord Warner** **Baroness Andrews** OBE
Home Office	**Baroness Scotland of Asthal** QC **Lord Bassam of Brighton**
International Development	**Baroness Amos** **Baroness Crawley**
Department for Constitutional Affairs/ Lord Chancellor's Department	Rt Hon **Lord Falconer of Thoroton** QC **Lord Filkin** **Lord Bassam of Brighton**
Scotland and Wales	**Lord Evans of Temple Guiting** CBE
Northern Ireland Office	Rt Hon **Lord Williams of Mostyn** QC **Baroness Farrington of Ribbleton**
Trade and Industry	**Lord Sainsbury of Turville** **Lord Evans of Temple Guiting** CBE
Transport	**Lord Davies of Oldham** **Lord Bassam of Brighton**
Treasury	Rt Hon **Lord McIntosh of Haringey** **Lord Davies of Oldham**
Work and Pensions	Rt Hon **Baroness Hollis of Heigham** DL **Baroness Andrews** OBE

Parliamentary Private Secretaries

Prime Minister

Rt Hon Tony Blair MP

David Hanson MP
020 7219 5064
E-mail: hansond@parliament.uk

Office of the Deputy Prime Minister

Rt Hon John Prescott MP

Dave Watts MP
020 7219 6325
E-mail: wattsd@parliament.uk

Rt Hon Nick Raynsford MP

Linda Gilroy MP
020 7219 4416
E-mail: gilroyl@parliament.uk

Rt Hon Keith Hill MP

Terry Rooney MP
020 7219 6407
E-mail: rooneyt@parliament.uk

Cabinet Office

Douglas Alexander MP

Lawrie Quinn MP
020 7219 4170
E-mail: brittainl@parliament.uk

Constitutional Affairs

Rt Hon Lord Falconer of Thoroton QC

Laura Moffatt MP
020 7219 3619
E-mail: clewerd@parliament.uk
Team PPS
Geraint Davies MP
020 7219 4599
E-mail: geraintdaviesmp@parliament.uk

Culture, Media and Sport

Rt Hon Tessa Jowell MP

Gordon Marsden MP
020 7219 1262
E-mail: marsdeng@parliament.uk

Rt Hon Richard Caborn MP

Ben Chapman MP
020 7219 1143
E-mail: chapmanb@parliament.uk

Rt Hon Estelle Morris MP

Howard Stoate MP
020 7219 4571
E-mail: hstoate@hotmail.com

Defence

Rt Hon Geoffrey Hoon MP

Liz Blackman MP
020 7219 2397
E-mail: lizblackman@email.labour.org.uk

Rt Hon Adam Ingram MP

Alan Campbell MP
020 7219 6619
E-mail: campbella@parliament.uk
Team PPS
Syd Rapson MP
020 7219 6351
E-mail: rapsons@parliament.uk

Education and Skills

Rt Hon Charles Clarke MP

Steve McCabe MP
020 7219 4842
E-mail: mccabes@parliament.uk

Rt Hon Margaret Hodge MBE MP

Michael John Foster MP
020 7219 6379
E-mail: fosterm@parliament.uk

David Miliband MP

Ian Cawsey MP
020 7219 5237
E-mail: ianmp@btclick.com

Alan Johnson MP

Bob Laxton MP
020 7219 4096
E-mail: laxtonb@parliament.uk
Team PPS
Meg Munn MP
020 7219 8316
E-mail: munnm@parliament.uk

Environment, Food and Rural Affairs

Rt Hon Margaret Beckett MP

Mark Hendrick MP
020 7219 4791
E-mail: hendrickm@parliament.uk

Rt Hon Alun Michael MP

Peter Bradley MP
020 7219 4112
E-mail: bradleyp@parliament.uk

Elliot Morley MP

Tony Cunningham MP
020 7219 8344
Team PPS
Nick Palmer MP
020 7219 2397

Foreign and Commonwealth Office

Rt Hon Jack Straw MP

Colin Pickthall MP
020 7219 5011
E-mail: pickthallc@parliament.uk

Rt Hon Baroness Symons of
    Vernham Dean

Mark Todd MP
020 7219 3549
E-mail: toddm@parliament.uk

Mike O'Brien MP

Eric Joyce MP
020 7219 6210

Dr Denis MacShane MP

Phyllis Starkey MP
020 7219 0456/6427
E-mail: starkeyp@miltonkeynes-sw.demon.co.uk
Team PPS
Roger Casale MP
020 7219 4565
E-mail: casaler@parliament.uk

Health

Rt Hon Dr John Reid MP

Mike Hall MP
020 7219 4001
E-mail: hallm@parliament.uk

Rt Hon John Hutton MP

Claire Ward MP
020 7219 4910
E-mail: wardc@parliament.uk

Rosie Winterton MP

Jim Knight MP
020 7219 8466
E-mail: jimknightmp@parliament.uk

Home Office

Rt Hon David Blunkett MP

Andy Burnham MP
020 7219 8250
E-mail: graham/m@parliament.uk

Beverley Hughes MP

Barry Gardiner MP
020 7219 4046
E-mail: gardinerb@parliament.uk

Baroness Scotland of Asthal QC

Shona McIsaac MP
020 7219 5801
E-mail: mcisaacs@parliament.uk

Hazel Blears MP

Dari Taylor MP
020 7219 4608
E-mail: greenr@parliament.uk

International Development

Rt Hon Baroness Amos

Tom Levitt MP
020 7219 6599
E-mail: tomlevittmp@parliament.uk

Hilary Benn MP

Ashok Kumar MP
020 7219 4460
E-mail: ashokkumarmp@parliament.uk

Law Officers

Rt Hon Lord Goldsmith QC
Rt Hon Harriet Harman QC MP

Vacant

Leader of the House

Commons:
Rt Hon Peter Hain MP

Martin Linton MP
020 7219 4619
E-mail: lintonm@parliament.uk

Lords:
Rt Hon Lord Williams of Mostyn QC

Vacant

Minister Without Portfolio and Labour Party Chair

Rt Hon Ian McCartney MP

Neil Turner MP
020 7219 4494
E-mail: turnern@parliament.uk

Northern Ireland

Rt Hon Paul Murphy MP

Gareth Thomas MP (Clwyd West)
020 7219 3516
E-mail: thomasg@parliament.uk

Rt Hon John Spellar MP

Tom Harris MP
020 7219 8237
E-mail: tomharrismp@parliament.uk

Jane Kennedy MP

Huw Irranca-Davies MP
020 7219 4027

Privy Council Office – see Leader of the House

Scotland – see Transport

Trade and Industry

Rt Hon Patricia Hewitt MP

Oona King MP
020 7219 5020
E-mail: silverv@parliament.uk

Stephen Timms MP

Ian Stewart MP
020 7219 6175
E-mail: ianstewartmp@parliament.uk

Mike O'Brien MP

Eric Joyce MP
020 7219 6210

Jacqui Smith MP

Andy Love MP
020 7219 5497
E-mail: lovea@parliament.uk
Equalities PPS
Jackie Lawrence MP
020 7219 2757
E-mail: leachv@parliament.uk
Team PPS
Andrew Miller MP
020 7219 3580
E-mail: millera@parliament.uk

Transport and Scotland

Rt Hon Alistair Darling MP

Ann Coffey MP
020 7219 4546
E-mail: coffeya@parliament.uk
David Stewart MP
020 7219 3586
E-mail: stewartd@parliament.uk

Kim Howells MP

David Borrow MP
020 7219 4126
E-mail: david.borrow@labour.co.uk

Treasury

Rt Hon Gordon Brown MP

Rt Hon Paul Boateng MP

Rt Hon Dawn Primarolo MP

Ruth Kelly MP

Ann Keen MP
020 7219 5623
E-mail: keena@parliament.uk
Helen Southworth MP
020 7219 3568
E-mail: southworthh@parliament.uk
Tom Watson MP
020 7219 8335
E-mail: watsont@parliament.uk
James Purnell MP
020 7219 8166
E-mail: basus@parliament.uk

Wales

Rt Hon Peter Hain MP

Chris Ruane MP
020 7219 6378
E-mail: ruanec@parliament.uk

Work and Pensions

Rt Hon Andrew Smith MP

Des Browne MP

Malcolm Wicks MP

Ivan Henderson MP
020 7219 3434
E-mail: hendersoni@parliament.uk
Kali Mountford MP
020 7219 4507
David Cairns MP
020 7219 8242

DodOnline
An Electronic Directory without rival . . .

MPs' biographies and photographs available with daily updates *via* the internet

For a *free* trial, call Yasmin Mirza, Aby Farsoun or Michael Mand on 020 7630 7643

Special Advisers

Prime Minister

See Prime Minister's Office

Office of the Deputy Prime Minister

Deputy Prime Minister and First Secretary of State
Rt Hon John Prescott MP

Joan Hammell
020 7944 8615
E-mail: joan.hammell@odpm.gsi.gov.uk
Ian McKenzie
020 7944 8615
E-mail: ian.mckenzie@odpm.gsi.gov.uk
Paul Hackett
020 7944 8615
E-mail: paul.hackett@odpm.gsi.gov.uk

Chief Whip's Office (Commons)

Rt Hon Hilary Armstrong MP

Sue Jackson
020 7219 4400
E-mail: jacksons@parliament.uk
Fiona Gordon
020 7219 4400
E-mail: gordonf@parliament.uk

Chief Whip's Office (Lords)

Rt Hon Lord Grocott

Margaret Ounsley
020 7219 1115
E-mail: ounsleym@parliament.uk

Constitutional Affairs

Rt Hon Lord Falconer of Thoroton QC

Garry Hart
020 7210 8590   Fax: 020 7210 0647
E-mail: garry.hart@dca.gsi.gov.uk

Culture, Media and Sport

Rt Hon Tessa Jowell MP

Bill Bush
020 7211 6010
E-mail: bill.bush@culture.gsi.gov.uk

Defence

Rt Hon Geoffrey Hoon MP

Richard Taylor
020 7218 2911
E-mail: public@ministers.mod.uk
Michael Dugher
020 7218 1964
E-mail: public@ministers.mod.uk

Education and Skills

Rt Hon Charles Clarke MP

Lisa Tremble
020 7925 6874
E-mail: lisa.tremble@dfes.gsi.gov.uk
Robert Hill
020 7925 6530
E-mail: robert.hill@dfes.gsi.gov.uk

Environment, Food and Rural Affairs

Rt Hon Margaret Beckett MP

Sheila Watson
020 7238 5378
E-mail: sheila.watson@defra.gsi.gov.uk
Nicci Collins
020 7238 5378
E-mail: nicci.collins@defra.gsi.gov.uk

Foreign and Commonwealth Office

Rt Hon Jack Straw MP

Ed Owen
020 7008 2117
E-mail: ed.owen@fco.gov.uk
Dr Michael Williams
020 7008 2112
E-mail: michael.williams@fco.gov.uk

Health

Rt Hon Dr John Reid MP

Prof Paul Corrigan
020 7210 5942 Fax: 020 7210 5613
E-mail: paul.corrigan@doh.gsi.gov.uk
Richard Olszewski
020 7210 5942
E-mail: richard.olszewski@doh.gsi.gov.uk
Steve Bates
020 7210 5945
E-mail: steve.bates@doh.gsi.gov.uk

Home Office

Rt Hon David Blunkett MP

Nick Pearce
020 7273 2713/2852
E-mail: nick.pearce@homeoffice.gsi.gov.uk
Katharine Raymond
020 7273 2713/2852
E-mail:
katharine.raymond@homeoffice.gsi.gov.uk
Matthew Seward
020 7273 2713/2852
E-mail: matthew.seward@homeoffice.gsi.gov.uk
Huw Evans
020 7273 2713/2852
E-mail: huw.evans@homeoffice.gsi.gov.uk

International Development

Rt Hon Baroness Amos

Alexander Evans
020 7023 0508
E-mail: alex.evans@homeoffice.gsi.gov.uk

Leader of the House

Commons:
Rt Hon Peter Hain MP

Phil Taylor
020 7210 1081
E-mail:
phil.taylor@CommonsLeader.x.gsi.gov.uk
Greg Power
020 7210 1084
E-mail:
greg.power@CommonsLeader.x.gsi.gov.uk

Lords:
Rt Hon Lord Williams of Mostyn QC

Matthew Seward
020 7276 1960
E-mail:
matthew.seward@cabinet-office.x.gsi.gov.uk

Lord Chancellor – see Department for Constitutional Affairs

Minister without Portfolio

Rt Hon Ian McCartney MP

Martin O'Donovan
020 7276 1093
E-mail:
martin.o'donovan@cabinet-office.x.gsi.gov.uk
Patrick Loughran
020 7276 1096
E-mail:
patrick.loughran@cabinet-office.x.gsi.gov.uk

Northern Ireland Office

Rt Hon Paul Murphy MP

Owen Smith
020 7210 6487
E-mail: owen.smith@nio.x.gsi.gov.uk

Privy Council Office

Rt Hon Lord Williams of Mostyn QC

Matthew Seward
020 7276 1960
E-mail: matthew.seward@pco.x.gsi.gov.uk

Scotland Office

Rt Hon Alistair Darling

Iain Gray
0131-244 9027
E-mail: iain.gray@scotland.gsi.gov.uk

Trade and Industry

Rt Hon Patricia Hewitt MP

Jim Godfrey
020 7215 6620
E-mail: jim.godfrey@dti.gsi.gov.uk
Roger Sharp
020 7215 6480
E-mail: roger.sharp@dti.gsi.gov.uk
Kitty Ussher
020 7215 6176
E-mail: kitty.ussher@dti.gsi.gov.uk
Deborah Lincoln
020 7215 3971
E-mail: deborah.lincoln@dti.gsi.gov.uk

Transport

Rt Hon Alistair Darling MP

Andrew Maugham
020 7944 4531
E-mail: special.advisers@dft.gsi.gov.uk
Tom Restrick
020 7944 4531
E-mail: special.advisers@dft.gsi.gov.uk

Treasury

Ed Balls
(Chief Economic Adviser to the Treasury)
020 7270 4941
E-mail: ed.balls@hm-treasury.gsi.gov.uk

Rt Hon Gordon Brown MP

Ian Austin
020 7270 1823
E-mail: ian.austin@hm-treasury.gsi.gov.uk
Spencer Livermore
020 7270 5027
E-mail:
spencer.livermore@hm-treasury.gsi.gov.uk
Sue Nye
020 7270 5012
E-mail: sue.nye@hm-treasury.gsi.gov.uk

Rt Hon Paul Boateng MP

Nicola Murphy
020 7270 1823
E-mail: nicola.murphy@hm-treasury.gsi.gov.uk

Wales Office

Rt Hon Peter Hain MP

Andrew Bold
029 2089 8549
E-mail: andrew.bold@wales.gsi.gov.uk

Work and Pensions

Rt Hon Andrew Smith MP

Chris Norton
020 7238 0886
E-mail: chris.norton@dwp.gsi.gov.uk
Tom Clark
020 7238 0886
E-mail: tom.clark@dwp.gsi.gov.uk

Ministerial Committees of the Cabinet

CIVIL CONTINGENCIES
Home Secretary *(Chair)* — Rt Hon **David Blunkett**

CRIMINAL JUSTICE SYSTEM
Home Secretary *(Chair)* — Rt Hon **David Blunkett**
Chief Secretary to the Treasury — Rt Hon **Paul Boateng**
Minister without Portfolio — Rt Hon **Ian McCartney**
Secretary of State for Constitutional Affairs — Rt Hon **Lord Falconer of Thoroton** QC
Attorney General — Rt Hon **Lord Goldsmith** QC
Minister for the Cabinet Office and
    Chancellor of the Duchy of Lancaster — **Douglas Alexander**
Solicitor General — Rt Hon **Harriet Harman** QC
Minister of State, Home Office — Rt Hon **Baroness Scotland of Asthal**
Parliamentary Under-Secretary,
    Department for Constitutional Affairs — **Christopher Leslie**

Crime Reduction Sub-committee
Home Secretary *(Chair)* — Rt Hon **David Blunkett**
Chief Secretary to the Treasury — Rt Hon **Paul Boateng**
Minister for the Cabinet Office and
    Chancellor of the Duchy of Lancaster — **Douglas Alexander**
Solicitor General — Rt Hon **Harriet Harman** QC
Minister of State, Office of the
    Deputy Prime Minister — Rt Hon **Keith Hill**
Minister of State, Home Office — **Hazel Blears**
Minister of State, Department for
    Environment, Food and Rural Affairs — Rt Hon **Alun Michael**
Minister of State, Department of Health — **Rosie Winterton**
Minister of State, Department of
    Trade and Industry — **Stephen Timms**
Minister of State, Department for
    Culture, Media and Sport — Rt Hon **Estelle Morris**
Minister of State, Department for
    Education and Skills — Rt Hon **Margaret Hodge**
Deputy Leader of the House of Commons — **Phil Woolas**
Parliamentary Under-Secretary,
    Department for Constitutional Affairs — **Christopher Leslie**
Parliamentary Under-Secretary for Scotland — **Anne McGuire**
Parliamentary Under-Secretary for Wales — **Don Touhig**
Parliamentary Under-Secretary,
    Department for Transport — **Tony McNulty**

Criminal Justice System Information Technology Sub-committee
Minister for the Cabinet Office and
    Chancellor of the Duchy of Lancaster *(Chair)* — **Douglas Alexander**
Attorney General — Rt Hon **Lord Goldsmith** QC
Minister of State, Home Office — Rt Hon **Baroness Scotland of Asthal**
Minister of State, Home Office — **Hazel Blears**
Economic Secretary to the Treasury — **John Healey**
Parliamentary Under-Secretary,
    Department for Constitutional Affairs — **Christopher Leslie**

CONSTITUTIONAL REFORM POLICY
Secretary of State for Constitutional Affairs
    (Chair) — Rt Hon **Lord Falconer of Thoroton** QC
Deputy Prime Minister and
    First Secretary of State — Rt Hon **John Prescott**

Chancellor of the Exchequer	Rt Hon **Gordon Brown**
Foreign Secretary	Rt Hon **Jack Straw**
Home Secretary	Rt Hon **David Blunkett**
Secretary of State for Transport and for Scotland	Rt Hon **Alistair Darling**
Secretary of State for Northern Ireland	Rt Hon **Paul Murphy**
Leader of the House of Lords	Rt Hon **Lord Williams of Mostyn** QC
Leader of the House of Commons and Secretary of State for Wales	Rt Hon **Peter Hain**
Chief Whip	Rt Hon **Hilary Armstrong**
Minister without Portfolio	Rt Hon **Ian McCartney**
Minister for the Cabinet Office and Chancellor of the Duchy of Lancaster	**Douglas Alexander**

House of Lords Reform Sub-committee

Secretary of State for Constitutional Affairs *(Chair)*	Rt Hon **Lord Falconer of Thoroton** QC
Deputy Prime Minister and First Secretary of State	Rt Hon **John Prescott**
Chancellor of the Exchequer	Rt Hon **Gordon Brown**
Foreign Secretary	Rt Hon **Jack Straw**
Home Secretary	Rt Hon **David Blunkett**
Secretary of State for Transport and for Scotland	Rt Hon **Alistair Darling**
Secretary of State for Northern Ireland	Rt Hon **Paul Murphy**
Leader of the House of Lords	Rt Hon **Lord Williams of Mostyn** QC
Chief Whip	Rt Hon **Hilary Armstrong**
Leader of the House of Commons and Secretary of State for Wales	Rt Hon **Peter Hain**
Minister without Portfolio	Rt Hon **Ian McCartney**
Government Chief Whip in the Lords	Rt Hon **Lord Grocott**
Minister for the Cabinet Office and Chancellor of the Duchy of Lancaster	**Douglas Alexander**
Parliamentary Under-Secretary, Department for Constitutional Affairs	**Lord Filkin** CBE

INTELLIGENCE SERVICES

Prime Minister *(Chair)*	Rt Hon **Tony Blair**
Deputy Prime Minister and First Secretary of State	Rt Hon **John Prescott**
Chancellor of the Exchequer	Rt Hon **Gordon Brown**
Foreign Secretary	Rt Hon **Jack Straw**
Home Secretary	Rt Hon **David Blunkett**
Secretary of State for Defence	Rt Hon **Geoff Hoon**

DOMESTIC AFFAIRS

Deputy Prime Minister and First Secretary of State *(Chair)*	Rt Hon **John Prescott**
Chancellor of the Exchequer	Rt Hon **Gordon Brown**
Home Secretary	Rt Hon **David Blunkett**
Secretary of State for Environment, Food and Rural Affairs	Rt Hon **Margaret Beckett**
Secretary of State for Transport and for Scotland	Rt Hon **Alistair Darling**
Secretary of State for Health	Rt Hon Dr **John Reid**
Secretary of State for Northern Ireland	Rt Hon **Paul Murphy**
Secretary of State for Defence	Rt Hon **Geoff Hoon**
Secretary of State for Work and Pensions	Rt Hon **Andrew Smith**

Leader of the House of Lords	Rt Hon **Lord Williams of Mostyn** QC
Secretary of State for Trade and Industry	Rt Hon **Patricia Hewitt**
Secretary of State for Culture, Media and Sport	Rt Hon **Tessa Jowell**
Chief Whip	Rt Hon **Hilary Armstrong**
Secretary of State for Education and Skills	Rt Hon **Charles Clarke**
Leader of the House of Commons and Secretary of State for Wales	Rt Hon **Peter Hain**
Chief Secretary to the Treasury	Rt Hon **Paul Boateng**
Minister without Portfolio	Rt Hon **Ian McCartney**
Secretary of State for Constitutional Affairs	Rt Hon **Lord Falconer of Thoroton** QC
Attorney General	Rt Hon **Lord Goldsmith** QC
Minister for the Cabinet Office and Chancellor of the Duchy of Lancaster	**Douglas Alexander**
Minister of State, Office of the Deputy Prime Minister	Rt Hon **Nick Raynsford**

Adult Basic Skills Sub-committee

Secretary of State for Education and Skills *(Chair)*	Rt Hon **Charles Clarke**
Minister for the Cabinet Office and Chancellor of the Duchy of Lancaster	**Douglas Alexander**
Minister of State, Department for Environment, Food and Rural Affairs	Rt Hon **Alun Michael**
Minister of State, Department for Culture, Media and Sport	Rt Hon **Estelle Morris**
Parliamentary Under-Secretary, Department for Work and Pensions	**Des Browne**
Economic Secretary to the Treasury	**John Healey**
Parliamentary Under-Secretary, Office of the Deputy Prime Minister	**Yvette Cooper**
Parliamentary Under-Secretary, Home Office	**Paul Goggins**
Parliamentary Under-Secretary, Department of Trade and Industry	**Lord Sainsbury of Turville**
Parliamentary Under-Secretary, Department of Health	**Stephen Ladyman**
Parliamentary Under-Secretary, Ministry of Defence	**Ivor Caplin**
Parliamentary Under-Secretary, Department for Education and Skills	**Ivan Lewis**

Active Communities and Community Cohesion Sub-committee

Home Secretary *(Chair)*	Rt Hon **David Blunkett**
Minister for the Cabinet Office and Chancellor of the Duchy of Lancaster	**Douglas Alexander**
Financial Secretary to the Treasury	**Ruth Kelly**
Minister of State, Department for Environment, Food and Rural Affairs	Rt Hon **Alun Michael**
Minister of State, Department of Health	**Rosie Winterton**
Minister of State, Department for Culture, Media and Sport	Rt Hon **Estelle Morris**
Parliamentary Under-Secretary, Office of the Deputy Prime Minister	**Yvette Cooper**
Parliamentary Under-Secretary, Department for Constitutional Affairs	**Lord Filkin** CBE
Parliamentary Under-Secretary, Home Office	**Fiona Mactaggart**
Parliamentary Under-Secretary, Department for Work and Pensions	Rt Hon **Baroness Hollis of Heigham** DL

Parliamentary Under-Secretary, Northern Ireland Office	**Ian Pearson**
Parliamentary Under-Secretary for Scotland	**Anne McGuire**
Parliamentary Under-Secretary for Wales	**Don Touhig**
Parliamentary Under-Secretary, Department of Trade and Industry	**Gerry Sutcliffe**
Parliamentary Under-Secretary, Department for Education and Skills	**Baroness Ashton of Upholland**

Drugs Policy Sub-committee

Home Secretary *(Chair)*	Rt Hon **David Blunkett**
Secretary of State for Health	Rt Hon Dr **John Reid**
Secretary of State for Education and Skills	Rt Hon **Charles Clarke**
Chief Secretary to the Treasury	Rt Hon **Paul Boateng**
Minister without Portfolio	Rt Hon **Ian McCartney**
Minister for the Cabinet Office and Chancellor of the Duchy of Lancaster	**Douglas Alexander**
Minister of State, Office of the Deputy Prime Minister	**Lord Rooker**
Parliamentary Under-Secretary, Foreign and Commonwealth Office	**Bill Rammell**
Parliamentary Under-Secretary, Home Office	**Caroline Flint**

Equality Sub-committee

Minister of State, Department of Trade and Industry *(Chair)*	Rt Hon **Jacqui Smith**
Minister for the Cabinet Office and Chancellor of the Duchy of Lancaster	**Douglas Alexander**
Financial Secretary to the Treasury	**Ruth Kelly**
Solicitor General	Rt Hon **Harriet Harman** QC
Minister of State, Northern Ireland Office	Rt Hon **John Spellar**
Parliamentary Under-Secretary, Department for Constitutional Affairs	**Lord Filkin** CBE
Parliamentary Under-Secretary, Department for Transport	**David Jamieson**
Parliamentary Under-Secretary, Home Office	**Fiona Mactaggart**
Parliamentary Under-Secretary, Department for Environment, Food and Rural Affairs	**Ben Bradshaw**
Parliamentary Under-Secretary, Department for Work and Pensions	**Maria Eagle**
Parliamentary Under-Secretary, Office of the Deputy Prime Minister	**Yvette Cooper**
Parliamentary Under-Secretary, Department of Health	**Melanie Johnson**
Parliamentary Under-Secretary for Scotland	**Anne McGuire**
Parliamentary Under-Secretary for Wales	**Don Touhig**
Parliamentary Under-Secretary, Department for Education and Skills	**Stephen Twigg**
Parliamentary Under-Secretary, Department of Trade and Industry	**Gerry Sutcliffe**

Energy Policy Sub-committee

Deputy Prime Minister and First Secretary of State *(Chair)*	Rt Hon **John Prescott**
Secretary of State for Environment, Food and Rural Affairs	Rt Hon **Margaret Beckett**
Secretary of State for Transport and for Scotland	Rt Hon **Alistair Darling**

Secretary of State for Trade and Industry	Rt Hon **Patricia Hewitt**
Chief Secretary to the Treasury	Rt Hon **Paul Boateng**
Leader of the House of Commons and Secretary of State for Wales	Rt Hon **Peter Hain**
Minister for the Cabinet Office and Chancellor of the Duchy of Lancaster	**Douglas Alexander**
Minister of State, Office of the Deputy Prime Minister	Rt Hon **Lord Rooker**
Minister of State, Foreign and Commonwealth Office	Rt Hon **Baroness Symons of Vernham Dean**
Minister of State, Department of Trade and Industry	**Stephen Timms**
Parliamentary Under-Secretary, Department for Environment, Food and Rural Affairs	**Lord Whitty**

Older People Sub-committee

Secretary of State for Work and Pensions *(Chair)*	Rt Hon **Andrew Smith**
Secretary of State for Health	Rt Hon Dr **John Reid**
Minister without Portfolio	Rt Hon **Ian McCartney**
Minister for the Cabinet Office and Chancellor of the Duchy of Lancaster	**Douglas Alexander**
Financial Secretary to the Treasury	**Ruth Kelly**
Minister of State, Home Office	Rt Hon **Baroness Scotland of Asthal**
Minister of State, Department for Environment, Food and Rural Affairs	Rt Hon **Alun Michael**
Minister of State, Department for Work and Pensions	**Malcolm Wicks**
Minister of State, Department for Education and Skills	Rt Hon **Alan Johnson**
Minister of State, Department of Trade and Industry	Rt Hon **Jacqui Smith**
Minister of State, Department for Culture, Media and Sport	Rt Hon **Richard Caborn**
Parliamentary Under-Secretary, Office of the Deputy Prime Minister	**Yvette Cooper**
Parliamentary Under-Secretary, Department for Constitutional Affairs	**Lord Filkin** CBE
Parliamentary Under-Secretary, Department for Transport	**Tony McNulty**
Parliamentary Under-Secretary, Northern Ireland Office	**Angela Smith**
Parliamentary Under-Secretary for Wales	**Don Touhig**
Parliamentary Under-Secretary for Scotland	**Anne McGuire**
Parliamentary Under-Secretary, Ministry of Defence	**Ivor Caplin**

Rural Renewal Sub-committee

Secretary of State for Environment, Food and Rural Affairs *(Chair)*	Rt Hon **Margaret Beckett**
Home Secretary	Rt Hon **David Blunkett**
Secretary of State for Transport and for Scotland	Rt Hon **Alistair Darling**
Secretary of State for Health	Rt Hon Dr **John Reid**
Secretary of State for Work and Pensions	Rt Hon **Andrew Smith**
Secretary of State for Trade and Industry	Rt Hon **Patricia Hewitt**
Secretary of State for Culture, Media and Sport	Rt Hon **Tessa Jowell**
Secretary of State for Education and Skills	Rt Hon **Charles Clarke**

Chief Secretary to the Treasury	Rt Hon **Paul Boateng**
Minister for the Cabinet Office and	
Chancellor of the Duchy of Lancaster	**Douglas Alexander**
Minister of State, Office of the	
Deputy Prime Minister	**Lord Rooker**
Minister of State, Department for	
Environment, Food and Rural Affairs	Rt Hon **Alun Michael**
Parliamentary Under-Secretary,	
Department for Constitutional Affairs	**Christopher Leslie**

Social Exclusion and Regeneration Sub-committee

Deputy Prime Minister and	
First Secretary of State *(Chair)*	Rt Hon **John Prescott**
Home Secretary	Rt Hon **David Blunkett**
Secretary of State for	
Environment, Food and Rural Affairs	Rt Hon **Margaret Beckett**
Secretary of State for Transport	
and for Scotland	Rt Hon **Alistair Darling**
Secretary of State for Health	Rt Hon Dr **John Reid**
Secretary of State for Defence	Rt Hon **Geoff Hoon**
Secretary of State for Work and Pensions	Rt Hon **Andrew Smith**
Secretary of State for Trade and Industry	Rt Hon **Patricia Hewitt**
Secretary of State for Culture,	
Media and Sport	Rt Hon **Tessa Jowell**
Secretary of State for Education and Skills	Rt Hon **Charles Clarke**
Chief Secretary to the Treasury	Rt Hon **Paul Boateng**
Secretary of State for Constitutional Affairs	Rt Hon **Lord Falconer of Thoroton** QC
Minister for the Cabinet Office and	
Chancellor of the Duchy of Lancaster	**Douglas Alexander**
Minister of State, Office of the	
Deputy Prime Minister	**Lord Rooker**

DEFENCE AND OVERSEAS POLICY

Prime Minister *(Chair)*	Rt Hon **Tony Blair**
Deputy Prime Minister and First Secretary of State	Rt Hon **John Prescott**
Chancellor of the Exchequer	Rt Hon **Gordon Brown**
Foreign Secretary	Rt Hon **Jack Straw**
Secretary of State for Defence	Rt Hon **Geoff Hoon**
Secretary of State for Trade and Industry	Rt Hon **Patricia Hewitt**
Secretary of State for International Development	Rt Hon **Baroness Amos**

Conflict Prevention in Sub-Saharan Africa Sub-committee

Secretary of State for International	
Development *(Chair)*	Rt Hon **Baroness Amos**
Foreign Secretary	Rt Hon **Jack Straw**
Secretary of State for Defence	Rt Hon **Geoff Hoon**
Chief Secretary to the Treasury	Rt Hon **Paul Boateng**

International Terrorism Sub-committee

Prime Minister *(Chair)*	Rt Hon **Tony Blair**
Deputy Prime Minister and	
First Secretary of State	Rt Hon **John Prescott**
Chancellor of the Exchequer	Rt Hon **Gordon Brown**
Foreign Secretary	Rt Hon **Jack Straw**
Home Secretary	Rt Hon **David Blunkett**
Secretary of State for Transport and for Scotland	Rt Hon **Alistair Darling**
Leader of the House of Lords	Rt Hon **Lord Williams of Mostyn** QC
Secretary of State for Defence	Rt Hon **Geoff Hoon**
Secretary of State for International Development	Rt Hon **Baroness Amos**

Consequence Management and Resilience Sub-committee

Home Secretary *(Chair)*	Rt Hon **David Blunkett**
Deputy Prime Minister and First Secretary of State	Rt Hon **John Prescott**
Secretary of State for Environment, Food and Rural Affairs	Rt Hon **Margaret Beckett**
Secretary of State for Transport and for Scotland	Rt Hon **Alistair Darling**
Secretary of State for Northern Ireland	Rt Hon **Paul Murphy**
Secretary of State for Defence	Rt Hon **Geoff Hoon**
Secretary of State for Trade and Industry	Rt Hon **Patricia Hewitt**
Chief Secretary to the Treasury	Rt Hon **Paul Boateng**
Leader of the House of Commons and Secretary of State for Wales	Rt Hon **Peter Hain**
Minister for the Cabinet Office and Chancellor of the Duchy of Lancaster	**Douglas Alexander**
Minister of State, Office of the Deputy Prime Minister	Rt Hon **Nick Raynsford**
Minister of State, Foreign and Commonwealth Office	Rt Hon **Baroness Symons of Vernham Dean**
Minister of State, Home Office	**Beverley Hughes**
Minister of State, Department for Work and Pensions	Rt Hon **Des Browne**

London Resilience Sub-committee

Minister of State, Office of the Deputy Prime Minister *(Chair)*	Rt Hon **Nick Raynsford**
Representatives of:	
Office of the Deputy Prime Minister	
HM Treasury	
Home Office	
Cabinet Office	
Department for Transport	
Government Office for London	

Protective and Preventive Security Sub-committee

Home Secretary *(Chair)*	Rt Hon **David Blunkett**
Deputy Prime Minister and First Secretary of State	Rt Hon **John Prescott**
Foreign Secretary	Rt Hon **Jack Straw**
Secretary of State for Environment, Food and Rural Affairs	Rt Hon **Margaret Beckett**
Secretary of State for Transport and for Scotland	Rt Hon **Alistair Darling**
Secretary of State for Health	Rt Hon Dr **John Reid**
Secretary of State for Northern Ireland	Rt Hon **Paul Murphy**
Secretary of State for Defence	Rt Hon **Geoff Hoon**
Secretary of State for Trade and Industry	Rt Hon **Patricia Hewitt**
Chief Secretary to the Treasury	Rt Hon **Paul Boateng**

Conflict Prevention outside Sub-Saharan Africa Sub-committee

Foreign Secretary *(Chair)*	Rt Hon **Jack Straw**
Secretary of State for Defence	Rt Hon **Geoff Hoon**
Chief Secretary to the Treasury	Rt Hon **Paul Boateng**
Secretary of State for International Development	Rt Hon **Baroness Amos**

ECONOMIC AFFAIRS, PRODUCTIVITY AND COMPETITIVENESS

Chancellor of the Exchequer *(Chair)*	Rt Hon **Gordon Brown**
Deputy Prime Minister and	
First Secretary of State	Rt Hon **John Prescott**
Home Secretary	Rt Hon **David Blunkett**
Secretary of State for	
Environment, Food and Rural Affairs	Rt Hon **Margaret Beckett**
Secretary of State for Transport	
and for Scotland	Rt Hon **Alistair Darling**
Secretary of State for Health	Rt Hon Dr **John Reid**
Secretary of State for Northern Ireland	Rt Hon **Paul Murphy**
Secretary of State for Defence	Rt Hon **Geoff Hoon**
Secretary of State for Work and Pensions	Rt Hon **Andrew Smith**
Leader of the House of Lords	Rt Hon **Lord Williams of Mostyn** QC
Secretary of State for Trade and Industry	Rt Hon **Patricia Hewitt**
Secretary of State for Education and Skills	Rt Hon **Charles Clarke**
Secretary of State for Culture, Media and Sport	Rt Hon **Tessa Jowell**
Chief Whip	Rt Hon **Hilary Armstrong**
Chief Secretary to the Treasury	Rt Hon **Paul Boateng**
Leader of the House of Commons and	
Secretary of State for Wales	Rt Hon **Peter Hain**
Minister without Portfolio	Rt Hon **Ian McCartney**
Secretary of State for Constitutional Affairs	Rt Hon **Lord Falconer of Thoroton** QC
Minister for the Cabinet Office and	
Chancellor of the Duchy of Lancaster	**Douglas Alexander**
Minister of State,	
Foreign and Commonwealth Office	**Mike O'Brien**

Employment Sub-committee

Chancellor of the Exchequer *(Chair)*	Rt Hon **Gordon Brown**
Secretary of State for Transport	
and for Scotland	Rt Hon **Alistair Darling**
Secretary of State for Health	Rt Hon Dr **John Reid**
Secretary of State for Northern Ireland	Rt Hon **Paul Murphy**
Secretary of State for Work and Pensions	Rt Hon **Andrew Smith**
Chief Secretary to the Treasury	Rt Hon **Paul Boateng**
Leader of the House of Commons and	
Secretary of State for Wales	Rt Hon **Peter Hain**
Minister for the Cabinet Office and	
Chancellor of the Duchy of Lancaster	**Douglas Alexander**
Minister of State, Department for	
Work and Pensions	**Des Browne**
Minister of State, Home Office	Rt Hon **Baroness Scotland of Asthal**
Parliamentary Under-Secretary,	
Office of the Deputy Prime Minister	**Yvette Cooper**
Parliamentary Under-Secretary,	
Department of Trade and Industry	**Gerry Sutcliffe**
Economic Secretary to the Treasury	**John Healey**

ENVIRONMENT

Deputy Prime Minister and	
First Secretary of State *(Chair)*	Rt Hon **John Prescott**
Foreign Secretary	Rt Hon **Jack Straw**
Home Secretary	Rt Hon **David Blunkett**
Secretary of State for	
Environment, Food and Rural Affairs	Rt Hon **Margaret Beckett**
Secretary of State for Transport	
and for Scotland	Rt Hon **Alistair Darling**

Secretary of State for Health	Rt Hon Dr **John Reid**
Secretary of State for Northern Ireland	Rt Hon **Paul Murphy**
Secretary of State for Defence	Rt Hon **Geoff Hoon**
Secretary of State for Trade and Industry	Rt Hon **Patricia Hewitt**
Secretary of State for Culture, Media and Sport	Rt Hon **Tessa Jowell**
Chief Whip	Rt Hon **Hilary Armstrong**
Secretary of State for Education and Skills	Rt Hon **Charles Clarke**
Chief Secretary to the Treasury	Rt Hon **Paul Boateng**
Leader of the House of Commons and Secretary of State for Wales	Rt Hon **Peter Hain**
Secretary of State for International Development	Rt Hon **Baroness Amos**
Minister for the Cabinet Office and Chancellor of the Duchy of Lancaster	**Douglas Alexander**
Minister of State, Department for Environment, Food and Rural Affairs	**Elliot Morley**
Parliamentary Under-Secretary, Office of the Deputy Prime Minister	**Phil Hope**

Green Ministers Sub-committee

Minister of State, Department for Environment, Food and Rural Affairs *(Chair)*	**Elliot Morley**
Secretary of State for Education and Skills	Rt Hon **Charles Clarke**
Minister for the Cabinet Office and Chancellor of the Duchy of Lancaster	**Douglas Alexander**
Solicitor General	Rt Hon **Harriet Harman** QC
Minister of State, Foreign and Commonwealth Office	**Denis MacShane**
Minister of State, Department of Trade and Industry	**Stephen Timms**
Minister of State, Department for Culture, Media and Sport	**Estelle Morris**
Parliamentary Under-Secretary, Office of the Deputy Prime Minister	**Phil Hope**
Economic Secretary to the Treasury	**John Healey**
Parliamentary Under-Secretary, Department for Constitutional Affairs	**Lord Filkin** CBE
Parliamentary Under-Secretary, Home Office	**Fiona Mactaggart**
Parliamentary Under-Secretary, Department for Environment, Food and Rural Affairs	**Lord Whitty**
Parliamentary Under-Secretary, Department for International Development	**Gareth R Thomas**
Parliamentary Under-Secretary, Department for Work and Pensions	Rt Hon **Baroness Hollis of Heigham** DL
Parliamentary Under-Secretary, Department for Transport	**Tony McNulty**
Parliamentary Under-Secretary, Department of Health	**Melanie Johnson**
Parliamentary Under-Secretary, Ministry of Defence	**Ivor Caplin**
Parliamentary Under-Secretary, Northern Ireland Office	**Angela Smith**
Parliamentary Under-Secretary for Scotland	**Anne McGuire**
Parliamentary Secretary for Wales	**Don Touhig**

EUROPEAN POLICY

Foreign Secretary *(Chair)*	Rt Hon **Jack Straw**
Deputy Prime Minister and First Secretary of State	Rt Hon **John Prescott**

Chancellor of the Exchequer	Rt Hon **Gordon Brown**
Home Secretary	Rt Hon **David Blunkett**
Secretary of State for Environment, Food and Rural Affairs	Rt Hon **Margaret Beckett**
Secretary of State for Transport and for Scotland	Rt Hon **Alistair Darling**
Secretary of State for Health	Rt Hon Dr **John Reid**
Secretary of State for Northern Ireland	Rt Hon **Paul Murphy**
Secretary of State for Defence	Rt Hon **Geoffrey Hoon**
Secretary of State for Work and Pensions	Rt Hon **Andrew Smith**
Leader of the House of Lords	Rt Hon **Lord Williams of Mostyn** QC
Secretary of State for Trade and Industry	Rt Hon **Patricia Hewitt**
Secretary of State for Culture, Media and Sport	Rt Hon **Tessa Jowell**
Chief Whip	Rt Hon **Hilary Armstrong**
Secretary of State for Education and Skills	Rt Hon **Charles Clarke**
Leader of the House of Commons and Secretary of State for Wales	Rt Hon **Peter Hain**
Minister without Portfolio	Rt Hon **Ian McCartney**
Secretary of State for International Development	Rt Hon **Baroness Amos**
Secretary of State for Constitutional Affairs	Rt Hon **Lord Falconer of Thoroton** QC
Attorney General	Rt Hon **Lord Goldsmith** QC
Minister for the Cabinet Office and Chancellor of the Duchy of Lancaster	**Douglas Alexander**
Minister of State, Foreign and Commonwealth Office	**Denis MacShane**

ENGLISH REGIONAL POLICY

Deputy Prime Minister and First Secretary of State *(Chair)*	Rt Hon **John Prescott**
Home Secretary	Rt Hon **David Blunkett**
Secretary of State for Environment, Food and Rural Affairs	Rt Hon **Margaret Beckett**
Secretary of State for Transport and for Scotland	Rt Hon **Alistair Darling**
Secretary of State for Health	Rt Hon Dr **John Reid**
Secretary of State for Northern Ireland	Rt Hon **Paul Murphy**
Secretary of State for Work and Pensions	Rt Hon **Andrew Smith**
Leader of the House of Lords	Rt Hon **Lord Williams of Mostyn** QC
Secretary of State for Trade and Industry	Rt Hon **Patricia Hewitt**
Secretary of State for Culture, Media and Sport	Rt Hon **Tessa Jowell**
Secretary of State for Education and Skills	Rt Hon **Charles Clarke**
Chief Whip	Rt Hon **Hilary Armstrong**
Leader of the House of Commons and Secretary of State for Wales	Rt Hon **Peter Hain**
Chief Secretary to the Treasury	Rt Hon **Paul Boateng**
Minister without Portfolio	Rt Hon **Ian McCartney**
Secretary of State for Constitutional Affairs	Rt Hon **Lord Falconer of Thoroton** QC
Attorney General	Rt Hon **Lord Goldsmith** QC
Minister of State, Office of the Deputy Prime Minister	Rt Hon **Nick Raynsford**

EUROPEAN UNION STRATEGY

Prime Minister *(Chair)*	Rt Hon **Tony Blair**
Deputy Prime Minister and First Secretary of State	Rt Hon **John Prescott**
Chancellor of the Exchequer	Rt Hon **Gordon Brown**
Foreign Secretary	Rt Hon **Jack Straw**

Secretary of State for	
Environment, Food and Rural Affairs	Rt Hon **Margaret Beckett**
Secretary of State for Education and Skills	Rt Hon **Charles Clarke**
Secretary of State for Trade and Industry	Rt Hon **Patricia Hewitt**
Secretary of State for Work and Pensions	Rt Hon **Andrew Smith**
Leader of the House of Commons and	
Secretary of State for Wales	Rt Hon **Peter Hain**
Secretary of State for Constitutional Affairs	Rt Hon **Lord Falconer of Thoroton** QC

LOCAL GOVERNMENT

Deputy Prime Minister and	
First Secretary of State *(Chair)*	Rt Hon **John Prescott**
Chancellor of the Exchequer	Rt Hon **Gordon Brown**
Home Secretary	Rt Hon **David Blunkett**
Secretary of State for	
Environment, Food and Rural Affairs	Rt Hon **Margaret Beckett**
Secretary of State for Transport	
and for Scotland	Rt Hon **Alistair Darling**
Secretary of State for Health	Rt Hon Dr **John Reid**
Secretary of State for Work and Pensions	Rt Hon **Andrew Smith**
Secretary of State for Trade and Industry	Rt Hon **Patricia Hewitt**
Secretary of State for Culture, Media and Sport	Rt Hon **Tessa Jowell**
Chief Whip	Rt Hon **Hilary Armstrong**
Secretary of State for Education and Skills	Rt Hon **Charles Clarke**
Chief Secretary to the Treasury	Rt Hon **Paul Boateng**
Leader of the House of Commons and	
Secretary of State for Wales	Rt Hon **Peter Hain**
Secretary of State for Constitutional Affairs	Rt Hon **Lord Falconer of Thoroton** QC
Minister for the Cabinet Office and	
Chancellor of the Duchy of Lancaster	**Douglas Alexander**
Minister of State, Office of the	
Deputy Prime Minister	Rt Hon **Nick Raynsford**

Local Government Performance Sub-committee

Minister of State, Office of the	
Deputy Prime Minister *(Chair)*	Rt Hon **Nick Raynsford**
Chief Secretary to the Treasury	Rt Hon **Paul Boateng**
Minister for the Cabinet Office and	
Chancellor of the Duchy of Lancaster	**Douglas Alexander**
Minister of State, Home Office	**Hazel Blears**
Minister of State, Department for	
Environment, Food and Rural Affairs	Rt Hon **Alun Michael**
Minister of State for Transport,	
Department for Transport	Dr **Kim Howells**
Minister of State, Department for	
Education and Skills	**David Miliband**
Minister of State, Department for	
Culture, Media and Sport	Rt Hon **Estelle Morris**
Parliamentary Under-Secretary,	
Department of Health	Dr **Stephen Ladyman**
Parliamentary Under-Secretary,	
Office of the Deputy Prime Minister	**Phil Hope**
Parliamentary Under-Secretary,	
Department for Work and Pensions	**Maria Eagle**
Parliamentary Under-Secretary,	
Department of Trade and Industry	**Gerry Sutcliffe**

JOINT CONSULTATIVE COMMITTEE WITH THE LIBERAL DEMOCRATS

Prime Minister *(Chair)*	Rt Hon **Tony Blair**

LEGISLATIVE PROGRAMME

Leader of the House of Commons and Secretary of State for Wales *(Chair)*	Rt Hon **Peter Hain**
Deputy Prime Minister and First Secretary of State	Rt Hon **John Prescott**
Secretary of State for Transport and for Scotland	Rt Hon **Alistair Darling**
Secretary of State for Northern Ireland	Rt Hon **Paul Murphy**
Leader of the House of Lords	Rt Hon **Lord Williams of Mostyn** QC
Chief Secretary to the Treasury	Rt Hon **Paul Boateng**
Chief Whip	Rt Hon **Hilary Armstrong**
Minister without Portfolio	Rt Hon **Ian McCartney**
Secretary of State for Constitutional Affairs	Rt Hon **Lord Falconer of Thoroton** QC
Government Chief Whip in the Lords	Rt Hon **Lord Grocott**
Minister for the Cabinet Office and Chancellor of the Duchy of Lancaster	**Douglas Alexander**
Attorney General	Rt Hon **Lord Goldsmith** QC
Advocate General	Dr **Lynda Clark** QC
Deputy Leader of the House of Commons	**Phil Woolas**
Parliamentary Under-Secretary for Wales	**Don Touhig**

NORTHERN IRELAND

Prime Minister *(Chair)*	Rt Hon **Tony Blair**
Deputy Prime Minister and First Secretary of State	Rt Hon **John Prescott**
Chancellor of the Exchequer	Rt Hon **Gordon Brown**
Foreign Secretary	Rt Hon **Jack Straw**
Home Secretary	Rt Hon **David Blunkett**
Secretary of State for Northern Ireland	Rt Hon **Paul Murphy**
Secretary of State for Defence	Rt Hon **Geoff Hoon**
Secretary of State for Constitutional Affairs	Rt Hon **Lord Falconer of Thoroton** QC

ORGANISED CRIME

Home Secretary *(Chair)*	Rt Hon **David Blunkett**
Chancellor of the Exchequer	Rt Hon **Gordon Brown**
Foreign Secretary	Rt Hon **Jack Straw**
Secretary of State for Trade and Industry	Rt Hon **Patricia Hewitt**
Secretary of State for Northern Ireland	Rt Hon **Paul Murphy**
Leader of the House of Commons and Secretary of State for Wales	Rt Hon **Peter Hain**
Secretary of State for Constitutional Affairs	Rt Hon **Lord Falconer of Thoroton** QC
Attorney General	Rt Hon **Lord Goldsmith** QC
Minister of State, Home Office	**Hazel Blears**

DEVOLUTION POLICY

Secretary of State for Constitutional Affairs *(Chair)*	Rt Hon **Lord Falconer of Thoroton** QC
Deputy Prime Minister and First Secretary of State	Rt Hon **John Prescott**
Home Secretary	Rt Hon **David Blunkett**
Secretary of State for Environment, Food and Rural Affairs	Rt Hon **Margaret Beckett**
Secretary of State for Transport and for Scotland	Rt Hon **Alistair Darling**
Secretary of State for Health	Rt Hon Dr **John Reid**

Secretary of State for Northern Ireland	Rt Hon **Paul Murphy**
Secretary of State for Work and Pensions	Rt Hon **Andrew Smith**
Leader of the House of Lords	Rt Hon **Lord Williams of Mostyn** QC
Secretary of State for Trade and Industry	Rt Hon **Patricia Hewitt**
Secretary of State for Culture, Media and Sport	Rt Hon **Tessa Jowell**
Chief Whip	Rt Hon **Hilary Armstrong**
Secretary of State for Education and Skills	Rt Hon **Charles Clarke**
Leader of the House of Commons and Secretary of State for Wales	Rt Hon **Peter Hain**
Minister without Portfolio	Rt Hon **Ian McCartney**
Chief Secretary to the Treasury	Rt Hon **Paul Boateng**
Attorney General	Rt Hon **Lord Goldsmith** QC
Advocate General	Dr **Lynda Clark** QC

REGULATORY ACCOUNTABILITY

Minister for the Cabinet Office and Chancellor of the Duchy of Lancaster *(Chair)*	**Douglas Alexander**
Secretary of State for Trade and Industry	Rt Hon **Patricia Hewitt**
Chief Secretary to the Treasury	Rt Hon **Paul Boateng**

PUBLIC SERVICES AND PUBLIC EXPENDITURE

Chancellor of the Exchequer *(Chair)*	Rt Hon **Gordon Brown**
Deputy Prime Minister and First Secretary of State	Rt Hon **John Prescott**
Secretary of State for Transport and for Scotland	Rt Hon **Alistair Darling**
Secretary of State for Work and Pensions	Rt Hon **Andrew Smith**
Leader of the House of Lords	Rt Hon **Lord Williams of Mostyn** QC
Secretary of State for Trade and Industry	Rt Hon **Patricia Hewitt**
Chief Secretary to the Treasury	Rt Hon **Paul Boateng**
Leader of the House of Commons and Secretary of State for Wales	Rt Hon **Peter Hain**
Minister without Portfolio	Rt Hon **Ian McCartney**
Secretary of State for Constitutional Affairs	Rt Hon **Lord Falconer of Thoroton** QC
Minister for the Cabinet Office and Chancellor of the Duchy of Lancaster	**Douglas Alexander**

Electronic Service Delivery Sub-committee

Chief Secretary to the Treasury *(Chair)*	Rt Hon **Paul Boateng**
Secretary of State for Trade and Industry	Rt Hon **Patricia Hewitt**
Secretary of State for Education and Skills	Rt Hon **Charles Clarke**
Minister without Portfolio	Rt Hon **Ian McCartney**
Minister for the Cabinet Office and Chancellor of the Duchy of Lancaster	**Douglas Alexander**
Minister of State, Department for Work and Pensions	**Des Browne**
Minister of State, Department of Trade and Industry	**Stephen Timms**
Minister of State, Home Office	Rt Hon **Baroness Scotland of Asthal**
Parliamentary Under-Secretary, Office of the Deputy Prime Minister	**Phil Hope**
Parliamentary Under-Secretary, Department for Transport	**David Jamieson**

Inspection Sub-committee

Chief Secretary to the Treasury *(Chair)*	Rt Hon **Paul Boateng**
Home Secretary	Rt Hon **David Blunkett**
Secretary of State for Health	Rt Hon Dr **John Reid**
Secretary of State for Education and Skills	Rt Hon **Charles Clarke**

Minister for the Cabinet Office and Chancellor of the Duchy of Lancaster	**Douglas Alexander**
Minister of State, Office of the Deputy Prime Minister	Rt Hon **Nick Raynsford**
Parliamentary Under-Secretary, Department for Constitutional Affairs	**Christopher Leslie**
Parliamentary Under-Secretary, Department for Work and Pensions	**Chris Pond**

SCIENCE POLICY

Secretary of State for Trade and Industry *(Chair)*	Rt Hon **Patricia Hewitt**
Home Secretary	Rt Hon **David Blunkett**
Secretary of State for Environment, Food and Rural Affairs	Rt Hon **Margaret Beckett**
Secretary of State for Transport and for Scotland	Rt Hon **Alistair Darling**
Secretary of State for Health	Rt Hon Dr **John Reid**
Secretary of State for Defence	Rt Hon **Geoff Hoon**
Secretary of State for Education and Skills	Rt Hon **Charles Clarke**
Leader of the House of Commons and Secretary of State for Wales	Rt Hon **Peter Hain**
Minister for the Cabinet Office and Chancellor of the Duchy of Lancaster	**Douglas Alexander**
Minister of State, Office of the Deputy Prime Minister	Rt Hon **Keith Hill**
Economic Secretary to the Treasury	**John Healey**
Minister of State, Foreign and Commonwealth Office	**Mike O'Brien**
Minister of State, Department for International Development	**Hilary Benn**
Minister of State, Department for Work and Pensions	**Malcolm Wicks**
Minister of State, Department for Culture, Media and Sport	Rt Hon **Estelle Morris**
Parliamentary Under-Secretary, Department of Trade and Industry	**Lord Sainsbury of Turville**
Parliamentary Under-Secretary, Northern Ireland Office	**Ian Pearson**

Biotechnology Sub-committee

Foreign Secretary *(Chair)*	Rt Hon **Jack Straw**
Secretary of State for Environment, Food and Rural Affairs	Rt Hon **Margaret Beckett**
Secretary of State for Health	Rt Hon Dr **John Reid**
Parliamentary Under-Secretary, Department for Work and Pensions	**Des Browne**
Economic Secretary to the Treasury	**John Healey**
Minister of State, Department for Environment, Food and Rural Affairs	**Elliot Morley**
Parliamentary Under-Secretary, Foreign and Commonwealth Office	**Bill Rammell**
Parliamentary Under-Secretary, Home Office	**Caroline Flint**
Parliamentary Under-Secretary, Department for International Development	**Gareth R Thomas**
Parliamentary Under-Secretary, Northern Ireland Office	**Angela Smith**

Parliamentary Under-Secretary for Wales	**Don Touhig**
Parliamentary Under-Secretary for Scotland	**Anne McGuire**
Parliamentary Under-Secretary,	
Department of Trade and Industry	**Lord Sainsbury of Turville**

WELFARE REFORM

Prime Minister *(Chair)*	Rt Hon **Tony Blair**
Deputy Prime Minister and	
First Secretary of State	Rt Hon **John Prescott**
Chancellor of the Exchequer	Rt Hon **Gordon Brown**
Secretary of State for Health	Rt Hon Dr **John Reid**
Secretary of State for Work and Pensions	Rt Hon **Andrew Smith**
Chief Secretary to the Treasury	Rt Hon **Paul Boateng**
Minister of State, Department for	
Work and Pensions	Rt Hon **Des Browne**

EUROPEAN AEROSPACE AND DEFENCE INDUSTRY

Secretary of State for Trade and Industry *(Chair)*	Rt Hon **Patricia Hewitt**
Secretary of State for Defence	Rt Hon **Geoff Hoon**
Chief Secretary to the Treasury	Rt Hon **Paul Boateng**
Minister of State,	
Foreign and Commonwealth Office	**Mike O'Brien**
Minister of State, Department of	
Trade and Industry	Rt Hon **Jacqui Smith**

CHILDREN AND YOUNG PEOPLE'S SERVICES

Chancellor of the Exchequer *(Chair)*	Rt Hon **Gordon Brown**
Home Secretary *(Chair)*	Rt Hon **David Blunkett**
Deputy Prime Minister and	
First Secretary of State	Rt Hon **John Prescott**
Secretary of State for	
Environment, Food and Rural Affairs	Rt Hon **Margaret Beckett**
Secretary of State for Transport	
and for Scotland	Rt Hon **Alistair Darling**
Secretary of State for Health	Rt Hon Dr **John Reid**
Secretary of State for Defence	Rt Hon **Geoff Hoon**
Secretary of State for Work and Pensions	Rt Hon **Andrew Smith**
Secretary of State for Culture,	
Media and Sport	Rt Hon **Tessa Jowell**
Secretary of State for Education and Skills	Rt Hon **Charles Clarke**
Secretary of State for Constitutional Affairs	Rt Hon **Lord Falconer of Thoroton** QC
Minister for the Cabinet Office and	
Chancellor of the Duchy of Lancaster	**Douglas Alexander**
Minister of State, Department for	
Education and Skills	Rt Hon **Margaret Hodge**
Economic Secretary to the Treasury	**John Healey**

Delivery of Services for Children, Young People and Families Sub-committee

Secretary of State for Education and Skills	
(Chair)	Rt Hon **Charles Clarke**
Home Secretary	Rt Hon **David Blunkett**
Secretary of State for Work and Pensions	Rt Hon **Andrew Smith**
Secretary of State for Health	Rt Hon Dr **John Reid**
Secretary of State for Culture,	
Media and Sport	Rt Hon **Tessa Jowell**
Chief Secretary to the Treasury	Rt Hon **Paul Boateng**
Minister of State, Department for	
Education and Skills	Rt Hon **Margaret Hodge**

Minister of State, Office of the Deputy Prime Minister	Rt Hon **Nick Raynsford**
Minister of State, Office of the Deputy Prime Minister	**Lord Rooker**
Parliamentary Under-Secretary, Department for Education and Skills	**Baroness Ashton of Upholland**

ANIMAL RIGHTS ACTIVISTS

Home Secretary *(Chair)*	Rt Hon **David Blunkett**
Solicitor General	Rt Hon **Harriet Harman** QC
Minister of State, Department for Education and Skills	Rt Hon **Alan Johnson**
Economic Secretary to the Treasury	**John Healey**
Parliamentary Under-Secretary, Home Office	**Caroline Flint**
Parliamentary Under-Secretary, Department for Environment, Food and Rural Affairs	**Ben Bradshaw**
Parliamentary Under-Secretary, Department of Health	**Lord Warner**
Parliamentary Under-Secretary, Northern Ireland Office	**Angela Smith**
Parliamentary Under-Secretary for Scotland	**Anne McGuire**
Parliamentary Under-Secretary for Wales	**Don Touhig**
Parliamentary Under-Secretary, Department of Trade and Industry	**Lord Sainsbury of Turville**

UNIVERSAL BANKING SERVICE

Secretary of State for Work and Pensions *(Chair)*	Rt Hon **Andrew Smith**
Chief Secretary to the Treasury	Rt Hon **Paul Boateng**
Minister for the Cabinet Office and Chancellor of the Duchy of Lancaster	**Douglas Alexander**
Minister of State, Department of Trade and Industry	**Stephen Timms**
Parliamentary Under-Secretary, Department for Work and Pensions	**Chris Pond**

SOCIAL AND ECONOMIC ASPECTS OF MIGRATION

Home Secretary *(Chair)*	Rt Hon **David Blunkett**
Deputy Prime Minister and First Secretary of State	Rt Hon **John Prescott**
Foreign Secretary	Rt Hon **Jack Straw**
Secretary of State for Environment, Food and Rural Affairs	Rt Hon **Margaret Beckett**
Secretary of State for Transport and for Scotland	Rt Hon **Alistair Darling**
Secretary of State for Health	Rt Hon Dr **John Reid**
Secretary of State for Work and Pensions	Rt Hon **Andrew Smith**
Secretary of State for Trade and Industry	Rt Hon **Patricia Hewitt**
Secretary of State for Culture, Media and Sport	Rt Hon **Tessa Jowell**
Secretary of State for Education and Skills	Rt Hon **Charles Clarke**
Leader of the House of Commons and Secretary of State for Wales	Rt Hon **Peter Hain**
Chief Secretary to the Treasury	Rt Hon **Paul Boateng**
Minister for the Cabinet Office and Chancellor of the Duchy of Lancaster	**Douglas Alexander**
Minister of State, Home Office	**Beverley Hughes**

GOVERNMENT'S RESPONSE TO PALIAMENTARY MODERNISATION

Leader of the House of Commons and Secretary of State for Wales *(Chair)*	Rt Hon **Peter Hain**
Deputy Prime Minister and First Secretary of State	Rt Hon **John Prescott**
Secretary of State for Environment, Food and Rural Affairs	Rt Hon **Margaret Beckett**
Secretary of State for Health	Rt Hon Dr **John Reid**
Leader of the House of Lords	Rt Hon **Lord Williams of Mostyn** QC
Secretary of State for Trade and Industry	Rt Hon **Patricia Hewitt**
Chief Whip	Rt Hon **Hilary Armstrong**
Secretary of State for Education and Skills	Rt Hon **Charles Clarke**
Chief Secretary to the Treasury	Rt Hon **Paul Boateng**
Minister without Portfolio	Rt Hon **Ian McCartney**
Government Chief Whip in the Lords	Rt Hon **Lord Grocott**
Deputy Leader of the House of Commons	**Phil Woolas**

THAMES GATEWAY

Prime Minister *(Chair)*	Rt Hon **Tony Blair**
Deputy Prime Minister and First Secretary of State	Rt Hon **John Prescott**
Chancellor of the Exchequer	Rt Hon **Gordon Brown**
Secretary of State for Environment, Food and Rural Affairs	Rt Hon **Margaret Beckett**
Secretary of State for Transport and for Scotland	Rt Hon **Alistair Darling**
Secretary of State for Health	Rt Hon Dr **John Reid**
Secretary of State for Trade and Industry	Rt Hon **Patricia Hewitt**
Secretary of State for Culture, Media and Sport	Rt Hon **Tessa Jowell**
Secretary of State for Education and Skills	Rt Hon **Charles Clarke**
Chief Secretary to the Treasury	Rt Hon **Paul Boateng**
Minister for the Cabinet Office and Chancellor of the Duchy of Lancaster	**Douglas Alexander**
Minister of State, Office of the Deputy Prime Minister	Rt Hon **Keith Hill**

ILLEGAL IMPORTS

Secretary of State for Environment, Food and Rural Affairs *(Chair)*	Rt Hon **Margaret Beckett**
Minister for the Cabinet Office and Chancellor of the Duchy of Lancaster	**Douglas Alexander**
Economic Secretary to the Treasury	**John Healey**
Minister of State, Home Office	**Beverley Hughes**
Minister of State for Transport, Department for Transport	Dr **Kim Howells**
Parliamentary Under-Secretary, Department for Environment, Food and Rural Affairs	**Lord Whitty**
Parliamentary Under-Secretary, Department of Health	**Melanie Johnson**
Parliamentary Under-Secretary, Department for Culture, Media and Sport	**Lord McIntosh of Haringey**

ELECTORAL POLICY

Leader of the House of Commons and Secretary of State for Wales *(Chair)*	Rt Hon **Peter Hain**
Secretary of State for Transport and for Scotland	Rt Hon **Alistair Darling**
Secretary of State for Health	Rt Hon Dr **John Reid**

Secretary of State for Trade and Industry	Rt Hon **Patricia Hewitt**
Secretary of State for Education and Skills	Rt Hon **Charles Clarke**
Minister without Portfolio	Rt Hon **Ian McCartney**
Chief Secretary to the Treasury	Rt Hon **Paul Boateng**
Secretary of State for Constitutional Affairs	Rt Hon **Lord Falconer of Thoroton** QC
Minister for the Cabinet Office and	
Chancellor of the Duchy of Lancaster	**Douglas Alexander**
Deputy Leader of the House of Commons	**Phil Woolas**
Minister of State, Office of the	
Deputy Prime Minister	Rt Hon **Nick Raynsford**

OLYMPIC GAMES

Foreign Secretary *(Chair)*	Rt Hon **Jack Straw**
Deputy Prime Minister and	
First Secretary of State	Rt Hon **John Prescott**
Secretary of State for Transport	
and for Scotland	Rt Hon **Alistair Darling**
Secretary of State for Trade and Industry	Rt Hon **Patricia Hewitt**
Secretary of State for Culture, Media and Sport	Rt Hon **Tessa Jowell**
Chief Secretary to the Treasury	Rt Hon **Paul Boateng**
Minister of State, Office of the	
Deputy Prime Minister	Rt Hon **Keith Hill**
Minister of State, Home Office	**Hazel Blears**
Minister of State, Department for	
Culture, Media and Sport	Rt Hon **Richard Caborn**

Visit the Vacher Dod Website . . .

www.DodOnline.co.uk

Political information updated daily

The Queen's Speech	House of Commons
Today's Business	House of Lords
This Week's Business	Scottish Parliament
Progress of Government Bills	National Assembly for Wales
Select Committees	Northern Ireland Assembly
Government and Opposition	Greater London Authority
Stop Press News	European Union

Check changes daily as they happen

The Opposition

Conservatives (official opposition)

Shadow Cabinet

Leader of the Opposition	Rt Hon **Iain Duncan Smith** MP
Deputy Leader of the Opposition and Shadow Secretary of State for Foreign and Commonwealth Affairs	Rt Hon **Michael Ancram** QC MP
Shadow Chancellor of the Exchequer	Rt Hon **Michael Howard** QC MP
Shadow Secretary of State for the Office of the Deputy Prime Minister	Rt Hon **David Davis** MP
Party Chairman	**Theresa May** MP
Shadow Secretary of State for Home Affairs	Rt Hon **Oliver Letwin** MP
Shadow Leader of the House of Lords	Rt Hon **Lord Strathclyde**
Shadow Secretary of State for Defence	Hon **Bernard Jenkin** MP
Shadow Secretary of State for Work and Pensions	**David Willetts** MP
Shadow Secretary of State for Health	Dr **Liam Fox** MP
Shadow Secretary of State for Trade and Industry	**Tim Yeo** MP
Shadow Secretary of State for Northern Ireland	**Quentin Davies** MP
Shadow Leader of the House of Commons	Rt Hon **Eric Forth** MP
Shadow Secretary of State for Culture, Media and Sport	**John Whittingdale** OBE MP
Shadow Secretary of State for Education and Skills	**Damian Green** MP
Shadow Secretary of State for Transport	**Tim Collins** CBE MP
Shadow Secretary of State for Environment, Food and Rural Affairs	**David Lidington** MP
Shadow Secretary of State for Local Government and the Regions	**Eric Pickles** MP
Shadow Secretary of State for Scotland	**Jacqui Lait** MP
Shadow Secretary of State for Wales	**Nigel Evans** MP
Shadow Secretary of State for International Development	**Caroline Spelman** MP
Shadow Chief Secretary to the Treasury	**Howard Flight** MP
Shadow Minister for Agriculture	**John Hayes** MP
Shadow Minister for Work and Pensions	**Oliver Heald** MP
Opposition Chief Whip (Commons)	Rt Hon **David Maclean** MP
Opposition Chief Whip (Lords)	Rt Hon **Lord Cope of Berkeley**

Visit the Vacher Dod Website . . .

www.DodonLine.co.uk

Opposition Frontbench Team

Leader of the Opposition   Rt Hon **Iain Duncan Smith** MP

CULTURE, MEDIA AND SPORT
Shadow Secretary of State   **John Whittingdale** OBE MP
Shadow Ministers   Rt Hon **Greg Knight** MP
                                                  Malcolm Moss MP
Lords   **Baroness Buscombe**
    Sport   **Lord Moynihan**

DEFENCE
Shadow Secretary of State   Hon **Bernard Jenkin** MP
Shadow Ministers   **Gerald Howarth** MP
                                                  Keith Simpson MP
                                                  Julian Lewis MP
    Homeland Security   **Patrick Mercer** OBE MP
Lords   **Lord Vivian**

OFFICE OF THE DEPUTY PRIME MINISTER (LOCAL GOVERNMENT AND THE REGIONS)
Shadow Secretary of State for
    Office of the Deputy Prime Minister with
    Shadow Ministerial responsibility for
    the Cabinet Office   Rt Hon **David Davis** MP
Shadow Secretary of State for Local
    Government and the Regions   **Eric Pickles** MP
Shadow Ministers   **Philip Hammond** MP
                                                  Geoffrey Clifton-Brown MP
Shadow Minister for the Cabinet Office   **Lord Saatchi**
Lords   **Baroness Wilcox**

EDUCATION AND SKILLS
Shadow Secretary of State   **Damian Green** MP
Shadow Ministers   **Tim Boswell** MP (Disability issues)
                                                  Graham Brady MP
    Children   **Eleanor Laing** MP
                                                  Charles Hendry MP
Lords   Rt Hon **Baroness Blatch** CBE

ENVIRONMENT, FOOD AND RURAL AFFAIRS
Shadow Secretary of State   **David Lidington** MP
Shadow Minister for Agriculture   **John Hayes** MP
Shadow Ministers   **James Gray** MP
                                                  Bill Wiggin
Lords   **Baroness Byford** DBE
                                                  Lord Dixon-Smith

FOREIGN AND COMMONWEALTH OFFICE
Shadow Secretary of State   Rt Hon **Michael Ancram** QC MP
Shadow Ministers   **Alan Duncan** MP
                                                  Richard Spring MP
Lords   Rt Hon **Lord Howell of Guildford**
                                                  Baroness Rawlings

HEALTH
Shadow Secretary of State   Dr **Liam Fox** MP
Shadow Ministers   **Simon Burns** MP
                                                  Tim Loughton MP
                                                  John Baron MP
                                                  Chris Grayling MP

Lords

Earl Howe
Lord McColl of Dulwich CBE
Baroness Noakes DBE

HOME OFFICE
Shadow Home Secretary

Rt Hon **Oliver Letwin** MP

Shadow Ministers

Dominic Grieve MP
James Paice MP
Humfrey Malins CBE MP
Julian Brazier MP

Lords

Baroness Anelay of St Johns
Rt Hon **Lord Roberts of Conwy**
Lord Hodgson of Astley Abbots CBE

INTERNATIONAL DEVELOPMENT
Shadow Secretary of State; Shadow Cabinet
Spokesperson for Women's Issues

Caroline Spelman MP

Shadow Ministers

Andrew Robathan MP

Lords

Baroness Rawlings

LAW OFFICERS' AND CONSTITUTIONAL AFFAIRS IN THE HOUSE OF COMMONS
Shadow Attorney-General*

Bill Cash MP

Shadow Lord Chancellor

Rt Hon **Lord Kingsland** QC TD DL

Shadow Solicitor General

Nick Hawkins MP

Lords

Baroness Buscombe

NORTHERN IRELAND
Shadow Secretary of State

Quentin Davies MP

Shadow Ministers

John Taylor MP

Lords

Lord Glentoran CBE DL

PRIVY COUNCIL OFFICE
Shadow Leader of the House of Commons

Rt Hon **Eric Forth** MP

Shadow Minister

David Cameron MP

SCOTLAND OFFICE
Shadow Secretary of State

Jacqui Lait MP

Shadow Minister

Peter Duncan MP

Lords

Duke of Montrose

SHADOW LEADER OF THE HOUSE OF LORDS

Rt Hon **Lord Strathclyde**

Deputy Shadow Leader

Rt Hon **Baroness Blatch** CBE

TRADE AND INDUSTRY
Shadow Secretary of State

Tim Yeo MP

Shadow Ministers

Henry Bellingham MP
Michael Fabricant MP
Laurence Robertson MP

Lords

Baroness Miller of Hendon MBE
Lord Hodgson of Astley Abbotts CBE

TRANSPORT
Shadow Secretary of State

Tim Collins CBE MP

Shadow Ministers

Christopher Chope OBE MP
Anne McIntosh MP

Lords

Viscount Astor

TREASURY
Shadow Chancellor of the Exchequer

Rt Hon **Michael Howard** QC MP

Shadow Chief Secretary

Howard Flight MP

Shadow Paymaster General

Stephen O'Brien MP

Shadow Financial Secretary

Mark Prisk MP

Lords

Lord Saatchi

WALES OFFICE

Shadow Secretary of State	Nigel Evans MP
Lords	Rt Hon **Lord Roberts of Conwy**

WORK AND PENSIONS

Shadow Secretary of State	David Willetts MP
Shadow Minister for Work and Pensions	Oliver Heald MP
Shadow Ministers	
People with disabilities	Nigel Waterson MP
	Paul Goodman MP
Lords	Rt Hon **Lord Higgins** KBE DL
	Baroness Noakes DBE

* Not a member of the Shadow Cabinet but attends at the invitation of the Leader.

Opposition Whips

HOUSE OF COMMONS

Chief Whip

Rt Hon **David Maclean** MP

Deputy Chief Whip

Patrick McLoughlin MP

Assistant Chief Whip

Peter Luff MP

Whips

Cheryl Gillan MP
Desmond Swayne MP
David Wilshire MP
John Randall MP
Robert Syms MP
Angela Watkinson MP
Mark Hoban MP
Mark Francois MP
Hugh Robertson MP
Mark Field MP
George Osborne MP

DodOnline

An Electronic Directory without rival . . .

MPs' biographies and photographs available with daily updates *via* the internet

For a *free* trial, call Yasmin Mirza, Aby Farsoun or Michael Mand on 020 7630 7643

Liberal Democrats
Shadow Cabinet

Leader	Rt Hon **Charles Kennedy** MP
Deputy Leader and Cabinet Office	Rt Hon **Alan Beith** MP
Treasury	**Matthew Taylor** MP
Chief Secretary to the Treasury	**David Laws** MP
Foreign Affairs	Rt Hon **Menzies Campbell** CBE QC MP
International Development	Dr **Jenny Tonge** MP
Home Office	**Simon Hughes** MP
Chair Parliamentary Party	**Mark Oaten** MP
Education and Skills	**Phil Willis** MP
Health	Dr **Evan Harris** MP
Transport	**Don Foster** MP
Office of the Deputy Prime Minister	**Edward Davey** MP
Environment	**Norman Baker** MP
Rural Affairs and Food	**Andrew George** MP
Work and Pensions	Prof **Steve Webb** MP
Defence	**Paul Keetch** MP
Trade and Industry	Dr **Vincent Cable** MP
Scotland	**John Thurso** MP
Wales and Northern Ireland	**Lembit Öpik** MP
Culture, Media and Sport	**Nick Harvey** MP
Leader in the House of Commons	**Paul Tyler** CBE MP
Chief Whip	**Andrew Stunell** OBE MP
Older People	**Paul Burstow** MP
Women's Issues	**Sandra Gidley** MP
Chair of Scottish Campaigns	**Mike Moore** MP
Leader in the House of Lords	Rt Hon **Baroness Williams of Crosby**
Chief Whip in the Lords	**Lord Roper**
Party President	**Lord Dholakia**
Chair of Campaigns and Communications Committee	**Lord Razzall**
Also a member of the Shadow Cabinet	Sir **Archy Kirkwood** MP

Whips

Chief Whip

Andrew Stunell OBE MP

Deputy Chief Whip

Sir Robert Smith MP

Whips

Tom Brake MP
Richard Younger-Ross MP
Alan Reid MP
Annette Brooke MP

Ulster Unionist Party (UUP)

Leader; Constitutional Affairs; Treasury	Rt Hon **David Trimble** MP
Chief Whip; Shadow Leader of the House; Education and Skills	**Roy Beggs** MP
Environment, Food and Rural Affairs; Cabinet Office; Transport; Local Government and the Regions	**David Burnside** MP
Defence; Trade and Industry; Work and Pensions	**Jeffrey Donaldson** MP
Home Affairs; Culture, Media and Sport; Youth and Women	**Lady Sylvia Hermon** MP
Foreign and Commonwealth; International Development; Health	Rev **Martin Smyth** MP
Leader in the House of Lords	**Lord Rogan**

Scottish National Party (SNP)

National Convener	**John Swinney** MSP
Senior Vice-Convener	**Roseanna Cunningham** MSP
Westminster Parliamentary Group Leader; Treasury; Constituency	**Alex Salmond** MP
Chief Whip; Transport; Rural Affairs; Culture, Media and Sport	**Peter Wishart** MP
Social Security and Pensions	**Annabelle Ewing** MP
Foreign Affairs	**Angus Robertson** MP
Trade and Industry; Health; Environment	**Mike Weir** MP

Plaid Cymru – The Party of Wales (PLC)

Parliamentary Leader; Housing; Home Affairs; Local Government; Tourism; Defence	**Elfyn Llwyd** MP
Whip; Environment and the Regions, Transport; Culture; Agriculture; Sustainable energy; Heritage; International Development	**Simon Thomas** MP
Work and Pensions; Social Security; Health; Disability	**Hywel Williams** MP
Economy and Taxation; Miners' compensation; Regeneration; Trade and Industry; Education and Skills	**Adam Price** MP

DodOnline
An Electronic Directory without rival ...

MPs' biographies and photographs available with daily updates *via* the internet

For a *free* trial, call Yasmin Mirza, Aby Farsoun or Michael Mand on 020 7630 7643

Lords Opposition Spokespeople and Whips

Conservatives

Leader of the Opposition	Rt Hon **Lord Strathclyde**
Deputy Leader of the Opposition	Rt Hon **Baroness Blatch** CBE
Shadow Lord Chancellor	Rt Hon **Lord Kingsland** QC TD DL
Chief Whip	Rt Hon **Lord Cope of Berkeley**
Deputy Chief Whip	**Baroness Seccombe** DBE JP
Whips	**Lord Luke**
	Viscount Bridgeman
	Lord Astor of Hever DL
	Baroness Hanham CBE
	Duke of Montrose
	Lord Vivian
	Lord Rotherwick
	Baroness Wilcox
	Earl Attlee
	Lord Hanningfield
	Lord Skelmersdale
Cabinet Office	**Lord Saatchi**
Whip	**Baroness Wilcox**
Culture, Media and Sport	**Baroness Buscombe**
Whips	**Baroness Seccombe** DBE JP
	Lord Luke
Defence	**Lord Vivian**
Whips	**Earl Attlee**
	Lord Astor of Hever
Education and Skills	Rt Hon **Baroness Blatch** CBE
Whips	**Baroness Seccombe** DBE JP
	Lord Rotherwick
Environment	**Lord Dixon-Smith**
Whips	**Duke of Montrose**
	Lord Hanningfield
Food and Rural Affairs	**Baroness Byford** DBE
Whips	**Duke of Montrose**
	Lord Hanningfield
Foreign and Commonwealth Office	Rt Hon **Lord Howell of Guildford**
	Baroness Rawlings
Whip	**Lord Astor of Hever** DL
Health	**Earl Howe**
	Lord McColl of Dulwich CBE
	Baroness Noakes DBE
Whip	**Lord Skelmersdale**
Home Office	**Baroness Anelay of St Johns** DBE
	Rt Hon **Lord Roberts of Conwy**
	Lord Hodgson of Astley Abbotts CBE
Whip	**Viscount Bridgeman**
International Development	**Baroness Rawlings**
Whip	**Lord Astor of Hever**
Legal Affairs	Rt Hon **Lord Kingsland** TD QC DL
	Baroness Buscombe
	Baroness Anelay of St Johns DBE
Whip	**Baroness Seccombe** DBE DL

Northern Ireland	**Lord Glentoran** CBE DL
Whip	**Viscount Bridgeman**
Office of the Deputy Prime Minister	
(Local Government and the Regions)	**Baroness Hanham**
Whip	**Lord Hanningfield**
Scotland	**Duke of Montrose**
Whip	**Baroness Hanham** CBE
Trade and Industry	**Baroness Miller of Hendon** MBE
	Lord Hodgson of Astley Abbotts CBE
Whip	**Baroness Wilcox**
Transport	**Viscount Astor**
Whips	**Lord Luke**
	Earl Attlee
Treasury	**Lord Saatchi**
Whip	**Baroness Wilcox**
Wales	Rt Hon **Lord Roberts of Conwy**
Whip	**Lord Luke**
Work and Pensions	Rt Hon **Lord Higgins** KBE DL
	Baroness Noakes DBE
Whips	**Lord Rotherwick**
	Lord Skelmersdale

Liberal Democrats

Leader	Rt Hon **Baroness Williams of Crosby**
Deputy Leader	**Lord McNally**
Chief Whip	**Lord Roper**
Deputy Chief Whip	**Lord Shutt of Greetland**
Whips	**Lord Addington**
	Baroness Harris of Richmond DL
	Earl of Mar and Kellie
Culture, Media and Sport	**Viscount of Falkland**
Sport	**Lord Addington**
Broadcasting	**Lord McNally**
Defence	**Lord Redesdale**
Education and Skills	**Baroness Sharp of Guildford**
Environment, Food and Rural Affairs	**Baroness Miller of Chilthorne Domer**
Agriculture	**Lord Livsey of Talgarth** CBE
Foreign and Commonwealth Affairs	**Lord Wallace of Saltaire**
	Lord Watson of Richmond
Africa	**Lord Avebury**
Europe	Rt Hon **Lord Maclennan of Rogart**
Health	**Lord Clement-Jones** CBE
Home Office	**Lord Dholakia** OBE DL
	Lord Thomas of Gresford OBE QC
	Baroness Walmsley
International Development	**Baroness Northover**
Lord Chancellor's Department	**Lord Goodhart** QC
Northern Ireland	**Lord Smith of Clifton**
	Baroness Harris of Richmond
	Lord Shutt of Greetland OBE

Office of the Deputy Prime Minister, Regional and Local Government	**Baroness Hamwee** **Baroness Maddock**
Scotland	**Earl of Mar and Kellie** DL
Trade and Industry	**Lord Razzall** CBE **Lord Sharman** OBE
Energy	**Lord Ezra** MBE
Transport	**Lord Bradshaw** **Baroness Scott of Needham Market**
Treasury	**Lord Newby** OBE
Pensions Policy	**Lord Oakeshott of Seagrove Bay**
Euro	**Lord Taverne QC**
Wales Office	**Lord Thomas of Gresford** OBE QC **Lord Carlile of Berriew** QC
Women's Issues	**Baroness Thomas of Walliswood** OBE DL
Work and Social Security	**Earl Russell** FBA
Social Services	**Baroness Barker**
Disability	**Lord Addington**

Lord Lester of Herne Hill QC, Lord Thomas of Gresford OBE QC and Lord Goodhart QC assist spokesmen on legal matters.

Cross-Bench Convener

Lord Craig of Radley GCB OBE

DodOnline

An Electronic Directory without rival . . .

MPs' biographies and photographs available with daily updates *via* the internet

For a *free* trial, call Yasmin Mirza, Aby Farsoun or Michael Mand on 020 7630 7643

Handbook of House of Commons Procedure

FOURTH EDITION

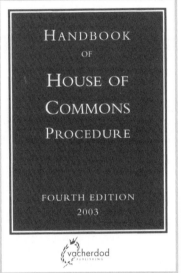

This book is an essential reference work for anyone who needs to understand the procedures of the House of Commons.

Inside you will find:

- Description of the House, its organisation, rules and privileges
- Business of the House and the new parallel Chamber in Westminster Hall
- Role of the Speaker and Chairmen
- The pattern of Parliaments, sessions, weeks and sitting days
- Parliamentary questions
- Rules of debate, procedures for Bills, Statutory Instruments and European legislation
- Functions and procedures of the select and standing committees of the House
- Glossary of parliamentary jargon
- A wealth of diagrams and tables to explain and illustrate throughout

To order call our Hotline now on 020 7630 7619

Vacher Dod Publishing
1 Douglas Street, London, SW1P 4PA
Tel: 020 7630 7619   Fax: 020 7233 7266
Email: subscriptions@vacherdod.co.uk
Website: www.DodonLine.co.uk

House of Commons

Visit the Vacher Dod Website...

- House of Commons
- House of Lords
- Stop Press News
- Today's Business
- This Week's Business
- Progress of Bills
- Select Committees
- Government and Opposition
- The Queen's Speech
- Terms and Procedures
- Government Departments
- Key Political Sites
- Scottish Parliament
- National Assembly for Wales
- Northern Ireland Assembly
- Greater London Authority
- European Union
- Archive

Political information updated daily

Vacher Dod Publishing
1 Douglas Street, London SW1P 4PA
Tel: 020 7630 7619   Fax: 020 7233 7266
E-mail: subscriptions@vacherdod.co.uk
Website: www.DodOnline.co.uk

Constituencies, MPs and Majorities

ENGLAND	529
SCOTLAND	72
WALES	40
NORTHERN IRELAND	18
	Total 659

Lab – Labour
Lab/Co-op – Labour Co-operative
Con – Conservative
Lib Dem – Liberal Democrats
UUP – Ulster Unionist Party
DUP – Democratic Unionist Party

SNP – Scottish National Party
PlC – Plaid Cymru
SF – Sinn Fein
SDLP – Social Democratic and Labour
Ind KHHC – Independent Kidderminster
    Hospital and Health Concern

			Majority
Aberavon	Hywel Francis	Lab	16,108
Aberdeen Central	Frank Doran	Lab	6,646
Aberdeen North	Malcolm Savidge	Lab	4,449
Aberdeen South	Anne Begg	Lab	4,388
Airdrie and Shotts	Helen Liddell	Lab	12,340
Aldershot	Gerald Howarth	Con	6,594
Aldridge-Brownhills	Richard Shepherd	Con	3,768
Altrincham and Sale West	Graham Brady	Con	2,941
Alyn and Deeside	Mark Tami	Lab	9,222
Amber Valley	Judy Mallaber	Lab	7,227
Angus	Mike Weir	SNP	3,611
Argyll and Bute	Alan Reid	Lib Dem	1,653
Arundel and South Downs	Howard Flight	Con	13,704
Ashfield	Geoff Hoon	Lab	13,268
Ashford	Damian Green	Con	7,359
Ashton under Lyne	David Heyes	Lab	15,518
Aylesbury	David Lidington	Con	10,009
Ayr	Sandra Osborne	Lab	2,545
Banbury	Tony Baldry	Con	5,219
Banff and Buchan	Alex Salmond	SNP	10,503
Barking	Margaret Hodge	Lab	9,534
Barnsley Central	Eric Illsley	Lab	15,130
Barnsley East and Mexborough	Jeffrey Ennis	Lab	16,789
Barnsley West and Penistone	Michael Clapham	Lab	12,352
Barrow and Furness	John Hutton	Lab	9,889
Basildon	Angela Smith	Lab	7,738
Basingstoke	Andrew Hunter	Con	880
Bassetlaw	John Mann	Lab	9,748
Bath	Don Foster	Lib Dem	9,894
Batley and Spen	Mike Wood	Lab	5,064
Battersea	Martin Linton	Lab	5,053
Beaconsfield	Dominic Grieve	Con	13,065
Beckenham	Jacqui Lait	Con	4,959
Bedford	Patrick Hall	Lab	6,157
Belfast East	Peter Robinson	DUP	7,117
Belfast North	Nigel Dodds	DUP	6,387

Belfast South	Rev Martin Smyth	UUP	5,399
Belfast West	Gerry Adams	SF	19,342
Berwick-upon-Tweed	Alan Beith	Lib Dem	8,458
Bethnal Green and Bow	Oona King	Lab	10,057
Beverley and Holderness	James Cran	Con	781
Bexhill and Battle	Gregory Barker	Con	10,503
Bexleyheath and Crayford	Nigel Beard	Lab	1,472
Billericay	John Baron	Con	5,013
Birkenhead	Frank Field	Lab	15,591
Birmingham Edgbaston	Gisela Stuart	Lab	4,698
Birmingham Erdington	Siôn Simon	Lab	9,962
Birmingham Hall Green	Steve McCabe	Lab	6,648
Birmingham Hodge Hill	Terry Davis	Lab	11,618
Birmingham Ladywood	Clare Short	Lab	18,143
Birmingham Northfield	Richard Burden	Lab	7,798
Birmingham Perry Barr	Khalid Mahmood	Lab	8,753
Birmingham Selly Oak	Dr Lynne Jones	Lab	10,339
Birmingham Sparkbrook and Small Heath	Roger Godsiff	Lab	16,246
Birmingham Yardley	Estelle Morris	Lab	2,576
Bishop Auckland	Derek Foster	Lab	13,926
Blaby	Andrew Robathan	Con	6,209
Blackburn	Jack Straw	Lab	9,249
Blackpool North and Fleetwood	Joan Humble	Lab	5,721
Blackpool South	Gordon Marsden	Lab	8,262
Blaenau Gwent	Llewellyn Smith	Lab	19,313
Blaydon	John McWilliam	Lab	7,809
Blyth Valley	Ronnie Campbell	Lab	12,188
Bognor Regis and Littlehampton	Nick Gibb	Con	5,643
Bolsover	Dennis Skinner	Lab	18,777
Bolton North East	David Crausby	Lab	8,422
Bolton South East	Dr Brian Iddon	Lab	12,871
Bolton West	Ruth Kelly	Lab	5,518
Bootle	Joe Benton	Lab	19,043
Boston and Skegness	Mark Simmonds	Con	515
Bosworth	David Tredinnick	Con	2,280
Bournemouth East	David Atkinson	Con	3,434
Bournemouth West	John Butterfill	Con	4,718
Bracknell	Andrew Mackay	Con	6,713
Bradford North	Terry Rooney	Lab	8,969
Bradford South	Gerry Sutcliffe	Lab	9,662
Bradford West	Marsha Singh	Lab	4,165
Braintree	Alan Hurst	Lab	358
Brecon and Radnorshire	Roger Williams	Lib Dem	751
Brent East	**By-election pending due to death of Paul Daisley**		
Brent North	Barry Gardiner	Lab	10,205
Brent South	Paul Boateng	Lab	17,380
Brentford and Isleworth	Ann Keen	Lab	10,318
Brentwood and Ongar	Eric Pickles	Con	2,821
Bridgend	Win Griffiths	Lab	10,046
Bridgwater	Ian Liddell-Grainger	Con	4,987
Brigg and Goole	Ian Cawsey	Lab	3,961
Brighton Kemptown	Dr Des Turner	Lab	4,922
Brighton Pavilion	David Lepper	Lab	9,643
Bristol East	Jean Corston	Lab	13,392
Bristol North West	Dr Doug Naysmith	Lab	10,887
Bristol South	Dawn Primarolo	Lab	14,181

Bristol West	Valerie Davey	Lab	4,426
Bromley and Chislehurst	Eric Forth	Con	9,037
Bromsgrove	Julie Kirkbride	Con	8,138
Broxbourne	Marion Roe	Con	8,993
Broxtowe	Dr Nick Palmer	Lab	5,873
Buckingham	John Bercow	Con	13,325
Burnley	Peter Pike	Lab	10,498
Burton	Janet Dean	Lab	4,849
Bury North	David Chaytor	Lab	6,532
Bury South	Ivan Lewis	Lab	12,772
Bury St Edmunds	David Ruffley	Con	2,503
Caernarfon	Hywel Williams	Pl C	3,511
Caerphilly	Wayne David	Lab	14,425
Caithness, Sutherland and Easter Ross	Viscount Thurso	Lib Dem	2,744
Calder Valley	Chris McCafferty	Lab	3,094
Camberwell and Peckham	Harriet Harman	Lab	14,123
Cambridge	Anne Campbell	Lab	8,579
Cannock Chase	Dr Tony Wayland Wright	Lab	10,704
Canterbury	Julian Brazier	Con	2,069
Cardiff Central	Jon Owen Jones	Lab	659
Cardiff North	Julie Morgan	Lab	6,165
Cardiff South and Penarth	Alun Michael	Lab	12,287
Cardiff West	Kevin Brennan	Lab	11,321
Carlisle	Eric Martlew	Lab	5,702
Carmarthen East and Dinefwr	Adam Price	Pl C	2,590
Carmarthen West and South Pembrokeshire	Nick Ainger	Lab	4,538
Carrick, Cumnock and Doon Valley	George Foulkes	Lab	14,856
Carshalton and Wallington	Tom Brake	Lib Dem	4,547
Castle Point	Bob Spink	Con	985
Central Fife	John MacDougall	Lab	10,075
Central Suffolk and North Ipswich	Michael Lord	Con	3,469
Ceredigion	Simon Thomas	Pl C	3,944
Charnwood	Stephen Dorrell	Con	7,739
Chatham and Aylesford	Jonathan Shaw	Lab	4,340
Cheadle	Patsy Calton	Lib Dem	33
Chelmsford West	Simon Burns	Con	6,261
Cheltenham	Nigel Jones	Lib Dem	5,255
Chesham and Amersham	Cheryl Gillan	Con	11,882
Chesterfield	Paul Holmes	Lib Dem	2,586
Chichester	Andrew Tyrie	Con	11,355
Chingford and Woodford Green	Iain Duncan Smith	Con	5,487
Chipping Barnet	Sydney Chapman	Con	2,701
Chorley	Lindsay Hoyle	Lab	8,444
Christchurch	Christopher Chope	Con	13,544
Cities of London and Westminster	Mark Field	Con	4,499
City of Chester	Christine Russell	Lab	6,894
City of Durham	Gerry Steinberg	Lab	13,441
City of York	Hugh Bayley	Lab	13,779
Cleethorpes	Shona McIsaac	Lab	5,620
Clwyd South	Martyn Jones	Lab	8,898
Clwyd West	Gareth Thomas	Lab	1,115
Clydebank and Milngavie	Tony Worthington	Lab	10,724
Clydesdale	Jimmy Hood	Lab	7,794
Coatbridge and Chryston	Tom Clarke	Lab	15,314
Colchester	Bob Russell	Lib Dem	5,553
Colne Valley	Kali Mountford	Lab	4,639

Congleton	Ann Winterton	Con	7,134
Conwy	Betty Williams	Lab	6,219
Copeland	Dr Jack Cunningham	Lab	4,964
Corby	Phil Hope	Lab	5,700
Cotswold	Geoffrey Clifton-Brown	Con	11,983
Coventry North East	Bob Ainsworth	Lab	15,751
Coventry North West	Geoffrey Robinson	Lab	10,874
Coventry South	Jim Cunningham	Lab	8,279
Crawley	Laura Moffatt	Lab	6,770
Crewe and Nantwich	Gwyneth Dunwoody	Lab	9,906
Crosby	Claire Curtis-Thomas	Lab	8,353
Croydon Central	Geraint Davies	Lab	3,984
Croydon North	Malcolm Wicks	Lab	16,858
Croydon South	Richard Ottaway	Con	8,697
Cumbernauld and Kilsyth	Rosemary McKenna	Lab	7,520
Cunninghame North	Brian Wilson	Lab	8,398
Cunninghame South	Brian Donohoe	Lab	11,230
Cynon Valley	Ann Clwyd	Lab	12,998
Dagenham	Jon Cruddas	Lab	8,693
Darlington	Alan Milburn	Lab	10,384
Dartford	Dr Howard Stoate	Lab	3,306
Daventry	Timothy Boswell	Con	9,649
Delyn	David Hanson	Lab	8,605
Denton and Reddish	Andrew Bennett	Lab	15,330
Derby North	Bob Laxton	Lab	6,982
Derby South	Margaret Beckett	Lab	13,855
Devizes	Michael Ancram	Con	11,896
Dewsbury	Ann Taylor	Lab	7,449
Don Valley	Caroline Flint	Lab	9,520
Doncaster Central	Rosie Winterton	Lab	11,999
Doncaster North	Kevin Hughes	Lab	15,187
Dover	Gwyn Prosser	Lab	5,199
Dudley North	Ross Cranston	Lab	6,800
Dudley South	Ian Pearson	Lab	6,817
Dulwich and West Norwood	Tessa Jowell	Lab	12,310
Dumbarton	John McFall	Lab	9,575
Dumfries	Russell Brown	Lab	8,834
Dundee East	Iain Luke	Lab	4,466
Dundee West	Ernie Ross	Lab	6,800
Dunfermline East	Gordon Brown	Lab	15,063
Dunfermline West	Rachel Squire	Lab	10,980
Durham North	Kevan Jones	Lab	18,683
Ealing North	Stephen Pound	Lab	11,837
Ealing Southall	Piara Khabra	Lab	13,683
Ealing, Acton and Shepherd's Bush	Clive Soley	Lab	10,789
Easington	John Cummings	Lab	21,949
East Antrim	Roy Beggs	UUP	128
East Devon	Hugo Swire	Con	8,195
East Ham	Stephen Timms	Lab	21,032
East Hampshire	Michael Mates	Con	8,890
East Kilbride	Adam Ingram	Lab	12,755
East Londonderry	Gregory Lloyd Campbell	DUP	1,901
East Lothian	Anne Picking	Lab	10,830
East Surrey	Peter Ainsworth	Con	13,203
East Worthing and Shoreham	Tim Loughton	Con	6,139
Eastbourne	Nigel Waterson	Con	2,154

Eastleigh	David Chidgey	Lib Dem	3,058
Eastwood	Jim Murphy	Lab	9,141
Eccles	Ian Stewart	Lab	14,528
Eddisbury	Stephen O'Brien	Con	4,568
Edinburgh Central	Alistair Darling	Lab	8,142
Edinburgh East and Musselburgh	Gavin Strang	Lab	12,168
Edinburgh North and Leith	Mark Lazarowicz	Lab	8,817
Edinburgh Pentlands	Dr Lynda Clark	Lab	1,742
Edinburgh South	Nigel Griffiths	Lab	5,499
Edinburgh West	John Barrett	Lib Dem	7,589
Edmonton	Andrew Love	Lab	9,772
Ellesmere Port and Neston	Andrew Miller	Lab	10,861
Elmet	Colin Burgon	Lab	4,171
Eltham	Clive Efford	Lab	6,996
Enfield North	Joan Ryan	Lab	2,291
Enfield Southgate	Stephen Twigg	Lab	5,546
Epping Forest	Eleanor Laing	Con	8,426
Epsom and Ewell	Christopher Grayling	Con	10,080
Erewash	Liz Blackman	Lab	6,932
Erith and Thamesmead	John Austin	Lab	11,167
Esher and Walton	Ian Taylor	Con	11,538
Exeter	Ben Bradshaw	Lab	11,759
Falkirk East	Michael Connarty	Lab	10,712
Falkirk West	Eric Joyce	Lab	8,532
Falmouth and Camborne	Candy Atherton	Lab	4,527
Fareham	Mark Hoban	Con	7,009
Faversham and Mid Kent	Hugh Robertson	Con	4,183
Feltham and Heston	Alan Keen	Lab	12,657
Fermanagh and South Tyrone	Michelle Gildernew	SF	53
Finchley and Golders Green	Rudi Vis	Lab	3,716
Folkestone and Hythe	Michael Howard	Con	5,907
Forest of Dean	Diana Organ	Lab	2,049
Foyle	John Hume	SDLP	11,550
Fylde	Michael Jack	Con	9,610
Gainsborough	Edward Leigh	Con	8,071
Galloway and Upper Nithsdale	Peter Duncan	Con	74
Gateshead East and Washington West	Joyce Quin	Lab	17,904
Gedling	Vernon Coaker	Lab	5,598
Gillingham	Paul Clark	Lab	2,272
Glasgow Anniesland	John Robertson	Lab	11,054
Glasgow Baillieston	James Wray	Lab	9,839
Glasgow Cathcart	Tom Harris	Lab	10,816
Glasgow Govan	Mohammad Sarwar	Lab	6,400
Glasgow Kelvin	George Galloway	Lab	7,260
Glasgow Maryhill	Ann McKechin	Lab	9,888
Glasgow Pollok	Ian Davidson	Lab	11,768
Glasgow Rutherglen	Thomas McAvoy	Lab	12,625
Glasgow Shettleston	David Marshall	Lab	9,818
Glasgow Springburn	Michael Martin	Speaker	11,378
Gloucester	Parmjit Dhanda	Lab	3,880
Gordon	Malcolm Bruce	Lib Dem	7,879
Gosport	Peter Viggers	Con	2,621
Gower	Martin Caton	Lab	7,395
Grantham and Stamford	Quentin Davies	Con	4,518
Gravesham	Chris Pond	Lab	4,862
Great Grimsby	Austin Mitchell	Lab	11,484

Great Yarmouth	Anthony David Wright	Lab	4,564
Greenock and Inverclyde	David Cairns	Lab	9,890
Greenwich and Woolwich	Nick Raynsford	Lab	13,433
Guildford	Sue Doughty	Lib Dem	538
Hackney North and Stoke Newington	Diane Abbott	Lab	13,651
Hackney South and Shoreditch	Brian Sedgemore	Lab	15,049
Halesowen and Rowley Regis	Sylvia Heal	Lab	7,359
Halifax	Alice Mahon	Lab	6,129
Haltemprice and Howden	David Davis	Con	1,903
Halton	Derek Twigg	Lab	17,428
Hamilton North and Bellshill	Dr John Reid	Lab	13,561
Hamilton South	Bill Tynan	Lab	10,775
Hammersmith and Fulham	Iain Coleman	Lab	2,015
Hampstead and Highgate	Glenda Jackson	Lab	7,876
Harborough	Edward Garnier	Con	5,252
Harlow	Bill Rammell	Lab	5,228
Harrogate and Knaresborough	Phil Willis	Lib Dem	8,845
Harrow East	Tony McNulty	Lab	11,124
Harrow West	Gareth Richard Thomas	Lab	6,156
Hartlepool	Peter Mandelson	Lab	14,571
Harwich	Ivan Henderson	Lab	2,596
Hastings and Rye	Michael Jabez Foster	Lab	4,308
Havant	David Willetts	Con	4,207
Hayes and Harlington	John McDonnell	Lab	13,466
Hazel Grove	Andrew Stunell	Lib Dem	8,435
Hemel Hempstead	Tony McWalter	Lab	3,742
Hemsworth	Jon Trickett	Lab	15,636
Hendon	Andrew Dismore	Lab	7,417
Henley	Boris Johnson	Con	8,458
Hereford	Paul Keetch	Lib Dem	968
Hertford and Stortford	Mark Prisk	Con	5,603
Hertsmere	James Clappison	Con	4,902
Hexham	Peter Atkinson	Con	2,529
Heywood and Middleton	Jim Dobbin	Lab	11,670
High Peak	Tom Levitt	Lab	4,489
Hitchin and Harpenden	Peter Lilley	Con	6,663
Holborn and St Pancras	Frank Dobson	Lab	11,175
Hornchurch	John Cryer	Lab	1,482
Hornsey and Wood Green	Barbara Roche	Lab	10,614
Horsham	Francis Maude	Con	13,666
Houghton and Washington East	Fraser Kemp	Lab	19,818
Hove	Ivor Caplin	Lab	3,171
Huddersfield	Barry Sheerman	Lab	10,046
Hull East	John Prescott	Lab	15,325
Hull North	Kevin McNamara	Lab	10,721
Hull West and Hessle	Alan Johnson	Lab	10,951
Huntingdon	Jonathan Djanogly	Con	12,792
Hyndburn	Greg Pope	Lab	8,219
Ilford North	Linda Perham	Lab	2,115
Ilford South	Mike Gapes	Lab	13,997
Inverness East, Nairn and Lochaber	David Stewart	Lab	4,716
Ipswich	Chris Mole	Lab	4,087
Isle of Wight	Andrew Turner	Con	2,826
Islington North	Jeremy Corbyn	Lab	12,958
Islington South and Finsbury	Chris Smith	Lab	7,280
Islwyn	Don Touhig	Lab	15,309
Jarrow	Stephen Hepburn	Lab	17,595

Keighley	Ann Cryer	Lab	4,005
Kensington and Chelsea	Michael Portillo	Con	8,771
Kettering	Phil Sawford	Lab	665
Kilmarnock and Loudoun	Desmond Browne	Lab	10,334
Kingston and Surbiton	Edward Davey	Lib Dem	15,676
Kingswood	Dr Roger Berry	Lab	13,962
Kirkcaldy	Lewis Moonie	Lab	8,963
Knowsley North and Sefton East	George Howarth	Lab	18,927
Knowsley South	Edward O'Hara	Lab	21,316
Lagan Valley	Jeffrey Donaldson	UUP	18,342
Lancaster and Wyre	Hilton Dawson	Lab	481
Leeds Central	Hilary Benn	Lab	14,381
Leeds East	George Mudie	Lab	12,643
Leeds North East	Fabian Hamilton	Lab	7,089
Leeds North West	Harold Best	Lab	5,236
Leeds West	John Battle	Lab	14,935
Leicester East	Keith Vaz	Lab	13,442
Leicester South	James Marshall	Lab	13,243
Leicester West	Patricia Hewitt	Lab	9,639
Leigh	Andy Burnham	Lab	16,362
Leominster	Bill Wiggin	Con	10,367
Lewes	Norman Baker	Lib Dem	9,710
Lewisham Deptford	Joan Ruddock	Lab	15,293
Lewisham East	Bridget Prentice	Lab	8,959
Lewisham West	Jim Dowd	Lab	11,920
Leyton and Wanstead	Harry Cohen	Lab	12,904
Lichfield	Michael Fabricant	Con	4,426
Lincoln	Gillian Merron	Lab	8,420
Linlithgow	Tam Dalyell	Lab	9,129
Liverpool Garston	Maria Eagle	Lab	12,494
Liverpool Riverside	Louise Ellman	Lab	13,950
Liverpool Walton	Peter Kilfoyle	Lab	17,996
Liverpool Wavertree	Jane Kennedy	Lab	12,319
Liverpool West Derby	Robert Wareing	Lab	15,853
Livingston	Robin Cook	Lab	10,616
Llanelli	Denzil Davies	Lab	6,403
Loughborough	Andy Reed	Lab	6,378
Louth and Horncastle	Sir Peter Tapsell	Con	7,554
Ludlow	Matthew Green	Lib Dem	1,630
Luton North	Kelvin Hopkins	Lab	9,977
Luton South	Margaret Moran	Lab	10,133
Macclesfield	Nicholas Winterton	Con	7,200
Maidenhead	Theresa May	Con	3,284
Maidstone and The Weald	Ann Widdecombe	Con	10,318
Makerfield	Ian McCartney	Lab	17,750
Maldon and Chelmsford East	John Whittingdale	Con	8,462
Manchester Blackley	Graham Stringer	Lab	14,464
Manchester Central	Tony Lloyd	Lab	13,742
Manchester Gorton	Gerald Kaufman	Lab	11,304
Manchester Withington	Keith Bradley	Lab	11,524
Mansfield	Alan Meale	Lab	11,038
Medway	Bob Marshall-Andrews	Lab	3,780
Meirionnydd Nant Conwy	Elfyn Llwyd	Pl C	5,684
Meriden	Caroline Spelman	Con	3,784
Merthyr Tydfil and Rhymney	Dai Havard	Lab	14,923
Mid Bedfordshire	Jonathan Sayeed	Con	8,066
Mid Dorset and Poole North	Annette Brooke	Lib Dem	384

Mid Norfolk	Keith Simpson	Con	4,562
Mid Sussex	Nicholas Soames	Con	6,898
Mid Ulster	Martin McGuinness	SF	9,953
Mid Worcestershire	Peter Luff	Con	10,627
Middlesbrough	Stuart Bell	Lab	16,330
Middlesbrough South and East Cleveland	Dr Ashok Kumar	Lab	9,351
Midlothian	David Hamilton	Lab	9,014
Milton Keynes North East	Brian White	Lab	1,829
Milton Keynes South West	Dr Phyllis Starkey	Lab	6,978
Mitcham and Morden	Siobhain McDonagh	Lab	13,785
Mole Valley	Sir Paul Beresford	Con	10,153
Monmouth	Huw Edwards	Lab	384
Montgomeryshire	Lembit Öpik	Lib Dem	6,234
Moray	Angus Robertson	SNP	1,744
Morecambe and Lunesdale	Geraldine Smith	Lab	5,092
Morley and Rothwell	Colin Challen	Lab	12,090
Motherwell and Wishaw	Frank Roy	Lab	10,956
Neath	Peter Hain	Lab	14,816
New Forest East	Dr Julian Lewis	Con	3,829
New Forest West	Desmond Swayne	Con	13,191
Newark	Patrick Mercer	Con	4,073
Newbury	David Rendel	Lib Dem	2,415
Newcastle-under-Lyme	Paul Farrelly	Lab	9,986
Newcastle upon Tyne Central	Jim Cousins	Lab	11,605
Newcastle upon Tyne East and Wallsend	Nick Brown	Lab	14,223
Newcastle upon Tyne North	Doug Henderson	Lab	14,450
Newport East	Alan Howarth	Lab	9,874
Newport West	Paul Flynn	Lab	9,304
Newry and Armagh	Séamus Mallon	SDLP	3,575
Normanton	William O'Brien	Lab	9,937
North Antrim	Rev Ian Paisley	DUP	14,224
North Cornwall	Paul Tyler	Lib Dem	9,832
North Devon	Nick Harvey	Lib Dem	2,984
North Dorset	Bob Walter	Con	3,797
North Down	Sylvia Hermon	UUP	7,324
North East Bedfordshire	Alistair Burt	Con	8,577
North East Cambridgeshire	Malcolm Moss	Con	6,373
North East Derbyshire	Harry Barnes	Lab	12,258
North East Fife	Menzies Campbell	Lib Dem	9,736
North East Hampshire	James Arbuthnot	Con	13,257
North East Hertfordshire	Oliver Heald	Con	3,444
North Essex	Bernard Jenkin	Con	7,186
North Norfolk	Norman Lamb	Lib Dem	483
North Shropshire	Owen Paterson	Con	6,241
North Southwark and Bermondsey	Simon Hughes	Lib Dem	9,632
North Swindon	Michael Wills	Lab	8,105
North Tayside	Pete Wishart	SNP	3,283
North Thanet	Roger Gale	Con	6,650
North Tyneside	Stephen Byers	Lab	20,568
North Warwickshire	Mike O'Brien	Lab	9,639
North West Cambridgeshire	Sir Brian Mawhinney	Con	8,101
North West Durham	Hilary Armstrong	Lab	16,333
North West Hampshire	Sir George Young	Con	12,009
North West Leicestershire	David Taylor	Lab	8,157
North West Norfolk	Henry Bellingham	Con	3,485
North Wiltshire	James Gray	Con	3,878
Northampton North	Sally Keeble	Lab	7,893

Northampton South	Tony Clarke	Lab	885
Northavon	Prof Steve Webb	Lib Dem	9,877
Norwich North	Dr Ian Gibson	Lab	5,863
Norwich South	Charles Clarke	Lab	8,816
Nottingham East	John Heppell	Lab	10,320
Nottingham North	Graham Allen	Lab	12,240
Nottingham South	Alan Simpson	Lab	9,989
Nuneaton	Bill Olner	Lab	7,535
Ochil	Martin O'Neill	Lab	5,349
Ogmore	Huw Irranca-Davies	Lab	5,721
Old Bexley and Sidcup	Derek Conway	Con	3,345
Oldham East and Saddleworth	Philip Woolas	Lab	2,726
Oldham West and Royton	Michael Meacher	Lab	13,365
Orkney and Shetland	Alistair Carmichael	Lib Dem	3,475
Orpington	John Horam	Con	269
Oxford East	Andrew Smith	Lab	10,344
Oxford West and Abingdon	Dr Evan Harris	Lib Dem	9,185
Paisley North	Irene Adams	Lab	9,321
Paisley South	Douglas Alexander	Lab	11,910
Pendle	Gordon Prentice	Lab	4,275
Penrith and The Border	David Maclean	Con	14,677
Perth	Annabelle Ewing	SNP	48
Peterborough	Helen Clark	Lab	2,854
Plymouth Devonport	David Jamieson	Lab	13,033
Plymouth Sutton	Linda Gilroy	Lab	7,517
Pontefract and Castleford	Yvette Cooper	Lab	16,378
Pontypridd	Dr Kim Howells	Lab	17,684
Poole	Robert Syms	Con	7,166
Poplar and Canning Town	Jim Fitzpatrick	Lab	14,108
Portsmouth North	Syd Rapson	Lab	5,134
Portsmouth South	Mike Hancock	Lib Dem	6,093
Preseli Pembrokeshire	Jackie Lawrence	Lab	2,946
Preston	Mark Hendrick	Lab	12,268
Pudsey	Paul Truswell	Lab	5,626
Putney	Tony Colman	Lab	2,771
Rayleigh	Mark Francois	Con	8,290
Reading East	Jane Griffiths	Lab	5,595
Reading West	Martin Salter	Lab	8,849
Redcar	Vera Baird	Lab	13,443
Redditch	Jacqui Smith	Lab	2,484
Regent's Park and Kensington North	Karen Buck	Lab	10,266
Reigate	Crispin Blunt	Con	8,025
Rhondda	Chris Bryant	Lab	16,047
Ribble Valley	Nigel Evans	Con	11,238
Richmond Park	Dr Jenny Tonge	Lib Dem	4,964
Richmond (Yorkshire)	William Hague	Con	16,319
Rochdale	Lorna Fitzsimons	Lab	5,655
Rochford and Southend East	Sir Teddy Taylor	Con	7,034
Romford	Andrew Rosindell	Con	5,977
Romsey	Sandra Gidley	Lib Dem	2,370
Rossendale and Darwen	Janet Anderson	Lab	4,970
Ross, Skye and Inverness West	Charles Kennedy	Lib Dem	12,952
Rother Valley	Kevin Barron	Lab	14,882
Rotherham	Dr Denis MacShane	Lab	13,077
Roxburgh and Berwickshire	Archy Kirkwood	Lib Dem	7,511
Rugby and Kenilworth	Andy King	Lab	2,877
Ruislip Northwood	John Wilkinson	Con	7,537

Runnymede and Weybridge	Philip Hammond	Con	8,360
Rushcliffe	Kenneth Clarke	Con	7,357
Rutland and Melton	Alan Duncan	Con	8,612
Ryedale	John Greenway	Con	4,875
Saffron Walden	Sir Alan Haselhurst	Con	12,004
Salford	Hazel Blears	Lab	11,012
Salisbury	Robert Key	Con	8,703
Scarborough and Whitby	Lawrie Quinn	Lab	3,585
Scunthorpe	Elliot Morley	Lab	10,372
Sedgefield	Tony Blair	Lab	17,713
Selby	John Grogan	Lab	2,138
Sevenoaks	Michael Fallon	Con	10,154
Sheffield Attercliffe	Clive Betts	Lab	18,844
Sheffield Brightside	David Blunkett	Lab	17,049
Sheffield Central	Richard Caborn	Lab	12,544
Sheffield Hallam	Richard Allan	Lib Dem	9,347
Sheffield Heeley	Meg Munn	Lab	11,704
Sheffield Hillsborough	Helen Jackson	Lab	14,569
Sherwood	Paddy Tipping	Lab	9,373
Shipley	Christopher Leslie	Lab	1,428
Shrewsbury and Atcham	Paul Marsden	Lab	3,579
Sittingbourne and Sheppey	Derek Wyatt	Lab	3,509
Skipton and Ripon	David Curry	Con	12,930
Sleaford and North Hykeham	Douglas Hogg	Con	8,622
Slough	Fiona Mactaggart	Lab	12,508
Solihull	John Mark Taylor	Con	9,407
Somerton and Frome	David Heath	Lib Dem	668
South Antrim	David Burnside	UUP	1,011
South Cambridgeshire	Andrew Lansley	Con	8,403
South Derbyshire	Mark Todd	Lab	7,851
South Dorset	Jim Knight	Lab	153
South Down	Eddie McGrady	SDLP	13,858
South East Cambridgeshire	Jim Paice	Con	8,990
South East Cornwall	Colin Breed	Lib Dem	5,375
South Holland and The Deepings	John Hayes	Con	11,099
South Norfolk	Richard Bacon	Con	6,893
South Ribble	David Borrow	Lab	3,802
South Shields	David Miliband	Lab	14,090
South Staffordshire	Sir Patrick Cormack	Con	6,881
South Suffolk	Tim Yeo	Con	5,081
South Swindon	Julia Drown	Lab	7,341
South Thanet	Dr Stephen Ladyman	Lab	1,792
South West Bedfordshire	Andrew Selous	Con	776
South West Devon	Gary Streeter	Con	7,144
South West Hertfordshire	Richard Page	Con	8,181
South West Norfolk	Gillian Shephard	Con	9,366
South West Surrey	Virginia Bottomley	Con	861
Southampton Itchen	John Denham	Lab	11,223
Southampton Test	Dr Alan Whitehead	Lab	11,207
Southend West	David Amess	Con	7,941
Southport	John Pugh	Lib Dem	3,007
Spelthorne	David Wilshire	Con	3,262
St Albans	Kerry Pollard	Lab	4,466
St Helens North	David Watts	Lab	15,901
St Helens South	Shaun Woodward	Lab	8,985
St Ives	Andrew George	Lib Dem	10,053
Stafford	David Kidney	Lab	5,032

Staffordshire Moorlands	Charlotte Atkins	Lab	5,838
Stalybridge and Hyde	James Purnell	Lab	8,859
Stevenage	Barbara Follett	Lab	8,566
Stirling	Anne McGuire	Lab	6,274
Stockport	Ann Coffey	Lab	11,569
Stockton North	Frank Cook	Lab	14,647
Stockton South	Dari Taylor	Lab	9,086
Stoke-on-Trent Central	Mark Fisher	Lab	11,845
Stoke-on-Trent North	Joan Walley	Lab	11,784
Stoke-on-Trent South	George Stevenson	Lab	10,489
Stone	William Cash	Con	6,036
Stourbridge	Debra Shipley	Lab	3,812
Strangford	Iris Robinson	DUP	1,110
Stratford-on-Avon	John Maples	Con	11,802
Strathkelvin and Bearsden	John Lyons	Lab	11,717
Streatham	Keith Hill	Lab	14,270
Stretford and Urmston	Beverley Hughes	Lab	13,271
Stroud	David Drew	Lab	5,039
Suffolk Coastal	John Gummer	Con	4,326
Sunderland North	Bill Etherington	Lab	13,354
Sunderland South	Chris Mullin	Lab	13,667
Surrey Heath	Nick Hawkins	Con	10,819
Sutton Coldfield	Andrew Mitchell	Con	10,104
Sutton and Cheam	Paul Burstow	Lib Dem	4,304
Swansea East	Donald Anderson	Lab	16,148
Swansea West	Alan John Williams	Lab	9,550
Tamworth	Brian Jenkins	Lab	4,598
Tatton	George Osborne	Con	8,611
Taunton	Adrian Flook	Con	235
Teignbridge	Rickie Younger-Ross	Lib Dem	3,011
Telford	David Wright	Lab	8,383
Tewkesbury	Laurence Robertson	Con	8,663
The Wrekin	Peter Bradley	Lab	3,587
Thurrock	Andrew Mackinlay	Lab	9,997
Tiverton and Honiton	Angela Browning	Con	6,284
Tonbridge and Malling	Sir John Stanley	Con	8,250
Tooting	Tom Cox	Lab	10,400
Torbay	Adrian Sanders	Lib Dem	6,708
Torfaen	Paul Murphy	Lab	16,280
Torridge and West Devon	John Burnett	Lib Dem	1,194
Totnes	Anthony Steen	Con	3,597
Tottenham	David Lammy	Lab	16,916
Truro and St Austell	Matthew Taylor	Lib Dem	8,065
Tunbridge Wells	Archie Norman	Con	9,730
Tweeddale, Ettrick and Lauderdale	Michael Moore	Lib Dem	5,157
Twickenham	Dr Vincent Cable	Lib Dem	7,655
Tyne Bridge	David Clelland	Lab	14,889
Tynemouth	Alan Campbell	Lab	8,678
Upminster	Angela Watkinson	Con	1,241
Upper Bann	David Trimble	UUP	2,058
Uxbridge	John Randall	Con	2,098
Vale of Clwyd	Chris Ruane	Lab	5,761
Vale of Glamorgan	John Smith	Lab	4,700
Vale of York	Anne McIntosh	Con	12,517
Vauxhall	Kate Hoey	Lab	13,018
Wakefield	David Hinchliffe	Lab	7,954
Wallasey	Angela Eagle	Lab	12,276

Walsall North	David Winnick	Lab	9,391
Walsall South	Bruce George	Lab	9,931
Walthamstow	Neil Gerrard	Lab	15,181
Wansbeck	Denis Murphy	Lab	13,101
Wansdyke	Dan Norris	Lab	5,613
Wantage	Robert Jackson	Con	5,600
Warley	John Spellar	Lab	11,850
Warrington North	Helen Jones	Lab	15,156
Warrington South	Helen Southworth	Lab	7,397
Warwick and Leamington	James Plaskitt	Lab	5,953
Watford	Claire Ward	Lab	5,555
Waveney	Bob Blizzard	Lab	8,553
Wealden	Charles Hendry	Con	13,772
Weaver Vale	Mike Hall	Lab	9,637
Wellingborough	Paul Stinchcombe	Lab	2,355
Wells	David Heathcoat-Amory	Con	2,796
Welwyn Hatfield	Melanie Johnson	Lab	1,196
Wentworth	John Healey	Lab	16,449
West Aberdeenshire and Kincardine	Robert Smith	Lib Dem	4,821
West Bromwich East	Tom Watson	Lab	9,763
West Bromwich West	Adrian Bailey	Lab	11,355
West Derbyshire	Patrick McLoughlin	Con	7,370
West Dorset	Oliver Letwin	Con	1,414
West Ham	Tony Banks	Lab	15,645
West Lancashire	Colin Pickthall	Lab	9,643
West Renfrewshire	Jim Sheridan	Lab	8,575
West Suffolk	Richard Spring	Con	4,295
West Tyrone	Pat Doherty	SF	5,040
West Worcestershire	Sir Michael Spicer	Con	5,374
Westbury	Andrew Murrison	Con	5,294
Western Isles	Calum MacDonald	Lab	1,074
Westmorland and Lonsdale	Tim Collins	Con	3,147
Weston-Super-Mare	Brian Cotter	Lib Dem	338
Wigan	Neil Turner	Lab	13,743
Wimbledon	Roger Casale	Lab	3,744
Winchester	Mark Oaten	Lib Dem	9,634
Windsor	Hon Michael Trend	Con	8,889
Wirral South	Ben Chapman	Lab	5,049
Wirral West	Stephen Hesford	Lab	4,035
Witney	David Cameron	Con	7,973
Woking	Humfrey Malins	Con	6,759
Wokingham	John Redwood	Con	5,994
Wolverhampton North East	Ken Purchase	Lab	9,965
Wolverhampton South East	Dennis Turner	Lab	12,464
Wolverhampton South West	Rob Marris	Lab	3,487
Woodspring	Dr Liam Fox	Con	8,798
Worcester	Michael John Foster	Lab	5,766
Workington	Tony Cunningham	Lab	10,850
Worsley	Terry Lewis	Lab	11,787
Worthing West	Peter Bottomley	Con	9,037
Wrexham	Ian Lucas	Lab	9,188
Wycombe	Paul Goodman	Con	3,168
Wyre Forest	Richard Taylor	Ind KHHC	17,630
Wythenshawe and Sale East	Paul Goggins	Lab	12,608
Yeovil	David Laws	Lib Dem	3,928
Ynys Môn	Albert Owen	Lab	800
Yorkshire East	Greg Knight	Con	4,682

MEMBERS' BIOGRAPHIES

A

ABBOTT, DIANE — Hackney North and Stoke Newington — *Lab majority 13,651*

Diane Julie Abbott. Born 27 September 1953; Daughter of late Reginald Abbott, welder, and late Mrs Julie Abbott, psychiatric nurse; Educated Harrow County Girls' Grammar School; Newnham College, Cambridge (BA history 1976); Married David Thompson 1991 (1 son) (marriage dissolved 1993). Administration trainee, Home Office 1976–78; Race relations officer, National Council for Civil Liberties 1978–80; Journalist, Thames Television 1980–82, TV AM 1982–84, freelance 1984–85; Principal press officer, Lambeth Council 1986–87; Equality officer, ACTT 1985–86; Member, RMT Parliamentary Campaigning Group 2002–. Westminster City Councillor 1982–86; Member Greater London Assembly advisory cabinet for women and equality 2000–. **House of Commons:** Member for Hackney North and Stoke Newington since June 1987; *Select Committees:* Member: Treasury and Civil Service 1989–97, Foreign Affairs 1997–2001, Entry Clearance Sub-Committee 1997–98. *Special Interests:* Small Businesses. *Countries of Interest:* Jamaica, Africa. Member, Labour Party National Executive Committee 1994–97. First black female MP; *Recreations:* Reading, cinema. Diane Abbott, MP, House of Commons, London, SW1A 0AA.

ADAMS, GERRY — Belfast West — *SF majority 19,342*

Gerry (Gerard) Adams. Born 6 October 1948; Son of Gerard Adams and Annie Hannaway; Educated St Mary's Christian Brothers' School, Belfast; Married Colette McArdle 1971 (1 son). Bartender; Founder member of the civil rights movement. **House of Commons:** Member for Belfast West 1983–92, and since May 1, 1997; Member, Northern Ireland Assembly 1981; Vice-President, Sinn Fein 1978–83, President 1983–; Member: Northern Ireland Forum 1996, new Northern Ireland Assembly for Belfast West 1998–. West Belfast Community Festival; Feile an Phobail; Member, PEN; *Publications: Before the Dawn, An Irish Voice, A Pathway to Peace, The Politics of Irish Freedom and Selected Writings, Falls Memories, Cage Eleven, The Street and Other Stories, An Irish Journal, Peace in Ireland – Towards a Lasting Peace;* Thorr Peace Prize 1996; *Sportsclubs:* Naomh Eoig; *Recreations:* Gaelic sports, Irish traditional music. Gerry Adams Esq, MP, House of Commons, London, SW1A 0AA *Tel:* 020 7219 3000. *Constituency:* 53 Falls Road, Belfast BT12 4PD *Tel:* 028 9022 3000.

ADAMS, IRENE — Paisley North — *Lab majority 9,321*

Irene Adams. Born 27 December 1947; Educated Stanley Green High School, Paisley; Married Allen Adams 1968 (MP 1979–90, died 1990) (1 son 2 daughters). Councillor: Paisley Town Council 1970, Renfrew District Council 1974–78, Strathclyde Regional Council 1979–84; JP. **House of Commons:** Member for Paisley North since November 29, 1990 by-election; *Select Committees:* Member: Catering 1991–95, Scottish Affairs 1997–2001; Member, Chairmen's Panel 1998–; Chair, Scottish Affairs 2001–; Member: Finance and Services 2001–, Liaison 2001–. Chair PLP Scottish Group –2001. *Recreations:* Reading, walking. Mrs Irene Adams, JP, MP, House of Commons, London, SW1A 0AA *Tel:* 020 7219 3564. *Constituency:* 10 Forbes Place, Paisley, PA1 1UT *Tel:* 0141–887 5949 *Fax:* 0141–887 8025 *E-mail:* contact@ireneadams-mp.new.labour.org.uk.

AINGER, NICK   Carmarthen West and South Pembrokeshire   Lab majority 4,538

Nick (Nicholas) Richard Ainger. Born 24 October 1949; Son of Richard John Wilkinson and Marjorie Isabel, née Dye; Educated Netherthorpe Grammar School, Staveley, Derbyshire; Married Sally Robinson 1976 (1 daughter). Marine and Port Services Ltd., Pembroke Dock 1977–92; Branch secretary, TGWU. Councillor, Dyfed County Council 1981–93; Vice-Chair, Dyfed County Council Labour Group 1989–92. **House of Commons:** Member for Pembroke 1992–97, and for Carmarthen West and South Pembrokeshire since May 1, 1997; Government Whip 2001–; PPS to Secretaries of State for Wales: Ron Davies 1997–98, Alun Michael 1998–99, Paul Murphy 1999–2001; *Select Committees:* Member: Broadcasting 1992–94, Welsh Affairs 1993–97; Member, Administration 2001–. *Special Interests:* Environment, Health. *Countries of Interest:* Ireland. Member: Amnesty International, RSPB; British-Irish Interparliamentary Body 1993–2001; Member, Dyfed Wildlife Trust. Nick Ainger Esq, MP, House of Commons, London, SW1A 0AA *Tel:* 020 7219 2241 *Fax:* 020 7219 2690. *Constituency:* Ferry Lane Works, Ferry Lane, Pembroke Dock, Dyfed, SA71 4RE *Tel:* 01646 684404 *Fax:* 01646 682954 *E-mail:* aingern@parliament.uk.

AINSWORTH, BOB   Coventry North East   Lab majority 15,751

Bob (Robert) William Ainsworth. Born 19 June 1952; Son of late Stanley and Pearl Ainsworth; Educated Foxford Comprehensive School, Coventry; Married Gloria Sandall 1974 (2 daughters). Sheet metal worker; fitter with Jaguar Cars, Coventry 1971–91; Member, MSF: Shop steward 1974, Senior steward and secretary of joint shop stewards 1980–91, Union Branch President 1983–87. Councillor, Coventry City Council 1984–93, Deputy Leader 1988–91, Chair, Finance Committee 1989–92. **House of Commons:** Member for Coventry North East since April 9, 1992; Opposition Whip 1995–97; Government Whip 1997–2001; Deputy Chief Whip 2003–; Parliamentary Under-Secretary of State, Department of the Environment, Transport and the Regions 2001; Parliamentary Under-Secretary of State for Anti-drugs Co-ordination and Organised Crime, Home Office 2001–03; *Select Committees:* Member: Accommodation and Works 2003–, Finance and Services 2003–, Selection 2003–. *Special Interests:* Industry, Environment, Taxation. *Countries of Interest:* France, India, Pakistan, USA. *Clubs:* Bell Green Working Men's; *Sportsclubs:* Broad Street Rugby Football Old Boys'; *Recreations:* Walking, chess, reading, cycling. Bob Ainsworth Esq, MP, House of Commons, London, SW1A 0AA *Tel:* 020 7219 4047. *Constituency:* Office 3, 3rd Floor, Coventry Point, Market Way, Coventry, CV1 1EA *Tel:* 024 7622 6707 *Fax:* 024 7655 3576 *E-mail:* ainsworthr@parliament.uk.

AINSWORTH, PETER   East Surrey   Con majority 13,203

Peter Michael Ainsworth. Born 16 November 1956; Son of late Lieutenant-Commander Michael Lionel Yeoward Ainsworth and Patricia Mary, née Bedford; Educated Bradfield College; Lincoln College, Oxford (MA English literature and language 1979); Married Claire Burnett 1981 (1 son 2 daughters). Research assistant to Sir John Stewart-Clark MEP 1979–81; Investment analyst, Laing & Cruickshank 1981–85; S G Warburg Securities 1985–92: Investment analyst 1985–87, Corporate finance 1987–92, Director 1990–92. Councillor, London Borough of Wandsworth 1986–94; Chair, Conservative Group on the Council 1990–92; Deputy Chair, Policy and Finance Committee. **House of Commons:** Member for East Surrey since April 9, 1992; Assistant Government Whip 1996–97; Opposition Deputy Chief Whip 1997–98; PPS: to Jonathan Aitken as Chief Secretary to the Treasury 1994–95, to Virginia Bottomley as Secretary of State for National Heritage 1995–96; Member, Shadow Cabinet 1998–2002; Shadow Secretary of State for: Culture, Media and Sport 1998–2001, Environment, Food and Rural Affairs 2001–02; *Select Committees:* Member: Consolidation Bills Joint Committee 1993–96, Environment 1993–94, Public Service 1993–96, Selection 1997–98; Chair, Environmental Audit 2003–. *Special Interests:* Economic Policy, Environment. Member, The Bow Group 1983–. *Country Life* Country MP of the Year 1994; *Green* Magazine Campaigning MP of the Year 1994; FRSA; *Sportsclubs:* MCC; *Recreations:* Family, music, gardening. Peter Ainsworth Esq, MP, House of Commons, London, SW1A 0AA *Tel:* 020 7219 5078 *Fax:* 020 7219 2527. *Constituency:* 2 Hoskins Road, Oxted, Surrey, RH8 9HT *Tel:* 01883 715782 *Fax:* 01883 730576 *E-mail:* kyprianouc@parliament.uk.

ALEXANDER, DOUGLAS   Paisley South   *Lab majority 11,910*

Douglas Garven Alexander. Born 26 October 1967; Son of Rev. Douglas N. Alexander and Dr. Joyce O. Alexander; Educated Park Mains High School, Erskine, Renfrewshire; Lester B. Pearson College, Vancouver, Canada; Edinburgh University (MA 1990, LLB 1993, Diploma in Legal Practice 1994); University of Pennsylvania, USA; Married Jacqueline Christian. Parliamentary researcher for Gordon Brown MP 1990–91; Solicitor: Brodies W.S. 1994–96, Digby Brown 1996–97; Member, TGWU. **House of Commons:** Contested Perth and Kinross 1995 by-election and Perth 1997 general election. Member for Paisley South since by-election November 6, 1997; Minister for E-Commerce and Competitiveness, Department of Trade and Industry 2001–02; Cabinet Office 2002–: Minister of State 2002–03, Minister for the Cabinet Office and Chancellor of the Duchy of Lancaster 2003–; *Special Interests:* Constitutional Reform, Economic Policy, Employment. General election campaign co-ordinator 1999–2001. *Publications:* Co-author *New Scotland, New Britain*, 1999; Notary Public; *Recreations:* Running, angling. Douglas Alexander Esq, MP, House of Commons, London, SW1A 0AA *Tel:* 020 7219 3000. *Constituency:* 2014 Mile End Mill, Abbey Mill Business Centre, Paisley, PA1 1JS *Tel:* 0141–561 0333 *Fax:* 0141–561 0334 *E-mail:* alexanderd@parliament.uk.

ALLAN, RICHARD   Sheffield Hallam   *LD majority 9,347*

Richard Beecroft Allan. Born 11 February 1966; Son of John Allan, retired, and Elizabeth Allan, doctor's receptionist; Educated Oundle School, Northants; Pembroke College, Cambridge (BA archaeology and anthropology 1988); Bristol Polytechnic (MSc information technology 1990); Married Louise Netley 1991 (1 daughter) (divorced). Field archaeologist in: Britain, France and Netherlands 1984–85, Ecuador 1988–89; Computer manager: Avon FHSA 1991–95, FHS 1995–97. Councillor, Avon County Council 1993–95, Deputy Group Leader of Liberal Democrats; Councillor, Bath City Council 1994–95. **House of Commons:** Member for Sheffield Hallam since May 1, 1997; Spokesperson for: Home and Legal Affairs (Community Relations and Urban Affairs) 1997–99, Education and Employment (Employment and Information Technology) 1999–2001, Trade and Industry (Information Technology) 2001–02, Cabinet Office (Information Technology) 2002–; *Select Committees:* Member, Home Affairs 1997–98; Chair, Information 1998–2001; Member: Finance and Services 1998–2001, Education and Employment 2000–01, Employment Sub-Committee 2001; Member: Liaison 1998–, Information 2001–, Liaison Sub-Committee 2002–. *Special Interests:* Information Technology, Heritage, Home Affairs, Education. *Countries of Interest:* Latin America especially Ecuador, USA, Kenya. Board Member, Parliamentary Office of Science and Technology (POST) 1997–; *Recreations:* Visiting sites of natural beauty and historical interest, walking. Richard Allan Esq, MP, House of Commons, London, SW1A 0AA *Tel:* 020 7219 1104 *Fax:* 020 7219 0971. *Constituency:* 85 Nether Green Road, Sheffield, S11 7EH *Tel:* 0114–230 9002 *Fax:* 0114–230 9614 *E-mail:* allanr@parliament.uk.

ALLEN, GRAHAM   Nottingham North   *Lab majority 12,240*

Graham William Allen. Born 11 January 1953; Son of Bill and Edna Allen; Educated Forest Fields Grammar School, Nottingham; City of London Polytechnic (BA politics and economics); Leeds University (MA political sociology); Married Allyson (1 daughter). Warehouseman 1974; Labour Party research officer 1979–83; Local government officer 1983–84; National co-ordinator, Political Fund ballots 1984–86; GMBATU research and education officer 1986–87. **House of Commons:** Member for Nottingham North since June 1987; Government Whip 1997–2001; Shadow Minister for: Social Security 1991–92, Constitutional Affairs 1992–94, Media and Broadcasting 1994–95, Transport 1995–96, Environment 1996–97; *Select Committees:* Member: Public Accounts 1988–91, Selection 2000–01. *Special Interests:* Economic Policy, Democratic Renewal. *Countries of Interest:* USA, Russia, China. *Publications: Reinventing Democracy*, 1995; *The Last Prime Minister*, 2001; *Clubs:* President Basford Hall Miners Welfare; *Sportsclubs:* Secretary, Lords and Commons Cricket XI; Member: Dunkirk Cricket, Bulwell Forest Golf; Vice-President Bulwell Cricket; *Recreations:* Playing and watching all sports, walking, cooking, oil painting. Graham Allen Esq, MP, House of Commons, London, SW1A 0AA *Tel:* 020 7219 5065. *Constituency Tel:* 0115–979 2344.

AMESS, DAVID   Southend West   *Con majority 7,941*

David Anthony Andrew Amess. Born 26 March 1952; Son of late James Amess and of Maud Amess; Educated St Bonaventure's Grammar School; Bournemouth College of Technology (BSc economics 1974); Married Julia Arnold 1983 (1 son 4 daughters). Junior school teacher 1970–71; Underwriter, Leslie Godwin Agency 1974–76; Accountancy personnel 1976–79; Senior consultant, Executemps Company Agency 1979–81; AA Recruitment Co 1981–87; Chair: Accountancy Solutions 1987–90, Accountancy Group 1990–96. Redbridge Council: Councillor 1982–86, Vice-chair, Housing Committee 1982–85. **House of Commons:** Contested Newham North West 1979 general election. Member for Basildon 1983–97, and for Southend West since May 1, 1997; PPS to Parliamentary under secretaries, DHSS: Edwina Currie 1987–88, Lord Skelmersdale 1988, to Michael Portillo: as Minister of State Department of Transport 1988–90, at Department of Environment 1990–92, as Chief Secretary to the Treasury 1992–94, as Secretary of State for Employment 1994–95, for Defence 1995–97; Sponsored: Horses and Ponies Bill 1984–85, Members of Parliament (Minimum Age) Bill 1984–85, Horses, Ponies and Donkeys Bill 1987–88, Abortion (Right of Conscience) (Amendment) Bill 1988–89, British Nationality (Hon. Citizenship) Bill 1988–89, Adoption (Amendment) Bill 1989–90, Dogs Bill 1989–90, Pet Animals (Amendment) Bill 1990–91, Protection Against Cruel Tethering Act 1988, Human Fertilisation (Choice) Bill 1992–93, Voluntary Personal Security Cards Bill 1992–93, Football Matches (Violent and Disorderly Conduct) Bill 1992–93, Newly Qualified Drivers Bill 1993–94, Coercion in Family Planning (Prohibition) Bill 1994–95, Freezing of Human Embryos Bill 1995–96, Abortion (Amendment) Bill 1996–97, Reform of Quarantine Regulations Bill 1997–98, Voluntary Personal Security Cards Bill 1997–98, The Warm Homes Act 2000; *Select Committees:* Member, Broadcasting 1994–97; Member: Health 1998–, Chairmen's Panel 2001–. *Special Interests:* Health, Education, Transport, Environment, Pro-Life Movement. *Countries of Interest:* USA, European Union, Middle East, Far East, Pacific Basin. Hon. Secretary, Conservative Friends of Israel 1998–. Founder Member, Wallenberg Appeal Foundation; President, 1912 Club 1996–; *Publications: The Basildon Experience*, 1995; Freeman, City of London; *Clubs:* Carlton, St Stephen's Constitutional; *Sportsclubs:* Kingswood Squash and Racketball; *Recreations:* Socialising, reading, writing, sports, modern music, keeping animals, gardening. David Amess Esq, MP, House of Commons, London, SW1A 0AA *Tel:* 020 7219 6387 *Fax:* 020 7219 2245. *Constituency:* Iveagh Hall, 67 Leigh Road, Leigh-on-Sea, Essex, SS9 1JW *Tel:* 01702 472391 *Fax:* 01702 480677 *E-mail:* amessd@parliament.uk.

ANCRAM, MICHAEL   Devizes   *Con majority 11,896*

Michael Andrew Foster Jude Kerr Ancram. Born 7 July 1945; Son of 12th Marquess of Lothian, KCVO, DL; Educated Ampleforth; Christ Church, Oxford (BA history 1966, MA); Edinburgh University (LLB 1968); Married Lady Jane Fitzalan-Howard 1975 (2 daughters). Advocate, Scottish Bar 1970, QC(Scot) 1996. DL, Roxburgh, Ettrick and Lauderdale 1990–. **House of Commons:** Contested West Lothian 1970 general election. Member for Berwickshire and East Lothian February-October 1974, for Edinburgh South 1979–87 and for Devizes since April 9, 1992; Frontbench Spokesperson for Constitutional Affairs, with overall responsibility for Scottish and Welsh issues 1997–98; Parliamentary Under-Secretary of State, Scottish Office 1983–87; Northern Ireland Office: Parliamentary Under-Secretary of State 1993–94, Minister of State 1994–97; Member, Shadow Cabinet 1997–; Deputy Chair, Conservative Party June-October 1998, Chair October 1998–2001; Deputy Leader of the Opposition 2001–; Shadow Secretary of State for Foreign and Commonwealth Affairs 2001–; *Select Committees:* Member, Public Accounts 1992–93. *Special Interests:* Housing, Defence, Agriculture. Chair, Conservative Party in Scotland 1980–83; Contested leadership 2001; Member Conservative Policy Board 2001–. Member, Board of Scottish Homes 1988–90; Heir to the marquessate; PC 1996; *Recreations:* Skiing, photography, folksinging. Rt Hon Michael Ancram, QC, DL, MP (Earl of Ancram), House of Commons, London, SW1A 0AA *Tel:* 020 7219 5072. *Constituency:* 116 High Street, Marlborough, Wiltshire, SN8 1LZ *Tel:* 01672 512675 *E-mail:* ancramm@parliament.uk.

ANDERSON, DONALD Swansea East *Lab majority 16,148*

Donald Anderson. Born 17 June 1939; Son of late David Robert Anderson, fitter and Eva, née Mathias; Educated Swansea Grammar School; University College, Swansea (BA modern history and politics 1960); Inner Temple (barrister 1969); Married Dr Dorothy Mary Trotman 1963 (3 sons). HM Diplomatic Service 1960–64; Lecturer in US and comparative government, University College of Wales, Swansea 1964–66; Called to the Bar, Inner Temple 1969–; Barrister, South Eastern Circuit 1970–97. Councillor, Royal Borough of Kensington and Chelsea 1970–75. **House of Commons:** Member for Monmouth 1966–70, and for Swansea East since October 1974; Opposition Frontbench Spokesperson for: Foreign and Commonwealth Affairs 1983–92, Defence, Disarmament and Arms Control 1993–94, Shadow Solicitor General 1994–96; PPS: to Minister of Defence (Administration) 1969–70, to Attorney General 1974–79; *Select Committees:* Member: Home Affairs 1994–95, Chairmen's Panel 1995–99, Entry Clearance Sub-Committee 1997–98; Chair, Foreign Affairs 1997–; Member, Liaison 1997–. *Special Interests:* Foreign Affairs, Housing Law, Transport, Wales, Environment. *Countries of Interest:* EU and accession countries, Norawy, France. Vice-chair, Welsh Labour Group 1969–70, Chair 1977–78. President, Gower Society 1976–78; Chair, Parliamentary Campaign for the Homeless and Rootless (CHAR) 1984–90; Vice-President, Institute of Environmental Health Officers 1984–95; Senior Vice-President, Association of European Parliamentarians for Southern Africa 1984–97; President, Swansea Male Choir; Vice-President, Morriston Orpheus Choir; Member, HAFOD Brotherhood; Director, Campaign for a Political Europe 1966–67; Member, Executive Committee, Commonwealth Parliamentary Association (CPA) UK Branch 1983–, Vice-chair 1987–88, Treasurer 1990–93, Special Representative 1989–90, Chair 1997–2001; Vice-chair, IPU 1985–88, Treasurer 1988–90 and 1993–95; Member, UK Delegation to North Atlantic Assembly 1992–, Leader 1997–2001; Member, Organisation for Security and Co-operation in Europe 1997–, Leader UK delegation 1997–98; Executive Committee Member, IPU British Group 1983–2001; Commander's Cross, Order of Merit, Federal Republic of Germany 1986; PC 2001; Hon. Fellow, University College of Wales, Swansea 1985–; Visiting Parliamentary Fellow, St Antony's College, Oxford 1999–2000; Freeman, City of Swansea 2000; *Sportsclubs:* Bonymaen RFC; *Recreations:* Walking, Church work. Rt Hon Donald Anderson, MP, House of Commons, London, SW1A 0AA *Tel:* 020 7219 3425 *Fax:* 020 7219 4801. *Constituency:* 42 High Street, Swansea, SA1 1LN *Tel:* 01792 655097 *Fax:* 01792 650766 *E-mail:* trotmang@parliament.uk.

ANDERSON, JANET Rossendale and Darwen *Lab majority 4,970*

Janet Anderson. Born 6 December 1949; Daughter of late Tom Anderson, Labour Party agent, and late Ethel Pearson; Educated Kingsfield Comprehensive School, Bristol; Polytechnic of Central London (Diploma in bi-lingual business studies); University of Nantes; Married Vincent William Humphreys 1972 (2 sons 1 daughter) (divorced). Secretary, *The Scotsman* and *The Sunday Times* 1971–74. **House of Commons:** Contested Rossendale and Darwen 1987 general election. Member for Rossendale and Darwen since April 9, 1992; Opposition Spokeswoman for Women 1996–97; Opposition Whip 1995–96; Government Whip 1997–98; Personal assistant: to Barbara Castle as MP and MEP 1974–81, to Jack Straw MP 1981–87; PPS to Margaret Beckett as Deputy Leader of the Labour Party 1992–93; Parliamentary Labour Party Representative, House of Commons Commission 1993–94; Parliamentary Under-Secretary of State, Department for Culture, Media and Sport (Minister for Tourism, Film and Broadcasting) 1998–2001; Member Joint Committee on House of Lords Reform 2002–; *Select Committees:* Member: Home Affairs 1994–95, Accommodation and Works 1997–98; Member: Catering 2001–, Joint Committee on House of Lords Reform 2002–, Home Affairs 2003–. *Special Interests:* Footwear, Textile Industries, Quotas for Women, Health, Constitution, Employment, Home Affairs, Culture, Media and Sport. *Countries of Interest:* France, Cyprus, Italy. Parliamentary Labour Party Campaign Organiser 1988–90; Vice-Chair, Labour Campaign for Electoral Reform; Steering Committee Member, Labour Women's Network; Secretary, Tribune Group 1993–96. Northern regional organiser, Shopping Hours Reform Council 1991–92; Hon. adviser, Emily's List UK; Member, Parliamentary Panel, Royal College of Nursing 1992–97; Vice-President, Association of District Councils; Fellow, Royal Society for the Arts; *Clubs:* Rosemount Working Men's, Stacksteads; *Recreations:* Playing the piano, listening to opera. Janet Anderson, MP, House of Commons, London, SW1A 0AA *Tel:* 020 7219 5375 *Fax:* 020 7219 2148. *Constituency:* 731 Bacup Road, Waterfoot, Rossendale, BB4 7EU *Tel:* 01706 220909 *E-mail:* andersonj@parliament.uk.

ARBUTHNOT, JAMES   North East Hampshire   *Con majority 13,257*

James Norwich Arbuthnot. Born 4 August 1952; Son of late Sir John Sinclair-Wemyss Arbuthnot, 1st Bt, MBE, TD, MP for Dover 1950–64 and Lady Arbuthnot; Educated Wellesley House, Broadstairs; Eton College; Trinity College, Cambridge (BA law 1974); Married Emma Broadbent 1984 (1 son 3 daughters). Called to the Bar, Inner Temple 1975 and Lincoln's Inn 1977. Councillor, Royal Borough of Kensington and Chelsea 1978–87. **House of Commons:** Contested Cynon Valley 1983 general election and 1984 by-election. Member for Wanstead and Woodford 1987–97 and for North East Hampshire since May 1, 1997; Assistant Government Whip 1992–94; Opposition Chief Whip 1997–2001; PPS: to Archie Hamilton as Minister of State for the Armed Forces 1988–90, to Peter Lilley as Secretary of State for Trade and Industry 1990–92; Parliamentary Under-Secretary of State, Department of Social Security 1994–95; Minister of State for Procurement, Ministry of Defence 1995–97; Member, Shadow Cabinet 1997–2001; Member Joint Committee on House of Lords Reform 2002–; *Select Committees:* Member, Joint Committee on House of Lords Reform 2002–. *Special Interests:* Taxation, Defence, Foreign Affairs, Law. Branch Chair, Putney Conservative Association 1975–77; Joint Deputy Chair, Chelsea Conservative Association 1980–82; President, Cynon Valley Conservative Association 1983–92. Heir presumptive to baronetcy; PC 1998; *Clubs:* Buck's; *Recreations:* Playing guitar, skiing, cooking. Rt Hon James Arbuthnot, MP, House of Commons, London, SW1A 0AA *Tel:* 020 7219 4649. *Constituency:* North East Hampshire Conservative Association, 14a Butts Road, Alton, Hampshire, GU34 1ND *Tel:* 01420 84122 *Fax:* 01420 84925.

ARMSTRONG, HILARY   North West Durham   *Lab majority 16,333*

Hilary Jane Armstrong. Born 30 November 1945; Daughter of late Ernest Armstrong, MP for Durham North West 1966–87, and of Hannah Armstrong; Educated Monkwearmouth Comprehensive School, Sunderland; West Ham College of Technology; Birmingham University (BSc sociology; Diploma in social work); Married Dr Paul Corrigan 1992. VSO teaching in Kenya 1967–69; Social worker, Newcastle Social Services 1970–73; Community worker, Southwick Neighbourhood Action Project 1973–75; Lecturer in community and youth work, Sunderland Polytechnic 1975–86; Secretary/Researcher for Ernest Armstrong MP (father) 1986–87; Chair, ASTMS Northern Division Council 1981–88. Councillor, Durham County Council 1985–88. **House of Commons:** Member for North West Durham since June 1987; Opposition Spokesperson on: Education 1988–92, Treasury and Economic Affairs 1994–95, The Environment and London 1995–97; Government Chief Whip (Parliamentary Secretary, HM Treasury) 2001–; PPS to John Smith, as Leader of the Opposition 1992–94; Minister of State, Department of the Environment, Transport and the Regions 1999–2001, (Minister for Local Government and Housing 1997–99, for Local Government and Regions 1999–2001); *Select Committees:* Member, Education 1998. *Special Interests:* Regional Development, World Development, Education, Environment. *Countries of Interest:* Central Africa, Kenya, South Africa, Tanzania, Uganda. Member: Labour Party National Executive Committee 1992–94, 1996–, Parliamentary Labour Party Parliamentary Committee. NCH Action for Children: Member NCH Board 1985–91, Vice-president 1991–97; Member, UNICEF National Committee 1995–97; Vice-Chair, The British Council 1994–97; PC 1999; *Recreations:* Theatre, reading. Rt Hon Hilary Armstrong, MP, House of Commons, London, SW1A 0AA *Tel:* 020 7219 5076. *Constituency:* North House, 17 North Terrace, Crook, Co Durham, DL15 9AZ *Tel:* 01388 767065 *Fax:* 01388 767923 *E-mail:* armstrongh@parliament.uk.

DodOnline
An Electronic Directory without rival...

MPs' biographies and photographs available with daily updates *via* the internet

For a *free* trial, call Yasmin Mirza, Aby Farsoun or Michael Mand on 020 7630 7643

ATHERTON, CANDY   Falmouth and Camborne   *Lab majority 4,527*

Candy (Candice) Kathleen Atherton. Born 21 September 1955; Daughter of late Denis Gordon Atherton, journalist, and Pamela Osborne, retired hairdresser/ salon owner/former Mayoress of Falmouth; Educated Convent of Sacred Hearts, Surrey; Midhurst Grammar School, Sussex; Polytechnic of North London (BA applied social studies 1985); Married Broderick Ross 2002. Researcher for Jo Richardson MP and Judith Hart MP 1981; Probation officer 1975; Launched women's magazine *Everywoman* 1985; Journalist for broadsheet newspapers 1980–; Press officer, Labour Party 1996; Member: NUJ, T&G. Councillor, London Borough of Islington 1986–92, Mayor 1989–90; Member, Islington Health Authority 1986–90. **House of Commons:** Contested Chesham and Amersham 1992 general election. Member for Falmouth and Camborne since May 1, 1997; *Select Committees:* Member: Education and Employment 1997–2001, Employment Sub-Committee 1997–2001; Member, Environment, Food and Rural Affairs 2002–. *Special Interests:* Environment, Disability, Health, Inland Waterways, Economic Regeneration. *Countries of Interest:* Southern Africa, East Africa, St Helena. Vice-Chair: South and West Group of Labour MPs 1997–99, South West Regional Group of Labour MPs 1999–. *Publications: Housing in Camden, Hackney and Islington,* 1975; Freeman, City of London 1990; *Clubs:* Falmouth Labour; *Sportsclubs:* Falmouth Golf Club; *Recreations:* Gliding, gig racing, ornithology. Candy Atherton, MP, House of Commons, London, SW1A 0AA *Tel:* 020 7219 4094 *Fax:* 020 7219 0982. *Constituency:* 4 Webber Hill, Falmouth, Cornwall, TR11 2BU *Tel:* 01326 314440 *Fax:* 01326 314415 *E-mail:* atherton@parliament.uk.

ATKINS, CHARLOTTE   Staffordshire Moorlands   *Lab majority 5,838*

Charlotte Atkins. Born 24 September 1950; Daughter of Ronald and Jessie Atkins; Educated Colchester County High School, Essex; London School of Economics (BSc economics 1973); London University (MA area studies 1974); Married Gus Brain 1990 (1 daughter). Assistant community relations officer, Luton CRC 1974–76; Research officer/head of research, UCATT 1976–80; Research/political officer, AUEW (TASS) 1980–84; Press officer/ parliamentary officer, COHSE/UNISON 1984–97; Member UNISON. Councillor, London Borough of Wandsworth 1982–86, Chief Whip and Deputy Leader of Labour Group 1983–86. **House of Commons:** Contested Eastbourne 1990 by-election. Member for Staffordshire Moorlands since May 1, 1997; Assistant Government Whip 2002–; PPS to Baroness Symons of Vernham Dean as Minister of State for Trade, Foreign and Commonwealth Office and Department of Trade and Industry and Deputy Leader of the House of Lords 2001–02; *Select Committees:* Member: Education and Employment 1997–2001, Education Sub-Committee 1997–2001, Selection 1997–2000. *Special Interests:* Civil Liberties, Education, Employment, Health, Agriculture, Trade. Member: National Policy Forum to 1998, National Women's Committee to 1998; Vice-chair West Midlands Regional Group of Labour MPs to 2002. Member, Liberty; *Publications:* Various articles in *Chartist* on parliamentary and equality issues; co-author *How to Select or Reselect Your MP*; *Recreations:* Family activities, theatre, keeping fit, cycling, conservation. Charlotte Atkins, MP, House of Commons, London, SW1A 0AA *Tel:* 020 7219 3591. *Constituency:* The former Police House, 15 Ravensclilte Road, Kidsgrove, Stoke on Trent, ST7 4ET *Tel:* 0121 569 1937.

ATKINSON, DAVID   Bournemouth East   *Con majority 3,434*

David Anthony Atkinson. Born 24 March 1940; Son of late Arthur Joseph and of the late Joan Margaret Atkinson; Educated St George's College, Weybridge; Southend College of Technology; College of Automobile and Aeronautical Engineering, Chelsea (Diplomas in automobile engineering and motor trade management 1972); Married Susan Nicola Pilsworth 1968 (1 son 1 daughter). Director: Chalkwell Motor Co Ltd 1963–72, David Graham Studios Ltd (printing, marketing, artwork, design) 1973–77. Councillor: Southend County Borough Council 1969–72, Essex County Council 1973–78. **House of Commons:** Contested Newham North West February 1974 and Basildon October 1974 general elections. Member for Bournemouth East since

November 1977 by-election; PPS to Paul Channon: as Minister of State for the Civil Service 1979–81, as Minister for the Arts 1981–83, as Minister of State for Trade 1983–86, as Secretary of State for Trade and Industry 1986–87; Author Licensing (Occasional Permissions) Act 1983; *Select Committees:* Member, Science and Technology 1997–98. *Special Interests:* Human Rights, Small Businesses, Mental Health, Foreign Affairs, Arts and Heritage, Space Technology. *Countries of Interest:* Russia, former USSR. Chair, National Young Conservatives 1970–71. National Chair/President, Christian Solidarity International (UK) 1979–97; UK Representative on the Council of Europe and Western Europe Union 1979–86 and 1987–, Leader, Conservative delegation 1997–, Chair, European Democratic Group 1998–; Chair, Council of Europe Committee for Non-Member Countries 1991–95; Chair, Western European Union Committee on Technology and Aerospace 2000–03; *Recreations:* Art and architecture, mountaineering. David Atkinson Esq, MP, House of Commons, London, SW1A 0AA *Tel:* 020 7219 3598 *Fax:* 020 7219 3847. *Constituency:* Bournemouth East Conservative Association, Haviland Road, Boscombe, Bournemouth, BH1 4JW *Tel:* 01202 397047 *E-mail:* atkinsond@parliament.uk.

ATKINSON, PETER   Hexham   *Con majority 2,529*

Peter Landreth Atkinson. Born 19 January 1943; Son of Major Douglas and Amy Atkinson; Educated Cheltenham College; Married Brione Darley 1976 (2 daughters). Journalist: various weekly newspapers, freelance news agency 1961–68; *The Journal*, Newcastle upon Tyne 1968–72; reporter, later news editor *The Evening Standard* 1972–82; Director of public affairs, British Field Sports Society 1983–92. Councillor, London Borough of Wandsworth 1978–82; Member, Wandsworth Health Authority 1982–89; Councillor, Suffolk County Council 1989–92. **House of Commons:** Member for Hexham since April 9, 1992; Opposition Whip: Agriculture, Scotland 1999–2000, Environment, Transport and the Regions 2000, Scotland, Social Security 2000–02, Home Office 2001–02; PPS: to Jeremy Hanley as Minister of State for the Armed Forces 1994, as Minister without Portfolio and Chair Conservative Party 1994–95, to Jeremy Hanley and Sir Nicholas Bonsor as Ministers of State, Foreign and Commonwealth Office 1995–96, to Lord Parkinson, as Chair Conservative Party 1997–99; *Select Committees:* Member: European Legislation 1992–97, Scottish Affairs 1992–97, Deregulation 1995–97, Chairmen's Panel 1997–99, Scottish Affairs 1997–2002; Member: Court of Referees 1997–, Chairmen's Panel 2002–, Catering 2002–, Procedure 2003–. *Special Interests:* Agriculture, Industry. *Countries of Interest:* Overseas Territories, Eastern Europe, USA. *Clubs:* Albert Edward (Hexham), Northern Counties (Newcastle upon Tyne); *Sportsclubs:* Tynedale Rugby; *Recreations:* Shooting, gardening, racing. Peter Atkinson Esq, MP, House of Commons, London, SW1A 0AA *Tel:* 020 7219 4128 *Fax:* 020 7219 2775. *Constituency:* 1 Meal Market, Hexham, Northumberland, NE46 1NF *Tel:* 01434 603777 *Fax:* 01434 601659 *E-mail:* atkinsonp@parliament.co.uk.

AUSTIN, JOHN   Erith and Thamesmead   *Lab majority 11,167*

John Eric Austin. Born 21 August 1944; Son of late Stanley Austin, electrician, and late Ellen Austin; Educated Glyn Grammar School, Epsom; Goldsmiths' College, London (Certificate in Community and Youth Work 1972); Bristol University (MA policy studies 1990); Married Linda Walker 1965 (divorced 1988) (2 sons 1 daughter). Medical laboratory technician 1961–63; Labour Party organiser/agent 1963–70; Social/community worker, London Borough of Bexley 1972–74; Director, Bexley Council for Racial Equality 1974–92; Member, MSF (AMICUS); Chair, MSF Parliamentary Group 1998–2000. Councillor, London Borough of Greenwich 1970–94: Chair, Social Services Committee 1974–78, Deputy Leader 1981–82, Leader 1982–87, Mayor 1987–88, 1988–89. **House of Commons:** Contested Woolwich 1987, as John Austin-Walker. Member for Woolwich 1992–97, and for Erith and Thamesmead since May 1, 1997 (contested as John Austin-Walker); *Select Committees:* Member, Health 1994–97; Member: Health 1997–, Unopposed Bills (Panel) 1998–. *Special Interests:* Health, Social Services, Mental Health, Equal Opportunities, Environment, Foreign Affairs. *Countries of Interest:* Eastern Europe, Ireland, Kurdistan, Middle East. Member, Labour Friends of Bosnia 1994–; Chair, Socialist Campaign Group of MPs 1994–97; Joint Vice-Chair, London Regional Group of Labour MPs 1996–98, 1999 Treasurer, Labour First Past the Post Group 1997–. Chairman, Greenwich MIND 1978–82; Chairman, Greenwich Community Health Council 1976–80;

National Chairman, Association of Community Health Councils for England and Wales 1980–82; Vice-Chairman: Association of London Authorities (ALA) 1983–87, London Strategic Policy Unit 1985–87; Chairman: London Boroughs Emergency Planning Information Committee 1985–87, British Caribbean Association 1999–, London Ecology Unit 1985–87; Member, Political Committee CWS (Retail South East) 1987–93; Environment spokesperson for ALA 1992–94; Member, Executive Committee Inter-Parliamentary Union British Group 1996–, Vice-chair 2000–2001, Chair 2001–; Vice-Chair, International Executive Parliamentary Association for Euro-Arab Co-operation 1997–; Co-Chair, Council for the Advancement of Arab British Understanding 1998–; Member, Executive Committee, Commonwealth Parliamentary Association UK Branch 1999–; Trustee (unpaid): The Adolescent and Children's Trust, Greenwich MIND; Unpaid Director: London Marathon Charitable Trust, Grossness Engines Trust; Trustee: Crossners Engines Trust, London Marathon Charitable Trust; *Clubs:* St Patrick's Social (Plumstead), Northumberland Heath Working Men's (Erith), Woolwich Catholic; *Recreations:* Gardening, cookery, running (including marathons). John Austin Esq, MP, House of Commons, London, SW1A 0AA *Tel:* 020 7219 5195 *Fax:* 020 7219 2706. *Constituency:* 301 Plumstead High Street, Plumstead, London, SE18 1JX *Tel:* 020 8311 4444 *Fax:* 020 8311 6666 *E-mail:* austinj@parliament.uk.

B

BACON, RICHARD   South Norfolk   *Con majority 6,893*

Richard Bacon. Born 3 December 1962; Educated King's School, Worcester; London School of Economics (BSc (Econ) politics and economics); Single. Investment banker Barclays 1986–89; Financial journalist Euromoney Publications plc 1993–94; Deputy director Management Consultancies Association 1994–96; Brunswick Public Relations 1996–99; Founder English Word Factory 1999–. **House of Commons:** Contested Vauxhall 1997 general election. Member for South Norfolk since June 7, 2001; *Select Committees:* Member: Public Accounts 2001–, European Scrutiny 2003–. *Special Interests:* Public Expenditure, Education, Health, Agriculture. Former chair Hammersmith Conservative Association; Co-founder Geneva Conservative general election voluntary agency. Member Amnesty International; *Recreations:* Music, words. Richard Bacon Esq, MP, House of Commons, London, SW1A 0AA *Tel:* 020 7219 8301 *Fax:* 020 7219 1784. *Constituency:* Grasmere, Denmark Street, Diss, Norfolk, IP22 3LE *Tel:* 01379 643728 *Fax:* 01379 650765.

BAILEY, ADRIAN   West Bromwich West   *Lab majority 11,355*

Adrian Bailey. Born 11 December 1945; Son of Edward Arthur Bailey, fitter and Sylvia Alice Bailey, née Bayliss; Educated Cheltenham Grammar School; Exeter University (BA economic history 1967) Loughborough College of Librarianship (postgraduate diploma in librarianship 1971); Married Jill Patricia Millard 1989 (1 stepson). Librarian, Cheshire County Council 1971–82; Political organiser, Co-operative Party 1982–2000; Contested Cheshire West 1979 European Parliament election; GMBATU 1982–2000. Sandwell Borough Council: Councillor 1991–, Chair finance 1992–97, Deputy leader of council 1997–2000. **House of Commons:** Contested South Worcester 1970 and Nantwich 1974 general elections, Wirral 1976 by-election. Member for West Bromwich West since November 23, 2000; *Select Committees:* Member: Northern Ireland Affairs 2001–, Unopposed Bills (Panel) 2001–. *Special Interests:* Co-operatives and Mutuals, Urban Regeneration, Animal Welfare (Anti Hunting with Dogs), Taxation, Economic Policy, Child Protection Policy. Secretary West Bromwich West constituency Labour Party 1993. *Recreations:* football, swimming, walking. Adrian Bailey Esq, MP, House of Commons, London, SW1A 0AA *Tel:* 020 7219 6060 *Fax:* 020 7219 1202. *Constituency:* Terry Duffy House, Thomas Street, West Bromich, West Midlands, BR70 6NT *Tel:* 01215 691926 *Fax:* 01215 691936 *E-mail:* baileya@parliament.uk.

BAIRD, VERA   Redcar — *Lab majority 13,443*

Vera Baird. Born 13 February 1951; Daughter of Jack Thomas and Alice Thomas, née Marsland; Educated Chadderton Grammar School for Girls; Newcastle Polytechnic (LLB law 1972); Open University (BA literature and history 1982); London Guildhall University (MA modern history in progress); Married David John Taylor-Gooby 1972 (divorced 1978); married Robert Brian Baird 1978 (widowed 1979) (2 stepsons). Called to the Bar 1975; Barrister Michael Mansfield QC's chambers; Visiting law fellow St Hilda's College, Oxford 1999; QC 2000; Vice-president Newcastle Polytechnic Student Union 1971; TGWU 1982–; ISTC 2001–. **House of Commons:** Contested Berwick 1983 general election. Member for Redcar since June 7, 2001; *Select Committees:* Member, Joint Committee on Human Rights 2001–. *Special Interests:* Human Rights, Civil Liberties, Equal Opportunities, Criminal Law, Regional Development, Regeneration, Social Entrepreneurism. *Countries of Interest:* East and South Africa, Tanzania, Ethiopia, Burma. Various constituency and branch offices Local Labour Parties; Member Fabian Society; Vice-chair Society of Labour Lawyers. Council Member Justice; Vice-President Association of Women Barristers; Vice-chair Fawcett Society 1998–2001; National Patron: Rape Crisis Foundation, Drug Rape Trust; Chair: Advisory Committee Liberty Research Project into Deaths in Custody, Labour Criminal Justice Forum; Member: Criminal Bar Association, British Academy of Forensic Science; Gray's Inn advocacy trainer; Team leader Home Office gender and criminal justice legislation project; *Publications:* Co-author: *The Judiciary* (Justice) 1992, *Response to Runciman* (Society of Labour Lawyers) 1993, *Negotiated Justice* (Justice) 1993, *Economical with the Proof* (Tooks Court) 1993; *Rape in Court* (Society of Labour Lawyers) 1998; Co-author, *Defending Battered Women who Kill* 2002; *Profile of Millicent Fawcett* (Fawcett Society) 2002; Co-author, *The Last Resort:* A Study of The Criminal Cases Review Commission, 2003; *Recreations:* Travel, reading, running. Vera Baird, QC, MP, House of Commons, London, SW1A 0AA *Tel:* 020 7219 8312 *Fax:* 020 7219 0371. *Constituency:* Unit 12, Redcar Station Business Centre, Station Road, Redcar, TS10 1RD *Tel:* 01642 471777 ext 312 *Fax:* 01642 484347 *E-mail:* bairdv@parliament.uk.

BAKER, NORMAN   Lewes — *LD majority 9,710*

Norman John Baker. Born 26 July 1957; Educated Royal Liberty School, Gidea Park; Royal Holloway College, London University (BA German 1978). Regional director, Our Price Records 1978–83; English as a foreign language teacher/lecturer 1985–97; Lib Dem environment campaigner, House of Commons 1989–90. Councillor: Lewes District Council 1987–99, Leader 1991–97, East Sussex County Council 1989–97. **House of Commons:** Contested Lewes 1992 general election. Member for Lewes since May 1, 1997; Spokesperson for: Environment and Transport: Genetic modification and environment 1997–99, Animal Welfare 1997–, Millennium Dome 1998–2001, Transport 1998–99, Consumer Affairs and Broadcasting 1999–2001, Home Affairs 2001–02; Liberal Democrat Shadow Environment Secretary 2002–; *Select Committees:* Member: Environmental Audit 1997–2000, European Legislation 1997–98, Broadcasting 2000–01, Joint Committee on Human Rights 2003–. *Special Interests:* Civil Liberties, Environment, Oppressed Minority Races. *Countries of Interest:* Tibet, Sweden. Member: Greenpeace, Amnesty International, Free Tibet, Liberty; Member, Human Rights Committee; *Publications:* Various environmental texts; *Recreations:* Walking, music. Norman Baker Esq, MP, House of Commons, London, SW1A 0AA *Tel:* 020 7219 2864 *Fax:* 020 7219 0445. *Constituency:* 204 High Street, Lewes, East Sussex, BN7 2NS *Tel:* 01273 480281 *Fax:* 01273 480287 *E-mail:* bakern@parliament.uk.

Visit the Vacher Dod Website . . .
www.DodOnline.co.uk

BALDRY, TONY   Banbury   *Con majority 5,219*

Tony (Antony) Brian Baldry. Born 10 July 1950; Son of Peter Baldry, consultant physician, and Oina, née Paterson; Educated Leighton Park School, Reading; Sussex University (BA social science 1972, LLB 1973); Lincoln's Inn (barrister 1975); Married Catherine Weir 1979 (1 son 1 daughter) (divorced 1996); married Pippa Isbell 2001. TA Officer 1971–83; Honorary Colonel RLC (TA); Construction industry; Barrister specialising in construction law, general commercial law and international arbitration 1975–. **House of Commons:** Contested Thurrock 1979 general election. Member for Banbury since June 1983; PA to Margaret Thatcher 1974 general election, served in her private office March-October 1975; PPS: to Lynda Chalker as Minister of State, FCO 1985–87, to John Wakeham, as Lord Privy Seal 1987–88, as Leader of the House 1987–89, as Lord President of The Council 1988–89, as Secretary of State for Energy 1989–90; Parliamentary Under-Secretary of State: Department of Energy 1990, Department of Environment 1990–94, Foreign and Commonwealth Office 1994–95; Minister of State, Ministry of Agriculture, Fisheries and Food 1995–97; *Select Committees:* Member: Trade and Industry 1997–2001, Standards and Privileges 2001; Chair, International Development 2001–; Member, Liaison 2001–. *Special Interests:* Employment, Youth Affairs, Legal Affairs, Overseas Aid and Development, European Union, Childcare. *Countries of Interest:* Asia, Africa, Caribbean, North America, Middle East. Chair, Conservative Parliamentary Mainstream Group 1997–2001; Member executive committee 1992 Committee 2001–. Vice-President, National Children's Homes 1981–83; Governor Commonwealth Institute 1997–; Deputy Chair, Conservative Group for Europe 1981–83; Executive Committee Member, IPU British Group: 1997–, Treasurer 2000–; Liveryman: Merchant Taylors Company, Stationers and Newspaper Makers Company, Arbitrators Company; Robert Schumann Silver Medal 1978; *Clubs:* Carlton, Farmers'; *Recreations:* Walking, gardening, beagling. Tony Baldry Esq, MP, House of Commons, London, SW1A 0AA *Tel:* 020 7219 4476 *Fax:* 020 7219 5826. *Constituency:* 16a North Bar, Banbury, Oxfordshire, OX16 0TS *Tel:* 01295 262341 *Fax:* 01295 263140 *E-mail:* baldryt@parliament.uk.

BANKS, TONY   West Ham   *Lab majority 15,645*

Tony (Anthony) Louis Banks. Born 8 April 1943; Son of Albert Banks; Educated State schools; York University (BA); London School of Economics; Married Sally Jones. Head of research, AUEW 1969–75; Assistant general secretary, Association of Broadcasting Staff 1976–83. Councillor, GLC 1970–77, 1981–86, Chairman 1985–86. **House of Commons:** Contested East Grinstead 1970, Newcastle North October 1974 and Watford 1979 general elections. Member for Newham North West 1983–97, and for West Ham since May 1, 1997; Opposition Spokesman on Social Security 1990–91; Opposition Front Bench Spokesman on: Transport 1992–93, Environment 1992–93; Political adviser to Judith Hart as Minister for Overseas Development 1975; Parliamentary Under-Secretary of State, Department of National Heritage/Department for Culture, Media and Sport (Minister for Sport) 1997–99; Resigned July 1999 reshuffle; *Select Committees:* Member: Procedure 1989–97, Procedure 1999–2001; Member, Accommodation and Works 2000–. *Special Interests:* Economics, Local and Regional Government, Media, Arts, Animal Welfare. *Countries of Interest:* Europe, Lithuania, Nicaragua, Panama, USA. Chair, London Group Labour MPs 1987–91. Member, Council of Europe, WEU 1989–91; Representative, UK Delegation to Council of Europe and Western Europe Union; *Recreations:* Soccer, trade union history. Tony Banks Esq, MP, House of Commons, London, SW1A 0AA *Tel:* 020 7219 3522. *Constituency:* 306 High Street, Stratford, London, E15 1AJ *Tel:* 020 8555 0036.

DodOnline
An Electronic Directory without rival ...

MPs' biographies and photographs available with daily updates *via* the internet

For a *free* trial, call Yasmin Mirza, Aby Farsoun or Michael Mand on 020 7630 7643

BARKER, GREGORY   Bexhill and Battle   *Con majority 10,503*

Gregory Leonard George Barker. Born 8 March 1966; Educated Steyning Grammar School; Lancing College, West Sussex; Royal Holloway College, London University (BA modern history, economics, history, politics 1987); Married Celeste Harrison 1992 (1 daughter 2 sons). Researcher Centre for Policy Studies 1987–89; Equity analyst Gerrard Vivian Gray 1988–90; Director International Pacific Securities 1990–97; Associate partner Brunswick Group Ltd 1997–98; Head investor communications Siberian Oil Company 1998–2000; Director Daric plc (Bartlett Merton) 1998–2001. **House of Commons:** Contested Eccles 1997 general election. Member for Bexhill and Battle since June 7, 2001; *Select Committees:* Member, Environmental Audit 2001–. *Special Interests:* Environment, Education, Overseas Development. *Countries of Interest:* US, Germany, Russia, Australia. Chair: Shoreham Young Conservatives 1982–83, Holloway Conservative Society 1986–87; Vice-chair: Hammersmith Conservative Association 1993–95, Wandsworth and Tooting Conservative Association 1997–98. Associate Centre for Policy Studies 1988–; Member British-German Forum; Honourable Artillery Company; *Clubs:* Carlton, Bexhill Conservative Club, Bexhill Racing Club; *Recreations:* Skiing, riding, horse racing. Gregory Barker Esq, MP, House of Commons, London, SW1A 0AA *Tel:* 020 7219 1852 *Fax:* 020 7219 1742. *Constituency:* Bexhill and Battle Conservative Association, Bexhill on Sea, East Sussex, TN40 1QJ *Tel:* 01424 219117 *Fax:* 01424 218367 *E-mail:* barkerg@parliament.uk.

BARNES, HARRY   North East Derbyshire   *Lab majority 12,258*

Harry (Harold) Barnes. Born 22 July 1936; Son of late Joseph and late Betsy Barnes; Educated Easington Colliery Secondary Modern School; Ryhope Grammar School; Ruskin College, Oxford (Diploma in economics and political science 1962); Hull University (BA philosophy and political studies 1965); Married Elizabeth Ann Stephenson 1963 (1 son 1 daughter). RAF national service 1954–56; Railway clerk 1952–54, 1956–60; Adult student 1960–65; Lecturer: in British government North Notts College of Further Education 1965–66, in political studies and industrial relations Sheffield University 1966–87; Member, National Administrative Council of Independent Labour Publications 1977–80, 1982–85; Director, Mature Matriculation Courses 1984–87 (Sheffield University); Member Amicus. **House of Commons:** Member for North East Derbyshire since June 1987; *Select Committees:* Member: European Legislation 1989–97, Members' Interests 1990–92; Member, Northern Ireland Affairs 1997–. *Special Interests:* European Union, Environment, Northern Ireland, Electoral Registration, Local and Regional Government, Conflict Resolution, Trade and Industry, Africa, Tobin tax. *Countries of Interest:* Ireland, Malta, Africa. Vice-Chair, East Midland Group of Labour MPs 1991–95; Campaign Officer, Central Regional Group, Labour MPs 1993–95; Hon. Treasurer, Central Region Group of Labour MPs 1997–99. Member, Standing Committees on: Local Government Finance, 1988, Employment and Football 1989, Student Loans 1990; Member, Standing Committee A on European Legislation 1990–97; Member, Standing Committees on: Northern Ireland Emergency Provisions 1991, Transport and Works 1992, Further and Higher Education 1992, Civil Rights (Disabled Persons) Bill 1994–95, Dog (Fouling of Land) Bill 1995–96, Pollution Prevention and Control Bill 1998–99, Road Traffic (Vehicle Testing) Bill 1998–99, Disability Rights Commission Bill 1998–99, Finance Bill 2000–01, Special Educational Needs and Disability Bill 2000–01, Electoral Fraud (Northern Ireland) Bill 2001–02, Justice (Northern Ireland) Bill 2001–02, Land Registration Bill 2001–02; Associate Member, British-Irish Parliamentary Body 1992–97, Full Member 1997–. Harry Barnes Esq, MP, House of Commons, London, SW1A 0AA *Tel:* 020 7219 4521 *Fax:* 020 7219 0667 *Tel (Constituency):* 01246 412588 *Fax (Constituency):* 01246 412588 *E-mail:* harrybarnes@parliament.uk.

Visit the Vacher Dod Website . . .

www.DodOnline.co.uk

BARON, JOHN Billericay *Con majority 5,013*

John Baron. Born 21 June 1959; Son of Raymond Arthur Ernest Baron and Kathleen Ruby (née Whittlestone); Educated Queens College, Taunton, Somerset; Jesus College, Cambridge (BA history and economics 1982); Royal Military College Sandhurst 1984; Married Thalia Anne Mayson, née Laird, architect (2 daughters). Captain Royal Regiment of Fusiliers 1984–87; Director: Henderson Private Investors Ltd 1987–99, Rothschild Asset Management 1999–2001. **House of Commons:** Contested Basildon 1997 general election. Member for Billericay since June 7, 2001; Shadow Spokesperson for Health 2002–03; Shadow Minister for Health 2003–; *Select Committees:* Member, Education and Skills 2001–02. *Special Interests:* Health, Education, Law and Order, Charity and Voluntary Sector, Small Businesses, European Affairs. Mentor, Prince's Trust; Director Two small Property Investment Companies; *Recreations:* Tennis, walking, history, family, cycling. John Baron Esq, MP, House of Commons, London, SW1A 0AA *Tel:* 020 7219 8138 *Fax:* 020 7219 1743. *Constituency:* 125 Bramble Tye, Noak Bridge, Basildon, SS15 5GR *Tel:* 01268 520765 *E-mail:* baronj@parliament.uk.

BARRETT, JOHN Edinburgh West *LD majority 7,589*

John Andrew Barrett. Born 11 February 1954; Son of late Andrew Barrett, building contractor, and late Elizabeth Mary, née Benert, librarian; Educated Forrester High School, Edinburgh; Telford College, Edinburgh; Napier Polytechnic, Edinburgh; Married Carol Pearson 1975 (1 daughter). Director: ABC Productions 1985–, Edinburgh International Film Festival 1995–2001, The EDI Group 1997–99, Edinburgh and Borders Screen Industries Office 1997–2001, Edinburgh Filmhouse 1997–2001; Contested Linlithgow 1999 Scottish Parliament election. Edinburgh City Council: Councillor 1995–, Group transport spokesman 1999–2001, Group economic development spokesman 1995–99, Group chair 1997–2000, Convener Edinburgh West local development committee 2000–01. **House of Commons:** Member for Edinburgh West since June 7, 2001; Scottish Liberal Democrat Spokesperson on Cross Border Transport 2001–; Liberal Democrat Spokesperson on International Development 2002–; *Select Committees:* Member, International Development 2002–. *Special Interests:* Air and Rail Safety, Energy, Overseas Aid and Development. *Countries of Interest:* Australia, Greece. Convener Lothian Region Liberal Democrats 1997–2000; Scottish Liberal Club: Chair 1995–2000, Vice-president 2000–; Election agent Donald Gorrie MP 1997. Member: Amnesty International, Greenpeace; Member European Standing Committee B 2003–; *Clubs:* National Liberal; *Recreations:* Music, cinema, travel, meeting people. John Barrett Esq, MP, House of Commons, London, SW1A 0AA *Tel:* 020 7219 8224 *Fax:* 020 7219 1762. *Constituency:* West Edinburgh Liberal Democrats, 11 Drum Brae Avenue, Edinburgh, EH12 8TE *Tel:* 0131 339 0339 *Fax:* 0131 476 7101 *E-mail:* barrettj@parliament.uk.

BARRON, KEVIN Rother Valley *Lab majority 14,882*

Kevin John Barron. Born 26 October 1946; Son of Richard Barron, retired and Edna Barron; Educated Maltby Hall Secondary Modern; Ruskin College, Oxford (Diploma in Labour studies 1977); Married Carol McGrath 1969 (1 son 2 daughters). National Coal Board 1962–83; AMICUS. **House of Commons:** Member for Rother Valley since June 1983; Opposition Spokesperson for: Energy 1988–92, Employment 1993–95, Health 1995–97; PPS to Neil Kinnock as Leader of the Opposition 1985–88; Sponsor private member's bill to ban advertising and promotion of tobacco products 1993, 94; *Select Committees:* Member, Environment 1992–93. *Special Interests:* Energy, Environment, Home Affairs, Health, Intelligence and Security. *Countries of Interest:* Bulgaria. Chair, Yorkshire Regional Group of Labour MPs 1987–. Member: General Medical Council 1999–, Intelligence and Security Committee; PC 2001; *Recreations:* Family life, football, fly fishing, photography, walking. Rt Hon Kevin Barron, MP, House of Commons, London, SW1A 0AA *Tel:* 020 7219 6306/4432 *Fax:* 020 7219 5952. *Constituency:* 9 Lordens Hill, Dinnington, Sheffield, S25 2QE *Tel:* 01909 568611 *Fax:* 01909 569974 *E-mail:* barronk@parliament.uk.

BATTLE, JOHN   Leeds West   *Lab majority 14,935*

John Dominic Battle. Born 26 April 1951; Son of John Battle, electrical engineer, and late Audrey Battle; Educated St Michael's College; Upholland College; Leeds University (BA English 1976); Married Mary Meenan 1977 (1 son 2 daughters). Research assistant 1979–83; National co-ordinator, Church Action on Poverty 1983–87. Councillor, Leeds City Council 1980–87. **House of Commons:** Contested Leeds North West 1983 general election. Member for Leeds West since June 1987; Opposition Spokesperson for the Environment (Shadow Minister of Housing) 1992–94; Labour Whip 1990; Shadow Minister for Housing 1993–94, Science and Technology 1994–95, Energy 1995–97; Minister of State: Department of Trade and Industry 1997–99, Foreign and Commonwealth Office 1999–2001; *Select Committees:* Member, Environment 1991–92; Member, International Development 2001–. *Special Interests:* Poverty and Wealth at Home and Abroad, Housing, Economic Policy, International Development, Science, Engineering. Joint Chair, British Trade International Board 1999–2001; *Publications: Tom McGuire*, 1992; PC 2002; *Recreations:* Folk music, poetry. Rt Hon John Battle, MP, House of Commons, London, SW1A 0AA *Tel:* 020 7219 4201. *Constituency:* 2a Conference Place, Leeds, West Yorkshire, LS12 3DZ *Tel:* 0113–231 0258 *Fax:* 0113–279 5850 *E-mail:* johnbattle@leedswest.freeserve.co.uk.

BAYLEY, HUGH   City of York   *Lab majority 13,779*

Hugh Bayley. Born 9 January 1952; Son of Michael Bayley, architect, and Pauline Bayley; Educated Haileybury; Bristol University (BSc politics 1974); York University (BPhil Southern African studies 1976); Married Fenella Jeffers 1984 (1 son 1 daughter). District officer, then National officer NALGO 1975–82; General secretary, International Broadcasting Trust 1982–86; York University: Lecturer in social policy 1986–97, Research fellow in health economics 1987–92; TGWU 1975–82, BECTU 1982–92, RMT 1992–2002, BECTU 2002–. Councillor, Camden Borough Council 1980–86; York Health Authority 1988–90. **House of Commons:** Contested York 1987 general election. Member for York 1992–97, and for City of York since May 1, 1997; PPS to Frank Dobson as Secretary of State for Health 1997–99; Parliamentary Under-Secretary of State, Department of Social Security 1999–2001; *Select Committees:* Member, Health 1992–97; Member, International Development 2001–. *Special Interests:* Health, Economic Policy, Environment, International Development, Defence, Media, Electoral Reform. *Countries of Interest:* Africa. Member, Executive Committee: Inter-Parliamentary Union – UK Branch 1997–99 and 2001–, Commonwealth Parliamentary Association – UK Branch 1997–99, 2001–; Member: UK Delegation to the North Atlantic Assembly 1997–99, UK Delegation to NATO Parliamentary Assembly 2001–, UK Delegation to the Organisation for Security and Co-operation in Europe's Parliamentary Assembly 2001–; *Publications: The Nation's Health*, 1995. Hugh Bayley Esq, MP, House of Commons, London, SW1A 0AA *Tel:* 020 7219 6824 *Fax:* 020 7219 0346. *Constituency:* 59 Holgate Road, York, YO2 4AA *Tel:* 01904 623713 *Fax:* 01904 623260 *E-mail:* dellaganal@parliament.uk.

BEARD, NIGEL   Bexleyheath and Crayford   *Lab majority 1,472*

(Christopher) Nigel Beard. Born 10 October 1936; Son of late Albert Leonard Beard, and late Irene Beard, née Bowes; Educated Castleford Grammar School; University College, London (BSc physics 1958); Married Jennifer Cotton 1969 (1 son 1 daughter). Central Policy Staff, MoD 1961–73; Chief planner, GLC 1973–74; Head, London Docklands Development Organisation 1974–79; Manager, innovation and new business development, ICI 1979–93; Group research and development manager, Zeneca 1993–97; Member, GMB. Member, SW Thames Regional Health Authority 1978–86; and Member Royal Marsden Hospital Board 1980–88. **House of Commons:** Contested Woking 1979, Portsmouth North 1983, Erith and Crayford 1992 general elections. Member for Bexleyheath and Crayford since May 1, 1997; *Select Committees:* Member, Science and Technology 1997–2000; Member: Unopposed Bills (Panel) 1998–, Treasury 2000–, Treasury Sub-Committee 2000–,

Chairmen's Panel 2002–. *Special Interests:* Defence, Foreign Affairs, Economy (Industrial Renewal), Technology, Inner Cities. *Countries of Interest:* France. Member: Labour Party Southern Region Executive 1981–95, Labour Party National Constitutional Committee 1994–98, Fabian Society. Board Member, Institute of Cancer Research 1986–88; Comprehensive School Governor 1974–1991; Member, Ecclesiastical Committee 1997–; *Publications: Use of Linear Programming in Planning and Analysis*, 1971; FRSA; *Clubs:* Athenaeum; *Recreations:* Reading, walking, classical music, modern art. Nigel Beard Esq, MP, House of Commons, London, SW1A 0AA *Tel:* 020 7219 5061 *Fax:* 020 7219 2708. *Constituency:* 50 Peareswood Road, Slade Green, Erith, Kent, DA8 2HP *Tel:* 01322 332261 *Fax:* 01322 332279 *E-mail:* beardn@parliament.uk.

BECKETT, MARGARET   Derby South   *Lab majority 13,855*

Margaret Mary Beckett. Born 15 January 1943; Daughter of late Cyril Jackson, carpenter, and Winifred Jackson, teacher; Educated Notre Dame High School, Manchester and Norwich; Manchester College of Science and Technology; John Dalton Polytechnic; Married Lionel Arthur Beckett 1979 (2 stepsons). Student apprentice in metallurgy, AEI Manchester 1961–66; Experimental officer, Department of Metallurgy, Manchester University 1966–70; Industrial policy researcher, Labour Party 1970–74; Principal researcher, Granada Television 1979–83; Political adviser, Ministry of Overseas Development 1974; Member: T&GWU 1964–, NUJ, BECTU. **House of Commons:** Contested Lincoln February 1974 general election. Member for Lincoln October 1974–79, and for Derby South since June 1983; Assistant Government Whip 1975–76; PPS to Judith Hart as Minister of Overseas Development 1974–75; Parliamentary Under-Secretary of State, Department of Education and Science 1976–79; Shadow Minister, Social Security 1984–89; Shadow Chief Secretary to the Treasury 1989–92; Shadow Leader, House of Commons and Campaign Co-ordinator 1992–94; Deputy Leader, Labour Party and Opposition 1992–94; Leader of Opposition May-July 1994; Shadow Secretary of State for Health 1994–95; Shadow President of the Board of Trade 1995–97; President of the Board of Trade and Secretary of State for Trade and Industry 1997–98; President of the Council and Leader of the House of Commons 1998–2001; Secretary of State for Environment, Food and Rural Affairs 2001–; *Select Committees:* Chair, Modernisation of the House of Commons 1998–2001. *Special Interests:* Industry. Secretary, Traders Council and Labour Party 1968–70; Member: Labour Party National Executive Committee 1980–81, 1985–86, 1988–97, Fabian Society, Tribune Group, Socialist Education Committee, Labour Women's Action Committee, Derby Co-op Party, Socialist Environment and Resources Association. Member: CND, Amnesty International, Anti-Apartheid Movement; *Publications: The Need For Consumer Protection*, 1972; *The National Enterprise Board*; *The Nationalisation of Shipbuilding, Ship Repair and Marine Engineering*; *Relevant sections of Labour's Programme*, 1972/73; *Renewing the NHS*, 1995; *Vision for Growth – A New Industrial Strategy for Britain*, 1996; PC 1993; *Recreations:* Cooking, reading, caravanning. Rt Hon Margaret Beckett, MP, House of Commons, London, SW1A 0AA *Tel:* 020 7219 3584 *Fax:* 020 7219 4780 *E-mail:* beckettm@parliament.uk.

BEGG, ANNE   Aberdeen South   *Lab majority 4,388*

Anne Begg. Born 6 December 1955; Daughter of David Begg, MBE, retired orthotist, and Margaret Catherine Begg, retired nurse; Educated Brechin High School; Aberdeen University (MA history and politics 1977); Aberdeen College of Education (Secondary Teaching Certificate 1978); Single. English and history teacher, Webster's High School, Kirriemuir 1978–88; English teacher, Arbroath Academy 1988–97, Member: Educational Institute of Scotland 1978–, EIS National Council 1990–95. **House of Commons:** Member for Aberdeen South since May 1, 1997; *Select Committees:* Member, Scottish Affairs 1997–2001; Member: Work and Pensions 2001–, Chairmen's Panel 2002–. *Special Interests:* Disability, Broadcasting, Welfare Reform, Social Inclusion, Genetics. Member, Labour Party National Executive Committee 1998–99; PLP Member, Labour Party Policy Forum. Patron: Scottish Motor Neuron Society, Angus Special Playscheme, National Federation of Shopmobility, Access to Training and Employment; Elected Member, General Teaching Council for Scotland 1994–97; Disabled Scot of the Year 1988; *Recreations:* Reading, cinema, theatre, public speaking. Anne Begg, MP, House of Commons, London, SW1A 0AA *Tel:* 020 7219 2140 *Fax:* 020 7219 1264. *Constituency:* 166 Market Street, Aberdeen, AB11 5PP *Tel:* 01224 252704 *Fax:* 01224 252705 *E-mail:* begga@parliament.uk.

BEGGS, ROY   East Antrim   *UUP majority 128*

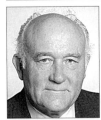

Roy (John Robert) Beggs. Born 20 February 1936; Son of John Beggs; Educated Ballyclare High School; Stranmillis Training College (CertEd 1956); Married Wilma Lorimer 1959 (2 sons 2 daughters). Assistant teacher, science department 1957–78; Vice-principal, Larne High School 1978–83; Member Ulster Farmers Union. Councillor, Larne Borough Council 1973–; Mayor of Larne 1978–83. **House of Commons:** Member for East Antrim since June 1983; Spokesperson for: Education, Trade and Industry 1983–97, Education and Employment, for Community Relations and Culture, Media and Sport 1997–2000, Education and Employment 2000–01, Education and Skills 2000–, Cabinet Office 2001–02; UUP Chief Whip 2000–; Member, Northern Ireland Assembly 1982–86; Chair, Economic Development Committee 1982–84; Shadow Leader of the House 2002–; *Select Committees:* Member, Northern Ireland Affairs 1997–. *Special Interests:* Education, Employment, National Heritage, Agriculture. *Countries of Interest:* USA, Brazil, China, Taiwan, Norway, Sweden, Denmark, France. Member, North Eastern Education and Library Board 1973–, Vice-chair 1981–84, Chair 1984–85; President, Northern Ireland Association of Education and Library Boards 1984–85; Member, House of Commons Public Accounts Commission 1983–; *Recreations:* Fishing. Roy Beggs Esq, MP, House of Commons, London, SW1A 0AA *Tel:* 020 7219 6305 *Fax:* 020 7219 2347. *Constituency:* 41 Station Road, Larne, Co Antrim, BT40 3AA *Tel:* 028 2827 3258 *Fax:* 028 2827 3007.

BEITH, ALAN   Berwick-upon-Tweed   *LD majority 8,458*

Alan James Beith. Born 20 April 1943; Son of late James Beith, foreman packer, and Joan Beith; Educated King's School, Macclesfield; Nuffield College, Oxford (BA philosophy, politics and economics 1964); Balliol College, Oxford (BLitt, MA 1964); Married Barbara Jean Ward 1965 (died 1998) (1 son deceased 1 daughter); married Baroness Maddock 2001. Politics lecturer, Newcastle University 1966–73; Association of University Teachers. Councillor: Hexham RDC 1969–74, Tynedale DC 1974–75. **House of Commons:** Contested Berwick-upon-Tweed 1970 general election. Member for Berwick-upon-Tweed since 1973 by-election; Liberal Spokesperson for Foreign Affairs 1985–87; Alliance Spokesperson on Foreign Affairs 1987; Liberal Treasury Spokesperson 1987; SLD Treasury Spokesperson 1988–89; Liberal Democrat: Treasury Spokesperson 1989–94, Home Affairs Spokesperson 1994–95, Spokesperson for: Police, Prison and Security Matters 1995–97, Home and Legal Affairs (Home Affairs) 1997–99, Cabinet Office 2001–02; Chief Whip, Liberal Party 1976–87; *Select Committees:* Member: House of Commons Commission 1979–97, Treasury and Civil Service 1987–94, Procedure 2000–01; Chair, Lord Chancellor's Department 2003–; Member, Liaison 2003–. *Special Interests:* Parliamentary and Constitutional Affairs, Architectural and Artistic Heritage. *Countries of Interest:* Canada, Scandinavia, Zimbabwe. Deputy Leader: Liberal Party 1985–88, Liberal Democrat 1992–2003. Member, Intelligence and Security Committee 1994–; Deputy Chair: Speaker's Committee on the Electoral Commission 2001–, Review Committee of Privy Counsellors of the Anti-terrorism, Crime and Security Act 2002–; Representative, Council of Europe Assembly 1976–84; Member, Western European Union Assembly 1976–84; Trustee, Historic Chapels Trust, 1995–: Chair 2002–; *Publications:* Co-author *Case for Liberal Party and Alliance*, 1983; *Faith and Politics*, 1987; PC 1992; Hon. DCL, Newcastle University 1998; *Clubs:* National Liberal; *Recreations:* Music, walking, boating. Rt Hon Alan Beith, MP, House of Commons, London, SW1A 0AA *Tel:* 020 7219 3540 *Fax:* 020 7219 5890. *Constituency:* 54 Bondgate Within, Alnwick, Northumberland, NE66 1JD *Tel:* 01665 602901 *Fax:* 01665 605700 *E-mail:* cheeseman@parliament.uk.

DodOnline
An Electronic Directory without rival . . .

MPs' biographies and photographs available with daily updates *via* the internet

For a *free* trial, call Yasmin Mirza, Aby Farsoun or Michael Mand on 020 7630 7643

BELL, STUART Middlesbrough · *Lab majority 16,330*

Stuart Bell. Born 16 May 1938; Son of late Ernest Bell, pitman and late Margaret Rose Bell; Educated Hookergate Grammar School; Council of Legal Education, Gray's Inn 1970; Married Margaret Bruce 1960 (1 son 1 daughter); married Margaret Allan 1980 (1 son). Barrister, called to the Bar, Gray's Inn 1970; Previously: colliery clerk, newspaper reporter, typist novelist; Conseil Juridique and International Lawyer Paris 1970–77; Member, General Municipal Boilermakers and Allied Trades Union. Councillor, Newcastle City Council 1980–83, Member: Finance, Health and Environment, Arts and Education Committee, Association of Metropolitan Authorities, Education Committee, Council of Local Education Authorities, Newcastle Area Health Authority (teaching). **House of Commons:** Contested Hexham 1979 general election. Member for Middlesbrough since June 1983; Opposition Frontbench Spokesperson for: Northern Ireland 1984–87, Trade and Industry 1992–97; PPS to Roy Hattersley as Deputy Leader of Opposition 1983–84; Second Church Estates Commissioner 1997–; *Select Committees:* Member, Liaison 2000–01; Chair, Finance and Services 2000–; Member, Liaison 2002–. *Special Interests:* Economic Policy, European Union, Middle East. *Countries of Interest:* Europe, USA, France. Member: Fabian Society, Society of Labour Lawyers. Member, House of Commons Commission 2000–; Founder member, British Irish Inter-Parliamentary Body 1990; Executive Member, British Group, Inter-Parliamentary Union 1992–95, Vice-Chair 1992–95; Vice-Chair, Interparliamentary Union; *Publications: Paris 69* 1973; *Days That Used to Be* 1975; *When Salem Came to the Boro* 1988; *Fabian Tract: How to Abolish the Lords* 1982; *Legal Tract: United States Customs Valuation* 1982; *The Children Act 1989 (annotated)* 1989; *Raising the Standard: The Case for First Past the Post* 1998; *Where Jenkins Went Wrong: A Further Case for First Past the Post* 1999; *Tony Really Loves Me* 2000; *Pathway to the Euro* 2002; *Binkie's Revolution* 2002; *The Honoured Society* 2003; Freeman, City of London; *Clubs:* Beefsteak, Pratts; *Recreations:* Writing short stories, novels and feature articles. Stuart Bell Esq, MP, House of Commons, London, SW1A 0AA *Tel:* 020 7219 6634 *Fax:* 020 7219 4873 *Tel (Constituency):* 01642 851252 *Fax (Constituency):* 01642 850170.

BELLINGHAM, HENRY North West Norfolk · *Con majority 3,485*

Henry Campbell Bellingham. Born 29 March 1955; Educated Eton College; Magdalene College, Cambridge (LLB 1977); Married Emma Whiteley 1993. Barrister, Middle Temple 1978–84. **House of Commons:** Member for Norfolk North West 1983–97. Contested Norfolk North West 1997 general election. Member for North West Norfolk since June 7, 2001; PPS to Malcolm Rifkind MP 1991–97; Shadow Minister for Trade and Industry 2002–; *Select Committees:* Member, Northern Ireland Affairs 2001–02; Member, Trade and Industry 2002–. *Special Interests:* Small Businesses, Agriculture, Defence, Northern Ireland, Eastern Europe, Tourism. Chairman Conservative Council on Eastern Europe 1989–93. President British Resorts Association 1993–97; *Recreations:* Country sports, golf, cricket. Henry Bellingham Esq, MP, House of Commons, London, SW1A 0AA *Tel:* 020 7219 8484 *Fax:* 020 7219 2844. *Constituency:* Greenland Fishery, Bridge Street, King's Lynn, Norfolk, PE31 6BZ *Tel:* 01553 773 023 *Fax:* 01485 600 292 *E-mail:* henrybellingham@hemscott.net.

BENN, HILARY Leeds Central · *Lab majority 14,381*

Hilary James Wedgwood Benn. Born 26 November 1953; Son of Tony Benn and late Caroline Middleton De Camp; Educated Holland Park Comprehensive School; Sussex University (BA Russian and East European studies 1974); Married Rosalind Retey 1973 (died 1979); married Sally Christina Clark 1982 (3 sons, 1 daughter). Research officer and latterly head of policy and communications, MSF 1975–97; Special Adviser to David Blunkett, as Secretary of State for Education and Employment 1997–99; Member: AMICUS, GMB; Trustee, Unions 21. London Borough of Ealing: Councillor 1979–99, Deputy Leader 1986–90, Chair, Education Committee 1986–90. **House of Commons:** Contested Ealing North 1983 and 1987 general elections.

Member for Leeds Central since June 10, 1999 by-election; Parliamentary Under-Secretary of State: Department for International Development 2001–02, for Community and Custodial Provision, Home Office 2002–03, Minister of State, Department for International Development 2003–; *Select Committees:* Member: Environment, Transport and Regional Affairs 1999–2001, Environment Sub-Committee 1999–2001. *Special Interests:* Home Affairs, International Development, Education, Employment, Trade Unions, Environment, Urban Policy. Member, Association of Metropolitan Authorities Education Committee 1986–90; Chair, Association of London Authorities Education Committee 1989–90; *Publications:* Contributor: *Beyond 2002: Long-term policies for Labour*, Profile Books 1999, *The Forces of Conservatism*, IPPR 1999; *Recreations:* Watching sport, gardening. Hilary Benn Esq, MP, House of Commons, London, SW1A 0AA *Tel:* 020 7219 5770 *Fax:* 020 7219 2639. *Constituency:* 2 Blenheim Terrace, Leeds, LS2 9JG *Tel:* 0113–244 1097 *Fax:* 0113–234 1176 *E-mail:* bennh@parliament.uk.

BENNETT, ANDREW   Denton and Reddish   *Lab majority 15,330*

Andrew Francis Bennett. Born 9 March 1939; Educated Birmingham University (BSocSc 1960); Married Gillian Lawley 1961 (2 sons 1 daughter). Geography teacher 1960–74; Member, National Union of Teachers. Councillor, Oldham Borough Council 1964–74. **House of Commons:** Contested Knutsford 1970 general election. Member for Stockport North February 1974–83 and Denton and Reddish since 1983; Opposition Front Bench Spokesman on Education 1983–88; *Select Committees:* Member: Social Security and Sittings of the House of Commons 1991–92, Environment 1992–97; Chairman, Joint and Select Committees on Statutory Instruments 1994–97; Member: Liaison 1994–97, Standing Orders Committee 1994–96; Chairman: Environment 1995–97, Environment Sub-Committee 1997–2001; Member, Transport Sub-Committee 1997–2001; Chairman: Transport, Local Government and the Regions 2001–02, Urban Affairs Sub-Committee 2001–02; Member, Transport Sub-Committee 2001–02; Member: Joint Committee on Statutory Instruments 1974–, Liaison 1997–; Chairman, Office of the Deputy Prime Minister: Housing, Planning and Local Government 2002–; Member, Urban Affairs Sub-Committee 2003–. *Recreations:* Photography, walking, climbing. Andrew Bennett Esq, MP, House of Commons, London, SW1A 0AA *Tel:* 020 7219 4155. *Constituency:* Constituency office, Denton Town Hall, Market Street, Denton, M34 2AP *Tel:* 0161–320 1504 *Fax:* 0161–320 1503 *E-mail:* bennett.andrew@pop3.poptel.org.uk.

BENTON, JOE   Bootle   *Lab majority 19,043*

Joseph Edward Benton. Born 28 September 1933; Son of late Thomas and Agnes Benton; Educated St Monica's Primary and Secondary School; Bootle Technical College; Married Doris Wynne 1959 (4 daughters). Joined RAF 1955, National Service; Apprentice fitter and turner 1949; Formerly with Pacific Steam Navigation Company as personnel manager; Girobank 1982–90; Member, RMT Parliamentary Campaigning Group 2002–. Sefton Borough Council: Councillor 1970–90, Leader, Labour Group 1985–90, Education spokesman 1977–86; JP, Bootle bench 1969. **House of Commons:** Member for Bootle since by-election November 8, 1990; Opposition Whip 1994–97; *Select Committees:* Member: Energy 1991–92, Speaker's Panel of Chairmen 1992–94, Education and Employment 1997–99, Education Sub-Committee 1997–99, Parliamentary Privilege (Joint Committee) 1997–2000, Chairmen's Panel 1998; Member, Chairmen's Panel 1998–. *Special Interests:* Education, Housing, Local and Regional Government, Health. Chairman of Governors, Hugh Baird College of Technology 1972–92; Working knowledge of Spanish; Member, Institute of Linguists; Affiliate Member, Institute of Personnel Management; *Recreations:* Reading, listening to classical music, squash, swimming. Joseph Benton Esq, JP, MP, House of Commons, London, SW1A 0AA *Tel:* 020 7219 6973. *Constituency:* 23A Oxford Road, Bootle, Liverpool, L20 9HJ *Tel:* 0151–933 8432 *Fax:* 0151–933 4746.

Visit the Vacher Dod Website . . .
www.DodOnline.co.uk

BERCOW, JOHN   Buckingham   *Con majority 13,325*

John Simon Bercow. Born 19 January 1963; Son of Brenda, née Bailey, and late Charles Bercow; Educated Finchley Manorhill School; Essex University (BA government 1985); Married. Credit analyst, Hambros Bank 1987–88; Public affairs consultant, Rowland Sallingbury Casey, Public Affairs Arm of Saatchi & Saatchi Group 1988–95; Board director, Rowland Consultancy 1994–95; Special adviser: to Jonathan Aitken as Chief Secretary to the Treasury 1995, to Virginia Bottomley as Secretary of State for National Heritage 1995–96. Lambeth Borough Council: Councillor, 1986–90, Deputy Leader, Conservative Opposition 1987–89. **House of Commons:** Contested Motherwell South 1987 and Bristol South 1992 general elections. Member for Buckingham since May 1, 1997; Opposition Spokesman for: Education and Employment 1999–2000, Work and Pensions 2002; Shadow Chief Secretary to the Treasury 2001–02; *Select Committees:* Member: Welsh Affairs 1997–98, Trade and Industry 1998–99; Member: Office of the Deputy Prime Minister: Housing, Planning and Local Government 2002–, Urban Affairs Sub-Committee 2003–. *Special Interests:* Education, Economic Policy, Small Businesses, Britain: EU relations. *Countries of Interest:* Israel, USA, Far East. Chair, University of Essex Conservative Association 1984–85; National Chair, Federation of Conservative Students 1986–87; Vice-Chair, Conservative Collegiate Forum 1987. Co-Director, Advanced Speaking and Campaigning Course; *Publications: Turning Scotland Around*, 1987; *Faster Moves Forward for Scotland*, 1987; *Recreations:* Tennis, squash, reading, swimming, music. John Bercow Esq, MP, House of Commons, London, SW1A 0AA *Tel:* 020 7219 3462. *Constituency:* Buckingham Constituency Conservative Association, Buckingham Road, Winslow, Buckingham, MK18 3DY *Tel:* 01296 714240 *Fax:* 01296 714273.

BERESFORD, PAUL   Mole Valley   *Con majority 10,153*

(Alexander) Paul Beresford. Born 6 April 1946; Son of Raymond and Joan Beresford; Educated Waimea College, Richmond, Nelson, New Zealand; Otago University, Dunedin, New Zealand; Married Julie Haynes (3 sons 1 daughter). Dental surgeon. Councillor, Wandsworth Borough Council 1978–94, Leader 1983–92. **House of Commons:** Member for Croydon Central 1992–97, and for Mole Valley since May 1, 1997; Parliamentary Under-Secretary of State, Department of the Environment 1994–97; *Select Committees:* Member: Education 1992–94, Procedure 1997–2001, Environment, Transport and Regional Affairs 2000–01, Environment Sub-Committee 2001, Transport Sub-Committee 2001, Transport, Local Government and the Regions 2001–02, Urban Affairs Sub-Committee 2001–02; Member: Office of the Deputy Prime Minister: Housing, Planning and Local Government 2002–, Urban Affairs Sub-Committee 2003–. *Special Interests:* Inner Cities, Housing, Education. *Countries of Interest:* Fiji, New Zealand, Samoa, Australia. Knighted 1990; BDS; *Recreations:* DIY, reading. Sir Paul Beresford, MP, House of Commons, London, SW1A 0AA *Tel:* 020 7219 5139. *Constituency:* Mole Valley Conservative Association, 86 South Street, Dorking, Surrey, RH4 2E2 *Tel:* 01306 883 312 *Fax:* 01306 885 194.

BERRY, ROGER   Kingswood   *Lab majority 13,962*

Roger Leslie Berry. Born 4 July 1948; Son of Sydney and Mary Joyce Berry; Educated Dalton County Junior School; Huddersfield New College; Bristol University (BSc economics 1970); Sussex University (DPhil economics 1977); Married Alison Delyth 1996. Temporary lecturer in economics, School of African and Asian Studies, Sussex University 1973–74; Associate fellow, Institute of Development Studies, Sussex University 1973–74; Lecturer in economics: University of Papua New Guinea 1974–78, Bristol University 1978–92; Contested Bristol 1984 European Parliament election; Member, MSF 1988–: chair parliamentary group 1997–98; Member, AUT 1978–. Avon County Council: Councillor 1981–92, Chair, Finance and Administration Committee 1983–86, Deputy Leader 1985–86, Leader, Labour Group 1986–92. **House of Commons:** Contested Weston-Super-Mare 1983 and Kingswood 1987 general elections. Member for Kingswood since April 9, 1992;

Select Committees: Member: Deregulation 1994–95, Trade and Industry 1995–97; Member, Trade and Industry 1997–. *Special Interests:* Economic Policy, Disability, Third World, Local and Regional Government. *Countries of Interest:* Lithuania, Italy, China. Chair South and West Group of Labour MPs 1997–. Trustee: Snowdon Award Scheme; Vice-President, Disabled Drivers' Association; Patron: Artsline, Circomedia; Director, Tribune Publications Ltd; *Publications:* Numerous journal and newspaper articles and pamphlets; Highland Park/Spectator Backbencher of the Year 1994; *Clubs:* Kingswood Labour; *Recreations:* Travel, food, cooking, gardening, reading. Dr Roger Berry, MP, House of Commons, London, SW1A 0AA *Tel:* 020 7219 4106 *Fax:* 020 7219 2205. *Constituency:* PO Box 130, Fishponds, Bristol, BS16 5FB *Tel:* 0117–956 1837 *Fax:* 0117–970 1363 *E-mail:* berryr@parliament.uk.

BEST, HAROLD   Leeds North West   *Lab majority 5,236*

Harold Best. Born 18 December 1937; Son of Fred and Marie Best; Educated Meanwood County School; Technical College; Married Mary Glyn 1960 (2 sons 2 daughters). Apprentice 1953–58; Contracting electrician 1958–66; Full-time trade union official 1966–78; Principal electrical technician Leeds Education Authority –1997; Member, RMT Parliamentary Campaigning Group 2002–. Councillor, West Yorkshire County Council 1981–86; Deputy Chair, West Yorkshire Police Authority 1982–86. **House of Commons:** Member for Leeds North West since May 1, 1997; *Select Committees:* Member, Joint Committee on Statutory Instruments 1999–2002; Member: Accommodation and Works 2001–, Environmental Audit 2001–. *Countries of Interest:* Italy, Portugal. Chair, North West Leeds Constituency Labour Party 1992–95. National Executive Committee Member, National Council for Civil Liberties 1994; Member: Amnesty International, Liberty National Executive Committee; Governor, two Leeds Schools; Chair, Headingley Network Community Group; Founder Member, Campaign Against Racial Discrimination, Leeds 1965; Member, European Standing Committee A 1998. Harold Best Esq, MP, House of Commons, London, SW1A 0AA *Tel:* 020 7219 6979 *Fax:* 020 7219 6979. *Constituency:* 7 Iveson Approach, Leeds, LS16 6LJ *Tel:* 0113–261 0002 *Fax:* 0113–261 0199 *E-mail:* harold.best@geo2.poptel.org.uk.

BETTS, CLIVE   Sheffield Attercliffe   *Lab majority 18,844*

Clive James Charles Betts. Born 13 January 1950; Son of late Harold and late Nellie Betts; Educated King Edward VII School, Sheffield; Pembroke College, Cambridge (BA economics and politics 1971). Economist, Trades Union Congress 1971–73; Local government economist: Derbyshire County Council 1973–74, South Yorkshire County Council 1974–86, Rotherham Borough Council 1986–91; Member, TGWU. Sheffield City Council: Councillor 1976–92, Chairman: Housing Committee 1980–86, Finance Committee 1986–88, Deputy Leader 1986–87, Leader 1987–92. **House of Commons:** Contested Sheffield Hallam October 1974 and Louth 1979 general elections. Member for Sheffield Attercliffe since April 9, 1992; Opposition Whip 1996–97; Assistant Government Whip 1997–98; Government Whip 1998–2001; *Select Committees:* Member: Treasury and Civil Service 1995–96, Treasury 1996–97, Selection 1997–2001, Transport, Local Government and the Regions 2001–02, Urban Affairs Sub-Committee 2001–02; Member: Office of the Deputy Prime Minister: Housing, Planning and Local Government 2002–, Urban Affairs Sub-Committee 2003–. *Special Interests:* Economic Policy, Local and Regional Government, Housing. *Countries of Interest:* Europe. Member, Labour Leader's Campaign Team with responsibility for Environment and Local Government 1995–96; Member, Labour Housing Group. Member, Anti-Apartheid Movement; Past Patron, National Association for Therapeutic Education; Patron: Mosborough Township Youth Project, British Deaf Sports Council; President, Mosborough Citizens' Advice Bureau; Past Vice-President, Energy from Waste Association; Vice-chair, Association of Metropolitan Authorities 1988–91; Chair, AMA Housing Committee 1985–89; Vice-president, LGA; Chair, South Yorkshire Pensions Authority 1989–92; *Recreations:* Supporting Sheffield Wednesday FC, playing squash, cricket, walking, real ale, scuba diving. Clive Betts Esq, MP, House of Commons, London, SW1A 0AA *Tel:* 020 7219 3588 *Fax:* 020 7219 2289. *Constituency:* 2nd Floor, Barkers Pool House, Burgess Street, Sheffield, S1 2HH *Tel:* 0114–273 4444 *Fax:* 0114–273 9666 *E-mail:* bettsc@parliament.uk.

BLACKMAN, ELIZABETH   Erewash   *Lab majority 6,932*

Liz (Elizabeth) Blackman. Born 26 September 1949; Educated Carlisle County High School for Girls; Prince Henry's Grammar School, Otley; Clifton College, Nottingham (BEd 1972); Married Derek Blackman (divorced 1999) (1 son 1 daughter). Head, Upper School, Bramcote Park Comprehensive, Nottingham; Member, GMB. Former Deputy Leader, Broxtowe Borough Council. **House of Commons:** Member for Erewash since May 1, 1997; PPS to Geoff Hoon as Secretary of State for Defence 2000–; *Select Committees:* Member: Treasury 1997–2001, Treasury Sub-Committee 1998–2001. *Special Interests:* Education, Economy, Economic Regeneration and Economic Disenfranchisement, Health, Disability, Defence. *Publications: Parliamentary Portions,* (charity recipe book) 1998; *Recreations:* Family, music, reading. Liz Blackman, MP, House of Commons, London, SW1A 0AA *Tel:* 020 7219 2397 *Fax:* 020 7219 4837. *Constituency:* 23 Barratt Lane, Attenborough, Nottingham, NG9 6AD *Tel:* 0115–922 4380 *Fax:* 0115–943 1860 *E-mail:* lizblackman@email.labour.org.uk.

BLAIR, TONY   Sedgefield   *Lab majority 17,713*

Tony (Anthony Charles Lynton) Blair. Born 6 May 1953; Son of Leo Charles Lynton Blair and late Hazel Elisabeth Blair; Educated Durham Choristers School; Fettes College, Edinburgh; St John's College, Oxford (MA law 1974); Married Cherie Booth 1980 (3 sons 1 daughter). Called to the Bar, Lincoln's Inn 1976; Barrister specialising in trade union and industrial law 1976–83; Sponsored until March 1996 by Transport and General Workers' Union. **House of Commons:** Contested Beaconsfield by-election May 1982. Member for Sedgefield since June, 1983; Opposition Spokesperson for: Treasury and Economic Affairs 1984–87, Trade and Industry 1987–88; Shadow Secretary of State for Energy 1988–89, Employment 1989–92, Shadow Home Secretary 1992–94; Leader, Labour Party 1994–; Leader of the Opposition 1994–97; Prime Minister, First Lord of the Treasury and Minister for the Civil Service May 1997–. Member, Parliamentary Labour Party Parliamentary Committee. Vice-President, Federation of Economic Development Authorities (FEDA); *Publications: New Britain: My Vision of a Young Country,* 1996; PC 1994; Charlemagne Prize 1999; Hon. DCL, Northumbria University 1995. Rt Hon Tony Blair, MP, House of Commons, London, SW1A 0AA *Tel:* 020 7219 5676. *Constituency:* Myrobella, Farfield Terrace, Trindon Colliery, Co Durham *Tel:* 01429 882202.

BLEARS, HAZEL   Salford   *Lab majority 11,012*

Hazel Anne Blears. Born 14 May 1956; Daughter of Arthur and Dorothy Blears; Educated Wardley Grammar School; Eccles VIth Form College; Trent Polytechnic (BA law 1977); Chester College of Law (Law Society part II 1978); Married Michael Halsall 1989. Trainee solicitor, Salford Council 1978–80; Private practice solicitor 1980–81; Solicitor: Rossendale Council 1981–83, Wigan Council 1983–85; Principal solicitor, Manchester City Council 1985–97; Branch Secretary, UNISON 1981–85; Member, TGWU. Councillor, Salford City Council 1984–92. **House of Commons:** Contested Tatton 1987, Bury South 1992 general elections. Member for Salford since May 1, 1997; PPS to Alan Milburn: as Minister of State, Department of Health 1998, as Chief Secretary, HM Treasury January-October 1999; Department of Health 2001–03: Parliamentary Under-Secretary of State for: Health 2001–02, Public Health 2002–03; Minister of State (Crime Reduction, Policing and Community Safety), Home Office 2003–; *Select Committees:* Member, European Legislation 1997–98. *Special Interests:* Employment, Health, Arts, Urban Regeneration. Vice-Chair North West Regional Group of Labour MPs 1997–98, Chair 1998–99; Member: North West Executive 1997–99, National Policy Forum 1997–2001, Leadership Campaign Team 1997–98; Labour Party Development Co-ordinator and Deputy to Ian McCartney 1998–2001; Leader Parliamentary Campaign Team 2003–. Chair Salford Community Health Council 1993–97; Trustee: Working Class Movement Library, Member Cooperative Action; *Publications: Making Healthcare Mutual,* Mutuo 2002; *Communities in Control,* Fabian Society 2003; *Recreations:* Dance, motorcycling. Hazel Anne Blears, MP, House of Commons, London, SW1A 0AA *Tel:* 020 7219 6595 *Fax:* 020 7219 0949. *Constituency:* Jubilee House, 51 The Crescent, Salford, Greater Manchester, M51 4WX *Tel:* 0161–925 0705 *Fax:* 0161–743 9173 *E-mail:* blearsh@parliament.uk.

BLIZZARD, BOB   Waveney
Lab majority 8,553

Bob (Robert John) Blizzard. Born 31 May 1950; Son of late Arthur Blizzard, signwriter, and late Joan Blizzard; Educated Culford School, Bury St Edmunds; Birmingham University (BA 1971); Married Lyn Chance 1978 (1 son 1 daughter). Teacher: Gravesend Secondary School 1973–75, Head of English, Crayford Secondary School, 1976–86, Head of English, Gorleston Secondary School, 1986–97; Member: NUT, GMB. Waveney District Council: Councillor 1987–97, Leader 1991–97; Vice-Chair, SCEALA 1995–97. **House of Commons:** Member for Waveney since May 1, 1997; PPS to: Baroness Hayman as Minister of State, Ministry of Agriculture, Fisheries and Food 1999–2001, Nick Brown as Minister of State, Department for Work and Pensions 2001–03; *Select Committees:* Member, Environmental Audit 1997–2000. *Special Interests:* Employment, Health, Education, Transport, Energy. *Clubs:* Royal Norfolk and Suffolk Yacht Club; Ronnie Scott's Jazz Club; 606 Jazz Club; *Recreations:* Walking, skiing, listening to jazz, watching cricket and rugby. Bob Blizzard Esq, MP, House of Commons, London, SW1A 0AA *Tel:* 020 7219 3880 *Fax:* 020 7219 3980. *Constituency:* 27 Milton Road East, Lowestoft, Suffolk, NR32 1NT *Tel:* 01502 514913 *Fax:* 01502 580694 *E-mail:* blizzardb@parliament.uk.

BLUNKETT, DAVID   Sheffield Brightside
Lab majority 17,049

David Blunkett. Born 6 June 1947; Son of late Arthur and Doris Blunkett; Educated Sheffield School for the Blind; Royal Normal College for the Blind; Shrewsbury Technical College; Sheffield Richmond College of Further Education (day release and evening courses); Sheffield University (BA political theory and institutions 1972); Huddersfield College of Education (PGCE 1973); Married Ruth Gwynneth Mitchell 1970 (3 sons) (divorced 1990). Office work, East Midlands Gas Board 1967–69; Tutor in industrial relations and politics, Barnsley College of Technology 1973–81; Shop steward GMB EMGB 1967–69; member, NATFHE 1973–87; member, UNISON 1973–. Councillor, Sheffield City Council 1970–1988, Chair, Social Services Committee 1976–80, Seconded as Leader 1980–87; Councillor, South Yorkshire County Council 1973–77; Chair, Race Relations Forum. **House of Commons:** Contested Sheffield Hallam February 1974 general election. Member for Sheffield Brightside since June 1987; Opposition Spokesperson for Environment (Local Government) 1988–92; Shadow Secretary of State for: Health 1992–94, Education 1994–95, Education and Employment 1995–97; Secretary of State for Education and Employment 1997–2001; Home Secretary 2001–; *Special Interests:* Local and Regional Government, Education, Economic and Democratic Planning. *Countries of Interest:* France, USA. Member, Labour Party National Executive Committee 1983–98; Labour Party: Vice-Chair 1992–93, Chair 1993–94. *Publications: Building from the Bottom*, 1983; *Democracy in Crisis – the Town Halls Respond*, 1987; *On a Clear Day* – (autobiography), 1995; updated 2002; *Politics and Progress*, 2001; PC 1997; *Recreations:* Walking, sailing, music, poetry. Rt Hon David Blunkett, MP, House of Commons, London, SW1A 0AA *Tel:* 020 7219 4043 *Fax:* 020 7219 5903. *Constituency:* 4th Floor, Palatine Chambers, Pinstone Street, Sheffield, S1 2HN *Tel:* 0114–273 5987 *Fax:* 0114–278 0384.

BLUNT, CRISPIN   Reigate
Con majority 8,025

Crispin Jeremy Rupert Blunt. Born 15 July 1960; Son of Major-General Peter Blunt and Adrienne Blunt; Educated Wellington College; Royal Military Academy, Sandhurst; University College, Durham University (BA politics 1984); Cranfield Institute of Technology (MBA 1991); Married Victoria Jenkins 1990 (1 son 1 daughter). Army Officer 1979–90; Regimental duty 13th/18th Royal Hussars (QMO) in England, Germany and Cyprus; District agent, Forum of Private Business 1991–92; Political consultant, Politics International 1993; Special Adviser to Malcolm Rifkind: as Secretary of State for Defence 1993–95, as Foreign Secretary 1995–97. **House of Commons:** Contested West Bromwich East 1992 general election. Member for Reigate since May 1, 1997; Opposition Spokesperson for Northern Ireland 2001–02; Shadow Minister for Trade and Industry 2002–03; *Select Committees:* Member: Defence 1997–2000, Environment, Transport and Regional Affairs 2000–01, Environment Sub-Committee 2000–01. *Special Interests:* Defence, Foreign Affairs, Environment, Energy. *Clubs:* Redhill Constitutional, Royal Automobile; *Sportsclubs:* Reigate Priory Cricket; *Recreations:* Cricket. Crispin Blunt Esq, MP, House of Commons, London, SW1A 0AA *Tel:* 020 7219 2254. *Constituency:* Reigate Conservative Association, 86a South Street, Dorking, Surrey, RH4 2EW *Tel:* 01306 888228 *Fax:* 01306 889228 *E-mail:* crispinbluntmp@parliament.uk.

BOATENG, PAUL   Brent South   *Lab majority 17,380*

Paul Boateng. Born 14 June 1951; Son of Kwaku Boateng, barrister, and Eleanor Boateng, teacher; Educated Achimota; Accra Academy; Apsley Grammar School, Ghana; Bristol University (LLB 1972); College of Law (solicitor 1975); Married Janet Olivia Alleyne 1980 (2 sons 3 daughters). Solicitor 1975; Barrister-at-law; Member GMB. Member GLC 1981–86: Chair, Police Committee 1981–86, Vice-Chair, Ethnic Minority Committee 1981–86. **House of Commons:** Contested Hertfordshire West 1983 general election. Member for Brent South since June 1987; Opposition Front Bench Spokesman on: Treasury and Economic Affairs 1989–92, Lord Chancellor's Department 1992–97; Parliamentary Under-Secretary of State, Department of Health 1997–98; Home Office: Minister of State (Minister for Criminal Policy) 1998–99, Minister of State and Deputy Home Secretary 1999–2001; Minister for Young People 2000–01; HM Treasury 2001–: Financial Secretary 2001–02, Chief Secretary 2002–; *Select Committees:* Member, Public Accounts 2001–02. *Special Interests:* Home Affairs, Housing, Inner Cities, Overseas Aid and Development, Environment. *Countries of Interest:* Africa, Caribbean, USA, Southern Africa. Member: Labour Party NEC Human Rights sub-committee 1979–83, Labour Party Joint Committee on Crime and Policing 1984–86. Chair: Afro-Caribbean Education Resource Project 1978–84, Westminster Community Relations Council 1979–81; Legal adviser, Scrap Sus Campaign 1977–81; Vice-President, Waltham Forest Community Relations Council 1981–; Home Office Advisory Council on Race Relations 1981–86; World Council of Churches Commission on programme to combat racism 1984–91; Vice-Moderator 1984–91; Police Training Council 1981–85; Executive NCCL 1980–86; Governor, Police Staff College Bramshill 1981–84; Board of English National Opera 1984–97; *Publications:* (contributor) *Reclaiming the Ground*; *Introduction to Sense and Sensibility: The Complete Jane Austen*; PC 1999; *Recreations:* Family, swimming, opera. Rt Hon Paul Boateng, MP, House of Commons, London, SW1A 0AA *Tel:* 020 7219 6816 *Fax:* 020 7219 4970 *E-mail:* boatengp@parliament.uk.

BORROW, DAVID   South Ribble   *Lab majority 3,802*

David Stanley Borrow. Born 2 August 1952; Son of James Borrow, retired training officer, and Nancy Borrow, secretary; Educated Mirfield Grammar School, Mirfield; Lanchester Polytechnic (BA economics 1973); Single. Clerk to Merseyside Valuation Tribunal 1983–97; Member, UNISON; Former Branch Vice-Chair; Member, AEEU. Councillor, Preston Borough Council 1987–98, Leader 1992–94, 1995–97. **House of Commons:** Contested Wyre 1992 general election. Member for South Ribble since May 1, 1997; PPS to Kim Howells as Minister of State, Department for Transport 2003–; *Select Committees:* Member: Agriculture 1999–2001, Radioactive Waste Policy Sub-Committee 2001–02; Member, Environment, Food and Rural Affairs 2001–. *Special Interests:* Regional Development, Local and Regional Government, Aerospace, Small Businesses. *Countries of Interest:* Southern Africa. Member: Fabian Society, Co-operative Party. President, Society of Clerks 1990–92 and 1996–97; Member: European Standing Committee A 1998, European Standing Committee C 1999–; TechIRRV. David Borrow Esq, MP, House of Commons, London, SW1A 0AA *Tel:* 020 7219 4126 *Fax:* 020 7219 4126. *Constituency:* Crescent House, 2–6 Sandy Lane, Leyland, Lancashire, PR25 2EB *Tel:* 01772 454727 *Fax:* 01772 422982 *E-mail:* borrowd@parliament.uk.

Visit the Vacher Dod Website . . .
www.DodOnline.co.uk

BOSWELL, TIMOTHY   Daventry   *Con majority 9,649*

Timothy Eric Boswell. Born 2 December 1942; Son of late Eric Boswell and Joan Boswell; Educated Marlborough College; New College, Oxford (MA classics 1965, Diploma in agricultural economics 1966); Married Helen Delahay, née Rees 1969 (3 daughters). Conservative Research Department 1966–73; Head, Economic Section 1970–73; Farmer 1974–87; Leicestershire, Northamptonshire and Rutland County Branch of NFU, County Chairman 1983; Part-time Special Adviser to Minister of Agriculture 1984–86. **House of Commons:** Contested Rugby February 1974 general election. Member for Daventry since June 1987; Opposition Spokesperson for: the Treasury June–December 1997, Trade and Industry December 1997–99, Education 1999–2001, Work and Pensions (People with Disabilities) 2001; Assistant Government Whip 1990–92; Government Whip 1992; PPS to Peter Lilley as Financial Secretary to Treasury 1989–90; Parliamentary Under-Secretary of State, Department for Education 1992–95; Parliamentary Secretary, Ministry of Agriculture, Fisheries and Food 1995–97; Shadow Minister for Education and Skills (People with Disabilities) 2002–; *Special Interests:* Agriculture, Finance, European Union. *Countries of Interest:* Europe. Daventry Constituency Conservative Association Treasurer 1976–79, Chairman 1979–83. Council of Perry Foundation 1967–90, President 1984–90; Member, Agricultural and Food Research Council 1988–90; *Clubs:* Farmers'; *Recreations:* Shooting. Timothy Boswell Esq, MP, House of Commons, London, SW1A 0AA *Tel:* 020 7219 3520 *Fax:* 020 7219 4919. *Constituency:* Lloyds Bank Chambers, North Street, Daventry, Northamptonshire, NN11 5PN *Tel:* 01327 703192 *Fax:* 01327 310263 *E-mail:* hodgesm@parliament.uk.

BOTTOMLEY, PETER   Worthing West   *Con majority 9,037*

Peter James Bottomley. Born 20 July 1944; Son of Sir James Bottomley, KCMG, HM Diplomatic Service, and Barbara Bottomley, social worker; Educated Comprehensive School, Washington DC; Westminster School, London; Trinity College, Cambridge (BA economics 1966, MA); Married Virginia Garnett (now MP as Virginia Bottomley) 1967 (1 son 2 daughters). Industrial sales, industrial relations, industrial economics; Member, TGWU. **House of Commons:** Contested Greenwich, Woolwich West February and October 1974 general election. Member for Greenwich, Woolwich West by-election 1975–83, for Eltham 1983–97, and for Worthing West since May 1, 1997; PPS: to Cranley Onslow as Minister of State, Foreign and Commonwealth Office 1982–83, to Norman Fowler as Secretary of State for Health and Social Security 1983–84; Parliamentary Under-Secretary of State: at Department of Employment 1984–86, at Department of Transport (Minister for Roads and Traffic) 1986–89, at Northern Ireland Office (Agriculture, Environment) 1989–90; PPS to Peter Brooke as Secretary of State for Northern Ireland September–November 1990; *Select Committees:* Member: Transport 1992–97, Standards and Privileges 1997–2002; Member: Unopposed Bills (Panel) 1997–, Lord Chancellor's Department 2003–. *Countries of Interest:* Southern Africa, El Salvador, USA. President, Conservative Trade Unionists 1978–80. Chairman, Family Forum 1980–82; Chairman, Church of England Children's Society 1982–84; Member, Council of NACRO; RIIA; Trustee, Christian Aid 1978–84; Fellow, Industry and Parliament Trust; Court Member, Drapers' Company; Gold Medal, Institute of the Motor Industry 1988; Fellow, Institute of Personnel Management 1985–; Fellow, Institute of Road Safety Officers; *Sportsclubs:* Former Parliamentary swimming and occasional dinghy sailing champion. Peter Bottomley Esq, MP, House of Commons, London, SW1A 0AA *Tel:* 020 7219 5060 *Fax:* 020 7219 1212 *E-mail:* bottomleyp@parliament.uk.

DodOnline
An Electronic Directory without rival …

MPs' biographies and photographs available with daily updates *via* the internet

For a *free* trial, call Yasmin Mirza, Aby Farsoun or Michael Mand on 020 7630 7643

BOTTOMLEY, VIRGINIA   South West Surrey   *Con majority 861*

Virginia Hilda Brunette Maxwell Bottomley. Born 12 March 1948; Daughter of late W. John Garnett CBE; Educated Putney High School; Essex University (BA sociology); London School of Economics (MSc social work and administration 1975); Married Peter Bottomley (now MP) 1967 (1 son 2 daughters). Behavioural scientist 1971–84; Researcher, Child Poverty Action Group 1971–73; Psychiatric social worker in South London, Social Policy Tutor 1973–74; Magistrate and Chair, Lambeth Juvenile Court 1974–84; Director, Mid Southern Water Company 1987–88; Chair, Not-for-Profit Practice, Odgers, Ray and Berndston (Executive Search); Member, Supervisory Board, Akzo Nobel NV. Magistrate in Inner London Juvenile Courts 1975–84; Chairman, Lambeth Juvenile Court 1980–84. **House of Commons:** Contested Isle of Wight in 1983 general election. Member for South West Surrey since May 3, 1984 by-election; PPS: to Chris Patten, as Minister of State, Department of Education and Science 1985–86, as Minister of State (Minister for Overseas Development), FCO 1986–87, to Sir Geoffrey Howe as Secretary of State for Foreign and Commonwealth Affairs 1987–88; Parliamentary Under-Secretary of State, Department of Environment 1988–89; Minister of State, Department of Health 1989–92; Secretary of State for: Health 1992–95, National Heritage 1995–97; *Select Committees:* Member: Foreign Affairs 1997–99, Entry Clearance Sub-Committee 1997–98. *Special Interests:* Health, Heritage, Home Office. Governor: London School of Economics 1985–, London Institute; Governor, Ditchley Foundation 1991–; Patron, Cruse Bereavement Care; President: Farnham Castle (Centre for International Briefing), Abbeyfield Society; Vice-President, Carers; Council Member, Prince of Wales International Business Leaders Forum; Lay Canon, Guildford Cathedral; Member, Medical Research Council 1987–88; Chair, Millennium Commission 1995–97; Government Co-Chair, Women's National Commission 1991–92; Vice-Chair, British Council Board 1997–2001; Fellow, Industry and Parliament Trust; *Publications:* Various articles on criminal justice, poverty and children; PC 1992; Honorary LLD (University of Portsmouth); Freeman, City of London 1988; *Recreations:* Grandchildren. Rt Hon Virginia Bottomley, MP, House of Commons, London, SW1A 0AA *Tel:* 020 7219 6499 *Fax:* 020 7219 6279. *Constituency:* 2 Royal Parade, Tilford Road, Hindhead, Surrey, GU26 6TD *Tel:* 01428 604526 *Fax:* 01428 667498 *E-mail:* bottomleyv@parliament.uk.

BRADLEY, KEITH   Manchester Withington   *Lab majority 11,524*

Keith John Charles Bradley. Born 17 May 1950; Son of late John Bradley and Mrs Beatrice Harris; Educated Bishop Vesey's Grammar School; Aston University (DipAcct 1970); Manchester Polytechnic (BA social science 1976); York University (MPhil social policy 1978); Married Rhona Ann Graham 1987 (2 sons 1 daughter). Charles Impey and Co, chartered accountants 1969–73; Research officer, Manchester City Council Housing Department 1978–81; Secretary, Stockport Community Health Council 1981–87; Member: MSF, UNISON. Councillor, Manchester City Council 1983–88, Chair, Environment and Consumer Services Committee 1984–88; City Council Director: Manchester Ship Canal Co 1984–87, Manchester Airport plc 1984–87. **House of Commons:** Member for Manchester Withington since June 1987; Opposition Spokesperson for: Social Security 1991–96, Transport 1996–97; Deputy Chief Whip 1998–2001; Parliamentary Under-Secretary of State, Department of Social Security 1997–98; Minister of State, Home Office 2001–02; *Select Committees:* Member: Agriculture 1989–92, Accommodation and Works 1998–2001, Finance and Services 1999–2001, Selection 1999–2001. *Special Interests:* Local and Regional Government, Housing, Health, Pensions, Poverty. Member, Co-op Party. PC 2001; *Recreations:* All sports, theatre, cinema. Rt Hon Keith Bradley, MP, House of Commons, London, SW1A 0AA *Tel:* 020 7219 2279 *Fax:* 020 7219 5901. *Constituency:* Investment House, 425 Wilmslow Road, Withington, Manchester, M20 4AF *Tel:* 0161–446 2047 *Fax:* 0161–445 5543 *E-mail:* keithbradleymp@parliament.uk.

Visit the Vacher Dod Website . . .
www.DodOnline.co.uk

BRADLEY, PETER   The Wrekin   *Lab majority 3,587*

Peter Charles Stephen Bradley. Born 12 April 1953; Son of Fred and Trudie Bradley; Educated Abingdon; Sussex University (BA American studies 1975); Married Annie Hart 2001 (twin son and daughter). Research director, Centre for Contemporary Studies 1979–85; Director, Good Relations 1985–93; Managing director, Millbank Consultants Ltd 1993–97; Member, MSF, GMB. Councillor, Westminster City Council 1986–96, Deputy Leader, Labour Group 1990–96. **House of Commons:** Member for The Wrekin since May 1, 1997; PPS to Alun Michael as Minister of State, Department for Environment, Food and Rural Affairs 2001–; *Select Committees:* Member, Public Administration 1997–99. *Special Interests:* Economic Policy, Transport, Education, Health, Housing, Rural Affairs. Chair, Rural Group of Labour MPs 1997–2001. Vice-President, UK Local Authority Forum of World Heritage Sites 1998–; *Publications:* Various research and press articles; *Sportsclubs:* Warwickshire County Cricket Club; *Recreations:* Playing cricket, watching football (especially Aston Villa) and rugby, walking. Peter Bradley Esq, MP, House of Commons, London, SW1A 0AA *Tel:* 020 7219 4112 *Fax:* 020 7219 0536. *Constituency:* Wrekin Labour Party, 19 Tan Bank, Wellington, Telford, TF1 1HJ *Tel:* 01952 240010 *Fax:* 01952 240455 *E-mail:* bradleyp@parliament.uk.

BRADSHAW, BEN   Exeter   *Lab majority 11,759*

Ben (Benjamin) Peter James Bradshaw. Born 30 August 1960; Son of late Canon Peter Bradshaw and late Daphne Bradshaw, teacher; Educated Thorpe St Andrew School, Norwich; Sussex University (BA German 1982); Freiburg University, Germany; Partner. Award-winning BBC reporter and presenter 1986–97; BBC Berlin correspondent during fall of Berlin Wall 1989–91; Reporter for 'World At One' and 'World This Weekend' on BBC Radio 4 1991–97; Member, NUJ. **House of Commons:** Member for Exeter since May 1, 1997; Introduced Pesticides Act (Private Member's Bill) 1998; PPS to John Denham as Minister of State, Department of Health 2000–01; Parliamentary Under-Secretary of State, Foreign and Commonwealth Office 2001–02; Parliamentary Secretary, Privy Council Office 2002–03; Parliamentary Under-Secretary of State, Department for Environment, Food and Rural Affairs 2003–: (Fisheries, Water and Nature Protection) 2003, (Minister for Nature Conservation and Fisheries) 2003–; *Select Committees:* Member: European Legislation 1997–98, European Legislation 1998, European Scrutiny 1998–2001. *Special Interests:* Foreign Affairs, Environment and Transport, Modernisation of Parliament. *Countries of Interest:* Europe – particularly Germany and Italy, USA. Labour Movement for Europe, Member: Labour Campaign for Electoral Reform, SERA, Christian Socialist Movement. *Publications:* Numerous for the BBC on domestic and foreign affairs; Argos Consumer Journalist of the Year 1989; Anglo-German Foundation Journalist of the Year 1990; Sony News Reporter Award 1993; Norfolk County Scholar; *Clubs:* Whipton Labour, Exeter; *Recreations:* Cycling, walking, cooking, music. Benjamin Bradshaw Esq, MP, House of Commons, London, SW1A 0AA *Tel:* 020 7219 6597 *Fax:* 020 7219 0950. *Constituency:* Labour HQ, 26B Clifton Hill, Exeter, Devon, EX1 2DJ *Tel:* 01392 424464 *Fax:* 01392 425630 *E-mail:* bradshawb@parliament.uk.

BRADY, GRAHAM   Altrincham and Sale West   *Con majority 2,941*

Graham Stuart Brady. Born 20 May 1967; Son of John Brady, accountant, and Maureen Brady, née Birch, medical secretary; Educated Altrincham Grammar School; Durham University (BA law 1989); Married Victoria Lowther 1992 (1 son, 1 daughter). Shandwick PLC public relations consultancy 1989–90; Centre for Policy Studies 1990–92; Public affairs director, The Waterfront Partnership public relations and strategic public affairs consultancy 1992–97. **House of Commons:** Member for Altrincham and Sale West since May 1, 1997; Opposition Spokesman for: Employment 2000–01, Schools 2001–; Opposition Whip (Trade and Industry, Cabinet Office) 2000; Parliamentary Private Secretary to Michael Ancram as Conservative Party Chairman 1999–2000; *Select Committees:* Member: Education and Employment 1997–2001, Employment Sub-Committee 1997–2001. *Special Interests:* Education, Health. *Countries of Interest:* Commonwealth,

Far East, British Overseas Territories. Chairman, Durham University Conservative Association 1987–88; National Union Executive Committee 1988; Chairman, Northern Area Conservative Collegiate Forum 1987–89; Vice-Chairman, East Berkshire Conservative Association 1993–95. Vice-Patron Friends of Rosie (research into children's cancer); Vice-President Altrincham Chamber of Trade Commerce and Industry 1997–; *Publications: Towards an Employees' Charter – and Away From Collective Bargaining* (Centre for Policy Studies), 1991; *Recreations:* Family, gardening, reading. Graham Brady Esq, MP, House of Commons, London, SW1A 0AA *Tel:* 020 7219 4604 *Fax:* 020 7219 1649. *Constituency:* Altrincham and Sale West Conservative Association, Thatcher House, Delahays Farm, Green Lane, Timperley, Cheshire, WA15 8QW *Tel:* 0161–904 8828 *Fax:* 0161–904 8868 *E-mail:* crowthers@parliament.uk.

BRAKE, TOM   Carshalton and Wallington   *LD majority 4,547*

Tom (Thomas Anthony) Brake. Born 6 May 1962; Son of Michael and Judy Brake; Educated Lycee International, St Germain-en-Laye, France; Imperial College, London (BSc physics 1983); Married Candida Goulden 1998 (1 daughter 1 son). Principal Consultant (IT), Cap Gemini. Councillor: London Borough of Hackney 1988–90, London Borough of Sutton 1994–98. **House of Commons:** Contested Carshalton and Wallington 1992 general election. Member for Carshalton and Wallington since May 1, 1997; Liberal Democrat Spokesperson for: Environment, Transport in London and Air Transport 1997–99, Environment, Transport, the Regions, Social Justice and London Transport 1999–2001; Transport, Local Government and the Regions 2001–02; Transport 2002–; Liberal Democrat Whip 2000–; *Select Committees:* Member: Environment, Transport and Regional Affairs 1997–2001, Environment Sub-Committee 1997–2001, Transport Sub-Committee 1999–2000, Accommodation and Works 2001–03; Member, Transport 2002–. *Special Interests:* Environment, Transport, Emergency Planning. *Countries of Interest:* France, Portugal, Russia, Australia. Member: Oxfam, Amnesty International, Greenpeace; *Sportsclubs:* Collingwood Athletic Club; *Recreations:* Sport, film, eating. Tom Brake Esq, MP, House of Commons, London, SW1A 0AA *Tel:* 020 7219 0924 *Fax:* 020 7219 6491. *Constituency:* Kennedy House, 5 Nightingale Road, Carshalton, Surrey, SM5 2DN *Tel:* 020 8255 8155 *Fax:* 020 8395 4453 *E-mail:* cwlibs@cix.co.uk.

BRAZIER, JULIAN   Canterbury   *Con majority 2,069*

Julian William Hendy Brazier. Born 24 July 1953; Son of Lieutenant Colonel Peter Hendy Brazier, retired, and Patricia Audrey Helen, née Stubbs; Educated Dragon School; Wellington College, Berks; Brasenose College, Oxford (Scholarship BA mathematics and philosophy 1975, MA); London Business School; Married Katherine Elizabeth Blagden 1984 (3 sons). TA 1972–82, 1989–92; Charter Consolidated Ltd 1975–84, economic research 1975–77, corporate finance 1977–81 and Secretary, executive committee of the Board 1981–84; Management consultant, H B Maynard International 1984–87. **House of Commons:** Contested Berwick-upon-Tweed 1983 general election. Member for Canterbury since June 1987; Opposition Whip 2001–02; PPS to Gillian Shephard as: Minister of State, Treasury 1990–92, Secretary of State for Employment 1992–93; Shadow Minister for: Work and Pensions 2002–03, Home Affairs 2003–; *Select Committees:* Member, Defence 1997–2001. *Special Interests:* Defence, Foreign Affairs Economics, Law and Order, Families, Countryside. *Countries of Interest:* Middle East, South Africa, USA, Australia, New Zealand, Russia. President, Conservative Family Campaign 1995–2001; Vice-chair Conservative Party Listening to Churches Programme 2000–. *Publications:* Co-author *Not Fit to Fight: The Cultural Subversion of the Armed Forces in Britain and America*, Social Affairs Unit 1999; Ten pamphlets on defence, social and economic issues (with Bow Group, Centre for Policy Studies and Conservative 2000); Territorial Decoration 1993; Highland Park/*The Spectator* Backbencher of the Year (jointly) 1996; *Clubs:* Travellers; *Recreations:* Cross-country running, science, philosophy. Julian Brazier Esq, TD, MP, House of Commons, London, SW1A 0AA *Tel:* 020 7219 5178 *Fax:* 020 7219 0643. *Constituency:* 128A John Wilson Business Park, Whitstable, Kent, CT5 3QT *Tel:* 01227 280277 *Fax:* 01227 280435.

BREED, COLIN   South East Cornwall   *LD majority 5,375*

Colin Edward Breed. Born 4 May 1947; Son of late Alfred and late Edith Violet Breed; Educated Torquay Boys Grammar School; Married Janet Courtiour 1968 (1 son 1 daughter). Manager, Midland Bank plc 1964–81; Managing director, Dartington and Co plc 1981–91; Director, Gemini Abrasives Ltd 1991–96. Councillor, Caradon District Council 1982–92; Mayor of Saltash 1989–90, 1995–96. **House of Commons:** Member for South East Cornwall since May 1, 1997; Liberal Democrat Spokesperson for: Competition and Consumer Affairs 1997–99, Competition 1999; Principal Spokesperson for Agriculture, Rural Affairs and Fisheries 1999–; Liberal Democrat Spokesperson for Environment, Food and Rural Affairs 2001–02; Liberal Democrat Spokesperson for Defence 2002–; *Select Committees:* Member: European Legislation 1998, Radioactive Waste Policy Sub-Committee 2001–02; Member: European Scrutiny 1998–, Environment, Food and Rural Affairs 2001–. *Special Interests:* Cornwall, Rural Affairs, Conflict Resolution, Middle East. Member, General Medical Council 1999–; Executive Committee Member, Council for Advancement of Arab-British Understanding; Chair, Princes Trust Volunteers (Devon); ACIB; *Sportsclubs:* St Mellion Golf and Country Club; *Recreations:* Watching sport, golf. Colin Breed Esq, MP, House of Commons, London, SW1A 0AA *Tel:* 020 7219 2588 *Fax:* 020 7219 5905. *Constituency:* Barras Street, Liskeard, Cornwall, PL14 6AD *Tel:* 01579 342150 *Fax:* 01579 347019 *E-mail:* colinbreedmp@aol.com.

BRENNAN, KEVIN   Cardiff West   *Lab majority 11,321*

Kevin Denis Brennan. Born 16 October 1959; Son of Michael John Brennan, retired steelworker and Beryl Marie, née Evans, school cook/cleaner; Educated St Alban's RC Comprehensive, Pontypool; Pembroke College, Oxford (BA philosophy, politics and economics 1982) (President Oxford Union 1982); University College of Wales, Cardiff (PGCE history 1985); Glamorgan University (MSc education management 1992); Married Amy Lynn Wack, poetry editor, 1988 (1 daughter). Cwmbran Community Press 1982–84: News editor, Volunteer organiser; Head of economics and business studies Radyr Comprehensive School 1985–94; Research officer to Rhodri Morgan MP 1995–99; Special adviser to Rhodri Morgan as First Minister National Assembly for Wales 2000–; NUT 1984–94; TGWU 1995–2001. Cardiff City Council: Vice-chair Finance 1991–92, Chair Finance 1993–96, Vice-chair Economic Development 1996–99, Chair Economic Scrutiny 1999–2001. **House of Commons:** Member for Cardiff West since June 7, 2001; *Select Committees:* Member, Public Administration 2001–. *Special Interests:* Economy, Constitutional Affairs. *Countries of Interest:* Ireland, Cyprus, Japan. Member: Fabian Society 1979–, Socialist Health Association, Bevan Foundation; Chair Cardiff West Constituency Labour Party 1998–2000; Executive Member Labour Campaign Electoral Reform. Chair Yes for Wales Cardiff 1997; *Clubs:* Canton Labour; *Recreations:* Rugby, golf, reading, cricket, music. Kevin Brennan Esq, MP, House of Commons, London, SW1A 0AA *Tel:* 020 7219 8156. *Constituency:* c/o Transport House, 1 Cathedral Road, Cardiff, CF11 9SD *Tel:* 029 2022 3207 *Fax:* 029 2023 0422.

BROOKE, ANNETTE   Mid Dorset and Poole North   *LD majority 384*

Annette Lesley Brooke. Born 7 June 1947; Daughter of Ernest Henry Kelly, bookbinder, and Edna Mabel Kelly; Educated Romford Technical College; London School of Ecnomics (BSc Econ 1968); Hughes Hall, Cambridge (Cert Ed 1969); Married Mike Brooke (2 daughters). Open University 1971–1991: Counsellor, Tutor: social sciences, economics; Various college posts: Reading, Aylesbury, Poole, Bournemouth; Head of economics Talbot Heath School Bournemouth 1984–94; Partner Broadstone Minerals; Owner Gemini shop Poole 1994–. Poole Borough Council 1986–2003: Councillor, Former member ALDC Standing Committee, Chair: Planning 1991–96, Education 1996–2000, Environmental Strategy Working Party 1995–97, Deputy leader ruling Liberal Democrat Group 1995–97, 1998–2000, Sheriff 1996–97, Mayor 1997–98, Deputy mayor 1998–99, Group leader 2000–01; Conference representative Mid Dorset and North Poole constituency.

House of Commons: Member for Mid Dorset and Poole North since June 7, 2001; Liberal Democrat Spokesperson for Home Affairs 2001–; Liberal Democrat Whip 2001–; *Select Committees:* Member, Public Administration 2001–. *Special Interests:* Young People, Home Affairs. *Countries of Interest:* Sudan. Beveridge Group. RSPB; Wessex Newfoundland Society; Former member South Wessex Area Environment Agency Advisory Group; Former Board member Dorset Careers; Former Vice-chair Poole Town Centre Management Board; Member European Standing Committee B 2001–02; *Recreations:* Gym, reading, shopping with daughters. Annette Brooke, MP, House of Commons, London, SW1A 0AA *Tel:* 020 7219 8473/8193 *Fax:* 020 7219 1898. *Constituency:* Broadstone Liberal Hall, 14 York Road, Broadstone, Dorset, BH18 8ET *Tel:* 01202 693555 *E-mail:* brookea@parliament.uk.

| BROWN, GORDON   Dunfermline East | Lab majority 15,063 |

Gordon Brown. Born 20 February 1951; Son of late Rev. Dr John Brown; Educated Kirkcaldy High School; Edinburgh University (MA 1972, PhD 1982); Married Sarah Macaulay 2000 (1 daughter deceased). Edinburgh University: Rector 1972–75, Temporary lecturer 1975–76; Lecturer in politics, Glasgow College of Technology 1976–80; Journalist, then editor, Scottish Television current affairs department 1980–83; Member, TGWU. **House of Commons:** Member for Dunfermline East since June, 1983; Opposition Front Bench Spokesman on Trade and Industry 1985–87; Shadow Spokesman for Trade and Industry 1989–92; Shadow Chief Secretary to The Treasury 1987–89; Shadow Chancellor of the Exchequer 1992–97; Chancellor of the Exchequer 1997–; *Special Interests:* Economic Policy, Employment, Health, Social Security, Scotland. Member, Scottish Executive Labour Party 1977–83; Chairman, Labour Party in Scotland 1983–84; Former Member, Labour Party National Executive Committee; Head, General Election Campaign (Strategy) 1999–2001. Joint Hon Treasurer (ex-officio), Commonwealth Parliamentary Association (CPA) UK Branch 1997–99, Joint Hon Secretary 1999–; *Publications:* Co-editor *Values, Visions and Voices: An Anthology of Socialism*; Co-author *John Smith: Life and Soul of the Party*; *Maxton*; *Where There is Greed*; PC 1996; *The Spectator*/Highland Park Parliamentarian of the Year 1997; Channel 4 and *The House* Magazine Speechmaker of the Year 1999; *Recreations:* Tennis, football, reading, writing. Rt Hon Gordon Brown, MP, House of Commons, London, SW1A 0AA *Tel:* 020 7219 6345. *Constituency:* 318–324 High Street, Cowdenbeath, Fife, KY4 9QS *Tel:* 01383 611702 *Fax:* 01383 611703.

| BROWN, NICK   Newcastle upon Tyne East and Wallsend | Lab majority 14,223 |

Nicholas H Brown. Born 13 June 1950; Educated Tunbridge Wells Technical High School; Manchester University (BA 1971). Proctor and Gamble advertising department; Legal adviser for northern region of GMBATU 1978–83. Councillor, Newcastle upon Tyne City Council 1980–83. **House of Commons:** Member for Newcastle upon Tyne East 1983–97, and for Newcastle upon Tyne East and Wallsend since May 1, 1997; Opposition Frontbench Spokesperson for: Legal Affairs 1985–92, Treasury and Economic Affairs 1988–94; Opposition Spokesperson for Health 1994–95; Opposition Deputy Chief Whip 1995–97; Government Chief Whip 1997–98; Deputy to Margaret Beckett as Shadow Leader of the Commons 1992–94; Minister of Agriculture, Fisheries and Food 1998–2001; Minister of State for Work, Department of Work and Pensions 2001–03; *Select Committees:* Member: Broadcasting 1994–95, Selection 1996–97. *Countries of Interest:* Australia, China, Japan, New Zealand, USA. PC 1997; Freeman, Newcastle 2001. Rt Hon Nicholas Brown, MP, House of Commons, London, SW1A 0AA *Tel:* 020 7219 4199. *Constituency:* Thorne House, 77/87 West Road, Newcastle upon Tyne, NE15 6RB *Tel:* 0191–272 0843 *E-mail:* wilkiec@parliament.uk.

Visit the Vacher Dod Website . . .
www.DodOnline.co.uk

BROWN, RUSSELL   Dumfries   *Lab majority 8,834*

Russell Brown. Born 17 September 1951; Son of late Howard Russell Brown and late Muriel Brown; Educated Annan Academy; Married Christine Calvert 1973 (2 daughters). Production supervisor ICI 1974–97; Member, TGWU 1974–: Branch Secretary and Branch Chair 1979–85. Councillor: Dumfries and Galloway Regional Council 1986–96, Annandale and Eskdale District Council 1988–96; Chair Public Protection Committee 1990–94; Councillor Dumfries and Galloway Unitary Council 1995–97; Member Dumfries and Galloway Tourist Board 1996–97. **House of Commons:** Member for Dumfries since May 1, 1997; PPS to Lord Williams of Mostyn as Leader of the House of Lords 2002–03; *Select Committees:* Member: European Legislation 1997–98, European Scrutiny 1998–99, Scottish Affairs 1999–2001; Member: Regulatory Reform 1999–, Joint Committee on Consolidation of Bills Etc 2001–, Standards and Privileges 2001–. *Special Interests:* Employment, Welfare State, Health and Safety Issues, Energy policy. *Countries of Interest:* European Union. Chair, Local Community Education Project 1991–97; *Recreations:* Sport (especially football). Russell Brown Esq, MP, House of Commons, London, SW1A 0AA *Tel:* 020 7219 4429 *Fax:* 020 7219 0922. *Constituency:* 5 Friars Vennel, Dumfries, DG1 2RQ *Tel:* 01387 247902 *Fax:* 01387 247903 *E-mail:* russell@brownmp.new.labour.org.uk.

BROWNE, DES   Kilmarnock and Loudoun   *Lab majority 10,334*

Des (Desmond) Henry Browne. Born 22 March 1952; Son of late Peter Browne, process worker, and of Maureen Browne, catering manageress; Educated Saint Michael's Academy, Kilwinning; Glasgow University (LLB 1975); Married Maura Taylor 1983 (2 sons). Qualified as solicitor 1976; Called to Scottish Bar 1993; Member UNISON. **House of Commons:** Contested Argyll and Bute 1992 general election. Member for Kilmarnock and Loudoun since May 1, 1997; PPS to: Donald Dewar as Secretary of State for Scotland 1998–99, Adam Ingram as Minister of State, Northern Ireland Office 2000; Parliamentary Under-Secretary of State, Northern Ireland Office 2001 03; Minister of State for Work, Department for Work and Pensions 2003–; *Select Committees:* Member: Northern Ireland Affairs 1997–98, Public Administration 1999–2000, Joint Committee on Human Rights 2001. *Special Interests:* Legal Affairs, Human Rights, Disability, Education, Northern Ireland, Constitution, International Affairs. *Countries of Interest:* France, South Africa, Colombia, Rwanda, Burundi. Secretary, Scottish Labour Party Working Party on Prison System 1988–. Council Member, Law Society of Scotland 1988–92; Member, Scottish Council For Civil Liberties 1976–; Chair: Children's Rights Group 1981–86, Scottish Child Law Centre 1988–92; *Publications:* Briefing Paper for MPs on Criminal Justice (Scotland) Bill 1980; Report for Lord MacAulay's Working Party on the Prison System 1990; *Recreations:* Sports, football, tennis, swimming, reading, computing. Des Browne Esq, MP, House of Commons, London, SW1A 0AA *Tel:* 020 7210 6489 *Fax:* 020 7219 2423. *Constituency:* Parliamentary Advice Centre, 32 Grange Street, Kilmarnock, KA1 2DD *Tel:* 01563 520267 *Fax:* 01563 539439 *E-mail:* browned@parliament.uk.

BROWNING, ANGELA   Tiverton and Honiton   *Con majority 6,284*

Angela Browning. Born 4 December 1946; Daughter of late Thomas and of Linda Pearson; Educated Reading College of Technology; Bournemouth College of Technology; Married David Browning 1968 (2 sons). Teacher home economics, Adult Education 1968–74; Auxiliary nurse 1976–77; Self-employed consultant, manufacturing industry 1977–85; Management consultant specialising in training, corporate communications and finance 1985–94; Director, Small Business Bureau 1985–94; Chairman, Women Into Business 1988–92; Member, Department of Employment Advisory Committee for Women's Employment 1989–92. **House of Commons:** Contested Crewe and Nantwich 1987 general election. Member for Tiverton 1992–97, and for Tiverton and Honiton since May 1, 1997; Opposition Spokesperson on Education and Employment (Education and Disability) 1997–98; PPS to Michael Forsyth as Minister of State, Department of

Employment 1993–94; Parliamentary Secretary, Ministry of Agriculture, Fisheries and Food 1994–97; Member, Shadow Cabinet 1999–2001: Shadow Secretary of State for Trade and Industry 1999–2000, Shadow Leader of the House 2000–01; *Select Committees:* Member: Agriculture 1992–93, Modernisation of the House of Commons 2000–01. *Special Interests:* Small Businesses, Education (Special Needs), Mental Health, Learning Disabilities. Vice-chairman Conservative Party 2001–. Member, National Autistic Society, Special Councillor 1993–; National Vice-President, Alzheimers Disease Society 1997–; Co-Chair The Women's National Commission 1995–97; Vice-President Institute of Sales and Marketing Management 1997–; Fellow, Institute of Sales and Marketing Management; *Recreations:* Theatre, supporting family of keen oarsmen, member of Thomas Hardy Society. Mrs Angela Browning, MP, House of Commons, London, SW1A 0AA *Tel:* 020 7219 5067. *Constituency Tel:* 01404 822103 *E-mail:* browningaf@parliament.uk.

BRUCE, MALCOLM   Gordon   *LD majority 7,879*

Malcolm Bruce. Born 17 November 1944; Son of David Bruce, former agricultural merchant and hotelier, retired and Kathleen Elmslie Bruce; Educated Wrekin College, Shropshire; St Andrews University (MA economics and political science); Strathclyde University (MSc marketing); CPE and Inns of Court School of Law; Married Jane Wilson 1969 (divorced 1992) (1 son 1 daughter); married Rosemary Vetterlein 1998 (1 daughter 1 son). Trainee journalist, Liverpool Post 1966–67; Boots section buyer 1968–69; Research and information officer, NE Scotland Development Authority 1971–75; Director, Noroil Publishing House (UK) Ltd. 1975–81; Joint editor/publisher, Aberdeen Petroleum Publishing 1981–84; Member, NUJ. **House of Commons:** Contested Angus North and Mearns October 1974, Aberdeenshire West 1979 general elections. Member for Gordon since June 1983; Liberal Spokesperson for Energy 1985–87; Scottish Liberal Spokesperson for Education 1986–87; Alliance Spokesperson for Employment 1987; Liberal Spokesperson for Trade and Industry 1987–88; SLD Spokesperson for Natural Resources (energy and conservation) 1988–89; Liberal Democrat Spokesperson for: The Environment and Natural Resources 1989–90, Scottish Affairs 1990–92, Trade and Industry 1992–94, The Treasury 1994–99; Chair, Liberal Democrat Parliamentary Party 1999–2001; Liberal Democrat Shadow Secretary of State on Environment, Food and Rural Affairs 2001–02; *Select Committees:* Member: Scottish Affairs 1990–92, Trade and Industry 1992–94, Treasury and Civil Service 1994–97, Treasury 1997–99, Standards and Privileges 1999–2001. *Special Interests:* Energy, Gas Industry, Oil Industry, Industrial Policy, Trade Policy, Deaf Children, Scottish Home Rule and Federalism. *Countries of Interest:* USA, Canada, South Africa, Zimbabwe, Eastern Europe, the Balkans, Hungary, Czech Republic, Baltic States, Scandinavia. Leader: Scottish Social and Liberal Democrats 1988–89, Liberal Democrats 1989–92; President Scottish Liberal Democrats 2000–. Vice-President, National Deaf Children's Society, President, Grampian Branch; Vice-President, Combined Heat and Power Association; Rector, Dundee University 1986–89; Member, UK Delegation Parliamentary Assembly of the Council of Europe/Western European Union 2000–; *Recreations:* Golf, cycling, walking, theatre and music. Malcolm Bruce Esq, MP, House of Commons, London, SW1A 0AA *Tel:* 020 7219 6233 *Fax:* 020 7219 2334. *Constituency:* 71 High Street, Inverurie, AB51 3QT *Tel:* 01467 623413 *Fax:* 01467 624994 *E-mail:* hendersonc@parliament.uk.

BRYANT, CHRIS   Rhondda   *Lab majority 16,047*

Chris (Christopher) John Bryant. Born 11 January 1962; Son of Rees Bryant and Anne Gracie, née Goodwin; Educated Cheltenham College; Mansfield College, Oxford (BA English 1983, MA); Ripon College, Cuddesdon (MA CertTheol 1986); Single. Church of England: Ordained Deacon 1986, Priest 1987; Curate All Saints High Wycombe 1986–89; Diocesan youth chaplain Diocese of Peterborough 1989–91; Agent Holborn and St Pancras Labour Party 1991–93; Local government development officer Labour Party 1993–94; London manager Common Purpose 1994–96; Freelance author 1996–98; Head European Affairs BBC 1998–2000; GMB 1991–94; MSF 1994–. London Borough of Hackney: Councillor 1993–98, Chief whip 1994–95. **House of Commons:** Contested Wycombe 1997 general election. Member for Rhondda since June 7, 2001; *Select Committees:* Member: Culture, Media and Sport 2001–, Joint Committee on House of Lords Reform 2002–.

Special Interests: Wales, European Affairs, Broadcasting, Information Economy. *Countries of Interest:* Spain, Latin America. Chair: Christian Socialist Movement 1993–98, Labour Movement for Europe 2002–. Associate of National Youth Theatre of Great Britain; *Publications: Reclaiming The Ground,* Hodder and Stoughton 1993; *John Smith: An Appreciation,* Hodder and Stoughton 1994; *Possible Dreams,* Hodder and Stoughton 1995; *Stafford Cripps: The First Modern Chancellor,* Hodder and Stoughton 1997; *Glenda Jackson: The Biography,* HarperCollins 1999; *Sportsclubs:* Ferndale RFC; *Recreations:* Swimming, theatre. Chris Bryant Esq, MP, House of Commons, London, SW1A 0AA *Tel:* 020 7219 8315 *Fax:* 020 7219 1792. *Constituency:* 5 Cemetery Rd, Porth, Rhondda, CF39 0LG *Tel:* 01443 687697 *Fax:* 01443 686405 *E-mail:* bryantc@parliament.uk.

BUCK, KAREN   Regent's Park and Kensington North   *Lab majority 10,266*

Karen Buck. Born 30 August 1958; Educated Chelmsford High School; London School of Economics (BSc Econ, MSc Econ, MA social policy and administration); Partner Barrie Taylor (1 son). Research and development worker, Outset (charity specialising in employment for disabled people) 1979–83; London Borough of Hackney: specialist officer developing services/employment for disabled people 1983–86, public health officer 1986–87; Labour Party Policy Directorate (Health) 1987–92; Labour Party Campaign Strategy Co-ordinator 1992–99; Member, TGWU. Councillor, Westminster City Council 1990–97; Member: Health Authority (late 1980s), Urban Regeneration Board; Chair, Westminster Early Years Development Partnership. **House of Commons:** Member for Regent's Park and Kensington North since May 1, 1997; *Select Committees:* Member: Social Security 1997–2001, Selection 1999–2001; Member, Work and Pensions 2001–. *Special Interests:* Housing, Urban Regeneration, Health Care, Welfare, Children. Chair, Constituency Labour Party; Chair, London Regional Group of Labour MPs 1999–. *Recreations:* Music: rock, soul, jazz, opera. Karen Buck, MP, House of Commons, London, SW1A 0AA *Tel:* 020 8968 7999 *Fax:* 020 8960 0150. *Constituency:* The Labour Party, 4(G) Shirland Mews, London, W9 3DY *Tel:* 020 8968 7999 *Fax:* 020 8960 0150 *E-mail:* k.buck@rpkn-labour.co.uk.

BURDEN, RICHARD   Birmingham Northfield   *Lab majority 7,798*

Richard Burden. Born 1 September 1954; Son of Kenneth Rodney Burden, engineer, and of late Pauline Burden, secretary; Educated Wallasey Technical Grammar School; Bramhall Comprehensive School; St John's College of Further Education, Manchester; York University (BA politics 1978); Warwick University (MA industrial relations 1979); Married Jane Slowey 2001 (1 stepson 2 stepdaughters). President, York University Students' Union 1976–77; NALGO: Branch Organiser, North Yorkshire 1979–81, West Midlands District Officer 1981–92; Member, TGWU 1979–; Sponsored by TGWU 1989–96. **House of Commons:** Contested Meriden 1987 general election. Member for Birmingham Northfield since April 9, 1992; PPS to Jeffrey Rooker: as Minister of State and Deputy Minister, Ministry of Agriculture, Fisheries and Food (Minister for Food Safety) 1997–99, as Minister of State, Department of Social Security (Minister for Pensions) 1999–2001; Adviser on Motor Sports to Richard Caborn, as Minister of State for Sport 2002–; *Select Committees:* Member, Trade and Industry 2001–. *Special Interests:* Industrial Policy – especially Motor and Motorsport Industries, Middle East, Poverty, Health, Constitution, Electoral Reform, Regeneration, Regional Government. *Countries of Interest:* Middle East, Europe. Founder member, Bedale Labour Party 1980; Member, Labour Middle East Council, Vice-Chair 1994–95; Member, Co-operative Party; Chair, Labour Campaign for Electoral Reform 1996–98, Vice-Chair 1998–; Member, Fabian Society. Co-chair, Parliamentary Advisory Council on Transport Safety (PACTS) 1995–98; Director, Northfield Community Development Association; Founded Joint Action for Water Services (Jaws) 1985 to oppose water privatisation, Secretary 1985–90; *Publications: Tap Dancing – Water, The Environment and Privatisation,* 1988; *Clubs:* Kingshurst Labour, Austin Sports and Social, Austin Branch British Legion; *Sportsclubs:* 750 Motor, Historic Sports Car Club; *Recreations:* Cinema, motor racing. Richard Burden Esq, MP, House of Commons, London, SW1A 0AA *Tel:* 020 7219 2318 *Fax:* 020 7219 2170. *Constituency:* Bournville College of Further Education, Bristol Road South, Birmingham, B31 1JR *Tel:* 0121–475 9295 *Fax:* 0121–476 2400 *E-mail:* burdenr@parliament.uk.

BURGON, COLIN Elmet   *Lab majority 4,171*

Colin Burgon. Born 22 April 1948; Son of Thomas Burgon, tailoring worker, and Winifred Burgon, school secretary; Educated St Charles School, Leeds; St Michael's College, Leeds; City of Leeds and Carnegie College; Divorced (1 daughter). Teacher; Local government policy and research officer; Member, GMB. **House of Commons:** Contested Elmet 1987 and 1992 general elections. Member for Elmet since May 1, 1997; *Select Committees:* Member: Joint Committee on Statutory Instruments 1997–99, Accommodation and Works 1999–2000, Procedure 1999–2001, Northern Ireland Affairs 2000–01. *Special Interests:* Youth Affairs, Planning Policy. *Countries of Interest:* USA, France, Italy, Spain. Former Secretary, Elmet Constituency Labour Party; Former Chair, Leeds Euro Constituency Labour Party. Member: Amnesty International, Friends of the Earth; Member, CPRE; *Recreations:* Football (Leeds United), walking, the countryside, history (military and American Civil War). Colin Burgon Esq, MP, House of Commons, London, SW1A 0AA *Tel:* 020 7219 6487. *Constituency:* 22A Main Street, Garforth, Leeds, LS25 1AA *Tel:* 0113–287 5198 *Fax:* 0113–287 5958.

BURNETT, JOHN Torridge and West Devon   *LD majority 1,194*

John Patrick Aubone Burnett. Born 19 September 1945; Son of late Lt-Col Aubone Burnett, OBE, and Joan Burnett (née Bolt); Educated Ampleforth College; Royal Marines Commando Training Centre; Britannia Royal Naval College, Dartmouth; College of Law, London; Married Elizabeth Sherwood, née de la Mare 1971 (2 sons 2 daughters). Royal Marines 1964–70: Troop Commander, 42 Commando in Borneo and Singapore, Troop Commander and Company Second-in-Command, 40 Commando in Far East and Middle East; Member, NFU. **House of Commons:** Contested Torridge and West Devon 1987 general election. Member for Torridge and West Devon since May 1, 1997; Spokesperson for Home and Legal Affairs: (Legal Affairs) 1997–, (Legal Affairs and Attorney General, Solicitor General, Lord Chancellor) 1999; *Select Committees:* Member: Joint Committee on Consolidation of Bills Etc 2001–, Procedure 2002–. *Special Interests:* Economic Policy, Defence, Agriculture. Member: Law Society, Devon and Exeter Law Society, Law Society's Revenue (Tax) Law Committee 1984–96, Council of Devon Cattle Breeders' Association, Royal Marine Association, Royal British Legion; *Recreations:* Breeding Devon cattle, walking, sport. John Burnett Esq, MP, House of Commons, London, SW1A 0AA *Tel:* 020 7219 5132. *Constituency:* Liberal Democrats, 21–25 St James Street, Okehampton, Devon, EX20 1DH *Tel:* 01837 55881 *Fax:* 01837 55694.

BURNHAM, ANDY Leigh   *Lab majority 16,362*

Andrew Murray Burnham. Born 7 January 1970; Son of Kenneth Roy Burnham, telecommunications engineer and Eileen Mary Burnham, née Murray; Educated St Aelred's RC High School, Merseyside; Fitzwilliam College, Cambridge (BA English 1991, MA); Married Marie-France van Heel 2000 (1 son 1 daughter). Researcher to Tessa Jowell MP 1994–97; Parliamentary officer NHS Confederation 1997; Administrator Football Task Force 1997–98; Special adviser to Chris Smith as Secretary of State for Culture, Media, and Sport 1998–2001; TGWU 1995–; UNISON 2000–. Chair Supporters Direct 2002–. **House of Commons:** Member for Leigh since June 7, 2001; PPS to David Blunkett as Home Secretary 2003–; *Select Committees:* Member, Health 2001–. *Special Interests:* Health, Sport, Media, Education, Crime. Member Co-operative Party. *Publications: Football in the Digital Age,* Mainstream Publishing 1999; *Supporters Direct – the changing face of the football business,* Frank Cass, 2000; *Clubs:* Lowton Labour Club; Leigh Catholic Club; *Recreations:* Fotball, cricket, rugby league, (Leigh RLFC, Everton FC). Andy Burnham Esq, MP, House of Commons, London, SW1A 0AA *Tel:* 020 7219 8250. *Constituency:* 10 Market Street, Leigh, Lancashire, WN7 1DS *Tel:* 01942 682353 *Fax:* 01942 682354 *E-mail:* grahamlm@parliament.uk.

BURNS, SIMON   Chelmsford West   *Con majority 6,261*

Simon Burns. Born 6 September 1952; Son of late Major B. S. Burns MC and Mrs Anthony Nash; Educated Christ the King School, Accra, Ghana; Stamford School; Worcester College, Oxford (BA history 1975); Married Emma Clifford 1982 (divorced) (1 son 1 daughter). Assistant to Sally Oppenheim, MP 1975–81; Director and company secretary, What to Buy for Business Ltd 1981–83; Conference organiser, Institute of Directors 1983–87. **House of Commons:** Contested Alyn and Deeside 1983 general election. Member for Chelmsford 1987–97, and for Chelmsford West since May 1, 1997; Opposition Spokesperson for: Social Security 1997-August 1998, Environment, Transport and the Regions (Planning, Housing and Construction) August 1998–99, Health 2001–; Assistant Government Whip 1994–95; Government Whip 1995–96; PPS: to Timothy Eggar as Minister of State: at Department of Employment 1989–90, at Department of Education and Science 1990–92, at Department of Trade and Industry 1992–93; to Gillian Shephard as Minister of Agriculture, Fisheries and Food 1993–94; Parliamentary Under-Secretary of State, Department of Health 1996–97; *Select Committees:* Member, Public Accounts 2000–01; Member, Health 1999–. *Special Interests:* Health. *Countries of Interest:* USA. Hon PhD Anglia University; *Clubs:* Essex; *Recreations:* Photography, American politics, reading. Simon Burns Esq, MP, House of Commons, London, SW1A 0AA *Tel:* 020 7219 6811. *Constituency:* 88 Rectory Lane, Chelmsford, Essex, CM1 1RF *Tel:* 01245 352872 *Fax:* 01245 344515.

BURNSIDE, DAVID   South Antrim   *UUP majority 1,011*

David Burnside. Born 24 August 1951; Son of Jack and Betty, née Carter, Burnside; Educated Coleraine Academical Institution; Queen's University Belfast politics and ancient history (BA 1973); Married Fiona Rennie 1999 (1 daughter (from first marriage)). Ulster Defence Regiment mid 1970s; Press officer Vanguard Unionist Party 1974–77; Director public relations Institute of Directors 1979–84; Director public affairs British Airways 1984–93; Chairman: New Century Holdings, David Burnside Associates 1993–. **House of Commons:** Member for South Antrim since June 7, 2001; UUP Spokesperson for: Defence 2001–02, Environment, Food and Rural Affairs 2001–, Culture, Media and Sport 2001–02, Cabinet Office 2002–, Transport 2002–; *Select Committees:* Member, Environment, Food and Rural Affairs 2001–. *Special Interests:* Constitution, Transport, Tourism, Sport. Delegate Ulster Unionist Council. Non-executive director: Northern Ireland Tourist Board 1990–93; The European Newspaper 1990–92; Founder and director Unionist information Office Great Britain; Founder patron Friends of the Union; Past master LOL 954; Sir knight RBP 309; Michelburne Club, Ballymoney A.B. of Derry; Aviation Club of Great Britain; General Service Medal Northern Ireland, Ulster Defence Regiment; Fellow Institute of Directors; *Clubs:* Carlton, Portballintrae Boat Club, Coleraine and District Motor Cycle Club; *Recreations:* Fishing, shooting, motorcycling. David Burnside Esq, MP, House of Commons, London, SW1A 0AA *Tel:* 020 7219 8493 *Fax:* 020 7219 2347. *Constituency:* 24 Fountain Street, Antrim, BT41 4BB *Tel:* 028 9446 1211 *Fax:* 028 9446 8988 *E-mail:* mckeem@parliament.uk.

BURSTOW, PAUL   Sutton and Cheam   *LD majority 4,304*

Paul Kenneth Burstow. Born 13 May 1962; Son of Brian Burstow, tailor, and Sheila Burstow; Educated Glastonbury High School For Boys; Carshalton College of Further Education; South Bank Polytechnic (BA business studies); Married Mary Kemm. Buyer Allied Shoe Repairs; Printing company, Chiswick; Organising Secretary, Organisation of Social Democrat Councillors 1986; Political Secretary, Association of Liberal Democrat Councillors 1996–97. Councillor, London Borough of Sutton 1986–, Chair, Environment Services 1988–96, Deputy Leader 1994–99. **House of Commons:** Contested Sutton and Cheam 1992 general election. Member for Sutton and Cheam since May 1, 1997; Liberal Democrat Spokesperson for: Disabled People 1997–98, Local Government (Social Services and Community Care) 1997–99, Local Government (Team Leader) 1997–99, Older People 1999–; *Select Committees:* Member, Health 2003–.

Special Interests: Environment, Disability, Community Safety, Ageing. Former Member: SDP/Liberal Alliance, London Regional Liberal Democrat Executive; Member, Federal Policy Committee 1988–90. *Clubs:* National Liberal; *Recreations:* Cooking, reading, cycling, walking, keeping fit. Paul Burstow Esq, MP, House of Commons, London, SW1A 0AA *Tel:* 020 7219 1196. *Constituency:* 312–314 High Street, Sutton, Surrey, SM1 1PR *Tel:* 020 8288 6555 *Fax:* 020 8288 6550.

BURT, ALISTAIR   North East Bedfordshire   *Con majority 8,577*

Alistair James Hendrie Burt. Born 25 May 1955; Son of James Hendrie Burt and Mina Christie Burt; Educated Bury Grammar School, Lancashire; St John's College, Oxford (BA jurisprudence 1977); Married Eve Alexandra Twite 1983 (1 son 1 daughter). Solicitor Private Practice 1980–98; Executive search consultant Whitehead Mann GKR 1997–2001. London Borough of Haringey 1982–84: Councillor, Conservative spokesman community affairs. **House of Commons:** Member for Bury North 1983–97. Contested Bury North 1997 general election. Member for North East Bedfordshire since June 7, 2001; Opposition Spokesperson for Education and Skills 2001–02; PPS to Kenneth Baker as Secretary of State for the Environment, for Education and Science and Chancellor of the Duchy of Lancaster 1985–90; Parliamentary Under-Secretary of State Department of Social Security 1992–95; Minister of State Department of Social Security and Minister for Disabled People 1995–97; Opposition Spokesperson for Education and Skills 2001–02; PPS to Iain Duncan Smith as Leader of the Opposition 2002–; *Select Committees:* Member: International Development 2001, Procedure 2001–02, Office of the Deputy Prime Minister: Housing, Planning and Local Government 2002; Member, International Development 2002–. *Special Interests:* Church Affairs, Trade and Industry, Third World, Foreign Affairs, Agriculture, Rural Affairs, Disability, Sport, Poverty, Social Affairs. Vice-President Tory Reform Group 1985–88; Chair Bow Group industry committee 1987–92. Secretary Parliamentary Christian Fellowship 1985–97; Patron Habitat for Humanity UK 1997–; Vice-president Headway Bedford 2000–; Council member Evangelical Alliance 2000–; Chair Enterprise Forum 1998–2001; Solicitors Part 2 1980; *Recreations:* Football, modern art, walking, outdoor leisure. Alistair Burt Esq, MP, House of Commons, London, SW1A 0AA *Tel:* 020 7219 8132. *Constituency:* Biggleswade Conservative Club, St Andrews Street, Biggleswade, Bedfordshire, SG18 8BA *Tel:* 01767 313 385 *Fax:* 01767 316 697 *E-mail:* burta@parliament.uk.

BUTTERFILL, JOHN   Bournemouth West   *Con majority 4,718*

John Valentine Butterfill. Born 14 February 1941; Son of late George Thomas, Lloyd's broker, and late Elsie Amelia, née Watts, Bank of England executive; Educated Caterham School; College of Estate Management, London (FRICS); Married Pamela Ross 1965 (1 son 3 daughters). Valuer, Jones Lang Wootton 1962–64; Senior executive, Hammerson Group 1964–69; Director, Audley Properties Ltd (Bovis Group) 1969–71; Managing Director, St Paul's Securities Group 1971–76; Senior partner, Curchod & Co. Chartered Surveyors 1977–92; President, European Property Associates 1977–; Contested London South Inner 1979 European Parliament election; Director: ISLEF Building and Construction Ltd 1985–91, Pavilion Services Group 1992–94. **House of Commons:** Contested Croydon North West 1981 by-election. Member for Bournemouth West since June 1983; PPS: to Cecil Parkinson: as Secretary of State for Energy 1988–89, as Secretary of State for Transport 1989–90, to Dr Brian Mawhinney as Minister of State, Northern Ireland Office 1991–92; *Select Committees:* Member: Trade and Industry 1992–2001; Member: Chairmen's Panel 1997–, Court of Referees 1997–, Unopposed Bills (Panel) 1997–. *Special Interests:* Trade and Industry, Tourism, Foreign Affairs, Environment, Housing, Health, Pensions. *Countries of Interest:* Spain, France, Germany, Scandinavia, Israel. Chair: Conservative Group for Europe 1989–92, Conservative Party Rules Committee 1997–; Member, Conservative Party Constitutional Committee 1998–; Vice-chair, Conservative Friends of Israel. Member, Council of Management PDSA 1990–; Founder Chairman, Guildford/Freiburg Town Twinning Association; Fellow, Royal Institution of Chartered Surveyors 1974; *Recreations:* Skiing, tennis, riding, bridge, music. John Butterfill Esq, MP, House of Commons, London, SW1A 0AA *Tel:* 020 7219 6383. *Constituency:* 135 Hankinson Road, Bournemouth, Dorset, BH9 1HR *Tel:* 01202 776607 *Fax:* 01202 521481.

BYERS, STEPHEN   North Tyneside   *Lab majority 20,568*

Stephen John Byers. Born 13 April 1953; Son of late Robert Byers, chief technician, RAF; Educated Chester City Grammar School; Chester College of Further Education; Liverpool Polytechnic (LLB); Single (1 son). Senior lecturer in law, Newcastle Polytechnic 1977–92; Member UNISON. North Tyneside Council: Councillor 1980–92, Chair, Education Committee 1982–85, Deputy Leader of the Council 1985–92. **House of Commons:** Contested Hexham 1983 general election. Member for Wallsend 1992–97, and for North Tyneside since May 1, 1997; Opposition Spokesperson for Education and Employment 1995–97; Opposition Whip 1994–95; Minister of State, Department for Education and Employment (Minister for School Standards) 1997–98; Chief Secretary, HM Treasury July-December 1998; Secretary of State for Trade and Industry December 1998–2001; Secretary of State for Transport, Local Government and the Regions 2001–02; *Select Committees:* Member, Home Affairs 1993–94. Member Labour Party National Policy Forum. Member, Business and Technician Education Council 1985–89; Chair, Association of Metropolitan Authorities Education Committee 1990–92; Leader, Council of Local Education Authorities 1990–92; Chair, National Employers' Organisation for Teachers 1990–92; PC 1998; Fellow, Royal Society of Arts. Rt Hon Stephen Byers, MP, House of Commons, London, SW1A 0AA *Tel:* 020 7219 4085. *Constituency:* 7 Palmersville, Great Lime Road, Forest Hall, Newcastle upon Tyne, NE12 9HW *Tel:* 0191–268 9111 *Fax:* 0191–268 9777 *E-mail:* byerss@parliament.uk.

C

CABLE, VINCENT   Twickenham   *LD majority 7,655*

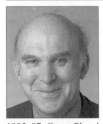

(John) Vincent Cable. Born 9 May 1943; Son of late Leonard Cable and of Edith Cable; Educated Nunthorpe Grammar School, York; Fitzwilliam College, Cambridge (President of Union) (BA natural science and economics 1966); Glasgow University (PhD international economics 1973); Widower (Dr Olympia Rebelo died 2001) (2 sons 1 daughter). Finance officer, Kenya Treasury 1966–68; Economics lecturer, Glasgow University 1968–74; Diplomatic Service 1974–76; Deputy Director, Overseas Development Institute 1976–83; Special Adviser to John Smith as Secretary of State for Trade 1979; Special Adviser, Commonwealth Secretariat 1983–90; Adviser to World Commission on Environment and Development (Brundtland Commission) 1985–87; Group Planning, Shell 1990–93; Head economics programme, Chatham House 1993–95; Chief economist, Shell International 1995–97. Councillor (Labour), Glasgow City Council 1971–74. **House of Commons:** Contested Glasgow Hillhead (Labour) 1970, York (SDP/Alliance) 1983 and 1987, Twickenham (Liberal Democrat) 1992 general elections. Member for Twickenham since May 1, 1997; Liberal Democrat Spokesperson for the Treasury (EMU and The City) 1997–99; Principal Spokesperson for Trade and Industry 1999–; *Select Committees:* Member: Treasury 1998–99, Treasury Sub-Committee 1998–99. *Special Interests:* Trade and Industry, Economic Policy, Foreign Affairs, European Union, Energy, Environment. *Countries of Interest:* India, Russia, China, Nigeria, Kenya. Ex-President London and South East Region United Nations Association; Patron Shooting Star Trust; *Publications:* Wide variety of books and pamphlets including: *Protectionism and Industrial Decline*, 1983, *Globalisation and Global Governance*, 1999; Journalism for the *Independent*; Visiting fellow, Nuffield College, Oxford; Special professor of economics, Nottingham University 1999; Research fellow, international economics, Royal Institute of International Affairs; *Recreations:* Ballroom and Latin dancing, classical music, walking. Dr Vincent Cable, MP, House of Commons, London, SW1A 0AA *Tel:* 020 7219 1106 *Fax:* 020 7219 1191. *Constituency:* 164c Heath Road, Twickenham, TW1 4BN *Tel:* 020 8892 0215 *Fax:* 020 8892 0218 *E-mail:* vincentcablemp@parliament.uk.

CABORN, RICHARD Sheffield Central — *Lab majority 12,544*

Richard George Caborn. Born 6 October 1943; Son of late George Caborn; Educated Hurlfield Comprehensive School; Granville College; Sheffield Polytechnic (engineering 1966); Married Margaret Hayes 1966 (1 son 1 daughter). Skilled engineer 1964–1979; MEP for Sheffield District 1979–84; Convenor of shop stewards AEEU. **House of Commons:** Member for Sheffield Central since June, 1983; Opposition Spokesperson for: Trade and Industry 1988–90, with special responsibility for Regional Policy 1990–92, National Competitiveness and Regulation 1995–97; Minister of State: Department of the Environment, Transport and the Regions (Minister for the Regions, Regeneration and Planning) 1997–99, Department of Trade and Industry (Minister for Trade) 1999–2001; Department for Culture, Media and Sport (Minister for Sport) 2001–; *Select Committees:* Chair, Trade and Industry 1992–95; Member, Liaison 1992–95. *Special Interests:* European Union, Trade Unions, Steel Industry. *Countries of Interest:* South Africa. Chair, Sheffield District Labour Party, served on Education Committee. Vice-President, Sheffield Trades Council 1968–79; Member, BBC Advisory Council 1975–78; Joint Chair, British Trade International Board 2000–01; Chair, European Parliament British Labour Party Group 1979–84; PC 1999; *Recreations:* Golf. Rt Hon Richard Caborn, MP, House of Commons, London, SW1A 0AA *Tel:* 020 7219 4211/6259 *Fax:* 020 7219 4866. *Constituency:* 2nd Floor, Barkers Pool House, Burgess Street, Sheffield, S1 2HF *Tel:* 0114–273 7947 *Fax:* 0114–275 3944 *E-mail:* lawrences@parliament.uk.

CAIRNS, DAVID Greenock and Inverclyde — *Lab majority 9,890*

(John) David Cairns. Born 7 August 1966; Educated Notre Dame High School, Greenock; Gregorian University, Rome; Franciscan Study Centre, Canterbury; Single. Priest 1991–94; Director Christian Socialist Movement 1994–97; Research assistant to Siobhan McDonagh MP 1997–2001; ISTC. London Borough of Merton 1998–2002: Councillor, Chief whip. **House of Commons:** Member for Greenock and Inverclyde since June 7, 2001; PPS to Malcolm Wicks as Minister of State, Department for Work and Pensions 2003–; *Select Committees:* Member, Joint Committee on Consolidation of Bills Etc 2001–. *Special Interests:* Defence, Employment, Welfare, Small Businesses. Member: Fabian Society, Christian Socialist Movement. Amnesty International; Member European Standing Committee B 2003–. David Cairns Esq, MP, House of Commons, London, SW1A 0AA *Tel:* 020 7219 8242. *Constituency:* The Parliamentary Office, 20 Union Street, Greenock, Inverclyde, PA16 8JL.

CALTON, PATSY Cheadle — *LD majority 33*

Patsy Calton. Born 19 September 1948; Daughter of John and late Joan Yeldon; Educated Wymondham College, Wymondham, Norfolk; University of Manchester Institute of Science and Technology (BSc biochemistry 1970); Manchester University (PGCE 1971); Married Clive Calton 1969 (2 daughters 1 son). Chemistry teacher Manchester Metropolitan Borough Council 1971–79; Human biology teacher Stockport Metropolitan Borough Council 1984–86; Chemistry teacher Stockport Metropolitan Borough Council 1987–89; Head of chemistry Cheshire County Council 1989–2001; NASUWT: Member 1993–2002, School representative 1998–2001, Associate Member 2002–. Stockport Metropolitan Borough Council: Councillor 1994–2002, Chair Environmental Health 1995–97, Deputy leader 1996–97, Chair Community Services 1997–99, Deputy leader 1998–2001, Chair Social Services 1999–2001. **House of Commons:** Contested Cheadle 1992, 1997 general elections. Member for Cheadle since June 7, 2001; Liberal Democrat Spokesperson for Northern Ireland 2001–02; Liberal Democrat Spokesperson for Health 2002–; *Select Committees:* Member, Administration 2001–. *Special Interests:* Environment, Transport, Community Services, Social Services, Science. *Countries of Interest:* Uganda, Cyprus. Chair Stockport Metropolitan Liberal Democrats 1993–96, 1997–2000; Member Liberal Democrat Federal Executive Committee 2001–. Executive member Stockport Cerebral Palsy Society 1994–; Chair, Travel Office Consumers' Panel; *Recreations:* Reading, gardening, running (London marathon 1999, 2001, 2002, 2003). Patsy Calton, MP, House of Commons, London, SW1A 0AA *Tel:* 020 7219 8471 *Fax:* 020 7219 1958. *Constituency:* Hillson House, 3 Gill Bent Road, Cheadle Hulme, Cheadle, Stockport, Cheshire, SK8 7LE *Tel:* 0161–486 1359 *Fax:* 0161–486 9005 *E-mail:* caltonp@parliament.uk.

CAMERON, DAVID   Witney   *Con majority 7,973*

David Cameron. Born 9 October 1966; Son of Ian Donald and Mary Fleur Cameron; Educated Eton College, Windsor; Brasenose College, Oxford (BA philosophy, politics, economics 1988); Married Samantha Sheffield 1996 (1 son). Conservative Research Department 1988–92: Head of Political Section, member Prime Minister's Question Time briefing team; Special adviser to: Norman Lamont as Chancellor of the Exchequer 1992–93, Michael Howard as Home Secretary 1993–94; Director of corporate affairs Carlton Communications plc 1994–2001; Member NFU. **House of Commons:** Contested Stafford 1997 general election. Member for Witney since June 7, 2001; Shadow Minister for Privy Council Office 2003–; *Select Committees:* Member, Home Affairs 2001–. *Special Interests:* Economy, Home Affairs, European Affairs. *Recreations:* Tennis, bridge, cooking. David Cameron Esq, MP, House of Commons, London, SW1A 0AA *Tel:* 020 7219 3475. *Constituency:* 10 Bridge Street, Witney, Oxfordshire, OX8 6HY *Tel:* 01993 702 302 *Fax:* 01993 776 639 *E-mail:* camerond@parliament.uk.

CAMPBELL, ALAN   Tynemouth   *Lab majority 8,678*

Alan Campbell. Born 8 July 1957; Son of Albert Campbell and Marian Campbell, née Hewitt; Educated Blackfyne Secondary School, Consett; Lancaster University (BA politics); Leeds University (PGCE); Newcastle Polytechnic (MA history); Married Jayne Lamont (1 son 1 daughter). Whitley Bay High School 1980–89; Hirst High School, Ashington, Northumberland: teacher 1989–97, head of sixth form, head of department. **House of Commons:** Member for Tynemouth since May 1, 1997; PPS to: Lord Macdonald of Tradeston as Minister for the Cabinet Office and Chancellor of the Duchy of Lancaster 2001–03, Adam Ingram as Minister of State, Ministry of Defence 2003–; *Select Committees:* Member, Public Accounts 1997–2001. *Special Interests:* Education, Constitutional Reform, Shipbuilding and Offshore Industries. Branch Secretary, Chair, Agent; Tynemouth Constituency Labour Party: Secretary, Campaign Co-ordinator; Hon. Secretary and Hon. Treasurer, Northern Group of Labour MPs 1999–; Member Seaside and Coastal Towns Group. *Recreations:* Family. Alan Campbell Esq, MP, House of Commons, London, SW1A 0AA *Tel:* 020 7219 6619 *Fax:* 020 7219 3006. *Constituency:* 99 Howard Street, North Shields, Tyne and Wear, NE30 1NA *Tel:* 0191–257 1927 *Fax:* 0191–257 6537 *E-mail:* campbella@parliament.uk.

CAMPBELL, ANNE   Cambridge   *Lab majority 8,579*

Anne Campbell. Born 6 April 1940; Daughter of late Frank Lucas, NHS clerical worker, and late Susan Lucas; Educated Penistone Grammar School, near Sheffield; Newnham College, Cambridge (MA mathematics 1962); Married Professor Archie Campbell 1963 (1 son 2 daughters). Assistant maths teacher: Herts and Essex High School, Bishops Stortford 1962–64, Girls' Grammar School, Cambridge 1964–65; Various part-time teaching posts 1965–70; Lecturer, then senior lecturer in statistics, Cambridgeshire College of Arts and Technology 1970–83; Head, Statistics and Data Processing, National Institute of Agricultural Botany, Cambridge 1983–92; Member, MSF. Councillor, Cambridgeshire County Council 1985–89. **House of Commons:** Member for Cambridge since April 9, 1992; PPS Department of Trade and Industry 1997–2003, to John Battle as Minister of State 1997–99, to Patricia Hewitt: as Minister for Small Business and E-Commerce 1999–2001, as Secretary of State for Trade and Industry 2001–03; *Select Committees:* Member, Science and Technology 1992–97. *Special Interests:* Education, Science Policy, Environment. Chair: South and East Group of Labour MPs 1997–99, Eastern Regional Group of Labour MPs 1999. Member, Greenpeace; Patron, Headway Cambridgeshire; Vice-President, United Nations Association, Cambridge City Branch; Patron: Addenbrooke's Kidney Patients Association Ltd, Cambridge Family and Divorce Centre; Vice-President: Cambridgeshire Beekeepers' Association, Cambridgeshire Association of Youth Clubs, Cambridgeshire Cricket Association; Honorary President, Cambridge Relate; Vice-President, The Multiple Sclerosis Society – Cambridge and District Branch;

Vice-Chair, Parliamentary Office of Science and Technology 1994–98; Patron, Cambridge Rowing Trust; *Publications: Calculations for Commercial Students*, 1972; Anglia Polytechnic University (PhD); Fellow: Institute of Statisticians 1987, Royal Statistical Society 1987, Royal Society of Arts 1992; *Recreations:* Gardening, tennis, mountain walking, skiing. Mrs Anne Campbell, MP, House of Commons, London, SW1A 0AA *Tel:* 020 7219 5089 *Fax:* 020 7219 2264. *Constituency:* Alex Wood Hall, Norfolk Street, Cambridge, CB1 2LD *Tel:* 01223 506500 *Fax:* 01223 311315 *E-mail:* campbella@parliament.uk.

CAMPBELL, GREGORY   East Londonderry   *DUP majority 1,901*

Gregory Lloyd Campbell. Born 15 February 1953; Son of James Campbell and Martha Joyce, née Robinson; Educated Londonderry Technical College; Magee College (extra-mural certificate political studies 1982); Married Frances Patterson 1979 (1 son 3 daughters). Civil servant 1972–82, 1986–94; Self-employed businessman 1994–. Councillor Londonderry City Council 1981–. **House of Commons:** Contested Foyle 1983, 1987, 1992 and East Londonderry 1997 general elections. Member for East Londonderry since June 7, 2001; Member: Northern Ireland Assembly 1982–86, Northern Ireland Forum for Political Dialogue 1996–98, New Northern Ireland Assembly 1998–2002, Enterprise, Trade and Investment Committee 1999–; Minister for Regional Development 2000–; *Select Committees:* Member: Transport, Local Government and the Regions 2001–02, Transport Sub-Committee 2001–02; Member, Transport 2002–. *Special Interests:* Economic Development, Tourism, Employment, Enterprise, Trade and Industry. Spokesman for Security 1994; Whip 1998; Treasurer; Senior Party Officer. *Publications:* Various publications; *Discrimination: The Truth*, 1987; *Discrimination: Where Now?*, 1993; *Ulster's Verdict on the Joint Declaration*, 1994; *Working Toward 2000*, 1998; *Recreations:* Football, music, reading. Gregory Campbell Esq, MP, House of Commons, London, SW1A 0AA *Tel:* 020 7219 8495. *Constituency:* 25 Bushmills Road, Coleraine, BT52 2BP *Tel:* 028 7032 7327 *Fax:* 028 7032 7328.

CAMPBELL, MENZIES   North East Fife   *LD majority 9,736*

(Walter) Menzies Campbell. Born 22 May 1941; Son of late George and Elizabeth Campbell; Educated Hillhead High School, Glasgow; Glasgow University (MA arts 1962, LLB law 1965, post graduate studies in international law 1966–67); Stanford University, California; Married Elspeth Mary Urquhart 1970. Called to the Bar (Scotland) 1968; QC (Scotland) 1982; Competed: 1964 (Tokyo) Olympics, 1966 Commonwealth Games (Jamaica); UK Athletics Team Captain 1965–66; UK 100 metres record holder 1967–74; Chair, Royal Lyceum Theatre Company, Edinburgh 1984–87. **House of Commons:** Contested Greenock and Port Glasgow February and October 1974, East Fife 1979, North East Fife 1983 general elections. Member for North East Fife since June 1987; Liberal Spokesperson for Arts, Broadcasting and Sport 1987–88; SLD Spokesperson for Defence, Sport 1988–89; Liberal Democrat Spokesperson for: Scotland (Legal Affairs, Lord Advocate) 1987–99, Defence and Disarmament, Sport 1989–94, Foreign Affairs and Defence, Sport 1994–97, Foreign Affairs (Defence and Europe) 1997–99; Principal Spokesperson for: Foreign Affairs 1999–, Defence 1999–2001; *Select Committees:* Member: Members' Interests 1988–90, Trade and Industry 1990–92, Defence 1992–97, Defence 1997–99. *Special Interests:* Defence, Foreign Affairs, Legal Affairs, Sport, Arts. *Countries of Interest:* Middle East, North America. Chair Scottish Liberal Party 1975–77; Member Liberal Democrat Peel Group 2001–; Deputy Leader Liberal Democrat Party 2003–. Member: Board of the British Council 1998–2002, Council of the Air League 1999–; Member: North Atlantic Assembly 1989–, UK Delegation, Parliamentary Assembly of OSCE 1992–97, 1999–; CBE 1987; PC 1999; Highland Park/*The Spectator* Member to Watch 1996; D. Univ. (Glasgow) 2001; *Clubs:* Reform; *Recreations:* All sports, theatre, music. Rt Hon Menzies Campbell, CBE, QC, MP, House of Commons, London, SW1A 0AA *Tel:* 020 7219 4446 *Fax:* 020 7219 0559. *Constituency:* 16 Millbank, Cupar, Fife, KY15 5EG *Tel:* 01334 656361 *Fax:* 01334 654045 *E-mail:* nefifelibdem@cix.co.uk.

Visit the Vacher Dod Website … **www.DodOnline.co.uk**

CAMPBELL, RONNIE   Blyth Valley   *Lab majority 12,188*

Ronnie Campbell. Born 14 August 1943; Son of Ronnie and Edna Campbell; Educated Ridley High School, Blyth; Married Deidre McHale 1967 (5 sons, including twins 1 daughter). Miner 1958–86; NUM Lodge Secretary, Bates Colliery, Blyth 1982–86; NUM Sponsored MP. Councillor: Blyth Borough Council 1969–74, Blyth Valley Council 1974–88. **House of Commons:** Member for Blyth Valley since June 1987; *Select Committees:* Member: Parliamentary Commissioner for Administration 1987–97, Public Administration 1997–2001; Member, Catering 2001–. Chair, Northern Regional Group of Labour MPs 1999–. *Recreations:* Furniture restoration, stamp collecting, antiques. Ronnie Campbell Esq, MP, House of Commons, London, SW1A 0AA *Tel:* 020 7219 4216 *Fax:* 020 7219 4358. *Constituency:* 42 Renwick Road, Blyth, Northumberland, NE24 2LQ *Tel:* 01670 363050/355192 *Fax:* 01670 363050 *E-mail:* ronniecampbellmp@btconnect.com.

CAPLIN, IVOR   Hove   *Lab majority 3,171*

Ivor Keith Caplin. Born 8 November 1958; Son of late Leonard Caplin, chartered accountant, and of Alma Caplin, market researcher; Educated King Edward's School, Witley; Brighton College of Technology (National Certificate in Business Studies 1979); Married Maureen Whelan 1985 (2 sons 1 daughter). Legal and General Assurance Society Ltd 1978–97, Quality manager, sales and marketing division 1993–97; Member, MSF. Councillor, Hove 1991–97, Leader 1995–97; Councillor, Brighton and Hove Council 1996–98, and Deputy Leader 1996–98. **House of Commons:** Member for Hove since May 1, 1997; Assistant Government Whip 2001–03; PPS to Margaret Beckett as President of the Council and Leader of the House of Commons 1998–2001; Parliamentary Under-Secretary of State (Minister for Veterans), Ministry of Defence 2003–; *Select Committees:* Member: Broadcasting 1997–98, Modernisation of the House of Commons 1998–2001. *Special Interests:* Finance, Heritage, Pensions, Sport, Arts, Local and Regional Government, Animal Welfare. *Countries of Interest:* Germany, Middle East, Netherlands. Chair, Hove Constituency Labour Party 1986–92; Member: Co-operative Party, Labour Friends of Israel. Member, League Against Cruel Sports; Member: CPA, IPU, British-American Parliamentary Group; Trustee, Old Market Trust, Hove; *Sportsclubs:* Vice-President, Lewes Priory Cricket Club, Brighton and Hove Cricket Club, Preston Nomads Cricket Club; *Recreations:* Football (Brighton and Hove Albion FC), music, cricket, eating out. Ivor Caplin Esq, MP, House of Commons, London, SW1A 0AA *Tel:* 020 7219 2146 *Fax:* 020 7219 0259. *Constituency:* Parliamentary Office, Town Hall, Norton Road, Hove, East Sussex, BN3 4AH *Tel:* 01273 292933 *Fax:* 01273 291054 *E-mail:* caplini@parliament.uk.

CARMICHAEL, ALISTAIR   Orkney and Shetland   *LD majority 3,475*

Alistair (Alexander Morrison) Carmichael. Born 15 July 1965; Son of Alexander Calder Carmichael, farmer and Mina, née McKay; Educated Islay High School, Argyll; Aberdeen University: Scots law: (LLB 1992), (Dip LP 1993); Married Kathryn Jane Eastham 1987 (2 sons). Hotel manager 1984–89; Procurator fiscal depute Procurator Fiscal Service 1993–96; Solicitor private practice 1996–2001. **House of Commons:** Contested Paisley South 1987 general election. Member for Orkney and Shetland since June 7, 2001; Scottish Liberal Democrat Spokesperson on the Energy Review 2001–02; Liberal Democrat Deputy Spokesperson for Northern Ireland 2002–; *Select Committees:* Member, International Development 2001–02; Member, Scottish Affairs 2001–. *Special Interests:* Transport, Agriculture, Fishing Industry, Criminal Justice, Energy. Elder Church of Scotland 1995–; *Recreations:* Amateur dramatics, music. Alistair Carmichael Esq, MP, House of Commons, London, SW1A 0AA *Tel:* 020 7219 8307 *Fax:* 020 7219 1787. *Constituency:* Orkney: 31 Broad Street, Kirkwall, Orkney, KW15 1DH, Shetland: 171 Commercial Street, Lerwick, ZE1 0HX *Tel:* 01856 876541 *Fax:* 01856 876162 *E-mail:* carmichaela@parliament.uk.

CASALE, ROGER   Wimbledon   *Lab majority 3,744*

Roger Mark Casale. Born 22 May 1960; Son of Edward and Jean Casale; Educated King's College, Wimbledon; Hurstpierpoint College, Sussex; Brasenose College, Oxford (BA philosophy, politics, economics 1982); Johns Hopkins, Bologna (MA international affairs 1994); Married Fernanda Miucci 1997 (2 daughters). Head, Training Institute 1984–92; University lecturer in European studies, Greenwich 1994–97; Member, GMB. **House of Commons:** Member for Wimbledon since May 1, 1997; Team PPS to Foreign and Commonwealth Office Ministers 2002–; *Select Committees:* Member: European Legislation 1997–98, European Legislation 1998–2001, European Scrutiny 1998–2003. *Special Interests:* Foreign Affairs, Treasury. *Countries of Interest:* Italy. Member Fabian Society. Honorary President: London and South East Direct Aid to Kosovo, Wimbledon Civic Forum; Member, Royal Institute of International Affairs; *Recreations:* Spending time with family and friends. Roger Casale Esq, MP, House of Commons, London, SW1A 0AA *Tel:* 020 7219 4565 *Fax:* 020 7219 0789. *Constituency:* Wimbledon Constituency Office, Nelson Hospital, Kingston Road, Wimbledon, London, SW20 8DB *Tel:* 020 8540 1012 *E-mail:* casaler@parliament.uk.

CASH, WILLIAM   Stone   *Con majority 6,036*

William Cash. Born 10 May 1940; Son of Paul Cash, MC (killed in action, 1944); Educated Stonyhurst College; Lincoln College, Oxford (MA); Married Bridget Mary Lee 1965 (2 sons 1 daughter). Solicitor, William Cash & Company. **House of Commons:** Member for Stafford 1984–97, and for Stone since May 1, 1997; Shadow Attorney General 2001–; *Select Committees:* Member: European Legislation 1985–97, European Legislation 1997–98; Member, European Scrutiny 1998–. *Special Interests:* European Union, Trade and Industry, Media, Small Businesses, Heritage, Africa, Debt Relief. *Countries of Interest:* East Africa, Europe. Chair, Friends of Bruges Group in the House of Commons 1989–. Vice-President, Conservative Small Business Bureau; Member, Standing Committees on: Financial Services 1985–86, Banking 1986–87; Founder and Chair, The European Foundation; *Publications: Against a Federal Europe*, 1991; *Europe – The Crunch*, 1992; *AEA – The Associated European Area*, 2000; *Clubs:* Beefsteak, Carlton, Vincent's (Oxford); *Sportsclubs:* Secretary, Lords and Commons Cricket Club 1988–92; *Recreations:* Local history, cricket, jazz. William Cash Esq, MP, House of Commons, London, SW1A 0AA *Tel:* 020 7219 6330 *Fax:* 020 7219 3935. *Constituency:* 50 High Street, Stone, Staffordshire, ST15 8AU *Tel:* 01785 811000 *Fax:* 01785 811000.

CATON, MARTIN   Gower   *Lab majority 7,395*

Martin Philip Caton. Born 15 June 1951; Son of William John Caton and Pauline Joan Caton, retired shopkeepers; Educated Newport (Essex) Grammar School; Norfolk School of Agriculture; Aberystwyth College of Further Education (National Certificate in Agriculture, Higher National Certificate in Applied Biology); Married Bethan Evans 1996 (2 step daughters). Agriculture research, Welsh Plant Breeding Station, Aberystwyth 1972–84; Political researcher to David Morris MEP 1984–97; Member, GMB; Former Section Treasurer/Membership Secretary, IPCS. Councillor: Mumbles Community Council 1986–90, Swansea City Council 1988–95, City and County of Swansea 1995–97. **House of Commons:** Member for Gower since May 1, 1997; *Select Committees:* Member: Welsh Affairs 1997–, Joint Committee on Consolidation of Bills Etc 2001–. *Special Interests:* Environment, Planning, Education, European Union. Member: Socialist Environmental Resources Association, Socialist Health Association, Welsh Regional Group of Labour MPs, Former Vice-chair, Chair 2002–. CND Cymru; *Recreations:* Reading, walking, theatre, thinking about gardening. Martin Caton Esq, MP, House of Commons, London, SW1A 0AA *Tel:* 020 7219 5111 *Fax:* 020 7219 0905. *Constituency:* 26 Pontardulais Road, Gorseinon, Swansea, SA4 4FE *Tel:* 01792 892100 *Fax:* 01792 892375 *E-mail:* martin.caton@politics.demon.co.uk.

CAWSEY, IAN   Brigg and Goole   *Lab majority 3,961*

Ian Cawsey. Born 14 April 1960; Son of Arthur Henry Cawsey and Edith Morrison Cawsey; Educated Wintringham School; Married Linda Mary Kirman 1987 (1 son 2 daughters). Computing/IT work Imperial Foods and Seven Seas Health Care 1977–87 Personal assistant to Elliot Morley, MP 1987–97; Member: ISTC, GMB. Councillor, Humberside County Council 1989–96; Chair, Humberside Police Authority 1993–97; Leader, North Lincolnshire Council 1995–97. **House of Commons:** Member for Brigg and Goole since May 1, 1997; PPS to: Lord Williams of Mostyn as Leader of the House of Lords 2001–02, David Miliband MP, Minister of State, Department for Education and Skills 2002–; *Select Committees:* Member, Home Affairs 1999–2001. *Special Interests:* Police, Local and Regional Government, Animal Welfare. *Countries of Interest:* Poland. Member Fabian Society. Member, Scunthorpe Hospitals Broadcasting Organisation; Vice-President: Federation of Economic Development Authorities (FEDA), Broughton Ex-Servicemen's Association; *Clubs:* Kinsley Labour, Ashby Mill Road, Old Goole Working Men's Club; *Recreations:* Football, playing in local 60s band 'The Moggies'. Ian Cawsey Esq, MP, House of Commons, London, SW1A 0AA *Tel:* 020 7219 5237 *Fax:* 020 7219 3047. *Constituency:* 7 Market Place, Brigg, North Lincolnshire, DN20 8HA *Tel:* 01652 651327, 01405 767744 *Fax:* 01652 657132, 01405 767733 *E-mail:* cawseyi@parliament.uk.

CHALLEN, COLIN   Morley and Rothwell   *Lab majority 12,090*

Colin Robert Challen. Born 12 June 1953; Son of Grenfell Stephen William Challen, quarry manager and Helen Mary Challen, née Swift; Educated Norton Secondary School; Malton Grammar School; Hull University (BA philosophy 1982); Single. RAF 1971–74; Supplier accountant RAF 1971–74; Postman Post Office 1974–78; Printer and publisher self-employed 1982–94; Marketing development worker Humberside Co-operative Development Agency 1991–93; GPMU; Member GMB. Hull City Council: Councillor 1986–94, Labour group secretary 1991–94. **House of Commons:** Contested Beverley 1992 general election. Member for Morley and Rothwell since June 7, 2001; *Select Committees:* Member: Environmental Audit 2001–, Joint Committee on Consolidation of Bills Etc 2001–. *Special Interests:* Economy, Environment, Pensions. *Countries of Interest:* Canada. Member Co-operative Party 1994–; Organiser Labour Party 1994–2000; Socialist Environment Resources Association (SERA) 1995–; Secretary: Morley South Labour Party 1998–2001, Leeds Co-operative Party 2000–. Member League Against Cruel Sports 1976–; *Publications: Price of Power: The Secret Funding of the Tory Party*, Vision London 1998; *Recreations:* Writing, art, rambling. Colin Challen Esq, MP, House of Commons, London, SW1A 0AA *Tel:* 020 7219 8260. *Constituency:* 2 Commercial Street, Morley, West Yorkshire, LS27 8HY *Tel:* 0113 238 1312.

CHAPMAN, BEN   Wirral South   *Lab majority 5,049*

Ben (James Keith) Chapman. Born 8 July 1940; Son of John Hartley and Elsie Vera Chapman; Educated Appleby Grammar School, Westmorland; Divorced (3 daughters); married Maureen Ann Byrne 1999. Pilot Officer, RAFVR 1959–61; Civil Servant: Ministry of Pensions and National Insurance 1958–62, Ministry of Aviation/BAA 1962–67, Rochdale Committee of Inquiry into Shipping 1967–70, Board of Trade 1970–74; First Secretary (Commercial) High Commission, Dar es Salaam, Tanzania 1974–78; First Secretary (Economic), High Commission, Accra, Ghana 1978–81; Assistant Secretary, Department of Trade and Industry 1981–87; Commercial Counsellor, Peking Embassy 1987–90; DTI North West: Director Merseyside and Deputy Regional Director 1991–93, Director Trade and Industry and Regional Director 1993–95; Director: On the Waterfront (Manchester) Ltd 1995–96, China Business Links Ltd 1995–97; Founder Consultant, Ben Chapman Associates 1995–97; Partner, The Pacific Practice 1996–97; Former Member, FDA; Member: UNISON, MSF, Amicus. **House of Commons:** Member for Wirral South since February 27, 1997 by-election; PPS to Richard Caborn: as Minister of State, Department of the Environment, Transport and the

Regions (Minister for the Regions, Regeneration and Planning) 1997–99, as Minister of State, Department of Trade and Industry 1999–2001, as Minister of State (Minister for Sport), Department for Culture, Media and Sport 2001–; *Special Interests:* Economic Development, Regional Development, Trade and Industry, Foreign Affairs. *Countries of Interest:* China, Pacific Rim, Turkey, Vietnam, Cuba. Director, Wirral Chamber of Commerce 1995–96; Hon Ambassador for: Cumbria 1995–, Merseyside 1997–; Council of Management, Lake District Summer Music Ltd 1996–97; Director, Heswall Society 1996–97; Hon Vice-President, Wirral Investment Network 1997–; Council member BESO; Fellow, Industry and Parliament Trust; *Recreations:* Opera, theatre, music, reading, walking. Ben Chapman Esq, MP, House of Commons, London, SW1A 0AA *Tel:* 020 7219 1143 *Fax:* 020 7219 1179. *Constituency:* 32 Bebington Road, New Ferry, Merseyside, CH62 5BQ *Tel:* 0151–643 8797 *Fax:* 0151–643 8546 *E-mail:* chapmanb@parliament.uk.

CHAPMAN, SYDNEY   Chipping Barnet   *Con majority 2,701*

Sydney Brookes Chapman. Born 17 October 1935; Son of late W. Dobson Chapman; Educated Rugby School; Manchester University (DipArch 1958, DipTP 1961); Married Claire McNab 1976 (2 sons 1 daughter) (divorced). Architect, planner, lecturer and occasional journalist; Director (Information), British Property Federation 1976–79. **House of Commons:** Contested Stalybridge and Hyde 1964 general election. Member for Birmingham Handsworth 1970–74, and for Chipping Barnet since May 1979; Assistant Government Whip 1988–90; Government Whip 1990–95; PPS: to Health and Social Security Ministers 1973–74; to Norman Fowler as Secretary of State for: Transport 1979–81, Social Services 1981–83; *Select Committees:* Member: Administration 1992–95, Accommodation and Works 1994–97, Public Service 1995–97; Chair, Accommodation and Works 1997–2001; Member: Finance and Services 1997–2001, Liaison 1997–2001; Member, Public Administration 2002–. *Special Interests:* Environment, Architectural Heritage, Conservation, Construction Industry, Inner Cities, Arboriculture. *Countries of Interest:* Belize, Seychelles. National Chair, Young Conservatives 1964–66; Senior Vice-Chair, North Western Area Conservatives and Unionist Associations 1966–70. Arboricultural Association: Vice-President 1973–83, President 1983–89; Instigator, National Tree Year 1973; Vice-President, RIBA 1974–75, Member of Council 1972–76; Vice-Chair, United and Cecil Club 1979–; President, London Green Belt Council 1984–89; Formerly Vice-Chair, Wildlife Link; Vice-President, Tree Council; Hon. Associate, British Veterinary Association; Former Vice-President, National Housing and Town Planning Council; Member, Sherlock Holmes Society of London; Formerly Member, Foreign Office Property Advisory Panel; Member, UK Delegation to Council of Europe and Western Europe Union 1997–; HM The Queen's Silver Jubilee Medal 1977; Knighted 1995; RIBA; FRTPI; FRSA; Hon. FRICS; Hon. MLI; Hon. FBEng; Hon. FFB; Hon. FIAS; *Clubs:* United and Cecil; *Recreations:* Tree spotting. Sir Sydney Chapman, MP, House of Commons, London, SW1A 0AA *Tel:* 020 7219 4542 *Fax:* 020 7219 2694. *Constituency:* Chipping Barnet Conservative Association, 163 High Street, Barnet, Hertfordshire, EN5 5SU *Tel:* 020 8449 7345 *Fax:* 020 8449 7346.

CHAYTOR, DAVID   Bury North   *Lab majority 6,532*

David Michael Chaytor. Born 3 August 1949; Educated Bury Grammar School; London University (BA 1970, MPhil 1979); Leeds University (PGCE 1976); Married (1 son 2 daughters). Various lecturing posts 1973–82; Senior staff tutor, Manchester College of Adult Education 1983–90; Head, Department of Continuing Education, Manchester College of Arts and Technology 1990–97; Member, TGWU. Councillor, Calderdale Council 1982–97, Chair: Education Committee, Highways Committee, Economic Development Committee. **House of Commons:** Contested Calder Valley 1987 and 1992 general elections. Member for Bury North since May 1, 1997; *Select Committees:* Member: Deregulation and Regulatory Reform 1997–2002, Environmental Audit 2000–01; Member: Education and Skills 2001–, Environmental Audit 2002–. *Special Interests:* Environment, Education, International Development, Transport. *Countries of Interest:* France, Albania, USA, Kazakhstan. *Clubs:* Rochdale Labour; *Recreations:* Walking, cycling, restoration of old buildings. David Chaytor Esq, MP, House of Commons, London, SW1A 0AA *Tel:* 020 7219 6625 *Fax:* 020 7219 0952. *Constituency:* Bury North Constituency Labour Party, 14A Market Street, Bury, Lancashire, BL9 0AJ *Tel:* 0161–764 2023 *Fax:* 0161–763 3410 *E-mail:* chaytord@parliament.uk.

CHIDGEY, DAVID   Eastleigh   *LD majority 3,058*

David Chidgey. Born 9 July 1942; Son of Major Cyril and Winifred Chidgey; Educated Brune Park County High School, Gosport; Portsmouth Polytechnic (Dip CivilEng 1965, CEng); Portsmouth Naval College; Married April Carolyn Idris-Jones 1964 (1 son 2 daughters). Consulting Civil Engineer; Senior Civil Engineer, Hampshire County Council 1964–73; Associate Partner, Brian Colquhoun and Partners 1973–93; Projects Director, West Africa and South East Asia 1978–87; Managing Director, Brian Colquhoun and Partners Ireland 1981–88; Chief Consultant to Dublin Transport Authority 1987–88; Contested Hampshire Central European Parliament (SLD) 1988 by-election and 1989 election; Associate Director, Thorburn Colquhoun 1994; Projects Director, Central Southern England. Winchester City Council: Councillor, Alresford 1987–91, Spokesperson for: Health and Works 1987–90, Amenities 1987–89, Director, Direct Works Organisation 1990–91. **House of Commons:** Contested Hampshire Central European Parliament (SLD) 1988 by-election and 1989 election. Contested Eastleigh (Lib Dem) 1992 general election. Member for Eastleigh since June 9, 1994 by-election; Spokesperson for: Employment 1994–95, Transport 1995–97, Trade and Industry 1997–99, Foreign Affairs 1999–; *Select Committees:* Member: Accommodation and Works 1998–2001, Standards and Privileges 2001; Member: Foreign Affairs 1999–, Chairmen's Panel 2001–, Joint Committee on Human Rights 2003–. *Special Interests:* Foreign Affairs, International Development, Transportation, Built Environment. *Countries of Interest:* Africa, Pacific Rim and South East Asia, Indian sub-continent, Middle East, Europe. Regional Chair, Hampshire and Wight Liberal Democrats 1992–94. Joint Founder and President, Association of Liberal Democrat Engineers and Applied Scientists; President, NSPCC Eastleigh Branch; Vice President Hampshire Society for the Blind; Patron: Macmillan Nurses Hampshire, Magpie Scanner Appeal, Institute of Mechanical Engineers, Southern, The CP Centre, Portsmouth; National Trust; Member, Worshipful Company of Carmen; Companion, Royal Aeronautical Society; Companion, Institute of Mechanical Engineers; FICE; FIEI; FIHT; MCIT; AConsEI; *Clubs:* National Liberal; *Sportsclubs:* Hampshire County Cricket; *Recreations:* Reading, golf, tennis, following cricket. David Chidgey Esq, MP, House of Commons, London, SW1A 0AA *Tel:* 020 7219 4298 *Fax:* 020 7219 2810. *Constituency:* 113 Leigh Road, Eastleigh, Hampshire, SO50 9DS *Tel:* 023 8062 0007 *Fax:* 023 8061 8245 *E-mail:* chidgeyd@parliament.uk.

CHOPE, CHRISTOPHER   Christchurch   *Con majority 13,544*

Christopher Chope. Born 19 May 1947; Son of late Judge Robert Chope and of Pamela Chope, née Durell; Educated St Andrew's School, Eastbourne; Marlborough College; St Andrew's University (LLB 1970); Married Christine Mary Hutchinson 1987 (1 son 1 daughter). Barrister, Inner Temple 1972; Consultant, Ernst and Young 1992–98. Councillor, London Borough Wandsworth 1974–83, Chair, Housing Committee 1978–79, Leader of the Council 1979–83. **House of Commons:** Member for Southampton Itchen 1983–92, and for Christchurch since May 1, 1997; Opposition Spokesperson for: the Environment, Transport and the Regions 1997–98, Trade and Industry 1998–99, the Treasury 2001–02; PPS to Peter Brooke, as Minister of State, HM Treasury 1986; Parliamentary Under-Secretary of State: at Department of the Environment 1986–90, at Department of Transport (Minister for Roads and Traffic) 1990–92; Shadow Minister of State for Transport 2002–; *Select Committees:* Member, Trade and Industry 1999–2002. Member, Executive Committee, Society of Conservative Lawyers 1983–86; Vice-Chair, Conservative Party 1997–98. Member: Health and Safety Commission 1992–97, Local Government Commission for England 1994–95; OBE 1982. Christopher Chope Esq, OBE, MP, House of Commons, London, SW1A 0AA *Tel:* 020 7219 5808. *Constituency:* 18a Bargates, Christchurch, Dorset *Tel:* 01202 474949 *Fax:* 01202 475548.

Visit the Vacher Dod Website . . .
www.DodOnline.co.uk

CLAPHAM, MICHAEL   Barnsley West and Penistone   *Lab majority 12,352*

Michael Clapham. Born 15 May 1943; Son of late Thomas Clapham, miner and Eva Ellen Clapham, née Winterbottom; Educated Darton Secondary Modern School; Barnsley Technical College; Leeds Polytechnic (BSc sociology 1973); Leeds University (PGCE 1974); Bradford University (MPhil industrial relations 1990); Married Yvonne Hallsworth 1965 (1 son 1 daughter). Miner 1958–69; Lecturer trade union studies, Whitwood FE College, Castleford 1974–77; Deputy Head, Comp Dept, Yorkshire Area NUM 1977–83; Head, Industrial Relations NUM 1983–92; NUM: Member 1958–, Claims Officer 1977–83, Head, Industrial Relations Department 1983–; Member, UCATT 1994–. Chair, Barnsley Crime Prevention Partnership 1995–, Chair, Barnsley MAP– Anti-Racist Strategy Body. **House of Commons:** Member for Barnsley West and Penistone since April 9, 1992; PPS to Alan Milburn as Minister of State, Department of Health May-November 1997 (resigned over benefit cuts); *Select Committees:* Member, Trade and Industry 1992–97. *Special Interests:* Coal Industry, Energy, Employment, Health, NATO, Eastern Europe. *Countries of Interest:* Tibet, Nepal, South Africa, Egypt, Bahrain, Eastern Europe. Member, Co-operative Party; Secretary, Higham Labour Party Branch 1981–83; Treasurer, Barnsley West and Penistone Constituency Labour Party 1983–92; Chair, Dodworth Labour Party Branch 1984–86. Member NATO Parliamentary Assembly 2000–; *Publications: The Case was made for Coal*, 1993 R Caherne; *The Miners and Clause IV*, 1994, Miners' Parliamentary Group; *Clubs:* Gilroyd Social Club; Dodworth Welfare Club; Wortley Hall; *Recreations:* Walking, gardening, reading. Michael Clapham Esq, MP, House of Commons, London, SW1A 0AA *Tel:* 020 7219 0477 *Fax:* 020 7219 5015. *Constituency:* 18 Regent Street, Barnsley, South Yorkshire, S70 2HG *Tel:* 01226 731244 *Fax:* 01226 779429 *E-mail:* claphamm@parliament.uk.

CLAPPISON, JAMES   Hertsmere   *Con majority 4,902*

James Clappison. Born 14 September 1956; Son of late Leonard Clappison, farmer, and Dorothy Clappison; Educated St Peter's School, York; The Queen's College, Oxford (BA philosophy, politics and economics 1978); Married Helen Margherita Carter 1984 (1 son 3 daughters). Barrister 1981–; Contested Yorkshire South 1989 European Parliament election. **House of Commons:** Contested Barnsley East 1987 general election, Bootle May and November 1990 by-elections. Member for Hertsmere since April 9, 1992; Opposition Spokesperson for: Home Affairs (Crime, Immigration and Asylums) 1997–99, Education and Employment 1999–2000, Treasury 2000–01; PPS to Baroness Blatch: as Minister of State, Department for Education 1992–94, Home Office 1994–95; Parliamentary Under-Secretary of State, Department of the Environment 1995–97; Shadow Financial Secretary, HM Treasury 2000–01; Shadow Minister for Work 2001–02; Shadow Minister for the Treasury 2002; *Select Committees:* Member: Health 1992–94, Members' Interests 1994–95; Member: Home Affairs 2002–, Lord Chancellor's Department 2003–. *Special Interests:* Home Affairs, Economic Policy, Health, Education. *Countries of Interest:* Israel. *Clubs:* United Oxford and Cambridge University, Carlton; *Recreations:* Bridge, walking. James Clappison Esq, MP, House of Commons, London, SW1A 0AA *Tel:* 020 7219 5027. *Constituency:* 104 High Street, London Colney, St Albans, Hertfordshire, AL2 1QL *Tel:* 01727 828221 *Fax:* 01727 828044 *E-mail:* clappisonj@parliament.uk.

CLARK, HELEN   Peterborough   *Lab majority 2,854*

Helen Rosemary Clark. Born 23 December 1954; Daughter of Phyllis May Dyche, ex infant headmistress, and George Henry Dyche, ex junior teacher; Educated Spondon Park Grammar, Derby; Bristol University (BA English literature 1976, MA medieval literature, PGCE 1979); Divorced (1 son 1 daughter); married Alan Clark 2001. Assistant teacher of English, Katharine Lady Berkeley Comprehensive, Gloucestershire 1979–82; 2nd in the English Department, Harrogate Ladies College 1983–88; Lecturer, North Thanet FE College, Broadstairs 1992–1993; Year Head, Rochester Grammar School For Girls 1993–97; Student Rep, NUT 1978–79; Member: NUT 1979–, TGWU 1989–; School Rep, NUT 1994–97; Member, RMT Parliamentary Campaigning

Group 2002–. **House of Commons:** Member for Peterborough since May 1, 1997 (contested the seat as Helen Brinton); *Select Committees:* Member: Environmental Audit 1997–, Unopposed Bills (Panel) 1998–, Broadcasting 2001–. *Special Interests:* Environment, Home Affairs, Health, Rural Affairs, Small Businesses. Member: Fabian Society 1988–97, Co-op Party 1988–97; Has held many posts in Labour Party and Co-operative Party; Kent county election organiser 1993. Volunteer: Alzheimer's Society, ASBAH, MIND-NCVO Parliamentary Secondment Scheme, Parliamentary Police Scheme; Member, Standing Committees on: Crime and Disorder Bill 1997–98, Water Bill 1999, Finance Bill 1999, Financial Services and Markets Bill 1999, Countryside and Rights of Way Bill 2000, Police and Criminal Justice Bill 2001, Proceeds of Crime 2002; *Publications:* Articles in: *Co-op Members News, Tribune, Fabian News, New Statesman & Society, Progress, Labour Weekly* Green Government; Various national newspapers and magazines; *Recreations:* Reading, modern film. Mrs Helen Clark, MP, House of Commons, London, SW1A 0AA *Tel:* 020 7219 4469 *Fax:* 020 7219 0951. *Constituency:* Unity Hall, Northfield Road, Peterborough, PE1 3QH *Tel:* 01733 703000 *Fax:* 01733 704000 *E-mail:* mosesi@parliament.uk.

CLARK, LYNDA   Edinburgh Pentlands   *Lab majority 1,742*

Lynda Clark. Born 26 February 1949; Educated Queens College, St Andrews University (LLB 1970); Edinburgh University (PhD 1975). Dundee University: part-time tutor 1971–73, lecturer in jurisprudence 1973–76; Advocate, Scots Bar 1977–89; QC 1989; Called to the English Bar 1990; Governing bencher Inner Temple 2000. **House of Commons:** Contested North East Fife 1992 general election. Member for Edinburgh Pentlands since May 1, 1997; Advocate General for Scotland 1999–; *Select Committees:* Member, Public Administration 1997–99. *Special Interests:* Constitutional Reform, Justice System, Health, Education, Pensions. Former Member: Scottish Legal Aid Board, Edinburgh University Court. Dr Lynda Clark, QC, MP, House of Commons, London, SW1A 0AA *Tel:* 020 7219 4492. *Constituency:* Constituency Office, 138 Lanark Road Office West, Edinburgh, EH14 5NY *Tel:* 0131 4497177 *E-mail:* ps/advocategeneral@scotland.gsi.gov.uk.

CLARK, PAUL   Gillingham   *Lab majority 2,272*

Paul Gordon Clark. Born 29 April 1957; Son of Gordon Thomas Clark, retired journalist, and of Sheila Gladys Clark, former Mayor of Gillingham; Educated Gillingham Grammar School; Keele University (BA economics and politics 1980); University of Derby (DMS 1997); Married Julie Hendrick 1980 (1 son 1 daughter). Centre manager, Trades Union Congress, National Education Centre 1986–97; AEEU: researcher to President and education officer 1980–86; Member: TUC, Amicus (Gillingham Branch). Councillor, Gillingham Borough Council 1982–90, Labour Group Leader 1988–90, Board Member of Thames Gateway Kent Partnership 2000–; Board Member Groundwork Medway/Swale 2001–. **House of Commons:** Contested Gillingham 1992 general election. Member for Gillingham since May 1, 1997; Assistant Government Whip 2003–; Joint PPS to Lord Irvine of Lairg as Lord Chancellor 1999–2001; PPS to Lord Falconer of Thoroton as Minister of State: Department for Transport, Local Government and the Regions (Minister for Housing, Planning and Regeneration 2001–02, for Criminal Justice System, Home Office 2002–03; *Special Interests:* Education, Transport, Environment, Regeneration. *Countries of Interest:* Europe, Eastern Europe, South East Asia. Member: European Standing Committee A 1998, European Standing Committee B 1998–2000; *Clubs:* Anchorians Association; *Recreations:* Historic buildings, reading. Paul Clark Esq, MP, House of Commons, London, SW1A 0AA *Tel:* 020 7219 5207 *Fax:* 020 7219 2545. *Constituency:* 62A Watling Street, Gillingham, Kent, ME7 2YN *Tel:* 01634 574261 *Fax:* 01634 574276 *E-mail:* clarkp@parliament.uk.

Visit the Vacher Dod Website . . .
www.DodOnline.co.uk

CLARKE, CHARLES   Norwich South   Lab majority 8,816

Charles Rodway Clarke. Born 21 September 1950; Son of late Sir Richard Clarke, KCB, and Lady Brenda Clarke; Educated Highgate School, London; King's College, Cambridge (BA maths and economics 1973); Married Carol Pearson 1984 (2 sons). Part-time adult education maths lecturer, City Literary Institute 1981–83; Organiser, Community Challenge Conference, Gulbenkian Fund 1981–82; Researcher to Neil Kinnock, MP 1981–83; Chief of Staff to Neil Kinnock, MP 1983–92; Chief Executive, Quality Public Affairs 1992–97; Sabbatical President, Cambridge Students' Union 1971–72; Member, National Union of Students' Executive, President 1975–77. Councillor, London Borough of Hackney 1980–86, Chair, Housing Committee, Vice-Chair, Economic Development. **House of Commons:** Member for Norwich South since May 1, 1997; Parliamentary Under-Secretary of State (School Standards), Department for Education and Employment 1998–99; Minister of State, Home Office 1999–2001; Labour Party Chair and Minister without Portfolio 2001–02; Member Joint Committee on House of Lords Reform 2002–; *Select Committees:* Member: Treasury 1997–98, Treasury Sub-Committee 1998. Chairman Labour Party 2002–. Organiser, Hackney People In Partnership 1978–80; PC 2001; *Clubs:* Norwich Labour; *Recreations:* Chess, reading, walking. Rt Hon Charles Clarke, MP, House of Commons, London, SW1A 0AA *Tel:* 020 7219 0945 *Fax:* 020 7219 0526. *Constituency:* Norwich Labour Party, 59 Bethel Street, Norwich, NR2 1NL *Tel:* 01603 219902 *Fax:* 01603 663502.

CLARKE, KENNETH   Rushcliffe   Con majority 7,357

Kenneth Clarke. Born 2 July 1940; Son of late Kenneth Clarke, watchmaker and jeweller, and Doris Clarke; Educated Nottingham High School; Gonville and Caius College, Cambridge (BA, LLB) (President, Cambridge Union 1963); Married Gillian Mary Edwards 1964 (1 son 1 daughter). Called to the Bar 1963; Member, Midland Circuit, practising from Birmingham; QC 1980; Non-executive Deputy Chair, Alliance UniChem 1997–; Director, Foreign & Colonial Investment Trust 1997–; Deputy Chair, British American Tobacco 1998–; Non-executive Chair: British American Racing (Holdings) Limited, Savoy Asset Management PLC; Director, Independent News and Media (UK). **House of Commons:** Contested Mansfield Notts 1964 and 1966 general elections. Member for Rushcliffe since June 1970; Opposition Spokesperson for: Social Services 1974–76, Industry 1976–79; Assistant Government Whip 1972–74; Government Whip 1973–74; PPS to Solicitor General 1971–72; Parliamentary Secretary, Ministry of Transport 1979–80; Parliamentary Under-Secretary of State, Department of Transport 1980–82; Minister for Health 1982–85; Paymaster General and Employment Minister 1985–87; Chancellor, Duchy of Lancaster (Minister of Trade and Industry) 1987–88; Secretary of State for: Health 1988–90, Education and Science 1990–92; Home Secretary 1992–93, Chancellor of the Exchequer 1993–97; *Select Committees:* Member, Joint Committee on House of Lords Reform 2002–. Chair: Cambridge University Conservative Association 1961, Federation Conservative Students 1963–65; Contested leadership June 1997 and 2001. Liveryman, The Clockmakers Company; PC 1984; Hon. LLD: Nottingham University 1989, Huddersfield University 1992, Nottingham Trent University 1995; Honorary Fellow, Gonville and Caius College, Cambridge; *Clubs:* Garrick; *Sportsclubs:* President, Nottinghamshire County Cricket Club; *Recreations:* Birdwatching, football, cricket, jazz. Rt Hon Kenneth Clarke, QC, MP, House of Commons, London, SW1A 0AA *Tel:* 020 7219 4528 *Fax:* 020 7219 4841. *Constituency:* Rushcliffe House, 17/19 Rectory Road, West Bridgford, Nottingham, NG2 6BE *Tel:* 0115–981 7224 *Fax:* 0115–981 7273 *E-mail:* clarkek@parliament.uk.

DodOnline
An Electronic Directory without rival . . .

MPs' biographies and photographs available with daily updates *via* the internet

For a *free* trial, call Yasmin Mirza, Aby Farsoun or Michael Mand on 020 7630 7643

CLARKE, TOM   Coatbridge and Chryston   *Lab majority 15,314*

Thomas Clarke. Born 10 January 1941; Son of late James Clarke; Educated Columba High School, Coatbridge; Scottish College of Commerce. Assistant Director, Scottish Council for Educational Technology (Scottish Film Council) 1966–82; Member, GMB. Councillor: Coatbridge Town Council 1964–74, Monklands District Council 1974–82; Provost of Monklands 1974–82; JP 1972; President, Convention of Scottish Local Authorities 1978–80. **House of Commons:** Member for Coatbridge and Airdrie by-election 1982–83, for Monklands West 1983–97, and for Coatbridge and Chryston since May 1, 1997; Principal Opposition Spokesperson for Development and Co-operation 1993–94; Author and Sponsor Disabled Persons (Services, Representation and Consultation) Act 1986; Shadow Minister for UK Personal Social Services 1987–92; Shadow Secretary of State for Scotland 1992–93, for International Development 1993–94; Shadow Cabinet Minister for Disabled People's Rights 1995–97; Minister of State (Film and Tourism), Department of National Heritage/for Culture, Media and Sport 1997–98; *Special Interests:* Film Industry, Foreign Affairs, Civil Service, Local and Regional Government. *Countries of Interest:* Central America, Philippines, Africa, Asia, Eastern Europe, USA, Peru, South Africa, Indonesia. Labour Member PAD Group to Iran, sponsored by Archbishop of Canterbury 1989; Led CPA delegations to Australia 2000; Observer Peruvian election 2001; Led IPU Rwanda 2002; Fellow, Industry and Parliament Trust; *Publications:* Director of award winning amateur film *Give us a Goal*, 1972; Joint chair, film review *A Bigger Picture*, 1998; CBE 1980; PC 1997; *Sportsclubs:* Coatbridge Municipal Golf; *Recreations:* Films, walking, reading, astrology. Rt Hon Thomas Clarke, CBE, JP, MP, House of Commons, London, SW1A 0AA *Tel:* 020 7219 5007 *Fax:* 020 7219 6094. *Constituency:* Municipal Buildings, Kildonan Street, Coatbridge, ML5 3LF *Tel:* 01236 600800 *Fax:* 01236 600808 *E-mail:* clarket@parliament.uk.

CLARKE, TONY   Northampton South   *Lab majority 885*

Tony (Anthony Richard) Clarke. Born 6 September 1963; Son of Walter Arthur Clarke, engineer, and late Joan Ada Iris Clarke; Educated Lings Upper School, Northampton; Institute of Training and Development; Institute of Safety and Health; Married Carole Chalmers (1 son 1 daughter). Social work trainer, Northamptonshire County Council; Disability training officer –1997; sponsored MP for CWU. Councillor, Northampton Borough Council 1991–99; Chair, Environment Services. **House of Commons:** Member for Northampton South since May 1, 1997; *Select Committees:* Member, Joint Committee on Consolidation of Bills Etc 1997–2001; Member, Northern Ireland Affairs 1999–. *Special Interests:* Environment, Leisure, Constitution, Sport, Local and Regional Government, Middle East. *Countries of Interest:* Europe, China, Palenstine. Director, East Midlands Sports Council Board; *Sportsclubs:* Director, Northampton Town FC; *Recreations:* Football, Travel. Tony Clarke Esq, MP, House of Commons, London, SW1A 0AA *Tel:* 020 7219 3000 *Fax:* 020 7219 2808. *Constituency:* 41 York Road, Northampton, NN1 5QJ *Tel:* 01604 250044 *Fax:* 01604 250055 *E-mail:* clarkea@parliament.uk.

CLELLAND, DAVID   Tyne Bridge   *Lab majority 14,889*

David Gordon Clelland. Born 27 June 1943; Son of Archibald Clelland and Ellen Clelland, née Butchart; Educated Kelvin Grove Boys School, Gateshead; Gateshead Technical College; Hebburn Technical College; Charles Trevelyan Technical College (City and Guilds and electrical technician courses); Married Maureen Potts 1965 (2 daughters) (divorced). Electrical fitter 1964–81; Local Government Association Secretary 1981–86; AEEU: Shop steward 1967–81. Chair, Gateshead Council Recreation Committee 1976–84; Secretary, Association of Councillors 1981–86; Vice-chair, Gateshead Health Authority 1982–84; Leader, Gateshead Council 1984–86. **House of Commons:** Member for Tyne Bridge since December 5, 1985 by-election; Opposition Whip 1995–97; Assistant Government Whip 1997–2001; Government Whip (Defence, International Development, North East) 2001; Adviser on Greyhounds to Richard Caborn, as Minister of State for Sport 2002–;

Select Committees: Member: Office of the Deputy Prime Minister: Housing, Planning and Local Government 2002–, Urban Affairs Sub-Committee 2003–. *Special Interests:* Local and Regional Government, Home Affairs, Transport, Environment, Employment, Energy, Devolution, Constitutional Reform (House of Lords). Northern Regional Group of Labour MPs: Hon. Secretary and Hon. Treasurer 1992–98, Vice-Chair 1999, Chair 2002–. *Recreations:* Golf, music, reading. David Clelland Esq, MP, House of Commons, London, SW1A 0AA *Tel:* 020 7219 3669 *Fax:* 020 7219 0328. *Constituency:* 19 Ravensworth Road, Dunston, Gateshead, Tyne and Wear, NE11 9AB *Tel:* 01914 200300 *Fax:* 01914 200301 *E-mail:* davidclellandmp@aol.com.

CLIFTON-BROWN, GEOFFREY   Cotswold   *Con majority 11,983*

Geoffrey Clifton-Brown. Born 23 March 1953; Son of Robert and Elizabeth Clifton-Brown; Educated Eton College; Royal Agricultural College, Cirencester (ARICS 1975); Married Alexandra Peto-Shepherd 1979 (1 son 1 daughter). Graduate estate surveyor, Property Services Agency, Dorchester 1975; Investment surveyor, Jones Lang Wootton 1975–79; Managing director, own farming business in Norfolk 1979–. **House of Commons:** Member for Cirencester and Tewkesbury 1992–97, and for Cotswold since May 1, 1997; Opposition Spokesperson for: Environment, Food and Rural Affairs 2001, Transport, Local Government and the Regions 2001–02, Local Government, Housing and Planning 2002–; Opposition Whip: Agriculture, Education and Employment: Scotland 1999–2001, Education and Employment, Defence 1999–2000, Culture, Media and Sport 1999–2000, Agriculture 2000, Environment, Transport and the Regions: Wales 2000–01, Private Members' Bills 2001; PPS to Douglas Hogg as Minister of Agriculture, Fisheries and Food 1995–97; *Select Committees:* Member: Environment 1992–97, Public Accounts 1997–99, Broadcasting 2000–01, Administration 2001. *Special Interests:* Economy, Taxation, Foreign Affairs, Environment, Agriculture. *Countries of Interest:* Brazil, France, Italy, Kashmir, Hong Kong. Chair, North Norfolk Constituency Association 1986–91. Vice-chair: Charities Property Association 1993–2002, Small Business Bureau 1995–, Euro Atlantic Group 1995–; Member: Eastern Area Executive and Agricultural Committees 1986–91; Liveryman, The Worshipful Company of Farmers; *Publications: Privatisation of the State Pension – Secure Funded Provision for all*, 1996; Fellowship, Royal Institute of Chartered Surveyors (FRICS) 2002; Freeman, City of London; *Clubs:* Carlton, Farmers'; *Recreations:* Fishing, other rural pursuits. Geoffrey Clifton-Brown Esq, MP, House of Commons, London, SW1A 0AA *Tel:* 020 7219 5147 *Fax:* 020 7219 2550. *Constituency:* 7 Rodney Road, Cheltenham, Gloucestershire, GL50 1HX *Tel:* 01242 514551 *Fax:* 01242 514949 *E-mail:* gcb@gcbmp.demon.co.uk.

CLWYD, ANN   Cynon Valley   *Lab majority 12,998*

Ann Clwyd. Born 21 March 1937; Daughter of Gwilym and Elizabeth Lewis; Educated Holywell Grammar School; The Queen's School, Chester; University College of Wales, Bangor; Married Owen Roberts 1963. Journalist; Broadcaster; MEP for Mid and West Wales 1979–84; Member: NUJ, TGWU. **House of Commons:** Contested Denbigh 1970 and Gloucester October 1974 general elections. Member for Cynon Valley since by-election May 3, 1984; Opposition Spokesperson for: Employment 1993–94, Foreign Affairs 1994–95; Shadow Minister of Education and Women's Rights 1987–88; Shadow Secretary of State for: International Development 1989–92, Wales July-November 1992, National Heritage 1992–93; Assistant to John Prescott as Deputy Leader of Labour Party 1994–95; *Select Committees:* Member, International Development 1997–. *Countries of Interest:* Iraq, Turkey, Iran, Russia, Cambodia, Vietnam, East Timor. Member Labour Party National Executive Committee 1983–84; Chair Tribune Group 1986–87; Member Parliamentary Labour Party Parliamentary Committee 1997–, Deputy Chair 2001–. Member, Arts Council 1975–79; Vice-Chair, Welsh Arts Council 1975–79; Royal Commission on NHS 1976–79; Inter-Parliamentary Union: Executive committee member, British Group, Member, Human Rights Commission; White Robe Gorsedd Member of Royal National Eisteddfod of Wales; Hon. Fellow, University of North Wales; *Recreations:* Walking, boating. Ann Clwyd, MP, House of Commons, London, SW1A 0AA *Tel:* 020 7219 6609. *Constituency:* 6 Dean Court, Aberdare, CF44 7BN *Tel:* 01685 871394 *E-mail:* clwyda@parliament.uk.

COAKER, VERNON   Gedling   *Lab majority 5,598*

Vernon Rodney Coaker. Born 17 June 1953; Son of Edwin Coaker; Educated Drayton Manor Grammar School, London; Warwick University (BA politics 1974); Trent Polytechnic (PGCE 1976); Married Jacqueline Heaton 1978 (1 son 1 daughter). Humanities teaching in Nottinghamshire: Manvers School 1976–82, Arnold Hill School 1982–89, Bramcote Park School 1989–95, Big Wood School 1995–97; Member, NUT. Councillor, Rushcliffe Borough Council 1983–97. **House of Commons:** Member for Gedling since May 1, 1997; Assistant Government Whip 2003–; PPS to: Stephen Timms: as Minister of State, Department of Social Security 1999, as Financial Secretary, HM Treasury 1999–2001, as Minister of State for School Standards, Department for Education and Skills 2001–02, as Minister of State for e-Commerce, Department of Trade and Industry 2002, Estelle Morris as Secretary of State for Education and Skills 2002, Tessa Jowell as Secretary of State for Culture, Media and Sport 2002–03; *Select Committees:* Member, Social Security 1998–99. *Special Interests:* Environment, Education, Welfare Reform, Foreign Policy, Sport. *Countries of Interest:* France, Kosovo, Macedonia, Angola. Member: League Against Cruel Sports, Friends of the Earth; Honorary Fellow UNICEF; Member, European Standing Committee B 1998; *Recreations:* Sport, walking. Vernon Coaker Esq, MP, House of Commons, London, SW1A 0AA *Tel:* 020 7219 6627. *Constituency:* 2A Parkyn Road, Daybrook, Nottingham, NG5 6BG *Tel:* 0115–920 4224 *Fax:* 0115–920 4500 *E-mail:* coakerv@parliament.uk.

COFFEY, ANN   Stockport   *Lab majority 11,569*

Ann Coffey. Born 31 August 1946; Daughter of late John Brown, MBE, Flight-Lieutenant, RAF, and of Marie Brown, nurse; Educated Nairn Academy; Bodmin and Bushey Grammar Schools; Polytechnic of South Bank, London (BSc sociology 1967); Walsall College of Education (Postgraduate Certificate in Education 1971); Manchester University (MSc psychiatric social work 1977); Married 1973 (marriage dissolved 1989) (1 daughter); married 1999. Trainee Social Worker, Walsall Social Services 1971–72; Social Worker: Birmingham 1972–73, Gwynedd 1973–74, Wolverhampton 1974–75, Stockport 1977–82, Cheshire 1982–88; Team Leader, Fostering, Oldham Social Services 1988–92; Member, USDAW. Stockport Metropolitan Borough Council: Councillor 1984–92, Leader of Labour Group 1988–92; Member, District Health Authority 1986–90. **House of Commons:** Contested Cheadle 1987 general election. Member for Stockport since April 9, 1992; Opposition Spokeswoman on Health 1996–97; Opposition Whip 1995–96; Joint PPS to Tony Blair as Prime Minister 1997–98; PPS to Alistair Darling as Secretary of State for: Social Security/Work and Pensions 1998–2002, Transport 2002–, Scotland 2003–; *Select Committees:* Member, Trade and Industry 1993–95; Member, Modernisation of the House of Commons 2000–. *Special Interests:* Health, Social Services, Voluntary Organisations. *Recreations:* Photography, drawing, cinema, swimming, reading. Ann Coffey, MP, House of Commons, London, SW1A 0AA *Tel:* 020 7219 4546 *Fax:* 020 7219 0770. *Constituency:* 207a Bramhall Lane, Stockport, SK2 6JA *Tel:* 0161 483 2600 *Fax:* 0161 483 1070 *E-mail:* coffeya@parliament.uk.

COHEN, HARRY   Leyton and Wanstead   *Lab majority 12,904*

Harry Cohen. Born 10 December 1949; Son of Emanuel and Anne Cohen; Educated George Gascoigne Secondary Modern; East Ham Technical College (part-time) Chartered Institute of Public Finance and Accountancy 1974; Birkbeck College, London University (MSc politics and administration 1995); Married Ellen Hussain 1978 (1 stepson 1 stepdaughter). Accountant and auditor, London Borough of Waltham Forest, Hackney and Haringey; Auditor, NALGO; Member, UNISON. Waltham Forest Borough Council: Councillor 1972–83, Chair, Planning Committee 1972–83, Secretary, Labour Group 1972–83; Member, Waltham Forest Area Health Authority 1972–83. **House of Commons:** Member for Leyton 1983–97, and for Leyton and Wanstead since May 1, 1997; *Select Committees:* Member, Defence 1997–2001. *Special Interests:* Defence, Equality,

Health, Transport, Ecology and Conservation, Animal Rights. *Countries of Interest:* Middle East, Central Europe, Eastern Europe, India, Pakistan, Bangladesh, Tibet. Vice-President, The Royal College of Midwives; Member, UK Delegation to North Atlantic Assembly 1992–; Chair, Sub-Committee for Economic Co-operation and Convergence with Central and Eastern Europe; Reserve, UK delegation to Organisation for Security and Co-operation in Europe 1997–2001; Member, CIPFA 1974; *Recreations:* Part-owner racing greyhound. Harry Cohen Esq, MP, House of Commons, London, SW1A 0AA *Tel:* 020 7219 6376/4137 *Fax:* 020 7219 0438 *E-mail:* cohenh@parliament.uk.

COLEMAN, IAIN   Hammersmith and Fulham   Lab majority 2,015

Iain Coleman. Born 18 January 1958; Son of late Ronald Coleman and Pamela Coleman; Educated Tonbridge School; Married Sally Powell (now DBE) (1 son). Senior administrative officer London Borough of Islington; Personal Assistant to Leader of Council London Borough of Ealing; Member, MSF. Councillor, Hammersmith and Fulham 1986–97, Leader 1991–96, Mayor 1996–97. **House of Commons:** Member for Hammersmith and Fulham since May 1, 1997; *Select Committees:* Member, Deregulation 1997–99. *Special Interests:* Housing, Sport, Asylum, Immigration. *Countries of Interest:* Ireland, France. Secretary London Regional Group of Labour MPs 1999–. Vice-Chair, Association of London Authorities 1993–95; *Sportsclubs:* Arsenal FC; *Recreations:* Football, opera, cooking, travel. Iain Coleman Esq, MP, House of Commons, London, SW1A 0AA *Tel:* 020 7219 4486 *Fax:* 020 7386 5415. *Constituency:* 28 Greyhound Road, London, W6 8NX *Tel:* 020 7381 5074 *Fax:* 020 7386 5415 *E-mail:* sheehanj@parliament.uk.

COLLINS, TIM   Westmorland and Lonsdale   Con majority 3,147

Tim William George Collins. Born 7 May 1964; Son of late William Collins, farmer and of Diana Collins, farmer; Educated Chigwell School, Essex; London School of Economics (BSc 1985); King's College, London (MA war studies 1986); Married Clare Benson 1997 (1 son). Conservative Research Department 1986–89; Special Adviser: to David Hunt and Michael Howard as Secretaries of State for the Environment 1989–90, to Michael Howard as Employment Secretary 1990–92; Press Secretary to John Major as Prime Minister 1992; Director of Communications, Conservative Party 1992–95; Member, Prime Minister's Policy Unit, Downing Street 1995; Senior Strategy Consultant, WCT Live Communications Ltd (commercial event management). **House of Commons:** Member for Westmorland and Lonsdale since May 1, 1997; Opposition Whip (Social Security, Trade and Industry) 1998–99; Vice-chair Conservative Party 1999–2001; Shadow Minister for the Cabinet Office 2001–02; *Select Committees:* Member: Agriculture 1997–98, Information 1998–2001. *Special Interests:* Defence, Media, Tourism, Constitution, Agriculture, European Union, Economic Policy, Employment, Northern Ireland. *Countries of Interest:* USA, Germany, Australia. Ex-officio Member, National Union Executive Committee 1992–95; Member Conservative Policy Board 2001–. CBE 1996; *Recreations:* Literature, cinema, heritage. Tim Collins Esq, CBE, MP, House of Commons, London, SW1A 0AA *Tel:* 020 7219 6673. *Constituency:* 112 Highgate, Kendal, Cumbria, LA9 4HE *Tel:* 01539 721010 *Fax:* 01539 733039 *E-mail:* listening@timcollins.co.uk.

COLMAN, TONY   Putney   Lab majority 2,771

Tony (Anthony) John Colman. Born 24 July 1943; Son of late William and Beatrice Colman; Educated Paston Grammar School, North Walsham, Norfolk; Magdalene College, Cambridge (BA history 1964, MA); Married Juliet Owen 1989 (2 sons plus 1 stepson 1 stepdaughter and 3 sons 1 daughter from previous marriages). Unilever (United Africa Company) 1964–69; Associated Fisheries Ltd 1969–71; Burton Group 1969–90, Main Board Director 1981–90; Director, London First Centre Ltd 1994–; 4ps: Chair 1996–8, Director 1998–; Member, GMB. Councillor, London Borough of Merton 1990–98, Leader of Council 1990–97. **House of Commons:** Contested South West Hertfordshire 1979 general election. Member for Putney since

May 1, 1997; Member Price Commission 1977–79; PPS to Adam Ingram as Minister of State, Northern Ireland Office 1998–2000; *Select Committees:* Member, Treasury 1997–98; Member, International Development 2000–. *Special Interests:* Agenda 21, Private Finance Initiative, Pension Funds, Global Warming, Sustainable Development, Corruption. *Countries of Interest:* Developing and transitional countries. Member: Labour Finance and Industry Group 1973–, Labour Party Enquiry into Education and Training in Europe 1991–93. Chair, Low Pay Unit 1990–98; Member, Prices Commission 1977–79; Vice-Chair, Association of London Authorities 1991–95; Director, London Arts Board 1994–98; Chair: UK Standing Committee Local Authority Pensions 1994–98, Public Private Partnership Program 1995–98; Director, CCLA 1995–98; Member Institute of Directors; Acting member IPW Sustainable Development Committee; Chair, Wimbledon Theatre Trust 1991–97; Industrial Fellow, Kingston University; FRSA 1983; Freeman, City of London 1997; *Clubs:* Reform, Winchester (Putney); *Recreations:* Swimming, theatre. Tony Colman Esq, MP, House of Commons, London, SW1A 0AA *Tel:* 020 7219 2843 *Fax:* 020 7219 1137. *Constituency:* 35 Felsham Road, London, SW15 1AY *Tel:* 020 8788 8961 *Fax:* 020 8785 2053 *E-mail:* colmant@parliament.uk.

CONNARTY, MICHAEL   Falkirk East   *Lab majority 10,712*

Michael Connarty. Born 3 September 1947; Son of late Patrick and Elizabeth Connarty; Educated St Patrick's High School, Coatbridge; Stirling University (BA economics 1972); Glasgow University; Jordanhill College of Education (DCE 1975); Married Margaret Doran 1969 (1 son 1 daughter). President, Student Association, Stirling University 1970–71; Chair, Stirling Economic Development Co. 1987–90; Teacher Economics and Modern Studies (secondary and special needs) 1976–92; Member: TGWU, EIS. Stirling District Council: Councillor 1977–90, Council leader 1980–90; JP 1977–90. **House of Commons:** Contested Stirling 1983 and 1987 general elections. Member for Falkirk East since April 9, 1992; PPS to Tom Clarke, as Minister of State, Department for Culture, Media and Sport (Film and Tourism) 1997–98; *Select Committees:* Member: European Directives Committee A (Agriculture, Environment, Health and Safety) 1993–97, Select Committee on Parliamentary Commissioner for Administration 1995–97, Information 1997–2001; Member, European Scrutiny 1998–. *Special Interests:* Economy and Enterprise, Local and Regional Government, European Union, Industry, Skills and Training, Youth Affairs, Crime, Drug Abuse, Small Businesses. *Countries of Interest:* Middle East, Central America, Australia, USA. Member, Labour Party Scottish Executive Committee 1981–82, 1983–92; Chair, LP Scottish Local Government Committee 1988–90; Member, LP Local Government Committee (UK) 1989–91; Vice-Chair, COSLA Labour Group 1988–90; Chair, Stirlingshire Co-operative Party 1990–92; Vice-Chair, Scottish Group of Labour MPs 1996–98, Chair 1998–99. Loch Lomond, Trossachs and Stirling Tourist Board: Financial Controller 1981–84, Member 1981–90; Member, Socialist Education Association 1978–; Central EIS President 1983–84; National Council EIS 1984–85; Rector, Stirling University 1983–84; Vice-Chair, Scottish Medical Aid for Palestinians 1988–95; Board Member, Parliamentary Office of Science and Technology (POST) 1997–; Life Member: International Parliamentary Union 1992–, Commonwealth Parliamentary Association 1992–; British American Parliamentary Group 1992–; *Recreations:* Family, music (jazz and classical), reading, walking. Michael Connarty Esq, MP, House of Commons, London, SW1A 0AA *Tel:* 020 7219 5071 *Fax:* 020 7219 2541. *Constituency:* Room 8, 5 Kerse Road, Grangemouth, FK3 8HQ *Tel:* 01324 474832 *Fax:* 01324 666811 *E-mail:* connartym@parliament.uk.

CONWAY, DEREK   Old Bexley and Sidcup   *Con majority 3,345*

Derek Conway. Born 15 February 1953; Son of Leslie Conway, superintendent of parks and crematoria and Florence Conway, housewife; Educated Beacon Hill Boys' School; Gateshead Technical College; Newcastle upon Tyne Polytechnic; Married Colette Elizabeth Mary Lamb 1980 (2 sons 1 daughter). Territorial Decoration (Territorial Army); Former advertising manager; Regional Director and Principal Organiser National Fund for Research into Crippling Diseases 1974–83; Chief executive Cats Protection League 1998–; Member Transport and General Workers Union 1968–71. Gateshead Borough Council 1974–87: Councillor, Deputy group leader 1974–82; Tyne and Wear Metropolitan County Council: Councillor 1977–83, Leader 1979–82,

Board Newcastle International Airport 1979–82; Member North of England Development Council 1979–83, Executive Board Washington Development Corporation 1979–83. **House of Commons:** Contested Durham October 1974, Newcastle upon Tyne East 1979 general elections. MP for Shrewsbury and Atcham 1983–97. Contested Shrewsbury 1997 general election. Member for Old Bexley and Sidcup since June 7, 2001; Assistant government whip 1993–94; Government whip 1993–97; PPS: to Minister of State for Wales 1988–91, to Minister of State for Employment 1992–93; *Select Committees:* Vice-chair, Defence 1991–93; Member: Accommodation and Works 1995–97, Administration 1995–97, Broadcasting 1995–97; Chair, Accommodation and Works 2001–; Member: Chairmen's Panel 2001–, Finance and Services 2001–, Liaison 2001–. *Special Interests:* Territorial Army, Defence, Voluntary Services, Animal Welfare, Foreign Affairs. Member National Executive Committee 1971–81; National vice-chair Young Conservatives 1972–74; Member General Purposes Committee 1972–84; Vice-chair Conservative National Local Government Committee 1979–83; Chair: Gateshead Association, Northern Area Young Conservatives; Vice-chair Northern Area Conservatives. Board member Newcastle Airport 1979–82; British Youth Council; Board of Northern Arts; Member Institute of Directors; Inter-Parliamentary Union: Former executive member, Former leader UK delegation, Vice-president 92nd conference, Vice-chair 1991–93, Treasurer 2001–; Freeman of City of London; Territorial Army decoration; *Recreations:* Walking, historical fiction. Derek Conway Esq, MP, House of Commons, London, SW1A 0AA *Tel:* 020 7219 3000. *Constituency:* 19 Station Road, Sidcup, Kent, DA15 7EB *Tel:* 020 8300 3471 *Fax:* 020 8300 9270.

COOK, FRANK   Stockton North   *Lab majority 14,647*

Frank (Francis) Cook. Born 3 November 1935; Son of late James Cook; Educated Corby School, Sunderland; De La Salle College, Manchester; Institute of Education, Leeds; Married Patricia Lundrigan 1959 (divorced) (1 son 3 daughters). Previously: Schoolmaster, Gravedigger, Butlins Redcoat, Barman, Brewery hand, Gardener, Postman, Steel works transport manager; Construction, planning, field, cost engineer, project manager; Member and Sponsored by MSF. **House of Commons:** Member for Stockton North since June 1983; Opposition Whip 1987–92; Deputy Speaker Westminster Hall 1999–2001, 2002–; *Select Committees:* Member: Procedure 1989–92, Defence 1992–97; Member, Chairmen's Panel 1997–. *Special Interests:* Engineering, Peace and Disarmament, Alternative Energy, Expatriate Workers, Pensioners' Rights, Education, Ecology, Race Relations, Landmine Victim Support, Landmine Eradication Measures, Child Protection and Safety, Shooters' Rights. *Countries of Interest:* North Korea, South Korea, Turkey, Laos. Member: NATO – Parliamentary Assembly 1987–2001, Vice-President 1998–2000; Organisation for Security and Co-operation in Europe Parliamentary Body 1991–2001; Trustee, Lucy Faithfull Foundation (for rehabilitation of sexual offenders); Fellow: Industry and Parliament Trust, Parliamentary Armed Services Trust; *Recreations:* Singing, climbing, fell-walking, swimming, supporting North East football. Frank Cook Esq, MP, House of Commons, London, SW1A 0AA *Tel:* 020 7219 4527 *Fax:* 020 7219 4303. *Constituency:* c/o The Health Centre, Queensway, Billingham, Teesside, TS23 2LA *Tel:* 01642 643288 *Fax:* 01642 803271 *E-mail:* cookf@parliament.uk.

COOK, ROBIN   Livingston   *Lab majority 10,616*

Robin (Robert) Finlayson Cook. Born 28 February 1946; Son of late Peter Cook; Educated Aberdeen Grammar School; Edinburgh University (MA English literature); Married Margaret Whitmore, medical consultant 1969 (2 sons) (divorced 1998); married Gaynor Regan, née Wellings 1998. Tutor-organiser, Workers' Educational Association 1970–74. Edinburgh Town Council: Councillor 1971–74, Chairman, Edinburgh Housing Committee 1973–74. **House of Commons:** Contested Edinburgh North 1970 general election. Member for Edinburgh Central 1974–83, and for Livingston since June 1983; Opposition Frontbench Spokesperson for: Treasury and Economic Affairs 1980–83, European and Community Affairs 1983–84; Spokesman on the City 1986–87; Shadow Secretary of State for: Health and Social Security 1987–92, Trade and Industry 1992–94, Foreign and Commonwealth Affairs 1994–97; Chair, NEC of Labour Party 1997; Secretary of State for Foreign and Commonwealth Affairs 1997–2001; Leader of the House of Commons and

President of the Council 2001–03; *Select Committees:* Chair, Modernisation of the House of Commons 2001–03. *Special Interests:* Welfare, Environment, Defence. Chair, Scottish Association of Labour Student Organisations 1966–67; Secretary, Edinburgh City Labour Party 1970–72; Labour Party Campaign Co-ordinator 1984–86; Former Member: Labour Party National Executive Committee, Labour Party National Policy Forum; Member Parliamentary Labour Party Parliamentary Committee 2001–. Member, House of Commons Commision 2001–03; Member, Executive Committee, Commonwealth Parliamentary Association (CPA) UK Branch 1999–; PC 1996; *The Spectator* Parliamentarian of the Year 1991, Debater of the Year 1996; *Recreations:* Reading, horse racing. Rt Hon Robin Cook, MP, House of Commons, London, SW1A 0AA *Tel:* 020 7219 4431. *Constituency:* 4 Newyear Field Farm, Hawk Brae, Ladywell, Livingston, EH54 6TW *Tel:* 01506 497961.

COOPER, YVETTE   Pontefract and Castleford   *Lab majority 16,378*

Yvette Cooper. Born 20 March 1969; Daughter of Tony and June Cooper; Educated Eggars Comprehensive; Balliol College, Oxford (BA philosophy, politics and economics 1990); Harvard University (Kennedy Scholar 1991); London School of Economics (MSc economics 1995); Married Ed Balls 1998 (1 daughter 1 son). Economic researcher for John Smith MP 1990–92; Domestic policy specialist, Bill Clinton presidential campaign 1992; Policy adviser to Labour Treasury teams 1992–94; Economic columnist/Leader writer, *The Independent* 1995–97; Member, TGWU, GMB. **House of Commons:** Member for Pontefract and Castleford since May 1, 1997; Parliamentary Under-Secretary of State for Public Health, Department of Health 1999–2002; Parliamentary Secretary, Lord Chancellor's Department 2002–03; Parliamentary Under-Secretary of State, Office of the Deputy Prime Minister 2003–; *Select Committees:* Member: Education and Employment 1997–99, Employment Sub-Committee 1997–99. *Special Interests:* Unemployment, Coal Industry, Poverty, Equal Opportunities. *Countries of Interest:* USA. *Recreations:* Swimming, painting, watching West Wing between Disney videos. Yvette Cooper, MP, House of Commons, London, SW1A 0AA *Tel:* 020 7219 5080 *Fax:* 020 7219 0912. *Constituency:* 2 Wesley Street, Castleford, West Yorkshire, WF10 1AE *Tel:* 01977 553388 *Fax:* 01977 553388 *E-mail:* coopery@parliament.uk.

CORBYN, JEREMY   Islington North   *Lab majority 12,958*

Jeremy Corbyn. Born 26 May 1949; Son of David Benjamin and Naomi Loveday Jocelyn Corbyn; Educated Adams Grammar School, Newport, Shropshire; (3 sons). Former full-time organiser, National Union of Public Employees; Also worked for Tailor and Garment workers and AUEW; NUPE sponsored MP; Member, RMT Parliamentary Campaigning Group 2002–. Haringey Borough Council: Chair: Community Development 1975–78, Public Works 1978–79, Planning 1980–81. **House of Commons:** Member for Islington North since June 1983; *Select Committees:* Member, Social Security 1991–97. *Special Interests:* People of Islington, Defence, Welfare State, NHS, Campaigning for Socialism in the Community and against Racism, Anti-Imperialism and Internationalism, Transport Safety, Environment, Irish Affairs, Liberation Islington Local Agenda 21. *Recreations:* Running, railways. Jeremy Corbyn Esq, MP, House of Commons, London, SW1A 0AA *Tel:* 020 7219 3545. *Constituency:* 213a Blackstock Road, London, N5 2LL *Tel:* 020 7226 5775.

DodOnline
An Electronic Directory without rival ...

MPs' biographies and photographs available with daily updates *via* the internet

For a *free* trial, call Yasmin Mirza, Aby Farsoun or Michael Mand on 020 7630 7643

CORMACK, PATRICK   South Staffordshire   *Con majority 6,881*

Patrick Thomas Cormack. Born 18 May 1939; Son of late Thomas C. Cormack, local government officer; Educated St James' Choir School; Havelock School, Grimsby; Hull University (BA English and history 1961); Married Kathleen Mary McDonald 1967 (2 sons). Industrial Consultant; Second master, St James' Choir School, Grimsby 1961–66; Training and education officer, Ross Group Ltd. 1966–67; Assistant housemaster, Wrekin College, Shropshire 1967–69; Head of history, Brewood Grammar School, Staffordshire 1969–70; Associate editor, *Time and Tide* 1977–79; Company director Historic House Hotels 1980–88, Aitken Dott 1984–90; Editor, *The House Magazine* 1983–; Visiting lecturer, University of Texas 1984; Visiting Parliamentary Fellowship, St Anthony's College, Oxford 1994; Visiting senior lecturer, Hull University 1994–; International President, *First* magazine 1994–; Governor, English Speaking Union 1999–. **House of Commons:** Contested Bolsover 1964 and Grimsby 1966 general elections. Member for Cannock 1970–74, for South-West Staffordshire 1974–83 and for South Staffordshire since June 1983; Spokesperson for Constitutional Affairs 1997–2000; PPS to the Joint Parliamentary Secretaries, Department of Health and Social Security 1970–73; Deputy to the Shadow Leader of the House of Commons 1997–2000; Opposition Spokesman on Constitutional Affairs 1997–2000; *Select Committees:* Member: House of Commons Services 1979–92, Speaker's Panel of Chairmen 1983–97; Chair, House of Commons Works of Art 1987–2001; Member: Accommodation and Works 1987–2001, Chairmen's Panel 1997–98, Modernisation of the House of Commons 1997–98, Parliamentary Privilege (Joint Committee) 1997–2000, Joint Committee on Human Rights 2001, Foreign Affairs 2001–03; Member: Joint Committee on Consolidation of Bills Etc 2001–, Standing Orders 2001–. *Special Interests:* Arts, Heritage, Defence and NATO, Parliamentary History, Education, Electoral Reform, Industrial Relations, Human Rights. *Countries of Interest:* Bosnia, former Soviet Union, Croatia, Finland, Netherlands, Lithuania, USA. Member, Council of Historical Association 1963–66; Founder and Vice-Chairman, Heritage in Danger 1974–97; Member, Historic Buildings Council 1979–84; Chairman, Council for Independent Education from 1980–95; Member: Royal Commission on Historical Manuscripts 1981–, General Synod of the Church of England 1995–; Governor, English Speaking Union 1999–; Member: Institute of Journalists 1979–89, Royal Commission on Historical Manuscripts 1981–, Lord Chancellor's Advisory Committee on Public Records 1982–87, House of Commons Commission 2002–; Director Parliamentary Broadcasting Unit; Vice-Chairman, De Burght Conference; Member, Council for Peace in the Balkans 1992–; Member, Executive Committee, Commonwealth Parliamentary Association (CPA) UK Branch 1997–99, Joint Vice-Chairman 1999–2000, Treasurer 2000–; Trustee Historic Churches Preservation Trust 1973–; History of Parliament Trust: Member 1979–, Trustee 1983–, Chairman 2001–; Museum of Garden History 1980–2000; Member Council of Winston Churchill Memorial Trust 1983–93; Vice-President Lincolnshire Historic Churches Trust 1997–; President Staffordshire Historic Churches Trust 1998–; Member, Worshipful Company of Glaziers; *Publications: Heritage in Danger*, 1976; *Right Turn*, 1978; *Westminster: Palace and Parliament*, 1981; *Castles of Britain* 1982; *Wilberforce – The Nation's Conscience*, 1983; *English Cathedrals 1984*; Hon. Citizen of Texas 1985; Knighted 1995; Commander of the Order of the Lion (Finland) 1998; Fellow, Society of Antiquaries 1978, Vice-President 1994–98; Freeman, City of London 1980; *Clubs:* Athenaeum; Chairman Works of Art Committee; *Recreations:* Walking, talking, fighting Philistines. Sir Patrick Cormack, MP, House of Commons, London, SW1A 0AA *Tel:* 020 7219 5514 *Fax:* 020 7219 6805. *Constituency:* The Firs, Codsall, Staffordshire, WV8 1BX *Tel:* 01902 844985 *Fax:* 01902 844949.

CORSTON, JEAN   Bristol East   *Lab majority 13,392*

Jean Corston. Born 5 May 1942; Daughter of late Laurie Parkin, trade union official, and late Eileen Parkin; Educated Yeovil Girls' High School; London School of Economics (LLB 1989); Inns of Court School of Law 1989–90; Open University; Married Christopher Corston 1961 (1 son 1 daughter); married Professor Peter Townsend 1985. Barrister; Member, TGWU. **House of Commons:** Member for Bristol East since April 9, 1992; PPS to David Blunkett as Secretary of State for Education and Employment 1997–2000; *Select Committees:* Member: Agriculture 1992–95, Home Affairs 1995–97; Chair, Joint Committee on Human Rights 2001–; Member, Liaison 2001–. *Special Interests:* Equal Opportunities, Disability, Human Rights, Complementary Medicine.

Countries of Interest: India, Kenya, USA. Organiser Taunton Labour Party 1974–76; South West Region Labour Party: Assistant regional organiser 1976–81, Regional organiser 1981–85; Assistant national agent Labour Party, London 1985–86; Secretary Labour Party Annual Conference Arrangements 1985–86; Parliamentary Labour Party: Deputy Chair 1997–98, 1999–2000, Chair 2001–. Associate Member, British-Irish Inter-Parliamentary Body 1998–2001, Member 2001–02; Member, Executive Committee, Commonwealth Parliamentary Association (CPA) UK Branch 1999–; Chair, Commonwealth Women Parliamentarians 2000; Trustee: ASDAN (Award Scheme Development Accreditation Network), Museum of Empire and Commonwealth; PC 2003; *Recreations:* Gardening, reading, walking, tap dancing. Rt Hon Jean Corston, MP, House of Commons, London, SW1A 0AA *Tel:* 020 7219 4575 *Fax:* 020 7219 4878. *Constituency:* PO Box 1105, Bristol, BS99 2DP *Tel:* 0117–939 9901 *Fax:* 0117–939 9902 *E-mail:* corstonj@parliament.uk.

COTTER, BRIAN   Weston-Super-Mare   *LD majority 338*

Brian Joseph Cotter. Born 24 August 1938; Son of late Michael Joseph and late Mary Cotter; Educated Downside School; London Polytechnic (business studies); Married Eyleen Patricia Wade 1963 (2 sons 1 daughter). Plasticable Ltd 1990–: Sales manager, Managing director. Councillor, Woking Borough Council 1986–90. **House of Commons:** Contested Weston-Super-Mare 1992 general election. Member for Weston-Super-Mare since May 1, 1997; Liberal Democrat Spokesperson for Trade and Industry: (Small Business) 1997–99, (Small Business) 1999–; *Select Committees:* Member, Regulatory Reform 1997–. *Special Interests:* Business, Tourism, Disability, Youth Affairs. *Countries of Interest:* China, Ireland. Member: Lib Dem Parliamentary Association, ASLDC, Green Liberal Democrat Association. *Publications: Creating an Entrepreneurial Culture,* 2001; *Clubs:* National Liberal; *Recreations:* Reading, walking, gardening, films. Brian Cotter Esq, MP, House of Commons, London, SW1A 0AA *Tel:* 020 7219 5127 *Fax:* 020 7219 2277. *Constituency:* 8a Alexandra Parade, Weston-super-Mare, North Somerset, BS23 1QT *Tel:* 01934 419200 *Fax:* 01934 419300 *E-mail:* brian@briancotter.org.

COUSINS, JIM   Newcastle upon Tyne Central   *Lab majority 11,605*

James MacKay Cousins. Born 23 February 1944; Son of late Charles John Cousins, printing trade worker, and late Grace Ellen Cousins; Educated New College, Oxford; London School of Economics; Married Anne Elizabeth (2 sons, 1 stepson, 1 stepdaughter). Industrial relations and research worker in industry 1967–72; Research worker, urban affairs and city labour markets 1972–82; Lecturer, Sunderland Polytechnic 1982–87; Amicus-MSF. Councillor, Wallsend Borough Council 1969–73; Tyne and Wear County Council: Councillor 1973–86, Deputy leader 1981–86. **House of Commons:** Member for Newcastle upon Tyne Central since June 1987; Opposition Spokesperson for: Trade and Industry 1992–94, Foreign and Commonwealth Affairs 1994–95; *Select Committees:* Member: Trade and Industry 1989–92, Public Service 1995–97; Member: Treasury 1997–, Treasury Sub-Committee 1998–. *Special Interests:* Financial Services. *Countries of Interest:* Czech Republic, Iran, Central Asian Republics. Chair, Northern Group of Labour MPs 1997–. *Recreations:* Composting. Jim Cousins Esq, MP, House of Commons, London, SW1A 0AA *Tel:* 020 7219 4204 *Fax:* 020 7219 6290. *Constituency:* 21 Portland Terrace, Newcastle upon Tyne, NE2 1QQ *Tel:* 0191–281 9888 *Fax:* 0191–281 3383 *E-mail:* jcousins@globalnet.co.uk.

DodOnline
An Electronic Directory without rival ...

MPs' biographies and photographs available with daily updates *via* the internet

For a *free* trial, call Yasmin Mirza, Aby Farsoun or Michael Mand on 020 7630 7643

COX, TOM   Tooting   *Lab majority 10,400*

Thomas Michael Cox. Born 19 January 1930; Educated state schools; London School of Economics. Electrical worker. Former Alderman, Fulham Borough Council. **House of Commons:** Contested Stroud 1966 general election. Member for Wandsworth Central 1970–74, and for Tooting since 1974; Assistant Government Whip 1974–77; Government Whip 1977–79. Member, UK Delegation of the Council of Europe and Western European Union; Representative, UK Delegation to Organisation for Security and Co-operation in Europe; Executive Member, Executive Committee, Commonwealth Parliamentary Association (CPA) UK Branch 1999–. Thomas Cox Esq, MP, House of Commons, London, SW1A 0AA *Tel:* 020 7219 5034. *Constituency:* Tooting Labour Party, 611 Garratt Lane, Earlsfield, London, SW18 4SU *E-mail:* contact@tooting-clp.new.labour.org.uk.

CRAN, JAMES   Beverley and Holderness   *Con majority 781*

James Douglas Cran. Born 28 January 1944; Son of late James and Jane Macdonald-Cran; Educated Ruthrieston School, Aberdeen (Dux Medallion Winner); King's College, Aberdeen University (MA 1968); Married Penelope Barbara Wilson 1973 (1 daughter). Conservative Research Department 1970–71; Secretary and Chief Executive, National Association of Pension Funds 1971–79; CBI: Northern Director 1979–84, West Midlands Director 1984–87. Councillor, London Borough of Sutton 1974–79, Chairman, Health and Housing Committee. **House of Commons:** Contested Glasgow Shettleston October 1974 and Gordon 1983 general elections. Member for Beverley 1987–97, and for Beverley and Holderness since May 1, 1997; Opposition Whip (Home Office, Northern Ireland: Northern and Yorkshire) 1997–98; Opposition Whip for Northern Ireland and Pairing Whip 1998–2001; Opposition Assistant Chief Whip 2001; PPS to Sir Patrick Mayhew as Secretary of State for Northern Ireland 1995–96; *Select Committees:* Member: Trade and Industry 1987–92, Northern Ireland Affairs 1994–95, Administration 1997–98, Selection 1998–2001; Member: Chairmen's Panel 2001–, Defence 2001–. *Special Interests:* Trade and Industry, Pensions, Regional Policy, European Union, Irish Affairs, Economic Policy. *Countries of Interest:* Canada, Europe, Hong Kong, Taiwan, USA, Mexico, China, New Zealand. Member of Court: Birmingham University 1984–87, Hull University 1987–; Treasurer, European Research Group 1994–97; Council of Europe and Western European Union 2001–; Fellow, Armed Forces Parliamentary Scheme 1992; Council Member, Pensions Trustee Forum 1992–95; Fellow, Industry and Parliament Trust 1994; OStJ; *Recreations:* Travelling, reading biographies and autobiographies, military history. James Cran Esq, MP, House of Commons, London, SW1A 0AA *Tel:* 020 7219 5069 *Fax:* 020 7219 2271. *Constituency:* 9 Cross Street, Beverley, East Yorkshire, HU17 9AX *Tel:* 01482 881316 *Fax:* 01482 861667 *E-mail:* cranp@parliament.uk.

CRANSTON, ROSS   Dudley North   *Lab majority 6,800*

Ross Frederick Cranston. Born 23 July 1948; Educated University of Queensland, Australia (BA 1969, LLB 1970); Harvard Law School, USA (LLM 1973); Oxford University (DPhil 1976, DCL 1998); Divorced. Barrister, Gray's Inn 1976; Professor of law, London University: Queen Mary College 1986–91, London School of Economics 1992–97; Assistant Recorder 1991–97; Recorder 1997–; Visiting Professor of Law, LSE 1997–; Practising barrister, Bencher, Gray's Inn 1998; QC 1998; Member: GMB, AUT. **House of Commons:** Contested Richmond, Yorkshire 1992 general election. Member for Dudley North since May 1, 1997; Solicitor General 1998–2001; *Select Committees:* Member: Home Affairs 1997–98, Home Affairs 1998; Member: Standards and Privileges 2001–, Lord Chancellor's Department 2003–. *Special Interests:* Home Affairs, Legal Affairs, Treasury. Consultant to Woolf Inquiry into Access to Justice 1994–96; Consultant (1988–97) to: UNCTAD, Commonwealth Secretariat, World Bank, IMF; Chair, Trustees of Public Concern at Work (The Whistleblowers Charity) 1996–97; *Publications: Regulating Business*, 1979; *Legal Foundations of the Welfare State*, 1985; *Legal Ethics and Professional Responsibility*, editor 1995; *Principles of Banking Law*, 1997, 2nd edition 2002; *Cranston's Consumers and the Law*, 3rd edition 2000. Ross Cranston Esq, QC, MP, House of Commons, London, SW1A 0AA *Tel:* 020 7219 5758 *Fax:* 020 7219 2726. *Constituency:* Holloway Chambers, 28 Priory Street, Dudley, West Midlands, DY1 1EZ *Tel:* 01384 233100 *Fax:* 01384 233 099.

CRAUSBY, DAVID   Bolton North East   *Lab majority 8,422*

David Crausby. Born 17 June 1946; Son of late Thomas Crausby, factory worker/club steward, and of Kathleen Crausby, cotton worker; Educated Derby Grammar School, Bury; Bury Technical College; Married Enid Noon 1965 (2 sons). Shop steward/works convenor, AEEU; Full-time works convenor 1978–97; Chair Amicus (AEEU) Group. Councillor, Bury Council 1979–92, Chair of Housing 1985–92. **House of Commons:** Contested Bury North 1987 and Bolton North East 1992 general elections. Member for Bolton North East since May 1, 1997; *Select Committees:* Member: Administration 1997–2001, Social Security 1999–2001; Member, Defence 2001–. *Special Interests:* Industrial Relations, Pensions, Housing, Defence. North West Regional Group PLP: Vice-chair 2000–01, Chair 2001–02. *Recreations:* Football. David Crausby Esq, MP, House of Commons, London, SW1A 0AA *Tel:* 020 7219 4092 *Fax:* 020 7219 3713. *Constituency:* 570 Blackburn Road, Astley Bridge, Bolton, BL1 6JN *Tel:* 01204 303340 *Fax:* 01204 304401.

CRUDDAS, JON   Dagenham   *Lab majority 8,693*

Jonathan Cruddas. Born 7 April 1962; Son of John, sailor, and Pat, housewife, Cruddas; Educated Oaklands RC Comprehensive, Warwick University 1981–88 (BSc, MA, PhD); University of Wisconsin, USA Visiting fellow 1987–88; Married Anna Mary Healy 1992 (1 son). Policy officer Labour Party Policy Directorate 1989–94; Chief assistant General Secretary Labour Party 1994–97; Deputy political secretary Prime Minister's political office Downing Street 1997–2001; TGWU 1989–2001: Branch secretary 1992–94. **House of Commons:** Member for Dagenham since June 7, 2001; *Special Interests:* Labour Law, Industrial Economy, Economic Regeneration. *Clubs:* Dagenham Working Men's, Dagenham Royal Naval Association; *Sportsclubs:* White Hart Dagenham Angling Society; *Recreations:* Golf, angling. Jon Cruddas Esq, MP, House of Commons, London, SW1A 0AA *Tel:* 020 7219 8161. *Constituency:* 10 Royal Parade, Church Street, Dagenham, Essex, RM10 9XB *Tel:* 020 8984 7854 *E-mail:* cruddasj@parliament.uk.

CRYER, ANN   Keighley   *Lab majority 4,005*

(Constance) Ann Cryer. Born 14 December 1939; Daughter of late Allen and Margaret Ann Place; Educated St John's Church of England Primary School; Spring Bank Secondary Modern, Darwen; Bolton Technical College (1955); Keighley Technical College (part-time) (1974); Married Bob Cryer, MP for Keighley and Bradford South 1963 (died 1994) (1 son John Cryer, MP 1 daughter). Clerk: ICI Ltd 1955–60, GPO 1960–64; Personal assistant, Bob Cryer, MP, MEP 1974–94; Member: TGWU, ASLEF 2000–, RMT Parliamentary Group 2002–. Member, Darwen Borough Council 1962–65; JP, Bradford Bench, appointed 1996 (now on the supplemented list); Member Bradford Cathedral Council 2000–. **House of Commons:** Member for Keighley since May 1, 1997; *Select Committees:* Member, Lord Chancellor's Department 2003–. *Special Interests:* Early Years Education, Health, Railways, Planning, Immigration, Human Rights of UK Asian Women – Campaigned against Forced Marriages. *Countries of Interest:* South Africa, Pakistan, Afghanistan, Palestine. Member, Co-operative Party 1965–; Chair, PLP CND Group 1997–. President, Keighley and Worth Valley Railway Preservation Society; Vice-president Friends of the Settle to Carlisle Railway; Patron Keighly Bus Museum Trust; Member: Friends of the Earth, CND, Brontë Society, Canon Collins Educational Trust for South Africa; Matron, Member, Social Security Appeal Tribunal 1987–96; Vice-president, Keighley Bus Museum; Delegate, Parliamentary Assembly of the Council of Europe 1997–2003; Member: Commonwealth Parliamentary Association 1997–, Equal Opportunities Committee 1998–2003 (Violence against women sub-committee), Culture and Education Committee 2000–03, Heritage Sub-committee, Media Sub-committee; Contributor to Canon Collins' Educational Trust for South Africa; *Publications:* Compiled *Boldness Be My Friend: Remembering Bob Cryer*, 1996; *Recreations:* Gardening, theatre, cinema, time with my six grandchildren, walking. Mrs Ann Cryer, MP, House of Commons, London, SW1A 0AA *Tel:* 020 7219 6649. *Constituency:* Bob Cryer House, 35 Devonshire Street, Keighley, West Yorkshire, BD21 2BH *Tel:* 01535 210083 *Fax:* 01535 210085 / 670049 *E-mail:* rowenc@parliament.uk.

CRYER, JOHN Hornchurch — Lab majority 1,482

John Cryer. Born 11 April 1964; Son of late Bob Cryer, MP and of Ann Cryer, MP (*qv*); Educated Oakbank School, Keighley; Hatfield Polytechnic (BA literature and history 1985); London College of Printing (Postgraduate Certificate in Print Journalism 1988); Married Narinder Bains 1994 (2 sons 1 daughter). Journalist with: *Tribune* 1992–96, *Morning Star* 1989–92; Freelance journalist with: *Labour Briefing* (editor), *Guardian*, *GMPU Journal*, *T&G Record*; Lloyd's of London Publications; Member: TGWU 1986–, NUJ 1988–, UCATT 1997–. **House of Commons:** Member for Hornchurch since May 1, 1997; *Select Committees:* Member, Deregulation and Regulatory Reform 1997–2002. *Special Interests:* Employment, Social Security, Education, Further Education, European Union, Health, Economic Policy, Industry, Coal Industry, Transport. *Countries of Interest:* Australia, India. Member, Executive of Labour Euro Safeguards Committee; Press officer, For Defend Clause Four Campaign 1995; Member, Co-operative Party; Secretary, Labour Against the Euro. Member: CND, Amnesty International, Transport on Water, Tibet Support Group, Keighley and Worth Valley Railway, RAF Hornchurch Association; Patron, St Francis Hospice; Amnesty International; *Publications:* Co-author with Ann Cryer, *Boldness be my Friend: Remembering Bob Cryer MP*, 1996; Many articles mainly in political publications; *Sportsclubs:* Member: House of Commons Cricket Club, House of Commons Rugby Club, House of Commons Boxing Club; *Recreations:* Swimming, reading, sport, old cars, cinema. John Cryer Esq, MP, House of Commons, London, SW1A 0AA *Tel:* 020 7219 1134 *Fax:* 020 7219 1183. *Constituency:* 11 Park Lane, Hornchurch, Essex, RM11 1BB *Tel:* 01708 742674 *Fax:* 01708 735576 *E-mail:* brunil@parliament.uk.

CUMMINGS, JOHN Easington — Lab majority 21,949

John Scott Cummings. Born 6 July 1943; Son of late George and Mary Cummings, née Cain; Educated Murton Council Infant, Junior, Senior Schools; Easington and Durham Technical Colleges 1958–62. Murton Colliery 1958–87, Colliery Electrician and Secretary 1967–87; Sponsored by NUM; Trustee NUM 1986–2000. Councillor, Easington Rural District Council 1970–73; Easington District Council: Councillor 1973–87, Chair 1975–76, Leader 1979–87; Member: Northumbrian Water Authority 1977–83, Peterlee and Aycliffe Development Corporation 1980–87. **House of Commons:** Member for Easington since June 1987; Opposition Whip (Northern and Overseas Development) 1994–97; *Select Committees:* Member: Environment, Transport and Regional Affairs 1997–2001, Environment Sub-Committee 1997–2001, Transport, Local Government and the Regions 2001–02, Urban Affairs Sub-Committee 2001–02; Member: Chairmen's Panel 2000–, Office of the Deputy Prime Minister: Housing, Planning and Local Government 2002–, Urban Affairs Sub-Committee 2003–. *Special Interests:* Energy, Environment, Coal Industry. *Countries of Interest:* Eastern Europe, Middle East, China. Chair, Northern Regional Group of Labour MPs 1999–. Vice-Chair, Coalfield Communities Campaign 1985–87; Member: Council of Europe 1992–, Western European Union 1992–; *Recreations:* Jack Russell terriers, walking, travel. John Cummings Esq, MP, House of Commons, London, SW1A 0AA *Tel:* 020 7219 5122. *Constituency:* Seaton Holme, Easington Village, County Durham, SR8 3BS *Tel:* 01915 273773.

CUNNINGHAM, JACK Copeland — Lab majority 4,964

Jack (John A.) Cunningham. Born 4 August 1939; Son of Andrew and Freda Cunningham; Educated Jarrow Grammar School; Bede College, Durham University (BSc chemistry 1962, PhD 1966); Married Maureen Appleby 1964 (1 son 2 daughters). Research fellow, Durham University 1966–68; Full-time Officer, GMWU 1969–70. DL, Cumbria 1991. **House of Commons:** Member for Whitehaven 1970–83, and for Copeland since June 1983; Opposition Frontbench Spokesperson for Industry 1979–83; PPS to James Callaghan as Foreign Secretary and Prime Minister 1974–76; Parliamentary Under-Secretary for Energy 1976–79; Shadow Environment Secretary 1983–89; Shadow Leader, House of Commons and Campaigns Co-ordinator 1989–92;

Shadow Secretary of State for: Foreign and Commonwealth Affairs 1992–94, Trade and Industry 1994–95, National Heritage 1995–97; Minister of Agriculture, Fisheries and Food 1997–98; Minister for the Cabinet Office, and Chancellor of the Duchy of Lancaster 1998–99; Commissioner, Millennium Commission 1998–99; Member Joint Committee on House of Lords Reform 2002–; *Select Committees:* Member, Privileges 1989–95; Chair, Joint Committee on House of Lords Reform 2002–. *Special Interests:* Regional Policy, Environment, Foreign Affairs, Industry. *Countries of Interest:* China, Japan, South Africa, Europe, USA. Fellow, Industry and Parliament Trust; PC 1993; *Recreations:* Fell-walking, gardening, music, reading, fishing, theatre. Rt Hon Dr Jack Cunningham, DL, MP, House of Commons, London, SW1A 0AA *Tel:* 020 7219 5222. *Constituency:* Ingwell Hall, Westlake Science and Technology Park, Moor Row, Cumbria, CA24 3JZ *Tel:* 01946 62024.

CUNNINGHAM, JAMES   Coventry South | Lab majority 8,279

Jim (James) Cunningham. Born 4 February 1941; Son of Adam and Elizabeth Cunningham; Educated Columbia High School, Coatbridge; Tillycoultry College, Ruskin Courses (Labour Movement, Industrial Law); Married Marion Douglas Podmore 1985 (1 son 1 stepson 1 daughter 1 stepdaughter). Engineer Rolls Royce 1965–88; MSF shop steward 1968–88. Coventry City Council: Councillor 1972–92, Chair, Consumer Services Committee 1975–77, Vice-Chair: Finance Committee 1975–77, 1979–82, 1985–88, Leisure Committee 1975–77, Chair 1979–82, Vice-Chair, Transportation and Highways Committee 1983–85, Chief Whip, Labour Group 1985–87, Deputy Leader of the Council 1987–88, Leader of the Council 1988–92. **House of Commons:** Member for Coventry South East 1992–97, and for Coventry South since May 1, 1997; *Select Committees:* Member: Home Affairs 1993–97, Trade and Industry 1997–2001, Chairmen's Panel 1998–2001; Member, Lord Chancellor's Department 2003–. *Special Interests:* Economic Policy, European Union, Industrial Relations, NHS. *Countries of Interest:* USA, Eastern Europe, Russia. Coventry South East CLP: Secretary 1976–77, Chair 1977–79. *Recreations:* Walking, reading, historical buildings. Jim Cunningham Esq, MP, House of Commons, London, SW1A 0AA *Tel:* 020 7219 6362 *Fax:* 020 7219 6362. *Constituency:* Rms 9–11 Palmer House, Palmer Lane, Burges, Coventry, CV1 1HL *Tel:* 024 7655 3159 *Fax:* 024 7655 3159.

CUNNINGHAM, TONY   Workington | Lab majority 10,850

Tony (Thomas Anthony) Cunningham. Born 16 September 1952; Son of late Daniel Cunningham, docker and Bessie Cunningham, née Lister; Educated Workington Grammar School; Liverpool University (BA history and politics 1975); Didsbury College (PGCE 1976); TESL; Married Anne Margaret Gilmore 1984 (1 daughter 1 stepdaughter 1 stepson). Teacher: Alsager Comprehensive School 1976–80, Mikunguni Trade School, Zanzibar 1980–82, Netherhall School, Maryport 1983–94; Chief executive Human Rights NGO 1999–2000; MEP for Cumbria and North Lancashire 1994–99. Contested North West Region 1999 European Parliament election; NUT 1976–94: Local secretary 1985–94; AEEU 1993–. Allerdale Borough Council: Councillor 1987–94, Leader 1992–94. **House of Commons:** Member for Workington since June 7, 2001; MEP Cumbria and North Lancashire 1994–99; PPS to Elliot Morley as Minister of State, Department for Environment, Food and Rural Affairs 2003–; *Select Committees:* Member: Catering 2001–, European Scrutiny 2001–. *Special Interests:* Third World, Education, Tourism, Sport, Small Businesses. *Countries of Interest:* Sub Saharan Africa. Patron: Mines Advisory Group 1994–, VSO 1994–, Several local charities; Member European Standing Committee C; MEP Cumbria and North Lancashire 1994–99; *Clubs:* Station Road Working Men's, John Street; *Recreations:* Sport, running, reading, Workington RFC. Tony Cunningham Esq, MP, House of Commons, London, SW1A 0AA *Tel:* 020 7219 8344 *Fax:* 020 7219 1947. *Constituency:* The Town Hall, Workington, CA14 2RS *Tel:* 01900 65815 *Fax:* 01900 68348 *E-mail:* cunninghamt@parliament.uk.

Visit the Vacher Dod Website . . .
www.DodOnline.co.uk

CURRY, DAVID   Skipton and Ripon   Con majority 12,930

David Maurice Curry. Born 13 June 1944; Son of Thomas Harold and late Florence Joan Curry (née Tyerman); Educated Ripon Grammar School; Corpus Christi College, Oxford (BA modern history 1966); Kennedy School of Government, Harvard University; Married Anne Helene Maude Roullet 1971 (1 son twin daughters). Newspaper Reporter, *Newcastle Journal* 1966–70; *Financial Times* 1970–79: world trade editor, international companies editor, Brussels correspondent, Paris correspondent; Freelance journalist; MEP for North East Essex 1979–89. Vice-President, Local Government Association; Board Member British Association for Central and Eastern Europe. **House of Commons:** Contested Morpeth February and October 1974 general elections. Member for Skipton and Ripon since June 1987; Conservative Spokesperson European Parliament Budget Committee 1984–89; Ministry of Agriculture, Fisheries and Food: Parliamentary Secretary 1989–92, Minister of State 1992–93; Minister of State, Department of the Environment for: Local Government and Planning 1993–94, Local Government, Housing and Urban Regeneration 1994–97; Shadow Minister of Agriculture, Fisheries and Food June-November 1997; *Select Committees:* Member: Agriculture 1998–2000, Public Accounts 1999–2000; Chair: Agriculture 2000–01, Radioactive Waste Policy Sub-Committee 2001–02; Member, Radioactive Waste Policy Sub-Committee 2002; Member, Liaison 2000–; Chair, Environment, Food and Rural Affairs 2001–. *Special Interests:* Agriculture, Foreign Affairs, Urban Issues and Local Government. *Countries of Interest:* Former Communist States in East and Central Europe, France. General rapporteur, EEC Budget for 1987; Director, British Association for Central and Eastern Europe; *Publications: The Conservative Tradition in Europe*, 1998; *Lobbying Government*, 1999; *The Sorcerer's apprentice: Government and Globalisation*, 2000; PC 1996; *Recreations:* Vegetable gardening, sailing. Rt Hon David Curry, MP, House of Commons, London, SW1A 0AA *Tel:* 020 7219 5164. *Constituency:* 19 Otley Street, Skipton, North Yorks, BD23 1DY *Tel:* 01756 792092 *Fax:* 01756 798742 *E-mail:* currydm@parliament.uk.

CURTIS-THOMAS, CLAIRE   Crosby   Lab majority 8,353

Claire Curtis-Thomas. Born 30 April 1958; Daughter of Joyce Curtis-Thomas; Educated Mynyddbach Comprehensive School For Girls, Swansea; Fareham Technical College, Hampshire (ONC mechanical engineering 1978); Cosham Technical College, Hampshire (HNC mechanical engineering 1980); University College of Wales, Cardiff (BSc mechanical engineering 1984); Aston University (MBA business administration 1996); Married Michael Jakub (1 son 2 daughters). Research assistant, University College of Wales, Cardiff 1984–86; Shell Chemicals: Site mechnical engineer 1986–88, Head, UK Supply and Distribution Ltd 1988–90, Head, environmental strategy 1990–92; Birmingham City Council: Head of research and development laboratory 1992–93, Head of strategy and business planning 1993–95; Dean, Faculty of Business and Engineering, University of Wales College, Newport 1996–97; Member, TGWU. Councillor, Crewe and Nantwich Borough Council 1995–97. **House of Commons:** Member for Crosby since May 1, 1997 (Contested the seat as Claire Curtis-Tansley); *Select Committees:* Member: Science and Technology 1997–2001, Regulatory Reform 2002; Member, Home Affairs 2003–. *Special Interests:* Economic Policy, Trade and Industry, Manufacturing and Engineering, Small Businesses. *Countries of Interest:* USA, India, South Africa, New Zealand. Member: Co-operative Party, Fabian Society, Labour Women's Network; Membership Secretary, Rossett and Marford Labour Party; Secretary, Eddisbury Constituency Labour Party; Vice-chair North West Regional Group of Labour MPs 2002–. Member: Soroptimist International, Amnesty International; Changed surname from Curtis-Tansley May 1997; Founder and president SETup (educational trust to promote science and engineering); CEng; FIMechE 1995; FCGI 2001; FICES; FIEE; *Recreations:* Family. Claire Curtis-Thomas, MP, House of Commons, London, SW1A 0AA *Tel:* 020 7219 4193 *Fax:* 020 7219 1540. *Constituency:* The Minster, 16 Beach Lawn, Waterloo, Liverpool, L22 8QA *Tel:* 0151–928 7250 *Fax:* 0151–928 9325 *E-mail:* curtisthomasc@parliament.uk.

Visit the Vacher Dod Website . . . **www.DodOnline.co.uk**

D

DALYELL, TAM   Linlithgow   *Lab majority 9,129*

Tam Dalyell. Born 9 August 1932; Son of late Gordon Dalyell, Indian Civil Servant and late Eleanor Dalyell; Educated Edinburgh Academy, Harecroft; Eton College; King's College, Cambridge (MA history and economics 1956); Moray House, Edinburgh; Married Kathleen Wheatley 1963 (1 son 1 daughter). National service, Royal Scots Greys 1950–52; History and maths teacher Bo'ness Academy 1956–60; Deputy director of studies, BI ship-school, Dunera, 1961–62; Member: EIS, RMT. **House of Commons:** Contested Roxburgh, Selkirk, Peebles 1959 general election. Member for West Lothian 1962–83, and for Linlithgow since June 1983; Opposition Spokesperson for Science 1980–82; PPS to Richard Crossman as Minister of Housing, Leader of the House of Commons and Secretary of State for Social Services 1964–65, 1967–70; MEP 1975–79; Father of the House 2001–; *Special Interests:* Science Policy, Central Economic Issues, Wildlife and Countryside Legislation, Kidney Transplantation, Rainforest Issues. *Countries of Interest:* Brazil, Burma, Indonesia, Libya, Democratic Republic of Congo, Iran, Iraq, Peru, Bolivia. Vice-Chair, Parliamentary Labour Party 1974–76; Member, Labour Party National Executive Committee 1985–86. Member, Socialist Bureau of the Parliamentary and Budget Committee 1975; Vice-Chair, Control Committee on Budgets of European Parliament 1976–79; *Publications: Case for Ship-Schools* 1959; *Ship-School Dunera* 1962; *Devolution: End of Britain,* 1977; *One Man's Falklands,* 1982; *A Science Policy for Britain,* 1983; *Thatcher's Torpedo,* 1983; *Misrule,* 1987; *Dick Crossman: a portrait,* 1989; Fellow, Royal Society of Edinburgh (FRSE) 2003; Rector Edinburgh University 2003–; Three honorary doctorates; *Recreations:* Hill-walking. Tam Dalyell Esq, MP, House of Commons, London, SW1A 0AA *Tel:* 020 7219 4343. *Constituency:* The Binns, Linlithgow, West Lothian, EH49 7NA *Tel:* 01506 834255.

DARLING, ALISTAIR   Edinburgh Central   *Lab majority 8,142*

Alistair Maclean Darling. Born 28 November 1953; Educated Loretto School; Aberdeen University (LLB 1976); Married Margaret McQueen Vaughan 1986 (1 son 1 daughter). Solicitor 1978–82; Advocate 1984–. Lothian Regional Council: Councillor 1982–87, Chair, Lothian Region Transport Committee 1986–87. **House of Commons:** Member for Edinburgh Central since June 1987; Opposition Spokesman on Home Affairs 1988–92; Opposition Front Bench Spokesman on Treasury, Economic Affairs and the City 1992–96; Shadow Chief Secretary to the Treasury 1996–97; Sponsored Solicitors (Scotland) Act 1988 (Private Member's Bill); Chief Secretary to the Treasury 1997–98; Secretary of State for: Social Security/Work and Pensions 1998–2002, Transport 2002–, Scotland 2003–; *Special Interests:* Transport, Education, Health, Economic Policy, Constitution. Member, Labour Party's Economic Commission 1994–97. PC 1997. Rt Hon Alistair Darling, MP, House of Commons, London, SW1A 0AA *Tel:* 020 7219 4584. *Constituency:* 15A Stafford Street, Edinburgh, EH3 7BU *Tel:* 0131–476 2552 *Fax:* 0131–467 3574 *E-mail:* sos@dtlr.gsi.gov.uk.

DAVEY, EDWARD   Kingston and Surbiton   *LD majority 15,676*

Edward Jonathon Davey. Born 25 December 1965; Son of late John George Davey, solicitor, and of late Nina Joan Davey (née Stanbrook), teacher; Educated Nottingham High School; Jesus College, Oxford (College President) (BA philosophy, politics and economics 1988); Birkbeck College, London (MSc economics 1993); Single, no children. Senior economics adviser to Liberal Democrat MPs 1989–93; Management consultant, Omega Partners 1993–97; Director, Omega Partners Postal 1996–97. **House of Commons:** Member for Kingston and Surbiton since May 1, 1997; Liberal Democrat Spokesperson for: the Treasury (Public Spending and Taxation) 1997–99, Economy 1999–2001, London 2000–, Shadow Spokesman for the Office of the Deputy Prime Minister 2002–; London Whip 1997–2000; Shadow Chief Secretary to the Treasury 2001–02;

Select Committees: Member: Procedure 1997–2000, Treasury 1999–2001, Treasury Sub-Committee 1999–2001. *Special Interests:* Taxation, Economics, Internet, Employment, Environment, Modernisation of Parliament. *Countries of Interest:* Latin America. Chair, Costing Group (costing all policies for manifesto) 1992 and 1997 general elections; Member, Federal Policy Committee 1994–95; Liberal Democrat Policy Group (Economics, Tax and Benefits and Transport); Member, Association of Liberal Democrat Councillors. *Publications: Making MPs Work for our Money: Reforming Budget Scrutiny* (2000, Centre for Reform); Royal Humane Society Honourable Testimonial; Chief Constable London Transport Police Commendation; Royal Humane Society; *Clubs:* Member National Liberal Club, Surbiton; *Recreations:* Music, walking, swimming. Edward Davey Esq, MP, House of Commons, London, SW1A 0AA *Tel:* 020 7219 3512 *Fax:* 020 7219 0250. *Constituency:* Liberal Democrats, 23A Victoria Road, Surbiton, Surrey, KT6 4JZ *Tel:* 020 8288 0161 *Fax:* 020 8288 1090 *E-mail:* daveye@parliament.uk.

DAVEY, VALERIE   Bristol West   *Lab majority 4,426*

Valerie Davey. Born 16 April 1940; Educated 3 state secondary schools; London University (PGCE 1963); Birmingham University (MA 1964); Married Graham Davey 1966 (1 son 2 daughters). Teacher, Tettenhall Comprehensive School, Wolverhampton; Teacher, Tanzania; Part-time Teacher, Further Education College, Filton, Bristol; Member, NUT. Avon County Council: Councillor 1981–96, Leader, Labour Group 1992–96; Former Member, Avon Health Authority. **House of Commons:** Member for Bristol West since May 1, 1997; *Select Committees:* Member: Education and Employment 1997–2001, Education Sub-Committee 1997–2001; Member, Education and Skills 2001–. *Special Interests:* Education, Health, Local and Regional Government, International Aid and Development, Small Businesses. *Countries of Interest:* East Africa (especially Tanzania), Cyprus. Member: Bristol University Court (formerly Member of Council), Amnesty International, ACTSA, Macular Disease Society; Member, European Standing Committee C 2003–; *Recreations:* Walking, gardens, reading, making marmalade. Mrs Valerie Davey, MP, House of Commons, London, SW1A 0AA *Tel:* 020 7219 3576 *Fax:* 020 7219 3658. *Constituency:* PO Box 1947, Bristol, BS99 2UG *Tel:* 0117–907 7464 *Fax:* 0117–907 7465 *E-mail:* valdavey@labourbriswest.demon.co.uk.

DAVID, WAYNE   Caerphilly   *Lab majority 14,425*

Wayne David. Born 1 July 1957; Son of David Haydn David, teacher, and Edna Amelia, née Jones, housewife; Educated Cynffig Comprehensive School, Kenfig Hill, Glamorgan; University College, Cardiff (BA history and Welsh history 1979); University College, Swansea economic history research 1979–82; University College, Cardiff (PGCE FE 1983); Married Catherine Thomas 1991. Teacher Brynteg Comprehensive School 1983–85; Tutor organiser Workers' Educational Association South Wales District 1985–89; Policy adviser youth policy Wales Youth Agency 1999–2001; MEP for South Wales 1989–94, South Wales Central 1994–99. Contested Rhondda 1999 National Assembly for Wales election; MSF1983–; AEEU 1998–. Cefn Cribwr Community Council 1985–91: Councillor, Chair 1986–87. **House of Commons:** Member for Caerphilly since June 7, 2001; *Select Committees:* Member, European Scrutiny 2001–. *Special Interests:* European Affairs, Economy, Education. *Countries of Interest:* Poland, Bulgaria. Vice-president Socialist Group European Parliament 1994–98; Leader European Parliamentary Labour Party 1994–98; Ex-officio Member of Labour Party NEC 1994–98. President: Aber Valley Male Voice Choir 2001–; Council for Wales of Voluntary Youth Services 2002–; UK Government link MP for Bulgaria; Vice-president Cardiff UN Association 1989–; *Publications:* Two pamphlets on the Future of Europe 1991 and 1993; Contributor: *The Future of Europe, Problems and Issues for the 21st Century*, 1996; Charles Morgan Prize in Welsh History 1979; Fellow Cardiff University 1995; *Clubs:* Bargoed Labour Club; *Recreations:* Music, playing the oboe. Wayne David Esq, MP, House of Commons, London, SW1A 0AA *Tel:* 020 7219 8152 *Fax:* 020 7219 1751. *Constituency:* Suite 5, St Fagans House, St Fagans Street, Caerphilly, CF83 1FZ *Tel:* 029 2088 1061 *Fax:* 029 2088 1954 *E-mail:* davidw@parliament.uk.

DAVIDSON, IAN   Glasgow Pollok   *Lab majority 11,268*

Ian Graham Davidson. Born 8 September 1950; Son of Graham Davidson and Elizabeth Crowe; Educated Jedburgh Grammar School; Galashiels Academy; Edinburgh University (MA); Jordanhill College; Married Morag Christine Anne Mackinnon 1978 (1 son 1 daughter). Sabbatical Chair National Association of Labour Students 1973–74; President Students' Association, Jordanhill College 1975–76; Researcher for Janey Buchan, MEP 1978–85; Project manager Community Service Volunteers 1985–92; Former chair MSF Parliamentary Group; Secretary: Trade Union Group of Labour MPs 1998–2002. Strathclyde Regional Council: Councillor 1978–92, Chair, Education Committee 1986–92. **House of Commons:** Member for Glasgow Govan 1992–97, and for Glasgow Pollok since May 1, 1997; *Select Committees:* Member, Selection 1997–99; Member, Public Accounts 1997–. *Special Interests:* Local and Regional Government, Commonwealth, International Development, Local Economic Development, Defence, Co-operative Movement, Trade and Industry, Trade Unions, Shipbuilding, Europe, Poverty, Euro (Against). *Countries of Interest:* Africa, Europe, Scandinavia, The Commonwealth, USA, Japan, Germany, British Overseas Territories. Former Chair Kelvingrove Constituency Labour Party; Former Executive: Glasgow Labour Party, Strathclyde Regional Labour Party; Member Co-operative Party; Secretary: Tribune Group, Trade Union Group of Labour MPs 1998–2002; Chair Co-operative Parliamentary Group 1998–99; Founder and Chair Labour Against The Euro 2002–; Vice-chair Scottish Regional Group of Labour MPs 2002–. Chair, COSLA Education Committee 1990–92; Chairman, COSLA Education Committee 1990–92; Member, New Europe Advisory Council; *Recreations:* Family, sport, distance running, swimming, rugby. Ian Davidson Esq, MP, House of Commons, London, SW1A 0AA *Tel:* 020 7219 3610 *Fax:* 020 7219 2238. *Constituency:* 1829 Paisley Road West, Glasgow, G52 3SS *Tel:* 0141–883 8338 *Fax:* 0141–883 4116 *E-mail:* iandavidsonmp@parliament.uk.

DAVIES, DENZIL   Llanelli   *Lab majority 6,403*

Denzil Davies. Born 9 October 1938; Educated Carmarthen Grammar School; Pembroke College, Oxford University (BA law 1962); Married 1963, Mary Ann Finlay (divorced 1988) (1 son 1 daughter). Lectured at Chicago 1963 and Leeds 1964 Universities; Called to Bar, Gray's Inn 1964. **House of Commons:** Member for Llanelli since June 18, 1970; Opposition Front Bench Spokesman on: The Treasury and Economic Affairs 1979–80, Foreign and Commonwealth Affairs 1980–81, Defence and Disarmament 1981–1983; Deputy Spokesman on Defence and Disarmament 1983–84; Chief Opposition Spokesman 1984–88; PPS to Secretary of State for Wales 1974–76; Minister of State, HM Treasury 1975–79; *Select Committees:* Member, Public Accounts 1992–97. *Special Interests:* Foreign Affairs, Treasury, Wales. PC 1978. Rt Hon Denzil Davies, MP, House of Commons, London, SW1A 0AA *Tel:* 020 7219 5197. *Constituency:* 22 Market Street, Llanelli, SA15 1YD *Tel:* 01554 756374.

DAVIES, GERAINT   Croydon Central   *Lab majority 3,984*

Geraint Richard Davies. Born 3 May 1960; Son of David Thomas Morgan Davies, civil servant, and of Betty Ferrer Davies; Educated Llanishen Comprehensive, Cardiff; JCR President, Jesus College, Oxford (BA philosophy, politics and economics 1982); Married Dr Vanessa Catherine Fry 1991 (3 daughters). Sales and Marketing Trainee; Group Product Manager, Unilever 1982–88; Marketing Manager, Colgate Palmolive Ltd 1988–89; Managing Partner, Pure Crete 1989–97; Member, GMB. Councillor, Croydon Council 1986–97: Chair, Housing Committee 1994–96, Leader of Council 1996–97. **House of Commons:** Contested Croydon South 1987 and Croydon Central 1992 general elections. Member for Croydon Central since May 1, 1997; Team PPS, Department for Constitutional Affairs 2003–; *Select Committees:* Member, Public Accounts 1997–. *Special Interests:* Treasury, Trade and Industry, Environment, Transport, Local and Regional Government, Housing. *Countries of Interest:* Wales, Crete. Chair, Labour Finance and Industry Group 1998–;

Member Co-op Party. Chair, London Boroughs Association Housing Committee 1994–96; Royal Humane Society Award for saving a man's life; *Clubs:* Ruskin House, Croydon; *Recreations:* Family, singing. Geraint Davies Esq, MP, House of Commons, London, SW1A 0AA *Tel:* 020 7219 4599 *Fax:* 020 7219 5962. *Constituency:* PO Box 679, Croydon, CR9 1UQ *Tel:* 020 8680 5833 *Fax:* 020 8686 2246 *E-mail:* geraintdaviesmp@parliament.uk.

DAVIES, QUENTIN   Grantham and Stamford   Con majority 4,518

Quentin Davies. Born 29 May 1944; Son of late Dr M I Davies, general practitioner, and the late Thelma Davies; Educated Dragon School, Oxford; Leighton Park; Gonville and Caius College, Cambridge (BA history 1966, MA); Harvard University, USA (Frank Knox Fellow); Married Chantal Tamplin 1983 (2 sons). HM Diplomatic Service 1967–74: 3rd Secretary, FCO 1967–69, 2nd Secretary, Moscow 1969–72, 1st Secretary, FCO 1972–74; Manager then assistant director, Morgan Grenfell & Co Ltd 1974–78; Director General and President, Morgan Grenfell France 1978–81; Director, Morgan Grenfell Co Ltd and certain group subsidiaries 1981–87, Consultant 1987–93; Consultant, National Westminster Securities plc 1993–99; Dewe Rogerson International 1987–94; Société Générale d'Entreprises 1999–2000; Director: Royal Bank of Scotland 1999–2002, Vinci 2000–, Norwest Holst 2000–. **House of Commons:** Contested Birmingham Ladywood 1977 by-election. Member for Stamford and Spalding 1987–97, and for Grantham and Stamford since May 1, 1997; Opposition Spokesperson for: Social Security 1998–99, the Treasury 1999–2000, Defence 2000–01; PPS to Angela Rumbold as Minister of State at: Department of Education and Science 1988–90, Home Office 1990–91; Shadow Minister for Pensions 1998–99; Shadow Paymaster General 1999–2000; Shadow Minister for Defence 2000–01; Shadow Secretary of State for Northern Ireland 2001–; *Select Committees:* Member: Treasury and Civil Service 1992–97, Standards and Privileges 1995–97, European Legislation 1997–98, Standards and Privileges 1997–98, Treasury 1997–98, European Legislation 1998–2001, European Scrutiny 1998. *Special Interests:* Trade and Industry, Finance, Agriculture, Health, Welfare, Pensions. *Countries of Interest:* Other EU, USA, Russia. Member of Executive Committee, Council for Economic Policy Research; Liveryman, Goldsmiths' Company; *Publications: Britain and Europe: A Conservative View,* 1996; *Clubs:* Beefsteak, Brooks's, Travellers', Grantham Conservative; *Recreations:* Reading, walking, skiing, travel. Quentin Davies Esq, MP, House of Commons, London, SW1A 0AA *Tel:* 020 7219 5518 *Fax:* 020 7219 2963. *Constituency:* Agent: Mrs Janice Thurston, Conservative Office, North Street, Bourne, Lincolnshire *Tel:* 01778 421498 *Fax:* 01778 394443.

DAVIS, DAVID   Haltemprice and Howden   Con majority 1,903

David Michael Davis. Born 23 December 1948; Son of late Ronald and Elizabeth Davis; Educated Bec Grammar School; Warwick University (BSc molecular science, computing science 1971); London Business School (MSc business studies 1973); Harvard Business School (AMP 1985); Married Doreen Cook 1973 (1 son 2 daughters). Joined Tate & Lyle 1974; Finance director, Manbré & Garton 1976–80; Managing director, Tate & Lyle Transport 1980–82; President, Redpath-Labatt joint venture 1982–84; Strategic planning director, Tate & Lyle 1984–87; Non-Executive director, Tate & Lyle 1987–90. **House of Commons:** Member for Boothferry 1987–97, and for Haltemprice and Howden since May 1, 1997; Assistant Government Whip 1990–93; PPS to Francis Maude as Financial Secretary to Treasury 1988–90; Parliamentary Secretary, Office of Public Service and Science 1993–94; Minister of State, Foreign and Commonwealth Office 1994–97; Chairman, Conservative Party 2001–02; Shadow Deputy Prime Minister with Shadow Ministerial responsibility for the Cabinet Office 2002–; *Select Committees:* Chair, Public Accounts 1997–2001; Member, Liaison 1998–2001. *Special Interests:* Health, Law and Order, Industry, Agriculture. Contested leadership 2001; Party Chairman 2001–; Member Conservative Policy Board 2001–. Member, Public Accounts Commission 1997–2001; *Publications: How to Turn Round a Company,* 1988; *The BBC Viewer's Guide to Parliament,* 1989; PC 1997; *Recreations:* Mountaineering, flying light aircraft, writing. Rt Hon David Davis, MP, House of Commons, London, SW1A 0AA *Tel:* 020 7219 5873. *Constituency:* Spaldington Court, Spaldington, Goole, East Yorkshire, DN14 7NG *Tel:* 01430 430365.

DAVIS, TERRY   Birmingham Hodge Hill   *Lab majority 11,618*

Terry Davis. Born 5 January 1938; Son of late Gordon and Gladys Davis; Educated King Edward VI Grammar School, Stourbridge; University College London (LLB 1960); University of Michigan, USA (MBA 1962); Married Anne Cooper 1963 (1 son 1 daughter). Company executive 1962–71; Manager in motor industry 1974–79; Member, MSF. Councillor, Yeovil Rural District Council 1967–68. **House of Commons:** Contested Bromsgrove 1970, February 1974 and October 1974 general elections. Member for Bromsgrove by-election 1971-February 1974. Contested Birmingham Stechford 1977 by-election. Member for Birmingham Stechford 1979–83, for Birmingham Hodge Hill since June 1983; Opposition Spokesperson for: NHS 1980–83, Treasury and Economic Affairs 1983–86, Trade and Industry 1986–87; Labour Whip for West Midlands 1979–80; *Select Committees:* Member, Public Accounts 1987–94; Member, European Scrutiny 2001–. *Countries of Interest:* Europe, USA, Canada, Australia. Member: Socialist Health Association, Fabian Society; Member, Advisory Council on Public Records 1989–94; Member, Review Committee of Privy Counsellors of the Anti-terrorism, Crime and Security Act 2002–; Member, British Delegation to Council of Europe Assembly and Western European Union Assembly 1992–; Leader, Labour Delegation 1995–2002; Chair: Rules Committee, Western European Union Assembly 1995–96, Economic Affairs and Development Committee, Council of Europe Assembly 1995–98; Leader, UK Delegation 1997–2002; Vice-President: Western European Union Assembly 1997–2001, Council of Europe Assembly 1998–2002; Executive Committee Member, IPU British Group 1998–; Chair Political Affairs Committee, Council of Europe Assembly 2000–02; Leader, Socialist Group, Council of Europe Assembly 2002–; PC 1999. Rt Hon Terry Davis Esq, MP, House of Commons, London, SW1A 0AA *Tel:* 020 7219 4509 *Fax:* 020 7219 6221. *Constituency Tel:* 0121–747 9500 *Fax:* 0121–747 9504.

DAWSON, HILTON   Lancaster and Wyre   *Lab majority 481*

(Thomas) Hilton Dawson. Born 30 September 1953; Son of late Harry Dawson, teacher, and Sally Dawson, teacher; Educated Ashington Grammar School, Northumberland; Warwick University (BA philosophy, politics 1975); Lancaster University (Diploma in social work 1982); Married Susan Williams 1973 (2 daughters). Clerk, Coventry County Council 1975–76; Kibbutz volunteer 1976–77; Warden, Northumberland Community Centre 1977–79; Unqualified Social Worker, Northumberland 1979–80; CQSW, Lancaster 1980–82; Social work manager, Lancashire 1983–97; Member, UNISON. Councillor, Lancaster City Council 1987–97. **House of Commons:** Member for Lancaster and Wyre since May 1, 1997; *Select Committees:* Member, Administration 1997–2001; Member, Lord Chancellor's Department 2003–. *Special Interests:* Children's Issues– Children's Rights, Locked Africa Children, Youth Justice, Park Homes Reform, Sudan, Angola, International Development, Social Work, Community Politics. *Countries of Interest:* Burundi, Sudan, Angola. *Recreations:* Keeping fit, family, arts. Hilton Dawson Esq, MP, House of Commons, London, SW1A 0AA *Tel:* 020 7219 4207 *Fax:* 020 7219 0699. *Constituency:* 15A Moor Lane, Lancaster, LA1 1QD *Tel:* 01524 380057 *E-mail:* dawsonh@parliament.uk.

DEAN, JANET   Burton   *Lab majority 4,849*

Janet Elizabeth Ann Dean. Born 28 January 1949; Daughter of late Harry and late Mary Gibson; Educated Winsford Verdin Grammar School; Married Alan Dean 1968 (deceased) (2 daughters). Bank clerk 1965–69; Clerk 1969–70; GMB. Member, South-East Staffordshire Health Authority 1981–90; Staffordshire County Council: Councillor 1981–97, Vice-Chair, Highways 1985–93, Vice-Chair, Social Services 1993–96; Councillor: East Staffordshire Borough Council 1991–97, Uttoxeter Town Council 1995–97; Mayor, East Staffordshire Borough Council 1996–97. **House of Commons:** Member for Burton since May 1, 1997; *Select Committees:* Member: Catering 1997–, Home Affairs 1999–. *Special Interests:* Health, Social Services, Education, Transport, Housing, Home Affairs, Hunting With Dogs (Against), Small Businesses. Vice-chair West Midlands

Regional Group of Labour MPs 2002–. School Governor 1979–97; Member: Arthritis and Rheumatism Council (Uttoxeter Branch), Uttoxeter Crime Prevention Panel, Lupus UK; Member: European Standing Committee A 1998–, European Standing Committee B until 2003; Chair, Burton Breweries Charitable Trust; *Recreations:* Dress-making, reading. Mrs Janet Dean, MP, House of Commons, London, SW1A 0AA *Tel:* 020 7219 6320 *Fax:* 020 7219 3010. *Constituency:* Suite 13, First Floor, Cross Street Business Centre, Cross Street, Burton upon Trent, DE14 1EF *Tel:* 01283 509166 *Fax:* 01283 569964 *E-mail:* mcgirrc@parliament.uk.

DENHAM, JOHN   Southampton Itchen   *Lab majority 11,223*

John Yorke Denham. Born 15 July 1953; Son of Edward and Beryl Denham; Educated Woodroffe Comprehensive School, Lyme Regis; Southampton University (President, Student's Union 1976–77) (BSc chemistry); Married Ruth Eleanore Dixon 1979 (1 son 1 daughter) (divorced). Advice worker, Energy Advice Agency, Durham 1977–78; Transport campaigner, Friends of the Earth 1978–79; Head of Youth Affairs, British Youth Council 1979–83; Campaigner, War on Want 1984–88; Consultant to various voluntary organisations 1988–92; Member MSF. Hampshire County Council: Councillor 1981–89, Spokesperson on Education 1985–89; Southampton City Council: Councillor 1989–92, Chairman Housing Committee 1990–92. **House of Commons:** Member for Southampton Itchen since April 9, 1992; Opposition Spokesperson for Social Security 1995–97; Department of Social Security: Parliamentary Under-Secretary of State 1997–98, Minister of State 1998–99; Minister of State: Department of Health 1999–2001, For Crime Reduction, Policing, Community Safety and Young People, Home Office 2001–03; *Select Committees:* Member, Environment 1993–95; Chair, Home Affairs 2003–; Member, Liaison 2003–. PC 2000. Rt Hon John Denham MP, House of Commons, London, SW1A 0AA *Tel:* 020 7219 4515. *Constituency:* 20–22 Southampton Street, Southampton, SO15 2ED *Tel:* 023 8033 9807 *Fax:* 023 8033 9907 *E-mail:* denhamj@parliament.uk.

DHANDA, PARMJIT   Gloucester   *Lab majority 3,880*

Parmjit Singh Dhanda. Born 17 September 1971; Son of Balbir Singh Dhanda, driving instructor and Satvinder Kaur Dhanda, hospital cleaner; Educated Mellow Lane Comprehensive, Hayes, Middlesex; Nottingham University (BEng electronic engineering 1993, MSc information technology 1995); Single. Labour Party organiser West London, Hampshire and Wiltshire 1996–98; TUC Trainer; Member Labour Party NEC Working Party on Equal Opportunities 1998–2001; Contested South East Region 1999 European Parliament election; Hillingdon Councillor, 1998–2002; Assistant national organiser Connect 1998–; Member: USDAW 1999–, TGWU. London Borough of Hillingdon 1998–2001: Councillor, Member: Labour Party National Policy Forum representitive, Education and Skills Policy Commission. **House of Commons:** Member for Gloucester since June 7, 2001; *Select Committees:* Member, Science and Technology 2001–. *Special Interests:* Science and Technology, Employment, European Affairs, Local and Regional Government. *Countries of Interest:* Indian Sub-continent, Europe. Agent general and local elections London Borough of Ealing 1996–98; Organiser Labour Party West London, Hampshire and Wiltshire 1996–98; Member: Fabian Society 1996–, Labour Housing Group 1996–, Co-operative Party 1996–, NEC working group on equal opportunities 1997–. Member Co-operative Party, Non-executive director Gloucester City Football Club; Member: European Standing Committee A 2003–, European Standing Committee B 2003; *Publications:* Former football writer for a football magazine; *Measuring distances using a gallium arsenide laser*, Nottingham University 1993; *Recreations:* Presenting newspaper review on satellite tv station, football, rugby, cricket, chess, writing. Parmjit Dhanda, MP, House of Commons, London, SW1A 0AA *Tel:* 020 7219 8240. *Constituency:* 1 Pullman Court, Great Western Road, Gloucester, GL1 3ND *Tel:* 01452 311870 *Fax:* 01452 311874 *E-mail:* dhandap@parliament.uk.

Visit the Vacher Dod Website . . .

www.DodOnline.co.uk

DISMORE, ANDREW   Hendon   *Lab majority 7,417*

Andrew Dismore. Born 2 September 1954; Son of late Ian Dismore, hotelier, and Brenda Dismore; Educated Bridlington Grammar School; Warwick University (LLB 1975); London School of Economics (LLM 1976); Guildford College of Law 1978. Education Department, GMWU 1976–78; Solicitor: Robin Thomson and Partners 1978–95, Russell Jones and Walker 1995–; Member, GMB. Councillor, Westminster City Council 1982–97, Leader, Labour Group 1990–97. **House of Commons:** Member for Hendon since May 1, 1997; *Select Committees:* Member: Accommodation and Works 1997–99, Social Security 1998–2001; Member: Standards and Privileges 2001–, Work and Pensions 2001–. *Special Interests:* Social Security, Health, Civil Justice, Rights of Victims of Accidents and Crime, Middle East, Cyprus, Greece. *Countries of Interest:* Greece, Cyprus, Israel, Middle East. Vice-chair, Friends of Israel. *Publications:* Various legal journals and articles; *Recreations:* Art, opera, travel, gardening. Andrew Dismore Esq, MP, House of Commons, London, SW1A 0AA *Tel:* 020 7219 4026 *Fax:* 020 7219 1279. *Constituency:* St George's Lodge, 79 The Burroughs, London, NW4 4AX *Tel:* 020 8202 2122 *Fax:* 020 8202 2124 *E-mail:* andrewdismoremp@parliament.uk.

DJANOGLY, JONATHAN   Huntingdon   *Con majority 12,792*

Jonathan Simon Djanogly. Born 3 June 1965; Son of Sir Harry Djanogly CBE and Carol Djanogly; Educated University College School; Oxford Polytechnic (BA law and politics 1987); Guildford College of Law (law finals 1988); Married Rebecca Jane Silk 1991 (1 son 1 daughter). Partner: SJ Berwin Solicitors 1988–, mail order retail business 1994–2002. Councillor Westminster City Council 1994–2001: Chairman: Traffic Committee 1995–96, Contracts 1996–97, Social Services Committee 1998–99, Environment Committee 1999–2000. **House of Commons:** Contested Oxford East 1997 general election. Member for Huntingdon since June 7, 2001; *Select Committees:* Member, Joint Committee on Statutory Instruments 2001–02; Member, Trade and Industry 2001–. *Special Interests:* Small Businesses, Trade, Environment, Rural Affairs, Transport, Planning. Chairman Oxford Polytechnic Conservative Association 1986–87; Vice-chairman Westminster North Conservative Association 1993–94. *Recreations:* Sport, arts, theatre, reading histories and biographies, Britain's countryside and heritage. Jonathan Djanogly Esq, MP, House of Commons, London, SW1A 0AA *Tel:* 020 7219 2367. *Constituency:* 8 Stukeley Road, Huntingdon, Cambridgeshire, PE29 6XG *Tel:* 01480 453062 *Fax:* 01480 453012.

DOBBIN, JIM   Heywood and Middleton   *Lab majority 11,670*

Jim Dobbin. Born 26 May 1941; Son of William Dobbin, miner, and Catherine Dobbin, née McCabe, mill worker; Educated St Columba's High, Cowdenbeath; St Andrew's High, Kirkcaldy; Napier College, Edinburgh (BSc bacteriology, virology 1970); Married Pat Russell 1964 (2 sons 2 daughters). Microbiologist, NHS 1966–94; Member, MSF. Councillor, Rochdale Metropolitan Borough Council 1983–92, 1994–97; Chairman of Housing 1986–90, Leader of Labour Group 1994–96, Deputy Leader 1990–92, Leader of Council 1996–97. **House of Commons:** Contested Bury North 1992 general election. Member for Heywood and Middleton since May 1, 1997; *Select Committees:* Member: European Legislation 1998, European Legislation 1998; Member: European Scrutiny 1998–, Joint Committee on Consolidation of Bills Etc 2001–. *Special Interests:* Local and Regional Government, Health, Housing, Transport, Small Businesses. *Countries of Interest:* America (North and South), Spain, Africa. Chair, Rochdale District Labour Party 1980–81: Executive Member, Rochdale Constituency Labour Party 1986–87; Hon Treasurer, North West Regional Group of Labour MPs 1999–. Amnesty International; Member: European Standing Committee A 1998–2003, European Standing Committee C 2002–; *Recreations:* Walking, football. Jim Dobbin Esq, MP, House of Commons, London, SW1A 0AA *Tel:* 020 7219 4530 *Fax:* 020 7219 2696. *Constituency:* 45 York Street, Heywood, Lancashire, OL10 4NN *Tel:* 01706 361135 *Fax:* 01706 361137.

DOBSON, FRANK   Holborn and St Pancras   Lab majority 11,175

Frank Dobson. Born 15 March 1940; Son of late James William Dobson, railwayman, and late Irene Dobson; Educated Archbishop Holgate's Grammar School, York; London School of Economics (BSc(Econ) 1962); Married Janet Mary Alker 1967 (1 daughter 2 sons). Worked at HQ of: CEGB 1962–70, Electricity Council 1970–75; Assistant Secretary, Office of Local Ombudsman 1975–79; RMT sponsored MP. Camden Borough Council: Councillor 1971–76, Leader of the Council 1973–75. **House of Commons:** Member for Holborn and St Pancras since May 1979; Opposition Spokesperson for Education 1981–83; Principal Opposition Spokesperson for: Energy 1989–92, Employment 1992–93, Transport and London 1993–94; Environment and London 1994–97; Shadow Health Minister 1983–87; Shadow Leader, House of Commons and Campaigns Co-ordinator 1987–89; Shadow Energy Secretary 1989–92; Shadow Employment Secretary 1992–93; Shadow Transport Secretary 1993–94; Shadow Minister for London 1993–97; Shadow Environment Secretary 1994–97; Secretary of State for Health 1997–99; *Special Interests:* Problems of Central London, Transport, Energy, Redistribution of Wealth, Government Reform. PC 1997; *Recreations:* Walking, theatre, watching cricket and football. Rt Hon Frank Dobson, MP, House of Commons, London, SW1A 0AA *Tel:* 020 7219 5040 *Fax:* 020 7219 6956. *Constituency:* 8 Camden Road, London, NW1 9DP *Tel:* 020 7267 1676 *Fax:* 020 7482 3950.

DODDS, NIGEL   Belfast North   DUP majority 6,387

Nigel Dodds. Born 20 August 1958; Son of Joseph Alexander Dodds, civil servant and Doreen Dodds, née McMahon; Educated Portora Royal School, Enniskillen; St John's College, Cambridge (BA law 1980); Queen's University, Belfast Institute of Professional Legal Studies (Cert PLS 1981); Married Diana Harris 1985 (2 sons 1 daughter). Barrister 1981–; European Parliament Secretariat 1984–96; Member of Senate, Queens University Belfast 1985–93. Belfast City Council: Councillor 1985–, Chair Finance and Personnel Committee 1985–87, Lord Mayor Belfast 1988–89, Vice-President Association of Local Authorities of Northern Ireland 1989–90, Chair Health and Environment Committee 1989–91, Lord Mayor Belfast 1991–92, Chair Development Committee 1997–99. **House of Commons:** Member for Belfast North since June 7, 2001; Chief Whip Democratic Unionist Party, House of Commons 2001–; Member: Northern Ireland Forum for Political Dialogue 1996–98, Northern Ireland Assembly 1998–: Minister for Social Development 1999–2000, 2001–02; *Special Interests:* European Affairs, Constitution, Social Policy. *Countries of Interest:* USA, France. OBE 1997. Nigel Dodds Esq, MP, House of Commons, London, SW1A 0AA *Tel:* 020 7219 8419 *Fax:* 020 7219 1972. *Constituency:* 210 Shore Road, Belfast, BT15 3QB *Tel:* 028 9077 4774 *Fax:* 028 9077 7685 *E-mail:* doddsn@parliament.uk.

DOHERTY, PAT   West Tyrone   SF majority 5,040

Pat Doherty. Born 18 July 1945; Married (2 sons 3 daughters). Site engineer 1975; Contested Donegal North East 1989 Dail general election, 1996 by-election and 1997 general election; Connaught/Ulster 1989 and 1994 European Parliament elections. Contested West Tyrone 1997 general election. **House of Commons:** Member for West Tyrone since June 7, 2001; *Special Interests:* Irish National Self-determination. Sinn Fein: Activist 1970–84; Director of Elections 1984–85; National organiser 1985–88; Vice-president 1988–, Leader of delegation to Dublin Forum for Peace and Reconciliation 1994–96, Member Castle Buildings talks team 1997–98, Spokesperson for Enterprise Trade and Investment 2000–. Founder member Local Credit Union 1992; New Northern Ireland Assembly 1998–: Member, Chair Enterprise, Trade and Investment Committee 1999–; *Recreations:* Walking, reading, building stone walls. Pat Doherty Esq, MP, House of Commons, London, SW1A 0AA *Tel:* 020 7219 3000. *Constituency:* 1A Melvin Road, Strabane, County Tyrone, BT82 9AE *Tel:* 028 7188 6464 *Fax:* 028 7188 0120.

DONALDSON, JEFFREY   Lagan Valley   *UUP majority 18,342*

Jeffrey Mark Donaldson. Born 7 December 1962; Son of James and Sarah Anne Donaldson; Educated Kilkeel High School; Castlereagh College (Diploma, Electrical Engineering 1982); Married Eleanor Cousins 1987 (2 daughters). Ulster Defence Regiment 1980–85; Agent to Enoch Powell, MP 1983–84; Personal assistant to Sir James Molyneaux, MP 1984–85; Member, Northern Ireland Assembly 1985–86; Partner, financial services and estate agency business 1986–96; Member, Northern Ireland Forum 1996–98; Former Member, AEEU. **House of Commons:** Member for Lagan Valley since May 1, 1997; Ulster Unionist Spokesperson for: Trade and Industry 2000–01, Environment, Transport and the Regions 2000–01, Treasury 2001–02, Transport, Local Government and the Regions 2001–02, Work and Pensions 2001–, Defence 2002–, Trade and Industry 2002–; Member, Northern Ireland Assembly 1985–86; Member, Northern Ireland Forum 1996–98; *Select Committees:* Member: Northern Ireland Affairs 1997–2000, Environment, Transport and Regional Affairs 2000–01, Transport Sub-Committee 2000–01; Member: Joint Committee on Statutory Instruments 2001–, Regulatory Reform 2001–. *Special Interests:* Northern Ireland, Christian Values, Constitution, Transport. *Countries of Interest:* USA, South Africa, Israel. Honorary Secretary, Ulster Unionist Council 1988–2000, Vice-President 2000–. Member: Evangelical Alliance, CARE, Tear Fund; *Recreations:* Hill-walking, reading, local history, church. Jeffrey Donaldson Esq, MP, House of Commons, London, SW1A 0AA *Tel:* 020 7219 3407 *Fax:* 020 7219 0696. *Constituency:* 2 Sackville Street, Wallace Avenue, Lisburn, Co Antrim, BT27 4AB *Tel:* 028 9266 8001 *Fax:* 028 9267 1845 *E-mail:* donaldsonjm@parliament.uk.

DONOHOE, BRIAN   Cunninghame South   *Lab majority 11,230*

Brian Harold Donohoe. Born 10 September 1948; Son of late George and Catherine Donohoe; Educated Irvine Royal Academy; Kilmarnock Technical College (National certificate engineering 1972); Married Christine Pawson 1973 (2 sons). Apprentice engineer, Ailsa Shipyard 1965–70; Hunterston Nuclear Power Station 1977; ICI Organics Division, draughtsman 1977–81; NALGO District Officer 1981–92; Convenor, Political and Education Committee TASS 1969–81; Secretary, Irvine Trades Council 1973–82; Member, TGWU Parliamentary Campaigning Group 1992–. Chair: Cunninghame Industrial Development Committee 1975–85, North Ayrshire and Arran Local Health Council 1977–79. **House of Commons:** Member for Cunninghame South since April 9, 1992; *Select Committees:* Member: Transport 1993–97, Environment, Transport and Regional Affairs 1997–2001, Environment Sub-Committee 1997–2001, Transport Sub-Committee 1997–2001, Transport, Local Government and the Regions 2001–02, Transport Sub-Committee 2001–02; Member, Transport 2002–. *Special Interests:* Health, Local and Regional Government, Transport, Small Businesses. *Countries of Interest:* Singapore, Indonesia, Malaysia, USA. Treasurer, Cunninghame South Constituency Labour Party 1983–91; Chair, Scottish Group of Labour MPs 1997–98. *Recreations:* Gardening. Brian Donohoe Esq, MP, House of Commons, London, SW1A 0AA *Tel:* 020 7219 6230 *Fax:* 020 7219 5388. *Constituency:* 17 Townhead, Irvine, Strathclyde, KA12 0BL *Tel:* 01294 276844 *Fax:* 01294 313463 *E-mail:* donohoeb@parliament.uk.

DORAN, FRANK   Aberdeen Central   *Lab majority 6,646*

Frank Doran. Born 13 April 1949; Son of Francis Anthony and Betty Hedges Doran; Educated Ainslie Park Secondary School; Leith Academy; Dundee University (LLB 1975); Married Patricia Ann Govan 1967 (divorced) (2 sons). Solicitor 1977–88; Contested North-East Scotland, European Parliament election 1984; Member, GMB 1983–. **House of Commons:** Member for Aberdeen South 1987–92 and for Aberdeen Central since May 1, 1997; Opposition Spokesperson for Energy 1988–92; PPS to Ian McCartney, MP: as Minister of State, Department of Trade and Industry (Competitiveness) 1997–99, as Minister of State, Cabinet Office 1999–2001; *Select Committees:* Member, Culture, Media and Sport 2001–. *Special Interests:* Energy, Childcare,

Families, Mental Health, Employment. GMB Westminster Parliamentary Group. Founder Member, Scottish Legal Action Group 1974; Chair, Dundee Association for Mental Health 1979–82; *Clubs:* Aberdeen Trades Council; *Recreations:* Cinema, art, football, sport. Frank Doran Esq, MP, House of Commons, London, SW1A 0AA *Tel:* 020 7219 3481. *Constituency:* 166 Market Street, Aberdeen, AB11 5PP *Tel:* 01224 252715 *Fax:* 01224 252716 *E-mail:* doranf@parliament.uk.

DORRELL, STEPHEN   Charnwood   *Con majority 7,739*

Stephen James Dorrell. Born 25 March 1952; Son of late Philip Dorrell, Company Director; Educated Uppingham School; Brasenose College, Oxford (BA law 1973); Married Penelope Anne Taylor 1980 (3 sons 1 daughter). Director, family industrial clothing firm 1975–87, 1997–. **House of Commons:** Contested Kingston-upon-Hull East October 1974 general election. Member for Loughborough 1979–97, and for Charnwood since May 1, 1997; Assistant Government Whip 1987–88; Government Whip 1988–90; PPS to Peter Walker as Secretary of State for Energy 1983–87; Parliamentary Under-Secretary of State, Department of Health 1990–92; Financial Secretary, HM Treasury 1992–94; Secretary of State for: National Heritage 1994–1995, Health 1995–97; Member, Shadow Cabinet 1997–98; Shadow Secretary of State for Education and Employment 1997–98; *Select Committees:* Honorary Member, Public Accounts 1992–94. *Special Interests:* Economics, Foreign Affairs. Chairman, Millennium Commission 1994–95; PC 1994; *Recreations:* Reading, theatre. Rt Hon Stephen Dorrell, MP, House of Commons, London, SW1A 0AA *Tel:* 020 7219 4472 *Fax:* 020 7219 5838. *Constituency:* 768 Melton Road, Thurmaston, Leicester, LE4 8BD *Tel:* 0116–260 8609 *Fax:* 0116–260 8700 *E-mail:* info@stephendorrell.org.uk.

DOUGHTY, SUE   Guildford   *LD majority 538*

Sue (Susan Kathleen) Doughty. Born 13 April 1948; Daughter of Ronald Thomas Powell, electrician, and Violet Olive Cooper, secretary; Educated Mill Mount Grammar School, York; Northumberland College of Education (CertEd 1969); Married David Vyvyan Orchard 1994 (2 sons 2 step-daughters). Teacher East Riding Yorkshire 1970–71; Work study analyst: Northern Gas 1971–75, CEGB 1975–76; O&M analyst Wilkinson Match 1976–77; Maternity break and charity activity 1977–82; Independent consultant 1982–88; IT project manager Thames Water 1989–98; Management consultant 1999; Contested London 1999 European Parliament election. **House of Commons:** Member for Guildford since June 7, 2001; Liberal Democrat Spokesperson for: Environment, Food and Rural Affairs 2001–02, Environment 2002–; *Select Committees:* Member, Environmental Audit 2001–. *Special Interests:* Environment, Waste Management, Care of the Elderly, International Development, NHS. *Countries of Interest:* Rwanda/Congo, Balkan States, Eritrea. Constituency chair Reading East Constituency Association 1995–98; Deputy chair Chilterns Region Liberal Democrats 1996–98. Chair Thatcham Children's Centre 1982–84; *Clubs:* National Liberal; Guildford County; *Recreations:* Gardening, music, travel, walking. Sue Doughty, MP, House of Commons, London, SW1A 0AA *Tel:* 020 7219 8482 *Fax:* 020 7219 8482. *Constituency:* The Hall, Woking Road, Guildford, Surrey, GU1 1QD *Tel:* 01483 306000 *Fax:* 01483 306031 *E-mail:* doughtys@parliament.uk.

DOWD, JIM   Lewisham West   *Lab majority 11,920*

Jim Dowd. Born 5 March 1951; Son of late James and Elfriede Dowd; Educated Sedgehill Comprehensive School, London; London Nautical School. Apprentice telephone engineer, GPO (now BT) 1967–72; Station manager, Heron Petrol Stations Ltd. 1972–73; Telecommunications engineer, Plessey Company 1973–92; Member: POEU 1967–72, MSF (ASTMS) 1973–. London Borough of Lewisham: Councillor 1974–94, Deputy Leader 1984–86, Chair, Finance Committee, Deputy Mayor 1987, 1990, Mayor 1992; Member, Lewisham and North Southwark District Health Authority. **House of Commons:** Contested Beckenham 1983 and Lewisham West 1987 general elections. Member for Lewisham West since April 9, 1992;

Opposition Spokesperson on Northern Ireland 1995–97; Opposition Whip for London 1993–95; Government Whip 1997–2001; *Select Committees:* Member, Health 2001–. *Special Interests:* NHS, Transport, Economic Policy, Industrial Policy, Environment, Housing, Animal Welfare, Human Rights. Member: International Fund for Animal Welfare, RSPB, WWFFN, Cats Protection League; Member, National Trust; *Clubs:* Bromley Labour Club; *Recreations:* Music, reading, theatre, Cornwall. Jim Dowd Esq, MP, House of Commons, London, SW1A 0AA *Tel:* 020 7219 4617 *Fax:* 020 7219 2686. *Constituency:* 43 Sunderland Road, Forest Hill, London, SE23 2PS *Tel:* 020 8699 2001 *Fax:* 020 8291 5607 *E-mail:* jimdowd.newlabour@care4free.net.

DREW, DAVID   Stroud   *Lab majority 5,039*

David Elliott Drew. Born 13 April 1952; Son of Ronald Montague Drew, company accountant, and late Maisie Joan Drew, hospital administrator; Educated Kingsfield School, Gloucestershire; Nottingham University (BA economics 1974); Birmingham University (PGCE 1976); Bristol Polytechnic (MA historical studies 1988); University of the West of England (MEd 1994); Married Anne Baker 1990 (2 sons 2 daughters). Economics and geography teacher, various schools in Warwickshire, Hertfordshire and Gloucestershire 1976–86; Lecturer, business education, Bristol Polytechnic/University of the West of England 1986–97; Member, NAS/UWT 1976–86, Branch secretary 1984–86; Member, NATFHE 1986–; Member, UNISON, then NUPE 1990–. Councillor: Stevenage Borough Council 1981–82, Stroud District Council 1987–95, Stonehouse Town Council 1987–, Gloucestershire County Council 1993–97. **House of Commons:** Contested Stroud 1992 general election. Member for Stroud since May 1, 1997; *Select Committees:* Member: Procedure 1997–2001, Modernisation of the House of Commons 1998–99, Agriculture 1999–2001, Radioactive Waste Policy Sub-Committee 2001–02; Member, Environment, Food and Rural Affairs 2001–. *Special Interests:* Housing, Poverty, Planning, Environment, Education, Agriculture, Rural Affairs, Small Businesses. *Countries of Interest:* South Africa, Sudan, Bangladesh. Member: Co-op Party 1980–, Christian Socialist Movement, Labour Party Rural Revival, Labour Campaign for Electoral Reform; Treasurer, Gloucestershire County Labour Party 1987–93; Secretary, Stroud Constituency Labour Party 1992–93. Member: Friends of the Earth, SERA, Greenpeace, ACTSA, Age Concern, Care and Repair, Stroud Small Business Club, St Cyr's Ministry Team, Charter 88, NHS Support Federation; Governor, Maidenhill School; Gloucestershire Association for Disability; Spent 20–25 days with MoD on "work experience" 1999 and 2002; *Publications:* Various IT related materials; *Sportsclubs:* Bristol Rugby Football Club, Forest Green FC; *Recreations:* Reading, watching rugby, football. David Drew Esq, MP, House of Commons, London, SW1A 0AA *Tel:* 020 7219 6479 *Fax:* 020 7219 0910. *Constituency:* 5A Lansdown, Stroud, Gloucestershire, G5 1BB *Tel:* 01453 764355 *Fax:* 01453 753756 *E-mail:* drewd@parliament.uk.

DROWN, JULIA   South Swindon   *Lab majority 7,341*

Julia Kate Drown. Born 23 August 1962; Daughter of David Drown, picture restorer, and Audrey, née Harris, nurse; Educated Hampstead Comprehensive; University College, Oxford (BA politics and economics 1985); Married Bill Child 1999 (1 son 1 daughter deceased). NHS accountancy trainee, Oxfordshire 1985–88; Unit accountant, Learning Disabilities, Oxfordshire 1989–90; Director, finance, contracts and information, Radcliffe Infirmary 1990–96; Member: UNISON (formerly NALGO), TGWU. Councillor, Oxfordshire County Council 1989–96, Labour Spokesperson/Deputy Spokesperson on Social Services 1990–96, Vice-Chair, Labour Group 1994–95; Director/Chair, Oxfordshire Co-operative Development Agency 1994–95. **House of Commons:** Member for South Swindon since May 1, 1997; *Select Committees:* Member: Health 1997–99, Information 2001; Member, Health 2001–. *Special Interests:* NHS, Social Services, International Development, Co-operative Movement, Small Businesses. *Countries of Interest:* Comoros. Member: Co-operative Party 1992–, Labour Women's Network 1996–. School Governor 1989–96; Member: World Development Movement, Amnesty International, Friends of the Earth, Greenpeace; Trust Board Member, Radcliffe Infirmary NHS Trust 1993–96; Member, Chartered Institute of Public Finance and Accountancy (CIPFA) 1988; *Recreations:* Family. Julia Drown, MP, House of Commons, London, SW1A 0AA *Tel:* 020 7219 2392 *Fax:* 020 7219 0266. *Constituency:* 13 Bath Road, Swindon, Wiltshire, SN1 4AS *Tel:* 01793 615444 *Fax:* 01793 644752 *E-mail:* juliadrownmp@parliament.uk.

DUNCAN, ALAN   Rutland and Melton   *Con majority 8,612*

Alan James Carter Duncan. Born 31 March 1957; Son of late Wing-Commander James Duncan, OBE, and Anne, née Carter; Educated Beechwood Park School, St Albans; Merchant Taylors' School, Northwood; St John's College, Oxford (BA philosophy, politics and economics 1979) (President, Oxford Union 1979); Harvard University (Kennedy Scholar). Graduate trainee, Shell International Petroleum 1979–81; Oil trader and adviser to governments and companies on oil supply, shipping and refining 1989–92; Visiting Fellow, St Antony's College, Oxford 2002–03. **House of Commons:** Contested Barnsley West and Penistone 1987 general election. Member for Rutland and Melton since April 9, 1992; Opposition Spokesperson for: Health 1998–99, Trade and Industry 1999–2001, Foreign and Commonwealth Affairs 2001–; PPS to Dr Brian Mawhinney: as Minister of State, Department of Health 1993–94, as Chairman Conservative Party 1995–97; Parliamentary Political Secretary to William Hague as Leader of the Conservative Party 1997–98; *Select Committees:* Member, Social Security 1992–95. *Special Interests:* International Trade, International Economics, Social Security, Middle East. Vice-Chairman Conservative Party 1997–98. Liveryman, Merchant Taylors' Company; *Publications:* Co-author: (CPC pamphlet) *Bearing the Standard: Themes for a Fourth Term*, 1991, *Who Benefits? Reinventing Social Security, An End to Illusions*, 1993, *Saturn's Children: How the State Devours Liberty, Prosperity and Virtue*, 1995; *Beware Blair*, 1997; Freeman, City of London; *Clubs:* Beefsteak; *Recreations:* Shooting, skiing. Alan Duncan Esq, MP, House of Commons, London, SW1A 0AA *Tel:* 020 7219 5204 *Tel (Constituency):* 01664 566444 *Fax (Constituency):* 01664 566555 *E-mail:* duncana@parliament.uk.

DUNCAN, PETER   Galloway and Upper Nithsdale   *Con majority 74*

Peter John Duncan. Born 10 July 1965; Son of late Ronald Duncan, draper and late Aureen Duncan; Educated Ardrossan Academy; Birmingham University (BCom 1985); Married Lorna Anne Forbes 1994 (1 son 1 daughter). Project manager Mackays Stores Ltd 1985–88; Director John Duncan and Son 1988–98; Freelance Business Consultant 1998–2001. **House of Commons:** Member for Galloway and Upper Nithsdale since June 7, 2001; PPS to Jacqui Lait, as Shadow Secretary of State for Scotland 2002–03; Shadow Minister for Scotland 2003–; *Select Committees:* Member, Scottish Affairs 2001–. *Special Interests:* Rural Affairs, E-business, Energy Policy. Vice-chair Birmingham University Conservatives 1984–85; Chairman Cunninghame North Constituency Association 1999–2001. *Recreations:* Golf, sailing, Scots rugby and English county cricket. Peter Duncan Esq, MP, House of Commons, London, SW1A 0AA *Tel:* 020 7219 8235 *Fax:* 020 7219 1768. *Constituency:* 110 Drumlanrig Street, Thornhill, Dumfries, DG3 5LU *Tel:* 01848 331725 *Fax:* 01848 331630 *E-mail:* duncanp@parliament.uk.

DUNCAN SMITH, IAIN   Chingford and Woodford Green   *Con majority 5,487*

(George) Iain Duncan Smith. Born 9 April 1954; Son of late Group Captain W. G. G. Duncan Smith, DSO, DFC, and Pamela, née Summers; Educated HMS Conway (Cadet School); University of Perugia, Italy; RMA Sandhurst; Dunchurch College of Management; Married Hon. Elizabeth Wynne Fremantle 1982 (2 sons 2 daughters). Commissioned, Scots Guards 1975; ADC to Major-General Sir John Acland, KCB, CBE, Commander of Commonwealth Monitoring Force in Zimbabwe 1979–81; GEC Marconi 1981; Director: Bellwinch Property 1988–89, Publishing Director Jane's Information Group 1989–92. **House of Commons:** Contested Bradford West 1987 general election. Member for Chingford 1992–97, and for Chingford and Woodford Green since May 1, 1997; Member, Shadow Cabinet 1997–; Shadow Secretary of State for: Social Security 1997–99, Defence 1999–2001; Leader of the Opposition 2001–; Leader, Conservative Party 2001–; *Select Committees:* Member: Administration 1993–97, Health 1993–95, Standards and Privileges 1995–97. *Special Interests:* Finance, Small Businesses, Transport, Defence, Environment. *Countries of Interest:* India, Italy, Sri Lanka, USA. Vice-Chair, Fulham Conservative Association 1991;

Chair Conservative Policy Board 2001–. *Publications:* Co-author *Who Benefits? Reinventing Social Security*; *Game, Set and Match?* (Maastricht); *Facing the Future* (Defence and Foreign and Commonwealth Affairs); *1994 and Beyond*; *A Response to Chancellor Kohl*; *A Race against time, Europe's growing vulnerablity to missile attack* 2002; PC 2001; Freeman, City of London 1993; *Recreations:* Cricket, rugby, tennis, sport in general, painting, theatre, family. Rt Hon Iain Duncan Smith, MP, House of Commons, London, SW1A 0AA. *Constituency:* 20A Station Road, Chingford, London, E4 7BE *Tel:* 020 8524 4344.

DUNWOODY, GWYNETH   Crewe and Nantwich   *Lab majority 9,906*

Gwyneth Patricia Dunwoody. Born 12 December 1930; Daughter of late Morgan Phillips, sometime General Secretary of the Labour Party and late Baroness Phillips; Married Dr. John Elliott Orr Dunwoody 1954 (marriage dissolved 1975) (2 sons 1 daughter). Director, Film Production Association of GB 1970–74. **House of Commons:** Contested Exeter 1964 general election. Member for Exeter 1966–70, for Crewe February 1974–83, and for Crewe and Nantwich since June 1983; Opposition Front Bench Spokesman on: Foreign and Commonwealth Affairs 1979–80, NHS 1980–83, Parliamentary Campaigning and Information 1983–84; Opposition Spokesman on Transport 1984–85; Parliamentary Secretary to Board of Trade 1967–70; MEP 1975–79; Deputy Speaker, Westminster Hall 1999–2000; *Select Committees:* Chairman, Transport Sub-Committee 1997–2001; Chairman (Transport), Environment, Transport and Regional Affairs 1997–2001; Member: Chairmen's Panel 1997–2001, Environment Sub-Committee 1997–2001; Chairman: Transport, Local Government and the Regions 2001–02, Transport Sub-Committee 2001–02; Member, Liaison 1997–; Chairman, Transport 2002–; Member, Liaison Sub-Committee 2002–. *Special Interests:* Transport, NHS, Arts. *Countries of Interest:* Botswana, Central Africa, East Africa, Middle East. Labour Friends of Israel: Former Chair, President 1993–95, Life President 1995–. Patron, BRAKE 1995–; Vice-President, Socialist International Women; Vice-Chairman, European Parliament Social Affairs Committee; *Recreations:* Reading, listening to music. Hon Gwyneth Dunwoody, MP, House of Commons, London, SW1A 0AA *Tel:* 020 7219 3490 *Fax:* 020 7219 6046. *Constituency:* 154 Nantwich Road, Crewe, CW2 6BG *Tel:* 01270 589132 *Fax:* 01270 589135.

E

EAGLE, ANGELA   Wallasey   *Lab majority 12,276*

Angela Eagle. Born 17 February 1961; Daughter of André Eagle, printworker, and late Shirley Eagle, dressmaker and student; Educated Formby High School; St John's College, Oxford (BA philosophy, politics and economics). COHSE 1984–: first as a researcher, then as National Press Officer, currently as Parliamentary Liaison Officer; Member: COHSE, NUJ. **House of Commons:** Member for Wallasey since April 9, 1992; Opposition Whip 1996–97; Parliamentary Under-Secretary of State: Department of the Environment, Transport and the Regions (Minister for Green Issues and Regeneration) 1997–98, Department of Social Security 1998–2001; Parliamentary Under-Secretary of State, Home Office 2001–02; *Select Committees:* Member: Members' Interests 1992–97, Employment 1994–96, Public Accounts 1995–97, Public Accounts 2002–03; Member: Treasury 2003–, Treasury Sub-committee 2003–. *Special Interests:* Economic Policy, NHS, Politics of Sport. Active at branch, women's section, general committee levels in Crosby Constituency 1978–80; Chairman: Oxford University Fabian Club 1980–83, National Conference of Labour Women 1991. Member, British Film Institute; *Publications:* Columnist and regular contributor to *Tribune*; *Recreations:* Chess, cricket, cinema. Angela Eagle, MP, House of Commons, London, SW1A 0AA *Tel:* 020 7219 4074. *Constituency:* 6 Manor Road, Liscard, Wallasey, Merseyside, CH45 4JB *Tel:* 01925 574 913 *E-mail:* eaglea@parliament.uk.

EAGLE, MARIA   Liverpool Garston   *Lab majority 12,494*

Maria Eagle. Born 17 February 1961; Daughter of André Eagle, printworker, and late Shirley Eagle, dressmaker and student; Educated St Peter's Church of England Primary School, Formby; Formby High School (Comprehensive); Pembroke College, Oxford (BA philosophy, politics and economics 1983); College of Law, London (Common Professional Exam, Law Society Finals 1990). Voluntary sector 1983–90; Articles of clerkship, Brian Thompson & Partners, Liverpool 1990–92; Goldsmith Williams, Liverpool 1992–95; Senior Solicitor, Steven Irving & Co, Liverpool 1994–97; Member GMB. **House of Commons:** Contested Crosby 1992 general election. Member for Liverpool Garston since May 1, 1997; PPS to John Hutton as Minister of State, Department of Health 1999–2001; Parliamentary Under-Secretary of State, (Minister for Disabled People) Department for Work and Pensions 2001–; *Select Committees:* Member, Public Accounts 1997–99. *Special Interests:* Transport, Housing, Employment. *Countries of Interest:* Nicaragua, USA, Australia. Campaigns organiser Crosby 1993–96; Campaigns organiser, Press officer, Merseyside West Euro Constituency Labour Party 1983–84; Constituency Labour Party secretary, Press officer, political education officer 1983–85. Played cricket for Lancashire as a Junior; Played chess for England and Lancashire; *Publications:* Co-author *High Time or High Tide for Labour Women*; *Recreations:* Cinema, chess, cricket. Maria Eagle, MP, House of Commons, London, SW1A 0AA *Tel:* 020 7219 5288 *Fax:* 020 7219 1157. *Constituency:* Unit House, Speke Boulevard, Liverpool, L24 9HZ *Tel:* 0151–448 1167 *Fax:* 0151–448 0976 *E-mail:* eaglem@parliament.uk.

EDWARDS, HUW   Monmouth   *Lab majority 384*

Huw William Edmund Edwards. Born 12 April 1953; Son of Rev Dr Ifor and Esme Edwards; Educated Eastfields High School, Mitcham, Surrey; Manchester Polytechnic (BA social science 1976); York University (MA social policy 1978, MPhil 1984); Single. Lecturer in social policy, Brighton Polytechnic/University 1988–97; Research consultant, Low Pay Unit 1988–97; Tutor, Open University 1988–89, 1993–96. **House of Commons:** Member for Monmouth 1991 by-election–1992, and from May 1, 1997; *Select Committees:* Member: Modernisation of the House of Commons 1997–98, Welsh Affairs 1997–2001; Member, Welsh Affairs 2002–. *Special Interests:* Health, Housing, Education, Wales, Constitutional Reform, Low Pay, Social Inequality. *Countries of Interest:* Wales, Japan. Member, Fabian Society; PLP Welsh Group: Chair 2000–01. Member: Amnesty International (Monmouth), One World Action, Shelter (Cymru), Gwalia Male Choir (London), London Welsh Association; Member, Gwent Wildlife Trust; *Publications: Low Pay in South Wales*, 1989; *Wales in the 1990s – Land of Low Pay*, 1995; Plus articles in new review of Low Pay Unit; *Clubs:* London Welsh Association; *Sportsclubs:* London Welsh AFC, Preston Park CC, Lords and Commons Cricket XI, Lords and Commons Rugby Football, Lords and Commons Skiing, Parliamentary Football; Vice President Monmouth Rugby. *Recreations:* Playing football, cricket, rugby, squash, skiing. Huw Edwards Esq, MP, House of Commons, London, SW1A 0AA *Tel:* 020 7219 3489 *Fax:* 020 7219 3949. *Constituency:* Constituency Office, 7 Agincourt Street, Monmouth, Monmouthshire, NP25 3DZ *Tel:* 01600 713537 *Fax:* 01600 712847 *E-mail:* edwardsh@parliament.uk.

DodOnline

An Electronic Directory without rival . . .

MPs' biographies and photographs available with daily updates *via* the internet

For a *free* trial, call Yasmin Mirza, Aby Farsoun or Michael Mand on 020 7630 7643

EFFORD, CLIVE   Eltham   *Lab majority 6,996*

Clive Efford. Born 10 July 1958; Son of Stanley Efford, retired civil servant and Mary Agnes Elizabeth Christina Efford, née Caldwell; Educated Walworth Comprehensive School; Southwark Further Education College; Married Gillian Vallins (3 daughters). Partner family-owned jewellery and watch repair business till 1987; Taxi driver 1987–97; Member, T&GWU. London Borough of Greenwich: Councillor 1986–98, Chair, Social Services, Health and Environment, Secretary Labour Group 1986–87; Chief Whip Labour Group 1990–91. **House of Commons:** Contested Eltham 1992 General Election. Member for Eltham since May 1, 1997; Presented two bills in Parliament on Energy efficiency and energy conservation; *Select Committees:* Member: Procedure 1997–2001, Standing Orders 1999–2000; Member, Transport 2002–. *Special Interests:* Welfare State, Health, Transport, Education, Environment, Local and Regional Government, Energy Conservation, Energy Efficiency, Energy from Waste, Waste Management, Recycling. Vice-chair London Group of Labour MPs 2001–02; Member Labour Friends of India. *Clubs:* Plumstead Co-op Club; CIU Club; Woolwich Catholic Club; *Recreations:* Football (FA Coaches Club). Clive Efford Esq, MP, House of Commons, London, SW1A 0AA *Tel:* 020 7219 4057. *Constituency:* Westmount Road, Eltham, London, SE9 *E-mail:* clive.efford@btinternet.com.

ELLMAN, LOUISE   Liverpool Riverside   *Lab majority 13,950*

Louise Joyce Ellman. Born 14 November 1945; Daughter of late Harold and Anne Rosenberg; Educated Manchester High School for Girls; Hull University (BA sociology 1967); York University (MPhil social administration 1972); Married Geoffrey Ellman 1967 (1 son 1 daughter). Member, T&GWU. Councillor, Lancashire County Council 1970–97, Leader, County Labour Group 1977–97, Leader of Council 1981–97; Councillor, West Lancashire District Council 1974–87; Vice-Chair, Lancashire Enterprises 1982–97; Founder Chair, Northwest Regional Association 1991–92, Vice-Chair 1996–97. **House of Commons:** Member for Liverpool Riverside since May 1, 1997; *Select Committees:* Member: Environment, Transport and Regional Affairs 1997–2001, Environment Sub-Committee 1997–2001, Transport, Local Government and the Regions 2001–02, Transport Sub-Committee 2001–02, Urban Affairs Sub-Committee 2001–02; Member, Transport 2002–. *Special Interests:* Regional Government, Local Government, Transport, Public Services, Arts, Middle East. Member, Co-op Party. Mrs Louise Ellman, MP, House of Commons, London, SW1A 0AA *Tel:* 020 7219 5210 *Fax:* 020 7219 2592. *Constituency:* First Floor, Threlfall Building, Trueman Street, Liverpool, L3 2EX *Tel:* 0151–236 2969 *Fax:* 0151–236 4301 *E-mail:* ellmanl@parliament.uk.

ENNIS, JEFFREY   Barnsley East and Mexborough   *Lab majority 16,789*

Jeffrey Ennis. Born 13 November 1952; Son of William, retired miner, and Jean Ennis; Educated Hemsworth Grammar School; Redland College, Bristol (CertEd, BEd 1975); Married Margaret Angela Knight 1980 (3 sons). Raw materials inspector, Lyons Bakery 1975–76; Primary teacher: Wolverhampton 1976–78, Hillsborough Primary School, Sheffield 1979–96; Member, TU 1975–; Representative, NASUWT at Hillsborough Primary 1979–96; Member, TGWU 1997–. Councillor, Barnsley Council 1980–96; Councillor, Barnsley Metropolitan Borough Council 1980–96, Deputy Leader 1988–95, Leader 1995–96; Chair, South Yorkshire Fire and Civil Defence Authority 1995–96. **House of Commons:** Member for Barnsley East from December 12, 1996 by-election–1997, and for Barnsley East and Mexborough since May 1, 1997; PPS to Tessa Jowell: as Minister for Public Health, Department of Health 1997–99, as Minister of State, Department for Education and Employment (Minister for Employment, Welfare to Work and Equal Opportunities) 1999–2001; *Select Committees:* Member, Education and Skills 2001–. *Special Interests:* Local and Regional Government, Environment, Education, Regeneration, Fire Service. *Countries of Interest:* Germany, Ukraine. Member, Co-operative Party. Chair: Barnsley Economic Regeneration Forum

1995–96, Barnsley City Challenge 1995–96, Barnsley Partnership Ltd 1995–96; Board member, Dearne Valley Partnership 1995–96; Board director, Barnsley and Doncaster and Training and Enterprise Council 1995–96; Member, British-Irish Inter-Parliamentary Body; *Clubs:* Member, British Legion; *Recreations:* Family activities, hill walking, sport, music, swimming, caravanning. Jeffrey Ennis Esq, MP, House of Commons, London, SW1A 0AA *Tel:* 020 7219 5008 *Fax:* 020 7219 2728. *Constituency:* Dearne Town Hall, Goldthorpe, Rotherham, South Yorkshire, S63 9EJ *Tel:* 01226 775080 *Fax:* 01226 775080 *E-mail:* ennisj@parliament.uk.

ETHERINGTON, BILL   Sunderland North   Lab majority 13,354

Bill (William) Etherington. Born 17 July 1941; Educated Redby Infant and Junior School; Monkwearmouth Grammar School; Married Irene Holton 1963 (2 daughters). Apprentice fitter, Austin & Pickersgill Shipyard 1957–63; Fitter, Dawdon Colliery 1963–83; Full-time official, NUM 1983–92; Member: AEU 1957–, NUM 1963–, National Executive Committee 1986–88, 1995–; Trustee, Mineworkers' Pension Scheme 1985–87; Representative, North Regional TUC 1985–92; NUM delegate, TUC 1990–91; Vice-President, North East Area NUM 1988–92; Member, RMT Parliamentary Campaigning Group 2002–. **House of Commons:** Member for Sunderland North since April 9, 1992; *Select Committees:* Member: Members' Interests 1994–95, Catering 1995–97,
Parliamentary Commissioner for Administration 1996–97, Court of Referees 1997–2001. *Special Interests:* Trades Union Legislation, Employment, Adult Education, Human Rights, Education, Equal Opportunities, NHS, Homelessness, Disability, Animal Welfare, Hunting with Dogs (Against), Fluoridation (Against). Various posts, including local ward treasurer 1978–87; GMC delegate 1978–87; CLP Executive Committee member 1981–87. UK Delegation to Council of Europe and Western Europe Union: Member 1997–, Deputy Leader 2001–; *Clubs:* Kelloe Working Men's, Durham City Labour; *Recreations:* Fell walking, motorcycling, watching soccer, local, industrial and transport history, reading. Bill Etherington Esq, MP, House of Commons, London, SW1A 0AA *Tel:* 020 7219 4603 *Fax:* 020 7219 1186. *Constituency:* 7 Bridge House, Bridge Street, Sunderland, SR1 1TE *Tel:* 0191–564 2489 *Fax:* 0191–564 2486.

EVANS, NIGEL   Ribble Valley   Con majority 11,238

Nigel Evans. Born 10 November 1957; Son of late Albert Evans, and of Betty Evans; Educated Dynevor School; University College of Wales, Swansea (BA politics 1979); Single. Management family retail newsagent and convenience store 1979–90. West Glamorgan County Council: Councillor 1985–91, Deputy Leader, Conservative Group 1990–91. **House of Commons:** Contested Swansea West 1987 general election, Pontypridd 1989 by-election, Ribble Valley 1991 by-election. Member for Ribble Valley since April 9, 1992; Opposition Spokesperson for: Constitutional Affairs (Scotland and Wales) 1997–99, Constitutional Affairs (Wales) 1999–2001; PPS: to David Hunt: as Secretary of State for Employment 1993–94, as
Chancellor of the Duchy of Lancaster 1994–95; to Tony Baldry as Minister of State, Ministry of Agriculture, Fisheries and Food 1995–96; to William Hague as Secretary of State for Wales 1996–97; Shadow Secretary of State for Wales 2001–; *Select Committees:* Member: Transport 1993, Public Service 1995–97. *Special Interests:* Education, Small Businesses, US Elections, Local and Regional Government, Defence, Agriculture, International Politics, European Affairs, Telecommunications, Space. *Countries of Interest:* Caribbean, Central America, Europe, USA, Asia, Far East, Australia, Egypt, Bahrain, Grand Caymen, Gibraltar. Chair, Conservative Welsh Parliamentary Candidates Policy Group 1990; President, Conservative North West Parliamentary Candidates Group 1991; Secretary, North West Conservative MPs 1992–97; Vice-Chair (Wales), Conservative Party 1999–2001. Has worked on three US presidential elections in New York, Florida and California; *Clubs:* Carlton, I.O.D., countryclubuk.com; *Recreations:* Tennis, swimming, running, theatre, cinema, arts. Nigel Evans Esq, MP, House of Commons, London, SW1A 0AA *Tel:* 020 7219 4165 *Fax:* 0870 131 3711. *Constituency:* 9 Railway View, Clitheroe, Lancashire, BB7 2HA *Tel:* 01200 425939 *Fax:* 01200 422904 *E-mail:* nigelmp@hotmail.com.

EWING, ANNABELLE   Perth   *SNP majority 48*

Annabelle Janet Ewing. Born 20 August 1960; Daughter of late Stewart Martin Ewing, and Dr Winifred Ewing, former MP, MEP and MSP; Educated Craigholme School, Glasgow; Glasgow University (LLB EC law 1981); John Hopkins University Bologna Center (Diploma advanced international relations 1982); Amsterdam University Europa Instituut (Diploma European integration 1983); Single. Apprentice lawyer Ruth Anderson and Company 1984–86; Stagiaire European Commission Legal Service 1987; Associate Lebrun de Smedt and Dassesse, Brussels 1987–89; Akin Gump, Brussels: Associate 1989–92, Contract partner 1993–96; Special counsel McKenna and Cuneo, Brussels 1996; Freelance EC lawyer 1997; Ewing and Company Solicitors, Glasgow: Associate 1998–99, Partner 1992–2001; Consultant, Leslie Wolfson and Co Solicitors, Glasgow 2001–; Member, Law Society of Scotland. **House of Commons:** Member for Perth since June 7, 2001; SNP Spokesperson for Work and Pensions and Home Affairs; *Special Interests:* Social Justice, European Affairs, Civil Liberties. Scottish National Party Brussels: Founder 1993–94, Honorary president. Member: Shelter, Amnesty International; Federation Small Business; Scottish Centre for Human Rights; *Publications:* Various publications on EC financial services law 1990–97; *Recreations:* Swimming, walking, reading, theatre, music, cinema. Annabelle Ewing, MP, House of Commons, London, SW1A 0AA *Tel:* 020 7219 8309 *Fax:* 020 7219 1788. *Constituency:* 55 Commissioner Street, Crieff, Perthshire PH7 3AY *Tel:* 01764 656611 *Fax:* 01764 656622 *E-mail:* ewinga@parliament.uk.

F

FABRICANT, MICHAEL   Lichfield   *Con majority 4,426*

Michael Fabricant. Born 12 June 1950; Son of late Isaac Nathan Fabricant, and of Helena Fabricant, née Freed; Educated Brighton, Hove and Sussex Grammar School, Brighton; Loughborough University (BSc economics and law 1973); Sussex University (MSc systems and econometrics 1974); Oxford University/London University/University of Southern California, Los Angeles, USA (PhD econometrics and economic forecasting 1975–78); Single. Economist and founder director, leading broadcast and communications group, manufacturing and commissioning electronics equipment to radio stations to 48 countries 1980–91; Adviser, Home Office on broadcasting matters; Staff, then freelance radio broadcaster and journalist 1968–80; Adviser to foreign governments on the establishment and management of radio stations, including the Russian Federation 1980–91; Has lived and worked extensively in Europe, Africa, the Far East, former Soviet Union, and the United States. **House of Commons:** Contested South Shields 1987 general election. Member for Mid-Staffordshire 1992–97, and for Lichfield since May 1, 1997; PPS to Michael Jack as Financial Secretary to the Treasury 1996–97; Shadow Minister for Trade and Industry 2003–; *Select Committees:* Member: European Legislation Scrutiny Committee B (Trade) 1992–97, National Heritage 1993–96, Culture, Media and Sport 1997–99, Catering 1999–2001, Home Affairs 1999–2001; Chair, Information 2001–03; Member: Culture, Media and Sport 2001–, Finance and Services 2001–, Liaison 2001–. *Special Interests:* Trade and Industry, Foreign Affairs, Broadcasting and Media, Technology. *Countries of Interest:* Russia, Israel, USA, Australia, Eastern Europe. Chairman, Brighton Pavilion Conservative Association 1985–88; Member, Conservative Way Forward; Associate Member, European Research Group; Member, Conservative Against a Federal Europe. Member: Council of the Institution of Electrical Engineers 1996–, Senate of the Engineering Council 1996–2002; Director Engineering and Technology Board 2002–; Presented Bills to strengthen economic and political ties between UK, United States, Canada, Australia and New Zealand; Promoted legislation to encourage the flying of the Union Flag; Promoted legislation to force the Government to undertake and publish regular financial cost-benefit analyses of Britain's membership of the European Union; Member: Inter-Parliamentary Union, Commonwealth Parliamentary Association; CEng; FIEE; *Clubs:* Rottingdean (Sussex); *Recreations:* Reading, music, fell-walking, skiing and listening to the Omnibus Edition of The Archers. Michael Fabricant Esq, MP, House of Commons, London, SW1A 0AA *Tel:* 020 7219 5022. *Constituency Tel:* 01543 417868.

FALLON, MICHAEL   Sevenoaks   *Con majority 10,154*

Michael Fallon. Born 14 May 1952; Son of late Martin Fallon, OBE, FRICS, and Hazel Fallon; Educated Epsom College, Surrey; St Andrews University (MA classics and ancient history 1974); Married Wendy Elisabeth Payne 1986 (2 sons). European Educational Research Trust 1974–75; Conservative Research Department 1975–79 (seconded to Opposition Whips Office, House of Lords 1975–77, EEC Desk Officer 1977–79); Secretary, Lord Home's Committee on Future of the House of Lords 1977–78; Joint Managing Director, European Consultants Ltd 1979–81; Assistant to Baroness Elles MEP 1979–83; Director, Quality Care Homes plc 1992–97; Chief Executive, Quality Care Developments Ltd 1996–97; Director: Just Learning Ltd 1996–, Banna Tyne Fitness Ltd 1999–2000, Just Learning Holdings 2001–, Just Learning Development Ltd 2001–. **House of Commons:** Contested Darlington by-election March 1983. Member for Darlington 1983–92, and for Sevenoaks since May 1, 1997; Frontbench Spokesperson for: Trade and Industry June-December 1997, the Treasury December 1997–98; Assistant Government Whip 1988–90; Government Whip (Lord Commissioner of HM Treasury) May-July 1990; PPS to Cecil Parkinson as Secretary of State for Energy 1987–88; Parliamentary Under-Secretary of State, Department of Education and Science 1990–92; *Select Committees:* Member, Treasury Sub-Committee 1999–2001; Member, Treasury 1999–; Chair, Treasury Sub-Committee 2001–. *Special Interests:* Constitution, Public Sector, Education, Energy. Non-Executive Director, International Care and Relief 1998–2003; Member: Higher Education Funding Council 1992–97, Deregulation Task Force 1994–97, Advisory Council, Social Market Foundation 1994–2000; *Publications: Brighter Schools,* Social Market Foundation 1993; *Clubs:* Academy. Michael Fallon Esq, MP, House of Commons, London, SW1A 0AA *Tel:* 020 7219 6482 *Fax:* 020 7219 6791. *Constituency:* 113 St John's Hill, Sevenoaks, TN13 3PF *Tel:* 01732 452261 *E-mail:* fallonm@parliament.uk.

FARRELLY, PAUL   Newcastle-under-Lyme   *Lab majority 9,986*

(Christopher) Paul Farrelly. Born 2 March 1962; Son of late Thomas Farrelly and Anne Farrelly, née King; Educated Wolstanton County Grammar School; Marshlands Comprehensive, Newcastle-Under-Lyme; St Edmund Hall, Oxford (BA philosophy, politics and economics 1984); Married Victoria Jane Perry 1998 (1 son 1 daughter). Manager corporate finance division Barclays De Zoete Wedd Ltd 1984–90; Reuters Ltd 1990–95: Correspondent, News editor; Deputy city and business editor *Independent on Sunday* 1995–97; City editor *The Observer* 1997–2001; NUJ; MSF. **House of Commons:** Contested Chesham and Amersham 1997 general election. Member for Newcastle-under-Lyme since June 7, 2001; *Select Committees:* Member, Joint Committee on Consolidation of Bills Etc 2001–. *Special Interests:* Education, Health, Employment, Trade and Industry, Regeneration, Investment, European Affairs, Pensions, Crime. Hornsey and Wood Green CLP: Secretary 1992–94, Vice-chair 1994–95; Newcastle-under-Lyme CLP 1998–: Campaign co-ordinator and organiser, Political education officer; Member Socialist Education Association. Member: Amnesty International, Greenpeace, Liberty; Member European Standing Committee B 2003–; *Clubs:* Holy Trinity Catholic Centre, Newcastle-Under-Lyme; *Sportsclubs:* Trentham RUFC, Finchley RFC; *Recreations:* Rugby, football, writing, biography, history, architecture. Paul Farrelly Esq, MP, House of Commons, London, SW1A 0AA *Tel:* 020 7219 8262 *Fax:* 020 7219 1986. *Constituency:* Waterloo Buildings, Dunkirk, Newcastle-under-Lyme, Staffordshire, ST5 2SW *Tel:* 01782 715033 *E-mail:* farrellyp@parliament.uk.

DodOnline
An Electronic Directory without rival . . .

MPs' biographies and photographs available with daily updates *via* the internet

For a *free* trial, call Yasmin Mirza, Aby Farsoun or Michael Mand on 020 7630 7643

FIELD, FRANK   Birkenhead   *Lab majority 15,591*

Frank Field. Born 16 July 1942; Son of late Walter Field; Educated St Clement Danes Grammar School; Hull University (BSc economics 1963). Teacher in further education 1964–69; Director: Child Poverty Action Group 1969–79, Low Pay Unit 1974–80. Councillor, Hounslow Borough Council 1964–68. **House of Commons:** Contested Buckinghamshire South 1966 general election. Member for Birkenhead since May 1979; Opposition Spokesperson for Education 1980–81; Minister of State, Department of Social Security (Welfare Reform) 1997–98; *Select Committees:* Chair, Social Security 1990–97; Member, Public Accounts 2002–. *Special Interests:* Poverty and Income Redistribution, Church Affairs. *Countries of Interest:* Poland. *Publications:* Publications on low pay, poverty and social issues since 1971; PC 1997; Honorary Doctorate of Science Southampton University 1996; Honorary Fellow South Bank University 2001; Honorary Doctorate of Law Warwick University. Rt Hon Frank Field, MP, House of Commons, London, SW1A 0AA *Tel:* 020 7219 5193 *Fax:* 020 7219 0601 *E-mail:* hendeyj@parliament.uk.

FIELD, MARK   Cities of London and Westminster   *Con majority 4,499*

Mark Christopher Field. Born 6 October 1964; Son of late Major Peter Charles Field and Ulrike Field, née Peipe, housewife; Educated Reading School; St Edmund Hall, Oxford law (MA 1987) (JCR President); College of Law, Chester (solicitors' finals 1988); Married Michèle Louise Acton 1994. Trainee solicitor 1988–90; Solicitor Freshfields 1990–92; Employment consultant 1992–94; Kellyfield Consulting 1994–2001: Director and former Co-owner. Councillor Royal London Borough of Kensington and Chelsea 1994–2002. **House of Commons:** Contested Enfield North 1997 general election. Member for Cities of London and Westminster since June 7, 2001; Opposition Whip 2003–; Association/Ward Officer Kensington and Chelsea and Islington North Associations 1989–99; Member Standing Committees: Proceeds of Crime Act 2001–02, Enterprise Act 2001–02, Finance Act 2001–02, Licensing Bill 2002–03; *Select Committees:* Member, Lord Chancellor's Department 2003–. *Special Interests:* Economy, Small Businesses, Employment, Culture, Media and Sport, Transport. *Countries of Interest:* USA, Germany. Freeman of Merchant Taylors Livery Company; *Publications:* Contributing Chapter to *A Blue Tomorrow* (Politicos 2001) and various articles for national newspapers on financial services, pensions and civil liberties issues; Freeman of the City of London; *Clubs:* City of London Club; *Recreations:* Football, cricket, motor-racing, popular/rock music. Mark Field Esq, MP, House of Commons, London, SW1A 0AA *Tel:* 020 7219 8160. *Constituency:* 90 Ebury Street, London, SW1W 9QD *Tel:* 020 7730 8181 *Fax:* 020 7730 4520 *E-mail:* fieldm@parliament.uk.

FISHER, MARK   Stoke-on-Trent Central   *Lab majority 11,845*

Mark Fisher. Born 29 October 1944; Son of late Sir Nigel Fisher, MC, MP 1950–83 and late Lady Gloria Flower; Educated Eton College; Trinity College, Cambridge (MA English literature 1966); Married Ingrid Hunt 1971 (divorced 1999) (2 sons 2 daughters). Documentary film producer and scriptwriter 1966–75; Principal, The Tattenhall Centre of Education 1975–83; Visiting Fellow, St Anthony's College, Oxford 2000–01; Member: NUT, MU. Staffordshire County Council: Councillor 1981–85, Chair, Libraries Committee 1981–83. **House of Commons:** Contested Leek 1979 general election. Member for Stoke-on-Trent Central since June 1983; Spokesperson on Arts and Media 1987–92; Frontbench Spokesperson for: The Citizen's Charter 1992–93, National Heritage 1993–97; Opposition Whip 1985–86; Parliamentary Under-Secretary of State: Department of National Heritage 1997, Department for Culture, Media and Sport 1997–98; *Select Committees:* Member, Treasury and Civil Service 1983–85. *Special Interests:* Urban Policy, Freedom of Information, Human Rights, Overseas Aid and Development, Broadcasting, Press, Cultural Policy, Arts. *Countries of Interest:* Hong Kong, Kashmir, Pakistan, Indonesia, Tunisia. Chair, Parliament First 2001–.

Deputy Pro-Chancellor, Keele University 1989–97; Member, BBC General Advisory Council 1987–97; Member of Council, Policy Studies Institute 1989–97; Member, Museums and Galleries Commission 1998–2000; Trustee: National Benevolent Fund for the Aged 1986–97, Education Extra 1992–97, Britten Pears Foundation 1998–, Estorick Foundation 2001–; *Publications: City Centres, City Cultures*, 1988; *Whose Cities?* (editor) 1991; *A New London*, 1992; Honorary Fellow: RIBA, Royal College of Art; Hon. FRIBA 1992; Hon. Fellow, Royal College of Art 1993. Mark Fisher Esq, MP, House of Commons, London, SW1A 0AA *Tel:* 020 7219 4502 *Fax:* 020 7219 4894. *Constituency:* Winton House, Stoke Road, Shelton, Stoke-on-Trent, ST4 2RW *Tel:* 01782 848468 *Fax:* 01782 845658 *E-mail:* fisherm@parliament.uk.

FITZPATRICK, JIM   Poplar and Canning Town   *Lab majority 14,108*

Jim (James) Fitzpatrick. Born 4 April 1952; Son of James and Jean Fitzpatrick; Educated Holyrood Senior Secondary, Glasgow; Married Jane Lowe 1980 (1 son 1 daughter) (divorced). Trainee, Tytrak Ltd, Glasgow 1970–73; Driver, Mintex Ltd, London 1973–74; Firefighter, London Fire Brigade 1974–97; Member: National Executive Council, Fire Brigades Union, GPMU Parliamentary Group. **House of Commons:** Member for Poplar and Canning Town since May 1, 1997; Assistant Government Whip 2001–02; Government Whip 2002–; PPS to Alan Milburn as Secretary of State for Health 1999–2001; *Select Committees:* Member Selection 2003–. *Special Interests:* Poverty, Regeneration, Racism, Fire, Animal Welfare. *Countries of Interest:* Bangladesh. Barking Constituency Labour Party: Voluntary Agent 1986–91, Chair 1989–90; Member, London Labour Executive 1988–2000; Chair, Greater London Labour Party 1991–2000; Hon. Treasurer, London Regional Group of Labour MPs 1999–2001. Patron Richard House Children's Hospice; Labour Animal Welfare Society; Fire Service: Long Service and Good Conduct Medal (20 years) 1994; Fire Brigade Long Service and Good Conduct Medal (20 years) 1994; *Recreations:* Reading, TV/film, football, West Ham United FC. Jim Fitzpatrick Esq, MP, House of Commons, London, SW1A 0AA *Tel:* 020 7219 5085/6215 *Fax:* 020 7219 2776 *E-mail:* fitzpatrickj@parliament.uk.

FITZSIMONS, LORNA   Rochdale   *Lab majority 5,655*

Lorna Fitzsimons. Born 6 August 1967; Daughter of Derek Fitzsimons and Barbara Jean Fitzsimons, née Taylor; Educated St James's Church of England, Wardle; Wardle High School, Rochdale; Rochdale College of Art and Design; Loughborough College of Art and Design (BA textile design 1988); Married Stephen Benedict Cooney 2000 (1 stepdaughter 1 stepson). Parliamentary Scheme (Army) 1998–99; Director: NUS Services 1990–94; Endsleigh Insurance 1992–94; Political consultant (associate director), The Rowland Company 1994–97; National Union of Students: Part-time executive member 1989–90; Vice-President, Education 1990–92; President 1992–94; Member, MSF. **House of Commons:** Member for Rochdale since May 1, 1997; PPS: to John Battle as Minister of State, Foreign and Commonwealth Office 2001, to Robin Cook as Leader of the House of Commons 2001–03; *Select Committees:* Member: Procedure 1997–2001, Modernisation of the House of Commons 1999–2003. *Special Interests:* Kashmir, Constitution (Electoral Reform, Modernisation of Parliament), Children's Services, Race, Islam, Health. *Countries of Interest:* USA, Kashmir, Pakistan, Bangladesh, Middle East. Member: Labour Campaign for Electoral Reform, Labour NEC Youth Committee 1990–94, LCC Executive 1994–97, Fabian Society, Labour Friends of Israel. Governor: Wardle High School 1982–83, Loughborough College of Art and Design 1988–89, Sheffield Hallam University 1995–96; Hansard Society 2000–; Vice-president British Dyslexia Association; Member, Further Education Funding Council Quality Committee 1993–94; Registered with The Sheffield Institute for Dyslexia; Chair, The European Students Forum 1992–93; Parliamentary Vice-Chair, Council for Education in the Commonwealth 1997–2002; Patron, Real Lancashire; Institute of Public Relations Young Communicator of the Year Award, 1996; *Recreations:* Music, walking, cooking, cinema, (watching) tennis. Lorna Fitzsimons, MP, House of Commons, London, SW1A 0AA *Tel:* 020 7219 3433. *Constituency:* 81 Durham Street, Rochdale, Greater Manchester, OL11 1LR *Tel:* 01706 644911 *Fax:* 01706 759826 *E-mail:* fitzsimonsl@parliament.uk.

FLIGHT, HOWARD   Arundel and South Downs   *Con majority 13,704*

Howard Emerson Flight. Born 16 June 1948; Son of late Bernard Thomas Flight and late Doris Mildred Emerson Flight; Educated Brentwood School, Essex; Magdalene College, Cambridge (MA economics 1969); University of Michigan, USA (MBA 1971); Married Christabel Diana Beatrice Norbury 1973 (1 son 3 daughters). Investment adviser, N M Rothschild 1971–73; Cayzer Ltd 1973–77; Manager: Wardley Ltd (HSBC) Hong Kong 1977–78; Merchant banking division, Hong Kong Bank, Bombay, India 1978–79; Director, investment division, Guinness Mahon 1979–86; Joint managing director, Guinness Flight Global Asset Management Ltd 1986–97; Chairman, Investec Asset Management 1998–; ACM Enchanced European Bond Trust 2000–. **House of Commons:** Contested Southwark (Bermondsey) February and October 1974 general elections. Member for Arundel and South Downs since May 1, 1997; Opposition Spokesperson for HM Treasury 1999–; Shadow Economic Secretary, HM Treasury 1999–2001; Shadow Paymaster General 2001–02; Shadow Chief Secretary to the Treasury 2002–; *Select Committees:* Member: Environment, Transport and Regional Affairs 1997–98, Environment Sub-Committee 1997–98, Social Security 1998–99. *Special Interests:* Taxation, Economic Policy, Farming, Charities, PFI, Venture Capital, EMU. *Countries of Interest:* India, South-East Asia, USA, China. Chair, Cambridge University Conservative Association 1968–69; Member, Tax Consultative Committee to HM Treasury 1988–92; Power Exchange Scholar 1969–71; Trustee, Elgar Foundation; Governor and Trustee Brentwood School; Liveryman, Carpenters' Company; *Publications: All You Need to Know About Exchange Rates,* 1988; FRSA; Freeman, City of London 1999; *Clubs:* Carlton, Pratt's; *Sportsclubs:* Marden (Skiing); *Recreations:* Skiing, classical music, antique collecting, gardening. Howard Flight Esq, MP, House of Commons, London, SW1A 0AA *Tel:* 020 7219 3461 *Fax:* 020 7219 2455. *Constituency:* Arundel and South Downs Conservative Association, The Town Hall, 38 High Street, Steyning, West Sussex, BN44 3YE *Tel:* 01903 816880 *Fax:* 01903 810348 *E-mail:* flighth@parliament.uk.

FLINT, CAROLINE   Don Valley   *Lab majority 9,520*

Caroline Louise Flint. Born 20 September 1961; Daughter of late Wendy Flint (née Beasley), clerical/shop employee; Educated Twickenham Girls School; Richmond Tertiary College; University of East Anglia (BA American history/literature and film studies); Marriage dissolved; married Phil Cole 2001 (1 son 1 daughter 1 stepson). Management trainee, GLC/ILEA 1984–85; Policy officer, ILEA 1985–87; Head, Women's Unit, National Union of Students 1988–89; Equal opportunities officer, Lambeth Council 1989–91; Welfare and staff development officer, Lambeth Council 1991–93; Senior researcher/Political officer, GMB Trade Union 1994–97; Member, GMB; Former shop steward: NALGO at GLC/LEA, GMB at Lambeth Council. **House of Commons:** Member for Don Valley since May 1, 1997; Joint PPS to the Ministers of State, Foreign and Commonwealth Office 1999–2001; PPS to: Peter Hain as Minister of State: Department of Trade and Industry 2001, Foreign and Commonwealth Office 2001–02, John Reid as Minister without Portfolio and Party Chair 2002–03, John Reid as Leader of the House of Commons and President of the Council 2003; Parliamentary Under-Secretary of State (Tackling Drugs, Reducing Organised and International Crime), Home Office 2003–; *Select Committees:* Member: Education and Employment 1997–99, Education Sub-Committee 1997–99, Modernisation of the House of Commons 2003; Member, Administration 2001–. *Special Interests:* Employment, Education and Training, Childcare, Welfare to Work, Family Friendly Employment, Crime, Anti-Social Behaviour, House of Commons Modernisation. National Women's Officer, Labour Students 1983–85; Executive Member, Labour Co-ordinating Committee 1984–85; Chair, Brentford and Isleworth Constituency Labour Party 1991–95; Branch Chair, Branch Secretary and GC Delegate; Facilitator, Labour National Policy Forums 1994–97; Associate Editor, *Renewal* 1995–2000; Member, Fabian Society; Member, Trade Union Group of Labour MPs. Member, Working For Childcare 1989–99, Chair 1991–95; Board member: Sure Start Denaby Main Partnership 2000–, Doncaster Early Years Development and Childcare Partnership 2001–; President, Denaby Utd FC 2001–; Member, GMB Group of MPs; Labour Party adviser to the Police Federation of England and Wales 1999; Member, Inter-Parliamentary Union 1997–; *Recreations:* Cinema, tennis, being with my family and friends. Caroline Flint, MP, House of Commons, London, SW1A 0AA *Tel:* 020 7219 4407 *Fax:* 020 7219 1277. *Constituency:* Room 10, 7 North Bridge Road, Doncaster, South Yorkshire, DN5 9AA *Tel:* 01302 366778 *Fax:* 01302 328833 *E-mail:* flintc@parliament.uk.

FLOOK, ADRIAN   Taunton   *Con majority 235*

Adrian John Richardson Flook. Born 9 July 1963; Educated King Edward's School, Bath; Colonel By High School, Ottawa, Canada; Oxford University (MA history 1985). Stockbroker 1985–97: Societe General Equities, Credit Lyonnais Securities, Baring Securities, SG Warburg Securities; Consultant Financial Dynamics Business Communications 1997–; BIFU 1992–2000. London Borough of Wandsworth 1994–: Councillor, Chair: Property Committee 1996–98, Environment Committee 1998–2000. **House of Commons:** Contested Pontefract and Castleford 1997 general election. Member for Taunton since June 7, 2001; *Select Committees:* Member, Culture, Media and Sport 2001–. *Special Interests:* Agriculture, Rural Affairs, European Affairs. Battersea Conservative Association: Vice-chair 1990–94, Deputy chair 1994–96; Member Selsdon Group 1998–. Member: Countryside Alliance, RSPB, Politeia 1997–; Supporter Cancer MacMilllan Somerset 2000–; *Clubs:* Wellington Conservative, Carlton; *Recreations:* Collecting water colours, rugby. Adrian Flook Esq, MP, House of Commons, London, SW1A 0AA *Tel:* 020 7219 8464. *Constituency:* 20a Staplegrove Road, Taunton, Somerset, TA1 1DQ *Tel:* 01823 286 106 *E-mail:* flooka@parliament.uk.

FLYNN, PAUL   Newport West   *Lab majority 9,304*

Paul Flynn. Born 9 February 1935; Son of late James and late Kathleen Flynn; Educated St Illtyd's College, Cardiff; University College of Wales, Cardiff; Married 2nd Samantha Cumpstone 1985 (1 stepson, 1 stepdaughter and 1 son and 1 daughter (deceased) from previous marriage). Chemist, steel industry 1962–83; Broadcaster, Gwent Community Radio 1983–84; Research officer for Llewellyn Smith, as Labour MEP for South Wales 1984–87. Councillor: Newport Council 1972–81, Gwent County Council 1974–83. **House of Commons:** Contested Denbigh October 1974 general election. Member for Newport West since June 1987; Opposition Spokesman on: Health and Social Security 1988–89, Social Security 1989–90; *Select Committees:* Member: Transport 1992–97, Welsh Affairs 1997–98. *Special Interests:* Health, Medicinal and Illegal Drugs, Social Security, Pensions, Animal Welfare, Devolution, Welsh Affairs, Constitutional Reform, Modernisation of Parliament. *Countries of Interest:* Baltic States, Eastern Europe, Hungary, Romania, Israel. Secretary, Welsh Group of Labour MPs 1997–. Board Member, Parliamentary Office of Science and Technology (POST) 1997–; Member, UK Delegation to Council of Europe and Western European Union 1997–; *Publications: Commons Knowledge. How to be a Backbencher*, 1997; *Baglu Mlaen (Staggering Forward)*, 1998; *Dragons Led by Poodles*, 1999; Campaign for Freedom of Information Award 1991; Highland Park/*The Spectator* Backbencher of the Year (jointly) 1996; *New Statesman* Best Website of an Elected Representative 2000–; *Recreations:* Local history, photography. Paul Flynn Esq, MP, House of Commons, London, SW1A 0AA *Tel:* 020 7219 3478 *Fax:* 020 7219 2433 *Tel (Constituency):* 01633 262348 *E-mail:* info@paulflynnmp.co.uk.

FOLLETT, BARBARA   Stevenage   *Lab majority 8,566*

(Daphne) Barbara Follett. Born 25 December 1942; Daughter of late William Vernon and late Charlotte Hubbard; Educated Sandford School, Addis Ababa, Ethiopia; Ellerslie Girls' High School, Cape Town; University of Cape Town (fine art); Open University (government); London School of Economics (BSc economic history 1993); Married Richard Turner 1963 (divorced 1971) (2 daughters); married Gerald Stonestreet 1971 (divorced 1974); married Les Broer 1974 (divorced 1985) (1 son); married Kenneth Martin Follett 1985 (1 stepson 1 stepdaughter). Part-time salesperson 1960–62: Ledger clerk, Barclays Bank of South Africa 1962–63; EFL teacher, Berlitz School of Languages 1964–66; Joint manager, fruit farm 1966–70; Acting regional secretary, South African Institute of Race Relations 1970–71; Regional manager, Kupugani 1971–74; National health education director, Kupugani 1975–78; Lecturer and assistant course organiser Centre for International Briefing 1980–84; Lecturer in cross-cultural communications 1985–87; Research associate, Institute of Public Policy Research 1993–96, Visiting Fellow 1993–; Director, EMILY's List UK 1993–;

Founding Patron, EQ 2000–; Member, Amicus/MSF. **House of Commons:** Contested Woking 1983, Epsom and Ewell 1987 general elections. Member for Stevenage since May 1, 1997; *Select Committees:* Member, International Development 1997–2001; Member, Modernisation of the House of Commons 2001–. *Special Interests:* Economic and Industrial Policy, Gender, Race Relations, Overseas Aid and Development, International Development, Trade and Industry, Housing, Film Industry, Small Businesses. *Countries of Interest:* Africa, France. Member: Fabian Society, SERA; Chair, Eastern Regional Group of Labour MPs 1999–. Member: ACTSA, Charter 88, CPAG, LCER, OWA, Fawcett Society, NAWO; Patron APEC; RSA; *Recreations:* Reading, Scrabble, photography, film, theatre and Star Trek. Barbara Follett, MP, House of Commons, London, SW1A 0AA *Tel:* 020 7219 2649 *Fax:* 020 7219 1158. *Constituency:* Stevenage Labour Party, 4 Popple Way, Stevenage, Herts, SG1 3TG *Tel:* 01438 222800 *Fax:* 01438 222292 *E-mail:* barbara@barbara-follett.org.uk.

FORTH, ERIC   Bromley and Chislehurst   *Con majority 9,037*

Eric Forth. Born 9 September 1944; Son of late William Forth and Aileen Forth; Educated Jordanhill College School, Glasgow; Glasgow University (MA politics and economics 1966); Married Linda St Clair 1967 (divorced 1994) (2 daughters); married Mrs Carroll Goff 1994 (1 stepson). Manager, industry (Ford, Deloitte, Dexion, Rank, Xerox) 1966–79; MEP for Birmingham North 1979–84. Councillor, Brentwood Urban District Council 1968–72. **House of Commons:** Contested Barking February and October 1974 general elections. Member for Mid Worcestershire 1983–97, and for Bromley and Chislehurst since May 1, 1997; Joint Parliamentary Under-Secretary of State for Industry and Consumer Affairs, Department of Trade and Industry 1988–90; Joint Parliamentary Under-Secretary of State, Department of Employment 1990–92; Department for Education: Parliamentary Under-Secretary of State for Schools 1992–94, Minister of State 1994–95; Minister of State, Department for Education and Employment 1995–97; Shadow Leader of the House 2001–; *Select Committees:* Member: Procedure 1999–2001, Standards and Privileges 1999–2001. *Special Interests:* Economic Policy, European Union, USA. *Countries of Interest:* Canada, USA, Australia, New Zealand. Member House of Commons Commission 2001–; PC 1997; Channel 4 and *The House Magazine* Opposition Politician of the Year 2000; *Clubs:* Bromley Conservative; *Recreations:* Cinema, political biographies. Rt Hon Eric Forth, MP, House of Commons, London, SW1A 0AA *Tel:* 020 7219 6344. *Constituency:* Bromley and Chislehurst Conservative Association, 5 White Horse Hill, Chislehurst, Kent, BR7 6DG *Tel:* 020 8295 2639 *E-mail:* forthe@parliament.uk.

FOSTER, DEREK   Bishop Auckland   *Lab majority 13,926*

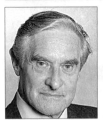

Derek Foster. Born 25 June 1937; Son of Joseph Foster, shipyard worker; Educated Bede Grammar School, Sunderland; Oxford University (BA philosophy, politics and economics 1960); Married Florence Anne Bulmer 1972 (3 sons 1 daughter). Ten years marketing in the private sector 1960–70; Durham County Council: Youth and community worker 1970–73, Further education organiser 1973–74; Assistant director of education, Sunderland Borough Council 1974–79; Member National Union of Teachers. Councillor, Sunderland County Borough Council 1972–74; Tyne and Wear County Council: Councillor 1973–77, Chair: Economic Development Committee 1974–76, North of England Development Council 1974–76, National Prayer Breakfast 1998–99, DL Durham 2001–. **House of Commons:** Member for Bishop Auckland since May 1979; Opposition Frontbench Spokesperson for Social Security 1982–83; Principal Opposition Spokesperson for the Duchy of Lancaster 1995–97; Opposition Whip 1981–82; Opposition Chief Whip 1985–95; PPS to Neil Kinnock as Leader of Opposition 1983–85; Member, Shadow Cabinet 1985–97; Shadow Chancellor of the Duchy of Lancaster 1995–97; *Select Committees:* Chair, Employment Sub-Committee 1997–2001; Chair (Employment), Education and Employment 1997–2001; Member: Education Sub-Committee 1997–2001, Liaison 1997–2001; Member, Standards and Privileges 2003–. *Special Interests:* Youth Affairs, Education and Training, Regional Policy, Socialist Enterprise, Transport, Economics, Finance, Small Businesses. *Countries of Interest:* USA, Japan. Ex-Officio Member, Labour Party National Executive Committee 1985–95; Member: Fabian Society, Christian Socialists Society; Chair, Labour Manufacturing Industry Group. Uniformed Member, Salvation Army; Vice-Chair, Youthaid 1979–83;

Vice-Chair, Youth Affairs Lobby 1984–86; Hon. President, British Youth Council 1984–86; Vice-President, Christian Socialist Movement 1985–; Member: Ecclesiastical Committee 1997–, National Advisory Board of the Salvation Army 1995–, Advisory Committee for the Registration of Political Parties 1998; Chair: Pioneering Care Partnership 1997–, North Regional Information Society Initiative 1997–2000, National Prayer Breakfast 1998; Non-Executive Director, Northern Informatics 1998–; Chair: Regional Electronics Economy Project 2000–, Bishop Auckland Development Company Ltd; Fellow, Industry and Parliament Trust; Trustee: Auckland Castle, National e-Learning Foundation; *Publications:* Articles in: *Guardian* newspaper, *Overview*; PC 1993; Companion of the Institution of Lighting Engineers 2001; *Sportsclubs:* Durham County Cricket; *Recreations:* Brass Bands, Male Voice Choirs, Cricket, Soccer. Rt Hon Derek Foster, MP, House of Commons, Room 32, Speakers House, London, SW1A 0AA *Tel:* 020 7219 3582/6500 *Fax:* 020 7219 2711. *Constituency:* Hackworth House, Byerley Road, Shildon, Co Durham, DL4 1HN *Tel:* 01388 777175 *Fax:* 01388 777175 *E-mail:* fosterderek@parliament.uk.

FOSTER, DON   Bath   *LD majority 9,894*

Don (Donald) Foster. Born 31 March 1947; Son of late John Anthony Foster, vicar and late Iris Edith Foster, née Ellison; Educated Lancaster Royal Grammar School; Keele University (BSc physics and psychology 1969, CEd 1969); Bath University (MEd 1981); Married Victoria Jane Dorcas Pettegree 1968 (1 son 1 daughter). Science teacher, Sevenoaks School, Kent 1969–75; Science project director, Resources for Learning Development Unit, Avon LEA 1975–80; Education lecturer, Bristol University 1980–89; Management consultant, Pannell Kerr Forster 1989–92. Avon County Council: Councillor, Cabot Ward, Bristol 1981–89, Chair, Education Committee 1987–89. **House of Commons:** Contested (Liberal/Alliance) Bristol East 1987 general election. Member for Bath since April 9, 1992; Spokesperson for: Education 1992–95, Education and Employment 1995–97; Principal Spokesperson for: Environment, Transport, the Regions and Social Justice 1999–2001, Transport, Local Government and the Regions 2001–02, Transport 2002–; *Select Committees:* Member: Education and Employment 1996–99, Education Sub-Committee 1997–99. *Special Interests:* Education, Local and Regional Government, Transport. *Countries of Interest:* Africa, Israel, Central Europe. President, Liberal Democrat Youth and Students 1993–95. Vice-Chair, National Campaign for Nursery Education 1993–99, President 1999–2001; President, British Association for Early Childhood Education 1998–2002; Executive, Association of County Councils 1985–89; Joint Hon. President, British Youth Council 1992–99; Vice-Chair, British Association for Central and Eastern Europe 1994–97; Trustee, Open School and Education Extra 1993–99; *Publications: Resource-based Learning in Science,* 1979; *Science With Gas,* 1981; Co-author: *Aspects of Science,* 1984, *Reading About Science,* 1984, *Nuffield Science,* 1986; *Teaching Science 11–13,* 1987; Numerous educational and political articles and pamphlets; Hon. Fellow, Bath College of High Education 1995; CPhys; MInstP; *Clubs:* National Liberal; *Recreations:* Classical music, travel, sport. Don Foster Esq, MP, House of Commons, London, SW1A 0AA *Tel:* 020 7219 5001 *Fax:* 020 7219 2695. *Constituency:* 31 James Street West, Bath, BA1 2BT *Tel:* 01225 338973 *Fax:* 01225 463630 *E-mail:* fosterd@parliament.uk.

FOSTER, MICHAEL JABEZ   Hastings and Rye   *Lab majority 4,308*

Michael Jabez Foster. Born 26 February 1946; Son of Dorothy Foster; Educated Hastings Secondary; Hastings Grammar School; Leicester University (LLM 1995); Married Rosemary Kemp 1969 (2 sons). Solicitor's clerk 1963–72; Legal executive 1972–80; Solicitor 1980–; Member and Legal Adviser to GMB. Councillor: Hastings County Borough Council 1971–74, Hastings Borough Council 1973–79, 1983–87, East Sussex County Council 1973–77, 1981–97; Member: Sussex Police Authority, East Sussex Health Authority; DL, East Sussex 1993–. **House of Commons:** Contested Hastings February and October 1974 and 1979 general elections. Member for Hastings and Rye since May 1, 1997; PPS: to Attorneys General John Morris 1999, Lord Williams of Mostyn 1999–2001, to Ross Cranston as Solicitor General 1999–2001, to Lord Goldsmith as Attorney General 2001–03, to Harriet Harman as Solicitor General 2001–03; *Select Committees:* Member, Social Security 1998–99; Member, Standards and Privileges 1997–. *Special Interests:* Health and Poverty, Animal Welfare, Taxation, Employment. *Countries of Interest:* United Kingdom.

Member: Society of Labour Lawyers, Christian Socialist Movement, Fabian Society. Member, The Child Poverty Action Group; Member: Methodist Church, European Standing Committee A 1998–, Law Society, The Chartered Institute of Arbitrators, Mensa, European Standing Committee B 2003; Member, National Trust; ACInArb; *Sportsclubs:* Amherst Tennis Club; *Recreations:* Lawn Tennis, Table Tennis. Michael Jabez Foster Esq, DL, MP (Hastings and Rye), House of Commons, London, SW1A 0AA *Tel:* 020 7219 1600 *Fax:* 020 7219 1393. *Constituency:* Ellen Draper Centre, 84 Bohemia Road, St Leonards on Sea, East Sussex, TN37 6RN *Tel:* 01424 460070 *Fax:* 01424 460072 *E-mail:* mp@1066.net.

FOSTER, MICHAEL JOHN   Worcester   Lab majority 5,766

Michael John Foster. Born 14 March 1963; Son of Brian William Foster, retired car worker, and Edna Foster, retired teacher; Educated Great Wyrley High School, Staffordshire; Wolverhampton Polytechnic (BA economics 1984); Wolverhampton University (PGCE 1995); Married Shauna Ogle 1985 (2 daughters 1 son). Financial planning and control department, Jaguar Cars Ltd: Financial analyst 1984–5, Senior analyst 1985–87, Manager 1989–91; Lecturer in accountancy, Worcester College of Technology 1991–97; Shop steward, TGWU 1986–88; Member, GMB, NATFHE. **House of Commons:** Member for Worcester since May 1, 1997; Introduced Private Members' Bill to Ban Hunting With Dogs 1997; On School Crossing Patrols 2000, since incorporated into Transport Act 2000; PPS to Margaret Hodge, Department for Education and Skills, as: Minister of State for Lifelong Learning and Higher Education 2001–03, Minister of State for Children 2003–; *Select Committees:* Member: Education and Employment 1999–2001, Education Sub-Committee 1999–2001. *Special Interests:* Trade and Industry, Education and Training, Hunting With Dogs (Against), Small Businesses. Agent, Mid Worcester 1992; Secretary, Constituency Labour Party, Worcester 1992–95. Patron Maggs Day Centre for Homeless People; President, Worcester City Mind Group; Associate of Chartered Institute of Management Accountants (ACMA); *Sportsclubs:* Worcestershire County Cricket Club, House of Commons Soccer and Cricket Teams; *Recreations:* Sport, gardening. Michael John Foster Esq, MP (Worcester), House of Commons, London, SW1A 0AA *Tel:* 020 7219 6379 *Fax:* 020 7219 6379. *Constituency:* Arboretum Lodge, 24 Sansome Walk, Worcester, WR1 1LX *Tel:* 01905 26504 *E-mail:* fosterm@parliament.uk.

FOULKES, GEORGE   Carrick, Cumnock and Doon Valley   Lab majority 14,856

George Foulkes. Born 21 January 1942; Son of late George Horace Foulkes, engineer and Jessie Foulkes; Educated Keith Grammar School, Banff; Haberdashers' Aske's School; Edinburgh University (BSc psychology 1964); Married Elizabeth Anna Hope 1970 (2 sons 1 daughter). President, Scottish Union of Students 1964–6; Director, ELEC 1966–68; Scottish organiser, European Movement 1968–69; Director, Enterprise Youth 1969–73; Director, Age Concern Scotland 1973–79; Member, GMB. Councillor: Edinburgh Corporation 1970–75, Lothian Regional Council 1974–79; Chair: Lothian Region Education Committee 1974–79, Education Committee of Convention of Scottish Local Authorities 1975–78; JP, Edinburgh 1975. **House of Commons:** Contested Edinburgh West 1970 and Edinburgh Pentlands October 1974 general elections. Member for South Ayrshire 1979–83 and for Carrick, Cumnock and Doon Valley since June 1983; Opposition Frontbench Spokesperson for: Europe 1983–85, Foreign and Commonwealth Affairs 1985–92, Defence, Disarmament and Arms Control 1992–93, Overseas Development 1994–97; Parliamentary Under-Secretary of State, Department of International Development 1997–2001; Minister of State, Scotland Office 2001–02; *Select Committees:* Member, Foreign Affairs 1980–83. *Special Interests:* International Development, Foreign Affairs, Devolution, Social Services, Tax Havens, Education, Aerospace, Aviation, Energy, Human Rights, Defence. *Countries of Interest:* Latin America, Canada, Netherlands, Eastern Europe. Chair, Labour Campaign for a Scottish Parliament–1997; Member, Co-operative Party. Member, Board of St Cuthbert's Co-op Association 1975–79; President, Edinburgh University SRC 1963–64; Rector's Assessor, University of Edinburgh 1968–71; Director, The Co-operative Press 1990–97; Chair, The John Wheatley Centre 1990–97; Delegate, Parliamentary Assemblies of the Council of Europe and Western European Union 1979–80; Vice-chair: UK-Netherlands Group of Inter-Parliamentary Union–1997, UK-Canadian Group of Commonwealth Parliamentary Association 1997; Treasurer, Anglo-Spanish Group of Inter-Parliamentary Union to 1997; Member: Executive UK

Branch of Commonwealth Parliamentary Association 1989–97, Executive British Section of Inter-Parliamentary Union 1989–97; Member, Commonwealth Parliamentary Association; *Publications:* Editor, *80 Years On* (History of Edinburgh University SRC); Chapters in: *Scotland – A Claim of Right, Football and the Commons People*; PC 2000; Wilberforce Medal 1998; *Recreations:* Boating, season ticket holder and shareholder Heart of Midlothian FC. Rt Hon George Foulkes, MP, House of Commons, London, SW1A 0AA *Tel:* 020 7219 3474 *Fax:* 020 7219 2407. *Constituency:* South Wing, Skerrington Farm, Glaisnock Road, Netherthird, Cumnock, KA18 3BU *Tel:* 01290 425859 *Fax:* 01290 424973 *E-mail:* foulkesg@parliament.uk.

FOX, LIAM   Woodspring   *Con majority 8,798*

Liam Fox. Born 22 September 1961; Son of William Fox, teacher, and Catherine Fox; Educated St Bride's High School, East Kilbride; Glasgow University (MB, ChB 1983, MROGP 1989); Single no children. General practitioner; Divisional surgeon, St John's Ambulance. **House of Commons:** Contested Roxburgh and Berwickshire 1987 general election. Member for Woodspring since April 9, 1992; Opposition Spokesperson for Constitutional Affairs, Scotland and Wales 1997–98; Frontbench Spokesperson for Constitutional Affairs, with overall responsibility for Scottish and Welsh issues 1998–99; Assistant Government Whip 1994–95; Government Whip 1995–96; PPS to Michael Howard as Home Secretary 1993–94; Parliamentary Under-Secretary of State, Foreign and Commonwealth Office 1996–97; Member, Shadow Cabinet 1998–; Shadow Secretary of State for Health 1999–; *Select Committees:* Member, Scottish Affairs 1992–93. *Special Interests:* Health, Economic Policy, Foreign Affairs. Secretary, West Country Conservative Members' Committee 1992–93. Member, Central Committee, Families for Defence 1987–89; President, Glasgow University Club 1982–83; Guest of US State Department, involving study of drug abuse problems in USA, and Republican Party campaigning techniques 1985; *Publications: Making Unionism Positive*, 1988; *Review of Health Reforms* (House of Commons Magazine), 1989; World Debating Competition, Toronto (Individual speaking prize) 1982; Best Speaker's Trophy, Glasgow University 1983; *Recreations:* Tennis, swimming, cinema, theatre. Dr Liam Fox, MP, House of Commons, London, SW1A 0AA *Tel:* 020 7219 4086 *Fax:* 020 7219 2617. *Constituency:* 71 High Street, Nailsea, North Somerset, BS48 1AW *Tel:* 01275 790090 *Fax:* 01275 790091.

FRANCIS, HYWEL   Aberavon   *Lab majority 16,108*

David Hywel Francis. Born 6 June 1946; Son of David Francis, miners' union official and Catherine Francis, housewife; Educated Whitchurch Grammar School, Cardiff; University of Wales, Swansea (BA history 1968, PhD 1978); Married Mair Georgina Price 1968 (1 daughter 2 sons (1 deceased)). Organisation department assistant TUC 1971–72; Senior research assistant University of Wales, Swansea 1972–74; Department of Adult Continuing Education University of Wales, Swansea: Tutor and lecturer 1974–86, Director 1987–99, Professor 1992–99; Special adviser Secretary of State for Wales 1999–2000; Contested South Wales West 1999 National Assembly for Wales election; Fellow National Centre for Public Policy University of Wales, Swansea 2000–01; Member: AUT 1974–2001, ISTC 2000–. **House of Commons:** Member for Aberavon since June 7, 2001; *Select Committees:* Member, Welsh Affairs 2001–. *Special Interests:* Disability Rights, Economic Development, Citizenship, European Affairs, Lifelong Learning. *Countries of Interest:* France, Italy, Ireland, Cuba, South Africa. Member: Socialist Education Association 1999–, Co-operative Party 1999–. Vice-president National Institute for Adult Continuing Education 1999–; Member Down's Syndrome Association, National Trust; Chair Paul Robeson Wales Trust 2001–; Vice-chair and Trustee, Bevan Foundation 2001–; Member European Standing Committee B 2003–; Vice-president, Friends of Cyprus; Founder and trustee Bevan Foundation Think-Tank 2000–; *Publications: The Fed: A history of the South Wales miners in the Twentieth Century*, Lawrence and Wishart 1980 reprint 1998; *Miners against Fascism*, Lawrence and Wishart 1984; *Communities and their Universities*, Lawrence and Wishart 1996; *Wales: A learning country*, Welsh Centre for Lifelong Learning 1999; Member of the Gorsedd of the National Eisteddfod 1986; Fellow Royal Society of The Arts (RSA) 1988; *Sportsclubs:* Aberavon RFC, Cwmavon RFC; *Recreations:* Walking, cycling, swimming, cinema. Hywel Francis Esq, MP, House of Commons, London, SW1A 0AA *Tel:* 020 7219 8121. *Constituency:* Eagle House, 2 Talbot Road, Port Talbot, SA13 1DH *Tel:* 01639 897333 *Fax:* 01639 891725 *E-mail:* francish@parliament.uk.

FRANCOIS, MARK   Rayleigh   *Con majority 8,290*

Mark Gino Francois. Born 14 August 1965; Son of Reginald Charles Francois, engineer and Anna Maria Francois, née Carloni, cook; Educated Nicholas Comprehensive School, Basildon; Bristol University (BA history 1986); King's College, London (MA war studies 1987); Married Karen Thomas 2000. TA 1983–89, commissioned 1985; Management trainee Lloyds Bank 1987; Market Access International Public Affairs Consultancy 1988–95: Consultant, Director; Public affairs consultant Francois Associates 1996–2001. Basildon District Council 1991–95: Councillor, Vice-chair Housing 1992–95. **House of Commons:** Contested Brent East 1997 general election. Member for Rayleigh since June 7, 2001; Opposition Whip 2002–;
Select Committees: Member, Environmental Audit 2001–. *Special Interests:* Defence, Local and Regional Government, Housing, Environment. Member: Royal United Services Institute for Defence Studies 1991–, International Institute for Strategic Studies 1999–, European Standing Committee A 2002–, European Standing Committee B until 2003; *Clubs:* Carlton, Rayleigh Conservative; *Recreations:* Reading, sports, military history, travel. Mark Francois Esq, MP, House of Commons, London, SW1A 0AA *Tel:* 020 7219 8311. *Constituency:* 25 Bellingham Lane, Rayleigh, Essex, SS6 7ED *Tel:* 01268 742 044 *Fax:* 01268 741 833.

G

GALE, ROGER   North Thanet   *Con majority 6,650*

Roger James Gale. Born 20 August 1943; Son of Richard Byrne Gale, solicitor, and Phyllis Mary Gale, née Rowell; Educated Hardye's School, Dorchester; Guildhall School of Music and Drama (LGSM&D 1963); Married Wendy Bowman 1964 (divorced 1967); married Susan Linda Sampson 1971 (divorced 1980) (1 daughter); married Susan Gabrielle Marks 1980 (2 sons). Freelance broadcaster 1963–; Programme director, Radio Scotland 1965; Personal assistant to general manager, Universal Films 1971–72; Freelance reporter, BBC Radio London 1972–73; Producer: Radio 1 *Newsbeat*, BBC Radio 4 *Today* 1973–76; Director, BBC Children's Television 1976–79; Senior producer, Children's Television, Thames TV;
Editor, Teenage Unit; Producer special projects, Thames TV 1979–83; Member: NUJ, Equity, BECTU. **House of Commons:** Contested Birmingham Northfield by-election 1982. Member for North Thanet since June 1983; PPS to Ministers of State for the Armed Forces: Archibald Hamilton 1992–93, Jeremy Hanley 1993–94; Vice-Chairman Conservative Party 2001–; *Select Committees:* Member, Home Affairs 1990–92; Member: Broadcasting 1997–, Chairmen's Panel 1997–. *Special Interests:* Education, Animal Welfare, Media, Broadcasting, Tourism, Leisure Industry, Licensed Trade. *Countries of Interest:* Cyprus, Cuba, Tunisia, Mongolia, Africa (Southern and Western). Vice-Chairman, Holborn and St Pancras Conservative Association 1971–72; Member, Greater London Young Conservative Committee 1972–82. Inaugural Fellowship, Police and Parliamentary Fellowship 1995; Fellow, Parliament and Armed Forces Fellowship, Post Graduate Fellowship 2001; Branch President, Arthritis Care; Branch Vice-President, St John's Ambulance; Hon. Associate, British Veterinary Association; Delegate, Council of Europe 1987–89; Delegate, Western European Union 1987–89; Fellow, Industry and Parliament Trust; Trustee: Children's Country Holidays Fund, 1st Margate (St John's) Scouts; LGSM&D; Freeman, City of London; *Clubs:* Farmer's; *Sportsclubs:* Kent County Cricket, Royal Temple Yacht; *Recreations:* Swimming, sailing. Roger Gale Esq, MP, House of Commons, London, SW1A 0AA *Tel:* 020 7219 4087 *Fax:* 020 7219 6828. *Constituency:* The Old Forge, 215a Canterbury Road, Birchington, Kent, CT7 9AH *Tel:* 01843 848588 *Fax:* 01843 844856 *E-mail:* galerj@parliament.uk.

GALLOWAY, GEORGE   Glasgow Kelvin   *Lab majority 7,260*

George Galloway. Born 16 August 1954; Son of George, engineer, and Sheila, née Reilly, factory worker; Educated Charleston Primary; Harris Academy; Married Elaine Fyffe 1979 (divorced 1999) (1 daughter); married Dr Amineh Abu-Zayyad 2000. General labourer, Garden Works, Dundee 1972; Production worker, Michelin Tyres 1973; Labour organiser 1977–83; General secretary, War on Want 1983–87; Member, TGWU 1973–; Sponsored by TGWU 1987–96. **House of Commons:** Member for Glasgow Hillhead 1987–97, and for Glasgow Kelvin since May 1, 1997; *Select Committees:* Member: Broadcasting 1997–99, Broadcasting 2000. *Special Interests:* Foreign Affairs, Defence, Scotland. Labour Party organiser, Dundee East and West Constituencies 1977–83; Chair, Scottish Labour Party 1980–81. General Secretary, War on Want 1983–87; *Publications: Downfall: The Ceausescus and the Romanian Revolution* (jointly) 1989; Hilal-i-Quaid-Azam, the highest civil award in Pakistan for services to the restoration of democracy in Pakistan 1990; Hilal-i-Pakistan for services to the people of Kashmir 1996; Kashmir Centres Europe Kashmir Award for work, efforts, support and services to the Kashmir cause 1998; *Clubs:* Groucho; *Recreations:* Football, sport, films, music. George Galloway Esq, MP, House of Commons, London, SW1A 0AA *Tel:* 020 7219 4084 *Fax:* 020 7219 2879. *Constituency:* 1274 Argyle Street, Glasgow, G3 7AA *Tel:* 0141 589 7127 *Fax:* 0141 589 7122 *E-mail:* gallowayg@parliament.uk.

GAPES, MIKE   Ilford South   *Lab majority 13,997*

Mike (Michael) John Gapes. Born 4 September 1952; Son of Frank Gapes, retired postal worker, and Emily Gapes, retired office worker; Educated Buckhurst Hill County High School; Fitzwilliam College, Cambridge (MA economics 1975); Middlesex Polytechnic, Enfield (Diploma in industrial relations 1976); Married Frances Smith 1992 (3 daughters). Voluntary Service Overseas (VSO) Teacher, Swaziland 1971–72; Secretary, Cambridge Students' Union 1973–74; National Organisation of Labour Students: Vice-chair 1975–76, Chair 1976–77; National student organiser, Labour Party 1977–80; Research officer, Labour Party International Department 1980–88; Senior international officer, Labour Party 1988–92; Member, TGWU. **House of Commons:** Contested Ilford North 1983 general election. Member for Ilford South since April 9, 1992; PPS: to Paul Murphy as Minister of State, Northern Ireland Office 1997–99, to Lord Rooker as Minister of State, Home Office 2001–02; *Select Committees:* Member: Foreign Affairs 1992–97, Defence 1999–2001. *Special Interests:* Defence, International Affairs, European Union, Economic Policy, Education. Deputy Chair, Parliamentary Labour Friends of Israel 1997–; Chair Co-op Party, Parliamentary Group 2000–01; Trade union liaison officer, London Group of Labour MPs 2001–; Member, Labour Friends of India. President, Redbridge United Chinese Association; Vice-President, Redbridge Chamber of Commerce 1992–; Member, Redbridge Racial Equality Council 1992–; Council Member Voluntary Service Overseas 1997–; Vice-Chair, Age Concern Redbridge 1997–; Trustee Parkside Community Association 1999–; Vice-President, Valentines Park Conservationists 2000–; Vice-President Council of European National Youth Committees 1977–79; Council Member Royal Institute of International Affairs 1996–99; Chair, Westminster Foundation for Democracy 2002; *Publications:* Contributor to several books and pamphlets; Fabian Society pamphlet: *After the Cold War*, 1990; *Sportsclubs:* Vice-President, Ilford Football Club; West Ham United Supporters' Club; *Recreations:* My family and when I get time watching football at West Ham, blues and jazz music. Mike Gapes Esq, MP, House of Commons, London, SW1A 0AA *Tel:* 020 7219 6485 *Fax:* 020 7219 0978 *E-mail:* gapesm@parliament.uk.

DodOnline
An Electronic Directory without rival . . .

MPs' biographies and photographs available with daily updates *via* the internet

For a *free* trial, call Yasmin Mirza, Aby Farsoun or Michael Mand on 020 7630 7643

GARDINER, BARRY   Brent North   *Lab majority 10,205*

Barry Strachan Gardiner. Born 10 March 1957; Son of late John Flannegan Gardiner, general manager, Kelvin Hall, and of late Sylvia Strachan, doctor; Educated Haileybury College; St Andrews (MA philosophy 1983); Harvard University (J. F. Kennedy Scholarship 1983–84); Cambridge University (research 1984–87); Married Caroline Smith 1979 (3 sons 1 daughter). Partner, Mediterranean Average Adjusting Co 1987–97; Occasional Lecturer, The Academy of National Economy, Moscow 1992–96; Member: MSF, GMB. Cambridge City Council: Councillor 1988–94, Chair of Finance, Mayor 1992–93. **House of Commons:** Member for Brent North since May 1, 1997; PPS to Beverley Hughes as Minister of State, Home Office 2002–; *Select Committees:* Member: Procedure 1997–2001, Public Accounts 1999–2002, Broadcasting 1998–2001; Member, Joint Committee on Consolidation of Bills Etc 2001–. *Special Interests:* Economic Policy, Trade and Industry, Education, Foreign Affairs. *Countries of Interest:* India, Sri Lanka, Russia, Georgia. Member, Labour Finance and Industry Group; Chair, Labour Friends of India 1999–2002, Secretary 2002–. Member, Amnesty International; Member, Shipwrights' Company; *Publications:* Various articles relating to shipping and maritime affairs; Articles on Political Philosophy in the *Philosophical Quarterly*; ACII; Freeman, City of London; *Clubs:* Royal Overseas League; *Recreations:* Walking, music, reading philosophy, bird-watching. Barry Gardiner Esq, MP, House of Commons, London, SW1A 0AA *Tel:* 020 7219 4046 *Fax:* 020 7219 2495 *E-mail:* gardinerb@parliament.uk.

GARNIER, EDWARD   Harborough   *Con majority 5,252*

Edward Henry Garnier. Born 26 October 1952; Son of late Colonel William d'Arcy Garnier, and Hon. Mrs Garnier; Educated Wellington College; Jesus College, Oxford 1971–74 (BA modern history 1974, MA); College of Law, London; Married Anna Caroline Mellows 1982 (2 sons 1 daughter). Barrister; Called to the Bar, Middle Temple 1976; QC 1995; Assistant Recorder 1998; Recorder 2000; Bencher, Middle Temple 2001. **House of Commons:** Contested Hemsworth 1987 general election. Member for Harborough since April 9, 1992; PPS: to Ministers of State, Foreign and Commonwealth Office, Alastair Goodlad 1994–95, David Davis 1994–95; to Sir Nicholas Lyell Attorney-General and Sir Derek Spencer as Solicitor-General 1995–97, to Roger Freeman as Chancellor of the Duchy of Lancaster 1996–97; Shadow Minister, Lord Chancellor's Department 1997–99; Shadow Attorney General 1999–2001; *Select Committees:* Member, Home Affairs 1992–95. *Special Interests:* Agriculture, Defence, Foreign Affairs, Education. Treasurer, Macleod Group of Conservative MPs 1995–97; Society of Conservative Lawyers: Vice-chairman 2003, Chairman, Executive Committee 2003–. Secretary, Foreign Affairs Forum 1988–92, Vice-Chairman 1992–; Director, Great Britain-China Centre 1998–; *Publications:* Co-author *Bearing the Standard: Themes for a Fourth Term*, 1991; *Facing the Future*, 1993; Contributor to *Halsbury's Laws of England*, 4th edition 1985; Visiting Parliamentary Fellow, St Antony's College, Oxford 1996–97; *Clubs:* Pratt's, Vincent's (Oxford); *Recreations:* Shooting, cricket, tennis, skiing, opera, biographical research. Edward Garnier Esq, QC, MP, House of Commons, London, SW1A 0AA *Tel:* 020 7219 6524. *Constituency:* 24 Nelson Street, Market Harborough, Leicestershire, LE16 9AY *Tel:* 01858 464146 *Fax:* 01858 410013 *E-mail:* garniere@parliament.uk.

GEORGE, ANDREW   St Ives   *LD majority 10,053*

Andrew Henry George. Born 2 December 1958; Son of Reginald Hugh George, horticulturist, and Diana May (née Petherick), teacher and musician; Educated Helston Grammar School; Helston School; Sussex University (BA cultural and community studies 1980); University College, Oxford (MSc agricultural economics 1981); Married Jill Elizabeth Marshall 1987 (1 son 1 daughter). Charity worker for various rural community development bodies, Nottinghamshire 1981–85, Cornwall 1985–97; Deputy director Cornwall Rural Community Council 1994–97. **House of Commons:** Contested St Ives 1992 general election. Member for St Ives since May 1, 1997; Liberal Democrat Spokesperson for: Agriculture, Fisheries, Food and Rural Affairs (Fisheries) 1997–, Social Security (Disabilities) 1999–2001; Shadow Fisheries Minister 1997–;

Agriculture Select Committee 1997–2000; Shadow Disabilities Minister 1999–2001; Regional Affairs Committee 2001–; PPS to Charles Kennedy as Leader of the Liberal Democrat Party 2001–02; Shadow Food and Rural Affairs Minister 2002–; *Select Committees:* Member, Agriculture 1997–2000. *Special Interests:* Third World, Cornwall, Economic Development, Housing, Fishing Industry, Agriculture, Social Exclusion, Devolution, Small Nations, Racism, Domestic Violence, Immigration, Environment, Minority Groups. *Countries of Interest:* All small nations. Member: Cornwall Rural Housing Association, Penwith Credit Union; Trustee, TRELYA; *Publications: Cornwall at the Crossroads,* 1989; *A View from the Bottom Left-hand Corner,* Patten Press 2002; Plus other publications and articles; *Sportsclubs:* Commons and Lords Cricket Club, Commons and Lords Rugby Club, Commons Football Team; *Recreations:* Cricket, football, rugby, tennis, swimming, writing, walking, Cornish culture, cycling, gardening, drawing, singing. Andrew George Esq, MP, House of Commons, London, SW1A 0AA *Tel:* 020 7219 4588 *Fax:* 020 7219 2324. *Constituency:* Knights Yard, Belgravia Street, Penzance, Cornwall, TR18 2EL *Tel:* 01736 360020 *Fax:* 01736 332866 *E-mail:* cooperu@parliament.uk.

GEORGE, BRUCE   Walsall South   *Lab majority 9,931*

Bruce Thomas George. Born 1 June 1942; Son of late Edgar Lewis George, former police officer and head of security, Wales National Coal Board and late Phyllis George; Educated Mountain Ash Grammar School; University of Wales (BA political theory and government 1964); Warwick University (MA comparative politics 1967); Married Lisa Toelle 1992. Assistant lecturer in politics, Glamorgan College of Technology 1964–66; Lecturer in politics, Manchester Polytechnic 1968–70; Senior lecturer in politics, Birmingham Polytechnic 1970–74; Tutor, Open University 1970–73; Visiting lecturer, Essex University 1983; Member GMB. **House of Commons:** Contested Southport 1970 general election. Member for Walsall South since February 1974; *Select Committees:* Chair, Defence 1997–; Member, Liaison 1997–. *Special Interests:* Defence, International Affairs, Housing, Health, Social Services, Private Security, Small Businesses. Member: RIIA, RUSI, International Institute of Strategic Studies, American Society for Industrial Security (UK); Patron: Institute of Security Management, Sister Dora Hospice Appeal Ltd, Hon. Adviser, Royal British Legion 1997; Councillor, Council for Arms Control; Former Chair, Mediterranean Special Group; Chair, Political Committee, North Atlantic Assembly 1983–94; Parliamentary Assembly of Organisation for Security and Co-operation in Europe 1992–: Chair, General (First) Committee on Political Affairs and Security 1994–, Leader, UK Delegation 1997–, Vice-President 1999–2002, President 2002; Fellow, Industry and Parliament Trust; *Publications:* Numerous books and articles on defence, foreign affairs and the private security industry; Editor, *Jane's NATO Handbook 1989–90, 1990–91, 1991–92*; *Private Security,* 2000; *Labour Party and Defence,* 1992; PC 2001; Hon. Fellow, University of Wales, Swansea 2001; *Sportsclubs:* Joint-Founder, House of Commons Football Club 1974; *Recreations:* Reading, supports Walsall Football Club. Rt Hon Bruce George, MP, House of Commons, London, SW1A 0AA *Tel:* 020 7219 4049/6610 *Fax:* 020 7219 3823. *Constituency:* 34 Bridge Street, Walsall, West Midlands, WS1 1HQ *Tel:* 01922 724960 *Fax:* 01922 621844 *E-mail:* georgeb@parliament.uk.

GERRARD, NEIL   Walthamstow   *Lab majority 15,181*

Neil Gerrard. Born 3 July 1942; Son of late Francis and Emma Gerrard, primary school teachers; Educated Manchester Grammar School; Wadham College, Oxford (BA natural science 1964); Chelsea College, London (MED 1973); Polytechnic of South Bank (DPSE 1983); Married Marian Fitzgerald 1968 (divorced 1983) (2 sons). Secondary schoolteacher, Queen Elizabeth's School, Barnet 1965–68; Chemistry and IT lecturer, Hackney College 1968–92; Member, GMB. London Borough of Waltham Forest: Councillor 1973–90, Leader, Labour Group 1983–90, Leader of Council 1986–90. **House of Commons:** Contested Chingford 1979 general election. Member for Walthamstow since April 9, 1992; PPS to: Dawn Primarolo as Financial Secretary, HM Treasury May-December 1997; *Select Committees:* Member: Deregulation 1995–97, Environment 1995–97, Environmental Audit 1999–2002; Member, Information 1997–. *Special Interests:*

Housing, Planning, Race Relations, Foreign Affairs, HIV/AIDS, Refugees/Asylum, Criminal Justice, Disability. *Countries of Interest:* Middle East, Sri Lanka, Kashmir, India. Secretary, PLP Civil Liberties Group. Former Board Member, SHAC; Former Board Member, Theatre Royal, Stratford, East London; Board of Trustees Leyton Orient Community Sports Programme; *Recreations:* Theatre, cinema, reading, music, sport. Neil Gerrard Esq, MP, House of Commons, London, SW1A 0AA *Tel:* 020 7219 6368 *Fax:* 020 7219 4899. *Constituency:* 23 Orford Road, Walthamstow, London, E17 9NL *E-mail:* gerrardn@parliament.uk.

GIBB, NICK   Bognor Regis and Littlehampton   *Con majority 5,643*

Nick (Nicolas) John Gibb. Born 3 September 1960; Son of late John McLean Gibb, civil engineer, and Eileen Mavern Gibb, retired schoolteacher; Educated Maidstone Boys' Grammar School; Roundhay School, Leeds; Thornes House School, Wakefield; Durham University (BA law 1981). Chartered accountant, specialising in taxation, KPMG, London 1984–97. **House of Commons:** Contested Stoke-on-Trent Central 1992 general election and Rotherham by-election 1994. Member for Bognor Regis and Littlehampton since May 1, 1997; Opposition Spokesperson for: the Treasury December 1998–99, Trade and Industry (Energy, Regulation, Company Law, Competition) 1999–2001, Transport, Local Government and the Regions 2001; *Select Committees:* Member: Social Security 1997–98, Treasury 1998, Treasury Sub-Committee 1998; Member, Public Accounts 2001–. *Special Interests:* Economics, Taxation, Education, Social Security. *Countries of Interest:* USA, Israel. *Publications: Maintaining Momentum,* Pamphlet on Tax Reform 1992; *Bucking the Market,* Pamphlet Opposing Membership of ERM 1990; *Duty to Repeal,* Pamphlet Calling for Abolition of Stamp Duty 1989; *Simplifying Taxes,* Pamphlet on Tax Reform 1987; Fellow, Institute of Chartered Accountants in England and Wales (FCA); *Recreations:* Long-distance running, skiing. Nick Gibb Esq, MP, House of Commons, London, SW1A 0AA *Tel:* 020 7219 6374 *Fax:* 020 7219 1395. *Constituency:* 110 London Road, Bognor Regis, West Sussex, PO21 1BD *Tel:* 01243 826410 *Fax:* 01243 842076.

GIBSON, IAN   Norwich North   *Lab majority 5,863*

Ian Gibson. Born 26 September 1938; Son of late William and Winifred Gibson; Educated Dumfries Academy; Edinburgh University (BSc genetics 1962, PhD); Married Elizabeth Frances Lubbock 1974 (2 daughters). University of East Anglia: lecturer 1965–71, senior lecturer 1971–97, dean of biology 1991–97; National Executive Committee, ASTMS/MSF 1972–96. Non-Executive Director Institute of Food Research; ESRG Science in Society Advisory Committee; Chair, Royal Institution's Science Media Centre; Royal Society Committee for Pulbic Understanding of Science. **House of Commons:** Contested Norwich North 1992. Member for Norwich North since May 1, 1997; Chair: Parliamentary Office of Science and Technology 1998–2001, Editorial Board 'pH7' The Parliamentary Health Magazine; *Select Committees:* Member, Science and Technology 1997–2001; Chair, Science and Technology 2001–; Member, Liaison 2002–. *Special Interests:* Science, Technology, Health, Environment, Higher Education. Chair, MSF Parliamentary Group 1998–2000. Trustee, Covent Garden Cancer Research Trust; Patron, Humane Research Trust; MIBiol; FIBiol; *Sportsclubs:* Football Supporters' Association; *Recreations:* Football. Dr Ian Gibson, MP, House of Commons, London, SW1A 0AA *Tel:* 020 7219 1100 *Fax:* 020 7219 2799. *Constituency:* Norwich Labour Centre, 59 Bethel Street, Norwich, NR1 1NL *Tel:* 01603 661144 *Fax:* 01603 663502 *E-mail:* gibsoni@parliament.uk.

DodOnline
An Electronic Directory without rival . . .

MPs' biographies and photographs available with daily updates *via* the internet

For a *free* trial, call Yasmin Mirza, Aby Farsoun or Michael Mand on 020 7630 7643

GIDLEY, SANDRA   Romsey   LD majority 2,370

Sandra Julia Gidley. Born 26 March 1957; Daughter of Frank Henry Rawson and Maud Ellen Rawson; Educated Eggars Grammar School, Alton, Hampshire; Afcent International, Brunssum, Netherlands; Windsor Girls School, Hamm, West Germany; Bath University (BPharm 1978); Married William Arthur Gidley 1979 (1 daughter 1 son). Pharmacist, Badham Chemists 1979–80; Pharmacy manager, G K Chemists 1980–81; Locum pharmacist 1982–92; Pharmacy manager, supermarkets 1992–2000. Councillor, Test Valley Borough Council 1995–2003; Mayor, Romsey Town 1997–98. **House of Commons:** Member for Romsey since May 4, 2000 by-election; Liberal Democrat Spokesperson for: Health and Women's Issues 2001–02, Women 2002–; Chair Gender Balance Task Force 2002–; *Select Committees:* Member, Health 2001–03. *Special Interests:* Health, Education. *Publications:* Entry in 2nd book of Mini Sagas; MRPharmS 1979; *Recreations:* Photography, travel, theatre, badminton. Sandra Gidley, MP, House of Commons, London, SW1A 0AA *Tel:* 020 7219 5986 *Fax:* 020 7219 2324. *Constituency:* 3a Victoria Place, Love Lane, Romsey, Hampshire *Tel:* 01794 511900 *Fax:* 01794 512538 *E-mail:* gidleys@parliament.uk.

GILDERNEW, MICHELLE   Fermanagh and South Tyrone   SF majority 53

Michelle Gildernew. Born 28 March 1970; Educated St Josephs PS, Caledon; St Catherine's College, Armagh; University of Ulster, Coleraine; Married (1 son). **House of Commons:** Member for Fermanagh and South Tyrone since June 7, 2001; Head of London Office 1997–98; New Northern Ireland Assembly 1998–2002; Member Employment and Learning Committee; Deputy chair Social Development Committee 1999–; Member Centre Committee 2000–; *Special Interests:* Housing, Rural Affairs, Education. Sinn Fein: Member: International Department, Inter-Party talks team, Former spokesperson women's issues, Press officer 1997; Head of London Office 1997–98; Spokesperson Social Development. *Sportsclubs:* Aghaloo GFC. Michelle Gildernew, MP, House of Commons, London, SW1A 0AA *Tel:* 020 7219 8162 *Fax:* 020 7219 6107. *Constituency:* 87 Main Street, Lisnaskea, Co Fermanagh, BT92 0JD *Tel:* 028 6772 3986 *Fax:* 028 6772 3643.

GILLAN, CHERYL   Chesham and Amersham   Con majority 11,882

Cheryl Gillan. Born 21 April 1952; Daughter of late Adam Mitchell Gillan, company director, and late Mona Gillan; Educated Cheltenham Ladies' College; College of Law; Chartered Institute of Marketing; Married John Coates Leeming 1985. International Management Group 1977–84; Director, British Film Year 1984–86; Senior marketing consultant, Ernst and Young 1986–91; Contested Greater Manchester Central 1989 European Parliament election; Marketing director, Kidsons Impey 1991–93; Consultant PKF 1999–. **House of Commons:** Member for Chesham and Amersham since April 9, 1992; Opposition Spokesperson for: Trade and Industry 1997–98, Foreign and Commonwealth Affairs 1998–2001, International Development 1998–2001; Opposition Whip 2001–03; PPS to Viscount Cranborne, as Leader of the House of Lords and Lord Privy Seal 1994–95; Parliamentary Under-Secretary of State, Department of Education and Employment 1995–97; *Select Committees:* Member: Science and Technology 1992–95, Procedure 1994–95. *Special Interests:* Industry, Space, International Affairs, Defence, Education, Employment. *Countries of Interest:* Former Soviet Union, Europe, Hungary, Poland, USA, Japan, Pacific Rim, China, Chairman, Bow Group 1987–88. Member, Executive Committee, Commonwealth Parliamentary Association (CPA) UK Branch 1998–; UK Representative, British Islands and Mediterranean region on CPA Executive 1999–; Member, NATO Parliamentary Assembly 2003–; Member, Worshipful Company of Marketors; FCIM; Freeman, City of London; *Clubs:* RAC; *Recreations:* Golf, music, gardening. Cheryl Gillan, MP, House of Commons, London, SW1A 0AA *Tel:* 020 7219 4061 *Fax:* 020 7219 2762. *Constituency:* 7B Hill Avenue, Amersham, Buckinghamshire, HP6 5BD *Tel:* 01494 721577 *E-mail:* gillanc@parliament.uk.

GILROY, LINDA   Plymouth Sutton   *Lab majority 7,517*

Linda Gilroy. Born 19 July 1949; Daughter of William and Gwendolen Jarvie; Educated Maynards, Exeter; Stirling High School; Edinburgh University (MA history 1971); Strathclyde University (postgraduate diploma, secretarial studies 1972); Married Bernard Gilroy 1986. Deputy director, Age Concern, Scotland 1972–79; Regional manager, Gas Consumers' Council 1979–96; Contested Devon and East Plymouth 1994 European Parliament election; Member, TGWU. **House of Commons:** Contested South-East Cornwall 1992 general election. Member for Plymouth Sutton since May 1, 1997; PPS to Nick Raynsford as Minister of State: Department for Transport, Local Government and the Regions 2001–02, Office of the Deputy Prime Minister 2002–; *Select Committees:* Member: European Legislation 1997–98, European Legislation 1998–2001, European Scrutiny 1998. *Special Interests:* Pensioners' Rights, Trade and Industry, Energy, Utility Regulation, Local and Regional Government, Small Businesses, Fair Trade. *Countries of Interest:* Turkey, Poland, New Zealand, Australia, America, Tanzania, Ghana. *Recreations:* Theatre, swimming, walking. Linda Gilroy, MP, House of Commons, London, SW1A 0AA *Tel:* 020 7219 4416 *Fax:* 020 7219 0987. *Constituency:* 65 Bretonside, Plymouth, PL4 0BD *Tel:* 01752 226626 *Fax:* 01752 221645 *E-mail:* gilroyl@parliament.uk.

GODSIFF, ROGER   Birmingham Sparkbrook and Small Heath   *Lab majority 16,246*

Roger Godsiff. Born 28 June 1946; Son of late George Godsiff, chargehand/fitter, and of Gladys Godsiff; Educated Catford Comprehensive School, London; Married Julia Brenda Morris 1977 (1 son 1 daughter). Banking 1965–70; Political Officer, APEX 1970–88; Senior research officer, GMB 1988–91; Member of and sponsored by GMB. London Borough of Lewisham: Councillor 1971–90, Labour Chief Whip 1974–77, Mayor 1977. **House of Commons:** Contested Birmingham Yardley 1983 general election. Member for Birmingham Small Heath 1992–97, and for Birmingham Sparkbrook and Small Heath since May 1, 1997; Adviser on Cricket to Richard Caborn, as Minister of State for Sport 2002–; *Special Interests:* European Union, Foreign Affairs, Sport, Recreation, Immigration. *Countries of Interest:* Indian Sub-Continent, America, Middle East, Asia. Member, Co-operative Party. Member, Executive Committee, IPU 1999–; *Sportsclubs:* Member, Charlton Athletic Supporters Club; *Recreations:* Sport in general, particularly football. Roger Godsiff Esq, MP, House of Commons, London, SW1A 0AA *Tel:* 020 7219 5191 *Fax:* 020 7219 2221. *Constituency:* 15D Lloyd Street, Small Heath, Birmingham, B10 0LH *Tel:* 0121–772 2383 *Fax:* 0121–772 2383 *E-mail:* godsiffr@parliament.uk.

GOGGINS, PAUL   Wythenshawe and Sale East   *Lab majority 12,608*

Paul Gerard Goggins. Born 16 June 1953; Son of John Goggins and late Rita Goggins; Educated St Bede's, Manchester; Ushaw College, Durham 1971–73; Birmingham Polytechnic (Certificate in Residential Care of Children and Young People 1976); Manchester Polytechnic (Certificate of Qualification in Social Work 1982); Married Wyn Bartley 1977 (2 sons 1 daughter). Child care worker, Liverpool Catholic Social Services 1974–75; Officer-in-Charge, local authority children's home, Wigan 1976–84; Project director, NCH Action For Children, Salford 1984–89; National director, Church Action On Poverty 1989–97; Member TGWU. Councillor, Salford City Council 1990–98. **House of Commons:** Member for Wythenshawe and Sale East since May 1, 1997; PPS to: John Denham as Minister of State: Department of Social Security 1998–99, Department of Health 1999–2000; David Blunkett: as Secretary of State for Education and Employment 2000–01, as Home Secretary 2001–03; Parliamentary Under-Secretary of State (Correctional Services and Reducing Re-offending), Home Office 2003–; *Select Committees:* Member, Social Security 1997–98. *Special Interests:* Poverty, Unemployment, Housing, Transport, Global Poverty, Democratic Renewal, Community Regeneration. Member CAFOD Board; Patron Trafford Crossroads; Hon. President Wythenshawe Mobile; Director Campus Ventures Ltd; Trustee Russian European Trust; *Recreations:* Watching Manchester City football team, walking, singing. Paul Goggins Esq, MP, House of Commons, London, SW1A 0AA *Tel:* 020 7219 5865 *Tel (Constituency):* 0161–499 7900 *Fax (Constituency):* 0161–499 7911 *E-mail:* gogginsp@parliament.uk.

GOODMAN, PAUL   Wycombe   *Con majority 3,168*

Paul Alexander Cyril Goodman. Born 17 November 1959; Son of Abel Goodman and Irene Goodman, née Rubens; Educated Cranleigh School, Surrey; York University (BA English literature 1981); Married Fiona Mary Ann Gill 1999. Public affairs executive Extel Consultancy 1984–85; Researcher Tom King MP 1985–87; Home news editor *Catholic Herald* 1990–91; Leader writer *Daily Telegraph* 1991–92; Reporter *Sunday Telegraph* 1992–95; *Daily Telegraph*: Comment editor 1995–2001, Leader writer 2001–; Member National Union of Students Executive Committee 1981–83. **House of Commons:** Member for Wycombe since June 7, 2001; PPS to David Davis, MP as Chairman of the Conservative Party 2001–02; Shadow Minister for Work and Pensions 2003–; *Select Committees:* Member: Regulatory Reform 2001–, Work and Pensions 2001–. *Special Interests:* Social Affairs. *Countries of Interest:* Kashmir. Chair Federation of Conservative Students 1983–84; Member policy unit Westminster Council 1988. Paul Goodman Esq, MP, House of Commons, London, SW1A 0AA *Tel:* 020 7219 5099 *Fax:* 020 7219 4614. *Constituency:* 150a West Wycombe Road, High Wycombe, Buckinghamshire, HP12 3AE *Tel:* 01494 521777 *Fax:* 01494 510042 *E-mail:* goodmanp@parliament.uk.

GRAY, JAMES   North Wiltshire   *Con majority 3,878*

James Whiteside Gray. Born 7 November 1954; Son of late Very Revd John R. Gray and Dr Sheila Gray; Educated Glasgow High School; Glasgow University (MA history 1975); Christ Church, Oxford (history thesis 1975–77); Married Sarah Ann Beale 1980 (2 sons 1 daughter). Honourable Artillery Company (TA) 1978–84; Member, HAC Court of Assistants 2002–; Management trainee, P & O 1977–78; Broker, senior broker then department manager, Anderson Hughes & Co Ltd (Shipbrokers) 1978–84; Member, The Baltic Exchange 1978–92, Pro Bono Member 1997–; Managing director, GNI Freight Futures Ltd, Senior Manager, GNI Ltd (Futures Brokers) 1984–1992; Director: Baltic Futures Exchange 1989–91, Westminster Strategy 1995–96; Union of Country Sports Workers. **House of Commons:** Contested Ross, Cromarty and Skye 1992 general election. Member for North Wiltshire since May 1, 1997; Opposition Spokesman for: Defence 2001–02, Defra 2002–; Opposition Whip 2000–01; Special Adviser to Michael Howard, John Gummer as Secretaries of State for Environment 1991–95; Shadow Minister for Environment, Food and Rural Affairs 2002–; *Select Committees:* Member: Environment, Transport and Regional Affairs 1997–2001, Environment Sub-Committee 1997–2001, Transport Sub-Committee 1997–2001; Member, Broadcasting 2001–. *Special Interests:* Housing, Local and Regional Government, Countryside, Agriculture, Defence, Scotland, Environment. *Countries of Interest:* America, China, Mongolia, Sri Lanka. Deputy Chairman, Wandsworth Tooting Conservative Association 1994–96. Governor, Hearnville Primary School, Balham 1989–92; Governor, Chestnut Grove Secondary School, Balham 1993–96; Vice-President, HAC Saddle Club; Consultant, British Horse Industry Confederation 1997–2001; Member: Armed Forces Parliamentary Scheme (Army) 1998, Post Graduate Scheme 2000–, Royal College of Defence Studies 2003–; President: Multiple Sclerosis Society, Association of British Riding Schools; Vice-chairman, Charitable Properties Association; Member, Honourable Artillery Company; *Publications: Financial Risk Management in the Shipping Industry*, 1985; *Futures and Options for Shipping*, 1987 (Winner of Lloyds of London Book Prize); *Shipping Futures*, 1990; Freeman, City of London 1978–; *Clubs:* President, Chippenham Constitutional 2000–; Wootton Bassett Conservative; *Sportsclubs:* Member, Avon Vale Foxhounds; *Recreations:* Riding Horses. James Gray Esq, MP, House of Commons, London, SW1A 0AA *Tel:* 020 7219 6237 *Fax:* 020 7219 1169. *Constituency:* North Wilts Conservative Association, 8 St Mary Street, Chippenham, Wiltshire, SN15 3JJ *Tel:* 01249 652851 *Fax:* 01249 448582 *E-mail:* jamesgray@parliament.uk.

Visit the Vacher Dod Website . . .
www.DodOnline.co.uk

GRAYLING, CHRISTOPHER   Epsom and Ewell   *Con majority 10,080*

Christopher Stephen Grayling. Born 1 April 1962; Educated Royal Grammar School, High Wycombe; Sidney Sussex College, Cambridge (BA history 1984); Married Susan Clare Dillistone 1987 (1 son 1 daughter). BBC News: Trainee 1985–86, Producer 1986–88; Programme editor Business Daily Channel 4 1988–91; Business development manager BBC Select 1991–93; Director: Charterhouse Prods Ltd 1993, Workhouse Ltd 1993–95, SSVC Group 1995–97; Change consultant and European marketing director Burson Marsteller 1997–2001. Councillor London Borough of Merton 1998–2002. **House of Commons:** Contested Warrington South 1997 general election. Member for Epsom and Ewell since June 7, 2001; Shadow Spokesperson for Health 2002–; Opposition Whip 2002; *Select Committees:* Member: Transport, Local Government and the Regions 2001–02, Transport Sub-Committee 2001–02, Urban Affairs Sub-Committee 2001–02, Transport 2002. *Special Interests:* Transport, Education, Health. Member Corporation of Merton College 1999–2001; Chair Epsom Victim Support; *Publications: The Bridgwater Heritage*, 1983; *A Land Fit for Heroes*, 1985; *Just Another Star?*, co-author 1987; *Insight Guide to the Waterways of Europe*, co-author 1989; *Recreations:* Golf, cricket. Christopher Grayling Esq, MP, House of Commons, London, SW1A 0AA *Tel:* 020 7219 8226. *Constituency:* 212 Barnett Wood Lane, Ashtead, Surrey, KT21 2DB *Tel:* 01372 271036 *Fax:* 01372 270906 *E-mail:* graylingc@parliament.uk.

GREEN, DAMIAN   Ashford   *Con majority 7,359*

Damian Howard Green. Born 17 January 1956; Son of Howard and late Audrey Green; Educated Reading School; Balliol College, Oxford (BA philosophy, politics and economics 1977, MA); President, Oxford Union 1997; Married Alicia Collinson 1988 (2 daughters). Financial journalist, BBC Radio 1978–82; Business producer, Channel 4 News 1982–84; News editor, business news, *The Times* 1984–85; Business editor, Channel 4 News, 1985–87; Programme presenter and city editor, *Business Daily* 1987–92; Special Adviser, Prime Minister's Policy Unit 1992–94; Public Affairs Consultant (Self-employed) 1995–97. **House of Commons:** Contested Brent East 1992 general election. Member for Ashford since 1997; Opposition Spokesperson for: Education and Employment 1998–99, Environment 1999–2001; Shadow Secretary of State for Education and Skills 2001–; *Select Committees:* Member: Culture, Media and Sport 1997–98, Procedure 1997–98. *Special Interests:* Economic Policy, Foreign Affairs, Media, Education, Employment, Rural Affairs. *Countries of Interest:* France, Italy. Vice-President, Tory Reform Group 1997–; Vice-Chair, Conservative Parliamentary Mainstream Group 1997–. Member, SPUC; Trustee, Community Development Foundations; *Publications: ITN Budget Fact Book*, 1984–85–86; *A Better BBC*, 1990; *The Cross-Media Revolution*, 1995; *Communities in the Countryside*, 1996; *Regulating the Media in the Digital Age*, 1997; *21st Century Conservatism*, 1998; *The Four Failures of the New Deal*, 1999; *Better Learning*, 2002; *Sportsclubs:* Fowlers FC, MCC; *Recreations:* Football, cricket, opera, cinema. Damian Green Esq, MP, House of Commons, London, SW1A 0AA *Tel:* 020 7219 3518 *Fax:* 020 7219 0904. *Constituency:* c/o Hardy House, The Street, Bethenden, Ashford, Kent, TN26 3AG *Tel:* 01233 820454 *Fax:* 01233 820111 *E-mail:* greend@parliament.uk.

GREEN, MATTHEW   Ludlow   *LD majority 1,630*

Matthew Green. Born 12 April 1970; Son of Roger Hector Green and Pamela Gillian Green, née Bolas; Educated Priory School, Shrewsbury, Shrewsbury sixth form college; Birmingham University (BA medieval studies 1991); Married Sarah Henthorn 1999. Sales and marketing Timber products industry 1991–96; Managing director Media relations and training consultancy 1996–. Councillor South Shropshire District Council 1994–95. **House of Commons:** Contested Wolverhampton South West 1997 general election. Member for Ludlow since June 7, 2001; Liberal Democrat Spokesperson for: Youth Affairs 2001–02, the Office of the Deputy Prime Minister 2002–; *Special Interests:* Agriculture, alternative energy, youth affairs. Vice-president, National

Executive Parliamentary Candidates Association. Member: European Standing Committee A, European Standing Committee B until 2003; *Publications:* Publisher *Who's Who of the Liberal Democrats*, 1998; *Clubs:* Liberal Club; *Recreations:* Rugby, cricket, hillwalking, rockclimbing. Matthew Green Esq, MP, House of Commons, London, SW1A 0AA *Tel:* 020 7219 8253 *Fax:* 020 7219 1778. *Constituency:* 33–34 High Street, Bridgnorth, Shropshire, WV16 4DB *Tel:* 01746 766465 *Fax:* 01746 765710 *E-mail:* greenm@parliament.uk.

GREENWAY, JOHN   Ryedale   *Con majority 4,875*

John Robert Greenway. Born 15 February 1946; Son of Bill and Kathleen Greenway; Educated Sir John Deane's Grammar School, Northwich; Hendon Police College; London College of Law; Married Sylvia Ann Gant 1974 (2 sons 1 daughter). Metropolitan Police Officer, stationed West End Central 1965–69; Insurance company representative 1970–72; Insurance broker and financial consultant 1973–. North Yorkshire County Council: Councillor 1985–87, Education and Schools Committees, Vice-chair, North Yorkshire Police Committee. **House of Commons:** Member for Ryedale since June 1987; Opposition Spokesperson for: Home Affairs (Police, Criminal Policy, Constitution, Data Protection, Electoral Policy, Gambling and Licensing) 1997–2000, Culture, Media and Sport (Sports; Tourism) 2000–03; PPS to Baroness Trumpington, as Minister of State, Ministry of Agriculture, Fisheries and Food 1991–92; *Select Committees:* Member, Home Affairs 1987–97. *Special Interests:* Law and Order, Personal Finance, Agriculture, Broadcasting, Sales Promotion and Marketing, Tourism. Member, 92 Group. Governor, York Theatre Royal 1985–87; Member, Standing Committees 1997–98 to Consider: Data Protection Bill, Registration of Political Parties Bill, Special Immigration Appeals Commissioners Bill; *Sportsclubs:* President, York City FC; *Recreations:* Opera, music, wine, travel. John Greenway Esq, MP, House of Commons, London, SW1A 0AA *Tel:* 020 7219 6397 *Fax:* 020 7219 6059. *Constituency:* 109 Town Street, Old Malton, North Yorkshire, YO17 0HD *Tel:* 01653 692023 *Fax:* 01653 696108 *E-mail:* greenwayj@parliament.uk.

GRIEVE, DOMINIC   Beaconsfield   *Con majority 13,065*

Dominic Charles Roberts Grieve. Born 24 May 1956; Son of late W. P. Grieve, MP 1964–83, and of late Evelyn Grieve, née Mijouain; Educated Westminster School; Magdalen College, Oxford (BA modern history, 1978, MA 1989); Central London Polytechnic (Diploma in law 1980); Married Caroline Hutton 1990 (2 sons and 1 son deceased). Territorial Army 1981–83. Councillor, London Borough of Hammersmith and Fulham 1982–86. **House of Commons:** Contested Norwood 1987 general election. Member for Beaconsfield since May 1, 1997; Opposition Spokesperson for: Constitutional Affairs and Scotland 1999–2001, Home Office 2001–; *Select Committees:* Member: Environmental Audit 1997–2001, Joint Committee on Statutory Instruments 1997–2001. *Special Interests:* Law and Order, Environment, Defence, Foreign Affairs, European Union, Constitution. *Countries of Interest:* France, Luxembourg. President, Oxford University Conservative Association 1997; Society of Conservative Lawyers: Chair Research Committee 1992–95, Chair Finance and General Purposes. Vice-Chair/Director, Hammersmith and Fulham MIND 1986–89; Lay visitor to police stations 1990–96; Member Council of: Franco-British Society, Luxembourg Society; Member, London Diocesan Synod of Church of England 1994–2000; Deputy Churchwarden; Member: National Trust, John Muir Trust; *Clubs:* Carlton; *Recreations:* Mountaineering, skiing, scuba diving, fell-walking, architecture and art. Dominic Grieve Esq, MP, House of Commons, London, SW1A 0AA *Tel:* 020 7219 6220 *Fax:* 020 7219 4803. *Constituency:* Disraeli House, 12 Aylesbury End, Beaconsfield, Buckinghamshire, HP9 1LW *Tel:* 01494 673745 *Fax:* 01494 670428 *E-mail:* grieved@parliament.uk.

Visit the Vacher Dod Website . . .

www.DodOnline.co.uk

GRIFFITHS, JANE   Reading East   *Lab majority 5,595*

Jane Griffiths. Born 17 April 1954; Daughter of late John Griffiths, advertising agent, and Pat Griffiths, née Thomas; Educated Cedars Grammar School, Leighton Buzzard; Durham University (BA Russian 1975); Married Andrew Tattersall 1999 (1 son 1 daughter from previous marriage). Linguist, GCHQ 1977–84; Asia Editor, BBC Monitoring 1984–97; Member, NUJ. Councillor, Reading Borough Council 1989–99. **House of Commons:** Member for Reading East since May 1, 1997; Adviser on Cycling to Richard Caborn, as Minister of State for Sport 2002–; *Select Committees:* Member, Public Accounts 1997–99. *Special Interests:* Transport, Environment, Waste, Urban Living. *Countries of Interest:* Korea, Japan, Mongolia, Former Soviet Bloc. Branch Chair 1990–92. Member, Transport 2000; Member, European Standing Committee B 1998–2002, 2003–; Member Standing Committees on: Government Resources and Accounts, Licensing (Young Persons), Race Relations (Amendment), Home Energy Conservation Bill; Member Parliamentary Assembly Council of Europe and Western European Union 2002–; Member, Ectopic Pregnancy Trust; *Publications:* Co-author *Bushido* 1988; *Recreations:* Cycling, urban living. Jane Griffiths, MP, House of Commons, London, SW1A 0AA *Tel:* 020 7219 4122 *Fax:* 020 7219 0719. *Constituency:* St Giles House, 10 Church Street, Reading, Berkshire, RG1 2SD *Tel:* 0118–957 3756 *Fax:* 0118–958 0949 *E-mail:* griffithsj@parliament.uk.

GRIFFITHS, NIGEL   Edinburgh South   *Lab majority 5,499*

Nigel Griffiths. Born 20 May 1955; Son of late Lionel Griffiths and of Elizabeth Griffiths; Educated Hawick High School; Edinburgh University (MA 1977); Moray House College of Education (1978); Married Sally McLaughlin 1979. City of Edinburgh District Council: Councillor 1980–87, Chair: Housing Committee, Decentralisation Committee 1986–87; Member: Edinburgh Festival Council 1984–87, Edinburgh Health Council 1982–87; Executive Member, Edinburgh Council of Social Service 1984–87. **House of Commons:** Member for Edinburgh South since June 1987; Opposition Spokesperson for Trade and Industry Specialising in International Trade and Consumer Affairs 1989–97; Opposition Whip 1987–89; Parliamentary Under-Secretary of State, Department of Trade and Industry 1997–: Competition and Consumer Affairs 1997–98, Small Business, Export Controls and Non-Proliferation 2001–03, Small Business and Enterprise 2003–; *Select Committees:* Member: Procedure 1999–2001, Public Accounts 1999–2001. *Special Interests:* Education, Housing, Health, Social Services, Disability, Scotland, Arts, Economic Policy, Small Businesses. President, EU Labour Club 1976–77; Member, Labour Party National Policy Forum 1999–. Rights Adviser, Mental Handicap Pressure Group 1979–87; Member, Wester Hailes School Council 1981; Secretary, Lothian Devolution Campaign 1978; Executive Member, Scottish Constitutional Convention 1988–90; Vice-President, Institute of Trading Standards Administration 1994–; Chair, Scottish Charities Kosovo Appeal 2000–; *Publications: Guide to Council Housing in Edinburgh*, 1981; *Council Housing on the Point of Collapse*, 1982; *Welfare Rights Survey*, 1981; *Welfare Rights Guide*, 1982, 1983, 1984, 1985, 1986; *Rights Guide for Mentally Handicapped People*, 1988; *300 Gains from the Labour Government*, 2000; *Recreations:* Travel, live entertainment, badminton, hill-walking and rock-climbing, architecture, reading, politics, scuba diving, flying. Nigel Griffiths Esq, JP, MP, House of Commons, London, SW1A 0AA *Tel:* 020 7219 3000. *Constituency:* 31 Minto Street, Edinburgh, EH9 2BT *Tel:* 0131–662 4520 *E-mail:* ngriffithsmp@parliament.uk.

DodOnline
An Electronic Directory without rival . . .

MPs' biographies and photographs available with daily updates *via* the internet

For a *free* trial, call Yasmin Mirza, Aby Farsoun or Michael Mand on 020 7630 7643

GRIFFITHS, WIN   Bridgend   *Lab majority 10,046*

Win (Winston) James Griffiths. Born 11 February 1943; Son of late Evan George Griffiths and late Rachel Elizabeth Griffiths; Educated Brecon Boys' Grammar School; University College of Wales, Cardiff (BA 1965, DipEd 1966); Married Elizabeth Ceri Gravell 1966 (1 son 1 daughter). Teacher: secondary school, Tanzania 1966–68, George Dixon Boys' Grammar School 1969–70, Barry Boys' Comprehensive School 1970–76; Head of history department, Cowbridge Comprehensive School 1976–79; Member, TGWU (ACTS). Vale of Glamorgan Borough Council: Councillor and Chair, Leisure Services Committee 1973–76; Member, St Andrew's Major Community Council 1974–79. **House of Commons:** Member for Bridgend since June 1987; Opposition Spokesperson for: The Environment 1990–92, Education 1992–94, Welsh Affairs 1994–97; MEP for South Wales 1979–89; Vice-President, European Parliament 1984–87; Parliamentary Under-Secretary of State, Welsh Office 1997–98; *Select Committees:* Member, Chairmen's Panel 2001–. *Special Interests:* Education, European Union, Disability, Overseas Aid and Development, Animal Welfare, Children, Health, Social Services, Human Rights, Green Issues. *Countries of Interest:* European Union, Tanzania, South Africa, Zimbabwe, Indonesia, Sierra Leone. Member: Labour Campaign for Electoral Reform; Secretary: Labour Movement for Europe 2002–. Member, Court of Governors: University College, Cardiff 1981–97, Museums and Galleries of Wales 1998–; Convention drawing up EU Charter of Fundamental Rights – representative of the House of Commons, December 1999-October 2000; *Publications:* Contributor to journal and book on European integration; *Recreations:* Reading, erstwhile marathon runner, cultivating pot plants, listening to music. Win Griffiths Esq, MP, House of Commons, London, SW1A 0AA *Tel:* 020 7219 4461 *Fax:* 020 7219 6052. *Constituency:* 47 Nolton Street, Bridgend, CF31 3AA *Tel:* 01656 645432 *Fax:* 01656 767551.

GROGAN, JOHN   Selby   *Lab majority 2,138*

John Grogan. Born 24 February 1961; Son of late John Martin Grogan and late Maureen Grogan; Educated St Michael's College, Leeds; St John's College, Oxford (BA modern history and economics 1982); Single. Communications co-ordinator, Leeds City Council 1987–94; Contested York European Parliament election 1989; Labour Party press officer, European Parliament, Brussels 1995; Self-employed conference organiser 1996–97; Member, GMB. **House of Commons:** Contested Selby 1987 and 1992 general elections. Member for Selby since May 1, 1997; *Select Committees:* Member: Northern Ireland Affairs 1997–2001, Joint Scrutiny Committee on Communications Bill 2002. *Special Interests:* Local and Regional Government, European Union, Economic Policy, Broadcasting, Sport, Liquor Licensing Reform, Small Businesses, Coal. *Countries of Interest:* Ukraine, Mongolia, Australia, New Zealand. Member: Fabian Society, Institute of Public Policy Research; John Smith Institute. *Recreations:* Football, running, cinema. John Grogan Esq, MP, House of Commons, London, SW1A 0AA *Tel:* 020 7219 4403 *Fax:* 020 7219 2676. *Constituency:* 58 Gowthorpe, Selby, North Yorkshire, YO8 4ET *Tel:* 01757 291152 *Fax:* 01757 291153 *E-mail:* selby@johngroganmp.u-net.com.

GUMMER, JOHN   Suffolk Coastal   *Con majority 4,326*

John Gummer. Born 26 November 1939; Son of late Canon Selwyn Gummer; Educated King's School, Rochester; Selwyn College, Cambridge (BA history 1961, MA 1971) (President of the Union 1962); Married Penelope Jane Gardner 1977 (2 sons 2 daughters). Former chairman, Siemssen Hunter Ltd; Since leaving office – Chairman, Sancroft International Ltd (corporate responsibility consultants); Chairman: Valpak Ltd, International Commission on Sustainable Consumption, Marine Stewardship Council; Director, Vivendi UK Ltd. Councillor, ILEA 1967–70. **House of Commons:** Contested Greenwich 1964 and 1966 general elections. Member for Lewisham West 1970–74, for Eye 1979–83, and for Suffolk Coastal since June 1983; Assistant Government Whip January 1981; Government Whip 1981–83; PPS: to Minister of Agriculture, Fisheries and Food 1971–72, to Secretary of State for Social Services 1979–81; Parliamentary Under-Secretary of State, Department of

Employment 1983; Minister of State, Department of Employment 1983–84; Paymaster General 1984–85; Minister of State, Ministry of Agriculture, Fisheries and Food 1985–88; Minister for Local Government 1988–89; Minister of Agriculture, Fisheries and Food 1989–93; Secretary of State for the Environment 1993–97; *Special Interests:* European Affairs, Environment. Chairman, Cambridge University Conservative Association 1961; Conservative Party: Vice-Chairman 1972–74, Chairman 1983–85; Chairman, Conservative Group for Europe 1997–2000. Member, General Synod of Church of England for St Edmundsbury and Ipswich Diocese 1978–92; *Publications: When the Coloured People Come*; *The Permissive Society*; Co-author *The Christian Calendar*; *Faith in Politics* 1987; PC 1985. Rt Hon John Gummer, MP, House of Commons, London, SW1A 0AA *Tel:* 020 7219 4591 *Fax:* 020 7219 5906. *Constituency:* Suffolk Coastal Conservative Association, National Hall, Sun Lane, Woodbridge, Suffolk, IP12 1EG *Tel:* 01394 380001 *Fax:* 01394 382570 *E-mail:* gummerj@parliament.uk.

H

HAGUE, WILLIAM   Richmond (Yorkshire)   *Con majority 16,319*

William Jefferson Hague. Born 26 March 1961; Son of Nigel and Stella Hague; Educated Wath-on-Dearne Comprehensive School; Magdalen College, Oxford (philosophy, politics and economics 1979–82) (President, Oxford Union 1981); INSEAD Business School, France 1985–86; Married Ffion Jenkins 1997. Shell UK 1982–83; McKinsey and Company 1983–88; Political adviser to Sir Geoffrey Howe as Chancellor of the Exchequer and Leon Brittan as Chief Secretary to the Treasury 1983; Political and economic adviser JCB 2001–; Non-executive director AES Engineering 2001–; Member Political Council of Terra Firma Capital Partners 2001–. **House of Commons:** Contested Wentworth 1987 general election. Member for Richmond, Yorks. since February 23, 1989 by-election; PPS to Norman Lamont as Chancellor of the Exchequer 1990–93; Department of Social Security: Joint Parliamentary Under-Secretary of State, 1993–94, Minister of State, (Minister for Social Security and Disabled People) 1994–95; Secretary of State for Wales 1995–97; Leader of the Opposition 1997–2001; Leader, Conservative Party 1997–2001; Member Joint Committee on House of Lords Reform 2002–; *Select Committees:* Member, Joint Committee on House of Lords Reform 2002–. *Special Interests:* Agriculture, Economic Policy. President Oxford University Conservative Association 1981; Leader Conservative Party June 1997–2001. International Democrat Union, Global Alliance of Conservative, Christian Democrat and like-minded parties: Chairman 1999–2002, Deputy Chairman 2002–; *Publications: Speaking with Conviction*, Conservative Policy Forum, October 1998; *I will Give you Back your Country*, Conservative Policy Forum, September 2000; *Biography of William Pitt the Younger* (Due to be published 2004); PC 1995; *The Spectator*/Highland Park Parliamentarian of the Year 1998; *Clubs:* Beefsteak, Carlton, Buck's, Pratt's, Budokwai, Mark's; *Recreations:* Walking, sailing, cross country, skiing, judo. Rt Hon William Hague, MP, House of Commons, London, SW1A 0AA *Tel:* 020 7219 4611. *Constituency:* c/o 67 High Street, Northallerton, North Yorkshire, DL7 8EG *Tel:* 01609 779093 *Fax:* 01609 778172.

HAIN, PETER   Neath   *Lab majority 14,816*

Peter Hain. Born 16 February 1950; Son of Walter and Adelaine Hain; Educated Pretoria Boys High School, South Africa; Emanuel School, Wandsworth, London; Queen Mary College, London University (BSc economics and political science 1973); Sussex University (MPhil 1976); Married Patricia Western 1975 (divorced) (2 sons); married Elizabeth Haywood 2003. Head of research, Union of Communication Workers 1976–91; Member, GMB. Health Authority Member 1981–87. **House of Commons:** Contested Putney 1983 and 1987 general elections. Member for Neath since by-election April 4, 1991; Opposition Spokesperson for Employment 1996–97; Opposition Whip 1995–96; Parliamentary Under-Secretary of State, Welsh Office 1997–99; Minister of State: Foreign and Commonwealth Office 1999–2001, Department of Trade and Industry

(Minister for Energy and Competitiveness) 2001; Foreign and Commonwealth Office (Minister for Europe) 2001–02; Government representative European Union Convention 2002–; Secretary of State for Wales 2002–; Leader of the House of Commons and Lord Privy Seal 2003–; *Select Committees:* Chair, Modernisation of the House of Commons 2003–. *Countries of Interest:* Southern Africa. Leader, Young Liberals 1971–73; Member: Co-op, Fabians. Leader, Stop the Seventy Tour 1969–70; Anti-Nazi League 1977–79; Member: CND, Anti-Apartheid Movement; School Governor 1981–90; Tribune Newspaper Board of Directors; *Publications:* 13 books including *Ayes to the Left: A future for socialism*, 1995; PC 2001; *Clubs:* Royal British Legion, Resolven; *Sportsclubs:* Resolven Rugby, Ynysygerwn Cricket; *Recreations:* Rugby, soccer, cricket, motor racing, rock and folk music. Rt Hon Peter Hain, MP, House of Commons, London, SW1A 0AA *Tel:* 020 7219 3925 *Fax:* 020 7219 3816. *Constituency:* 39 Windsor Road, Neath, SA11 1NB *Tel:* 01639 630152 *Fax:* 01639 641196 *E-mail:* hainp@parliament.uk.

HALL, MIKE   Weaver Vale   Lab majority 9,637

Michael Hall. Born 20 September 1952; Son of late Thomas Hall, maintenance engineer, and of late Veronica Hall, mail order clerk; Educated St Damian's Secondary Modern School; Padgate College of Higher Education (Teacher's Certificate 1977); North Cheshire College (BEd 1987); University College of Wales, Bangor (Diploma in Education 1989); Married Lesley Gosling 1975 (1 son). Scientific assistant, chemical industry 1969–73; Teacher of history and physical education, Bolton LEA 1977–85; Support teacher, Halton Community Assessment Team 1985–92. Warrington Borough Council: Councillor 1979–93; Chair: Environmental Health Committee 1981–84, Finance Sub-Committee 1984–85, Policy and Resources Committee 1985–92; Council Leader 1985–92. **House of Commons:** Member for Warrington South 1992–97, and for Weaver Vale since May 1, 1997; Assistant Government Whip 1998–2001; PPS to: Ann Taylor as Leader of the House and President of the Council 1997–98, Secretaries of State for Health: Alan Milburn 2001–03, John Reid 2003–; *Select Committees:* Member: Public Accounts 1992–97, Modernisation of the House of Commons 1997–98, Administration 1999–2001. *Special Interests:* Poverty, Education, Local and Regional Government, Home Affairs, Health. *Countries of Interest:* Czech Republic. *Sportsclubs:* Lymm Lawn Tennis and Croquet, Owley Wood Sports and Social Club; *Recreations:* Tennis, walking, cooking, reading. Michael Hall Esq, MP, House of Commons, London, SW1A 0AA *Tel:* 020 7219 4001. *Constituency:* Room 17, Castle Park, Frodsham, Cheshire, WA6 6UJ *Tel:* 01928 735000 *Fax:* 01928 735250 *E-mail:* halll@parliament.uk.

HALL, PATRICK   Bedford   Lab majority 6,157

Patrick Hall. Born 20 October 1951; Son of Frank Hall, architect and Josie Hall, teacher; Educated Bedford Modern School; Birmingham University (BA geography 1970); Oxford Polytechnic (post graduate diploma town planning 1979). Local government planning officer Bedford 1975–91; Bedford Town Centre co-ordinator 1991–97; Member, NALGO 1974–97. Councillor, Bedfordshire County Council 1989–97; Member, North Bedfordshire Community Health Council 1988–97. **House of Commons:** Contested North Bedfordshire 1992 general election. Member for Bedford since May 1, 1997; *Select Committees:* Member: Joint Committee on Consolidation of Bills Etc 1997–2001, European Scrutiny 1999–2001, Radioactive Waste Policy Sub-Committee 2001–02; Member, Environment, Food and Rural Affairs 2001–. Hon. Secretary, Eastern Regional Group of Labour MPs 1999–. Chair Bedford Door to Door Dial-a-Ride 1989–97; *Recreations:* Squash, gardens. Patrick Hall Esq, MP, House of Commons, London, SW1A 0AA *Tel:* 020 7219 3605 *Fax:* 020 7219 3987. *Constituency:* 5 Mill Street, Bedford, MK40 3EX *Tel:* 01234 262699 *Fax:* 01234 272981 *E-mail:* hallp@parliament.uk.

Visit the Vacher Dod Website . . .
www.DodOnline.co.uk

HAMILTON, DAVID Midlothian   *Lab majority 9,014*

David Hamilton. Born 24 October 1950; Son of David Hamilton and Agnes Gardner; Educated Dalkeith High School; Married Jean Trench Macrae 1969 (2 daughters). Miner National Coal Board 1965–84; Employment training scheme supervisor Midlothian Council 1987–89; Placement and training officer Craigmillar Festival Society 1989–92; Chief executive Craigmillar Opportunities Trust 1992–2000; NUM 1965–87, 2001–: Delegate 1976–87, Joint union chair 1981–87, Chair numerous committees; TGWU 1987–2000; Member, RMT Parliamentary Campaigning Group 2002–. Midlothian Council: Convenor Strategic Services Committee 1995–2000, Cabinet member Strategic Services Portfolio 2000–01; Convention of Scottish Local Authorities (COSLA): Chair Economic Development, Planning and Transport Committee 1997–99, Spokesman Economic Development and Tourism 1999–2001; Midlothian Chamber of Commerce –2002; Midlothian Enterprise Trust –2002; Midlothian Innovation Technology Trust 2002–. **House of Commons:** Member for Midlothian since June 7, 2001; *Select Committees:* Member: Broadcasting 2001–, Procedure 2001–, Scottish Affairs 2003–. *Special Interests:* Economic Development, Transport, Social Inclusion. *Countries of Interest:* EU, USA, Gibraltar, Cyprus. Member, European Standing Committee A 2003–; *Clubs:* Dalkeith Miners Welfare; *Recreations:* Films, theatre. David Hamilton Esq, MP, House of Commons, London, SW1A 0AA *Tel:* 020 7219 8257 *Fax:* 020 7219 3606. *Constituency:* PO Box 11, 95 High Street, Dalkeith, Midlothian, EH22 1AX *Tel:* 0131–654 1585 *Fax:* 0131–654 1586 *E-mail:* hamiltonda@parliament.uk.

HAMILTON, FABIAN Leeds North East   *Lab majority 7,089*

Fabian Hamilton. Born 12 April 1955; Son of late Mario Uziell-Hamilton, solicitor, and Adrianne Uziell-Hamilton (Her Honour Judge Uziell-Hamilton); Educated Brentwood School, Brentwood, Essex; York University (BA social sciences); Married Rosemary Ratcliffe 1980 (1 son 2 daughters). Taxi driver 1978–79; graphic designer 1979–94; consultant and dealer, Apple Macintosh computer systems 1994–97; Member: SLADE 1978–82, NGA 1982–91, GPMU 1991–. Councillor, Leeds City Council 1987–98, Chair: Race Equality Committee 1988–94, Economic Development Committee 1994–96, Education Committee 1996–97. **House of Commons:** Contested Leeds North East 1992 general election. Member for Leeds North East since May 1, 1997; *Select Committees:* Member, Administration 1997–2001; Member, Foreign Affairs 2001–. *Special Interests:* Education, Economic Development and Small Businesses, Racism, International Development, Alternative Fuels. *Countries of Interest:* Middle East, Europe, Southern Africa, Caribbean and Indian sub-continent, Cyprus. Member Co-op Party; Vice-chair Labour Friends of Israel. Member Poale Zion; Governor Northern School of Contemporary Dance; Trustee, National Heart Research Fund; Trustee National Heart Research Fund; *Recreations:* Film, opera, cycling, computers, photography. Fabian Hamilton Esq, MP, House of Commons, London, SW1A 0AA *Tel:* 020 7219 3493 *Fax:* 020 7219 4945. *Constituency:* 6 Queenshill Approach, Leeds, LS17 6AY *Tel:* 0113–237 0022 *Fax:* 0113–237 0404 *E-mail:* fabian@leedsne.co.uk.

HAMMOND, PHILIP Runnymede and Weybridge   *Con majority 8,360*

Philip Hammond. Born 4 December 1955; Son of Bernard Lawrence Hammond, AMICE, retired civil engineer and local government officer; Educated Shenfield School, Brentwood, Essex; University College, Oxford (MA politics, philosophy and economics 1977); Married June 29, 1991, Susan Carolyn Williams-Walker (2 daughters 1 son). Assistant to Chair then marketing manager, Speywood Laboratories Ltd 1977–81; Director, Speywood Medical Ltd 1981–83; Established and ran medical equipment manufacturing and distribution companies 1983–94; Director, Castlemead Ltd 1984–; Director, various medical equipment manufacturing companies 1983–96; Partner, CMA Consultants 1993–95; Director, Castlemead Homes Ltd 1994–; Consultant to Government of Malawi 1995–97. **House of Commons:** Contested Newham North East by-election 1994. Member for Runnymede and Weybridge since May 1, 1997; Opposition Spokesperson for:

Health and Social Services 1998–2001, Trade and Industry 2001–02; Shadow Minister of State, Office of the Deputy Prime Minister 2002–; *Select Committees:* Member: Environment, Transport and Regional Affairs 1998, Transport Sub-Committee 1998, Trade and Industry 2002; Member, Unopposed Bills (Panel) 1997–. *Special Interests:* Economic Policy, International Trade, European Union, Defence, Social Security, Transport, Housing and Planning, Energy, Health. *Countries of Interest:* Latin America, Germany, Italy, Southern and Eastern Africa. East Lewisham Conservative Association: Executive Council Member 1982–89, Chair 1989–96; Member, Greater London Area Executive Council 1989–96; Vice-Chair, Greenwich and Lewisham Conservative Action Group 1993–94. Member, European Standing Committee B 1997–1998; *Clubs:* Carlton; *Recreations:* Travel, cinema, walking. Philip Hammond Esq, MP, House of Commons, London, SW1A 0AA *Tel:* 020 7219 4055 *Fax:* 020 7219 5851. *Constituency:* Runnymede, Spelthorne and Weybridge, Conservative Association, 55 Cherry Orchard, Staines, Middlesex, TW18 2DQ *Tel:* 01784 453544 *Fax:* 01784 466109 *E-mail:* hammondp@parliament.uk.

HANCOCK, MIKE   Portsmouth South   *LD majority 6,093*

Mike (Michael) Thomas Hancock. Born 9 April 1946; Son of Thomas William Hancock and Margaret Eva Hancock (née Cole); Married Jacqueline Elliott 1967 (1 son 1 daughter). Director, BBC Daytime; District Officer for Hampshire, Isle of Wight and Channel Islands Mencap 1989–97; Contested (Liberal Democrat) Wight and Hampshire South European Parliamentary election 1994. Councillor, Portsmouth City Council 1971, Fratton Ward 1973–, Leader, Liberal Democrat Group 1989–97, Chair, Planning and Economic Development Committee; Councillor, Hampshire County Council 1973–97, Leader of the Opposition 1977–81, 1989–93, Leader 1993–97. **House of Commons:** Contested Portsmouth South (SDP) 1983, (SDP/Alliance) 1987 general elections. Member (SDP) for Portsmouth South 1984–87. Member for Portsmouth South since May 1, 1997; Spokesperson for: Foreign Affairs, Defence and Europe (Defence) 1997–99; Environment, Transport, the Regions and Social Justice (Planning) 2000–01; *Select Committees:* Member, Public Administration 1997–99; Member: Defence 1999–, Chairmen's Panel 2000–. *Special Interests:* European Affairs, Defence, Sport. Member: Labour Party 1968–81, Social Democrat Party 1981–87, Liberal Democrat Party 1987–. Chairman, Southern Branch, NSPCC 1989–92; Vice-Chairman, Portsmouth Docks 1992–2002; Council of Europe, Western European Union, NATO; Trustee, Royal Marine Museum; *Publications: Council of Europe Report on International Abduction of children by one of the parents,* 2002; CBE 1992; *Recreations:* Supporter Portsmouth Football Club. Mike Hancock Esq, CBE, MP, House of Commons, London, SW1A 0AA *Tel:* 020 7219 5180 *Fax:* 020 7219 2496. *Constituency:* 1A Albert Road, Southsea, Hampshire, PO5 2SE *Tel:* 023 9286 1055 *Fax:* 023 9283 0530 *E-mail:* portsmouthldp@cix.co.uk.

HANSON, DAVID   Delyn   *Lab majority 8,605*

David George Hanson. Born 5 July 1957; Son of Brian Hanson, retired fork lift driver and Glenda Hanson, retired wages clerk; Educated Verdin Comprehensive School, Winsford, Cheshire; Hull University (BA drama 1978, Certificate of Education 1980); Married Margaret Mitchell 1986 (2 sons 2 daughters). Vice-President, Hull University Students' Union 1978–79; Trainee, Co-operative Union 1980–81; Manager, Plymouth Co-operative 1981–82; Various posts with The Spastics Society 1982–89; Contested Cheshire West 1984 European Parliament election; Director, Re-Solv (The Society for the Prevention of Solvent Abuse) 1989–92; Member: T&G, MSF. Councillor: Vale Royal Borough Council 1983–91, Northwich Town Council 1987–91; Vale Royal Borough Council: Chair, Economic Development Committee 1988–89, Labour Leader 1989–91, Leader of Council. **House of Commons:** Contested Eddisbury 1983 and Delyn 1987 general elections; Member for Delyn since April 9, 1992; Assistant Government Whip 1998–99; PPS to Alastair Darling as Chief Secretary to the Treasury 1997–98; Parliamentary Under-Secretary of State, Wales Office 1999–2001; PPS to Tony Blair as Prime Minister 2001–; *Select Committees:* Member: Welsh Affairs 1992–95, Public Service 1995–97. *Special Interests:* Foreign Affairs, Health, Heritage, Local and Regional Government, Solvent Abuse, Treasury, Small Businesses. *Countries of Interest:* South Africa, Cyprus. Member, Leadership Campaign Team 1994–97. *Recreations:* Football, cinema, family. David Hanson Esq, MP, House of Commons, London, SW1A 0AA *Tel:* 020 7219 5064 *Fax:* 020 7219 2671. *Constituency:* 64 Chester Street, Flint, Flintshire, CH6 5DH *Tel:* 01352 763159 *Fax:* 01352 730140 *E-mail:* hansond@parliament.uk.

HARMAN, HARRIET   Camberwell and Peckham   *Lab majority 14,123*

Harriet Harman. Born 30 July 1950; Daughter of late John Bishop Harman, and of Anna Harman; Educated St Paul's Girls' School; York University (BA politics 1978); Married Jack Dromey 1982 (2 sons 1 daughter). Legal officer, National Council for Civil Liberties 1978–82. **House of Commons:** Member for Peckham 1982–1997, and for Camberwell and Peckham since May 1, 1997; Spokesperson on Health 1987–92; Shadow Minister, Social Services 1984, 1985–87; Shadow Chief Secretary to the Treasury 1992–94; Shadow Secretary of State for: Employment 1994–95, Health 1995–96; Social Security 1996–97; Secretary of State for Social Security and Minister for Women 1997–98; Solicitor General, Law Officers' Department 2001–; *Special Interests:* Women, Social Services, Provision for under 5s, Law, Domestic Violence, Civil Liberties. Member, Labour Party National Executive Committee 1993–98. Chair, Childcare Commission 1999–; PC 1997, QC 2001. Rt Hon Harriet Harman, QC MP, House of Commons, London, SW1A 0AA *Tel:* 020 7219 4218 *Fax:* 020 7219 4877 *E-mail:* harmanh@parliament.uk.

HARRIS, EVAN   Oxford West and Abingdon   *LD majority 9,185*

Evan Harris. Born 21 October 1965; Son of Prof Frank Harris, CBE, former Dean of Medicine, Leicester University, and Brenda Harris, formerly scientific officer; Educated Liverpool Blue Coat Secondary School; Harvard High School, North Hollywood, USA; Wadham College, Oxford (BA physiology 1988); Oxford University Medical School (BM, BCh 1991); Divorced. NHS Hospital Doctor 1991–94; Public Health Registrar (Hon) 1994–97; BMA National Council 1994–97; Junior Doctors Committee Executive 1995–97. **House of Commons:** Member for Oxford West and Abingdon since May 1, 1997; Spokesperson for: NHS 1997–99, Higher Education, Science and Women's Issues 1999–2001, Health 2001–; *Select Committees:* Member, Education and Employment 1999–2001. *Special Interests:* Health, Civil Liberties, Voting Systems, Asylum, Science, Medical Ethics. *Countries of Interest:* Israel, South Africa, USA. Member, Oxford West and Abingdon SDP and Lib Dem Executive Committee 1986–97; Hon. President, Lib Dems for Gay and Lesbian Rights 2000–. Member: Central Oxford Research Ethics Committee 1995–98, Oxford Diocesan Board of Social Responsibility 1998–; *Clubs:* National Liberal; *Recreations:* TV, squash, Bridge, chess. Dr Evan Harris, MP, House of Commons, London, SW1A 0AA *Tel:* 020 7219 5128 *Fax:* 020 7219 2346. *Constituency:* The Old Jam Factory, 27 Park End Street, Oxford, OX1 1HU *Tel:* 01865 245584 *Fax:* 01865 245589 *E-mail:* harrise@parliament.uk.

HARRIS, TOM   Glasgow Cathcart   *Lab majority 10,816*

Tom (Thomas) Harris. Born 20 February 1964; Son of Tom Harris, lorry/taxi driver, and Rita Harris, née Ralston, office clerk; Educated Garnock Academy, Kilbirnie, Ayrshire; Napier College, Edinburgh (HND journalism 1986); Married 1998 (1 son). Trainee reporter *East Kilbride News* 1986–88; Reporter *Paisley Daily Express* 1988–90; Press officer: Scottish Labour Party 1990–92, Strathclyde Regional Council 1993–96; Senior media officer Glasgow City Council 1996; Public relations manager East Ayrshire Council 1996–98; Chief public relations and marketing officer Strathclyde Passenger Transport Executive 1998–2001; NUJ 1984–97; UNISON 1997–. **House of Commons:** Member for Glasgow Cathcart since June 7, 2001; PPS to John Spellar as Minister of State, Northern Ireland Office 2003–; *Select Committees:* Member, Science and Technology 2001–. *Special Interests:* Welfare Reform, Transport, Economy, Foreign Affairs, Northern Ireland. *Countries of Interest:* USA, Israel. Member, Labour Friends of Israel. *Clubs:* Cathcart Labour Social, Castlemilk; *Recreations:* Astronomy, cinema, hillwalking. Tom Harris Esq, MP, House of Commons, London, SW1A 0AA *Tel:* 020 7219 8237 *Fax:* 020 7219 1769. *Constituency:* Constituency Office, The Couper Institute, 86 Clarkston Road, Cathcart, Glasgow, G44 3DA *Tel:* 0141 6376447 *Fax:* 0141 6379625 *E-mail:* tomharrismp@parliament.uk.

HARVEY, NICK   North Devon   *LD majority 2,984*

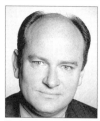

Nick (Nicholas) Barton Harvey. Born 3 August 1961; Son of Frederick Harvey, civil servant, and Christine Harvey, teacher; Educated Queen's College, Taunton; Middlesex Polytechnic (BA business studies 1983); Married Kate Fox (1 daughter). President, Middlesex Polytechnic Students' Union 1981–82; Communications and marketing executive: Profile PR Ltd 1984–86, Dewe Rogerson Ltd 1986–91; Communications Consultant 1989–92; Former Member NUJ. **House of Commons:** Contested Enfield Southgate (Liberal/Alliance) 1987 general election. Member for North Devon since April 9, 1992; Liberal Democrat Spokesperson for: Transport 1992–94, Trade and Industry 1994–97, Constitution (English Regions) 1997–99; Principal Spokesperson for: Health 1999–2001, Culture, Media and Sport 2001–; *Select Committees:* Trade and Industry 1994–95. *Special Interests:* Economics, European Union. National Vice-Chair, Union of Liberal Students 1981–82; Chair of Candidates Committee 1993–98; Chair of Campaigns and Communications 1994–99. Vice-President, Federation of Economic Development Authorities (FEDA) 2000–; Honorary Doctorate, Middlesex University 2000; *Recreations:* Travel, football, walking, music. Nick Harvey Esq, MP, House of Commons, London, SW1A 0AA *Tel:* 020 7219 6232. *Constituency:* 23 Castle Street, Barnstaple, North Devon, EX31 1DR *Tel:* 01271 328631 *Fax:* 01271 345664 *E-mail:* harveyn@parliament.uk.

HASELHURST, ALAN   Saffron Walden   *Con majority 12,004*

Sir Alan Gordon Barraclough Haselhurst. Born 23 June 1937; Son of late John Haselhurst; Educated King Edward VI School, Birmingham; Cheltenham College; Oriel College, Oxford; Married Angela Margaret Bailey 1977 (2 sons 1 daughter). Secretary, Treasurer, Librarian, Oxford Union Society 1959–60; Executive chemicals and plastics industry 1960–70; Public affairs consultant 1974–97. **House of Commons:** Member for Middleton and Prestwich 1970-February 1974, and for Saffron Walden from July 7, 1977 by-election; PPS to Mark Carlisle as Secretary of State, Education and Science 1979–81; Chair, Ways and Means and Deputy Speaker 1997–; *Select Committees:* Member: European Legislation 1982–97, Catering 1991–97, Transport 1992–97; Chair of Ways and Means: Court of Referees 1997–, Unopposed Bills (Panel) 1997–; Chairman of Ways and Means (ex officio): Chairmen's Panel 1997–, Standing Orders 1998–. *Special Interests:* Education, Aerospace, Aviation, Youth Affairs, European Union, Agriculture, Community Development. *Countries of Interest:* USA, South Africa, Australia. President, Oxford University Conservative Association 1958; National Chair, Young Conservative Movement 1966–68; Deputy Chair, Conservative Group for Europe 1982–85. Chair, Commonwealth Youth Exchange Council 1978–81; Chair of Trustees, Community Projects Foundation 1986–97; Fellow, Industry and Parliament Trust 1979; *Publications: Occasionally Cricket,* Queen Anne Press 1999; *Eventually Cricket,* Queen Anne Press 2001; Knighted 1995; PC 1999; *Clubs:* MCC; *Sportsclubs:* Essex County Cricket Club, Executive Committee Member 1996–; *Recreations:* Hi-fi, watching cricket, gardening. Rt Hon Sir Alan Haselhurst, MP, House of Commons, London, SW1A 0AA *Tel:* 020 7219 5214 *Fax:* 020 7219 5600. *Constituency:* The Old Armoury, Saffron Walden, Essex, CB10 1JN *Tel:* 01799 506349 *Fax:* 01799 506047 *E-mail:* haselhursta@parliament.uk.

HAVARD, DAI   Merthyr Tydfil and Rhymney   *Lab majority 14,923*

David Stewart Havard. Born 7 February 1950; Son of Eileen, former shop worker and family carer and late Edward (Ted) Havard, former miner; Educated Secondary modern school, Treharris; Grammar Technical, Quakers Yard, Edwardsville; Comprehensive school, Afon Taf; St Peter's College, Birmingham (Certificate in Education); Warwick University (MA industrial relations); Married Julia Watts 1986 (separated). Member Armed Forces Parliamentary Scheme (Army) 2002; MSF full time officer: Studies tutor 1971–75, Researcher 1975–79, Education 1975–82, Official 1989–, Delegation leader: Wales Labour Party, Conferences; Wales secretary; AMICUS. **House of Commons:** Member for Merthyr Tydfil and Rhymney since June 7, 2001;

Select Committees: Member, Regulatory Reform 2001–. *Special Interests:* Education, Lifelong Learning, Health, Cancer and Blood, Industrial Relations and Working Conditions. Constituency Labour Party; Wales Labour Party Joint Policy Committee. Merthyr Tydfil Credit Union; BHS; RSPB; Member European Standing Committee C; *Publications:* Contributor to academic publications on trade union and economic development; *Clubs:* Aberfan Social and Democratic; *Recreations:* Hillwalking, horse riding, birdwatching, Commons and Lords Rugby team. Dai Havard Esq, MP, House of Commons, London, SW1A 0AA *Tel:* 020 7219 8255 *Fax:* 020 7219 1449. *Constituency:* Room 3, First Floor, Venture Wales Building, Merthyr Tydfil Industrial Park, Pentrebach, Merthyr Tydfil, CF48 4DR *Tel:* 01443 693924 *Fax:* 01443 692905 *E-mail:* havardd@parliament.uk.

HAWKINS, NICK   Surrey Heath   Con majority 10,819

Nicholas John Hawkins. Born 27 March 1957; Son of Dr Arthur Ernest (PhD) and Patricia Jean Hawkins, née Papworth; Educated Bedford Modern School; Lincoln College, Oxford (MA jurisprudence 1978); Middle Temple, Inns of Court School of Law 1979; Married Angela Margaret Turner 1979 (divorced 2000) (2 sons 1 daughter); married Jennifer Frances Cassar 2001 (1 stepdaughter, 1 stepson). Hon Lt Col, Armed Forces Parliamentary Scheme 2000–02; Barrister, Chambers in Birmingham and Northampton 1979–86; Consultant 1986–87; Company Legal adviser, Access (The Joint Credit Card Co. Ltd) 1987–89; Group Legal adviser, Lloyds Abbey Life plc 1989–92; Door tenant London Chambers 1995–99; Member, NATSOPA 1976–77. **House of Commons:** Contested Huddersfield 1987 general election. Member for Blackpool South 1992–97, and for Surrey Heath since May 1, 1997; Opposition Spokesman for: Lord Chancellor's Department 1999–2001, 2002–03, Home Affairs 2000–03, International Development 2001–02; Government Whip, Armed Forces Bill Committee 1996; PPS: to James Arbuthnot and Nicholas Soames, Ministers of State, Ministry of Defence 1995–96, to Virginia Bottomley as Secretary of State for National Heritage 1996–97; Political aide, to Gillian Shepherd as Shadow Leader of the House and as Shadow Secretary of State, Department of the Environment, Transport and the Regions 1997–99; *Select Committees:* Member: Transport 1992–95, Home Affairs 1998–99. *Special Interests:* Defence, Home Affairs, Law and Order, Trade and Industry, Finance, Insurance, Financial Services, Environment, Transport, Education, Tourism, Sport, Small Businesses. *Countries of Interest:* Numerous. Vice-Chair, Rochford Constituency Conservative Association, Essex 1988–91; Bow Group 1990–92, Campaign Director 1991–92, Chair 1992–93. Area Chair, Business Support Group, Marie Curie Cancer Care 1991–97; Sponsor, Parliamentary Events, Association of Medical Research Charities; Founder Patron, Knight Foundation for Cystic Fibrosis; Supporter, Children with Special Needs Foundation; Hon. Major, Armed Forces Parliamentary Scheme 1997–98; Hon Lt Col 2001; Bar Association for Commerce, Finance and Industry: Chair International Committee 1989–92, Chair 1993–94; Member, International Practice Committee, Bar Council 1989–91; Co-Sponsor, Event for Coopers' Company 1999; *Publications:* Co-author *1992 – The Single Market in Insurance*, 1990; Author *Competitive Sport in Schools*, 1994; *Televising Sport – Responding to Debate*, 1996; *Bringing Order to the Law*, 1997; *Populist Conservatism*, 1998; Various articles on transport history and employment/legal matters; Eastern Area CPC Public Speaking Competition Winner 1990; *Sportsclubs:* Surrey CCC, Lords Taverners, MCC, Camberley RFC; *Recreations:* Cricket, theatre, music, other sports including swimming, rugby union, soccer. Nick Hawkins Esq, MP, House of Commons, London, SW1A 0AA *Tel:* 020 7219 6329 *Fax:* 020 7219 2693. *Constituency:* Curzon House, Church Road, Windlesham, Surrey, GU20 6BH *Tel:* 01252 372200 *Fax:* 01252 3772200.

HAYES, JOHN   South Holland and The Deepings   Con majority 11,099

John Henry Hayes. Born 23 June 1958; Son of late Henry John and Lily Hayes; Educated Colfe's Grammar School, London; Nottingham University (BA politics, PGCE history/English 1977–82); Married Susan Hopewell 1997 (1 son). IT company 1983–99, (director 1986–97, non-executive director 1997–99). Councillor, Nottinghamshire County Council 1985–98, Conservative Spokesperson for Education 1988–97, Former Chair, County Conservative Group's Campaigns Committee. **House of Commons:** Contested Derby North East 1987, 1992 general elections. Member for South Holland and The Deepings since May 1, 1997; Opposition Spokesperson for Education and Employment 2000–01; Opposition Pairing Whip 2001–02;

Shadow Minister for Agriculture 2002–; *Select Committees:* Member: Agriculture 1997–99, Education and Employment 1998–99, Education and Employment 1999–2000, Education Sub-Committee 1999–2000, Selection 2001–02, Administration 2001–02. *Special Interests:* Education, Elections and Campaigning, Political Ideas and Philosophy, Local Government, Agriculture, Commerce and Industry, Welfare of the Elderly and Disabled. *Countries of Interest:* England, Italy, USA, Spain. Former Chair Young Conservatives; Vice-chair, Conservatives Against Federal Europe; Vice-chair Conservative Party 1999–2000; Member 1992 Group. Countryside Member NFU; Countryside Alliance, SPUC; Patron Headway Cambridgeshire; *Publications: Representing Rural Britain – Blair's Bogus Claim,* Conservative Policy Forum 2000; *Answer the Question: Prime Ministerial Accountability and the Rule of Parliament,* Politeia 2000; *Tony B. Liar,* Conservative Party 2001; *Clubs:* Carlton, Spalding; *Recreations:* The arts, many sports, gardening, antiques, history, good food and wine. John Hayes Esq, MP, House of Commons, London, SW1A 0AA *Tel:* 020 7219 1389 *Fax:* 020 7219 2273. *Constituency:* 20 Station Street, Spalding, Lincolnshire, PE11 1EB *Tel:* 01775 713905 *Fax:* 01775 713905 *E-mail:* unterhaltera@parliament.uk.

HEAL, SYLVIA   Halesowen and Rowley Regis   *Lab majority 7,359*

Sylvia Lloyd Heal. Born 20 July 1942; Daughter of late John Lloyd Fox, steelworker, and Ruby Fox; Educated Elfed Secondary Modern School, Buckley, North Wales; Coleg Harlech, University College of Wales, Swansea (BSc Econ 1968); Married Keith Heal 1965 (1 son 1 daughter). Medical records clerk 1957–63; Social worker: Department of Employment 1968–70, National Health Service 1980–90; National officer, Carers National Association 1992–97; Member, GMB. JP. **House of Commons:** Member for Mid Staffordshire 1990 by-election–1992. Member for Halesowen and Rowley Regis since May 1, 1997; Shadow Minister of Health 1991–92; Deputy Shadow Minister for Women 1991–92; PPS to Secretaries of State for Defence: Lord Robertson of Port Ellen 1997–99, Geoffrey Hoon 1999–2000; First Deputy Chairman, Ways and Means and Deputy Speaker 2000–; *Select Committees:* Member, Education and Science 1990–91; First Deputy Chair of Ways and Means: Court of Referees 2000–, Unopposed Bills (Panel) 2000–; First Deputy Chairman of Ways and Means (ex officio): Chairmen's Panel 2000–, Standing Orders 2000–. *Special Interests:* Health Education, Equal Opportunities. Council Member, ASA 1992–97; Member: Action for South Africa (ACTSA); NATO Parliamentary Assembly 1997–2000; *Clubs:* London-Welsh Association, Rowley and Blackheath Labour Club, Halesowen Royal British Legion; *Recreations:* Walking, gardening, listening to male voice choirs. Mrs Sylvia Heal, MP, House of Commons, London, SW1A 0AA *Tel:* 020 7219 2317 *Fax:* 020 7219 0956. *Constituency:* Municipal Buildings, Barrs Road, Cradley Heath, West Midlands, B64 7JX *Tel:* 0121–569 4646 *Fax:* 0121–569 4647.

HEALD, OLIVER   North East Hertfordshire   *Con majority 3,444*

Oliver Heald. Born 15 December 1954; Son of late J A Heald, chartered engineer and Joyce Heald, née Pemberton, teacher; Educated Reading School; Pembroke College, Cambridge (MA law 1976); Married Christine Whittle 1979 (1 son 2 daughters). Barrister, Middle Temple 1977–. **House of Commons:** Contested Southwark and Bermondsey 1987 general election. Member for North Hertfordshire 1992–97, and for North East Hertfordshire since May 1, 1997; Opposition Spokesperson for: Home Affairs 2000–01, Health 2001–02; Opposition Whip 1997–2000; PPS: to Sir Peter Lloyd as Minister of State, Home Office 1994, to William Waldegrave as Minister of Agriculture, Fisheries and Food 1994–95; Parliamentary Under-Secretary of State, Department of Social Security 1995–97; Sponsored Private Member's Bill: Insurance Companies (Reserves) Act 1995; Shadow Minister for Work and Pensions 2002–; *Select Committees:* Member: Employment 1992–94, Administration 1998–2000. *Special Interests:* Industrial Relations, Environment, Law and Order, Pensions. Chair, North Hertfordshire Conservative Association 1984–86; Vice-President, Southwark and Bermondsey Conservative Association 1988–93, President 1993–98, Patron 1998–. *Recreations:* Sport, family. Oliver Heald Esq, MP, House of Commons, London, SW1A 0AA. *Tel (Constituency):* 01763 247640 *Fax (Constituency):* 01763 247640 *E-mail:* healdo@parliament.uk.

HEALEY, JOHN   Wentworth   *Lab majority 16,449*

John Healey. Born 13 February 1960; Son of Aidan Healey, prison service, and Jean Healey, teacher; Educated Lady Lumley's Comprehensive School, Pickering; St Peter's School, York; Christ's College, Cambridge (BA 1982); Married Jackie Bate 1993 (1 son). Journalist/deputy editor, *The House Magazine* 1983–84; Disability campaigner for three national charities 1984–90; Tutor, Open University Business School 1989–92; Campaigns manager, Issue Communications 1990–92; Head of communications, MSF Union 1992–94; Campaigns and communications director, TUC 1994–97; Member, GMB. **House of Commons:** Contested Ryedale 1992 general election. Member for Wentworth since May 1, 1997; PPS to Gordon Brown as Chancellor of the Exchequer 1999–2001; Parliamentary Under-Secretary of State for Adult Skills, Department for Education and Skills 2001–02; Economic Secretary, HM Treasury 2002–; *Select Committees:* Member: Education and Employment 1997–99, Employment Sub-Committee 1997–99. *Special Interests:* Employment, Trade Unions, Economic Regeneration, Industrial Relations, Disability, Local and Regional Government. *Recreations:* Family. John Healey Esq, MP, House of Commons, London, SW1A 0AA *Tel:* 020 7219 5170/2448 *Fax:* 020 7219 2451. *Constituency:* 79 High Street, Wath-upon-Deane, Rotherham, South Yorkshire, S63 7QB *Tel:* 01709 875943 *Fax:* 01709 874207 *E-mail:* healeyj@parliament.uk.

HEATH, DAVID   Somerton and Frome   *LD majority 668*

David William St John Heath. Born 16 March 1954; Son of Eric and Pamela Heath; Educated Millfield School, Street; St John's College, Oxford (MA physiological sciences 1976); City University (ophthalmic optics 1979); Married Caroline Netherton 1987 (1 son 1 daughter). Qualified optician in practice 1979–85; Parliamentary consultant, Worldwide Fund for Nature 1990–91; Consultant to various NGOs/Charities; Member, Audit Commission 1995–97. Councillor, Somerset County Council 1985–97, Leader of Council 1985–89; Chairman, Avon and Somerset Police Authority 1993–96. **House of Commons:** Contested Somerton and Frome 1992 general election. Member for Somerton and Frome since May 1, 1997; Spokesperson for: Foreign Affairs 1997–99, Agriculture, Rural Affairs and Fisheries 1999–2001, Work and Pensions 2001–02, Science 2001–, Lord Chancellor's Department 2002–, Home Office 2002–; *Select Committees:* Member: Foreign Affairs 1997–98, Foreign Affairs 1997–99, Entry Clearance Sub-Committee 1998; Member: Science and Technology 2001–, Standards and Privileges 2001–. *Special Interests:* Education, Local and Regional Government, Rural Affairs, Environment, Home Affairs. *Countries of Interest:* Europe, France, Balkans. Member: Liberal Party National Executive 1988–89, Liberal Democrats Federal Executive 1990–92, 1993–95. Member, Witham Friary Friendly Society; Vice-Chair: Association of County Councils 1994–97, Committee of Local Police Authorities 1993–97; Member, Audit Commission 1994–97; Member: Council of Local Authorities and Regions of Europe 1993–97, Parliamentary Assembly of the Organisation for Security and Co-operation in Europe (OSCE) 1997–; CBE 1989; FRSA; FADO; *Clubs:* National Liberal; *Recreations:* Cricket, rugby football, until recently pig breeding. David Heath Esq, CBE, MP, House of Commons, SW1A 0AA *Tel:* 020 7219 6245 *Fax:* 020 7219 5939. *Constituency:* 14 Catherine Hill, Frome, Somerset, BA11 1BZ *Tel:* 01373 473618 *Fax:* 01373 455152 *E-mail:* davidheath@davidheath.co.uk.

HEATHCOAT-AMORY, DAVID   Wells   *Con majority 2,796*

David Heathcoat-Amory. Born 21 March 1949; Son of late Brigadier Roderick Heathcoat-Amory, MC; Educated Eton College; Christ Church College, Oxford (MA philosophy, politics and economics); Married Linda Adams 1978 (2 sons, 1 deceased 1 daughter). Qualified as chartered accountant 1974; Assistant finance director, British Technology Group 1980–83. **House of Commons:** Contested Brent South 1979 general election. Member for Wells since June 1983; Assistant Government Whip 1988–89; Government Whip July-October 1989; Deputy Chief Whip 1992–93; PPS: to Norman Lamont as Financial Secretary to the Treasury 1985–87, to Douglas Hurd as Home Secretary 1987–88; Parliamentary Under-Secretary of State: at Department of

Environment 1989–90, at Department of Energy 1990–92; Minister of State, Foreign and Commonwealth Office 1993–94; Paymaster General 1994–96; Member, Shadow Cabinet 1997–2001; Shadow Chief Secretary to the Treasury 1997–2000; Shadow Secretary of State for Trade and Industry 2000–01; Parliamentary representative European Union Convention 2002–; *Select Committees:* Member: Broadcasting 1992–93, Finance and Services 1992–93. *Special Interests:* Industrial Policy, Agriculture, Forestry, Arms Control, Energy, European Union. Treasurer, West Country Group of Conservative MPs 1983–85. PC 1996; FCA 1980; *Recreations:* Fishing, shooting, music. Rt Hon David Heathcoat-Amory, MP, House of Commons, London, SW1A 0AA *Tel:* 020 7219 3543. *Constituency:* Priory Lodge, 7 Priory Road, Wells, Somerset, BA5 1SR *Tel:* 01749 673146 *Fax:* 01749 670783.

HENDERSON, DOUG   Newcastle upon Tyne North   Lab majority 14,450

Douglas Henderson. Born 9 June 1949; Son of John Henderson, railwayman, and Joy Henderson; Educated Waid Academy, Fife; Central College, Glasgow (economics); Strathclyde University, Glasgow (economics 1973); Married Janet Graham 1974 (divorced) (1 son 1 daughter); married Geraldine Daly 2002. Apprentice, Rolls-Royce, Glasgow 1966–68; British Rail clerk, London 1969–70; Research officer GMWU, Glasgow 1973; Scottish organiser GMB 1975–85, Organiser Newcastle 1985–87. **House of Commons:** Member for Newcastle upon Tyne North since June 1987; Opposition Spokesperson on: Trade and Industry 1988–92, The Environment (Local Government) 1992–94, Citizen's Charter 1994–95, Home Affairs 1995–97; Minister of State (Europe), Foreign and Commonwealth Office 1997–98; Minister of State for the Armed Forces, Ministry of Defence 1998–99; *Special Interests:* Economic Policy, Industrial Policy, Employment, IT Industry. *Countries of Interest:* former Soviet Union, USA, Middle East. *Clubs:* Lemington Labour, Newburn Memorial, Dinnington; *Sportsclubs:* Elswick Harriers, Cambuslang Harriers; *Recreations:* Athletics, mountaineering, cross-country skiing. Douglas Henderson Esq, MP, House of Commons, London, SW1A 0AA *Tel:* 020 7219 5017. *Constituency Tel:* 0191–286 2024 *E-mail:* douglas@newcastle-north-clp.new.labour.org.uk.

HENDERSON, IVAN   Harwich   Lab majority 2,596

Ivan Henderson. Born 7 June 1958; Stepson of late Michael Bloice, son of Margaret Bloice; Educated Sir Anthony Deane Comprehensive; Trade Union Courses – Political/Health and Safety; Married 1st (1 son 1 daughter); married Jo'Anne Atkinson 1992. Former Dock Operative, Harwich International Port; Union organiser, Docks; Member, T&GWU (formerly NUR/RMT): Shop steward 1984, Executive officer 1991–94, Member, Political and Transport Committee, Former President, RMT Anglia District Council. Councillor: Harwich Town Council 1986–97, Tendring District Council 1995–97. **House of Commons:** Member for Harwich since May 1, 1997; PPS to: Keith Bradley as Minister of State, Home Office 2001–02, Lord Rooker as Minister of State, Office of the Deputy Prime Minister 2002–, Andrew Smith as Secretary of State for Work and Pensions 2003–; *Select Committees:* Member, Joint Committee on Statutory Instruments 1999–2002. *Special Interests:* Transport, Employment, Health, Shipping, Animal Welfare. Member: Young Socialists, Executive Member, Harwich Constituency Labour Party; Member, Co-operative Party. President, Clacton and District Chamber of Trade & Commerce; Hon Membership, Harwich Royal Navy Association; Member: Trade's Council – Harwich Hospital Review Committee, European Standing Committee C 1999–; Worked with International Transport Federation; European Works Council; *Sportsclubs:* Harwich and Parkeston Football Club; Vice-President: Harwich and Dovercourt Cricket Club, Clacton Cricket Club; *Recreations:* Football, golf. Ivan Henderson Esq, MP, House of Commons, London, SW1A 0AA *Tel:* 020 7219 3434 *Fax:* 020 7219 3434. *Constituency:* Kingsway House, 21 Kingsway, Dovercourt, Essex, CO12 3AB *Tel:* 01255 552859 *Fax:* 01255 556771 *E-mail:* hendersoni@parliament.uk.

Visit the Vacher Dod Website . . .
www.DodOnline.co.uk

HENDRICK, MARK   Preston   *Lab majority 12,268*

Mark Phillip Hendrick. Born 2 November 1958; Son of Brian Francis Hendrick, timber worker, and Jennifer, née Chapman, clerk/typist; Educated Salford Grammar School; Liverpool Polytechnic (BSc electrical and electronic engineering 1982); Manchester University (MSc computer science 1985, CertEd 1992); Volkshochschule, Hanau, Germany ('Zertifikat Deutsch als Fremdsprache'); Single. Student engineer Ministry of Defence 1979; Werk student AEG Telefunken 1981; Science and Engineering Research Council 1982–84, 1985–88; Lecturer in electronics and software design, Stockport college 1990–94; MEP Lancashire Central 1994–99: Member Economic and Monetary Affairs and Industrial Policy committee 1994–99; Substitute: Foreign Affairs, Security and Defence Policy committee 1994–97, Member European Parliamentary Committee for Relations with Japan 1994–99; Environment, Public Health and Consumer Protection committee 1997–99; Member GMB. Councillor Salford City Council 1987–95; Representative Salford City Council as an alternate director Manchester Airport plc 1987–94; Vice-chair: planning committee 1987–94, management services committee 1990–94, policy committee 1992–94, education committee 1992–94; Hon vice-president Central and West Lancashire chamber of commerce and industry 1994–96, 2001–. **House of Commons:** Member for Preston since November 23, 2000; PPS to Margaret Beckett as Secretary of State for Environment, Food and Rural Affairs 2003–; *Select Committees:* Member, European Scrutiny 2001–. *Special Interests:* Foreign Affairs, Defence, European Affairs, Economic and Industrial Affairs, International Development. *Countries of Interest:* USA, Japan, Germany, Poland, Hungary. Branch secretary, Salford Co-operative Party 1984–94; Chair Eccles constituency Labour party 1990–94; Member, Preston and District Co-operative Party 1994–. *Publications: The euro and Co-operative Enterprise: Co-operating with the euro,* Co-operative Press Ltd 1998; *Changing States: A Labour Agenda for Europe,* Mandarin Paperbacks 1996; CEng; MIEE; Chartered Electrical Engineer; *Clubs:* Deepdale Labour; *Sportsclubs:* Penwortham Sports and Social; *Recreations:* football, boxing, chess. Mark Hendrick Esq, MP, House of Commons, London, SW1A 0AA *Tel:* 020 7219 4791 *Fax:* 020 7219 5220. *Constituency:* 6 Sedgwick Street, Preston, Lancashire, PR1 1TP *Tel:* 01772 883575 *Fax:* 01772 887188 *E-mail:* hendrickm@parliament.uk.

HENDRY, CHARLES   Wealden   *Con majority 13,772*

Charles Hendry. Born 6 May 1959; Educated Rugby School; Edinburgh University (BCom business studies 1981); Married Sallie Moores, née Smith 1995 (2 sons 1 stepson 1 stepdaughter). Account director Ogilvy and Mather PR 1982–88; Special adviser to: John Moore as Secretary of State for Social Services 1988, Antony Newton at Departments of Social Security and Trade and Industry 1988–90; at Burson-Marsteller: Senior counsellor public affairs 1990–92, Associate director public relations; Chief executive Agenda Group 1999–2001; Agenda Group: Chief executive 1999–01, Non-executive chair 2001–. **House of Commons:** Contested Clackmannan 1983, Mansfield 1987 general elections. Member for High Peak 1992–1997. Contested High Peak 1997 general election. Member for Wealden since June 7, 2001; Opposition Whip 2001–02; PPS: to William Hague and Lord Mackay of Ardbrecknish as Ministers of State, Department of Social Security 1994–95, to Gillian Shephard as Secretary of State for Education and Employment 1995; Vice-chair Conservative Party 1995–97; Shadow Minister for Young People 2002–; *Select Committees:* Member: Procedure 1992–95, Northern Ireland Affairs 1994–97. *Special Interests:* Trade and Industry, Youth Policy, Training, Urban Regeneration, Social Affairs, Housing, Homelessness, Rural Affairs, Agriculture. *Countries of Interest:* USA, Europe, Southern Africa. President Edinburgh University Conservative Association 1979–80; Vice-chair: Scottish Federation of Conservative Students 1980–81, Battersea Conservative Association 1981–83; Chief of staff Leader of Opposition 1997; Head of Business liaison, Conservative Party 1997–99. President British Youth Council 1992–97; Development board member Tusk Force 1992–98; Patron The Big Issue Foundation 1995–; Member European Standing Committee B 1992–95; Joint honorary president British Youth Council 1992–; Trustee: Drive for Youth 1989–98, UK Youth Parliament 2002–, Resources for Autism; *Recreations:* Tennis, skiing, family, opera, rugby, travel. Charles Hendry Esq, MP, House of Commons, London, SW1A 0AA *Tel:* 020 7219 8333. *Constituency:* Wealden Conservative Association, The Granary, Bales Green Farm, Arlington, East Sussex, BN27 6SH *Tel:* 01323 489289 *E-mail:* hendryc@parliament.uk.

HEPBURN, STEPHEN   Jarrow   *Lab majority 17,595*

Stephen Hepburn. Born 6 December 1959; Son of Peter and Margaret Hepburn; Educated Springfield Comprehensive, Jarrow; Newcastle University (BA). Labourer, South Tyneside Metropolitan Borough Council; Research assistant to Don Dixon MP; Member, UCATT. Councillor, South Tyneside Council 1985–, Deputy Leader 1990–97; Chair, Tyne & Wear Pensions 1989–97. **House of Commons:** Member for Jarrow since May 1, 1997; Government representative on football 2002–; *Select Committees:* Member: Administration 1997–2001, Defence 1999–2001. *Special Interests:* Small Businesses. *Clubs:* Neon CIU, Jarrow, Iona Catholic Club, Hebburn; *Sportsclubs:* President, Jarrow FC, Patron, Jarrow Roofing FC; *Recreations:* Soccer, music, art. Stephen Hepburn Esq, MP, House of Commons, London, SW1A 0AA *Tel:* 020 7219 4134. *Constituency:* 136/137 Tedlo Business Centre, Jarrow, Tyne and Wear, NE32 3DT *Tel:* 0191–420 0648 *Fax:* 0191–489 7531 *E-mail:* hepburns@parliament.uk.

HEPPELL, JOHN   Nottingham East   *Lab majority 10,320*

John Heppell. Born 3 November 1948; Son of late Robert Heppell, miner, and late Helen Heppell; Educated Rutherford Grammar School; South East Northumberland Technical College; Ashington Technical College; Married Eileen Golding 1974 (2 sons 1 daughter). Fitter: NCB 1964–70 and for number of firms in Nottingham area 1970–75; British Rail: Diesel fitter 1975–78, Workshop supervisor 1978–89; GMB. Councillor, Nottinghamshire County Council 1981–93; Assistant Whip 1982; Vice-Chair, Environment Committee 1983; Chair: East Midlands Airport 1985, Resources Committee 1986, Deputy Leader, Nottinghamshire County Council 1989–92; Former Chair, Equal Opportunities Committee; Former Chair, Greater Nottingham LRT Board; Former Vice-Chair, Policy Committee. **House of Commons:** Member for Nottingham East since April 9, 1992; Government Whip 2001–; PPS to: Lord Richard as Lord Privy Seal and Leader of the House of Lords 1997–98, John Prescott as Deputy Prime Minister and Secretary of State for the Environment, Transport and the Regions 1998–2001; *Select Committees:* Member, Selection 2001–. *Special Interests:* Equal Opportunities, Transport, Local and Regional Government. *Countries of Interest:* India, Pakistan, Cyprus. *Recreations:* Walking, reading, swimming, birdwatching. John Heppell Esq, MP, House of Commons, London, SW1A 0AA *Tel:* 020 7219 4095 *Fax:* 020 7219 2969. *Constituency:* 9 Trinity Square, Nottingham, NG1 4AF *Tel:* 0115–947 4132 *Fax:* 0115–947 2029 *E-mail:* tanvirj@parliament.uk.

HERMON, SYLVIA   North Down   *UUP majority 7,324*

Sylvia Hermon. Born 11 August 1955; Robert and Mary Paisley; Educated Dungannon High School for Girls; Aberstwyth University, Wales (law 1977); Part II Solicitors' Qualifying Examinations 1978; Married Sir John Hermon OBE QPM 1988 (2 sons). Lecturer European, international and constitutional law Queen's University, Belfast 1978–88. **House of Commons:** Member for North Down since June 7, 2001; UUP Spokesperson for: Home Affairs 2001–, Trade and Industry 2001–02, Youth and Women's Issues 2001–, Culture, Media and Sport 2002–; *Special Interests:* Policing, Human Rights, European Affairs, Health, Education. Author and committee member addressing Patten Report Criminal Justice Review 2000; Ulster Unionist Executive 1999; Constituency chair North Down Unionist Constituency Association 2001–. Chair North Down Support Group Marie Curie Cancer Care 1998–; Member Friends of Bangor Community Hospital 2000–; *Publications: A Guide to EEC Law in Northern Ireland*, SLS Legal Publications (NI) 1986; *Recreations:* Fitness training, swimming, ornithology, letter writing, proof reading. Lady Hermon, MP, House of Commons, London, SW1A 0AA *Tel:* 020 7219 8491 *Fax:* 020 7219 1969. *Constituency:* 17a Hamilton Road, Bangor, BT20 4LF *Tel:* 028 9127 5858 *Fax:* 028 9127 5747 *E-mail:* jamisons@parliament.uk.

HESFORD, STEPHEN   Wirral West
Lab majority 4,035

Stephen Hesford. Born 27 May 1957; Son of Bernard and Nellie Hesford; Educated Urmston Grammar School; Bradford University (BSc social science 1978); Central London Polytechnic (LLM 1980); Married Elizabeth Anne Henshall 1984 (2 sons). Barrister 1981–97; Assistant to Joan Lestor, MP 1992–93; Branch Equal Opportunities Officer, GMB. Vice-Chair, North Manchester Community Health Council. **House of Commons:** Contested Suffolk South 1992 general election. Member for Wirral West since May 1, 1997; *Select Committees:* Member: Deregulation 1997–98, Northern Ireland Affairs 1998–99, Health 1999–2001. *Special Interests:* Economic Policy, Health, Social Services, Pensions, Education, Small Businesses. *Countries of Interest:* France. Member, Fabian Society; NEC Member, Socialist Health Association. Member: Greenpeace, Amnesty International, Child Poverty Action Group; Member, European Standing Committee C 1999–; Fellow: Royal Institue of Public Health and Hygiene, Society of Public Health; *Sportsclubs:* Life Member, Lancashire Cricket Club; *Recreations:* Sport, music, reading. Stephen Hesford Esq, MP, House of Commons, London, SW1A 0AA *Tel:* 020 7219 6227 *Fax:* 020 7219 4953. *Constituency:* 140 Ford Road, Upton, Wirral, Merseyside, CH49 0TQ *Tel:* 0151–522 0531 *Fax:* 0151–522 0558 *E-mail:* hesfords@parliament.uk.

HEWITT, PATRICIA   Leicester West
Lab majority 9,639

Patricia Hope Hewitt. Born 2 December 1948; Daughter of Sir Lenox Hewitt, OBE and Lady Hope Hewitt; Educated Canberra Girls' Grammar School; Newnham College, Cambridge (BA English literature 1970); Married William Jack Birtles 1981 (1 son 1 daughter). Public relations officer, Age Concern 1971–73; National Council for Civil Liberties: Women's rights officer 1973–74, General Secretary 1974–83; To Neil Kinnock as Leader of the Opposition: Press secretary 1983–87, Policy co-ordinator 1987–89; Deputy director, Institute for Public Policy Research 1989–94; Director of research, Andersen Consulting (now Accenture) 1994–97; Member: MSF, TGWU. Chair, Council for Science and Technology. **House of Commons:** Contested Leicester East 1983 general election. Member for Leicester West since May 1, 1997; Economic Secretary, HM Treasury 1998–99; Minister of State, Department of Trade and Industry (Minister for Small Business and E-Commerce) 1999–2001; Secretary of State for Trade and Industry, Minister for Women and Equality and e-Minister in Cabinet 2001–; *Select Committees:* Member: Social Security 1997–98, Social Security 1998. *Special Interests:* Social Security, Employment, Family Policy, Information Technology. *Countries of Interest:* Australia, South Africa, India. Member: Labour Women's Advisory Committee 1976–82, Labour Campaign for Social Justice, Fabian Society. Governor, Kentish Town Primary School 1993–96; Member: CPAG, Liberty; Member, Secretary of State's Advisory Committee on the Employment of Women 1976–83; Vice-Chair: Commission on Social Justice 1992–94, British Council Board 1997–98; Advisory Board, International Human Rights League; Trustee, Institute for Public Policy Research 1995–98; *Publications:* Numerous, including books, pamphlets and articles for academic, specialist and popular journals. Also regular contributor on radio and television programmes; Visiting fellow, Nuffield College, Oxford; PC 2001; Fellow, Royal Society for the Arts; *Recreations:* Gardening, music, theatre. Rt Hon Patricia Hewitt, MP, House of Commons, London, SW1A 0AA. *Constituency:* Janner House, Woodgate, Leicester, LE3 5GH *Tel:* 0116–251 6160 *Fax:* 0116–251 0482 *E-mail:* hewittph@parliament.uk.

DodOnline
An Electronic Directory without rival . . .

MPs' biographies and photographs available with daily updates *via* the internet

For a *free* trial, call Yasmin Mirza, Aby Farsoun or Michael Mand on 020 7630 7643

HEYES, DAVID   Ashton under Lyne   Lab majority 15,518

David Alan Heyes. Born 2 April 1946; Son of Harold Heyes, police officer and Lilian Heyes, née Crowe; Educated Blackley Technical High School, Manchester; Open University (BA social sciences 1987); Married Judith Egerton-Gallagher 1968 (1 son 1 daughter). Local Government Officer Manchester City Council 1962–74; Greater Manchester Council 1974–86, Oldham Metropolitan Borough Council 1987–90; Self-employed Computer graphics 1990–95; Development worker, Voluntary Action Manchester 1993–95; Deputy district manager Manchester Citizens Advice Bureau service 1995–2001; Member UNISON (formerly NALGO) 1962–. Oldham Metropolitan Borough Council: Councillor 1992–, Labour Group Secretary 1993–2000, Chair Personnel Committee 1994–2000, Vice-chair Policy Committee 1999–2000. **House of Commons:** Member for Ashton-Under-Lyne since June 7, 2001; *Select Committees:* Member, Public Administration 2001–. *Special Interests:* Social Exclusion, Health, Education, Work and Pensions, Local and Regional Government. David Heyes Esq, MP, House of Commons, London, SW1A 0AA *Tel:* 020 7219 8129 *Fax:* 020 7219 1738. *Constituency:* St. Michael's Court, St. Michael's Square, Stamford Street, Ashton-Under-Lyne, OL6 6XN *Tel:* 0161–331 9307 *Fax:* 0161–330 9420 *E-mail:* heyesd@parliament.uk.

HILL, KEITH   Streatham   Lab majority 14,270

(Trevor) Keith Hill. Born 28 July 1943; Son of Ernest Hill, printer, and Ida Hill, textile machine operative; Educated City of Leicester Boys' Grammar School; Corpus Christi College, Oxford (MA philosophy, politics and economics 1965); University College of Wales, Aberystwyth (DipEd (Wales) 1966); Married Lesley Ann Sheppard 1972. Research assistant in politics, Leicester University 1966–68; Belgian government scholar, Brussels 1968–69; Lecturer in politics, Strathclyde University 1969–73; Research officer, Labour Party International Department 1974–76; Political Liaison Officer National Union of Rail, Maritime and Transport Workers (formerly NUR) 1976–92. **House of Commons:** Contested Blaby 1979 general election. Member for Streatham since April 9, 1992; Assistant Government Whip 1998–99; Deputy Chief Whip (Treasurer of HM Household) 2001–03; PPS to Hilary Armstrong, as Minister of State (Minister for Local Government and Housing) 1997–98, Parliamentary Under-Secretary of State, Department of Environment, Transport and the Regions 1999–2001; Minister of State for Housing and Planning, Office of the Deputy Prime Minister 2003–; *Select Committees:* Member: Transport 1992–97, Accommodation and Works 2001–03, Selection 2001–03; Member, Finance and Services 2001–. *Special Interests:* Transport, European Union, Environment. *Countries of Interest:* Europe, Africa. London Campaigner, Leadership Campaigns Team 1995; *Publications: Belgium* in *European Political Parties* 1969; *Belgium: Political Change in A Segmented Society* in *Electoral Behaviour* 1974; PC 2003; *Recreations:* Walking, books, films, music. Rt Hon Keith Hill, MP, House of Commons, London, SW1A 0AA *Tel:* 020 7219 6980 *Fax:* 020 7219 2565 *E-mail:* hillk@parliament.uk.

HINCHLIFFE, DAVID   Wakefield   Lab majority 7,954

David Martin Hinchliffe. Born 14 October 1948; Son of late Robert Hinchliffe, leading railman, and late Muriel Hinchliffe; Educated Cathedral Secondary School, Wakefield; Wakefield Technical College; Leeds Polytechnic (CQSW 1971); Bradford University (MA social work and community work 1978); Cert Ed; Married Julia North 1982 (1 son 1 daughter). Social worker, Leeds 1968–79; Social work tutor, Kirklees MDC 1980–87; Member UNISON. Councillor: Wakefield City Council 1971–74, Wakefield Metropolitan District Council 1979–88. **House of Commons:** Member for Wakefield since June 1987; Opposition Front Bench Spokesman on Health (Shadow Minister for Personal Social Services and Community Care) 1992–95; Adviser on Rugby League to Richard Caborn, as Minister of State for Sport 2002–; *Select Committees:* Member, Health 1990–92; Chair, Health 1997–; Member, Liaison 1997–. *Special Interests:* NHS, Social Services. *Publications: Rugby's Class War* (London League Publications) 2000; *A Westminster XIII* (London League Publications) 2002; *Sportsclubs:* Vice-President, Wakefield Trinity RLFC; *Recreations:* Rugby League, researching family history, inland waterways. David Hinchliffe Esq, MP, House of Commons, London, SW1A 0AA *Tel:* 020 7219 3000.

HOBAN, MARK   Fareham   *Con majority 7,009*

Mark Hoban. Born 31 March 1964; Son of Tom Hoban, general manager and Maureen Hoban, née Orchard, housewife; Educated St Leonards RC Comprehensive School, Durham; London School of Economics (BSc Econ 1985); Married Fiona Jane Barrett 1994. Pricewaterhouse Coopers 1985–: Chartered accountant, Manager 1990–92, Senior manager 1992–. **House of Commons:** Contested South Shields 1997 general election. Member for Fareham since June 7, 2001; Opposition Whip 2002–; *Select Committees:* Member, Science and Technology 2001–03. *Special Interests:* Economy, Trade and Industry, Education, Health. General election campaign manager 1987, 1992; Southampton Itchen Conservative Association: Treasurer 1989–91, Political vice-chair 1991–93; Finance officer Itchen, Test and Avon European Constituency Council 1993–95. Member: European Standing Committee A 2001–, European Standing Committee B 2001–03; Associate of Institute of Chartered Accountants of England and Wales 1988; *Recreations:* Cooking, reading, travel, entertaining. Mark Hoban Esq, MP, House of Commons, London, SW1A 0AA *Tel:* 020 7219 8228. *Constituency:* 14 East Street, Fareham, Hampshire, PO16 0BN *Tel:* 01329 233573 *Fax:* 01329 234197 *E-mail:* hobanm@parliament.co.uk.

HODGE, MARGARET   Barking   *Lab majority 9,534*

Margaret Eve Hodge. Born 8 September 1944; Daughter of Hans and Lisbeth Oppenheimer; Educated Bromley High School; Oxford High School; London School of Economics (BSc economics 1966); Married Andrew Watson 1968 (divorced 1978) (1 son 1 daughter); married Henry Hodge OBE 1978 (2 daughters). Teaching and market research 1966–73; Senior consultant, Price Waterhouse 1992–94; Member, TGWU. Councillor, London Borough of Islington 1973–94, Chair, Housing Committee 1975–79, Deputy Leader of Council 1981–82, Leader 1982–92. **House of Commons:** Member for Barking since June 9, 1994 by-election; Parliamentary Under-Secretary of State (Employment and Equal Opportunities), Department for Education and Employment 1998–2001; Department for Education and Skills 2001–: Minister of State for: Lifelong Learning and Higher Education 2001–03, Lifelong Learning, Further and Higher Education 2003, Children 2003–; *Select Committees:* Member: Deregulation 1996–97, Education and Employment 1996–97; Chair, Education Sub-Committee 1997–98; Chair (Education): Education and Employment 1997–98, Education Sub-Committee 1997–98; Joint Chair, Education and Employment 1997–98; Member: Employment Sub-Committee 1997–98, Liaison 1997–98. *Special Interests:* Education, Local and Regional Government, Housing, Inner Cities, Democratic Reform, London Government. Member, Labour Party Local Government Committee 1983–92; Chair: London Group of Labour MPs 1995–98, Fabians 1997–98. Member, Home Office Advisory Committee on Race Relations 1988–92; Director: University College, Middlesex Hospitals; Governor, London School of Economics 1990–2001; Chair, Association of London Authorities 1984–92; Vice-Chair, AMA 1991–92; *Publications: Quality, Equality and Democracy*; *Beyond the Town Hall*; Fabian pamphlet on London Government, *Not Just the Flower Show*; Contributed chapters to a number of books as well as articles in numerous journals and newspapers; MBE 1978; PC 2003; Hon. Fellow, University of North London; Hon. DCL, City 1993; *Recreations:* Family, opera, piano, travel, cooking. Rt Hon Margaret Hodge, MBE, MP, House of Commons, London, SW1A 0AA *Tel:* 020 7219 6666. *Constituency Tel:* 020 8594 1333 *Fax:* 020 8594 1131 *E-mail:* haywoodmw@parliament.uk.

DodOnline
An Electronic Directory without rival . . .

MPs' biographies and photographs available with daily updates *via* the internet

For a *free* trial, call Yasmin Mirza, Aby Farsoun or Michael Mand on 020 7630 7643

HOEY, KATE Vauxhall
Lab majority 13,018

Kate (Catharine) Letitia Hoey. Born 21 June 1946; Daughter of Thomas and Letitia Hoey; Educated Belfast Royal Academy; Ulster College of Physical Education (teaching diploma 1964); City of London College, London (BSc economics 1968); Single. Senior lecturer, Kingsway College 1976–85; Educational adviser to Arsenal Football Club 1985–89; Member, GMB. Councillor: Hackney Borough Council 1978–82, Southwark Borough Council 1988–89. **House of Commons:** Contested Dulwich 1983 and 1987 general elections. Member for Vauxhall since June 15, 1989 by-election; Member, Opposition team on Citizen's Charter and Women 1992–93; PPS to Frank Field as Minister of State, Department of Social Security 1997–98; Parliamentary Under-Secretary of State: Home Office (Metropolitan Police, European Union, Judicial Co-operation) 1998–99, Department for Culture, Media and Sport (Minister for Sport) 1999–2001; *Select Committees:* Member: Broadcasting 1991–97, Social Security 1994–97. *Special Interests:* Countryside, Sport, Foreign Affairs, Housing. *Countries of Interest:* Angola, Bosnia, Oman. *Publications:* Occasional articles on sport in the press; *The Spectator*/Highland Park Debater of the Year Award 1998; University of Ulster Distinguished Graduate 2000; *Sportsclubs:* Hon Vice-President Surrey County Cricket Club. Kate Hoey, MP, House of Commons, London, SW1A 0AA *Tel:* 020 7219 5989 *Fax:* 020 7219 5985.

HOGG, DOUGLAS Sleaford and North Hykeham
Con majority 8,622

Douglas Martin Hogg. Born 5 February 1945; Son of late Baron Hailsham of St Marylebone, former Lord Chancellor; Educated Eton College; Christ Church, Oxford (MA history 1968) (President, Oxford Union 1966); Married Hon. Sarah Boyd-Carpenter (cr. Baroness Hogg, 1995) 1968 (*qv*) (1 son 1 daughter). Called to the Bar, Lincoln's Inn 1968 (Kennedy Law Scholar); QC 1990. **House of Commons:** Member for Grantham 1979–97, and for Sleaford and North Hykeham since May 1, 1997; Government Whip 1983–84; PPS to Leon Brittan Chief as Secretary to the Treasury 1982–83; Parliamentary Under-Secretary, Home Office 1986–89; Minister of State at: Department of Trade and Industry (Minister for Industry and Enterprise) 1989–90, Foreign and Commonwealth Office 1990–95; Minister of Agriculture, Fisheries and Food 1995–97; *Select Committees:* Member, Home Affairs 1997–98. QC 1990; PC 1992. Rt Hon Douglas Hogg QC, MP (Viscount Hailsham), House of Commons, London, SW1A 0AA *Tel:* 020 7219 3444 *Fax:* 020 7219 4123. *Constituency:* Sleaford and North Hykeham Conservative Association, 6 Market Place, Sleaford, Lincolnshire, NG34 7SD *Tel:* 01529 419000 *Fax:* 01529 419019 *E-mail:* hoggd@parliament.uk; edwardsa@parliament.uk.

HOLMES, PAUL Chesterfield
LD majority 2,586

Paul Holmes. Born 16 January 1957; Son of Frank Holmes, plumber, and Dorothy, née Uttley, cutlery worker; Educated Firth Park School, Sheffield; York University (BA history 1978); Sheffield University (PGCE 1979); Married Raelene Palmer 1978 (2 daughters 1 son). History teacher Chesterfield 1979–84; Head of department Buxton 1984–90; Head of sixth form Buxton 1988–2000; Union Rep ATL 1989–99; NASUWT 1999–2001. Councillor Chesterfield Borough Council 1987–95, 1999–2003; Vice-president LGA 2001–. **House of Commons:** Member for Chesterfield since June 7, 2001, Liberal Democrat Spokesperson for Disability Issues 2001–02, Disability Issues and Work and Pensions 2002–; *Select Committees:* Member, Education and Skills 2001–. *Special Interests:* Education, Health, Pensions, Law and Order, Human Rights, Constitutional Reform, International Affairs. *Countries of Interest:* Laos, Thailand, France, New Zealand, Ireland. Campaigner Local party; Election agent and organiser Tony Rogers 1992, 1997; Agent: Euro election 1994, Numerous Council elections. Chair Walton and West Community Forum, Chesterfield 2000–01; Member: Amnesty International, National Trust; Working with UNICEF on Campaign Against Child Exploitation; *Recreations:* Running (marathon), history, reading, archaeology. Paul Holmes Esq, MP, House of Commons, London, SW1A 0AA *Tel:* 020 7219 8158 *Fax:* 020 7219 1754. *Constituency:* 69 West Gardens, Chesterfield, Derbyshire, S40 1BA *Tel:* 01246 234879 *Fax:* 01246 206333 *E-mail:* holmesr@parliament.uk.

HOOD, JIMMY   Clydesdale   *Lab majority 7,794*

James Hood. Born 16 May 1948; Son of William Hood, retired miner, and Bridget Hood (deceased); Educated Lesmahagow Higher Grade School, Coatbridge; Nottingham University; Married Marion Stewart McCleary 1967 (1 son 1 daughter). Mining engineer 1964–87; Member, NUM 1964–: Official 1973–87, Leader of Nottinghamshire striking miners in 1984–85 national miners' strike; Member, AEEU 1996–. Councillor, Newark and Sherwood District Council 1979–87. **House of Commons:** Member for Clydesdale since June 1987; *Select Committees:* Member, European Legislation 1987–97; Chair, European Legislation 1992–98; Member: Liaison 1992–97, Defence 1997–2001; Member: Chairmen's Panel 1997–, Liaison 1997–; Chair, European Scrutiny 1998–. *Special Interests:* NHS, Home Affairs, Agriculture, Environment, Energy, Housing, Education, Alcohol Abuse and Under-age Drinking, European Union, Defence. Member Scottish Parliamentary Group of Labour MPs; Member, Co-operative Party. Fellow, Industry and Parliament Trust; Armed Forces Parliamentary Scheme; *Clubs:* Lesmahagow Miners; *Recreations:* Gardening, reading, writing. James Hood Esq, MP, House of Commons, London, SW1A 0AA *Tel:* 020 7219 4585 *Fax:* 020 7219 5872. *Constituency:* c/o Council Offices, South Vennel, Lanark, ML11 7JT *Tel:* 01555 673177 *Fax:* 01555 673188 *E-mail:* hoodj@parliament.uk.

HOON, GEOFFREY   Ashfield   *Lab majority 13,268*

Geoff (Geoffrey) William Hoon. Born 6 December 1953; Son of Ernest and June Hoon; Educated Nottingham High School; Jesus College, Cambridge (BA law 1976, MA); Married Elaine Ann Dumelow 1981 (1 son 2 daughters). Lecturer in law, Leeds University 1976–82; Visiting professor of law, University of Louisville, USA 1980–81; Practising barrister 1982–84; MEP for Derbyshire 1984–94; Member TGWU. **House of Commons:** Member for Ashfield since April 9, 1992; Opposition Spokesperson for Trade and Industry 1995–97; Opposition Whip 1994–95; Lord Chancellor's Department: Parliamentary Secretary 1997–98, Minister of State 1998–99; Minister of State, Foreign and Commonwealth Office 1999; Secretary of State for Defence 1999–; *Special Interests:* Economic Policy, European Union, Constitution, Defence. *Countries of Interest:* Europe, USA, Far East. Chair, European Parliament Delegation for relations with: China 1986–89, United States 1989–93; PC 1999; *Recreations:* Sport, football and running, cinema, music. Rt Hon Geoff Hoon, MP, House of Commons, London, SW1A 0AA *Tel:* 020 7219 3477 *Fax:* 020 7219 2428. *Constituency:* 8 Station Street, Kirkby-in-Ashfield, Nottinghamshire, NG17 7AR *Tel:* 01623 720399 *Fax:* 01623 720398 *E-mail:* public@ministers.mod.uk.

HOPE, PHIL   Corby   *Lab majority 5,700*

Phil (Philip) Ian Hope. Born 19 April 1955; Son of A. G. (Bob) Hope, former police commander, and Grace Hope; Educated Wandsworth Comprehensive, London; St Luke's College, Exeter University (BEd 1978); Married Allison Butt 1980 (1 son 1 daughter). Secondary school science teacher, Kettering School for Boys 1978–79; Youth policy adviser, National Council for Voluntary Organisations 1979–82; Head, Young Volunteer Resources Unit, National Youth Bureau 1982–85; Management/community work consultant, Framework 1985–97; Director, Framework in Print Publishing Co-operative; Member, NUT 1978–79; Member, MSF 1979–. Councillor, Kettering Borough Council 1983–87, Deputy Leader, Labour Group 1986–87; Councillor, Northamptonshire County Council 1993–97, Chair, Equal Opportunities Sub-Committee 1993–97, Chair, Labour Group 1993–97. **House of Commons:** Contested Kettering 1992 general election. Member for Corby since May 1, 1997; PPS to: Nick Raynsford as Minister of State, Department of the Environment, Transport and the Regions 1999–2001, John Prescott as Deputy Prime Minister and First Secretary of State 2001–03; Parliamentary Under-Secretary of State, Office of the Deputy Prime Minister 2003–; *Select Committees:* Member, Public Accounts 1997–98; Member, Selection 1999–. *Special Interests:* Youth Affairs, Social Inclusion, Community Regeneration. National Adviser on Youth Policy 1982–87;

Member, Co-operative Party 1982–; Delegate to National Conference; Member, Labour Party Leadership Campaign Team 1997–99. Member, Corby MIND; President: Corby Accommodation Project, Thrapston Volunteer Centre; Member: Wine Society Co-operative, Midlands Co-operative Society; Non-voting Member: Catalyst Corby Urban Regeneration, Challenge Corby Education Action Zone; Member: National Advisory Group on Personal, Social and Health Education (DfEE), Development Awareness Working Group (DfID); Member, Commonwealth Parliamentary Association 1997–; *Publications:* Author/co-author of many publications including: *Making the Best Use of Consultants*, 1993; *Education for Parenthood*, 1994; *Analysis and Action on Youth Health*, 1995; *Performance Appraisal*, 1995; *Sportsclubs:* Corby Tennis Centre; *Recreations:* Tennis, juggling, gardening. Phil Hope Esq, MP, House of Commons, London, SW1A 0AA *Tel:* 020 7219 4075 *Fax:* 020 7219 2964. *Constituency:* 2nd Floor, Chisholm House, Queen's Square, Corby, Northamptonshire, NN17 1PD *Tel:* 01536 443325 *Fax:* 01536 269462 *E-mail:* hopep@parliament.uk.

HOPKINS, KELVIN   Luton North   *Lab majority 9,977*

Kelvin Peter Hopkins. Born 22 August 1941; Son of late Professor Harold Horace Hopkins, FRS, physicist and mathematician, and Joan Avery Frost, medical secretary; Educated Queen Elizabeth's Grammar School, High Barnet; Nottingham University (BA politics, economics and mathematics with statistics); Married Patricia Langley 1965 (1 son 1 daughter). TUC Economic Department 1969–70, 1973–77; Policy and research officer, NALGO/UNISON 1977–94; Member, GMB; Delegate, Luton Trades Union Council. Councillor, Luton Borough 1972–76. **House of Commons:** Contested Luton North 1983 general election. Member for Luton North since May 1, 1997; Adviser on Yachting to Richard Caborn, as Minister of State for Sport 2002–; *Select Committees:* Member, Broadcasting 1999–2001; Member, Public Administration 2002–. *Special Interests:* Economic Policy, Employment, Transport, Arts. *Countries of Interest:* France, Sweden. Vice-Chair, Central Region Labour Party 1995–96. Governor, Luton Sixth Form College; Chair of Governors, Luton College of Higher Education 1985–89; Member: Mary Seacole House, Luton, Wine Society, Hon. Vice-President, UK Carrom Federation; Member, European Standing Committee B 1998–; *Publications:* Various NALGO publications; Hon. Fellow, Luton University 1993; *Clubs:* Luton Socialist, Lansdowne (Luton); *Sportsclubs:* Luton Town Football Club, UK Carrom Federation; *Recreations:* Music, photography, sailing on the Norfolk Broads. Kelvin Hopkins Esq, MP, House of Commons, London, SW1A 0AA *Tel:* 020 7219 6670 *Fax:* 020 7219 0957. *Constituency:* 3 Union Street, Luton, Bedfordshire, LU1 3AN *Tel:* 01582 488208 *Fax:* 01582 480990.

HORAM, JOHN   Orpington   *Con majority 269*

John Rhodes Horam. Born 7 March 1939; Son of Sydney and Catherine Horam; Educated Silcoates School, Wakefield; St Catharine's College, Cambridge (MA economics 1960); Married Judith Jackson 1987 (2 sons from previous marriage). Market research officer, Rowntree & Co. 1960–62; Leader and feature writer: *Financial Times* 1962–65, *The Economist* 1965–68; Managing director: Commodities Research Unit Ltd 1968–70, 1983–87; CRU Holdings Ltd. 1988–92; Deputy chair, CRU International Ltd 1992–95, 1997–. **House of Commons:** Contested (Labour) Folkstone and Hythe 1966 general election. Member for Gateshead West 1970–83 (Labour 1970–81, SDP 1981–83). Contested Newcastle upon Tyne Central (SDP/Alliance) 1983 general election. Member for Orpington since April 9, 1992; Labour Spokesperson for Economic Affairs 1979–81; SDP Spokesperson 1981–83; Parliamentary Under-Secretary of State, Department of Transport 1976–79; Parliamentary Secretary, Office of Public Service July–November 1995; Parliamentary Under-Secretary of State, Department of Health 1995–97; *Select Committees:* Member, Public Accounts 1992–95; Chair, Environmental Audit 1997–2003; Member: Liaison 1997–, Environmental Audit 1997–. *Special Interests:* Economic Policy, Transport, Health, Environment. *Publications:* *Making Britain Competitive*, 1993; *Clubs:* Orpington Conservative; *Recreations:* Opera, ballet, gardening, walking. John Horam Esq, MP, House of Commons, London, SW1A 0AA *Tel:* 020 7219 6328 *Fax:* 020 7219 3806. *Constituency:* 6 Sevenoaks Road, Orpington, Kent, BR6 9JJ *Tel:* 01689 820347 *Fax:* 01689 890429 *E-mail:* horamj@parliament.uk.

HOWARD, MICHAEL   Folkestone and Hythe   *Con majority 5,907*

Michael Howard. Born 7 July 1941; Son of late Bernard and Hilda Howard; Educated Llanelli Grammar School; Peterhouse, Cambridge (MA economics, LLB 1963); Married Sandra Paul 1975 (1 son 1 daughter and 1 step-son). Called to the Bar, Inner Temple 1964; QC 1982; Junior Counsel to the Crown 1980–82. **House of Commons:** Contested Liverpool Edge Hill 1966 and 1970 general elections. Member for Folkestone and Hythe since June 1983; PPS to Sir Patrick Mayhew as Solicitor-General 1984–85; Parliamentary Under-Secretary of State, Trade and Industry 1985–87; Minister for: Local Government 1987–88, Water and Planning 1988–89, Housing and Planning 1989–90; Secretary of State for: Employment 1990–92, The Environment 1992–93, The Home Department 1993–97; Contested Leadership of the Conservative Party June 1997; Member, Shadow Cabinet 1997–99, 2001–; Shadow Secretary of State for Foreign and Commonwealth Affairs 1997–99; Shadow Chancellor of the Exchequer 2001–; *Special Interests:* Home Affairs, Foreign Affairs. *Countries of Interest:* USA. Chair: Bow Group 1970, Coningsby Club 1972–73; Member Conservative Policy Board 2001–. Chair Atlantic Partnership; PC 1990; *Clubs:* Carlton, Pratt's; *Recreations:* Football and baseball. Rt Hon Michael Howard, QC, MP, House of Commons, London, SW1A 0AA *Tel:* 020 7219 5493 *Fax:* 020 7219 5322. *Constituency:* Folkestone and Hythe Conservative Association, 4 Westcliff Gardens, Folkestone, Kent, CT20 1SP *Tel:* 01303 253524 *Fax:* 01303 251061 *E-mail:* howardm@parliament.uk.

HOWARTH, ALAN   Newport East   *Lab majority 9,874*

Alan Howarth. Born 11 June 1944; Son of late T. E. B. Howarth, MC, TD, and Margaret Howarth (née Teakle); Educated Rugby School; King's College, Cambridge (BA history 1965); Married Gillian Chance 1967 (divorced 1996) (2 sons 2 daughters). Senior research assistant to Field-Marshal Montgomery on *A History of Warfare* 1965–67; Assistant master, Westminster School 1968–74; Personal assistant to Chair Conservative Party 1975–79; Director, Conservative Research Department 1979–81; Member, GMB. **House of Commons:** Member for Stratford-on-Avon (Conservative – June 1983 to Oct 1995, Labour – Oct 1995 to May 1997), and for Newport East since May 1, 1997; Assistant Government Whip, 1987–88; Government Whip 1988–89; PPS to Sir Rhodes Boyson as Minister of State, Northern Ireland Office and Department of Environment 1985–87; Parliamentary Under-Secretary of State, Department for Education and Science 1989–92; Resigned from the Conservative Party and joined the Labour Party, October 1995; Parliamentary Under-Secretary of State: Department for Education and Employment (Employment and Equal Opportunities) 1997–98, Department for Culture, Media and Sport (Minister for the Arts) 1998–2001; *Select Committees:* Member: National Heritage 1992–93, Social Security 1996–97. *Special Interests:* Economic Policy, Employment, Education, Charities, Voluntary Sector, Social Security, Arts. Vice-Chair, Conservative Party 1980–81. *Publications:* Co-author of *Changing Charity*, 1984; *Montgomery at Close Quarters*, 1986; *Save Our Schools*, 1986; *The Arts: The Next Move Forward*, 1987; CBE 1982; PC 2000; *Recreations:* Books, arts, hill walking. Rt Hon Alan Howarth CBE, MP, House of Commons, London, SW1A 0AA *Tel:* 020 7219 5077 *Fax:* 020 7219 0444. *Constituency:* Ringland Labour Club, Ringland, Newport, Gwent, NP19 9PS *Tel:* 01633 277910/273111 *Fax:* 01633 282793.

HOWARTH, GEORGE   Knowsley North and Sefton East   *Lab majority 18,927*

George Howarth. Born 29 June 1949; Educated Schools in Huyton; Liverpool Polytechnic (BA social sciences 1977); Married Julie Rodgers 1977 (2 sons 1 daughter). Engineering apprentice 1966–70; Engineer 1970–75; Teacher 1975–80; Co-operative Development Services 1980–82; Chief executive Walm Co-operative Centre 1982–86; AEU; Chief executive, Wales TUC sponsored co-op. centre, Cardiff 1984–86. Councillor, Huyton Urban District Council 1971–75; Knowsley Borough Council: Councillor 1975–86, Deputy Leader 1982–83. **House of Commons:** Member Knowsley North November 13, 1986 by-election–1997, and for Knowsley North and Sefton East since May 1, 1997; Opposition Spokesperson for: the Environment 1989–92; Environmental

Protection 1993–94; Home Affairs 1994–97; Parliamentary Under-Secretary of State: Home Office (Minister for Fire and Emergency Planning, Liquor, Drugs and Elections) 1997–99, Northern Ireland Office 1999–2001; *Select Committees:* Member, Public Accounts 2002–. *Special Interests:* Housing, Environment. Chair, Knowsley South Labour Party 1981–85; Secretary, Knowsley Borough District Labour Party 1977–80; Member, North West Region Executive, Labour Party 1981–84. *Recreations:* Coarse fishing, family, reading. George Howarth Esq, MP, House of Commons, London, SW1A 0AA *Tel:* 020 7219 6902. *Constituency:* 149 Cherryfield Drive, Kirkby, Merseyside, L32 8SE *Tel:* 0151–546 9918 *Fax:* 0151–546 9918 *E-mail:* georgehowarthmp@hotmail.com.

HOWARTH, GERALD Aldershot   *Con majority 6,594*

Gerald Howarth. Born 12 September 1947; Son of Mary and late James Howarth, retired company director; Educated Bloxham School, Banbury (Scholar); Southampton University (BA English 1969); Married Elizabeth Squibb 1973 (1 daughter 2 sons). Commissioned RAFVR 1968; Assistant manager, loan syndication Bank of America International Ltd 1971–77; European Arab Bank 1977–81: Manager and personal assistant to group managing director 1979, Manager, loan syndications 1980; Loan syndication manager responsible for arranging project and other loans in Africa, Middle East and South America, Standard Chartered Bank plc 1981–83; Joint managing director, Taskforce Communications 1993–95; Member, National Union of Seamen 1966. London Borough Council of Hounslow: Councillor 1982–83, Shadow Vice-chair, Environmental Planning Committee 1982–83, Member, Finance and General Purposes Committee. **House of Commons:** Member for Cannock and Burntwood 1983–92, and for Aldershot since May 1, 1997; Opposition Spokesman on Defence 2002–; PPS to Michael Spicer: as Parliamentary Under-Secretary of State, Department of Energy 1987–90, as Minister of State, Department of the Environment (Minister for Housing and Construction) 1990; to Sir George Young as Minister of State, Department of the Environment 1990–91, to Margaret Thatcher, MP December 1991-April 1992; *Select Committees:* Member, Home Affairs 1997–2001; Member, Defence 2001–. *Special Interests:* Aerospace, Aviation, Defence, Media, Privatisation. *Countries of Interest:* Germany, Russia, South Africa, Chile, Pakistan. Member, Greater London Area CPC Advisory Committee; Vice-Chairman, City Conservative Forum 1981–84; Founder Member, No Turning Back Group; Chairman, 92 Group of Conservative MPs 2001–; Member Executive 1922 Committee 2000–02. General Secretary, Society for Individual Freedom 1969–71; Director, Freedom Under Law; Britannia Airways Parliamentary Pilot of the Year 1988; Fellow, Industry and Parliament Trust; *Publications:* Co-author *No Turning Back*, 1985, and further publications by the Group; *Clubs:* Aldershot Conservative; *Recreations:* Flying, tennis, DIY, family. Gerald Howarth Esq, MP, House of Commons, London, SW1A 0AA *Tel:* 020 7219 5650 *Fax:* 020 7219 1198. *Constituency:* Conservative Club, Victoria Road, Aldershot, Hampshire, GU11 1JX *Tel:* 01252 323637 *Fax:* 01252 323637 *E-mail:* geraldhowarth@parliament.uk.

HOWELLS, KIM Pontypridd   *Lab majority 17,684*

Kim Scott Howells. Born 27 November 1946; Son of late Glanville Howells and of Joan Glenys Howells; Educated Mountain Ash Grammar School; Hornsey College of Art; Cambridge CAT (BA English and history 1974); Warwick University (PhD UK coal Industry (1937–57) 1979); Married Eirlys Davies 1983 (2 sons 1 daughter). Research officer, Coalfield History Project, University College of Wales, Swansea 1979–82; Freelance radio and television presenter and writer 1986–89; Research officer and newspaper editor, NUM South Wales Area 1982–89; Member GPMU. **House of Commons:** Member for Pontypridd since February 23, 1989 by-election; Opposition Spokesperson for: Development and Co-operation 1993–94, Foreign Affairs 1994, Home Affairs 1994–95, Trade and Industry 1995–97; Parliamentary Under-Secretary of State: Department for Education and Employment (Life-long Learning) 1997–98, Department of Trade and Industry 1998–2001 (Consumer and Corporate Affairs 1999–2000, Competition and Consumer Affairs 2000–2001); Parliamentary Under-Secretary of State (Minister for Tourism, Film and Broadcasting), Department for Culture, Media and Sport 2001–03; Minister of State for Transport, Department for Transport 2003–; *Select Committees:* Member: Welsh Affairs 1989–90, Environment 1990–92, Public Accounts 1993–94.

Special Interests: Energy, Environment, Foreign Affairs, Transnational Broadcasting, Arts, Intellectural Property, Small Businesses. *Countries of Interest:* Germany, Italy, Latin America, Switzerland, USA, South Africa, Austria, Romania. President: Arthritis Care, Pontypridd, Taff Ely Drugs Support Group; Vice-President, Travol Pontypridd; Patron, Dragon Swimming Club for Disabled; Member, British Mountaineering Council; *Publications:* Various, on 20th century industrial history and economics and politics of energy; Honorary Doctorate, Anglia Polytechnic University 1998; *Sportsclubs:* Llantwit Fadre Cricket, Hopkinstown Cricket, Pontypridd Rugby Football, Pontypridd Cricket Club, British Mountaineering Council; *Recreations:* Writing, films, jazz, mountain climbing, painting, cycling. Dr Kim Howells, MP, House of Commons, London, SW1A 0AA *Tel:* 020 7219 5813 *Fax:* 020 7219 5526. *Constituency:* 16 Tyfica Road, Pontypridd, Mid Glamorgan, CF37 2DA *Tel:* 01443 402551 *Fax:* 01443 485628 *E-mail:* raybouldc@parliament.uk.

HOYLE, LINDSAY   Chorley   *Lab majority 8,444*

Lindsay Harvey Hoyle. Born 10 June 1957; Son of Baron Hoyle (*qv*) and late Pauline Hoyle; Educated Anderton County Primary; Lords College, Bolton; Horwich FE; Bolton TIC (City & Guilds Construction); Married Catherine Swindley (2 daughters). Company director; Shop steward; Member, MSF. Councillor, Adlington Town Council 1980–98; Councillor, Chorley Borough Council 1980–98; Chair, Economic Development, Deputy Leader 1994–97; Mayor of Chorley 1997–98. **House of Commons:** Member for Chorley since May 1, 1997; *Select Committees:* Member: Catering 1997–, Trade and Industry 1998–. *Special Interests:* Trade and Industry, Sport, Defence, Small Businesses, Agriculture. *Countries of Interest:* Gibraltar, Falkland Islands, British Overseas Territories. Member, Royal Lancashire Agricultural Society; Former Chairman, Chorley Rugby League; Armed Forces Parliamentary Scheme (Royal Marines) 1998–; Member, Cuerdon Valley Trust; *Sportsclubs:* Member: Adlington Cricket Club, Chorley Cricket Club; *Recreations:* Cricket, Rugby League. Hon Lindsay Hoyle, MP, House of Commons, London, SW1A 0AA *Tel:* 020 7219 3515 *Fax:* 020 7219 3831. *Constituency:* 35–39 Market Street, Chorley, Lancashire, PR7 2SW *Tel:* 01257 271555.

HUGHES, BEVERLEY   Stretford and Urmston   *Lab majority 13,271*

Beverley June Hughes. Born 30 March 1950; Daughter of late Norman Hughes and Doris Hughes; Educated Ellesmere Port Girls' Grammar School; Manchester University (BSc 1971, MSc 1978); Liverpool University (Diploma in applied social studies 1974); Married Thomas McDonald 1973 (2 daughters 1 son). Trainee probation officer, Merseyside 1971; Probation officer, Merseyside 1972; Manchester University: Research associate 1976; Lecturer 1981, Senior lecturer and head of department 1993–97; Member USDAW. Trafford Metropolitan Borough Council: Councillor 1986, Labour Group Deputy Leader 1990, Labour Group Leader 1992, Council Leader 1995–97; Director: Trafford Park Development Corporation 1992–97, Manchester Airport plc 1995–97. **House of Commons:** Member for Stretford and Urmston since May 1, 1997; PPS to Hilary Armstrong as Minister of State, Department of the Environment, Transport and the Regions (Minister for Local Government and Housing) 1998–99; Parliamentary Under-Secretary of State, Department of the Environment, Transport and the Regions 1999–2001; Home Office 2001–: Parliamentary Under-Secretary of State 2001–02, Minister of State 2002–: for Citizenship, Immigration and Community Cohesion 2002–03, (Citizenship, Immigration and Counter Terrorism) 2003–; *Select Committees:* Member, Home Affairs 1997–98. *Special Interests:* Economic Regeneration, Investment, Local and Regional Government, Health and Community Care, Families, Regional Development, Education, Criminal Justice, Child Protection and Safety. *Publications: Older People and Community Care: Critical Theory and Practice,* 1995; Numerous academic and professional publications; *Recreations:* Jazz, fell-walking. Beverley Hughes, MP, House of Commons, London, SW1A 0AA *Constituency:* c/o House of Commons *Tel:* 0161 749 9120 *Fax:* 0161 749 9121 *E-mail:* hughesb@parliament.uk.

Visit the Vacher Dod Website . . . **www.DodOnline.co.uk**

HUGHES, KEVIN   Doncaster North   Lab majority 15,187

Kevin Michael Hughes. Born 15 December 1952; Son of Leonard Hughes, retired coal miner, and Annie Hughes, retired school assistant; Educated local schools; Sheffield University, Department of Extra Mural Studies (industrial relations, trade union history, economics and politics); Married Lynda Saunders 1972 (1 son 1 daughter). Coal miner 1970–90; Branch delegate, Brodsworth NUM 1981–90; Member, Yorkshire NUM Executive Committee 1983–87. Councillor, Doncaster Borough Council 1986–92; Chair, Social Services Committee 1987–92. **House of Commons:** Member for Doncaster North since April 9, 1992; Opposition Whip 1996–97; Assistant Government Whip 1997–2001; *Select Committees:* Member, European Legislation 1994–96. *Special Interests:* Social Services, Childcare, Elderly. Secretary/Agent: Don Valley CLP 1980–83 Doncaster North 1983–89. Hon. President, DIAL (Doncaster); Fellow, Industry and Parliament Trust 1995; *Clubs:* Doncaster Trades and Labour, Skellow Grange Workingmen's; *Recreations:* Golf, walking, listening to opera. Kevin Hughes Esq, MP, House of Commons, London, SW1A 0AA *Tel:* 020 7219 4107 *Fax:* 020 7219 2521. *Constituency:* Bentley Training Centre, High Street, Bentley, Doncaster, DN5 0AA *Tel:* 01302 873974 *Fax:* 01302 876176 *E-mail:* khughes@mplink.co.uk.

HUGHES, SIMON   North Southwark and Bermondsey   LD majority 9,632

Simon Henry Ward Hughes. Born 17 May 1951; Son of late James Henry Hughes and of Sylvia Hughes (née Ward); Educated Llandaff Cathedral School, Cardiff; Christ College, Brecon; Selwyn College, Cambridge (BA law 1973, MA); Inns of Court School of Law; College of Europe, Bruges (Certificate in Higher European Studies 1975); Single. Barrister Called to the Bar, Inner Temple 1974; In practice 1978–. GLC candidate 1981; Southwark Borough Council candidate 1982. **House of Commons:** Member for Southwark and Bermondsey by-election February 1983–97, and for North Southwark and Bermondsey since May 1, 1997; Liberal Spokesperson for the Environment 1983–88; Alliance Spokesperson for Health January–June 1987; Spokesman for: Education, Science and Training 1989–92, Environment and Natural Resources 1992–94, Urban Affairs and Young People 1994–97, The Church of England 1988–97, Health and Social Welfare 1995–97, Health (Future of NHS) 1997–99; Principal Spokesperson for Home and Legal Affairs 1999–; Liberal Democrat Deputy Whip 1989–99; *Select Committees:* Member: Ecclesiastical Committee 1987–97, Accommodation and Works 1992–97. *Special Interests:* Human Rights, Civil Liberties, Youth Affairs, Social Affairs, Housing, Environment. *Countries of Interest:* South Africa, Sierra Leone, Commonwealth, Peru. President, National League of Young Liberals 1986–92, Vice-President, Liberal Democrat Youth and Students 1983–86, President 1992–; Vice-Chair, Southwark and Bermondsey Liberal Association 1981–83; Former Chair, Liberal Party's Home Affairs Panel; Member, Association of Liberal Lawyers. London mayoral candidate 2002, 2004; Trainee, EEC Brussels 1976; Trainee and member Secretariat, Directorate and Commission on Human Rights, Council of Europe, Strasbourg 1976–77; Chair, Thames Festival Trust; *Publications:* Co-author *Human Rights in Western Europe – The Next 30 Years*, 1981; *The Prosecutorial Process in England and Wales*, 1981; *Across the Divide – Liberal Values for Defence and Disarmament*, 1986; *Pathways to Power*, 1992; *Who Goes Where – Asylum: Opportunity not Crisis*, 2002; Honorary Fellow, South Bank University; *Clubs:* Redriff (Rotherhithe); *Recreations:* Music, theatre, history, sport (Millwall and Hereford football clubs, Glamorgan county cricket club and Wales rugby football union), the countryside and open air. Simon Hughes Esq, MP, House of Commons, London, SW1A 0AA *Tel:* 020 7219 6256 *Fax:* 020 7219 6567 *Tel (Constituency):* 020 7403 2860 *Fax (Constituency):* 020 7378 9670 *E-mail:* simon@simonhughesmp.org.uk.

Visit the Vacher Dod Website . . .
www.DodOnline.co.uk

HUMBLE, JOAN   Blackpool North and Fleetwood   *Lab majority 5,721*

(Jovanka) Joan Humble. Born 3 March 1951; Daughter of John Piplica and Dora Piplica; Educated Greenhead Grammar School, Keighley; Lancaster University (BA history 1972); Married Paul Humble 1972 (2 daughters). Civil servant, Department of Health and Social Security and Inland Revenue 1972–77; Housewife 1977–85; Member, TGWU. Councillor, Lancashire County Council 1985–97, Chair, Lancashire Social Services 1990–97; JP, Preston Bench. **House of Commons:** Member for Blackpool North and Fleetwood since May 1, 1997; *Select Committees:* Member, Social Security 1998–2001; Member, Work and Pensions 2001–. *Special Interests:* Social Services, Education, Economic Regeneration, Small Businesses. Member: Co-operative Party, Christian Socialist Movement; Hon. Secretary, North West Regional Group of Labour MPs 1999–. School Governor 1982–97; Member, European Standing Committee A 1998; *Recreations:* Reading, gardening, cooking. Mrs Joan Humble, MP, House of Commons, London, SW1A 0AA *Tel:* 020 7219 5025 *Fax:* 020 7219 2755. *Constituency:* 216 Lord Street, Fleetwood, Lancashire, FY7 6SW *Tel:* 01253 877346 *Fax:* 01253 777236 *E-mail:* sue@humblemp.freeserve.co.uk.

HUME, JOHN   Foyle   *SDLP majority 11,550*

John Hume. Born 18 January 1937; Son of Samuel Hume and Annie Hume, née Doherty; Educated Rosemount Primary School, Derry; St Columb's College, Derry; National University of Ireland (BA French and history 1958); St Patrick's College, Maynooth (MA 1964); Married Patricia Hone 1960 (2 sons 3 daughters). French and history teacher 1958–66; President, Credit Union League of Ireland 1964–68; MP for Foyle, Northern Ireland Parliament 1969–72; Associate Fellow, Centre for International Affairs, Harvard 1976; Research Fellow in European Studies, Trinity College, Dublin 1976–77; Member (SDLP) for Londonderry: Northern Ireland Assembly 1973–75, Minister of Commerce Northern Ireland 1974; Northern Ireland Constitutional Convention 1975–76, MEP for Northern Ireland 1979–; Northern Ireland Assembly 1982–86; Member: New Ireland Forum 1983–84, Northern Ireland Forum 1996–98, New Northern Ireland Assembly 1998–2001; Lifelong Director Credit Union League of Ireland; Member, SIPTU (Services, Industrial, Professional and Technical Union). **House of Commons:** Member for Foyle since June 1983; *Special Interests:* European Union, Third World, Poverty, Credit Unions, Northern Ireland, Conflict Resolution. *Countries of Interest:* Belgium, Europe, France, USA. SDLP: Founder Member, Deputy Leader 1970–79, Leader 1979–2001. Director National Democratic Institute (USA); Committee supervising Philippine election 1983; *Publications: Personal Views – Politics, Peace and Reconciliation in Ireland,* 1996; Numerous awards internationally, especially for human rights, including recently European of the Year Award; International Human Rights Award 1996; Global Citizens Award 1998; The Nobel Peace Prize (jointly) 1998; Martin Luther King Award 1999; Légion d'Honneur 1999; Ghandi Award 2001; Fr Mychal Judge Humanitarian Award 2002; Golden Plate Award, American Academy of Achievement 2002; 20 honorary doctorates from British, Irish, French and American universities; Freeman City of Londonderry 2000. John Hume Esq, MP, House of Commons, London, SW1A 0AA *Tel:* 020 7219 3485. *Constituency:* 5 Bayview Terrace, Derry, BT48 7EE *Tel:* 028 7126 5340 *Fax:* 028 7136 3423.

DodOnline

An Electronic Directory without rival ...

MPs' biographies and photographs available with daily updates *via* the internet

For a *free* trial, call Yasmin Mirza, Aby Farsoun or Michael Mand on 020 7630 7643

HUNTER, ANDREW Basingstoke *Con* majority 880*

Andrew Robert Frederick Hunter. Born 8 January 1943; Son of late Squadron-Leader Roger Hunter, DFC MBE and late Winifred Mary née Nelson; Educated St George's School, Harpenden; Durham University (BA theology 1966, MA history 1968); Jesus College, Cambridge (Diploma in education 1967); Westcott House, Cambridge; Married Janet Bourne 1972 (died 2002) (1 son 1 daughter). TAVR, resigned commission 1983; President, Office Furniture 1969; Assistant master, St Martin's, Northwood 1970–71; Assistant master, Harrow School 1971–83. **House of Commons:** Contested Southampton Itchen 1979 general election. *Conservative member for Basingstoke 1983–2002, Independent Conservative since October 2002; PPS to Lord Elton, Minister of State, Department of Environment 1985–86; Sponsored Private Members' Bills: Control of Smoke Pollution Act 1989, Timeshare Act 1992, Noise and Statutory Nuisance (Amendment) Act 1993, Dogs (Fouling of Land) Act 1996 Road Traffic (Vehicle Testing Act) 1999; *Select Committees:* Member: Environment 1986–92, Agriculture 1993–94, Northern Ireland Affairs 1994–2001, Environment, Food and Rural Affairs 2001. *Special Interests:* Environment, Agriculture, Northern Ireland, Southern Africa. *Countries of Interest:* Ireland, southern Africa. Vice-President, National Prayer Book Society 1987–; Member: National Farmers' Union, Countryside Alliance; Honorary Member, Society of the Sealed Knot 1990–; *Publications: The Betrayal of British Ulster*, 2002; *Clubs:* St Stephen's Constitutional, Pratt's, Carlton; *Recreations:* Horse riding, watching cricket and rugby football, collecting model soldiers. Andrew Hunter Esq, MP, House of Commons, London, SW1A 0AA *Tel:* 020 7219 5216 *Tel (Constituency):* 01635 47445 *Fax (Constituency):* 01635 40532 *E-mail:* andrewhunter@parliament.uk.

HURST, ALAN Braintree *Lab majority 358*

Alan Arthur Hurst. Born 2 September 1945; Son of late George Hurst; Educated Westcliff High School; Liverpool University (BA history); Married Hilary Burch 1976 (2 sons 1 daughter). Partner Law, Hurst and Taylor, law firm 1980–. Councillor, Southend Borough Council 1980–96: Labour Group Leader 1990–95, Deputy Leader of Council 1994–95; Councillor, Essex County Council 1993–98. **House of Commons:** Member for Braintree since May 1, 1997; *Select Committees:* Member, Agriculture 1997–2001; Member, Chairmen's Panel 2001–. *Special Interests:* Agriculture, Conservation, Rural Affairs, Pensions. Member, Law Society; Former President, Southend Law Society; President, Brain Valley Archaeological Society; Patron: Silver End Friendship Club, Braintree Operatic Society; *Clubs:* Reform; *Recreations:* Bird watching, local history. Alan Hurst Esq, MP, House of Commons, London, SW1A 0AA *Tel:* 020 7219 4068 *Fax:* 020 7219 2655. *Constituency:* The Labour Hall, Collingwood Road, Witham, Essex, CM8 2EE *Tel:* 01376 520128 *Fax:* 01376 517709.

HUTTON, JOHN Barrow and Furness *Lab majority 9,889*

John Hutton. Born 6 May 1955; Son of late George Hutton, salesman and general labourer, and Rosemary Hutton, orthoptist; Educated Westcliff High School, Southend; Magdalen College, Oxford (BA law 1976, BCL 1978); Married Rosemary Caroline Little 1978 (divorced 1993) (3 sons 1 daughter and 1 son deceased). Research associate, Templeton College, Oxford 1980–81; Senior law lecturer, Newcastle Polytechnic 1981–92; Contested Cumbria and North Lancashire 1989 European Parliament election; Member GMB. **House of Commons:** Contested Penrith and the Border 1987 general election. Member for Barrow and Furness since April 9, 1992; PPS to Margaret Beckett: as President of the Board of Trade and Secretary of State for Trade and Industry 1997–98, as President of the Council and Leader of the House of Commons 1998; Department of Health: Parliamentary Under-Secretary of State 1998–99, Minister of State for Health 1999–; *Select Committees:* Member, Home Affairs 1994–97. *Special Interests:* Defence, Welfare State, Home Affairs, Legal Affairs. PC 2001; *Clubs:* Cemetery Cottages Workingmen's (Barrow-in-Furness); *Recreations:* Cricket, football, films, music, history. Rt Hon John Hutton, MP, House of Commons, London, SW1A 0AA *Tel:* 020 7219 6228. *Constituency:* 22 Hartington Street, Barrow-in-Furness, Cumbria, LA14 5SL *Tel:* 01229 431204 *Fax:* 01229 432016 *E-mail:* huttonj@parliament.uk.

I

IDDON, BRIAN   Bolton South East   *Lab majority 12,871*

Brian Iddon. Born 5 July 1940; Son of late John Iddon and late Violet Iddon; Educated Christ Church Boys' School, Southport; Southport Technical College; Hull University (BSc chemistry 1961, PhD organic chemistry 1964, DSc 1981); Married Merrilyn-Ann Muncaster 1965 (marriage dissolved 1989) (2 daughters); married Eileen Harrison, née Barker 1995 (2 stepsons). Durham University: temporary lecturer 1964–65, senior demonstrator 1965–66 in organic chemistry; Salford University: lecturer 1966–78, senior lecturer 1978–86, reader 1986–97 in organic chemistry; Member, Association of University Teachers. Councillor, Bolton Metropolitan District Council 1977–98, Hon. Alderman 1998–, Housing Committee: Vice-Chair, 1980–82, Chair, 1986–96. **House of Commons:** Member for Bolton South East since May 1, 1997; *Select Committees:* Member, Environmental Audit 1997–2000; Member, Science and Technology 2000–. *Special Interests:* Housing, Science and Technology, Health, Education (HE/FE in particular). *Countries of Interest:* Europe, Africa, India, Pakistan, Kashmir, Middle East. Member: North West Group of the Labour Party, Arts For Labour, Co-operative Party, Labour Middle East Council, Labour Friends of Remploy, Labour Housing Group, Labour PLP Keep The Link Group. Member, Amnesty International; Local patron, Kids Club Network (Bolton-Bury Branch); National patron, Society of Registration Officers; Patron, Bully Free Zone Programme; Member: IPU, CPA; *Publications:* two books, research papers, research communications, major reviews, articles in magazines and a number of papers presented orally at conferences; FRSC; CChem; *Clubs:* Member, Bradford Ward Labour Institute; Honorary Membership, Derby Ward Labour Club; Member, Rumworth Labour Club; Our Lady of Lourdes Social Club; *Recreations:* Philately, gardening, cricket (spectator). Dr Brian Iddon, MP, House of Commons, London, SW1A 0AA *Tel:* 020 7219 4064/2096 *Fax:* 020 7219 2653. *Constituency:* 60 St Georges Road, Bolton, BL1 2DD *Tel:* 01204 371202 *Fax:* 01204 371374 *E-mail:* iddonb@parliament.uk.

ILLSLEY, ERIC   Barnsley Central   *Lab majority 15,130*

Eric Illsley. Born 9 April 1955; Son of John and Maud Illsley; Educated Barnsley Holgate Grammar School; Leeds University (LLB 1977); Married Dawn Webb 1978 (2 daughters). Yorkshire Area NUM: Compensation officer 1978–81, Assistant head of general department 1981–84, Head of general department and chief administration officer 1984–87; Member, MSF. **House of Commons:** Member for Barnsley Central since June 1987; Opposition Spokesperson for: Health 1994–95, Local Government 1995, Northern Ireland 1995–97; Labour Whip 1991–94; *Select Committees:* Member, Procedure 1991–97; Chair, Entry Clearance Sub-Committee 1997–98; Member: Foreign Affairs 1997–, Procedure 1997–, Chairmen's Panel 2000–. *Special Interests:* Trade Unions, Mining, Energy, Social Security, Glass Industry. *Countries of Interest:* Australia, France. Secretary, Barnsley Constituency Labour Party 1981–83, Treasurer 1980–81; Secretary and election agent, Yorkshire South European Labour Party 1984–86; Member, Mining Group of MPs 1987–97; Hon. Treasurer, Yorkshire Regional Group of Labour MP 1997–. Patron, Barnsley Alzheimer's Disease Society; Member, Executive Committee: IPU 1997–, Commonwealth Parliamentary Association (CPA) UK Branch 1997–; *Recreations:* Gymnasium. Eric Illsley Esq, MP, House of Commons, London, SW1A 0AA *Tel:* 020 7219 3501 *Fax:* 020 7219 4863. *Constituency:* 18 Regent Street, Barnsley, S70 2HG *Tel:* 01226 730692 *Fax:* 01226 779429 *E-mail:* illsleye@parliament.uk.

Visit the Vacher Dod Website . . .
www.DodOnline.co.uk

INGRAM, ADAM   East Kilbride   Lab majority 12,755

Adam Paterson Ingram. Born 1 February 1947; Son of Bert Ingram, fitter, and Louisa Ingram; Educated Cranhill Senior Secondary School; Married Maureen McMahon 1970. Computer programmer/systems analyst 1967–77; Full-time trade union official 1977–87; Full-time union official, NALGO 1977–87; Member of Parliament supported by TGWU 1987–. District Councillor, East Kilbride 1980–87, Leader 1984–87. **House of Commons:** Contested Strathkelvin and Bearsden 1983 general election. Member for East Kilbride since June 1987; Opposition Spokesperson for: Social Security 1993–95, Trade and Industry 1995–97; Opposition Whip for Scottish Affairs and Treasury Matters 1988–89; PPS to Neil Kinnock as Leader of the Opposition 1988–92;

Minister of State: Northern Ireland Office 1997–2001, for the Armed Forces, Ministry of Defence 2001–; *Select Committees:* Member, Trade and Industry 1992–93. *Special Interests:* Energy, Aerospace, Defence, Northern Ireland. *Countries of Interest:* USA, Japan, South Africa. Chair, East Kilbride Constituency Labour Party 1981–85. PC 1999; *Recreations:* Fishing, cooking, reading. Rt Hon Adam Ingram, MP, House of Commons, London, SW1A 0AA *Tel:* 020 7219 4093. *Constituency:* Parliamentary Office, Civic Centre, East Kilbride, G74 1AB *Tel:* 01355 806016 *E-mail:* adam_ingram@compuserve.com.

IRRANCA-DAVIES, HUW   Ogmore   Lab majority 5,721

Huw Irranca-Davies. Born 22 January 1963; Son of Gerwin Davies and Teresa Davies, née Griffiths; Educated Gowerton Comprehensive School; Swansea Institute of Higher Education (MSc European leisure resort management); Married Joanna Irranca 1990 (3 sons). Leisure facility management; Senior lecturer and course director, business faculty, Swansea Institute of Higher Education 1996–2002; Member, GMB. **House of Commons:** Contested Brecon and Radnorshire 2001 general election. Member for Ogmore since by-election February 14, 2002; PPS to Jane Kennedy as Minister of State, Northern Ireland Office 2003–; *Select Committees:* Member: Joint Committee on Statutory Instruments 2002–, Procedure 2002–. *Special Interests:* Police

Reform, Social Justice, European Union. *Countries of Interest:* Middle East, Northern Ireland. Vice-president, Neath Constituency Labour Party –2002; Secretary, Ystalyfera branch –2002. Member, Bevan Foundation; Trustee and director, Charitable Trust (community regeneration); *Clubs:* Chair, Ogmore Valley Male Voice Choir; *Sportsclubs:* President, Maesteg Celtic Cricket Club; *Recreations:* Hill-walking, cycling, most sport, family. Huw Irranca-Davies Esq, MP, House of Commons, London, SW1A 0AA *Tel:* 020 7219 4027 *Fax:* 020 7219 0134 *Tel (Constituency):* 01656 737777 *Fax (Constituency):* 01656 737788 *E-mail:* irrancadaviesh@parliament.uk.

J

JACK, MICHAEL   Fylde   Con majority 9,610

(John) Michael Jack. Born 17 September 1946; Son of late Ralph Jack and Florence Edith Jack; Educated Bradford Grammar School; Bradford Technical College; Leicester University (BA economics 1968, MPhil transport economics 1970); Married Alison Jane Musgrave 1976 (2 sons). Manager transport and brands Proctor and Gamble 1971–75; PA to Lord Rayner 1975–76; Marks and Spencer 1975–80; Director, L. O. Jeffs Ltd (Part of Northern Foods from 1986) 1981–87. Member, Mersey Regional Health Authority 1984–87. **House of Commons:** Contested Newcastle Central February 1974. Member for Fylde since June 1987; Opposition Spokesperson for Health June-November 1997; PA to James Prior, MP 1979 general election; PPS to John Gummer: as Minister for

Local Government 1988–89, as Minister of Agriculture, Fisheries and Food 1989–90; Joint Parliamentary Under-Secretary of State for Social Security 1990–92; Minister of State at: Home Office 1992–93,

Ministry of Agriculture, Fisheries and Food 1993–95; Financial Secretary, HM Treasury 1995–97; Member, Shadow Cabinet 1997–98; Shadow Minister of Agriculture, Fisheries and Food November 1997-August 1998; *Select Committees:* Member: Agriculture 1999–2001, Radioactive Waste Policy Sub-Committee 2001–02; Chair, Radioactive Waste Policy Sub-Committee 2002; Member, Environment, Food and Rural Affairs 2001–; Chair, Information 2003–. *Special Interests:* Health, Nuclear Industry, Horticulture, Sheltered Housing, Aerospace, Transport, Agriculture. *Countries of Interest:* China, USA, Italy. National Chair, Young Conservatives 1976. Member, Eastern Electricity Consultative Council 1979; Member: European Standing Committee C 1999–, Tax Law Rewrite Committee 1999–; PC 1997; Freeman, City of London; *Recreations:* Boule, motorsport, dinghy sailing, growing vegetables. Rt Hon Michael Jack, MP, House of Commons, London, SW1A 0AA *Tel:* 020 7219 3000. *Constituency:* Universal, Fairfield, Bradshaw Lane, Greenhalgh, Kirkham, Preston, PR4 3JA *Tel:* 01772 671533 *Fax:* 01772 671534.

JACKSON, GLENDA   Hampstead and Highgate   *Lab majority 7,876*

Glenda Jackson. Born 9 May 1936; Daughter of Harry and Joan Jackson; Educated West Kirby County Grammar School for Girls; RADA; Married Roy Hodges 1958 (marriage dissolved 1976) (1 son). Actress: Plays include: *The Idiot* 1962, *Love's Labour's Lost*, *Hamlet* 1965, *Three Sisters* 1967, *Hedda Gabler* 1975; Films include: *Women in Love*, *Mary, Queen of Scots*, *A Touch of Class*; Television includes *Elizabeth R* 1971; Member, Royal Shakespeare Company 1963–67, 1979–80. Member, Greater London Assembly advisory cabinet for homelessness 2000–. **House of Commons:** Member for Hampstead and Highgate since April 9, 1992; Opposition Spokeswoman on Transport 1996–97; Parliamentary Under-Secretary of State, Department of the Environment, Transport and the Regions 1997–99; Resigned in July 1999 reshuffle; *Special Interests:* Overseas Aid and Development, Housing, Environment. Member: Anti-Apartheid Movement, Amnesty International, Has campaigned for: Oxfam, Shelter, Friends of the Earth; President, The National Toy Libraries Association; CBE 1978; Best film actress awards: Variety Clubs of Great Britain 1971, 1975, 1978, NY Film critics 1971, Oscar 1971, 1974; *Recreations:* Cooking, gardening, reading Jane Austen. Glenda Jackson, CBE, MP, House of Commons, London, SW1A 0AA *Tel:* 020 7219 4008 *Fax:* 020 7219 2112.

JACKSON, HELEN   Sheffield Hillsborough   *Lab majority 14,569*

Helen Jackson. Born 19 May 1939; Daughter of late Stanley Price, further education adviser, and late Katherine Price, health visitor; Educated Berkhamsted School for Girls; St Hilda's College, Oxford (BA modern history 1960, MA); C. F. Mott College of Education (Postgraduate teaching certificate 1972); Married Keith Jackson 1960 (divorced 1998) (2 sons 1 daughter). Assistant librarian, The Queen's College, Oxford 1960–61; Assistant teacher, City of Stoke-on-Trent 1961–62; Infant, junior, special needs and mathematics teacher: Lancashire Education Authority 1972–74, Sheffield Education Authority 1974–80; Member, TGWU (constituency sponsored by UCATT). Councillor: Huyton Urban District Council 1973–74, Sheffield City Council 1980–91; Chair: Public Works Committee 1981–83, Employment and Economic Development Committee 1983–91, Sheffield Economic Regeneration Committee 1987–91; Board Member: Sheffield Partnerships Ltd 1988–91, Sheffield Science Park 1988–91, Sheffield Development Corporation 1989–90; Founder Member and Chair, Centre for Local Economic Strategies. **House of Commons:** Member for Sheffield Hillsborough since April 9, 1992; PPS to Secretaries of State of State for Northern Ireland: Marjorie Mowlam 1997–99, Peter Mandelson 1999–2001, John Reid January to June 2001; *Select Committees:* Member: Environment 1992–97, Modernisation of the House of Commons 1997–2001, Transport, Local Government and the Regions 2001–02, Transport Sub-Committee 2001–02, Transport 2002. *Special Interests:* Environment, Women, Northern Ireland, Transport, International Women's Agenda, Africa. *Countries of Interest:* Africa, Europe. Member: Labour Party "Britain of the World" Policy Commission, Labour Party National Policy Forum 1998–, Labour Party National Executive Committee 1999–; Vice-chair, Parliamentary Labour Party 2001–02; Member, Parliamentary Labour Party Parliamentary Committee 2001–. Child Care; Voluntary work as playgroup organiser;

School governor; Occasional research work for Liverpool Council Social Services 1962–70; UK representative to AWEPA 1997–; Member, British-Irish Interparliamentary Group 2001–; *Recreations:* Walking, music. Helen Jackson, MP, House of Commons, London, SW1A 0AA *Tel:* 020 7219 4587 *Fax:* 020 7219 2442. *Constituency:* Hillsborough Library, Middlewood Road, Sheffield, S6 4HD *Tel:* 0114–232 2439 *Fax:* 0114–285 5808 *E-mail:* jacksonh@parliament.uk.

JACKSON, ROBERT   Wantage   *Con majority 5,600*

Robert Victor Jackson. Born 24 September 1946; Son of late Maurice Henry Jackson; Educated Falcon College, Rhodesia; St Edmund Hall, Oxford (modern history 1968); All Souls College, Oxford (MA) (President, Oxford Union 1967); Married Caroline Frances Harvey 1975 (MEP as Caroline Jackson 1994–) (1 son deceased). MEP for Upper Thames 1979–83. Councillor, Oxford City Council 1969–71. **House of Commons:** Contested Manchester Central October 1974 general election. Member for Wantage since June 1983; Political adviser: to Willie Whitelaw as Secretary of State for Employment 1973–74, to Sir Christopher Soames as EC Commissioner 1974–76; Chef de Cabinet to Basil De Ferranti, as President of EEC Economic and Social Committee 1976–78; Special Adviser to Lord Soames as Governor of Rhodesia 1980; Parliamentary Under-Secretary of State: at Department of Education and Science 1987–90, at Department of Employment 1990–92; Parliamentary Secretary, Office of Public Service and Science 1992–93; *Select Committees:* Member, Science and Technology 1999–2001; Member, Education and Skills 2002–. *Special Interests:* European Union, Agriculture, Science, Foreign Affairs. *Countries of Interest:* Europe, Arab World. Treasurer, Conservative Parliamentary Mainstream Group 2000–. EP Rapporteur on EEC Budget 1983; Member, UK Delegation Parliamentary Assembly of the Council of Europe and Assembly of Western European Union 2000–01; *Publications: The Round Table: The Commonwealth Journal of International Affairs,* 1970–74; *South Asian Crisis, Pakistan, Bangladesh,* 1974; *The European Parliament: a Guide for Direct Elections,* 1978; Editor: *International Affairs,* 1979–80; Fellow, All Souls College, Oxford 1968–75; *Recreations:* Walking, gardening, singing. Robert Jackson Esq, MP, House of Commons, London, SW1A 0AA *Tel:* 020 7219 4557 *Fax:* 020 7219 0480. *Constituency:* Orchard House, Portway, Wantage, Oxfordshire, OX13 5HR *Tel:* 01235 769090 *Fax:* 01235 224833 *E-mail:* jacksonr@parliament.uk.

JAMIESON, DAVID   Plymouth Devonport   *Lab majority 13,033*

David Charles Jamieson. Born 18 May 1947; Son of late Frank Jamieson, engineer, and of Eileen Jamieson; Educated Tudor Grange Grammar School, Solihull; St Peter's College, Birmingham 1967–70; Open University (BA social science and education management 1976–81); Married Patricia Hofton 1971 (2 sons 1 daughter). Assistant teacher, mathematics, Riland-Bedford School, Sutton Coldfield 1970–76; Head of mathematics, Crown Hills Community College, Leicester 1976–81; Senior vice-principal, The John Kitto Community College, Plymouth 1981–92. Solihull Borough Council: Councillor 1970–74, Vice-Chairman, Housing Committee 1973–74. **House of Commons:** Contested Birmingham Hall Green February 1974 and Plymouth Drake 1987 general elections. Member for Plymouth Devonport since April 9, 1992; Assistant Government Whip 1997–98; Government Whip 1998–2001; Promoted as Private Member's Bill: Activity Centres (Young Persons' Safety) Act 1995; Parliamentary Under-Secretary of State for Transport, Department for Transport 2001–; *Select Committees:* Member: Education 1992–96, Education and Employment 1996–97, Accommodation and Works 1998–2001. *Special Interests:* Education. Vice-President, National Association for Gifted Children; *Recreations:* Music, classic cars, gardening. David Jamieson Esq, MP, House of Commons, London, SW1A 0AA *Tel:* 020 7219 6252 *Fax:* 020 7219 2388. *Constituency Tel:* 01752 704677 *Fax:* 01752 704677 *E-mail:* david.jamieson@dtlr.gsi.gov.uk.

Visit the Vacher Dod Website . . .
www.DodOnline.co.uk

JENKIN, BERNARD   North Essex   *Con majority 7,186*

Bernard Jenkin. Born 9 April 1959; Son of Rt Hon. Baron Jenkin of Roding (*qv*); Educated Highgate School; William Ellis School; Corpus Christi College, Cambridge (BA English literature 1982) (President, Cambridge Union Society 1982); Married Anne Strutt 1988 (2 sons). Previously employed by: Ford Motor Co Ltd and 3i plc; Manager, Legal and General Ventures Ltd 1989–92; Adviser, Legal and General Group plc 1992–95. Chairman, Matching Parish Council 1985–87. **House of Commons:** Contested Glasgow Central in 1987 General Election. Member for North Colchester 1992–97, and for North Essex since May 1, 1997; Opposition Spokesperson for: Constitutional Affairs, Scotland and Wales 1997–98, Environment, Transport and the Regions (Roads and Environment) 1998; Political Adviser to Leon Brittan MP 1986–88; PPS to Michael Forsyth as Secretary of State for Scotland 1995–97; Shadow Minister for Transport 1998–2001; Member, Shadow Cabinet 1999–; Shadow Secretary of State for Defence 2001–; *Select Committees:* Member, Social Security 1993–97. *Special Interests:* Economic Policy, Trade, European Union, Defence, Foreign Affairs. *Countries of Interest:* USA, New Zealand, Singapore, Chile, France, Germany. Governor, Central Foundation Girls' School ILEA 1985–89; Governor, London Goodenough Trust for Overseas Graduates 1992–; Member, European Standing Committee B 1992–97; *Publications:* Co-author *Who Benefits: Reinventing Social Security*, 1993; *A Conservative Europe: 1994 and beyond*, 1994; *Fairer Business Rates*, 1996; *Clubs:* Colchester Conservative; *Recreations:* Sailing, music (especially opera), fishing, family, DIY. Hon. Bernard Jenkin, MP, House of Commons, London, SW1A 0AA *Tel:* 020 7219 4029 *Fax:* 020 7219 5963. *Constituency:* North Essex Conservative Association, 167B London Road, Stanway, Colchester, Essex, CO3 5PB *Tel:* 01206 717900 *Fax:* 01206 717909 *E-mail:* jenkinb@parliament.uk.

JENKINS, BRIAN   Tamworth   *Lab majority 4,598*

Brian Jenkins. Born 19 September 1942; Son of late Hiram and Gladys Jenkins; Educated Kingsbury High School, Tamworth; Coventry College; Coleg Harlech; London School of Economics (BSc econ 1980); Wolverhampton Polytechnic (PGCE 1981); Married Joan Dix 1963 (1 son 1 daughter). Instrument mechanic, CEGB 1961–68; Industrial engineer, Jaguar Cars 1968–73; Percy Lane 1973–75; Student 1975–81; College lecturer: Isle of Man College 1981–83, Tamworth College 1983–96; GMB. Councillor, Tamworth Borough Council, Mayor 1993–94. **House of Commons:** Contested South East Staffordshire 1992 general election. Member for South East Staffordshire by-election April 11, 1996–97, and for Tamworth since May 1, 1997; PPS: to Joyce Quin, as Minister of State, Home Office (Minister for Prisons, Probation and Europe) 1997–98, to Joyce Quin, Derek Fatchett and Tony Lloyd as Ministers of State, Foreign and Commonwealth Office 1998–99, to Joyce Quin, Geoff Hoon and Tony Lloyd as Ministers of State, Foreign and Commonwealth Office 1999, to Joyce Quin, as Minister of State and Deputy Minister, Ministry of Agriculture, Fisheries and Food 1999–2001; *Select Committees:* Member, Broadcasting 2001–03; Member: Unopposed Bills (Panel) 1997–, Standing Orders 1998–, Public Accounts 2001–. *Special Interests:* Trade and Industry, Training, Housing. *Countries of Interest:* Europe, North America. School governor; *Clubs:* Tamworth Royal British Legion; *Recreations:* Music, reading, watching sport. Brian Jenkins Esq, MP, House of Commons, London, SW1A 0AA *Tel:* 020 7219 6622 *Fax:* 020 7219 0169. *Constituency:* 31c Market Street, Tamworth, Staffordshire, B79 7LR *Tel:* 01827 311957 *Fax:* 01827 311958 *E-mail:* jenkinsb@parliament.uk.

DodOnline
An Electronic Directory without rival ...

MPs' biographies and photographs available with daily updates *via* the internet

For a *free* trial, call Yasmin Mirza, Aby Farsoun or Michael Mand on 020 7630 7643

JOHNSON, ALAN   Hull West and Hessle   *Lab majority 10,951*

Alan Arthur Johnson. Born 17 May 1950; Son of Stephen Arthur and late Lillian May Johnson; Educated Sloane Grammar School, Chelsea; Married Judith Cox 1968 (divorced) (1 son 2 daughters); married Laura Jane Patient 1991 (1 son). Postman 1968–87; Local Officer, Slough UCW 1974–81; Union of Communication Workers: Branch Official 1976, Executive Council 1981–87, National Officer 1987–93, General Secretary 1993–95; Member, General Council, TUC 1993–95; Executive Member, Postal, Telegraph and Telephone International 1993–97; Director, Unity Bank Trust plc 1993–97; Joint General Secretary, Communication Workers Union 1995–97; Member, CWU. **House of Commons:** Member for Hull West and Hessle since May 1, 1997; PPS to Dawn Primarolo: as Financial Secretary, HM Treasury 1997–99, as Paymaster General, HM Treasury 1999; Department of Trade and Industry 1999–2003: Parliamentary Under-Secretary of State (Competitiveness) 1999–2001, Minister of State 2001–03: Minister for Employment Relations and Regions 2001–02, Minister for Employment Relations, Industry and the Regions 2002–03; Minister of State for Lifelong Learning, Further and Higher Education, Department for Education and Skills 2003–; *Select Committees:* Member, Trade and Industry 1997–98. *Special Interests:* Education, Electoral Reform, Employment, Post Office. Member: Eton and Slough Labour Party GMC 1976–87, Southern Regional Executive of Labour Party 1981–87, Member, Labour Party National Executive Committee 1995–97, Labour Campaign for Electoral Reform. Member, World Executive, Postal, Telegraph and Telephone International (PTTI) 1993–97; PC 2003; *Recreations:* Tennis, cooking, reading, Radio 4, music. Rt Hon Alan Johnson, MP, House of Commons, London, SW1A 0AA *Tel:* 020 7219 5227 *Fax:* 020 7219 5856. *Constituency:* Goodwin Resource Centre, Icehouse Road, Hull, HU3 2HQ *Tel:* 01482 219211 *Fax:* 01482 219211 *E-mail:* johnsona@parliament.uk.

JOHNSON, BORIS   Henley   *Con majority 8,458*

(Alexander) Boris de Pfeffel Johnson. Born 19 June 1964; Son of Stanley Patrick Johnson and Charlotte Johnson, née Fawcett; Educated Eton College; Balliol College, Oxford (BA literae humaniores 1987); Married Marina Wheeler 1993 (2 sons 2 daughters). Trainee reporter: *Times, Wolverhampton Express, Star* 1987–88; *Daily Telegraph:* Leader and feature writer 1988–89, EC correspondent Brussels 1989–94, Assistant editor 1994–99; Political columnist *Spectator* 1994–95; Chief political commentator *Daily Telegraph*; Editor *Spectator* 1999–. **House of Commons:** Contested Clwyd South 1997 general election. Member for Henley since June 7, 2001. Patron Downside UP Moscow 2000–; Member European Standing Committee B 2003–; *Publications:* Numerous radio and television broadcasts and publications *Friends, Voters, Countrymen,* 2001; *What the Papers Say* Commentator of the Year 1997; *Clubs:* Beefsteak; *Recreations:* Painting, poetry, tennis, skiing, rugby, cricket. Boris Johnson Esq, MP, House of Commons, London, SW1A 0AA *Tel:* 020 7219 8244. *Constituency:* 8 Gorwell, Watlington, Oxfordshire, OX49 5QE *Tel:* 01491 612 852 *Fax:* 01491 612 001.

JOHNSON, MELANIE   Welwyn Hatfield   *Lab majority 1,196*

Melanie Jane Johnson. Born 5 February 1955; Daughter of David Johnson, retired civil engineer, and Angela Johnson, retired pharmacist, Educated Clifton High School, Bristol; University College, London (BA philosophy and ancient Greek 1976); King's College, Cambridge (Postgraduate research); Partner William Jordan (twin daughters 1 son). Member relations officer, Cambridge Co-op 1981–88; Retail administration manager, Cambridge Co-op 1988–90; Assistant general manager, quality assurance, Cambridge FHSA 1990–92; Schools inspector, OFSTED 1993–97; Contested Cambridgeshire 1994 European Parliament election; Member, UNISON. Councillor, Cambridgeshire County Council 1981–97; JP 1994–. **House of Commons:** Member for Welwyn Hatfield since May 1, 1997; HM Treasury: PPS to Barbara Roche as Financial Secretary 1999, Economic Secretary 1999–2001; Parliamentary Under-Secretary of State for: Competition, Consumers and Markets, Department of Trade and Industry 2001–03, Public Health, Department of Health 2003–; *Select Committees:* Member: Public Administration 1997–98, Home Affairs 1998–99. *Special Interests:* Business, Employment, Education, Health, Child Protection and Safety. Vice-Chair, Eastern Regional Group of Labour MPs 1999. *Recreations:* Family, gardening, a wide range of classical and rock music, films. Melanie Johnson, MP, House of Commons, London, SW1A 0AA. *Constituency:* 2 Queensway House, Hatfield, Hertfordshire, AL10 0LW *Tel:* 01707 262920 *Fax:* 01707 262834 *E-mail:* melaniej@netcomuk.co.uk.

JONES, HELEN   Warrington North   *Lab majority 15,156*

Helen Mary Jones. Born 24 December 1954; Daughter of late Robert Edward Jones and of Mary Scanlan; Educated St Werburgh's Primary School; Ursuline Convent, Chester; University College, London (BA); Chester College; Liverpool University (MEd); Manchester Metropolitan University; Married Michael Vobe 1988 (1 son). Teacher of English; Development officer, MIND; Justice and peace officer, Liverpool Archdiocese; Solicitor; Contested Lancashire Central 1984 European Parliament election; MSF: Labour Party Liaison Officer, North West Coast Region, Former Member: National Women's Committee, National Appeals Panel. Councillor, Chester City Council 1984–91. **House of Commons:** Contested Shropshire North 1983, Ellesmere Port and Neston 1987 general elections. Member for Warrington North since May 1, 1997; *Select Committees:* Member: Catering 1997–98, Public Administration 1998–2000, Education and Employment 1999–2001, Education Sub-Committee 1999–2000, Standing Orders 1999–2000; Member: Unopposed Bills (Panel) 1999–, Standing Orders 2001–. *Special Interests:* Education, Health. *Recreations:* Gardening, reading, cooking. Helen Jones, MP, House of Commons, London, SW1A 0AA *Tel:* 020 7219 4048. *Constituency:* Gilbert Wakefield House, 67 Bewsey Street, Warrington, WA2 7JQ *Tel:* 01925 232480 *Fax:* 01925 232239 *E-mail:* jonesh@parliament.uk.

JONES, JON OWEN   Cardiff Central   *Lab majority 659*

Jon Owen Jones. Born 19 April 1954; Son of Gwynfor Owen Jones, retired optical salesman and former miner, and Dorothy Jones, retired teacher; Educated Ysgol Gyfun Rhydfelin; University of East Anglia (BSc biology 1975); University College of Wales, Cardiff (PGCE 1976); Married Allison Mary Clement 1989 (2 sons 1 daughter). Teacher of biology and science in comprehensive schools 1977–92; President: Caerphilly NUT 1983, Mid Glamorgan NUT 1984. Cardiff City Council: Councillor 1987–92, Vice-chair, Finance Committee 1987–91, Chair, Economic Development Committee 1990–92. **House of Commons:** Contested Cardiff Central in 1987 general election. Member for Cardiff Central since April 9, 1992; Opposition Welsh/Agricultural Whip 1993–97; Transport Whip 1994–97; Government Whip 1997–98; Parliamentary Under-Secretary of State, Welsh Office 1998–99; *Select Committees:* Member, Welsh Affairs 1992–93; Chair, Information 1997–98; Member, Information 1998; Member, Environmental Audit 1999–. *Special Interests:* Environment, Wales, Education. Secretary, Cardiff Central Labour Party 1984–85; Chair Welsh Regional Group of Labour MPs 2002–03; Member, Co-operative Party. Chair, Campaign for Welsh Assembly 1988–91; *Clubs:* Roath Labour; *Recreations:* Walking, cooking, natural history, watching rugby, family, golf. Jon Owen Jones Esq, MP, House of Commons, London, SW1A 0AA *Tel:* 020 7219 4531 *Fax:* 020 7219 2698. *Constituency:* 50A Crwys Road, Cathays, Cardiff, CF24 4NN *Tel:* 029 2063 5811 *Fax:* 029 2063 5814 *E-mail:* jon@jonowen99.freeserve.co.uk.

DodOnline
An Electronic Directory without rival . . .

MPs' biographies and photographs available with daily updates *via* the internet

For a *free* trial, call Yasmin Mirza, Aby Farsoun or Michael Mand on 020 7630 7643

JONES, KEVAN   Durham North — *Lab majority 18,683*

Kevan Jones. Born 25 April 1964; Educated Portland Comprehensive, Worksop, Nottinghamshire; Newcastle upon Tyne Polytechnic (BA government and public policy). GMB: Political officer 1989–2001, Regional organiser 1992–99, Senior organiser 1999–2001. Newcastle City Council 1990–2001: Councillor, Former deputy leader, Group Council Cabinet member for Development, Chief whip, Chair: Public Health, Development and Transport. **House of Commons:** Member for Durham North since June 7, 2001; *Select Committees:* Member, Defence 2001–. *Special Interests:* Regeneration, Transport, Employment, Regional Policy, Local and Regional Government, Defence. Parliamentary assistant N H Brown MP 1985–89; Northern Region Labour Party: Chair 1998–2000, Vice-chair 2000–. Patron Chester Le Street Mind 2001–; Member European Cities Environment Committee 1994–99; *Clubs:* Sacriston Workingmens Club; *Recreations:* Golf. Kevan Jones Esq, MP, House of Commons, London, SW1A 0AA *Tel:* 020 7219 8219. *Constituency:* Co-operative Buildings, Plawsworth Road, Sacriston, Co Durham *Tel:* 0191 371 8834 *Fax:* 0191 371 8834 *E-mail:* kevanjonesmp@parliament.uk.

JONES, LYNNE   Birmingham Selly Oak — *Lab majority 10,339*

Lynne Mary Jones. Born 26 April 1951; Daughter of late Stanley Stockton and of Jean Stockton; Educated Bartley Green Girls' Grammar School; Birmingham University (BSc 1972, PhD biochemistry 1979); Birmingham Polytechnic (Postgraduate diploma in housing studies 1987); Married (2 sons). Biochemistry research fellow, Birmingham University 1972–86; Housing association manager 1987–92; Member, MSF. Birmingham City Councillor 1980–94, Chair, Housing Committee 1984–87. **House of Commons:** Member for Birmingham Selly Oak since April 9, 1992; *Select Committees:* Member: Science and Technology 1992–97, Science and Technology 1997–2001. *Special Interests:* Economic Policy, Science, Social Security, Housing, Small Businesses. *Countries of Interest:* Mozambique. Member: Liberty, Greenpeace, CND, Amnesty International; *Publications:* Regular columns in *Roof* magazine, Pensions Management; Contributions to: *Tribune*, Campaign Group News (available via own website); Spectator "Backbencher to Watch" 1998; *Recreations:* Family, cycling. Dr Lynne Jones, MP, House of Commons, London, SW1A 0AA *Tel:* 020 7219 4190 *Fax:* 020 7219 3870. *Constituency:* The Cotteridge Church, 24 Pershore Road South, Birmingham, B30 3AS *Tel:* 0121–486 2808 *Fax:* 0121–486 2808 *E-mail:* jonesl@parliament.uk.

JONES, MARTYN   Clwyd South — *Lab majority 8,898*

Martyn Jones. Born 1 March 1947; Son of Vernon, engine driver, and Violet Jones; Educated Grove Park Grammar School, Wrexham; Liverpool College of Commerce; Liverpool Polytechnic (CIBiol) 1966–67; Trent Polytechnic (MIBiol) 1968–69; Married Rhona Bellis 1974 (divorced 1991) (1 son 1 daughter). Microbiologist, Wrexham Lager Beer Co. 1969-June 1987; Member, TGWU 1974–; Vice-Chair, TGWU Parliamentary Group 2000–01; Chair TGWU Parliamentary Group 2001–. Councillor, Clwyd County Council 1981–89. **House of Commons:** Member for Clwyd South West 1987–97, and for Clwyd South since May 1, 1997; Opposition Spokesperson for Food, Agricultural and Rural Affairs 1994–95; Opposition Whip 1988–92; *Select Committees.* Member: Agriculture 1988–94, Speaker's Panel of Chairmen 1993–94, Agriculture 1996–97; Chair, Welsh Affairs 1997–; Member, Liaison 1997–. *Special Interests:* Science, Ecology, Agriculture. *Countries of Interest:* Wales, Spain, USA. Chair, Clwyd County Party 1979–81; Member: Christian Socialist Movement, Socialist Environment and Resources Association, Fabian Society. Member, SERA; Council Member: Royal College of Veterinary Surgeons, National Rifle Association; Vice-President, Federation of Economic Development Authorities (FEDA); *Recreations:* Backpacking, first aid, target shooting. Martyn Jones Esq, MP, House of Commons, London, SW1A 0AA *Tel:* 020 7219 3417 *Fax:* 020 7219 2815. *Constituency:* Foundry Buildings, Gutter Hill, Johnstown, Wrexham, LL14 1LU *Tel:* 01978 845938 *Fax:* 01978 843392.

JONES, NIGEL   Cheltenham   *LD majority 5,255*

Nigel Jones. Born 30 March 1948; Son of late A. J. Jones, and of Nora Jones; Educated Prince Henry's Grammar School, Evesham; Married Katy Grinnell 1981 (1 son twin daughters). Clerk; Computer operator, Westminster Bank 1965–67; Computer programmer, ICL Computers 1967–70; Systems analyst, Vehicle and General Insurance 1970–71; Systems programmer, Atkins Computing 1971; Systems designer; Consultant; Project manager, ICL Computers 1971–92. Councillor, Gloucestershire County Council 1989–93. **House of Commons:** Contested Cheltenham 1979 general election. Member for Cheltenham since April 9, 1992; Liberal Democrat Spokesperson for: England, Local Government and Housing 1992–93, Science and Technology 1993–, Consumer Affairs 1995–97, National Heritage, Constitution and Civil Service (Sport) 1997, Culture, Media, Sport, and Civil Service (Sport) 1997–99, Trade and Industry (Science and Technology) 1997–99, International Development 1999–; *Select Committees:* Member: Broadcasting 1994–97, Standards and Privileges 1995–97, Science and Technology 1997–99, International Development 1999–2001; Member, Public Accounts 2002–. *Special Interests:* Trade and Industry, Transport, Restructuring of Defence Industries, Information Technology, Sport, International Development. *Countries of Interest:* Middle East, Africa, Malawi, Botswana, Ghana, Zimbabwe, Zambia, Lesotho, Swaziland, Tanzania, Uganda, Kenya, UAE, Bahrain, Kuwait. Member, Executive Committee: Inter-Parliamentary Union British Group 1997–, Commonwealth Parliamentary Association UK Branch 1999–, Governing Body British Association for Central and Eastern Europe 1996–; *Clubs:* National Liberal; *Sportsclubs:* Gloucestershire County Cricket Club, Cheltenham Town FC Season Ticket Holder; *Recreations:* Watching Swindon Town and Cheltenham Town Football Club, playing cricket, gardening. Nigel Jones Esq, MP, House of Commons, London, SW1A 0AA *Tel:* 020 7219 4415 *Fax:* 020 7219 2537. *Constituency:* 16 Hewlett Road, Cheltenham, Gloucestershire, GL52 6AA *Tel:* 01242 224889 *Fax:* 01242 256658 *E-mail:* nigeljonesmp@cix.co.uk.

JOWELL, TESSA   Dulwich and West Norwood   *Lab majority 12,310*

Tessa Jowell. Born 17 September 1947; Daughter of Dr. Kenneth Palmer, and of Rosemary Palmer, radiographer; Educated St Margaret's School, Aberdeen; Aberdeen (MA), Edinburgh University; Goldsmith's College, London University; Married Roger Jowell 1970 (divorced 1977); married David Mills 1979 (1 son 1 daughter, 3 stepchildren). Child care officer, London Borough of Lambeth 1969–71; Psychiatric social worker, Maudsley Hospital 1972–74; Assistant director, MIND 1974–86; Director: Community care special action project, Birmingham 1987–90, Joseph Rowntree Foundation, Community Care Programme 1990–92; Senior visiting research fellow: Policy Studies Institute 1987–90, King's Fund Institute 1990–92; Member: TGWU, MSF. Councillor, London Borough of Camden 1971–86; Vice-Chair, then Chair, Social Services Committee of Association of Metropolitan Authorities 1978–86; Mental Health Act Commission 1985–90; Chair, Millennium Commission. **House of Commons:** Contested Ilford North 1978 by-election and 1979 general election. Member for Dulwich 1992–97, and for Dulwich and West Norwood since May 1, 1997; Frontbench Opposition Spokesperson on: Women 1995–96, Health 1994–95, 1996–97; Opposition Whip 1994–95; Minister of State: Department of Health (Minister for Public Health) 1997–99, Department for Education and Employment (Minister for Employment, Welfare to Work and Equal Opportunities) 1999–2001; Minister for Women 1999–2001; Secretary of State for Culture, Media and Sport 2001–; *Select Committees:* Member: Social Security –1992, Health 1992–94. *Countries of Interest:* Italy. Governor, National Institute for Social Work 1985–97; Member: Central Council for Training and Education in Social Work 1983–89; *Publications:* Various articles on social policy; PC 1998; Visiting Fellow, Nuffield College, Oxford; *Recreations:* Gardening, family, reading. Rt Hon Tessa Jowell, MP, House of Commons, London, SW1A 0AA *Tel:* 020 7219 3409 *Fax:* 020 7219 2702. *Constituency:* 264 Rosendale Road, London SE24 9DL *Tel:* 020 8333 1372 *E-mail:* jowellt@parliament.uk.

Visit the Vacher Dod Website . . . **www.DodOnline.co.uk**

JOYCE, ERIC   Falkirk West   *Lab majority 8,532*

Eric Joyce. Born 13 October 1960; Son of late Leslie Robert Joyce and Sheila McKay, née Christie; Educated Perth Academy; Royal Military Academy, Sandhurst; Stirling University: (BA religious studies 1986); Bath University (MA education 1994); Keele University (MBA education 1995); Married Rosemary Jones 1991 (twin daughters). Private, Black Watch Regiment 1978–81; Officer 1987–99; Commission for Racial Equality 1999–2000; Member UNISON. **House of Commons:** Member for Falkirk West since December 21, 2000; PPS to Mike O'Brien as Minister of State, Foreign and Commonwealth Office 2003–; *Select Committees:* Member: Procedure 2001–, Scottish Affairs 2001–. *Special Interests:* Foreign Affairs, International Development (especially Education Issues), Defence, Trade and Industry (especially Oil and Gas, GM Crops), Higher Education, Asylum and Immigration. *Countries of Interest:* Argentina, Turkey, USA, China. Executive Member, Fabian Society 1998–. *Publications: Arms and the Man – Renewing the Armed Services* (Fabian Society) 1997; *Now's the Hour: New Thinking for Holyrood* (Fabian Society) 1999; *Clubs:* Camelon Labour Club; *Recreations:* Climbing, judo, most sports. Eric Joyce Esq, MP, House of Commons, London, SW1A 0AA *Tel:* 020 7219 6210 *Fax:* 020 7219 2090. *Constituency:* The Studio, Burnfoot Lane, Falkirk, FK1 5BH *Tel:* 01324 638919 *Fax:* 01324 679449 *E-mail:* ericjoycemp@parliament.uk.

K

KAUFMAN, GERALD   Manchester Gorton   *Lab majority 11,304*

Gerald Bernard Kaufman. Born 21 June 1930; Son of Louis and Jane Kaufman; Educated Leeds Council Schools; Leeds Grammar School; The Queen's College, Oxford (MA philosophy, politics and economics 1953). Assistant general secretary, Fabian Society 1954–55; Political staff, *Daily Mirror* 1955–64; Political correspondent, *New Statesman* 1964–65; Parliamentary press liaison officer, Labour Party 1965–70; Member, GMB. **House of Commons:** Contested Bromley 1955 and Gillingham 1959 general elections. Member for Ardwick 1970–1983, and for Manchester Gorton since 1983; Opposition Frontbench Spokesperson for the Environment 1979–80; Parliamentary Under-Secretary of State for the Environment 1974–75; Parliamentary Under-Secretary, Department of Industry 1975; Minister of State, Department of Industry 1975–79; Shadow Environment Secretary 1980–83; Shadow Home Secretary 1983–87; Shadow Foreign Secretary 1987–92; *Select Committees:* Chair, National Heritage 1992–97; Member, Liaison 1992–97; Chair, Culture, Media and Sport 1997–; Member, Liaison 1997–. Member: Labour Party National Executive 1991–92, Fabian Society. Member, Royal Commission on Lords Reform February 1999–January 2000; *Publications:* Co-author, *How to Live Under Labour*, 1964; Editor, *The Left*, 1966; *To Build the Promised Land*, 1973; *How to Be a Minister*, 1980; Editor, *Renewal*, 1983; *My Life in the Silver Screen*, 1985; *Inside the Promised Land*, 1986; *Meet Me In St Louis*, 1994; *How to Be a Minister*, (updated and revised edition) 1997; PC 1978; Hilal-i-Pakistan 1999; *Sportsclubs:* President: Gorton and District Sunday Football League; *Recreations:* Cinema, theatre, opera, concerts, travel. Rt Hon Gerald Kaufman, MP, House of Commons, London, SW1A 0AA *Tel:* 020 7219 5145 *Fax:* 020 7219 6825. *Constituency:* Gorton Labour Club, Kirk Street, Manchester 18 *Tel:* 0161–248 0073 *Fax:* 0161–248 0073.

Visit the Vacher Dod Website . . .
www.DodOnline.co.uk

KEEBLE, SALLY   Northampton North   *Lab majority 7,893*

Sally Keeble. Born 13 October 1951; Daughter of Sir Curtis Keeble, GCMG, and Lady Keeble; Educated Cheltenham Ladies' College; St Hugh's College, Oxford (BA theology 1973); University of South Africa (BA sociology 1981); Married Andrew Hilary Porter 1990 (1 son 1 daughter). Journalist: *Daily News*, Durban, South Africa 1973–79, *Birmingham Post* 1978–83; Press officer, Labour Headquarters 1983–84; Assistant director, External Relations, ILEA 1984–86; Head of communications, GMB 1986–90; Public affairs consultant 1995–97; Member: National Union of Journalists. Councillor, Southwark Council 1986–94, Leader 1990–93. **House of Commons:** Member for Northampton North since May 1, 1997; PPS to Hilary Armstrong as Minister of State, Department of the Environment, Transport and the Regions (Minister for Local Government and Regions) 1999–2001; Parliamentary Under-Secretary of State: Department for Transport, Local Government and the Regions 2001–02, Department for International Development 2002–03; *Select Committees:* Member, Agriculture 1997–99. *Special Interests:* Economic Policy, Home Affairs, Education, Local and Regional Government, Financial Services. *Countries of Interest:* North Africa, South Africa, USA. *Publications: Citizens Look At Congress Profiles*, 1971; *Flat Broke*, 1984; *Collectors Corner*, 1986; *Feminism, Infertility and New Reproductive Technologies*, 1994; *Conceiving Your Baby, How Medicine Can Help*, 1995; *Recreations:* Antiques, walking, writing. Sally Keeble, MP, House of Commons, London, SW1A 0AA *Tel:* 020 7219 4039 *Fax:* 020 7219 2642. *Constituency:* Unit 5, Barratt Building, Kingsthorpe Road, Northampton, NN2 6EZ *Tel:* 01604 27803 *Fax:* 01604 27805 *E-mail:* keebles@parliament.uk.

KEEN, ALAN   Feltham and Heston   *Lab majority 12,657*

Alan Keen. Born 25 November 1937; Son of late Jack and Gladys Keen; Educated St William Turner's School, Redcar, Cleveland; Married Ann Fox 1980 (now MP as Ann Keen) (2 sons 1 daughter). Part-time tactical scout (assessing opposition tactics) Middlesbrough FC 1967–85; Miscellaneous positions in private industry and commerce, mainly in the fire protection industry 1963–92; Member, GMB. Councillor, London Borough of Hounslow 1986–90. **House of Commons:** Member for Feltham and Heston since April 9, 1992; *Select Committees:* Member: Deregulation 1995–96, Education 1995–96; Member, Culture, Media and Sport 1997–. *Special Interests:* Commerce, Industry, Foreign Affairs, Development, Democracy, Defence, Sport, Culture. Co-operative Party MPs 1992–; Secretary, Labour First Past the Post Group 1997–. *Clubs:* Feltham Labour, Heston Catholic Social, Hanworth British Legion; *Sportsclubs:* Joint Secretary, Lords and Commons Cricket 1997–; *Recreations:* Playing and listening to music, Association football, athletics, cricket, jazz enthusiast. Alan Keen Esq, MP, House of Commons, London, SW1A 0AA *Tel:* 020 7219 2819 *Fax:* 020 7219 0985. *Constituency:* Labour Party Office, Manor Place, Feltham, Middlesex, TW14 9BT *Tel:* 020 8890 4489 *Fax:* 020 8893 2606 *E-mail:* alankeenmp@parliament.uk.

KEEN, ANN   Brentford and Isleworth   *Lab majority 10,318*

Ann Keen. Born 26 November 1948; Daughter of late John Fox, and of Ruby Fox; Educated Elfed Secondary Modern, Clwyd; Surrey University (PGCEA); Married Alan Keen (now MP) 1980 (2 sons 1 daughter). Registered Nurse 1976; Head, Faculty of Advanced Nursing, Queen Charlotte's College, Hammersmith 1992; General Secretary, Community and District Nursing Association 1994; Member, GMB. **House of Commons:** Contested Brentford and Isleworth 1987 and 1992 general elections. Member for Brentford and Isleworth since May 1, 1997; PPS to: Frank Dobson as: Secretary of State for Health 1999, at HM Treasury 2000–01, Gordon Brown as Chancellor of the Exchequer 2001–; *Select Committees:* Member, Health 1997–99. *Special Interests:* Health, Child Poverty, International Development. *Countries of Interest:* South Africa, Cyprus. Hon. Professor of Nursing, Thames Valley University; CancerBACUP Paliamentary Figure of the Year; *Clubs:* Ewloe Social and Working Men's; *Sportsclubs:* Nurse/Physiotherapist, the House of Commons' Football Team; *Recreations:* Theatre, music, football. Mrs Ann Keen, MP, House of Commons, London, SW1A 0AA *Tel:* 020 7219 5623 *Fax:* 020 7219 2233. *Constituency:* Brentford and Isleworth Labour Party, 367 Chiswick High Road, London, W4 4AG *Tel:* 020 8995 7289 *Fax:* 020 8742 1004 *E-mail:* keena@parliament.uk.

KEETCH, PAUL   Hereford   *LD majority 968*

Paul Stuart Keetch. Born 21 May 1961; Son of late John Norton, engineer, and late Agnes (née Hughes); Educated Hereford High School for Boys; Hereford Sixth Form College; Married Claire Elizabeth Baker 1991 (1 son). Self-employed business consultant 1979–95; Non-executive director, London Computer Company 1996–. Councillor, Hereford City Council 1983–86. **House of Commons:** Member for Hereford since May 1, 1997; Spokesperson for: Health 1997, Education and Employment (Employment and Training) 1997–99, Defence 1999–; *Select Committees:* Member: Education and Employment 1997–99, Education Sub-Committee 1997–99, Employment Sub-Committee 1997–99, Catering 1998–99, Environmental Audit 2000–01.

Special Interests: National Heritage, Defence, Foreign Affairs. *Countries of Interest:* Former Soviet Union, Eastern Bloc countries, Eastern Europe. Joined Liberal Party 1975; Member Liberal Democrat Federal Executive Committee 2001–. Member: National Development Board, British Dyslexia Association 1993–; OSCE Observer, Albanian Elections 1996; Adviser, Lithuanian Local and National Elections 1995, 1996; Member, Council of The Electoral Reform Society; *Clubs:* Hereford Liberal, Herefordshire Farmers', National Liberal; *Sportsclubs:* Herefordshire County Cricket Club; *Recreations:* Cricket (watching), swimming, entertaining friends at home, country walks with my wife and son. Paul Keetch Esq, MP, House of Commons, London, SW1A 0AA *Tel:* 020 7219 5163 *Fax:* 020 7219 1184. *Constituency:* 39 Widemarsh Street, Hereford, HR4 9EA *Tel:* 01432 341483 *Fax:* 01432 378111 *E-mail:* paulkeetch@cix.co.uk.

KELLY, RUTH   Bolton West   *Lab majority 5,518*

Ruth Maria Kelly. Born 9 May 1968; Daughter of Bernard James Kelly, pharmacist, and Gertrude Anne Kelly, teacher; Educated Sutton High School; Westminster School; Queen's College, Oxford (BA philosophy, politics and economics 1989); London School of Economics (MSc economics 1992); Married Derek John Gadd 1996 (1 son 3 daughters). Economics writer, *The Guardian* 1990–94; Deputy head, Inflation Report Division, Bank of England 1994–97; Member, MSF. **House of Commons:** Member for Bolton West since May 1, 1997; PPS to Nick Brown as Minister of Agriculture, Fisheries and Food 1998–2001; HM Treasury 2001–: Economic Secretary 2001–02, Financial Secretary 2002–; *Select Committees:* Member: Treasury 1997–98,

Treasury Sub-Committee 1998; Member, Public Accounts 2002–. *Special Interests:* Economic Policy, European Affairs, Social Policy, Welfare Reform, Employment, Families. *Countries of Interest:* France, Spain. Bethnal Green and Stepney/Bow Constituency Labour Party: Treasurer 1994–96, Ward Secretary 1994–96; Bolton West Constituency Labour Party. Tower Hamlets Anti-Racist Committee; *Publications:* Various Pamphlets on Finance and Taxation and family policy; *Recreations:* Walking, writing. Ruth Kelly, MP, House of Commons, London, SW1A 0AA *Tel:* 020 7219 3496 *Fax:* 020 7219 2211. *Constituency:* Studio 4, Horwich Business Centre, 86 Lee Lane, Horwich, Bolton, BL6 7AE *Tel:* 01204 693351 *Fax:* 01204 693383 *E-mail:* kellyr@parliament.uk.

KEMP, FRASER   Houghton and Washington East   *Lab majority 19,818*

Fraser Kemp. Born 1 September 1958; Son of William and Mary Kemp; Educated Washington Comprehensive; Married Patricia Mary Byrne 1989 (2 sons 1 daughter). Civil servant 1975–81; Full-time Labour Party organiser, Leicester 1981–84; Assistant regional organiser, East Midlands 1984–86; Regional secretary, West Midlands 1986–94; National Labour Party general election co-ordinator 1994–96; Full-time branch secretary CPSA 1975–80; Member: GMB, AEEU. **House of Commons:** Member for Houghton and Washington East since May 1, 1997; Assistant Government Whip 2001–; *Select Committees:* Member: Public Administration 1997–99, Selection 1997–99.

Special Interests: Technology, Motor Industry, Small Businesses. *Countries of Interest:* Australia. Secretary: National Annual Labour Party Conference Arrangements Committee 1993–96, Labour's National General Election Planning Group 1994–96; Secretary, Labour's NEC

Campaigns and Elections Committee 1995–96. Vice-chair, Herrington Burn YMCA; Honorary president, Northguard Roman Research and Living History Society; Honorary member, North East Chamber of Commerce; President, Washington MIND; Patron, The Friends of Houghton Parish Church Trust; Member, Beamish Development Trust (North of England Open Air Museum); *Clubs:* Usworth and District Workmens and Institute (Washington); Hetton; *Sportsclubs:* Member, Houghton and Peterlee Athletics Club; *Recreations:* People. Fraser Kemp Esq, MP, House of Commons, London, SW1A 0AA *Tel:* 020 7219 5181 *Fax:* 020 7219 2536. *Constituency:* 14 Nesham Place, Church Street, Houghton-Le-Spring, Tyne and Wear, DH5 8AG *Tel:* 0191–584 9266 *Fax:* 0191–584 8329 *E-mail:* kempf@parliament.uk.

KENNEDY, CHARLES   Ross, Skye and Inverness West   *LD majority 12,952*

Charles Peter Kennedy. Born 25 November 1959; Son of Ian Kennedy, crofter and Mary MacVarish MacEachen; Educated Lochaber High School, Fort William; Glasgow University (MA politics, philosophy and English 1982); Indiana University (1982–83); Married Sarah Gurling 2002. President, Glasgow University Union 1980–81; Winner, British Observer Mace Debating Tournament 1982; Journalist with BBC Highland, at Inverness 1982. **House of Commons:** Member for Ross, Cromarty and Skye 1983–97, and for Ross, Skye and Inverness West since May 1, 1997; Alliance Spokesman for Social Security 1987; SDP Spokesman for: Scotland and Social Security 1987–88, Trade and Industry 1988–89; Liberal Democrat Spokesman for: Health 1989–92, European Union Affairs 1992–97, Agriculture, Fisheries, Food and Rural Affairs 1997–99; Leader, Liberal Democrat Party 1999–; *Select Committees:* Member, Standards and Privileges 1997–99. *Special Interests:* Scotland, Social Policy, Broadcasting, European Union. Chair Glasgow University Social Democratic Club 1979–80; President Liberal Democrat Party 1990–94; Member Liberal Democrat: Federal Executive Committee, Policy Committee. Associate Member, Scottish Crofters Union; *Publications: The Future of Politics,* 2000; PC 1999; *The Spectator* Member to Watch Award 1989; Channel 4 and *The House* Magazine, Political Humourist of the Year Award 1999; Doctorate Glasgow University 2001; *Clubs:* National Liberal; *Recreations:* Reading, writing, music, swimming, golf, journalism, broadcasting. Rt Hon Charles Kennedy, MP, House of Commons, London, SW1A 0AA *Tel:* 020 7219 6226 *Fax:* 020 7219 4881. *Constituency:* 1a Montague Row, Inverness, IV3 5DX *Tel:* 01463 714377 *Fax:* 01463 714380 *E-mail:* rossldp@cix.co.uk.

KENNEDY, JANE   Liverpool Wavertree   *Lab majority 12,319*

Jane Kennedy. Born 4 May 1958; Daughter of Clifford Hodgson, engineer, and of Barbara Hodgson; Educated Haughton School, Darlington; Queen Elizabeth Sixth Form College; Liverpool University; Married Malcolm Kennedy 1977 (divorced 1998) (2 sons). Residential child care officer, Liverpool City Council (LCC) 1979–83; Care assistant, LCC Social Services 1983–88; Branch Secretary, NUPE 1983–88, Area Organiser 1988–92. **House of Commons:** Member for Liverpool Broadgreen 1992–97, and for Liverpool Wavertree since May 1, 1997; Opposition Whip 1995–97; Assistant Government Whip 1997–98; Government Whip 1998–99; Parliamentary Secretary, Lord Chancellor's Department 1999–2001; Minister of State, Northern Ireland Office 2001–; *Select Committees:* Member: Social Security 1992–94, Administration 1997–99. *Special Interests:* Local and Regional Government, Public Services, Social Security, Foreign Affairs. *Countries of Interest:* Middle East and South East Asia. Chair, Labour Friends of Israel 1997–98. Member, Governing Body: Liverpool Polytechnic 1986–88, Oldham Sixth Form College 1990–92; Member: Ramblers' Association, Youth Hostelling Association; Fellow, Industry and Parliament Trust; PC 2003; *Recreations:* Walking, training Belgian Shepherd dogs, horse-riding. Rt Hon Jane Kennedy, MP, House of Commons, London, SW1A 0AA. *Constituency:* 1st Floor, Threlfall Building, Trueman Street, Liverpool, L3 2EX *Tel:* 0151–236 1117 *Fax:* 0151–236 0067 *E-mail:* jane.kennedy@nio.x.gsi.gov.uk.

Visit the Vacher Dod Website . . .
www.DodOnline.co.uk

KEY, ROBERT Salisbury

Con majority 8,703

(Simon) Robert Key. Born 22 April 1945; Son of late Rt Rev. Maurice Key, former Bishop of Truro; Educated Salisbury Cathedral School; Sherborne School; Clare College, Cambridge (BA economics 1966, MA, CertEd 1967); Married Susan Priscilla Bright, née Irvine 1968 (1 son 2 daughters). Assistant master: Loretto School, Edinburgh 1967–69, Harrow School (economics department) 1969–83; Member, then Associate member, Association of Teachers and Lecturers 1967–; Vice-Chair, Wembley Branch ASTMS 1975–80. **House of Commons:** Contested Camden, Holborn and St Pancras South 1979 general election. Member for Salisbury since June 1983; Opposition Spokesperson for: Defence 1997–2001, Trade and Industry 2001–02; Political Secretary to Edward Heath 1984–85; PPS: to Alick Buchanan-Smith as Minister of State for Energy 1985–87, to Christopher Patten: as Minister for Overseas Development 1987–89, as Secretary of State for the Environment 1989–90; Parliamentary Under-Secretary of State: at Department of the Environment 1990–92, at Department of National Heritage 1992–93 at Department of Transport (Minister for Roads and Traffic) 1993–94; Shadow Minister for International Development 2002–03; *Select Committees:* Member: Health 1994–95, Defence 1995–97; Member, Science and Technology 2003–. *Special Interests:* Education, Arts, Foreign Affairs, Defence, Agriculture. *Countries of Interest:* France, Turkey, USA. Treasurer, Conservative Candidates' Association 1976–79; Chair, Harrow Central Conservative Association 1980–82; Vice-Chair, London Central Euro-Constituency 1980–82; Member: Conservative Party National Advisory Committee on Education 1979–82, Executive Committee National Union of Conservative Party 1980–83. Chair, Governors of School at Great Ormond Street Children's Hospital 1976–79; Governor, Sir William Collins Comprehensive School 1976–79; Member of Council, Gap Activity Projects 1970–82; Member: UK National Commission for UNESCO 1984–85, Medical Research Council 1989–90; Member, Executive Council, Inter Parliamentary Union British Branch 1986–90; Chair, Council for Education in the Commonwealth 1985–87; Substitute, UK Delegation to Council of Europe and Western Europe Union 1996–97; Founding Chairman, the Alice Trust for Autistic Children 1977–80; *Publications: Reforming our Schools,* 1988; Hon. Fellow, College of Preceptors 1989–; *Recreations:* Singing, cooking, countryside. Robert Key Esq, MP, House of Commons, London, SW1A 0AA *Tel:* 020 7219 6501 *Fax:* 020 7219 4865. *Constituency:* The Morrison Hall, 12 Brown Street, Salisbury, Wiltshire, SP1 1HE *Tel:* 01722 323050 *Fax:* 01722 327080 *E-mail:* rob@robertkey.com.

KHABRA, PIARA Ealing Southall

Lab majority 13,683

Piara Singh Khabra. Born 20 November 1924; Educated Khalsa High School, Mahilpur, Punjab, India; Punjab University (BA social sciences 1951, BEd); Whitelands College, Putney (Diploma in Teaching 1968); Married Beulah Marian. Served Indian Armed Corps 1942–46; Clerical work, British Oxygen 1964–66; Class Teacher for Children aged 7–11, ILEA 1968–80; Community worker 1981–91; Chairman, Ealing law centre 1983–90; Member, MSF. Councillor, London Borough of Ealing 1978–82; JP 1977–. **House of Commons:** Member for Ealing Southall since April 9, 1992; *Select Committees:* Member, Members' Interests 1994–97; Member, International Development 1997–. *Special Interests:* Employment, Education, Race Relations, European Union, International Development. *Countries of Interest:* India. Chair, Indian Workers' Association, Southall, Middlesex; Member Quadripartite Committee 2000–2001; *Recreations:* Reading, watching football. Piara Khabra Esq, JP, MP, House of Commons, London, SW1A 0AA *Tel:* 020 7219 5010/5918 *Fax:* 020 7219 5699. *Constituency:* 49 B The Broad Way, Southall, Middlesex, UB1 1JY *Tel:* 020 8571 1003 *Fax:* 020 8571 1003.

DodOnline
An Electronic Directory without rival ...

MPs' biographies and photographs available with daily updates *via* the internet

For a *free* trial, call Yasmin Mirza, Aby Farsoun or Michael Mand on 020 7630 7643

KIDNEY, DAVID   Stafford   *Lab majority 5,032*

David Neil Kidney. Born 21 March 1955; Son of late Neil Bernard and Doris Kidney; Educated Longton High School; Sixth Form College, Stoke-on-Trent; Bristol University (LLB law 1976); Married Elaine Dickinson 1978 (1 son 1 daughter). Solicitor: Hanley, Stoke-on-Trent 1977–79, Stafford 1979–97; Member, MSF (now "AMICUS"). Councillor: Checkley Parish Council 1983–87, Stafford Borough Council 1987–97. **House of Commons:** Member for Stafford since May 1, 1997; Team Parliamentary Private Secretary to Ministers of State, Department for Environment, Food and Rural Affairs 2002–03; *Select Committees:* Member: Treasury 1998–2001, Treasury Sub-Committee 1998–2001; Member, Modernisation of the House of Commons 2001–. *Special Interests:* Children, Housing, Environment. *Countries of Interest:* Britain. Member, Society of Labour Lawyers. Member: British Agencies for Adoption and Fostering, Law Society; Fellow, Industry and Parliament Trust; *Recreations:* Chess, bridge. David Kidney Esq, MP, House of Commons, London, SW1A 0AA *Tel:* 020 7219 6472 *Fax:* 020 7219 0919. *Constituency:* Labour Rooms, Meyrick Road, Stafford, ST17 4DG *Tel:* 01785 224444/250356 *Fax:* 01785 250357 *E-mail:* kidneyd@parliament.uk.

KILFOYLE, PETER   Liverpool Walton   *Lab majority 17,996*

Peter Kilfoyle. Born 9 June 1946; Son of late Edward and Ellen Kilfoyle; Educated St Edward's College, Liverpool; Durham University; Christ's College, Liverpool; Married Bernadette Slater 1968 (2 sons 3 daughters). Labourer 1965–70, 1973–75; Student 1970–73; Teacher 1975–85; Member MSF. **House of Commons:** Member for Liverpool Walton since July 4, 1991 by-election; Opposition Spokesperson for: Education 1994–96, Education and Employment 1996–97; Opposition Whip 1992–94; Parliamentary Secretary: Office of Public Service 1997–98, Cabinet Office 1998–99; Parliamentary Under-Secretary of State, Ministry of Defence 1999–2000; *Special Interests:* Foreign Affairs, Commonwealth, Employment, Education. *Countries of Interest:* Australia, Latin America, The Commonwealth. Labour Party organiser 1986–91. *Publications: Left Behind: Lessons from Labour's Heartlands* (Politico's), 2000; *Recreations:* Reading, music, spectator sport. Peter Kilfoyle Esq, MP, House of Commons, London, SW1A 0AA *Tel:* 020 7219 2591 *Fax:* 020 7219 2356. *Constituency:* 69/71 County Road, Walton, Liverpool, L4 3QD *Tel:* 0151–284 4150 *E-mail:* kilfoylep@parliament.uk.

KING, ANDY   Rugby and Kenilworth   *Lab majority 2,877*

Andy (Andrew) King. Born 14 September 1948; Son of late Charles King, labourer, and of late Mary King; Educated St John the Baptist School, Uddingston; Coatbridge Technical College; Missionary Institute, London; Hatfield Polytechnic; Stevenage College; Nene College, Northants (CQSW, CMS); Married Semma Ahmet 1975 (1 daughter). Former: Labourer, Postal officer, Apprentice motor vehicle mechanic; Social work manager, Northamptonshire County Council 1989–97; Member, UNISON. Member, Warwickshire Police Authority 1989–97; Councillor, Warwickshire County Council 1989–98, Chair, Social Services Committee 1993–96; Councillor, Rugby Borough Council 1995–98. **House of Commons:** Member for Rugby and Kenilworth since May 1, 1997; *Select Committees:* Member, Social Security 1999–2001; Member, Regulatory Reform 1999–. *Special Interests:* Health, Law and Order, Social Services, Home Affairs, Small Businesses. *Countries of Interest:* Ethiopia, New Zealand, Brazil, Turkey, Australia, China. Member, Co-operative Party; Treasurer, Rugby and Kenilworth Constituency Labour Party 1984–88; Member, Christian Socialist Movement. Member, British Association of Social Workers; Vice-Chair, Rugby Parkinsons Disease Society; Member Co-operative Party; *Sportsclubs:* Rugby Golf Club; President, Rugby Town Junior FC; Hillmorton Ex-servicemen's Club; *Recreations:* Golf, football, dominoes, theatre. Andy King Esq, MP, House of Commons, London, SW1A 0AA *Tel:* 020 7219 1386 *Fax:* 020 7219 5855. *Constituency:* 12 Regent Place, Rugby, Warwickshire, CV21 2PN *Tel:* 01788 575504 *Fax:* 01788 575506 *E-mail:* kinga@parliament.uk.

KING, OONA   Bethnal Green and Bow   *Lab majority 10,057*

Oona King. Born 22 October 1967; Daughter of Preston King, professor of political science, and of Hazel King, teacher; Educated Haverstock Comprehensive Secondary School; York University (BA politics 1990); Berkeley-University of California (Scholarship); Married Tiberio Santomarco 1994. Researcher, Socialist Group, European Parliament 1990; Political assistant to Glyn Ford MEP, as Leader, EPLP 1991–93; John Smith's Labour Party leadership campaign team 1992; Freelance speech-writer/ghost writer 1993–94; Political assistant to Glenys Kinnock MEP 1994–95; Trade Union Organiser, GMB Southern Region 1995–97; Southern Region Equality Officer, GMB. **House of Commons:** Member for Bethnal Green and Bow since May 1, 1997; PPS to: Stephen Timms as Minister of State, Department of Trade and Industry 2002–03, Patricia Hewitt as Secretary of State, Department of Trade and Industry 2003–; *Select Committees:* Member: International Development 1997–2001, Transport, Local Government and the Regions 2001–02, Urban Affairs Sub-Committee 2001–02. *Special Interests:* Race Relations, Employment, Education, Health, Development, Equal Opportunities, Housing, European Affairs, Electoral Reform, Poverty. *Countries of Interest:* Bangladesh, Nicaragua, USA, Italy, France, South Africa, Rwanda and Great Lakes Region (Africa). Member, Fabian Society; Joint Vice-Chair, London Regional Group of Labour MPs 1997–; Chair, Labour Campaign for Electoral Reform. Member: Oxfam, Amnesty International, Jewish Council for Racial Equality (J-Core), One World Action, UNICEF; Vice-chair British Council 2001–; Patron: Positive Care Link, Council for Education in the World, Riverside Gallery; Member, 1990 Trust, Toynbee Hall; Vice-Chair, British Council 1999–; Patron, Dane Ford Trust; *Recreations:* Music, cinema. Oona King, MP, House of Commons, London, SW1A 0AA *Tel:* 020 7219 5020 *Fax:* 020 7219 2798. *Constituency:* Bethnal Green and Bow Labour Party Constituency Office, 349 Cambridge Heath Road, London, E2 9RA *Tel:* 020 7613 2274 *Fax:* 020 7613 2014 *E-mail:* silverv@parliament.uk.

KIRKBRIDE, JULIE   Bromsgrove   *Con majority 8,138*

Julie Kirkbride. Born 5 June 1960; Daughter of late Henry Raymond Kirkbride and Barbara Kirkbride (née Bancroft); Educated Highlands School, Halifax; Girton College, Cambridge (BA economics and history 1981, MA); Graduate School of Journalism, University of California 1982–83; Married Andrew Mackay MP 1997 (1 son). Researcher, Yorkshire Television 1983–86; Producer, BBC News and Current Affairs 1986–89; ITN 1989–92; Political correspondent, *Daily Telegraph* 1992–96; Social affairs editor, *Sunday Telegraph* 1996. **House of Commons:** Member for Bromsgrove since May 1, 1997; *Select Committees:* Member, Social Security 1997–99; Member: Catering 1998–, Culture, Media and Sport 1999–. *Special Interests:* Taxation, European Union, Social Security, Law and Order, Health. Vice-President, The Cambridge Union Society 1981. International Republican Institute Lecturer in Romania 1995; Member, Executive Committee: Commonwealth Parliamentary Association (CPA) UK Branch 1999–, Inter-Parliamentary Union 2001–; Rotary Foundation Scholar 1982–83; *Recreations:* Walking, opera. Julie Kirkbride, MP, House of Commons, London, SW1A 0AA *Tel:* 020 7219 6417. *Constituency:* Conservative Association, 37 Worcester Road, Bromsgrove, Worcestershire *Tel:* 01527 872135 *Fax:* 01527 575019.

KIRKWOOD, ARCHY   Roxburgh and Berwickshire   *LD majority 7,511*

Archy Kirkwood. Born 22 April 1946; Son of David Kirkwood; Educated Cranhill School; Heriot-Watt University (BSc pharmacy 1971); Married Rosemary Chester 1972 (1 son 1 daughter). Solicitor; Notary Public. **House of Commons:** Member for Roxburgh and Berwickshire since June 1983; Liberal Spokesman on: Health, Social Services and Social Security 1985–87; Alliance Spokesman on Overseas Development 1987; Liberal Spokesman on Scotland 1987–88; Convenor and Spokesman on Welfare and Social Security 1989–94; Liberal Democrat Shadow Leader of the House 1994–97; Spokesman on Community Care 1994–97; Liberal Democrat Deputy Chief Whip 1989–92, Chief Whip 1992–97; Aide to David Steel 1971–75, 1977–78;

Sponsored: Access to Personal Files Act 1987 (Private Member's Bill), Access to Medical Reports Act 1988 (Private Member's Bill); *Select Committees:* Member: Finance and Services 1992–97, Liaison 1992–97, Selection 1992–97; Chair, Social Security 1997–2001; Member: Court of Referees 1997–, Liaison 1997–; Chair, Work and Pensions 2001–. *Special Interests:* Freedom of Information, Health, Social Security, Human Rights. Social and Liberal Democrat Convenor on Welfare, Health and Education 1988–89. Member House of Commons Commission 1997–; Joseph Rowntree Reform Trust: Trustee 1985–, Chair 1999–; *Publications:* Co-author *Long Term Care – a Framework for Reform*; Kt 2003; Rowntree Political Fellow 1971; *Recreations:* Music, photography. Sir Archy Kirkwood, MP, House of Commons, London, SW1A 0AA *Tel:* 020 7219 6523 *Fax:* 020 7219 6437 *E-mail:* kirkwooda@parliament.uk.

KNIGHT, GREG   Yorkshire East   Con majority 4,682

Greg (Gregory) Knight. Born 4 April 1949; Son of Albert George Knight, company director, and Isabel, née Bell; Educated Alderman Newton's Grammar School, Leicester; College of Law, London; College of Law, Guildford. Solicitor 1973–89, 1997–; Business consultant 1997–2001. Councillor Leicester City Council 1976–79; Leicestershire County Council 1977–83, Councillor, Chair: Haymarket Theatre Finance Committee 1979, Public Protection Committee 1981. **House of Commons:** Member for Derby North 1983–97. Contested Derby North 1997 general election. Member for Yorkshire East since June 7, 2001; Assistant Government Whip 1989–90; Government Whip 1990–93; Government Deputy Chief Whip 1993–96; PPS to David

Mellor QC: as Minister of State Foreign Office 1987–88, as Minister of State Health 1988–89; Minister of State Department of Trade and Industry 1996–97; Deputy Shadow Leader of the House 2002–03; Shadow Minister for Culture, Media and Sport 2003–; *Select Committees:* Member, Televising Proceedings of the House 1989–92; Chair, House of Commons Services 1993–2002; Member: Broadcasting 1993–96, Finance and Services 1993–96; Member, Modernisation of the House of Commons 2001–. *Special Interests:* Consumer Issues, Information Technology, Music, Arts, Home Affairs. *Countries of Interest:* USA. Chair: South Leicester Young Conservatives 1970–72, Leicester and Leicestershire Young Conservatives 1972–73; Vice-chair Conservative Parliamentary Candidates Association 1997–2001. Executive Committee Member, British-American Parliamentary Group 2001–; *Publications:* Co-author *Westminster Words* 1988; *Honourable Insults* 1990; *Parliamentary Sauce* 1993; *Right Honourable Insults* 1998; PC 1995; *Clubs:* Bridlington Conservative; *Recreations:* Classic and vintage cars, music. Rt Hon Greg Knight, MP, House of Commons, London, SW1A 0AA *Tel:* 0845 0900203. *Constituency:* 3 Tennyson Avenue, Bridlington, East Yorkshire, YO15 2EU *Tel:* 01262 674074 *E-mail:* secretary@gregknight.com.

KNIGHT, JIM   South Dorset   Lab majority 153

Jim Knight. Born 6 March 1965; Son of Philip John Knight, accountant and Hilary Jean Howlett, née Harper, craftswoman; Educated Eltham College, London; Fitzwilliam College, Cambridge (BA geography, social and political sciences 1987); Married Anna Wheatley 1989 (1 daughter 1 son). Manager Central Studio Basingstoke 1988–90; Director: West Wiltshire Arts Centre Ltd 1990–91, Dentons Directories Ltd 1991–2001; Contested South West Region 1999 European Parliament election; MSF 1995–: Branch chair 1997–2001; AEEU 1998–; GMB 2001–. Frome Town Council: Councillor 1993–2001, Mayor 1998–2001; Mendip District Council: Councillor 1997–2001, Deputy leader 1999–2001, Labour group leader 1999–2001. **House of Commons:**

Contested South Dorset 1997 general election. Member for South Dorset since June 7, 2001; PPS to Rosie Winterton as Minister of State, Department of Health 2003–; *Select Committees:* Member, Defence 2001–. *Special Interests:* Foreign Policy, International Development, Families, Arts, Sport. *Countries of Interest:* Belarus, Iran, Iraq, Taiwan. Various posts Local constituency party 1990–. *Recreations:* Football, tennis, cooking, cycling. Jim Knight Esq, MP, House of Commons, London, SW1A 0AA *Tel:* 020 7219 8466 *Fax:* 020 7219 1976. *Constituency:* A32 Winfrith Technology Centre, Dorset, DT2 8DH *Tel:* 01305 853408 *Fax:* 01305 854643 *E-mail:* jimknightmp@parliament.uk.

KUMAR, ASHOK   Middlesbrough South and East Cleveland   *Lab majority 9,351*

Ashok Kumar. Born 28 May 1956; Educated Rykenld School for Boys; Derby and District College of Art and Technology; Aston University (BSc chemical engineering 1978, MSc process analysis and development 1980, PhD fluid mechanics 1982). Research fellow, Imperial College, London 1982–85; Research scientist, British Steel 1985–97; Member: Association of University Teachers 1982–84, Steel and Industrial Managers' Union 1984–. Councillor, Middlesbrough Borough Council 1987–97. **House of Commons:** Member for Langbaurgh 1991 by-election – 1992, and for Middlesbrough South and East Cleveland since May 1, 1997; PPS to Hilary Benn as Minister of State, Department for International Development 2003–; *Select Committees:* Member: Science and Technology 1997–2001, Deregulation and Regulatory Reform 1999–2002, Chairmen's Panel 2000–01; Member, Trade and Industry 2001–. *Special Interests:* Trade and Industry, Education, Local and Regional Government, Small Businesses. *Countries of Interest:* Japan, USA, India, Korea, Kazakhstan, Bahrain. Vice-chair Northern Regional Group of Labour MPs 2002–. Member: Institute of Energy Middlesbrough Law Centre 1985–95; Fellow Institution of Chemical Engineers; Board Member, Parliamentary Office of Science and Technology (POST) 1997–; Vice-President, Federation of Economic Development Authorities (FEDA) 1997–; *Publications:* Articles in scientific and mathematical journals; *Sportsclubs:* Marton Cricket Club; *Recreations:* Listening to music, reading history and philosophy books, playing badminton and cricket. Dr Ashok Kumar, MP, House of Commons, London, SW1A 0AA *Tel:* 020 7219 4460. *Constituency:* 6–8 Wilson Street, Guisborough, Cleveland, TS14 6NA *Tel:* 01287 610878 *Fax:* 01287 631894 *E-mail:* ashokkumarmp@parliament.uk.

L

LADYMAN, STEPHEN   South Thanet   *Lab majority 1,792*

Stephen John Ladyman. Born 6 November 1952; Son of Frank Ladyman, engineer, and of Winifred Ladyman; Educated Birkenhead Institute; Liverpool Polytechnic (BSc applied biology 1971–75); Strathclyde University (PhD for research into isotopic abundances in soil development 1975–79); Married Janet Baker 1994 (1 daughter 2 stepsons 1 stepdaughter). Computer manager, Pfizer Central Research; Member USDAW. Councillor, Thanet District Council 1995–99, Chair, Labour Group 1995–97, Chair, Finance Committee 1995–97. **House of Commons:** Contested Wantage 1987 general election. Member for South Thanet since May 1, 1997; PPS to Adam Ingram as Minister of State for the Armed Forces, Ministry of Defence 2001–03; Liaison MP for the Netherlands; Parliamentary Under-Secretary of State for Health, Department of Health 2003–; *Select Committees:* Member: Environment, Transport and Regional Affairs 1999–2001, Transport Select Committee 1999–2001, Transport Sub-Committee 2000–01. *Special Interests:* Environment, Economics, Industry, Science and Technology, Nuclear Power, Research, Defence, Small Businesses, Autism, Selective Education. *Countries of Interest:* Netherlands, China. Former Chair, Thanet South Constituency Labour Party; Member, Fabian Society. Member: European Standing Committee B 1997–99, European Standing Committee C 1999–2003; *Recreations:* Football, family, golf, house renovation. Dr Stephen Ladyman, MP, House of Commons, London, SW1A 0AA *Tel:* 020 7219 6946 *Fax:* 020 7219 6839. *Constituency:* 28 Newington Road, Ramsgate, Kent, CT12 6EE *Tel:* 01843 852696 *Fax:* 01843 852689 *E-mail:* ladymans@parliament.uk.

Visit the Vacher Dod Website . . .
www.DodOnline.co.uk

LAING, ELEANOR   Epping Forest   Con majority 8,426

Eleanor Laing. Born 1 February 1958; Daughter of late Matthew Pritchard and Betty, née McFarlane; Educated St Columba's School, Kilmacolm, Renfrewshire; Edinburgh University (BA, LLB) (First Woman President of Union); Married Alan Laing 1983 (1 son). Practised law in Edinburgh, City of London and industry; Special Adviser to John MacGregor: as Secretary of State for Education 1989–90, as Leader of the House of Commons 1990–92, as Secretary of State for Transport 1992–94. **House of Commons:** Contested Paisley North 1987 general election. Member for Epping Forest since May 1, 1997; Opposition Spokesperson for: Constitutional Affairs and Scotland 2000–01, Education and Skills 2001–03; Opposition Whip: (Constitutional, Education and Employment) 1999, (Social Security; Trade and Industry) 1999, (International Development; Trade and Industry; Wales) 1999–2000; Shadow Minister for Children 2003–; *Select Committees:* Member: Education and Employment 1997–98, Employment Sub-Committee 1997–98, Environment, Transport and Regional Affairs 1998–99, Transport Sub-Committee 1998–99. *Special Interests:* Education, Transport, Economic Policy, Constitution, Devolution. *Countries of Interest:* Australia, Gibraltar, USA, New Zealand. *Recreations:* Theatre, music, golf. Mrs Eleanor Laing, MP, House of Commons, London, SW1A 0AA *Tel:* 020 7219 4203 *Fax:* 020 7219 0980. *Constituency:* Thatcher House, 4 Meadow Road, Loughton, Essex, IG10 4HX *Tel:* 020 8508 6608 *Fax:* 020 8508 8099.

LAIT, JACQUI   Beckenham   Con majority 4,959

Jacqui Lait. Born 16 December 1947; Daughter of late Graham Lait and of Margaret Lait; Educated Paisley Grammar School; Strathclyde University (BA business 1967); Married Peter Jones 1974. Public relations, Jute Industries Ltd 1968–70; Visnews Ltd 1970–74; Government Information Service 1974–79; Parliamentary adviser, Chemical Industries Association 1980–84; Parliamentary consultant – own business 1984–92; Contested Strathclyde West 1984 European Parliament election. Chair, City and East London Family Health Services Authority 1987–91. **House of Commons:** Contested Tyne Bridge 1985 by-election. Member for Hastings and Rye 1992–97, and for Beckenham since November 20, 1997 by-election; Opposition Spokesperson for Pensions 2000–01; Assistant Government Whip 1996–97; Opposition Whip 1999–2000; PPS: to Parliamentary Under-Secretaries of State, Department of Social Security 1994–95, to William Hague as Secretary of State for Wales 1995–96; Shadow Secretary of State for Scotland 2001–; *Select Committees:* Member: Health 1992–93, Scottish Affairs 1994–95, Deregulation 1997–2001, Catering 1998–99, Science and Technology 1998–99, Catering 2001–02. *Special Interests:* Trade and Industry, European Union, Health. *Countries of Interest:* Australia, Europe, South Africa, USA. First woman in the Conservative Whips Office 1996–97; Chair, British Section, European Union of Women 1990–92; *Recreations:* Walking, swimming, theatre, food and wine. Mrs Jacqui Lait, MP, House of Commons, London, SW1A 0AA *Tel:* 020 7219 1375 *Fax:* 020 7219 0141. *Constituency:* c/o BCCA, 31 Beckenham Road, Beckenham, Kent, BR3 4PR *Tel:* 020 8663 1425 *E-mail:* jacquilaitmp@parliament.uk.

LAMB, NORMAN   North Norfolk   LD majority 483

Norman Peter Lamb. Born 16 September 1957; Son of late Hubert Horace Lamb, professor of climatology and Beatrice Moira Lamb, née Milligan, nurse; Educated George Abbot School, Guildford, Surrey; Wymondham College, Wymondham, Norfolk; Leicester University (LLB 1980); Qualified as solicitor 1984; Married Mary Elizabeth Green 1984 (2 sons). Norwich City Council: Trainee solicitor 1982–84, Senior assistant solicitor 1984–85; Steele and Company Norfolk: Solicitor 1986–87; Partner Steele and Company Norfolk 1987–2001; Consultant 2001–. Norwich City Council: Councillor 1987–91, Group leader 1989–91. **House of Commons:** Contested North Norfolk 1992, 1997 general elections. Member for North Norfolk since June 7, 2001; Liberal Democrat Spokesperson for: International Development 2001–02, the Treasury 2002–; *Select Committees:* Member: Treasury 2003–, Treasury Sub-Committee 2003–.

Special Interests: Employment, Social Affairs, Constitution, Environment, Housing. *Countries of Interest:* United States, South Africa. Chair Tottenham Liberals 1980–81; Norwich South Liberals 1985–87. Member: European Standing Committee A, European Standing Committee B until 2003; *Publications: Remedies in the Employment Tribunal,* Sweet and Maxwell 1998; *Clubs:* Member, National Liberal Club; *Recreations:* Walking, five-a-side football. Norman Lamb Esq, MP, House of Commons, London, SW1A 0AA *Tel:* 020 7219 8480 *Fax:* 020 7219 1963. *Constituency:* 15 Market Place, North Walsham, Norfolk, NR28 9BP *Tel:* 01692 403752 *Fax:* 01692 500818 *E-mail:* normanlamb@hotmail.com.

LAMMY, DAVID   Tottenham   *Lab majority 16,916*

David Lammy. Born 19 July 1972; Son of Rosalind Lammy, council officer; Educated The King's School, Peterborough; School of Oriental and African Studies, London University (LLB 1993); Harvard Law School, USA (LLM 1997); Single. Barrister, 3 Serjeants Inn, Philip Naughton QC 1994–96; Attorney, Howard Rice Nemerovsky Canada Falk & Rabkin 1997–98; Barrister, D J Freeman 1998–2000; member Amicus. Member: Greater London Assembly 2000, Archbishops' Council 1999–2002. **House of Commons:** Member for Tottenham since by-election June 22, 2000; PPS to Estelle Morris as Secretary of State for Education and Skills 2001–02; Parliamentary Under-Secretary of State: Department of Health 2002–03, Department for Constitutional Affairs 2003–; *Select Committees:* Member: Procedure 2001, Public Administration 2001. *Special Interests:* Health, Treasury (Regeneration), Arts and Culture, Education, International Development. *Countries of Interest:* USA, Caribbean, Latin America, Africa. Member: Fabian Society, Society of Labour Lawyers, Christian Socialist Movement. Former part-time volunteer Free Representation Unit; Member, Christian Socialist Movement; Trustee ActionAid; *Publications: Leading Together*; *Clubs:* Home House; The Honourable Society of Lincoln's Inn; *Recreations:* Film, live music, Spurs FC. David Lammy Esq, MP, House of Commons, London, SW1A 0AA *Tel:* 020 7219 0767 *Fax:* 020 7219 0357 *E-mail:* lammyd@parliament.uk.

LANSLEY, ANDREW   South Cambridgeshire   *Con majority 8,403*

Andrew David Lansley. Born 11 December 1956; Son of Thomas Lansley, OBE, and Irene Lansley; Educated Brentwood School; Exeter University (BA politics 1979) (President, Guild of Students 1977–78); First marriage dissolved (3 daughters); married Sally Low 2001. Department of Industry (Department of Trade and Industry 1984–87) 1979–87; Private secretary to Secretary of State, at Department of Trade and Industry 1984–85; Principal Private Secretary, to Norman Tebbit as Chancellor of the Duchy of Lancaster 1985–87; Policy director, British Chambers of Commerce 1987–89; Deputy director-general, British Chambers of Commerce 1989–95; Director, Conservative Research Department 1990–95; Director, Public Policy Unit 1995–97. Vice-President, Local Government Association. **House of Commons:** Member for South Cambridgeshire since May 1, 1997; Vice-chair Conservative Party 1998–99; Member, Shadow Cabinet 1999–2001; Shadow Minister for the Cabinet Office and Policy Renewal 1999–2001, Shadow Chancellor of the Duchy of Lancaster 1999–2001; *Select Committees:* Member, Health 1997–98; Member, Trade and Industry 2001–. *Special Interests:* Trade and Industry, Economic Policy, Small Businesses, Health, Local and Regional Government, Police, Film Industry. *Countries of Interest:* USA, Japan, Egypt, Israel, France, Germany, South Africa. A Vice-Chairman, Conservative Party (with responsibility for Policy Renewal) 1998–99. Patron: ASPIRE (Spinal injury), STRADA (Stroke and Action for Dysphasic Adults, Cambridge), Headway (Brain injury); Member, National Union Executive Committee 1990–95; Patron: Cambridgeshire Small Business Group, International Centre for Child Studies; *Publications: A Private Route,* 1988; *Conservatives and the Constitution* (with R. Wilson), 1997; CBE 1996; *Recreations:* Spending time with my children, films, biography, history, cricket. Andrew Lansley Esq, CBE, MP, House of Commons, London, SW1A 0AA *Tel:* 020 7219 2538 *Fax:* 020 7219 6835. *Constituency:* 153 St Neots Road, Harwick, Cambridge, CB3 7QJ *Tel:* 01954 212707 *Fax:* 01954 212707 *E-mail:* lansleya@parliament.uk.

LAWRENCE, JACKIE   Preseli Pembrokeshire   *Lab majority 2,946*

Jackie Lawrence. Born 9 August 1948; Daughter of the late Sidney and Rita Beale; Educated Upperthorpe School, Darlington, County Durham; Upperthorpe College; Open University; Married David Lawrence 1968 (2 sons 1 daughter). Assistant to Nick Ainger, MP; TSB Bank plc; Member, TGWU. Leader, Labour Group, Pembrokeshire County Council 1995–97; Councillor, Dyfed County Council 1993–96; Member, Dyfed Powys Police Authority 1994–97; Member, Pembrokeshire Coast National Park Committee 1993–95. **House of Commons:** Member for Preseli Pembrokeshire since May 1, 1997; Equalities PPS, Department of Trade and Industry 2003–; *Select Committees:* Member, Welsh Affairs 1997–99; Member, Trade and Industry 2001–. *Special Interests:* Small Businesses, Environment. Election Agent, Pembroke County Constituency 1992; Secretary, Pembroke Constituency Labour Party 1992–95; Chair, Pembroke Constituency Labour Party 1995–96; Hon. Treasurer, Welsh Regional Group of Labour MPs 1999, Hon. Secretary 1999–. Member: RSPB, Amnesty International; Life Member Commonwealth Parliamentary Association; *Recreations:* Walking, photography. Jackie Lawrence, MP, House of Commons, London, SW1A 0AA *Tel:* 020 7219 2757. *Constituency:* Fulke Street, Milford Haven, Pembrokeshire, SA73 2HH *Tel:* 01646 697969 *Fax:* 01646 698830 *E-mail:* lawrencej@parliament.uk.

LAWS, DAVID   Yeovil   *LD majority 3,928*

David Anthony Laws. Born 30 November 1965; Son of DA Laws and Mrs MT Davies; Educated St George's College, Weybridge, Surrey; King's College, Cambridge (BA economics 1987); Single. Vice-president JP Morgan and Company 1987–92; Barclays de Zoete Wedd Ltd 1992–94: Managing director, Head US Dollar and Sterling treasuries 1992–94. **House of Commons:** Contested Folkestone and Hythe 1997 general election. Member for Yeovil since June 7, 2001; Liberal Democrat Spokesperson for Defence 2001–02; Liberal Democrat Shadow Chief Secretary to the Treasury 2002–; *Select Committees:* Member: Treasury 2001–03, Treasury Sub-Committee 2001–03. *Special Interests:* Economy, Education, Pensions, Public Service Reform. *Countries of Interest:* Egypt, Jordan, France. Liberal Democrat Parliamentary Party: Economics adviser 1994–97, Director of Policy and Research 1997–99. Winner 1984 Observer Mace National Schools Debating Competition; *Recreations:* Running, rugby, reading, desert regions. David Laws Esq, MP, House of Commons, London, SW1A 0AA *Tel:* 020 7219 8413 *Fax:* 020 7219 8188. *Constituency:* 94 Middle Street, Yeovil, Somerset, BA20 1LT *Tel:* 01935 425 025 *Fax:* 01935 433 652 *E-mail:* lawsd@parliament.uk.

LAXTON, BOB   Derby North   *Lab majority 6,982*

Bob Laxton. Born 7 September 1944; Son of Alan and Elsie Laxton; Educated Woodlands Secondary School; Derby College of Art and Technology; Married (1 son from previous marriage). TU branch officer, Communication Workers' Union; Telecommunications engineer, BT plc 1961–; Member, Communication Workers' Union. Derby City Council: Councillor 1979–97; Council Leader 1986–88, 1994–97; Chair, East Midlands LGA to 1997. **House of Commons:** Member for Derby North since May 1, 1997; Member Trade and Industry Select Committee 1997–2001; PPS to Alan Johnson as Minister of State, Department of Trade and Industry 2001–; *Select Committees:* Member, Trade and Industry 1997–2001. *Special Interests:* Local and Regional Government. *Countries of Interest:* Middle East, USA. Member Labour Middle East Council. Labour Party Conference Debate, Local Government 1995; *Recreations:* Hill walking. Bob Laxton Esq, MP, House of Commons, London, SW1A 0AA *Tel:* 020 7219 4096 *Fax:* 020 7219 2329. *Constituency:* 1st Floor, Abbots Hill Chamber, Gower Street, Derby, DE1 1SD *Tel:* 01332 206699 *Fax:* 01332 206444 *E-mail:* laxtonb@parliament.uk.

LAZAROWICZ, MARK   Edinburgh North and Leith   *Lab majority 8,817*

Marek Jerzy Lazarowicz. Born 8 August 1953; Son of Jerzy Witold Lazarowicz and Ivy Lazarowicz, née Eacott; Educated St Benedicts School, London; St Andrews University (MA moral philosophy and medieval history 1976); Edinburgh University (LLB 1992); Diploma Legal Practice 1993; Married Caroline Elizabeth Johnston 1993 (1 daughter 3 sons). Organiser Scottish Education and Action for Development 1978–80; General secretary British Youth Council Scotland 1980–82; Organiser Scottish Education and Action for Development 1982–86; Advocate 1996–; TGWU 1978–. City of Edinburgh District Council 1980–96: Councillor, Leader of Council 1986–93; Councillor City of Edinburgh Council 1999–2001. **House of Commons:** Contested Edinburgh Pentlands 1987 and 1992 general elections. Member for Edinburgh North and Leith since June 7, 2001; *Select Committees:* Member, Scottish Affairs 2001–03; Member: Regulatory Reform 2002–, Environment, Food and Rural Affairs 2002–. *Special Interests:* Environment, Transport, Consumer Issues, Co-operative Issues, Constitution, Finance, Economy, Small Businesses. Member Co-operative Party; Chair Scottish Labour Party 1989–90; Member: Socialist Environment and Resources Association (SERA), SERA Parliamentary Group. *Publications:* Co-author *The Scottish Parliament: An Introduction*, T and T Clark 1999, 1st edition 1999, 2nd edition 2000; Various articles, papers and pamphlets on political and legal issues; *Recreations:* Jogging, walking. Mark Lazarowicz Esq, MP, House of Commons, London, SW1A 0AA *Tel:* 020 7219 8199. *Constituency:* 86–88 BrunswickStreet, Edinburgh, EH7 5HU *Tel:* 0131 557 0577 *Fax:* 0131 557 5759 *E-mail:* lazarowiczm@parliament.uk.

LEIGH, EDWARD   Gainsborough   *Con majority 8,071*

Edward Julian Egerton Leigh. Born 20 July 1950; Son of late Sir Neville Leigh, KCVO, former Clerk to the Privy Council; Educated Oratory School, Berkshire; French Lycee, London; Durham University (BA history 1972) (President of Union); Married Mary Goodman 1984 (3 sons 3 daughters). Member: Conservative Research Department 1973–75, Private Office of Margaret Thatcher as Leader of the Opposition 1976–77; Barrister, Inner Temple 1977–; Fellow, Institute of Arbitrators 1999–. Councillor: Richmond Borough Council 1974–78, GLC 1977–81. **House of Commons:** Contested Teesside, Middlesbrough October 1974 general election. Member for Gainsborough and Horncastle 1983–97, and for Gainsborough since May 1, 1997; PPS to John Patten as Minister of State, Home Office 1990; Parliamentary Under-Secretary of State, Department of Trade and Industry 1990–93; *Select Committees:* Member: Social Security 1995–97, Agriculture 1996–97, Deregulation 1997, Social Security 1997–2000, Public Accounts 2000–01; Chair, Public Accounts 2001–; Member, Liaison 2001–. *Special Interests:* Defence, Foreign Affairs, Agriculture, Families. Former Chair Durham University Conservative Association; Member governing council Conservative Christian Fellowship. Chair, National Council for Civil Defence 1979–83; Director, Coalition For Peace Through Security 1981–83; Fellow, Industry and Parliament Trust; *Publications: Right Thinking,* 1982; *Onwards from Bruges,* 1989; *Choice and Responsibility – The Enabling State,* 1990; Knight of Honour and Devotion of the Sovereign Military Order of Malta; *Recreations:* Walking, reading. Edward Leigh Esq, MP, House of Commons, London, SW1A 0AA *Tel:* 020 7219 6480 *Fax:* 020 7219 4883. *Constituency:* 23 Queen Street, Market Rasen, Lincolnshire *Tel:* 01673 844501 *Fax:* 01673 844501; 01673 849003 *E-mail:* leighe@parliament.uk.

DodOnline
An Electronic Directory without rival . . .

MPs' biographies and photographs available with daily updates *via* the internet

For a *free* trial, call Yasmin Mirza, Aby Farsoun or Michael Mand on 020 7630 7643

LEPPER, DAVID   Brighton Pavilion   *Lab majority 9,643*

David Lepper. Born 15 September 1945; Son of late Harry Lepper, lorry driver, and late Maggie Lepper; Educated Gainsborough Secondary Modern, Richmond; Wimbledon Secondary School; Kent University (BA English and American literature 1968); Sussex University (PGCE, postgraduate certificate in media education 1992); Polytechnic of Central London (postgraduate diploma in film 1978); Married Jeane Stroud 1966 (1 son 1 daughter). Secondary school English and media studies teacher 1969–96; Member, NUT 1969–. Councillor, Brighton Council 1980–96: Council Leader 1986–97, Mayor 1993–94, Brighton and Hove Council 1996–97. **House of Commons:** Member for Brighton
Pavilion since May 1, 1997; *Select Committees:* Member: Broadcasting 1997–2001, Public Administration 1999–2001, Radioactive Waste Policy Sub-Committee 2001–02; Chair, Broadcasting 2001–; Member: Environment, Food and Rural Affairs 2001–, Finance and Services 2001–, Liaison 2001–. *Special Interests:* Environment and Housing, Leasehold Reform, Community and Economic Regeneration, Town Centre Issues, Cyprus, Small Businesses. *Countries of Interest:* France, Italy, Japan, Cyprus. Member: Fabian Society, Socialist Education Association, Socialist Health Association, SERA, Labour Animal Welfare Society. Board Member, Alzheimer's and Related Dementia Sufferers Society, Brighton (ARDIS); Member: Alzheimer's Disease Society, Brighton MENCAP; Patron: Brighton Age Concern, Brighton Cares; Hon. President, Brighton and Hove Schools Rugby Association; Fellow, Sussex University Society; Member: CPA 1997–, IPU; Trustee ARDIS (local dementia charity); *Publications: John Wayne*, 1986; Contributor to British Film Institute publications and other film journalism; *Clubs:* Brighton Trades and Labour; *Recreations:* Music, cinema, reading fiction and poetry, watching professional cycling. David Lepper Esq, MP, House of Commons, London, SW1A 0AA *Tel:* 020 7219 4421 *Fax:* 020 7219 5814. *Constituency:* John Saunders House, 179 Preston Road, Brighton, East Sussex, BN1 6AG *Tel:* 01273 551532 *Fax:* 01273 550617.

LESLIE, CHRISTOPHER   Shipley   *Lab majority 1,428*

Christopher Leslie. Born 28 June 1972; Son of Michael and Dania Leslie; Educated Bingley Grammar School; Leeds University (BA politics and parliamentary studies 1994, MA industrial and labour studies 1996); Single. Office administrator 1994–96; Political research assistant 1996–97; Member: TGWU, GMB. Councillor, Bradford City Council 1994–98. **House of Commons:** Member for Shipley since May 1, 1997; PPS to Lord Falconer as Minister of State, Cabinet Office 1998–2001; Parliamentary Secretary, Cabinet Office 2001–02; Parliamentary Under-Secretary of State for: Local Government and the Regions, Office of the Deputy Prime Minister 2002–03, Department for Constitutional Affairs 2003–; *Select Committees:* Member,
Public Accounts 1997–98. *Special Interests:* Industrial Policy, Economic Policy, Environment, Local and Regional Government. *Recreations:* Travel, tennis, cinema, art. Christopher Leslie Esq, MP, House of Commons, London, SW1A 0AA *Tel:* 020 7219 4424 *Fax:* 020 7219 2832. *Constituency:* 33 Saltaire Road, Shipley, BD18 3HH *Tel:* 01274–401300 *Fax:* 01274–401313 *E-mail:* lesliec@parliament.uk.

LETWIN, OLIVER   West Dorset   *Con majority 1,414*

Oliver Letwin. Born 19 May 1956; Son of Professor William Letwin and late Dr Shirley Robin Letwin; Educated Eton College; Trinity College, Cambridge (BA history 1978, MA, PhD philosophy 1982); London Business School; Married Isabel Grace Davidson 1984 (1 son 1 daughter). Visiting fellow (Procter Fellow), Princeton University, USA 1980–81; Research fellow, Darwin College, Cambridge 1981–82; Special adviser to Sir Keith Joseph as Secretary of State for Education 1982–83; Special adviser, Prime Minister's Policy Unit 1983–86; N. M. Rothschild & Son, Merchant Bank 1986–: Manager 1986, Assistant Director 1987, Director 1991–2003, Managing Director 2003–. **House of Commons:** Contested Hackney North 1987, Hampstead and Highgate
1992 general elections. Member for West Dorset since May 1, 1997; Opposition Spokesperson for:

Constitutional Affairs, Scotland and Wales 1998–99, the Treasury 1999–2000; Shadow Financial Secretary 1999–2000; Shadow Chief Secretary to the Treasury 2000–01; Shadow Home Secretary 2001–; *Select Committees:* Member, Deregulation 1998–99. *Special Interests:* Economics, Employment, Education. *Countries of Interest:* Eastern Europe, Africa. Member, Conservative Disability Group. Patron, Joseph Weld Hospice; Member, European Standing Committee B 1998; *Publications: Ethics, Emotion and the Unity of the Self,* 1985; *Aims of Schooling,* 1986; *Privatising the World,* 1989; *Drift to Union,* 1989; *The Purpose of Politics,* 1999; Plus Articles and Reviews in learned and popular journals; Privy Counsellor 2002; Fellow, Royal Society of Arts; *Clubs:* St Stephen's Constitutional; Carlyle; *Recreations:* Ski-ing, sailing, tennis, reading, writing books. Rt Hon Oliver Letwin, MP, House of Commons, London, SW1A 0AA *Tel:* 020 7219 4192 *Fax:* 020 7219 0622. *Constituency:* Chapel House, Dorchester Road, Maiden Newton, Dorset, DT2 0BG *Tel:* 01300 321188 *Fax:* 01300 321233.

LEVITT, TOM   High Peak   *Lab majority 4,489*

Tom Levitt. Born 10 April 1954; Son of John and Joan Levitt; Educated Westwood High School, Leek; Lancaster University (BSc biological sciences 1975); Oxford University (PGCE 1976); Married Teresa Sledziewska 1983 (1 daughter). Teacher: Wiltshire County Council 1976–79, Gloucestershire County Council 1980–91; Contested Cotswolds 1989 European Parliament election; Supply teacher, Staffordshire County Council 1991–95; Sensory awareness trainer 1993–97; Consultant, Access for People With Sensory Impairments 1993–97; Member, NUT 1975–; School representative, NUT 1977–79, 1984–90; Local association president, NUT 1985; County division president, NUT 1988; Member: NUPE 1988–94, GMB 1995–. Councillor: Cirencester Town 1983–87, Stroud District 1990–92, Derbyshire County 1993–97, Vice-Chair, Education 1994–95. **House of Commons:** Contested Stroud 1987 and High Peak 1992 general elections. Member for High Peak since May 1, 1997; PPS to: Barbara Roche as Minister of State: Home Office 1999–2001, Cabinet Office 2001–02, Office of the Deputy Prime Minister 2002–03, Baroness Amos as Secretary of State for International Development 2003–; *Select Committees:* Member, Standards and Privileges 1997–. *Special Interests:* Disability, Education, Local and Regional Government, Quarrying, Voluntary Sector, Anti-Hunting. *Countries of Interest:* Western Europe, Poland. Member, SERA. Member: Friends of Buxton Museum; British Deaf Association; League Against Cruel Sports; Friends of the Earth; Amnesty International; SEA; Member, Global Organisation of Parliamentarians Against Corruption; Trustee, Royal National Institute for Deaf People 1998–; *Publications:* Local Government Management Board: *Sound Policies,* 1994, *Sound Practice,* 1995, *Clear Access,* 1996; *Sportsclubs:* Tideswell Cricket Club; *Recreations:* Cricket, walking, theatre. Tom Levitt Esq, MP, House of Commons, London, SW1A 0AA *Tel:* 020 7219 6599 *Fax:* 020 7219 0935. *Constituency:* 20 Hardwick Street, Buxton, Derbyshire, SK17 6DH *Tel:* 01298 71111 *Fax:* 01298 71522 *E-mail:* tomlevittmp@parliament.uk.

LEWIS, IVAN   Bury South   *Lab majority 12,772*

Ivan Lewis. Born 4 March 1967; Son of Joe and Gloria Lewis; Educated William Hulme Grammar School; Stand College; Bury Further Education College; Married Juliette Fox 1990 (2 sons). Coordinator, Contact Community Care Group 1986–89; Community care manager, Jewish Social Services 1989–92; Chief executive, Manchester Jewish Federation 1992–97; Member, MSF. Councillor, Bury Metropolitan Borough Council 1990–98; Chairman, Social Services Committee 1991–95. **House of Commons:** Member for Bury South since May 1, 1997; PPS to Stephen Byers as Secretary of State for Trade and Industry 1999–2001; Parliamentary Under-Secretary of State, Department for Education and Skills: for Young People and Learning 2001–02, for Adult Learning and Skills 2002, for Young People and Adult Skills 2002–03, for Skills and Vocational Education 2003–; *Select Committees:* Member: Deregulation 1997–99, Health 1999. *Special Interests:* Health, Crime, Education. *Countries of Interest:* Israel, USA. Chair, Bury South Labour Party 1991–96; Vice-Chair, Labour Friends of Israel 1997–. Chair, Bury MENCAP 1989–92; Member, Bury Carers Partnership Management Committee; Founder Member, Coordinator and Chair, Contact Community Care Group 1986–92; Trustee, Holocaust Educational Trust; *Recreations:* Keen supporter of Manchester City FC. Ivan Lewis Esq, MP, House of Commons, London, SW1A 0AA *Tel:* 020 7219 6404 *Fax:* 020 7219 6866. *Constituency:* 381 Bury New Road, Prestwich, Manchester, M25 1AV *Tel:* 0161–773 5500 *Fax:* 0161–773 7959 *E-mail:* heneghanp@parliament.uk; ivanlewis@burysouth.fsnet.co.uk.

LEWIS, JULIAN   New Forest East   *Con majority 3,829*

Julian Murray Lewis. Born 26 September 1951; Son of Samuel Lewis and late Hilda Lewis; Educated Dynevor Grammar School, Swansea; Balliol College, Oxford (MA philosophy and politics 1977); St Antony's College, Oxford (DPhil strategic studies 1981). Seaman, HM Royal Naval Reserve 1979–82; Doctoral research (strategic studies) 1975–77, 1978–81; Secretary, Campaign for Representative Democracy 1977–78; Research director and director, Coalition for Peace Through Security 1981–85; Director, Policy Research Associates 1985–; Deputy director, Conservative Research Department 1990–96. Hon Vice-president, British Military Powerboat Trust; Hon Vice-president, Calshot Association. **House of Commons:** Contested Swansea West 1983 general election. Member for New Forest East since May 1, 1997; Shadow Spokesman for Defence 2002–; Opposition Whip 2001–02; *Select Committees:* Member: Welsh Affairs 1998–2001, Defence 2000–01. *Special Interests:* Defence, Security, Foreign Affairs, European Affairs. *Countries of Interest:* Western Europe, Central and Eastern Europe, Russia. Treasurer, Oxford University Conservative Association 1971; Secretary, Oxford Union 1972; Honorary Vice-President, Greater London and West London Young Conservatives 1980s; Executive member 1922 Committee 2001. Member: RNLI, Medical Charities; Joint organiser of campaign against militant infiltration of the Labour Party 1977–78; Hon Vice-President, British Military Powerboat Trust; *Publications: Changing Direction: British Military Planning for Post-War Strategic Defence, 1942–1947,* 1988 (second edition 2003); *Who's Left? An Index of Labour MPs and Left-Wing Causes, 1985–1992,* 1992; *Labour's CND Cover-Up,* 1992; *The Liberal Democrats: The Character of Their Politics,* 1993; *What's Liberal? Liberal Democrat Quotations and Facts,* 1996; *Clubs:* Athenaeum, Hon president Totton Conservative; *Recreations:* History, fiction, films, music, photography. Dr Julian Lewis, MP, House of Commons, London, SW1A 0AA *Tel:* 020 7219 3000. *Constituency:* New Forest East Conservative Association, 3 The Parade, Southampton Road, Cadnam, Hampshire, SO40 2NG *Tel:* 023 8081 4817.

LEWIS, TERRY   Worsley   *Lab majority 11,787*

Terry Lewis. Born 29 December 1935; Son of Andrew Lewis, dockworker; Educated Our Lady of Mount Carmel School, Salford; Technical college; Married Audrey Clarke 1958 (1 son and 1 son deceased). RAMC 1954–56; Local government 1976–84; Personnel officer 1979–83; Sponsored by TGWU. Deputy leader, Bolton Borough Council 1980–83: Chair, Education Committee 1981–83. **House of Commons:** Member for Worsley since June 1983; *Select Committees:* Member: Environment 1991–92, Members' Interests 1992–97, Standards and Privileges 1997–2001. *Special Interests:* Local and Regional Government, Employment. *Recreations:* Football spectating. Terry Lewis Esq, MP, House of Commons, London, SW1A 0AA *Tel:* 020 7219 3479. *Constituency:* Emlyn Hall, Emlyn Street, Worsley, Greater Manchester, M28 3JZ *Tel:* 0161–703 8017 *Fax:* 0161–703 8346.

LIDDELL, HELEN   Airdrie and Shotts   *Lab majority 12,340*

Helen Lawrie Liddell. Born 6 December 1950; Daughter of Hugh and Bridget Reilly; Educated St Patrick's High School, Coatbridge; Strathclyde University (BA economics 1972); Married Dr Alistair Liddell 1972 (1 son 1 daughter). Economics correspondent, BBC Scotland 1976–77; General secretary, Labour Party in Scotland 1977–88; Director, personnel and public affairs, Scottish Daily Record and Sunday Mail (1986) Ltd 1988–92; Chief executive, Business Venture Programme 1993–94; Scottish TUC: Head of economics department 1971–75, Assistant secretary 1975–76; Member GMB. **House of Commons:** Contested Fife East October 1974 general election. Member for Monklands East from June 30, 1994 by-election–1997, and for Airdrie and Shotts since May 1, 1997; Opposition Spokesperson on Scotland 1995–97; Economic Secretary, HM Treasury 1997–98; Minister of State: Scottish Office (Minister for Education) 1998–99, Department of the Environment, Transport and the Regions (Minister for Transport) 1999, Department of Trade and Industry

(Minister for Energy and Competitiveness in Europe) 1999–2001; Secretary of State for Scotland 2001–03; *Special Interests:* Media, Scottish Affairs, Economic Policy, Trade and Industry, Small Businesses. *Countries of Interest:* USA, Europe, Russia. Chair, Independent Review into the future of the Scottish Symphony Orchestra and Orchestra of Scottish Opera 1993–94; Vice-chair, Rehab Scotland 1990–92; Chair, UN5O: Scotland 1994; *Publications: Elite,* 1990; PC 1998; *Recreations:* Cooking, hill-walking, music, writing. Rt Hon Helen Liddell, MP, House of Commons, London, SW1A 0AA *Tel:* 020 7219 6507 *Fax:* 020 7219 3390. *Constituency:* 115 Graham Street, Airdrie, Lanarkshire, ML6 6DE *Tel:* 01236 748777 *Fax:* 01236 748666.

LIDDELL-GRAINGER, IAN   Bridgwater   Con majority 4,987

Ian Richard Peregrine Liddell-Grainger. Born 23 February 1959; Son of David Liddell-Grainger, farmer, and Ann Grainger; Educated Wellesley House School, Kent; Millfield School, Somerset; South of Scotland Agricultural College Edinburgh (National Certificate of Agriculture); Married Jill Nesbitt 1959 (1 son 2 daughters). Major Fusiliers TA; Family farm Berwickshire 1980–85; Managing director property management and development companies group 1985–; Contested Tyne and Wear 1994 European Parliament election. Councillor: Tynedale District Council 1989–95, Northern Area Council 1992–95. **House of Commons:** Contested Torridge and Devon West 1997 general election. Member for Bridgwater since June 7, 2001; *Select Committees:* Member: Public Administration 2001–, Scottish Affairs 2002–. *Special Interests:* Business, Economy, Defence, Rural Affairs, Farming. Member Conservative agricultural forum; Chair Corbridge Branch Hexham Association 1992–94; President Tyne Bridge Conservative Association 1993–96. Northern industrial representative European Parliament; Member House of Lords rural economy group; Adviser to chair: Foreign Affairs Select Committee, Defence Select Committee; *Recreations:* Walking, travel, skiing, family. Ian Liddell-Grainger Esq, MP, House of Commons, London, SW1A 0AA *Tel:* 020 7219 8149. *Constituency:* 16 Northgate, Bridgwater, Somerset, TA6 3EU *Tel:* 01278 458383 *Fax:* 01278 433613 *E-mail:* ianlg@parliament.uk.

LIDINGTON, DAVID   Aylesbury   Con majority 10,009

David Lidington. Born 30 June 1956; Son of Roy and Rosa Lidington; Educated Haberdashers' Aske's School, Elstree; Sidney Sussex College, Cambridge (MA history, PhD); Married Helen Parry 1989 (4 sons). British Petroleum 1983–86; Rio Tinto Zinc 1986–87; Special Adviser to Douglas Hurd: at Home Office 1987–89, at Foreign and Commonwealth Office 1989–90; Senior Consultant, The Public Policy Unit 1991–92. **House of Commons:** Contested Vauxhall 1987 general election. Member for Aylesbury since April 9, 1992; Opposition Spokesperson for Home Affairs 1999–2001; PPS: to Michael Howard as Home Secretary 1994–97, to William Hague as Leader of the Opposition 1997–99; Shadow Financial Secretary 2001–02; Shadow Minister for Agriculture and the Fisheries 2002; Shadow Secretary of State for Environment, Food and Rural Affairs 2002–; *Select Committees:* Member, Education 1992–96. *Countries of Interest:* Europe, Hong Kong. Various offices in: Cambridge University (Chairman), Enfield North Conservative Association; Conservative Christian Fellowship: Member governing council, Deputy chair board of directors. *Clubs:* Aylesbury Conservative; *Recreations:* History, choral singing, reading. David Lidington Esq, MP, House of Commons, London, SW1A 0AA *Tel:* 020 7219 3432 *Fax:* 020 7219 2564. *Constituency:* 100 Walton Street, Aylesbury, Buckinghamshire, HP21 7QP *Tel:* 01296 482102 *Fax:* 01296 398481 *E-mail:* davidlidingtonmp@parliament.uk

Visit the Vacher Dod Website . . .
www.DodOnline.co.uk

LILLEY, PETER Hitchin and Harpenden *Con majority 6,663*

Peter Bruce Lilley. Born 23 August 1943; Son of Arnold and Lilian (née Elliott) Lilley; Educated Dulwich College; Clare College, Cambridge (BA natural sciences and economic sciences 1965); Married Gail Ansell 1979. Economic adviser on underdeveloped countries 1966–72; Investment adviser on North Sea oil and other energy industries 1972–84; Consultant director, Conservative Research Department 1979–83; Partner, W Greenwell & Co 1979–86; Director: Great Western Resources Ltd 1985–87, Greenwell Montague Stockbrokers 1986–87 (Head, oil investment department); Fleming Claverhouse Investment Trust 1997–. Member, School of Management Advisory Board, Southampton University 2002–. **House of Commons:** Contested Haringey, Tottenham October 1974 general election. Member for St Albans 1983–97, and for Hitchin and Harpenden since May 1, 1997; Joint PPS: to Lord Bellwin, as Minister of State for Local Government, Department of the Environment and William Waldegrave as Parliamentary Under-Secretary of State, Department of Environment June-November 1984, to Nigel Lawson, as Chancellor of the Exchequer 1984–87; Economic Secretary to the Treasury 1987–89; Financial Secretary to the Treasury 1989–90; Secretary of State for: Trade and Industry 1990–92, Social Security 1992–97; Contested Leadership of the Conservative Party June 1997; Member, Shadow Cabinet 1997–99; Shadow Chancellor of the Exchequer 1997–98; Deputy Leader of the Opposition (with overall responsibility for development of party policy) 1998–99; *Special Interests:* Economic Policy, European Union, Education, Race Relations. *Countries of Interest:* France. Chair, Bow Group 1973–75. *Publications: You Sincerely Want to Win? – Defeating Terrorism in Ulster*, 1972; *Lessons for Power*, 1974; Co-author, *Delusions of Income Policy*, 1977; Contributor, *End of the Keynesian Era*, 1980; *Thatcherism, the Next Generation*, 1989; *The Mais Lecture Benefits and Costs: Securing the Future of the Social Security*, 1993; *Patient Power*, 2000; *Common Sense on Cannabis* (Social Market Foundation) 2001; *Taking Liberties* (Adam Smith Institute) 2002; PC 1990; *Clubs:* Carlton, Beefsteak. Rt Hon Peter Lilley, MP, House of Commons, London, SW1A 0AA *Tel:* 020 7219 4577 *Fax:* 020 7219 3840. *Constituency:* Riverside House, 1 Place Farm, Wheathampstead, Hertfordshire, AL4 8SB *Tel:* 01582 834344 *Fax:* 01582 834884 *E-mail:* lilleyp@parliament.uk.

LINTON, MARTIN Battersea *Lab majority 5,053*

Martin Linton. Born 11 August 1944; Son of Sydney Linton and late Karin Linton; Educated Christ's Hospital, Sussex; Pembroke College, Oxford (MA philosophy, politics and economics 1963–66); Université de Lyon; Married Kathy Stanley 1975 (died 1995) (2 daughters). Journalist on: *Daily Mail* 1966–71, *Financial Times* 1971, *Labour Weekly* 1971–79, *Daily Star* 1980–81, *The Guardian* 1981–97; Member: NUJ 1966–97, GMB. Councillor, London Borough of Wandsworth 1971–82, Chairman, Recreation Committee 1971–77. **House of Commons:** Member for Battersea since May 1, 1997; PPS to: Baroness Blackstone as Minister of State (Minister for the Arts), Department for Culture, Media and Sport 2001–03, Peter Hain as Leader of the House of Commons 2003–; *Select Committees:* Member, Home Affairs 1997–2001; Member: Administration 2001–, Modernisation of the House of Commons 2003–. *Special Interests:* Arts, Housing, Education, Culture, Political Finance, Media Influence, Voting Systems. *Countries of Interest:* Sweden. Joined Labour Party 1968; Chairman, Constituency Labour Party 1994–96. President, Battersea Arts Centre; Treasurer, British Swedish Parliamentary Association; *Publications: Get Me Out Of Here*, 1980; *The Swedish Road to Socialism*, 1984; *Labour Can Still Win*, 1988; *The Guardian Guide to the House of Commons*, (editor) 1992; *What's wrong with first-past-the-post?*, 1993; *Money and Votes*, 1994; *Was It The Sun Wot Won It?*, 1995; Editor, *Guardian Election Guide*, 1997; *Making Votes Count*, 1998; *Beyond 2002*, 2000; *Recreations:* Playing music, watching football (Fulham FC). Martin Linton Esq, MP, House of Commons, London, SW1A 0AA *Tel:* 020 7219 4619 *Fax:* 020 7219 5728. *Constituency:* 177 Lavender Hill, London, SW11 5TE *Tel:* 020 7207 3060 *Fax:* 020 7207 3063 *E-mail:* lintonm@parliament.uk.

Visit the Vacher Dod Website . . .

www.DodOnline.co.uk

LLOYD, TONY   Manchester Central   *Lab majority 13,742*

Tony (Anthony) Joseph Lloyd. Born 25 February 1950; Son of late Sydney Lloyd, lithographic printer; Educated Stretford Grammar School; Nottingham University (maths); Manchester Business School (business administration); Married Judith Ann Tear 1974 (1 son 3 daughters). University lecturer. Councillor, Trafford District Council 1979–84. **House of Commons:** Member for Stretford 1983–97, and for Manchester Central since May 1, 1997; Opposition Spokesperson for: Transport 1988–89, Employment 1988–92, 1993–94, Education (responsible for co-ordinating policies on education and training) 1992–94, The Environment and London 1994–95, Foreign and Commonwealth Affairs 1995–97; Minister of State, Foreign and Commonwealth Office 1997–99; *Special Interests:* Civil Liberties, Disarmament, Immigration, Race Relations, Industrial Policy, Human Rights, Overseas Aid and Development. *Countries of Interest:* Former Soviet Union, Guatemala, Japan, Poland. Member Parliamentary Labour Party Parliamentary Committee 2001–. Member, UK Delegation Parliamentary Assembly of the Council of Europe/Western European Union 2000–; *Recreations:* Family. Tony Lloyd Esq, MP, House of Commons, London, SW1A 0AA *Tel:* 020 7219 3488 *Fax:* 020 7219 2585. *Constituency:* 10 Swan Street, Manchester, M4 5JN *Tel:* 0161–819 2828 *Fax:* 0161–839 6875 *E-mail:* contact@tonylloydmp.co.uk.

LLWYD, ELFYN   Meirionnydd Nant Conwy   *Pl C majority 5,684*

Elfyn Llwyd. Born 26 September 1951; Son of late Huw Meirion and Hefina Hughes; Educated Dyffryn Conwy School; Llanrwst Grammar School; University College of Wales, Aberystwyth (LLB law 1974); College of Law, Chester (Solicitor); Married Eleri Llwyd 1974 (1 son 1 daughter). Solicitor until 1997; President, Gwynedd Law Society 1990–91; Barrister, Gray's Inn 1997–. **House of Commons:** Member for Meirionnydd Nant Conwy since April 9, 1992; Spokesperson for: Transport 1992–94, Trade and Industry 1992–94, Northern Ireland 1997–99, Housing 1997–, Local Government 1997–, Tourism 1997–, Home Affairs 1999–, Defence 2001–; Plaid Cymru Parliamentary Whip 1995–2001; Leader, Plaid Cymru Parliamentary Party 1997–; *Select Committees:* Member: Welsh Affairs 1992–97, Welsh Affairs 1998–2001. *Special Interests:* Civil Liberties, Agriculture, Tourism, Home Affairs. *Countries of Interest:* Spain, Scotland, USA, Wales, Greece. Member, Plaid Cymru Policy Cabinet 1994–, Parliamentary Leader 1997–. Council member, NSPCC Wales; Patron Abbeyfield Wales; Member, Parliamentary Panel UNICEF; Hon member, Gorsedd of Bards 1998; Council member, University of Wales, Aberystwyth; Council member, University of Wales School of Medicine; Chair, Dolgellau Hatchery Trust; *Sportsclubs:* President: Estimaner Angling Association, Betws-y-Coed Football Club, Llanuwchllyn Football Club, Bala Rugby Club; Vice-President, Dolgellau Old Grammarians' Rugby Club; *Recreations:* Pigeon breeding, choral singing, rugby, fishing, cycling. Elfyn Llwyd Esq, MP, House of Commons, London, SW1A 0AA *Tel:* 020 7219 3555 *Fax:* 020 7219 2633. *Constituency:* Adeiladau Glyndwr, Heol Glyndwr, Dolgellau, Gwynedd, LL40 1BD *Tel:* 01341 422661 *Fax:* 01341 423990 *E-mail:* llwyde@parliament.uk.

LORD, MICHAEL   Central Suffolk and North Ipswich   *Con majority 3,469*

Michael Lord. Born 17 October 1938; Son of late John Lord, schoolmaster; Educated William Hulme's Grammar School, Manchester; Christ's College, Cambridge (MA agriculture 1962); Married Jennifer Margaret Childs 1965 (1 son 1 daughter). Farmer and taught agriculture 1962–66; Director, Power Line Maintenance Ltd 1966–68; Founded Lords Tree Services Ltd 1968; Aboricultural Consultant 1983. North Bedfordshire Borough Council: Councillor 1974–77, Chair, Policy Commission 1974–77; Bedfordshire County Council: Councillor 1981–83, Chair, Further Education Committee 1981–83. **House of Commons:** Contested Manchester Gorton 1979 general election. Member for Central Suffolk 1983–97, and for Central Suffolk and North Ipswich since May 1, 1997; PPS to: John MacGregor, as Minister of Agriculture, Fisheries and Food 1984–85, as Chief Secretary to the Treasury 1985–87; Second Deputy Chairman, Ways and Means and Deputy Speaker 1997–;

Select Committees: Member, Parliamentary Commissioner for Administration 1990–97; Second Deputy Chair of Ways and Means, Court of Referees 1997–; Second Deputy Chairman of Ways and Means (ex officio): Chairmen's Panel 1997–, Standing Orders 1998–; Second Deputy Chair of Ways and Means, Unopposed Bills (Panel) 2000–. *Special Interests:* Agriculture, Forestry, Environment. Vice-President, The Arboricultural Association, President 1989–95; Captain, Parliamentary Golfing Society 1999–2002; Cambridge Rugby Blue; Parliamentary delegate, The Council of Europe and the Western European Union 1987–91; Member, Executive Committee, Inter Parliamentary Union (IPU) British Group 1995–97; KB 2001; FArbA; *Recreations:* Golf, sailing, gardening. Sir Michael Lord MP, House of Commons, London, SW1A 0AA *Tel:* 020 7219 5055 *Fax:* 020 7219 2931. *Constituency:* Central Suffolk and North Ipswich Conservative Association, 19 The Business Centre, Earl Soham, Woodbridge, Suffolk, IP13 7SA *Tel:* 01728 685148 *Fax:* 01728 685157.

LOUGHTON, TIM   East Worthing and Shoreham   *Con majority 6,139*

Timothy Paul Loughton. Born 30 May 1962; Son of Reverend Michael Loughton and Pamela Dorothy Loughton; Educated The Priory School, Lewes, Sussex; Warwick University (BA classical civilisation 1983); Clare College, Cambridge (Research Mesopotamian archaeology 1983–84); Married Elizabeth Juliet MacLauchlan 1992 (1 son 2 daughters). Fund manager, Fleming Private Asset Management, City of London 1984–, Director 1992–2000; Formerly BIFU. **House of Commons:** Contested Sheffield Brightside 1992 general election. Member for East Worthing and Shoreham since May 1, 1997; Opposition Spokesperson for: Environment, Transport and the Regions (Regeneration; Poverty; Regions; Housing) 2000–01, Health 2001–; *Select Committees:* Member, Environmental Audit 1997–2001. *Special Interests:* Finance, Foreign Affairs, Home Affairs, Education (Special Needs), Environmental Taxation, Environment and Housing, Disability, Animal Welfare, Health. *Countries of Interest:* Latin America, Middle East, Indian subcontinent. Chair Lewes Young Conservatives 1978; Vice-chair: Sussex Young Conservatives 1979, Lewes Constituency Conservative Association 1979, South East Area Young Conservatives 1980; Secretary Warwick University Conservative Association 1981–82; Member Cambridge University Conservative Association 1983–84; Member Bow Group 1985–92; Vice-chair Battersea Conservative Association 1990–91; Member London Area Conservative Executive Committee 1993–96; Life Vice-President Sheffield Brightside Constituency Association 1993–; Deputy Chair Battersea Constituency Conservative Association 1994–96; Executive Committee Member, Selsdon Group 1994–; Member Carlton Club Political Committee 1994–; Chair Conservative Disability Group 1998–. Member: Sussex Archaeological Society, Society of Sussex Downsmen, RNLI, RSPCA, British Museum Society, Centre for Policy Studies, Institute of Economic Affairs, Tibet Action (UK), Court of Sussex University; Patron: League of Friends of Worthing Hospital, St Barnabas Hospice, Worthing, Patron, Worthing Hockey Club; President Adur Art Club; General election PA to Tim Eggar MP 1987; Member: Burns committee Financial Services and Markets Bill 1999, Standing committee Financial Services and Markets Bill 1999–, Standing committee Local Government Bill 2000–, Homes Bill 2001–, Homelessness Bill 2001–, European Standing committee C 1999–2001; Lecturer, English Wine and Stock Exchange; Adoption and Children Bill November 2001-May 2002; Member: Royal Institute International Affairs, CPA, IPU; MSi(Dip); *Clubs:* Carlton; *Sportsclubs:* Patron, Worthing Hockey; *Recreations:* Skiing, tennis, hockey, wine, archaeology. Timothy Loughton Esq, MP, House of Commons, London, SW1A 0AA *Tel:* 020 7219 4471 *Fax:* 020 7219 0461. *Constituency:* Haverfield House, 4 Union Place, Worthing, West Sussex, BN11 1LG *Tel:* 01903 235168 *Fax:* 01903 219755 *E-mail:* loughtont@parliament.uk.

DodOnline

An Electronic Directory without rival . . .

MPs' biographies and photographs available with daily updates *via* the internet

For a *free* trial, call Yasmin Mirza, Aby Farsoun or Michael Mand on 020 7630 7643

LOVE, ANDREW   Edmonton   *Lab majority 9,772*

Andrew Love. Born 21 March 1949; Son of late James Love and Olive Love; Educated Greenock High School; Strathclyde University (BSc physics); Association of Chartered Institute of Secretaries; Married Ruth Rosenthal 1983. Parliamentary Officer, Co-operative Party; Member (branch chairman 1980–83), TGWU; National Executive Member, NACO 1989–92. Councillor, London Borough of Haringey 1980–86. **House of Commons:** Contested Edmonton 1992 general election. Member for Edmonton since May 1, 1997; PPS to Jacqui Smith as Minister of State: Department of Health 2001–03, Department of Trade and Industry 2003–; *Select Committees:* Member, Public Accounts 1997–2001; Member, Regulatory Reform 1999–. *Special Interests:* Housing, Regeneration, Health, Mutuality, Small Businesses. *Countries of Interest:* France, Cyprus, Sri Lanka, Lebanon. Chair: Hornsey and Wood Green Labour Party 1987–89, Policy Committee, Greater London Labour Party 1990–94, Co-operative Parliamentary Group 1999–. Member, NETRHA 1986–90; Vice-chair, North London FE College 1987–90; Member, St Pancras Housing Association; Vice-Patron, Helen Rollason Cancer Appeal 1999–; Trustee, ICOF; ACIS; *Sportsclubs:* Muswell Hill Golf Club; *Recreations:* History, opera, cinema, golf. Andrew Love Esq, MP, House of Commons, London, SW1A 0AA *Tel:* 020 7219 6377 *Fax:* 020 7219 6623. *Constituency:* Broad House, 205 Fore Street, Edmonton, London, N18 2TZ *Tel:* 020 8803 0574 *Fax:* 020 8807 1673 *E-mail:* lovea@parliament.uk.

LUCAS, IAN   Wrexham   *Lab majority 9,188*

Ian Colin Lucas. Born 18 September 1960; Son of Colin Lucas, process engineer and Alice Lucas, cleaner; Educated Greenwell Comprehensive School, Gateshead; Royal Grammar School, Newcastle upon Tyne; New College, Oxford jurisprudence (BA 1982); College of Law, Christleton law (Solicitor's Final Exam 1983); Married Norah Anne Sudd 1986 (1 daughter 1 son). Russell-Cooke Porter and Chapman Solicitors: Articled clerk, assistant solicitor 1983–86; Solicitor's Admission 1985; Assistant Solicitor: Percy Hughes and Roberts 1986–87, Lees Moore and Price 1987–89, Roberts Moore Nicholas Jones 1989–92, DR Crawford 1992–97; Principal Crawford Lucas 1997–2000; Partner Stevens Lucas, Oswestry 2000–01; MSF 1996–. Member Gresford Community Council, Wrexham 1987–91. **House of Commons:** Contested Shropshire North 1997 general election. Member for Wrexham since June 7, 2001; *Select Committees:* Member, Procedure 2001–02; Member: Environmental Audit 2001–, Transport 2003–. *Special Interests:* Economy, European Affairs, Health, Education, Environment, Small Businesses. *Countries of Interest:* Germany, Japan, USA, India, Zimbabwe. Chair Wrexham Labour Party 1992–93; Vice-chair North Shropshire Labour Party 1993–2000; Society of Labour Lawyers 1996–; Fabian Society 2000–. Homeless in Oswestry Action Project 1993–2000: Chair, Committee member; Secretary Memorial Hall, Oswestry 1997–2000; *Recreations:* History, film, football, cricket, painting. Ian Lucas Esq, MP, House of Commons, London, SW1A 0AA *Tel:* 020 7219 8346. *Constituency:* 2 Mount Street, Wrexham, LL13 8DN *Tel:* 01978 355 743 *Fax:* 01978 310 051 *E-mail:* lucasi@parliament.uk.

LUFF, PETER   Mid Worcestershire   *Con majority 10,627*

Peter James Luff. Born 18 February 1955; Son of late Thomas Luff, master printer, and late Joyce Luff; Educated Windsor Grammar School; Corpus Christi College, Cambridge (BA economics 1976, MA); Married Julia Jenks 1982 (1 son 1 daughter). Research assistant to Peter Walker MP 1977–80; Head of private office to Edward Heath MP 1980–82; Company secretary, family stationery business, Luff & Sons Ltd to 1987; Account director, director and managing director, Good Relations Public Affairs Ltd 1982–87; Assistant managing director, Good Relations Ltd 1990–92; Senior consultant, Lowe Bell Communications 1989–90. **House of Commons:** Contested Holborn and St Pancras 1987 general election. Member for Worcester 1992–97, and for Mid Worcestershire since May 1, 1997; Opposition Whip 2000–: Home Office and Health 2000–01, Treasury, 2000–, Foreign Affairs 2001–02; Assistant Chief Whip 2002–; PPS: to Tim Eggar as Minister of State,

Department of Trade and Industry 1993–96, to Lord Mackay of Clashfern as Lord Chancellor 1996–97, to Ann Widdecombe as Minister for Prisons, Home Office 1996–97; *Select Committees:* Member: Welsh Affairs 1992–97, Transport 1993, Consolidation Etc Joint Bills Committee 1995–97, Public Service 1996–97; Chair, Agriculture 1997–2000; Member, Liaison 1997–2000; Member: Information 2001–, Selection 2002–, Administration 2002–. *Special Interests:* Railways, Trade and Industry, Rural Affairs, Performing Arts, International Development. *Countries of Interest:* Hong Kong, Falkland Islands, Israel, India, Mongolia. Chairman, Conservative Parliamentary Friends of India 2001–. Patron: Conservative Students 1995–98, Worcestershire ME Support Group; Vice-President: Severn Valley Railway 1997–, Evesham Rowing Club 1997–, Droitwich Canals Trust 1997–; Chairman, Worcester Cathedral Council; Member, Joseph Rowntree Inquiry into Planning for Housing 1992–94; Member, Armed Forces Parliamentary Scheme (Royal Navy) 1996, 2002; Member, Executive Committee, Commonwealth Parliamentary Association; *Publications: Supporting Excellence – Funding Dance and Drama Students* (Bow Group), 1995; Fellow, Institute of Public Relations; *Sportsclubs:* Worcestershire County Cricket; *Recreations:* Steam railways, theatre, photography, shooting, diving. Peter Luff Esq, MP, House of Commons, London, SW1A 0AA. *Constituency Tel:* 01905 763952 *Fax:* 01905 763952 *E-mail:* luffpj@parliament.uk.

LUKE, IAIN   Dundee East   *Lab majority 4,466*

Iain Malone Luke. Born 8 October 1951; Educated Dundee University (MA modern history and political science 1980); Edinburgh University (Diploma in business administration 1981); Jordanhill Teacher Training College (TQFE 1989); Married. Assistant collector taxes 1969–74; Dundee College of Further Education 1983–: Lecturer, Senior lecturer, Team leader; GMB. Councillor Dundee District Council 1984–96; Dundee City Council 1996–: Councillor, Convener cultural services 1988–90, Council leader 1990–92, Convener economic development 1991–96, Convener housing 1996–, Group chair. **House of Commons:** Member for Dundee East since June 7, 2001; *Select Committees:* Member: Administration 2001–, Broadcasting 2001–, Procedure 2001–. *Special Interests:* Dundee's Economic Prosperity, Housing, Scotland, Britain: EU relations, Social Inclusion. Council member National Trust for Scotland; Joint co-ordinator Dundee William McGonagall Centenary; Board member Dundee Contemporary Arts; Cleghorn Housing Association; Board Member Scottish Policy Forum 1998–2000; Member European Standing Committee C; *Recreations:* Football (Dundee FC), reading. Iain Luke Esq, MP, House of Commons, London, SW1A 0AA *Tel:* 020 7219 8165 *Fax:* 020 7219 1758. *Constituency:* Dundee Parliamentary Office, 57 Blackscroft, Dundee, DD4 6AT *Tel:* 01382 466700 *Fax:* 01382 466719 *E-mail:* lukei@parliament.uk.

LYONS, JOHN   Strathkelvin and Bearsden   *Lab majority 11,717*

John Lyons. Born 11 July 1949; Educated Woodside Secondary; Stirling University (MSc human resource management 2000); Partner (1 daughter 1 son). Mechanical engineer various organisations 1971–88; Trade Union officer NUPE, UNISON 1988–2001; Health Board member Forth Valley Health Board 1999–2001; AEEU 1965–1988; UNISON 1988–2001. **House of Commons:** Member for Strathkelvin and Bearsden since June 7, 2001; *Select Committees:* Member: Public Accounts 2001; Member: Broadcasting 2001–, Public Administration 2001–, Scottish Affairs 2001–. *Special Interests:* NHS, Local and Regional Government, Education, Voluntary Sector, Social Security, Pensions, International Development, Minimum Wage, Employment, Small Businesses, Employment. *Countries of Interest:* Cyprus. Member Forth Valley Health Board; *Recreations:* Hillwalking, reading. John Lyons Esq, MP, House of Commons, London, SW1A 0AA *Tel:* 020 7219 8325 *Fax:* 020 7219 1798. *Constituency:* 1 Dalrymple Court, Kirkintilloch, Glasgow, G66 3AA *Tel:* 0141–776 5403 *Fax:* 0141–776 3239 *E-mail:* lyonsj@parliament.uk.

Visit the Vacher Dod Website . . .
www.DodOnline.co.uk

M

McAVOY, THOMAS   Glasgow Rutherglen   *Lab majority 12,625*

Thomas McLaughlin McAvoy. Born 14 December 1943; Son of late Edward McAvoy, steelworker, and late Frances McLaughlin McAvoy; Educated Secondary Schools; Married Eleanor Kerr 1968 (4 sons). Shop steward, AEU 1974–87. Chair, Rutherglen Community Council 1980–82; Strathclyde regional councillor for Rutherglen and Toryglen 1982–87. **House of Commons:** Member for Glasgow Rutherglen since June 1987; Opposition Whip 1991–93, 1996–97; Government Whip (Pairing Whip) 1997–; *Select Committees:* Member, Northern Ireland Affairs 1994–96; Member, Finance and Services 1997–. *Special Interests:* Social Services. *Countries of Interest:* Ireland, USA. Member, Co-operative Party. Chair: Fernhill Tenants Association 1980–82, Rutherglen Federation of Tenants Associations 1980–82; PC 2003. Rt Hon Thomas McAvoy, MP, House of Commons, London, SW1A 0AA *Tel:* 020 7219 5009. *Constituency:* Cambuslang Training and Enterprise Centre, 1–15 Main Street, Cambuslang, G72 7EX *Tel:* 0141–641 6394 *Fax:* 0141–642 0126.

McCABE, STEPHEN   Birmingham Hall Green   *Lab majority 6,648*

Steve (Stephen) James McCabe. Born 4 August 1955; Son of James and Margaret McCabe; Educated Port Glasgow, Senior Secondary; Moray House College, Edinburgh (Diploma in Social Studies 1977, Certificate Qualification Social Work 1977); Bradford University (MA social work 1986); Married Lorraine Lea Clendon 1991 (1 son 1 daughter). Social work with young offenders 1977–85; Lecturer in social work NE Worcestershire College 1989–91; Part-time researcher British Association of Social Workers 1989–91; Part-time child protection social worker 1989–91; Central Council for Education in Social Work 1991–97; Member, MSF; Shop steward, NALGO 1978–82. Birmingham City Council: Councillor 1990–98, Chair, Transportation Committee 1993–96. **House of Commons:** Member for Birmingham Hall Green since May 1, 1997; PPS to Charles Clarke as Secretary of State for Education and Skills 2003–; *Select Committees:* Member, Deregulation 1997–99; Member: Northern Ireland Affairs 1998–, Joint Committee on House of Lords Reform 2002–. *Special Interests:* Community Care, Transport, Economic Issues, Police and Security Issues. School Governor; *Sportsclubs:* Local Cricket Club; *Recreations:* Reading, football, hill walking. Steve McCabe Esq, MP, House of Commons, London, SW1A 0AA *Tel:* 020 7219 4842/3509 *Fax:* 020 7219 0367. *Constituency:* c/o The Labour Party, 14–16 Bristol Street, Birmingham, B5 7AF *Tel:* 0121–622 6761 *Fax:* 0121–666 7322 *E-mail:* mccabes@parliament.uk.

McCAFFERTY, CHRISTINE   Calder Valley   *Lab majority 3,094*

Chris (Christine) McCafferty. Born 14 October 1945; Daughter of late John and late Dorothy Livesley; Educated Whalley Range Grammar School For Girls, Manchester; Footscray High School, Melbourne, Australia; Married 1st, Michael McCafferty (1 son), married 2nd, David Tarlo. Welfare worker (Disabled), CHS Manchester 1963–70; Education welfare officer, Manchester Education Committee 1970–72; Registrar of marriages, Bury Registration District 1978–80; Project worker, Calderdale Well Woman Centre 1989–96; Member: NALGO 1967–81, MSF 1994–. Calderdale MBC: Councillor 1991–97, Chair, woman's advisory group 1991–93, disabilities advisory group 1991–93, adoption panel 1992–96; Member: Independent Education Appeals Panel 1991–97, Independent Advisory Panel 1991–97, Calderdale District Council 1991–, Hebden Royd Town Council 1991–95; Chair/Spokesperson, social services 1993–96; Executive of North Region Association for the Blind 1993–96; Member: West Yorkshire Police Authority 1994–97, West Yorkshire Police Complaints Committee 1994–97; Chair: Brighouse Police Community Forum 1994–97, Sowerby Bridge Police Community Forum 1994–97; Advisory Board, Queen Mary and Westfield College Public Policy Seminars. **House of Commons:** Member for Calder Valley since May 1, 1997;

Select Committees: Member, Procedure 1997–99; Member, International Development 2001–. *Special Interests:* Health, Social Services, International Development. *Countries of Interest:* Gambia, India, Australia, Yemen. Member, Co-op Party 1990–. Member: Calderdale Well Women Centre, Redwater Arts; Governor/press officer, Central St School 1988–92; Founder member/chair, Calderdale Domestic Violence Forum 1989–97; Governor, Luddenden Dene School 1993–95; West Yorkshire Lay Prison Visitor 1994–97; Founder member/chair, Calderdale Valley Cancer Support Group; Director, Royd Regeneration Ltd; Trustee, Trades Club Building Hebden Bridge; Member, Political Advisory Committee, Environmental Industries Commission; Parliamentary Member, Council of Europe 1999; Member: Social Health and Family Committee, Sub Committee for Children; Parliamentary Member, Western European Union 1999–; Member, Rules and Procedures Committee; Trustee, Trades Club Building, Hebden Bridge 1992–; Director, Royd Regeneration Ltd 1996–; *Recreations:* Swimming, reading, caravanning. Chris McCafferty, MP, House of Commons, London, SW1A 0AA *Tel:* 020 7219 5026 *Fax:* 020 7219 7269. *Constituency:* 15 Heptonstall Road, Hebden Bridge, West Yorkshire, HX4 6AZ *Tel:* 01422 843713 *Fax:* 01422 846713 *E-mail:* mccafferty@btinternet.com.

McCARTNEY, IAN   Makerfield   *Lab majority 17,750*

Ian McCartney. Born 25 April 1951; Son of Hugh McCartney, Labour MP; Educated State Schools; Divorced (1 son deceased 2 daughters), married 2nd Ann Parkes, née Kevan 1988. Secretary to Roger Stott MP 1979–87; TGWU: Branch secretary 1968, Shop steward 1970; Chair, TGWU Parliamentary Group. Wigan Borough Councillor 1982–87. **House of Commons:** Member for Makerfield since June 1987; Opposition Front Bench Spokesperson for: National Health Service 1992–94, Employment 1994–96, Education and Employment (Chief Employment Spokesperson) 1996–97; Minister of State: Department of Trade and Industry 1997–99, Cabinet Office 1999–2001; Minister of State for Pensions, Department for Work and Pensions 2001–03;

Minister without Portfolio and Party Chair 2003–; *Select Committees:* Member, Social Security 1991–92. *Special Interests:* Local and Regional Government, Fire Service, Civil Defence, Health and Safety Issues, NHS, Social Services, Employment. *Countries of Interest:* Australia. Labour Party full-time officer 1973; Member, Labour Party National Executive Committee 1996–; Member, PLP General Election Campaign (Country) 1999–; Chair, Labour Party National Policy Forum 2002–; Member, Labour Party Joint Policy Commission. Chair, Children's Wheelchair Fund; Vice-President, BARLA (British Amateur Rugby League Association); PC 1999; *Clubs:* Platt Bridge Labour; *Recreations:* Wigan Rugby League. Rt Hon Ian McCartney, MP, House of Commons, London, SW1A 0AA *Tel:* 020 7219 4503. *Constituency:* 1st Floor, Gerrard Winstanley House, Crawford Street, Wigan, Greater Manchester, WN1 1NJ *Tel:* 01942 824029 *Fax:* 01942 492746.

McDONAGH, SIOBHAIN   Mitcham and Morden   *Lab majority 13,785*

Siobhain McDonagh. Born 20 February 1960; Daughter of Cumin and Breda McDonagh, née Doogue, retired builder and nurse; Educated Holy Cross Convent, New Malden; Essex University (BA government 1981); Single, no children. Clerical officer, DHSS 1981–83; Housing Benefits assistant 1983–84; Receptionist, Homeless Persons Unit, London Borough of Wandsworth 1984–86; Housing adviser 1986–88; Development co-ordinator, Battersea Church Housing Trust 1988–97; Member, GMB. Councillor, London Borough of Merton 1982–1997, Chair, Housing Committee 1990–95. **House of Commons:** Contested Mitcham and Morden 1987 and 1992 general elections. Member for Mitcham and Morden since May 1, 1997; *Select Committees:* Member, Social Security 1997–98; Member, Health 2000–. *Special Interests:* Health, Housing, Quality of Life, Welfare Reform. Former Governor, Liberty Middle School and Tamworth Manor High School, Mitcham; Member: South Mitcham Community Centre, Colliers Wood Community Centre, Grenfell Housing Association, Merton MIND; Vice-President QUIT (smoking cessation charity); Made first Conference Speech aged 23; Trustee Mitcham Garden Village; *Recreations:* Travel, friends, music. Siobhain McDonagh, MP, House of Commons, London, SW1A 0AA *Tel:* 020 7219 4678 *Fax:* 020 7219 0986. *Constituency:* 1 Crown Road, Morden, Surrey, SM4 5DD *Tel:* 020 8542 4835 *Fax:* 020 8544 0377 *E-mail:* mcdonaghs@parliament.uk.

MacDONALD, CALUM   Western Isles   *Lab majority 1,074*

Calum A MacDonald. Born 7 May 1956; Son of Malcolm MacDonald, crofter and weaver and Donella MacDonald; Educated Bayble School; Nicholson Institute, Stornoway; Edinburgh University; University of California (PhD). Former teaching fellow in political philosophy, University of California at Los Angeles. **House of Commons:** Member for Western Isles since June 1987; PPS to Donald Dewar as Secretary of State for Scotland May-December 1997; Parliamentary Under-Secretary of State, Scottish Office (Minister for Housing, Transport and European Affairs) December 1997–99; *Select Committees:* Member, Agriculture 1987–92. *Countries of Interest:* Former Soviet Union, Europe, USA. Calum MacDonald Esq, MP, House of Commons, London, SW1A 0AA *Tel:* 020 7219 2780. *Constituency:* 4 South Beach Street, Stornoway, Isle of Lewis *Tel:* 01851 704684.

McDONNELL, JOHN   Hayes and Harlington   *Lab majority 13,466*

John Martin McDonnell. Born 8 September 1951; Son of late Robert and Elsie McDonnell; Educated Great Yarmouth Grammar School, Burnley Technical College; Brunel University (BSc government and politics); Birkbeck College, London University (MSc politics and sociology); Married Cynthia Pinto 1995 (1 son 2 daughters). Shopfloor production worker 1968–73; Assistant head, social insurance department, National Union of Mineworkers 1977–78; Researcher, TUC 1978–82; Head of policy unit, London Borough of Camden 1985–87; Chief Executive: Association of London Authorities 1987–95, Association of London Government 1995–97; Former Shop Steward, UNISON; Member, RMT Parliamentary Campaigning Group 2002–. GLC Councillor 1981–86: Chair Finance Committee, Deputy Leader. **House of Commons:** Member for Hayes and Harlington since May 1, 1997; *Select Committees:* Member, Deregulation and Regulatory Reform 1999–2002; Member, Unopposed Bills (Panel) 1999–. *Special Interests:* Economics, Local and Regional Government, Irish Affairs, Environment, Aviation. *Countries of Interest:* Ireland, Kenya, Gambia, Tanzania, Punjab. Member: Labour Party Animal Welfare Society, Labour Party Committee on Ireland, Labour Party CND; Chair: Labour Party Irish Society, Socialist Campaign Group of MPs; Member: UNISON Group, RMT Group. Member: Liberty, Action for South Africa, Hayes and Harlington Community Centre, League Against Cruel Sports, Hayes Football Club, Hayes Cricket Club, Friends of Lake Farm, Friends of Hitherbroom Park, Barra Hall Regeneration Committee, Rosedale Park; Member, Friends of Ireland – Coalition in support of Belfast Agreement; Chair, Britain and Ireland Human Rights Centre; Member, London Wildlife Trust; *Publications:* Editor, *Labour Herald*; Contributor to: *Campaign Group News*, *Tribune*, *Red Pepper*, *Labour Briefing*; *Clubs:* Member: Hayes Irish Society, Hayes and Harlington Workingmens, Hayes and Harlington History Society, Hayes and Harlington Community Centre; *Sportsclubs:* Hillingdon Outdoor Activities Centre; Wayfarer Sailing Association; Vice-president, Hayes Football Club; Patron, Hayes Cricket Club; *Recreations:* Sailing, football, cycling, gardening, theatre, cinema. John McDonnell Esq, MP, House of Commons, London, SW1A 0AA. *Constituency:* Pump Lane, Hayes, Middlesex, UB3 3NB *Tel:* 020 8569 0010 *Fax:* 020 8569 0109 *E-mail:* office@john-mcdonnell.net.

MACDOUGALL, JOHN   Central Fife   *Lab majority 10,075*

John William MacDougall. Born 8 December 1947; Son of William MacDougall, process worker and Barbara, housewife; Educated Templehall Secondary Modern School, Kirkcaldy, Fife; Rosyth Naval Dockyard College; Glenrothes Technical College; Fife College (Diploma industrial management); Married Cathy 1968 (1 son 1 daughter). Former board member Glenrothes Development Corporation, Member GMBA. Former chair Rosyth Dockyard and Naval Base Co-ordinating Committee; Former Leader Controlling Group COSLA; Fife Regional Council: Councillor 1982, Leader of Administration 1987–96, Chair Policy and Resources Committee 1989–96, Convener 1996-May 2001; Justice of the Peace. **House of Commons:** Member for Central Fife since June 7, 2001; *Select Committees:* Member: Joint Committee on Consolidation of Bills Etc 2001–, Administration 2002–, Regulatory Reform 2003–. Honorary president Fife Express Group for Mental Health;

Member Scottish Old Age Pensioners Association; Organiser Fife Charity Shield; Former member: Scottish Broadcasting Authority, Scottish Constitutional Convention; Leader Inquiry into Financial Irregularities in European Community; Bureau member Assembly of the European Regions 1992; Member Scottish Valuation Advisory Council 1992–96; Chair East of Scotland European Consortium 1993–96; Assembly of the European Regions: Former vice-president, Former treasurer; Member: Consultative Assembly British Section Council of European Municipalities, European Network Group COSLA; Founder member East of Scotland European Consortium; Alternate delegate Congress of Local and Regional Authorities of European Union; Convention of Scottish Local Authorities: Delegate, Member: policy executive, European and International Affairs Committee; Delegate International Union of Local Authorities; Vice-president Development of CPMR/AER relations Assembly of the European Regions 1998–; Member: St Andrews University Court, St Andrews Joint Liaison Committee, Fife Economic Forum, Forth Road Bridge Joint Board; Alternate director East Neuk Ltd; Former chair and director Burntisland Initiative Recreational Trust Ltd; Chair and director Community Business Fife Ltd 1988–92; St Andrews Links Trust: Trustee 1996–98, Vice-chair 1998–2001; Director Fife Enterprise Ltd; Commonwealth Parliamentary Association; Inter Parliamentary Union; Honorary president: Fife Historic Buildings Trust, Wemyss Caves Preservation Trust; Institute of Industrial Managers; *Recreations:* Cycling, walking, sport. John MacDougall Esq, MP, House of Commons, London, SW1A 0AA *Tel:* 020 7219 8233. *Constituency:* 5 Hanover Court, Glenrothes, Fife, KY7 6SB *E-mail:* macdougallj@parliament.uk.

McFALL, JOHN   Dumbarton   *Lab majority 9,575*

John McFall. Born 4 October 1944; Son of late John and Jean McFall; Educated Paisley College of Technology; Strathclyde University (BSc chemistry, MBA); Open University (BA education); Married (4 children). Mathematics and chemistry teacher; Assistant head teacher –1987. **House of Commons:** Member for Dumbarton since June 1987; Opposition Spokesperson for Scottish Affairs (with responsibilities for Industry, Economic Affairs, Employment and Training, Home Affairs, Transport and Roads, Agriculture, Fisheries and Forestry) 1992–97; Opposition Whip 1989–91; Government Whip 1997–98; Parliamentary Under-Secretary of State, Northern Ireland Office 1998–99 (Minister for Education, Training and Employment, Health and Community Relations 1998–99, for Economy and Education 1999); *Select Committees:* Member: Public Administration 2000–01, Public Administration 2001; Chair, Treasury 2001–; Member: Liaison 2001–, Treasury Sub-Committee 2001–. *Special Interests:* Defence, Education, Economic Policy, Co-operative Development. *Countries of Interest:* Latin America, Middle East, Romania. Member, Co-operative Party. *Recreations:* Jogging, golf, reading. John McFall Esq, MP, House of Commons, London, SW1A 0AA *Tel:* 020 7219 3521. *Constituency:* 125 College Street, Dumbarton, G82 1NH *E-mail:* mcfallj@parliament.uk.

McGRADY, EDDIE   South Down   *SDLP majority 13,858*

Eddie (Edward) K McGrady. Born 3 June 1935; Son of late Michael and Lilian McGrady; Educated St Patrick's High School, Downpatrick; Married Patricia Swail 1959 (2 sons 1 daughter). Partner M B McGrady & Co., Chartered Accountants (retired 1998). Downpatrick Urban District Council: Councillor 1961–73, Chair 1964–73; Down District Council: Councillor 1973–89, Chair 1975. **House of Commons:** Contested South Down in 1979 and 1983 general elections and 1986 by-election. Member for South Down since June 1987; Spokesperson for: Housing, Local Government, Environment; Chief Whip, SDLP 1979–; Member: Northern Ireland Assembly 1973, Minister for Co-ordination 1974, Northern Ireland Assembly 1982–86, Northern Ireland Forum 1996–98, Northern Ireland Assembly 1998–2002, Northern Ireland Policing Board; *Select Committees:* Member, Northern Ireland Affairs 1997–. *Special Interests:* Northern Ireland, Constitutional Issues. *Countries of Interest:* Ireland, USA. Founder Member and First Chairman, SDLP 1970–72; SDLP Parliamentary Group Leader 2002–. Fellow, Institute Chartered Accountants (FCA); *Recreations:* Walking, gardening. Eddie McGrady Esq, MP, House of Commons, London, SW1A 0AA *Tel:* 020 7219 4481. *Constituency:* 32 Saul Street, Downpatrick, County Down, BT30 6NQ *Tel:* 028 4461 2882 *Fax:* 028 4461 9574 *E-mail:* e.mcgrady@sdlpire.

McGUINNESS, MARTIN   Mid Ulster   *SF majority 9,953*

Martin McGuinness. Born 23 May 1950; Educated Christian Brothers' Technical College. Sinn Fein Chief negotiator mid–1980s–; Member, Northern Ireland Assembly 1982, 1998–; Sinn Fein representative to the Dublin Forum for Peace and Reconciliation 1994–95; Minister for Education, Northern Ireland Assembly 1999–. **House of Commons:** Contested Foyle 1983, 1987 and 1992 general elections. Member for Mid Ulster since May 1, 1997; *Special Interests:* South Africa. *Recreations:* Cooking, walking, reading, fly fishing. Martin McGuinness Esq, MP, House of Commons, London, SW1A 0AA *Tel:* 020 7219 3000. *Constituency:* 32 Burn Road, Cookstown, Co Tyrone, BT80 8DN *Tel:* 028 8676 5850 *Fax:* 028 8676 6734.

McGUIRE, ANNE   Stirling   *Lab majority 6,274*

Anne Catherine McGuire. Born 26 May 1949; Daughter of late Albert Long, railway signalman, and late Agnes Long, shop worker; Educated Our Lady of St Francis Secondary School, Glasgow; Glasgow University (MA politics with history 1971); Notre Dame College of Education (Diploma in Secondary Education 1975); Married Len McGuire 1972 (1 son 1 daughter). Teacher, Supply, history/modern studies 1982–84; Development Worker/Senior Manager, Voluntary Sector, Community Service Volunteers 1984–93; Depute Director, Scottish Council for Voluntary Organisations 1993–97; National Executive, GMB 1987–91. Councillor, Strathclyde Regional Council 1980–82. **House of Commons:** Member for Stirling since May 1, 1997; Assistant Government Whip 1998–2001; Government Whip 2001–02; PPS to Donald Dewar as Secretary of State for Scotland December 1997–98; Parliamentary Under-Secretary of State: Scotland Office 2002–03, Department for Constitutional Affairs 2003–; *Select Committees:* Member, European Legislation 1997–98. *Special Interests:* European Union, Rural Development, Urban Regeneration. *Countries of Interest:* USA, Germany. Member: Labour Party Scottish Executive 1984–97; Chair, Labour Party Scotland 1992–93. *Recreations:* Learning Gaelic, reading, walking. Mrs Anne McGuire, MP, House of Commons, London, SW1A 0AA *Tel:* 020 7219 5014 *Fax:* 020 7219 2503. *Constituency:* 22 Viewfield Street, Stirling, FK8 1UA *Tel:* 01786 446515 *Fax:* 01786 446513 *E-mail:* mcguirea@parliament.uk.

McINTOSH, ANNE   Vale of York   *Con majority 12,517*

Anne Caroline Ballingall McIntosh. Born 20 September 1954; Daughter of Dr Alastair McIntosh, retired medical practitioner, and Mrs Grethe-Lise McIntosh; Educated Harrogate College; Edinburgh University (LLB 1977); Århus University, Denmark (European Law); Married John Harvey 1992. Trainee, EEC Competition Directorate 1978; Legal adviser, Didier and Associates, Brussels 1979–80; Apprentice, Scottish Bar, Edinburgh 1980–82; Admitted to Faculty of Advocates June 1982; Advocate, practising with Community Law Office, Brussels 1982–83; Adviser, European Democratic Group, principally on Transport, Youth Education, Culture, Tourism, Relations with Scandinavia, Austria and Yugoslavia 1983–89; MEP for Essex North East 1989–94, and for Essex North and Suffolk South 1994–99. **House of Commons:** Contested Workington, Cumbria 1987 general election. Member of Parliament for Vale of York since May 1, 1997; Opposition Spokesperson for Culture, Media and Sport 2001–02; Shadow Minister for Transport 2002–; *Select Committees:* Member: Environment, Transport and Regional Affairs 1999–2001, Transport Sub-Committee 1999–2001, Transport, Local Government and the Regions 2001–02, Transport Sub-Committee 2001–02, Urban Affairs Sub-Committee 2001–02; Member, European Scrutiny 2000–. *Special Interests:* Transport, Legal Affairs, Animal Welfare. *Countries of Interest:* Eastern Europe, Scandinavia. President Yorkshire First – Enterprise in Yorkshire; Member, European Standing Committee C 1999–2001; Member, European Parliament for: Essex North East 1989–94, Essex North and Suffolk South 1994–99; Assistant Whip, European Democratic Group 1989–92, Conservative Spokesman on Transport and Tourism 1992–99, Member, European People's Party 1992–99, Bureau Member 1994–97, Rapporteur on Air Transport, relations with third world countries and Trans-European Road Networks, EU Competition Policy,

Air Transport Safety, Co-Chair, European Transport Safety Council 1994–99; President, Anglia Enterprise in Europe 1989–99; Fellow Industry and Parliament Trust 1995; Graduate Armed Forces Parliamentary Scheme, Royal Navy 2000; Honorary Doctorate of Laws Anglia Polytechnic University 1997; *Clubs:* Yorkshire Agricultural Society; Royal Over-seas League; *Recreations:* Swimming, walking, cinema. Anne McIntosh, MP, House of Commons, London, SW1A 0AA *Tel:* 020 7219 3541 *Fax:* 020 7219 0972. *Constituency:* Vale of York Conservative Association, Thirsk Conservative Club, Westgate, Thirsk, North Yorkshire, YO7 1QS *Tel:* 01845 523835 *Fax:* 01845 527507 *E-mail:* mcintosha@parliament.uk.

McISAAC, SHONA   Cleethorpes   *Lab majority 5,620*

Shona McIsaac. Born 3 April 1960; Daughter of Angus McIsaac, retired chief petty officer, and Isa, née Nicol, school dinner lady; Educated SHAPE School, Belgium; Barne Barton Secondary Modern, Plymouth; Stoke Damerel High, Plymouth; Durham University (BSc geography 1981); Married Peter John Keith 1994. Senior sub-editor, *Chat*; Deputy chief-sub-editor, *Bella*; Chief sub-editor, *Woman*; Freelance food writer; Member, NUJ, USDAW. Councillor, London Borough of Wandsworth 1990–98. **House of Commons:** Member for Cleethorpes since May 1, 1997; PPS to: Ministers of State, Northern Ireland Office: Adam Ingram 2000–01, Jane Kennedy 2001–03, Baroness Scotland of Asthal as Minister of State, Home Office 2003–; *Select Committees:* Member, Standards and Privileges 1997–2001. *Special Interests:* Finance, Taxation, Benefits, Crime. Member, Northern Ireland Grand Committee; *Publications:* Various non-political work-related publications; *Recreations:* Football, food, travel, cycling, archaeology of the UK, soap operas. Shona McIsaac, MP, House of Commons, London, SW1A 0AA *Tel:* 020 7219 5801 *Fax:* 020 7219 3047. *Constituency:* Immingham Resource Centre, Margaret Street, Immingham, NE Lincolnshire, DN40 1LE *Tel:* 01469 574324 *Fax:* 01469 510842 *E-mail:* mcisaacs@parliament.uk.

MACKAY, ANDREW   Bracknell   *Con majority 6,713*

Andrew James MacKay. Born 27 August 1949; Son of late Robert and Olive Mackay; Educated Solihull School; Married Diana Joy Kinchin 1974 (1 son 1 daughter) (divorced 1996); married Julie Kirkbride MP 1997 (1 son). Consultant to various public companies. **House of Commons:** Member for Birmingham Stechford 1977 by-election–1979. Member for Berkshire East 1983–97, and for Bracknell since May 1, 1997; Assistant Government Whip 1992–94; Government Whip 1994–96; Deputy Chief Whip 1996–97; PPS to Tom King as Secretary of State: for Northern Ireland 1986–89, for Defence 1989–92; Sponsored Licensing (Retail Sales) Act 1988 (Private Member's Bill); Member, Shadow Cabinet 1997–2001; Shadow Secretary of State for Northern Ireland 1997–2001; *Select Committees:* Member: Procedure 1994–95, Selection 1994–97; Member, Standards and Privileges 2002–. *Special Interests:* Foreign Affairs, Industry, Environment. Chair, Solihull Young Conservative 1971–74; Vice-Chair, Solihull Conservative Association 1971–74; Member, Conservative Party National Executive 1979–82. Chair, *Britain in Europe* Meriden Branch 1975 (Referendum); PC 1998; *Recreations:* Golf, tennis, good food, travel. Rt Hon Andrew Mackay, MP, House of Commons, London, SW1A 0AA *Tel:* 020 7219 2989 *Fax:* 020 7219 4123. *Constituency:* 10 Millbanke Court, Millbanke Way, Western Road, Bracknell, Berkshire, RG12 1RP *Tel:* 01344 868286 *E-mail:* mackaya@parliament.uk.

DodOnline
An Electronic Directory without rival . . .

MPs' biographies and photographs available with daily updates *via* the internet

For a *free* trial, call Yasmin Mirza, Aby Farsoun or Michael Mand on 020 7630 7643

McKECHIN, ANN   Glasgow Maryhill   *Lab majority 9,888*

Ann McKechin. Born 22 April 1961; Daughter of William McKechin and Anne McKechin (neé Coyle); Educated Sacred Heart High School, Paisley; Paisley Grammar School; Strathclyde University (LLB Scots law 1981); Single. Solicitor 1983–; Pacitti Jones Solicitors, Glasgow 1986–2000: Solicitor, Partner 1990–2000; Contested West of Scotland list 1999 Scottish Parliament election; T.G.W.U. **House of Commons:** Member for Glasgow Maryhill since June 7, 2001; *Select Committees:* Member: Information 2001–, Scottish Affairs 2001–, Standing Orders 2001–. *Special Interests:* International Development, Economics, Small Businesses. *Countries of Interest:* Rwanda, Africa. Glasgow Kelvin Labour Party: Constituency secretary 1995–98, Women's officer 2000–01. Member Co-operative Party; World Development Movement 1998–: Scottish representative 1998–2001, Council member 1999–; Member, Management Board, Mercycorps/Aid International Scotland 2003–; *Recreations:* Dancing, films, art history. Ann McKechin, MP, House of Commons, London, SW1A 0AA *Tel:* 020 7219 8239 *Fax:* 020 7219 1770 *Tel (Constituency):* 0141–946 1300 *Fax (Constituency):* 0141–946 1412 *E-mail:* mckechina@parliament.uk.

McKENNA, ROSEMARY   Cumbernauld and Kilsyth   *Lab majority 7,520*

Rosemary McKenna. Born 8 May 1941; Daughter of late Cornelius Harvey, publican, and late Mary Susan Crossan, chrome polisher and shopkeeper; Educated St Augustine's Comprehensive, Glasgow; Notre Dame College of Education (Diploma in Primary Education 1974); Married James Stephen McKenna 1963 (3 sons 1 daughter). Member AEEU, now AMICUS. Councillor, Cumbernauld and Kilsyth District Council 1984–96, Leader and Convenor of Policy and Resources 1984–88, Provost 1988–92, Leader 1992–94; Member: Cumbernauld Development Corporation 1985–97, Scottish Enterprise 1993–96, 1996–97. **House of Commons:** Member for Cumbernauld and Kilsyth since May 1, 1997; Joint PPS to Ministers of State, Foreign and Commonwealth Office 1999–2001; PPS to Brian Wilson as Minister of State, Foreign and Commonwealth Office 2001; *Select Committees:* Member: Joint Committee on Statutory Instruments 1997–99, Scottish Affairs 1997–98, Catering 1998–99, European Legislation 1998, European Legislation 1998–2001, European Scrutiny 1998–99; Member: Culture, Media and Sport 2001–, Procedure 2001–. *Special Interests:* Constitutional Reform, Democratic Renewal and Inclusive Politics, Libraries, Internet. *Countries of Interest:* France, USA. Chair, Constituency Party 1979–85; Member, Scottish Executive and National Local Government Committee 1994–98. Chair, SLIC (Scottish Libraries and Information Council) 1998–2002; Member, Convention of Scottish Local Authorities 1984–96, Vice-President 1992–94, President 1994–96; Member, EU Committee of the Regions 1993–97; Chair, Ad-Hoc Committee on Equality Issues until 1997; Chair, Scotland Europa 1994–96; Chair, UK and European Standing Committees of Women Elected Members of the Council of European Municipalities and Regions 1995–98; Cumbernauld Theatre Trust 1984–95; CBE; *Recreations:* Reading, family gatherings, travel. Mrs Rosemary McKenna, CBE, MP, House of Commons, London, SW1A 0AA *Tel:* 020 7219 4135 *Fax:* 020 7219 2544. *Constituency:* Lennox House, Lennox Road, Cumbernauld, Glasgow, G67 ILL *Tel:* 01236 457788 *Fax:* 01236 457313 *E-mail:* mckennar@parliament.uk.

MACKINLAY, ANDREW   Thurrock   *Lab majority 9,997*

Andrew MacKinlay. Born 24 April 1949; Son of Daniel and Monica Mackinlay; Educated Salesian College, Chertsey, Surrey; Diploma in municipal administration 1968; Married Ruth Segar 1972 (2 sons 1 daughter). Local government officer with Surrey County Council 1965–75; NALGO Official 1975–92; Contested London South and Surrey East 1984 European Parliament election; Member: NALGO 1965–75; TGWU. Councillor, London Borough of Kingston upon Thames 1971–78. **House of Commons:** Contested Kingston-upon-Thames, Surbiton February and October 1974, Croydon Central 1983 and Peterborough 1987 general elections. Member for Thurrock since April 9, 1992; Opposition Whip 1993–94; *Select Committees:* Member, Transport 1992–97;

Member: Foreign Affairs 1997–, Unopposed Bills (Panel) 1997–. *Special Interests:* Constitution, Devolution, Electoral Reform, Police, Ports Industry, River Thames, Transport, Channel Islands, Isle of Man, Irish Affairs, Elderly, Environment. *Countries of Interest:* Poland, Belgium, France, Baltic States, Czech/Slovak Republics, Hungary, Falkland Islands, Gibraltar, USA, Ireland. Member Parliamentary Labour Party Parliamentary Committee 2001–. Armed Forces Parliamentary Scheme (Royal Marines) 1997–98; Member, Parliamentary Delegation to OSCE; Associate Member, Chartered Institute of Secretaries and Administrators; *Sportsclubs:* Patron, Tilbury Football Club; *Recreations:* Visiting and studying First World War battlefields in France and Belgium, collecting Labour and Trade Union ephemera and memorabilia; non-league soccer, Ireland. Andrew Mackinlay Esq, MP, House of Commons, London, SW1A 0AA *Tel:* 020 7219 6819. *Constituency:* MPs Office, Civic Square, Tilbury, Essex, RM18 8ZZ *Tel:* 01375 850359.

MACLEAN, DAVID   Penrith and The Border   Con majority 14,677

David MacLean. Born 16 May 1953; Educated Fortrose Academy; Aberdeen University. **House of Commons:** Member for Penrith and The Border since July 1983 by-election; Assistant Government Whip 1987–89; Government Whip 1988–89; Opposition Chief Whip 2001–; Parliamentary Secretary, Ministry of Agriculture, Fisheries and Food 1989–92; Minister of State: at Department of the Environment 1992–93, at Home Office 1993–97. PC 1995. Rt Hon David Maclean, MP, House of Commons, London, SW1A 0AA *Tel:* 020 7219 6494.

McLOUGHLIN, PATRICK   West Derbyshire   Con majority 7,370

Patrick Allan McLoughlin. Born 30 November 1957; Son of Patrick Alphonsos McLoughlin; Educated Cardinal Griffin Comprehensive School, Cannock; Staffordshire College of Agriculture; Married Lynne Patricia Newman 1984 (1 son 1 daughter). Agricultural worker 1974–79; Various positions with National Coal Board 1979–86. Councillor: Cannock Chase District Council 1980–87, Staffordshire County Council 1981–87. **House of Commons:** Contested Wolverhampton South East 1983 general election. Member for West Derbyshire since May 8, 1986 By-election; Assistant Government Whip 1995–96; Government Whip 1996–97; Opposition Pairing Whip 1997–98; Opposition Deputy Chief Whip 1998–; PPS: to Angela Rumbold as Minister of State, Department of Education 1987–88, to Lord Young of Graffham, as Secretary of State for Trade and Industry 1988–89; Parliamentary Under-Secretary of State, Department of Transport (Minister for Aviation and Shipping) 1989–92; Joint Parliamentary Under-Secretary of State, Department of Employment 1992–93; Parliamentary Under-Secretary of State for Trade and Technology, Department of Trade and Industry 1993–94; *Select Committees:* Member: Broadcasting 1994–95, National Heritage 1994–95, Selection 1997–2001; Member: Finance and Services 1998–, Accommodation and Works 2001–. *Special Interests:* Agriculture, Education. National Vice-Chair, Young Conservatives 1982–84. Patrick McLoughlin Esq, MP, House of Commons, London, SW1A 0AA *Tel:* 020 7219 3511. *Constituency Tel:* 01332 558125 *Fax:* 01332 541509 *E-mail:* mcloughlinp@parliament.uk.

DodOnline

An Electronic Directory without rival . . .

MPs' biographies and photographs available with daily updates *via* the internet

For a *free* trial, call Yasmin Mirza, Aby Farsoun or Michael Mand on 020 7630 7643

McNAMARA, KEVIN   Hull North   Lab majority 10,721

(Joseph) Kevin McNamara. Born 5 September 1934; Son of late Patrick McNamara; Educated St Mary's College, Crosby; Hull University (LLB 1956, PGCE 1957); Married Nora Jones 1960 (4 sons 1 daughter). Head of history and government, St Mary's Grammar School, Hull 1958–64; Lecturer in law, Hull College of Commerce 1964–66; Secretary, Parliamentary Group TGWU 1974–2001. **House of Commons:** Contested Bridlington 1964 general election. Member for Kingston-upon-Hull North 1966–74, for Kingston-upon-Hull Central February 1974–83, and for Hull North since June 1983; Opposition Spokesperson for Defence (Armed Forces) 1983–87; Principal Spokesperson for Northern Ireland 1987–94; Opposition Spokesperson for the Civil Service 1994–95; *Select Committees:* Member: Joint Committee on Human Rights 2001–, Standards and Privileges 2001–. *Special Interests:* Northern Ireland, Human Rights. *Countries of Interest:* Ireland. Secretary, National Association of Labour Student Organisations 1956–57. Member UK Delegation to North Atlantic Assembly 1984–88; UK Delegation to Council of Europe and Western European Union: Member 1996–, Legal Affairs and Human Rights Committee, Chair Sub-Committee for the election of Judges to the European Court of Human rights, Deputy chair Defence Committee; Vice-chair British-Irish Inter-Parliamentary Body 1997–; *Recreations:* Family, reading, walking. Kevin McNamara Esq, MP, House of Commons, London, SW1A 0AA *Tel:* 020 7219 5194 *Fax:* 020 7219 3398. *Constituency:* 145 Newland Park, Hull, HU5 2DX *Tel:* 01482 448170 *Fax:* 01482 441505 *E-mail:* kevinmcnamaramp@parliament.uk.

McNULTY, TONY   Harrow East   Lab majority 11,124

Tony McNulty. Born 3 November 1958; Son of James Anthony McNulty, self-employed builder, and of Eileen McNulty; Educated Salvatorian College; Stanmore Sixth Form College; Liverpool University (BA political theory and institutions 1981); Virginia Polytechnic Institute and State University, USA (MA political science 1982); Married Christine Gilbert. Lecturer, Business School, Polytechnic/University of North London 1983–97; Member: NUPE 1983–90, NATHE 1983–97. Councillor, London Borough of Harrow 1986–97, Deputy Leader, Labour Group 1990–95, Leader 1995–97. **House of Commons:** Contested Harrow East 1992 general election. Member for Harrow East since May 1, 1997; Assistant Government Whip 1999–2001; Government Whip 2001–02; PPS to David Blunkett as Secretary of State for Education and Employment with responsibility for post–16 provision 1997–99; Parliamentary Under-Secretary: Housing, Planning and Regeneration, Office of the Deputy Prime Minister 2002–03, Department for Transport 2003–; *Special Interests:* Education, Health, Local and Regional Government, Regeneration, London. *Countries of Interest:* Ireland, France, Germany. Member: Socialist Educational Association, Fabian Society; Co-founder, Labour Friends of India; Member, Labour Friends of Israel. *Publications:* Various academic papers; *Clubs:* Wealdstone CIU; *Recreations:* Reading, theatre, rugby, cinema, football, gaelic games. Tony McNulty Esq, MP, House of Commons, London, SW1A 0AA *Tel:* 020 7219 4108 *Fax:* 020 7219 2417. *Constituency:* 18 Byron Road, Wealdstone, Harrow, HA3 7ST *Tel:* 020 8427 2100 *Fax:* 020 8424 2319 *E-mail:* mcnultyt@parliament.uk.

MacSHANE, DENIS   Rotherham   Lab majority 13,077

Denis MacShane. Born 21 May 1948; Educated Merton College, Oxford (MA modern history); London University (PhD international economics); Married Nathalie Pham 1987 (1 son 4 daughters). BBC producer 1969–77; Policy director, International Metal Workers' Federation 1980–92; Director, European Policy Institute 1992–94; President, National Union of Journalists 1978–79. **House of Commons:** Contested Solihull October 1974 general election. Member for Rotherham since May 5, 1994 By-Election; PPS: to Joyce Quin, Derek Fatchett and Tony Lloyd as Ministers of State, Foreign and Commonwealth Office 1997–99, to Geoff Hoon as Minister of State, Foreign and Commonwealth Office 1999; Joint PPS to the Ministers of State for

Foreign and Commonwealth Affairs 1999–2001–; Foreign and Commonwealth Office 2001–: Parliamentary Under-Secretary of State 2001–02, Minister of State 2002–; *Select Committees:* Member, Deregulation 1996–97. *Special Interests:* International Economics, European Union, Manufacturing. *Countries of Interest:* Europe, East and South East Asia. *Publications:* Several books on international politics; *Recreations:* Family, walking. Dr Denis MacShane, MP, House of Commons, London, SW1A 0AA *Tel:* 020 7219 4060 *Fax:* 020 7219 6888. *Constituency:* 4 Hall Grove, Rotherham, S60 2BS *Tel:* 01709 367793 *Fax:* 01709 835622.

MACTAGGART, FIONA   Slough   *Lab majority 12,508*

Fiona Mactaggart. Born 12 September 1953; Daughter of late Sir Ian Mactaggart and of late Rosemary Belhaven; Educated London University: King's College (BA English 1975), Goldsmiths' College (Postgraduate Teaching Certificate 1987), Institute of Education (MA 1993). Vice-President, National Secretary, National Union of Students 1978–81; Press and Public Relations Officer, National Council for Voluntary Organisations 1981; General Secretary, Joint Council for the Welfare of Immigrants 1982–86; Primary school teacher 1987–92; Public Relations Officer, private property company 1992; Lecturer in primary education, Institute of Education 1992–97; Former Member: TGWU 1982–86, NUJ, ASTMS 1981; Member: NUT 1987–92, AUT 1992–1997, GMB 1997–. London Borough of Wandsworth: Councillor, Shaftesbury Ward 1986–90, Leader, Labour Group 1988–90. **House of Commons:** Member for Slough since May 1, 1997; PPS to Chris Smith as Secretary of State for Culture, Media and Sport December 1997–2001; Parliamentary Under-Secretary of State (Race Equality, Community Policy and Civil Renewal), Home Office 2003–; *Select Committees:* Member, Public Administration 1997–98. *Special Interests:* Human Rights, Civil Liberties, Home Affairs, Education, Arts. Member, Fabian Society. Chair, Liberty 1994–96, Editorial Board, Renewal; *Recreations:* Walking, talking, reading, the arts, watching television. Fiona Mactaggart, MP, House of Commons, London, SW1A 0AA *Tel:* 020 7219 3416 *Fax:* 020 7219 0989. *Constituency:* 29 Church Street, Slough, Berkshire, SL1 1PL *Tel:* 01753 518161 *Fax:* 01753 550293 *E-mail:* mactaggartf@parliament.uk.

McWALTER, TONY   Hemel Hempstead   *Lab majority 3,742*

Tony McWalter. Born 20 March 1945; Son of late Joe McWalter, painter/decorator, and late Ann McWalter; Educated St Benedict's, Ealing; University College of Wales, Aberystwyth (BSc pure maths 1967, BSc philosophy 1968); McMaster University, Canada (MA philosophy 1968); University College, Oxford (BPhil philosophy 1971, MLitt 1983); Married Karen Omer 1991 (1 son 2 daughters). Parliamentary Armed Forces Scheme (Royal Navy) 2000–01; School teacher, Cardinal Wiseman Secondary School 1963–64; Long-distance lorry driver, E. H. Paterson Ltd 1964–67; Teaching Fellow, McMaster University, Canada 1968–69; Lecturer: Thames Polytechnic 1972–74, Hatfield Polytechnic/University of Hertfordshire 1974–97; Contested Hertfordshire 1984 and Bedfordshire South 1989 European Parliament elections; Member, TGWU; Branch Chair, NATFHE 1979–87; Polytechnics Panel, NATFHE 1984–89. Councillor, North Hertfordshire District Council 1979–83. **House of Commons:** Contested St Albans 1987 and North Luton 1992 general elections. Member for Hemel Hempstead since May 1, 1997; *Select Committees:* Member, Northern Ireland Affairs 1997–2000; Member, Science and Technology 2001–. *Special Interests:* Local and Regional Government, Green Issues, Political Ideas and Philosophy, Science and Technology, Economic Theory. *Countries of Interest:* Ireland, Canada, USA, Mozambique, Sri Lanka. Member: UNA, The Samaritans 1971–81, Greenpeace, Friends of the Earth, Compassion in World Farming, Amnesty International, World Development Movement, CND; School Governor 1983–93; *Publications:* Co-editor *Kant and His Influence*, 1990; *Recreations:* Club tennis, family pursuits, contract bridge, philosophy, theatre, the Arts, croquet. Tony McWalter Esq, MP, House of Commons, London, SW1A 0AA *Tel:* 020 7219 4547 *Fax:* 020 7219 0563. *Constituency:* 7A Marlowes, Hemel Hempstead, Herts, HP1 1LA *Tel:* 01442 251251 *Fax:* 01442 241268 *E-mail:* mcwaltert@parliament.uk.

McWILLIAM, JOHN   Blaydon   *Lab majority 7,809*

John David McWilliam. Born 16 May 1941; Son of late Alexander McWilliam, post office engineer; Educated Leith Academy; Heriot-Watt College; Napier College of Science and Technology; Ruskin College, Oxford; Married Lesley Catling 1965 (2 daughters); married Mary McLoughlin 1994 (divorced 1997); married Helena Maughan 1998. Telecommunications engineer; Branch Secretary and Regional Council Member, CWU. Councillor, Edinburgh City Council 1970–75; City Treasurer, Edinburgh 1974–75; Member: Commission for Local Authority Accounts, Scotland 1974–78; Scottish Council for Technical Education 1994–98. **House of Commons:** Member for Blaydon since May 1979; Opposition Whip 1984–87; Deputy Shadow Leader of the House 1983–84; Deputy Speaker Westminster Hall 1999–2001, 2002–; *Select Committees:* Member: Defence 1987–97, Speaker's Panel of Chairmen 1987–97, Defence 1997–99, Liaison 1997–99; Chair, Selection 1997–; Member: Chairmen's Panel 1997–, Liaison 2000–. *Special Interests:* Defence, Technology, Education. *Countries of Interest:* Canada, Former Yugoslavia, New Zealand, USA, former Eastern Europe. Vice-Chair, Pitcom 1987–97; Chair, Pitcom 1997–; *Recreations:* Reading, angling, listening to music. John McWilliam Esq, MP, House of Commons, London, SW1A 0AA *Tel:* 020 7219 4020 *Fax:* 020 7219 6536. *Constituency:* 15 Shibdon Road, Blaydon on Tyne, NE21 5AF *Tel:* 0191–414 2488 *Fax:* 0191–414 8036.

MAHMOOD, KHALID   Birmingham Perry Barr   *Lab majority 8,753*

Khalid Mahmood. Former engineer; AEEU; Former adviser Danish International Trade Union. Birmingham City Council 1990–93: Councillor, Chair Race Relations. **House of Commons:** Member for Birmingham Perry Barr since June 7, 2001; *Select Committees:* Member, Broadcasting 2001–. Local Constituency Labour Party: Secretary, Vice-chair; Member: Socialist Health Association, Socialist Education Association; Labour Finance and Industry Group: National member, Midlands branch executive member. Adviser President of the Olympic Council Asia; Former school governor: Local primary school, Further education college; Member of governing body: Neighbourhood forum, South Birmingham CHC. Khalid Mahmood Esq, MP, House of Commons, London, SW1A 0AA *Tel:* 020 7219 8141. *Constituency:* 1 George Street, West Bromwich, West Midlands, B70 6NT *Tel:* 0121 569 1937.

MAHON, ALICE   Halifax   *Lab majority 6,129*

Alice Mahon. Born 28 September 1937; Daughter of late Thomas Edward Reginald Bottomley, bus driver, and late Edna Bottomley; Educated Grammar school; Bradford University (BA social policy and administration 1979); Married 1st (divorced) (2 sons); married 2nd Tony Mahon 1972. Worked in NHS; Nursing auxiliary for 10 years; Higher education 1980; Taught trade union studies at Bradford College 1980–87; Activist with NUPE (now UNISON); Member, RMT Parliamentary Campaigning Group 2002–. Calderdale Borough Councillor 1982–87. **House of Commons:** Member for Halifax since June 1987; PPS to Chris Smith as Secretary of State: for National Heritage 1997, for Culture, Media and Sport to December 1997; *Select Committees:* Member, Health 1991–97. *Special Interests:* Health, Employment, Local and Regional Government, Trade Unions, Defence. *Countries of Interest:* Balkans, Russia, Europe. UK Delegate, Nato Parliamentary Assembly 1992–; *Recreations.* Family. Mrs Alice Mahon, MP, House of Commons, London, SW1A 0AA *Tel:* 020 7219 4464 *Fax:* 020 7219 2450. *Constituency:* 2 West Parade, Halifax, West Yorkshire, HX1 2TA *Tel:* 01422 251800 *Fax:* 01422 251888 *E-mail:* mahona@parliament.uk.

Visit the Vacher Dod Website . . .
www.DodOnline.co.uk

MALINS, HUMFREY   Woking   *Con majority 6,759*

Humfrey Jonathan Malins. Born 31 July 1945; Son of Rev P. Malins and late Lilian Joan Malins; Educated St John's School, Leatherhead; Brasenose College, Oxford (MA jurisprudence 1967); Married Lynda Petman 1979 (1 son 1 daughter). Deputy Metropolitan Stipendiary Magistrate 1992–97; Recorder of the Crown Court 1996–. Mole Valley District Council: Member 1973–82, Chairman, Housing Committee 1980–81. **House of Commons:** Contested Liverpool Toxteth February and October 1974, East Lewisham 1979 general elections. Member for Croydon North West 1983–92, and for Woking since May 1, 1997; Opposition Spokesperson for Home Affairs 2001–03; PPS: to Tim Renton as Minister of State, Home Office 1987–89, to Virginia Bottomley as Minister of State, Department of Health 1989–92; Shadow Minister for Home Affairs 2003–; *Select Committees:* Member: Chairmen's Panel 1998–2001, Member, Home Affairs 1997–2002. *Special Interests:* Penal Affairs and Policy, Criminal Law Reform, European Union, Sport. *Countries of Interest:* Pakistan, Kashmir. Conservative Back Bench Legal Committee: Secretary 1983–86, Vice-Chair 1986–87. Chair, Trustees Immigration Advisory Service 1993–96; CBE 1997; *Clubs:* Vincents, Oxford, Walton Heath Golf, Richmond RFC; *Sportsclubs:* Captain, Parliamentary Golf Society; *Recreations:* Rugby, golf, gardening, family. Humfrey Malins Esq, CBE, MP, House of Commons, London, SW1A 0AA *Tel:* 020 7219 4169/020 7219 1189 *Fax:* 020 7219 2624. *Constituency:* Woking Constituency Conservative Association, Churchill House, Chobham Road, Woking, Surrey, GU21 4AA *Tel:* 01483 773384 *Fax:* 01483 770060 *E-mail:* malinsh@parliament.uk.

MALLABER, JUDY   Amber Valley   *Lab majority 7,227*

Judy Mallaber. Born 10 July 1951; Daughter of late Kenneth Mallaber, librarian, and of late Margaret Joyce Mallaber, librarian; Educated North London Collegiate School; St Anne's College, Oxford (BA). Research officer, National Union of Public Employees 1975–85; Local government information unit 1985–96, Director 1987–95; Member, UNISON; Research Officer, NUPE 1975–85. **House of Commons:** Member for Amber Valley since May 1, 1997; *Select Committees:* Member: Education and Employment 1997–2001, Employment Sub-Committee 1997–2001, Treasury 2001, Treasury Sub-Committee 2001. *Special Interests:* Economic Policy, Local and Regional Government, Education, Equal Opportunities, Employment. Labour Party posts include: Constituency Chair, Greater London Labour Party Regional Executive; Chair, Labour Research Department 1991–94; Vice-chair East Midlands Regional Group of Labour MPs 2002–. Member: Action for Southern Africa, Liberty, Friends of the Earth, Amnesty; Advisory Council Member, Northern College for Adult Education, Barnsley; *Clubs:* Anvil, Ironville; *Recreations:* Cinema, theatre, reading, family and friends. Judy Mallaber, MP, House of Commons, London, SW1A 0AA *Tel:* 020 7219 3428. *Constituency:* Prospect House, Nottingham Road, Ripley, Derbyshire, DE5 3AZ *Tel:* 01773 512792 *Fax:* 01773 742393.

MALLON, SEAMUS   Newry and Armagh   *SDLP majority 3,575*

Séamus Mallon. Born 17 August 1936; Son of late Francis and Jane Mallon; Educated Abbey Grammar School, Newry; St Joseph's College of Education, Belfast; Married Gertrude Cush 1966 (1 daughter). Headmaster, St James Primary School, Markethill 1960–73; Member: Northern Ireland Assembly 1973–74, Northern Ireland Convention 1975–76, Irish Senate 1982, New Ireland Forum 1983–84, Northern Ireland Forum 1996–98, new Northern Ireland Assembly 1998–; Deputy First Minister, Northern Ireland Assembly 1998–2001; Irish National Teachers' Organisation. Councillor, Armagh District Council 1973–86. **House of Commons:** Contested Newry and Armagh, June 1983 general election. Member for Newry and Armagh since by-election January 23, 1986; Spokesperson for Justice 1978–; *Select Committees:* Member, Agriculture 1987–92. *Special Interests:* Justice, Social Services. *Countries of Interest:* Australia, USA. Party Deputy Leader 1979-November 2001. Member, British-Irish Inter-Parliamentary Body 1986–;

Publications: Adam's Children; Regular contributor to *Tribune*; Hon LLD, Queen's University, Belfast 1999; Hon LLD, National Council for Education Awards, Dublin 2000; Hon LLD, National University of Ireland 2002; *Sportsclubs:* Member, House of Commons Golf Society; *Recreations:* Angling, horse racing. Séamus Mallon Esq, MP, House of Commons, London, SW1A 0AA *Tel:* 020 7219 4018. *Constituency:* 2 Bridge Street, Newry, County Down, BT35 8AE *Tel:* 028 3025 2999 *Fax:* 028 3026 7828.

MANDELSON, PETER   Hartlepool   *Lab majority 14,571*

Peter Benjamin Mandelson. Born 21 October 1953; Son of late George Mandelson, and of Hon. Mary Joyce Morrison, daughter of late Baron Morrison of Lambeth; Educated Hendon County Grammar School; St Catherine's College, Oxford (BA philosophy, politics and economics 1976); Single. Producer LWT 1982–85; Director of Campaigns and Communications, Labour Party 1985–90; Industrial consultant, SRU Group 1990–92; Economic Department TUC 1977–78; Member, GMB. Councillor, London Borough of Lambeth 1979–82. **House of Commons:** Member for Hartlepool since April 9, 1992; Opposition Spokesperson for: The Civil Service 1995–96, Election Planning 1996–97; Opposition Whip 1994–95; Minister without Portfolio, Cabinet Office 1997–98; Secretary of State for Trade and Industry July-December 1998, for Northern Ireland 1999–2001. *Countries of Interest:* Europe, USA, Asia, Africa. Chair, PLP General Election Campaign (Planning) 1999–2001. Chairman: British Youth Council 1978–80, Policy Network 2001–; President, Central School of Speech and Drama 2001–; *Publications: Youth Employment: causes and cures*, 1977; *Broadcasting and Youth*, 1980; Co-author *The Blair Revolution – Can New Labour Deliver*, 1996; "The Blair Revolution Revisited" 2002–; PC 1998; Hon Fellow, St Catherine's College, Oxford; *Recreations:* Cinema, theatre, physical exercise. Rt Hon Peter Mandelson, MP, House of Commons, London, SW1A 0AA *Tel:* 020 7219 2632 *Fax:* 020 7219 4525 *Tel (Constituency):* 01429 264956.

MANN, JOHN   Bassetlaw   *Lab majority 9,748*

John Mann. Born 10 January 1960; Son of James Mann and Brenda Cleavin; Educated Bradford Grammar School; Manchester University (BA Econ 1982); Married Joanna White 1985 (2 daughters 1 son). Head research and education AEU 1988–90; National training officer TUC 1990–95; Liaison officer National Trade Union and Labour Party 1995–2000; Director Abraxas Communications Ltd 1998–2002; Contested East Midlands 1999 European Parliament election; AEEU 1985–. Councillor London Borough of Lambeth 1986–90. **House of Commons:** Member for Bassetlaw since June 7, 2001; *Select Committees:* Member, Information 2001–. *Special Interests:* Small Businesses, Training, Economic Regeneration, Sport. *Publications: Labour and Youth: The Missing Generation*, Fabian Society 1985; *MIPD; Clubs:* IPD, YHA, Manton Miners; *Recreations:* Football, cricket, fellwalking. John Mann Esq, MP, House of Commons, SW1A 0AA *Tel:* 020 7219 8130. *Constituency:* 68a Carlton Road, Worksop, S80 1PH *Tel:* 01909 506 200.

MAPLES, JOHN   Stratford-on-Avon   *Con majority 11,802*

John Maples. Born 22 April 1943; Educated Marlborough College; Downing College, Cambridge (BA law 1964, MA); Harvard Business School; Married Jane Corbin 1986 (1 son 1 daughter). Barrister at Law 1965–; Called to Bar 1965. Council member Royal Institute of International Affairs. **House of Commons:** Member for Lewisham West 1983–92, and for Stratford-upon-Avon since May 1, 1997; PPS to Norman Lamont as Chief Secretary to the Treasury 1987–90; Economic Secretary, Treasury 1990–92; Member, Shadow Cabinet 1997–2000; Shadow Secretary of State for: Health 1997–98, Defence 1998–99, Foreign and Commonwealth Affairs 1999–2000; *Select Committees:* Member, Foreign Affairs 2000–. *Special Interests:* Foreign Affairs, Health, Economy. Deputy Chair, Conservative Party 1994–95. Joint Vice-Chair, British-American Parliamentary International Group 1999–. John Maples Esq, MP, House of Commons, London, SW1A 0AA *Tel:* 020 7219 5495 *Fax:* 020 7219 2829. *Constituency:* 3 Trinity Street, Stratford upon Avon, CV37 6BL *Tel:* 01789 292723 *Fax:* 01789 415866 *E-mail:* maplesj@parliament.uk.

MARRIS, ROB   Wolverhampton South West   *Lab majority 3,487*

Robert Marris. Born 8 April 1955; Son of Dr Charles Marris, radiologist, and Margaret Marris, JP; Educated St Edward's School, Oxford; University of British Columbia (BA sociology and history 1976, MA history 1979); Birmingham Polytechnic (law: Common Professional Examination 1983, Law Society Finals 1984); Partner Julia Pursehouse 1984. Firefighter British Columbia Forest Service 1974; Labourer Walter Derkaz and Company 1975; Trucker Eaton and Company 1977–79; Bus driver British Columbia Metro Transit 1979–82; Manby and Steward: Articled clerk 1985–87, Solicitor 1987–88; Solicitor Thompsons 1988–2001; TGWU 1985–. **House of Commons:** Member for Wolverhampton South West since June 7, 2001; *Select Committees:* Member, Work and Pensions 2001–. *Special Interests:* Manufacturing, Industry, Transport, Environment. *Countries of Interest:* Canada. Member: Greenpeace 1975–, Foundation for Conductive Education 1990–; Member: New Democratic Party Canada 1980–82, European Standing Committee A 2003–, European Standing Committee B 2003; *Clubs:* Springvale Club, Bilston; Birmingham TUC; *Recreations:* Canadiana, football (Wolverhampton Wanderers FC). Rob Marris Esq, MP, House of Commons, London, SW1A 0AA *Tel:* 020 7219 8342. *Constituency:* 41 Bath Road, Wolverhampton, WV1 4EW *Tel:* 01902 771166 *E-mail:* marrisr@parliament.uk.

MARSDEN, GORDON   Blackpool South   *Lab majority 8,262*

Gordon Marsden. Born 28 November 1953; Son of late George Henry Marsden and Joyce Marsden; Educated Stockport Grammar School; New College, Oxford (MA history 1976); London University (combined historical studies 1976–80); Harvard University 1978–79. Open University tutor/associate lecturer, arts faculty 1977–97; Public relations consultant 1980–85; Chief public affairs adviser to English Heritage 1984–85; Member, GMB/APEX. **House of Commons:** Contested Blackpool South 1992. Member for Blackpool South since May 1, 1997; PPS to: Lord Irvine of Lairg as Lord Chancellor 2001–03, Tessa Jowell as Secretary of State for Culture, Media and Sport 2003–; *Select Committees:* Member: Deregulation 1997–99, Education and Employment 1998–2001, Education Sub-Committee 1998–2001. *Special Interests:* Heritage, Education, International Affairs, Social Affairs, Disability, Human Rights. *Countries of Interest:* USA, Russia, Caribbean, Eastern Europe. Joined Labour Party 1971; Joined Fabian Society 1975; Chairman, Young Fabians 1980–81; Fabian Society: Vice-Chair, Chair, Research and and Public Committee 1998–2000, Chair 2000–01. Member, Association of British Editors; Editor, *New Socialist* 1989–90; Judge, Ford Conservation Awards UK 1990–97; Board Member, Institute of Historical Research 1996–; President, British Resorts Association 1998–; Member, National Trust; Trustee, Dartmouth Street Trust; Board, History Today Trust; Advisory Board, Institute of Historical Research; *Publications: Victorian Values* (ed.) 1990; Contributor to *The History Debate*, 1990; *Victorian Values*, 2nd edition 1998; *Low Cost Socialism*, 1997; Contributor to *The English Question*, Fabian Society 2000; *International History of Censorship*, 2001; Gibbs Prize in History 1975; Kennedy Scholar, Harvard 1978–79; *Recreations:* Theatre, early music and medieval culture, swimming, heritage sites, architecture. Gordon Marsden Esq, MP, House of Commons, London, SW1A 0AA *Tel:* 020 7219 1262 *Fax:* 020 7219 5859. *Constituency:* 304 Highfield Road, Blackpool, Lancashire, FY4 3JX *Tel:* 01253 344143 *Fax:* 01253 344940 *E-mail:* marsdeng@parliament.uk.

MARSDEN, PAUL   Shrewsbury and Atcham   *Lab majority 3,579**

Paul William Barry Marsden. Born 18 March 1968; Son of late Tom Marsden and of Audrey Marsden; Educated Helsby High School; Mid-Cheshire College of Further Education (National Diploma in Building Studies 1986); Teesside Polytechnic 1990; Open University (Professional Certificate in Management, Professional Diploma in Management 1995); Newcastle College (Diploma in Business Excellence 2000); Married Shelly Somerville 1994 (2 sons). Quality manager: Taylor Woodrow Group 1990–94, Natwest Bank 1994–96, Mitel Telecom 1996–97. Director, Shrewsbury Citizens Advice Bureau. **House of Commons:** *Labour Member for Shrewsbury and Atcham 1997–2001, Liberal Democrat Member for Shrewsbury and Atcham 2001–;

Liberal Democrat Shadow Health Minister 2002–; Spokesperson for Mental Health, Children's Health, Prison Health and Patient Focus; *Select Committees:* Member, Agriculture 1997–2001. *Special Interests:* Health, International Affairs, Agriculture, Rural Affairs, Environment, Education, Economy. *Countries of Interest:* USA, Europe, Africa. Personal assistant to Parliamentary candidate in Cheshire 1987 general election; Key organiser for Parliamentary candidate in Halifax 1992; Campaign manager/social secretary, Teesside Labour Party 1986–90; Branch secretary/GC delegate, Huddersfield CLP 1990–91; Member, National Executive Committee, Young Fabians 1990. Member: English Heritage, Shropshire Chamber of Commerce, Training and Enterprise, Greenpeace 2001–; Agriculture and Rural Economy Committee of Country Landowners Association; Vice-President: Offa's Dyke Association, Heart of Wales Line Travellers Association; Patron, Shropshire and Wrekin ME Support Group; Supporter, Shropshire and Mid-Wales Hospice; Member: Institute of Management, Institute of Directors, Health Bill Standing Committee 1999; Member: Commonwealth Parliamentary Association, British-American Parliamentary Group, United Nations Association; *Publications:* Contributor *Voices for Peace* 2001; MIMgt, MInstD; *Recreations:* Marathon running, reading, cinema, organic gardening, being with my family, archaeology. Paul Marsden Esq, MP, House of Commons, London, SW1A 0AA *Tel:* 020 7219 2300 *Fax:* 020 7219 0963. *Constituency:* Talbot House, Market Street, Shrewsbury, SY1 1LG *Tel:* 01743 341422 *Fax:* 01743 341261 *E-mail:* marsdenp@parliament.uk.

MARSHALL, DAVID Glasgow Shettleston   *Lab majority 9,818*

David Marshall. Born 7 May 1941; Educated Larbert High School; Denny High School; Falkirk High School; Woodside Senior Secondary School, Glasgow; Married Christina Stewart 1968 (2 sons 1 daughter). Office worker; Shepherd; Tram and bus conductor; Member, TGWU 1960–; Chairman, TGWU Group of 33 MPs 1987–88. Councillor, Glasgow Corporation 1972–75; Strathclyde Regional Council: Councillor 1974–79, Chief Whip 1974–76, Member, Local Authorities Conditions of Service Advisory Board 1975–79; Chair: Manpower Committee of Convention of Scottish Local Authorities 1976–79, Manpower Committee 1978–79. **House of Commons:** Member for Glasgow Shettleston since May 1979; Sponsored Solvent Abuse (Scotland) Act as private member's bill 1983; *Select Committees:* Member, Transport 1985–92; Chair, Transport 1987–92; Member: Liaison 1987–92, Scottish Affairs 1994–97; Chair, Scottish Affairs 1997–2001; Member, Liaison 1997–2001; Member, Unopposed Bills (Panel) 1997–. *Special Interests:* Aviation, Foreign Affairs, Poverty, Scottish Affairs, Transport. Labour Party Organiser, Glasgow 1969–71; Hon. Secretary and Hon. Treasurer, Scottish Group of Labour MPs 1981–2001. Vice-chair, Inter-Parliamentary Union (IPU) British Group 1994–97, Chair 1997–2000; Member, Executive Committee, Commonwealth Parliamentary Association (CPA) UK Branch 1997–99, Joint Vice-Chair 1999–2000; *Recreations:* Gardening, music. David Marshall Esq, MP, House of Commons, London, SW1A 0AA *Tel:* 020 7219 5134. *Constituency Tel:* 0141–778 8125.

MARSHALL, JAMES Leicester South   *Lab majority 13,243*

James Marshall. Born 13 March 1941; Son of late Fred Marshall and Mrs Lilian Marshall; Educated Sheffield City Grammar School; Leeds University (PhD 1968); Married Shirley Ellis 1962 (divorced) (1 son 1 daughter); married Sue Carter 1986. Research scientist, Wool Industries Research Association 1963–67; Lecturer, Leicester Polytechnic 1968–74. Councillor, Leeds City 1965–68; Leicester City Council: Councillor 1971–76, Chair, Finance Committee 1972–74, Leader 1974. **House of Commons:** Contested the Harborough division of Leicestershire 1970 and Leicester South February 1974 general elections. Member for Leicester South October 1974–83 and since June 1987; Opposition Spokesman on: Home Affairs 1982–83, Northern Ireland 1988–92; Assistant Government Whip 1977–79; *Select Committees:* Member: European Legislation 1997–98, European Legislation 1998–2001; Member, European Scrutiny 1998–. *Special Interests:* Housing, Education, Local and Regional Government. Labour Leader, Association of District Councils 1974; Member, British Delegation to the Council of Europe and WEU. James Marshall Esq, MP, House of Commons, London, SW1A 0AA *Tel:* 020 7219 5187. *Constituency:* 57 Regent Road, Leicester, CE1 6BF *Tel:* 0116–254 6900 *Fax:* 0116–255 3651.

MARSHALL-ANDREWS, ROBERT   Medway   *Lab majority 3,780*

Bob (Robert) Graham Marshall-Andrews. Born 10 April 1944; Son of late Robin and late Eileen Marshall; Educated Mill Hill School; Bristol University (LLB 1966); Married Gillian Diana Elliott 1968 (1 son 1 daughter). Called to the Bar, Gray's Inn 1967, QC 1987, Bencher 1996; Recorder of the Crown Court 1982; Occasional novelist. **House of Commons:** Contested Richmond 1974 and Medway 1992. Member for Medway since May 1, 1997; *Select Committees:* Member, Joint Committee on Consolidation of Bills Etc 1997–2001. *Special Interests:* Economic Policy, Environment, Civil Liberties, Parliamentary Democracy. *Countries of Interest:* East Africa, USA. Member, Society of Labour Lawyers. Former Head Governor, Grey Court School; Vice-chair Theatre Council 1998–; Trustee: George Adamson Wildlife Trust 1988–, Geffreye Museum 1990–; *Publications:* Palace of Wisdom, 1989/1990; *A Man Without Guilt* 2002; Observer Mace 1967; Spectactor Parliamentary Award 1997; *Sportsclubs:* Vice-President, Old Millhillians Rugby; *Recreations:* Theatre, reading, watching rugby, writing, walking, travel. Bob Marshall-Andrews Esq, QC, MP, House of Commons, London, SW1A 0AA *Tel:* 020 7219 6920 *Fax:* 020 7219 2933. *Constituency:* Moat House, 1 Castle Hill, Rochester, Kent, ME1 1QQ *Tel:* 01634 814687 *Fax:* 01634 831294 *E-mail:* marshallandrewsr@parliament.uk.

MARTIN, MICHAEL   Glasgow Springburn   *Speaker majority 11,378*

Michael John Martin. Born 3 July 1945; Son of Michael Martin, merchant seaman and Mary McNeil, school cleaner; Educated St Patrick's Boys' School, Glasgow; Married Mary McLay 1966 (1 son 1 daughter). Metal worker, Rolls-Royce Engineering 1960–76; Full-time trades union official 1976–79; Shop Steward AUEW 1970–74; Trade union organiser, NUPE 1976–79; Member, AEEU (Craft Sector); Sponsored as MP by AEEU. Councillor: Glasgow Corporation 1973–74, Glasgow District Council 1974–79. **House of Commons:** Member for Glasgow Springburn since May 1979; PPS to Denis Healey as Deputy Leader of the Labour Party 1980–83; First Deputy Chairman, Ways and Means (Deputy Speaker) 1997–2000; Speaker 2000–; *Select Committees:* Chair: Chairmen's Panel 1987–2000, Scottish Grand Committee 1987–97; Member, Speaker's Panel of Chairmen 1987–97; Chair: Administration 1992–97, Liaison 1993–97; Member: Court of Referees 1997–2000, Unopposed Bills (Panel) 1997–2000, Standing Orders 1998–2000. *Special Interests:* Trade and Industry, Drug Abuse, Industrial Relations, Equal Opportunities, Care of the Elderly, Human Rights. *Countries of Interest:* Italy, Canada, USA. Fellow, Industry and Parliament Trust; PC 2000; *Recreations:* Hillwalking, folk music, local history, playing the Highland Pipes and member of the College of Piping. Rt Hon Michael Martin, MP, House of Commons, London, SW1A 0AA *Tel:* 020 7219 5300/4111 *Fax:* 020 7219 6901 *Tel (Constituency):* 0141–762 2329 *Fax (Constituency):* 0141–762 1519.

MARTLEW, ERIC   Carlisle   *Lab majority 5,702*

Eric Anthony Martlew. Born 3 January 1949; Son of late George and Mary Jane Martlew; Educated Harraby School, Carlisle; Carlisle College 1966–67; Married Elsie Barbara Duggan 1970. Nestlé Co. 1966–87: Laboratory technician, Personnel manager; Member TGWU. Councillor, Carlisle County Borough Council 1972–74; Cumbria County Council: Councillor 1973–88, Chair 1983–85; East Cumbria Health Authority: Member 1975–88, Chairman 1977–79. **House of Commons:** Member for Carlisle since June 1987; Opposition Front Bench Spokesman on Defence, Disarmament and Arms Control with special responsibilities for the RAF 1992–95; Opposition Whip 1996–97; Shadow Defence Minister 1992–97; PPS: to Dr David Clark as Chancellor of the Duchy of Lancaster 1997–98, to Baroness Jay of Paddington as Lord Privy Seal, Leader of the Lords and Minister for Women 1998–2001; *Select Committees:* Member, Environment, Food and Rural Affairs 2001–02. *Special Interests:* Transport, Health, Social Services, Agriculture, Defence. Vice-president Chartered Institute Environmental Health; Vice-patron Carlisle MIND; Patron Cumbria Deaf Association; Hon council member Rural Buildings Preservation Trust 1997–; Trustee, Parliamentary Pension Fund 1999–; *Recreations:* Photography, fell-walking, horse-racing, watching rugby league. Eric Martlew Esq, MP, House of Commons, London, SW1A 0AA *Tel:* 020 7219 4114 *Fax:* 020 7219 6898. *Constituency:* 3 Chatsworth Square, Carlisle, Cumbria, CA1 1HB *Tel:* 01228 511395 *Fax:* 01228 819798.

MATES, MICHAEL   East Hampshire *Con majority 8,890*

Michael John Mates. Born 9 June 1934; Son of Claude John Mates; Educated Blundell's School; King's College, Cambridge; Married Mary Rosamund Paton 1959 (divorced 1980) (2 sons 2 daughters); married Rosellen Bett 1982 (divorced 1995) (1 daughter). Army service 1954–74: 2nd Lieutenant RUR 1955; Queen's Dragoon Guards, RAC 1961, Major 1967, Lieutenant-Colonel 1973, Resigned commission 1974. **House of Commons:** Member for Petersfield October 1974–83, East Hampshire since June 1983; Minister of State, Northern Ireland Office 1992–93; *Select Committees:* Chair, Defence 1987–92; Chair, Northern Ireland Affairs 2001–; Member, Liaison 2001–. *Special Interests:* Defence, Northern Ireland, Home Affairs. UK Delegate, NATO Parliamentary Assembly; Liveryman, Farriers' Company 1975, Master 1986–87; *Clubs:* MCC, Garrick; *Recreations:* Music. Michael Mates Esq, MP, House of Commons, London, SW1A 0AA *Tel:* 020 7219 5166 *Fax:* 020 7219 4884. *Constituency:* 14A Butts Road, Alton, Hampshire, GU34 1ND *Tel:* 01420 84122 *E-mail:* matesm@parliament.uk.

MAUDE, FRANCIS   Horsham *Con majority 13,666*

Francis Anthony Aylmer Maude. Born 4 July 1953; Son of late Baron Maude of Stratford-upon-Avon, PC (Life Peer), author and journalist, and late Lady Maude; Educated Abingdon School; Corpus Christi, Cambridge (MA history 1976) (Hulse Prize and Avory Studentship); College of Law (Forster Boulton Prize and Inner Temple Law Scholarship 1977); Married Christina Jane Hadfield 1984 (2 sons 3 daughters). Called to Bar, Inner Temple 1977; Practising barrister 1977–85; Head of global privatisation, Salomon Bros International 1992–93; Managing Director, global privatisation, Morgan Stanley & Co Ltd 1993–97; Chairman, Deregulation Task Force 1993–97; Non-executive Director: Asda Group plc 1993–99, Benfield Reinsurance Ltd 1994–99, Gartmore Shared Equity Trust 1997–99, Benfield Group plc 1999–, Deputy chair 2003–, Businesses for Sale Company plc 2000–2002; Chairman: Prestbury Holdings PLC, Jubilee Investment Trust plc. Councillor, Westminster City Council 1978–84. **House of Commons:** Member for North Warwickshire 1983–92, and for Horsham since May 1, 1997; Government Whip 1985–87; PPS to Peter Morrison, as Minister of State for Employment 1984; Minister for Corporate and Consumer Affairs, Department of Trade and Industry 1987–89; Minister of State, Foreign and Commonwealth Office 1989–90; Financial Secretary to the Treasury 1990–92; Member, Shadow Cabinet 1997–2001; Shadow Secretary of State: for National Heritage 1997, for Culture, Media and Sport 1997–98; Shadow Chancellor of the Exchequer 1998–2000; Shadow Secretary of State for Foreign and Commonwealth Affairs 2000–01; *Select Committees:* Member, Public Accounts 1990–92. Chairman, Governors of Abingdon School 1994–; PC 1992; *Recreations:* Skiing, reading, opera. Rt Hon Francis Maude, MP, House of Commons, London, SW1A 0AA *Tel:* 020 7219 2494 *Fax:* 020 7219 0638. *Constituency:* Gough House, Madeira Avenue, Horsham, West Sussex, RH12 1AB *Tel:* 01403 242000 *Fax:* 01403 210600 *E-mail:* francismaudemp@parliament.uk.

MAWHINNEY, BRIAN   North West Cambridgeshire *Con majority 8,101*

Brian Stanley Mawhinney. Born 26 July 1940; Son of Frederick Stanley Arnot and Coralie Jean Mawhinney; Educated Royal Belfast Academical Institution; Queen's University, Belfast (BSc physics 1963); Michigan University, USA (MSc radiation biology 1964); London University (PhD radiation biology 1968); Married Betty Louise Oja 1965 (2 sons 1 daughter). Assistant professor of radiation research, Iowa University, USA 1968–1970; Lecturer (subsequently senior lecturer), Royal Free Hospital School of Medicine 1970–84; Life Member, AUT. **House of Commons:** Contested Teeside Stockton October 1974 general election. Member for Peterborough 1979–97, and for North West Cambridgeshire since May 1, 1997; PPS: to Barney Hayhoe as Minister of State at the Treasury 1982–84; to Tom King: as Secretary of State for Employment 1983–85, for Northern Ireland 1984–86; Northern Ireland Office: Parliamentary Under-Secretary of State 1986–90,

Minister of State, 1990–92; Minister of State, Department of Health 1992–94; Secretary of State for Transport 1994–95; Minister without Portfolio 1995–97; Member, Shadow Cabinet 1997–98: Shadow Home Secretary 1997–98; *Special Interests:* Health, Northern Ireland, Anglo-American Relations, Trade and Industry. *Countries of Interest:* Middle East, USA. National President Conservative Trade Unionists 1987–90; Chair Conservative Party 1995–97; Member governing council Conservative Christian Fellowship. Member: National Council, National Society for Cancer Relief 1981–85, General Synod 1985–90; President, Peterborough Association for the Blind; Member, Council, World Relief; Chairman Football League 2003–; Member, Medical Research Council 1979–83; Member, Review Committee of Privy Counsellors of the Anti-terrorism, Crime and Security Act 2002–; Trustee, Boston University, USA; Fellow, Industry and Parliament Trust; *Publications:* Co-author *Conflict and Christianity in Northern Ireland* 1972; *In the Firing Line – Politics, Faith, Power and Forgiveness,* 1999; PC 1994; Kt 1997; *Sportsclubs:* Member, Etton Furze Golf Club; *Recreations:* Sport, reading. Rt Hon Sir Brian Mawhinney, MP, House of Commons, London, SW1A 0AA *Tel:* 020 7219 6205 *Fax:* 020 7219 2737. *Constituency:* 18 Peterborough Road, Wansford, Cambridgeshire, PE6 6JN *Tel:* 01780 783869; 01733 261868 *Fax:* 01780 783770; 01733 266887.

MAY, THERESA   Maidenhead   *Con majority 3,284*

Theresa Mary May. Born 1 October 1956; Daughter of late Rev Hubert Brasier and late Zaidee Brasier; Educated Wheatley Park Comprehensive School; St Hugh's College, Oxford (BA geography 1977, MA); Married Philip John May 1980. Association for Payment Clearing Services 1985–97: Various posts latterly senior adviser, international affairs. Councillor, London Borough of Merton 1986–94. **House of Commons:** Contested North-West Durham 1992 general election and Barking 1994 by-election. Member for Maidenhead since May 1, 1997; Opposition Spokeswoman for Education and Employment (schools, disabled people and women) 1998–99; Shadow Cabinet Spokeswoman for Women's Issues 1999–2001; Shadow Schools Minister 1998–99; Member, Shadow Cabinet 1999–; Shadow Secretary of State for: Education and Employment 1999–2001, Transport, Local Government and the Regions 2001–02, Transport 2002; Chairman, Conservative Party 2002–; *Select Committees:* Member: Education and Employment 1997–98, Education Sub-Committee 1997–99. *Special Interests:* Education, Disability, Local Government. Chair, Conservative Disability Group 1997–98. PC 2003; Fellow, Royal Geographical Society; *Clubs:* Maidenhead Conservative; *Recreations:* Walking, cooking. Rt Hon Theresa May, MP, House of Commons, London, SW1A 0AA *Tel:* 020 7219 5206 *Fax:* 020 7219 1145. *Constituency:* Maidenhead Conservative Association, 2 Castle End Farm, Ruscombe, Berkshire, RG10 9XQ *Tel:* 0118 934 5433 *Fax:* 0118 934 5288 *E-mail:* mayt@parliament.uk.

MEACHER, MICHAEL   Oldham West and Royton   *Lab majority 13,365*

Michael H Meacher. Born 4 November 1939; Son of late George H. Meacher; Educated Berkhamsted School, Hertfordshire; New College, Oxford (BA Greats 1962); LSE (social administration Diploma 1963); Married Molly Christine Reid 1962 (divorced 1987) (2 sons 2 daughters); married Lucianne Sawyer, née Craven 1988. Secretary, Danilo Dolci Trust 1964; Sembal research fellow in social gerontology, Essex University 1965–66; Lecturer in social administration: York University 1966–69, London School of Economics 1970; Visiting professor to Department of Sociology, Surrey University 1980–86; Member, UNISON. **House of Commons:** Contested Colchester 1966 general election and Oldham West 1968 by-election. Member for Oldham West 1970–97, and for Oldham West and Royton since May 1, 1997; Principal Opposition Frontbench Spokesperson for: Health and Social Security 1983–87, Employment 1987–89, Social Security 1989–92, Overseas Development and Co-operation 1992–93, Citizen's Charter and Science 1993–94, Transport 1994–95, Education and Employment 1995–96, Environmental Protection 1996–97; Parliamentary Under-Secretary of State: Department of Industry 1974–75, Department of Health and Social Security 1975–76, Department of Trade 1976–79; Member, Shadow Cabinet 1983–97; Minister of State: Department of the Environment, Transport and the Regions (Minister for the Environment) 1997–2001, Department for Environment, Food and Rural Affairs (Environment) 2001–02, (Environment and

Agri-Environment) 2002–03; *Select Committees:* Member, Environmental Audit 1998; Member, Environmental Audit 1997–. *Special Interests:* Economics and Social Policy, Redistribution of Income and Wealth, Industrial Democracy, Civil Liberties, Housing. Candidate for Deputy Leadership, Labour Party 1983; Member, Labour Party National Executive Committee 1983–89. Fellow, Industry and Parliament Trust; *Publications: The Care of Old People,* Fabian Society 1969; *Taken For A Ride: Special Residential Homes for the Elderly Mentally Infirm: A Study of Separatism in Social Policy,* 1972; *Socialism with a Human Face – the Political Economy in the 1980s,* 1982; *Diffusing Power – The key to Socialist Revival,* 1992; Numerous articles and pamphlets on social and economic policy; PC 1997; *Recreations:* Sport, music, reading. Rt Hon Michael Meacher, MP, House of Commons, London, SW1A 0AA *Tel:* 020 7219 4532/6461 *Fax:* 020 7219 5945. *Constituency:* 11 Church Lane, Oldham, Lancashire, OL1 3AN *Tel:* 0161–626 5779 *Fax:* 0161–626 8572 *E-mail:* massonm@parliament.uk.

MEALE, ALAN   Mansfield   *Lab majority 11,038*

(Joseph) Alan Meale. Born 31 July 1949; Son of late Albert Henry Meale, and of Elizabeth Meale; Educated St Joseph Roman Catholic School, Bishop Auckland; Durham University; Ruskin College, Oxford; Sheffield Hallam University; Married Diana Gilhespy 1983 (2 children). Author; editor; development officer; researcher for MPs Barbara Castle, Tony Benn, Dennis Skinner, Albert Booth; Parliamentary and political adviser to Michael Meacher as Principal Opposition Front Bench Spokesman on Health and Social Security 1984–87; National employment development officer, NACRO 1977–80; Assistant to Ray Buckton, General Secretary of ASLEF 1979–84; Sponsored by MSF. Former Deputy Leader, Local Authority. **House of Commons:** Member for Mansfield since June 1987; Opposition Whip 1992–94; PPS to John Prescott: as Deputy Leader of the Labour Party 1994–97, as Deputy Prime Minister and Secretary of State for the Environment, Transport and the Regions 1997–98; Parliamentary Under-Secretary of State, Department of the Environment, Transport and the Regions 1998–99; Adviser on Horse Racing to Richard Caborn, as Minister of State for Sport 2002–; *Select Committees:* Member: European Legislation 1988–90, Home Affairs 1990–92, Court of Referees 1997–98, Court of Referees 1999–2001. *Special Interests:* Home Affairs, Transport, Health, Social Security, Drug Abuse, Human Rights, Environment, Poverty, Sport, Unemployment, Media, Music. *Countries of Interest:* Cyprus. Chair, PLP East Midlands and Central Groups 1988–95; Former Vice-Chair, PLP Employment Committee; Member, Co-operative Party. Parliamentary Representative, SSAFA 1990–94; Member, War Pensions Board 1990–; Author; Parliamentary Representative, SSAFA (Armed Forces Social Welfare Organisation) 1989–95 Member, War Pensions Board 1989–97; Chair, British Cyprus Committee; Vice-Chair, Parliamentary Ukraine Committee; Fellow and Postgraduate Fellow of the Industry and Parliament Trust; Founder, Former Chair, Executive Member, Parliamentary Beer Industries Committee; Treasurer, CPA Cyprus Group (British Section); Former Executive Member: Commonwealth Parliamentary Association (CPA), Inter-Parliamentary Union (IPU); Member, UK Delegation Parliamentary Assembly of the Council of Europe/Western European Union 2000–; Fellow and Postgraduate Fellow, Industry and Parliament Trust; Honorary Citizenship: of Morphou, Cyprus, of Mansfield, Ohio (USA); Honorary Senatorship of Louisiana (USA); Freeman, State of Louisiana, USA; Freeman, City of: Mansfield, Ohio, USA; Morphou, Cyprus; *Sportsclubs:* Mansfield Town FC; *Recreations:* Reading, writing, arts, politics, sports, Mansfield Football Club, Cyprus. Alan Meale Esq, MP, House of Commons, London, SW1A 0AA *Tel:* 020 7219 4159. *Constituency:* 5 Clumber Street, Mansfied, Nottinghamshire, NG18 1NT *Tel:* 01623 660531 *Fax:* 01623 420495 *E-mail:* enquiries@alanmeale.co.uk.

MERCER, PATRICK   Newark   *Con majority 4,073*

Patrick John Mercer. Born 26 June 1956; Son of Rt Rev Eric Arthur John Mercer (Bishop of Exeter) and Rosemary, née Denby; Educated King's School, Chester; Exeter College, Oxford (MA modern history 1980); Royal Military Academy, Sandhurst (commission 1995); Married Catriona Jane Beaton (publisher) 1990 (1 son). The Worcestershire and Sherwood Foresters Regiment 1974–99: Second Lieutenant to Colonel (mentioned in Despatches 1982), gallery commendation 1991; Regular Army Officer 1974–99: Head of strategy Army Training and Recruiting Agency, Commanding officer The Sherwood Foresters, Bosnia, Canada, Tidworth, Operational service in the Balkans and Ulster; Reporter, BBC Radio 4 'Today' Programme 1999;

Freelance journalist 2000–01; Member, King's College London mission to East Timor 2000. Governor, Tuxford Comprehensive School. **House of Commons:** Member for Newark since June 7, 2001; Shadow Minister for Homeland Security 2003–; *Select Committees:* Member, Defence 2001–. *Special Interests:* Agriculture, Prisons, Defence, Northern Ireland. *Countries of Interest:* Ukraine, Russia, Israel, Serbia, Bosnia. Passed Staff College (psc) 1988; *Publications: Give Them a Volley and Charge*, Spellmount 1997; *Inkermann: The Soldier's Battle*, Osprey 1997; MBE 1993; OBE 1997; *Clubs:* Newark Working Men's, Newark Conservative, Army and Navy; *Recreations:* Painting, walking, bird-watching, history, country sports. Patrick Mercer Esq, MP, House of Commons, London, SW1A 0AA *Tel:* 020 7219 8477. *Constituency:* Newark and Retford Conservative Association, Belvedere, London Road, Newark, Nottinghamshire, NG24 1TN *Tel:* 01636 612837 *Fax:* 01636 703 269.

MERRON, GILLIAN Lincoln   *Lab majority 8,420*

Gillian Merron. Born 12 April 1959; Educated Wanstead High School; Lancaster University (BSc management sciences 1981). Business development adviser 1982–85; Local government officer 1985–87; Appointed Official, National Union of Public Employees (now UNISON) 1987–97; Senior officer for Lincolnshire, UNISON 1995–97; Member, UNISON. **House of Commons:** Member for Lincoln since May 1, 1997; Assistant Government Whip 2002–; Sponsored, Football Sponsorship Levy Bill 1997; PPS: to Ministers of State, Ministry of Defence: Doug Henderson, MP (Minister for the Armed Forces) 1998–99, Baroness Symons of Vernham Dean (Minister for Defence Procurement) 1999–2001, to Dr John Reid as Secretary of State for Northern Ireland 2001–02; *Select Committees:* Member, Trade and Industry 1997–98. *Special Interests:* Economy, Employment, Low Pay, Business, Crime, Police. Constituency Party Officer; Vice-chair, Regional Labour Party Executive; Vice-chair, Central Region Group of Labour MPs 1997–99; Chair, East Midlands Regional Group of Labour MPs 1999–2002. Member: Amnesty International, Cats Protection League, Action for Southern Africa (formerly Anti Apartheid); Co-ordinated the Shadow Cabinet Central Region Campaign in General and European Elections 1992; Member, Armed Forces Parliamentary Scheme (RAF) 1997–98; Member, Standing Committee National Minimum Wage Bill, Northern Ireland Arms Decommissioning, Local Authority Tendering, New Northern Ireland Assembly (Elections) Order 1998– Football (Offences and Disorder) Bill Armed Forces Discipline Bill; Fellow-Elect, Industry and Parliament Trust Board Member, Westminster Foundation for Democracy 1998–2001; *Recreations:* Football, walking, films, Lincoln City Football Club. Gillian Merron, MP, House of Commons, London, SW1A 0AA *Tel:* 020 7219 4031 *Fax:* 020 7219 0489. *Constituency:* Grafton House, 32 Newland, Lincoln, LN1 1XJ *Tel:* 01522 888688 *Fax:* 01522 888686 *E-mail:* merrong@parliament.uk.

MICHAEL, ALUN   Cardiff South and Penarth   *Lab majority 12,287*

Alun Michael. Born 22 August 1943; Son of late Leslie Michael and of Elizabeth Michael; Educated Colwyn Bay Grammar School; Keele University (BA); Married Mary Crawley 1966 (2 sons 3 daughters). Journalist, *South Wales Echo* 1966–72; Youth Worker, Cardiff City Council 1972–74; Youth and Community Worker, South Glamorgan CC 1974–87; AM for Mid and West Wales region 1999–2000; Member, GMB; Former Member: TGWU, CYWU; Branch Secretary, National Union of Journalists 1967–70; General Secretary, Welsh Association of FE and Youth Service Officers 1973–75. JP, Cardiff 1972–; Chair, Cardiff Juvenile Bench 1986–87; Cardiff City Council: Councillor 1973–89, Past Chair: Finance Committee, Planning Committee, Economic Development Committee 1987–89. **House of Commons:** Member for Cardiff South and Penarth since June 1987; Opposition Spokesperson for: Welsh Affairs 1988–92, Home Affairs 1992–97; The Voluntary Sector 1994–97; Opposition Whip 1987–88; Minister of State, Home Office (Minister for Criminal Policy also responsible for Police and the Voluntary Sector) 1997–98; Secretary of State for Wales 1998–99; Minister of State, Department for Environment, Food and Rural Affairs: (Rural Affairs) 2001–02, (Rural Affairs and Urban Quality of Life) 2002–03, Rural Affairs and Local Environmental Quality 2003–; *Special Interests:* Local and Regional Government, Housing, Youth Work, Juvenile Justice, Voluntary Sector, Community Development, Economic Development, Co-operative Development, Political Ideas and Philosophy. *Countries of Interest:* Germany, South Africa, Israel,

Canada, Somalia, USA, Japan. Former Chair, Co-operative Group of MPs; Member, National Executive, Co-operative Party (representing Wales); Member, Christian Socialist Movement. National Vice-President, Youth Hostels Association; Member of Board, Crime Concern 1993–97; Member: Commonwealth Parliamentary Association (CPA) (delegation to South Africa and Canada), Inter-Parliamentary Association (IPA); *Publications:* Contributor, *Restoring Faith in Politics,* 1966, *Challenges to a Challenging Faith,* 1995; Editor, *Tough on Crime and Tough on the Causes of Crime,* 1997, *Building the Future Together,* 1997; PC 1998; *Clubs:* Penarth Labour, Grange Stars (Cardiff), Earlswood (Cardiff); *Sportsclubs:* Penarth and Dinas Runners; *Recreations:* Long-distance walking, running, reading, opera, music. Rt Hon Alun Michael, JP, MP, House of Commons, London, SW1A 0AA *Tel:* 020 7219 5980 *Fax:* 020 7219 5930. *Constituency:* PO Box 453, Cardiff, CF11 9YN *Tel:* 029 2022 3533 *Fax:* 029 2022 9936/9947 *E-mail:* alunmichaelmp@parliament.uk.

MILBURN, ALAN   Darlington   *Lab majority 10,384*

Alan Milburn. Born 27 January 1958; Son of Evelyn Metcalfe, former NHS secretary; Educated John Marlay School, Newcastle; Stokesley Comprehensive School; Lancaster University (BA history); Newcastle University; Partner, Ruth Briel (2 sons). Senior business development officer, North Tyneside Council 1990–92; Co-ordinator, Trade Union Studies Information Unit, Newcastle 1984–90; Co-ordinator, Sunderland Shipyards Campaign 1988–89; President, North East Region, MSF Union 1990–92. **House of Commons:** Member for Darlington since April 9, 1992; Opposition Spokesperson for: Health 1995–96, Treasury and Economic Affairs (Shadow Economic Secretary) 1996–97; Minister of State, Department of Health 1997–98; Chief Secretary, HM Treasury December 1998–99; Secretary of State for Health 1999–2003; *Select Committees:* Member, Public Accounts 1994–95. *Special Interests:* Economic Policy, Industry, Regional Policy, Crime, Health. Chair, Newcastle Central Constituency Labour Party 1988–90; Member, Northern Region Labour Party Executive Committee 1990–92. *Publications: Jobs and Industry, the North Can Make It,* 1986; *Plan for the North,* 1987; *The Case for Regional Government,* 1989; PC 1998; *Recreations:* Cricket, football, music, cinema. Rt Hon Alan Milburn, MP, House of Commons, London, SW1A 0AA *Tel:* 020 7219 3594. *Constituency:* 123 Victoria Road, Darlington, County Durham, DL1 5JH *Tel:* 01325 380366 *Fax:* 01325 381341.

MILIBAND, DAVID   South Shields   *Lab majority 14,090*

David Wright Miliband. Born 15 July 1965; Son of Ralph and Marion Miliband (née Kozak); Educated Haverstock Comprehensive School; Corpus Christi College, Oxford (BA philosophy, politics and economics 1987); Massachusetts Institute of Technology (MSc political science 1989); Married Louise Shackelton 1998. Parliamentary officer National Council for Voluntary Organisations 1987–88; Research fellow Institute for Public Policy Research 1989–94; Secretary Commission on Social Justice 1992–94; Head of Policy Office, Leader of the Opposition 1994–97; Head of Prime Minister's Policy Unit 1997–2001; TGWU 1989–. **House of Commons:** Member for South Shields since June 7, 2001; Minister of State for School Standards, Department for Education and Skills 2002–; *Special Interests:* Education, Employment. Secretary, Social Justice Commission; Founder Centre for European Reform; *Publications:* Editor *Reinventing the Left,* Polity Press 1994; Co-editor *Paying for Inequality,* Rivers Oram Press 1994; *Clubs:* Whiteleas Social, Cleadon Social; *Sportsclubs:* President, South Shields Football Club. David Miliband Esq, MP, House of Commons, London, SW1A 0AA *Tel:* 020 7219 8320. *Constituency:* South Shields Constituency Labour Party, Ede House, 143 Westoe Road, South Shields, Tyne and Wear, NE33 3PD *Tel:* 0191 456 8910 *Fax:* 0191 456 5842.

Visit the Vacher Dod Website . . .
www.DodOnline.co.uk

MILLER, ANDREW   Ellesmere Port and Neston   *Lab majority 10,861*

Andrew Miller. Born 23 March 1949; Son of late Ernest and Daphne Miller; Educated Hayling Island Secondary School; Highbury Technical College; London School of Economics (diploma in industrial relations 1977); Married Frances Ewan (2 sons 1 daughter). Technician, Portsmouth Polytechnic, analyst in geology 1967–76; Regional official, MSF (formerly ASTMS) 1977–92; Member MSF 1968–. **House of Commons:** Member for Ellesmere Port and Neston since April 9, 1992; Chair Leadership Campaign Team 1997–98; PPS to Ministers, Department of Trade and Industry 2001–; Member, First Steps Team working with the Foreign Office to promote relations with EU and prospective EU member states with specific responsibility for Hungary and Malta 2001–; *Select Committees:* Member: Information 1992–97, Science and Technology 1992–97, Information 1997–2001, Joint Committee on Human Rights 2001. *Special Interests:* Industry, Economic Policy, Science and Technology, Communications and Information Technology, Pensions. *Countries of Interest:* Europe, China, USA, Malta, Hungary. Member: Labour Party, NW Regional Executive Committee 1984–92; President, Computing for Labour 1993–; Chair: Leadership Campaign Team 1997–98, North West Group of Labour MPs 1997–98; Member, Scientists for Labour 1997–. Patron: Road Peace, Chester Childbirth Trust, Parents Against Drug Abuse; *Sportsclubs:* Vice-President: Alvanley Cricket Club, Chester and Ellesmere Port Athletics Club; *Recreations:* Walking, photography, tennis, cricket. Andrew Miller Esq, MP, House of Commons, London, SW1A 0AA *Tel:* 020 7219 3580 *Fax:* 020 7219 3796. *Constituency:* Whitby Hall Lodge, Stanney Lane, Ellesmere Port, Cheshire, CH65 6QY *Tel:* 0151–357 3019 *Fax:* 0151–356 8226 *E-mail:* millera@parliament.uk.

MITCHELL, ANDREW   Sutton Coldfield   *Con majority 10,104*

Andrew John Bower Mitchell. Born 23 March 1956; Son of Sir David Mitchell, vintner and politician, and Pam Mitchell; Educated Rugby School; Jesus College, Cambridge (MA history 1978); Married Sharon Denise Bennet 1985 (2 daughters). UN Peacekeeping Forces Cyprus: 1st Royal Tank Regiment (SSLC); International and corporate finance Lazard Brothers and Company Ltd 1979–87; Lazard Brothers: Consultant 1987–92, Director 1997–; Director: Miller Insurance Group 1997–2001, Financial Dynamics Holdings 1997–; Senior strategy adviser: Boots 1997–2000, Andersen Consulting/Accenture 1997–; Director Commer Group 1998–2002; Supervisory board member The Foundation 1999–. Member Islington Health Authority 1985–87. **House of Commons:** Contested Sunderland South 1983 general election. Member for Gedling 1987–97. Contested Gedling 1997 general election. Member for Sutton Coldfield since June 7, 2001; Assistant Government Whip 1992–93; Government Whip 1993–95; PPS: to William Waldegrave, Foreign and Commonwealth Office 1988–90, to John Wakeham as Secretary of State for Energy 1990–92; Vice-chair Conservative Party 1992–93; Parliamentary Under-Secretary of State Department of Social Security 1995–97; *Select Committees:* Member: Members' Interests 1994–95, Work and Pensions 2001–03; Member: Modernisation of the House of Commons 2002–. *Special Interests:* Health, Defence, Economy, Pensions. Chair Cambridge University Conservative Association 1977; Islington North Conservatives 1983–85: President, Chair; Secretary One Nation Group of Conservative MPs 1989–92. English Speaking Union Council International Debate Council 1998–; Council of management GAP 1999–; Council SOS SAHEL 1992–; Liveryman, Vintner's Company; *Clubs:* Carlton, Chair Coningsby 1984–85; *Recreations:* Music, windsurfing, skiing, walking. Andrew Mitchell Esq, MP, House of Commons, London, SW1A 0AA *Tel:* 020 7219 8516. *Constituency:* Sutton Coldfield Conservative Association, 36 High Street, Sutton Coldfield, B72 1UP *Tel:* 0121 354 2229 *Fax:* 0121 321 1762.

DodOnline
An Electronic Directory without rival . . .

MPs' biographies and photographs available with daily updates *via* the internet

For a *free* trial, call Yasmin Mirza, Aby Farsoun or Michael Mand on 020 7630 7643

MITCHELL, AUSTIN   Great Grimsby   Lab majority 11,484

Austin Vernon Mitchell. Born 19 September 1934; Son of Richard Vernon Mitchell, Dyer; Educated Woodbottom Council School; Bingley Grammar School; Manchester University (BA history 1956); Nuffield College, Oxford (MA, DPhil 1963); Married Patricia Dorothea Jackson (divorced) (2 daughters); married Linda Mary McDougall (1 son 1 daughter). Lecturer in history, Otago University, Dunedin, New Zealand 1959–63; Senior lecturer in politics, University of Canterbury, Christchurch, NZ 1963–67; Official fellow, Nuffield College, Oxford 1967–69; Journalist: Yorkshire Television 1969–71, BBC 1972, Yorkshire Television 1973–77; Political commentator, Sky Television's Target programme 1989–98; Associate editor, *The House Magazine*; GMB, NUJ.

House of Commons: Member for Grimsby 1977–83 and for Great Grimsby since June 1983; Opposition Spokesperson for Trade and Industry 1988–89; Former Opposition Whip; PPS to John Fraser as Minister of State for Prices and Consumer Protection 1977–79; *Select Committees:* Member, Agriculture 1997–2001; Member, Environment, Food and Rural Affairs 2001–. *Special Interests:* Economics, Media, Fishing Industry, Agriculture, Poverty, Accountancy, Legal Reform, European Union, Electoral Reform, Constitutional Reform, Small Businesses. *Countries of Interest:* Canada, Iceland, New Zealand, France, Germany, China, Hong Kong, Nigeria. Member, Executive Council Fabian Society; Vice-chair Labour Campaign for Electoral Reform; Chair: Labour Euro-Safeguards Campaign, Labour Economic Policy Group. Vice-Chair, Hansard Society; Member: Hairdressing Council, Advisory Council, National Fishing Heritage Centre, Public Accounts Commission 1997–; Vice-President, Federation of Economic Development Authorities (FEDA); President, Debating Group; Member, Royal Institute of International Affairs; Joint Secretary, Esperanto Parliamentary Group; Fellow, Industry and Parliament Trust; *Publications: New Zealand Politics in Action 1962; Government by Party, 1966; Whigs in Opposition, 1815–30,* 1969; *Politics and People in New Zealand,* 1970; *Half Gallon Quarter Acre Pavlova – Paradise,* 1974; *Can Labour Win Again,* 1979; *Yes Maggie there is an Alternative; Westminster Man,* 1982; *The Case for Labour,* 1983; *Four Years in the Death of the Labour Party,* 1983; *Yorkshire Jokes* 1988; *Teach Thissen Tyke* 1988; *Britain, Beyond the Blue Horizon,* 1989; *Competitive Socialism,* 1989; *Election '45,* 1995; *Accounting for Change,* 1993; *Corporate Governance Matters,* 1996; *The Common Fisheries Policy, End or Mend?,* 1996; Co-author *Last Time: Labour's Lessons from the Sixties* 1997; *Farewell My Lords,* 1999; Co-author *Parliament in Pictures* 1999; *Pavlova Paradise Revisited* 2002; Order of New Zealand 1991; New Zealand Order of Merit for Services to New Zealand interests in the UK; *Recreations:* Photography, contemplating exercise. Austin Mitchell Esq, MP, House of Commons, London, SW1A 0AA *Tel:* 020 7219 4559 *Fax:* 020 7219 4843. *Constituency:* 15 New Cartergate, Grimsby, NE Lincs, DN31 1RB *Tel:* 01472 342145 *Fax:* 01472 251484 *E-mail:* mitchellav@parliament.uk.

MOFFATT, LAURA   Crawley   Lab majority 6,770

Laura Jean Moffatt. Born 9 April 1954; Daughter of Stanley and Barbara Field; Educated Hazelwick School, Crawley; Crawley College of Technology (pre nursing course); Married Colin Moffatt 1975 (3 sons). State Registered Nurse, Crawley Hospital (1975–97); Member, UNISON. Crawley Borough Council: Councillor 1984–96, Mayor 1989–90, Chair, Environmental Services 1987–96. **House of Commons:** Member for Crawley since May 1, 1997; PPS to: Lord Irvine of Lairg as Lord Chancellor 2001–03, Lord Falconer of Thoroton as Secretary of State for Constitutional Affairs 2003–; *Select Committees:* Member, Defence 1997–2001. *Special Interests:* Health, Housing, Aerospace, Aviation, Defence, AIDS, Drug Abuse. Member, Lioness Club; Director, Furniaid (registered charity to provide furniture for needy); President, Relate; *Recreations:* Family, friends, walking, pets, swimming. Mrs Laura Moffatt, MP, House of Commons, London, SW1A 0AA *Tel:* 020 7219 3619 *Fax:* 020 7219 3619. *Constituency:* 6 The Broadway, Crawley, West Sussex, RH10 1DS *Tel:* 01293 526005 *Fax:* 01293 527610 *E-mail:* clewerd@parliament.uk.

Visit the Vacher Dod Website . . .
www.DodOnline.co.uk

MOLE, CHRIS   Ipswich   *Lab majority 4,087*

Chris Mole. Born 16 March 1958; Educated Dulwich College; University of Kent, Canterbury (BSc electronics 1979); Married Shona Gibb 1996 (2 sons). Technologist Plessey Research 1979–81; Research manager BT Labs 1981–98; Member Connect 1980–2001. Leader Suffolk County Council 1993–2001; Deputy leader EEDA 1998–2001. **House of Commons:** Member for Ipswich since by-election November 22, 2001; *Select Committees:* Member: Joint Committee on Statutory Instruments 2002–, Office of the Deputy Prime Minister: Housing, Planning and Local Government 2002–, Regulatory Reform 2002–, Urban Affairs Sub-Committee 2003–. *Special Interests:* Local and Regional Government, European Affairs, Transport. *Recreations:* Reading, films, music. Chris Mole Esq, MP, House of Commons, London, SW1A 0AA *Tel:* 020 7219 4171 *Fax:* 0870 1305681. *Constituency:* 33 Silent Street, Ipswich, Suffolk, IP1 1TF *Tel:* 01473 281559 *Fax:* 01473 217489 *E-mail:* molec@parliament.uk.

MOONIE, LEWIS   Kirkcaldy   *Lab majority 8,963*

Lewis Moonie. Born 25 February 1947; Son of late George Moonie, retired accountant, and of Eva Moonie; Educated Grove Academy, Dundee; St Andrews University (MB, ChB 1970); Edinburgh University (DPM 1975, MRCPsych 1979, MSc Community Medicine 1981, MFCM 1984); Married Sheila Ann Burt 1971 (2 sons). Registrar training in psychiatry 1973–75; Full-time research clinical pharmacologist and medical adviser in pharmaceutical industry in Netherlands, Switzerland and Edinburgh 1975–80; Trainee Community Medicine, Fife Health Board 1980–84; Community Medicine specialist, Fife Health Board 1984–87; Member: TGWU, MSF. Councillor, Fife Regional Council 1982–86; Chair, Advisory Committee on War Pensions. **House of Commons:** Member for Kirkcaldy since June 1987; Opposition Frontbench Spokesperson for: Technology, Trade and Industry 1989–92, Science and Technology 1992–94, Trade and Industry 1994–95, Broadcasting and Telecommunications 1995–97; Parliamentary Under-Secretary of State, (Minister for Veterans), Ministry of Defence 2000–03; *Select Committees:* Member, Public Accounts Commission 1995–97; Chair, Finance and Services 1997–2000; Member: Liaison 1997–2000, Treasury 1998–2000, Treasury Sub-Committee 1998–2000. *Special Interests:* Industry, Technology, Economic Policy, Defence. Member, Co-operative Party. Member, House of Commons Commission 1997–2000; *Recreations:* Fishing, walking, golf. Dr Lewis Moonie, MP, House of Commons, London, SW1A 0AA *Tel:* 020 7219 4097. *Constituency:* John Smith House, 145 West Regent Street, Glasglow, G2 4RE *Tel:* 0141–572 6900 *E-mail:* mooniel@parliament.uk.

MOORE, MICHAEL   Tweeddale, Ettrick and Lauderdale   *LD majority 5,157*

Michael Kevin Moore. Born 3 June 1965; Son of Reverend W. Haisley Moore, Church of Scotland minister, and Jill Moore, physiotherapist; Educated Strathallan School; Jedburgh Grammar School; Edinburgh University (MA politics and modern history 1987); Single. Research assistant to Archy Kirkwood, MP 1987–88; Coopers and Lybrand, Edinburgh 1988–97; Manager, Corporate Finance Practice 1993–97. **House of Commons:** Member for Tweeddale, Ettrick and Lauderdale since May 1, 1997; Spokesperson for: Scotland (Industry, Employment, Health and Environment) 1997–99, Transport 1999–2001, Scotland 2001, Deputy Spokesperson for Foreign Affairs 2001–; *Select Committees:* Member, Scottish Affairs 1997–99. *Special Interests:* Business, Employment, Housing. Campaign Chair, 1999 and 2003 Scottish Parliament elections; Parliamentary Group Convener 2000–01; Scottish MP representative Liberal Democrat Policy Committee 2001–02; Deputy Leader Scottish Liberal Democrats 2003–. Member Amnesty International; Governor and Vice-chair Westminster Foundation for Democracy; Board Member Scotland in Europe 2003–; Scottish Spokesman on Business and Employment 1995–99; Institute of Chartered Accountants of Scotland 1991; *Sportsclubs:* Jed-Forest Rugby Club; *Recreations:* Rugby, hill-walking, music, films. Michael Moore Esq, MP, House of Commons, London, SW1A 0AA *Tel:* 020 7219 2236 *Fax:* 020 7219 0263. *Constituency:* Tweeddale, Ettrick and Lauderdale Liberal Democrats, 11 Island Street, Galashiels, Borders, TD1 1NZ *Tel:* 01896 663650 *Fax:* 01896 663655 *E-mail:* michaelmoore@cix.co.uk.

MORAN, MARGARET   Luton South   *Lab majority 10,133*

Margaret Moran. Born 24 April 1955; Daughter of late Patrick (Jack) Moran, caretaker and of Mary, née Murphy, home care worker; Educated St Ursula's, South London; St Mary's, Strawberry Hill, Twickenham; Birmingham University (BSocSc 1978). Director, Housing Association; Housing, local government, social services and education; Former national president, NALGO Housing Association Branch. Councillor, London Borough of Lewisham 1984–97, Leader 1993–95, Chair, Housing Committee (6 years). **House of Commons:** Contested Carshalton and Wallington 1992. Member for Luton South since May 1, 1997; Assistant Government Whip 2003–; PPS to: Gavin Strang as Minister of State (in Cabinet), Department of the Environment, Transport and the Regions (Minister for Transport) 1997–98, Dr Mo Mowlam as Minister for the Cabinet Office 1999–2001, Baroness Morgan of Huyton as Minister of State, Cabinet Office 2001, Barbara Roche as Minister of State for Women 2001–02, Andrew Smith as Secretary of State for Work and Pensions 2002–03; *Select Committees:* Member: Northern Ireland Affairs 1998, Public Administration 1999–2000; Member, Information 2001–. *Special Interests:* Economy and Employment, Welfare, Housing and Urban Regeneration, Childcare, E-Issues. *Countries of Interest:* Northern Ireland, Kashmir, Spain, Bangladesh, Ireland. Member: Labour National Policy Forum, Labour Women's Network, Labour Housing Group. School governor: Denbigh Infants and Juniors, Luton, Cardinal Newman School, Luton; Luton Day Centre for the Homeless; Patron, Homes for Homeless People; Vice-Chair: Association of London Local Authorities, Association of Metropolitan Authorities; Chair, AMA Housing Committee; *Recreations:* Visiting historic sites, rambling, cinema. Margaret Moran, MP, House of Commons, London, SW1A 0AA *Tel:* 020 7219 5049 *Fax:* 020 7219 5094. *Constituency:* 3 Union Street, Luton, Bedfordshire *Tel:* 01582 731882 *Fax:* 01582 731885 *E-mail:* moranm@parliament.uk.

MORGAN, JULIE   Cardiff North   *Lab majority 6,165*

Julie Morgan. Born 2 November 1944; Daughter of late Jack Edwards and Grace Edwards; Educated Dinas Powys Primary School; Howell's School, Llandaff, Cardiff; King's College, London University (BA English 1965); Manchester University; Cardiff University (Postgraduate Diploma in Social Administration, CQSW); Married Rhodri Morgan 1967 (now First Minister National Assembly for Wales) (1 son 2 daughters). Principal officer and development officer, West Glamorgan County Council 1983–87; Senior social worker, Barry Social Services 1985–87; Assistant director, Child Care, Barnados 1987–; Member, TGWU. Councillor: South Glamorgan Council 1985–96, Cardiff Council 1996; Member, Probation Committee. **House of Commons:** Contested Cardiff North 1992 General Election. Member for Cardiff North since May 1, 1997; *Select Committees:* Member, Administration 2001; Member: Welsh Affairs 1997–, Administration 2002–. *Special Interests:* Equal Opportunities, Social Services, Childcare. *Countries of Interest:* Nicaragua. Hon. Treasurer: Welsh Regional Group of Labour MPs 1999–, Parliamentary Labour Party Women's Group. Chair of Governors, Albany Road School; Member: Welsh Refugee Council, Race Equality Council, Nicaragua Solidarity Campaign; Permanent Waves, Women's Arts Association; *Recreations:* Swimming, walking. Mrs Julie Morgan, MP, House of Commons, London, SW1A 0AA *Tel:* 020 7219 6960 *Fax:* 020 7219 0960. *Constituency:* Cardiff North Constituency Office, 17 Plasnewydd, Whitchurch, Cardiff, CF14 1NR *Tel:* 029 2062 4166 *Fax:* 029 2062 3661.

MORLEY, ELLIOT   Scunthorpe   *Lab majority 10,372*

Elliot Morley. Born 6 July 1952; Son of Anthony Morley and late Margaret Morley; Educated St Margaret's High School, Liverpool; Hull College of Education (BEd 1975); Married Patricia Hunt 1975 (1 son 1 daughter). Teacher Greatfield High School, Hull 1975–87; Former President, Hull Teachers Association. Hull City Council: Councillor 1979–86, Chair, City Transport Committee 1981–85, Former deputy traffic commissioner, NE Region; Member, NIJC of Municipal Bus Industries; Executive member, Federation of Public Passenger Employers 1981–86. **House of Commons:** Contested Beverley 1983 general election. Member for Glanford and Scunthorpe 1987–97, and for Scunthorpe since May 1, 1997; Opposition Spokesperson for Food, Agriculture and Rural Affairs with special responsibility for animal welfare 1989–97; Parliamentary

Secretary, Ministry of Agriculture, Fisheries and Food (Minister for Fisheries and the Countryside) 1997–2001; Department for Environment, Food and Rural Affairs 2001–: Parliamentary Under-Secretary 2001–03: (Minister for Fisheries and the Countryside) 2001–02, (Minister for Fisheries, Water and Nature Protection) 2002–03; Minister of State for Environment and Agri-Environment 2003–; *Select Committees:* Member, Agriculture 1987–89. *Special Interests:* Education, Transport, Local and Regional Government, Green Issues, Countryside. *Countries of Interest:* Africa, Cyprus. Parliamentary Convener, Socialist Environmental Resources Association 1989–91; Steel Group of MPs. Former Council member, RSPB, BTO; Vice-President, Wildlife Link; President, South Humber and North Lincolnshire RSPCA; Vice-President: Steel Action, Federation of Economic Development Agencies, Association of Drainage Authorities; Vice-President: Federation of Economic Development Authorities (FEDA), Association of Drainage Authorities, Wildlife and Countryside Link; Former Council Member, British Trust for Ornithology; Trustee, Birds of the Humber Trust; Hon. Fellow, Lincolnshire and Humberside University; *Recreations:* Ornithology, travel, conservation, countryside issues, scuba-diving. Elliot Morley Esq, MP, House of Commons, London, SW1A 0AA. *Constituency:* Kinsley Labour Club, Cole Street, Scunthorpe, Lincolnshire, DN15 6QS *Tel:* 01724 842000 *Fax:* 01724 281734 *E-mail:* emorleymp@aol.com.

MORRIS, ESTELLE   Birmingham Yardley   Lab majority 2,576

Estelle Morris. Born 17 June 1952; Daughter of Rt Hon Charles Morris, DL, MP and of Pauline Morris; Educated Whalley Range High School, Manchester; Coventry College of Education (BEd); Single. Teacher, Sidney Stringer School and Community College 1974–92; Member: NUT, GMBU. Councillor, Warwick District Council 1979–91; Leader, Labour Group 1982–89. **House of Commons:** Member for Birmingham Yardley since April 9, 1992; Opposition Spokesperson for Education and Employment 1995–97; Opposition Whip 1994–95; Department for Education and Employment: Parliamentary Under-Secretary of State, (School Standards) 1997–98, Minister of State (Minister for School Standards) 1998–2001; Secretary of State for Education and Skills 2001–02; Minister of State (Minister for the Arts), Department for Culture, Media and Sport 2003–; *Special Interests:* Education and Training, Housing, Local and Regional Government. PC 1999; Honorary Degree, Doctor of Laws, Warwick University 2003. Rt Hon Estelle Morris, MP, House of Commons, London, SW1A 0AA *Tel:* 020 7219 3000 *Tel (Constituency):* 0121 706 6418 *Fax (Constituency):* 0121 706 8327 *E-mail:* morrise@parliament.uk.

MOSS, MALCOLM   North East Cambridgeshire   Con majority 6,373

Malcolm Douglas Moss. Born 6 March 1943; Son of late Norman Moss and Annie Moss, née Gay; Educated Audenshaw Grammar School; St John's College, Cambridge (BA geography 1965, MA); Married Vivien Lorraine Peake 1965 (died 1997) (2 daughters); married Sonya Alexandra McFarlin, née Evans 2000. Blundell's School: Assistant master 1966–68, Head of department, geography and economics 1968–70; Barwick Associates Ltd: Insurance consultant 1971–72, General manager 1972–74; Mandrake Associates Ltd: Co-Founder and director 1974–94, Managing director 1986–88; Chairman: Mandrake Group plc 1986–88, Mandrake Associates Ltd 1988–93. Wisbech Town Councillor 1979–87; Fenland District Councillor 1983–87; Cambridgeshire County Councillor 1985–87. **House of Commons:** Member for North East Cambridgeshire since June 1987; Opposition Spokesperson for: Northern Ireland November 1997–1999; Agriculture, Fisheries and Food 1999–2001, Local Government and the Regions 2001–02; Opposition Whip 1997; PPS: to Tristan Garel-Jones as Minister of State, Foreign and Commonwealth Office 1991–93, to Sir Patrick Mayhew as Secretary of State for Northern Ireland 1993–94; Parliamentary Under-Secretary of State, Northern Ireland Office 1994–97; Shadow Minister for: Transport 2002, Culture, Media and Sport 2002–; *Select Committees:* Member, Energy 1989–91. *Special Interests:* Energy, Education, Housing, Small Businesses, Financial Services, Rural Development. *Countries of Interest:* France, Switzerland, USA, South Africa, Botswana. Larmor Award, St John's College; Trustee, Angles Theatre and Arts Centre, Wisbech; *Sportsclubs:* Member, Lords and Commons: Ski Club, Tennis Club; *Recreations:* Amateur dramatics, gardening, skiing, tennis. Malcolm Moss Esq, MP, House of Commons, London, SW1A 0AA *Tel:* 020 7219 6933 *Fax:* 020 7219 6840. *Constituency:* 111 High Street, March, Cambridgeshire, PE15 9LH *Tel:* 01354 656541 *Fax:* 01354 660417 *E-mail:* mossm@parliament.uk.

MOUNTFORD, KALI   Colne Valley   Lab majority 4,639

Kali Mountford. Born 12 January 1954; Educated Crewe Grammar School for Girls; Crewe and Alsager College (DipHE) (BA philosophy, psychology, sociology 1988); (1 son 1 daughter). Member, CPSA 1975–97: Shop steward 1983–95, Branch secretary 1985–90, Regional secretary 1987–92, Department Employment Whitley Council Secretary 1988–95, Branch chair 1990–92, Trades Council Executive 1990–95. Councillor, Sheffield City Council 1992–96: Vice-Chair, Economic Development 1992–94, Chair, Personnel 1994–95, Deputy Chair, Finance 1995, Chair, Finance 1995–96. **House of Commons:** Member for Colne Valley since May 1, 1997; PPS to Des Browne as Minister of State, Department for Work and Pensions 2003–; *Select Committees:* Member: Social Security 1998–99, Treasury 2001–03, Treasury Sub-Committee 2001–03. *Special Interests:* Social Security, Employment, Textiles, Agriculture, Finance, Small Businesses. Member, Labour Party (Sheffield Brightside): General Management Committee 1985–95, Women's Officer 1989–91, Euro Constituency Vice-Chair 1989–91, Campaign Co-ordinator 1992, Recruitment Officer 1992–93. Member: Sheffield Co-ordinating Committee Against Unemployment 1992–94, National Centre for Popular Music 1994–95; Vice-Chair: CAB 1998–, Victim Support 1998–; President, Mehfal-E-Niswan 2000–; Member, Sheffield Race Equality Council 1993–95. Kali Mountford, MP, House of Commons, London, SW1A 0AA *Tel:* 020 7219 4507 *Fax:* 020 7219 2906. *Constituency:* Civic Hall, New Street, Slaithwaite, Huddersfield, HD7 5AB *Tel:* 01484 840100 *Fax:* 01484 840101.

MUDIE, GEORGE   Leeds East   Lab majority 12,643

George Mudie. Born 6 February 1945; Educated Local state schools; Married (2 children). Trade Union Official. Former Leader, Leeds City Council. **House of Commons:** Member for Leeds East since April 9, 1992; Opposition Whip 1994–97; Pairing and Accommodation Whip 1995–97; Deputy Chief Whip (Treasurer of HM Household) 1997–98; Parliamentary Under-Secretary of State (Lifelong Learning), Department for Education and Employment 1998–99; *Select Committees:* Member: Accommodation and Works 1992–98, Public Accounts 1994–95, Selection 1995–97, Finance and Services 1997–98, Selection 1997–98, Finance and Services 1998–99, Selection 1998–99; Member: Treasury 2001–, Treasury Sub-Committee 2001–. *Clubs:* Harehills Labour; *Recreations:* Watching football. George Mudie Esq, MP, House of Commons, London, SW1A 0AA *Tel:* 020 7219 5889. *Constituency:* 242 Brooklands Avenue, Leeds, LS14 6NW.

MULLIN, CHRIS   Sunderland South   Lab majority 13,667

Chris Mullin. Born 12 December 1947; Son of Leslie and Teresa Mullin; Educated St Joseph's College, Ipswich; Hull University (LLB 1969); Married Nguyen Thi Ngoc 1987 (2 daughters). Author; Journalist; travelled extensively in Asia; BBC World Service 1974–78; *Tribune* 1978–84, editor 1982–84; Member: NUJ, MSF. **House of Commons:** Contested Devon North 1970, Kingston Upon Thames February 1974 general elections. Member for Sunderland South since June 1987; Parliamentary Under-Secretary of State: Department of the Environment, Transport and the Regions 1999–2001, Department for International Development 2001, Foreign and Commonwealth Office 2003–; *Select Committees:* Member, Home Affairs 1992–97; Chair, Home Affairs 1997–99, 2001–03; Member: Liaison 1997–99, 2001–03; Member, Liaison Sub-Committee 2002–. *Special Interests:* Media Ownership, Justice. *Countries of Interest:* Cambodia, Tibet, Vietnam. Member Parliamentary Labour Party Parliamentary Committee 1997–99, 2001–. *Publications: How to Select or Reselect your MP,* 1981; *The Tibetans,* 1981; *A Very British Coup,* 1982; *Error of Judgement,* 1986; *The Last Man Out of Saigon,* 1986; *The Year of the Fire Monkey,* 1991; Channel 4 and House Award for Questioner of the Year 1999; Hon. LLD, City University, London; *Recreations:* Walking, gardening. Chris Mullin Esq, MP, House of Commons, London, SW1A 0AA *Tel:* 020 7219 3440. *Constituency:* 3 The Esplanade, Sunderland, Tyne and Wear, SR2 7BQ *Tel:* Sunderland Office: 0191–567 2848 *Fax:* 0191–510 1063 *E-mail:* mullinc@parliament.uk.

MUNN, MEG   Sheffield Heeley   *Lab majority 11,704*

Margaret Patricia Munn. Born 24 August 1959; Daughter of late Reginald Edward Munn, representative and Lillian Munn, née Seward, retired nurse tutor; Educated Rowlinson Comprehensive School, Sheffield; York University (BA languages 1981); Nottingham University (MA social work 1986); Certificate of Qualification in Social Work 1986; Certificate in Management Studies 1995; Diploma in Management Studies 1997; Married Dennis Bates 1989. Social work assistant, Berkshire County Council 1981–84; Nottinghamshire County Council: Social worker 1986–90, Senior social worker 1990–92; District manager, Barnsley Metropolitan Council 1992–96; Children's services manager, Wakefield Metropolitan District Council 1996–99; Assistant Director, City of York Council 1999–2000; UNISON 1981–96; Shop steward NALGO 1982–84; GMB 1997–. Councillor Nottingham City Council 1987–91. **House of Commons:** Member for Sheffield Heeley since June 7, 2001; Team PPS, Department for Education and Skills 2003–; *Select Committees:* Member, Procedure 2001–02; Member, Education and Skills 2001–. *Special Interests:* Social Welfare, Social Affairs, Co-operative Issues, European Affairs, Small Businesses. Member Co-operative Party 1975–; Chair Women's Parliamentary Labour Party. *Recreations:* Tennis, swimming, reading. Meg Munn, MP, House of Commons, London, SW1A 0AA *Tel:* 020 7219 8316 *Fax:* 020 7219 1793. *Constituency:* 2nd Floor, Barkers Pool House, Burgess Street, Sheffield, S1 2HF *Tel:* 0114 263 4004 *Fax:* 0114 263 4334 *E-mail:* munnm@parliament.uk.

MURPHY, DENIS   Wansbeck   *Lab majority 13,101*

Denis Murphy. Born 2 November 1948; Son of late John Murphy and of Josephine Murphy; Educated St Cuthberts Grammar School, Newcastle upon Tyne; Northumberland College (electrical engineering 1967); Married Nancy Moffat 1969 (separated) (1 son 1 daughter). Apprentice electrician 1965–69; Underground electrician, Ellington Colliery 1969–94; Member, National Union of Mineworkers (Craft Section) 1965–; General Secretary, Northumberland Colliery Mechanics Association 1989–97. Wansbeck District Council: Councillor 1990–97, Chair of Planning, Leader of Council 1994–97. **House of Commons:** Member for Wansbeck since May 1, 1997; *Select Committees:* Member, Regulatory Reform 1998–. *Special Interests:* Economic Development, Transport. Chair, Board of Governors, Northumberland Aged Mineworkers Homes Association; *Recreations:* Cycling, walking. Denis Murphy Esq, MP, House of Commons, London, SW1A 0AA *Tel:* 020 7219 6474. *Constituency:* 94 Station Road, Ashington, Northumberland, NE63 8RN *Tel:* 01670 523100 *Fax:* 01670 521655.

MURPHY, JIM   Eastwood   *Lab majority 9,141*

Jim (James) Murphy. Born 23 August 1967; Son of Jim Murphy, pipe-fitter, and Anne Murphy, secretary; Educated Bellarmine Secondary School, Glasgow; Milnerton High School, Cape Town; Strathclyde University; Married Claire Cook (1 daughter 1 son). Director, Endsleigh Insurance 1994–96; Project Manager, Scottish Labour Party 1996–97; President: NUS (Scotland) 1992–94, NUS 1994–96; Member, GMB. **House of Commons:** Member for Eastwood since May 1, 1997; Assistant Government Whip 2002–03, Government Whip 2003–; PPS to Helen Liddell as Secretary of State for Scotland 2001–02; *Select Committees:* Member, Public Accounts 1999–2001. *Special Interests:* Economy, International Affairs, Defence, Consumer Issues, Sport. *Countries of Interest:* Southern Africa, Middle East. Vice-Chair, Labour Friends of Israel 1997–01, Chair 2001–02; Member, Co-operative Party. Fellow, Royal Society of Arts; *Sportsclubs:* Bonnington Golf; *Recreations:* Football, travelling in Scotland, cinema, horse-racing, golf. Jim Murphy Esq, MP, House of Commons, London, SW1A 0AA *Tel:* 020 7219 4615 *Fax:* 020 7219 5657. *Constituency:* 238 Ayr Road, Newton Mearns, East Renfrewshire, G77 6AA *Tel:* 0141 577 0100 *Fax:* 0141 616 3613.

 Paul Peter Murphy. Born 25 November 1948; Son of late Ronald and late Marjorie Murphy; Educated St Francis School, Abersychan; West Monmouth School, Pontypool; Oriel College, Oxford (MA modern history); Single. Management trainee, CWS 1970–71; Lecturer in government, Ebbw Vale College of Further Education 1971–87; Member, TGWU. Torfaen Borough Council: Councillor 1973–87, Chair, Finance Committee 1976–86. **House of Commons:** Contested Wells 1979 general election. Member for Torfaen since June 1987; Opposition Spokesman on: Welsh Affairs 1988–94, Northern Ireland 1994–95, Foreign Affairs 1995, Defence, Disarmament and Arms Control 1995–97; Minister of State, Northern Ireland Office (Minister for Political Development) 1997–99; Secretary of State for Wales 1999–2002; Secretary of State for Northern Ireland 2002–; *Special Interests:* Local and Regional Government, Wales, Education, Housing, Foreign Affairs, Northern Ireland. Secretary, Torfaen Constituency Labour Party 1971–87; Chair, Welsh Group of Labour MPs 1996–97. Former school and college governor; Former Treasurer, Anglo-Austrian Society; Member, Royal Institute of International Affairs 1997–; Knight of St Gregory (Papal Award); PC 1999; Hon. Fellow, Oriel College, Oxford 2001; *Recreations:* Classical music, cooking. Rt Hon Paul Murphy, MP, House of Commons, London, SW1A 0AA *Tel:* 020 7219 3463. *Constituency:* 73 Upper Trosnant Street, Pontypool, Torfaen, NP4 8AU *Tel:* 01495 750078 *Fax:* 01495 752584 *E-mail:* hunta@parliament.uk.

 Andrew William Murrison. Born 24 April 1961; Son of William Murrison and Marion Murrison, née Horn; Educated Harwich High School; The Harwich School; Bristol University medicine: (MB CHB 1984), (MD 1995); Cambridge Universty medicine (DPH 1996); Married Jennifer Jane Munden 1994 (5 daughters). Surgeon Commander Royal Navy 1981–2000; Principal Medical Officer HM Naval Base Portsmouth 1996–99; Staff Officer, Commander-In-Chief Fleet 1999–2000; Locum Consultant Occupational Physician Gloucestershire Royal Hospital and GP 2000–01. Westbury and District Community Trust 2002–. **House of Commons:** Member for Westbury since June 7, 2001; Research assistant Lord Freeman 2000–; *Select Committees:* Member, Science and Technology 2001–. *Special Interests:* Health, Defence. Election agent Local Constituency Party 1997–98. Representative Hampshire Area Council: Royal College of Physicians: Member International Medical Committee, Faculty of Occupational Medicine: Board member, Examiner; Member European Standing Committee C; Lions; *Publications: Investors in Communities* (Bow Group) 2000; Gilbert Blane Medal 1994; MFOM 1994; *Clubs:* Warminster Conservative Club, Royal British Legion, Vice-president, Trowbridge White Ensign Association; Member Standing Committee on NHS Reform Bill 2001–02; *Recreations:* Sailing, skiing. Dr Andrew Murrison, MP, House of Commons, London, SW1A 0AA *Tel:* 020 7219 8337 *Fax:* 020 7219 1944. *Constituency:* Lovemead House, Roundstone Street, Trowbridge, Wiltshire, BA14 8DG *Tel:* 01225 752 141 *Fax:* 01225 776 942 *E-mail:* murrisona@parliament.uk.

DodOnline
An Electronic Directory without rival ...
MPs' biographies and photographs available with daily updates *via* the internet

For a *free* trial, call Yasmin Mirza, Aby Farsoun or Michael Mand on 020 7630 7643

N

NAYSMITH, DOUG   Bristol North West   *Lab majority 10,887*

Doug (John Douglas) Naysmith. Born 1 April 1941; Son of late James Naysmith and late Ina Vass; Educated Musselburgh Burgh School; George Heriots School, Edinburgh; Heriot-Watt University (biology); Edinburgh University (BSc zoology 1965, PhD surgical science 1970); Married Caroline Hill 1966 (separated) (1 son 1 daughter). Research assistant, Edinburgh University 1966–69; Post-doctoral fellow, Yale University 1969–70; Research immunologist, Beecham Research Laboratories 1970–72; Bristol University: Research associate, Fellow, lecturer in immunology, Pathology Department 1972–92; Contested 1979 European Parliament election; Bristol University Administrator, Registrar's Office 1992–97; Past President and Secretary, Bristol AUT. Bristol City Council: Councillor 1981–98, Past Chair: Docks Committee, Health and Environmental Services Committee, Health Policy Committee, Port of Bristol Authority 1986–91; Past Labour Group Whip; Past member, Avon FPC; Past member, Bristol CHC. **House of Commons:** Contested Cirencester and Tewekesbury 1987, Bristol North West 1992 general elections. Member for Bristol North West since May 1, 1997; Chair Bristol Co-operative Party 1990–97; Member Co-operative Party NEC 1994–96; *Select Committees:* Member, Social Security 1999–2001; Member: Regulatory Reform 1998–, Health 2001–. *Special Interests:* Health, Co-operative Development, Local and Regional Government, International Development, Science, Education, Ports and Shipping. Chair Bristol District Labour Party 1991–97; President Socialist Health Association 1991–97; National Vice-President Socialist Health Association 1997–2000; Co-operative Group of MPs 1997–. Member: Citizens Advice Bureau, CND, WDM; Member Council of Europe and WEU 1997–99; Past treasurer International Union of Immunology Societies; Past secretary European Federation of Immunology Societies; Member, Wildlife Trust; Trustee, Jenner Trust; *Publications:* Various scientific papers and book chapters; FRSM; FIBiol; *Recreations:* Music, theatre, films, preserving paddle steamers. Dr Doug Naysmith, MP, House of Commons, London, SW1A 0AA *Tel:* 020 7219 4187 *Fax:* 020 7219 2602. *Constituency:* Unit 6, Greenway Business Centre, Doncaster Road, Bristol, BS10 5PY *Tel:* 0117–950 2385 *Fax:* 0117–950 5302 *E-mail:* naysmithd@parliament.uk.

NORMAN, ARCHIE   Tunbridge Wells   *Con majority 9,730*

Archie John Norman. Born 1 May 1954; Son of Dr Archie Norman, physician, and Dr Aleida Elisabeth Norman; Educated Charterhouse; University of Minnesota, Minneapolis, USA (MBA 1971, MA economics 1972); Emmanuel College, Cambridge (Exhibitioner, BA economics 1975); Harvard Business School 1977–79; Married Vanessa Mary Peet 1983 (1 daughter). Citibank NA 1975–77; Partner, McKinsey & Co Inc 1979–86; Group finance director, Kingfisher plc 1986–91; Non-executive director: British Rail 1992–94, Railtrack plc 1994–2000, Geest plc 1988–91; Chief executive, Asda Group plc 1991–96; Chair: Asda Group plc 1996–99, Energis 2002–. **House of Commons:** Member for Tunbridge Wells since May 1, 1997; Opposition Spokesperson for Europe 1999–2000; Member, Shadow Cabinet 2000–01; Shadow Secretary of State for Environment, Transport and the Regions 2000–01; Introduced Private Members' Bill on Company Directors' Performance and Compensation Bill 2003; *Special Interests:* Business, Transport, Agriculture, Countryside. Chair: Cambridge University Conservative Association 1975, East Region Federation of Conservative Students 1975; Council Member, Federation of Conservative Students 1975–76; President, West Yorkshire (Conservative) Businessmen's Association 1990–96; Vice-Chair, Conservative Party (with responsibility for organisation) 1997–98, Chief executive and Deputy chair 1998–99. DTI Deregulation Taskforce 1994–; ACISE Government Committee on Business and the Environment 1995–96; Member, Council of the Industrial Society; Fellow, Marketing Society; Hon. Degree, Leeds Metropolitan University; *Recreations:* Farming, music, opera, tennis, football. Archie Norman Esq, MP, House of Commons, London, SW1A 0AA *Tel:* 020 7219 5156 *Fax:* 020 7219 6050. *Constituency:* 84 London Road, Tunbridge Wells, Kent, TN1 1EA *Tel:* 01892 522581 *Fax:* 01892 522582.

NORRIS, DAN   Wansdyke   *Lab majority 5,613*

Dan Norris. Born 28 January 1960; Son of David Norris and June Norris (née Allen); Educated State schools; Sussex University (MSW). Former child protection officer; Member, GMB. Councillor: Bristol City Council 1989–92, 1995–97, Avon County Council 1994–96. **House of Commons:** Member for Wansdyke since May 1, 1997; Assistant Government Whip 2001–03; *Special Interests:* Freedom of Information, Child Protection and Safety, Animal Welfare. Member: Co-op Party, Labour Leader's Campaign Team with responsibility for Health 1998–99, General Election Campaign Team with responsibility for campaigning against the Liberal Democrats 1999–. *Publications:* Various publications on prevention and reduction of violence; Hon. Fellow, School of Cultural and Community Studies, Sussex University; *Clubs:* Radstock Working Men's; *Recreations:* Photography. Dan Norris Esq, MP, House of Commons, London, SW1A 0AA *Tel:* 020 7219 6395 *Tel (Constituency):* 01454 857406 *Fax (Constituency):* 01454 857382.

O

OATEN, MARK   Winchester   *LD majority 9,634*

Mark Oaten. Born 8 March 1964; Son of Ivor and Audrey Oaten; Educated Queen's Comprehensive School, Watford; Hatfield Polytechnic (BA history, Diploma in International Public Relations 1986); Married Belinda Fordham 1992 (2 daughters). Director Oasis Radio, Hertfordshire 1988–97; Consultant Shandwick Public Affairs 1988–92; Managing Director Westminster Public Relations 1996–97; Managing Director Westminster Communications Ltd 1996–97. Councillor, Watford Borough Council 1986–94, Liberal Democrat Group Leader. **House of Commons:** Contested Watford 1992 general election. Member for Winchester since May 1, 1997. (His two-vote victory was declared invalid and a by-election held in November 1997 convincingly confirmed him in the seat); Liberal Democrat Spokesperson for: Social Security and Welfare (Disabled People) 1997–99, Foreign Affairs and Defence (Foreign Affairs) 1999–2000, Foreign Affairs and Defence (Europe) 2000–01, Cabinet Office 2001–03; PPS to Charles Kennedy as Leader of the Liberal Democrat Party 1999–2001; *Select Committees:* Member, Public Administration 1999–2001. Chair: Parliamentary Party 2001–, Liberal Democrat Peel Group 2001–. Member, European Standing Committee C 1999–2000; *Recreations:* Gardening, swimming. Mark Oaten Esq, MP, House of Commons, London, SW1A 0AA *Tel:* 020 7219 2703 *Fax:* 020 7219 2389. *Constituency:* 13 City Road, Winchester, Hampshire, SO23 8SD *Tel:* 01962 622212 *Fax:* 01962 863300 *E-mail:* oatenm@parliament.uk.

O'BRIEN, MIKE   North Warwickshire   *Lab majority 9,639*

Michael O'Brien. Born 19 June 1954; Son of late Timothy O'Brien and Mary O'Brien, née Toomey; Educated St George's School; Blessed Edward Oldcorne School; North Staffs Polytechnic (BA history and politics, PGCE); Married Alison Joy Munro 1987 (2 daughters). Trainee solicitor 1977–80; Teacher training 1980–81; Lecturer in law, Colchester College of Further and Higher Education 1981–87; In practice as solicitor 1987–92; Branch secretary, NATFHE 1989–90. **House of Commons:** Contested Ruislip Northwood 1983 and North Warwickshire 1987 general elections. Member for North Warwickshire since April 9, 1992; Opposition Spokesperson for Treasury and Economic Affairs 1995–96; Shadow Economic Secretary to the Treasury 1996–97; Parliamentary Under-Secretary of State, Home Office 1997–2001; Foreign and Commonwealth Office 2002–: Parliamentary Under-Secretary of State 2002–03, Minister of State for Trade and Foreign Affairs (also DTI) 2003–; *Select Committees:* Member: Home Affairs 1992–93, Treasury and Civil Service 1993–95. *Special Interests:* West Midlands Industry, Police, Coal Industry. Parliamentary Adviser to Police Federation of England and Wales 1993–96; *Clubs:* Bedworth Ex Servicemen's, Woodend Workingmen's; Ansley Social Club; *Recreations:* Spending time with family. Michael O'Brien Esq, MP, House of Commons, London, SW1A 0AA *Tel:* 020 7219 3000. *Constituency:* 92 King Street, Bedworth, Warwickshire, CV12 8JF *Tel:* 024 7631 5084.

O'BRIEN, STEPHEN   Eddisbury   *Con majority 4,568*

Stephen Rothwell O'Brien. Born 1 April 1957; Son of David O'Brien, retired businessman and Rothy O'Brien, shopowner and retired nurse; Educated Loretto School, Mombasa, Kenya; Handbridge School, Chester; Heronwater School, Abergele, N Wales; Sedbergh School, Cumbria; Emmanuel College, Cambridge (law 1979, MA); College of Law, Chester (Professional Qualification 1980); Married Gemma Townshend 1986 (2 sons 1 daughter). Armed Forces Parliamentary Scheme (Army) 2001–03; Articles, Freshfields (Solicitors, City of London) 1981–83, Senior Managing Solicitor 1983–88; Redland plc 1988–98: Group secretary and director, Strategy and Corporate Affairs, Director of UK and overseas operations, Member, Group Executive Committee, Deputy chairman, Redland Tile and Brick (Northern Ireland 1995–98), Executive Director, Redland Clay Tile (Mexico1994–98); International business consultant 1998–. **House of Commons:** Member for Eddisbury since July 22, 1999; Opposition Whip 2001–02; Private Member's Bill, Honesty in Food Labelling 1999–2000, re-introduced 2002–03; PPS to: Francis Maude as Shadow Foreign Secretary 2000, Michael Ancram as Chairman Conservative Party 2000–01; Acting Director Office Leader of Conservative Party, Iain Duncan Smith 2001; Shadow Financial Secretary to the Treasury 2002; Shadow Paymaster General 2002–; *Select Committees:* Member: Education and Employment 1999–2001, Education Sub-Committee 1999–2001. *Special Interests:* Economy, Trade and Industry, Agriculture and the Rural Economy, Housing, Infrastructure, Transport, Northern Ireland, Foreign Affairs, Education, Constitutional Affairs. *Countries of Interest:* Ireland, East African countries, Australia, New Zealand, Mexico, USA. Chairman, Chichester Conservative Association 1998–99; Executive committee member, Westminster Candidates Association 1998–99; Special adviser, Conservative Business Liaison Unit (construction sector) 1998–2001; Member, National Membership Committee of the Conservative Party 1999–2001. Non-executive director, Cambridge University Careers Service 1992–99; Member CBI SE Regional Council 1995–98; Chairman Public and Parliamentary Affairs Committee BMP (UK Building Materials Producers) 1995–99; Non-executive director, City of London Sinfornia 2001–; Founder Member, Brazil-UK Joint Business Council 1994; Council of Members, Scottish Business in the Community 1995–98; Member: British-Irish Inter-Parliamentary Body 2000–, International Parliamentary Union 1999–, Commonwealth Parliamentary Association 1999–; FCIS; *Clubs:* Institute of Chartered Secretaries and Administrators, Law Society, Winsford Constitutional and Conservative, Cheshire Pitt Club; *Recreations:* Music (piano), fell-walking, golf. Stephen O'Brien Esq, MP, House of Commons, London, SW1A 0AA *Tel:* 020 7219 6315 *Fax:* 020 7219 0584. *Constituency:* Eddisbury Conservative Association, 4 Church Walk, High Street, Tarporley, Cheshire, CW6 0AJ *Tel:* 01829 733243 *Fax:* 01829 733243 *E-mail:* obriens@parliament.uk.

O'BRIEN, WILLIAM   Normanton   *Lab majority 9,937*

William O'Brien. Born 25 January 1929; Educated State schools; Leeds University; Married Jean Scofield (3 daughters). Coalminer 1946–83; Member, NUM 1945–. Councillor: Knottingly Urban District Council 1952–85, West Riding County Council 1964–74; Member, Yorkshire Water Authority 1973–83; Wakefield Council: Councillor 1973–83, Former Deputy Leader, Chairman, Finance and General Purposes Committee; JP, Wakefield Division. **House of Commons:** Member for Normanton since June 1983; Opposition Spokesperson for: Environment (Local Government) 1988–92, Northern Ireland 1992–96; *Select Committees:* Member: Environment, Transport and Regional Affairs 1997–2001, Transport Sub-Committee 1997–2001, Transport, Local Government and the Regions 2001–02, Transport Sub-Committee 2001–02, Urban Affairs Sub-Committee 2001–02; Member: Chairmen's Panel 1998–, Standing Orders 1998–, Office of the Deputy Prime Minister: Housing, Planning and Local Government 2002–, Urban Affairs Sub-Committee 2003–. *Special Interests:* Local and Regional Government, Water Industry, Energy, Transport. Member, Public Accounts Commission 1997–; Executive Committee Member, IPU British Group; Fellow, Industry and Parliament Trust; *Recreations:* Reading, organising. William O'Brien Esq, MP, House of Commons, London, SW1A 0AA *Tel:* 020 7219 3492 *Fax:* 020 7219 0301. *Constituency Tel:* 01977 709868; 01924 826225 *Fax:* 01977 599830; 01924 826225.

O'HARA, EDWARD Knowsley South

Lab majority 21,316

Edward O'Hara. Born 1 October 1937; Son of late Robert and Clara O'Hara, née Davies; Educated Liverpool Collegiate School; Magdalen College, Oxford (MA literae humaniores 1962); Married Lillian Hopkins 1962 (2 sons 1 daughter). Lecturer/principal lecturer in higher education: C.F. Mott College 1970–75, City of Liverpool College of Higher Education 1975–85, Liverpool Polytechnic 1985–90; Member, Association of Teachers and Lecturers. Councillor, Knowsley Borough Council 1975–91. **House of Commons:** Member for Knowsley South since September 27, 1990 by-election; Deputy Speaker Westminster Hall 2001–; *Select Committees:* Member: Education 1992–96, Speaker's Panel of Chairmen 1993–97, Education and Employment 1996–97; Member, Chairmen's Panel 1997–. *Special Interests:* Local and Regional Government, Regional Development, European Union, Education, Housing, Emergency Planning, Animal Welfare, Ageing Issues. *Countries of Interest:* CIS, Cyprus, Germany, Greece, Japan, USA. Member: Socialist Education Association, Co-operative Party, Fabian Society. Member: Merseyside Arts Association 1976–79, Board of management, Royal Liverpool Philharmonic Society 1987–90, Board of management, National Foundation for Educational Research 1987–90; Governor, Knowsley Community College 1991–; Vice-President, *TS Iron Duke* (Huyton) 1994–; President, Knowsley South Juniors Football Club 1997–; Merseyside delegate to Régions Européenes de Tradition Industrielle 1989–90, Permanent Committee, Assembly of European Regions 1989–90, Member, Labour Movement in Europe 1990–, Council of Europe 1997–; Patron, Marilyn Houlton MND Trust 1991–; Community Development Foundation: Trustee 1992–, Chair 1997–; Vice-Chair, National Wild Flower Centre Development Trust 1996–; Patron Knowsley Arts Trust 1999–; *Recreations:* Theatre, literature, music (classical, jazz, folk – especially Rembetiko), watching soccer, Greek language and culture. Edward O'Hara Esq, MP, House of Commons, London, SW1A 0AA *Tel:* 020 7219 5232 *Fax:* 020 7219 4952. *Constituency:* 69 St. Mary's Road, Huyton, Merseyside, L36 5SR *Tel:* 0151 489 8021 *Fax:* 0151 449 3873 *E-mail:* oharae@parliament.uk.

OLNER, BILL Nuneaton

Lab majority 7,535

William John Olner. Born 9 May 1942; Son of late C. William Olner, coalminer, and late Lillian Olner; Educated Atherstone Secondary Modern School; North Warwickshire Technical College (City and Guilds Mechanical Engineering); Married Gillian Everitt 1962. Engineer; Skilled machinist, Rolls Royce, Coventry 1957–92; Apprenticed with Armstrong Siddeley Motors 1967–72; Member, AEU/AMICUS and branch secretary 1972–. Nuneaton Borough Council: Councillor 1971–92, Chair, Planning Committee 1974–76, Deputy Leader 1980–82, Leader 1982–87, Chair, Policy and Resources Committee 1982–86, Mayor 1987–88, Chair, Environmental Health Committee 1990–92. **House of Commons:** Member for Nuneaton since April 9, 1992; *Select Committees:* Member: Environment 1995–97, Environment, Transport and Regional Affairs 1997–2001, Environment Sub-Committee 1997–2001, Transport Sub-Committee 1997–2001, Standing Orders 1998–99, Standing Orders 2000–01; Member: Chairmen's Panel 1998–, Foreign Affairs 2001–. *Special Interests:* Engineering, Local and Regional Government. *Countries of Interest:* France, USA, China, Ghana, Australia. Chair, various school governing bodies; Joint Vice-Chair, Executive Committee, Commonwealth Parliamentary Association (CPA) UK Branch 1995–99, Member, 1999–; Freeman, City of Coventry; *Recreations:* Local Hospice Movement, walking, current affairs, television. William Olner Esq, MP, House of Commons, London, SW1A 0AA *Tel:* 020 7219 4154. *Constituency:* 171 Queens Road, Nuneaton, Warwickshire *Tel:* 02476 642222 *Fax:* 02476 642223 *E-mail:* olnerb@parliament.uk.

DodOnline
An Electronic Directory without rival . . .

MPs' biographies and photographs available with daily updates *via* the internet

For a *free* trial, call Yasmin Mirza, Aby Farsoun or Michael Mand on 020 7630 7643

O'NEILL, MARTIN   Ochil   *Lab majority 5,349*

Martin John O'Neill. Born 6 January 1945; Son of John O'Neill, fitter and turner; Educated Trinity Academy, Edinburgh; Heriot-Watt University (BA economics); Moray House College of Education, Edinburgh; Married Elaine Marjorie Samuel 1973 (2 sons). Insurance Clerk 1963–67; President, Scottish Union of Students 1970–71. **House of Commons:** Contested Edinburgh North October 1974 general election. Member for Stirlingshire East and Clackmannan 1979–83, for Clackmannan 1983–97, and for Ochil since May 1, 1997; Opposition Front Bench Spokesman on: Scotland 1980–84, Defence and Disarmament and Arms Control 1984–88; Principal Opposition Front Bench Spokesman on Defence 1988–92; Opposition Front Bench Spokesman on Trade and Industry (Energy) 1992–95; *Select Committees:* Chair, Trade and Industry 1995–97; Chair, Trade and Industry 1995–; Member, Liaison 1997–. *Special Interests:* Education, Defence, Trade and Industry. *Countries of Interest:* Argentina. Labour Party Member since 1963; Held most Party positions in Constituency and Local Government Organisations. *Recreations:* Cinema, jazz. Martin O'Neill Esq, MP, House of Commons, London, SW1A 0AA *Tel:* 020 7219 5059 *Fax:* 020 7219 5907. *Constituency:* 49 High Street, Alloa, Clackmannanshire, FK10 1JF *Tel:* 01259 721536 *Fax:* 01259 216761 *E-mail:* cartere@parliament.uk.

ÖPIK, LEMBIT   Montgomeryshire   *LD majority 6,234*

Lembit Öpik. Born 2 March 1965; Son of Dr Uno Öpik and Liivi Öpik; Educated Royal Belfast Academical Institution; Bristol University (BA philosophy 1987) (President Union 1985–86); Single. Procter and Gamble Ltd: Brand assistant/Assistant brand manager 1988–91, Corporate training and organisation development manager 1991–96, Global human resources training manager 1996–97; Contested Northumbria 1994 European Parliament election; National Union of Students Executive 1987–88. Councillor, Newcastle upon Tyne City Council 1992. **House of Commons:** Contested Newcastle Central 1992 general election. Member for Montgomeryshire since May 1, 1997; Spokesperson for: Northern Ireland 1997–, Welsh Affairs 1997–2001, Young People 1997–2002, Wales 2001–; *Select Committees:* Member, Agriculture 1999–2001. *Special Interests:* Transport, Education and Youth, Aerospace. *Countries of Interest:* Eastern Europe, China, Fiji. Member: Federal Executive Committee of Liberal Democrats 1991–, Federal Finance Administration Committee 1997–; Welsh Vice-President, Liberal Democrat Federal Party 1999–; Member, Federal Executive Committee 2001–; Leader: Welsh Liberal Democrat Parliamentary Party 2001–, Welsh Liberal Democrats 2001–. President: Shropshire Astronomical Society; Clive Motorcycle Club; Fellow, Royal Astronomical Society; Member, Welsh Grand Committee 1997–; *Publications:* Contributor to Patrick Moore's *2001 Astronomy Yearbook*; *Recreations:* Aviation, military history, astronomy, films. Lembit Öpik Esq, MP, House of Commons, London, SW1A 0AA *Tel:* 020 7219 1144 *Fax:* 020 7219 2210. *Constituency:* Montgomeryshire Liberal Democrats, 3 Park Street, Newtown, Powys, SY16 1EE *Tel:* 01686 625527 *Fax:* 01686 628891 *E-mail:* opikl@parliament.uk.

ORGAN, DIANA   Forest of Dean   *Lab majority 2,049*

Diana Mary Organ. Born 21 February 1952; Daughter of Jack, company director, and Vera Pugh, voluntary organiser; Educated Edgbaston Church of England College for Girls, Birmingham; St Hugh's College, Oxford (BA geography 1973); Bath University School of Education (PGCE 1974); Bristol Polytechnic (Diploma in Special Education 1981); Married Richard Thomas Organ 1975 (2 daughters). Assistant teacher special needs 1974–77; Deputy head teacher, St Germans, Cornwall 1977–79; Head of special needs unit, Somerset 1979–82; Supply special school, Somerset 1982–88; Assistant English teacher, Somerset 1988–92; Contested Somerset and Dorset West 1989 European Parliament election; Political researcher, Oxfordshire County Council 1992–95; Member: NUT, NUPE (now UNISON). **House of Commons:** Contested Gloucestershire West 1992 general election. Member for Forest of Dean since May 1, 1997;

Select Committees: Member: Agriculture 1997–99, Joint Committee on Statutory Instruments 1997–99, Culture, Media and Sport 1999–2001, Radioactive Waste Policy Sub-Committee 2001–02; Member, Environment, Food and Rural Affairs 2001–. *Special Interests:* Education, Transport, Rural Affairs, Libraries, Further Education, Women's Health, Small Businesses. *Countries of Interest:* India, Tibet, China, Mongolia. Secretary Constituency Labour Party; Member 1987–89: South-West Women's Committee 1989–, South-West Regional Executive 1992–, Labour REC 1990–92, 300 Group, Co-op Party. Member, Amnesty International; School governor; Political Board Member, TV South West; Labour Party Conference Debates: Nuclear Energy 1990, Defence 1992, Transport 1993, Education 1994, Rural issues 1995; *Recreations:* Swimming, sailing, tennis, gardening, cinema. Mrs Diana Organ, MP, House of Commons, London, SW1A 0AA *Tel:* 020 7219 5498 *Fax:* 020 7219 6860. *Constituency:* St Annals House, Bellevue Centre, Cinderford, Gloucestershire, GL14 1AB *Tel:* 01594 826835 *Fax:* 01594 827892 *E-mail:* organd@parliament.uk.

OSBORNE, GEORGE   Tatton   *Con majority 8,611*

George Gideon Oliver Osborne. Born 23 May 1971; Son of Sir Peter George Osborne Bt, founder and chairman Osborne and Little plc and Felicity Alexandra Osborne, née Loxton-Peacock, foodshop owner; Educated St Paul's School, London; Davidson College, North Carolina USA 1990; Magdalen College, Oxford (BA modern history 1993, MA); Married Frances Victoria Howell 1998 (1 son). Freelance journalist *Sunday* and *Daily Telegraph* 1993; Head of political section Conservative Research Department 1994–95; Special adviser Ministry of Agriculture, Fisheries and Food 1995–97; Political Office, 10 Downing Street 1997; Secretary Shadow Cabinet 1997–2001; Political secretary to William Hague MP as Leader of Opposition 1997–2001. **House of Commons:** Member for Tatton since June 7, 2001; Opposition Whip 2003–; *Select Committees:* Member: Public Accounts 2001–, Transport 2002–. *Special Interests:* Economy, Taxation, Foreign Affairs, Education, Law and Order. *Countries of Interest:* USA, Hungary, South Africa. Vice-president, East Cheshire Hospice; Member Public Accounts Commission 2002–; Dean Rusk Scholarship 1990; Magdalen College Scholarship 1992; *Recreations:* Cinema, theatre, walking, observing American politics. George Osborne Esq, MP, House of Commons, London, SW1A 0AA *Tel:* 020 7219 8329/8214. *Constituency:* Tatton Conservative Association, Manchester Road, Knutsford, Cheshire, WA16 0LT *Tel:* 01565 632181 *Fax:* 01565 632182.

OSBORNE, SANDRA   Ayr   *Lab majority 2,545*

Sandra Osborne. Born 23 February 1956; Daughter of Thomas Clark, labourer, and Isabella Clark, shop worker, meat factory worker, cleaner and laundry worker; Educated Camphill Senior Secondary, Paisley; Anniesland College; Jordanhill College; Strathclyde University (Diploma in community education 1990, Diploma in equality and discrimination 1991, MSc equality and discrimination 1992); Married Alastair Osborne 1982 (2 daughters). Member, TGWU; Former Branch Secretary, TGWU. Councillor, Kyle and Carrick District Council 1990–95; South Ayrshire Council: Councillor 1994–97, Convener, Community Services (Housing and Social Work) –1997. **House of Commons:** Member for Ayr since May 1, 1997; PPS to: Ministers of State for Scotland: Brian Wilson 1999–2001, George Foulkes 2001–02, Helen Liddell as Secretary of State for Scotland 2002–03; *Select Committees:* Member: Information 1997–2000, Scottish Affairs 1998–99. *Special Interests:* Women, Housing, Poverty. *Countries of Interest:* All countries. Vice-chair, Scottish Regional Group of Labour MPs 1998–99, Chair 1999–. Women's Aid; Member: European Standing Committee A, European Standing Committee B until 2003; *Recreations:* Reading and television. Mrs Sandra Osborne, MP, House of Commons, London, SW1A 0AA *Tel:* 020 7219 6402. *Constituency:* Constituency Office, Damside, Ayr, KA8 8ER *Tel:* 01292 262906 *Fax:* 01292 885661 *E-mail:* osbornes@parliament.uk.

Visit the Vacher Dod Website . . .
www.DodOnline.co.uk

OTTAWAY, RICHARD   Croydon South   *Con majority 8,697*

Richard Geoffrey James Ottaway. Born 24 May 1945; Son of late Professor Christopher Ottaway and of Grace Ottaway; Educated Backwell School, Somerset; Bristol University (LLB 1974); Married Nicola Kisch 1982. Officer in the Royal Navy 1961–70, Serving on: HMSs Beechampton, Nubian and Eagle 1967–70; Admitted solicitor 1977, specialising in international, maritime and commercial law; Partner, William A. Crump & Son 1981–87; Director, Coastal States Petroleum (UK) Ltd 1988–95. **House of Commons:** Member for Nottingham North 1983–87. Contested Nottingham North 1987 general election. Member for Croydon South since April 9, 1992; Opposition Spokesperson for: Local Government and London 1997–99, Defence 1999–2000; Treasury 2000–01; Government Whip 1995–97; Opposition Whip June-November 1997; PPS: to Ministers of State, Foreign and Commonwealth Office 1985–87, to Michael Heseltine: as President of the Board of Trade and Secretary of State for Trade and Industry 1992–95, as Deputy Prime Minister and First Secretary of State 1995; *Select Committees:* Member, Procedure 1996–97; Member: Standards and Privileges 2001–, Foreign Affairs 2003–. *Special Interests:* Defence, Industry, Commerce, World Population. *Countries of Interest:* Malaysia, Singapore. Vice-chair Conservative Party (with responsibility for local government) 1998–99; Chair Executive Committee, Society of Conservative Lawyers 2000–03. Member, Population Concern; London mayoral nominee 2002; *Publications:* Papers on international and maritime law, global pollution, London, privatisation, debt and international fraud; *Recreations:* Yacht racing, jazz, skiing. Richard Ottaway Esq, MP, House of Commons, London, SW1A 0AA *Tel:* 020 7219 6392 *Fax:* 020 7219 2256. *Constituency:* Croydon South Conservative Association, 36 Brighton Road, Purley, Surrey, CR8 2LG *Tel:* 020 8660 0491 *Fax:* 020 8763 9686 *E-mail:* ottawayrgj@parliament.uk.

OWEN, ALBERT   Ynys Môn   *Lab majority 800*

Albert Owen. Born 10 August 1959; Son of late William Owen and late Doreen, née Wood; Educated Holyhead County Comprehensive School, Anglesey; Coleg Harlech (Diploma industrial relations 1994); York University (BA politics 1997); Married Angela Margaret Magee 1983 (2 daughters). Merchant seafarer 1976–92; Welfare rights and employment adviser 1995–97; Centre manager Isle of Anglesey County Council 1997–; Contested Ynys Môn 1999 National Assembly for Wales election; RMT 1976–92: Health and safety officer 1985–87, Ferry sector national panel 1987–92; NUS 1992–97: Welfare officer 1992–94; UNISON 1997–2001. Town councillor 1997–99. **House of Commons:** Member for Ynys Môn since June 7, 2001; *Select Committees:* Member: Accommodation and Works 2001–, Welsh Affairs 2001–. *Special Interests:* Welsh Affairs, Welfare, Economic Development. *Countries of Interest:* Ireland, Cyprus. Chair Local branch 1987–92; Constituency Labour Party: Treasurer 1991–92, Vice-chair 1992–96; Press officer 1996–2000. Member Greenpeace 1982–90; Director Homeless project 1998–; Member Institute of Welsh Affairs 1999–; Governor Coleg Harlech 1999–2001; Member management committee WEA North Wales 1999–2001; Chair Anglesey Regeneration Partnership 2000–01; *Sportsclubs:* Holyhead Sailing Club; *Recreations:* Cycling, walking, cooking, gardening. Albert Owen Esq, MP, House of Commons, London, SW1A 0AA *Tel:* 020 7219 8415 *Fax:* 020 7219 1951. *Constituency:* 18/18a Thomas Street, Holyhead, Anglesey, LL65 1RR *Tel:* 01407 765750 *Fax:* 01407 764336 *E-mail:* owena@parliament.uk.

DodOnline

An Electronic Directory without rival . . .

MPs' biographies and photographs available with daily updates *via* the internet

For a *free* trial, call Yasmin Mirza, Aby Farsoun or Michael Mand on 020 7630 7643

P

PAGE, RICHARD South West Hertfordshire Con majority 8,181

Richard Lewis Page. Born 22 February 1941; Son of late Victor Charles Page; Educated Hurstpierpoint College; Luton Technical College (HNC mechanical engineering 1962); Married Madeleine Ann Brown 1964 (1 son 1 daughter). Apprentice, Vauxhall Motors 1959–63; Page Holdings 1964–: chairman 1985–95, 1997–. Councillor, Banstead Urban District Council 1968–71; Governor, Foundation for Western Democracy 1997–99. **House of Commons:** Contested Workington February and October 1974 general elections. Member for Workington November 1976 by-election -May 1979. Member for South West Hertfordshire since December 1979; Opposition Spokesperson for Trade and Industry 2000–01; PPS to John Biffen as Leader of the House 1982–87; Parliamentary Under-Secretary of State, Department of Trade and Industry 1995–97; *Select Committees:* Member: Public Accounts 1987–95, Public Accounts 1997–2000. *Special Interests:* Small Businesses, Horses, Scientific Research and Development, Trade and Industry. *Countries of Interest:* Middle East, Eastern Europe. Chair, International Office Conservative Central Office 1998–2000. Hon. National Treasurer, Leukaemia Research Fund 1987–95; Member, Investment Committee LRF 1997–; Governor, Rickmansworth Masonic School for Girls 1984–95, 2002–; Liveryman, The Pattenmakers Company 1979–; Freeman, City of London; *Recreations:* Shooting, horse racing. Richard Page Esq, MP, House of Commons, London, SW1A 0AA *Tel:* 020 7219 5032 *Fax:* 020 7219 2775. *Constituency:* SW Herts Conservative Association, Scotsbridge House, Scots Hill, Rickmansworth, Hertfordshire, WD3 3BB *Tel:* 01923 771781 *Fax:* 01923 710211.

PAICE, JIM South East Cambridgeshire Con majority 8,990

Jim (James) Edward Thornton Paice. Born 24 April 1949; Son of late Edward Paice and of Winifred Paice; Educated Framlingham College; Writtle Agricultural College (National Diploma in Agriculture 1970); Married Ava Patterson 1973 (2 sons). Farm manager 1970–73; Farmer and contractor 1973–79; Training manager, later general manager, Framlingham Management and Training Services Ltd 1979–87, Non-executive director, 1987–89; Director, United Framlingham Farmers Ltd 1989–94. Suffolk Coastal District Council: Councillor 1976–87, Chair 1982–83. **House of Commons:** Contested Caernarvon 1979 general election. Member for South East Cambridgeshire since June 1987; Opposition Spokesperson for: Agriculture, Fisheries and Food 1997–2001, Home Affairs 2001–; PPS: to Baroness Trumpington, as Minister of State, Ministry of Agriculture, Fisheries and Food 1989–90, to John Selwyn Gummer: as Minister of Agriculture, Fisheries and Food 1990–93, as Secretary of State for the Environment 1993–94; Parliamentary Under-Secretary of State: Department of Employment 1994–95, Department for Education and Employment 1995–97; *Special Interests:* Small Businesses, Employment, Agriculture, Rural Affairs, Training, Waste Management. *Countries of Interest:* Europe, New Zealand. UK delegate, EEC Council of Young Farmers 1974–78; Fellow, Writtle University College; *Recreations:* Shooting, conservation. Jim Paice Esq, MP, House of Commons, London, SW1A 0AA *Tel:* 020 7219 4101. *Constituency:* Snailbridge House, The Moor, Fordham, Nr Ely, Cambridgeshire, CB7 5LU *Tel:* 07638 721526 *Fax:* 07638 721526 *E-mail:* paicejet@parliament.uk.

PAISLEY, IAN North Antrim DUP majority 14,224

Ian Richard Kyle Paisley. Born 6 April 1926, Son of late Rev. J. Kyle Paisley; Educated Ballymena Model School; Ballymena Technical High School; South Wales Bible College; Reformed Presbyterian Theological College, Belfast; Married Eileen Emily Cassells 1956 (twin sons 3 daughters). Ordained 1946; Minister, Martyrs Memorial Free Presbyterian Church 1946–; Moderator, Free Presbyterian Church of Ulster 1951–; Founded *Protestant Telegraph* 1966; Member, Northern Ireland Assembly 1973–74; Co-chair, World Congress of Fundamentalists 1978; MEP for Northern Ireland 1979–; Elected to second Northern Ireland Assembly 1982; MP (Protestant Unionist) for Bannside, Co. Antrim, Parliament of Northern Ireland (Stormont) 1970–72;

Leader of Opposition 1972; Member: Northern Ireland Forum 1996–98, Northern Ireland Assembly 1998–. **House of Commons:** Member for North Antrim since June 1970; Spokesman for Constitutional Affairs; *Special Interests:* Foreign Affairs, Religious Affairs, Constitution. Leader (co-founder), Democratic Unionist Party 1971–. President, Whitefield College of the Bible, Laurencetown 1980; Member, Constitutional Convention 1975–76; Member: Rex Committee, Political Committee, European Parliament; *Publications:* Author of several publications; *Recreations:* History, Antiquarian book collecting. Rev Ian Paisley, MP, House of Commons, London, SW1A 0AA *Tel:* 020 7219 3457. *Constituency:* 46 Hill Street, Ballymena, BT43 6BH *Tel:* 028 2564 1421 *Fax:* 028 2564 1421.

PALMER, NICK   Broxtowe   *Lab majority 5,873*

Nick (Nicholas) Palmer. Born 5 February 1950; Son of late Reginald and Irina Palmer; Educated International Schools, Vienna and Copenhagen; Copenhagen University (mathematics and computing 1967–72); Birkbeck College, London University (PhD mathematics 1975); Married Fiona Hunter 2000. Computing jobs with medical and pharmaceutical organisations; Head of internet services, Novartis, Switzerland 1995–97; Contested East Sussex and South Kent 1995 European Parliament election; Sponsor on fair trade issues for Department of Trade and Industry; Health and safety officer, MSF Brighton 1975–76. **House of Commons:** Contested Chelsea 1983 general election. Member for Broxtowe since May 1, 1997; Team PPS, Department for Environment, Food and Rural Affairs 2003–; *Select Committees:* Member: Administration 1998–2002, European Scrutiny 1998–2001, Northern Ireland Affairs 1999–2001; Member: Treasury 2001–, Treasury Sub-Committee 2001–. *Special Interests:* Economy, Taxation, Fair Trade, Development, Animal Welfare. *Countries of Interest:* Scandinavia, Switzerland. National Executive Member, Labour Animal Welfare Society 1999–. Member: Compassion in World Farming, World Development Movement, Cats Protection League (Patron), United Nations Association; Member, Danish 1975–77 and Swiss 1994– Social Democrats; Worked on Draft Swiss Social Democrat Economic Programme; Member, European Standing Committee B 1998–; *Publications: The Comprehensive Guide to Board Wargaming,* 1977; *The Best of Board Wargaming,* 1980; *Beyond the Arcade,* 1984; *Parliamentary Portions,* 1998; *Recreations:* Postal and computer games. Dr Nick Palmer, MP, House of Commons, London, SW1A 0AA *Tel:* 020 7219 2397 *Fax:* 020 7219 5205. *Constituency:* 23 Barratt Lane, Attenborough, Nottingham, NG9 6AD *Tel:* 0115–943 0721 *Fax:* 0115–943 1860 *E-mail:* nickmpl@aol.com.

PATERSON, OWEN   North Shropshire   *Con majority 6,241*

Owen William Paterson. Born 24 June 1956; Son of late Alfred Dobell Paterson and Cynthia Marian Paterson; Educated Radley College; Corpus Christi College, Cambridge (MA history 1978); Married Hon. Rose Ridley 1980 (2 sons 1 daughter). British Leather Co Ltd: Sales director 1985–93, Managing director 1993–99. **House of Commons:** Contested Wrexham 1992 general election. Member for North Shropshire since May 1, 1997; Opposition Whip 2000–01: Agriculture, Culture, Media and Sport, Legal 2000–01, Agriculture, Culture and Sport, Legal Affairs 2001; PPS to Iain Duncan Smith as Leader of the Opposition 2001–; *Select Committees:* Member: Welsh Affairs 1997–2001, European Scrutiny 1999–2000, Agriculture 2000–01. *Special Interests:* Trade, Industry, Agriculture, Foreign Affairs. *Countries of Interest:* Western and Eastern Europe, USA, China, India. Member: 92 Group 1997–, Conservative Friends of Israel 1997–, Conservative Way Forward 1997–, Conservative 2000 1997–; Vice-President, Conservatives Against a Federal Europe 1998–2001, Member, No Turning Back Group 1998–. Director, Orthopaedic Institute Ltd, Oswestry; President, Ellesmere Cadet Force; Member, Countryside Alliance; Member: European Standing Committee A 1998–2001, Welsh Grand Committee 1998–2000; President, Cotance (European Tanners' Confederation) 1996–98; Member: World League For Freedom and Democracy 1997–, Inter-Parliamentary Union 1997–, Commonwealth Parliamentary Association 1997–; Member, Advisory Board, European Foundation 1998–; Liveryman, Leathersellers' Company; *Sportsclubs:* Patron, Oswestry Cricket Club; Member, Shropshire Cricket Club. Owen Paterson Esq, MP, House of Commons, London, SW1A 0AA *Tel:* 020 7219 5186 *Fax:* 020 7219 3955. *Constituency:* Sambrook Hall, Noble Street, Wem, Shropshire, SY4 5DT *Tel:* 01939 235222 *Fax:* 01939 232220 *E-mail:* patersono@parliament.uk.

PEARSON, IAN   Dudley South   *Lab majority 6,817*

Ian Pearson. Born 5 April 1959; Son of late Phares and of Pauline Pearson; Educated Brierley Hill Grammar School; Balliol College, Oxford (BA philosophy, politics and economics 1980); Warwick University (MA industrial relations 1983, PhD industrial and business studies 1987); Married Annette Sandy 1988 (2 daughters 1 son). Deputy Director, Urban Trust 1987–88; Business and economic development consultant 1988–89; Joint chief executive, West Midlands Enterprise Board 1989–94; Member, TGWU. Councillor, Dudley Borough Council 1984–87. **House of Commons:** Member for Dudley West December 15, 1994 by-election–1997, and for Dudley South since May 1, 1997; Assistant Government Whip 2001–02, Government Whip 2002–; PPS to Geoffrey Robinson as Paymaster General, HM Treasury 1997–98; Parliamentary Under-Secretary of State, Northern Ireland Office 2002–; *Select Committees:* Member: Deregulation 1996–97, Treasury 1996–97, Education and Employment 1999–2001, Employment Sub-Committee 1999–2001. *Special Interests:* Economic and Industrial Policy, Regional Development, Regeneration, Further and Higher Education. *Countries of Interest:* Central and Eastern Europe, India, USA, Canada. Local Government Policy Research Officer for the Labour Party 1985–87. Patron, Black Country Headway and Wordsley Kidney Patients Association; Chairman, Redhouse Cone Trust; *Publications: Universities and Innovation: Meeting the Challenge* 2000; *Sportsclubs:* Stourbridge RFC, West Bromwich Albion FC; *Recreations:* Rugby, literature, architecture. Ian Pearson Esq, MP, House of Commons, London, SW1A 0AA *Tel:* 020 7219 6462 *Fax:* 020 7219 0390. *Constituency:* 139 High Street, Brierley Hill, West Midlands, DY5 3BU *Tel:* 01384 482123 *Fax:* 01384 482209 *E-mail:* pearsoni@parliament.uk.

PERHAM, LINDA   Ilford North   *Lab majority 2,115*

Linda Perham. Born 29 June 1947; Daughter of George Sidney Conroy and Edith, née Overton; Educated Mary Datchelor Girls' School, Camberwell, London; Leicester University (BA classics 1969); Ealing Technical College (Postgraduate Diploma of the Library Association 1970); Married Raymond Perham 1972 (2 daughters). Library assistant, London Borough of Southwark 1966; Information officer, GLC Research Library 1970–72; City of London Polytechnic: Archives librarian 1972–76, Staff development librarian 1976–78; Cataloguer, Fawcett Library 1981–92; Bibliographical librarian, Epping Forest College 1992–97; Local organiser, GLC Staff Association 1970–78; Chair, Joint Union Committee, City of London Polytechnic 1975–78; Member, Unison (NALGO) 1985–. Member, Redbridge Community Health Council 1984–88; JP 1990–; London Borough of Redbridge: Councillor 1989–97, Mayor 1994–95, Chair, Highways Committee 1995–96, Leisure Committee 1996–97. **House of Commons:** Member for Ilford North since May 1, 1997; *Select Committees:* Member, Accommodation and Works 1997–2001; Member: Trade and Industry 1998–, Court of Referees 2002–. *Special Interests:* Leisure, Environment, Education, Transport, Age Discrimination, Corporate Social Responsibility. *Countries of Interest:* Italy, Greece, Spain, Cyprus, USA, Israel, Saudi Arabia, India. Constituency Secretary, Ilford North Labour Party 1987–91; Member, Socialist Educational Association; Vice-chair, Labour Friends: of Israel 2001–, of India 2001–. Patron, Haven House Foundation (Children's Hospice Project); President, Hainault Forest Community Association; Postnatal support organiser, National Childbirth Trust 1979–85; *Publications: Directory of GLC Library Resources*, 1970, 2nd ed 1971; *Greater London Council Publications 1965–71*, 1972; *Libraries of London*, 1973; *How To Find Out In French*, 1977; MCILIP; *Recreations:* Art, cinema, theatre, organising quizzes, watching tennis. Linda Perham, MP, House of Commons, London, SW1A 0AA *Tel:* 020 7219 5853 *Fax:* 020 7219 1161. *Constituency:* Suite 501, Coventry House, Ilford, Essex, IG1 4GR *Tel:* 020 8554 3070 *Fax:* 020 8518 0394 *E-mail:* lindaperhammp@parliament.uk.

Visit the Vacher Dod Website . . .
www.DodOnline.co.uk

PICKING, ANNE   East Lothian   *Lab majority 10,830*

Anne Picking. Born 30 March 1958; Daughter of Frank and late Wilma Moffat; Educated Woodmill High Comprehensive School; Married David Adair Harold Picking 1984 (1 son). Fife Health Board: Nursing assistant 1975–77, Pupil nurse 1977–78, Enrolled nurse 1978–80; Northern Ireland Eastern Health and Social Service: Student nurse 1980–81, Staff nurse 1982–83; East Kent Community Health Care Trust 1984–: Staff nurse, Nursing sister; COHSE 1975–: Member NEC 1990–; UNISON 1975–: Member NEC 1999–2000, National President 1999–2000. Ashford Borough Council 1994–98: Chair Health Committee, Vice-chair Finance Committee, Group chair. **House of Commons:** Member for East Lothian since June 7, 2001; *Select Committees:* Member: Accommodation and Works 2001–, Modernisation of the House of Commons 2001–. *Special Interests:* Health, Social Justice, Economy, Small Businesses. Member NEC Labour Party. Member European Standing Committee B 2003–; Registered Nurse; *Clubs:* Prestonpans Labour, William Harvey Hospital Social. Anne Picking, MP, Room 38, Upper Committee Corridor North, House of Commons, London, SW1A 0AA *Tel:* 020 7219 8220 *Fax:* 020 7219 1760. *Constituency:* East Lothian Labour Party, 65 High Street, Tranent, East Lothian, EH33 1LN *Tel:* 01875 614 990 *Fax:* 01875 613 562 *E-mail:* pickinga@parliament.uk.

PICKLES, ERIC   Brentwood and Ongar   *Con majority 2,821*

Eric Pickles. Born 20 April 1952; Son of late Jack and Constance Pickles; Educated Greenhead Grammar School; Leeds Polytechnic; Married Irene 1976. Bradford Metropolitan District Council: Councillor 1979–91, Chairman: Social Services Committee 1982–84, Education Committee 1984–86, Leader of Conservative Group 1987–91; Member, Yorkshire Regional Health Authority 1982–90. **House of Commons:** Member for Brentwood and Ongar since April 9, 1992; Opposition Spokesperson for Social Security 1998–2001; Shadow Minister for Transport 2001–02; Shadow Secretary of State for Local Government and the Regions 2002–; *Select Committees:* Member: Environment 1992–93, Transport 1995–97, Environment, Transport and Regional Affairs 1997–98, Transport Sub-Committee 1997–98. *Special Interests:* Housing, Health, Social Services, Local and Regional Government. *Countries of Interest:* Eastern Europe, India, Poland, USA. Member, Conservative Party National Union Executive Committee 1975–97; National Chairman, Young Conservatives 1980–81; Member, Conservative Party National Local Government Advisory Committee 1985–; Local Government Editor, Newsline 1990–; Deputy Leader, Conservative Group on Association of Metropolitan Authorities 1989–91; Vice-Chairman, Conservative Party 1993–97. Chair, National Local Government Advisory Committee 1992–95; Member, One Nation Forum 1987–91; Chair Joint Committee Against Racism 1982–87; *Clubs:* Carlton; *Recreations:* Films, opera, serious walking, golf. Eric Pickles Esq, MP, House of Commons, London, SW1A 0AA *Tel:* 020 7219 4428. *Constituency:* 19 Crown Street, Brentwood, Essex *Tel:* 01277 210725 *Fax:* 01277 202221.

PICKTHALL, COLIN   West Lancashire   *Lab majority 9,643*

Colin Pickthall. Born 13 September 1944; Son of Francis and Edith Pickthall; Educated Ulverston Grammar School; University College of Wales, Bangor (BA English literature and history 1966); Lancaster University (MA modern literature 1968); Married Judith Ann Tranter 1973 (2 daughters). Assistant master, Ruffwood Comprehensive School, Kirkby, Liverpool 1967–70; Lecturer in English, head of modern European cultural studies, Edge Hill College, Ormskirk, Lancashire 1970–92; Member, USDAW; Chair, USDAW MPs Group. Councillor, Ormskirk, Lancashire County Council 1989–92. **House of Commons:** Contested West Lancashire 1987 general election; Member for West Lancashire since April 9, 1992; PPS to: Alun Michael as Minister of State, Home Office (Minister for Criminal Policy) 1997–98, Jack Straw: as Home Secretary 1999–2000, 2001, as Foreign Secretary 2001–; *Select Committees:* Member, Agriculture 1992–97. *Special Interests:* Home Affairs, Agriculture and Rural Affairs, Education, Environment, Foreign Affairs.

Countries of Interest: Canada, France. Hon. Secretary, North West Group of Labour MPs 1997–99. President: West Lancashire Arthritis Care, West Lancashire Mencap; *Clubs:* Skelmersdale British Legion; *Sportsclubs:* Dalton-in-Furness Cricket; *Recreations:* Fell-walking, cricket, Shakespeare, gardening, literature. Colin Pickthall Esq, MP, House of Commons, London, SW1A 0AA *Tel:* 020 7219 5011 *Fax:* 020 7219 2354. *Constituency:* 127 Burscough Street, Ormskirk, Lancashire, L39 2EP *Tel:* 01695 570094 *Fax:* 01695 570094 *E-mail:* pickthallc@parliament.uk.

PIKE, PETER   Burnley   *Lab majority 10,498*

Peter Leslie Pike. Born 26 June 1937; Son of late Leslie Henry Pike; Educated Hinchley Wood County Secondary School; Kingston Technical College (evening classes); Married Sheila Lillian Bull 1962 (2 daughters). Royal Marines, national service 1956–58; Clerk: Midland Bank 1958–62, Twinings Tea 1962–63; Labour Party organiser 1963–73; Final Inspector, Mullards (Simonstone) Ltd 1973–83; Shop Steward, GMB 1976–83. Councillor, Merton and Morden Urban District Council 1962–63; Burnley Borough Council: Councillor 1976–84, Group Leader 1980–83. **House of Commons:** Member for Burnley since June 1983; Opposition Spokesperson for: Rural Affairs 1990–92, Environment (Housing) 1992–94; *Select Committees:* Member: Deregulation 1995–97, Procedure 1995–97; Chair, Regulatory Reform 1997–; Member: Liaison 1997–, Modernisation of the House of Commons 1997–, Chairmen's Panel 2001–. *Special Interests:* Local and Regional Government, Energy, Employment, Trade and Industry, Pensions, NHS, Environment. *Countries of Interest:* Bangladesh, Brazil, India, Pakistan, Romania, Southern Africa. Member, Executive Committee, Commonwealth Parliamentary Association (CPA) UK Branch 1999–; *Clubs:* Byerden House Socialist; *Recreations:* Burnley Football Club supporter, member of National Trust. Peter Pike Esq, MP, House of Commons, London, SW1A 0AA *Tel:* 020 7219 3514 *Fax:* 020 7219 3872. *Constituency:* 2 Victoria Street, Burnley, Lancashire, BB11 1DD *Tel:* 01282 450840 *Fax:* 01282 839623 *E-mail:* peterpikemp@parliament.uk.

PLASKITT, JAMES   Warwick and Leamington   *Lab majority 5,953*

James Andrew Plaskitt. Born 23 June 1954; Son of late Ronald Edmund Plaskitt, and Phyllis Irene Plaskitt; Educated Pilgrim School, Bedford; University College, Oxford (MA philosophy, politics and economics 1976, MPhil); Single. Politics lecturer: University College 1977–78, Christ Church, Oxford 1984–87; Business analyst, Brunel University 1981–84; Member, MSF. Councillor, Oxfordshire County Council 1985–97, Leader 1990–96. **House of Commons:** Contested Witney 1992 general election. Member for Warwick and Leamington since May 1, 1997; *Select Committees:* Member: Joint Committee on Consolidation of Bills Etc 1997–2001, Financial Services (Joint Committee) 1998–99; Member: Treasury 1999–, Treasury Sub-Committee 1999–. *Special Interests:* Constitution, European Union, Education, Local and Regional Government, Welfare Reform, Economic Policy. *Countries of Interest:* All EU, USA. *Publications:* Contributor, *Beyond 2002 – A Programme for Labour's Second Term,* 1999. James Plaskitt Esq, MP, House of Commons, London, SW1A 0AA *Tel:* 020 7219 6207 *Fax:* 020 7219 4993. *Constituency:* First Floor, 2A Leam Terrace, Leamington Spa, Warwickshire, CV31 1BB *Tel:* 01926 831151 *Fax:* 01926 338838 *E-mail:* plaskittj@parliament.uk.

POLLARD, KERRY   St Albans   *Lab majority 4,466*

Kerry Patrick Pollard. Born 27 April 1944; Son of late Patrick Joseph Pollard, and Iris Betty Pollard; Educated Thornleigh Grammar School, Bolton; Open University (BA industrial relations and urban regeneration); Married Maralyn Murphy 1966 (5 sons 2 daughters). Process/development engineer, British Gas 1960–92; Co-ordinator, Homes for Homeless People 1992–; Director, Cherry Tree Housing Association 1992–97; Member: UNISON, MSF. Councillor: Hertfordshire County Council 1989, St Albans District Council 1982, 1992–94; JP 1984. **House of Commons:** Member for St Albans since May 1, 1997; *Select Committees:* Member: Education and Employment 2001, Employment Sub-Committee 2001; Member, Education and Skills 2000–.

Special Interests: Housing, Social Services, Small Businesses. *Countries of Interest:* Ireland, Morocco, Bangladesh, Zambia. Vice-Chair, Eastern Regional Group of Labour MPs 1999–. President, St Albans Community Forum; Chairman, St Albans into the 21st Century; Director, Open Door Trust; Fellow, Royal College of Midwives 2003; *Sportsclubs:* St Albans City Football Club; *Recreations:* Relaxing with my family. Kerry Pollard Esq, MP, House of Commons, London, SW1A 0AA *Tel:* 020 7219 4537. *Constituency:* 28 Alma Road, St Albans, Hertfordshire, AL1 3BW *Tel:* 01727 761031 *Fax:* 01727 761032.

POND, CHRIS   Gravesham   *Lab majority 4,862*

Chris Pond. Born 25 September 1952; Son of late Charles Richard and late Doris Violet Pond; Educated Minchenden School, Southgate; Sussex University (BA economics 1974); Married Carole Tongue 1990 (divorced 1999) (1 daughter); married Lorraine. Research assistant (economics) Birkbeck College, London 1974–75; Research officer, Low Pay Unit 1975–79; Lecturer in economics, Civil Service College 1979–80; Director, Low Pay Unit 1980–97; Visiting lecturer in economics, University of Kent 1981–82; Visiting professor/Research fellow, Surrey University 1984–86; Consultant, Open University 1987–88, 1991–92; 'Expert' DGV European Commission 1996; Member, TGWU. **House of Commons:** Contested

Welwyn-Hatfield 1987 general election. Member for Gravesham since May 1, 1997; PPS to Dawn Primarolo as Paymaster General, HM Treasury 1999–2003; Parliamentary Under-Secretary of State (Work), Department for Work and Pensions 2003–; *Select Committees:* Member, Social Security 1997–99. *Special Interests:* Employment, Social Policy, Poverty. *Countries of Interest:* European Union, USA, Eastern Europe, India (Punjab). Member, Editorial Board, Charity Magazine 1995–96; Former Member, Management Committees of Unemployment Unit and Child Poverty Action Group; Chair, Low Pay Unit (unpaid) 1998–99; Expert, Directorate-general V Social Policy, European Commission; *Publications: Inflation and Low Incomes,* 1975; *Trade Unions and Taxation,* 1976; *To Him Who Hath,* 1977; *The Poverty Trap: a study in statistical sources,* 1978; *Taxing Wealth Inequalities,* 1980; *Taxation & Social Policy,* 1981; *Low Pay: Labour's Response,* 1983; *The Changing Distribution of Income, Wealth & Poverty, in Restructuring Britain,* 1989; *Old and New Poverty: the challenge for reform,* (Rivers Oram Press, London) 1995; Co-author *Beyond 2001: Long Term Policies for Labour, The European Dimension in an Inclusive Society* (IPPR) 1998; Plus numerous contributions to other publications, together with articles published in magazines and newspapers; Hon. Visiting Professor, Middlesex University; Fellow, Royal Society of Arts 1994–95; *Sportsclubs:* Gravesend Road Runners and Athletics Club (14 marathons completed); *Recreations:* Running, reading. Chris Pond Esq, MP, House of Commons, London, SW1A 0AA *Tel:* 020 7219 6493 *Fax:* 020 7219 0946. *Constituency:* 24 Overcliffe, Gravesend, Kent, DA11 0EH *Tel:* 01474 354725 *Fax:* 01474 351679 *E-mail:* pondc@parliament.uk.

POPE, GREG   Hyndburn   *Lab majority 8,219*

Gregory Pope. Born 29 August 1960; Son of late Samuel Pope, ambulance officer, and of Sheila Pope; Educated St Mary's College Roman Catholic Grammar School, Blackburn; Hull University (BA politics 1981); Married Catherine Fallon 1985 (2 sons 1 daughter). Vice-President, Hull University Students Union 1981–82; Co-ordinator, Blackburn Trade Union Centre for the unemployed 1983–85; Paperworker, Star newspaper, Blackburn 1985–87; Local government officer, Lancashire County Council 1987–92. Councillor: Hyndburn Borough Council 1984–88, Blackburn Borough Council 1989–91. **House of Commons:** Contested Ribble Valley 1987 general election. Member for Hyndburn since April 9, 1992; Opposition Whip 1995–97; Assistant

Government Whip 1997–99; Government Whip 1999–2001; *Select Committees:* Member, Education 1994–95; Member, Foreign Affairs 2001–. *Special Interests:* Education, Housing, Foreign Affairs. *Clubs:* Accrington Old Band (CIU); *Recreations:* Walking, chess, music, watching Blackburn Rovers FC. Gregory Pope Esq, MP, House of Commons, SW1A 0AA *Tel:* 020 7219 5842 *Fax:* 020 7219 0685. *Constituency:* 149 Blackburn Road, Accrington, Lancs, BB5 0AA *Tel:* 01254 382283 *Fax:* 01254 398089 *E-mail:* popegj@parliament.uk.

PORTILLO, MICHAEL   Kensington and Chelsea   *Con majority 8,771*

Michael Denzil Xavier Portillo. Born 26 May 1953; Son of late Luis Gabriel Portillo, and of Cora Blyth; Educated Harrow County School for Boys; Peterhouse, Cambridge (MA history 1975); Married Carolyn Claire Eadie 1982. Conservative Research Department 1976–79; Special adviser to David Howell, MP, as Secretary of State for Energy 1979–81; Oil industry consultant 1981–83; Special adviser to: Cecil Parkinson, MP, as Secretary of State for Trade and Industry 1983, Nigel Lawson, MP, as Chancellor of the Exchequer 1983–84; Presenter: *Portillo's Progress* Channel 4 1998, BBC TV programme in series *Great Railway Journeys* 1999, BBC Radio programme: *The Legacy of Division* 2000, *Barca and the General* 2002; BBC TV Programmes *Art that shook the World: Richard Wagner's Ring* and *Portillo in England* 2002; Non-executive director, BAE Systems 2002–. **House of Commons:** Contested Birmingham Perry Barr June 1983. Member for Enfield Southgate 1984–97, for Kensington and Chelsea since November 25, 1999 by-election; Government Whip October 1986–87; PPS to Secretary of State for Transport 1986; Parliamentary Under-Secretary of State DHSS 1987–88; Minister of State: at Department of Transport 1988–90, at Department of Environment (Minister for Local Government and Inner Cities) 1990–92; Chief Secretary to HM Treasury 1992–94; Secretary of State for: Employment 1994–95, Defence 1995–97; Member, Shadow Cabinet 2000–01; Shadow Chancellor of the Exchequer 2000–01. Contested leadership 2001. Chair Sinfonia 21 chamber orchestra; Commissioner International Commission for Missing Persons in the Former Yugoslavia 1998–; PC 1992; *Clubs:* Carlton, Savile, Beefsteak. Rt Hon Michael Portillo, MP, House of Commons, London, SW1A 0AA *Tel:* 020 7219 6212 *Fax:* 020 7219 1208. *Constituency:* 1a Chelsea Manor Street, Chelsea, London, SW3 5RP *Tel:* 020 7352 0102/3 *Fax:* 020 7351 5885.

POUND, STEPHEN   Ealing North   *Lab majority 11,837*

Stephen Pelham Pound. Born 3 July 1948; Son of Pelham Pound, journalist, and Dominica Pound, teacher; Educated Hertford Grammar School; London School of Economics (BSc economics 1979, Diploma in industrial relations 1981) (Sabbatical President of Union 1981–82); Married Maggie Griffiths 1976 (1 son 1 daughter). Armed Forces Parliamentary Scheme (Navy); Seaman 1964–66; Bus conductor 1966–68; Hospital porter 1969–79; Student 1979–84; Housing officer 1984–97; Branch Secretary, 640 Middlesex Branch, COHSE 1975–79; Branch Officer, T&GWU (ACTS) 1990–96. Councillor, London Borough of Ealing 1982–98, Mayor 1995–96. **House of Commons:** Member for Ealing North since May 1, 1997; *Select Committees:* Member, Broadcasting 1997–2001; Member, Northern Ireland Affairs 1999–. *Special Interests:* Housing, Transport. *Countries of Interest:* Ireland. Labour Friends of India. Director, Hanwell Community Centre; Trustee, Charity of Wm Hobbayne (Hanwell); *Clubs:* St Joseph's Catholic Social, Hanwell; *Sportsclubs:* Fulham FC Supporters Club; *Recreations:* Watching football, playing cricket, snooker, jazz, gardening, collecting comics. Stephen Pound Esq, MP, House of Commons, London, SW1A 0AA *Tel:* 020 7219 1140 *Fax:* 020 7219 5982 *E-mail:* stevepoundmp@parliament.uk.

PRENTICE, BRIDGET   Lewisham East   *Lab majority 8,959*

Bridget Prentice. Born 28 December 1952; Daughter of late James Corr, joiner, and of Bridget Corr, clerical worker; Educated Our Lady and St Francis School, Glasgow; Glasgow University (MA English literature and modern history 1973), London University (PGCE 1974); South Bank University (LLB 1992); Married Gordon Prentice (now MP) 1975 (divorced 2000). Rector's assessor, Glasgow University 1972–73; London Oratory School: English and history teacher 1974–86, Head of careers 1984–86; Head of careers, John Archer School 1986–88. London Borough of Hammersmith and Fulham: Councillor 1986–92, Chair: Public Services Committee 1987–90, Labour Group 1986–89; JP 1985–. **House of Commons:** Contested Croydon Central 1987 general election. Member for Lewisham East since April 9, 1992; Opposition Whip 1995–97; Assistant Government Whip 1997–98, 2003–; PPS to: Brian Wilson as Minister of State, Department of Trade and

Industry (Minister for Trade) 1998–99, Lord Irvine of Lairg as Lord Chancellor 1999–2001; *Select Committees:* Member: Prliamentary Commissioner for Administration 1992–96, Home Affairs 2001–03; Member, Court of Referees 2002–. *Special Interests:* Education, Training, Constitutional Reform, Human Rights, Home Affairs. *Countries of Interest:* South Africa, USA. Chair, Fulham Constituency Labour Party 1982–85; Leadership Campaign Team Co-ordinator 1995–96. Director, Fire Protection Association 2001–03; *Recreations:* Reading, music, crosswords, gardening, my cat, badminton (qualified coach), football. Bridget Prentice, MP, House of Commons, London, SW1A 0AA *Tel:* 020 7219 3503 *Fax:* 020 7219 5581. *Constituency:* 82 Lee High Road, London, SE13 5PF *Tel:* 020 8852 3995 *Fax:* 020 8852 2386; 020 7219 1286 *E-mail:* info@bridgetprenticemp.org.uk.

PRENTICE, GORDON   Pendle   *Lab majority 4,275*

Gordon Prentice. Born 28 January 1951; Son of late William Prentice, and of late Esther Prentice; Educated George Heriot's School, Edinburgh; Glasgow University (MA politics and economics 1972); Married Bridget Corr 1975 (now MP as Bridget Prentice) (divorced 2000). Labour Party Policy Directorate 1982–92; Member, TGWU. London Borough of Hammersmith and Fulham: Councillor 1982–90, Deputy Leader, Labour Group 1982–84, Leader 1984–88. **House of Commons:** Member for Pendle since April 9, 1992; PPS to Gavin Strang as Minister of State (in Cabinet), Department of the Environment, Transport and the Regions (Minister for Transport) May-December 1997; *Select Committees:* Member: Statutory Instruments 1993–97, Deregulation 1995–97,

Agriculture 1996–97, Modernisation of the House of Commons 1999–2001; Member, Public Administration 2001–. *Special Interests:* Countryside, Agriculture, Manufacturing, Low Pay, Poverty, Regional Policy, Small Businesses. *Countries of Interest:* Pakistan, China, Korea, Australia, New Zealand, Canada. Member: Labour Party National Policy Forum 1999–2001, Parliamentary Labour Party Parliamentary Committee 2001–. Executive Committee Member: Inter-Parliamentary Union (IPU) British Group, Member, British Delegation to Council of Europe and WEU 2001–; *Recreations:* Cooking, hillwalking. Gordon Prentice Esq, MP, House of Commons, London, SW1A 0AA *Tel:* 020 7219 4011. *Constituency:* 33 Carr Road, Nelson, Lancashire, BB9 7JS *Tel:* 01282 695471 *Fax:* 01282 614097 *E-mail:* prenticeg@parliament.uk.

PRESCOTT, JOHN   Hull East   *Lab majority 15,325*

John Leslie Prescott. Born 31 May 1938; Son of late John Herbert Prescott, railway controller and late Phyllis Prescott; Educated Ellesmere Port Secondary Modern School; Ruskin College, Oxford (DipEcon/Pol 1965); Hull University (BSc Econ 1968); Married Pauline Tilston 1961 (2 sons). Steward in the Merchant Navy 1955–63; Union Official, National Union of Seamen 1968–70; TU Official, National Union of Seamen, RMT (resigned 2002). **House of Commons:** Contested Southport 1966 general election. Member for Kingston-upon-Hull East June 18, 1970–83 and for Hull East 1983; Opposition Frontbench Spokesperson for: Transport 1979–81, Regional Affairs and Devolution 1981–83; Shadow Secretary of State for Transport 1983–84;

Employment 1984–87, Energy 1987–89, Transport 1988–93, Employment 1993–94; PPS to Peter Shore as Secretary of State for Trade 1974–76; Member, Shadow Cabinet 1983–97; Deputy Prime Minister 1997–; Secretary of State for the Environment, Transport and the Regions 1997–2001; First Secretary of State 2001–. Deputy Leader, Labour Party 1994–; Member: National Executive Committee of the Labour Party, Parliamentary Labour Party Parliamentary Committee; Deputy Leader, Labour Party National Executive Committee 1997–. Member, Council of Europe 1972–75; Delegate, EEC Parliamentary 1975; Leader, Labour Party Delegation to European Parliament 1976–79; PC 1994; North of England Zoological Society Gold Medal 1999; Priyadarshni Award 2002; *Recreations:* Jazz, theatre, music, aqua diving. Rt Hon John Prescott, MP, House of Commons, London, SW1A 0AA *Tel:* 020 7219 3618. *Constituency:* 430 Holderness Road, Hull, HU9 3DW *Tel:* 01482 702698 *E-mail:* john.prescott@odpm.gsi.gov.uk.

Visit the Vacher Dod Website . . .
www.DodOnline.co.uk

PRICE, ADAM   Carmarthen East and Dinefwr   Pl C majority 2,590

Adam Price. Born 23 September 1968; Educated Amman Valley Comprehensive School; Saarland University; Cardiff University (BA European community studies 1991); Single. Research associate University of Wales, Cardiff Department of City and Regional Planning 1991–93; Menter an Busnes: Project manager 1993–95, Executive manager 1995–96, Executive director 1996–98; Executive director Newidiem economic development consultancy 1998–. **House of Commons:** Contested Gower 1992 general election. Member for Carmarthen East and Dinefwr since June 7, 2001; Plaid Cymru Spokesperson for Economy and Taxation, Miners' Compensation, Regeneration, Trade and Industry, Education and Skills 2001–; *Select Committees:* Member, Welsh Affairs 2001–. *Special Interests:* Economy, Regional Development, International Development, Culture, Education. *Publications: Quiet Revolution? Language, Culture and Economy in the Nineties* (Menter a Busnes) 1994; *The Diversity Dividend* (European Bureau for Lesser used Languages) 1996; *Rebuilding our Communities: A New Agenda for the Valleys*, 1993; Co-author *The other Wales: The Case for Objective 1 Funding Post 1999* (Institute of Welsh Affairs) 1998; *The Welsh Renaissance: Innovation and Inward Investment in Wales* (Regional Ind Research) 1992; *The Collective Entrepreneur* (Institute for Welsh Affairs); Spectator Inquisitor of the Year 2002; *Clubs:* Ammanford Working Men's Social; *Recreations:* Contemporary culture, good friends, good food, travel. Adam Price Esq, MP, House of Commons, London, SW1A 0AA *Tel:* 020 7219 8486 *Fax:* 020 7219 3705. *Constituency:* Plaid Cymru Office, 37 Wind Street, Ammanford, Carmarthenshire, SA18 3DN *Tel:* 01269 597 677 *Fax:* 01269 591 344 *E-mail:* pricea@parliament.uk.

PRIMAROLO, DAWN   Bristol South   Lab majority 14,181

Dawn Primarolo. Born 2 May 1954; Educated Thomas Bennett Comprehensive School, Crawley; Bristol Polytechnic (BA social science 1984); Bristol University; Married 1972 (divorced) (1 son); married Thomas Ian Ducat 1990. Secretary 1972–73; Secretary and advice worker, Law Centre, East London; Secretary, Avon County Council 1975–78; Voluntary work 1978–81; Mature student 1981–87; Member UNISON. Councillor, Avon County Council 1985–87. **House of Commons:** Member for Bristol South since June 1987; Opposition Frontbench Spokesperson on: Health 1992–94, Treasury and Economic Affairs 1994–97; HM Treasury: Financial Secretary 1997–99, Paymaster General 1999–; *Select Committees:* Member: Members' Interests 1990–92, Public Accounts 1997–98. *Special Interests:* Education, Housing, Social Security, Health, Economic Policy, Equal Opportunities. Patron Terence Higgins Trust; PC 2002. Rt Hon Dawn Primarolo, MP, House of Commons, London, SW1A 0AA *Tel:* 020 7219 5202. *Constituency:* PO Box 1002, Bristol, BS99 1WH *Tel:* 0117–909 0063 *Fax:* 0117–909 0064 *E-mail:* dawn.primarolo@hm-treasury.gov.uk.

PRISK, MARK   Hertford and Stortford   Con majority 5,603

Mark Michael Prisk. Born 12 June 1962; Son of Michael Raymond, chartered surveyor, and Irene June Prisk, née Pearce; Educated Truro School, Cornwall; Reading University (BSc land management 1983); Married Lesley Jane Titcomb 1989. Graduate surveyor Knight Frank 1983–85; Derrick Wade & Waters 1985–91: Senior surveyor 1985–89, Director 1989–91; Principal: The Mark Prisk Connection 1991–97, mpý, consultancy 1997–2001. **House of Commons:** Contested Newham North West 1992 and Wansdyke 1997 general elections. Member for Hertford and Stortford since June 7, 2001; Shadow Financial Secretary 2002–; *Select Committees:* Member, Welsh Affairs 2001–. *Special Interests:* Defence, Planning, Development, Small Businesses. *Countries of Interest:* Italy, China. Member Young Conservatives 1978–83; Chair Reading University Conservatives 1981–82; National vice-chair Federation of Conservative Students 1982–83; Deputy chair Hertfordshire Area 1999–2000. Member Prince's Trust; Founding chair Youth For Peace Through NATO 1983–86; Founder East Hertfordshire Business Forum; Chair Hertfordshire Countryside Partnership;

Creator Charter for Hertfordshire's Countryside; Parliamentary Chairman, First Defence 2002–; Member Royal Institute of Chartered Surveyors; *Sportsclubs:* Saracens RFC, Middlesex CCC; *Recreations:* Music, piano, rugby, cricket, walking, running. Mark Prisk Esq, MP, House of Commons, London, SW1A 0AA *Tel:* 020 7219 6358 *Fax:* 020 7219 1774. *Constituency:* Hertford and Stortford Conservatives, Unit 4, Swains Mill, Crane Mead, Ware, Hertfordshire, SG12 9PY *Tel:* 01920 462 182 *Fax:* 01920 485 805 *E-mail:* hunterj@parliament.uk.

PROSSER, GWYN   Dover   *Lab majority 5,199*

Gwyn Mathews Prosser. Born 27 April 1943; Son of late Glyn Prosser and of Doreen Prosser; Educated Dunvant Secondary Modern; Swansea Technical School; Swansea College of Technology (National Diploma, Mechanical Engineering, First Class Certificate of Competency, Marine Engineering); Married Rhoda McLeod 1972 (1 son 2 daughters). Merchant Navy cadet engineer 1960–64; Seagoing engineer, BP 1964–67, Blue Funnel 1967–71; Chief engineer, BR Shipping 1971–74; Test and guarantee engineer, Kincaid of Greenock 1974–77; Port engineer, Aramco, Saudi Arabia 1977–78; Chief engineer: Anscar 1978–79, Sealink Ferries at Dover 1979–92; Social survey interviewer, Civil Service 1993–96; Former member, NUMAST NEC; Political officer, MSF, South East Kent. Councillor, Dover District Council 1987–97; Kent County Council: Councillor 1989–97, Co-Chair, Economic Development and President, European Affairs 1993–97. **House of Commons:** Member for Dover since May 1, 1997; *Select Committees:* Member: Information 2000–, Home Affairs 2001–. *Special Interests:* Transport, Shipping, Economic Development, Environment, Asylum, Immigration. *Countries of Interest:* Hungary. Director, East Kent Women's Refuge; Member: Greenpeace, Kent Against Live Animal Exports; Organising opposition, Channel Tunnel Bill; Member, Parliamentary Assembly of: Council of Europe 1997–2001, Western European Union 1997–2001; Trustee, Numerous Local Charities; MIMarE; CEng; *Recreations:* Hill walking, swimming, awaiting revival of Welsh rugby. Gwyn Prosser Esq, MP, House of Commons, London, SW1A 0AA *Tel:* 020 7219 3704. *Constituency:* 26 Coombe Valley Road, Dover, Kent, CT17 0EP *Tel:* 01304 214484 *Fax:* 01304 214486 *E-mail:* prosserg@parliament.uk.

PUGH, JOHN   Southport   *LD majority 3,007*

John David Pugh. Born 28 June 1948; Educated Prescott Grammar School; Maidstone Grammar School; Durham University (BA philosophy 1971); (MA, MEd, MPhil, PhD logic); Married Annette Sangar 1971 (1 son 3 daughters). Merchant Taylors Boys School, Crosby 1983–: Teacher, Head of philosophy; Member ATL. Sefton Metropolitan Borough Council 1987–: Councillor, Group leader 1992–, Leader 2000–, Member: Local Joint Consultative Committee, Cabinet, Council, Joint Consultative Committee for Teaching Staff, Management Board Committee, Sefton Borough Partnership, Southport South Area Committee; Substitute member Social Services Ratification Committee; Former member Merseyside Police Authority; Member: North West Arts Board, Merseyside Partnership; Drector local airport. **House of Commons:** Member for Southport since June 7, 2001; Liberal Democrat Spokesperson on Education 2002–; *Select Committees:* Member: Transport, Local Government and the Regions 2001–02, Transport Sub-Committee 2001–02, Urban Affairs Sub-Committee 2001–02; Member: Office of the Deputy Prime Minister: Housing, Planning and Local Government 2002–, Urban Affairs Sub-Committee 2003–. *Special Interests:* Local and Regional Government, Elderly, Education, Transport. Former chair Southport Liberal Democrat Association. Member Stapleton Philosophy Society, Liverpool University; Supporter: Oxfam, ActionAid; *Publications: Christian Understanding of God,* 1990; *Recreations:* Philosophy society Liverpool University, weightlifting, reading, football, computers. Dr John Pugh, MP, House of Commons, London, SW1A 0AA *Tel:* 020 7219 8318. *Constituency:* 27 The Walk, Southport, Lancashire, PR8 4BG *Tel:* 01704 569 025.

Visit the Vacher Dod Website . . .
www.DodOnline.co.uk

PURCHASE, KEN   Wolverhampton North East   *Lab majority 9,965*

Kenneth Purchase. Born 8 January 1939; Son of late Albert Purchase, diecaster, and late Rebecca Purchase, cleaner; Educated Springfield Secondary Modern School; Wolverhampton Polytechnic (BA social science 1981); Married Brenda Sanders 1960 (2 daughters). Apprentice toolmaker, foundry industry 1956–60; Experimental component development, aerospace industry 1960–68; Toolroom machinist, motor industry 1968–76; Property division, Telford Development Corporation 1977–80; Housing Department, Walsall Metropolitan Borough Council 1981–82; Business Development Adviser, Black Country CDA Ltd 1982–92; Member, TGWU (ACTSS). Councillor: Wolverhampton County Borough Council 1970–74; Wolverhampton Metropolitan Borough Council 1973–90; Member: Wolverhampton Health Authority 1978–82, 1985–87, 1988–90, Wolverhampton Community Health Council 1990–92. **House of Commons:** Contested Wolverhampton North East 1987 general election. Member for Wolverhampton North East since April 9, 1992; PPS to Robin Cook: as Foreign Secretary 1997–2001, as Leader of the House of Commons and President of the Council 2001–03; *Select Committees:* Member, Trade and Industry 1993–97. *Special Interests:* Trade and Industry, Health, Education, Foreign Affairs, Small Businesses. Sponsored by Co-operative Party. *Recreations:* Listening to jazz. Kenneth Purchase Esq, MP, House of Commons, London, SW1A 0AA *Tel:* 020 7219 3602 *Fax:* 020 7219 2110. *Constituency:* 492a Stafford Road, Wolverhampton, WV10 6AN *Tel:* 01902 397698 *Fax:* 01902 397538 *E-mail:* kenpurchasemp@parliament.uk.

PURNELL, JAMES   Stalybridge and Hyde   *Lab majority 8,859*

James Purnell. Born 2 March 1970; Son of John Purnell, chartered accountant and Janet Purnell, teacher and civil servant; Educated Lycee International, St Gerrain en Laye, France; College Pierre et Marie Curie, Le Pecq, France; Royal Grammar School, Guildford; Balliol College, Oxford (BA philosophy, politics, economics 1991); Single. Researcher Tony Blair, Shadow Employment Secretary 1989–92; Strategy consultant Hydra Associates 1992–94; Research fellow media and communications project Institute for Public Policy Research 1994–95; Head corporate planning BBC 1995–97; Special adviser culture, media, sport and knowledge economy, Tony Blair, Prime Minister 1997–2001; Amicus – AEEU. London Borough of Islington: Councillor, Chair Housing Committee, Chair Early Years Committee. **House of Commons:** Member for Stalybridge and Hyde since June 7, 2001; PPS to Ruth Kelly as Financial Secretary, HM Treasury 2003–; *Select Committees:* Member, Work and Pensions 2001–. *Special Interests:* Economy, Education, Housing, Culture, Poverty, Sport, Welfare, Employment, Pensions. *Countries of Interest:* Israel, India. Local Constituency Party: Former Ward secretary, Membership secretary, Treasurer, Delegate; Member: Co-operative Party, Fabian Society; Chair, Labour Friends of Israel 2002–. Board member: Young Vic Theatre, Enterprise Europe; *Publications:* Various publications for IPPR; *Clubs:* Stalybridge Labour; *Recreations:* Football, cinema, theatre, golf. James Purnell Esq, MP, House of Commons, London, SW1A 0AA *Tel:* 020 7219 8166 *Fax:* 020 7219 1287. *Constituency:* Hyde Town Hall, Market Street, Hyde, Cheshire, SK14 1HL *Tel:* 0161–367 8077 *Fax:* 0161–367 0050 *E-mail:* purnellj@parliament.uk.

Q

QUIN, JOYCE   Gateshead East and Washington West   *Lab majority 17,904*

Joyce Gwendolen Quin. Born 26 November 1944; Daughter of late Basil Godfrey Quin, schoolmaster, and late Ida Quin, née Ritson, teacher; Educated Whitley Bay Grammar School; Newcastle University (BA French 1967); LSE (MSc international relations 1969). Lecturer in French, Bath University 1972–76; Tutor and lecturer in French and politics, Durham University 1976–79; MEP for Tyne and Wear 1979–89; Member, TGWU. **House of Commons:** Member for Gateshead East 1987–97, and for Gateshead East and Washington West since May 1, 1997; Opposition Spokesperson for Trade and Industry 1989–92; Opposition Spokesperson for: Employment 1992–93, Foreign and Commonwealth Affairs 1993–97; Minister of State: Home Office 1997–98,

Foreign and Commonwealth Office 1998–99; Minister of State and Deputy Minister, Ministry of Agriculture, Fisheries and Food 1999–2001; Member Joint Committee on House of Lords Reform 2002–; *Select Committees:* Member, Joint Committee on House of Lords Reform 2002–. *Special Interests:* European Affairs, Industrial Policy, Regional Policy. *Countries of Interest:* Europe (including Eastern Europe). Research officer, International Department, Labour Party HQ 1969–72; Chair Parliamentary Labour Party Regional Government Group 2001–. Member, Review Committee of Privy Counsellors of the Anti-terrorism, Crime and Security Act 2002–; PC 1998; Hon. Fellow: Sunderland Polytechnic 1986, St Mary's College, University of Durham 1996; *Recreations:* North-East local history, walking, music, reading, cycling, playing Northumbrian pipes. Rt Hon Joyce Quin, MP, House of Commons, London, SW1A 0AA *Tel:* 020 7219 4009. *Constituency:* Design Works, William Street, Felling, Gateshead, Tyne & Wear, NE10 0JP *Tel:* 0191–469 6006 *Fax:* 0191–469 6009.

QUINN, LAWRIE   Scarborough and Whitby   *Lab majority 3,585*

Lawrie Quinn. Born 25 December 1956; Son of late Jimmy and Sheila Quinn; Educated Pennine Way Schools, Carlisle; Harraby School, Carlisle; Hatfield Polytechnic (BSc civil engineering 1979); Married Ann Eames 1983. British Rail/ Railtrack London NE 1979–97: civil engineer 1979–94, project manager 1994–97; TSSA: branch secretary 1986–96, York P&T branch. Councillor, North Yorkshire County Council 1989–93, Member: Highways Committee, Policy and Resources Committee, Planning Committee. **House of Commons:** Member for Scarborough and Whitby since May 1, 1997; PPS to Douglas Alexander as Minister of State: Department of Trade and Industry 2001–02, Cabinet Office 2002–; *Special Interests:* Trade and Industry, Transport,
Devolution, Constitution, Tourism, Deep Sea Fishing Industry, Forestry, Small Businesses. *Countries of Interest:* USA, Brazil, Saudi Arabia, Japan, South Africa, Australia, Canada, Palestine. Member: Fabian Society, Labour Campaigning for Electoral Reform, SERA; Chair, North Yorkshire and City of York 1984–96 Member, Yorkshire and the North Regional Executive 1988–96. Member: Governing Board, York Sixth Form College 1989–93, Transport 2000; Vice-president, North Yorks Moors Railway; Member: European Standing Committee A 1998–, European Standing Committee B until 2003; Permanent Way Institution; Hon. Life Member, Association of Civil Engineering Trainees; Institution of Civil Engineers Engineering Council; MICE 1986; CEng 1986; *Clubs:* Cvil Service; *Recreations:* Reading, photography, biographies, theatre, internet, Carlisle United football team, travel, cookery. Lawrie Quinn Esq, MP, House of Commons, London, SW1A 0AA *Tel:* 020 7219 4170 *Fax:* 020 7219 2477. *Constituency:* 53 Westborough, Scarborough, North Yorkshire, YO11 1TU *Tel:* 01723 507000 *Fax:* 01723 507008 *E-mail:* brittainl@parliament.uk.

R

RAMMELL, BILL   Harlow   *Lab majority 5,228*

Bill Ernest Rammell. Born 10 October 1959; Son of William Ernest and Joan Elizabeth Rammell; Educated Burnt Mill Comprehensive, Harlow; University College of Wales, Cardiff (BA French and politics 1982); Married Beryl Jarhall 1983 (1 son 1 daughter). President, Cardiff University SU 1982–83; Management trainee, British Rail 1983–84; Regional officer, NUS 1984–87; Head of youth services, Basildon Council 1987–89; General manager, Kings College, London SU 1989–94; Senior university business manager, London University 1994–; Member, MSF. Councillor, Harlow Council 1985–97; Former Member, Local Government Information Unit. **House of Commons:** Member for Harlow since May 1, 1997; Assistant Government Whip 2002; PPS
to Tessa Jowell as Secretary of State for Culture, Media and Sport 2001–02; Parliamentary Under-Secretary of State, Foreign and Commonwealth Office 2002–; *Select Committees:* Member: Education and Employment 1997–99, European Legislation 1997–98, European Legislation 1998–2001, European Scrutiny 1998–2000, European Scrutiny 2000–01. *Special Interests:* Education, Housing, Economic

Policy, European Affairs, Media, Sport, Electoral Reform, Health. *Countries of Interest:* France, Sweden, USA, Germany, Hungary, Netherlands. Former Chair, CLP; Chair, Labour Movement for Europe 1999–. Member, Community Health Council; Chair, Community Safety Group; Member, European Standing Committee B 1998–; Vice-chair The European Movement 2001–; *Recreations:* Family, friends, sport, reading. Bill Rammell Esq, MP, House of Commons, London, SW1A 0AA *Tel: Fax:* 020 7219 2804. *Constituency:* Rooms 4–6, 1st Floor, Market House, The High, Harlow, Essex, CM20 1BL *Tel:* 01279 439706 *Fax:* 01279 446899 *E-mail:* rammellb@parliament.uk.

RANDALL, JOHN   Uxbridge   *Con majority 2,098*

(Alexander) John Randall. Born 5 August 1955; Son of late Alec Albert Randall, company director, and of Joyce Margaret Randall (née Gore); Educated Rutland House School, Hillingdon; Merchant Taylors School, Moor Park; School of Slavonic and East European Studies, London University (BA Serbo-Croat 1979); Married Katherine Frances Gray 1986 (2 sons 1 daughter). Randall's of Uxbridge: Sales assistant, Buyer, Director 1980–, Managing director 1988–97; Tour leader, Birdquest Holidays and Limosa Holidays as specialist ornithologist 1986–97. **House of Commons:** Member for Uxbridge since July 31, 1997 by-election; Opposition Whip 2000–03: Social Security; Culture, Media and Sport 2000, Defence, Education and Employment 2000–2001, Home Office 2001, Foreign Affairs 2001–02, Transport 2002–03; Opposition Whip 2003–; *Select Committees:* Member: Deregulation 1997–2001, Environment, Transport and Regional Affairs 1998–2000, Environment Sub-Committee 1998–2000; Member, Transport 2003–. *Special Interests:* Environment, Trade and Industry, Foreign Affairs. Hon. Treasurer, Uxbridge Conservative Association 1994, Chairman 1994–97. Chair: Uxbridge Retailers' Association to 1997, Cowley Residents' Association to 1997; Member: Uxbridge Town Centre Steering Committee to 1997, Royal Society for the Protection of Birds, British Ornithologists Union; *Clubs:* Uxbridge Conservative; *Sportsclubs:* Vice-President: Uxbridge Cricket Club, Uxbridge Rugby Football Club, Saracens Rugby Football Club, Member, Middlesex County Cricket Club; *Recreations:* Local history, ornithology, theatre, opera, travel, music (plays piano), Uxbridge FC supporter, Cricket, Rugby. John Randall Esq, MP, House of Commons, London, SW1A 0AA *Tel:* 020 7219 3400 *Fax:* 020 7219 2590. *Constituency:* 36 Harefield Road, Uxbridge, Middlesex, UB8 1PH *Tel:* 01895 239465 *Fax:* 01895 253105 *E-mail:* randallj@parliament.uk.

RAPSON, SYD   Portsmouth North   *Lab majority 5,134*

Syd (Sydney) Norman John Rapson. Born 17 April 1942; Son of late Sidney Rapson and of Doris Rapson, née Fisher, adopted by Lily and Sidney Rapson (grandparents); Educated Southsea and Paulsgrove Secondary Modern; Portsmouth Dockyard College (City and Guilds); National Council of Labour Colleges; Married Phyllis Edna Rapson, née Williams 1967 (1 daughter 1 son). Ministry of Defence: apprentice aircraft fitter, MoD 1958–63; aircraft fitter 1963–96; industrial technician 1997; AEEU 1960–: Shop steward 1965–97, Convenor 1979–97, National delegate, District president. Freeman of the City of London 1991; Councillor, Portsmouth City Council 1971–97: Lord Mayor 1990–91, Deputy Leader 1994–95; Councillor, Hampshire County Council 1973–77; Hon. Alderman, City of Portsmouth 1997–. **House of Commons:** Contested Portsmouth South 1992. Member for Portsmouth North since May 1, 1997; Team PPS, Ministry of Defence 2003–; *Select Committees:* Member: Accommodation and Works 1997–, Unopposed Bills (Panel) 1998–, Defence 2001 . *Special Interests:* Leisure, Economic Development, Defence, Local and Regional Government. *Countries of Interest:* America, Germany, Australia. Member, Co-operative Party; Joined Labour Party 1968; Chair, Portsmouth South Constituency 1970–71; Member, Parliamentary Armed Forces Scheme (Royal Marines) 1998–99. Member: Britain Australia Society Portsmouth Branch 1984–, Vice-president Portsmouth/Sydney Sister Link Committee 1984–, Vice-president Portsmouth/Duisburg Friendship Committee 1991–, Portsmouth Haifa Friendship Committee 1991–, Council of Europe, Parliamentary Assembly 1998–2001, Council of Europe Science and Technology Committee 1998–2001, Western European Union 1998–2001, Western European Union Defence Committee 1998–2001; Former non-executive member, Portsmouth Healthcare NHS Trust; *Publications: New Missions for European Armed*

278   HOUSE OF COMMONS

Forces and their Collective Capabilities Required for their Implementation Western European Union Document 1987; BEM 1984; Imperial Service Medal 1998; Freeman, City of London; Honorary Alderman, Portsmouth City Council 1997–; *Clubs:* President: Model Engineering Society (Portsmouth), Portsmouth District Angling Society; *Sportsclubs:* Former President, Portsmouth Athletic Club 1991–96; *Recreations:* Swimming, gardening. Syd Rapson Esq, BEM, MP, House of Commons, London, SW1A 0AA *Tel:* 020 7219 6351/6248 *Fax:* 020 7219 0915. *Constituency:* 79 Washbrook Road, Paulsgrove, Portsmouth, Hampshire, PO6 3SB *Tel:* 023 9242 1165 *Fax:* 023 9242 1165 *E-mail:* rapsons@parliament.uk.

RAYNSFORD, NICK   Greenwich and Woolwich   *Lab majority 13,433*

Nick (Wyvill Richard Nicolls) Raynsford. Born 28 January 1945; Son of late Wyvill and Patricia Raynsford; Educated Repton School; Sidney Sussex College, Cambridge (BA history 1966, MA); Chelsea School of Art (diploma in art and design 1972); Married Anne Jelley 1968 (3 daughters). Director, SHAC, the London Housing Aid Centre 1976–86; Member GMB. London Borough of Hammersmith and Fulham: Councillor 1971–75. **House of Commons:** Member for Fulham 1986 by-election –1987. Member for Greenwich 1992–97, and for Greenwich and Woolwich since May 1, 1997; Opposition Spokesperson for: Transport and London 1993–94, Housing, Construction and London 1994–97; Former PPS to Roy Hattersley; Department of the Environment,
Transport and the Regions 1997–2001: Parliamentary Under-Secretary of State 1997–99, Minister of State (Minister for Housing and Planning) 1999–2001; Minister of State (Minister for Local Government and the Regions), Department for Transport, Local Government and the Regions 2001–02; Office of the Deputy Prime Minister 2002–: Minister of State for: Local Government and the Regions 2002–03, Local and Regional Government 2003–; *Select Committees:* Member, Environment 1992–93. *Special Interests:* Housing, Social Policy, Transport, Environment. *Countries of Interest:* Europe. *Publications: A Guide to Housing Benefit*, 1982; Contributor to journals including *Building, Housing* and *New Statesman*; PC 2001; *Recreations:* Photography, walking, golf. Rt Hon Nick Raynsford MP, House of Commons, London, SW1A 0AA *Tel:* 020 7219 2773 *Fax:* 020 7219 2619. *Constituency:* 32 Woolwich Road, London, SE10 0JU *Tel:* 020 7219 5895 *Fax:* 020 7219 2619 *E-mail:* raynsfordn@parliament.uk.

REDWOOD, JOHN   Wokingham   *Con majority 5,994*

John Alan Redwood. Born 15 June 1951; Son of William and Amy Redwood (née Champion); Educated Kent College, Canterbury; Magdalen College, Oxford (MA modern history 1971); St Antony's College, Oxford (DPhil modern history 1975); Married Gail Felicity Chippington 1974 (1 son 1 daughter). Fellow, All Souls College, Oxford 1972–87; Tutor and lecturer 1972–73; Investment analyst, Robert Fleming & Co. 1974–77; N. M. Rothschild: Bank clerk 1977–78, Manager 1978–79, Assistant director 1979–80, Director, investment division 1980–83, Overseas corporate finance director and head of international (non-UK) privatisation 1986–87; Norcros
plc: Non-executive director 1985–87, Chair 1987–89; Chair, Mabey Securities 1999–; Visiting professor Middlesex University Business School 2000–; Non-executive director, BNB plc 2001–. Councillor, Oxfordshire County Council 1973–77. **House of Commons:** Contested Southwark Peckham 1981 by-election. Member for Wokingham since June 1987; Parliamentary Under-Secretary of State for Corporate Affairs, Department of Trade and Industry 1989–90; Minister of State 1990–92; Minister of State, Department of the Environment (Minister for Local Government) 1992–93; Secretary of State for Wales 1993–95; Contested Leadership of the Conservative Party 1995 and 1997; Member, Shadow Cabinet 1997–2000; Shadow Secretary of State for: Trade and Industry 1997–99, Environment, Transport and the Regions 1999–2000; *Special Interests:* Popular Capitalism, European Affairs, Constitution, Euro. *Countries of Interest:* USA. Governor, Oxford Polytechnic 1973–77; Governor of various schools in West Oxfordshire and Inner London 1973–82; Investment Committee, All Souls College Oxford; Adviser, Treasury and Civil Service Select Committee 1981; Head, Prime Minister's policy unit 1983–85; *Publications: Reason, Ridicule and Religion*, (Thames & Hudson) 1976; *Public Enterprise in Crisis*, (Blackwell) 1980; *Going for Broke*, (Blackwell) 1984; *Popular Capitalism*, (Routledge) 1987; *The Global Marketplace*, (HarperCollins) 1993; *Our Currency, Our Country*,

(Penguin) 1997; Several books and articles, especially on wider ownership and popular capitalism; *The Death of Britain*, (Macmillan) 1999; *Stars and Strife*, (Macmillan) 2001; *Just Say No*, (Politicos) 2001; *Third Way Which Way?* (Middlesex) 2002; PC 1993; *Sportsclubs:* Lords and Commons Cricket; *Recreations:* Village cricket, water sports. Rt Hon John Redwood, MP, House of Commons, London, SW1A 0AA *Tel:* 020 7219 4073. *Constituency:* 30 Rose Street, Wokingham, Berkshire, RG40 3SU *Tel:* 0118–962 9501 *Fax:* 0118–962 9323 *E-mail:* redwoodj@parliament.uk.

REED, ANDREW   Loughborough

Lab majority 6,378

Andy (Andrew) John Reed. Born 17 September 1964; Son of James Donald Reed and Margaret Ann Reed; Educated Riverside Junior, Birstall, Leicestershire; Stonehill High School, Birstall, Leicestershire; Longslade Community College, Birstall, Leicestershire; Leicester Polytechnic (BA public administration 1997); Married Sarah Elizabeth Chester 1992. Parliamentary assistant to Keith Vaz MP 1987–88; Urban regeneration, Leicester City Council 1988–90; Leicestershire County Council: economic development unit 1990–94, European affairs adviser 1994–97; NALGO 1988–: UNISON 1990–, Steward, Convenor, Executive, Leicestershire County Council, Conference Delegate, Service Conditions Officer. Councillor: Birstall Parish Council 1987–92, Charnwood Borough Council 1995–97, Chair, Economic Development 1995–97; Vice-chair, Loughborough Town Partnership 1995–97; Board Member, Business Link Loughborough 1995–99. **House of Commons:** Contested Loughborough 1992 general election. Member for Loughborough since May 1, 1997; PPS: at Department for Culture, Media and Sport 2000–01, to Margaret Beckett as Secretary of State for Environment, Food and Rural Affairs 2001–03; *Special Interests:* Economic Regeneration, Unemployment, Lifelong Learning, Education, Vocational Training, Sport, International Development, Co-operatives. *Countries of Interest:* South Africa, Germany, Ethiopia. Loughborough Constituency Labour Party: Chair 1988–92, Regional executive 1993–94; Member, East Midlands PLP; East Midlands Regional Group of Labour MPs: Vice-chair 1999–2002, Chair 2002–. *Sportsclubs:* Leicester Rugby Football Club, Birstall Rugby Football Club: player and president; *Recreations:* Rugby, tennis, volleyball, any sport. Andy Reed Esq, MP, House of Commons, London, SW1A 0AA *Tel:* 020 7219 3529 *Fax:* 020 7219 2405. *Constituency:* Unity House, Fennel Street, Loughborough, Leceistershire, LE11 1UQ *Tel:* 01509 261226 *Fax:* 01509 230579 *E-mail:* andy@andyreedmp.org.uk.

REID, ALAN   Argyll and Bute

LD majority 1,653

Alan Reid. Born 7 August 1954; Son of James Reid and Catherine, née Steele; Educated Prestwick Academy; Ayr Academy; Strathclyde University (BSc maths 1975); Jordanhill College (teacher training qualification 1976); Bell College (computer data processing 1979); Single. Strathclyde Regional Council: Maths teacher 1976–77, Computer programmer 1977–85; Computer project programmer Glasgow University 1985–; EIS 1976–77; NALGO 1977–85; AUT 1985–. Renfrew District Council 1988–96: Councillor, Group secretary. **House of Commons:** Contested Paisley South 1990 by-election, 1992 general election, Dumbarton 1997 general election. Member for Argyll and Bute since June 7, 2001; Scottish Liberal Democrat Spokesperson on the Common Fisheries Policy 2001–; Liberal Democrat Whip 2002–; *Select Committees:* Member, Broadcasting 2001–. *Special Interests:* Environment, Employment, Fuel Tax, Health, Fishing Industry, Local Issues, Elderly, Farming, Rural Development, International Affairs. Scottish Liberal Democrats 1981–: Various posts, Vice-convener 1994–98, Member executive committee; Election agent George Lyon Scottish Parliament election 1999. *Recreations:* Chess, football, walking, reading, television. Alan Reid Esq, MP, House of Commons, London, SW1A 0AA *Tel:* 020 7219 8127 *Fax:* 020 7219 1737. *Constituency:* 44 Hillfoot Street, Dunoon, Argyll, PA23 7DT *Tel:* 01369 704840 *Fax:* 01369 701212.

Visit the Vacher Dod Website . . .
www.DodOnline.co.uk

REID, JOHN   Hamilton North and Bellshill   *Lab majority 13,561*

John Reid. Born 8 May 1947; Son of late Thomas Reid, postman, and of Mary Reid, factory worker; Educated St Patrick's Senior Secondary School, Coatbridge; Stirling University (MA history 1978, PhD economic history 1987); Married Cathie McGowan 1969 (died 1998) (2 sons); Married Carine Adler 2002. Fellow Armed Forces Parliamentary Scheme; Scottish research officer, Labour Party 1979–83; Adviser to Neil Kinnock as Leader of the Labour Party 1983–85; Scottish organiser, Trade Unionists for Labour 1985–87; Member, TGWU. **House of Commons:** Member for Motherwell North 1987–97, and for Hamilton North and Bellshill since May 1, 1997; Deputy Shadow Spokesperson for Children 1989–90; Opposition Spokesperson for Defence, Disarmament and Arms Control 1990–97; Shadow Deputy Secretary of State for Defence 1995–97; Minister of State, Ministry of Defence (Minister for the Armed Forces) 1997–98; Minister of State, Department of the Environment, Transport and the Regions (Minister for Transport) 1998–99; Secretary of State for Scotland 1999–2001; Secretary of State for Northern Ireland 2001–02; Minister without Portfolio and Party Chair 2002–03; Leader of the House of Commons and President of the Council 2003; Secretary of State for Health 2003–; *Select Committees:* Chair, Modernisation of the House of Commons 2003. *Special Interests:* Foreign Affairs, Defence, Economy. Former Member Labour Party National Executive Committee. Fellow, Armed Services Parliamentary Scheme 1990–; PC 1998; *Recreations:* Football, crosswords. Rt Hon Dr John Reid, MP, House of Commons, London, SW1A 0AA *Tel:* 020 7219 4040 *Fax:* 020 7219 2771. *Constituency:* Parliamentary Office, Montrose House, 154 Montrose Crescent, Hamilton, ML3 6LL *Tel:* 01698 454672 *Fax:* 01698 424732.

RENDEL, DAVID   Newbury   *LD majority 2,415*

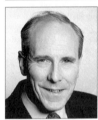

David Digby Rendel. Born 15 April 1949; Son of late Alexander Rendel, CBE and of Elizabeth Rendel; Educated Eton College; Magdalen College and St Cross College, Oxford (BA physics and philosophy 1971); Married Dr Susan Taylor 1974 (3 sons). Volunteer teacher in Cameroon and Uganda, Voluntary Service Overseas 1967–68; Operational research analyst, Shell International 1974–76; Financial analyst, British Gas 1976–77; Various analytical and management posts (finance and computing), Esso Petroleum 1977–90. Councillor: Newbury District Council 1987–95, St John's Ward 1987–91, Craven Ward 1991–95; Chairman: Finance and Property Sub-Committee 1991–92, Recreation and Amenities Committee 1992–93. **House of Commons:** Contested Hammersmith Fulham 1979, Fulham 1983, Newbury 1987 and 1992 general elections. Member for Newbury since May 6, 1993 by-election; Spokesperson for: Housing 1993–94, Local Government in England 1993–97, Local Government and Housing 1997, Social Security and Welfare 1997–99; Education and Skills (Higher Education) 2001–; *Select Committees:* Member: Accommodation and Works 1997–98, Procedure 2001–02; Member, Public Accounts 1999–. Member: Association of Liberal Democrat Councillors, Liberal Democrat Parliamentary Candidates Association, Green Liberal Democrats. Patron, Cats Protection; Member, Oxford Boat Race crew 1974; *Recreations:* Family, sport, music, travel. David Rendel Esq, MP, House of Commons, London, SW1A 0AA *Tel:* 020 7219 3495 *Fax:* 020 7219 2941. *Constituency:* Kendrick House, Wharf Street, Newbury, Berkshire, RG14 5AP *Tel:* 01635 581048 *Fax:* 01635 581049 *E-mail:* kovars@parliament.uk.

ROBATHAN, ANDREW   Blaby   *Con majority 6,209*

Andrew Robert George Robathan. Born 17 July 1951; Son of late Douglas and Sheena Robathan (née Gimson); Educated Merchant Taylors' School, Northwood; Oriel College, Oxford (BA modern history 1973, MA); RMA, Sandhurst; Army Staff College (psc 1984); Married Rachael Maunder 1991 (1 son 1 daughter). Regular Army Officer, Coldstream Guards 1974–89; Rejoined Army for Gulf War January-April 1991; BP 1991–92. Councillor, London Borough of Hammersmith and Fulham 1990–92. **House of Commons:** Member for Blaby since April 9, 1992; PPS to Iain Sproat, as Minister of State, Department of National Heritage 1995–97; Shadow Minister for: Trade and Industry 2002–03, International Development 2003–; *Select Committees:*

Chris Baker / Private Sort

Member: Employment 1992–94, International Development 1997–2002. *Special Interests:* International Development, Environment, Transport, Defence, Northern Ireland, Conservation. *Countries of Interest:* Caucasus, Africa. Trustee, Halo Trust; Freeman, Merchant Taylors Company; Freeman, City of London; *Recreations:* Mountain walking, skiing, wild life, shooting. Andrew Robathan Esq, MP, House of Commons, London, SW1A 0AA *Tel:* 020 7219 3550. *Constituency:* Blaby Conservative Association, 35 Lutterworth Road, Blaby, Leicestershire, LE8 4DW *Tel:* 0116–277 9992 *Fax:* 0116–278 6664.

ROBERTSON, ANGUS   Moray   *SNP majority 1,744*

Angus Robertson. Born 28 September 1969; Educated Broughton High School, Edinburgh; Aberdeen University (MA politics and international relations 1991); Partner. News editor Austrian Broadcasting Corporation 1991–99; Reporter BBC Austria 1992–99; Contributor: National Public Radio USA, Radio Telefís Eireann, Ireland, Deutsche Welle, Germany; Consultant in media skills, presentation skills and political affairs with Communications Skills International (CSI) 1994–2001; NUJ. **House of Commons:** Contested Midlothian 1999 Scottish Parliament election. Member for Moray since June 7, 2001; SNP Spokesperson for Foreign Affairs; SNP Westminster Spokesperson for Defence and Europe 2001–; *Select Committees:* Member, European Scrutiny 2001–. *Special Interests:* European Affairs, External Affairs, Defence, International Development, Youth Affairs. *Countries of Interest:* Austria, Germany, Norway, Ireland, USA. Member National Executive Young Scottish Nationalists 1986; National organiser Federation of Student Nationalists 1988; Member SNP International Bureau; Deputy SNP spokesperson for Constitutional and External Affairs 1998–99; European policy adviser SNP Group Scottish Parliament; Shadow Scottish Minister for Foreign Affairs 2001–. *Recreations:* Sport, current affairs, history, travel, socialising, cinema. Angus Robertson Esq, MP, House of Commons, London, SW1A 0AA *Tel:* 020 7219 8259. *Constituency:* Moray Parliamentary Office, 9 Wards Road, Elgin, IV30 1NL *Tel:* 01343 551 111 *Fax:* 01343 556 355 *E-mail:* angus.robertson@snp.org.

ROBERTSON, HUGH   Faversham and Mid Kent   *Con majority 4,183*

Hugh Michael Robertson. Born 9 October 1962; Son of George Patrick Robertson, headmaster, and June Miller Robertson, née McBryde; Educated King's School, Canterbury; Reading University (BSc land management 1985); Royal Military Academy Sandhurst (commissioned 1986); Married Anna Copson 2002. Army officer The Life Guards 1985–95; Army Officer 1985–95; Schroder Investment Management 1995–2001: Assistant director 1999–2000. **House of Commons:** Member for Faversham and Mid Kent since June 7, 2001; Opposition Whip 2002–; Special adviser security Shadow Northern Ireland Secretary 1998–2001; *Special Interests:* Defence, Foreign Affairs, Agriculture, Fruit Farming. *Countries of Interest:* China, Singapore, Middle East, Balkans. Armourers and Brasiers Prize 1986; Sultan of Brunei's Personal Order of Merit 1992; Fellow Royal Geographical Society; *Clubs:* Cavalry and Guards; *Sportsclubs:* Playing Member MCC; *Recreations:* Cricket, hockey, skiing. Hugh Robertson, Esq, MP, House of Commons, London, SW1A 0AA *Tel:* 020 7219 8230 *Fax:* 020 7219 1765. *Constituency:* 8 Faversham Road, Lenham, Kent, ME17 2PN *Tel:* 01622 850 574 *Fax:* 01622 850 294 *E-mail:* robertsonh@parliament.uk.

ROBERTSON, JOHN   Glasgow Anniesland   *Lab majority 11,054*

John Robertson. Born 17 April 1952; Educated Shawlands Academy; Langside College (ONC electrical engineering 1983); Stow College (HNC electrical engineering 1985); Married Eleanor Wilkins Munro 1973 (3 daughters). GPO/ Post Office/ British Telecom/ BT 1969–2000: technical officer 1973–87, special faults investigation officer 1987–91, customer service manager 1991–95, field manager 1995–99, local customer manager 1999–2000; Member: NCU/POEU/CWU 1969–90, STE/Connect 1991–; CWU/NCU: political and education officer, Glasglow Branch 1986–90; Connect: chair West of Scotland 1997–2000. **House of Commons:** Member for Glasgow Anniesland since November 23, 2000; *Select Committees:* Member: Scottish Affairs 2001–,

European Scrutiny 2003–. *Special Interests:* Small Businesses. Chair Anniesland constituency Labour party 1995–2000; Former election agent to Donald Dewar MP, MSP; Secretary, Glasgow Group of MPs. Member European Standing Committee B until 2003; Commonwealth Parliamentary Association; International Parliamentary Union; *Sportsclubs:* Cambus Athletic Football Club, Garrowhill Cricket Club; *Recreations:* reading, music, football, cricket. John Robertson Esq, MP, House of Commons, London, SW1A 0AA *Tel:* 020 7219 6964. *Constituency:* 131 Dalsetter Avenue, Drumchapel, Glasgow, G15 8TE *Tel:* 0141 944 7298.

ROBERTSON, LAURENCE   Tewkesbury   Con majority 8,663

Laurence Anthony Robertson. Born 29 March 1958; Son of James Robertson, former colliery electrician, and Jean Robertson (née Larkin); Educated St James' Church of England Secondary School; Farnworth Grammar School; Bolton Institute of Higher Education (Management Services Diploma); Married Susan Lees 1989 (2 stepdaughters). Warehouse assistant 1976–77; Work study engineer 1977–83; Industrial management consultant 1983–89; Factory owner 1987–88; Charity fundraising, public relations and special events consultant 1988–. **House of Commons:** Contested Makerfield 1987, Ashfield 1992 general elections. Member for Tewkesbury since May 1, 1997; Opposition Whip 2001–03; Shadow Minister for Trade and Industry 2003–; *Select Committees:* Member: Environmental Audit 1997–99, Joint Committee on Consolidation of Bills Etc 1997–2001, European Scrutiny 1999–2002, Social Security 1999–2001, Education and Skills 2001. *Special Interests:* Overseas Aid, Constitution, European Affairs, Education, Economic Policy, Law and Order, Countryside. *Countries of Interest:* UK, USA, Ethiopia, other African countries. Former Member, Conservative 2000 Foundation; Former Member, Conservative Way Forward; Vice-Chair, Association of Conservative Clubs (ACC) 1997–2000. *Publications: Europe: the Case Against Integration,* 1991; *The Right Way Ahead,* 1995; *Recreations:* Horses and horseracing, golf, other sports (completed 6 marathons), reading, writing, countryside. Laurence Robertson Esq, MP, House of Commons, London, SW1A 0AA *Tel:* 020 7219 4196 *Fax:* 020 7219 2325. *Constituency:* Tewkesbury Conservative Association, Lloyds Bank Chambers, Abbey Terrace, Winchcombe, Gloucestershire, GL54 5LL *Tel:* 01242 602388 *Fax:* 01242 604364 *E-mail:* robertsonl@parliament.uk.

ROBINSON, GEOFFREY   Coventry North West   Lab majority 10,874

Geoffrey Robinson. Born 25 May 1938; Son of late Robert Norman Robinson and late Dorothy Jane Robinson; Educated Emanuel School, London; Clare College, Cambridge; Yale University, USA; Married Marie Elena Giorgio 1967 (1 daughter 1 son). Labour Party research assistant 1965–68; Senior executive, Industrial Reorganisation Corporation 1968–70; Financial controller, British Leyland 1970–72; Managing director, Leyland Innocenti 1972–73; Chief executive, Jaguar Cars Coventry 1974–75; Chief executive (unpaid), Triumph Motorcycles (Meriden) Ltd 1978–80; Director, West Midlands Enterprise Board 1982–85; Chief executive, TransTec plc 1986–97; Member, T&G. **House of Commons:** Member for Coventry North West since March 1976 by-election; · Opposition Front Bench Spokesman on: Science 1982–83, Trade and Industry and Regional Affairs 1983–87; Paymaster General, HM Treasury 1997–98; *Special Interests:* Regional Policy, Industry, Economic Policy, New Technology. *Countries of Interest:* France, Germany, Italy, USA. *Publications: The Unconventional Minister: My Life in New Labour; Recreations:* Motorcars, gardens, architecture, football. Geoffrey Robinson Esq, MP, House of Commons, London, SW1A 0AA *Tel:* 020 7219 4504 *Fax:* 020 7219 0984. *Constituency:* Transport House, Short Street, Coventry, CV1 2LS *Tel:* 024 7625 7870 *Fax:* 024 7625 7813 *E-mail:* geoffrey@newstatesman.co.uk.

Visit the Vacher Dod Website . . .
www.DodOnline.co.uk

ROBINSON, IRIS Strangford *DUP majority 1,110*

Iris Robinson. Born 6 September 1949; Daughter of Joseph Collins and Mary McCartney; Educated Knockbreda Intermediate School; Castlereagh Technical College; Married Peter Robinson (later MP) 1970 (2 sons 1 daughter). Castlereagh Borough Council 1989–: Mayor Castlereagh 1992, 1995, 2000. **House of Commons:** Member for Strangford since June 7, 2001; New Northern Ireland Assembly 1998–2002; *Special Interests:* Health. Spokesperson Health, Social Services and Public Safety; Whip. Fundraiser Multiplesclerosis; Chair Staff and Office Accommodation; Director: Ballybeen Square Regeneration Board, Tullycarnet Community Enterprises Ltd; Member: Dundonald International Icebowl Board, Central Services Committee; *Recreations:* Interior design. Iris Robinson, MP, House of Commons, London, SW1A 0AA *Tel:* 020 7219 8323 *Fax:* 020 7219 1797. *Constituency:* Constituency Office, 2(B) James Street, Newtownards, BT23 4DY *Tel:* 028 9182 7701 *Fax:* 028 9182 7703 *E-mail:* iris.robinson@ukgateway.net.

ROBINSON, PETER Belfast East *DUP majority 7,117*

Peter David Robinson. Born 29 December 1948; Son of late David McCrea Robinson and of Sheila Robinson; Educated Annadale Grammar School; Castlereagh College of Further Education; Married Iris Collins (later MP as Iris Robinson) 1970 (2 sons 1 daughter). Estate agent; Member, Northern Ireland Assembly 1982–86; Deputy Leader, Democratic Unionist Party: resigned 1987, re-elected 1988; Member: Northern Ireland Forum 1996–98, new Northern Ireland Assembly 1998–; Minister for Regional Development, Northern Ireland Assembly 1999–. Castlereagh Borough Council: Councillor 1977–, Alderman 1977, Deputy Mayor 1978, Mayor 1986. **House of Commons:** Member for Belfast East since May 1979 (resigned seat December 1985 in protest against Anglo-Irish Agreement; re-elected January 1986); Spokesman for Constitutional Affairs; *Select Committees:* Member, Northern Ireland Affairs 1994–97; Member, Northern Ireland Affairs 1997–. *Special Interests:* Housing, Shipbuilding, Community Care, Aerospace, Aviation, International Terrorism. Foundation Member, Ulster Democratic Unionist Party, Party Executive Member 1973–; Secretary, Central Executive Committee 1974–79; General Secretary 1975. Member, NI Sports Council; *Publications: The North Answers Back*; *Capital Punishment for Capital Crime*; *Savagery and Suffering*; *Self-inflicted*; *Ulster the Prey*; *Ulster – The facts*; *Carson Man of Action*; *A War to be Won*; *It's Londonderry*; *Ulster in Peril*; *Give me Liberty*; *Hands off the UDR*; *Their cry was 'No Surrender'*; *IRA-Sinn Fein*; *The Union under Fire*; *Recreations:* Golf, bowling, breeding Koi carp. Peter Robinson Esq, MP, House of Commons, London, SW1A 0AA *Tel:* 020 7219 3506 *Fax:* 020 7219 5854. *Constituency:* Strandtown Hall, 96 Belmont Road, Belfast, BT4 3DE *Tel:* 028 9047 3111 *Fax:* 028 9047 1797 *E-mail:* info@dup.org.uk.

ROCHE, BARBARA Hornsey and Wood Green *Lab majority 10,614*

Barbara Roche. Born 13 April 1954; Daughter of Barnet and Hannah Margolis; Educated Comprehensive school; Lady Margaret Hall, Oxford University (BA philosophy, politics and economics 1972–75); Married Patrick Roche 1977 (1 daughter). Barrister, called to the Bar 1977. **House of Commons:** Contested Surrey South West by-election 1984 and Hornsey and Wood Green 1987 general election. Member for Hornsey and Wood Green since April 9, 1992; Opposition Spokesperson on Trade and Industry 1995–97; Spokesperson Women's Issues 2001–03; Opposition Whip 1994–95; PPS to Margaret Beckett as deputy leader of Labour Party 1993–94; Parliamentary Under-Secretary of State, Department of Trade and Industry 1997–99; Financial Secretary, HM Treasury 1999; Minister of State, Home Office 1999–2001; Minister of State (Social Exclusion) Office of the Deputy Prime Minister 2001– and Deputy Minister for Women, Cabinet Office 2001–02; Minister of State for Social Exclusion, Regional Co-ordination, Neighbourhood Renewal, Homelessness, Women and Equality, Office of the Deputy Prime Minister 2002–03; *Select Committees:* Member: Home Affairs 1992–94, Public Accounts 1999. *Special Interests:* Home Affairs, Legal Reform, Environment. *Countries of Interest:* Cyprus, Israel. *Clubs:* Wood Green Labour; *Recreations:* Theatre, family. Barbara Roche, MP, House of Commons, London, SW1A 0AA. *Constituency:* 28 Middle Lane, London, N8 8PL *Tel:* 020 8348 8668.

ROE, MARION   Broxbourne   *Con majority 8,993*

Marion Audrey Roe. Born 15 July 1936; Daughter of late William and Grace Keyte (née Bocking); Educated Bromley High School; Croydon High School (both Girls Public Day School Trust); English School of Languages, Vevey, Switzerland; Married James Kenneth Roe 1958 (1 son 2 daughters). Councillor, London Borough of Bromley 1975–78; GLC Councillor, Ilford North 1977–86: served on every Committee of the Council; GLC Representative, General Services Committee of the Association of Metropolitan Authorities 1978–81; UK Representative, Conference of Local and Regional Authorities of Europe 1978–81; Member, South East Thames Regional Health Authority 1980–83. **House of Commons:** Contested Barking 1979 general election. Member for Broxbourne since June 1983; Promoted: Prohibition of Female Circumcision Act 1985 (Private Member's Bill); PPS to: David Mitchell as: Parliamentary Under-Secretary of State for Transport 1985–86, Minister of State for Transport 1986, John Moore as Secretary of State for Transport 1986–87; Parliamentary Under-Secretary of State, Department of Environment 1987–88; *Select Committees:* Member: Procedure 1990–92, Administration 1991–97, Sittings of the House 1991–92; Chair, Health 1992–97; Member: Liaison 1992–97, Health 2000–01; Chair, Administration 1997–; Member: Chairmen's Panel 1997–, Finance and Services 1997–, Liaison 1997–. *Special Interests:* Health, Horticulture, Environment. *Countries of Interest:* Angola, Canada, Seychelles, South Africa, USA. Vice-President, Greater London Young Conservative Group 3 1977–80; Member, Conservative Women's National Committee Working Party on Women; Numerous Conservative Party Organisations. Vice-President, Women's Nationwide Cancer Control Campaign 1985–; BBC's General Advisory Council 1986–87; Numerous organisations concerned primarily with women, health and horticulture; Member, Department of Employment's Advisory Committee on Women's Employment 1989–92; Vice-President, Association of District Councils 1994–; Member, Armed Forces Parliamentary Scheme 1998; Chair, Conservative House of Commons Benevolent Fund 1998–99; Parliamentary Consultant to the Horticultural Trades Association 1990–95; UK Representative on Commonwealth Observer Group Monitoring Elections in the Seychelles and Angola 1992–; Substitute Member, UK Delegation to Parliamentary Assemblies of Council of Europe and WEU 1989–92; Member, Executive Committee: Commonwealth Parliamentary Association (CPA) UK Branch 1997–, Vice-Chair 2002–03, British Group of the Inter-Parliamentary Union (IPU) 1997–, Vice-Chair 1998–2001; Fellow, Industry and Parliament Trust 1990; Managing Trustee, Parliamentary Contributory Pension Fund 1990–97; Freeman, Worshipful Company of Gardeners 1990, Liveryman 1993; *Publications: The Labour Left in London – A Blueprint for a Socialist Britain,* CPC 1985; FRSA 1990; Hon. Member, Institute of Horticulture 1993; Hon. Fellowship, Professional Business and Technical Management 1995; Freeman, City of London 1981; *Recreations:* Ballet and opera. Mrs Marion Roe, MP, House of Commons, London, SW1A 0AA *Tel:* 020 7219 3528 *Fax:* 020 7219 4992. *Constituency:* Broxbourne Parliamentary Conservative Association, 76 High Street, Hoddesdon, Hertfordshire, EN11 8ET *Tel:* 01992 479972 *Fax:* 01992 479973.

ROONEY, TERRY   Bradford North   *Lab majority 8,969*

Terence Rooney. Born 11 November 1950; Son of late Eric and Frances Rooney; Educated Buttershaw Comprehensive School; Bradford College; Married Susanne Chapman 1969 (1 son 2 daughters). Commercial insurance broker; Welfare rights worker; Member: GPMU, UNISON. Bradford City Council: Councillor 1983–91, Chair, Labour Group 1988–91, Deputy Leader 1990–91. **House of Commons:** Member for Bradford North since November 8, 1990 by-election; PPS to: Michael Meacher as Minister of State: Department of the Environment, Transport and the Regions (Minister for the Environment) 1997–2001, Department for Environment, Food and Rural Affairs 2001–02, Keith Hill as Minister of State, Office of the Deputy Prime Minister 2003–; *Select Committees:* Member, Broadcasting 1991–97; Member, Joint Committee on House of Lords Reform 2002–. *Special Interests:* Public Sector Housing, Poverty, Industrial Relations. *Countries of Interest:* Pakistan, India, Bangladesh. Campaign co-ordinator, Bradford West Labour Party in 1983 general election campaign; Hon. secretary, Yorkshire Regional Group of Labour MPs 1991–2001. Member: Low Pay Unit, Unemployment Unit; Trustee, Bierley Community Association; *Recreations:* Crosswords, football, tennis. Terence Rooney Esq, MP, House of Commons, London, SW1A 0AA *Tel:* 020 7219 6407 *Fax:* 020 7219 5275. *Constituency:* 76 Kirkgate, Bradford, West Yorkshire, BD1 1SZ *Tel:* 01274 777821 *Fax:* 01274 777817 *E-mail:* rooneyt@parliament.uk.

ROSINDELL, ANDREW   Romford   *Con majority 5,977*

Andrew Richard Rosindell. Born 17 March 1966; Son of Frederick William Rosindell, tailor and Eileen Rosina Clark, pianist; Educated Marshalls Park Comprehensive School, Romford. Central Press Features London 1984–86; Freelance journalist 1986–97; Parliamentary researcher Vivian Bendall MP 1986–97; Director and International Director European Foundation 1997–2001. London Borough of Havering 1990–2002: Councillor, Member Standing Advisory Council on Religious Education 1990–2000, Vice-chairman Housing Committee 1996–97; Chairman North Romford Community Area Forum 1998–2002. **House of Commons:** Contested Glasgow Provan 1992 and Thurrock 1997 general elections. Member for Romford since June 7, 2001; *Select Committees:* Member: Regulatory Reform 2001–, Joint Committee on Statutory Instruments 2002–. *Special Interests:* British Overseas Territories, Foreign Affairs, European Affairs, Law and Order, Defence, Local and Regional Government, Dog issues, Gibraltar. *Countries of Interest:* Overseas Territories, Nordic countries, Australia, New Zealand, USA, Canada, Israel, South Africa, Eastern Europe. Chair: Romford Young Conservatives 1983–84, Greater London Young Conservatives 1987–88, National Young Conservatives 1993–94, Chase Cross Ward Romford 1988–99, Romford Conservative Association 1998–2001; International secretary Young Conservatives United Kingdom 1991–98; National Union Executive Committee Conservative Party: Member 1986–88, 1992–94; President Havering Park Ward Conservatives 2000–; Member: Conservative Christian Fellowship. Co-ordinator Freedom Training Programme 1993–; Vice-president Romford and District Scout Association; Hon member East Anglia Staffordshire Bull Terrier Club; North Romford Community Association; Patron Justice for Dogs; Honorary member Konservativ Ungdom, Denmark 1988–; Chairman European Young Conservatives 1993–97; Executive Secretary International Young Democrat Union 1994–98; International Democrat Union Executive member 1998–2002, Chairman International Young Democrat Union 1998–2002; *Publications:* Co-author *Defending Our Great Heritage*, 1993; *Clubs:* Romford Conservative and Constitutional; Royal Air Forces Association; Romford Royal British Legion. Andrew Rosindell Esq, MP, House of Commons, London, SW1A 0AA *Tel:* 020 7219 8475 *Fax:* 020 7219 1960. *Constituency:* 85 Western Road, Romford, Essex, RM1 3LS *Tel:* 01708 766700 *Fax:* 01708 707163 *E-mail:* andrew@rosindell.com.

ROSS, ERNIE   Dundee West   *Lab majority 6,800*

Ernie Ross. Born 27 July 1942; Educated St John's Junior Secondary School; Married 1964 (2 sons 1 daughter). Quality control engineer, Timex Ltd 1970–79; Member, MSF. Former Chair, Westminster Foundation for Democracy. **House of Commons:** Member for Dundee West since May 1979; *Select Committees:* Member: Education and Employment 1996–97, Standards and Privileges 1996–97, Foreign Affairs 1997–99; Member: Court of Referees 1997–, Standing Orders 1997–. *Special Interests:* Social Services, Defence, Industry, Employment, Education, Small Businesses. *Countries of Interest:* Bangladesh, Former Soviet Union, Cuba, Cyprus, Latin America, Middle East, South Africa, USA. UK Delegation to Organisation for Security and Co-operation in Europe; *Recreations:* Football, cricket. Ernie Ross Esq, MP, House of Commons, London, SW1A 0AA *Tel:* 020 7219 3480. *Constituency:* 57 Blackscroft, Dundee, DD4 6AT *Tel:* 01382 466700 *Fax:* 01382 466719 *E-mail:* rosse@parliament.uk.

ROY, FRANK   Motherwell and Wishaw   *Lab majority 10,956*

Frank Roy. Born 29 August 1958; Son of late James Roy, settler manager, and Esther McMahon, home-help; Educated St Joseph's High School, Motherwell; Our Lady's High School, Motherwell; Motherwell College (HNC marketing 1994); Glasgow Caledonian University (BA consumer and management studies 1994); Married Ellen Foy 1977 (1 son 1 daughter). Ravenscraig Steelworker 1977–91; Personal assistant to Helen Liddell, MP 1994–97; Member, GMB; Shop steward, ISTC 1983–90. **House of Commons:** Member for Motherwell and Wishaw since May 1, 1997; PPS: to Helen Liddell as Minister of State, Scottish Office (Minister for Education) 1998–99, to Secretaries of State for Scotland: Dr John Reid 1999–2001, Helen Liddell 2001;

Select Committees: Member, Social Security 1997–98; Member, Defence 2001–. *Special Interests:* Employment, Social Welfare. *Countries of Interest:* Europe, USA. Parliamentary election agent to Dr Jeremy Bray 1987–92; Vice-President, Federation of Economic Development Authorities (FEDA); *Recreations:* Football, reading, music. Frank Roy Esq, MP, House of Commons, London, SW1A 0AA *Tel:* 020 7219 6467. *Constituency:* Constituency Office, 265 Main Street, Wishaw, Lanarkshire, ML2 7NE *Tel:* 01698 303040 *Fax:* 01698 303060 *E-mail:* royf@parliament.uk.

RUANE, CHRIS   Vale of Clwyd   *Lab majority 5,761*

Chris Ruane. Born 18 July 1958; Son of late Michael Ruane, labourer, and Esther Ruane; Educated Ysgol Mair RC, Rhyl Primary; Blessed Edward Jones Comprehensive, Rhyl; University College of Wales, Aberystwyth (BSc economics 1979); Liverpool University (PGCE 1980); Married Gill Roberts 1994 (2 daughters). Primary school teacher 1982–97, Deputy head 1991–97; National Union of Teachers: School Rep 1982–97, President, West Clwyd 1991, Vale of Clwyd 1997. Councillor, Rhyl Town Council 1988–99. **House of Commons:** Contested Clwyd North West 1992 general election. Member for Vale of Clwyd since May 1, 1997; PPS to Peter Hain as Secretary of State for Wales 2002–; *Select Committees:* Member, Welsh Affairs 1999–2002. *Special Interests:* Anti-Poverty, Human Rights, Education, Environment. *Countries of Interest:* Belize. Member: Labour Group of Seaside MPs 1997–; Rural Group of Labour MPs. Member: Welfare Benefits Shop Management Committee, Steering Group forming Vale of Clwyd Credit Union; Founder Member: Rhyl Anti Apartheid 1987, Rhyl and District Amnesty International Group 1991, Rhyl Environmental Association 1988, President; *Recreations:* Cooking, walking, reading, humour. Chris Ruane Esq, MP, House of Commons, London, SW1A 0AA *Tel:* 020 7219 6378 *Fax:* 020 7219 6090. *Constituency:* 45–47 Kinmel Street, Rhyl, Clwyd, LL18 1AG *Tel:* 01745 354626 *Fax:* 01745 334827 *E-mail:* ruanec@parliament.uk.

RUDDOCK, JOAN   Lewisham Deptford   *Lab majority 15,293*

Joan Ruddock. Born 28 December 1943; Daughter of late Kenneth Anthony and Eileen Anthony; Educated Pontypool Grammar School for Girls; Imperial College, London University (BSc botany 1965); Married Keith Ruddock 1963 (separated 1990, died 1996). Director: research and publications, Shelter, National Campaign for Homeless 1968–73, Oxford Housing Aid Centre 1973–77; Special programmes officer (MSC) for unemployed young people, Berkshire County Council 1977–79; Manager, Citizens Advice Bureau, Reading 1979–86; Member, TGWU. **House of Commons:** Contested Newbury 1979 general election. Member for Lewisham Deptford since June 1987; Opposition Spokesperson for: Transport 1989–92, Home Affairs 1992–94, Environmental Protection 1994–97; Private Members' Bill on flytipping – Control of Pollution Act (amendment) 1989; Parliamentary Under-Secretary of State for Women 1997–98; Promoted: Ten Minute Rule Bill 1999, Prophylactic Mastectomy Registry Presentation Bill 1999, Organic Food and Farming Targets Bill 1999, Ten Minute Rule Bill 2000, Sex Discrimination (Amendment) No. 2, Ten Minute Rule Bill 2002, Waste Bill, Private Members' Bill – Municipal Waste, Recycling Bill 2003; *Select Committees:* Member, Modernisation of the House of Commons 2001–. *Special Interests:* Environment, Women, Foreign Affairs. *Countries of Interest:* Afghanistan, South Africa. Chairperson, CND 1981–85; Member, British Delegation to Council of Europe and Western European Union 1988–89; Inter-Parliamentary Union 2001–; Hon. Fellow: Goldsmith's College, London University; Laban Centre, London; ARCS (1965); *Recreations:* Travel, music, gardening. Joan Ruddock, MP, House of Commons, London, SW1A 0AA *Tel:* 020 7219 6206 *Fax:* 020 7219 6045 *E-mail:* alexanderh@parliament.uk.

Visit the Vacher Dod Website . . .

www.DodOnline.co.uk

RUFFLEY, DAVID   Bury St Edmunds   *Con majority 2,503*

David Ruffley. Born 18 April 1962; Son of Jack Laurie Ruffley solicitor and Yvonne Grace, née Harris; Educated Bolton Boys' School; Queens' College, Cambridge (BA law 1985); Single. Clifford Chance Solicitors, London 1985–91; Special adviser to Ken Clarke, MP as: Secretary of State for Education and Science 1991–92, Home Secretary 1992–93, Chancellor of the Exchequer 1993–96; Strategic Economic Consultant to the Conservative Party 1996–97; Vice-President, Small Business Bureau 1996–. **House of Commons:** Member for Bury St Edmunds since May 1, 1997; *Select Committees:* Member, Public Administration 1997–99; Member: Treasury 1998–, Treasury Sub-Committee 1999–. *Special Interests:* Treasury, Home Affairs, Education, Broadcasting. *Countries of Interest:* USA, China, France. Patron, Bury St Edmunds Constitutional Club; Patron, West Suffolk Voluntary Association for the Blind; Unpaid adviser: to 'Catch 'em Young' young offenders project 1992, to Grant Maintained Schools Foundation 1996–97; Patron, Bury St Edmunds Town Trust; *Sportsclubs:* Patron, Bury St Edmunds and District Football League; Member, Stowmarket FC, The Suffolk Golf and Country Club; *Recreations:* Football, cinema, golf, thinking. David Ruffley Esq, MP, House of Commons, London, SW1A 0AA *Tel:* 020 7219 2880 *Fax:* 020 7219 3998. *Constituency:* Bury St Edmunds Conservative Association, 3 Woolhall Street, Bury St Edmunds, IP33 1LA *Tel:* 01284 754072 *Fax:* 01284 763515 *E-mail:* davidruffleymp@parliament.uk.

RUSSELL, BOB   Colchester   *LD majority 5,553*

Bob (Robert Edward) Russell. Born 31 March 1946; Son of late Ewart Russell and late Muriel Russell (née Sawdy); Educated St Helena Secondary Boys, Colchester; North-East Essex Technical College (Proficiency Certificate, National Council for the Training of Journalists 1966); Married Audrey Blandon 1967 (twin sons 1 daughter, 1 daughter deceased). Trainee reporter, *Essex County Standard* and *Colchester Gazette* 1963–66; News editor, *Braintree and Witham Times* 1966–68; Editor, *Maldon and Burnham Standard* 1968–69; Sub-editor: London *Evening News* 1969–72, London *Evening Standard* 1972–73; Press officer, BT Eastern Region 1973–85; Publicity information officer, Essex University 1986–97; Branch secretary, North-Essex, National Union of Journalists 1967–68. Councillor, Colchester Borough Council 1971–2002: Mayor 1986–87, Council Leader 1987–91. **House of Commons:** Member for Colchester since May 1, 1997; Liberal Democrat Spokesperson for: Home and Legal Affairs 1997–99, Sport 1999–; Liberal Democrat Whip 1999–2002, 2003–; *Select Committees:* Member: Home Affairs 1998–2001, Catering 2000–01; Member, Home Affairs 2001–. *Special Interests:* Environment, Local and Regional Government, Sport, Transport, Animal Welfare, Voluntary sector, Youth organisations. *Countries of Interest:* St Helena. Member: Labour Party 1966, SDP May 1981, Liberal Democrats since formation. Member: Oxfam, Colchester and East Essex Co-operative Society, Colchester Credit Union, The Ramblers Association; Honorary Alderman of Colchester; Journalists Prize, NEETC 1965; *Sportsclubs:* Colchester United Football Club; *Recreations:* Local history, walking, camping, watching Colchester Utd FC. Bob Russell Esq, MP, House of Commons, London, SW1A 0AA *Tel:* 020 7219 5150 *Fax:* 020 7219 2365. *Constituency:* Magdalen Hall, Wimpole Road, C01 2DE *Tel:* 01206 506600 *Fax:* 01206 506610.

RUSSELL, CHRISTINE   City of Chester   *Lab majority 6,894*

Christine Margaret Russell. Born 25 March 1945; Daughter of late John Alfred William Carr, farmer, and Phyllis Carr; Educated Spalding High School; London School of Librarianship; Polytechnic of North West London (Professional Librarianship Qualification, ALA 1970); Married Dr James Russell 1971 (divorced 1991) (1 son 1 daughter). Librarian: London Borough of Camden 1967–70, Glasgow University 1970–71, Dunbartonshire County Council 1971–73; Personal assistant to: Lyndon Harrison, MEP 1989–91, Brian Simpson, MEP 1992–94; Co-ordinator of Advocacy Project, MIND 1994–97; Member, GMB. JP 1980–; Chester City Council: Councillor 1980–97, Chair, Development Committee 1990–97. **House of Commons:** Member for City of

Chester since May 1, 1997; *Select Committees:* Member: Environmental Audit 1999–2001, Transport, Local Government and the Regions 2001–02, Urban Affairs Sub-Committee 2001–02; Member: Office of the Deputy Prime Minister: Housing, Planning and Local Government 2002–, Urban Affairs Sub-Committee 2003–. *Special Interests:* Transport, Environment, Education, Urban Regeneration, Arts, International Development. *Countries of Interest:* Mozambique, South Africa, Middle East, Romania, Central America. Chester Constituency Labour Party: Agent 1986–95, Chair/President 1989–92. President, Chester Women's Hostel Association; Elected member, Citizens Advice Bureau; Member, Magistrates Association; Among other broadcasts, On The Record: General Election 1992; ALA, JP; *Recreations:* Cinema, football, walking, art and architecture. Mrs Christine Russell, MP, House of Commons, London, SW1A 0AA *Tel:* 020 7219 6398 *Fax:* 020 7219 0943. *Constituency:* York House, York Street, Chester, CH1 3LR *Tel:* 01244 400174 *Fax:* 01244 400487 *E-mail:* russellcm@parliament.uk.

RYAN, JOAN   Enfield North   *Lab majority 2,291*

Joan Ryan. Born 8 September 1955; Daughter of Michael Joseph Ryan and Dolores Marie, née Joyce; Educated St Josephs Secondary School, Notre Dame High School; City of Liverpool College (BA history, sociology 1979); Polytechnic of the South Bank (MSc sociology 1981); Married 2nd Martin Hegarty (1 son 1 daughter). Member: AEEU, NUT. Councillor, Barnet Council 1990–98, Deputy Leader 1994–98, Chair, Policy and Resources Committee 1994. **House of Commons:** Member for Enfield North since May 1, 1997; Assistant Government Whip 2002–03, Government Whip 2003–; PPS to Andrew Smith: as Minister of State, Department for Education and Employment (Minister for Employment, Welfare to Work and Equal Opportunities) 1998–99, as Chief Secretary to the Treasury 1999–02; *Select Committees:* Member, Selection 2001–. *Special Interests:* Investment, NHS, Local and Regional Government, Employment, Regeneration, Health. *Countries of Interest:* Cyprus, Ireland, Israel. Chair: Finchley Constituency Labour Party 1992–96, London North European Constituency 1994–97. School Governor: Lea Valley High School, Chase Side Primary School; Patron: Enfield Lock Village Fair, North London LUPUS, Capel Players; Trustee, Riders For Health; Patron, Nightingale Community Hospice Trust; *Recreations:* Swimming, reading, music, visiting historic buildings. Joan Ryan, MP, House of Commons, London, SW1A 0AA *Tel:* 020 7219 6502 *Fax:* 020 7219 2335. *Constituency:* 180 High Street, Enfield, EN3 4EU *Tel:* 020 8805 9470 *Fax:* 020 8804 0754 *E-mail:* ryanj@parliament.uk.

S

SALMOND, ALEX   Banff and Buchan   *SNP majority 10,503*

Alex Elliot Anderson Salmond. Born 31 December 1954; Son of Robert and the late Mary Salmond; Educated Linlithgow Academy; St Andrew's University (MA economics and history); Married Moira French McGlashan 1981. Assistant agriculture and fisheries economist, Department of Agriculture and Fisheries (Scotland) 1978–80; Assistant economist, Royal Bank of Scotland 1980–82; Oil economist 1982–87; Economist 1984–87. **House of Commons:** Member for Banff and Buchan since June 1987; MSP for Banff and Buchan 1999–2001; Parliamentary Spokesperson for: Constitution, Economy, Trade and Industry, Fishing 1992–97, Constitution; Fishing 1997–, Treasury 2001–; *Special Interests:* Fishing Industry, Agriculture, Energy, Third World, Scottish Economy. *Countries of Interest:* Europe. SNP National Executive: Member 1981–, Vice-chair 1985–87, Deputy Leader 1987, Senior Vice-convener 1988–90, National convener 1990–2000; Leader Westminster Parliamentary Group 2001–. Hon. Vice-President, Scottish Centre for Economic and Social Research; Visiting Professor of Economics, Strathclyde University; *Recreations:* Golf, reading, football. Alex Salmond Esq, MP, House of Commons, London, SW1A 0AA *Tel:* 020 7219 3494. *Constituency:* 17 Maiden Street, Peterhead, Aberdeenshire, AB42 1EE *Tel:* 01779 470444 *Fax:* 01779 474460 *E-mail:* asmp.peterhead@snp.org.

SALTER, MARTIN   Reading West   *Lab majority 8,849*

Martin John Salter. Born 19 April 1954; Son of Raymond and Naomi Salter; Educated Grammar school; Sussex University; Married Natalie O'Toole. Co-ordinator, Reading Centre for the Unemployed 1986–86; Regional manager, Co-operative Home Services housing association 1987–96; Member, TGWU; Former shop steward: TGWU, UCATT. Reading Borough Council: Councillor 1984–96, Chair Leisure Committee 1986–88, Deputy Leader 1987–96. **House of Commons:** Contested Reading East 1987 general election. Member for Reading West since May 1, 1997; Parliamentary Adviser on Shooting and Fishing to Richard Caborn, as Minister of State for Sport 2002–; *Select Committees:* Member, Northern Ireland Affairs 1997–99; Member, Modernisation of the House of Commons 2001–. *Special Interests:* Environment, Local and Regional Government, Housing, Northern Ireland, Human Rights. *Countries of Interest:* India, Pakistan, Ireland. Member, Co-operative Party; Organiser, Network of Labour Councils in South 1987–94; Joint Vice-Chair, South and West Group of Labour MPs 1997–98; Chair, South East Regional Group of Labour MPs 1998–; Representative, South East PLP Campaign Team 1999–. Member: Greenpeace, National Trust, Amnesty International, Angling Conservation Association, Green Lanes Environmental Action Movement; Patron: Cystinosis Foundation, Berkshire Multiple Sclerosis Centre; Secretary, Punjab Human Rights Sub Group; Vice-President, Supporters Trust, Reading Football Club; *Publications:* Various articles in national and local press, Fabian Review and Punch; *Sportsclubs:* Reading and District Angling Association and other Fishing Clubs; *Recreations:* Angling, walking, football. Martin Salter Esq, MP, House of Commons, London, SW1A 0AA *Tel:* 020 7219 2416 *Fax:* 020 7219 2749. *Constituency:* 413 Oxford Road, Reading, Berkshire, RG30 1HA *Tel:* 0118–954 6782 *Fax:* 0118–954 6784 *E-mail:* salterm@parliament.uk.

SANDERS, ADRIAN   Torbay   *LD majority 6,708*

Adrian Mark Sanders. Born 25 April 1959; Son of John Sanders, insurance official, and of Helen, nurse; Educated Torquay Boys' Grammar School; Married Alison Nortcliffe 1992. Parliamentary officer, Liberal Democrat Whips' Office 1989–90; Association of Liberal Democrat Councillors 1990–92; Policy officer, National Council for Voluntary Organisations 1992–93; Worked for Paddy Ashdown, MP and Party Leader 1992–93, organised his tour of Britain 1993; Southern Association of Voluntary Action Groups for Europe 1993–97; Contested Devon and East Plymouth 1994 European Parliament election. Councillor, Torbay Borough Council 1984–86. **House of Commons:** Contested Torbay 1992 general election. Member for Torbay since May 1, 1997; Spokesperson for: Housing 1997–2001, Environment, Transport, the Regions and Social Justice 1999–2001, Transport, Local Government and the Regions (Local Government) 2001–02; Liberal Democrat Spokesperson for Tourism 2002–; Liberal Democrat Whip 1997–2001; *Select Committees:* Member, Joint Committee on Consolidation of Bills Etc 1997–2001. *Special Interests:* Local and Regional Government, Voluntary Sector, Tourism. *Countries of Interest:* USA. Vice-President, National League of Young Liberals 1985; Political secretary, Devon and Cornwall Regional Liberal Party 1983–84; Information officer, Association of Liberal Councillors 1986–89. Member: Paignton Preservation Society, Diabetes UK; Director (non-pecuniary), Southern Association of Voluntary Action Groups; Member: CPA, IPU, British American Parliamentary Group; *Clubs:* Paignton Club; *Recreations:* Football. Adrian Sanders Esq, MP, House of Commons, London, SW1A 0AA *Tel:* 020 7219 6304 *Fax:* 020 7219 3963. *Constituency:* 69 Belgrave Road, Torquay, Devon, TQ2 5HZ *Tel:* 01803 200036 *Fax:* 01803 200031 *E-mail:* asanders@cix.co.uk.

DodOnline
An Electronic Directory without rival . . .

MPs' biographies and photographs available with daily updates *via* the internet

For a *free* trial, call Yasmin Mirza, Aby Farsoun or Michael Mand on 020 7630 7643

SARWAR, MOHAMMED   Glasgow Govan   *Lab majority 6,400*

Mohammad Sarwar. Born 18 August 1952; Son of Mohammad Abdullah and Rushida Abdullah; Educated University of Faisalabad, Pakistan (BA political science); Married Perveen Sarwar 1976 (3 sons 1 daughter). Director, United Wholesale Ltd 1983–97; Member, GMB. Councillor: Glasgow District Council 1992–95, Glasgow City Council 1995–97. **House of Commons:** Member for Glasgow Govan since May 1, 1997; *Select Committees:* Member, Scottish Affairs 1999–. *Special Interests:* Housing, Employment, Economic Policy, Devolution, International Affairs, International Development, British Shipbuilding, Pensioners' Rights, Senior Citizens. *Countries of Interest:* Pakistan, Middle East, Developing World. Member: Scottish Labour Executive 1994–97, Scottish Labour Gala Fund-raising Dinner Organising Committee; Constituency Labour Party: Former Branch Chair, Membership Secretary, Trades Union Liaison Officer; Scottish Regional Group of Labour MPs: Former Vice-chair, Chair 2002–. Scottish Conference, Racism Debate 1994; BBC Scotland, Frontline Scotland 1995; BBC Newsnight 1995; Several appearances Reporting Scotland 1995–96; *Recreations:* Family and friends, charitable work, abseiling. Mohammad Sarwar Esq, MP, House of Commons, London, SW1A 0AA *Tel:* 020 7219 5024/0547 *Fax:* 020 7219 5898. *Constituency:* 247 Paisley Road West, Glasgow, G51 1NE *Tel:* 0141–427 5250 *Fax:* 0141–427 5938 *E-mail:* sarwar@sarwar.org.uk.

SAVIDGE, MALCOLM   Aberdeen North   *Lab majority 4,449*

Malcolm Kemp Savidge. Born 9 May 1946; Son of late David Gordon Madgwick Savidge and of the late Jean Kirkpatrick, née Kemp; Educated Wallington County Grammar School For Boys, Surrey; Aberdeen University (MA 1970); Aberdeen College of Education (Teaching Certificate 1972). Clerk 1970–71; Secondary school teacher Nottingham and Scotland 1970–97: Maths teacher, Kincorth Academy, Aberdeen 1973–97; Educational Institute of Scotland: National Executive 1982–84, National Council 1980–86, 1989–90; Member, Transport and General Workers Union. Aberdeen City Council: Councillor 1980–96, Vice-Chair, Labour Group 1980–88, Libraries Convenor 1984–87, 1988–94, Finance Convenor and Deputy Leader of the Council 1994–96; JP 1984–96. **House of Commons:** Contested Kincardine and Deeside 1991 by-election, 1992 general election. Member for Aberdeen North since May 1, 1997; *Select Committees:* Member, Environmental Audit 1997–. *Special Interests:* International Affairs, Foreign Affairs, Defence, Non-Proliferation and Disarmament, Scotland, Constitution, Northern Ireland, International Development. Member: Scottish Executive of the Labour Party 1993–94, Co-op Party. Governor: Aberdeen College of Education 1980–87, Robert Gordon Institute of Technology 1980–88; Member: Scientists For Global Responsibility, Amnesty International; Royal United Services Institute for Defence Studies; Member, United Nations Association; Hon. Fellow, Robert Gordon University, Aberdeen 1997; FRGU; *Recreations:* Exploring life, spectator sport, crosswords and puzzles, reading, real ale, the Arts, heraldry. Malcolm Savidge Esq, MP, House of Commons, London, SW1A 0AA *Tel:* 020 7219 3570 *Fax:* 020 7219 2398. *Constituency:* Aberdeen Constituency Office, 166 Market Street, Aberdeen, AB11 5PP *Tel:* 01224 252708 *Fax:* 01224 252712 *E-mail:* mksavidge@aol.com.

SAWFORD, PHIL   Kettering   *Lab majority 665*

Phil (Philip) Andrew Sawford. Born 26 June 1950; Son of John William Sawford and Audrey Kathleen Sawford; Educated Kettering Grammar School; Ruskin College, Oxford (Diploma 1982); Leicester University (BA social sciences 1985); Married Rosemary Stokes 1971 (2 sons). Apprentice carpenter/joiner, Moulton; British Steel Corporation, Corby 1977–80; Wellingborough Community Relations Council; Training partnership, Wellingborough 1985–97; Member, GMB. Councillor, Desborough Town Council 1977–97, Chair 1985; Councillor, Kettering Borough Council 1979–83, 1986–97, Leader 1991–97. **House of Commons:** GMB supported candidate. Contested Wellingborough 1992 general election. Member for Kettering since May 1, 1997;

Select Committees: Member: Information 1997–2001, Environmental Audit 2000–01, Environment, Food and Rural Affairs 2001–03. *Special Interests:* Education, Employment, Rural Affairs. *Countries of Interest:* France. Branch secretary, District party chair, political education organiser, Constituency vice-chair, Annual conference delegate and various other capacities 1971–97. Member: CND, Co-op Party, League Against Cruel Sports; Member, Institute of Personnel and Development; MCIPD; *Recreations:* Playing guitar, music, reading. Phil Sawford Esq, MP, House of Commons, London, SW1A 0AA *Tel:* 020 7219 6213 *Fax:* 020 7219 6174. *Constituency:* 1A Headlands, Kettering, Northamptonshire, NN15 7ER *Tel:* 01536 411900 *Fax:* 01536 410742 *E-mail:* philsawfordMP@parliament.uk.

SAYEED, JONATHAN   Mid Bedfordshire   *Con majority 8,066*

Jonathan Sayeed. Born 20 March 1948; Son of late M M Sayeed, chartered electrical engineer, and L S Sayeed; Educated Britannia Royal Naval College, Dartmouth; Royal Naval Engineering College, Manadon, Plymouth; Married Nicola Anne Power 1980 (2 sons). Royal Navy and Royal Naval Reserve 1964–74; Founder director, Wade Emerson & Co Ltd 1974–82; Chair and chief executive, Calmady Insurance Services Ltd 1982–83; Chair, Ranelagh Ltd 1992–96; Non-executive, director Love Lane Investments Ltd (Holding Company) 1992–96; Chair, Training Division Corporate Services Group plc 1996–97. **House of Commons:** Member for Bristol East 1983–92, for Mid Bedfordshire since May 1, 1997; Opposition Spokesperson for Environment, Food and Rural Affairs 2001–03; PPS to Lord Belstead as Paymaster General 1991–92; Member Chairman's Panel 2000–01; *Select Committees:* Member: Broadcasting 1997–2001, Chairmen's Panel 2000–01; Member Chairman's Panel 2003–. President, Bristol East Conservative Association. Vice-President, Primrose Appeal, Bedford Hospital, East Bedfordshire Charity Cricket Shield, Royal British Legion Shefford Branch; *Clubs:* Carlton; *Recreations:* Golf, sailing, tennis, skiing, flying, classical music, books, architecture. Jonathan Sayeed Esq, MP, House of Commons, London, SW1A 0AA *Tel:* 020 7219 2355 *Fax:* 020 7219 1670. *Constituency:* Mid-Bedfordshire Conservative Association, St Michaels Close, High Street, Shefford, Bedfordshire, SG17 5DD *Tel:* 01462 811992 *Fax:* 01462 811010 *E-mail:* wolffea@parliament.uk.

SEDGEMORE, BRIAN   Hackney South and Shoreditch   *Lab majority 15,049*

Brian Sedgemore. Born 17 March 1937; Son of late Charles John Sedgemore; Educated State Schools; Oxford University (MA philosophy, politics and economics 1961, Diploma in Public and Social Administration 1962); Married Audrey Reece 1966 (divorced) (1 son); remarried 2002. RAF national service 1956–58; Principal, Ministry of Housing and Local Government 1962–66; Private secretary to Robert Mellish as Parliamentary Secretary to Minister of Housing 1964–66; Barrister 1966–74; Granada TV 1979–83; Member, NUJ. Councillor, Wandsworth Council 1971–74, Chair, Community Relations 1971–74. **House of Commons:** Member for Luton West February 1974–79 and for Hackney South and Shoreditch since June 1983; PPS to Tony Benn as Secretary of State for Energy 1977–79; *Select Committees:* Member: Treasury and Civil Service 1987–96, Treasury 1996–97, Treasury 1997–2001, Treasury Sub-Committee 1998–2001. *Special Interests:* Economic Policy. *Countries of Interest:* Europe, USA. Member: Fabian Society, Co-operative Party. Member: World Development Movement, London Brook; Chair, East London Committee, Sanctuary Housing Association; Member, Defence of Literature and Arts; Member, Writers Guild of Great Britain; *Publications:* Contributor to *Tribune*; *The How and Why of Socialism*, 1977; *Mr Secretary of State* (fiction), 1979; *The Secret Constitution*, 1980; *Power Failure* (fiction), 1985; *Big Bang 2000*, 1986; *Pitless Pursuit* (fiction), 1994; *Insider's Guide to Parliament*, 1995; *Sportsclubs:* Vice-President, Esher RFC, Stockwood Park RFC; *Recreations:* Music, sleeping on the grass, art, sport. Brian Sedgemore Esq, MP, House of Commons, London, SW1A 0AA *Tel:* 020 7219 3410 *Fax:* 020 7219 5969. *Constituency:* 17 Sutton Square, Urswick Road, Hackney, London, E9 6EQ *Tel:* 020 8533 1305 *Fax:* 020 8533 3392 *E-mail:* sedgemoreb@parliament.uk.

SELOUS, ANDREW   South West Bedfordshire   *Con majority 776*

Andrew Edmund Armstrong Selous. Born 27 April 1962; Son of Commander Gerald Selous, and Miranda Selous, née Casey; Educated London School of Economics (BSc Econ industry and trade 1984); Married Harriet Victoria Marston 1993 (3 daughters). TA officer Honourable Artillery Company, Royal Regiment of Fusiliers 1981–94; Director CNS Electronics Ltd 1988–94; Underwriter Great Lakes Re (UK) plc 1991–. **House of Commons:** Contested Sunderland North 1997 general election. Member for South West Bedfordshire since June 7, 2001; *Select Committees:* Member, Work and Pensions 2001–. *Special Interests:* Trade and Industry, Social Affairs, Families, Defence, Homelessness. Bow Group 1982–; Chairman, Conservative Christian Fellowship 2001–. Supporter and fundraiser 1990–: CARE, Shaftesbury, CRISIS; *Publications: Lessons from the Frontline,* private pamphlet for CCF 1997; ACII 1993; Chartered Insurer 1998; *Clubs:* Leighton Buzzard Conservative, Dunstable Conservative; *Recreations:* Family, walking, tennis, bridge. Andrew Selous Esq, MP, House of Commons, London, SW1A 0AA *Tel:* 020 7219 8134 *Fax:* 020 7219 1741 *Tel (Constituency):* 01582 662 821 *Fax (Constituency):* 01582 476619 *E-mail:* selousa@parliament.uk.

SHAW, JONATHAN   Chatham and Aylesford   *Lab majority 4,340*

Jonathan Rowland Shaw. Born 3 June 1966; Son of Alan James Shaw and Les Percival; Educated Vinters Boys School, Maidstone; West Kent College of FE (Diploma in Social Care); Bromley College (Certificate in Social Services 1990); Married Sue Gurmin 1990 (1 son 1 daughter). Social worker, Kent Council; Member, UNISON. Councillor, Rochester 1993–98, Chair, Community Development Committee 1995. **House of Commons:** Member for Chatham and Aylesford since May 1, 1997; *Select Committees:* Member, Environmental Audit 1997–2001; Member, Education and Skills 2001–. *Special Interests:* Community Development, Economic Development, Housing, Welfare. Member, Fabian Society. *Recreations:* All music especially folk music, reading, walking, family. Jonathan Shaw Esq, MP, House of Commons, London, SW1A 0AA *Tel:* 020 7219 6919 *Fax:* 020 7219 0938. *Constituency:* 411 High Street, Chatham, Kent, ME4 4NM *Tel:* 01634 811573 *Fax:* 01634 811006 *E-mail:* shawj@parliament.uk.

SHEERMAN, BARRY   Huddersfield   *Lab majority 10,046*

Barry John Sheerman. Born 17 August 1940; Son of late Albert William and Florence Sheerman; Educated Hampton Grammar School; Kingston Technical College; London School of Economics (BSc economics 1965); London University (MSc 1967); Married Pamela Elizabeth Brenchley 1965 (1 son 3 daughters). Lecturer, University College of Wales, Swansea 1966–79; Member, AUT, MSF. Member Loughon and Llin Valley Unitary District Council 1972–79. **House of Commons:** Contested Taunton October 1974 general election. Member for Huddersfield East 1979–83, for Huddersfield since June 1983; Opposition Spokesperson for: Employment and Education 1983–88, Home Affairs 1988–92, Disabled People's Rights 1992–94; Shadow Minister for: Education and Employment 1983–87, Home Affairs deputy to Roy Hattersley 1987–92, Disability 1992–94; *Select Committees:* Chair, Education Sub-Committee 1999–2001; Chair (Education), Education and Employment 1999–2001; Member, Employment Sub-Committee 2000–01; Member, Liaison 1999–; Chair, Education and Skills 2001–; Member, Liaison Sub-Committee 2002–. *Special Interests:* Trade, Industry, Finance, Further Education, Education, Economy. *Countries of Interest:* European Union, South America, USA. Member, Co-operative Party; Chair, Labour Forum for Criminal Justice. Chair: Parliamentary Advisory Council on Transport Safety 1981–, Urban Mines 1995–, Networking for Industry 1995–; Governor, LSE 1995–; Chair, Cross-Party Advisory Group on Preparation for EMU 1998–; Vice-Chair, Joint Pre-Legislative Committee Investigating the Financial Services and Markets Bill 1998–; Chair, Interparle (Parliamentary Communication Across Europe) 1997–; World Bank Business Partnership for Development Global Road Safety Partnership (GRSP);

Chair, National Educational Research and Development Trust; Fellow, Industry and Parliament Trust; Director and Trustee, National Children's Centre; *Publications:* Co-author, *Harold Laski: A Life on the Left*, 1993; FRSA, FRGS; *Sportsclubs:* Member, Royal Commonwealth Club; *Recreations:* Walking, biography, films. Barry Sheerman Esq, MP, House of Commons, London, SW1A 0AA *Tel:* 020 7219 5037 *Fax:* 020 7219 2404. *Constituency:* Labour Party, 6 Cross Church Street, Huddersfield, West Yorkshire, HD1 2PT *Tel:* 01484 451382 *Fax:* 01484 451334 *E-mail:* sheermanb@parliament.uk.

SHEPHARD, GILLIAN   South West Norfolk   *Con majority 9,366*

Gillian Patricia Shephard. Born 22 January 1940; Daughter of Reginald and Bertha Watts; Educated North Walsham Girls' High School; St Hilda's College, Oxford (BA modern languages 1961, MA); Married Thomas Shephard 1975 (2 stepsons). Education Officer and Schools Inspector, Norfolk County Council 1963–75; Anglia TV 1975–77. JP 1973– Norfolk County Council: Councillor 1977–89, Deputy Leader 1982–87, Chair: Social Services Committee 1978–83, West Norfolk Health Authority 1981–85, Education Committee 1983–85, Norwich Health Authority 1985–87, DL Norfolk 2003–. **House of Commons:** Member for South West Norfolk since June 1987; PPS to Peter Lilley as Economic Secretary to the Treasury 1988–89; Parliamentary Under-Secretary of State, Department of Social Security 1989–90; Minister of State, HM Treasury 1990–92; Secretary of State for Employment 1992–93; Minister of Agriculture, Fisheries and Food 1993–94; Secretary of State for: Education 1994–95; Education and Employment 1995–97; Shadow Leader of the House of Commons 1997–98; Shadow Chancellor of the Duchy of Lancaster 1997–98; Shadow Secretary of State for the Environment, Transport and the Regions 1998–99; *Select Committees:* Member, Modernisation of the House of Commons 1997–98; Member, Environment, Food and Rural Affairs 2001–. *Special Interests:* The Constitution, Education, Agriculture and Rural Affairs. *Countries of Interest:* France, Latin America. Joint Deputy Chairman Conservative Party 1991–92; Head Conservative Candidates Development Unit 2001–; Deputy Chairman Conservative Party 2002–. Part-time lecturer, Workers' Educational Association and Cambridge Extra Mural Board 1965–87; Government Co-Chairman, Women's National Commission 1990; Member, House of Commons Commission 1997–99; Member, Franco-British Council; *Publications: Reforming Local Government* 1999; *Shephard's Watch* 2000; PC 1992; Hon. Fellow, St Hilda's College, Oxford 1991; *Clubs:* The Norfolk Club; *Recreations:* Music, gardening, France. Rt Hon Gillian Shephard, MP, House of Commons, London, SW1A 0AA *Tel:* 020 7219 2898 *Fax:* 020 7219 1438. *Constituency:* 17A Lynn Road, Downham Market, Norfolk, PE38 4NJ *Tel:* 01366 385072 *E-mail:* foxl@parliament.uk.

SHEPHERD, RICHARD   Aldridge-Brownhills   *Con majority 3,768*

Richard Charles Scrimgeour Shepherd. Born 6 December 1942; Son of late Alfred Shepherd and Davida Sophia, neé Wallace; Educated London School of Economics; John Hopkins School of Advanced International Studies (MSc economics). Director, retail food business in London Underwriter, Lloyd's 1974–94. **House of Commons:** Contested Nottingham East February 1974 general election. Member for Aldridge-Brownhills since May 1979; Personal assistant to Edward Taylor MP (Glasgow Cathcart) October 1974 general election; Introduced four Private Member's Bills: The Crown Immunity Bill 1986, Protection of Official Information Bill 1988, The Referendum Bill 1992, Public Interest Disclosure Bill; *Select Committees:* Member, Public Administration 1997–2000; Member: Modernisation of the House of Commons 1997–, Joint Committee on Human Rights 2001–. Co-Chair, Campaign for Freedom of Information, Member, South East Economic Planning Council 1970–74; The *Spectator's* Award as: Backbencher of the Year 1987, Parliamentarian of the Year 1995; Campaign for Freedom of Information 1988; *Clubs:* Carlton, Beefsteak, Chelsea Arts. Richard Shepherd Esq, MP, House of Commons, London, SW1A 0AA *Tel:* 020 7219 5004. *Constituency:* 82 Walsall Road, Aldridge, Walsall, WS9 0JW *Tel:* 01922 451449 *Fax:* 01922 458078.

Visit the Vacher Dod Website . . .
www.DodOnline.co.uk

SHERIDAN, JIM   West Renfrewshire   *Lab majority 8,575*

James Sheridan. Born 24 November 1952; Educated St Pius Secondary School; Married Jean McDowell 1977 (1 son 1 daughter). Print room assistant Beaverbrook Newspapers 1967–70; Semi-skilled painter Barcley Curle 1970–74; M/C operator Bowater Containers 1974–79; Semi-skilled painter Yarrow Shipbuilders 1982–84; Material handler Pilkington Optronics 1984–99; TGWU 1984–: Convener 1984–99, Stand down official 1998–99. Renfrewshire Council: Councillor 1999–, Vice-convener Social Work, Chair Scrutiny Board. **House of Commons:** Member for West Renfrewshire since June 7, 2001; *Select Committees:* Member: Information 2001–, Broadcasting 2003–. *Special Interests:* Foreign Affairs, Defence, Employment, Welfare, Social Affairs. *Clubs:* Inchinnan Community Association; *Recreations:* Keep fit, golf, football. Jim Sheridan, Esq, MP, House of Commons, London, SW1A 0AA *Tel:* 020 7219 8314. *Constituency:* 21 John Wood Street, Port Glasgow, PA14 5HU *Tel:* 01475 791826 *Fax:* 01475 791829.

SHIPLEY, DEBRA   Stourbridge   *Lab majority 3,812*

Debra Shipley. Born 22 June 1957; Educated Kidderminster High School; Kidderminster College; Oxford Polytechnic (BA history of art and anthropology 1980); London University (MA history of art and architecture 1990). Writer and Lecturer; Member, GMB. **House of Commons:** Member for Stourbridge since May 1, 1997; Initiated Private Member's Bill for Protection of Children Act 1999; *Select Committees:* Member, Social Security 1999; Member, Culture, Media and Sport 2001–. *Special Interests:* Children, elderly, architecture. *Countries of Interest:* Mongolia, Portugal. Former Board Member, Opportunities For Volunteering; Member, Amnesty; Patron, Headway Blackcountry; Member, Co-op; Member; Western European Union Defence Committee 1998–99, Council of Europe 1998–99; *Publications:* 17 books; *Recreations:* Walking, cooking/eating. Debra Shipley, MP, House of Commons, London, SW1A 0AA *Tel:* 020 7219 3053 *Tel (Constituency):* 01384 374356.

SHORT, CLARE   Birmingham Ladywood   *Lab majority 18,143*

Clare Short. Born 15 February 1946; Daughter of late Frank and Joan Short; Educated St Francis JI School, Handsworth; St Paul's Grammar, Birmingham; Keele University; Leeds University (BA political science 1968); Married Andrew Moss 1964 (divorced 1971) (1 son); married Alex Lyon (MP 1966–83) 1982 (died 1993). Civil servant, Home Office 1970–75; Director: AFFOR – Community organisation concerned with race and urban deprivation in Handsworth 1976–77, Youth Aid 1979–83, Unemployment unit 1981–83; Member, UNISON. **House of Commons:** Member for Birmingham Ladywood since June 1983; Spokesperson for Employment 1985–88; Opposition Spokesperson for Social Security 1989–91; Opposition Frontbench Spokesperson for: Environmental Protection 1992–93, Women 1993–95; Principal Opposition Spokesperson for Transport 1995–96; Shadow Minister for Overseas Development 1996–97; Vice-Chair, Parliamentary Labour Party 1997–99; Secretary of State for International Development 1997–2003; *Special Interests:* Unemployment, Race Relations, Immigration, Low Pay, Home Affairs, Northern Ireland, Women. Member, Labour Party National Executive Committee 1988–98. Chair, Human Rights Committee of Socialist International 1996–98; PC 1997; *Recreations:* Swimming, family, friends. Rt Hon Clare Short, MP, House of Commons, London, SW1A 0AA *Tel: Fax:* 020 7219 2586.

Visit the Vacher Dod Website . . .
www.DodOnline.co.uk

SIMMONDS, MARK   Boston and Skegness   *Con majority 515*

Mark Jonathan Mortlock Simmonds. Born 12 April 1964; Son of Neil Mortlock Simmonds, teacher, and Mary Griffith Simmonds, née Morgan, teacher; Educated Worksop College, Nottinghamshire; Trent Polytechnic (BSc urban estate surveying 1986); Married Lizbeth Josefina Hanomancin-Garcia 1994 (2 daughters, 1 son). Surveyor Savills 1986–88; Partner Strutt and Parker 1988–96; Director Hillier Parker 1997–99; Chairman Mortlock Simmonds Brown 1999–. London Borough of Wandsworth 1990–94: Councillor, Chairman: Property Committee 1991–92, Housing Committee 1992–94. **House of Commons:** Contested Ashfield 1997 general election. Member for Boston and Skegness since June 7, 2001; *Select Committees:* Member, Environmental Audit 2001–02; Member, Education and Skills 2001–. *Special Interests:* Economy, Education, Agriculture, Foreign Affairs. *Countries of Interest:* Latin America. Member Royal Institution of Chartered Surveyors 1987; *Clubs:* Naval and Military; *Sportsclubs:* Honky Tonk Cricket; *Recreations:* Reading, history, rugby, tennis, family. Mark Simmonds Esq, MP, House of Commons, London, SW1A 0AA *Tel:* 020 7219 6254 *Fax:* 020 7219 1746. *Constituency:* The Conservative Association, Main Ridge West, Boston, Lincolnshire, PE21 6QQ *Tel:* 01205 751414 *Fax:* 01205 751414 *E-mail:* mark.simmondsmp@virgin.net.

SIMON, SION   Birmingham Erdington   *Lab majority 9,962*

Siôn Llewelyn Simon. Born 23 December 1968; Son of Jeffrey Simon and Anne Loverini Owen, née Jones; Educated Handsworth Grammar School, Birmingham; Magdalen College, Oxford (BA philosophy, politics and economics 1990); Divorced (2 daughters 1 son). Research assistant George Robertson MP 1990–93; Senior manager Guinness PLC 1993–95; Freelance 1995–97; Labour Party general election HQ 1997; Columnist *Daily Telegraph* 1997–Oct 2001; Associate editor *The Spectator* 1997–; Columnist: *Daily Express* 1998, *News of the World* 2000–; TGWU 1990–96, AEEU 1997–, NUJ 1997–. **House of Commons:** Member for Birmingham Erdington since June 7, 2001; *Select Committees:* Member, Public Accounts 2003–. *Special Interests:* Social Democracy, Urban Regeneration, Crime, European Affairs. *Countries of Interest:* USA, Italy, France, Japan, Australia, Spain. Action for Victims of Medical Accidents 1997–: Board member, Trustee; Founder board secretary Choroideremia Research Foundation Inc 1999. Siôn Simon Esq, MP, House of Commons, London, SW1A 0AA *Tel:* 020 7219 8140 *Fax:* 020 7219 5856. *Constituency:* 50a Reservoir Road, Erdington, Birmingham, B23 6DG *Tel:* 0121 373 1147 *Fax:* 0121 382 6347 *E-mail:* simons@parliament.uk.

SIMPSON, ALAN   Nottingham South   *Lab majority 9,989*

Alan Simpson. Born 20 September 1948; Son of Reg and Marjorie Simpson; Educated Bootle Grammar School; Nottingham Trent Polytechnic (BSc economics 1971); Divorced (2 sons 1 daughter); married 2001 (1 stepdaughter). President, Students' Union, Nottingham Polytechnic 1969–70; Assistant General Secretary, Nottingham Council of Voluntary Service 1970–74; set up first pilot project for the national non-custodial treatment of offenders programme 1971–74; Community worker, Inner city anti-vandalism project 1974–78; Research Officer, Nottingham Racial Equality Council 1979–92; Member, UNISON. **House of Commons:** Contested Nottingham South in 1987 general election. Member for Nottingham South since April 9, 1992; Adviser on Tennis to Richard Caborn, as Minister of State for Sport 2002–; *Select Committees:* Member, Environment, Food and Rural Affairs 2003–. *Special Interests:* Environment, Economics, Disarmament, Food Safety, GM Issues, Fuel Poverty. Board Member, Tribune Newspaper 1996–; Vice-chair Socialist Campaign of Labour MPs: Secretary, 1995–2001, Treasurer SCG 2001–02; Chair, Labour Against the War. Member: CND; *Publications:* Author of books on: common security, community development, housing, employment, policing policies, Europe, racism; 1999 Green Ribbon Award, Environment Back Bencher of the Year; *Recreations:* Tennis, cricket, football (also a lifelong supporter of Everton FC), vegetarian cooking, music (eclectic taste), reading. Alan Simpson Esq, MP, House of Commons, London, SW1A 0AA *Tel:* 020 7219 4534. *Constituency:* Vernon House, 18 Friar Lane, Nottingham, NG1 6DQ *Tel:* 0115–956 0460 *Fax:* 0115–956 0445 *E-mail:* simpsona@parliament.uk.

SIMPSON, KEITH   Mid Norfolk   *Con majority 4,562*

Keith Robert Simpson. Born 29 March 1949; Son of Harry Simpson and Jean Betty, née Day; Educated Thorpe Grammar School, Norfolk; Hull University (BA history 1970); King's College, University of London (PGCE 1965); Married Pepita Hollingsworth 1984 (1 son). London University OTC 1970–72; Honorary Colonel Royal Military Police T.A. Senior lecturer in war studies, RMA Sandhurst 1973–86; Head of foreign affairs and defence section, Conservative Research Department 1987–88; Special adviser to George Younger and Tom King as Secretaries of State for Defence 1988–90; Director, Cranfield Security Studies Institute, Cranfield University 1991–97. **House of Commons:** Contested Plymouth Devonport 1992 general election. Member for Mid Norfolk since May 1, 1997; Opposition Spokesperson for: Defence 1998–99, Environment, Food and Rural Affairs 2001–02; Opposition Whip 1999–2001: Home Office, Culture, Media and Sport: Wales 1999, Treasury, Health 1999–2000, Home Office, International Development 2000, Health, Treasury 2000–01; Shadow Minister for Defence 2002–; *Select Committees:* Member: Catering 1998, Environment, Food and Rural Affairs 2001–02. *Special Interests:* Foreign Affairs, Defence, Education, Farming, Countryside. *Countries of Interest:* USA, Germany, France, Poland. National Vice-chair, Federation of Conservative Students 1971–72. Member: International Institute for Strategic Studies, Royal United Services Institute for Defence Studies, British Field Sports Society, British Commission for Military History; Council Member, SSAFA 1997–; Member, European Standing Committee A 1998; *Publications: The Old Contemptibles,* 1981; Joint Editor *A Nations in Arms,* 1985; *History of the German Army,* 1985; Editor *The War the Infantry Knew 1914–1919,* 1986; *Clubs:* Norfolk; *Recreations:* Walking dogs, reading, visiting restaurants, cinema, collecting and consuming malt whiskies, observing ambitious people. Keith Simpson Esq, MP, House of Commons, London, SW1A 0AA *Tel:* 020 7219 4053 *Fax:* 020 7219 0975. *Constituency:* Mid Norfolk Conservative Association, The Stable, Church Farm, Attlebridge, Norwich, Norfolk NR9 5ST *Tel:* 01603 865763 *Fax:* 01603 865762 *E-mail:* keithsimpsonmp@parliament.uk.

SINGH, MARSHA   Bradford West   *Lab majority 4,165*

Marsha Singh. Born 11 October 1954; Son of Harbans Singh and late Kartar Kaur; Educated Belle Vue Boys Upper School; Loughborough University (BA languages, politics and economics of modern Europe 1976); Married Sital Kaur 1971 (widowed 2001) (1 son 1 daughter). Senior development manager, Bradford Community Health 1990–97; Member, UNISON. **House of Commons:** Member for Bradford West since May 1, 1997; *Select Committees:* Member, Home Affairs 1997–. *Special Interests:* European Union, Health, Education, Small Businesses. Chair: Bradford West Labour Party 1986–91, 1996–97, District Labour Party 1992. *Recreations:* Chess, bridge, reading. Marsha Singh Esq, MP, House of Commons, London, SW1A 0AA *Tel:* 020 7219 4625 *Fax:* 020 7219 0965. *Constituency:* Bradford West Constituency Office, 2nd Floor, 76 Kirkgate, Bradford, West Yorkshire, BD1 1SZ *Tel:* 01274 402220.

SKINNER, DENNIS   Bolsover   *Lab majority 18,777*

Dennis Skinner. Born 11 February 1932; Son of Edward Skinner; Educated Tupton Hall Grammar School; Ruskin College, Oxford; Married Mary Parker 1960 (1 son 2 daughters). Miner 1949–70; President, Derbyshire Miners 1966–70. Clay Cross UDC 1960–70; County Councillor, Derbyshire 1964–70; Former President, Derbyshire UDC Association. **House of Commons:** Member for Bolsover since 1970; *Special Interests:* Inland Waterways, Energy, Economic Policy, Environment, Anti-Common Market, Third World. President, North East Derbyshire Constituency Labour Party 1968–71; Member, Labour Party National Executive Committee 1978–92, 1994–98, 1999–; Vice-Chair, Labour Party 1987–88, Chair 1988–89. Former Member, Scarsdale Valuation Panel; *Recreations:* Cycling, tennis, athletics (watching). Dennis Skinner Esq, MP, House of Commons, London, SW1A 0AA *Tel:* 020 7219 5107 *Fax:* 020 7219 0028. *Constituency:* 1 Elmhurst Close, South Normanton, Derbyshire *Tel:* 01773 581027.

SMITH, ANDREW   Oxford East   Lab majority 10,344

Andrew David Smith. Born 1 February 1951; Son of late David E. C. Smith and Georgina H. J. Smith; Educated Reading Grammar School; St John's College, Oxford (BA 1972, BPhil economics, politics, sociology 1974); Married Valerie Lambert 1976 (1 son). Member relations officer, Oxford and Swindon Co-op Society 1979–87; Member, Union Shop, Distributive and Allied Workers. Oxford City Councillor 1976–87; Chairman: Recreation and Amenities Committee 1980–83, Planning Committee 1985–87. **House of Commons:** Contested Oxford East 1983. Member for Oxford East since June 1987; Opposition Spokesman on Education 1988–92; Opposition Frontbench Spokesman on Treasury and Economic Affairs 1992–96; Shadow Chief Secretary to the Treasury 1994–96; Shadow Secretary of State for Transport 1996–97; Minister of State, Department for Education and Employment (Minister for Employment, Welfare to Work and Equal Opportunities) 1997–99; Chief Secretary to the Treasury 1999–2002; Secretary of State for Work and Pensions 2002–; *Select Committees:* Member, Health and Social Services 1987–88. *Special Interests:* Car Industry, Education, Retail Industry, Transport, Employment. *Countries of Interest:* Europe. Member, Labour Party Economy Policy Commission; Member Parliamentary Labour Party Parliamentary Committee 1999–2002. Chair of governors, Oxford Polytechnic/Oxford Brookes University 1987–93; PC 1997; Hon. Doctorate, Oxford Brookes University; *Clubs:* Blackbird Leys Community Association; *Sportsclubs:* President Blackbird Leys Youth Football Club. Rt Hon Andrew Smith, MP, House of Commons, London, SW1A 0AA *Tel:* 020 7219 4512 *Fax:* 020 7219 2965. *Constituency:* 21 Templars Square, Cowley, Oxford, OX4 3UZ *Tel:* 01865 772893 *Fax:* 01865 772916 *E-mail:* andrewsmith.mp@virgin.net.

SMITH, ANGELA   Basildon   Lab majority 7,738

Angela Evans Smith. Born 7 January 1959; Daughter of Patrick Evans, factory worker, and Emily, née Russell, supervisor of church pre-school; Educated Chalvedon Comprehensive, Basildon; Leicester Polytechnic (BA public administration); Married Nigel Smith 1978. Trainee accountant, London Borough of Newham 1982–83; League Against Cruel Sports, finally head of political and public relations 1983–95; Research assistant to Alun Michael MP 1995–97; Member: TGWU, AEEU. Essex County Council: Councillor 1989–97, Chief Whip 1993–96, Lead Spokesperson, Fire and Public Protection Committee 1993–96. **House of Commons:** Contested Southend West 1987 general election. Member for Basildon since May 1, 1997; Assistant Government Whip 2001–; Joint PPS to Paul Boateng as Minister of State, Home Office 1999–2001; Parliamentary Under-Secretary of State, Northern Ireland Office 2002–; *Special Interests:* Home Affairs, Animal Welfare, International Development, Employment. *Countries of Interest:* Cuba, Germany, USA. Voluntary Representative for Traidcraft; Patron: Basildon Home Start, Basildon Co-op Development Agency, Basildon Women's Refuge, Vange United Youth FC, Basildon Age Concern, Burned Children's Club. Angela Smith, MP, House of Commons, London, SW1A 0AA *Tel:* 020 7219 6273 *Fax:* 020 7219 0926. *Constituency:* Cornwallis House, Howard Chase, Basildon, Essex, SS14 3BB *Tel:* 01268 284830 *Fax:* 01268 284831 *E-mail:* flackk@parliament.uk.

SMITH, CHRIS   Islington South and Finsbury   Lab majority 7,280

Chris (Christopher) Robert Smith. Born 24 July 1951; Son of Colin Smith, civil servant and Gladys Smith, teacher; Educated George Watson's College, Edinburgh; Pembroke College, Cambridge (BA English 1972, PhD 1979) (President, Cambridge Union 1972); Harvard University (Kennedy Scholar 1975–76). The Housing Corporation 1976–77, Shaftesbury Society Housing Association 1977–80, Society for Co-operative Dwellings 1980–83; Branch Secretary, ASTMS 1977–80, Branch Chairman 1980–83. Islington Borough Council: Councillor 1978–83, Chief Whip 1978–79, Chair of Housing 1981–83. **House of Commons:** Contested Epsom and Ewell 1979 general election. Member for Islington South and Finsbury since June 1983; London Labour Whip 1986–87; Shadow Treasury Minister 1987–92; Shadow Secretary of State for:

Environmental Protection 1992–94, National Heritage 1994–95, Social Security 1995–96, Health 1996–97; Sponsored Environment and Safety Information Act 1988 (Private Member's Bill); Secretary of State: for National Heritage May-July 1997, for Culture, Media and Sport July 1997–2001; Chair, Millennium Commission 1997–2001; *Select Committees:* Member, Environment 1983–86. *Special Interests:* Culture, Media, Sport, Housing, Local and Regional Government, Foreign Affairs, Environment, Civil Liberties, Criminal Justice, Economic Policy, Social Security, Health. *Countries of Interest:* Cyprus, Europe, Hong Kong, USA, Australia, New Zealand, China. Vice-president, Christian Socialist Movement 1987–; Secretary, Tribune Group 1984–88, Chair 1988–89; Chair, Labour Campaign for Criminal Justice 1985–88; Chair, Board of *Tribune* newspaper 1990–93; Member, Executive of Fabian Society 1990–97, Vice-Chair 1995–96, Chair 1996–97; President, SERA 1992–; Chair, Board of New Century Magazine 1993–96. Member: Shelter Board 1986–92, Executive of National Council for Civil Liberties 1986–88; Board Member Sadlers Wells Theatre 1986–92, Governor 1992–97; Vice-President Wildlife Link 1986–90; Executive Committee National Trust 1994–96; Trustee: John Muir Trust 1992–97, The Wordsworth Trust 2001–, Chairman 2002–; Board Member: Royal National Theatre 2001–, Donmar Warehouse 2001–, Terrence Higgins Trust 2001–, The Poetry Archive 2002–; Co-opted Member Council for National Parks 1980–89; Honorary Fellow of Royal Institute of British Architects 2000–; Member Committee on Standards in Public Life 2001–; Senior Adviser The Walt Disney Company 2001–; Member, Review Committee of Privy Counsellors of the Anti-terrorism, Crime and Security Act 2002–; Chairman Classic FM Consumer Panel 2001–; Senior Associate Judge Institute, Cambridge University 2001–; Visiting Professor, The London Institute 2002–; Director, Clore Programme for Cultural Leadership 2003–; Trustee, John Muir Trust 1991–97; Executive Committee, National Trust 1995–97; Trustee, Wordsworth Trust 2001–; *Publications: National Parks,* Fabian Society 1977; *New Questions for Socialism,* Fabian Society 1996; *Creative Britain,* Faber 1998; PC 1997; Hon Fellow, Royal Institute of British Architects 2000; *Recreations:* Mountaineering, literature, theatre, music, art. Rt Hon Chris Smith, MP, House of Commons, London, SW1A 0AA *Tel:* 020 7219 5119 *Fax:* 020 7219 5820. *Constituency:* 65 Barnsbury Street, London, N1 1EJ *Tel:* 020 7607 8373 *Fax:* 020 7607 8299 *E-mail:* barans@parliament.uk.

SMITH, GERALDINE   Morecambe and Lunesdale   *Lab majority 5,092*

Geraldine Smith. Born 29 August 1961; Daughter of John and Ann Smith; Educated Morecambe High School; Lancaster and Morecambe College (Diploma business studies 1978); Single. Postal officer 1980–97; Member, Communication Workers Union 1980–: positions including area representative. Councillor, Lancaster City Council 1991–97; Chair: Coastal Protection, Economic Development and Tourism Policy. **House of Commons:** Member for Morecambe and Lunesdale since May 1, 1997; *Select Committees:* Member, Deregulation 1997–99; Member, Science and Technology 2001–. *Special Interests:* Economic Regeneration, Tourism, Public/Private Partnerships, Small Businesses. *Countries of Interest:* Ireland, Eastern Europe. Various positions including constituency secretary; North West Regional Group of Labour MPs: Former Vice-chair, Chair 2002–. Member, European Standing Committee C 1999–2002; UK substitute delegate, Council of Europe 1999–; Delegate to the Council of Europe; *Recreations:* Playing chess, walking and campaigning. Geraldine Smith, MP, House of Commons, London, SW1A 0AA *Tel:* 020 7219 5816 *Fax:* 020 7219 0977. *Constituency:* Morecambe and Lunesdale CLP, Labour Party Offices, 26–28 Victoria Street, Morecambe, Lancashire, LA4 4AJ *Tel:* 01524 411367 *Fax:* 01524 411369 *E-mail:* smithg@parliament.uk.

SMITH, JACQUI   Redditch   *Lab majority 2,484*

Jacqui (Jacqueline) Smith. Born 3 November 1962; Daughter of Michael L. Smith, headteacher, and Jill Smith, retired teacher; Educated Dyson Perrins High School, Malvern, Worcs; Hertford College, Oxford University (BA philosophy, politics and economics 1984); Worcester College of Higher Education (PGCE 1986); Married Richard Timney 1987 (2 sons). Economics teacher, Arrow Vale High School, Redditch 1986–88; Teacher, Worcester Sixth Form College 1988–90; Head of economics, GNVQ co-ordinator, Haybridge High School, Hagley 1990–97; Member: NUT, GMB. Councillor, Redditch Borough Council 1991–97. **House of Commons:** Member for Redditch since May 1, 1997; Parliamentary Under-Secretary of State, Department for

Education and Employment 1999–2001; Minister of State for: Community, Department of Health 2001–03, Minister of State for Industry and the Regions and Deputy Minister for Women and Equality, Department of Trade and Industry 2003–; *Select Committees:* Member: Treasury 1998–99, Treasury Sub-Committee 1998–99. *Special Interests:* Industry, Education and Training, Economic Policy, Social Services. Member: Amnesty International, ALTSA; Member, British East-West Centre; Member, Worcester Nature Conservation Trust; PC 2003; *Recreations:* Family, football, theatre. Rt Hon Jacqui Smith, MP, House of Commons, London, SW1A 0AA *Tel:* 020 7219 5190. *Constituency:* Unit 16, 1st Floor, Greenlands Business Centre, Studley Road, Redditch, B98 7HD *Tel:* 01527 523355 *Fax:* 01527 523355 *E-mail:* smithjj@parliament.uk.

SMITH, JOHN   Vale of Glamorgan   *Lab majority 4,700*

John William Patrick Smith. Born 17 March 1951; Son of John and Margaret Smith; Educated Penarth Grammar School; Gwent College of Higher Education; University College of Wales, Cardiff (BSc economics); Married Kathleen Mulvaney 1971 (2 sons 1 daughter). RAF 1967–71; Carpenter and joiner, Vale Borough Council 1971–76; Mature student 1976–81; University tutor (UCC) 1981–85; Senior lecturer in business studies 1985–89; Campaign manager, Gwent Image Partnership, chief executive 1992–; Member: MSF 1970–, TASS, NATFHE, AUT, NUPE, UCATT. Vale of Glamorgan Borough Council: Councillor 1979–91, Opposition Finance and Housing Spokesperson 1979–87, Labour Group Secretary 1981–83, Labour Group Leader 1983–88. **House of Commons:** Contested Vale of Glamorgan 1987 general election. Member for Vale of Glamorgan 1989–92 and since May 1, 1997; PPS to Roy Hattersley as Deputy Leader of Labour Party 1989–92; Contributed to: Trade Union Bill, Armed Forces Bill, Barry Old Harbour Bill, Seat Belt Regulation; PPS to Dr John Reid: as Minister of State, Ministry of Defence (Minister for the Armed Forces) 1997–98, Department of the Environment, Transport and the Regions (Minister of Transport) 1998–99; *Select Committees:* Member: Welsh Affairs 1990–92, Welsh Affairs 2000–01. *Special Interests:* Economic Development, Industrial Relations, Transport Safety, Defence, Deep Vein Thrombosis in Air Travellers. Chair, Young Socialists 1967–94; Member: Vale of Glamorgan CLP 1972–, Welsh Executive 1985–89, 1996–; Chair, Wales Labour Party 1988–89; Member, National Policy Forum 1996; Former Vice-chair, Welsh Parliamentary Labour Party. Hon. Vice-President: Imperial Cancer Foundation, Rail Users Federation, Local Arthritis Care; President, Local Leisure and Community Centre; Team Manager, Valley and Vale Arts; Advisory Council on Transport Safety 1989–92; Member: Commonwealth Parliamentary Association (CPA), UK Delegation to North Atlantic Assembly; *Recreations:* Reading, walking, camping, boating. John Smith Esq, MP, House of Commons, London, SW1A 0AA *Tel:* 020 7219 3589. *Constituency:* 115 High Street, Barry *Tel:* 01446 743769 *Fax:* 01446 743769 *E-mail:* smithj@parliament.uk.

SMITH, LLEWELLYN   Blaenau Gwent   *Lab majority 19,313*

Llewellyn Thomas Smith. Born 16 April 1944; Son of late Ernest Smith, and of Cissie Smith; Educated Greenfields Secondary Modern School; Colleg Harlech; Cardiff University (BSc, MSc); Married December 13, 1969, Pamela Williams (2 sons 1 daughter). Labourer; computer operator; tutor-organiser, Worker's Educational Association; MEP for South East Wales 1984–94; Member, TGWU. **House of Commons:** Member for Blaenau Gwent since April 9, 1992. *Countries of Interest:* Cuba. Member: CND, Socialist Education Association; Vice-President, Anti-Apartheid Wales; *Publications:* Co-author: *Bombing Ahead With Disarmament*, 1990, *The Politics of Poverty*, 1993. Llewellyn Smith Esq, MP, House of Commons, London, SW1A 0AA *Tel:* 020 7219 6433. *Constituency:* 23 Beaufort Street, Brynmawr, Gwent, NP3 4AQ *Tel:* 01495 313345.

Visit the Vacher Dod Website . . .
www.DodOnline.co.uk

SMITH, ROBERT   West Aberdeenshire and Kincardine   *LD majority 4,821*

Robert Smith. Born 15 April 1958; Son of late Sir (William) Gordon Smith, Bt, VRD, and of Diana Lady Smith; Educated Merchant Taylors' School, Northwood; Aberdeen University (BSc); Married Fiona Anne Cormack MD 1993 (3 daughters). Family estate manager until 1997. Councillor, Aberdeenshire Council 1995–97; JP 1997. **House of Commons:** Contested (SDP/Liberal Alliance) Aberdeen North 1987 general election. Member for West Aberdeenshire and Kincardine since May 1, 1997; Spokesperson for Scotland 1999–2001; Liberal Democrat Whip 1999–2001, Deputy Chief Whip 2001–; *Select Committees:* Member, Scottish Affairs 1999–2001; Member: Procedure 2001–, Standing Orders 2001–, Trade and Industry 2001–, Unopposed Bills (Panel) 2001–, Accommodation and Works 2003–. *Special Interests:* Electoral Reform, Offshore Oil and Gas Industry, Rural Affairs. General Council Assessor, Aberdeen University 1994–98; Director, Grampian Transport Museum 1995–97; Vice-convener, Grampian Joint Police Board 1995–97; Member, Electoral Reform Society; Member, European Standing Committee A 2000–01; *Clubs:* Royal Yacht Squadron, Royal Thames Yacht; *Recreations:* Hill-walking, sailing. Sir Robert Smith, Bt, MP, House of Commons, London, SW1A 0AA *Tel:* 020 7219 3531 *Fax:* 020 7219 4526. *Constituency:* 6 Dee Street, Banchory, Kincardineshire, AB31 5ST *Tel:* 01330 820330 *Fax:* 01330 820338 *E-mail:* bobsmith@cix.co.uk.

SMYTH, MARTIN   Belfast South   *UUP majority 5,399*

(William) Martin Smyth. Born 15 June 1931; Son of late James Smyth, JP; Educated Methodist College, Belfast; Magee University College, Londonderry; Trinity College, Dublin (BA general arts 1953, BD 1961); Presbyterian College, Dublin 1955; San Francisco Theological Seminary 1979–80; Married Kathleen Johnston 1957 (2 daughters and 1 daughter deceased). Assistant Minister, Finaghy Presbyterian Church, Belfast 1953–57; Minister: Raffrey Church 1957–63, Alexandra Presbyterian Church 1963–82. **House of Commons:** Member for Belfast South since by-election March 1982; Spokesperson for: Health and Social Services 1992–97, Health and Family Policy 1997–2000, Health, Social Security, Youth and Women's Issues 2000–01, Foreign and Commonwealth Affairs 2001–, International Development 2001–, Health 2001–; Chief Whip 1996–2000; Member, Northern Ireland Constitutional Convention 1975; Northern Ireland Assembly: Member for Belfast South 1982–86; Chair, Health and Social Services Committee 1983–84, Finance and Personnel Committee 1984–86; Sponsored Disabled Persons (Northern Ireland) Act, 1989 (Private Member's Bill); Graduate, Police Services Parliamentary Scheme 1999; Contested Ulster Unionist Party Leadership March 2000; *Select Committees:* Member, Health 1990–97; Member, Northern Ireland Affairs 2001–. *Special Interests:* World Protestantism, Health, Social Services, Education, Foreign Affairs, Human Rights, Transport. *Countries of Interest:* Brazil, Canada, Malawi, Morocco, New Zealand, Taiwan, USA, India, Australia. Chair, Ulster Unionist Executive Committee 1972–74; Ulster Unionist Council: Vice-President 1974–2000, Honorary Secretary 2000–01, President 2001–. Grand Master: Grand Orange Lodge of Ireland 1972–96, Grand Orange Council of the World 1973–82; Chairman, Belfast No. 1 School Management Committee 1972–80; President, Orange Council of the World 1985–88; Member European Standing Committee C 2001–; Member, Executive Committee: IPU (UK Branch) 1985–92, 1994–, Commonwealth Parliamentary Association (CPA) UK Branch 1989–; Fellow, Industry and Parliament Trust 1987; *Publications:* Editor *Faith For Today*, 1961; Pamphlets: *In Defence of Ulster*; *The Battle for Northern Ireland*; *A Federated People*; *Till Death Us Do Part*; *Why Presbyterian?*; *Recreations:* Travel, photography, reading. Rev Martin Smyth, MP, House of Commons, London, SW1A 0AA *Tel:* 020 7219 4098 *Fax:* 020 7219 2347. *Constituency:* 117 Cregagh Road, Belfast, BT6 0LA *Tel:* 028 9045 7009 *Fax:* 028 9045 0837 *E-mail:* mckeem@parliament.uk.

Visit the Vacher Dod Website . . .
www.DodOnline.co.uk

SOAMES, NICHOLAS   Mid Sussex   *Con majority 6,898*

Nicholas Soames. Born 12 February 1948; Son of late Baron and Lady Soames; Educated Eton College; Married Catherine Weatherall 1981 (divorced 1988) (1 son), married Serena Smith 1993 (1 daughter). Lieutenant, 11th Hussars 1967–72; Equerry to Prince of Wales 1970–72; Stockbroker 1972–74; PA to: Sir James Goldsmith 1974–76, US Senator Mark Hatfield 1976–78; Assistant director, Sedgwick Group 1979–81. **House of Commons:** Contested Dumbartonshire Central 1979 general election. Member for Crawley 1983–97, and for Mid Sussex since May 1, 1997; PPS: to John Gummer as Minister of State for Employment and Chairman of the Conservative Party 1984–86; to Nicholas Ridley as Secretary of State for the Environment 1987–89; Joint Parliamentary Secretary, Ministry of Agriculture, Fisheries and Food 1992–94; Minister of State for the Armed Forces, Ministry of Defence 1994–97; *Select Committees:* Member, Public Administration 1999; Member, Joint Committee on Consolidation of Bills Etc 2001–. *Special Interests:* Defence, Foreign Affairs, Trade and Industry, Aerospace, Aviation, Agriculture and Countryside matters. *Clubs:* White's, Turf, Pratt's; *Recreations:* Country pursuits. Hon Nicholas Soames, MP, House of Commons, London, SW1A 0AA *Tel:* 020 7219 4184 *Fax:* 020 7219 2998. *Constituency:* 5 Hazelgrove Road, Haywards Heath, West Sussex, RH16 3PH *Tel:* 01444 452590 *Fax:* 01444 415766 *E-mail:* soamesn@parliament.uk.

SOLEY, CLIVE   Ealing, Acton and Shepherd's Bush   *Lab majority 10,789*

Clive Stafford Soley. Born 7 May 1939; Educated Downshall Secondary Modern, Ilford; Newbattle Abbey Adult Education College; Strathclyde University (BA politics and psychology 1968); Southampton University (Diploma applied social studies 1970); Living with partner (1 son 1 daughter). RAF national service 1959–61; British Council, London and Madrid 1968–69; Probation officer and senior probation officer, Inner London Probation Service 1970–79. **House of Commons:** Member for Hammersmith North 1979–83, for Hammersmith 1983–97, and for Ealing, Acton and Shepherds Bush since May 1, 1997; Opposition Spokesperson on: Northern Ireland 1982–85, Home Affairs 1985–87, Housing and Local Government 1987–89, Housing and Planning 1989–92; Member Joint Committee on House of Lords Reform 2002–; *Select Committees:* Member, Northern Ireland Affairs 1994–97; Chair, Northern Ireland Affairs 1995–97; Member, Modernisation of the House of Commons 1997–2001; Member, Joint Committee on House of Lords Reform 2002–; Member, Select Committee on Lord Chancellor's Department 2003–. *Special Interests:* Environment, Housing, Penal Affairs and Policy, Civil Liberties, Northern Ireland, Foreign Policy. *Countries of Interest:* China, South East Asia. Chair: Labour Campaign for Criminal Justice 1983–97, Parliamentary Labour Party 1997–2001; Member, Labour Party National Executive Committee 1998–2001; Chair, London Selection Board for Labour candidate for Mayor 1999. Chair, Alcohol Education Centre –1984; Member of several House of Commons Committees including: Prevention of Terrorism Bill 1983–84, Criminal Justice Bill 1987–99, Housing Bill 1987–88, Local Government and Housing Bill 1988–89, Planning and Compensation Bill 1990–91, Freedom and Responsibility of the Press 1992–93; International Observer at: first National Elections in Mongolia 1990, Peruvian General Election 1995; Fellow, Industry and Parliament Trust; *Publications:* Chapter: The Politics of the Family in *Rewriting the Sexual Contract*; co-author, *Regulating the Press* 2000; *Recreations:* Walking, photography, scuba diving. Clive Soley Esq, MP, House of Commons, London, SW1A 0AA *Tel:* 020 7219 5490 *Fax:* 020 7219 5974. *Constituency:* Ruskin Hall, 16 Church Road, London, W3 8PP *Tel:* 020 8992 5614 *Fax:* 020 8752 1200 *E-mail:* macleodn@parliament.uk.

DodOnline
An Electronic Directory without rival ...

MPs' biographies and photographs available with daily updates *via* the internet

For a *free* trial, call Yasmin Mirza, Aby Farsoun or Michael Mand on 020 7630 7643

SOUTHWORTH, HELEN   Warrington South
Lab majority 7,397

Helen Mary Southworth. Born 13 November 1956; Educated Larkhill Convent School; Lancaster University (BA); Married Edmund Southworth (1 son). Director, Age Concern (St Helens); Non-executive director, St Helens and Knowsley Health Authority; Representative on the Community Health Council for 8 years; Member, MSF. Councillor, St Helens Borough Council 1994–98, Chair, Leisure Committee 1994–96; Non-executive Member, St Helens and Knowsley Health Authority. **House of Commons:** Contested Wirral South general election 1992. Member for Warrington South since May 1, 1997; PPS to Paul Boateng as: Financial Secretary to the Treasury 2001–02, Chief Secretary to the Treasury 2002–; *Select Committees:* Member: Procedure 1997–99, Trade and Industry 1998–2001. *Special Interests:* Health, Housing, Democracy, Small Businesses. *Countries of Interest:* Denmark, Sweden, Finland. Governor, Age Concern; Director, Grosvenor Housing Association; Council Member, St Helen's College; Member, Sankey Canal Restoration Society; Trustee, History of Parliament Trust; *Publications:* Co-author, *National Standards for Day Care Provision*; *Recreations:* Family, gardening, painting, walking the dog. Helen Southworth, MP, House of Commons, London, SW1A 0AA *Tel:* 020 7219 3568 *Fax:* 020 7219 2115. *Constituency:* 33 Cairo Street, Warrington, WA1 1EH *Tel:* 01925 240002 *Fax:* 01925 632614 *E-mail:* southworthh@parliament.uk.

SPELLAR, JOHN   Warley
Lab majority 11,850

John Francis Spellar. Born 5 August 1947; Son of late William David Spellar, and of Phyllis Kathleen Spellar; Educated Dulwich College, London; St Edmund's Hall, Oxford (BA philosophy, politics and economics 1969); Married Anne Rosalind Wilmot 1981 (1 daughter). National Officer, Electrical, Electronic, Telecommunication and Plumbing Union 1969–97. **House of Commons:** Contested Bromley 1970 general election. Member for Birmingham Northfield from October 28, 1982 by-election to June 1983. Contested Birmingham Northfield 1987 general election. Member for Warley West 1992–97, and for Warley since May 1, 1997; Opposition Spokesperson for: Northern Ireland 1994–95, Defence, Disarmament and Arms Control 1995–97; Opposition Whip 1992–94; Ministry of Defence: Parliamentary Under-Secretary of State 1997–99, Minister of State for the Armed Forces 1999–2001; Minister of State (Minister for Transport), Department of Transport, Local Government and the Regions 2001–02; Minister of State for: Transport, Department for Transport 2002–03; Northern Ireland Office 2003–; *Special Interests:* Energy, Electronics Industry, Motor Industry, Construction Industry. *Countries of Interest:* Australia, Israel, USA. PC 2001; *Clubs:* Rowley Regis and Blackheath Labour; *Recreations:* Gardening. Rt Hon John Spellar, MP, House of Commons, London, SW1A 0AA *Tel:* 020 7219 0674/5800 *Fax:* 020 7219 2113. *Constituency:* Brandhall Labour Club, Tame Road, Oldbury, West Midlands, B68 0JT *Tel:* 0121 423 2933 *E-mail:* spellarj@parliament.uk.

SPELMAN, CAROLINE   Meriden
Con majority 3,784

Caroline Alice Spelman. Born 4 May 1958; Daughter of late Marshall and Helen Margaret Cormack; Educated Herts and Essex Grammar School for Girls; Queen Mary College, London University (BA European studies 1980); Married Mark Spelman 1987 (2 sons 1 daughter). Sugar Beet commodity secretary, National Farmers Union 1981–84; Deputy director, International Confederation of European Beetgrowers, Paris 1984–89; Research fellow, Centre for European Agricultural Studies 1989–93; Director, Spelman, Cormack and Associates, Food and Biotechnology Consultancy 1989–. **House of Commons:** Contested Bassetlaw 1992 general election. Member for Meriden since May 1, 1997; Opposition Spokesperson for: Health 1999–2001, Women's Issues 1999; Opposition Whip (Agriculture; Environment, Transport and the Regions) 1998–99; Shadow Secretary of State for International Development 2001–; Shadow Minister for Women 2001–; *Select Committees:* Member, Science and Technology 1997–98. *Special Interests:* Environment, Agriculture, International Development. *Countries of Interest:* France, Germany, India, Pakistan.

Co-opted member executive committee Conservative Women's National Council; Member board of directors governing council Conservative Christian Fellowship. Board Member, Parliamentary Office of Science and Technology (POST) 1997–2001; Trustee: Snowdon Awards Scheme for Disabled, Oxford Kilburn Club for Deprived Inner City Kids; *Publications: A Green and Pleasant Land*, Bow Group Paper 1994; *Clubs:* Parliamentary Choir; *Sportsclubs:* Member: Knowle and Dorridge Tennis Club, Lords and Commons Ski Club, Lords and Commons Tennis Club; *Recreations:* Tennis, skiing, cooking, gardening. Caroline Spelman, MP, House of Commons, London, SW1A 0AA *Tel:* 020 7219 4189 *Fax:* 020 7219 0378. *Constituency:* 2 Manor Road, Solihull, West Midlands, B91 2BH *Tel:* 0121–711 2955 *Fax:* 0121–711 2955 *E-mail:* spelmanc@parliament.uk.

SPICER, MICHAEL   West Worcestershire   *Con majority 5,374*

(William) Michael Hardy Spicer. Born 22 January 1943; Son of late Brigadier L. H. Spicer; Educated Wellington College; Emmanuel College, Cambridge (MA economics 1964); Married Patricia Ann Hunter 1967 (1 son 2 daughters). Assistant to editor The Statist 1964–66; Conservative Research Department 1966–68; Director, Conservative Systems Research Centre 1968–70, Managing director, Economic Models Limited 1970–80. **House of Commons:** Contested Easington 1966 and 1970 general elections. Member for South Worcestershire 1974–97, and for West Worcestershire since May 1, 1997; PPS to Sally Oppenheim as Minister for Trade and Consumer Affairs 1979–81; Parliamentary Under-Secretary of State for Transport 1984–87; Aviation Minister 1985–87; Parliamentary Under-Secretary of State, Department of Energy 1987–90; Minister of State, Housing and Planning, Department of Environment 1990; *Select Committees:* Member, Treasury 1997–2001; Chair: Treasury Sub-Committee 1999–2001. *Special Interests:* Economic Policy. *Countries of Interest:* USA. Conservative Party: Vice-Chair 1981–83, Deputy Chair 1983–84, Board member 2001–. Governor, Wellington College 1992–; Chairman, European Research Group 1992–2001; Joint chairman, Congress of Democracy; Chairman, Parliamentary and Scientific Committee 1996–99; *Publications: A Treaty Too Far: A New Policy For Europe*, 1992; *The Challenge from the East: The Rebirth of the West*, 1996; Six novels; Knighted 1996; *Clubs:* Pratts, Garrick; *Recreations:* Tennis, writing novels, painting, bridge. Sir Michael Spicer, MP, House of Commons, London, SW1A 0AA *Tel:* 020 7219 3491. *Constituency:* 209a Worcester Road, Malvern Link, Malvern, Worcestershire, WR14 1SP *Tel:* 01684 573469 *Fax:* 01684 575280.

SPINK, BOB   Castle Point   *Con majority 985*

Bob (Robert) M Spink. Born 1 August 1948; Son of George, panel beater, and Brenda; Educated Holycroft School, Keighley; Manchester University; Cranfield University (PhD, CDipAF, BSc engineering, MSc industrial engineering); Married Janet Mary Barham 1968 (3 sons 1 daughter). RAF 1964–66 (invalided); Engineer EMI Electronics Ltd 1966–77; Industrial and management consultant 1977–80; Director and co-owner Seafarer Navigation International Ltd 1980–84; Management consultant Harold Whitehead and Partners 1984–92; Director: Bournemouth International Airport plc 1989–93, Harold Whitehead and Partners 1997–; Member 1966–75: DATA, TASS, AUEW. Dorset County Council 1985–93: Councillor, Member Dorset Police Authority 1985–93, Deputy group leader 1989–90, Chair Education Policy Committee 1989–93. **House of Commons:** Member for Castle Point 1992–1997. Contested Castle Point 1997 general election. Member for Castle Point since June 7, 2001; PPS: to Ann Widdecombe as Minister of State for Employment 1994–95, as Minister of State Home Office 1995–97, to John Watts as Minister of State for Railways, Roads and Local Transport, Department of Transport 1997; Private member's bill on underage drinking; *Select Committees:* Member, Education and Skills 2001; Member, Science and Technology 2001–. *Special Interests:* Employment, Trade and Industry, Education, Elderly, Britain's Sovereignty. Joint chair UNA UNESCO Working Committee 1992–97; BLISS; Parliamentary Office of Science and Technology: Board member 1993–97, Director; *Recreations:* Marathons, pottery, gardening. Bob Spink, MP, House of Commons, London, SW1A 0AA *Tel:* 020 7219 8468 *Fax:* 020 7219 1956. *Constituency:* 8 Green Road, Benfleet, Essex *Tel:* 01268 792992 *E-mail:* spinkr@parliament.uk.

SPRING, RICHARD   West Suffolk   *Con majority 4,295*

Richard Spring. Born 24 September 1946; Son of late H. J. A. Spring and of late Marjorie Watson-Morris; Educated Rondebosch, Cape; University of Cape Town; Magdalene College, Cambridge; Married Hon. Jane Henniker-Major 1979 (divorced 1993) (1 son 1 daughter). Merrill Lynch Ltd 1971–86, Vice-President 1976–86; Deputy managing director, Hutton International Associates 1986–88; Executive director, Shearson Lehman Hutton 1988–90; Managing director, Xerox Furman Selz 1990–92. **House of Commons:** Contested Ashton-under-Lyne 1983 general election. Member for Bury St Edmunds 1992–97, and for West Suffolk since May 1, 1997; Opposition Spokesperson for: Culture, Media and Sport November 1997–2000, Foreign Affairs 2000–; PPS: to Sir Patrick Mayhew as Secretary of State for Northern Ireland 1994–95, to Tim Eggar, as Minister for Trade and Industry 1995–96, to Nicholas Soames and James Arbuthnot as Ministers of State, Ministry of Defence 1996–97; *Select Committees:* Member: Employment 1992–94, Health 1995–96, Northern Ireland Affairs 1995–97, Deregulation 1997. *Countries of Interest:* Spain, South Africa, USA, Middle East, China, Pacific Rim. Various offices in Westminster Conservative Association 1976–87, including CPC Chair 1990; Vice-Chair, Conservative Industrial Fund 1993–96. Deputy-Chairman, Small Business Bureau 1992–; *Publications:* Contributed to *Fairer Business Rates* Conservative Backbench Committee on Smaller Businesses, July 1996; *Clubs:* Boodle's; *Recreations:* Country pursuits, tennis, swimming. Richard Spring Esq, MP, House of Commons, London, SW1A 0AA *Tel:* 020 7219 5192. *Constituency:* 4a Exeter Road, Newmarket, Suffolk, CB8 8LT *Tel:* 01638 669391 *Fax:* 01638 669410.

SQUIRE, RACHEL   Dunfermline West   *Lab majority 10,980*

Rachel Squire. Born 13 July 1954; Daughter of Louise Anne Squire; Educated Godolphin and Latymer Girls' School; Durham University (BA anthropology 1975); Birmingham University (CQSW 1978); Married Allan Lee Mason 1984. Social worker, Birmingham City Council 1975–81; Area officer, NUPE: Liverpool 1981–82, Ayrshire 1982–83, Renfrewshire 1983–85, All of Scotland Education Officer 1985–92; Trade union official 1981–92; Member, UNISON. **House of Commons:** Member for Dunfermline West since April 9, 1992; PPS to Ministers of State, Department for Education and Employment: Stephen Byers 1997–98, Estelle Morris 1998–2001; *Select Committees:* Member: Procedure 1992–97, European Legislation 1994–97, Modernisation of the House of Commons 1997–99; Member, Defence 2001–. *Special Interests:* Defence, NHS, Community Care, Foreign Affairs. *Countries of Interest:* Scandinavia, Europe, Former Eastern Bloc, Russia, Korea. Head, Scottish Labour Party's Task Force on Community Care 1993–97; Member, Labour Movement in Europe; Chair, Scottish Policy Forum, Labour Party 1998–2002. Member: Amnesty International, Workers Educational Association, Council for Scotland Archaeology, Historic Scotland, Camping and Caravanning Club; Patron, Brain Tumour Action; Dunfermline Home-Start; Advisory Board Member, Dunfermline Core Clubhouse; Honorary Vice President, Royal British Legion (Scotland) Dunfermline Branch; Labour Representative, Commission on Future of Scotland's Voluntary Sector; Fellow, Industry and Parliament Trust (BAe); Member, National Trust (Scotland); Fellow (Navy), Armed Forces Parliamentary Scheme 1993–94, 2001–; *Recreations:* Archaeology, reading, cooking. Rachel Squire, MP, House of Commons, London, SW1A 0AA *Tel:* 020 7219 5144. *Constituency:* Parliamentary Office, Music Hall Lane, Dunfermline, KY12 7NG *Tel:* 01383 622889 *Fax:* 01383 623500.

DodOnline
An Electronic Directory without rival...

MPs' biographies and photographs available with daily updates *via* the internet

For a *free* trial, call Yasmin Mirza, Aby Farsoun or Michael Mand on 020 7630 7643

STANLEY, JOHN   Tonbridge and Malling — *Con majority 8,250*

John P Stanley. Born 19 January 1942; Educated Repton School; Lincoln College, Oxford; Married Susan Giles 1968 (1 son 1 daughter 1 son deceased). Conservative Research Department 1967–68; Research Associate, Institute for Strategic Studies 1968–69; Rio Tinto-Zinc Corp. Ltd 1969–79. **House of Commons:** Contested Newton 1970 general election. Member for Tonbridge and Malling since February 1974; PPS to Margaret Thatcher as Leader of the Opposition 1976–79; Minister for Housing and Construction 1979–83; Minister for the Armed Forces 1983–87; Minister of State, Northern Ireland Office 1987–88; *Select Committees:* Member: Foreign Affairs 1992–97, Entry Clearance Sub-Committee 1997–98; Member, Foreign Affairs 1997–. Member, Executive Committee, Commonwealth Parliamentary Association (CPA) UK Branch 1999–; PC 1984; Knighted 1988; *Recreations:* Music and the arts, sailing. Rt Hon Sir John Stanley, MP, House of Commons, London, SW1A 0AA *Tel:* 020 7219 4506. *Constituency:* 91 High Street, West Malling, Maidstone, Kent, ME19 6NA *Tel:* 01732 842794 *Fax:* 01732 873960.

STARKEY, PHYLLIS   Milton Keynes South West — *Lab majority 6,978*

Phyllis Margaret Starkey. Born 4 January 1947; Daughter of late Dr John and Catherine Hooson Williams; Educated Perse School for Girls, Cambridge; Lady Margaret Hall, Oxford (BA biochemistry 1970); Clare Hall, Cambridge (PhD 1974); Married Hugh Walton Starkey 1969 (2 daughters). Research scientist: Strangeways Laboratory, Cambridge 1974–81, Sir William Dunn School of Pathology, Oxford 1981–84; University lecturer in obstetrics, Oxford University and fellow, Somerville College 1984–93; Science policy administrator, Biotechnology and Biological Sciences Research Council 1993–97; Parliamentary fellow, St Antony's College, Oxford 1997–98; Member: AUT 1974–93, MSF 1992–, PTC 1993–97. Oxford City Council: Councillor 1983–97, Leader 1990–93, Chair of Transport 1985–88, Chair of Finance 1988–90, 1993–96. **House of Commons:** Member for Milton Keynes South West since May 1, 1997; Team PPS, Foreign and Commonwealth Office 2001–02; PPS to Denis MacShane as Minister of State, Foreign and Commonwealth Affairs 2002–; *Select Committees:* Member: Modernisation of the House of Commons 1997–99, Foreign Affairs 1999–2001. *Special Interests:* Science, Health, Environment and Transport, Local Democracy and Regional Devolution, Foreign Affairs, Middle East. *Countries of Interest:* Palestine, France, North Africa, Middle East. Vice-Chair, South East Regional Group of Labour MPs 1998–. Chair, Local Government Information Unit 1992–97; Representative of Labour Councillors on National Policy Forum 1995–97; Board Member, Parliamentary Office of Science and Technology (POST) 1997–, Chair 2002–; Trustee, Theatres Trust; *Publications:* Seventy scientific papers 1977–96; K M Stott Prize, Newnham College, Cambridge 1974; *Recreations:* Gardening, cinema, walking, family. Dr Phyllis Starkey, MP, House of Commons, London, SW1A 0AA *Tel:* 020 7219 0456/6427 *Fax:* 020 7219 6865. *Constituency:* The Labour Hall, Newport Road, New Bradwell, Milton Keynes, MK13 0AA *Tel:* 01908 225522 *Fax:* 01908 320731 *E-mail:* starkeyp@miltonkeynes-sw.demon.co.uk.

STEEN, ANTHONY   Totnes — *Con majority 3,597*

Anthony David Steen. Born 22 July 1939; Son of late Stephen Steen; Educated Westminster School; Gray's Inn, London University; Married Carolyn Padfield 1966 (1 son 1 daughter). Called to the Bar 1962; Barrister, Gray's Inn; Youth leader and social worker; Founder, Task Force (Young helping the old) with Government grant 1964, First Director 1964–68; As community worker initiated Young Volunteer Force, Government Urban Development Foundation, First Director 1968–74; Lecturer in law, Ghana High Commission and Council of Legal Education 1964–67; Ministry of Defence Court Martials Defence Counsel; Adviser to Federal and Provincial Canadian Governments on unemployment and youth problems 1970–71. **House of Commons:** Member for Liverpool Wavertree 1974–83, for South Hams 1983–97, and for Totnes since May 1, 1997; PPS to Peter Brooke as Secretary of State for National Heritage 1992–94;

Select Committees: Member: Environment 1989–92, House of Commons Catering 1991–95, European Legislation 1997–98, European Legislation 1998, Public Administration 2001–02; Member: Regulatory Reform 1997–, European Scrutiny 1998–, Joint Committee on Consolidation of Bills Etc 2001–. *Special Interests:* Urban and Rural Regeneration, Community Care, Youth Affairs, Conservation, Heritage, Fishing Industry, Agriculture, Deregulation and Scrutiny of EU Directives, Affordable Housing, Environmental Pollution and Social and Community Work. *Countries of Interest:* Middle East, St Helena, West Indies. Appointed by the Prime Minister to generate new activity amongst MPs in constituency work 1994; Conservative Central Office Co-ordinator for Critical Seats 1982–87; Joint National Chairman, Impact 80s Campaign 1980–82; Chair, Minority Party Unit 1999–2000. Founder of two national charities; Vice-President: International Centre for Child Studies, Association of District Councils, Malborough with South Huish Horticultural Society; Advisory tutor to the School of Environment, Polytechnic of Central London 1982–83; Patron, Kidscape; Member, Council for Christians and Jews; Trustee of: Education Extra, Dartington International Summer School; *Publications: New Life for Old Cities,* 1981; *Tested Ideas for Political Success,* 1983, 7th ed, 1993; *Public Land Utilisation Management Schemes (PLUMS),* 1988; *Clubs:* Royal North Cape, Royal Automobile; *Sportsclubs:* Lords and Commons Cycle, Lords and Commons Tennis; *Recreations:* Piano playing, cycling and tennis. Anthony Steen Esq, MP, House of Commons, London, SW1A 0AA *Tel:* 020 7219 5045 *Fax:* 020 7219 6586. *Constituency:* TCCA, Station Road, Totnes, Devon, TQ9 5HW *Tel:* 01803 866064 *Fax:* 01803 867236 *E-mail:* steena@parliament.uk.

STEINBERG, GERRY   City of Durham   *Lab majority 13,441*

Gerry Steinberg. Born 20 April 1945; Son of late Harry and Esther Steinberg; Educated Whinney Hill Secondary Modern School; Durham Johnston Grammar School; Sheffield College of Education (Teachers Certificate); Newcastle Polytechnic (Certificate Education of Backward Children); Married Margaret Thornton 1969 (1 son 1 daughter). Teacher, Hexham Camp School 1966–69; Elemore Hall 1969–75, Deputy head 1975–79; Head teacher, Whitworth House School 1979–87; Member: TGWU, NUT. Councillor, Durham City Council 1976–87. **House of Commons:** Member for City of Durham since June 1987; *Select Committees:* Member: Education 1987–96, Education and Employment 1997–98, Education Sub-Committee 1997–98,
Catering 1998–2001; Member, Public Accounts 1998–. *Special Interests:* Education, Local and Regional Government, Animal Welfare. Secretary, Durham CLP and Agent to Dr Mark Hughes, MP 1973–83; Secretary, Durham City Labour Group 1981–87; Vice-Chair, Northern Group of Labour MPs 1997–98, Chair 1998–99. President, RSPCA Durham; *Clubs:* Sherburn Village Workman's, Brandon Village Workman's, Crossgate Workman's, Neville's Cross Workman's, New Durham Workman's; *Recreations:* All sport, supporting Sunderland AFC, dog walking, reading, jogging. Gerry Steinberg Esq, MP, House of Commons, London, SW1A 0AA *Tel:* 020 7219 6909 *Fax:* 020 7219 5901. *Constituency:* 4b Millennium Place, Durham, DH1 1WA *Tel:* 0191–386 0166 *Fax:* 0191–383 0047.

STEVENSON, GEORGE   Stoke-on-Trent South   *Lab majority 10,489*

George William Stevenson. Born 30 August 1938; Son of Harold Stevenson, miner and Elsie Stevenson, née Bryan, pottery worker; Educated Queensberry Road Secondary Modern School; Married Doreen June Parkes 1958 (died 1989) (2 sons 1 daughter); married Pauline Margaret Barber 1991 (4 stepchildren). Pottery industry 1953–57; Mining industry 1957–66; MEP for Staffordshire East 1984–94: Chair, British Labour Group 1987–88; Contested Stoke-on-Trent mayoral election 2002; TGWU Shop steward 1968; Chair, 5/24 Branch TGWU 1975–83. Deputy Leader, Stoke-on-Trent City Council 1972–83, Chair, Highways Committee; Deputy Leader, Staffordshire County Council 1981–85, Former Chair, Social Services and Establishment
Committees. **House of Commons:** Member for Stoke-on-Trent South since April 9, 1992; *Select Committees:* Member: Agriculture 1992–96, European Legislation 1996–97, Environment, Transport and Regional Affairs 1997–2001, Transport Sub-Committee 1997–2001, Chairmen's Panel 1998, Transport, Local Government and the Regions 2001–02, Transport Sub-Committee 2001–02; Member: Chairmen's Panel 1998–, Transport 2002–. *Special Interests:* Transport, Energy, Human Rights, Education. *Countries of Interest:* India, Kashmir, Pakistan, Sri Lanka, Tibet, Nepal, Bangladesh. Member: Amnesty International,

ACTSA; Member: European Standing Committee B 1998, European Standing Committee A 1998–2003; Vice-President, Federation of Economic Development Authorities (FEDA); *Recreations:* Walking, travel, reading. George Stevenson Esq, MP, House of Commons, London, SW1A 0AA *Tel:* 020 7219 5012 *Fax:* 020 7219 2688. *Constituency:* 2A Stanton Road, Meir, Stoke-on-Trent, Staffs, ST3 6DD *Tel:* 01782 593393 *Fax:* 01782 593430 *E-mail:* stevensonp@parliament.uk.

STEWART, DAVID   Inverness East, Nairn and Lochaber   Lab majority 4,716

David Stewart. Born 5 May 1956; Son of John Stewart, retired postal executive, and Alice Stewart; Educated Inverness High School; Paisley College (BA 1978); Stirling University (Postgraduate diploma in social work and CQSW 1981); Open University Business School (Prof Dip Mgt 1996); Married Linda MacDonald 1982 (1 son 1 daughter 1 son deceased). Social worker and social work manager 1980–97; Member, UNISON. Councillor: Nithsdale Council, Dumfries 1984–86, Inverness District Council 1988–96. **House of Commons:** Contested Inverness, Nairn and Lochaber 1987 and 1992 general elections. Member for Inverness East, Nairn and Lochaber since May 1, 1997; PPS to Alistair Darling as Secretary of State for Transport and for Scotland 2003–; *Select Committees:* Member, Scottish Affairs 1997–99; Member, Work and Pensions 2001–. *Special Interests:* Rural Affairs, Local and Regional Government, Health, International Development, Social Security, Defence, Oil Industry, Gas Industry, Small Businesses. *Countries of Interest:* USA, Italy. Member, Scottish Executive Labour Party 1985–95; Scottish Group of Labour MPs: Executive Member 1999–2001, Secretary 2001–. Governor, Eden Court Theatre 1992–96; Patron, Shopmobility Highland; Member: Interparliamentary Union, British American Group; Trustee, Highland Homeless at Christmas; Director, Inverness Caledonian Thistle Trust; *Sportsclubs:* Inverness Caledonian Thistle Football Club; *Recreations:* Football, films, fitness, American political biographies. David Stewart Esq, MP, House of Commons, London, SW1A 0AA *Tel:* 020 7219 3586 *Fax:* 020 7219 5687. *Constituency:* Queensgate Business Centre, 1/3 Fraser Street, Inverness, IV1 1DY *Tel:* 01463 237441 *Fax:* 01463 237661 *E-mail:* stewartd@parliament.uk.

STEWART, IAN   Eccles   Lab majority 14,528

Ian Stewart. Born 28 August 1950; Son of John and Helen; Educated Calder St Secondary, Blantyre; Alfred Turner Secondary Modern, Irlam, nr Manchester; Stretford Technical College 1966–69; Manchester Metropolitan University (MPhil Management of Change in progress); Married Merilyn Holding 1968 (2 sons 1 daughter). Regional full-time officer, Transport and General Workers Union for 20 years; Member, Transport and General Workers 1966–. **House of Commons:** Member for Eccles since May 1, 1997; PPS to: Ministers of State, Department of Trade and Industry: Brian Wilson 2001–03, Stephen Timms 2003–; *Select Committees:* Member: Deregulation and Regulatory Reform 1997–2001, Information 1998–2001. *Special Interests:* Employment, Education and Training, Economics, Trade and Industry, Investment, Regional Development, Information Technology, Democracy, International Affairs, Small Businesses. *Countries of Interest:* EU, Central and Eastern Europe, China, USA, Commonwealth. Member: International Society of Industrial Relations, UK Society of Industrial Tutors, Manchester Industrial Relations Society; Founder, European Foundation for Social Partnership and Continuing Training Initiatives; Secretary, House of Commons Football Team; Member: Society of International Industrial Relations, UK China Forum (Industry Group); Executive Member, Great Britain-China Centre; *Publications: Youth Unemployment and Government Training Strategies*, 1981; Visiting fellow, Salford University; *Recreations:* Tai-Chi, painting, research into philosophical religious and life systems, scientific and medical developments. Ian Stewart Esq, MP, House of Commons, London, SW1A 0AA *Tel:* 020 7219 6175 *Fax:* 020 7219 0903. *Constituency:* Eccles Parliamentary Office, Eccles Town Hall, Church Street, Eccles, Greater Manchester, M30 0EL *Tel:* 0161–707 4688 *Fax:* 0161–789 8065 *E-mail:* ianstewartmp@parliament.uk.

Visit the Vacher Dod Website . . .
www.DodOnline.co.uk

STINCHCOMBE, PAUL   Wellingborough   *Lab majority 2,355*

Paul David Stinchcombe. Born 25 April 1962; Son of Lionel and Pauline Stinchcombe; Educated High Wycombe Royal Grammar School; Trinity College, Cambridge (BA law 1983); Harvard Law School, USA (LLM 1984); Married Suzanne Gardiner 1990 (2 sons 1 daughter). Barrister, specialising in environmental law and judicial review 1986–; Member: GMB, MSF. London Borough of Camden: Councillor 1990–94, Chair Labour Group 1992–94; Member, Board of Management: Arlington House 1990–91, Central London Law Centre 1990–94. **House of Commons:** Member for Wellingborough since May 1, 1997; Member Joint Committee on House of Lords Reform 2002–; *Select Committees:* Member: Procedure 1997–99, Home Affairs 1998–2001, Environment, Food and Rural Affairs 2001; Member, Joint Committee on House of Lords Reform 2002–. *Special Interests:* Environment, Civil Liberties, Home Affairs, especially drugs, prisons and crime. *Countries of Interest:* Kenya, India, Philippines. Member: Christian Socialist Movement, Society of Labour Lawyers. Member: Friends of the Earth, Liberty; Trustee: Prison Reform Trust, Wellingborough MIND; *Publications: Law Reform For All,* 1996; Senior Scholar, Trinity College, Cambridge; Frank Knox Fellow, Harvard Law School; Megarry Scholar, Lincoln's Inn; *Clubs:* Rushden Working Men's; *Recreations:* Football, cricket, golf. Paul Stinchcombe Esq, MP, House of Commons, London, SW1A 0AA *Tel:* 020 7219 4066. *Constituency:* 49 Oxford Street, Wellingborough, Northamptonshire, NN8 4JH *Tel:* 01933 279022 *Fax:* 01933 279025.

STOATE, HOWARD   Dartford   *Lab majority 3,306*

Howard Geoffrey Stoate. Born 14 April 1954; Son of late Alvan Stoate, engineer, and late Maisie Stoate, teacher; Educated Kingston Grammar School; King's College, London University (MBBS 1974, MSc, FRCOG); Married Deborah Dunkerley 1979 (2 sons). Junior hospital doctor 1977–81; GP, Bexley Heath 1982–; GP tutor, Queen Mary's Hospital, Sidcup 1989–; Chair, Bexley Ethics Research Committee 1995–97; Member: MPU, MSF. Councillor, Dartford Borough Council 1990–99, Chair, Finance and Corporate Business 1995–99. **House of Commons:** Contested Old Bexley and Sidcup 1987, Dartford 1992 general elections; Member for Dartford since May 1, 1997; PPS to: John Denham as Minister of State, Home Office 2001–03, Estelle Morris as Minister of State, Department for Culture, Media and Sport 2003–; *Select Committees:* Member, Health 1997–2001. *Special Interests:* Health, Education, Environment, Home Affairs. *Countries of Interest:* Spain. Vice-Chair, DCLP 1984–91; Chair, LP Branch 1985–97; Vice-Chair, Dartford Fabian Society. Governor, Dartford Grammar School 1996–2000; Vice-Chair, Regional Graduate Education Board 1997–; Member, British Medical Association; *Publications:* Many medical publications, particularly on health screening; *All's Well that Starts Well – A Strategy for Children's Health,* Fabian Society, 2002; MBBS MSc FRCGP; *Sportsclubs:* Emsworth Sailing Club; *Recreations:* Running, sailing, reading, music. Dr Howard Stoate, MP, House of Commons, London, SW1A 0AA *Tel:* 020 7219 4571 *Fax:* 020 7219 6820. *Constituency:* Civic Centre, Home Gardens, Dartford, Kent, DA1 1DR *Tel:* 01322 343234 *Fax:* 01322 343235.

STRANG, GAVIN   Edinburgh East and Musselburgh   *Lab majority 12,168*

Gavin Steel Strang. Born 10 July 1943; Son of James S. Strang, tenant farmer; Educated Morrison's Academy; Edinburgh University (BSc 1964); Churchill College, Cambridge University (DipAgriSci 1965); Edinburgh University (PhD 1968); Married Bettina Morrison, née Smith 1973 (1 son, 2 stepsons). Member, Tayside Economic Planning Consultative Group 1966–68; Scientist, Agricultural Research Council 1968–70; Member, TGWU. **House of Commons:** Member for Edinburgh East 1970–97, and for Edinburgh East and Musselburgh since May 1, 1997; Opposition Frontbench Spokesperson for: Agriculture 1979–82, Employment 1987–89, Food, Agriculture and Rural Affairs 1992–97; Parliamentary Under-Secretary of State for Energy February–October 1974; Parliamentary Secretary to Ministry of Agriculture 1974–79; Minister of State (in Cabinet),

Department of the Environment, Transport and the Regions (Minister for Transport) 1997–98; *Select Committees:* Member: Agriculture, Science and Technology, Scottish Affairs. *Special Interests:* Agriculture, Transport, Fishing Industry, AIDS. *Countries of Interest:* Europe. PC 1997; *Recreations:* Swimming, golf, watching football, walking in the countryside. Rt Hon Gavin Strang, MP, House of Commons, London, SW1A 0AA *Tel:* 020 7219 5155. *Constituency:* 54 Portobello High Street, Edinburgh, EH15 1DA *Tel:* 0131–669 6002 *E-mail:* daviesk@parliament.uk.

STRAW, JACK   Blackburn   *Lab majority 9,249*

Jack (John Whitaker) Straw. Born 3 August 1946; Son of Walter Arthur Straw; Educated Brentwood School; Leeds University (LLB 1967); Inns of Court School of Law 1972; Married Alice Perkins 1978 (1 son 1 daughter). President, National Union of Students 1969–71; Called to the Bar, Inner Temple 1972; Practised as Barrister 1972–74; Special adviser: to Barbara Castle, MP as Secretary of State for Social Services 1974–76, to Peter Shore, MP as Secretary of State for the Environment 1976–77; Member, staff of Granada Television *World in Action* 1977–79; Elected Master of Bench of the Inner Temple 1997; Member, GMB. Councillor, Islington Borough Council 1971–78; ILEA: Member 1971–74, Deputy Leader 1973. **House of Commons:** Contested Tonbridge and Malling February 1974 general election. Member for Blackburn since May 1979; Opposition Front Bench Spokesman on: Treasury and Economic Affairs 1980–83, Environment 1983–87; Shadow Education Secretary 1987–92; Shadow Environment Secretary 1992–94; Shadow Home Secretary 1994–97; Home Secretary 1997–2001; Foreign Secretary 2001–; *Special Interests:* Education, Taxation, Economic Policy, Local and Regional Government, Police, European Union. Member, Labour Party National Executive Committee 1994–95. Member of Council Lancaster University 1989–92; Governor: Blackburn College 1990–, Pimlico School 1994–2000, Chair 1995–98; Joint Vice-Chair, British-American Parliamentary International Group 1999–; *Publications: Policy and Ideology*, 1993; PC 1997; Visiting fellow, Nuffield College, Oxford 1990–98; Hon. LLD, Leeds University 1999; Fellow, Royal Statistical Society 1995–; *Sportsclubs:* Hon Vice-President Blackburn Rovers FC 1998; *Recreations:* Cooking, walking, music, watching Blackburn Rovers. Rt Hon Jack Straw, MP, House of Commons, London, SW1A 0AA *Tel:* 020 7219 3000. *Constituency:* Richmond Chambers, Richmond Road, Blackburn, BB1 7AS *Tel:* 01254 52317 *Fax:* 01254 682213.

STREETER, GARY   South West Devon   *Con majority 7,144*

Gary Streeter. Born 2 October 1955; Son of Kenneth Victor, farmer, and Shirley Streeter; Educated Tiverton Grammar School; King's College, London (LLB 1977); Married Janet Vanessa Stevens 1978 (1 son 1 daughter). Solicitor; Partner, Foot and Bowden, Plymouth 1984–98, specialist in company and employment law. Plymouth City Council: Councillor 1986–92, Chairman, Housing Committee 1989–91. **House of Commons:** Member for Plymouth Sutton 1992–97, and for South West Devon since May 1, 1997; Opposition Spokesperson for: Foreign Affairs 1997–98, Europe 1997–98; Assistant Government Whip 1995–96; PPS: to Sir Derek Spencer as Solicitor General 1993–95, to Sir Nicholas Lyell as Attorney-General 1994–95; Parliamentary Secretary, Lord Chancellor's Department 1996–97; Shadow Secretary of State for International Development 1998–2001; *Select Committees:* Member, Environment 1992–93; Member: Office of the Deputy Prime Minister: Housing, Planning and Local Government 2002–, Urban Affairs Sub-Committee 2003–. *Special Interests:* Law and Order, Family Moral and Social Affairs, Developing World. Chair board of directors governing council Conservative Christian Fellowship; Vice-Chair Conservative Party 2001–02. *Recreations:* Watching cricket and rugby, family. Gary Streeter Esq, MP, House of Commons, London, SW1A 0AA *Tel:* 020 7219 4070 *Fax:* 020 7219 2414. *Constituency Tel:* 01752 335666 *Fax:* 01752 338401 *E-mail:* mail@garystreeter.co.uk.

Visit the Vacher Dod Website . . .
www.DodOnline.co.uk

STRINGER, GRAHAM   Manchester Blackley   *Lab majority 14,464*

Graham Stringer. Born 17 February 1950; Son of late Albert Stringer, railway clerk, and Brenda Stringer, shop assistant; Educated Moston Brook High School; Sheffield University (BSc chemistry 1971); Married 2nd Kathryn Carr 1999 (1 son 1 stepson 1 stepdaughter). Analytical chemist; Chair of Board, Manchester Airport plc 1996–97; Branch officer and shop steward, MSF. Councillor, Manchester City Council 1979–98, Leader 1984–96. **House of Commons:** Member for Manchester Blackley since May 1, 1997; Government Whip 2001–02; Parliamentary Secretary, Cabinet Office 1999–2001; *Select Committees:* Member: Environment, Transport and Regional Affairs 1997–99, Transport Sub-Committee 1997–99; Member, Transport 2002–. *Special Interests:* Urban Regeneration, House of Lords Reform, Revitalising Local Democracy, New Aviation and Airports. Hon. RNCM; *Sportsclubs:* Member: Manchester Tennis and Racquet Club, Cheetham Hill Cricket Club. Graham Stringer Esq, MP, House of Commons, London, SW1A 0AA *Tel:* 020 7219 6055. *Constituency:* Constituency Office, 4th Floor, Mancat Moston Campus, Ashley Lane, Moston, Manchester, M9 4WU *Tel:* 0161–202 6600 *Fax:* 0161–202 6626 *E-mail:* stringerg@parliament.uk.

STUART, GISELA   Birmingham Edgbaston   *Lab majority 4,698*

Gisela Gschaider Stuart. Born 26 November 1955; Daughter of late Martin Gschaider and Liane Krompholz; Educated Realschule Vilsbiburg; Manchester Polytechnic; London University (LLB); Married Robert Scott Stuart 1980 (divorced 2000) (2 sons). Deputy Director, London Book Fair 1983; Translator; Lawyer and lecturer, Worcester College of Technology and Birmingham University 1992–1997. **House of Commons:** Member for Birmingham Edgbaston since May 1, 1997; PPS to Paul Boateng as Minister of State, Home Office 1998–99; Parliamentary Under-Secretary of State, Department of Health 1999–2001; Parliamentary representative Convention on Future of Europe 2002–; *Select Committees:* Member, Social Security 1997–98; Member, Foreign Affairs 2001–. *Special Interests:* Pension Law, Constitutional Reform, European Union. Gisela Stuart, MP, House of Commons, London, SW1A 0AA *Tel:* 020 7219 5051 *Tel (Constituency):* 0121–428 5011 *Fax (Constituency):* 0121–428 5073.

STUNELL, ANDREW   Hazel Grove   *LD majority 8,435*

(Robert) Andrew Stunell. Born 24 November 1942; Son of late Robert George Stunell and Trixie Stunell; Educated Surbiton Grammar School; Manchester University (architecture RIBA Pt. II exemption 1963); Liverpool Polytechnic; Married Gillian Chorley 1967 (3 sons 2 daughters). Architectural assistant: CWS Manchester 1965–67, Runcorn New Town 1967–81; Freelance architectural assistant 1981–85; Various posts including political secretary, Association of Liberal Democrat Councillors (ALDC) 1985–97; Head of Service 1989–96; Member, NALGO: New Towns Whitley Council 1977–81. Councillor: Chester City Council 1979–90, Cheshire County Council 1981–91, Stockport Metropolitan Borough Council 1994–2002. **House of Commons:** Contested City of Chester 1979, 1983, 1987, Hazel Grove 1992 general elections. Member for Hazel Grove since May 1, 1997; Liberal Democrat Spokesperson for Energy 1997–; Deputy Chief Whip 1997–2001; Chief Whip 2001–02; *Select Committees:* Member: Broadcasting 1997–2000, Procedure 1997–2001, Unopposed Bills (Panel) 1997–2001, Standing Orders 1998–2001; Member: Modernisation of the House of Commons 1997–, Finance and Services 2001–, Selection 2001–. *Special Interests:* Local Democracy and Regional Devolution, Third World, Race Relations, Energy, Climate Change. *Countries of Interest:* All. Various local and national party offices 1977–; Member: Liberal Democrat Federal Executive Committee 2001–, Liberal Democrat Federal Conference Committee 2001–. Member: United Nations Association 1959–, Romiley Methodist Church; President, Goyt Valley Rail Users Association; NW Constitutional Convention 1999–; Vice-chair, Association of County Councils 1985–90; Vice-president, Local Government Association 1997–; *Publications: Life In The Balance*, 1986; *Budgeting For Real*, 1984, 2nd edition 1994, 3rd edition 1999; *Thriving In The Balance*, 1995; *Open Active & Effective*, 1995;

Local Democracy Guaranteed, 1996; *Energy – Clean and Green to 2050*, 1999; *Nuclear Waste-Cleaning up the Mess*, 2001; OBE 1995; *Recreations:* Theoretical astronomy, camping, table tennis. Andrew Stunell Esq, OBE, MP, House of Commons, London, SW1A 0AA *Tel:* 020 7219 5223 *Fax:* 020 7219 2302. *Constituency:* Liberal Democrat HQ, 68A Compstall Road, Romiley, Stockport, Greater Manchester, SK6 4DE *Tel:* 0161–406 7070 *Fax:* 0161–494 2425.

SUTCLIFFE, GERRY   Bradford South   *Lab majority 9,662*

Gerry Sutcliffe. Born 13 May 1953; Son of Henry and Margaret Sutcliffe; Educated Cardinal Hinsley Grammar School, Bradford; Married Maria Holgate 1972 (3 sons). Salesperson 1969–72; Display advertising, *Bradford Telegraph and Argus* 1972–75; Field printers, Bradford 1975–80; Deputy Branch Secretary, SOGAT/GPMU 1980–94; Member: Yorkshire and Humberside Trade Union Friends of Labour, Regional TUC. Bradford City Council: Councillor 1982–94, Leader 1992–94. **House of Commons:** Member for Bradford South since by-election June 9, 1994; Assistant Government Whip 1999–2001; Government Whip 2000–03; PPS to Harriet Harman as Secretary of State for Social Security and Minister for Women 1997–98; PPS to Stephen Byers: as Chief Secretary, HM Treasury July-December 1998, as Secretary of State for Trade and Industry 1999; Parliamentary Under-Secretary of State for Employment Relations, Competition and Consumers, Department of Trade and Industry 2003–; *Select Committees:* Member: Public Accounts 1996–98, Unopposed Bills (Panel) 1997–99, Selection 2001–03. *Special Interests:* Employment, Local and Regional Government. *Countries of Interest:* Pakistan, Bangladesh, India, European Union. Member, Regional Labour Party Executive; Vice-chair, Yorkshire Regional Group of Labour MPs 1997–. School governor; Member: Friends of the Earth, Amnesty International; Patron Catholic Housing Aid (CHAS); *Recreations:* Sport, music. Gerry Sutcliffe Esq, MP, House of Commons, London, SW1A 0AA *Tel:* 020 7219 3247 *Fax:* 020 7219 1227. *Constituency:* 3rd Floor, 76 Kirkgate, Bradford BD1 1SZ *Tel:* 01274 400007 *Fax:* 01274 400020 *E-mail:* sutcliffeg@parliament.uk.

SWAYNE, DESMOND   New Forest West   *Con majority 13,191*

Desmond Angus Swayne. Born 20 August 1956; Son of George Joseph Swayne and Elisabeth McAlister Swayne, née Gibson; Educated Drumley House, Ayrshire; Bedford School; St Mary's College, St Andrews University (MA theology 1980); Married Moira Cecily Teek 1987 (1 son 2 daughters). Major, Territorial Army; Schoolmaster, 'A' level economics: Charterhouse 1980–81, Wrekin College 1982–87; Manager, Risk Management Systems, Royal Bank of Scotland 1988–96. **House of Commons:** Contested Pontypridd 1987, West Bromwich West 1992 general elections. Member for New Forest West since May 1, 1997; Opposition Spokesperson for: Health 2001, Defence 2001–02; Opposition Whip 2002–; *Select Committees:* Member: Scottish Affairs 1997–2001, Social Security 1999–2001; Member, Procedure 2002–. Countryside Alliance; TD; *Clubs:* Cavalry and Guards; *Sportsclubs:* Serpentine Swimming Club; *Recreations:* Territorial Army. Desmond Swayne Esq, MP, House of Commons, London, SW1A 0AA *Tel:* 020 7219 4886. *Constituency:* 4 Cliff Crescent, Marine Drive, Barton-on-Sea, New Milton, Hampshire, BH25 7EB *Tel:* 023 8081 4554 *Fax:* 023 8081 2019.

SWIRE, HUGO   East Devon   *Con majority 8,195*

Hugo George William Swire. Born 30 November 1959; Son of Humphrey Roger Swire and Philippa Sophia Swire, née Montgomerie; Educated St Aubyns School; Eton College; St Andrews University; Royal Military Academy Sandhurst; Married Alexandra (Sasha) Petrushka Mina Nott 1996 (2 daughters). Commissioned 1st Battalion Grenadier Guards 1979–83; Joint managing director International News Services and Prospect Films 1983–85; Financial consultant Streets Financial Ltd 1985–87; Head of development National Gallery 1988–92; Sotheby's: Deputy director 1992–97, Director 1997–2003. **House of Commons:** Contested Greenock and Inverclyde 1997 general election. Member for East Devon since June 7, 2001; *Select Committees:*

Member, Northern Ireland Affairs 2002–. *Special Interests:* The arts, Tourism, Field Sports, Agriculture, Architectural Heritage, Defence, Foreign Affairs, Rural Affairs, Northern Ireland, Housing. *Countries of Interest:* Lebanon, Oman, Slovenia. Charity auctioneer and fundraiser for numerous charities; Member European Standing Committee C; Advisory Committee, The Airey Neave Trust; Fellow Royal Society of Arts; *Clubs:* White's, Pratt's, Beefsteak; *Recreations:* Country pursuits, skiing, tennis, gardening, reading, travel, arts. Hugo Swire Esq, MP, House of Commons, London, SW1A 0AA *Tel:* 020 7219 8163 *Fax:* 020 7219 1895. *Constituency:* Conservative Campaign HQ, 45 Imperial Road, Exmouth, Devon, EX8 1DQ *Tel:* 01395 264 251 *Fax:* 01395 272 205.

SYMS, ROBERT   Poole   *Con majority 7,166*

Robert Andrew Raymond Syms. Born 15 August 1956; Son of Raymond Syms, builder, and Mary Syms, teacher; Educated Colston's School, Bristol; Married Nicola Guy 1991 (divorced 1999); married Fiona Mellersh 2000 (1 daughter 1 son). Director, family building, plant hire and property group, based in Chippenham, Wiltshire 1978–. Councillor: North Wiltshire District Council 1983–87, Wiltshire County Council 1985–97; Member, Wessex Regional Health Authority 1988–90. **House of Commons:** Contested Walsall North 1992 general election. Member for Poole since May 1, 1997; Opposition Spokesperson for Environment, Transport and Regions 1999–2001; Opposition Whip 2003–; PPS to Michael Ancram as Chair Conservative Party 1999–2000; Vice-Chair Conservative Party 2001–; *Select Committees:* Member: Health 1997–2000, Procedure 1998–99, Transport 2002–03. *Special Interests:* Economic Policy, Constitution, Local and Regional Government. *Countries of Interest:* USA, most of English speaking world. North Wiltshire Conservative Association: Treasurer 1982–84, Deputy Chair 1983–84, Chair 1984–86. Member, North Wiltshire Enterprise Agency 1986–90; Member, Calne Development Project Trust 1986–97; Fellow of the Chartered Institute of Building (FCIOTS); *Recreations:* Reading, music. Robert Syms Esq, MP, House of Commons, London, SW1A 0AA *Tel:* 020 7219 4601. *Constituency:* Poole Conservative Association, 38 Sandbanks Road, Poole, Dorset, BH14 8BX *Tel:* 01202 739922 *Fax:* 01202 739944.

T

TAMI, MARK   Alyn and Deeside   *Lab majority 9,222*

Mark Richard Tami. Born 3 October 1962; Son of Michael John Tami and Patricia Tami; Educated Enfield Grammar School; Swansea University (BA history 1985); Married Sally Ann Daniels 1994 (2 sons). AEEU: Head of research and communications 1992–99, Head of policy 1999–2001; Member AEEU 1986–; Member TUC General Council 1999–2001. **House of Commons:** Member for Alyn and Deeside since June 7, 2001; *Select Committees:* Member, Northern Ireland Affairs 2001–. *Special Interests:* Manufacturing, Aerospace, Small Businesses. Treasurer, Labour Friends of Australia. Member European Standing Committee B 2003–; *Publications:* Co-author *Votes for All*, Fabian Society pamphlet, 2000; *Sportsclubs:* Glamorgan County Cricket; *Recreations:* Football (Norwich City), cricket, fishing, antiques. Mark Tami Esq, MP, House of Commons, London, SW1A 0AA *Tel:* 020 7219 8174 *Fax:* 020 7219 1943. *Constituency:* Deeside Enterprise Centre, Rowleys Drive, Shotton, Deeside, Flintshire, CH5 1PP *Tel:* 01244 819854 *Fax:* 01244 823548 *E-mail:* tamim@parliament.uk.

Visit the Vacher Dod Website ...
www.DodOnline.co.uk

TAPSELL, PETER   Louth and Horncastle   Con majority 7,554

Peter H B Tapsell. Born 1 February 1930; Son of late Eustace Tapsell and late Jessie Tapsell (née Hannay); Educated Tonbridge School; Merton College, Oxford (BA modern history 1953, MA); Diploma in Economics 1954; Married The Hon. Cecilia Hawke, daughter of 9th Baron Hawke 1963 (divorced 1971) (1 son deceased); married Gabrielle Mahieu 1974. Subaltern Army national service in Middle East 1948–50; Royal Sussex Regiment; Personal Assistant to Prime Minister (Anthony Eden) 1955; Member, London Stock Exchange 1957–90; Adviser to central banks and international companies 1960–; Partner, James Capel and Co 1960–90. **House of Commons:** Contested Wednesbury February 1957 by-election. Member for Nottingham West 1959–64, for Horncastle 1966–83, for Lindsey East 1983–97, and for Louth and Horncastle since May 1, 1997; Opposition Frontbench Spokesperson for: Foreign and Commonwealth Affairs 1976–77, Treasury and Economic Affairs 1977–78; *Special Interests:* Foreign Affairs, Economics and Finance. *Countries of Interest:* Third World. Council Member, Institute of Fiscal Studies; Vice-President, Tennyson Society; Council Member, Business Advisory Committee of UN Organisation; Longest serving Conservative MP; Member: Trilateral Commission 1979–98, Business Advisory Council of the UN, International Investment Advisory Board to Brunei Government 1976–83; Hon Deputy Chair, Mitsubishi Trust Oxford Foundation; Brunei Dato 1971; Hon Life Member 6th Squadron RAF 1971; Knighted 1985; Spectator Backbencher of the Year 1993; Honorary Postmaster, Merton College, Oxford 1953; Honorary Fellow, Merton College, Oxford 1989; *Clubs:* Athenaeum, Carlton, Hurlingham; *Recreations:* Overseas travel, walking in mountains, reading, history. Sir Peter Tapsell, MP, House of Commons, London, SW1A 0AA *Tel:* 020 7219 4477 *Fax:* 020 7219 0976. *Constituency:* Cannon Street House, Cannon Street, Louth, Lincolnshire *Tel:* 01507 603713 *Fax:* 01507 602154.

TAYLOR, ANN   Dewsbury   Lab majority 7,449

Ann Taylor. Born 2 July 1947; Daughter of late John Walker and Doreen Bowling; Educated Bolton School; Bradford University (BSc 1969); Sheffield University (MA 1977); Married David Taylor 1966 (1 son 1 daughter). Part-time tutor, Open University 1971–74; Monitoring officer, Housing Corporation 1985–87; Member: Association of University Teachers GMB. Holmfirth UDC 1972–74. **House of Commons:** Contested Bolton West February 1974 general election. Member for Bolton West October 1974–83, contested Bolton North East 1983 general election. Member for Dewsbury since June 1987; Opposition Frontbench Spokesperson for: Education 1979–81, Housing 1981–83, Home Office 1987–88, Environment 1988–92; Citizen's Charter 1994–95; Government Whip 1977–79; Government Chief Whip 1998–2001; PPS: to Fred Mulley as Secretary of State for Education and Science 1975–76, as Secretary of State for Defence 1976–77; Shadow Secretary of State for Education 1992–94; Shadow Chancellor of the Duchy of Lancaster 1994–95; Shadow Leader of the House 1994–97; President of the Council and Leader of the House of Commons 1997–98; *Select Committees:* Member, Standards and Privileges 1995–97; Chair, Modernisation of the House of Commons 1997–98; Member, Parliamentary Privilege (Joint Committee) 1997–2000. *Special Interests:* Education, Home Office. Member: House of Commons Commission 1994–98, Public Accounts Commission 1997–98; Chair Intelligence and Security Committee 2001–; *Publications:* Choosing Our Future – Practical Politics of the Environment, 1992; PC 1997; Hon. Fellow, Birkbeck College, London University; Hon. Doctorate, Bradford University. Rt Hon Ann Taylor, MP, House of Commons, London, SW1A 0AA *Tel:* 020 7219 4400. *Constituency:* Dewsbury Business and Media Centre, Wellington Road East, Dewsbury, West Yorkshire, WF13 1HF *Tel:* 01924 324999 *Fax:* 01924 324998.

DodOnline
An Electronic Directory without rival ...

MPs' biographies and photographs available with daily updates *via* the internet

For a *free* trial, call Yasmin Mirza, Aby Farsoun or Michael Mand on 020 7630 7643

TAYLOR, DARI   Stockton South   *Lab majority 9,086*

Dari (Daria Jean) Taylor. Born 13 December 1944; Daughter of late Daniel Jones, MP for Burnley 1959–83, and late Phyllis Jones; Educated Ynyshir Girls' School; Burnley Municipal College; Nottingham University (BA politics); Durham University (MA social policy); Married David E Taylor 1970 (1 daughter). Assistant lecturer, Basford College of Further Education 1970–71; Lecturer, Westbridgeford College of Further Education 1971–81; Lecturer (PT), North Tyneside College of Further Education 1986–87; General Municipal and Boilermakers 1990: Research Support 1990, Regional Education Officer, Northern Region 1993–97; Regional/Local Representative NATFHE; Member, General Municipal and Boilermakers (GMB); Trade Union Support and Information Unit. Councillor, Sunderland Metropolitan Council 1986–97. **House of Commons:** Member for Stockton South since May 1, 1997; PPS to: Parliamentary Under Secretaries Lewis Moonie and Lord Bach, Ministry of Defence 2001–03, Hazel Blears as Minister of State, Home Office 2003–; *Select Committees:* Member, Defence 1997–99. *Special Interests:* Economic Policy, Industry, Education, Housing, Defence. *Countries of Interest:* Europe, Africa, USA. Leadership Campaign Team. Member, Domestic Violence Multi-Agency; Supporter: NSPCC, NSPCA, Children's Society; *Recreations:* Choral singing, walking, travelling. Dari Taylor, MP, House of Commons, London, SW1A 0AA *Tel:* 020 7219 4608 *Fax:* 020 7219 6876. *Constituency:* 109 Lanehouse Road, Thornaby on Tees, TS17 8AB *Tel:* 01642 604546 *Fax:* 01642 608395 *E-mail:* mchughd@parliament.uk.

TAYLOR, DAVID   North West Leicestershire   *Lab majority 8,157*

David Leslie Taylor. Born 22 August 1946; Son of late Leslie Taylor, civil servant, and Eileen Mary Taylor, retired postal worker; Educated Ashby-de-la-Zouch Boys Grammar School; Leicester Polytechnic and Lanchester Polytechnic (Chartered Public Finance Accountant 1970); Open University (BA maths and computing 1974); Married Pamela Caunt 1969 (4 daughters 1 son deceased). Accountant and Computer Manager, Leicestershire County Council 1977–97; Department steward and auditor, NALGO (now UNISON) 1985–97. Councillor, North West Leicestershire District Council 1981–87, 1992–95; Councillor, Heather Parish Council 1987–, Chair 1996–97, 2001–02; JP, Ashby-de-la-Zouch 1985–. **House of Commons:** Contested North West Leicestershire 1992 general election. Member for North West Leicestershire since May 1, 1997; *Select Committees:* Sub-Committee Staff, Environment Sub-Committee –2001; Member, Modernisation of the House of Commons 1999–2001; Member: Environment, Food and Rural Affairs 2001–, Chairmen's Panel 2002–. *Special Interests:* Housing, Low Pay, Rural Affairs, Environment, Safer Communities (Crime), Small Businesses. *Countries of Interest:* France. Member, Labour Campaign for Electoral Reform. Member: CPRE, Greenpeace, Friends of the Earth, Magistrates Association; Member, Chartered Institute of Public Finance and Accountancy (Prize Winner in Accountancy Final Exams); *Clubs:* Ibstock Working Mens; Coalville Labour; Hugglescote Working Mens; Ibstock Town Cricket; *Sportsclubs:* President, Heather Sparkenhoe Cricket Club; *Recreations:* Running, Cycling. David Taylor Esq, MP, House of Commons, London, SW1A 0AA *Tel:* 020 7219 4567 *Fax:* 020 7219 6808. *Constituency:* Labour Office, 17 Hotel Street, Coalville, Leicestershire, LE67 3EQ *Tel:* 01530 814372 *Fax:* 01530 813833 *E-mail:* taylordl@parliament.uk.

TAYLOR, IAN   Esher and Walton   *Con majority 11,538*

Ian Colin Taylor. Born 18 April 1945; Son of late Horace Stanley Taylor and late Beryl Harper; Educated Whitley Abbey School, Coventry; Keele University (BA economics, politics and modern history 1967); LSE (research scholar 1967–69); Married Hon Carole Alport 1974 (2 sons). Hill Samuel & Co 1969–71; Stirling & Co 1971–75; Banque Pommier, Paris 1975–76; Shenley International Finance 1976–80; Director, Mathercourt Securities Ltd 1980–91; Corporate Finance Consultant; Executive Director, Interregnum PLC; Director, Next Fifteen Group PLC; Chair: Screen PLC, Radioscape Ltd, Speed-Trap Ltd. **House of Commons:** Contested Coventry South East 1974 general election. Member for Esher 1987–97, and for Esher and Walton since May 1, 1997;

Opposition Spokesperson for Northern Ireland June-November 1997; PPS to William Waldegrave as: Minister of State, Foreign and Commonwealth Office 1988–90, as Secretary of State for Health 1990–92, as Chancellor of the Duchy of Lancaster, Minister for Public Services and Science 1992–94; Parliamentary Under Secretary of State, Department of Trade and Industry (Minister for Science and Technology) 1994–97; *Select Committees:* Member: Foreign Affairs 1987–89, Science and Technology 1998–2001. *Special Interests:* European Union, Economy, Science and Technology. *Countries of Interest:* Former Soviet Union, France, Germany, Middle East, Scandinavia, USA. National Chair, Federation of Conservative Students 1968–69; Chair, European Union of Christian Democratic and Conservative Students 1969–70; Member, Conservative National Union Executive and other national committees 1966–75, 1990–95; National Chair, Conservative Group for Europe 1985–88; Vice-Chair, Association of Conservative Clubs 1988–92; Chair, Conservative Foreign and Commonwealth Council 1990–95. Chair, Commonwealth Youth Exchange Council 1980–84, Vice-President 1984–; Patron, UK Centre for European Education 1991–94; Governor, Westminster Foundation for Democracy 1992–94; Member, Royal Society for International Affairs; Governor, Research into Ageing 1997–2001; Council Member, Anglo-German Foundation 1999–; Governor for British Association for Central and Eastern Europe 1997–2000; Member, Finance Bill Standing Committees 1987–94; Board Member, Parliamentary Office of Science and Technology (POST) 1997–; Council Member, Parliamentary Information Technology Committee; Director, EURIM (European Informatics Market) 1999–; Chair: European Movement 2001–, Tory Europe Network 2002–; Adviser, Broadband Stakeholders Group 2002–; Trustee, Painshill Park Trust 1998–; Worshipful Company of Information Technologists 1998–; *Publications: Fair Shares for all the Workers,* 1988; *Releasing the Community Spirit – The Active Citizen,* 1990; *A Community of Employee Shareholders,* 1992; *The Positive Europe,* 1993; *Escaping the Protectionist Trap,* 1995; *Net-Working,* 1996; *Conservative Tradition in Europe,* 1996; *Science, Government and Society,* 1998; *Restoring the Balance,* 2000; *Full Steam Ahead,* 2001; *Federal Britain in a Federal Europe,* 2001; *Europe: Our Case,* 2002; *Shaping The New Europe – The British Opportunity* (EUW) 2002; MBE 1974; Associate, Institute of Investment Management and Research 1972–; Clubs: Buck's, IOD, Commonwealth; *Recreations:* Country walks, shooting, cigars, opera. Ian Taylor Esq, MBE, MP, House of Commons, London, SW1A 0AA *Tel:* 020 7219 5221 *Fax:* 020 7219 5492. *Constituency:* Cheltonian House, Portsmouth Road, Esher, Surrey, KT10 9AA *Tel:* 01372 469105 *Fax:* 01372 469091 *E-mail:* taylori@parliament.uk.

TAYLOR, JOHN   Solihull   *Con majority 9,407*

John Mark Taylor. Born 19 August 1941; Son of late Wilfred and Eileen Martha Taylor; Educated Bromsgrove School; College of Law. Senior Partner, John Taylor & Co., Solicitors; MEP for Midlands East 1979–84. Councillor, Solihull County Borough Council 1971–74; West Midlands County Council: Councillor 1973–86, Leader of Opposition 1975–77, Leader of Council 1977–79; Member, West Midland Economic Planning Council 1977–79. **House of Commons:** Contested Dudley East February and October 1974 general elections. Member for Solihull since June 1983; Opposition Spokesperson for Northern Ireland 1999–2001, 2003–; Assistant Government Whip 1988–89; Government Whip 1989–92; Opposition Whip 1997–99; PPS to Kenneth Clarke: as Chancellor of the Duchy of Lancaster and Minister for Trade and Industry 1987–88; Parliamentary Secretary, Lord Chancellor's Department 1992–95; Parliamentary Under-Secretary of State, Department of Trade and Industry 1995–97; *Select Committees:* Member, Modernisation of the House of Commons 2001–02. *Special Interests:* Environment, European Union, Care of Ancient Monuments, Legal Affairs, Trade and Industry. *Countries of Interest:* USA. Member, Conservative Friends of Israel. Chair, Solihull Business Enterprise; President, Shirley Citizens' Advice Bureau; President, Park View Association; Founder chair, Solihull Institute for Medical Training and Research; Life member, English Heritage; Shoreline (Life) member, RNLI; Deputy Chair, Association of Metropolitan Authorities 1978–79; European Parliament 1979–84: Group Budget Spokesman 1979–81, Group Deputy Chair 1981–82, Council of Europe and WEU 1997; Life Member, National Trust; *Clubs:* MCC; *Sportsclubs:* Bromsgrove Martlets Cricket Club, Hampton-in-Arden Cricket Club, Olton Cricket Club, Olton Golf Club, Warwickshire County Cricket Club; *Recreations:* Fellowship, cricket, golf, reading. John M Taylor Esq, MP, House of Commons, London, SW1A 0AA *Tel:* 020 7219 4146 *Fax:* 020 7219 1243. *Constituency:* Northampton House, Poplar Road, Solihull, West Midlands, B91 3AP *Tel:* 0121–704 3071 *Fax:* 0121–705 6388.

TAYLOR, MATTHEW   Truro and St Austell   *LD majority 8,065*

Matthew Owen John Taylor. Born 3 January 1963; Son of Ken Taylor, TV author, and Jill Taylor, née Black; Educated Treliske School, Truro; University College School, London; Lady Margaret Hall, Oxford (BA politics, philosophy and economics 1986, MA). Sabbatical President, Oxford University Student Union 1985–86; Economic researcher, Parliamentary Liberal Party, attached to David Penhaligan MP 1986–87. **House of Commons:** Member for Truro March 12, 1987 by-election –1997 and for Truro and St Austell since May 1, 1997; Liberal Spokesperson for Energy 1987–88; Liberal Democrat Spokesperson for: England (Local Government, Housing and Transport) 1988–89, Trade and Industry 1989–90, Education 1990–92, Citizen's Charter 1992–94; Principal Spokesperson for: Environment 1994–97, the Environment and Transport 1997–99, Economy 1999–; *Select Committees:* Member: Broadcasting 1992–94, Environment 1995–97, Environmental Audit 1997. Chair, Liberal Democrat Campaigns and Communications 1989–95. Matthew Taylor Esq, MP, House of Commons, London, SW1A 0AA *Tel:* 020 7219 6686 *Fax:* 020 7219 4903. *Constituency:* Liberal Democrats, 10 South Street, St Austell, Cornwall, PL25 5BH *Tel:* 01726 63443 *Fax:* 01726 68457 *E-mail:* holbyi@parliament.uk.

TAYLOR, RICHARD   Wyre Forest   *Ind KHHC majority 17,630*

Richard Thomas Taylor. Born 7 July 1934; Son of Thomas Taylor, cotton spinner and Mabel Taylor, née Hickley; Educated The Leys School, Cambridge; Clare College, Cambridge (BA natural sciences 1956); Westminster Medical School (BChir 1959, MB 1960); Married Elizabeth Ann Brett 1962 (divorced 1986) (2 daughters 1 son); married Christine Helen Miller 1990 (1 daughter). Medical officer RAF 1961–64; House physician and surgeon 1959–61; St Stephen's Hospital, London: Senior house physician 1964–65, Medical registrar 1965–66; Westminster Hospital: Medical registrar 1966–67, Senior medical registrar 1967–72; Consultant in general medicine with special interest in rheumatology Kidderminster General Hospital and Droitwich Centre for Rheumatic Diseases 1972–95; BMA 1959–2001. **House of Commons:** Member for Wyre Forest since June 7, 2001; *Select Committees:* Member, Health 2001–. *Special Interests:* National Health Service. League of Friends of Kidderminster Hospital 1975–2001: Member, Chair 1996–2001; Chair: Save Kidderminster Hospital Campaign 1997–2000, Health Concern 2000–01; Royal Horticultural Society; Club Lotus; Severn Valley Railway; Royal Society of Medicine; Royal Society for the Protection of Birds; National Trust; English Heritage; Institute of Advanced Motorists; Worcester Wildlife Trust; *Publications:* Papers on drug treatment of rheumatic diseases etc in various medical journals 1968–73; MRCP 1965; FRCP 1979; *Recreations:* Family, ornithology, gardening, classic cars. Dr Richard Taylor, MP, House of Commons, London, SW1A 0AA *Tel:* 020 7219 4598 *Fax:* 020 7219 1967. *Constituency:* Gavel House, 137 Franche Road, Kidderminster, DY11 5AP *Tel:* 01562 753333 *E-mail:* pricemah@parliament.uk.

TAYLOR, TEDDY   Rochford and Southend East   *Con majority 7,034*

Teddy (Edward Macmillan) Taylor. Born 18 April 1937; Son of late Edward Taylor and Minnie H Taylor, née Murray; Educated The High School of Glasgow; Glasgow University (MA economics and politics 1958); Married Sheila Duncan 1970 (2 sons 1 daughter). Commercial editorial staff, *Glasgow Herald* October 1958-April 1959; Industrial relations officer, Clyde Shipbuilders' Association 1959–1964. Councillor, Glasgow Town Council 1959–64. **House of Commons:** Contested Glasgow Springburn 1959 general election. Member for Glasgow Cathcart 1964–79, for Southend East from March 13, 1980 by-election–1997, and for Rochford and Southend East since May 1, 1997; Shadow Spokesperson for: Trade 1977, Scottish Affairs 1977–79; Parliamentary Under-Secretary of State, Scottish Office 1970–71 (resigned over Government decision to join EC) and 1974; Shadow Secretary of State for: Trade 1976–, Scotland 1977–79; *Select Committees:* Member: Treasury 1997–2001, Treasury Sub-Committee 1998–2001. *Special Interests:* Temperance

Movement, European Union, Home Affairs, Environment. *Countries of Interest:* Libya, Pakistan. Council of Europe and the Western European Union; *Publications: Hearts of Stone* (novel), 1970; Knighted 1991; *Recreations:* Golf, chess, history. Sir Teddy Taylor, MP, House of Commons, London, SW1A 0AA *Tel:* 020 7219 3476 *Fax:* 020 7219 4828. *Constituency:* Suite 1, Strand House, 742 Southchurch Road, Southend, Essex, SS1 2PS *Tel:* 01702 600460 *Fax:* 01702 600460 *E-mail:* dayea@parliament.uk.

THOMAS, GARETH   Clwyd West   *Lab majority 1,115*

Gareth Thomas. Born 25 September 1954; Son of late William Thomas, toolmaker, and Megan H Thomas; Educated Rock Ferry High School, Birkenhead; University College of Wales, Aberystwyth (LLB 1976); Council of Legal Education, London 1977; Married Sioned Wyn Jones 1987 (1 daughter 1 son); married Joanne Warlow (1 daughter 1 son). Insurance industry in UK and overseas; Formerly loss adjuster: Toplis and Harding Guardian Royal Exchange; Barrister 1986–: Oriel Chambers, Liverpool 1986–99, Arden Chambers, London 1999–, Gray's Inn; Member, Amicus. Councillor, Flintshire County Council 1995–97. **House of Commons:** Member for Clwyd West since May 1, 1997; PPS to Paul Murphy: as Secretary of State for Wales 2001–02, as Secretary of State for Northern Ireland 2002–; *Select Committees:* Member: Welsh Affairs 1997–2000, Social Security 1999–2001, Joint Committee on Human Rights 2001. *Special Interests:* Constitutional Reform, Human Rights, Social Security, Legal Affairs, Criminal Justice, Police, Agriculture, Small Businesses. *Countries of Interest:* West Indies, South America. Member: Society of Labour Lawyers, Fabian Society. Member: Amnesty International, Local Credit Union; ACII; *Recreations:* Gardening, the arts, walking, restoring, old buildings. Gareth Thomas Esq, MP (Clwyd West), House of Commons, London, SW1A 0AA *Tel:* 020 7219 3516/2003 *Fax:* 020 7219 1263. *Constituency:* 5 Wynnstay Road, Colwyn Bay, Conwy, LL29 8NB *Tel:* 01492 531154 *Fax:* 01492 535731 *E-mail:* thomasg@parliament.uk.

THOMAS, GARETH RICHARD   Harrow West   *Lab majority 6,156*

Gareth Richard Thomas. Born 15 July 1967; Educated Hatch End High School; Lowlands College; University College of Wales, Aberystwyth (BSc (Econ) politics 1988); King's College, London (MA imperial and Commonwealth studies 1996); University of Greenwich (PGCE 1992). Member, AEEU. Councillor, Harrow 1990–97, Labour Group Whip 1996–96. **House of Commons:** Member for Harrow West since May 1, 1997; Member Environmental Audit Select Committee 1997–99; PPS to Charles Clarke: as Minister of State, Home Office 1999–2001, as Minister without Portfolio and Party Chair 2001–02, as Secretary of State for Education and Skills 2002–03; Sponsored Private Member's Bill, Industrial and Provident Societies Bill 2002; Parliamentary Under-Secretary of State, Department for International Development 2003–; *Select Committees:* Member, Environmental Audit 1997–99. *Special Interests:* Energy, Mutuals, Health, Environment. *Countries of Interest:* Europe, Norway, India, Sri Lanka. Member: Fabian Society, SERA; Chair Co-operative Party 2000–. Vice-Chair, Association of Local Government Social Services Committee; *Publications: At the Energy Crossroads* Policies for a Low Carbon Economy, Fabian Society, June 2001; *From Margins to Mainstream – Making Social Resposibility Part of Corporate Culture*, 2002; *Clubs:* United Services Club, Pinner; *Recreations:* Canoeing, running, rugby union. Gareth R Thomas Esq, MP (Harrow West), House of Commons, London, SW1A 0AA *Tel:* 020 7219 6436. *Constituency:* 132 Blenheim Road, West Harrow, Middlesex, HA2 7AA *Tel:* 020 8861 1300 *E-mail:* thomasgr@parliament.uk.

DodOnline
An Electronic Directory without rival …

MPs' biographies and photographs available with daily updates *via* the internet

For a *free* trial, call Yasmin Mirza, Aby Farsoun or Michael Mand on 020 7630 7643

THOMAS, SIMON   Ceredigion   *Pl C majority 3,944*

Simon Thomas. Born 28 December 1963; Educated Aberdare Boys Grammar/Comprehensive School; University College of Wales, Aberystwyth (BA Welsh 1985); College of Librarianship, Aberystwyth (post-graduate diploma 1988); Married Gwen Davies 1997 (1 son 1 daughter). Assistant curator National Library of Wales 1986–92; Policy and research officer Taff-Ely borough council 1992–94; Community development worker 1994–97; Rural development manager Jigso rural regeneration agency 1997–2000. Councillor, Ceredigion County Council 1999–2000. **House of Commons:** Member for Ceredigion since by-election February 3, 2000; Plaid Cymru Spokesperson for: Environment, Food and Rural Affairs and the Regions, Transport, International Development, Culture 2000–, Media and Sport, Energy 2000–01, Agriculture, Sustainable Energy, Heritage, International Development 2001–; Parliamentary whip 2001–; *Select Committees:* Member: Environmental Audit 2000–, Catering 2001–. Director for Policy and Research, Plaid Cymru's National Executive 1995–98. Simon Thomas Esq, MP, House of Commons, London, SW1A 0AA *Tel:* 020 7219 5021 *Fax:* 020 7219 3705. *Constituency:* 8 Water Street, Aberaeron, Ceredigion, SA46 0DG *Tel:* 01545 571688 *Fax:* 01545 571567 *E-mail:* thomassi@parliament.uk.

THURSO, JOHN   Caithness, Sutherland and Easter Ross   *LD majority 2,744*

John Archibald Sinclair Thurso. Born 10 September 1953; Son of late Robin, 2nd Viscount Thurso and Margaret, née Robertson; Educated Eton College; Westminster Technical College (HCIMA membership exam 1974); Married Marion Ticknor, née Sage 1976 (2 sons 1 daughter). Director: Lancaster Hotel 1981–85, Cliveden House Ltd 1985–93; Non-executive director, Savoy Hotel plc 1993–98; Managing director Fitness and Leisure Holdings Ltd 1995–2001; Chair: Thurso Fisheries Ltd 1995–, Scrabster Harbour Trust 1996–2001; Director: Profile Recruitment and Management Ltd 1996–2002, Walker Greenbank plc 1997–2002, Anton Mosiman Ltd 1997–2002; Deputy Chairman, Millennium and Copthorn's Hotels plc 2002–. **House of Commons:** Member for Caithness, Sutherland and Easter Ross since June 7, 2001; Liberal Democrat Lords spokesperson for: Tourism 1996–99, Food 1998–99; Scottish Liberal Democrat Spokesperson on Tourism 2001–; Liberal Democrat Spokesperson for Scotland 2001–; Liberal Democrat Whip 2001–02; *Select Committees:* Member, Lords Refreshment Sub-Committee 1997–99; Member, Culture, Media and Sport 2001–. *Special Interests:* Tourism, House of Lords Reform. Member Liberal Democrat Party Federal Policy Committee 1999–2001. Chair: Bucks Game Conservancy 1990–92, BHA Clubs Panel 1992–1996, Master Innholders Association 1995–97; President Licensed Victuallers Schools 1996–97; President and Fellow, Tourism Society 1999–; Patron: Hotel Catering and International Management Association 1997–2003, Institute of Management Services 1998–; President: Academy of Food and Wine Service 1998–, Tourism Society 2000–; Chair UK Springboard Festival Year 2000; Liveryman Innholders' Company 1997; *Publications: Tourism Tomorrow*, 1998; FHCIMA 1991; FInstD 1997; Freeman City of London 1991; *Clubs:* Brook's, New Edinburgh. Viscount Thurso, MP, House of Commons, London, SW1A 0AA *Tel:* 020 7219 8154 *Fax:* 020 7219 3797. *Constituency:* Thurso East Mains, Thurso, Caithness, KW14 8HN *Tel:* 01847 892600 *E-mail:* thursoj@parliament.uk.

TIMMS, STEPHEN   East Ham   *Lab majority 21,032*

Stephen Timms. Born 29 July 1955; Son of late Ronald James Timms, engineer, and of Margaret Joyce Timms, retired school teacher; Educated Farnborough Grammar School, Hampshire; Emmanuel College, Cambridge (MA mathematics 1977, MPhil operational research 1978); Married Hui-Leng Lim 1986. Computer and telecommunications industry; Logica Ltd 1978–86; Ovum Ltd 1986–94; Member, MSF. Little Ilford Ward, London Borough of Newham: Councillor 1984–97, Leader of the Council 1990–94, Former Chair, Economic Development Committee, Chair, Planning Committee 1987–90; Board Member, East London Partnership (now East London Business Alliance) 1990–; Stratford Development Partnership 1992–94; Chair, Race Education and Employment Forum. **House of Commons:** Member for Newham North East from June 9, 1994 by-election–1997, and for East Ham since May 1, 1997; PPS to Andrew Smith as Minister of State, Department for Education and Employment 1997–98; Joint PPS to Marjorie Mowlam, as Secretary of State for Northern Ireland 1998; Parliamentary Under-Secretary of State, Department of Social Security 1998–99, Minister of State 1999; Financial Secretary, HM Treasury 1999–2001; Minister of State: For School Standards, Department for Education and Skills 2001–02, For Energy, E-Commerce and Postal Services, Department of Trade and Industry 2002–; *Select Committees:* Member: Treasury 1996–97, Public Accounts 1999–2001. *Special Interests:* Economic Policy, Urban Regeneration, Telecommunications, Employment, Christian Socialism. Joint Vice-Chair, Christian Socialist Movement 1995–98. *Publications: Broadband Communications: The Commercial Impact*, 1987. Stephen Timms Esq, MP, House of Commons, London, SW1A 0AA *Tel:* 020 7219 4000 *Fax:* 020 7219 2949 *E-mail:* stephen@stephentimmsmp.org.uk.

TIPPING, PADDY Sherwood   *Lab majority 9,373*

Paddy Tipping. Born 24 October 1949; Son of late Ernest Tipping, newsagent, and late Margaret Tipping, clerk; Educated Hipperholme Grammar School; Nottingham University (BA philosophy 1972, MA applied social science 1978); Married Irene Margaret Quinn 1970 (2 daughters). Social worker, Nottingham and Nottinghamshire 1972–79; Project Leader, Church of England Children's Society, Nottingham 1979–83; Member, UNISON. Councillor, Nottinghamshire County Council 1981–93; Director: Nottinghamshire Co-operative Development Agency 1983–93, Nottingham Development Enterprise 1987–93. **House of Commons:** Contested Rushcliffe 1987 general election. Member for Sherwood since April 9, 1992; PPS to Jack Straw as Home Secretary 1997–99; Parliamentary Secretary, Privy Council Office 1999–2001; *Select Committees:* Member, Parliamentary Commissioner for Administration 1996–97; Member, Environment, Food and Rural Affairs 2001–. *Special Interests:* Local and Regional Government, Energy, Education, Police, Workers' Co-operatives, Rural Affairs, Agriculture, Environment. *Countries of Interest:* Former Soviet Union. Member, Co-operative Party; Chair: Central Region Group of Labour MPs 1997–2001, East Midlands Group of Labour MPs until 1999. Vice-President, The Ramblers' Association; Member: Industry and Parliament Trust, Armed Forces Parliamentary Trust; *Clubs:* Clipstone Miners' Welfare; *Recreations:* Family, gardening, running, walking. Paddy Tipping Esq, MP, House of Commons, London, SW1A 0AA *Tel:* 020 7219 5044 *Fax:* 020 7219 3641. *Constituency:* Sherwood Parliamentary Office, 1st Floor, Council Offices, Watnall Road, Hucknall, Nottinghamshire, NG15 7LA *Tel:* 0115–964 0314 *Fax:* 0115–968 1639.

TODD, MARK South Derbyshire   *Lab majority 7,851*

Mark Wainwright Todd. Born 29 December 1954; Son of Matthew and Viv Todd; Educated Sherborne School; Emmanuel College, Cambridge (BA history 1976); Married Sarah Margaret Dawson 1979 (1 son). Longman Group, latterly Addison Wesley Longman 1977–96: Managing Director: Longman Industry and Public Service Management 1988–92, Longman Cartermill 1990–92, Director: Information Technology 1992–94, Operations 1994–96; ASTMS (now AMICUS), union chairman at employers: Cambridge City Council 1980–92: Deputy Leader 1982–87, Leader of Council 1987–90. **House of Commons:** Member for South Derbyshire since May 1, 1997; PPS to Baroness Symons of Vernham Dean as Deputy Leader of the Lords and Minister of State, FCO and DTI 2002–; *Select Committees:* Member: Agriculture 1997–2001, Environment, Food and Rural Affairs 2001–02. *Special Interests:* Business, Economics, Local and Regional Government, Environment, Agriculture, Transport. *Countries of Interest:* Europe, Third World. Member: Greenpeace, Royal Society of Arts and Manufacture; Director, Cambridge and District Co-operative Society 1986–89; FRSA; *Recreations:* Reading, cinema. Mark Todd Esq, MP, House of Commons, London, SW1A 0AA *Tel:* 020 7219 3549 *Fax:* 020 7219 4935. *Constituency:* 37 Market Street, Church Gresley, Swadlincote, Derbyshire, DE11 9PR *Tel:* 01283 551573 *Fax:* 01283 210640 *E-mail:* toddm@parliament.uk.

TONGE, JENNY   Richmond Park   *LD majority 4,964*

Jenny (Jennifer) Louise Tonge. Born 19 February 1941; Daughter of late Sidney Smith, school teacher, and late Violet Smith, school teacher; Educated Dudley Girls' High School; University College, London (MB, BS 1964); Married Keith Tonge 1964 (2 sons 1 daughter). General practice/family planning 1968–78; Senior medical officer, Women's Services (Ealing) 1982–87; Manager, Community Health Services (Ealing) 1992–96; SW Thames Representative, BMA Public and Community Health Committee 1992–96. Councillor, London Borough of Richmond-on-Thames 1981–90, Chair, Social Services 1981–86. **House of Commons:** Contested Richmond and Barnes 1992 general election. Member for Richmond Park since May 1, 1997; Liberal Democrat Spokesperson for: International Development 1997–; *Select Committees:* Member, International Development 1997–99. *Special Interests:* Health, Environment, Social Services, International Development. *Countries of Interest:* Sudan, India, Pakistan, Colombia, Rwanda, Afghanistan. Chair, Richmond and Barnes Liberal Party 1978–80. Chair, Governors of Waldegrave School 1981–86; Member: RSPB, Amnesty International, Action For South Africa, Karuna Trust, Project Hope (UK); OSCE: Parliamentary Assembly Delegate 1998–2000, Rescue 2000–; Trustee, Off the Record, Richmond; School – James Smellie Gold Medal; Hon. Fellow Faculty of Family Planning (FFFP) of Royal College of Obstetricians and Gynaecologists; MFFP; FRIPHH; Visiting Parliamentary Fellow, St Anthony's College, Oxford 1999–2000; *Sportsclubs:* Hon. Member, Richmond Football Club (Rugby). Dr Jenny Tonge, MP, House of Commons, London, SW1A 0AA *Tel:* 020 7219 4596 *Fax:* 020 7219 4596. *Constituency:* Old Station Works, 119–123 Sandycombe Lane, Richmond, Surrey, TW9 2ER *Tel:* 020 8332 7919 *Fax:* 020 8332 7919 *E-mail:* tonge@cix.compulink.co.uk.

TOUHIG, DON   Islwyn   *Lab majority 15,309*

Don (James Donnelly) Touhig. Born 5 December 1947; Son of late Michael and Catherine Touhig; Educated St Francis School, Abersychan; Mid Gwent College; Married Jennifer Hughes 1968 (2 sons 2 daughters). Journalist 1968–76; Editor, Free Press of Monmouthshire 1976–90; General manager and editor in chief, Free Press Group of Newspapers 1988–92; General manager (business development), Bailey Group 1992–93, Bailey Print 1993–95; Member, TGWU. Councillor, Gwent County Council 1973–95; Chair, Finance Committee 1992–94. **House of Commons:** Contested Richmond and Barnes 1992 general election. Member for Islwyn since February 16, 1995 by-election; Assistant Government Whip 1999–2001; Public Interest Disclosure (Private Member's Bill) 1995; PPS to Gordon Brown as Chancellor of the Exchequer 1997–99; Parliamentary Under-Secretary of State: Wales Office 2001–03, Department for Constitutional Affairs 2003–; *Select Committees:* Member, Welsh Affairs 1996–97. *Special Interests:* Treasury, Employment, Health, Education, Local and Regional Government. Hon. Secretary, Welsh Regional Group of Labour MPs 1995–99; Member, Labour Leadership Campaign Team (responsible for Devolution in Wales) 1996–97; Member, Co-Operative Party; Chair, Co-operative Parliamentary Group 1999. Past President, South Wales Newspaper Society; Member: MENSA, MENCAP. Amnesty International, Credit Union; President: Home Start, Islwyn Drug and Alcohol Project, National Old Age Pensioners Association of Wales, Caerphilly County Borough Access Group; Member, European Standing Committee B 1995–96; Trustee, Medical Council on Alcoholism; Papal Knight of the Order of St Sylvester; *Recreations:* Reading, cooking for family and friends, music, walking. Don Touhig Esq, MP, House of Commons, London, SW1A 0AA *Tel:* 020 7219 6435 *Fax:* 020 7219 2070. *Constituency:* 6 Woodfieldside Business Park, Penmaen Road, Pontllanfraith, Blackwood, Gwent, NP12 2DG *Tel:* 01495 231990 *Fax:* 01495 231959 *E-mail:* don.touhig@wales.gsi.gov.uk.

Visit the Vacher Dod Website . . .
www.DodOnline.co.uk

TREDINNICK, DAVID   Bosworth   Con majority 2,280

David Tredinnick. Born 19 January 1950; Son of Stephen Victor Tredinnick and Evelyn Mabel, née Wates; Educated Eton College; Mons Officer Cadet School; Graduate School of Business; Cape Town University (MBA 1975); St John's College, Oxford (MLitt 1987); Married Rebecca Shott 1983 (1 son 1 daughter). 2nd Lieutenant Grenadier Guards 1968–71; Trainee, E. B. Savory Milln & Co. (Stockbrokers) 1972–73; Account executive, Quadrant Int. 1974; Salesman, Kalle Infotech UK 1976; Sales manager, Word Right Word Processing 1977–78; Consultant, Baird Communications NY 1978–79; Marketing manager, QI Europe Ltd 1979–81; Manager, Malden Mitcham Properties 1981–87. **House of Commons:** Contested Cardiff South and Penarth 1983 general election. Member for Bosworth since June 1987; PPS to Sir Wyn Roberts as Minister of State, Welsh Office 1991–94; *Select Committees:* Chair, Joint Committee on Statutory Instruments 1997–; Member, Liaison 1997–. *Special Interests:* Complementary and Alternative Medicine, Health Care, Diet and Nutrition, Foreign Affairs, Home Affairs, Police, Law and Order, Environment. *Countries of Interest:* Eastern Europe. Chair, British Atlantic Group of Young Politicians 1989–91; Future of Europe Trust 1991–95; *Recreations:* Golf, skiing, tennis, windsurfing, sailing. David Tredinnick Esq, MP, House of Commons, London, SW1A 0AA *Tel:* 020 7219 4514 *Fax:* 020 7219 4901. *Constituency:* Bosworth Conservative Association, 10a Priory Walk, Hinckley, Leicestershire, LE10 1HU *Tel:* 01455 635741 *Fax:* 01455 612023 *E-mail:* tredinnickd@parliament.uk.

TREND, MICHAEL   Windsor   Con majority 8,889

Michael St John Trend. Born 19 April 1952; Son of late Rt Hon. Baron Trend, GCB, CVO and Patricia Charlotte Shaw; Educated Westminster School; Oriel College, Oxford (MA Oxon); Married Jill Kershaw 1987 (1 son 2 daughters). Journalist; Editor; Broadcaster; Contested North East London 1989 European Parliament election; Chief leader writer, *Daily Telegraph* 1990–92. **House of Commons:** Member for Windsor and Maidenhead 1992–97, and for Windsor since May 1, 1997; Opposition Front Bench Spokesman for: Foreign and Commonwealth Affairs 1998–99, Social Security 1999–2000; PPS; to Tim Yeo as Minister of State, Department of Environment 1993–94, to Brian Mawhinney: as Minister of State, Department of Health 1992–94, as Secretary of State for Transport 1994–95; *Select Committees:* Member, Health 1992–93; Member, Public Administration 2000–. *Special Interests:* Education, Health, Defence, Foreign Affairs. Deputy Chair, Conservative Party 1995–98; Head of Conservative Party International Office 2000–. CBE 1997; *Recreations:* Hill walking, cricket, playing the organ. Hon Michael Trend, CBE, MP, House of Commons, London, SW1A 0AA *Tel:* 020 7219 6929 *Fax:* 020 7219 5946. *Constituency:* 87 St Leonards Road, Windsor, Berkshire, SL4 3BZ *Tel:* 01753 678693 *Fax:* 01753 832774.

TRICKETT, JON   Hemsworth   Lab majority 15,636

Jon Trickett. Born 2 July 1950; Son of Laurence and Rose Trickett; Educated Roundhay School, Leeds; Hull University (BA politics); Leeds University (MA political sociology); Married Sarah Balfour 1993 (1 son 2 daughters). Plumber/builder 1974–86; Member, GMB Union; Member, RMT Parliamentary Campaigning Group 2002–. Leeds City Council: Councillor 1984–96, Chair: Finance Committee 1985–88, Housing Committee 1988–89, Leader of the Council 1989–96 **House of Commons:** Member for Hemsworth since February 1, 1996 By-election; PPS to Peter Mandelson: as Minister without Portfolio 1997–98, as Secretary of State for Trade and Industry July–December 1998; *Select Committees:* Member: Education and Employment 2001, Employment Sub-Committee 2001; Member: Unopposed Bills (Panel) 1997–, Public Accounts 2001–. *Special Interests:* Economic Policy, Finance, Industry, Sport. *Countries of Interest:* Middle East, France, USA. *Clubs:* British Cycling Federation; *Sportsclubs:* Member: British Cycling Federation, West Riding Sailing Club; Hon Life Member, Cyclists' Touring Club; *Recreations:* Cycle racing, windsurfing. Jon Trickett Esq, MP, House of Commons, London, SW1A 0AA *Tel:* 020 7219 5074 *Fax:* 020 7219 2133. *Constituency:* 18 Market Street, Hemsworth, Pontefract, West Yorkshire, WF9 5LB *Tel:* 01977 722290 *Fax:* 01977 722290 *E-mail:* trickettj@parliament.uk.

TRIMBLE, DAVID   Upper Bann   *UUP majority 2,058*

(William) David Trimble. Born 15 October 1944; Son of late William and Ivy Trimble; Educated Bangor Grammar School; Queen's University, Belfast (LLB); Married Daphne Orr 1978 (2 sons 2 daughters). Queen's University, Belfast: Lecturer in Law 1968–77, Senior Lecturer 1977–90; Member, South Belfast, Northern Ireland Constitutional Convention 1975–76; Elected to the Northern Ireland Forum 1996–98; Elected to the Northern Ireland Assembly 1998–; First Minister, Northern Ireland Assembly 1998-July 2001, November 2001–03. **House of Commons:** Member for Upper Bann since May 17, 1990 by-election; UUP Spokesperson for: Constitutional Affairs, Treasury 2002–. Chair, Lagan Valley Unionist Association 1985–90; Leader, Ulster Unionist Party 1995–. Chair, Ulster Society 1985–90; PC 1998; Nobel Peace Prize (jointly) 1998; Channel 4 and *The House* Magazine, Major Political Achievement 1999; St Angela's Peace and Justice Group Award 2002; *Recreations:* Music, reading. Rt Hon David Trimble, MP, House of Commons, London, SW1A 0AA *Tel:* 020 7219 6987 *Fax:* 020 7219 0575. *Constituency:* 2 Queen Street, Lurgan, BT66 8BQ *Tel:* 028 3832 8088 *Fax:* 028 3832 2343 *E-mail:* trimbled@parliament.uk.

TRUSWELL, PAUL   Pudsey   *Lab majority 5,626*

Paul Anthony Truswell. Born 17 November 1955; Son of John Truswell, retired foundryman, and Olive Truswell, retired cleaner; Educated Firth Park Comprehensive School; Leeds University (BA history 1977); Married Suzanne Evans (2 sons). Journalist, Yorkshire Post Newspapers 1977–88; Local government officer, Wakefield MDC 1988–97; Member: UNISON, NUJ. Councillor, Leeds City Council 1982–97; Member: Leeds Eastern Health Authority 1982–90, Leeds Community Health Council 1990–92, Leeds Family Health Services Authority 1992–96. **House of Commons:** Member for Pudsey since May 1, 1997; *Select Committees:* Member, Environmental Audit 1997–99. *Special Interests:* Health, Social Services, Environment. *Clubs:* Civil Service, Guiseley Factory Workers; *Recreations:* Cinema, Cricket, Tennis, Badminton, Photography. Paul Truswell Esq, MP, House of Commons, London, SW1A 0AA *Tel:* 020 7219 3504 *Fax:* 020 7219 2252. *Constituency:* 10A Greenside, Pudsey, West Yorkshire, LS28 8PU *Tel:* 0113–229 3553 *Fax:* 0113–229 3800.

TURNER, ANDREW   Isle of Wight   *Con majority 2,826*

Andrew John Turner. Born 24 October 1953; Son of Eustace Albert Turner, schoolmaster, and Joyce Mary Turner, née Lowe, schoolmistress; Educated Rugby School; Keble College, Oxford (BA geography 1976, MA 1981); Birmingham University (PGCE 1977); Henley Management College; Single. Teacher economics and geography comprehensive schools 1977–84; Conservative Research Department specialist: education, trade and industry 1984–86; Special Adviser Secretary of State for Social Services 1986–88; Director Grant-Maintained Schools Foundation 1988–97; Contested Birmingham East 1994 European Parliament election; Education consultant 1997–2001; Head of policy and resources, education department, London Borough of Southwark 2000–01. Councillor Oxford City Council 1979–96; Sheriff of Oxford 1994–95. **House of Commons:** Contested Hackney South and Shoreditch 1992 and Isle of Wight 1997 general elections. Member for Isle of Wight since June 7, 2001; Sponsored Animal Welfare (Journey to Slaughter) Bill 2001; *Select Committees:* Member, Education and Skills 2001–. *Special Interests:* Education, Social Services, Economy, Constitution. Party worker ward and constituency level; Campaign co-ordinator DHSS Ministers general election 1987; Appointee party education policy groups for general elections: 1987, 1992, 2001; Vice-president Association of Conservative Clubs 2002–. Fellow of Royal Society of Arts; *Clubs:* United Oxford and Cambridge University; *Recreations:* Walking, old movies, avoiding gardening. Andrew Turner Esq, MP, House of Commons, London, SW1A 0AA *Tel:* 020 7219 8490. *Constituency:* 24 The Mall, Carisbrooke Road, Newport, PO30 1BW *Tel:* 01983 530808 *Fax:* 01983 822266.

TURNER, DENNIS   Wolverhampton South East   *Lab majority 12,464*

Dennis Turner. Born 26 August 1942; Son of late Thomas Herbert and Mary Elizabeth Turner; Educated Stonefield Secondary School, Bilston; Bilston College of Further Education; Married Patricia Narroway 1976 (1 son 1 daughter). Director, Springvale Co-operative, sports, social and leisure centre 1981–; Chair, Midlands Iron and Steel Trades Confederation Conference 1974–76. Councillor: Wolverhampton Borough Council 1966–86, West Midlands County Council 1973–86; Chair: Wolverhampton Social Services Committee 1973–79, Higher Education Committee 1974–81, Economic Development Committee 1979–84, Theatre Committee 1980–82, Deputy Leader 1980–86; Director, Black Country Co-operative Development Agency 1983–88; Chair Housing Committee 1985–86. **House of Commons:** Contested Halesowen and Stourbridge February and October 1974 general elections. Member for Wolverhampton South East since June 1987; Opposition Whip 1992–97; PPS to Secretaries of State for International Development: Clare Short 1997–2003, Baroness Amos 2003; *Select Committees:* Member, Education 1988–94; Chair, Catering 1997–2001; Member: Court of Referees 1997–, Finance and Services 1997–, Liaison 1998–; Chair, Catering 2001–. *Special Interests:* Education, Social Services, Housing, International Development, Small Businesses. *Countries of Interest:* South Africa, The Commonwealth, British Overseas Territories. Member, Co-operative Party; Chair, Parliamentary Labour Party Local Government Group 1997–99; PLP West Midlands Group: Vice-chair 1997–2001, Chair 2001–. President: Bilston Community Association, Wolverhampton Deaf Children's Society; Vice-President: Wolverhampton MENCAP, Wolverhampton Race Equality Council; Member, Executive Committee: IPU (British Branch); Commonwealth Parliamentary Association (CPA) UK Branch 1999–, Vice-Chair; Trustee-Secretary, Bradley Old People's Trust; *Clubs:* New Springvale Sports and Social (Bilston); *Recreations:* Tasting traditional ales, all card games. Dennis Turner Esq, MP, House of Commons, London, SW1A 0AA *Tel:* 020 7219 4210. *Constituency:* Springvale Club, Millfields Road, Bilston, West Midlands, WV14 0QR *Tel:* 01902 492364 *Fax:* 01902 494074.

TURNER, DES   Brighton Kemptown   *Lab majority 4,922*

Des (Desmond Stanley) Turner. Born 17 July 1939; Son of late Stanley M. M. Turner and of Elsie Turner; Educated Luton Grammar School; Imperial College, London (BSc botany 1961, MSc biochemistry 1962); University College, London (PhD biochemistry 1972); Brighton Polytechnic (PGCE); Married Lynne Rogers 1997 (1 daughter from previous marriage). Medical researcher; Teacher; Partner in independent brewery; Past Member: AUT, TGWU, NUT; Member, MSF (AMICUS). Councillor: East Sussex County Council 1985–96, Brighton Borough Council 1994–96, Brighton and Hove Unitary Council 1996–99. **House of Commons:** Contested Mid-Sussex 1979 general election. Member for Brighton Kemptown since May 1, 1997; *Select Committees:* Member, Science and Technology 1997–. *Special Interests:* Health, Social Services, Employment, Disability, Housing, Science Policy, Animal Welfare, Fuel Poverty and Renewable Energy. *Countries of Interest:* Europe, Peru. Member: Age Concern, East Sussex, Shelter, LACS, CFAW, Terence Higgins Trust, Brighton Housing Trust, Brighton and Hove ME Group; Parliamentary observer: Albanian elections 1997, Bosnian elections 1998; Member, Brighton Housing Trust; *Publications:* Research papers and reviews; R. D. Lawrence Memorial Fellow, British Diabetic Association 1970–72; ARCS; *Sportsclubs:* Polytechnic Fencing Club, Brighton Marina Yacht Club; *Recreations:* Sailing, fencing. Dr Des Turner, MP, *Tel:* 020 7219 4024, *Constituency:* 179 Preston Road, Brighton, BN1 6AG *Tel:* 01273 330610 *Fax:* 01273 500966 *E-mail:* turnerd@parliament.uk.

DodOnline
An Electronic Directory without rival . . .
MPs' biographies and photographs available with daily updates *via* the internet

For a *free* trial, call Yasmin Mirza, Aby Farsoun or Michael Mand on 020 7630 7643

TURNER, NEIL   Wigan   *Lab majority 13,743*

Neil Turner. Born 16 September 1945; Educated Carlisle Grammar School; Married Susan 1971 (1 son). Quantity surveyor, Fairclough Builders (later AMEC) 1967–94; Operations manager, North Shropshire District Council 1995–97; Member, MSF. Councillor, Wigan County Borough Council 1972–74; Wigan Metropolitan Borough Council: Councillor 1975–2000, Vice-Chair, Highways and Works Committee 1978–80, Chair 1980–97, Chair, Best Value Review Panel 1998–99. **House of Commons:** Contested Oswestry 1970 general election. Member for Wigan since September 23, 1999 by-election; PPS to Ian McCartney as: Minister of State, Department for Work and Pensions 2001–03, Minister without Portfolio and Party Chair 2003–; *Select Committees:* Member, Public Administration 2000–01. *Special Interests:* Local and Regional Government, Housing. Former Member, Sale Young Socialists. Vice-Chair, Public Services Committee, Association of Metropolitan Authorities 1987–95, Chair 1995–97; Vice-Chair, Local Government Association Quality Panel 1997–98, Chair 1998–99; *Recreations:* Keen follower of Wigan Rugby League Club, naval history. Neil Turner Esq, MP, House of Commons, London, SW1A 0AA *Tel:* 020 7219 4494. *Constituency:* Gerrard Winstanley House, Crawford Street, Wigan, Greater Manchester, WN1 1NG *Tel:* 01942 242047 *Fax:* 01942 828008 *E-mail:* turnern@parliament.uk.

TWIGG, DEREK   Halton   *Lab majority 17,428*

Derek Twigg. Born 9 July 1959; Son of Kenneth and Irene Twigg; Educated Bankfield High School, Widnes; Halton College of Further Education; Married Mary Cassidy 1988 (1 son 1 daughter). Civil servant, Department for Education and Employment 1975–96; Political consultant 1996–; PCS: Branch secretary, Branch chair 1978–84; Member GMB. Councillor, Cheshire County Council 1981–85; Halton Borough Council: Councillor 1983–97, Chair of Housing 1988–93, Chair of Finance 1993–96, Education Spokesperson 1996–97. **House of Commons:** Member for Halton since May 1, 1997; Assistant Government Whip 2002–03, Government Whip 2003–; PPS: to Helen Liddell: as Minister of State, Department of the Environment, Transport and the Regions (Minister for Transport) 1999, as Minister of State, Department of Trade and Industry (Minister for Energy and Competitiveness in Europe) 1999–2001; to Stephen Byers as Secretary of State for Transport, Local Government and the Regions 2001–02; *Select Committees:* Member, Public Accounts 1998–99. *Special Interests:* Economy, Education, Health and Poverty, Housing, Small Businesses. *Countries of Interest:* Greece. Member, European Standing Committee B 1997–98; *Recreations:* Various sporting activities, hill walking, reading history. Derek Twigg Esq, MP, House of Commons, London, SW1A 0AA *Tel:* 020 7219 3554. *Constituency:* F2 Moor Lane Business Centre, Moor Lane, Widnes, Cheshire, WA8 7AQ *Tel:* 0151–424 7030 *Fax:* 0151–495 3800 *E-mail:* twiggd@parliament.uk.

TWIGG, STEPHEN   Enfield Southgate   *Lab majority 5,546*

Stephen Twigg. Born 25 December 1966; Son of Ian David Twigg and late Jean Barbara Twigg; Educated Southgate Comprehensive; Balliol College, Oxford (BA politics and economics 1988); Single. Former President, National Union of Students; Former Parliamentary Officer: Amnesty International UK, NCVO; Former Research Assistant to Margaret Hodge, MP for Barking; Former Political Consultant, Rowland Sallingbury Casey; General Secretary, Fabian Society 1996–97; Member, AMICUS-MSF. Councillor, London Borough of Islington 1992–97; Chief Whip 1994–96; Deputy Leader 1996. **House of Commons:** Member for Enfield Southgate since May 1, 1997; Parliamentary Secretary, Privy Council Office 2001–02; Parliamentary Under-Secretary of State, Department for Education and Skills: for Young People and Learning 2002, for Schools 2002–; *Select Committees:* Member: Modernisation of the House of Commons 1998–2000, Education and Employment 1999–2001, Employment Sub-Committee 1999–2001. *Special Interests:* Education, Electoral Reform, Local and Regional Government, Foreign Affairs. *Countries of Interest:* Israel, Cyprus. Executive Member, Fabian Society; Chair: Labour Campaign for Electoral Reform –2001, Labour Friends of Israel –2001. Member: Amnesty International, Stonewall, League Against Cruel Sports;

Governor: Merryhills Primary School, Southgate School, Middlesex University Court; Principal Patron, Theatre Company; Hon President, British Youth Council; Patron, Principal Theatre Co; Member, Holocaust Educational Trust; *Publications:* Co-author *The Cross We Bear: Electoral Reform in Local Government*, 1997; *Clubs:* National Liberal; *Sportsclubs:* Southgate Cricket. Stephen Twigg Esq, MP, House of Commons, London, SW1A 0AA *Tel:* 020 7219 6554 *Fax:* 020 7219 0948. *Constituency:* 3 Chase Side, Southgate, London, N14 3BP *Tel:* 020 8245 5151 *Fax:* 020 8245 0022 *E-mail:* twiggs@parliament.uk.

TYLER, PAUL   North Cornwall   *LD majority 9,832*

Paul Archer Tyler. Born 29 October 1941; Son of Oliver and Grace Tyler; Educated Sherborne School; Exeter College, Oxford (BA modern history 1963, MA); Married Nicola Mary Ingram 1970 (1 daughter 1 son). Director, public affairs, Royal Institute of British Architects 1972–73; Board member, Shelter: National Campaign for the Homeless 1975–76; Managing director, Cornwall Courier Newspaper Group 1976–81; Public affairs division, Good Relations plc: Executive director 1982–84, Chief executive 1984–86, Chair 1986–87; Senior consultant, Public Affairs 1987–92; Director, Western Approaches Public Relations Ltd 1987–92; Contested (SLD) Cornwall and Plymouth 1989 European Parliament election. Councillor, Devon County Council 1964–70; Member, Devon and Cornwall Police Authority 1965–70; Vice-Chair, Dartmoor National Park Committee 1965–70. **House of Commons:** Contested (Liberal) Totnes 1966 and Bodmin 1970 general elections. Member for Bodmin February-October 1974. Contested Bodmin 1979 general election and Beaconsfield 1982 by-election. Member (Liberal Democrat) for North Cornwall since April 9, 1992; Spokesperson for: Agriculture and Rural Affairs 1992–97, Agriculture, Tourism, Transport and Rural Affairs 1994–96, Food 1997–99; Chief Whip 1997–2001; Shadow Leader of the House 1997–; Member Joint Committee on House of Lords Reform 2002–; *Select Committees:* Member: Procedure 1992–97, Finance and Services 1997–2001, Parliamentary Privilege (Joint Committee) 1997–2000, Procedure 1997–98, Selection 1997–2001; Member: Modernisation of the House of Commons 1997–, Joint Committee on House of Lords Reform 2002–. *Special Interests:* Tourism, Rural Affairs, Constitutional Reform. Chair: Devon and Cornwall Region Liberal Party 1981–82, Liberal Party National Executive Committee 1983–86; Campaign adviser to David Steel, MP in 1983 and 1987 general elections. Vice-President: British Resorts Association, Youth Hostels Association, Action for Communities in Rural England; Chair, CPRE Working Party on the future of the village 1974–81; Vice-President, Federation of Economic Development Authorities (FEDA); Vice-President, British Trust for Conservation Volunteers; *Publications:* Co-author *Power to the Provinces*, 1968; *A New Deal for Rural Britain*, 1978; *Country Lives, Country Landscapes*, 1996; CBE 1985; *Recreations:* Sailing, gardening, walking. Paul Tyler Esq, CBE, MP, House of Commons, London, SW1A 0AA *Tel:* 020 7219 6355 *Fax:* 020 7219 4870. *Constituency:* Church Stile, Launceston, Cornwall, PL15 8AT *Tel:* 01566 777123 *Fax:* 01566 772122 *E-mail:* williamssa@parliament.uk.

TYNAN, BILL   Hamilton South   *Lab majority 10,775*

Bill Tynan. Born 18 August 1940; Son of late James and Mary Tynan; Educated St Mungo's Academy, Glasgow; Stow College (City and Guilds Certificate mechanical engineering 1960); Married Elizabeth Mathieson 1964 (3 daughters). Toolmaker apprenticeship 1956–61; Press toolmaker 1961–88; Full-time union official: district secretary, regional office and political officer 1988–99; AEEU 1965–: Convenor 1965–75, Shop steward various companies 1965–88, local and national posts, Scottish Political Secretary 1991–98; Treasurer, Scottish Trade Union Labour Liaison Committee 1997 98, AEU: National committee delegate, Rules revision delegate; Chair Standing Orders Committee; Treasurer AEEU MP Group 2001–. **House of Commons:** Member for Hamilton South since September 23, 1999 by-election; *Select Committees:* Member, Scottish Affairs 1999–2001; Member: European Scrutiny 2001–, Northern Ireland Affairs 2001–. *Special Interests:* Employment Law, Social Security, Equal Opportunities, Social Inclusion, Energy, International Development. Constituency and Scottish Labour Party posts; Member Labour's Scottish Policy Forum 1997–99; Chair Scottish Regional Group of Labour MPs 2001–02. *Recreations:* Golf, watching football, diy, gardening. Bill Tynan, Esq, MP, House of Commons, London, SW1A 0AA *Tel:* 020 7219 6285 *Fax:* 020 7219 1295. *Constituency:* 154 Montrose Crescent, Hamilton, South Lanarkshire, ML3 6LL *Tel:* 01698 454925 *Fax:* 01698 454926 *E-mail:* tynanb@parliament.uk.

TYRIE, ANDREW   Chichester   *Con majority 11,355*

Andrew Tyrie. Born 15 January 1957; Son of the late Derek and Patricia Tyrie; Educated Felstead School, Essex; Trinity College, Oxford (BA philosophy, politics and economics 1979 MA); College of Europe, Bruges (Diploma in economics 1980); Wolfson College, Cambridge (MPhil international relations 1981). Group head office, British Petroleum 1981–83; Adviser to Chancellors of the Exchequer: Nigel Lawson 1986–89, John Major 1989–90, Fellow, Nuffield College, Oxford 1990–91; Senior economist, European Bank for Reconstruction and Development 1992–97. **House of Commons:** Contested Houghton and Washington 1992 general election. Member for Chichester since May 1, 1997; *Select Committees:* Member: Joint Committee on Consolidation of Bills Etc 1997–2001, Public Administration 1997–2001; Member: Treasury 2001–, Treasury Sub-Committee 2001–. *Special Interests:* European Union, Economic Policy. Member, Public Accounts Commission 1997–; Member, Inter-Parliamentary Union; *Publications:* Various works on economic and monetary union in Europe and other European issues; *The Prospects for Public Spending*, 1996; *Reforming the Lords: a Conservative Approach*, 1998; *Sense on EMU*, 1998; Co-author *Leviathan at Large: The New Regulator for the Financial Markets*, 2000; *Mr Blair's Poodle: An Agenda for Reviving the House of Commons*, 2000; *Back from the Brink*, 2001; Co-author, *Statism by Stealth: New Labour, New Collectivism*, 2002; *Axis of Instability: America, Britain and the New World Order after Iraq*, 2003; *Clubs:* MCC, RAC, Chichester Yacht Club; *Recreations:* Golf. Andrew Tyrie Esq, MP, House of Commons, London, SW1A 0AA *Tel:* 020 7219 6371 *Fax:* 020 7219 0625. *Constituency:* Chichester Conservative Association, 145 St Pancras, Chichester, West Sussex, PO19 4LH *Tel:* 01243 783519 *Fax:* 01243 536848 *E-mail:* marsha@parliament.uk.

V

VAZ, KEITH   Leicester East   *Lab majority 13,442*

Keith Vaz. Born 26 November 1956; Son of Merlyn Verona Vaz, mother and teacher; Educated St Joseph's Convent, Aden; Latymer Upper School, Hammersmith; Gonville and Caius College, Cambridge (BA law 1979, MA 1987, MCFI 1988); College of Law, London; Married Maria Fernandes 1993 (1 son, 1 daughter). Articled clerk, Richmond Council 1980–82; Solicitor 1982; Senior solicitor, Islington LBC 1982–85; Contested Surrey West 1984 European Parliament election; Solicitor: Highfields and Belgrave Law Centre 1985–87, North Leicester Advice Centre 1986–87; Contested Surrey West 1994 European Parliament elections; Member, UNISON 1985–. **House of Commons:** Contested Richmond and Barnes 1983 general election. Member for Leicester East since June 1987; Opposition Front Bench Spokesman on: The Environment 1992–97; PPS to: John Morris as Attorney General 1997–99, Solicitors General Lord Falconer of Thoroton 1997–98, Ross Cranston 1998–99; Parliamentary Secretary, Lord Chancellor's Department 1999; Minister of State, Foreign and Commonwealth Office (Minister for Europe) 1999–2001; *Select Committees:* Member, Home Affairs 1987–92; Member, Lord Chancellor's Department 2003–. *Special Interests:* Education, Legal Services, Local and Regional Government, Race Relations, Urban Policy, Small Businesses. *Countries of Interest:* India, Pakistan, Yemen, Bangladesh, Oman. Chair: Labour Party Race Action Group 1983–, Unison Group 1990–99; Tribune Group: Vice-chair 1992, Treasurer 1994; Labour Party Regional Executive 1994–96. President, Leicester and South Leicestershire RSPCA 1988–99; Patron, Gingerbread 1990–; National Advisory Committee, Crime Concern; Patron, Asian Business Club 1998–1999; President: Asian Business Network 1998–1999, Patron, Asian Doners Appeal 2000–; Several local organisations; Member, Standing Committees on: Immigration Bill 1987–88, Legal Aid Bill 1988, Children's Bill 1988–89, Football Spectators Bill 1989, National Health Service and Community Care Bill 1989–90, Courts and Legal Services Bill 1990, Armed Forces Bill 1990–91, Promoter, Race Relations Remedies Act 1994; Governor, Commonwealth Institute 1998–99; Board Member, The British Council 1999–; Member, Executive Committee Inter-Parliamentary Union 1993–94; *Publications:* Co-author *Law Reform Now*, 1996; *Clubs:* Safari (Leicester); *Recreations:* Tennis. Keith Vaz Esq, MP, House of Commons, London, SW1A 0AA *Tel:* 020 7219 6419 *Fax:* 020 7219 5743. *Constituency:* 144 Uppingham Road, Leicester LE5 0QF *Tel:* 0116–212 2028.

VIGGERS, PETER   Gosport   *Con majority 2,621*

Peter J Viggers. Born 13 March 1938; Son of late John Sidney Viggers and Evelyn Viggers; Educated Portsmouth Grammar School; Trinity Hall, Cambridge (history and law 1961, MA); College of Law, Guildford 1967; Married Dr Jennifer Mary McMillan 1968 (2 sons 1 daughter). National service RAF pilot 1956–58; Territorial Army Officer 1962–67; Solicitor 1967; Chair and director of companies in banking, oil, hotels, textiles, pharmaceuticals, venture capital 1970–79; Member Council of Lloyd's of London 1992–95; Chair: Tracer Petroleum Corporation 1996–98, Lloyd's Pension Fund 1996–. **House of Commons:** Member for Gosport since February 1974; PPS: to Sir Ian Percival as Solicitor General 1979–83, to Peter Rees as Chief Secretary to the Treasury 1983–85; Parliamentary Under-Secretary of State (Industry Minister), Northern Ireland Office 1986–89; *Select Committees:* Member: Defence 1992–97, Armed Forces Bill 1996, Defence 2000–01. *Special Interests:* Finance, Trade and Industry, Defence, Local Hospitals. *Countries of Interest:* Japan, South East Asia, USA, China, Central and Eastern Europe. Chair, Cambridge University Conservative Association 1960. RNLI: National Committee 1979–, Vice-President 1989–; Chairman Governors of St Vincent College, Gosport 1993–97; Member: European Standing Committee A 1998–, European Standing Committee B until 2003; UK Delegate, North Atlantic Assembly 1981–86, 1992–; Chair: Sub-Committee on Central and Eastern Europe 1999–2000, Political Committee 2000–; Fellow Industry and Parliament Trust; Trustee Royal Navy Submarine Museum Appeal; Patron Bridgeworks Trust; *Publications: Reserve Forces*, RUSI Journal, 2003; *Clubs:* Boodle's; President, Gosport Conservative; *Sportsclubs:* House of Commons Yacht Club: Member, Commodore 1982–83, Admiral 1997–99; *Recreations:* Beagling, opera, travel. Peter Viggers Esq, MP, House of Commons, London, SW1A 0AA *Tel:* 020 7219 5081 *Fax:* 020 7219 3985. *Constituency:* Gosport Conservative Association, 167 Stoke Road, Gosport, Hampshire, PO12 1SE *Tel:* 023 9258 8400 *Fax:* 023 9252 7624.

VIS, RUDI   Finchley and Golders Green   *Lab majority 3,716*

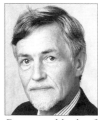

Rudi (Rudolf) Jan Vis. Born 4 April 1941; Son of late Laurens Vis, insurance broker, and late Helena Vis; Educated High School, Alkmaar, The Netherlands; University of Maryland, USA (BSc economics 1970); London School of Economics (MSc economics 1972); Brunel University (PhD economics 1976); Married Joan Hanin 1982 (divorced) (1 son); married Jacqueline Suffling 2001 (twin sons). Dutch armed services 1960–64; Administrator US Air Force, Madrid 1964–66; Night manager, Hotel Fleissis, Amsterdam 1966; University of Maryland, USA 1966–70; Principal lecturer, economics, North East London Polytechnic/University of East London 1971–97; Member: NATFHE 1971–94, MSF 1994–. Councillor, London Borough of Barnet 1986–98. **House of Commons:** Member for Finchley and Golders Green since May 1, 1997; *Special Interests:* Finance, European Union, Economics, Defence, Elderly, Small Businesses. *Countries of Interest:* All. Member: Co-op Party 1971–, SERA 1986–, Labour Movement in Europe 1997–, Labour Friends of Israel 1997–, Labour Friends of India 1997–, European Movement 1999–. Member: CND 1971–, Friends of the Earth 1978–, Friends of Cyprus 1997–, UNA 1998–, Friends of Israel 1977–; Member: Howard League for Penal Reform 1986–, European Standing Committee A 1998–, Finchley Society 1998–, Council for the Advancement of Arab-British Understanding 2000–, European Standing Committee B until 2003; Member: Council of Europe, Western European Union; Member: College Farm Finchley, Hendon Youth Club; Hon. Doctorate, Schiller International University 1997; *Recreations:* Walking through London. Dr Rudi Vis, MP, House of Commons, London, SW1A 0AA *Tel.* 020 7219 4562 *Fax:* 020 7219 0565. *Constituency:* Labour Party Constituency Office, 38 Church Lane, London N2 8DT *Tel:* 020 8883 0411 *Fax.* 020 8883 0411 *E-mail:* visr@parliament.uk.

Visit the Vacher Dod Website . . .
www.DodOnline.co.uk

W

WALLEY, JOAN   Stoke-on-Trent North   *Lab majority 11,784*

Joan Lorraine Walley. Born 23 January 1949; Daughter of late Arthur and late Mary Emma Walley; Educated Biddulph Grammar School; Hull University (BA social administration); University College of Wales, Swansea (Diploma in community work development); Married Jan Ostrowski 1981 (2 sons). Alcoholics recovery project 1970–73; Local government officer: Swansea City Council 1974–78, Wandsworth Council 1978–79; NACRO development officer 1979–82; Member, UNISON. Lambeth Council: Councillor 1981–85, Chair, Health and Consumer Services Committee. **House of Commons:** Member for Stoke-on-Trent North since June 1987; Opposition Spokesperson on: Environmental Protection and Development 1988–90, Transport 1990–95; *Select Committees:* Member: Trade and Industry 1995–97, Trade and Industry 1997–98; Member, Environmental Audit 1997–. *Special Interests:* Environment, Health, Small Businesses. *Countries of Interest:* Eastern Europe. Member: SERA, SEA. Vice-President, Institute Environmental Health Officers; President: West Midlands Home and Water Safety Council, City of Stoke on Trent Primary School Sports Association; Member, Armed Forces Parliamentary Scheme (RAF); *Clubs:* Fegg Hayes Sports and Social; *Recreations:* Walking, swimming, music, football. Joan Walley, MP, House of Commons, London, SW1A 0AA *Tel:* 020 7219 4524 *Fax:* 020 7219 4397. *Constituency:* Unit 5, Burslem Enterprise Centre, Moorland Road, Burslem, Stoke-on-Trent, ST6 1JN *Tel:* 01782 577900 *Fax:* 01782 836462 *E-mail:* walleyj@parliament.uk.

WALTER, ROBERT   North Dorset   *Con majority 3,797*

Robert Walter. Born 30 May 1948; Educated Lord Weymouth School, Warminster; Aston University, Birmingham (BSc 1971); Married Sally Middleton 1970 (died 1995) (2 sons 1 daughter); married Barbara Gorna 2000. Former Farmer; Sheep farm, South Devon; Director and Vice-President, Aubrey G Lanston and Co 1986–97; Member, London Stock Exchange 1983–86; Visiting lecturer in East-West trade, Westminster University. **House of Commons:** Contested Bedwelty 1979. Member for North Dorset since May 1, 1997; Opposition Spokesperson for Constitutional Affairs (Wales) 1999–2001; *Select Committees:* Member: Health 1997–99, European Scrutiny 1998–99; Member: Unopposed Bills (Panel) 1997–, International Development 2001–. *Special Interests:* Agriculture, Health. Chair: Aston University Conservative Association 1967–69, Westbury Constituency Young Conservative 1973–76, Conservative Foreign Affairs Forum 1986–88, Member: Carlton Club Political Committee 1991–99, National Union Executive Committee 1992–95, Conservative Group for Europe: Chair 1992–95, Vice-President 1997–2000. Founder Chair, Wiltshire Europe Society; Member: National Farmers Union, National Sheep Association, Royal Agricultural Society of England; Member, European Standing Committee B 1998–; Former Chairman, European Democrat Forum; Member: British-Irish Inter-Parliamentary Body 1997, Assembly of Western European Union 2001–, Parliamentary Assembly of Council of Europe 2001–; Liveryman, Worshipful Company of Needlemakers 1983; Freeman, City of London 1983; *Recreations:* Sailing. Robert Walter Esq, MP, House of Commons, London, SW1A 0AA *Tel:* 020 7219 6981 *Fax:* 020 7219 2608. *Constituency:* The Stables, White Cliff Gardens, Blandford Forum, Dorset, DT11 7BU *Tel:* 0845 123 2785 *Fax:* 01258 459 614 *E-mail:* walterr@parliament.uk.

DodOnline

An Electronic Directory without rival . . .

MPs' biographies and photographs available with daily updates *via* the internet

For a *free* trial, call Yasmin Mirza, Aby Farsoun or Michael Mand on 020 7630 7643

WARD, CLAIRE   Watford   *Lab majority 5,555*

Claire Margaret Ward. Born 9 May 1972; Daughter of Frank and Catherine Ward; Educated Loreto College, St Albans, Hertfordshire; University of Hertfordshire (LLB 1993); Brunel University (MA 1994 Britain and the European Union); College of Law, London; Single. Part-time clerical and secretarial work 1985–95; Trainee Solicitor 1995–98; Solicitor 1998–; Member, TGWU 1987–; Winner: South East TUC Mike Perkins Memorial Award for Young Trade Unionists 1989, TGWU National Youth Award 1990; Delegate, TGWU Biennial Delegate Conference 1991. Councillor, Elstree and Boreham Wood Town Council 1994–97, Mayor 1996–97, Former Vice-chair, Leisure and Entertainments Committee. **House of Commons:** Member for Watford since May 1, 1997; PPS to John Hutton as Minister of State, Department of Health 2001–; *Select Committees:* Member, Culture, Media and Sport 1997–2001. *Special Interests:* Transport, Education, Employment, Home Affairs, Culture, Media, Sport. *Countries of Interest:* St Lucia. Member, Co-operative Party and CRS Ltd 1987–; Youth Representative, Labour Party National Executive Committee 1991–95; Chair: Boreham Wood Branch Labour Party 1991–97, Hertsmere Constituency Labour Party 1992–96; Member, Central Region Executive Committee 1993; Member: London Region CRS Political Committee 1993–2001, Co-operative Party Parliamentary Panel 1994–95; Member, Labour Party National Policy Commissions on: Democracy and Citizenship 1992–95, Social Policy 1992–95, Equalities 1992–95, Environment 1992–95; Member: Fabian Society, Society of Labour Lawyers. Board Member, Howard League for Penal Reform 2000–; Youngest Woman MP; Patron, Young European Movement; *Clubs:* Reform; *Recreations:* Cinema, reading, restaurants, Watford Football Club. Claire Ward, MP, House of Commons, London, SW1A 0AA *Tel:* 020 7219 4910 *Fax:* 020 7219 0468. *Constituency:* 270 St Albans Road, Watford, Hertfordshire, WD24 6PE *Tel:* 01923 213579 *Fax:* 01923 213595 *E-mail:* wardc@parliament.uk.

WAREING, ROBERT   Liverpool West Derby   *Lab majority 15,853*

Robert Nelson Wareing. Born 20 August 1930; Son of late Robert and Florence Patricia Wareing; Educated Ranworth Square Council School, Liverpool; Alsop High School, Liverpool; Bolton College of Education (Teacher's Certificate 1957); External student, London University (BSc economics 1956); Married Betty Coward 1962 (died 1989). RAF 1948–50; Local government officer, Liverpool Corporation 1946–48, 1950–56; Lecturer: Brooklyn Technical College 1957–59, Wigan and District Mining and Technical College 1959–63, Liverpool College of Commerce 1963–64, Liverpool City Institute of Further Education 1964–72; Principal lecturer/deputy head adult education, Central Liverpool College of FE 1972–83; Member: AMICUS, RMT Parliamentary Campaigning Group 2002–. Merseyside County Council: Councillor 1981–86, Chairman, Economic Development Committee 1981–83, Chief Whip, Labour Group 1981–83. **House of Commons:** Contested Berwick-upon-Tweed 1970 general election and Liverpool Edge Hill 1979 by-election and general election of 1979. Member for Liverpool, West Derby since June 1983; Assistant Opposition Whip 1987–92; *Select Committees:* Member, Foreign Affairs 1992–97. *Special Interests:* Economic and Foreign Affairs, Regional Economic Policy, Disability, Tranquilliser Addiction, Motor Industry, Airports Policy. *Countries of Interest:* Russia, Yugoslavia, Germany, Latin America, Eastern Europe, Far East. President, Liverpool District Labour Party 1972–73, 1974–81. Member, Hansard Society; Vice-President, AMA 1984–97; *Clubs:* Dovecot Labour (Liverpool); Royal Navy Club, Kirkby, Merseyside; *Recreations:* Watching soccer, concert-going, ballet, motoring, travel. Robert Wareing Esq, MP, House of Commons, London, SW1A 0AA *Tel:* 020 7219 3482 *Fax:* 020 7219 6187. *Constituency:* 74a Mill Lane, Liverpool, L12 *Tel:* 0151–256 9111 *Fax:* 0151–226 0285 *E-mail:* wareingr@parliament.uk.

Visit the Vacher Dod Website . . .
www.DodOnline.co.uk

WATERSON, NIGEL   Eastbourne *Con majority 2,154*

Nigel Christopher Waterson. Born 12 October 1950; Son of late James Waterson and Katherine Mahon; Educated Leeds Grammar School; The Queen's College, Oxford (BA law 1971, MA); Married Gisela Guettler 1979 (divorced); married Bernadette Anne O'Halloran 1989 (divorced); married Dr Barbara Judge 1999. Solicitor; Barrister; Founder and senior partner of law firm, Waterson Hicks; Research assistant to Sally Oppenheim, MP 1972–73. Councillor, London Borough of Hammersmith and Fulham 1974–78. **House of Commons:** Contested Islington South and Finsbury 1979 general election. Member for Eastbourne since April 9, 1992; Opposition Spokesperson for: Local Government and Housing 1999–2001, Trade and Industry 2001–02; Opposition Whip: Social Security, Health, Legal, Lord Chancellor; Eastern 1997–98, Home Office, Culture, Media and Sport 1998–99; PPS to: Gerry Malone as Minister of State, Department of Health 1995–96, Michael Heseltine as Deputy Prime Minister 1996–97; Shadow Minister for People with Disabilities 2003–; *Select Committees:* Member: Joint Committee on Statutory Instruments 1992–97, National Heritage 1995–96; Member, Work and Pensions 2003–. *Special Interests:* Health, Foreign Affairs, Tourism, Shipping, Energy. *Countries of Interest:* USA, Greece, France. President, Oxford University Conservative Association 1970; Chair, Bow Group 1986–87; Chair: Hammersmith Conservative Association 1987–90, Hammersmith and Fulham Joint Management Committee 1988–90; Member, CPC Advisory Committee 1986–90; Hon. Patron, Bow Group 1993–95. School governor 1986–88; Member, Management Committee of Stonham Housing Association Hostel for Ex-Offenders 1988–90; Vice-Chair, Eastbourne Branch of BLESMA; Member: IPU, CPA; *Clubs:* Eastbourne Constitutional; *Sportsclubs:* Guards' Polo, Sussex County Cricket Club; *Recreations:* Sailing, reading, music. Nigel Waterson Esq, MP, House of Commons, London, SW1A 0AA *Tel:* 020 7219 4576 *Fax:* 020 7219 2561. *Constituency:* Eastbourne Conservative Association, 179 Victoria Drive, Eastbourne, East Sussex, BN20 8QJ *Tel:* 01323 720776 *Fax:* 01323 410994 *E-mail:* watersonn@parliament.uk.

WATKINSON, ANGELA   Upminster *Con majority 1,241*

Angela Eileen Watkinson. Born 18 November 1941; Daughter of Edward John Ellicott and Maisie Eileen Ellicott, née Thompson; Educated Wanstead County High School; Anglia University (HNC public administration 1989); Married Roy Michael Watkinson 1961 (1 son 2 daughters). Bank of New South Wales 1958–64; Family career break 1964–76; Special school secretary Essex County Council 1976–88; London Borough of Barking and Dagenham: Clerk to school governing bodies 1988, Committee clerk 1988–89; Committee manager Basildon District Council 1989–94. Councillor, Group secretary, Committee chair: London Borough of Havering 1994–98, Essex County Council 1997–2001. **House of Commons:** Member for Upminster since June 7, 2001; Opposition Whip 2002–; *Select Committees:* Member: Home Affairs 2001–02, European Scrutiny 2002. *Special Interests:* Education, Law and Order, Families, European Affairs, Constitution, Local and Regional Government. *Countries of Interest:* Sweden, USA. Secretary: Upminster Ward 1988–93, Emerson Park Ward 1993–96: Chair 1996–2001; Upminster Conservative Association: Executive member 1988–99, Executive officer 1997–99; Billericay Conservative Association: Executive Member 1997–, Vice-president 1999–; Member: Monday Club 1996–2001, Conservative Councillors Association 1998–, Conservative Way Forward Group 1998–, Conservative Christian Fellowship 1999–, Conservative Friends of Israel 2001–, 1922 Committee 2001–. Patron: RSPCA 1986–2000, Redwings Horse Sanctuary 1976–; Subscriber European Foundation 1998–; *Recreations:* Working, family, reading, music, dining, crosswords, visiting stately homes and gardens, animal sanctuaries. Angela Watkinson, MP, House of Commons, London, SW1A 0AA *Tel:* 020 7219 8470 *Fax:* 020 7219 1957. *Constituency:* 23 Butts Green Road, Hornchurch, Essex, RM11 2JS *Tel:* 01708 475252 *Fax:* 01708 470495 *E-mail:* watkinsona@parliament.uk.

Visit the Vacher Dod Website . . .
www.DodOnline.co.uk

WATSON, TOM   West Bromwich East   *Lab majority 9,763*

Tom Watson. Born 8 January 1967; Son of Anthony Watson, social worker, and Linda Watson, née Pearce, social worker; Educated King Charles I, Kidderminster; Married Siobhan Corby 2001. Marketing officer Save the Children 1987–88; Account executive Advertising agency 1988–90; AEEU 1995–: Member, National political officer 1997–. **House of Commons:** Member for West Bromwich East since June 7, 2001; PPS to Dawn Primarolo as Paymaster General, HM Treasury 2003–; *Select Committees:* Member, Home Affairs 2001–03. *Special Interests:* Industry, Manufacturing, Law and Order, Small Businesses. *Countries of Interest:* USA, Japan, Australia. Labour Party: National Development Officer (Youth) 1993–98, Former research assistant, National Co-ordinator Labour Campaign for First Past the Post 1997–; Director: Tribune 2000–, The Policy Network 2000–. English Heritage; *Publications:* Co-author *Votes for All*, Fabian Society pamphlet 2000; *Clubs:* West Bromwich Labour; *Recreations:* Supporter of Kidderminster Harriers FC, walking, Playstation 2. Tom Watson Esq, MP, House of Commons, London, SW1A 0AA *Tel:* 020 7219 8335. *Constituency:* 1 Thomas Street, West Bromwich, B70 6NT *Tel:* 0121–569 1904 *Fax:* 0121–569 1936 *E-mail:* watsont@parliament.uk.

WATTS, DAVID   St Helens North   *Lab majority 15,901*

David Leonard Watts. Born 26 August 1951; Son of Leonard and Sarah Watts; Educated Seel Road Secondary Modern School; Married Avril Davies 1972 (2 sons). Labour Party organiser; Research assistant to Angela Eagle MP 1992–93 and John Evans MP 1993–97; Shop steward, United Biscuits AEU. St Helens MBC: Councillor 1979–97, Deputy Leader 1990–93, Leader 1993–97; Chair: Education Development Committee 1979–83, Economic Development Committee 1983–90. **House of Commons:** Member for St Helens North since May 1, 1997; PPS to: John Spellar: as Minister of State for the Armed Forces, Ministry of Defence 1999–2001, as Minister of Transport, Department for Transport, Local Government and the Regions 2001–02, as Minister of State, Department for Transport 2002–03, John Prescott as Deputy Prime Minister 2003–; *Select Committees:* Member, Finance and Services 1997–2001. *Special Interests:* Regional Policy, Education, Training. PLP North West Regional Group: Vice-chair 1999–2000, Chair 2000–01. Vice-chair, Association of Metropolitan Authorities; UK President, Euro Group of Industrial Regions 1989–93; *Recreations:* Watching football and rugby, reading. David Watts Esq, MP, House of Commons, London, SW1A 0AA *Tel:* 020 7219 6325. *Constituency:* Ann Ward House, 1 Milk Street, St Helens, Merseyside, WA10 1PX *Tel:* 01744 623416 *Fax:* 01744 623417 *E-mail:* wattsd@parliament.uk.

WEBB, STEVE   Northavon   *LD majority 9,877*

Steve (Steven) John Webb. Born 18 July 1965; Son of Brian and Patricia Webb; Educated Dartmouth High School, Birmingham; Hertford College, Oxford (BA philosophy, politics and economics 1983, MA); Married Helen Edwards 1993 (1 daughter 1 son). Researcher then programme director, Institute for Fiscal Studies 1986–95; Professor of social policy, University of Bath 1995–. **House of Commons:** Member for Northavon since May 1, 1997; Spokesperson for Social Security and Welfare (Pensions) 1997–99; Principal Spokesperson for: Social Security 1999–2001, Work and Pensions 2001–; *Special Interests:* Social Affairs, Welfare, Third World, Internet. Member: Liberal Democrat Tax and Benefits Working Group, Liberal Democrat Costings Group, Liberal Democrat Policy Committee. Member: Oxfam, Amnesty International, World Development Movement; Member, Commission on Social Justice; Specialist Adviser to Social Security Select Committee; *Publications:* Include: *Beyond The Welfare State*, 1990, Co-author *For Richer, For Poorer*, 1994, *Inequality in the UK*, 1997. Prof Steve Webb, MP, House of Commons, SW1A 0AA *Tel:* 020 7219 4378 *Fax:* 020 7219 1110. *Constituency:* Poole Court, Poole Court Drive, Yate, Bristol BS37 5PP *Tel:* 01454 322100.

WEIR, MIKE   Angus   SNP majority 3,611

Michael Fraser Weir. Born 24 March 1957; Son of James Gordon Weir, electrician, and Elizabeth Mary, née Fraser, hospital cook; Educated Arbroath High School; Aberdeen University (LLB 1979); Married Anne Elizabeth Jack 1985 (2 daughters). Solicitor: Charles Wood and Son 1981–83, Myers and Wills 1983–84; Solicitor and partner J and DG Shiell 1984–2001. Angus District Council 1984–88: Councillor, Convener General Purposes Committee 1984–88. **House of Commons:** Contested Aberdeen South 1987 general election. Member for Angus since June 7, 2001; *Select Committees:* Member, Scottish Affairs 2001–. *Special Interests:* Disability, European Affairs, Rural Affairs, Health, Education, Employment, Legal Affairs, International Development. Various posts Local party. Law Society of Scotland 1981; *Recreations:* History, organic gardening. Mike Weir Esq, MP, House of Commons, London, SW1A 0AA *Tel:* 020 7219 8125 *Fax:* 020 7219 1746. *Constituency:* SNP Office, 16 Brothock Bridge, Arbroath, Angus, DD11 1AT *Tel:* 01241 874522 *Fax:* 01241 879350 *E-mail:* weirm@parliament.uk.

WHITE, BRIAN   Milton Keynes North East   Lab majority 1,829

Brian Arthur Robert White. Born 5 May 1957; Son of William Edward White and Elinor White; Educated Methodist College, Belfast; Married Leena Lindholm (2 stepsons). Civil servant, HM Customs and Excise; IT consultant; Systems analyst, Abbey National; Member, MSF. Councillor, Milton Keynes Borough Council 1987–97, former Deputy Leader; Councillor, Buckinghamshire County Council 1994–97. **House of Commons:** Member for Milton Keynes North East since May 1, 1997; *Select Committees:* Member, Joint Committee on Consolidation of Bills Etc 1997–2001; Member: Joint Committee on Statutory Instruments 1999–, Public Administration 1999–, Regulatory Reform 1999–. *Special Interests:* Environment, Transport, Economic Policy, European Union, International Trade, Information Technology, Animal Welfare, Third World Debt, Modernising Government, Small Businesses, Regulatory Issues. Member, Milton Keynes Energy Association; Agent, Milton Keynes South West general election 1992; Local Government Association: Member, Policy and Strategy Committee, Chair, Planning Committee, Secretary, Labour Group; *Recreations:* Reading, ten-pin bowling. Brian White Esq, MP, House of Commons, London, SW1A 0AA *Tel:* 020 7219 3435 *Fax:* 020 7219 2887. *Constituency:* Labour Hall, Newport Road, New Bradwell, Milton Keynes, MK13 0AA *Tel:* 01908 313933 *Fax:* 01908 311713 *E-mail:* whitebar@parliament.uk.

WHITEHEAD, ALAN   Southampton Test   Lab majority 11,207

Alan Patrick Vincent Whitehead. Born 15 September 1950; Educated Isleworth Grammar School, Isleworth, Middlesex; Southampton University (BA politics and philosophy 1973, PhD political science 1976); Married Sophie Wronska 1979 (1 son 1 daughter). Director, Outset 1979–83, Deputy 1976–79; Director, BIIT 1983–92; Professor of public policy, Southampton Institute 1992–97; Member, UNISON (formerly NUPE). Councillor, Southampton City Council 1980–92, Leader 1984–92. **House of Commons:** Contested Southampton Test 1983, 1987, 1992 general elections. Member for Southampton Test since May 1, 1997; Joint PPS to David Blunkett as Secretary of State for Education and Employment 1999–2000; PPS to Baroness Blackstone as Minister for Education and Employment 1999–2001; Parliamentary Under-Secretary of State, Department for Transport, Local Government and the Regions 2001–02; *Select Committees:* Member: Environment, Transport and Regional Affairs 1997–99, Environment Sub-Committee 1997–99; Member, Lord Chancellor's Department 2003–. *Special Interests:* Environment, Local and Regional Government, Further Education, Education, Constitution, Transport. *Countries of Interest:* Poland, France, Estonia, Lithuania. Member, Labour Party National Policy Forum 1999–2001. Director/Board Member, Southampton Environment Centre; Vice-President, Local Government Association 1998–; Director, Southampton Environment Centre; *Publications:* Various chapters, articles and papers including:

Co-author *TUPE – the EU's Revenge on the Iron Lady*, 1994; *Spain, European Regions and City States*, 1995; *Rational Actors and Irrational Structures*, 1995; *Local Government Finance – Accountancy or Accountability?*, 1995; Joint editor, *Beyond 2002: Long-Term Policies for Labour*; Visiting professor, Southampton Institute 1997–; *Recreations:* Football (playing and watching), writing, tennis. Dr Alan Whitehead, MP, House of Commons, London, SW1A 0AA *Tel:* 020 7219 6338 *Fax:* 020 7219 0918. *Constituency:* Southampton Labour Party, 20–22 Southampton Street, Southampton, SO15 1ED *Tel:* 023 8023 1942 *Fax:* 023 8023 1943 *E-mail:* whiteheada@parliament.uk.

WHITTINGDALE, JOHN   Maldon and Chelmsford East   *Con majority 8,462*

John Flasby Lawrance Whittingdale. Born 16 October 1959; Son of late John Whittingdale and of Margaret Whittingdale; Educated Sandroyd School, Wiltshire; Winchester College; University College, London (BSc economics 1982); Married Ancilla Murfitt 1990 (1 son 1 daughter). Head, political section, Conservative research department 1982–84; Special adviser to Secretary of State for Trade and Industry 1984–87; Manager, N. M. Rothschild & Sons 1987; Political secretary to Margaret Thatcher as Prime Minister 1988–90; Private secretary to Margaret Thatcher 1990–92. **House of Commons:** Member for South Colchester and Maldon 1992–97, and for Maldon and Chelmsford East since May 1, 1997; Opposition Spokesperson for the Treasury (Tax, VAT and Duties; EU Budget and other EU Issues) 1998–99; Opposition Whip 1997–98; PPS to Eric Forth: as Minister of State for Education 1994–95, as Minister of State for Education and Employment 1994–96; Parliamentary private secretary to William Hague as Leader of the Opposition 1999–2001; Shadow Secretary of State for Trade and Industry 2001–02; Shadow Secretary of State for Culture, Media and Sport 2002–; *Select Committees:* Member: Health 1993–97, Information 1997–98, Trade and Industry 2001. *Special Interests:* Broadcasting and Media. *Countries of Interest:* Israel, USA, Korea, Malaysia, Japan. Mensa; *Publications: New Policies for the Media*, 1995; OBE 1990; *Clubs:* Essex; *Recreations:* Cinema, music. John Whittingdale Esq, OBE, MP, House of Commons, London, SW1A 0AA *Tel:* 020 7219 3557 *Fax:* 020 7219 2522. *Constituency:* Maldon and East Chelmsford Conservative Association, 120B High Street, Maldon, Essex, CM9 5ET *Tel:* 01621 855663 *Fax:* 01621 855217 *E-mail:* jwhittingdale.mp@tory.org.uk.

WICKS, MALCOLM   Croydon North   *Lab majority 16,858*

Malcolm Wicks. Born 1 July 1947; Son of Arthur Wicks and of late Daisy Wicks; Educated Elizabeth College, Guernsey; North West London Polytechnic; London School of Economics (BSc sociology); Married Margaret Baron 1968 (1 son 2 daughters). Fellow, Department of Social Administration, York University 1968–70; Research worker, Centre for Environmental Studies 1970–72; Lecturer in social administration, Brunel University 1970–74; Social policy analyst, Urban Deprivation Unit, Home Office 1974–77; Lecturer in social policy, Civil Service College 1977–78; Research director and secretary, Study Commission on the Family 1978–83; Director, Family Policy Studies Centre 1983–92. **House of Commons:** Contested Croydon North West 1987 general election. Member for Croydon North West 1992–97, and for Croydon North since May 1, 1997; Opposition Spokesperson for Social Security 1995–97; Parliamentary Under-Secretary of State (Lifelong Learning), Department for Education and Employment 1999–2001; Department for Work and Pensions 2001–: Parliamentary Under-Secretary of State (Work) 2001–03, Minister of State for Pensions 2003–; *Select Committees:* Member: Social Security 1994–96, Social Security 1997–98; Chair, Education Sub-Committee 1998–99, Chair (Education), Education and Employment 1998–99; Member, Liaison 1998–99. *Special Interests:* Social Policy, Welfare State, Education. *Countries of Interest:* Australia, Europe, New Zealand. *Publications:* Several publications and articles on social policy and welfare including: *Old and Cold: hypothermia and social policy*, 1978; *Government and Urban Poverty*, 1983 (co-author); *A Future for All: do we need a welfare state?* 1987; *Family Change and Future Policy*, 1990 (co-author); *A New Agenda* (jointly) IPPR, 1993; *Clubs:* Ruskin House Labour (Croydon); *Recreations:* Music, walking, gardening, very occasional white water rafting. Malcolm Wicks Esq, MP, House of Commons, SW1A 0AA *Tel:* 020 7219 4554 *Fax:* 020 7219 2795. *Constituency:* 84 High Street, Thornton Heath, Surrey, CR7 8LF *Tel:* 020 8665 1214 *Fax:* 020 8683 0179 *E-mail:* wicksm@parliament.uk.

WIDDECOMBE, ANN   Maidstone and The Weald   *Con majority 10,318*

Ann Noreen Widdecombe. Born 4 October 1947; Daughter of late James Murray Widdecombe CB, OBE, retired Director General in Ministry of Defence, and of Rita Widdecombe; Educated La Sainte Union Convent, Bath; Birmingham University (BA Latin 1969); Lady Margaret Hall, Oxford (BA philosophy, politics and economics 1972, MA); Single. With Unilever in marketing 1973–75; Senior administrator, London University 1975–1987; Member, Association of University Teachers 1978–83. Councillor, Runnymede District Council 1976–78. **House of Commons:** Contested Burnley 1979, Plymouth Devonport 1983 general elections. Member for Maidstone 1987–97, and for Maidstone and The Weald since May 1, 1997; Introduced Abortion Amendment Bill 1988–89; PPS to Tristan Garel-Jones as Minister of State, Foreign and Commonwealth Office 1990; Joint Parliamentary Under-Secretary of State, Department of Social Security 1990–93; Department of Employment: Joint Parliamentary Under-Secretary of State 1993–94, Minister of State 1994–95; Minister of State, Home Office 1995–97; Member, Shadow Cabinet 1998–2001; Shadow Secretary of State for Health 1998–99; Shadow Home Secretary 1999–2001; *Select Committees:* Member: Health and Social Security 1989–90, Standards and Privileges 1997, Chairmen's Panel 1998; Member: Chairmen's Panel 2001–, Home Affairs 2002–. *Special Interests:* Abortion, Health, Defence, Prisons. *Countries of Interest:* Singapore. Vice-chair, National Association of Conservative Graduates 1974–76. Founding Member and Vice-Chair, Women and Families for Defence; National Patron, Life; Member, Gas Consumers Council 1984–86; *Publications:* Various publications including *A Layman's Guide to Defence*, 1984; *Outspoken and Inspired*, 1999; *The Clematis Tree*, 2000; *An Act of Treachery*, 2002; PC 1997; Highland Park/*The Spectator* Minister of the Year 1996; Talk Radio, Straight Talker of the Year 1997; *Clubs:* The Carlton; *Recreations:* Reading, researching Charles II's escape, writing. Rt Hon Ann Widdecombe, MP, House of Commons, London, SW1A 0AA *Tel:* 020 7219 5091 *Fax:* 020 7219 2413. *Constituency:* 3 Albion Place, Maidstone, Kent, ME14 5DY *Tel:* 01622 752463 *Fax:* 01622 844330 *E-mail:* widdecombea@parliament.uk.

WIGGIN, BILL   Leominster   *Con majority 10,367*

William David Wiggin. Born 4 June 1966; Son of Sir Jerry Wiggin and Mrs Rosie Dale Harris; Educated Eton College; University College of North Wales (BA economics 1988); Married Camilla Chilvers 1999. Trader UBS 1991–93; Associate director currency options sales Dresdner Kleinwort Benson 1994–98; Manager structured products Commerzbank 1998–; Contested North West region 1999 European Parliament election. **House of Commons:** Contested Burnley 1997 general election. Member for Leominster since June 7, 2001; Shadow Minister for Environment, Food and Rural Affairs 2003–; *Select Committees:* Member, Transport, Local Government and the Regions 2001–02; Member: Welsh Affairs 2001–, Environment, Food and Rural Affairs 2002–. *Special Interests:* Defence, Agriculture, Treasury, Environment. Vice-chair Hammersmith and Fulham Conservative Association 1995–97. Supporter NSPCC; Governor Hammersmith and West London College 1995–98; Trustee, Violet Eveson Charitable Trust; Goldsmiths Company; Freeman of City of London; *Clubs:* Hurlingham, Annabels, Pratt's; *Recreations:* Motorcycles, diving, fencing, country sports. Bill Wiggin Esq, MP, House of Commons, London, SW1A 0AA. *Constituency:* 8 Corn Square, Leominster, Herefordshire, HR6 8LR *Tel:* 01568 612 565 *Fax:* 01568 610 320 *E-mail:* billwigginmp@parliament.uk.

DodOnline

An Electronic Directory without rival ...

MPs' biographies and photographs available with daily updates *via* the internet

For a *free* trial, call Yasmin Mirza, Aby Farsoun or Michael Mand on 020 7630 7643

WILKINSON, JOHN   Ruislip Northwood   *Con majority 7,537*

John Arbuthnot Du Cane Wilkinson. Born 23 September 1940; Son of late Denys Wilkinson, schoolmaster, and late Gillian, née Nairn, university lecturer; Educated Eton College (King's Scholar); RAF College, Cranwell 1961; Churchill College, Cambridge (BA history 1965); University of Aix/Marseilles (Diploma) 1961; Married Paula Adey 1969 (divorced 1987) (1 daughter); married Cecilia Cienfuegos 1987 (1 son). Commissioned into RAF from Cranwell 1961; Qualified French interpreter in RAF 1961; Flying instructor: No. 8 FTS 1962; Trooper, 21 SAS Regiment (Artists') TA 1963–65; Qualified flying instructor, RAF College, Cranwell 1966–67; ADC to Commander, 2nd Allied Tactical Air Force, Germany 1967; Head of university department, Conservative Central Office 1967–68; Aviation specialist, Conservative Research Department 1969; Senior administration officer (Anglo/French Jaguar Project), Preston Division BAC 1969–70; Correspondence tutor, Open University 1970–71; Chief flying instructor, Skywork Ltd, Stansted 1974–75; Sales manager, Brooklands Aviation 1975; Personal assistant to Chairman, BAC 1976–77; Sales manager, Executive Air Services 1978–79; Chairman, EMC Communications Ltd 1987–98. **House of Commons:** Member for Bradford West 1970-February 1974. Contested Bradford West October 1974 general election. Member for Ruislip Northwood since May 1979; PPS: to Minister of State for Industry 1979–80, to John Nott as Secretary of State for Defence 1981–82; Whip withdrawn over European Communities Finance Bill 1994–1995; *Select Committees:* Member, Defence 1987–90; Chair, Armed Forces Bill (Special Select Committee) 1990–91. *Special Interests:* International Affairs, Defence, Aerospace, Air Transport, European Union, Industry, London, Immigration and Race Relations. *Countries of Interest:* Latin America, Baltic States, Ukraine, Philippines and ASEAN States, Indo-Pakistan Sub Continent. Chairman, Anglo/Asian Conservative Society 1979–82. Chairman: European Freedom Council 1982–90, Horn of Africa Council 1984–88; Commonwealth War Graves Commissioner 1997–; President, London Green Belt Council 1997–; Member, European Standing Committee B 1998–; London mayoral nominee 1998, 2002; Delegate, Council of Europe and WEU 1979–90; Chairman: Aerospace Committee, WEU 1986–89, Space Sub-Committee, Council of Europe 1984–88; Member, UK Delegation Parliamentary Assembly of the Council of Europe/Western European Union 2000–; Leader, FederatedGroup of European and Christian Democrat MPs Assembly of WEU 2000–02; Chief Whip European Democrat Group Council of Europe 2001–; Vice-Chairman British Group of the Interparliamentary Union 2001–; Chairman: Migration Sub-committee Council of Europe 2001–, Defence Committee, Assembly of WEU 2002–; Fellow, Industry and Parliament Trust 1993; Armed Forces Parliamentary Scheme, Royal Marines 1993; Parliamentary Police Service Scheme 2002; *Publications:* Co-author *The Uncertain Ally*, 1982; *British Defence: A Blueprint for Reform*, 1987; Hilal-i-Quaid-i-Azam (HQA) Pakistan 1989; Cross of Land of Mary (Estonia) 1999; Companion, Royal Aeronautical Society; *Recreations:* Travel in South America. John Wilkinson Esq, MP, House of Commons, London, SW1A 0AA *Tel:* 020 7219 5165 *Fax:* 020 7219 4850. *Constituency:* 20B High Street, Northwood, Middlesex, HA6 1BN *Tel:* 01923 835383 *Fax:* 01923 814514 *E-mail:* johnwilkinsonmp@parliament.uk.

WILLETTS, DAVID   Havant   *Con majority 4,207*

David Lindsay Willetts. Born 9 March 1956; Son of John and Hilary Willetts; Educated King Edward's School, Birmingham; Christ Church, Oxford (BA philosophy, politics and economics 1978); Married Hon. Sarah Butterfield 1986 (1 son 1 daughter). HM Treasury 1978–84; Private secretary to Financial Secretary 1981–82; Principal, Monetary Policy Division 1982–84; Prime Minister's Downing Street Policy Unit 1984–86; Director of Studies, Centre for Policy Studies 1987–92; Consultant director, Conservative Research Department 1987–92; Director: Retirement Security Ltd 1988–94, Electra Corporate Ventures Ltd 1988–94; Visiting Fellow, Nuffield College, Oxford 1999–; Member, Global Commission on Ageing 2000–. Member: Lambeth and Lewisham Family Practitioners' Committee 1987–90, Parkside Health Authority 1988–90, Social Security Advisory Committee 1989–92. **House of Commons:** Member for Havant since April 9, 1992; Opposition Spokesman on Education and Employment (Employment) 1997–98; Assistant Government Whip 1994–95; Government Whip July-November 1995; PPS to Sir Norman Fowler as Chairman of Conservative Party 1993–94; Parliamentary Secretary, Office of Public Service 1995–96;

Paymaster General, Office of Public Service July-December 1996; Shadow Secretary of State for: Education and Employment 1998–99, Social Security 1999–2001, Work and Pensions 2001–; *Select Committees:* Member, Social Security 1992–93. *Special Interests:* Economic Policy, Health, Social Security, Education. *Countries of Interest:* USA, Germany. Chair, Conservative Research Department 1997; Member Conservative Policy Board 2001–. *Publications: Modern Conservatism,* 1992; *Civic Conservatism,* 1994; *Blair's Gurus,* 1996; *Why Vote Conservative,* 1997; *Welfare to Work,* 1998; *After the Landslide,* 1999; *Browned-off: What's Wrong with Gordon Brown's Social Policy* 2000; Co-author *Tax Credits: Do They Add Up?* 2002; *Clubs:* Hurlingham; *Recreations:* Swimming, reading. David Willetts Esq, MP, House of Commons, London, SW1A 0AA *Tel:* 020 7219 4570 *Fax:* 020 7219 2567. *Constituency:* c/o Havant Conservative Association, 19 South Street, Havant, Hampshire, PO9 1BU *Tel:* 023 9249 9746 *Fax:* 023 9249 8753.

WILLIAMS, ALAN   Swansea West   *Lab majority 9,550*

Alan John Williams. Born 14 October 1930; Son of Emlyn Williams, coal miner; Educated Cardiff High School; Cardiff College of Technology (BSc economics, London 1954); University College, Oxford (BA philosophy, politics and economics); Married Patricia Rees 1957 (2 sons 1 daughter). Lecturer in economics, Welsh College of Advanced Technology; Member, Association of Teachers at Technical Institutes, affiliated to NUT 1958–; Member, Transport Salaried Staff Association (TSSA). **House of Commons:** Contested Poole 1959 general election. Member for Swansea West since October 15, 1964; Opposition Spokesman on: Industry 1970–71, Higher Education 1971–72, Consumer Affairs 1973–74; Opposition Frontbench Spokesperson for: Wales 1979–80, Industry and Consumer Affairs 1979–87, The Civil Service 1980–83; PPS to Edward Short as Postmaster General 1966–67; Joint Parliamentary Secretary, Ministry of Technology 1969–70; Parliamentary Under-Secretary of State, Department of Economic Affairs 1967–69; Minister of State for: Prices and Consumer Protection 1974–76, Industry 1976–79; Shadow Secretary of State for Wales 1987–88; Deputy Shadow Leader of the House and Campaigns Co-ordinator 1983–87; *Select Committees:* Member: Public Accounts 1990–97, Privileges 1994–97, Parliamentary Privilege (Joint Committee) 1997–2000, Standards and Privileges 1997–2003; Member, Public Accounts 1997–; Chair: Liaison 2001–, Liaison (Liaison Sub-Committee) 2002–. *Special Interests:* Regional Policy, Industrial Policy, Employment, Micro-Technology. Member: Fabian Society, Co-operative Party; Chair, Welsh Parliamentary Labour Group 1966–67. Member: Public Accounts Committee 1990–, Lord Chancellor's Advisory Council on Committee Records 1995–; Chairman, Public Accounts Commission 1997–; Council of Europe and Western European 1966–67; Chair, Welsh Branch of British-Russia Centre 1995–2001; Member, North Atlantic Alliance 1997–2001; PC January 1977; Freeman, City of Swansea; *Clubs:* Clyne Golf; *Recreations:* Golf. Rt Hon Alan Williams, MP, House of Commons, London, SW1A 0AA *Tel:* 020 7219 3449 *Fax:* 020 7219 6943. *Constituency:* Alexandra House, 42 High Street, Swansea, SA1 1LM *Tel:* 01792 655097 *Fax:* 01792 655097 *E-mail:* batchelore@parliament.uk.

WILLIAMS, BETTY   Conwy   *Lab majority 6,219*

Betty Williams. Born 31 July 1944; Daughter of late Griffith Williams and of Elizabeth Williams; Educated Ysgol Dyffryn Nantlle, Penygroes; Normal College, Bangor (BA communications 1995); Evan Glyn Williams (2 sons). Secretarial 1961–71; Freelance journalist/media researcher 1995–97; Member, T&GWU. Councillor: Parish/Community 1967–83, District Council 1970–91, County Council 1976–93; Mayor, Arfon Borough Council 1990–91; Former Member: Gwynedd Health Authority, Snowdonia National Park Committee (Northern). **House of Commons:** Contested Caernarfon 1983, Conwy 1987 and 1992 general elections. Member for Conwy since May 1, 1997; *Select Committees:* Member, Welsh Affairs 1997–. *Special Interests:* Social Services, Health, Health Education, Environmental Health, Consumer Issues, Education (Special Needs), Railways, Small Businesses. *Countries of Interest:* Malta, Romania, India. Vice-chair Welsh Regional Group of Labour MPs 2002–. Chair, Governors of Special School in Caernarfon; Former Governor: Normal College, Bangor, Gwynedd Technical College; Former Chair, National Eisteddfod Local Finance Committee; Chair: Victims' Support, Arfon Carers' Committee; Christian Aid Organiser; Vice-President,

University of Wales, Bangor 2002–; Member, Gas Consumers' Council for Wales; Deacon, Seion C Talysarn; Commonwealth Parliamentary Association; Inter-Parliamentary Union; Hon President, Tyddyn Bach Trust; Hon Fellow University of Wales, Bangor 2000; HTV Student of the Year; National Eisteddfod Prize for video production; John Evans Memorial Prize; Y Cymro Prize 1994–95; *Recreations:* Eisteddfodau, opera, hymn singing festivals, sheep dog trials. Betty Williams, MP, House of Commons, London, SW1A 0AA *Tel:* 020 7219 5052 *Fax:* 020 7219 2759. *Constituency Tel:* 01248 680097 *E-mail:* bettywilliamsmp@parliament.uk.

WILLIAMS, HYWEL   Caernarfon   *Pl C majority 3,511*

Hywel Williams. Born 14 May 1953; Son of Robert Williams and Jennie Page Williams, shopkeepers; Educated Glan y Môr School, Pwllheli; University of Wales: Cardiff (BSc psychology 1974), Bangor (CQSW social work 1979); Divorced (3 daughters). Social worker: Mid Glamorgan County Council 1974–76, Gwynedd County Council 1976–84; North Wales Social Work Practice Centre University of Wales Bangor 1985–94: Project worker 1985–94, Head of centre 1991–94; Freelance lecturer consultant and author Social work and social policy 1994–; Contested Clwyd South 1999 National Assembly for Wales election; NALGO 1974–84; NUPE 1974–84; UCAC 1984–94. **House of Commons:** Member for Caernarfon since June 7, 2001; Plaid Cymru Spokesperson for Work and Pensions, Social Security, Health, Disability 2001–; *Special Interests:* Social Affairs, Social Security, Social Work, Language Issues, Kurdish Issues. *Countries of Interest:* Turkey. Policy developer Social security and policy for older people Plaid Cymru 1999–; Plaid Cymru policy cabinet 1999–. Member: Welsh Committee Central Council for Education and Training in Social Work, European Standing Committee B 2002–; *Publications: Social Work in Action in the 1980s STI* (Contributor); *Geirfa Gwaith Cymdeithasol/ A Social Work Vocabulary*, University of Wales Press 1988; *Geirfa Gwaith Plant/ Child Care Terms*, University of Wales Press 1993 (General Editor); *Gwaith Cymdeithasol a'r Iaith Gymraeg/ Social Work and the Welsh Language*, University of Wales Press/CCETSW; *Llawlyfr Hyfforddi a Hyfforddwyr/ An Index of Trainers and Training*, AGWC 1994; *Gofal – Pecyn Adnoddau a Hyfforddi Gofal yn y Gymuned yng Nghymru/ A Training and Resource Pack for Community Care in Wales*, CCETSW Cymru 1998; Contributor, *Speaking the Invisible*, National Assembly for Wales 2002; *Recreations:* Reading, cinema, walking, kite flying. Hywel Williams Esq, MP, House of Commons, London, SW1A 0AA *Tel:* 020 7219 8150 *Fax:* 020 7219 3705. *Constituency:* 8 Castle Street, Caernarfon, Gwynedd *Tel:* 01286 672 076 *Fax:* 01286 672 003.

WILLIAMS, ROGER   Brecon and Radnorshire   *LD majority 751*

Roger Hugh Williams. Born 22 January 1948; Educated Christ College; Cambridge University (BA agriculture 1969); Married Penelope James (1 daughter 1 son). Farmer 1969–; Contested Carmarthen West and South Pembrokeshire 1999 National Assembly for Wales election; Former chair Brecon and Radnorshire NFU; Member Farmers Union of Wales. Councillor Powys County Council 1981–; Brecon Beacons National Park 1985–: Councillor, Chair 1991–95. **House of Commons:** Member for Brecon and Radnorshire since June 7, 2001; Liberal Democrat Spokesperson for Rural Affairs 2002–; *Select Committees:* Member, Welsh Affairs 2001–. *Special Interests:* Agriculture, Education, Economic Development. Former member Development Board for Rural Wales; Chair Mid Wales Agri-Food Partnership; Member Country Landowners and Business Association; Former vice-chair Powys TEC; Lay school inspector; *Recreations:* Sport, walking, nature conservation. Roger Williams Esq, MP, House of Commons, London, SW1A 0AA *Tel:* 020 7219 8145. *Constituency:* 99 The Street, Brecon, Powys, LD3 7LS *Tel:* 01874 625 739 *Fax:* 01874 625 635 *E-mail:* brecrad@cix.co.uk.

Visit the Vacher Dod Website . . .
www.DodOnline.co.uk

WILLIS, PHIL   Harrogate and Knaresborough   *LD majority 8,845*

Phil (Philip George) Willis. Born 30 November 1941; Son of late George Willis, postman, and of late Norah, nurse; Educated Burnley Grammar School; City of Leeds and Carnegie College (Cert Ed 1963); Birmingham University (BPhil education 1978); Married Heather Sellars 1974 (1 son 1 daughter). Head teacher, Ormesby School, Cleveland 1978–82; Head teacher, John Smeaton Community High School, Leeds 1983–97; Member, Secondary Heads Association. Harrogate Borough Council: Councillor 1988–99, First Liberal Democrat Leader 1990–97; North Yorkshire County Council: Councillor 1993–97, Deputy Group Leader 1993–97. **House of Commons:** Member for Harrogate and Knaresborough since May 1, 1997; Liberal Democrat Spokesperson for Education and Employment (Further, Higher and Adult Education) 1997–99; Principal Spokesperson for: Education and Employment 1999–2000, Education and Skills 2000–; North, Midlands and Wales Whip 1997–99; *Select Committees:* Member: Education and Employment 1999–2000, Education Sub-Committee 1999–2000. *Special Interests:* Inclusive Education, Health, Local and Regional Government, Northern Ireland, Gibraltar. *Countries of Interest:* Ireland. Member: Charter 88, Friends of the Earth, Amnesty International; Times Educational Supplement 'Man of the Year' 2002; *Sportsclubs:* Leeds United Football Club; *Recreations:* Theatre, music, dance (especially ballet), football (Leeds United). Phil Willis Esq, MP, House of Commons, London, SW1A 0AA *Tel:* 020 7219 5709 *Fax:* 020 7219 0971. *Constituency:* Ashdown House, Station Parade, Harrogate, North Yorkshire, HG1 5BR *Tel:* 01423 528888 *Fax:* 01423 505700 *E-mail:* johnfox@cix.co.uk.

WILLS, MICHAEL   North Swindon   *Lab majority 8,105*

Michael David Wills. Born 20 May 1952; Son of late Stephen Wills and Elizabeth Wills; Educated Haberdashers Aske's, Elstree; Clare College, Cambridge (BA History 1973); Married Jill Freeman 1984 (3 sons 2 daughters). Third secretary later second secretary, HM Diplomatic Service 1976–80; Researcher, later producer, London Weekend Television 1980–84; Director, Juniper Productions TV production company 1984–97; Member, TGWU. **House of Commons:** Member for North Swindon since May 1, 1997; Parliamentary Under-Secretary of State: Department of Trade and Industry (Minister for Small Firms, Trade and Industry) 1999, Department for Education and Employment 1999–2001; Parliamentary Secretary, Lord Chancellor's Department 2001–02; Parliamentary Under-Secretary of State, Home Office 2002–03: for Criminal Justice System IT 2002, (Information Technology in the Criminal Justice System) 2003. Chair, Non-Ministerial Cross-Party Advisory Group on Preparation for the EMU 1998–. Michael Wills Esq, MP, House of Commons, London, SW1A 0AA *Tel:* 020 7219 4399. *Constituency:* People's Centre, Beech Avenue, Swindon, SN2 1JT *Tel:* 01793 481016 *Fax:* 01793 524483.

WILSHIRE, DAVID   Spelthorne   *Con majority 3,262*

David Wilshire. Born 16 September 1943; Educated Kingswood School, Bath; Fitzwilliam College, Cambridge (BA geography 1965, MA); Married Margaret Weeks 1967 (separated 2000) (1 son, 1 daughter deceased). Built up own group of small businesses; Worked for MEPs 1979–85; Partner, Western Political Research Services 1979–2000; Co-director, Political Management Programme, Brunel University 1985–90; Partner, Moorlands Research Services 2000–. Wansdyke District Council: Councillor 1976–87, Leader 1981–87; Councillor Avon County Council 1977–81. **House of Commons:** Member for Spelthorne since June 1987; Opposition Whip 2001–; PPS: to Alan Clark as Minister for Defence Procurement 1991–92, to Peter Lloyd as Minister of State, Home Office 1992–94; *Select Committees:* Member: Northern Ireland Affairs 1994–97, Foreign Affairs 1997–2000, Entry Clearance Sub-Committee 1997–98. *Special Interests:* Foreign Affairs, Aviation, Local and Regional Government, Political Process, Northern Ireland. Member, British-Irish Inter-Parliamentary Body 1990–2001; Treasurer, IPU British Branch 1997–2000; Substitute Member, Assembly of Council of Europe 1997–2001; Vice-Chairman, CPA UK Branch 1998–99; *Publications: Scene from the Hill*; *Recreations:* Gardening, wine and cider-making. David Wilshire Esq, MP, House of Commons, London, SW1A 0AA *Tel:* 020 7219 3534 *Fax:* 020 7219 5852. *Constituency:* 55 Cherry Orchard, Staines, Middx, TW8 2DQ *Tel:* 01784 450822 *Fax:* 01784 466109.

WILSON, BRIAN   Cunninghame North   *Lab majority 8,398*

Brian Wilson. Born 13 December 1948; Son of late John Forrest Wilson and Marion MacIntyre; Educated Dunoon Grammar School; Dundee University (MA history 1970); University College, Cardiff (MA journalism studies 1971); Married Joni Buchanan 1981 (2 sons 1 daughter). Journalist; Founding editor and publisher, *West Highland Free Press* 1972–97; Contributor to: *The Guardian, Glasgow Herald* and others; Member USDW. **House of Commons:** Contested Ross and Cromarty October 1974, Inverness 1979 and Western Isles 1983 general elections. Member for Cunninghame North since June 1987; Opposition Spokesperson for: Scotland 1988–92, Citizen's Charter and Women July–November 1992, Transport November 1992–94, Trade and Industry 1994–95, Transport 1995–96, Election Planning 1996–97; Minister of State: Scottish Office (Minister for Education and Industry) 1997–98, Department of Trade and Industry (Minister for Trade) 1998–99; Minister of State: Scotland Office 1999–2001, Foreign and Commonwealth Office 2001, Department of Trade and Industry 2001–: Minister for Industry and Energy 2001–02, Minister for Energy and Construction 2002–03. *Publications: Celtic: A Century with Honour*, 1988; PC 2003; First winner, Nicholas Tomalin Memorial Award for outstanding journalism; *Spectator* Parliamentarian of the Year 'New Member' Award 1990; FRSA (Scot); *Clubs:* Garnock Labour, Soho House; *Sportsclubs:* Kilbirnie Place Golf. Rt Hon Brian Wilson, MP, House of Commons, London, SW1A 0AA *Tel:* 020 7219 1053. *Constituency:* 37 Main Street, Kilbirnie, Ayrshire, KA25 7BX *Tel:* 01505 682847 *Fax:* 01505 684648.

WINNICK, DAVID   Walsall North   *Lab majority 9,391*

David Winnick. Born 26 June 1933; Son of late E. G. and Rose Winnick; Educated Secondary school; London School of Economics (diploma social administration 1974); Married Bengisu Rona 1968 (divorced 1984). Administrative Employee; Association of Professional, Executive, Clerical & Computer Staff (APEX): Member of Executive Council 1978–88, Vice-President 1983–88. Councillor: Willesden Borough Council 1959–64, Brent Borough Council 1964–66. **House of Commons:** Contested Harwich 1964 general election. Member for Croydon South 1966–70. Contested Croydon Central October 1974 general election and Walsall North 1976 by-election. Member for Walsall North since May 1979; *Select Committees:* Member, Procedure 1989–97; Member, Home Affairs 1997–. Chair, United Kingdom Immigrants Advisory Service 1984–90; British Co-Chair, British-Irish Inter-Parliamentary Body 1997–. David Winnick Esq, MP, House of Commons, London, SW1A 0AA *Tel:* 020 7219 5003 *Fax:* 020 7219 0257. *Constituency:* Bellamy House (Mondays, Wednesday and Friday mornings), Wilkes Street, Willenhall, West Midlands, WV13 2BS *Tel:* 01902 605020 *Fax:* 01902 637372.

WINTERTON, ANN   Congleton   *Con majority 7,134*

(Jane) Ann Winterton. Born 6 March 1941; Daughter of late Joseph Robert Hodgson and Ellen Jane Hodgson; Educated Erdington Grammar School for Girls; Married Nicholas Winterton (now MP, later Sir) 1960 (2 sons 1 daughter). **House of Commons:** Member for Congleton since June, 1983; Opposition Spokesman for National Drug Strategy 1998–2001; Shadow Minister for Agriculture and Fisheries 2001–02; *Select Committees:* Member: Agriculture 1987–97, Chairmen's Panel 1992–98, Social Security 2000–01; Member, Unopposed Bills (Panel) 1997–. *Special Interests:* Textile Industries, Pharmaceutical and Chemical Industries, Agriculture, Transport, Fisheries. *Countries of Interest:* Austria, Namibia, South Africa, USA. Member, West Midlands Conservative Women's Advisory Committee 1969–71. Vice-President: Townswomen's Guilds, East Cheshire and St Luke's Hospices; Patron: East Cheshire National Osteoporosis Group, East Cheshire NSPCC, VISYON; President, Congleton Division of the St. John Ambulance; Joint Master, South Staffordshire Hunt 1959–64; Fellow, Industry and Parliament Trust; *Recreations:* Cinema, theatre, music, tennis, riding, skiing. Ann Winterton, MP, House of Commons, London, SW1A 0AA *Tel:* 020 7219 3585 *Fax:* 020 7219 6886. *Constituency:* Riverside, Mountbatten Way, Congleton, Cheshire, CW12 1DY *Tel:* 01260 278866 *Fax:* 01260 271212 *E-mail:* wintertona@parliament.uk.

WINTERTON, NICHOLAS   Macclesfield   *Con majority 7,200*

Nicholas Winterton. Born 31 March 1938; Son of late Norman Harry Winterton; Educated Bilton Grange Preparatory School; Rugby School; Married Ann Hodgson (now MP as Ann Winterton) 1960 (2 sons 1 daughter). Army national service 1957–59; Sales executive trainee, Shell-Mex BP Ltd 1959–60; Sales and general manager, Stevens & Hodgson Ltd 1960–71. Warwickshire County Council: Councillor 1967–72, Chair, County Youth Service Sub-Committee 1969–72, Deputy Chair, Education Committee 1970–72. **House of Commons:** Contested Newcastle-under-Lyme October 1969 by-election and 1970 general election. Member for Macclesfield since by-election Sept 30, 1971; Deputy Speaker Westminster Hall 1999–2001, 2002–; Chairman: Health Select Committee 1990–92, Procedure Committee 1997–; Member, Speaker's Panel of Chairmen, Modernisation and Liaison Committee; *Select Committees:* Chair, Health 1991–92; Member, Liaison 1997–98; Chair, Procedure 1997–; Member: Chairmen's Panel 1997–, Modernisation of the House of Commons 1997–, Liaison 1998–, Standing Orders 1998–, Liaison Sub-Committee 2002–. *Special Interests:* Local and Regional Government, NHS, Sport, Recreation, Paper Industries, Textile Industries, Foreign Affairs, Media, Pharmaceutical and Chemical Industries. *Countries of Interest:* South Africa, Indonesia, Taiwan, USA, Denmark, Sweden, Austria, Namibia, Zimbabwe. Patron: International Centre for Child Care Studies, Macclesfield District Sheepdog Trials Association, East Cheshire Branch, NSPCC, Macclesfield Silk Brass, Macclesfield Just Drop In Centre, Macclesfield Advanced Motorists, Poynton Male Voice Choir; Chair, Zimbabwe Rhodesia Relief Fund; President: Macclesfield Riding for the Disabled Branch, Macclesfield Handicapped Social Club, Macclesfield Branch of RNLI, Friends of Pallotti Day Care Centre, Rossendale Trust, Macclesfield Access Group, King Edward Musical Society, Fermain Youth Club, Poynton Youth and Community Centre, Bollington Light Opera Group, Macclesfield Majestic Theatre Group; Macclesfield Branch Multiple Sclerosis Society, Hon. Vice-president Macclesfield and District Council for Voluntary Service; Vice-president: Macclesfield Division of St John Ambulance Brigade, East Cheshire Hospice, Macclesfield and Congleton District Scout Council, Cheshire County Scout Association, Poynton Horticultural and Agricultural Society, Macclesfield Canal Society, North Cheshire Cruising Club, Poynton Vemon Building Society Brass Band; Chair, Executive Committee of Anglo/Austrian Society 1999–2000; Hon. Vice-President: National Association of Master Bakers, Confectioners and Caterers, The Royal College of Midwives; Vice-President, National Association of Local Councils; Hon Member Macclesfield and District Lions Club; Member of Council, League for Exchange of Commonwealth Teachers 1979–92; Member, Executive Committee: Commonwealth Parliamentary Association (CPA) UK Branch 1997–, Inter-Parliamentary Union, UK Branch; Fellow, Industry and Parliament Trust –2001; Past Upper Bailiff and Member of the Court of Assistants, Worshipful Company of Weavers; Knight Bachelor 2002; Freeman, City of London; Freeman, Borough of Macclesfield; *Clubs:* Cavalry and Guards, Lighthouse, Old Boys and Park Green Macclesfield; *Sportsclubs:* Hon. Vice-president: Bollington Bowling Club, Bollington Cricket Club, Macclesfield Cricket Club, Prince Albert Angling Society; President: Macclesfield Hockey Club, New Century Bowman, Macclesfield Satellite Swimming Club, Disley Amalgamated Sports Club; Hon life member Macclesfield Rugby Union Football Club; Hon Vice-president, Poynton Sports Club; *Recreations:* Squash, tennis, swimming, jogging, skiing. Sir Nicholas Winterton KT, MP, House of Commons, London, SW1A 0AA *Tel:* 020 7219 4402. *Constituency:* Macclesfield Conservative and Unionist Association, West Bank Road, Macclesfield, Cheshire, SK10 3DU *Tel:* 01625 422848 *Fax:* 01625 617066.

DodOnline

An Electronic Directory without rival ...

MPs' biographies and photographs available with daily updates *via* the internet

For a *free* trial, call Yasmin Mirza, Aby Farsoun or Michael Mand on 020 7630 7643

WINTERTON, ROSIE Doncaster Central
Lab majority 11,999

Rosie Winterton. Born 10 August 1958; Daughter of Gordon Winterton, teacher, and late Valerie Winterton, teacher; Educated Doncaster Grammar School; Hull University (BA history 1979). Constituency personal assistant to John Prescott, MP 1980–86; Parliamentary officer: Southwark Council 1986–88, Royal College of Nursing 1988–90; Managing Director, Connect Public Affairs 1990–94; Head of private office of John Prescott as Deputy Leader of Labour Party 1994–97; Branch Officer, TGWU 1998–99; Member: NUJ, TGWU. **House of Commons:** Member for Doncaster Central since May 1, 1997; Parliamentary Secretary, Lord Chancellor's Department 2001–03; Minister of State, Department of Health 2003–; *Special Interests:* Regional Policy, Employment, Transport, Housing, Home Affairs. Member, Labour Party Strategic Campaign Committee; Representative, PLP on the National Policy Forum of the Labour Party. Member, Amnesty International; Leader, Leadership Campaign Team 1998–99; Chair, Transport and General Workers' Parliamentary Group 1998–99; Former Member, Standing Committees: Local Government Finance (Supplementary Credit Approvals) Bill, Regional Development Agencies Bill; Member Standing Committees: Transport Bill January 2000, Finance Bill April 2000; Intelligence and Security Committee January 2000–; *Clubs:* Doncaster Trades and Labour, Intake Social, Doncaster Catholic; *Recreations:* Sailing, reading. Rosie Winterton, MP, House of Commons, London, SW1A 0AA *Tel:* 020 7219 0925 *Fax:* 020 7219 4581. *Constituency:* Guildhall Advice Centre, Old Guildhall Yard, Doncaster, South Yorkshire, DN1 1QW *Tel:* 01302 735241 *Fax:* 01302 735242 *E-mail:* wintertonr@parliament.uk.

WISHART, PETER North Tayside
SNP majority 3,283

Peter Wishart. Born 9 March 1962; Son of late Alex Wishart, former dockyard worker and Nan Irvine, retired teacher; Educated Queen Anne High School, Dunfermline, Fife; Moray House College of Education (Dip CommEd 1984); Married Carrie Lindsay 1990 (1 son). Musician Big Country 1981; Community worker Central Region 1984–85; Musician Runrig 1985–2001; Musicians Union 1985–. **House of Commons:** Member for North Tayside since June 7, 2001; SNP Chief Whip 2001–; *Special Interests:* Drugs Issues, Justice and Equality, Arts and Culture. *Countries of Interest:* Scandinavia, Germany. Member: National Council 1997–, NEC 1999–; Executive vice-convener fundraising SNP 1999–2001. Patron West Fife Cultural Initiative; Director Fast Forward Positive Lifestyle 1992–2001; Campaign Committee Scotland Against Drugs 1997–99; *Recreations:* Music, hillwalking, travel. Peter Wishart Esq, MP, House of Commons, London, SW1A 0AA *Tel:* 020 7219 8303. *Constituency:* 35 Perth Street, Blairgowrie, Perthshire, PH10 6DL *Tel:* 01250 876 576 *Fax:* 01250 876 991 *E-mail:* wishartp@parliament.uk.

WOOD, MIKE Batley and Spen
Lab majority 5,064

Mike Wood. Born 3 March 1946; Son of late Rowland L. Wood, foundry worker, and Laura M. Wood, retired cleaner; Educated Nantwich and Acton Grammar School, Nantwich, Cheshire; Salisbury/Wells Theological College (Cert Theol 1974); Leeds University (CQSW 1981); Leeds Metropolitan University (BA history and politics 1989); Married 2nd Christine O'Leary 1999 (1 son 1 daughter from previous marriage; 2 stepdaughters). Probation officer, social worker, community worker 1965–97; Trade unionist 1962–; Member: UNISON, GMB. Kirklees Metropolitan District Council: Councillor 1980–88, Deputy Leader of Council 1986–87. **House of Commons:** Contested Hexham 1987 general election. Member for Batley and Spen since May 1, 1997; *Select Committees:* Member, Broadcasting 1997–98. *Special Interests:* Poverty, Housing, Transport, Environmental Issues and World Development, Small Businesses. *Countries of Interest:* France, Indian Sub-continent. Member, Labour Friends of India. Former Director, Housing Charity; *Publications: Probation Hostel Directory*, 1980; *Recreations:* Sport, music, ornithology, walking. Mike Wood Esq, MP, House of Commons, London, SW1A 0AA *Tel:* 020 7219 4125. *Constituency:* Tom Myer's House, 9 Cross Crown Street, Cleckheaton, West Yorkshire, BD19 3HW *Tel:* 01274 335233 *Fax:* 01274 335235 *E-mail:* mike.wood@geo2.poptel.org.uk.

WOODWARD, SHAUN   St Helens South   *Lab majority 8,985**

Shaun Anthony Woodward. Born 26 October 1958; Son of Dennis George Woodward and Joan Lillian, née Nunn; Educated Bristol Grammar School; Jesus College, Cambridge (MA English literature); Married Camilla Davan Sainsbury 1987 (1 son 3 daughters). BBC TV News and Current Affairs 1982–98; Director of communications, Conservative Party 1991–92; Member, AEEU. **House of Commons:** *Conservative Member for Witney May 1, 1997-December 1999, Labour Member December 1999-June 2001, for St Helens South since June 7, 2001; Opposition Frontbench Spokesperson for Environment, Transport and the Regions 1999; *Select Committees:* Member: Broadcasting 1997–99, European Legislation 1997–99, European Scrutiny 1998–99, Foreign Affairs 1999, Broadcasting 2000–01; Member, Joint Committee on Human Rights 2001–. *Special Interests:* Finance, Environment, Education, Culture, Children's Issues, European Affairs, Race Relations and Civil Rights, Regeneration, International Development, Speaker's Advisory Committee on Works of Art. *Countries of Interest:* USA, France, Germany, Italy, China and Australia. Director: English National Opera 1998–2001, Marine Stewardship Council 1998–2001; Former Member, Foundation Board, RSC; Trustee, Childline; Vice-President, St Helens District Council for Voluntary Service; Honorary President, St Helens Millennium Centre; *Publications:* Co-author: *Tranquillisers*, 1983, *Ben: The Story of Ben Hardwick*, 1984, *Drugwatch*, 1985; Visiting professor, Queen Mary and Westfield College, London University; Visiting fellow, John F. Kennedy School of Government, Harvard University; *Recreations:* Opera, tennis, reading, gardening, architecture. Shaun Woodward Esq, MP, House of Commons, London, SW1A 0AA *Tel:* 020 7219 2680 *Fax:* 020 7219 0979. *Constituency:* 1st Floor, Century House, Hardshaw Street, St Helens, WA10 1QW *Tel:* 01744 24226 *Fax:* 01744 24306 *E-mail:* shaunwoodward@email.labour.org.uk.

WOOLAS, PHILIP   Oldham East and Saddleworth   *Lab majority 2,726*

Philip James Woolas. Born 11 December 1959; Son of Dennis and Maureen Woolas; Educated Nelson Grammar School; Walton Lane High School; Nelson and Colne College; Manchester University (BA philosophy 1981); Married Tracey Allen 1988 (2 sons). President, National Union of Students 1984–86; BBC Newsnight producer 1988–90; Channel 4 News producer 1990; Head of communication, GMB 1991–97; Member, GMB. **House of Commons:** Contested Littleborough and Saddleworth by-election 1995. Member for Oldham East and Saddleworth since May 1, 1997; Assistant Government Whip 2001–02; Government Whip 2002–03; PPS to Lord Macdonald of Tradeston, as Minister of State for Transport, Department of the Environment, Transport and the Regions (Minister for Transport) 1999–2001; Deputy Leader of the House of Commons, Privy Council Office 2003–; *Special Interests:* Employment, Economics, Media, Trade and Industry, Benzodiazipines. *Countries of Interest:* Kashmir and Jammu. Chair, Tribune Newspaper 1997–2001; Deputy Leader, Leadership Campaign Team 1997–99. RTS Award for Political Coverage 1990; *Sportsclubs:* Lancashire County Cricket Club, Manchester United Football Club; *Recreations:* Photography. Philip Woolas Esq, MP, House of Commons, London, SW1A 0AA *Tel:* 020 7219 1149 *Fax:* 020 7219 0992. *Constituency:* 11 Church Lane, Oldham, Lancashire, OL1 3AN *Tel:* 0161–624 4248 *Fax:* 0161–626 8572 *E-mail:* woolasp@parliament.uk.

DodOnline

An Electronic Directory without rival . . .

MPs' biographies and photographs available with daily updates *via* the internet

For a *free* trial, call Yasmin Mirza, Aby Farsoun or Michael Mand on 020 7630 7643

WORTHINGTON, TONY   Clydebank and Milngavie   *Lab majority 10,724*

Tony Worthington. Born 11 October 1941; Son of late Malcolm and Monica Worthington; Educated City School, Lincoln; York and Durham Universities; London School of Economics (BA sociology 1966); Glasgow University (MEd 1977); Married Angela Oliver 1966 (1 son 1 daughter). Lecturer: HM Borstal, Dover 1962–66, Monkwearmouth College of F.E., Sunderland 1967–71, Jordanhill College of Education 1971–87; Member GMB. Clydebank North: Regional Councillor 1974–87, Chair, Finance Committee 1986–87. **House of Commons:** Member for Clydebank and Milngavie since June 1987; Opposition Spokesman for Scotland on: Education, Employment, Training and Social Work 1989–92, Development and Co-operation 1992–93; Opposition Spokesman on: Foreign and Commonwealth Affairs 1993–94, Northern Ireland 1995–97; Parliamentary Under-Secretary of State, Northern Ireland Office 1997–98; *Select Committees:* Member: Home Affairs 1987–88, International Development 1999–2001; Member, International Development 2001–. *Special Interests:* International Development, Employment, Asbestos Issues. *Countries of Interest:* Africa, Middle East, Eastern Europe. Board Director, Parliamentarians Network on World Band 2000–; Member Executive Council, Parliamentarians for Global Action; *Recreations:* Gardening. Tony Worthington Esq, MP, House of Commons, London, SW1A 0AA *Tel:* 020 7219 3507 *Fax:* 020 7219 3507. *Constituency:* 24 Cleddans Crescent, Handgate, Clydebank, Dunbartonshire, G81 5NW *Tel:* 01389 873195 *Fax:* 01389 873195 *E-mail:* worthingtont@parliament.uk.

WRAY, JAMES   Glasgow Baillieston   *Lab majority 9,839*

James Wray. Born 28 April 1938; Son of late Harold Wray and the late Elizabeth Wray; Educated St Bonaventure's, Gorbals; Married Laura Walker 1999 (1 son; 1 son 2 daughters from previous marriages). Member of Committee, TGWU. Councillor, Glasgow Corporation 1972–75; Councillor, Strathclyde Regional Council 1976–88. **House of Commons:** Member for Glasgow Provan 1987–97, and for Glasgow Baillieston since May 1, 1997; *Special Interests:* Social Services, Education, Foreign Affairs. Parliamentary agent for Frank McElhone MP 1969–82; Former Parliamentary election agent for Robert McTaggart MP. Leader: Anti-Dampness campaign, Anti-Eviction campaign, Anti-Fluoridation campaign, Gorbals rent strike; Substitute, UK Delegation to Council of Europe and Western Europe Union; *Sportsclubs:* Hon. President, Scottish Pro-Amateur Ex-Boxers Association; President: Kelvin Amateur Boxing Club, Strathclyde Community Boxers Club; *Recreations:* Boxing. James Wray Esq, MP, House of Commons, London, SW1A 0AA *Tel:* 020 7219 4606 *Fax:* 020 7219 2008. *Constituency:* 12 Sunningdale Avenue, Newton Mearns, Glasgow, G77 5PD *Tel:* 0141 639 1966 *Fax:* 0141 639 9235 *E-mail:* fisht@parliament.uk.

WRIGHT, ANTHONY DAVID   Great Yarmouth   *Lab majority 4,564*

Anthony David Wright. Born 12 August 1954; Son of late Arthur Wright and of Jean Wright; Educated Hospital Secondary modern school, Great Yarmouth; City and Guilds Mechanical Engineer apprentice 1969–73; Married Barbara Fleming 1988 (1 son 1 daughter 1 stepdaughter). Engineering apprentice 1970–74; Engineer 1974–83; Labour Party organiser/agent 1983–97; Member: AMICUS, GMB. Great Yarmouth Borough Council: Councillor 1980–82, 1986–98, Leader of Council 1996–97. **House of Commons:** Member for Great Yarmouth since May 1, 1997; PPS to Ruth Kelly as Financial Secretary to the Treasury 2002–03; *Select Committees:* Member, Public Administration 2000–02. *Special Interests:* Local and Regional Government, Trade and Industry. *Countries of Interest:* Cyprus. Member European Standing Committee C 1999–; Director Seachange Trust 1995–. Anthony David Wright Esq, MP (Great Yarmouth), House of Commons, London, SW1A 0AA *Tel:* 020 7219 3447 *Fax:* 020 7219 2304. *Constituency:* 21 Euston Road, Great Yarmouth, Norfolk, NR30 1DZ *Tel:* 01493 332291 *Fax:* 01493 332189 *E-mail:* wrighta@parliament.uk.

WRIGHT, TONY WAYLAND   Cannock Chase   *Lab majority 10,704*

Anthony Wayland Wright. Born 11 March 1948; Son of Frank and Maud Wright; Educated Desborough Primary School; Kettering Grammar School; London School of Economics (BSc economics 1970); Harvard University (Kennedy Scholar 1970–71); Balliol College, Oxford (DPhil 1973); Married Moira Elynwy Phillips 1973 (3 sons and 1 son deceased). Lecturer in politics, University College of North Wales, Bangor 1973–75; School of Continuing Studies, Birmingham University: Lecturer, Senior lecturer, Reader in politics 1975–92; AUT. Chair, South Birmingham Community Health Council 1983–85. **House of Commons:** Contested Kidderminster 1979 general election. Member for Cannock and Burntwood 1992–97, and for Cannock Chase since May 1, 1997; PPS to the Lord Irvine of Lairg, as Lord Chancellor 1997–98; *Select Committees:* Member: Parliamentary Commissioner for Administration 1992–96, Public Service 1995–97; Chair, Public Administration 1999–; Member: Liaison 1999–, Liaison Sub-Committee 2002–. *Special Interests:* Education, Health, Environment, Constitution. Executive Member, Fabian Society. Parent Governor, St Laurence Church Schools, Northfield, Birmingham 1989–92; Co-Chair, Campaign for Freedom of Information 1997–99; *Publications:* Include: *G. D. H. Cole and Socialist Democracy,* 1979; *Local Radio and Local Democracy,* 1982; *British Socialism,* 1983; *Socialisms: Theories and Practices,* 1986; *R. H. Tawney,* 1987; *Matters of Death and Life: A Study of Bereavement Support in Hospitals,* 1988; *Consuming Public Services,* 1990 (editor); *Contemporary Political Ideologies,* 1993 (editor); *Subjects and Citizens,* 1993; *Socialisms: Old and New,* 1996; *The People's Party,* 1997; *Who Can I Complain To?,* 1997; *Why Vote Labour?,* 1997; Joint Editor, *The Political Quarterly; The New Social Democracy,* 1999 (joint editor); *The British Political Process,* 2000 (editor); *The English Question,* 2000 (joint editor); Hon professor, Birmingham University 1999–; *Recreations:* Tennis, football, secondhand bookshops, walking, gardening. Dr Anthony Wayland Wright, MP (Cannock Chase), House of Commons, London, SW1A 0AA *Tel:* 020 7219 5029/5583 *Fax:* 020 7219 2665. *Constituency:* 6A Hallcourt Crescent, Cannock, Staffordshire, WS11 3AB *Tel:* 01543 467810 *Fax:* 01543 467811 *E-mail:* wrightt@parliament.uk.

WRIGHT, DAVID   Telford   *Lab majority 8,383*

David Wright. Born 22 December 1966; Son of Kenneth William Wright and Heather Wright, née Wynn; Educated Wrockwardine Wood Comprehensive School, Telford, Shropshire; New College, Telford, Shropshire; Wolverhampton Polytechnic (BA humanities 1988); Married Lesley Insole 1996. Housing strategy manager Sandwell Metropolitan Borough Council 1988–2001; Member TGWU 1988–. Councillor Wrekin District Council 1989–97; Oakengates Town Council 1989–2000: Councillor, Former chair. **House of Commons:** Member for Telford since June 7, 2001; *Select Committees:* Member, Administration 2001–02; Member: Environmental Audit 2001–, Procedure 2001–. *Special Interests:* Development of Housing and Regeneration Strategy, Regional Development, Sports Development, Hunting with Dogs (Against), Poverty. *Countries of Interest:* France, USA. Various former positions: Wrekin and Telford Constituency Labour Parties, Oakengates Branch Labour Party. Member Chartered Institute of Housing (MCIH); *Clubs:* Member: Wrockwardine Wood and Trench Labour, Dawley Social; *Recreations:* Football (Telford United and Shrewsbury Town), local history, visiting medieval towns. David Wright Esq, MP, House of Commons, London, SW1A 0AA *Tel:* 020 7219 8331 *Fax:* 020 7219 1979. *Constituency:* Suite 1, Matthew Webb House, High Street, Dawley, Telford, TF4 2RL *Tel:* 01952 507747 *Fax:* 01952 506064 *E-mail:* wrightda@parliament.uk.

Visit the Vacher Dod Website . . .

www.DodOnline.co.uk

WYATT, DEREK   Sittingbourne and Sheppey   *Lab majority 3,509*

Derek Wyatt. Born 4 December 1949; Son of late Reginald and Margaret Wyatt; Educated Westcliff County High School; Colchester Royal Grammar School; St Luke's College, Exeter (Certificate of Education 1971); Open University (BA art and architecture 1978); St Catherine's College, Oxford (research 1981–82); Married Joanna Willett (1 daughter 1 son). Director and a Publisher, William Heinemann 1986–88; Head of Programmes, Wire TV 1994–95; Director, Computer Channel, BSkyB 1995–97. Councillor, London Borough of Haringey 1994–96, Chairman, Alexandra Palace and Parks 1994–96. **House of Commons:** Member for Sittingbourne and Sheppey since May 1, 1997; Adviser on Rugby Union to Richard Caborn, as Minister of State for Sport 2002–; *Select Committees:* Member, Culture, Media and Sport 1997–. *Special Interests:* Venture Capital, Internet, British Council, Foreign Affairs, Media, Money Laundering. *Countries of Interest:* Southern Africa, Middle East, China. Member: RSPB, Amnesty International; Founder: Campaign for Fair Play 1985, Women's Sports Foundation (UK) 1985; Founder Oxford Internet Institute 2000; Trustee Major Stanley's, Oxford University 1993–; Fellow: Industry and Parliament Trust (Motorola) 1998–2001, Parliament Voluntary Sector Trust (Raleigh International) 1999–2001; Worshipful Company of Information Technologists; *Publications:* 5 books to date including: *Wisecracks From The Movies,* 1987, *Rugby DisUnion,* 1995; United Nations Commendation (Apartheid in Sport) 1987; FRSA; Freeman, City of London; *Clubs:* RAC, Vincents (Oxford); *Sportsclubs:* Charlton Athletic FC, Penguin International RFC (Executive); Played Rugby for Oxford University, Barbarians and England; *Recreations:* Reading, sport, writing, travel, jazz. Derek Wyatt, MP, House of Commons, London, SW1A 0AA *Tel:* 020 7219 5238 *Fax:* 020 7219 5520. *Constituency:* 29 Park Road, Sittingbourne, Kent, ME10 1DR *Tel:* 01795 477277 *Fax:* 01795 479558 *E-mail:* wyattd@parliament.uk.

Y

YEO, TIM   South Suffolk   *Con majority 5,081*

Timothy Stephen Kenneth Yeo. Born 20 March 1945; Son of late Dr Kenneth John Yeo; Educated Charterhouse; Emmanuel College, Cambridge (MA history 1968); Married Diane Helen Pickard 1970 (1 son 1 daughter). Cambridge University Air Squadron 1964–67; Assistant treasurer, Bankers Trust Company 1970–73; Director: Worcester Engineering Co. Ltd 1975–86, The Spastics Society 1980–83, Univent plc 1995–, Genus plc 2002–. **House of Commons:** Contested Bedwelty February 1974 general election. Member for South Suffolk since June 1983; Opposition Spokesperson for Environment, Transport and the Regions (Local Government, Regions, Planning and Housing) 1997–98; PPS to Douglas Hurd: as Home Secretary 1988–89, as Foreign and Commonwealth Secretary 1989–90; Joint Parliamentary Under-Secretary of State at: Department of the Environment 1990–92, Department of Health 1992–93; Minister of State for Environment and Countryside, Department of the Environment 1993–94; Shadow Minister of Agriculture, Fisheries and Food 1998–2001; Shadow Secretary of State for: Culture, Media and Sport 2001–02, Trade and Industry 2002–; *Select Committees:* Member: Social Services 1986–88, Employment 1994–96, Treasury 1996–97. *Special Interests:* Health, Economic Policy, Unemployment, Charity Reform, Rural Affairs. Vice-Chair, Conservative Party (with responsibllity for Local Government) 1998. Chair, Charities VAT Reform Group 1981–88; President, Charities Tax Reform Group 1988–90; Vice-President, International Voluntary Service 1984; Chair, Tadworth Court Trust 1984–91; Golf Correspondent Country Life 1994–; Trustee, Tanzania Development Trust 1980–97; Fellow, Industry and Parliament Trust; *Publications:* Public Accountancy and Aquisition of Charities 1983; *Clubs:* Royal St George's (Sandwich), Royal and Ancient Golf Club of St Andrews, MCC, Sunningdale Golf; *Sportsclubs:* Captain, Parliamentary Golfing Society 1991–95; *Recreations:* Golf, skiing. Timothy Yeo Esq, MP, House of Commons, London, SW1A 0AA *Tel:* 020 7219 6366 *Fax:* 020 7219 4857. *Constituency:* 43 High Street, Hadleigh, Suffolk, IP7 5AB *Tel:* 01473 823435 *Fax:* 01473 823536 *E-mail:* timyeomp@parliament.uk.

YOUNG, GEORGE   North West Hampshire   *Con majority 12,009*

George Young. Born 16 July 1941; Son of Sir George Young, 5th Bt, CMG, and Elizabeth Young, née Knatchbull-Hugessen; Educated Eton College; Christ Church, Oxford (BA philosophy, politics and economics 1963, MA); Surrey University (MPhil economics 1971); Married Aurelia Nemon-Stuart 1964 (2 sons 2 daughters). Economic adviser, Post Office 1969–74. Councillor, London Borough of Lambeth 1968–71; GLC Councillor for Ealing 1970–73; Chair, Acton Housing Association 1972–79. **House of Commons:** Member for Ealing Acton 1974–97, and for North West Hampshire since May 1, 1997; Opposition Whip 1976–79; Government Whip July-November 1990; Parliamentary Under-Secretary of State at: Department of Health and Social Services 1979–81, Department of Environment 1981–86; Department of Environment: Minister for Housing and Planning 1990–93, Minister for Housing, Inner Cities and Construction 1993–94; Financial Secretary, HM Treasury 1994–95; Secretary of State for Transport 1995–97; Member, Shadow Cabinet 1997–2000; Shadow Secretary of State for Defence 1997–98; Shadow Leader of the House of Commons 1998–99; Shadow Chancellor of the Duchy of Lancaster 1998–99; Shadow Leader of the House of Commons and Constitutional Affairs 1999–2000; *Select Committees:* Member: Public Accounts 1994–95, Modernisation of the House of Commons 1998–2000; Chair, Standards and Privileges 2001–; Member: Liaison 2001–, Selection 2001–, Liaison Sub-Committee 2002–. *Special Interests:* Housing, Disability, Health Education, Consitutional Reform. 6th Baronet, created 1813, succeeded his father 1960; Trustee, Guinness Trust 1986–90; *Publications: Tourism – Blessing or Blight*, 1970; PC 1993; *Recreations:* Bicycling, opera. Rt Hon Sir George Young, Bt, MP, House of Commons, London, SW1A 0AA *Tel:* 020 7219 6665 *Fax:* 020 7219 2566. *Constituency:* 2 Church Close, Andover, Hampshire, SP10 1DP *Tel:* 01264 401401 *Fax:* 01264 391155 *E-mail:* sirgeorge@sirgeorgeyoung.org.uk.

YOUNGER-ROSS, RICHARD   Teignbridge   *LD majority 3,011*

Richard Alan Younger-Ross. Born 29 January 1953; Son of late Arthur George Ross and Patricia Ross; Educated Walton-on-Thames Secondary Modern School; Ewell Technical College (HNC building construction 1976); Married Susan Younger 1982. Architectural assistant various architectural practices 1970–90; Design consultant self-employed 1990–2001. **House of Commons:** Contested Chislehurst 1987 and Teignbridge 1992, 1997 general elections. Member for Teignbridge since June 7, 2001; Liberal Democrat Whip 2002–03; *Special Interests:* Economy, Trade and Industry. *Countries of Interest:* USA, Kurdistan. Organising vice-chair NLYL 1979; Parliamentary researcher 1981; Secretary-general YLM 1981–82; Economics spokesperson south west 1994–97. Member: Anti-Slavery International, British Kurdish Friendship Society, Howard League for Penal Reform; Member European Standing Committee C; *Recreations:* Cooking, riding, folk music, gardening, football (Arsenal FC). Richard Younger-Ross Esq, MP, House of Commons, London, SW1A 0AA *Tel:* 020 7219 8479. *Constituency:* 70 Queen Street, Newton Abbot, Devon, TQ12 2ET *Tel:* 01626 202626 *Fax:* 01626 202016 *E-mail:* yrossr@parliament.uk.

DodOnline

An Electronic Directory without rival ...

MPs' biographies and photographs available with daily updates *via* the internet

For a *free* trial, call Yasmin Mirza, Aby Farsoun or Michael Mand on 020 7630 7643

MPs' Political Interests

The interests listed are supplied to Dod by MPs themselves.

Abortion
Widdecombe, Ann *(Con)*

Accountancy
Mitchell, Austin *(Lab)*

Adult Education
Etherington, Bill *(Lab)*

Aerospace
Borrow, David *(Lab)*
Foulkes, George *(Lab/Co-op)*
Haselhurst, Sir Alan *(Con)*
Howarth, Gerald *(Con)*
Ingram, Adam *(Lab)*
Jack, Michael *(Con)*
Moffatt, Laura *(Lab)*
Öpik, Lembit *(Lib Dem)*
Robinson, Peter *(DUP)*
Soames, Nicholas *(Con)*
Tami, Mark *(Lab)*
Wilkinson, John *(Con)*

Affordable Housing
Steen, Anthony *(Con)*

Africa
Barnes, Harry *(Lab)*
Cash, William *(Con)*
Jackson, Helen *(Lab)*

Age Discrimination
Perham, Linda *(Lab)*

Ageing
Burstow, Paul *(Lib Dem)*
O'Hara, Edward *(Lab)*

Agenda 21
Colman, Tony *(Lab)*

Agriculture
Ancram, Michael *(Con)*
Atkins, Charlotte *(Lab)*
Atkinson, Peter *(Con)*
Bacon, Richard *(Con)*
Beggs, Roy *(UUP)*
Bellingham, Henry *(Con)*
Boswell, Timothy *(Con)*
Burnett, John *(Lib Dem)*
Burt, Alistair *(Con)*
Carmichael, Alistair *(Lib Dem)*

Clifton-Brown, Geoffrey *(Con)*
Collins, Tim *(Con)*
Curry, David *(Con)*
Davies, Quentin *(Con)*
Davis, David *(Con)*
Drew, David *(Lab/Co-op)*
Evans, Nigel *(Con)*
Flook, Adrian *(Con)*
Garnier, Edward *(Con)*
George, Andrew *(Lib Dem)*
Gray, James *(Con)*
Green, Matthew *(Lib Dem)*
Greenway, John *(Con)*
Hague, William *(Con)*
Haselhurst, Sir Alan *(Con)*
Hayes, John *(Con)*
Heathcoat-Amory, David *(Con)*
Hendry, Charles *(Con)*
Hood, Jimmy *(Lab)*
Hoyle, Lindsay *(Lab)*
Hunter, Andrew *(Ind)*
Hurst, Alan *(Lab)*
Jack, Michael *(Con)*
Jackson, Robert *(Con)*
Jones, Martyn *(Lab)*
Key, Robert *(Con)*
Leigh, Edward *(Con)*
Llwyd, Elfyn *(Plaid Cymru)*
Lord, Michael *(Con)*
McLoughlin, Patrick *(Con)*
Marsden, Paul *(Lib Dem)*
Martlew, Eric *(Lab)*
Mercer, Patrick *(Con)*
Mitchell, Austin *(Lab)*
Mountford, Kali *(Lab)*
Norman, Archie *(Con)*
O'Brien, Stephen *(Con)*
Paice, Jim *(Con)*
Paterson, Owen *(Con)*
Pickthall, Colin *(Lab)*
Prentice, Gordon *(Lab)*
Robertson, Hugh *(Con)*
Salmond, Alex *(SNP)*
Shephard, Gillian *(Con)*
Simmonds, Mark *(Con)*
Soames, Nicholas *(Con)*
Spelman, Caroline *(Con)*
Steen, Anthony *(Con)*
Strang, Gavin *(Lab)*
Swire, Hugo *(Con)*
Thomas, Gareth *(Lab)*

Tipping, Paddy *(Lab)*
Todd, Mark *(Lab)*
Walter, Robert *(Con)*
Wiggin, Bill *(Con)*
Williams, Roger *(Lib Dem)*
Winterton, Ann *(Con)*

AIDS
Moffatt, Laura *(Lab)*
Strang, Gavin *(Lab)*

Air and Rail Safety
Barrett, John *(Lib Dem)*

Air Transport
Wilkinson, John *(Con)*

Airports Policy
Wareing, Robert *(Lab)*

Alcohol Abuse and Under-age Drinking
Hood, Jimmy *(Lab)*

Alternative Energy
Cook, Frank *(Lab)*
Green, Matthew *(Lib Dem)*
Hamilton, Fabian *(Lab)*

Anglo-American Relations
Mawhinney, Sir Brian *(Con)*

Angola
Dawson, Hilton *(Lab)*

Animal Welfare
Banks, Tony *(Lab)*
Caplin, Ivor *(Lab)*
Cawsey, Ian *(Lab)*
Cohen, Harry *(Lab)*
Conway, Derek *(Con)*
Dowd, Jim *(Lab)*
Etherington, Bill *(Lab)*
Fitzpatrick, Jim *(Lab)*
Flynn, Paul *(Lab)*
Foster, Michael Jabez *(Lab)*
Gale, Roger *(Con)*
Griffiths, Win *(Lab)*
Henderson, Ivan *(Lab)*
Loughton, Tim *(Con)*
McIntosh, Anne *(Con)*
Norris, Dan *(Lab)*
O'Hara, Edward *(Lab)*

Palmer, Dr Nick *(Lab)*
Russell, Bob *(Lib Dem)*
Smith, Angela *(Lab/Co-op)*
Steinberg, Gerry *(Lab)*
Turner, Dr Des *(Lab)*
White, Brian *(Lab)*

Anti-Common Market
Skinner, Dennis *(Lab)*

Anti-Hunting
Bailey, Adrian *(Lab/Co-op)*
Levitt, Tom *(Lab)*

**Anti-Imperialism and
  Internationalism**
Corbyn, Jeremy *(Lab)*

Anti-Poverty
Ruane, Chris *(Lab)*

Anti-Social Behaviour
Flint, Caroline *(Lab)*

Arboriculture
Chapman, Sydney *(Con)*

**Architectural and Artistic
  Heritage**
Beith, Alan *(Lib Dem)*
Chapman, Sydney *(Con)*
Shipley, Debra *(Lab)*
Swire, Hugo *(Con)*

Arms Control
Heathcoat-Amory, David
  (Con)

Arts
Atkinson, David *(Con)*
Banks, Tony *(Lab)*
Blears, Hazel *(Lab)*
Campbell, Menzies *(Lib Dem)*
Caplin, Ivor *(Lab)*
Cormack, Sir Patrick *(Con)*
Dunwoody, Gwyneth *(Lab)*
Ellman, Louise *(Lab/Co-op)*
Fisher, Mark *(Lab)*
Griffiths, Nigel *(Lab)*
Hopkins, Kelvin *(Lab)*
Howarth, Alan *(Lab)*
Howells, Dr Kim *(Lab)*
Key, Robert *(Con)*
Knight, Greg *(Con)*
Knight, Jim *(Lab)*
Lammy, David *(Lab)*

Linton, Martin *(Lab)*
Mactaggart, Fiona *(Lab)*
Russell, Christine *(Lab)*
Swire, Hugo *(Con)*
Wishart, Peter *(SNP)*

Asbestos Issues
Worthington, Tony *(Lab)*

Asylum and Immigration
Coleman, Iain *(Lab)*
Harris, Dr Evan *(Lib Dem)*
Joyce, Eric *(Lab)*
Prosser, Gwyn *(Lab)*

Autism
Ladyman, Dr Stephen *(Lab)*

Aviation
Foulkes, George
  (Lab/Co-op)
Haselhurst, Sir Alan *(Con)*
Howarth, Gerald *(Con)*
McDonnell, John *(Lab)*
Marshall, David *(Lab)*
Moffatt, Laura *(Lab)*
Robinson, Peter *(DUP)*
Soames, Nicholas *(Con)*
Wilshire, David *(Con)*

Benefits
McIsaac, Shona *(Lab)*

Benzodiazipines
Woolas, Philip *(Lab)*

Britain's Sovereignty
Spink, Bob *(Con)*

British Council
Wyatt, Derek *(Lab)*

British Overseas Territories
Rosindell, Andrew *(Con)*

Broadcasting
Begg, Anne *(Lab)*
Bryant, Chris *(Lab)*
Fabricant, Michael *(Con)*
Fisher, Mark *(Lab)*
Gale, Roger *(Con)*
Greenway, John *(Con)*
Grogan, John *(Lab)*
Kennedy, Charles *(Lib Dem)*
Ruffley, David *(Con)*
Whittingdale, John *(Con)*

Built Environment
Chidgey, David *(Lib Dem)*

Business
Cotter, Brian *(Lib Dem)*
Johnson, Melanie *(Lab)*
Liddell-Grainger, Ian *(Con)*
Merron, Gillian *(Lab)*
Moore, Michael *(Lib Dem)*
Norman, Archie *(Con)*
Todd, Mark *(Lab)*

**Campaigning for Socialism
  in the Community and
  against Racism**
Corbyn, Jeremy *(Lab)*

Cancer and Blood
Havard, Dai *(Lab)*

Car Industry
Smith, Andrew *(Lab)*

Care of Ancient Monuments
Taylor, Mark John *(Con)*

Channel Islands
Mackinlay, Andrew *(Lab)*

**Charity and Voluntary
  Sector**
Baron, John *(Con)*
Flight, Howard *(Con)*
Howarth, Alan *(Lab)*
Yeo, Tim *(Con)*

Child Poverty
Keen, Ann *(Lab)*

Child Protection and Safety
Bailey, Adrian *(Lab/Co-op)*
Cook, Frank *(Lab)*
Hughes, Beverley *(Lab)*
Johnson, Melanie *(Lab)*
Norris, Dan *(Lab)*

Childcare
Baldry, Tony *(Con)*
Doran, Frank *(Lab)*
Flint, Caroline *(Lab)*
Hughes, Kevin *(Lab)*
Moran, Margaret *(Lab)*
Morgan, Julie *(Lab)*

Children
Buck, Karen *(Lab)*

Dawson, Hilton *(Lab)*
Fitzsimons, Lorna *(Lab)*
Griffiths, Win *(Lab)*
Kidney, David *(Lab)*
Shipley, Debra *(Lab)*
Woodward, Shaun *(Lab)*

Christian Socialism
Timms, Stephen *(Lab)*

Christian Values
Donaldson, Jeffrey *(UUP)*

Church Affairs
Burt, Alistair *(Con)*
Field, Frank *(Lab)*

Citizenship
Francis, Hywel *(Lab)*

Civil Defence
McCartney, Ian *(Lab)*

Civil Justice
Dismore, Andrew *(Lab)*

Civil Liberties
Atkins, Charlotte *(Lab)*
Baird, Vera *(Lab)*
Baker, Norman *(Lib Dem)*
Ewing, Annabelle *(SNP)*
Harman, Harriet *(Lab)*
Harris, Dr Evan *(Lib Dem)*
Hughes, Simon *(Lib Dem)*
Lloyd, Tony *(Lab)*
Llwyd, Elfyn *(Plaid Cymru)*
Mactaggart, Fiona *(Lab)*
Marshall-Andrews, Bob
   (Lab)
Meacher, Michael *(Lab)*
Smith, Chris *(Lab)*
Soley, Clive *(Lab)*
Stinchcombe, Paul *(Lab)*

Civil Service
Clarke, Tom *(Lab)*

Climate Change
Stunell, Andrew *(Lib Dem)*

Co-operative Development
McFall, John *(Lab/Co-op)*
Michael, Alun
   (Lab/Co-op)
Naysmith, Dr Doug
   (Lab/Co-op)

Co-operative Issues
Lazarowicz, Mark *(Lab/Co-op)*
Munn, Meg *(Lab/Co-op)*

Co-operative Movement
Bailey, Adrian *(Lab/Co-op)*
Davidson, Ian *(Lab/Co-op)*
Drown, Julia *(Lab)*
Reed, Andy *(Lab/Co-op)*

Coal Industry
Clapham, Michael *(Lab)*
Cooper, Yvette *(Lab)*
Cryer, John *(Lab)*
Cummings, John *(Lab)*
Grogan, John *(Lab)*
O'Brien, Mike *(Lab)*

Commerce
Hayes, John *(Con)*
Keen, Alan *(Lab/Co-op)*
Ottaway, Richard *(Con)*

Commonwealth
Davidson, Ian *(Lab/Co-op)*
Kilfoyle, Peter *(Lab)*

**Communications and
   Information Technology**
Miller, Andrew *(Lab)*

Community Care
McCabe, Steve *(Lab)*
Robinson, Peter *(DUP)*
Squire, Rachel *(Lab)*
Steen, Anthony *(Con)*

Community Development
Burstow, Paul *(Lib Dem)*
Calton, Patsy *(Lib Dem)*
Dawson, Hilton *(Lab)*
Goggins, Paul *(Lab)*
Haselhurst, Sir Alan *(Con)*
Hope, Phil *(Lab/Co-op)*
Michael, Alun *(Lab/Co-op)*
Shaw, Jonathan *(Lab)*

**Complementary and
   Alternative Medicine**
Corston, Jean *(Lab)*
Tredinnick, David *(Con)*

Conflict Resolution
Barnes, Harry *(Lab)*
Breed, Colin *(Lib Dem)*
Hume, John *(SDLP)*

Conservation
Chapman, Sydney *(Con)*
Hurst, Alan *(Lab)*
Robathan, Andrew *(Con)*
Steen, Anthony *(Con)*

Constitution
Alexander, Douglas *(Lab)*
Anderson, Janet *(Lab)*
Brennan, Kevin *(Lab)*
Browne, Des *(Lab)*
Burden, Richard *(Lab)*
Burnside, David *(UUP)*
Campbell, Alan *(Lab)*
Clark, Dr Lynda *(Lab)*
Clarke, Tony *(Lab)*
Collins, Tim *(Con)*
Darling, Alistair *(Lab)*
Dodds, Nigel *(DUP)*
Donaldson, Jeffrey *(UUP)*
Edwards, Huw *(Lab)*
Fallon, Michael *(Con)*
Fitzsimons, Lorna *(Lab)*
Flynn, Paul *(Lab)*
Grieve, Dominic *(Con)*
Holmes, Paul *(Lib Dem)*
Hoon, Geoff *(Lab)*
Laing, Eleanor *(Con)*
Lamb, Norman *(Lib Dem)*
Lazarowicz, Mark *(Lab/Co-op)*
McGrady, Eddie *(SDLP)*
McKenna, Rosemary *(Lab)*
Mackinlay, Andrew *(Lab)*
Mitchell, Austin *(Lab)*
O'Brien, Stephen *(Con)*
Paisley, Rev Ian*(DUP)*
Plaskitt, James *(Lab)*
Prentice, Bridget *(Lab)*
Quinn, Lawrie *(Lab)*
Redwood, John *(Con)*
Robertson, Laurence *(Con)*
Savidge, Malcolm *(Lab)*
Shephard, Gillian *(Con)*
Stuart, Gisela *(Lab)*
Syms, Robert *(Con)*
Thomas, Gareth *(Lab)*
Turner, Andrew *(Con)*
Tyler, Paul *(Lib Dem)*
Watkinson, Angela *(Con)*
Whitehead, Dr Alan *(Lab)*
Wright, Dr Tony Wayland *(Lab)*
Young, Sir George *(Con)*

Construction Industry
Chapman, Sydney *(Con)*
Spellar, John *(Lab)*

Consumer Issues
Knight, Greg *(Con)*
Lazarowicz, Mark *(Lab/Co-op)*
Murphy, Jim *(Lab)*
Williams, Betty *(Lab)*

Cornwall
Breed, Colin *(Lib Dem)*
George, Andrew *(Lib Dem)*

Corporate Social Responsibility
Perham, Linda *(Lab)*

Corruption
Colman, Tony *(Lab)*

Countryside
Brazier, Julian *(Con)*
Gray, James *(Con)*
Hoey, Kate *(Lab)*
Morley, Elliot *(Lab)*
Norman, Archie *(Con)*
Prentice, Gordon *(Lab)*
Robertson, Laurence *(Con)*
Simpson, Keith *(Con)*

Credit Unions
Hume, John *(SDLP)*

Crime
Burnham, Andy *(Lab)*
Connarty, Michael *(Lab)*
Farrelly, Paul *(Lab)*
Flint, Caroline *(Lab)*
Lewis, Ivan *(Lab)*
McIsaac, Shona *(Lab)*
Merron, Gillian *(Lab)*
Milburn, Alan *(Lab)*
Simon, Siôn *(Lab)*

Criminal Justice
Baird, Vera *(Lab)*
Carmichael, Alistair *(Lib Dem)*
Gerrard, Neil *(Lab)*
Hughes, Beverley *(Lab)*
Malins, Humfrey *(Con)*
Smith, Chris *(Lab)*
Thomas, Gareth *(Lab)*

Culture
Anderson, Janet *(Lab)*
Field, Mark *(Con)*
Fisher, Mark *(Lab)*
Keen, Alan *(Lab/Co-op)*
Linton, Martin *(Lab)*

Price, Adam *(Plaid Cymru)*
Purnell, James *(Lab)*
Smith, Chris *(Lab)*
Ward, Claire *(Lab)*
Woodward, Shaun *(Lab)*

Cyprus
Dismore, Andrew *(Lab)*
Lepper, David *(Lab/Co-op)*

Deaf Children
Bruce, Malcolm *(Lib Dem)*

Debt Relief
Cash, William *(Con)*

Deep Sea Fishing Industry
Quinn, Lawrie *(Lab)*

Deep Vein Thrombosis in Air Travellers
Smith, John *(Lab)*

Defence
Ancram, Michael *(Con)*
Arbuthnot, James *(Con)*
Bayley, Hugh *(Lab)*
Beard, Nigel *(Lab)*
Bellingham, Henry *(Con)*
Blackman, Liz *(Lab)*
Blunt, Crispin *(Con)*
Brazier, Julian *(Con)*
Burnett, John *(Lib Dem)*
Cairns, David *(Lab)*
Campbell, Menzies *(Lib Dem)*
Cohen, Harry *(Lab)*
Collins, Tim *(Con)*
Conway, Derek *(Con)*
Cook, Robin *(Lab)*
Corbyn, Jeremy *(Lab)*
Crausby, David *(Lab)*
Davidson, Ian *(Lab/Co-op)*
Duncan Smith, Iain *(Con)*
Evans, Nigel *(Con)*
Foulkes, George *(Lab/Co-op)*
Francois, Mark *(Con)*
Galloway, George *(Lab)*
Gapes, Mike *(Lab/Co-op)*
Garnier, Edward *(Con)*
George, Bruce *(Lab)*
Gillan, Cheryl *(Con)*
Gray, James *(Con)*
Grieve, Dominic *(Con)*
Hammond, Philip *(Con)*
Hancock, Mike *(Lib Dem)*
Hawkins, Nick *(Con)*

Hendrick, Mark *(Lab/Co-op)*
Hood, Jimmy *(Lab)*
Hoon, Geoff *(Lab)*
Howarth, Gerald *(Con)*
Hoyle, Lindsay *(Lab)*
Hutton, John *(Lab)*
Ingram, Adam *(Lab)*
Jenkin, Bernard *(Con)*
Jones, Kevan *(Lab)*
Joyce, Eric *(Lab)*
Keen, Alan *(Lab/Co-op)*
Keetch, Paul *(Lib Dem)*
Key, Robert *(Con)*
Ladyman, Dr Stephen *(Lab)*
Leigh, Edward *(Con)*
Lewis, Dr Julian *(Con)*
Liddell-Grainger, Ian *(Con)*
McFall, John *(Lab/Co-op)*
McWilliam, John *(Lab)*
Mahon, Alice *(Lab)*
Martlew, Eric *(Lab)*
Mates, Michael *(Con)*
Mercer, Patrick *(Con)*
Mitchell, Andrew *(Con)*
Moffatt, Laura *(Lab)*
Moonie, Lewis *(Lab/Co-op)*
Murphy, Jim *(Lab)*
Murrison, Andrew *(Con)*
O'Neill, Martin *(Lab)*
Ottaway, Richard *(Con)*
Prisk, Mark *(Con)*
Rapson, Syd *(Lab)*
Reid, Dr John *(Lab)*
Robathan, Andrew *(Con)*
Robertson, Angus *(SNP)*
Robertson, Hugh *(Con)*
Rosindell, Andrew *(Con)*
Ross, Ernie *(Lab)*
Savidge, Malcolm *(Lab)*
Selous, Andrew *(Con)*
Sheridan, Jim *(Lab)*
Simpson, Keith *(Con)*
Smith, John *(Lab)*
Soames, Nicholas *(Con)*
Squire, Rachel *(Lab)*
Stewart, David *(Lab)*
Swire, Hugo *(Con)*
Taylor, Dari *(Lab)*
Trend, Hon Michael *(Con)*
Viggers, Peter *(Con)*
Vis, Rudi *(Lab)*
Widdecombe, Ann *(Con)*
Wiggin, Bill *(Con)*
Wilkinson, John *(Con)*

Defence and NATO
Cormack, Sir Patrick *(Con)*

Democracy
Allen, Graham *(Lab)*
Hodge, Margaret *(Lab)*
Goggins, Paul *(Lab)*
Keen, Alan *(Lab/Co-op)*
McKenna, Rosemary *(Lab)*
Southworth, Helen *(Lab)*
Stewart, Ian *(Lab)*

Deregulation and Scrutiny of EU Directives
Steen, Anthony *(Con)*

Developing World
Streeter, Gary *(Con)*

Development
Keen, Alan *(Lab/Co-op)*
King, Oona *(Lab)*
Palmer, Dr Nick *(Lab)*
Prisk, Mark *(Con)*

Devolution
Clelland, David *(Lab)*
Flynn, Paul *(Lab)*
Foulkes, George *(Lab/Co-op)*
George, Andrew *(Lib Dem)*
Laing, Eleanor *(Con)*
Mackinlay, Andrew *(Lab)*
Quinn, Lawrie *(Lab)*
Sarwar, Mohammad *(Lab)*

Diet and Nutrition
Tredinnick, David *(Con)*

Disability
Atherton, Candy *(Lab)*
Begg, Anne *(Lab)*
Berry, Dr Roger *(Lab)*
Blackman, Liz *(Lab)*
Browne, Des *(Lab)*
Burstow, Paul *(Lib Dem)*
Burt, Alistair *(Con)*
Corston, Jean *(Lab)*
Cotter, Brian *(Lib Dem)*
Etherington, Bill *(Lab)*
Francis, Hywel *(Lab)*
Gerrard, Neil *(Lab)*
Griffiths, Nigel *(Lab)*
Griffiths, Win *(Lab)*
Hayes, John *(Con)*
Healey, John *(Lab)*
Levitt, Tom *(Lab)*
Loughton, Tim *(Con)*
Marsden, Gordon *(Lab)*
May, Theresa *(Con)*

Turner, Dr Des *(Lab)*
Wareing, Robert *(Lab)*
Weir, Mike *(SNP)*
Young, Sir George *(Con)*

Disarmament
Lloyd, Tony *(Lab)*
Simpson, Alan *(Lab)*

Dog issues
Rosindell, Andrew *(Con)*

Domestic Violence
George, Andrew *(Lib Dem)*
Harman, Harriet *(Lab)*

Drug Abuse
Connarty, Michael *(Lab)*
Martin, Michael *(The Speaker)*
Meale, Alan *(Lab)*
Moffatt, Laura *(Lab)*
Wishart, Peter *(SNP)*

Dundee's Economic Prosperity
Luke, Iain *(Lab)*

E-business
Duncan, Peter *(Con)*

E-Issues
Moran, Margaret *(Lab)*

Early Years Education
Cryer, Ann *(Lab)*

Eastern Europe
Bellingham, Henry *(Con)*
Clapham, Michael *(Lab)*

Ecology
Cohen, Harry *(Lab)*
Cook, Frank *(Lab)*
Jones, Martyn *(Lab)*

Economic and Democratic Planning
Blunkett, David *(Lab)*

Economic and Foreign Affairs
Wareing, Robert *(Lab)*

Economic and Industrial Affairs
Hendrick, Mark *(Lab/Co-op)*

Economic and Industrial Policy
Follett, Barbara *(Lab)*
Pearson, Ian *(Lab)*

Economic Development
Campbell, Gregory Lloyd *(DUP)*
Chapman, Ben *(Lab)*
Francis, Hywel *(Lab)*
George, Andrew *(Lib Dem)*
Hamilton, David *(Lab)*
Michael, Alun *(Lab/Co-op)*
Murphy, Denis *(Lab)*
Owen, Albert *(Lab)*
Prosser, Gwyn *(Lab)*
Rapson, Syd *(Lab)*
Shaw, Jonathan *(Lab)*
Smith, John *(Lab)*
Williams, Roger *(Lib Dem)*

Economic Development and Small Businesses
Hamilton, Fabian *(Lab)*

Economic Policy
Ainsworth, Peter *(Con)*
Alexander, Douglas *(Lab)*
Allen, Graham *(Lab)*
Bailey, Adrian *(Lab/Co-op)*
Battle, John *(Lab)*
Bayley, Hugh *(Lab)*
Bell, Stuart *(Lab)*
Bercow, John *(Con)*
Berry, Dr Roger *(Lab)*
Betts, Clive *(Lab)*
Bradley, Peter *(Lab)*
Brown, Gordon *(Lab)*
Burnett, John *(Lib Dem)*
Cable, Dr Vincent *(Lib Dem)*
Clappison, James *(Con)*
Collins, Tim *(Con)*
Cran, James *(Con)*
Cryer, John *(Lab)*
Cunningham, Jim *(Lab)*
Curtis-Thomas, Claire *(Lab)*
Dalyell, Tom *(Lab)*
Darling, Alistair *(Lab)*
Dowd, Jim *(Lab)*
Eagle, Angela *(Lab)*
Flight, Howard *(Con)*
Forth, Eric *(Con)*
Fox, Dr Liam *(Con)*
Gapes, Mike *(Lab/Co-op)*
Gardiner, Barry *(Lab)*
Green, Damian *(Con)*

Griffiths, Nigel *(Lab)*
Grogan, John *(Lab)*
Hague, William *(Con)*
Hammond, Philip *(Con)*
Henderson, Doug *(Lab)*
Hesford, Stephen *(Lab)*
Hoon, Geoff *(Lab)*
Hopkins, Kelvin *(Lab)*
Horam, John *(Con)*
Howarth, Alan *(Lab)*
Jenkin, Bernard *(Con)*
Jones, Dr Lynne *(Lab)*
Keeble, Sally *(Lab)*
Kelly, Ruth *(Lab)*
Laing, Eleanor *(Con)*
Lansley, Andrew *(Con)*
Leslie, Christopher *(Lab)*
Liddell, Helen *(Lab)*
Lilley, Peter *(Con)*
McCabe, Steve *(Lab)*
McFall, John *(Lab/Co-op)*
Mallaber, Judy *(Lab)*
Marshall-Andrews, Bob *(Lab)*
Milburn, Alan *(Lab)*
Miller, Andrew *(Lab)*
Moonie, Lewis *(Lab/Co-op)*
Plaskitt, James *(Lab)*
Primarolo, Dawn *(Lab)*
Rammell, Bill *(Lab)*
Robertson, Laurence *(Con)*
Robinson, Geoffrey *(Lab)*
Sarwar, Mohammad *(Lab)*
Sedgemore, Brian *(Lab)*
Skinner, Dennis *(Lab)*
Smith, Chris *(Lab)*
Smith, Jacqui *(Lab)*
Spicer, Sir Michael *(Con)*
Straw, Jack *(Lab)*
Syms, Robert *(Con)*
Taylor, Dari *(Lab)*
Timms, Stephen *(Lab)*
Trickett, Jon *(Lab)*
Tyrie, Andrew *(Con)*
White, Brian *(Lab)*
Willetts, David *(Con)*
Yeo, Tim *(Con)*

Economic Regeneration
Atherton, Candy *(Lab)*
Blackman, Liz *(Lab)*
Cruddas, Jon *(Lab)*
Healey, John *(Lab)*
Hughes, Beverley *(Lab)*
Humble, Joan *(Lab)*
Mann, John *(Lab)*
Reed, Andy *(Lab/Co-op)*
Smith, Geraldine *(Lab)*

Economics
Banks, Tony *(Lab)*
Davey, Edward *(Lib Dem)*
Dorrell, Stephen *(Con)*
Foster, Derek *(Lab)*
Gibb, Nick *(Con)*
Harvey, Nick *(Lib Dem)*
Ladyman, Dr Stephen *(Lab)*
Letwin, Oliver *(Con)*
McDonnell, John *(Lab)*
McKechin, Ann *(Lab)*
McWalter, Tony *(Lab/Co-op)*
Mitchell, Austin *(Lab)*
Simpson, Alan *(Lab)*
Stewart, Ian *(Lab)*
Tapsell, Sir Peter *(Con)*
Todd, Mark *(Lab)*
Vis, Rudi *(Lab)*
Woolas, Philip *(Lab)*

Economics and Social Policy
Meacher, Michael *(Lab)*

Economy
Beard, Nigel *(Lab)*
Blackman, Liz *(Lab)*
Brennan, Kevin *(Lab)*
Cameron, David *(Con)*
Challen, Colin *(Lab)*
Clifton-Brown, Geoffrey *(Con)*
Connarty, Michael *(Lab)*
David, Wayne *(Lab)*
Field, Mark *(Con)*
Harris, Tom *(Lab)*
Hoban, Mark *(Con)*
Laws, David *(Lib Dem)*
Lazarowicz, Mark *(Lab/Co-op)*
Liddell-Grainger, Ian *(Con)*
Lucas, Ian *(Lab)*
Maples, John *(Con)*
Marsden, Paul *(Lib Dem)*
Merron, Gillian *(Lab)*
Mitchell, Andrew *(Con)*
Moran, Margaret *(Lab)*
Murphy, Jim *(Lab)*
O'Brien, Stephen *(Con)*
Osborne, George *(Con)*
Palmer, Dr Nick *(Lab)*
Picking, Anne *(Lab)*
Price, Adam *(Plaid Cymru)*
Purnell, James *(Lab)*
Reid, Dr John *(Lab)*
Sheerman, Barry *(Lab/Co-op)*
Simmonds, Mark *(Con)*
Taylor, Ian *(Con)*
Turner, Andrew *(Con)*

Twigg, Derek *(Lab)*
Younger-Ross, Richard
   (Lib Dem)

Education
Allan, Richard *(Lib Dem)*
Amess, David *(Con)*
Armstrong, Hilary *(Lab)*
Atkins, Charlotte *(Lab)*
Bacon, Richard *(Con)*
Barker, Gregory *(Con)*
Baron, John *(Con)*
Beggs, Roy *(UUP)*
Benn, Hilary *(Lab)*
Benton, Joe *(Lab)*
Bercow, John *(Con)*
Beresford, Sir Paul *(Con)*
Blackman, Liz *(Lab)*
Blizzard, Bob *(Lab)*
Blunkett, David *(Lab)*
Bradley, Peter *(Lab)*
Brady, Graham *(Con)*
Browne, Des *(Lab)*
Burnham, Andy *(Lab)*
Campbell, Alan *(Lab)*
Campbell, Anne *(Lab)*
Caton, Martin *(Lab)*
Chaytor, David *(Lab)*
Clappison, James *(Con)*
Clark, Dr Lynda *(Lab)*
Clark, Paul *(Lab)*
Coaker, Vernon *(Lab)*
Cook, Frank *(Lab)*
Cormack, Sir Patrick *(Con)*
Cryer, John *(Lab)*
Cunningham, Tony *(Lab)*
Darling, Alistair *(Lab)*
Davey, Valerie *(Lab)*
David, Wayne *(Lab)*
Dean, Janet *(Lab)*
Drew, David *(Lab/Co-op)*
Edwards, Huw *(Lab)*
Efford, Clive *(Lab)*
Ennis, Jeffrey *(Lab)*
Etherington, Bill *(Lab)*
Evans, Nigel *(Con)*
Fallon, Michael *(Con)*
Farrelly, Paul *(Lab)*
Flint, Caroline *(Lab)*
Foster, Derek *(Lab)*
Foster, Don *(Lib Dem)*
Foster, Michael John *(Lab)*
Foulkes, George *(Lab/Co-op)*
Gale, Roger *(Con)*
Gapes, Mike *(Lab/Co-op)*
Gardiner, Barry *(Lab)*

Garnier, Edward *(Con)*
Gibb, Nick *(Con)*
Gidley, Sandra *(Lib Dem)*
Gildernew, Michelle
    (Sinn Fein)
Gillan, Cheryl *(Con)*
Grayling, Christopher *(Con)*
Green, Damian *(Con)*
Griffiths, Nigel *(Lab)*
Griffiths, Win *(Lab)*
Hall, Mike *(Lab)*
Hamilton, Fabian *(Lab)*
Haselhurst, Sir Alan *(Con)*
Havard, Dai *(Lab)*
Hawkins, Nick *(Con)*
Hayes, John *(Con)*
Heath, David *(Lib Dem)*
Hermon, Sylvia *(UUP)*
Hesford, Stephen *(Lab)*
Heyes, David *(Lab)*
Hoban, Mark *(Con)*
Hodge, Margaret *(Lab)*
Holmes, Paul *(Lib Dem)*
Hood, Jimmy *(Lab)*
Howarth, Alan *(Lab)*
Hughes, Beverley *(Lab)*
Humble, Joan *(Lab)*
Iddon, Dr Brian *(Lab)*
Jamieson, David *(Lab)*
Johnson, Alan *(Lab)*
Johnson, Melanie *(Lab)*
Jones, Helen *(Lab)*
Jones, Jon Owen *(Lab/Co-op)*
Keeble, Sally *(Lab)*
Key, Robert *(Con)*
Khabra, Piara *(Lab)*
Kilfoyle, Peter *(Lab)*
King, Oona *(Lab)*
Kumar, Dr Ashok *(Lab)*
Laing, Eleanor *(Con)*
Lammy, David *(Lab)*
Laws, David *(Lib Dem)*
Letwin, Oliver *(Con)*
Levitt, Tom *(Lab)*
Lewis, Ivan *(Lab)*
Lilley, Peter *(Con)*
Linton, Martin *(Lab)*
Lucas, Ian *(Lab)*
Lyons, John *(Lab)*
McFall, John *(Lab/Co-op)*
McLoughlin, Patrick *(Con)*
McNulty, Tony *(Lab)*
Mactaggart, Fiona *(Lab)*
McWilliam, John *(Lab)*
Mallaber, Judy *(Lab)*
Marsden, Gordon *(Lab)*

Marsden, Paul *(Lib Dem)*
Marshall, James *(Lab)*
May, Theresa *(Con)*
Miliband, David *(Lab)*
Morley, Elliot *(Lab)*
Morris, Estelle *(Lab)*
Moss, Malcolm *(Con)*
Murphy, Paul *(Lab)*
Naysmith, Dr Doug
    (Lab/Co-op)
O'Brien, Stephen *(Con)*
O'Hara, Edward *(Lab)*
O'Neill, Martin *(Lab)*
Öpik, Lembit *(Lib Dem)*
Organ, Diana *(Lab)*
Osborne, George *(Con)*
Perham, Linda *(Lab)*
Pickthall, Colin *(Lab)*
Plaskitt, James *(Lab)*
Pope, Greg *(Lab)*
Prentice, Bridget *(Lab)*
Price, Adam *(Plaid Cymru)*
Primarolo, Dawn *(Lab)*
Pugh, John *(Lib Dem)*
Purchase, Ken *(Lab/Co-op)*
Purnell, James *(Lab)*
Rammell, Bill *(Lab)*
Reed, Andy *(Lab/Co-op)*
Robertson, Laurence *(Con)*
Ross, Ernie *(Lab)*
Ruane, Chris *(Lab)*
Ruffley, David *(Con)*
Russell, Christine *(Lab)*
Sawford, Phil *(Lab)*
Sheerman, Barry *(Lab/Co-op)*
Shephard, Gillian *(Con)*
Simmonds, Mark *(Con)*
Simpson, Keith *(Con)*
Singh, Marsha *(Lab)*
Smith, Andrew *(Lab)*
Smith, Jacqui *(Lab)*
Smyth, Rev Martin *(UUP)*
Spink, Bob *(Con)*
Steinberg, Gerry *(Lab)*
Stevenson, George *(Lab)*
Stewart, Ian *(Lab)*
Stoate, Dr Howard *(Lab)*
Straw, Jack *(Lab)*
Taylor, Ann *(Lab)*
Taylor, Dari *(Lab)*
Tipping, Paddy *(Lab)*
Touhig, Don *(Lab/Co-op)*
Trend, Hon Michael *(Con)*
Turner, Andrew *(Con)*
Turner, Dennis *(Lab/Co-op)*
Twigg, Derek *(Lab)*

Twigg, Stephen *(Lab)*
Vaz, Keith *(Lab)*
Ward, Claire *(Lab)*
Watkinson, Angela *(Con)*
Watts, David *(Lab)*
Weir, Mike *(SNP)*
Whitehead, Dr Alan *(Lab)*
Wicks, Malcolm *(Lab)*
Willetts, David *(Con)*
Williams, Roger *(Lib Dem)*
Woodward, Shaun *(Lab)*
Wray, James *(Lab)*
Wright, Dr Tony Wayland
    (Lab)

Education (Special Needs)
Browning, Angela *(Con)*
Loughton, Tim *(Con)*
Williams, Betty *(Lab)*

Elderly
Doughty, Sue *(Lib Dem)*
Hayes, John *(Con)*
Hughes, Kevin *(Lab)*
Mackinlay, Andrew *(Lab)*
Martin, Michael *(Speaker)*
Pugh, John *(Lib Dem)*
Reid, Alan *(Lib Dem)*
Shipley, Debra *(Lab)*
Spink, Bob *(Con)*
Vis, Rudi *(Lab)*

Elections and Campaigning
Hayes, John *(Con)*

Electoral Reform
Bayley, Hugh *(Lab)*
Burden, Richard *(Lab)*
Cormack, Sir Patrick *(Con)*
Johnson, Alan *(Lab)*
King, Oona *(Lab)*
Mackinlay, Andrew *(Lab)*
Mitchell, Austin *(Lab)*
Rammell, Bill *(Lab)*
Smith, Robert *(Lib Dem)*
Twigg, Stephen *(Lab)*

Electoral Registration
Barnes, Harry *(Lab)*

Electronics Industry
Spellar, John *(Lab)*

Emergency Planning
Brake, Tom *(Lib Dem)*
O'Hara, Edward *(Lab)*

Employment
Alexander, Douglas *(Lab)*
Anderson, Janet *(Lab)*
Atkins, Charlotte *(Lab)*
Baldry, Tony *(Con)*
Beggs, Roy *(UUP)*
Benn, Hilary *(Lab)*
Blears, Hazel *(Lab)*
Blizzard, Bob *(Lab)*
Brown, Gordon *(Lab)*
Brown, Russell *(Lab)*
Cairns, David *(Lab)*
Campbell, Gregory Lloyd
  (DUP)
Clapham, Michael *(Lab)*
Clelland, David *(Lab)*
Collins, Tim *(Con)*
Cryer, John *(Lab)*
Davey, Edward *(Lib Dem)*
Dhanda, Parmjit *(Lab)*
Doran, Frank *(Lab)*
Eagle, Maria *(Lab)*
Etherington, Bill *(Lab)*
Farrelly, Paul *(Lab)*
Field, Mark *(Con)*
Flint, Caroline *(Lab)*
Foster, Michael Jabez *(Lab)*
Gillan, Cheryl *(Con)*
Green, Damian *(Con)*
Healey, John *(Lab)*
Henderson, Doug *(Lab)*
Henderson, Ivan *(Lab)*
Hewitt, Patricia *(Lab)*
Hopkins, Kelvin *(Lab)*
Howarth, Alan *(Lab)*
Johnson, Alan *(Lab)*
Johnson, Melanie *(Lab)*
Jones, Kevan *(Lab)*
Kelly, Ruth *(Lab)*
Khabra, Piara *(Lab)*
Kilfoyle, Peter *(Lab)*
King, Oona *(Lab)*
Lamb, Norman *(Lib Dem)*
Letwin, Oliver *(Con)*
Lewis, Terry *(Lab)*
Lyons, John *(Lab)*
Lyons, John *(Lab)*
McCartney, Ian *(Lab)*
Mahon, Alice *(Lab)*
Mallaber, Judy *(Lab)*
Merron, Gillian *(Lab)*
Miliband, David *(Lab)*
Moore, Michael *(Lib Dem)*
Mountford, Kali *(Lab)*
Paice, Jim *(Con)*
Pike, Peter *(Lab)*

Pond, Chris *(Lab)*
Purnell, James *(Lab)*
Reid, Alan *(Lib Dem)*
Ross, Ernie *(Lab)*
Roy, Frank *(Lab)*
Ryan, Joan *(Lab)*
Sarwar, Mohammad *(Lab)*
Sawford, Phil *(Lab)*
Sheridan, Jim *(Lab)*
Smith, Andrew *(Lab)*
Smith, Angela *(Lab/Co-op)*
Spink, Bob *(Con)*
Stewart, Ian *(Lab)*
Sutcliffe, Gerry *(Lab)*
Timms, Stephen *(Lab)*
Touhig, Don *(Lab/Co-op)*
Turner, Dr Des *(Lab)*
Ward, Claire *(Lab)*
Weir, Mike *(SNP)*
Williams, Alan John *(Lab)*
Winterton, Rosie *(Lab)*
Woolas, Philip *(Lab)*
Worthington, Tony *(Lab)*

Employment Law
Tynan, Bill *(Lab)*

EMU
Flight, Howard *(Con)*

Energy
Barrett, John *(Lib Dem)*
Barron, Kevin *(Lab)*
Blizzard, Bob *(Lab)*
Blunt, Crispin *(Con)*
Brown, Russell *(Lab)*
Bruce, Malcolm *(Lib Dem)*
Cable, Dr Vincent *(Lib Dem)*
Carmichael, Alistair *(Lib Dem)*
Clapham, Michael *(Lab)*
Clelland, David *(Lab)*
Cummings, John *(Lab)*
Dobson, Frank *(Lab)*
Doran, Frank *(Lab)*
Duncan, Peter *(Con)*
Efford, Clive *(Lab)*
Fallon, Michael *(Con)*
Foulkes, George *(Lab/Co-op)*
Gilroy, Linda *(Lab/Co-op)*
Hammond, Philip *(Con)*
Heathcoat-Amory, David *(Con)*
Hood, Jimmy *(Lab)*
Howells, Dr Kim *(Lab)*
Illsley, Eric *(Lab)*
Ingram, Adam *(Lab)*
Moss, Malcolm *(Con)*

O'Brien, William *(Lab)*
Pike, Peter *(Lab)*
Salmond, Alex *(SNP)*
Skinner, Dennis *(Lab)*
Spellar, John *(Lab)*
Stevenson, George *(Lab)*
Stunell, Andrew *(Lib Dem)*
Thomas, Gareth Richard
  (Lab/Co-op)
Tipping, Paddy *(Lab)*
Tynan, Bill *(Lab)*
Waterson, Nigel *(Con)*

Engineering
Battle, John *(Lab)*
Cook, Frank *(Lab)*
Olner, Bill *(Lab)*

Enterprise
Campbell, Gregory Lloyd
  (DUP)

Environment
Ainger, Nick *(Lab)*
Ainsworth, Bob *(Lab)*
Ainsworth, Peter *(Con)*
Amess, David *(Con)*
Anderson, Donald *(Lab)*
Armstrong, Hilary *(Lab)*
Atherton, Candy *(Lab)*
Austin, John *(Lab)*
Baker, Norman *(Lib Dem)*
Barker, Gregory *(Con)*
Barnes, Harry *(Lab)*
Barron, Kevin *(Lab)*
Bayley, Hugh *(Lab)*
Benn, Hilary *(Lab)*
Blunt, Crispin *(Con)*
Boateng, Paul *(Lab)*
Brake, Tom *(Lib Dem)*
Burstow, Paul *(Lib Dem)*
Butterfill, John *(Con)*
Cable, Dr Vincent *(Lib Dem)*
Calton, Patsy *(Lib Dem)*
Campbell, Anne *(Lab)*
Caton, Martin *(Lab)*
Challen, Colin *(Lab)*
Chapman, Sydney *(Con)*
Chaytor, David *(Lab)*
Clark, Helen *(Lab)*
Clark, Paul *(Lab)*
Clarke, Tony *(Lab)*
Clelland, David *(Lab)*
Clifton-Brown, Geoffrey *(Con)*
Coaker, Vernon *(Lab)*
Cook, Robin *(Lab)*

Corbyn, Jeremy *(Lab)*
Cummings, John *(Lab)*
Cunningham, Dr Jack *(Lab)*
Davey, Edward *(Lib Dem)*
Davies, Geraint *(Lab)*
Djanogly, Jonathan *(Con)*
Doughty, Sue *(Lib Dem)*
Dowd, Jim *(Lab)*
Drew, David *(Lab/Co-op)*
Duncan Smith, Iain *(Con)*
Efford, Clive *(Lab)*
Ennis, Jeffrey *(Lab)*
Francois, Mark *(Con)*
George, Andrew *(Lib Dem)*
Gibson, Dr Ian *(Lab)*
Gray, James *(Con)*
Grieve, Dominic *(Con)*
Griffiths, Jane *(Lab)*
Gummer, John *(Con)*
Hawkins, Nick *(Con)*
Heald, Oliver *(Con)*
Heath, David *(Lib Dem)*
Hill, Keith *(Lab)*
Hood, Jimmy *(Lab)*
Horam, John *(Con)*
Howarth, George *(Lab)*
Howells, Dr Kim *(Lab)*
Hughes, Simon *(Lib Dem)*
Hunter, Andrew *(Ind)*
Jackson, Glenda *(Lab)*
Jackson, Helen *(Lab)*
Jones, Jon Owen *(Lab/Co-op)*
Kidney, David *(Lab)*
Ladyman, Dr Stephen *(Lab)*
Lamb, Norman *(Lib Dem)*
Lawrence, Jackie *(Lab)*
Lazarowicz, Mark *(Lab/Co-op)*
Leslie, Christopher *(Lab)*
Lord, Michael *(Con)*
Lucas, Ian *(Lab)*
McDonnell, John *(Lab)*
Mackay, Andrew *(Con)*
Mackinlay, Andrew *(Lab)*
Marris, Rob *(Lab)*
Marsden, Paul *(Lib Dem)*
Marshall-Andrews, Bob *(Lab)*
Meale, Alan *(Lab)*
Perham, Linda *(Lab)*
Pickthall, Colin *(Lab)*
Pike, Peter *(Lab)*
Prosser, Gwyn *(Lab)*
Randall, John *(Con)*
Raynsford, Nick *(Lab)*
Reid, Alan *(Lib Dem)*
Robathan, Andrew *(Con)*
Roche, Barbara *(Lab)*

Roe, Marion *(Con)*
Ruane, Chris *(Lab)*
Ruddock, Joan *(Lab)*
Russell, Bob *(Lib Dem)*
Russell, Christine *(Lab)*
Salter, Martin *(Lab)*
Simpson, Alan *(Lab)*
Skinner, Dennis *(Lab)*
Smith, Chris *(Lab)*
Soley, Clive *(Lab)*
Spelman, Caroline *(Con)*
Stinchcombe, Paul *(Lab)*
Stoate, Dr Howard *(Lab)*
Taylor, David *(Lab/Co-op)*
Taylor, Mark John *(Con)*
Taylor, Sir Teddy *(Con)*
Thomas, Gareth Richard
  (Lab/Co-op)
Tipping, Paddy *(Lab)*
Todd, Mark *(Lab)*
Tonge, Dr Jenny *(Lib Dem)*
Tredinnick, David *(Con)*
Truswell, Paul *(Lab)*
Walley, Joan *(Lab)*
White, Brian *(Lab)*
Whitehead, Dr Alan *(Lab)*
Wiggin, Bill *(Con)*
Wood, Mike *(Lab)*
Woodward, Shaun *(Lab)*
Wright, Dr Tony Wayland
  (Lab)

Environment and Housing
Lepper, David *(Lab/Co-op)*
Loughton, Tim *(Con)*

Environment and Transport
Bradshaw, Ben *(Lab)*
Starkey, Dr Phyllis *(Lab)*

Environmental Health
Williams, Betty *(Lab)*

**Environmental Pollution and
  Social and Community
  Work**
Steen, Anthony *(Con)*

Environmental Taxation
Loughton, Tim *(Con)*

Equal Opportunities
Austin, John *(Lab)*
Baird, Vera *(Lab)*
Cohen, Harry *(Lab)*
Cooper, Yvette *(Lab)*

Corston, Jean *(Lab)*
Etherington, Bill *(Lab)*
Heal, Sylvia *(Lab)*
Heppell, John *(Lab)*
King, Oona *(Lab)*
Mallaber, Judy *(Lab)*
Martin, Michael *(The Speaker)*
Morgan, Julie *(Lab)*
Primarolo, Dawn *(Lab)*
Tynan, Bill *(Lab)*

Euro
Redwood, John *(Con)*

Euro (Against)
Davidson, Ian *(Lab/Co-op)*

European Affairs
Baron, John *(Con)*
Bryant, Chris *(Lab)*
Cameron, David *(Con)*
David, Wayne *(Lab)*
Davidson, Ian *(Lab/Co-op)*
Dhanda, Parmjit *(Lab)*
Dodds, Nigel *(DUP)*
Evans, Nigel *(Con)*
Ewing, Annabelle *(SNP)*
Farrelly, Paul *(Lab)*
Flook, Adrian *(Con)*
Francis, Hywel *(Lab)*
Gummer, John *(Con)*
Hancock, Mike *(Lib Dem)*
Hendrick, Mark *(Lab/Co-op)*
Hermon, Sylvia *(UUP)*
Kelly, Ruth *(Lab)*
King, Oona *(Lab)*
Lewis, Dr Julian *(Con)*
Lucas, Ian *(Lab)*
Mole, Chris *(Lab)*
Munn, Meg *(Lab/Co-op)*
Quin, Joyce *(Lab)*
Rammell, Bill *(Lab)*
Redwood, John *(Con)*
Robertson, Angus *(SNP)*
Robertson, Laurence *(Con)*
Rosindell, Andrew *(Con)*
Simon, Siôn *(Lab)*
Watkinson, Angela *(Con)*
Weir, Mike *(SNP)*
Woodward, Shaun *(Lab)*

European Union
Baldry, Tony *(Con)*
Barnes, Harry *(Lab)*
Bell, Stuart *(Lab)*
Bercow, John *(Con)*

Boswell, Timothy *(Con)*
Cable, Dr Vincent *(Lib Dem)*
Caborn, Richard *(Lab)*
Cash, William *(Con)*
Caton, Martin *(Lab)*
Collins, Tim *(Con)*
Connarty, Michael *(Lab)*
Cran, James *(Con)*
Cryer, John *(Lab)*
Cunningham, Jim *(Lab)*
Forth, Eric *(Con)*
Gapes, Mike *(Lab/Co-op)*
Godsiff, Roger *(Lab)*
Grieve, Dominic *(Con)*
Griffiths, Win *(Lab)*
Grogan, John *(Lab)*
Hammond, Philip *(Con)*
Harvey, Nick *(Lib Dem)*
Haselhurst, Sir Alan *(Con)*
Heathcoat-Amory, David *(Con)*
Hill, Keith *(Lab)*
Hood, Jimmy *(Lab)*
Hoon, Geoff *(Lab)*
Hume, John *(SDLP)*
Irranca-Davies, Huw *(Lab)*
Jackson, Robert *(Con)*
Jenkin, Bernard *(Con)*
Kennedy, Charles *(Lib Dem)*
Khabra, Piara *(Lab)*
Kirkbride, Julie *(Con)*
Lait, Jacqui *(Con)*
Lilley, Peter *(Con)*
Luke, Iain *(Lab)*
McGuire, Anne *(Lab)*
MacShane, Dr Denis *(Lab)*
Malins, Humfrey *(Con)*
Mitchell, Austin *(Lab)*
O'Hara, Edward *(Lab)*
Plaskitt, James *(Lab)*
Singh, Marsha *(Lab)*
Straw, Jack *(Lab)*
Stuart, Gisela *(Lab)*
Taylor, Ian *(Con)*
Taylor, Mark John *(Con)*
Taylor, Sir Teddy *(Con)*
Tyrie, Andrew *(Con)*
Vis, Rudi *(Lab)*
White, Brian *(Lab)*
Wilkinson, John *(Con)*

Expatriate Workers
Cook, Frank *(Lab)*

Fair Trade
Gilroy, Linda *(Lab/Co-op)*
Palmer, Dr Nick *(Lab)*

Families
Brazier, Julian *(Con)*
Doran, Frank *(Lab)*
Hewitt, Patricia *(Lab)*
Hughes, Beverley *(Lab)*
Kelly, Ruth *(Lab)*
Knight, Jim *(Lab)*
Leigh, Edward *(Con)*
Selous, Andrew *(Con)*
Streeter, Gary *(Con)*
Watkinson, Angela *(Con)*

Family Friendly
Employment
Flint, Caroline *(Lab)*

Farming
Flight, Howard *(Con)*
Liddell-Grainger, Ian *(Con)*
Reid, Alan *(Lib Dem)*
Simpson, Keith *(Con)*

Field Sports
Swire, Hugo *(Con)*

Film Industry
Clarke, Tom *(Lab)*
Follett, Barbara *(Lab)*
Lansley, Andrew *(Con)*

Finance
Boswell, Timothy *(Con)*
Caplin, Ivor *(Lab)*
Davies, Quentin *(Con)*
Duncan Smith, Iain *(Con)*
Foster, Derek *(Lab)*
Hawkins, Nick *(Con)*
Lazarowicz, Mark
  (Lab/Co-op)
Loughton, Tim *(Con)*
McIsaac, Shona *(Lab)*
Mountford, Kali *(Lab)*
Sheerman, Barry *(Lab/Co-op)*
Trickett, Jon *(Lab)*
Viggers, Peter *(Con)*
Vis, Rudi *(Lab)*
Woodward, Shaun *(Lab)*

Financial Services
Cousins, Jim *(Lab)*
Hawkins, Nick *(Con)*
Keeble, Sally *(Lab)*
Moss, Malcolm *(Con)*

Fire
Fitzpatrick, Jim *(Lab)*

Fire Service
Ennis, Jeffrey *(Lab)*
McCartney, Ian *(Lab)*

Fishing Industry
Carmichael, Alistair
  (Lib Dem)
George, Andrew *(Lib Dem)*
Mitchell, Austin *(Lab)*
Reid, Alan *(Lib Dem)*
Salmond, Alex *(SNP)*
Steen, Anthony *(Con)*
Strang, Gavin *(Lab)*
Winterton, Ann *(Con)*

Fluoridation (Against)
Etherington, Bill *(Lab)*

Food Safety
Simpson, Alan *(Lab)*

Footwear
Anderson, Janet *(Lab)*

Forced Marriages
Cryer, Ann *(Lab)*

Foreign Affairs
Anderson, Donald *(Lab)*
Arbuthnot, James *(Con)*
Atkinson, David *(Con)*
Austin, John *(Lab)*
Beard, Nigel *(Lab)*
Blunt, Crispin *(Con)*
Bradshaw, Ben *(Lab)*
Brazier, Julian *(Con)*
Burt, Alistair *(Con)*
Butterfill, John *(Con)*
Cable, Dr Vincent *(Lib Dem)*
Campbell, Menzies *(Lib Dem)*
Casale, Roger *(Lab)*
Chapman, Ben *(Lab)*
Chidgey, David *(Lib Dem)*
Clarke, Tom *(Lab)*
Clifton-Brown, Geoffrey *(Con)*
Coaker, Vernon *(Lab)*
Conway, Derek *(Con)*
Cunningham, Dr Jack *(Lab)*
Curry, David *(Con)*
Davies, Denzil *(Lab)*
Dorrell, Stephen *(Con)*
Fabricant, Michael *(Con)*
Foulkes, George *(Lab/Co-op)*
Fox, Dr Liam *(Con)*
Galloway, George *(Lab)*
Gardiner, Barry *(Lab)*

Garnier, Edward *(Con)*
Gerrard, Neil *(Lab)*
Godsiff, Roger *(Lab)*
Green, Damian *(Con)*
Grieve, Dominic *(Con)*
Hanson, David *(Lab)*
Harris, Tom *(Lab)*
Hendrick, Mark *(Lab/Co-op)*
Hoey, Kate *(Lab)*
Howard, Michael *(Con)*
Howells, Dr Kim *(Lab)*
Jackson, Robert *(Con)*
Jenkin, Bernard *(Con)*
Joyce, Eric *(Lab)*
Keen, Alan *(Lab/Co-op)*
Keetch, Paul *(Lib Dem)*
Kennedy, Jane *(Lab)*
Key, Robert *(Con)*
Kilfoyle, Peter *(Lab)*
Knight, Jim *(Lab)*
Leigh, Edward *(Con)*
Lewis, Dr Julian *(Con)*
Loughton, Tim *(Con)*
Mackay, Andrew *(Con)*
Maples, John *(Con)*
Marshall, David *(Lab)*
Murphy, Paul *(Lab)*
O'Brien, Stephen *(Con)*
Osborne, George *(Con)*
Paisley, Rev Ian *(DUP)*
Paterson, Owen *(Con)*
Pickthall, Colin *(Lab)*
Pope, Greg *(Lab)*
Purchase, Ken *(Lab/Co-op)*
Randall, John *(Con)*
Reid, Dr John *(Lab)*
Robertson, Angus *(SNP)*
Robertson, Hugh *(Con)*
Rosindell, Andrew *(Con)*
Ruddock, Joan *(Lab)*
Savidge, Malcolm *(Lab)*
Sheridan, Jim *(Lab)*
Simmonds, Mark *(Con)*
Simpson, Keith *(Con)*
Smith, Chris *(Lab)*
Smyth, Rev Martin *(UUP)*
Soames, Nicholas *(Con)*
Soley, Clive *(Lab)*
Squire, Rachel *(Lab)*
Starkey, Dr Phyllis *(Lab)*
Swire, Hugo *(Con)*
Tapsell, Sir Peter *(Con)*
Tredinnick, David *(Con)*
Trend, Hon Michael *(Con)*
Twigg, Stephen *(Lab)*
Waterson, Nigel *(Con)*

Wilshire, David *(Con)*
Winterton, Sir Nicholas *(Con)*
Wray, James *(Lab)*
Wyatt, Derek *(Lab)*

Forestry
Heathcoat-Amory, David *(Con)*
Lord, Michael *(Con)*
Quinn, Lawrie *(Lab)*

Freedom of Information
Fisher, Mark *(Lab)*
Kirkwood, Sir Archy
  (Lib Dem)
Norris, Dan *(Lab)*

Fruit Farming
Robertson, Hugh *(Con)*

Fuel Poverty
Simpson, Alan *(Lab)*
Turner, Dr Des *(Lab)*

Fuel Tax
Reid, Alan *(Lib Dem)*

**Further and Higher
  Education**
Cryer, John *(Lab)*
Organ, Diana *(Lab)*
Pearson, Ian *(Lab)*
Sheerman, Barry *(Lab/Co-op)*
Whitehead, Dr Alan *(Lab)*

Gas Industry
Bruce, Malcolm *(Lib Dem)*
Stewart, David *(Lab)*

Gender
Follett, Barbara *(Lab)*

Genetics
Begg, Anne *(Lab)*

Gibraltar
Rosindell, Andrew *(Con)*
Willis, Phil *(Lib Dem)*

Glass Industry
Illsley, Eric *(Lab)*

Global Poverty
Goggins, Paul *(Lab)*

Global Warming
Colman, Tony *(Lab)*

GM Issues
Joyce, Eric *(Lab)*
Simpson, Alan *(Lab)*

Government Reform
Dobson, Frank *(Lab)*

Greece
Dismore, Andrew *(Lab)*

Green Issues
Griffiths, Win *(Lab)*
McWalter, Tony *(Lab/Co-op)*
Morley, Elliot *(Lab)*

Health
Ainger, Nick *(Lab)*
Amess, David *(Con)*
Anderson, Janet *(Lab)*
Atherton, Candy *(Lab)*
Atkins, Charlotte *(Lab)*
Austin, John *(Lab)*
Bacon, Richard *(Con)*
Baron, John *(Con)*
Barron, Kevin *(Lab)*
Bayley, Hugh *(Lab)*
Benton, Joe *(Lab)*
Blackman, Liz *(Lab)*
Blears, Hazel *(Lab)*
Blizzard, Bob *(Lab)*
Bottomley, Virginia *(Con)*
Bradley, Keith *(Lab)*
Bradley, Peter *(Lab)*
Brady, Graham *(Con)*
Brown, Gordon *(Lab)*
Buck, Karen *(Lab)*
Burden, Richard *(Lab)*
Burnham, Andy *(Lab)*
Burns, Simon *(Con)*
Butterfill, John *(Con)*
Clapham, Michael *(Lab)*
Clappison, James *(Con)*
Clark, Helen *(Lab)*
Clark, Dr Lynda *(Lab)*
Coffey, Ann *(Lab)*
Cohen, Harry *(Lab)*
Cryer, Ann *(Lab)*
Cryer, John *(Lab)*
Darling, Alistair *(Lab)*
Davey, Valerie *(Lab)*
Davies, Quentin *(Con)*
Davis, David *(Con)*
Dean, Janet *(Lab)*
Dismore, Andrew *(Lab)*
Dobbin, Jim *(Lab/Co-op)*
Donohoe, Brian *(Lab)*

Edwards, Huw *(Lab)*
Efford, Clive *(Lab)*
Farrelly, Paul *(Lab)*
Fitzsimons, Lorna *(Lab)*
Flynn, Paul *(Lab)*
Fox, Dr Liam *(Con)*
George, Bruce *(Lab)*
Gibson, Dr Ian *(Lab)*
Gidley, Sandra *(Lib Dem)*
Grayling, Christopher *(Con)*
Griffiths, Nigel *(Lab)*
Griffiths, Win *(Lab)*
Hall, Mike *(Lab)*
Hammond, Philip *(Con)*
Hanson, David *(Lab)*
Harris, Dr Evan *(Lib Dem)*
Havard, Dai *(Lab)*
Henderson, Ivan *(Lab)*
Hermon, Sylvia *(UUP)*
Hesford, Stephen *(Lab)*
Heyes, David *(Lab)*
Hoban, Mark *(Con)*
Holmes, Paul *(Lib Dem)*
Horam, John *(Con)*
Iddon, Dr Brian *(Lab)*
Jack, Michael *(Con)*
Johnson, Melanie *(Lab)*
Jones, Helen *(Lab)*
Keen, Ann *(Lab)*
King, Andy *(Lab)*
King, Oona *(Lab)*
Kirkbride, Julie *(Con)*
Kirkwood, Sir Archy *(Lib Dem)*
Lait, Jacqui *(Con)*
Lammy, David *(Lab)*
Lansley, Andrew *(Con)*
Lewis, Ivan *(Lab)*
Loughton, Tim *(Con)*
Love, Andrew *(Lab/Co-op)*
Lucas, Ian *(Lab)*
McCafferty, Chris *(Lab)*
McDonagh, Siobhain *(Lab)*
McNulty, Tony *(Lab)*
Mahon, Alice *(Lab)*
Maples, John *(Con)*
Marsden, Paul *(Lib Dem)*
Martlew, Eric *(Lab)*
Mawhinney, Sir Brian *(Con)*
Meale, Alan *(Lab)*
Milburn, Alan *(Lab)*
Mitchell, Andrew *(Con)*
Moffatt, Laura *(Lab)*
Murrison, Andrew *(Con)*
Naysmith, Dr Doug
  (Lab/Co-op)
Picking, Anne *(Lab)*

Pickles, Eric *(Con)*
Primarolo, Dawn *(Lab)*
Purchase, Ken *(Lab/Co-op)*
Rammell, Bill *(Lab)*
Reid, Alan *(Lib Dem)*
Robinson, Iris *(DUP)*
Roe, Marion *(Con)*
Ryan, Joan *(Lab)*
Singh, Marsha *(Lab)*
Smith, Chris *(Lab)*
Smyth, Rev Martin *(UUP)*
Southworth, Helen *(Lab)*
Starkey, Dr Phyllis *(Lab)*
Stewart, David *(Lab)*
Stoate, Dr Howard *(Lab)*
Thomas, Gareth Richard
  (Lab/Co-op)
Tonge, Dr Jenny *(Lib Dem)*
Touhig, Don *(Lab/Co-op)*
Tredinnick, David *(Con)*
Trend, Hon Michael *(Con)*
Truswell, Paul *(Lab)*
Turner, Dr Des *(Lab)*
Walley, Joan *(Lab)*
Walter, Robert *(Con)*
Waterson, Nigel *(Con)*
Weir, Mike *(SNP)*
Widdecombe, Ann *(Con)*
Willetts, David *(Con)*
Williams, Betty *(Lab)*
Willis, Phil *(Lib Dem)*
Wright, Dr Tony Wayland
  (Lab)
Yeo, Tim *(Con)*

Health and Community Care
Hughes, Beverley *(Lab)*

Health and Poverty
Foster, Michael Jabez *(Lab)*
Twigg, Derek *(Lab)*

Health and Safety Issues
Brown, Russell *(Lab)*
McCartney, Ian *(Lab)*

Health Education
Heal, Sylvia *(Lab)*
Williams, Betty *(Lab)*
Young, Sir George *(Con)*

Heritage
Allan, Richard *(Lib Dem)*
Beggs, Roy *(UUP)*
Bottomley, Virginia *(Con)*
Caplin, Ivor *(Lab)*

Cash, William *(Con)*
Cormack, Sir Patrick *(Con)*
Hanson, David *(Lab)*
Keetch, Paul *(Lib Dem)*
Marsden, Gordon *(Lab)*
Steen, Anthony *(Con)*

Higher Education
Gibson, Dr Ian *(Lab)*
Iddon, Dr Brian *(Lab)*
Joyce, Eric *(Lab)*

HIV/AIDS
Gerrard, Neil *(Lab)*

Home Affairs
Allan, Richard *(Lib Dem)*
Anderson, Janet *(Lab)*
Barron, Kevin *(Lab)*
Benn, Hilary *(Lab)*
Boateng, Paul *(Lab)*
Bottomley, Virginia *(Con)*
Brooke, Annette *(Lib Dem)*
Cameron, David *(Con)*
Clappison, James *(Con)*
Clark, Helen *(Lab)*
Clelland, David *(Lab)*
Cranston, Ross *(Lab)*
Dean, Janet *(Lab)*
Hall, Mike *(Lab)*
Hawkins, Nick *(Con)*
Heath, David *(Lib Dem)*
Hood, Jimmy *(Lab)*
Howard, Michael *(Con)*
Hutton, John *(Lab)*
Keeble, Sally *(Lab)*
King, Andy *(Lab)*
Knight, Greg *(Con)*
Llwyd, Elfyn *(Plaid Cymru)*
Loughton, Tim *(Con)*
Mactaggart, Fiona *(Lab)*
Mates, Michael *(Con)*
Meale, Alan *(Lab)*
Pickthall, Colin *(Lab)*
Prentice, Bridget *(Lab)*
Roche, Barbara *(Lab)*
Ruffley, David *(Con)*
Short, Clare *(Lab)*
Smith, Angela *(Lab/Co-op)*
Stinchcombe, Paul *(Lab)*
Stoate, Dr Howard *(Lab)*
Taylor, Ann *(Lab)*
Taylor, Sir Teddy *(Con)*
Tredinnick, David *(Con)*
Ward, Claire *(Lab)*
Winterton, Rosie *(Lab)*

Homelessness
Etherington, Bill *(Lab)*
Hendry, Charles *(Con)*
Selous, Andrew *(Con)*

Horses
Page, Richard *(Con)*

Horticulture
Jack, Michael *(Con)*
Roe, Marion *(Con)*

**House of Commons
   Modernisation**
Flint, Caroline *(Lab)*

House of Lords Reform
Clelland, David *(Lab)*
Stringer, Graham *(Lab)*
Thurso, Viscount *(Lib Dem)*

Housing
Ancram, Michael *(Con)*
Battle, John *(Lab)*
Benton, Joe *(Lab)*
Beresford, Sir Paul *(Con)*
Betts, Clive *(Lab)*
Boateng, Paul *(Lab)*
Bradley, Keith *(Lab)*
Bradley, Peter *(Lab)*
Buck, Karen *(Lab)*
Butterfill, John *(Con)*
Coleman, Iain *(Lab)*
Crausby, David *(Lab)*
Davies, Geraint *(Lab)*
Dean, Janet *(Lab)*
Dobbin, Jim *(Lab/Co-op)*
Dowd, Jim *(Lab)*
Drew, David *(Lab/Co-op)*
Eagle, Maria *(Lab)*
Edwards, Huw *(Lab)*
Follett, Barbara *(Lab)*
Francois, Mark *(Con)*
George, Andrew *(Lib Dem)*
George, Bruce *(Lab)*
Gerrard, Neil *(Lab)*
Gildernew, Michelle
   (Sinn Fein)
Goggins, Paul *(Lab)*
Gray, James *(Con)*
Griffiths, Nigel *(Lab)*
Hammond, Philip *(Con)*
Hendry, Charles *(Con)*
Hodge, Margaret *(Lab)*
Hoey, Kate *(Lab)*
Hood, Jimmy *(Lab)*

Howarth, George *(Lab)*
Hughes, Simon *(Lib Dem)*
Iddon, Dr Brian *(Lab)*
Jackson, Glenda *(Lab)*
Jenkins, Brian *(Lab)*
Jones, Dr Lynne *(Lab)*
Kidney, David *(Lab)*
King, Oona *(Lab)*
Lamb, Norman *(Lib Dem)*
Linton, Martin *(Lab)*
Love, Andrew
   (Lab/Co-op)
Luke, Iain *(Lab)*
McDonagh, Siobhain *(Lab)*
Marshall, James *(Lab)*
Meacher, Michael *(Lab)*
Michael, Alun *(Lab/Co-op)*
Moffatt, Laura *(Lab)*
Moore, Michael *(Lib Dem)*
Moran, Margaret *Lab)*
Morris, Estelle *(Lab)*
Moss, Malcolm *(Con)*
Murphy, Paul *(Lab)*
O'Brien, Stephen *(Con)*
O'Hara, Edward *(Lab)*
Osborne, Sandra *(Lab)*
Pickles, Eric *(Con)*
Pollard, Kerry *(Lab)*
Pope, Greg *(Lab)*
Pound, Stephen *(Lab)*
Primarolo, Dawn *(Lab)*
Purnell, James *(Lab)*
Rammell, Bill *(Lab)*
Raynsford, Nick *(Lab)*
Robinson, Peter *(DUP)*
Salter, Martin *(Lab)*
Sarwar, Mohammad *(Lab)*
Shaw, Jonathan *(Lab)*
Smith, Chris *(Lab)*
Soley, Clive *(Lab)*
Southworth, Helen *(Lab)*
Swire, Hugo *(Con)*
Taylor, Dari *(Lab)*
Taylor, David *(Lab/Co-op)*
Turner, Dennis
   (Lab/Co-op)
Turner, Dr Des *(Lab)*
Turner, Neil *(Lab)*
Twigg, Derek *(Lab)*
Winterton, Rosie *(Lab)*
Wood, Mike *(Lab)*
Wright, David *(Lab)*
Young, Sir George *(Con)*

Housing Law
Anderson, Donald *(Lab)*

Human Rights
Atkinson, David *(Con)*
Baird, Vera *(Lab)*
Browne, Des *(Lab)*
Cormack, Sir Patrick *(Con)*
Corston, Jean *(Lab)*
Dowd, Jim *(Lab)*
Etherington, Bill *(Lab)*
Fisher, Mark *(Lab)*
Foulkes, George *(Lab/Co-op)*
Griffiths, Win *(Lab)*
Hermon, Sylvia *(UUP)*
Holmes, Paul *(Lib Dem)*
Hughes, Simon *(Lib Dem)*
Kirkwood, Sir Archy
   (Lib Dem)
Lloyd, Tony *(Lab)*
McNamara, Kevin *(Lab)*
Mactaggart, Fiona *(Lab)*
Marsden, Gordon *(Lab)*
Martin, Michael *(The Speaker)*
Meale, Alan *(Lab)*
Prentice, Bridget *(Lab)*
Ruane, Chris *(Lab)*
Salter, Martin *(Lab)*
Smyth, Rev Martin *(UUP)*
Stevenson, George *(Lab)*
Thomas, Gareth *(Lab)*

Hunting with Dogs (Against)
Dean, Janet *(Lab)*
Etherington, Bill *(Lab)*
Foster, Michael John *(Lab)*
Wright, David *(Lab)*

Immigration
Coleman, Iain *(Lab)*
Cryer, Ann *(Lab)*
George, Andrew *(Lib Dem)*
Godsiff, Roger *(Lab)*
Lloyd, Tony *(Lab)*
Prosser, Gwyn *(Lab)*
Short, Clare *(Lab)*
Wilkinson, John *(Con)*

Inclusive Education
Willis, Phil *(Lib Dem)*

Industrial Relations
Cormack, Sir Patrick *(Con)*
Crausby, David *(Lab)*
Cunningham, Jim *(Lab)*
Havard, Dai *(Lab)*
Heald, Oliver *(Con)*
Healey, John *(Lab)*
Martin, Michael *(The Speaker)*

Meacher, Michael *(Lab)*
Rooney, Terry *(Lab)*
Smith, John *(Lab)*

Industry
Ainsworth, Bob *(Lab)*
Atkinson, Peter *(Con)*
Beckett, Margaret *(Lab)*
Bruce, Malcolm *(Lib Dem)*
Burden, Richard *(Lab)*
Connarty, Michael *(Lab)*
Cruddas, Jon *(Lab)*
Cryer, John *(Lab)*
Cunningham, Dr Jack *(Lab)*
Davis, David *(Con)*
Dowd, Jim *(Lab)*
Gillan, Cheryl *(Con)*
Heathcoat-Amory, David
    (Con)
Henderson, Doug *(Lab)*
Keen, Alan *(Lab/Co-op)*
Ladyman, Dr Stephen *(Lab)*
Leslie, Christopher *(Lab)*
Lloyd, Tony *(Lab)*
Mackay, Andrew *(Con)*
Marris, Rob *(Lab)*
Milburn, Alan *(Lab)*
Miller, Andrew *(Lab)*
Moonie, Lewis *(Lab/Co-op)*
Ottaway, Richard *(Con)*
Paterson, Owen *(Con)*
Quin, Joyce *(Lab)*
Robinson, Geoffrey *(Lab)*
Ross, Ernie *(Lab)*
Sheerman, Barry
    (Lab/Co-op)
Smith, Jacqui *(Lab)*
Taylor, Dari *(Lab)*
Trickett, Jon *(Lab)*
Watson, Tom *(Lab)*
Wilkinson, John *(Con)*
Williams, Alan John *(Lab)*

Information Economy
Bryant, Chris *(Lab)*

Information Technology
Allan, Richard *(Lib Dem)*
Hewitt, Patricia *(Lab)*
Jones, Nigel *(Lib Dem)*
Knight, Greg *(Con)*
Stewart, Ian *(Lab)*
White, Brian *(Lab)*

Infrastructure
O'Brien, Stephen *(Con)*

Inland Waterways
Atherton, Candy *(Lab)*
Skinner, Dennis *(Lab)*

Inner Cities
Beard, Nigel *(Lab)*
Beresford, Sir Paul *(Con)*
Boateng, Paul *(Lab)*
Chapman, Sydney *(Con)*
Hodge, Margaret *(Lab)*

Insurance
Hawkins, Nick *(Con)*

Intellectural Property
Howells, Dr Kim *(Lab)*

Intelligence and Security
Barron, Kevin *(Lab)*

International Affairs
Browne, Des *(Lab)*
Gapes, Mike *(Lab/Co-op)*
George, Bruce *(Lab)*
Gillan, Cheryl *(Con)*
Holmes, Paul *(Lib Dem)*
Marsden, Gordon *(Lab)*
Marsden, Paul *(Lib Dem)*
Murphy, Jim *(Lab)*
Reid, Alan *(Lib Dem)*
Sarwar, Mohammad *(Lab)*
Savidge, Malcolm *(Lab)*
Stewart, Ian *(Lab)*
Wilkinson, John *(Con)*

International Development
Battle, John *(Lab)*
Bayley, Hugh *(Lab)*
Benn, Hilary *(Lab)*
Chaytor, David *(Lab)*
Chidgey, David *(Lib Dem)*
Davey, Valerie *(Lab)*
Davidson, Ian *(Lab/Co-op)*
Dawson, Hilton *(Lab)*
Doughty, Sue *(Lib Dem)*
Drown, Julia *(Lab)*
Follett, Barbara *(Lab)*
Foulkes, George *(Lab/Co-op)*
Hamilton, Fabian *(Lab)*
Hendrick, Mark *(Lab/Co-op)*
Jones, Nigel *(Lib Dem)*
Joyce, Eric *(Lab)*
Keen, Ann *(Lab)*
Khabra, Piara *(Lab)*
Knight, Jim *(Lab)*
Lammy, David *(Lab)*

Luff, Peter *(Con)*
Lyons, John *(Lab)*
McCafferty, Chris *(Lab)*
McKechin, Ann *(Lab)*
Naysmith, Dr Doug
    (Lab/Co-op)
Price, Adam *(Plaid Cymru)*
Reed, Andy *(Lab/Co-op)*
Robathan, Andrew *(Con)*
Robertson, Angus *(SNP)*
Russell, Christine *(Lab)*
Sarwar, Mohammad *(Lab)*
Savidge, Malcolm *(Lab)*
Smith, Angela *(Lab/Co-op)*
Spelman, Caroline *(Con)*
Stewart, David *(Lab)*
Tonge, Dr Jenny *(Lib Dem)*
Turner, Dennis *(Lab/Co-op)*
Tynan, Bill *(Lab)*
Weir, Mike *(SNP)*
Woodward, Shaun *(Lab)*
Worthington, Tony *(Lab)*

International Economics
Duncan, Alan *(Con)*
MacShane, Dr Denis *(Lab)*

International Politics
Evans, Nigel *(Con)*

International Terrorism
Robinson, Peter *(DUP)*

International Trade
Duncan, Alan *(Con)*
Hammond, Philip *(Con)*
White, Brian *(Lab)*

**International Women's
    Agenda**
Jackson, Helen *(Lab)*

Internet
Davey, Edward *(Lib Dem)*
McKenna, Rosemary *(Lab)*
Steve Webb, Prof *(Lib Dem)*
Wyatt, Derek *(Lab)*

Investment
Farrelly, Paul *(Lab)*
Hughes, Beverley *(Lab)*
Ryan, Joan *(Lab)*
Stewart, Ian *(Lab)*

Irish Affairs
Corbyn, Jeremy *(Lab)*

Cran, James *(Con)*
Doherty, Pat *(Sinn Fein)*
McDonnell, John *(Lab)*
Mackinlay, Andrew *(Lab)*

Islam
Fitzsimons, Lorna *(Lab)*

Isle of Man
Mackinlay, Andrew *(Lab)*

IT Industry
Henderson, Doug *(Lab)*

Justice
Mallon, S,amus *(SDLP)*
Mullin, Chris *(Lab)*

Justice and Equality
Wishart, Peter *(SNP)*

Justice System
Clark, Dr Lynda *(Lab)*

Juvenile Justice
Michael, Alun *(Lab/Co-op)*

Kashmir
Fitzsimons, Lorna *(Lab)*

Kidney Transplantation
Dalyell, Tam *(Lab)*

Kurdish Issues
Williams, Hywel *(Plaid Cymru)*

Labour Law
Cruddas, Jon *(Lab)*

**Landmine Eradication
  Measures**
Cook, Frank *(Lab)*

Landmine Victim Support
Cook, Frank *(Lab)*

Language Issues
Williams, Hywel *(Plaid
  Cymru)*

Law and Order
Baron, John *(Con)*
Brazier, Julian *(Con)*
Davis, David *(Con)*
Greenway, John *(Con)*
Grieve, Dominic *(Con)*

Hawkins, Nick *(Con)*
Heald, Oliver *(Con)*
Holmes, Paul *(Lib Dem)*
King, Andy *(Lab)*
Kirkbride, Julie *(Con)*
Osborne, George *(Con)*
Robertson, Laurence *(Con)*
Rosindell, Andrew *(Con)*
Streeter, Gary *(Con)*
Tredinnick, David *(Con)*
Watkinson, Angela *(Con)*
Watson, Tom *(Lab)*

Learning Disabilities
Browning, Angela *(Con)*

Leasehold Reform
Lepper, David *(Lab/Co-op)*

Legal Affairs
Arbuthnot, James *(Con)*
Baldry, Tony *(Con)*
Browne, Des *(Lab)*
Campbell, Menzies *(Lib Dem)*
Cranston, Ross *(Lab)*
Harman, Harriet *(Lab)*
Hutton, John *(Lab)*
McIntosh, Anne *(Con)*
Mitchell, Austin *(Lab)*
Roche, Barbara *(Lab)*
Taylor, Mark John *(Con)*
Thomas, Gareth *(Lab)*
Vaz, Keith *(Lab)*
Weir, Mike *(SNP)*

Leisure
Clarke, Tony *(Lab)*
Gale, Roger *(Con)*
Perham, Linda *(Lab)*
Rapson, Syd *(Lab)*

**Liberation Islington Local
  Agenda 21**
Corbyn, Jeremy *(Lab)*

Libraries
McKenna, Rosemary *(Lab)*
Organ, Diana *(Lab)*

Licensed Trade
Gale, Roger *(Con)*

Lifelong Learning
Francis, Hywel *(Lab)*
Havard, Dai *(Lab)*
Reed, Andy *(Lab/Co-op)*

Liquor Licensing Reform
Grogan, John *(Lab)*

**Local and Regional
  Government**
Banks, Tony *(Lab)*
Barnes, Harry *(Lab)*
Benton, Joe *(Lab)*
Berry, Dr Roger *(Lab)*
Betts, Clive *(Lab)*
Blunkett, David *(Lab)*
Borrow, David *(Lab)*
Bradley, Keith *(Lab)*
Caplin, Ivor *(Lab)*
Cawsey, Ian *(Lab)*
Clarke, Tom *(Lab)*
Clarke, Tony *(Lab)*
Clelland, David *(Lab)*
Connarty, Michael *(Lab)*
Davey, Valerie *(Lab)*
Davidson, Ian *(Lab/Co-op)*
Davies, Geraint *(Lab)*
Dhanda, Parmjit *(Lab)*
Dobbin, Jim *(Lab/Co-op)*
Donohoe, Brian *(Lab)*
Efford, Clive *(Lab)*
Ellman, Louise *(Lab/Co-op)*
Ennis, Jeffrey *(Lab)*
Evans, Nigel *(Con)*
Foster, Don *(Lib Dem)*
Francois, Mark *(Con)*
Gilroy, Linda *(Lab/Co-op)*
Gray, James *(Con)*
Grogan, John *(Lab)*
Hall, Mike *(Lab)*
Hanson, David *(Lab)*
Hayes, John *(Con)*
Healey, John *(Lab)*
Heath, David *(Lib Dem)*
Heppell, John *(Lab)*
Heyes, David *(Lab)*
Hodge, Margaret *(Lab)*
Hughes, Beverley *(Lab)*
Jones, Kevan *(Lab)*
Keeble, Sally *(Lab)*
Kennedy, Jane *(Lab)*
Kumar, Dr Ashok *(Lab)*
Lansley, Andrew *(Con)*
Laxton, Bob *(Lab)*
Leslie, Christopher *(Lab)*
Levitt, Tom *(Lab)*
Lewis, Terry *(Lab)*
Lyons, John *(Lab)*
McCartney, Ian *(Lab)*
McDonnell, John *(Lab)*
McNulty, Tony *(Lab)*

McWalter, Tony *(Lab/Co-op)*
Mahon, Alice *(Lab)*
Mallaber, Judy *(Lab)*
Marshall, James *(Lab)*
May, Theresa *(Con)*
Michael, Alun *(Lab/Co-op)*
Mole, Chris *(Lab)*
Morley, Elliot *(Lab)*
Morris, Estelle *(Lab)*
Murphy, Paul *(Lab)*
Naysmith, Dr Doug
  (Lab/Co-op)
O'Brien, William *(Lab)*
O'Hara, Edward *(Lab)*
Olner, Bill *(Lab)*
Pickles, Eric *(Con)*
Pike, Peter *(Lab)*
Plaskitt, James *(Lab)*
Pugh, John *(Lib Dem)*
Rapson, Syd *(Lab)*
Rosindell, Andrew *(Con)*
Russell, Bob *(Lib Dem)*
Ryan, Joan *(Lab)*
Salter, Martin *(Lab)*
Sanders, Adrian *(Lib Dem)*
Smith, Chris *(Lab)*
Starkey, Dr Phyllis *(Lab)*
Steinberg, Gerry *(Lab)*
Stewart, David *(Lab)*
Straw, Jack *(Lab)*
Stunell, Andrew *(Lib Dem)*
Sutcliffe, Gerry *(Lab)*
Syms, Robert *(Con)*
Tipping, Paddy *(Lab)*
Todd, Mark *(Lab)*
Touhig, Don *(Lab/Co-op)*
Turner, Neil *(Lab)*
Twigg, Stephen *(Lab)*
Vaz, Keith *(Lab)*
Watkinson, Angela *(Con)*
Whitehead, Dr Alan *(Lab)*
Willis, Phil *(Lib Dem)*
Wilshire, David *(Con)*
Winterton, Sir Nicholas
  (Con)
Wright, David Anthony *(Lab)*

**Local Economic
  Development**
Davidson, Ian *(Lab/Co-op)*

Local Hospitals
Viggers, Peter *(Con)*

Local Issues
Reid, Alan *(Lib Dem)*

Locked Africa Children
Dawson, Hilton *(Lab)*

London
Dobson, Frank *(Lab)*
Hodge, Margaret *(Lab)*
McNulty, Tony *(Lab)*
Wilkinson, John *(Con)*

Low Pay
Edwards, Huw *(Lab)*
Merron, Gillian *(Lab)*
Prentice, Gordon *(Lab)*
Short, Clare *(Lab)*
Taylor, David *(Lab/Co-op)*

Manufacturing
Curtis-Thomas, Claire *(Lab)*
MacShane, Dr Denis *(Lab)*
Marris, Rob *(Lab)*
Prentice, Gordon *(Lab)*
Tami, Mark *(Lab)*
Watson, Tom *(Lab)*

Media
Anderson, Janet *(Lab)*
Banks, Tony *(Lab)*
Bayley, Hugh *(Lab)*
Burnham, Andy *(Lab)*
Cash, William *(Con)*
Collins, Tim *(Con)*
Field, Mark *(Con)*
Gale, Roger *(Con)*
Green, Damian *(Con)*
Howarth, Gerald *(Con)*
Liddell, Helen *(Lab)*
Linton, Martin *(Lab)*
Meale, Alan *(Lab)*
Mitchell, Austin *(Lab)*
Mullin, Chris *(Lab)*
Rammell, Bill *(Lab)*
Smith, Chris *(Lab)*
Ward, Claire *(Lab)*
Winterton, Sir Nicholas
  (Con)
Woolas, Philip *(Lab)*
Wyatt, Derek *(Lab)*

Media Ownership
Mullin, Chris *(Lab)*

Medical Ethics
Harris, Dr Evan *(Lib Dem)*

Medicinal and Illegal Drugs
Flynn, Paul *(Lab)*

Mental Health
Atkinson, David *(Con)*
Austin, John *(Lab)*
Browning, Angela *(Con)*
Doran, Frank *(Lab)*

Micro-Technology
Williams, Alan John *(Lab)*

Middle East
Bell, Stuart *(Lab)*
Breed, Colin *(Lib Dem)*
Burden, Richard *(Lab)*
Clarke, Tony *(Lab)*
Dismore, Andrew *(Lab)*
Duncan, Alan *(Con)*
Ellman, Louise *(Lab/Co-op)*
Starkey, Dr Phyllis *(Lab)*

Minimum Wage
Lyons, John *(Lab)*

Mining
Illsley, Eric *(Lab)*

Minority Groups
George, Andrew *(Lib Dem)*

Modernisation of Parliament
Bradshaw, Ben *(Lab)*
Davey, Edward *(Lib Dem)*
Fitzsimons, Lorna *(Lab)*
Flynn, Paul *(Lab)*
White, Brian *(Lab)*

Money Laundering
Wyatt, Derek *(Lab)*

Motor Industry
Kemp, Fraser *(Lab)*
Spellar, John *(Lab)*
Wareing, Robert *(Lab)*

Music
Knight, Greg *(Con)*
Meale, Alan *(Lab)*

Mutuality
Love, Andrew *(Lab/Co-op)*

Mutuals
Thomas, Gareth Richard
  (Lab/Co-op)

National Health Service
Corbyn, Jeremy *(Lab)*

Cunningham, Jim *(Lab)*
Doughty, Sue *(Lib Dem)*
Dowd, Jim *(Lab)*
Drown, Julia *(Lab)*
Dunwoody, Gwyneth *(Lab)*
Eagle, Angela *(Lab)*
Etherington, Bill *(Lab)*
Hinchliffe, David *(Lab)*
Hood, Jimmy *(Lab)*
Lyons, John *(Lab)*
McCartney, Ian *(Lab)*
Pike, Peter *(Lab)*
Ryan, Joan *(Lab)*
Squire, Rachel *(Lab)*
Taylor, Richard *(Ind KHHC)*
Winterton, Sir Nicholas *(Con)*

NATO
Clapham, Michael *(Lab)*

New Aviation and Airports
Stringer, Graham *(Lab)*

New Technology
Robinson, Geoffrey *(Lab)*

**Non-Proliferation and
    Disarmament**
Savidge, Malcolm *(Lab)*

Northern Ireland
Barnes, Harry *(Lab)*
Bellingham, Henry *(Con)*
Browne, Des *(Lab)*
Collins, Tim *(Con)*
Donaldson, Jeffrey *(UUP)*
Harris, Tom *(Lab)*
Hume, John *(SDLP)*
Hunter, Andrew *(Ind)*
Ingram, Adam *(Lab)*
Jackson, Helen *(Lab)*
McGrady, Eddie *(SDLP)*
McNamara, Kevin *(Lab)*
Mates, Michael *(Con)*
Mawhinney, Sir Brian *(Con)*
Mercer, Patrick *(Con)*
Murphy, Paul *(Lab)*
O'Brien, Stephen *(Con)*
Robathan, Andrew *(Con)*
Salter, Martin *(Lab)*
Savidge, Malcolm *(Lab)*
Short, Clare *(Lab)*
Soley, Clive *(Lab)*
Swire, Hugo *(Con)*
Willis, Phil *(Lib Dem)*
Wilshire, David *(Con)*

Nuclear Industry
Jack, Michael *(Con)*
Ladyman, Dr Stephen *(Lab)*

**Offshore Oil and Gas
    Industry**
Joyce, Eric *(Lab)*
Smith, Robert *(Lib Dem)*

Oil Industry
Bruce, Malcolm *(Lib Dem)*
Stewart, David *(Lab)*

Oppressed Minority Races
Baker, Norman *(Lib Dem)*

**Overseas Aid and
    Development**
Baldry, Tony *(Con)*
Barker, Gregory *(Con)*
Barrett, John *(Lib Dem)*
Boateng, Paul *(Lab)*
Fisher, Mark *(Lab)*
Follett, Barbara *(Lab)*
Griffiths, Win *(Lab)*
Jackson, Glenda *(Lab)*
Lloyd, Tony *(Lab)*
Robertson, Laurence *(Con)*

Paper Industries
Winterton, Sir Nicholas *(Con)*

Park Homes Reform
Dawson, Hilton *(Lab)*

**Parliamentary and
    Constitutional Affairs**
Beith, Alan *(Lib Dem)*

Parliamentary Democracy
Marshall-Andrews, Bob *(Lab)*

Parliamentary History
Cormack, Sir Patrick *(Con)*

Peace and Disarmament
Cook, Frank *(Lab)*

Penal Affairs and Policy
Malins, Humfrey *(Con)*
Soley, Clive *(Lab)*

Pensions
Bradley, Keith *(Lab)*
Butterfill, John *(Con)*
Caplin, Ivor *(Lab)*

Challen, Colin *(Lab)*
Clark, Dr Lynda *(Lab)*
Colman, Tony *(Lab)*
Cook, Frank *(Lab)*
Cran, James *(Con)*
Crausby, David *(Lab)*
Davies, Quentin *(Con)*
Farrelly, Paul *(Lab)*
Flynn, Paul *(Lab)*
Gilroy, Linda *(Lab/Co-op)*
Heald, Oliver *(Con)*
Hesford, Stephen *(Lab)*
Holmes, Paul *(Lib Dem)*
Hurst, Alan *(Lab)*
Laws, David *(Lib Dem)*
Lyons, John *(Lab)*
Miller, Andrew *(Lab)*
Mitchell, Andrew *(Con)*
Pike, Peter *(Lab)*
Purnell, James *(Lab)*
Sarwar, Mohammad *(Lab)*
Stuart, Gisela *(Lab)*

People of Islington
Corbyn, Jeremy *(Lab)*

Performing Arts
Luff, Peter *(Con)*

Personal Finance
Greenway, John *(Con)*

**Pharmaceutical and
    Chemical Industries**
Winterton, Ann *(Con)*
Winterton, Sir Nicholas *(Con)*

Planning
Burgon, Colin *(Lab)*
Caton, Martin *(Lab)*
Cryer, Ann *(Lab)*
Djanogly, Jonathan *(Con)*
Drew, David *(Lab/Co-op)*
Gerrard, Neil *(Lab)*
Prisk, Mark *(Con)*

Police
Cawsey, Ian *(Lab)*
Hermon, Sylvia *(UUP)*
Irranca-Davies, Huw *(Lab)*
Lansley, Andrew *(Con)*
McCabe, Steve *(Lab)*
Mackinlay, Andrew *(Lab)*
Merron, Gillian *(Lab)*
O'Brien, Mike *(Lab)*
Straw, Jack *(Lab)*

Thomas, Gareth *(Lab)*
Tipping, Paddy *(Lab)*
Tredinnick, David *(Con)*

Political Finance
Linton, Martin *(Lab)*

**Political Ideas and
Philosophy**
Hayes, John *(Con)*
McWalter, Tony *(Lab/Co-op)*
Michael, Alun *(Lab/Co-op)*

Political Process
Wilshire, David *(Con)*

Politics of Sport
Eagle, Angela *(Lab)*

Popular Capitalism
Redwood, John *(Con)*

Ports and Shipping
Mackinlay, Andrew *(Lab)*
Naysmith, Dr Doug
(Lab/Co-op)

Post Office
Johnson, Alan *(Lab)*

Poverty
Battle, John *(Lab)*
Bradley, Keith *(Lab)*
Burden, Richard *(Lab)*
Burt, Alistair *(Con)*
Cooper, Yvette *(Lab)*
Davidson, Ian *(Lab/Co-op)*
Drew, David *(Lab/Co-op)*
Field, Frank *(Lab)*
Fitzpatrick, Jim *(Lab)*
Goggins, Paul *(Lab)*
Hall, Mike *(Lab)*
Hume, John *(SDLP)*
King, Oona *(Lab)*
Marshall, David *(Lab)*
Meale, Alan *(Lab)*
Mitchell, Austin *(Lab)*
Osborne, Sandra *(Lab)*
Pond, Chris *(Lab)*
Prentice, Gordon *(Lab)*
Purnell, James *(Lab)*
Rooney, Terry *(Lab)*
Wood, Mike *(Lab)*
Wright, David *(Lab)*

Press
Fisher, Mark *(Lab)*

Prisons
Mercer, Patrick *(Con)*
Stinchcombe, Paul *(Lab)*
Widdecombe, Ann *(Con)*

Private Finance Initiative
Colman, Tony *(Lab)*
Flight, Howard *(Con)*

Private Security
George, Bruce *(Lab)*

Privatisation
Howarth, Gerald *(Con)*

Pro-Life Movement
Amess, David *(Con)*

Provision for under 5s
Harman, Harriet *(Lab)*

Public Expenditure
Bacon, Richard *(Con)*

Public Sector
Fallon, Michael *(Con)*

Public Sector Housing
Rooney, Terry *(Lab)*

Public Services
Ellman, Louise *(Lab/Co-op)*
Kennedy, Jane *(Lab)*
Laws, David *(Lib Dem)*

Public/Private Partnerships
Smith, Geraldine *(Lab)*

Quality of Life
McDonagh, Siobhain *(Lab)*

Quarrying
Levitt, Tom *(Lab)*

Quotas for Women
Anderson, Janet *(Lab)*

Race Relations
Cook, Frank *(Lab)*
Fitzpatrick, Jim *(Lab)*
Fitzsimons, Lorna *(Lab)*
Follett, Barbara *(Lab)*
George, Andrew *(Lib Dem)*
Gerrard, Neil *(Lab)*
Hamilton, Fabian *(Lab)*
Khabra, Piara *(Lab)*

King, Oona *(Lab)*
Lilley, Peter *(Con)*
Lloyd, Tony *(Lab)*
Short, Clare *(Lab)*
Stunell, Andrew *(Lib Dem)*
Vaz, Keith *(Lab)*
Woodward, Shaun *(Lab)*

Railways
Cryer, Ann *(Lab)*
Luff, Peter *(Con)*
Williams, Betty *(Lab)*

Rainforest Issues
Dalyell, Tam *(Lab)*

Recreation
Godsiff, Roger *(Lab)*
Winterton, Sir Nicholas
(Con)

Recycling
Efford, Clive *(Lab)*

Redistribution of Wealth
Dobson, Frank *(Lab)*
Meacher, Michael *(Lab)*

Refugees/Asylum
Gerrard, Neil *(Lab)*

Regeneration
Baird, Vera *(Lab)*
Burden, Richard *(Lab)*
Clark, Paul *(Lab)*
Ennis, Jeffrey *(Lab)*
Farrelly, Paul *(Lab)*
Fitzpatrick, Jim *(Lab)*
Jones, Kevan *(Lab)*
Love, Andrew *(Lab/Co-op)*
McNulty, Tony *(Lab)*
Pearson, Ian *(Lab)*
Ryan, Joan *(Lab)*
Woodward, Shaun *(Lab)*

Regional Development
Armstrong, Hilary *(Lab)*
Baird, Vera *(Lab)*
Borrow, David *(Lab)*
Chapman, Ben *(Lab)*
Hughes, Beverley *(Lab)*
O'Hara, Edward *(Lab)*
Pearson, Ian *(Lab)*
Price, Adam *(Plaid Cymru)*
Stewart, Ian *(Lab)*
Wright, David *(Lab)*

Regional Policy
Burden, Richard *(Lab)*
Cran, James *(Con)*
Cunningham, Dr Jack *(Lab)*
Ellman, Louise *(Lab/Co-op)*
Foster, Derek *(Lab)*
Jones, Kevan *(Lab)*
Milburn, Alan *(Lab)*
Prentice, Gordon *(Lab)*
Quin, Joyce *(Lab)*
Robinson, Geoffrey *(Lab)*
Wareing, Robert *(Lab)*
Watts, David *(Lab)*
Williams, Alan John *(Lab)*
Winterton, Rosie *(Lab)*

Regulatory Issues
White, Brian *(Lab)*

Religious Affairs
Paisley, Rev Ian *(DUP)*

Research
Ladyman, Dr Stephen *(Lab)*

**Restructuring of Defence
  Industries**
Jones, Nigel *(Lib Dem)*

Retail Industry
Smith, Andrew *(Lab)*

**Revitalising Local
  Democracy**
Stringer, Graham *(Lab)*

**Rights of Victims of
  Accidents and Crime**
Dismore, Andrew *(Lab)*

River Thames
Mackinlay, Andrew *(Lab)*

Rural Affairs
Bradley, Peter *(Lab)*
Breed, Colin *(Lib Dem)*
Burt, Alistair *(Con)*
Clark, Helen *(Lab)*
Djanogly, Jonathan *(Con)*
Drew, David *(Lab/Co-op)*
Duncan, Peter *(Con)*
Flook, Adrian *(Con)*
Gildernew, Michelle
  (Sinn Fein)
Green, Damian *(Con)*
Heath, David *(Lib Dem)*

Hendry, Charles *(Con)*
Hurst, Alan *(Lab)*
Liddell-Grainger, Ian *(Con)*
Luff, Peter *(Con)*
McGuire, Anne *(Lab)*
Marsden, Paul *(Lib Dem)*
Moss, Malcolm *(Con)*
Organ, Diana *(Lab)*
Paice, Jim *(Con)*
Reid, Alan *(Lib Dem)*
Sawford, Phil *(Lab)*
Smith, Robert *(Lib Dem)*
Stewart, David *(Lab)*
Swire, Hugo *(Con)*
Taylor, David *(Lab/Co-op)*
Tipping, Paddy *(Lab)*
Tyler, Paul *(Lib Dem)*
Weir, Mike *(SNP)*
Yeo, Tim *(Con)*

Safer Communities (Crime)
Taylor, David *(Lab/Co-op)*

**Sales Promotion and
  Marketing**
Greenway, John *(Con)*

Science
Battle, John *(Lab)*
Calton, Patsy *(Lib Dem)*
Campbell, Anne *(Lab)*
Dalyell, Tam *(Lab)*
Gibson, Dr Ian *(Lab)*
Harris, Dr Evan *(Lib Dem)*
Jackson, Robert *(Con)*
Jones, Dr Lynne *(Lab)*
Jones, Martyn *(Lab)*
Naysmith, Dr Doug
  (Lab/Co-op)
Page, Richard *(Con)*
Starkey, Dr Phyllis *(Lab)*
Turner, Des *(Lab)*

Science and Technology
Dhanda, Parmjit *(Lab)*
Iddon, Dr Brian *(Lab)*
Ladyman, Dr Stephen *(Lab)*
McWalter, Tony *(Lab/Co-op)*
Miller, Andrew *(Lab)*
Taylor, Ian *(Con)*

Scotland
Brown, Gordon *(Lab)*
Galloway, George *(Lab)*
Gray, James *(Con)*
Griffiths, Nigel *(Lab)*

Kennedy, Charles *(Lib Dem)*
Liddell, Helen *(Lab)*
Luke, Iain *(Lab)*
Marshall, David *(Lab)*
Salmond, Alex *(SNP)*
Savidge, Malcolm *(Lab)*

**Scottish Home Rule and
  Federalism**
Bruce, Malcolm *(Lib Dem)*

Security
Lewis, Dr Julian *(Con)*

Selective Education
Ladyman, Dr Stephen *(Lab)*

Senior Citizens
Sarwar, Mohammad *(Lab)*

Sheltered Housing
Jack, Michael *(Con)*

Shipbuilding
Campbell, Alan *(Lab)*
Davidson, Ian *(Lab/Co-op)*
Robinson, Peter *(DUP)*
Sarwar, Mohammad *(Lab)*

Shipping
Henderson, Ivan *(Lab)*
Prosser, Gwyn *(Lab)*
Waterson, Nigel *(Con)*

Shooters' Rights
Cook, Frank *(Lab)*

Skills and Training
Connarty, Michael *(Lab)*

Small Businesses
Abbott, Diane *(Lab)*
Atkinson, David *(Con)*
Baron, John *(Con)*
Bellingham, Henry *(Con)*
Bercow, John *(Con)*
Borrow, David *(Lab)*
Browning, Angela *(Con)*
Cairns, David *(Lab)*
Cash, William *(Con)*
Clark, Helen *(Lab)*
Connarty, Michael *(Lab)*
Cunningham, Tony *(Lab)*
Curtis-Thomas, Claire *(Lab)*
Davey, Valerie *(Lab)*
Dean, Janet *(Lab)*

Djanogly, Jonathan *(Con)*
Dobbin, Jim *(Lab/Co-op)*
Donohoe, Brian *(Lab)*
Drew, David *(Lab/Co-op)*
Drown, Julia *(Lab)*
Duncan Smith, Iain *(Con)*
Evans, Nigel *(Con)*
Field, Mark *(Con)*
Follett, Barbara *(Lab)*
Foster, Derek *(Lab)*
Foster, Michael John *(Lab)*
George, Bruce *(Lab)*
Gilroy, Linda *(Lab/Co-op)*
Griffiths, Nigel *(Lab)*
Grogan, John *(Lab)*
Hanson, David *(Lab)*
Hawkins, Nick *(Con)*
Hepburn, Stephen *(Lab)*
Hesford, Stephen *(Lab)*
Howells, Dr Kim *(Lab)*
Hoyle, Lindsay *(Lab)*
Humble, Joan *(Lab)*
Jones, Dr Lynne *(Lab)*
Kemp, Fraser *(Lab)*
King, Andy *(Lab)*
Kumar, Dr Ashok *(Lab)*
Ladyman, Dr Stephen *(Lab)*
Lansley, Andrew *(Con)*
Lawrence, Jackie *(Lab)*
Lazarowicz, Mark *(Lab/Co-op)*
Lepper, David *(Lab/Co-op)*
Liddell, Helen *(Lab)*
Love, Andrew *(Lab/Co-op)*
Lucas, Ian *(Lab)*
Lyons, John *(Lab)*
McKechin, Ann *(Lab)*
Mann, John *(Lab)*
Mitchell, Austin *(Lab)*
Moss, Malcolm *(Con)*
Mountford, Kali *(Lab)*
Munn, Meg *(Lab/Co-op)*
Organ, Diana *(Lab)*
Page, Richard *(Con)*
Paice, Jim *(Con)*
Picking, Anne *(Lab)*
Pollard, Kerry *(Lab)*
Prentice, Gordon *(Lab)*
Prisk, Mark *(Con)*
Purchase, Ken *(Lab/Co-op)*
Quinn, Lawrie *(Lab)*
Robertson, John *(Lab)*
Ross, Ernie *(Lab)*
Singh, Marsha *(Lab)*
Smith, Geraldine *(Lab)*
Southworth, Helen *(Lab)*
Stewart, David *(Lab)*

Stewart, Ian *(Lab)*
Tami, Mark *(Lab)*
Taylor, David *(Lab/Co-op)*
Thomas, Gareth *(Lab)*
Turner, Dennis *(Lab/Co-op)*
Twigg, Derek *(Lab)*
Vaz, Keith *(Lab)*
Vis, Rudi *(Lab)*
Walley, Joan *(Lab)*
Watson, Tom *(Lab)*
White, Brian *(Lab)*
Williams, Betty *(Lab)*
Wood, Mike *(Lab)*

Small Nations
George, Andrew *(Lib Dem)*

Social Affairs
Burt, Alistair *(Con)*
Goodman, Paul *(Con)*
Hendry, Charles *(Con)*
Hughes, Simon *(Lib Dem)*
Lamb, Norman *(Lib Dem)*
Marsden, Gordon *(Lab)*
Munn, Meg *(Lab/Co-op)*
Selous, Andrew *(Con)*
Sheridan, Jim *(Lab)*
Steve Webb, Prof *(Lib Dem)*
Williams, Hywel *(Plaid Cymru)*

Social Democracy
Simon, Siôn *(Lab)*

Social Entrepreneurism
Baird, Vera *(Lab)*

Social Exclusion
George, Andrew *(Lib Dem)*
Heyes, David *(Lab)*

Social Inclusion
Begg, Anne *(Lab)*
Hamilton, David *(Lab)*
Hope, Phil *(Lab/Co-op)*
Luke, Iain *(Lab)*
Tynan, Bill *(Lab)*

Social Inequality
Edwards, Huw *(Lab)*

Social Justice
Ewing, Annabelle *(SNP)*
Irranca-Davies, Huw *(Lab)*
Picking, Anne *(Lab)*

Social Policy
Dodds, Nigel *(DUP)*

Kelly, Ruth *(Lab)*
Kennedy, Charles *(Lib Dem)*
Pond, Chris *(Lab)*
Raynsford, Nick *(Lab)*
Wicks, Malcolm *(Lab)*

Social Security
Brown, Gordon *(Lab)*
Cryer, John *(Lab)*
Dismore, Andrew *(Lab)*
Duncan, Alan *(Con)*
Flynn, Paul *(Lab)*
Gibb, Nick *(Con)*
Hammond, Philip *(Con)*
Hewitt, Patricia *(Lab)*
Howarth, Alan *(Lab)*
Illsley, Eric *(Lab)*
Jones, Dr Lynne *(Lab)*
Kennedy, Jane *(Lab)*
Kirkbride, Julie *(Con)*
Kirkwood, Sir Archy *(Lib Dem)*
Lyons, John *(Lab)*
Meale, Alan *(Lab)*
Mountford, Kali *(Lab)*
Primarolo, Dawn *(Lab)*
Smith, Chris *(Lab)*
Stewart, David *(Lab)*
Thomas, Gareth *(Lab)*
Tynan, Bill *(Lab)*
Willetts, David *(Con)*
Williams, Hywel *(Plaid Cymru)*

Social Services
Austin, John *(Lab)*
Calton, Patsy *(Lib Dem)*
Coffey, Ann *(Lab)*
Dean, Janet *(Lab)*
Drown, Julia *(Lab)*
Foulkes, George *(Lab/Co-op)*
George, Bruce *(Lab)*
Griffiths, Nigel *(Lab)*
Griffiths, Win *(Lab)*
Harman, Harriet *(Lab)*
Hesford, Stephen *(Lab)*
Hinchliffe, David *(Lab)*
Hughes, Kevin *(Lab)*
Humble, Joan *(Lab)*
King, Andy *(Lab)*
McAvoy, Thomas *(Lab/Co-op)*
McCafferty, Chris *(Lab)*
McCartney, Ian *(Lab)*
Mallon, S,amus *(SDLP)*
Martlew, Eric *(Lab)*
Morgan, Julie *(Lab)*
Pickles, Eric *(Con)*

Pollard, Kerry *(Lab)*
Ross, Ernie *(Lab)*
Smith, Jacqui *(Lab)*
Smyth, Rev Martin *(UUP)*
Tonge, Dr Jenny *(Lib Dem)*
Truswell, Paul *(Lab)*
Turner, Andrew *(Con)*
Turner, Dennis *(Lab/Co-op)*
Turner, Dr Des *(Lab)*
Williams, Betty *(Lab)*
Wray, James *(Lab)*

Social Welfare
Munn, Meg *(Lab/Co-op)*
Roy, Frank *(Lab)*

Social Work
Dawson, Hilton *(Lab)*
Williams, Hywel *(Plaid Cymru)*

Socialist Enterprise
Foster, Derek *(Lab)*

Solvent Abuse
Hanson, David *(Lab)*

South Africa
McGuinness, Martin
   (Sinn Fein)

Southern Africa
Hunter, Andrew *(Ind)*

Space
Evans, Nigel *(Con)*
Gillan, Cheryl *(Con)*

Space Technology
Atkinson, David *(Con)*

Sport
Burnham, Andy *(Lab)*
Burnside, David *(UUP)*
Burt, Alistair *(Con)*
Campbell, Menzies *(Lib Dem)*
Caplin, Ivor *(Lab)*
Clarke, Tony *(Lab)*
Coaker, Vernon *(Lab)*
Coleman, Iain *(Lab)*
Cunningham, Tony *(Lab)*
Godsiff, Roger *(Lab)*
Grogan, John *(Lab)*
Hancock, Mike *(Lib Dem)*
Hawkins, Nick *(Con)*
Hoey, Kate *(Lab)*
Hoyle, Lindsay *(Lab)*

Jones, Nigel *(Lib Dem)*
Keen, Alan *(Lab/Co-op)*
Knight, Jim *(Lab)*
Malins, Humfrey *(Con)*
Mann, John *(Lab)*
Meale, Alan *(Lab)*
Murphy, Jim *(Lab)*
Purnell, James *(Lab)*
Rammell, Bill *(Lab)*
Reed, Andy *(Lab/Co-op)*
Russell, Bob *(Lib Dem)*
Smith, Chris *(Lab)*
Trickett, Jon *(Lab)*
Ward, Claire *(Lab)*
Winterton, Sir Nicholas *(Con)*
Wright, David *(Lab)*

Steel Industry
Caborn, Richard *(Lab)*

Sudan
Dawson, Hilton *(Lab)*

Sustainable Development
Colman, Tony *(Lab)*

Tax Havens
Foulkes, George *(Lab/Co-op)*

Taxation
Ainsworth, Bob *(Lab)*
Arbuthnot, James *(Con)*
Bailey, Adrian *(Lab/Co-op)*
Clifton-Brown, Geoffrey
   (Con)
Davey, Edward *(Lib Dem)*
Flight, Howard *(Con)*
Foster, Michael Jabez *(Lab)*
Gibb, Nick *(Con)*
Kirkbride, Julie *(Con)*
McIsaac, Shona *(Lab)*
Osborne, George *(Con)*
Palmer, Dr Nick *(Lab)*
Straw, Jack *(Lab)*

Technology
Beard, Nigel *(Lab)*
Fabricant, Michael *(Con)*
Gibson, Dr Ian *(Lab)*
Kemp, Fraser *(Lab)*
McWilliam, John *(Lab)*
Moonie, Lewis *(Lab/Co-op)*

Telecommunications
Evans, Nigel *(Con)*
Timms, Stephen *(Lab)*

Temperance Movement
Taylor, Sir Teddy *(Con)*

Territorial Army
Conway, Derek *(Con)*

Textile Industries
Anderson, Janet *(Lab)*
Mountford, Kali *(Lab)*
Winterton, Ann *(Con)*
Winterton, Sir Nicholas *(Con)*

Third World
Berry, Dr Roger *(Lab)*
Burt, Alistair *(Con)*
Cunningham, Tony *(Lab)*
George, Andrew *(Lib Dem)*
Hume, John *(SDLP)*
Salmond, Alex *(SNP)*
Skinner, Dennis *(Lab)*
Stunell, Andrew *(Lib Dem)*
Steve Webb, Prof *(Lib Dem)*
White, Brian *(Lab)*

Tobin tax
Barnes, Harry *(Lab)*

Tourism
Bellingham, Henry *(Con)*
Burnside, David *(UUP)*
Butterfill, John *(Con)*
Campbell, Gregory Lloyd
   (DUP)
Collins, Tim *(Con)*
Cotter, Brian *(Lib Dem)*
Cunningham, Tony *(Lab)*
Gale, Roger *(Con)*
Greenway, John *(Con)*
Hawkins, Nick *(Con)*
Llwyd, Elfyn *(Plaid Cymru)*
Quinn, Lawrie *(Lab)*
Sanders, Adrian *(Lib Dem)*
Smith, Geraldine *(Lab)*
Swire, Hugo *(Con)*
Thurso, Viscount *(Lib Dem)*
Tyler, Paul *(Lib Dem)*
Waterson, Nigel *(Con)*

Town Centre Issues
Lepper, David *(Lab/Co-op)*

Trade
Atkins, Charlotte *(Lab)*
Bruce, Malcolm *(Lib Dem)*
Djanogly, Jonathan *(Con)*
Jenkin, Bernard *(Con)*

Paterson, Owen *(Con)*
Sheerman, Barry *(Lab/Co-op)*

Trade and Industry
Barnes, Harry *(Lab)*
Burt, Alistair *(Con)*
Butterfill, John *(Con)*
Cable, Dr Vincent *(Lib Dem)*
Campbell, Gregory Lloyd
　(DUP)
Cash, William *(Con)*
Chapman, Ben *(Lab)*
Cran, James *(Con)*
Curtis-Thomas, Claire *(Lab)*
Davidson, Ian *(Lab/Co-op)*
Davies, Geraint *(Lab)*
Davies, Quentin *(Con)*
Fabricant, Michael *(Con)*
Farrelly, Paul *(Lab)*
Follett, Barbara *(Lab)*
Foster, Michael John *(Lab)*
Gardiner, Barry *(Lab)*
Gilroy, Linda *(Lab/Co-op)*
Hawkins, Nick *(Con)*
Hendry, Charles *(Con)*
Hoban, Mark *(Con)*
Hoyle, Lindsay *(Lab)*
Jenkins, Brian *(Lab)*
Jones, Nigel *(Lib Dem)*
Kumar, Dr Ashok *(Lab)*
Lait, Jacqui *(Con)*
Lansley, Andrew *(Con)*
Liddell, Helen *(Lab)*
Luff, Peter *(Con)*
Martin, Michael *(The Speaker)*
Mawhinney, Sir Brian *(Con)*
O'Brien, Stephen *(Con)*
O'Neill, Martin *(Lab)*
Page, Richard *(Con)*
Pike, Peter *(Lab)*
Purchase, Ken *(Lab/Co-op)*
Quinn, Lawrie *(Lab)*
Randall, John *(Con)*
Selous, Andrew *(Con)*
Soames, Nicholas *(Con)*
Spink, Bob *(Con)*
Stewart, Ian *(Lab)*
Taylor, Mark John *(Con)*
Viggers, Peter *(Con)*
Woolas, Philip *(Lab)*
Wright, David Anthony *(Lab)*
Younger-Ross, Richard
　(Lib Dem)

Trade Unions
Benn, Hilary *(Lab)*

Caborn, Richard *(Lab)*
Davidson, Ian *(Lab/Co-op)*
Etherington, Bill *(Lab)*
Healey, John *(Lab)*
Illsley, Eric *(Lab)*
Mahon, Alice *(Lab)*

Training
Hendry, Charles *(Con)*
Jenkins, Brian *(Lab)*
Mann, John *(Lab)*
Paice, Jim *(Con)*
Prentice, Bridget *(Lab)*
Watts, David *(Lab)*

Tranquilliser Addiction
Wareing, Robert *(Lab)*

Transnational Broadcasting
Howells, Dr Kim *(Lab)*

Transport
Amess, David *(Con)*
Anderson, Donald *(Lab)*
Blizzard, Bob *(Lab)*
Bradley, Peter *(Lab)*
Brake, Tom *(Lib Dem)*
Burnside, David *(UUP)*
Calton, Patsy *(Lib Dem)*
Carmichael, Alistair
　(Lib Dem)
Chaytor, David *(Lab)*
Chidgey, David *(Lib Dem)*
Clark, Paul *(Lab)*
Clelland, David *(Lab)*
Cohen, Harry *(Lab)*
Cryer, John *(Lab)*
Darling, Alistair *(Lab)*
Davies, Geraint *(Lab)*
Dean, Janet *(Lab)*
Djanogly, Jonathan *(Con)*
Dobbin, Jim *(Lab/Co-op)*
Dobson, Frank *(Lab)*
Donaldson, Jeffrey *(UUP)*
Donohoe, Brian *(Lab)*
Dowd, Jim *(Lab)*
Duncan Smith, Iain *(Con)*
Dunwoody, Gwyneth *(Lab)*
Eagle, Maria *(Lab)*
Efford, Clive *(Lab)*
Ellman, Louise *(Lab/Co-op)*
Field, Mark *(Con)*
Foster, Derek *(Lab)*
Foster, Don *(Lib Dem)*
Goggins, Paul *(Lab)*
Grayling, Christopher *(Con)*

Griffiths, Jane *(Lab)*
Hamilton, David *(Lab)*
Hammond, Philip *(Con)*
Harris, Tom *(Lab)*
Hawkins, Nick *(Con)*
Henderson, Ivan *(Lab)*
Heppell, John *(Lab)*
Hill, Keith *(Lab)*
Hopkins, Kelvin *(Lab)*
Horam, John *(Con)*
Jack, Michael *(Con)*
Jackson, Helen *(Lab)*
Jones, Kevan *(Lab)*
Jones, Nigel *(Lib Dem)*
Laing, Eleanor *(Con)*
Lazarowicz, Mark
　(Lab/Co-op)
McCabe, Steve *(Lab)*
McIntosh, Anne *(Con)*
Mackinlay, Andrew *(Lab)*
Marris, Rob *(Lab)*
Marshall, David *(Lab)*
Martlew, Eric *(Lab)*
Meale, Alan *(Lab)*
Mole, Chris *(Lab)*
Morley, Elliot *(Lab)*
Murphy, Denis *(Lab)*
Norman, Archie *(Con)*
O'Brien, Stephen *(Con)*
O'Brien, William *(Lab)*
Öpik, Lembit *(Lib Dem)*
Organ, Diana *(Lab)*
Perham, Linda *(Lab)*
Pound, Stephen *(Lab)*
Prosser, Gwyn *(Lab)*
Pugh, John *(Lib Dem)*
Quinn, Lawrie *(Lab)*
Raynsford, Nick *(Lab)*
Robathan, Andrew *(Con)*
Russell, Bob *(Lib Dem)*
Russell, Christine *(Lab)*
Smith, Andrew *(Lab)*
Smyth, Rev Martin *(UUP)*
Stevenson, George *(Lab)*
Strang, Gavin *(Lab)*
Todd, Mark *(Lab)*
Ward, Claire *(Lab)*
White, Brian *(Lab)*
Whitehead, Dr Alan *(Lab)*
Winterton, Ann *(Con)*
Winterton, Rosie *(Lab)*
Wood, Mike *(Lab)*

Transport Safety
Corbyn, Jeremy *(Lab)*
Smith, John *(Lab)*

Treasury
Casale, Roger *(Lab)*
Cranston, Ross *(Lab)*
Davies, Denzil *(Lab)*
Davies, Geraint *(Lab)*
Hanson, David *(Lab)*
Lammy, David *(Lab)*
Ruffley, David *(Con)*
Touhig, Don *(Lab/Co-op)*
Wiggin, Bill *(Con)*

Unemployment
Cooper, Yvette *(Lab)*
Goggins, Paul *(Lab)*
Meale, Alan *(Lab)*
Reed, Andy *(Lab/Co-op)*
Short, Clare *(Lab)*
Yeo, Tim *(Con)*

Urban and Rural Regeneration
Steen, Anthony *(Con)*

Urban Policy
Benn, Hilary *(Lab)*
Curry, David *(Con)*
Fisher, Mark *(Lab)*
Griffiths, Jane *(Lab)*
Vaz, Keith *(Lab)*

Urban Regeneration
Bailey, Adrian *(Lab/Co-op)*
Blears, Hazel *(Lab)*
Buck, Karen *(Lab)*
Hendry, Charles *(Con)*
McGuire, Anne *(Lab)*
Russell, Christine *(Lab)*
Simon, Siôn *(Lab)*
Stringer, Graham *(Lab)*
Timms, Stephen *(Lab)*

US Elections
Evans, Nigel *(Con)*

USA
Forth, Eric *(Con)*

Utility Regulation
Gilroy, Linda *(Lab/Co-op)*

Venture Capital
Flight, Howard *(Con)*
Wyatt, Derek *(Lab)*

Vocational Training
Reed, Andy *(Lab/Co-op)*

Voluntary Sector
Coffey, Ann *(Lab)*
Conway, Derek *(Con)*
Howarth, Alan *(Lab)*
Levitt, Tom *(Lab)*
Lyons, John *(Lab)*
Michael, Alun *(Lab/Co-op)*
Russell, Bob *(Lib Dem)*
Sanders, Adrian *(Lib Dem)*

Voting Systems
Harris, Dr Evan *(Lib Dem)*
Linton, Martin *(Lab)*

Wales
Anderson, Donald *(Lab)*
Bryant, Chris *(Lab)*
Davies, Denzil *(Lab)*
Edwards, Huw *(Lab)*
Flynn, Paul *(Lab)*
Jones, Jon Owen *(Lab/Co-op)*
Murphy, Paul *(Lab)*
Owen, Albert *(Lab)*

Waste Management
Doughty, Sue *(Lib Dem)*
Efford, Clive *(Lab)*
Griffiths, Jane *(Lab)*
Paice, Jim *(Con)*

Water Industry
O'Brien, William *(Lab)*

Welfare
Begg, Anne *(Lab)*
Buck, Karen *(Lab)*
Cairns, David *(Lab)*
Coaker, Vernon *(Lab)*
Cook, Robin *(Lab)*
Davies, Quentin *(Con)*
Harris, Tom *(Lab)*
Kelly, Ruth *(Lab)*
McDonagh, Siobhain *(Lab)*
Moran, Margaret *(Lab)*
Owen, Albert *(Lab)*
Plaskitt, James *(Lab)*
Purnell, James *(Lab)*
Shaw, Jonathan *(Lab)*
Sheridan, Jim *(Lab)*
Webb, Prof Steve *(Lib Dem)*

Welfare State
Brown, Russell *(Lab)*
Corbyn, Jeremy *(Lab)*
Efford, Clive *(Lab)*
Hutton, John *(Lab)*
Wicks, Malcolm *(Lab)*

Welfare to Work
Flint, Caroline *(Lab)*

West Midlands Industry
O'Brien, Mike *(Lab)*

Wildlife and Countryside Legislation
Dalyell, Tam *(Lab)*

Women
Harman, Harriet *(Lab)*
Jackson, Helen *(Lab)*
Osborne, Sandra *(Lab)*
Ruddock, Joan *(Lab)*
Short, Clare *(Lab)*

Women's Health
Organ, Diana *(Lab)*

Work and Pensions
Heyes, David *(Lab)*

Workers' Co-operatives
Tipping, Paddy *(Lab)*

World Development
Armstrong, Hilary *(Lab)*

World Population
Ottaway, Richard *(Con)*

World Protestantism
Smyth, Rev Martin *(UUP)*

Youth Affairs
Baldry, Tony *(Con)*
Brooke, Annette *(Lib Dem)*
Burgon, Colin *(Lab)*
Connarty, Michael *(Lab)*
Cotter, Brian *(Lib Dem)*
Foster, Derek *(Lab)*
Green, Matthew *(Lib Dem)*
Haselhurst, Sir Alan *(Con)*
Hendry, Charles *(Con)*
Hope, Phil *(Lab/Co-op)*
Hughes, Simon *(Lib Dem)*
Michael, Alun *(Lab/Co-op)*
Robertson, Angus *(SNP)*
Russell, Bob *(Lib Dem)*
Steen, Anthony *(Con)*

Youth Justice
Dawson, Hilton *(Lab)*

MPs' educational backgrounds

	Labour	%	Conservative	%	Lib Dem	%	Total (includes other parties)	%
State schools								
Secondary	118	28.6	14	8.4	13	25.0	158	24.0
Grammar/Academy	159	38.6	33	19.9	17	32.7	216	32.8
Comprehensive	60	14.6	6	3.6	5	9.6	73	11.1
Public school	62	15.0	103	62.0	14	26.9	184	27.9
Further and higher education								
FE College	36	8.7	6	3.6	4	7.7	55	8.3
HE College/Poly	34	8.3	11	6.6	8	15.4	54	8.2
Universities	303	73.5	139	83.7	36	69.2	493	74.8
Total	**373**	**90.5**	**156**	**94.0**	**48**	**92.3**	**602**	**91.4**
Oxbridge	79	19.2	81	48.8	14	26.9	176	26.7

MPs by age groups (at 2001 general election)

	Labour	%	Conservative	%	Lib Dem	%	Total	%
Under 30	4	1.0	0	0.0	0	0.0	4	0.6
30–39	36	8.7	24	14.5	14	26.9	80	12.1
40–49	146	35.4	66	39.8	14	26.9	235	35.7
50–59	165	40.0	54	32.5	21	40.4	247	37.5
60–69	53	12.9	21	12.7	3	5.8	83	12.6
Over 70	8	1.9	1	0.6	0	0.0	10	1.5
Average	**50.35**		**49.25**		**47.23**		**49.83**	

MPs with Local Government experience

		%
Labour	273	66.3
Conservative	51	30.7
Lib Dem	34	65.4
Others	9	31.0
Total	**367**	**55.7**

DodOnline

An Electronic Directory without rival . . .

MPs' biographies and photographs available with daily updates *via* the internet

For a *free* trial, call Yasmin Mirza, Aby Farsoun or Michael Mand on 020 7630 7643

MPs' occupational backgrounds

Professions	Labour	Conservative	Lib Dem	Total (includes other parties)
Barrister	22	19	2	45
Solicitor	15	12	4	33
Doctor/Dentist/Medical	2	3	4	10
Architect/Surveyor	1	5	1	9
Chartered engineer	4	2	1	7
Accountant	4	3	1	9
Civil servant/Local government	21	1	0	24
Armed forces	1	7	0	8
Social/Charity worker	39	3	2	45
Scientific worker	7	0	0	7
Health professional	6	0	0	6
Total	**122**	**55**	**15**	**203**
(Percentage)	29.6%	33.1%	28.8%	30.8%
Teaching				
University	32	0	6	40
College	27	2	0	29
School	40	5	5	53
Others/Research	7	2	0	9
Total	**106**	**9**	**11**	**131**
(Percentage)	25.7%	5.4%	21.2%	19.9%
Business				
Company director	2	21	4	27
Company executive	10	17	4	32
Commerce/Insurance	5	16	2	23
Management/Clerical	23	5	4	34
General business	3	1	0	4
Self-employed	3	5	2	10
Total	**46**	**65**	**16**	**130**
(Percentage)	11.2%	39.2%	30.8%	19.7%
Miscellaneous				
Misc white collar	3	1	0	7
Political organiser/Researcher	26	17	5	50
Trade union official	37	0	0	37
Publisher/Journalist/Broadcaster	27	11	3	43
Farmer/Landowner	0	6	2	8
Housewife/Husband	1	1	0	2
Total	**94**	**36**	**10**	**147**
(Percentage)	22.8%	21.7%	19.2%	22.3%
Manual workers				
Miner	10	1	0	11
Skilled worker	24	0	0	26
Semi-/Unskilled worker	10	0	0	11
Total	**44**	**1**	**0**	**48**
(Percentage)	10.7%	0.6%	0.0%	7.3%

Women MPs

ABBOTT Diane
ADAMS Irene
ANDERSON Janet
ARMSTRONG Rt Hon Hilary
ATHERTON Candy
ATKINS Charlotte
BAIRD Vera
BECKETT Rt Hon Margaret
BEGG Anne
BLACKMAN Elizabeth
BLEARS Hazel
BOTTOMLEY Rt Hon Virginia
BROOKE Annette
BROWNING Angela
BUCK Karen
CALTON Patsy
CAMPBELL Anne
CLARK Helen
CLARK Dr Lynda
CLWYD Ann
COFFEY Ann
COOPER Yvette
CORSTON Jean
CRYER Ann
CURTIS-THOMAS Claire
DAVEY Valerie
DEAN Janet
DOUGHTY Sue
DROWN Julia
DUNWOODY Hon Gwyneth
EAGLE Angela
EAGLE Maria
ELLMAN Louise
EWING Annabelle
FITZSIMONS Lorna
FLINT Caroline
FOLLETT Barbara
GIDLEY Sandra
GILDERNEW Michelle
GILLAN Cheryl
GILROY Linda
GRIFFITHS Jane
HARMAN Rt Hon Harriet
HEAL Sylvia
HERMON Lady Sylvia
HEWITT Rt Hon Patricia
HODGE Rt Hon Margaret
HOEY Kate
HUGHES Beverley
HUMBLE Joan
JACKSON Glenda
JACKSON Helen

JOHNSON Melanie
JONES Helen
JONES Dr Lynne
JOWELL Rt Hon Tessa
KEEBLE Sally
KEEN Ann
KELLY Ruth
KENNEDY Rt Hon Jane
KING Oona
KIRKBRIDE Julie
LAING Eleanor
LAIT Jacqui
LAWRENCE Jackie
LIDDELL Rt Hon Helen
McCAFFERTY Christine
McDONAGH Siobhain
McGUIRE Anne
McINTOSH Anne
McISAAC Shona
McKECHIN Ann
McKENNA Rosemary
MACTAGGART Fiona
MAHON Alice
MALLABER Judy
MAY Theresa
MERRON Gillian
MOFFATT Laura
MORAN Margaret
MORGAN Julie
MORRIS Rt Hon Estelle
MOUNTFORD Kali
MUNN Meg
ORGAN Diana
OSBORNE Sandra
PERHAM Linda
PICKING Anne
PRENTICE Bridget
PRIMAROLO Rt Hon Dawn
QUIN Rt Hon Joyce
ROBINSON Iris
ROCHE Barbara
ROE Marion
RUDDOCK Joan
RUSSELL Christine
RYAN Joan
SHEPHARD Rt Hon Gillian
SHIPLEY Debra
SHORT Rt Hon Clare
SMITH Angela
SMITH Geraldine
SMITH Rt Hon Jacqui
SOUTHWORTH Helen

SPELMAN Caroline
SQUIRE Rachel
STARKEY Dr Phyllis
STUART Gisela
TAYLOR Rt Hon Ann
TAYLOR Dari
TONGE Dr Jennifer

WALLEY Joan
WARD Claire
WATKINSON Angela
WIDDECOMBE Rt Hon Ann
WILLIAMS Betty
WINTERTON Ann
WINTERTON Rosie

THE 300 GROUP

PO Box 166, Horsham RH13 9YS   Tel: 01403 733797   Fax: 01403 734432

The 300 Group is an all party campaign for more women in Parliament, Local Government and all areas of public life. Its members are women and men from all walks of life across the country. It encourages and trains women to seek and hold public office and to participate in public decision making processes at all levels.

Chair: Rhian Chilcott, *Finance Director:* Sara Phillp, *Directors:* Carolyn Hilder, Ann Swain

Women MPs 1945–2001

	Conservative	Labour	Lib Dem	Others	Total
1945	1	21	1	1	24
1950	6	14	1	0	21
1951	6	11	0	0	17
1955	10	14	0	0	24
1959	12	13	0	0	25
1964	11	18	0	0	29
1966	7	19	0	0	26
1970	15	10	0	1	26
1974 (Feb)	9	13	0	1	23
1974 (Oct)	7	18	0	2	27
1979	8	11	0	0	19
1983	13	10	0	0	23
1987	17	21	2	1	41
1992	20	37	2	1	60
1997	13	101	3	3	120
2001	14	95	5	4	118

MPs' Membership of other Assemblies

Gerry Adams	Northern Ireland Assembly
Gregory Campbell	Northern Ireland Assembly
Nigel Dodds	Northern Ireland Assembly
Pat Doherty	Northern Ireland Assembly
Michelle Gildernew	Northern Ireland Assembly
John Hume	European Parliament
Edward McGrady	Northern Ireland Assembly
Martin McGuinness	Northern Ireland Assembly
Séamus Mallon	Northern Ireland Assembly
Rev Ian Paisley	Northern Ireland Assembly, European Parliament
Iris Robinson	Northern Ireland Assembly
Peter Robinson	Northern Ireland Assembly
David Trimble	Northern Ireland Assembly

Select Committees (as at July 2003)

The current structure of Select Committees was established in 1979 with the aim of "improving the scrutiny of the expenditure, administration and policy of the main government departments and certain public bodies". The range of inquiries has grown dramatically over the years and tends to reflect matters of current concern and occasional controversy.

Each Department of State is shadowed by a Select Committee. In addition to the departmentally-related select committees there are a number of domestic committees which concern themselves with the day-to-day running of the House, such as the finance and services committee and the broadcasting committee. More recently the work of the Standards and Privileges Committee has come to the forefront with its scrutiny of allegations of misconduct made against individual MPs.

Departmental Committees

CULTURE, MEDIA AND SPORT

Appointed 16 July 2001

Members: (11) Gerald Kaufman (Chair), Chris Bryant, Frank Doran, Michael Fabricant, Adrian Flook, Alan Keen, Julie Kirkbride, Rosemary McKenna, Debra Shipley, John Thurso, Derek Wyatt

Officers: Fergus Reid (Clerk), Olivia Davidson (Second Clerk), Anita Fuki (Committee Assistant), Fiona Mearns (Secretary)

DEFENCE

Appointed 16 July 2001

Members: (11) Bruce George (Chair), James Cran, David Crausby, Mike Hancock, Gerald Howarth, Kevan Jones, Jim Knight, Patrick Mercer, Syd Rapson, Frank Roy, Rachel Squire

Officers: Mark Hutton (Clerk), Steven Mark (Second Clerk), Dr John Gearson (Committee Specialist), Simon Fiander (Audit Adviser), Fiona Channon (Committee Assistant), Sue Monaghan (Secretary)

OFFICE OF THE DEPUTY PRIME MINISTER: HOUSING, PLANNING AND LOCAL GOVERNMENT

Members: (11) Andrew Bennett (Chairman), John Bercow, Paul Beresford, Clive Betts, David Clelland, John Cummings, Chris Mole, Bill O'Brien, John Pugh, Christine Russell, Gary Streeter

Officers: Kate Emms (Committee Clerk), Libby Preston (Second Clerk), Ben Kochan (Committee Specialist), Claire O'Shaughnessy (Committee Specialist), Ian Hook (Committee Assistant), Emma Carey (Committee Secretary)

Urban Affairs Sub-Committee

Members: (11) Andrew Bennett, John Bercow, Paul Beresford, Clive Betts, David Clelland, John Cummings, Chris Mole, Bill O'Brien, John Pugh, Christine Russell, Gary Streeter

Officers: Kate Emms (Clerk), Libby Preston (Clerk), Claire O'Shaughnessy (Committee Specialist), Ben Kochan (Committee Specialist), Ian Hook (Committee Assistant), Emma Carey (Committee Secretary)

EDUCATION AND SKILLS

Appointed 16 July 2001

Members: (11) Barry Sheerman (Chair), David Chaytor, Valerie Davey, Jeff Ennis, Paul Holmes, Robert Jackson, Meg Munn, Kerry Pollard, Jonathan Shaw, Mark Simmonds, Andrew Turner

Officers: David Lloyd (Clerk), Annabel Jones (Second Clerk), Sara Eustace (Committee Specialist), Pam Fisher (Committee Assistant), Catherine Jackson (Secretary)

ENVIRONMENT, FOOD AND RURAL AFFAIRS

Appointed 16 July 2001

Members: (17) David Curry (Chair), Candy Atherton, David Borrow, Colin Breed, David Burnside, David Drew, Patrick Hall, Michael Jack, Mark Lazarowicz, David Lepper, Austin Mitchell, Diana Organ, Gillian Shephard, Alan Simpson, David Taylor, Paddy Tipping, Bill Wiggin

Officers: Gavin Devine (Clerk), Tim Jarvis (Second Clerk), Richard Kelly (Committee Specialist), Katherine Trumper (Committee Specialist), Mark Oxborough (Committee Assistant), Louise Combs (Committee Assistant), Anne Woolhouse (Secretary)

FOREIGN AFFAIRS

Appointed 19 July 2001

Members: (11) Donald Anderson (Chair), David Chidgey, Fabian Hamilton, Eric Illsley, Andrew Mackinlay, John Maples, Bill Olner, Richard Ottaway, Greg Pope, John Stanley, Gisela Stuart

Officers: Steve Priestley (Clerk), Geoffrey Farrar (Second Clerk), Elizabeth Sellwood (Committee Specialist), Jane Appleton (Committee Assistant), Andrew Boyd (Office Clerk), Sheryl Bertasius (Secretary)

HEALTH

Appointed 16 July 2001

Members: (11) David Hinchliffe (Chair), David Amess, John Austin, Andy Burnham, Simon Burns, Paul Burstow, Jim Dowd, Julia Drown, Siobhain McDonagh, Doug Naysmith, Richard Taylor

Officers: John Benger (Clerk), Jenny McCullough (Second Clerk), Laura Hilder (Committee Specialist), Frank McShane (Committee Assistant), Anne Browning (Secretary)

HOME AFFAIRS

Appointed 16 July 2001

Members: (11) John Denham (Chair), Janet Anderson, David Cameron, James Clappison, Claire Curtis-Thomas, Janet Dean, Gwyn Prosser, Bob Russell, Marsha Singh, Ann Widdecombe, David Winnick

Officers: Dr Robin James (Clerk), Sarah Ioannou (Second Clerk), Amy Fitzgerald (Committee Specialist), Ian Thomson (Committee Assistant), Melanie Barklem (Secretary)

INTERNATIONAL DEVELOPMENT

Appointed 16 July 2001

Members: (11) Tony Baldry (Chair), John Barrett, John Battle, Hugh Bayley, Alistair Burt, Ann Clwyd, Tony Colman, Piara Khabra, Chris McCafferty, Robert Walter, Tony Worthington

Officers: Alistair Doherty (Clerk), Sarah Hartwell (Second Clerk), Dr Alan Hudson (Committee Specialist), Katie Phelan (Committee Assistant), Wanda Wilson (Secretary)

LORD CHANCELLOR'S DEPARTMENT

Appointed 28 January 2003

Members: (11) Alan Beith (Chair), Peter Bottomley, James Clappison, Ross Cranston, Ann Cryer, Jim Cunningham, Hilton Dawson, Mark Field, Clive Soley, Keith Vaz, Alan Whitehead

Officers: Huw Yardley (Clerk), Richard Poureshagh (Committee Assistant), Julie Storey (Secretary)

NORTHERN IRELAND AFFAIRS

Appointed 19 July 2001

Members: (13) Michael Mates (Chair), Adrian Bailey, Harry Barnes, Roy Beggs, Tony Clarke, Stephen McCabe, Edward McGrady, Stephen Pound, Peter Robinson, Martin Smyth, Hugo Swire, Mark Tami, Bill Tynan

Officers: Elizabeth Hunt (Clerk), Tony Catinella (Committee Assistant), Camilla Brace (Secretary)

SCIENCE AND TECHNOLOGY

Members: *(11)* Ian Gibson (Chair), Parmjit Dhanda, Tom Harris, David Heath, Brian Iddon, Robert Key, Tony McWalter, Andrew Murrison, Geraldine Smith, Bob Spink, Desmond Turner

Officers: Chris Shaw (Clerk), Nerys Welfoot (Second Clerk), Dr Alun Roberts (Committee Specialist), Ana Ferreira (Committee Assistant), Simali Shah (Secretary)

SCOTTISH AFFAIRS

Appointed 16 July 2001

Members: *(11)* Irene Adams (Chair), Alistair Carmichael, Peter Duncan, David Hamilton, Eric Joyce, Ian Liddell-Grainger, John Lyons, Ann McKechin, John Robertson, Mohammed Sarwar, Michael Weir

Officers: John Whatley (Clerk), Diane Nelson (Committee Assistant), Cynthia Benjamin (Secretary)

TRADE AND INDUSTRY

Appointed 16 July 2001

Members: *(11)* Martin O'Neill (Chair), Henry Bellingham, Roger Berry, Richard Burden, Jonathan Djanogly, Lindsay Hoyle, Ashok Kumar, Andrew Lansley, Jackie Lawrence, Linda Perham, Robert Smith

Officers: Elizabeth Flood (Clerk), David Lees (Second Clerk), Dr Philip Larkin (Committee Specialist), Clare Genis (Committee Assistant), Rowena McDonald (Secretary)

TRANSPORT

Members: *(11)* Gwyneth Dunwoody (Chairman), Tom Brake, Gregory Campbell, Brian H Donohoe, Clive Efford, Louise Ellman, Ian Lucas, George Osborne, John Randall, George Stevenson, Graham Stringer

Officers: Eve Samson (Committee Clerk), John Patterson (Second Clerk), Dr Greg Marsden (Committee Specialist), Frances Allingham (Committee Assistant), Lis McCracken (Secretary)

TREASURY

Appointed 16 July 2001

Members: *(11)* John McFall (Chair), Nigel Beard, Jim Cousins, Angela Eagle, Michael Fallon, Norman Lamb, George Mudie, Nick Palmer, James Plaskitt, David Ruffley, Andrew Tyrie

Officers: Crispin Poyser (Clerk), Alex Kidner (Second Clerk), Lis Partridge (Committee Assistant), Dominic Lindley (Committee Specialist), George Hodgson (Committee Specialist), Amanda Waller (Secretary)

Treasury Sub-Committee

Appointed 16 July 2001

Members: *(11)* Michael Fallon (Chair), Nigel Beard, Jim Cousins, Angela Eagle, Norman Lamb, John McFall, George Mudie, Nick Palmer, James Plaskitt, David Ruffley, Andrew Tyrie

Officers: Alex Kidner (Clerk), Dominic Lindley (Committee Specialist), George Hodgson (Committee Specialist), Lis Partridge (Committee Assistant), Amanda Waller (Secretary)

WELSH AFFAIRS

Appointed 16 July 2001

Members: *(11)* Martyn Jones (Chair), Martin Caton, Huw Edwards, Hywel Francis, Julie Morgan, Albert Owen, Adam Price, Mark Prisk, Bill Wiggin, Betty Williams, Roger Williams

Officers: James Davies (Clerk), Paul Derrett (Committee Assistant), Sarah Colebrook (Secretary)

WORK AND PENSIONS

Appointed 16 July 2001

Members: (11) Archy Kirkwood (Chair), Anne Begg, Karen Buck, Andrew Dismore, Paul Goodman, Joan Humble, Rob Marris, James Purnell, Andrew Selous, David Stewart, Nigel Waterson

Officers: Phil Moon (Clerk), Mick Hillyard (Second Clerk), Maxine Hill (Committee Specialist), Kevin Candy (Committee Assistant), Emily Lumb (Secretary)

Domestic Committees

ACCOMMODATION AND WORKS

Appointed 16 July 2001

Members: (9) Derek Conway (Chair), Bob Ainsworth, Tony Banks, Harold Best, Patrick McLoughlin, Albert Owen, Anne Picking, Syd Rapson, Robert Smith

Officers: Tom Goldsmith (Clerk), Michelle Edney (Secretary)

ADMINISTRATION

Appointed 16 July 2001

Members: (9) Marion Roe (Chair), Nick Ainger, Patsy Calton, Caroline Flint, Martin Linton, Peter Luff, Iain Luke, John MacDougall, Julie Morgan

Officers: Tom Goldsmith (Clerk), Michelle Edney (Secretary)

BROADCASTING

Appointed 16 July 2001

Members: (10) David Lepper (Chair), Helen Clark, Roger Gale, James Gray, David Hamilton, Iain Luke, John Lyons, Khalid Mahmood, Alan Reid, Jim Sheridan

Officers: Gordon Clarke (Clerk), Lynda Young (Secretary)

CATERING

Appointed 19 July 2001

Members: (9) Dennis Turner (Chair), Janet Anderson, Peter Atkinson, Ronnie Campbell, Tony Cunningham, Janet Dean, Lindsay Hoyle, Julie Kirkbride, Simon Thomas

Officers: Gordon Clarke (Clerk), Dawn Summers (Secretary)

INFORMATION

Appointed 16 July 2001

Members: (9) Michael Jack (Chair), Richard Allan, Neil Gerrard, Peter Luff, Ann McKechin, John Mann, Margaret Moran, Gwyn Prosser, Jim Sheridan

Officers: Gordon Clarke (Clerk), Dawn Summers (Secretary)

Other Committees

ENVIRONMENTAL AUDIT

Appointed 16 July 2001

Members: (16) Peter Ainsworth (Chair), Gregory Barker, Harold Best, Colin Challen, David Chaytor, Helen Clark, Sue Doughty, Mark Francois, John Horam, Jon Owen Jones, Ian Lucas, Michael Meacher, Malcolm Savidge, Simon Thomas, Joan Walley, David Wright

Officers: Jessica Mulley (Clerk), Eric Lewis (Committee Specialist), Emma Downing (Committee Specialist), Anna O'Rourke (Committee Assistant), Caroline McElwee (Secretary)

EUROPEAN SCRUTINY

Appointed 16 July 2001

Members: (16) Jimmy Hood (Chair), Richard Bacon, Colin Breed, William Cash,
Michael Connarty, Tony Cunningham, Wayne David, Terry Davis, Jim Dobbin, Mark Hendrick,
Anne McIntosh, Jim Marshall, Angus Robertson, John Robertson, Anthony Steen, Bill Tynan

Officers: Dorian Gerhold (Clerk), Jane Fox (Second Clerk), Terry Byrne (Clerk Adviser), Dr
Gunmar Beck (Clerk Adviser), Josephine Eldred (Clerk Adviser), David Griffiths (Clerk Adviser),
Rosemary Melling (Clerk Adviser), Jackie Ahrens (Committee Assistant), Keely Bishop (Secretary),
Susan Ramsay (Secretary), Liz Booth (Secretary), Joanne Larcombe (Secretary), Bryan Dye
(Assistant), Allen Mitchell (Document Registrar)

JOINT COMMITTEE ON HOUSE OF LORDS REFORM

Appointed 28 November 2002

Members: (24) Lord Archer of Sandwell, Viscount Bledisloe, Brooke of Alverthorpe, Lord Carter,
Lord Forsyth of Drumlean, Baroness Gibson of Market Rasen, Lord Goodhart, Lord Howe of
Aberavon, Lord Oakeshott of Seagrove Bay, Baroness O'Cathain, Earl of Selborne, Lord
Weatherill, Jack Cunningham (Chair), Janet Anderson, James Arbuthnot, Chris Bryant,
Kenneth Clarke, William Hague, Stephen McCabe, Joyce Quin, Terry Rooney, Clive Soley,
Paul Stinchcombe, Paul Tyler

Officers: Malcolm Jack (Commons Clerk), David Beamish (Lords Clerk), Julia Kalogerides
(Commons Secretary), Zana Paul (Lords Secretary)

JOINT COMMITTEE ON HUMAN RIGHTS

Appointed 16 July 2001

Members: (12) Lord Bowness, Lord Lester of Herne Hill, Lord Parekh, Baroness Perry of
Southwark, Baroness Prashar, Baroness Whitaker, Jean Corston (Chair), Vera Baird, David Chidgey,
Kevin McNamara, Richard Shepherd, Shaun Woodward

Officers: Paul Evans (Clerk, Commons), Thomas Elias (Clerk, Lords), Roisin Pillay (Committee
Specialist), Professor David Feldman (Legal Adviser), Diane Ward (Committee Assistant, Lords),
Duma Langton (Committee Assistant, Commons), Pam Morris (Secretary)

MODERNISATION OF THE HOUSE OF COMMONS

Appointed 16 July 2001

Members: (15) Peter Hain (Chair), Ann Coffey, Barbara Follett, David Kidney, Greg Knight,
Martin Linton, Andrew Mitchell, Anne Picking, Peter Pike, Joan Ruddock, Martin Salter,
Richard Shepherd, Andrew Stunell, Paul Tyler, Nicholas Winterton

Officers: George Cubie (Clerk), Tom Healey (Clerk), Susan Morrison (Committee Assistant)

PROCEDURE

Appointed 16 July 2001

Members: (13) Nicholas Winterton (Chair), Peter Atkinson, John Burnett, David Hamilton,
Eric Illsley, Huw Irranca-Davies, Eric Joyce, Iain Luke, Rosemary McKenna, Tony McWalter,
Robert Smith, Desmond Swayne, David Wright

Officers: Simon Patrick (Clerk), Charlotte Littleboy (Second Clerk), Susan Morrison (Committee
Assistant)

PUBLIC ACCOUNTS

Appointed 16 July 2001

Members: (16) Edward Leigh (Chair), Richard Bacon, Ian Davidson, Geraint Davies, Frank Field,
Nick Gibb, George Howarth, Brian Jenkins, Nigel Jones, Ruth Kelly, George Osborne,
David Rendel, Sion Simon, Gerry Steinberg, Jon Trickett, Alan Williams

Officers: Nick Wright (Clerk), Christine Randall (Committee Assistant), Ronnie Jefferson (Secretary)

PUBLIC ADMINISTRATION

Appointed 16 July 2001

Members: (11) Tony Wright (Cannock Chase) (Chair), Kevin Brennan, Annette Brooke, Sydney Chapman, David Heyes, Kelvin Hopkins, Ian Liddell-Grainger, John Lyons, Gordon Prentice, Michael Trend, Brian White

Officers: Phillip Aylett (Clerk), Clive Porro (Second Clerk), Chris Carrington (Committee Specialist), Jackie Recardo (Committee Assistant), Jenny Pickard (Secretary)

REGULATORY REFORM

Appointed 16 July 2001

Members: (16) Peter Pike (Chair), Russell Brown, Brian Cotter, Jeffrey Donaldson, Paul Goodman, Dai Havard, Andy King, Mark Lazarowicz, Andrew Love, John MacDougall, Chris Mole, Denis Murphy, Doug Naysmith, Andrew Rosindell, Anthony Steen, Brian White

Officers: Martyn Atkins (Clerk), Alan Preston (Legal Adviser), Fiona McClean (Committee Specialist), Brian Dye (Committee Assistant), Liz Booth (Secretary)

SELECTION

Appointed 16 July 2001

Members: (9) John McWilliam (Chair), Bob Ainsworth, Jim Fitzpatrick, John Heppell, Phil Hope, Peter Luff, Joan Ryan, Andrew Stunell, George Young

Officers: Siân Jones (Clerk), Robert Bartram (Committee Assistant)

STANDARDS AND PRIVILEGES

Appointed 16 July 2001

Members: (11) George Young (Chair), Russell Brown, Ross Cranston, Andrew Dismore, Derek Foster, Michael Jabez Foster, David Heath, Tom Levitt, Andrew Mackay, Kevin McNamara, Richard Ottaway

Officers: Dr Christopher Ward (Clerk), Mike Clark (Second Clerk), Lisa Hasell (Secretary)

JOINT COMMITTEE ON STATUTORY INSTRUMENTS

Appointed 16 July 2001

Members: (14) Lord Brougham and Vaux, Lord Greenway, Lord Hardy of Wath, Lord Lea of Crondall, Lord Mancroft, Earl Russell, Lord Skelmersdale, David Tredinnick (Chair), Andrew Bennett, Jeffrey Donaldson, Huw Irranca-Davies, Chris Mole, Andrew Rosindell, Brian White

Officers: Martyn Atkins (Clerk Commons), Anna Murphy (Clerk Lords), Alan Preston (Committee Specialist), Anwar Akbar (Committee Specialist), Jane Lauder (Secretary)

Internal Committees

CHAIRMEN'S PANEL

Appointed 26 June 2001

Members: (32) Alan Haselhurst (Chairman of Ways and Means (ex officio), Sylvia Heal (First Deputy Chairman of Ways and Means (ex officio), Michael Lord (Second Deputy Chairman of Ways and Means (ex officio), Irene Adams, David Amess, Peter Atkinson, Nigel Beard, Anne Begg, Joe Benton, John Butterfill, David Chidgey, Derek Conway, Frank Cook, James Cran, John Cummings, Roger Gale, Win Griffiths, Mike Hancock, Jimmy Hood, Alan Hurst, Eric Illsley, John McWilliam, Bill O'Brien, Edward O'Hara, Bill Olner, Peter Pike, Marion Roe, Jonathan Sayeed, George Stevenson, David Taylor, Ann Widdecombe, Nicholas Winterton

Officers: Frank Cranmer (Clerk)

JOINT COMMITTEE ON CONSOLIDATION OF BILLS ETC

Commons appointed 12 December 2001 and Lords 14 March 2002

Members: (24) Lord Acton, Lord Brightman, Lord Campbell of Alloway, Lord Christopher, Viscount Colville of Culross, Earl of Dundee, Baroness Fookes, Lord Janner of Braunstone, Baroness Mallalieu, Lord Phillips of Sudbury, Lord Razzall, Lord Hobhouse of Woodborough (Chairman), Russell Brown, John Burnett, David Cairns, Martin Caton, Colin Challen, Patrick Cormack, Jim Dobbin, Paul Farrelly, Barry Gardiner, John MacDougall, Nicholas Soames, Anthony Steen

Officers: Tom Mohan (Clerk Lords), Tracey Garratty (Clerk Commons)

COURT OF REFEREES

Appointed 14 February 2002

Members: (10) Alan Haselhurst (Chair of Ways and Means), Sylvia Heal (First Deputy Chair of Ways and Means), Michael Lord (Second Deputy Chair of Ways and Means), Peter Atkinson, John Butterfill, Archy Kirkwood, Linda Perham, Bridget Prentice, Ernie Ross, Dennis Turner

Officers: Frank Cranmer (Clerk of the Court), John Vaux (Counsel to the Speaker)

FINANCE AND SERVICES

Appointed 19 November 2001

Members: (12) Stuart Bell (Chair), Irene Adams, Bob Ainsworth, Derek Conway, Michael Fabricant, Keith Hill, David Lepper, Thomas McAvoy, Patrick McLoughlin, Marion Roe, Andrew Stunell, Dennis Turner

Officers: Robert Rogers (Clerk), Michelle Owens (Secretary)

LIAISON

Members: (36) Alan Williams (Chair), Irene Adams, Richard Allan, Donald Anderson, Tony Baldry, Alan Beith, Stuart Bell, Andrew Bennett, Derek Conway, Jean Corston, David Curry, John Denham, Gwyneth Dunwoody, Michael Fabricant, Bruce George, Ian Gibson, David Hinchliffe, Jimmy Hood, John Horam, Martyn Jones, Gerald Kaufman, Archy Kirkwood, Edward Leigh, David Lepper, John McFall, John McWilliam, Michael Mates, Martin O'Neill, Peter Pike, Marion Roe, Barry Sheerman, David Tredinnick, Dennis Turner, Nicholas Winterton, Tony Wright, George Young

Officers: George Cubie (Clerk), Robert Wilson (Clerk), Annie Power (Secretary), Catherine Close (Secretary)

Liaison Sub-Committee

Appointed 31 January 2002

Members: (8) Alan Williams (Chair), Richard Allan, Gwyneth Dunwoody, Chris Mullin, Barry Sheerman, Nicholas Winterton, Tony Wright, George Young

Officers: George Cubie (Clerk), Robert Wilson (Clerk), Annie Power (Secretary), Catherine Close (Secretary)

STANDING ORDERS

Appointed 24 October 2001

Members: (11) Alan Haselhurst (Chairman of Ways and Means (ex officio), Sylvia Heal (First Deputy Chairman of Ways and Means (ex officio), Michael Lord (Second Deputy Chairman of Ways and Means (ex officio), Patrick Cormack, Brian Jenkins, Helen Jones, Ann McKechin, Bill O'Brien, Ernie Ross, Robert Smith, Nicholas Winterton

Officers: Mike Hennessy (Clerk)

UNOPPOSED BILLS (PANEL)

Appointed 17 October 2001

Members: (20) Alan Haselhurst (Chair of Ways and Means), Sylvia Heal (First Deputy Chair of Ways and Means), Michael Lord (Second Deputy Chair of Ways and Means), John Austin, Adrian Bailey, Nigel Beard, Peter Bottomley, John Butterfill, Helen Clark, Philip Hammond, Brian Jenkins, Helen Jones, John McDonnell, Andrew Mackinlay, David Marshall, Syd Rapson, Robert Smith, Jon Trickett, Robert Walter, Ann Winterton

Officers: Mike Hennessy (Clerk)

European Standing Committees

There are three European Standing Committees to consider such documents as are referred to them by the European Legislation Committee, Committee A, B and C. Each committee has 13 Members who are appointed by the Committee of Selection for the whole session of Parliament. The Chairman is appointed by the Speaker on an ad hoc basis. Any Member may attend and speak in a sitting of a Committee but cannot vote. Following Committee debate, the Scrutiny process is completed by the Government moving a motion in the House, which is usually (but need not be) the same as that agreed by the Committee. This is not debatable, and amendments may be tabled and, if selected by the Speaker, voted on.

European Standing Committee A

Members: (13) Janet Dean, Parmjit Dhanda, Michael Jabez Foster, Mark Francois, Matthew Green, David Hamilton, Mark Hoban, Norman Lamb, Rob Marris, Sandra Osborne, Lawrie Quinn, Peter Viggers, Dr Rudi Vis

European Standing Committee B

Members: (13) John Barrett, David Cairns, Paul Farrelly, Dr Hywel Francis, Jane Griffiths, Kelvin Hopkins, Boris Johnson, Dr Nick Palmer, Anne Picking, Mark Tami, Robert Walter, John Wilkinson, Hywel Williams

European Standing Committee C

Members: (13) Tony Cunningham, Valerie Davey, Jim Dobbin, Dai Havard, Ivan Henderson, Stephen Hesford, Michael Jack, Iain Luke, Dr Andrew Murrison, Rev Martin Smyth, Hugo Swire, Anthony D Wright, Richard Younger-Ross

DodOnline

An Electronic Directory without rival...

MPs' biographies and photographs available with daily updates *via* the internet

For a *free* trial, call Yasmin Mirza, Aby Farsoun or Michael Mand on 020 7630 7643

Party Committees

Parliamentary Labour Party

REGIONAL GROUPS 2002–03

East Midlands
Chair: Andy Reed MP; *Vice-Chair:* Judy Mallaber MP; *Hon Treasurer:* Tom Levitt MP; *Clerk:* Tim Nuthall

Eastern
Chair: Barbara Follett MP; *Vice-Chair:* Kerry Pollard MP; *Hon Secretary:* Patrick Hall MP; *Clerk:* Catherine Jackson

London
Chair: Karen Buck MP; *Vice-Chairs:* Clive Efford MP, Oona King MP; *Hon Secretary:* Iain Coleman MP; *Hon Treasurer:* Andrew Dismore MP; *Clerk:* Catherine Jackson

North West
Chair: Geraldine Smith MP; *Vice-Chair:* Claire Curtis-Thomas MP; *Hon Secretary:* Joan Humble MP; *Hon Treasurer:* Jim Dobbin MP; *Clerk:* David Arnold

Northern
Chair: David Clelland MP; *Vice-Chair:* Ashok Kumar MP; *Hon Secretary/Treasurer:*
Alan Campbell MP; *Clerk:* Tim Nuthall

Scottish
Chair: Mohammed Sarwar MP; *Vice-Chair:* Ian Davidson MP; *Hon Secretary/Treasurer:* David Stewart MP; *Clerk:* David Arnold

South East
Chair: Martin Salter MP; *Vice-Chair:* Phyllis Starkey MP; *Hon Secretary:* Jonathan Shaw MP; *Clerk:* David Arnold

South West
Chair: Roger Berry MP; *Vice-Chair:* Candy Atherton MP; *Clerk:* Catherine Jackson

Welsh
Chair: Martin Caton MP; *Vice-Chair:* Betty Williams MP; *Hon Secretary:* Jackie Lawrence MP; *Hon Treasurer:* Julie Morgan MP; *Clerk:* David Arnold

West Midlands
Chair: Dennis Turner MP; *Vice-Chair:* Janet Dean MP; *Clerk:* Tim Nuthall

Yorkshire
Chair: Kevin Barron MP; *Vice-Chair:* Kali Mountford MP; *Hon Secretary:* Lawrie Quinn MP; *Hon Treasurer:* Eric Illsley MP; *Clerk:* Tim Nuthall

DEPARTMENTAL COMMITTEES 2003

Cabinet Office
Chair: Brian White MP; *Vice-Chair:* Lord Brooke of Alverthorpe

Culture, Media and Sport
Chairs: Barry Gardiner MP, Diana Organ MP; *Vice-Chairs:* Gareth Thomas MP *(Harrow West)*, Lord Dubs; *Hon Secretary:* Joan Humble MP

Defence
Chair: John Smith MP; *Vice-Chairs:* Nigel Beard MP, Lord Davies of Coity; *Hon Secretary:* Syd Rapson MP

Education and Skills
Chair: Valerie Davey MP; *Vice-Chairs:* David Chaytor MP, Chris Mole MP, Lord Puttnam; *Hon Secretary:* Judy Mallaber MP

Environment, Food and Rural Affairs
Chair: Paddy Tipping MP; *Vice-Chairs:* David Drew MP, Diana Organ MP, Lord Hoyle

Foreign and Commonwealth Affairs
Chair: Ernie Ross MP; *Vice-Chairs:* Ann Clwyd MP, Greg Pope MP, Baroness Ramsay of Cartvale; *Hon Secretary:* Tony Cunningham MP

Health and Social Services
Chair: Kevin Hughes MP; *Vice-Chairs:* Doug Naysmith MP, Phyllis Starkey MP, Baroness Howells of St Davids; *Hon Secretary:* Howard Stoate MP

Home Affairs
Chair: Fiona Mactaggart MP; *Vice-Chairs:* Stephen Hesford MP, Baroness Gibson of Market Rasen; *Hon Secretary:* Helen Jones MP

International Development
Chair: Hugh Bayley MP; *Vice-Chairs:* Paul Goggins MP, Ann McKechin MP, Baroness Whitaker; *Hon Secretary:* Oona King MP

Legal and Constitutional Affairs
Chair: David Kidney MP; *Vice-Chairs:* Vera Baird MP, Lord Graham of Emonton; *Hon Secretary:* Stephen Hesford MP

Office of the Deputy Prime Minister
Chair: Neil Turner MP; *Vice-Chairs:* Andy Love MP, Chris Mole MP, Baroness Gould of Potternewton

Northern Ireland
Chair: Helen Jackson MP; *Vice-Chairs:* Harry Barnes MP, Kevin McNamara MP, Lord Dubs; *Hon Secretary:* Stephen McCabe MP

Parliamentary Affairs
Chair: Margaret Moran MP; *Vice-Chairs:* John McWilliam MP, Lord Campbell-Savours; *Hon Secretary:* Anne Campbell MP

Trade and Industry
Chair: David Borrow MP; *Vice-Chairs:* Andy Burnham MP, Barbara Follett MP; *Hon Secretary:* Gareth Thomas MP *(Harrow West)*

Transport
Chair: Geraint Davies MP; *Vice-Chairs:* Brian Donohoe MP, Jane Griffiths MP, Lord Lea of Crondall; *Hon Secretary:* Lawrie Quinn MP

Treasury
Chair: Jim Cunningham MP; *Vice-Chairs:* Kali Mountford MP, James Plaskitt MP, Lord Sheldon; *Hon Secretary:* Claire Curtis-Thomas MP

Work and Pensions
Chair: Terry Rooney MP; *Vice-Chairs:* Kali Mountford MP, Tom Levitt MP; *Hon Secretary:* Wayne David MP

Women
Chair: Fiona Mactaggart; *Vice-Chairs:* Lorna Fitzsimmons MP, Barbara Follett MP, Baroness Gould of Potternewton; *Hon Secretary:* Joan Ruddock MP

Visit the Vacher Dod Website . . .
www.DodOnline.co.uk

Conservative Party

1922 COMMITTEE

When in Government, the 1922 is comprised of all the back benchers of the Party; the Whips come to the weekly meetings by invitation. Otherwise, Government Ministers do not regularly attend.

In Opposition, the membership extends to all members of the Parliamentary Party whether front or back benchers.

Conservative Peers are invited to all 1922 meetings.

The 1922 conducts the early stages of leadership elections in the Party and the Chair has the role of the Returning Officer throughout the process which includes a vote by the entire countrywide membership of the Tory Party.

Chairman: Sir Michael Spicer MP
Vice-Chairmen: Mrs Marion Roe MP, Sir Nicholas Winterton MP
Treasurer: John Butterfill MP
Secretaries: Anthony Steen MP, Sir Paul Beresford MP
Executives: Sir Sydney Chapman MP, Sir Patrick Cormack MP, Michael Fabricant MP, Edward Garnier QC MP, Rt Hon David Heathcoat-Amory MP, Rt Hon Michael Jack MP, Hon Nicholas Soames MP, John Taylor MP, David Tredinnick MP, Andrew Turner MP, Peter Viggers MP, Robert Walter MP, Bill Wiggin MP

Conservative Party Policy Groups

AGRICULTURE/ENVIRONMENT (INCLUDING TRANSPORT, LOCAL GOVERNMENT AND THE REGIONS)
Chairman: David Lidington MP
Vice-Chairs: Bill Wiggin MP, Greg Barker MP
Other Shadow Minister: John Hayes MP (Agriculture)
Secretary: Bill Wiggin MP

ECONOMIC AFFAIRS/PENSIONS/SOCIAL AFFAIRS (INCLUDING TREASURY, ENERGY, TRADE AND INDUSTRY, WORK AND PENSIONS)
Chairman: Andrew Mitchell MP
Other Shadow Ministers: David Willetts MP and John Bercow MP (Work and Pensions); Tim Yeo MP, James Clappison MP (Work)
Vice-Chairman: Andrew Mitchell MP
Secretary: David Ruffley MP

DEFENCE/FOREIGN AFFAIRS (INCLUDING INTERNATIONAL DEVELOPMENT)
Chairman: Rt Hon Michael Ancram QC MP
Vice-Chairs: Hugo Swire MP, Ian Liddell-Grainger MP
Other Shadow Ministers: Hon Bernard Jenkin MP (Defence); Caroline Spelman MP (International Development)
Secretary: Mark Prisk MP

PUBLIC SERVICES/HOME AFFAIRS (INCLUDING CONSTITUTION, HOME OFFICE, HEALTH, EDUCATION AND SKILLS, CULTURE, MEDIA AND SPORT, NORTHERN IRELAND, SCOTLAND, WALES)
Chairman: Oliver Letwin MP
Vice-Chairs: David Amess MP, Andrew Turner MP
Other Shadow Ministers: Quentin Davies MP (Northern Ireland); Jacqui Lait MP (Scotland); Nigel Evans MP (Wales); Rt Hon Lord Strathclyde (Lords); John Whittingdale MP (Culture, Media and Sport)
Secretary: David Cameron MP

Officers and Officials

House of Commons Commission

The House of Commons Commission is responsible for the management of the House, including the employment of its staff and the provision of services by the six departments of the House. The Commission delegates some of its functions to the Board of Management and to individual heads of departments.

Members
The Speaker (Rt Hon Michael Martin MP), Chairman
Leader of the House (Rt Hon Peter Hain MP)
Rt Hon Eric Forth MP (Shadow Leader)
Sir Archy Kirkwood MP (Liberal Democrat, spokesman for the Commission)
Stuart Bell MP (Labour)
Sir Patrick Cormack MP (Conservative)

Secretary to the Commission: Robert Rogers

Audit Committee
Rt Hon Eric Forth MP
Sir Archy Kirkwood MP
Sir Thomas Legg KCB QC
David Taylor FCA

Secretary to the Audit Committee: Mark Egan

SPEAKER AND DEPUTY SPEAKERS
The Speaker is the presiding officer of the Commons, whose main responsibility is to maintain order in debates and apply the rules and traditions of the House. The Chairman of Ways and Means is the principal deputy Speaker. The Speaker and Deputy Speakers are normally drawn equally from the government and opposition sides of the House and do not take part in divisions. By tradition, the Speaker, once elected, renounces party allegiance for the remainder of his or her career.

The Speaker — Rt Hon **Michael Martin** MP
Chairman of Ways and Means — Rt Hon Sir **Alan Haselhurst** MP (Con)
First Deputy Chairman — Mrs **Sylvia Heal** MP (Lab)
Second Deputy Chairman — Sir **Michael Lord** MP (Con)

Speaker's Secretary — **Roger Daw**
Speaker's Chaplain — Rev Canon **Robert Wright**
Secretary to the Chairman of Ways and Means — **Mike Hennessy**

Deputy Speakers, Westminster Hall — Sir **Nicholas Winterton** MP (Con)
John McWilliam MP (Lab)
Frank Cook MP (Lab)
Edward O'Hara MP (Lab)

OFFICE OF THE CLERK
Tel: 020 7219 1707
Clerk of the House and Chief Executive: Roger Sands
Head of Office and Secretary to the Board of Management: Richard Ware DPhil
Communications Adviser: Liz Parratt
Private Secretary to the Clerk: Mark Egan
Freedom of Information Officer: Judy Wilson

DEPARTMENT OF THE CLERK OF THE HOUSE
Clerk of the House: Roger Sands (020 7219 3758)
Clerk Assistant: Douglas Millar
Personnel Enquiries: Susan Pamphlett (020 7219 6585)

Legislation Service
Clerk of Legislation: Malcolm Jack PhD
Clerk of Delegated Legislation: Liam Laurence Smyth
Clerk of Bills, Examiner of Petitions for Private Bills and Taxing Officer: Frank Cranmer
Public Bill Office (Tel: 020 7219 6758): Alan Sandall, David Harrison, Colin Lee, Richard Cooke, Tracey Garratty
Private Bill Office: Sîan Jones
Clerk at National Parliament Office, Brussels: Nick Walker

See also European Scrutiny and Deregulation under Select Committees

Committee Office
Clerk of Committees: George Cubie CB
Clerk of Domestic Committees: Robert Rogers
Principal Clerks of Select Committees: Robert Wilson, David Natzler, David Doig
Tel: 020 7219 4300

For full details of staff attached to particular committees, see the earlier pages on Select Committees

Journal Office
William Proctor *(Clerk of the Journals),* Simon Patrick, Tom Healey, Mike Clark, Charlotte Littleboy *(Clerk of Public Petitions)*
Tel: 020 7219 3320

Table Office
Helen Irwin *(Principal Clerk),* Roger Phillips, Chris Stanton, Lynn Gardner, Kenneth Fox, Carol Oxborough, Karen McClelland, Lynn Lewis *(Editorial Supervisor)*
Tel: 020 7219 3305

Overseas Office
Jacqy Sharpe *(Principal Clerk),* James Rhys *(Delegation Secretary)*, Shona McGlashan *(Delegation Secretary)*, Rosie Challis *(Inward Visits Manager)*
Tel: 020 7219 3728

Legal Services Office
John Vaux *(Speaker's Counsel)*, Alan Preston, Michael Carpenter, Anwar Akbar, Peter Brooksbank, Veronica Daly *(Legal Clerk)*, Gunnar Beck
Tel: 020 7219 3776

Vote Office and Parliamentary Bookshop
John Collins *(Deliverer),* Frank Hallett, Owen Sweeney, Robert Brook, Sheila Mitchell *(Parliamentary Bookshop Manager)*
Tel: 020 7219 3631 or 3890 (Bookshop)

DEPARTMENT OF THE SERJEANT AT ARMS
Serjeant at Arms: Michael Cummins
Head of Finance: Philip Collins
Executive Officer: Jill Pay

Serjeant's Operations Directorate
Deputy Serjeant at Arms: Muir Morton
Assistant Serjeants at Arms: Philip Wright, James Robertson, Mark Harvey
Clerk in Charge and Accommodation Co-ordinator: Judy Scott Thomson
Human Resources Manager: Judith Welham

Parliamentary Estates Directorate
Director of Estates: Henry Webber
Project Sponsor: Andy Makepeace

Parliamentary Works Services Directorate
Director of Parliamentary Works Services: John Sellars

Parliamentary Communications Directorate
Director of Communications: Matthew Taylor
Operations and Customer Services Manager: Janet Kilby
Planning and Programmes Manager: Simon Dawe

General Services
Head of Security: Chief Superintendent Gregory Roylance
Postmaster: Mark Pearce

OFFICIAL REPORT (HANSARD)
Editor: Bill Garland
Deputy Editors: Lorraine Sutherland *(House)*, Catherine Fogarty *(Personnel, Finance and Administration)*, Vivian Widgery *(Committees)*
Tel: 020 7219 4786 and 5290

HOUSE OF COMMONS LIBRARY
Librarian: Priscilla Baines
Library Directors: Keith Cuninghame, (Human Resources), Robert Clements (Research Services), Edward Wood (Information Systems), Robert Twigger (Parliamentary and Reference Services), Betty McInnes (PIMS Project)
Library Business Manager: Jane Hough
Head of Information Systems: Paul Ryan
*Head of Library Resources Section:*Dora Clark
Parliamentary OnLine Indexing Service (Polis): Felicity Whittle
Reference and Reader Services: Chris Pond PhD, Helen Holden, Keith Parry, John Prince, Greg Howard (deposited papers)

Research Sections
Business and Transport: Julia Lourie, Fiona Poole, Philippa Carling, Antony Seely, Christopher Blair PhD, Tim Edmonds
Economic Policy and Statistics: Patsy Richards PhD, Grahame Allen, Dominic Webb, Ian Townsend, Edward Potton
Home Affairs: Grahame Danby PhD, Sally Broadbridge, Lorraine Conway, Arabella Thorp, Catherine Fairbain, Pat Strickland, Gabrielle Garton Grimwood
International Affairs and Defence: Carole Andrews, Vaughne Miller, Paul Bowers PhD, Tim Youngs, Christine Fretten, Claire Taylor, Irina Isakova
Parliament and Constitution: Chris Sear, Isobel White, Ruth Winstone
Science and Environment: Christopher Barclay, Donna Gore PhD, Dr Alex Sleator, Brenda Brevitt, Stephen McGinness PhD, Elena Ares PhD
Social and General Statistics: Richard Cracknell, Gavin Berman, Adam Mellows-Facer, David Knott, Ross Young, Matthew Whitaker
Social Policy: Christine Gillie, Jo Roll, Wendy Wilson, Susan Hubble, Steven Kennedy, Tim Jarrett

House of Commons Information Office
Head of Office: Bryn Morgan
Editor of Weekly Information Bulletin: Richard Woodward
Education Officer: Chris Weeds
Tel enquiries: 020 7219 4272   Fax: 020 7219 5839
E-mail: heinfo@parliament.uk   Website: www.parliament.uk

DEPARTMENT OF FINANCE AND ADMINISTRATION
Director of Finance and Administration: Andrew Walker
Director of Operations and Head of Fees Office: Archie Cameron
Director of Financial Management: Chris Ridley
Director of Personnel Policy: Susan Craig
Director of Internal Review Services: Richard Russell
Director of Business Development: Elizabeth Honer
Policy Adviser (Members' Allowances): Heather Wood
Head of Occupational Health, Safety and Welfare Services: Vacant
Travel Office Manager: John Jones

REFRESHMENT DEPARTMENT
Director of Catering Services: Sue Harrison
Operations Managers: Robert Gibbs, Della Herd
Tel: 020 7219 3686

BROADCASTING AND MEDIA
Director of Parliamentary Broadcasting: Barbara Long (020 7219 5848)
Parliamentary Press Gallery inquiries: 020 7219 4700
Communications Adviser, Office of the Clerk: Liz Parratt (020 7219 8978)
House of Commons Information Office: 020 7219 4272

Parliamentary Commissioner for Standards

Parliamentary Commissioner for Standards: Sir Philip Mawer
Registrar of Members' Interests: Alda Barry
Tel: 020 7219 0320   Fax: 020 7219 0490
E-mail: mawerp@parliament.uk

Parliamentary Office of Science and Technology (POST)

Chair: Dr Phyllis Starkey, MP
Director: Prof David Cope
Tel: 020 7219 2848   Website: www.parliament.ukpost/home.htm

DodOnline

An Electronic Directory without rival . . .

MPs' biographies and photographs available with daily updates *via* the internet

For a *free* trial, call Yasmin Mirza, Aby Farsoun or Michael Mand on 020 7630 7643

General Election 2001

dodonline.co.uk

The UK's leading political website from Vacher Dod Publishing . . .

DodOnline is the premier service designed for those at the forefront of their fields with a need for accurate and updated political knowledge. Simple to use, with thousands of contacts at your fingertips, as well as a mass of supporting information – and the ability to interactively tailor the service to your needs.

Extensive coverage of: Westminster, Scotland, Wales, Northern Ireland, European Union and the GLA.

- Full biographies with photographs
- Fully printable and searchable
- Comprehensive contact database
- Export names and addresses for mail merge

- Personal notepad and search facility
- Constituency profiles
- General election and by-election results
- Events as they happen

Call Yasmin Mirza, Aby Farsoun or Michael Mand now on 020 7630 7643 for a instant free trial

Vacher Dod Publishing
1 Douglas Street, London, SW1P 4PA
Tel: 020 7630 7619
Fax: 020 7233 7266
E-mail: subscriptions@vacherdod.co.uk
Website: www.DodOnline.co.uk

Polling Results

Con: Conservative
DUP: Democratic Unionist Party
Ind KHHC: Independent Kidderminster Hospital and Health Concern
Lab: Labour
Lab/Co-op: Labour Co-operative
Lib Dem: Liberal Democrat
Pl C: Plaid Cymru
SDLP: Social Democratic and Labour Party
SF: Sinn Fein
SNP: Scottish National Party
Speaker: The Speaker
UUP: Ulster Unionist Party

AL: Asian League; **Alliance:** Alliance Party of Northern Ireland; **Anti-CF:** Anti-corruption Forum; **BNP:** British National Party; **CD:** Christian Democratic Party; **Choice:** People's Choice; **CMEP:** Church of the Militant Elvis Party; **Comm GB:** Communist Party of Great Britain; **CPA:** Christian People's Alliance; **DCSP:** Direct Customer Service Party; **DWSB:** Defend the Welfare State against Blairism; **EC:** Extinction Club; **FDP:** Fancy Dress Party; **Free:** Free Party; **Green:** Green Party; **Ind:** Independent; **IOW:** Isle of Wight Party; **Jam:** Jam Wrestling Party; **JLDP:** John Lilburne Democratic Party; **JP:** Justice Party; **LCA:** Legalise Cannabis Alliance; **LEDP:** Lower Excise Duty Party; **Left All:** Left Alliance; **Lib:** Liberal Party; **LibP:** Liberated Party; **Loony:** Official Monster Raving Loony Party; **Marxist:** Marxist Party; **Meb Ker:** Mebyon Kernow (The Party for Cornwall); **Mus:** Muslim Party; **New Brit:** New Britain Party; **NF:** National Front; **NIUP:** Northern Ireland Unionist Party; **NIWC:** Northern Ireland Women's Coalition; **NMB:** New Millennium Bean Party; **None:** None; **PCP:** Pensioner Coalition Party; **PDP:** Progressive Democratic Party; **PJP:** People's Justice Party; **PP:** Pacifist Party; **Pro-Euro Con:** Pro Euro Conservative Party; **ProLife:** Pro-Life Alliance; **PUP:** Progressive Unionist Party; **Qari:** Qari; **Reform 2000:** Reform 2000; **RefUK:** Reform UK; **RMGB:** Residents and Motorists of Great Britain; **RNRL:** Rock 'N' Roll Loony Party; **RP:** Ratepayer; **SA:** Socialist Alliance; **SAP:** Socialist Alternative Party; **SFRP:** Scottish Freedom Referendum Party; **SLP:** Socialist Labour Party; **SSP:** Scottish Socialist Party; **Stuck:** Stuckist Party; **Sun Rad:** Sunrise Radio; **SUP:** Scottish Unionist Party; **TCP:** CountrySide Party; **TGP:** Grey Party; **Third:** Third Way; **TP:** Truth Party; **UKIP:** UK Independence Party; **UKP:** United Kingdom Pathfinders; **UKU:** United Kingdom Unionist; **UPP:** Unrepresented Peoples Party; **UTW:** Ulster Third Way; **VYP:** Vote for Yourself Party; **Wessex Reg:** Wessex Regionalists; **WRP:** Workers' Revolutionary Party

ABERAVON

		%	+/- %
Francis, H. Lab	19,063	63.1	-8.2
Turnbull, L. Pl C	2,955	9.8	+4.0
Davies, C. LD	2,933	9.7	-1.6
Miraj, A. Con	2,296	7.6	-0.3
Tutton, A. RP	1,960	6.5	
Beany, C. NMB	727	2.4	
Chapman, M. SA	256	0.8	
Lab majority	16,108		53.36%
Electorate	49,524		
Total Vote	30,190		60.96

Lab Hold (6.1% from Lab to Pl C)

ABERDEEN CENTRAL

		%	+/- %
*Doran, F. Lab	12,025	45.5	-4.3
Gault, W. SNP	5,379	20.4	+4.2
Anderson, E. LD	4,547	17.2	+4.0
Whyte, S. Con	3,761	14.2	-5.3
Cumbers, A. SSP	717	2.7	
Lab majority	6,646		25.15%
Electorate	50,190		
Total Vote	26,429		52.66

*Member of last parliament
Lab Hold (4.2% from Lab to SNP)

ABERDEEN NORTH

		%	+/- %
*Savidge, M. Lab	13,157	43.3	-4.5
Allan, A. SNP	8,708	28.7	+6.9
Donaldson, J. LD	4,991	16.4	+2.3
Cowling, R. Con	3,047	10.0	-5.0
Foreman, S. SSP	454	1.5	
Lab majority	4,449		14.66%
Electorate	52,876		
Total Vote	30,357		57.41

*Member of last parliament
Lab Hold (5.7% from Lab to SNP)

ABERDEEN SOUTH

		%	+/- %
*Begg, A. Lab	14,696	39.8	+4.6
Yuill, I. LD	10,308	27.9	+0.3
Macdonald, M. Con	7,098	19.2	-7.1
Angus, I. SNP	4,293	11.6	+1.9
Watt, D. SSP	495	1.3	
Lab majority	4,388		11.89%
Electorate	59,025		
Total Vote	36,890		62.50

*Member of last parliament
Lab Hold (2.1% from LD to Lab)

WEST ABERDEENSHIRE AND KINCARDINE

		%	+/- %
*Smith, R. LD	16,507	43.5	+2.5
Kerr, T. Con	11,686	30.8	-4.1
Hutchens, K. Lab	4,669	12.3	+3.2
Green, J. SNP	4,634	12.2	-0.8
Manley, A. SSP	418	1.1	
LD majority	4,821		12.72%
Electorate	61,391		
Total Vote	37,914		61.76

*Member of last parliament
LD Hold (3.3% from Con to LD)

AIRDRIE AND SHOTTS

		%	+/- %
*Liddell, H. Lab	18,478	58.2	-3.6
Lindsay, A. SNP	6,138	19.3	-5.1
Love, J. LD	2,376	7.5	+3.3
McIntosh, G. Con	1,960	6.2	-2.7
Dempsey, M. SUP	1,439	4.5	
McGuigan, K. SSP	1,171	3.7	
Herriot, C. SLP	174	0.5	
Lab majority	12,340		38.88%
Electorate	58,349		
Total Vote	31,736		54.39

*Member of last parliament
Lab Hold (0.7% from SNP to Lab)

ALDERSHOT

		%	+/- %
*Howarth, G. Con	19,106	42.2	-0.5
Collett, A. LD	12,512	27.6	-2.8
Akehurst, L. Lab	11,394	25.2	+1.0
Rumsey, D. UKIP	797	1.8	+0.3
Stacey, A. Green	630	1.4	
Pendragon, K. Ind	459	1.0	
Hope, A. Loony	390	0.9	
Con majority	6,594		14.56%
Electorate	78,255		
Total Vote	45,288		57.87

*Member of last parliament
Con Hold (1.2% from LD to Con)

ALDRIDGE-BROWNHILLS

		%	+/- %
*Shepherd, R. Con	18,974	50.2	+3.0
Geary, I. Lab	15,206	40.2	-1.5
Howes, M. LD	3,251	8.6	-2.6
Rothery, J. SA	379	1.0	
Con majority	3,768		9.97%
Electorate	62,361		
Total Vote	37,810		60.63

*Member of last parliament
Con Hold (2.3% from Lab to Con)

ALTRINCHAM AND SALE WEST

		%	+/- %
*Brady, G. Con	20,113	46.2	+3.0
Baugh, J. Lab	17,172	39.4	-0.8
Gaskell, C. LD	6,283	14.4	+1.8
Con majority	2,941		6.75%
Electorate	71,861		
Total Vote	43,568		60.63

*Member of last parliament
Con Hold (1.9% from Lab to Con)

ALYN AND DEESIDE

		%	+/- %
Tami, M. Lab	18,525	52.3	-9.6
Isherwood, M. Con	9,303	26.3	+3.5
Burnham, D. LD	4,585	12.9	+3.2
Coombs, R. Pl C	1,182	3.3	+1.6
Armstrong-Braun, K. Green	881	2.5	
Crawford, W. UKIP	481	1.4	
Cooksey, M. Ind	253	0.7	
Davies, G. Comm GB	211	0.6	
Lab majority	9,222		26.04%
Electorate	60,478		
Total Vote	35,421		58.57

Lab Hold (6.5% from Lab to Con)

AMBER VALLEY

		%	+/- %
*Mallaber, J. Lab	23,101	51.9	-2.8
Shaw, A. Con	15,874	35.7	+2.2
Smith, K. LD	5,538	12.4	+4.7
Lab majority	7,227		16.24%
Electorate	73,798		
Total Vote	44,513		60.32

*Member of last parliament
Lab Hold (2.5% from Lab to Con)

ANGUS

		%	+/- %
Weir, M. SNP	12,347	35.3	-13.0
Booth, M. Con	8,736	25.0	+0.3
McFatridge, I. Lab	8,183	23.4	+7.7
Nield, P. LD	5,015	14.3	+4.9
Wallace, B. SSP	732	2.1	
SNP majority	3,611		10.31%
Electorate	59,004		
Total Vote	35,013		59.34

SNP Hold (6.7% from SNP to Con)

EAST ANTRIM

		%	+/- %
*Beggs, R. UUP	13,101	36.4	-2.4
Wilson, S. DUP	12,973	36.0	+16.6
Mathews, J. Alliance	4,483	12.5	-7.7
O'Connor, D. SDLP	2,641	7.3	+2.7
Mason, R. Ind	1,092	3.0	
Graffin, J. SF	903	2.5	+0.9
Greer, A. Con	807	2.2	-4.6
UUP majority	128		0.36%
Electorate	60,897		
Total Vote	36,000		59.12

*Member of last parliament
UUP Hold (9.5% from UUP to DUP)

NORTH ANTRIM

		%	+/- %
*Paisley, I. DUP	24,539	49.9	+3.3
Scott, L. UUP	10,315	21.0	-2.7
Farren, S. SDLP	8,283	16.8	+1.0
Kelly, J. SF	4,822	9.8	+3.5
Dunlop, J. Alliance	1,258	2.6	-3.6
DUP majority	14,224		28.90%
Electorate	74,451		
Total Vote	49,217		66.11

*Member of last parliament
DUP Hold (3.0% from UUP to DUP)

SOUTH ANTRIM

		%	+/- %
Burnside, D. UUP	16,366	37.1	-20.4
*McCrea, W. DUP	15,355	34.8	
McKee, S. SDLP	5,336	12.1	-4.1
Meehan, M. SF	4,160	9.4	+3.9
Ford, D. Alliance	1,969	4.5	-7.2
Boyd, N. NIUP	972	2.2	
UUP majority	1,011		2.29%
Electorate	70,651		
Total Vote	44,158		62.50

*Member of last parliament

ARGYLL AND BUTE

		%	+/- %
Reid, A. LD	9,245	29.9	-10.3
Raven, H. Lab	7,592	24.5	+8.9
Petrie, D. Con	6,436	20.8	+1.8
Samuel, A. SNP	6,433	20.8	-2.4
Divers, D. SSP	1,251	4.0	
LD majority	1,653		5.34%
Electorate	49,897		
Total Vote	30,957		62.04

LD Hold (9.6% from LD to Lab)

ARUNDEL AND SOUTH DOWNS

		%	+/- %
*Flight, H. Con	23,969	52.2	-0.9
Deedman, D. LD	10,265	22.4	-3.4
Taylor, C. Lab	9,488	20.7	+2.4
Perrin, R. UKIP	2,167	4.7	+1.8

Con majority	13,704		29.86%
Electorate	70,956		
Total Vote	45,889		64.67

*Member of last parliament
Con Hold (1.3% from LD to Con)

ASHFIELD

		%	+/- %
*Hoon, G. Lab	22,875	58.1	-7.0
Leigh, J. Con	9,607	24.4	+4.2
Smith, B. LD	4,428	11.3	+1.6
Harby, C. Ind	1,471	3.7	
Watson, G. SA	589	1.5	
Howse, K. SLP	380	1.0	
Lab majority	13,268		33.72%
Electorate	73,540		
Total Vote	39,350		53.51

*Member of last parliament
Lab Hold (5.6% from Lab to Con)

ASHFORD

		%	+/- %
*Green, D. Con	22,739	47.4	+6.0
Adams, J. Lab	15,380	32.1	+0.4
Fitchett, K. LD	7,236	15.1	-4.6
Boden, R. Green	1,353	2.8	+1.6
Waller, D. UKIP	1,229	2.6	
Con majority	7,359		15.35%
Electorate	76,699		
Total Vote	47,937		62.50

*Member of last parliament
Con Hold (2.8% from Lab to Con)

ASHTON-UNDER-LYNE

		%	+/- %
Heyes, D. Lab	22,340	62.5	-5.0
Charlesworth, T. Con	6,822	19.1	+0.1
Fletcher, K. LD	4,237	11.8	+2.1
Woods, R. BNP	1,617	4.5	
Rolland, N. Green	748	2.1	
Lab majority	15,518		43.39%
Electorate	72,820		
Total Vote	35,764		49.11

Lab Hold (2.6% from Lab to Con)

AYLESBURY

		%	+/- %
*Lidington, D. Con	23,230	47.3	+3.1
Jones, P. LD	13,221	26.9	-2.6
White, K. Lab	11,388	23.2	+1.0
Harper, J. UKIP	1,248	2.5	
Con majority	10,009		20.39%
Electorate	80,002		
Total Vote	49,087		61.36

*Member of last parliament
Con Hold (2.9% from LD to Con)

AYR

		%	+/- %
*Osborne, S. Lab	16,801	43.6	-4.9
Gallie, P. Con	14,256	37.0	+3.2
Mather, J. SNP	4,621	12.0	-0.6
Ritchie, S. LD	2,089	5.4	+0.7
Stewart, J. SSP	692	1.8	
Smith, J. UKIP	101	0.3	
Lab majority	2,545		6.60%
Electorate	55,630		
Total Vote	38,560		69.32

*Member of last parliament
Lab Hold (4.0% from Lab to Con)

BANBURY

		%	+/- %
*Baldry, T. Con	23,271	45.2	+2.3
Sibley, L. Lab	18,052	35.0	+0.2
Worgan, T. LD	8,216	15.9	-0.8
Cotton, B. Green	1,281	2.5	+1.6
Harris, S. UKIP	695	1.3	+0.7
Con majority	5,219		10.13%
Electorate	84,374		
Total Vote	51,515		61.06

*Member of last parliament
Con Hold (1.0% from Lab to Con)

BANFF AND BUCHAN

		%	+/- %
*Salmond, A. SNP	16,710	54.2	-1.5
Wallace, S. Con	6,207	20.1	-3.7
Harris, E. Lab	4,363	14.2	+2.3
Herbison, D. LD	2,769	9.0	+3.0
Rowan, A. SSP	447	1.5	
Davidson, E. UKIP	310	1.0	
SNP majority	10,503		34.09%
Electorate	56,669		
Total Vote	30,806		54.36

*Member of last parliament
SNP Hold (1.1% from Con to SNP)

BARKING

		%	+/- %
*Hodge, M. Lab	15,302	60.9	-4.9
Weatherley, M. Con	5,768	23.0	+5.4
Keppetipola, A. LD	2,450	9.8	+0.3
Tolman, M. BNP	1,606	6.4	+3.7
Lab majority	9,534		37.94%
Electorate	55,229		
Total Vote	25,126		45.49

*Member of last parliament
Lab Hold (5.1% from Lab to Con)

BARNSLEY CENTRAL

		%	+/- %
*Illsley, E. Lab	19,181	69.6	-7.4
Hartley, A. LD	4,051	14.7	+5.2
McCord, I. Con	3,608	13.1	+3.3
Rajch, H. SA	703	2.6	
Lab majority	15,130		54.93%
Electorate	60,086		
Total Vote	27,543		45.84

*Member of last parliament
Lab Hold (6.3% from Lab to LD)

BARNSLEY EAST AND MEXBOROUGH

		%	+/- %
*Ennis, J. Lab	21,945	67.5	-5.6
Brook, S. LD	5,156	15.9	+5.5
Offord, M. Con	4,024	12.4	+1.0
Robinson, T. SLP	722	2.2	-0.6
Savage, G. UKIP	662	2.0	
Lab majority	16,789		51.64%
Electorate	65,655		
Total Vote	32,509		49.51

*Member of last parliament
Lab Hold (5.6% from Lab to LD)

BARNSLEY WEST AND PENISTONE

		%	+/- %
*Clapham, M. Lab	20,244	58.6	-0.7
Rowe, W. Con	7,892	22.8	+4.5
Crompton, M. LD	6,428	18.6	+0.6
Lab majority	12,352		35.74%
Electorate	65,291		
Total Vote	34,564		52.94

*Member of last parliament
Lab Hold (2.6% from Lab to Con)

BARROW AND FURNESS

		%	+/- %
*Hutton, J. Lab	21,724	55.7	-1.6
Airey, J. Con	11,835	30.3	+3.1
Rabone, B. LD	4,750	12.2	+3.3
Smith, J. UKIP	711	1.8	
Lab majority	9,889		25.34%
Electorate	64,746		
Total Vote	39,020		60.27

*Member of last parliament
Lab Hold (2.4% from Lab to Con)

BASILDON

		%	+/- %
*Smith, A. Lab	21,551	52.7	-3.1
Schofield, D. Con	13,813	33.8	+3.0
Smithard, J. LD	3,691	9.0	+0.3
Mallon, F. UKIP	1,397	3.4	
Duane, D. SA	423	1.0	
Lab majority	7,738		18.93%
Electorate	74,121		
Total Vote	40,875		55.15

*Member of last parliament
Lab Hold (3.0% from Lab to Con)

BASINGSTOKE

		%	+/- %
*Hunter, A. Con	20,490	42.7	-0.6
Hartley, J. Lab	19,610	40.9	+1.7
Sollitt, S. LD	6,693	13.9	-3.1
Graham, K. UKIP	1,202	2.5	
Con majority	880		1.83%
Electorate	75,300		
Total Vote	47,995		63.74

*Member of last parliament
Con Hold (1.2% from Con to Lab)

BASSETLAW

		%	+/- %
Mann, J. Lab	21,506	55.3	-5.8
Holley, A. Con	11,758	30.2	+5.5
Taylor, N. LD	4,942	12.7	+2.4
Meloy, K. SLP	689	1.8	
Lab majority	9,748		25.06%
Electorate	68,417		
Total Vote	38,895		56.85

Lab Hold (5.7% from Lab to Con)

BATH

		%	+/- %
*Foster, D. LD	23,372	50.5	+2.0
Fox, A. Con	13,478	29.1	-2.1
Hawkings, M. Lab	7,269	15.7	-0.7
Boulton, M. Green	1,469	3.2	+2.1
Tettenborn, A. UKIP	708	1.5	+0.9
LD majority	9,894		21.37%
Electorate	71,371		
Total Vote	46,296		64.87

*Member of last parliament
LD Hold (2.1% from Con to LD)

BATLEY AND SPEN

		%	+/- %
*Wood, M. Lab	19,224	49.9	+0.5
Peacock, E. Con	14,160	36.7	+0.4
Pinnock, K. LD	3,989	10.3	+1.5
Lord, C. Green	595	1.5	+0.7
Burton, A. UKIP	574	1.5	
Lab majority	5,064		13.14%
Electorate	63,665		
Total Vote	38,542		60.54

*Member of last parliament
Lab Hold (0.0% from Con to Lab)

BATTERSEA

		%	+/- %
*Linton, M. Lab	18,498	50.3	-0.5
Shersby, L. Con	13,445	36.5	-2.9
Vitelli, S. LD	4,450	12.1	+4.7
Barber, T. Ind	411	1.1	
Lab majority	5,053		13.73%
Electorate	67,495		
Total Vote	36,804		54.53

*Member of last parliament
Lab Hold (1.2% from Con to Lab)

BEACONSFIELD

		%	+/- %
*Grieve, D. Con	22,233	52.8	+3.5
Lathrope, S. Lab	9,168	21.8	+1.7
Lloyd, S. LD	9,117	21.6	+0.3
Moffatt, A. UKIP	1,626	3.9	+3.0
Con majority	13,065		31.07%
Electorate	68,894		
Total Vote	42,114		61.03

*Member of last parliament
Con Hold (0.9% from Lab to Con)

BECKENHAM

		%	+/- %
*Lait, J. Con	20,618	45.3	+2.8
Watts, R. Lab	15,659	34.4	+1.0
Feakes, A. LD	7,308	16.0	-2.1
Moran, K. Green	961	2.1	
Pratt, C. UKIP	782	1.7	+0.8
Winfield, R. Lib	234	0.5	-0.8
Con majority	4,959		10.88%
Electorate	72,241		
Total Vote	45,562		63.07

*Member of last parliament
Con Hold (0.9% from Lab to Con)

BEDFORD

		%	+/- %
*Hall, P. Lab	19,454	47.9	-2.7
Attenborough, N. Con	13,297	32.8	-0.9
Headley, M. LD	6,425	15.8	+3.5
Rawlins, R. Ind	973	2.4	
Lo Bianco, J. UKIP	430	1.1	
Lab majority	6,157		15.17%
Electorate	67,762		
Total Vote	40,579		59.88

*Member of last parliament
Lab Hold (0.9% from Con to Lab)

MID BEDFORDSHIRE

		%	+/- %
*Sayeed, J. Con	22,109	47.4	+1.4
Valentine, J. Lab	14,043	30.1	-2.4
Mabbutt, G. LD	9,205	19.7	+2.9
Laurence, C. UKIP	1,281	2.7	
Con majority	8,066		17.29%
Electorate	70,794		
Total Vote	46,638		65.88

*Member of last parliament
Con Hold (1.9% from Lab to Con)

NORTH EAST BEDFORDSHIRE

		%	+/- %
Burt, A. Con	22,586	49.9	+5.6
Ross, P. Lab	14,009	31.0	-1.6
Rogerson, D. LD	7,409	16.4	+2.1
Hill, R. UKIP	1,242	2.7	
Con majority	8,577		18.96%
Electorate	69,877		
Total Vote	45,246		64.75

Con Hold (3.6% from Lab to Con)

SOUTH WEST BEDFORDSHIRE

		%	+/- %
Selous, A. Con	18,477	42.1	+1.4
Date, A. Lab	17,701	40.4	-0.1
Pantling, M. LD	6,473	14.8	+0.5
Wise, T. UKIP	1,203	2.7	
Con majority	776		1.77%
Electorate	70,666		
Total Vote	43,854		62.06

Con Hold (0.8% from Lab to Con)

BELFAST EAST

		%	+/- %
*Robinson, P. DUP	15,667	42.5	-0.1
Lemon, T. UUP	8,550	23.2	-2.1
Alderdice, D. Alliance	5,832	15.8	-8.0
Ervine, D. PUP	3,669	10.0	
O'Donnell, J. SF	1,237	3.4	+1.3
Farren, C. SDLP	880	2.4	+0.8
Dick, T. Con	800	2.2	-0.2
Bell, J. WRP	123	0.3	
Weiss, G. VYP	71	0.2	
DUP majority	7,117		19.32%
Electorate	58,455		
Total Vote	36,829		63.00

*Member of last parliament
DUP Hold (1.0% from UUP to DUP)

BELFAST NORTH

		%	+/- %
Dodds, N. DUP	16,718	40.8	
Kelly, G. SF	10,331	25.2	+5.0
Maginness, A. SDLP	8,592	21.0	+0.6
Walker, C. UUP	4,904	12.0	-39.8
Delaney, M. WRP	253	0.6	
Weiss, G. VYP	134	0.3	
DUP majority	6,387		15.60%
Electorate	60,941		
Total Vote	40,932		67.17

DUP Gain

BELFAST SOUTH

		%	+/- %
*Smyth, M. UUP	17,008	44.8	+8.8
McDonnell, A. SDLP	11,609	30.6	+6.3
McWilliams, M. NIWC	2,968	7.8	
Maskey, A. SF	2,894	7.6	+2.5
Rice, G. Alliance	2,042	5.4	-7.6
Purvis, D. PUP	1,112	2.9	
Lynn, P. WRP	204	0.5	
Weiss, G. VYP	115	0.3	
UUP majority	5,399		14.23%
Electorate	59,436		
Total Vote	37,952		63.85

*Member of last parliament
UUP Hold (1.3% from SDLP to UUP)

BELFAST WEST

		%	+/- %
*Adams, G. SF	27,096	66.1	+10.2
Attwood, A. SDLP	7,754	18.9	-19.8
Smyth, E. DUP	2,641	6.4	
McGimpsey, C. UUP	2,541	6.2	+2.8
Lowry, J. WRP	736	1.8	
Kerr, D. UTW	116	0.3	
Weiss, G. VYP	98	0.2	
SF majority	19,342		47.20%
Electorate	59,617		
Total Vote	40,982		68.74

*Member of last parliament
SF Hold (15.0% from SDLP to SF)

BERWICK-UPON-TWEED

		%	+/- %
*Beith, A. LD	18,651	51.4	+5.9
Sanderson, G. Con	10,193	28.1	+4.0
Walker, M. Lab	6,435	17.7	-8.5
Pearson, J. UKIP	1,029	2.8	+2.0
LD majority	8,458		23.30%
Electorate	56,918		
Total Vote	36,308		63.79

*Member of last parliament
LD Hold (0.9% from Con to LD)

BETHNAL GREEN AND BOW

		%	+/- %
*King, O. Lab	19,380	50.5	+4.1
Bakth, S. Con	9,323	24.3	+3.2
Ludlow, J. LD	5,946	15.5	+3.5
Bragga, A. Green	1,666	4.3	+2.5
Davidson, M. BNP	1,211	3.2	-4.3
Delderfield, D. New Brit	888	2.3	
Lab majority	10,057		26.18%
Electorate	77,478		
Total Vote	38,414		49.58

*Member of last parliament
Lab Hold (0.5% from Con to Lab)

BEVERLEY AND HOLDERNESS

		%	+/- %
*Cran, J. Con	19,168	41.3	+0.2
Langford, P. Lab	18,387	39.6	+0.8
Willie, S. LD	7,356	15.9	-2.6
Wallis, S. UKIP	1,464	3.2	+1.8
Con majority	781		1.68%
Electorate	74,741		
Total Vote	46,375		62.05

*Member of last parliament
Con Hold (0.3% from Con to Lab)

BEXHILL AND BATTLE

		%	+/- %
Barker, G. Con	21,555	48.1	0.0
Hardy, S. LD	11,052	24.7	-0.8
Moore-Williams, A. Lab	8,702	19.4	+1.3
Farage, N. UKIP	3,474	7.8	+6.2
Con majority	10,503		23.45%
Electorate	69,010		
Total Vote	44,783		64.89

Con Hold (0.4% from LD to Con)

OLD BEXLEY AND SIDCUP

		%	+/- %
Conway, D. Con	19,130	45.4	+3.4
Dickson, J. Lab	15,785	37.5	+2.4
Ford, B. LD	5,792	13.7	-2.4
Cronin, J. UKIP	1,426	3.4	+2.4
Con majority	3,345		7.94%
Electorate	67,841		
Total Vote	42,133		62.11

Con Hold (0.5% from Lab to Con)

BEXLEYHEATH AND CRAYFORD

		%	+/- %
*Beard, N. Lab	17,593	43.6	-1.9
Evennett, D. Con	16,121	39.9	+1.5
O'Hare, N. LD	4,476	11.1	-0.1
Smith, C. BNP	1,408	3.5	+2.6
Dunford, J. UKIP	780	1.9	+1.1
Lab majority	1,472		3.65%
Electorate	63,580		
Total Vote	40,378		63.51

*Member of last parliament
Lab Hold (1.7% from Lab to Con)

BILLERICAY

		%	+/- %
Baron, J. Con	21,608	47.4	+7.6
Campbell, A. Lab	16,595	36.4	-0.9
Bellard, F. LD	6,323	13.9	-1.9
Yeomans, N. UKIP	1,072	2.4	
Con majority	5,013		10.99%
Electorate	78,528		
Total Vote	45,598		58.07

Con Hold (4.3% from Lab to Con)

BIRKENHEAD

		%	+/- %
*Field, F. Lab	20,418	70.5	-0.3
Stewart, B. Con	4,827	16.7	+1.5
Wood, R. LD	3,722	12.8	+3.8
Lab majority	15,591		53.82%
Electorate	60,026		
Total Vote	28,967		48.26

*Member of last parliament
Lab Hold (0.9% from Lab to Con)

BIRMINGHAM EDGBASTON

		%	+/- %
*Stuart, G. Lab	18,517	49.1	+0.5
Hastilow, N. Con	13,819	36.6	-2.0
Davies, N. LD	4,528	12.0	+2.3
Gretton, J. Pro-Euro Con	454	1.2	
Brackenbury, S. SLP	431	1.1	
Lab majority	4,698		12.45%
Electorate	67,405		
Total Vote	37,749		56.00

*Member of last parliament
Lab Hold (1.2% from Con to Lab)

BIRMINGHAM ERDINGTON

		%	+/- %
Simon, S. Lab	17,375	56.8	-2.0
Lodge, O. Con	7,413	24.2	-3.3
Johnson, S. LD	3,602	11.8	+1.6
Shore, M. NF	681	2.2	
Godward, S. SA	669	2.2	
Nattrass, M. UKIP	521	1.7	
Sambrook-Marshall, J. SLP	343	1.1	
Lab majority	9,962		32.55%
Electorate	65,668		
Total Vote	30,604		46.60

Lab Hold (0.6% from Con to Lab)

BIRMINGHAM HALL GREEN

		%	+/- %
*McCabe, S. Lab	18,049	54.6	+1.1
White, C. Con	11,401	34.5	+1.1
Singh, P. LD	2,926	8.8	-0.8
Johnson, P. UKIP	708	2.1	
Lab majority	6,648		20.09%
Electorate	57,563		
Total Vote	33,084		57.47

*Member of last parliament
Lab Hold (0.0% from Lab to Con)

BIRMINGHAM HODGE HILL

		%	+/- %
*Davis, T. Lab	16,901	63.9	-1.7
Lewis, D. Con	5,283	20.0	-4.0
Dow, C. LD	2,147	8.1	-0.4
Windridge, L. BNP	889	3.4	
Hussain, P. PJP	561	2.1	
Cridge, D. SA	284	1.1	
Vivian, H. UKIP	275	1.0	
Khan, A. Mus	125	0.5	
Lab majority	11,618		43.90%
Electorate	55,254		
Total Vote	26,465		47.90

*Member of last parliament
Lab Hold (1.2% from Con to Lab)

BIRMINGHAM LADYWOOD

		%	+/- %
*Short, C. Lab	21,694	68.9	-5.2
Prentice, B. Con	3,551	11.3	-2.0
Chaudhry, M. LD	2,586	8.2	+0.3
Ditta, A. PJP	2,112	6.7	
Virdee, S. SLP	443	1.4	
Hussain, M. Mus	432	1.4	
Caffery, J. ProLife	392	1.2	
Nattrass, A. UKIP	283	0.9	
Lab majority	18,143		57.61%
Electorate	71,113		
Total Vote	31,493		44.29

*Member of last parliament
Lab Hold (1.6% from Lab to Con)

BIRMINGHAM NORTHFIELD

		%	+/- %
*Burden, R. Lab	16,528	56.0	-1.5
Purser, N. Con	8,730	29.6	+1.6
Sword, T. LD	3,322	11.2	+0.8
Rogers, S. UKIP	550	1.9	
Walder, C. SA	193	0.7	
Carpenter, Z. SLP	151	0.5	
Chaffer, A. Comm GB	60	0.2	
Lab majority	7,798		26.40%
Electorate	55,922		
Total Vote	29,534		52.81

*Member of last parliament
Lab Hold (1.5% from Lab to Con)

BIRMINGHAM PERRY BARR

		%	+/- %
Mahmood, K. Lab	17,415	46.5	-16.5
Binns, R. Con	8,662	23.1	+1.4
Hunt, J. LD	8,566	22.9	+13.0
Jouhl, A. SLP	1,544	4.1	
Johnson, C. SA	465	1.2	
Nattrass, N. UKIP	352	0.9	
Roche, M. Marxist	221	0.6	
Davidson, R. Mus	192	0.5	
Lab majority	8,753		23.39%
Electorate	71,121		
Total Vote	37,417		52.61

Lab Hold (9.0% from Lab to Con)

BIRMINGHAM SELLY OAK

		%	+/- %
*Jones, L. Lab	21,015	52.4	-3.2
Hardeman, K. Con	10,676	26.6	-1.1
Osborne, D. LD	6,532	16.3	+4.2
Smith, B. Green	1,309	3.3	
Williams, S. UKIP	568	1.4	
Lab majority	10,339		25.78%
Electorate	71,237		
Total Vote	40,100		56.29

*Member of last parliament
Lab Hold (1.0% from Lab to Con)

BIRMINGHAM SPARKBROOK AND SMALL HEATH

		%	+/- %
*Godsiff, R. Lab	21,087	57.5	-6.7
Afzal, Q. LD	4,841	13.2	+3.9
Hussain, S. PJP	4,770	13.0	
Hussain, I. Con	3,948	10.8	-6.7
Mohammed, G. Ind	662	1.8	
Vincent, W. UKIP	634	1.7	
Aziz, A. Mus	401	1.1	
Mirza, S. SA	304	0.8	
Lab majority	16,246		44.33%
Electorate	74,358		
Total Vote	36,647		49.28

*Member of last parliament
Lab Hold (5.3% from Lab to LD)

BIRMINGHAM YARDLEY

		%	+/- %
*Morris, E. Lab	14,083	46.9	-0.1
Hemming, J. LD	11,507	38.3	+5.4
Roberts, B. Con	3,941	13.1	-4.7
Ware, A. UKIP	329	1.1	+0.7
Wren, C. SLP	151	0.5	
Lab majority	2,576		8.58%
Electorate	52,444		
Total Vote	30,011		57.22

*Member of last parliament
Lab Hold (2.7% from Lab to LD)

BISHOP AUCKLAND

		%	+/- %
*Foster, D. Lab	22,680	58.8	-7.1
McNish, F. Con	8,754	22.7	+2.5
Foote Wood, C. LD	6,073	15.7	+6.4
Bennett, C. Green	1,052	2.7	
Lab majority	13,926		36.12%
Electorate	67,368		
Total Vote	38,559		57.24

*Member of last parliament
Lab Hold (4.8% from Lab to Con)

BLABY

		%	+/- %
*Robathan, A. Con	22,104	46.4	+0.6
Morgan, D. Lab	15,895	33.4	-0.4
Welsh, G. LD	8,286	17.4	+2.5
Scott, E. BNP	1,357	2.8	+1.9
Con majority	6,209		13.03%
Electorate	73,732		
Total Vote	47,642		64.62

*Member of last parliament
Con Hold (0.5% from Lab to Con)

BLACKBURN

		%	+/- %
*Straw, J. Lab	21,808	54.1	-0.9
Cotton, J. Con	12,559	31.2	+6.6
Patel, I. LD	3,264	8.1	-2.4
Baxter, D. UKIP	1,185	2.9	
Cullen, T. SLP	559	1.4	0.0
Nichol, J. SA	532	1.3	
Morris, P. Ind	377	0.9	
Lab majority	9,249		22.96%
Electorate	72,611		
Total Vote	40,284		55.48

*Member of last parliament
Lab Hold (3.7% from Lab to Con)

BLACKPOOL NORTH AND FLEETWOOD

		%	+/- %
*Humble, J. Lab	21,610	50.8	-1.4
Vincent, A. Con	15,889	37.3	+1.8
Bate, S. LD	4,132	9.7	+1.1
Porter, J. UKIP	950	2.2	
Lab majority	5,721		13.44%
Electorate	74,456		
Total Vote	42,581		57.19

*Member of last parliament
Lab Hold (1.6% from Lab to Con)

BLACKPOOL SOUTH

		%	+/- %
*Marsden, G. Lab	21,060	54.3	-2.7
Morris, D. Con	12,798	33.0	-1.4
Holt, D. LD	4,115	10.6	+2.1
Cowell, V. UKIP	819	2.1	
Lab majority	8,262		21.30%
Electorate	74,311		
Total Vote	38,792		52.20

*Member of last parliament
Lab Hold (0.7% from Lab to Con)

BLAENAU GWENT

		%	+/- %
*Smith, L. Lab	22,855	72.0	-7.4
Rykala, A. Pl C	3,542	11.2	+5.9
Townsend, E. LD	2,945	9.3	+0.6
Williams, H. Con	2,383	7.5	+0.9
Lab majority	19,313		60.88%
Electorate	53,353		
Total Vote	31,725		59.46

*Member of last parliament
Lab Hold (6.7% from Lab to Pl C)

BLAYDON

		%	+/- %
*McWilliam, J. Lab	20,340	54.8	-5.1
Maughan, P. LD	12,531	33.8	+10.0
Watson, M. Con	4,215	11.4	-1.8
Lab majority	7,809		21.06%
Electorate	64,574		
Total Vote	37,086		57.43

*Member of last parliament
Lab Hold (7.6% from Lab to LD)

BLYTH VALLEY

		%	+/- %
*Campbell, R. Lab	20,627	59.7	-4.5
Reid, J. LD	8,439	24.4	+2.0
Daley, W. Con	5,484	15.9	+2.5
Lab majority	12,188		35.28%
Electorate	62,641		
Total Vote	34,550		55.16

*Member of last parliament
Lab Hold (3.2% from Lab to LD)

BOGNOR REGIS AND LITTLEHAMPTON

		%	+/- %
*Gibb, N. Con	17,602	45.2	+1.0
O'Neill, G. Lab	11,959	30.7	+2.2
Peskett, P. LD	6,846	17.6	-6.4
Stride, G. UKIP	1,779	4.6	+1.3
Cheyne, L. Green	782	2.0	
Con majority	5,643		14.48%
Electorate	66,903		
Total Vote	38,968		58.25

*Member of last parliament
Con Hold (0.6% from Con to Lab)

BOLSOVER

		%	+/- %
*Skinner, D. Lab	26,249	68.6	-5.4
Massey, S. Con	7,472	19.5	+2.8
Bradley, M. LD	4,550	11.9	+2.6
Lab majority	18,777		49.06%
Electorate	67,237		
Total Vote	38,271		56.92

*Member of last parliament
Lab Hold (4.1% from Lab to Con)

BOLTON NORTH EAST

		%	+/- %
*Crausby, D. Lab	21,166	54.3	-1.8
Winstanley, M. Con	12,744	32.7	+2.3
Perkins, T. LD	4,004	10.3	+0.4
McIver, K. Green	629	1.6	
Lowe, L. SLP	407	1.0	-0.3
Lab majority	8,422		21.62%
Electorate	69,514		
Total Vote	38,950		56.03

*Member of last parliament
Lab Hold (2.1% from Lab to Con)

BOLTON SOUTH EAST

		%	+/- %
*Iddon, B. Lab	21,129	61.9	-7.0
Rashid, H. Con	8,258	24.2	+4.5
Harasiwka, F. LD	3,941	11.5	+2.8
Kelly, W. SLP	826	2.4	
Lab majority	12,871		37.69%
Electorate	68,140		
Total Vote	34,154		50.12

*Member of last parliament
Lab Hold (5.7% from Lab to Con)

BOLTON WEST

		%	+/- %
*Kelly, R. Lab	19,381	47.0	-2.5
Stevens, J. Con	13,863	33.6	-1.5
Ronson, B. LD	7,573	18.4	+7.6
Toomer, D. SA	397	1.0	
Lab majority	5,518		13.39%
Electorate	66,033		
Total Vote	41,214		62.41

*Member of last parliament
Lab Hold (0.5% from Lab to Con)

BOOTLE

		%	+/- %
*Benton, J. Lab	21,400	77.6	-5.3
Murray, J. LD	2,357	8.5	+2.8
Symes, J. Con	2,194	8.0	-0.5
Flynn, D. SLP	971	3.5	
Glover, P. SA	672	2.4	
Lab majority	19,043		69.01%
Electorate	55,910		
Total Vote	27,594		49.35

*Member of last parliament
Lab Hold (4.1% from Lab to LD)

BOSTON AND SKEGNESS

		%	+/- %
Simmonds, M. Con	17,298	42.9	+0.5
Bird, E. Lab	16,783	41.6	+0.6
Moffatt, D. LD	4,994	12.4	-4.2
Wakefield, C. UKIP	717	1.8	
Harrison, M. Green	521	1.3	
Con majority	515		1.28%
Electorate	69,010		
Total Vote	40,313		58.42

Con Hold (0.1% from Con to Lab)

BOSWORTH

		%	+/- %
*Tredinnick, D. Con	20,030	44.4	+3.8
Furlong, A. Lab	17,750	39.4	+0.7
Ellis, J. LD	7,326	16.2	-1.6
Con majority	2,280		5.05%
Electorate	69,992		
Total Vote	45,106		64.44

*Member of last parliament
Con Hold (1.5% from Lab to Con)

BOURNEMOUTH EAST

		%	+/- %
*Atkinson, D. Con	15,501	43.3	+1.9
Garratt, A. LD	12,067	33.7	+2.3
Nicholson, P. Lab	7,107	19.9	-1.3
Chamberlaine, G. UKIP	1,124	3.1	+1.3
Con majority	3,434		9.59%
Electorate	60,454		
Total Vote	35,799		59.22

*Member of last parliament
Con Hold (0.2% from Con to LD)

BOURNEMOUTH WEST

		%	+/- %
*Butterfill, J. Con	14,417	42.8	+1.2
Stokes, D. Lab	9,699	28.8	+4.3
Hornby, F. LD	8,468	25.2	-2.6
Blake, C. UKIP	1,064	3.2	+2.5
Con majority	4,718		14.02%
Electorate	62,038		
Total Vote	33,648		54.24

*Member of last parliament
Con Hold (1.5% from Con to Lab)

BRACKNELL

		%	+/- %
*Mackay, A. Con	22,962	46.6	-0.7
Keene, J. Lab	16,249	33.0	+3.2
Earwicker, R. LD	8,424	17.1	+1.7
Boxall, L. UKIP	1,266	2.6	
Roberts, D. ProLife	324	0.7	+0.2
Con majority	6,713		13.64%
Electorate	81,118		
Total Vote	49,225		60.68

*Member of last parliament
Con Hold (2.0% from Con to Lab)

BRADFORD NORTH

		%	+/- %
*Rooney, T. Lab	17,419	49.7	-6.3
Iqbal, Z. Con	8,450	24.1	-1.5
Ward, D. LD	6,924	19.8	+5.3
Brayshaw, J. BNP	1,613	4.6	
Schofield, S. Green	611	1.7	
Lab majority	8,969		25.61%
Electorate	66,454		
Total Vote	35,017		52.69

*Member of last parliament
Lab Hold (2.4% from Lab to Con)

BRADFORD SOUTH

		%	+/- %
*Sutcliffe, G. Lab	19,603	55.8	-0.9
Tennyson, G. Con	9,941	28.3	+0.3
Wilson Fletcher, A. LD	3,717	10.6	-0.7
North, P. UKIP	783	2.2	
Kelly, A. SLP	571	1.6	
Siddique, A. SA	302	0.9	
Riseborough, G. DWSB	220	0.6	
Lab majority	9,662		27.50%
Electorate	68,449		
Total Vote	35,137		51.33

*Member of last parliament
Lab Hold (0.6% from Lab to Con)

BRADFORD WEST

		%	+/- %
*Singh, M. Lab	18,401	48.0	+6.4
Riaz, M. Con	14,236	37.1	+4.1
Robinson, J. Green	2,672	7.0	+5.1
Khan, A. LD	2,437	6.4	-8.4
Hussain, I. UKIP	427	1.1	
Khokhar, F. AL	197	0.5	
Lab majority	4,165		10.85%
Electorate	71,622		
Total Vote	38,370		53.57

*Member of last parliament
Lab Hold (1.2% from Con to Lab)

BRAINTREE

		%	+/- %
*Hurst, A. Lab	21,123	42.0	-0.7
Newmark, B. Con	20,765	41.3	+1.2
Turner, P. LD	5,664	11.3	-0.3
Abbott, J. Green	1,241	2.5	+1.2
Nolan, B. LCA	774	1.5	
Cole, C. UKIP	748	1.5	
Lab majority	358		0.71%
Electorate	78,362		
Total Vote	50,315		64.21

*Member of last parliament
Lab Hold (0.9% from Lab to Con)

BRECON AND RADNORSHIRE

		%	+/- %
Williams, R. LD	13,824	36.8	-4.0
Aubel, F. Con	13,073	34.8	+5.9
Irranca-Davies, H. Lab	8,024	21.4	-5.3
Parri, B. Pl C	1,301	3.5	+2.0
Mitchell, I. Ind	762	2.0	
Phillips, E. UKIP	452	1.2	
Nicholson, R. Ind	80	0.2	
LD majority	751		2.00%
Electorate	53,247		
Total Vote	37,516		70.46

LD Hold (4.9% from LD to Con)

BRENT EAST

		%	+/- %
Daisley, P. Lab	18,325	63.2	-4.1
Gauke, D. Con	5,278	18.2	-4.1
Bhatti, N. LD	3,065	10.6	+2.8
Aspis, S. Green	1,361	4.7	
Macken, S. ProLife	392	1.4	+0.7
Cremer, I. SLP	383	1.3	-0.0
Tanna, A. UKIP	188	0.6	
Lab majority	13,047		45.00%
Electorate	58,095		
Total Vote	28,992		49.90

Lab Hold (0.01% from Lab to Con)

BRENT NORTH

		%	+/- %
*Gardiner, B. Lab	20,149	59.4	+8.7
Allott, P. Con	9,944	29.3	-10.8
Lorber, P. LD	3,846	11.3	+3.2
Lab majority	10,205		30.07%
Electorate	58,789		
Total Vote	33,939		57.73

*Member of last parliament
Lab Hold (9.8% from Con to Lab)

BRENT SOUTH

		%	+/- %
*Boateng, P. Lab	20,984	73.3	+0.3
Selvarajah, C. Con	3,604	12.6	-3.3
Hughes, H. LD	3,098	10.8	+3.1
McDonnell, M. SA	491	1.7	
Mac Stiofain, T. RMGB	460	1.6	
Lab majority	17,380		60.69%
Electorate	55,891		
Total Vote	28,637		51.24

*Member of last parliament
Lab Hold (1.8% from Con to Lab)

BRENTFORD AND ISLEWORTH

		%	+/- %
*Keen, A. Lab	23,275	52.3	-5.2
Mack, T. Con	12,957	29.1	-2.6
Hartwell, A. LD	5,994	13.5	+5.2
Ferriday, N. Green	1,324	3.0	+1.8
Ingram, G. UKIP	412	0.9	+0.2
Faith, D. SA	408	0.9	
Khaira, A. Ind	144	0.3	
Lab majority	10,318		23.18%
Electorate	84,049		
Total Vote	44,514		52.96

*Member of last parliament
Lab Hold (1.3% from Lab to Con)

BRENTWOOD AND ONGAR

		%	+/- %
*Pickles, E. Con	16,558	38.0	-7.4
*Bell, M. Ind	13,737	31.5	
Kendall, D. LD	6,772	15.6	-10.7
Johnson, D. Lab	5,505	12.6	-9.5
Gulleford, K. UKIP	611	1.4	+0.5
Pryke, P. Ind	239	0.5	
Bishop, D. CMEP	68	0.2	
Appleton, T. Ind	52	0.1	
Con majority	2,821		6.48%
Electorate	64,693		
Total Vote	43,542		67.15

*Member of last parliament

BRIDGEND

		%	+/- %
*Griffiths, W. Lab	19,423	52.5	-5.6
Brisby, T. Con	9,377	25.3	+2.5
Barraclough, J. LD	5,330	14.4	+2.9
Mahoney, M. Pl C	2,653	7.2	+3.4
Jeremy, S. ProLife	223	0.6	
Lab majority	10,046		27.15%
Electorate	61,496		
Total Vote	37,006		60.18

*Member of last parliament
Lab Hold (4.0% from Lab to Con)

BRIDGWATER

		%	+/- %
Liddell-Grainger, I. Con	19,354	40.4	+3.5
Thorn, I. LD	14,367	30.0	-3.6
Monteith, W. Lab	12,803	26.8	+2.0
Gardner, V. UKIP	1,323	2.8	
Con majority	4,987		10.42%
Electorate	74,079		
Total Vote	47,847		64.59

Con Hold (3.6% from LD to Con)

BRIGG AND GOOLE

		%	+/- %
*Cawsey, I. Lab	20,066	48.9	-1.3
Stewart, D. Con	16,105	39.2	+2.7
Nolan, D. LD	3,796	9.2	-0.8
Bloom, G. UKIP	688	1.7	
Kenny, M. SLP	399	1.0	
Lab majority	3,961		9.65%
Electorate	64,647		
Total Vote	41,054		63.50

*Member of last parliament
Lab Hold (2.0% from Lab to Con)

BRIGHTON KEMPTOWN

		%	+/- %
*Turner, D. Lab	18,745	47.8	+1.3
Theobald, G. Con	13,823	35.3	-3.6
Marshall, J. LD	4,064	10.4	+0.7
Miller, H. Green	1,290	3.3	
Chamberlain-Webber, J. UKIP	543	1.4	
McLeod, J. SLP	364	0.9	+0.2
Dobbs, D. Free	227	0.6	
Cook, E. ProLife	147	0.4	
Lab majority	4,922		12.56%
Electorate	67,621		
Total Vote	39,203		57.97

*Member of last parliament
Lab Hold (2.4% from Con to Lab)

BRIGHTON PAVILION

		%	+/- %
*Lepper, D. Lab	19,846	48.7	-5.9
Gold, D. Con	10,203	25.1	-2.6
Berry, R. LD	5,348	13.1	+3.6
Taylor, K. Green	3,806	9.3	+6.8
Fyvie, I. SLP	573	1.4	
Dobbs, B. Free	409	1.0	
Hutchin, S. UKIP	361	0.9	+0.5
Paragallo, M. ProLife	177	0.4	
Lab majority	9,643		23.68%
Electorate	69,200		
Total Vote	40,723		58.85

*Member of last parliament
Lab Hold (1.6% from Lab to Con)

BRISTOL EAST

		%	+/- %
*Corston, J. Lab	22,180	55.0	-1.9
Lo Presti, J. Con	8,788	21.8	-1.6
Niblett, B. LD	6,915	17.1	+2.4
Collard, G. Green	1,110	2.8	
Marsh, R. UKIP	572	1.4	
Langley, M. SLP	438	1.1	-0.5
Pryor, A. SA	331	0.8	
Lab majority	13,392		33.20%
Electorate	70,279		
Total Vote	40,334		57.39

*Member of last parliament
Lab Hold (0.2% from Lab to Con)

BRISTOL NORTH WEST

		%	+/- %
*Naysmith, D. Lab	24,236	52.1	+2.2
Hansard, C. Con	13,349	28.7	-0.6
Tyzack, P. LD	7,387	15.9	+2.7
Carr, D. UKIP	1,140	2.5	
Horrigan, V. SLP	371	0.8	-0.1
Lab majority	10,887		23.42%
Electorate	76,903		
Total Vote	46,483		60.44

*Member of last parliament
Lab Hold (1.4% from Con to Lab)

BRISTOL SOUTH

		%	+/- %
*Primarolo, D. Lab	23,299	56.9	-3.1
Eddy, R. Con	9,118	22.3	+1.1
Main, J. LD	6,078	14.8	+1.4
Vowles, G. Green	1,233	3.0	+1.6
Drummond, B. SA	496	1.2	
Prasad, C. UKIP	496	1.2	
Shorter, G. SLP	250	0.6	
Lab majority	14,181		34.61%
Electorate	72,490		
Total Vote	40,970		56.52

*Member of last parliament
Lab Hold (2.1% from Lab to Con)

BRISTOL WEST

		%	+/- %
*Davey, V. Lab	20,505	36.8	+1.6
Williams, S. LD	16,079	28.9	+0.9
Chesters, P. Con	16,040	28.8	-4.0
Devaney, J. Green	1,961	3.5	+2.2
Kennedy, B. SLP	590	1.1	+0.7
Muir, S. UKIP	490	0.9	
Lab majority	4,426		7.95%
Electorate	84,821		
Total Vote	55,665		65.63

*Member of last parliament
Lab Hold (0.4% from LD to Lab)

BROMLEY AND CHISLEHURST		%	+/- %
*Forth, E. Con	21,412	49.5	+3.2
Polydorou, S. Lab	12,375	28.6	+3.4
Payne, G. LD	8,180	18.9	-4.8
Bryant, R. UKIP	1,264	2.9	+0.7
Con majority	9,037		20.90%
Electorate	68,763		
Total Vote	43,231		62.87
*Member of last parliament			
Con Hold (0.1% from Con to Lab)			

BROMSGROVE		%	+/- %
*Kirkbride, J. Con	23,640	51.7	+4.6
McDonald, P. Lab	15,502	33.9	-3.8
Rowley, M. LD	5,430	11.9	0.0
Gregory, I. UKIP	1,112	2.4	+2.0
Con majority	8,138		17.81%
Electorate	68,081		
Total Vote	45,684		67.10
*Member of last parliament			
Con Hold (4.2% from Lab to Con)			

BROXBOURNE		%	+/- %
*Roe, M. Con	20,487	54.1	+5.3
Prendergast, D. Lab	11,494	30.4	-4.3
Davies, J. LD	4,158	11.0	-0.3
Harvey, M. UKIP	858	2.3	
Cope, J. BNP	848	2.2	+0.9
Con majority	8,993		23.76%
Electorate	67,897		
Total Vote	37,845		55.74
*Member of last parliament			
Con Hold (4.8% from Lab to Con)			

BROXTOWE		%	+/- %
*Palmer, N. Lab	23,836	48.6	+1.6
Latham, P. Con	17,963	36.7	-0.8
Watts, D. LD	7,205	14.7	+2.8
Lab majority	5,873		11.98%
Electorate	73,665		
Total Vote	49,004		66.52
*Member of last parliament			
Lab Hold (1.2% from Con to Lab)			

BUCKINGHAM		%	+/- %
*Bercow, J. Con	24,296	53.7	+3.9
Seddon, M. Lab	10,971	24.2	-0.5
Wilson, I. LD	9,037	20.0	-4.7
Silcock, C. UKIP	968	2.1	
Con majority	13,325		29.43%
Electorate	65,270		
Total Vote	45,272		69.36
*Member of last parliament			
Con Hold (2.2% from Lab to Con)			

BURNLEY		%	+/- %
*Pike, P. Lab	18,195	49.3	-8.6
Frost, R. Con	7,697	20.9	+0.6
Wright, P. LD	5,975	16.2	-1.2
Smith, S. BNP	4,151	11.3	
Buttrey, R. UKIP	866	2.3	
Lab majority	10,498		28.46%
Electorate	66,270		
Total Vote	36,884		55.66
*Member of last parliament			
Lab Hold (4.6% from Lab to Con)			

BURTON		%	+/- %
*Dean, J. Lab	22,783	49.0	-2.0
Punyer, M. Con	17,934	38.6	-0.8
Fletcher, D. LD	4,468	9.6	+1.1
Crompton, I. UKIP	984	2.1	
Roberts, J. ProLife	288	0.6	
Lab majority	4,849		10.44%
Electorate	75,194		
Total Vote	46,457		61.78
*Member of last parliament			
Lab Hold (0.6% from Lab to Con)			

BURY NORTH		%	+/- %
*Chaytor, D. Lab	22,945	51.2	-0.6
Walsh, J. Con	16,413	36.6	-0.9
Hackley, B. LD	5,430	12.1	+3.9
Lab majority	6,532		14.58%
Electorate	71,108		
Total Vote	44,788		62.99
*Member of last parliament			
Lab Hold (0.1% from Con to Lab)			

BURY SOUTH		%	+/- %
*Lewis, I. Lab	23,406	59.2	+2.3
Le Page, N. Con	10,634	26.9	-5.4
Pickstone, T. LD	5,499	13.9	+5.5
Lab majority	12,772		32.30%
Electorate	67,276		
Total Vote	39,539		58.77
*Member of last parliament			
Lab Hold (3.9% from Con to Lab)			

BURY ST EDMUNDS		%	+/- %
*Ruffley, D. Con	21,850	43.5	+5.1
Ereira, M. Lab	19,347	38.5	+0.8
Williams, R. LD	6,998	13.9	-4.3
Howlett, J. UKIP	831	1.7	
Brundle, M. Ind	651	1.3	
Benwell, M. SLP	580	1.2	
Con majority	2,503		4.98%
Electorate	76,146		
Total Vote	50,257		66.00
*Member of last parliament			
Con Hold (2.2% from Lab to Con)			

CAERNARFON		%	+/- %
Williams, H. Pl C	12,894	44.4	-6.7
Eaglestone, M. Lab	9,383	32.3	+2.8
Naish, B. Con	4,403	15.2	+2.9
Ab-Owain, M. LD	1,823	6.3	+1.4
Lloyd, I. UKIP	550	1.9	
Pl C majority	3,511		12.08%
Electorate	46,850		
Total Vote	29,053		62.01
Pl C Hold (4.8% from Pl C to Lab)			

CAERPHILLY		%	+/- %
David, W. Lab	22,597	58.2	-9.6
Whittle, L. Pl C	8,172	21.0	+11.4
Simmonds, D. Con	4,413	11.4	+0.6
Roffe, R. LD	3,649	9.4	+1.2
Lab majority	14,425		37.32%
Electorate	67,593		
Total Vote	38,883		57.18
Lab Hold (10.4% from Lab to Pl C)			

CAITHNESS, SUTHERLAND AND EASTER ROSS

		%	+/- %
Thurso, J. LD	9,041	36.4	+0.8
Meighan, M. Lab	6,297	25.3	-2.5
Macadam, J. SNP	5,273	21.2	-1.8
Rowantree, R. Con	3,513	14.1	+3.3
Mabon, K. SSP	544	2.2	
Campbell, J. Ind	199	0.8	
LD majority	2,744		11.03%
Electorate	40,811		
Total Vote	24,867		60.93

LD Hold (1.6% from Lab to LD)

CALDER VALLEY

		%	+/- %
*McCafferty, C. Lab	20,244	42.7	-3.4
Robson-Catling, S. Con	17,150	36.2	+1.1
Taylor, M. LD	7,596	16.0	+1.3
Hutton, S. Green	1,034	2.2	+1.3
Nunn, J. UKIP	729	1.5	
Lockwood, P. LCA	672	1.4	
Lab majority	3,094		6.52%
Electorate	69,870		
Total Vote	47,425		67.88

*Member of last parliament
Lab Hold (2.3% from Lab to Con)

CAMBERWELL AND PECKHAM

		%	+/- %
*Harman, H. Lab	17,473	69.6	+0.3
McCarthy, D. LD	3,350	13.3	+2.1
Morgan, J. Con	2,740	10.9	-1.0
Poorun, S. Green	805	3.2	
Mulrenan, J. SA	478	1.9	
Adams, B. SLP	188	0.7	-1.7
Sweeney, F. WRP	70	0.3	-0.1
Lab majority	14,123		56.26%
Electorate	53,687		
Total Vote	25,104		46.76

*Member of last parliament
Lab Hold (0.9% from Lab to LD)

CAMBRIDGE

		%	+/- %
*Campbell, A. Lab	19,316	45.1	-8.3
Howarth, D. LD	10,737	25.1	+8.9
Stuart, G. Con	9,829	22.9	-3.0
Lawrence, S. Green	1,413	3.3	+2.0
Senter, H. SA	716	1.7	
Baynes, L. UKIP	532	1.2	
Underwood, C. ProLife	232	0.5	+0.2
Courtney, M. WRP	61	0.1	-0.1
Lab majority	8,579		20.03%
Electorate	70,664		
Total Vote	42,836		60.62

*Member of last parliament
Lab Hold (8.6% from Lab to LD)

NORTH EAST CAMBRIDGESHIRE

		%	+/- %
*Moss, M. Con	23,132	48.1	+5.1
Owen, D. Lab	16,759	34.9	+1.0
Renaut, R. LD	6,733	14.0	-2.4
Stevens, J. UKIP	1,189	2.5	
Hoey, T. ProLife	238	0.5	
Con majority	6,373		13.26%
Electorate	79,891		
Total Vote	48,051		60.15

*Member of last parliament
Con Hold (2.0% from Lab to Con)

NORTH WEST CAMBRIDGESHIRE

		%	+/- %
*Mawhinney, B. Con	21,895	49.8	+1.7
Cox, A. Lab	13,794	31.4	-0.8
Taylor, A. LD	6,957	15.8	+0.7
Hudson, B. UKIP	881	2.0	+1.5
Hall, D. Ind	429	1.0	
Con majority	8,101		18.43%
Electorate	71,247		
Total Vote	43,956		61.70

*Member of last parliament
Con Hold (1.3% from Lab to Con)

SOUTH CAMBRIDGESHIRE

		%	+/- %
*Lansley, A. Con	21,387	44.2	+2.2
Taylor, A. LD	12,984	26.9	+1.0
Herbert, J. Lab	11,737	24.3	-0.8
Saggers, S. Green	1,182	2.4	
Davies, H. UKIP	875	1.8	+1.3
Klepacka, A. ProLife	176	0.4	
Con majority	8,403		17.38%
Electorate	72,095		
Total Vote	48,341		67.05

*Member of last parliament
Con Hold (0.6% from LD to Con)

SOUTH EAST CAMBRIDGESHIRE

		%	+/- %
*Paice, J. Con	22,927	44.2	+1.2
Brinton, S. LD	13,937	26.9	+1.8
Inchley, A. Lab	13,714	26.4	-0.1
Scarr, N. UKIP	1,308	2.5	
Con majority	8,990		17.33%
Electorate	81,663		
Total Vote	51,886		63.54

*Member of last parliament
Con Hold (0.3% from Con to LD)

CANNOCK CHASE

		%	+/- %
*Wright, T. Lab	23,049	56.1	+1.3
Smithers, G. Con	12,345	30.1	+2.9
Reynolds, S. LD	5,670	13.8	+5.1
Lab majority	10,704		26.07%
Electorate	73,467		
Total Vote	41,064		55.89

*Member of last parliament
Lab Hold (0.8% from Lab to Con)

CANTERBURY

		%	+/- %
*Brazier, J. Con	18,711	41.5	+2.8
Thornberry, E. Lab	16,642	36.9	+5.6
Wales, P. LD	8,056	17.8	-5.9
Dawe, H. Green	920	2.0	+1.0
Moore, L. UKIP	803	1.8	+1.3
Con majority	2,069		4.58%
Electorate	74,144		
Total Vote	45,132		60.87

*Member of last parliament
Con Hold (1.4% from Con to Lab)

CARDIFF CENTRAL

		%	+/- %
*Jones, J. Lab	13,451	38.6	-5.1
Willott, J. LD	12,792	36.7	+11.8
Walker, G. Con	5,537	15.9	-4.2
Grigg, R. Pl C	1,680	4.8	+1.3
Bartley, S. Green	661	1.9	
Goss, J. SA	283	0.8	

Hughes, F. UKIP	221	0.6	
Jeremy, M. ProLife	217	0.6	
Lab majority	659		1.89%
Electorate	59,785		
Total Vote	34,842		58.28

*Member of last parliament
Lab Hold (8.4% from Lab to LD)

CARDIFF NORTH

		%	+/- %
*Morgan, J. Lab	19,845	45.9	-4.6
Watson, A. Con	13,680	31.6	-2.0
Dixon, J. LD	6,631	15.3	+4.4
Jobbins, S. Pl C	2,471	5.7	+3.2
Hulston, D. UKIP	613	1.4	
Lab majority	6,165		14.26%
Electorate	62,634		
Total Vote	43,240		69.04

*Member of last parliament
Lab Hold (1.3% from Lab to Con)

CARDIFF SOUTH AND PENARTH

		%	+/- %
*Michael, A. Lab	20,094	56.2	+2.8
Kelly Owen, M. Con	7,807	21.8	+1.1
Berman, R. LD	4,572	12.8	+3.4
Haines, L. Pl C	1,983	5.5	+2.4
Callan, J. UKIP	501	1.4	
Bartlett, D. SA	427	1.2	
Savoury, A. ProLife	367	1.0	
Lab majority	12,287		34.37%
Electorate	62,627		
Total Vote	35,751		57.09

*Member of last parliament
Lab Hold (0.8% from Con to Lab)

CARDIFF WEST

		%	+/- %
Brennan, K. Lab	18,594	54.6	-5.8
Davies, A. Con	7,273	21.3	-0.2
Gasson, J. LD	4,458	13.1	+2.2
Bowen, D. Pl C	3,296	9.7	+4.8
Jenking, J. UKIP	462	1.4	
Lab majority	11,321		33.22%
Electorate	58,348		
Total Vote	34,083		58.41

Lab Hold (2.8% from Lab to Con)

CARLISLE

		%	+/- %
*Martlew, E. Lab	17,856	51.2	-6.3
Mitchelson, A. Con	12,154	34.8	+5.8
Guest, J. LD	4,076	11.7	+1.2
Paisley, C. LCA	554	1.6	
Wilcox, P. SA	269	0.8	
Lab majority	5,702		16.33%
Electorate	58,811		
Total Vote	34,909		59.36

*Member of last parliament
Lab Hold (6.0% from Lab to Con)

CARMARTHEN EAST AND DINEFWR

		%	+/- %
Price, A. Pl C	16,130	42.4	+7.7
*Williams, A. Lab	13,540	35.6	-7.3
Thomas, D. Con	4,912	12.9	+0.9
Evans, D. LD	2,815	7.4	-0.2
Squires, M. UKIP	656	1.7	
Pl C majority	2,590		6.81%
Electorate	54,035		
Total Vote	38,053		70.42

*Member of last parliament
Pl C Gain (7.5% from Lab to Pl C)

CARMARTHEN WEST AND SOUTH PEMBROKESHIRE

		%	+/- %
*Ainger, N. Lab	15,349	41.6	-7.6
Wilson, R. Con	10,811	29.3	+2.7
Griffiths, L. Pl C	6,893	18.7	+6.0
Jeremy, W. LD	3,248	8.8	+0.6
Phillips, I. UKIP	537	1.5	
Turner, N. DCSP	78	0.2	
Lab majority	4,538		12.29%
Electorate	56,518		
Total Vote	36,916		65.32

*Member of last parliament
Lab Hold (5.1% from Lab to Con)

CARRICK, CUMNOCK AND DOON VALLEY

		%	+/- %
*Foulkes, G. Lab	22,174	55.3	-4.5
Millar, G. Con	7,318	18.2	+1.3
Wilson, T. SNP	6,258	15.6	-1.1
Rodger, A. LD	2,932	7.3	+2.0
McFarlane, A. SSP	1,058	2.6	
McDaid, J. SLP	367	0.9	
Lab majority	14,856		37.04%
Electorate	64,919		
Total Vote	40,107		61.78

*Member of last parliament
Lab Hold (2.9% from Lab to Con)

CARSHALTON AND WALLINGTON

		%	+/- %
*Brake, T. LD	18,289	45.0	+6.8
Andrew, K. Con	13,742	33.8	+0.3
Cooper, M. Lab	7,466	18.4	-5.5
Dixon, S. Green	614	1.5	-0.7
Haley, M. UKIP	501	1.2	-0.8
LD majority	4,547		11.20%
Electorate	67,339		
Total Vote	40,612		60.31

*Member of last parliament
LD Hold (3.3% from Con to LD)

CASTLE POINT

		%	+/- %
Spink, R. Con	17,738	44.6	+4.5
*Butler, C. Lab	16,753	42.1	-0.3
Boulton, P. LD	3,116	7.8	-1.4
Hurrell, R. UKIP	1,273	3.2	
Roberts, D. Ind	663	1.7	
Searle, N. TP	223	0.6	
Con majority	985		2.48%
Electorate	68,108		
Total Vote	39,766		58.39

*Member of last parliament
Con Gain (2.4% from Lab to Con)

CENTRAL FIFE – see under Fife

CENTRAL SUFFOLK AND NORTH IPSWICH – see under Suffolk

CEREDIGION

		%	+/- %
*Thomas, S. Pl C	13,241	38.3	-3.4
Williams, M. LD	9,297	26.9	+10.4
Davies, P. Con	6,730	19.4	+4.6
Grace, D. Lab	5,338	15.4	-8.9
Pl C majority	3,944		11.40%
Electorate	56,125		
Total Vote	34,606		61.66

*Member of last parliament
Pl C Hold (6.9% from Pl C to LD)

CHARNWOOD

		%	+/- %
*Dorrell, S. Con	23,283	48.2	+1.8
Sheahan, S. Lab	15,544	32.2	-3.8
King, S. LD	7,835	16.2	+3.4
Bye, J. UKIP	1,603	3.3	
Con majority	7,739		16.03%
Electorate	75,073		
Total Vote	48,265		64.29

*Member of last parliament
Con Hold (2.8% from Lab to Con)

CHATHAM AND AYLESFORD

		%	+/- %
*Shaw, J. Lab	19,180	48.3	+5.2
Holden, S. Con	14,840	37.3	-0.1
Lettington, D. LD	4,705	11.8	-3.2
Knopp, G. UKIP	1,010	2.5	+1.5
Lab majority	4,340		10.92%
Electorate	69,759		
Total Vote	39,735		56.96

*Member of last parliament
Lab Hold (2.6% from Con to Lab)

CHEADLE

		%	+/- %
Calton, P. LD	18,477	42.4	+4.7
*Day, S. Con	18,444	42.3	-1.4
Dawber, H. Lab	6,086	14.0	-1.8
Cavanagh, V. UKIP	599	1.4	
LD majority	33		0.08%
Electorate	69,001		
Total Vote	43,606		63.20

*Member of last parliament
LD Gain (3.1% from Con to LD)

CHELMSFORD WEST

		%	+/- %
*Burns, S. Con	20,446	42.5	+1.9
Longden, A. Lab	14,185	29.5	+3.1
Robinson, S. LD	11,197	23.3	-5.9
Burgess, E. Green	837	1.7	+1.0
Wedon, K. UKIP	785	1.6	+1.1
Philbin, H. LCA	693	1.4	
Con majority	6,261		13.01%
Electorate	78,073		
Total Vote	48,143		61.66

*Member of last parliament
Con Hold (0.6% from Con to Lab)

CHELTENHAM

		%	+/- %
*Jones, N. LD	19,970	47.7	-1.7
Garnham, R. Con	14,715	35.2	-1.1
Erlam, A. Lab	5,041	12.0	+1.9
Bessant, K. Green	735	1.8	
Hanks, D. Loony	513	1.2	+0.5
Carver, J. UKIP	482	1.2	+0.6
Gates, A. ProLife	272	0.7	+0.2
Everest, R. Ind	107	0.3	
LD majority	5,255		12.56%
Electorate	67,563		
Total Vote	41,835		61.92

*Member of last parliament
LD Hold (0.3% from LD to Con)

CHESHAM AND AMERSHAM

		%	+/- %
*Gillan, C. Con	22,867	50.5	+0.1
Ford, J. LD	10,985	24.3	+0.4
Hulme, K. Lab	8,497	18.8	-0.9
Harvey, I. UKIP	1,367	3.0	+1.8
Wilkins, N. Green	1,114	2.5	
Duval, G. ProLife	453	1.0	

Con majority	11,882		26.24%
Electorate	70,021		
Total Vote	45,283		64.67

*Member of last parliament
Con Hold (0.2% from Con to LD)

CITY OF CHESTER

		%	+/- %
*Russell, C. Lab	21,760	48.5	-4.5
Jones, D. Con	14,866	33.1	-1.1
Dawson, T. LD	6,589	14.7	+5.2
Weddell, A. UKIP	899	2.0	
Rogers, G. Ind	763	1.7	
Lab majority	6,894		15.36%
Electorate	70,382		
Total Vote	44,877		63.76

*Member of last parliament
Lab Hold (1.7% from Lab to Con)

CHESTERFIELD

		%	+/- %
Holmes, P. LD	21,249	47.8	+8.3
Race, R. Lab	18,663	42.0	-8.8
Hitchcock, S. Con	3,613	8.1	-1.1
Robinson, J. SA	437	1.0	
Harrison, W. SLP	295	0.7	
Rawson, C. Ind	184	0.4	
LD majority	2,586		5.82%
Electorate	73,252		
Total Vote	44,441		60.67

LD Gain (8.5% from Lab to LD)

CHICHESTER

		%	+/- %
*Tyrie, A. Con	23,320	47.0	+0.6
Ravenscroft, L. LD	11,965	24.1	-4.8
Barlow, C. Lab	10,627	21.4	+4.2
Denny, D. UKIP	2,380	4.8	+3.4
Graham, G. Green	1,292	2.6	
Con majority	11,355		22.90%
Electorate	77,703		
Total Vote	49,584		63.81

*Member of last parliament
Con Hold (2.7% from LD to Con)

CHINGFORD AND WOODFORD GREEN

		%	+/- %
*Duncan Smith, I. Con	17,834	48.2	+0.7
Webb, J. Lab	12,347	33.4	-1.2
Beanse, J. LD	5,739	15.5	0.0
Griffin, J. BNP	1,062	2.9	+0.5
Con majority	5,487		14.84%
Electorate	63,252		
Total Vote	36,982		58.47

*Member of last parliament
Con Hold (1.0% from Lab to Con)

CHIPPING BARNET

		%	+/- %
*Chapman, S. Con	19,702	46.4	+3.4
Welfare, D. Lab	17,001	40.0	-0.9
Hooker, S. LD	5,753	13.6	+1.2
Con majority	2,701		6.36%
Electorate	70,217		
Total Vote	42,456		60.46

*Member of last parliament
Con Hold (2.1% from Lab to Con)

CHORLEY

		%	+/- %
*Hoyle, L. Lab	25,088	52.3	-0.7
Booth, P. Con	16,644	34.7	-1.2
Fenn, S. LD	5,372	11.2	+2.7
Frost, J. UKIP	848	1.8	

Lab majority	8,444		17.61%
Electorate	77,036		
Total Vote	47,952		62.25

*Member of last parliament
Lab Hold (0.3% from Con to Lab)

CHRISTCHURCH		%	+/- %
*Chope, C. Con	27,306	55.1	+8.7
Webb, D. LD	13,762	27.8	-14.8
Begg, J. Lab	7,506	15.1	+8.2
Strange, M. UKIP	993	2.0	+0.9
Con majority	13,544		27.32%
Electorate	73,447		
Total Vote	49,567		67.49

*Member of last parliament
Con Hold (11.7% from LD to Con)

CITIES OF LONDON AND WESTMINSTER – see under London

CITY OF CHESTER – see under Chester

CITY OF DURHAM – see under Durham

CITY OF YORK – see under York

CLEETHORPES		%	+/- %
*McIsaac, S. Lab	21,032	49.6	-2.0
Howd, S. Con	15,412	36.3	+2.9
Smith, G. LD	5,080	12.0	+0.6
Hatton, J. UKIP	894	2.1	
Lab majority	5,620		13.25%
Electorate	68,398		
Total Vote	42,418		62.02

*Member of last parliament
Lab Hold (2.5% from Lab to Con)

CLWYD SOUTH		%	+/- %
*Jones, M. Lab	17,217	51.4	-6.7
Biggins, T. Con	8,319	24.8	+1.8
Edwards, D. Pl C	3,982	11.9	+5.5
Griffiths, D. LD	3,426	10.2	+0.9
Theunissen, E. UKIP	552	1.6	
Lab majority	8,898		26.56%
Electorate	53,680		
Total Vote	33,496		62.40

*Member of last parliament
Lab Hold (4.3% from Lab to Con)

VALE OF CLWYD		%	+/- %
*Ruane, C. Lab	16,179	50.0	-2.7
Murphy, B. Con	10,418	32.2	+2.4
Rees, G. LD	3,058	9.5	+0.7
Williams, J. Pl C	2,300	7.1	+1.2
Campbell, W. UKIP	391	1.2	+0.5
Lab majority	5,761		17.81%
Electorate	50,842		
Total Vote	32,346		63.62

*Member of last parliament
Lab Hold (2.5% from Lab to Con)

CLWYD WEST		%	+/- %
*Thomas, G. Lab	13,426	38.8	+1.7
James, J. Con	12,311	35.6	+3.1
Williams, E. Pl C	4,453	12.9	-0.6
Feeley, B. LD	3,934	11.4	-1.4
Guest, M. UKIP	476	1.4	

Lab majority	1,115		3.22%
Electorate	53,886		
Total Vote	34,600		64.2

*Member of last parliament
Lab Hold (0.7% from Lab to Con)

CLYDEBANK AND MILNGAVIE		%	+/- %
*Worthington, T. Lab	17,249	53.1	-2.1
Yuill, J. SNP	6,525	20.1	-1.1
Ackland, R. LD	3,909	12.0	+1.6
Jardine, K. Con	3,514	10.8	-1.7
Brennan, D. SSP	1,294	4.0	
Lab majority	10,724		33.01%
Electorate	51,979		
Total Vote	32,491		62.51

*Member of last parliament
Lab Hold (0.5% from Lab to SNP)

CLYDESDALE		%	+/- %
*Hood, J. Lab	17,822	46.6	-5.9
Wright, J. SNP	10,028	26.2	+4.1
Newton, K. Con	5,034	13.2	-3.1
Craig, M. LD	4,111	10.8	+2.4
Cockshott, P. SSP	974	2.5	
MacKay, D. UKIP	253	0.7	
Lab majority	7,794		20.39%
Electorate	64,423		
Total Vote	38,222		59.33

*Member of last parliament
Lab Hold (5.0% from Lab to SNP)

COATBRIDGE AND CHRYSTON		%	+/- %
*Clarke, T. Lab	19,807	65.3	-3.0
Kearney, P. SNP	4,493	14.8	-2.2
Tough, A. LD	2,293	7.6	+2.1
Ross-Taylor, P. Con	2,171	7.2	-1.4
Sheridan, L. SSP	1,547	5.1	
Lab majority	15,314		50.52%
Electorate	52,178		
Total Vote	30,311		58.09

*Member of last parliament
Lab Hold (0.4% from Lab to SNP)

COLCHESTER		%	+/- %
*Russell, B. LD	18,627	42.6	+8.2
Bentley, K. Con	13,074	29.9	-1.5
Fegan, C. Lab	10,925	25.0	-5.6
Lord, R. UKIP	631	1.4	
Overy-Owen, L. TGP	479	1.1	
LD majority	5,553		12.70%
Electorate	77,958		
Total Vote	43,736		56.10

*Member of last parliament
LD Hold (4.8% from Con to LD)

COLNE VALLEY		%	+/- %
*Mountford, K. Lab	18,967	40.4	-0.9
Davies, P. Con	14,328	30.5	-2.2
Beever, G. LD	11,694	24.9	+2.3
Plunkett, R. Green	1,081	2.3	+1.4
Quarmby, A. UKIP	917	2.0	+1.1
Lab majority	4,639		9.87%
Electorate	74,192		
Total Vote	46,987		63.33

*Member of last parliament
Lab Hold (0.6% from Con to Lab)

CONGLETON

		%	+/- %
*Winterton, A. Con	20,872	46.3	+5.1
Flanagan, J. Lab	13,738	30.5	+2.9
Lloyd-Griffiths, D. LD	9,719	21.6	-8.2
Young, W. UKIP	754	1.7	+0.2
Con majority	7,134		15.82%
Electorate	71,975		
Total Vote	45,083		62.64

*Member of last parliament
Con Hold (1.1% from Lab to Con)

CONWY

		%	+/- %
*Williams, B. Lab	14,366	41.8	+6.8
Logan, D. Con	8,147	23.7	-0.6
Macdonald, V. LD	5,800	16.9	-14.3
Owen, A. Pl C	5,665	16.5	+9.6
Barham, A. UKIP	388	1.1	
Lab majority	6,219		18.10%
Electorate	54,637		
Total Vote	34,366		62.9

*Member of last parliament
Lab Hold (3.7% from Con to Lab)

COPELAND

		%	+/- %
*Cunningham, J. Lab	17,991	51.8	-6.4
Graham, M. Con	13,027	37.5	+8.3
Gayler, M. LD	3,732	10.7	+1.5
Lab majority	4,964		14.28%
Electorate	53,526		
Total Vote	34,750		64.92

*Member of last parliament
Lab Hold (7.3% from Lab to Con)

CORBY

		%	+/- %
*Hope, P. Lab	23,283	49.3	-6.1
Griffith, A. Con	17,583	37.2	+3.8
Scudder, K. LD	4,751	10.1	+2.6
Gillman, I. UKIP	855	1.8	+0.9
Dickson, A. SLP	750	1.6	
Lab majority	5,700		12.07%
Electorate	72,594		
Total Vote	47,222		65.05

*Member of last parliament
Lab Hold (5.0% from Lab to Con)

NORTH CORNWALL

		%	+/- %
*Tyler, P. LD	28,082	52.0	-1.1
Weller, J. Con	18,250	33.8	+4.3
Goodman, M. Lab	5,257	9.7	+0.3
Protz, S. UKIP	2,394	4.4	
LD majority	9,832		18.21%
Electorate	84,090		
Total Vote	53,983		64.20

*Member of last parliament
LD Hold (2.7% from LD to Con)

SOUTH EAST CORNWALL

		%	+/- %
*Breed, C. LD	23,756	45.9	-1.2
Gray, A. Con	18,381	35.5	-0.3
Stevens, W. Lab	6,429	12.4	-0.4
Palmer, G. UKIP	1,978	3.8	+1.3
George, K. Meb Ker	1,209	2.3	+1.3
LD majority	5,375		10.39%
Electorate	79,090		
Total Vote	51,753		65.44

*Member of last parliament
LD Hold (0.4% from LD to Con)

COTSWOLD

		%	+/- %
*Clifton-Brown, G. Con	23,133	50.3	+4.0
Lawrence, A. LD	11,150	24.2	+1.3
Wilkins, R. Lab	10,383	22.6	-0.1
Stopps, J. UKIP	1,315	2.9	
Con majority	11,983		26.06%
Electorate	68,140		
Total Vote	45,981		67.48

*Member of last parliament
Con Hold (1.3% from LD to Con)

COVENTRY NORTH EAST

		%	+/- %
*Ainsworth, B. Lab	22,739	61.0	-5.2
Bell, G. Con	6,998	18.8	-0.6
Sewards, G. LD	4,163	11.2	+3.1
Nellist, D. SA	2,638	7.1	
Sheppard, E. BNP	737	2.0	
Lab majority	15,751		42.27%
Electorate	73,998		
Total Vote	37,265		50.36

*Member of last parliament
Lab Hold (2.3% from Lab to Con)

COVENTRY NORTH WEST

		%	+/- %
*Robinson, G. Lab	21,892	51.4	-5.4
Fairburn, A. Con	11,018	25.9	-0.4
Penlington, N. LD	5,832	13.7	+3.2
Oddy, C. Ind	3,159	7.4	
Benson, M. UKIP	650	1.5	
Lab majority	10,874		25.56%
Electorate	76,652		
Total Vote	42,551		55.51

*Member of last parliament
Lab Hold (2.5% from Lab to Con)

COVENTRY SOUTH

		%	+/- %
*Cunningham, J. Lab	20,125	50.2	-0.7
Wheeler, H. Con	11,846	29.5	+0.5
McKee, V. LD	5,672	14.1	+4.9
Windsor, R. SA	1,475	3.7	
Rogers, I. Ind	564	1.4	
Logan, T. SLP	414	1.0	
Lab majority	8,279		20.65%
Electorate	72,527		
Total Vote	40,096		55.28

*Member of last parliament
Lab Hold (0.6% from Lab to Con)

CRAWLEY

		%	+/- %
*Moffatt, L. Lab	19,488	49.3	-5.7
Smith, H. Con	12,718	32.2	+0.4
Seekings, L. LD	5,009	12.7	+4.5
Galloway, B. UKIP	1,137	2.9	+2.2
Staniford, C. Loony	383	1.0	
Khan, A. JP	271	0.7	+0.2
Stewart, K. SLP	260	0.7	
Hirsch, M. SA	251	0.6	
Lab majority	6,770		17.13%
Electorate	71,626		
Total Vote	39,517		55.17

*Member of last parliament
Lab Hold (3.0% from Lab to Con)

CREWE AND NANTWICH

		%	+/- %
*Dunwoody, G. Lab	22,556	54.3	-3.9
Potter, D. Con	12,650	30.4	+3.5
Cannon, D. LD	5,595	13.5	+1.7
Croston, R. UKIP	746	1.8	

Lab majority	9,906		23.84%
Electorate	69,040		
Total Vote	41,547		60.18

*Member of last parliament
Lab Hold (3.7% from Lab to Con)

CROSBY

		%	+/- %
*Curtis-Thomas, C. Lab	20,327	55.1	+4.1
Collinson, R. Con	11,974	32.5	-2.3
Drake, T. LD	4,084	11.1	-0.4
Holt, M. SLP	481	1.3	
Lab majority	8,353		22.66%
Electorate	57,190		
Total Vote	36,866		64.46

*Member of last parliament
Lab Hold (3.2% from Con to Lab)

CROYDON CENTRAL

		%	+/- %
*Davies, G. Lab	21,643	47.2	+1.6
Congdon, D. Con	17,659	38.5	-0.1
Booth, P. LD	5,156	11.2	+0.4
Feisenberger, J. UKIP	545	1.2	+0.7
Miller, L. BNP	449	1.0	
Cartwright, J. Loony	408	0.9	
Lab majority	3,984		8.69%
Electorate	77,568		
Total Vote	45,860		59.12

*Member of last parliament
Lab Hold (0.9% from Con to Lab)

CROYDON NORTH

		%	+/- %
*Wicks, M. Lab	26,610	63.5	+1.4
Allison, S. Con	9,752	23.3	-3.9
Lawman, S. LD	4,375	10.4	+2.7
Smith, A. UKIP	606	1.4	+0.7
Madgwick, D. SA	539	1.3	
Lab majority	16,858		40.25%
Electorate	76,575		
Total Vote	41,882		54.69

*Member of last parliament
Lab Hold (2.6% from Con to Lab)

CROYDON SOUTH

		%	+/- %
*Ottaway, R. Con	22,169	49.2	+1.9
Ryan, G. Lab	13,472	29.9	+4.6
Gallop, A. LD	8,226	18.3	-2.9
Garner, K. UKIP	998	2.2	+1.6
Samuel, M. Choice	195	0.4	+0.3
Con majority	8,697		19.30%
Electorate	73,372		
Total Vote	45,060		61.41

*Member of last parliament
Con Hold (1.4% from Con to Lab)

CUMBERNAULD AND KILSYTH

		%	+/- %
*McKenna, R. Lab	16,144	54.4	-4.3
McGlashan, D. SNP	8,624	29.0	+1.2
O'Donnell, J. LD	1,934	6.5	+2.7
Ross, A. Con	1,460	4.9	-1.9
McEwan, K. SSP	1,287	4.3	+3.3
Taylor, T. SFRP	250	0.8	
Lab majority	7,520		25.32%
Electorate	49,739		
Total Vote	29,699		59.71

*Member of last parliament
Lab Hold (2.9% from Lab to SNP)

CUNNINGHAME NORTH

		%	+/- %
*Wilson, B. Lab	15,571	46.0	-4.2
Martin, C. SNP	7,173	21.2	+2.8
Wilkinson, R. Con	6,666	19.7	-3.7
Chmiel, R. LD	3,060	9.0	+3.5
Scott, S. SSP	964	2.9	
McDaid, L. SLP	382	1.1	-0.1
Lab majority	8,398		24.83%
Electorate	54,993		
Total Vote	33,816		61.49

*Member of last parliament
Lab Hold (3.5% from Lab to SNP)

CUNNINGHAME SOUTH

		%	+/- %
*Donohoe, B. Lab	16,424	58.4	-4.3
Kidd, B. SNP	5,194	18.5	-2.3
Paterson, P. Con	2,782	9.9	-0.2
Boyd, J. LD	2,094	7.4	+2.9
Byrne, R. SSP	1,233	4.4	
Cochrane, R. SLP	382	1.4	-0.0
Lab majority	11,230		39.95%
Electorate	49,982		
Total Vote	28,109		56.24

*Member of last parliament
Lab Hold (1.0% from Lab to SNP)

CYNON VALLEY

		%	+/- %
*Clwyd, A. Lab	17,685	65.6	-4.1
Cornelius, S. Pl C	4,687	17.4	+6.8
Parry, I. LD	2,541	9.4	-0.9
Waters, J. Con	2,045	7.6	+0.8
Lab majority	12,998		48.22%
Electorate	48,629		
Total Vote	26,958		55.44

*Member of last parliament
Lab Hold (5.4% from Lab to Pl C)

DAGENHAM

		%	+/- %
Cruddas, J. Lab	15,784	57.2	-8.5
White, M. Con	7,091	25.7	+7.2
Gee-Turner, A. LD	2,820	10.2	+2.7
Hill, D. BNP	1,378	5.0	+2.5
Hamilton, B. SA	262	0.9	
Siggins, R. SLP	245	0.9	
Lab majority	8,693		31.52%
Electorate	59,340		
Total Vote	27,580		46.48

Lab Hold (7.8% from Lab to Con)

DARLINGTON

		%	+/- %
*Milburn, A. Lab	22,479	56.3	-5.2
Richmond, T. Con	12,095	30.3	+2.0
Adamson, R. LD	4,358	10.9	+3.7
Docherty, A. SA	469	1.2	
Platt, C. Ind	269	0.7	
Rose, A. SLP	229	0.6	
Lab majority	10,384		26.03%
Electorate	64,354		
Total Vote	39,899		62.00

*Member of last parliament
Lab Hold (3.6% from Lab to Con)

DARTFORD

		%	+/- %
*Stoate, H. Lab	21,466	48.0	-0.6
Dunn, B. Con	18,160	40.6	+0.3
Morgan, G. LD	3,781	8.5	-0.9
Croucher, M. UKIP	989	2.2	
Davenport, K. FDP	344	0.8	+0.2
Lab majority	3,306		7.39%
Electorate	71,758		
Total Vote	44,740		62.35

*Member of last parliament
Lab Hold (0.5% from Lab to Con)

DAVENTRY

		%	+/- %
*Boswell, T. Con	27,911	49.2	+2.9
Quigley, K. Lab	18,262	32.2	-2.2
Calder, J. LD	9,130	16.1	+1.2
Baden, P. UKIP	1,381	2.4	+1.7
Con majority	9,649		17.02%
Electorate	86,510		
Total Vote	56,684		65.52

*Member of last parliament
Con Hold (2.5% from Lab to Con)

DELYN

		%	+/- %
*Hanson, D. Lab	17,825	51.5	-5.7
Brierley, P. Con	9,220	26.6	+0.6
Jones, T. LD	5,329	15.4	+5.2
Rowlinson, P. Pl C	2,262	6.5	+2.7
Lab majority	8,605		24.84%
Electorate	54,732		
Total Vote	34,636		63.28

*Member of last parliament
Lab Hold (3.2% from Lab to Con)

DENTON AND REDDISH

		%	+/- %
*Bennett, A. Lab	21,913	65.2	-0.2
Newman, P. Con	6,583	19.6	-1.7
Fletcher, R. LD	4,152	12.4	-0.9
Cadwallender, A. UKIP	945	2.8	
Lab majority	15,330		45.63%
Electorate	69,236		
Total Vote	33,593		48.52

*Member of last parliament
Lab Hold (0.8% from Con to Lab)

DERBY NORTH

		%	+/- %
*Laxton, B. Lab	22,415	50.9	-2.3
Holden, B. Con	15,433	35.0	+0.8
Charlesworth, B. LD	6,206	14.1	+5.1
Lab majority	6,982		15.85%
Electorate	75,926		
Total Vote	44,054		58.02

*Member of last parliament
Lab Hold (1.5% from Lab to Con)

DERBY SOUTH

		%	+/- %
*Beckett, M. Lab	24,310	56.4	+0.2
Spencer, S. Con	10,455	24.3	-0.9
Hanson, A. LD	8,310	19.3	+4.9
Lab majority	13,855		32.16%
Electorate	76,708		
Total Vote	43,075		56.15

*Member of last parliament
Lab Hold (0.5% from Con to Lab)

NORTH EAST DERBYSHIRE

		%	+/- %
*Barnes, H. Lab	23,437	55.6	-4.8
Hollingsworth, J. Con	11,179	26.5	+1.3
Higginbottom, M. LD	7,508	17.8	+3.5
Lab majority	12,258		29.10%
Electorate	71,527		
Total Vote	42,124		58.89

*Member of last parliament
Lab Hold (3.1% from Lab to Con)

SOUTH DERBYSHIRE

		%	+/- %
*Todd, M. Lab	26,338	50.7	-3.8
Hakewill, J. Con	18,487	35.6	+4.3
Eagling, R. LD	5,233	10.1	+1.1
Blunt, J. UKIP	1,074	2.1	+1.0
Liversuch, P. SLP	564	1.1	
Taylor, J. Ind	249	0.5	
Lab majority	7,851		15.11%
Electorate	81,217		
Total Vote	51,945		63.96

*Member of last parliament
Lab Hold (4.1% from Lab to Con)

WEST DERBYSHIRE

		%	+/- %
*McLoughlin, P. Con	24,280	48.0	+5.9
Clamp, S. Lab	16,910	33.4	-0.1
Beckett, J. LD	7,922	15.7	-1.8
Bavester, S. UKIP	672	1.3	+0.5
Delves, N. Loony	472	0.9	+0.4
Goodall, R. Ind	333	0.7	
Con majority	7,370		14.57%
Electorate	74,651		
Total Vote	50,589		67.77

*Member of last parliament
Con Hold (3.0% from Lab to Con)

DEVIZES

		%	+/- %
*Ancram, M. Con	25,159	47.2	+4.4
Thorpe, J. Lab	13,263	24.9	+0.7
Frances, H. LD	11,756	22.1	-4.5
Wood, A. UKIP	1,521	2.9	+1.8
Kennedy, L. Ind	1,078	2.0	
Potter, V. Loony	472	0.9	
Con majority	11,896		22.34%
Electorate	82,925		
Total Vote	53,249		64.21

*Member of last parliament
Con Hold (1.9% from Lab to Con)

EAST DEVON

		%	+/- %
Swire, H. Con	22,681	47.4	+4.0
Dumper, T. LD	14,486	30.3	+1.2
Starr, P. Lab	7,974	16.7	-1.0
Wilson, D. UKIP	2,696	5.6	+4.8
Con majority	8,195		17.13%
Electorate	69,542		
Total Vote	47,837		68.79

Con Hold (1.4% from LD to Con)

NORTH DEVON

		%	+/- %
*Harvey, N. LD	21,784	44.2	-6.5
Allen, C. Con	18,800	38.2	-1.3
Gale, V. Lab	4,995	10.1	+0.4
Knapman, R. UKIP	2,484	5.0	
Bown, A. Green	1,191	2.4	
LD majority	2,984		6.06%
Electorate	72,100		
Total Vote	49,254		68.31

*Member of last parliament
LD Hold (2.6% from LD to Con)

SOUTH WEST DEVON

		%	+/- %
*Streeter, G. Con	21,970	46.8	+3.9
Mavin, C. Lab	14,826	31.6	+2.7
Hutty, P. LD	8,616	18.4	-5.4
Bullock, R. UKIP	1,492	3.2	+2.3
Con majority	7,144		15.23%
Electorate	70,922		
Total Vote	46,904		66.13

*Member of last parliament
Con Hold (0.6% from Lab to Con)

TORRIDGE AND WEST DEVON

		%	+/- %
*Burnett, J. LD	23,474	42.2	+0.3
Cox, G. Con	22,280	40.0	+1.5
Brenton, D. Lab	5,959	10.7	-1.7
Edwards, R. UKIP	2,674	4.8	+1.7
Quinn, M. Green	1,297	2.3	
LD majority	1,194		2.14%
Electorate	78,976		
Total Vote	55,684		70.51

*Member of last parliament
LD Hold (0.6% from LD to Con)

DEWSBURY

		%	+/- %
*Taylor, A. Lab	18,524	50.5	+1.1
Cole, R. Con	11,075	30.2	+0.1
Cuthbertson, I. LD	4,382	12.0	+1.7
Smith, R. BNP	1,632	4.5	-0.7
Smithson, B. Green	560	1.5	+0.6
Peace, D. UKIP	478	1.3	
Lab majority	7,449		20.32%
Electorate	62,345		
Total Vote	36,651		58.79

*Member of last parliament
Lab Hold (0.5% from Con to Lab)

DON VALLEY

		%	+/- %
*Flint, C. Lab	20,009	54.6	-3.6
Browne, J. Con	10,489	28.6	+4.0
Smith, P. LD	4,089	11.2	+1.4
Wilde, T. Ind	800	2.2	
Cooper, D. UKIP	777	2.1	
Ball, N. SLP	466	1.3	-1.1
Lab majority	9,520		25.99%
Electorate	66,787		
Total Vote	36,630		54.85

*Member of last parliament
Lab Hold (3.8% from Lab to Con)

DONCASTER CENTRAL

		%	+/- %
*Winterton, R. Lab	20,034	59.1	-3.0
Meggitt, G. Con	8,035	23.7	+2.7
Southcombe, M. LD	4,390	12.9	+3.5
Gordon, D. UKIP	926	2.7	+1.7
Terry, J. SA	517	1.5	
Lab majority	11,999		33.39%
Electorate	65,690		
Total Vote	33,902		51.61

*Member of last parliament
Lab Hold (2.9% from Lab to Con)

DONCASTER NORTH

		%	+/- %
*Hughes, K. Lab	19,788	63.1	-6.7
Kapoor, A. Con	4,601	14.7	-0.1
Ross, C. LD	3,323	10.6	+2.1
Williams, M. Ind	2,926	9.3	
Wallis, J. UKIP	725	2.3	

Lab majority	15,187		48.42%
Electorate	62,124		
Total Vote	31,363		50.48

*Member of last parliament
Lab Hold (3.3% from Lab to Con)

MID DORSET AND POOLE NORTH

		%	+/- %
Brooke, A. LD	18,358	42.0	+2.7
*Fraser, C. Con	17,974	41.1	+0.4
Selby Bennett, J. Lab	6,765	15.5	-0.3
Mager, J. UKIP	621	1.4	
LD majority	384		0.88%
Electorate	66,675		
Total Vote	43,718		65.57

*Member of last parliament
LD Gain (1.1% from Con to LD)

NORTH DORSET

		%	+/- %
*Walter, R. Con	22,314	46.7	+2.4
Gasson, E. LD	18,517	38.7	-0.4
Wareham, M. Lab	5,334	11.2	+0.9
Jenkins, P. UKIP	1,019	2.1	+0.6
Duthie, J. LEDP	391	0.8	
Bone, C. Ind	246	0.5	
Con majority	3,797		7.94%
Electorate	71,412		
Total Vote	47,821		66.96

*Member of last parliament
Con Hold (1.4% from LD to Con)

SOUTH DORSET

		%	+/- %
Knight, J. Lab	19,027	42.0	+6.0
*Bruce, I. Con	18,874	41.6	+5.5
Canning, A. LD	6,531	14.4	-5.8
Moss, L. UKIP	913	2.0	+0.3
Lab majority	153		0.34%
Electorate	68,115		
Total Vote	45,345		66.57

*Member of last parliament
Lab Gain (0.2% from Con to Lab)

WEST DORSET

		%	+/- %
*Letwin, O. Con	22,126	44.6	+3.5
Green, S. LD	20,712	41.8	+4.1
Hyde, R. Lab	6,733	13.6	-4.1
Con majority	1,414		2.85%
Electorate	71,291		
Total Vote	49,571		69.53

*Member of last parliament
Con Hold (0.3% from Con to LD)

DOVER

		%	+/- %
*Prosser, G. Lab	21,943	48.8	-5.7
Watkins, P. Con	16,744	37.2	+4.4
Hook, A. LD	5,131	11.4	+3.5
Speakman, L. UKIP	1,142	2.5	+1.7
Lab majority	5,199		11.56%
Electorate	68,994		
Total Vote	44,960		65.17

*Member of last parliament
Lab Hold (5.0% from Lab to Con)

NORTH DOWN

		%	+/- %
Hermon, S. UUP	20,833	56.0	+24.9
*McCartney, R. UKU	13,509	36.3	+1.3
Farrell, M. SDLP	1,275	3.4	-1.0
Robertson, J. Con	815	2.2	-2.8
Carter, C. Ind	444	1.2	
McConvey, E. SF	313	0.8	
UUP majority	7,324		19.69%
Electorate	63,212		
Total Vote	37,189		50.58

*Member of last parliament
UUP Gain (11.8% from UKU to UUP)

SOUTH DOWN

		%	+/- %
*McGrady, E. SDLP	24,136	46.3	-6.6
Murphy, M. SF	10,278	19.7	+9.4
Nesbitt, D. UUP	9,173	17.6	-15.2
Wells, J. DUP	7,802	15.0	
Campbell, B. Alliance	685	1.3	-2.1
SDLP majority	13,858		26.61%
Electorate	73,519		
Total Vote	52,074		70.83

*Member of last parliament
SDLP Hold (8.0% from SDLP to SF)

DUDLEY NORTH

		%	+/- %
*Cranston, R. Lab	20,095	52.1	+0.9
Griffiths, A. Con	13,295	34.5	+3.1
Burt, R. LD	3,352	8.7	+0.5
Darby, S. BNP	1,822	4.7	
Lab majority	6,800		17.63%
Electorate	68,964		
Total Vote	38,564		55.92

*Member of last parliament
Lab Hold (1.1% from Lab to Con)

DUDLEY SOUTH

		%	+/- %
*Pearson, I. Lab	18,109	49.8	-6.8
Sugarman, J. Con	11,292	31.1	+1.6
Burt, L. LD	5,421	14.9	+4.0
Westwood, J. UKIP	859	2.4	
Thompson, A. SA	663	1.8	
Lab majority	6,817		18.76%
Electorate	65,578		
Total Vote	36,344		55.42

*Member of last parliament
Lab Hold (4.2% from Lab to Con)

DULWICH AND WEST NORWOOD

		%	+/- %
*Jowell, T. Lab	20,999	54.9	-6.1
Vineall, N. Con	8,689	22.7	-1.5
Pidgeon, C. LD	5,805	15.2	+4.4
Jones, J. Green	1,914	5.0	
Kelly, B. SA	839	2.2	
Lab majority	12,310		32.19%
Electorate	71,621		
Total Vote	38,246		53.40

*Member of last parliament
Lab Hold (2.3% from Lab to Con)

DUMBARTON

		%	+/- %
*McFall, J. Lab	16,151	47.5	-2.1
Robertson, I. SNP	6,576	19.3	-3.9
Thompson, E. LD	5,265	15.5	+7.9
Ramsay, P. Con	4,648	13.7	-4.0
Robertson, L. SSP	1,354	4.0	+3.3

Lab majority	9,575		28.17%
Electorate	55,643		
Total Vote	33,994		61.09

*Member of last parliament
Lab Hold (0.8% from SNP to Lab)

DUMFRIES

		%	+/- %
*Brown, R. Lab	20,830	48.9	+1.4
Charteris, J. Con	11,996	28.2	+0.1
Ross Scott, J. LD	4,955	11.6	+0.6
Fisher, G. SNP	4,103	9.6	-2.4
Dennis, J. SSP	702	1.6	
Lab majority	8,834		20.74%
Electorate	63,571		
Total Vote	42,586		66.99

*Member of last parliament
Lab Hold (0.6% from Con to Lab)

DUNDEE EAST

		%	+/- %
Luke, I. Lab	14,635	45.2	-5.9
Hosie, S. SNP	10,159	31.4	+4.9
Donnelly, A. Con	3,900	12.0	-3.7
Lawrie, R. LD	2,784	8.6	+4.5
Duke, H. SSP	879	2.7	+2.1
Lab majority	4,466		13.80%
Electorate	56,535		
Total Vote	32,367		57.25

Lab Hold (5.5% from Lab to SNP)

DUNDEE WEST

		%	+/- %
*Ross, E. Lab	14,787	50.6	-3.2
Archer, G. SNP	7,987	27.3	+4.1
Hail, I. Con	2,656	9.1	-4.1
Dick, E. LD	2,620	9.0	+1.3
McFarlane, J. SSP	1,192	4.1	+3.0
Lab majority	6,800		23.25%
Electorate	53,760		
Total Vote	29,242		54.39

*Member of last parliament
Lab Hold (3.8% from Lab to SNP)

DUNFERMLINE EAST

		%	+/- %
*Brown, G. Lab	19,487	64.8	-2.0
Mellon, J. SNP	4,424	14.7	-0.8
Randall, S. Con	2,838	9.4	-0.6
Mainland, J. LD	2,281	7.6	+1.7
Jackson, A. SSP	770	2.6	
Dunsmore, T. UKIP	286	1.0	
Lab majority	15,063		50.07%
Electorate	52,811		
Total Vote	30,086		56.97

*Member of last parliament
Lab Hold (0.6% from Lab to SNP)

DUNFERMLINE WEST

		%	+/- %
*Squire, R. Lab	16,370	52.8	-0.2
Goodall, B. SNP	5,390	17.4	-1.8
McPhate, R. LD	4,832	15.6	+2.0
Mackie, J. Con	3,166	10.2	-2.4
Stewart, C. SSP	746	2.4	
Harper, A. UKIP	471	1.5	
Lab majority	10,980		35.45%
Electorate	54,293		
Total Vote	30,975		57.05

*Member of last parliament
Lab Hold (0.8% from SNP to Lab)

CITY OF DURHAM

		%	+/- %
*Steinberg, G. Lab	23,254	56.1	-7.2
Woods, C. LD	9,813	23.7	+8.4
Cartmell, N. Con	7,167	17.3	-0.2
Williamson, C. UKIP	1,252	3.0	
Lab majority	13,441		32.40%
Electorate	69,610		
Total Vote	41,486		59.60

*Member of last parliament
Lab Hold (7.8% from Lab to LD)

DURHAM NORTH

		%	+/- %
Jones, K. Lab	25,920	67.2	-3.1
Palmer, M. Con	7,237	18.8	+4.3
Field, C. LD	5,411	14.0	+3.0
Lab majority	18,683		48.44%
Electorate	67,755		
Total Vote	38,568		56.92

Lab Hold (3.7% from Lab to Con)

NORTH WEST DURHAM

		%	+/- %
*Armstrong, H. Lab	24,526	62.5	-6.2
Clouston, W. Con	8,193	20.9	+5.6
Ord, A. LD	5,846	14.9	+4.1
Hartnell, J. SLP	661	1.7	
Lab majority	16,333		41.64%
Electorate	67,294		
Total Vote	39,226		58.29

*Member of last parliament
Lab Hold (5.9% from Lab to Con)

EALING NORTH

		%	+/- %
*Pound, S. Lab	25,022	55.7	+2.0
Walker, C. Con	13,185	29.3	-7.9
Fruzza, F. LD	5,043	11.2	+4.2
Seibe, A. Green	1,039	2.3	+1.4
Moss, D. UKIP	668	1.5	+0.2
Lab majority	11,837		26.33%
Electorate	78,169		
Total Vote	44,957		57.51

*Member of last parliament
Lab Hold (4.9% from Con to Lab)

EALING SOUTHALL

		%	+/- %
*Khabra, P. Lab	22,239	47.5	-12.5
Kawczynski, D. Con	8,556	18.3	-2.5
Lit, A. Sun Rad	5,764	12.3	
Sharma, B. LD	4,680	10.0	-0.4
Cook, J. Green	2,119	4.5	+2.8
Dhillon, S. Ind	1,214	2.6	
Choudhry, M. Ind	1,166	2.5	
Brar, H. SLP	921	2.0	-1.9
Bhutta, M. Qari	169	0.4	
Lab majority	13,683		29.22%
Electorate	82,928		
Total Vote	46,828		56.47

*Member of last parliament
Lab Hold (5.0% from Lab to Con)

EALING, ACTON AND SHEPHERD'S BUSH

		%	+/- %
*Soley, C. Lab	20,144	54.1	-4.2
Greening, J. Con	9,355	25.1	-0.7
Tod, M. LD	6,171	16.6	+5.8
Grant, N. SA	529	1.4	
Lawrie, A. UKIP	476	1.3	+0.5
Rule, C. SLP	301	0.8	-0.5
Ng, R. ProLife	225	0.6	+0.1

Lab majority	10,789		29.00%
Electorate	70,924		
Total Vote	37,201		52.45

*Member of last parliament
Lab Hold (1.8% from Lab to Con)

EASINGTON

		%	+/- %
*Cummings, J. Lab	25,360	76.8	-3.4
Lovel, P. Con	3,411	10.3	+1.8
Ord, C. LD	3,408	10.3	+3.1
Robinson, D. SLP	831	2.5	
Lab majority	21,949		66.49%
Electorate	61,532		
Total Vote	33,010		53.65

*Member of last parliament
Lab Hold (2.6% from Lab to Con)

EAST ANTRIM – see under Antrim

EAST DEVON – see under Devon

EAST HAM

		%	+/- %
*Timms, S. Lab	27,241	73.1	+8.5
Campbell, P. Con	6,209	16.7	+0.6
Fox, B. LD	2,600	7.0	+0.5
Finlayson, R. SLP	783	2.1	-4.7
Pandhal, J. UKIP	444	1.2	
Lab majority	21,032		56.42%
Electorate	71,255		
Total Vote	37,277		52.31

*Member of last parliament
Lab Hold (3.9% from Con to Lab)

EAST HAMPSHIRE – see under Hampshire

EAST KILBRIDE

		%	+/- %
*Ingram, A. Lab	22,205	53.3	-3.3
Buchanan, A. SNP	9,450	22.7	+1.8
Hawthorn, E. LD	4,278	10.3	+3.0
McCulloch, M. Con	4,238	10.2	-1.8
Stevenson, D. SSP	1,519	3.6	
Lab majority	12,755		30.59%
Electorate	66,572		
Total Vote	41,690		62.62

*Member of last parliament
Lab Hold (2.5% from Lab to SNP)

EAST LONDONDERRY – see under Londonderry

EAST LOTHIAN

		%	+/- %
Picking, A. Lab	17,407	47.2	-5.5
Mair, H. Con	6,577	17.8	-2.1
Hayman, J. LD	6,506	17.6	+7.1
Brown, H. SNP	5,381	14.6	-1.1
White, D. SSP	624	1.7	
Herriot, J. SLP	376	1.0	
Lab majority	10,830		29.37%
Electorate	58,987		
Total Vote	36,871		62.51

Lab Hold (1.7% from Lab to Con)

EAST SURREY – see under Surrey

EAST WORTHING AND SHOREHAM – see under Worthing

EASTBOURNE

		%	+/- %
*Waterson, N. Con	19,738	44.1	+2.0
Berry, C. LD	17,584	39.3	+0.9
Roles, G. Lab	5,967	13.3	+0.8
Jones, B. UKIP	907	2.0	+1.5
Williamson, M. Lib	574	1.3	-0.1
Con majority	2,154		4.81%
Electorate	73,756		
Total Vote	44,770		60.70

*Member of last parliament
Con Hold (0.5% from LD to Con)

EASTLEIGH

		%	+/- %
*Chidgey, D. LD	19,360	40.7	+5.6
Burns, C. Con	16,302	34.3	+0.6
Jaffa, S. Lab	10,426	21.9	-4.9
Challis, S. UKIP	849	1.8	+1.0
Lyn, M. Green	636	1.3	
LD majority	3,058		6.43%
Electorate	74,603		
Total Vote	47,573		63.77

*Member of last parliament
LD Hold (2.5% from Con to LD)

EASTWOOD

		%	+/- %
*Murphy, J. Lab	23,036	47.6	+7.9
Robertson, R. Con	13,895	28.7	-4.8
Steele, A. LD	6,239	12.9	+1.2
Maxwell, S. SNP	4,137	8.6	-4.5
Murray, P. SSP	814	1.7	
Tayan, M. Ind	247	0.5	
Lab majority	9,141		18.90%
Electorate	68,297		
Total Vote	48,368		70.82

*Member of last parliament
Lab Hold (6.4% from Con to Lab)

ECCLES

		%	+/- %
*Stewart, I. Lab	21,395	64.5	-2.2
Caillard, P. Con	6,867	20.7	+2.0
Boyd, R. LD	4,920	14.8	+4.1
Lab majority	14,528		43.78%
Electorate	68,764		
Total Vote	33,182		48.25

*Member of last parliament
Lab Hold (2.1% from Lab to Con)

EDDISBURY

		%	+/- %
*O'Brien, S. Con	20,556	46.3	+3.8
Eyres, B. Lab	15,988	36.0	-4.1
Roberts, P. LD	6,975	15.7	+2.5
Carson, D. UKIP	868	2.0	
Con majority	4,568		10.29%
Electorate	69,181		
Total Vote	44,387		64.16

*Member of last parliament
Con Hold (3.9% from Lab to Con)

EDINBURGH CENTRAL

		%	+/- %
*Darling, A. Lab	14,495	42.1	-4.9
Myles, A. LD	6,353	18.5	+5.4
Orr, A. Con	5,643	16.4	-4.8
McKee, I. SNP	4,832	14.1	-1.7
Farmer, G. Green	1,809	5.3	+3.8
Williamson, K. SSP	1,258	3.7	
Lab majority	8,142		23.68%
Electorate	66,089		
Total Vote	34,390		52.04

*Member of last parliament
Lab Hold (5.2% from Lab to LD)

EDINBURGH EAST AND MUSSELBURGH

		%	+/- %
*Strang, G. Lab	18,124	52.6	-1.0
Munn, R. SNP	5,956	17.3	-1.8
Peacock, G. LD	4,981	14.5	+3.7
Finnie, P. Con	3,906	11.3	-4.1
Durkin, D. SSP	1,487	4.3	
Lab majority	12,168		35.32%
Electorate	59,241		
Total Vote	34,454		58.16

*Member of last parliament
Lab Hold (0.4% from SNP to Lab)

EDINBURGH NORTH AND LEITH

		%	+/- %
Lazarowicz, M. Lab	15,271	45.9	-1.0
Tombs, S. LD	6,454	19.4	+6.4
Stewart, K. SNP	5,290	15.9	-4.2
Mitchell, I. Con	4,626	13.9	-3.9
Grant, C. SSP	1,334	4.0	+3.2
Jacobsen, D. SLP	259	0.8	
Lab majority	8,817		26.53%
Electorate	62,731		
Total Vote	33,234		52.98

Lab Hold (3.8% from Lab to LD)

EDINBURGH PENTLANDS

		%	+/- %
*Clark, L. Lab	15,797	40.6	-2.4
Rifkind, M. Con	14,055	36.1	+3.7
Walker, D. LD	4,210	10.8	+0.8
Gibb, S. SNP	4,210	10.8	-2.2
Mearns, J. SSP	555	1.4	
McMurdo, W. UKIP	105	0.3	+0.1
Lab majority	1,742		4.47%
Electorate	60,484		
Total Vote	38,932		64.37

*Member of last parliament
Lab Hold (3.1% from Lab to Con)

EDINBURGH SOUTH

		%	+/- %
*Griffiths, N. Lab	15,671	42.2	-4.7
MacLaren, M. LD	10,172	27.4	+9.7
Buchan, G. Con	6,172	16.6	-4.7
Williams, H. SNP	3,683	9.9	-3.0
Fox, C. SSP	933	2.5	
Hendry, L. LCA	535	1.4	
Lab majority	5,499		14.80%
Electorate	64,437		
Total Vote	37,166		57.68

*Member of last parliament
Lab Hold (7.2% from Lab to LD)

EDINBURGH WEST

		%	+/- %
Barrett, J. LD	16,719	42.4	-0.9
Alexandra, E. Lab	9,130	23.1	+4.3
Whyte, I. Con	8,894	22.5	-5.4
Smith, A. SNP	4,047	10.3	+1.4
Scott, B. SSP	688	1.7	
LD majority	7,589		19.22%
Electorate	62,503		
Total Vote	39,478		63.16

LD Hold (2.6% from LD to Lab)

EDMONTON

		%	+/- %
*Love, A. Lab	20,481	58.9	-1.4
Burrows, D. Con	10,709	30.8	+0.6
Taylor, D. LD	2,438	7.0	+0.7
Rolph, G. UKIP	406	1.2	+0.6

		%	+/- %
Basarik, E. Reform 2000	344	1.0	
Medwell, H. SA	296	0.9	
Saxena, R. Ind	100	0.3	
Lab majority	9,772		28.10%
Electorate	61,788		
Total Vote	34,774		56.28

*Member of last parliament
Lab Hold (1.0% from Lab to Con)

ELLESMERE PORT AND NESTON

		%	+/- %
*Miller, A. Lab	22,964	55.3	-4.3
Williams, G. Con	12,103	29.1	+0.1
Kelly, S. LD	4,828	11.6	+2.7
Crocker, H. UKIP	824	2.0	
Nicholls, G. Green	809	1.9	
Lab majority	10,861		26.15%
Electorate	68,147		
Total Vote	41,528		60.94

*Member of last parliament
Lab Hold (2.2% from Lab to Con)

ELMET

		%	+/- %
*Burgon, C. Lab	22,038	48.0	-4.4
Millard, A. Con	17,867	38.9	+2.7
Kirk, M. LD	5,001	10.9	+2.2
Spence, A. UKIP	1,031	2.2	
Lab majority	4,171		9.08%
Electorate	70,121		
Total Vote	45,937		65.51

*Member of last parliament
Lab Hold (3.6% from Lab to Con)

ELTHAM

		%	+/- %
*Efford, C. Lab	17,855	52.8	-1.8
Massey, S. Con	10,859	32.1	+1.0
Morris, M. LD	4,121	12.2	+3.7
Jones, T. UKIP	706	2.1	
Graham, A. Ind	251	0.7	
Lab majority	6,996		20.70%
Electorate	57,554		
Total Vote	33,792		58.71

*Member of last parliament
Lab Hold (1.4% from Lab to Con)

ENFIELD NORTH

		%	+/- %
*Ryan, J. Lab	17,888	46.7	-4.0
De Bois, N. Con	15,597	40.7	+4.4
Leighter, H. LD	3,355	8.8	-0.2
Johns, R. BNP	605	1.6	+0.3
Hall, B. UKIP	427	1.1	+0.1
Akerman, M. ProLife	241	0.6	
Course, R. None	210	0.5	
Lab majority	2,291		5.98%
Electorate	67,204		
Total Vote	38,323		57.02

*Member of last parliament
Lab Hold (4.2% from Lab to Con)

ENFIELD SOUTHGATE

		%	+/- %
*Twigg, S. Lab	21,727	51.8	+7.6
Flack, J. Con	16,181	38.6	-2.5
Hoban, W. LD	2,935	7.0	-3.7
Graham-Leigh, E. Green	662	1.6	
Freshwater, R. UKIP	298	0.7	
Malakouna, A. Ind	105	0.3	
Lab majority	5,546		13.23%
Electorate	65,957		
Total Vote	41,908		63.54

*Member of last parliament
Lab Hold (5.1% from Con to Lab)

EPPING FOREST

		%	+/- %
*Laing, E. Con	20,833	49.1	+3.6
Naylor, C. Lab	12,407	29.3	-6.3
Heavens, M. LD	7,884	18.6	+5.2
Smith, A. UKIP	1,290	3.0	
Con majority	8,426		19.87%
Electorate	72,645		
Total Vote	42,414		58.39

*Member of last parliament
Con Hold (5.0% from Lab to Con)

EPSOM AND EWELL

		%	+/- %
Grayling, C. Con	22,430	48.1	+2.5
Mansell, C. Lab	12,350	26.5	+2.1
Vincent, J. LD	10,316	22.1	-0.7
Webster-Gardiner, G. UKIP	1,547	3.3	+2.3
Con majority	10,080		21.61%
Electorate	74,266		
Total Vote	46,643		62.81

Con Hold (0.2% from Lab to Con)

EREWASH

		%	+/- %
*Blackman, E. Lab	23,915	49.2	-2.5
Gregor MacGregor, N. Con	16,983	34.9	-1.6
Garnett, M. LD	5,586	11.5	+2.9
Smith, L. UKIP	692	1.4	
Belshaw, S. BNP	591	1.2	
Seerius, R. Loony	428	0.9	
Waldock, P. SLP	401	0.8	0.0
Lab majority	6,932		14.26%
Electorate	78,484		
Total Vote	48,596		61.92

*Member of last parliament
Lab Hold (0.4% from Lab to Con)

ERITH AND THAMESMEAD

		%	+/- %
*Austin, J. Lab	19,769	59.3	-2.8
Brooks, M. Con	8,602	25.8	+5.6
Kempton, J. LD	3,800	11.4	-0.6
Dhillon, H. SLP	1,180	3.5	
Lab majority	11,167		33.48%
Electorate	66,371		
Total Vote	33,351		50.25

*Member of last parliament
Lab Hold (4.2% from Lab to Con)

ESHER AND WALTON

		%	+/- %
*Taylor, I. Con	22,296	49.0	-0.9
McGowan, J. Lab	10,758	23.6	+0.9
Marsh, M. LD	10,241	22.5	+2.1
Collignon, B. UKIP	2,236	4.9	+3.9
Con majority	11,538		25.34%
Electorate	73,541		
Total Vote	45,531		61.91

*Member of last parliament
Con Hold (0.9% from Con to Lab)

NORTH ESSEX

		%	+/- %
*Jenkin, B. Con	21,325	47.4	+3.5
Hawkins, P. Lab	14,139	31.5	-1.7
Ellis, T. LD	7,867	17.5	-2.1
Curtis, G. UKIP	1,613	3.6	+1.2
Con majority	7,186		15.99%
Electorate	71,605		
Total Vote	44,944		62.77

*Member of last parliament
Con Hold (2.6% from Lab to Con)

EXETER

		%	+/- %
*Bradshaw, B. Lab	26,194	49.8	+2.3
Jobson, A. Con	14,435	27.4	-1.2
Copus, R. LD	6,512	12.4	-5.6
Morrish, D. Lib	2,596	4.9	+1.6
Edwards, P. Green	1,240	2.4	+1.3
Stuart, J. UKIP	1,109	2.1	+1.1
Choules, F. SA	530	1.0	
Lab majority	11,759		22.35%
Electorate	81,946		
Total Vote	52,616		64.21

*Member of last parliament
Lab Hold (1.7% from Con to Lab)

FALKIRK EAST

		%	+/- %
*Connarty, M. Lab	18,536	55.0	-1.1
Hutton, I. SNP	7,824	23.2	-0.7
Stevenson, B. Con	3,252	9.6	-4.3
Utting, K. LD	2,992	8.9	+3.7
Weir, T. SSP	725	2.2	
Stead, R. SLP	373	1.1	
Lab majority	10,712		31.78%
Electorate	57,633		
Total Vote	33,702		58.48

*Member of last parliament
Lab Hold (0.2% from Lab to SNP)

FALKIRK WEST

		%	+/- %
*Joyce, E. Lab	16,022	51.9	-7.5
Kerr, D. SNP	7,490	24.2	+0.8
Murray, S. Con	2,321	7.5	-4.6
O'Donnell, H. LD	2,203	7.1	+2.0
Buchanan, B. Ind	1,464	4.7	
McAlpine, M. SSP	707	2.3	
Lynch, H. Ind	490	1.6	
Forbes, R. SLP	194	0.6	
Lab majority	8,532		27.62%
Electorate	53,585		
Total Vote	30,891		57.65

*Member of last parliament
Lab Hold (4.2% from Lab to SNP)

FALMOUTH AND CAMBORNE

		%	+/- %
*Atherton, C. Lab	18,532	39.6	+5.7
Serpell, N. Con	14,005	29.9	+1.1
Brazil, J. LD	11,453	24.5	-0.7
Browne, J. UKIP	1,328	2.8	+2.2
Wasley, H. Meb Ker	853	1.8	+1.4
Holmes, P. Lib	649	1.4	+0.4
Lab majority	4,527		9.67%
Electorate	72,833		
Total Vote	46,820		64.28

*Member of last parliament
Lab Hold (2.3% from Con to Lab)

FAREHAM

		%	+/- %
Hoban, M. Con	21,389	47.1	+0.2
Carr, J. Lab	14,380	31.6	+4.7
Pritchard, H. LD	8,503	18.7	-0.9
O'Brien, W. UKIP	1,175	2.6	
Con majority	7,009		15.42%
Electorate	84,150		
Total Vote	45,447		62.50

Con Hold (2.2% from Con to Lab)

FAVERSHAM AND MID KENT

		%	+/- %
Robertson, H. Con	18,739	45.6	+1.3
Birchall, G. Lab	14,556	35.5	-0.5
Sole, M. LD	5,529	13.5	+1.1
Gascoyne, J. UKIP	828	2.0	+1.1
Kemp, P. Green	799	1.9	+1.2
Davidson, N. RNRL	600	1.5	
Con majority	4,183		10.19%
Electorate	67,995		
Total Vote	41,051		60.37

Con Hold (0.9% from Lab to Con)

FELTHAM AND HESTON

		%	+/- %
*Keen, A. Lab	21,406	59.2	-0.5
Mammatt, L. Con	8,749	24.2	-2.8
Darley, A. LD	4,998	13.8	+4.7
Cheema, S. SLP	651	1.8	
Prachar, W. Ind	204	0.6	
Khaira, A. Ind	169	0.5	
Lab majority	12,657		34.99%
Electorate	73,229		
Total Vote	36,177		49.40

*Member of last parliament
Lab Hold (1.1% from Con to Lab)

FERMANAGH AND SOUTH TYRONE

		%	+/- %
Gildernew, M. SF	17,739	34.1	+11.0
Cooper, J. UUP	17,686	34.0	-17.5
Gallagher, T. SDLP	9,706	18.7	-4.2
Dixon, W. Ind	6,843	13.2	
SF majority	53		0.10%
Electorate	66,640		
Total Vote	51,974		77.99

SF Gain (14.2% from UUP to SF)

CENTRAL FIFE

		%	+/- %
MacDougall, J. Lab	18,310	56.3	-2.3
Alexander, D. SNP	8,235	25.3	+0.3
Riches, E. LD	2,775	8.5	+2.1
Balfour, J. Con	2,351	7.2	-1.8
Balfour, M. SSP	841	2.6	
Lab majority	10,075		30.99%
Electorate	59,597		
Total Vote	32,512		54.55

Lab Hold (1.3% from Lab to SNP)

NORTH EAST FIFE

		%	+/- %
*Campbell, M. LD	17,926	51.7	+0.4
Scott-Hayward, M. Con	8,190	23.6	-2.9
Brennan, C. Lab	3,950	11.4	+1.1
Murray-Browne, K. SNP	3,596	10.4	-0.5
White, K. SSP	610	1.8	
Von Goetz, L. LCA	420	1.2	
LD majority	9,736		28.06%
Electorate	61,900		
Total Vote	34,692		56.05

*Member of last parliament
LD Hold (1.7% from Con to LD)

FINCHLEY AND GOLDERS GREEN

		%	+/- %
*Vis, R. Lab	20,205	46.3	+0.2
Marshall, J. Con	16,489	37.8	-2.0
Teather, S. LD	5,266	12.1	+0.8
Dunn, M. Green	1,385	3.2	+2.0
de Roeck, J. UKIP	330	0.8	+0.3

Lab majority	3,716		8.51%
Electorate	76,178		
Total Vote	43,675		57.34

*Member of last parliament
Lab Hold (1.1% from Con to Lab)

FOLKESTONE AND HYTHE

		%	+/- %
*Howard, M. Con	20,645	45.0	+6.0
Carroll, P. LD	14,738	32.1	+5.3
Catterall, A. Lab	9,260	20.2	-4.7
Baker, J. UKIP	1,212	2.6	+1.9
Con majority	5,907		12.88%
Electorate	71,507		
Total Vote	45,855		64.13

*Member of last parliament
Con Hold (0.4% from LD to Con)

FOREST OF DEAN

		%	+/- %
*Organ, D. Lab	19,350	43.4	-4.8
Harper, M. Con	17,301	38.8	+3.2
Gayler, D. LD	5,762	12.9	+0.6
Pickering, S. Green	1,254	2.8	
Prout, A. UKIP	661	1.5	
Morgan, G. Ind	279	0.6	
Lab majority	2,049		4.59%
Electorate	66,240		
Total Vote	44,607		67.34

*Member of last parliament
Lab Hold (4.0% from Lab to Con)

FOYLE

		%	+/- %
*Hume, J. SDLP	24,538	50.2	-2.3
McLaughlin, M. SF	12,988	26.6	+2.6
Hay, W. DUP	7,414	15.2	-6.4
Davidson, A. UUP	3,360	6.9	
Murray-Kavanagh, C. Alliance	579	1.2	-0.5
SDLP majority	11,550		23.63%
Electorate	70,943		
Total Vote	48,879		68.90

*Member of last parliament
SDLP Hold (2.5% from SDLP to SF)

FYLDE

		%	+/- %
*Jack, M. Con	23,383	52.3	+3.4
Stockton, J. Lab	13,773	30.8	-0.9
Begg, J. LD	6,599	14.8	+0.1
Brown, L. UKIP	982	2.2	
Con majority	9,610		21.48%
Electorate	73,460		
Total Vote	44,737		60.90

*Member of last parliament
Con Hold (2.1% from Lab to Con)

GAINSBOROUGH

		%	+/- %
*Leigh, E. Con	19,555	46.2	+3.1
Rhodes, A. Lab	11,484	27.1	-1.7
Taylor, S. LD	11,280	26.7	-1.5
Con majority	8,071		19.07%
Electorate	65,870		
Total Vote	42,319		64.25

*Member of last parliament
Con Hold (2.4% from Lab to Con)

GALLOWAY AND UPPER NITHSDALE

		%	+/- %
Duncan, P. Con	12,222	34.0	+3.5
Fleming, M. SNP	12,148	33.8	-10.1
Sloan, T. Lab	7,258	20.2	+3.9
Wallace, N. LD	3,698	10.3	+3.9
Harvey, A. SSP	588	1.6	
Con majority	74		0.21%
Electorate	53,254		
Total Vote	35,914		67.44

Con Gain (6.8% from SNP to Con)

GATESHEAD EAST AND WASHINGTON WEST

		%	+/- %
*Quin, J. Lab	22,903	68.1	-3.9
Beadle, R. LD	4,999	14.9	+4.1
Campbell, E. Con	4,970	14.8	+0.6
Rouse, M. UKIP	743	2.2	
Lab majority	17,904		53.26%
Electorate	64,041		
Total Vote	33,615		52.49

*Member of last parliament
Lab Hold (4.0% from Lab to LD)

GEDLING

		%	+/- %
*Coaker, V. Lab	22,383	51.1	+4.3
Bullock, J. Con	16,785	38.3	-1.2
Gillam, A. LD	4,648	10.6	+0.7
Lab majority	5,598		12.78%
Electorate	68,519		
Total Vote	43,816		63.95

*Member of last parliament
Lab Hold (2.7% from Con to Lab)

GILLINGHAM

		%	+/- %
*Clark, P. Lab	18,782	44.5	+4.7
Butcher, T. Con	16,510	39.1	+3.2
Hunt, J. LD	5,755	13.6	-5.4
Scholefield, A. UKIP	933	2.2	+1.0
Thomas, W. SA	232	0.5	
Lab majority	2,272		5.38%
Electorate	70,901		
Total Vote	42,212		59.54

*Member of last parliament
Lab Hold (0.7% from Con to Lab)

VALE OF GLAMORGAN

		%	+/- %
*Smith, J. Lab	20,524	45.4	-8.5
Inkin, S. Con	15,824	35.0	+0.7
Smith, D. LD	5,521	12.2	+3.0
Franks, C. Pl C	2,867	6.3	+3.8
Warry, N. UKIP	448	1.0	
Lab majority	4,700		10.40%
Electorate	67,774		
Total Vote	45,184		66.67

*Member of last parliament
Lab Hold (4.6% from Lab to Con)

GLASGOW ANNIESLAND

		%	+/- %
*Robertson, J. Lab	15,102	56.5	-5.3
Thoms, G. SNP	4,048	15.1	-2.0
McGinty, C. LD	3,244	12.1	+4.9
Connell, S. Con	2,651	9.9	-1.5
McCarthy, C. SSP	1,486	5.6	+4.9
McGavigan, K. SLP	191	0.7	
Lab majority	11,054		41.37%
Electorate	52,703		
Total Vote	26,722		50.70

*Member of last parliament
Lab Hold (1.8% from Lab to SNP)

GLASGOW BAILLIESTON

		%	+/- %
*Wray, J. Lab	14,200	61.0	-4.6
McNeill, L. SNP	4,361	18.7	-0.4
Comrie, D. Con	1,580	6.8	-1.0
McVicar, J. SSP	1,569	6.7	+3.7
Dundas, C. LD	1,551	6.7	+2.8
Lab majority	9,839		42.30%
Electorate	48,741		
Total Vote	23,261		47.72

*Member of last parliament
Lab Hold (2.2% from Lab to SNP)

GLASGOW CATHCART

		%	+/- %
Harris, T. Lab	14,902	54.4	-3.0
Docherty, J. SNP	4,086	14.9	-3.6
Cook, R. Con	3,662	13.4	+0.6
Henery, T. LD	3,006	11.0	+4.1
Stevenson, R. SSP	1,730	6.3	+4.9
Lab majority	10,816		39.49%
Electorate	51,518		
Total Vote	27,386		53.16

Lab Hold (0.3% from SNP to Lab)

GLASGOW GOVAN

		%	+/- %
*Sarwar, M. Lab	12,464	49.3	+5.2
Neary, K. SNP	6,064	24.0	-11.1
Stewart, B. LD	2,815	11.1	+5.2
Menzies, M. Con	2,167	8.6	-0.2
McGartland, W. SSP	1,531	6.1	+3.8
Foster, J. Comm GB	174	0.7	
Mirza, B. Ind	69	0.3	
Lab majority	6,400		25.31%
Electorate	53,471		
Total Vote	25,284		47.29

*Member of last parliament
Lab Hold (8.2% from SNP to Lab)

GLASGOW KELVIN

		%	+/- %
*Galloway, G. Lab	12,014	44.8	-6.1
Mayberry, T. LD	4,754	17.7	+3.6
Rankin, F. SNP	4,513	16.8	-4.5
Rankin, D. Con	2,388	8.9	-1.9
Ritchie, H. SSP	1,847	6.9	+5.7
Shand, T. Green	1,286	4.8	
Lab majority	7,260		27.09%
Electorate	59,820		
Total Vote	26,802		44.80

*Member of last parliament
Lab Hold (4.9% from Lab to LD)

GLASGOW MARYHILL

		%	+/- %
McKechin, A. Lab	13,420	60.4	-4.6
Dingwall, A. SNP	3,532	15.9	-1.1
Callison, S. LD	2,372	10.7	+3.5
Scott, G. SSP	1,745	7.8	+6.4
Towler, G. Con	1,162	5.2	-0.7
Lab majority	9,888		44.48%
Electorate	54,635		
Total Vote	22,231		40.69

Lab Hold (1.8% from Lab to SNP)

GLASGOW POLLOK

		%	+/- %
*Davidson, I. Lab	15,497	61.3	+1.4
Ritchie, D. SNP	4,229	16.7	-1.1
Baldassara, K. SSP	2,522	10.0	+1.1
Nelson, I. LD	1,612	6.4	+2.9
O'Brien, R. Con	1,417	5.6	-0.4

Lab majority	11,268		44.58%
Electorate	48,745		
Total Vote	25,277		51.86

*Member of last parliament
Lab Hold (1.4% from SNP to Lab)

GLASGOW RUTHERGLEN

		%	+/- %
*McAvoy, T. Lab	16,760	57.4	-0.1
McLaughlin, A. SNP	4,135	14.2	-1.1
Jackson, D. LD	3,689	12.6	-1.9
Macaskill, M. Con	3,301	11.3	+2.0
Bonnar, B. SSP	1,328	4.5	+3.8
Lab majority	12,625		43.22%
Electorate	51,855		
Total Vote	29,213		56.34

*Member of last parliament
Lab Hold (0.5% from SNP to Lab)

GLASGOW SHETTLESTON

		%	+/- %
*Marshall, D. Lab	13,235	64.7	-8.5
Byrne, J. SNP	3,417	16.7	+2.7
Kane, R. SSP	1,396	6.8	+5.0
Hutton, L. LD	1,105	5.4	+1.4
Murdoch, C. Con	1,082	5.3	-0.2
Ritchie, M. SLP	230	1.1	
Lab majority	9,818		47.97%
Electorate	51,006		
Total Vote	20,465		40.12

*Member of last parliament
Lab Hold (5.6% from Lab to SNP)

GLASGOW SPRINGBURN

		%	+/- %
*Martin, M. Speaker	16,053	66.6	-4.8
Bain, S. SNP	4,675	19.4	+2.9
Leckie, C. SSP	1,879	7.8	+6.5
Houston, D. SUP	1,289	5.3	
Silvester, R. Ind	208	0.9	
Speaker majority	11,378		47.20%
Electorate	54,632		
Total Vote	24,104		44.12

*Member of last parliament
Speaker Gain

GLOUCESTER

		%	+/- %
Dhanda, P. Lab	22,067	45.8	-4.2
James, P. Con	18,187	37.7	+2.0
Bullamore, T. LD	6,875	14.3	+3.8
Lines, T. UKIP	822	1.7	+0.9
Smyth, S. SA	272	0.6	
Lab majority	3,880		8.05%
Electorate	81,206		
Total Vote	48,223		59.38

Lab Hold (3.1% from Lab to Con)

GORDON

		%	+/- %
*Bruce, M. LD	15,928	45.5	+2.9
Milne, N. Con	8,049	23.0	-3.0
Kemp, R. SNP	5,760	16.5	-3.5
Thorpe, E. Lab	4,730	13.5	+3.2
Sangster, J. SSP	534	1.5	
LD majority	7,879		22.51%
Electorate	60,059		
Total Vote	35,001		58.28

*Member of last parliament
LD Hold (3.0% from Con to LD)

GOSPORT		%	+/- %
*Viggers, P. Con	17,364	43.6	0.0
Williams, R. Lab	14,743	37.1	+6.4
Roberts, R. LD	6,011	15.1	-4.5
Bowles, J. UKIP	1,162	2.9	
Chetwynd, K. SLP	509	1.3	
Con majority	2,621		6.59%
Electorate	69,626		
Total Vote	39,789		57.15

*Member of last parliament
Con Hold (3.2% from Con to Lab)

GOWER		%	+/- %
*Caton, M. Lab	17,676	47.3	-6.5
Bushell, J. Con	10,281	27.5	+3.7
Waye, S. LD	4,507	12.1	-0.9
Caiach, S. Pl C	3,865	10.3	+5.2
Shrewsbury, T. Green	607	1.6	
Hickery, D. SLP	417	1.1	
Lab majority	7,395		19.80%
Electorate	58,936		
Total Vote	37,353		63.38

*Member of last parliament
Lab Hold (5.1% from Lab to Con)

GRANTHAM AND STAMFORD		%	+/- %
*Davies, Q. Con	21,329	46.1	+3.3
Robinson, J. Lab	16,811	36.3	-1.4
Carr, J. LD	6,665	14.4	+1.9
Swain, M. UKIP	1,484	3.2	+2.2
Con majority	4,518		9.76%
Electorate	75,500		
Total Vote	46,289		61.31

*Member of last parliament
Con Hold (2.3% from Lab to Con)

GRAVESHAM		%	+/- %
*Pond, C. Lab	21,773	49.9	+0.2
Arnold, J. Con	16,911	38.8	-0.1
Parmenter, B. LD	4,031	9.2	+1.5
Jenner, W. UKIP	924	2.1	
Lab majority	4,862		11.14%
Electorate	69,588		
Total Vote	43,639		62.71

*Member of last parliament
Lab Hold (0.1% from Con to Lab)

GREAT GRIMSBY – see under Grimsby

GREAT YARMOUTH		%	+/- %
*Wright, A. Lab	20,344	50.4	-3.0
Reynolds, C. Con	15,780	39.1	+3.5
Leeke, M. LD	3,392	8.4	-2.6
Poole, B. UKIP	850	2.1	
Lab majority	4,564		11.31%
Electorate	69,131		
Total Vote	40,366		58.39

*Member of last parliament
Lab Hold (3.2% from Lab to Con)

GREENOCK AND INVERCLYDE		%	+/- %
Cairns, D. Lab	14,929	52.5	-3.6
Brodie, C. LD	5,039	17.7	+3.9
Murie, A. SNP	4,248	14.9	-3.6
Haw, A. Con	3,000	10.6	-0.9
Landels, D. SSP	1,203	4.2	

	Lab majority	9,890	34.80%
	Electorate	47,884	
	Total Vote	28,419	59.35

Lab Hold (3.8% from Lab to LD)

GREENWICH AND WOOLWICH		%	+/- %
*Raynsford, N. Lab	19,691	60.5	-2.9
Forsdyke, R. Con	6,258	19.2	+0.7
Pyne, R. LD	5,082	15.6	+3.1
Gain, S. UKIP	672	2.1	
Paton, K. SA	481	1.5	
Sharkey, M. SLP	352	1.1	
Lab majority	13,433		41.29%
Electorate	62,565		
Total Vote	32,536		52.00

*Member of last parliament
Lab Hold (1.8% from Lab to Con)

GREAT GRIMSBY		%	+/- %
*Mitchell, A. Lab	19,118	57.9	-1.9
Cousins, J. Con	7,634	23.1	+1.0
de Freitas, A. LD	6,265	19.0	+0.9
Lab majority	11,484		34.78%
Electorate	63,157		
Total Vote	33,017		52.28

*Member of last parliament
Lab Hold (1.5% from Lab to Con)

GUILDFORD		%	+/- %
Doughty, S. LD	20,358	42.6	+8.4
*St Aubyn, N. Con	19,820	41.4	-1.1
Still, J. Lab	6,558	13.7	-3.8
Porter, S. UKIP	736	1.5	+0.8
Morris, J. PP	370	0.8	
LD majority	538		1.12%
Electorate	76,296		
Total Vote	47,842		62.71

*Member of last parliament
LD Gain (4.8% from Con to LD)

HACKNEY NORTH AND STOKE NEWINGTON		%	+/- %
*Abbott, D. Lab	18,081	61.0	-4.1
Dye, P. Con	4,430	15.0	-2.0
Ece, M. LD	4,170	14.1	+3.9
Chong, C. Green	2,184	7.4	+3.1
Chandan, S. SLP	756	2.6	
Lab majority	13,651		46.00%
Electorate	60,444		
Total Vote	29,621		47.75

*Member of last parliament
Lab Hold (0.2% from Lab to Con)

HACKNEY SOUTH AND SHOREDITCH		%	+/- %
*Sedgemore, B. Lab	19,471	64.2	+4.8
Vickers, A. LD	4,422	14.6	-0.4
White, P. Con	4,180	13.8	+0.5
Prosper, C. SA	1,401	4.6	
Koksal, S. Reform 2000	471	1.6	
Beavis, I. Comm GB	259	0.9	-0.0
Rogers, W. WRP	143	0.5	+0.1
Lab majority	15,049		49.59%
Electorate	63,990		
Total Vote	30,347		47.42

*Member of last parliament
Lab Hold (2.6% from LD to Lab)

HALESOWEN AND ROWLEY REGIS

		%	+/- %
*Heal, S. Lab	20,804	53.0	-1.1
Jones, L. Con	13,445	34.2	+1.4
Harley, P. LD	4,089	10.4	+1.9
Sheath, A. UKIP	936	2.4	
Lab majority	7,359		18.74%
Electorate	66,012		
Total Vote	39,274		59.50

*Member of last parliament
Lab Hold (1.2% from Lab to Con)

HALIFAX

		%	+/- %
*Mahon, A. Lab	19,800	49.0	-5.3
Walsh, J. Con	13,671	33.8	+1.7
Durkin, J. LD	5,878	14.6	+2.6
Martinek, H. UKIP	1,041	2.6	+1.0
Lab majority	6,129		15.17%
Electorate	70,426		
Total Vote	40,390		57.35

*Member of last parliament
Lab Hold (3.5% from Lab to Con)

HALTEMPRICE AND HOWDEN

		%	+/- %
*Davis, D. Con	18,994	43.2	-0.8
Neal, J. LD	17,091	38.9	+10.1
Howell, L. Lab	6,898	15.7	-7.9
Robinson, J. UKIP	945	2.2	+1.5
Con majority	1,903		4.33%
Electorate	66,733		
Total Vote	43,928		65.83

*Member of last parliament
Con Hold (5.4% from Con to LD)

HALTON

		%	+/- %
*Twigg, D. Lab	23,841	69.2	-1.7
Davenport, C. Con	6,413	18.6	+0.9
Walker, P. LD	4,216	12.2	+4.9
Lab majority	17,428		50.56%
Electorate	63,742		
Total Vote	34,470		54.08

*Member of last parliament
Lab Hold (1.3% from Lab to Con)

HAMILTON NORTH AND BELLSHILL

		%	+/- %
*Reid, J. Lab	18,786	61.8	-2.2
Stephens, C. SNP	5,225	17.2	-1.9
Frain-Bell, B. Con	2,649	8.7	-1.7
Legg, K. LD	2,360	7.8	+2.7
Blackall, S. SSP	1,189	3.9	
Mayes, S. SLP	195	0.6	
Lab majority	13,561		44.60%
Electorate	53,539		
Total Vote	30,404		56.79

*Member of last parliament
Lab Hold (0.2% from Lab to SNP)

HAMILTON SOUTH

		%	+/- %
*Tynan, B. Lab	15,965	59.7	-5.9
Wilson, J. SNP	5,190	19.4	+1.8
Oswald, J. LD	2,388	8.9	+3.8
Richardson, N. Con	1,876	7.0	-1.6
Mitchell, G. SSP	1,187	4.4	
Murdoch, J. UKIP	151	0.6	
Lab majority	10,775		40.27%
Electorate	46,665		
Total Vote	26,757		57.34

*Member of last parliament
Lab Hold (3.9% from Lab to SNP)

HAMMERSMITH AND FULHAM

		%	+/- %
*Coleman, I. Lab	19,801	44.3	-2.5
Carrington, M. Con	17,786	39.8	+0.1
Burden, J. LD	5,294	11.8	+3.1
Dias, D. Green	1,444	3.2	+2.2
Roberts, G. UKIP	375	0.8	+0.5
Lab majority	2,015		4.51%
Electorate	79,303		
Total Vote	44,700		56.37

*Member of last parliament
Lab Hold (1.3% from Lab to Con)

EAST HAMPSHIRE

		%	+/- %
*Mates, M. Con	23,950	47.6	-0.4
Booker, B. LD	15,060	29.9	+1.8
Burfoot, B. Lab	9,866	19.6	+2.5
Coles, S. UKIP	1,413	2.8	+1.9
Con majority	8,890		17.68%
Electorate	78,802		
Total Vote	50,289		63.82

*Member of last parliament
Con Hold (1.1% from Con to LD)

NORTH EAST HAMPSHIRE

		%	+/- %
*Arbuthnot, J. Con	23,379	53.2	+2.3
Plummer, M. LD	10,122	23.0	+0.3
Jones, B. Lab	8,744	19.9	+3.8
Mellstrom, G. UKIP	1,702	3.9	+3.0
Con majority	13,257		30.17%
Electorate	71,304		
Total Vote	43,947		61.63

*Member of last parliament
Con Hold (1.0% from LD to Con)

NORTH WEST HAMPSHIRE

		%	+/- %
*Young, G. Con	24,374	50.1	+4.9
Mumford, M. Lab	12,365	25.4	+1.8
Bentley, A. LD	10,329	21.2	-2.9
Oram, S. UKIP	1,563	3.2	+0.7
Con majority	12,009		24.69%
Electorate	78,793		
Total Vote	48,631		61.72

*Member of last parliament
Con Hold (1.5% from Lab to Con)

HAMPSTEAD AND HIGHGATE

		%	+/- %
*Jackson, G. Lab	16,601	46.9	-10.5
Mennear, A. Con	8,725	24.6	-2.6
Simpson, J. LD	7,273	20.5	+8.1
Cornwell, A. Green	1,654	4.7	
Cooper, M. SA	559	1.6	
McDermott, B. UKIP	316	0.9	+0.6
Xnunoftheabove, S. None	144	0.4	
Teale, M. ProLife	92	0.3	
Klein, A. Ind	43	0.1	
Lab majority	7,876		22.24%
Electorate	71,084		
Total Vote	35,407		49.81

*Member of last parliament
Lab Hold (4.0% from Lab to Con)

HARBOROUGH

		%	+/- %
*Garnier, E. Con	20,748	44.7	+2.9
Hope, J. LD	15,496	33.4	+3.9
Jethwa, R. Lab	9,271	20.0	-5.2
Knight, D. UKIP	912	2.0	
Con majority	5,252		11.31%
Electorate	73,300		
Total Vote	46,427		63.34

*Member of last parliament
Con Hold (0.5% from Con to LD)

HARLOW

		%	+/- %
*Rammell, B. Lab	19,169	47.8	-6.3
Halfon, R. Con	13,941	34.8	+2.7
Spenceley, L. LD	5,381	13.4	+4.0
Bennett, T. UKIP	1,223	3.0	+2.3
Hobbs, J. SA	401	1.0	
Lab majority	5,228		13.03%
Electorate	67,196		
Total Vote	40,115		59.70

*Member of last parliament
Lab Hold (4.5% from Lab to Con)

HARROGATE AND KNARESBOROUGH

		%	+/- %
*Willis, P. LD	23,445	55.6	+4.0
Jones, A. Con	14,600	34.6	-3.8
MacDonald, A. Lab	3,101	7.4	-1.4
Brown, B. UKIP	761	1.8	
Cornforth, J. ProLife	272	0.6	
LD majority	8,845		20.97%
Electorate	65,159		
Total Vote	42,179		64.73

*Member of last parliament
LD Hold (3.9% from Con to LD)

HARROW EAST

		%	+/- %
*McNulty, T. Lab	26,590	55.3	+2.8
Wilding, P. Con	15,466	32.2	-3.3
Kershaw, G. LD	6,021	12.5	+4.3
Lab majority	11,124		23.14%
Electorate	81,575		
Total Vote	48,077		58.94

*Member of last parliament
Lab Hold (3.0% from Con to Lab)

HARROW WEST

		%	+/- %
*Thomas, G. Lab	23,142	49.6	+8.1
Finkelstein, D. Con	16,986	36.4	-2.8
Noyce, C. LD	5,995	12.9	-2.6
Kefford, P. UKIP	525	1.1	
Lab majority	6,156		13.20%
Electorate	73,505		
Total Vote	46,648		63.46

*Member of last parliament
Lab Hold (5.4% from Con to Lab)

HARTLEPOOL

		%	+/- %
*Mandelson, P. Lab	22,506	59.1	-1.6
Robinson, A. Con	7,935	20.9	-0.5
Boddy, N. LD	5,717	15.0	+1.0
Scargill, A. SLP	912	2.4	
Cameron, I. Ind	557	1.5	
Booth, J. Ind	424	1.1	
Lab majority	14,571		38.29%
Electorate	67,654		
Total Vote	38,051		56.24

*Member of last parliament
Lab Hold (0.5% from Lab to Con)

HARWICH

		%	+/- %
*Henderson, I. Lab	21,951	45.6	+6.9
Sproat, I. Con	19,355	40.2	+3.7
Wilcock, P. LD	4,099	8.5	-4.6
Finnegan-Butler, T. UKIP	2,463	5.1	
Lawrance, C. Ind	247	0.5	
Lab majority	2,596		5.40%
Electorate	77,590		
Total Vote	48,115		62.01

*Member of last parliament
Lab Hold (1.6% from Con to Lab)

HASTINGS AND RYE

		%	+/- %
*Foster, M. Lab	19,402	47.1	+12.7
Coote, M. Con	15,094	36.6	+7.5
Peters, G. LD	4,266	10.3	-17.6
Coomber, A. UKIP	911	2.2	+1.2
Phillips, S. Green	721	1.7	
Bargery, G. Ind	486	1.2	
Ord-Clarke, J. Loony	198	0.5	+0.2
McLean, B. RNRL	140	0.3	
Lab majority	4,308		10.45%
Electorate	70,734		
Total Vote	41,218		58.27

*Member of last parliament
Lab Hold (2.6% from Con to Lab)

HAVANT

		%	+/- %
*Willetts, D. Con	17,769	43.9	+4.2
Guthrie, P. Lab	13,562	33.5	+1.5
Cole, H. LD	7,508	18.6	-3.8
Jacks, K. Green	793	2.0	
Cuell, T. UKIP	561	1.4	
Stanley, R. Ind	244	0.6	
Con majority	4,207		10.40%
Electorate	70,246		
Total Vote	40,437		57.56

*Member of last parliament
Con Hold (1.3% from Lab to Con)

HAYES AND HARLINGTON

		%	+/- %
*McDonnell, J. Lab	21,279	65.7	+3.7
McLean, R. Con	7,813	24.1	-3.1
Boethe, N. LD	1,958	6.0	-1.4
Burch, G. BNP	705	2.2	
Kennedy, W. SAP	648	2.0	
Lab majority	13,466		41.56%
Electorate	57,561		
Total Vote	32,403		56.29

*Member of last parliament
Lab Hold (3.4% from Con to Lab)

HAZEL GROVE

		%	+/- %
*Stunell, A. LD	20,020	52.0	-2.5
Bargery, N. Con	11,585	30.1	-0.4
Miller, M. Lab	6,230	16.2	+4.3
Price, G. UKIP	643	1.7	+1.1
LD majority	8,435		21.92%
Electorate	65,105		
Total Vote	38,478		59.10

*Member of last parliament
LD Hold (1.0% from LD to Con)

HEMEL HEMPSTEAD

		%	+/- %
*McWalter, T. Lab	21,389	46.6	+0.9
Ivey, P. Con	17,647	38.5	-0.6
Stuart, N. LD	5,877	12.8	+0.5
Newton, B. UKIP	970	2.1	
Lab majority	3,742		8.16%
Electorate	72,743		
Total Vote	45,883		63.08

*Member of last parliament
Lab Hold (0.8% from Con to Lab)

HEMSWORTH

		%	+/- %
*Trickett, J. Lab	23,036	65.4	-5.2
Truss, E. Con	7,400	21.0	+3.2
Waller, E. LD	3,990	11.3	+2.5
Turek, P. SLP	801	2.3	
Lab majority	15,636		44.39%
Electorate	67,948		
Total Vote	35,227		51.84

*Member of last parliament
Lab Hold (4.2% from Lab to Con)

HENDON

		%	+/- %
*Dismore, A. Lab	21,432	52.5	+3.1
Evans, R. Con	14,015	34.3	-2.7
Casey, W. LD	4,724	11.6	+0.7
Crosbie, J. UKIP	409	1.0	+0.5
Taylor, S. WRP	164	0.4	+0.1
Stewart, M. PDP	107	0.3	
Lab majority	7,417		18.16%
Electorate	78,212		
Total Vote	40,851		52.23

*Member of last parliament
Lab Hold (2.9% from Con to Lab)

HENLEY

		%	+/- %
Johnson, B. Con	20,466	46.1	-0.3
Bearder, C. LD	12,008	27.0	+2.3
Matthews, J. Lab	9,367	21.1	-1.6
Collings, P. UKIP	1,413	3.2	
Tickell, O. Green	1,147	2.6	+1.6
Con majority	8,458		19.05%
Electorate	69,081		
Total Vote	44,401		64.27

Con Hold (1.3% from Con to LD)

HEREFORD

		%	+/- %
*Keetch, P. LD	18,244	40.9	-7.1
Taylor, V. Con	17,276	38.7	+3.4
Hallam, D. Lab	6,739	15.1	+2.6
Easton, C. UKIP	1,184	2.7	
Gillett, D. Green	1,181	2.6	
LD majority	968		2.17%
Electorate	70,305		
Total Vote	44,624		63.47

*Member of last parliament
LD Hold (5.2% from LD to Con)

HERTFORD AND STORTFORD

		%	+/- %
Prisk, M. Con	21,074	44.7	+0.6
Speller, S. Lab	15,471	32.8	+1.4
Goldspink, M. LD	9,388	19.9	+2.2
Rising, S. UKIP	1,243	2.6	+0.4
Con majority	5,603		11.88%
Electorate	75,141		
Total Vote	47,176		62.78

Con Hold (0.4% from Con to Lab)

NORTH EAST HERTFORDSHIRE

		%	+/- %
*Heald, O. Con	19,695	44.1	+2.4
Gibbons, I. Lab	16,251	36.4	+0.6
Kingman, A. LD	7,686	17.2	-1.0
Virgo, M. UKIP	1,013	2.3	
Con majority	3,444		7.71%
Electorate	68,718		
Total Vote	44,645		64.97

*Member of last parliament
Con Hold (0.9% from Lab to Con)

SOUTH WEST HERTFORDSHIRE

		%	+/- %
*Page, R. Con	20,933	44.3	-1.7
Dale, G. Lab	12,752	27.0	-0.9
Featherstone, E. LD	12,431	26.3	+4.0
Dale-Mills, C. UKIP	847	1.8	
Goffin, J. ProLife	306	0.6	
Con majority	8,181		17.31%
Electorate	73,264		
Total Vote	47,269		64.52

*Member of last parliament
Con Hold (0.4% from Con to Lab)

HERTSMERE

		%	+/- %
*Clappison, J. Con	19,855	47.8	+3.5
Broderick, H. Lab	14,953	36.0	-2.2
Thompson, P. LD	6,300	15.2	+2.3
Dry, J. SLP	397	1.0	
Con majority	4,902		11.81%
Electorate	68,780		
Total Vote	41,505		60.34

*Member of last parliament
Con Hold (2.9% from Lab to Con)

HEXHAM

		%	+/- %
*Atkinson, P. Con	18,917	44.6	+5.8
Brannen, P. Lab	16,388	38.6	+0.4
Latham, P. LD	6,380	15.0	-2.4
Patterson, A. UKIP	728	1.7	-0.8
Con majority	2,529		5.96%
Electorate	59,807		
Total Vote	42,413		70.92

*Member of last parliament
Con Hold (2.7% from Lab to Con)

HEYWOOD AND MIDDLETON

		%	+/- %
*Dobbin, J. Lab	22,377	57.7	-0.0
Hopkins, M. Con	10,707	27.6	+4.6
Greenhalgh, I. LD	4,329	11.2	-4.5
Burke, P. Lib	1,021	2.6	+1.1
West, C. CD	345	0.9	
Lab majority	11,670		30.09%
Electorate	73,005		
Total Vote	38,779		53.12

*Member of last parliament
Lab Hold (2.3% from Lab to Con)

HIGH PEAK

		%	+/- %
*Levitt, T. Lab	22,430	46.6	-4.2
Chapman, S. Con	17,941	37.3	+1.8
Ashenden, P. LD	7,743	16.1	+4.9
Lab majority	4,489		9.33%
Electorate	73,833		
Total Vote	48,114		65.17

*Member of last parliament
Lab Hold (3.0% from Lab to Con)

HITCHIN AND HARPENDEN

		%	+/- %
*Lilley, P. Con	21,271	47.3	+1.5
Amos, A. Lab	14,608	32.5	-0.6
Murphy, J. LD	8,076	18.0	-2.1
Saunders, J. UKIP	606	1.3	
Rigby, P. Ind	363	0.8	
Con majority	6,663		14.83%
Electorate	67,196		
Total Vote	44,924		66.86

*Member of last parliament
Con Hold (1.1% from Lab to Con)

HOLBORN AND ST PANCRAS

		%	+/- %
*Dobson, F. Lab	16,770	53.9	-11.2
Green, N. LD	5,595	18.0	+5.5
Serelli, R. Con	5,258	16.9	-1.0
Whitley, R. Green	1,875	6.0	
Udwin, C. SA	971	3.1	
Brar, J. SLP	359	1.2	
Nielsen, M. UKIP	301	1.0	
Lab majority	11,175		35.90%
Electorate	68,205		
Total Vote	31,129		45.64

*Member of last parliament
Lab Hold (8.3% from Lab to LD)

SOUTH HOLLAND AND THE DEEPINGS

		%	+/- %
*Hayes, J. Con	25,611	55.4	+6.2
Walker, G. Lab	14,512	31.4	-1.9
Hill, G. LD	4,761	10.3	-5.3
Charlesworth, M. UKIP	1,318	2.9	
Con majority	11,099		24.02%
Electorate	73,922		
Total Vote	46,202		62.50

*Member of last parliament
Con Hold (4.0% from Lab to Con)

HORNCHURCH

		%	+/- %
*Cryer, J. Lab	16,514	46.4	-3.8
Squire, R. Con	15,032	42.3	+5.0
Lea, S. LD	2,928	8.2	+0.4
Webb, L. UKIP	893	2.5	
Durant, D. Third	190	0.5	-0.1
Lab majority	1,482		4.17%
Electorate	61,185		
Total Vote	35,557		58.28

*Member of last parliament
Lab Hold (4.4% from Lab to Con)

HORNSEY AND WOOD GREEN

		%	+/- %
*Roche, B. Lab	21,967	49.9	-11.9
Featherstone, L. LD	11,353	25.8	+14.5
Hollands, J. Con	6,921	15.7	-6.2
Forbes, J. Green	2,228	5.1	+2.7
Christian, L. SA	1,106	2.5	
Rule, E. SLP	294	0.7	-0.5
Ataman, E. Reform 2000	194	0.4	
Lab majority	10,614		24.09%
Electorate	75,974		
Total Vote	44,063		58.00

*Member of last parliament
Lab Hold (13.2% from Lab to LD)

HORSHAM

		%	+/- %
*Maude, F. Con	26,134	51.5	+0.7
Carr, H. LD	12,468	24.6	-0.2
Sully, J. Lab	10,267	20.2	+1.5
Miller, H. UKIP	1,472	2.9	+1.5
Duggan, J. None	429	0.8	
Con majority	13,666		26.92%
Electorate	79,604		
Total Vote	50,770		63.78

*Member of last parliament
Con Hold (0.5% from LD to Con)

HOUGHTON AND WASHINGTON EAST

		%	+/- %
*Kemp, F. Lab	24,628	73.2	-3.2
Devenish, T. Con	4,810	14.3	+1.4
Ormerod, R. LD	4,203	12.5	+4.8

Lab majority	19,818	58.91%
Electorate	67,946	
Total Vote	33,641	49.51

*Member of last parliament
Lab Hold (2.3% from Lab to Con)

HOVE

		%	+/- %
*Caplin, I. Lab	19,253	45.9	+1.3
Langston, J. Con	16,082	38.3	+1.9
De Souza, H. LD	3,823	9.1	-0.5
Ballam, A. Green	1,369	3.3	+1.9
Richards, A. SA	531	1.3	
Franklin, R. UKIP	358	0.9	+0.4
Donovan, N. Lib	316	0.8	
Dobbshead, S. Free	196	0.5	
Major, T. Ind	60	0.1	
Lab majority	3,171		7.55%
Electorate	70,889		
Total Vote	41,988		59.23

*Member of last parliament
Lab Hold (0.3% from Lab to Con)

HUDDERSFIELD

		%	+/- %
*Sheerman, B. Lab	18,840	53.2	-3.2
Baverstock, P. Con	8,794	24.9	+3.9
Bentley, N. LD	5,300	15.0	-2.2
Phillips, J. Green	1,254	3.5	+1.4
Longman, J. UKIP	613	1.7	
Hellawell, G. SA	374	1.1	
Randall, G. SLP	208	0.6	
Lab majority	10,046		28.39%
Electorate	64,350		
Total Vote	35,383		54.99

*Member of last parliament
Lab Hold (3.6% from Lab to Con)

HULL EAST

		%	+/- %
*Prescott, J. Lab	19,938	64.6	-6.7
Swinson, J. LD	4,613	14.9	+5.1
Verma, S. Con	4,276	13.8	+0.1
Jenkinson, J. UKIP	1,218	3.9	
Muir, L. SLP	830	2.7	
Lab majority	15,325		49.64%
Electorate	66,397		
Total Vote	30,875		46.50

*Member of last parliament
Lab Hold (5.9% from Lab to LD)

HULL NORTH

		%	+/- %
*McNamara, K. Lab	16,364	57.2	8.7
Butterworth, S. LD	5,643	19.7	+5.1
Charlson, P. Con	4,902	17.1	+2.1
Robinson, T. UKIP	655	2.3	
Smith, R. SA	490	1.7	
Wagner, C. LCA	478	1.7	
Veasey, C. Ind	101	0.4	
Lab majority	10,721		37.44%
Electorate	62,938		
Total Vote	28,633		45.49

*Member of last parliament
Lab Hold (6.9% from Lab to LD)

HULL WEST AND HESSLE

		%	+/- %
*Johnson, A. Lab	16,880	58.4	-0.3
Sharp, J. Con	5,929	20.5	+2.4
Wastling, A. LD	4,364	15.1	-3.1
Cornforth, J. UKIP	878	3.0	
Harris, D. Ind	512	1.8	
Skinner, D. SLP	353	1.2	
Lab majority	10,951		37.87%
Electorate	63,077		
Total Vote	28,916		45.84

*Member of last parliament
Lab Hold (1.4% from Lab to Con)

HUNTINGDON

		%	+/- %
Djanogly, J. Con	24,507	49.9	-5.4
Pope, M. LD	11,715	23.9	+9.1
Sulaiman, T. Lab	11,211	22.8	-0.6
Norman, D. UKIP	1,656	3.4	+2.8
Con majority	12,792		26.06%
Electorate	80,335		
Total Vote	49,089		61.11

Con Hold (7.3% from Con to LD)

HYNDBURN

		%	+/- %
*Pope, G. Lab	20,900	54.7	-0.9
Britcliffe, P. Con	12,681	33.2	+1.3
Greene, B. LD	3,680	9.6	+1.0
Tomlin, J. UKIP	982	2.6	
Lab majority	8,219		21.49%
Electorate	66,533		
Total Vote	38,243		57.48

*Member of last parliament
Lab Hold (1.1% from Lab to Con)

ILFORD NORTH

		%	+/- %
*Perham, L. Lab	18,428	45.8	-1.6
Bendall, V. Con	16,313	40.5	-0.2
Stollar, G. LD	4,717	11.7	+1.4
Levin, M. UKIP	776	1.9	
Lab majority	2,115		5.26%
Electorate	68,893		
Total Vote	40,234		58.40

*Member of last parliament
Lab Hold (0.7% from Lab to Con)

ILFORD SOUTH

		%	+/- %
*Gapes, M. Lab	24,619	59.6	+1.1
Kumar, S. Con	10,622	25.7	-4.4
Scott, R. LD	4,647	11.3	+5.0
Khan, H. UKIP	1,407	3.4	
Lab majority	13,997		33.90%
Electorate	76,025		
Total Vote	41,295		54.32

*Member of last parliament
Lab Hold (2.8% from Con to Lab)

INVERNESS EAST, NAIRN AND LOCHABER

		%	+/- %
*Stewart, D. Lab	15,605	36.8	+2.9
MacNeil, A. SNP	10,889	25.6	-3.3
Kenton, P. LD	9,420	22.2	+4.7
Jenkins, R. Con	5,653	13.3	-4.2
Arnott, S. SSP	894	2.1	
Lab majority	4,716		11.11%
Electorate	67,264		
Total Vote	42,461		63.13

*Member of last parliament
Lab Hold (3.1% from SNP to Lab)

IPSWICH

		%	+/- %
*Cann, J. Lab	19,952	51.3	-1.4
Wild, E. Con	11,871	30.5	-0.6
Gilbert, T. LD	5,904	15.2	+3.0
Vinyard, W. UKIP	624	1.6	+1.2
Leech, P. SA	305	0.8	
Gratton, S. SLP	217	0.6	
Lab majority	8,081		20.79%
Electorate	68,198		
Total Vote	38,873		57.00

*Member of last parliament
Lab Hold (0.4% from Lab to Con)

ISLE OF WIGHT

		%	+/- %
Turner, A. Con	25,223	39.7	+5.7
*Brand, P. LD	22,397	35.3	-7.5
Gardiner, D. Lab	9,676	15.2	+2.1
Lott, D. UKIP	2,106	3.3	+1.9
Holmes, D. Ind	1,423	2.2	
Scivier, P. Green	1,279	2.0	+1.3
Murray, P. IOW	1,164	1.8	
Spensley, J. SLP	214	0.3	
Con majority	2,826		4.45%
Electorate	103,654		
Total Vote	63,482		61.24

*Member of last parliament
Con Gain (6.6% from LD to Con)

ISLINGTON NORTH

		%	+/- %
*Corbyn, J. Lab	18,699	61.9	-7.4
Willoughby, L. LD	5,741	19.0	+5.4
Rands, N. Con	3,249	10.8	-2.2
Ashby, C. Green	1,876	6.2	+2.0
Cook, S. SLP	512	1.7	
Hassan, E. Reform 2000	139	0.5	
Lab majority	12,958		42.88%
Electorate	61,970		
Total Vote	30,216		48.76

*Member of last parliament
Lab Hold (6.4% from Lab to LD)

ISLINGTON SOUTH AND FINSBURY

		%	+/- %
*Smith, C. Lab	15,217	53.9	-8.6
Sharp, K. LD	7,937	28.1	+6.8
Morgan, N. Con	3,860	13.7	+0.7
Booth, J. SA	817	2.9	
McCarthy, T. Ind	276	1.0	
Thomson, C. Stuck	108	0.4	
Lab majority	7,280		25.80%
Electorate	59,516		
Total Vote	28,215		47.41

*Member of last parliament
Lab Hold (7.7% from Lab to LD)

ISLWYN

		%	+/- %
*Touhig, D. Lab	19,505	61.5	-12.6
Etheridge, K. LD	4,196	13.2	+4.8
Thomas, L. Pl C	3,767	11.9	+5.6
Howells, P. Con	2,543	8.0	+0.2
Taylor, P. None	1,263	4.0	
Millington, M. SLP	417	1.3	
Lab majority	15,309		48.31%
Electorate	51,230		
Total Vote	31,691		61.86

*Member of last parliament
Lab Hold (8.7% from Lab to LD)

JARROW		%	+/- %
*Hepburn, S. Lab	22,777	66.1	+1.2
Selby, J. LD	5,182	15.0	+4.0
Wood, D. Con	5,056	14.7	-0.3
Badger, A. UKIP	716	2.1	
Le Blond, A. Ind	391	1.1	
Bissett, J. None	357	1.0	
Lab majority	17,595		51.03%
Electorate	62,467		
Total Vote	34,479		55.20

*Member of last parliament
Lab Hold (1.4% from Lab to LD)

KEIGHLEY		%	+/- %
*Cryer, A. Lab	20,888	48.2	-2.4
Cooke, S. Con	16,883	39.0	+2.2
Doyle, M. LD	4,722	10.9	+1.1
Cassidy, M. UKIP	840	1.9	
Lab majority	4,005		9.24%
Electorate	68,331		
Total Vote	43,333		63.42

*Member of last parliament
Lab Hold (2.3% from Lab to Con)

KENSINGTON AND CHELSEA		%	+/- %
*Portillo, M. Con	15,270	54.4	+0.8
Stanley, S. Lab	6,499	23.2	-4.8
Falkner, K. LD	4,416	15.7	+0.5
Stephenson, J. Green	1,168	4.2	
Hockney, N. UKIP	416	1.5	0.0
Quintavalle, J. ProLife	179	0.6	
Crab, G. Jam	100	0.4	
Con majority	8,771		31.27%
Electorate	64,893		
Total Vote	28,048		43.22

*Member of last parliament
Con Hold (2.8% from Lab to Con)

KETTERING		%	+/- %
*Sawford, P. Lab	24,034	44.7	+1.4
Hollobone, P. Con	23,369	43.5	+0.5
Aron, R. LD	5,469	10.2	-0.5
Mahoney, B. UKIP	880	1.6	
Lab majority	665		1.24%
Electorate	78,946		
Total Vote	53,752		68.09

*Member of last parliament
Lab Hold (0.5% from Con to Lab)

KILMARNOCK AND LOUDOUN		%	+/- %
*Browne, D. Lab	19,926	52.9	+3.1
Brady, J. SNP	9,592	25.5	-9.1
Reece, D. Con	3,943	10.5	-0.3
Stewart, J. LD	3,177	8.4	+4.4
Muir, J. SSP	1,027	2.7	
Lab majority	10,334		27.44%
Electorate	61,048		
Total Vote	37,665		61.70

*Member of last parliament
Lab Hold (6.1% from SNP to Lab)

KINGSTON AND SURBITON		%	+/- %
*Davey, E. LD	29,542	60.2	+23.5
Shaw, D. Con	13,866	28.2	-8.3
Woodford, P. Lab	4,302	8.8	-14.3
Spruce, C. Green	572	1.2	
Burns, A. UKIP	438	0.9	+0.1

Hayball, J. SLP	319	0.6	
Middleton, J. UPP	54	0.1	
LD majority	15,676		31.93%
Electorate	72,683		
Total Vote	49,093		67.54

*Member of last parliament
LD Hold (15.9% from Con to LD)

KINGSWOOD		%	+/- %
*Berry, R. Lab	28,903	54.9	+1.1
Marven, R. Con	14,941	28.4	-1.6
Greenfield, C. LD	7,747	14.7	+1.9
Smith, D. UKIP	1,085	2.1	
Lab majority	13,962		26.51%
Electorate	80,532		
Total Vote	52,676		65.41

*Member of last parliament
Lab Hold (1.4% from Con to Lab)

KIRKCALDY		%	+/- %
*Moonie, L. Lab	15,227	54.1	+0.5
Somerville, S. SNP	6,264	22.2	-0.7
Campbell, S. Con	3,013	10.7	-3.0
Weston, A. LD	2,849	10.1	+1.5
Kinnear, D. SSP	804	2.9	
Lab majority	8,963		31.83%
Electorate	51,559		
Total Vote	28,157		54.61

*Member of last parliament
Lab Hold (0.6% from SNP to Lab)

KNOWSLEY NORTH AND SEFTON EAST		%	+/- %
*Howarth, G. Lab	25,035	66.7	-3.2
Chapman, K. Con	6,108	16.3	-1.0
Roberts, R. LD	5,173	13.8	+2.7
Waugh, R. SLP	574	1.5	-0.2
Rossiter, T. Ind	356	0.9	
Jones, D. Ind	271	0.7	
Lab majority	18,927		50.45%
Electorate	70,781		
Total Vote	37,517		53.00

*Member of last parliament
Lab Hold (1.1% from Lab to Con)

KNOWSLEY SOUTH		%	+/- %
*O'Hara, E. Lab	26,071	71.3	-5.9
Smithson, D. LD	4,755	13.0	+4.7
Jemetta, P. Con	4,250	11.6	-1.0
Fogg, A. SLP	1,068	2.9	
McNee, M. Ind	446	1.2	
Lab majority	21,316		58.26%
Electorate	70,681		
Total Vote	36,590		51.77

*Member of last parliament
Lab Hold (5.3% from Lab to LD)

LAGAN VALLEY		%	+/- %
*Donaldson, J. UUP	25,966	56.5	+1.1
Close, S. Alliance	7,624	16.6	-0.6
Poots, E. DUP	6,164	13.4	-0.1
Lewsley, P. SDLP	3,462	7.5	-0.2
Butler, P. SF	2,725	5.9	+3.4
UUP majority	18,342		39.93%
Electorate	72,671		
Total Vote	45,941		63.22

*Member of last parliament
UUP Hold (0.9% from Alliance to UUP)

WEST LANCASHIRE

		%	+/- %
*Pickthall, C. Lab	23,404	54.5	-5.9
Myers, J. Con	13,761	32.0	+3.0
Thornton, J. LD	4,966	11.6	+4.4
Hill, D. Ind	523	1.2	
Braid, D. Ind	317	0.7	
Lab majority	9,643		22.44%
Electorate	73,046		
Total Vote	42,971		58.83

*Member of last parliament
Lab Hold (4.4% from Lab to Con)

LANCASTER AND WYRE

		%	+/- %
*Dawson, H. Lab	22,556	43.1	+0.3
Barclay, S. Con	22,075	42.2	+1.6
Scott, E. LD	5,383	10.3	-1.3
Whitelegg, J. Green	1,595	3.0	+1.7
Whittaker, J. UKIP	741	1.4	+0.2
Lab majority	481		0.92%
Electorate	78,964		
Total Vote	52,350		66.30

*Member of last parliament
Lab Hold (0.6% from Lab to Con)

LEEDS CENTRAL

		%	+/- %
*Benn, H. Lab	18,277	66.9	-2.7
Richmond, V. Con	3,896	14.3	+0.5
Arnold, S. LD	3,607	13.2	+2.0
Burgess, D. UKIP	775	2.8	
Johnston, S. SA	751	2.8	
Lab majority	14,381		52.67%
Electorate	65,653		
Total Vote	27,306		41.59

*Member of last parliament
Lab Hold (1.6% from Lab to Con)

LEEDS EAST

		%	+/- %
*Mudie, G. Lab	18,290	62.9	-4.5
Anderson, B. Con	5,647	19.4	+0.8
Jennings, B. LD	3,923	13.5	+3.2
Northgreaves, R. UKIP	634	2.2	
King, M. SLP	419	1.4	
Socrates, P. None	142	0.5	
Lab majority	12,643		43.51%
Electorate	56,552		
Total Vote	29,055		51.38

*Member of last parliament
Lab Hold (2.6% from Lab to Con)

LEEDS NORTH EAST

		%	+/- %
*Hamilton, F. Lab	19,540	49.1	-0.0
Rhys, O. Con	12,451	31.3	-2.6
Brown, J. LD	6,325	15.9	+2.0
Foote, C. Left All	770	1.9	
Miles, J. UKIP	382	1.0	
Muir, C. SLP	173	0.4	-0.6
Zaman, M. Ind	132	0.3	
Lab majority	7,089		17.82%
Electorate	64,263		
Total Vote	39,773		61.89

*Member of last parliament
Lab Hold (1.3% from Con to Lab)

LEEDS NORTH WEST

		%	+/- %
*Best, H. Lab	17,794	41.9	+2.0
Pritchard, A. Con	12,558	29.6	-2.5
Hall-Matthews, D. LD	11,431	26.9	+3.3
Jones, S. UKIP	668	1.6	
Lab majority	5,236		12.33%
Electorate	72,941		
Total Vote	42,451		58.20

*Member of last parliament
Lab Hold (2.3% from Con to Lab)

LEEDS WEST

		%	+/- %
*Battle, J. Lab	19,943	62.1	-4.5
Hopkins, K. Con	5,008	15.6	-1.9
Finlay, D. LD	3,350	10.4	+1.4
Blackburn, D. Green	2,573	8.0	+5.8
Finley, W. UKIP	758	2.4	
Nowosielski, N. Lib	462	1.4	-0.1
Lab majority	14,935		46.54%
Electorate	64,342		
Total Vote	32,094		49.88

*Member of last parliament
Lab Hold (1.3% from Lab to Con)

LEICESTER EAST

		%	+/- %
*Vaz, K. Lab	23,402	57.6	-7.9
Mugglestone, J. Con	9,960	24.5	+0.5
Athwal, H. LD	4,989	12.3	+5.3
Roberts, D. SLP	837	2.1	+1.1
Potter, C. BNP	772	1.9	
Bennett, S. Ind	701	1.7	
Lab majority	13,442		33.06%
Electorate	65,526		
Total Vote	40,661		62.05

*Member of last parliament
Lab Hold (4.2% from Lab to Con)

LEICESTER SOUTH

		%	+/- %
*Marshall, J. Lab	22,958	54.5	-3.5
Hoile, R. Con	9,715	23.1	-0.7
Gill, P. LD	7,243	17.2	+3.4
Layton, M. Green	1,217	2.9	
Gardner, A. SLP	676	1.6	+0.3
Ladwa, K. UKIP	333	0.8	
Lab majority	13,243		31.42%
Electorate	72,674		
Total Vote	42,142		57.99

*Member of last parliament
Lab Hold (1.4% from Lab to Con)

LEICESTER WEST

		%	+/- %
*Hewitt, P. Lab	18,014	54.2	-1.0
Shaw, T. Con	8,375	25.2	+1.5
Vincent, A. LD	5,085	15.3	+1.1
Gough, M. Green	1,074	3.2	+1.8
Kirkpatrick, S. SLP	350	1.1	-0.1
Score, S. SA	321	1.0	
Lab majority	9,639		29.02%
Electorate	65,267		
Total Vote	33,219		50.90

*Member of last parliament
Lab Hold (1.2% from Lab to Con)

NORTH WEST LEICESTERSHIRE

		%	+/- %
*Taylor, D. Lab	23,431	52.1	-4.3
Weston, N. Con	15,274	33.9	+3.0
Fraser-Fleming, C. LD	4,651	10.3	+1.7
Nattrass, W. UKIP	1,021	2.3	
Nettleton, R. Ind	632	1.4	
Lab majority	8,157		18.12%
Electorate	68,414		
Total Vote	45,009		65.79

*Member of last parliament
Lab Hold (3.6% from Lab to Con)

LEIGH

		%	+/- %
Burnham, A. Lab	22,783	64.5	-4.4
Oxley, A. Con	6,421	18.2	+2.6
Atkins, R. LD	4,524	12.8	+1.6
Kelly, W. SLP	820	2.3	
Best, C. UKIP	750	2.1	
Lab majority	16,362		46.35%
Electorate	71,054		
Total Vote	35,298		49.68

Lab Hold (3.5% from Lab to Con)

LEOMINSTER

		%	+/- %
Wiggin, B. Con	22,879	49.0	+3.7
Downie, C. LD	12,512	26.8	-1.0
Hart, S. Lab	7,872	16.8	
Hart, S. Lab	7,872	16.8	-0.6
Bennett, P. Green	1,690	3.6	+1.5
Kingsley, C. UKIP	1,590	3.4	+2.2
Haycock, J. Ind	186	0.4	
Con majority	10,367		22.19%
Electorate	68,695		
Total Vote	46,729		68.02

Con Hold (2.4% from LD to Con)

LEWES

		%	+/- %
*Baker, N. LD	25,588	56.3	+13.1
Sinnatt, S. Con	15,878	34.9	-5.6
Richards, P. Lab	3,317	7.3	-3.3
Harvey, J. UKIP	650	1.4	+0.9
LD majority	9,710		21.37%
Electorate	66,332		
Total Vote	45,433		68.49

*Member of last parliament
LD Hold (9.4% from Con to LD)

LEWISHAM, DEPTFORD

		%	+/- %
*Ruddock, J. Lab	18,915	65.0	-5.8
McCartney, C. Con	3,622	12.4	-2.3
Wiseman, A. LD	3,409	11.7	+2.8
Johnson, D. Green	1,901	6.5	
Page, I. SA	1,260	4.3	
Lab majority	15,293		52.54%
Electorate	60,275		
Total Vote	29,107		48.29

*Member of last parliament
Lab Hold (1.8% from Lab to Con)

LEWISHAM EAST

		%	+/- %
*Prentice, B. Lab	16,116	53.6	-4.7
McInnes, D. Con	7,157	23.8	-2.1
Buxton, D. LD	4,937	16.4	+5.3
Roberts, B. BNP	1,005	3.3	
Kysow, J. SA	464	1.5	
Link, M. UKIP	361	1.2	
Lab majority	8,959		29.82%
Electorate	56,657		
Total Vote	30,040		53.02

*Member of last parliament
Lab Hold (1.3% from Lab to Con)

LEWISHAM WEST

		%	+/- %
*Dowd, J. Lab	18,816	61.1	-0.9
Johnson, G. Con	6,896	22.4	-1.5
Thomas, R. LD	4,146	13.5	+3.7
Pearson, F. UKIP	485	1.6	
Long, N. Ind	472	1.5	

Lab majority	11,920	38.68%
Electorate	59,176	
Total Vote	30,815	52.07

*Member of last parliament
Lab Hold (0.3% from Con to Lab)

LEYTON AND WANSTEAD

		%	+/- %
*Cohen, H. Lab	19,558	58.0	-2.8
Heckels, E. Con	6,654	19.7	-2.5
Wilcock, A. LD	5,389	16.0	+0.9
Gunstock, A. Green	1,030	3.1	
Labern, S. SA	709	2.1	
Skaife D'Ingerthorpe, M. UKIP	378	1.1	
Lab majority	12,904		38.27%
Electorate	61,818		
Total Vote	33,718		54.54

*Member of last parliament
Lab Hold (0.2% from Con to Lab)

LICHFIELD

		%	+/- %
*Fabricant, M. Con	20,480	49.1	+6.2
Machray, M. Lab	16,054	38.5	-3.9
Bennion, P. LD	4,462	10.7	-0.6
Phazey, J. UKIP	684	1.6	
Con majority	4,426		10.62%
Electorate	63,794		
Total Vote	41,680		65.34

*Member of last parliament
Con Hold (5.1% from Lab to Con)

LINCOLN

		%	+/- %
*Merron, G. Lab	20,003	53.9	-1.0
Talbot, C. Con	11,583	31.2	+0.2
Gabriel, L. LD	4,703	12.7	+1.8
Doughty, R. UKIP	836	2.3	
Lab majority	8,420		22.68%
Electorate	66,299		
Total Vote	37,125		56.00

*Member of last parliament
Lab Hold (0.6% from Con to Lab)

LINLITHGOW

		%	+/- %
*Dalyell, T. Lab	17,207	54.4	+0.2
Sibbald, J. SNP	8,078	25.5	-1.3
Lindhurst, G. Con	2,836	9.0	-3.6
Oliver, M. LD	2,628	8.3	+2.4
Cornock, E. SSP	695	2.2	
Cronin, L. RNRL	211	0.7	
Lab majority	9,129		28.84%
Electorate	54,603		
Total Vote	31,655		57.97

*Member of last parliament
Lab Hold (0.8% from SNP to Lab)

LIVERPOOL GARSTON

		%	+/- %
*Eagle, M. Lab	20,043	61.4	+0.1
Keaveney, P. LD	7,549	23.1	+4.1
Sutton, H. Con	5,059	15.5	-0.2
Lab majority	12,494		38.27%
Electorate	65,094		
Total Vote	32,651		50.16

*Member of last parliament
Lab Hold (2.0% from Lab to LD)

LIVERPOOL RIVERSIDE

		%	+/- %
*Ellman, L. Lab	18,201	71.4	+0.9
Marbrow, R. LD	4,251	16.7	+3.4
Edwards, J. Con	2,142	8.4	-1.1
Wilson, C. SA	909	3.6	
Lab majority	13,950		54.70%
Electorate	74,827		
Total Vote	25,503		34.08

*Member of last parliament
Lab Hold (1.2% from Lab to LD)

LIVERPOOL WALTON

		%	+/- %
*Kilfoyle, P. Lab	22,143	77.8	-0.6
Reid, K. LD	4,147	14.6	+3.4
Horgan, S. Con	1,726	6.1	-0.3
Forest, P. UKIP	442	1.6	
Lab majority	17,996		63.24%
Electorate	66,237		
Total Vote	28,458		42.96

*Member of last parliament
Lab Hold (2.0% from Lab to LD)

LIVERPOOL WAVERTREE

		%	+/- %
*Kennedy, J. Lab	20,155	62.7	-1.7
Newby, C. LD	7,836	24.4	+2.8
Allen, G. Con	3,091	9.6	-1.1
Lane, M. SLP	359	1.1	
O'Brien, M. SA	349	1.1	
Miney, N. UKIP	348	1.1	
Lab majority	12,319		38.33%
Electorate	72,555		
Total Vote	32,138		44.29

*Member of last parliament
Lab Hold (2.3% from Lab to LD)

LIVERPOOL WEST DERBY

		%	+/- %
*Wareing, R. Lab	20,454	66.2	-5.0
Radford, S. Lib	4,601	14.9	+5.3
Moloney, P. LD	3,366	10.9	+1.9
Clare, B. Con	2,486	8.0	-0.6
Lab majority	15,853		51.29%
Electorate	67,921		
Total Vote	30,907		45.50

*Member of last parliament
Lab Hold (5.1% from Lab to Lib)

LIVINGSTON

		%	+/- %
*Cook, R. Lab	19,108	53.0	-1.9
Sutherland, G. SNP	8,492	23.6	-3.9
Mackenzie, G. LD	3,969	11.0	+4.3
Mowat, I. Con	2,995	8.3	-1.1
Milne, W. SSP	1,110	3.1	
Kingdon, R. UKIP	359	1.0	
Lab majority	10,616		29.46%
Electorate	64,852		
Total Vote	36,033		55.56

*Member of last parliament
Lab Hold (1.0% from SNP to Lab)

LLANELLI

		%	+/- %
*Davies, D. Lab	17,586	48.6	-9.3
Jones, D. Pl C	11,183	30.9	+11.9
Hayes, S. Con	3,442	9.5	-2.6
Rees, K. LD	3,065	8.5	-0.7
Cliff, J. Green	515	1.4	
Willock, J. SLP	407	1.1	

Lab majority	6,403	17.69%
Electorate	58,148	
Total Vote	36,198	62.25

*Member of last parliament
Lab Hold (10.6% from Lab to Pl C)

CITIES OF LONDON AND WESTMINSTER

		%	+/- %
Field, M. Con	15,737	46.3	-0.9
Katz, M. Lab	11,238	33.1	-2.0
Horwood, M. LD	5,218	15.4	+3.1
Charlton, H. Green	1,318	3.9	
Merton, C. UKIP	464	1.4	+0.8
Con majority	4,499		13.24%
Electorate	71,935		
Total Vote	33,975		47.23

Con Hold (0.5% from Lab to Con)

EAST LONDONDERRY

		%	+/- %
Campbell, G. DUP	12,813	32.1	+6.5
*Ross, W. UUP	10,912	27.4	-8.2
Dallat, J. SDLP	8,298	20.8	-0.9
Brolly, F. SF	6,221	15.6	+6.5
Boyle, Y. Alliance	1,625	4.1	-2.3
DUP majority	1,901		4.77%
Electorate	60,215		
Total Vote	39,869		66.21

*Member of last parliament
DUP Gain (7.4% from UUP to DUP)

LOUGHBOROUGH

		%	+/- %
*Reed, A. Lab	22,016	49.7	+1.2
Lyon, N. Con	15,638	35.3	-2.4
Simons, J. LD	5,667	12.8	+1.0
Bigger, J. UKIP	933	2.1	
Lab majority	6,378		14.41%
Electorate	70,078		
Total Vote	44,254		63.15

*Member of last parliament
Lab Hold (1.8% from Con to Lab)

LOUTH AND HORNCASTLE

		%	+/- %
*Tapsell, P. Con	21,543	48.5	+5.0
Bolland, D. Lab	13,989	31.5	+1.8
Martin, F. LD	8,928	20.1	-4.4
Con majority	7,554		16.99%
Electorate	71,556		
Total Vote	44,460		62.13

*Member of last parliament
Con Hold (1.6% from Lab to Con)

LUDLOW

		%	+/- %
Green, M. LD	18,620	43.2	+13.5
Taylor-Smith, M. Con	16,990	39.4	-3.0
Knowles, N. Lab	5,785	13.4	-12.0
Gaffney, J. Green	871	2.0	+0.3
Gutteridge, P. UKIP	858	2.0	+1.2
LD majority	1,630		3.78%
Electorate	63,514		
Total Vote	43,124		67.90

LD Gain (8.3% from Con to LD)

LUTON NORTH

		%	+/- %
*Hopkins, K. Lab	22,187	56.7	+2.1
Sater, A. Con	12,210	31.2	-3.1
Hoyle, B. LD	3,795	9.7	+0.6
Brown, C. UKIP	934	2.4	+0.9

Lab majority	9,977		25.50%
Electorate	65,998		
Total Vote	39,126		59.28

*Member of last parliament
Lab Hold (2.6% from Con to Lab)

LUTON SOUTH

		%	+/- %
*Moran, M. Lab	21,719	55.2	+0.3
Henderson, G. Con	11,586	29.4	-1.9
Martins, R. LD	4,292	10.9	+1.3
Scheimann, M. Green	798	2.0	+1.3
Lawman, C. UKIP	578	1.5	+0.7
Hearne, J. SA	271	0.7	
Bolton, R. WRP	107	0.3	
Lab majority	10,133		25.75%
Electorate	70,349		
Total Vote	39,351		55.94

*Member of last parliament
Lab Hold (1.1% from Con to Lab)

MACCLESFIELD

		%	+/- %
*Winterton, N. Con	22,284	48.9	-0.7
Carter, S. Lab	15,084	33.1	-0.6
Flynn, M. LD	8,217	18.0	+1.3
Con majority	7,200		15.79%
Electorate	73,123		
Total Vote	45,585		62.34

*Member of last parliament
Con Hold (0.1% from Con to Lab)

MAIDENHEAD

		%	+/- %
*May, T. Con	19,506	45.0	-4.8
Newbound, K. LD	16,222	37.4	+11.2
O'Farrell, J. Lab	6,577	15.2	-2.9
Cooper, D. UKIP	741	1.7	+1.2
Clarke, L. Loony	272	0.6	
Con majority	3,284		7.58%
Electorate	69,837		
Total Vote	43,318		62.03

*Member of last parliament
Con Hold (8.0% from Con to LD)

MAIDSTONE AND THE WEALD

		%	+/- %
*Widdecombe, A. Con	22,621	49.6	+5.5
Davis, M. Lab	12,303	27.0	+0.8
Wainman, A. LD	9,064	19.9	-2.5
Botting, J. UKIP	978	2.1	+1.5
Hunt, N. Ind	611	1.3	
Con majority	10,318		22.64%
Electorate	74,002		
Total Vote	45,577		61.59

*Member of last parliament
Con Hold (2.4% from Lab to Con)

MAKERFIELD

		%	+/- %
*McCartney, I. Lab	23,879	68.5	-5.1
Brooks, J. Con	6,129	17.6	+2.2
Crowther, D. LD	3,990	11.4	+3.1
Jones, M. SA	858	2.5	
Lab majority	17,750		50.92%
Electorate	68,457		
Total Vote	34,856		50.92

*Member of last parliament
Lab Hold (3.6% from Lab to Con)

MALDON AND CHELMSFORD EAST

		%	+/- %
*Whittingdale, J. Con	21,719	49.2	+0.6
Kennedy, R. Lab	13,257	30.1	+1.3
Jackson, J. LD	7,002	15.9	-3.5
Harris, G. UKIP	1,135	2.6	+0.7
Schwarz, W. Green	987	2.2	+0.9
Con majority	8,462		19.19%
Electorate	69,201		
Total Vote	44,100		63.73

*Member of last parliament
Con Hold (0.4% from Con to Lab)

MANCHESTER BLACKLEY

		%	+/- %
*Stringer, G. Lab	18,285	68.9	-1.1
Stanbury, L. Con	3,821	14.4	-0.8
Riding, G. LD	3,015	11.4	+0.4
Barr, K. SLP	485	1.8	
Reissmann, K. SA	461	1.7	
Bhatti, A. Anti-CF	456	1.7	
Lab majority	14,464		54.53%
Electorate	59,111		
Total Vote	26,523		44.87

*Member of last parliament
Lab Hold (0.1% from Lab to Con)

MANCHESTER CENTRAL

		%	+/- %
*Lloyd, T. Lab	17,812	68.7	-2.3
Hobson, P. LD	4,070	15.7	+3.4
Powell, A. Con	2,328	9.0	-2.8
Hall, V. Green	1,018	3.9	
Sinclair, R. SLP	484	1.9	-0.5
Brosnan, T. ProLife	216	0.8	
Lab majority	13,742		53.00%
Electorate	66,268		
Total Vote	25,928		39.13

*Member of last parliament
Lab Hold (2.9% from Lab to LD)

MANCHESTER GORTON

		%	+/- %
*Kaufman, G. Lab	17,099	62.8	-2.5
Pearcey, J. LD	5,795	21.3	+3.8
Causer, C. Con	2,705	9.9	-1.8
Bingham, B. Green	835	3.1	+1.2
Bhatti, R. UKIP	462	1.7	
Muir, K. SLP	333	1.2	-0.2
Lab majority	11,304		41.51%
Electorate	63,834		
Total Vote	27,229		42.66

*Member of last parliament
Lab Hold (3.1% from Lab to LD)

MANCHESTER WITHINGTON

		%	+/- %
*Bradley, K. Lab	19,239	54.9	-6.7
Zalzala, Y. LD	7,715	22.0	+8.4
Samways, J. Con	5,349	15.3	-4.1
Valentine, M. Green	1,539	4.4	
Clegg, J. SA	1,208	3.4	
Lab majority	11,524		32.88%
Electorate	67,480		
Total Vote	35,050		51.94

*Member of last parliament
Lab Hold (7.5% from Lab to LD)

MANSFIELD

		%	+/- %
*Meale, A. Lab	21,050	57.1	-7.3
Wellesley, W. Con	10,012	27.2	+6.0
Hill, T. LD	5,790	15.7	+4.7
Lab majority	11,038		29.95%
Electorate	66,733		
Total Vote	36,852		55.22

*Member of last parliament
Lab Hold (6.7% from Lab to Con)

MEDWAY

		%	+/- %
*Marshall-Andrews, R. Lab	18,914	49.0	+0.1
Reckless, M. Con	15,134	39.2	+2.3
Juby, G. LD	3,604	9.3	-0.8
Sinclaire, N. UKIP	958	2.5	+1.6
Lab majority	3,780		9.79%
Electorate	64,934		
Total Vote	38,610		59.46

*Member of last parliament
Lab Hold (1.1% from Lab to Con)

MEIRIONNYDD NANT CONWY

		%	+/- %
*Llwyd, E. Pl C	10,459	49.6	-1.1
Jones, D. Lab	4,775	22.7	-0.4
Francis, L. Con	3,962	18.8	+2.8
Raw-Rees, D. LD	1,872	8.9	+1.9
Pl C majority	5,684		26.98%
Electorate	32,969		
Total Vote	21,068		63.90

*Member of last parliament
Pl C Hold (0.4% from Pl C to Lab)

MERIDEN

		%	+/- %
*Spelman, C. Con	21,246	47.7	+5.7
Shawcroft, C. Lab	17,462	39.2	-1.8
Hicks, N. LD	4,941	11.1	-1.9
Adams, R. UKIP	910	2.0	
Con majority	3,784		8.49%
Electorate	73,787		
Total Vote	44,559		60.39

*Member of last parliament
Con Hold (3.7% from Lab to Con)

MERTHYR TYDFIL AND RHYMNEY

		%	+/- %
Havard, D. Lab	19,574	61.8	-14.9
Hughes, R. Pl C	4,651	14.7	+8.7
Rogers, S. LD	2,385	7.5	+0.1
Cuming, R. Con	2,272	7.2	+0.8
Edwards, J. Ind	1,936	6.1	
Evans, K. SLP	692	2.2	
Lewis, A. ProLife	174	0.5	
Lab majority	14,923		47.10%
Electorate	54,919		
Total Vote	31,684		57.69

Lab Hold (11.8% from Lab to Pl C)

MID BEDFORDSHIRE – see under Bedfordshire

MID DORSET AND POOLE NORTH – see under Dorset

MID NORFOLK – see under Norfolk

MID SUSSEX – see under Sussex

MID ULSTER – see under Ulster

MID WORCESTERSHIRE – see under Worcestershire

MIDDLESBROUGH

		%	+/- %
*Bell, S. Lab	22,783	67.6	-3.9
Finn, A. Con	6,453	19.1	+2.0
Miller, K. LD	3,512	10.4	+1.9
Kerr-Morgan, G. SA	577	1.7	
Anderson, K. SLP	392	1.2	
Lab majority	16,330		48.43%
Electorate	67,662		
Total Vote	33,717		49.83

*Member of last parliament
Lab Hold (2.9% from Lab to Con)

MIDDLESBROUGH SOUTH AND EAST CLEVELAND

		%	+/- %
*Kumar, A. Lab	24,321	55.3	+0.6
Harpham, B. Con	14,970	34.0	-0.9
Parrish, L. LD	4,700	10.7	+3.2
Lab majority	9,351		21.26%
Electorate	71,542		
Total Vote	43,991		61.49

*Member of last parliament
Lab Hold (0.7% from Con to Lab)

MIDLOTHIAN

		%	+/- %
Hamilton, D. Lab	15,145	52.7	-0.8
Goldie, I. SNP	6,131	21.3	-4.2
Bell, J. LD	3,686	12.8	+3.7
Traquair, R. Con	2,748	9.6	-1.3
Goupillot, B. SSP	837	2.9	
Holden, T. ProLife	177	0.6	
Lab majority	9,014		31.38%
Electorate	48,625		
Total Vote	28,724		59.07

Lab Hold (1.7% from SNP to Lab)

MILTON KEYNES NORTH EAST

		%	+/- %
*White, B. Lab	19,761	42.0	+2.5
Rix, M. Con	17,932	38.1	-0.9
Yeoward, D. LD	8,375	17.8	+0.4
Phillips, M. UKIP	1,026	2.2	
Lab majority	1,829		3.88%
Electorate	72,909		
Total Vote	47,094		64.59

*Member of last parliament
Lab Hold (1.7% from Con to Lab)

MILTON KEYNES SOUTH WEST

		%	+/- %
*Starkey, P. Lab	22,484	49.5	-4.2
Stewart, I. Con	15,506	34.2	+0.7
Mohammad, N. LD	4,828	10.6	-1.3
Francis, A. Green	957	2.1	
Davies, C. UKIP	848	1.9	
Denning, P. LCA	500	1.1	
Bradbury, D. SA	261	0.6	
Lab majority	6,978		15.38%
Electorate	72,823		
Total Vote	45,384		62.32

*Member of last parliament
Lab Hold (2.5% from Lab to Con)

MITCHAM AND MORDEN

		%	+/- %
*McDonagh, S. Lab	22,936	60.4	+2.1
Stokes, H. Con	9,151	24.1	-5.6
Harris, N. LD	3,820	10.1	+2.5

Walsh, T. Green	926	2.4	+1.6
Tyndall, J. BNP	642	1.7	+0.6
Roberts, A. UKIP	486	1.3	+1.0
Lab majority	13,785		36.31%
Electorate	65,671		
Total Vote	37,961		57.80

*Member of last parliament
Lab Hold (3.8% from Con to Lab)

MOLE VALLEY		%	+/- %
*Beresford, P. Con	23,790	50.5	+2.5
Savage, C. LD	13,637	29.0	-0.3
Redford, D. Lab	7,837	16.6	+1.9
Walters, R. UKIP	1,333	2.8	+2.0
Newton, W. ProLife	475	1.0	
Con majority	10,153		21.57%
Electorate	68,316		
Total Vote	47,072		68.90

*Member of last parliament
Con Hold (1.4% from LD to Con)

MONMOUTH		%	+/- %
*Edwards, H. Lab	19,021	42.8	-5.0
Evans, R. Con	18,637	41.9	+2.7
Parker, N. LD	5,080	11.4	+1.9
Hubbard, M. Pl C	1,068	2.4	+1.3
Rowlands, D. UKIP	656	1.5	
Lab majority	384		0.86%
Electorate	62,280		
Total Vote	44,462		71.39

*Member of last parliament
Lab Hold (3.8% from Lab to Con)

MONTGOMERYSHIRE		%	+/- %
*Opik, L. LD	14,319	49.4	+3.5
Jones, D. Con	8,085	27.9	+1.8
Davies, P. Lab	3,443	11.9	-7.3
Senior, D. Pl C	1,969	6.8	+1.8
Rowlands, D. UKIP	786	2.7	
Davies, R. ProLife	210	0.7	
Taylor, R. None	171	0.6	
LD majority	6,234		21.51%
Electorate	44,243		
Total Vote	28,983		65.51

*Member of last parliament
LD Hold (0.9% from Con to LD)

MORAY		%	+/- %
Robertson, A. SNP	10,076	30.3	-11.2
Munro, C. Lab	8,332	25.1	+5.2
Spencer-Nairn, F. Con	7,677	23.1	-4.5
Gorn, L. LD	5,224	15.7	+6.8
Anderson, N. SSP	821	2.5	
Jappy, W. Ind	802	2.4	
Keynon, N. UKIP	291	0.9	
SNP majority	1,744		5.25%
Electorate	58,008		
Total Vote	33,223		57.27

SNP Hold (8.2% from SNP to Lab)

MORECAMBE AND LUNESDALE		%	+/- %
*Smith, G. Lab	20,646	49.6	+0.7
Nuttall, D. Con	15,554	37.3	+0.6
Cotton, C. LD	3,817	9.2	-2.2
Beaman, G. UKIP	935	2.2	
Adams, C. Green	703	1.7	

Lab majority	5,092		12.22%
Electorate	68,159		
Total Vote	41,655		61.11

*Member of last parliament
Lab Hold (0.1% from Con to Lab)

MORLEY AND ROTHWELL		%	+/- %
Challen, C. Lab	21,919	57.0	-1.5
Schofield, D. Con	9,829	25.6	-0.8
Golton, S. LD	5,446	14.2	+3.1
Bardsley, J. UKIP	1,248	3.2	
Lab majority	12,090		31.45%
Electorate	71,880		
Total Vote	38,442		53.48

Lab Hold (0.3% from Lab to Con)

MOTHERWELL AND WISHAW		%	+/- %
*Roy, F. Lab	16,681	56.2	-1.2
McGuigan, J. SNP	5,725	19.3	-3.2
Nolan, M. Con	3,155	10.6	-0.4
Brown, I. LD	2,791	9.4	+3.0
Smellie, S. SSP	1,260	4.2	
Watt, C. SLP	61	0.2	-2.0
Lab majority	10,956		36.92%
Electorate	52,418		
Total Vote	29,673		56.61

*Member of last parliament
Lab Hold (1.0% from SNP to Lab)

NEATH		%	+/- %
*Hain, P. Lab	21,253	60.7	-12.8
Llewelyn, A. Pl C	6,437	18.4	+10.3
Davies, D. LD	3,335	9.5	+3.2
Devine, D. Con	3,310	9.5	+0.8
Pudner, H. SA	483	1.4	
Brienza, G. ProLife	202	0.6	
Lab majority	14,816		42.31%
Electorate	56,001		
Total Vote	35,020		62.53

*Member of last parliament
Lab Hold (11.6% from Lab to Pl C)

NEW FOREST EAST		%	+/- %
*Lewis, J. Con	17,902	42.4	-0.5
Dash, B. LD	14,073	33.4	+1.1
Goodfellow, A. Lab	9,141	21.7	-3.1
Howe, W. UKIP	1,062	2.5	
Con majority	3,829		9.08%
Electorate	66,723		
Total Vote	42,178		63.21

*Member of last parliament
Con Hold (0.8% from Con to LD)

NEW FOREST WEST		%	+/- %
*Swayne, D. Con	24,575	55.7	+5.2
Bignell, M. LD	11,384	25.8	-2.0
Onuegbu, C. Lab	6,481	14.7	+0.4
Clark, M. UKIP	1,647	3.7	+0.6
Con majority	13,191		29.92%
Electorate	67,725		
Total Vote	44,087		65.10

*Member of last parliament
Con Hold (3.6% from LD to Con)

NEWARK

		%	+/- %
Mercer, P. Con	20,983	46.5	+7.1
*Jones, F. Lab	16,910	37.5	-7.8
Harding-Price, D. LD	5,970	13.2	+1.8
Haxby, D. Ind	822	1.8	
Thomson, I. SA	462	1.0	
Con majority	4,073		9.02%
Electorate	71,061		
Total Vote	45,147		63.53

*Member of last parliament
Con Gain (7.4% from Lab to Con)

NEWBURY

		%	+/- %
*Rendel, D. LD	24,507	48.2	-4.7
Benyon, R. Con	22,092	43.5	+5.6
Billcliffe, S. Lab	3,523	6.9	+1.4
Gray-Fisk, D. UKIP	685	1.3	+0.8
LD majority	2,415		4.75%
Electorate	75,490		
Total Vote	50,807		67.30

*Member of last parliament
LD Hold (5.2% from LD to Con)

NEWCASTLE-UNDER-LYME

		%	+/- %
Farrelly, P. Lab	20,650	53.4	-3.1
Flynn, M. Con	10,664	27.6	+6.1
Roodhouse, J. LD	5,993	15.5	+1.5
Fyson, R. Ind	773	2.0	
Godfrey, P. UKIP	594	1.5	
Lab majority	9,986		25.82%
Electorate	65,739		
Total Vote	38,674		58.83

Lab Hold (4.6% from Lab to Con)

NEWCASTLE UPON TYNE CENTRAL

		%	+/- %
*Cousins, J. Lab	19,169	55.0	-4.2
Psallidas, S. LD	7,564	21.7	+6.7
Ruff, A. Con	7,414	21.3	-2.2
Potts, G. SLP	723	2.1	
Lab majority	11,605		33.28%
Electorate	67,970		
Total Vote	34,870		51.30

*Member of last parliament
Lab Hold (5.4% from Lab to LD)

NEWCASTLE UPON TYNE EAST AND WALLSEND

		%	+/- %
*Brown, N. Lab	20,642	63.1	-8.1
Ord, D. LD	6,419	19.6	+9.0
Troman, T. Con	3,873	11.8	-2.1
Gray, A. Green	651	2.0	
Narang, H. Ind	563	1.7	
Carpenter, B. SLP	420	1.3	-0.3
Levy, M. Comm GB	126	0.4	-0.0
Lab majority	14,223		43.50%
Electorate	61,494		
Total Vote	32,694		53.17

*Member of last parliament
Lab Hold (8.5% from Lab to LD)

NEWCASTLE UPON TYNE NORTH

		%	+/- %
*Henderson, D. Lab	21,874	60.1	-2.0
Smith, P. Con	7,424	20.4	+1.0
Soult, G. LD	7,070	19.4	+4.9
Lab majority	14,450		39.73%
Electorate	63,208		
Total Vote	36,368		57.54

*Member of last parliament
Lab Hold (1.5% from Lab to Con)

NEWPORT EAST

		%	+/- %
*Howarth, A. Lab	17,120	54.7	-2.9
Oakley, I. Con	7,246	23.2	+1.8
Cameron, A. LD	4,394	14.0	+3.6
Batcup, M. Pl C	1,519	4.9	+2.9
Screen, E. SLP	420	1.3	-3.9
Reynolds, N. UKIP	410	1.3	
Griffiths, R. Comm GB	173	0.6	
Lab majority	9,874		31.56%
Electorate	56,456		
Total Vote	31,282		55.41

*Member of last parliament
Lab Hold (2.4% from Lab to Con)

NEWPORT WEST

		%	+/- %
*Flynn, P. Lab	18,489	52.7	-7.8
Morgan, W. Con	9,185	26.2	+1.8
Watkins, V. LD	4,095	11.7	+2.0
Salkeld, A. Pl C	2,510	7.2	+5.5
Moelwyn Hughes, H. UKIP	506	1.4	+0.6
Cavill, T. BNP	278	0.8	
Lab majority	9,304		26.54%
Electorate	59,742		
Total Vote	35,063		58.69

*Member of last parliament
Lab Hold (4.8% from Lab to Con)

NEWRY AND ARMAGH

		%	+/- %
*Mallon, S. SDLP	20,784	37.4	-5.6
Murphy, C. SF	17,209	30.9	+9.9
Berry, P. DUP	10,795	19.4	
McRoberts, S. UUP	6,833	12.3	-21.5
SDLP majority	3,575		6.43%
Electorate	72,466		
Total Vote	55,621		76.75

*Member of last parliament
SDLP Hold (7.8% from SDLP to SF)

MID NORFOLK

		%	+/- %
*Simpson, K. Con	23,519	44.8	+5.2
Zeichner, D. Lab	18,957	36.1	-1.2
Clifford-Jackson, V. LD	7,621	14.5	-0.5
Agnew, S. UKIP	1,333	2.5	
Reeve, P. Green	1,118	2.1	-0.1
Con majority	4,562		8.68%
Electorate	79,046		
Total Vote	52,548		66.48

*Member of last parliament
Con Hold (3.2% from Lab to Con)

NORTH NORFOLK

		%	+/- %
Lamb, N. LD	23,978	42.7	+8.4
*Prior, D. Con	23,495	41.8	+5.3
Gates, M. Lab	7,490	13.3	-11.7
Sheridan, M. Green	649	1.2	
Simison, P. UKIP	608	1.1	
LD majority	483		0.86%
Electorate	80,061		
Total Vote	56,220		70.22

*Member of last parliament
LD Gain (1.5% from Con to LD)

NORTH WEST NORFOLK

		%	+/- %
Bellingham, H. Con	24,846	48.5	+7.0
*Turner, G. Lab	21,361	41.7	-2.1
Mack, I. LD	4,292	8.4	-1.2
Durrant, I. UKIP	704	1.4	
Con majority	3,485		6.81%
Electorate	77,387		
Total Vote	51,203		66.16

*Member of last parliament
Con Gain (4.6% from Lab to Con)

SOUTH NORFOLK

		%	+/- %
Bacon, R. Con	23,589	42.2	+2.0
Lee, A. LD	16,696	29.9	+1.6
Wells, M. Lab	13,719	24.5	-1.5
Ross-Wagenknecht, S. Green	1,069	1.9	+1.1
Neal, J. UKIP	856	1.5	+0.9
Con majority	6,893		12.32%
Electorate	82,710		
Total Vote	55,929		67.62

Con Hold (0.2% from LD to Con)

SOUTH WEST NORFOLK

		%	+/- %
*Shephard, G. Con	27,633	52.2	+10.2
Hanson, A. Lab	18,267	34.5	-3.3
Dean, G. LD	5,681	10.7	-3.2
Smith, I. UKIP	1,368	2.6	
Con majority	9,366		17.69%
Electorate	83,903		
Total Vote	52,949		63.11

*Member of last parliament
Con Hold (6.7% from Lab to Con)

NORMANTON

		%	+/- %
*O'Brien, W. Lab	19,152	56.1	-4.5
Smith, G. Con	9,215	27.0	+3.4
Pearson, S. LD	4,990	14.6	+2.2
Appleyard, T. SLP	798	2.3	
Lab majority	9,937		29.09%
Electorate	65,392		
Total Vote	34,155		52.23

*Member of last parliament
Lab Hold (3.9% from Lab to Con)

NORTH ANTRIM – see under Antrim

NORTH CORNWALL – see under Cornwall

NORTH DEVON – see under Devon

NORTH DORSET – see under Dorset

NORTH DOWN – see under Down

NORTH EAST BEDFORDSHIRE –
see under Bedfordshire

NORTH EAST CAMBRIDGESHIRE – see under Cambridgeshire

NORTH EAST DERBYSHIRE –
see under Derbyshire

NORTH EAST FIFE – see under Fife

NORTH EAST HAMPSHIRE –
see under Hampshire

NORTH EAST HERTFORDSHIRE –
see under Hertfordshire

NORTH ESSEX – see under Essex

NORTH NORFOLK – see under Norfolk

NORTH SHROPSHIRE – see under Shropshire

NORTH SOUTHWARK AND BERMONDSEY –
see under Southwark

NORTH SWINDON – see under Swindon

NORTH TAYSIDE – see under Tayside

NORTH THANET – see under Thanet

NORTH TYNESIDE – see under Tyneside

NORTH WARWICKSHIRE –
see under Warwickshire

NORTH WEST CAMBRIDGESHIRE –
see under Cambridgeshire

NORTH WEST DURHAM – see under Durham

NORTH WEST HAMPSHIRE –
see under Hampshire

NORTH WEST LEICESTERSHIRE –
see under Leicestershire

NORTH WEST NORFOLK – see under Norfolk

NORTH WILTSHIRE – see under Wiltshire

NORTHAMPTON NORTH

		%	+/- %
*Keeble, S. Lab	20,507	49.4	-3.3
Whelan, J. Con	12,614	30.4	-3.0
Church, R. LD	7,363	17.7	+5.0
Torbica, D. UKIP	596	1.4	+0.5
White, G. SA	414	1.0	
Lab majority	7,893		19.02%
Electorate	73,836		
Total Vote	41,494		56.20

*Member of last parliament
Lab Hold (0.2% from Lab to Con)

NORTHAMPTON SOUTH

		%	+/- %
*Clarke, T. Lab	21,882	42.9	+0.5
Vara, S. Con	20,997	41.1	0.0
Simpson, A. LD	6,355	12.5	+1.4
Clark, D. UKIP	1,237	2.4	+0.4
Harvey, T. LibP	362	0.7	
Johnson, C. ProLife	196	0.4	
Lab majority	885		1.73%
Electorate	83,848		
Total Vote	51,029		60.86

*Member of last parliament
Lab Hold (0.2% from Con to Lab)

NORTHAVON

		%	+/- %
*Webb, S. LD	29,217	52.4	+10.0
Ruxton, C. Con	19,340	34.7	-4.3
Hall, R. Lab	6,450	11.6	-4.1
Carver, C. UKIP	751	1.3	
LD majority	9,877		17.71%
Electorate	78,840		
Total Vote	55,758		70.72

*Member of last parliament
LD Hold (7.1% from Con to LD)

NORWICH NORTH

		%	+/- %
*Gibson, I. Lab	21,624	47.4	-2.3
Mason, K. Con	15,761	34.6	+2.1
Toye, M. LD	6,750	14.8	+2.2
Tinch, R. Green	797	1.7	
Cheyney, G. UKIP	471	1.0	
Betts, M. Ind	211	0.5	
Lab majority	5,863		12.85%
Electorate	77,158		
Total Vote	45,614		59.12

*Member of last parliament
Lab Hold (2.3% from Lab to Con)

NORWICH SOUTH

		%	+/- %
*Clarke, C. Lab	19,367	45.5	-6.2
French, A. Con	10,551	24.8	+1.1
Aalders-Dunthorne, A. LD	9,640	22.6	+4.0
Holmes, A. Green	1,434	3.4	+1.9
Buffry, A. LCA	620	1.5	
Manningham, E. SA	507	1.2	
Mills, T. UKIP	473	1.1	
Lab majority	8,816		20.70%
Electorate	65,792		
Total Vote	42,592		64.74

*Member of last parliament
Lab Hold (3.7% from Lab to Con)

NOTTINGHAM EAST

		%	+/- %
*Heppell, J. Lab	17,530	59.0	-3.3
Allan, R. Con	7,210	24.3	+0.8
Ball, T. LD	3,874	13.0	+2.9
Radcliff, P. SA	1,117	3.8	
Lab majority	10,320		34.71%
Electorate	65,339		
Total Vote	29,731		45.50

*Member of last parliament
Lab Hold (2.0% from Lab to Con)

NOTTINGHAM NORTH

		%	+/- %
*Allen, G. Lab	19,392	64.5	-1.2
Wright, M. Con	7,152	23.8	+3.5
Lee, R. LD	3,177	10.6	+2.6
Botham, A. SLP	321	1.1	
Lab majority	12,240		40.74%
Electorate	64,281		
Total Vote	30,042		46.74

*Member of last parliament
Lab Hold (2.3% from Lab to Con)

NOTTINGHAM SOUTH

		%	+/- %
*Simpson, A. Lab	19,949	54.5	-0.8
Manning, W. Con	9,960	27.2	-0.5
Mulloy, K. LD	6,064	16.6	+3.7
Bartrop, D. UKIP	632	1.7	
Lab majority	9,989		27.29%
Electorate	72,274		
Total Vote	36,605		50.65

*Member of last parliament
Lab Hold (0.1% from Lab to Con)

NUNEATON

		%	+/- %
*Olner, B. Lab	22,577	52.1	-4.1
Lancaster, M. Con	15,042	34.7	+3.8
Ferguson, T. LD	4,820	11.1	+2.3
James, B. UKIP	873	2.0	+1.6
Lab majority	7,535		17.40%
Electorate	72,101		
Total Vote	43,312		60.07

*Member of last parliament
Lab Hold (4.0% from Lab to Con)

OCHIL

		%	+/- %
*O'Neill, M. Lab	16,004	45.3	+0.3
Brown, K. SNP	10,655	30.2	-4.2
Campbell, A. Con	4,235	12.0	-2.6
Edie, P. LD	3,253	9.2	+4.0
Thomson, P. SSP	751	2.1	
Approaching, F. Loony	405	1.1	
Lab majority	5,349		15.15%
Electorate	57,554		
Total Vote	35,303		61.34

*Member of last parliament
Lab Hold (2.3% from SNP to Lab)

OGMORE

		%	+/- %
*Powell, R. Lab	18,833	62.0	-11.9
Pulman, A. Pl C	4,259	14.0	+7.0
Lewis, I. LD	3,878	12.8	+3.6
Hill, R. Con	3,383	11.1	+1.4
Lab majority	14,574		48.02%
Electorate	52,185		
Total Vote	30,353		58.16

*Member of last parliament
Lab Hold (9.5% from Lab to Pl C)

OLD BEXLEY AND SIDCUP – see under Bexley

OLDHAM EAST AND SADDLEWORTH

		%	+/- %
*Woolas, P. Lab	17,537	38.6	-3.1
Sykes, H. LD	14,811	32.6	-2.8
Heeley, C. Con	7,304	16.1	-3.6
Treacy, M. BNP	5,091	11.2	
Little, B. UKIP	677	1.5	
Lab majority	2,726		6.00%
Electorate	74,511		
Total Vote	45,420		60.96

*Member of last parliament
Lab Hold (0.1% from Lab to LD)

OLDHAM WEST AND ROYTON

		%	+/- %
*Meacher, M. Lab	20,441	51.2	-7.6
Reed, D. Con	7,076	17.7	-5.7
Griffin, N. BNP	6,552	16.4	
Ramsbottom, M. LD	4,975	12.4	+0.6
Roney, D. Green	918	2.3	
Lab majority	13,365		33.44%
Electorate	69,409		
Total Vote	39,962		57.57

*Member of last parliament
Lab Hold (1.0% from Lab to Con)

ORKNEY AND SHETLAND

		%	+/- %
Carmichael, A. LD	6,919	41.3	-10.6
Mochrie, R. Lab	3,444	20.6	+2.3
Firth, J. Con	3,121	18.7	+6.4
Mowat, J. SNP	2,473	14.8	+2.1
Andrews, P. SSP	776	4.6	
LD majority	3,475		20.77%
Electorate	31,909		
Total Vote	16,733		52.44

LD Hold (6.5% from LD to Lab)

ORPINGTON

		%	+/- %
*Horam, J. Con	22,334	43.9	+3.3
Maines, C. LD	22,065	43.3	+7.7
Purnell, C. Lab	5,517	10.8	-7.0
Youles, J. UKIP	996	2.0	+1.1

Con majority	269		0.53%
Electorate	74,423		
Total Vote	50,912		68.41

*Member of last parliament
Con Hold (2.2% from Con to LD)

OXFORD EAST

		%	+/- %
*Smith, A. Lab	19,681	49.4	-7.4
Goddard, S. LD	9,337	23.4	+8.7
Potter, C. Con	7,446	18.7	-3.3
Singh, P. Green	1,501	3.8	+1.7
Lister, J. SA	708	1.8	
Gardner, P. UKIP	570	1.4	+0.9
Ahmed, F. SLP	274	0.7	
Hodge, L. ProLife	254	0.6	
Mylvaganam, P. Ind	77	0.2	
Lab majority	10,344		25.96%
Electorate	71,357		
Total Vote	39,848		55.84

*Member of last parliament
Lab Hold (8.1% from Lab to LD)

OXFORD WEST AND ABINGDON

		%	+/- %
*Harris, E. LD	24,670	47.8	+4.9
Matts, E. Con	15,485	30.0	-2.6
Kirk, G. Lab	9,114	17.7	-2.5
Woodin, M. Green	1,423	2.8	+1.6
Watney, M. UKIP	451	0.9	+0.5
Shreeve, S. Ind	332	0.6	
Twigger, R. EC	93	0.2	
LD majority	9,185		17.81%
Electorate	79,915		
Total Vote	51,568		64.53

*Member of last parliament
LD Hold (3.8% from Con to LD)

PAISLEY NORTH

		%	+/- %
*Adams, I. Lab	15,058	55.5	-4.0
Adam, G. SNP	5,737	21.1	-0.8
Hook, J. LD	2,709	10.0	+3.0
Stevenson, C. Con	2,404	8.9	-0.7
Halfpenny, J. SSP	982	3.6	
Graham, R. ProLife	263	1.0	-0.6
Lab majority	9,321		34.33%
Electorate	47,994		
Total Vote	27,153		56.58

*Member of last parliament
Lab Hold (1.6% from Lab to SNP)

PAISLEY SOUTH

		%	+/- %
*Alexander, D. Lab	17,830	58.4	+0.9
Lawson, B. SNP	5,920	19.4	-4.0
O'Malley, B. LD	3,178	10.4	+1.0
Cossar, A. Con	2,301	7.5	-1.1
Curran, F. SSP	835	2.7	+2.3
Graham, P. ProLife	346	1.1	
O'Donnell, T. Ind	126	0.4	
Lab majority	11,910		39.00%
Electorate	53,351		
Total Vote	30,536		57.24

*Member of last parliament
Lab Hold (2.4% from SNP to Lab)

PENDLE

		%	+/- %
*Prentice, G. Lab	17,729	44.6	-8.7
Skinner, R. Con	13,454	33.9	+3.6
Whipp, D. LD	5,479	13.8	+2.2
Jackson, C. BNP	1,976	5.0	
Cannon, G. UKIP	1,094	2.8	

Lab majority	4,275		10.76%
Electorate	62,870		
Total Vote	39,732		63.20

*Member of last parliament
Lab Hold (6.1% from Lab to Con)

PENRITH AND THE BORDER

		%	+/- %
*Maclean, D. Con	24,302	54.9	+7.3
Walker, G. LD	9,625	21.8	-4.9
Boaden, M. Lab	8,177	18.5	-3.1
Lowther, T. UKIP	938	2.1	
Gibson, M. LCA	870	2.0	
Moffat, J. Ind	337	0.8	
Con majority	14,677		33.17%
Electorate	68,605		
Total Vote	44,249		64.50

*Member of last parliament
Con Hold (6.1% from LD to Con)

PERTH

		%	+/- %
Ewing, A. SNP	11,237	29.7	-6.7
Smith, E. Con	11,189	29.6	+0.3
Dingwall, M. Lab	9,638	25.5	+0.7
Harris, V. LD	4,853	12.8	+4.8
Byrne, F. SSP	899	2.4	
SNP majority	48		0.13%
Electorate	61,497		
Total Vote	37,816		61.49

SNP Hold (3.5% from SNP to Con)

PETERBOROUGH

		%	+/- %
*Brinton, H. Lab	17,975	45.1	-5.2
Jackson, S. Con	15,121	38.0	+2.8
Sandford, N. LD	5,761	14.5	+3.8
Fairweather, J. UKIP	955	2.4	+1.7
Lab majority	2,854		7.17%
Electorate	64,874		
Total Vote	39,812		61.37

*Member of last parliament, now sitting as Helen Clark
Lab Hold (4.0% from Lab to Con)

PLYMOUTH DEVONPORT

		%	+/- %
*Jamieson, D. Lab	24,322	58.3	-2.6
Glen, J. Con	11,289	27.1	+2.9
Baldry, K. LD	4,513	10.8	+0.1
Parker, M. UKIP	958	2.3	+1.4
Staunton, T. SA	334	0.8	
Hawkins, R. SLP	303	0.7	
Lab majority	13,033		31.24%
Electorate	73,666		
Total Vote	41,719		56.63

*Member of last parliament
Lab Hold (2.7% from Lab to Con)

PLYMOUTH SUTTON

		%	+/- %
*Gilroy, L. Lab	19,827	50.7	+0.6
Colvile, O. Con	12,310	31.5	+1.2
Connett, A. LD	5,605	14.3	+0.5
Whitton, A. UKIP	970	2.5	+1.4
Leary, H. SLP	361	0.9	
Lab majority	7,517		19.24%
Electorate	68,438		
Total Vote	39,073		57.09

*Member of last parliament
Lab Hold (0.3% from Lab to Con)

PONTEFRACT AND CASTLEFORD

		%	+/- %
*Cooper, Y. Lab	21,890	69.7	-6.0
Singleton, P. Con	5,512	17.6	+4.0
Paxton, W. LD	2,315	7.4	0.0
Burdon, J. UKIP	739	2.4	
Bolderson, T. SLP	605	1.9	
Gill, J. SA	330	1.1	
Lab majority	16,378		52.17%
Electorate	63,181		
Total Vote	31,391		49.68

*Member of last parliament
Lab Hold (5.0% from Lab to Con)

PONTYPRIDD

		%	+/- %
*Howells, K. Lab	22,963	59.9	-3.9
Hancock, B. Pl C	5,279	13.8	+7.3
Dailey, P. Con	5,096	13.3	+0.4
Brooke, E. LD	4,152	10.8	-2.6
Warry, S. UKIP	603	1.6	
Biddulph, J. ProLife	216	0.6	
Lab majority	17,684		46.16%
Electorate	66,891		
Total Vote	38,309		57.27

*Member of last parliament
Lab Hold (5.6% from Lab to Pl C)

POOLE

		%	+/- %
*Syms, R. Con	17,710	45.1	+3.0
Watt, D. Lab	10,544	26.9	+5.3
Westbrook, N. LD	10,011	25.5	-5.3
Bass, J. UKIP	968	2.5	+1.4
Con majority	7,166		18.27%
Electorate	64,644		
Total Vote	39,233		60.69

*Member of last parliament
Con Hold (1.1% from Con to Lab)

POPLAR AND CANNING TOWN

		%	+/- %
*Fitzpatrick, J. Lab	20,866	61.2	-2.0
Marr, R. Con	6,758	19.8	+4.8
Sugden, A. LD	3,795	11.1	+0.8
Borg, P. BNP	1,733	5.1	-2.2
Boomla, K. SA	950	2.8	
Lab majority	14,108		41.37%
Electorate	84,593		
Total Vote	34,102		45.36

*Member of last parliament
Lab Hold (3.4% from Lab to Con)

PORTSMOUTH NORTH

		%	+/- %
*Rapson, S. Lab	18,676	50.7	+3.5
Day, C. Con	13,542	36.7	-0.9
Sanders, D. LD	3,795	10.3	-0.3
McCabe, W. UKIP	559	1.5	+0.9
Bundy, B. Ind	294	0.8	
Lab majority	5,134		13.93%
Electorate	64,256		
Total Vote	36,866		57.37

*Member of last parliament
Lab Hold (2.2% from Con to Lab)

PORTSMOUTH SOUTH

		%	+/- %
*Hancock, M. LD	17,490	44.6	+5.1
Warr, P. Con	11,397	29.1	-2.1
Heaney, G. Lab	9,361	23.9	-1.4
Molyneux, J. SA	647	1.6	
Tarrant, M. UKIP	321	0.8	+0.5

LD majority	6,093		15.54%
Electorate	77,095		
Total Vote	39,216		50.87

*Member of last parliament
LD Hold (3.6% from Con to LD)

PRESELI PEMBROKESHIRE

		%	+/- %
*Lawrence, J. Lab	15,206	41.3	-6.9
Crabb, S. Con	12,260	33.3	+5.6
Sinnett, R. Pl C	4,658	12.7	+6.3
Dauncey, A. LD	3,882	10.6	-2.5
Bowen, P. SLP	452	1.2	
Jones, H. UKIP	319	0.9	
Lab majority	2,946		8.01%
Electorate	54,283		
Total Vote	36,777		67.75

*Member of last parliament
Lab Hold (6.3% from Lab to Con)

PRESTON

		%	+/- %
*Hendrick, M. Lab	20,540	57.0	-3.8
O'Hare, G. Con	8,272	23.0	+1.0
Chadwick, B. LD	4,746	13.2	-1.5
Patel, B. Ind	1,241	3.4	
Merrick, R. Green	1,019	2.8	
Braid, D. Ind	223	0.6	
Lab majority	12,268		34.04%
Electorate	72,650		
Total Vote	36,041		49.61

*Member of last parliament
Lab Hold (2.4% from Lab to Con)

PUDSEY

		%	+/- %
*Truswell, P. Lab	21,717	48.1	-0.0
Procter, J. Con	16,091	35.6	-0.7
Boddy, S. LD	6,423	14.2	+0.2
Sewards, D. UKIP	944	2.1	
Lab majority	5,626		12.45%
Electorate	71,576		
Total Vote	45,175		63.11

*Member of last parliament
Lab Hold (0.3% from Con to Lab)

PUTNEY

		%	+/- %
*Colman, T. Lab	15,911	46.5	+0.8
Simpson, M. Con	13,140	38.4	-0.5
Burrett, A. LD	4,671	13.6	+2.9
Wild, P. UKIP	347	1.0	+0.5
Windsor, Y. ProLife	185	0.5	
Lab majority	2,771		8.09%
Electorate	60,643		
Total Vote	34,254		56.48

*Member of last parliament
Lab Hold (0.7% from Con to Lab)

RAYLEIGH

		%	+/- %
Francois, M. Con	21,434	50.1	+0.4
Clark, P. Lab	13,144	30.7	+1.8
Williams, G. LD	6,614	15.5	-4.3
Morgan, C. UKIP	1,581	3.7	
Con majority	8,290		19.38%
Electorate	70,653		
Total Vote	42,773		60.54

Con Hold (0.7% from Con to Lab)

READING EAST

		%	+/- %
*Griffiths, J. Lab	19,538	44.8	+2.1
Tanswell, B. Con	13,943	32.0	-3.2
Dobrashian, T. LD	8,078	18.5	-0.0
Kennet, M. Green	1,053	2.4	
Thornton, A. UKIP	525	1.2	+0.7
Williams, D. SA	394	0.9	
Hammerson, P. Ind	94	0.2	
Lab majority	5,595		12.83%
Electorate	74,637		
Total Vote	43,625		58.45

*Member of last parliament
Lab Hold (2.6% from Con to Lab)

READING WEST

		%	+/- %
*Salter, M. Lab	22,300	53.1	+8.0
Reid, S. Con	13,451	32.0	-6.9
Martin, P. LD	5,387	12.8	+0.1
Black, D. UKIP	848	2.0	+1.5
Lab majority	8,849		21.08%
Electorate	71,089		
Total Vote	41,986		59.06

*Member of last parliament
Lab Hold (7.4% from Con to Lab)

REDCAR

		%	+/- %
Baird, V. Lab	23,026	60.3	-7.1
Main, C. Con	9,583	25.1	+2.0
Wilson, S. LD	4,817	12.6	+3.1
Taylor, J. SLP	772	2.0	
Lab majority	13,443		35.19%
Electorate	67,150		
Total Vote	38,198		56.88

Lab Hold (4.5% from Lab to Con)

REDDITCH

		%	+/- %
*Smith, J. Lab	16,899	45.6	-4.2
Lumley, K. Con	14,415	38.9	+2.8
Ashall, M. LD	3,808	10.3	-0.7
Flynn, G. UKIP	1,259	3.4	
Armstrong, R. Green	651	1.8	
Lab majority	2,484		6.71%
Electorate	62,565		
Total Vote	37,032		59.19

*Member of last parliament
Lab Hold (3.5% from Lab to Con)

REGENT'S PARK AND KENSINGTON NORTH

		%	+/- %
*Buck, K. Lab	20,247	54.6	-5.3
Wilson, P. Con	9,981	26.9	-2.0
Boyle, D. LD	4,669	12.6	+4.1
Miller, P. Green	1,268	3.4	
Mieville, C. SA	459	1.2	
Crisp, A. UKIP	354	1.0	
Regan, C. Ind	74	0.2	
Lab majority	10,266		27.71%
Electorate	75,886		
Total Vote	37,052		48.83

*Member of last parliament
Lab Hold (1.6% from Lab to Con)

REIGATE

		%	+/- %
*Blunt, C. Con	18,875	47.8	+4.0
Charleton, S. Lab	10,850	27.5	-0.3
Kulka, J. LD	8,330	21.1	+1.1
Smith, S. UKIP	1,062	2.7	+2.1
Green, H. RefUK	357	0.9	
Con majority	8,025		20.33%
Electorate	65,023		
Total Vote	39,474		60.71

*Member of last parliament
Con Hold (2.1% from Lab to Con)

WEST RENFREWSHIRE

		%	+/- %
Sheridan, J. Lab	15,720	46.9	+0.4
Puthucheary, C. SNP	7,145	21.3	-5.2
Sharpe, D. Con	5,522	16.5	-2.1
Hamblen, C. LD	4,185	12.5	+4.8
Nunnery, A. SSP	925	2.8	
Lab majority	8,575		25.60%
Electorate	52,889		
Total Vote	33,497		63.33

Lab Hold (2.8% from SNP to Lab)

RHONDDA

		%	+/- %
Bryant, C. Lab	23,230	68.3	-6.1
Wood, L. Pl C	7,183	21.1	+7.8
Hobbins, P. Con	1,557	4.6	+0.8
Cox, G. LD	1,525	4.5	-1.2
Summers, G. Ind	507	1.5	
Lab majority	16,047		47.19%
Electorate	56,091		
Total Vote	34,002		60.62

Lab Hold (7.0% from Lab to Pl C)

SOUTH RIBBLE

		%	+/- %
*Borrow, D. Lab	21,386	46.4	-0.4
Owens, A. Con	17,584	38.1	+0.5
Alcock, M. LD	7,150	15.5	+4.9
Lab majority	3,802		8.24%
Electorate	73,794		
Total Vote	46,120		62.50

*Member of last parliament
Lab Hold (0.5% from Lab to Con)

RIBBLE VALLEY

		%	+/- %
*Evans, N. Con	25,308	51.5	+4.8
Carr, M. LD	14,070	28.6	-6.4
Johnstone, M. Lab	9,793	19.9	+4.2
Con majority	11,238		22.85%
Electorate	74,319		
Total Vote	49,171		66.16

*Member of last parliament
Con Hold (5.6% from LD to Con)

RICHMOND (YORKSHIRE)

		%	+/- %
*Hague, W. Con	25,951	58.9	+10.1
Tinnion, F. Lab	9,632	21.9	-5.9
Forth, E. LD	7,890	17.9	-0.5
Staniforth, M. Loony	561	1.3	
Con majority	16,319		37.06%
Electorate	65,360		
Total Vote	44,034		67.37

*Member of last parliament
Con Hold (8.0% from Lab to Con)

RICHMOND PARK

		%	+/- %
*Tonge, J. LD	23,444	47.7	+3.0
Harris, T. Con	18,480	37.6	-1.9
Langford, B. Lab	5,541	11.3	-1.3
Page, J. Green	1,223	2.5	
St John Howe, P. UKIP	348	0.7	
Perrin, R. Ind	115	0.2	
LD majority	4,964		10.10%
Electorate	72,251		
Total Vote	49,151		68.03

*Member of last parliament
LD Hold (2.5% from Con to LD)

ROCHDALE

		%	+/- %
*Fitzsimons, L. Lab	19,406	49.2	-0.2
Rowen, P. LD	13,751	34.9	-5.1
Cohen, E. Con	5,274	13.4	+4.6
Harvey, N. Green	728	1.8	
Mohammed, S. None	253	0.6	
Lab majority	5,655		14.35%
Electorate	69,506		
Total Vote	39,412		56.70

*Member of last parliament
Lab Hold (2.4% from LD to Lab)

ROCHFORD AND SOUTHEND EAST

		%	+/- %
*Taylor, T. Con	20,058	53.6	+4.8
Dandridge, C. Lab	13,024	34.8	-4.9
Newton, S. LD	2,780	7.4	-2.0
Hedges, A. Green	990	2.6	
Lynch, B. Lib	600	1.6	-0.6
Con majority	7,034		18.78%
Electorate	70,328		
Total Vote	37,452		53.25

*Member of last parliament
Con Hold (4.9% from Lab to Con)

ROMFORD

		%	+/- %
Rosindell, A. Con	18,931	53.0	+11.4
*Gordon, E. Lab	12,954	36.3	-6.9
Meyer, N. LD	2,869	8.0	+0.1
Ward, S. UKIP	533	1.5	
McAllister, F. BNP	414	1.2	-0.1
Con majority	5,977		16.74%
Electorate	60,040		
Total Vote	35,701		59.46

*Member of last parliament
Con Gain (9.1% from Lab to Con)

ROMSEY

		%	+/- %
*Gidley, S. LD	22,756	47.0	+17.5
Raynes, P. Con	20,386	42.1	-3.9
Roberts, S. Lab	3,986	8.2	-10.3
McCabe, A. UKIP	730	1.5	-2.0
Large, D. LCA	601	1.2	
LD majority	2,370		4.89%
Electorate	72,574		
Total Vote	48,459		66.77

*Member of last parliament
LD Gain (10.7% from Con to LD)

ROSS, SKYE AND INVERNESS WEST

		%	+/- %
*Kennedy, C. LD	18,832	54.1	+15.4
Crichton, D. Lab	5,880	16.9	-11.8
Urquhart, J. SNP	4,901	14.1	-5.5
Laing, A. Con	3,096	8.9	-2.0
Scott, E. Green	699	2.0	+1.2
Topp, S. SSP	683	2.0	
Anderson, P. UKIP	456	1.3	
Crawford, J. TCP	265	0.8	
LD majority	12,952		37.21%
Electorate	55,915		
Total Vote	34,812		62.26

*Member of last parliament
LD Hold (13.6% from Lab to LD)

ROSSENDALE AND DARWEN

		%	+/- %
*Anderson, J. Lab	20,251	48.7	-5.0
Lee, G. Con	15,281	36.7	+4.5
Dunning, B. LD	6,079	14.6	+4.0
Lab majority	4,970		11.94%
Electorate	70,683		
Total Vote	41,611		58.87

*Member of last parliament
Lab Hold (4.7% from Lab to Con)

ROTHER VALLEY

		%	+/- %
*Barron, K. Lab	22,851	62.1	-5.5
Duddridge, J. Con	7,969	21.7	+5.0
Knight, W. LD	4,603	12.5	+0.9
Cutts, D. UKIP	1,380	3.7	
Lab majority	14,882		40.44%
Electorate	69,174		
Total Vote	36,803		53.20

*Member of last parliament
Lab Hold (5.2% from Lab to Con)

ROTHERHAM

		%	+/- %
*MacShane, D. Lab	18,759	63.9	-7.4
Powell, R. Con	5,682	19.4	+5.1
Hall, C. LD	3,117	10.6	+0.2
Griffith, P. UKIP	730	2.5	
Penycate, D. Green	577	2.0	
Smith, F. SA	352	1.2	
Bartholomew, G. JLDP	137	0.5	
Lab majority	13,077		44.55%
Electorate	57,931		
Total Vote	29,354		50.67

*Member of last parliament
Lab Hold (6.2% from Lab to Con)

ROXBURGH AND BERWICKSHIRE

		%	+/- %
*Kirkwood, A. LD	14,044	48.8	+2.3
Turnbull, G. Con	6,533	22.7	-1.2
Maxwell Stuart, C. Lab	4,498	15.6	+0.7
Campbell, R. SNP	2,806	9.7	-1.6
Millar, A. SSP	463	1.6	
Neilson, P. UKIP	453	1.6	+1.0
LD majority	7,511		26.08%
Electorate	47,515		
Total Vote	28,797		60.61

*Member of last parliament
LD Hold (1.7% from Con to LD)

RUGBY AND KENILWORTH

		%	+/- %
*King, A. Lab	24,221	45.0	+2.0
Martin, D. Con	21,344	39.7	-2.6
Fairweather, G. LD	7,444	13.8	-0.4
Garratt, P. UKIP	787	1.5	
Lab majority	2,877		5.35%
Electorate	79,764		
Total Vote	53,796		67.44

*Member of last parliament
Lab Hold (2.3% from Con to Lab)

RUISLIP NORTHWOOD

		%	+/- %
*Wilkinson, J. Con	18,115	48.8	-1.5
Travers, G. Lab	10,578	28.5	-4.4
Cox, M. LD	7,177	19.3	+3.1
Lee, G. Green	724	1.9	
Edward, I. BNP	547	1.5	
Con majority	7,537		20.29%
Electorate	60,777		
Total Vote	37,141		61.11

*Member of last parliament
Con Hold (1.5% from Lab to Con)

RUNNYMEDE AND WEYBRIDGE		%	+/- %
*Hammond, P. Con	20,646	48.7	+0.1
Briginshaw, J. Lab	12,286	29.0	-0.5
Bushill, C. LD	6,924	16.3	0.0
Browne, C. UKIP	1,332	3.1	+1.9
Gilman, C. Green	1,238	2.9	
Con majority	8,360		19.70%
Electorate	75,569		
Total Vote	42,426		56.14

*Member of last parliament
Con Hold (0.3% from Lab to Con)

RUSHCLIFFE		%	+/- %
*Clarke, K. Con	25,869	47.5	+3.2
Fallon, P. Lab	18,512	34.0	-2.2
Hargreaves, J. LD	7,385	13.6	-0.7
Brown, K. UKIP	1,434	2.6	+2.0
Baxter, A. Green	1,236	2.3	
Con majority	7,357		13.51%
Electorate	81,847		
Total Vote	54,436		66.51

*Member of last parliament
Con Hold (2.7% from Lab to Con)

RUTLAND AND MELTON		%	+/- %
*Duncan, A. Con	22,621	48.1	+2.3
O'Callaghan, M. Lab	14,009	29.8	+0.8
Lee, K. LD	8,386	17.8	-1.4
Baker, P. UKIP	1,223	2.6	+1.0
Davies, C. Green	817	1.7	
Con majority	8,612		18.30%
Electorate	73,264		
Total Vote	47,056		64.23

*Member of last parliament
Con Hold (0.8% from Lab to Con)

RYEDALE		%	+/- %
*Greenway, J. Con	20,711	47.2	+3.4
Orrell, K. LD	15,836	36.1	+2.7
Ellis, D. Lab	6,470	14.7	-3.2
Feaster, S. UKIP	882	2.0	+0.1
Con majority	4,875		11.11%
Electorate	66,849		
Total Vote	43,899		65.67

*Member of last parliament
Con Hold (0.4% from LD to Con)

SAFFRON WALDEN		%	+/- %
*Haselhurst, A. Con	24,485	48.9	+3.6
Tealby-Watson, E. LD	12,481	24.9	-1.9
Rogers, T. Lab	11,305	22.6	+1.1
Glover, R. UKIP	1,769	3.5	+2.4
Con majority	12,004		23.99%
Electorate	76,724		
Total Vote	50,040		65.22

*Member of last parliament
Con Hold (2.7% from LD to Con)

ST ALBANS		%	+/- %
*Pollard, K. Lab	19,889	45.4	+3.4
Elphicke, C. Con	15,423	35.2	+2.0
Rijke, N. LD	7,847	17.9	-3.1
Sherwin, C. UKIP	602	1.4	
Lab majority	4,466		10.21%
Electorate	66,040		
Total Vote	43,761		66.26

*Member of last parliament
Lab Hold (0.7% from Con to Lab)

ST HELENS NORTH		%	+/- %
*Watts, D. Lab	22,977	61.1	-3.8
Pearce, S. Con	7,076	18.8	+1.5
Beirne, J. LD	6,609	17.6	+4.8
Whatham, S. SLP	939	2.5	+0.8
Lab majority	15,901		42.29%
Electorate	71,313		
Total Vote	37,601		52.73

*Member of last parliament
Lab Hold (2.6% from Lab to Con)

ST HELENS SOUTH		%	+/- %
*Woodward, S. Lab	16,799	49.7	-18.9
Spencer, B. LD	7,814	23.1	+9.7
Rotherham, L. Con	4,675	13.8	-1.1
Thompson, N. SA	2,325	6.9	
Perry, M. SLP	1,504	4.4	
Slater, B. UKIP	336	1.0	
Murphy, M. Ind	271	0.8	
Braid, D. Ind	80	0.2	
Lab majority	8,985		26.58%
Electorate	65,741		
Total Vote	33,804		51.42

*Member of last parliament
Lab Hold (14.3% from Lab to LD)

ST IVES		%	+/- %
*George, A. LD	25,413	51.6	+7.1
Richardson, J. Con	15,360	31.2	0.0
Morris, W. Lab	6,567	13.3	-1.9
Faulkner, M. UKIP	1,926	3.9	+2.9
LD majority	10,053		20.41%
Electorate	74,256		
Total Vote	49,266		66.35

*Member of last parliament
LD Hold (3.6% from Con to LD)

SALFORD		%	+/- %
*Blears, H. Lab	14,649	65.1	-3.9
Owen, N. LD	3,637	16.2	+5.9
King, C. Con	3,446	15.3	-2.1
Grant, P. SA	414	1.8	
Wallace, S. Ind	216	1.0	
Masterson, R. Ind	152	0.7	
Lab majority	11,012		48.91%
Electorate	54,152		
Total Vote	22,514		41.58

*Member of last parliament
Lab Hold (4.9% from Lab to LD)

SALISBURY		%	+/- %
*Key, R. Con	24,527	46.6	+3.7
Emmerson-Peirce, Y. LD	15,824	30.1	-2.1
Mallory, S. Lab	9,199	17.5	-0.1
Wood, M. UKIP	1,958	3.7	-2.0
Soutar, H. Green	1,095	2.1	+1.0
Con majority	8,703		16.54%
Electorate	80,527		
Total Vote	52,603		65.32

*Member of last parliament
Con Hold (2.9% from LD to Con)

SCARBOROUGH AND WHITBY

		%	+/- %
*Quinn, L. Lab	22,426	47.2	+1.6
Sykes, J. Con	18,841	39.6	+3.4
Pearce, T. LD	3,977	8.4	-5.8
Dixon, J. Green	1,049	2.2	
Jacob, J. UKIP	970	2.0	
Murray, T. ProLife	260	0.5	
Lab majority	3,585		7.54%
Electorate	75,213		
Total Vote	47,523		63.18

*Member of last parliament
Lab Hold (0.9% from Lab to Con)

SCUNTHORPE

		%	+/- %
*Morley, E. Lab	20,096	59.8	-0.6
Theobald, B. Con	9,724	28.9	+2.6
Tress, B. LD	3,156	9.4	+1.0
Cliff, M. None	347	1.0	
Patterson, D. Ind	302	0.9	
Lab majority	10,372		30.85%
Electorate	59,367		
Total Vote	33,625		56.64

*Member of last parliament
Lab Hold (1.6% from Lab to Con)

SEDGEFIELD

		%	+/- %
*Blair, T. Lab	26,110	64.9	-6.3
Carswell, D. Con	8,397	20.9	+3.1
Duffield, A. LD	3,624	9.0	+2.5
Spence, A. UKIP	974	2.4	
Gibson, B. SLP	518	1.3	+0.3
Driver, S. RNRL	375	0.9	
John, H. Ind	260	0.6	
Lab majority	17,713		44.00%
Electorate	64,925		
Total Vote	40,258		62.01

*Member of last parliament
Lab Hold (4.7% from Lab to Con)

SELBY

		%	+/- %
*Grogan, J. Lab	22,652	45.1	-0.8
Mitchell, M. Con	20,514	40.8	+1.7
Wilcock, J. LD	5,569	11.1	-1.0
Kenwright, H. Green	902	1.8	
Lewis, B. UKIP	635	1.3	+0.3
Lab majority	2,138		4.25%
Electorate	77,391		
Total Vote	50,272		64.96

*Member of last parliament
Lab Hold (1.3% from Lab to Con)

SEVENOAKS

		%	+/- %
*Fallon, M. Con	21,052	49.4	+4.0
Humphreys, C. Lab	10,898	25.6	+1.0
Gray, C. LD	9,214	21.6	-2.5
Hawkins, L. UKIP	1,155	2.7	
Ellis, M. UKP	295	0.7	
Con majority	10,154		23.83%
Electorate	66,649		
Total Vote	42,614		63.94

*Member of last parliament
Con Hold (1.5% from Lab to Con)

SHEFFIELD ATTERCLIFFE

		%	+/- %
*Betts, C. Lab	24,287	67.8	+2.5
Perry, J. Con	5,443	15.2	-0.9
Smith, G. LD	5,092	14.2	-1.5
Arnott, P. UKIP	1,002	2.8	

Lab majority	18,844		52.60%
Electorate	67,697		
Total Vote	35,824		52.92

*Member of last parliament
Lab Hold (1.7% from Con to Lab)

SHEFFIELD BRIGHTSIDE

		%	+/- %
*Blunkett, D. Lab	19,650	76.9	+3.4
Wilson, M. Con	2,601	10.2	+1.8
Firth, A. LD	2,238	8.8	-5.8
Wilson, B. SA	361	1.4	
Morris, R. SLP	354	1.4	-0.0
Suter, M. UKIP	348	1.4	
Lab majority	17,049		66.72%
Electorate	54,134		
Total Vote	25,552		47.20

*Member of last parliament
Lab Hold (0.8% from Con to Lab)

SHEFFIELD CENTRAL

		%	+/- %
*Caborn, R. Lab	18,477	61.4	-2.2
Qadar, A. LD	5,933	19.7	+2.5
Brelsford, N. Con	3,289	10.9	-1.0
Little, B. Green	1,008	3.4	+0.7
Riley, N. SA	754	2.5	
Hadfield, D. SLP	289	1.0	
Schofield, C. UKIP	257	0.9	
Driver, M. WRP	62	0.2	0.0
Lab majority	12,544		41.72%
Electorate	60,765		
Total Vote	30,069		49.48

*Member of last parliament
Lab Hold (2.4% from Lab to LD)

SHEFFIELD HALLAM

		%	+/- %
*Allan, R. LD	21,203	55.4	+4.1
Harthman, J. Con	11,856	31.0	-2.1
Furniss, G. Lab	4,758	12.4	-1.1
Arnott, L. UKIP	429	1.1	
LD majority	9,347		24.44%
Electorate	58,982		
Total Vote	38,246		64.84

*Member of last parliament
LD Hold (3.1% from Con to LD)

SHEFFIELD HEELEY

		%	+/- %
Munn, M. Lab	19,452	57.0	-3.7
Willis, D. LD	7,748	22.7	+1.4
Abbott, C. Con	4,864	14.2	-1.4
Unwin, R. Green	774	2.3	
Fischer, B. SLP	667	2.0	
Dunn, D. UKIP	634	1.9	
Lab majority	11,704		34.28%
Electorate	61,949		
Total Vote	34,139		55.11

Lab Hold (2.6% from Lab to LD)

SHEFFIELD HILLSBOROUGH

		%	+/- %
*Jackson, H. Lab	24,170	56.8	-0.0
Commons, J. LD	9,601	22.6	-3.3
King, G. Con	7,801	18.3	+3.8
Webb, P. UKIP	964	2.3	
Lab majority	14,569		34.25%
Electorate	74,180		
Total Vote	42,536		57.34

*Member of last parliament
Lab Hold (1.6% from LD to Lab)

SHERWOOD

		%	+/- %
*Tipping, P. Lab	24,900	54.2	-4.3
Lewis, B. Con	15,527	33.8	+5.1
Harris, P. LD	5,473	11.9	+3.3
Lab majority	9,373		20.42%
Electorate	75,558		
Total Vote	45,900		60.75

*Member of last parliament
Lab Hold (4.7% from Lab to Con)

SHIPLEY

		%	+/- %
*Leslie, C. Lab	20,243	44.0	+0.6
Senior, D. Con	18,815	40.9	+3.1
Wright, H. LD	4,996	10.9	-4.2
Love, M. Green	1,386	3.0	
Whitaker, W. UKIP	580	1.3	
Lab majority	1,428		3.10%
Electorate	69,576		
Total Vote	46,020		66.14

*Member of last parliament
Lab Hold (1.3% from Lab to Con)

SHREWSBURY AND ATCHAM

		%	+/- %
*Marsden, P. Lab	22,253	44.6	+7.6
McIntyre, A. Con	18,674	37.4	+3.4
Rule, J. LD	6,173	12.4	-12.6
Curteis, H. UKIP	1,620	3.2	+2.4
Bullard, E. Green	931	1.9	
Gollins, J. Ind	258	0.5	
Lab majority	3,579		7.17%
Electorate	74,964		
Total Vote	49,909		66.58

*Member of last parliament
Lab Hold (2.1% from Con to Lab)

NORTH SHROPSHIRE

		%	+/- %
*Paterson, O. Con	22,631	48.6	+8.4
Ion, M. Lab	16,390	35.2	-0.7
Jephcott, B. LD	5,945	12.8	-7.6
Trevanion, D. UKIP	1,165	2.5	
Maxfield, R. Ind	389	0.8	
Con majority	6,241		13.42%
Electorate	71,700		
Total Vote	46,520		64.88

*Member of last parliament
Con Hold (4.6% from Lab to Con)

SITTINGBOURNE AND SHEPPEY

		%	+/- %
*Wyatt, D. Lab	17,340	45.8	+5.2
Lee, A. Con	13,831	36.5	+0.2
Lowe, E. LD	5,353	14.1	-4.2
Young, M. RNRL	673	1.8	
Oakley, R. UKIP	661	1.7	+0.7
Lab majority	3,509		9.27%
Electorate	65,824		
Total Vote	37,858		57.51

*Member of last parliament
Lab Hold (2.5% from Con to Lab)

SKIPTON AND RIPON

		%	+/- %
*Curry, D. Con	25,736	52.4	+5.8
Bateman, B. LD	12,806	26.1	+0.9
Dugher, M. Lab	8,543	17.4	-5.0
Holdsworth, N. UKIP	2,041	4.2	
Con majority	12,930		26.32%
Electorate	74,326		
Total Vote	49,126		66.10

*Member of last parliament
Con Hold (2.5% from LD to Con)

SLEAFORD AND NORTH HYKEHAM

		%	+/- %
*Hogg, D. Con	24,190	49.7	+5.7
Donnelly, E. Lab	15,568	32.0	-2.3
Arbon, R. LD	7,894	16.2	+1.0
Ward-Barrow, M. UKIP	1,067	2.2	
Con majority	8,622		17.70%
Electorate	75,033		
Total Vote	48,719		64.93

*Member of last parliament
Con Hold (4.0% from Lab to Con)

SLOUGH

		%	+/- %
*Mactaggart, F. Lab	22,718	58.3	+1.6
Coad, D. Con	10,210	26.2	-3.1
Kerr, K. LD	4,109	10.5	+3.2
Haines, T. Ind	859	2.2	
Lane, J. UKIP	738	1.9	
Nazir, C. Ind	364	0.9	
Lab majority	12,508		32.07%
Electorate	73,008		
Total Vote	38,998		53.42

*Member of last parliament
Lab Hold (2.3% from Con to Lab)

SOLIHULL

		%	+/- %
*Taylor, J. Con	21,935	45.4	+0.8
Byron, J. LD	12,528	26.0	+0.7
O'Brien, B. Lab	12,373	25.6	+1.3
Moore, A. UKIP	1,061	2.2	
Pyne, S. ProLife	374	0.8	-0.3
Con majority	9,407		19.49%
Electorate	76,298		
Total Vote	48,271		63.27

*Member of last parliament
Con Hold (0.1% from LD to Con)

SOMERTON AND FROME

		%	+/- %
*Heath, D. LD	22,983	43.6	+4.1
Marland, J. Con	22,315	42.4	+3.1
Perkins, A. Lab	6,113	11.6	-4.7
Bridgwood, P. UKIP	919	1.7	+1.2
Pollock, J. Lib	354	0.7	
LD majority	668		1.27%
Electorate	75,815		
Total Vote	52,684		69.49

*Member of last parliament
LD Hold (0.5% from Con to LD)

SOUTH ANTRIM – see under Antrim

SOUTH CAMBRIDGESHIRE – see under Cambridgeshire

SOUTH DERBYSHIRE – see under Derbyshire

SOUTH DORSET – see under Dorset

SOUTH DOWN – see under Down

SOUTH EAST CAMBRIDGESHIRE – see under Cambridgeshire

SOUTH EAST CORNWALL – see under Cornwall

SOUTH HOLLAND AND THE DEEPINGS – see under Holland

SOUTH NORFOLK – see under Norfolk

SOUTH RIBBLE – see under Ribble

SOUTH SHIELDS

		%	+/- %
Miliband, D. Lab	19,230	63.2	-8.3
Gardner, J. Con	5,140	16.9	+2.3
Grainger, M. LD	5,127	16.8	+8.0
Hardy, A. UKIP	689	2.3	
Nettleship, R. Ind	262	0.9	
Lab majority	14,090		46.28%
Electorate	61,112		
Total Vote	30,448		49.82

Lab Hold (5.3% from Lab to Con)

SOUTH STAFFORDSHIRE –
see under Staffordshire

SOUTH SUFFOLK – see under Suffolk

SOUTH SWINDON – see under Swindon

SOUTH THANET – see under Thanet

SOUTH WEST BEDFORDSHIRE –
see under Bedfordshire

SOUTH WEST DEVON – see under Devon

SOUTH WEST HERTFORDSHIRE –
see under Hertfordshire

SOUTH WEST NORFOLK – see under Norfolk

SOUTH WEST SURREY – see under Surrey

SOUTHAMPTON ITCHEN

		%	+/- %
*Denham, J. Lab	22,553	54.5	-0.3
Nokes, C. Con	11,330	27.4	-1.0
Cooper, M. LD	6,195	15.0	+3.3
Rose, K. UKIP	829	2.0	+1.7
Marsh, G. SA	241	0.6	
Holmes, M. SLP	225	0.5	-0.6
Lab majority	11,223		27.13%
Electorate	78,066		
Total Vote	41,373		53.00

*Member of last parliament
Lab Hold (0.4% from Con to Lab)

SOUTHAMPTON TEST

		%	+/- %
*Whitehead, A. Lab	21,824	52.5	-1.7
Gueterbock, R. Con	10,617	25.5	-2.5
Shaw, J. LD	7,522	18.1	+4.4
Rankin-Moore, G. UKIP	792	1.9	+1.5
Abel, M. SA	442	1.1	
Bahia, P. SLP	378	0.9	
Lab majority	11,207		26.96%
Electorate	75,485		
Total Vote	41,575		55.08

*Member of last parliament
Lab Hold (0.3% from Con to Lab)

SOUTHEND WEST

		%	+/- %
*Amess, D. Con	17,313	46.3	+7.6
Fisher, P. Lab	9,372	25.1	+2.3
de Ste Croix, R. LD	9,319	24.9	-8.2
Lee, R. UKIP	1,371	3.7	+2.3
Con majority	7,941		21.25%
Electorate	64,328		
Total Vote	37,375		58.10

*Member of last parliament
Con Hold (2.6% from Lab to Con)

SOUTHPORT

		%	+/- %
Pugh, J. LD	18,011	43.8	-4.3
Jones, L. Con	15,004	36.5	+0.5
Brant, P. Lab	6,816	16.6	+4.4
Green, D. Lib	767	1.9	+1.1
Kelley, G. UKIP	555	1.3	
LD majority	3,007		7.31%
Electorate	70,259		
Total Vote	41,153		58.57

LD Hold (2.4% from LD to Con)

**NORTH SOUTHWARK AND
BERMONDSEY**

		%	+/- %
*Hughes, S. LD	20,991	56.9	+8.3
Abrams, K. Lab	11,359	30.8	-9.5
Wallace, E. Con	2,800	7.6	+0.6
Jenkins, R. Green	752	2.0	
Shore, L. NF	612	1.7	
McWhirter, R. UKIP	271	0.7	
Davies, J. Ind	77	0.2	
LD majority	9,632		26.13%
Electorate	73,529		
Total Vote	36,862		50.13

*Member of last parliament
LD Hold (8.9% from Lab to LD)

SPELTHORNE

		%	+/- %
*Wilshire, D. Con	18,851	45.1	+0.2
Shaw, A. Lab	15,589	37.3	-0.9
Rimmer, M. LD	6,156	14.7	+1.6
Squire, R. UKIP	1,198	2.9	+2.0
Con majority	3,262		7.80%
Electorate	68,731		
Total Vote	41,794		60.81

*Member of last parliament
Con Hold (0.6% from Lab to Con)

STAFFORD

		%	+/- %
*Kidney, D. Lab	21,285	48.0	+0.4
Cochrane, P. Con	16,253	36.6	-2.6
Pinkerton, J. LD	4,205	9.5	-1.1
Bradford, R. UKIP	2,315	5.2	
Hames, M. RNRL	308	0.7	
Lab majority	5,032		11.34%
Electorate	67,934		
Total Vote	44,366		65.31

*Member of last parliament
Lab Hold (1.5% from Con to Lab)

STAFFORDSHIRE MOORLANDS

		%	+/- %
*Atkins, C. Lab	20,904	49.0	-3.2
Hayes, M. Con	15,066	35.3	+2.8
Redfern, J. LD	5,928	13.9	+1.8
Gilbert, P. UKIP	760	1.8	
Lab majority	5,838		13.69%
Electorate	66,760		
Total Vote	42,658		63.90

*Member of last parliament
Lab Hold (3.0% from Lab to Con)

SOUTH STAFFORDSHIRE

		%	+/- %
*Cormack, P. Con	21,295	50.5	+0.5
Kalinauckas, P. Lab	14,414	34.2	-0.5
Harrison, J. LD	4,891	11.6	+0.3
Lynch, M. UKIP	1,580	3.7	
Con majority	6,881		16.31%
Electorate	69,959		
Total Vote	42,180		60.29

*Member of last parliament
Con Hold (0.5% from Lab to Con)

STALYBRIDGE AND HYDE

		%	+/- %
Purnell, J. Lab	17,781	55.5	-3.4
Reid, A. Con	8,922	27.8	+3.3
Jones, B. LD	4,327	13.5	+1.5
Bennett, F. UKIP	1,016	3.2	
Lab majority	8,859		27.64%
Electorate	66,265		
Total Vote	32,046		48.36

Lab Hold (3.4% from Lab to Con)

STEVENAGE

		%	+/- %
*Follett, B. Lab	22,025	51.9	-3.5
Quar, G. Con	13,459	31.7	-1.1
Davies, H. LD	6,027	14.2	+5.3
Glennon, S. SA	449	1.1	
Losonczi, A. Ind	320	0.8	
Bell, S. ProLife	173	0.4	0.0
Lab majority	8,566		20.18%
Electorate	69,203		
Total Vote	42,453		61.35

*Member of last parliament
Lab Hold (1.2% from Lab to Con)

STIRLING

		%	+/- %
*McGuire, A. Lab	15,175	42.2	-5.2
Mawdsley, G. Con	8,901	24.8	-7.7
Macaulay, F. SNP	5,877	16.4	+3.0
Freeman, C. LD	4,208	11.7	+5.5
Mullen, C. SSP	1,012	2.8	
Ruskell, M. Green	757	2.1	
Lab majority	6,274		17.46%
Electorate	53,097		
Total Vote	35,930		67.67

*Member of last parliament
Lab Hold (1.3% from Con to Lab)

STOCKPORT

		%	+/- %
*Coffey, A. Lab	20,731	58.6	-4.3
Allen, J. Con	9,162	25.9	+3.6
Hunter, M. LD	5,490	15.5	+4.9
Lab majority	11,569		32.70%
Electorate	66,395		
Total Vote	35,383		53.29

*Member of last parliament
Lab Hold (3.9% from Lab to Con)

STOCKTON NORTH

		%	+/- %
*Cook, F. Lab	22,470	63.4	-3.4
Vigar, A. Con	7,823	22.1	+3.3
Wallace, M. LD	4,208	11.9	+1.0
Wennington, W. Green	926	2.6	
Lab majority	14,647		41.34%
Electorate	64,629		
Total Vote	35,427		54.82

*Member of last parliament
Lab Hold (3.3% from Lab to Con)

STOCKTON SOUTH

		%	+/- %
*Taylor, D. Lab	23,414	53.0	-2.3
Devlin, T. Con	14,328	32.4	-0.6
Fletcher, S. LD	6,012	13.6	+4.5
Coombes, L. SA	455	1.0	
Lab majority	9,086		20.55%
Electorate	70,337		
Total Vote	44,209		62.85

*Member of last parliament
Lab Hold (0.8% from Lab to Con)

STOKE-ON-TRENT CENTRAL

		%	+/- %
*Fisher, M. Lab	17,170	60.7	-5.6
Clark, J. Con	5,325	18.8	+2.1
Webb, G. LD	4,148	14.7	+2.7
Wise, R. Ind	1,657	5.9	
Lab majority	11,845		41.86%
Electorate	59,750		
Total Vote	28,300		47.36

*Member of last parliament
Lab Hold (3.8% from Lab to Con)

STOKE-ON-TRENT NORTH

		%	+/- %
*Walley, J. Lab	17,460	58.0	-7.2
Browning, B. Con	5,676	18.8	-1.3
Jebb, H. LD	3,580	11.9	+1.2
Wanger, C. Ind	3,399	11.3	
Lab majority	11,784		39.13%
Electorate	57,998		
Total Vote	30,115		51.92

*Member of last parliament
Lab Hold (2.9% from Lab to Con)

STOKE-ON-TRENT SOUTH

		%	+/- %
*Stevenson, G. Lab	19,366	53.8	-8.2
Bastiman, P. Con	8,877	24.6	+2.3
Coleman, C. LD	4,724	13.1	+2.9
Knapper, A. Ind	1,703	4.7	
Batkin, S. BNP	1,358	3.8	+2.5
Lab majority	10,489		29.11%
Electorate	70,032		
Total Vote	36,028		51.45

*Member of last parliament
Lab Hold (5.2% from Lab to Con)

STONE

		%	+/- %
*Cash, W. Con	22,395	49.1	+2.2
Palfreyman, J. Lab	16,359	35.8	-3.8
McKeown, B. LD	6,888	15.1	+3.0
Con majority	6,036		13.22%
Electorate	68,847		
Total Vote	45,642		66.29

*Member of last parliament
Con Hold (3.0% from Lab to Con)

STOURBRIDGE

		%	+/- %
*Shipley, D. Lab	18,823	47.1	-0.0
Eyre, S. Con	15,011	37.6	+1.8
Bramall, C. LD	4,833	12.1	-2.2
Knotts, J. UKIP	763	1.9	
Atherton, M. SLP	494	1.2	
Lab majority	3,812		9.55%
Electorate	64,610		
Total Vote	39,924		61.79

*Member of last parliament
Lab Hold (0.9% from Lab to Con)

STRANGFORD

		%	+/- %
Robinson, I. DUP	18,532	42.8	+12.6
McNarry, D. UUP	17,422	40.3	-4.0
McCarthy, K. Alliance	2,902	6.7	-6.4
McCarthy, D. SDLP	2,646	6.1	-0.6
Johnston, L. SF	930	2.2	+0.9
Wilson, C. NIUP	822	1.9	
DUP majority	1,110		2.57%
Electorate	72,192		
Total Vote	43,254		59.92

DUP Gain (8.3% from UUP to DUP)

STRATFORD-ON-AVON

		%	+/- %
*Maples, J. Con	27,606	50.3	+2.0
Juned, S. LD	15,804	28.8	+3.2
Hussain, M. Lab	9,164	16.7	-3.9
Mole, R. UKIP	1,184	2.2	
Davies, M. Green	1,156	2.1	
Con majority	11,802		21.49%
Electorate	83,757		
Total Vote	54,914		65.56

*Member of last parliament
Con Hold (0.6% from Con to LD)

STRATHKELVIN AND BEARSDEN

		%	+/- %
Lyons, J. Lab	19,250	46.4	-6.5
Macdonald, G. LD	7,533	18.2	+8.4
Smith, C. SNP	6,675	16.1	-0.2
Roxburgh, M. Con	6,635	16.0	-4.1
Telfer, W. SSP	1,393	3.4	
Lab majority	11,717		28.24%
Electorate	62,869		
Total Vote	41,486		66.14

Lab Hold (7.4% from Lab to LD)

STREATHAM

		%	+/- %
*Hill, K. Lab	21,041	56.9	-5.9
O'Brien, R. LD	6,771	18.3	+4.8
Hocking, S. Con	6,639	17.9	-3.8
Sajid, M. Green	1,641	4.4	
Tucker, G. SA	906	2.4	
Lab majority	14,270		38.57%
Electorate	76,021		
Total Vote	36,998		48.67

*Member of last parliament
Lab Hold (5.3% from Lab to LD)

STRETFORD AND URMSTON

		%	+/- %
*Hughes, B. Lab	23,836	61.1	+2.6
Mackie, J. Con	10,565	27.1	-3.4
Bridges, J. LD	3,891	10.0	+1.8
Price, J. Ind	713	1.8	
Lab majority	13,271		34.02%
Electorate	71,222		
Total Vote	39,005		55.00

*Member of last parliament
Lab Hold (3.0% from Con to Lab)

STROUD

		%	+/- %
*Drew, D. Lab	25,685	46.6	+3.9
Carmichael, N. Con	20,646	37.4	-0.5
Beasley, J. LD	6,036	10.9	-4.5
Cranston, K. Green	1,913	3.5	-0.5
Blake, A. UKIP	895	1.6	
Lab majority	5,039		9.13%
Electorate	78,818		
Total Vote	55,175		70.00

*Member of last parliament
Lab Hold (2.2% from Con to Lab)

CENTRAL SUFFOLK AND NORTH IPSWICH

		%	+/- %
*Lord, M. Con	20,924	44.4	+1.8
Jones, C. Lab	17,455	37.1	+1.2
Elvin, A. LD	7,593	16.1	-4.5
Wright, J. UKIP	1,132	2.4	
Con majority	3,469		7.36%
Electorate	74,200		
Total Vote	47,104		63.48

*Member of last parliament
Con Hold (0.3% from Lab to Con)

SUFFOLK COASTAL

		%	+/- %
*Gummer, J. Con	21,847	43.3	+4.8
Gardner, N. Lab	17,521	34.8	+2.0
Schur, T. LD	9,192	18.2	-3.2
Burn, M. UKIP	1,847	3.7	
Con majority	4,326		8.58%
Electorate	75,963		
Total Vote	50,407		66.36

*Member of last parliament
Con Hold (1.4% from Lab to Con)

SOUTH SUFFOLK

		%	+/- %
*Yeo, T. Con	18,748	41.4	+4.1
Young, M. Lab	13,667	30.2	+0.9
Munt, T. LD	11,296	24.9	-2.8
Allen, D. UKIP	1,582	3.5	
Con majority	5,081		11.22%
Electorate	68,456		
Total Vote	45,293		66.16

*Member of last parliament
Con Hold (1.6% from Lab to Con)

WEST SUFFOLK

		%	+/- %
*Spring, R. Con	20,201	47.6	+6.7
Jefferys, M. Lab	15,906	37.5	+0.4
Martlew, R. LD	5,017	11.8	-2.2
Burrows, W. UKIP	1,321	3.1	
Con majority	4,295		10.12%
Electorate	70,129		
Total Vote	42,445		60.52

*Member of last parliament
Con Hold (3.2% from Lab to Con)

SUNDERLAND NORTH

		%	+/- %
*Etherington, W. Lab	18,685	62.7	-5.6
Harris, M. Con	5,331	17.9	+1.2
Lennox, J. LD	3,599	12.1	+1.7
Herron, N. Ind	1,518	5.1	
Guynan, D. BNP	687	2.3	
Lab majority	13,354		44.78%
Electorate	60,846		
Total Vote	29,820		49.01

*Member of last parliament
Lab Hold (3.4% from Lab to Con)

SUNDERLAND SOUTH

		%	+/- %
*Mullin, C. Lab	19,921	63.9	-4.2
Boyd, J. Con	6,254	20.1	+1.2
Greenfield, M. LD	3,675	11.8	+0.2
Dobbie, J. BNP	576	1.8	
Moore, J. UKIP	470	1.5	+0.0
Warner, R. Loony	291	0.9	
Lab majority	13,667		43.82%
Electorate	64,577		
Total Vote	31,187		48.29

*Member of last parliament
Lab Hold (2.7% from Lab to Con)

EAST SURREY

		%	+/- %
*Ainsworth, P. Con	24,706	52.5	+2.4
Pursehouse, J. LD	11,503	24.4	+2.0
Tanner, J. Lab	8,994	19.1	-2.1
Stone, A. UKIP	1,846	3.9	+2.9
Con majority	13,203		28.06%
Electorate	74,338		
Total Vote	47,049		63.29

*Member of last parliament
Con Hold (0.2% from LD to Con)

SURREY HEATH		%	+/- %
*Hawkins, N. Con	22,401	49.7	-1.9
Lelliott, M. LD	11,582	25.7	+3.9
Norman, J. Lab	9,640	21.4	+0.3
Hunt, N. UKIP	1,479	3.3	+2.1
Con majority	10,819		23.99%
Electorate	75,858		
Total Vote	45,102		59.46

*Member of last parliament
Con Hold (2.9% from Con to LD)

SOUTH WEST SURREY		%	+/- %
*Bottomley, V. Con	22,462	45.3	+0.7
Cordon, S. LD	21,601	43.6	+3.8
Whelton, M. Lab	4,321	8.7	-0.7
Clark, T. UKIP	1,208	2.4	+1.7
Con majority	861		1.74%
Electorate	70,570		
Total Vote	49,592		70.27

*Member of last parliament
Con Hold (1.5% from Con to LD)

MID SUSSEX		%	+/- %
*Soames, N. Con	21,150	46.2	+2.7
Wilkins, L. LD	14,252	31.1	+0.5
Mitchell, P. Lab	8,693	19.0	+0.3
Holdsworth, P. UKIP	1,126	2.5	+1.3
Berry, P. Loony	601	1.3	
Con majority	6,898		15.05%
Electorate	70,623		
Total Vote	45,822		64.88

*Member of last parliament
Con Hold (1.1% from LD to Con)

SUTTON AND CHEAM		%	+/- %
*Burstow, P. LD	19,382	48.8	+6.5
Maitland, O. Con	15,078	38.0	+0.1
Homan, L. Lab	5,263	13.2	-2.2
LD majority	4,304		10.84%
Electorate	63,648		
Total Vote	39,723		62.41

*Member of last parliament
LD Hold (3.2% from Con to LD)

SUTTON COLDFIELD		%	+/- %
Mitchell, A. Con	21,909	50.4	-1.8
Pocock, R. Lab	11,805	27.2	+3.3
Turner, M. LD	8,268	19.0	-0.3
Nattrass, M. UKIP	1,186	2.7	
Robinson, I. Ind	284	0.7	
Con majority	10,104		23.25%
Electorate	71,856		
Total Vote	43,452		60.47

Con Hold (2.6% from Con to Lab)

SWANSEA EAST		%	+/- %
*Anderson, D. Lab	19,612	65.2	-10.2
Ball, J. Pl C	3,464	11.5	+8.1
Speht, R. LD	3,064	10.2	+1.3
Morris, P. Con	3,026	10.1	+0.8
Young, J. Green	463	1.5	
Jenkins, T. UKIP	443	1.5	
Lab majority	16,148		53.70%
Electorate	56,821		
Total Vote	30,072		52.92

*Member of last parliament
Lab Hold (9.1% from Lab to Pl C)

SWANSEA WEST		%	+/- %
*Williams, A. Lab	15,644	48.7	-7.5
Harper, M. Con	6,094	19.0	-1.5
Day, M. LD	5,313	16.6	+2.0
Titherington, I. Pl C	3,404	10.6	+4.0
Lewis, R. UKIP	653	2.0	
Shrewsbury, M. Green	626	2.0	
Thraves, A. SA	366	1.1	
Lab majority	9,550		29.75%
Electorate	57,520		
Total Vote	32,100		55.81

*Member of last parliament
Lab Hold (3.0% from Lab to Con)

NORTH SWINDON		%	+/- %
*Wills, M. Lab	22,371	52.9	+3.1
Martin, N. Con	14,266	33.7	-0.1
Nation, D. LD	4,891	11.6	-1.4
Lloyd, B. UKIP	800	1.9	
Lab majority	8,105		19.15%
Electorate	70,471		
Total Vote	42,328		60.06

*Member of last parliament
Lab Hold (1.6% from Con to Lab)

SOUTH SWINDON		%	+/- %
*Drown, J. Lab	22,260	51.3	+4.5
Coombs, S. Con	14,919	34.4	-1.4
Brewer, G. LD	5,165	11.9	-2.5
Sharp, V. UKIP	713	1.6	
Gillard, R. RNRL	327	0.8	
Lab majority	7,341		16.92%
Electorate	72,439		
Total Vote	43,384		59.89

*Member of last parliament
Lab Hold (2.9% from Con to Lab)

TAMWORTH		%	+/- %
*Jenkins, B. Lab	19,722	49.0	-2.8
Gunter, L. Con	15,124	37.6	+0.8
Pinkett, J. LD	4,721	11.7	+3.7
Sootheran, P. UKIP	683	1.7	+1.0
Lab majority	4,598		11.42%
Electorate	69,596		
Total Vote	40,250		57.83

*Member of last parliament
Lab Hold (1.8% from Lab to Con)

TATTON		%	+/- %
Osborne, G. Con	19,860	48.1	+10.7
Conquest, S. Lab	11,249	27.3	
Ash, M. LD	7,685	18.6	
Sheppard, M. UKIP	769	1.9	
Sharratt, P. Ind	734	1.8	
Allinson, V. Ind	505	1.2	
Batchelor, W. Ind	322	0.8	
Hunt, J. Ind	154	0.4	
Con majority	8,611		20.86%
Electorate	64,954		
Total Vote	41,278		63.55

TAUNTON

		%	+/- %
Flook, A. Con	23,033	41.7	+3.0
*Ballard, J. LD	22,798	41.3	-1.4
Govier, A. Lab	8,254	14.9	+1.4
Canton, M. UKIP	1,140	2.1	
Con majority	235		0.43%
Electorate	81,651		
Total Vote	55,225		67.64

*Member of last parliament
Con Gain (2.2% from LD to Con)

NORTH TAYSIDE

		%	+/- %
Wishart, P. SNP	15,441	40.1	-4.8
Fraser, M. Con	12,158	31.6	-4.2
Docherty, T. Lab	5,715	14.8	+3.6
Robertson, J. LD	4,365	11.3	+3.2
Adams, R. SSP	620	1.6	
MacDonald, T. Ind	220	0.6	
SNP majority	3,283		8.52%
Electorate	61,645		
Total Vote	38,519		62.49

SNP Hold (0.3% from SNP to Con)

TEIGNBRIDGE

		%	+/- %
Younger-Ross, R. LD	26,343	44.4	+5.7
*Nicholls, P. Con	23,332	39.3	+0.1
Bain, C. Lab	7,366	12.4	-5.6
Exmouth, P. UKIP	2,269	3.8	+1.3
LD majority	3,011		5.08%
Electorate	85,533		
Total Vote	59,310		69.34

*Member of last parliament
LD Gain (2.8% from Con to LD)

TELFORD

		%	+/- %
Wright, D. Lab	16,854	54.6	-3.2
Henderson, A. Con	8,471	27.4	0.0
Wiggin, S. LD	3,983	12.9	+1.1
Brookes, N. UKIP	1,098	3.6	
Jeffries, M. SA	469	1.5	
Lab majority	8,383		27.15%
Electorate	59,431		
Total Vote	30,875		51.95

Lab Hold (1.6% from Lab to Con)

TEWKESBURY

		%	+/- %
*Robertson, L. Con	20,830	46.1	+0.3
Dhillon, K. Lab	12,167	26.9	+0.7
Martin, S. LD	11,863	26.2	-1.8
Vernall, C. None	335	0.7	
Con majority	8,663		19.17%
Electorate	70,465		
Total Vote	45,195		64.14

*Member of last parliament
Con Hold (0.2% from Con to Lab)

NORTH THANET

		%	+/- %
*Gale, R. Con	21,050	50.3	+6.2
Stewart Laing, J. Lab	14,400	34.4	-4.0
Proctor, S. LD	4,603	11.0	-0.4
Moore, I. UKIP	980	2.3	+1.4
Shortt, D. Ind	440	1.1	
Holmes, T. NF	395	0.9	
Con majority	6,650		15.88%
Electorate	71,012		
Total Vote	41,868		58.96

*Member of last parliament
Con Hold (5.1% from Lab to Con)

SOUTH THANET

		%	+/- %
*Ladyman, S. Lab	18,002	45.7	-0.5
MacGregor, M. Con	16,210	41.1	+1.3
Voizey, G. LD	3,706	9.4	-2.3
Baldwin, W. Ind	770	2.0	
Eccott, T. UKIP	502	1.3	-0.1
Franklin, B. NF	242	0.6	
Lab majority	1,792		4.54%
Electorate	61,680		
Total Vote	39,432		63.93

*Member of last parliament
Lab Hold (0.9% from Lab to Con)

THURROCK

		%	+/- %
*Mackinlay, A. Lab	21,121	56.5	-6.8
Penning, M. Con	11,124	29.8	+3.0
Lathan, J. LD	3,846	10.3	+2.2
Sheppard, C. UKIP	1,271	3.4	+1.6
Lab majority	9,997		26.76%
Electorate	76,180		
Total Vote	37,362		49.04

*Member of last parliament
Lab Hold (4.9% from Lab to Con)

TIVERTON AND HONITON

		%	+/- %
*Browning, A. Con	26,258	47.1	+5.7
Barnard, J. LD	19,974	35.8	-2.7
Owen, I. Lab	6,647	11.9	-0.9
Langmaid, A. UKIP	1,281	2.3	
Burgess, M. Green	1,030	1.8	+1.0
Roach, J. Lib	594	1.1	-0.0
Con majority	6,284		11.26%
Electorate	79,880		
Total Vote	55,784		69.83

*Member of last parliament
Con Hold (4.2% from LD to Con)

TONBRIDGE AND MALLING

		%	+/- %
*Stanley, J. Con	20,956	49.4	+1.4
Hayman, V. Lab	12,706	29.9	+2.7
Canet, M. LD	7,605	17.9	-1.3
Croucher, L. UKIP	1,169	2.8	+1.7
Con majority	8,250		19.44%
Electorate	65,979		
Total Vote	42,436		64.32

*Member of last parliament
Con Hold (0.7% from Con to Lab)

TOOTING

		%	+/- %
*Cox, T. Lab	20,332	54.1	-5.6
Nicoll, A. Con	9,932	26.4	-0.7
James, S. LD	5,583	14.9	+5.5
Ledbury, M. Green	1,744	4.6	+3.5
Lab majority	10,400		27.67%
Electorate	68,447		
Total Vote	37,591		54.92

*Member of last parliament
Lab Hold (2.4% from Lab to Con)

TORBAY

		%	+/- %
*Sanders, A. LD	24,015	50.5	+10.9
Sweeting, C. Con	17,307	36.4	-3.2
McKay, J. Lab	4,484	9.4	-5.4
Booth, G. UKIP	1,512	3.2	-0.5
Winwrite, P. Ind	251	0.5	
LD majority	6,708		14.10%
Electorate	76,072		
Total Vote	47,569		62.53

*Member of last parliament
LD Hold (7.0% from Con to LD)

TORFAEN		%	+/- %
*Murphy, P. Lab	21,883	62.1	-7.0
Evans, J. Con	5,603	15.9	+3.6
Masters, A. LD	3,936	11.2	-1.0
Smith, S. Pl C	2,720	7.7	+5.3
Vipass, B. UKIP	657	1.9	
Bell, S. SA	443	1.3	
Lab majority	16,280		46.19%
Electorate	61,110		
Total Vote	35,242		57.67

*Member of last parliament
Lab Hold (5.3% from Lab to Con)

TORRIDGE AND WEST DEVON –
see under Devon

TOTNES		%	+/- %
*Steen, A. Con	21,914	44.5	+8.0
Oliver, R. LD	18,317	37.2	+2.3
Wildy, T. Lab	6,005	12.2	-4.2
MacKinlay, C. UKIP	3,010	6.1	+4.3
Con majority	3,597		7.30%
Electorate	72,548		
Total Vote	49,246		67.88

*Member of last parliament
Con Hold (2.8% from LD to Con)

TOTTENHAM		%	+/- %
*Lammy, D. Lab	21,317	67.5	-1.8
Fernandes, U. Con	4,401	13.9	-1.8
Khan, M. LD	3,008	9.5	-1.3
Budge, P. Green	1,443	4.6	+1.8
Bennett, W. SA	1,162	3.7	
Shefki, U. Reform 2000	270	0.9	
Lab majority	16,916		53.53%
Electorate	65,568		
Total Vote	31,601		48.20

*Member of last parliament
Lab Hold (0.0% from Lab to Con)

TRURO AND ST AUSTELL		%	+/- %
*Taylor, M. LD	24,296	48.3	-0.2
Bonner, T. Con	16,231	32.3	+5.8
Phillips, D. Lab	6,889	13.7	-1.6
Wonnacott, J. UKIP	1,664	3.3	+2.3
Jenkin, C. Meb Ker	1,137	2.3	+1.5
Lee, J. Ind	78	0.2	
LD majority	8,065		16.04%
Electorate	79,219		
Total Vote	50,295		63.49

*Member of last parliament
LD Hold (3.0% from LD to Con)

TUNBRIDGE WELLS		%	+/- %
*Norman, A. Con	19,643	48.9	+3.7
Brown, K. LD	9,913	24.7	-5.0
Carvell, I. Lab	9,332	23.2	+2.8
Webb, V. UKIP	1,313	3.3	+2.7
Con majority	9,730		24.20%
Electorate	65,730		
Total Vote	40,201		61.16

*Member of last parliament
Con Hold (4.3% from LD to Con)

TWEEDDALE, ETTRICK AND LAUDERDALE		%	+/- %
*Moore, M. LD	14,035	42.3	+11.0
Geddes, K. Lab	8,878	26.7	-0.7
Brocklehurst, A. Con	5,118	15.4	-6.7

Thomson, R. SNP	4,108	12.4	-4.7
Lockhart, N. SSP	695	2.1	
Hein, J. Lib	383	1.2	+0.2
LD majority	5,157		15.53%
Electorate	52,430		
Total Vote	33,217		63.35

*Member of last parliament
LD Hold (5.9% from Lab to LD)

TWICKENHAM		%	+/- %
*Cable, V. LD	24,344	48.7	+3.6
Longworth, N. Con	16,689	33.4	-4.3
Rogers, D. Lab	6,903	13.8	-1.8
Maciejowska, J. Green	1,423	2.8	
Hollebone, R. UKIP	579	1.2	
LD majority	7,655		15.33%
Electorate	75,225		
Total Vote	49,938		66.38

*Member of last parliament
LD Hold (4.0% from Con to LD)

TYNE BRIDGE		%	+/- %
*Clelland, D. Lab	18,345	70.5	-6.3
Cook, J. Con	3,456	13.3	+2.2
Wallace, J. LD	3,213	12.3	+4.4
Fitzpatrick, J. SLP	533	2.0	
Robson, S. SA	485	1.9	
Lab majority	14,889		57.19%
Electorate	58,900		
Total Vote	26,032		44.20

*Member of last parliament
Lab Hold (4.3% from Lab to Con)

TYNEMOUTH		%	+/- %
*Campbell, A. Lab	23,364	53.2	-2.1
Poulsen, K. Con	14,686	33.5	+0.1
Reid, P. LD	5,108	11.6	+2.8
Rollings, M. UKIP	745	1.7	+0.8
Lab majority	8,678		19.77%
Electorate	65,184		
Total Vote	43,903		67.35

*Member of last parliament
Lab Hold (1.1% from Lab to Con)

NORTH TYNESIDE		%	+/- %
*Byers, S. Lab	26,027	69.5	-3.3
Ruffell, M. Con	5,459	14.6	+0.9
Reed, S. LD	4,649	12.4	+1.9
Taylor, A. UKIP	770	2.1	
Burnett, P. SA	324	0.9	
Capstick, W. SLP	240	0.6	
Lab majority	20,568		54.89%
Electorate	64,914		
Total Vote	37,469		57.72

*Member of last parliament
Lab Hold (2.1% from Lab to Con)

WEST TYRONE		%	+/- %
Doherty, P. SF	19,814	40.8	+10.0
*Thompson, W. UUP	14,774	30.4	-4.1
Rodgers, B. SDLP	13,942	28.7	-3.3
SF majority	5,040		10.39%
Electorate	60,739		
Total Vote	48,530		79.90

*Member of last parliament
SF Gain (7.1% from UUP to SF)

MID ULSTER

		%	+/- %
*McGuinness, M. SF	25,502	51.1	+11.0
McCrea, I. DUP	15,549	31.1	-5.2
Haughey, E. SDLP	8,376	16.8	-5.3
Donnelly, F. WRP	509	1.0	
SF majority	9,953		19.93%
Electorate	61,390		
Total Vote	49,936		81.34

*Member of last parliament
SF Hold (8.1% from DUP to SF)

UPMINSTER

		%	+/- %
Watkinson, A. Con	15,410	45.5	+6.0
*Darvill, K. Lab	14,169	41.9	-4.3
Truesdale, P. LD	3,183	9.4	-0.1
Murray, T. UKIP	1,089	3.2	
Con majority	1,241		3.67%
Electorate	56,932		
Total Vote	33,851		59.46

*Member of last parliament
Con Gain (5.2% from Lab to Con)

UPPER BANN

		%	+/- %
*Trimble, D. UUP	17,095	33.5	-10.1
Simpson, D. DUP	15,037	29.5	+18.0
O'Hagan, D. SF	10,771	21.1	+9.0
Kelly, D. SDLP	7,607	14.9	-9.3
French, T. WRP	527	1.0	
UUP majority	2,058		4.03%
Electorate	72,574		
Total Vote	51,037		70.32

*Member of last parliament
UUP Hold (14.0% from UUP to DUP)

UXBRIDGE

		%	+/- %
*Randall, J. Con	15,751	47.1	+3.6
Salisbury-Jones, D. Lab	13,653	40.9	-1.0
Royce, C. LD	3,426	10.3	-0.6
Cannons, P. UKIP	588	1.8	
Con majority	2,098		6.28%
Electorate	58,068		
Total Vote	33,418		57.55

*Member of last parliament
Con Hold (2.3% from Lab to Con)

VALE OF CLWYD – see under Clwyd

VALE OF GLAMORGAN –
see under Glamorgan

VALE OF YORK – see under York

VAUXHALL

		%	+/- %
*Hoey, K. Lab	19,738	59.1	-4.7
Bottrall, A. LD	6,720	20.1	+4.1
Compton, G. Con	4,489	13.4	-1.8
Collins, S. Green	1,485	4.4	+2.2
Bennett, T. SA	853	2.6	
Boyd, M. Ind	107	0.3	
Lab majority	13,018		38.99%
Electorate	74,474		
Total Vote	33,392		44.84

*Member of last parliament
Lab Hold (4.4% from Lab to LD)

WAKEFIELD

		%	+/- %
*Hinchliffe, D. Lab	20,592	49.9	-7.5
Karran, T. Con	12,638	30.6	+2.2
Dale, D. LD	5,097	12.4	+1.2
Greenwood, S. Green	1,075	2.6	
Cannon, J. UKIP	677	1.6	

Aziz, A. SLP	634	1.5
Griffiths, M. SA	541	1.3
Lab majority	7,954	19.28%
Electorate	75,750	
Total Vote	41,254	54.46

*Member of last parliament
Lab Hold (4.8% from Lab to Con)

WALLASEY

		%	+/- %
*Eagle, A. Lab	22,718	60.8	-3.8
Rennie, L. Con	10,442	28.0	+4.1
Reisdorf, P. LD	4,186	11.2	+2.9
Lab majority	12,276		32.87%
Electorate	64,889		
Total Vote	37,346		57.55

*Member of last parliament
Lab Hold (3.9% from Lab to Con)

WALSALL NORTH

		%	+/- %
*Winnick, D. Lab	18,779	58.1	+1.5
Pitt, M. Con	9,388	29.1	+1.5
Heap, M. LD	2,923	9.0	-0.3
Mayo, J. UKIP	812	2.5	
Church, D. SA	410	1.3	
Lab majority	9,391		29.06%
Electorate	65,981		
Total Vote	32,312		48.97

*Member of last parliament
Lab Hold (0.0% from Lab to Con)

WALSALL SOUTH

		%	+/- %
*George, B. Lab	20,574	59.0	+1.1
Bird, M. Con	10,643	30.5	-1.2
Tomlinson, B. LD	2,365	6.8	+0.5
Bennett, D. UKIP	974	2.8	
Smith, P. SA	343	1.0	
Lab majority	9,931		28.46%
Electorate	62,626		
Total Vote	34,899		55.73

*Member of last parliament
Lab Hold (1.1% from Con to Lab)

WALTHAMSTOW

		%	+/- %
*Gerrard, N. Lab	21,402	62.2	-1.0
Boys Smith, N. Con	6,221	18.1	-2.2
Dunphy, P. LD	5,024	14.6	+0.9
Donovan, S. SAP	806	2.3	
Phillips, W. BNP	389	1.1	
Mayer, G. UKIP	298	0.9	
Duffy, B. ProLife	289	0.8	
Lab majority	15,181		44.09%
Electorate	64,403		
Total Vote	34,429		53.46

*Member of last parliament
Lab Hold (0.6% from Con to Lab)

WANSBECK

		%	+/- %
*Murphy, D. Lab	21,617	57.8	-7.7
Thompson, A. LD	8,516	22.8	+6.8
Lake, R. Con	4,774	12.8	-1.2
Kirkup, M. Ind	1,076	2.9	
Best, N. Green	954	2.5	+0.4
Attwell, G. UKIP	482	1.3	
Lab majority	13,101		35.01%
Electorate	63,149		
Total Vote	37,419		59.26

*Member of last parliament
Lab Hold (7.3% from Lab to LD)

WANSDYKE

		%	+/- %
*Norris, D. Lab	23,206	46.8	+2.8
Watt, C. Con	17,593	35.5	+0.2
Coleshill, G. LD	7,135	14.4	-2.4
Hayden, F. Green	958	1.9	
Sandell, P. UKIP	655	1.3	+0.5
Lab majority	5,613		11.33%
Electorate	70,850		
Total Vote	49,547		69.93

*Member of last parliament
Lab Hold (1.3% from Con to Lab)

WANTAGE

		%	+/- %
*Jackson, R. Con	19,475	39.6	-0.2
Beer, S. Lab	13,875	28.2	-0.7
Fawcett, N. LD	13,776	28.0	+1.5
Brooks-Saxl, D. Green	1,062	2.2	+1.0
Tolstoy, N. UKIP	941	1.9	+1.1
Con majority	5,600		11.40%
Electorate	76,129		
Total Vote	49,129		64.53

*Member of last parliament
Con Hold (0.3% from Lab to Con)

WARLEY

		%	+/- %
*Spellar, J. Lab	19,007	60.5	-3.3
Pritchard, M. Con	7,157	22.8	-1.3
Cockings, R. LD	3,315	10.6	+0.8
Dardi, H. SLP	1,936	6.2	
Lab majority	11,850		37.72%
Electorate	58,065		
Total Vote	31,415		54.10

*Member of last parliament
Lab Hold (1.0% from Lab to Con)

WARRINGTON NORTH

		%	+/- %
*Jones, H. Lab	24,026	61.7	-0.4
Usher, J. Con	8,870	22.8	-1.2
Smith, R. LD	5,232	13.4	+3.1
Kirkham, J. UKIP	782	2.0	
Lab majority	15,156		38.95%
Electorate	72,445		
Total Vote	38,910		53.71

*Member of last parliament
Lab Hold (0.4% from Con to Lab)

WARRINGTON SOUTH

		%	+/- %
*Southworth, H. Lab	22,419	49.3	-2.9
Mosley, C. Con	15,022	33.0	+0.5
Barlow, R. LD	7,419	16.3	+3.2
Kelley, J. UKIP	637	1.4	
Lab majority	7,397		16.26%
Electorate	74,283		
Total Vote	45,497		61.25

*Member of last parliament
Lab Hold (1.7% from Lab to Con)

WARWICK AND LEAMINGTON

		%	+/- %
*Plaskitt, J. Lab	26,108	48.8	+4.3
Campbell Bannerman, D. Con	20,155	37.6	-1.2
Forbes, L. LD	5,964	11.1	-0.7
Kime, A. SA	664	1.2	
Warwick, G. UKIP	648	1.2	
Lab majority	5,953		11.12%
Electorate	81,515		
Total Vote	53,539		65.68

*Member of last parliament
Lab Hold (2.7% from Con to Lab)

NORTH WARWICKSHIRE

		%	+/- %
*O'Brien, M. Lab	24,023	54.1	-4.3
Parsons, G. Con	14,384	32.4	+1.2
Powell, W. LD	5,052	11.4	+3.9
Flynn, J. UKIP	950	2.1	+1.2
Lab majority	9,639		21.71%
Electorate	73,825		
Total Vote	44,409		60.15

*Member of last parliament
Lab Hold (2.8% from Lab to Con)

WATFORD

		%	+/- %
*Ward, C. Lab	20,992	45.3	-0.0
McManus, M. Con	15,437	33.3	-1.5
Hames, D. LD	8,088	17.4	+0.7
Kingsley, D. Green	900	1.9	
Stewart-Mole, E. UKIP	535	1.2	
Berry, J. SA	420	0.9	
Lab majority	5,555		11.98%
Electorate	75,872		
Total Vote	46,372		61.12

*Member of last parliament
Lab Hold (0.7% from Con to Lab)

WAVENEY

		%	+/- %
*Blizzard, B. Lab	23,914	50.7	-5.3
Scott, L. Con	15,361	32.6	-1.9
Young, D. LD	5,370	11.4	+2.4
Aylett, B. UKIP	1,097	2.3	
Elliott, G. Green	983	2.1	
Mallin, R. SA	442	0.9	
Lab majority	8,553		18.13%
Electorate	76,585		
Total Vote	47,167		61.59

*Member of last parliament
Lab Hold (1.7% from Lab to Con)

WEALDEN

		%	+/- %
Hendry, C. Con	26,279	49.8	0.0
Murphy, S. LD	12,507	23.7	-2.0
Fordham, K. Lab	10,705	20.3	+3.1
Riddle, K. UKIP	1,539	2.9	+2.0
Salmon, J. Green	1,273	2.4	
Thornton, C. PCP	453	0.9	
Con majority	13,772		26.11%
Electorate	83,940		
Total Vote	52,756		62.85

Con Hold (1.0% from LD to Con)

WEAVER VALE

		%	+/- %
*Hall, M. Lab	20,611	52.5	-3.9
Cross, C. Con	10,974	27.9	-0.6
Griffiths, N. LD	5,643	14.4	+2.1
Cooksley, M. Ind	1,484	3.8	
Bradshaw, J. UKIP	559	1.4	
Lab majority	9,637		24.54%
Electorate	68,236		
Total Vote	39,271		57.55

*Member of last parliament
Lab Hold (1.7% from Lab to Con)

WELLINGBOROUGH

		%	+/- %
*Stinchcombe, P. Lab	23,867	46.8	+2.6
Bone, P. Con	21,512	42.2	-1.6
Gaskell, P. LD	4,763	9.3	-0.0
Ellwood, A. UKIP	864	1.7	+0.4
Lab majority	2,355		4.62%
Electorate	77,323		
Total Vote	51,006		65.96

*Member of last parliament
Lab Hold (2.1% from Con to Lab)

WELLS

		%	+/- %
*Heathcoat-Amory, D. Con	22,462	43.8	+4.4
Oakes, G. LD	19,666	38.3	-0.1
Merryfield, A. Lab	7,915	15.4	-2.7
Reed, A. UKIP	1,104	2.2	
Bex, C. Wessex Reg	167	0.3	
Con majority	2,796		5.45%
Electorate	74,189		
Total Vote	51,314		69.17

*Member of last parliament
Con Hold (2.3% from LD to Con)

WELWYN HATFIELD

		%	+/- %
*Johnson, M. Lab	18,484	43.2	-3.9
Shapps, G. Con	17,288	40.4	+3.9
Cooke, D. LD	6,021	14.1	+0.5
Biggs, M. UKIP	798	1.9	
Pinto, F. ProLife	230	0.5	0.0
Lab majority	1,196		2.79%
Electorate	67,004		
Total Vote	42,821		63.91

*Member of last parliament
Lab Hold (3.9% from Lab to Con)

WENTWORTH

		%	+/- %
*Healey, J. Lab	22,798	67.5	-4.8
Roberts, M. Con	6,349	18.8	+3.8
Wildgoose, D. LD	3,652	10.8	+1.6
Wilkinson, J. UKIP	979	2.9	
Lab majority	16,449		48.70%
Electorate	64,033		
Total Vote	33,778		52.75

*Member of last parliament
Lab Hold (4.3% from Lab to Con)

WEST ABERDEENSHIRE AND KINCARDINE –
see under Aberdeenshire

WEST BROMWICH EAST

		%	+/- %
Watson, T. Lab	18,250	55.9	-1.3
McFarlane, D. Con	8,487	26.0	+1.6
Garrett, I. LD	4,507	13.8	-1.1
Grey, S. UKIP	835	2.6	
Johal, S. SLP	585	1.8	
Lab majority	9,763		29.89%
Electorate	61,180		
Total Vote	32,664		53.39

Lab Hold (1.4% from Lab to Con)

WEST BROMWICH WEST

		%	+/- %
*Bailey, A. Lab	19,352	60.8	+37.5
Bissell, K. Con	7,997	25.1	
Smith, S. LD	2,168	6.8	
Salvage, J. BNP	1,428	4.5	
Walker, K. UKIP	499	1.6	
Singh, B. SLP	396	1.2	
Lab majority	11,355		35.66%
Electorate	66,765		
Total Vote	31,840		47.69

*Member of last parliament
Lab Gain (6.2% from Con to Lab)

WEST DERBYSHIRE – see under Derbyshire

WEST DORSET – see under Dorset

WEST HAM

		%	+/- %
*Banks, T. Lab	20,449	69.9	-3.0
Kamall, S. Con	4,804	16.4	+1.4
Fox, P. LD	2,166	7.4	0.0
Chandler-Oatts, J. Green	1,197	4.1	
Batten, G. UKIP	657	2.2	
Lab majority	15,645		53.45%
Electorate	59,828		
Total Vote	29,273		48.93

*Member of last parliament
Lab Hold (2.2% from Lab to Con)

WEST LANCASHIRE – see under Lancashire

WEST RENFREWSHIRE – see under Renfrewshire

WEST SUFFOLK – see under Suffolk

WEST TYRONE – see under Tyrone

WEST WORCESTERSHIRE –
see under Worcestershire

WESTBURY

		%	+/- %
Murrison, A. Con	21,299	42.1	+1.5
Vigar, D. LD	16,005	31.6	+1.7
Cardy, S. Lab	10,847	21.4	+0.3
Booth-Jones, C. UKIP	1,261	2.5	+1.1
Gledhill, B. Green	1,216	2.4	
Con majority	5,294		10.46%
Electorate	76,137		
Total Vote	50,628		66.50

Con Hold (0.1% from Con to LD)

WESTERN ISLES

		%	+/- %
*MacDonald, C. Lab	5,924	45.0	-10.6
Nicholson, A. SNP	4,850	36.9	+3.5
Taylor, D. Con	1,250	9.5	+2.8
Horne, J. LD	849	6.5	+3.4
Telfer, J. SSP	286	2.2	
Lab majority	1,074		8.16%
Electorate	21,706		
Total Vote	13,159		60.62

*Member of last parliament
Lab Hold (7.0% from Lab to SNP)

WESTMORLAND AND LONSDALE

		%	+/- %
*Collins, T. Con	22,486	46.9	+4.7
Farron, T. LD	19,339	40.4	+7.0
Bateson, J. Lab	5,234	10.9	-9.7
Gibson, R. UKIP	552	1.2	
Bell, T. Ind	292	0.6	
Con majority	3,147		6.63%
Electorate	70,637		
Total Vote	47,903		67.24

*Member of last parliament
Con Hold (1.1% from Con to LD)

WESTON-SUPER-MARE

		%	+/- %
*Cotter, B. LD	18,424	39.5	-0.6
Penrose, J. Con	18,086	38.7	+1.0
Kraft, D. Lab	9,235	19.8	+1.9
Lukins, W. UKIP	650	1.4	
Peverelle, C. Ind	206	0.4	
Sibley, R. Ind	79	0.2	
LD majority	338		0.72%
Electorate	74,322		
Total Vote	46,680		62.81

*Member of last parliament
LD Hold (0.8% from LD to Con)

WIGAN		%	+/- %
*Turner, N. Lab	20,739	61.7	-6.8
Page, M. Con	6,996	20.8	+3.9
Beswick, T. LD	4,970	14.8	+4.8
Lowe, D. SA	886	2.6	
Lab majority	13,743		40.91%
Electorate	64,040		
Total Vote	33,591		52.45

*Member of last parliament
Lab Hold (5.4% from Lab to Con)

NORTH WILTSHIRE		%	+/- %
*Gray, J. Con	24,090	45.5	+1.7
Pym, H. LD	20,212	38.2	+0.4
Garton, J. Lab	7,556	14.3	0.0
Dowdney, N. UKIP	1,090	2.1	+1.4
Con majority	3,878		7.32%
Electorate	78,625		
Total Vote	52,948		67.34

*Member of last parliament
Con Hold (0.7% from LD to Con)

WIMBLEDON		%	+/- %
*Casale, R. Lab	18,806	45.7	+3.0
Hammond, S. Con	15,062	36.6	+0.1
Pierce, M. LD	5,341	13.0	-3.6
Thacker, R. Green	1,007	2.4	+1.5
Glencross, R. CPA	479	1.2	
Bell, M. UKIP	414	1.0	
Lab majority	3,744		9.11%
Electorate	63,930		
Total Vote	41,109		64.30

*Member of last parliament
Lab Hold (1.5% from Con to Lab)

WINCHESTER		%	+/- %
*Oaten, M. LD	32,282	54.6	+12.5
Hayes, A. Con	22,648	38.3	-3.8
Wyeth, S. Lab	3,498	5.9	-4.6
Martin, J. UKIP	664	1.1	+0.4
Rous, H. Wessex Reg	66	0.1	
LD majority	9,634		16.29%
Electorate	83,532		
Total Vote	59,158		70.82

*Member of last parliament
LD Hold (8.1% from Con to LD)

WINDSOR		%	+/- %
*Trend, M. Con	19,900	47.3	-0.9
Pinfield, N. LD	11,011	26.1	-2.5
Muller, M. Lab	10,137	24.1	+5.8
Fagan, J. UKIP	1,062	2.5	+1.9
Con majority	8,889		21.11%
Electorate	73,854		
Total Vote	42,110		57.02

*Member of last parliament
Con Hold (0.8% from LD to Con)

WIRRAL SOUTH		%	+/- %
*Chapman, B. Lab	18,890	47.4	-3.5
Millard, T. Con	13,841	34.8	-1.6
Gilchrist, P. LD	7,087	17.8	+7.4
Lab majority	5,049		12.68%
Electorate	60,653		
Total Vote	39,818		65.65

*Member of last parliament
Lab Hold (0.9% from Lab to Con)

WIRRAL WEST		%	+/- %
*Hesford, S. Lab	19,105	47.2	+2.3
Lynch, C. Con	15,070	37.2	-1.8
Holbrook, S. LD	6,300	15.6	+2.9
Lab majority	4,035		9.97%
Electorate	62,294		
Total Vote	40,475		64.97

*Member of last parliament
Lab Hold (2.1% from Con to Lab)

WITNEY		%	+/- %
Cameron, D. Con	22,153	45.0	+2.0
Bartlet, M. Lab	14,180	28.8	-1.8
Epps, G. LD	10,000	20.3	+0.5
Stevenson, M. Green	1,100	2.2	+1.1
Beadle, B. Ind	1,003	2.0	
Dukes, K. UKIP	767	1.6	+0.2
Con majority	7,973		16.20%
Electorate	74,612		
Total Vote	49,203		65.95

Con Hold (1.9% from Lab to Con)

WOKING		%	+/- %
*Malins, H. Con	19,747	46.0	+7.6
Hilliar, A. LD	12,988	30.3	+3.0
Hussain, S. Lab	8,714	20.3	-0.7
Harvey, M. UKIP	1,461	3.4	+2.4
Con majority	6,759		15.75%
Electorate	71,254		
Total Vote	42,910		60.22

*Member of last parliament
Con Hold (2.3% from LD to Con)

WOKINGHAM		%	+/- %
*Redwood, J. Con	20,216	46.1	-4.0
Longton, R. LD	14,222	32.4	+1.1
Syed, M. Lab	7,633	17.4	+0.6
Carstairs, F. UKIP	897	2.0	
Owen, T. Loony	880	2.0	+0.3
Con majority	5,994		13.67%
Electorate	68,430		
Total Vote	43,848		64.08

*Member of last parliament
Con Hold (2.5% from Con to LD)

WOLVERHAMPTON NORTH EAST		%	+/- %
*Purchase, K. Lab	18,984	60.3	+1.0
Miller, M. Con	9,019	28.6	+0.7
Bourne, S. LD	2,494	7.9	+2.6
McCartney, T. UKIP	997	3.2	
Lab majority	9,965		31.64%
Electorate	59,616		
Total Vote	31,494		52.83

*Member of last parliament
Lab Hold (0.1% from Con to Lab)

WOLVERHAMPTON SOUTH EAST		%	+/- %
*Turner, D. Lab	18,409	67.4	+3.7
Pepper, A. Con	5,945	21.8	+1.6
Wild, P. LD	2,389	8.8	-0.7
Barry, J. NF	554	2.0	
Lab majority	12,464		45.66%
Electorate	53,243		
Total Vote	27,297		51.27

*Member of last parliament
Lab Hold (1.0% from Con to Lab)

WOLVERHAMPTON SOUTH WEST

		%	+/- %
Marris, R. Lab	19,735	48.3	-2.1
Chambers, D. Con	16,248	39.7	-0.2
Dixon, M. LD	3,425	8.4	+0.2
Walker, W. Green	805	2.0	
Hope, J. UKIP	684	1.7	
Lab majority	3,487		8.53%
Electorate	65,909		
Total Vote	40,897		62.05

Lab Hold (1.0% from Lab to Con)

WOODSPRING

		%	+/- %
*Fox, L. Con	21,297	43.7	-0.8
Stevens, C. Lab	12,499	25.6	+4.9
Eldridge, C. LD	11,816	24.2	-6.1
Shopland, D. Ind	1,412	2.9	
Lawson, R. Green	1,282	2.6	+1.4
Crean, F. UKIP	452	0.9	
Con majority	8,798		18.04%
Electorate	71,018		
Total Vote	48,758		68.66

*Member of last parliament
Con Hold (2.8% from Con to Lab)

WORCESTER

		%	+/- %
*Foster, M. Lab	21,478	48.6	-1.5
Adams, R. Con	15,712	35.5	-0.2
Chandler, P. LD	5,578	12.6	+0.1
Chamings, R. UKIP	1,442	3.3	+1.5
Lab majority	5,766		13.04%
Electorate	71,255		
Total Vote	44,210		62.04

*Member of last parliament
Lab Hold (0.7% from Lab to Con)

MID WORCESTERSHIRE

		%	+/- %
*Luff, P. Con	22,937	51.1	+3.7
Bannister, D. Lab	12,310	27.4	-1.5
Browne, R. LD	8,420	18.8	+0.1
Eaves, A. UKIP	1,230	2.7	+1.5
Con majority	10,627		23.67%
Electorate	72,055		
Total Vote	44,897		62.31

*Member of last parliament
Con Hold (2.6% from Lab to Con)

WEST WORCESTERSHIRE

		%	+/- %
*Spicer, M. Con	20,597	46.0	+0.9
Hadley, M. LD	15,223	34.0	-3.3
Azmi, W. Lab	6,275	14.0	-1.7
Morris, I. UKIP	1,574	3.5	
Victory, M. Green	1,138	2.5	+0.5
Con majority	5,374		11.99%
Electorate	66,769		
Total Vote	44,807		67.11

*Member of last parliament
Con Hold (2.1% from LD to Con)

WORKINGTON

		%	+/- %
Cunningham, T. Lab	23,209	55.5	-8.7
Stoddard, T. Con	12,359	29.6	+5.1
Francis, I. LD	5,214	12.5	+4.4
Peacock, J. LCA	1,040	2.5	
Lab majority	10,850		25.94%
Electorate	65,965		
Total Vote	41,822		63.40

Lab Hold (6.9% from Lab to Con)

WORSLEY

		%	+/- %
*Lewis, T. Lab	20,193	57.1	-5.1
Ellwood, T. Con	8,406	23.8	-0.5
Bleakley, R. LD	6,188	17.5	+3.9
Entwistle, D. SLP	576	1.6	
Lab majority	11,787		33.33%
Electorate	69,300		
Total Vote	35,363		51.03

*Member of last parliament
Lab Hold (2.3% from Lab to Con)

EAST WORTHING AND SHOREHAM

		%	+/- %
*Loughton, T. Con	18,608	43.2	+2.7
Yates, D. Lab	12,469	29.0	+5.0
Elgood, P. LD	9,876	22.9	-7.6
McCulloch, J. UKIP	1,195	2.8	+1.0
Baldwin, C. LCA	920	2.1	
Con majority	6,139		14.25%
Electorate	71,890		
Total Vote	43,068		59.91

*Member of last parliament
Con Hold (1.1% from Con to Lab)

WORTHING WEST

		%	+/- %
*Bottomley, P. Con	20,508	47.5	+1.3
Walsh, J. LD	11,471	26.5	-4.6
Butcher, A. Lab	9,270	21.5	+5.2
Cross, T. UKIP	1,960	4.5	+2.5
Con majority	9,037		20.91%
Electorate	72,419		
Total Vote	43,209		59.67

*Member of last parliament
Con Hold (3.0% from LD to Con)

THE WREKIN

		%	+/- %
*Bradley, P. Lab	19,532	47.1	+0.1
Rees-Mogg, J. Con	15,945	38.4	-1.8
Jenkins, I. LD	4,738	11.4	-1.4
Brookes, D. UKIP	1,275	3.1	
Lab majority	3,587		8.65%
Electorate	65,781		
Total Vote	41,490		63.07

*Member of last parliament
Lab Hold (1.0% from Con to Lab)

WREXHAM

		%	+/- %
Lucas, I. Lab	15,934	53.0	-3.1
Elphick, F. Con	6,746	22.5	-1.4
Davies, R. LD	5,153	17.1	+3.9
Evans, M. Pl C	1,783	5.9	+2.7
Brookes, J. UKIP	432	1.4	
Lab majority	9,188		30.58%
Electorate	50,465		
Total Vote	30,048		59.54

Lab Hold (0.9% from Lab to Con)

WYCOMBE

		%	+/- %
Goodman, P. Con	19,064	42.4	+2.5
Shafique, C. Lab	15,896	35.3	-0.1
Tomlin, D. LD	7,658	17.0	-1.5
Cooke, C. UKIP	1,059	2.4	
Laker, J. Green	1,057	2.4	+1.0
Fitton, D. Ind	240	0.5	
Con majority	3,168		7.04%
Electorate	74,297		
Total Vote	44,974		60.53

Con Hold (1.3% from Lab to Con)

WYRE FOREST		%	+/- %
Taylor, R. Ind KHHC	28,487	58.1	
*Lock, D. Lab	10,857	22.1	-26.6
Simpson, M. Con	9,350	19.1	-17.1
Millington, J. UKIP	368	0.8	+0.2
Ind KHHC majority	17,630		35.93%
Electorate	72,152		
Total Vote	49,062		68.00

*Member of last parliament
Ind KHHC Gain (42.3% from Lab to Ind KHHC)

WYTHENSHAWE AND SALE EAST		%	+/- %
*Goggins, P. Lab	21,032	60.0	+1.9
Fildes, S. Con	8,424	24.0	-1.1
Tucker, V. LD	4,320	12.3	-0.1
Crookes, L. Green	869	2.5	
Shaw, F. SLP	410	1.2	-0.9
Lab majority	12,608		35.97%
Electorate	72,127		
Total Vote	35,055		48.60

*Member of last parliament
Lab Hold (1.5% from Con to Lab)

YEOVIL		%	+/- %
Laws, D. LD	21,266	44.2	-4.6
Forgione, M. Con	17,338	36.0	+8.4
Conway, P. Lab	7,077	14.7	-0.2
Boxall, N. UKIP	1,131	2.3	
Begg, A. Green	786	1.6	+0.3
Prior, A. Lib	534	1.1	
LD majority	3,928		8.16%
Electorate	75,977		
Total Vote	48,132		63.35

LD Hold (6.4% from LD to Con)

YNYS MÔN		%	+/- %
Owen, A. Lab	11,906	35.0	+1.8
Williams, E. Pl C	11,106	32.6	-6.8
Fox, A. Con	7,653	22.5	+1.0
Bennett, N. LD	2,772	8.1	+4.3
Wykes, F. UKIP	359	1.1	
Donald, N. Ind	222	0.7	
Lab majority	800		2.35%
Electorate	53,398		
Total Vote	34,018		63.71

Lab Gain (4.3% from Pl C to Lab)

CITY OF YORK		%	+/- %
*Bayley, H. Lab	25,072	52.3	-7.7
McIntyre, M. Con	11,293	23.5	-1.2
Waller, A. LD	8,519	17.8	+6.6
Shaw, B. Green	1,465	3.1	+1.5
Ormston, F. SA	674	1.4	
Bate, R. UKIP	576	1.2	+0.7
Cambridge, G. Loony	381	0.8	
Lab majority	13,779		28.72%
Electorate	80,431		
Total Vote	47,980		59.65

*Member of last parliament
Lab Hold (3.2% from Lab to Con)

VALE OF YORK		%	+/- %
*McIntosh, A. Con	25,033	51.6	+6.9
Jukes, C. Lab	12,516	25.8	-0.6
Stone, G. LD	9,799	20.2	-3.6
Thornber, P. UKIP	1,142	2.4	
Con majority	12,517		25.81%
Electorate	73,335		
Total Vote	48,490		66.12

*Member of last parliament
Con Hold (3.8% from Lab to Con)

YORKSHIRE EAST		%	+/- %
Knight, G. Con	19,861	45.9	+3.2
Simpson-Laing, T. Lab	15,179	35.0	-0.8
Hardy, M. LD	6,300	14.5	-4.0
Pearson, T. UKIP	1,661	3.8	
Dessoy, P. Ind	313	0.7	
Con majority	4,682		10.81%
Electorate	72,052		
Total Vote	43,314		60.11

Con Hold (2.0% from Lab to Con)

DodOnline

An Electronic Directory without rival . . .

MPs' biographies and photographs available with daily updates *via* the internet

For a *free* trial, call Yasmin Mirza, Aby Farsoun or Michael Mand on 020 7630 7643

Geographical whereabouts of constituencies

Aberavon	South Wales
Aberdeen Central	North East Scotland
Aberdeen North	North East Scotland
Aberdeen South	North East Scotland
West Aberdeenshire and Kincardine	North East Scotland
Airdrie and Shotts	North Lanarkshire
Aldershot	Hampshire
Aldridge-Brownhills	West Midlands
Altrincham and Sale West	Greater Manchester
Alyn and Deeside	Flintshire
Amber Valley	Derbyshire
Angus	East Scotland
East Antrim	Northern Ireland
North Antrim	Northern Ireland
South Antrim	Northern Ireland
Argyll and Bute	Northern Scotland
Arundel and South Downs	West Sussex
Ashfield	Nottinghamshire
Ashford	Kent
Ashton under Lyne	Greater Manchester
Aylesbury	Buckinghamshire
Ayr	Southern Scotland
Banbury	Oxfordshire
Banff and Buchan	Aberdeenshire
Barking	East London
Barnsley Central	South Yorkshire
Barnsley East and Mexborough	South Yorkshire
Barnsley West and Penistone	South Yorkshire
Barrow and Furness	Cumbria
Basildon	Essex
Basingstoke	Hampshire
Bassetlaw	Nottinghamshire
Bath	Somerset
Batley and Spen	West Yorkshire
Battersea	South London
Beaconsfield	Buckinghamshire
Beckenham	Kent
Bedford	Southern England
Mid Bedfordshire	Southern England
North East Bedfordshire	Southern England
South West Bedfordshire	Southern England
Belfast East	Northern Ireland
Belfast North	Northern Ireland
Belfast South	Northern Ireland
Belfast West	Northern Ireland
Berwick-upon-Tweed	Northumberland
Bethnal Green and Bow	East London
Beverley and Holderness	East Yorkshire
Bexhill and Battle	Kent
Old Bexley and Sidcup	London
Bexleyheath and Crayford	London
Billericay	Essex
Birkenhead	Merseyside
Birmingham Edgbaston	West Midlands

Birmingham Erdington	West Midlands
Birmingham Hall Green	West Midlands
Birmingham Hodge Hill	West Midlands
Birmingham Ladywood	West Midlands
Birmingham Northfield	West Midlands
Birmingham Perry Barr	West Midlands
Birmingham Selly Oak	West Midlands
Birmingham Sparkbrook and Small Heath	West Midlands
Birmingham Yardley	West Midlands
Bishop Auckland	County Durham
Blaby	Leicestershire
Blackburn	Lancashire
Blackpool North and Fleetwood	Lancashire
Blackpool South	Lancashire
Blaenau Gwent	South Wales
Blaydon	Tyne and Wear
Blyth Valley	Northumberland
Bognor Regis and Littlehampton	West Sussex
Bolsover	Derbyshire
Bolton North East	Greater Manchester
Bolton South East	Greater Manchester
Bolton West	Greater Manchester
Bootle	Merseyside
Boston and Skegness	Lincolnshire
Bosworth	Leicestershire
Bournemouth East	Dorset
Bournemouth West	Dorset
Bracknell	Berkshire
Bradford North	West Yorkshire
Bradford South	West Yorkshire
Bradford West	West Yorkshire
Braintree	Essex
Brecon and Radnorshire	Powys
Brent East	North London
Brent North	North London
Brent South	North London
Brentford and Isleworth	London
Brentwood and Ongar	Essex
Bridgend	South Wales
Bridgwater	Somerset
Brigg and Goole	Lincolnshire
Brighton Kemptown	East Sussex
Brighton Pavilion	East Sussex
Bristol East	South West England
Bristol North West	South West England
Bristol South	South West England
Bristol West	South West England
Bromley and Chislehurst	Kent
Bromsgrove	Worcestershire
Broxbourne	Hertfordshire
Broxtowe	Nottinghamshire
Buckingham	Southern England
Burnley	Lancashire
Burton	Staffordshire
Bury North	Greater Manchester
Bury South	Greater Manchester

Bury St Edmunds	East Anglia
Caernarfon	North Wales
Caerphilly	South Wales
Caithness, Sutherland and Easter Ross	Northern Scotland
Calder Valley	West Yorkshire
Camberwell and Peckham	South London
Cambridge	East Anglia
North East Cambridgeshire	East Anglia
North West Cambridgeshire	East Anglia
South Cambridgeshire	East Anglia
South East Cambridgeshire	East Anglia
Cannock Chase	Staffordshire
Canterbury	Kent
Cardiff Central	South Central Wales
Cardiff North	South Central Wales
Cardiff South and Penarth	South Central Wales
Cardiff West	South Central Wales
Carlisle	Cumbria
Carmarthen East and Dinefwr	Mid West Wales
Carmarthen West and South Pembrokeshire	South West Wales
Carrick, Cumnock and Doon Valley	Southern Scotland
Carshalton and Wallington	London
Castle Point	Essex
Ceredigion	Mid West Wales
Charnwood	Leicestershire
Chatham and Aylesford	Kent
Cheadle	Greater Manchester
Chelmsford West	Essex
Cheltenham	Gloucestershire
Chesham and Amersham	Buckinghamshire
City of Chester	Cheshire
Chesterfield	Derbyshire
Chichester	West Sussex
Chingford and Woodford Green	London
Chipping Barnet	London
Chorley	Lancashire
Christchurch	Dorset
Cleethorpes	Lincolnshire
Clwyd South	North Wales
Vale of Clwyd	North Wales
Clwyd West	North Wales
Clydebank and Milngavie	Dunbartonshire
Clydesdale	South Lanarkshire
Coatbridge and Chryston	Central Scotland
Colchester	Essex
Colne Valley	West Yorkshire
Congleton	Cheshire
Conwy	North Wales
Copeland	Cumbria
Corby	Northamptonshire
North Cornwall	South West England
South East Cornwall	South West England
Cotswold	Gloucestershire
Coventry North East	West Midlands
Coventry North West	West Midlands
Coventry South	West Midlands

Crawley	West Sussex
Crewe and Nantwich	Cheshire
Crosby	Merseyside
Croydon Central	London
Croydon North	London
Croydon South	London
Cumbernauld and Kilsyth	North Lanarkshire
Cunninghame North	North Ayrshire
Cunninghame South	North Ayrshire
Cynon Valley	South Wales
Dagenham	London
Darlington	County Durham
Dartford	Kent
Daventry	Northamptonshire
Delyn	Flintshire
Denton and Reddish	Greater Manchester
Derby North	East Midlands
Derby South	East Midlands
North East Derbyshire	East Midlands
South Derbyshire	East Midlands
West Derbyshire	East Midlands
Devizes	Wiltshire
East Devon	South West England
North Devon	South West England
South West Devon	South West England
Torridge and West Devon	South West England
Dewsbury	West Yorkshire
Don Valley	South Yorkshire
Doncaster Central	South Yorkshire
Doncaster North	South Yorkshire
Mid Dorset and Poole North	South West England
North Dorset	South West England
South Dorset	South West England
West Dorset	South West England
Dover	Kent
North Down	Northern Ireland
South Down	Northern Ireland
Dudley North	West Midlands
Dudley South	West Midlands
Dulwich and West Norwood	London
Dumbarton	West Scotland
Dumfries	Southern Scotland
Dundee East	North East Scotland
Dundee West	North East Scotland
Dunfermline East	Mid Scotland and Fife
Dunfermline West	Mid Scotland and Fife
City of Durham	North East England
Durham North	North East England
North West Durham	North East England
Ealing North	West London
Ealing Southall	West London
Ealing, Acton and Shepherds Bush	West London
Easington	County Durham
East Ham	East London
East Kilbride	South Lanarkshire
East Lothian	South East Scotland

Eastbourne	East Sussex
Eastleigh	Hampshire
Eastwood	East Renfrewshire
Eccles	Greater Manchester
Eddisbury	Cheshire
Edinburgh Central	Lothians
Edinburgh East and Musselburgh	Lothians
Edinburgh North and Leith	Lothians
Edinburgh Pentlands	Lothians
Edinburgh South	Lothians
Edinburgh West	Lothians
Edmonton	North London
Ellesmere Port and Neston	Cheshire
Elmet	West Yorkshire
Eltham	London
Enfield North	North London
Enfield Southgate	North London
Epping Forest	Essex
Epsom and Ewell	Surrey
Erewash	Derbyshire
Erith and Thamesmead	London
Esher and Walton	Surrey
North Essex	South East England
Exeter	Devon
Falkirk East	Central Scotland
Falkirk West	Central Scotland
Falmouth and Camborne	Cornwall
Fareham	Hampshire
Faversham and Mid Kent	Kent
Feltham and Heston	London
Fermanagh and South Tyrone	Northern Ireland
Central Fife	Mid Scotland
North East Fife	Mid Scotland
Finchley and Golders Green	North London
Folkestone and Hythe	Kent
Forest of Dean	Gloucestershire
Foyle	Northern Ireland
Fylde	Lancashire
Gainsborough	Lincolnshire
Galloway and Upper Nithsdale	Dumfries and Galloway
Gateshead East and Washington West	Tyne and Wear
Gedling	Nottinghamshire
Gillingham	Kent
Vale of Glamorgan	South Wales
Glasgow Anniesland	West Central Scotland
Glasgow Baillieston	West Central Scotland
Glasgow Cathcart	West Central Scotland
Glasgow Govan	West Central Scotland
Glasgow Kelvin	West Central Scotland
Glasgow Maryhill	West Central Scotland
Glasgow Pollok	West Central Scotland
Glasgow Rutherglen	West Central Scotland
Glasgow Shettleston	West Central Scotland
Glasgow Springburn	West Central Scotland
Gloucester	South West England
Gordon	North Eastern Scotland

Gosport	Hampshire
Gower	South Wales
Grantham and Stamford	Lincolnshire
Gravesham	Kent
Great Yarmouth	Norfolk
Greenock and Inverclyde	West Scotland
Greenwich and Woolwich	South East London
Great Grimsby	Lincolnshire
Guildford	Surrey
Hackney North and Stoke Newington	North London
Hackney South and Shoreditch	North London
Halesowen and Rowley Regis	West Midlands
Halifax	West Yorkshire
Haltemprice and Howden	East Yorkshire
Halton	Cheshire
Hamilton North and Bellshill	Lanarkshire
Hamilton South	South Lanarkshire
Hammersmith and Fulham	West London
East Hampshire	Southern England
North East Hampshire	Southern England
North West Hampshire	Southern England
Hampstead and Highgate	North London
Harborough	Leicestershire
Harlow	Essex
Harrogate and Knaresborough	North Yorkshire
Harrow East	London
Harrow West	London
Hartlepool	County Durham
Harwich	Essex
Hastings and Rye	Kent
Havant	Hampshire
Hayes and Harlington	London
Hazel Grove	Greater Manchester
Hemel Hempstead	Hertfordshire
Hemsworth	West Yorkshire
Hendon	London
Henley	Oxfordshire
Hereford	Midlands
Hertford and Stortford	Southern England
North East Hertfordshire	South East England
South West Hertfordshire	South East England
Hertsmere	Hertfordshire
Hexham	Northumberland
Heywood and Middleton	Greater Manchester
High Peak	Derbyshire
Hitchin and Harpenden	Hertfordshire
Holborn and St Pancras	Central London
South Holland and The Deepings	Lincolnshire
Hornchurch	London
Hornsey and Wood Green	North London
Horsham	West Sussex
Houghton and Washington East	Tyne and Wear
Hove	East Sussex
Huddersfield	West Yorkshire
Hull East	East Yorkshire
Hull North	East Yorkshire

Hull West and Hessle	East Yorkshire
Huntingdon	Cambridgeshire
Hyndburn	Lancashire
Ilford North	East London
Ilford South	East London
Inverness East, Nairn and Lochaber	Northern Scotland
Ipswich	Suffolk
Isle of Wight	Southern England
Islington North	North London
Islington South and Finsbury	North London
Islwyn	South Wales
Jarrow	Tyne and Wear
Keighley	West Yorkshire
Kensington and Chelsea	Central London
Kettering	Northamptonshire
Kilmarnock and Loudoun	East Ayrshire
Kingston and Surbiton	London
Kingswood	Gloucestershire
Kirkcaldy	Fife
Knowsley North and Sefton East	Merseyside
Knowsley South	Merseyside
Lagan Valley	Northern Ireland
West Lancashire	North West England
Lancaster and Wyre	North West England
Leeds Central	West Yorkshire
Leeds East	West Yorkshire
Leeds North East	West Yorkshire
Leeds North West	West Yorkshire
Leeds West	West Yorkshire
Leicester East	East Midlands
Leicester South	East Midlands
Leicester West	East Midlands
North West Leicestershire	East Midlands
Leigh	Greater Manchester
Leominster	Herefordshire
Lewes	East Sussex
Lewisham East	South East London
Lewisham West	South East London
Lewisham, Deptford	South East London
Leyton and Wanstead	North East London
Lichfield	Staffordshire
Lincoln	East Midlands
Linlithgow	West Lothian
Liverpool Garston	Merseyside
Liverpool Riverside	Merseyside
Liverpool Walton	Merseyside
Liverpool Wavertree	Merseyside
Liverpool West Derby	Merseyside
Livingston	West Lothian
Llanelli	Carmarthenshire
Cities of London and Westminster	Central London
East Londonderry	Northern Ireland
Loughborough	Leicester
Louth and Horncastle	Lincolnshire
Ludlow	Shropshire
Luton North	Bedfordshire

Luton South	Bedfordshire
Macclesfield	Cheshire
Maidenhead	Berkshire
Maidstone and The Weald	Kent
Makerfield	Greater Manchester
Maldon and Chelmsford East	Essex
Manchester Blackley	North West England
Manchester Central	North West England
Manchester Gorton	North West England
Manchester Withington	North West England
Mansfield	Nottinghamshire
Medway	Kent
Meirionnydd Nant Conwy	North Wales
Meriden	West Midlands
Merthyr Tydfil and Rhymney	South Wales
Middlesbrough	North Yorkshire
Middlesbrough South and East Cleveland	North Yorkshire
Midlothian	South East Scotland
Milton Keynes North East	Buckinghamshire
Milton Keynes South West	Buckinghamshire
Mitcham and Morden	London
Mole Valley	Surrey
Monmouth	South East Wales
Montgomeryshire	Powys
Moray	North Eastern Scotland
Morecambe and Lunesdale	Lancashire
Morley and Rothwell	West Yorkshire
Motherwell and Wishaw	North Lanarkshire
Neath	South Wales
New Forest East	Hampshire
New Forest West	Hampshire
Newark	Nottinghamshire
Newbury	Berkshire
Newcastle upon Tyne Central	North East England
Newcastle upon Tyne East and Wallsend	North East England
Newcastle upon Tyne North	North East England
Newcastle-under-Lyme	North East England
Newport East	South Wales
Newport West	South Wales
Newry and Armagh	Northern Ireland
Mid Norfolk	East Anglia
North Norfolk	East Anglia
North West Norfolk	East Anglia
South Norfolk	East Anglia
South West Norfolk	East Anglia
Normanton	West Yorkshire
Northampton North	East Midlands
Northampton South	East Midlands
Northavon	Gloucestershire
Norwich North	East Anglia
Norwich South	East Anglia
Nottingham East	East Midlands
Nottingham North	East Midlands
Nottingham South	East Midlands
Nuneaton	Warwickshire
Ochil	Eastern Central Scotland

Ogmore	South Wales
Oldham East and Saddleworth	Greater Manchester
Oldham West and Royton	Greater Manchester
Orkney and Shetland	Northern Scotland
Orpington	London
Oxford East	Southern England
Oxford West and Abingdon	Southern England
Paisley North	Renfrewshire
Paisley South	Renfrewshire
Pendle	Lancashire
Penrith and The Border	Cumbria
Perth	Central Scotland
Peterborough	Cambridgeshire
Plymouth Devonport	Devon
Plymouth Sutton	Devon
Pontefract and Castleford	West Yorkshire
Pontypridd	South Wales
Poole	Dorset
Poplar and Canning Town	East London
Portsmouth North	Hampshire
Portsmouth South	Hampshire
Preseli Pembrokeshire	Mid West Wales
Preston	Lancashire
Pudsey	West Yorkshire
Putney	West London
Rayleigh	Essex
Reading East	Berkshire
Reading West	Berkshire
Redcar	North Yorkshire
Redditch	Worcestershire
Regents Park and Kensington North	Central London
Reigate	Surrey
West Renfrewshire	West Scotland
Rhondda	South Wales
South Ribble	Lancashire
Ribble Valley	Lancashire
Richmond (Yorkshire)	Northern England
Richmond Park	South West London
Rochdale	Greater Manchester
Rochford and Southend East	Essex
Romford	London
Romsey	Hampshire
Ross, Skye and Inverness West	Northern Scotland
Rossendale and Darwen	Lancashire
Rother Valley	South Yorkshire
Rotherham	South Yorkshire
Roxburgh and Berwickshire	Scottish Borders
Rugby and Kenilworth	Warwickshire
Ruislip Northwood	West London
Runnymede and Weybridge	Surrey
Rushcliffe	Nottinghamshire
Rutland and Melton	East Midlands
Ryedale	North Yorkshire
Saffron Walden	Essex
St Albans	Hertfordshire
St Helens North	Merseyside

St Helens South	Merseyside
St Ives	Cornwall
Salford	Greater Manchester
Salisbury	Wiltshire
Scarborough and Whitby	North Yorkshire
Scunthorpe	East Riding of Yorkshire
Sedgefield	County Durham
Selby	North Yorkshire
Sevenoaks	Kent
Sheffield Attercliffe	South Yorkshire
Sheffield Brightside	South Yorkshire
Sheffield Central	South Yorkshire
Sheffield Hallam	South Yorkshire
Sheffield Heeley	South Yorkshire
Sheffield Hillsborough	South Yorkshire
Sherwood	Nottinghamshire
Shipley	West Yorkshire
Shrewsbury and Atcham	Shropshire
North Shropshire	West Midlands
Sittingbourne and Sheppey	Kent
Skipton and Ripon	North Yorkshire
Sleaford and North Hykeham	Lincolnshire
Slough	Berkshire
Solihull	West Midlands
Somerton and Frome	Somerset
South Shields	Tyne and Wear
Southampton Itchen	Hampshire
Southampton Test	Hampshire
Southend West	Essex
Southport	Merseyside
North Southwark and Bermondsey	South London
Spelthorne	Surrey
Stafford	West Midlands
Staffordshire Moorlands	West Midlands
South Staffordshire	West Midlands
Stalybridge and Hyde	Greater Manchester
Stevenage	Hertfordshire
Stirling	Central Scotland
Stockport	Greater Manchester
Stockton North	County Durham
Stockton South	County Durham
Stoke-on-Trent Central	West Midlands
Stoke-on-Trent North	West Midlands
Stoke-on-Trent South	West Midlands
Stone	Staffordshire
Stourbridge	West Midlands
Strangford	Northern Ireland
Stratford-on-Avon	Warwickshire
Strathkelvin and Bearsden	East Dunbartonshire
Streatham	South London
Stretford and Urmston	Greater Manchester
Stroud	Gloucestershire
Central Suffolk and North Ipswich	East Anglia
Suffolk Coastal	East Anglia
South Suffolk	East Anglia
West Suffolk	East Anglia

Sunderland North	Tyne and Wear
Sunderland South	Tyne and Wear
East Surrey	South East England
Surrey Heath	South East England
South West Surrey	South East England
Mid Sussex	South East England
Sutton and Cheam	London
Sutton Coldfield	West Midlands
Swansea East	South West Wales
Swansea West	South West Wales
North Swindon	Wiltshire
South Swindon	Wiltshire
Tamworth	Staffordshire
Tatton	Cheshire
Taunton	Somerset
North Tayside	Central East Scotland
Teignbridge	Devon
Telford	Shropshire
Tewkesbury	Gloucestershire
North Thanet	Kent
South Thanet	Kent
Thurrock	Essex
Tiverton and Honiton	Devon
Tonbridge and Malling	Kent
Tooting	South London
Torbay	Devon
Torfaen	South Wales
Totnes	Devon
Tottenham	North London
Truro and St Austell	Cornwall
Tunbridge Wells	Kent
Tweeddale, Ettrick and Lauderdale	South East Scotland
Twickenham	London
Tyne Bridge	Tyne and Wear
Tynemouth	Tyne and Wear
North Tyneside	Tyne and Wear
West Tyrone	Northern Ireland
Mid Ulster	Northern Ireland
Upminster	East London
Upper Bann	Northern Ireland
Uxbridge	London
Vauxhall	South London
Wakefield	West Yorkshire
Wallasey	Merseyside
Walsall North	West Midlands
Walsall South	West Midlands
Walthamstow	North London
Wansbeck	Northumberland
Wansdyke	Somerset
Wantage	Oxfordshire
Warley	West Midlands
Warrington North	Cheshire
Warrington South	Cheshire
Warwick and Leamington	West Midlands
North Warwickshire	West Midlands
Watford	Hertfordshire

Waveney	Suffolk
Wealden	East Sussex
Weaver Vale	Cheshire
Wellingborough	Northamptonshire
Wells	Somerset
Welwyn Hatfield	Hertfordshire
Wentworth	South Yorkshire
West Bromwich East	West Midlands
West Bromwich West	West Midlands
West Ham	East London
Westbury	Wiltshire
Western Isles	Northern Scotland
Westmorland and Lonsdale	Cumbria
Weston-Super-Mare	Somerset
Wigan	Greater Manchester
North Wiltshire	South West England
Wimbledon	South West London
Winchester	Hampshire
Windsor	Berkshire
Wirral South	Merseyside
Wirral West	Merseyside
Witney	Oxfordshire
Woking	Surrey
Wokingham	Berkshire
Wolverhampton North East	West Midlands
Wolverhampton South East	West Midlands
Wolverhampton South West	West Midlands
Woodspring	Somerset
Worcester	West Midlands
Mid Worcestershire	West Midlands
West Worcestershire	West Midlands
Workington	Cumbria
Worsley	Greater Manchester
East Worthing and Shoreham	West Sussex
Worthing West	West Sussex
The Wrekin	Shropshire
Wrexham	North Wales
Wycombe	Buckinghamshire
Wyre Forest	Worcestershire
Wythenshawe and Sale East	Greater Manchester
Yeovil	Somerset
Ynys Môn	Anglesey
City of York	North East England
Vale of York	North East England
Yorkshire East	North East England

DodOnline

An Electronic Directory without rival . . .

Constituency Profiles available with regular updates *via* the internet

For a *free* trial, call Yasmin Mirza, Aby Farsoun or Michael Mand on 020 7630 7643

State of the Parties

	2001 General Election	May 2001	1997 General Election
Labour*	412	418	418
Conservative	166	162	165
Liberal Democrat	52	47	46
Ulster Unionist Party	6	9	10
Democratic Unionist Party	5	3	2
Scottish National Party	5	6	6
Plaid Cymru	4	4	4
Sinn Fein	4	2	2
Social Democratic and Labour Party	3	3	3
Independent Kidderminster Hospital and Health Concern	1		
Independent		3	1
United Kingdom Unionist		1	1
The Speaker	1	1	1
Total	**659**	**659**	**659**

*Includes 29 Labour/Co-operative MPs

Share of the vote

	Seats	Gains	Losses	Net	Votes	% of votes
Lab	412	2	8	−6	10,724,549	40.68%
Con	166	9	8	+1	8,357,586	31.70%
LibDem	52	8	2	+6	4,814,027	18.26%
SNP	5	0	1	−1	464,314	1.76%
UKIP	0	0	0	0	390,159	1.48%
UUP	6	1	5	−4	216,839	0.82%
PlC	4	1	1	0	195,893	0.74%
DUP	5	3	0	+3	181,999	0.69%
SF	4	2	0	+2	175,933	0.67%
SDLP	3	0	0	0	169,865	0.64%
Other	1	1	2	−1		
The Speaker	1					

DodOnline

An Electronic Directory without rival ...

MPs' biographies and photographs available with daily updates *via* the internet

For a *free* trial, call Yasmin Mirza, Aby Farsoun or Michael Mand on 020 7630 7643

Changes since 7 June 2001 General Election

State of Parties (August 2003)

Labour*	410	Social Democratic and Labour Party	3
Conservative	163	Independent Unionist	3
Liberal Democrats	53	Independent Kidderminster Hospital	
Democratic Unionist Party	5	and Health Concern	1
Scottish National Party	5	Independent	1
Plaid Cymru	4	Vacant (by-election pending)	1
Sinn Fein	4	Speaker	1
Ulster Unionist Party	3		
		Total seats	659

*Includes 29 Labour/Co-operative MPs

(Includes the three Deputy Speakers)

DEATHS

		Died
Jamie Cann	Ipswich – Labour	15 October 2001
Sir Raymond Powell	Ogmore – Labour	7 December 2001
Paul Daisley	Brent East – Labour	19 June 2003

By-elections

Ipswich

22 November 2001 due to the death of the Labour MP Jamie Cann

Lab	Chris Mole	11,881
Con	Paul West	7,794
Lib Dem	Tessa Munt	6,146

Christian People's Alliance Dave Cooper 581, United Kingdom Independence Party Jonathan Wright 276, Green Party Tony Slade 255, Legalise Cannabis Alliance John Ramirez 236, Socialist Alliance Peter Leech 152, English Independence Party Nicholas Winskill 84

Lab majority 4,087 – Lab hold
Electorate 68,244 – Total vote 27,477 – Poll 40.26%

Ogmore

14 February 2002 due to the death of the Labour MP Sir Raymond Powell

Lab	Huw Irranca-Davies	9,548
PlC	Bleddyn Hancock	3,827
Lib Dem	Veronica Watkins	1,608

Conservative Guto Bebb 1,377, Socialist Labour Chris Herriot 1,152, Green Jonathan Spink 250, Socialist Alliance Jeff Hurford 205, Official Monster Raving Loony Party Leslie Edwards 187, New Millennium Bean Party 122, Independent David Braid 100

Lab majority 5,721 – Lab hold
Electorate 52,209 – Total vote 18,410 – Poll 35.3%

Electoral Dates

The Representation of the People Act 1983 sets out the timetable for parliamentary elections. In the case of a General Election, the last day for the delivery of nomination papers is the sixth day after the date of the proclamation summoning the new Parliament, and the poll is held in every constituency on the eleventh day after the last day for delivery of nomination papers. In the case of a by-election, the last day for the delivery of nomination papers is fixed by the Returning Officer and must be not earlier than the third day after the date of publication of the notice of election nor later than the seventh day after that on which the writ is received. Polling takes place on the day fixed by the Returning Officer, which is not earlier than the ninth nor later than the eleventh day after the last day for delivery of nomination papers. In calculating these dates, a Sunday, a Saturday, Christmas Eve, Christmas Day, Maundy Thursday, Good Friday, a bank holiday and a day appointed for public thanksgiving or mourning are disregarded.

Parliamentary Franchise

A person resident in the United Kingdom on the annual qualifying date of 15 October is entitled to be entered on the register of electors if he or she is (a) a British or other Commonwealth citizen or a citizen of the Republic of Ireland, and
(b) is at least 18 years of age (or will become 18 during the currency of the register) and is not otherwise disqualified. Under the Representation of the People Act 1985, certain British citizens resident abroad may also vote in parliamentary elections.

Since 1999 hereditary peers, who were previously barred from voting in general elections, have been allowed to do so if they no longer sit in the Lords.

Parliamentary Candidates

A candidate must be at least 21 years old. Since 1999 hereditary peers who no longer sit in the House of Lords have been allowed to stand as candidates for the Commons.

Each candidate must deposit £500 with the Returning Officer at the time of nomination. This sum is returned when he has taken the oath, if elected, or if he is not elected but has polled 5% of the number of votes polled, otherwise the deposit is forefeited.

The maximum expenditure which may be incurred by a candidate is £5,483 plus, in a county constituency, 6.2p and, in a borough constituency, 4.6p for every entry in the Register of Electors to be used at the election (as first published). The sum in the case of a by-election is £100,000.

The Returning Officer's expenses are paid by the Treasury.

Number of Voters

In December 2002 there was a total of 44,363,353 names on the parliamentary electoral register of the United Kingdom. This is broken down as follows: England 37,179,095; Scotland 3,887,059; Wales 2,225,599; and Northern Ireland 1,071,600.

Visit the Vacher Dod Website . . .

www.DodOnline.co.uk

House of Lords

London SW1A 0PW 020 7219 3000 Information Office Tel: 020 7219 3107
Website: www.parliament.uk

Membership

Since the passing of the House of Lords Act, 1999, the majority of members, over 500, are life peers. In addition, there is a minority of life peers who are Lords of Appeal in Ordinary.

The Archbishops of Canterbury and York and the Bishops of London, Durham and Winchester are ex-officio members of the Lords, while the remaining 21 Bishops who are members sit by rotation according to seniority; these are known as Lords Spiritual.

Ninety hereditary peers still sit by virtue of election by their fellow peers. In addition, some 15 hereditary peers have been created life peers.

There are two hereditary office holders who are members of the House under the House of Lords Act, 1999: the Duke of Norfolk as Earl Marshal, and the Marquess of Cholmondeley as Lord Great Chamberlain.

Summary

(August 2003)

		Viscounts	16
Archbishops	2	Bishops	24
Dukes	2	Barons/Lords	510
Marquess	2	Baronesses	112
Earls and Countesses	26	Lady	1
Women Peers by Succession (ie 1 Countess, 2 Baronesses and 1 Lady)	4	Hereditary Peers who have received Life Peerages	14

Party affiliation

(August 2003)

Conservative	211	Liberal Democrat	65
Labour	186	Others*	44
Crossbencher	179		

*Includes Lords Spiritual, two hereditary royal office holders, peers who have not declared any party affiliation, peers on leave of absence and a peer disqualified by bankruptcy.

House of Lords Appointments Commission

House of Lords Appointments Commission, 35 Great Smith Street, London SW1P 3BQ
General enquiries: 020 7276 2300   *Information pack:* 020 7276 2315
Website: www.lordsappointments.gov.uk

The Appointments Commission is a non-statutory advisory non-departmental public body. It has two main functions: to make recommendations for non-party-political peers; and to vet for propriety all nominations for peerages, including those from the political parties.

Chairman: Lord Stevenson of Coddenham
  CBE
Independent Members: Angela Sarkis CBE,
  Dame Deirdre Hine DBE, Felicity Huston
Members nominated by the political parties:
  Rt Hon Baroness Dean of Thornton-le-Fylde
  (Labour),

Rt Hon Lord Hurd of Westwell CH CBE
  (Conservative), Lord Dholakia OBE DL
  (Liberal Democrat)
  Secretary to the Commission: Jim Barron

PEERS' BIOGRAPHIES

A

ABERDARE, LORD

ABERDARE (4th Baron, UK), Morys George Lyndhurst Bruce; cr. 1873. Born 16 June 1919. Son of 3rd Baron, GBE; educated Winchester College; New College, Oxford (MA). Married Maud Helen Sarah Dashwood 1946 (4 sons). Major, Welsh Guards 1939–46. DL, Dyfed 1985. *Career:* Chairman: Albany Life Assurance Co Ltd 1975–92, Metlife (UK) Ltd 1986–92. *House of Lords:* First entered House of Lords 1957; Minister of State, Department of Health and Social Security 1970–74; Minister without Portfolio 1974; Chairman of Committees 1976–92; Deputy Speaker 1976–2001; Deputy Chairman of Committees 1992–2001; Elected hereditary peer 1999–. Chairman, Broadcasting 1978–92. President: Welsh National Council of YMCAs 1963–2000, Kidney Research Unit for Wales Foundation 1970–2000, National Association of Leagues of Hospital Friends 1978–85, Queen's Club 1993–96. Hon. LLD, University of Wales 1985. Chairman, The Football Trust 1979–98. Prior for Wales, Order of St John 1957–88; Bailiff Grand Cross, Order of St John 1974; PC 1974; KBE 1984. *Publications: The Story of Tennis* (1959); *The Willis Faber Book of Tennis and Rackets* (1980); *The J.T. Faber Book of Tennis and Rackets* (2001). *Recreations:* Real tennis. *Sportsclubs:* All England Lawn Tennis, Jesters, Queens. *Clubs:* Lansdowne, MCC, Boodle's. Rt Hon the Lord Aberdare, KBE, DL, 26 Crown Lodge, 12 Elystan Street, London, SW3 3PP; House of Lords, London, SW1A 0PW *Tel:* 020 7219 6925.

ACKNER, LORD

ACKNER (Life Baron), Desmond James Conrad Ackner; cr. 1986. Born 18 September 1920. Son of late Dr Conrad Ackner; educated Highgate School; Clare College, Cambridge (BA economics and law 1941). Married Joan Spence, née Evans 1946 (1 son 2 daughters). Served in Royal Artillery 1941–42; Admiralty Naval Law branch 1942–45. *Career:* Called to Bar, Middle Temple 1945; QC 1961; Recorder of Swindon 1962–71; Judge of Courts of Appeal, Jersey and Guernsey 1967–71; Member, General Council of the Bar 1957–61, 1963–70, Treasurer 1964–66, Vice-Chairman 1966–68, Chairman 1968–70; Judge of High Court of Justice, Queen's Bench Division 1971–80; Lord Justice of Appeal 1980–86; Lord of Appeal in Ordinary 1986–92. Member, House of Lords Select Committees on: Murder and Life Imprisonment 1988–89, Science and Technology Subcommittee on Digital Images as Evidence 1997–98. President, Senate of the Four Inns of Court 1983–84; Deputy Treasurer, Middle Temple 1983; Treasurer 1984; President, Society of Sussex Downsmen 1993–96, Vice-President 1996–. Hon. Fellow, Clare College 1984. Member, British Council 1991–; President, Arbitration Appeal Panel of the Securities and Futures Authority 1993–2002; Appeal Commissioner, Personal Investment Authority 1994–2002. Kt 1971; PC 1980. *Special Interests:* Law, Alternative Dispute Resolutions, Prisons, Administration of Justice, Human Rights, Independence of the Judiciary, *Recreations:* Theatre, concerts. Raised to the peerage as Baron Ackner, of Sutton in the County of West Sussex 1986. Rt Hon the Lord Ackner, House of Lords, London, SW1A 0PW *Tel:* 020 7219 3243; 4 Pump Court, Temple, London, EC4Y 7AN *Tel:* 020 7353 2656.

Visit the Vacher Dod Website . . .
www.DodOnline.co.uk

ACTON, LORD   Labour

ACTON (4th Baron, UK), Richard Gerald Lyon-Dalberg-Acton; cr. 1869; (Life) Baron Acton of Bridgnorth 2000; 11th Bt of Aldenham (E) 1644. Born 30 July 1941. Son of 3rd Baron, CMG, MBE, TD and Hon. Daphne Strutt, daughter of 4th Baron Rayleigh, DL; educated St George's College, Salisbury, Rhodesia; Trinity College, Oxford (BA history 1963, MA). Married Hilary Juliet Sarah Cookson 1965 (died 1973) (1 son); married Judith Garfield Todd 1974 (divorced 1987); married Patricia Nassif 1988. *Career:* Management trainee, Amalgamated Packaging Industries Ltd 1964–66; Coutts and Co. Bankers, London 1967–74, Director 1970–74; Called to Bar, Inner Temple 1976; Practising Barrister 1977–81; Senior Law Officer, Ministry of Justice, Legal and Parliamentary Affairs, Harare, Zimbabwe 1981–85. *House of Lords:* First entered House of Lords 1989. Member: Select Committee on Constitution 2001–, Consolidation Bills Joint Committee 2002–. Member: Commonwealth Parliamentary Association, Inter-Parliamentary Union. Patron: MIND Jubilee Appeal 1996–, The Mulberry Bush School 1998–; Sponsor, British Defence and Aid Fund for Southern Africa 1980–94; Member: Oxford Brookes University Court 1999–. Patron APEX Trust 2002–; Patron Frank Longford Charitable Trust 2002–. *Publications:* Co-author *To Go Free: A Treasury of Iowa's Legal Heritage*, 1995 (Benjamin F. Shambaugh Award 1996); *A Brit Among the Hawkeyes*, 1998; Contributor to: *Outside In: African American History in Iowa 1838–2000*, 2001; Other anthologies and periodicals. *Special Interests:* Anglo-American Relations, Southern Africa, Mental Health, Penal Affairs and Policy. *Recreations:* Reading, travel. Created a life peer as Baron Acton of Bridgnorth, of Aldenham in the County of Shropshire 2000. The Lord Acton, 152 Whitehall Court, London, SW1A 2EL *Tel:* 020 7839 3077 *Fax:* 020 7839 3077; 100 Red Oak Lane, SE Cedar Rapids, Iowa 52403, USA *Tel:* 001(319) 362 6181 *Fax:* 001(319) 362 6181 *E-mail:* r.acton@prodigy.net.

ADDINGTON, LORD   Liberal Democrat

ADDINGTON (6th Baron, UK), Dominic Bryce Hubbard; cr. 1887. Born 24 August 1963. Son of 5th Baron; educated The Hewett School, Norwich; Aberdeen University (MA history 1988). Married Elizabeth Ann Morris 1999. *Career:* Charity fundraiser and counsellor Apex Trust 1991–94; Consultant Milton Broadway, Events Company 1996–99. *House of Lords:* First entered House of Lords 1986; Elected hereditary peer 1999–. Liberal Democrat Whip 2002–. Liberal Democrat Spokesperson for: Disability 1994–, Sport 1995–. Vice-President: British Dyslexia Association, UK Sports Association (Sport for those with learning disabilities); Patron Adult Dyslexia Organisation. Apex Trust fund raiser 1990–; Vice-President Apex Trust 2001–. *Special Interests:* Education, Prison Reform, Disabilities, Sport. *Recreations:* Rugby football, portrait painting. *Sportsclubs:* Vice-President: Lonsdale Sporting Club, Lakenham Hewett Rugby Club; Playing Captain Commons and Lords Rugby Football Club. *Clubs:* National Liberal. The Lord Addington, House of Lords, London, SW1A 0PW *Tel:* 020 7219 4443 *E-mail:* addingtond@parliament.uk.

ADEBOWALE, LORD   Crossbencher

ADEBOWALE (Life Baron), Victor Olufemi Adebowale; cr 2001. Born 21 July 1962; educated Thornes House School, Wakefield; Polytechnic of East London. Separated. *Trades Union:* Member UNISON. *Career:* Housing administration London Borough of Newham 1983–86; Management posts housing associations 1986–90; Director of alcohol recovery project 1990–95; Chief executive Centre Point youth social exclusion charity 1995–2001; Member: Social Exclusion Unit Policy Action, New Deal Task Force 1997–; Central London Partnership, Training Skills 2001–; Chief executive Turning Point 2001–. Honorary doctorate. CBE 2000. *Recreations:* Poetry writing, reading, music. Raised to the peerage as Baron Adebowale, of Thornes in the County of West Yorkshire 2001. The Lord Adebowale CBE, House of Lords, London, SW1A 0PW *E-mail:* victor.a@virgin.net.

AHMED, LORD — Labour

AHMED (Life Baron), Nazir Ahmed; cr. 1998. Born 24 April 1957. Son of late Haji Sain Mohammed and Rashem Bibi; educated Spurley Hey Comprehensive School, Rotherham; Thomas Rotherham College, Rotherham; Sheffield Hallam University (BA public administration 1992). Married Sakina Bibi 1974 (2 sons 1 daughter). *Trades Union:* Member, USDAW; Chairman, Sheffield Private Branch 1996–98; Member, Political Committee 1996–98. Councillor, Rotherham Metropolitan Borough Council 1990–2000; JP, Rotherham 1992–2000. *Career:* Company director 1990–; Business development manager, Kilnhurst Business Park 1991–; Naz and Brothers Properties, Shalimar International Ltd; Consultant on International Affairs to Nestlé, UK; Consultant to Nesco Foods plc. Member, House of Lords' Offices: Library and Computers Sub-Committee 2000–01, Refreshment Sub-Committee 2001–. Member: IPU, CPA. Member, Kashmir Policy Group; Al-Hamd Trust-International Disabled Network; Al-Shifa, Pakistan; Amnesty International; Khattak Medical College, Pakistan; Layton Rehmatula Trust, Pakistan; Chinese Muslim Charity, Kuwait; SAHARA, Pakistan; The Alma Hospital Trust; Patron: Kashmiri Journalist Association Mirpur, Jammu and Kashmir Human Rights Commission, Mirpur Friendship Association. Chair, South Yorkshire Labour Party 1994–98; Vice-chair, South Yorkshire Euro-constituency Party 1996–98. Founder, British Muslim Councillors Forum 1992–98; Association of British Hujjaj; British Heart Foundation; Co-Op Party; FACE Advice Centre, Rotherham; Magistrates Association; Unity Centre, Rotherham; Yemeni Development Foundation, UK; Patron: Kashmiri and Pakistani Professional Association, British Hujjaj Association, Young Pakistani Doctors' Association, SAARC Foundation; Board Member: Board of Advisers for the Pakistan Institute of Legislative Development and Transparency (PILDAT), Board of Trustees of the Jinnah Institute (London), President of South Yorkshire Victim Support. Trusteeships: Fazaldad Human Rights Organisation, Zindagi Trust – Charity for underprivileged children. *Special Interests:* Human Rights, Kashmiri Right of Self Determination, Conflict resolution, Race Relations, Relations with Muslim countries, Dialogue of Civilisation, Education, Immigration, Minorities Rights. *Recreations:* Volleyball. Raised to the peerage as Baron Ahmed, of Rotherham in the County of South Yorkshire 1998. The Lord Ahmed, House of Lords, London, SW1A 0PW *Tel:* 020 7219 1396 *Fax:* 020 7219 1384 *E-mail:* ahmedn@parliament.uk.

ALDERDICE, LORD — Liberal Democrat

ALDERDICE (Life Baron), John Thomas Alderdice; cr. 1996. Born 28 March 1955. Son of Reverend David Alderdice and Annie Margaret Helena, née Shields; educated Ballymena Academy; Queen's University, Belfast (MB BCh BAO 1978). Married Joan Margaret Hill 1977 (2 sons 1 daughter). *Trades Union:* British Medical Association. Councillor, Belfast City Council 1989–97; Member, Belfast Education and Library Board 1993–97. *Career:* Consultant psychiatrist in psychotherapy, Eastern Health and Social Services Board 1988–; Hon. Lecturer, Faculty of Medicine, Queen's University, Belfast 1991–99, Hon. Senior Lecturer 1999; Executive Medical Director, South and East Belfast Health and Social Services Trust 1993–97. Member Procedure Committee 2003–. Member, Commonwealth Parliamentary Association (President Northern Ireland Assembly Branch). Executive Committee, Alliance Party 1984–98, Chair, Policy Committee 1985–87; Vice-Chair, Alliance Party March 1987-October 1987, Party Leader 1987–98; Executive Committee, European Liberal Democrat and Reform Party 1987–, Treasurer 1995–99, Vice-President 1999–; Candidate (NI) in European Parliament Election 1989; Leader, Alliance Delegation at Inter-Party and Inter-Governmental Talks on the Future of Northern Ireland 1991–98; Vice-President, Liberal International 1992–99, Deputy President 2000–; Chair, Liberal International Human Rights Committee 1999–; Member Liberal Democrats Federal Policy Committee 2001–. Patron Northern Ireland Institute of Human Relations. Galloway Medal (National Schizophrenia Fellowship, NI) 1987; John F Kennedy Profiles in Courage Award 1998; W. Averell Harriman Democracy Award 1998; Silver Medal of Congress of Peru 1999; Medal of Honour, College of Medicine of Peru, 1999. Hon. Fellow, Royal College of Physicians of Ireland, Hon. Professor, Faculty of Medicine, University of San Marcos, Peru, Hon. Fellow Royal College of Psychiatrists, Hon. Affiliate British Psychoanalytical Society. Trustee, Ulster Museum 1993–97. Contested Belfast East (Alliance Party) 1987 and 1992 general elections; Leader, Alliance Delegation,

Forum for Peace and Reconciliation, Dublin Castle 1994–97; Member, Northern Ireland Forum 1996–98; Leader, Alliance Delegation to Northern Ireland Multiparty Talks 1996–98; Elected to the Northern Ireland Assembly (as one of the members for Belfast East) 1998–; Speaker of the Northern Ireland Assembly 1998–. FRCPsych. City of Baltimore, USA 1991. *Publications:* Various professional articles on eating disorders, psychotherapy and ethics, the psychology of conflict and terrorism, many political papers and articles. *Special Interests:* Northern Ireland, Psychoanalysis and Political Conflict Resolution, Mental Health. *Recreations:* Reading, music, gastronomy. *Sportsclubs:* Bentley Drivers' Club. *Clubs:* National Liberal, Ulster Reform (Belfast). Raised to the peerage as Baron Alderdice, of Knock in the City of Belfast 1996. The Lord Alderdice, House of Lords, London, SW1A 0PW *Tel:* 020 7219 5050 *E-mail:* alderdicej@parliament.uk.

ALEXANDER OF WEEDON, LORD   Conservative

ALEXANDER OF WEEDON (Life Baron), Robert Scott Alexander; cr. 1988. Born 5 September 1936. Son of late Samuel James Alexander and Hannah May Alexander; educated Brighton College; King's College, Cambridge (MA English law 1959), Honorary Fellow 2002. Married Marie Anderson 1985 (2 sons 2 daughters). *Career:* Called to the Bar, Middle Temple 1961, Bencher 1979; QC (NSW Australia) 1983; Vice-Chairman, Bar Council 1984–85, Chairman 1985–86; Judge of the Courts of Appeal of Jersey and Guernsey 1985–88; Chairman: Panel on Takeovers and Mergers 1987–89, National Westminster Bank plc 1989–99; Non-Executive Director: RTZ Corporation plc 1991–96, International Stock Exchange of the UK and Republic of Ireland 1991–93; Deputy Chairman, Securities and Investments Board 1994–96; Member, Government's Panel on Sustainable Development 1994–; Chairman, Royal Shakespeare Company 2000–. Chancellor, Exeter University 1998–. *House of Lords:* Chair Audit Committee 2002–. Chairman: Delegated Powers Scrutiny Committee 1995–97, Select Committee on Delegated Powers and Deregulation 1997–2002. President International Monetary Conference 1996–97. Governor, Wycombe Abbey School 1986–92; Chairman, Council of Justice. Four honorary law doctorates. Trustee, National Gallery 1986–93; Chairman, Trustees of Crisis 1988–96. Member, Independent Commission on Voting Reform 1998; Chairman, Inquiry into Tonnage Tax 1999. *Publications: The Voice of the People: A Constitution for Tomorrow,* 1997. *Special Interests:* Law, Legal Profession, City, Arts. *Recreations:* Cricket, tennis, theatre. *Sportsclubs:* President, MCC 2000–01. *Clubs:* Garrick, MCC. Raised to the peerage as Baron Alexander of Weedon, of Newcastle-under-Lyme in the County of Staffordshire 1988. The Lord Alexander of Weedon, QC, House of Lords, London, SW1A 0PW *Tel:* 020 7219 3000; 22/23 Gayfere Street, London, SW1P 3HP.

ALLEN OF ABBEYDALE, LORD   Crossbencher

ALLEN OF ABBEYDALE (Life Baron), Philip Allen; cr. 1976. Born 8 July 1912. Son of late Arthur Allen; educated King Edward VII School, Sheffield; Queens' College, Cambridge (BA history 1933, MA). Married Marjorie Brenda Coe 1938 (died 2002). *Career:* Entered Home Office 1934; Served in Offices of War Cabinet 1943–44; Deputy Secretary, Ministry of Housing and Local Government 1955–60; Deputy Under-Secretary of State, Home Office 1960–62; Second Secretary, HM Treasury 1963–66; Permanent Under-Secretary of State, Home Office 1966–72. Chairman Select Committee on a Bill of Rights 1977–78; Member Select Committee on Privileges. Chairman, Council of Royal Holloway and Bedford New College, London University 1985–92, Visitor 1992–97; Chairman: National Council of Social Service 1973–77, MENCAP 1982–88. Hon. Fellow: Queens' College, Cambridge, Royal Holloway and Bedford New College. Chairman, Occupational Pensions Board 1973–78; Member: Security Commission 1973–91, Royal Commission on Standards of Conduct in Public Life 1974–76, Royal Commission on Compensation for Personal Injury 1973–78, Tribunal of Inquiry into Crown Agents 1978–82; Chief Counting Officer, EEC referendum 1975; Chairman, Gaming Board 1977–85. CB 1954; KCB 1964; GCB 1970. Raised to the peerage as Baron Allen of Abbeydale, of the City of Sheffield 1976. The Lord Allen of Abbeydale, GCB, Holly Lodge, Middle Hill, Englefield Green, Surrey, TW20 0JP *Tel:* 01784 432291.

ALLENBY OF MEGIDDO, VISCOUNT   Crossbencher

ALLENBY OF MEGIDDO (3rd Viscount, UK), Michael Jaffray Hynman Allenby; cr. 1919. Born 20 April 1931. Son of 2nd Viscount; educated Eton College; RMA, Sandhurst. Married Sara Margaret Wiggin 1965 (1 son). Commissioned 11th Hussars as 2nd Lieutenant 1951; Served Malaya and Cyprus, as ADC to Governor 1956–58; Brigade Major, 51 Brigade, Hong Kong 1967–70; Commanded The Royal Yeomanry (TA) 1974–77; GSO1 Instructor, Nigerian Staff College, Kaduna, Nigeria 1977–79. *Career:* Director, Quickrest Ltd 1987–91. *House of Lords:* First entered House of Lords 1984; Deputy Speaker 1997–; Deputy Chairman of Committees 1997–; Elected hereditary peer 1999–. Member, Select Committees on: House of Lords' Offices 1997–99, Procedure Committee 1999–2002. Chairman, The International League for The Protection of Horses 1997–99, Vice-President 1999–. *Special Interests:* Defence, Animal Welfare. *Recreations:* Horses, sailing. *Clubs:* Naval and Military. The Viscount Allenby of Megiddo, House of Lords, London, SW1A 0PW *Tel:* 020 7219 3497.

ALLI, LORD   Labour

ALLI (Life Baron), Waheed Alli; cr. 1998. Born 16 November 1964; educated Norbury Manor School, South London. Gay with Partner. *Career:* Director, Atomic TV Poland 1992–98; Founder Joint Managing Director, Planet 24 Television; Managing Director, Planet 24 Products Ltd (later Castaway Television Productions); Numerous directorships of radio, television and entertainment companies; Director Carlton Television 1999–2001; Managing Director, Carlton Productions 1999–2001; Director English National Ballet 2001–. Member: Panel 2000, Creative Industries Task Force, Board of the Teacher Training Agency 1997–98. Member Fabian Society Commission 2002–. Raised to the peerage as Baron Alli, of Norbury in the London Borough of Croydon 1998. The Lord Alli, House of Lords, London, SW1A 0PW *Tel:* 020 7219 8658.

ALTON OF LIVERPOOL, LORD   Crossbencher

ALTON OF LIVERPOOL (Life Baron), David Patrick Paul Alton; cr. 1997. Born 15 March 1951. Son of late Frederick Alton, car worker with Ford Motor Company, and Bridget Mulroe; educated Edmund Campion School, Hornchurch; Christ's College, Liverpool (teaching certificate in history and divinity 1972); St Andrews University (philosophy and theology, fellowship 1996–97). Married Elizabeth Bell 1988 (3 sons 1 daughter). Councillor, Liverpool City Council 1972–80: Chair, Housing Committee and Deputy Leader of Council 1978; Councillor, Merseyside County Council 1973–77. *Career:* Teacher 1972–74, then with children with special needs 1974–79; Local Government 1972–80, including Deputy Leader of Liverpool City Council; Professor of citizenship, Liverpool John Moores University 1997–. *House of Commons:* Contested Liverpool Edge Hill February and October 1974 general elections; MP for Liverpool Edge Hill 1979–83, and for Liverpool Mossley Hill 1983–97 (Liberal 1979–88, Liberal Democrat 1988–97); Parliamentary Chair, Council for Education in the Commonwealth 1983–87. Liberal Chief Whip 1985–87, Liberal Spokesperson for Home Affairs and Environment 1979–85; Alliance Spokesperson for Northern Ireland 1985–88. Member: IPU, CPA. Member: IPU, CPA. National President, National League of Young Liberals 1976; Chair: Liberal Policy Committee 1981–83, Candidates Committee 1984–87. Patron: Karen Action Group, Zoe's Place, Francis House Children's Hospice, Network of Access and Child Contact Centres, Council for Advancement of Deaf People, Mersey Kidney Research Trust, Crisis (for the homeless); National Vice-President, LIFE; Vice-President, Liverpool YMCA; Founder member: Jubilee Campaign 1987, Epiphany Trust 1989, Movement for Christian Democracy 1990; President, Liverpool Branch, NSPCC; Vice-president, Merseyside Council for Voluntary Service; Chair: Liverpool Royal Hospital Forget-Me-Not Cancer Appeal, Banner Ethical Investment Fund; Member: Wavertree Society, The Catholic Writers Guild, The Royal Horticultural Society; Chairman, Tolkien Library Appeal; Member: Catholic Bishops Bio-Ethics Committee, Liverpool John Moores University Ethical Review Committee;

Director Merseyside Special Investment Fund. Trustee The Catholic Central Library; Meta Trust (Burmese Education); Bernard Braine Memorial Fund; Partners In Hope (Russian Street Children); Merseyside Lord Lieutenant's Charitable Fund. Visiting Fellowship, St Andrews University (School of Philosophy and Public Affairs and St Mary's College). Knight of the Sacred Military Constantinian Order of St George 2002. *Publications: What Kind of Country*, 1987; *Whose Choice Anyway – the Right to Life*, 1988; *Faith in Britain*, 1991; *Signs of Contradiction*, 1996; *Life After Death*, 1997; *Citizen Virtues*, 1998; *Citizen 2000*, 2000; *Pilgrim Ways*, 2001; Columnist The Universe. *Special Interests:* Pro Life, Environment, Housing, Inner Cities, Refugees, Human Rights, Northern Ireland, Citizenship. *Recreations:* Walking, reading, theatre. Raised to the peerage as Baron Alton of Liverpool, of Mossley Hill in the County of Merseyside 1997. The Lord Alton of Liverpool, House of Lords, London, SW1A 0PW *Tel:* 020 7219 3551 *Fax:* 020 7219 3551 *E-mail:* davidalton@mail.com.

AMOS, BARONESS   Labour

AMOS (Life Baroness), Valerie Ann Amos; cr. 1997. Born 13 March 1954. Daughter of Michael and Eunice Amos; educated Townley Grammar School for Girls; Warwick University (BA sociology 1976); Birmingham University (MA cultural studies 1977); University of East Anglia (doctoral research). *Career:* With London Boroughs: Lambeth 1981–82, Camden 1983–85, Hackney 1985–89, Head of Training, Head of Management Services; Chief Executive, Equal Opportunities Commission 1989–94; Director, Amos Fraser Bernard 1995–98. *House of Lords:* Parliamentary Under-Secretary of State, Foreign and Commonwealth Office 2001–03; Secretary of State for International Development 2003–. Government Whip 1998–2001. Government Spokesperson for: Social Security 1998–2001, International Development 1998–, Women's Issues 1998–2001, Foreign and Commonwealth Office 2001–03. Co-opted Member, European Union Sub-committee F (Social Affairs, Education and Home Affairs) 1997–98; Member, Committee of Selection 2000–. Council Member, Institute of Employment Studies 1993–98; Chair, Board of Governors, Royal College of Nursing Institute 1994–98; Director, Hampstead Theatre 1995–98. Honorary professorship; Three honorary doctorates. Deputy Chair, Runnymede Trust 1990–98; Trustee, Institute of Public Policy Research 1994–98; Non-Executive Director, UCLH Trust; Chair, Afiya Trust 1996–98; Trustee: VSO 1997–98, Project Hope 1997–98. PC 2003. Raised to the peerage as Baroness Amos, of Brondesbury in the London Borough of Brent 1997. Rt Hon the Baroness Amos, House of Lords, London, SW1A 0PW *Tel:* 020 7219 4120 *E-mail:* amosv@parliament.uk.

AMPTHILL, LORD   Crossbencher

AMPTHILL (4th Baron, UK), Geoffrey Denis Erskine Russell; cr. 1881. Born 15 October 1921. Son of 3rd Baron, CBE; educated Stowe School. Married Susan Mary Winn 1946 (divorced 1971) (2 sons 1 daughter and 1 son deceased); married Elisabeth Anne Marie Mallon 1972 (divorced 1987). Irish Guards 1941–46, Captain 1944. *Career:* General manager, Fortnum & Mason 1947–51; Chair, New Providence Hotel Co. Ltd 1951–65; Managing Director, theatre owning and producing companies 1953–71; Director, Dualvest plc 1980–87; Director, United Newspapers plc 1981–96, Deputy Chair 1991–96; Director, Express Newspapers plc 1985–98, Deputy Chair 1989–98; Chair, London's Helicopter Emergency Service 1992–97. *House of Lords:* First entered House of Lords 1976; Deputy Chair of Committees 1980–92, 1997–, Chair 1992–94; Deputy Speaker 1982–; Elected hereditary peer 1999–. Member or Chair, Select Committees on Offices, Finance and Administration 1979–94; Chair, Refreshment Sub-committee 1980–92; Chair, Select Committees on: Channel Tunnel Bill 1987–88, Rail Link Bill 1996; Member, Delegated Powers and Deregulation Committee 1997–2000. CBE 1986; PC 1995. *Clubs:* Garrick. Rt Hon the Lord Ampthill, CBE, 6 North Court, Great Peter Street, London, SW1P 3LL *Tel:* 020 7233 0133 *Fax:* 020 7233 0122; House of Lords, London, SW1A 0PW *Tel:* 020 7219 0173 *Fax:* 020 7219 2916.

Visit the Vacher Dod Website . . . **www.DodOnline.co.uk**

ANDREWS, BARONESS · Labour

ANDREWS (Life Baroness), (Elizabeth) Kay Andrews; cr. 2000. Born 16 May 1943; educated Lewis School for Girls, Hengoed, Ystradmynach; University College of Wales, Aberystwyth (BA international politics 1964); Sussex University (MA political sociology 1966, DPhil history and social studies of science 1975). Married Professor Roy MacLeod 1970 (divorced 1992). *Career:* Fellow, Science Policy Research Unit, Sussex University 1968–70; Parliamentary Clerk 1970–85; Policy adviser to Neil Kinnock as Leader of the Opposition 1985–92; Director, Education Extra 1992–2002. Government Whip 2002–. Government Spokesperson for: Health 2002–, Work and Pensions 2002–, Education and Skills 2003–. OBE 1998. Fellow, Royal Society of Arts.
Publications: Articles and books on science and education policy, social policy and out of school learning; *Extra Learning* (Kogan Page) 2001. *Special Interests:* Education and Social Policy, International Development, The Arts, Science Policy. Raised to the peerage as Baroness Andrews, of Southover in the County of East Sussex 2000. The Baroness Andrews, OBE, Education Extra, 17 Old Ford Road, Bethnal Green, London, E2 9PL *Tel:* 020 8709 9900 *E-mail:* andrewsk@parliament.uk.

ANELAY OF ST JOHNS, BARONESS · Conservative

ANELAY OF ST JOHNS (Life Baroness) Joyce Anne Anelay; cr. 1996. Born 17 July 1947. Daughter of late Stanley Charles Clarke and of Annette Marjorie Clarke; educated Enfield County School; Bristol University (BA history 1968); London University Institute of Education (CertEd 1969); Brunel University (MA public and social administration 1982). Married Richard Alfred Anelay QC 1970. JP, NW Surrey 1985–97. *Career:* History secondary teacher, St David's School, Ashford, Middlesex 1969–74. Opposition Whip 1997–98. Opposition Spokesperson for: Agriculture 1997–98, Culture, Media and Sport December 1998–2002, Home Affairs 1997–98, Social Security 1997–99, Home Affairs 2002–, Legal Affairs 2003–. Co-opted Member, European Union Sub-committee E (Law and Institutions) 1997–98; Member, Procedure Committee 1997–2000. Chair, SE Area Conservative Women's Committee 1987–90; Member, National Union Executive Committee of the Conservative Party 1987–97, Vice-chair, SE Area Executive Committee 1990–93; Chair, Women's National Committee 1993–96, Vice-President, National Union 1996–97. Voluntary adviser, Woking Citizens' Advice Bureau 1976–85, Chair 1988–93, President 1996–; Chair, Governors, Hermitage First and Middle Schools 1981–88. Hon. DSocSci, Brunel 1997. Member: Social Security Appeal Tribunal 1983–96, Social Security Advisory Committee for Great Britain and Northern Ireland 1989–96, Women's National Commission 1991–94, Child Support Appeal Tribunal 1993–96, Patron Restaurant Association of Great Britain 1999–. OBE 1990; DBE 1995. FRSA. *Special Interests:* Social Security, Home Affairs. *Recreations:* Golf, reading. *Sportsclubs:* Woking Golf. Raised to the peerage as Baroness Anelay of St Johns, of St Johns in the County of Surrey 1996. The Baroness Anelay of St Johns, DBE, House of Lords, London, SW1A 0PW *Tel:* 020 7219 3237 *E-mail:* anelayj@parliament.uk.

ARCHER OF SANDWELL, LORD · Labour

ARCHER OF SANDWELL (Life Baron), Peter Kingsley Archer; cr. 1992. Born 20 November 1926. Son of late Cyril Kingsley Archer and May Archer; educated Wednesbury Boys' High School; London School of Economics (LLM 1950); University College, London (BA philosophy 1952). Married Margaret Irene Smith 1954 (1 son). *Career:* Called to the Bar, Gray's Inn 1952, Bencher 1974, QC, Recorder of the Crown Court 1981–98. *House of Commons:* Contested Hendon South 1959 and Brierley Hill 1964 general elections; MP (Labour) for Rowley Regis and Tipton 1966–74; PPS to Attorney-General Sir Elwyn Jones 1967–70; MP (Labour) for Warley West 1974–92; Solicitor General 1974–79; Member, Shadow Cabinet 1981–87. Opposition Spokesperson for: Legal Affairs 1981–82, Trade, Prices and Consumer Protection 1982–83, Northern Ireland 1983–87. Opposition Spokesperson for Foreign Affairs 1992–97. Member, Select Committees on: European Affairs (Sub-Committee E) 1993–96, the Scrutiny of Delegated Powers, Delegated Powers and

Deregulation 1997–99, Parliamentary Privilege (Joint Committee) 1999; Chairman, Select Committee on Freedom of Information Bill 1999; Member: Select Committee on Registration of Interests 2001, Joint Committee on House of Lords Reform 2002–, Intelligence and Security Committee. Chair, Society of Labour Lawyers 1971–74, 1980–93; President, Fabian Society 1993–; Joint President, Society of Labour Lawyers 1993–; Member, Labour Party Departmental Committees for: Home Affairs 1992–, Foreign Affairs 1992–, Defence 1992–. Chair, Amnesty International (British Section) 1971–74; President: Methodist Homes for the Aged 1993–, World Disarmament Campaign 1994–, UNA (London Region) 1999–2000. One honorary doctorate, One honorary fellowship. President, One World Trust. Chair: Council on Tribunals 1992–99, Enemy Property Compensation Panel 1998–, Member, Intelligence and Security Committee 1999–. PC 1977. Freeman: Metropolitan Borough of Sandwell, State of Maryland. *Publications: The Queen's Courts* 1956; *Communism and the Law* 1963; *The International Protection of Human Rights* 1967; Co-author *Freedom at Stake* 1966; *Purpose in Socialism* 1973; Editor, *Social Welfare and the Citizen* 1957; Editor, *More Law Reform Now* 1983. *Special Interests:* Human Rights, Law Reform, Northern Ireland, World Government, Conservation, Third World. *Recreations:* Music, writing, gardening. Raised to the peerage as Baron Archer of Sandwell, of Sandwell in the County of West Midlands 1992. Rt Hon the Lord Archer of Sandwell, QC, Highcroft, Hill View Road, Wraysbury, Staines, Middlesex, TW19 5EQ *Tel:* 01784 483136 *Fax:* 01784 483136; House of Lords, London, SW1A 0PW *Tel:* 020 7219 3223.

ARCHER OF WESTON-SUPER-MARE, LORD   Non-affiliated

ARCHER OF WESTON-SUPER-MARE (Life Baron), Jeffrey Howard Archer; cr. 1992. Born 15 April 1940. Son of late William and Lola Archer; educated Wellington School, Somerset; Brasenose College, Oxford. Married Mary Doreen Weeden 1966 (2 sons). Councillor, GLC for Havering 1966–70. *Career:* Athletics Blues 1963–65; Gymnastics Blue 1963; Represented Great Britain in athletics 1966; Author, Playwright and Auctioneer. *House of Commons:* MP (Conservative) for Louth 1969–74. Deputy Chairman, Conservative Party 1985–86; President, Conservative Party London Clubs 1998–99. *Publications:* Plays: *Beyond Reasonable Doubt*, 1987; *Exclusive*, 1990; *The Accused*, 2000; Novels/short stories: *Not a Penny More, Not a Penny Less*, 1975; *Shall We Tell the President?* 1977; *Kane and Abel*, 1979; *A Quiver Full of Arrows* (short stories), 1980; *The Prodigal Daughter*, 1982; *First Among Equals*, 1984; *A Matter of Honour*, 1986; *A Twist in the Tale* (short stories) 1988; *As the Crow Flies*, 1991; *Honour Among Thieves*, 1993; *Twelve Red Herrings* (short stories), 1994; *The Fourth Estate*, 1996; *Collected Short Stories*, 1997; *The Eleventh Commandment*, 1998; *To Cut a Long Story Short*, 2000. *Recreations:* Theatre, cricket, auctioneering, art. *Sportsclubs:* President, Somerset AAA 1973–99; Vice-President, Cambridge City RFU; President, World Snooker Association 1997–99. *Clubs:* MCC. Raised to the peerage as Baron Archer of Weston-super-Mare, of Mark in the County of Somerset 1992. The Lord Archer of Weston-super-Mare, The Penthouse, 93 Albert Embankment, London, SE1 7TY; The Old Vicarage, Grantchester, Cambridge, CB3 9ND *E-mail:* jeffrey.archer@jeffreyarcher.co.uk.

ARMSTRONG OF ILMINSTER, LORD   Crossbencher

ARMSTRONG OF ILMINSTER (Life Baron), Robert Temple Armstrong; cr. 1988. Born 30 March 1927. Son of late Sir Thomas Armstrong, musician and late Hester Muriel, née Draper; educated Dragon School; Eton College (King's Scholar); Christ Church, Oxford (Scholar) (BA classical mods 1947, literae humaniores 1949). Married Serena Mary Benedicta Chance 1953 (2 daughters) (divorced 1985, she died 1994); married (Mary) Patricia Carlow 1985. *Career:* Assistant Principal, HM Treasury 1950–55; Private Secretary to: Reginald Maudling as Economic Secretary to the Treasury 1953–54, Rab Butler as Chancellor of the Exchequer 1954–55; Principal, Treasury 1955–57; Secretary, Radcliffe Committee on Working of Monetary System 1957–59; Returned to Treasury as Principal 1959–64; Secretary, Armitage Committee on Pay of Postmen 1964; Assistant Secretary: Cabinet Office 1964–66, Treasury 1967–68; Principal Private Secretary to Roy Jenkins as Chancellor of the Exchequer 1968; Under-Secretary (Home Finance), Treasury 1968–70; Principal Private Secretary to Prime Minister 1970–75; Home Office: Deputy Under Secretary of State, 1975–77,

Permanent Under Secretary of State 1977–79; Secretary of the Cabinet 1979–87; Head of the Home Civil Service 1981–87; Director various companies 1988–97; Director, Royal Opera House 1988–93; Chairman: Biotechnology Investments Ltd 1989–2000, Bristol and West plc (formerly Building Society) 1993–97; Forensic Investigative Associates plc 1997–; Director, Bank of Ireland 1997–2001; Director, 3i Bioscience Investment Trust plc 2000–2001. Chancellor, Hull University 1994–. Member, Select Committee on European Union, Sub-Committee A (Economic and Financial Affairs) 2000–. Member of Council, Musicians Benevolent Fund; Royal United Kingdom Benevolent Association. Honorary doctorate. Fellow of Eton College 1979–94; Member: RVW Trust 1958–, Rhodes Trust 1975–97, Pilgrim Trust 1987–2002; Chair: Board of Trustees, V & A Museum 1988–98, Hestercombe Gardens Trust 1996–, Leeds Castle Foundation 2001–; Board of Governors: Royal Northern College of Music 2000–. Hon. Student, Christ Church, Oxford 1985; Hon. Bencher, Inner Temple 1985. CB 1974; CVO 1975; KCB 1978; GCB 1983. Freeman, City of London. Honorary Member, Salters' Company. *Special Interests:* Arts, museums and galleries, public service. *Recreations:* music. *Clubs:* Brooks's, Garrick. Raised to the peerage as Baron Armstrong of Ilminster, of Ashill in the County of Somerset 1988. The Lord Armstrong of Ilminster, GCB, CVO, House of Lords, London, SW1A 0PW *Tel:* 020 7219 4983 *Fax:* 020 7219 1259 *E-mail:* armstrongr@parliament.uk.

ARRAN, EARL OF — Conservative

ARRAN (9th Earl of, I), Arthur Desmond Colquhoun Gore; cr. 1762; 9th Viscount Sudley and Baron Saunders (I) 1758; 5th Baron Sudley (UK) 1884; 11th Bt of Castle Gore (I) 1662. Born 14 July 1938. Son of 8th Earl. Sits as Baron Sudley; educated Eton College; Balliol College, Oxford (MA English literature 1960). Married Eleanor Van Cutsem 1974 (2 daughters). Served Grenadier Guards, national service, commissioned 1958–60. *Career:* Assistant manager *Daily Mail* 1972–73; Managing Director, Clark Nelson 1973–74; Assistant general manager, *Daily Express* and *Sunday Express* June-November 1974; Director, Waterstone & Co Ltd 1984–87; Parliamentary consultant to the waste industry 1995–; Non-executive Director: HMV (EMI) 1995–98, SWEL (the Economy and Inward Investment of the West Country), Bonham's (Auctioneers) 1998–2001. *House of Lords:* First entered House of Lords 1983; Parliamentary Under-Secretary of State for: The Armed Forces, Ministry of Defence 1989–92, Northern Ireland Office 1992–94, Department of the Environment January-July 1994; Elected hereditary peer 1999–. Government Whip 1987–89; Government Deputy Chief Whip July 1994-January 1995. Spokesperson for: The Home Office, DES and DHSS 1987–89, Department of the Environment 1988–89. Chairman, Children's Country Holidays Fund 1999. *Special Interests:* Media, Charity, Sport, Foreign Affairs. *Recreations:* Tennis, golf, croquet, shooting and gardening. *Clubs:* Turf, Beefsteak, Pratt's, White's, Annabels. The Earl of Arran, House of Lords, London, SW1A 0PW *Tel:* 020 7219 5353.

ASHCROFT, LORD — Conservative

ASHCROFT (Life Baron), Michael Anthony Ashcroft; cr. 2000. *Career:* Company Director; Chairman, Carlisle Holdings Ltd; Former Belize Ambassador to the UN. Senior Party Treasurer, Conservative Party 1998–2001. KCMG 2000. Raised to the peerage as Baron Ashcroft, of Chichester in the county of West Sussex. The Lord Ashcroft, KCMG, House of Lords, London, SW1A 0PW *Tel:* 020 7219 3000.

ASHDOWN OF NORTON-SUB-HAMDON, LORD — Liberal Democrat

ASHDOWN OF NORTON-SUB-HAMDON (Life Baron), Jeremy John Ashdown; cr. 2001. Born 2 / February 1941. Son of late Lieutenant Colonel John W. R. D. Ashdown; educated Bedford School. Married Mary Jane Donne Courtenay 1961 (1 son 1 daughter). Royal Marines Officer (Captain) 1959–72 with Commando Units in Far East, Middle East and Belfast; Commanded Unit of Special Boat Service in Far East. *Career:* Studied Chinese (Mandarin) at Hong Kong Language School 1967–70; 1st class interpreter, Chinese; First Secretary, UK Mission (Foreign Office) to UN in Geneva 1971–76; Westland Helicopters, Yeovil 1976–78; Morlands, Yeovil 1978–81; Youth Officer, Dorset County Council 1981–83; High Representative for Bosnia and Herzegovina 2002–.

House of Commons: Contested Yeovil 1979 general election; Member for Yeovil 1983–2001; Leader: Social and Liberal Democrats 1988–89, Liberal Democrats 1988–99. Liberal Spokesperson for Trade and Industry 1985–87; Alliance Spokesperson for Education and Science 1987; Liberal Spokesperson for Education and Science 1987–88; Spokesperson for Northern Ireland 1988–92. Peace Implementation Council and European Union Special Representative for Bosnia 2002–. PC 1989; KBE 2000. *Publications: Citizens' Britain: A Radical Agenda for the 1990s,* 1989; *Beyond Westminster: Finding Hope in Britain,* 1992; *The Ashdown Diaries: Volume One,* 2000, *Volume Two,* 2001. *Special Interests:* Youth Affairs, Foreign Affairs, Defence, Industry, New Technology. *Recreations:* Gardening, classical music, hill walking, wine making. *Clubs:* National Liberal. Raised to the peerage as Baron Ashdown of Norton-sub-Hamdon, of Norton-sub-Hamdon in the County of Somerset 2001. Rt Hon the Lord Ashdown of Norton-sub-Hamdon, KBE, House of Lords, London, SW1A 0PW *Tel:* 020 7219 1430.

ASHLEY OF STOKE, LORD   Labour

ASHLEY OF STOKE (Life Baron), Jack Ashley; cr. 1992. Born 6 December 1922. Son of late Jack Ashley; educated St Patrick's Elementary School, Widnes; Ruskin College, Oxford (Diploma economics and political science 1948); Gonville and Caius College, Cambridge (BA economics 1951) (President of Union). Married Pauline Crispin 1951 (3 daughters). *Trades Union:* National Executive Council, Clerical Workers Union 1945; Shop steward convenor 1946. Councillor, Widnes Borough Council 1945–47. *Career:* Labourer and crane driver 1935–46; BBC radio producer 1951–57; Commonwealth Fund Fellow 1955; BBC senior television producer 1957–66. *House of Commons:* Contested Finchley 1951; MP (Labour) for Stoke-on-Trent South 1966–92; PPS to Secretary of State for: Economic Affairs 1967–70, Health and Social Security 1974–79. Chancellor, Staffordshire University 1993–2002. Member, Labour Party National Executive Committee 1976–78. Member, General Advisory Council, BBC 1967–69; President: Royal College of Speech and Language Therapists 1995–2001, Royal National Institute for Deaf, Defeating Deafness, British Tinnitus Association; National Cochlea Implant Users Association. *Spectator* and *Oldie,* Campaigner of the Year 2000; People of the Year Awards Life-Time Achievement Award (jointly) 2000. Twelve honorary degrees. CH 1975; PC 1979. Stoke on Trent; Honorary Alderman-Widnes, Halton, Cheshire. *Publications: Journey into Silence* (autobiography) 1973; *Acts of Defiance,* 1992. *Special Interests:* Disability, Health, Medical Drugs, Poverty, Disadvantaged, Human Rights. *Recreations:* Playing with grandchildren, all sports. *Sportsclubs:* Patron, Widnes Rugby League Club. Raised to the peerage as Baron Ashley of Stoke, of Widnes in the County of Cheshire 1992. Rt Hon the Lord Ashley of Stoke, CH, House of Lords, London, SW1A 0PW *Tel:* 01372 723784 *Fax:* 01372 749283 *E-mail:* ashleyj@parliament.uk.

ASHTON OF UPHOLLAND, BARONESS   Labour

ASHTON OF UPHOLLAND (Life Baroness), Catherine Margaret Ashton; cr. 1999. Born 20 March 1956. Daughter of late Harold and Clare Ashton; educated Upholland Grammar School; Bedford College, London University (BSc Econ 1977). Married Peter Kellner 1988 (1 son, 1 daughter, 1 stepson, 2 stepdaughters). Chairman, Hertfordshire Health Authority 1998–2001. *Career:* Administrative Officer, CND 1977–79; The Coverdale Organisation 1979–81; Central Council for Education and Training in Social Work 1981–83; Director of Community Development and Public Affairs, Business in the Community 1983–89; Public Policy Adviser 1989–, seconded by London First to Home Office 1998–99; Adviser, Lattice Foundation 2000–01. *House of Lords:* Parliamentary Under-Secretary of State, Department for Education and Skills: for Early Years and School Standards 2001–02, for Early Years and Childcare 2002, for Sure Start 2002– (also Department for Work and Pensions). Government Spokesperson for Education and Skills 2001–. Member, British American Parliamentary Group. Advisory Board Member, "Can Do" Network; Vice President, National Council for One Parent Families; Patron, Grove Hospice, St Albans. Trustee, Verulamium Museum 2000–. *Special Interests:* Policy Implementation. *Recreations:* Swimming, theatre, cooking. *Clubs:* Royal Commonwealth Society. Raised to the peerage as Baroness Ashton of Upholland, of St Albans in the County of Hertfordshire 1999. The Baroness Ashton of Upholland, House of Lords, London, SW1A 0PW *Tel:* 020 7925 6391 *E-mail:* ashton.ps@dfes.gsi.gov.uk.

ASTOR, VISCOUNT Conservative

ASTOR (4th Viscount, UK), William Waldorf Astor; cr. 1917; 4th Baron Astor (UK) 1916. Born 27 December 1951. Son of 3rd Viscount and Hon. Sarah Katharine Elinor Norton, daughter of 6th Baron Grantley; educated Eton College. Married Mrs Annabel Sheffield, née Jones 1976 (2 sons 1 daughter). *Career:* Citibank, New York 1970–72; Observer, USA 1972; Westminster Press 1973–74; Director: UK and US Property and Investment Companies 1974–84, Blakeney Hotels and Cliveden Hotels 1984–90; Director: Chorion Plc 1996–, Urbium Plc 2002–. *House of Lords:* First entered House of Lords 1972; Parliamentary Under-Secretary of State: Department of Social Security 1993–94, Department of National Heritage 1994–95; Elected hereditary peer 1999–. Government Whip 1990–93. Spokesperson for: Department of Environment 1990–91, Home Office 1991–92, Department of National Heritage 1992–93; Opposition Spokesperson for: Home Office 1997–2001, Education and Employment 1999–2001, Transport, Local Government and the Regions 2001–02, Transport 2002–. Trustee, Stanley Spencer Gallery, Cookham. *Clubs:* White's, Turf. The Viscount Astor, Ginge Manor, Nr Wantage, Oxfordshire, OX12 8QT *Tel:* 01235 833228.

ASTOR OF HEVER, LORD Conservative

ASTOR OF HEVER (3rd Baron, UK), John Jacob Astor; cr. 1956. Born 16 June 1946. Son of 2nd Baron, and late Lady Irene Haig, daughter of Field Marshal 1st Earl Haig, KT, GCB, OM, GCVO, KCIE; educated Eton College. Married Fiona Harvey 1970 (divorced 1990) (3 daughters); married Hon. Elizabeth Mackintosh 1990 (1 son 1 daughter). Lieutenant, The Life Guards 1966–70. DL Kent 1996–. *Career:* President, Astor Enterprises Inc. 1986–. *House of Lords:* First entered House of Lords 1984; Elected hereditary peer 1999–. Opposition Whip 1998–. Member, Personal Bills –2000, Finance and Staff Sub-Committee 1998–2001. Member of Executive, Association of Conservative Peers 1996–98. President, Sevenoaks Westminster Patrons Club 1991–; Governor, Cobham Hall School 1992–96; President: Earl Haig Branch, Royal British Legion 1994–, Kent Federation of Amenity Societies 1995–, Motorsport Industry Association 1995–, RoSPA 1996–99, RoSPA Advanced Drivers Association 1997–; Patron, Aquarian Opera 1999–, Royal British Legion, Kent 2002–. Trustee: Astor of Hever Trust 1986–, Astor Foundation 1988–, Rochester Cathedral Trust 1988–; Patron, Edenbridge Music and Arts Trust 1989–; Trustee, Canterbury Cathedral Trust 1992–; Patron: Bridge Trust 1993–, Kent Youth Trust 1994–; President, Eden Valley Museum Trust 1998–, New School at West Health 2001–, Conservatives in Paris. Chair, Council of the Order of St John for Kent 1987–97. Member, Goldsmiths' Company. *Special Interests:* France, Motorsport Industry, Defence. *Clubs:* White's. The Lord Astor of Hever, DL, House of Lords, London, SW1A 0PW *Tel:* 020 7219 5475 *Fax:* 020 7219 5979 *E-mail:* astorjj@parliament.uk.

ATTENBOROUGH, LORD Labour

ATTENBOROUGH (Life Baron), Richard Samuel Attenborough; cr. 1993. Born 29 August 1923. Son of late Frederick Attenborough; educated Wyggeston Grammar School, Leicester; Leverhulme scholarship to Royal Academy of Dramatic Art. Married Sheila Sim 1945 (1 son 2 daughters). Served RAF 1943–46. *Career:* Actor, producer and director; Appeared in a number of productions on the London stage including: *Brighton Rock* 1943, *The Mousetrap* 1952–54, *The Rape of the Belt* 1957–58; Film appearances include: *In Which We Serve, Brighton Rock, London Belongs to Me, The Guinea Pig, Morning Departure, The Ship That Died of Shame, I'm Alright Jack, The League of Gentlemen, The Angry Silence* (also co-produced), *The Dock Brief, The Great Escape, Seance On a Wet Afternoon* (also produced, BAFTA Award), *Guns at Batasi* (BAFTA Award), *The Flight of the Phoenix, The Sand Pebbles* (Hollywood Golden Globe), *Dr Dolittle* (Hollywood Golden Globe), *10 Rillington Place, The Chess Players, Jurassic Park, Miracle on 34th Street, Lost World, Elizabeth I*; Produced: *Whistle Down the Wind, The L-Shaped Room*; Directed: *Young Winston* (Hollywood Golden Globe), *A Bridge Too Far, Magic, A Chorus Line*; Produced and directed:

Oh! What a Lovely War (BAFTA Award, Hollywood Golden Globe), *Gandhi* (8 Oscars, 5 BAFTA Awards, 5 Hollywood Golden Globes), *Cry Freedom, Chaplin, Shadowlands* (BAFTA Award); *In Love and War; Grey Owl*; Chairman, Capital Radio 1972–92, Life President 1992–; Chairman: Goldcrest Films and Television Ltd 1982–87, Channel Four Television 1987–92, Deputy Chairman 1980–86. Pro-Chancellor, Sussex University 1970–, Chancellor 1998–. Member, chair, president numerous organisations in arts, theatre, film including: Chairman, Royal Academy of Dramatic Art 1970–, Mem. Council 1963–; President, Muscular Dystrophy Group of Great Britain 1971–, Vice-President 1962–71; President, The Gandhi Foundation 1983–, Patron, Goodwill Ambassador for Unicef 1987–; Chairman, European Script Fund 1988–96, Hon. President 1996–; President, Combined Theatrical Charities Appeals Council 1988–, Chairman 1964–88; President, Arts for Health 1989–; Patron, Richard Attenborough Centre for Disability and the Arts, Leicester University 1990–; President, National Film and TV School 1997–, Governor 1970–81. *Evening Standard* Film Award, 40 years service to British Cinema 1983; Martin Luther King Jr Peace Prize 1983; European Film Awards Award of Merit for Humanitarianism in Film Making 1988; Shakespeare Prize for Outstanding Contribution to European Culture 1992; Praemium Imperiale 1998; BBC/BAFTA Lifetime Achievement Award 1999; EMMA Award 2001. Ten honorary doctorates and fellowships. President, The Actors' Charitable Trust 1988–, Chairman 1956–88; Trustee: King George V Fund for Actors and Actresses 1973–, Help a London Child 1975–, Tate Gallery 1976–82 and 1994–96; Chairman, UK Trustees Waterford-Kamhlaba School Swaziland 1976–, Governor 1987–; Trustee: Motability 1977–, Tate Foundation 1986–. CBE 1967; Kt 1976; Padma Bhushan, India 1983; Commandeur, Ordre des Arts et des Lettres, France 1985; Chevalier, Legion d'Honneur, France 1988. Fellow: BAFTA 1983, BFI 1992. Freeman, City of Leicester 1990. *Publications: In Search of Gandhi*, 1982; *Richard Attenborough's Chorus Line* (with Diana Carter) 1986; *Cry Freedom, A Pictorial Record*, 1987. *Special Interests:* Arts, Education, Disability, Underdeveloped Countries. *Recreations:* Collecting paintings and sculpture, listening to music, watching football and reading the newspapers. *Sportsclubs:* Director, Chelsea Football Club 1969–82, Life Vice-President 1993–. *Clubs:* Garrick, Beefsteak. Raised to the peerage as Baron Attenborough, of Richmond upon Thames in the London Borough of Richmond upon Thames 1993. The Lord Attenborough, CBE, Old Friars, Richmond Green, Richmond upon Thames, Surrey, TW9 1NH *Tel:* 020 8940 7234.

ATTLEE, EARL   Conservative

ATTLEE (3rd Earl, UK), John Richard Attlee; cr. 1955; Viscount Prestwood. Born 3 October 1956. Son of 2nd Earl; educated Stowe School. Married Celia Jane Plummer 1993 (divorced). Major, REME TA, All Arms Pool and Watchkeepers. *Career:* President, The Heavy Transport Association 1994–; British Direct Aid: In-Country Director (Rwanda) 1995–96. *House of Lords:* First entered House of Lords 1994; Elected hereditary peer 1999–. Opposition Whip 1997–99, 2002–. Opposition Spokesperson for: Defence June-Oct 1997, Environment, Transport and the Regions (Transport) June-Oct 1997, Northern Ireland June-Oct 1997, December 1998-June 1999, Defence 1998–2001, Trade and Industry 1998–99, Transport 1999–2001. Trustee, Attlee Foundation.
Special Interests: Engineering, Defence, Transport, Overseas Aid and Development. The Earl Attlee, House of Lords, London, SW1A 0PW *Tel:* 020 7219 6071 *E-mail:* attleej@parliament.uk.

AVEBURY, LORD   Liberal Democrat

AVEBURY (4th Baron, UK), Eric Reginald Lubbock; cr. 1900; 7th Bt of Lamas (UK) 1806. Born 29 September 1928. Son of late Hon. Maurice Lubbock, son of 1st Baron, PC, DL, and late Hon. Mary Katharine Adelaide Stanley; educated Upper Canada College, Toronto; Harrow School; Balliol College, Oxford (BA engineering 1949). Married Kina Maria O'Kelly de Gallagh, 1953 (2 sons 1 daughter) (divorced 1983); married Lindsay Stewart 1985 (1 son). Second Lieutenant, Welsh Guards 1949–51. *Career:* Rolls-Royce aero-engine division 1951–55; Production Engineering Ltd (Management consultant) 1955–60; Charterhouse Group 1960–62; Director, C.L. Projects Ltd 1968–. *House of Commons:* MP (Liberal) for Orpington 1962–70. Liberal Whip 1963–70. *House of Lords:* First entered House of Lords 1971; Elected hereditary peer 1999–. Liberal Democrat Spokesperson for: Race Relations and Immigration 1971–83, Foreign and Commonwealth Affairs 1998–.

Member: House of Lords' Offices Library and Computers Sub-Committee; Religious Offences Committee 2002–03. President: Fluoridation Society 1972–84, Conservation Society 1973–81, London Bach Society, Steinitz Bach Players 1984–95; Vice-President Steinitz Bach Players 1995–; Patron: Angulimala, Buddhist Prison Chaplaincy 1990–, Kurdish Human Rights Project 1993–, British Campaign for East Timor 1994–; Advisory Committee on the Education of Romany and other travellers 2001–. Member: Speaker's Conference on Electoral Law 1963–65, Royal Commission on Standards of Conduct in Public Life 1975–76. Hilal-i-Quaid-i-Azam (Pakistan) 1990. MInstMechE; FBCS; CEng. *Publications: The Energy Crisis – Growth, Stability or Collapse*, 1973; *Alcohol – Politics and Practicalities*, 1981; *Authority and Accountability*, 1986; *Desolated and Profaned*, 1992; *A Desolation called Peace*, 1993; *Iran: The Subjection of Women*, 1995; *Iran: State of Terror*, 1996; *A Positive Legal Duty: the liberation of the people of East Timor* in *Self Determination*, ed Donald Clark and Roloo William, MacMillan, 1996; *Iran: Fatal Writ*, 2000. *Special Interests:* Human Rights, Gypsies, Prisons. The Lord Avebury, 26 Flodden Road, London, SE5 9LH *Tel:* 020 7274 4617 *Fax:* 020 7738 7864 *E-mail:* ericavebury@hotmail.com.

B

BACH (Life Baron), William Stephen Goulden Bach; cr. 1998. Born 25 December 1946. Son of late Stephen Bach, CBE, and late Joan Bach; educated Westminster School; New College, Oxford (BA English 1968). Married Caroline Jones 1984 (1 daughter plus 2 children from previous marriage). *Trades Union:* Member, TGWU 1977–. Leicester City Council: Councillor 1976–87, Chief Whip, Labour Group 1981–83, Councillor, Lutterworth Town Council 1991–99; Mayor, Lutterworth 1993–94; Harborough District Council: Councillor 1995–99, Chair, Contracts Services Committee 1995–97; Chief Whip, Labour Group 1995–98. *Career:* Called to the Bar, Middle Temple 1972, Tenant Barristers' Chambers 1975–2000, Head of Chambers 1996–99; Served on a number of circuit and local court and bar committees over many years. *House of Lords:* Parliamentary Secretary, Lord Chancellor's Department 2000–01, Parliamentary Under-Secretary of State (Minister for Defence Procurement), Ministry of Defence 2001–. Government Whip 1999–2000. Government Spokesperson for: Home Office 1999–2000, Lord Chancellor's Department 1999–2000, Education and Employment 1999–2000, Defence 2001–. Member, European Communities Sub Committee E (Laws and Institutions) 1998–99. Executive Committee Member, Society of Labour Lawyers; Elected Member, Labour Party: National Policy Forum 1998–99, Economic Policy Commission 1998–99; Member: Co-operative Party, Fabian Society; Chair and Co-Founder, Society of Labour Lawyers, East Midlands; Chair: Harborough District Labour Party 1989–95, Northants and Blaby Euro Constituency GC 1992–99. Council Member, Leicester University 1980–99; Court Member, 1980–. Contested (Labour): Gainsborough 1979, Sherwood 1983 and 1987 general elections. *Special Interests:* Crime and Criminal Justice, Local Government, USA Affairs, Sport. *Recreations:* Playing and watching football and cricket, supporting Leicester City FC, American crime writing. *Sportsclubs:* Leicester City FC, Leicestershire CCC; Founder Member and President, Walcote Cricket Club. Raised to the peerage as Baron Bach, of Lutterworth in the County of Leicestershire 1998. The Lord Bach, Ministry of Defence, Room 200, Old War Office, Whitehall, London, SW1A 2GU *Tel:* 020 7218 6621; House of Lords, London, SW1A 0PW *Tel:* 020 7222 2597 *E-mail:* mindp@dpa.mod.uk.

DodOnline
An Electronic Directory without rival . . .

Peers' biographies and photographs available with daily updates *via* the internet

For a *free* trial, call Yasmin Mirza, Aby Farsoun or Michael Mand on 020 7630 7643

BAGRI, LORD   Conservative

BAGRI (Life Baron), Raj Kumar Bagri; cr. 1997. Born 24 August 1930. Son of late Sohan Lal Bagri. Married Usha Maheshwary 1954 (1 son 1 daughter). *Career:* Founder and Chairman, Metdist Group 1970–; Chairman, The London Metal Exchange Limited 1993–2002, Director 1983–2002, Vice-Chairman 1990–92, Honorary President 2003–. Member: Advisory Committee of The Prince's Youth Business Trust, Governing Body of School of Oriental and African Studies; Chairman, Bagri Foundation. Two honorary doctorates. Chairman, Trustees of The Rajiv Gandhi (UK) Foundation; Trustee, Sangam. CBE 1995. *Recreations:* Fine art, classical music, antiques. *Clubs:* MCC. Raised to the peerage as Baron Bagri, of Regent's Park in the City of Westminster 1997. The Lord Bagri, CBE, 80 Cannon Street, London, EC4N 6EJ; House of Lords, London, SW1A 0PW *Tel:* 020 7219 5353.

BAKER OF DORKING, LORD   Conservative

BAKER OF DORKING (Life Baron), Kenneth Wilfred Baker; cr. 1997. Born 3 November 1934. Son of late Wilfred Michael Baker, OBE; educated St Paul's School, London; Magdalen College, Oxford (BA history 1958) (Secretary of Union). Married Mary Elizabeth Gray-Muir 1963 (1 son 2 daughters). National Service 1953–55 (Lieutenant in Gunners). Councillor, Twickenham Borough Council 1960–62. *House of Commons:* Contested Poplar 1964, Acton 1966 general elections; MP (Conservative) for Acton 1968–70, St Marylebone 1970–83 and for Mole Valley June 1983–97; PPS to Minister of State, Department of Employment 1970–72; Parliamentary Secretary, Civil Service Department 1972–74; Minister of State for Industry and Information Technology 1981–84; Minister for Local Government 1984–85; Secretary of State: for The Environment 1985–86, for Education and Science 1986–89; Chancellor of the Duchy of Lancaster 1989–90; Secretary of State for the Home Department 1990–92. Chair Information Committee 2003–. Chairman, Conservative Party 1989–90. Chairman: Hansard Society 1978–81, Museum of British History 1995–. Hon. Degree, Richmond College, The American University in London. PC 1984; CH 1992. *Publications: I Have No Gun But I Can Spit,* 1980; *London Lines,* 1982; *The Faber Book of English History in Verse,* 1988; *Unauthorised Versions: Poems and their Parodies,* 1990; *The Faber Book of Conservatism,* 1993; *The Turbulent Years: My Life in Politics,* 1993; *The Prime Ministers – An Irreverent Political History in Cartoons,* 1995; *Kings and Queens: An Irreverent Cartoon History of the British Monarchy,* 1996; *The Faber Book of War Poetry,* 1996; *Children's English History in Verse,* 2000; *The Faber Book of Landscape Poetry,* 2000. *Special Interests:* Education, History, Information Technology. *Recreations:* Collecting books, collecting political cartoons. *Clubs:* Athenaeum, Garrick. Raised to the peerage as Baron Baker of Dorking, of Iford in the County of East Sussex 1997. Rt Hon the Lord Baker of Dorking, CH, House of Lords, London, SW1A 0PW *Tel:* 020 7219 4434 *Fax:* 020 7219 8640 *E-mail:* bakerk@parliament.uk.

BALDWIN OF BEWDLEY, EARL   Crossbencher

BALDWIN OF BEWDLEY (4th Earl, UK), Edward Alfred Alexander Baldwin; cr. 1937; Viscount Corvedale. Born 3 January 1938. Son of 3rd Earl and late Joan Elspeth, née Tomes; educated Eton College; Trinity College, Cambridge (BA modern languages and law 1961, MA, CertEd 1970). Married Sarah James 1970 (died 2001) (3 sons). Army national service 1956–58; 2nd Lieutenant, Intelligence Corps 1957–58. *Career:* Schoolmaster: Christ's Hospital 1970–74; Hemel Hempstead School 1974–77; Education officer: Leicestershire 1978–80, Oxfordshire 1980–87. *House of Lords:* First entered House of Lords 1976; Elected hereditary peer 1999–. Co-opted Member, Select Committee on Science and Technology Sub-Committee I (Complementary and Alternative Medicine) 2000. Chairman, British Acupuncture Accreditation Board 1990–98; Former Member, Research Council for Complementary Medicine. *Special Interests:* Complementary Medicine, Medicine, Environment, Education. *Recreations:* Mountains, tennis, music. *Clubs:* MCC. The Earl Baldwin of Bewdley, Manor Farm House, Godstow Road, Upper Wolvercote, Oxford, OX2 8AJ *Tel:* 01865 552683 *Fax:* 01865 552683.

BARBER, LORD

BARBER (Life Baron), Anthony Perrinott Lysberg Barber; cr. 1974. Born 4 July 1920. Son of late John Barber, CBE, Company director of Doncaster; educated Retford Grammar School, Nottinghamshire; Oriel College, Oxford (MA). Married Jean Patricia Asquith 1950 (died 1983) (2 daughters); married Rosemary Surgenor, née Youens 1989. Served 1939–45, Commissioned Army, seconded RAF pilot (mentioned in despatches) (P.O.W. 1942–45) (Germany). DL, West Yorkshire 1987. *Career:* Called to the Bar, Inner Temple 1948; Chairman, Standard Chartered Bank plc. 1974–87; Director, BP 1979–88. *House of Commons:* Contested Doncaster 1950 general election; MP (Conservative) for: Doncaster 1951–64, Altrincham and Sale 1965–74; PPS, Air Ministry 1952; PPS to Harold Macmillan as Prime Minister 1958; Economic Secretary to the Treasury 1959–62; Financial Secretary to Treasury 1962–63; Minister of Health and member of the Cabinet 1963–64; Chancellor of the Duchy of Lancaster and member of the Cabinet June-July 1970; Chancellor of the Exchequer 1970–74. Government Whip 1955; Lord Commissioner HM Treasury (Government Whip) 1957–58. Chairman, Conservative Party 1967–70. Member, Falkland Islands Enquiry (Franks Committee) 1982; British Member, Eminent Persons Group on South Africa 1986; Chairman, RAF Benevolent Fund 1991–96. Hon. Fellow, Oriel College 1973. TD, PC 1963. *Publications:* Memoirs: *Taking the Tide. Clubs:* Carlton, Royal Air Force. Raised to the peerage as Baron Barber, of Wentbridge in the County of West Yorkshire 1974. Rt Hon the Lord Barber, TD, DL, House of Lords, London, SW1A 0PW *Tel:* 020 7219 5353.

BARBER OF TEWKESBURY, LORD

BARBER OF TEWKESBURY (Life Baron), Derek Coates Barber; cr. 1992. Born 17 June 1918. Son of late Thomas Smith-Barber; educated Royal Agricultural College, Cirencester. Married 1st, (divorced 1981); married Rosemary Jennifer Brougham Pearson 1983. Served in Second World War (invalided). Councillor, Cheltenham Rural District Council 1948–52. *Career:* Farmer in Gloucestershire; Various posts, Ministry of Agriculture, Fisheries and Food 1946–72; Environment consultant to Humberts, Chartered Surveyors 1972–93. Member, House of Lords Select Committees on: European Communities, Sub-Committee D (Food and Agriculture) 1993–96, Sustainable Development 1994–95. Chairman, Royal Society for the Protection of Birds 1976–81, Vice-President 1981–97, President 1990–91; President, Gloucestershire Naturalists' Society 1981–; Vice-President, Ornithological Society of the Middle East 1987–97; President: Royal Agricultural Society of England 1991–92, British Pig Association 1995–97. Bledisloe Gold Medal for distinguished service to UK agriculture 1967; RSPB Gold Medal for services to bird conservation 1982; RASE Gold Medal for services to agriculture 1991; Massey-Ferguson Award for Services to agriculture. Hon. DSc, Bradford University 1986. Council Member, British Trust for Ornithology 1987–90; President: Rare Breeds Survival Trust 1991–95 and 1997–99, The Hawk and Owl Trust 1991–96. Chairman: BBC Central Agricultural Advisory Committee 1974–80, Countryside Commission 1981–91; Member, Ordnance Survey Advisory Board 1982–85; Chairman: Booker Countryside Advisory Board 1990–96, The National Forest Advisory Board 1991–96. Kt 1984. Hon. Fellow, Royal Agricultural Society of England 1986; Fellow: Royal Agricultural Societies (FRAgS) 1991, Institute of Agricultural Management (FIAgrM) 1992, Royal Agricultural College (FRAC) 2000. *Publications:* Joint Author of books on agriculture as well as contributing to journals on farming and wildlife. *Special Interests:* Farming, Forestry, Environment. *Recreations:* Birds, farming. *Clubs:* Farmers'. Raised to the peerage as Baron Barber of Tewkesbury, of Gotherington in the County of Gloucestershire 1992. The Lord Barber of Tewkesbury, House of Lords, London, SW1A 0PW *Tel:* 020 7219 5353,

DodOnline
An Electronic Directory without rival . . .

Peers' biographies and photographs available with daily updates *via* the internet

For a *free* trial, call Yasmin Mirza, Aby Farsoun or Michael Mand on 020 7630 7643

BARKER, BARONESS   Liberal Democrat

BARKER (Life Baroness); Elizabeth Jean Barker; cr. 1999. Born 31 January 1961. Daughter of Horace Felstead Barker and Lillian Taylor Patrick; educated Dalziel High School, Motherwell, Lanarkshire, Scotland; Broadway School, Oldham, Lancashire; Southampton University (BSc(SocSci) psychology). *Trades Union:* Member, ACCTS. *Career:* Age Concern England; Project co-ordinator, Opportunities for Volunteering Programme 1983–88, Grants officer 1988–92, Field officer based in London 1992–; Management consultant, Age Concern organisations. Liberal Democrat Spokesperson for: Pensions 2000–02, Social Services 2000–. Member, Union of Liberal Students 1979–83, Chair 1982–83; Member: Liberal Party National Executive 1982–83, Liberator Collective which produces *Liberator* magazine 1983–96, Liberal Assembly Committee 1984–97, Federal Policy Committee 1997–; Chair, Liberal Democrat Federal Conference Committee 1997–; Member: Future of Social Services Policy Working Group, Freedom and Fairness for Women Policy Working Group; It's About Freedom – Liberal Democracy Policy Working Group. Trustee, Andy Lawson Memorial Fund. *Special Interests:* Health, Social Services, Ageing, Poverty, Civil Liberties. Raised to the peerage as Baroness Barker, of Anagach in Highland 1999. The Baroness Barker, House of Lords, London, SW1A 0PW *Tel:* 020 7219 2955.

BARNETT, LORD   Labour

BARNETT (Life Baron), Joel Barnett; cr. 1983. Born 14 October 1923. Son of late Louis and Ettie Barnett; educated Elementary school; Manchester Central High School; Correspondence course, qualified as Accountant. Married Lilian Goldstone 1949 (1 daughter). RASC 1939–45. Councillor, Prestwich Council 1956–59; JP, Manchester Bench 1960. *Career:* Accountant; Senior partner, J. C. Allen & Co (now Hacker Young) until 1974; Vice-Chair, BBC 1986–93; Chair, British Screen Finance Ltd 1986–97; Member, International Advisory Board of Unisys Inc. 1989–96; Chair: Education Broadcasting Services Trust Ltd 1993–, Origin (UK) Ltd 1996– (Now Atos Origin (UK) Ltd.), Mercury Recycling Ltd 1996– (Now Mercury Recycling Group Plc 2001–), Helping Hands plc 1997–98; Previously Chairman and Director of a number of public limited companies. *House of Commons:* Contested (Labour) Runcorn 1959 general election; MP (Labour) for Heywood and Royton 1964–83; Chief Secretary to the Treasury 1974–79; Member of Cabinet, February 1977–79. Official Opposition Spokesperson for Financial and Economic matters 1970–74. Official Frontbench Spokesperson for Treasury Affairs 1983–86. Chair, Sub-Committee A of European Communities Select Committee (Economic and Financial Affairs, Trade and External Relations) 1995–97, 1997–98; Member, Select Committees on: European Communities 1997–2000, Monetary Policy of the Bank of England/Economic Affairs 1998–2001; Economic Affairs 2001, House 2003–. Member, Fabian Society. Chair, Hansard Society 1984–90; President, Royal Institute of Public Administration (RIPA) 1988–91; Chair, Mansfield 2010 1993–97. Hon. LLD, Strathclyde University 1983; Hon. Fellow, Birkbeck College, London University. Trustee: Victoria and Albert Museum 1983–97, Open University Foundation 1995–. Chairman, Building Society Ombudsman Council 1986–96. PC 1975. FACCA. *Publications: Inside the Treasury,* 1982. *Recreations:* Walking, reading, theatre, good food, watching Manchester United. Raised to the peerage as Baron Barnett, of Heywood and Royton in Greater Manchester 1983. Rt Hon the Lord Barnett, 7 Hillingdon Road, Whitefield, Manchester, M45 7QQ; House of Lords, London, SW1A 0PW *Tel:* 020 7219 5440 *E-mail:* barnettj@parliament.uk.

BASSAM OF BRIGHTON, LORD   Labour

BASSAM OF BRIGHTON (Life Baron), (John) Steven Bassam; cr. 1997. Born 11 June 1953. Son of late Sydney Stevens and of Enid Bassam; educated Sussex University (BA history 1975); Kent University (MA social work 1979). *Trades Union:* Member, UNISON. Councillor: Brighton Borough Council 1983–97, Leader 1987–96, Brighton and Hove Council 1996–99, Leader 1996–99; Head of Environmental Health and Consumer Issues, Local Government Association 1997–99. *Career:* Social worker, East Sussex County Council 1976–77; Legal adviser, North Lewisham Law Centre 1979–83; Research officer Camden Council 1983–84; Head of environmental health, Trading Standards AMA 1988–97; Consultant adviser, KPMG Capital 1997–99. *House of Lords:*

Parliamentary Under-Secretary of State, Home Office 1999–2001. Government Whip 2001–. Government Spokesperson for: Home Office 1999–, Cabinet Office 2001–, Lord Chancellor's Department 2001–, Office of the Deputy Prime Minister 2002. Alumni Fellow Sussex University 2001. Fellow, Brighton College 2002. Contested Brighton Kemptown (Lab) 1987. *Recreations:* Cricket, walking, running. *Sportsclubs:* Preston Village Cricket Club. Raised to the peerage as Baron Bassam of Brighton, of Brighton in the County of East Sussex 1997. The Lord Bassam of Brighton, House of Lords, London, SW1A 0PW *Tel:* 020 7219 4918; Longstone, 25 Church Place, Brighton, BN2 5JN.

BEAUMONT OF WHITLEY, LORD   Green

BEAUMONT OF WHITLEY (Life Baron), Timothy Wentworth Beaumont; cr. 1967. Born 22 November 1928. Son of late Major Michael Wentworth Beaumont, TD, DL, MP and Hon. Faith Pease, daughter of 1st Baron Gainford, PC, DL; educated Gordonstoun School; Christ Church, Oxford (MA agriculture 1952); Westcott House, Cambridge. Married Mary Rose Wauchope 1955 (1 son 2 daughters and 1 son deceased). *Trades Union:* Member, NUJ 1970–80. *Career:* Ordained 1955; Assistant chaplain, Hong Kong Cathedral 1955–57; Vicar of Christchurch, Kowloon Tong, Hong Kong 1957–59; Owner of various periodicals including: *Time & Tide*, 1960–62, *New Christian*, 1965–70; Chair, Studio Vista Ltd. (book publishers) 1963–68; Member, Parliamentary Assembly Council of Europe and Western European Union 1974–78; Leader, British Liberal Delegation 1977–78; Vice-Chair, Council of Europe Liberal Group 1977–78; Vicar of St Philip's and St Luke's churches, Kew 1986–91; Joint organiser, Southwark Diocese Spiritual Direction Course 1994–96. Liberal Spokesperson for the Arts, Education, the Environment 1983–86; Liberal Democrat Spokesperson for Conservation and Countryside 1993–99; Green Party Spokesperson, especially for Agriculture 2000–. Member, Select Committee on Sustainable Development 1994–95; Co-opted Member, Select Committee on European Communities Sub-Committee C (Environment, Public Health and Consumer Protection) 1997–2000; Member, Ecclesiastical Committee 1997–2002. Hon. Treasurer, Liberal Party 1965–66; Chair, Liberal Party 1967–68, President 1969–70; Editor, *New Outlook* 1972–74; Chair: Liberal Party Education Panel 1972–74, Liberal Party General Election Committee 1974; Co-ordinator, The Green Alliance 1978–80; Director of Policy Promotion, Liberal Party 1980–82; Member, Liberal Democrat Party National Policy Committee 1992–95; Member, Green Party Policy Committee 2000–. Chair, Institute of Research into Mental Retardation 1972–74; President, British Federation of Film Societies 1974–79. The 1999 Green Ribbon Special Lifetime Achievement Award; Green Futures Award for Lifetime Service to the Green Movement 2000. Trustee, The Environmental Research Trust. *Publications: Where shall I put my Cross? exercising Christian responsibility in politics*, 1987; *The End of the Yellow Brick Road: Ways and Means to the Sustainable Society*, 1997. *Special Interests:* Ecological Economics, Poverty, Environment. *Recreations:* Crime fiction, gardening. Raised to the peerage as Baron Beaumont of Whitley, of Child's Hill in the County of Greater London 1967. The Lord Beaumont of Whitley, 40 Elms Road, London, SW4 9EX *Tel:* Home: 020 7498 8664 *Fax:* 020 7720 2904; House of Lords, London, SW1A 0PW *E-mail:* beaumontt@parliament.uk.

BELL, LORD   Conservative

BELL (Life Baron), Timothy John Leigh Bell; cr. 1998. Born 18 October 1941. Son of late Arthur Bell and of Greta Bell; educated Queen Elizabeth's Grammar School, Barnet, Herts. Married Virginia Wallis Hornbrook 1988 (1 son 1 daughter) *Career:* ABC Television 1959–61; Colman Prentis and Varley 1961–63; Hobson Bates 1963–66; Geers Gross 1966–70; Managing Director, Saatchi and Saatchi 1970–75; Chairman and Managing Director, Saatchi and Saatchi Compton 1975–85; Group Chief Executive, Lowe Howard-Spink Campbell Ewald 1985–87; Deputy Chairman, Lowe Hoard-Spink and Bell 1987–89; Chairman, Lowe Bell Communications 1987–; Chairman, Chime Communications plc 1994–. Member: Public Relations Committee, Greater London Fund for the Blind 1979–86, Council, Royal Opera House 1982–85; Chairman, Charity Projects 1984–93, President 1993–; Member: Public Affairs, World Wide Fund for Nature 1985–88, Council, School of Communication Arts 1985–87; Director, Centre for Policy Studies 1989–92; Chairman, Conservative Party Keep the œ Campaign 1999–. Governor, British Film Institute 1983–86;

Special Adviser: to Chairman, National Coal Board 1984–86, to South Bank Board 1985–86. Kt 1990. FIPA, FIPR. *Special Interests:* Golf, Music. *Sportsclubs:* Prince Edward Yacht Club Sydney, RAC. Raised to the peerage as Baron Bell, of Belgravia in the City of Westminster 1998. The Lord Bell, 14 Curzon Street, London, W1J 5HN *Tel:* 020 7495 4044 *Fax:* 020 7491 9860; House of Lords, London, SW1A 0PW *Tel:* 020 7219 5353 *E-mail:* lord.bell@bell-pottinger.co.uk.

BELSTEAD, LORD   Conservative

BELSTEAD (2nd Baron, UK), John Julian Ganzoni; cr. 1938; (Life) Baron Ganzoni 1999; 2nd Bt of Ipswich (UK) 1929. Born 30 September 1932. Son of 1st Baron, DL; educated Eton College; Christ Church, Oxford (MA history 1953). JP for Borough of Ipswich 1962; DL, Suffolk 1979–94, Lord Lieutenant 1994–2002; Chairman, The Parole Board 1992–97. *House of Lords:* First entered House of Lords 1958; Parliamentary Under-Secretary of State: Department of Education and Science 1970–1973, Northern Ireland Office 1973–74, Home Office 1979–82; Minister of State: Foreign and Commonwealth Office 1982–83, Ministry of Agriculture, Fisheries and Food 1983–87, Department of Environment 1987–88; Deputy Leader of House of Lords 1983–87; Lord Privy Seal and Leader of the House of Lords 1987–90; Paymaster General and Deputy to the Secretary of State for Northern Ireland 1990–92. Government Spokesperson for: Trade and Industry 1982–84, Employment 1984–85, Arts and Civil Service 1985–87. Chair: Association of Governing Bodies of Public Schools 1974–79, Independent Schools Joint Committee 1977–79. PC 1983. *Sportsclubs:* All England Lawn Tennis. *Clubs:* MCC, Boodle's. Created a life peer as Baron Ganzoni, of Ipswich in the County of Suffolk 1999. Rt Hon the Lord Belstead, House of Lords, London, SW1A 0PW *Tel:* 020 7219 8682 *Tel:* 01473 735278 *Fax:* 01473 735003.

BERKELEY, LORD   Labour

BERKELEY (18th Baron, E), Anthony Fitzhardinge Gueterbock; cr. 1421; (Life) Baron Guerterbock 2000. Born 20 September 1939. Son of late Brigadier Ernest Adolphus Leopold Gueterbock, and late Hon. Cynthia Ella Gueterbock; educated Eton College; Trinity College, Cambridge (MA mechanical sciences 1991). Married Diana Christine (Dido) Townsend 1965 (2 sons 1 daughter); married Rosalind Julia Georgina Clarke 1999. *Career:* Civil engineer Sir Alexander Gibb and Partners 1961–67; Chairman, George Wimpey plc 1967–87; Public affairs manager, Eurotunnel 1987–95; Chairman: Piggyback Consortium 1995–98, Rail Freight Group 1997–. *House of Lords:* First entered House of Lords 1992. Opposition Whip 1996–97. Opposition Spokesperson for Transport 1996–97. Member, European Communities Committee 1997–99; Co-opted Member, Select Committee on European Communities Sub-Committee B (Energy, Industry and Transport) 1997–99. President: United Kingdom Marine Pilots Association, Road Danger Reduction Forum, Aviation Environment Federation; Board member Partnership Sourcing Limited. Honorary degree. OBE 1989. MICE, FRSA. *Special Interests:* Transport, environment. *Recreations:* Sailing, skiing. Created a life peer as Baron Gueterbock, of Cranford in the London Borough of Hillingdon 2000. The Lord Berkeley, OBE, House of Lords, London, SW1A 0PW *Tel:* 020 7219 0611 *Fax:* 020 7219 5761 *Tel:* 07710 431542 *E-mail:* tony@rfg.org.uk.

BERNSTEIN OF CRAIGWEIL, LORD   Labour

BERNSTEIN OF CRAIGWEIL (Life Baron), Alexander Bernstein; cr. 2000. Born 15 March 1936. Son of late Cecil Bernstein and of Myra Bernstein; educated Stowe School; St John's College, Cambridge (BA economics 1959). Married Vanessa Anne Mills 1962 (1 son 1 daughter) (divorced 1993); married Angela Mary Serota 1995. *Career:* Director, Granada Group plc 1964–96, Chairman 1979–96; Director, Waddington Galleries 1966–; Joint managing director, Granada Television 1971–75. Member of Court: Salford University 1976–87, Manchester University 1983–98; Chairman Royal Exchange Theatre 1983–94, Member National Theatre Development Council 1996–98; Chairman Old Vic Theatre Trust 1998–2002. Hon DLitt, Salford 1981; Hon LLD,

Manchester 1996. Trustee: Granada Foundation 1968–, Trusthouse Charitable Foundation 1996–. *Recreations:* Modern art, skiing, gardening. Raised to the peerage as Baron Bernstein of Craigweil, of Craigweil in the County of West Sussex 2000. The Lord Bernstein of Craigweil, House of Lords, London, SW1A 0PW *Tel:* 020 7219 8629.

BEST, LORD   Crossbencher

BEST (Life Baron), Richard Stuart Best; cr. 2001. Born 22 June 1945. Son of late Walter Stuart Best DL, JP and late Frances Mary, née Chignell; educated Shrewsbury School; Nottingham University (BA social administration 1967). Married Belinda Stemp 1978 (2 daughters 2 sons). Chairman, Hull Partnership Liaison Board 2003–. *Career:* Director: British Churches Housing Trust 1970–73, National Foundation of Housing Associations 1973–88, Joseph Rowntree Foundation 1988–, Joseph Rowntree Housing Trust 1988–; Commissioner, Rural Development Commission 1989–98. House of Lords Audit Committee 2002–. Honorary Degree, Sheffield University 2003. OBE 1988. Hon. Fellow RIBA 2001; Hon Member, Chartered Institute of Housing 2003. *Publications:* Contributor to various books and numerous articles for magazines and journals. *Special Interests:* Housing, regeneration, social policy. *Clubs:* Travellers Club. Raised to the peerage as Baron Best, of Godmanstone in the County of Dorset 2001. The Lord Best, OBE, 40 Water End, York, YO30 6WP *Tel:* 01904 615901 *Fax:* 01904 620072 *E-mail:* richard.best@jrf.org.uk.

BHATIA, LORD   Crossbencher

BHATIA (Life Baron), Amirali Alibhai Bhatia; cr. 2001. Born 18 March 1932; educated Schools in Tanzania, India. Married Nurbanu Amersi Kanji 1954 (3 daughters). *Career:* Chair and managing director Forbes Campbell International Ltd 1980–2001; Director Cashey Finance Ltd 1985–2001; Chair: Forbes Trust 1985–, Ethnic Minority Foundation 1999–. Member Religious Offences Committee 2002–. Chair: The Forbes Trust, Local Investment Fund, Hospice Arts; Chair and Co-founder: Ethnic Minority Foundation (EMF), Council of Ethnic Minorty Voluntary Sector Organisations (CEMVO); Trustee: St. Christopher's Hospice, Project Fullemploy, PRIAE, Aston Mansfield. UK Charity Awards Personality of the Year 2001. Former Trustee: Oxfam, High/Scope Educational Research Foundation, USA, Community Development Foundation, Cities in Schools, Charities Evaluation Services. Former board member, Tower Hamlets College, National Lottery Charities Board, London First, London East Training and Enterprise Council, International Alert, Chair, SITPRO (Simpler Trades Procedures Board). OBE 1997. FRSA. *Recreations:* Swimming, walking, reading, music. *Clubs:* Commonwealth Club, Institute of Directors. Raised to the peerage as Baron Bhatia, of Hampton in the London Borough of Richmond upon Thames 2001. The Lord Bhatia, OBE, Forbes House, 9 Artillery Lane, London, E1 7LP *Tel:* 020 7377 8484 *Fax:* 020 7377 0032 *E-mail:* abhatia@casley.co.uk.

BIFFEN, LORD   Conservative

BIFFEN (Life Baron) (William) John Biffen; cr. 1997. Born 3 November 1930. Son of late Victor W. Biffen; educated Dr Morgan's Grammar School, Bridgwater; Jesus College, Cambridge (BA history 1953). Married Sarah Wood, née Drew 1979 (1 stepson 1 stepdaughter). DL, Shropshire 1993–. *Career:* Tube Investments Ltd. 1953–60; Economist Intelligence Unit 1960–61; Member Board: Glynwed International 1987–2000, Rockware Group 1988–91, J Bibby & Sons 1988–97; Barlow International plc 1997–2001. *House of Commons:* Contested (Conservative) Coventry East 1959 general election; MP (Conservative) for Oswestry by-election 1961–83 and for Shropshire North 1983–97; Chief Secretary to the Treasury 1979–81; Secretary of State for Trade 1981–82; Lord President of the Council 1982–83; Leader of the House of Commons 1982–87; Lord Privy Seal 1983–87. Vice-Chair, Federation of University Conservative and Unionist Associations. Trustee, London Clinic –2002. PC 1979. *Publications: Inside the House of Commons,* 1989. *Special Interests:* EU and its enlargement. Raised to the peerage as Baron Biffen, of Tanat in the County of Shropshire 1997. Rt Hon the Lord Biffen, DL, House of Lords, London, SW1A 0PW *Tel:* 020 7219 6476.

BILLINGHAM, BARONESS   Labour

BILLINGHAM (Life Baroness), Angela Theodora Billingham; cr. 2000. Born 31 July 1939. Daughter of late Theodore and Eva Case; educated Aylesbury Grammar School; College of Education (London); Department of Education, Oxford University (MEd). Married Peter Billingham 1962 (died 1992) (2 daughters). *Trades Union:* Member: NUT, GMB. Councillor: Banbury Borough Council 1970–74, Cherwell District Council 1974–84: Leader of Labour Group; Mayor of Banbury 1976; JP 1976–; Councillor, Oxfordshire County Council 1993–94. *Career:* Teacher 1960–90; Examiner for Education Board 1990–95; MEP for Northamptonshire and Blaby 1994–99: Former Rapporteur on: Postal Services, Strategy for Motor Fuel Emission, Services of General Interest (Public Services); Former Chief Whip, Socialist Group; Chair, Catalyst Corby urban regeneration company 2001–. Member, European Union Committee 2000–; EU Sub-committee D (Environment, Agriculture, Public Health and Consumer Protection) 2000–. Patron: Supporters Direct (football and all professional sport), CSCS (Centre for supporting comprehensive education in the UK). Former Member, Sports Council; Contested Banbury 1992 general election; Chair, Banbury and District Sport for the Disabled; Member, Special Olympics. *Special Interests:* Europe, Education, Health, Sport. *Recreations:* Family, tennis, cinema, bridge, gardening. *Sportsclubs:* Former Captain, Oxfordshire County Tennis Team; Member, Cumberland Lawn Tennis and Squash Club. Raised to the peerage as Baroness Billingham, of Banbury in the County of Oxfordshire 2000. The Baroness Billingham, House of Lords, London, SW1A 0PW *Tel:* 020 7219 5353.

BINGHAM OF CORNHILL, LORD   Crossbencher

BINGHAM OF CORNHILL (Life Baron), Thomas Henry Bingham; cr. 1996. Born 13 October 1933. Son of late Dr Thomas Bingham and Dr Catherine Bingham; educated Sedbergh School; Balliol College, Oxford (MA, Gibbs Scholar in modern history 1956). Married Elizabeth Loxley 1963 (2 sons 1 daughter). 2nd Lieutenant, Royal Ulster Rifles 1952–54; London Irish Rifles (TA) 1954–59. *Career:* Called to the Bar, Gray's Inn 1959, Bencher 1979; Standing Junior Counsel to Department of Employment 1968–72; QC 1972; Recorder of the Crown Court 1975–80; Leader, Investigation into the supply of petroleum products to Rhodesia 1977–78; Judge of the High Court of Justice, Queen's Bench Division and Judge of the Commercial Court 1980–86; Lord Justice of Appeal 1986–92; Chairman: King's Fund Working Parties into Statutory Registration of Osteopaths and Chiropractors 1989–93, Inquiry into the Supervision of the Bank of Credit and Commerce 1991–92; Interceptions Commissioner 1992–94; Master of the Rolls 1992–96; Lord Chief Justice of England and Wales 1996–2000; Senior Lord of Appeal in Ordinary 2000–; Member, Lord Chancellor's Law Reform Committee. Governor, Sedbergh School 1978–88; Chairman, Council of Legal Education 1982–86; Fellow, Winchester 1983–93; Governor, Atlantic College 1984–89; Visitor, Balliol College, Oxford 1986–; Advisory Council, Centre for Commercial Law Studies, Queen Mary and Westfield College, London University 1989–92; Visitor, Royal Postgraduate Medical School 1989–99; Advisory Council on Public Records 1992–96; President, British Records Association 1992–96; Visitor, Nuffield College, Oxford 1992–96; Royal Commission of Historical Manuscripts 1994–2003; Visitor: Darwin College, Cambridge 1996–2000, Templeton College, Oxford 1996–. Six honorary doctorates; Five honorary fellowships, including Balliol College, Oxford. Trustee, Pilgrim Trust 1991–; Magna Carta Trust 1992–96; Butler Trust 2001–. Hon. Bencher, Inn of Court, Northern Ireland 1993, Hon. Bencher, Inner Temple 2000, Hon. Bencher, Middle Temple 2002. Kt 1980; PC 1986. Drapers Company. *Publications:* Assistant Editor, *Chitty on Contracts* (22nd edition), 1961; *The Business of Judging* (OUP) 2000. *Clubs:* Athenaeum. Raised to the peerage as Baron Bingham of Cornhill 1996. Rt Hon the Lord Bingham of Cornhill, House of Lords, London, SW1A 0PW *Tel:* 020 7219 3134.

Visit the Vacher Dod Website...
www.DodOnline.co.uk

BIRT, LORD   Crossbencher

BIRT (Life Baron), John Birt; cr. 2000. Born 10 December 1944. Son of Leo and Ida Birt; educated St Mary's College, Liverpool; St Catherine's College, Oxford (BA engineering science 1966, MA). Married Jane Frances Lake 1965 (1 son 1 daughter). *Career:* Producer, Nice Time 1968–69; Joint editor, World in Action 1969–70; Producer, The Frost Programme 1971–72; Executive producer, Weekend World 1972–74; London Weekend Television: Head of current affairs 1974–77, Controller of features and current affairs 1977–81, Director of programmes 1981–87; BBC: Deputy Director-General 1987–92, Director-General 1992–2000. Member, Wilton Park Academic Council 1980–83; Vice-President, Royal Television Society 1994–2001 (Fellow 1989). Emmy Award, US National Academy of Television, Arts and Sciences 1995. Two honorary university fellowships, three honorary doctorates. Visiting Fellow, Nuffield College, Oxford 1991–99. Kt 1998. *Recreations:* Walking, cinema, football. Raised to the peerage as Baron Birt, of Liverpool in the County of Merseyside 2000. The Lord Birt, House of Lords, London, SW1A 0PW *Tel:* 020 7219 5353.

BLACK OF CROSSHARBOUR, LORD   Conservative

BLACK OF CROSSHARBOUR (Life Baron), Conrad Moffat Black; cr 2001. Born 25 August 1944. Son of George M Black and Jean Elizabeth Riley; educated Carleton University, Canada (BA history and political science 1965); Laval University, Canada (LLL law 1970); McGill University, Canada (MA history 1973). Married Shirley Gail Hishon 1978 (divorced 1992) (2 sons 1 daughter); married Barbara Amiel 1992. *Career:* Chair Sterling Newspapers Ltd 1971–; President Argus Corporation Ltd 1978–79; Chair: Argus Corporation Ltd 1979–, Hollinger Inc, USA 1985–, Hollinger International Inc, Canada 1986–, Telegraph Group Ltd, London 1985–. Hudson Institute; Bilderberg Meetings, International Institute of Strategic Studies, Trilateral Commission on Foreign Relations (New York). Four honorary doctorates from Canadian universities. Order of Canada 1990; PC (Canada) 1992; Knight Commander of the Order of St Gregory the Great (Holy See) 2001. *Publications: A Life in Progress,* 1993; *Duplessis,* 1997, revised as *Render unto Caesar,* 1998. *Clubs:* Athenaeum, Beefsteak, Garrick, Whites. Raised to the peerage as Baron Black of Crossharbour, of Crossharbour in the London Borough of Tower Hamlets 2001. The Lord Black of Crossharbour OC PC (Canada), Telegraph Group Ltd, 1 Canada Square, Canary Wharf, London, E14 5DT *Tel:* 020 7538 6219 *Fax:* 020 7513 2510; House of Lords, London, SW1A 0PW *E-mail:* cblack@hollingermail.com.

BLACKSTONE, BARONESS   Labour

BLACKSTONE (Life Baroness), Tessa Ann Vosper Blackstone; cr. 1987. Born 27 September 1942. Daughter of late Geoffrey Blackstone and of Joanna, née Vosper; educated Ware Grammar School; London School of Economics (BScSoc 1964, PhD). Married Tom Evans 1963 (divorced 1975) (1 son 1 daughter). *Career:* Associate lecturer, Enfield College 1965–66; Assistant lecturer then lecturer, Department of Social Administration, London School of Economics 1966–75; Fellow, Centre for Studies in Social Policy 1972–74; Adviser, Central Policy Review Staff, Cabinet Office 1975–78; Professor of educational administration, University of London Institute of Education 1978–83; Deputy education officer (resources), Inner London Education Authority 1983–86; Fellow, Policy Studies Institute 1987; Master, Birkbeck College, London University October 1987–97. *House of Lords:* Minister of State: Department for Education and Employment (Minister of State for Education and Employment) 1997–2001, Department for Culture, Media and Sport (Minister of State for the Arts) 2001–03. Opposition Spokesperson for: Education and Science 1988–96, Treasury Matters 1990–91; Principal Opposition Spokesperson for Education and Science 1990–92; Opposition Spokesperson for Trade and Industry 1992–96; Principal Opposition Spokesperson for Foreign Affairs 1992–97; Government Spokesperson for: Education and Employment 1997–2001, Culture, Media and Sport 2001–03. Chair and Founder Member, Institute for Public Policy Research 1988–97; Member of Board, Royal Opera House 1987–97, Chairman, Ballet Board 1991–97.

Seven honorary doctorates. Member, Board of Trustees, The Natural History Museum 1992–97. Chair, General Advisory Council of BBC 1987–91. PC 2001. *Publications: A Fair Start*, 1971; Co-author *Inside the Think Tank: Advising the Cabinet* 1971–84, 1988; *The Academic Labour Market*, 1974 (co-author); Co-author *Educational Policy and Educational Inequality*, 1982, *Disadvantage and Education*, 1982, *Response to Adversity*, 1983, *Prison and Penal Reform*, 1992, *Race Relations in Britain*, 1998. *Special Interests:* Education, Social Policy, Foreign Affairs, Arts. *Recreations:* Tennis, walking, ballet, opera, cinema. Raised to the peerage as Baroness Blackstone, of Stoke Newington in the County of Greater London 1987. Rt Hon the Baroness Blackstone, Department for Culture, Media and Sport, 2–4 Cockspur Street, London, SW1Y 5DH *Tel:* 020 7211 6200 *Fax:* 020 7925 5011; House of Lords, London, SW1A 0PW *Tel:* 020 7219 5409 *E-mail:* tessa.blackstone@culture.gsi.gov.uk.

BLACKWELL, LORD   Conservative

BLACKWELL (Life Baron), Norman Roy Blackwell; cr. 1997. Born 29 July 1952. Son of Albert and Frances Blackwell; educated Latymer Upper School, London; Royal Academy of Music (Junior Exhibitioner); Trinity College, Cambridge (BA natural sciences 1973, MA); Wharton Business School, University of Pennsylvania (AM, MBA 1975, PhD finance and economics 1976). Married Brenda Clucas 1974 (3 sons 2 daughters). Board Member, Office of Fair Trading 2003–. *Career:* Plessey Company 1976–78; Partner, McKinsey & Co 1978–95, Partner 1984; Special Adviser, Prime Minister's Policy Unit 1986–87, Head 1995–97; Director, Group Development, NatWest Group 1997–2000; Director, Dixons Group 2000–03; Chair, Centre for Policy Studies 2000–; Special Adviser, KPMG Corporate Finance 2000–; Director: The Corporate Services Group 2000–, Slough Estates 2001–; Chair: SmartStream Technologies Ltd 2001–, Akers Biosciences Inc 2002–03; Director, Standard Life Assurance 2003–. Member Joint Committee on Tax Simplification 2001–. *Publications: Funding the Basic State Pension* (CPS), 2001; *Towards Smaller Government* (CPS), 2001; *Better Healthcare for all* (CPS), 2002; *A defining moment? – the European Constitutional Convention* (CPS) 2003. *Recreations:* Classical music, walking. *Clubs:* Carlton, Royal Automobile. Raised to the peerage as Baron Blackwell, of Woodcote in the County of Surrey 1997. The Lord Blackwell, House of Lords, London, SW1A 0PW *Tel:* 020 7694 3724 *E-mail:* blackwelln@parliament.uk.

BLAKE, LORD   Conservative

BLAKE (Life Baron), Robert Norman William Blake; cr. 1971. Born 23 December 1916. Son of late William Joseph Blake and late Norah Lindley, née Daynes; educated King Edward VI School, Norwich; Magdalen College, Oxford (BA philosophy, politics and economics 1938). Married Patricia Mary Waters 1953 (died 1995), (3 daughters). Served Royal Artillery 1939–46 (despatches 1944); POW Italy 1942–44, escaped 1944. Councillor (Conservative), Oxford City Council 1957–64; JP, Oxford City 1964–85. *Career:* Student and Tutor in Politics, Christ Church, Oxford 1947–68; Provost, The Queen's College, Oxford 1968–87; Pro Vice-Chancellor Oxford University 1971–87; Director Channel Four Television 1983–87. Member, Association of Conservative Peers 1971–. High Steward, Westminster Abbey 1989–99. Hon. Student, Christ Church, Oxford 1977; Hon. Fellow: The Queen's College, Oxford 1987, Pembroke College, Cambridge 1992; Four honorary DLitts from British and American Universities. Trustee, British Museum 1978–88; Rhodes Trustee 1971–87, Chairman 1983–87; Beit Trustee 1973–99. Member, Royal Commission on Historical Manuscripts 1975–97, Chairman 1982–89; President Electoral Reform Society 1986–93. Fellow, British Academy 1967. Member: Dyers' Company 1947–, Prime Warden 1976–77. *Publications:* Several books including: *The Unknown Prime Minister, Bonar Law*, 1955; *Disraeli*, 1966; *The Conservative Party from Peel to Churchill*, 1970 (re-issued as *Peel to Thatcher*, 1985 and *Peel to Major*, 1997); *A History of Rhodesia*, 1977; *The Decline of Power 1915–64*, 1985; *Winston Churchill, a Pocket Biography*, 1998; *Jardine Matheson, Traders of the Far East*, 1999. *Special Interests:* Electoral Reform, Education, Foreign Affairs. *Recreations:* Writing and reading. *Clubs:* Vincent's (Oxford), United Oxford and Cambridge University, Beefsteak, Pratt's, Norfolk (Norwich). Raised to the peerage as Baron Blake, of Braydeston in the County of Norfolk 1971. The Lord Blake, Riverview House, Brundall, Norfolk, NR13 5LA *Tel:* 01603 712133.

BLAKER, LORD   Conservative

BLAKER (Life Baron), Peter Allan Renshaw Blaker; cr. 1994. Born 4 October 1922. Son of late Cedric Blaker, CBE, MC, ED and Louisa Douglas Chapple; educated Shrewsbury School; Toronto University (BA classics 1943); New College, Oxford (MA jurisprudence 1952). Married Jennifer Dixon 1953 (1 son 2 daughters). Served with Argyll and Sutherland Highlanders of Canada 1942–46 (wounded; Captain). *Career:* Admitted Solicitor 1948; Called to the Bar, Lincoln's Inn 1952; HM Foreign Service 1953–64, serving in Cambodia, Canada, the UN Disarmament Conference in Geneva and London; Private secretary to the Minister of State, Foreign Office 1962–64, attended the signing of the Nuclear Test Ban Treaty, Moscow 1963; Chair, Royal Ordnance Factories 1972–74; Chairman of Governors, Welbeck College 1972–74. *House of Commons:* MP (Conservative), Blackpool South 1964–92; PPS to Chancellor of the Exchequer 1970–72; Parliamentary Under-Secretary of State: Army, Ministry of Defence 1972–74, Foreign and Commonwealth Office 1974; Minister of State: FCO 1979–81, Armed Forces, MoD 1981–83 including Chairmanship, Admiralty, Army and RAF Boards. Opposition Whip 1966–67. Hon. Secretary, Franco-British Parliamentary Relations Committee 1975–79. Governor Atlantic Institute 1978–79. Vice-President, Conservative Foreign and Commonwealth Council 1983–92, Patron 1992–. Chair of Governors, Welbeck College 1972–74; Member of Council: Britain-Russia Centre (formerly GB-USSR Ass) 1974–78 and 1992–2000, Vice-Chair 1983–92; Royal Institute for International Affairs (Chatham House) Council 1977–79, 1986–90; Council for Arms Control 1983–92; Freedom Association 1984–97. Trustee, Institute for Negotiation and Conciliation 1984–92. Vice-Chair, Peace Through NATO 1983–93; Member: Public Accounts Commission 1987–92, Intelligence and Security Committee 1996–97. PC 1983; KCMG 1983. *Publications: Coping with the Soviet Union*, 1977; *Small is Dangerous: micro states in a macro world*, 1984. *Special Interests:* Foreign Affairs, Commonwealth, Defence, Tourism. *Recreations:* Opera, tennis, sailing. Raised to the peerage as Baron Blaker, of Blackpool in the County of Lancashire and of Lindfield in the County of West Sussex 1994. Rt Hon the Lord Blaker, KCMG, House of Lords, London, SW1A 0PW *Tel:* 020 7219 8679.

BLATCH, BARONESS   Conservative

BLATCH (Life Baroness), Emily May Blatch; cr. 1987. Born 24 July 1937. Daughter of late Stephen and Sarah Triggs; educated Prenton Girls School, Birkenhead. Married John Richard Blatch 1963 (1 son 1 twin son and daughter and 1 son deceased). Women's Royal Air Force, Air Traffic Control 1955–59. Councillor, Cambridgeshire County Council 1977–89, Leader 1981–85; Member, Peterborough Development Corporation 1984–88. *Career:* Air Traffic Control (Civilian) 1959–63. *House of Lords:* Parliamentary Under-Secretary of State, Department of Environment 1990–91; Minister of State (Heritage) 1991–92; Minister of State: Department for Education 1992–94, Home Office 1994–97; Shadow Minister for Education 1997–2000; Deputy Leader of the Opposition 2000–. Government Whip 1990. Opposition Spokesperson for Education and Skills 1998–. Member: House of Lords' Offices 2000–02, Procedure Committee 2000–, Committee of Selection 2000. Member, Association of Conservative Peers. Vice President, Local Government Association; Member, European Economic and Social Committee 1986–87; President, National Benevolent Institute 1988–; National Vice-President, Alzheimer's Disease Society; Patron: English Schools Orchestra, Huntingdon Male Voice Choir; President Cathedral Camps; Member: Air League Council, Air Cadet Council; Trustee: Royal Air Force Museum, Dorman Museum Appeal. Rotarian Paul Harris Fellow 1992; Hon. LLD, Teesside University 1997. Trustee: Dorman Museum, RAF Museum. CBE 1983; PC 1993. FRSA 1985. *Special Interests:* Local Government Management, Education, Anglo-American Relations. *Recreations:* Family, music, theatre. *Clubs:* Royal Air Force. Raised to the peerage as Baroness Blatch, of Hinchingbrooke, in the County of Cambridgeshire 1987. Rt Hon the Baroness Blatch, CBE, House of Lords, London, SW1A 0PW *Tel:* 020 7219 6712 *E-mail:* blatche@parliament.uk.

Visit the Vacher Dod Website . . .
www.DodOnline.co.uk

BLEASE, LORD — Labour

BLEASE (Life Baron), William John Blease; cr. 1978. Born 28 May 1914. Son of late William John Blease; educated Public elementary school; Technical College, Belfast; National Council Labour Colleges; Workers' Educational Associations (student and voluntary executive member). Married Sarah Evelyn Caldwell 1939 (died 1995) (3 sons 1 daughter). *Trades Union:* Divisional Councillor, Union Shop Workers 1948–59; Northern Ireland Officer, Irish Congress of Trade Unions 1959–75. JP, County Borough of Belfast 1974–. *Career:* Apprentice to provision trade 1930; Branch manager Co-op 1939. Opposition Whip 1979–84. Opposition Spokesperson for Northern Ireland Affairs 1979–83. Parliamentary Labour Party, Northern Ireland Committee Member 1999. Member: British-Irish Inter-Parliamentary Body 1990–2001, CPA, IPU. Member: Northern Ireland Labour Party 1939–87, Labour Party 1949–. President, Northern Ireland Hospice 1980–85, Vice-President 1985–95, Patron 1995–; Member, Board of Governors, St MacNissi's College 1981–91; President: Northern Ireland Care and Resettlement of Offenders (NICRO) 1982–84, Northern Ireland Festival of Youth Society 1982–84, Belfast East Group for Disabled 1983–88; Patron, Northern Ireland Widows' Association 1985–90; Member, Board of Co-operative Development Agency Northern Ireland 1987–91, Patron 1991–2000; President, Belfast Housing Aid 1988–95; Member of Management Board, Rathgael Child Care and Youth Treatment Centre 1989–93; Patron, Action Cancer 1994–; Joint President, Northern Ireland Forum on Industrial Relations (NIFIR) 1994–2000; Hon. President, Institute of Management (Belfast Branch) 1995–2001; Duke of Edinburgh Award, Northern Ireland and Honorary Member 1979–. New Ireland University Peace Trophy 1971–74; Ford Foundation Travel Award, USA 1958. Hon. DLitt, New University of Ulster 1972; Hon. LLD, Queen's University Belfast 1982. Trustee, Belfast Charitable Trust for Integrated Education 1984–88; Member, Board of Trustees, TSB Foundation (Northern Ireland) 1986–94. Northern Ireland Economic Council 1964–75; Member, Independent Broadcasting Authority 1974–79; Research Fellow, New University of Ulster (NUU) 1976–78; Member, Standing Commission on Human Rights 1977–79; Rapporteur to EEC on Cross Border Communications Study on Londonderry-Donegal 1978–79; Chair, Community Service Order Committee 1979–80. Fellow, British Institute of Management 1981. *Publications:* Encyclopaedia of Labour Law Vol 1, *The Trade Union – Movement in Northern Ireland*, 1995. *Recreations:* Gardening, reading. Raised to the peerage as Baron Blease, of Cromac in the City of Belfast 1978. The Lord Blease, House of Lords, London, SW1A 0PW *Tel:* 020 7219 5859 *Fax:* 020 7219 5979.

BLEDISLOE, VISCOUNT — Crossbencher

BLEDISLOE (3rd Viscount, UK), Christopher Hiley Ludlow Bathurst; cr. 1935; 3rd Baron Bledisloe (UK) 1918. Born 24 June 1934. Son of 2nd Viscount, QC; educated Eton College; Trinity College, Oxford. Married Elizabeth Mary Thompson 1962 (2 sons 1 daughter) (divorced 1986). 2nd Lieutenant, 11th Hussars (PAO) 1954–55. *Career:* Called to Bar Gray's Inn 1959; QC 1978. *House of Lords:* First entered House of Lords 1979; Elected hereditary peer 1999–. Member Select Committees on: European Union 1999–, European Union Sub-Committee E (Law and Institutions), Procedure –2002; Member Joint Committee on House of Lords Reform 2002–. Trustee, Equitas. *Clubs:* Garrick. The Viscount Bledisloe, QC, Lydney Park, Gloucestershire, GL15 6BT *Tel:* 01594 842566; Fountain Court, Temple, London, EC4Y 9DH *Tel:* 020 7583 3335.

DodOnline

An Electronic Directory without rival ...

Peers' biographies and photographs available with daily updates *via* the internet

For a *free* trial, call Yasmin Mirza, Aby Farsoun or Michael Mand on 020 7630 7643

BLOOD, BARONESS   Crossbencher

BLOOD (Life Baroness), May Blood; cr. 1999. Born 26 May 1938. Daughter of late William and Mary Blood; educated Linfield Secondary, Belfast. Single. *Trades Union:* Member, TGWU. Non-Executive Director North West Health and Social Services; Queen's University Senate Body 2002. *Career:* Cutting Supervisor, Blackstaff Mill 1952–90; Community Worker, Gt Shankill Partnership 1990–98. Citizen's Global Circle, Boston. UK Council Trustee, Barnardos; Committee Member, Barnardos (NI); Federation Board, Groundwork UK; Board Member, Groundwork (NI); Chair, Intergrated Education Fund. Catherine Dunpfy Peace Global Citizens Awards 1997; Frank Cousins Peace Award 1999. Three honorary doctorates from Northern Ireland. Groundwork Northern Ireland; Northern Ireland Voluntary Trust. MBE 1996. *Special Interests:* Women's Issues, Low Pay, Working Class Issues, Family, Children. *Recreations:* Reading, gardening. Raised to the peerage as Baroness Blood, of Blackwatertown in the County of Armagh 1999. The Baroness Blood, MBE, 7 Blackmountain Place, Belfast, BT13 3TT *Tel:* 028 9032 6514; Alessie Centre, 60 Shankhill Road, Belfast, BT13 2BD *Tel:* 028 9087 4000 *Fax:* 028 9087 4009 *E-mail:* wendy@earlyyears.org.uk.

BLYTH OF ROWINGTON, LORD   Conservative

BLYTH OF ROWINGTON (Life Baron), James Blyth; cr. 1995. Born 8 May 1940. Son of Daniel and Jane Blyth; educated Spiers School; Glasgow University (BA history 1963, MA). Married Pamela Anne Campbell Dixon 1967 (1 daughter and 1 son deceased). *Career:* Mobil Oil Company 1963–69; General Foods Ltd 1969–71; Mars Ltd 1971–74; General Manager: Lucas Batteries Ltd 1974–77, Lucas Aerospace Ltd 1977–81; Head of Defence Sales, Ministry of Defence 1981–85; Non-executive Director, Imperial Group plc 1984–86; Managing Director, Plessey Electronic Systems 1985–86; Chief Executive, The Plessey Co plc 1986–87; Non-executive Director, Cadbury-Schweppes plc 1986–90; Director and Chief Executive, The Boots Company plc 1987–2000, Deputy Chairman 1994–98, Chairman 1998–2000–; Non-executive Director: British Aerospace 1990–94, Anixter Inc 1995–; Director: NatWest Group 1998–2000, Diageo plc 1999–, Chairman 2000–; Senior adviser Greenhill and Company 2000–02, Partner 2002–. Governor, London Business School 1987–96. Hon. LLD, Nottingham University 1992; Hon. Fellow, London Business School 1997. Chairman, Advisory panel on Citizen's Charter 1991–97. Kt 1985. Liveryman, Coachmakers' and Coach Harness Makers' Company. *Recreations:* Skiing, tennis, paintings, theatre. *Sportsclubs:* The Queen's Club. *Clubs:* East India, Devonshire, Sports and Public Schools. Raised to the peerage as Baron Blyth of Rowington, of Rowington in the County of Warwickshire 1995. The Lord Blyth of Rowington, Diageo plc, 8 Henrietta Place, London, W1G 0NB *E-mail:* chairmans.office@diageo.com.

BOOTHROYD, BARONESS   Crossbencher

BOOTHROYD (Life Baroness), Betty Boothroyd; cr. 2001. Born 8 October 1929. Daughter of late Archibald and Mary Boothroyd; educated Dewsbury College of Commerce and Art. Councillor, Hammersmith Borough Council 1965–68. *Career:* Personal/political assistant to: Barbara Castle 1956–58, Lord Walston as Minister of State, Foreign and Commonwealth Office 1962–73; Legislative Assistant, US congressman Silvio O Conte 1960–62; Member of European Parliament July 1975-March 1977. *House of Commons:* Contested Leicester South East 1957 by-election, Peterborough 1959 general election, Nelson & Colne 1968 by-election, Rossendale 1970 general election. Labour Member for West Bromwich 1973–74 and for West Bromwich West 1974–2000; Second Deputy Chairman of Ways and Means and Deputy Speaker 1987–92; Speaker 1992–2000. Assistant Government Whip 1974–76. Chancellor Open University 1994–. Member, Labour Party National Executive Committee 1981–87. Chancellor, Open University 1994–. *The Spectator* Parliamentarian of the Year Award 1992; Personality of the Year 1993; Communicator of the Year 1994.

10 honorary degrees, including Oxford, Cambridge and St Andrews. Chairman, House of Commons Commission 1992–2000. PC 1992. Freedom: Metropolitan Borough of Sandwell, Metropolitan Borough of Kirklees, City of London. Worshipful Company of Feltmakers 1994, Worshipful Company of Glovers of London 2001 (Special Member), Worshipful Company of Lightmongers 2001 (Special Member). *Publications:* Autobiography 2001. *Clubs:* Reform, University Women's. Raised to the peerage as Baroness Boothroyd, of Sandwell in the County of West Midlands 2001. Rt Hon the Baroness Boothroyd, House of Lords, London, SW1A 0PW *Tel:* 020 7219 8673.

BORRIE, LORD   Labour

BORRIE (Life Baron), Gordon Johnson Borrie; cr. 1995. Born 13 March 1931. Son of Stanley Borrie; educated John Bright Grammar School, Llandudno; Manchester University (LLB 1950, LLM 1952). Married Dorene Toland 1960. National Service with Army Legal Services, HQ British Commonwealth Forces in Korea 1952–54. *Career:* Barrister-at-Law and Harmsworth Scholar of the Middle Temple; Called to the Bar, Middle Temple 1952, Bencher 1980; Practiced as barrister in London 1954–57; Lecturer and later senior lecturer, College of Law 1957–64; Birmingham University: senior lecturer in law 1965–68, professor of English law and Director, Institute of Judicial Administration 1969–76, Dean of Faculty of law 1974–76, Hon professor of law 1989–; Member: Parole Board for England and Wales 1971–74, CNAA Legal Studies Board 1971–76; Member, Equal Opportunities Commission 1975–76; Director General of Fair Trading 1976–92; Director: Woolwich Building Society 1992–2000, Three Valleys Water 1992–2003, Chair Commission on Social Justice 1992–94; Director: Mirror Group 1993–99, TeleWest 1994–2001; Chair Direct Marketing Authority 1997–2001; Director, Vivendi Water 1998–2003; Chair: Accountancy Foundation 2000–03, Advertising Standards Authority 2001–. Member: European Union Committee 1997–2000, European Union Sub-committee E (Law and Institutions) 1996–2000. Governor, Birmingham College of Commerce 1966–70; Member: Circuit Advisory Committee, Birmingham Group of Courts 1972–74, Council, Consumers' Association 1972–75, Consumer Protection Advisory Committee 1973–76; Vice-President, Institute of Trading Standards Administration 1985–92 and 1997–, President 1992–97; Patron, Public Concern at Work; Jubilee Patron, MIND; Access to Justice Advisory Board, NSPCC; President, Money Advice Trust. Six honorary law doctorates. Contested (Labour): Croydon North East 1955, Ilford South 1959 general elections. Kt 1982, QC 1986. Fellow: Chartered Institute of Arbitrators, Royal Society of Arts. *Publications: Commercial Law,* 1962; Co-author: *The Consumer, Society and the Law,* 1963, *Law of Contempt,* 1973; *The Development of Consumer Law and Policy* (Hamlyn Lectures) 1984. *Recreations:* Gastronomy, playing the piano, travel. *Clubs:* Garrick, Reform, Pratt's. Raised to the peerage as Baron Borrie, of Abbots Morton in the County of Hereford and Worcester 1995. The Lord Borrie, QC, Manor Farm, Abbots Morton, Worcestershire, WR7 4NA *Tel:* 01386 792330; 4 Brick Court, Temple, London, EC4Y 9AD *Tel:* 020 7353 4434.

BOSTON OF FAVERSHAM, LORD   Crossbencher

BOSTON OF FAVERSHAM (Life Baron), Terence George Boston; cr. 1976. Born 21 March 1930. Son of late George Thomas and Kate Boston; educated Woolwich Polytechnic School; King's College, London University (Inter LLB law 1953). Married Margaret Joyce Head 1962. Commissioned RAF; National Service 1950–52. *Career:* BBC: news sub-editor 1957–60; senior producer, current affairs 1960–64; Called to the Bar, Inner Temple 1960; Head of Chambers (1 Gray's Inn Square) 1973–1983; UK Delegate, UN General Assembly 1976–78; QC 1981; Chairman: TVS Entertainment plc 1980–90, TVS Television Ltd 1986–90, TVS Music Ltd 1983–90. *House of Commons:* Contested Wokingham 1955 and 1959 general elections; MP (Labour) for Kent, Faversham division 1964–70; PPS: to Minister of Public Building and Works 1964–66, to Minister of Power 1966–68, to Minister of Transport 1968–69. Assistant Government Whip 1969–70. *House of Lords:* Minister of State, Home Office 1979; Principal Deputy Chairman of Committees 1992–1994; Chairman of Committees 1994–1997, 1997–2000; Deputy Speaker 1991–; Deputy Chairman of Committees 2001–. Opposition Spokesperson for: Home Office Affairs 1979–84, Defence 1984–86. Member, Select Committee on the Committee work of the House of Lords 1991–92; Chairman: Select

Committee on the European Communities 1992–94, House of Lords' Offices 1994–97, 1997–2000; and other Domestic Select Committees. Member: National Committee Young Socialists (then Labour League of Youth) 1949–51, Executive Committee, International Union of Socialist Youth 1950. Lords' Member, Parliamentary Broadcasting Unit Limited 1994–97, 1997–2000. *Publications:* Co-author *Do We Need A Bill of Rights?*, 1980. *Recreations:* Fell-walking, opera. Raised to the peerage as Baron Boston of Faversham, of Faversham in the County of Kent 1976. The Lord Boston of Faversham, QC, House of Lords, London, SW1A 0PW *Tel:* 020 7219 5605.

BOWNESS, LORD — Conservative

BOWNESS (Life Baron), Peter Spencer Bowness; cr. 1996. Born 19 May 1943. Son of late Hubert Bowness and of Doreen Bowness; educated Whitgift School, Croydon; Law Society School of Law, College of Law. Married 1969 (divorced 1983) (1 daughter); married Mrs Patricia Jane Cook 1984 (1 stepson). Hon. Colonel, 151 (Greater London) Transport Regiment, Royal Corps of Transport (Volunteers) 1988–93. Councillor, London Borough of Croydon 1968–98, Leader 1976–94, Mayor 1979–80; Deputy Chair, Association of Metropolitan Authorities 1978–80; Chair, London Boroughs Association 1978–94; DL, Greater London 1981–; Member: Audit Commission 1983–95, London Residuary Body 1985–93, National Training Task Force 1989–92. *Career:* Admitted Solicitor 1966; Partner, Weightman Sadler, Solicitors, Purley, Surrey 1970–2002; Consultant, Streeter Marshall Solicitors, Warlingham/Purley/Croydon 2002–. *House of Lords:* House of Lords representative to Convention to Draft an EU Charter of Fundamental Rights 1999–2000. Opposition Spokesperson for Environment, Transport and the Regions (Local Government) 1997–98. Chair, Joint Committee on Draft Local Government (Organisation and Standards) Bill 1999; Member: European Union Sub-committee C (Common Foreign and Security Policy) 2000–, Select Committee on Chinook ZD567 2001–02, Human Rights Joint Commitee 2002–. Member, IPU. Member: UK Delegation to Congress of Regional and Local Authorities of Europe (Council of Europe) 1990–98, UK Delegation to the Committee of the Regions of the EU (COR) 1994–98; Member of the Bureau and of Transport and Telecommunications Commission and of Institutional Affairs Commission (COR) 1994–98; Vice-President, European People's Party Group COR 1994–98. Governor, Whitgift Foundation 1982–96; Member, Royal Society for the Protection of Birds. CBE 1981; Kt 1987. Freeman, City of London 1984; Honorary Freeman, London Borough of Croydon 2002. *Special Interests:* Local Government, Europe, London. *Recreations:* Travel, gardening. Raised to the peerage as Baron Bowness, of Warlingham in the County of Surrey and of Croydon in the London Borough of Croydon 1996. The Lord Bowness, CBE, DL, House of Lords, London, SW1A 0PW *Tel:* 020 7219 2575; Three Gables, 10 Westview Road, Warlingham, Surrey, CR6 9JD *Tel:* 01883 624546 *Fax:* 0870 133107 *E-mail:* bowness@globalnet.co.uk; pbowness@streetermarshall.com; bownessp@parliament.uk.

BOYCE, LORD — Crossbencher

BOYCE (Life Baron), Michael Cecil Boyce; cr. 2003. Born 2 April 1943. Son of Commander Hugh Boyce DSC RN and late Madeleine, née Manley; educated Hurstpierpoint College; Britannia Royal Naval College, Dartmouth. Married Harriette Gail Fletcher 1971 (separated 1994) (1 son 1 daughter). Royal Navy 1961–2003: Served HM Submarines Anchorite, Valiant and Conqueror 1965–72; Commanded HM Submarines Oberon 1973–74, Opossum 1974–75, Superb 1979–81, HMS Brilliant 1983–84, Captain Submarine Sea Training 1984–86; Royal College of Defence Studies 1988; Senior Naval Officer Middle East 1989; Director Naval Staff Duties 1989–91; Flag Officer Sea Training 1991–92, Surface Flotilla 1992–95; Commander Anti-Submarine Warfare Striking Force 1992–94; Second Sea Lord and Commander-in-Chief Naval Home Command 1995–97; Commander-in-Chief Fleet and Eastern Atlantic Area and Commander Naval Forces North Western Europe 1977–98; First Sea Lord and Chief of Naval Staff 1988–2001; Chief of the Defence Staff 2001–03. OBE 1982; KCB 1995; GCB 1999; KStJ 2002; Commander, Legion of Merit (US) 2003. Raised to the peerage as Baron Boyce, of Pimlico in the City of Westminster 2003. Admiral the Lord Boyce GCB OBE, House of Lords, London, SW1A 0PW; c/o Naval Secretary, Victory Building, HM Naval Base, Portsmouth, Hampshire, PO1 3ZS.

BRABAZON OF TARA, LORD   Crossbencher

BRABAZON OF TARA (3rd Baron, UK), Ivon Anthony Moore-Brabazon; cr. 1942. Born 20 December 1946. Son of 2nd Baron, CBE; educated Harrow School. Married Harriet Frances de Courcy Hamilton 1979 (1 son 1 daughter). DL, Isle of Wight 1993–. *Career:* Member, Stock Exchange 1972–84. *House of Lords:* First entered House of Lords 1977; Parliamentary Under-Secretary of State, Department of Transport 1986–89; Minister of State: Foreign and Commonwealth Office 1989–90, Department of Transport 1990–92; Elected hereditary peer 1999–; Principal Deputy Chairman of Committees 2001–02; Chairman of Committees 2002–; Deputy Speaker 2002–. Government Whip 1984–86. House of Lords Spokesperson for: Transport 1984–85, Trade and Industry, Treasury and Energy 1985–86; Opposition Spokesperson on Environment, Transport and the Regions (Transport) 1998–2000. Member European Communities Sub-Committee B 1993–97; Member Select Committees on: Public Service 1996–97, House of Lords' Offices/House Committee 2001–, Chair 2003–, Procedure 2001–, Chair 2003–; Chair: European Union 2001–02, Hybrid Instruments 2003–, Liaison 2003–, Personal Bills 2003–, Privileges 2003–, Procedure 2003–, Selection 2003–, Standing Orders (Private Bills) 2003–. President, United Kingdom Warehousing Association 1992–; Deputy Chair, Foundation for Sport and the Arts 1992–; Council Member, Shipwrecked Mariners' Society 1993–; President, Natural Gas Vehicles Association 1995–97; Deputy President, Institute of the Motor Industry 1997–98, President 1998–; President, British International Freight Association 1997–98. Director, Parliamentary Advisory Council for Transport Safety. Fellow, Institute of the Motor Industry 1997–. *Special Interests:* Transport. *Recreations:* Sailing, golf. *Clubs:* Royal Yacht Squadron (Cowes). The Lord Brabazon of Tara, DL, House of Lords, London, SW1A 0PW *Tel:* 020 7219 6796 *E-mail:* brabazoni@parliament.uk.

BRADSHAW, LORD   Liberal Democrat

BRADSHAW (Life Baron), William Peter Bradshaw; cr. 1999. Born 9 September 1936. Son of late Leonard Charles and Ivy Doris Bradshaw; educated Slough Grammar School; Reading University (BA political economy 1957, MA 1960). Married Jill Hayward 1957 (died 2002) (1 son 1 daughter). National Service 1957–59. Councillor, Oxfordshire County Council 1993; Member, Thames Valley Police Authority 1993–95 and 1997–, Vice-Chairman 1999–2003; Member: Commission for Integrated Transport –2001 British Railways Board (Shadow Strategic Rail Authority) 1999–2001. *Career:* Management trainee, British Rail Western Region 1959; Various appointments, London and West of England Division; Divisional manager, Liverpool 1973; Chief operating manager, London Midland Region Crewe 1976; Deputy general manager, LM Region 1977; Chief operations manager, BR Headquarters 1978; Director, Policy Unit 1980; General manager, Western Region BR 1983–85; Professor of transport management, Salford University 1986–92; Chair, Ulsterbus and Citybus Ltd Belfast 1987–93; Special Adviser to Transport Select Committee 1992–97. Liberal Democrat Spokesperson for Transport 2001–. Member European Union, Sub-Committee B (Energy Industry and Transport) 2000–01. Trustee, Oxford Preservation Trust –2000. FCIT. *Publications:* Many chapters and articles on transport issues. *Special Interests:* Transport, Environment, Planning, Police. *Recreations:* Growing hardy perennial plants, playing member of a brass band. *Clubs:* National Liberal. Raised to the peerage as Baron Bradshaw, of Wallingford in the County of Oxfordshire 1999. Professor the Lord Bradshaw, House of Lords, London, SW1A 0PW *Tel:* 020 7219 8621.

DodOnline

An Electronic Directory without rival ...

Peers' biographies and photographs available with daily updates *via* the internet

For a *free* trial, call Yasmin Mirza, Aby Farsoun or Michael Mand on 020 7630 7643

BRAGG, LORD   Labour

BRAGG (Life Baron), Melvyn Bragg; cr. 1998. Born 6 October 1939. Son of Stanley and Mary Ethel Bragg; educated Nelson-Thomlinson Grammar School, Wigton; Wadham College, Oxford (BA modern history 1961, MA). Married Marie-Elisabeth Roche 1961 (died 1971) (1 daughter); married Catherine Mary Haste 1973 (1 son 1 daughter). *Career:* BBC radio and TV producer 1961–67; Novelist 1964–; Writer and broadcaster 1967–; Presenter, BBC TV series: *2nd House* 1973–77, *Read All About It* 1976–77; Presenter and editor: *The South Bank Show* for ITV 1978–, *Start the Week* for Radio 4 1988–98; Controller of arts, London Weekend Television 1990–, Head of Arts 1982–90; Chairman, Border Television 1990–95, Deputy Chairman 1985–90; Governor, London School of Economics 1997; *In Our Time* for Radio 4 1998–. Chancellor, Leeds University 1999–. Member, Arts Council; Chairman, Literature Panel of Arts Council 1977–80; President: Cumbrians for Peace 1982–86, Northern Arts 1983–87, National Campaign for the Arts 1986–, NAW 2000–, MIND 2001–; Chairman RNIB Talking Books 2000–. RTS Gold Medal; John Llewllyn-Rhys Memorial Award for *Without a City Wall*; PEN Awards for Fiction for *The Hired Man*; Richard Dimbleby Award for Outstanding Contribution to Television 1987; Ivor Novello Award for Best Musical *The Hired Man* 1985; Numerous prizes for *The South Bank Show* including a record four Prix Italias; TRIC Award: Radio Programme of the Year for *Start the Week* 1990, Radio Personality of the Year for *Start the Week* 1991; WHS Literary Award for *The Soldier's Return*. Twelve honorary doctorates, four honorary fellowships. Fellow: Royal Society of Literature, Royal Television Society. *Publications: For Want of a Nail*, 1965; *The Second Inheritance*, 1966; *Without a City Wall*, 1968; *The Hired Man*, 1969; *A Place in England*, 1970; *The Nerve*, 1971; *Josh Lawton*, 1972; *The Silken Net*, 1974; *A Christmas Child*, 1976; *Speak for England*, 1976; *Mardi Gras*, (musical) 1976; *Orion*, (TV play) 1977; *Autumn Manoeuvres*, 1978; *Kingdom Come*, 1980; *Love and Glory*, 1983; *Land of the Lakes*, 1983; *Laurence Olivier*, 1984; *The Hired Man*, (musical) 1984; *The Maid of Buttermere*, 1987; *Rich: The Life of Richard Burton*, 1988; *A Time to Dance*, 1990; *Crystal Rooms*, 1992; *King Lear in New York*, (play) 1992; *The Seventh Seal: a study of Ingmar Bergman*, 1993; *Credo*, 1996; *On Giants' Shoulders*, 1998; *The Soldier's Return*, 1999; *A Son of War*, 2001; Screenplays: *Isadora; Jesus Christ Superstar; Clouds of Glory* (with Ken Russell). *Recreations:* Walking, books. *Clubs:* Garrick. Raised to the peerage as Baron Bragg, of Wigton in the County of Cumbria 1998. The Lord Bragg, 12 Hampstead Hill Gardens, London, NW3 2PL.

BRAMALL, LORD   Crossbencher

BRAMALL (Life Baron), Edwin Noel Westby Bramall; cr. 1987. Born 18 December 1923. Son of late Major Edmund Haselden Bramall and late Katharine Bridget Bramall, née Westby; educated Eton College; Army Staff College; Imperial Defence College. Married Dorothy Avril Wentworth, née Albemarle Vernon 1949 (1 son 1 daughter). Joined Army in ranks 1942; Commissioned into KRRC 1943; Served in North West Europe 1944–45; Occupation of Japan 1946–47; Instructor, School of Infantry 1949–51; PSC 1952; GS02 Div HQ and Company Commander, Middle East 1953–58; Instructor, Army Staff College 1958–61; Brevet Leiutenant Colonel 1961; On staff of Lord Mountbatten with special responsibilty for reorganisation of MoD 1963–64; CO, 2 Green Jackets KRRC, Malaysia, during Indonesian confrontation 1965–66; Commander, 5th Airportable BDE 1967–69; IDC 1970; GOC, 1st Division BAOR 1971–73; Lt Gen. 1973; Commander, British Forces, Hong Kong 1973–76; Colonel Commandant, 3rd Battalion Royal Green Jackets 1973–84; General 1976; Commander-in-Chief, UK Land Forces 1976–78; Colonel, 2nd Goorkas 1976–86; Vice-Chief of Defence Staff (Personnel and Logistics) 1978–79; Chief of the General Staff 1979–82; ADC (General) 1979–82; Field Marshal 1982; Chief of the Defence Staff 1982–85. Lord Lieutenant, Greater London 1986–98; JP 1986. Vice-President, SSAFA 1985–; Star and Garter Home 1985–; President: Greater London TAVRA 1986–98, Gurkha Brigade Association 1987–97, London Playing Fields Society 1990–, Greater London Association of Disabled People 1986–98, Age Concern Greater London 1986–91, Not Forgotten Association 1985–, Order of St John 1986–98. Trustee, Imperial War Museum 1983–, Chairman 1990–98. Member, Council of Radley College 1985–. MC 1945; OBE (Mil) 1965; KCB 1974; GCB (Mil) 1979; KG 1990; K St J 1986. Freeman, City of London. Hon Freeman, The Skinners' Company; Hon Freeman, Company of Fire Fighters. *Publications:* Co-Author *The Chiefs*

– The Story of the UK Chiefs of Staff. Special Interests: Defence, Hong Kong, Foreign Affairs, Education. *Recreations:* Cricket, painting, shooting, travel. *Sportsclubs:* I Zingari, Free Foresters, St Emedoc Golf Club. *Clubs:* Travellers', Army and Navy, Pratt's, MCC (President 1988–89), (Hon Life Vice President 1997–). Raised to the peerage as Baron Bramall, of Bushfield in the County of Hampshire 1987. Field Marshal the Lord Bramall, KG, GCB, OBE, MC, House of Lords, London, SW1A 0PW *Tel:* 020 7219 5353.

BRENNAN, LORD   Labour

BRENNAN (Life Baron), Daniel Joseph Brennan; cr. 2000. Born 19 March 1942. Son of late Daniel and Mary Brennan; educated St Bede's Grammar School, Bradford; Manchester University (LLB 1964). Married Pilar Sanchez 1968 (4 sons). *Career:* Called to the Bar, Gray's Inn 1967 (Bencher 1993); Crown Court Recorder 1982–; QC 1985; Member, Criminal Injuries Compensation Board 1989–97; Deputy High Court Judge 1994–; Chair, General Council of the Bar, 1999; Independent Assessor to Home Office on Miscarriages of Justice 2001–. Member Select Committees on: European Union 2000–, EU Sub-committee E (Law and Institutions) 2000–, Animals in Scientific Procedures 2001–02; Chinook Enquiry 2001–02. UK Bar Delegate to CCBE; Councillor of the International Bar Association. President of the Catholic Union of Great Britain 2001–. Two honorary doctorates. Cruz de Honor of the Order of St Raimond de Penafort, Spain 2000. FRSA. *Publications:* General editor *Bullen and Leake on Pleadings*, 2001. *Clubs:* Garrick. Raised to the peerage as Baron Brennan, of Bibury in the Country of Gloucestershire 2000. The Lord Brennan, QC, Matrix Chambers, Griffin Building, Gray's Inn, London, WC1R 5LN *Tel:* 020 7404 3447 *Fax:* 020 7404 3448 *E-mail:* danbrennan@matrixlaw.co.uk.

BRETT, LORD   Labour

BRETT (Life Baron), William Henry Brett; cr. 1999. Born 6 March 1942. Son of late William and Mary Brett; educated Radcliffe Secondary Technical College. Married Jean Valerie 1961 (divorced 1986) (1 son 1 daughter); married Janet Winters 1994 (2 daughters). *Trades Union:* Member: APEX 1960–99, IPMS 1974–. Councillor, London Borough of Lewisham 1964–68. *Career:* Various administrative positions, British Rail 1958–64; Administrative assistant, Transport Salaried Staffs Association 1965–67; North West organiser, National Union of Bank Employees 1966–68; Divisional officer, Association of Scientific Technical and Managerial Staffs 1968–74; Institution of Professionals, Managers and Specialists: Assistant General Secretary 1980–89, General Secretary 1989–99; Member: Executive Committee, Public Services International 1989–99, General Council, Trades Union Congress 1989–99; International Labour Organisation (ILO), Geneva 1992–2003: Member, Governing Body, Vice-Chairman 1993–2003, Chair, Worker Group 1993–2002, Chair, Governing Body 2002–03. FRSA. *Publications: International Labour in the 21st Century*, 1994. *Special Interests:* Human Rights, Development, Economics, Labour Issues. *Recreations:* Reading, walking. *Clubs:* Lydd War Memorial Institute. Raised to the peerage as Baron Brett, of Lydd in the County of Kent 1999. The Lord Brett, 310 Nelson House, Dolphin Square, London, SW1 *Tel:* 020 7219 6151; Sycamore House, 2 Mill Road, Lydd, Romney Marsh, Kent, TN29 9EP *Tel:* 01797 321597 *Fax:* 01797 322148 *E-mail:* brettw@parliament.uk.

DodOnline
An Electronic Directory without rival …

Peers' biographies and photographs available with daily updates *via* the internet

For a *free* trial, call Yasmin Mirza, Aby Farsoun or Michael Mand on 020 7630 7643

BRIDGE OF HARWICH, LORD   Crossbencher

BRIDGE OF HARWICH (Life Baron), Nigel Cyprian Bridge; cr. 1980. Born 26 February 1917. Son of late Commander C. D. C. Bridge, RN; educated Marlborough College. Married Margaret Swinbank 1944 (1 son 2 daughters). Army Service 1940–46, Commissioned KRRC 1941. *Career:* Called to the Bar, Inner Temple 1947, Bencher 1964, Treasurer 1986; Junior Counsel to Treasury (Common Law) 1964–68; Judge of High Court, Queen's Bench Division 1968–75; Presiding Judge, Western Circuit 1972–74; Lord Justice of Appeal 1975–80; Lord of Appeal in Ordinary 1980–92. Chairman, Ecclesiastical Committee (Joint Committee of both Houses of Parliament) 1981–92. Hon. Fellow: American College of Trial Lawyers 1984, Wolfson College, Cambridge 1989. Member, Security Commission 1977–85, Chairman 1982–85; Chairman, Church of England Synodical Government Review 1993–97. Kt 1968; PC 1975. Raised to the peerage as Baron Bridge of Harwich, of Harwich in the County of Essex 1980. Rt Hon the Lord Bridge of Harwich, House of Lords, London, SW1A 0PW *Tel:* 020 7219 0673.

BRIDGEMAN, VISCOUNT   Conservative

BRIDGEMAN (3rd Viscount, UK), Robin John Orlando Bridgeman; cr. 1929. Born 5 December 1930. Son of late Brigadier Hon. Geoffrey Bridgeman, MC, FRCS, second son of 1st Viscount; educated Eton College. Married Victoria Harriet Lucy Turton 1966 (3 sons 1 daughter). 2nd Lieutenant, The Rifle Brigade 1950–51. *Career:* Chartered accountant; Partner, Henderson Crosthwaite and Co., Stockbrokers 1973–86; Director: The Bridgeman Art Library Limited 1972–, Guinness Mahon and Co. Ltd 1988–90, Nestor-BNA plc 1988–. *House of Lords:* First entered House of Lords 1982; Elected hereditary peer 1999–. Opposition Whip 1998–; Former Member: Joint Committee on Statutory Instruments, European Communities, Sub-Committee C (Environment, Public Health and Consumer Protection), Member Select Committee on House of Lords' Offices 2001–02. Chair, Friends of Lambeth Palace Library; Treasurer, New England Company. Special Trustee, Hammersmith and Queen Charlotte's Hospital Authority 1992–2000; Treasurer, Florence Nightingale Aid in Sickness Trust; Chair, Hospital of St John and St Elizabeth; Trustee: Music at Winchester, Winchester Theatre Fund; Treasurer, The New England Company. Knight of Malta. CA. *Special Interests:* Health, Social Services, Environment, Home Affairs, Local Government. *Recreations:* Gardening, music, shooting, skiing. *Clubs:* Beefsteak, MCC, Pitt. The Viscount Bridgeman, 19 Chepstow Road, London, W2 5BP *Tel:* 020 7727 5400 *Fax:* 020 7792 9178 *E-mail:* bridgemanr@parliament.uk.

BRIDGES, LORD   Crossbencher

BRIDGES (2nd Baron, UK), Thomas Edward Bridges; cr. 1957. Born 27 November 1927. Son of 1st Baron, KG, PC, GCB, GCVO, MC, and late Hon. Katharine Dianthe Farrer, daughter of 2nd Baron Farrer; educated Eton College; New College, Oxford (MA modern history 1951). Married Rachel Mary Bunbury 1953 (2 sons 1 daughter). Commissioned in Royal Signals 1946–48. Vice-President, Council for National Parks 2000–. *Career:* Entered HM Foreign Service 1951; Served in Bonn, Berlin, Rio de Janeiro, Athens and Moscow, Private Secretary (Overseas Affairs) to the Prime Minister 1972–74; Royal College of Defence Studies 1975; Minister (Commercial) at British Embassy, Washington, DC 1976–79; Deputy Secretary, Foreign and Commonwealth Office 1979–82; HM Ambassador to Italy 1983–87; Non-executive director, Consolidated Gold Fields plc 1988–90; Member E Anglian Regional Committee, National Trust 1988–97; Independent Board Member, Securities and Futures Authority Ltd 1989–97; Director British Rail (Anglia) 1989–92; Vice-President Council for National Parks 2000–. *House of Lords:* First entered House of Lords 1969; Elected hereditary peer 1999–. Member, Select Committee on the European Communities 1988–92, 1994–98. Chair UNICEF-UK 1989–97. Chairman, UK National Committee for UNICEF 1989–97; Chairman, British-Italian Society 1991–97, Hon. Vice-President 1998–; President, Dolmetsch Foundation. Trustee, Rayne Foundation; Member Hon Committee William Walton Trust 2000–. GCMG 1988. FRSA. *Clubs:* Athenaeum. The Lord Bridges, GCMG, 56 Church Street, Orford, Woodbridge, Suffolk, IP12 2NT *Tel:* 01394 450235.

BRIGGS, LORD   Crossbencher

BRIGGS (Life Baron), Asa Briggs; cr. 1976. Born 7 May 1921. Son of late William Walker Briggs; educated Keighley Grammar School; Sidney Sussex College, Cambridge (BA history 1940); London School of Economics (BSc Econ 1941). Married Susan Anne Banwell 1955 (2 sons 2 daughters). *Career:* Professor of modern history, Leeds University 1955–61; Sussex University: Professor of history, 1961–76, Vice-Chancellor, 1967–76; Provost, Worcester College, Oxford 1976–91. Chancellor, Open University 1979–94. Chairman: European Institute of Education and Social Policy, Paris, 1976–84, Eurydice Consultative Committee, 1996–2002; Vice-chairman, United Nations University 1997–80. President: Social History Society, Victorian Society, Ephemera Society. Marconi Medal for Services to the study of Broadcasting, 1975; French Academy Medal for Architecture, 1982. Chairman, Trustees of the Royal Pavilion, Brighton 1981–; Trustee, Glyndebourne Arts Trust 1966–91; Member, Civic Trust 1976–86. Chairman: Committee on Nursing 1970–72, Advisory Board Redundant Churches 1983–88, Commonwealth of Learning Board 1988–93. Fellow, British Academy; American Academy of Arts and Sciences. Member, Spectacle Makers Company. *Publications:* Various historical works including six volumes on history of British broadcasting: 3 Volumes of a Victorian Trilogy, republished by the Polio Society, *Michael Young, Social Entrepeneur*, 2001. *Special Interests:* Education, Social Policy. *Recreations:* Travel. *Clubs:* Beefsteak, United Oxford and Cambridge University. Raised to the peerage as Baron Briggs, of Lewes in the County of East Sussex 1976. The Lord Briggs, The Caprons, Keere Street, Lewes, East Sussex, BN7 1TY *Tel:* 01273 474704 *Fax:* 01273 474704.

BRIGHTMAN, LORD   Crossbencher

BRIGHTMAN (Life Baron), John Anson Brightman; cr. 1982. Born 20 June 1911. Son of late William Henry Brightman; educated Marlborough College; St John's College, Cambridge (BA law 1932). Married Roxane Ambatielo 1945 (1 son). Able seaman, merchant navy 1939–40; RNVR (Lieutenant-Commander) 1940–46; Anti-submarine warfare base, Tobermory; North Atlantic and Mediterranean convoys; Royal Naval Staff College, Greenwich; Assistant Naval Attaché, Ankara; Staff, South East Asia Command. *Career:* Called to the Bar, Lincoln's Inn 1932; Member, General Council of the Bar 1956–60, 1966–70; QC 1961; Bencher of Lincoln's Inn 1966; Attorney General of the Duchy of Lancaster 1969–70; Judge of the High Court of Justice, Chancery Division 1970–79; Judge of National Industrial Relations Court 1971–74; Lord Justice of Court of Appeal 1979–82; Lord of Appeal in Ordinary 1982–86. Chairman: Select Committee on Parochial and Small Charities 1983–84, Joint Committee on Consolidation Bills 1983–86, Select Committees on: Infant Life Preservation 1986–88, Bristol Urban Development 1988, Spitalfields Market 1989 British Waterways 1991–92, Special Standing Committee on Property Law 1994, Special Public Bill Committeees on: Private International Law 1995, Family Homes and Domestic Violence 1995. Chairman, Tancred's Foundation 1982–96; Member Advisory Committee, Institute of Advanced Legal Studies 2000–. Honorary Fellowship RGS 2001. Honorary Fellow, St John's College, Cambridge 1982. Member: Tax Law Review Committee's Working Party on Parliamentary Procedures for the enactment of Rewritten Tax Law 1996, Joint Committee on: Tax Simplification Bills 2001–, Consolidation Bills 2001–; Member Ecclesiastical Committee 1997–. Kt 1970; PC 1979. FRGS 1993. *Publications: Historical Sites in Franz Josef Land*, 1997; *Drafting Quagmires*, 2002. *Special Interests:* ARCTIC: Greenland, Franz Josef Land, Spitsbergen, Legislative Drafting in Plain English. *Sportsclubs:* Bar Yacht. *Clubs:* Geographical Club. Raised to the peerage as Baron Brightman, of Ibthorpe in the County of Hampshire 1982. Rt Hon the Lord Brightman, 30 Onslow Gardens, London, SW7 3AH *Tel:* 020 7584 8488 *Fax:* 01264 736280; House of Lords, London, SW1A 0PW *Tel:* 020 7219 2034 *Fax:* 020 7219 5979.

Visit the Vacher Dod Website . . .
www.DodOnline.co.uk

BRIGSTOCKE, BARONESS — Conservative

BRIGSTOCKE (Life Baroness), Heather Renwick Brigstocke; cr. 1990. Born 2 September 1929. Daughter of late Squadron-Leader J. R. Brown, DFC and Mrs. M. J. C. Brown; educated Abbey School, Reading; Girton College, Cambridge (BA classics, archaeology and anthropology 1950, MA). Married Geoffrey Brigstocke 1952 (died 1974) (3 sons 1 daughter); married Lord Griffiths, MC (*qv*) 2000. *Career:* Classics mistress, Francis Holland School, London 1951–53; Part-time classics mistress, Godolphin and Latymer School 1954–60; Part-time Latin teacher, National Cathedral School, Washington DC 1962–64; Headmistress, Francis Holland School, London 1965–74; High Mistress, St. Paul's Girls' School, London 1974–89; Non-executive Director, London Weekend Television 1982–90; Member, Programme Advisory Board 1990–93; Independent national director, Times Newspapers Holdings 1990–; Non-executive director, Burberry's 1993–96; Associate director, Great Universal Stores 1993–96. Member, House of Lords Library Sub-Committee 1991–93. Past and present senior posts in numerous organisations, especially educational establishments, including: Governor: Imperial College of Science, Technology and Medicine 1991–99; Member, European Cultural Foundation (UK Committee) 1992–99; Chairman, English Speaking Union 1993–99. Trustee: National Gallery 1975–82, Kennedy Memorial Trust 1980–85, City Technology Colleges Trust 1987–2000; Chairman: Thames LWT Telethon Trust 1990, The Menerva Educational Trust 1991–93; Council Member, National Literacy Trust 1993–; Trustee, The Great Britain Sasakawa Foundation 1994–. Member, Modern Foreign Languages Working Group 1989–90; Commissioner, Museums and Galleries Commission 1992–2000; Hon. Bencher, The Inner Temple 1992–. CBE 2000. *Special Interests:* Education, Health, Broadcasting, Museums and Galleries. Raised to the peerage as Baroness Brigstocke, of Kensington in the Royal Borough of Kensington and Chelsea 1990. The Baroness Brigstocke, CBE, House of Lords, London, SW1A 0PW *Tel:* 020 7219 3000.

BRITTAN OF SPENNITHORNE, LORD — Conservative

BRITTAN OF SPENNITHORNE (Life Baron), Leon Brittan; cr. 2000. Born 25 September 1939. Son of late Dr Joseph Brittan and Mrs Rebecca Brittan; educated Haberdashers' Aske's School; Trinity College, Cambridge (BA English and law 1961, MA) (President of Cambridge Union); Yale University, USA (Henry Fellow 1961–62). Married Diana Peterson 1980 (2 step-daughters). *Career:* Called to the Bar, Inner Temple 1962; QC 1978; Bencher 1983; European Commission: Member 1989–99, Vice President 1989–93 and 1995–99; Vice-Chairman, UBS Warburg/UBS Investment Banking 2000–; Consultant, Herbert Smith 2000–; Advisory Director, Unilever 2000–; Distinguished Visiting Scholar, Yale University 2000–02. *House of Commons:* Contested North Kensington 1966 and 1970; MP (Conservative) for Cleveland and Whitby February 1974–83 and for Richmond, North Yorkshire 1983–88; Minister of State, Home Office 1979–81; Chief Secretary to HM Treasury 1981–83; Home Secretary 1983–85; Secretary of State for Trade and Industry 1985–86. Opposition Spokesperson for: Devolution 1976–79, Employment 1978–79. Chancellor, Teesside University 1993–. Chair: Cambridge University Conservative Association 1960, Bow Group 1964–65; Editor, *Crossbow* 1966–68; Chairman: Society of Conservative Lawyers 1986–88, Conservative Group for Europe 2000–03. Seven honorary doctorates from England and Korea. PC 1981; Kt 1989. *Publications: Defence and Arms Control in a Changing Era*, 1988; *European Competition Policy*, 1992; *The Europe We Need*, 1994; *A Diet of Brussels*, 2000; has written and contributed to various Conservative and other pamphlets and lectures. *Recreations:* Opera, art, cricket, walking. *Clubs:* Carlton, MCC, White's, Pratt's. Raised to the peerage as Baron Brittan of Spennithorne, of Spennithorne in the County of North Yorkshire 2000. Rt Hon the Lord Brittan of Spennithorne, QC, House of Lords, London, SW1A 0PW *Tel:* 020 7219 8670.

DodOnline
An Electronic Directory without rival ...

Peers' biographies and photographs available with daily updates *via* the internet

For a *free* trial, call Yasmin Mirza, Aby Farsoun or Michael Mand on 020 7630 7643

BROOKE OF ALVERTHORPE, LORD   Labour

BROOKE OF ALVERTHORPE (Life Baron), Clive Brooke; cr. 1997. Born 21 June 1942. Son of John and Mary Brooke; educated Thornes House School, Wakefield. Married Lorna Hopkin Roberts 1967. *Trades Union:* Member, Public and Commercial Services Union (PCS). Member Pensions Compensation Board 1996–; Government Partner Director NATS Limited 2001–. *Career:* Inland Revenue Staff Federation: Assistant Secretary 1964–82, Deputy General Secretary 1982–88, General Secretary 1988–95; Joint General Secretary, Public Services Tax and Commerce Union 1996–98; Member, TUC: General Council 1989–96, Executive Committee 1993–96. Chairman, Select Committee on European Communities Sub-Committee B (Energy, Industry and Transport) 1999–2002; Member, Select Committee on European Union 1999–2002; Joint Committee on the House of Lords Reform –2002. Member, Labour Departmental Committees for: Cabinet Office 1998–; Department of Trade and Industry 2001–; Department for Transport 2002–. Member: IPA, CPA. Member: Labour Party, Fabian Society. Patron: Community Initiatives Foundation; European Association for the Treatment of Addiction (UK) 2001–; Sparrow Foundation 2002–; Federation of Drug and Alcohol Practitioners 2003–. Trustee: Community Service Volunteers 1989–, Duke of Edinburgh's Study Conference 1993–, Institute for Public Policy Research 1997–, London Dorchester Committee Trust; Patron ADAPT Trust 1999–; Action on Addiction 2002–. Member: House of Commons Speaker's Commission on Citizenship 1988, Council of Churches for Britain and Ireland Enquiry into Unemployment and the Future of Work 1995–97. FRSA. *Special Interests:* Employment, Transport, Drug and Alcohol Issues. *Recreations:* Travel, community services, politics, church affairs, sailing. Raised to the peerage as Baron Brooke of Alverthorpe, of Alverthorpe in the County of West Yorkshire 1997. The Lord Brooke of Alverthorpe, House of Lords, London, SW1A 0PW *Tel:* 020 7219 0478 *Fax:* 020 7219 6715 *E-mail:* brookec@parliament.uk.

BROOKE OF SUTTON MANDEVILLE, LORD   Conservative

BROOKE OF SUTTON MANDEVILLE (Life Baron), Peter Leonard Brooke; cr 2001. Born 3 March 1934. Son of late Baroness Brooke of Ystradfellte, DBE and late Lord Brooke of Cumnor, PC, CH; educated Marlborough College; Balliol College, Oxford (BA mods and greats 1957, MA 1961); Harvard Business School (MBA 1959); Commonwealth (Harkness) Fund Fellow, Harvard. Married Joan Margaret Smith (died 1985) (3 sons and 1 son deceased); married Lindsay Allinson 1991. Royal Engineers. Chair: Churches Conservation Trust 1995–98, Building Societies Ombudsman Council 1996–2001. *Career:* Research Associate, IMEDE, Lausanne 1960–61; Swiss Correspondent, *Financial Times* 1960–61; Spencer Stuart Management Consultants 1961–79, served in: New York 1969–71, Brussels 1971–72, Chair 1974–79. *House of Commons:* Member (Conservative) for City of London and Westminster South 1977–97, and for Cities of London and Westminster 1997–2001; Parliamentary Under-Secretary of State, Department of Education and Science 1983–85; HM Treasury: Minister of State 1985–87, Paymaster General 1987–89; Secretary of State for: Northern Ireland 1989–92, National Heritage 1992–94. Government Whip 1979–83. Member Delegated Powers and Regulatory Reform Committee 2003–. Member British-Irish Inter Parliamentary Body 1997–. Chair, Conservative Party 1987–89. Council, London University 1995–, Deputy Chair 2001–02, Chair and Pro-Chancellor 2002–; President, British Antique Dealers Association 1995–; President British Art Market Federation 1996–. Senior Fellow, Royal College of Art 1987; Presentation Fellow, King's College, London 1989; Honorary Fellow, Queen Mary and Westfield College 1996; Hon D Litt Westminster University 1999; Hon D Litt London Guildhall University 2001. Wordsworth Trust 1975–: Trustee 1975–2001, Fellow 2001–; Trustee Marlburian Club. PC 1988; CH 1992. Fellow: Society of Antiquaries, Securities Institute 1998. Member, Drapers' Company. *Recreations:* Churches, conservation, cricket, visual arts. *Sportsclubs:* I Zingari. *Clubs:* Beefsteak, Brooks's, City Livery, MCC, St George's (Hanover Sq) Conservative, Coningsby (President), St. Andrew's Youth Club (President). Raised to the peerage as Baron Brooke of Sutton Mandeville, of Sutton Mandeville in the County of Wiltshire 2001. Rt Hon the Lord Brooke of Sutton Mandeville, CH, PC, House of Lords, London, SW1A 0PW *Tel:* 020 7219 2150 *Fax:* 020 7219 8602.

BROOKEBOROUGH, VISCOUNT

BROOKEBOROUGH (3rd Viscount, UK), Alan Henry Brooke; cr. 1952; 7th Bt of Cole Brooke (UK) 1822. Born 30 June 1952. Son of 2nd Viscount, PC; educated Harrow School; Millfield School; Royal Agricultural College, Cirencester. Married Janet Elizabeth Cooke 1980. Commission, 17th/21st Lancers 1971; Transferred to: Ulster Defence Regiment 1977, Royal Irish Regiment 1992; Lieutenant-Colonel 1993; Hon. Colonel, 4th/5th Battalion, The Royal Irish Rangers 1997–. DL, Co. Fermanagh 1987–; High Sheriff, Co. Fermanagh 1995. *Career:* Non-Executive Director: Green Park Health Care Trust 1993–2001, Basel International (Jersey); Personal Lord in Waiting to HM The Queen 1997–; Board Member, Northern Ireland Policing Board 2001–. *House of Lords:* First entered House of Lords 1987; Elected hereditary peer 1999–. Member: Select Committee on European Communities 1998–2002, Sub-Committee D (Agriculture and Food) 1989–93, 1994–97, Sub-Committee B (Energy, Industry and Transport) 1998–2002, Procedure Committee 2003–. Vice-President, Somme Association 1990–; President, Army Benevolent Fund, Northern Ireland 1995–. Fellow, Industry and Parliament Trust. DL. *Special Interests:* Northern Ireland, Agriculture, Tourism, Defence, Health. *Recreations:* Shooting, fishing, gardening, sailing. *Clubs:* Cavalry and Guards, Pratt's, Farmers'. The Viscount Brookeborough, DL, Colebrooke Park, Brookeborough, Enniskillen, Co. Fermanagh, BT94 4DW *Tel:* 028 8953 1402 *Fax:* 028 8953 1686.

BROOKMAN, LORD

BROOKMAN (Life Baron), David Keith Brookman; cr. 1998. Born 3 January 1937. Son of George Henry Brookman, MM and Blodwin Brookman; educated Nantyglo Grammar School, Gwent. Married Patricia Worthington 1958 (3 daughters). *Trades Union:* Member: TUC Educational Advisory Committee for Wales 1976–82, Trades Union Congress 1992–99; European Coal and Steel Committee (ECCC) 1992–2002; International Metal Workers (IMF); President, Iron and Steel Non-Ferrous Department 1992–99. RAF national service 1955–57. *Career:* Steel worker, Richard Thomas and Baldwin, Ebbw Vale 1953–55, 1957–73; Iron and Steel Trades Confederation: Divisional organiser 1973–85, Assistant General Secretary 1985–93, General Secretary 1993–99; Board Member, British Steel (Industry)/UK Steel Enterprise 1993–. Honorary Secretary, International Metalworkers' Federation (British Section) 1993–99: President, International Metalworkers' Federation, Iron, Steel and Non-Ferrous Metals Department 1993–99. Labour Party: Member: Executive Committee, Wales 1982–85, National Constitutional Committee 1987–91, NEC 1991–92. Governor, Gwent College of Higher Education 1980–84. Trustee, Julian Melchett Trust 1985–95. Member: Joint Industrial Council for Slag Industry 1985–93, British Steel Joint Accident Prevention Advisory Committee 1985–93, British Steel Advisory Committee on Education and Training 1986–93, Executive Council, European Metalworkers Federation 1985–95; Member, National T.U. Steel Co-ordinating Committee 1991–, Chairman 1993–; Member, European Coal and Steel Community Consultative Committee 1993–; Joint Secretary: British Steel Strip Trade Board 1993–98, British Steel Joint Standing Committee 1993–98, British Steel European Works Council 1996–99. *Recreations:* Cricket, rugby, reading, keep-fit, golf. *Sportsclubs:* Harpenden Common Golf Club. *Clubs:* Reform. Raised to the peerage as Baron Brookman, of Ebbw Vale in the County of Gwent 1998. The Lord Brookman, 4 Bassett Close, Redbourn, Hertfordshire, AL3 2JY *Tel:* 01582 792066 (Home).

DodOnline

An Electronic Directory without rival . . .

Peers' biographies and photographs available with daily updates *via* the internet

For a *free* trial, call Yasmin Mirza, Aby Farsoun or Michael Mand on 020 7630 7643

BROOKS OF TREMORFA, LORD Labour

BROOKS OF TREMORFA (Life Baron), John Edward Brooks; cr. 1979. Born 12 April 1927. Son of Edward George Brooks; educated Elementary schools; Coleg Harlech. Married 1948 (1 son 1 daughter) (divorced 1956); married Margaret Pringle 1958 (2 sons). Councillor, South Glamorgan County Council 1973–93, Leader 1973–77, 1986–92, Chairman 1981–82; Member, Cardiff Bay Development Corporation 1987–, currently Deputy Chairman; DL, South Glamorgan 1994–. Opposition Spokesperson for Defence 1980–81. Former Member, Joint Committee on Statutory Instruments. Secretary, Cardiff South East Labour Party 1966–; Parliamentary agent to James Callaghan MP 1970 and 1979 general elections; Chairman, Labour Party, Wales 1978–79. Steward, British Boxing Board of Control 1986–, Vice-Chairman 1999–; Chairman: Welsh Sports Hall of Fame 1988–, Sportsmatch Wales 1992–. Hon Fellowship, University of Wales Institute, Cardiff (UWIC). Contested Barry (Labour) February and October 1974 general elections. *Recreations:* Reading, most sports. Raised to the peerage as Baron Brooks of Tremorfa, of Tremorfa in the County of Glamorgan 1979. The Lord Brooks of Tremorfa, DL, 46 Kennerleigh Road, Rumney, Cardiff, CF3 9BJ *Tel:* 01222 791848.

BROUGHAM AND VAUX, LORD Conservative

BROUGHAM AND VAUX (5th Baron, UK), Michael John Brougham; cr. 1860. Born 2 August 1938. Son of 4th Baron; educated Lycée Jaccard, Lausanne; Millfield School; Northampton Institute of Agriculture. Married Olivia Susan Gray 1963 (divorced 1967 and who died 1986) (1 daughter); married Catherine Gulliver 1969 (divorced 1981) (1 son). *House of Lords:* First entered House of Lords 1967; Deputy Chair of Committees 1993–97, 1997–; Deputy Speaker 1995–; Elected hereditary peer 1999–. Member, Select Committees on: House of Lords' Offices 1997–99, Hybrid Instruments 1999–2001, Statutory Instruments Joint Committee 2001–. Vice-chair, Association of Conservative Peers 1998–2002, 2003–. President, Royal Society for the Prevention of Accidents 1986–89, Vice-President 1999–; Chair: The Tax Payers' Society 1989–91, European Secure Vehicle Alliance 1992–; President, National Health Safety Groups Council 1994–. CBE 1995. *Special Interests:* Road Safety, Transport, Motor Industry, Aviation. *Recreations:* Photography, bridge, shooting. The Lord Brougham and Vaux, CBE, 11 Westminster Gardens, Marsham Street, London, SW1P 4JA; House of Lords, London, SW1A 0PW *Tel:* 020 7219 5452.

BROWNE OF MADINGLEY, LORD Crossbencher

BROWNE OF MADINGLEY (Life Baron), John Philip Browne; cr 2001. Born 20 February 1948; educated King's School, Ely; St John's College, Cambridge (BA physics 1969, MA); Stanford University, USA (MS business 1980). Single. *Career:* British Petroleum 1966–; Group chief executive BP Amoco plc 1998–; Vice-president Prince of Wales Business Leaders Forum; Chairman Judge Institue Advisory Board; Numerous non-executive directorships, including Intel Corporation and Goldman Sachs. Member and former chair, British-American Chamber of Commerce; Chairman Advisory Board, Tsinghua School of Economics and Management; Director, Catalyst; Member Advisory Board, Freshfields Bruckhaus Deringer; Chairmans Council, DaimlerChrysler. Council member Foundation for Science and Technology. Royal Academy of Engineering Prince Philip medal for outstanding contribution to engineering 1999; Institute of Energy Melchett Medal 2001; Institute of Management Gold Medal 2001. Eleven honorary doctorates; Four honorary fellowships. Trustee: British Museum, Chicago Symphony Orchestra Honorary. Knighthood 1998. FREng. *Recreations:* Opera, Photography, Pre-Columbian Art. *Clubs:* Athenaeum, Savile. Raised to the peerage as Baron Browne of Madingley, of Cambridge in the County of Cambridgeshire 2001. The Lord Browne of Madingley, House of Lords, London, SW1A 0PW *Tel:* 020 7219 5353.

BROWNE-WILKINSON, LORD   Crossbencher

BROWNE-WILKINSON (Life Baron), Nicolas Christopher Henry Browne-Wilkinson; cr. 1991. Born 30 March 1930. Son of late Canon A. R. Browne-Wilkinson; educated Lancing College; Magdalen College, Oxford (BA). Married Ursula de Lacy Bacon 1955 (died 1987) (3 sons 2 daughters); married Mrs Hilary Tuckwell 1990. *Career:* Called to the Bar, Lincoln's Inn 1953, Bencher 1977; Junior Counsel: to Registrar of Restrictive Trading Agreements 1964–66, to Attorney-General in Charity Matters 1966–72, in bankruptcy to Department of Trade and Industry 1966–72; QC 1972; Judge of the Courts of Appeal of Jersey and Guernsey 1976–77; Judge of the High Court, Chancery Division 1977–83; President, Employment Appeal Tribunal 1981–83; Lord Justice of Appeal 1983–85; President, Senate of the Inns of Court and the Bar 1984–86; Vice-Chancellor of the Supreme Court 1985–91; Lord of Appeal in Ordinary 1991–2000; Senior Law Lord 1998–2000. Chair Privileges Committee Lords' Interests Sub-committee 2003–. Hon. Fellow: St Edmund Hall, Oxford 1987, Magdalen College, Oxford 1993; American College of Trial Lawyers; University of East Anglia 2000. Member, Review Committee of Privy Counsellors of the Anti-terrorism, Crime and Security Act 2002–. PC 1983. *Recreations:* Gardening, music. Raised to the peerage as Baron Browne-Wilkinson, of Camden in the London Borough of Camden 1991. Rt Hon the Lord Browne-Wilkinson, House of Lords, London, SW1A 0PW *Tel:* 020 7219 1639.

BRUCE OF DONINGTON, LORD   Labour

BRUCE OF DONINGTON (Life Baron), Donald William Trevor Bruce; cr. 1974. Born 3 October 1912. Son of late W. T. Bruce; educated The Grammar School, Donington, Lincolnshire. Married Joan Butcher 1939 (1 son 2 daughters and 1 daughter deceased) (divorced 1980), married Mrs Cyrena Shaw Heard 1981. Served Royal Signals 1939; Major 1942; General Staff 1943–45. *Career:* Chartered Accountant; Economist; Member, European Parliament 1975–79. *House of Commons:* MP (Labour), Portsmouth North Division 1945–50; PPS to Minister of Health 1945–50; Contested The Wrekin 1959, 1963. Opposition Spokesman on: Trade and Industry 1985–88, The Treasury 1979–85, 1988–90. Member: House of Lords Select Committee on the European Community 1982–97, Select Committee on House of Lords' Offices 1997–81. Specialist on EU matters 1990–. FCA. *Publications:* Co-author *The State of the Nation*, 1998. *Special Interests:* Finance, Industry, Economic Policy, European Union. *Recreations:* Swimming. Raised to the peerage as Baron Bruce of Donington, of Rickmansworth in the County of Hertfordshire 1974. The Lord Bruce of Donington, House of Lords, London, SW1A 0PW *Tel:* 020 7219 3172.

BULLOCK, LORD   Crossbencher

BULLOCK (Life Baron), Alan Louis Charles Bullock; cr. 1976. Born 13 December 1914. Son of late Rev. Frank Bullock; educated Bradford Grammar School; Wadham College, Oxford. Married Hilda Handy 1940 (3 sons 1 daughter and 1 daughter deceased). *Career:* Fellow, Dean and Tutor in Modern History, New College Oxford 1945–52; Founding Master, St. Catherine's College, Oxford 1960–80; Vice-Chancellor, Oxford University 1969–73. Foreign Member, American Academy of Arts and Sciences; Chairman, Friends of the Ashmolean Museum. Five honorary doctorates. Chairman, National Advisory Council on the Training and Supply of Teachers 1963–65. Kt 1972; Chevalier, Legion D'Honneur (France) 1970; Commander's Cross of the Order of Merit (Germany) 1995. FBA 1967. *Publications: Hitler, A Study in Tyranny; The Liberal Tradition; The Life and Times of Ernest Bevin; Hitler and Stalin: Parallel Lives; Fontana Dictionary of Modern Thought* (revised edition) 1999; *Ernest Bevin* (abridged version) 2002. Raised to the peerage as Baron Bullock, of Leafield in the County of Oxfordshire 1976. The Lord Bullock, St. Catherine's College, Oxford, OX1 3UJ.

Visit the Vacher Dod Website . . .
www.DodOnline.co.uk

BURLISON, LORD Labour

BURLISON (Life Baron), Thomas Henry Burlison; cr. 1997. Born 23 May 1936. Son of Robert and Georgina Burlison; educated Edmondsley, Co. Durham. Married Valerie Stephenson 1981 (2 sons 1 daughter). *Trades Union:* Member, GMB. RAF 1959–61. Councillor Chester-le-Street Rural District Council 1970–74; DL, Tyne and Wear 1997–. *Career:* Panel beater 1951–57; Professional footballer 1953–65; General and Municipal Workers' Union, then General, Municipal, Boilermakers and Allied Trades Union, later GMB: Regional officer 1965–78, Regional secretary 1978–91, Deputy general secretary 1991–. Government Whip (Lord in Waiting) 1999–2001. Government Spokesperson for: Cabinet Office 1999–2001, Defence 1999–2001, Home Office 1999–2000, Health 2000–01. Member House Committee 2003–. Member: Council of Europe, Western European Union. NEC 1987–96; Treasurer, Labour Party 1992–96. Honorary President, Hartlepool United F.C. *Recreations:* Gardening. Raised to the peerage as Baron Burlison, of Rowlands Gill in the County of Tyne and Wear 1997. The Lord Burlison, DL, High Point, West Highhorse Close, Rowlands Gill, Tyne and Wear, NE39 1AL; House of Lords, London, SW1A 0PW *Tel:* 020 7219 5168.

BURNHAM, LORD Conservative

BURNHAM (6th Baron), Hugh John Frederick Lawson; cr. 1903; 6th Bt of Hall Barn and Peterborough Court (UK) 1892. Born 15 August 1931. Son of Major-General 4th Baron, CB, DSO, MC, TD, DL; educated Eton College; Balliol College, Oxford (BA philosophy, politics and economics 1954, MA). Married Hilary Hunter 1955 (1 son 2 daughters). Late Scots Guards. *Career: Daily Telegraph* 1954–86, Deputy Managing Director 1984–86. *House of Lords:* First entered House of Lords 1993; Deputy Speaker 1995–2001, 2002–; Deputy Chair of Committees 1995–2001, 2002–; Elected hereditary peer 1999–. Opposition Deputy Chief Whip 1997–2001. Opposition Spokesman for Defence 1997–2001. Member: Procedure Committee 1997–2000, House of Lords Offices: Library and Computer Sub-Committee 2001–, Refreshment Sub-Committee. Director General, King George's Fund for Sailors 1988–93; Younger Brother of Trinity House 1998. Provincial Grand Master, Buckinghamshire Freemasons; Lords' Member, Parliamentary Broadcasting Unit 2000–. *Special Interests:* Freemasonry. *Recreations:* Horse racing, shooting, sailing. *Clubs:* Pratt's, Royal Yacht Squadron (Cowes), Royal Ocean Racing,Turf. The Lord Burnham, Woodlands Farm, Burnham Road, Beaconsfield, Buckinghamshire, HP9 2SF *Tel:* 01494 674531 *Fax:* 01494 674531; House of Lords, London, SW1A 0PW *Tel:* 020 7219 6906 *Fax:* 020 7219 1444.

BURNS, LORD Crossbencher

BURNS (Life Baron), Terence Burns; cr. 1998. Born 13 March 1944. Son of Patrick and Doris Burns; educated Houghton-le-Spring Grammar School; Manchester University (BA economics 1965). Married Anne Elizabeth Powell 1969 (1 son 2 daughters). *Career:* London Business School: Research posts 1965–70, Lecturer in economics 1970–74, senior lecturer 1974–79, Director, LBS Centre for Economic Forecasting 1976–79, Professor of economics 1979, Fellow 1989; Member, HM Treasury Academic Panel 1976–79; Chief Economic Adviser to the Treasury and Head of the Government Economic Service 1980–91; Visiting Fellow, Nuffield College, Oxford 1989–97; Permanent Secretary, HM Treasury 1991–98; Visiting Professor, Durham University 1995–; Non-executive Director: Legal and General Group plc 1999–2001, Pearson plc 1999–, The British Land Company plc 2000–; Chair: National Lottery Commission 2000–01, Glas Cymru (Welsh Water) 2001, Abbey National plc 2002–. Member, Select Committee on Monetary Policy of the Bank of England/Economic Affairs 1998–; Chair, Financial Services and Markets Joint Committee 1999. Vice-President, Society of Business Economists 1985–98, President 1998–; Vice-President, Royal Economic Society 1992–; Board Member, Manchester Business School 1992–98; Non-executive Director, Queens Park Rangers FC 1996–2001; Governor: Royal Academy of Music 1998–, National Institute of Economic and Social Research. Four honorary degrees. Trustee, Montererai Choir and Orchestra 1998–.

Member: Scottish Fee Support Review, 1998–2000, The Hansard Society Commission on the Scrutiny Role of Parliament 1999–; Chair, Committee of Inquiry into Hunting with Dogs in England and Wales 2000. Kt 1983; GCB 1995. Fellow, London Business School 1989–. *Publications: The Interpretation and Use of Economic Predictions* (*Proceedings of the Royal Society*, London, A 407), 1986; *The UK Government's Financial Strategy* (*Keynes and Economic Policy*), 1988. *Recreations:* Watching football, music, golf. *Sportsclubs:* Ealing Golf, Royal St George's Golf; President, Civil Service Golf Society. *Clubs:* Reform. Raised to the peerage as Baron Burns, of Pitshanger in the London Borough of Ealing 1998. The Lord Burns, GCB, Abbey National plc, Abbey House, Baker Street, London, NW1 6XL *E-mail:* terry.burns@abbeynational.co.uk.

BUSCOMBE, BARONESS — Conservative

BUSCOMBE (Life Baroness), Peta Jane Buscombe; cr. 1998. Born 12 March 1954; educated Hinchley Wood School, Hinchley Wood, Surrey; Rosebery Grammar School, Epsom, Surrey; Inns of Court School of Law; Columbia Law School, New York. Married Philip John Buscombe 1980 (twin sons, 1 daughter). Councillor, South Oxfordshire District Council 1995–99. *Career:* Called to the Bar, Inner Temple 1977; Director R Buxton textile marketing company 1977–79; Legal adviser Dairy Trade Federation 1979–80; Barclays Bank 1980–84: Legal counsel New York, Head Office lawyer and inspector, London Legal Adviser and Assistant Secretary Institute of Practitioners in Advertising 1984–87. Opposition Spokesperson for: Law Officers and Lord Chancellor's Department 1999–, Social Security 1999–2001, Trade and Industry 1999–2000, 2001; Cabinet Office 2000–01, Home Office 2001–02, 2003– Culture, Media and Sport 2002–. Member, IPU. Foundation for International and Commercial Arbitration and Alternative Dispute Resolution. Vice-chairman, Conservative Party 1997–99; President, Slough Conservative Association 1997–2001; Patron Inns of Court School of Law Conservative Association. Contested (Conservative) Slough 1997 general election. *Special Interests:* Law and Order, Trade and Industry, Legal Affairs. *Recreations:* Gardening, boating, tennis, theatre, cinema, shooting. *Sportsclubs:* Rock sailing. Raised to the peerage as Baroness Buscombe, of Goring in the County of Oxfordshire 1998. The Baroness Buscombe, House of Lords, London, SW1A 0PW *Tel:* 020 7219 5356 *E-mail:* buscombep@parliament.uk.

BUTLER OF BROCKWELL, LORD — Crossbencher

BUTLER OF BROCKWELL (Life Baron) (Frederick Edward) Robin Butler; cr. 1998. Born 3 January 1938. Son of late Bernard and Nora Butler; educated Harrow School; University College, Oxford (BA literae humaniores 1961, MA). Married Gillian Lois Galley 1962 (1 son 2 daughters). *Career:* Joined HM Treasury 1961; Private Secretary to Financial Secretary to Treasury 1964–65; Secretary, Budget Committee 1965–69; Seconded to Cabinet Office as Member, Central Policy Review Staff 1971–72; Private Secretary: to Edward Heath MP as Prime Minister 1972–74, to Harold Wilson MP as Prime Minister 1974–75; Returned to HM Treasury as Assistant Secretary, General Expenditure Intelligence Division 1975; Under Secretary, General Expenditure Policy Group 1977–80; Principal Establishment Officer 1980–82; Principal Private Secretary to Margaret Thatcher as Prime Minister 1982–85; Second Permanent Secretary, Public Expenditure, HM Treasury 1985 87; Secretary of the Cabinet and Head of the Home Civil Service 1988–98; Master, University College, Oxford 1998–. Governor, Harrow School 1975–91, Chairman of Governors 1988–91; Chairman of Governors, Dulwich College 1997–2003. Hon. Degrees: Cranfield University, Exeter University, Aston University, London University, Southern Methodist University, USA. Rhodes Trust 2001–. Member, Royal Commission on the Reform of the House of Lords 1999. CVO 1986; KCB 1988; GCB 1992; KG 2003. Hon. Member, The Salters' Company. *Recreations:* Competitive games. *Sportsclubs:* President, Oxford University Rugby Football Member: Fritford Heath Golf, St Enodoc Golf, Dulwich and Sydenham Hill Golf. *Clubs:* Athenaeum, Brooks's, Beefsteak, Anglo-Belgian, MCC; President, Oxford University Rugby Football; Member: Fritford Heath Golf, Dulwich and Sydenham Hill Golf. Raised to the peerage as Baron Butler of Brockwell, of Herne Hill in the London Borough of Lambeth 1998. The Lord Butler of Brockwell, KG, GCB, CVO, University College, Oxford, OX1 4BH *E-mail:* lord.butler@univ.ox.ac.uk.

BUXTON OF ALSA, LORD Conservative

BUXTON OF ALSA (Life Baron), Aubrey Leland Oakes Buxton; cr. 1978. Born 15 July 1918. Son of late Leland Wilberforce Buxton; educated Ampleforth College; Trinity College, Cambridge. Married Pamela Birkin 1946 (died 1983) (2 sons 4 daughters); married Mrs Kathleen Peterson 1988. Served RA 1939–45; In Burma 1942–45. High Sheriff, Essex 1972; DL, Essex 1975–85. *Career:* Chief Executive Anglia TV Group 1958–86; Extra Equerry to HRH the Duke of Edinburgh 1964–97; Member, Countryside Commission 1968–72; Member, Royal Commission on Pollution 1970–75; Chairman: Independent Television News Ltd 1980–86, Oxford Scientific Films Ltd 1982–86; Member, Nature Conservancy Council 1984–86; Chairman: Anglia Television Group 1986–88, Survival Anglia 1986–92. Treasurer, Zoological Society 1976–83; President, Falkland Islands Foundation 1990–96; Vice-president, Royal Society for the Protection of Birds 1980–. Trustee of the British Museum (Natural History) 1971–73; British Trustee, World Wildlife Fund; Trustee, Wildfowl Trust; Founder Buxton Conservation Trust. MC 1943 Mentioned in Despatches 1942; KCVO 1996. *Recreations:* Travel, natural history, painting, conservation. *Clubs:* White's. Raised to the peerage as Baron Buxton of Alsa, of Stiffkey in the County of Norfolk 1978. The Lord Buxton of Alsa, KCVO, MC, Old Hall Farm, Stiffkey, Norfolk, NR23 1QJ *Tel:* 01328 830351.

BYFORD, BARONESS Conservative

BYFORD (Life Baroness), Hazel Byford; cr. 1996. Born 14 January 1941. Daughter of late Sir Cyril Osborne, Conservative MP for Louth 1945–69, and Lady Osborne; educated St Leonard's School, St Andrews; Moulton Agricultural College, Northampton. Married C. Barrie Byford 1962 (1 daughter and 1 son deceased). *Career:* Farmer. Opposition Whip 1997–98. Opposition Spokesperson for: Agriculture December 1998–2002, Environment 1998–2003, Food and Rural Affairs 1998–. Chairman, National Committee, Conservative Women 1990–93; Vice-President, National Union of Conservative and Unionist Associations 1993–95, President 1996–97. WRVS Leicestershire 1961–96, County Organiser 1972–76; Member: CLA, NFU; Patron: Institute of Agricultural Secretaries and Administrators 2000–, Rural Stress Information Network 2001–, VIRSA 1998–, National Farm Attractions Network 2002–. Lay Canon of Leicester Cathedral 2003–; Associate Member, Royal Agricultural Society 2003–. Member: Transport Users' Consultative Committee 1989–94, Rail Users' Consultative Committee 1994–95. DBE 1994. *Recreations:* Golf, reading, bridge. *Clubs:* Farmers'. Raised to the peerage as Baroness Byford, of Rothley in the County of Leicestershire 1996. The Baroness Byford, DBE, House of Lords, London, SW1A 0PW *Tel:* 020 7219 3095 *E-mail:* byfordh@Parliament.uk.

C

CAITHNESS, EARL OF Conservative

CAITHNESS (20th Earl of, S), Malcolm Ian Sinclair; cr. 1455; Lord Berriedale; 15th Bt of Canisbay (NS) 1631. Born 3 November 1948. Son of 19th Earl, CVO, CBE, DSO; educated Marlborough College; Royal Agricultural College, Cirencester. Married Diana Caroline Coke 1975 (died 1994) (1 son 1 daughter). *Career:* Savills 1972–78; Brown and Mumford 1978–80; Director of various companies 1980–84; Director: Victoria Soames Ltd, Residential Property Consultants, and other companies. *House of Lords:* First entered House of Lords 1969; Parliamentary Under-Secretary of State, Department of Transport 1985–86; Minister of State: Home Office 1986–88, Department of Environment 1988–89; Paymaster General and Treasury

Minister 1989–90; Minister of State: Foreign and Commonwealth Office 1990–92, for Aviation and Shipping, Department of Transport 1992–94; Elected hereditary peer 1999–. Government Whip 1984–85. Government Spokesperson on: DHSS 1984–85, Scotland 1984–86. Member: House of Lords' Offices Committee 1997–2000, Procedure Committee. Chief Executive Clan Sinclair Trust; The Queen Elizabeth Castle of Mey Trust. PC 1990, FRICS. FRICS. Rt Hon the Earl of Caithness, House of Lords, London, SW1A 0PW *Tel:* 020 7219 5442.

CALLAGHAN OF CARDIFF, LORD   Labour

CALLAGHAN OF CARDIFF (Life Baron), Leonard James Callaghan; cr. 1987. Born 27 March 1912. Son of late James Callaghan, RN, and Charlotte, née Cundy; educated Portsmouth Northern Secondary School. Married Audrey Elizabeth Moulton 1938 (1 son 2 daughters). *Trades Union:* Member, GMBU; Hon. Member, NUM (South Wales); Life Member, IRSF. Served with Royal Navy during Second World War. *Career:* Inland Revenue 1929–36; Assistant secretary, Inland Revenue Staff Federation 1936–50; Consultant to police federations of England, Wales and Scotland 1955–64. *House of Commons:* MP (Labour) for South Cardiff 1945–50, for Cardiff South East 1950–83, and for Cardiff South and Penarth 1983–87; Parliamentary Secretary, Ministry of Transport 1947–50; Parliamentary and Financial Secretary to the Admiralty 1950–51; Chancellor of the Exchequer 1964–67; Home Secretary 1967–1970; Foreign and Commonwealth Secretary 1974–76; Prime Minister and First Lord of the Treasury 1976–79; Leader of the Opposition 1979–80. Member, The Interaction Council. Member, National Executive Labour Party 1957–80, Treasurer 1967–76, Chairman 1973. Chair, Advisory Committee on Protection of the Sea 1952–63, President 1963–2002, Founding President 2002–; President: United Kingdom Pilots Association 1963–76, International Maritime Pilots Association 1971–76, University College of Wales, Swansea 1986–95, Cardiff Community Housing Association –2002; Patron, Cardiff Community Housing Association 2002–. Hubert H Humphrey International Award 1978. Hon. Fellow, Nuffield College, Oxford 1967 and three other universities; honorary doctorates from nine universities in UK, India and Japan. Member: Cambridge Commonwealth Trust, Pegasus Trust, Inner Temple. Visiting Fellow, Nuffield College, Oxford 1956–67; Hon. Bencher, Inner Temple 1976. PC 1964; Grand Cross First Class of the Order of Merit of the Federal Republic of Germany 1979; KG 1987; Order of the Nile, Egypt. Cardiff 1975, Sheffield 1979, Portsmouth 1991, Swansea 1993. *Publications: A House Divided: the dilemma of Northern Ireland,* 1973; *Time and Chance* (autobiography) 1987. *Special Interests:* Agriculture, Farming. *Clubs:* Athenaeum. Raised to the peerage as Baron Callaghan of Cardiff, of the City of Cardiff in the County of South Glamorgan 1987. Rt Hon the Lord Callaghan of Cardiff, KG, House of Lords, London, SW1A 0PW *Tel:* 020 7219 5802.

CAMERON OF LOCHBROOM, LORD   Crossbencher

CAMERON OF LOCHBROOM (Life Baron), Kenneth John Cameron; cr. 1984. Born 11 June 1931. Son of late Hon. Lord Cameron, KT, DSC; educated The Edinburgh Academy; Corpus Christi, Oxford (MA history 1955); Edinburgh University (LLB 1958). Married Jean Pamela Murray 1964 (2 daughters). Served RNVR 1950–62; Commissioned 1951. *Career:* Called to the Scottish Bar 1958; QC (Scot) 1972; Advocate Depute 1981–84; Senator, College of Justice in Scotland 1989–2003; Lord of Appeal. *House of Lords:* Lord Advocate 1984–89. President, Pensions Appeal Tribunal (Scotland) 1976–84; Chairman, Royal Fine Art Commission for Scotland 1995–. FRSE (Fellow of Royal Society of Edinburgh). *Special Interests:* Law, Local Government, Arts. *Recreations:* Fishing, music, sailing. *Clubs:* Scottish Arts (Edinburgh), New (Edinburgh). Raised to the peerage as Baron Cameron of Lochbroom, of Lochbroom in the District of Ross and Cromarty 1984. Rt Hon the Lord Cameron of Lochbroom, QC, House of Lords, London, SW1A 0PW *Tel:* 020 7219 3000.

Visit the Vacher Dod Website . . .
www.DodOnline.co.uk

CAMPBELL OF ALLOWAY, LORD   Conservative

CAMPBELL OF ALLOWAY (Life Baron), Alan Robertson Campbell; cr. 1981. Born 24 May 1917. Son of late John Kenneth Campbell and Juliet Pinner; educated Aldenham School, Hertfordshire; Ecole des Sciences Politiques, Paris 1934; Trinity Hall, Cambridge (BA economics and law 1938). Married Vivien de Kantzow 1957. Second Lieutenant (Royal Artillery Supplementary Reserve), BEF 1939–40; PoW Colditz 1940–45. *Career:* Called to the Bar, Inner Temple 1939; QC 1965; Bencher 1972; Recorder of the Crown Court 1976–89. Member: Privileges Committee 1982–2000, Murder and Life Imprisonment Committee 1988–89, Consolidation of Bills Joint Committee 1999–, Hybrid Instruments Committee 2000–, Human Rights Joint Committee 2000–02; Ecclesiastical Committee 2000–. Member, Association of Conservative Peers. Consultant to Council of Europe on Industrial Espionage 1965–74. Chair, Legal Research Committee of Society of Conservative Lawyers 1968–80; Co-Patron, Inns of Court School of Law Conservatives 1996–99. Member, Management Committee of UK Association for European Law 1975–89; Vice-President, Association des Juristes Franco-Britanniques 1989–91; President, Colditz Association 1978–. Member: Law Advisory Panel of British Council 1974–79, Scottish Peers' Association. ERD 1996. *Publications:* Co-author *Restrictive Trade Practices and Monopolies,* 1956, 2nd edn 1966, Supplements 1 and 2 1965; *Restrictive Trading Agreements in the Common Market,* 1964, Supplement 1965; *Common Market Law,* vols 1 and 2 1969, vol 3 1973, Supplement 1975; *Industrial Relations Act,* 1971; *EC Competition Law,* 1980; *Trade Unions and the Individual,* 1980. *Special Interests:* Industrial Relations, European Union, Restrictive Trade Practices and Monopolies, Constitutional Affairs. *Clubs:* Beefsteak, Carlton, Pratt's. Raised to the peerage as Baron Campbell of Alloway, of Ayr in the District of Kyle and Carrick 1981. The Lord Campbell of Alloway, ERD, QC, House of Lords, London, SW1A 0PW *Tel:* 020 7219 3147 *E-mail:* campbella@parliament.uk.

CAMPBELL OF CROY, LORD   Conservative

CAMPBELL OF CROY (Life Baron), Gordon Thomas Calthrop Campbell; cr. 1974. Born 8 June 1921. Son of late Major-General J. A. Campbell, DSO and Bar; educated Wellington. Married Nicola Madan 1949 (2 sons 1 daughter). Served Regular Army 1939–46; Instructor at OCTU, Larkhill; Major, 15th Scottish Division 1942 (MC 1944 and Bar 1945); Wounded and disabled 1945. DL, Nairn 1985–98; Vice-Lord Lieutenant of Nairn 1988–98. *Career:* HM Foreign Service 1946–57; Foreign Office 1946–49; UK Permanent Mission UN, New York 1949–52; Private secretary to Secretary to the Cabinet 1954–56; British Embassy, Vienna 1956–57; Partner, Holme Rose Farms and Estate; Consultant to Chevron Corporation 1975–94; Chair, Stoic Insurance Services 1980–93; Director, Alliance and Leicester Building Society 1985–92, Chairman of its Scottish Board to 1994; In retirement, lecturing to the armed forces in the UK and abroad on Second World War battles. *House of Commons:* MP (Conservative), Moray and Nairn 1959–74; Under-Secretary of State for Scotland 1963–64; Secretary of State for Scotland 1970–74. Assistant Government Whip 1961–62; Government Whip and Scottish Whip 1962–63. Opposition Spokesperson for: Defence 1966–68, Scotland (Shadow Cabinet) 1969–70. Opposition Frontbench Spokesperson for many subjects 1975–79. Member, and co-opted to its sub-committees at other times, Select Committee on the European Communities 1975–93; Co-opted to Sub-Committee, Select Committee on Science and Technology 1989–92; Member, Select Committee on Delegated Powers 1993–95. Vice-President and Acting Chair, Advisory Committee on Pollution of the Sea 1980–82, Chair 1987–89; Chair for Scotland of the International Year of Disabled People 1981; Office-bearer in several organisations for the disabled; President, Anglo-Austrian Society 1991–98. Trustee, Thomson Foundation 1980–99. Chair, Scottish Council of Independent Schools 1976–80. MC 1944 and Bar 1945; PC 1970; Gold Grand Cross With Star (Austria). First Fellow, Nuffield Provincial Hospitals Trust, Queen Elizabeth The Queen Mother Fellowship 1980. *Publications: Disablement in the UK, Problems and Prospects,* 1981. *Special Interests:* Foreign Affairs, Defence, Environment, Consumer Affairs. *Recreations:* Music, natural history. Raised to the peerage as Baron Campbell of Croy, of Croy in the County of Nairn 1974. Rt Hon the Lord Campbell of Croy, MC, Flat 907, Howard House, Dolphin Square, London, SW1V 3PQ *Tel:* 020 7219 5353; House of Lords, London, SW1A 0PW *Tel:* 020 7219 5353 *Fax:* 020 7219 5979.

CAMPBELL-SAVOURS, LORD

CAMPBELL-SAVOURS (Life Baron), Dale Norman Campbell-Savours; cr 2001. Born 23 August 1943. Son of late John Lawrence; educated Keswick School; The Sorbonne, Paris. Married Gudrun Kristin Runolfsdottir 1970 (3 sons). Councillor, Ramsbottom Urban District Council 1972–74. *Career:* Former Company director, clock and metal component manufacturing company. *House of Commons:* Contested Darwen February and October 1974 general elections, Workington 1976 by-election; Member for Workington 1979–2001. Opposition Frontbench Spokesperson for: Development and Co-operation 1991–92, Food, Agriculture and Rural Affairs 1992–94, Resigned from Front Bench because of ill health. *Publications: The Case for the Supplementary Vote*, 1990; *The Case for The University of the Lakes*, 1995. *Special Interests:* Investigative Political and Social Work, Education and Health Reform, Application of Industrial Democracy, Member of Cumbria Remuneration Panel. *Recreations:* Trout fishing, music. *Clubs:* Labour Club, Workington. Raised to the peerage as Baron Campbell-Savours, of Allerdale in the County of Cumbria 2001. The Lord Campbell-Savours, House of Lords, London, SW1A 0PW *Tel:* 020 7219 3513.

CANTERBURY, LORD ARCHBISHOP OF

CANTERBURY (104th Archbishop of), Rowan Douglas Williams. Born 14 June 1950. Son of Aneurin and Nancy Williams; educated Dynevor School, Swansea; Christ's College, Cambridge (BA theology 1971, MA); Christ Church and Wadham Colleges, Oxford (DPhil 1975, DD 1989). Married (Hilary) Jane Paul 1981 (1 son 1 daughter). *Career:* Lecturer, College of the Resurrection, Mirfield 1975–77; Ordained priest 1978; Tutor and director of studies, Westcott House, Cambridge 1977–80; Canon theologian, Leicester Cathedral 1981–92; Honorary curate, Chesterton St George, Ely 1980–83; Divinity lecturer, Cambridge 1980–86; Fellow and dean Clare College, Cambridge 1984–86; Lady Margaret professor of divinity and canon of Christ Church, Oxford 1986–92; Bishop of Monmouth 1992–2002; Archbishop of Wales 2000–02; Archbishop of Canterbury 2002–. Three honorary fellowships, including Clare College, Cambridge; Honorary doctorates from British, German and US universities; Fellow British Academy 1990. *Publications: The Wound of Knowledge*, 1979; *Resurrection*, 1982; *The Truce of God*, 1983; Co-author *Beginning Now: Peacemaking Theology*, 1984; *Arius: heresy and tradition*, 1987; Editor *The Making of Orthodoxy*, 1989; *Teresa of Avila*, 1991; *Open to Judgement*, 1994; *After Silent Centuries*, 1994; *Sergii Bulgakov: towards a Russian political theology*, 1999; *On Christian Theology*, 1999; *Lost Icons: Reflections on Cultural Bereavement*, 2000; *Christ on Trial*, 2000; Co-editor *Love's Redeemimg Work*, 2001; *Remembering Jerusalem*, 2001; *Ponder these Things*, 2002. *Special Interests:* Children and Family Issues, Middle East. *Recreations:* Reading, listening to music. *Clubs:* Athenaeum. Most Rev and Right Hon the Archbishop of Canterbury, Lambeth Palace, London, SE1 7JU *Tel:* 020 7898 1200 *Fax:* 020 7261 9836.

CAREY OF CLIFTON, LORD

CAREY OF CLIFTON (Life Baron), George Leonard Carey; cr 2002. Born 13 November 1935. Son of late George and Ruby Carey; educated Bifrons School, Barking; King's College, London (PhD); London College of Divinity (ALCD, BD, MTh). Married Eileen Harmsworth Hood 1960 (2 sons 2 daughters). *Career:* Curate of St Mary's, Islington 1962–66; Lecturer: Oakhill Theological College 1966–70, St John's College, Nottingham; Occasional teacher at Nottingham University 1970–75; Vicar of St Nicholas Church, Durham 1975–82; Principal, Trinity Theological College, Bristol 1982–87; Bishop of Bath and Wells 1987–91; Archbishop of Canterbury 1991–2002; Entered the House of Lords 1991. President: Worldwide Anglican Communion, World Conference for Religion and Peace; Honorary President International Council for Christians and Jews. Eleven honorary doctrates. PC 1991. Fellow of: King's College, London, Christchurch University College, Canterbury. Freeman: City of London, Bath, Wells. Honorary Liveryman, The Scriveners' Company. *Publications: I Believe in Man*, 1975; *God Incarnate*, 1976; Co-author *The Great Acquittal*, 1980;

The Meeting of the Waters, 1985; *The Church in the Market Place*, 1984; *The Gate of Glory*, 1986; *The Message of the Bible*, 1986; *The Great God Robbery*, 1989; *I Believe*, 1991; *Sharing a Vision*, 1993; *Spiritual Journey*, 1994; Co-author *My Journey, Your Journey*, 1996; *Canterbury Letters to the Future*, 1998; *Jesus 2000*, 1999. *Recreations:* Family life, music, poetry, reading, walking. *Clubs:* Athenaeum, Nobodies. Raised to the peerage as Baron Carey of Clifton, of Clifton in the City and Council of Bristol 2002. Rt Rev and Rt Hon the Lord Carey of Clifton, House of Lords, London, SW1A 0PW.

CARLILE OF BERRIEW, LORD   Liberal Democrat

CARLILE OF BERRIEW (Life Baron), Alexander Charles Carlile; cr. 1999. Born 12 February 1948. Son of Dr Erwin Falik; educated Epsom College; King's College, London University (LLB, AKC 1969, FKC 2003); Council of Legal Education. Married Frances Soley 1968 (3 daughters). Member of Council of Justice. *Career:* Called to the Bar, Gray's Inn 1970, Bencher 1992; QC 1984; Crown Court Recorder 1986–; Honorary Recorder of the City of Hereford 1996–; Deputy High Court Judge 1998–. *House of Commons:* Contested (Lib) Flint East, February 1974 and 1979 general elections; MP (Lib) for Montgomery 1983–88, (Lib Dem) 1988–97. Liberal Spokesperson for Home Affairs, Law 1985–88; Alliance Spokesperson for Legal Affairs 1987; SLD Spokesperson for Foreign Affairs 1988–89; Liberal Democrat Spokesperson for: Legal Affairs 1989–90, Trade and Industry 1990–92, Wales 1992–97, Employment 1992–94, Health 1994–95, Justice, Home Affairs and Immigration 1995–97. Liberal Democrat Spokesperson for Wales 2001–. Chair, Welsh Liberal Party 1980–82; Leader, Welsh Liberal Democrat Party 1992–97; President, Liberal Democrats Wales 1997–99. Patron, National Depression Campaign. Fellow, King's College, London (FKC) 2003. Trustee Nuffield Trust, Council Member and Trustee, NACRO; Trustee: Rekindle Charity (mental health), White Ensign Association Ltd; Member Epsom College Development Board. Lay member, General Medical Council 1989–99; Member, Advisory Council on Public Records 1989–95; Non-executive Director, Wynnstay Group plc. Fellow: Institute of Advanced Legal Studies, Industry and Parliament Trust, King's College. *Publications:* Various Articles. *Special Interests:* Home Affairs, Agriculture, Legal Affairs, United Nations, Central and Eastern Europe, Arts, Wales, Mental Health, Medical Profession. *Recreations:* Family, politics, theatre, food, Association Football. *Clubs:* Athenaeum. Raised to the peerage as Baron Carlile of Berriew, of Berriew in the County of Powys 1999. The Lord Carlile of Berriew, QC, 9–12 Bell Yard, London, WC2A 2LF *Tel:* 020 7400 1800 *Fax:* 020 7681 1250 *E-mail:* carlilea@parliament.uk.

CARLISLE OF BUCKLOW, LORD   Conservative

CARLISLE OF BUCKLOW (Life Baron), Mark Carlisle; cr. 1987. Born 7 July 1929. Son of late Philip and Mary Carlisle; educated Radley College; Manchester University (LLB 1953). Married Sandra Joyce Des Voeux 1959 (1 daughter). National service as 2nd Lieutenant, Royal Army Education Corps 1948–50. DL, Cheshire 1983–. *Career:* Called to the Bar Gray's Inn 1954, Entrance Scholar Junior; Northern Circuit; Practised in Manchester from February 1954; Member of Bar Council 1966–70; QC 1971; Recorder 1976–98; Chair, Criminal Injuries Compensation Board 1989–2000; Judge of the Courts of Appeal of Jersey and Guernsey 1990–99; Chair, Manchester and London Investment Trust plc 1997–2000. *House of Commons:* Contested (Conservative) St. Helens 1958 and 1959 general elections; MP (Conservative) for Runcorn 1964–83, for Warrington South 1983–87: Under-Secretary of State, Home Office 1970–72; Minister of State, Home Office 1972–74; Secretary of State for Education and Science 1979–81. Hon. Treasurer, Commonwealth Parliamentary Association 1982–85, Vice-Chairman (UK Branch) 1985–87. Chair: Federation of University Conservative and Union Associations 1953–54, Society of Conservative Lawyers 1996–2001. Trustee, The Foundation for Children with Leukaemia; Chairman, The Drugwatch Trust. Member: Home Office Advisory Council on the Penal System 1966–70, BBC Advisory Council 1975–79; Chairman: Parole Review Committee 1987–88, Prime Minister's Advisory Committee on Business Appointments for Crown Servants 1988–1998, Commonwealth Observer Group to the Elections in Lesotho 1993. PC 1979. *Special Interests:* Penal Affairs and Policy, Education, Law, Human Rights. *Recreations:* Golf. *Clubs:* Garrick, St James' (Manchester). Raised to the peerage as Baron Carlisle of Bucklow, of Mobberley in the County of Cheshire 1987. Rt Hon the Lord Carlisle of Bucklow, QC, DL, 3 Holt Gardens, Blakeley Lane, Mobberley, Cheshire, WA16 7LH *Tel:* 01565 872275 *Fax:* 01565 872775.

CARNEGY OF LOUR, BARONESS   Conservative

CARNEGY OF LOUR (Life Baroness), Elizabeth Patricia Carnegy of Lour; cr. 1982. Born 28 April 1925. Daughter of late Lieutenant-Colonel U. E. C. Carnegy of Lour, DSO, MC, DL, and of late Violet Carnegy, MBE; educated Downham School, Essex. Single. Co-opted Education Committee, Angus County Council 1967–75; Honorary Sheriff 1969–84; Councillor, Tayside Regional Council 1974–82; Convener, Education Committee 1976–82; DL, Angus 1988–2001; Chair, Tayside Committee on Medical Research Ethics 1990–93. *Career:* Farmer 1956–89. Member: House of Lords European Communities Select Committee 1993–96, Sub-committee D (Agriculture and Food) 1990–93, Sub-committee E (Law and Institutions) 1993–97; Delegated Powers and Regulatory Reform Select Committee 2001–. Member, Association of Conservative Peers, Vice-Chairman 1990–94. Served Cavendish Laboratory, Cambridge 1943–46; Girl Guides Association: Training adviser, Scotland 1958–62, Commonwealth HQ 1963–65, President for Scotland 1979–89; Formerly Member, Visiting Committee Noranside Borstal Institution; Member, Council and Finance Committee of Open University 1984–96; Honorary President, Scottish Library Association 1989–92, Honorary Member 1996–; Member of Court, St Andrews University 1991–96. Three honorary doctorates. Member, Administration Council, Royal Jubilee Trusts 1984–88. Chair, Working Party on Professional Training in Community Education Scotland 1975–77; Commissioner, Manpower Services Commission 1979–82; Member, Scottish Council for Tertiary Education 1979–84; Chairman, Manpower Services Commission Committee for Scotland 1980–83; Member, Scottish Economic Council 1980–93; Chair, Scottish Council for Education 1981–88; Hon. Fellow, Scottish Community Education Council 1993. FRSA. *Special Interests:* Education, European Union, Local Government, Scottish Affairs, Countryside, Medical Research Ethics, Constitution, Health Service. *Clubs:* Lansdowne, New (Edinburgh). Raised to the peerage as Baroness Carnegy of Lour, of Lour in the District of Angus 1982. The Baroness Carnegy of Lour, DL, Lour, Forfar, Angus, DD8 2 LR *Tel:* 01307 820237 *Tel:* 020 7219 8671.

CARR OF HADLEY, LORD   Conservative

CARR OF HADLEY (Life Baron), (Leonard) Robert Carr; cr. 1976. Born 11 November 1916. Son of late Ralph Edward Carr; educated Westminster School; Gonville and Caius College, Cambridge (BA natural science 1938). Married Joan Kathleen Twining 1943 (2 daughters and 1 son deceased). *Career:* Director, John Dale Ltd 1948–55, Chairman 1958–63, 1965–70; Member, London Board Scottish Union and National Insurance Co. 1958–63; Director, S. Hoffnung & Co. 1958–63, 1965–70, 1974–80; Deputy Chairman, Metal Closures Group Ltd 1960–63, 1965–70, Director 1965–70; Director, Securicor Ltd and Security Services Ltd 1961–63, 1965–70, 1974–85; Member, Norwich Union Insurance Group (London Advisory Board) 1965–70, 1974–76; Director, SGB Group Ltd 1974–86; Member of Council, CBI 1976–78; Director, Prudential Assurance Co. 1976–85, Chairman 1980–85; Chairman, CBI Education and Training Committee 1977–82; Director: Cadbury Schweppes Ltd 1979–87, Prudential Corporation 1979–89, Chairman 1980–85; Chairman, CBI Special Programme Unit 1981–84; Chairman, Business in the Community 1984–87; Advisory Director: P. A. Strategy Partners 1985–87, Lek Partnership 1987–95. *House of Commons:* MP (Conservative) for: Mitcham 1950–74, Sutton Carshalton 1974–76; PPS to Anthony Eden as: Secretary of State for Foreign Affairs 1951–55, Prime Minister 1955; Parliamentary Secretary, Ministry of Labour 1955–58; Secretary for Technical Co-operation 1963–64; Secretary of State for Employment 1970–72; Lord President of the Council and Leader of the House of Commons 1972; Home Secretary 1972–74. Opposition Spokesperson for: Aviation 1965–67, Labour 1967–70, Treasury 1974–75. Opposition Spokesman on Economics, Industrial and Home Affairs 1976–79. Member, House of Lords Select Committee on the European Communities 1990–93. Imperial College of Science and Technology 1959–63, 1976–87; Vice-President, Birmingham Settlement; Vice-President, CORDA (Coronary Artery Disease Research Association). Fellow: Imperial College 1985, Gonville and Caius College 2001. PC 1963. Companion: British Institute of Management, Institute of Personel Management. *Publications:* Co-author: *One Nation*, 1950, *Change is our Ally*, 1954, *The Responsible Society*, 1958, *One Europe*, 1965. *Recreations:* Lawn tennis, music, gardening. *Sportsclubs:* President, Surrey County Cricket Club 1985–86; Vice-President, All England Lawn Tennis Club 1990–. *Clubs:* Brooks's, MCC. Raised to the peerage as Baron Carr of Hadley, of Monken Hadley in the County of Greater London 1976. Rt Hon the Lord Carr of Hadley, 14 North Court, Great Peter Street, London, SW1P 3LL.

CARRINGTON, LORD   Conservative

CARRINGTON (6th Baron, I), Peter Alexander Rupert Carington; cr. 1796; 6th Baron Carrington (GB) 1797; (Life) Baron Carington of Upton 1999. Born 6 June 1919. Son of 5th Baron, DL, and late Hon. Sybil Marion Colville, daughter of 2nd Viscount Colville of Culross; educated Eton College; RMC, Sandhurst. Married Iona McClean 1942 (1 son 2 daughters). Major, Grenadier Guards, served North West Europe 1940–46. JP, Bucks 1948; DL, Bucks 1951. *Career:* UK High Commissioner in Australia 1956–59; Chairman, GEC 1983–84; Secretary-General, NATO 1984–88; Chairman, Christies International plc 1988–93; Director, The Telegraph plc 1990–; Chairman, EC Peace Conference on Yugoslavia 1991–92. Chancellor, Reading University 1992–. *House of Lords:* First entered House of Lords 1940; Joint Parliamentary Secretary, Ministry of Agriculture and Fisheries 1951–54; Parliamentary Secretary, Ministry of Defence 1954–56; First Lord of the Admiralty 1959–63; Minister without Portfolio and Leader of the House of Lords October 1963-October 1964; Leader of Opposition 1964–70, 1974–79; Secretary of State for Defence 1970–74; Minister of Aviation Supply 1971–74; Secretary of State for: Energy January-February 1974, Foreign and Commonwealth Affairs 1979–82. Opposition Whip 1947–51. Chairman, Conservative Party 1972–74. President, The Pilgrims 1983–2002; Elder Brother, Trinity House 1984; President, VSO 1993–98. Hon. LLD, Cambridge 1981; Hon. Fellow, St Antony's College, Oxford 1982, plus 12 honorary degrees from universities in the United Kingdom and abroad. Trustee, Cambridge Commonwealth Trust 1982–; Chairman of Trustees, Victoria and Albert Museum 1983–88; Trustee: The Dulverton Trust 1981–, The Royal Fine Art Commission 1987–, Museum of Garden History 1990–, Daiwa Anglo Japanese Foundation 1989, Winston Churchill Memorial Trust –2001. Hon. Bencher of the Middle Temple 1983–; Chancellor of the Order of St Michael and St George 1984–94; Chancellor of the Most Noble Order of the Garter 1994–. MC 1945; PC 1959; CH 1983; KG 1985; GCMG 1988. *Publications: Reflect on Things Past* (autobiography) 1988. *Clubs:* Pratt's, White's. Created a life peer as Baron Carington of Upton, of Upton in the County of Nottinghamshire 1999. Rt Hon the Lord Carrington, KG, GCMG, CH, MC, DL, The Manor House, Bledlow, Princes Risborough, Buckinghamshire, HP27 9PB *Tel:* 01844 343499; 32A Ovington Square, London, SW3 1LR *Tel:* 020 7584 1476 *Fax:* 020 7823 9051 *E-mail:* lc@lordcarrington.demon.co.uk.

CARTER, LORD   Labour

CARTER (Life Baron), Denis Victor Carter; cr. 1987. Born 17 January 1932. Son of late Albert and Annie Carter; educated Xaverian College, Brighton; East Sussex College of Agriculture 1954–55; Essex College of Agriculture (Queen's Prize of the Royal Agricultural Society of England and Fream Memorial Prize) 1955–57; Worcester College, Oxford (BLitt 1976). Married Teresa Mary Greengoe 1957 (1 daughter and 1 son deceased). National Service, Egypt 1950–52. Member, Northfield Committee of enquiry into ownership and occupancy of agricultural land 1977–79; JP 1966–70. *Career:* Audit clerk 1949–50, 1953; Farmworker 1953–54; Agricultural education 1954–57; Founder and director, Agricultural Accounting and Management Co. (AKC Ltd) 1957–97; Director: United Oilseeds Marketing Ltd 1972–97, WE and DT Cave Ltd 1976–97; Partner, Drayton Farms 1976–97; Executive producer, Link Television programme for people with disabilities 1988–97. *House of Lords:* Deputy Chair of Committees 1997–; Deputy Speaker 1999–. Opposition Whip 1987–92; Deputy Opposition Chief Whip 1990–92; Government Chief Whip (Captain of the Honourable Corps of the Gentlemen at Arms) 1997–2002. Opposition Spokesperson for: Agriculture 1987–97, Social Security 1988–97, Health (Community Care) 1989–97; Government Spokesperson for: Agriculture 2001, Food and Farming 2001–02. Member: European Communities Sub-committee D 1987–92, House of Lords' Offices 1997–2002, Procedure 1997–2002, House of Lords' Offices Administration and Works Sub-Committee 1997–2002, Refreshment Sub-Committee 1997–2002, Committee of Selection 1997–2002, Privileges 1997–2002, Joint Select Committee on House of Lords Reform 2002–, European Union Sub-committee D (Environment, Agriculture, Public Health and Consumer Protection) 2003–. Member, Council of Royal Agricultural Society of England 1994–97. Honorary doctorate, Essex University. Trustee: Farmers' Club 1985–97, Rural Housing Trust 1991–97, John Arlott Memorial Trust 1993–97. Contested (Labour) Basingstoke 1970 general election; MAFF Senior Research Fellowship in Agricultural Marketing, Oxford 1970–72; Member, Central Council for

Agricultural and Horticultural Co-operation 1977–80; Chair: BBC Central Agricultural Advisory Committee 1985–89, UK Co-operative Council 1993–97. PC 1997. Fellow, Institute of Agricultural Management 1992–; Fellow in Business Administration, Royal Agricultural College Fellow, Royal Agricultural Societies. *Special Interests:* Agriculture, Rural Affairs, Disability, Community Care, Health, Football. *Recreations:* Walking, reading, supporting Southampton FC. *Clubs:* Farmers' (Chairman 1982). Raised to the peerage as Baron Carter, of Devizes in the County of Wiltshire 1987. Rt Hon the Lord Carter, House of Lords, London, SW1A 0PW *Tel:* 020 7219 1300 *Fax:* 020 7219 8733.

CAVENDISH OF FURNESS, LORD — Conservative

CAVENDISH OF FURNESS (Life Baron), Richard Hugh Cavendish; cr. 1990. Born 2 November 1941. Son of late Captain Richard Edward Osborne Cavendish, DL; educated Eton College. Married Grania Mary Caulfeild 1970 (1 son 2 daughters). Councillor, Cumbria County Council 1985–90; High Sheriff of Cumbria 1978; DL, Cumbria 1988. *Career:* International merchanting and banking in London 1961–71; Chairman, Holker Estate Group of Companies 1971–; Commissioner for the Historic Buildings and Monuments Commission (English Heritage) 1992–98; Director, UK Nirex Ltd 1993–99. Government Whip 1990–92. Member, Select Committee on: the Croydon Tramlink Bill 1992–93, European Union Sub-committee B (Energy, Industry and Transport) 2000–, European Union 2001–. Member, Association of Conservative Peers. Chairman, Morecambe and Lonsdale Conservative Association 1975–78. Chairman of Governors, St. Anne's School, Windermere 1983–89; Chairman, Lancashire and Cumbria Foundation for Medical Research 1994–. Trustee, St Mary's Hospice, Ulveston 1987–. Fellow, Royal Society of Arts 1988. Liveryman, Fishmongers' Company. *Special Interests:* Education, Environment, Local Issues, Industry, Foreign Affairs, Drug and Alcohol Rehabilitation, Agriculture, Forestry. *Recreations:* Gardening, National Hunt racing, shooting, reading, travel. *Clubs:* Brooks's, White's, Pratt's, Beefsteak. Raised to the peerage as Baron Cavendish of Furness, of Cartmel in the County of Cumbria 1990. The Lord Cavendish of Furness, DL, Holker Hall, Cark-in-Cartmel, Cumbria, LA11 7PL *Tel:* 01539 558220 *Tel:* Office: 01539 558123 *Fax:* 01539 558776 *E-mail:* cavendish@holker.co.uk.

CHADLINGTON, LORD — Conservative

CHADLINGTON (Life Baron), Peter Selwyn Gummer; cr. 1996. Born 24 August 1942. Son of late Canon Selwyn Gummer and late Sybille, née Mason; educated King's School, Rochester, Kent; Selwyn College, Cambridge (BA, MA). Married Lucy Rachel Dudley-Hill 1982 (1 son 3 daughters). *Career:* Portsmouth and Sunderland Newspaper Group Ltd 1964–65; Viyella International 1965–66; Hodgkinson and Partners 1966–67; Industrial and Commercial Finance Corporation 1967–74; Chairman, Shandwick International plc 1974–2000; Non-Executive Director: CIA Group plc 1990–94, Halifax Building Society/plc 1994–2001; Chairman, International Public Relations 1998–2000; Director, Black Box Music Ltd 1999–2001; Director, Walbrook Club 1999–2001; Chief Executive, Huntsworth plc 2000–. Member, Select Committee on the European Union Sub-Committee B (Energy, Industry and Transport) 2000–. Chairman, Royal Opera House 1996–97; Council Member, Cheltenham Ladies College 1998–; Chairman, Action on Addiction 2000–. Honorary Fellow, Bournemouth University 1999–. Chairman, Understanding Industry Trust 1991–95; Trustee, Atlantic Partnership 1999–; Board of Trustees, American University 1999–. Member: NHS Policy Board 1991–95, Arts Council of England 1991–96; Chairman, National Lottery Advisory Board for Arts and Film 1994–96; Non-Executive Director, Oxford Resources 1999–; Non-Executive Chairman, guideforlife.com 1999–2000. FRSA; FIPR. Freeman, City of London. *Publications:* Various articles and booklets on public relations. *Recreations:* Opera, rugby, cricket. *Clubs:* Garrick, MCC, Carlton, White's. Raised to the peerage as Baron Chadlington, of Dean in the County of Oxfordshire 1996. The Lord Chadlington, House of Lords, London, SW1A 0PW, *Tel:* 020 7408 2232.

Visit the Vacher Dod Website . . . **www.DodOnline.co.uk**

CHALFONT, LORD   Crossbencher

CHALFONT (Life Baron), Alun Arthur Gwynne Jones; cr. 1964. Born 5 December 1919. Son of late Arthur Gwynne Jones; educated West Monmouth School; School of Slavonic Studies, London University (BA Russian language 1955). Married Mona Mitchell 1948 (1 daughter deceased). Commissioned as 2nd Lieutenant in South Wales Borderers 1940; Served in Burma and afterwards in Cyprus, Malaya and East Africa; Has held various intelligence appointments; Graduate of: Army Staff College 1950, Joint Service Staff College 1958; Resigned commission as Brevet Lieutenant-Colonel in 1961 upon appointment as Defence Correspondent of *The Times*; Hon. Colonel, University of Wales Officer Training Corps 1992–95. *Career:* Director: Shandwick plc 1979–94, IBM (UK) 1983–90, Lazard Bros & Co Ltd 1983–91; Chair, Vickers Shipbuilding and Engineering Ltd 1987–95; Deputy Chair, Independent Broadcasting Authority 1989–90; Chair: Radio Authority 1991–95, Marlborough Stirling 1994–99; Director, Television Corporation 1996–2001; Chair, Southern Mining Corp 1997–99. *House of Lords:* Minister of State for Foreign Affairs 1964–70. Opposition Spokesperson on Defence and Foreign Affairs 1970–73. Member Select Committees on: House of Lords' Offices –2002, Procedure 2003–. President: Hispanic and Luso Brazilian Council 1972–79, European Atlantic Group 1983–90. President: Llangollen International Music Festival 1978–87, RNID 1980–87, Freedom in Sport 1982–88; Member: Royal Academy of Morocco, Pilgrims Society. MC 1957; OBE (Mil) 1961; PC 1964; Grand Officer, Order of the Southern Cross (Brazil) 1976. FRSA. Freeman, City of London. Member, Paviors' Company. *Publications:* Several books including: *The Great Commanders*, 1973; *Montgomery of Alamein*, 1976; *Waterloo: A Battle of Three Armies*, 1979; *Star Wars*, 1985; *Defence of the Realm*, 1987; *By God's Will*, 1989; *The Shadow of My Hand*, 2000. *Special Interests:* Defence, Foreign Affairs. *Recreations:* Music. *Sportsclubs:* London Welsh RFC, Llanelli RFC. *Clubs:* Garrick, City Livery. Raised to the peerage as Baron Chalfont, of Llantarnam, in the County of Monmouth 1964. Rt Hon the Lord Chalfont, OBE, MC, House of Lords, London, SW1A 0PW *Tel:* 020 7219 6807.

CHALKER OF WALLASEY, BARONESS   Conservative

CHALKER OF WALLASEY (Life Baroness), Lynda Chalker; cr. 1992. Born 29 April 1942. Daughter of late Sidney Henry James Bates, and late Marjorie Kathleen Randell; educated Roedean School, UK; Heidelberg University (Technical German 1961); London University; Central London Polytechnic (Statistics 1965). Married Eric Robert Chalker 1967 (divorced 1973); Married Clive Landa 1981 (separated 2001). Hon. Colonel, Royal Logistic Corps (156 Transport Regiment NW). *Career:* Unilever's Research Bureau Ltd 1963–69; Shell Mex and BP 1969–72; Executive director (International) Opinion Research International Ltd 1972–74; Independent Consultant on Africa and Development 1997–. *House of Commons:* MP (Conservative) for Wallasey February 1974–92; Parliamentary Under-Secretary of State, Department of Health and Social Security 1979–82; Parliamentary Under-Secretary of State, Department of Transport 1982–83, Minister of State 1983–86; Minister of State, Foreign and Commonwealth Office with special responsibility for: Europe, International trade, Economic relations, Personnel 1986–89, Sub-Saharan Africa and The Commonwealth 1986–97; Deputy to Foreign Secretary 1987–97, Minister for Overseas Development 1989–92. Opposition spokesman on Social Services 1976–79. *House of Lords:* Minister of Overseas Development and Minister for Africa and Commonwealth, Foreign and Commonwealth Office 1992–97. Chairman Presidential Advisory Council on Investment for Nigeria 2001–. National Vice-Chairman, Young Conservatives 1970–71. President and Chairman, Board of Management of London School of Hygiene and Tropical Medicine. Nine honorary degrees. Member, BBC Advisory Committee 1974–79. PC 1987. Fellow, Royal Statistical Society. *Publications: Police in Retreat*, 1968; *Unhappy Families*, 1972; *We're Richer than We Think*, 1978; *Africa – Turning the Tide*, 1989. *Special Interests:* Voluntary Sector, European Co-operation, Africa, Overseas Aid and Development, Trade, Transport. *Recreations:* Theatre, cooking, gardening, jazz. *Clubs:* Royal Oversea Club, St James. Raised to the peerage as Baroness Chalker of Wallasey, of Leigh-on-Sea in the County of Essex 1992. Rt Hon the Baroness Chalker of Wallasey, House of Lords, London, SW1A 0PW *Tel:* 020 7219 5098 *E-mail:* lchalker@africamatters.com.

CHAN, LORD   Crossbencher

CHAN (Life Baron), Michael Chew Koon Chan; cr. 2001. Born 6 March 1940. Son of James Chieu Kim Chan and Rosie Chan; educated Raffles Institution, Singapore; Guy's Hospital Medical School (MB, BS 1964). Married Irene Wei-Len Chee 1965 (1 daughter 1 son). Non-executive director: Wirral and West Cheshire Community NHS Trust 1999–2002, Birkenhead and Wallasey Primary Care Trust 2002–. *Career:* Consultant paediatrician, Fazakerley Hospital, Liverpool 1976–94; Consultant and senior lecturer, Liverpool School of Tropical Medicine 1976–94; Member, Home Secretary's Standing Advisory Council on Race Relations 1986–90; Commissioner, Commission for Racial Equality 1990–95; Director, NHS Ethnic Health Unit 1994–97; Visiting Professor, Liverpool University 1996–; Chair, Chinese in Britain Forum 1996–; Adviser on ethnic health: NHS executive NW region 2000–02, Commission for Health Improvement 2001–02; Member, Press Complaints Commission 2002–; Chair, Acupuncture Regulatory Working Group, Department of Health 2002–03. Chair: of Council, Chinese Overseas Christian Mission 1982–, Wirral Multicultural Organisation 1997–, Malaria Consortium 2003–. Heinz Fellow, British Paediatric Association (now Royal College of Paediatrics and Child Health) 1974–75. MFPHM (1996). Chair Afiya Trust 1998–. Chair, British Council Consultant on Training in maternal and child health 1986–84; Member, Sentencing Advisory Panel, Lord Chancellor's Department and Home Office 1999–. MBE 1991. FRCP (London), FRCPCH, FRACP, MFPHM. *Publications:* Co-editor *Diseases of Children in the Tropics and Sub-Tropics* (E Arnold) 4th edition 1991; Chapter on Health in *The Future of Multi-Ethnic Britain: the Parekh Report*, 2000. *Special Interests:* Community Participation, Mother and Child Health in North India, Race Relations in Britain. *Recreations:* Travel, Chinese cooking. Raised to the peerage as Baron Chan, of Oxton in the County of Merseyside 2001. Professor the Lord Chan, MBE, House of Lords, London, SW1A 0PW *Tel:* 020 7219 8726 *E-mail:* chanm@parliament.uk.

CHANDOS, VISCOUNT   Labour

CHANDOS (3rd Viscount, UK), Thomas Orlando Lyttelton; cr. 1954; (Life) Baron Lyttelton of Aldershot 2000. Born 12 February 1953. Son of 2nd Viscount; educated Eton College; Worcester College, Oxford (BA). Married Arabella Sarah Bailey 1985 (2 sons 1 daughter). *Career:* Director: Kleinwort Benson 1985–93, Botts & Company Limited 1993–98, Capital and Regional Properties plc 1993–, Cine-UK Limited 1995–, Video Networks Limited 1996–99, Chairman: Lopex plc 1997–99, Mediakey plc 1998–2000, Capital and Regional plc 2000–; Director: Global Natural Energy plc 2000–, Northbridge (UK) Limited 2001–. *House of Lords:* First entered House of Lords 1982. Formerly SDP Spokesperson for Finance and Trade; Opposition Spokesman on Treasury and Economic Affairs 1995–97. Director, English National Opera 1995–; Governor, National Film and Television School 1996–2001; President, National Kidney Research Fund 2001–; Director, Social Market Foundation 2001–. Trustee: 21st Century Learning Initiative 1995–, Education Low-Priced Sponsored Texts 1996–99. Created a life peer as Baron Lyttelton of Aldershot, of Aldershot in the County of Hampshire 2000. The Viscount Chandos, House of Lords, London, SW1A 0PW; Northbridge UK Ltd, 9 Park Place, London, SW1A 1LP *E-mail:* tom@northbridgefunds.com.

CHAPPLE, LORD   Crossbencher

CHAPPLE (Life Baron), Francis Joseph Chapple; cr. 1985. Born 8 August 1921. Born 1921. Son of late Frank Chapple; educated Elementary School. Married Joan Nicholls 1944 (died 1994) (2 sons); married Phyllis Luck 1999. *Trades Union:* Member, Electrical Trade Union 1937–83; Shop Steward and Branch Official; General Secretary, Electrical, Electronic, Telecommunication and Plumbing Union 1966–84; Member, General Council of the TUC 1971–83, Chairman 1982–83, Gold Badge of Congress 1983. Member, Select Committee on Sustainable Development 1994–95. Member: Royal Commission on Environmental Pollution 1973–77, Horserace Totalisator Board 1976–90, NEDC 1979–83. *Publications: Sparks Fly* (autobiography) 1984. *Recreations:* Pigeon racing. Raised to the peerage as Baron Chapple, of Hoxton in Greater London 1985. The Lord Chapple, House of Lords, London, SW1A 0PW *Tel:* 020 7219 5353.

CHESTER, LORD BISHOP OF   Non-affiliated

CHESTER (Bishop of), Peter Robert Forster. Born 16 March 1950. Thomas and Edna Forster; educated Tudor Grange Grammar School for Boys, Solihull; Merton College, Oxford (MA chemistry 1973); Edinburgh University (BD theology 1977, PhD 1985). Married Elisabeth Anne Stevenson 1978 (2 sons 2 daughters). *Career:* Assistant Curate, Mossley Hill Parish Church, Liverpool 1980–82; Senior Tutor, St John's College, Durham 1983–91; Vicar, Beverley Minster 1991–96; Bishop of Chester 1996–; Took his seat in the House of Lords 2001. *Recreations:* Gardening, crafts, hens. *Clubs:* Penn Club. Rt Rev Dr the Lord Bishop of Chester, Bishop's House, Abbey Square, Chester, CH1 2JD *Tel:* 01244 350864 *Fax:* 01244 314187 *E-mail:* bpchester@chester.anglican.org.

CHILVER, LORD   Conservative

CHILVER (Life Baron), (Amos) Henry Chilver; cr. 1987. Born 30 October 1926. Son of late Amos Henry Chilver; educated Southend High School; Bristol University. Married Claudia Grigson 1959 (3 sons 2 daughters). Chairman, Milton Keynes Development Corporation 1983–92. *Career:* Railway Engineer 1947–48; Research Assistant, then Assistant Lecturer, then Lecturer, Bristol University 1948–54; Demonstrator then Lecturer, Cambridge University 1954–61; Professor Civil Engineering, UCL 1961–69; Vice-Chancellor, Cranfield Institute of Technology 1970–89; Chairman, English China Clays plc 1989–95; Non-executive Director: ICI 1990–93, Zeneca 1993–95; Chairman, RJB Mining 1993–97. Fellow, Corpus Christi College, Cambridge 1958–61. Chairman, Universities Funding Council 1988–91. *Special Interests:* Education, Industry, Environment. *Clubs:* Athenaeum, United Oxford and Cambridge University. Raised to the peerage as Baron Chilver, of Cranfield in the County of Bedfordshire 1987. The Lord Chilver, House of Lords, London, SW1A 0PW *Tel:* 020 7219 3000.

CHITNIS, LORD   Crossbencher

CHITNIS (Life Baron), Pratap Chidamber Chitnis; cr. 1977. Born 1 May 1936. Son of late Dr Chidamber N. Chitnis; educated Stonyhurst College; Birmingham University (BA); University of Kansas (MA). Married Anne Brand 1964 (1 son deceased). *Career:* Administration Assistant, National Coal Board 1958–59; Secretary, The Joseph Rowntree Social Service Trust 1969–75, Chief Executive and Director, 1975–88; Member, Community Relations Commission 1970–77; Member, BBC Asian Programme Advice Committee 1972–77, Chairman 1979–83; Chairman, Refugee Action 1981–86; Chairman, British Refugee Council 1986–89. Liberal Party Organisation: Local Government Officer 1960–62, Agent, Orpington By-election 1962, Training Officer 1962–64, Press Officer 1964–66; Head, Liberal Party Organisation 1966–69. Raised to the peerage as Baron Chitnis, of Ryedale in the County of North Yorkshire 1977. The Lord Chitnis, House of Lords, London, SW1A 0PW *Tel:* 020 7219 5353.

CHOLMONDELEY, MARQUESS OF   Crossbencher

CHOLMONDELEY (7th Marquess of, UK), David George Philip Cholmondeley; cr. 1815; 10th Earl of Cholmondeley (E) 1706; 7th Earl of Rocksavage (UK) 1815; 10th Viscount Malpas (E) 1706; 11th Viscount Cholmondeley (I) 1661; 10th Baron Cholmondeley (E) 1689; 10th Baron Newburgh (GB) 1716; 10th Baron Newborough (I) 1715. Born 27 June 1960. Son of 6th Marquess, GCVO, MC, DL; educated Eton College; Sorbonne. *Career:* Page of Honour to HM The Queen 1974–76; Joint Hereditary Lord Great Chamberlain of England (acting for the reign of Queen Elizabeth II) since 1990. *House of Lords:* First entered House of Lords 1990. Most Hon the Marquess of Cholmondeley, Office: 10 St. James's Place, London, SW1A 1PE *Tel:* 020 7408 0418; House of Lords, London, SW1A 0PW.

CHORLEY, LORD   Crossbencher

CHORLEY (2nd Baron, UK), Roger Richard Edward Chorley; cr. 1945. Born 14 August 1930. Son of 1st Baron, QC; educated Stowe School, Buckinghamshire; Gonville and Caius College, Cambridge (BA natural sciences and economics 1953). Married Ann Elizabeth Debenham 1964 (2 sons). *Career:* Coopers and Lybrand 1954–90: Partner 1967–89. *House of Lords:* First entered House of Lords 1978; Elected hereditary peer 2001–. Member, Select Committees on: Science and Technology, Remote Sensing and Digital Mapping 1983, UK Space Policy 1987, Greenhouse Effect 1989, Innovation in Manufacturing Industry 1990; Member, Select Committee on Sustainable Development 1994–95. Four honorary degrees. Member: Finance Committee National Trust 1970–90, Council and Executive Committee 1989–96; Chairman, National Trust 1991–96. Member: Royal Commission on the Press 1974–77, Ordnance Survey Review Committee 1978–79; Board Member, Royal National Theatre 1980–91; Board Member, British Council 1981–99, Deputy-Chairman 1991–99; Member: Top Salaries Review Body 1981–91, Ordnance Survey Advisory Board 1982–85; Chairman, Committee on Handling of Geographic Information 1985–87; Member, Natural Environment Research Council 1988–94. Fellow, Institute of Chartered Accountants 1959; President, Royal Geographical Society 1987–90; Hon. Fellow, Royal Institute of Chartered Surveyors 1995. *Special Interests:* Heritage, Countryside, environment. *Recreations:* Mountains. *Clubs:* Alpine. The Lord Chorley, House of Lords, London, SW1A 0PW *Tel:* 020 7219 5353.

CHRISTOPHER, LORD   Labour

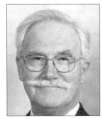

CHRISTOPHER (Life Baron), Anthony (Tony) Martin Grosvenor Christopher; cr. 1998. Born 25 April 1925. Son of late George and Helen Christopher; educated Cheltenham Grammar School; Westminster College of Commerce. Married Adela Joy Thompson 1962. *Trades Union:* Member, TUC General Council 1976–89, Chairman 1988–89; Member, TUC Committees: Economic Committee 1977–89, Education Committee 1977–85, Media Committee 1979–89, Chair, 1985–89, International Committee 1982–89, Finance and General Purposes Committee 1983–89, Education and Training Committee 1985–86, Employment and Organisation Committees 1985–89. RAF 1944–48. *Career:* Articled Pupil, Agricultural Valuers, Gloucester 1941–44; Inland Revenue 1948–57; Inland Revenue Staff Federation: Assistant Secretary 1957–60, Assistant General Secretary 1960–74, Joint General Secretary 1975, General Secretary 1976–88; Chairman, TU Fund Managers Ltd 1983, Director 1981–; Industrial and Public Affairs Consultant 1988–. Member, Select Committees on: European Communities Sub-Committee D (Agriculture, Fisheries and Food) 1999–2002, Joint Committee on Consolidation of Bills 2000–, Audit Committee 2003–. Members' Auditor, International Confederation of Free Trades Unions 1984–. Trustee: NACRO 1956–98, Trades Union Unit Trust Charitable Trust 1981–, Commonwealth Trades Union Council Charitable Trust 1985–89, Save The Children Fund 1985–90; Trustee, Institute for Public Policy Research 1989–94, Treasurer 1990–94, Douglas Houghton Memorial Fund 1998–. Member, Council, NACRO 1956–98, Chairman 1973–98; Director, Civil Service Building Society 1958–87, Chairman 1978–87; Member: Inner London Probation and After-care Committee 1966–79, Tax Reform Committee 1974–80, Royal Commission on Distribution of Income and Wealth 1978–79, Independent Broadcasting Authority 1978–83; Chairman, Tyre Industry Economic Development Council 1983–86; Member: Council of Institute of Manpower Studies 1984–89, Economic and Social Research Council 1985–88; Vice-President, Building Societies Association 1985–90; Director, Birmingham Midshires Building Society 1987–88; Member: General Medical Council 1989–94, Audit Commission 1989–95, Broadcasting Complaints Commission 1989–97; Former member of several other committees, inquiries and working parties. CBE 1984. FRSA 1989. *Publications:* Co-author: *Policy for Poverty,* 1970; *The Wealth Report,* 1979; *The Wealth Report 2,* 1982. *Special Interests:* Agriculture, Financial Services, Pensions, Penal Affairs and Policy, Economics, Industry. *Recreations:* Gardening, Dog walking. *Clubs:* Beefsteak, Wig and Pen, Royal Automobile. Raised to the peerage as Baron Christopher, of Leckhampton in the County of Gloucestershire 1998. The Lord Christopher, CBE, TU Fund Managers Ltd, Congress House, Great Russell Street, London, WC1B 3LQ.

Visit the Vacher Dod Website . . .
www.DodOnline.co.uk

CLARK OF KEMPSTON, LORD   Conservative

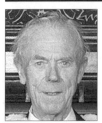

CLARK OF KEMPSTON (Life Baron), William Gibson Haig Clark; cr. 1992. Born 18 October 1917. Son of late Hugh Clark; educated London. Married Irene Dorothy Rands 1944 (died 2003) (2 sons and 1 son and 1 daughter deceased). Served in Army in UK and India 1941–46, Major. Councillor, Wandsworth Borough Council 1949–53. *House of Commons:* Contested (Conservative) Northampton 1955 general election; MP (Conservative) for: Nottingham South 1959–66, Surrey East 1970–74, Croydon South 1974–92. Frontbench Spokesperson for Trade, Finance and Economics 1964–66. Former Member, Procedure Committee. Chairman: Clapham Conservative Association 1949–52, Mid-Bedforshire Conservative Association 1956–59; Joint Treasurer, Conservative Party 1974–75; Deputy Chairman, Conservative Party 1975–77. Hon. National Director, £2 million Carrington Appeal 1967; Chairman, Anglo-Austrian Society 1983–98, Patron 1998–; President, The City Group for Smaller Companies (Cisco) 1993–98. Fellow, Industry and Parliament Trust; Trustee, Carlton Club. Kt 1980; Order of the Golden Fleece (Austria) 1989; PC 1990; Grand Decoration of Honour in Gold with Star (Austria) 1994. Member, Chartered Association of Certified Accountants 1941. Freeman, City of London. *Special Interests:* Finance, Industry, Trade and Industry, Housing, Cane Sugar, Insurance. *Recreations:* Reading. *Clubs:* Buck's, Carlton. Raised to the peerage as Baron Clark of Kempston, of Kempston in the County of Bedfordshire 1992. Rt Hon the Lord Clark of Kempston, The Clock House, Box End, Bedford, MK43 8RT *Tel:* 01234 852361; 3 Barton Street, London, SW1P 3NG *Tel:* 020 7222 5759.

CLARK OF WINDERMERE, LORD   Labour

CLARK OF WINDERMERE (Life Baron), David George Clark; cr. 2001. Born 19 October 1939. Son of George Clark; educated Windermere Grammar School; Manchester University (BA economics 1963, MSc 1965) Sheffield University (PhD 1978). Married Christine Kirby 1970 (1 daughter). *Trades Union:* Member, UNISON. *Career:* Forester 1956–57; Laboratory worker in textile mill 1957–59; Student teacher, Salford 1959–60; President, University of Manchester Union 1963–64; Lecturer in public administration, Salford University 1965–70; Chair Forestry Commission 2001–. *House of Commons:* Contested Manchester Withington Division 1966 general election; Member for Colne Valley 1970–74, and for South Shields 1979–2001; Chancellor of the Duchy of Lancaster 1997–98. Opposition Spokesperson for: Agriculture, Fisheries and Food 1972–74, Defence 1980–81, The Environment 1981–87, Food, Agricultural and Rural Affairs 1987–92, Defence, disarmament and arms control 1992–97. UK Delegation of the North Atlantic Assembly 1980–: Member 1980–97, 1998–, Leader 2001–. Executive Member, National Trust 1980–94; Trustee: Vindolanda Trust 1983–, History of Parliament Trust 1986–. Chair, Atlantic Council of the UK 1998–2003. PC 1997. Borough of South Tyneside 1999. *Publications: Industrial Manager,* 1966; *Colne Valley: Radicalism to Socialism,* 1981; *Victor Grayson: Labour's Lost Leader,* 1985; *We do not want The Earth,* 1992. *Special Interests:* Open Spaces. *Recreations:* Gardening, fell-walking, reading, watching football. Raised to the peerage as Baron Clark of Windermere, of Windermere in the County of Cumbria 2001. Rt Hon the Lord Clark of Windermere, House of Lords, London, SW1A 0PW *Tel:* 020 7219 8890.

CLARKE OF HAMPSTEAD, LORD   Labour

CLARKE OF HAMPSTEAD (Life Baron), Anthony James Clarke; cr. 1998. Born 17 April 1932. Son of Henry Walter and Elizabeth Clarke; educated St Dominics Roman Catholic School, Kentish Town; Ruskin College, Oxford. Married Josephine Ena Turner 1954 (1 son and 1 daughter). *Trades Union:* UPW: Committee Member 1953, Branch Secretary 1962–69; Member: London Trades Council 1965–69 (EC Member 1967–68), TUC Disputes Panel 1972–93, TUC SE Regional Council 1974–79, London Council of Post Office Unions 1975–79, Midlands Council of Post Office Unions 1975–79. National Service, Royal Signals 1950–52; TA and Army Emergency Reserve 1952–68. Councillor, London Borough of Camden 1971–78. *Career:* Post Office:

Telegraph boy, Postman, Postman higher grade (sorter); Full-time trade union officer, UPW 1979–93; Editor, UPW journal (*The Post*) 1979; Deputy General Secretary, UPW 1981–93. Member, Committees on: Procedure –2002, Religious Offences 2002–03. Organiser and Lecturer, Postal and Telegraph International (PTTI) in Malaysia and India. Member: Hampstead Labour Party 1954–86, Executive Committee, Labour Friends of Israel 1972–2001, Labour Party National Executive Committee 1983–93, St Albans Labour Party 1986–2003, Chair, The Labour Party 1992–93; Governor, Westminster Foundation for Democracy 1992–98. Governor, Quentin Kynaston Comprehensive School (ILEA) 1973–78; Executive Committee Member, Camden Committee for Community Relations 1974–81; Chairman, Camden Council of Social Services 1978–87; Management Committee Member: Hampstead Old People's Homes, Newstead Old People's Home. Trustee, Post Office Pension Funds 1991–97; Founder Member and Trustee, One World Action. Contested (Labour) Camden Hampstead February and October 1974 general elections. Knight of St Gregory (Papal Order) 1994; CBE 1998. *Special Interests:* Overseas Aid and Development, Industrial Relations. *Recreations:* Arsenal FC, *The Archers*, reading. Raised to the peerage as Baron Clarke of Hampstead, of Hampstead in the London Borough of Camden 1998. The Lord Clarke of Hampstead, CBE, House of Lords, London, SW1A 0PW.

CLEMENT-JONES, LORD — Liberal Democrat

CLEMENT-JONES (Life Baron), Timothy Francis Clement-Jones; cr. 1998. Born 26 October 1949. Son of late Maurice Llewelyn Clement-Jones; educated Haileybury; Trinity College, Cambridge (MA economics and law 1971). Married Dr Vicky Yip 1973 (died 1987); married Jean Whiteside 1994 (1 son). *Career:* Solicitor; Head of Legal Services, London Weekend Television 1980–83; Legal Director, Grand Metropolitan Retailing 1984–86; Group Company Secretary and Legal Adviser, Kingfisher plc 1986–95; Chair: Context Group Ltd 1997–, DLA Upstream, the public affairs practice of DLA 1999–. Liberal Democrat Spokesperson for Health 1998–. Chairman, Association of Liberal Lawyers 1981–86; Member, Liberal Democrat National Executive 1988–98; Chairman, Liberal Democrat Party Federal Finance Committee 1991–98; Director, Liberal Democrat Campaign for the European Parliamentary elections 1994; Chairman, Liberal Democrat London 2000 Mayoral and Assembly Campaign. Chairman and Director, Crime Concern 1988–99; Member, Council of the London Lighthouse 1989–93; Director, Brixton City Challenge 1994–98; Chairman, Women Returners Network. Trustee: Cancer BACUP, Lambeth Crime Prevention Trust; Chair trustees Treehouse school for autistic children. CBE 1988. FRSA; FIPR. *Recreations:* Travelling, eating, talking, reading, walking, diving. *Clubs:* Royal Automobile. Raised to the peerage as Baron Clement-Jones, of Clapham in the London Borough of Lambeth 1998. The Lord Clement-Jones, CBE, House of Lords, London, SW1A 0PW *Tel:* 020 7219 3660.

CLINTON-DAVIS, LORD — Labour

CLINTON-DAVIS (Life Baron), Stanley Clinton Clinton-Davis; cr. 1990. Born 6 December 1928. Son of Sidney and Lily Davis; educated Hackney Down School, London Mercer's School; King's College, London University (LLB 1950). Married Frances Jane Lucas 1954 (1 son 3 daughters). *Trades Union:* Member General and Municipal. Councillor, London Borough of Hackney 1959–71, Mayor 1968–69. *Career:* Admitted solicitor 1953; President, UN Selection Committee for the Sasakawa Environment Project 1989–97; Consultant on European law and affairs with S. J. Berwin & Co. solicitors 1989–97, 1998–. *House of Commons:* Contested (Labour): Portsmouth, Langstone in 1955, Yarmouth in 1959 and 1964 general elections; MP (Labour) for Hackney Central 1970–83; Parliamentary Under-Secretary of State, Department of Trade 1974–79. Opposition Spokesperson for: Trade, prices and consumer protection 1979–81, Foreign affairs 1981–83. *House of Lords:* Minister of State, Department of Trade and Industry (Minister for Trade) 1997–98. Opposition Spokesperson for Transport 1990–97; Supporting Spokesperson for: Trade and Industry 1990–96, Foreign Affairs 1990–97. Member Select Committee on Liaison 2001–. Member, Parliamentary Assembly of the Council of Europe and the Assembly of the Western European Union 2000–. Member, Royal Institute for International Affairs. Member, Executive Council, National Association of Labour Student Organisations 1949–50; Joint President, Society of Labour Lawyers. President, Hackney Branch,

Multiple Sclerosis Society; Patron, Hackney Association for the Disabled; Former President: UK Pilots (Marine), Institute of Travel Management; President British Airline Pilots Association; Former President Aviation Environment Federation; Vice-President, Chartered Institute of Environmental Health; Joint Chair, Europe 21. Awarded first medal by Eurogroup for Animal Welfare 1988. Fellow, Queen Mary and Westfield College; Hon. Doctorate Polytechnic University of Bucharest; Hon. ACA Degree; Fellow King's College London. Trustee, Bernt Carlsson Trust 1989–. Member, Commission of the European Communities 1985–89; Chair, Advisory Committee on Pollution of the Sea 1984–85, 1989–97; Member: Council of Justice, Council of British Maritime League 1989–; Chair, Refugee Council 1989–97; Former President, Association of Municipal Authorities (AMA); Member, Advisory Panel of CIS Environ Trust. Grand Cross, Order of Leopold II (Belgium) for services to the EC 1990; PC 1998. Fellow, Chartered Institution of Water and Environmental Management. *Special Interests:* Transport, Environment, Foreign Affairs, Law, Civil Liberties, International Trade. *Recreations:* Association football, golf, political biographies. *Sportsclubs:* Hendon Golf Club. *Clubs:* Former Member Royal Overseas League. Raised to the peerage as Baron Clinton-Davis, of Hackney in the London Borough of Hackney 1990. Rt Hon the Lord Clinton-Davis, House of Lords, London, SW1A 0PW *Tel:* 020 7219 6203.

CLYDE, LORD   Crossbencher

CLYDE (Life Baron), James John Clyde; cr. 1996. Born 29 January 1932. Son of late Rt Hon. Lord Clyde; educated Edinburgh Academy; Corpus Christi College, Oxford (BA literae humaniores 1954); Edinburgh University (LLB 1959). Married Ann Clunie Hoblyn 1963 (2 sons). Army national service (Intelligence Corps) 1954–56. *Career:* Called to the Scottish Bar 1959; QC (Scot) 1971; Advocate-Depute 1973–74; Chancellor to the Bishop of Argyll and the Isles 1972–85; Judge of the Courts of Appeal of Jersey and Guernsey 1979–85; Senator of the College of Justice in Scotland 1985–96; Lord of Appeal in Ordinary 1996–2001; Elected as Honorary Master of the Bench of the Middle Temple 1996. Chairman, Joint Select Committee on Consolidation of Bills 1998–2001. Leader of the UK Delegation to the Consultative Committee of the Bars of Europe. Director, Edinburgh Academy 1979–88; Vice-President, Royal Blind Asylum and School 1987–; Hon. President, Scottish Young Lawyers' Association 1988–97; Governor, Napier Polytechnic and University 1989–93; Chairman, Governors, St George's School for Girls 1989–97; Assessor to the Chancellor of Edinburgh University and Vice-Chairman of Court 1989–97; Convenor, Children in Scotland 2003–. DUniv, Heriot-Watt 1991; DLitt, Napier University 1995; Hon. Fellow Corpus Christi College, Oxford 1996 DUniv, Edinburgh University 1997. Trustee: St Mary's Music School 1976–92, National Library of Scotland 1977–93; Chairman, Special Trustees of St Mary's Hospital, Paddington 1997–99; Chairman, Statute Law Society 2000–2002. Contested (Conservative) Dundee East February 1974 general election; Chair: Medical Appeal Tribunal 1974–85, Committee of Investigation for Scotland on Agricultural Marketing 1984–85, Scottish Valuation Advisory Council 1987–96, Member 1972–96, The Europa Institute 1990–97, Orkney Children Inquiry 1991–92, Scottish Lawyers European Group 1981–84. PC 1996. *Publications:* Co-editor *Armour on Valuation*, 5th ed. 1985; Co-author *Judicial Review*, 2000. *Recreations:* Music, gardening. *Clubs:* New (Edinburgh). Raised to the peerage as Baron Clyde, of Briglands in Perthshire and Kinross 1996. Rt Hon the Lord Clyde, 12 Dublin Street, Edinburgh, EH1 3PP *Tel:* 0131-556 7114; House of Lords, London, SW1A 0PW.

COBBOLD, LORD   Crossbencher

COBBOLD (2nd Baron, UK), David Antony Fromanteel Lytton Cobbold; cr. 1960. Born 14 July 1937. Son of 1st Baron, KG, PC, GCVO, DL, and Lady Hermione Bulwer-Lytton, daughter of 2nd Earl of Lytton, KG, PC, GCSI, GCIE, DL; educated Eton College; Trinity College, Cambridge (BA moral sciences 1960). Married Christine Elizabeth Stucley 1961 (3 sons 1 daughter). Pilot Officer, RAF 1955–57. DL, Hertfordshire 1993–. *Career:* Bank of London and South America 1962–72; Chairman and Managing Director, Lytton Enterprises Ltd 1971–; Treasurer, Finance for Industry Ltd 1974–79; Manager, Treasury Division BP Finance International 1979–87; Director: Hill Samuel Bank Ltd 1988–89; Head of Treasury and Financial Markets, TSB England and Wales plc and Hill Samuel Bank Ltd 1988–89; Managing Director, Gaiacorp UK Ltd 1989–94;

Director: Close Brothers Group plc 1993–2000, Stevenage Leisure Ltd 1998–2000. *House of Lords:* First entered House of Lords 1987; Elected hereditary peer 2000–. Member Advisory Panel on Works of Art 2003–. Historic Houses Association: Member, Executive Committee 1974–97, Treasurer 1988–97; Member, Association for Monetary Union in Europe 1991–2002; President, University of Hertfordshire Development Committee 1991–; Member, Board of Governors, University of Hertfordshire 1993–; Governor, European Union of Historic Houses Association 1993–97. Chairman, Stevenage Community Trust 1991–; Trustee, Pilgrim Trust 1993–; Director: Shuttleworth Trust 1998–2000, English Sinfonia Ltd 1998–2000. Assumed by deed poll the additional surname of Lytton before his patronymic; Contested: (Liberal) Bishop Auckland October 1974 general election, Hertfordshire European Parliament election 1979; Responsible for upkeep and public opening of Knebworth House, Hertfordshire 1970–2001. Fellow, Association of Corporate Treasurers 1983–. *Special Interests:* China, European Monetary Union, Historic Buildings. *Recreations:* Theatre, travel. The Lord Cobbold, DL, House of Lords, London, SW1A 0PW *Tel:* 01438 812261 *Fax:* 01438 817455 *E-mail:* lordcobbold@knebworthhouse.com.

COCKFIELD, LORD   Conservative

COCKFIELD (Life Baron), (Francis) Arthur Cockfield; cr. 1978. Born 28 September 1916. Son of Lieutenant Charles Francis Cockfield, killed in the battle of the Somme 1916; educated Dover Grammar School; London School of Economics (LLB 1938, BSc economics 1942). Married Aileen Monica Mudie 1970 (died 1992). *Career:* Called to the Bar, Inner Temple, 1942; HM Customs and Excise 1933; Estate Duty Office 1935; Secretaries' Office Board of Inland Revenue 1938, Assistant Secretary 1945; Director, Statistics and Intelligence 1945–52; Commissioner of Inland Revenue 1951–52; Finance Director, Boots Pure Drug Co. 1953–61, Managing Director and Chairman of Executive Committee 1961–67 (retired); Member, NEDC 1962–64, 1982–83; Adviser on Taxation Policy to Chancellor of the Exchequer 1970–73; Chairman, Price Commission 1973–77; Vice-President, Commission of the European Communities 1985–89; Adviser, Peat Marwick McLintock 1989–93. *House of Lords:* Minister of State, Treasury, June 1979–82; Secretary of State for Trade 1982–1983; Chancellor of the Duchy of Lancaster 1983–84. Government Spokesperson on Trade and Industry and for the Treasury 1983–84. Member, County Governors, Nottingham University 1963–67. Hon. Fellow, LSE 1972–; four honorary doctorates. Kt 1974; PC 1982; Grand Cross, Order of Leopold II (Belgium) 1989. President, The Royal Statistical Society 1968–69. *Publications: The European Union: Creating the Single Market,* 1994. Raised to the peerage as Baron Cockfield, of Dover in the County of Kent 1978. Rt Hon the Lord Cockfield, House of Lords, London, SW1A 0PW *Tel:* 020 7219 5416.

COE, LORD   Conservative

COE (Life Baron), Sebastian Newbold Coe; cr. 2000. Born 29 September 1956. Son of Peter and Angela Coe; educated Tapton Secondary Modern School, Sheffield; Abbeydale Grange School; Loughborough University (BSc economics and social history 1979). Married Nicola McIrvine 1990 (2 sons 2 daughters). *Career:* Athlete; Sports Council: Member 1983–89, Vice-Chairman 1986–89; Member: Athletes and Medical Commission, International Olympic Committee, Health Education Authority 1987–92; Associate Member, Academy of Sport (France) 1982; Steward, British Boxing Board of Control 1994–; Company director; President, Amateur Athletics Association 2000– Sports columnist *Daily Telegraph*; Founding member Laureus World Sports Academy 2000; Global adviser to Nike 2001–; Athletics commentator Channel 7, Australia. *House of Commons:* Member for Falmouth and Camborne 1992–97; PPS: to Roger Freeman: as Minister of State for Defence Procurement 1994–95, as Chancellor of the Duchy of Lancaster and Minister of Public Service 1995–96, to Nicholas Soames as Minister of State for the Armed Forces 1994–95, to Michael Heseltine as First Secretary of State and Deputy Prime Minister 1995–96; Private Secretary to William Hague as Leader of the Opposition 1997–2001. Assistant Government Whip 1996–97. Has won gold and silver medals at the Moscow Olympic Games 1980 and Los Angeles Olympic Games 1984; European Champion for 800m Stuttgart, 1986; Set nine world records; BBC Sport Personality of the Year 1979; Sportswriters' Sportsman of the Year: 1979, 1980, 1981, 1984. Hon. DSc, Hull University 1988; Hon. LLD, Sheffield University. MBE 1982; OBE 1990. *Special Interests:* Health, Foreign Affairs, Education, Environment, Economy, The Voluntary Movement. *Recreations:* Jazz, theatre, reading. *Clubs:* Carlton, East India. Raised to the peerage as Baron Coe, of Ranmore in the County of Surrey 2000. The Lord Coe, OBE, House of Lords, London, SW1A 0PW.

COHEN OF PIMLICO, BARONESS   Labour

COHEN OF PIMLICO (Life Baroness), Janet Cohen; cr. 2000. Born 4 July 1940. Daughter of late George Edric Neel and of Mary Isabel Neel; educated South Hampstead High Shool; Newnham College, Cambridge (BA law 1962) (Associate Fellow 1988–91). Married James Lionel Cohen 1971 (2 sons 1 daughter). *Trades Union:* Member, First Division Association 1969–82. *Career:* Articled clerk, Frere Cholmeley 1963–65; admitted solicitor 1965; Consultant: ABT Associates, USA 1965–67, John Laing Construction 1968–69; Department of Trade and Industry: principal 1969–78, assistant secretary 1978–82; Assistant director, Charterhouse Bank Ltd 1982–88, Director 1988–2000; Chairman, Café Pelican Ltd 1984–90; Director, Yorkshire Building Society 1991–94, Vice-Chairman 1994–99; Non-executive director: BPP Holdings 1994–2002, non-executive chairman 2002–, Waddington plc 1994–97, London and Manchester Assurance 1997–98, United Assurance 1999–2000, Defence Logistics Organisation 1999–, ISI Ltd 1998–2002, London Stock Exchange 2001–. Member: Joint Committee on Tax Simplification 2001–, Select Committee B on the European Union, Joint Committee on Draft Communications Bill 2002 (prelegislative scrutiny). Co-ordinating Committee of Labour Peers. Member, Sheffield Development Corporation 1993–97; Governor, BBC 1994–99. Hon DLitt, Humberside 1995. Member Schools Examination and Assessment Council 1990–93. *Publications:* As Janet Neel: *Death's Bright Angel*, 1988; *Death on Site*, 1989; *Death of a Partner*, 1991; *Death among the Dons*, 1993; *A Timely Death*, 1999; *To Die For*, 1998; *O Gentle Death*, 2000; As Janet Cohen: *The Highest Bidder*, 1992; *Children of a Harsh Winter*, 1994. *Recreations:* Restaurants, writing. Raised to the peerage as Baroness Cohen of Pimlico, in the City of Westminster 2000. The Baroness Cohen of Pimlico, House of Lords, London, SW1A 0PW *Tel:* 020 7219 3000.

COLVILLE OF CULROSS, VISCOUNT   Crossbencher

COLVILLE OF CULROSS (4th Viscount, UK), John Mark Alexander Colville; cr. 1902; 13th Lord Colville of Culross (S) 1604; 4th Baron Colville of Culross (UK) 1885. Born 19 July 1933. Son of 3rd Viscount, DL; educated Rugby School; New College, Oxford (BA law 1957, MA 1963). Married Mary Elizabeth Webb-Bowen 1958 (4 sons) (divorced 1973); married Margaret Birgitta, Viscountess Davidson 1974 (1 son). Lieutenant, Grenadier Guards (RARO). *Career:* Called to the Bar, Lincoln's Inn 1960; QC 1978; UK Representative, UN Commission on Human Rights 1980–83; Special Rapporteur on Guatemala 1983–87; Chair, Mental Health Act Commission 1983–87; Bencher 1986; Chair, Parole Board for England and Wales 1988–92; Recorder 1990–93; Judge, South Eastern Circuit 1993–99; Member, UN Human Rights Committee 1996–2000; Assistant Surveillance Commissioner 2001–. *House of Lords:* First entered House of Lords 1954; Minister of State, Home Office 1972–74; Elected hereditary peer 1999–. Member: Joint Select Committee on Consolidation of Bills 1998–, Liaison Committee 1999–; Chair, Select Committee on Religious Offences 2002–03. Hon. Fellow, New College, Oxford 1997; Hon. DCL, University of East Anglia 1998. Member, Queen's Bodyguard for Scotland, Royal Company of Archers. The Viscount Colville of Culross, QC, The Manor House, West Lexham, King's Lynn, Norfolk, PE32 2QN.

COLWYN, LORD   Conservative

COLWYN (3rd Baron, UK), (Ian) Anthony Hamilton-Smith; cr. 1917; 3rd Bt of Colwyn Bay (UK) 1912. Born 1 January 1942. Son of 2nd Baron; educated Cheltenham College; St Bartholomew's Hospital and Royal Dental Hospital, London University (BDS London University 1966, LDS, RCS (England) 1966). Married Sonia Jane Morgan 1964 (1 son 1 daughter) (divorced 1976); married Nicola Jeanne Tyers 1977 (2 daughters). *Trades Union:* Member, Musicians' Union. *Career:* Dental practice; Chair, Dental Protection Ltd. 1995–2001; Non-executive director: Medical Protection Society 1989–2002, Project Hope 1996–2001; Bandleader, Lord Colwyn Organisation; Chair, RAW FM (Radio) 1998–99; Chair, Banbury Local Radio 2003–. *House of Lords:* First entered House of Lords 1967; Elected hereditary peer 1999–. Member, Select Committees on:

Medical Ethics 1993–97, Finance and Staff 1997–2002, Administration and Works 1997–2002, House of Lords' Offices 1997–2002; Chair Refreshment Sub-Committee 1997–; Co-opted Member, Select Committee on Science and Technology Sub-Committee I (Complementary and Alternative Medicine) 2000. FDI Federation Dentaire International. Member, Conservative Medical Society. President: Natural Medicines Society 1988–, Huntington's Disease Association 1991–98, Society for Advancement of Anaesthesia in Dentistry 1993–98, Arterial Health Foundation 1993–, Metropolitan Branch, British Dental Association 1994–95; Council Member, Medical Protection Society 1994–. Member, Eastman Research Institute Trust 1990–2001; Fellow, Industry and Parliament Trust. CBE 1989. Member, Royal Society of Medicine; Fellow, Institute of Directors 1999–2001. *Publications:* Various articles on Anaesthesia in Dentistry. *Special Interests:* Broadcasting, Health, Complementary Medicine, Arts, Sport, Cycling. *Recreations:* Bandleader, music, riparian pursuits, golf. *Sportsclubs:* Cheltenham Rugby, Colwyn Bay Rugby. The Lord Colwyn, CBE, 53 Wimpole Street, London, W1G 8YH *Tel:* 020 7935 6809 *E-mail:* colwyna@parliament.uk.

CONDON, LORD   Crossbencher

CONDON (Life Baron) Paul Leslie Condon QPM; cr 2001; educated St Peter's College, Oxford. Married (2 sons 1 daughter). *Career:* Police service 1967–2000: Assistant Chief Constable of Kent 1984–87, Metropolitan Police 1987–88: Deputy Assistant Commissioner 1987–88, Assistant Commissioner 1988–89; Chief Constable of Kent 1989–93; Commissioner Metropolitan Police 1993–2000; Director International Cricket Council anti-corruption unit 2000–. Queen's Police Medal 1989; Knighthood 1994. Raised to the peerage as Baron Condon, of Langton Green in the County of Kent. The Lord Condon, QPM, House of Lords, London, SW1A 0PW *Tel:* 020 7219 3617.

CONSTANTINE OF STANMORE, LORD   Conservative

CONSTANTINE OF STANMORE (Life Baron), Theodore Constantine; cr. 1981. Born 15 March 1910. Son of late Leonard Constantine; educated Acton College, London. Married Sylvia Mary Legge-Pointing 1935 (died 1990) (1 son 1 daughter). Served Royal Auxiliary Air Force, Fighter Command 1939–45 (Air Efficiency Award 1945). High Sheriff, Greater London 1967; DL, Greater London 1967. *Career:* Secretary to Managing Director, Calders Ltd 1926–28; Personal Assistant to Managing Director, Pedestros Ltd 1928–31; Adminstration Manager, A.T. Betts & Co Ltd 1931–34; General Manager, Allen and Hanburys (Acoustic Division) 1934–39; Director, Allen and Hanburys (Acoustics) Ltd 1945–50; Chief Executive, Bonochord Ltd 1950–63; Deputy Chairman, Henry C. Stephens Ltd 1964–66; Chairman: Waterman Pen Co. Ltd 1966–68, Anscon Ltd 1966–, London Private Health Group plc 1981–85, Health Care Services plc 1985; Director, Stratstone Ltd 1985–92. Chairman, National Union Conservative Party 1968, President 1980; Work for Conservative party as constituency Chairman, area Chairman, Member National Executive Committee, Policy Committee, National Advisory Committee on publicity. Trustee, Sir John Wolstenholme Charity 1962–89. AE 1945; CBE 1956; Kt 1964. Freeman, City of London 1949. Master, Worshipful Company of Coachmakers 1975. *Recreations:* Reading, walking, watching motor racing. *Clubs:* Carlton. Raised to the peerage as Baron Constantine of Stanmore, of Stanmore in Greater London 1981. The Lord Constantine of Stanmore, CBE, AE, DL, House of Lords, London, SW1A 0PW *Tel:* 020 7219 5353.

DodOnline
An Electronic Directory without rival ...

Peers' biographies and photographs available with daily updates *via* the internet

For a *free* trial, call Yasmin Mirza, Aby Farsoun or Michael Mand on 020 7630 7643

COOKE OF ISLANDREAGH, LORD   Crossbencher

COOKE OF ISLANDREAGH (Life Baron), Victor Alexander Cooke; cr. 1992. Born 18 October 1920. Son of Victor and Alice Cooke; educated Marlborough College; Trinity College, Cambridge (MA mechanical sciences tripos 1941). Married Alison Sheila Casement 1951 (2 sons 1 daughter). Engineer Officer, Royal Navy 1940–46. DL, Co. Antrim 1970–96. *Career:* Henry R. Ayton Ltd, Belfast 1946–89, Chairman 1970–89; Chairman: Belfast Savings Bank 1963, Springvale EPS 1964–2000; Chairman, Harland & Wolff Ltd 1980–81, Director 1970–87; Director, Northern Ireland Airports 1970–85; Senator, Parliament of Northern Ireland 1960–68. Member, Northern Ireland Economic Council 1974–78; Belfast Harbour Commissioner 1968–79; Commissioner of Irish Lights 1983–96, Chair 1990–92; Member, The Foyle, Carlingford and Irish Lights Commission, North/South Ministerial Council 2000–. OBE 1981. CEng; FIMechE. *Special Interests:* Manufacturing Industries, Energy, Maritime Affairs. *Recreations:* Sailing, shooting. Raised to the peerage as Baron Cooke of Islandreagh, of Islandreagh in the County of Antrim 1992. The Lord Cooke of Islandreagh, OBE, House of Lords, London, SW1A 0PW *Tel:* 020 7219 8504.

COOKE OF THORNDON, LORD   Crossbencher

COOKE OF THORNDON (Life Baron), Robin Brunskill Cooke; cr. 1996. Born 9 May 1926. Son of late Hon. Philip Brunskill Cooke, MC, Judge of the Supreme Court of New Zealand, and of Valmai Digby Gore; educated Wanganui Collegiate School, New Zealand; Victoria University College, Wellington, New Zealand (LLM law 1950); Clare College, Cambridge (research 1950–51); Gonville and Caius College, Cambridge (MA 1954, PhD constitutional, administrative and procedural law 1955). Married Phyllis Annette Miller 1952 (3 sons). *Career:* Travelling scholarship in law, New Zealand 1950; Fellow, Gonville and Caius College, Cambridge 1952–56; Called to the Bar, Inner Temple 1954; Practised at New Zealand Bar 1955–72; QC 1964; Chairman, Commission of Inquiry into Housing 1970–71; Judge of the Supreme Court 1972–1976; President, Court of Appeal of: Samoa 1982, 1994–; Cook Islands 1981, 1982, Kiribati 1995–; Judge of the Supreme Court of Fiji 1995–2000; Administrator, Government of New Zealand for periods in 1986, 1992, 1993 and 1995; Judge, Court of Appeal of New Zealand 1976–86, President 1986–96; Member: Advisory Board, Centre for Independence of Judges and Lawyers 1989–, Judicial Committee, Privy Council 1977–2001; Commission Member representing New Zealand, International Commission of Jurists 1993–; Lord of Appeal, U.K. 1996–2001; Non-permanent Judge Court of Final Appeal of Hong Kong 1997–. Member International Bar Association. Special Status Member, The American Law Institute 1993–; Life Member, Lawasia; Patron, Cricket Wellington, New Zealand. Yorke Prize, University of Cambridge 1954. Hon. Fellow, Gonville and Caius College, Cambridge 1982; Hon. LLD: Victoria University of Wellington 1989, Cambridge University 1990; Hon. DCL, Oxford University 1991. Hon. Bencher, Inner Temple 1985–; Visiting Fellow, All Souls, Oxford 1990; Hon. Fellow, New Zealand Legal Research Foundation 1993–; Distinguished Visiting Fellow, Victoria University of Wellington 1998–. Kt 1977; Privy Counsellor 1977; KBE 1986; ONZ 2002. *Publications: Portrait of a Profession* (Centennial Book of New Zealand Law Society), 1969 (editor); *The Laws of New Zealand*, Editor-in-Chief 1990–; Sultan Azlan Shah Lecture, Malaysia 1990; Peter Allan Memorial Lecture, Hong Kong 1994; *Turning Points of the Common Law* (Hamlyn Lectures), 1996; Many articles in law journals and papers at international law conferences; Peter Taylor Memorial Lecture 2001. *Recreations:* Theatre, watching cricket, *The Times* crossword. *Sportsclubs:* Wellington Golf (NZ). *Clubs:* Oxford and Cambridge, London; Wellington (NZ); Wellington Golf (NZ). Raised to the peerage as Baron Cooke of Thorndon, of Wellington in New Zealand and of Cambridge in the County of Cambridgeshire 1996. Rt Hon the Lord Cooke of Thorndon, ONZ, KBE, PC, 4 Homewood Crescent, Karori, Wellington 6005, New Zealand *Tel:* 00 64 4 4768 059; Lords of Appeal Corridor, House of Lords, London, SW1A 0PW *Tel:* 020 7219 3202 *E-mail:* ddensem@attglobal.net.

Visit the Vacher Dod Website . . . **www.DodOnline.co.uk**

COPE OF BERKELEY, LORD — Conservative

COPE OF BERKELEY (Life Baron), John Ambrose Cope; cr. 1997. Born 13 May 1937. Son of late George Cope, MC, FRIBA; educated Oakham School, Rutland. Married Djemila Payne 1969 (2 daughters). National Service (Commissioned RA) 1955–57, subsequently TA. *Career:* Chartered accountant. *House of Commons:* Contested Woolwich East 1970 general election; MP (Conservative) for Gloucestershire South February 1974–83 and for Northavon 1983–97; Minister of State for: Employment with special responsibility for Small Firms 1987–89, Northern Ireland Office 1989–90; Paymaster General, HM Treasury 1992–94. Government Whip 1979–83; Deputy Chief Whip 1983–87. *House of Lords:* Deputy Chairman of Committees 2001–; Deputy Speaker 2002–. Opposition Chief Whip 2001–. Opposition Spokesperson for Home Affairs 1998–2001. Member Select Committees on: Procedure 2000–02, House of Lords' Offices 2001–02; House of Lords Offices Administration and Works Sub-committee/Committee 2001–, Liaison 2003–. Member, UK Parliamentary Delegation to Council of Europe and Western European Union 1995–97. Conservative Party: Deputy Chair 1990–92, Hon. Joint Treasurer 1991–92. Commissioner, Royal Hospital Chelsea 1992–94. Patron, The Vigilant Trust. PC 1988; Kt 1991. FCA. *Clubs:* Carlton, Beefsteak, Tudor House (Chipping Sodbury). Raised to the peerage as Baron Cope of Berkeley, of Berkeley in the County of Gloucestershire 1997. Rt Hon the Lord Cope of Berkeley, House of Lords, London, SW1A 0PW *Tel:* 020 7219 2249 *E-mail:* copej@parliament.uk.

CORBETT OF CASTLE VALE, LORD — Labour

CORBETT OF CASTLE VALE (Life Baron), Robin Corbett; cr. 2001. Born 22 December 1933. Son of late Thomas Corbett, foundry worker; educated Holly Lodge Grammar School, Smethwick, Staffordshire. Married Val Hudson, née Jonas 1970 (1 son 2 daughters). *Trades Union:* Member, National Executive Council, National Union of Journalists 1964–69. RAF national service 1951–53. Member, Wilton Park Academic Council; Chair, Castle Vale Neighbourhood Management Board. *Career:* Journalist; Assistant editor, *Farmer's Weekly* 1968–70; Editorial staff development executive, ICP Magazines 1970–73; Senior labour adviser, IPC Magazines 1973–74; Communications consultant 1979–83. *House of Commons:* Member for Hemel Hempstead 1974–79, and for Birmingham Erdington 1983–2001. West Midlands Labour Whip 1984–87. Opposition Deputy Spokesperson for Home Affairs 1987–92; Opposition Spokesperson for: National Heritage, Broadcasting and Press 1992–94, Disabled People's Rights 1994–95. Member European Union Sub-committee F (Social Affairs, Education and Home Affairs) 2003–. Member, Parliamentary Labour Party Campaign Unit 1984–85. Chair, Farm Animal Welfare Co-ordinating Executive 1975–87; Member, Committee for the Reform of Animal Experiments; Director, Rehab UK 1998–. Fellow, Industry and Parliament Trust. *Publications: Can I Count on Your Support?* (for Save the Children Fund, with wife), 1986; *Tales from the Campaign Trail* (co-author, for Save the Children Fund). *Special Interests:* Home Affairs, Police, Civil Liberties, Motor Industry, Manufacturing, Disabled/Disability, Children's Rights, Alternative Energy, Environment, Agriculture, Animal Welfare, Press. *Recreations:* Being with friends, concerts, theatre, radio. *Clubs:* Castle Vale Residents', Forget-Me-Not. Raised to the peerage as Baron Corbett of Castle Vale, of Erdington in the County of West Midlands 2001. The Lord Corbett of Castle Vale, House of Lords, London, SW1A 0PW *Tel:* 020 7219 3420 *E-mail:* corbettr@parliament.uk.

DodOnline
An Electronic Directory without rival . . .

Peers' biographies and photographs available with daily updates *via* the internet

For a *free* trial, call Yasmin Mirza, Aby Farsoun or Michael Mand on 020 7630 7643

COURTOWN, EARL OF Conservative

COURTOWN (9th Earl of, I), James Patrick Montagu Burgoyne Winthrop Stopford; cr. 1762; Viscount Stopford; 9th Baron Courtown (I) 1758; 8th Baron Saltersford (GB) 1796. Born 19 March 1954. Son of 8th Earl, OBE, TD. Sits as Baron Saltersford; educated Eton College; Berkshire College of Agriculture; Royal Agricultural College, Cirencester. Married Elisabeth Dunnett 1985 (1 son 2 daughters). *Career:* Land agent: Bruton Knowles, Gloucester 1987–90, John German, Shrewsbury 1990–93. *House of Lords:* First entered House of Lords 1975; Elected hereditary peer 1999–. Government Whip 1995–97; Opposition Whip 1997–2000. Government Spokesperson for the Home Office, Scotland and Transport 1995–97. Member, Select Committee on Bodmin Moor Commons Bill 1994. *Special Interests:* Agriculture, Environment, Property, Landscape Industry, West Country. *Recreations:* Fishing, shooting, skiing. The Earl of Courtown, House of Lords, London, SW1A 0PW.

COVENTRY, LORD BISHOP OF Non-affiliated

COVENTRY (Bishop of), Colin James Bennetts. Born 9 September 1940. Son of James Thomas Bennetts and Winifred, née Couldry; educated Battersea Grammar School; Jesus College, Cambridge (BA modern and medieval languages and theology 1963); Ridley Hall, Cambridge. Married Veronica Leat 1966 (2 sons 2 daughters). *Career:* Curate St Stepehen, Tonbridge 1965–69; Chaplain to Oxford pastorate 1969–73; Chaplain Jesus College, Oxford 1973–80; Vicar St Andrew, Oxford 1980–90; Canon residentiary Chester Cathedral 1990–94; Area bishop of Buckingham 1994–98; Co-chair Springboard 1995–2001; Bishop of Coventry 1998–; Took his seat in the House of Lords 2002. Rt Rev the Lord Bishop of Coventry, Bishop's House, 23 Davenport Road, Coventry, CV5 6DT *Tel:* 024 7667 2244 *Fax:* 024 7671 3271 *E-mail:* bishcov@btconnect.com.

COX, BARONESS Conservative

COX (Life Baroness), Caroline Anne Cox; cr. 1983. Born 6 July 1937. Daughter of late Robert John McNeill Love, FRCS, FACS, and late Dorothy Ida Borland; educated Channing School, Highgate, London; London Hospital (SRN 1958) London University external student (BSc Soc 1967, MSc Econ 1969). Married Dr Murray Newall Cox 1959 (died 1997) (2 sons 1 daughter). *Career:* Staff nurse, Edgware General Hospital 1960; Polytechnic of North London: lecturer, senior lecturer and principal lecturer, 1969–74, Head, Department of Sociology 1974–77; Director, Nursing Education Research Unit, Chelsea College, London University 1977–84; Fellow, Royal College of Nursing, Vice-President, 1990–. Chancellor, Bournemouth University 1992–2001. *House of Lords:* Deputy Speaker 1986–; Deputy Chair of Committees 1986–. Government Whip 1985. Standing Conference on Women's Organisations, Vice-President, Girl Guides Association; Director, Educational Research Trust; Patron: Medical Aid for Poland Fund, Physicians for Human Rights, UK; Non-executive Director: Andrei Sakarov Foundation; Board of Management/President, Hon. Christian Solidarity Worldwide UK; International Representative, Elam Ministries; IUS et Lex-Poland Foundation. Wilberforce Award 1995; Fridej of Nansen International Foundation Award. 12 honorary doctorates and fellowships. President: Tushinskaya Children's Hospital Trust, London Bible College, Dean Close School; Trustee: MERLIN (Medical Emergency Relief International), Siberian Medical University, The Nuffield Trust, The Trusthouse Charitable Foundation. Commander Cross of the Order of Merit of the Republic of Poland 1990. RGN; FRCN; Hon. FRCS 1997. *Publications:* Former Co-editor, International Journal of Nursing Studies; Author of numerous publications on education and health care, including: Co-editor, *A Sociology of Medical Practice*, 1975; Co-author, *The Rape of Reason: The Corruption of the Polytechnic of North London*, 1975; *The Right to Learn*, 1982; *Sociology: A Guide for Nurses, Midwives and Health Visitors*, 1983; Editor, *Trajectories of Despair: Misdiagnosis and Maltreatment of Soviet Orphans*, 1991; Co-author: *Ethnic Cleansing in Progress: War in Nagorno Karabakh*, 1993, *Made to Care: The Case for Residential and Village Communities for People with a Mental*

Handicap, 1995, *Remorse: The Most Dreadful Sentiment* in *Remorse and Reparation*, Ed. Murray Cox, 1998, *The 'West', Islam and Islamism: is ideological Islam compatible with liberal democracy?*, 2003. *Special Interests:* Human Rights, Humanitarian Aid, Education, Health, Nursing. *Recreations:* Campanology, hill walking, Tennis. *Sportsclubs:* Cumberland Lawn Tennis. *Clubs:* Royal Over-Seas League. Raised to the peerage as Baroness Cox, of Queensbury in Greater London 1983. The Baroness Cox, House of Lords, London, SW1A 0PW *Tel:* 020 8204 7336 *Fax:* 020 8204 5661 *E-mail:* ccox@ertnet.demon.co.uk.

CRAIG OF RADLEY, LORD   Crossbencher

CRAIG OF RADLEY (Life Baron), David Brownrigg Craig; cr. 1991. Born 17 September 1929. Son of late Major Francis Brownrigg Craig and Hannah Olivia (Olive) Craig; educated Radley College; Lincoln College, Oxford (BA pure maths 1951, MA). Married June Derenburg 1955 (1 son 1 daughter). Commissioned into RAF 1951; Flying instructor on Meteors and Hunter pilot in Fighter Command; CO, No. 35 Squadron 1963–65; Military Assistant to Chief of the Defence Staff 1965–68; Group Captain 1968; Station CO, RAF College, Cranwell 1968–70; ADC to HM The Queen 1969–71; Director, Plans and Operations, HQ Far East Command 1970–71; OC, RAF Akrotiri (Cyprus) 1972–73; Assistant Chief of Air Staff (Operations) Ministry of Defence 1975–78; Air Officer Commanding No 1 Group 1978–80; Vice-Chief of Air Staff 1980–82; Air Officer Commanding-in-Chief Strike Command and Commander-in-Chief UK Air Forces 1982–85; Chief of the Air Staff 1985–88; Air ADC to HM The Queen 1985–88; Marshal of the Royal Air Force 1988; Chief of the Defence Staff 1988–91. *House of Lords:* Convenor of Cross-Bench Peers 1999–. Member: Science and Technology Committee 1993–98, House of Lords Offices Committee 2000–02, House of Lords Offices Finance and Staff Sub-committee, 2000–02, Administration and Works Sub-committee 2000–02, Privileges Committee 2000–, Liaison Committee 2000–, Procedure Committee 2000–, Committee of Selection 2000–, House Committee 2002–, Administration and Works Committee 2002–. Chair of Council King Edward VII Hospital (Sister Agnes); Vice-Chair, RAF Benevolent Fund. Hon. Fellow, Lincoln College, Oxford 1984; Hon. DSc, Cranfield Institute of Technology 1988. OBE (Mil) 1967; CB 1978; KCB 1981; GCB (Mil) 1984. FRAeS. *Special Interests:* Defence. *Recreations:* Golf, fishing, shooting, woodwork. *Clubs:* President, Royal Air Force 2001–. Raised to the peerage as Baron Craig of Radley, of Helhoughton in the County of Norfolk 1991. Marshal of the Royal Air Force The Lord Craig of Radley, GCB, OBE, House of Lords, London, SW1A 0PW *Tel:* 020 7219 2200 *Fax:* 020 7219 0670 *E-mail:* craigd@parliament.uk.

CRAIGAVON, VISCOUNT   Crossbencher

CRAIGAVON (3rd Viscount, UK), Janric Fraser Craig; cr. 1927; 3rd Bt of Craigavon (UK) 1918. Born 9 June 1944. Son of 2nd Viscount; educated Eton College; London University (BA, BSc). *Career:* Chartered accountant. *House of Lords:* First entered House of Lords 1974; Elected hereditary peer 1999–. Member, Hybrid Instruments 1993–97, 1999–. Member, Executive Committee Anglo-Austrian Society. Former Trustee now Adviser, Progress Educational Trust. Commander of the Order of the Lion (Finland) 1998; Commander of the Royal Order of the Polar Star (Sweden) 1999. The Viscount Craigavon, 54 Westminster Mansions, 1 Little Smith Street, London, SW1P 3DQ *Tel:* 020 7222 1949.

CRATHORNE, LORD   Conservative

CRATHORNE (2nd Baron, UK), (Charles) James Dugdale; cr. 1959; 2nd Bt of Crathorne (UK) 1945. Born 12 September 1939. Son of 1st Baron, PC, TD; educated Eton College; Trinity College, Cambridge (MA fine arts 1963). Married Sylvia Mary Montgomery 1970 (1 son 2 daughters). DL, County of Cleveland 1983–96; DL, County of North Yorkshire 1996–98, Lord Lieutenant 1999–; JP 1999–. *Career:* Impressionist painting department, Sotheby & Co. 1963–66; Assistant to president, Parke-Bernet Galleries, New York 1966–69; Independent fine art consultancy, James Dugdale & Associates 1969–; Lecture tours to the USA 1969–; Director, Blakeney Hotels Ltd 1979–96; Lecture series *Aspects of England*, in Metropolitan Museum, New York 1981;

Australian bicentennial lecture tour 1988; Director: Woodhouse Securities Ltd 1988–99, Cliveden plc 1996–99, Cliveden Ltd 1999–2002, Hand Picked Hotels 2000–01. *House of Lords:* First entered House of Lords 1977; Elected hereditary peer 1999–. Member, Conservative Advisory Group on Arts and Heritage 1988–99. Council RSA 1982–88; Editorial Board of the House Magazine 1983–; Member University Court of Leeds University 1985–97; Executive Committee, Georgian Group 1985–, Chair 1990–99; Governor Queen Margaret's School York Ltd. 1986–99; President: Yarm Civic Society 1987–, Cleveland Family History Society 1988–, Cleveland Sea Cadets 1988–; Hambleton District of CPRE 1988–; Patron Cleveland Community Foundation 1990–; Deputy Chair Joint Committee of National Amenity Societies 1993–96, Chair 1996–99; President Cleveland and North Yorkshire Magistrates' Association 1997–; President North Yorkshire County Scout Council 1999–; Vice-President: The Public Monuments and Sculpture Association 1997–, Yorkshire and Humberside RFCA 1999–; Patron British Red Cross North Yorkshire Branch 1999–; Vice-president North of England RFCA 2001–. Queen's Golden Jubilee Medal 2002. Trustee, Georgian Theatre Royal, Richmond, Yorkshire 1970–; Trustee, Captain Cook Birthplace Museum Trust 1978–, Chair 1993–; Yorkshire Regional Committee, National Trust 1988–94; Vice-President, Cleveland Wildlife Trust 1989–; Patron, Attingham Trust for the Study of the British Country House 1990–; Trustee, National Heritage Memorial Fund 1992–95. KStJ 1999; Queen's Golden Jubilee Medal 2002. FRSA 1972. *Publications:* Articles in *The Connoisseur* and *Apollo*; *Edouard Vuillard*, 1967; *Cliveden, the Place and the People*, 1995; *The Royal Crescent Book of Bath*, 1998; Co-Author: *Tennant's Stalk*, 1973; *A Present from Crathorne*, 1989; Co-Photographer *Parliament in Pictures*, 1999. *Special Interests:* Visual and Performing Arts, Country Houses. *Recreations:* Photography, jazz, collecting, country pursuits, travel with the family. *Clubs:* Brooks's. The Lord Crathorne, Crathorne House, Yarm, North Yorkshire, TS15 0AT *Tel:* 01642 700431 *Fax:* 01642 700632; House of Lords, London, SW1A 0PW *Tel:* 020 7219 5224 *Fax:* 020 7219 2772 *E-mail:* james@jcrathorne.fsnet.co.uk.

CRAWFORD AND BALCARRES, EARL OF   Conservative

CRAWFORD (29th Earl of, S), cr. 1398, AND BALCARRES (12th Earl of, S), cr. 1651; Robert Alexander Lindsay; Lord Lindsay of Crawford before 1143. Lord Lindsay (S) 1633; Lord Balniel (S) 1651; 5th Baron Wigan (UK) 1826; (Life) Baron Balniel 1974. Born 5 March 1927. Son of 28th Earl, KT, GBE; educated Eton College; Trinity College, Cambridge. Married Ruth Beatrice Meyer-Bechtler 1949 (2 sons 2 daughters). Served with Grenadier Guards 1945–48. DL, Fife –2002. *Career:* President, Rural District Council Association for England and Wales 1959–65; Chair, National Association for Mental Health 1963–70; Director, National Westminster Bank 1975–89; Vice-Chairman, Sun Alliance & London Insurance 1975–91; Chair, Historic Buildings Council for Scotland 1976–83; First Commissioner of the Crown Estate 1980–85; Chair, Royal Commission on the Ancient and Historical Monuments of Scotland 1985–95; Chair, Board of the National Library of Scotland 1991–2000; Lord Chamberlain to HM Queen Elizabeth the Queen Mother 1992–2002. *House of Commons:* MP (Conservative) for: Hertford 1955–74, Welwyn and Hatfield March-October 1974; PPS: to Financial Secretary to the Treasury 1955–56, to Minister of Housing and Local Government 1956–59; Minister of State for Defence 1970–72, Minister of State, Foreign and Commonwealth Affairs 1972–74. Principal Opposition Frontbench Spokesperson for Health and Social Security 1967–70. *House of Lords:* First entered House of Lords 1975. Premier Earl of Scotland on Union Roll; Head of the House of Lindsay. PC 1972; KT 1996; GCVO 2002. Created a life peer as Baron Balniel, of Pitcorthie in the County of Fife 1974. Rt Hon the Earl of Crawford and Balcarres, KT, GCVO, House of Lords, London, SW1A 0PW *Tel:* 020 7219 5353.

CRAWLEY, BARONESS   Labour

CRAWLEY (Life Baroness), Christine Mary Crawley; cr. 1998. Born 9 January 1950. Daughter of Thomas Louis Quinn and Joan Ryan; educated Notre Dame Catholic Secondary Girls School, Plymouth; Digby Stuart Training College, Roehampton. Married (1 son 2 daughters). *Trades Union:* Member: MSF, UNISON. Former Town and District Councillor in South Oxfordshire. *Career:* Former Teacher and Youth Theatre Leader; MEP for Birmingham East 1984–99, Chair: Women's National Commission 1999–2002, West Midlands Regional Cultural Consortium 1999–2002. Government Whip 2002–. Government Spokesperson for: Defence 2002–, Foreign and Commonwealth Office 2002–, International Development 2002–. Member: European Union Committee –2000, European Union Sub-committee A (Economic and Financial Affairs, Trade and External Relations) 2000–01. Member: Fabian Society, Co-operative Party, Labour Movement in Europe;

Deputy Leader, EP Labour Party with responsibility for links with the Labour Government in UK 1994–98; Member, Socialist Group Bureau in European Parliament 1994–98. Member, Amnesty International. Contested Staffordshire South East 1983 general election; Chair, Regional Cultural Consortium – West Midlands. Fellow, Royal Society of Arts. *Publications:* Contributions to a number of publications including *Changing States – Labour Agenda for Europe*; Articles on women's rights and equality policy. *Special Interests:* Women's Rights, Equal Opportunities, European Union. *Recreations:* Latin American literature, amateur dramatics, attending local football matches in Birmingham. Raised to the peerage as Baroness Crawley, of Edgbaston in the County of West Midlands 1998. The Baroness Crawley, House of Lords, London, SW1A 0PW *Tel:* 020 7219 4650 *E-mail:* ccrawley@enterprise.net.

CRICKHOWELL, LORD   Conservative

CRICKHOWELL (Life Baron), Roger Nicholas Edwards; cr. 1987. Born 25 February 1934. Son of late Ralph Edwards, CBE, FSA; educated Westminster School; Trinity College, Cambridge (BA history 1952, MA). Married Ankaret Healing 1963 (1 son 2 daughters). National service (Second Lieutenant) Royal Welch Fusiliers; Lieutenant, TA. *Career:* Member of Lloyds 1963–2002; Chair: ITNET Plc, HTV Group Ltd 1997–2002; Former Director: William Brandts Ltd and Associated Companies, A L Sturge Holdings Ltd, PA International & Sturge Underwriting Agency Ltd, Associated British Ports Holdings plc, Anglesey Mining plc; Globtik Tankers Ltd, Committee of Automobile Association 1988–98; Chair: National Rivers Authority Advisory Committee 1988–89, National Rivers Authority 1989–96. *House of Commons:* MP (Conservative) for Pembroke 1970–87; Secretary of State for Wales, May 1979–87. Member, Procedure Committee 2000–; Co-opted Member, EU Sub-committee D (Environment, Agriculture, Public Health and Consumer Protection) 2000–; Member, Joint Committee on the Draft Communications Bill 2002. President: Cardiff University of Wales 1988–98, South East Wales Arts Association 1988–94. Hon. Fellow, Cardiff University of Wales, Doctor of Law, Glamorgan University. Chair, Cardiff Bay Opera House Trust 1993–97. PC 1979. Fishmongers' Company. *Publications: Opera House Lottery – Zaha Hadid and The Cardiff Bay Project*, 1997; *Westminster, Wales and Water*, 1999. *Special Interests:* Environment, Economic Policy, Urban Policies, Arts, Broadcasting. *Clubs:* Brooks's, Cardiff and County (Cardiff). Raised to the peerage as Baron Crickhowell, of Pont Esgob in the Black Mountains and County of Powys 1987. Rt Hon the Lord Crickhowell, 4 Henning St, London, SW11 3DR *Tel:* 020 7350 2568; Pont Esgob Mill, Fforest Coalpit, Nr Abergavenny, Gwent, NP7 7LS *E-mail:* ncrickhowell@aol.com.

CROHAM, LORD   Crossbencher

CROHAM (Life Baron), Douglas Albert Vivian Allen; cr. 1978. Born 15 December 1917. Son of Albert John Allen (killed in action 1918); educated Wallington County Grammar School for Boys; London School of Economics (BSc(Econ) statistics 1938). Married Sybil Eileen Allegro 1941 (died 1994) (2 sons 1 daughter). *Trades Union:* Member, First Division Association (FDA). Served Royal Artillery 1940–45. *Career:* Joined Home Civil Service, Board of Trade 1939; Treasury 1948, Assistant Secretary 1949–58; Under-Secretary, Ministry of Health 1958–60; Treasury 1960–64, Third Secretary 1962; Department of Economic Affairs 1964–68, Permanent Secretary 1966–68; Permanent Secretary, Treasury 1968–74; Permanent Secretary, Civil Service Department and Head of Home Civil Service 1974–77; Chairman: British National Oil Corporation 1982–86, Guinness Peat Group plc 1982–87, Trinity Insurance Ltd 1987–92. Member, Select Committee on the Public Service 1996–97. President, Institute for Fiscal Studies 1978–92; Chairman, Anglo-German Foundation 1982–98; President, British Institute of Energy Economics 1986–94; Vice-President, Anglo-German Association, Governor: London School of Economics, Wallington County Grammar School. Hon. DSocSc, Southampton University. Member, Institute of Directors; Companion, Institute of Management. CB 1963; KCB 1967; GCB 1973. Fellow, Royal Society of Arts. *Special Interests:* Finance, Economic Policy, Energy. *Recreations:* Woodwork, Bridge. *Clubs:* Reform, Civil Service. Raised to the peerage as Baron Croham, of the London Borough of Croydon 1978. The Lord Croham, GCB, 9 Manor Way, South Croydon, Surrey, CR2 7BT *Tel:* 020 8688 0496.

CUCKNEY, LORD
Conservative

CUCKNEY (Life Baron), John Graham Cuckney; cr. 1995. Born 12 July 1925. Son of late Air Vice-Marshal E. J. Cuckney, CB, CBE, DSC and Bar, and Lilian, née Williams; educated Shrewsbury School; St Andrews University (MA 1947). Married 2nd, Muriel Boyd 1960. War service with Royal Northumberland Fusiliers, King's African Rifles, followed by attachment to War Office (Civil Assistant General Staff) 1947–57. *Career:* Director, Lazard Brothers & Co. 1964–70, 1988–90; Independent Member, Railway Policy Review Committee 1966–67; Chairman, Mersey Docks and Harbour Board 1970–72; Chief Executive (Second Permanent Secretary), Property Services Agency, Department of the Environment 1972–74; Senior Crown Agent and Chairman, Crown Agents for Overseas Governments and Administrations 1974–78; Chairman: International Military Services (an MoD company) 1974–85, EDC for Building 1976–80, Port of London Authority 1977–79, Thomas Cook Group Ltd 1978–88; Director, Midland Bank plc 1978–88; Council, British Executive Service Overseas 1981–84; Chairman: Brooke Bond Group plc 1981–84, International Maritime Bureau of International Chamber of Commerce 1981–85, John Brown plc 1983–86, Westland Group 1985–89; Deputy Chairman, TI Group plc 1985–90; Chairman, Royal Insurance Holdings plc 1985–94; Director: Brixton Estate plc 1985–96, SBAC 1986–89; Chairman: 3i Group plc 1987–92, Understanding Industry Trust 1988–91, NEDC Working Party on European Public Purchasing 1990–92; Vice-Chairman, Glaxo Wellcome plc 1990–95; Adviser to the Secretary of State for Social Security on the Maxwell pensions affair and founder Chairman of the Maxwell Pensioners' Trust 1992–95; Controller, ROH Development Land Trust 1993–96; Chairman, The Orion Publishing Group Ltd 1994–97. Member, Select Committees on: Science and Technology Sub-Committee II on the Innovation Exploitation Barrier 1996–97, Public Service 1996–97, Monetary Policy of the Bank of England/Economic Affairs 2000–02. Governor, Centre for International Briefing, Farnham Castle 1974–84; Elder Brother of Trinity House 1980–; Vice-President, Liverpool School of Tropical Medicine 1985–93. Hon. DSc, Bath 1991; Hon. LLD, St Andrews 1993. Trustee, RAF Museum 1987–99. Kt 1978. Freeman, City of London 1977. *Special Interests:* City, Economic Policy. *Clubs:* Athenaeum. Raised to the peerage as Baron Cuckney, of Millbank in the City of Westminster 1995. The Lord Cuckney, House of Lords, London, SW1A 0PW *Tel:* 020 7219 5353.

CULLEN OF WHITEKIRK, LORD
Crossbencher

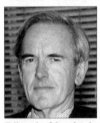

CULLEN OF WHITEKIRK (Life Baron), (William) Douglas Cullen; cr. 2003. Born 18 November 1935. Son of late Sheriff K D Cullen and G M Cullen; educated Dundee High School; St Andrews University (MA classics 1957); Edinburgh Uniiversity (LLB 1960). Married Rosamond Downer 1961 (2 sons 2 daughters). *Career:* Called to Scottish Bar 1960; Standing junior counsel to HM Customs and Excise 1970–73; QC (Scotland) 1973; Advocate-Depute 1978–81; Senator College of Justice in Scotland 1986–; Lord Justice Clerk and President of the Second Division of Court of Session 1977–2001; Chair Medical Appeal Tribunal 1977–86; Court of Inquiry into Piper Alpha disaster 1988–90; Review of Business of Outer House of Court of Session 1995; Tribunal of Inquiry into shootings at Dunblane Primary School 1996; Ladbroke Grove Rail Inquiry 1999–2001; Lord Justice General of Scotland and Lord President of the Court of Session 2001–. PC 1997. Raised to the peerage as Baron Cullen of Whitekirk, of Whitekirk in East Lothian 2003. Rt Hon the Lord Cullen of Whitekirk, House of Lords, London, SW1A 0PW; Parliament House, Edinburgh, EH1 1RQ *Tel:* 0131–240 6701 *Fax:* 0131–240 6704 *E-mail:* amaxwell@scotcourts.gov.uk.

DodOnline
An Electronic Directory without rival . . .

Peers' biographies and photographs available with daily updates *via* the internet

For a *free* trial, call Yasmin Mirza, Aby Farsoun or Michael Mand on 020 7630 7643

CUMBERLEGE, BARONESS — Conservative

CUMBERLEGE (Life Baroness), Julia Frances Cumberlege; cr. 1990. Born 27 January 1943. Daughter of Dr L U Camm and Mrs M G G Camm; educated Convent of the Sacred Heart, Tunbridge Wells. Married Patrick Cumberlege 1961 (3 sons). Chair, Brighton Health Authority 1981–88; Councillor, Lewes District Council 1966–79, Leader 1977–78; Councillor, East Sussex County Council 1974–85, Chair, Social Services Committee 1979–82; Chair, South West Thames Regional Health Authority 1988–92; JP, East Sussex 1973–85; DL, East Sussex 1986–; Vice-Lord Lieutenant 1992; Chair, St George's Medical School Council 2000–. *Career:* Executive director, MJM Healthcare Solutions 1997–2001; Non-executive director Huntsworth plc 2001–03; Consultant, Quo Health 2001–; Founded Cumberlege Connections April 2001. *House of Lords:* Joint Parliamentary Under-Secretary of State, Department of Health 1992–97. Opposition Spokesperson for Health 1997. Member Stem Cell Research Committee –2002. Vice-President: Royal College of Nursing 1989–, Pre-School Playgroups Association 1989–91; Council Member Brighton Polytechnic 1987–89; Chair of Council, St George's Hospital Medical School 1988–92; Governor, Chailey Heritage School and Hospital 1982–88; President: Age Concern Sussex 1993–, Sussex Care for the Carers 1996–, Member of Council: Sussex University 2001–, Vice-President, Royal College of Midwives 2001; Chair, HR Remunerations Committee, Cancer Research UK. DUniv: Surrey University 1990, Brighton University 1994. Trustee: Chailey Heritage, Cancer Link, Cancer Research UK; Patron, National Childbirth Trust. Council Member, National Association of Health Authorities 1982–88, Vice-chair 1984–87, Chair 1987–88; Member, Press Council 1984–90; Chair, Review of Community Nursing for England 1985; Member: DHSS Expert Advisory Group on AIDS 1987–89, NHS Policy Board for England 1989–; Council Member, UK Central Council for Nursing, Midwifery and Health Visiting 1989–92; CBE 1985. Fellow, Royal Society of Arts 1989. *Special Interests:* Local Government, National Health Service, Media, Education. *Recreations:* Other people's gardens, bicycling. *Clubs:* Royal Society of Medicine. Raised to the peerage as Baroness Cumberlege, of Newick in the County of East Sussex 1990. The Baroness Cumberlege, CBE, DL, Snells Cottage, The Green, Newick, Lewes, East Sussex, BN8 4LA *Tel:* 01825 722154 *Fax:* 01825 723873 *E-mail:* cumberlegej@parliament.uk.

CURRIE OF MARYLEBONE, LORD — Crossbencher

CURRIE OF MARYLEBONE (Life Baron), David Anthony Currie; cr. 1996. Born 9 December 1946. Son of late Kennedy Currie and of Marjorie Currie; educated Battersea Grammar School; Manchester University (BSc maths 1968); Birmingham University (MSoc Sci Econs 1971); London University (PhD economics 1978). Married Shaziye Gazioglu 1975 (2 sons) (divorced 1992); married Angela Mary Piers Dumas 1995 (1 stepson). *Career:* Economist, Hoare Govett 1971–72; Lecturer, reader and professor of economics, Queen Mary College, London University 1972–88; Visiting scholar, International Monetary Fund 1987; London Business School: Professor of economics 1988–2000, Research dean 1989–92, Governor 1989–95, 1999–2000, Deputy principal 1992–95, Deputy dean, External Relations 1999–2000; Director: Joseph Rowntree Reform Trust 1991–2002, International Schools of Business Management 1992–95; Visiting professor, European University Institute 1992–95; Director: Gas and Electricity Markets Authority 2000–02, Charter 88 1994–98, Member: Terra Firma, Advisory Board of Nomura Private Finance Group 2000–02, Advisory Board, Terra Firma Capital Partners 2002–, Dean, City University Business School 2001–; Director Abbey National plc 2001–02; Chairman, Ofcom 2002–. Honorary fellowship and doctorate. Research fellow, Centre for Economic Policy Research 1983–98; Houblon Norman resident fellow, Bank of England 1985–86; Member. Retail Price Index Advisory Committee 1992–95, Treasury's Panel of Independent Forecasters 1992–95, Management Board OFGEM 1999–2000. FRSA. *Publications: Advances in Monetary Economics*, 1985; Co-author: *The Operation and Regulation of Financial Markets*, 1986, *Macroeconomic Interactions Between North and South*, 1988, *Rules, Reputation and Macroeconomic Policy Co-ordination*, 1993, *EMUs Problems in the Transition to a Single European Currency*, 1995, *North-South Linkages and International Macroeconomic Policy*, 1995; *The Pros and Cons of EMU*, 1997; *Will the Euro Work?*, 1998; Articles in journals. *Special Interests:* Economic Policy, Media and Communications, Regulation. *Recreations:* Music (playing the cello), literature, swimming. Raised to the peerage as Baron Currie of Marylebone, of Marylebone in the City of Westminster 1996. Professor the Lord Currie of Marylebone, City University Business School, Frobisher Crescent, Barbican, London, EC2Y 8HB *Tel:* 020 7040 8601.

D

DAHRENDORF, LORD   Liberal Democrat

DAHRENDORF (Life Baron), Ralf Dahrendorf; cr. 1993. Born 1 May 1929. Son of late Gustav Dahrendorf and of Lina Dahrendorf; educated in Hamburg and Berlin; Hamburg University (Drphil philosophy and classics 1952) Postgraduate studies at London School of Economics 1952–54 (Leverhulme Research Scholar 1953–54, PhD 1956). *Career:* Fellow at Center for Advanced Study in the Behavioural Sciences, Palo Alto, USA 1957–58; Professor of Sociology: Hamburg 1957–60, Tubingen 1960–64, Konstanz 1966–69; Parliamentary Secretary of State, Federal German Ministry of Foreign Affairs 1969–70; Member, EEC, Brussels 1970–74; Director, London School of Economics 1974–84, Governor 1986–; Professor of Social Science, Konstanz University 1984–86; Non-Exec Director, Glaxo Holdings plc 1984–92; Visiting Professor at several European and North American Universities; Visiting Scholar, Russell Sage Foundation, New York 1986–87; Warden, St Antony's College, Oxford 1987–97; Chairman, Newspaper Publishing plc 1992–93; Non-Executive Director, Bank Gesellschaft Berlin 1996–2001. Co-opted Member, European Communities Committee Sub-Committee A (Economic and Financial Affairs, Trade and External Relations) 1997–99; Member: Delegated Powers and Deregulation Committee 1997–2001, Stem Cell Research Committee 2001–02; Chair Delegated Powers and Regulatory Reform Committee 2002–. Chairman, Council for Charitable Support 1995–. Hon. Fellow, London School of Economics 1970; Fellow, St Antony's College, Oxford 1976; 28 honorary degrees from universities in Great Britain, Ireland, Belgium, Italy, Malta, the United States, Canada, Argentina, Israel and France and Bulgaria. Trustee: Ford Foundation 1976–88, Charities Aid Foundation. Adopted British nationality 1988; Member: Hansard Society Commission on Electoral Reform 1975–76, Royal Commission on Legal Services 1976–79, Committee to Review Functioning of Financial Institutions 1977–80. Holder of decorations from Senegal, Germany, Luxembourg, Austria, Belgium, Spain and Italy; KBE 1982. FBA 1977; FRSA 1977; Hon. FRCS 1982. Freeman, City of London 1998. *Publications:* Several works on philosophy, sociology and politics, including: *Marx in Perspective*, 1953; *Class and Class Conflict*, 1959; *Society and Democracy in Germany*, 1966; *Essays on the Theory of Society*, 1968; *The New Liberty*, 1975; *On Britain*, 1982; *Law and Order*, 1985; *The Modern Social Conflict*, 1988; *Reflections on the Revolution in Europe*, 1990; *A History of the London School of Economics and Political Science 1895–1995*, 1995; *After 1989*, 1997; many of which have been translated into several European and Asian languages. *Clubs:* Reform, Garrick. Raised to the peerage as Baron Dahrendorf, of Clare Market in the City of Westminster 1993. The Lord Dahrendorf, KBE, House of Lords, London, SW1A 0PW *Tel:* 020 7219 3170.

DARCY DE KNAYTH, BARONESS   Crossbencher

DARCY DE KNAYTH (Baroness, 18th in line, E), Davina Marcia Ingrams; cr. 1332. Born 10 July 1938. Daughter of 17th Baron (Viscount Clive), son of 4th Earl of Powis; educated St. Mary's School, Wantage, Oxfordshire; Italy; Sorbonne, Paris. Married Rupert George Ingrams 1960 (died 1964) (1 son 2 daughters). *House of Lords:* First entered House of Lords 1969; Elected hereditary peer 1999–. Member: European Communities Sub-committee C 1985–88, Select Committee on murder and life imprisonment 1988–89, House of Lords' Offices Refreshment Sub-committee 2000–02, Administration and Works 2003–. President: SKILL (National Bureau for Students with Disabilities), DDA Disabled Ramblers; Vice-President: GRANGE (Centre for People with Disabilities) WAMDSAD (Windsor, Ascot, Maidenhead and District Sports Association for Disabled People); Patron: Artsline, DEMAND, IPSEA (Independent Panel for Special Education Advice), GLAD (Greater London Action on Disability); Member: JCMDP (Joint Committee on Mobility for Disabled People), WAMU (Windsor and Maidenhead Users Group). Member, Independent Broadcasting Authority General Advisory Council 1987–90. DBE 1996. *Special Interests:* Disability. *Recreations:* Theatre, cinema. *Sportsclubs:* Stoke Paraplegic Athletics Club, Windsor, Ascot, Maidenhead and District Sports Association for Disabled People. The Baroness Darcy de Knayth, DBE, Camley Corner, Stubbings, Maidenhead, Berkshire, SL6 6QW *Tel:* 01628 822935.

DAVID, BARONESS   Labour

DAVID (Life Baroness), Nora Ratcliff David; cr. 1978. Born 23 September 1913. Daughter of late George Blockley Blakesley, JP; educated Ashby-De-La-Zouch Girls' Grammar School; St. Felix School, Southwold; Newnham College, Cambridge (BA English 1935, MA). Married Richard William David 1935 (died 1993) (2 sons 2 daughters). Councillor: Cambridge City Council 1964–67, 1968–74, Cambridgeshire County Council 1974–78; Member of Board, Peterborough Development Corporation 1976–78; JP, Cambridge City 1965–. Government Whip 1978–79; Opposition Whip 1979–83; Opposition Deputy Chief Whip 1983–87. Opposition Spokesperson for: Education 1979–85, the Environment 1985–87, Education 1987–97. Member: Select Committee on European Communities 1990–94, Sub-Committee on Social and Consumer Affairs 1989–94, Sub-Committee on Agriculture 1993–97. Member: CPA, IPU. Hon. Fellow: Newnham College, Cambridge 1986, Anglia Polytechnic University 1989; Hon. DLitt, Staffordshire University 1995. *Special Interests:* Education, Environment, Home Affairs, Children. *Recreations:* Walking, swimming, theatre, travel. Raised to the peerage as Baroness David, of Romsey in the City of Cambridge 1978. The Baroness David, 50 Highsett, Cambridge, CB2 1NZ *Tel:* 01223 350376 *Fax:* 020 7219 5979; Cove, New Polzeath, Cornwall, PL27 6UF *Tel:* 01208 863310 *E-mail:* davidn@parliament.uk.

DAVIES OF COITY, LORD   Labour

DAVIES OF COITY (Life Baron), (David) Garfield Davies; cr. 1997. Born 24 June 1935. Son of late David and Lizzie Davies; educated Heolgam Secondary Modern School; Bridgend Technical College (part-time). Married Marian Jones 1960 (4 daughters). *Trades Union:* Member, TUC General Council 1986–97, Chairman, International Committee 1992–94; Spokesperson on International Affairs 1994–97; Member: Executive Board, International Confederation of Free Trade Unions 1992–97, Executive Committee, European Trade Union Confederation 1992–97; Governor, Birmingham College of Food, Tourism and Creative Studies 1995–99. RAF 1956–58. Parish Councillor 1963–69; Councillor, Penybont RDC 1966–69; JP, Ipswich 1972–78. *Career:* Junior operative, electrical apprentice and electrician, British Steel Corporation, Port Talbot 1950–69; USDAW: Area organiser, Ipswich 1969–73, Deputy division officer, London/Ipswich 1973–78, National officer, Manchester 1978–85, General Secretary 1986–97. Member: IPU, CPU. Member, Employment Appeal Tribunal. CBE 1996. *Special Interests:* Health Service, Education, Industrial Relations. *Recreations:* Most sport, swimming, jogging, family, reading, golf. *Sportsclubs:* Lancashire CCC, Stockport County AFC. *Clubs:* Reform. Raised to the peerage as Baron Davies of Coity, of Penybont in the County of Mid Glamorgan 1997. The Lord Davies of Coity, CBE, 64 Dairyground Road, Bramhall, Stockport, Cheshire, SK7 2QW *Tel:* 0161–439 9548.

DAVIES OF OLDHAM, LORD   Labour

DAVIES OF OLDHAM (Life Baron), Bryan Davies; cr. 1997. Born 9 November 1939. Son of late George and Beryl Davies; educated Redditch High School, Worcs; University College, London (BA history 1961); Institute of Education (PGCE 1962); London School of Economics (BSc economics 1968). Married Monica Shearing 1963 (2 sons 1 daughter). *Trades Union:* Divisional Executive Officer, NATFHE 1967–74; Member, TGWU 1979–. *Career:* History teacher, Latymer School 1962–65; History and social science lecturer, Middlesex Polytechnic, Enfield 1965–74; Secretary, Parliamentary Labour Party and Shadow Cabinet 1979–92. *House of Commons:* Contested Norfolk Central 1966 and Newport West 1983 general elections; MP (Labour) for Enfield North 1974–1979 and for Oldham Central and Royton 1992–97. Assistant Government Whip 1978–79. Opposition Spokesperson for: Education 1993–95, Education and Employment 1995–97. Government Whip 2000–. Government Spokesperson for: Home Office 2000–02, Education and Skills 2001–03, Culture, Media and Sport 2001–, Transport 2002–. Chair, Culture, Media and Sport 1992–99

Member, Education, Transport and Economic Affairs Committees 1997–. President, Royal Society for the Prevention of Accidents (RoSPA) 1999–2000. Honorary Doctorate, Middlesex University 1996. Member, Medical Research Council 1977–79; Chair, Further Education Funding Council 1998–2000. *Special Interests:* Economic Policy, Employment, Training, Education, Arts, Transport. *Recreations:* Sport, literature. Raised to the peerage as Baron Davies of Oldham, of Broxbourne in the County of Hertfordshire 1997. The Lord Davies of Oldham, House of Lords, London, SW1A 0PW *Tel:* 020 7219 1475 *Fax:* 01992 300166.

DEAN OF HARPTREE, LORD   Conservative

DEAN OF HARPTREE (Life Baron), (Arthur) Paul Dean; cr. 1993. Born 14 September 1924. Son of late Arthur Percival Dean and of Jessie Margaret Dean; educated Ellesmere College, Shropshire; Exeter College, Oxford (BA modern history 1950, BLitt). Married Doris Ellen Webb 1957 (died 1979), married Mrs Peggy Parker 1980 (died 2002). Served Second World War 1939–45, Captain, Welsh Guards, ADC to Commander, 1st British Corps in Germany. *Career:* Farmer 1950–56; Resident Tutor, Swinton Conservative College 1957; Conservative Research Department 1957–64, Assistant Director 1962–64; Member, Commonwealth Parliamentary Association, UK Branch Executive Committee 1975–92; Former Director: Charterhouse Pensions Ltd, Watney, Mann and Truman Holdings Ltd, Grand Metropolitan Brewing, Foods, Leisure and Retailing Ltd. *House of Commons:* Contested (Conservative) Pontefract 1962 by-election; MP (Conservative): for Somerset North 1964–83, for Woodspring 1983–92; Parliamentary Under-Secretary of State, Department of Health and Social Security 1970–74; Deputy Chairman of Ways and Means and Deputy Speaker 1982–92. Frontbench Spokesperson for Health and Social Security 1969–70. *House of Lords:* Deputy Speaker 1995–; Deputy Chair of Committees 1995–. Member, Select Committees on: Procedure 1995, Delegated Legislation 1995–97, Delegated Powers and Deregulation 1997–2000, House of Lords Offices 2001–02. Member Executive Committee, Association of Conservative Peers 1995–98. Kt 1985; PC 1991. *Special Interests:* Constitutional Affairs, Health, Social Security. *Recreations:* Fishing, walking, gardening. *Clubs:* United Oxford and Cambridge University. Raised to the peerage as Baron Dean of Harptree, of Wedmore in the County of Somerset 1993. Rt Hon the Lord Dean of Harptree, Archer's Wyck, Knightcott, Banwell, Weston-Super-Mare, BS29 6HS *Tel:* 020 7219 3160; House of Lords, London, SW1A 0PW.

DEAN OF THORNTON-LE-FYLDE, BARONESS   Labour

DEAN OF THORNTON-LE-FYLDE (Life Baroness), Brenda McDowall; cr. 1993. Born 29 April 1943. Daughter of Hugh and Lillian Dean; educated St Andrew's Junior School, Eccles; Stretford High School for Girls. Married Keith Desmond McDowall, CBE 1988 (2 step-daughters). *Trades Union:* Member: TUC General Council 1985–92, Graphical, Paper and Media Union 1959–. *Career:* SOGAT, Administrative Secretary 1959–72, Assistant Secretary, Manchester Branch 1972–76, Secretary 1976–83, Member, National Executive Council 1977–83, President, SOGAT '82 1983–85, General-Secretary 1985–91; Deputy General Secretary, Graphical, Paper and Media Union 1991–92. Opposition Whip 1996–97. Opposition Spokesperson for: Employment 1994–96, National Heritage 1996–97. Co-opted Member, Select Committee on European Communities Sub-Committee B (Energy, Industry and Transport) 1995–97, 1997–98. Council Member: Association for Business Sponsorship of the Arts 1990–96, City University 1991–96; Governor, Ditchley Foundation 1992–; Member, Board of Council, London School of Economics 1994–99; Member of Council, Open University 1995–98. Six honorary degrees. Non-Executive Board Member, University College London Hospitals NHS Trust 1993–98; Trustee: Industry and Parliament Trust, Inveresk plc Pension Fund 1996–2001, The Prince's Foundation 1999–. Co-Chair, Women's National Commission 1985–87; Member: Printing and Publishing Training Board 1974–82, Supplementary Benefits Commission 1976–80, Price Commission 1977–79, Occupational Pensions Board 1983–87, General Advisory Council, BBC 1984–88, NEDC 1989–92, Employment Appeal Tribunal 1991–93; Member, Independent Committee for Supervision of Telephone Information Services 1991–93, Chair 1993–99; Non-Executive Director, Inveresk plc 1993–96; Member: Armed Forces Pay Review Body 1993–94,

Press Complaints Commission 1993–98, Broadcasting Complaints Commission 1993–94; Non-Executive Director: Chamberlain Phipps plc 1994–96, Takecare plc 1995–98; Member, Committee of Inquiry into Future of Higher Education 1996–97; Chair: Housing Corporation 1997–, Armed Forces Pay Review Body 1999–; Member: Royal Commission on the Reform of the House of Lords 1999, General Insurance Standards Council 1999–, House of Lords Appointments Commission 2000–; Chair, Freedom to Fly Coalition 2002–; Member, Senior Salaries Review Body. PC 1998. FRSA. *Special Interests:* Industry, Media, Arts Sponsorship, Women's Issues, Telecommunications, Pensions, Housing. *Recreations:* Sailing, family, theatre, cooking. *Sportsclubs:* Royal Cornwall Yacht. *Clubs:* Reform. Raised to the peerage as Baroness Dean of Thornton-le-Fylde, of Eccles in the County of Greater Manchester 1993. Rt Hon the Baroness Dean of Thornton-le-Fylde, House of Lords, London, SW1A 0PW *Tel:* 020 7219 6907.

DEARING, LORD   Crossbencher

DEARING (Life Baron), Ronald Ernest Dearing; cr. 1998. Born 27 July 1930. Son of late E. H. A. Dearing; educated Doncaster Grammar School; Hull University (BSc economics 1954); London Business School (Sloan Fellow 1968). Married Margaret Patricia Riley 1954 (2 daughters). RAF 1949–51. *Career:* Ministry of Labour and National Service 1946–49; Ministry of Power 1949–62; HM Treasury 1962–64; Ministry of Power, Ministry of Technology, Department of Trade and Industry 1965–72; Regional Director, Northern Region, DTI 1972–74; Under-Secretary, DTI later Department of Industry 1972–75, Deputy Secretary 1975–80; Deputy Chair, Post Office Corporation 1980–81, Chair 1981–87; Chair: CNAA 1987–88, County Durham Development Company 1987–90; Chair: Polytechnics and Colleges Funding Council 1988–93, Northern Development Company 1990–94; Non-Executive Director: Ericsson Ltd 1991–94, Whitbread 1987–90, IMI 1987–92, Prudential 1987–91, British Coal 1988–91; Chair: Council of National Academic Awards 1986–88, Polytechnic Colleges Funding Council 1998–91, Universities' Funding Council 1991–93, High Education Funding Council for England 1992–93, Camelot Group 1993–95, Financial Reporting Council 1989–94, School Curriculum and Assessment Authority 1993–96; Non Executive Director, SDX plc 1995–98; Chair: National Committee of Enquiry into Higher Education 1996–97, Write Away 1996–99; University for Industry 1998–2000, Committe on Church of England Schools 2000–01, Ufi 1998–2000, Christs College Guildford Governing Body 2002–. Chancellor, Nottingham University 1993–2000. Member: Council Industrial Society 1985–98, Governing Council London Business School 1985–89; Chair, Accounting Standards Review Committee 1987–88; Member, Council, Durham University 1988–91; Chair: Financial Reporting Council 1989–94, London Education Business Partnership 1989–92, Northern Sinfonia Appeals Committee 1993–94; President, Institute of Direct Marketing 1994–98; Chair, Committee of Inquiry into Higher Education 1996–97; Member, Council Melbourne University 1997–99; Chair, LGA Hearings and Regional Government 1999–2000; Vice-President, Local Government Association 1999–; President, Council of Church Colleges 1999–2002; Patron: UFI, Write Away 1999–, Church Colleges Association. Gold Medal of British Institute of Management 1994. Fourteen honorary doctorates and fellowships. Trustee, Higher Education Policy Institution 2002–. CB 1979; Kt 1984. Hon. FEng 1992. Freeman, City of London 1982. *Publications: The National Curriculum and its Assessment,* 1993; *Review of Qualifications for 16–19 Year Olds,* 1996. *Special Interests:* Education, Post Office, Regional Government. *Recreations:* Gardening, DIY. *Clubs:* Athenaeum. Raised to the peerage as Baron Dearing, of Kingston upon Hull in the County of the East Riding of Yorkshire 1998. The Lord Dearing, Kt, CB, Athenaeum Club, London, SW1; House of Lords, London, SW1A 0PW *Tel:* 020 7219 8725 *E-mail:* ronald.dearing@blueyonder.co.uk.

DodOnline
An Electronic Directory without rival . . .

Peers' biographies and photographs available with daily updates *via* the internet

For a *free* trial, call Yasmin Mirza, Aby Farsoun or Michael Mand on 020 7630 7643

DEEDES, LORD   Conservative

DEEDES (Life Baron), William Francis Deedes; cr. 1986. Born 1 June 1913. Son of late William Herbert Deedes; educated Harrow School. Married Evelyn Hilary Branfoot 1942 (1 son 3 daughters and 1 son deceased). Served with 12th KRRC 1939–44. DL, Kent 1962. *Career:* Journalist with the *Morning Post* and *Daily Telegraph* 1931–; Editor, *The Daily Telegraph* 1974–86. *House of Commons:* MP (Conservative) for Ashford 1950–74; Parliamentary Secretary, Ministry of Housing and Local Government 1954–55; Parliamentary Under-Secretary of State, Home Office 1955–57; Minister without Portfolio 1962–64. Chairman, One Nation Group 1970–74. Trustee: CARE International UK, African Medical and Research Foundation (AmREF); Member, Mines Advisory Group (MAE). Hon. DCL, University of Kent. MC 1944; PC 1962; KBE 1999. *Publications: The Drugs Epidemic*, 1970. *Special Interests:* Race Relations, Agriculture, Media, Home Office Affairs, Overseas Aid and Development. *Recreations:* Golf. *Clubs:* Carlton, Beefsteak, Royal and Ancient (St Andrews). Raised to the peerage as Baron Deedes, of Aldington in the County of Kent 1986. Rt Hon the Lord Deedes, KBE, MC, DL, New Hayters, Aldington, Kent, TN25 7DT *Tel:* 01233 720269 *Tel:* Office: 020 7538 5000.

DELACOURT-SMITH OF ALTERYN, BARONESS   Labour

DELACOURT-SMITH OF ALTERYN (Life Baroness), Margaret Delacourt-Smith; cr. 1974. Born 5 April 1916. Daughter of late F. J. Hando; educated Newport High School for Girls; St Anne's College, Oxford (BA modern languages (French) 1937, MA). Married Charles Smith, later Baron Delacourt-Smith, PC 1939 (died 1972) (1 son 2 daughters), married Professor Charles Blackton 1978. Raised to the peerage as Baroness Delacourt-Smith of Alteryn, of Alteryn in the County of Gwent 1974. The Baroness Delacourt-Smith of Alteryn, House of Lords, London, SW1A 0PW *Tel:* 020 7219 5353.

DENHAM, LORD   Conservative

DENHAM (2nd Baron, UK), Bertram Stanley Mitford Bowyer; cr. 1937; 10th Bt of Denham (E) 1660; 2nd Bt of Weston Underwood (UK) 1933. Born 3 October 1927. Son of 1st Baron, MC; educated Eton College; King's College, Cambridge (BA English literature 1951). Married Jean McCorquodale 1956 (3 sons 1 daughter). *Career:* Countryside Commissioner 1993–99. *House of Lords:* First entered House of Lords 1948; Elected hereditary peer 1999–. Government Whip 1961–64, 1970–71; Opposition Whip 1964–70; Deputy Chief Whip 1972–74; Opposition Deputy Chief Whip 1974–78; Opposition Chief Whip 1978–79; Government Chief Whip 1979–91. Member Procedure Committee 2003–. Extra Lord in Waiting to HM The Queen 1998–. PC 1981; KBE 1991. *Publications: The Man Who Lost His Shadow*, 1979; *Two Thyrdes*, 1983; *Foxhunt*, 1988; *Black Rod*, 1997; *A Thing of Shreds and Patches* (a read anthology of own selection of light verse) 2000. *Recreations:* Field sports. *Clubs:* White's, Pratt's, Garrick. Rt Hon the Lord Denham, KBE, The Laundry Cottage, Weston Underwood, Olney, Buckinghamshire, MK46 5JZ *Tel:* 01234 711535 *Tel:* 020 7219 6056 *Fax:* 020 7219 6056.

DERBY, LORD BISHOP OF   Non-affiliated

DERBY (6th Bishop of), Jonathan Sansbury Bailey. Born 24 February 1940. Son of late Walter Bailey, and of Audrey Sansbury Bailey; educated Quarry Bank High School, Liverpool; Trinity College, Cambridge (BA history and theology 1961, MA). Married Rev Susan Bennett-Jones 1965 (3 sons). *Career:* Assistant Curate: Sutton, St Helens, Lancashire 1965–68, St Paul, Warrington 1968–71; Warden, Marrick Priory 1971–76; Vicar of Wetherby, West Yorkshire 1976–82; Archdeacon of Southend and Bishop's Officer for Industry and Commerce, Diocese of Chelmsford 1982–92; Suffragan Bishop of Dunwich 1992–95; Bishop of Derby 1995–; Clerk of the Closet to HM The Queen 1996–; Took his seat in the House of Lords 1999; Chair of Churches Main Committee 2002–. *Recreations:* Theatre, music, beekeeping, carpentry. *Clubs:* Oxford and Cambridge University. Rt Rev the Lord Bishop of Derby, Bishop's Office, Derby Church House, Full Street, Derby, DE1 3DR *Tel:* 01332 346744 *Fax:* 01332 295810 *E-mail:* bishopderby@clara.net.

DESAI, LORD — Labour

DESAI (Life Baron), Meghnad Jagdishchandra Desai; cr. 1991. Born 10 July 1940. Son of late Jagdishchandra and Mandakini Desai; educated University of Bombay (BA economics 1958, MA 1960); University of Pennsylvania (PhD economics 1964). Married Gail Graham Wilson 1970 (1 son 2 daughters) (separated 1995). *Trades Union:* Member, AUT. *Career:* Associate specialist, Department of Agricultural Economics, University of California, Berkeley, California 1963–65; London School of Economics: Lecturer in Economics 1965–77, Senior Lecturer 1977–80, Reader 1980–83, Professor 1983–, Convenor, Economics Department 1987–90, Head, Development Studies Institute 1990–95, Director, Centre for the Study of Global Governance 1992–. Opposition Whip 1991–94. Opposition Spokesperson for: Health 1991–93, Treasury and Economic Affairs 1992–93. Member: Science and Technology 1993–94, European Affairs Sub Committee A 1995–97; Co-opted Member, Select Committee on European Communities Sub-Committee A (Economic and Financial Affairs, Trade and External Relations) 1997–2000; Member, Delegated Powers Scruntiny Committee 2001–. Member, Executive Committee, IPU British Group 1995–. Member: One World Action; Association of University Teachers. Four honorary doctorates. Member Tribune Newspaper. Member, Marshall Aid Commission until 1998. FRSA. *Publications:* Author of several publications on economics. *Special Interests:* Economic Policy, Education, Development. *Recreations:* Reading, writing, cricket. Raised to peerage as Baron Desai, of St Clement Danes in the City of Westminster 1991. Professor the Lord Desai, London School of Economics, Houghton Street, Aldwych, London, WC2A 2AE *Tel:* 020 7955 7489 *Fax:* 020 7955 7591; 501 Raleigh House, Dolphin Square, London, SW1V 3NF *Tel:* 020 7798 8673 *E-mail:* m.desai@lse.ac.uk.

DHOLAKIA, LORD — Liberal Democrat

DHOLAKIA (Life Baron), Navnit Dholakia; cr. 1997. Born 4 March 1937. Son of Permananddas Mulji Dholakia and Shantabai Permananddas Dholakia; educated Indian public schools in Moshi, Arusha, Tabora and Morogoro in Tanzania; Institute of Science, Bhavnager, Gujarat, India; Brighton Technical College. Married Ann McLuskie 1967 (2 daughters). Councillor, County Borough of Brighton 1961–64; JP, Mid Sussex 1978; Member, Sussex Police Authority 1991–94; DL, West Sussex 1999–. *Career:* Medical laboratory technician, Southlands Hospital, Shoreham-by-Sea 1960–66; Development officer, National Committee for Commonwealth Immigrants 1966–68; Senior development officer, Community Relations Commission 1968–74, Principal Officer and Secretary 1974–76; Commission for Racial Equality 1976–94: head, administration of justice section 1984–94; Member, Police Complaints Authority 1994–98. *House of Lords:* Member, House of Lords Appointments Commission 2000–. Liberal Democrat Deputy Whip 1998–2002. Liberal Democrat Spokesperson for Home Affairs 1998–. Co-opted Member, European Communities Sub-Committee F (Social Affairs, Education and Home Affairs) 1997–2000; House of Lords Offices Committee. Chair: Brighton Young Liberals 1959–62; Brighton Liberal Association 1962–64; Secretary, Race and Community Relations Panel, Liberal Party 1969–74; Member: Liberal Democrat Federal Policy Committee 1996–97, Federal Executive Committee; President: Liberal Democrat Party 2000–, Liberal Democrat Federal Conference Committee 2001–. Member, Lord Hunt's Committee on Immigration and Youth Service 1967–69; Secretary, Race and Community Relations Panel, Liberal Party 1969–74; Member, Board of Visitors, HM Prison Lewes 1978–95; Council Member, National Association of Care and Resettlement of Offenders 1984–, Chairman 1998–; Council Member Save The Children Fund 1986–99; Member, Home Office Inter-departmental Committee on Racial Attacks and Harassment 1987–92; Chair, Race Issues Advisory Committee of the National Association of Care and Resettlement of Offenders 1989–; Member, Ethnic Minority Advisory Committee of the Judicial Studies Board 1992–96; Council Member The Howard League of Penal Reform 1992–2002; Editorial Board, The Howard Journal of Criminology 1993–; Member: Lord Carlisle's Committee on Parole Systems Review, Home Secretary's Race Forum 1999–; Vice Chair, Policy Research Institute on Aging and Ethnicity. Asian of the Year 2000. Member: Governing Body, Commonwealth Institute 1999–, House of Lords Appointments Commission 2000–. OBE 1994. *Publications:* Various articles on criminal justice matters. *Recreations:* Photography, travel, gardening, cooking exotic dishes. Raised to the peerage as Baron Dholakia, of Waltham Brooks in the County of West Sussex 1997. The Lord Dholakia, OBE, DL, House of Lords, London, SW1A 0PW *Tel:* 020 7219 5203 *Fax:* 020 7219 2082 *E-mail:* dholakian@parliament.uk.

DIAMOND, LORD — Labour

DIAMOND (Life Baron), John Diamond; cr. 1970. Born 30 April 1907. Son of late Rev. Solomon Diamond; educated Leeds Grammar School. Married (2 sons 2 daughters). *Career:* Practised as Chartered Accountant from 1931–64 Managing Director, Capital and Provincial News Theatres 1951–57. *House of Commons:* MP (Labour): for Manchester, Blackley 1945–51, (contested Manchester, Blackley 1955 general election), for Gloucester 1957–70; PPS to Minister of Works 1946; Chief Secretary to the Treasury 1964–70; Cabinet Minister 1968–70. *House of Lords:* Principal Deputy Chairman Committees 1974. Hon. Treasurer, Fabian Society 1950–64; Trustee, Social Democratic Party 1981–82; Leader of SDP in the House of Lords 1982–88. Council Member, London Philharmonic Orchestra 1972–74. Hon. LLD, Leeds 1978. Director, Sadler's Wells Trust 1957–64; Chairman of Trustees, Industry and Parliament Trust 1977–82. Member, General Nursing Council (Chairman of Financial and General Purposes Committee) 1947–53; Hon. Treasurer, The European Movement 1973–74; Chairman, Royal Commission on Distribution of Income and Wealth 1974–79; Chairman, Civil Service Advisory Committee on Business Appointments 1975–88. PC 1965. FCA. *Publications: Public Expenditure in Practice*, 1975; Co-author *Socialism The British Way*, 1948. *Recreations:* Music, gardening, classical languages. Raised to the peerage as Baron Diamond, of the City of Gloucester 1970. Rt Hon the Lord Diamond, Aynhoe, Doggetts Wood Lane, Chalfont St. Giles, Buckinghamshire, HP8 4TH *Tel:* 01494 763229.

DIXON, LORD — Labour

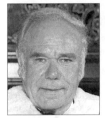

DIXON (Life Baron), Donald Dixon; cr. 1997. Born 6 March 1929. Son of late Albert Dixon, shipyard worker; educated Ellison Street Elementary School, Jarrow. Married Doreen Morad 1979 (1 son 1 daughter). *Trades Union:* Member, GMWU and Branch Secretary. Royal Engineers 1947–49. Councillor: Jarrow Borough Council 1963–74, South Tyneside Metropolitan District Council 1974–81; DL, Tyne and Wear 1997–. *Career:* Previously shipyard worker 1944–79. *House of Commons:* MP (Labour) for Jarrow May 1979–97. Opposition Deputy Chief Whip 1987–96. Member, House of Lords' Offices Committee. Member, Local Co-operative Group 1979–97; Chair, Northern Group Labour MPs 1989. PC 1996. Freeman: Jarrow 1972, South Tyneside 1997. *Special Interests:* Trade Unions, Ships and Shipbuilding, Maritime Affairs, Housing, Transport, Social Services. *Recreations:* Football, reading, boxing. *Clubs:* Jarrow Ex-Servicemen's, Jarrow Labour. Raised to the peerage as Baron Dixon, of Jarrow in the County of Tyne and Wear 1997. Rt Hon the Lord Dixon, DL, 1 Hillcrest, Jarrow, Tyne and Wear, NE32 4DP *Tel:* 0191–489 7635 *Tel:* 020 7219 0078 *Fax:* 020 7219 4124 *E-mail:* dixond@parliament.uk.

DIXON-SMITH, LORD — Conservative

DIXON-SMITH (Life Baron), Robert William Dixon-Smith; cr. 1993. Born 30 September 1934. Son of late Dixon and Alice Winifred Smith; educated Oundle School; Writtle Agricultural College, Essex. Married Georgina Janet Cook 1960 (1 son 1 daughter). Second Lieutenant, King's Dragoon Guards (National Service) 1956–57. Councillor, Essex County Council 1965–93, Chairman 1986–89; DL, Essex 1986. *Career:* Farmer. Opposition Spokesperson for: Environment, Transport and the Regions (Local Government) December 1998–2001, Home Affairs 2001–02, Environment 2003–. Member, Select Committees on: Science and Technology 1994–97, European Communities 1994–97. Governor, Writtle Agricultural College 1967–94, Chair 1973–85; Chair, Governors of Anglia Polytechnic University 1993–94 (formerly Anglia Polytechnic), Governor 1973–2000. Honorary Doctorate, Anglia Polytechnic University; Fellow, Writtle College. Member, Association of County Councils 1983–93, Chairman 1992–93. Liveryman, Farmers' Company 1990. *Special Interests:* Agriculture, Environment, Transport. *Recreations:* Country sports, golf. Raised to the peerage as Baron Dixon-Smith, of Bocking in the County of Essex 1993. The Lord Dixon-Smith, DL, Home: Lyons Hall, Braintree, Essex, CM7 9SH *Tel:* 01376 326834; Office: Houchins, Coggeshall, Colchester, Essex, CO6 1RT *Tel:* 01376 561448.

DONALDSON OF LYMINGTON, LORD   Crossbencher

DONALDSON OF LYMINGTON (Life Baron), John Francis Donaldson; cr. 1988. Born 6 October 1920. Son of late Malcolm Donaldson, FRCS, FRCOG; educated Charterhouse; Trinity College, Cambridge (MA 1949, MA (Oxon) 1982). Married Dorothy Mary Warwick (now Dame Mary Donaldson, GBE) 1945 (1 son 2 daughters). Commissioned, Royal Signals 1941; Served with: Guards Armoured Divisional Signals in UK and North West Europe 1942–45, Military Government, Schleswig-Holstein 1945–46. Councillor, Croydon Borough Council 1949–53. *Career:* Called to Bar, Middle Temple 1946; Harmsworth Law Scholar 1946; Bencher 1966; Member, General Council of the Bar 1956–61, 1962–66; QC 1961; Judge of the High Court, Queen's Bench Division 1966–79; President, National Industrial Relations Court 1971–74; Lord Justice of Appeal 1979–82; Master of the Rolls 1982–92. Member Procedure Committee 2003–. Hon. Member, Association of Average Adjusters 1966, Chairman 1981; President, British Maritime Law Association 1979–95, Vice-President 1969–78; President, British Insurance Law Association 1979–81, Deputy President 1978–79; Governor, Sutton's Hospital in Charterhouse 1981–84; Visitor: UCL 1982–92, Nuffield College, Oxford 1982–92, London Business School 1986–92; President, Council, Inns of Court 1987–90; Hon. Life Member, The Law Society 1994. Thomas Gray Memorial Trust Silver Medal for services to shipping 1995. Hon. Fellow, Trinity College, Cambridge 1983; Four honorary doctorates. Chairman: Financial Law Panel 1993–2002, Inquiry into pollution from merchant shipping 1993–94, Lord Donaldson's Assessment (Derbyshire) 1995; Chairman, Review of: Salvage and Intervention Command and Control 1997–98, Four Year Strategy for HM Coastguard 1999. Kt 1966; PC 1979. Fellow, Chartered Institute of Arbitrators 1980, President 1980–83. City of London. Honorary Freeman, Drapers Company 1994; Honorary Liveryman 2000. *Special Interests:* Law and the Administration of Justice, Maritime Safety. *Recreations:* Travel. *Sportsclubs:* Royal Lymington Yacht; Royal Cruising Club. Raised to the peerage as Baron Donaldson of Lymington, of Lymington in the County of Hampshire 1988. Rt Hon the Lord Donaldson of Lymington, House of Lords, London, SW1A 0PW *Tel:* Home: 020 7588 6610 *Fax:* 020 7588 6610 *Tel:* 01590 675716 *Fax:* 01590 675716 *E-mail:* donaldsonj@parliament.uk.

DONOUGHUE, LORD   Labour

DONOUGHUE (Life Baron), Bernard Donoughue; cr. 1985. Born 8 September 1934. Son of late Thomas Joseph Donoughue; educated Campbell Secondary Modern School, Northampton; Northampton Grammar School; Lincoln College, Oxford (BA history 1957); Nuffield College, Oxford (DPhil 1963); Harvard University, USA. Married Carol Ruth Goodman 1959 (2 sons 2 daughters) (divorced 1989). *Trades Union:* Member, GMBW. *Career:* Editorial staff, *The Economist* 1959–60; Senior research officer, Political and Economic Planning Institute 1960–63; Senior lecturer, London School of Economics 1963–74; Senior policy adviser to Prime Minister 1974–79; Development director, Economist Intelligence Unit 1979–81; Assistant editor, *The Times* 1981–82; Head of research and investment policy, Grieveson Grant and Co. 1982–86; Head of international research and Director, Kleinwort Grieveson Securities Ltd 1986–88; Executive Vice-chair, LBI 1988–91; Director, Towcester Racecourse Ltd 1992–97; Visiting Professor of Government LSE 2000–. *House of Lords:* Parliamentary Secretary, Ministry of Agriculture, Fisheries and Food (Minister for Farming and the Food Industry) 1997–99. Opposition Spokesperson for: Energy 1991–92, Treasury Affairs 1991–92, National Heritage 1992–97. Member Committee on Stem Cell Research 2001–02. Chair Executive, London Symphony Orchestra 1979–91, Patron 1989–95; Consultant Member, House Industry Confederation 1999–; Chair, British Horseracing Board Committee on VAT 2000–03. Hon. Fellow, Lincoln College, Oxford; Hon. LLD, Leicester; Hon. Fellow, LSE. Member: Dorneywood Trust, Victoria County History of Northamptonshire, International League for Protection of Horses. Member: Sports Council 1965–71, Commission of Enquiry into Association Football 1966–68, London Arts Board 1992–97; Vice-President, Comprehensive Schools Association. FRHS. *Publications:* Books on history and politics including: *Trade Unions in a Changing Society*, 1963; *British Politics and the American Revolution*, 1964; *The People into Parliament*, 1966; *Herbert Morrison*, 1973; *Prime Minister*, 1987; *The Heat of the Kitchen*, 2003. *Special Interests:* Arts, Finance, Sport. *Recreations:* Music, theatre, sport. *Sportsclubs:* Houses of Parliament Cricket Club. *Clubs:* Pratt's, Farmers', 1795. Raised to the peerage as Baron Donoughue, of Ashton in the County of Northamptonshire 1985. The Lord Donoughue, House of Lords, London, SW1A 0PW *Tel:* 020 7219 3000 *Fax:* 020 7730 7332.

DORMAND OF EASINGTON, LORD   Labour

DORMAND OF EASINGTON (Life Baron), John Donkin Dormand; cr. 1987. Born 27 August 1919. Son of Bernard and Mary Dormand; educated Wellfield Grammar School; Bede College, Durham University 1940; Loughborough College 1947; Harvard University 1954; St Peter's College, Oxford 1957. Married Doris Robinson, née Pearson 1963 (1 stepson 1 stepdaughter). *Trades Union:* Member: APEX (GMB), NUT. *Career:* Teacher 1940–48; Education adviser 1948–52, 1959–63; Education officer: NCB 1957–59, Easington Rural District Council 1963–70. *House of Commons:* MP (Labour) for Easington 1970–87. Assistant Government Whip 1974; Government Whip 1974–79; Opposition Whip 1979–81. *House of Lords:* Labour Peers' Representative on Parliamentary Committee (Shadow Cabinet) 1994–97. Member: Select Committee on Nationalised Industries 1970–73, Select Committee on Committee Structure of House of Lords June-December (chairman) 1991; House of Lords Liaison Committee 1992–97, Procedure Committee. Education, Trade and Industry, Sport, Tourism, Film Industry. Chair, Parliamentary Labour Party 1981–87. Fulbright Scholar, Harvard University, USA 1953–54. Hon. Fellow, St Peter's College, Oxford; Hon Graduate, Loughborough University. *Special Interests:* Education, Coal Industry, Regional Policy, Local Government, Tourism, Film Industry. *Recreations:* Music, sport, films. *Sportsclubs:* Houghton Rugby Union Club, Burmoor Cricket Club, Durham County Cricket Club, Durham County Rugby Union Club. *Clubs:* Peterlee Labour, Easington Workmen's. Raised to the peerage as Baron Dormand of Easington, of Easington in the County of Durham 1987. The Lord Dormand of Easington, House of Lords, London, SW1A 0PW *Tel:* 020 7219 5419.

DUBS, LORD   Labour

DUBS (Life Baron), Alfred Dubs; cr. 1994. Born 5 December 1932. Born 1932; educated London School of Economics (BSc Econ). Married (1 son 1 daughter). *Trades Union:* Member, TGWU. Councillor, Westminster City Council 1971–78; Chair, Westminster Community Relations Council 1972–77; Member, Kensington, Chelsea and Westminster Area Health Authority 1975–78; Non-executive Director, Pathfinder NHS Trust 1995–97. *Career:* Former local government officer; Director, Refugee Council 1988–95; Member, Broadcasting Standards Council 1988–94, Deputy Chairman 1994–97; Deputy Chair, ITC 2000; Chair, Broadcasting Standards Commission 2001–. *House of Commons:* Contested (Labour): Cities of London and Westminster 1970, Hertfordshire South February and October 1974 general elections; MP (Labour) for: Battersea South 1979–83, Battersea 1983–87; contested Battersea 1987 and 1992 general elections. Opposition Spokesperson for Home Affairs 1983–87. *House of Lords:* Parliamentary Under-Secretary of State, Northern Ireland Office (Minister for Environment and Agriculture) 1997–99; Chair Labour Party in Lords 2000–. Opposition Whip 1995–97. Opposition Spokesperson for: The Environment (Health and Safety) 1996–97, Energy 1996–97. Member, Select Committees on: Relations between Central and Local Government 1995–96, European Community 1996–97, European Union Sub-committee: D (Environment, Agriculture, Public Health and Consumer Protection) 2001–02, F (Social Affairs, Education and Home Affairs) 2003–, European Union 2003–. Member, The Co-operative Party; Chairman, Fabian Society 1993–94. Chair: Liberty 1990–92, Broadcasting Standards Commission 2001–. Trustee: Action Aid 1989–97, Immigration Advisory Service 1992–97. *Publications: Lobbying: An Insider's Guide to the Parliamentary Process,* 1989. *Special Interests:* Civil Liberties, Penal Reform, Race Relations, Immigration, Health Service, Ireland, Human Rights. *Recreations:* Walking in the Lake District. Raised to the peerage as Baron Dubs, of Battersea in the London Borough of Wandsworth 1994. The Lord Dubs, House of Lords, London, SW1A 0PW *Tel:* 020 7219 3590 *E-mail:* dubsa@parliament.uk.

DUNDEE, EARL OF   Conservative

DUNDEE (12th Earl of, S), Alexander Henry Scrymgeour; cr. 1660; Viscount Dudhope (S) 1641; Lord Scrymgeour (S) 1641; Lord Inverkeithing (S) 1660; Baron Glassary (UK) 1954. Born 5 June 1949. Son of 11th Earl, PC, DL; educated Eton College; St Andrews University. Married Siobhan Mary Llewellyn 1979 (1 son 3 daughters). *House of Lords:* First entered House of Lords 1983; Elected hereditary peer 1999–. Government Whip 1986–89. Government Spokesperson for Home Affairs, Energy, Scottish

Affairs 1986–89. Member: European Communities Sub-Committee A (Economic Affairs) 1989–92, European Communities Sub-Committee F (Social Affairs, Education and Home Affairs) 1997–2000, Joint Committee on Consolidation of Bills 2000–. UK delegate to Organisation for Security and Co-operation in Europe 1992–97; Member: Council of Europe parliament 1992–99, Western European parliament 1992–99. Hereditary Banner Bearer for Scotland; Contested (Conservative) Hamilton By-election 1978. *Clubs:* White's, New (Edinburgh). The Earl of Dundee, House of Lords, London, SW1 0PW *Tel:* 020 7219 6781.

DUNN, BARONESS   Crossbencher

DUNN (Life Baroness), Lydia Dunn; cr. 1990. Born 29 February 1940. Daughter of late Yen Chuen Yih Dunn and Bessie Dunn; educated St Paul's Convent School, Hong Kong; College of the Holy Names, Oakland, California; University of California, Berkeley, California. Married Michael Thomas CMG QC 1988. *Career:* Member, Legislative Council, Hong Kong 1976–88, Senior Member 1985–88; Director: John Swire & Sons (HK) Ltd 1978–2003, Mass Transit Railway Corporation 1979–85; Chair: Special Committee on Land Supply 1981–83, Prince Philip Dental Hospital 1981–87; Director, Hong Kong & Shanghai Banking Corporation Ltd 1981–96, Deputy Chairman 1992–96; Director: Swire Pacific Ltd 1981–, Kowloon Canton Railway Corporation 1982–84; Member, Hong Kong Executive Council 1982–95, Senior Member 1988–95; Chair, Hong Kong Trade Development Council 1983–91; Deputy Chair, Executive Committee, Commonwealth Parliamentary Association, Hong Kong Branch 1985–88; Director, Cathay Pacific Airways Ltd 1985–97; Director, HSBC Holdings plc 1990, Non-Executive Deputy Chair 1992–; Director: Volvo AB 1991–93, Christies International plc 1996–98; Executive Director, John Swire & Sons Ltd 1996–; Director, General Electric Company/Marconi plc 1997–2002; Adviser to Board, Cathay Pacific Airways Ltd 1997–2002; Christies Fine Art Limited 1998–2000. Member: General Committee, Federation of Hong Kong Industries 1978–83, World Wildlife Fund Hong Kong 1982–85, Hong Kong/Japan Business Co-operation Committee 1983–95, Hong Kong/US Economic Co-operation Committee 1984–93, The International Council of the Asia Society 1986–96, Hong Kong Association, United Kingdom 1991–, Chair 2001–. Prime Minister of Japan's Trade Award 1987; *To Peace and Commerce* Award, USA Secretary of Commerce 1988. Hon. LLD: Chinese University of Hong Kong 1984, Hong Kong University 1991, University of British Columbia, Canada 1991, University of Leeds 1994; Hon. DSc, University of Buckingham 1995; Hon. Fellow, London Business School 2000. Industry Committee of the Animal Health Trust 1996–1999; Swire Educational Trust 1997–. OBE 1978; CBE 1983; DBE 1989. Fellow: Institute of Directors 1989–, The Royal Society for the Encouragement of Arts, Manufacturers and Commerce 1989–. *Publications: In the Kingdom of the Blind,* 1983. *Recreations:* Art, antiques. *Clubs:* Hong Kong, Hong Kong Jockey. Raised to the peerage as Baroness Dunn, of Hong Kong Island in Hong Kong and of Knightsbridge in the Royal Borough of Kensington and Chelsea 1990. The Baroness Dunn, DBE, John Swire and Sons Ltd, Swire House, 59 Buckingham Gate, London, SW1E 6AJ *Tel:* 020 7834 7717 *Fax:* 020 7828 9029.

DURHAM, LORD BISHOP OF   Non-affiliated

DURHAM (94th Bishop of), (Tom) Nicholas Thomas Wright. Born 1 December 1948. Son of Nicholas I. Wright and Rosemary Wright, nee Forman; educated Sedbergh School; Exeter College, Oxford (BA literae humaniores 1971, BA theology 1973, MA 1975); Merton College, Oxford (DPhil theology 1981, DD 2000). Married Maragret Fiske 1971 (2 sons 2 daughters). *Career:* Merton College, Oxford 1975–78: Junior Research Fellow and College Tutor in Theology, Junior Chaplain 1976–78, Acting Theology Lecturer 1977–78; Fellow and Chaplain, College Tutor in Theology, Downing College, Cambridge 1978–81; Assistant Professor of New Testament Language and Literature, McGill University, Canada 1981–86; New Testament Studies Lecturer, Oxford University and Fellow, Tutor and Chaplain Worcester College 1986–92; Dean of Lichfield 1993–99; Canon of Westminster 2000–03; Bishop of Durham 2003–; Took his seat in the House of Lords 2003. Hon. DD Aberdeen 2000; Hon. Fellow, Downing College, Cambridge 2003; Hon. DLitt, Gordon College, Massachusetts 2003. *Publications:* Numerous books and articles on theological subjects. *Recreations:* Golf, hillwalking, poetry, music. Rt Rev the Lord Bishop of Durham, Auckland Castle, Bishop Auckland, Co. Durham, DL14 7NR *Tel:* 01388 602576 *Fax:* 01388 605264 *E-mail:* bishop.of.durham@durham.anglican.org.

E

EAMES, LORD   Crossbencher

EAMES (Life Baron), Robert Henry Alexander Eames; cr. 1995. Born 27 April 1937. Son of William and Mary Eames; educated Belfast Royal Academy; Methodist College, Belfast; Queen's University, Belfast (LLB 1957); Trinity College, Dublin (PhD theology 1963). Married Ann Christine Daly 1966 (2 sons). *Career:* Research scholar and tutor, Faculty of Laws, Queen's University 1960–63; Curate assistant, Bangor Parish Church 1963–66; Rector of St Dorothea's, Belfast 1966–74; Examining Chaplain to the Bishop of Down 1973; Rector of St Mark's, Dundela 1974–75; Bishop of Derry and Raphoe 1975–80; Bishop of Down and Dromore 1980–86; Archbishop of Armagh and Primate of All Ireland 1986–; Select Preacher, Oxford University 1987; Chair: Commission on Communion and Women in the Episcopate 1988–, Commission on Inter-Anglican Relations 1988–; Select Preacher, Cambridge University 1990; Chair, Inter-Anglican Theological and Doctrinal Commission 1991; Select Preacher, Edinburgh University 1993; Chair, Inter-Anglican Finance Committee 1997–; Select Preacher St Andrews University 2001–. Member Advisory Panel on Works of Art 2003–. Member, Anglican International Consultative Council. Governor, Church Army 1985–; Chairman: Board of Governors, Royal School, Armagh, Armagh Observatory and Planetarium. Seven honorary doctorates from British and Irish universities. Hon. Bencher, Lincoln's Inn 1998; Member, Institute of Advanced Drivers. Freeman, City of London 1989. *Publications: A Form of Worship for Teenagers*, 1965; *The Quiet Revolution – Irish Disestablishment*, 1970; *Through Suffering*, 1973; *Thinking through Lent*, 1978; *Through Lent*, 1984; *Chains to be Broken*, 1992; Contributor to: Irish Legal Quarterly, Criminal Law Review, New Divinity, Cambridge Law Review. *Special Interests:* Northern Ireland, Social Issues, Community Care, Broadcasting. *Recreations:* Sailing, rugby union, reading, travel. *Sportsclubs:* Member: Strangford Lough Yacht Club, Co Down, Royal Yachting Association. *Clubs:* Kildare Street and University (Dublin). Raised to the peerage as Baron Eames, of Armagh in the County of Armagh 1995. Most Rev the Lord Eames, Lord Archbishop of Armagh and Primate of All Ireland, The See House, Cathedral Close, Armagh, Co. Armagh, BT61 7EE *Tel:* 028 3752 7144 (office) *Fax:* 028 3752 7823 *Tel:* 028 3752 2851 (home) *E-mail:* archbishop@armagh.anglican.org.

EATWELL, LORD   Labour

EATWELL (Life Baron), John Leonard Eatwell; cr. 1992. Born 2 February 1945. Son of late Harold Jack Eatwell, and late Mary Eatwell; educated Headlands Grammar School, Swindon; Queens' College, Cambridge (BA economics 1967, MA); Harvard University (PhD economics 1975). Married Hélène Seppain 1970 (divorced) (2 sons 1 daughter). *Trades Union:* Member, Association of University Teachers. *Career:* Teaching fellow, Graduate School of Arts and Sciences, Harvard University 1968–69; Research fellow, Queens' College, Cambridge 1969–70; Fellow of Trinity College, Cambridge 1970–96; Assistant lecturer, Faculty of Economics and Politics, Cambridge University 1975–77, Lecturer 1977–2002; Director, Cambridge Endowment for Research in Finance, and Professor of Financial Policy, Cambridge University 2002–; Visiting professor of economics, New School for Social Research, New York 1982–96; Economic adviser to Neil Kinnock as Leader of the Labour Party 1985–92; Trustee, Institute for Public Policy Research 1988–, Secretary 1988–97, Chairman 1997–2001; Chairman, Extemporary Dance Theatre 1990; Non-executive Director: Anglia Television Group Ltd 1994–2001, Cambridge Econometrics Ltd 1996–; Director, Securities and Futures Authority 1997–2002; President, Queens' College, Cambridge 1997–; Chairman, British Screen 1997–2000; Member, Board of Directors of the Royal Opera House 1998–; Chair, British Library 2001–; Director, Cambridge Endowment for Research in Finance 2002–. Opposition Spokesperson for: Trade and Industry 1992–96, Treasury and Economic Affairs 1992–93; Principal Opposition Spokesperson for Treasury and Economic Affairs 1993–97. Member, Joint Committee on the Financial Services and Markets Bill, 1999. Chair: Crusaid, the national fundraiser for AIDS 1993–98, Commercial Radio Companies Association 2000–. Governor, Contemporary Dance Trust 1991–95; Director, Arts Theatre Trust, Cambridge 1991–98. *Publications:* Co-author *An Introduction to Modern Economics*, 1973;

Whatever happened to Britain?, 1982; Co-author *Keynes's Economics and the Theory of Value and Distribution*, 1983; *The New Palgrave: A Dictionary of Economics*, 4 vols, 1987; *The New Palgrave Dictionary of Money and Finance*, 3 vols, 1992; Editor *Global Unemployment: Loss of Jobs in the '90s*, 1996; Co-author *Not Just Another Accession: The Political Economy of EU Enlargement to the East*, 1997; *Understanding Globalisation: The Nation-State, Democracy and Economic Policies in the New Epoch*, 1998; *Global Finance at Risk: The Case for International Regulation*, 2000; *Hard Budgets and Soft States: Social Policy Choices in Central and Eastern Europe*, 2000; Articles in scientific journals and other collected works. *Special Interests:* Economics, Trade and Industry, Arts. *Recreations:* Classical and contemporary dance, rugby union football. *Sportsclubs:* Lords and Commons RUFC. *Clubs:* Harvard Club of New York City. Raised to the peerage as Baron Eatwell, of Stratton St Margaret in the County of Wiltshire 1992. The Lord Eatwell, The President's Lodge, Queens' College, Cambridge, CB3 9ET *Tel:* 01223 335532 *Fax:* 01223 335555 *E-mail:* president@quns.cam.ac.uk.

ECCLES OF MOULTON, BARONESS   Conservative

ECCLES OF MOULTON (Life Baroness), Diana Catherine Eccles; cr. 1990. Born 4 October 1933. Daughter of late Raymond and Margaret Sturge; educated St. James's School, West Malvern; Open University (BA 1979). Married Hon. John Dawson Eccles 1955 (Now 2nd Viscount Eccles, CBE) (1 son 3 daughters). Member, Teesside Urban Development Corporation 1987–98; Chairman: Ealing District Health Authority 1988–93, Ealing, Hammersmith and Hounslow Health Authority 1993–2000; DL, North Yorkshire 1998–. *Career:* Voluntary work, Middlesbrough Community Council 1955–58; Partner in graphic design business 1963–77; Member, North Eastern Electricity Board 1974–85; Vice-Chairman, National Council for Voluntary Organisations 1981–87; Lay Member, Durham University Council 1981–, Vice-Chairman 1985–; Chairman, Tyne Tees Television Programme Consultative Council 1982–84; Member: Advisory Council on Energy Conservation (Department of Energy) 1982–84, Widdicombe Inquiry into Local Government 1985–86, Home Office Advisory Panel on Licences for Experimental Community Radio 1985–86, British Rail Eastern Board 1986–92; Director: Tyne Tees Television 1986–94, J. Sainsbury plc 1986–95, Yorkshire Electricity Group plc 1990–97; Member, Unrelated Live Transplant Regulatory Authority 1990–99; Director: National and Provincial Building Society 1991–96, Times Newspapers Holdings Ltd 1998–, Opera North 1998–. Member, Committee on Animals in Scientific Procedures 2001–02. Hon. DCL, Durham 1995. Trustee: Charities Aid Foundation 1982–89, York Minster Trust Fund 1989–99; Member, British Heart Foundation 1989–98. Raised to the peerage as Baroness Eccles of Moulton, of Moulton in the County of North Yorkshire 1990. The Viscountess Eccles, Lady Eccles of Moulton, DL, 5 St John's House, 30 Smith Square, London, SW1P 3HF *Tel:* 020 7222 4040; Moulton Hall, Richmond, North Yorkshire, DL10 6QH *Tel:* 01325 377227.

EDEN OF WINTON, LORD   Conservative

EDEN OF WINTON (Life Baron), John Benedict Eden; cr 1983; 9th Bt of West Auckland (E) 1672; 7th Bt of Maryland (GB) 1776. Born 15 September 1925. Son of Sir Timothy Eden, 8th and 6th Bt; educated Eton College; St Paul's School, USA. Married Belinda Jane Pascoe 1958 (2 sons 2 daughters) (divorced 1974); married Margaret Ann, Viscountess Strathallan, née Gordon 1977. Served British and Indian Armies 1943–47; Lieutenant, Rifle Brigade, seconded to 2nd King Edward's Own Goorkha Rifles and the Gilgit Scouts. *Career:* Former Chairman of various plcs; Chairman, Lady Eden's School Ltd –2001; Member, Timken Company International Advisory Board –2001. *House of Commons:* Contested Paddington North 1953 by-election; MP (Conservative) for Bournemouth West 1954–83; Minister of State, Ministry of Technology June-October 1970; Minister for Industry 1970–72; Minister of Posts and Telecommunications 1972–74. Former opposition Spokesman on Defence (RAF) and Power. Former Member: WEU, NATO Parliamentarians, Council of Europe; Rapporteur, Cultural Affairs Committee. President, Wessex Area Council, National Union of Conservative and Unionist Associations 1974–77; Hon. Life Vice-President, Association of Conservative Clubs Ltd. President, Independent Schools Association 1969–71; Chairman, The British

Lebanese Association 1990–98; Vice-President, International Tree Foundation to 1998. Chairman, The Royal Armouries Board of Trustees 1986–94. PC 1972. Hon. Freeman: Annapolis, Maryland, USA 1976, Bournemouth 1984. *Recreations:* Gardening, trees, shooting. *Clubs:* Boodle's, Pratt's. Raised to the peerage as Baron Eden of Winton, of Rushyford in the County of Durham 1983. Rt Hon the Lord Eden of Winton, House of Lords, London, SW1A 0PW *Tel:* 020 7219 5353.

ELDER, LORD — Labour

ELDER (Life Baron), Thomas Murray Elder; cr. 1999. Born 9 May 1950; educated Kirkcaldy High School; Edinburgh University (MA economic history). *Career:* Bank of England 1972–80; Labour Party Scotland 1984–92, General Secretary 1988–92; Chief of Staff to John Smith, MP 1992–94; Special Adviser, Scottish Office 1997–99. *House of Commons:* Contested (Labour) Ross, Cromarty and Skye 1983 general election. Member, Select Committee on Monetary Policy of the Bank of England/Economic Affairs 2000–. *Recreations:* Walking, reading, opera. Raised to the peerage as Baron Elder, of Kirkcaldy in Fife 1999. The Lord Elder, House of Lords, London, SW1A 0PW *Tel:* 020 7219 8512.

ELIS-THOMAS, LORD — Crossbencher

ELIS-THOMAS (Life Baron), Dafydd Elis Elis-Thomas; cr. 1992. Born 18 October 1946; educated Ysgol Dyffryn Conwy; University College of Wales (PhD). Married Elen M. Williams 1970 (3 sons) (marriage dissolved); married Mair Parry Jones 1993. *Career:* Tutor in Welsh Studies, Coleg Harlech 1971–74; Has subsequently taught at: The University College of North Wales, Bangor, Aberystwyth, Cardiff, The Open University; Has been a broadcaster on BBC Wales, HTV, S4C, Radio Wales; Consultant to 1999: S4C, The Welsh Development Agency, The Rural Initiative Programme, The Assembly of European Regions, The Government of Catalonia; Chairman, Screen Wales; Director and Deputy Chairman, Cynefin Environmental; Director and Chairman, New Media Agency; Director: Oriel Mostyn, National Botanical Gardens, MFM Marcher. *House of Commons:* Contested Conway 1970 general election; MP (Plaid Cymru) for: Meirionnydd February 1974–83, Meirionnydd Nant Conwy 1974–92. Member: Select Committee on European Communities 1997–98, Select Committee on European Communities Sub-Committee C (Environment, Public Health and Consumer Protection) 1997–98. President, Plaid Cymru 1984–91. President, Hay-on-Wye Literature Festival; Vice-President –1999: Snowdonia National Park Society –1999, Abbeyfield –1999. Trustee –1999: Big Issue Foundation –1999, Theatr Bara Caws –1999; Patron, Prince of Wales Trust – Bro; Member, Wales Committee of National Trust. Member –1999: Welsh Arts Council –1999, Welsh Film Council –1999, Welsh Film Board –1999, BBC General Consultative Council –1999; Chairman, Welsh Language Board 1993–96, 1996–99; Fellow, International Centre for Intercultural Studies, Institute of Education, London; AM for the Constituency of Meirionnydd Nant Conwy since May 6, 1999 (contested the seat as Dafydd Elis-Thomas); Presiding Officer (The Speaker) National Assembly for Wales May 1999–, Surname changed from Thomas to Elis-Thomas by deed poll 1992. *Recreations:* Welsh literature and art, music, theatre, films, hill and mountain walking, swimming, jogging. Raised to the peerage as Baron Elis-Thomas, of Nant Conwy in the County of Gwynedd 1992. The Lord Elis-Thomas, AM, 3 Lon Warfield, Caernarfon, Gwynedd, LL55 1LA; Pen y Ceunant, Betws y Coed, Conwy, LL24 0SL *E-mail:* dafydd.elis-thomas@wales.gsi.gov.uk.

ELLES, BARONESS — Conservative

ELLES (Life Baroness), Diana Louie Elles; cr. 1972. Born 19 July 1921. Daughter of late Colonel Stewart Newcombe, DSO; educated Private Schools, London, Paris, Florence; London University (BA French 1941). Married Neil Patrick Moncrieff Elles 1945 (1 son 1 daughter). Served in WAAF 1941–45; Flight Officer 1944. *Career:* Called to the Bar, Lincoln's Inn, 1956; Voluntary care committee worker, Kennington 1956–72; UK delegate, United Nations General Assembly 1972; Member, UN Sub-Commission for Prevention of Discrimination and Protection of Minorities 1973–74; International Chairman, European Union of Women 1973–79; UK delegate to European Parliament 1973–75; UN Special Rapporteur on Human Rights 1975–79; Member

European Parliament for Thames Valley 1979–89: Vice-President, European Parliament 1982–1987, Group Spokesperson, Political Affairs Northern Ireland 1980–1987, Chair, Legal Affairs Committee 1987–89. Opposition Spokesperson 1975–79. Member: European Communities Select Committee 1989–94, Ad Hoc Sub-Committee on 1996 Inter-Governmental Conference 1995–97, Sub-Committee E on Law and Institutions 1994–97, Co-opted Member 1997–99. Member: International Bar Association, International Law Association, IPU. Chairman, Conservative Party International Office 1973–78. Council Member, Royal Institute of International Affairs 1977–86; Governor, British Institute Florence 1986–96, Chairman, Board of Governors 1994–96, Life Governor 1996–; Governor, Reading University 1986–96. Trustee: Industry and Parliament Trust 1985–96, Caldecott Community 1990–97. Hon. Bencher, Lincoln's Inn 1993. *Publications: UN Human Rights of Non-Citizens*, 1984; Contribution to: *Legal Issues of the Maastricht Treaty*, 1995, *European and World Trade Law*, 1996; *Procedural Aspects of Competition Law*, 1975; articles on EC law. *Special Interests:* Foreign Affairs. *Recreations:* Reading, music. Raised to the peerage as Baroness Elles, of the City of Westminster 1972. The Baroness Elles, 75 Ashley Gardens, London, SW1P 1HG *Tel:* 020 7219 3149 *Fax:* 020 7931 0046; Villa Fontana, Ponte del Giglio, Lucca, Italy *Tel:* 00 39 05833 94158.

ELLIOTT OF MORPETH, LORD — Conservative

ELLIOTT OF MORPETH (Life Baron), (Robert) William Elliott; cr. 1985. Born 11 December 1920. Son of late Richard Elliott; educated Edward VI Grammar School, Morpeth. Married Catherine Jane Morpeth 1956 (1 son 4 daughters inc twins). DL, Northumberland 1982. *Career:* Director: Corporate Trade Finance plc 1970–73, Sino French Holdings (Hong Kong) 1980–; Chair, United Artists Communications (North East) 1980–95; Director: Port of Tyne Authority 1982–91, Ferguson Industrial Holdings plc; Chair: Metro Radio Group 1981–94, Newcastle and Gateshead Water Company 1983–93; Non-Executive Director, T. Cowie 1987–95; Vice-Chair, Lyonaisse UK 1994–99. *House of Commons:* Contested (Conservative): Morpeth by-election 1954, General election 1955; MP (Conservative) for Newcastle upon Tyne North 1957–83; PPS to: Joint Parliamentary Secretaries, Ministry of Transport and Civil Aviation 1958–59, Under-Secretary, Home Office 1959–60, Minister of State, Home Office 1960–61, Secretary for Technical Co-operation 1961–63. Assistant Government Whip 1963–64; Opposition Whip 1964; Government Whip June–September 1970. *House of Lords:* Deputy Speaker 1992–2002; Deputy Chair of Committees 1997–2002. Vice-Chairman, Conservative Party Organisation 1970–74. President, Water Companies Association 1975–92; Chairman, Tyneside Save The Children. Kt 1974. *Special Interests:* Regional Policy. *Recreations:* Country life, family. *Clubs:* Northern Counties (Newcastle upon Tyne). Raised to the peerage as Baron Elliott of Morpeth, of Morpeth in the County of Northumberland and of the City of Newcastle-upon-Tyne 1985. The Lord Elliott of Morpeth, DL, House of Lords, London, SW1A 0PW *Tel:* 020 7219 3000 *Tel:* 020 7730 7619.

ELTON, LORD — Conservative

ELTON (2nd Baron, UK), Rodney Elton; cr. 1934. Born 2 March 1930. Son of 1st Baron; educated Eton College; New College, Oxford (MA modern history 1953). Married Anne Frances Tilney 1958 (1 son 3 daughters) (divorced 1979), married Richenda Gurney 1979. *Trades Union:* Assistant Masters Association 1962–69. 2nd Lieutenant, The Queens Bays 1950; Captain, Queen's Own Warwickshire and Worcestershire Yeomanry 1959; Major, Leicestershire and Derbyshire Yeomanry 1970. *Career:* Farming 1957–73; Assistant mastership (history): Loughborough Grammar School 1962–67, Fairham Comprehensive School for Boys 1967–69; Lecturer, Bishop Lonsdale College of Education 1969–72; Director: Overseas Exhibitions Ltd 1977–79, Building Trades Exhibition Ltd 1977–79; Director and Deputy Chairman, Andry Montgomery Ltd 1987–; Licensed Lay Minister, Church of England 1998–; Founded the DIVERT Trust 1993; Chairman, Quality and Standards Committee, City and Guilds of London Institute 1999–. *House of Lords:* First entered House of Lords 1973; Parliamentary Under-Secretary of State for: Northern Ireland 1979–81, Department of Health and Social Security September 1981–82, Home Office 1982–84; Minister of State: Home Office 1984–85, Department of the Environment 1985–86; Deputy Chairman of Committees 1997–; Deputy Speaker 1999–; Elected hereditary peer (office holder) 1999–. Opposition Whip 1974–76.

Opposition Spokesperson 1976–79. Member, Select Committee on: Scrutiny of Delegated Powers 1994–97, House of Lords' Offices 2000–02, Constitution 2003–, Ecclesiastical Committee 2003–. Deputy Chair, Association of Conservative Peers 1988–93. Chairman, Intermediate Treatment Fund 1990–93; Vice-President, Institute of Trading Standards Administration. Trustee: The Airey Neave Trust 1991–96, City Parochial Foundation and Trust for London 1991–97; Chairman, DIVERT Trust 1993–99, President 1999–2001. Contested (Conservative) Loughborough division of Leicestershire 1966 and 1970 general elections; Member, Boyd Commission (South Rhodesia Independence Elections) 1979; Chairman, Financial Intermediaries Managers & Brokers Regulatory Association 1987–90; Member, Panel on Takeovers and Mergers 1988–90; Chairman, Inquiry into Discipline in Schools (The Elton Report) 1988. TD 1970. *Special Interests:* Juvenile Justice, Education. *Recreations:* Painting. *Clubs:* Beefsteak, Pratt's, Cavalry and Guards. The Lord Elton, TD, House of Lords, London, SW1A 0PW *Tel:* 020 7219 3165.

ELYSTAN-MORGAN, LORD   Crossbencher

ELYSTAN-MORGAN (Life Baron), Dafydd Elystan Elystan-Morgan; cr. 1981. Born 7 December 1932. Son of late Dewi Morgan, Journalist; educated Ardwyn Grammar School; University of Wales, Aberystwyth (LLB). Married Alwen Roberts 1959 (1 son 1 daughter). *Career:* Called to the Bar 1971 (Gray's Inn); Partner in North Wales firm of solicitors 1958–68; Recorder of the Wales and Chester Circuit 1983–1987; Judge of the Wales and Chester Circuit 1987–. *House of Commons:* MP (Labour) for Cardigan 1966–74; Joint Under-Secretary of State, Home Office April 1968–70. Deputy Opposition Spokesman: Home Affairs 1970–72, Welsh Affairs 1972–74. Opposition Spokesman on Home Affairs and Legal Affairs 1983–87. Chairman, Welsh Parliamentary Party 1964, 1974. President, Association of Welsh Local Authorities 1970–74. Raised to the peerage as Baron Elystan-Morgan, of Aberteifi in the County of Dyfed 1981. The Lord Elystan-Morgan, Carreg Afon, Dolau, Bow Street, Dyfed.

EMERTON, BARONESS   Crossbencher

EMERTON (Life Baroness), Audrey Caroline Emerton; cr. 1997. Born 10 September 1935. Daughter of late George Emerton, and of Lily Emerton; educated Tunbridge Wells Grammar School; St George's Hospital; Battersea College of Technology. Single. DL, Kent 1992–. *Career:* Senior Tutor, St George's Hospital, London SW1 1965–68; County nursing officer, St John Ambulance, Kent 1967–85, County Commissioner 1985–88; Principal nursing officer, Education, Bromley Hospital Management Committee 1968–70; Chief nursing officer, Tunbridge Wells and Leybourne Hospital Management Committee 1970–73; Regional nursing officer, SE Thames RHA 1973–91; Chief nursing officer, St John Ambulance 1988–96, Chairman, Medical Board 1993–96; Vice-Chairman, Brighton Health Care NHS Trust 1993–94, Chairman 1994–2000; St John Ambulance 1996–2002: Chief Officer, Care in the Community, 1996–98, Chancellor, Chief Commander 1998–2002. Member Science and Technology Sub-committee I (Fighting Infection) 2003–. President, Association of Nurse Administrators 1979–82; Chair: English National Board for Nursing, Midwifery and Health Visiting 1983–85, United Kingdom Central Council for Nursing, Midwifery and Health Visiting 1985–93, Nurses Welfare Service 1991–96; Hon. Vice-President, Royal College of Nursing 1994–99; Member, Court of Sussex University 1996–98; Lay Member, General Medical Council 1996–2001; Chair, Association of Hospital and Community Friends 2003–. Five honorary doctorates. Chair, Care Committee, Kent Community Housing Trust 1992–98; Trustee, Kent Community Housing Trust 1993–98; Member, Burdett Nursing Trust 2001–; Trustee, Defence Medical Welfare Service 2001–. CStJ 1978; DBE 1989; DStJ 1993. Fellow, Royal Society of Arts. *Special Interests:* Health – Social Care, Voluntary Services. *Recreations:* Walking, travel, reading. Raised to the peerage as Baroness Emerton, of Tunbridge Wells in the County of Kent and of Clerkenwell in the London Borough of Islington 1997. The Baroness Emerton, DBE, DL, Carlton House, 3 Strettitt Gardens, East Peckham, Tonbridge, Kent, TN12 SE5 *Tel:* 01622 872659 *Fax:* 01622 873241 *E-mail:* audrey.emerton@sja.org.uk.

Visit the Vacher Dod Website . . .
www.DodOnline.co.uk

ERROLL, EARL OF   Crossbencher

ERROLL (24th Earl of, S), Merlin Sereld Victor Gilbert Hay; cr. 1452. 25th Lord Hay (S) 1429, 24th Lord Slains (S) 1452; 12th Bt of Moncreiffe of that Ilk (NS) 1685; 28th Hereditary Lord High Constable of Scotland, 1314; 32nd Chief of The Hays since 1160 (Celtic Title) Mac Garadh Mhor. Born 20 April 1948. Son of Sir Iain Moncreiffe of that Ilk, 11th Bt and Diana Denyse, Countess of Erroll (23rd in line); educated Eton College; Trinity College, Cambridge. Married Isabelle Jacqueline Laline Astell 1982 (2 sons 2 daughters). TA 1975–90; Hon. Colonel, RMPTA 1992–97. *Career:* Hayway Partners (Marketing) 1991–; Computer Consultant until 1993; Group Director Applications and Development, Girovend Holdings plc 1993–94; Chairman, CRC Ltd 1995–. *House of Lords:* First entered House of Lords 1978; Elected hereditary peer 1999–. Member, Library and Computers Sub-Committee 1999–2001; Board Member of Parliamentary Office of Science and Technology 2000–; Council Member: PITCOM, EURIM; Member Information Committee 2003–. Council Member: PITCOM, EURIM. Page to the Lord Lyon 1956; Lieutenant, Atholl Highlanders 1974; Member, Queens Body Guard for Scotland, Royal Company of Archers. OStJ 1977. Freeman, City of London. Member, Court of Assistants of Fishmongers' Company, Prime Warden 2000–01. *Special Interests:* Defence, ICT, Science, Scotland, Environment. *Recreations:* Country pursuits. *Clubs:* White's, Pratt's, Puffin's (Edinburgh). The Earl of Erroll, Woodbury Hall, Everton, Sandy, Bedfordshire, SG19 2HR *Tel:* 01767 650251 *E-mail:* errollm@parliament.uk.

EVANS OF PARKSIDE, LORD   Labour

EVANS OF PARKSIDE (Life Baron), John Evans; cr. 1997. Born 19 October 1930. Son of late James and Margaret Evans; educated Jarrow Central School. Married Joan Slater 1959 (2 sons 1 daughter). *Trades Union:* Joined AEU 1951. Royal Engineers 1949–50. Hebburn Urban District Council: Councillor 1962–74, Chair 1972–73, Leader 1969–74; Councillor, South Tyneside Metropolitan District Council 1973–74. *Career:* Tyneside Shipyard Worker. *House of Commons:* MP (Labour) for Newton February 1974–83 and for St. Helens North 1983–97; PPS to Leader of Opposition Michael Foot 1980–83; Shadow Employment Minister 1983–87. Government Whip 1978–1979; Opposition Whip 1979–80. Member, Administration and Works Sub-Committee, House of Lords Offices Committee 2000–. UK Member, European Parliament 1975–78; Chair, European Parliament Policy and Transport Committee 1976–78. Political Secretary, National Union of Labour and Socialist Clubs 1981–96; Member, National Executive Committee of the Labour Party 1982–96; Labour Party: Vice-Chair 1990–91, Chair 1991–92. Freeman, Metropolitan Borough of St Helens 1997. *Special Interests:* Employment, Energy, Transport, Manufacturing Industries, Industrial Relations, Licensed Trade. *Recreations:* Gardening, watching Rugby League and Association Football. Raised to the peerage as Baron Evans of Parkside, of St Helens in the County of Merseyside 1997. The Lord Evans of Parkside, 6 Kirkby Road, Culcheth, Warrington, Cheshire, WA3 4BS.

EVANS OF TEMPLE GUITING, LORD   Labour

EVANS OF TEMPLE GUITING (Life Baron), Matthew Evans; cr. 2000. Born 7 August 1941. Son of late George Ewart Evans and Florence Ellen Evans; educated Friends' School, Saffron Walden; London School of Economics (BSc economics 1963). Married Elizabeth Mead 1966 (2 sons) (marriage dissolved 1991); married Caroline Michel 1991(2 sons 1 daughter). *Career:* Bookselling 1963–64; Faber & Faber Ltd 1964–, Managing Director 1972–93, Chairman 1981–; Director, Which? Ltd 1997–2000. Government Whip 2002–. Government Spokesperson for: Office of the Deputy Prime Minister 2002–, Scotland Office 2002–03, Wales Office 2002–03, Constitutional Affairs/Lord Chancellor's Department (Scotland and Wales) 2003–, Trade and Industry 2003–. Governor, BFI 1982–97 (Vice-Chairman 1996–97); Member: Council, Publishers Association 1978–84, Franco-British Society 1981–2003; Chairman: National Book League 1982–84, English Stage Company 1984–90. Hon. DLitt, Sunderland. Member, Literary Advisory Panel, British Council 1986–97;

Chairman, Library and Information Commission 1995–98; Member: Arts Council National Lottery Advisory Panel 1997–, University for Industry Advisory Group 1997, Sir Richard Eyre's Working Group on Royal Opera House 1997, Arts and Humanities Research Board 1998–2003; Chairman, Museums, Libraries and Archives Council 2000–03. CBE 1998. FRSA 1990; Hon FRCA 1999; Hon FLA 1999. *Clubs:* Groucho. Raised to the peerage as Baron Evans of Temple Guiting, of Temple Guiting in the County of Gloucestershire 2000. The Lord Evans of Temple Guiting, CBE, 36 Chapel Street, SW1X 7DD *E-mail:* evansm@parliament.uk.

EVANS OF WATFORD, LORD   Labour

EVANS OF WATFORD (Life Baron), David Charles Evans; cr. 1998. Born 30 November 1942. Son of Arthur Charles Evans and Phyllis Connie Evans; educated Hampden Secondary School; Watford College of Technology. Married June Scaldwell 1966 (1 son 1 daughter). *Trades Union:* GPMU. *Career:* Apprentice printer, Stone and Cox Ltd 1957; Sales executive and sales director at various printers; Centurion Press: Founder 1971, Chair, and of subsidiary companies in UK, Netherlands and the USA –2002; Chair: Personnel Publications Ltd, Centurion Publishing Ltd, Senate Consulting Ltd, Senate Holdings bv, Indigo Publishing Ltd; Non-executive Chief Executive Officer Union Income Benefit Holdings plc 2001–; Non-executive director: Yoo Media plc 2002–, Partnership Sourcing Ltd. *House of Lords:* Departmental Liaison Peer for the DTI 1999–. Member, House of Lords Offices' Library and Computers Sub-committee 2000–02. Honorary Fellow, Cancer Research UK; Chair, CT Spiral Scanner Appeal, Watford Hospital; Member of Benevolent Committee, The Royal British Legion. Trustee, Royal Air Force Museum. Assisted in the creation of the One World group (now One World Action); Voluntary lecturer for the Postal Telegraph and Telephone International in trade union studies and media public relations; Non-executive Director Hendon Museum Enterprises Ltd. Fellow: Chartered Institute of Marketing, City and Guilds Institute. Member, Worshipful Company of Marketors. *Special Interests:* Industrial Relations, Current Affairs, Education, Travel, Voluntary Sector. *Recreations:* Theatre, the arts, reading, travel. *Clubs:* Mortons. Raised to the peerage as Baron Evans of Watford, of Chipperfield in the County of Hertfordshire 1998. The Lord Evans of Watford, House of Lords, London, SW1A 0PW *Tel:* 020 7219 6184 *Fax:* 020 7219 1733 *E-mail:* lordevans@senateconsulting.co.uk.

EWING OF KIRKFORD, LORD   Labour

EWING OF KIRKFORD (Life Baron), Harry Ewing; cr. 1992. Born 20 January 1931. Son of late William Ewing; educated Beath High School, Cowdenbeath. Married Margaret Greenhill 1954 (1 son 1 daughter). *Trades Union:* Active trade unionist, AUEW, Member No. 1 District Council 1958–61; Various offices within Union of Post Office Workers 1962–71. RAF 1949–51. DL, Fife 1995–. *House of Commons:* Contested (Labour) East Fife 1970 general election; MP (Labour) for: Stirling and Falkirk 1971–74, Stirling, Falkirk and Grangemouth 1974–83, Falkirk East 1983–92; Parliamentary Under-Secretary of State, Scottish Office (with special responsibility for Devolution matters) 1974–79. Opposition Frontbench Spokesperson for: Scotland 1979–84, Trade and Industry 1984–85, Scotland 1985–87. Opposition Spokesperson for: Scottish Office Affairs 1992–96, Transport 1993–96, Energy 1994–95. Member: Council of Europe 1987–92, Western European Union 1987–92. Has held many local and national positions in the Co-operative Movement. Chairman, Scottish Disability Foundation 1992–; Non-executive Director, Kirkcaldy Acute Hospitals NHS Trust 1994–96; Chairman, Fife Healthcare NHS Trust 1996–98. Hon. DU, University of Stirling 1998. Joint Chairman, Scottish Constitutional Convention 1990–96; Chairman, Ewing Enquiry into the availability of housing for wheelchair disabled in Scotland November 1993, report published April 1994. *Special Interests:* Health, Social Services. *Recreations:* Gardening, bowls. Raised to the peerage as Baron Ewing of Kirkford, of Cowdenbeath in the District of Dunfermline 1992. The Lord Ewing of Kirkford, DL, Gowanbank, 45 Glenlyon Road, Leven, Fife, KY8 4AA *Tel:* 01333 426123.

EZRA, LORD   Liberal Democrat

EZRA (Life Baron), Derek Ezra; cr. 1983. Born 23 February 1919. Son of late David Ezra; educated Monmouth School; Magdalene College, Cambridge. Married Julia Elizabeth Wilkins 1950. Army Service 1939–47. *Career:* National Coal Board 1947–82: marketing department 1947–65, Director General of Marketing 1960–65, Board member 1965–67, Deputy Chair 1967–71; Chair 1971–82, Chair: Energy and Technical Services Group plc 1990–99, AHS-Emstar plc 1966–99, Sheffield Heat & Power Ltd 1985–2000; Director, Aran Energy plc 1984–95; Chair, Throgmorton Trust 1985–90; Director: Solvay SA 1979–89, Redland plc 1981–89; Member, International Advisory Board: Banca del Lavoro 1981–2000, Creditanstalt Bankverein 1981–91; Member: Advisory Board, Petrofina SA 1981–90, Advisory Committee, Energy International SA 1975–90. Former Liberal Democrat Spokesperson for Economic Affairs; Spokesperson for Energy 1998–. Chairman, EU Sub-committee B 1985–88; Member, Select Committee on Monetary Policy of the Bank of England 1998–99. Former President, Coal Industry Society. Two honorary doctorates. Former President, British Standards Institution; President, Institute of Trading Standards Administration 1987–92; Former President, Keep Britain Tidy Group; Former Patron, Neighbourhood Energy Action; Patron (Past President), Combustion Engineering Association. MBE (Mil) 1945; Kt 1974; Italian Order of Merit 1979; Luxembourg Order of Merit 1981; Officer, Légion d'Honneur 1981. *Publications: Coal and Energy,* 1978; *The Energy Debate,* 1983. *Clubs:* National Liberal. Raised to the peerage as Baron Ezra, of Horsham in the County of West Sussex 1983. The Lord Ezra, MBE, House of Lords, London, SW1A 0PW *Tel:* 020 7219 3180.

F

FALCONER OF THOROTON, LORD   Labour

FALCONER OF THOROTON (Life Baron), Charles Leslie Falconer; cr. 1997. Born 19 November 1951. Son of John Leslie Falconer and of late Anne Mansel Falconer; educated Trinity College, Glenalmond; Queens' College, Cambridge. Married Marianna Catherine Thoroton Hildyard 1985 (3 sons 1 daughter). *Career:* Called to the Bar, Inner Temple 1974; QC 1991. *House of Lords:* Solicitor General 1997–98; Minister of State: Cabinet Office 1998–2001, Department for Transport, Local Government and the Regions (Minister for Housing, Planning and Regeneration) 2001–02, For Criminal Justice, Sentencing and Law Reform, Home Office 2002–03; Secretary of State for Constitutional Affairs and Lord Chancellor 2003–. Government Spokesperson for: Cabinet Office 1998–2001, Northern Ireland, Transport, Local Government and the Regions 2001–02, Home Office 2002–03, Constitutional Affairs/Lord Chancellor's Department 2003–. Elected Master, Bench of the Inner Temple 1997. PC 2003. Raised to the peerage as Baron Falconer of Thoroton, of Thoroton in the County of Nottinghamshire 1997. Rt Hon the Lord Falconer of Thoroton, QC, House of Lords, London, SW1A 0PW *Tel:* 020 7219 5159.

FALKENDER, BARONESS   Labour

FALKENDER (Life Baroness), Marcia Matilda Falkender; cr. 1974. Born 10 March 1932. Daughter of late Harry Field; educated Northampton High School for Girls; Queen Mary College, London University (BA history). Married George Edmund Charles Williams 1955 (divorced 1961). *Career:* Secretary to General Secretary Labour Party HQ 1955–56; Private secretary to Harold Wilson MP 1956–64; Political secretary and head of political office to Harold Wilson as Leader of the Labour Party and Prime Minister 1964–70 and 1974–76; Columnist, *Mail on Sunday* 1983–88; Local director, Cheltenham and Gloucester Building Society, Peckham; Director: South London Investment Mortgage Corporation 1986–91, Canvasback Productions 1988–91, Regent (GM) Laboratories 1996–. Lay Governor, Queen Mary and Westfield College, London University 1987–93.

Formerly President, UN Unifem UK Trust; Trustee: The Silver Trust 1986–, Women Aid. Member: Film Industry Working Party 1975, Film Industry Action Committee 1977–85, British Screen Advisory Council 1985–, Royal Society of Arts. CBE. *Publications: Inside No. 10*, 1972; *Perspective on Downing Street*, 1983. *Special Interests:* Exports, Health, Breast Cancer, British Film Industry. *Recreations:* Films. *Clubs:* Reform. Raised to the peerage as Baroness Falkender, of West Haddon in the County of Northamptonshire 1974. The Baroness Falkender, CBE, Highcliffe, Northampton Road, Blisworth, Northants, NN7 3DN *Tel:* 020 7402 8570.

FALKLAND, VISCOUNT OF   Liberal Democrat

FALKLAND (15th Viscount of, S), Lucius Edward William Plantagenet Cary; cr. 1620; Lord Cary. Born 8 May 1935. Son of 14th Viscount; educated Wellington College. Married Caroline Butler 1962 (divorced 1990) (1 son 2 daughters and 1 daughter deceased); married Nicole Mackey 1990 (1 son). 2nd Lieutenant, 8th Hussars. *Career:* Journalist, Theatrical agent, Chartered shipbroker; Chief executive, C T Bowring Trading (Holdings) Ltd 1974–80; Marketing consultant 1980–86. *House of Lords:* First entered House of Lords 1984; Elected hereditary peer 1999–; Deputy Chair of Committees 2000–. Liberal Democrat Deputy Whip 1988–2001. Liberal Democrat Spokesperson for: National Heritage 1995–97, Culture, Media and Sport 1997–. Member: Overseas Trade Committee 1984–85, House of Lords' Offices Refreshment Sub-committee 2000–. *Special Interests:* Developing World, Film Industry, Alcohol and Drug Addiction, Transport, Motorcycle Industry. *Recreations:* Golf, cinema, motorcycling, reading. *Sportsclubs:* Sunningdale Golf. *Clubs:* Brooks's. The Viscount of Falkland, House of Lords, London, SW1A 0PW *Tel:* 020 7219 3230.

FARRINGTON OF RIBBLETON, BARONESS   Labour

FARRINGTON OF RIBBLETON (Life Baroness), Josephine Farrington; cr. 1994. Born 29 June 1940. Daughter of late Ernest Joseph Cayless, and of Dorothy Cayless. Married Michael James Farrington 1960 (3 sons). Councillor: Preston Borough Council 1973–76, Lancashire County Council 1977–; Chair, Education Committee 1981–91; Chair of County Council 1992–93. *Career:* Member, Council of Europe Standing Conference of Local and Regional Authorities 1981–94 and of new Congress; Chair, Culture, Education, Media and Sport Committee 1988–94; International observer at local elections in Poland, Ukraine and Albania; Member, Committee of the Regions – EU; Chairman, Education and Training 1994; Currently Chair, Association of County Councils; Service as: Education Spokesperson, Chair, Policy Committee, Labour Group Deputy and Leader; Has served on Burnham Primary and Secondary and Further Education Committees; Member, National Advisory Body for Public Sector Higher Education. Opposition Whip 1995–97; Government Whip 1997–. Government Spokesperson for: Environment, Transport and the Regions (Local Government) 1997–2001, Northern Ireland 1997–, Wales Office –2002, Environment and Rural Affairs 2001–, Cabinet Office 2001–02, Women's Issues/Equality Agenda –2003. UK Woman of Europe 1994. Contested (Labour) Lancashire West 1983 general election. *Recreations:* Reading. Raised to the peerage as Baroness Farrington of Ribbleton, of Fulwood in the County of Lancashire 1994. The Baroness Farrington of Ribbleton, House of Lords, London, SW1A 0PW *Tel:* 020 7219 3104.

FAULKNER OF WORCESTER, LORD   Labour

FAULKNER OF WORCESTER (Life Baron), Richard Oliver Faulkner; cr. 1999. Born 22 March 1946. Son of late Harold and Mabel Faulkner; educated Merchant Taylors' School, Northwood; Worcester College, Oxford (BA philosophy, politics and economics 1967, MA). Married Susan Heyes 1968 (2 daughters). Councillor, Merton Borough Council 1971–78. *Career:* Research assistant and journalist, Labour Party 1967–69; Public relations officer, Construction Industry Training Board 1969–70; Editor, *Steel News* 1971; Account director, F J Lyons (Public Relations) Ltd 1971–73; Director, PPR International 1973–76; Government relations adviser to various companies, unions, councils and bodies 1973–99; Co-founder, *The House*

Magazine parliamentary journal; Communications Adviser to Leader of the Opposition and Labour Party (unpaid) in general elections 1987, 1992, 1997; Communications adviser to the Bishop at Lambeth 1990; Deputy chair, Citigate Westminster 1997–99 (Joint Managing Director, Westminster Communications Group 1989–97); Director, Cardiff Millennium Stadium plc 1997–2002; Strategy adviser: Littlewoods Leisure 1999–, Incepta Group plc 1999–, Director, Sponsorship Consultancy Ltd. 2002–, Director, Gamcare 2003–. *House of Lords:* Departmental Liaison Peer: Department of the Environment, Transport and the Regions 2000–01, Cabinet Office 2001–. Member: European Union Sub-committee B (Energy, Industry and Transport) 2000–, House of Lords' Offices 2001–02. Member, CPA IPU. Member: Football League Enquiry into Membership Schemes 1984, Sports Council 1986–88, Anti-hooliganism Committee 1987–90; Chair: Women's Football Association 1988–91, Sports Grounds Initiative 1995–2000; Associate Director, Oxford United Football Club 2002–; Director, Brighton and Hove Albion Football Club 1997–2002; Former Director, Wimbledon and Crystal Palace Football Clubs; Vice-Chair, Transport 2000 Ltd 1986–99, Vice-President 2001–; Elected member, The Dons Trust 2002–03; Chair, Worcester College Appeal Campaign 1996–2003; Vice-Chair, Football Task Force 1997–99; Patron, Roy Castle Lung Cancer Foundation 1999–; Member, Court of University of Luton 1999–; Patron, The TERRE Initiative 1999–2002; Member: Safer Sports Grounds Panel 2000–01, Home Office Working Group on football disorder 2000–02; President ROSPA 2001–; Member, Railway Heritage Committee 2002–. Honorary Fellow, Worcester College, Oxford 2002 Honorary Doctor of Law, Luton University 2003. Trustee, Football Trust 1979–82, Secretary 1983–86, First Deputy Chairman 1986–98; Trustee, Foundation for Sport and the Arts 2000–. Contested (Labour) Devizes 1970, February 1974, Monmouth October 1974, Huddersfield West 1979 general elections. *Special Interests:* Transport, Sport, Human Rights. *Recreations:* Travelling by railway, collecting Lloyd George memorabilia, tinplate trains, watching Association Football. *Clubs:* Reform. Raised to the peerage as Baron Faulkner of Worcester, of Wimbledon in the London Borough of Merton 1999. The Lord Faulkner of Worcester, House of Lords, London, SW1A 0PW *Tel:* 020 7219 8503 *Fax:* 020 7219 1460 *E-mail:* faulknerro@parliament.uk.

FEARN, LORD   Liberal Democrat

FEARN (Life Baron), Ronnie Cyril Fearn; cr. 2001. Born 6 February 1931. Son of late James Fearn and late Martha Ellen Fearn; educated Norwood School; King George V Grammar School, Southport. Married Joyce Dugan 1955 (1 son 1 daughter). *Trades Union:* Member, Association of Liberal Democrat Trade Unionists. Royal Navy national service 1950–51. Councillor and Leader of Lib Dem Group: Southport Borough Council 1963–74, Merseyside Metropolitan County Council 1974–86; Councillor, Sefton Metropolitan Borough Council 1974–. *Career:* Banking, Royal Bank of Scotland 1947–87. *House of Commons:* Member for Southport: Liberal 1987–88, Liberal Democrat 1988–92; Contested Southport 1992 general election; Member for Southport 1997–2001. Deputy Whip 1988–90. Liberal Democrat Spokesperson for: Health, Tourism, Housing, Transport 1989–92, National Heritage, Constitution and Civil Service (Tourism) 1997, Culture, Media, Sport and Civil Service (Tourism) 1997–99, Culture, Media and Sport (Tourism) 1999–. Member European Union Sub-committee B (Energy, Industry and Transport) 2003–. Member: IPU, CPA, Liberal International. Voluntary Youth Leader in Southport for 21 years; President, Local Carers' Association; Local President, Sue Ryder Association; Member: All Souls' Dramatic Club, Hon. Member, LIFE; President, Southport M.E. Society. Southport Offshore Life Boat, Southport Gladstone Liberal Club. OBE 1985. Fellow, Chartered Institute of Bankers. *Special Interests:* Tourism, Health, Transport, Leisure, Local Government. *Recreations:* Amateur dramatics, badminton, athletics, community work. *Sportsclubs:* Southport and Waterloo Athletic Club. *Clubs:* National Liberal. Raised to the peerage as Baron Fearn, of Southport in the County of Merseyside 2001. The Lord Fearn, OBE, House of Lords, London, SW1A 0PW *Tel:* 020 7219 5116 *Tel:* 01704 228577 *Fax:* 01704 508635.

DodOnline
An Electronic Directory without rival . . .

Peers' biographies and photographs available with daily updates *via* the internet

For a *free* trial, call Yasmin Mirza, Aby Farsoun or Michael Mand on 020 7630 7643

FELDMAN, LORD   Conservative

FELDMAN (Life Baron), Basil Feldman; cr. 1996. Born 23 September 1926. Son of late Philip and Tilly Feldman; educated Grocers' School; SE London Technical College. Married Gita Julius 1952 (2 sons 1 daughter). *Career:* Chair, Martlet Services Group Ltd 1973–81; Member, Post Office Users' National Council 1978–81; Chair, The Clothing Little Neddy 1978–85; Underwriting Member of Lloyds 1979–97; Chair: Solport Ltd 1980–85, Better Made in Britain 1983–98; Director, The Young Entrepreneurs Fund 1985–94; Member, English Tourist Board 1986–96; Chair: The Quality Mark 1987–92, Shopping Hours Reform Council 1988–94, Better Business Opportunities 1990–98, Market Opportunities Advisory Group, Department of Trade and Industry 1991–93. Deputy Chairman, National Union of Conservative and Unionist Associations, Greater London Area 1975–78, Chairman 1978–81, President 1981–85, Vice President 1985–; Vice Chairman, National Union of the Conservative Party 1982–85, Chairman 1985–86, Vice-President 1986–; Member, National Union Executive Committee 1975–99, Chairman 1991–96; Joint National Chairman, Conservative Party's Impact 80s Campaign 1982–87; Vice-President, Greater London Young Conservatives 1975–77; Has held various other posts within the Conservative Party including Party Treasurer 1996–. Governor, Sports Aid Foundation 1990–2002; Founder/Chairman, The London Arts Season 1993–96; Chairman: The Festival of Arts and Culture 1995–96, Conservative National Golf Tournament Charitable Settlement. Adopted Member: GLC Housing Management Committee 1973–77, GLC Arts Board 1976–81. Kt 1982. FRSA 1987. Freeman, City of London 1983. *Publications:* Several publications, booklets and pamphlets for the Conservative Party; *Constituency Campaigning*, 1977; *Some Thoughts on Job Creation*, (for NEDO) 1984. *Special Interests:* Industry, Arts, Construction Industry, Retail Industry, Import Substitution, Tourism, Sport. *Recreations:* Golf, tennis, theatre, opera, travel. *Clubs:* Carlton, Garrick. Raised to the peerage as Baron Feldman, of Frognal in the London Borough of Camden 1996. The Lord Feldman, House of Lords, London, SW1A 0PW *Tel:* 020 7219 0661.

FELLOWES, LORD   Crossbencher

FELLOWES (Life Baron), Robert Fellowes; cr. 1999. Born 11 December 1941. Son of late Sir William Fellowes, KCVO and Lady Fellowes; educated Eton College. Married Lady Jane Spencer, daughter of 8th Earl Spencer, LVO, and Hon. Mrs Shand Kydd 1978 (1 son 2 daughters). Short Service Commission, Scots Guards 1960–63. *Career:* Director, Allen Harvey & Ross Ltd 1968–77; Assistant Private Secretary to HM The Queen 1977–86, Deputy Private Secretary 1986–90, Private Secretary 1990–99; Vice-Chairman, Barclays Private Banking 1999–2000, Chairman 2000–; Non-executive Director, South African Breweries 1999–; Chairman (Consultant)/Degremont UK 2003–. Member Constitution Committee 2001–. Vice-Chairman, Commonwealth Institute 2000–; Member, Council of St George's House, Windsor 2001–. Rhodes Trust 2001–, Winston Churchill Memorial Trust 2001–; Chair Prison Reform Trust 2001–. LVO 1983; CB 1987; KCVO 1989; PC 1990; KCB 1991; GCVO 1996; GCB 1998; QSO 1999. Liveryman, Goldsmith's Company. *Recreations:* Golf, watching cricket, reading. *Clubs:* White's, Pratt's, MCC, Royal Overseas League. Raised to the peerage as Baron Fellowes, of Shotesham in the County of Norfolk 1999. Rt Hon the Lord Fellowes, GCB, GCVO, House of Lords, London, SW1A 0PW *Tel:* 020 7219 5353.

DodOnline

An Electronic Directory without rival . . .

Peers' biographies and photographs available with daily updates *via* the internet

For a *free* trial, call Yasmin Mirza, Aby Farsoun or Michael Mand on 020 7630 7643

FERRERS, EARL
Conservative

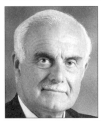

FERRERS (13th Earl, GB), Robert Washington Shirley; cr. 1711; Viscount Tamworth; 19th Bt of Staunton Harold (E) 1611. Born 8 June 1929. Son of 12th Earl; educated Winchester College; Magdalene College, Cambridge (MA agriculture 1953). Married Annabel Mary Carr 1951 (2 sons 3 daughters). Coldstream Guards, Malaya 1949. DL, Norfolk 1983. *Career:* Trustee, East Anglian Trustee Savings Bank 1957–75; Trustee, Trustee Savings Bank of Eastern England 1975–79, Chairman 1977–79; Member, Central Board Trustee Savings Bank 1977–79; Director: Central Trustee Savings Bank Ltd 1978–79, TSB Trustcard Ltd 1978–79; Director, Norwich Union Insurance Group 1975–79, 1983–88; Member, Governing Body of Rothamsted Agricultural Experimental Station 1984–88; Director, Economic Forestry Group plc 1985–88. *House of Lords:* First entered House of Lords 1954; Parliamentary Secretary to Ministry of Agriculture, Fisheries and Food 1974; Member, Armitage Committee on Political Activities of Civil Servants 1976; Joint Deputy Leader of the Opposition 1976–79; Minister of State, Ministry of Agriculture, Fisheries and Food 1979–83; Deputy Leader 1979–83, 1988–97; Minister of State, Home Office 1988–94; Minister of State, Department of Trade and Industry (Minister for Small Firms and Consumer Affairs) 1994–95; Minister of State, Department of the Environment (Minister for the Environment and Countryside) 1995–97; Elected hereditary peer 1999–. Opposition Whip 1964–67; Government Whip 1962–64, 1971–74. Member Select Committees on: Procedure 1988–2000, Privileges Lords' Interests Sub-committee 2001–. Member, Council of Hurstpierpoint College 1959–68; High Steward, Norwich Cathedral 1979–; Member, Council of Food from Britain 1985–88; Fellow, Winchester College 1988–2003; Sub-Warden, Winchester College 1998–2003. Director, The Chatham Historic Dockyard Trust 1984–88. Chairman: Royal Commission on Historical Monuments (England) 1984–88, British Agricultural Export Council 1984–88. PC 1982. *Recreations:* Shooting, music, travel. *Clubs:* Beefsteak. Rt Hon the Earl Ferrers, DL, Park Lodge, Hedenham, Norfolk, NR35 2LE *Tel:* 01508 482250 *Fax:* 01508 482332; House of Lords, London, SW1A 0PW *Tel:* 020 7219 3204.

FILKIN, LORD
Labour

FILKIN (Life Baron), David Geoffrey Nigel Filkin; cr. 1999. Born 1 July 1944. Son of late Donald Geoffrey and Winifred Filkin; educated King Edward VI School, Birmingham; Clare College, Cambridge (MA history 1966); Manchester University (DipTP 1972); Birmingham University (post graduate study). Married Elizabeth Tompkins 1974 (3 daughters) (divorced 1994). *Career:* Teacher on VSO, Ghana 1966–67; Town planner, Redditch Development Corporation (New Town) 1969–72; Manager, Brent Housing Aid Centre, London Borough of Brent 1972–75; Deputy Chief Executive, Merseyside Improved Housing 1975–79; Borough housing officer, Ellesmere Port and Neston Borough Council 1979–82; Director of housing, London Borough of Greenwich 1982–88; Chief Executive, Reading Borough Council 1988–91; Secretary, Association of District Councils 1991–97; Local government adviser to Joseph Rowntree Foundation 1997–2001; Director, New Local Government Network 1997–2001; Policy analyst and writer 1997–2001. *House of Lords:* Parliamentary Under-Secretary of State: for Race Equality, Community and European and International Policy, Home Office 2002–03, Department for Constitutional Affairs 2002–03. Government Whip 2001–02. Government Spokesperson for: Transport, Local Government and the Regions 2001–02, Health 2001–02, Home Office 2002–03, Constitutional Affairs/Lord Chancellor's Department 2003–. Member House of Lords Offices Finance and Staffing Sub Committee 2000–01. Trustee, The Parliament Choir. CBE 1997. Former Member of Royal Town Planning Institute; Former Associate Member of Institute of Housing. *Publications: Best Value for the Public; Political Leadership of Best Value; Partnerships for Best Value; Modernising Local Government; Starting to Modernise; Achieving Best Value; Towards a New Localism; Winning the e-Revolution; Strategic Partnering for Local Services. Special Interests:* Policy Development, Policy Implementation, Housing, West Africa, Southern Africa. *Recreations:* Founder of the Parliament Choir and Chairman 1999–2001, music, walking, swimming, singing, church. Raised to the peerage as Baron Filkin, of Pimlico in the City of Westminster 1999. The Lord Filkin, CBE, House of Lords, London, SW1A 0PW *Tel:* 020 7219 0640 *E-mail:* gfilkin1@aol.com.

FINLAY OF LLANDAFF, BARONESS   Crossbencher

FINLAY OF LLANDAFF (Life Baroness), Ilora Gillian Finlay; cr 2001. Born 23 February 1949. Daughter of Charles Beaumont Benoy Downman and Thaïs Helèna, née Barakan; educated Wimbledon High School, London; St Mary's Hospital, London University (MB BS 1972). Married Andrew Yule Finlay 1972 (1 son 1 daughter). *Trades Union:* Member British Medical Association. Non-executive Director Gwent Health Authority 1995–2001; Cancer Research UK Science Committee 2002–. *Career:* General practitioner 1981–86; Palliative medicine 1987–; Marie Curie Cancer Care 1987–; Member Expert Advisory Group on Cancers 1993–97, Chairman Association for Palliative Medicine 1995–98; Velindre NHS Trust Cancer Centre, Cardiff 1994–; National Cancer Forum 1997–2000; Vice-dean School of Medicine, University of Wales College of Medicine 2000–; President Medical Women's Federations 2001–02. Member: Procedure Committee 2003–, Science and Technology Sub-committee I (Fighting Infection) 2003–, Science and Technology Sub-committee II (Science and the Regional Development Agencies) 2003–. Welsh Woman of the Year 1996–97. Hon Doctor of Science, University of Glamorgan; Hon Fellow, Cardiff University; Johanna Bijtel Professor, Gröningen University, Netherlands 2000–02. FRCP, FRCGP. *Publications:* Co-author *Care of the Dying – a clinical handbook* (Churchill Livingstone) 1984; Co-editor: *Medical Humanities*, (BMJ Press) 2001, *The Effective Management of Cancer Pain* (Aesculapius Medical Press) 2000, 2nd edition 2001; Many chapters in books and papers on palliative medicine, medical education, ethics and service provision. *Special Interests:* Women's Careers, Medical Ethics. *Clubs:* Royal Society of Medicine. Raised to the peerage as Baroness Finlay of Llandaff, of Llandaff in the County of South Glamorgan 2001. The Baroness Finlay of Llandaff, House of Lords, London, SW1A 0PW *Tel:* 020 7219 6693 *E-mail:* finlayig@cardiff.ac.uk.

FISHER OF REDNAL, BARONESS   Labour

FISHER OF REDNAL (Life Baroness), Doris Mary Fisher; cr. 1974. Born 13 September 1919. Daughter of late Frederick Satchwell, BEM; educated Birmingham Schools; Fircroft College. Married Joseph Fisher 1939 (died 1978) (2 daughters). Councillor, Birmingham City Council 1952–74: Past Chair Housing Committee; JP, Birmingham 1961; Formerly Member, Warrington New Town Development Corporation; Member, New Towns Staff Commission 1976–79. *Career:* Member, European Parliament 1975–79. *House of Commons:* Contested Birmingham Ladywood 1969 by-election; MP (Labour) for Birmingham, Ladywood 1970–74. Opposition Whip 1983–84. Opposition Spokesperson for the Environment 1983–84. National President, Women's Co-op Guild 1961–62. Chairman, Baskerville Special School 1981–89; Warden, Birmingham Assay Office 1981–89; President, Birmingham Royal Institute of Blind (now Focus) 1982–; Member, Hallmarking Council 1989–94; President, Motability Midlands 1989–95; Governor, Hunters Hill Special School, Bromsgrove; President, The British Fluoridation Society 1993–; Midland Area Chairman: NSPCC 1993–, Macmillan Nurses 1995–; Patron, St Basil's Young Homeless, Birmingham. Formerly Member, General Medical Council. Hon. Doctor, University of Central England, Birmingham 1998. *Special Interests:* Housing, Local Government. *Recreations:* Swimming. Raised to the peerage as Baroness Fisher of Rednal, of Rednal in the City of Birmingham 1974. The Baroness Fisher of Rednal, 60 Jacoby Place, Priory Road, Edgbaston, Birmingham, B5 7UW.

FITT, LORD   Independent Socialist

FITT (Life Baron), Gerard Fitt; cr. 1983. Born 9 April 1926. Son of late George Fitt; educated in Belfast. Married Susan Doherty 1947 (died 1996) (5 daughters and 1 daughter deceased). Councillor, Dock Ward, Belfast Corporation 1958. *Career:* Merchant Seaman 1941–53; Member (Irish Labour) Parliament of Northern Ireland, Dock Division of Belfast 1962–72; Member (SDLP), North Belfast, Northern Ireland Assembly 1973–75; Deputy Chief Executive of the Northern Ireland Executive 1974. *House of Commons:* MP for Belfast West as: Republican Labour 1966–70, SDLP 1970–79, Socialist 1979–83. Raised to the peerage as Baron Fitt, of Bell's Hill in the County of Down 1983. The Lord Fitt, House of Lords, London, SW1A 0PW *Tel:* 020 7219 6701.

FLATHER, BARONESS   Conservative

FLATHER (Life Baroness), Shreela Flather; cr. 1990. Daughter of Aftab and Krishna Rai; educated University College, London (LLB 1956). Married Gary Denis Flather 1965 (2 sons). JP, Maidenhead 1971–90 (Crown Supplemental List); Councillor, Royal Borough of Windsor and Maidenhead 1976–91, Deputy Mayor 1985–86, Mayor 1986–87; DL, Berkshire 1994–. *Career:* Called to the Bar, Inner Temple 1962; Infant teacher, ILEA 1965–67; Teacher of English as second language, Altwood Comprehensive School, Maidenhead 1968–74; Teacher of English as second language, Broadmoor Hospital 1974–78; Member, Committee of Management, Servite Houses Ltd 1987–94; UK Member, Economic and Social Committee European Community 1987–90; Director, Meridian Broadcasting (MAI) Ltd 1990–2000; Chairman, Alcohol Education and Research Council 1995–2001; Director: Marie Stopes International 1996–, Cable Corporation 1997–2000; Fellow, University College, London; Director Kiss FM and Magic FM 1999–2002; Chair and Director, Club Asia 2002–. Member: European Communities Sub-Committee C 1990–95, Select Committee on Medical Ethics 1993–94. UK Representative on EU Advisory Commission on Racism and Xenophobia 1995–97. Member, Conservative Women's National Committee 1978–88; Member, Anglo-Asian Conservative Society 1979–83; Resigned the Conservative Whip December 1998, rejoined November 1999. Senior posts in numerous organisations involved in refugee, community, carer, race relations and prison work, including Member: Commission for Racial Equality 1980–86, Social Security Advisory Committee 1987–90; Vice-Chair, The Refugee Council 1991–94; Governor, Commonwealth Institute 1993–98; Joint President, Family Planning Association 1995–98; Board Member and Chair Ethics and Equal Opportunities Committees Broadmoor Hospital 1984–98; Patron Cedar Centre (community centre Isle of Dogs). *Asian Who's Who* Asian of the Year 1996. Hon. DUniv, Open University 1994. Trustee: Hillingdon Hospital 1990–98, Rajiv Gandhi (UK) Foundation 1993–2002; Member: Council of the Winston Churchill Memorial Trust 1993–, Council of St George's House, Windsor Castle 1996–2002; Chair Memorial Gates Trust (memorial on Constitution Hill) 1998–2003; Member Council of University College London 2000–; Seva Mandir (providing water in Rajsthan). Member, BBC South and East Regional Advisory Council 1987–89. FRSA. *Special Interests:* Race Relations, European Union. *Recreations:* Reading, cinema, travel. Raised to the peerage as Baroness Flather, of Windsor and Maidenhead in the Royal County of Berkshire 1990. The Baroness Flather, DL, Triveni, Ascot Road, Maidenhead, Berkshire, SL6 2HT *Tel:* 01628 625408 *Fax:* 01628 675355.

FLOWERS, LORD   Crossbencher

FLOWERS (Life Baron), Brian Hilton Flowers; cr. 1979. Born 13 September 1924. Son of late Rev. Harold Joseph Flowers; educated Bishop Gore Grammar School, Swansea; Gonville and Caius College, Cambridge (MA); Birmingham University (DSc). Married Mary Frances Behrens 1951 (2 step-sons). *Career:* Anglo-Canadian Atomic Energy Project (Tube Alloys) 1944–46; Research in nuclear physics and atomic energy at Atomic Energy Research Establishment (AERE), Harwell 1946–50; Department of mathematical physics, Birmingham University 1950–52; Head of theoretical physics division, AERE, Harwell 1952–58; Manchester University: Professor of theoretical physics 1958–61, Langworthy Professor of physics 1961–72; Chairman, Science Research Council 1967–73; London University: Rector, Imperial College 1973–85, Vice-Chancellor 1985–90. Chancellor, Manchester University 1994–2001. Member, House of Lords Select Committee on Science and Technology 1980–93, 1994–97, Chairman 1989–93, Co-opted Member 2000–; Member, Select Committees on: Science and Technology Sub-Committee II (Aircraft Cabin Environment/Innovations in Computer Processors) 2000–02, Science and Technology Sub-Committee IIA (Human Genetic Databases) 2000–02. Chair: Computer Board for Universities and Research Council 1966–70, Member, Atomic Energy Authority 1971–81; President, Institute of Physics 1972–74; Chair, Royal Commission on Environmental Pollution 1973–76; President: European Science Foundation 1974–80, National Society for Clean Air 1977–79; Chair: Commission on Energy and the Environment 1978–81, University of London Working Party on future of medical and dental teaching resources 1979–80, Committee of Vice-Chancellors and Principals for 1983–85; Member of Council, Academia Europaea 1988–91; Member of Council and Vice-Chairman, Royal Postgraduate Medical School 1990–97; Member of Management Board,

London School of Hygiene and Tropical Medicine 1991–95, Chairman 1994–95; Governor, Middlesex University 1992–2001; Chair, Committee of Enquiry into the Academic Year 1992–93. 16 honorary doctorates; 4 honorary university fellowships. Managing Trustee, Nuffield Foundation 1982–98, Chairman 1987–98. Vice-Chairman, Parliamentary Office of Science and Technology (POST) 1998–. Kt 1969; Officier de la Légion d'Honneur (France), 1981. FRS 1961. *Publications:* Co-author *Properties of Matter*, 1970; *An Introduction to Numerical Methods C++*, 1995; Contributions to scientific periodicals on scientific structure of atomic nucleus, nuclear reations, science policy, energy and the environment. *Special Interests:* Higher Education, Science and Technology, Environment. *Recreations:* Music, walking, gardening, computing. Raised to the peerage as Baron Flowers, of Queen's Gate in the City of Westminster 1979. The Lord Flowers, 53 Athenaeum Road, London, N20 9AL *Tel:* 020 8446 5993 *E-mail:* fofqg@clumsies.demon.co.uk.

FOOKES, BARONESS   Conservative

FOOKES (Life Baroness), Janet Evelyn Fookes; cr. 1997. Born 21 February 1936. Daughter of late Lewis Aylmer Fookes, retired company director, and late Evelyn Margery, née Holmes; educated Hastings and St. Leonards Ladies' College; Hastings High School for Girls; Royal Holloway College, London University (BA history 1957). County Borough of Hastings: Councillor 1960–61, 1963–70, Chairman, Education Committee 1967–70; Member, Council of Stonham Housing Association 1980–92. *Career:* History and English teacher in independent schools 1958–70. *House of Commons:* MP (Conservative) for Merton and Morden 1970–74, and for Plymouth Drake 1974–97; Deputy Speaker and Second Deputy Chairman of Ways and Means 1992–97; Sponsored as Private Member's Bill: Sexual Offences Act 1985, Dangerous Dogs Act 1989. *House of Lords:* Deputy Chair of Committees 2002–; Deputy Speaker 2002–. Member: Joint Select Committee on Consolidation of Bills 2000–, Select Committee on Hybrid Instruments 2002–. Member, Association of Conservative Peers. Member: Commonwealth War Graves Commission 1987–97, Council of Management, College of St Mark and St John 1989–, Royal Horticultural Society, National Art Collections Fund, National Trust, The Woodland Trust; Patron, Plymouth Workroute 1998–; Governor, Kelly College, Tavistock 2002–. DLitt, University of Plymouth (hc); Hon. Fellow, Royal Holloway College. Fellow, Industry and Parliament Trust. Member, Armed Forces Parliamentary Scheme 2001–. DBE 1989. Freeman, City of Plymouth 2000. *Special Interests:* Penal Affairs and Policy, Health including Mental Health, Defence, Animal Welfare, Equal Opportunities, Housing. *Recreations:* Keep fit exercises, swimming, gardening, theatre, Yoga, opera, scuba diving. *Sportsclubs:* Westminster Gymnasium. Raised to the peerage as Baroness Fookes, of Plymouth in the County of Devon 1997. The Baroness Fookes, DBE, House of Lords, London, SW1A 0PW *Tel:* 020 7219 5353 (Lords' Message Bureau) *Fax:* 020 7219 5979 (House of Lords).

FORSYTH OF DRUMLEAN, LORD   Conservative

FORSYTH OF DRUMLEAN (Life Baron), Michael Bruce Forsyth; cr. 1999. Born 16 October 1954. Son of John T. Forsyth; educated Arbroath High School; St Andrews University (MA). Married Susan Jane Clough 1977 (1 son 2 daughters). Councillor, Westminster City Council 1978–83. *Career:* Director, Robert Fleming & Co Ltd 1997–2000; J P Morgan 2000–: Vice-chair investment banking Europe 2000–, Deputy Chairman 2002–. *House of Commons:* MP (Conservative) for Stirling 1983–97; PPS to the Foreign Secretary 1986–87; Parliamentary Under-Secretary of State, Scottish Office 1987–90; Minister of State at: Scottish Office with responsibility for Health, Education, Social Work and Sport 1990–92, Department of Employment 1992–94, Home Office 1994–95; Secretary of State for Scotland 1995–97. Member, Select Committee on Monetary Policy of the Bank of England 2000–01; Member Joint Committee on House of Lords Reform 2002–. President, St Andrews University Conservative Association 1973–76; Member, Executive Committee National Union of Conservative and Unionist Associations 1975–77; Chair: Federation of Conservative Students 1976–77, Scottish Conservative Party 1989–90. Patron, Craighalbent Centre for Children with motor impairments; Member: Development Board, National Portrait Gallery, Commission on Strengthening Parliament 1999–2000. Highland Park/*The Spectator* Parliamentarian of the Year 1996;

Member to Watch 1993. Vice-President, Students' Representative Council, St Andrew's University 1974–75. PC 1995; Kt 1997. *Publications:* Various Pamphlets on Privatisation and Local Government. *Special Interests:* Local Government, Privatisation, Economics, Health Care, Mental Handicap, Environment, Constitution. *Recreations:* Mountaineering, photography, gardening, fly-fishing, astronomy. Raised to the peerage as Baron Forsyth of Drumlean, of Drumlean in Stirling 1999. Rt Hon the Lord Forsyth of Drumlean, House of Lords, London, SW1A 0PW *Tel:* 020 7219 4479.

FORTE, LORD · Conservative

FORTE (Life Baron), Charles Forte; cr. 1982. Born 26 November 1908. Son of late Rocco Giovanni and Maria Luigia Forte; educated Alloa Academy; Dumfries College; Mamiani, Rome. Married Irene Chierico 1943 (1 son 5 daughters). *Career:* Honorary Consul-General for San Marino –1996; Chief Executive, Forte plc 1971–78, Deputy Chair 1970–78, Executive Chair 1979–92, President 1992–96; Member, London Tourist Board. Kt 1970. *Publications: Forte* (autobiography) 1986. *Recreations:* Golf, fishing, shooting. *Sportsclubs:* Member New Zealand Golf. *Clubs:* Carlton, Caledonian. Raised to the peerage as Baron Forte, of Ripley in the County of Surrey 1982. The Lord Forte, House of Lords, London, SW1A 0PW *Tel:* 020 7235 6244.

FOSTER OF THAMES BANK, LORD · Crossbencher

FOSTER OF THAMES BANK (Life Baron), Norman Robert Foster; cr. 1999. Born 1 June 1935; educated Burnage Grammar School; School of Architecture, Manchester University (DipArch, CertTP 1961); School of Architecture, Yale University (MArch 1962); Henry Fellowship and Guest Fellow, Jonathan Edwards College, Yale School of Architecture 1962. Married Wendy Ann Cheesman 1964 (4 sons) (died 1989); married Dr Elena Ochoa 1996 (1 daughter 1 son). National service, Royal Air Force 1953–55. *Career:* Private practice, Team Four 1963–67; Foster Associates, later Foster and Partners (Chairman) 1967–; Collaboration with Richard Buckminster Fuller 1968–83; Member Council AA 1969–71; RIBA Visiting Board of Education 1971 and External Examiner 1971–73; Vice-president, Architectural Association 1974; Consultant architect to University of East Anglia 1978–87; Member Council RCA 1981; Trustee, Architecture Foundation 1991–99; Hon. Professor, University of Buenos Aires 1997; Visiting Professor, Urban Research, Bartlett School of Architecture, London 1998. Member, The Norman Foster Foundation; Council Member: Architectural Association, London 1969–71; Royal College of Art, London 1981. RIBA Silver Medal 1959; Heywood Medal 1959; Builders Association Scholarship 1959; Manchester Society of Architects Bronze Medal 1959; Walpamur Design Prize 1959; Batsford Essay Prize 1959; RIBA Royal Gold Medal 1983; Japan Design Foundation Award 1987; Grosse Kunstpreis Award, Akademie der Kunst, Berlin 1989; The Chicago Architecture Award 1990; Academie d'Architecture, France Gold Medal 1991; Mies van der Rohe Pavilion Award 1991; Arnold W Brunner Memorial Prize, American Academy and Institute of Arts and Letters 1992; Cultural Foundation Madrid Award for Barcelona Tower 1993; American Institute of Architects Gold Medal 1994; Universidad Internacional 'Menendez Pelayo' Santander, Spain Gold Medal 1995; MIPIM Man of the Year Award 1996; The 'Building' Award Construction Personality of the Year Award 1996; Premi a la millor tasca de promoció international de Barcelona Award 1997; Chartered Society of Designers Silver Medal 1997; Prince Philip Designers Prize 1997; Berliner Zeitung Kultur-preis 1998, German-British Forum Special Prize 1998; Pritzker Architecture Prize – 21st Laureate 1999; Walpole Medal of Excellence 1999; Le Prix Européen de l'Architecture de la Fondation Européene de la Culture Pro Europa 1999; Special Prize 4th International Biennal of Architecture, São Paolo 1999; 5th South Bank Show Award Visual Arts Award 2001; Auguste Perret Prize 2002. Twelve honorary degrees and doctorates. Kt 1990; Officer of the Order of the Arts and Letters – Ministry of Culture, France 1994; Order of North Rhine Westphalia 1995; OM 1997; Commander's Cross of the Order of Merit of the Federal Republic of Germany 1999. RIBA 1965; FCSD 1975; IBM Fellow Aspen Conf 1980; RA 1983; Hon. BDA 1983: Hon. FAIA 1980; Member, International Academy of Architecture, Sofia, Bulgaria 1988; RDI 1988; Member, French Order of Architects 1989; Associate, Academie Royale de Belgique 1990; Hon. Fellow Institution of Structural Engineers 1991; Hon. Fellow, Kent Institute of Art and Design 1994; Member, Department of Architecture Akademie der Künste 1994; Foreign Member, Royal

Academy of Fine Arts Sweden 1995; Hon.FEng 1995; Member, European Academy of Sciences and Art 1996; Foreign Hon. Member, American Academy of Arts and Sciences 1996; Hon. Fellowship of the Royal Incorporation of Architects in Scotland 2000; Hon. Fellow Institution for Civil Engineers 2001. *Publications: Buildings and Projects: Foster Associates Volumes 1, 2, 3, 4*, 1989–96; *Norman Foster Sketches*, 1992; *Sir Norman Foster* 1997; *Norman Foster: Selected and Current Works*, 1997; *Rebuilding The Reichstag*, 1999; *On Foster. Foster On*, 2000; *Foster*, 2001. *Recreations:* Flying, skiing, running. *Clubs:* Athenaeum, The China Club, Hong Kong. Raised to the peerage as Baron Foster of Thames Bank, of Reddish in the County of Greater Manchester 1999. The Lord Foster of Thames Bank, OM, Foster and Partners, Riverside Three, 22 Hester Road, London, SW11 4AN *Tel:* 020 7738 0455 *Fax:* 020 7738 1107/8 *E-mail:* enquiries@fosterandpartners.com.

FOWLER, LORD   Conservative

FOWLER (Life Baron), (Peter) Norman Fowler; cr. 2001. Born 2 February 1938. Son of late N. F. Fowler and Katherine Fowler; educated King Edward VI School, Chelmsford; Trinity Hall, Cambridge (BA economics and law 1961, MA). Married Fiona Poole, née Donald 1979 (2 daughters). Commissioned national service, Essex Regiment 1956–58. *Career: The Times*: Special Correspondent 1961–66, Home Affairs Correspondent 1966–70; Non-executive director NFC plc 1990–97; Non-executive chair: Midland Independent Newspapers 1991–98, National House Building Council 1992–98, Regional Independent Media 1998–, Numart Ltd 1998–, Aggregate Industries plc 2000–. *House of Commons:* Conservative member for Nottingham South 1970–74, and for Sutton Coldfield February 1974–2001; PPS to Secretary for Northern Ireland 1972–74; Minister of Transport 1979–81; Secretary of State for: Transport January-September 1981, Social Services 1981–87, Employment 1987–90; Member, Shadow Cabinet 1997–99; Shadow Secretary of State for: the Environment, Transport and the Regions 1997–98, the Home Department 1998–99. Opposition Spokesperson on Home Affairs 1974–75; Chief Opposition Spokesperson on: Social Services 1975–76, Transport 1976–79. Chair, Cambridge University Conservative Association 1960; Editorial Board, *Crossbow* 1962–70; Council Member, Bow Group 1967–69; Vice-Chair, North Kensington Conservative Association 1967–68; Chair: East Midlands Conservative Political Centre 1970–73, Conservative Party 1992–94. PC 1979; Knighted 1990. *Publications: After the Riots*, 1979; *Ministers Decide*, 1991. *Clubs:* Hurlingham. Raised to the peerage as Baron Fowler, of Sutton Coldfield in the County of West Midlands 2001. Rt Hon the Lord Fowler, House of Lords, London, SW1A 0PW *Tel:* 020 7219 3525.

FRASER OF CARMYLLIE, LORD   Conservative

FRASER OF CARMYLLIE (Life Baron), Peter Lovat Fraser; cr. 1989. Born 29 May 1945. Son of late George Robson Fraser, Church of Scotland Minister; educated Loretto School, Musselburgh; Gonville and Caius College, Cambridge (BA law 1966, LLM 1967); Edinburgh University. Married Fiona Macdonald Mair 1969 (1 son 2 daughters). *Career:* Called to the Scottish Bar 1969–; Lecturer in constitutional law, Heriot-Watt University 1972–74; Standing junior counsel in Scotland to Foreign and Commonwealth Office 1979; QC (Scot) 1982 Solicitor General for Scotland 1982–89; Chair, International Petroleum Exchange 1999–2000. *House of Commons:* Contested (Conservative) Aberdeen North October 1974 general election; MP (Conservative) for: Angus South 1979–83, Angus East 1983–87; PPS to George Younger as Secretary of State for Scotland 1981–82; Solicitor General for Scotland 1982–87. *House of Lords:* Lord Advocate 1989–92; Minister of State: Scottish Office 1992–95, Department of Trade and Industry 1995–97; Deputy Leader of the Opposition 1997–98. Opposition Spokesperson for Trade and Industry 1997–98. Member: House of Lords' Offices 1997–98; European Union Sub Committee E 1999–. Chair, Scottish Conservative Lawyers Reform Group 1976. Hon. Professor of Law, Dundee University. Fellow, Industry and Parliament Trust. Hon. Bencher of Lincoln's Inn 1989; Hon. President, Chartered Institute of Arbitrators 2001. PC 1989. *Recreations:* Skiing, golf. *Clubs:* New Club (Edinburgh); Pratt's. Raised to the peerage as Baron Fraser of Carmyllie, of Carmyllie in the District of Angus 1989. Rt Hon the Lord Fraser of Carmyllie, QC, Slade House, Carmyllie, by Arbroath, Angus, DD11 2RE *E-mail:* lordfraser@hotmail.

FREEMAN, LORD — Conservative

FREEMAN (Life Baron), Roger Norman Freeman; cr. 1997; PC 1993. Born 27 May 1942. Son of Norman James Freeman, CBE and Marjorie Hilda Freeman; educated Whitgift School; Balliol College, Oxford (BA philosophy, politics and economics 1964); Institute of Chartered Accountants, England and Wales (ACA 1968). Married Jennifer Margaret Watson 1969 (1 son 1 daughter). *Career:* Managing Director, Bow Publications Ltd 1968–69; Partner, Lehman Bros 1969–86; Director, Martini & Rossi UK Ltd and Baltic Leasing Group plc to May 1986; Partner, PricewaterhouseCoopers, Corporate Finance Division 1997–98, Adviser 1999–; Chair: Corporate Finance Advisory Board 2001–, Thales PLC 1999–; Director Thales SA 1999–; Member, advisory panel IDDAS Ltd 2002–. *House of Commons:* Contested Don Valley 1979; MP (Conservative) for Kettering 1983–97; Parliamentary Under-Secretary of State: for the Armed Forces 1986–88, at the Department of Health 1988–90; Minister of State for: Public Transport, Department of Transport 1990–94, Defence Procurement, Ministry of Defence 1994–95; Chancellor of the Duchy of Lancaster and Cabinet Minister for Public Service 1995–97. Co-opted Member Science and Technology Sub-committee II (Innovations in Computer Processors/Microprocessing/Science and the Regional Development Agencies) 2002–. Member of the Executive, Association of Conservative Peers. President, Oxford University Conservative Association 1964; Treasurer, Bow Group 1967–68; Chief Financial Officer, Conservative Central Office 1984–86; Vice-Chairman, Conservative Party July-December 1997; Special Adviser on Candidates, Conservative Party December 1997–2001. President: Council of the Reserve Forces and Cadets Association 1999–, British International Freight Association 1999–2002; Vice-president, British Horse Society. Companion, Royal Aeronautical Society. Chair, Busoga Trust. PC 1993. Fellow, Institute of Chartered Accountants, England and Wales. *Publications: Fair Deal for Water*, 1986; *Democracy in the Digital Age*, 1997; *All Change, British Railway Privatisation*, 2000. *Clubs:* Carlton, Kennel. Raised to the peerage as Baron Freeman, of Dingley in the County of Northamptonshire 1997. Rt Hon the Lord Freeman, House of Lords, London, SW1A 0PW *Tel:* 020 7219 6364 *E-mail:* freemanr@parliament.uk.

FREYBERG, LORD — Crossbencher

FREYBERG (3rd Baron, UK), Valerian Bernard Freyberg; cr. 1951. Born 15 December 1970. Son of Colonel 2nd Baron, OBE, MC, and Ivry Perronelle Katharine, daughter of Cyril Harrower Guild; educated Eton College; Camberwell College of Arts 1989–94. Married Harriet Atkinson 2002. Member Design Council 2001–. *Career:* Sculptor. *House of Lords:* First entered House of Lords 1994; Elected hereditary peer 1999–. Member, House of Lords Library and Computers Sub-Committee 1995–98; Member, House of Lords Offices Sub-Committee: Advisory Panel on Works of Art 1999–2002. Vice-chairman, Royal Naval Division, Memorial Committee. *Special Interests:* Visual Arts. *Recreations:* Beekeeping, music. The Lord Freyberg, House of Lords, London, SW1A 0PW *Tel:* 020 7219 3881 *E-mail:* freybergv@parliament.uk.

FYFE OF FAIRFIELD, LORD — Labour

FYFE OF FAIRFIELD (Life Baron), George Lennox Fyfe; cr. 2000. Born 10 April 1941. Son of the late George and Elizabeth Fyfe; educated Alloa Academy; Co-operative College, Loughborough. Married Ann Clark Asquith 1965 (died 1999) (1 daughter). JP, Perthshire 1972–75. *Career:* General manager, Kirriemuir Co-operative Society 1966–68; Regional manager, Scottish Co-operative Society 1968–72; Group general manager, CWS 1972–75; Chief executive, Leicestershire Co-operative Society 1975–95; Director, Shoefayre Ltd 1981–2000, Chairman 1984–2000; Director, CWS 1981–2000, Vice-Chairman 1986–89, Chairman 1993–2000; Director: Co-operative Insurance Society Ltd 1982–2000, Central TV-East 1983–92; Co-operative Bank plc: Director 1986–2000, Deputy Chairman 1996–2000; Chief executive, Midlands Co-operative Society 1995–2000; Chairman, Unity Trust Bank 2000–; President, Co-operative Congress 2001. Co-opted member, European Union Sub-committee D (Environment, Agriculture,

Public Health and Consumer Protection) 2000–. Member, Central Committee of International Co-operative Alliance 1989–2000. Member, East Midlands Economic Planning Council 1976–79; Member, Court of Leicester University. Companion, Institute of Management. *Special Interests:* Mutuality, Co-operative Movement, Transport, Economic Affairs. *Recreations:* History, reading, music, classic cars. *Clubs:* Member: Reform, Royal Automobile, The Farmers. Raised to the peerage as Baron Fyfe of Fairfield, of Sauchie in Clackmannanshire 2000. The Lord Fyfe of Fairfield, House of Lords, London, SW1A 0PW *Tel:* 020 7219 8630.

G

GALE, BARONESS — Labour

GALE (Life Baroness), Anita Gale; cr. 1999. Born 28 November 1940. Daughter of late Arthur Victor Gale, coalminer and late Lilian Maud Gale, housewife; educated Treherbert Secondary Modern School; Pontypridd Technical College 1970–73; University College of Wales, Cardiff (BSc Econ politics 1976). Married Morcom Holmes 1959 (divorced 1983) (2 daughters). *Trades Union:* Shop Steward, Tailors and Garment Workers' Union 1967–70; GMB: Member 1976–, Chair Wales and South West Section 1986–99, Equal Opportunities Officer 1991–99. *Career:* Sewing machinist, clothing factory 1956–57; Shop assistant 1957–59; Sewing machinist 1965–69; Women's Officer and Assistant Organiser, Wales Labour Party 1976–84; General Secretary, Wales Labour Party 1984–99. Member House of Lords Offices, Library and Computers Sub-Committee. IPU. Member, Labour Women's Network National Committee; Vice-Chair, Labour Animal Welfare Society; Member Welsh Labour Women's Committee. Member: Ramblers Association, H. S. Chapman Society; President, Treherbert and District Branch British Legion. *Special Interests:* Animal Welfare, Women's Issues, Children's Rights, Wales, Devolution, Anti Smoking, Environment. *Recreations:* Swimming, walking, keep fit, gardening. Raised to the peerage as Baroness Gale, of Blaenrhondda in the County of Mid Glamorgan 1999. The Baroness Gale, House of Lords, London, SW1A 0PW *Tel:* 020 7219 8511.

GALLACHER, LORD — Labour/Co-operative

GALLACHER (Life Baron), John Gallacher; cr. 1983. Born 7 May 1920. Son of late William Gallacher; educated St Patrick's High School, Dumbarton; Co-operative College, Loughborough 1946–48. Married Freda Vivian Chittenden 1947 (1 son). *Trades Union:* Former Member, National Association of Co-operative Officials. RAF 1940–45. *Career:* Chartered Secretary; President, Enfield Highway Co-operative Society 1954–68; Secretary, International Co-operative Alliance 1964–68; Sectional Secretary, Co-operative Union 1968–73; Parliamentary Secretary, Co-operative Union 1973–83. Opposition Whip 1985–92. Opposition Frontbench Spokesperson for Agriculture, Food, Forestry and Fisheries 1987–97. Chairman, Sub-Committee on Common Agricultural Policy and Fisheries 1984–87; Co-opted Member, Select Committee on European Communities Sub-Committee D (Agriculture, Fisheries and Food) 1997–99. Member, Economic and Social Committee of the European Communities 1978–82. Member, Co-operative Party. President, Institute of Meat 1983–86. Hon. Freeman, The Worshipful Company of Butchers. *Special Interests:* European Union. Raised to the peerage as Baron Gallacher, of Enfield in Greater London 1983. The Lord Gallacher, House of Lords, London, SW1A 0PW *Tel:* 020 7219 5353.

Visit the Vacher Dod Website ...
www.DodOnline.co.uk

GARDNER OF PARKES, BARONESS   Conservative

GARDNER OF PARKES (Life Baroness), (Rachel) Trixie Anne Gardner; cr. 1981. Born 17 July 1927. Daughter of late Hon. J. J. Gregory McGirr and late Rachel McGirr, OBE, LC; educated Monte Sant Angelo College, North Sydney; East Sydney Technical College; Sydney University (BDS 1954); Cordon Bleu de Paris (Diplome 1956). Married Kevin Anthony Gardner 1956 (3 daughters). Councillor, Westminster City Council 1968–78; Lady Mayoress of Westminster 1987–88; Member, Westminster, Kensington and Chelsea Area Health Authority 1974–81; JP, North Westminster 1971–97 Councillor, GLC for: Havering 1970–73, Enfield-Southgate 1977–86; Vice-Chairman, North East Thames Regional Health Authority 1990–94. *Career:* Came to UK 1954; Dentist in general practice 1955–90; British Chairman, European Union of Women 1978–82; UK representative on the UN Status of Women Commission 1982–88; Director: Gateway Building Society 1987–88, Woolwich Building Society 1988–93; Chairman (UK), Plan International 1989–2003; Chairman, Royal Free Hampstead NHS Trust 1994–97. *House of Lords:* Deputy Chair of Committees 1999–2002; Deputy Speaker 1999–2002. Member House of Lords' Offices Library and Computers Sub-committee 2001–. Elected Member, Executive of Inter-Parliamentary Union to 1997; UK representative to Euro-Mediterranean Women's Forum 2000–. Governor: National Heart Hospital 1974–90, Eastman Dental Hospital 1971–80; Hon. President, War Widows' Association of Great Britain 1984–87; President, British Fluoridation Society 1990–93; Chairman, The Cook Society 1996; President Married Women's Association 1998–; Hon. National Vice-President British Legion Women's Section 2001–. DU, Middlesex 1997. Chairman, Suzy Lamplugh Trust 1993–96. Member, Inner London Executive Council NHS 1966–71; Standing Dental Advisory Committee for England and Wales 1968–76; Contested (Conservative) Blackburn 1970, North Cornwall February 1974 general elections; Chairman, London Canals' Consultative Committee 1970–73; Member, Inland Waterways Amenity Advisory Council 1971–74; Member, Industrial Tribunal Panel for London 1974–97; Department of Employment's Advisory Committee on Women's Employment 1980–89; North Thames Gas Consumer Council 1980–82; Elected to General Dental Council 1984–86, 1987–91; Member, London Electricity Board 1984–90; Trustee, Parliamentary Advisory Council on Transport Safety 1992–98; Honorary Vice-President, British Legion, Women's Section 2001–; Vice-President, National House Building Council 1992–. AM (Order of Australia) 2003. Former Fellow, Institute of Directors. Freeman, City of London 1992. *Special Interests:* Transport, Housing, Health, Planning, Energy. *Recreations:* Family life, gardening, needlework, travel. Raised to the peerage as Baroness Gardner of Parkes, of Southgate in Greater London and of Parkes in the State of New South Wales and Commonwealth of Australia 1981. The Baroness Gardner of Parkes, House of Lords, London, SW1A 0PW *Tel:* 020 7219 6611 *Fax:* 020 7219 5979 *E-mail:* gardnert@parliament.uk.

GAREL-JONES, LORD   Conservative

GAREL-JONES (Life Baron), (William Armand Thomas) Tristan Garel-Jones; cr. 1997. Born 28 February 1941. Son of Bernard Garel-Jones; educated King's School, Canterbury; Madrid University. Married Catalina Garrigues 1966 (4 sons 1 daughter). *Career:* In business on the Continent 1960–70; Merchant banker 1971–74; Managing Director, UBS Warburg. *House of Commons:* Personal Assistant to Michael Roberts, MP at Cardiff North in February 1970 general election; Contested Caernarvon February 1974, and Watford October 1974 general elections; Personal Assistant to Lord Thorneycroft 1978–79; MP (Conservative) for Watford 1979–97; PPS to Barney Hayhoe as Minister of State, Civil Service Department March 1981–82; Minister of State, Foreign and Commonwealth Office 1990–93. Assistant Government Whip 1982–83; Government Whip 1983–89; Deputy Chief Whip 1989–90. PC 1992. *Recreations:* Book collecting. *Clubs:* Beefsteak. Raised to the peerage as Baron Garel-Jones, of Watford in the County of Hertfordshire 1997. Rt Hon the Lord Garel-Jones, House of Lords, London, SW1A 0PW *Tel:* 020 7219 8639.

Visit the Vacher Dod Website . . . www.DodOnline.co.uk

GAVRON, LORD   Labour

GAVRON (Life Baron), Robert Gavron; cr. 1999. Born 13 September 1930. Son of Nathaniel and Leah Gavron; educated Leighton Park School; St Peter's College, Oxford (BA jurisprudence 1953, MA). Married Hannah Fyvel 1955 (died 1965) (2 sons); married Nicolette Coates 1967 (2 daughters) (divorced 1987); married Katharine Gardiner, née Macnair 1989. RAEC, National Service 1949–50. *Career:* Called to the Bar, Middle Temple 1955; Founded St Ives Group 1964, Director 1964–98, Chairman 1964–93; Director: Octopus Publishing plc 1975–87, Electra Management plc 1981–92; Proprietor, The Carcanet Press Ltd 1983–; Chairman: The Folio Society 1982–, National Gallery Co Ltd (formerly National Gallery Publications Ltd) 1996–98, Guardian Media Group plc 1997–2000. Member, House of Lords Offices Sub-Committee: Advisory Panel on Works of Art 2000–02, Works of Art Committee 2002–. Chairman, Open College of the Arts 1991–96; Director, Royal Opera House 1992–98; Governor, LSE 1997–. Hon. Fellow, St Peter's College, Oxford 1992; Hon. PhD, Thames Valley University 1997. Trustee: National Gallery 1994–2001, Scott Trust 1997–2000, Paul Hamlyn Foundation; Chair of Trustees, Robert Gavron Charitable Trust. CBE 1990. Hon. Fellow: Royal College of Art 1990, Royal Society of Literature 1996. *Publications:* (jointly) *The Entrepreneurial Society*, 1998. *Clubs:* Groucho, MCC. Raised to the peerage as Baron Gavron, of Highgate in the London Borough of Camden 1999. The Lord Gavron, CBE, 44 Eagle Street, London, WC1R 4FS *Tel:* 020 7400 4300.

GEDDES, LORD   Conservative

GEDDES (3rd Baron, UK), Euan Michael Ross Geddes; cr. 1942. Born 3 September 1937. Son of 2nd Baron, KBE, DL; educated Rugby School; Gonville and Caius College, Cambridge (BA history 1961, MA); Harvard Business School 1969. Married Gillian Butler 1966 (died 1995) (1 son 1 daughter); married Susan Margaret Hunter, née Carter 1996. Royal Navy 1956–58; Lieutenant-Commander, RNR (Rtd). *Career:* Chair: Trinity College London 1992–, Chrome Castle Ltd 2000–; Director Trinity College of Music and other Companies. *House of Lords:* First entered House of Lords 1975; Elected hereditary peer 1999–; Deputy Chair of Committees 2000–; Deputy Speaker 2002–. Member: European Union Committee 1994–2000, Sub-committee A 1985–90, 2000–; Member, Sub-committee B 1990–94, 1995–99, Chair 1996–99; Member: Science and Technology Sub-committee 1 1990–92, Refreshment Sub-committee 2000–, Procedure Committee 2003–. Member, Executive of Association of Conservative Peers 1999–, Treasurer 2000–. Hon. FTCL. *Special Interests:* Shipping, Anglo-Chinese Relations, Hong Kong, South East Asia, Immigration, Energy, Transport, Industry, Tourism. *Recreations:* Golf, music, bridge, gardening, skiing, shooting. *Sportsclubs:* Aldeburgh Golf, Hong Kong Golf. *Clubs:* Brooks's, Hong Kong, Noblemen and Gentlemen's Catch. The Lord Geddes, House of Lords, London, SW1A 0PW *Tel:* 020 7219 6400 *Fax:* 020 7219 5979 *E-mail:* lordgeddes@aol.com.

GERAINT, LORD   Liberal Democrat

GERAINT (Life Baron), Geraint Wyn Howells; cr. 1992. Born 15 April 1925. Son of late David and Mary Howells; educated Ardwyn Grammar School, Aberystwyth. Married Mary Olwen Hughes, née Griffiths 1957 (2 daughters). *Career:* Farmer; Vice-Chairman, British Wool Marketing Board 1971–83; Chairman, Wool Producers of Wales 1977–87. *House of Commons:* MP (Liberal) for: Cardigan 1974–83, Ceredigion and Pembroke North 1983–92 (Liberal Democrat 1989–92). Spokesperson for: Welsh Affairs 1985–87, Agriculture 1987–92. *House of Lords:* Deputy Speaker 1995–98; Deputy Chair of Committees 1997–98. Spokesperson for Welsh Rural Affairs 1974–2001. Past President, Royal Welsh Show, Bulith Wells, Powys; Chairman, Bronglais Hospital Cancer Appeal Fund, Aberystwyth. Fellow University College of Wales, Aberystwyth 2002. Extra Lord in Waiting to HM The Queen 1998–. FRAgS. *Special Interests:* Agriculture, Wales, Devolution of Power, Language and Culture, Rural Affairs, Third World. *Recreations:* Rugby, walking. *Sportsclubs:* London Welsh RFC Ltd, Aberstwyth Football Club. *Clubs:* National Liberal, St David's (London), London Welsh. Raised to the peerage as Baron Geraint, of Ponterwyd in the County of Dyfed 1992. The Lord Geraint, Glennydd, Ponterwyd, Sir Aberteifi, SY23 3LB *Tel:* 01970 85258.

GLENARTHUR, LORD   Conservative

GLENARTHUR (4th Baron, UK), Simon Mark Arthur; cr. 1918; 4th Bt of Carlung (UK) 1903. Born 7 October 1944. Son of 3rd Baron, OBE, DL; educated Eton College. Married Susan Barry 1969 (1 son 1 daughter). Commissioned 10th Royal Hussars (PWO) 1963; ADC to High Commissioner, Aden 1964–65; Captain 1970; Major 1973; Retired 1975; Major, The Royal Hussars (PWO) TAVR 1976–80. DL, Aberdeenshire 1988. *Career:* Captain, British Airways Helicopters Ltd 1976–82; Director: Aberdeen and Texas Corporate Finance Ltd 1977–82, ABTEX Computer Systems Ltd 1979–82; Senior Executive, Hanson plc 1989–96; Deputy Chairman, Hanson Pacific Ltd 1994–98; Director, Whirly Bird Services Ltd 1995–; Consultant, British Aerospace 1989–99; President, National Council for Civil Protection 1991–2003; Chairman, British Helicopter Advisory Board 1992–; Director, Lewis Group plc 1993–94; Consultant, Chevron UK Ltd 1994–97; Director, Millennium Chemicals Inc 1996–; Consultant: Hanson plc 1996–99, Imperial Tobacco Group plc 1996–98; Chairman: European Helicopter Association 1996–2003, International Federation of Helicopter Associations 1997–2003; Governor, Nuffield Hospitals 2000–; Commissioner, Royal Hospital, Chelsea 2001–; Consultant, Audax Trading Ltd 2001–02, Director 2003–; Director, The Medical Defence Union 2002–. *House of Lords:* First entered House of Lords 1976; Parliamentary Under-Secretary of State: DHSS 1983–85, Home Office 1985–86; Minister of State: Scottish Office 1986–87, Foreign and Commonwealth Office 1987–89; Elected hereditary peer 1999–. Lord in Waiting (Government Whip) 1982–83. Government Spokesperson for: the Treasury 1982–85, Home Office, Employment and Industry 1982–83; Government Spokesman for Defence 1983–89. Council Member, The Air League 1994–; Member, National Employers Liaison Committee for HM Reserve Forces 1996–2002; Chairman, National Employer Advisory Board for Britain's Reserve Forces 2002–. Chairman, St Mary's Hospital, Paddington, NHS Trust 1991–98; Special Trustee, St Mary's Hospital, Paddington 1991–2000. Member (Ensign) of the Queen's Bodyguard for Scotland (Royal Company of Archers); Honorary Colonel, 306 Field Hospital (Volunteer) 2001–. Fellow, Royal Aeronautical Society 1992. Freeman, City of London 1996. Freeman, Guild of Air Pilots and Air Navigators 1992, Liveryman 1996. *Special Interests:* Aviation, Foreign Affairs, Defence, Penal Policy, Health, Scotland. *Recreations:* Field sports, gardening, choral singing, organ playing, antique barometers. *Clubs:* Cavalry and Guards, Pratt's. The Lord Glenarthur, DL, PO Box 11012, Banchory, Kincardineshire, AB31 6ZJ *Tel:* 01330 844467 *Fax:* 01330 844465 *E-mail:* glenarth@northbrae.co.uk.

GLENTORAN, LORD   Conservative

GLENTORAN (3rd Baron, UK), (Thomas) Robin Valerian Dixon; cr. 1939; 5th Bt of Ballymenoch (UK) 1903. Born 21 April 1935. Son of 2nd Baron, PC, KBE, and late Lady Diana Wellesley, daughter of 3rd Earl Cowley; educated Eton College; Grenoble University, France. Married Rona Colville 1959 (3 sons) (divorced 1975); married Alwyn Mason 1979 (divorced 1988); married Mrs Margaret Rainey 1990. Grenadier Guards 1954–66, retired as Major. DL, Co. Antrim 1995. *Career:* Managing Director, Redland (NI) Ltd 1971–95, Chair 1995–98; Chair, Roofing Industry Alliance 1997–2003; Non-executive Director NHBC 2001–. *House of Lords:* First entered House of Lords 1995; Elected hereditary peer 1999–. Opposition Spokesperson for: Northern Ireland 1999–, Environment, Food and Rural Affairs 2001–03. Member, British/Irish Parliamentary Body. Member, The Sports Council for Northern Ireland 1980–87; Founder Chairman, Ulster Games Foundation 1983–90; Commissioner, Irish Lighthouse Service 1986–; President, British Bobsleigh Association 1987–; Chairman, Northern Ireland Tall Ships Council 1987–91, Regional Chairman, British Field Sports Society 1990–96; Chairman: Positively Belfast 1992–96, Growing a Green Economy (reporting to Minister for the Environment, NIO) 1993–95; Member, Millennium Commission 1994–; Chairman, Northern Ireland Classic Golf Promotions 1996–99; Member, Countryside Alliance; Hon. Member (RSUA) Royal Society of Ulster Architect. Olympic gold medallist (bobsleigh) 1964. MBE 1969; CBE 1992. Liveryman, Worshipful Company of Tylers and Bricklayers. *Special Interests:* Sport, Environment, Northern Ireland, Army, Maritime Affairs. *Recreations:* Sailing, golf, travel, music, arts. *Sportsclubs:* Royal Portrush Golf, Irish Cruising, Soto Grande Golf Club. *Clubs:* Royal Cruising, Carlton, Royal Yacht Squadron (Cowes); Royal Portrush Golf, Irish Cruising, Royal Soto Grande Golf. The Lord Glentoran, CBE, DL, Drumadarragh House, Ballyclare, Co. Antrim, BT39 0TA *Tel:* 028 9334 0222; 16 Westgaet Terrace, London, SW10 9BJ *Tel:* 020 7370 7190 *Fax:* 020 7341 0023 *E-mail:* rg@glentoran.demon.co.uk (Home); glentoranr@parliament.uk (Office).

GLOUCESTER, LORD BISHOP OF   Non-affiliated

GLOUCESTER (39th Bishop of), David Edward Bentley. Born 7 August 1935. Son of William and Florence Bentley; educated Great Yarmouth Grammar School; Leeds University (BA English 1956); Westcott House, Cambridge. Married Clarice Lahmers 1962 (2 sons 2 daughters). Second Lieutenant, 5th Regiment, Royal Horse Artillery. *Career:* Deacon 1960; Priest 1961; Curate: St Ambrose, Bristol 1960–62, Holy Trinity with St Mary, Guildford 1962–66; Rector: Headley, Bordon 1966–73, Esher 1973–86; Bishop of Lynn 1986–93; Rural Dean of Emly 1977–82; Chairman: Guildford Diocesan House of Clergy 1977–86, Guildford Diocesan Council of Social Responsibility 1980–86; Hon. Canon, Guildford Cathedral 1980–86; Member, various church committees on recruitment and selection 1987–; Warden, Community of All Hallows, Ditchingham 1989–93; Bishop of Gloucester 1993–; Took his seat in the House of Lords 1998. Hon PhD Gloucestershire University 2002. *Recreations:* Music, sport, especially cricket, theatre, family. *Sportsclubs:* Vice President, Gloucestershire CCC. *Clubs:* MCC. Rt Rev the Lord Bishop of Gloucester, Bishopscourt, Pitt Street, Gloucester, GL1 2BQ *Tel:* 01452 524598 *E-mail:* bshpglos@star.co.uk.

GOFF OF CHIEVELEY, LORD   Crossbencher

GOFF OF CHIEVELEY (Life Baron), Robert Lionel Archibald Goff; cr. 1986. Born 12 November 1926. Son of late Lieutenant Colonel L. T. Goff and Isobel Goff; educated Eton College; New College, Oxford (BA law 1950, MA 1953, DCL 1972). Married Sarah Cousins 1953 (1 son 2 daughters and 1 son deceased). Served Scots Guards 1945–48. *Career:* Fellow and tutor, Lincoln College, Oxford 1951–55; Called to Bar, Inner Temple 1951; Bencher 1975; QC 1967; In practice at the Bar 1956–75; Member, General Council of the Bar 1971–74; Recorder 1974–75; Judge of the High Court, Queen's Bench Division 1975–82; Judge i/c Commercial Court 1979–81; Lord Justice of Appeal 1982–86; Lord of Appeal in Ordinary 1986–98; Second Senior Law Lord 1994–96; Senior Law Lord 1996–98. Chairman, Sub-Committee E, House of Lords Select Committee on European Communities 1986–88. Chair, Council of Legal Education 1975–82; President, Chartered Institute of Arbitrators 1986–91; Chair: Court of London University 1986–91; British Institute of International and Comparative Law 1986–2001, President 2001–; Chair: Oxford Institute of European and Comparative Law 1995–2001; President, New College Society 1999–2001; High Steward, Oxford University 1991–2001. Three honorary Oxford fellowships; five honorary doctorates. Kt 1975; PC 1982 Grand Cross (First Class) of the Order of Merit (Germany) 1999. DCL 1972 FBA 1987. *Publications:* Co-author *The Law of Restitution,* 1966. *Special Interests:* Comparative Law. Raised to the peerage as Baron Goff of Chieveley, of Chieveley in the Royal County of Berkshire 1986. Rt Hon the Lord Goff of Chieveley, House of Lords, London, SW1A 0PW *Tel:* 020 7219 3202 *Fax:* 020 7219 6156.

GOLDING, BARONESS   Labour

GOLDING (Life Baroness), (Llinos) Llin Golding; cr. 2001. Born 21 March 1933. Daughter of late Ness Edwards, MP; educated Caerphilly Girls Grammar School. Married Dr Roland Lewis 1957 (1 son 2 daughters); married John Golding MP 1980 (died 1999). *Trades Union:* Former NUPE Branch Secretary. Member, North Staffs District Health Authority 1983–87. *Career:* Member, Society of Radiographers 1953–; Secretary and assistant to second husband, when an MP. *House of Commons:* Member for Newcastle-under-Lyme 1986–2001; Member of Opposition team on: Social Security 1992–93, Children and Families 1993–95, Food, Agriculture and Rural Affairs 1995–97. Opposition Whip 1987–92. Executive Committee Member, IPU British Group. Secretary, Newcastle Staffs and District Trades Council 1976–86; Former Member, District Manpower Services Committee; Member: BBC Advisory Committee 1989–92, Commonwealth War Graves Commission 1992–. *Special Interests:* Health Service, Trade Unions, Children, Racing, Gambling. *Recreations:* Fishing. Raised to the peerage as Baroness Golding, of Newcastle-under-Lyme in the County of Staffordshire 2001. The Baroness Golding, House of Lords, London, SW1A 0PW *Tel:* 020 7219 4209.

GOLDSMITH, LORD
Labour

GOLDSMITH (Life Baron), Peter Henry Goldsmith; cr. 1999. Born 5 January 1950. Son of late Sydney Elland Goldsmith, and of Myra Nurick; educated Quarry Bank High School, Liverpool; Gonville and Caius College, Cambridge (MA law 1971); University College, London (LLM 1972). Married Joy Elterman 1974 (3 sons 1 daughter). *Career:* Called to the Bar, Gray's Inn 1972; In Practice 1972–; QC 1987; Recorder of the Crown Court 1991–; Chairman, Bar Council of England and Wales 1995; Member, Paris Bar (Avocat a la Cour) 1997. *House of Lords:* Attorney General 2001–. Government Spokesperson for Law Officers' Departments 2001–. Prime Minister's Representative on Convention for a Charter of Fundamental Rights of the EU 1999–2000. Executive Committee Member, Great Britain China Centre 1996–2001; Council Member, Public Concern at Work 1996–2001. Fellow, University College London. Chairman, Bar Council International Relations Committee 1996; Member, Financial Reporting Review Panel 1995–2000, Chairman 1997–2000; Chairman, IBA Standing Committee on Globalisation 1996–98; Founder and Chairman, Bar Pro Bono Unit 1996–2001, President 2001–; Various offices held in international law organisations, including American Law Institute 1996–; Co-Chairman, IBA Human Pro Rights Institute 1998–2001. PC 2002. *Publications: Contributions to legal esson collections.* Raised to the peerage as Baron Goldsmith, of Allerton in the County of Merseyside 1999. Rt Hon the Lord Goldsmith, QC, 9 Buckingham Gate, London, SW1E 6JP *Tel:* 020 7219 2405; Fountain Court Chambers, Fountain Court, Temple, London, EC4 *Tel:* 020 7583 3335 *Fax:* 020 7353 0329 *E-mail:* lslo@gtnet.gov.uk.

GOODHART, LORD
Liberal Democrat

GOODHART (Life Baron), William Howard Goodhart; cr. 1997. Born 18 January 1933. Son of late Professor Arthur Goodhart, Hon. KBE, QC, FBA; educated Eton College; Trinity College, Cambridge (Scholar, MA law 1956); Harvard Law School (Commonwealth Fund Fellow, LLM 1958). Married Hon Celia McClare Herbert 1966 (1 son 2 daughters). Second Lieutenant, Oxford and Bucks Light Infantry 1951–53 (National Service). Member, Committee on Standards in Public Life 1997–. *Career:* Called to the Bar, Lincoln's Inn 1957, QC 1979–, Bencher 1986–; Director, Bar Mutual Indemnity Fund Ltd 1988–97. Liberal Democrat Spokesperson for: Lord Chancellor's Department 2000–, Pensions 1998–2001. Co-opted Member, Select Committee on European Communities Sub-Committee E 1997–2001; Member, Select Committees on: Delegated Powers and Regulatory Reform 1998–2002, European Communities 1998–2001, Freedom of Information Bill 1999; Joint Committee on Tax Simplification 2000–03, Procedure 2001–; Joint Committee on Reform of the House of Lords 2002–. Member, International Commission of Jurists 1993–, Executive Committee 1995–2002; Committee Officer, Human Rights Institute 1995–2000. Chairman: SDP Council Arrangements Committee 1982–88, Liberal Democrat Conference Committee 1988–91, Liberal Democrat Lawyers Association 1988–91; Member, Liberal Democrat Policy Committee 1988–97, Vice-Chairman 1995–97. Justice: Member of Council 1972–, Vice-Chair, Executive Committee 1978–88, Chair, Executive Committee 1988–94, Vice-Chair of Council 1999–; Member: Trust Law Committee 1994–, Tax Law Review Committee 1994–2003; Council Member, Royal Institute of International Affairs, 1999–2002. Trustee, Airey Neave Trust 1999–. Contested: Kensington (SDP) 1983, (SDP/Alliance) 1987 general elections, (Lib Dem) July 1988 by-election, Oxford West and Abingdon (Lib Dem) 1992 general election; Member: Council of Legal Education 1986–92, Conveyancing Standing Committee, Law Commission 1987–89; Has led reporting missions on human rights to Hong Kong 1991, Kashmir 1993, Israel and the West Bank 1994, Kenya 1996 and Sri Lanka 1997. Kt 1989. *Publications: Co-author, Specific Performance,* 1986 (2nd ed. 1996); Contributor to *Halsbury's Laws of England;* also articles in legal journals. *Special Interests:* Human Rights. *Recreations:* Walking, skiing. *Clubs:* Brooks's, Century Association (New York). Raised to the peerage as Baron Goodhart, of Youlbury in the County of Oxfordshire 1997. The Lord Goodhart, QC, 11 Clarence Terrace, London, NW1 4RD *Tel:* 020 7262 1319 *Fax:* 020 7723 5851; Youlbury House, Boars Hill, Oxford, OX1 5HH *Tel:* 01865 735477 *E-mail:* goodhartw@parliament.uk.

Visit the Vacher Dod Website . . . **www.DodOnline.co.uk**

GORDON OF STRATHBLANE, LORD · Labour

GORDON OF STRATHBLANE (Life Baron), James Stuart Gordon; cr. 1997. Born 17 May 1936. Son of late James and Elsie Gordon, née Riach; educated St Aloysius' College, Glasgow; Glasgow University (MA classics 1958). Married Margaret Anne Stevenson 1971 (2 sons 1 daughter). *Career:* Political editor, STV 1965–73; Managing Director, Radio Clyde 1973–96; Scottish Advisory Board, BP 1990–; Chief Executive, Scottish Radio Holdings 1991–96, Chair 1996–; Vice-Chair, Melody Radio 1991–97; Director: Clydeport Holdings 1992–98, Johnston Press plc 1996–, AIM Trust plc 1996–; Chair, Scottish Tourist Board 1998–2001; Chair, RAJAR (Radio Audience Research) 2003–. Member, Scottish Development Agency 1981–90; Chair, Scottish Exhibition Centre 1983–89; Member: Court of University of Glasgow 1984–97, Committee of Enquiry into Teachers' Pay and Conditions 1986, Member, Scottish Tourist Board 1997–, Chair 1998–2001; Chair, Advisory Group on Listed Events 1997–98; Member, Independent Review Panel on Funding of BBC 1998–99; Board Member, British Tourist Authority 1998–2001. Sony Award for outstanding services to radio 1984; Fellow, Radio Academy 1994; Lord Provost's Award for Public Service in Glasgow 1994. Hon. DLitt, Glasgow Caledonian 1994; DUniv, Glasgow University 1998. Trustee: National Galleries of Scotland 1998–2001, John Smith Memorial Trust 1995–. Contested East Renfrewshire (Lab) 1964 general election. CBE 1984. *Special Interests:* Broadcasting, Tourism, Constitutional Affairs. *Recreations:* Skiing, walking, genealogy, golf. *Sportsclubs:* Buchanan Castle Golf, Prestwick Golf. *Clubs:* New (Edinburgh), Glasgow Art. Raised to the peerage as Baron Gordon of Strathblane, of Deil's Craig in Stirling 1997. The Lord Gordon of Strathblane, CBE, Deil's Craig, Strathblane, Glasgow, G63 9ET *Tel:* 01360 770604 *Fax:* 01360 770637 *Tel:* 07711 223149 *E-mail:* gordonj@parliament.uk.

GOSCHEN, VISCOUNT · Conservative

GOSCHEN (4th Viscount, UK), Giles John Harry Goschen; cr. 1900. Born 16 November 1965. Son of 3rd Viscount, KBE; educated Eton College. Married Sarah Penelope Horsnail 1991 (1 daughter). *Career:* Deutsche Bank 1997–2000; Director, Barchester Advisory 2000–02. *House of Lords:* First entered House of Lords 1986; Parliamentary Under-Secretary of State, Department of Transport 1994–97; Elected hereditary peer 1999–. Government Whip 1992–94. Government Spokesperson for Environment, Employment, Social Security, Transport and Trade and Industry 1992–94; Opposition Spokesperson for Environment, Transport and the Regions (Transport) 1997. Member House of Lords' Offices Finance and Staff Sub-committee 2001–02. *Clubs:* Air Squadron, Pratt's. The Viscount Goschen, House of Lords, London, SW1A 0PW *Tel:* 020 7219 3198.

GOUDIE, BARONESS · Labour

GOUDIE (Life Baroness), Mary Teresa Goudie; cr. 1998. Born 2 September 1946. Daughter of Martin and Hannah Brick; educated Our Lady of The Visitation, Greenford; Our Lady of St Anselm, Hayes. Married James Goudie QC 1969 (2 sons). *Trades Union:* Member: APEX, GMB. Councillor, London Borough of Brent 1971–78, Chair, Housing and Planning Committees, Deputy Whip. *Career:* Assistant Director, Brent People's Housing Association 1977–81; Director: The Hansard Society for Parliamentary Government 1985–90, *The House Magazine* (weekly journal of the Houses of Parliament and the Parliamentary Information Unit) 1989–90; European director of public affairs, World Wide Fund for Nature (UK) 1990–95; Independent public affairs consultant 1995–98; Strategic and management consultant 1998–. Co-opted member, European Union Sub-committee E (Law and Institutions) 1998–2000; Member Select Committees on: Procedure 2001, House of Lords' Offices Finance and Staff Sub-committee 2002–, Information Committee 2003–. Member: Labour Movement in Europe, Inter-Parliamentary Union, British-American Parliamentary Group. Member Labour Parliamentary general election campaign team 1998–2001; Secretary, Labour Solidarity Campaign 1981–87; Vice-Chair Labour Peers 2001–; Member: Society of Labour Lawyers,

Fabian Society, Smith Institute. Chair, Family Courts' Consortium; Secretary, Industry Forum Scotland; Community Service Volunteers, Scotland. Honorary doctorate, Napier University 2000. Patron: National Childbirth Trust, Northern Ireland Community Foundation. *Special Interests:* Europe, Ireland, Scotland, Regional Development, Children, Charity Law. *Recreations:* Family, travelling, gardening, food and wine, art. *Clubs:* Reform. Raised to the peerage as Baroness Goudie, of Roundwood in the London Borough of Brent 1998. The Baroness Goudie, House of Lords, London, SW1A 0PW *Tel:* 020 7219 5880 *Fax:* 020 7219 6258.

GOULD OF POTTERNEWTON, BARONESS — Labour

GOULD OF POTTERNEWTON (Life Baroness), Joyce Brenda Gould; cr. 1993. Born 29 October 1932. Daughter of late Sydney and Fanny Manson; educated Roundhay High School for Girls; Bradford Technical College. Married Kevin Gould 1952 (1 daughter) (separated). *Trades Union:* Member: TGWU, GMW. *Career:* Pharmaceutical dispenser 1952–65; Organiser, Pioneer Women 1965; Clerical worker 1966–69; Labour Party 1969–93: Assistant regional organiser 1969–75, Assistant national agent and chief women's officer 1975–85, Director of organisation 1985–93; Secretary, National Joint Committee of Working Women's Organisations 1975 85; Member, Jenkins Commission 1977–98; Chair, Independent Advisory Group on Sexual Health 2003–. *House of Lords:* Deputy Chair of Committees 2002–; Deputy Speaker 2002–. Opposition Whip 1994–97; Government Whip (Social Security, Health and Women) May-December 1997. Opposition Spokesperson for: Citizen's Charter 1994–96, Women 1996–97. Member: Select Committee on Finance and Staffing 1994–97, European Select Committee, Sub-Committee C (Environmental Affairs) 1994–97; Member Constitution Committee 2001–. Vice-chair, Labour Party Departmental Committees for: Women 2001–, Office of the Deputy Prime Minister 2003–. Vice-President, Socialist International Women 1978–85; Member: Council of Europe and Education and Cultural Committee 1993–95, WEU and Parliamentary and Public Relations Committee, CPA, IPU. Member: Regional Women's Advisory Committee, National Labour Women's Committee, Plant Committee on Electoral Systems; Chair, Computing for Labour; Member: Fabian Society, Labour Electoral Reform Association, Bevan Society, Labour Heritage, Arts for Labour. Secretary: National Joint Committee of Working Women, Yorkshire National Council for Civil Liberties; Committee Member, Campaign Against Racial Discrimination; Executive Member, Joint Committee Against Racism; Member, Management Committee, Grand Theatre, Leeds; Senior posts various charities; Member: Fawcett Society, Howard League, Yorkshire Society; Council Member: Hansard Society, Constitution Unit; President: Family Planning Association, Epilepsy Action. Hon. Degree, Bradford University 1997. Chair and Trustee, Mary MacArthur Holiday Trust; Trustee and Director: Diarama Arts, Studio Upstairs, Yigol Allon Trust; Fellow, Industry and Parliamentary Trust. Executive Member, Women's National Commission; Member: Department of Employment Women's Advisory Committee, Home Office Committee on Electoral Matters, Commission on Conduct of Referendums, Independent Commission on Electoral System 1997–98. *Publications:* Include *Women and Health* (editor); pamphlets on Feminism, Socialism and Sexism, Women's Right to Work, Violence in Society; articles and reports on Women's Rights, Electoral systems – their practices and procedures. *Special Interests:* Women's Equality, Constitutional Affairs, Electoral Affairs, Race Relations, Population and Development, Disabled, Sexual Health. *Recreations:* Theatre, cinema, reading. Raised to the peerage as Baroness Gould of Potternewton, of Leeds in the County of West Yorkshire 1993. The Baroness Gould of Potternewton, 6 College Street, Brighton, BN2 1JG *Tel:* 01273 607474.

GRABINER, LORD — Labour

GRABINER (Life Baron), Anthony Stephen Grabiner; cr. 1999. Born 21 March 1945. Son of late Ralph and Freda Grabiner (née Cohen); educated Central Foundation Boys' Grammar School, London EC2; London School of Economics (LLB 1966, LLM 1967); Lincoln's Inn (Hardwicke Scholar 1966, Droop Scholar 1968). Married Jane Portnoy 1983 (3 sons 1 daughter). *Career:* Called to the Bar, Lincoln's Inn 1968; Standing Junior Counsel to Department of Trade, Export Credits Guarantee Department 1976–81; Junior Counsel to the Crown 1978–81; QC 1981; Bencher 1989; Recorder of the Crown Court 1990–99; Deputy High Court Judge 1994–; Non-executive director Next plc 2002; Non-executive chairman, Arcadia Group Limited 2002–;

Bank of England Financial Services Law Committee 2002–. Member Select Committees on: Religious Offences 2002–, European Union Sub-committee E (Law and Institutions) 2003–. Member, Court of Governors, LSE 1991–, Vice-Chairman 1993–98, Chairman 1998–. *Publications:* Co-editor, *Sutton and Shannon on Contract*, 7th edition 1970; Contributor, *Banking Documents to Encyclopedia of Forms and Precedents*, 5th edition 1986; *The Informal Economy* (March 2000) Report to Chancellor of the Exchequer. *Special Interests:* Law Reform, Commercial and Company Law, City, Pensions, Higher Education. *Recreations:* Golf, theatre, reading. *Sportsclubs:* Brocket Hall Golf. *Clubs:* Garrick. Raised to the peerage as Baron Grabiner, of Aldwych in the City of Westminster 1999. The Lord Grabiner, QC, 1 Essex Court, Temple, London, EC4Y 9AR *Tel:* 020 7583 2000 *Fax:* 020 7583 0118; House of Lords, London, SW1A 0PW *E-mail:* mdoyle@oeclaw.co.uk.

GRAHAM OF EDMONTON, LORD — Labour/Co-operative

GRAHAM OF EDMONTON (Life Baron), Thomas Edward Graham; cr. 1983. Born 26 March 1925. Son of Thomas Edward Graham; educated Elementary School; WEA Co-operative College 1964; Open University (BA 1976). Married Margaret Golding 1950 (2 sons). *Trades Union:* Member, National Association of Co-operative Officials. Corporal, Royal Marines 1943–46. Councillor and Labour leader, Enfield Borough Council 1961–68; Chair, Housing and Redevelopment Committee 1961–68; President, Co-operative Congress 1987–. *Career:* Various posts within the Co-operative Movement 1939–74. *House of Commons:* Contested (Labour and Co-operative) Enfield West 1966 general election; MP (Labour and Co-operative) for Enfield, Edmonton 1974–83; PPS to Alan Williams as Minister of State, Department of Prices and Consumer Affairs 1974–76. Government Whip 1976–79. Spokesperson for the Environment 1981–83. *House of Lords:* Deputy Speaker 1990–97; Deputy Chair of Committees 1997–2000. Opposition Whip 1983–90, Opposition Chief Whip 1990–97. Opposition Spokesperson for the Environment, Northern Ireland and Defence 1983–90; Opposition Spokesperson for National Heritage (Tourism) 1990–95. Member: Refreshments Sub-committee 1990–2000, Privileges Committee 2000–. Member, Refreshments Committee 1990–. Chair, Labour Peers Group 1997–2000. Member, Co-operative Party 1997–2000. President, Institute of Meat; Patron, Ancient Order of Foresters. Hon. Degree of Master of Open University 1989. PC 1998. Fellow: Institute of British Management, Royal Society of Arts. Freeman, Worshipful Company of Butchers. *Special Interests:* Local Government, Consumer Affairs, Environment. *Recreations:* Gardening, reading, relaxing. Raised to the peerage as Baron Graham of Edmonton, of Edmonton in Greater London 1983. Rt Hon the Lord Graham of Edmonton, 2 Clerks Piece, Loughton, Essex, IG10 1NR *Tel:* 020 8508 9801; House of Lords, London, SW1A 0PW *Tel:* 020 7219 6704 *Fax:* 020 7219 0035.

GRAY OF CONTIN, LORD — Conservative

GRAY OF CONTIN (Life Baron), (James Hector Northey) Hamish Gray; cr. 1983. Born 28 June 1927. Son of late James Northey Gray, JP, and late Mrs M. E. Gray; educated Inverness Royal Academy. Married Judith W Brydon 1953 (2 sons 1 daughter). Served Queens Own Cameron Highlanders 1945–48. Served Highland Chamber of Commerce 1943–70; Inverness Town Council 1965–70; DL, Lochaber, Inverness, Badenoch and Strathspey 1989–96, Vice-Lord Lieutenant 1994–96; Lord Lieutenant of Inverness 1996–2002; JP, Inverness 1996–. *Career:* Company director 1950–70; Business and parliamentary consultant 1987–2000; Non-executive director 1995–2002. *House of Commons:* MP (Conservative) Ross and Cromarty 1970–83; Successfully piloted Education Scotland (Mentally Handicapped) Bill through Parliament 1974; Minister of State for Energy 1979–83. Assistant Government Whip 1971–73; Government Whip 1973–74; Opposition Whip 1974–75. Opposition Spokesperson for Energy 1975–79. *House of Lords:* Minister of State, Scottish Office 1983–86. Government Spokesperson for Employment 1983–84; Principal Government Spokesperson for Energy 1984–86. Member, Select Committees on: Channel Tunnel 1986–87, Relations between Central and Local Government 1995–96. President, British Romanian Chamber of Commerce 1999–. Hon. President: National Charities, Energy Action Scotland 1987–97; Hon. Vice-President: Neighbourhood Energy Action 1987–98, National Energy Action 1987–98. PC 1982. *Recreations:* Golf, cricket, walking, gardening, reading. Raised to the peerage as Baron Gray of Contin, of Contin in the District of Ross and Cromarty 1983. Rt Hon the Lord Gray of Contin, House of Lords, London, SW1A 0PW *Tel:* 020 7219 3177.

GREAVES, LORD   Liberal Democrat

GREAVES (Life Baron), Anthony Robert Greaves; cr. 2000. Born 27 July 1942. Son of late Geoffrey Lawrence Greaves and of Moyra Louise Greaves; educated Queen Elizabeth Grammar School, Wakefield; Hertford College, Oxford (BA geography 1963). Married Heather Ann Baxter 1968 (2 children). Councillor: Colne Borough Council 1971–74, Pendle Borough Council 1973–92, 1994–98 Lancashire County Council 1973–97. *Career:* Teacher; Lecturer; Organising secretary, Association of Liberal Councillors; Manager, Liberal Party Publications; Book dealer. Liberal Democrat Spokesperson for: Environment, Food and Rural Affairs 2001–03, Deputy Prime Minister, Regional and Local Government 2003. Co-opted member, European Union Sub-committee F (Social Affairs, Education and Home Affairs) 2000–; Member, Standing Orders (Private Bills) Committee 2000–. Contested Nelson and Colne February and October 1974, Pendle 1997 general elections. *Publications:* Co-author *Merger: The Inside Story*, 1989. *Recreations:* Climbing, mountaineering, botany, cycling. Raised to the peerage as Baron Greaves, of Pendle in the County of Lancashire 2000. The Lord Greaves, 3 Hartington Street, Winewall, Colne, Lancashire, BB8 8DB *Tel:* 01282 864346; House of Lords, London, SW1A 0PW *Tel:* 020 7219 8620 *E-mail:* greavesa@parliament.uk.

GREENE OF HARROW WEALD, LORD   Labour

GREENE OF HARROW WEALD (Life Baron), Sidney Francis Greene; cr. 1974. Born 12 February 1910. Son of late Frank Greene; educated elementary schools. Married Masel Elizabeth Carter 1936 (3 daughters). *Trades Union:* General Secretary, National Union of Railwaymen 1957–75; Member, General Council of TUC 1957–75. JP, London 1941–65. *Career:* Joined railway service 1924; Director: Bank of England 1970–78, RTZ Corporation 1975–80, Times Newspapers 1975–82. Member, National Economic Development Council 1962–75. Raised to the peerage as Baron Greene of Harrow Weald, of Harrow in the County of Greater London 1974. The Lord Greene of Harrow Weald, CBE, 26 Kynaston Wood, Boxtree Road, Harrow Weald, Middlesex, HA3 6UA.

GREENFIELD, BARONESS   Crossbencher

GREENFIELD (Life Baroness) Professor Susan Adele Greenfield; cr 2001. Born 1 October 1950. Daughter of Reginald Meyer Greefield and Doris Margaret Winifred Thorpe; educated Godolphin and Latymer School for Girls, London; St Hilda's College, Oxford (BA experimental psychology 1973, DPhil pharmacology 1977, MA 1978); Honorary Fellowship, St Hilda's College, Oxford 1999. Married Peter William Atkins 1991. *Career:* Professor of pharmacology, Oxford University 1966–; Travelling scholarship to Israel ('Bridge in Britain') 1970; Medical Research Council (MRC) research scholarship, pharmacology department, Oxford 1973–76; Dame Catherine Fulford Senior Scholarship, St Hugh's College, Oxford 1974; J.H. Burn Trust Scholarship, pharmacology department, Oxford 1977; MRC training fellowship, physiology department, Oxford 1977–81; Royal Society study visit award, College de France, Paris 1978; MRC-INSERM exchange fellowship, College de France, Paris 1979–80; Junior research fellowship, Green College, Oxford 1981–84; Lecturer in synaptic pharmacology, Oxford 1985–96; Tutorial fellowship in medicine, Lincoln College, Oxford 1985–98; Deputy director, Squibb Projects 1988–95; Gresham Chair of Physic, Gresham College, London 1995–99; Visiting fellow, Neurosciences Institute, La Jolla, USA 1995; Distinguished visiting scholar, Queen's University, Belfast 1996; Senior research fellowship, Lincoln College 1998; Director: The Royal Institution of Great Britain 1998–, Synaptica Ltd 1998–. Vice-President, Association of Woman in Science and Engineering 2001; Oxford University Society; Physiological Society; The New York Academy of Sciences; Patron: Oxford Dementia Centre, Oxford Brookes University, West Berkshire Neurological Alliance, Motor Neurone Disease Association, Oxford International Bio-Medical Centre, Mentor Foundation UK, Federation of Women Graduates, National Schizophrenic Foundation. Woman of Distinction of the Year (Jewish Care) 1998; The Royal Society Michael Faraday Award 1998; *Observer* Woman of the Year 2000. 21 honorary degrees. Trustee, Science Museum 1998. Chair, Women in Science Group 2002. CBE 2000. Honorary Fellowship, Royal College of Physicians 2000. *Publications:* Over 150 peer-reviewed scientific papers; Co-editor *Mindwaves:*

Thoughts on Intelligence, Identity and Consciousness, Basil Blackwell 1987; Co-author *Journey to the Centres of the Brain*, BBC Education Publishers 1994; Editor: *The Human Mind Explained*, Reader's Digest (USA); Cassell (UK) 1994; *The Human Brain: A Guided Tour*, Weidenfeld & Nicholson/Basic Books 1997, Paperback Phoenix Press (1998); *Brainpower*, Ivy Press 1999; *The Private Life of the Brain*, Penguin (UK) 2000; *Brain Story*, BBC Books 2000. *Recreations:* Aerobics, travel. *Clubs:* Athenaeum. Raised to the peerage as Baroness Greenfield, of Ot Moor in the County of Oxfordshire 2001. Professor the Baroness Greenfield, CBE, Department of Pharmacology, Mansfield Road, Oxford, OX1 3QT *Tel:* 01865 271852 *Fax:* 01865 271853 *E-mail:* susan.greenfield@pharm.ox.ac.uk.

GREENGROSS, BARONESS   Crossbencher

GREENGROSS (Life Baroness), Sally Ralea Greengross; cr. 2000. Born 29 June 1935; educated Brighton and Hove High School; London School of Economics (BA 1972). Married Sir Alan Greengross 1959 (1 son 3 daughters). *Career:* Formerly a linguist, executive in industry, lecturer and researcher; Age Concern England: Assistant Director 1977–82, Deputy Director 1982–87, Director-General (formerly Director) 1987–2000; Vice-President (Europe), International Federation on Ageing 1987–2001, (Secretary General 1982–87); Joint Chair, Age Concern Institute of Gerontology, King's College London 1987–2000; Chair, Experience Corps 2001–; Executive Chair, International Longevity Centre UK 1999–. Co-opted member, European Union Sub-committee F (Social Affairs, Education and Home Affairs) 2000–. Member, Advisory Council, European Movement 1992–; Independent Member, UN and WHO Networks on Ageing 1983–2000; Vice-Chair, Britain in Europe 2000–. Patron, Action on Elder Abuse 1994–; Vice-President, EXTEND 1996. UK Woman of Europe 1990. Six honorary degrees. Trustee, Help Age International. Past and current member several advisory bodies concerned with the elderly. OBE 1993. FRSH 1994; FRSA 1994. *Publications:* Consultant, *Journal of Educational Gerontology*, 1987–; Editor, *Ageing: an adventure in living*, 1985; has edited and contributed to other publications on ageing issues and social policy. *Recreations:* Countryside, music. *Clubs:* Reform, Hurlingham. Raised to the peerage as Baroness Greengross, of Notting Hill in the Royal Borough of Kensington and Chelsea 2000. The Baroness Greengross, OBE, House of Lords, London, SW1A 0PW *Tel:* 020 7219 5494 *Fax:* 020 7219 5979 *E-mail:* greengrossS@parliament.uk.

GREENWAY, LORD   Crossbencher

GREENWAY (4th Baron, UK), Ambrose Charles Drexel Greenway; cr. 1927; 4th Bt of Stanbridge Earls (UK) 1919. Born 21 May 1941. Son of 3rd Baron; educated Winchester College. Married Rosalynne Peta Schenk, née Fradgley 1985. *Career:* Marine Photographer; Shipping Consultant. *House of Lords:* First entered House of Lords 1975; Elected hereditary peer 1999–; Member, Committee on Statutory Instruments 2000–. President, Cruise Europe 1996–. Younger Brother, Trinity House 1987; Chairman, The Marine Society 1994–2000; Vice-President, Sail Training Association 1995–. *Publications:* Soviet Merchant Ships, 1976; Comecon Merchant Ships, 1978; A Century of Cross-Channel Passenger Ferries, 1981; A Century of North Sea Passenger Steamers, 1986. *Special Interests:* Shipping, Marine Industry. *Recreations:* Sailing. *Clubs:* House of Lords Yacht. The Lord Greenway, House of Lords, London, SW1A 0PW *Tel:* 020 7219 4943.

GREGSON, LORD   Labour

GREGSON (Life Baron), John Gregson; cr. 1975. Born 29 January 1924. Son of late John Gregson. Single. DL, County of Greater Manchester 1979. *Career:* Fairey Engineering 1939–94: Board Member 1966, Managing Director 1978–94, retired as non-executive director, Fairey Holding 1994; Non-executive director: British Steel plc 1976–94, Otto-Simon Carves Ltd 1995, Innvotech Ltd. Member: Science and Technology 1980–97, Sustainable Development 1994–97. Honorary Life President, Labour Finance and Industry Group. Member, Court of UMIST 1976–; Vice-President, Association of Metropolitan Authorities 1984; Member Council, University of Manchester Institute of Science and Technology; President, Defence Manufacturers

Association 1984–2000; Chair, Waste Management Industry Training and Advisory Board 1989–2002; Member, National Rivers Authority 1991–95; Member, Court of University of Manchester 1995–97. Four honorary doctorates. Hon. Fellow: Royal Academy of Engineering, Institute of Civil Engineers 1987; AMCT; CIMgt. *Recreations:* Mountaineering, ski-ing, sailing, gardening. Raised to the peerage as Baron Gregson, of Stockport in the County of Greater Manchester 1975. The Lord Gregson, DL, 12 Rosemont Road, Richmond, Surrey, TW10 6QL.

GRENFELL, LORD   Crossbencher

GRENFELL (3rd Baron, UK), Julian Pascoe Francis St Leger Grenfell; cr. 1902; (Life) Baron Grenfell of Kilvey 2000. Born 23 May 1935. Son of 2nd Baron, CBE, TD; educated Eton College; King's College, Cambridge 1959 (President of the Union 1959). Married Loretta Reali 1961 (divorced 1970) (1 daughter); married Gabrielle Raab 1970 (divorced 1987) (2 daughters); married Mrs Elizabeth Porter 1987 (divorced 1992); married Mrs Dagmar Langbehn Debreil, née Langbehn 1993. 2nd Lieutenant, KRRC (60th Rifles) 1954–56; Captain, Queen's Royal Rifles, TA 1963. *Career:* Television reporter, ATV Ltd 1960–63; With World Bank: Washington DC 1965–69, Paris 1969–74; Representative of the World Bank to the United Nations 1974–81; Senior adviser, The World Bank, Washington, DC 1983–90; Head of external affairs, European Office of the World Bank 1990–95. *House of Lords:* First entered House of Lords 1976; Principal Deputy Chairman of Committees 2002–; Deputy Speaker 2002–. Member, European Union Sub-committee A (Economic and Financial Affairs, Trade and External Relations) 1996–99, 2000–Chair, 1999, 2000–; Member, European Union Select Committee 1999, 2000–, Chair 2003–; Member Procedure Committee 2003–. Member, UK Delegation to the Parliamentary Assemblies of the Council of Europe and Western European Union 1997–99. *Publications: Margot* (novel), 1987. *Special Interests:* European Affairs, Economic Policy. *Recreations:* Walking, European history. *Clubs:* Royal Green Jackets. Created a life peer as Baron Grenfell of Kilvey, of Kilvey in the County of Swansea 2000. The Lord Grenfell, House of Lords, London, SW1A 0PW *Tel:* 020 7219 3601 *Fax:* 020 7219 6715 *E-mail:* grenfellj@parliament.uk.

GRIFFITHS, LORD   Crossbencher

GRIFFITHS (Life Baron), (William) Hugh Griffiths; cr. 1985. Born 26 September 1923. Son of late Sir Hugh Griffiths, CBE; educated Charterhouse; St John's College, Cambridge. Married Evelyn Krefting 1949 (died March 1998) (1 son 3 daughters); married The Baroness Brigstocke (*qv*) 2000. Commissioned Welsh Guards 1942. *Career:* Called to the Bar, Inner Temple 1949; QC 1964; Recorder of: Margate 1962–64, Cambridge 1964–70; Judge of the High Court of Justice, Queen's Bench Division 1971–80; Lord Justice of Appeal 1980–85; Lord of Appeal in Ordinary 1985–93. Hon Member, Canadian Bar Association 1981; Hon Fellow, American Institute of Judicial Administration 1985; American College of Trial Lawyers 1988. President, Bar Association for Commerce, Finance and Industry. Hon LLD: University of Wales 1987; De Montfort University 1993. Chairman, Security Commission 1985–92. MC 1944; Kt 1971; PC 1980. *Recreations:* Golf, cricket, fishing. *Clubs:* Garrick, MCC (President 1990), Royal and Ancient (St Andrews) (Captain 1993). Raised to the peerage as Baron Griffiths, of Govilon in the County of Gwent 1985. Rt Hon the Lord Griffiths, MC, House of Lords, London, SW1A 0PW *Tel:* 020 7219 3202.

DodOnline

An Electronic Directory without rival . . .

Peers' biographies and photographs available with daily updates *via* the internet

For a *free* trial, call Yasmin Mirza, Aby Farsoun or Michael Mand on 020 7630 7643

GRIFFITHS OF FFORESTFACH, LORD   Conservative

GRIFFITHS OF FFORESTFACH (Life Baron), Brian Griffiths; cr. 1991. Born 27 December 1941. Son of Ivor Winston and Phyllis Mary Griffiths; educated Dynevor Grammar School; London School of Economics (BScEcon 1963, MScEcon 1965). Married Rachel Jane Jones 1965 (1 son 2 daughters). *Career:* Lecturer in economics, London School of Economics 1965–76; Professor of banking and Director of Centre, Banking and International Finance, City University 1977–82; Dean, Business School The City University 1982–85; Director, Bank of England 1983–85; Head, Prime Minister's Policy Unit and Special Adviser to The Rt Hon. Margaret Thatcher MP 1985–90; Director: Thorn EMI 1990–96, Herman Miller Inc. 1991–, Times Newspapers Ltd 1991–; Chair, Schools Examinations and Assessment Council 1991–93; International Adviser, Goldman Sachs 1991–; Vice-Chair, Goldman Sachs (International) 1991–; Director: Servicemaster 1992–, HTV 1992–93, Telewest 1995–98, English, Welsh, Scottish Railway 1996–; Chair: Trillium 1998–2000, Trillium Land Securities 2000–, Westminster Health Care 1999–2002. Member: European Union, Sub-Committee F (Social Affairs, Education and Home Affairs) 1999–, Religious Offences Committee 2002–. Chairman, Centre for Policy Studies 1991–2001; Member, board of directors Conservative Christian Fellowship. DSc The City University 1999; Fellow, Trinity College, Carmarthen 1996–. Freeman, City of London. *Publications:* Several books on economics including: *The Creation of Wealth,* 1984; *Morality and the Market Place,* 1989. *Special Interests:* Economic Policy, Education, Broadcasting, Social Policy. *Clubs:* Garrick. Raised to the peerage as Baron Griffiths of Fforestfach, of Fforestfach in the County of West Glamorgan 1991. The Lord Griffiths of Fforestfach, House of Lords, London, SW1A 0PW *Tel:* 020 7219 5353.

GROCOTT, LORD   Labour

GROCOTT (Life Baron), Bruce Joseph Grocott; cr. 2001. Born 1 November 1940. Son of late Reginald and Helen Grocott; educated Hemel Hempstead Grammar School; Leicester University (BA politics 1962); Manchester University (MA economics 1966). Married Sally Ridgway 1965 (2 sons). *Trades Union:* Member: NUJ, TGWU. Councillor, Bromsgrove Urban District Council 1971–74. *Career:* Administrative officer, LCC 1963–64; Tutor in politics, Manchester University 1964–65; Lecturer then senior lecturer in politics, Birmingham Polytechnic 1965–72; Principal lecturer, North Staffs Polytechnic 1972–74; Presenter then producer, Central Television 1979–87. *House of Commons:* Contested South West Hertfordshire 1970, Lichfield and Tamworth February 1974 general elections; Member (Labour) for Lichfield and Tamworth October 1974–79; Contested Lichfield and Tamworth 1979, The Wrekin 1983 general elections; Member for The Wrekin 1987–97, and for Telford 1997–2001; PPS to John Silkin: as Minister for Planning and Local Government 1975–76, as Minister of Agriculture 1976–78; Deputy Shadow Leader of the House and Deputy Campaigns Co-ordinator 1987–92; PPS to Tony Blair: as Leader of the Labour Party 1994–2001, as Prime Minister 1997–2001. Opposition Frontbench Spokesperson for Foreign and Commonwealth Affairs 1992–93. *House of Lords:* Deputy Chair of Committees 2002–; Deputy Speaker 2002–. Government Whip 2001–02; Chief Whip 2002–. Government Spokesperson for: Defence 2001–02, Foreign and Commonwealth Office 2001–02, International Development 2001–02, Work and Pensions 2001–02. Member: House of Lords' Offices 2002, Committee for Privileges 2002–, Procedure Committee 2002–, Committee of Selection 2002–, House of Lords' Offices Administration and Works Sub-committee 2002–, Refreshment Committee 2003–. PC. *Special Interests:* Foreign Affairs, Media, Health Service, Machinery of Government. *Recreations:* Steam railways, sport. *Clubs:* Trench Labour. Raised to the peerage as Baron Grocott, of Telford in the County of Shropshire 2001. Rt Hon the Lord Grocott, House of Lords, London, SW1A 0PW *Tel:* 020 7219 5058.

Visit the Vacher Dod Website . . .
www.DodOnline.co.uk

GUILDFORD, LORD BISHOP OF
Non-affiliated

GUILDFORD (8th Bishop of), John Warren Gladwin. Born 30 May 1942. Son of late Thomas and Muriel Gladwin; educated Hertford Grammar School; Churchill College, Cambridge (BA history and theology, MA 1965); St John's College, Durham (DipTheol 1969). Married Lydia Elizabeth Adam 1981. *Career:* Assistant Curate, St John the Baptist, Kirkheaton, Huddersfield 1967–71; Tutor, St John's College, Durham and Hon. Chaplain to Students, St Nicholas Church, Durham 1971–77; Director, Shaftesbury Project on Christian Involvement in Society 1977–82; Secretary, General Synod Board for Social Responsibility 1982–88; Prebendary, St Paul's Cathedral 1984–88; Provost of Sheffield 1988–94; Member, General Synod of the Church of England 1990–; Bishop of Guildford 1994–; Took his seat in the House of Lords 1999. Member Select Committee on Administration and Works 2003–. President, Church's National Housing Coalition; Chairman, Board of Christian Aid; Member, Archbishop's Council. Freeman, City of London. *Publications: God's People in God's World*, 1979; *The Good of the People*, 1988; *Love and Liberty*, 1998. *Recreations:* Gardening, travel, bee keeping. *Clubs:* Ronnie Scott's. Rt Rev the Lord Bishop of Guildford, Willow Grange, Woking Road, Guildford, Surrey, GU4 7QS *Tel:* 01483 590500 *Fax:* 01483 590501 *E-mail:* bishop.john@cofeguildford.org.uk.

GUTHRIE OF CRAIGIEBANK, LORD
Crossbencher

GUTHRIE OF CRAIGIEBANK (Life Baron), Charles Ronald Llewelyn Guthrie GCB LVO OBE; cr 2001. Born 17 November 1938; educated Harrow School; Royal Military Academy, Sandhurst (commission 1959). Married Catherine Worrall 1972 (2 sons). *Career:* 2nd lieutenant to captain Welsh Guards 1959–65; Captain 22 Special Air Service 1965–69; Lieutenant colonel Welsh Guards 1977–80; Brigadier 4th Armoured Brigade 1982–84; Major General 2 Infantry Division 1986–87; Lieutenant General 1 (BR) Corps 1987–91; Commander-in-chief British Army of the Rhine 1992–94; Ministry of Defence: Chief of the General Staff 1994–97, Chief of the Defence Staff 1997–2001. International Institute of Strategic Studies; Centre for Strategic and International Studies, Washington. President: Army Benevolent Fund, Federation of London Youth Clubs, Action Research. Fellow, King's College London 2002, Visiting Professor 2001–. Colonel, The Life Guards and Gold Stick, Colonel Commandant Special Air Service. LVO 1977; OBE 1980; KCB 1990; GCB 1994; Commander Legion of Merit, USA 2001. Painter Stainers. *Special Interests:* Defence, International Relations. *Recreations:* Tennis, opera, travel. *Sportsclubs:* All-England Lawn Tennis, Queen's. *Clubs:* White's, Beefsteak. Raised to the peerage as Baron Guthrie of Craigiebank, of Craigiebank in the City of Dundee 2001. General the Lord Guthrie of Craigiebank, GCB, LVO, OBE, N M Rothschild & Son Ltd, New Court, St Swithins Lane, London, EC4P 4DU *Tel:* 020 7280 5468 *E-mail:* lord.guthrie@rothschild.co.uk.

H

HABGOOD, LORD
Crossbencher

HABGOOD (Life Baron), John Stapylton Habgood; cr. 1995. Born 23 June 1927. Son of late Arthur Henry Habgood, DSO, MB, BCH, and late Vera Chetwynd-Stapylton; educated Eton College; King's College, Cambridge (BA natural sciences and physiology 1948, PhD 1952); Cuddesdon Theological College, Oxford. Married Rosalie Mary Anne Boston 1961 (2 sons 2 daughters). *Career:* Demonstrator in pharmacology, Cambridge University 1950–53; Curate, St Mary Abbots, Kensington 1954–56; Vice-principal, Westcott House, Cambridge 1956–62; Rector, St John's Church, Jedburgh 1962–67; Principal, Queen's College, Birmingham 1967–73; Bishop of Durham 1973–83; First entered the House of Lords 1973; Archbishop of York 1983–95. Pro-Chancellor, York University 1985–90. Member, Select Committee on Medical Ethics 1993–94.

Member, World Council of Churches 1983–91; Moderator of Church and Society Sub-Unit 1983–90. Patron, National Family Mediation 1990–; Vice-President, Population Concern 1991–2000; Patron: Action for Disability 1991–, Encephalitis Support Group 2000–. 10 honorary doctorates from UK and USA; honorary fellow King's College, Cambridge. Chairman, UK Xenotransplantation Interim Regulatory Authority 1997–2003; Member, Round Table on Sustainable Development 1997–99. PC 1983. *Publications: Religion and Science*, 1964; *A Working Faith*, 1980; *Church and Nation in a Secular Age*, 1983; *Confessions of a Conservative Liberal*, 1988; *Making Sense*, 1993; *Faith and Uncertainty*, 1997; *Being A Person*, 1998; *Varieties of Unbelief*, 2000; *The Concept of Nature*, 2002. *Special Interests:* Science, Medicine, Ethics. *Recreations:* Painting, carpentry. *Clubs:* Athenaeum. Raised to the peerage as Baron Habgood, of Calverton in the County of Buckinghamshire 1995. Rt Rev and Rt Hon the Lord Habgood, 18 The Mount, Malton, North Yorkshire, YO17 7ND.

HAMWEE, BARONESS   Liberal Democrat

HAMWEE (Life Baroness), Sally Rachel Hamwee; cr. 1991. Born 12 January 1947. Daughter of late Alec and Dorothy Hamwee; educated Manchester High School for Girls; Girton College, Cambridge (BA law 1969, MA). Councillor, London Borough of Richmond upon Thames 1978–98; Chair, Planning Committee 1983–87; Vice-chair, Policy and Resources Committee 1987–91; Chair, London Planning Advisory Committee 1986–94; Member, Greater London Authority 2000–; Deputy Chair of Assembly 2000–01, 2001–; Chair of Assembly 2001–02. *Career:* Admitted Solicitor 1972; Partner, Clintons Solicitors 1984–. Liberal Democrat Spokesperson for: Local Government 1991–98, Housing and Planning 1993–98, Local Government and Planning 1998–2000; Principal Spokesperson for: Environment, Transport and the Regions 1999–2000, Local Government and the Regions 2001–. Member, House of Lords Select Committee on Relations between Central and Local Government 1995–96, Joint Select Committee on Draft Local Government Bill 1999. Past President, ALDC (Liberal Democrat Councillors' and Campaigners' Association); Member: National Executive, Liberal Party 1987–88, Federal Executive, Liberal Democrats 1989–91, Federal Policy Committee 1996–98. Member of Council, Parents for Children 1977–86; Legal adviser, The Simon Community 1980–; Member of Council, Refuge 1991–; Chair, Xfm Ltd 1996–98; Member of Council, Family Policy Studies Centre –2001; President, Town and Country Planning Association; Member, Joseph Rowntree Foundation Inquiry, Planning for Housing 1991–. *Special Interests:* Local Government, Planning, London, Arts, Media, Housing. Raised to the peerage as Baroness Hamwee, of Richmond upon Thames in the London Borough of Richmond upon Thames 1991. The Baroness Hamwee, 101A Mortlake High Street, London, SW14 8HQ *Tel:* 020 8878 1380; House of Lords, London, SW1A 0PW *Tel:* 020 7219 3239 *E-mail:* sally.hamwee@london.gov.uk.

HANHAM, BARONESS   Conservative

HANHAM (Life Baroness), Joan Brownlow Hanham; cr. 1999. Born 23 September 1939. Daughter of late Alfred and Mary Spark (née Mitchell); educated Hillcourt School, Dublin. Married Dr Iain William Ferguson Hanham FRCP FRCR 1964 (1 son 1 daughter). Royal Borough of Kensington and Chelsea: Councillor 1970–, Mayor 1983–84, Chairman: Town Planning Committee 1984–86, Social Services Committee 1987–89, Policy and Resources Committee 1989–, Leader of the Council 1989–2000; Chairman, Policy Committee, London Boroughs Association 1991–95; JP: City of London Commission 1984, Inner London Family Proceedings Court 1992. Opposition Whip 2000–. Opposition Spokesperson for: Transport, Local Government and the Regions 2001–02, Local Government and the Regions 2002, Local Government, Planning, Housing and the Regions 2003–. Member Select Committee on Procedure –2002. Member, Committee of the Regions. Director, London First 1996–99; Governor: Sir John Cass Foundation 1996–99, Sir John Cass Primary School 1997–99. Vice-president Commonwealth Institute 1999–; Special Trustee St Mary's NHS Trust. Member, Mental Health Act Commission 1983–90; Non-Executive Member, North West Thames Regional Health Authority 1983–94; Chairman, St Mary's Hospital NHS Trust 2000–; Vice-President Commonwealth Institute; Friend University of Grenada. CBE 1997. Freeman, City of London 1984. *Special Interests:* Local Government, Health, Justice, Environment. *Recreations:* Music, travel. *Clubs:* Hurlingham. Raised to the peerage as Baroness Hanham, of Kensington in the Royal Borough of Kensington and Chelsea 1999. The Baroness Hanham, CBE, House of Lords, London, SW1A 0PW *Tel:* 020 7219 3237.

HANNAY OF CHISWICK, LORD   Crossbencher

HANNAY OF CHISWICK (Life Baron), David Hugh Alexander Hannay GCMG; cr 2001. Born 28 September 1935. Son of late Julian George Hannay and late Eileen Millicent Hannay; educated Winchester College; New College, Oxford (BA modern history 1959). Married Gillian Rosemary Rex 1961 (4 sons). *Trades Union:* First Division Association. *Career:* Foreign and Commonwealth Office (FCO) 1959–2003: London 1959–60; Language student Tehran 1960–61; Oriental secretary Kabul 1961–63; Second secretary FCO 1963–65; First secretary Brussels (EC) 1965–70; Brussels negotiating team 1970–72; Chef de Cabinet to Vice-President EC Commission 1973–77; FCO 1977–84: head of energy, science and space department 1977–79, head of Middle East department 1979, assistant under secretary EC 1979–84; Minister Washington 1984–85; Ambassador, permanent representative to the EC 1985–90; Ambassador, permanent representative to the UN, New York 1990–95; Special Representative for Cyprus, London 1996–2003. Pro-chancellor Birmingham University 2001–. Member European Union Sub-committee A (Economic and Financial Affairs, Trade and External Relations) 2001–, European Union Committee 2003–. Adviser to Executive Committee of World Federation of United Nations Associations 1995–2000; Advisory Board: Centre for European Reform, Prospect, European Foreign Affairs Review; EDHEC Business School (France) 2002–; Salzburg Seminar 2002–; TANGGUH Independent Advisory Panel. Honorary Fellow New College, Oxford; Hon DLitt Birmingham University. CMG 1981 KCMG 1986 GCMG 1995. *Publications:* Editor *Britain's Entry into the European Community, Report on the Negotiations*, 1970–72. *Recreations:* Travel, photography, gardening, grandchildren. *Clubs:* Travellers. Raised to the peerage as Baron Hannay of Chiswick, of Bedford Park in the London Borough of Ealing 2001. The Lord Hannay of Chiswick, 3 The Orchard, London, W4 1JZ *Tel:* 020 8987 9012 *Fax:* 020 8987 9012.

HANNINGFIELD, LORD   Conservative

HANNINGFIELD (Life Baron), Paul Edward Winston White; cr. 1998. Born 16 September 1940. Son of Edward Ernest William White and Irene Joyce Gertrude White (née Williamson; educated King Edward VI Grammar School, Chelmsford; Nuffield Scholarship for Agriculture (research in USA specialising in marketing in farming). DL Essex 1991–; Councillor Essex County Council 1970–, various positions from 1973–98 including Chair of Education Committee, Chair 1989–92, Leader of the Council 1998–99, 2001–, Conservative Group Leader. *Career:* Farmer. Opposition Whip 2003–. President, Assembly of European Regions Sub-Commission 1990–; Conservative Group Leader, Committee of the Regions, Member 1994–; Chair, Enlargement Group, EU Committee of the Regions. Member, Chelmsford Conservative Party Executive 1962–; Chairman: Conservative Party (Stock Area) 1968–75, Conservative Party Eastern Area Local Government Advisory Committee 1995–98, Conservative Party National Local Government Advisory Committee, Conservative Councillors Association Steering Committee; Board Member, Conservative Party representing local government; Member, Conservative Party National Union Executive. Member, National Executive, NFU 1965; Association of County Councils: Member 1981–97, Chair of Education Committee 1989–93, Conservative Leader 1995–97. Chair: Council of Local Education Authorities (CLEA) 1990–92; Eastern Region Further Education Funding Council 1992–97; Deputy Chair and Conservative Group Leader, Local Government Association; Chair and co-founder Localis Think Tank 2001–. Honorary doctorate. Chairman, Chelmsford Young Farmers 1962; Member, Court of Essex University; Governor, Brentwood School, Essex. *Publications:* Several contributions to local government journals. *Recreations:* Botany, current affairs, travel, food and wine. Raised to the peerage as Baron Hanningfield, of Chelmsford in the County of Essex 1998. The Lord Hanningfield, DL, House of Lords, London, SW1A 0PW *Tel:* 020 7219 8680 *E-mail:* lord.hanningfield@essexcc.gov.uk.

Visit the Vacher Dod Website . . .
www.DodOnline.co.uk

HANSON, LORD   Conservative

HANSON (Life Baron), James Edward Hanson; cr. 1983. Born 20 January 1922. Son of late Robert Hanson, CBE. Married Geraldine Kaelin 1959 (2 sons 1 step-daughter). Second World War army service 1939–46. *Career:* Director Hanson Transport Group Ltd 1946–; Chair: Hanson plc 1965–97, Hanson Transport Group Ltd 1965–96, Trident Television Ltd 1972–76, 1984–85, Director 1970–85; Director, Hanson Capital Ltd 2000–. Life Trustee of University of Southern California 2002. Member, Court of Patrons, Royal College of Surgeons of England 1991. Hon. LLD, Leeds 1984; Hon. DBA, Huddersfield 1991; Hon. Fellow: St Peter's College, Oxford 1996, Royal College of Radiologists 1998. Kt 1976. Hon. Liveryman, Worshipful Company of Saddlers. *Special Interests:* Industry. *Clubs:* Brooks's, Huddersfield Borough, The Brook (New York), Toronto (Canada). Raised to the peerage as Baron Hanson, of Edgerton in the County of West Yorkshire 1983. The Lord Hanson, 28 Old Brompton Road, Box 164, London, SW7 3SS *Tel:* 020 7245 6996 *Fax:* 020 7245 9900.

HARDIE, LORD   Crossbencher

HARDIE (Life Baron), Andrew Rutherford Hardie; cr 1997. Born 8 January 1946. Son of Andrew Rutherford and Elizabeth Currie Hardie; educated St Modan's High School, Stirling; Edinburgh University (MA, LLB). Married Catherine Storrar Elgin 1971 (2 sons 1 daughter). *Career:* Solicitor 1971; Member, Faculty of Advocates 1973; Advocate Depute 1979–83; QC (Scot) 1985 Treasurer, Faculty of Advocates 1989–94, Dean 1994–97; Senator of the College of Justice in Scotland 2000–; Honorary Bencher, Lincoln's Inn; Lord of Appeal. *House of Lords:* Lord Advocate 1997–2000; Lord Advocate, Scottish Executive 1999–2000. PC 1997. *Special Interests:* Childcare. *Recreations:* Cricket. Raised to the peerage as Baron Hardie, of Blackford in the City of Edinburgh 1997. Rt Hon the Lord Hardie, High Court of Justiciary and Court of Session, Parliament House, Parliament Square, Edinburgh, EH1 1RF.

HARDY OF WATH, LORD   Labour

HARDY OF WATH (Life Baron), Peter Hardy; cr. 1997. Born 17 July 1931. Son of late Lawrence Hardy, miner – colliery overman official; educated Wath upon Dearne Grammar School, Yorkshire; Westminster College, London (Teacher's Certificate 1953); College of Preceptors (education theory 1962) (licentiate); Sheffield University (curricular studies 1965–66); Leeds University (Europe 1996–97). Married Margaret Ann Brookes 1954 (2 sons). *Trades Union:* Sponsored by NACODS 1983–97; Hon. Life Member, UNISON. RAF national service 1949–51 and reserve service; Completed Parliamentary attachment to RAF 1992. Councillor, Wath upon Dearne Urban District Council 1960–70, Chair 1968, ex-officio JP; Chairman/Governor, Wath upon Dearne Grammar School 1960–70; DL, South Yorkshire 1997–. *Career:* Teacher, South Yorkshire 1953–70; Lexborough County Secondary School 1960–70: Head of English department 1960–64, Head of lower school 1964–70. *House of Commons:* Contested Scarborough and Whitby 1964 and Sheffield Hallam 1966 general elections; MP (Labour) for Rother Valley 1970–83 and for Wentworth 1983–97; Sponsored: The Badgers Act 1973, The Conservation of Wild Creatures and Wild Plants Act 1975, The Protection of Birds (Amendment) Act 1976, The Education (Northern Ireland) Act 1978; PPS to: Secretary of State for the Environment 1974–76, Foreign and Commonwealth Secretary 1976–79. *House of Lords:* Sponsor, Waste Minimisation Bill 1998. Member Select Committee on Statutory Instruments (Joint Committee) 1997–. Chairman, Defence Group. Hon. Member, Council of European Parliamentary Assembly. Chairman and Rapporteur, Committee on Environment, Council of Europe 1977–97; Chairman, Sub-committee National Environment 1978–86, 1990–95; Vice-Chair, Socialist Group WEU 1979–83; Leader, Labour delegation to Council of Europe and WEU 1983–96; Vice-Chair, Socialist Group of Council of Europe 1983–95; Chair, Council of Europe Committee on Environment 1986–89; Leader, Labour delegation to OSCE 1992–97; Rapporteur, Committee on Defence (WEU) 1993–97.

Member: Council of RSPB 1985–89, Central Executive NSPCC 1986–94; Vice-President, South Yorkshire Foundation; Hon. Member, Kennel Club 1992; President, South Yorkshire, North Derbyshire and Peak District Branch, CPRE; President, Air Training Corps Squadron, Rotherham; President, CPRE Peak District and South Yorkshire branch 1997–. Green Ribbon Award for Services to Conservation 1997. Patron, Yorkshire Wildlife Trust; Fellow, Industry and Parliament Trust. Involved in campaign to improve hedgerow protection for fifteen years; Member Ecclesiastical Committee 1993–. Liveryman, Guild of Fuellers 2001. *Publications: Lifetime of Badgers*, 1975. *Special Interests:* Wildlife, Conservation, Foreign Affairs, Home Affairs, Defence, Energy. *Recreations:* Wildlife observation, dogs, occasionally judging dogs. *Clubs:* Kennel; Royal Air Force. Raised to the peerage as Baron Hardy of Wath, of Wath upon Dearne in the County of South Yorkshire 1997. The Lord Hardy of Wath, DL, House of Lords, London, SW1A 0PW *Tel:* 020 7219 1465.

HARRIS OF HARINGEY, LORD   Labour

HARRIS OF HARINGEY (Life Baron), Jonathan Toby Harris; cr. 1998. Born 11 October 1953. Son of late Professor Harry Harris, FRS and Muriel Harris; educated Haberdashers' Aske's School, Elstree; Trinity College, Cambridge (BA natural sciences and economics 1975) (President of the Union 1974). Married Ann Sarah Herbert 1979 (2 sons 1 daughter). *Trades Union:* Member, Amicus. London Borough of Haringey: Councillor 1978–2002, Chair, Social Services Committee 1982–87, Leader of the Council 1987–99; Member: London Ambulance Service NHS Trust 1998–, London Pension Fund Authority 1998–2000, Metropolitan Police Committee 1998–2000; Member, Greater London Authority for Brent and Harrow 2000–; Chair, Metropolitan Police Authority 2000–. *Career:* Economics Division, Bank of England 1975–79; Electricity Consumers' Council 1979–86, Deputy Director 1983–86; Director, Association of Community Health Councils for England and Wales 1987–98; Senior Associate, The Kings Fund 1998–; Consultant adviser to: Harrogate Management Centre 1998–, Infolog Training 1998–, Vantage Point 1998–2001, KPMG 1999–, DEMSA 2001–03, Wyeth Pharmaceuticals 2001–, National Grid Transco 2003–. Member, Finance and Staff Sub-Committee, House of Lords Offices Committee 2000–02. Committee of the Regions of EU: Member 1994–98, Alternate Member 1998–2002. Chair: Cambridge University Labour Club 1973, Young Fabian Group 1976–77, Hornsey Labour Party 1978, 1979, 1980; Member: Labour Party National Policy Forum 1992–, Labour Party Local Government Committee 1993–, Greater London Labour Party Regional Board 1993–. Governor, National Institute for Social Work 1986–94; Board Member, London First 1993–2002; Executive Council Member, RNIB 1993–94; Member, Court of Middlesex University 1995–. Honorary doctorate, Middlesex University 1999. Trustee: Evening Standard Blitz Memorial Appeal 1995–99, Help for Health Trust 1995–97, The Learning Agency 1996–98; Chair, English National Stadium Trust 1997–. Deputy Chair, National Fuel Poverty Forum 1981–86; Deputy Chair, AMA 1991–97, Chair, Social Services Committee 1986–93; Member: London Drug Policy Forum 1990–98, National Nursery Examination Board 1992–94, Home Office Advisory Council on Race Relations 1992–97; Chair, Association of London Authorities 1993–95, Deputy Chair 1990–93, Chair, Social Services Committee 1984–88; Chair: Local Government Anti-Poverty Unit 1994–97, Association of London Government 1995–2000; Member: Joint London Advisory Panel 1996–1997, Executive, Local Government Association 1999–, Executive, Association of Police Authorities 2000–. FRSA. Freeman, City of London 1998. *Publications:* Co-author *Why Vote Labour?*, 1979; Contributor to *Economics of Prosperity*, 1980; Co-editor *Energy and Social Policy*, 1983; Contributor to *Rationing in Action*, 1993 and *Whistleblowing in the Health Service: accountability, law and professional practice*, 1994. *Recreations:* Reading, walking. Raised to the peerage as Baron Harris of Haringey, of Hornsey in the London Borough of Haringey 1998. The Lord Harris of Haringey, 4 Beatrice Road, London, N4 4PD *E-mail:* toby.harris@london.gov.uk.

DodOnline
An Electronic Directory without rival . . .

Peers' biographies and photographs available with daily updates *via* the internet

For a *free* trial, call Yasmin Mirza, Aby Farsoun or Michael Mand on 020 7630 7643

HARRIS OF HIGH CROSS, LORD   Crossbencher

HARRIS OF HIGH CROSS (Life Baron), Ralph Harris; cr. 1979. Born 10 December 1924. Son of late W. H. Harris and Lilian Vallé; educated Tottenham Grammar School; Queens' College, Cambridge (Foundation Scholar) (MA economics 1947). Married José Jeffery 1949 (1 daughter and 2 sons deceased). *Career:* Political economy lecturer, St Andrew's University 1949–56; Leader writer, Glasgow Herald 1956; General Director, Institute of Economic Affairs 1957–87, Chair, Institute of Economic Affairs 1987–89, Director, Times Newspapers Holdings Ltd 1988–2001; Chair, Bruges Group 1989–91; Founder President, Institute of Economic Affairs 1990–; Joint Chair, International Centre for Research into Economic Transformation (Moscow) 1990–95. Member, Political Economy Club; Chairman, FOREST 1989–2001; President, Mont Pelerin Society 1982–84. Free Enterprise Award 1976. DSc honoris causa, Buckingham University 1984. Trustee: Wincott Foundation 1969, McWhirter Foundation 1975–, Centre for Research into Communist Economies 1984–95, Civitas 1999–. Contested: Kirkcaldy (Liberal Unionist) 1951, Edinburgh Central (Conservative) 1955 general elections. *Publications:* Co-author several publications including: *Hire Purchase in a Free Society*, 1958; *Advertising in a Free Society*, 1959; *Choice in Welfare*, 1963, 1965, 1970; *Not from Benevolence*, 1977; Author *The Coming Confrontation*, 1978; *Over-ruled on Welfare*, 1979; Author *End of Government*, 1980; *Challenge of a Radical Reactionary*, 1980; *No Prime Minister!*, 1985; *Morality and Markets*, 1986; *Beyond the Welfare State*, 1988. *Special Interests:* European Union, Economic Policy, Social Policy. *Recreations:* Word processing, reading, sea swimming. Raised to the peerage as Baron Harris of High Cross, of Tottenham in the County of Greater London 1979. The Lord Harris of High Cross, 5 Cattley Close, Wood Street, Barnet, Hertfordshire, EN5 4SN *Tel:* 020 8449 6212.

HARRIS OF PECKHAM, LORD   Conservative

HARRIS OF PECKHAM (Life Baron), Philip Charles Harris; cr. 1996. Born 15 September 1942. Son of Charles Harris, MC and Ruth Harris; educated Streatham Grammar School. Married Pauline Norma Chumley 1960 (3 sons 1 daughter). *Career:* Chairman, Harris Queensway plc 1964–88, Chief Executive 1987–88; Non-executive director: Great Universal Stores 1986–, Fisons plc 1986–94; Chairman: Harris Ventures Ltd 1988–, C. W. Harris Properties 1988–97; Non-executive director, Molyneux Estates 1990–95; Chairman, Carpetright plc 1993–. Deputy Chairman, Conservative Party Treasurers 1993. Member, United Medical and Dental Schools of Guy's and St Thomas's Hospitals, Governor 1983–98; Member, Court of Patrons, Royal College of Gynaecologists 1984–; University of London Court 1990–94; Council Member 1994–96; Prostate Cancer Charity; University College London Council 1996–99; NSPCC National Appeal Board and Executive Committee 1998–; Deputy Chair, Full-Stop Campaign 1998–; President, Friends of Guy's Hospital 1999–. Hambro Business Man of the Year 1983. Two honorary doctorates. Chair, Generation Trust, Guy's Hospital 1984–; National Hospital for Neurology and Neurosurgery Development Foundation 1984–92; Westminster Abbey Trust 1987–96; Chair, Guy's and Lewisham NHS Trust 1991–93; Deputy Chair, Lewisham NHS Trust 1993–97; Tavistock Trust for Aphasia 1993–2003; Royal Academy of Arts 1999–; Outward Bound Trust 2001–03. Harris City Technology College 1989–; Bacon's City Technology College 1990–; Harris HospisCare, South Bromley 2002–; The Academy of Peckham 2003–. Kt 1985. Hon. Fellow, Royal College of Radiologists 1992; Four honorary University Fellowships. Freeman, City of London 1992. Liveryman, Broderers' Company 1992. *Recreations:* Football, cricket, show jumping, tennis. Raised to the peerage of Baron Harris of Peckham, of Peckham in the London Borough of Southwark 1996. The Lord Harris of Peckham, Amberley House, New Road, Rainham, Essex, RM13 8QN *Tel:* 01708 527730 *Fax:* 01708 630970.

Visit the Vacher Dod Website . . .
www.DodOnline.co.uk

HARRIS OF RICHMOND, BARONESS   Liberal Democrat

HARRIS OF RICHMOND (Life Baroness), Angela Felicity Harris; cr. 1999. Born 4 January 1944. Daughter of late Rev. G H Hamilton Richards and Eva Richards; educated Canon Slade Grammar School, Bolton; Ealing Hotel and Catering College. Married 2nd John Philip Roger Harris 1976 (1 son from previous marriage). Councillor, Richmond Town Council 1978–81, 1991–99, Mayor 1993–94; Councillor, Richmondshire District Council 1979–89, Chair 1987–88; Councillor, North Yorkshire County Council 1981–2001, Chair 1991–92; JP 1982–98; Non-executive Director, Northallerton NHS Trust 1990–97; DL, North Yorkshire 1994; Chair North Yorkshire Police Authority 1994–2001; Deputy Chair, National Association of Police Authorities 1997–2001. Liberal Democrat Whip 2000–. Liberal Democrat Deputy Spokesperson for: Home Office 2002, Northern Ireland 2003–. Member: European Union Committee 2000–, European Union Sub-committee F (Social Affairs, Education and Home Affairs) 2000–, Chair 2000–, House of Lords Offices Committee –2002, Refreshment Committee 2003–. Member: British-American Parliamentary Group, Inter-parliamentary Union. Patron: Hospice Homecare, Northallerton, Trauma International, Lister House (Royal British Legion), Member, Court of the University of York 1996–; President, National Association of Chaplains to the Police. Contested European Parliament elections 1999. Honorary Alderman, North Yorkshire County Council –2002. *Special Interests:* Police, Northern Ireland. *Recreations:* Music, political biographies. Raised to the peerage as Baroness Harris of Richmond, of Richmond in the County of North Yorkshire 1999. The Baroness Harris of Richmond, DL, House of Lords, London, SW1A 0PW *Tel:* 020 7219 6709 *E-mail:* harrisa@parliament.uk.

HARRISON, LORD   Labour

HARRISON (Life Baron), Lyndon Henry Arthur Harrison; cr. 1999. Born 28 September 1947. Son of late Charles and Edith Harrison; educated Oxford School; Warwick University (BA English and American studies 1970); Sussex University (MA American studies 1971); Keele University (MA American studies 1978). Married Hilary Plank 1980 (1 son 1 daughter). *Trades Union:* Member, GMB. Cheshire County Council: Councillor 1981–90, Chairman: Libraries Committee 1982, 1984–89, Tourism Committee 1985–89, Further Education Committee 1984–89. *Career:* Research officer, UMIST Union, Manchester 1975–78; Union manager, North East Wales Institute, Clwyd 1978–89; MEP for Cheshire West 1989–94, and for Cheshire West and Wirral 1994–99; Secretary, European Parliamentary Labour Party 1991–94. *House of Lords:* Departmental Liaison Peer for Northern Ireland 1999–2001. Member: European Union Select Committee Sub-Committee C (Common Foreign and Security Policy) 1999–, Select Committee on Delegated Powers and Regulatory Reform 2003–. Member: British-American Parliamentary Group, IPU. Deputy Chairman, North West Tourist Board 1986–89; Vice-President, Association of County Councils 1990–97. *Special Interests:* Small Business, Tourism, Monetary Union, Children. *Recreations:* Chess, the arts, sport. Raised to the peerage as Baron Harrison, of Chester in the County of Cheshire 1999. The Lord Harrison, House of Lords, London, SW1A 0PW *Tel:* 020 7219 6424.

HASKEL, LORD   Labour

HASKEL (Life Baron), Simon Haskel; cr. 1993. Born 8 October 1934. Son of late Isaac and Julia Haskel; educated Sedbergh School; Salford College of Advanced Technology (ARTCS textile technology 1955). Married Carole Lewis 1962 (1 son 1 daughter). National service commission, Royal Artillery 1957. *Career:* Joined Perrotts Ltd 1961; Chairman, Perrotts Group plc and associated companies 1973–97. *House of Lords:* Deputy Chair of Committees 2002–; Deputy Speaker 2002–. Opposition Whip 1994–97; Government Whip 1997–98. Opposition Spokesperson for Trade and Industry 1994–97; Spokesperson for: Social Security 1997–98, Trade and Industry 1997–98, the Treasury 1997–98. Member Select Committees on: Science and Technology 1994–97, 1999–2002, Procedure, Science and Technology Sub-committee I (Fighting Infection) 2002–.

Vice-chairman, Trade and Industry Committee 2003–. Founder Member, Labour Party Industry 1972 Group, Secretary 1976–81; Secretary, Labour Finance and Industry Group 1982–90, Chairman 1990–96. Chair, Thames Concerts Society 1982–90; Patron: Chronic Disease Research Foundation 1999–, Society of Operations Engineers 2000–; President, Environment Industries Commission 2000–; International President, Textile Institute 2002–; President, Jewish Policy research 2002–. Trustee: Lord and Lady Haskel Charitable Foundation, Israel Diaspora Trust 1998–; Chair of Trustees, The Smith Institute 1998–. Member, Joint Committee on Financial Services and Markets Bill. *Special Interests:* Trade and Industry, Science and Technology. *Recreations:* Music, cycling. *Sportsclubs:* Cyclists' Touring, Tandem. Raised to the peerage as Baron Haskel, of Higher Broughton in the County of Greater Manchester 1993. The Lord Haskel, House of Lords, London, SW1A 0PW *Tel:* 020 7219 4076 *E-mail:* haskel@blueyonder.co.uk.

HASKINS, LORD — Labour

HASKINS (Life Baron), Christopher Robin Haskins; cr. 1998. Born 30 May 1937. Son of Robin and Margaret Haskins; educated St Columba's College, Dublin; Trinity College, Dublin (BA modern history 1959). Married Gilda Horsley 1959 (3 sons 2 daughters). *Career:* Ford Motor Company, Dagenham 1960–62; Northern Foods 1962–, Chair 1986–2002; Non-executive chair Express Dairies 1998–2002; Board member Yorkshire Forward Regional Development Agency 1998–; Rural Recovery Co-ordinator 2001. Member European Union Sub-committee D (Environment, Agriculture, Public Health and Consumer Protection) 2003–. Six honorary doctorates. Trustee: Runnymede Trust 1989–98, Demos 1993–2000, Civil Liberties Trust 1997–99, Legal Assistance Trust 1998–, Lawes Agricultural Trust 2000–, Business Dynamics 2002–. Member: Commission for Social Justice 1992–94, UK Round Table on Sustainable Development 1995–97, Hampel Committee on Corporate Governance 1996–97, New Deal Advisory Task Force 1997–2001; Chairman, Better Regulation Task Force 1997–2002; Director, Yorkshire Television. *Special Interests:* Europe, Food and Agriculture, the Countryside. Raised to the peerage as Baron Haskins, of Skidby in the County of the East Riding of Yorkshire 1998. The Lord Haskins, 46 Main Street, Quarryside Farm, Skidby, Nr Cottingham, East Yorkshire, HU16 5TG *Tel:* 01482 842692 *Fax:* 01482 845249 *E-mail:* gshaskins@aol.com.

HATTERSLEY, LORD — Labour

HATTERSLEY (Life Baron), Roy Sydney George Hattersley; cr. 1997. Born 28 December 1932. Son of late Frederick Roy Hattersley; educated Sheffield City Grammar School; Hull University (BSc economics). Married Molly Loughran 1956. *Trades Union:* Member, NUJ. Councillor, Sheffield City Council 1957–65. *House of Commons:* Contested Sutton Coldfield 1959 general election; MP (Labour) for Birmingham Sparkbrook 1964–97; PPS to Minister of Pensions October 1964-February 1967; Parliamentary Secretary, Ministry of Labour March 1967-March 1968; Parliamentary Under-Secretary of State, Department of Employment and Productivity March 1968-August 1969; Minister of Defence for Administration August 1969–70; Minister of State, Foreign and Commonwealth Affairs 1974–76; Secretary of State for Prices and Consumer Protection September 1976–79; Deputy Leader, Labour Party 1983–92. Opposition Spokesman on: Defence 1972, Education and Science 1972–74; Principal Opposition Frontbench Spokesperson for: the Environment May 1979-December 1980, Home Affairs Dec 1980–83, Treasury and Economic Affairs October 1983–87, Home Affairs June 1987–92. PC 1975. *Publications: Nelson,* 1974; *Goodbye to Yorkshire,* (essays) 1976; *Politics Apart,* 1982; *Press Gang,* 1983; *A Yorkshire Boyhood,* 1983; *Endpiece Revisited,* (essays) 1985; *Choose Freedom: the future for Democratic Socialism,* 1987; *Economic Priorities for a Labour Government,* 1987; *The Maker's Mark* (novel), 1990; *In that Quiet Earth,* (novel) 1991; *Between Ourselves,* (essays) 1993; *Who Goes Home? Scenes from a Political Life,* 1995; *Fifty Years On,* 1997; *Buster's Diaries,* 1998; *Blood and Fire, the Story of William and Catherine Booth and their Salvation Army,* 1999. *Recreations:* Writing, watching football and cricket. *Clubs:* Garrick. Raised to the peerage as Baron Hattersley, of Sparkbrook in the County of West Midlands 1997. Rt Hon the Lord Hattersley, House of Lords, London, SW1A 0PW *Tel:* 020 7219 5353 *E-mail:* roy.hattersley@ukgateway.net.

HAYHOE, LORD — Conservative

HAYHOE (Life Baron), (Bernard) Barney John Hayhoe; cr. 1992. Born 8 August 1925. Son of late Frank and Catherine Hayhoe; educated State schools; Croydon and Borough Polytechnics (Higher National Certificate, mechanical engineering 1944). Married Ann Gascoigne, née Thornton 1962 (2 sons 1 daughter). *Career:* Tool room apprentice 1941–44; Technical and engineering appointments in Ministry of Supply and Ministry of Aviation 1944–63; Associate Director, Ariel Foundation 1963–65; Head of Research Section, Conservative Research Department 1965–70; Director: Portman Building Society 1987–96, Abbott Laboratories Inc. 1989–96. *House of Commons:* MP (Conservative) for: Heston and Isleworth 1970–74, Brentford and Isleworth 1974–92; PPS to Lord President of the Council and Leader of the House of Commons 1972–74; Parliamentary Under-Secretary of State for Defence (Army) 1979–81; Minister of State: Civil Service Department January-November 1981, Treasury 1981–85; Minister of State for Health, DHSS 1985–86. Opposition Spokesperson on Employment 1974–79. Member, Select Committee on the Public Service 1997–98. Member, Association of Conservative Peers Executive Committee 1995–98. Joint Secretary, Conservative Group for Europe 1970, Vice-Chairman 1973–76; Chairman, The Hansard Society 1991–94. Governor, Birkbeck College 1976–79; President, Help The Hospices 1992–98. Fellow, Birkbeck College 1993. Chairman, Guy's and St Thomas' NHS Trust 1993–95; Trustee: The Tablet Trust 1989–, British Brain and Spine Foundation 1992–2001, Liver Research Trust 1994–. PC 1985; Kt 1987. CEng; FIMechE. *Clubs:* Garrick. Raised to the peerage as Baron Hayhoe, of Isleworth in the London Borough of Hounslow 1992. Rt Hon the Lord Hayhoe, 20 Wool Road, London, SW20 0HW *Tel:* 020 8947 0037 *Fax:* 020 8944 0603.

HAYMAN, BARONESS — Labour

HAYMAN (Life Baroness), Helene Valerie Hayman; cr. 1996. Born 26 March 1949. Daughter of late Maurice and Maude Middleweek; educated Wolverhampton Girls' High School; Newnham College, Cambridge (BA law 1969) (President of Union 1969). Married Martin Heathcote Hayman 1974 (4 sons). Member, Bloomsbury Health Authority 1985–88; Vice-Chair: Bloomsbury Health Authority 1988–90, Bloomsbury and Islington Health Authority 1991–92. *Career:* With Shelter, National Campaign for the Homeless 1969–71; Social Services Department, London Borough of Camden 1971–74; Deputy Director, National Council for One Parent Families 1974; Member, Royal College of Gynaecologists Ethics Committee 1982–97; Member, University College London/University College Hospital Committee on Ethics of Clinical Investigation 1987–97, Vice Chair 1990–97; Member, Council, University College, London 1992–97; Chair, Whittington Hospital NHS Trust 1992–97. *House of Commons:* Contested Wolverhampton South West February 1974 general election; MP (Labour) for Welwyn and Hatfield, October 1974–79. *House of Lords:* Parliamentary Under-Secretary of State: Department of the Environment, Transport and the Regions (Minister for Roads) 1997–98, Department of Health 1998–99; Minister of State, Ministry of Agriculture, Fisheries and Food 1999–2001. Opposition Spokesperson for Health 1996–97. Chair, Cancer Research UK 2001–, Board of Trustees, Royal Botanical Gardens, Kew, Board Member, Roadsafe. Two honorary fellowships; Honorary doctorate. Member, Review Committee of Privy Counsellors of the Anti-terrorism, Crime and Security Act 2002–. PC 2001. *Special Interests:* Health, Education. Raised to the peerage as Baroness Hayman, of Dartmouth Park in the London Borough of Camden 1996. Rt Hon the Baroness Hayman, House of Lords, London, SW1A 0PW *Tel:* 020 7219 5083.

DodOnline
An Electronic Directory without rival . . .

Peers' biographies and photographs available with daily updates *via* the internet

For a *free* trial, call Yasmin Mirza, Aby Farsoun or Michael Mand on 020 7630 7643

HEALEY, LORD — Labour

HEALEY (Life Baron), Denis Winston Healey; cr. 1992. Born 30 August 1917. Son of late William Healey; educated Bradford Grammar School; Balliol College, Oxford (BA mods and greats 1940, MA). Married Edna May Edmunds 1945 (1 son 2 daughters). *Trades Union:* Member, GMB. Served North Africa and Italy in Second World War (mentioned in despatches, MBE), Major RE. *Career:* President, Birkbeck College 1989–99. *House of Commons:* Contested (Labour) Pudsey and Otley 1945 general election; MP (Labour) for: South East Leeds 1952–55, Leeds East 1955–92; Member, Shadow Cabinet 1959–64, 1970–74, 1979–87; Secretary of State for Defence 1964–70; Chancellor of the Exchequer 1974–79. Opposition Spokesperson for Foreign Affairs 1983–87. Member, Council for Global Energy Studies 1989–. Secretary, International Department, Labour Party 1945–52; Member, Labour Party National Exec Committee 1970–75; Deputy Leader, Labour Party 1980–83. President, National Trust Appeal Yorkshire Moors and Dales 1985–95; Member, Council for Global Energy Studies 1981–89; President, Birkbeck College 1993–99. Hon. Fellow, Balliol College, Oxford 1979; three honorary degrees; Hon. Fellow, Birkbeck College 1999. Chairman, IMF Interim Committee 1977–79. MBE (Mil) 1945; PC 1964; CH 1979; Grand Cross of Order of Merit (Germany) 1979. Freeman, City of Leeds 1991. *Publications:* Several political works and Fabian essays; *Healey's Eye,* 1980; *The Time of My Life,* (autobiography) 1989; *When Shrimps Learn to Whistle* (essays), 1990; *My Secret Planet* (anthology) 1992; *Denis Healey's Yorkshire Dales,* 1995; *Healey's World,* 2002. *Special Interests:* Foreign Affairs, Defence, Arts. *Recreations:* Music, painting photography, gardening. Raised to the peerage as Baron Healey, of Riddlesden in the County of West Yorkshire 1992. Rt Hon the Lord Healey, CH, MBE, House of Lords, London, SW1A 0PW *Tel:* 020 7219 3155.

HENLEY, LORD — Conservative

HENLEY (8th Baron, I), Oliver Michael Robert Eden; cr. 1799; 6th Baron Northington (UK) 1885. Born 22 November 1953. Son of 7th Baron. Sits as Baron Northington; educated Dragon School, Oxford; Clifton College, Bristol; Durham University (BA modern history 1975). Married Caroline Patricia Sharp 1984 (3 sons 1 daughter). Councillor, Cumbria County Council 1986–89. *Career:* Called to the Bar, Middle Temple 1977. *House of Lords:* First entered House of Lords 1977; Joint Parliamentary Under-Secretary of State: Department of Social Security 1989–93, Department of Employment 1993–94, Ministry of Defence 1994–95; Minister of State, Department of Education and Employment 1995–97; Deputy Speaker 1999–; Deputy Chairman of Committees 1999–2001; Elected hereditary peer 1999–. Government Whip February-July 1989; Opposition Chief Whip December 1998–2001. Opposition Spokesperson for: Defence 1997, Education and Employment 1997, Treasury 1997–98, Home Affairs 1997–98, Constitutional Affairs December 1998-June 1999, Cabinet Office June 1999–2000, Government Spokesperson for Health 1989. Member Select Committees on: Selection 1999–2001, House of Lords' Offices –2001, House of Lords' Offices Administration and Works Sub-committee –2001, Procedure –2001, Privileges –2002, European Union Sub-committee E (Law and Institutions) 2003–. Chair, Penrith and the Border Conservative Association 1987–89, President 1989–94. President, Cumbria Association of Local Councils 1981–89. *Clubs:* Brooks's, Pratt's. The Lord Henley, Scaleby Castle, Carlisle, Cumbria, CA6 4LN; House of Lords, London, SW1A 0PW *Tel:* 020 7219 3108 *E-mail:* henleyo@parliament.uk.

DodOnline
An Electronic Directory without rival ...

Peers' biographies and photographs available with daily updates *via* the internet

For a *free* trial, call Yasmin Mirza, Aby Farsoun or Michael Mand on 020 7630 7643

HEREFORD, LORD BISHOP OF   Non-affiliated

HEREFORD (103rd Bishop of), John Keith Oliver. Born 14 April 1935. Son of Walter and Ivy Oliver; educated Westminster School; Gonville and Caius College, Cambridge (MA theology 1959, MLitt 1963); Westcott House. Married Meriel Moore 1961 (2 sons 1 daughter). *Career:* Assistant Curate, Hilborough Group of Parishes, Norfolk 1964–68; Chaplain and Assistant Master, Eton College 1968–72; Team Rector: South Molton Group of Parishes, Devon 1973–82, Parish of Central Exeter 1982–85; Archdeacon of Sherborne 1985–90; Bishop of Hereford 1990–; Chairman, Advisory Board of Ministry 1993–; Took his seat in the House of Lords 1997. Spokesman for the Bench of Bishops on Environmental, Agricultural and Transport Issues. President, Herefordshire CPRE 1995–2001; Chairman, West Midlands Churches' Forum 1999–2001. Trustee, Eveson Charitable Trust; President, River Wye Preservation Trust. *Publications: The Church and Social Order*, 1968; Contributions to: *Theology, Crucible. Special Interests:* Transport, Environment. *Recreations:* Railways, music, architecture, motorcycling, walking. *Sportsclubs:* Worcester County Cricket Club. *Clubs:* United Oxford and Cambridge University. Rt Rev the Lord Bishop of Hereford, Bishop's House, The Palace, Hereford, HR4 9BN.

HESELTINE, LORD   Conservative

HESELTINE (Life Baron), Michael Ray Dibdin Heseltine; cr. 2001. Born 21 March 1933. Son of late Colonel R. D. Heseltine; educated Shrewsbury School; Pembroke College, Oxford (President of the Union). Married Anne Williams 1962 (1 son 2 daughters). *Career:* Chairman: Haymarket Press (Magazine Publishers) 1964–70, Haymarket Publishing Group 1999–. *House of Commons:* Contested Gower 1959 and Coventry North 1964 general elections; Member for Tavistock 1966–74, and for Henley February 1974–2001; Parliamentary Secretary, Ministry of Transport June-October 1970; Parliamentary Under-Secretary of State, Department of the Environment October 1970–72; Minister for Aerospace and Shipping, DTI 1972–74; Secretary of State for: the Environment 1979–83, Defence 1983–86; Contested Leadership of the Conservative Party November 1990; Secretary of State for the Environment 1990–92; President of the Board of Trade and Secretary of State for Trade and Industry 1992–95; Deputy Prime Minister and First Secretary of State 1995–97. Opposition Spokesperson for: Industry 1974–76, The Environment 1976–79. International Advisory Council for The Federation of Korean Industries. Chair, Conservative Mainstream Group; President, Conservative Group for Europe. Hon. Fellow, Pembroke College 1986; Hon. LLD, Liverpool University 1990; Two honorary university fellowships. Member, The Millennium Commission 1994–; Chairman, Anglo/Chinese Forum 1998–. CH 1997; PC 1979. *Publications: Where There's a Will* 1987; *The Challenge of Europe: Can Britain Win?* 1989; *Life in the Jungle – the autobiography* 2000. *Clubs:* Carlton. Raised to the peerage as Baron Heseltine, of Thenford in the County of Northamptonshire 2001. Rt Hon the Lord Heseltine, House of Lords, London, SW1A 0PW *Tel:* 020 7219 5353.

HIGGINS, LORD   Conservative

HIGGINS (Life Baron), Terence Langley Higgins; cr. 1997. Born 18 January 1928. Son of late Reginald and Rose Higgins; educated Alleyn's School, Dulwich; Gonville and Caius College, Cambridge (MA) (President of Union 1958); Yale University, USA. Married Rosalyn Cohen 1961 (later QC and DBE) (1 son 1 daughter). Served in the RAF 1946–48. DL, West Sussex 1988. *Career:* New Zealand Shipping Co., in UK and New Zealand 1948–55; British Olympic Team 1948, 1952; Commonwealth Games Team 1950; Economic Specialist, Unilever Ltd 1958–64; Economic Consultant, Lex Services Group plc 1975–; Director: Warne Wright Group 1976–84, Lex Service Group 1980–92; First Choice Holidays plc (formerly Owners Abroad plc) 1991–97; Chairman and Trustee, Lex Services Pension Fund 1994–. *House of Commons:* MP (Conservative) for Worthing 1964–97; Minister of State, Treasury 1970–72; Financial Secretary, Treasury 1972–74. Opposition Frontbench Spokesperson for Treasury and Economic Affairs 1967–70;

Opposition Spokesperson for: Treasury and Economic Affairs 1974, Trade 1974–76. Opposition Spokesperson for: Social Security/Work and Pensions 1997–, the Treasury 1997–2001. Former Treasurer, Cambridge University Conservative Association. Governor: Dulwich College 1980–95, National Institute Economic Social Research 1988–, Alleyn's School, Dulwich 1995–99. Trustee, Industry and Parliament Trust 1987–92. Council, Royal Institute of International Affairs 1980–85; Council, Institute of Advanced Motorists 1980–97, Fellow 1997; Council, National Institute for Economic and Social Research 1980–. PC 1979; KBE 1993. Freeman, Worthing 1997. *Special Interests:* Finance, Social Security, Transport, Sport. *Recreations:* Golf. *Sportsclubs:* Royal Blackheath Golf, Koninklijke Haagsche Golf. *Clubs:* Hawk's (Cambridge), Reform, Yale Club of London. Raised to the peerage as Baron Higgins, of Worthing in the County of West Sussex 1997. Rt Hon the Lord Higgins, KBE, DL, House of Lords, London, SW1A 0PW *Tel:* 020 7219 4164 *E-mail:* higginst@parliament.uk.

HILL-NORTON, LORD   Crossbencher

HILL-NORTON (Life Baron), Peter John Hill-Norton; cr. 1979. Born 8 February 1915. Son of late Captain Martin John Norton and late Mrs M. B. Gooch; educated Royal Naval Colleges, Dartmouth and Greenwich; Technical Naval School (Master Mariner). Married Margaret Eileen Linstow 1936 (1 son 1 daughter). Served Second World War 1939–45, Arctic convoys and NW approaches; Commander 1948; Captain 1952; Naval Attaché, Argentina, Uruguay and Paraguay 1953–55; Commanded: HMS Decoy 1956–57, HMS Ark Royal 1959–61; Second Sea Lord and Chief of Naval Personnel January–August 1967; Vice-Chief of Naval Staff 1967–68; Commander-in-Chief, Far East 1969–70; First Sea Lord 1970–71; Chief of Defence Staff 1971–73; Chairman, NATO Military Committee 1974–77. Friends of Osborne House; President Sea Cadet Association. CB 1964; KCB 1967; GCB (Mil) 1970. Freeman, City of London 1973. Liveryman, Worshipful Company of Shipwrights. *Publications: No Soft Options,* 1978; *Sea Power,* 1982. *Special Interests:* Defence, UFOs. *Recreations:* Gardening. *Clubs:* Army and Navy, Royal Navy of 1765. Raised to the peerage as Baron Hill-Norton, of South Nutfield in the County of Surrey 1979. Admiral of the Fleet the Lord Hill-Norton, GCB, Cass Cottage, Hyde, Fordingbridge, Hampshire, SP6 2QH.

HILTON OF EGGARDON, BARONESS   Labour

HILTON OF EGGARDON (Life Baroness), Jennifer Hilton; cr. 1991. Born 12 January 1936. Daughter of late John Robert Hilton, CMG, and of Margaret Frances Hilton; educated Bedales School, Hampshire; Manchester University (BA psychology 1970, MA 1971); London University (Diplomas in criminology 1973, history of art 1980). *Career:* Joined Metropolitan Police as Constable 1956; Manchester University (Police Scholarship) 1967–71; National Police Staff College, directing staff; Metropolitan Police Management Services 1975–76; Superintendent/Chief Superintendent 1977–83; Senior Command Course, National Staff College 1979; New Scotland Yard 1983–87; North West London, responsible for Complaints/Discipline, Personnel, Community Relations 1987–88; Peel Centre, Hendon, responsible for all Metropolitan Police Training 1988–90; Retired 1990; Member of: ACPOs Executive Committee, Equal Opportunities, Extended Interview Panel, Various Home Office Committees. *House of Lords:* Trustee, House of Lords Collection Trust 2000–. Opposition Whip 1991–95. Opposition Spokesperson for: the Environment 1991–97, Home Affairs 1994–97. Member, European Union Sub-committee D (Environment) 1991–97, Chair 1995–97; Member Select Committees on: Science and Technology 1992–95, European Union 1997–99; Chair: European Union Sub-Committee C (Environment, Public Health and Consumer Protection) 1997–99, Advisory Panel on Works of Art 1998–, Member: European Union Sub-committee C (Common Foreign and Security Policy) 2000–, Chair 2000–01, House of Lords' Offices –2002, House of Lords' Offices Administration and Works Sub-committee –2002. Lords Labour Delegate to OSCE Parliamentary Assembly. QPM 1989. *Publications: The Gentle Arm of the Law,* 1967; Co-author *Individual Development and Social Experience,* 1974. *Special Interests:* Environment, Race Relations, Criminal Justice. *Recreations:* Gardening, travel, art. Raised to the peerage as Baroness Hilton of Eggardon, of Eggardon in the County of Dorset 1991. The Baroness Hilton of Eggardon, QPM, House of Lords, London, SW1A 0PW *Tel:* 020 7219 3182.

HOBHOUSE OF WOODBOROUGH, LORD — Crossbencher

HOBHOUSE OF WOODBOROUGH (Life Baron), John Stewart Hobhouse; cr. 1998. Born 31 January 1932; educated Christ Church, Oxford (BCL 1955, MA 1958). Married Susannah Roskill 1959 (2 sons 1 daughter). *Career:* Called to the Bar, Inner Temple 1955; QC 1973; Judge of the High Court, Queen's Bench Division 1982–93; Lord Justice of Appeal 1993–98; Lord of Appeal in Ordinary 1998–. Member Joint Select Committee on Consolidation of Bills 1999–, Chair 2002–; Member House of Lords' Offices Library and Computers Sub-committee 2001–03. Kt 1982; PC 1993. Raised to the peerage as Baron Hobhouse of Woodborough, of Woodborough in the County of Wiltshire 1998. Rt Hon the Lord Hobhouse of Woodborough, House of Lords, London, SW1A 0PW *Tel:* 020 7219 3137.

HODGSON OF ASTLEY ABBOTTS, LORD — Conservative

HODGSON OF ASTLEY ABBOTTS (Life Baron), Robin Granville Hodgson; cr. 2000. Born 25 April 1942. Son of late Henry Edward Hodgson, and of Natalie Beatrice Hodgson; educated Shrewsbury School; Oxford University (BA modern history 1964); Wharton School of Finance, Pennsylvania University (MBA 1969). Married Fiona Ferelith Allom 1982 (3 sons 1 daughter and 1 twin son deceased). *Career:* Investment Banker, New York and Montreal 1964–67; Industry in Birmingham 1969–72; Director: Johnson Brothers & Co Ltd Walsall 1970–, Granville Baird Group 1972– (Group Chief Executive 1979–95, Chairman 1995–2002), Domnick Hunter plc 1989–2002, Staffordshire Building Society 1995–, Community Hospitals plc 1995–2001, Securities and Futures Authority 1993–2001, Wolverhampton and Dudley Breweries Plc. 2002–; Chair: Rostrum Fund Managers 2000–, Market Touch plc 2001–02, Nova Capital Management 2002–, Carbo plc 2002–. *House of Commons:* Contested (Conservative) Walsall North, February and October 1974 general elections; MP for Walsall North November 1976–79. Opposition Spokesperson for: Home Office 2002–, Trade and Industry 2002–. National Union of Conservative Associations: Member: Executive Committee 1988–98, General Purpose Committee 1990–98, Vice-President 1995–96, Chairman 1996–98; Chairman, National Conservative Convention 1998–2000; Deputy Chairman, Conservative Party 1998–2000. Trustee: Shrewsbury School, St Peter's College, Oxford; Chair of Trustees, Conservative and Unionist Agents Superannuation Fund. Member: Council for the Securities Industry 1980–85, Securities and Investment Board 1985–89, West Midlands Industrial Development Board 1989–97. CBE 1992. Liveryman, Goldsmith's Company 1983. *Publications: Britain's Home Defence Gamble*, 1978. *Recreations:* Squash, fishing, theatre. Raised to the peerage as Baron Hodgson of Astley Abbotts, of Nash in the County of Shropshire 2000. The Lord Hodgson of Astley Abbotts, CBE, 15 Scarsdale Villas, London, W8 6PT *Tel:* 020 7937 2964; Nash Court, Ludlow, Shropshire, SY8 3DG *Tel:* 01584 811677 *E-mail:* hodgsonr@parliament.uk.

HOFFMANN, LORD — Crossbencher

HOFFMANN (Life Baron), Leonard Hubert Hoffmann; cr. 1995. Born 8 May 1934; educated South African College School, Cape Town; University of Cape Town (BA); The Queen's College, Oxford (Rhodes Scholar, MA, BCL, Vinerian Law Scholar). Married Gillian Lorna Sterner 1957 (2 daughters). *Career:* Advocate of Supreme Court of South Africa 1958–60; Stowell Civil Law Fellow, University College, Oxford 1961–73; Called to the Bar, Gray's Inn 1964; Bencher 1984; Member, Royal Commission on Gambling 1976–78; QC 1977; Judge of the Courts of Appeal of Jersey and Guernsey 1980–85; Member, Council of Legal Education 1983–92, Chairman 1989–92; Judge of the High Court of Justice, Chancery Division 1985–92; Lord Justice of Appeal 1992–95; Lord of Appeal in Ordinary 1995–. Member, Select Committee on European Committees; Chairman, Select Committee on European Communities Sub-Committee E (Law and Institutions) 1997–. President, British-German Jurists Association 1991–; Director, English National Opera 1985–90, 1991–94. Hon. Fellow, The Queen's College, Oxford 1992; Hon. DCL: City University 1992, University of the West of England 1995. Kt 1985; PC 1992. *Publications: The South African Law of Evidence*, 1963. Raised to the peerage as Baron Hoffmann, of Chedworth in the County of Gloucestershire 1995. Rt Hon the Lord Hoffmann, House of Lords, London, SW1A 0PW; Surrey Lodge, 23 Keats Grove, London, NW3 2RS.

HOGG, BARONESS   Conservative

HOGG (Life Baroness), Sarah Elizabeth Mary Hogg; cr. 1995. Born 14 May 1946. Daughter of late Rt Hon Baron Boyd-Carpenter; educated St Mary's Convent, Ascot; Lady Margaret Hall, Oxford (BA philosophy, politics and economics 1967). Married Douglas Martin Hogg, QC, MP (*qv*) 1968 (1 son 1 daughter). *Career:* On staff of *The Economist* 1967–81, Literary Editor 1970–77, Economics Editor 1977–81; Economics Editor, *The Sunday Times* 1981–82; Presenter, Channel 4 News 1982–83; Economics Editor and Deputy Executive Editor, Finance and Industry, *The Times* 1984–86; Assistant Editor and Business and City Editor, *The Independent* 1986–89; Economics Editor, *The Daily Telegraph* and *The Sunday Telegraph* 1989–90; Head, Prime Minister's Policy Unit, with rank of Second Permanent Secretary 1990–95; Director: London Broadcasting Company 1982–90, Royal National Theatre 1988–91; London Economics 1995–96, Chairman 1997–99; Foreign and Colonial Smaller Companies Trust 1995–2002, Chair 1997–2002; NPI 1996–99; International Advisory Board, National Westminster Bank 1995–98; Advisory Board, Bankinter 1995–98; Director: The Energy Group 1996–98, GKN 1996–; Director, 3i 1997–, Deputy Chair 2000–01, chair 2002–; Director: Scottish Eastern Investment Trust 1998–99, Martin Currie Portfolio Trust 1999–2002, P&O 1999–2000; Chairman, Frontier Economics 1999–; Director, P&O Princess Cruises 2000–03; Governor, BBC 2000–; Carnival Corporation and Carnival plc 2003–. Member Select Committee on: Science and Technology 1996–99, Monetary Policy of the Bank of England/Economic Affairs 2000–. Fellow, Eton College 1996–; Governor, Centre for Economic Policy Research 1985–92; Council Member: Royal Economic Society 1996–, Institute for Fiscal Studies 1996–, Hansard Society for Parliamentary Government 1996–2000, Lincolnshire Foundation 1996–98; Lincoln University 2001–. Wincott Foundation Financial Journalist of the Year 1985. Four honorary degrees and doctorates. Trustee, St Mary's School, Ascot. *Publications:* Co-author *Too Close to Call*, 1995. Raised to the peerage as Baroness Hogg, of Kettlethorpe in the County of Lincolnshire 1995. The Baroness Hogg, House of Lords, London, SW1A 0PW *Tel:* 020 7219 5417.

HOGG OF CUMBERNAULD, LORD   Labour

HOGG OF CUMBERNAULD (Life Baron), Norman Hogg; cr. 1997. Born 12 March 1938. Son of late Norman Hogg, CBE, DL, LLD, JP and late Mary Hogg; educated Ruthrieston Secondary School, Aberdeen. Married Elizabeth McCall, née Christie 1964. *Trades Union:* Member: NALGO 1953–67, TGWU 1967–. Chairman, Bus Appeals Body 2000–. *Career:* Local government officer, Aberdeen Corporation 1953–67; District officer, Scottish District, National and Local Government Officers Association 1967–79. *House of Commons:* MP (Labour) for Dunbartonshire East 1979–83 and for Cumbernauld and Kilsyth 1983–97. Scottish Labour Whip 1982–83; Opposition Deputy Chief Whip 1983–87. Opposition Spokesperson for Scottish Affairs 1987–88. Chair, Scottish Parliamentary Labour Group 1981–82. *House of Lords:* Deputy Speaker 2002–; Deputy Chair of Committees 2002–. Member, Select Committee on Delegated Powers and Regulatory Reform 1999–2002. Member, Fabian Society 1984–. Member, Transport Users Consultative Committee for Scotland 1977–79; Hon. President, YMCA Scotland 1998–; Patron, Scottish Centre for Children with Motor Impairments 1998–. Hon LLD, Aberdeen University 1999. Church of Scotland Trust 2001–. Chairman, Scottish Peers Association 2002–. Appointed Lord High Commissioner to the 1998 and 1999 General Assembly of the Church of Scotland. *Special Interests:* Public Transport, Local Government, Constitutional Affairs. *Clubs:* Royal Overseas League. Raised to the peerage as Baron Hogg of Cumbernauld, of Cumbernauld in North Lanarkshire 1997. The Lord Hogg of Cumbernauld, House of Lords, London, SW1A 0PW *Tel:* 020 7219 4214; 61 Argyll Place, Aberdeen, AB25 2HU *Tel:* 01224 635862 *Fax:* 01224 648314 *E-mail:* hoggn@parliament.uk.

Visit the Vacher Dod Website . . .
www.DodOnline.co.uk

HOLLICK, LORD   Labour

HOLLICK (Life Baron), Clive Richard Hollick; cr. 1991. Born 20 May 1945. Son of late Leslie Hollick, and of Olive Hollick; educated Taunton's School, Southampton; Nottingham University (BA sociology 1966). Married Susan Cross 1977 (3 daughters). University Air Squadron. *Career:* Joined Hambros Bank 1967, Director 1973–96; Managing Director, MAI plc 1974–96; Director, Mills and Allen Ltd. 1975–89; Chairman, Shepperton Studios Ltd. 1976–84; Member, National Bus Company 1984–91; Director: Logica plc 1987–91, Avenir Havas Media SA (France) 1988–92, National Opinion Polls Ltd. 1989–97, Satellite Information Services 1990–94; Chairman, Meridian Broadcasting 1991–96; Director, British Aerospace 1992–97; Member, Financial Law Panel 1993–97; Director, Anglia Television 1994–97; Member, Commission on Public Policy and British Business 1995–97; Director, United Broadcasting and Entertainment Ltd 1995–; Chief Executive, United Business Media plc 1996–; Special Adviser to Margaret Beckett as President of the Board of Trade 1997–98; Director: Express Newspapers plc 1998–2000, TRW Inc 2000–02, DIAGEO plc 2001–, Honeywell International Inc 2003–. Member, Science and Technology Sub-Committee I, Information Superhighway 1995–96. Governor, London School of Economics and Political Science 1997–. Hon. LLD, Nottingham University 1993. Founding Trustee, Institute for Public Policy Research 1988. Chair, South Bank Board 2002–. *Special Interests:* Business, Economic Policy, Constitutional Affairs, Transport. *Recreations:* Reading, countryside, cinema, theatre, tennis. Raised to the peerage as Baron Hollick, of Notting Hill in the Royal Borough of Kensington and Chelsea 1991. The Lord Hollick, United Business Media plc, Ludgate House, 245 Blackfriars Road, London, SE1 9UY *Tel:* 020 7921 5000 *Fax:* 020 7921 5043.

HOLLIS OF HEIGHAM, BARONESS   Labour

HOLLIS OF HEIGHAM (Life Baroness), Patricia Lesley Hollis; cr. 1990. Born 24 May 1941; educated Plympton Grammar School; Cambridge University (BA history 1962, MA); University of California and Columbia University, New York (Harkness Fellow 1962–64); Nuffield College, Oxford (MA, DPhil). Married Professor James Martin Hollis FBA 1965 (died 1998) (2 sons). *Trades Union:* Member, AUT. Councillor Norwich City Council 1968–91; Member: BBC Regional Advisory Council 1973–79, East Anglian Planning Council 1975–79, Regional Health Authority 1979–83; Councillor, Norfolk County Council 1981–85; Leader Norwich City Council 1983–88; Member The Press Council 1988–90, Commissioner English Heritage 1988–91; Member DL, Norfolk 1994–. *Career:* University of East Anglia: Lecturer 1967, Senior lecturer 1979, Reader 1985, Dean 1988–90; Founder-director, Radio Broadland 1983–97. *House of Lords:* Parliamentary Under-Secretary of State 1997–: Department of Social Security 1997–2001, (Minister for Children and the Family), Department for Work and Pensions 2001–. Opposition Whip 1990–95. Opposition Spokesperson for Environment and Social Security 1990–97; Government Spokesperson for: Social Security 1997–2001, Work and Pensions 2001–. Patron: Chatterbox, Norwich, Norfolk Millennium Carers, Norfolk Rural Art. Three honorary doctorates; Honorary fellow, Girton College, Cambridge. Patron, St Martin's Housing Trust. Contested (Labour) Great Yarmouth February and October 1974, 1979 general elections; National Commissioner, English Heritage 1988–91; Former Vice-President: Association of District Councils, Association of Metropolitan Authorities, Environmental Health Officers, National Federation of Housing Associations. DL 1994, PC 1999. Fellow, Royal Historical Society. *Publications:* *The Pauper Press*, 1970; *Class and Class Conflict 1815–50*, 1973; *Pressure from Without*, 1974, *Women in Public, 1850–1900*, 1979; *Robert Lowry, Radical and Chartist*, 1979; *Ladies Elect: women in English Local Government 1865–1914*, 1987; *Jennie Lee: a Life*, 1997. *Special Interests:* Local Government, Education, Media, Heritage, Health. *Recreations:* Boating, singing, domesticity. Raised to the peerage as Baroness Hollis of Heigham, of Heigham in the City of Norwich 1990. Rt Hon the Baroness Hollis of Heigham, DL, 30 Park Lane, Norwich, Norfolk, NR2 3EE *Tel:* 01603 621990; House of Lords, London, SW1A 0PW *Tel:* 020 7219 6784 *E-mail:* psl@dwp.gsi.gov.uk.

Visit the Vacher Dod Website . . . **www.DodOnline.co.uk**

HOLME OF CHELTENHAM, LORD   Liberal Democrat

HOLME OF CHELTENHAM (Life Baron), Richard Gordon Holme; cr. 1990. Born 27 May 1936. Son of late Jack Richard Holme; educated Royal Masonic School, Bushey, Hertfordshire; St. John's College, Oxford (MA law 1956). Married Kay Mary Powell 1958 (2 sons 2 daughters). Commissioned, 10th Gurkha Rifles 1954. *Career:* Marketing trainee and manager, Unilever 1959–63; Marketing director, Penguin Books Ltd. 1963–65; Chairman, BPC Publishing 1967–69; Executive Vice-President, CRM Inc 1970–74; Chairman: Threadneedle Publishing Group 1988–98, Hollis Directories 1989–98, DPR Publishing Ltd 1993–98, Brassey's Ltd 1995–98; Director, RTZ Corporation plc (now RioTinto plc) 1995–98; CRA Ltd (now RioTinto Ltd) 1996–98; Deputy Chairman, Independent Television Commission 1999; Chairman, Broadcasting Standards Commission 1999–2000. Chancellor, University of Greenwich 1998–. Liberal Democrat Spokesperson for Northern Ireland 1991–99. Constitution Committee. President, Liberal Party 1980–81; Vice-Chairman, Policy Committee, Liberal Democrat Party 1989–. Chairman, English College Foundation in Prague 1991–; Board Member, Campaign for Oxford 1990–; Council Member, Cheltenham Ladies College 1994–, Chairman, College Council 1998–2000. Hon. Fellow, St John's College, Oxford. Contested (Liberal): East Grinstead 1964 general election and 1965 by-election, Braintree 1974, Cheltenham 1983, 1987 general elections; Director, National Committee for Electoral Reform 1975–85; Member of Council, The Hansard Society 1979–, Vice-Chair 1990–2000, Chair 2001–; Chair: Constitutional Reform Centre 1985–92, ICC Environment Commission 1999–; Advisory Board, British American Project 1999–; Member, Review Committee of Privy Counsellors of the Anti-terrorism, Crime and Security Act 2002–. CBE 1983; PC 2000. *Special Interests:* Constitutional Reform, Industry, Environment, Foreign Affairs, Broadcasting. *Recreations:* Walking, opera, collecting books. *Sportsclubs:* RAC. *Clubs:* Brooks's, Reform. Raised to the peerage as Baron Holme of Cheltenham, of Cheltenham in the County of Gloucestershire 1990. Rt Hon the Lord Holme of Cheltenham, CBE, House of Lords, London, SW1A 0PW *Tel:* 020 7219 5434.

HOME, EARL OF   Conservative

HOME (15th Earl of, S), David Alexander Cospatrick Douglas-Home; cr. 1604; Lord Dunglass; 20th Lord Home (S) 1473; 5th Baron Douglas (UK) 1875. Born 20 November 1943. Son of 14th Earl, KT, PC, DL, who disclaimed the earldom 1963, and who was subsequently made a life peer as Baron Home of the Hirsel 1974; educated Eton College; Christ Church, Oxford (BA philosophy, politics and economics 1966). Married Jane Margaret Williams-Wynne 1972 (1 son 2 daughters). *Career:* Director, Douglas and Angus Estates 1966–, Chairman 1995–; Director: Morgan Grenfell & Co. Ltd. 1974–99, Arab-British Chamber of Commerce 1975–84; Director, Morgan Grenfell (Asia) Ltd. 1978–82, Deputy Chair 1979–82; Director: Arab Bank Investment Co. 1979–87, Agricultural Mortgage Corporation plc 1979–93; Director, Tandem Group plc (formerly EFG plc) 1981–96, Chair 1993–96; Chair: Morgan Grenfell Export Services 1984–98, Morgan Grenfell (Scotland) 1986–98, Committee for Middle East Trade 1986–92, Morgan Grenfell International Ltd 1987–98; Director: Deutsche Morgan Grenfell Hong Kong Ltd (name changed from Morgan Grenfell Asia (Hong Kong) Ltd May 1996) 1989–99, Deutsche Morgan Grenfell Asia Holdings Pte Ltd (name changed from Morgan Grenfell Asia Holdings Pte Ltd May 1996) 1989–99, K & N Kenanga Holdings Bhd 1993–99; Non-Executive Director, Grosvenor Estate Holdings 1993–; Director: Kenanga DMG Futures Sdn Bhd 1995–99 (name changed to Kenanga Deutsche Futures Sdn Bhd September 1998–), Deutsche Morgan Grenfell Group plc 1996–99; Chair: Coutts and Company 1999–, Coutts Switzerland Ltd 2000–, Man Ltd 2000–. *House of Lords:* First entered House of Lords 1995; Elected hereditary peer 1999–. Opposition Frontbench Spokesperson for: Trade 1997–98, the Treasury 1997–98. Governor: Ditchley Foundation 1977–, Commonwealth Institute 1988–98; Council Member: Royal Agricultural Society of England 1990–, Glenalmond College 1995–; President, British Malaysian Society 2001–. Trustee: Grosvenor Estate 1993–, The Royal Agricultural Society of England 1999–. Member, Export Guarantee Advisory Council, ECGD 1988–93. CBE 1991; CVO 1997. Fellow, Chartered Institute of Bankers 1999–. *Special Interests:* Foreign Affairs, Scottish Affairs, Industry, Agriculture. *Recreations:* Outdoor sports. *Clubs:* Turf, Caledonian Westminster Business. The Earl of Home, CVO, CBE, 99 Dovehouse Street, London, SW3 6JZ *Tel:* 020 7352 9060 *Fax:* 020 7753 1066; The Hirsel, Coldstream, Berwickshire, TD12 4LP *Tel:* 01890 882345.

HOOPER, BARONESS   Conservative

HOOPER (Life Baroness), Gloria Dorothy Hooper; cr. 1985. Born 25 May 1939. Daughter of late Frederick Hooper and late Frances Hooper, née Maloney; educated La Sainte Union Convent; Royal Ballet School; Southampton University (BA law 1960); Universidad Central, Ecuador (Rotary Foundation Fellow). Single. *Career:* Assistant to chief registrar, John Lewis Partnership 1960–61; Editor, Current Law, Sweet & Maxwell, Law Publishers 1961–62; Information officer, Winchester City Council 1962–67; Assistant solicitor, Taylor and Humbert 1967–72; Legal adviser, Slater Walker France S.A. 1972–73; Partner, Taylor and Humbert (Solicitors), Now Taylor, Joynson Garrett 1974–84; Member, European Parliament (Conservative) for Liverpool 1979–84: Vice-chair, Committee on Environment, Public Health and Consumer Protection, Deputy chief whip, European Democratic Group. *House of Commons:* Member European Parliament (Conservative) for Liverpool 1979–84; Vice-chair, Committee on Environment, Public Health and Consumer Protection; Deputy chief whip, European Democratic Group. *House of Lords:* Parliamentary Under-Secretary of State, Department of: Education and Science 1987–88, Energy 1988–89, Health 1989–92; Deputy Speaker 1993–; Deputy Chairman of Committees 1993–; PPS to William Hague as Leader of the Opposition 1999–2001. Government Whip 1985–87. Member, Association of Conservative Peers. Member: IPU, CPA. Member, The Law Society; President: British Educational Equipment and Supplies Association, Canning House (Hispanic and Luso Brazilian Council), Waste Watch, European Foundation For Heritage Skills. Trustee/Governor: Royal Academy of Dance, Centre for Global Energy Studies, National Museums and Galleries of Merseyside Development Trust; Fellow and Trustee, Industry and Parliament Trust. CMG (Companion of Order of St Michael and St George); Order of Francisco de Miranda (Venezuela); Order of Boyaca Gran Cruz (Colombia). Fellow: Royal Geographical Society, RSA. *Special Interests:* European Union, Latin America, Inner Cities. *Recreations:* Theatre, travel. *Clubs:* In and Out Club. Raised to the peerage as Baroness Hooper, of Liverpool and St James's in the City of Westminster 1985. The Baroness Hooper, House of Lords, London, SW1A 0PW *Tel:* 020 7219 5489.

HOOSON, LORD   Liberal Democrat

HOOSON (Life Baron), (Hugh) Emlyn Hooson; cr. 1979. Born 26 March 1925. Son of late Hugh Hooson, farmer and Elsie Hooson; educated Denbigh Grammar School; University College of Wales, Aberystwyth (LLB 1948); Gray's Inn. Married Shirley Margaret Wynne Hamer 1950 (2 daughters). Royal Navy 1943–46. *Career:* Called to the Bar, Gray's Inn 1949; Deputy Chair: Flintshire Quarter Sessions 1960–72, Merioneth Quarter Sessions 1960–67, Chair 1967–72; Bencher, Gray's Inn 1968, Vice Treasurer 1985, Treasurer 1986; Recorder of Merthyr Tydfil 1971; Recorder of Swansea July 1971; Leader of Wales and Chester Circuit 1971–74; Recorder of Crown Courts 1972–91; Non-executive Director, Laura Ashley plc 1985–95, Chair: Severn River Crossing plc 1991–2000 Laura Ashley plc 1995–96. *House of Commons:* MP (Liberal) for Montgomeryshire 1962–79. Spokesperson for Defence, Foreign Affairs, Home Affairs, Legal Affairs, Agriculture and Welsh Affairs 1962–79. British Delegate to the Atlantic Assembly (formerly NATO Parliamentarians) 1962–79; Member, Political Committee of North Atlantic Assembly 1962–79, Vice-Chairman 1975–79; Rapporteur, Working Party on East-West Relations 1974–79. Liberal Democrat Spokesperson for: Legal Affairs, Agriculture and European Affairs 1979–96, Welsh Affairs 1996–2001. European and International Affairs; Vice-chair, Political Committee, North Atlantic Assembly 1975–79. Welsh Liberal Party: Leader 1966–79, President 1983–86. President: Royal National Eisteddfod of Wales, Newtown 1965, Llangollen International Eisteddfod 1987–93, Wales International 1995–98, Royal National Eisteddfod of Wales, Denbigh 2001–. Hon. Professorial Fellow, University of Wales, Aberystwyth 1971–; Hon. Doctor of Law, University of Wales 2003. Chair, Trustees of Laura Ashley Foundation 1986–97. QC 1960. *Special Interests:* Law, Constitutional Affairs, Agriculture, Defence, Wales, Europe, International Affairs. *Recreations:* Music, theatre, reading, walking. Raised to the peerage as Baron Hooson, of Montgomery in the County of Powys and Colomendy in the County of Clwyd 1979. The Lord Hooson, QC, Summerfield Park, Llanidloes, Powys *Tel:* 01686 412298; House of Lords, London, SW1A 0PW *Tel:* 020 7219 5226.

HOPE OF CRAIGHEAD, LORD Crossbencher

HOPE OF CRAIGHEAD (Life Baron), James Arthur David Hope; cr. 1995. Born 27 June 1938. Son of late Arthur Henry Cecil Hope, OBE, WS; educated Edinburgh Academy; Rugby School; St John's College, Cambridge (Scholarship 1956, BA 1962, MA 1978); Edinburgh University (LLB 1965). Married Katharine Mary Kerr 1966 (twin sons 1 daughter). National service, Seaforth Highlanders 1957–59. *Career:* Admitted Faculty of Advocates 1965; Standing Junior Counsel in Scotland to Board of Inland Revenue 1974–78; Advocate-Depute 1978–82; QC (Scotland) 1978; Legal Chairman, Pensions Appeal Tribunal 1985–86; Chairman, Medical Appeal Tribunals 1985–86; Dean, Faculty of Advocates 1986–89; Lord Justice General of Scotland and Lord President of the Court of Session 1989–96; Lord of Appeal in Ordinary 1996–. Chancellor, Strathclyde University 1998–. Member, Select Committee on European Communities 1998–2001; Chairman, Sub-Committee E (Law and Institutions) 1998–2001. President, The Stair Society 1993–; Council Member, Commonwealth Magistrates' and Judges' Association 1998–; President, International Criminal Law Association 2000–. Hon. LLD: Aberdeen 1991, Strathclyde 1993, Edinburgh 1995; Hon. Fellow, St John's College, Cambridge 1995; Fellow, Strathclyde University 2000; Fellow, Royal Society of Edinburgh 2003. Board of Trustees, National Library of Scotland 1989–1996; Member, University of Strathclyde Charitable Foundation 1998–2001. Hon. Bencher: Gray's Inn 1989, Inn of Court of Northern Ireland 1995. PC 1989. *Publications:* Co-editor *Gloag and Henderson's Introduction to the Law of Scotland*, 6th–9th eds 1956–1987; *Armour on Valuation for Rating*, 4th–5th eds 1871 and 1985; Co-author *The Rent (Scotland) Act, 1984*, 1986; Contributor *Stair Memorial Encyclopaedia of Scots Law*; *Gloag and Henderson's The Law of Scotland*, 11th ed 2002. *Recreations:* Walking, ornithology, music. *Clubs:* New (Edinburgh). Raised to the peerage as Baron Hope of Craighead, of Bamff in the District of Perth and Kinross 1995. Rt Hon the Lord Hope of Craighead, 34 India Street, Edinburgh, EH3 6HB *Tel:* 0131–225 8245 *Fax:* 0131–225 8245; Law Lords Corridor, House of Lords, London, SW1A 0PW *Tel:* 020 7219 3202 *Fax:* 020 7219 6156 *E-mail:* hopejad@parliament.uk (London); craighead@dial.pipex.com (home).

HOWARTH OF BRECKLAND, BARONESS Crossbencher

HOWARTH OF BRECKLAND (Life Baroness), Valerie Georgina Howarth OBE; cr 2001; educated Abbeydale Girls School; Leicester University. *Career:* Former director of social services London Borough of Brent; Founder King's Cross Homeless Project and London Homeless Forum; Chief executive Childline charity; Vice-chair John Grooms disability charity 1995–; Member Food Standards Agency 2000–; Member National Care Standards Commission 2001–. OBE 1999. Raised to the peerage as Baroness Howarth of Breckland, of Parson Cross in the County of South Yorkshire 2001. The Baroness Howarth of Breckland, OBE, House of Lords, London, SW1A 0AA *Tel:* 020 7219 8744.

HOWE, EARL Conservative

HOWE (7th Earl, UK), Frederick Richard Penn Curzon; cr. 1821; 8th Viscount Curzon (UK) 1802; 9th Baron Howe (GB) 1788; 8th Baron Curzon (GB) 1794. Born 29 January 1951. Son of late Commander Chambré George William Penn Curzon, RN, grandson of 3rd Earl, GCVO, CB, and of late Mrs Jane Victoria Curzon (née Fergusson); educated Rugby School; Christ Church, Oxford (MA literae humaniores 1973). Married Elizabeth Helen Stuart 1983 (1 son 3 daughters). *Trades Union:* Member, NFU. *Career:* Arable and dairy farmer; Director: Adam & Company plc 1987–90, Provident Life Association Ltd 1988–91; Barclays Bank plc 1973–87, Senior manager 1984–87; Chair, LAPADA 1999–; Director, Andry Montgomery Ltd 2000–. *House of Lords:* First entered House of Lords 1984; Parliamentary Secretary, Ministry of Agriculture, Fisheries and Food 1992–95; Parliamentary Under-Secretary of State, Ministry of Defence 1995–97; Elected hereditary peer 1999–. Government Whip 1991–92. Opposition Spokesperson for: Defence May-October 1997, Health October 1997–. Governor, King William IV Naval Foundation 1984–; Vice-President, National Society for Epilepsy 1984–86, President 1986–; President; Chilterns Branch RNLI 1985–, South Bucks Association for the Disabled 1984–; Member, RNLI Council 1997–; Patron, Demand 1999–; Patron, The Chiltern Society 2001–. Governor, The Trident Trust 1985–; Trustee: Milton's Cottage 1986, Sir William Borlase's Grammar School, Marlow 1998–, Restoration of Appearance and Function Trust (RAFT) 1999–. President, CPRE (Penn Country Branch) 1986–92. Associate, Chartered Institute of Bankers 1976–. *Special Interests:* Agriculture, Penal Affairs and Policy, Finance. *Recreations:* Gardening, music, writing. The Earl Howe, House of Lords, London, SW1A 0PW *Tel:* 020 7219 5427 *E-mail:* howef@parliament.uk.

HOWE OF ABERAVON, LORD   Conservative

HOWE OF ABERAVON (Life Baron), (Richard Edward) Geoffrey Howe; cr. 1992. Born 20 December 1926. Son of late Benjamin Edward Howe; educated Winchester College; Trinity Hall, Cambridge (Scholar, MA law 1951, LLB). Married Elspeth Rosamund Shand (now Baroness Howe of Idlicote) 1953 (1 son 2 daughters). Lieutenant, Royal Signals 1945–48; Seconded to E African Signals 1947–48. *Career:* Called to the Bar, Middle Temple 1952, QC 1965, Bencher 1969, Reader 1993; Deputy Chair, Glamorgan Quarter Sessions 1966–70; Director: AGB Research Group 1974–79, Sun Alliance and Insurance Group 1974–79, EMI Ltd 1976–79, BICC plc 1991–97, Glaxo Wellcome 1991–96; Special Adviser on European and International Affairs to law firm of Jones, Day, Reavis and Pogue 1991–2001; International Advisory Councils of: J. P. Morgan & Co. 1992–2001; Stanford University's Institute for International Studies 1991–; Visitor at the School of Oriental and African Studies, London University 1991–2001; Chair, Framlington Russian Investment Fund 1994–2003; Fuji International European Advisory Board 1996–2003; Carlyle European Advisory Board 1996–2001; Chairman, Steering Committee Inland Revenue Tax Law Rewrite Project 1997–. *House of Commons:* Contested (Conservative) Aberavon 1955 and 1959 general elections; MP (Conservative) for: Bebington 1964–66, Reigate 1970–74, Surrey East 1974–92; Solicitor-General 1970–72; Minister for Trade and Consumer Affairs, Department of Trade and Industry 1972–74; Chancellor of the Exchequer 1979–83; Secretary of State for Foreign and Commonwealth Affairs 1983–89; Lord President of the Council, Leader of the House of Commons and Deputy Prime Minister 1989–90. Opposition Spokesperson for: Social Services 1974–75, Treasury and Economic Affairs 1975–79. Member Joint Committee on House of Lords Reform 2002–. Chairman, Interim Committee International Monetary Fund 1982–83. Chairman: Cambridge University Conservative Association 1951, Bow Group 1955; Managing Director, Crossbow 1957–60, Editor 1960–62. Member, General Council of the Bar 1957–61; Visitor, School of Oriental and African Studies 1991–2001; President: Great Britain-China Centre 1992–, The Academy of Experts 1996–. Joseph Bech Memorial Prize, Luxembourg 1993. Two honorary doctorates, three honorary university fellowships; Visiting Fellow, John F Kennedy School of Government, Harvard University, USA 1991–92; Hon. Fellow, Trinity Hall, Cambridge 1992; Herman Phleger Visiting Professor, Stanford Law School, USA 1992–93. Trustee, Thomson Foundation 1991–. President, Consumers' Association 1993–. Kt 1970; PC 1972; Grand Cross of the Order of Merit (Portugal) 1987; Grand Cross of the Order of Merit of the Federal Republic of Germany 1992; CH 1996; Order of Public Service (Ukraine) 2001. Hon. Fellow: American Bar Foundation 2000–, Chartered Institute of Taxation 2000–. Freeman, Borough of Port Talbot 1992 (now Neath Port Talbot). *Publications: Conflict of Loyalty,* 1994; Various political pamphlets for the Bow Group and Conservative Political Centre. *Recreations:* Photography. *Clubs:* Athenaeum, Garrick. Raised to the peerage as Baron Howe of Aberavon, of Tandridge in the County of Surrey 1992. Rt Hon the Lord Howe of Aberavon, Kt, CH, QC, House of Lords, London, SW1A 0PW *Tel:* 020 7219 6986 *E mail:* howeg@parliament.uk.

DodOnline

An Electronic Directory without rival . . .

Peers' biographies and photographs available with daily updates *via* the internet

For a *free* trial, call Yasmin Mirza, Aby Farsoun or Michael Mand on 020 7630 7643

HOWE OF IDLICOTE, BARONESS   Crossbencher

BARONESS HOWE OF IDLICOTE (Life Baroness), Elspeth Rosamund Morton the Lady Howe of Aberavon CBE; cr 2001. Born 8 February 1932. Daughter of late Philip Morton Shand and Sybil Mary Shand; educated Bath High School; Wycombe Abbey; London School of Economics (BSc social science and administration 1985). Nee Shand: married Geoffrey Howe (later Sir Geoffrey, then Lord Howe of Aberavon) 1953 (2 daughters 1 son). Co-opted member Inner London Education Authority 1967–70; Vice-president Institute of Business Ethics Advisory Council 2002–. *Career:* JP 1964–90; Chair Inner London Juvenile Court 1970–90; Member: Briggs Committee on the Future of the Nursing Profession 1970–72, Parole Board for England and Wales 1972–75; Deputy Chair Equal Opportunities Commission 1975–79; President Federation of Recruitment and Services 1980–94; Governor: London School of Economics 1985–, Open University 1985–2003; Vice-chair Council of the Open University 2001–03; Chair BOC Foundation for the Environment 1990–2003; Institute of Business Ethics' Advisory Council: Member 1990–2001, Vice-President 2002–; Board member Business in the Community 1992–98, Chairman of BITC's opportunity 2000 Target Team 1990–99; Chair Archbishop's Commission on Cathedrals 1992–94; Member Department of Employment working group on women's issues 1992–97; Chair Broadcasting Standards Commission 1993–99; President UK Committee of UNICEF 1993–2002. Seven honorary doctorates; Honorary Fellow London School of Economics 2001. CBE 1999. *Publications: Under Five,* (CPC) 1966; *Women and Credit,* (Equal Opportunities Commission) 1978; *Women at the Top,* (Hansard Society) 1990. *Special Interests:* Equal Opportunities, Education, Environment, Law, Third Age, Broadcasting. *Recreations:* Bridge, theatre, grandchildren. *Clubs:* Royal Society of Arts. Raised to the peerage as Baroness Howe of Idlicote, of Shipston-on-Stour in the County of Warwickshire 2001. The Baroness Howe of Idlicote, CBE, House of Lords, London, SW1A 0PW *Tel:* 020 7219 6581 *Fax:* 020 7219 5979 *E-mail:* howee@parliament.uk.

HOWELL OF GUILDFORD, LORD   Conservative

HOWELL OF GUILDFORD (Life Baron), David Arthur Russell Howell; cr. 1997. Born 18 January 1936. Son of late Arthur Howell, retired Army Officer and Businessman; educated Eton College; King's College, Cambridge (BA economics 1959, MA). Married Davina Wallace 1967 (1 son 2 daughters). Second Lieutenant, 2nd Btn Coldstream Guards 1954–56. *Career:* Economic section, HM Treasury 1959–60; Leader writer, *Daily Telegraph* 1960–64; Director: Monks Investment Trust plc, Advisory Director, UBS-Warburg 1997–2000. *House of Commons:* Contested (Conservative) Dudley 1964 general election; MP (Conservative) for Guildford 1966–97; Parliamentary Secretary, Civil Service Department 1970–72; Parliamentary Under-Secretary of State: Department of Employment 1971–72, Northern Ireland Office March-November 1972; Minister of State: Northern Ireland Office 1972–74, Department of Energy 1974; Secretary of State for: Energy 1979–81, Transport 1981–83. Government Whip 1970–71. Opposition Spokesperson for Foreign and Commonwealth Affairs 2000–. Member: Select Committee on European Communities Sub-Committee B (Energy, Industry and Transport) 1997–99, Select Committee on European Communities 1999–2000. Member, Trilateral Commission. Chairman, Bow Group 1962; Editor, "Crossbow" 1962–64; Director, Conservative Political Centre 1964–66. Member: Royal Institute of International Affairs (Chatham House), Development Council and Trustee, Shakespeare Globe Theatre. Trustee, Shakespeare's Globe Theatre. Visiting Fellow, Nuffield College, Oxford 1992–2000; Chairman, UK-Japan 21st Century Group 1990–2000. PC 1979. Liveryman, Clothworkers' Company. *Publications:* Co-author *Principles in Practice,* 1960; *The Conservative Opportunity,* 1965; *Freedom and Capital,* 1981; *Blind Victory: a study in income, wealth and power,* 1986; *The Edge of Now,* 2000. *Special Interests:* Economics, International Finance, Energy, Oil, Foreign Affairs. *Recreations:* Writing, travel, golf, do-it-yourself. *Clubs:* Beefsteak. Raised to the peerage as Baron Howell of Guildford, of Penton Mewsey in the County of Hampshire 1997. Rt Hon the Lord Howell of Guildford, House of Lords, London, SW1A 0PW *Tel:* 020 7219 5415 *Fax:* 020 7219 0304 *E-mail:* howelld@parliament.uk.

Visit the Vacher Dod Website . . . **www.DodOnline.co.uk**

HOWELLS OF ST DAVIDS, BARONESS — Labour

HOWELLS OF ST DAVIDS (Life Baroness), Rosalind Patricia-Anne Howells; cr 1999. Born 10 January 1931; educated St Joseph's Convent, Grenada; South West London College; City University, Washington DC (community and race relations). Married John Charles Howells 1955 (2 daughters). *Career:* Former community and equal opportunities worker, with Moonshot Youth Club, Community Industry, then to Greenwich Racial Equality Council as equal opportunities director until retirement. Chair, Lewisham Racial Equality Council; Ex-Chair: Charlton Consortium, Carnival Liaison Committee, Greater London Action on Race Equality; Director, Smithville Associates; President, Grenada Convent Past Pupils Association; Patron: Grenada Arts Council, Mediation Service; Member, Court of Governors, University of Greenwich; Former Vice-Chair, London Voluntary Services Council; Has served on various committees including: Advisory Committee to the Home Secretary, Commonwealth Countries League, Greenwich Police/Community Consultative Group. Hansib Publications Award; The Voice Newspaper Community Award. Hon. DUniv, Greenwich 1998. Trustee: West Indian Standing Conference, Museum of Ethnic Arts, Women of the Year Committee, Stephen Lawrence Charitable Trust, City Parochial Foundation. Has been an active campaigner for justice in the field of race relations: The New Cross Fire, Roland Adams Campaign, Stephen Lawrence Family Campaign, SUS Campaign. OBE 1993. *Special Interests:* Community Relations. *Recreations:* Food, music of all kinds, cricket, football. Raised to the peerage as Baroness Howells of St Davids, of Charlton in the London Borough of Greenwich 1999. The Baroness Howells of St Davids, OBE, House of Lords, London, SW1A 0PW *Tel:* 020 8852 9808 *Fax:* 020 8297 1975.

HOWIE OF TROON, LORD — Labour

HOWIE OF TROON (Life Baron), William Howie; cr. 1978. Born 2 March 1924. Son of late Peter Howie; educated Marr College, Troon; Royal Technical College, Glasgow (BSc civil engineering 1944). Married Mairi Sanderson 1951 (2 daughters 2 sons). *Trades Union:* Life Member, NUJ. *Career:* Civil engineer; Journalist and publisher; Director: Internal relations of Thomas Telford Ltd, publishers 1976–95, Seto 1996–2001; Consultant, George S Hall Ltd, building services engineer 1999–. *House of Commons:* Contested Cities of London and Westminster 1959; MP (Labour) for Luton 1963–70. Pro-Chancellor, City University 1984–91. Member of House of Lords Select Committees on: Science and Technology 1992–95, 1997–2001, the European Communities 1995–97; Co-opted Member, Select Committee on European Communities Sub-Committee B (Energy, Industry and Transport) 1997–98; Member, Select Committee on Science and Technology: Sub-Committee II (Science and Society) 1999–2000, Sub-Committee I (Complementary and Alternative Medicine) 2000; Member European Union Sub-committee B (Energy, Industry and Transport) 2003–. Member: Council of Institution of Civil Engineers 1965–68, Council of City University 1968–91; Vice-President, Periodical Publishers Association. Institution of Civil Engineers Garth Watson Medal. Hon. DSc, City University; Hon. LLD, Strathclyde. Fellow, Industry and Parliamentary Trust. Member, Committee of Inquiry into Engineering Profession 1977–79. Fellow, Institution of Civil Engineers; Member, Society of Engineers and Scientists (France); Hon. Fellow: Institution of Standard Engineers, Association of Building Engineers. *Publications:* Co-author *Public Sector Purchasing*, 1968; *Trade Unions and the Professional Engineer*, 1977; *Trade Unions in Construction*, 1981; Co-editor *Thames Tunnel to Channel Tunnel*, 1987. *Special Interests:* Construction Industry, Professional Engineers, Higher Education. Raised to the peerage as Baron Howie of Troon, of Troon, Kyle and Carrick 1978. The Lord Howie of Troon, 34 Temple Fortune Lane, London, NW11 7UL *Tel:* 020 8455 0492 *Fax:* 020 8455 0492.

DodOnline
An Electronic Directory without rival . . .

Peers' biographies and photographs available with daily updates *via* the internet

For a *free* trial, call Yasmin Mirza, Aby Farsoun or Michael Mand on 020 7630 7643

HOYLE, LORD — Labour

HOYLE (Life Baron), (Eric) Douglas Harvey Hoyle; cr. 1997. Born 17 February 1930. Son of late William Hoyle; educated Adlington School; Horwich Technical College. Married Pauline Spencer 1952 (died 1991) (1 son). *Trades Union:* Vice-President, ASTMS 1972–74, President 1977–81, Vice-President 1981–85, President 1985–88; Merged with TASS 1988; Joint President, MSF 1988–90, President 1990–91. JP 1958; Former Member, North West Regional Health Authority. *Career:* British Rail 1945–51; AEI 1951–53; Sales engineer, C. Weston Ltd, Salford 1953–74; Chair, Warrington Rugby League plc 1999–. *House of Commons:* Contested (Labour) Clitheroe 1964, Nelson and Colne 1970 and February 1974 general elections; MP (Labour) for: Nelson and Colne October 1974–79, Warrington 1981–83, Warrington North 1983–97. Member, Labour Party National Executive 1978–82, 1983–85; Chair, Parliamentary Labour Party 1992–97. Government Whip 1997–99. Government Spokesperson for: Defence 1997–99, Home Office 1997–99, Agriculture 1997–99. Member, Parliamentary Labour Party Parliamentary Committee 2001–. Member Parliamentary Labour Party Committee 2001–. *Special Interests:* Trade, Employment, Industrial Relations, Health, Immigration, Arts. *Recreations:* Cricket, theatre, cinema, sport. *Sportsclubs:* President: Adlington Cricket Club 1974–, Chorley Rugby League Club 1989–96, Warrington Rugby League Supporters Club 1990–. Raised to the peerage as Baron Hoyle, of Warrington in the County of Cheshire 1997. The Lord Hoyle, House of Lords, London, SW1A 0PW *Tel:* 020 7219 3196.

HUGHES OF WOODSIDE, LORD — Labour

HUGHES OF WOODSIDE (Life Baron), Robert Hughes; cr. 1997. Born 3 January 1932; educated Robert Gordon's College, Aberdeen; Benoni High School, Transvaal; Pietermaritzburgh Technical College, Natal. Married Ina Margaret Miller 1957 (2 sons 3 daughters). *Trades Union:* Member, AMICUS. Councillor, Aberdeen Town Council 1962–71; Former Member, North East Scotland Regional Hospital Board. *Career:* Emigrated to South Africa 1947; Returned UK 1954; CF Wilson and Co (1932) Ltd, Aberdeen. Draughtsman 1954–64, Chief draughtsman 1964–70. *House of Commons:* Contested North Angus and Mearns 1959 general election; MP (Labour) for Aberdeen North 1970–97; Parliamentary Under-Secretary of State, Scottish Office 1974–75; Piloted the Rating (Disabled Persons) Act 1978 to Statute as Private Members Bill; Chair, Select Committee, Scottish Affairs 1991–94. Opposition Spokesperson for: Transport November 1981–83, Agriculture, Fisheries and Food 1983–84, Transport 1984–88. Vice-chair Tribune Group of MPs 1984–85. Chairman, Aberdeen City Labour Party 1963–69. Founder Member, CND; Vice-Chair, Anti-Apartheid Movement 1976, Chair 1977–94; Chair Action for Southern Africa (ACTSA) 1994–98, Hon President 1998–; Hon President, Mozambique, Angola Committee (MAC) 2001–. Trustee, Canon Collins Education Trust for Southern Africa 1996–. Member, General Medical Council 1976–81. *Special Interests:* Anti-Apartheid Work, Agriculture, Fishing Industry, Transport, Health Service, Overseas Aid and Development. *Recreations:* Fishing, golf. Raised to the peerage as Baron Hughes of Woodside, of Woodside in the City of Aberdeen 1997. The Lord Hughes of Woodside, House of Lords, London, SW1A 0PW *Tel:* 020 7219 1451 *E-mail:* hughesr@parliament.uk.

HUNT OF CHESTERTON, LORD — Labour

HUNT OF CHESTERTON (Life Baron), Julian Charles Roland Hunt; cr. 2000. Born 5 September 1941. Son of Roland Charles Hunt, CMG; educated Westminster School; Trinity College, Cambridge (BA engineering 1963, PhD engineering 1967); Warwick University. Married Marylla Ellen Shephard 1965 (1 son 2 daughters). *Trades Union:* Member, AUT. Councillor, Cambridge City Council 1971–74, Leader Labour Group 1972. *Career:* Post-doctoral research, Cornell University, USA 1967; Research officer, Central Electricity Research Laboratories 1968–70; Cambridge University: Fellow 1966–, Senior research fellow 1998–99; Trinity College: Lecturer in applied mathematics and in engineering 1970–78, Reader in fluid mechanics 1978–90, Professor 1990–92,

Hon Professor 1992–; Visiting Professor: Colorado State University, USA 1980, National Center for Atmospheric Research, Boulder, Colorado, USA 1983; Founder Director, Cambridge Environmental Research Ltd 1986–91, Director 1997–, Chair 2000–; Chief Executive, Meteorological Office 1992–97; Visiting Scientist, Cerfacs, Toulouse, France 1997, 1998; Visiting Professor: Arizona State University, USA 1997–98, Stanford University, USA 1998, Delft University of Technology 1998–; Professor in climate modelling, University College, London 1999–. Member Select Committee on: Animals in Scientific Procedures 2001–02, Science and Technology Sub-committee II (Innovations in Microprocessing) 2002–. GLOBE (Global Legislation for better Environment). Chair ACOPS (Advisory Committee on the Protection of the Sea) 2001–. European Geophysical Society, LF Richardson Medal 2001. Six honorary doctorates from England, France and Sweden. Chair Advisory Committee for Protection of the Sea. Member: Management board, European Research Community for Flow Turbulence and Combustion 1988–95, Executive council, World Meteorological Organisation 1992–97; President, Institute of Mathematics and its Applications 1993–95; Member of Council, Royal Society 1998–99; Vice-president, National Society of Clean Air 2001–. CB 1998. FRS 1989. *Publications:* Articles in mathematical and scientific publications and newspapers, edited three volumes. *Special Interests:* Environment, Science, Government – Civil Service Issues, Informational Aspects. *Recreations:* Swimming, cinema. *Clubs:* Meteorological. Raised to the peerage as Baron Hunt of Chesterton, of Chesterton in the County of Cambridgeshire 2000. Professor the Lord Hunt of Chesterton, CB, Department of Space and Climate Physics, University College, Gower Street, London, WC1E 6BT *E-mail:* jcrh@mssl.ucl.ac.uk.

HUNT OF KINGS HEATH, LORD — Labour

HUNT OF KINGS HEATH (Life Baron), Philip Alexander Hunt; cr. 1997. Born 19 May 1949. Son of late Rev. Philip Hunt and Muriel Hunt; educated City of Oxford High School; Oxford School; Leeds University (BA political studies 1970). Married 1974 (divorced) (1 daughter); married Selina Ruth Stewart 1988 (3 sons 1 daughter). *Trades Union:* Member, Unison. Councillor, Oxford City Council 1973–79; Member, Oxfordshire Area Health Authority 1975–77; Councillor, Birmingham City Council 1980–82. *Career:* Oxford Regional Hospital Board 1972–74; Nuffield Orthopaedic Centre 1974–75; Secretary, Edgware/Hendon Community Health Council 1975–78; National Association of Health Authorities: Assistant Secretary 1978–79, Assistant Director 1979–84, Director 1984–90; Director, National Association of Health Authorities and Trusts 1990–96; Chief Executive, NHS Confederation 1996–97. *House of Lords:* Parliamentary Under-Secretary of State, Department of Health 1999–2003. Government Whip 1998–99. Government Spokesperson for: Education and Employment 1998–99, Health 1998–2003. Member, Joint Select Committee on Consolidation of Bills 1998. Council, International Hospital Federation 1986–91. Council, Association for Public Health 1992, Co-Chairman 1994–98; President, Family Planning Association 1997–98. OBE 1993. *Special Interests:* Devolution, Transport, Environment. *Recreations:* Cycling, swimming, Birmingham City FC, music. *Sportsclubs:* Warwickshire CCC. Raised to the peerage as Baron Hunt of Kings Heath, of Birmingham in the County of West Midlands 1997. The Lord Hunt of Kings Heath, OBE, House of Lords, London, SW1A 0PW *Tel:* 020 7210 5826 *Fax:* 020 7210 5066.

HUNT OF TANWORTH, LORD — Crossbencher

HUNT OF TANWORTH (Life Baron), John Joseph Benedict Hunt; cr. 1980. Born 23 October 1919. Son of late Major A. L. Hunt and Daphne Hunt, née Ashton Case; educated Downside School; Magdalene College, Cambridge (BA history). Married Hon Magdalen Robinson 1941 (died 1971) (2 sons and 1 daughter deceased); married Lady Madeleine Frances Hume 1973. Served Royal Naval Volunteer Reserve 1940–45. *Career:* Entered Home Civil Service 1946; Dominions Office 1946; Private Secretary to Parliamentary Under-Secretary 1947; Second Secretary, UK High Commission Ceylon 1948–50; Private Secretary to Secretary of Cabinet and Permanent Secretary to Treasury and Head of Civil Service 1956–58; Assistant Secretary, Commonwealth Relations Office 1958; Cabinet Office 1960; HM Treasury 1962–67; Deputy Secretary 1968; First Civil Service Commissioner, Civil Service Department 1968–71; Third Secretary, Treasury 1971–72;

Second Permanent Secretary, Cabinet Office 1972–73; Secretary of the Cabinet 1973–79; Chairman, Banque Nationale de Paris plc 1980–97; Director, IBM (UK) Ltd 1980–90; Advisory Director, Unilever 1980–90; Director, Prudential Corporation plc 1980–92, Chairman: Disasters Emergency Committee 1981–89, Inquiry into Cable Expansion and Broadcasting Policy 1982, Tablet Publishing Co. Ltd 1984–96, Director 1984–99, Prudential Corporation plc 1985–90, European Policy Forum 1992–98, Council 1992–. Member, Sub-Committee A of House of Lords European Communities Committee 1992–95, Chairman 1993–97; Member, House of Lords European Communities Committee 1993–96; Chairman, House of Lords Select Committee on Central and Local Government Relations 1995–96. Chair, Ditchley Foundation 1983–91; President, The Local Government Association 1997–2001. Hon. Fellow, Magdalene College, Cambridge 1977. CB 1968; KCB 1973; GCB 1977; Officier, Légion d'Honneur (France) 1987; Knight Commander with Star of the Order of Pius IX 1997. *Recreations:* Gardening. Raised to the peerage as Baron Hunt of Tanworth, of Stratford-on-Avon in the County of Warwickshire 1980. The Lord Hunt of Tanworth, GCB, 8 Wool Road, London, SW20 0HW *Tel:* 020 8947 7640 *Fax:* 020 8947 4879 *E-mail:* madjon1919@hotmail.com.

HUNT OF WIRRAL, LORD   Conservative

HUNT OF WIRRAL (Life Baron), David James Fletcher Hunt; cr. 1997. Born 21 May 1942. Son of late Alan Nathaniel Hunt, OBE, shipping agent and late Jessie Edna Ellis Hunt; educated Liverpool College; Montpellier University, France; Bristol University (LLB 1965); Guildford College of Law (LLB). Married Paddy Orchard 1973 (2 sons 2 daughters). *Career:* Solicitor; Beachcroft Wansbroughs: Partner 1968–, Senior Partner 1996–, Chair Beachcroft Wansbroughs Consulting 2002–; Director BET Omnibus Services Ltd 1980–81. *House of Commons:* Contested Bristol South 1970 and Kingswood 1974; MP (Conservative) for Wirral 1976–83 and for Wirral West 1983–97; PPS: to Secretary of State for Trade 1979–81, to Secretary of State for Defence 1981; Parliamentary Under-Secretary of State, Department of Energy 1984–87; Minister of State, Department of the Environment (Minister for Local Government and Inner Cities) 1989–90; Secretary of State: for Wales 1990–93, for Employment 1993–94; Chancellor of the Duchy of Lancaster and Minister for Public Service and Science 1994–95. Assistant Government Whip 1981–83; Government Whip 1983–84; Deputy Government Chief Whip 1987–89. Opposition Spokesperson for Shipping and Shipbuilding 1977–79. Member: Offices Committee 1999–2001, European Communities Committee, Sub-Committee E (Law and Institutions) 1999–2002, House Committee 2003–. Chair British Atlantic Group of Young Politicians 1979–81; President Atlantic Association for Young Political Leaders 1981–83. Chair, Bristol University Conservative Association 1964–65; National Vice-Chair, Federation of Conservative Students 1965–66; Chair: Bristol City CPC 1965–68, Bristol Federation of Young Conservatives; Member: General Purposes Committee, National Union Executive 1967–76, 1983–89; Vice-Chair, Bristol Conservative Association 1970; Chair, National Young Conservatives 1972–73; Vice-Chair, National Union 1974–76; Vice-President, European Conservative and Christian Democratic Youth Community; Vice-Chair, Conservative Party 1983–84; President, Tory Reform Group 1991–97. Member, Government Advisory Committee on Pop Festivals 1972–75; Governor: European Youth Foundation at Strasbourg 1972–75, English Speaking Union 1998–, Deputy Chair 2000–. Trustee, Holocaust Educational Trust; President: Hoylake Cottage Hospital Trust, Arrowe Park Sick Children's Fund. Chair, British Youth Council 1971–74; Member, South West Economic Planning Council 1972–76; President, British Youth Council 1978–80. MBE 1973; PC 1990. *Recreations:* Cricket, walking. *Clubs:* Hurlingham. Raised to the peerage as Baron Hunt of Wirral, of Wirral in the County of Merseyside 1997. Rt Hon the Lord Hunt of Wirral, MBE, Senior Partner, Beachcroft Wansbroughs, 100 Fetter Lane, London, EC4A 1BN *Tel:* 020 7894 6066 *Fax:* 020 7894 6153 *E-mail:* lordhunt@bwlaw.co.uk.

DodOnline
An Electronic Directory without rival . . .

Peers' biographies and photographs available with daily updates *via* the internet

For a *free* trial, call Yasmin Mirza, Aby Farsoun or Michael Mand on 020 7630 7643

HURD OF WESTWELL, LORD · Conservative

HURD OF WESTWELL (Life Baron), Douglas Richard Hurd; cr. 1997. Born 8 March 1930. Son of late Baron Hurd (Life Peer); educated Eton College; Trinity College, Cambridge (MA history 1952, President, Cambridge Union 1952). Married Tatiana Eyre 1960 (3 sons) (divorced 1982); married Judith Smart 1982 (1 son 1 daughter). 2nd Lieutenant, Royal Artillery 1948–49. *Career:* HM Foreign Service, Peking 1954–6; UN, New York 1956–60, Rome 1963–66; Conservative Research Department 1966–68; Deputy Chairman Natwest Markets 1995–98; Chair British Invisibles 1997–2000; Deputy Chairman Coutts & Co 1998–; Chair CEDR (Council for Effective Dispute Resolutions) 2001–; Senior Adviser Hawkpoint Partners. *House of Commons:* MP (Conservative) for Mid Oxon 1974–83 and for Witney 1983–97; Political Secretary to Edward Heath MP 1968–74; Minister of State for: Foreign and Commonwealth Office 1979–83, Home Office 1983–84; Secretary of State for: Northern Ireland 1984–85, The Home Department 1985–89, Foreign and Commonwealth Affairs 1989–95; Contested Leadership of the Conservative Party November 1990. Opposition Spokesman on Europe 1976–79. Honorary doctorate. Trustee, Prayer Book Society 1989–; Prison Reform Trust: Chair 1997–2001, Hon President 2001–. Vice-President, The Falkland Islands Association 1996–2000, President 2000–; Member: The Constitutional Commission 1998–99, Royal Commission on the Reform of the House of Lords 1999; High Steward, Westminster Abbey 1999–, House of Lords Appointments Commission 2000–; Chair, Archbishop of Canterbury's Review 2000–01. CBE 1974; PC 1982; CH 1996. *Publications: The Arrow War,* 1967; *Truth Game,* 1972; *Vote to Kill,* 1975; *An End to Promises,* 1979; Co-author *Send Him Victorious,* 1968; *The Smile on the Face of the Tiger,* 1969; *Scotch on the Rocks,* 1971; *War Without Frontiers,* 1982; Co-author *Palace of Enchantments,* 1985; *The Search for Peace,* 1997; *The Shape of Ice,* 1998; *Ten Minutes to Turn the Devil,* 1999; *Image in the Water,* 2001. *Recreations:* Writing novels. *Clubs:* Beefsteak, Travellers', Pratt's. Raised to the peerage as Baron Hurd of Westwell, of Westwell in the County of Oxfordshire 1997. Rt Hon the Lord Hurd of Westwell, CH, CBE, House of Lords, London, SW1A 0PW *Tel:* 020 7219 3535.

HUSSEY OF NORTH BRADLEY, LORD · Crossbencher

HUSSEY OF NORTH BRADLEY (Life Baron) Marmaduke James Hussey; cr. 1996. Born 29 August 1923. Son of late Eric Robert James Husssey, CMG, and of Mrs Christine Hussey; educated Rugby; Honorary Fellow Trinity College, Oxford (Scholar, BA history 1942, MA). Married Lady Susan Waldegrave 1959 (1 son 1 daughter). Served Second World War, with Grenadier Guards in Italy (wounded). *Career:* Associated Newspapers 1949, Director 1964; Managing Director, Harmsworth Publications 1967–70; Thomson Organisation Executive Board 1971; Chief Executive and Managing Director, Times Newspapers Ltd 1971–80, Director 1982–86; Director, Colonial Mutual Group 1982–96; Joint Chairman, Great Western Radio 1985–86; Director, William Collins plc 1985–89, MAID plc 1996–2000; Chairman: Ruffer Investment Management 1996–2000, Casweb Ltd. Member: Select Committee on European Communities 1997–, Select Committee on European Communities Sub-Committee A (Economic and Financial Affairs, Trade and External Relations) 1997–, Joint Committee on Draft Communications Bill 2002. Member: Board of British Council 1983–96, Government Working Party on Artificial Limb and Appliance Centres in England 1984–86; Chairman: Royal Marsden Hospital 1985–98, BBC 1986–96; Member, Management and Education Committees, King Edward's Hospital Fund for London 1987–; President, Royal Bath and West of England Society 1990–91; Chairman, King's Fund London Committee 1996; President, Iris Fund for Prevention of Blindness 1998–; Various positions held in these charities: BLESMA, British Legion, Cheshire Homes. Hon. Fellow, Trinity College, Oxford 1989. Trustee: Rhodes Trust 1972–91, Royal Academic Trust 1988–97. *Publications: Chance Governs All – A Memoir. Clubs:* Brooks's. Raised to the peerage as Baron Hussey of North Bradley, of North Bradley in the County of Wiltshire 1996. The Lord Hussey of North Bradley, Flat 15, 47 Courtfield Road, London, SW7 4DB *Tel:* 020 7370 1414; Waldegrave House, Chewton Mendip, near Bath, Somerset, BA3 4PD *Tel:* 01761 241289.

Visit the Vacher Dod Website ... www.DodOnline.co.uk

HUTCHINSON OF LULLINGTON, LORD　　　　　Liberal Democrat

HUTCHINSON OF LULLINGTON (Life Baron), Jeremy Nicolas Hutchinson; cr. 1978. Born 28 March 1915. Son of late St John Hutchinson, KC; educated Stowe School; Magdalen College, Oxford (BA philosophy, politics and economics 1937, MA). Married Peggy Ashcroft (later DBE) 1940 (1 son 1 daughter) (divorced 1966, she died 1991); married June Osborn 1966. RNVR 1939–46. *Career:* Called to the Bar, Middle Temple 1939; QC 1961; Bencher 1963; Recorder of Bath 1962–72; Recorder of Crown Court 1973–76; Professor of Law, Royal Academy of Arts 1988–. Trustee, Tate Gallery 1977–80, Chairman 1980–84. Member: Committee on Immigration Appeals 1966–68, Committee on Identification Procedures 1974–76; Vice-Chairman, Arts Council of Great Britain 1976–78. *Clubs:* MCC. Raised to the peerage as Baron Hutchinson of Lullington, of Lullington in the County of East Sussex 1978. The Lord Hutchinson of Lullington, QC, House of Lords, London, SW1A 0PW *Tel:* 020 7219 5874.

HUTTON, LORD　　　　　Crossbencher

HUTTON (Life Baron), (James) Brian Edward Hutton; cr. 1997. Born 29 June 1931. Son of late James and Mabel Hutton; educated Shrewsbury School; Balliol College, Oxford (BA jurisprudence 1953); Queen's University, Belfast. Married Mary Gillian Murland 1975 (died 2000) (2 daughters); married Rosalind Ann Nickols 2001 (2 stepsons 1 stepdaughter). *Career:* Called to Northern Ireland Bar 1954; Junior Counsel to Attorney-General for Northern Ireland 1969; QC (NI) 1970; Called to English Bar 1972; Legal Adviser to Ministry of Home Affairs (NI) 1973; Senior Crown Counsel in NI 1973–79; Member, Joint Law Enforcement Commission 1974; Bencher, Inn of Court of Northern Ireland 1974; Judge of the High Court of Justice (NI) 1979–88; Lord Chief Justice of Northern Ireland 1988–97; Lord of Appeal in Ordinary 1997–. President, Northern Ireland Association for Mental Health 1983–90; Visitor of the University of Ulster 1999–. Hon. Fellow, Balliol College, Oxford 1988; Hon. LLD, Queen's University, Belfast 1992. Deputy Chairman, Boundary Commission (NI) 1985–88; Hon. Bencher: Inner Temple 1988, King's Inn, Dublin 1988. PC 1988; Kt 1988. Raised to the peerage as Baron Hutton, of Bresagh in the County of Down 1997. Rt Hon the Lord Hutton, House of Lords, London, SW1A 0PW *Tel:* 020 7219 3202.

HYLTON, LORD　　　　　Crossbencher

HYLTON (5th Baron), Raymond Hervey Jolliffe; cr. 1866; 5th Bt of Merstham (UK) 1821. Born 13 June 1932. Son of 4th Baron; educated Eton College; Trinity College, Oxford (MA history 1955). Married Joanna de Bertodano 1966 (4 sons 1 daughter). National Service, commissioned Coldstream Guards 1951–52. DL, Somerset 1975–90; Councillor, Frome RDC 1968–72. *Career:* Assistant Private Secretary to the Governor-General of Canada 1960–62. *House of Lords:* First entered House of Lords 1967; Private Members Bills: Sexual Offences (Amendment) Bill, Overseas Domestic Workers (Protection) Bill; Elected hereditary peer 1999–. Chairman, MICOM – Moldova Initiatives Committee of Management 1994. Associated in various capacities since 1962 with: Abbeyfield Society, Catholic Housing Aid Society, The London Housing Aid Centre, National Federation of Housing Associations, Age Concern, L'Arche Ltd, Royal MENCAP, Foundation for Alternatives, Christian College for Adult Education, Mendip Wansdyke Local Enterprise Group, Hugh of Witham Foundation, Action around Bethlehem Children with Disability (ABCD); President, Northern Ireland Association for Care and Resettlement of Offenders 1988–; Housing Associations Charitable Trust. Hon. DSc, Southampton University 1994. Associated in various capacities since 1962 with: Acorn Christian Healing Trust; Chairman, St Francis and St Sergius Trust Fund (for the churches and youth in Russia) 1993–2001; Vice-chairman, Partners in hope (Young people at risk in Russia); Trustee and governor, Ammerdown Study Centre, near Bath. ARICS 1960. *Special Interests:* Northern Ireland, Housing, British-Irish Relations, Human Rights, Prisons, Penal Affairs and Policy, Middle East, Europe, Former Soviet Union, Conflict Resolution, Peace Building. *Clubs:* Lansdowne. The Lord Hylton, House of Lords, London, SW1A 0PW *Tel:* 020 7219 3883 *Fax:* 020 7219 5979.

I

IMBERT, LORD
Crossbencher

IMBERT (Life Baron), Peter Michael Imbert; cr. 1999. Born 27 April 1933. Son of late William Henry Imbert, and of Frances May (née Hodge); educated Harvey Grammar School, Folkestone; Holborn College of Law, Languages and Commerce. Married Iris Dove 1956 (1 son 2 daughters). DL, Greater London 1994–98, Lord Lieutenant 1998–; JP 1998. *Career:* Joined Metropolitan Police 1953; Metropolitan Police Anti-Terrorist Squad 1973–75; Police negotiator at Balcombe Street siege December 1975; Assistant Chief Constable, Surrey Constabulary 1976, Deputy Chief Constable 1977; Chief Constable, Thames Valley Police 1979–85; Secretary, National Crime Committee-ACPO Council 1980–83, Chairman 1983–85; Deputy Commissioner, Metropolitan Police 1985–87, Commissioner 1987–93; Leader, International Criminal Justice Delegation to Russia 1993; Visiting International Fellow, Australian Police Staff College 1994 and 1997; Non-executive director: Securicor 1994–2000, Camelot plc 1994–2001; Non-executive chair Retainagroup 1995–2002; Has lectured on terrorism and siege situations in UK, Europe, Australia and Canada; Chair, Capital Eye Security 1997–. President, Richmond Horse Show 1993–98; Governor, Harvey Grammar School 1994–. Hon. DLitt, Reading University 1987. Trustee, Queen Elizabeth Foundation of St Catharine's 1988–2001; Chairman, Surrey CCC Youth Trust 1993–96. Member: General Advisory Council, BBC 1980–87, Criminal Justice Consultative Committee 1992–93, Ministerial Advisory Group, Royal Parks 1993–99, Public Policy Committee, RAC 1993–, Mental Health Foundation, Committee of Inquiry into Care in the Community for the Severely Mentally Ill 1994. QPM 1980; Kt 1988. CIMgt (CBIM 1982). Freeman: City of London, New Romney, Kent. Guild of Security Professionals. *Special Interests:* Police, Criminal Justice. *Recreations:* Bridge, golf, grandchildren. *Clubs:* RAC, Saints and Sinners Club, London. Raised to the peerage as Baron Imbert, of New Romney in the County of Kent 1999. The Lord Imbert, QPM, JP, The Lieutenancy Office, 18th Floor, City Hall, PO Box 240, Victoria Street, London, SW1E 6QP *Tel:* 020 7641 3259 *Fax:* 020 7641 2429.

INGE, LORD
Crossbencher

INGE (Life Baron), Peter Anthony Inge; cr. 1997. Born 5 August 1935. Son of late Raymond and Grace Inge; educated Summer Fields; Wrekin College; RMA, Sandhurst. Married Letitia Marion Beryl Thornton-Berry 1960 (2 daughters). Army Officer 1956–97; Commissioned Green Howards 1956; Served Hong Kong, Malaya, Germany, Libya and UK; ADC to GOC, 4 Division 1960–61; Adjutant, 1 Green Howards 1963–64; Student, Staff College 1966; Ministry of Defence 1967–69; Company Commander, 1 Green Howards 1969–70; Student, Joint Services Staff College 1971; BM, 11 Armoured Brigade 1972; Instructor, Staff College 1973–74; CO, 1 Green Howards 1974–76; Commandant, Junior Division, Staff College 1977–79; Commander, Task Force C/4 Armoured Brigade 1980–81; Chief of Staff, HQ 1 (BR) Corps 1982–83; Colonel, The Green Howards 1982–94; GOC, NE District and Commander 2nd Infantry Division 1984–86; Director General, Logistic Policy (Army), Ministry of Defence 1986–87; Commander, 1st (Br) Corps 1987–89; Colonel Commandant, Royal Military Police 1987–92; Commander, Northern Army Group and C-in-C, BAOR 1989–92; ADC General to HM The Queen 1991–94; Chief of the General Staff 1992–94; Field Marshal 1994; Chief of the Defence Staff 1994–97; Constable, HM Tower of London 1996–2001. DL, North Yorkshire 1994. Member, Select Committee Sub-Committee C European Union 1999–. Member, International Institute for Strategic Studies; President British German Officers Association. Commissioner Royal Hospital, Chelsea; Member of Council, King Edward VII's Hospital Sister Agnes. Hon. DCL, University of Newcastle upon Tyne. St George's House; Deputy Chair, Historic Royal Palaces; Marlborough College Council. KCB 1988; GCB (Mil) 1992; KG 2001. Freeman, City of London. *Special Interests:* Defence. *Recreations:* Cricket, walking, music, reading. *Clubs:* Boodle's, Beefsteak, Army and Navy, MCC. Raised to the peerage as Baron Inge, of Richmond in the County of North Yorkshire 1997. Field Marshal The Lord Inge, KG, GCB, DL, House of Lords, London, SW1A 0PW *Tel:* 020 7219 8706.

INGLEWOOD, LORD   Conservative

INGLEWOOD (2nd Baron, UK), (William) Richard Fletcher-Vane; cr. 1964. Born 31 July 1951. Son of 1st Baron, TD, DL And Mary, neé Proby; educated Eton College; Trinity College, Cambridge (MA); Cumbria College of Agriculture and Forestry. Married Cressida Pemberton-Pigott 1986 (1 son 2 daughters). Member, Lake District Special Planning Board 1984–90; Chairman, Development Control Committee 1985–89; Member, North West Water Authority 1987–89; DL, Cumbria 1993. *Career:* Called to the Bar, Lincoln's Inn 1975; MEP (Conservative) for Cumbria and Lancashire North 1989–94: British Conservative Group spokesperson, Legal Affairs Committee 1989–94; Chief Whip, British Conservative section EPP Group 1994; MEP (Conservative) for North West Region 1999–: Leader NW Conservative MEPs 1999–; Vice-President, EP-China Delegation; British Conservative Spokesperson: Legal Affairs Committee 1999–, Constitutional Affairs Committee 2001–, Chairman, CN Group 2002–. *House of Lords:* First entered House of Lords 1989; Parliamentary Under-Secretary of State, Department of National Heritage 1995–97; Elected hereditary peer 1999–. Government Whip 1994–95; Government Deputy Chief Whip January-July 1995. Opposition Spokesperson for: National Heritage 1997; Environment, Transport and the Regions 1997–98. Contested (Conservative), Houghton and Washington 1983 general election; Contested (Conservative), Durham 1984 European Parliament election. MRICS, FSA. Liveryman, Skinners' Company. *Special Interests:* Rural Affairs, Agriculture, Environment, Europe, Local Government, Regional Policy, Legal Affairs, Media, Arts. *Clubs:* Travellers', Pratt's. The Lord Inglewood, MEP, DL, Hutton-in-the-Forest, Penrith, Cumbria, CA11 9TH *Tel:* 017684 84500 *Fax:* 017684 84571.

IRVINE OF LAIRG, LORD   Labour

IRVINE OF LAIRG (Life Baron), Alexander Andrew Mackay Irvine; cr. 1987. Born 23 June 1940. Son of Alexander and Margaret Christina Irvine; educated Inverness Royal Academy, Hutchesons' Boys' Grammar School, Glasgow; Glasgow University (MA, LLB); Christ's College, Cambridge (Scholar, BA, LLB). Married Alison Mary McNair 1974 (2 sons). *Career:* University lecturer, London School of Economics 1965–69; Called to the Bar, Inner Temple 1967; QC 1978; Head, 11 King's Bench Walk Chambers 1981–97; Bencher of the Inner Temple, 1985; Recorder 1985–88; Deputy High Court Judge 1987–97. *House of Lords:* Shadow Lord Chancellor 1992–97; Lord Chancellor 1997–2003. Opposition Spokesperson for Legal Affairs and Home Affairs 1987–92; Government Spokesperson for Legal Affairs and Lord Chancellor's Department 1997–2003. Member, Select Committees on: House of Lords' Offices 1997–2002, Procedure 1997–. Joint President: British-American Parliamentary Group, CPA, IPU. Vice-Patron, World Federation of Mental Health. President, Magistrates Association; Chair, Glasgow 2001 Committee; Member, Committee of the Slade School of Fine Art 1990–. George and Thomas Hutcheson Award 1998. Hon. Fellow, Christ's College, Cambridge 1996; Hon. LLD, Glasgow 1997; Hon. Doctorate, Siena 2000; Fellowship, LSE 2000; Member, Polish Bar 2000. Foundation Trustee, Whitechapel Art Gallery 1990–97; Trustee: John Smith Memorial Trust 1992–97, Hunterian Collection 1997–; Joint President, Industry and Parliament Trust 1997–. Contested (Labour) Hendon North 1970 general election; Church Commissioner; Hon. Bencher, Inn of Court of Northern Ireland 1998. PC 1997. Hon. Fellow, Society for Advanced Legal Studies; Fellow, US College of Trial Lawyers 1998–. *Publications:* Articles on constitutional and legal topics in legal journals. *Special Interests:* Legal Affairs, Home Affairs, Constitutional Affairs. *Recreations:* Collecting paintings, travel, reading, cinema and theatre. *Clubs:* Garrick. Raised to the peerage as Baron Irvine of Lairg, of Lairg in the District of Sutherland 1987. Rt Hon the Lord Irvine of Lairg, House of Lords, London, SW1A 0PW *Tel:* 020 7219 3232 *Fax:* 020 7219 4711.

Visit the Vacher Dod Website . . .
www.DodOnline.co.uk

ISLWYN, LORD   Labour

ISLWYN (Life Baron), Roy (Royston) John Hughes; cr. 1997. Born 9 June 1925. Son of late John Hughes, Miner; educated Pontllanfraith Grammar School, Gwent; Ruskin College, Oxford. Married Marion Appleyard 1957 (3 daughters). *Trades Union:* Numerous offices in TGWU from 1959; Chair, Parliamentary Group TGWU 1968–69, 1979–82. Served 2nd Btn, Welch Regiment. Coventry City Councillor 1962–66; DL, Gwent 1992–. *House of Commons:* MP (Labour) for Newport 1966–83 and for Newport East 1983–97. Opposition Frontbench Spokesperson for Welsh Affairs 1984–88. Member, Executive British Group, Inter Parliamentary Union 1986–92, Treasurer 1991; Member, Council of Europe 1990–97. Secretary, Coventry Borough Labour Party 1962–66; Chair, Welsh Parliamentary Party 1969–70. Chair, Welsh Grand Committee 1982–84, 1990–97; Spokesperson, Pensioners' Convention 1998–. *Special Interests:* Steel, Motor Industry, Sport, Road Programme, International Affairs. *Recreations:* Rugby, soccer, cricket, gardening. *Sportsclubs:* Vice-President: Crawshay's (Wales) Rugby XV 1991–, Glamorgan County Cricket Club; Life Member Newport RFC. *Clubs:* RAC, Pontllanfraith Workingmens Club. Raised to the peerage as Baron Islwyn, of Casnewydd in the County of Gwent 1997. The Lord Islwyn, DL, Chapel Field, Chapel Lane, Abergavenny, Gwent, NP7 7BT *Tel:* 01873 856502.

J

JACOBS, LORD   Liberal Democrat

JACOBS (Life Baron) (David) Anthony Jacobs; cr. 1997. Born 13 November 1931. Born November 1931. Son of Ridley and Ella Jacobs; educated Clifton College; London University (BCom 1951). Married Evelyn Felicity Patchett 1954 (1 son 1 daughter). *Career:* Chairman: Nig Securities Group 1957–72, Tricoville Group 1961–90, 1992–94, British School of Motoring 1973–90. *House of Lords:* Member of Liberal Democrat Party. Member, House of Lords Offices Sub-Committee: Advisory Panel on Works of Art 2000–02. Joint Treasurer, Liberal Party 1984–87; Vice-President, Social and Liberal Democrats 1988, Member, Federal Executive 1988. Chairman, Board of Governors, Haifa University, Israel. Crown Estate Paving Commissioner. Kt 1988. FCA. *Recreations:* Golf, reading, theatre, opera, travel. *Sportsclubs:* Coombe Hill Golf (Surrey). Raised to the peerage as Baron Jacobs, of Belgravia in the City of Westminster 1997. The Lord Jacobs, 9 Nottingham Terrace, London, NW1 4QB *Tel:* 020 7486 6323.

JAMES OF HOLLAND PARK, BARONESS   Conservative

JAMES OF HOLLAND PARK (Life Baroness), Phyllis Dorothy James; cr. 1991. Born 3 August 1920. Daughter of late Sydney and Dorothy James; educated Cambridge High School for Girls. Married Connor Bantry White 1941 (died 1964) (2 daughters). JP, Willesden and Inner London 1979–84. *Career;* Administrator, National Health Service 1949–68; Civil Servant: appointed Principal, Home Office 1968, Police Department 1968–72, Criminal Policy Department 1972–79; Governor, BBC 1988–93; Member, Arts Council 1988–92, Chairman, Literature Advisory Panel 1988–92; Board Member, British Council 1988–93. Chair: Booker Panel of Judges 1987, President, Society of Authors 1997–; Lay Patron, Prayer Book Society. Seven honorary doctorates, three honorary fellowships. OBE 1983. Fellow, Royal Society of Literature 1987; FRSA. *Publications:* As P.D. James: *Cover her Face*, 1962; *A Mind to Murder*, 1963; *Unnatural Causes*, 1967; *Shroud for a Nightingale*, 1971; *The Maul and the Pear Tree* (with T.A. Critchley), 1971; *An Unsuitable Job for a Woman*, 1972; *The Black Tower*, 1975; *Death of an Expert Witness*, 1977; *Innocent Blood*, 1980; *The Skull Beneath the Skin*, 1982; *A Taste for Death*, 1986; *Devices and Desires*, 1989;

The Children of Men, 1992; *Original Sin*, 1994; *A Certain Justice*, 1997; *Time to be in Earnest*, 1999; *Death in Holy Orders*, 2001; *The Murder Room*, 2003. *Special Interests:* Literature, Arts, Criminal Justice, Broadcasting. *Recreations:* Reading, exploring churches, walking by the sea. *Clubs:* Detection. Raised to the peerage as Baroness James of Holland Park, of Southwold in the County of Suffolk 1991. The Baroness James of Holland Park, OBE, c/o Greene and Heaton Ltd, 37 Goldhawk Road, London, W12 8QQ.

JANNER OF BRAUNSTONE, LORD   Labour

JANNER OF BRAUNSTONE (Life Baron), Greville Ewan Janner; cr. 1997. Born 11 July 1928. Son of late Baron Janner (Life Peer) and late Lady Janner, CBE; educated Bishop's College School, Canada; St Paul's School, London; Trinity Hall, Cambridge (MA economics and law 1952); Harvard Post-Graduate Law School, USA 1953. Married Myra Sheink 1955 (died 1996) (1 son 2 daughters). *Trades Union:* Member, NUJ (London Freelance Branch); Hon. Member, NUM, Leicester. National Service 1946–48, RA, BAOR, War Crimes Investigator. *Career:* Former President, Cambridge Union; Called to the Bar, Middle Temple 1954; QC 1971; Non-executive director, Ladbroke plc 1986–95; Chairman, JSB Group and Effective Presentational Skills 1987–97;
President, REACH 1989–. *House of Commons:* Contested Wimbledon 1955; MP (Labour) for Leicester North-West 1970–74, and for Leicester West 1974–97. Member, Joint Select Committee on Consolidation of Bills 1998–. Former Chairman, Cambridge University Labour Club; International Secretary, National Association of Labour Students 1952; Labour Friends of: Israel, India. President: Board of Deputies of British Jews 1979–85, Commonwealth Jewish Council 1982–; Founder/President, Interparliamentary Council Against Anti-Semitism 1985–; Vice-President, World Jewish Congress 1991–; Founder and President, Maimonides Foundation 1995–; Vice-President: Association of Jewish Ex-Servicemen, Association for Jewish Youth. Order of Lithuanian Grand Duke Gediminas. Hon. PhD, Haifa University; Hon. LLD, De Montfort University. Chair: Holocaust Educational Trust, Lord Forte Charitable Trust; Joint President Minorities Foundation. Fellow, Institute of Personnel Management and Development. Freeman, City of London. *Publications:* Many books including: *Janner's Complete Speechmaker* (6th edition); *One Hand Alone Cannot Clap*, 1998. *Special Interests:* Employment Law, Industrial Relations, Jewish Causes, Human Rights, Consumer Protection, Commonwealth, India, Middle East. *Recreations:* Swimming, member of the Magic Circle and International Brotherhood of Magicians, languages. Raised to the peerage as Baron Janner of Braunstone, of Leicester in the County of Leicestershire 1997. The Lord Janner of Braunstone, QC, House of Lords, London, SW1A 0PW *Tel:* 020 7219 5353.

JAUNCEY OF TULLICHETTLE, LORD   Crossbencher

JAUNCEY OF TULLICHETTLE (Life Baron), Charles Eliot Jauncey; cr. 1988. Born 8 May 1925. Son of late Captain John Henry Jauncey, DSO, RN; educated Radley College; Christ Church, Oxford (BA jurisprudence 1947); Glasgow University (LLB 1949). Married Jean Graham 1948 (2 sons 1 daughter) (divorced 1969); married Elizabeth Ballingal 1973 (divorced 1977); married Camilla Cathcart 1977 (1 daughter). Served in Second World War 1943–46, Sub-Lieutenant RNVR. *Career:* Advocate, Scottish Bar 1949; Standing Junior Counsel to Admiralty 1954; QC (Scotland) 1963; Kintyre Pursuivant of Arms 1955–71; Sheriff Principal of Fife and Kinross 1971–74; Judge of the Courts of Appeal of Jersey and Guernsey 1972–79; Senator of the
College of Justice in Scotland 1979–88; Lord of Appeal in Ordinary 1988–96. Member Constitution Committee 2002–; Chairman, Chinook Committee 2001–02. Member: Queen's Body Guard for Scotland, Royal Company of Archers 1951, Historic Buildings Council for Scotland 1972–92. PC 1998. *Recreations:* Shooting, fishing, genealogy, bicycling. *Clubs:* Royal (Perth). Raised to the peerage as Baron Jauncey of Tullichettle, of Comrie in the District of Perth and Kinross 1988. Rt Hon the Lord Jauncey of Tullichettle, Tullichettle, Comrie, Crieff, Perthshire, PH6 2HU.

Visit the Vacher Dod Website . . . **www.DodOnline.co.uk**

JAY OF PADDINGTON, BARONESS   Labour

JAY OF PADDINGTON (Life Baroness), Margaret Ann Jay; cr. 1992. Born 18 November 1939. Daughter of Rt Hon. Baron Callaghan of Cardiff, KG (*qv*); educated Blackheath High School; Somerville College, Oxford (BA philosophy, politics and economics 1961). Married Hon Peter Jay 1961 (divorced 1986) (1 son 2 daughters); married Professor Michael W Adler, CBE 1994. *Trades Union:* Member, NUJ. Member, Kensington and Chelsea and Westminster Health Authority 1993–97; Former Member, Central Research and Development Committee for the NHS. *Career:* Various production posts with BBC Television in current affairs and further education 1965–77; Former reporter for: BBC Television's *Panorama*, Thames Television's *This Week*; Founder director, The National AIDS Trust 1988–92; Non-executive Director: Carlton Television to 1997, Scottish Power to 1997, Independent News and Media UK 2001–, BT 2001–. *House of Lords:* Minister of State, Department of Health 1997–98; Deputy Leader, House of Lords 1997–98; Leader of the House of Lords and Minister for Women (Lord Privy Seal) 1998–2001. Opposition Whip 1992–95. Opposition Spokesperson for Health 1992–97, Principal Opposition Spokesperson 1995–97, Government Spokesperson for Women's Issues 1998–2001. Member: Medical Ethics Committee 1993–94, House of Lords' Offices Committee 1997–. Former Member, President World Bank International Advisory Group on Health; Member, International Advisory Board Independent News and Media 2002–. Member Labour Party Donations Committee 2002–. Former Chair: National Association of League of Hospital Friends, North Thames Regional Committee for Research and Development in the NHS; Former Member of Council, The Overseas Development Institute; Former Governor, South Bank University; Former Member, Governing Board: Queen Charlotte's Maternity Hospital, Chelsea Hospital for Women; Chair, Overseas Development Institute 2002–. Two honorary degrees. Chair, Overseas Development Institute 2002–. PC 1998. *Publications: How Rich Can We Get?*, 1972; *Battered – The Story of Child Abuse* (joint author), 1986. *Special Interests:* Health, Overseas Aid and Development, Media, Broadcasting. Raised to the peerage as Baroness Jay of Paddington, of Paddington in the City of Westminster 1992. Rt Hon the Baroness Jay of Paddington, House of Lords, London, SW1A 0PW *Tel:* 020 7219 4912.

JEGER, BARONESS   Labour

JEGER (Life Baroness), Lena May Jeger; cr. 1979. Born 19 November 1915. Daughter of late Charles and Alice Chivers; educated Southgate County School; Birkbeck College, London (BA Hon Fellow 1994). Married Dr Santo Jeger 1948 (died 1953), formerly MP for Holborn and St Pancras South. *Trades Union:* Life Member NUJ. Councillor: St Pancras Borough Council 1945–59, London County Council 1951–54. *Career:* Formerly employed at the Ministry of Information and Foreign Office; Assistant editor in Moscow of *British Ally*, a newspaper published by the British Government for issue in the Soviet Union; Staff writer on *The Guardian* 1959–64; UK representative on the Status of Women Commission of UN 1967; Member, Consultative Assembly of the Council of Europe and of Western European Union 1969–71. *House of Commons:* MP (Labour) for Holborn and St Pancras South 1953–59, 1964–79; Chairman, Government's Working Party on Sewage Disposal 1969–70. Opposition Spokesman on: Health 1983–86, Social Security 1983–90. Member of: CPA, IPU. Member, National Executive Committee of the Labour Party 1960–61, 1968–80; Chairman, Labour Party 1979–80. Raised to the peerage as Baroness Jeger, of St Pancras in the County of Greater London 1979. The Baroness Jeger, 9 Cumberland Terrace, Regents Park, London, NW1 4HS

DodOnline
An Electronic Directory without rival …

Peers' biographies and photographs available with daily updates *via* the internet

For a *free* trial, call Yasmin Mirza, Aby Farsoun or Michael Mand on 020 7630 7643

JELLICOE, EARL   Conservative

JELLICOE (2nd Earl, UK), George Patrick John Rushworth Jellicoe; cr. 1925; Viscount Brocas; Viscount Jellicoe (UK) 1918; (Life) Baron Jellicoe of Southampton 1999. Born 4 April 1918. Son of Admiral of the Fleet 1st Earl, GCB, OM, GCVO; educated Winchester College; Trinity College, Cambridge (Exhibitioner, BA history 1939). Married Patricia Christine O'Kane 1944 (2 sons 2 daughters) (divorced 1966); married Philippa Dunne 1966 (1 son 2 daughters). Served in Middle East 1941–45 (despatches thrice, DSO, MC), No 8 Commando, Coldstream Guards, SAS and SBS, Lieutenant-Colonel. *Career:* HM Foreign Service 1947–58, serving in Washington, Brussels and Baghdad (Deputy Secretary General, The Baghdad Pact); Chairman: Greece Fund 1988–94, European Capital 1991–95; Director, Tate & Lyle plc 1973–93, Chairman 1978–83; Director, Sothebys 1973–93; Chairman: Davy Corporation 1985–90, Booker Tate 1988–91; Director: Smiths Industries 1973–86, S. G. Warburg 1964–70, 1973–88, Morgan Crucible 1974–88; President, East European Trade Council, Chairman 1986–90; Chairman, British Overseas Trade Board 1983–86. Chancellor, Southampton University 1984–95. *House of Lords:* First entered House of Lords 1939; Joint Parliamentary Secretary, Ministry of Housing and Local Government 1961–62; Minister of State, Home Office 1962–63; First Lord of the Admiralty 1963–64; Minister of Defence for the Royal Navy April-October 1964; Deputy Leader of Opposition 1967–70; Lord Privy Seal, Leader of the House of Lords and Minister for the Civil Service Department 1970–73. Government Whip (Lord in Waiting) January-June 1961. Former Chairman, Select Committee on Committees. Chair, Council, King's College, London 1977–84; President: Anglo-Hellenic League 1978–86, Patron 1986–, London Chamber of Commerce and Industry 1979–82; Chair, Medical Research Council 1982–90; President: UK Crete Veterans Association 1990–01; British Heart Foundation 1992–95, Royal Geographical Society 1993–97, The Geographical Club 1993–97, SAS Regimental Association 1996–2000, Patron 2000–. Hon. Degrees: Kings College, London, Southampton University, University of Southampton, Long Island, USA. President, Kennet and Avon Canal Trust 1987–94. DSO 1942; MC 1944; PC 1963; KBE 1986; French Legion d'Honneur; Croix de Guerre; Greek Order of Honour; Greek War Cross. Hon. Fellow, Royal Scottish Geographical Society 1997; FRS. Freeman, City of Athens. Member, Mercers' Company. *Special Interests:* Foreign Affairs, Education, Environment, Arts. *Recreations:* Travel. *Sportsclubs:* Ski Club of Great Britain. *Clubs:* Brooks's, Special Forces. Created a life peer as Baron Jellicoe of Southampton, of Southampton in the County of Hampshire 1999. Rt Hon the Earl Jellicoe, KBE, DSO, MC, FRS, Tidcombe Manor, Tidcombe, Nr Marlborough, Wiltshire, SN8 3SL *Tel:* 01264 731225 *Fax:* 01264 731418; Flat 5, 97 Onslow Square, London, SW7 3LU *Tel:* 020 7584 1551.

JENKIN OF RODING, LORD   Conservative

JENKIN OF RODING (Life Baron), Charles Patrick Fleeming Jenkin; cr. 1987. Born 7 September 1926. Son of late Charles Jenkin, industrial chemist; educated Clifton College; Jesus College, Cambridge (BA law 1951). Married Alison Monica Graham 1952 (2 sons 2 daughters). Served in the Cameron Highlanders, including service abroad 1945–48. Councillor, Hornsey Borough Council 1960–63. *Career:* Called to the Bar Middle Temple 1952; Practising barrister 1952–57; Distillers Co. Ltd 1957–70; Adviser, Andersen Consulting, Management Consultants 1985–96; Member, UK Advisory Board, National Economic Research Associates Inc. 1985–98; Chair, Target Finland Ltd 1987–96; Director, Friends Provident Life Office, Chair 1988–98; Member, Supervisory Board, Achmea Holding NV (Netherlands) 1992–98; UK Co-Chair, UK-Japan 2000 Group 1986–90, Board Member 1990–99; Non-executive Director, Crystalate Holdings plc 1987–90, Chair 1988–90; Chair, Lamco Paper Sales Ltd 1987–93; Adviser, Sumitomo Trust and Banking Co. Ltd 1989–; Member, International Advisory Board, Marsh and McLennan Group of Companies (US) 1993–99; Adviser, Thames Estuary Airport Co. Ltd. 1992–; Senior Vice-President, World Congress on Urban Growth and the Environment (Hong Kong) 1992–94. *House of Commons:* MP (Conservative) for Wanstead and Woodford 1964–87; Financial Secretary to the Treasury 1970–72; Chief Secretary to the Treasury 1972–74; Mininster for Energy 1974; Secretary of State for: Social Services 1979–81, Industry September 1981–83, the Environment 1983–85. Opposition Spokesperson for Treasury, Trade and Economic Affairs October 1965; Opposition Spokesperson for the Treasury 1967–70; Member, Shadow

Cabinet and Opposition Spokesperson for: Energy 1974–76, Social Services 1976–79. Member: House of Lords Offices Committee and Finance and Staffing Sub-Committee 1991–94, Select Committee on: Sustainable Development 1994–95, Science and Technology 1997–2001; Chair, Select Committee on Science and Technology Sub-Committee II (Science and Society) 1999–2000; Member, Science and Technology Sub-Committee: II (Aircraft Cabin Environment) 2000–01, IIA (Human Genetic Databases) 2000–01. Vice-President, Parliamentary and Scientific Committee 2003–. Executive Committee Member, ACP 1996–2000. Member: CPA, IPU. Member, Bow Group from 1951; President: Conservative Greater London Area Education Committee 1967–80, Conservative Greater London Area CPC Committee 1981–83, National CPC Committee 1982–85; Vice-President, Greater London Area Conservatives 1987–89, President 1989–93; President, Saffron Walden Constituency Conservative Association 1994–2003. Numerous charitable and voluntary organisations, including: Council member, Guide Dogs for the Blind Association 1987–97; Deputy Chair, Imperial Cancer Research Fund 1994–97; Joint President, Association of London Government 1995–; Vice-President, Foundation for Science and Technology 1996–97, Chair 1997–; Vice-President, Local Government Association 1997–; President, Association for Science Education, 2002–03. Fellow, Queen Mary and Westfield College 1991–; Two honorary doctorates; Fellow, College of Optometrists 2003–. Chair, Westfield College Trust 1989–2000; Patron: Redbridge Community Trust 1992–95, St Clare Hospice Trust 1992–; Chair, Forest Healthcare NHS Trust 1992–97; Trustee: Monteverdi Choir and Orchestra 1992–2001, Conservative Agents Superannuation Fund 1992–2000; Patron, London North-East Community Foundation 1995–; Trustee, St Andrews Prize Trust 2001–. PC 1973. Honorary Fellow Royal Society of Edinburgh 2001–. Freeman, City of London 1985; Hon. Freeman, London Borough of Redbridge 1988. *Special Interests:* Economic Policy, Industry, Science, Technology, Health, Disabled, Energy, Housing, Planning, Financial Services. *Recreations:* Gardening, DIY, bricklaying, sailing, music. *Clubs:* West Essex Conservative Club. Raised to the peerage as Baron Jenkin of Roding, of Wanstead and Woodford in Greater London 1987. Rt Hon the Lord Jenkin of Roding, House of Lords, London, SW1A 0PW *Tel:* 020 7219 6966 *Fax:* 020 7219 0759 *E-mail:* jenkinp@parliament.uk.

JENKINS OF PUTNEY, LORD — Labour

JENKINS OF PUTNEY (Life Baron), Hugh Gater Jenkins; cr. 1981. Born 27 July 1908. Son of late Joseph Walter Jenkins, dairyman and late Florence Gater; educated Enfield Grammar School. Married Marie Crosbie 1936 (died 1989); married Helena Maria Pavlidis 1991 (died 1994). *Trades Union:* Trade unionist since 1930; Member: Prudential Staff Union 1930–40, MSF 1947–, Actors Equity 1948–. Flight-Lieutenant, Royal Air Force during Second World War. London County Councillor 1958–64, Member, Town Planning Committee. *Career:* Prudential Assurance Company 1930–40, Assistant-Superintendent 1935–40; Research and publicity officer, National Union of Bank Employees 1946–50; Former editor, *The Bank Officer*; Assistant general secretary, Actors' Equity to 1964. *House of Commons:* Contested (Labour) Enfield West 1950, Mitcham 1955 general elections; MP (Labour) for Wandsworth, Putney division October 15, 1964–79; Minister for the Arts 1974–76. Opposition Spokesperson for the Arts 1973–74; Former Member, Public Records Committee. Member, Tribune Group. Member: CPA, IPU. Opposition Spokesperson for the Arts 1981–83. Member: CPA, IPU. Member, British-American Security Information Committee. Member, London Labour Party Executive Committee; Chairman, Victory For Socialism; Vice-Chairman, Labour Action For Peace. Former Chair, now Vice-President, Campaign for Nuclear Disarmament; Director Summer Schools Fabian Society. President, Theatres Trust. Life-President, Theatres Advisory Council; Former Member: The Arts Council, The National Theatre Board. Burma Star. *Publications; The Culture Gap*, 1980; *Rank and File*, 1981; As well as radio plays (DDC Radio Four), various pamphlets and contributions to journals and newspapers. *Special Interests:* Disarmament, Arts, Trade Unions, Media, Nuclear Disarmament. *Recreations:* Avoiding retirement, writing, listening, talking, viewing, reading, concert and theatre-going. *Clubs:* Progressive League. Raised to the peerage as Baron Jenkins of Putney, of Wandsworth in Greater London 1981. The Lord Jenkins of Putney, House of Lords, London, SW1A 0PW *Tel:* 020 7219 6706 *Tel:* 020 8788 0371.

Visit the Vacher Dod Website . . . **www.DodOnline.co.uk**

JOFFE, LORD   Crossbencher

JOFFE (Life Baron), Joel Goodman Joffe; cr. 2000. Born 12 May 1932. Son of Abraham and Dena Joffe; educated Marist Brothers' College, Johannesburg, South Africa; University of Witwatersrand (BCom, LLB 1955). Married Vanetta Pretorius 1962 (3 daughters). *Career:* Admitted Solicitor, Johannesburg 1956; Called to the Bar, South Africa 1962; Human Rights lawyer 1958–65; Director and secretary, Abbey Life Assurance Company 1965–70; Director, Joint Managing Director and Deputy Chairman, Allied Dunbar, Life Assurance Company 1971–91; Chair, Swindon Private Hospital 1982–87; Oxfam: Hon. Secretary 1982–85, Executive Committee Chairman 1985–93, Chair 1995–2001; Chair The Giving Campaign 2001–. Chair: Swindon Health Authority 1988–93, Swindon and Marlborough NHS Trust 1993–95. Three honorary doctorates. Chair, Allied Dunbar Charitable Trust 1974–93; Trustee: Action for Disability and Development 1984–98, Oxfam 1979–2001: Canon Collins Educational Trust for Southern Africa 1985–, Legal Assistance Trust for Southern Africa 1995–, International Alert 1994–2000, The Smith Institute 1999–, Management Accountancy for NGOs 2000–, J&G and VLJ Charitable Trusts 1968–. Member, Royal Commission on Long Term Care for the Elderly 1997–98, Special Adviser to the South African Minister of Transport 1997–98. CBE 1999. *Publications: The Rivonia Trial*, 1995. *Special Interests:* Human Rights, Developing World, Financial Services, Consumer Protection. *Recreations:* Tennis. *Clubs:* Royal Commonwealth Society. Raised to the peerage as Baron Joffe, of Liddington in the County of Wiltshire 2000. The Lord Joffe, CBE, Liddington Manor, Liddington, Swindon, Wiltshire, SN4 0HD *Tel:* 01793 790203 *Fax:* 01793 791144.

JONES, LORD   Labour

JONES (Life Baron), (Stephen) Barry Jones; cr. 2001. Born 26 June 1937. Son of late Stephen Jones, steelworker, and late Grace Jones; educated Hawarden Grammar School; Teacher training, Normal College, Bangor, North Wales. Married Janet Davies (1 son). *Trades Union:* Regional officer, National Union of Teachers. *Career:* Head of English department, Deeside Secondary School, Flintshire. *House of Commons:* Contested Northwich, Cheshire 1966 general election; Labour member for East Flint 1970–83, and for Alyn and Deeside 1983–2001; PPS to Denis Healey as Chancellor of the Exchequer 1972–74; Parliamentary Under-Secretary of State for Wales 1974–79; Member, Shadow Cabinet 1983–92. Opposition Front Bench Spokesman on Employment 1980–83. Member European Union Sub-committee A (Economic and Financial Affairs, Trade and External Relations) 2003–. Member, Delegation of Council of Europe and Western European Union 1971–74. Former Member, Executive of Labour Party, Wales. Governor: National Museum of Wales, National Library of Wales; Life Member, Liverpool Royal Philharmonic Society; Friend of: The Royal Academy, The Tate Gallery, Museums and Galleries of Merseyside; Member, National Trust. Member, Prime Minister's Intelligence and Security Committee 1994–97, 1997–; Vice-President, Federation of Economic Development Authorities; Chairman, Diocesan Education Board (St Asaph); President, Flintshire Alzheimers Society; Trustee, Winnicot Clinic; President, Deeside Hospital League of Friends. PC 1999. *Special Interests:* Manufacturing Industry. *Recreations:* Soccer, cricket, watching tennis. Raised to the peerage as Baron Jones, of Deeside in the County of Clwyd 2001. Rt Hon the Lord Jones, House of Lords, London, SW1A 0PW *Tel:* 020 7219 3556.

JOPLING, LORD   Conservative

JOPLING (Life Baron), (Thomas) Michael Jopling; cr. 1997. Born 10 December 1930. Son of Mark Jopling; educated Cheltenham College; King's College, Newcastle upon Tyne (BSc agriculture Durham 1952). Married Gail Dickinson 1958 (2 sons). Councillor, Thirsk Rural District Council 1958–64; DL: Cumbria 1991–97, North Yorkshire 1998–. *Career:* Farmer. *House of Commons:* Contested (Conservative) Wakefield 1959 general election; MP (Conservative) for Westmorland 1964–83 and for Westmorland and Lonsdale 1983–97; Sponsored Private Member's Bill on Parish Councils 1969; PPS to Minister of Agriculture, Fisheries and Food 1970–71; Member, Shadow Cabinet 1975–76; Minister of Agriculture, Fisheries and Food 1983–87;

Sponsored Private Member's Bills on: Children's Seat Belts 1990, Antarctica 1994. Assistant Whip 1971–73; Government Whip 1973–74; Chief Whip 1979–83. Opposition Spokesman for Agriculture 1974–79. Co-opted Member, European Union Sub-committee D (Agriculture, Fisheries and Food) 1997–99; Member: European Union 1999–, European Union Sub-committee C (Common Foreign and Security Policy) 1999–, Chairman 2000–. Committee Member, Association of Conservative Peers 1997–2000. Executive Committee, UK Branch of CPA 1974–79, 1987–97, Vice-Chairman 1977–78; UK Delegate, North Atlantic Assembly 1987–97; Executive, CPA HQ 1988–89; Leader of UK Delegation, OSCE Parliamentary Assembly 1991–97, UK Delegate 2000–01; President, EU Councils of Agriculture and Fishery Ministers 1996; Executive Committee, UK Branch IPU 1999–; UK representative to NATO Parliamentary Assembly 2002–. Member, National Council of NFU 1962–65; President, Auto Cycle Union 1990–; President, Despatch Association 2002–. Hon. DCL, Newcastle 1992. Fellow, Industry and Parliament Trust. PC 1979. *Clubs:* Buck's, Royal Automobile. Raised to the peerage as Baron Jopling, of Ainderby Quernhow in the County of North Yorkshire 1997. Rt Hon the Lord Jopling, DL, Ainderby Hall, Thirsk, North Yorkshire, YO7 4HZ; House of Lords, London, SW1A 0PW *Tel:* 020 7219 0801.

JORDAN, LORD — Labour

JORDAN (Life Baron), William Brian Jordan; cr. 2000. Born 28 January 1936. Son of Walter and Alice Jordan; educated Secondary Modern School, Birmingham. Married Jean Ann Livesey 1958 (3 daughters). *Trades Union:* Member of: AAEEU England Amicus. Board Member, English Partnerships 1993–2002. *Career:* Convenor of shop stewards, Guest, Keen and Nettlefold 1966; full time AUEW divisional organiser 1976; President, AEU, then AEEU 1986–95; Member, TUC General Council 1986–95; General Secretary, ICFTU (International Confederation of Free Trade Unions) 1995–2002. President: European Metal Workers Federation 1986–95, International Metal Workers Federation 1986–95; UN High Panel on Youth Employment 2001–; UN Global Compact Advisory Council 2001. Governor: LSE 1987–2002, Manchester Business School 1987–92, BBC 1988–98, Victim Support Advisory Committee, Winston Churchill Trust. DUniv, Central England 1993; Hon. DSc, Cranfield 1995. Member: NEDC 1986–92, Engineering Industry Training Board 1986–91, Council, Industrial Society 1987–. CBE 1992. *Recreations:* Reading, watching football. Raised to the peerage as Baron Jordan, of Bournville in the County of West Midlands 2000. The Lord Jordan, CBE, House of Lords, London, SW1A 0PW *Tel:* 020 7219 5648; 352 Heath Road, South Northfield, Birmingham, B31 2BH *Tel:* 0121 475 7319 *Fax:* 0121 478 9485 *E-mail:* ji@dial.pipex.com.

JUDD, LORD — Labour

JUDD (Life Baron), Frank Ashcroft Judd; cr. 1991. Born 28 March 1935. Son of late Charles Judd, CBE, and late Helen Judd, JP; educated City of London School; London School of Economics (BSc economics 1956). Married Christine Elizabeth Willington 1961 (2 daughters). *Trades Union:* Member: AMICUS, GMB. Short Service Commission, RAF 1957–59. *Career:* General Secretary, International Voluntary Service 1960–66; Associate director, International Defence and Aid Fund for Southern Africa 1979–80; Director, Voluntary Service Overseas 1980–85; Director, Oxfam 1985–91; Chair, International Council of Voluntary Agencies 1985–90; Non-executive Director, Portsmouth Harbour Renaissance; Consultant (professional) to De Montfort University on international and community action issues. *House of Commons:* Contested (Labour): Sutton and Cheam 1959, Portsmouth West 1964 general elections; MP (Labour) for: Portsmouth West 1966–74 for, Portsmouth North 1974–79; PPS to: Minister of Housing 1967–70, Leader of Opposition 1970–72; Parliamentary Under-Secretary of State (Navy) Ministry of Defence 1974–76; Minister of State: Overseas Development 1976–77, Foreign and Commonwealth Office 1977–79. Opposition Defence Spokesperson (Navy) 1972–74. Member, Parliamentary Delegation to Council of Europe and WEU 1969–72. Opposition Spokesperson for Foreign Affairs 1991–92; Principal Opposition Spokesperson for: Development and Co-operation 1992–97, Education 1992–94; Opposition Spokesperson for Defence 1995–97. Co-opted Member, Select Committee on European Communities Sub-Committee D (Environment, Agriculture, Public Health and Consumer Protection) 1997–2001; Member: Procedure Committee 2001–, Ecclesiastical Committee 2002–. Member, Parliamentary Delegation to Council of

Europe and WEU 1997–; Chair: Rapporteur and Co-Chair Ad Hoc Committee on Chechnya of the Council of Europe 1999–2003. Former Member: Commission on Global Governance, WHO Task Force on Health and Development, Justice Richard Goldstone's Commission on Human Duties and Responsibilities. Member, Fabian Society, former Chair; Member, Christian Socialist Movement. President, YMCA (England); President, Friends of the Royal Naval Museum; Member of the Court: London School of Economics and Political Science, Lancaster University, Vice-President: Intermediate Technology Group, Council for National Parks; United Nations Association Member: Royal Institute for International Affairs, Oxfam Association; Convenor, Social Responsibility Forum of Churches Together in Cumbria and North Lancashire; Hon lecturer, University of East Anglia. Five honorary doctorates/fellowships. Trustee: Saferworld, The Ruskin Foundation, Member, North West Regional Committee of the National Trust. Member: British Council. FRSA. Freeman, City of Portsmouth 1995. *Publications:* Co-author: *Radical Future*, 1967; *Purpose in Socialism*, 1973; *Imaging Tomorrow*, 2000; Also various articles on current affairs. *Special Interests:* Foreign Affairs, Third World, Defence, Education, Refugees, Migration, Race Relations, Penal Affairs, Environment Policy. *Recreations:* Walking, family holidays. *Clubs:* Royal Commonwealth Society. Raised to the peerage as Baron Judd, of Portsea in the County of Hampshire 1991. The Lord Judd, House of Lords, London, SW1A 0PW *Tel:* 020 7219 3205 *Fax:* 020 7630 7135 *Tel:* 020 7630 7135.

K

KEITH OF CASTLEACRE, LORD   Conservative

KEITH OF CASTLEACRE (Life Baron), Kenneth Alexander Keith; cr.1980. Born 30 August 1916. Son of late Edward Charles Keith; educated Rugby School. Married Lady Ariel Olivia Winifred Baird 1946 (1 son 1 daughter) (divorced 1958); married Mrs Nancy Hayward 1962 (divorced 1972, she died 1990); married Mrs Marie Hanbury 1973 (died 2001); married Mrs Penelope de Laszlo 2002. 2nd Lieutenant, Welsh Guards 1939; Lieutenant-Colonel 1945; Served in North Africa, Italy, France and Germany; (despatches, Croix de Guerre with Silver Star). *Career:* Trained as a chartered accountant; Merchant Banker; Assistant to Director General, Political Intelligence Department, Foreign Office 1945–46; Director: Philip Hill and Partners 1947–51, Eagle Star Insurance Co. 1955–75; Vice-Chairman, BEA 1964–71; Member, NEDC 1964–71; Chairman, Economic Planning Council for East Anglia 1965–70; Director, National Provincial Bank 1967–69; Chairman, Hill Samuel Group Ltd 1970–80; Director, British Airways 1971–72; Chairman, Philip Hill Investment Trust Ltd 1972–87; Chairman and Chief Executive, Rolls-Royce Ltd 1972–80; Member, CBI/NEDC Liaison Committee 1974–78, Vice-Chairman, Beecham Group Ltd 1974–87, Director, Standard Telephones & Cables Ltd 1977–89, Member, National Defence Industries Council to January 1980; Chairman, Standard Telephones & Cables Ltd 1985–1989; Chairman, Beecham Group Ltd 1986–87; Member: SBAC, Defence Industries Council. Vice-President, Engineering Employers' Federation to January 1980; Governor, National Institute of Economic and Social Research; President, British Standards Institute 1989–94. Kt 1969. Hon. Companion, Royal Aeronautical Society 1979. *Special Interests:* Agriculture. *Recreations:* Shooting, golf. *Sportsclubs:* Royal Ancient Golf Club, St Andrews, Fife. *Clubs:* White's, Links (New York). Raised to the peerage as Baron Keith of Castleacre, of Swaffham in the County of Norfolk 1980. The Lord Keith of Castleacre, The Wicken House, Castle Acre, Norfolk, PE32 2BP *Tel:* 01760 755225 *E-mail:* wicken@c-acre.u-net.com.

DodOnline
An Electronic Directory without rival ...

Peers' biographies and photographs available with daily updates *via* the internet

For a *free* trial, call Yasmin Mirza, Aby Farsoun or Michael Mand on 020 7630 7643

KELVEDON, LORD — Conservative

KELVEDON (Life Baron), (Henry) Paul Guinness Channon; cr. 1997. Born 9 October 1935. Son of late Sir Henry Channon, MP and of late Lady Honor Svejdar, daughter of 2nd Earl of Iveagh, KG, CB, CMG; educated Eton College; Christ Church, Oxford. Married Mrs Ingrid Olivia Georgia Guinness, née Wyndham 1963 (1 son 1 daughter, 1 daughter deceased). 2nd Lieutenant, Royal Horse Guards (The Blues) 1955–56. *House of Commons:* MP (Conservative) for Southend West 1959–97; PPS: to Minister of Power 1959–60, to Home Secretary 1960–62, to First Secretary of State July 1962, to Foreign Secretary 1963–64; Joint Parliamentary Secretary to the Minister of Housing and Local Government June-October 1970; Joint Parliamentary Under-Secretary of State, Department of the Environment 1970–72; Minister of State for Northern Ireland 1972; Minister for Housing and Construction 1972–74; Minister of State, Civil Service Department 1979–81; Minister for: The Arts 1981–83, Trade 1983–86; Secretary of State for: Trade and Industry 1986–87, Transport 1987–89. Opposition Spokesman on: Arts and Amenities 1967–70, Price and Consumer Affairs February-November 1974, The Environment 1974–75. Deputy Leader, Conservative Group on Council of Europe 1976–79. Chairman, British Association for Central and Eastern Europe 1992–. PC 1980. *Clubs:* White's, Buck's. Raised to the peerage as Baron Kelvedon, of Ongar in the County of Essex 1997. Rt Hon the Lord Kelvedon, House of Lords, London, SW1A 0PW *Tel:* 020 7219 5353.

KENNEDY OF THE SHAWS, BARONESS — Labour

KENNEDY OF THE SHAWS (Life Baroness), Helena Ann Kennedy; cr. 1997. Born 12 May 1950. Daughter of late Joshua Kennedy and of Mary Kennedy; educated Holyrood Secondary School, Glasgow; Council of Legal Education. Partner Roger Iain Mitchell 1977–84 (1 son); married Dr Iain Louis Hutchison 1986 (1 son 1 daughter). *Career:* Called to the Bar, Gray's Inn 1972; Established Chambers at: Garden Court 1974, Tooks Court 1984, Doughty Street 1990; Queen's Counsel 1991; Bencher of Gray's Inn 1999. Chancellor, Oxford Brookes University 1994–2001. IBA's International Task Force on Terrorism 2001–02. Member: National Board, Women's Legal Defence Fund 1989–91, Council, Howard League for Penal Reform 1989–, Hampstead Theatre Board 1989–98, Bar Council 1990–93, Committee, Association of Women Barristers 1991–92; Chair: British Council 1998–, London International Festival of Theatre 1993–2002, Human Genetics Commission 2000–, Advisory Council of the World Bank Institute; Member Independent Newspaper Board. Women's Network Award for her work on women and justice 1992; UK Woman of Europe Award 1995; National Federation of Women's Institutes Making a World of Difference Award Institutes for her work on equal rights 1996; The Times Newspaper (Joint) Lifetime Achievement Award 1997. 18 honorary law doctorates. Board Member, City Limits Magazine 1982–84; Chairman, Haldane Society 1983–86, Vice-President 1986–; Broadcaster: First female moderator, Hypotheticals (Granada) on surrogate motherhood and artificial insemination; Presenter: Heart of the Matter, BBC 1987, Putting Women in the Picture, BBC2 1987, Time Gentlemen Please, BBC Scotland 1994; Has also presented many other television programmes; Board Member: New Statesman 1990–96, Counsel Magazine 1990–; Chairman, Charter '88 1992–97; Chairman, Standing Committee for Youth Justice, NACRO 1993–. Fellow, Royal Society of Arts; Hon. Fellow: Institute of Advanced Legal Studies 1997, City and Guilds London Institute, Institute of Advanced Legal Studies; Hon Member Paris-based Academie Universelle des Cultures. *Publications:* Co-author: *The Bar on Trial*, 1978, *Child Abuse Within the Family*, 1984, *Balancing Acts*, 1989; *Eve was Framed*, 1992; Leader of enquiry into health, environmental and safety aspects of Atomic Weapons Establishment *Secrecy Versus Safety*, 1994; *Learning Works* Official report for the FEFC on widening participation in Further Education, 1997; *Inquiry into Violence in Penal Institutions for Young People*, report published 1995; Lectures; Has contributed articles on law, civil liberties and women. *Recreations:* Theatre, spending time with family and friends. Raised to the peerage as Baroness Kennedy of The Shaws, of Cathcart in the City of Glasgow 1997. The Baroness Kennedy of The Shaws, QC, c/o Hilary Hard, 12 Athelstan Close, Harold Wood, Essex, RM3 0QJ.

KILCLOONEY, LORD   Crossbencher

KILCLOONEY (Life Baron), John David Taylor; cr. 2001. Born 24 December 1937. Son of late George David Taylor, architect, and late Georgina Taylor (née Baird); educated Royal School, Armagh; Queen's University, Belfast (BSc applied science and technology 1950). Married Mary Frances Todd 1970 (1 son 5 daughters). Leader, Ulster Unionists in Castlereagh Borough Council 1989–94. *Career:* Company director; Chairman, Alpha Newspaper Group (19 newspapers in Northern Ireland); MP (South Tyrone) Stormont 1965–73; Parliamentary Secretary, Ministry of Home Affairs, Northern Ireland 1969–70; Minister of State, Home Affairs 1970–72; Member: for Fermanagh and South Tyrone, Northern Ireland Assembly 1973–75, for North Down, Northern Ireland Constitutional Convention 1976–77, for North Down, Northern Ireland Assembly 1982–86; MEP (Northern Ireland) 1979–89; Northern Ireland Forum 1996–98; New Northern Ireland Assembly 1998–2003. *House of Commons:* Member for Strangford 1983–2001. Spokesperson for: Trade and Industry 1992–97, Foreign and Commonwealth Affairs 1997–2001. Member for Northern Ireland, European Parliament 1979–89; Member: Council of Europe 1998–, Western European Union 1998–. Chair: Queen's University Conservative and Unionist Association 1959–60, Ulster Young Unionist Council 1961–62; Hon. Secretary, Ulster Unionist Party 1994–96, Deputy Leader 1995–2001. Chair, Gosford Housing Association; Member, Board of Charles Sheils Charity Homes; Governor, The Royal School, Armagh. Eastern Mediterranean University, Famagusta (PhD International Relations 1999). PC (Northern Ireland) 1970. AMICEI; AMInstHE. *Publications: Ulster – The Economic Facts. Special Interests:* Irish Politics, European Union, Regional Policy, Agriculture. *Recreations:* Antiques, Irish Art, Travelling, Horticulture. *Sportsclubs:* Ards Football Club. *Clubs:* Farmers (London), County (Armagh). Raised to the peerage as Baron Kilclooney, of Armagh in the County of Armagh 2001. Rt Hon the Lord Kilclooney, House of Lords, London, SW1A 0PW *Tel:* 020 7219 6443 *Fax:* 020 7219 0575 *Tel:* 020 7931 7211 *Fax:* 028 3752 2409.

KILPATRICK OF KINCRAIG, LORD   Crossbencher

KILPATRICK OF KINCRAIG (Life Baron), Robert Kilpatrick; cr. 1996. Born 29 July 1926. Son of late Robert Kilpatrick; educated Buckhaven High School; Edinburgh University (MB, ChB 1949, MD 1960) (Ettles Scholar, Leslie Gold Medallist). Married Elizabeth Gibson Page Forbes 1950 (2 sons 1 daughter). *Career:* Medical Registrar, Edinburgh 1951–54; Sheffield University: Lecturer 1955–66, Professor of Clinical Pharmacology and Therapeutics 1966–75, Dean, Faculty of Medicine 1971–74; Member, General Medical Council 1972–76, 1979–, President 1989–95; Chairman, Society of Endocrinology 1975–78; Chairman, Advisory Committee on Pesticides 1975–87; Leicester University 1975–89: Dean, Faculty of Medicine 1975–89, Professor and Head of Department of Clinical Pharmacology and Therapeutics 1975–83, Professor of Medicine 1984–89; President, British Medical Association 1997–98. Dr hc Edinburgh 1987; Hon. LLD, Dundee 1992; Hon. DSc; Hull 1994, Leicester 1994; Hon. LLD, Sheffield 1995. CBE 1979; Kt 1986. FRCP (Ed) 1963; FRCP 1975; FRCPGlas 1991; Hon. FRCS, 1995; Hon. FRCP, Dublin 1995; Hon. FRCS, Edinburgh 1996; Hon. RC Path. 1996; Hon. FRCP (Ed) 1996; FRSE 1998. *Publications:* Several articles in medical and scientific journals. *Special Interests:* Health, Education, Professional Self-Regulation. *Recreations:* Golf. *Clubs:* Royal and Ancient (St Andrews), New (Edinburgh). Raised to the peerage as Baron Kilpatrick of Kincraig, of Dysart in the District of Kirkcaldy 1996. The Lord Kilpatrick of Kincraig, CBE, 12 Wester Coates Gardens, Edinburgh, EH12 5LT *Tel:* 0131–337 7304.

DodOnline
An Electronic Directory without rival ...

Peers' biographies and photographs available with daily updates *via* the internet

For a *free* trial, call Yasmin Mirza, Aby Farsoun or Michael Mand on 020 7630 7643

KIMBALL, LORD — Conservative

KIMBALL (Life Baron), Marcus Richard Kimball; cr. 1985. Born 18 October 1928. Son of late Major Lawrence Kimball; educated Eton College; Trinity College, Cambridge (BA history 1951). Married June Mary Fenwick 1956 (2 daughters). Captain, Leicestershire and Derbyshire Yeomanry (TA). Member, Rutland County Council 1955–62; DL, Leicestershire 1984–97, Rutland 1997–. *Career:* Director, The Royal Trust Bank 1970–93; Elected to the Council of Lloyd's of London 1982–90; Chairman, South East Assured Tenancies plc 1989–96; Chairman, British Greyhound Racing Fund Ltd 1993–96. *House of Commons:* Contested (Conservative) Derby South 1955; MP (Conservative) for Gainsborough 1956–83. Member of: Liaison Committee 1998–, Procedure Committee 1999–2002. Chairman, East Midlands Area Young Conservatives 1954–58. Privy Council Representative, Royal College of Veterinary Surgeons 1969–82; Chairman: British Field Sports Society 1966–82, Firearms Consultation Committee 1989–94; President: National Light Horse Breeding Society 1990–91, Olympia International Show Jumping Championship 1991–2000; President, British Field Sports Society 1996–98, Deputy President 1998–. Chairman, University of Cambridge Veterinary School Trust 1989–97. Kt 1981. Hon. Associate, Royal College of Veterinary Surgeons 1982. *Special Interests:* Finance, Agriculture. *Recreations:* Fishing, hunting, shooting. *Clubs:* White's, Pratt's. Raised to the peerage as Baron Kimball, of Easton in the County of Leicestershire 1985. The Lord Kimball, DL, Great Easton Manor, Market Harborough, Leicestershire, LE16 8TB *Tel:* 01536 770333 *Fax:* 01536 770453.

KING OF BRIDGWATER, LORD — Conservative

KING OF BRIDGWATER (Life Baron), Tom (Thomas) Jeremy King; cr. 2001. Born 13 June 1933; educated Rugby School; Emmanuel College, Cambridge (MA classics, archaeology and anthropology 1956). Married Jane Tilney 1960 (1 son 1 daughter). Army national service 1952–53; service in East Africa; TA 1953–56. *Career:* E. S. and A. Robinson Ltd, Bristol 1956–69, Divisional General Manager 1964–69; Chair Sale, Tilney & Co Ltd industrial holding company 1971–79; Non-executive Director, Electra Investment Trust 1992–; Chairman, London International Exhibition Centre plc 1994–. *House of Commons:* Conservative Member for Bridgwater 1970 by-election–2001; PPS to Christopher Chataway: as Minister of Posts and Telecommunications 1970–72, as Minister for Industrial Development 1972–74; Minister for Local Government and Environmental Services 1979–83; Secretary of State for: Environment January-June 1983, Transport June-October 1983, Employment 1983–85, Northern Ireland 1985–89, Defence 1989–92. Opposition Spokesperson for: Industry 1975–76, Energy 1976–79. Chair, Intelligence and Security Committee 1994–2001. PC 1979; CH 1992. *Recreations:* Cricket, skiing. Raised to the peerage as Lord King of Bridgwater, of Bridgwater in the County of Somerset 2001. Rt Hon the Lord King of Bridgwater, CH, House of Lords, London, SW1A 0PW *Tel:* 020 7219 4467.

KING OF WARTNABY, LORD — Conservative

KING OF WARTNABY (Life Baron), John Leonard King; cr. 1983. Son of late Albert John King and Kathleen King. Married Lorna Sykes 1941 (died 1969) (3 sons 1 daughter); married Hon. Isabel Monckton 1970 *Career:* Founded: Whitehouse Industries Ltd 1945, Ferrybridge Industries Ltd; Chairman, Pollard Ball & Roller Bearing Co Ltd 1961–69; Babcock International Group plc (firstly Babcock and Wilcox Ltd, secondly Babcock International plc, thirdly FKI Babcock plc and fourthly Babcock International Group plc) 1970–, President 1994–; Dennis Motor Holdings Ltd 1970–72; NEDC Finance Committee, Review Board for Government Contracts 1975–78; SKF (UK) Ltd 1976–89; British Nuclear Associates Ltd 1978–89; British Airways 1981–93, President 1993–, President Emeritus; Numerous directorships, especially in aviation companies, in USA and UK; Member: Advisory Committee, Optima Fund Management LP, USA, Advisory Council, Westinghouse Electric Europe. Chairman, British Olympics Appeal Committee 1975–78;

MacMillan Appeal for Continuing Care (Cancer Relief) 1977–78; Alexandra Rose Day 1980–85; Committee Member, Ranfurly Library Service; MFH Badsworth Foxhounds 1949–58; Duke of Rutlands Foxhounds (Belvoir) 1958–72, Chairman 1972–; President: Brooklands Club, British Show Jumping Association. Hon. Dr Hum., Gardner-Webb College (USA) 1980; Hon. Dr of Science, Cranfield Institute of Technology; Hon. City and Guilds Insignia Award in Technology. Trustee: Royal Opera House Trust, Liver Research Unit, Blenheim Foundation; Advisory Council, Prince's Youth Business Trust. Kt 1979; Commander of the Royal Order of the Polar Star (Sweden) 1983. ARAeS 1982 (President Heathrow Branch); FCIT 1982; FBIM; Companion, Royal Aeronautical Society 1985–87. Freedom, City of London 1984. *Recreations:* Field sports, fox hunting, shooting, fishing. *Clubs:* White's, Pratt's, The Brook (New York). Raised to the peerage as Baron King of Wartnaby, of Wartnaby in the County of Leicestershire 1983. The Lord King of Wartnaby, Wartnaby, Melton Mowbray, Leicestershire, LE14 3HY *Tel:* 01664 822549 *Fax:* 01664 822231.

KING OF WEST BROMWICH, LORD   Labour

KING OF WEST BROMWICH (Life Baron), Tarsem King; cr. 1999. Born 24 April 1937. Son of Ujagar Singh, and Dalip Kaur; educated Khalsa High School, Dosanjh, Kalan, Punjab, India; Punjab University, India (BA mathematics 1958); National Foundry College, Wolverhampton (Diploma in foundry technology and management 1964); Aston University, Birmingham (Postgraduate diploma in management studies 1965); Teacher Training College, Wolverhampton (Teachers' Certificate 1968); Essex University (MSc statistics and operational research 1972). Married Mrs Mohinder Kaur 1957 (1 son). *Trades Union:* Member, NUT. Councillor, Sandwell Metropolitan Borough Council 1979–: Deputy Mayor 1982–83, Deputy Leader 1992–97, Leader 1997–; JP, West Bromwich 1987– Mayor 2001–02. *Career:* Laboratory assistant, Coneygre Foundry 1960–62; Foundry trainee, Birmid Group of Companies 1964–65; Teacher, Churchfields School, West Bromwich 1968–74; Deputy head, mathematics department, Great Barr School, Birmingham 1974–90; Managing Director, Sandwell Polybags Ltd 1990–. Member: Hybrid Instruments Committee 1999–, Select Committee on European Union, Sub-Committee F (Social Affairs, Education and Home Affairs) 2000–. Co-operative Party Sponsored Councillor; Secretary, West Bromwich Ward Branch Labour Party; Treasurer: Sandwell Local Government Committee, Executive Member, West Bromwich East GC. Member Black Country Consortium; Vice-Chair Faith in Sandwell Organisation; Vice-President, West Bromwich and District YMCA. Doctorate of education Wolverhampton University. Member, South Staffordshire Water Company Charitable Trust. Represents Sandwell in: West Midlands Local Goverment Association, West Midlands Regional Chamber Member EU Committee of the Regions (COR). MSc; CEd; DipFTM; DMS; MBIM. *Special Interests:* Local Government, Education, Small Businesses. *Recreations:* Reading, music. Raised to the peerage as Baron King of West Bromwich, of West Bromwich in the County of West Midlands 1999. The Lord King of West Bromwich, Sandwell MBC, Sandwell Council House, PO Box 2374, Oldbury, West Midlands, B69 3DE *Tel:* 0121–532 5688 *Fax:* 0121–532 5688; 27 Roebuck Lane, West Bromwich, B70 6QP *E-mail:* lordking@sandwellmbcfsnet.co.uk.

KINGSDOWN, LORD   Crossbencher

KINGSDOWN (Life Baron), Robin (Robert) Leigh-Pemberton; cr. 1993. Born 5 January 1927. Son of late Robert Douglas Leigh-Pemberton, MBE, MC; educated St Peter's Court, Broadstairs; Eton College; Trinity College, Oxford (MA greats 1950). Married 1953, Rosemary Davina, OBE, daughter of late Lieutenant-Colonel D. W. A. W. Forbes, MC and late Dowager Marchioness of Exeter (4 sons and 1 son deceased). Served Grenadier Guards 1945–48; Hon. Colonel: Kent and Sharpshooters Yeomanry Squadron 1979–92, 265 (Kent and County of London Yeomanry) Signal Squadron (V) 1979–92, 5th Volunteer Battalion, The Queen's Regiment 1987–93. Councillor, Kent County Council 1961–77, Chair 1972–75; JP, Kent 1961–75; DL, Kent 1970–72, Vice-Lord-Lieutenant 1972–82, Lord Lieutenant 1982–2002. *Career:* Called to Bar, Inner Temple 1954; Director, National Westminster Bank 1972–83, Deputy Chairman 1974–77, Chairman 1977–83; Director, Birmid Qualcast 1966–83, Chairman 1975–77; Director, University Life Assurance Society 1967–78; Member, South East Planning Council 1972–74; Director, Redland Ltd 1972–83; Member: Prime Minister's

Committee on Local Government Rules of Conduct 1973–74, Medway Ports Authority 1974–76, Committee on Police Pay 1977–79; Director, Equitable Life Assurance Society 1979–83; Member, National Economic Development Council 1982–92, Governor, Bank of England 1983–93; Non-Executive Director: Hambros plc 1993–98, Glaxo Wellcome plc 1993–96, Redland plc 1993–98, Foreign and Colonial Investment Trust 1993–98. Pro-Chancellor, University of Kent 1977–83. Seneschal, Canterbury Cathedral 1983–; Governor, Ditchley Foundation 1987–2001. Hon. DCL, Kent 1983; Hon. Fellow, Trinity College, Oxford 1984; Hon. DLitt: City 1988, Loughborough 1990. Trustee, Glyndebourne Arts Trust 1977–83. Hon. Bencher, Inner Temple 1983. PC 1987; KG 1994. FRSA 1977–2002; FBIM 1977. Liveryman, Mercers' Company; Hon Liveryman, Skinners' Company. *Special Interests:* Countryside and Country Life. *Recreations:* Country life, The Arts. *Sportsclubs:* Kent County Cricket, Royal St George Golf (Sandwich). *Clubs:* Brooks's, Cavalry and Guards. Raised to the peerage as Baron Kingsdown, of Pemberton in the County of Lancashire 1993. Rt Hon the Lord Kingsdown, KG, Torry Hill, Sittingbourne, Kent, ME9 0SP *Tel:* 01795 830258 *Fax:* 01795 830268 *E-mail:* lord.kingsdown@btinternet.com.

KINGSLAND, LORD — Conservative

KINGSLAND (Life Baron), Christopher James Prout; cr. 1994. Born 1 January 1942. Son of late Frank Yabsley Prout, MC and bar, and of Doris Lucy, née Osborne; educated Sevenoaks School; Manchester University (BA); The Queen's College, Oxford (Scholar, BPhil, DPhil). TA Officer (Major); OU OTC 1966–74; 16/5 The Queen's Royal Lancers 1974–82; 3rd Armoured Division 1982–88; RARO 1988–. DL, Shropshire 1997–. *Career:* English Speaking Union Fellow, Columbia University, New York 1963–64; Staff member, IBRD (UN) Washington DC 1966–69; Leverhulme Fellow and lecturer in law, Sussex University 1969–79; Barrister-at-Law, Called to the Bar Middle Temple 1972, QC 1988, Bencher 1996; Recorder of the Crown Court (Wales and Chester Circuit) 1997–. *House of Lords:* Shadow Lord Chancellor 1997–. Chairman, Select Committee on European Communities Sub-Committee F 1996–97. President, Shropshire and West Midlands Agricultural Show 1993. Grande Médaille de la Ville de Paris 1988; Schuman Medal 1995. MEP (Conservative) for Shropshire and Stafford 1979–94; Deputy Whip, European Democratic Group (EDG) 1979–82; Chief Whip, EDG 1983–87; Chairman, Parliamentary Committee, Legal Affairs 1987; Leader, Conservative MEPs 1987–94; Chairman and Leader, EDG 1987–92; Vice-Chairman, European People's Party Parliamentary Group 1992–94; Contested Herefordshire and Shropshire 1994 European Parliament election. TD 1987; QC 1988; Kt 1990; PC 1994; DL 1997. Master, Shrewsbury Drapers Company 1995. *Publications: Market Socialism in Yugoslavia,* 1985; (contributed) Vols 8, 51 and 52, *Halsbury's Law of England* (4th ed.); Miscellaneous lectures, pamphlets, chapters and articles. *Recreations:* Boating, gardening, musical comedy, the turf. *Clubs:* White's, Pratt's, Beefsteak, Royal Ocean Racing, Royal Yacht Squadron (Cowes). Raised to the peerage as Baron Kingsland, of Shrewsbury in the County of Shropshire 1994. Rt Hon the Lord Kingsland, QC, TD, DL, House of Lords, London SW1A 0PW *Tel:* 020 7219 5412.

KIRKHAM, LORD — Conservative

KIRKHAM (Life Baron), Graham Kirkham; cr. 1999. Born 14 December 1944. Son of Tom and Elsie Kirkham; educated Maltby Grammar School. Married Pauline Fisher 1965 (1 son and 1 daughter). *Career:* Executive Chairman, DFS Furniture Company Plc, Founded Company in 1969, Listed on UK Stock Exchange 1993. Member Administration and Works Committee 2003–. Chairman, Conservative Party Treasurers 1997. Member: Duke of Edinburgh's Award Scheme, Duke of Edinburgh's International Award Scheme, Chairman, Joint Funding Board; Vice-president, The Blue Cross. Hon. Member, Emmanuel College, Cambridge 1995 Hon. Doctorate, Bradford University 1997. Trustee, Outward Bound Trust; Member: Animal Health Trust (Hon. Fellow 1997), The Prince's Youth Business Trust. Kt 1995, CVO 2001. Raised to the peerage as Baron Kirkham, of Old Cantley in the County of South Yorkshire 1999. The Lord Kirkham, CVO, DFS Furniture Company plc, Bentley Moor Lane, Adwick-le-Street, Doncaster, DN6 7BD.

Visit the Vacher Dod Website . . . **www.DodOnline.co.uk**

KIRKHILL, LORD   Labour

KIRKHILL (Life Baron), John Farquharson Smith; cr. 1975. Born 7 May 1930. Son of late Alexander Findlay Smith and Ann Farquharson. Married Frances Mary Walker Reid 1965. *Career:* Lord Provost, Aberdeen 1971–75; Chairman, North of Scotland Hydro-Electric Board 1979–82. *House of Lords:* Minister of State, Scottish Office 1975–78. Member, Assemblies of the Council of Europe and of WEU 1987–; Chairman, Legal Affairs and Human Rights Committee of the Parliamentary Assembly of the Council of Europe 1991–95. Hon. LLD, Aberdeen University 1974. Raised to the peerage as Baron Kirkhill, in the District of the City of Aberdeen 1975. The Lord Kirkhill, 3 Rubislaw Den North, Aberdeen, AB15 4AL.

KNIGHT OF COLLINGTREE, BARONESS   Conservative

KNIGHT OF COLLINGTREE (Life Baroness) (Joan Christabel) Jill Knight; cr. 1997. Born 9 July 1927. Daughter of late A. E. Christie; educated King Edward Grammar School, Birmingham. Married James Montague Knight 1947 (died 1986) (2 sons). Councillor, Northampton County Borough Council 1956–66. *Career:* Director: Computeach International Ltd 1985–2002, Heckett Multiserv plc 1999–2002. *House of Commons:* Contested Northampton 1959 and 1964 general elections; MP (Conservative) for Birmingham Edgbaston 1966–97. Member: European Union Sub-committee F (Social Affairs, Education and Home Affairs) 2000–, Personal Bills Committee 2000–. Vice-chairman, Association of Conservative Peers 2002–. Member, Parliamentary Assembly of the Council of Europe and the Assembly of the Western European Union 1977–88, 1999–; Chairman: WEU Relations with Parliaments Committee 1984–88, Member again 1999–; British IPU 1994–97. National Chair, Lifeline 1974–84; Vice-President, Townswomen's Guilds 1989–95. Hon. DSc, Aston University 1998. MBE 1964; DBE 1985. San Francisco. *Publications: About the House*, 1995. *Special Interests:* Health, Social Security, Childcare, Industry, Council of Europe and Western European Union. *Recreations:* Antique collecting, tapestry work, singing, theatre, cooking. Raised to the peerage as Baroness Knight of Collingtree, of Collingtree in the County of Northamptonshire 1997. The Baroness Knight of Collingtree, DBE, House of Lords, London, SW1A 0PW *Tel:* 020 7219 4470.

KNIGHTS, LORD   Crossbencher

KNIGHTS (Life Baron), Philip Douglas Knights; cr. 1987. Born 3 October 1920. Son of late Thomas James Knights, market gardener and late Ethel Ginn, schoolteacher; educated East Grinstead County School; King's School, Grantham; Police Staff College. Married Jean Burman 1945. RAF 1943–45. DL, West Midlands 1985. *Career:* Police Cadet, Lincolnshire Constabulary 1937; Seconded to the Home Office in 1946; Superintendent 1955; Chief Superintendent 1957; Assistant Chief Constable, Birmingham 1959; Deputy Commandant, Police Staff College, Bramshill 1962–66; Deputy Chief Constable, Birmingham 1970; Chief Constable, Sheffield and Rotherham Constabulary 1972, responsible for Police Force of the newly created County of South Yorkshire 1974; Chief Constable, West Midlands Police 1975–85; Member, Departmental Committee, chaired by Lord Devlin, which reported in 1976 on Identification Procedures; Formerly Adviser, Police and Fire Committee of the Association of Municipal Authorities; Vice-President, Association of Metropolitan Authorities. Past President, Association of Chief Police Officers; Member: Council of Aston University 1985–98, Council of Cambridge Institute of Criminology 1986–. Hon. DSc, Aston University 1996. Trustee, Police Foundation 1979–98. QPM 1964; OBE 1971; CBE 1976; Kt 1980. Companion, British Institute of Management 1977. *Special Interests:* Law and Order, Police, Inner Cities, Local Government. *Recreations:* Gardening, reading, travel, sport. *Sportsclubs:* Vice-President, Warwickshire County Cricket Club. *Clubs:* Royal Over-Seas League. Raised to the peerage as Baron Knights, of Edgbaston in the County of West Midlands 1987. The Lord Knights, CBE, QPM, DL, 11 Antringham Gardens, Edgbaston, Birmingham, B15 3QL *Tel:* 0121–455 0057.

L

LAING OF DUNPHAIL, LORD — Conservative

LAING OF DUNPHAIL (Life Baron), Hector Laing; cr. 1991. Born 12 May 1923. Son of late Hector Laing and Margaret Norris Grant; educated Loretto School, Musselburgh; Jesus College, Cambridge (agriculture). Married Marian Clare Laurie 1950 (3 sons). Served Scots Guards 1942–47 Captain (American Bronze Star, mentioned in despatches). *Career:* Director, McVitie and Price 1947, Chairman 1963; Director, United Biscuits 1953, Managing Director 1964; Chairman, United Biscuits (Holdings) plc 1972–90, Life President 1990–99; Director, Bank of England 1973–91; Chairman: Food and Drink Industries Council 1977–79, City and Industrial Liaison Council 1985–90; Director: Grocery Manufacturers of America 1984–90, Exxon Corporation Inc 1984–94. Joint Treasurer, Conservative Party 1988–93. Governor, Wycombe Abbey School 1981–93; Chairman, Scottish Business in the Community 1982–90; President, Goodwill 1983–92; Joint Chairman, The Per Cent Club 1986–90; Chairman, Business in the Community 1987–92; President, The Weston Spirit 1989–95; Member, Advisory Board, Phillips Son and Neale 1990–93; President, Trident 1992–95. Hon. Doctorates: Stirling University 1984, Heriot-Watt University 1986; Hon. Fellow, Jesus College, Cambridge 1988; Fellow of the Royal Society of Edinburgh. Chairman of Trustees, The Lambeth Fund 1983–96; Trustee, Royal Botanic Gardens Kew Foundation 1991–97. Kt 1978. *Recreations:* Walking, gardening. *Clubs:* White's. Raised to the peerage as Baron Laing of Dunphail, of Dunphail in the County of Moray 1991. The Lord Laing of Dunphail, High Meadows, Gerrards Cross, Buckinghamshire, SL9 8ST *Tel:* 01753 882437 *Fax:* 01753 885106.

LAIRD, LORD — Crossbencher

LAIRD (Life Baron), John Dunn Laird; cr. 1999. Born 23 April 1944. Son of late Dr Norman D Laird, OBE, sometime Northern Ireland MP, and of late Councillor Mrs Margaret Laird; educated Royal Belfast Academical Institution. Married Caroline Ethel Ferguson (1 son 1 daughter). *Career:* Bank official 1963–67; Bank inspector 1967–68; Computer programmer 1968–73; PR consultant 1973–76; Chairman, John Laird Public Relations 1976–; Visiting professor of public relations, University of Ulster 1993–. Member, Ulster Unionist Party. Governor, Royal Belfast Academical Institution. MP for St Annes, Belfast, Northern Ireland Parliament 1970–73; Member for West Belfast: Northern Ireland Assembly 1973–75, Northern Ireland Convention 1975–76; Member, North/South Language Implementation Board 1999–; Chairman of the Ulster/Scots Agency 1999–. Fellow, Institute of Public Relations 1991. *Publications:* Videos: *Trolley Bus Day in Belfast*, 1992, *Swansong of Steam in Ulster*, 1994, *Twilight of Steam in Ulster* 1995. *Special Interests:* Transport, Dyslexia, Ulster Scots Activity. *Recreations:* Local history, railways, cricket. *Sportsclubs:* Member Instonians, Belfast. Raised to the peerage as Baron Laird, of Artigarvan in the County of Tyrone 1999. The Lord Laird, 104 Holywood Road, Belfast, BT4 1ND *Tel:* 028 9047 1282 *Fax:* 028 9065 6022.

LAMING, LORD — Crossbencher

LAMING (Life Baron), William Herbert Laming; cr. 1998. Born 19 July 1936. Son of William and Lillian Laming; educated Durham University (applied social sciences 1958–60); Rainer House 1960–61; London School of Economics 1964–65. Married Aileen Margaret Pollard 1962. DL, Hertfordshire 1999–. *Career:* Nottingham Probation Service: Probation officer 1961–66, Senior probation officer 1966–68; Assistant chief probation Officer, Nottingham City and County Probation Service 1968–71; Hertfordshire County Council Social Services: Deputy Director 1971–75, Director 1975–91; Chief Inspector, Social Services Inspectorate, Department of Health 1991–98; Chair: Independent Inquiry for Somerset Health Authority 1989, Review of

Management of the Prison Service 1999–2000, Independent Statutory Inquiry following the murder of Victoria Climbie 2001–03. Member Select Committees on: House of Lords' Offices 2000–02, Ecclesiastical Committee 2003–. President, Association of Directors of Social Services 1982–83; President and Patron of Social Care Charities. Three honorary doctorates. CBE 1985; Kt 1996. Freeman, City of London 1996. *Publications: Lessons from America: the balance of services in social care*, 1985. Raised to the peerage as Baron Laming, of Tewin in the County of Hertfordshire 1998. The Lord Laming, CBE, DL, 1 Firs Walk, Tewin Wood, Welwyn, Hertfordshire, AL6 0NY *Tel:* 01438 798574.

LAMONT OF LERWICK, LORD   Conservative

LAMONT OF LERWICK (Life Baron), Norman Stewart Hughson Lamont; cr. 1998. Born 8 May 1942. Son of late Daniel Lamont and Helen Irene Lamont; educated Loretto School (Scholar); Fitzwilliam College, Cambridge (BA economics 1965) (President of Union 1964). Married Rosemary White 1971 (separated 1999) (1 son 1 daughter). *Career:* NM Rothschild and Sons Ltd 1968–79, 1990–93, Director: Rothschild Asset Management 1978, NM Rothschild and Sons 1993–95; Banker 1968–79, Director 1993–95, Jupiter European Investment Trust 1994–2000; Adviser to: Monsanto Corporation 1994–99, Romanian Government 1995–97; Chair: Indonesia Fund 1995–2001, Archipelago Fund 1995–2000, East European Food Fund 1995–; Director: Balli Group plc 1995–, Cie International de Participations Bancaires et Financieres 1999–, Banca Commerciala Robank 2000–, European Growth and Income Trust 2000–, Jupiter Finance and Income Trust 2000–; Adviser to Rotch Property Group Ltd 2001–; Director, Scottish Annuity and Life Holdings Ltd 2002–. *House of Commons:* Contested Kingston-upon-Hull East 1970 general election; MP (Conservative) for Kingston-upon-Thames 1972–97; PPS to Norman St John Stevas, MP, as Minister for the Arts 1974; Parliamentary Under-Secretary of State, Department of Energy 1979–81; Minister of State, Department of Trade and Industry 1981–85; Minister for Defence Procurement, Ministry of Defence 1985–86; Financial Secretary to HM Treasury 1986–89; Chief Secretary to HM Treasury 1989–90; Chancellor of the Exchequer 1990–93; Contested Harrogate and Knaresborough 1997 general election. Opposition Spokesman on: Prices and Consumer Affairs 1975–76, Industry 1976–79. Member: Select Committee on European Union 1999–, Europan Communities Committee Sub-Committee A (Economic and Financial Affairs, Trade and External Relations). Chairman, Bow Group 1971–72; Vice-President, Bruges Group 1994–2003, Co-chairman 2003–. PC 1986. *Publications: Sovereign Britain*, 1995; *In Office*, 1999. *Special Interests:* Economics, European Union, Foreign Affairs. *Recreations:* Theatre, history, ornithology. *Clubs:* Garrick, Beefsteak, White's. Raised to the peerage as Baron Lamont of Lerwick, of Lerwick in the Shetland Islands 1998. Rt Hon the Lord Lamont of Lerwick, Balli Group plc, 5 Stanhope Gate, London, W1K 1AH *Tel:* 020 7306 2138.

LANE, LORD   Crossbencher

LANE (Life Baron), Geoffrey Dawson Lane; cr. 1979. Born 17 July 1918. Son of late Percy Albert Lane and late Mary Lane (née Dawson); educated Shrewsbury; Trinity College, Cambridge (BA classical tripos and law tripos 1939). Married Jan Macdonald 1944 (1 son). Served in RAF 1939–45. *Career:* Called to the Bar, Gray's Inn 1946; QC 1962; Bencher 1966; Recorder of Bedford 1963–66; Judge of the High Court of Justice, Queen's Bench Division 1966–74; Lord Justice of Appeal 1974–79; Lord of Appeal in Ordinary 1979–80; Lord Chief Justice of England 1980–92; Elected an Honorary Master of the Bench of the Inner Temple July 1980. Hon. DCL, Cambridge; Hon. Fellow, Trinity College, Cambridge. Former Member, Prison Reform Trust. AFC 1943, Kt 1966, PC 1974. Raised to the peerage as Baron Lane, of St Ippollitts in the County of Hertfordshire 1979. Rt Hon the Lord Lane, AFC, House of Lords, London, SW1A 0PW *Tel:* 020 7219 5353.

Visit the Vacher Dod Website...
www.DodOnline.co.uk

LANE OF HORSELL, LORD Conservative

LANE OF HORSELL (Life Baron), Peter Stewart Lane; cr. 1990. Born 29 January 1925. Son of late Leonard George Lane; educated Sherborne School. Married Doris Florence Botsford 1951 (died 1969) (2 daughters). Sub-Lieutenant, RNVR 1943–46. JP, Surrey. *Career:* Senior Partner, BDO Binder Hamlyn, Chartered Accountants 1979–92; Chairman, Brent International 1985–95; Deputy Chairman, More O'Ferrall 1985–97; Deputy Chairman, Automated Security (Holdings) 1992–94, Chairman 1994–96; Director, Attwoods 1992–94, Chairman 1994. Member, Select Committees on: the Public Service 1996–, House of Lords' Offices 1997–98. National Union of Conservative Associations: Vice-President 1984–, Chairman 1983–84, Chairman Executive Committee 1986–91. Governor, Nuffield Nursing Homes Trust 1985–96, Chairman 1993–96; Trustee, Chatham Historic Dockyard Trust 1992–. Kt 1984. FCA. Freeman, City of London. *Publications:* Co-author *Maw on Corporate Governance*, 1994. *Clubs:* Boodle's, MCC, Beefsteak. Raised to the peerage as Baron Lane of Horsell, of Woking in the County of Surrey 1990. The Lord Lane of Horsell, Rossmore, Pond Road, Woking, Surrey, GU22 0JY.

LANG OF MONKTON, LORD Conservative

LANG OF MONKTON (Life Baron), Ian Bruce Lang; cr. 1997. Born 27 June 1940. Son of late James Lang, DSC; educated Lathallan School, Montrose; Rugby School; Sidney Sussex College, Cambridge (BA history 1962). Married Sandra Montgomerie 1971 (2 daughters). DL, Ayrshire and Arran 1998–. *Career:* Non-Executive Director, Marsh and Mclennan Companies Inc and other companies; Chair: Murray tmt PLC, BFS US Special Opportunities Trust plc, Second Scottish National Trust plc, Thistle Mining Inc. *House of Commons:* Contested Ayrshire Central 1970 and Glasgow Pollok February 1974 general elections; MP (Conservative) for Galloway 1979–83 and for Galloway and Upper Nithsdale 1983–97; Parliamentary Under-Secretary of State: at Department of Employment 1986, at Scottish Office 1986–87; Minister of State, Scottish Office 1987–90; Secretary of State for Scotland 1990–95; President of the Board of Trade and Secretary of State for Trade and Industry 1995–97. Assistant Government Whip 1981–83; Government Whip 1983–86. Member, Constitution Committee 2001–. Governor, Rugby School 1997–; President, The Association for the Protection of Rural Scotland 1998–2001; Chairman, Patrons of the National Galleries of Scotland 1999–; Hon President St Columba's School, Renfrewshire 2000–. Member, Queen's Bodyguard for Scotland, Royal Company of Archers 1974–. Officer of the Order of St John 1974; PC 1990. *Publications: Blue Remembered Years*, 2002. *Sportsclubs:* Prestwick Golf Club. *Clubs:* Pratt's. Raised to the peerage as Baron Lang of Monkton, of Merrick and the Rhinns of Kells in Dumfries and Galloway 1997. Rt Hon the Lord Lang of Monkton, DL, House of Lords, London, SW1A 0PW *Tel:* 020 7219 5792.

LAWSON OF BLABY, LORD Conservative

LAWSON OF BLABY (Life Baron), Nigel Lawson; cr. 1992. Born 11 March 1932. Son of late Ralph Lawson and late Joan Elisabeth, née Davis; educated Westminster School; Christ Church, Oxford (Scholar, BA philosophy, politics and economics 1954). Married Vanessa Mary Salmon 1955 (1 son 2 daughters and 1 daughter deceased) (divorced 1980, she died 1985); married Thérèse Mary Maclear 1980 (1 son 1 daughter). Served Royal Navy 1954–56. *Career:* Member, editorial staff, *Financial Times* 1956–60; City Editor, *Sunday Telegraph* 1961–63; Special Assistant to Sir Alec Douglas-Home, as Prime Minister 1963–64; *Financial Times* columnist and BBC broadcaster 1965; Editor, *The Spectator* 1966–70; Chair, Central Europe Trust (CET) 1990–; Director, Barclays Bank plc 1990–98. *House of Commons:* Contested (Conservative) Eton and Slough 1970 general election; MP (Conservative) for Blaby February 1974–92; Financial Secretary to the Treasury 1979–81; Secretary of State for Energy 1981–83; Chancellor of the Exchequer 1983–89. Opposition Whip 1976–77. Opposition Spokesperson for Treasury and Economic Affairs 1977–79.

Hon. Student, Christ Church, Oxford 1996. President, British Insititute of Energy Economics 1995–. PC 1981. *Publications:* Co-author *The Power Game*, 1976; *The View from Number 11: Memoirs of a Tory Radical*, 1992; Co-author *The Nigel Lawson Diet Book*, 1996. *Clubs:* Garrick, Pratt's, Beefsteak. Raised to the peerage as Baron Lawson of Blaby, of Newnham in the County of Northamptonshire 1992. Rt Hon the Lord Lawson of Blaby, House of Lords, London, SW1A 0PW *Tel:* 020 7219 5353.

LAYARD, LORD — Labour

LAYARD (Life Baron) (Peter) Richard Grenville Layard; cr. 2000. Born 15 March 1934. Son of Dr John Layard and Doris Layard; educated Eton College; King's College, Cambridge (BA); London School of Economics (MSc Econ). Married Molly Meacher 1991. *Trades Union:* Member, Association of University Teachers. *Career:* History master London secondary schools 1959–61; Senior research officer, Robbins Committee on Higher Education 1961–63; London School of Economics 1964–: Deputy Director, Higher Education Research Unit 1964–74, Lecturer in economics 1968–75, Reader in economics of labour 1975–80, Head, Centre for Labour Economics 1974–90, Professor of Economics 1980–; Director, Centre for Economic Performance 1990–; Economic Consultant to the Russian Government 1991–97; Consultant: Department for Education and Employment 1997–2001, Cabinet Office 2001. Member, European Union Sub-Committee A (Economic and Financial Affairs, Trade and External Relations) –2002. Member, UGC 1985–89; Chairman, Employment Institute 1987–92. *Publications:* Co-author: *The Causes of Graduate Unemployment in India*, 1969; *The Impact of Robbins: Expansion in Higher Education*, 1969; *Qualified Manpower and Economic Performance*, 1971; Editor, *Cost-Benefit Analysis*, 1973, 2nd ed 1994; Co-author: *Microeconomic Theory*, 1978; *The Causes of Poverty*, 1978; Author of: *More Jobs, Less Inflation*, 1982; *How to Beat Unemployment*, 1986; Co-author: *Handbook of Labour Economics*, 1986; *The Performance of the British Economy*, 1988; *Unemployment: Macroeconomic Performance and the Labour Market*, 1991; *Reform in Eastern Europe*, 1991; *East-West Migration: the alternatives*, 1992; *Post-Communist Russia: pain and progress*, 1993; *Macroeconomics: a text for Russia*, 1994; *The Coming Russian Boom*, 1996; Author of *What Labour Can Do*, 1997; Co-author *Emerging from Communism: Lessons from Russia, China and Eastern Europe*, 1998; Author of: *Tackling Unemployment*, 1999; *Tackling Inequality*, 1999; Co-author *What the Future Holds*, 2001. *Recreations:* Walking, tennis, the clarinet. Raised to the peerage as Baron Layard, of Highgate in the London Borough of Haringey 2000. Professor the Lord Layard, Centre for Economic Performance, London School of Economics, Houghton Street, London WC2A 2AE *Tel:* 020 7955 7281 *E-mail:* r.layard@lse.ac.uk.

LEA OF CRONDALL, LORD — Labour

LEA OF CRONDALL (Life Baron), David Edward Lea; cr. 1999. Born 2 November 1937. Son of late Edward and Lilian Lea; educated Farnham Grammar School; Christ's College, Cambridge (MA economics 1961). *Trades Union:* Member, T&GWU 1962–. National Service, Royal Horse Artillery 1955–57. *Career:* Inaugural Chair, Cambridge University, Students Representative Council 1961; Economist Intelligence Unit 1961–63; Trades Union Congress: Research/Economic Department 1964–67, Assistant Secretary, Economic and Social Affairs 1968–70, Head, Economic and Social Affairs 1970–77, Assistant General Secretary 1978–99. Member, European Communities Committee Sub-Committee A (Economic and Financial Affairs, Trade and External Relations) 2000–; Joint Committee on Statutory Instruments 2000–. Vice-chair, Parliamentary Labour Party Committee on Transport. Chair, Farnham Roads Action. Trustee, Employment Policy Institute 1982–2000. Member: DTI Inward Investment Mission in Japan 1974, Channel Tunnel Advisory Committee 1974–75, Bullock Committee on Industrial Democracy 1975–77, Royal Commission on the Distribution of Income and Wealth 1975–79, Delors Committee on Economic and Social Concepts in the Community 1977–79, Energy Commission 1977–79, UN Commission on Transnational Corporations 1977–82, NEDC Committee on Finance for Industry 1978–82, Led TUC Mission to Study Employment and Technology in the USA 1980; Chair, European TUC Economic Committee 1980–90; Vice-President, ETUC 1997–99; Member, Franco-British Council 1982–99; Governor, National Institute of Economic and Social Research; Editorial Board Member, New Economy

(IPPR) 1991–99; Member, Retail Prices Index Advisory Committee 1985–99; Secretary, TUC Nuclear Energy Review Body 1986–88; Member: Kreisky Commission on Employment Issues in Europe 1987–89, Tripartite Mission EU, Japan 1990, European TUC Executive Committee and Steering Group 1991–99, European Social Dialogue Joint Steering Committee 1992–, UK Delegation Earth Summit, Rio 1992; Secretary, TUC Task Force on Representation at Work 1994–99; Member, Round Table on Sustainable Development (sub Group of the Round Table) 1995–99; Chair, Sub-Group on Sustainable Business – A Stakeholder Approach (sub Group of the Round Table) 1997–98; Member: Trade Union and Sustainable Development Advisory Committee 1998–99, Advisory Committee on Vehicle Emissions 1998–99, EU High Level Group on Benchmarking 1998–99, Treasury Advisory Committee on EMU 1998–99, Central Arbitration Committee 2000–; Council Member, Britain in Europe 2000–. OBE 1968. *Publications: Trade Unionism*, 1966; *Industrial Democracy*, 1974; *Trade Unions and Multinational Companies. Special Interests:* Council. *Recreations:* Tennis, music, theatre, skiing. *Sportsclubs:* Bourne Club, Farnham, Lords/Commons Tennis and Ski Clubs. Raised to the peerage as Baron Lea of Crondall, of Crondall in the County of Hampshire 1999. The Lord Lea of Crondall, OBE, South Court, Crondall, Nr Farnham, Surrey, GU10 5QF *Tel:* 01252 850711 *Fax:* 01252 850711; 17 Ormonde Mansions, 106 Southampton Row, London, WC1B 4BP *Tel:* 020 7405 6237 *E-mail:* lead@parliament.uk.

LEICESTER, LORD BISHOP OF   Non-affiliated

LEICESTER (Bishop of), Tim (Timothy) John Stevens. Born 31 December 1946. Son of late Ralph and Ursula Stevens; educated Chigwell School; Selwyn College, Cambridge (BA classics 1968, MA English 1972); Ripon Hall, Oxford (Diploma in theology). Married Wendi Kathleen Price 1973 (1 daughter 1 son). *Career:* Senior management trainee, BOAC 1968–72; Second Secretary, Foreign and Commonwealth Office 1972–75; Ordained 1976; Curate East Ham 1976–79; Team vicar Upton Park 1979–80; Team rector Canvey Island 1980–88; Bishop of Chelmsford's urban officer 1988–91; Archdeacon of West Ham 1991–95; Bishop suffragan of Dunwich 1995–99; Bishop of Leicester 1999–; Took his seat in the House of Lords 2003. Two honorary doctorates. *Recreations:* Cricket, golf, walking in Yorkshire. Rt Rev the Lord Bishop of Leicester, Bishop's Lodge, 10 Springfield Road, Leicester, LE2 3BD *Tel:* 0116–270 8985 *Fax:* 0116–270 3288 *E-mail:* bptim@leicester.anglican.org.

LESTER OF HERNE HILL, LORD   Liberal Democrat

LESTER OF HERNE HILL (Life Baron), Anthony Paul Lester; cr. 1993. Born 3 July 1936. Son of late Harry Lester, and of Kate Lester; educated City of London School; Trinity College, Cambridge (MA history and law 1962); Harvard Law School (LLM 1964). Married Catherine Elizabeth Debora Wassey 1971 (1 son 1 daughter). 2nd Lieutenant, Royal Artillery 1955–57 (National Service). *Career:* Called to Bar, Lincoln's Inn 1963; QC 1975, QC (NI) 1984; Bencher 1985; Called to Bar of Northern Ireland 1984; Irish Bar 1983; Special Adviser to: Home Secretary 1974–76, Special Adviser to Standing Advisory Commission on Human Rights in Northern Ireland 1975–77; Hon. Visiting Professor, University College London 1983–; Recorder of the Crown Court 1987–93. Member: House of Lords Procedure Committee 1995–97, European Communities Select Committee Sub-Committees E: Law and Institutions 1995–97, 1999–, 1996 Inter-Governmental Conference 1995–97, European Communities Select Committee Sub-Committee F (Social Affairs, Education and Home Affairs) 1997–99, Joint Committee on Human Rights 2001–. Member, International Advisory Board, Open Society Institute. Founder member, Social Democrat Party; President, Liberal Democrat Lawyers' Association. President, Interights (International Centre for the Legal Protection of Human Rights) 1991–; Governor, British Institute of Human Rights; Board of Governors, James Allen's Girls' School 1987–93; Member, Council of Justice; Executive Committee, European Roma Rights Center, Co-Chair 1998–2001; Member, Board of Directors, Salzburg Seminar 1996–2000; Governor, Westminster School 1998–2001. Liberty Human Rights Lawyer of the Year Award 1997. Hon. DUniv, The Open University; Hon. DLitt: University of Ulster, University of South Bank; Hon. Life Fellow, University College London 1998; HD Durham University 2001. Hon Member, American Academy of Arts and Sciences 2002. Member, American Law Institute 1985–; Hon. Fellow, Society for Advanced

Legal Studies 1998–. *Publications: Justice in the American South*, (Amnesty International) 1964; Co-editor *Shawcross and Beaumont on Air Law*, 3rd edition 1964; Co-author *Race and Law*, 1972; Numerous articles on human rights law and constitutional reform; Contributor to other legal publications; Editor-in-Chief, *Butterworths Human Rights Cases*; Member, Editorial Board of *Public Law*; Consultant Editor and Contributor, *Halsbury's Laws of England*, 4th edition, reissued 1996, title on 'Constitutional Law and Human Rights'; Co-editor *Butterworths Human Rights Law and Practice*, 1999. *Special Interests:* Human Rights, Constitutional Reform, Law Reform, Equality and Non-Discrimination, Media, European Political Integration. *Recreations:* Walking, golf, sailing, watercolours. *Sportsclubs:* Member: Dulwich and Sydenham Hill Golf Club, Bounty Golf Club. *Clubs:* RAC; Bantry Golf Club. Raised to the peerage as Baron Lester of Herne Hill, of Herne Hill in the London Borough of Southwark 1993. The Lord Lester of Herne Hill, QC, The Odysseus Trust, 193 Fleet Street, London, EC4A 2AH *E-mail:* lestera@parliament.uk.

LEVENE OF PORTSOKEN, LORD   Crossbencher

LEVENE OF PORTSOKEN (Life Baron), Peter Keith Levene; cr. 1997. Born 8 December 1941. Son of late Maurice and Rose Levene; educated City of London School; Manchester University (BA economics 1963). Married Wendy Fraiman 1966 (2 sons 1 daughter). Hon. Col. Comdt, Royal Logistic Corps 1993–. Member (Candlewick Ward), Court of Common Council, City of London 1983–84, Alderman (Portsoken Ward) 1984–; JP, City of London 1984–2002; Sheriff, City of London 1995–96; Lord Mayor of London 1998–99. *Career:* Joined United Scientific Holdings 1963, Managing Director 1968–85, Chair 1982–85; Member, SE Asia Trade Advisory Group 1979–83; Council Member, Defence Manufacturers' Association 1982–85, Chair 1984–85; Personal Adviser to the Secretary of State for Defence 1984; Chief of Defence Procurement, Ministry of Defence 1985–91; UK National Armaments Director 1988–91; Chair, European National Armaments Directors 1989–90; Personal Adviser to Secretary of State for the Environment 1991–92, Chair, Docklands Light Railway Ltd 1991–94; Deputy Chair, Wasserstein Perella & Co Ltd 1991–94; Personal Adviser to Chancellor of the Exchequer on Competition and Purchasing 1992; Member, Citizen's Charter Advisory Panel 1992–93; Personal Adviser to the President of the Board of Trade 1992–95; Adviser to the Prime Minister on Efficiency and Effectiveness 1992–97; Chair and Chief Executive, Canary Wharf Ltd 1993–96; Senior Adviser, Morgan Stanley & Co Ltd 1996–98; Director Haymarket Group Ltd 1997–; Chair: Bankers Trust International plc 1998–99, Investment Banking Europe Deutsche Bank 1999–2001; Vice-chair Deutsche Bank AG London 2001–02; Director J. Sainsbury plc 2001–; Chair: General Dynamics UK Ltd. 2001–, World Trade Centre Disaster Fund (UK) 2001–, Lloyd's 2002–. Chancellor, City University 1998–99. Governor, City of London School for Girls 1984–85; Member, Board of Management, London Homes for the Elderly 1984–93, Chairman 1990–93; Governor, City of London School 1986–. Fellow, Queen Mary and Westfield College 1995; Hon. DSc, City University 1998. Chairman, Bevis Marks Trust. KBE 1989; KSt.J 1998; Commandeur, Ordre National du Merite (France) 1996; Knight Commander Order of Merit (Germany) 1998; Middle Cross Order of Merit (Hungary) 1999. CIMgt; FCIPS. Liveryman, Carmen's Company 1984–, Master 1992–93; Liveryman, Information Technologists 1992–. *Recreations:* Ski-ing, watching football, travel. *Clubs:* Guildhall, City Livery, Royal Automobile. Raised to the peerage as Baron Levene of Portsoken, of Portsoken in the City of London 1997. The Lord Levene of Portsoken, KBE, House of Lords, London, SW1A 0PW *Tel:* 020 7327 6556 *Fax:* 020 7327 5926 *E-mail:* peter.levene@lloyds.com.

LEVY, LORD   Labour

LEVY (Life Baron), Michael Abraham Levy; cr. 1997. Born 11 July 1944. Son of Samuel and Annie Levy; educated Hackney Downs Grammar School; F.C.A. 1966. Married Gilda Altbach 1967 (1 son 1 daughter). *Career:* Lubbock Fine (Chartered Accountants) 1961–66; Principal, M. Levy & Co. 1966–69; Partner, Wagner Prager Levy & Partners 1969–73; Chairman, Magnet Group of Companies 1973–88; Vice-Chairman: Phonographic Performance Ltd 1979–84, British Phonographic Industry Ltd 1984–87; Chairman: D & J Securities Ltd 1988–92, M & G Records Ltd 1992–97, Chase Music Ltd (formerly M & G Music Ltd) 1992–, Wireart Ltd 1992–; Global Consultancy Services. *House of Lords:* Personal Envoy to the Prime Minister and Adviser on the Middle East. Member, Labour Party Donations Committee 2002–. National Campaign Chair, United Joint Israel Appeal 1982–85, Honorary Vice-President 1994–2000, Honorary President 2000–; Member, World Board of Governors of the Jewish Agency 1990–95; Member, Keren Hayesod World Board of Governors 1991–95; Governor, Jews Free School 1990–95, Hon. President 1995–2001, President 2001; Chair, Jewish Care 1992–97, President 1998–; World Chair, Youth Aliyah Committee of Jewish Agency Board of Governors 1991–95; Chair: Chief Rabbinate Awards for Excellence 1992–, Foundation for Education 1993–; Vice Chairman Central Council for Jewish Social Services 1994–; Chair Jewish Care Community Foundation 1995–; Member: World Commission on Israel-Diaspora Relations 1995–, International Board of Governors of the Peres Centre for Peace 1997–; Member: Advisory Council to the Foreign Policy Centre 1997–, Foreign and Commonwealth Office Panel 2000 1998–; President, Community Service Volunteers 1998–; Member, National Council for Voluntary Organisations Advisory Committee 1998–; Member, Community Legal Service Champions Panel 1999–; Patron, Save A Child's Heart Foundation 2000–; Member Honorary Committee, Israel Britain and the Commonwealth Association 2000–; Executive Committee Member of Chai-Lifeline 2001–; Hon. Patron Cambridge University Jewish Society 2002–. B'nai B'rith First Lodge Award 1994; Friends of the Hebrew University of Jerusalem Scopus Award 1998. Honorary Doctorate, Middlesex University 1999. Patron, Prostate Cancer Charitable Trust 1997–; Trustee, Holocaust Education Trust 1998–; Patron, Friends of Israel Educational Trust 1998–; Chairman of Board of Trustees, New Policy Network Foundation 2000–; Patron, Simon Marks Jewish Primary School Trust 2002–. Chairman, British Music Industry Awards Committee 1992–95; Patron, British Music Industry Awards 1995–. FCA 1966. *Special Interests:* Voluntary Sector, Social Welfare, Education, Middle East Peace Process. *Recreations:* Tennis, swimming. Raised to the peerage as Baron Levy, of Mill Hill in the London Borough of Barnet 1997. The Lord Levy, House of Lords, London, SW1A 0PW *E-mail:* ml@lmalvy.demon.co.uk.

LEWIS OF NEWNHAM, LORD   Crossbencher

LEWIS OF NEWNHAM (Life Baron), Jack Lewis; cr. 1989. Born 13 February 1928. Son of late Robert Lewis; educated Barrow Grammar School; London University (BSc chemistry 1949, DSc 1961); Nottingham University (PhD chemistry 1952); Manchester University (MSc chemistry 1964); Sidney Sussex College, Cambridge (MA chemistry 1970, ScD chemistry 1977). Married Elfreida Mabel Lamb 1951 (1 son 1 daughter). *Career:* Chemistry lecturer: Sheffield University 1954–56, Imperial College, London 1956–57; Chemistry lecturer/reader, University College, London 1957–61; Professor of chemistry: Manchester University 1961–67, University College, London 1967–70, Cambridge University 1970–95; Member, Cambridge University 1970–; First Warden, Robinson College, Cambridge 1975–2001; Member, Council of SERC 1979–84; Member, Council, Royal Society 1982–84, 1996–98, Vice-President 1983–84; Chair, Visiting Committee, Cranfield Institute of Technology 1982–92; Chair, Royal Commission on Environmental Pollution 1986–92; President, Royal Society of Chemistry 1986–88; Science Representative for UK on NATO Science Committee 1986–98; Director, The BOC Foundation 1990–2003; Member, Council, Royal Society of Chemistry 1992–95, 1996–98; President, National Society for Clean Air and Environmental Protection 1993–95; Chair, ESART Board 1998–. Member: Science and Technology Sub-committee II 1990–91, 1995–97, 2001–, European Communities Sub-committee F 1991–92, Science and Technology Sub-committee I 1992–93, European Union Sub-committee C 1993–95 (Chair), European Union Sub-committee B 1995–97; Co-opted Member, European Union: Sub-committee B (Energy, Industry and Transport) 1997–2001, Sub-committee C 1997–2001; Member: Science and Technology Sub-committee II (Aircraft Cabin Environment) 2000, Science and Technology Committee 2000 , Science and Technology Sub-committee I (Fighting Infection) 2002–, Science and Technology Sub-committee II (Innovations in Computer Processors/Microprocessing/Science and the Regional Development Agencies) 2002–. Patron, Student Community Action Development Unit 1985–; Foreign Member: American Academy of Arts and Sciences 1983, American Philosophical Society 1994, Accademia Nazionale dei Lincei, Italy 1995, Polish Academy of Arts and Sciences 1996–; Hon. Member, Society of Chemical Industry 1996; Chair, The Leys School Governors 1997–2002; President, Arthritis Research Campaign 1998–; Hon. Fellow, Royal Society of Chemistry 1998–. Hon. Fellow, Sidney Sussex College, Fellow 1970–77; 18 honorary doctorates from the UK, Canada, Hong Kong, France and Ireland; 3 honorary university fellowships. Chair, Executive Committee of the Cambridge Overseas Trust 1988–; Trustee: Kennedy Memorial Trust 1989–99, Croucher Foundation 1989–98. Hon. President, Environmental

Industries Commission 1996–2000; Chair, Standing Committee on Structural Safety 1998–2002; European Union Sub-committee D 2003–. FRS 1973, Kt 1982; Chevalier dans l'Ordre des Palmes Académiques; Commander Cross of the Order of Merit of the Republic of Poland. Fellow, Indian National Science Academy 1985; Foreign Associate, National Academy of Sciences, USA 1987; Foreign Fellow, Bangladesh Academy of Sciences 1992; FRSA. *Publications:* Some 50 papers and review articles. *Special Interests:* Education, Environment. *Recreations:* Music, walking. *Clubs:* United Oxford and Cambridge University. Raised to the peerage as Baron Lewis of Newnham, of Newnham in the County of Cambridgeshire 1989. Professor the Lord Lewis of Newnham, Robinson College, Grange Road, Cambridge, CB3 9AN *Tel:* 01223 339198 *E-mail:* jl219@cam.ac.uk.

LINDSAY, EARL OF   Conservative

LINDSAY (16th Earl of, S), James Randolph Lindesay-Bethune; cr. 1633; Viscount Garnock (S) 1703; Lord Lindsay of the Byres (S) 1445; Lord Parbroath (S) 1633; Lord Kilbirnie, Kingsburn and Drumry (S) 1703. Born 19 November 1955. Son of 15th Earl and Hon. Mary-Clare Douglas Scott Montagu, daughter of 2nd Baron Montagu of Beaulieu, KCIE, CSI, DL; educated Eton College; Edinburgh University (BA economic history 1978, MA); University of California, Davis (Land use). Married Diana Mary Chamberlayne-Macdonald 1982 (2 sons 3 daughters inc. twins). Board Member, Cairngorms Partnership 1998–. *Career:* President, International Tree Foundation 1995–; Chair, Assured British Meat Ltd (ABM) 1997–2001; Chair, Scottish Quality Salmon 1999–; Non-Executive Director, UA Group plc 1998–; Chair: UA Properties Ltd 1999–2000, UA Forestry Ltd 1999–2000, Genesis Quality Assurance Ltd 2001–02, Elmwood College Board of Management 2001–; Managing Director, Marine Stewardship Council International 2001–; Non-Executive Director, Mining (Scotland) Ltd 2001–; Chair, United Kingdom Accreditation Service 2002–. *House of Lords:* First entered House of Lords 1989; Parliamentary Under-Secretary of State, Scottish Office 1995–97; Elected hereditary peer 1999–. Government Whip January-July 1995. Opposition Spokesperson for Agriculture, Fisheries and Food, Environment, Transport and the Regions (Green Issues) June-October 1997. Member: European Communities Sub-Committee C (Environment and Social Affairs) 1993–95, 1997–98, Select Committee on Sustainable Development 1994–95. Inter-Parliamentary Union Committee on Environment 1993–95, Vice-Chairman 1994–95. Chairman: Landscape Foundation 1992–95, RSPB Scotland 1998–; Council Member, RSPB (UK) 1998–. Green Ribbon Political Award 1995. Director West Highland Rail Heritage Trust Ltd 1998–. Member: Secretary of State's Advisory Group on Sustainable Development 1998–99, UK Round Table on Sustainable Development Sub-Group: Sustainability – Devolved and Regional Dimensions 1998–99. Hon. Fellow, Institute of Wastes Management (IWM) 1998–; Fellow, Royal Agricultural Societies (FRAgS) 2003. *Special Interests:* Environment, Transport, Energy, Food Industry. *Clubs:* New (Edinburgh). The Earl of Lindsay, Lahill, Upper Largo, Fife, KY8 6JE *Tel:* 01333 360251.

LINKLATER OF BUTTERSTONE, BARONESS   Liberal Democrat

LINKLATER OF BUTTERSTONE (Life Baroness), Veronica Linklater; cr. 1997. Born 15 April 1943. Daughter of Lieutenant-Colonel Archibald Michael Lyle, OBE, JP, DL and late Hon. Elizabeth Sinclair, daughter of 1st Viscount Thurso, KT, PC, CMG; educated Cranborne Chase School; Sussex University (degree 1962); London University (DipSoc Admin 1966). Married Magnus Duncan Linklater 1967 (2 sons 1 daughter). *Career:* Childcare Officer London Borough of Tower Hamlets 1967–68; Co-Founder Visitors Centre Pentonville Prison 1971–77; Governor, three Islington Schools 1970–85; Children's panel member, Edinburgh 1989–97. President, The Society of Friends of Dunkeld Cathedral 1989–; Vice-Chairman, Pushkin Prizes, Scotland 1989–; Founder and Chair, The New School, Butterstone Ltd 1991–; Patron, The Airborne Initiative (Scotland) Ltd 1998–; Member, The Beattie Committee on post-school provision for young people with special needs 1997–98; Patron, The National Schizophrenia Fellowship, Scotland 2000–; Foundation Patron, QM University College, Edinburgh 2001–; Member of the Scottish Committee, Barnado's 2001; Assessor to the Chancellor, Napier University Court 2001; The Visitors Centre, Pentonville Prison. Two honorary doctorates. Member: The Butler Trust 1983–87 Administrator, Trustee then Vice President 2001–;

Trustee Chair of the Social Development Sector, The Esmée Fairbairn Foundation 1991; Trustee The Young Musicians Trust 1993–97; Committee member Gulliver Award for the Performing Arts in Scotland 1990–96; Director, The Maggie Keswick Jencks Cancer Caring Trust 1997; Prison Reform Trust, Winchester prison project 1981–82; Patron: University of the Highlands and Islands 1999–2001, Liberating Scots Trust, Patron, The Sutherland Trust 1993–; Appeal Patron, Hopetown House Preservation Trust 2001–; Patron of the Family and Parenting Institute 2002–. Contested (Lib Dem) Perth and Kinross by-election 1995. *Special Interests:* Education, Youth Affairs, Penal Affairs and Policy. *Recreations:* Family, music, theatre, reading. Raised to the peerage as Baroness Linklater of Butterstone, of Riemore in Perth and Kinross 1997. The Baroness Linklater of Butterstone, 5 Drummond Place, Edinburgh, EH3 6PH *Tel:* 0131 557 5705 *Fax:* 0131 557 9757 *E-mail:* v.linklater@talk21.com.

LIPSEY, LORD   Labour

LIPSEY (Life Baron), David Lawrence Lipsey; cr. 1999. Born 21 April 1948. Son of late Lawrence Lipsey, and of Penlope Lipsey; educated Bryanston School; Magdalen College, Oxford (BA philosophy, politics and economics 1970). Married Margaret Robson 1982 (1 daughter, 2 stepsons). *Career:* Research assistant, GMWU 1970–72; Political adviser to Anthony Crosland (in Opposition, DoE and FCO) 1972–77; Adviser to 10 Downing Street 1977–79; Journalist, *New Society* 1979–80, Editor 1986–88; Journalist, then economics editor, *Sunday Times* 1980–86; Founder/deputy editor, *Sunday Correspondent* 1988–90; Associate (Acting deputy editor) *Times* 1990–92; Journalist, political editor, public policy editor, *Economist* 1992–99; Public interest director, Personal Investment Authority 1994–2000; Member of Council, Advertising Standards Authority; Chair: Shadow Racing Trust, Make Votes Count, Social Market Foundation, Inpower plc; Non-executive director, LWT. Secretary, Streatham Labour Party 1970–72; Chair, Fabian Society 1982–83. Advisory Council: Constitution Unit, Centre for the Study of Gambling, Salford University, Centre for Research into Election and Social Trends; ESRC External Affairs Committee; Trustee Retired Greyhound Trust. Chair Social Market Foundation 2001–. Member: Jenkins Commission on Electoral Reform 1998; Royal Commission on Long-term Care of the Elderly 1998–99, Davies Panel on BBC Licence Fee 1999. Visiting Fellow, London School of Economics. *Publications: Labour and Land*, 1972; *The Socialist Agenda*, Editor 1981; *The Name of the Rose*, 1992; *The Secret Treasury*, 2000. *Special Interests:* Horse Racing, Financial Regulation, Electoral Reform, Broadcasting, Machinery of Government, Psephology, Greyhound Welfare. *Recreations:* Golf, racing, opera, swimming. *Sportsclubs:* Wimbledon Park Golf Club, South London Swimming Club. Raised to the peerage as Baron Lipsey, of Tooting Bec in the London Borough of Wandsworth 1999. The Lord Lipsey, 94 Drewstead Road, London, SW16 1AG *Tel:* 020 8677 7446 *Fax:* 020 8677 7446 *E-mail:* lipseyd@parliament.uk.

LISTOWEL, EARL OF   Crossbencher

LISTOWEL (6th Earl of, I), Francis Michael Hare; cr. 1822; 6th Viscount Ennismore and Listowel (I) 1816; 6th Baron Ennismore (I) 1800; 4th Baron Hare (UK) 1869. Born 28 June 1964. Son of 5th Earl, PC, GCMG. Sits as Baron Hare; educated Westminster School; Queen Mary and Westfield College, London (BA English literature 1992). *House of Lords:* First entered House of Lords 1997; Elected hereditary peer 1999–. Member, Library and Computers Sub-Committee, House of Lords Offices Committee 2000–02. *Special Interests:* Young Under-privileged. *Recreations:* Singing, music, art. *Clubs:* Reform. The Earl of Listowel, House of Lords, London, SW1A 0PW *E-mail:* listowelf@parliament.uk.

DodOnline
An Electronic Directory without rival . . .

Peers' biographies and photographs available with daily updates *via* the internet

For a *free* trial, call Yasmin Mirza, Aby Farsoun or Michael Mand on 020 7630 7643

LIVERPOOL, EARL OF — Conservative

LIVERPOOL (5th Earl of, UK), Edward Peter Bertram Savile Foljambe; cr. 1905; Viscount Hawkesbury; 5th Baron Hawkesbury (UK) 1893. Born 14 November 1944. Son of Captain Peter George William Savile Foljambe; educated Shrewsbury School; Perugia University, Italy (art and Italian). Married Lady Juliana Noel 1970 (2 sons) (divorced 1994); married Comtesse Marie-Ange de Pierredon 1995 (divorced 2001); Married Georgina Lederman 2002. *Career:* Managing director, Melbourns Brewery Ltd, Stamford, Lincolnshire 1971–76, Joint chair and managing director 1977–87; Director: Hilstone Developments Ltd 1986–91, Hart Hambleton plc 1986–92, Rutland Properties Ltd 1987–, J W Cameron & Co Ltd 1987–91; Chair and managing director, Maxador Ltd 1987–1997; Chairman, Rutland Management Ltd 1997–. *House of Lords:* First entered House of Lords 1969; Elected hereditary peer 1999–. *Recreations:* Flying, golf, shooting. *Clubs:* Turf, Pratt's, Air Squadron. The Earl of Liverpool, House of Lords, London, SW1A 0PW *Tel:* 020 7219 5406 *Fax:* 020 7219 2082 *E-mail:* liverpoole@parliament.uk.

LIVERPOOL, LORD BISHOP OF — Non-affiliated

LIVERPOOL (Bishop of), James Jones. Born 18 August 1948. Son of Major James Jones and Helen Jones; educated Duke of York's Royal Military School, Dover; Exeter University (BA theology 1970) (Kitchener Scholar); PGCE in drama and RE 1971; Wycliffe Hall, Oxford. Married Sarah Marrow (3 daughters). *Career:* Teacher of RE and Latin, Sevenoaks School 1970–74; Ran one of first Community Service programmes in schools (Sevenoaks VSU); Co-founder of first Volunteer Bureau in England; Producer at Scripture Union 1975–81; Curate, then Associate Vicar, Christ Church with Emmanuel, Clifton (Diocese of Bristol); Visiting lecturer in media studies at Trinity College, Bristol; Vicar of Emmanuel Church, South Croydon (Diocese of Southwark) 1990–94; Bishop of Southwark's Examining Chaplain, Bishop's Selector; Bishop of Hull (Diocese of York) 1994–98; Bishop of Liverpool 1998–; Took his seat in the House of Lords 2003. Two honorary doctorates. *Publications: Finding God,* (Darton, Longman and Todd) 1987; *The Power and the Glory,* (Darton, Longman and Todd) 1994; *Why do people suffer?,* (Lion), 1996; *People of the Blessing,* (Bible Reading Fellowship), 1998; *The Moral Leader* (IVP) 2002; *Jesus and the Earth* (SPCK) 2003; Various articles for newspapers (including *The Times, The Guardian, The Independent, The Daily Telegraph and Daily Mail*); Broadcast on *Thought for the Day,* on the *Today* programme, *The Word on the Street* (seven TV programmes for BBC1, Easter 99), various other TV and radio programmes. *Special Interests:* Urban regeneration, Role of the voluntary sector in community renewal, Value of the family to social cohesion, Engagement of the Christian faith with contemporary culture. *Recreations:* Opera, swimming, holidays in France. Rt Rev Dr the Lord Bishop of Liverpool, Bishop's Lodge, Woolton Park, Liverpool, L25 6DT *Tel:* 0151–421 0831 *Fax:* 0151–428 3055 *E-mail:* bishopslodge@liverpool.anglican.org.

LIVSEY OF TALGARTH, LORD — Liberal Democrat

LIVSEY OF TALGARTH (Life Baron), Richard Arthur Lloyd Livsey; cr. 2001. Born 2 May 1935. Son of late Arthur Norman and Lilian Maisie Livsey (neé James); educated Talgarth C.P. School, Bedales School; Seal Hayne Agricultural College (NDA diploma in farm management); Reading University (MSc agricultural management). Married Irene Earsman 1964 (2 sons 1 daughter). *Career:* Agricultural development officer, ICI 1961–67; Farm manager, Blairdrummond Estate, Perthshire 1967–71; Senior lecturer in farm management, Welsh Agricultural College, Llanbadarn Fawr, Aberystwyth 1971–85. *House of Commons:* Contested (Liberal) Perth and East Perthshire 1970, Pembroke 1979, Brecon and Radnor 1983 general elections; Member for Brecon and Radnor from July 1985 by-election to 1992 (Liberal 1985–88, Lib Dem 1988–92), and for Brecon and Radnorshire 1997–2001: Served on Housing Bill Committee 1988, Water Privatisation Bill 1989. Spokesperson for: Agriculture 1985–87, Welsh Affairs 1987–92; Principal Spokesperson for Wales 1997–2001 and on Wales Bill; Leading to Wales Act and creation of National Assembly for Wales.

Liberal Democrat Spokesperson for Environment, Food and Rural Affairs 2002–. Member European Union Sub-committee D (Environment, Agriculture, Public Health and Consumer Protection) 2003–. Leader, Welsh Liberal Democrats 1988–92, 1997–2001; Member: Constitution Reform Strategy Committee 1997–99, Liberal Democrats Policy Committee 1997–2001, Welsh Liberal Democrats Executive 1982–2001. CBE 1994. *Special Interests:* Agriculture, Wales, Democratic and Constitutional Reform. *Recreations:* Cricket, fishing, cycling. Raised to the peerage as Baron Livsey of Talgarth, of Talgarth in the County of Powys 2001. The Lord Livsey of Talgarth, CBE, House of Lords, London, SW1A 0PW *Tel:* 020 7219 6234.

LLOYD OF BERWICK, LORD — Crossbencher

LLOYD OF BERWICK (Life Baron), Anthony John Leslie Lloyd; cr. 1993. Born 9 May 1929. Son of late Edward John Boydell Lloyd; educated Eton College; Trinity College, Cambridge (MA classics and law 1952). Married Jane Helen Violet Shelford 1960. Served Coldstream Guards (National Service) 1948. DL, East Sussex 1983–; Member: Top Salaries Review Body 1971–77, Committee on Royal Peculiars 2001. *Career:* Called to Bar, Inner Temple 1955; QC 1967; Bencher 1976; Attorney-General to Prince of Wales 1969–77; Judge of the High Court of Justice, Queen's Bench Division 1978–84; Lord Justice of Appeal 1984–93; Vice-chair, Security Commission 1985–92, Chair 1992–99; Lord of Appeal in Ordinary 1993–98; Treasurer, Inner Temple 1999–. Joint Committee on Consolidation 1994–97; Member Select Committee on: House of Lords' Offices 2001–02, House and Lords House Committee 2002–. Director, Royal Academy of Music 1979–98; Vice-President, Corporation of the Sons of the Clergy 1996–. Choate Fellow, Harvard 1952; Fellow Peterhouse 1953; Hon. Fellow, Peterhouse 1981. Trustee: Glyndebourne Arts Trust 1973–, Chairman 1975–94, Smith Charity 1971–91. Chairman: Ecclesiastical Committee 2002–. Kt 1978; PC 1984. Hon. FRAM 1985. Hon. Member, Salters' Company 1988–, Master 2000–01. *Publications: Report of Inquiry into Legislation on Terrorism,* 1995. *Recreations:* Music, carpentry. *Clubs:* Brooks's. Raised to the peerage as Baron Lloyd of Berwick, of Ludlay in the County of East Sussex 1993. Rt Hon the Lord Lloyd of Berwick, DL, House of Lords, London, SW1A 0PW *Tel:* 020 7219 3169.

LLOYD OF HIGHBURY, BARONESS — Crossbencher

LLOYD OF HIGHBURY (Life Baroness), June Kathleen Lloyd; cr. 1996. Born 1 January 1928. Daughter of late Arthur Cresswell Lloyd, MBE, and late Lucy Bevan Lloyd; educated Royal School, Bath; Bristol University (MD); Durham University (DPH). *Career:* Junior hospital appointments in Bristol, Oxford and Newcastle 1951–57; Resident fellow and lecturer on child health, Birmingham University 1958–65; Senior lecturer, reader in paediatrics, Institute of Child Health 1965–73; Professor of Paediatrics, London University 1973–75; Professor of child health, St George's Medical School, London University 1975–85; Visiting examiner in paediatrics in Universities in the UK and abroad; Nuffield Professor of Child Health, British Postgraduate Medical Federation, London University 1985–92, currently Emeritus Professor; Past Chairman, Department of Health Advisory Committee on Gene Therapy. Member of Paediatric Associations in: Finland, France, Switzerland, Germany, USA, Sri Lanka, Australia. Member, Royal College of Physicians, London 1982–85, 1986–88; President, British Paediatric Association 1988–91. Hon. DSc: Bristol 1991, Birmingham 1993. DBE 1990. *Publications:* Several articles in scientific journals. *Recreations:* Cooking, gardening, walking. Raised to the peerage as Baroness Lloyd of Highbury, of Highbury in the London Borough of Islington 1996. The Baroness Lloyd of Highbury, DBE, House of Lords, London, SW1A 0PW *Tel:* 020 7219 5353.

Visit the Vacher Dod Website . . .
www.DodOnline.co.uk

LLOYD-WEBBER, LORD

Conservative

LLOYD-WEBBER (Life Baron), Andrew Lloyd Webber; cr. 1997. Born 22 March 1948. Son of late William Southcombe Lloyd Webber, CBE, DMus, FRCM, FRCO, and late Jean Hermione Johnstone; educated Westminster School; Magdalen College, Oxford; Royal College of Music. Married Sarah Jane Tudor 1971 (1 son 1 daughter) (divorced 1983); married Sarah Brightman 1984 (divorced 1990); married Madeleine Astrid Gurdon 1991 (2 sons, 1 daughter). *Career:* Composer: Requiem, a setting of the Latin Requiem Mass 1985, Variations (based on A minor Caprice No 24 by Paganini) 1977, symphonic version 1986, Joseph and the Amazing Technicolour Dreamcoat (with lyrics by Timothy Rice) 1968, rev 1973, 1991, Jesus Christ Superstar (with lyrics by Timothy Rice) 1970, rev 1996, Gumshoe (film score) 1971, The Odessa File (film score) 1974, Jeeves (with lyrics by Alan Ayckbourn) 1975, Evita (with lyrics by Timothy Rice) 1976, (stage version 1978), Tell Me On a Sunday (with lyrics by Don Black) 1980, Cats (based on poems by T. S. Eliot) 1981, Song and Dance (with lyrics by Don Black) 1982, Starlight Express (with lyrics by Richard Stillgoe) 1984, Requiem Mass 1985, The Phantom of the Opera (with lyrics by Charles Hart and Richard Stilgoe) 1986, Aspects of Love (with lyrics by Don Black and Charles Hart) 1989, Sunset Boulevard (with lyrics by Don Black and Christopher Hampton) 1993, By Jeeves (with lyrics by Alan Ayckbourn) 1996, Whistle Down The Wind (with lyrics by Jim Steinman) 1996, The Beautiful Game (with lyrics by Ben Elton) 2000; Producer: Joseph and the Amazing Technicolor Dreamcoat 1973, 1974, 1978, 1980, 1991, Jeeves Takes Charge 1975, Cats 1981, Song and Dance 1982, Daisy Pulls it Off 1983, 2002, The Hired Man 1984, Starlight Express 1984, On Your Toes 1984, The Phantom of the Opera 1986, Café Puccini 1986, The Resistable Rise of Arturo Ui 1987, Lend Me a Tenor 1988, Aspects of Love 1989, Shirley Valentine (Broadway) 1989, La Bete 1992, Sunset Boulevard 1993, By Jeeves 1996, Jesus Christ Superstar 1996, 1998, Whistle Down the Wind 1996, 1998, The Beautiful Game 2000, Bombay Dreams 2002; Film scores: Gumshoe 1971, The Odessa File 1974, additional music, Evita 1996. Member, Offices Sub-Committee: Advisory Panel on Works of Art 2000–. Star on the Hollywood Walk of Fame 1993; The American Society of Composers, Authors and Publishers Triple Play Award 'First recipient'; Six Tony Awards; Five Drama Desk Awards; Three Grammy Awards; Six Laurence Olivier Awards; Praemium Imperial Award for Music 1995; Richard Rodger's Award for contributions to excellence in Musical Theatre 1996; Oscar and Golden Globe for Best Original Song *You Must Love Me* from Evita the movie; London Critics' Circle Award for Best Musical *The Beautiful Game*, 2000. Member, Open Churches Trust. Kt 1992. FRCM 1988. *Publications: Evita*, (with Tim Rice) 1978; *Cats* the book of the musical, 1981; *Joseph and the Amazing Technicolor Dreamcoat*, (with Tim Rice) 1982; *The Complete Phantom of the Opera*, 1987; *The Complete Aspects of Love*, 1989; *Sunset Boulevard: From Movie to Musical*, 1993. *Special Interests:* Art, Architecture. *Recreations:* Architecture, art, food and wine. Raised to the peerage as Baron Lloyd-Webber, of Sydmonton in the County of Hampshire 1997. The Lord Lloyd-Webber, 22 Tower Street, London, WC2H 9NS.

LOCKWOOD, BARONESS

Labour

LOCKWOOD (Life Baroness), Betty Lockwood; cr. 1978. Born 22 January 1924. Daughter of late Arthur Lockwood; educated East Borough Girls School, Dewsbury; Ruskin College, Oxford. Married Lieutenant-Colonel Cedric Hall 1978 (died 1988). Member, Leeds Development Corporation 1988–95; DL, West Yorkshire 1987. *Career:* Assistant Agent, Reading 1948–50; Secretary-Agent, Gillingham Labour Party 1950–52; Yorkshire Regional Women's Officer, Labour Party 1952–67; Chief Woman Officer and Assistant National Agent, Labour Party 1967–75; Chair, Equal Opportunities Commission 1975–83; Chair, European Advisory Committee on Equal Opportunities for Women and Men 1982–83; Member, Council of Advertising Standards Authority 1983–92; Member, Council of Europe and WEU 1992–94. Pro-Chancellor, Bradford University 1987–97, Chancellor 1997–. *House of Lords:* Deputy Speaker 1990–; Deputy Chair of Committees 1990–. Member Select Committees on: Science and Technology 1983–89, European Communities 1985–93; Chair, Sub-committee on Social and Community Affairs 1990–93; Member House of Lords' Offices Finance and Staff Sub-committee 2001–02. President, Birkbeck College, London University 1983–89; Member of Council: Bradford University 1983–, Leeds University 1985–91;

President, Hillcroft College 1987–94; Chair, National Coal Mining Museum for England 1995–. Hon. DLitt, Bradford 1981; Hon. Dr of Law, Strathclyde University 1985; Hon. Fellow: UMIST 1986, Birkbeck College, University of London 1987; Hon. Dr of University Leeds Metropolitan University 1999. Fellow, Industry and Parliament Trust. Hon. Fellow: UMIST 1986, Birkbeck College 1987, RSA 1987, City and Guilds 2000. *Special Interests:* Sex Equality, Education, Industrial Training, Training, Industry. *Recreations:* Enjoying the North Yorkshire Dales, opera. *Clubs:* Soroptimist International. Raised to the peerage as Baroness Lockwood, of Dewsbury in the County of West Yorkshire 1978. The Baroness Lockwood, DL, 6 Sycamore Drive, Addingham, Nr Ilkley, West Yorkshire, LS29 0NY *Tel:* 01943 831098.

LOFTHOUSE OF PONTEFRACT, LORD — Labour

LOFTHOUSE OF PONTEFRACT (Life Baron), Geoffrey Lofthouse; cr. 1997. Born 18 December 1925. Son of late Ernest Lofthouse; educated Featherstone Secondary School; Leeds University (day release economics and politics). Married Sarah Onions 1946 (died 1985) (1 daughter). *Trades Union:* Member, NUM. JP Pontefract 1970; Pontefract Borough Council: Councillor 1962–74, Leader of Council, Mayor of Pontefract 1967–68; Wakefield Metropolitan District Council: Councillor 1973–79, First Chair 1974, Chair: Housing Committee 1975–79, Wakefield Area Health Authority 1998–. *Career:* Personnel Manager, NCB Fryston 1970–78. *House of Commons:* MP (Labour) for Pontefract and Castleford 1978 by-election –1997; First Deputy Chair Ways and Means 1992–97. *House of Lords:* Deputy Chair of Committees 1999–. Vice-President, Wakefield District Labour Party 1974–78. Member: Division Education Executive Committee, All Governing/Managing Bodies of Pontefract Schools; Chairman: Primary Schools' Managers, Pontefract Carleton High School Governing Body; Patron, Heartlink. Knighted 1995. Fellow, Institute of Personnel Development 1984–. *Publications: A Very Miner MP* (Autobiography), 1986 *From Coal Sack to Woolsack* (Autobiography), 1999. *Special Interests:* Housing, Industrial Relations, Energy, Local Government, Human Rights. *Recreations:* Rugby League and cricket. *Sportsclubs:* Vice-President, Featherstone Rovers RLFC; President, British Amateur Rugby League Association; Vice-Chairman, Policy Making Board of Rugby Football League. Raised to the peerage as Baron Lofthouse of Pontefract, of Pontefract in the County of West Yorkshire 1997. The Lord Lofthouse of Pontefract, 67 Carleton Crest, Pontefract, West Yorkshire, WF8 2QR *Tel:* 01977 704275.

LONDON, LORD BISHOP OF — Non-affiliated

LONDON (132nd Bishop of), Richard John Carew Chartres. Born 11 July 1947. Son of late Richard Chartres and of Charlotte Chartres; educated Hertford Grammar School; Trinity College, Cambridge (MA history 1968); Cuddesdon Theological College, Oxford; Lincoln Theological College (BD (Lambeth). Married Caroline Mary McLintock 1982 (2 sons 2 daughters). *Career:* Deacon 1973; Priest 1974; Assistant Curate, St Andrew's, Bedford 1973–75; Bishop's Domestic Chaplain, St Albans 1975–80; Archbishop of Canterbury's Chaplain 1980–84; Vicar, St Stephen with St John, Westminster 1984–92; Director of Ordinands for the London Area 1985–92; Gresham Professor of Divinity 1986–92; Area Bishop of Stepney 1992–95; Bishop of London 1995–; Prelate of the Most Excellent Order of the British Empire 1995–; Prelate of the Imperial Society of Knights Bachelor; Took his seat in the House of Lords 1996; Dean of HM Chapels Royal 1996–, Chair, Church Heritage Forum. Member: Central Committee Conference of European Churches, Joint Liaison Group with RC Bishops' Conference of Europe. Member: The Court of the City University, The Ecclesiological Society; Bencher of the Middle Temple; Ecclesiastical Patron, The Prayer Book Society; Chaplain to the Order of St John. Hon. DD: London, City, Brunel Universities; Hon. DLitt, Guildhall London. Member: St Ethelburga's Centre for Reconciliation and Peace, St Catherine's Foundation, St Andrew's Trust. PC 1996. FSA, 1999. Freeman, City of London. Liveryman, Merchant Taylors' Company; Hon. Freeman: Weavers' Company, Leathersellers' Company, Drapers' Company, Woolmen Company, Vintners. *Publications: A Brief History of Gresham College,* 1997. *Special Interests:* London, Environment. *Recreations:* Family. *Clubs:* Garrick. Rt Rev and Rt Hon the Lord Bishop of London, The Old Deanery, Dean's Court, London, EC4V 5AA *Tel:* 020 7248 6233 *E-mail:* bishop@londin.clara.co.uk.

LUCAS OF CRUDWELL AND DINGWALL, LORD
Conservative

LUCAS OF CRUDWELL (11th Baron, E) cr. 1663, and DINGWALL (de facto 8th Lord, 14th but for the attainder) (S) 1609; Ralph Matthew Palmer. Born 7 June 1951. Son of late Major Hon. Robert Jocelyn Palmer, MC, and Anne Rosemary, Baroness Lucas of Crudwell (10th in line); educated Eton College; Balliol College, Oxford (BA physics 1972). Married Clarissa Marie Lockett 1978 (1 son 1 daughter) (divorced 1995); married Amanda Atha 1995 (died 2000); married Antonia Rubinstein 2001. *Career:* Articles with various firms once part of Arthur Andersen 1972–76; With S. G. Warburg & Co. Ltd 1976–88; Director of various companies, principally those associated with the Good Schools Guide. *House of Lords:* First entered House of Lords 1991; Elected hereditary peer 1999–. Government Whip 1994–97. Government Spokesperson for: Department of Education 1994–95, Department of Social Security and the Welsh Office 1994–97, Ministry of Agriculture, Fisheries and Food and Department of the Environment 1995–97; Opposition Spokesperson for: Agriculture, Fisheries and Food 1997, Constitutional Affairs, Scotland and Wales (Wales) 1997, Environment, Transport and the Regions (Environment) 1997, International Development 1997–98. Member Select Committees on: Animals in Scientific Procedures 2001–02, House of Lords' Offices Library and Computers Sub-committee. Aplastic Anaemia Trust; Safe Ground. FCA. Liveryman, Mercers' Company. *Special Interests:* Education, Liberty, Trade and Industry, Finance. The Lord Lucas of Crudwell and Dingwall, House of Lords, London, SW1A 0PW *Tel:* 020 7219 4177 *E-mail:* lucasr@parliament.uk.

LUCE, LORD
Crossbencher

LUCE (Life Baron), Richard Napier Luce; cr. 2000. Born 14 October 1936. Son of late Sir William Luce; educated Wellington College, Berkshire; Christ's College, Cambridge (BA history 1960); Wadham College, Oxford (overseas civil service course 1961). Married Rose Nicholson 1961 (2 sons). DL, West Sussex 1991–. *Career:* Army national service 1955–57; District officer, Kenya 1961–63; Marketing manager: Gallaher Ltd 1963–65, Spirella 1965–67; Director, National Innovations Centre 1967–71; Vice-president, Institute of Patentees and Inventors 1974–79; Non-executive director, European Advisory Board, Corning Glass International SA 1976–79; Chair, Courtenay Stewart International Limited 1975–79; Non-executive director: Booker Tate 1991–96, Meridian Broadcasting 1991–97; Vice-chancellor, Buckingham University 1992–96; Governor and Commander-in-chief, Gibraltar 1997–2000; Lord Chamberlain of the Queen's Household 2000–. *House of Commons:* Contested Hitchin 1970; Conservative MP for West Sussex, Arundel and Shoreham 1971–74 and for Shoreham 1974–92; PPS to Minister for Trade and Consumer Affairs 1972–74; Opposition Whip 1974–75; Parliamentary Under-Secretary of State for Foreign and Commonwealth Affairs 1979–81; Minister of State, Foreign and Commonwealth Office 1981–82 (resigned April 1982 on Falklands issue), 1983–85; Minister for Arts (Minister of State, Privy Council Office) 1985–90; Minister of State for Civil Service. Opposition Spokesperson for Foreign and Commonwealth Affairs 1977–79. Chair: Atlantic Council of UK 1991–96, Commonwealth Foundation 1992–96. President, Voluntary Art Network 1993–; Member court of governors, Royal Shakespeare Theatre 1994–2002; President of the Royal Overseas League 2002–. Trustee, Geographers' A-Z Map Trust 1993–; Emeritus trustee Royal Academy of Arts; Member Board of Trustees: Royal Collection Trust. PC 1986; Kt 1991; GCVO 2000. *Recreations:* Walking, reading, piano, painting. *Clubs:* RAC; Royal Overseas League. Raised to the peerage as Baron Luce, of Adur in the County of West Sussex 2000. Rt Hon the Lord Luce, GCVO DL, Lord Chamberlain, Buckingham Palace, London SW1A 1AA *Tel:* 020 7024 4262.

DodOnline
An Electronic Directory without rival . . .

Peers' biographies and photographs available with daily updates *via* the internet

For a *free* trial, call Yasmin Mirza, Aby Farsoun or Michael Mand on 020 7630 7643

LUDFORD, BARONESS   Liberal Democrat

LUDFORD (Life Baroness), Sarah Ann Ludford; cr. 1997. Born 14 March 1951. Daughter of Joseph Campbell Ludford and Valerie Kathleen, née Skinner; educated Portsmouth High School for Girls; London School of Economics (BSc (Econ) international history 1972, MSc (Econ) European studies 1976); Inns of Court School of Law. Married Stephen Hitchins. Councillor, London Borough of Islington 1991–99. *Career:* Department of the Environment 1972–73; Independent Broadcasting Authority 1973–75; Called to the Bar, Gray's Inn 1979; Official, European Commission, Brussels 1979–85; European adviser, Lloyd's of London 1985–87; American Express Europe 1987–90; Freelance European consultant 1990–99; Liberal Democrat MEP for London Region 1999–: Vice-President Anti-racism intergroup, European Liberal Democrat (ELDR) group spokesperson for justice and home affairs, Vice-president, European Parliament's South-East Europe delegation. Member, Royal Institute of International Affairs (Chatham House); Contested (Lib Dem) Hampshire East and Wight 1984, London Central 1989 and 1994, Islington North 1992 European Parliament elections, Islington South and Finsbury 1997 general election. *Special Interests:* Europe, Local Government, Justice and Home Affairs. *Recreations:* Theatre, ballet, gardening. *Clubs:* National Liberal. Raised to the peerage as Baroness Ludford, of Clerkenwell in the London Borough of Islington 1997. The Baroness Ludford, MEP, 36 St Peter's Street, London, N1 8JT *E-mail:* sludfordmep@cix.co.uk.

LUKE, LORD   Conservative

LUKE (3rd Baron, UK), Arthur Charles St John Lawson Johnston; cr. 1929. Born 13 January 1933. Son of 2nd Baron; educated Eton College; Trinity College, Cambridge (BA history 1954). Married Silvia Maria Roigt 1959 (1 son 2 daughters) (divorced 1971); married Sarah Louise Hearne OBE 1971 (1 son). County Councillor for Bedfordshire 1965–70; High Sheriff, Bedfordshire 1969–70; DL, Bedfordshire 1989. *Career:* Various managerial positions, Bovril Ltd 1955–71; Fine art dealer in watercolours 18th, 19th, 20th century 1972–. *House of Lords:* First entered House of Lords 1996; Elected hereditary peer 1999–. Opposition Whip 1997–. Opposition Spokesperson for: Culture, Media and Sport, Wales, Transport. Member Select Committees on: Hybrid Instruments 2001–, Advisory Panel on Works of Art 2003–. President, National Association of Warehouse-keepers 1962–78; Member, Court of Corporation of Sons of the Clergy 1980–; Commander, St John's Ambulance Brigade, Bedfordshire 1983–90; Member: CLA, Game Conservancy Association, Countryside Alliance. KStJ. Freeman, City of London. Junior Warden, Drapers' Company 1993, Member of Court 1993–, Second Master Warden 1999–2000, Master Warden 2000–01, Master 2001–02. *Special Interests:* Art, Heritage, Church Affairs, Military History, River Thames, Tourism, Defence, Motoring. *Recreations:* Watching cricket, shooting, fishing, watching motor sports. *Clubs:* MCC. The Lord Luke, Odell Manor, Bedfordshire, MK43 7BB *Tel:* 01234 720416 *Fax:* 01234 721311; House of Lords, London, SW1A 0PW *Tel:* 020 7219 3703 *Tel:* 020 7219 3703 *E-mail:* lukea@parliament.uk.

LYELL, LORD   Conservative

LYELL (3rd Baron), Charles Lyell; cr. 1914; 3rd Bt of Kinnordy (UK) 1894. Born 27 March 1939. Son of 2nd Baron, VC; educated Eton College; Christ Church, Oxford (MA 1962). 2nd Lieutenant Scots Guards 1957 59. DL, Angus 1988. *Career:* Chartered Accountant. *House of Lords:* First entered House of Lords 1960; Parliamentary Under-Secretary of State for Northern Ireland 1984–89; Deputy Speaker; Deputy Chair of Committees 1993–; Elected hereditary peer 1999–. Opposition Whip 1974–79; Government Whip 1979–1984. Government Spokesperson for: Health and Social Security, The Treasury 1982, Scotland 1982–84, Foreign Office Affairs 1983–84. Member: North Atlantic Assembly 1973–79, UK Delegation to North Atlantic Assembly 1994–97. Member, Queen's Bodyguard for Scotland, Royal Company of Archers. *Sportsclubs:* Chairman, Lords and Commons Ski Club 1990–93. *Clubs:* Turf, White's. The Lord Lyell, DL, 20 Petersham Mews, London, SW7 5NR *Tel:* 020 7584 9419; Kinnordy House, Kirriemuir, Angus, DD8 5ER *Tel:* 01575 572848.

M

McALPINE OF WEST GREEN, LORD — Independent Conservative

McALPINE OF WEST GREEN (Life Baron), Robert Alistair McAlpine; cr. 1984. Born 14 May 1942. Son of late Baron McAlpine of Moffat (Life Peer); educated Stowe School. Married Sarah Alexandra Baron 1964 (2 daughters) (divorced 1979); married Romilly Hobbs 1980 (1 daughter) (divorced 2001); married Anthena Malpas 2002. *Career:* Joined Sir Robert McAlpine and Sons Ltd 1958, Director 1963–95; Treasurer, European League for Economic Co-operation 1974–75, Vice-President 1975–; Director, ICA 1972–73; Member, Arts Council of GB 1981–82. Hon. Treasurer, European Democratic Union 1978–88; Hon. Treasurer, Conservative and Unionist Party 1975–90, jointly 1981–90, Deputy Chairman 1979–83. Vice-President, Friends Ashmolean Museum 1969–; Greater London Arts Association 1971–77; Vice-Chairman, Contemporary Arts Society 1973–80; President, British Waterfowl Association 1978–81, Patron since 1981; Member, Council, English Stage Co. 1973–75; Governor: Polytechnic of the South Bank 1981–82, Stowe School 1981–83; President, Medical College of St. Bartholomew's Hospital 1993–. Trustee, Royal Opera House Trust 1974–80. Chairman, The Referendum Movement 1997. *Publications: The Servant*, 1992; *Journal of a Collector*, 1994; *Letters to a Young Politician*, 1995; *Once a Jolly Bagman*, 1997; *The New Machiavelli*, 1997; *Collecting and Display*, 1998; *Bagman to Swagman*, 1999; *The Essential Guide to Collectibles*, 2002. *Recreations:* The arts, horticulture, aviculture, agriculture. *Clubs:* Garrick, Pratt's. Raised to the peerage as Baron McAlpine of West Green, of West Green in the County of Hampshire 1984. The Lord McAlpine of West Green, Sir Robert McAlpine & Sons Ltd, 40 Bernard Street, London, WC1N 1LE.

MACAULAY OF BRAGAR, LORD — Labour

MACAULAY OF BRAGAR (Life Baron), Donald Macaulay; cr. 1989. Born 14 November 1933. Son of late John and Henrietta Macaulay; educated Hermitage School, Helensburgh; Clydebank High School; Glasgow University (MA history, logic, French 1950, LLB 1956). Married Mary Morrison 1962 (2 daughters). National Service, RASC 1958–60. Member, Bryden Committee on Identification following Devlin Report. *Career:* Solicitor 1960–62; Called to Scottish Bar 1963; Advocate Depute (Crown Prosecutor) 1967–70, 1973–74; Standing Junior Counsel to Highlands and Islands Development Board; Chairman, SACRO 1993–96; Chairman, Supreme Court Legal Aid Committee; Member, Central Legal Aid Committee both during 1970s; Member, Criminal Injuries Compensation Board; Scottish Chairman, Committee for Abolition of Paybeds in NHS; Founder Member and former Chairman, Advocates' Criminal Law Group. Former Opposition Spokesperson for Scottish Legal Affairs. Member, Select Committees on: Computers, Crofting. Contested (Labour) Inverness 1970 General Election. *Special Interests:* Scottish Law, Education, Local Government, Sport, Theatre. *Recreations:* Art, music, theatre, football, golf, running. Raised to the peerage as Baron Macaulay of Bragar, of Bragar in the County of Ross and Cromarty 1989. The Lord Macaulay of Bragar, QC, Belmont, 2 South Morton Street, Edinburgh, EH15 2NB *Tel:* 0131–669 6419 *Fax:* 0131–669 0484; Advocates' Library, Parliament House, Edinburgh *E-mail:* macaulayd@parliament.uk.

McCARTHY, LORD — Labour

McCARTHY (Life Baron), William Edward John McCarthy; cr. 1976. Born 30 July 1925. Son of Edward McCarthy; educated Holloway County School; Ruskin College, Oxford; Merton College, Oxford (BA philosophy, politics and economics 1957); Nuffield College, Oxford (MA, DPhil industrial relations 1961). Married Margaret Godfrey 1956. *Trades Union:* Member, Association of University Teachers. *Career:* Research Director, Royal Commission on Trade Union & Employers Associations 1965–68; Fellow, Nuffield College 1969–; Chairman, Railway National Staff Tribunal 1974–85; Member, ACAS Arbitrational Panel 1975–; Associate Fellow, Templeton College 1980–; Member, Civil Service Arbitration Tribunal 1994–;

Formerly Special Commissioner, Equal Opportunities Commission; Member, TUC's Independent Review Committee; Chairman, TUC Working Party on new National Daily; Former Director, Harland and Wolff, Belfast. Opposition Spokesperson for Employment 1979–97. Member, Select Committee on Unemployment 1980–82. Member Labour Peers: Trade and Industry Group 1979–, Trade Union Group 1979–. Member Labour Party: Job Creation Group 1979–, Education and Employment Group 1979–, Culture, Media and Sport Committee 1979–. Member: Society for Theatre Research, Institute of Employment Rights. Research Fellow, Nuffield College 1959–63; Academic adviser Ruskin College 1976–; Member Civil Service Arbitration Tribunal 1984–. Fellow, Chartered Institute of Personnel and Development 1989. *Publications:* Numerous books and articles on industrial relations and labour economics. *Special Interests:* Industrial Relations and Labour Economics, Theatre. *Recreations:* Theatre, ballet, gardening, theatrical history, opera. *Clubs:* Reform. Raised to the peerage as Baron McCarthy, of Headington in the City of Oxford 1976. The Lord McCarthy, Nuffield College, Oxford, OX1 1NF *Tel:* 01865 278554 *Fax:* 01865 762016; 4 William Orchard Close, Oxford, OX3 9DR *Tel:* 01865 762016 *Fax:* 01865 762016.

McCLUSKEY, LORD — Crossbencher

McCLUSKEY (Life Baron), John Herbert McCluskey; cr. 1976. Born 12 June 1929. Son of late Francis John McCluskey and Margaret McCluskey (née Doonan); educated St Bede's College, Manchester; Holy Cross Academy, Edinburgh; Edinburgh University (Harry Dalgety Bursar 1948, Vans Dunlop Scholar, MA arts 1950, LLB 1952). Married Ruth Friedland 1956 (2 sons 1 daughter). Royal Air Force 1952–54 (Sword of Honour, Spitalgate OCTU 1953). *Career:* Admitted to Faculty of Advocates 1955; QC (Scot) 1967; Sheriff Principal of Dumfries and Galloway 1973–74; Senator of the College of Justice in Scotland 1984–; Reith Lecturer 1986. *House of Lords:* Solicitor-General for Scotland 1974–79. Opposition Spokesperson for Scottish Legal Affairs 1979–84. Vice-Chair: International Bar Association, IBA Human Rights Institute 1995–2000. Chair: Scottish Association for Mental Health 1985–94, Fairbridge in Scotland 1995–97, Age Concern Scotland 1999–2001. Hon. LLD, Dundee 1989. Chair, John Smith Memorial Trust. *Publications: Law, Justice and Democracy*, 1987; *Criminal Appeals*, 1992, 2nd edition 2000. *Special Interests:* Mental Health, Human Rights. *Recreations:* Tennis, swimming. *Sportsclubs:* Edinburgh Sports. *Clubs:* Royal Air Force. Raised to the peerage as Baron McCluskey, of Churchhill in the District of the City of Edinburgh 1976. The Lord McCluskey, LLD, Parliament House, Edinburgh, EH1 1RQ *Tel:* 0131–225 2595.

McCOLL OF DULWICH, LORD — Conservative

McCOLL OF DULWICH (Life Baron), Ian McColl; cr. 1989. Born 6 January 1933. Son of late Frederick and Winifred McColl; educated Hutchesons' Grammar School, Glasgow; St Paul's School, London (Foundation Scholarship in Classics); London University: Master of Surgery 1965, MB BS 1957. Married Dr Jean Lennox, née McNair 1960 (1 son 2 daughters). *Career:* Consultant surgeon and Sub Dean, St Bartholomew's Hospital 1967–71; Professor and Director of Surgery, Guy's Hospital 1971–98; Professor of Surgery, University of London 1971–98; Consultant Surgeon to the Army 1980–98; Chairman, Government Working Party on Artificial Limbs and Wheelchair Service 1984–86; Vice-Chairman, Disablement Services Authority 1987–91; Chairman, Department of Surgery of the United Medical Schools of Guy's and St Thomas' Hospital 1988–92. *House of Lords:* PPS to John Major as Prime Minister 1994–97; Deputy Speaker 1994–97, 1998–2002; Deputy Chairman of Committees 1994–97, 1998–2002. Opposition Spokesperson for Health 1997–. Member, House of Lords Select Committees on: European Communities, Sub-Committee F (Environment) 1991–94, Medical Ethics 1993–94; Member, Select Committees on: Science and Technology 2000–, Science and Technology Sub-Committee IIA (Human Genetic Databases) 2000–01, Science and Technology Sub-Committee II (Aircraft Cabin Environment) 2001; Science and Technology Sub-committee I (Systematic Biology and Biodiversity/Fighting Infection) 2002–. Member, Backbench Committee on Disablement 1989–. Member, Executive Committee, CPA UK Branch 1999–. Vice-chairman, International Board of Mercy Ships. Member governing council Conservative Christian Fellowship. Chair, U.K. Board of Mercy Ships; Governor-at-large for England, Board of Governors,

American College of Surgeons 1982–86; President, Mildmay Mission Hospital 1985–; Member of Council, Royal College of Surgeons 1986–94; President: Society of Minimally Invasive Surgery 1991–94, National Association of Limbless Disabled 1992–; Vice-President, John Groom's Association for Disabled People 1992–; President: The Hospital Saving Association 1994–2001, Association of Endoscopic Surgery of Great Britain and Ireland, Leprosy Mission 1996–. George and Thomas Hutchesons Award 2000; Fellow of King's College, London 2001. Research Fellow, Harvard Medical School 1967. CBE 1997. FRCS; FRCSE; FACS; FKC. Master, Worshipful Company of Barbers. *Publications: Intestinal Absorption in Man*, 1976; *NHS Data Book*, 1984; *Government Report on Artificial Limb and Appliance Centre Service*, 1986; As well as articles in medical journals. *Special Interests:* Disability, Higher Education, Health Service, Forestry, Medicine, Health. *Recreations:* Forestry. *Sportsclubs:* Palace of Westminster. *Clubs:* Royal College of Surgeons. Raised to the peerage as Baron McColl of Dulwich, of Bermondsey in the London Borough of Southwark 1989. Professor the Lord McColl of Dulwich, CBE, House of Lords, London, SW1A 0PW *E-mail:* mccolli@parliament.uk.

MACDONALD OF TRADESTON, LORD — Labour

MACDONALD OF TRADESTON (Life Baron), Angus John Macdonald; cr. 1998. Born 20 August 1940. Son of late Colin and Jean Macdonald; educated Allan Glen's School, Glasgow; Apprenticeship, Marine engineer. Married Teen McQuaid 1963 (2 daughters). *Career:* Marine fitter 1955–63; Circulation manager, *Tribune* 1964–65; Feature writer, *The Scotsman* 1965–67; Granada Television 1967–85; Chair: Scottish Media Group plc 1996–98 (Director of Programmes 1985–90, Managing Director 1990–96), Taylor and Francis plc 1997–98; Board Member, Bank of Scotland plc; GMTV. *House of Lords:* Parliamentary Under-Secretary of State, Scottish Office (Minister of Business and Industry) 1998–99; Minister of State, Department of the Environment, Transport and the Regions (Minister for Transport) 1999–2001; Minister for the Cabinet Office and Chancellor of the Duchy of Lancaster 2001–03. Government Spokesperson for: the Scottish Office 1998–99, Environment, Transport and the Regions 1999–2001, Cabinet Office 2001–03, Transport 2002–03. Chair: Edinburgh International Television Festival 1976, ITV Broadcasting Board 1992–94, Edinburgh Film Festival 1994–96; Member, Press and Broadcasting Advisory Committee, Ministry of Defence 1994–95; Vice-President, Royal Television Society 1994–98; Chair, Cairngorms Partnership 1997–98; Board Member Scottish Enterprise 1997–98; Governor: British Film Institute, National Film and Television School. BAFTA Award, Best Factual Television (*World in Action*) 1973; BAFTA Scotland Lifetime Achievement Award 1997; Scottish Business Elite 'Corporate Leader of the Year' and 'Chairman of the Year' 1997. DUniv, Stirling 1992; DLit: Napier 1997, Robert Gordon 1998; DUniv, Glasgow 2001. CBE 1997; PC 1999. *Publications: Camera: Victorian eyewitness*, 1979. *Recreations:* Words, pictures, music, sports, hills. *Clubs:* Royal Automobile. Raised to the peerage as Baron Macdonald of Tradeston, of Tradeston in the County of Glasgow 1998. Rt Hon the Lord Macdonald of Tradeston, CBE, House of Lords, London, SW1A 0PW *Tel:* 020 7219 2239.

MACFARLANE OF BEARSDEN, LORD — Conservative

MACFARLANE OF BEARSDEN (Life Baron), Norman Somerville Macfarlane; cr. 1991. Born 5 March 1926. Son of late Daniel Robertson Macfarlane; educated High School of Glasgow. Married Marguerite Campbell 1953 (1 son 4 daughters). Served in Palestine with RA 1945–47. DL, Dumbartonshire 1993. *Career:* Founded N. S. Macfarlane & Co. Ltd. 1949, becoming Macfarlane Group (Clansman) plc 1973, Managing Director 1973–90, Chair 1973–98, Honorary Life President 1998; Member, Council CBI Scotland 1975–81; Chair, The Fine Art Society plc 1976–98, Honorary Life President 1998–; Underwriting Member, Lloyd's 1978–99; Member, Board of Scottish Development Agency 1979–87; Member, Royal Fine Art Commission for Scotland 1980–82; Director, Edinburgh Fund Managers plc 1980–97; Chair, Glasgow Development Agency (Formerly Glasgow Action) 1985–92; Director, Clydesdale Bank plc 1980–96, Deputy Chair 1993–96; Director, General Accident Fire & Life Assurance Corporation 1984–96; Chair: Amercian Trust plc 1984–97, United Distillers UK plc 1989–96, Hon. Life President 1996–, Guinness plc 1987–89, Joint Deputy Chair, 1989–92; Lord High Commissioner to the General Assembly of the Church of Scotland

1992, 1993 and 1997; Chair Roger Billcliffe Fine Art Ltd 1991–. President: Stationers Association of Great Britain and Ireland 1965, Royal Glasgow Institute of the Fine Arts 1976–87; Director, Scottish National Orchestra 1977–82; Member, Court of Glasgow University 1979–87; Scottish Ballet: Director 1975–87, Vice-chair 1983–87, President 2001–; Hon. President, Chas Rennie McIntosh Society 1988–; President, High School of Glasgow 1992–; Patron, Scottish Licensed Trade Association (SLTA) 1992–; Regent, Royal College of Surgeons of Edinburgh 1997–; Hon. President Glasgow School of Art 2001–; Hon Patron, Queen's Park Football Club; Vice-president Professional Golfers Association. Seven honorary doctorates/fellowships. Trustee: National Heritage Memorial Fund 1984–97, National Galleries of Scotland 1986–97. Kt 1983; KT 1996. Hon. FRIAS 1984; Hon. RSA 1987; Hon. RGI 1987; Hon. SCOTVEC 1991; Hon. FRCPS (Glasgow) 1992. *Special Interests:* The arts. *Recreations:* Golf, cricket, theatre, art. *Sportsclubs:* Glasgow Golf, North Berwick Golf, Honorary Company of Edinburgh Golfers. *Clubs:* Royal Scottish Automobile (Glasgow), New (Edinburgh). Raised to the peerage as Baron Macfarlane of Bearsden, in the District of Bearsden and Milngavie 1991. The Lord Macfarlane of Bearsden, KT, DL, Macfarlane Group (Clansman) plc, 21 Newton Place, Glasgow, G3 7PY.

McFARLANE OF LLANDAFF, BARONESS — Crossbencher

McFARLANE OF LLANDAFF (Life Baroness), Jean Kennedy McFarlane; cr. 1979. Born 1 April 1926. Daughter of late Dr James McFarlane; educated Howell's School, Llandaff; Bedford and Birkbeck Colleges, London University (MA manpower studies 1969, BSc(Soc) 1967, HV Tut Cert 1960). *Career:* Staff Nurse, St. Bartholomew's Hospital, London 1950–51; Health visitor, Cardiff City 1953–59; Tutor, Royal College of Nursing, London 1960–62; Education Officer, Royal College of Nursing, Birmingham 1962–66; Research Project Leader, Royal College of Nursing, London 1967–69; Director of Education, Royal College of Nursing, London 1969–71; Senior Lecturer in Nursing, University of Manchester 1971–74; Professor and Head of Department of Nursing, University of Manchester 1974–88; Member: General Synod, Church of England 1990–94, General Synod Review of Synodical Government Group 1993–97. Member Select Committees on: Priorities in Medical Research 1987–88, Medical Ethics 1993–94, Medical Research and the NHS Reforms 1994–95, Resistance to Antimicrobial Agents 1997–98, Administration and Works 2003–. Six honorary doctorates; Two honorary fellowships. Member: Royal Commission on NHS 1976–79, Commonwealth War Graves Commission 1983–88; Govenor: Howell's School Denbeigh 1984–88, St Martins College Lancaster 1994–97; Patron, Dixie Grammar School Market Bosworth 1996–. FRCN; SRN; SCM; Hon RCN (Austr); Hon FRCP. *Publications: The Proper Study of the Nurse – Critique of methods for establishing criteria of quality for nursing care*, Rea 1970; *Essays on Nursing*, KEF 1980; Co-author: *Multi-disciplinary Clinical Teams*, KEF 1980 *Hospitals in the NHS*, KEF 1980, *The Practice of Nursing using the Nursing Process*, 1982. *Special Interests:* Health, Education. *Recreations:* Music, Theology. Raised to the peerage as Baroness McFarlane of Llandaff, of Llandaff in the County of South Glamorgan 1979. The Baroness McFarlane of Llandaff, House of Lords, London, SW1A 0PW; 5 Dovercourt Avenue, Heaton Mersey, Stockport, SK4 3QB *Tel:* 0161–432 8367.

MacGREGOR OF PULHAM MARKET, LORD — Conservative

MacGREGOR OF PULHAM MARKET (Life Baron), John Roddick Russell MacGregor; cr. 2001. Born 14 February 1937. Son of late Dr N. S. R. and Mrs MacGregor; educated Merchiston Castle School, Edinburgh; St Andrews University (MA economics and history 1959); King's College, London University (LLB 1962). Married Jean Mary Elizabeth Dungey 1962 (1 son 2 daughters). *Career:* Administrator, London University 1961–62; Editorial staff, *New Society* 1962–63; Special assistant to Sir Alec Douglas-Home, MP 1963–64; Head of private office of Edward Heath, MP 1965–68; Business executive in the City 1968–79; Director: Hill Samuel Registrars Ltd 1971–79, Hill Samuel & Co. Ltd 1973–79; Deputy Chair, Hill Samuel & Co. Ltd 1994–96; Director: Associated British Foods 1994–, Slough Estates 1995–, Unigate (now Uniq) 1996–; Director, Friends Provident 1998–; Member of Supervisory Board, DAF Trucks NV 2000–. *House of Commons:* Conservative Member for South Norfolk February 1974–2001; Parliamentary Under-Secretary of State for Industry 1981–83; Minister of State, Ministry of Agriculture, Fisheries and Food 1983–85;

Chief Secretary to the Treasury 1985–87; Minister of Agriculture, Fisheries and Food 1987–89; Secretary of State for Education and Science 1989–90; Lord President of the Council and Leader of the House of Commons 1990–92; Secretary of State for Transport 1992–94. Conservative Opposition Whip 1977–79; Government Whip 1979–81. Member Select Committee on Constitution 2002–. Chair: Young Conservative External Relations Committee 1959–62, Bow Group 1961–62; First President, Conservative and Christian Democratic Youth Community 1965. Member: Council of King's College, London 1996–2002, Inner Magic Circle, West Buckland School Foundation; Patron, New London Orchestra. Fellow, King's College, London; Hon. LLD, Westminster University. Member, Council of Institute of Directors 1995–; Vice-President, Association of County Councils 1995–97; Member, Committee on Standards in Public Life 1997–; Trustee, Foundation of Business Responsibilities 1996–; Deputy Chairman, Governing Bodies Association (now Association of Governing Bodies of Independent Schools) 1998–; Member: Independent Schools Council 1998–, Norwich Cathedral Council 2002–. OBE 1971; PC 1985. *Special Interests:* Economic and Financial Matters, Agriculture, Education, Industry, Housing, Countryside. *Recreations:* Music, gardening, travel, conjuring. Raised to the peerage as Baron MacGregor of Pulham Market, of Pulham Market in the County of Norfolk 2001. Rt Hon the Lord MacGregor of Pulham Market, OBE, House of Lords, London, SW1A 0PW *Tel:* 020 7219 4439.

McINTOSH OF HARINGEY, LORD   Labour

McINTOSH OF HARINGEY (Life Baron), Andrew Robert McIntosh; cr. 1983. Born 30 April 1933. Son of late Professor Albert William McIntosh, OBE, and late Jenny McIntosh (née Britton); educated Royal Grammar School, High Wycombe; Jesus College, Oxford (BA philosophy, politics and economics 1954); Ohio State University (University fellow in Economics). Married Naomi Ellen Kelly, née Sargant 1962 (2 sons). *Trades Union:* Member GMB. Councillor: Borough of Hornsey 1963–64, London Borough of Haringey 1964–68; Greater London Council 1973–83, Leader of the Opposition 1980–81. *Career:* Market Research Society: Editor of journal 1963–67, Chair 1972–73, President 1995–98; IFF Research Ltd: Managing director 1965–81, Chair 1981–88, Deputy Chair 1988–97; Principal (Honorary), Working Men's College, London 1988–97. *House of Lords:* Deputy Leader of the Opposition 1992–97; Deputy Chair of Committees 1997–2001; Deputy Speaker 1999–2002; Parliamentary Under-Secretary of State (Minister for Media and Heritage), Department for Culture, Media and Sport 2003–. Deputy Chief Whip (Captain of HM Body Guard of the Yeomen of the Guard) 1997–2003. Opposition Spokesperson for: Education and Science 1985–87, The Environment 1987–92, Home Affairs 1992–97; Government Spokesperson for: the Treasury 1997–, Trade and Industry 1998–2003, Culture, Media and Sport 1997–2001, Scotland Office 2001–02, Transport 2002–03, Culture, Media and Sport 2003–. Member, Committee of Selection 2000–. Chair, Fabian Society 1985–86. President Abbeyfield North London Housing Society. Chair Dartmouth Street Trust. Chair, Association for Neighbourhood Councils 1974–80. PC 2002. *Recreations:* Cooking, reading, music. Raised to the peerage as Baron McIntosh of Haringey, of Haringey in the County of Greater London 1983. Rt Hon the Lord McIntosh of Haringey, 27 Hurst Avenue, London, N6 5TX *Tel:* 020 8340 1496 *Fax:* 020 8348 4641; Department for Culture, Media and Sport, 2–4 Cockspur Street, London, SW1Y 5DH *E-mail:* mcintoshar@parliament.uk.

McINTOSH OF HUDNALL, BARONESS   Labour

McINTOSH OF HUDNALL (Life Baroness), Genista Mary McIntosh; cr. 1999. Born 23 September 1946. Daughter of late Geoffrey and Maire Tandy; educated Hemel Hempstead Grammar School; York University (BA philosophy and sociology 1968). Married Neil Scott Wishart McIntosh 1971 (1 son 1 daughter) (divorced 1990). *Career:* Press Secretary, York Festival of Arts 1968–69; Royal Shakespeare Company: Casting Director 1972–77, Planning Controller 1977–84, Senior Administrator 1986–90, Associate Producer 1990; Executive Director, Royal National Theatre 1990-January 1997 and October 1997–2002; Chief Executive, Royal Opera House, Covent Garden 1997; Principal, Guildhall School of Music and Drama 2002–03; Board Member: Almeida Theatre, The Roundhouse Trust, Southbank Sinfonia, Royal National Theatre Foundation. Member House of Lords Offices Sub-Committee: Advisory Panel on Works of Art 2000–02;

Member Commitee on Stem Cell Research 2001–02. Three honorary degrees; One honorary fellowship, Goldsmith's College 2003. Trustee: National Endowment for Science, Technology and Arts, Peggy Ramsay Foundation; Patron, Helena Kennedy Bursary Scheme; Trustee: Mustardseed Arts Trust, Nicholas Hytner Charitable Trust. FRSA. *Special Interests:* Arts, Public Health, Prison Reform, Education. *Recreations:* Gardening, music. Raised to the peerage as Baroness McIntosh of Hudnall, of Hampstead in the London Borough of Camden 1999. The Baroness McIntosh of Hudnall, Royal National Theatre, Upper Ground, London, SE1 9PX *Tel:* 020 7452 3347 *Fax:* 020 7452 3350.

MACKAY OF CLASHFERN, LORD   Conservative

MACKAY OF CLASHFERN (Life Baron), James Peter Hymers Mackay; cr. 1979. Born 2 July 1927. Son of late James Mackay, Railwayman; educated George Heriot's School, Edinburgh; Edinburgh University (MA mathematics and natural philosophy 1948, LLB 1955); Trinity College, Cambridge (BA maths 1952). Married Elizabeth Gunn Hymers 1958 (1 son 2 daughters). *Career:* Lecturer in mathematics, St Andrews University 1948–50; Advocate 1955; QC (Scotland) 1965; Sheriff Principal, Renfrew and Argyll 1972–74; Vice-Dean, Faculty of Advocates 1973–76, Dean of Faculty 1976–79; Director, Stenhouse Holdings Ltd 1976–78; Part-time Member, Scottish Law Commission 1976–79; Member, Insurance Brokers' Registration Council 1978–79; Senator of the College of Justice in Scotland 1984–85; Lord of Appeal in Ordinary 1985–87; Editor, *Halsbury's Laws of England* 1998–. Chancellor, Heriot-Watt University 1991–. *House of Lords:* Lord Advocate 1979–84; Lord High Chancellor 1987–97. Government Spokesperson for Legal Affairs in Scotland 1983–84. Member Select Committee on Privileges. Elder Brother, Trinity House. Hon. Fellow: Trinity College, Cambridge, Girton College, Cambridge; and other Universities' Honorary Degrees. Chair, Conservative Party Constitutional Commission 1998–99. PC 1979; KT 1997. Hon. Fellow: Royal College of Surgeons of Edinburgh 1989, Royal Society of Edinburgh, RICE, Royal College of Physicians Edinburgh 1990, Royal College of Obstetrics and Gynaecology, Chartered Institute of Taxation. Hon. Freeman, Woolman's Company. *Publications:* General Editor-in-chief, Halesbury's Laws of England 1999–. *Clubs:* New (Edinburgh), Caledonian, Athenaeum. Raised to the peerage as Baron Mackay of Clashfern, of Eddrachillis in the District of Sutherland 1979. Rt Hon the Lord Mackay of Clashfern, KT, House of Lords, London, SW1A 0PW *Tel:* 020 7219 3169.

MACKAY OF DRUMADOON, LORD   Crossbencher

MACKAY OF DRUMADOON (Life Baron), Donald Sage Mackay; cr. 1995. Born 30 January 1946. Son of late Rev. Donald George Mackintosh Mackay and late Jean Margaret Mackay; educated George Watson's Boys' College, Edinburgh; Edinburgh University (LLB 1966, LLM 1968); University of Virginia, USA (LLM 1969). Married Lesley Ann Waugh 1979 (1 son 2 daughters). *Career:* Law apprentice 1969–71; Solicitor with Allan McDougall & Co., SSC, Edinburgh 1971–76; Called to the Scottish Bar 1976; Advocate Depute 1982–85; QC (Scot) 1987–; Member, Criminal Injuries Compensation Board 1989–95; Solicitor-General for Scotland 1995; Senator of the College of Justice in Scotland 2000–; Lord of Appeal. *House of Lords:* Lord Advocate 1995–97. Government Spokesperson for Legal Affairs and for the Home and Scottish Offices 1995–97; Opposition Spokesperson for: Constitutional Affairs, Scotland 1997–2000, Home Affairs 1997–2000, Lord Advocate's Department 1997–99. PC 1996. *Recreations:* Golf, gardening, Isle of Arran. *Sportsclubs:* Commons and Lords Rugby Club, Shiskine Golf and Tennis Club. *Clubs:* Western (Glasgow). Raised to the peerage as Baron Mackay of Drumadoon, of Blackwaterfoot in the District of Cunninghame 1995. Rt Hon the Lord Mackay of Drumadoon, Parliament House, Edinburgh, EH1 1RF *Tel:* 0131–225 2595 *Fax:* 0131–240 6704; 39 Hermitage Gardens, Edinburgh, EH10 6AZ *Tel:* 0131–447 1412 *Fax:* 0131–447 9863 *E-mail:* lord.mackay@scotcourts.gov.uk.

Visit the Vacher Dod Website . . . **www.DodOnline.co.uk**

MACKENZIE OF CULKEIN, LORD   Labour

MACKENZIE OF CULKEIN (Life Baron), Hector Uisdean MacKenzie; cr. 1999. Born 25 February 1940. Son of late George MacKenzie, principal lighthouse keeper, and late Williamina Budge, née Sutherland; educated Isle of Erraid Public School, Argyll; Aird Public School, Isle of Lewis; Nicolson Institute, Stornoway; Portree High School, Skye; Leverndale School of Nursing, Glasgow; West Cumberland School of Nursing, Whitehaven. Married Anna Morrison 1961 (1 son 3 daughters) (divorced 1991). *Trades Union:* Member, UNISON. Sergeant, 1st Cadet Btn Queen's Own Cameron Highlanders. *Career:* Student nurse, Leverndale Hospital 1958–61; Assistant lighthouse keeper, Clyde Lighthouses Trust 1961–64; West Cumberland Hospital: Student nurse 1964–66, Staff nurse 1966–69; Confederation of Health Service Employees: Assistant regional secretary 1969, Regional secretary, Yorkshire and East Midlands 1970–74, National officer 1974–83, Assistant General Secretary 1983–87, General Secretary 1987–93; Associate General Secretary, UNISON 1993–2000; Company secretary, UIA Insurance ltd 1996–2000; President, TUC 1998–99; Senior Vice-President, TUC 1999–2000. *House of Lords:* Departmental liaison peer at Scotland Office 2001–. First Substitute Member, World Executive of Public Services International 1987–; British-American Parliamentary Group; Inter-Parliamentary Union (British Group). Member: Labour Party Policy Forum 1997–2000, Labour Party Policy Commission on Health 1998–2000. Governor Member, RNLI; Hon. Secretary, Wallington Branch, RNLI; Governor Member, Marine Society; Member, RSPB. Lindsay Robertson Gold Medal for Nurse of the Year 1966. Member, National Trust for Scotland. RGN; RMN. *Publications:* Various articles in nursing and specialist health service press. *Special Interests:* Health, Nursing, Defence, Aviation, Maritime Affairs, Land Reform. *Recreations:* Reading, Celtic music, shinty, aviation. *Clubs:* St Elpheges, Wallington; Ruskin Club, Croydon. Raised to the peerage as Baron MacKenzie of Culkein, of Assynt in Highland 1999. The Lord MacKenzie of Culkein, House of Lords, London, SW1A 0PW *Tel:* 020 7219 8515 *Fax:* 020 7219 5979 *E-mail:* mackenzieh@parliament.uk.

MACKENZIE OF FRAMWELLGATE, LORD   Labour

MACKENZIE OF FRAMWELLGATE (Life Baron), Brian Mackenzie; cr. 1998. Born 21 March 1943. Son of Frederick Mackenzie and Lucy Mackenzie (née Ward); educated Eastbourne Boys' School, Darlington; London University (LLB 1974); FBI National Academy, Quantico, USA (Graduate 1985). Married Jean Seed 1965 (2 Sons). *Trades Union:* Member, Police Federation of England and Wales 1963–80; National President, Police Superintendents' Association 1995–98; Member, National Association of Retired Police Officers (NARPO) 1998–. *Career:* Durham Constabulary 1963–98: Chief Superintendent 1989–98. Member: FBI National Academy Associates, International Association of Chiefs of Police. President, Association of Police Superintendents of England and Wales 1995–98; Patron: Kid Scape, St Oswald's Hospice, Finchale Training College, Durham; President, Security Industry Council (JSIC) 2000–; Vice-president Defence Manufacturers' Association (DMA) 2000–. Honorary Billetmaster, City of Durham. OBE 1998. *Special Interests:* Police, Home Affairs, Legal Affairs. *Recreations:* Herpetology, after-dinner speaking, swimming, fitness, singing. *Clubs:* Dunelm, Durham City. Raised to the peerage as Baron Mackenzie of Framwellgate, of Durham in the County of Durham 1998. The Lord Mackenzie of Framwellgate, OBE, House of Lords, London, SW1A 0PW *Tel:* 020 7219 8632 *Fax:* 020 7219 8602 *E-mail:* mackenzieb@parliament.uk.

DodOnline
An Electronic Directory without rival ...

Peers' biographies and photographs available with daily updates *via* the internet

For a *free* trial, call Yasmin Mirza, Aby Farsoun or Michael Mand on 020 7630 7643

MACKIE OF BENSHIE, LORD   Liberal Democrat

MACKIE OF BENSHIE (Life Baron), George Yull Mackie; cr. 1974. Born 10 July 1919. Son of late Maitland Mackie, OBE, LLD; educated Aberdeen Grammar School; Aberdeen University. Married Lindsay Sharp 1944 (died 1985) (3 daughters and 1 son deceased); married Jacqueline Lane, née Rauch 1988. *Trades Union:* Member, NFU. Served with RAF 1940–46; Squadron-Leader 1944; DSO 1944; DFC 1944; Air Staff 1944–45. *Career:* Farming in Angus 1945–89; Former Chair: Perth and Angus Fruit Growers Ltd, Caithness Glass Ltd; Benshie Cattle Company Ltd; Cotswold Wine Ltd 1983–85; Rector, Dundee University 1980–83; Member Council of Europe and WEU 1986. *House of Commons:* Contested (Liberal) South Angus 1959 general election; MP (Liberal) Caithness and Sutherland 1964–66. Scottish Whip 1964–66. Spokesperson for Economic Affairs 1964–66. Liberal Democrat Spokesperson for Agriculture and Scottish Affairs –2000. Member, European Union Committee: Sub-Committee D 1975–95, Sub-Committee C 1998–99, Sub-Committee D (Environment, Agriculture, Public Health and Consumer Protection) 2000–. Executive Committee Member, IPU British Group; Member, CPA. Scottish Liberal Party: Chair 1965–70, President 1983–88. Member, Scottish Farmers Union; Former President, Royal Agricultural and Highlands Society, currently Vice-President. Hon. LLD, Dundee University 1982. DSO 1944; DFC 1944; CBE 1971. *Publications: Policy for Scottish Agriculture* 1963. *Special Interests:* Agriculture. *Recreations:* Golf, social life. *Clubs:* Garrick, Farmers', Royal Air Force. Raised to the peerage as Baron Mackie of Benshie, of Kirriemuir in the County of Angus 1974. The Lord Mackie of Benshie, CBE, DSO, DFC, Benshie Cottage, Oathlaw, By Forfar, Angus, DD8 3PQ *Tel:* 01307 850376; House of Lords, London, SW1A 0PW *Tel:* 020 7219 3179.

MACLAURIN OF KNEBWORTH, LORD   Conservative

MACLAURIN OF KNEBWORTH (Life Baron), Ian Charter MacLaurin; cr. 1996. Born 30 March 1937. Son of late Arthur George and Evelina Florence MacLaurin; educated Malvern College. Married Ann Margaret Collar 1961 (died 1999) (1 son 2 daughters); married Paula Brooke 2002. National Service, RAF Flight Command 1956–58. Dep Lord Lt, Hertfordshire 1992–. *Career:* Tesco plc: Joined 1959, Director 1970, Managing Director 1973–85, Deputy Chairman 1983–85, Chairman 1985–97; Director, Enterprise Oil 1984–90; Non-Executive Director: National Westminster Bank plc 1990–96, Gleneagles Hotels plc 1992–97, Vodafone Group plc 1997– (Chairman 1998–), Whitbread plc 1997–2001. Chancellor, University of Hertfordshire 1996–. Chairman, Food Policy Group, Retail Consortium 1980–84; Committee Member, MCC 1986–; President, Institute of Grocery Distribution 1989–92; Governor and Chairman of Council, Malvern College. Hon DPhil, Stirling 1987; Hon LLD, University of Hertfordshire; Hon Fellow, University of Wales; Hon Doctrate, University of Bradford. Trustee, Royal Opera House Trust 1992. Chairman, UK Sports Council, resigned 1997; Chairman, England and Wales Cricket Board (formerly Test and County Cricket Board) 1996–2002. Kt 1989. FRSA 1986; FIM 1987; Hon. FCGI 1992. Freeman, City of London 1981. Liveryman, The Carmen's Company 1982–. *Publications: Tiger by the Tail,* 1999. *Recreations:* Golf. *Sportsclubs:* President, Brocket Hall Golf. *Clubs:* MCC, Harry's Bar, Annabel's; President, Brocket Hall Golf; Royal and Ancient Golf Club; Royal St George's, Rye. Raised to the peerage as Baron MacLaurin of Knebworth, of Knebworth in the County of Hertfordshire 1996. The Lord MacLaurin of Knebworth, DL, 14 Great College Street, London, SW1P 3RX *Tel:* 020 7233 2203 *Fax:* 020 7233 0438.

MACLENNAN OF ROGART, LORD   Liberal Democrat

MACLENNAN OF ROGART (Life Baron), Robert Adam Ross Maclennan; cr 2001. Born 26 June 1936. Son of late Sir Hector Maclennan; educated Glasgow Academy; Balliol College, Oxford (BA history 1958, MA); Trinity College, Cambridge (LLB 1962); Columbia University, New York. Married Mrs Helen Noyes 1968 (1 son 1 daughter and 1 stepson). *Career:* Barrister. *House of Commons:* MP for Caithness and Sutherland, firstly as Labour, then as SDP and as a Liberal Democrat 1966–97, and as a Liberal Democrat for Caithness, Sutherland and Easter Ross 1997–2001; PPS to: George Thomson, as Minister without Portfolio 1967–69, as Chancellor of the Duchy of Lancaster 1969–70; Parliamentary Under-Secretary of State, Department of Prices and Consumer

Protection 1974–79; Resigned the Labour Party and joined the Social Democrats 1981. Additional Opposition Spokesperson for: Scottish Affairs 1970–71, Defence 1971–72; Opposition Frontbench Spokesperson for Foreign and Commonwealth Affairs 1980–81; SDP Spokesperson for: Agriculture, Fisheries and Food 1981–87, Home and Legal Affairs 1983–87, Northern Ireland 1983–87, Scotland (jointly) 1982–87; Alliance Spokesperson for Agriculture and Fisheries and Food 1987; Liberal Democrat Spokesperson for Home Affairs and National Heritage 1988–94; Spokesperson for Constitutional Affairs (Arts and Broadcasting) 1994–97; Principal Liberal Democrat Spokesperson for Constitutional Affairs and Culture 1997–2001. Liberal Democrat Spokesperson for Europe 2001–. Member Select Committee on European Union Sub-committee C (Common Foreign and Security Policy) 2002–. Leader, SDP 1987–88; President, Liberal Democrat Party 1994–98. Council member: Association of British Orchestras. Alternate National Parliamentary Representative European Convention 2002–. PC 1997. Freeman, Caithness. *Publications:* Librettos: *The Lie,* 1992, *Friend of The People,* 1999. *Special Interests:* Constitutional Reform, European Union, Rural Affairs, Arts. *Recreations:* Theatre, music, visual arts. *Clubs:* Brooks's. Raised to the peerage as Baron Maclennan of Rogart, of Rogart in Sutherland 2001. Rt Hon the Lord Maclennan of Rogart, House of Lords, London, SW1A 0PW *Tel:* 020 7129 4133 *E-mail:* maclennanr@parliament.uk.

McNALLY, LORD   Liberal Democrat

McNALLY (Life Baron), Tom McNally; cr. 1995. Born 20 February 1943. Son of late John and Elizabeth McNally; educated College of St Joseph, Blackpool; University College, London (BSc economics 1966) (President, Students Union 1965–66). Married Eileen Powell 1970 (divorced 1990); married Juliet Lamy Hutchinson 1990 (2 sons 1 daughter). *Trades Union:* Vice-President, National Union of Students 1966–67. *Career:* Political Adviser to: James Callaghan as Secretary of State for Foreign and Commonwealth Affairs 1974–76, Prime Minister 1976–79; Public Affairs Adviser, GEC 1983–84; Director-General, Retail Consortium, Director, British Retailers Association 1985–87; Head of Public Affairs, Hill & Knowlton 1987–93; Head of Public Affairs, Shandwick 1993–96, Vice-Chair Weber Shandwick 1996–. *House of Commons:* MP (Labour 1979–81, SDP 1981–83) for Stockport South; Contested (SDP) Stockport 1983 general election. SDP Spokesperson for Education and Sport 1981–83. *House of Lords:* Deputy Leader Liberal Democrats 2001–. Spokesperson for: Broadcasting and Trade and Industry 1996–97, Home Affairs 1998–2002, Media 2002–. Member Select Committee on: Public Service 1996–97, Freedom of Information 1999, Joint Committee on Draft Communications Bill 2002. Assistant General Secretary, The Fabian Society 1966–67; Labour Party Researcher 1967–68; International Secretary, Labour Party 1969–74. Fellow, University College, London 1995. Trustee of Verulamium Museum, St Albans; Fellow of Parliament Industry Trust 1981. Fellow, University College, London 1995; Fellow of the Institute of Public Relations (FIPR) 2000. *Special Interests:* Trade and Industry, Broadcasting, Retail Industry, Tourism, Leisure Industries, Foreign Affairs. *Recreations:* Playing and watching sport, reading political biographies. *Clubs:* National Liberal. Raised to the peerage as Baron McNally, of Blackpool in the County of Lancashire 1995. The Lord McNally, House of Lords, London, SW1A 0PW *Tel:* 020 7219 5443 *E-mail:* tmcnally@webershandwick.com.

MADDOCK, BARONESS   Liberal Democrat

MADDOCK (Life Baroness), Diana Maddock; cr. 1997. Born 19 May 1945. Daughter of late Reginald Derbyshire and of Margaret Evans; educated Brockenhurst Grammar School; Shenstone Training College (Cert Ed 1966); Portsmouth Polytechnic (CertEd, Postgraduate linguistics diploma 1978). Married Robert Frank Maddock 1966 (2 daughters); married Rt Hon Alan Beith MP 2001. Portswood Ward, Southampton City Council: Councillor 1984–93, Leader, Liberal Democrat Group. *Career:* Geography teacher Weston Park Girls' School, Southampton 1966–69, English as second language teacher: Extra-mural department, Stockholm University 1969–72, Sholing Girls' School, Southampton 1972–73, Anglo-Continental School of English, Bournemouth 1973–76, Greylands School of English (part time) 1990–91. *House of Commons:* Contested Southampton Test 1992 general election; MP (Liberal Democrat) for Christchurch by-election 1993–97; Sponsored as Private Member's Bill, Home Energy Conservation Act 1995. Liberal Democrat

Spokesperson for Housing, Women's Issues and Family Policy 1994–97. Liberal Democrat Spokesperson for Housing 1998–. Member Select Committee on: European Union Sub-committee D (Environment, Agriculture, Public Health and Consumer Protection) 2001–, European Union 2002–. President, Liberal Democrat Party 1998–2000. President, National Housing Forum 1997–; Vice-President, National Housing Federation 1997–; Member, Board of Corporation, Brockenhurst College; Vice-President: National Energy Action, National Home Improvement Council. Trustee: National Energy Foundation, Richard Newitt Trust, Wessex Medical Trust. Member, Standing Committees for: Finance Bill 1994, Housing Bill 1996. *Special Interests:* Education, Local Government, Housing, Environment. *Recreations:* Theatre, music, reading, travel. *Clubs:* National Liberal. Raised to the peerage as Baroness Maddock, of Christchurch in the County of Dorset 1997. The Baroness Maddock, House of Lords, London, SW1A 0PW *Tel:* 020 7219 1625 *E-mail:* maddockd@parliament.uk.

MAGINNIS OF DRUMGLASS, LORD   Crossbencher

MAGINNIS OF DRUMGLASS (Life Baron), Kenneth Wiggins Maginnis; cr 2001. Born 21 January 1938. Son of late Gilbert and Margaret Maginnis, née Wiggins; educated Royal School, Dungannon; Stranmillis Teacher Training College, Belfast 1958. Married Joy Stewart 1961 (2 sons 2 daughters). 8 Battalion, Ulster Defence Regiment (Substantive Major) 1970–81. Dungannon District Council: Councillor 1981–93, 2001–, Member, Southern Health and Social Services Council 1989–93, Chair, Finance and Personnel Committee. *Career:* Teacher: Cookstown Secondary School 1959–60, Drumglass Primary School, Dungannon 1960–66; Principal, Pomeroy Primary School 1966–82. *House of Commons:* Contested Fermanagh and South Tyrone by-election August 1981; MP (UUP) for Fermanagh and South Tyrone 1983–2001; (Resigned December 1985 in protest against the Anglo-Irish Agreement; Re-elected by-election January 23, 1986); Member: Northern Ireland Assembly 1982, Northern Ireland Forum 1996–98. Spokesperson for: Defence and Home Office 1997–2000, Defence, Trade and Industry 2000–01. Vice-President, Ulster Unionist Council. Chair, Moygashel Regeneration Group; Director, Fermanagh Business Initiative (FBI). *Special Interests:* Terrorism and Internal Security, Defence. *Recreations:* Rugby. *Sportsclubs:* President, Dungannon Rugby Club 2001–02. *Clubs:* Ulster Reform. Raised to the peerage as Baron Maginnis of Drumglass, of Carnteel in the County of Tyrone 2001. The Lord Maginnis of Drumglass, House of Lords, London, SW1A 0PW *E-mail:* ken@southtyrone.fsnet.co.uk.

MALLALIEU, BARONESS   Labour

MALLALIEU (Life Baroness), Ann Mallalieu; cr. 1991. Born 27 November 1945. Daughter of late Sir William Mallalieu and Lady Mallalieu; educated Holton Park Girls' Grammar School, Wheatley, Oxfordshire; Newnham College, Cambridge (MA, LLM law 1968). Married Timothy Felix Harold Cassel (later Sir Timothy Bt) 1979 (2 daughters). *Trades Union:* Society of Labour Lawyers. Exmoor National Park Consultative Forum. *Career:* Called to the Bar, Inner Temple 1970; Elected Member, General Council of the Bar 1973–75; Recorder 1985–94; Bencher 1992. Opposition Spokesperson for: Home Affairs 1992–97, Legal Affairs 1992–97. Member, Joint Select Committee on Consolidation of Bills 1998–. Member, Society of Labour Lawyers; Chairman, Leave Country Sports Alone Labour Support Campaign. President: Countryside Alliance May 1998–, British Hawking Association 1999–. Hon. Fellow, Newnham College, Cambridge 1992. Chairman, Suzy Lamplugh Trust 1996–2000. Chairman, Council of the Ombudsman for Corporate Estate Agents 1993–2000. *Special Interests:* Law, Home Affairs, Agriculture, Environment. *Recreations:* Hunting, poetry, sheep, fishing. Raised to the peerage as Baroness Mallalieu, of Studdridge in the County of Buckinghamshire 1991. The Baroness Mallalieu, QC, House of Lords, London, SW1A 0PW *Tel:* 020 7219 5157.

Visit the Vacher Dod Website...
www.DodOnline.co.uk

MANCHESTER, LORD BISHOP OF   Non-affiliated

MANCHESTER (11th Bishop of), Nigel Simeon McCulloch. Born 17 January 1942. Born Crosby, Liverpool. Son of late Pilot Officer Kenneth McCulloch, RAFVR, and of late Audrey McCulloch; educated Liverpool College; Selwyn College, Cambridge (Kitchener Scholar, BA theology 1964, MA); Cuddesdon College, Oxford. Married Celia Hume Townshend 1974 (2 daughters). *Career:* Ordained 1966; Curate of Ellesmere Port 1966–70; Chaplain of Christ's College, Cambridge 1970–73; Director of Theological Studies, Christ's College, Cambridge 1970–75; Diocesan Missioner, Norwich Diocese 1973–78; Rector of St Thomas' and St Edmund's, Salisbury 1978–86; Archdeacon of Sarum 1979–86; Prebendary of: Ogbourne, Salisbury Cathedral 1979–86, Wanstrow, Wells Cathedral 1986–92; Bishop Suffragan of Taunton 1986–92; Canon Emeritus, Salisbury Cathedral 1989; Member, House of Bishops, General Synod of Church of England 1990–; Bishop of Wakefield 1992–2002; Chairman: Church of England Communications Unit 1993–99, Church of England Mission, Evangelism and Renewal Committee 1990–99; Took his seat in the House of Lords 1997; Lord High Almoner to HM The Queen 1997–; General Synod Religion in Broadcasting Group 1999–; Church of England Statistics Review Group 1999–2001; Bishop of Manchester 2002–. National Chaplain, Royal British Legion; Board Member, Royal School of Church Music 1984–; Chaplain, St John Council: Somerset 1987–91, West and South Yorkshire 1991–2002; Chairman, Somerset County Scout Association 1988–92; President: Central Yorkshire Scouts 1992–2002, CALCB 1997–2000. Chairman, Sandford St Martin Trust 1999–. *Publications: A Gospel to Proclaim,* 1992; *Barriers to Belief,* 1995. *Special Interests:* Broadcasting and Communications. *Recreations:* Music, walking in the Lake District. *Clubs:* Athenaeum. Rt Rev the Lord Bishop of Manchester, Bishopscourt, Bury New Road, Manchester, M7 4LE *Tel:* 0161–792 2096 *Fax:* 0161–792 6826 *E-mail:* bishop@bishopscourt.manchester.anglican.org.

MANCROFT, LORD   Conservative

MANCROFT (3rd Baron, UK), Benjamin Lloyd Stormont Mancroft; cr. 1937; 3rd Bt of Mancroft (UK) 1932. Born 16 May 1957. Son of 2nd Baron, KBE, TD and of late Diana, née Lloyd; educated Eton College. Married Emma Peart 1990 (2 sons 1 daughter). *Career:* Chairman: Inter Lotto (UK) Ltd 1995–, Scratch-n-Win Lotteries Ltd 1995–98; Non-executive director St Martin's Magazines plc. *House of Lords:* First entered House of Lords 1987; Elected hereditary peer 1999–. Member: Select Committee on Broadcasting 1992–94, House of Lords Offices Sub-Committee: Advisory Panel on Works of Art 2000–02; Procedure Committee 2000–02, Joint Committee on Statutory Instruments 2002–. Member, Executive Association of Conservative Peers 1989–94, 1999–. President European Association for the Treatment of Addiction. Member, Executive of National Union of Conservative Associations 1989–94. Joint Master, Vale of White Horse Fox Hounds 1987–89; Chair, Addiction Recovery Foundation 1989–; Director, Phoenix House Housing Association 1991–96, Vice-Chairman 1992–96; Deputy Chair, British Field Sports Society 1992–97; Chair, Drug and Alcohol Foundation 1994–; President, Alliance of Independent Retailers 1996–; Director, Countryside Alliance 1997–. Patron, Sick Dentists' Trust 1991–; Board Member, Mentor Foundation; Patron, Osteopathic Centre for Children; Chair, Mentor (UK) 2001–. *Special Interests:* Drug Addiction, Alcoholism, Rural Affairs. *Recreations:* Hunting, stalking, shooting, fishing. *Clubs:* Pratt's. The Lord Mancroft, House of Lords, London, SW1A 0PW *Tel:* 020 7219 3249; 502 Drake House, Dolphin Square, London, SW1V 3NW *E-mail:* mancroft@iluk.co.uk.

MAR, COUNTESS OF   Crossbencher

MAR (Countess of, 31st in line, S), Margaret of Mar; cr. 1114, precedence 1404; Lady Garioch (24th in line, S) 1320. Born 19 September 1940. Daughter of 30th Earl; educated Kenya High School for Girls, Nairobi; Lewes County Grammar School for Girls. Married Edwin Noel Artiss 1959 (1 daughter) (divorced 1976); married John Salton 1976 (divorced 1981); married John Jenkin 1982. *Trades Union:* Vice-President, Association of Members of the Immigration Appeal Tribunal. *Career:* Civil Service clerical officer 1959–63; Post Office/British Telecom sales superintendent 1969–82. *House of Lords:* First entered House of Lords 1975; Deputy Chair of Committees 1997–; Deputy Speaker 1999–; Elected hereditary peer 1999–. Co-opted Member,

Select Committee on European Communities Sub-Committee C (Environment, Public Health and Consumer Protection) 1997–99; Sub-committee D (Environment, Agriculture, Public Health and Consumer Protection) 2001–. Numerous charitable organisations, especially ones involved in health. Laurent Perrier/Country Life Parliamentarian of the Year 1996; BBC Wildlife Magazine Green Ribbon Award 1997; Spectator 'Peer of the Year' 1997. Holder of the Premier Earldom of Scotland; Recognised in the surname "of Mar" by warrant of the Court of the Lord Lyon 1967, when she abandoned her second Christian name of Alison. *Special Interests:* Health Service, Social Security, Agriculture, Environment, Pesticides, Food standards. *Recreations:* Gardening, goat keeping, reading. *Clubs:* Farmers'. The Countess of Mar, St Michael's Farm, Great Witley, Worcester, WR6 6JB *Tel:* 01299 896608 *E-mail:* marm@parliament.uk.

MAR AND KELLIE, EARL OF   Scottish Liberal Democrat

MAR (14th Earl of, S); cr. 1565, AND KELLIE (16th Earl of, S); cr. 1619, James Thorne Erskine; 16th Viscount Fentoun (S) 1606; 19th Lord Erskine (S) 1429; 16th Lord Erskine of Dirleton (S) 1604; 16th Lord Dirleton (S) 1606; (Life) Baron Erskine of Alloa Tower 2000. Born 10 March 1949. Son of 13th Earl; educated Eton College; Moray House College of Education (Diploma in Social Work, Diploma in Youth and Community Work 1971); Inverness College (Certificate in Building 1988). Married Mary Irene Mooney, née Kirk 1974 (1 stepson 4 stepdaughters). *Trades Union:* NALGO 1973–76. RAuxAF Pilot Officer 1979–82, Flying Officer 1982–86; Royal Naval Auxiliary Service 1986–88. DL, Clackmannan 1991–. *Career:* Community service volunteer, York 1967–68; Youth worker, Craigmillar 1971–73; Senior social worker, Sheffield District Council 1973–76; Social worker: Grampian Regional Council 1976–78, Highland Regional Council 1978–87, HM Prison, Inverness 1979–81; Youth worker, Merkinch Centre 1982; Community service offenders supervisor, Inverness 1983–87; Slater, Kincardine 1989–91; Project worker, SACRO 1991–93; Canoe builder 1993–; Estate worker 1993–; Non-Executive Director, Clackmannanshire Enterprise. *House of Lords:* First entered House of Lords 1993; Chair, Strathclyde Tram Inquiry 1996; Commissioner, Burrell Collection (Lending) Inquiry 1997. Liberal Democrat Whip 2002–. Liberal Democrat Spokesperson for Scotland 2001–. Member Select Committee on: Transfer of Crofting Estates (Scotland) Bill 1996, The Constitution 2001–; Religious Offences 2002–03. Hon. Vice-President, Scottish Canoe Association. Chair, Clackmannanshire Heritage Trust. Premier Viscount of Scotland; Hereditary Keeper of Stirling Castle; Page of Honour to HM the Queen 1962, 1963 (Order of Thistle page); Contested Ochil Scottish Parliament election 1999. *Special Interests:* Scotland, Prisons, Probation, Social Policy, Devolution, Energy, Transport. *Recreations:* Canoeing, hillwalking, cycling, Alloa Tower, boat building. *Clubs:* Farmers'. Created a life peer as Baron Erskine of Alloa Tower, of Alloa in Clackmannanshire 2000 but known as Earl of Mar and Kellie. The Earl of Mar and Kellie, DL, Hilton Farm, Alloa, Clackmannan, FK10 3PS.

MARLESFORD, LORD   Conservative

MARLESFORD (Life Baron), Mark Shuldham Schreiber; cr. 1991. Born 11 September 1931. Son of late John Shuldham Schreiber, AE, DL; educated Eton College; Trinity College, Cambridge (BA economics 1956, MA). Married 1969, Gabriella Federica, daughter of Count Teodoro Veglio di Castelletto d'Uzzone (2 daughters). National Service, Coldstream Guards, 2nd Lieutenant 1950–51. Councillor, East Suffolk County Council 1968–70; DL, Suffolk 1991–. *Career:* Fisons Ltd 1957–63; Conservative Research Department 1963–70; Special Adviser to HM Government 1970–74; Special Adviser to Leader of the Opposition 1974–75; Editorial consultant, *The Economist* 1974–91 (Lobby correspondent 1976–91); Member: Countryside Commission 1980–92, Rural Development Commission 1985–93; Director, Eastern Group plc 1990–96; Adviser to Mitsubishi Corporation International NV 1990–2003; An independent national director of Times Newspaper Holdings 1991–; Adviser to Board of John Swire and Sons Ltd 1992–; Chair, Council for the Protection of Rural England 1993–98; Adviser to Sit Investment Associates, Minneapolis, USA 2001–. Member European Union Sub-Committee A (Economic and Financial Affairs, Trade and External Relations) 2000–. President: Suffolk ACRE 1995–, Suffolk Preservation Society 1997–. *Special Interests:* Hong Kong, China, Conservation. *Recreations:* Planting trees and hedges, collecting minerals. *Clubs:* Pratt's. Raised to the peerage as Baron Marlesford, of Marlesford in the County of Suffolk 1991. The Lord Marlesford, DL, Marlesford Hall, Woodbridge, Suffolk, IP13 0AU *E-mail:* marlesford@parliament.uk.

MARSH, LORD Crossbencher

MARSH (Life Baron), Richard William Marsh; cr. 1981. Born 14 March 1928. Son of late William Marsh; educated Jennings School, Swindon; Ruskin College, Oxford. Married Evelyn Mary Andrews 1950 (divorced 1973) (2 sons); married Caroline Dutton 1973 (died 1975); married Hon Felicity McFadzean 1979. *Trades Union:* Health services officer, National Union of Public Employees 1951–59. *Career:* Chair: British Rail Board 1970–75, Newspaper Publishers Association 1975–83, Allied Investments Ltd 1977–81, British Iron and Steel Consumers Council 1977–82, Strategy International Ltd 1978–84; Director, Imperial Life of Canada, Toronto 1980–97; Chair: Lee Cooper Group plc 1982–88, Mannington Management Services Ltd 1981–99; Deputy Chair, TV-AM Ltd 1981, Chair 1982–86; Chair, China & Eastern Investment Co., Hong Kong 1987–96; Executive Chair: Laurentian Holding Company, Laurentian Life, Montreal 1989–95; Chair, British Industry Committee on South Africa Ltd 1989–95; Chair, British Income and Growth Trust Ltd 1993–. *House of Commons:* MP (Labour) for Greenwich 1959–70; Parliamentary Secretary, Ministry of Labour 1964–65; Joint Parliamentary Secretary, Ministry of Technology 1965–66; Minister of Power 1966–68; Minister of Transport 1968–70. Member, Select Committee on: European Union 1997–2000, European Union Sub-committee B (Energy, Industry and Transport) 1997–2000, Privileges 2001–. Chair, Special Trustees of Guy's Hospital 1982–96. PC 1966; Kt 1976. FCIT; FInstD; FInstM. *Special Interests:* Industry, Economic Policy, Financial Services, Far East. Raised to the peerage as Baron Marsh, of Mannington in the County of Wiltshire 1981. Rt Hon the Lord Marsh, House of Lords, London, SW1A 0PW *Tel:* 020 7219 6525.

MARSHALL OF KNIGHTSBRIDGE, LORD Crossbencher

MARSHALL OF KNIGHTSBRIDGE (Life Baron), Colin Marsh Marshall; cr. 1998. Born 16 November 1933. Son of Leslie and Florence Marshall; educated University College School, Hampstead. Married Janet Cracknell 1958 (1 daughter). *Career:* Orient Steam Navigation Co 1951–58; Hertz Corporation in USA, Canada, Mexico, UK, Netherlands, Belgium 1958–64; Avis Inc 1964–79: President and Chief Executive Officer 1976–79; Norton Simon Inc 1979–81; Sears Holdings Ltd 1981–83; Director: British Airways Helicopters Limited 1983–86, BEA Airtours Limited 1983–87; Chair, British Airways Associated Companies Limited 1983–97; British Airways 1983–: Chief Exective 1983–95, Deputy Chair 1989–93, Chair 1993–; Chair: British Caledonian Airways Limited 1988–91, British Caledonian Group plc 1988–97; Director, several banking and airline companies; Deputy Chair, British Telecommunications plc 1996–2001; Chair: Inchcape plc 1996–2000, Invensys plc 1998–2003. Member, British Tourist Authority 1986–1993; Vice-Chair, World Travel and Tourism Council 1990–99; Governor, Ashridge Management College 1991–99; President, Chartered Institute of Marketing 1991–96; Deputy Chair, London First 1993–98; Chair: International Advisory Board British American Business Council 1994–96, London First Centre 1994–98; President: CBI 1996–98, Commonwealth Youth Exchange Council 1998–; Chair: London Development Partnership 1998–2000, Britain in Europe 1999–, Council of Royal Institute of International Affairs (Chatham House) 1999–2003; Vice-president London First 2002–. Eleven honorary doctorates. Trustee, RAF Museum 1991–2000; The Conference Board 1996–, Chair 2000–03; Chair, Royal Armouries Development Trust 2000–. Kt 1987. FCIT; FCIM. Freeman, City of London. Liveryman: Company of Information Technologists, Guild of Airline Pilots and Navigators. *Recreations:* Tennis. *Sportsclubs:* Queen's, All England Lawn Tennis and Croquet. *Clubs:* Royal Automobile. Raised to the peerage as Baron Marshall of Knightsbridge, of Knightsbridge in the City of Westminster 1998. The Lord Marshall of Knightsbridge, Chairman, British Airways plc, Waterside (HBB 3), PO Box 365, Harmondsworth, Middlesex, UB7 0GB *Tel:* 020 8738 5107/5105 *Fax:* 020 8738 9801 *E-mail:* anne.p.hensman@britishairways.com.

Visit the Vacher Dod Website...
www.DodOnline.co.uk

MASHAM OF ILTON, BARONESS   Crossbencher

MASHAM OF ILTON (Life Baroness), Susan Lilian Primrose Cunliffe-Lister; cr. 1970. Born 14 April 1935. Daughter of late Major Sir Ronald Sinclair, 8th Bt, TD, DL; educated Heathfield School, Ascot; London Polytechnic. Married Lord Masham, now 2nd Earl of Swinton 1959 (1 son 1 daughter both adopted). Member: Peterlee and Newton Aycliffe Corporation 1973–85; Yorkshire Regional Health Authority 1982–90; DL, North Yorkshire 1991–; Member, North Yorkshire Family Health Service Authority 1990–96. *Career:* Voluntary social work/health matters. Member, Select Committee on Science and Technology Sub-Committee on Resistance to Anti-Microbial Agents 1997–98. President, North Yorkshire Red Cross 1963–88, Patron 1989–; Former and current president, patron, chair, member of numerous charities, especially in areas of health and disability. Eleven honorary degrees. Council Member, Winston Churchill Trust 1980–; Patron: International Spinal Research Trust, Northern Counties Trust for People Living with HIV/AIDS; Animal Health Trust; John Mordaunt Trust; Yorkshire Wildlife Trust. Chair: Home Office Crime Prevention Working Group on Young People and Alcohol 1987, Howard League Inquiry into Girls in Prison. Hon. Fellowship: RCGP 1981, Chartered Society of Physiotherapy 1996. Freedom, Borough of Harrogate 1989. *Publications: The World Walks By. Special Interests:* Health, Disability, Penal Affairs and Policy, Drug Abuse. *Recreations:* Breeding Highland ponies, gardening, swimming. Raised to the peerage as Baroness Masham of Ilton, of Masham in the North Riding of the County of Yorkshire 1970. The Countess of Swinton, Baroness Masham of Ilton, DL, Dykes Hill House, Masham, Nr Ripon, North Yorkshire, HG4 4NS *Tel:* 01765 689241 *Fax:* 01765 688184; 46 Westminster Gardens, Marsham Street, London, SW1P 4JG *Tel:* 020 7834 0700 *Fax:* 020 7834 6126 *E-mail:* baroness.masham@breathemail.net.

MASON OF BARNSLEY, LORD   Labour

MASON OF BARNSLEY (Life Baron), Roy Mason; cr. 1987. Born 18 April 1924. Son of late Joseph Mason, miner; educated Carlton and Royston Elementary Schools; London School of Economics (TUC Scholarship 1951–52). Married Marjorie Sowden 1945 (2 daughters). *Trades Union:* Member, Yorkshire Miners' Council 1949–53; Chairman, Parliamentary Triple Alliance of Miners, Railway and Steel Union MPs 1979–80. DL, South Yorkshire 1992–. *Career:* Coal Miner 1938–53; Member, Council of Europe and Western European Union 1970–71. *House of Commons:* Labour candidate for Bridlington 1951–53; MP (Labour) for: Barnsley 1953–83, Barnsley Central 1983–87; Minister of State (Shipping), Board of Trade 1964–67; Minister of Defence Equipment 1967–1968; Postmaster General April-June 1968; Minister of Power 1968–69; President, Board of Trade 1969–70; Chair: Yorkshire Group of Labour MPs 1970–74, 1981–84, Miners Group of Labour MPs 1973–74, 1980–81; Secretary of State for: Defence 1974–76, Northern Ireland 1976–79. Opposition Spokesperson for Defence and Post Office Affairs 1960–64; Principal Opposition Spokesperson for Board of Trade Affairs 1970–74; Principal Opposition Spokesperson for Agriculture, Fisheries and Food 1979–81. Chair: Yorkshire Group of Labour MPs 1970–74, 1981–84, Miners' Group of MPs 1973–74, 1980–81. Member, Council of Europe 1970–71. President, Yorkshire Salmon and Trout Association, Member, National Council; President, Yorkshire Water Colour Society; Vice-President, South Yorkshire Foundation (Charity); Chairman, Barnsley Business and Innovation Centre Ltd; Member, National Council of The Scouts Association. DUniv, Hallam University, Sheffield. Chairman, Prince's Youth Business Trust, South Yorkshire 1987–2002. Member: National Rivers Authority Advisory Committee 1988, National Rivers Authority 1989–92; President, Lords and Commons Pipe and Cigar Club; Convener of Lords and Commons Flying Fishing Club. PC 1968. *Publications: Paying the Price* (autobiography), 1999. *Special Interests:* Coal Industry, Human Rights, Northern Ireland, Defence, Anti-Pollution Matters. *Recreations:* Fly-fishing, golf, tie designing (cravatology), specialist philately. *Sportsclubs:* President, Lords and Commons Fly Fishing Club. *Clubs:* Life Membership: Carlton Village Working Men's Club, Barnsley Gawber Road Working Men's Club, Barnsley Trades and Labour Club. Raised to the peerage as Baron Mason of Barnsley, of Barnsley in South Yorkshire 1987. Rt Hon the Lord Mason of Barnsley, DL, 12 Victoria Avenue, Barnsley, South Yorkshire, S70 2BH.

MASSEY OF DARWEN, BARONESS   Labour

MASSEY OF DARWEN (Life Baroness), Doreen Elizabeth Massey; cr. 1999. Born 5 September 1938. Daughter of late Jack and Mary Ann Hall (née Sharrock); educated Darwen Grammar School; Birmingham University (BA French 1961, DipEd 1962); London University (MA health education 1985). Married Dr Leslie Massey 1966 (2 sons 1 daughter). *Trades Union:* Former Member: NUT, MSF. School Governor; Lady Taverner 2003–. *Career:* Graduate service overseas, Gabon 1962–63; French teacher South Hackney School 1964–67; French and English teacher Springside School, Philadelphia 1967–69; Running community playgroup 1970–77, Teacher/Head of year/Senior teacher in charge of health education, Walsingham School, London 1979–83; Adviser in personal, social and health education, Inner London Education Authority 1983–85; Director of training, Family Planning Association 1981–89; Director of Young People's Programme, Health Education Authority 1985–87; Director, FPA 1989–94; Independent Consultant in Health Education 1994–2001; Chair, National Treatment Agency 2002–. Member: House of Lords' Offices Administration and Works Sub-committee 2001–, Religious Offences Committee 2002–. Member: Brook Advisory Centres, Family Planning Association, Opera North, English National Opera, Royal Shakespeare Company, Sex Education Forum. Advisory Council for Alcohol and Drug Education; Trust for the Study of Adolescence. Member Ecclesiastical Committee 2000–. FRSA. *Publications: Teaching About HIV/AIDS,* 1988; Co-author *Sex Education Factpack,* 1988; *Sex Education: Why, What and How,* 1988; Editor *The Sex Education Source Book,* 1995; *Lovers' Guide Encyclopaedia,* 1996; articles on health education in a variety of journals. *Special Interests:* Education, Health, International Development, Children and Young People, Sport. *Recreations:* Theatre, opera, reading, walking, yoga, travel, sports. Raised to the peerage as Baroness Massey of Darwen, of Darwen in the County of Lancashire 1999. The Baroness Massey of Darwen, 66 Lessar Avenue, London, SW4 9HQ *Tel:* 020 7219 8653 *E-mail:* masseyd@parliament.uk.

MAY OF OXFORD, LORD   Crossbencher

MAY OF OXFORD (Life Baron), Robert McCredie May; cr 2001. Born 8 January 1936. Son of Henry Wilkinson May and Kathleen Mitchell, née McCredie; educated Sydney Boys' High School; Sydney University, Australia (BSc theoretical physics 1957, PhD 1959). Married Judith Feiner 1962 (1 daughter). *Career:* Gordon Mackay Lecturer in Applied Mathematics, Harvard University, USA 1959–61; Sydney University: Senior lecturer 1961–64, Reader 1964–69, Professor of Theoretical Physics; Princeton University, USA: Class of 1877 Professor of Zoology 1973–88, Vice-president for research 1977–88; Royal Society Research Professor, Oxford University and Imperial College, London 1988–; Chair Trustees Natural History Museum 1993–98; Chief Scientific Adviser to the UK Government and Head of UK Office of Science and Technology 1995–2000; President, The Royal Society 2000–. Numerous, including: Royal Swedish Academy of Science, Crafoord Prize 1996, Balzan Prize 1998, Blue Planet Prize 2001. Numerous honorary degrees, including Uppsalla, Princeton, Sydney, Yale. Executive Trustees, Nuffield Foundation; Foundation Trustees, Gate Cambridge University Trust. Kt 1996, Companion Order of Australia (AC) 1998, OM 2002. Fellow: Royal Society 1979, Australian Academy of Sciences 1991, US National Academy of Sciences 1992. *Publications:* Several hundred scientific papers; Scientific journalism for journals, radio and television; *Stability and Complexity in Model Ecosystems* (Princeton University Press) 1973, 2000; Co-author *Infectious Diseases of Humans: Dynamics and Control* (OUP) 1991; Editor: *Large Scale Ecology and Conservation Biology* (Blackwell) 1994, *Extinction Rates* (OUP) 1995, *Evolution of Biological Diversity* (OUP) 1999; Co-author *Virus Dynamics: the Mathematical Foundations of Immunology and Virology* (OUP) 2000. *Recreations:* Hiking, running, tennis. *Sportsclubs:* Oxford University Tennis. Raised to the peerage as Baron May of Oxford, of Oxford in the County of Oxfordshire. The Lord May of Oxford, OM, House of Lords, London, SW1A 0PW *Tel:* 020 7219 6958.

Visit the Vacher Dod Website . . .
www.DodOnline.co.uk

MAYHEW OF TWYSDEN, LORD   Conservative

MAYHEW OF TWYSDEN (Life Baron), Patrick Barnabas Burke Mayhew; cr. 1997. Born 11 September 1929. Son of late A. G. H. Mayhew, MC, and the late Sheila M. B. Mayhew, née Roche; educated Tonbridge School; Balliol College, Oxford (BA jurisprudence 1953, MA). Married Jean Elizabeth Gurney OBE 1963 (4 sons). National service 1948–49, commissioned 4th/7th Royal Dragoon Guards; Captain, Army Emergency Reserve 1954–65. President: Tunbridge Wells Sea Cadets 1976–, West Kent College of Further Education 1997, National Fruit Show 1999–, Kent Scouts Council 2000–; Chairman, Rochester Cathedral Council 2000–; Deputy Lieutenant for Kent 2001–. *Career:* Called to the Bar Middle Temple 1955; QC 1972; Bencher 1976; Reader 2000. *House of Commons:* Contested (Conservative) Camberwell-Dulwich 1970; MP (Conservative) for Tunbridge Wells 1974–97; Parliamentary Under Secretary of State, Department of Employment 1979–81; Minister of State, Home Office 1981–83; Solicitor-General 1983–87; Attorney General 1987–92; Secretary of State for Northern Ireland 1992–97. Member, Select Committees on: Deregulation and Devolved Legislation 1997–2001, Parliamentary Privilege (Joint Committee) 1997–99, European Union Sub-committee E (Law and Institutions) 2001–, Delegated Powers and Regulatory Reform 2003–. Executive Member, Association Conservative Peers 1998–. President, The Airey Neave Trust 1997–; Trustee, Rochester Cathedral Appeal 1985–2000. Chair, Minister's Advisory Committee on Business Appointments 1999–. Kt 1983; PC 1986. Liveryman, Worshipful Company of Skinners 1956–; Hon. Liveryman, Worshipful Company of Poulterers, 2001. *Special Interests:* Northern Ireland, Criminal Justice Policy, Constitutional Matters, Defence. *Recreations:* Country life, travel, reading. *Clubs:* Pratt's, Beefsteak, Garrick, Tunbridge Wells Constitutional. Raised to the peerage as Baron Mayhew of Twysden, of Kilndown in the County of Kent 1997. Rt Hon the Lord Mayhew of Twysden, QC, House of Lords, London, SW1A 0PW *Tel:* 020 7219 5858.

MERLYN-REES, LORD   Labour

MERLYN-REES (Life Baron), Merlyn Merlyn-Rees; cr. 1992. Born 18 December 1920. Son of late L. D. Rees; educated Harrow Weald Grammar School; Goldsmiths' College (President, Students' Union 1940); London School of Economics (BSc economics and economic history 1949, MSc economics 1954). Married Colleen Faith Cleveley 1949 (3 sons). Served RAF 1941–46; Demobilised as Squadron-Leader. Member, Committee to examine Section 2 of Official Secrets Act 1971; Member, Franks' Committee of Enquiry on Falkland Islands 1982. *Career:* Economics and history teacher, Harrow Weald Grammar School 1949–60; Economics lecturer, Luton College of Technology 1962–63. *House of Commons:* Contested (Labour) Harrow East in: 1955, 1959 general elections, By-election 1959; MP (Labour) for: Leeds South1963–83, Morley and South Leeds 1983–92; PPS to Chancellor of the Exchequer 1964–65; Parliamentary Under-Secretary of State: Ministry of Defence, for the Army 1965–66, for the Royal Air Force 1966–68, Home Office 1968–70; Member, Shadow Cabinet 1972–74; Secretary of State for Northern Ireland 1974–76; Home Secretary 1976–79. Opposition Frontbench Spokesperson for Northern Ireland 1972; Principal Frontbench Spokesperson on: Home Affairs 1979–80, Energy 1980–82, Industry and Employment Co-ordination 1982–83. Chancellor, University of Glamorgan 1993–2002. Member, Select Committees on: the Civil Service 1996–97, Delegated Powers and Deregulation 1997–2000, Public Service 1997–2000, Parliamentary Privilege (Joint Committee) 1997–. Member: CPA, IPU, British American Parliamentary Group. Organiser, Festival of Labour 1960–62. Hon. LLD, Wales 1987; Fellow, Polytechnic of Wales 1989, Hon. LLD, Leeds 1992; Honorary doctorate, University of Glamorgan 2002. Assumed the surname of Merlyn-Rees in lieu of his patronymic 1992; President, Video Standards Council 1990–. PC 1974. *Publications: The Public Sector in the Mixed Economy*, 1973; *Northern Ireland: A Personal Perspective*, 1985. *Special Interests:* Housing, Education, Penal Reform. *Recreations:* Reading, theatre. Raised to the peerage as Baron Merlyn-Rees, of Morley and South Leeds in the County of West Yorkshire and of Cilfynydd in the County of Mid Glamorgan 1992. Rt Hon the Lord Merlyn-Rees, House of Lords, London, SW1A 0PW *Tel:* 020 7219 5422.

Visit the Vacher Dod Website . . . www.DodOnline.co.uk

METHUEN, LORD   Liberal Democrat

METHUEN (7th Baron), Robert Alexander Holt Methuen; cr. 1838. Born 22 July 1931. Son of 5th Baron; educated Shrewsbury School; Trinity College, Cambridge (BA engineering 1957). Married Mary Catherine Jane Hooper 1958 (2 daughters) (divorced 1993); married Margrit Andrea Hadwiger 1994. *Career:* Design engineer, Westinghouse Brake and Signal Company 1957–67; Computer systems engineer: IBM UK Ltd 1968–75, Rolls-Royce plc 1975–94; Retired. *House of Lords:* First entered House of Lords 1994; Deputy Chair of Committees 1999–2001; Elected hereditary peer 1999–. Member: European Communities Sub-Committee B (Energy, Industry and Transport) 1995–99, Channel Tunnel Rail Link 1996, House of Lords' Offices Administration and Works Sub-committee 1997–2001, Science and Technology 1999–; Science and Technology Sub-committee II (Aircraft Cabin Environment) 2000; House of Lords' Offices Library and Computers Sub-committee 2000–; Science and Technology Sub-committee II (innovations in microprocessing/Science and the Regional Development Agencies) 2002–. Patron, Lady Margaret Hungerford Charity. *Recreations:* Walking, horse trekking, industrial archaeology. The Lord Methuen, House of Lords, London, SW1A 0PW *Tel:* 020 7219 1220.

MICHIE OF GALLANACH, BARONESS   Liberal Democrat

MICHIE OF GALLANACH (Life Baroness), (Janet) Ray Michie; cr. 2001. Born 4 February 1934. Daughter of late Lord and Lady Bannerman of Kildonan; educated Aberdeen High School for Girls; Lansdowne House, Edinburgh; Edinburgh College of Speech Therapy (MCST 1955). Married Dr Iain Michie FRCP 1957 (2 daughters and 1 daughter deceased). *Trades Union:* Member: Scottish National Farmers Union, Scottish Crofting Foundation. *Career:* Area speech therapist, Argyll and Clyde Health Board 1977–87. *House of Commons:* Contested Argyll 1979, Argyll and Bute 1983 general elections; MP (Liberal Democrat) for Argyll and Bute 1987–2001. Liberal Spokeswoman for Transport and Rural Development 1987–88; Liberal Democrat Spokeswoman for: Women's Issues 1988–94, Scotland 1988–97, (Scottish Team) for Agriculture, Community Care, Rural Affairs and National Heritage 1997–99. Vice-Chair, Scottish Liberal Party 1976–78; Chair, Scottish Liberal Democrats 1992–93; Deputy Leader, Scottish Liberal Democrats 1997–99. Vice-President, Royal College of Speech and Language Therapists 1996–01; Hon. President, CFA (Clyde Fishermens Association); Member: An Comunn Gaidhealach, Scottish Constitutional Convention. Hon. Associate, National Council of Women of GB. *Special Interests:* Constitutional Reform, Home Rule for Scotland, Farming, Crofting, Gaelic language, Health, EU Political Institutions, Education. *Recreations:* Golf, swimming, gardening, watching rugby. *Clubs:* National Liberal. Raised to the peerage as Baroness Michie of Gallanach, of Oban in Argyll and Bute 2001. The Baroness Michie of Gallanach, House of Lords, London, SW1A 0PW *Tel:* 020 7219 6879 *Fax:* 01631 730 610 *Tel:* 01631 730 610 *E-mail:* margaret.wills@virgin.net.

MILLER OF CHILTHORNE DOMER, BARONESS   Liberal Democrat

MILLER OF CHILTHORNE DOMER (Life Baroness), Susan Elisabeth Miller; cr. 1998. Born 1 January 1954. Daughter of Frederick Oliver Meddows Taylor and Norah Langham; educated Sidcot School, Winscombe, Somerset; Oxford Polytechnic (book publishing 1975). Married John Miller 1980 (divorced 1998) (2 daughters 1 deceased); married Humphrey Temperley 1999. Councillor: Chilthorne Domer Parish Council 1987, South Somerset District Council 1991–98, Leader 1996–98; Councillor, Somerset County Council 1997–; LGA Executive, European and International. *Career:* In publishing: David & Charles, Weidenfeld & Nicolson, Penguin Books 1975–79; Bookshop owner 1979–89. Liberal Democrat Spokesperson for: Agriculture and Rural Affairs 1999–2001, Environment, Food and Rural Affairs 2001–. Member, European Communities Sub Committee D (Agriculture, Fisheries and Food) 1998–2002. Member, IPU. Chairman, Somerset Food Links; Vice-President: Council of National Parks, British Trust for Conservation Volunteers. Fellow, Joint University (Exeter and Bournemouth). Patron, Somerset Trust for Sustainable Development Yeovil Arts Centre. *Publications: Stuck or Spiked – What Happened to eco-labelling in UK* 2002. *Special Interests:* Environment, Street Children. *Recreations:* Walking, reading, friends, sailing. Raised to the peerage as Baroness Miller of Chilthorne Domer, of Chilthorne Domer in the County of Somerset 1998. The Baroness Miller of Chilthorne Domer, House of Lords, London, SW1A 0PW *Tel:* 020 7219 6042 *E-mail:* millers@parliament.uk.

MILLER OF HENDON, BARONESS   Conservative

MILLER OF HENDON (Life Baroness), Doreen Miller; cr. 1993. Born 13 June 1933. Daughter of Bernard and Hetty Feldman; educated Brondesbury and Kilburn High School; London School of Economics. Married Henry Lewis Miller 1955 (3 sons). JP, Brent 1971; Chairman, Barnet Family Health Services Authority 1990–94. *Career:* Managing Director/Chairman Universe Beauty Club Ltd 1972–88; Managing Director Cosmetic Club Interactive GmbH (Germany) 1974–88; Managing Director Universe Beauty Club (Pty) Australia 1976–88; Director group of property investment companies. Government Whip 1994–97; Opposition Whip 1997–99. Spokesperson for: Health 1995–97, Education and Employment 1996–97, Trade and Industry 1996–97, Office of Public Service 1996, Environment 1996–97; Opposition Spokesperson for: Environment, Transport and the Regions 1997–2000, Department of Trade and Industry 1997–, Employment 2000–03, Education and Skills 2001–03. Greater London Area Conservative and Unionist Associations: Joint Treasurer 1990–93, Chairman 1993–96, President 1996–98; Member, Conservative Board of Finance and its Training and Fund Raising Sub-Committees 1990–93; President, Hampstead and Highgate Women's Committee 1993–96; Member, Conservative Women's National and General Purposes Committees 1993–96, Patron 1996–; President, Greenwich and Woolwich Conservative Association 1996–; Patron: Eltham and Woolwich Conservative Association 1996–, Hackney North Conservative Association 1996–, North Thanet Conservative Association 1996–, Hendon Conservative Association 2000–. National Chairman and Executive Director, 300 Group 1985–88; Chairman, Women into Public Life Campaign 1986–92; Human rights adviser, Soroptomist International 1987–90; Chairman, National Association of Hospital and Community Friends 1997–2003. Patron, Minerva Educational Trust. Contested (Conservative): London South Inner, 1984 European Parliament elections, ILEA 1986; Non-Executive Director, Crown Agents 1990–94; Member, Monopolies and Mergers Commission 1992–93. MBE, 1989. Fellow, Institute of Marketing; FRSA. *Publications: Let's Make Up* (1974). *Special Interests:* Women's Issues, Health, Law and Order, Small Businesses. *Recreations:* Reading, football, politics. *Clubs:* Carlton. Raised to the peerage as Baroness Miller of Hendon, of Gore in the London Borough of Barnet 1993. The Baroness Miller of Hendon, MBE, House of Lords, London, SW1A 0PW *Tel:* 020 7219 3164 *Fax:* 020 7219 3164 *E-mail:* millerd@parliament.uk.

MILLETT, LORD   Crossbencher

MILLETT (Life Baron), Peter Julian Millett; cr. 1998. Born 23 June 1932. Son of late Denis Millett and Adele Millett; educated Harrow School; Trinity Hall, Cambridge (Scholar, MA classics and law 1954). Married Ann Mireille Harris 1959 (2 sons and 1 son deceased). Flying Officer, RAF, National Service 1955–57. *Career:* Called to the Bar: Middle Temple 1955, Lincoln's Inn 1959 (Bencher 1980), Singapore 1976, Hong Kong 1979; At Chancery Bar 1958–86; Examiner and lecturer in practical conveyancing, Council of Legal Education 1962–76; Junior counsel to Department of Trade and Industry in Chancery matters 1967–73; Member, General Council of the Bar 1971–75; Outside Member, Law Commission on working party on co-ownership of the matrimonial home 1972–73; QC 1973; Member, Department of Trade Insolvency Law Review Committee 1977–82; Judge of the High Court of Justice 1986–94; Lord Justice of Appeal 1994–98; Lord of Appeal in Ordinary 1998–; Non-Permanent Judge of the Court of Final Appeal, Hong Kong 2000–. Member, Insol International. President, West London Synagogue of British Jews 1991–95. Hon. Fellow, Trinity Hall, Cambridge; honorary doctorate London University. Kt 1986; PC 1994. *Publications:* Has contributed to several legal publications including *Halsbury's Law of England*; Editor in Chief, *Encyclopaedia of Forms and Precedents. Recreations:* Philately, bridge, *The Times* crossword. *Clubs:* Home House. Raised to the peerage as Baron Millett, of St Marylebone in the City of Westminster 1998. Rt Hon the Lord Millett, House of Lords, London, SW1A 0PW *Tel:* 020 7219 6380 *E-mail:* lordmillett@02.co.uk.

Visit the Vacher Dod Website . . .
www.DodOnline.co.uk

MISHCON, LORD   Labour

MISHCON (Life Baron), Victor Mishcon; cr. 1978. Born 14 August 1915. Son of late Rabbi Arnold and Queenie Mishcon; educated City of London School. Married Joan Estelle Monty 1976 (2 sons 1 daughter by former marriage). Served HM Forces during Second World War. Councillor, Lambeth Borough Council 1945–49, Chair, Finance Committee; Councillor, LCC 1946–65, Chair 1954–55; Councillor, GLC, Chair, General Purposes Committe 1964–67; Member, ILEA 1964–67; DL, Greater London 1954. *Career:* Solicitor, Senior Partner Mishcon De Reya 1988–92, Consultant 1992–; Member: National Theatre Board 1965–90, South Bank Theatre Board 1966–67; Vice-President, Board of Deputies of British Jews 1967–73; Vice-Chair, Council of Christians and Jews 1976–77; Former Member, various Government Committees. Principal Opposition Spokesperson for: Home Affairs 1983–90, Legal Affairs 1990–93. Hon. LLD, Birmingham University 1991; Hon. Fellow, University College, London 1993. Contested (Labour): North West Leeds 1950, Bath 1951, Gravesend 1955, 1959 general elections. Commander, Royal Swedish Order of North Star 1954; Star of Ethiopia 1954; QC (Hon) 1992; Star of Jordan 1995. Raised to the peerage as Baron Mishcon, of Lambeth in Greater London 1978. The Lord Mishcon, QC, DL, Summit House, 12 Red Lion Square, London, WC1R 4QD.

MITCHELL, LORD   Labour

MITCHELL (Life Baron), Parry Andrew Mitchell; cr. 2000. Born 6 May 1943. Son of late Leon Mitchell and Rose Mitchell; educated Christ's College Grammar School, London; London University (BSc economics 1964); Graduate School of Business, Columbia University, New York (MBA 1966). Married 1st (divorced) (1 daughter); married Hannah Lowy 1988 (twin sons). *Career:* Information technology entrepreneur; Founder, Syscap plc. Member: House of Lords' Offices Library and Computers Sub-committee 2001–, Science and Technology Sub-committee II (Innovations in Computer Processors/ Microprocessors/Science and the Regional Development Agencies) 2002–, Science and Technology Committee 2003–. e-Learning Foundation; Jewish Association for Business Ethics. Lowy Mitchell Foundation. *Special Interests:* Information Technology, Small Business. *Recreations:* Scuba diving, theatre, jazz, opera. Raised to the peerage as Baron Mitchell, of Hampstead in the London Borough of Camden 2000. The Lord Mitchell, House of Lords, London, SW1A 0PW *Tel:* 020 7433 3238 *Fax:* 020 7431 5734 *E-mail:* parrym@mac.com.

MOLYNEAUX OF KILLEAD, LORD   Crossbencher

MOLYNEAUX OF KILLEAD (Life Baron), James Henry Molyneaux; cr. 1997. Born 27 August 1920. Son of late William Molyneaux; educated Aldergrove School, Co. Antrim. RAF 1941–46. JP, Co. Antrim 1957–86; Antrim County Councillor 1964–73. *House of Commons:* MP (UUP) for Antrim South 1970–83 and for Lagan Valley 1983–97. Spokesman, Treasury 1995–97. Spokesperson for Northern Ireland. Hon. Secretary, South Antrim Unionist Association 1964–70; Chairman, Antrim division Unionist Association 1971–74; Leader: United Ulster Unionist Coalition 1974–77, Ulster Unionist Parliamentary Party 1974–95, Ulster Unionist Party 1979–95. Vice-Chairman, Eastern Special Care Hospital Committee 1966–73; Chairman: Antrim Mental Health Branch 1967–70, Crumlin Branch, Royal British Legion 1985–99; Sovereign Grand Master, British Commonwealth Royal Black Institution 1971–98; Vice-President, Federation of Economic Development Authorities. PC 1983; KBE 1996. *Special Interests:* Constitutional Affairs, Mental Health, Local Government. *Recreations:* Gardening, music. Raised to the peerage as Baron Molyneaux of Killead, of Killead in the County of Antrim 1997. Rt Hon the Lord Molyneaux of Killead, KBE, House of Lords, London, SW1A 0PW *Tel:* 020 7219 6707.

Visit the Vacher Dod Website . . . www.DodOnline.co.uk

MONRO OF LANGHOLM, LORD — Conservative

MONRO OF LANGHOLM (Life Baron), Hector Seymour Peter Monro; cr. 1997. Born 4 October 1922. Son of late Captain Alastair Monro, Queens Own Cameron Highlanders; educated Canford School; King's College, Cambridge. Married Elizabeth Anne Welch 1949 (died 1994) (2 sons); married Mrs Doris Kaestner 1994. Served RAF 1941–46; RAuxAF 1947–54; Hon. Air Commodore 1982–2000; Hon. Inspector General RAuxAF 1989–2000. Councillor, Dumfries County Council 1952–67; JP Dumfries 1972–; DL, Dumfriesshire 1973–. *Career:* Farming 1947–; Chair and Director Century Aluminium 1966–70. *House of Commons:* MP (Conservative) for Dumfries 1964–97; Parliamentary Under-Secretary of State: for Scotland 1971–74, at Department of Environment and Minister for Sport 1979–81; Joint Parliamentary Under-Secretary of State, Scottish Office 1992–95. Opposition Whip 1967–70; Government Whip 1970–71. Opposition Spokesperson for: Scottish Affairs 1974–75, Sport 1974–79. Chairman, Dumfriesshire Conservative Association 1958–63. Chairman, Dumfries and Galloway Police Committee; Area Executive, NFU; Member, Nature Conservancy Council 1982–91; President: Auto Cycle Union 1983–90, National Small-bore Rifle Association 1987–92. Member, Queen's Bodyguard for Scotland, Royal Company of Archers. AE 1953; Knighted 1981; PC 1995. FRAGS. *Special Interests:* Scotland, Agriculture, Aviation, Defence, Sport, Recreation, Heritage. *Recreations:* Sport, flying, shooting, music. *Sportsclubs:* Scottish Rugby Union: Member 1957–77, Vice-President 1975, President 1976–77. *Clubs:* MCC, Royal Scottish Automobile (Glasgow), Royal Air Force, Royal and Ancient (St Andrews). Raised to the peerage as Baron Monro of Langholm, of Westerkirk in Dumfries and Galloway 1997. Rt Hon the Lord Monro of Langholm, AE, DL, Williamwood, Kirtlebride, Lockerbie, Dumfries, DG11 3LN *Tel:* 01461 500 213.

MONSON, LORD — Crossbencher

MONSON (11th Baron, GB), John Monson; cr. 1728; 15th Bt of Carlton (E) 1611. Born 3 May 1932. Son of 10th Baron; educated Eton College; Trinity College, Cambridge (BA 1954). Married Emma Devas 1955 (3 sons). *House of Lords:* First entered House of Lords 1961; Elected hereditary peer 1999–. Member, Administration and Works Sub-Committee, House of Lords Offices Committee 2000–02. President, Society for Individual Freedom. The Lord Monson, The Manor House, South Carlton, Nr Lincoln, LN1 2RN *Tel:* 01522 730263.

MONTAGU OF BEAULIEU, LORD — Conservative

MONTAGU OF BEAULIEU (3rd Baron, UK), Edward John Barrington Douglas-Scott-Montagu; cr. 1885. Born 20 October 1926. Son of 2nd Baron, KCIE, CSI, DL; educated St Peter's Court, Broadstairs; Ridley College; St Catharines, Ontario; Eton College; New College, Oxford (history). Married Belinda Crossley 1959 (1 son 1 daughter) (divorced 1974); married Fiona Herbert 1974 (1 son). Lieutenant, Grenadier Guards 1945–48. *Career:* Author, museum founder, historic house entrepreneur; Founded Montagu Motor Museum 1952, which became the National Motor Museum 1972, Founder and editor, *Veteran and Vintage Magazine* 1956–79; President, Fédération Internationale des Voitures Anciennes 1980–83; Development Commissioner 1980–84; First Chair, Historic Buildings and Monuments Commission (English Heritage) 1984–92; Chair: Report on Britain's Historic Buildings: A Policy for their Future Use, English Tourist Board's Committee of Enquiry publishing Britain's Zoos. *House of Lords:* First entered House of Lords 1947; Elected hereditary peer 1999–. Member: Commission Historique Internationale de FIA (Federation Internationale de l'Automobile), International Council of Museums. President, Southern Tourist Board; President Emeritus, Tourism Society; President, United Kingdom Vineyards Association; Chancellor, Wine Guild UK; President: Historic Commercial Vehicle Society, Disabled Drivers Motor Club, Millennium Institute of Journalists; First President: Historic Houses Association 1973–78, European

Union of Historic Houses Associations 1978–81; President: Museums Association 1982–84, Federation of British Historic Vehicle Clubs 1988–; Hon Vice-President, Veteran Car Club of Great Britain. Hon. DTech. Chair National Motor Museum Trust; President British Military Powerboat Trust. Officer, Order of St John. FRSA; FMA; Hon. RICS; FMI; FIMI; FIPR. Freeman, City of London. *Publications: More Equal than Others*; *Gilt and the Gingerbread*; *Jaguar: A Biography*; *Daimler Century*, 1995, *Wheels Within Wheels – an Unconventional Life*, 2000; and many other motoring books and books on motoring history and historic houses. *Special Interests:* Heritage, Museums and Galleries, Road Transport, Motor Industry, Tourism. *Recreations:* Water and field sports, theatre, cinema, music. *Sportsclubs:* Commodore, Beaulieu River Sailing Club; Vice-Commodore, House of Lords Yacht Club; Commodore, Nelson Boat Owners' Club. *Clubs:* RAC, Beefsteak. The Lord Montagu of Beaulieu, Palace House, Beaulieu, Brockenhurst, Hampshire, SO42 7ZN *Tel:* 01590 614 701 (direct) *Fax:* 01590 612623; Flat 11, Wyndham House, Bryanston Square, London, W1H 2DS *Tel:* 020 7262 2603 *Fax:* 020 7724 3262 *E-mail:* lord.montagu@beaulieu.com.uk.

MONTROSE, DUKE OF   Conservative

MONTROSE (8th Duke of, S), James Graham; cr. 1707; Marquis of Montrose (S) 1644; Marquess of Graham and Buchanan (S) 1707; Earl of Montrose (S) 1505; Earl of Kincardine (S) 1707; Earl Graham (GB) 1722; Viscount Dundaff (S) 1707; Lord Graham (S) 1445; Lord Aberuthven, Mugdock and Fintrie (S) 1707; Baron Graham (GB) 1722; 12th Bt of Braco (NS) 1625. Born 6 April 1935. Son of 7th Duke and late Isobel Veronica, daughter of late Lieutenant-Colonel Thomas Sellar, CMG, DSO; educated Loretto School, Musselburgh. Married Catherine Elizabeth MacDonnell, née Young 1970 (2 sons 1 daughter). Chair, Buchanan Community Council 1982–93; Vice-Chair, Secretary of State's Working Party for Loch Lomond and the Trossachs. *House of Lords:* First entered House of Lords 1995; Elected hereditary peer 1999–. Opposition Whip 2001–. Opposition Spokesperson for Scotland 2001–. Member: CPA, IPU. Member: Council of Scottish National Farmers Union 1981–90, Royal Scottish Pipers Society, Royal Highland and Agricultural Society, President 1997–98, Scottish Landowners Federation. Member, Queen's Bodyguard for Scotland (Royal Company of Archers) 1965–, Brigadier 1986–2001, Ensign 2001–; Hereditary Sheriff, Dunbartonshire. OStJ 1978. *Special Interests:* Europe, Agriculture, Rural Affairs. *Recreations:* Walking, shooting, golf. *Clubs:* Farmers. The Duke of Montrose, Auchmar, Drymen, Glasgow, G63 0AG *E-mail:* montrosej@parliament.uk.

MOORE OF LOWER MARSH, LORD   Conservative

MOORE OF LOWER MARSH (Life Baron), John Edward Michael Moore; cr. 1992. Born 26 November 1937. Son of late Edward Moore; educated Licensed Victuallers' School, Slough; London School of Economics (BSc Econ 1961). Married Sheila Sarah Tillotson 1962 (2 sons 1 daughter). National Service with Royal Sussex Regiment in Korea 1955–57, Commissioned. Councillor, London Borough of Merton 1971–74. *Career:* Chairman, Dean Witter (International) Ltd 1975–79, Director 1968–79; Advisory Board Member, Marvin and Palmer Inc. 1989–; Director, Monitor Inc. 1990–, Chairman, European Executive Committee; Member, Advisory Board, Sir Alexander Gibb & Co. 1990–95; Chairman, Credit Suisse Asset Management 1992–2000; Director: Swiss American NY Inc 1992–96, GTECH 1993–2001, Blue Circle Industries plc 1993–2001, Camelot Holdings plc 1993–98; Director, Rolls-Royce plc 1994–, Deputy Chairman 1996–; Supervisory Board Member, ITT Automotive Europe GMBH, Germany 1994–97; Director: Central European Growth Fund Ltd 1995–2000, BEA (NY) 1996–98, TIG Holdings Inc (NY) 1997–99, Private Client Bank (Zurich) 1999–. *House of Commons:* MP (Conservative) Croydon Central February 1974–92; Parliamentary Under-Secretary of State for Energy 1979–83; Economic Secretary to the Treasury June-October 1983; Financial Secretary to the Treasury 1983–86; Secretary of State for: Transport 1986–87, Social Services 1987–88, Social Security 1988–89. Chairman, Conservative Association, LSE 1958; Chairman, Stepney Green Conservative Association 1968; Vice-Chairman, Conservative Party with responsibility for Youth 1975–79. President, Student Union, LSE 1959–60; Member, Court of Governors, LSE 1977–2002; Council Member, Institute of Directors 1991–95. Chairman, Energy Savings Trust 1992–95, President 1995–2001. PC 1986. *Clubs:* Royal Automobile. Raised to the peerage as Baron Moore of Lower Marsh, of Lower Marsh in the London Borough of Lambeth 1992. Rt Hon the Lord Moore of Lower Marsh, House of Lords, London, SW1A 0PW *Tel:* 020 7219 5353.

MOORE OF WOLVERCOTE, LORD   Crossbencher

MOORE OF WOLVERCOTE (Life Baron), Philip Brian Cecil Moore; cr. 1986. Born 6 April 1921. Son of late Cecil Moore, ICS; educated Dragon School; Cheltenham College; Brasenose College, Oxford (Classical Exhibitioner 1940). Married Joan Ursula Greenop 1945 (2 daughters). RAF Bomber Command, POW 1942–45. *Career:* Entered Home Civil Service 1947; Assistant Private Secretary to First Lord of the Admiralty 1950–51; Principal Private Secretary to First Lord of the Admiralty 1957–58; Deputy UK Commissioner and Deputy British High Commissioner, Singapore 1961–65; Chief of Public Relations, Ministry of Defence 1965–66; Assistant Private Secretary to HM The Queen 1966–72, Deputy Private Secretary 1972–77, Private Secretary 1977–86; Permanent Lord-in-Waiting to HM The Queen 1990–. Hon. Fellow, Brasenose College, Oxford. CMG 1966; CB 1973; KCVO 1976; PC 1977; KCB 1980; GCVO 1983; GCB 1985; QSO 1986. *Special Interests:* Foreign Affairs, Defence, Church Affairs. *Recreations:* Golf, shooting, fishing. *Sportsclubs:* England Rugby International; Rugby and Hockey Blues for Oxford; Cricket for Oxfordshire. *Clubs:* MCC. Raised to the peerage as Baron Moore of Wolvercote, of Wolvercote in the City of Oxford 1986. Rt Hon the Lord Moore of Wolvercote, GCB, GCVO, CMG, QSO, Hampton Court Palace, East Molesey, Surrey, KT8 9AU *Tel:* 020 7943 4695.

MORAN, LORD   Crossbencher

MORAN (2nd Baron, UK), (Richard) John McMoran Wilson; cr. 1943. Born 22 September 1924. Son of 1st Baron, MC, MD, FRCP, and late Dorothy, née Dufton; educated Eton College; King's College, Cambridge. Married Shirley Rowntree, née Harris 1948 (2 sons 1 daughter). Served RNVR 1943–45; Ordinary Seaman, HMS Belfast 1943; Sub-Lieutenant, Motor Torpedo Boats and HM Destroyer Oribi 1944–45. *Career:* Foreign Office 1945; Served in Ankara, Tel Aviv, Rio de Janeiro, Washington and South Africa; Head of West African Department, Foreign Office 1968–73; Concurrently non-resident Ambassador to Chad 1970–73; Ambassador to: Hungary 1973–76, Portugal 1976–81; High Commissioner to Canada 1981–84. *House of Lords:* First entered House of Lords 1977; Elected hereditary peer 1999–. Member: Industry Sub-Committee of European Communities Committee 1984–86, Environmental Sub-Committee of European Communities Committee 1986–91, Sub-Committee of the Science and Technology Committee on the Scientific Base of the Nature Conservancy Council 1990, Agriculture Sub-Committee of European Communities Committee 1991–95, Sub-Committee of the Science and Technology Committee on Fish Stocks 1995, Sub-Committee on the 1996 Inter-Governmental Conference 1995–97; Co-opted Member, Select Committee on European Communities Sub-Committee D (Agriculture, Fisheries and Food) 1997–2000. Chair, Wildlife and Countryside Link 1990–95; Council Member, RSPB 1992–94, Vice-President 1996–97; President, Welsh Salmon and Trout Angling Association 1988–95, 2000–; Chair, Salmon and Trout Association 1997–2000, Executive Vice-President 2000–; Chair, Fisheries Policy and Legislation Working Group (The Moran Committee) 1997–. Vice-Chairman, Atlantic Salmon Trust 1988–95; President, Radnorshire Wildlife Trust 1994–. Chairman, National Rivers Authority Regional Fisheries Advisory Committee for the Welsh Region 1989–94. CMG 1970; KCMG 1981; Grand Cross Order of the Infante, Portugal 1978. *Publications: C.B. – A Life of Sir Henry Campbell-Bannerman*, 1973 (Whitbread Award for Biography); *Fairfax*, 1985. *Recreations:* Fly-fishing, bird-watching. *Clubs:* Flyfishers' (President 1987–88). The Lord Moran, KCMG, House of Lords, London, SW1A 0PW *Tel:* 020 7219 5353.

DodOnline
An Electronic Directory without rival ...

Peers' biographies and photographs available with daily updates *via* the internet

For a *free* trial, call Yasmin Mirza, Aby Farsoun or Michael Mand on 020 7630 7643

MORGAN (Life Baron), Kenneth Owen Morgan; cr. 2000. Born 16 May 1934. Son of late David James and Margaret Morgan, neé Owen; educated Aberdyfi Council School; University College School, Hampstead; Oriel College, Oxford (BA modern history 1955, MA, DPhil 1958, DLitt 1985). Married Jane Keeler 1973 (died 1992) (1 son 1 daughter). *Trades Union:* Member, AUT to 1995. *Career:* Lecturer, later Senior Lecturer in History, University College of Wales, Swansea 1958–66; Visiting Fellow, Columbia University 1962–63, Visiting Professor 1965; Fellow and Praelector, modern history and politics, The Queen's College, Oxford 1966–89; Visiting Professor, University of South Carolina 1972; O'Donnell lecturer, University of Wales 1981–82; Neale Lecturer, University College, London 1986; Principal, then Vice-Chancellor, University College of Wales, Aberystwyth and Professor University of Wales 1989–95, Senior Vice-Chancellor 1993–95, Emeritus Professor 1999; Lloyd George Memorial lecturer 1993; Visiting lecturer, University of Texas (Austin) 1994, 1999; Faculty lecturer, Oxford University 1995–; BBC (Wales) Lecturer 1995; Prothero Lecturer, Royal Historical Society 1996; Callaghan lecturer, University College of Wales, Swansea 1996; Visiting Professor, Witwatersrand University, South Africa 1997, 1998 and 2000; British Academy lecturer 1998; Benjamin Meaker Visiting Professor, Bristol University 2000; Merlyn-Rees lecturer, Glamorgan University 2002. Member Select Committee on the Constitution 2001–. Life member, British-American Parliamentary Group 2000. Chairman, Curatorium, Celtic Studies Centre, Tubingen University 1998–; President, Committee for Advanced Studies, Rouen University 2002–. Vice-President, Hon Secretary, Cymmrodorion, Llafur, International Eisteddfod of Llangollen. ACLS Fellowship, Columbia University 1962–63. Five honorary university fellowships; Two honorary doctorates. Trustee: St. Deiniol's, Harvarden 1989–96, History of Parliament Trust 2002–. Member: Board of Celtic Studies 1972–2003, Council, Royal Historical Society 1983–86, Council, National Library of Wales 1991–95; Academic assessor, Leverhulme Devolution project 1999–2002; Chairman, Fabian Society Commission 2002–03. FRHistS 1964; FBA 1983; FRSA 2003. *Publications:* Editor, *Welsh History Review* 1961–2003; *Wales in British Politics,* 1963; *David Lloyd George: Welsh radical as world statesman,* 1963; *Freedom or Sacrilege?,* 1967; *Keir Hardie,* 1967; *The Age of Lloyd George,* 1971; Editor *Lloyd George Family Letters,* 1973; *Lloyd George,* 1974; *Keir Hardie, Radical and Socialist,* 1975 (Arts Council prize); *Consensus and Disunity,* 1979; Co-author *Portrait of a Progressive,* 1980; *Rebirth of a Nation: Wales 1880–1980,* 1981 (Arts Council prize); *David Lloyd George,* 1981; *Labour in Power, 1945–1951,* 1984; Editor *The Oxford Illustrated History of Britain,* 1984; *Labour People,* 1987; Editor *The Oxford History of Britain,* 1988, new edn. 2001; *The Red Dragon and the Red Flag,* 1989; *The People's Peace,* 1990, new edn 2001; Co-editor *Twentieth Century British History,* 1994–99; *Modern Wales: politics, places and people,* 1995; *Britain and Europe,* 1995; Editor *The Young Oxford History of Britain and Ireland,* 1996; *Callaghan: a life,* 1997; Co-editor *Crime, Protest and Police in Modern British Society,* 1999; *The Twentieth Century,* 2000; *The Great Reform Act,* 2001; Author and editor of many other works, as well as articles and reviews; Frequent broadcaster on history, politics and Welsh affairs. *Special Interests:* Education, Europe, Foreign Affairs, Constitutional Reform, Civil Liberties. *Recreations:* Music, travel, sport (cricket), architectural history. *Sportsclubs:* Member Middlesex County Cricket Club. *Clubs:* Reform. Raised to the peerage as Baron Morgan, of Aberdyfi in the County of Gwynedd 2000. Professor the Lord Morgan, The Croft, 63 Millwood End, Long Hanborough, Witney, Oxfordshire, OX29 8BP *Tel:* 01993 881341 *Fax:* 01993 881341 *E-mail:* k.morgan@online.rednet.co.uk.

DodOnline
An Electronic Directory without rival . . .

Peers' biographies and photographs available with daily updates *via* the internet

For a *free* trial, call Yasmin Mirza, Aby Farsoun or Michael Mand on 020 7630 7643

MORGAN OF HUYTON, BARONESS — Labour

MORGAN OF HUYTON (Life Baroness), Sally Morgan; cr. 2001. Born 28 June 1959. Daughter of Albert Edward Morgan and Margaret Morgan; educated Belvedere School for Girls, Liverpool; Van Mildert College, Durham University (BA geography 1980); King's College, London (PGCE 1981); Institute of Education, London (MA education 1988). Married John Lyons 1984 (2 sons). *Trades Union:* Member GMB. Councillor, Wandsworth Borough Council 1986–90. *Career:* Secondary school geography teacher 1981–85; Labour Party: Student organiser 1985–88, Key seats organiser 1989–92, Director of campaigns and elections 1993–95, Head of party liaison to Tony Blair as Leader of the Opposition 1995–97; Political secretary to Tony Blair as Prime Minister 1997–2001; Director, government and political relations 2001–. *House of Lords:* Minister of State, Cabinet Office 2001. Government Spokesperson for Women's Issues, Cabinet Office 2001. *Special Interests:* Women's Issues, Education, Health. *Recreations:* Gardening, family, cooking, theatre. Raised to the peerage as Baroness Morgan of Huyton, of Huyton in the County of Merseyside 2001. The Baroness Morgan of Huyton, House of Lords, London, SW1A 0PW *Tel:* 020 7219 5500.

MORRIS OF ABERAVON, LORD — Labour

MORRIS OF ABERAVON (Life Baron), John Morris; cr. 2001. Born 5 November 1931. Son of late D W Morris and late M O A Lewis, formerly Morris; educated Ardwyn School, Aberystwyth; University College of Wales, Aberystwyth; Gonville and Caius College, Cambridge (LLM). Married Margaret Lewis 1959 (3 daughters). *Trades Union:* Member, GMB. Commissioned Welch Regiment and served Royal Welch Fusiliers. *Career:* Called to the Bar, Gray's Inn 1954; QC 1973; Recorder of Crown Court 1982–97; Bencher, Gray's Inn 1984. *House of Commons:* Labour member for Aberavon 1959–2001; Parliamentary Secretary to the Ministry of Power 1964–1966; Joint Parliamentary Secretary, Ministry of Transport 1966–1968; Minister of Defence for Equipment 1968–70; Secretary of State for Wales 1974–79; Opposition Attorney General 1979–81, 1983–97; Attorney General 1997–99. Principal Opposition Frontbench Spokesperson for Legal Affairs 1979–81, 1983–97. Chancellor, University of Glamorgan 2001–. Member Select Committee on European Union Sub-committee C (Common Foreign and Security Policy) 2002–. Member: UK Delegation Consultative Assemblies Council of Europe and WEU 1963–64, 1982–83, UK Delegates North Atlantic Assembly 1970. President, London Welsh Association 2001–; Member: Prince's Trust Council (Cymru) 2002–, Prime Minister's Advisory Committee on Business Appointments 2002–. Hon. LLD, University of Wales; Hon. Fellow: University College, Aberystwyth, Trinity College, Carmarthen, University College, Swansea; Gonville and Caius College, Cambridge. Chair, Joint Review of British Railways 1966–67; Chair, National Road Safety Advisory Council 1967–68; Committee Member, Implementation of Nolan Report 1997; Chancellor, University of Glamorgan 2001–. PC 1970; Knighted 1999; KG 2003. Freeman, Borough of Port Talbot 1992. *Sportsclubs:* Vice-President, Aberavon RFC. Raised to the peerage as Baron Morris of Aberavon, of Aberavon in the County of West Glamorgan and of Ceredigion in the County of Dyfed 2001. Rt Hon the Lord Morris of Aberavon, KG QC, House of Lords, London, SW1A 0PW *Tel:* 020 7219 3470.

MORRIS OF MANCHESTER, LORD — Labour

MORRIS OF MANCHESTER (Life Baron), Alfred Morris; cr. 1997. Born 23 March 1928. Son of late George Henry Morris and late Jessie, née Murphy; educated Manchester Elementary School; Matriculated by means of evening school tuition; Ruskin College, Oxford 1949–50; St Catherine's College, Oxford (BA modern history 1953, MA); Department of Education, Manchester University (DipEd 1954). Married Irene Jones 1950 (2 sons 2 daughters). *Trades Union:* Life Member, GMB. Served in the army, mainly in the Middle East 1946–48. *Career:* Manchester schoolteacher and university extension lecturer in social history 1954–56; Industrial relations officer, Electricity Supply Industry 1956–64. *House of Commons:* Contested Liverpool, Garston 1951 and Manchester Wythenshawe 1959; MP (Labour/Co-operative) for Manchester Wythenshawe 1964–97;

PPS: to Minister of Agriculture, Fisheries and Food 1964–1967, to Leader of the House of Commons 1968–70; Parliamentary Under-Secretary of State, Department of Health and Social Security with special responsibility for the Disabled 1974–79; UK and the world's first Minister for Disabled People; Promoted three Acts of Parliament as Private Member: Chronically Sick and Disabled Persons Act 1970, Food and Drugs (Milk) Act 1970, Police Act 1972; Chair: Managing Trustees, Parliamentary Contributory Pension Fund 1983–97, House of Commons Members' Fund 1983–97. Opposition Spokesperson for Social Services 1970–74; Principal Opposition Spokesperson for the Rights of Disabled People 1979–92. Treasurer, IPU British Group 1968–74; Joint-Treasurer, British-American Parliamentary Group 1983–97; Chair, ANZAC Group of MPs and Peers 1972–97, President 1997. Member, Executive Committee, CPA UK Branch 1999–; first British parliamentarian to be co-opted on to a US congressional committee of inquiry (the congressional committee of inquiry into Gulf War illness). British representative, UN advisory Council on the International Year of Disabled People; Chairman, World Planning Group appointed to draft *Charter for the 1980s* (1978–80) and *Charter for the New Millennium* for disabled people world-wide (1998–2000); Life Patron, Rehabilitation International 2001. National Chair, Labour League of Youth 1950–52; Chair, Parliamentary Cooperative Group 1970–71, 1983–85; President, Co-operative Congress 1995–96. Member, General Advisory Council, BBC 1968–74, 1979–97; Vice-President, Rehab UK 1995–; President: Society of Chiropodists and Pediatrists 1997; Haemophilia Society 1999–. First-ever recipient, Field Marshal Lord Harding Award for outstanding services to disabled people 1971; Louis Braille Memorial Award of the National Federation of the Blind for distinguished services to blind people 1971; Rotary International Paul Harris Fellow; Earl of Snowdon Award for expanding the rights of disabled people 1997; Automobile Association Award for work of immeasurable value to disabled road users 1998; People of the Year Awards 2000: Life-Time Achievement Award (jointly with Lord Ashley), Henry Kessler Award "for inspired leadership and outstanding achievement in the service of disabled people around the world" Rehabilitation International Word Congress, Brazil 2000. 3 honorary degrees. Chair, Managing Trustees, Parliamentary Contributory Pension Scheme and House of Commons Members' Fund 1983–97; Trustee, Hallé Orchestra 2001–; Trustee of many charities for disabled people. PC 1979; Queen's Service Order (QSO) awarded by Government of New Zealand 1989; Order of Australia (AO) 1991. Hon. Associate, British Veterinary Association; Hon. Fellow, Association of Building Engineers 2000. *Publications: Human Relations in Industry*, 1963; *The Growth of Parliamentary Scrutiny by Committee*, 1971; *VAT: A Tax on the Consumer*, 1972; Contributor to numerous books on the problems and needs of disabled people. *Special Interests:* The problems and needs of disabled people; Co-operative Movement, Regional Development, Airport Policy, Science and Technology. *Recreations:* Tennis, gardening, chess, snooker. Raised to the peeerage as Baron Morris of Manchester, of Manchester in the County of Greater Manchester 1997. Rt Hon the Lord Morris of Manchester, AO, QSO, House of Lords, London, SW1A 0PW *Tel:* 020 7219 6795.

MOSER, LORD   Crossbencher

MOSER (Life Baron), Claus Adolf Moser KCB CBE; cr 2001. Born 24 November 1922. Son of Dr Ernest Moser and Lotte Moser; educated Frensham Heights School, Surrey; London School of Economics (BSc(Econ) statistics 1943). Married Mary Oxlin 1949 (2 daughters 1 son). *Trades Union:* Association of University Teachers 1946–67. *Career:* London School of Economics 1946–67: eventually professor of social statistics; Head of Government Statistical Service 1967–78; Vice-chair N M Rothschild 1978–84; Warden Wadham College, Oxford 1984–93; British Museum 1988–: trustee 1988–2001, Chair BM Development Trust 1994–; Chair Basic Skills Agency 1997–2002. Open University of Israel. Chair: Royal Opera House, Oxford Playhouse, Music at Oxford, London Symphony Orchestra Education Committee, "The Economist", Equity and Law and other companies. Sixteen honorary doctorates; Three honorary university fellowships. Adviser, Paul Hamlyn Trust; Trustee, Rayne Foundation. CBE 1965, FBA 1969, KCB 1973. *Publications:* Numerous articles in statistics professional journals; *The Measurement of Levels of Living: with special reference to Jamaica* (HMSO, London) 1957; *Survey Methods in Social Investigations* (William Heineman Ltd) 1958; Co-author *A Survey of Social Conditions in England and Wales: as illustrated by statistics* (Clarendon Press) 1958; *British Towns: a statistical study of their social and economic conditions* (Oliver and Boyd, Edinburgh and London) 1961; Co-author *The Impact of Robbins* (Penguin, London) 1969. *Special Interests:* Arts, Education, Social Policy. *Recreations:* Music. *Clubs:* Garrick. Raised to the peerage as Baron Moser, of Regents Park in the London Borough of Camden 2001. The Lord Moser, KCB, CBE, The British Museum Development Trust, 91 Great Russell Street, London NW1 7EE *Tel:* 020 7636 5765 *Fax:* 020 7636 5779.

MOWBRAY AND STOURTON, LORD   Conservative

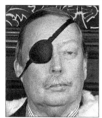

MOWBRAY (26th Baron, E), Charles Edward Stourton; cr. 1283; 27th Baron SEGRAVE (E) 1283; 23rd Baron STOURTON (E) 1448. Born 11 March 1923. Son of 25th Baron, MC, Premier Baron of England; educated Ampleforth College; Christ Church, Oxford. Married Hon. Jane de Yarburgh-Bateson 1952 (died 1998) (2 sons); married Joan, Lady Holland, née Street 1999. Served as Lieutenant, 2nd Armoured Battalion Grenadier Guards 1943–45; Wounded in France 1944; Invalided. Councillor, Niddesdale RDC 1954–61. *Career:* Director, Securicor (Scotland) Ltd 1964–70; Chairman, Government Picture Buying Committee 1972–74; Director: EIRC Holdings Ltd (Jersey), Ghadeco (UK) Ltd 1986–; Chairman, Thames Estuary Airport Company Ltd 1993–;
Member, Parliamentary Delegation to Bicentennial Celebrations in Washington DC. *House of Lords:* First entered House of Lords 1965; Elected hereditary peer 1999–. Opposition Whip 1967–70, 1974–78; Deputy Chief Opposition Whip 1978–79; Government Whip 1970–74, 1979–80. Spokesperson for Department of the Environment 1970–74, Departments of Environment and Transport and Arts 1979–80. Member, Select Committee for Privileges 1992–99. Patron, Normandy Veterans Association Tayside and Mearns Branch. Recipient, 1976 Bicentennial Year Award of Baronial Order of Magna Carta (USA). Trustee, College of Arms Trust 1975–. CBE 1982; Knight of Sovereign and Military Order of Malta; Vice-president British Association. *Clubs:* Turf, White's, Pratt's, Roxburghe, Pilgrims. The Lord Mowbray and Stourton, CBE, 23 Warwick Square, London, SW1V 2AB; Marcus, By Forfar, Angus, DD8 3QH *Tel:* 01307 850219.

MOYNIHAN, LORD   Conservative

MOYNIHAN (4th Baron, UK), Colin Berkeley Moynihan; cr. 1929; 4th Bt of Carr Manor (UK) 1922. Born 13 September 1955. Son of 2nd Baron, OBE, TD; educated Monmouth School (Music Scholar); University College, Oxford (BA philosophy, politics and economics 1977, MA 1982) (President of the Union). Married Gaynor-Louise Metcalf 1992 (2 sons 1 daughter). Director, Canterbury Festival 1999–2001. *Career:* Personal assistant to chairman, Tate and Lyle Ltd 1978–80; Manager, Tate and Lyle Agribusiness 1980–82; Chief Executive, Ridgways Tea and Coffee Merchants 1982–83, Chair 1983–87; Chair, CMA Consultants 1993–; Managing Director, Independent Power Corporation plc 1996–2001; Chair and Chief Executive, Consort Resources Group of Companies
2000–; Director: Rowan Group of Companies, Clipper Windpower UK Ltd 2001–; Council Member Institute of Petroleum 2001–03. *House of Commons:* MP (Conservative) for Lewisham East 1983–92; Chair, Bow Group Trade and Industry Standing Committee 1983–87; PPS: to Minister of Health 1985, to Paymaster-General 1985–87; Parliamentary Under-Secretary of State: at Department of Environment (Minister for Sport) 1987–90, at Department of Energy 1990–92. *House of Lords:* First entered House of Lords 1997; Elected hereditary peer 1999–; Shadow Minister for Sport 2003–. Senior Opposition Spokesperson on Foreign and Commonwealth Affairs 1997–2000. Member, The Bow Group 1978–. Governor, Sports Aid Foundation (London and South East) 1980–82. Oxford Double Blue, Rowing and Boxing 1976 and 1977; World Gold Medal for Lightweight Rowing, International Rowing Federation 1978; Olympic Silver Medal for Rowing 1980; World Silver Medal for Rowing 1981. J A Fiddian Research Scholarship, Brasenose College, Oxford 1997. Freeman, City of London 1978. Liveryman, Worshipful Company of Haberdashers 1981; Court of Assistants 2003–. *Special Interests:* Foreign Affairs, Trade and Industry, Sport, Inner Cities, Refugees, Overseas Aid and Development. *Recreations:* Reading, sport, music. *Sportsclubs:* London Rowing, Leander. *Clubs:* Brooks's, Vincent's (Oxford). The Lord Moynihan, House of Lords, London, SW1A 0PW *Tel:* 020 7340 0100 *Fax:* 020 7340 0179 *E-mail:* cbm@dial.pipex.com.

DodOnline
An Electronic Directory without rival . . .

Peers' biographies and photographs available with daily updates *via* the internet

For a *free* trial, call Yasmin Mirza, Aby Farsoun or Michael Mand on 020 7630 7643

MURRAY OF EPPING FOREST, LORD   Labour

MURRAY OF EPPING FOREST (Life Baron), Lionel Murray; cr. 1985. Born 2 August 1922; educated State schools; Queen Mary College, London University; New College, Oxford (BA philosophy, politics and economics 1947). Married Heather Woolf 1945 (2 sons 2 daughters). *Trades Union:* Member TGWU. Wartime service with King's Shropshire Light Infantry. *Career:* TUC 1947–84, General Secretary 1973–84. Vice-President ICFTU 1973–84. President, Friends of Epping Forest; Vice-President: Wesley's Chapel, National Youth Theatre, National Children's Home; Patron: St Clare's Hospice, Shropshire Society. Hon. Fellow, New College, Oxford 1975; six honorary doctorates/fellowships. President: Friends of Ironbridge Museum Trust, Friends of Epping Forest; Vice-Patron, Winged Fellowship Trust. OBE 1966; PC 1976. *Special Interests:* Children, Homeless, Disability. *Recreations:* Theatre, music, looking at Epping Forest. Raised to the peerage as Baron Murray of Epping Forest, of Telford in the County of Shropshire 1985. Rt Hon the Lord Murray of Epping Forest, OBE, 29 The Crescent, Loughton, Essex, IG10 4PY *Tel:* Home: 020 8508 4425.

MURTON OF LINDISFARNE, LORD   Conservative

MURTON OF LINDISFARNE (Life Baron), (Henry) Oscar Murton; cr. 1979. Born 8 May 1914. Son of late H E C Murton and Mrs E M Murton, née Renton; educated Uppingham School. Married Constance Frances Connell 1939 (died 1977) (1 son and 1 daughter deceased 1986); married Pauline Teresa Keenan 1979. Commissioned TA 1934 in Royal Northumberland Fusiliers; Army Staff Course, Camberley 1938–39; General Staff 1939–46; Lieutenant-Colonel. Councillor, Poole Borough Council 1961–64; Member, Herrison (Dorchester) Hospital Management Committee until 1974; JP, Borough of Poole 1963, latterly Supplemental List Inner London. *Career:* Managing Director, Private Limited Company with Department Stores NE England 1949–57. *House of Commons:* MP (Conservative) for Poole 1964–79; Introduced Highways (Amendment) Act 1965, PPS to Minister of Local Government and Development 1970–71; Deputy Chairman, Ways and Means 1973–76; Chairman, Ways and Means and the Deputy Speaker House of Commons 1976–79. Assistant Government Whip 1971; Government Whip (Lord Commissioner to the Treasury) 1972–73. *House of Lords:* Deputy Chair of Committees 1981–; Deputy Speaker 1983–; Introduced Access to Neighbouring Land Act 1992. Member, Joint Select Committee of Lords and Commons on Private Bill Procedure 1987–88. President, Poole Conservative Association 1983–95. Chancellor, Primrose League 1983–88. C-In-C's Commendations 1942, 1944; TD 1947 (Clasp 1951). OBE (Mil) 1946; PC 1976. Freeman, City of London. Freeman, Wax Chandlers Company; Past-Master, Clockmakers Company. *Special Interests:* Defence. *Recreations:* Sailing, painting. Raised to the peerage as Baron Murton of Lindisfarne, of Hexham in the County of Northumberland 1979. Rt Hon the Lord Murton of Lindisfarne, OBE, TD, 49 Carlisle Mansions, Carlisle Place, London, SW1P 1HY *Tel:* 020 7834 8226.

MUSTILL, LORD   Crossbencher

MUSTILL (Life Baron), Michael John Mustill; cr. 1992. Born 10 May 1931. Son of late Clement William and Marion Mustill; educated Oundle School; St John's College, Cambridge (LLD 1992). Married Beryl Davies 1960 (divorced 1983); married Mrs Caroline Phillips 1991 (2 sons 1 step-daughter). Served Royal Artillery 1949–51. *Career:* Called to the Bar, Gray's Inn 1955; Bencher 1976; QC 1968; Deputy Chairman, Hampshire Quarter Sessions 1971; Chairman, Civil Service Appeal Tribunal 1971–78; Recorder of the Crown Court 1972–78; Judge of the High Court, Queen's Bench Division 1978–85; Presiding Judge, NE Circuit 1981–84; Chairman: Judicial Studies Board 1985–89, Departmental Committee on Law of Arbitration 1985–90; Lord Justice of Appeal 1985–92; Lord of Appeal in Ordinary 1992–97. Member, House of Lords Select Committee on Medical Ethics 1993–. Kt 1978; PC 1985. FBA. *Publications:* Several legal works and articles in legal journals. Raised to the peerage as Baron Mustill, of Pateley Bridge in the County of North Yorkshire 1992. Rt Hon the Lord Mustill, Essex Court Chambers, 24 Lincoln's Inn Fields, London, WC2A 3EG.

N

NASEBY, LORD Conservative

NASEBY (Life Baron), Michael Wolfgang Laurence Morris; cr. 1997. Born 25 November 1936. Son of late Cyril Laurence Morris, FRIBA and Margaret Morris; educated Bedford School; St Catharine's College, Cambridge (BA economics 1960, MA). Married Ann Appleby 1960 (2 sons 1 daughter). National service pilot (RAF and NATO) 1955–57. London Borough of Islington: Councillor 1968–74, Leader 1969–71, Alderman 1971–74. *Career:* Marketing manager, Reckitt and Colman Group 1960–64; Director: Service Advertising 1964–71, Benton & Bowles Ltd 1971–81. *House of Commons:* Contested Islington North 1966 general election; MP (Conservative) for Northampton South 1974–97; PPS to Minister of State, Northern Ireland 1979–81; Chair Ways and Means and Deputy Speaker 1992–97. Member Standing Orders (Private Bills) Committee 2003–. Member, Council of Europe and Western European Union 1983–91. Chair of Governors, Bedford School 1989–2003; Chair, Progressive Supranuclear Palsy Charity 1994–2001. Chair, Northamptonshire Victoria County History Trust. PC 1994. *Publications: Helping The Exporter*, 1967; Co-author *Marketing Below The Line*, 1970; *The Disaster of Direct Labour*, 1978. *Special Interests:* Energy, Health Service, Exports, Marketing, Parliamentary Procedure, National Lottery, South East Asia, particularly Sri Lanka. *Recreations:* Golf, tennis, shooting, forestry, budgerigars. *Sportsclubs:* John O'Gaunt Golf, Port Stanley Golf, All England Lawn Tennis, Royal St George's Golf, Lords Taverners, Northamptonshire County Cricket (Committee). *Clubs:* Carlton, Northampton Town and Country, MCC. Raised to the peerage as Baron Naseby, of Sandy in the County of Bedfordshire 1997. Rt Hon the Lord Naseby, Caesar's Camp, Sandy, Bedfordshire, SG19 2AD *Tel:* 01767 680388 *Fax:* 01767 692099.

NEILL OF BLADEN, LORD Crossbencher

NEILL OF BLADEN (Life Baron), Francis Patrick Neill; cr. 1997. Born 8 August 1926. Son of late Sir Thomas Neill, JP, and late Lady (Annie) Neill; educated Highgate School; Magdalen College, Oxford (BA law 1950, MA); All Souls College, Oxford (BCL 1951). Married Caroline Susan Debenham 1954 (4 sons 2 daughters). Served Rifle Brigade 1944–47 (Captain); GSO III (Training) British Troops, Egypt 1947. *Career:* Fellow, All Souls, Oxford 1950–77, Sub-Warden 1972–74, Warden 1977–95, Hon Fellow 1995–; Called to the Bar, Gray's Inn 1951, QC 1966, Bencher 1971, Vice-Treasurer 1989, Treasurer 1990; Lecturer in Air Law, LSE 1955–58; Member, Bar Council 1967–71, Vice-Chairman 1973–74, Chairman 1974–75; Chairman, Senate of the Inns of Court and the Bar 1974–75; Recorder of the Crown Court 1975–78; Judge of the Courts of Appeal of Jersey and Guernsey 1977–94; Chairman: Press Council 1978–83, Council for the Securities Industry 1978–85; Chairman, Justice – All Souls Committee for Review of Administrative Law 1978–87; Hon. Professor of Legal Ethics, Birmingham University 1983–84; Vice-Chancellor, Oxford University 1985–89; Chairman, DTI Committee of Inquiry into Regulatory Arrangements at Lloyd's 1986–87; Vice-Chairman, Committee of Vice-Chancellors and Principals of the Universities of the United Kingdom 1987–90; Independent National Director, Times Newspaper Holdings 1988–97; Chairman: Feltrim Loss Review Committee at Lloyd's 1991–92, Committee on Standards in Public Life 1997–2001; Visitor, Buckingham University 1997–, Member: Select Committee on European Union 2003–, European Union Sub-committee E (Law and Institutions) 2003–. Hon. Fellow, Magdalen College, Oxford 1988; Three honorary law doctorates (Hull, Oxford, Buckingham). Kt 1983. *Publications: Administrative Justice: some necessary reforms*, (OUP 1988). *Recreations:* Music, forestry. *Clubs:* Athenaeum, Garrick, Beefsteak. Raised to the peerage as Baron Neill of Bladen, of Briantspuddle in the County of Dorset 1997. The Lord Neill of Bladen, QC, Serle Court, 6 New Square, Lincoln's Inn, London, WC2A 3QS *E-mail:* pneill@serlecourt.co.uk.

NEWBY, LORD   Liberal Democrat

NEWBY (Life Baron), Richard Mark Newby; cr 1997. Born 14 February 1953. Son of Frank and Kathleen Newby; educated Rothwell Grammar School; St Catherine's College, Oxford (BA philosophy, politics and economics 1974, MA). Married Ailsa Ballantyne Thomson 1978 (2 sons). *Career:* HM Customs and Excise: Administration trainee 1974; Private secretary to Permanent Secretary 1977–79; Principal, Planning Unit 1979–81; Secretary, SDP Parliamentary Committee 1981; Joined SDP headquarters staff 1981; National Secretary, SDP 1983–88, Executive 1988–90; Director, Corporate Affairs, Rosehaugh plc 1991; Director, Matrix Communications Consultancy Ltd 1992–99; Chair: Reform Publications Ltd 1993–, Director, Centre for Reform; Director, Flagship Group Ltd 1999–2001; Chief of Staff to Charles Kennedy, MP 1999–; Chairman, Live Consulting 2001–. Liberal Democrat Spokesperson for: Trade and Industry 1998–2000, The Treasury 1998–. Member Select Committees on Monetary Policy of the Bank of England/Economic Affairs 1998–. Secretary, Yorkshire and the Humber Peers Group. Deputy Chair, Liberal Democrat General Election Team 1995–97; Liberal Democrat Campaigns and Communications Committee. Trustee: Allachy Trust, Coltstaple Trust. Member Ecclesiastical Committee 2002–. OBE 1990. *Special Interests:* Europe, Regional Development. *Recreations:* Football, cricket, tennis. *Sportsclubs:* MCC. *Clubs:* Reform, MCC. Raised to the peerage as Baron Newby, of Rothwell in the County of West Yorkshire 1997. The Lord Newby, OBE, 179 Fentiman Road, London, SW8 1JY *Tel:* 07802 887606 *Fax:* 020 7735 3191; House of Lords, London, SW1A 0PW *Tel:* 020 7219 8501 *E-mail:* newbyr@parliament.uk.

NEWCASTLE, LORD BISHOP OF   Non-affiliated

NEWCASTLE (Bishop of), (John) Martin Wharton. Born 6 August 1944. Son of John and Marjorie Wharton; educated Ulverston Grammar School; Van Mildert College, Durham (BA economics, politics, sociology 1969); Linacre College, Oxford (BA theology 1971, MA); Ripon Hall, Oxford. Married Marlene Olive Duckett 1970 (1 daughter 2 sons). *Career:* Curate: St Peter Spring Hill, Birmingham 1972–75, St John the Baptist, Croydon 1975–77; Director of Pastoral Studies, Ripon College, Cuddesdon, Oxford 1977–83; Director of Ministry and Training, Diocese of Bradford and Residentiary Canon of Bradford Cathedral 1983–92; Bishop of Kingston upon Thames 1992–97; Bishop of Newcastle 1997–; Took his seat in the House of Lords 2002–. Norcare; Abbeyfield, Newcastle upon Tyne; Shaw; SPCK. St Hilda's Trust; Northumbria Historic Churches Trust; The Hild Bede Trust; Shepherds Law Hermitage Trust; Newcastle Diocesan Society. *Publications:* Co-author *Knowing Me, Knowing You*, SPCK 1993. *Recreations:* Cricket, football, rugby. *Sportsclubs:* Lancashire County Cricket Club. Rt Rev the Lord Bishop of Newcastle, Bishop's House, 29 Moor Road South, Newcastle upon Tyne, NE3 1PA *Tel:* 0191–285 2220 *Fax:* 0191–284 6933 *E-mail:* bishop@newcastle.anglican.org.

NEWTON OF BRAINTREE, LORD   · Conservative

NEWTON OF BRAINTREE (Life Baron), Antony Harold Newton; cr. 1997. Born 29 August 1937. Son of Harold Newton; educated Friend's School, Saffron Walden; Trinity College, Oxford (BA philosophy, politics and economics). Married Janet Huxley 1962 (2 daughters) (divorced 1986); married Patricia Gilthorpe 1986 (1 stepson 2 stepdaughters). Chair, Council on Tribunals. *Career:* President, Oxford Union Society 1959; Debating tour in US 1960; Conservative Research Department 1961–74; Head, economic section 1965–70; Assistant director 1970–74. *House of Commons:* Contested Sheffield Brightside 1970 general election; MP (Conservative) for Braintree 1974–97; Parliamentary Under-Secretary of State, Department of Health and Social Security 1982–84; Minister for the Disabled 1983; Minister of State for Social Security and the Disabled 1983–86; Minister for Health 1986–88; Chancellor of the Duchy of Lancaster (Minister of Trade and Industry) 1988–89; Secretary of State for Social Security 1989–92; Lord President of the Council and Leader of the House of Commons 1992–97. Assistant Government Whip 1979–81; Government Whip

1981–82. President, Oxford University Conservative Association 1958; Secretary, Bow Group 1962–64. Member, Review Committee of Privy Counsellors of the Anti-terrorism, Crime and Security Act 2002–. OBE 1972; PC 1988. *Special Interests:* Tax, Social Security, Pensions, Disability, Health, Social Services. Raised to the peerage as Baron Newton of Braintree, of Coggeshall in the County of Essex 1997. Rt Hon the Lord Newton of Braintree, OBE, House of Lords, London, SW1A 0PW *Tel:* 020 7219 5878.

NICHOLLS OF BIRKENHEAD, LORD   Crossbencher

NICHOLLS OF BIRKENHEAD (Life Baron), Donald James Nicholls; cr. 1994. Born 25 January 1933. Son of late William Greenhow and Eleanor Jane Nicholls; educated Birkenhead School; Liverpool University (LLB 1956); Trinity Hall, Cambridge (BA Law Tripos, LLB 1958). Married Jennifer Mary Thomas 1960 (2 sons 1 daughter). *Career:* Called to the Bar, Middle Temple 1958; Bencher 1981, Treasurer 1997; In practice, Chancery Bar 1958–83; QC 1974; Judge of the High Court of Justice, Chancery Division 1983–86; Lord Justice of Appeal 1986–91; Vice-Chancellor of the Supreme Court 1991–94; Lord of Appeal in Ordinary 1994–; Member, Senate of Inns of Court and the Bar 1974–76; Chair, Lord Chancellor's Advisory Committee on Legal Education and Conduct 1996–97; Non-permanent member of the Court of Final Appeal of Hong Kong 1998–. Chairman, Select Committee on Parliamentary Privilege (Joint Committee) 1997–99. President, Birkenhead School 1986–; Patron, Cayman Islands Law School 1994–. Hon. Fellow, Trinity Hall, Cambridge 1986; Hon. LLD, Liverpool University 1987. Kt 1983; PC 1986. *Recreations:* Walking, history, music. *Clubs:* Athenaeum (Trustee). Raised to the peerage as Baron Nicholls of Birkenhead, of Stoke D'Abernon in the County of Surrey 1994. Rt Hon the Lord Nicholls of Birkenhead, House of Lords, London, SW1A 0PW *Tel:* 020 7219 3202.

NICHOLSON OF WINTERBOURNE, BARONESS   Liberal Democrat

NICHOLSON OF WINTERBOURNE (Life Baroness), Emma Harriet Nicholson; cr. 1997. Born 16 October 1941. Daughter of late Sir Godfrey Nicholson, 1st and last Bt and late Lady Katharine Lindsay, daughter of 27th Earl of Crawford, KT, PC; educated Portsdown Lodge School, Bexhill; St Mary's School, Wantage; The Royal Academy of Music (LRAM 1962, ARCM). Married Sir Michael Harris Caine 1987 (died 1999) (2 step-children and 1 ward/foster son). *Career:* ICL 1961–64; Computer Consultant, John Tyzack and Partners 1964–69; Computer Management Consultant, McLintock Mann and Whinney Murray 1969–74; Save the Children Fund 1974–85, Director of Fundraising 1977–85; Consultant inter alia Dr Barnardos, Westminster Children's Hospital, The Duke of Edinburgh's Award Scheme, Foster Parents Plan 1985–87; Visiting Fellow, St Antony's College, Oxford 1995–96, Senior Associate Member 1997–98, 1998–99; MEP for the South East Region 1999–: Whip, Liberal Democrat Party 1999–01; Vice Chair, Foreign Affairs, Human Rights, Common Security and Defence Policy Committee 1999–; Rapporteur for Romania for Iraq. *House of Commons:* Contested Blyth 1979: MP for Devon West and Torridge 1987–97; Resigned from the Conservative Party December 1995 and joined the Liberal Democrats; PPS to Michael Jack, MP, as Minister of State: at Home Office 1992–93, at Ministry of Agriculture, Fisheries and Food 1993–95, at The Treasury 1995. Liberal Democrat Spokesperson for Overseas Development and Human Rights 1996–97. Former Treasurer, Positive European Group (Conservative). Member, Liberal Democrat Foreign Affairs Team 1997–; Front Bench Spokesperson for Data Protection 1998–. Member, Select Committee for Employment 1990–92, Treasurer Positive European Group 1990–95. Vice-Chair Conservative Party 1983–87; Member Liberal Democrat: Federal Executive Committee –2003, Peel Group 2001–. Many and varied past honorary positions with UK registered charities helping the disadvantaged; Chair AMAR International Charitable Foundation. Hon. Doctorate, University of North London. Trustee, chair, fellow, member of a number of charitable trusts, particularly ones concerned with refugees, children, the elderly and the disabled. LRAM; ARCM; FRSA; Hon D. Freeman, Worshipful Company of Information Technologists. *Publications: Why Does the West Forget?*, 1993; *Secret Society – Inside and Outside the Conservative Party*, 1996; as well as various articles and pamphlets. *Clubs:* Reform. Raised to the peerage as Baroness Nicholson of Winterbourne, of Winterbourne in the Royal County of Berkshire 1997. The Baroness Nicholson of Winterbourne, MEP, House of Lords, London, SW1A 0PW; European Parliament, Rue Wiertz, 104 Brussels, Belgium *E-mail:* enicholson@europarl.eu.int.

NICKSON, LORD   Crossbencher

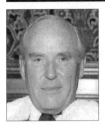

NICKSON (Life Baron), David Wigley Nickson; cr. 1994. Born 27 November 1929. Son of late Geoffrey Wigley Nickson and of late Janet Mary Dobie; educated Eton College; RMA, Sandhurst. Married Helen Louise Cockcraft 1952 (3 daughters). Commissioned Coldstream Guards 1949–54. DL, Stirling and Falkirk 1982–97, Vice-Lieutenant 1997–. *Career:* Joined William Collins Sons & Co. Ltd publishers 1954, Director 1961–85, Joint Managing Director 1967, Vice-Chairman 1976–83, Group Managing Director 1979–82; Director, Scottish United Investors plc 1970–83; Director, General Accident Fire and Life Assurance Corporation plc 1971–98, Deputy Chairman 1993–98; Member, Scottish Committee, Design Council 1978–81; Chairman, CBI in Scotland 1979–81; Member, Scottish Economic Council 1980–95; Director, Clydesdale Bank plc 1981–89, 1990–98, Deputy Chairman 1990–91, Chairman 1991–98; Director, Scottish & Newcastle Breweries plc 1981–95, Deputy Chairman 1982–83, Chairman 1983–89; Chairman, Pan Books Ltd 1982; Director, Radio Clyde plc 1982–85; Chairman, Countryside Commission for Scotland 1983–85; Director, Edinburgh Investment Trust plc 1983–94; Member, NEDC 1985–88; President, CBI 1986–88; Director, Hambro's plc 1989–98; Chairman: Senior Salaries Review Body 1989–95, Scottish Development Agency 1989–92; Director, National Australia Bank Ltd 1991–96; Chairman, Scottish Enterprise 1992–94. Chancellor, Glasgow Caledonian University 1993–2002. President, Association of Scottish District Salmon Fishery Boards 1989–92, President 1996–; Chair, Scottish Advisory Committee, Imperial Cancer Research Fund 1994–2002, Life Governor. DUniversity: Stirling University 1986, Napier University 1991, Paisley University 1992; Hon. Dr., Glasgow Caledonian University 1993. Atlantic Salmon Trust: Member, Council of Management 1982–, Chairman 1989–95, Vice-President 1995–; Trustee: Prince's Youth Business Trust 1987–90, Game Conservancy 1988–91, Princess Royal's Trust for Carers 1990–94. Ensign, Queen's Body Guard for Scotland, The Royal Company of Archers; Chairman, Secretary of State for Scotland's Scottish Salmon Strategy Task Force 1996–; Independent Adviser, Secretary of State for Scotland's Appointments Committee 1996–99. CBE 1981; KBE 1987. CIMgt; FRSE 1987. Freeman, City of London. Hon. Freeman, Fishmongers' Company 1999–. *Recreations:* Fishing, shooting, birdwatching. *Clubs:* Boodle's, MCC, Flyfishers'. Raised to the peerage as Baron Nickson, of Renagour in the District of Stirling 1994. The Lord Nickson, KBE, House of Lords, London, SW1A 0PW *Tel:* 020 7219 5353 *Tel:* 01786 841614 *Fax:* 01786 841062.

NICOL, BARONESS   Labour

NICOL (Life Baroness), (Olive Mary) Wendy Nicol; cr. 1982. Born 21 March 1923. Daughter of late James and Harriet Rowe-Hunter; educated Cahir School, Ireland. Married Alexander Douglas Ian Nicol 1947 (2 sons 1 daughter). JP, Cambridge Bench 1972–86; Cambridge City Council 1972–82, Deputy Mayor 1974, Chairman, Environment Committee 1978–82. *Career:* Inland Revenue 1942–44; Admiralty 1944–48; United Charities 1967–86; Supplementary Benefits Tribunal 1976–78; Co-operative Board 1976–85, President 1981–85 Careers Service Consultative Panel 1978–81. *House of Lords:* Deputy Speaker 1995–2002, Deputy Chair of Committees 1995–2002. Opposition Whip 1983–87; Opposition Deputy Chief Whip 1987–89. Member, Opposition Frontbench Environment Team with responsibility for Green issues 1983–92; Opposition Spokesperson for Energy 1988–89. Member, Select Committees on: European Communities 1986–91, Science and Technology 1990–93, Environment and Social Affairs Sub-Committee of EC Committee 1993–95, Sustainable Development 1994–95; Member, Ecclesiastical Committee 1990–96; Member, Select Committees on: House of Lords' Offices, Offices Library and Computers Sub-Committee –2000, Science and Technology Sub-Committee on Management of Nuclear Waste 1998–99, Animals in Scientific Procedures 2001–02, Privileges Lords' Interests Sub-committee 2003–. Member, Labour Party Departmental Committees for: Agriculture 1997–, Environment 1997–. Member, Co-operative Party. Various School Governing Bodies and other public service areas, including Granta Housing Association; Council Member, RSPB 1989–94; Vice-President: Marine Conservation Society, Vice-President, Youth Hostels Association, RSPB, Council for National Parks. Member, Lord Chancellor's Advisory Committee 1982–88; Vice-President: Council for National Parks 1995–, Association of Municipal Authorities, Association of District Councils; Board Member, Parliamentary Office of Science and Technology

(POST) 1998–2000. FRGS 1990. *Special Interests:* Commerce, Conservation, Environment, Energy, Forestry. *Recreations:* Reading, walking, gardening. Raised to the peerage as Baroness Nicol, of Newnham in the County of Cambridge 1982. The Baroness Nicol, 39 Granchester Road, Newnham, Cambridge, CB3 9ED *Tel:* 01223 323733; House of Lords, London, SW1A 0PW *Tel:* 020 7219 6705.

NOAKES, BARONESS — Conservative

NOAKES (Life Baroness), Sheila Valerie Noakes; cr. 2000. Born 23 June 1949. Daughter of Albert and Iris Masters; educated Eltham Hill Grammar School; Bristol University (LLB 1970). Married (Colin) Barry Noakes 1985. Member: Inland Revenue Management Board 1992–99, NHS Policy Board 1992–95, Chancellor of the Exchequer's Private Finance Panel 1993–97; Commissioner, Public Works Loan Board 1995–2001; Member, Public Services Productivity Panel 1998–2000. *Career:* Joined Peat Marwick Mitchell & Co 1970, Partner KPMG (formerly Peat Marwick Mitchell & Co, then KPMG Peat Marwick) 1983–2000; seconded to HM Treasury 1979–81; seconded to Department of Health, as Director of Finance, NHS Management Executive 1988–91; a Director, Bank of England 1994–2001, senior non-executive director 1998–2001; Non-executive director: Carpetright plc 2001–, Solutions in Staffing and Software PLC 2001–, Hanson plc 2001–; English National Opera 2001–; John Laing plc 2002–. Opposition Spokesperson for: Health 2001–, Work and Pensions 2001–. Governor: London Business School 1998–2001, Eastbourne College 2000–; Member: Board of Companions, Institute of Management 1996–2002, Council, Institute of Chartered Accountants of England and Wales 1987–2002, President 1999–2000, Board, Social Market Foundation 2002–. Three honorary doctorates. Trustee Reuters Founder Share Company 1998–. DBE 1996. FCA; CIMgt. Freeman, City of London. Worshipful Company of Chartered Accountants. *Special Interests:* Health, Public finance, Trade and Industry, Public service management, Horse-racing, Rural issues. *Recreations:* Ski-ing, horse racing, opera, early classical music. *Clubs:* Farmers'. Raised to the peerage as Baroness Noakes, of Goudhurst in the County of Kent 2000. The Baroness Noakes, DBE, House of Lords, London, SW1A 0PW *Tel:* 020 7219 5230 *Fax:* 020 7219 4215 *E-mail:* noakess@parliament.uk.

NOLAN, LORD — Crossbencher

NOLAN (Life Baron), Michael Patrick Nolan; cr. 1994. Born 10 September 1928. Son of James Thomas Nolan and Jane, née Walsh; educated Ampleforth College; Wadham College, Oxford (BA jurisprudence 1952). Married Margaret Noyes 1953 (1 son 4 daughters). Served Royal Artillery 1947–49; TA 1949–55. *Career:* Called to the Bar, Middle Temple 1953; Bencher 1975; QC 1968; Member, Bar Council 1973–74; Member, Sandilands Committee on Inflation Accounting 1973–75; Called to the Bar, Northern Ireland 1974; QC (Northern Ireland) 1974; Member, Senate of Inns of Court and Bar 1974–81, Treasurer 1977–79; Recorder of the Crown Court 1975–82; Judge, High Court of Justice, Queen's Bench Division 1982–91; Presiding Judge, Western Circuit 1985–88; Lord Justice of Appeal 1991–94; Lord of Appeal in Ordinary 1994–98; Chair, Committee on Standards in Public Life 1994–97; Commissioner, Interception of Communications Act 1985, 1994–2000; Chair Independent Committee on Review of Child Protection in the Catholic Church in England and Wales 2000–01. Chancellor, Essex University 1997–2002. Chair Select Committee on Privileges Lords' Interests Sub-committee 2001–02. Member, Governing Body, Convent of the Sacred Heart, Woldingham 1973–83; Chairman, Board of Institute of Advanced Legal Studies 1994–2000. Hon. Fellow, Wadham College, Oxford 1992; six honorary doctorates. Kt 1982; PC 1991. *Recreations:* Family, friends, fishing. *Clubs:* Army and Navy, MCC. Raised to the peerage as Baron Nolan, of Brasted in the County of Kent 1994. Rt Hon the Lord Nolan, House of Lords, London, SW1A 0PW *Tel:* 020 7219 1639.

DodOnline
An Electronic Directory without rival …

Peers' biographies and photographs available with daily updates *via* the internet

For a *free* trial, call Yasmin Mirza, Aby Farsoun or Michael Mand on 020 7630 7643

NORFOLK, DUKE OF   Non-affiliated

NORFOLK (18th Duke of, E), Edward William Fitzalan-Howard; cr. 1483; 29th Earl of Arundel (E) 1139/1289; Earl of Surrey (E) 1483; 16th Earl of Norfolk (E) 1644; 13th Baron Beaumont (E) 1309; 20th Baron Maltravers (E) 1330; 16th Baron FitzAlan, Clun, and Oswaldestre (E) 1627; 5th Baron Howard of Glossop (UK) 1869; DL. Born 2 December 1956. Son of Major-General 17th Duke, KG, GCVO, CB, MC, DL; educated Ampleforth College; Lincoln College, Oxford (BA philosophy, politics and economics 1978, MA). Married Georgina Susan Temple Gore 1987 (3 sons 2 daughters). DL, West Sussex, 2002–. *Career:* Chairman: Sigas Ltd 1979–88, Parkwood Group Ltd 1989–2002. *House of Lords:* Entered House of Lords 2002. Premier Duke and Earl of England; Earl Marshal and Hereditary Marshal and Chief Butler of England. *Recreations:* Ski-ing, motor-racing, shooting. *Clubs:* British Racing Drivers Club (Silverstone). The Duke of Norfolk, DL, Arundel Castle, Arundel, West Sussex, BN18 9AB *Tel:* 01903 883400 *Fax:* 01903 884482.

NORTHBOURNE, LORD   Crossbencher

NORTHBOURNE (5th Baron, UK), Christopher George Walter James; cr. 1884; 6th Bt of Langley Hall (GB) 1791. Born 18 February 1926. Son of 4th Baron; educated Eton College; Magdalen College, Oxford (MA 1959). Married Marie Sygne Claudel 1959 (3 sons 1 daughter). DL Kent 1996–. *Career:* Farmer and businessman; Chair, Betteshanger Farms Ltd; Director: Plantation and General Investment plc to 1995, Center Parks plc to 1995. *House of Lords:* First entered House of Lords 1982; Elected hereditary peer 1999–. Independent Spokesperson for Education and Children especially disadvantaged and excluded children. Former Member, Select Committee on European Communities Sub-Committees C and D. Member, Anglo French Parliamentary Group. Deputy Chair, Toynbee Hall; Chair: Parenting Support Forum –1999, Stepney Children's Fund; Governor, Wye College –1999. Council, Caldecott Community/Toynbee Hall. FRICS. *Special Interests:* Education, Disadvantaged and Excluded Children, Family, Agriculture, Horticulture. *Recreations:* Painting, sailing, gardening. *Clubs:* Brooks's, Royal Yacht Squadron (Cowes), House of Lords Yacht Club. The Lord Northbourne, DL, 11 Eaton Place, London, SW1X 8BN *Tel:* 020 7235 6790 *Tel:* Office 020 7235 6224 *Fax:* Office 020 7235 6224.

NORTHBROOK, LORD   Conservative

NORTHBROOK (6th Baron, UK), Francis Thomas Baring; cr. 1866; 8th Bt of The City of London (GB) 1793. Born 21 February 1954. Son of 5th Baron; educated Winchester College; Bristol University (BA 1976). Married Amelia Taylor 1987 (3 daughters). *Career:* Trainee accountant, Dixon Wilson & Co. 1976–80; Baring Bros & Co. Ltd 1981–89; Senior investment manager, Taylor Young Investment Management Ltd 1990–93; Investment fund manager, Smith and Williamson 1993–95; Managing director, Cabincity Ltd 1995–; Director, Mars Asset Management 1996–. *House of Lords:* First entered House of Lords 1990; Elected hereditary peer 1999–. Opposition Whip 1999–2000. Trustee, Winchester Medical Trust. *Special Interests:* City, Agriculture, Foreign Affairs. *Recreations:* Cricket, Skiing, Shooting. *Clubs:* White's. The Lord Northbrook, House of Lords, London, SW1A 0PW *Tel:* 020 7219 4090.

NORTHESK, EARL OF   Conservative

NORTHESK (14th Earl of, S), David John MacRae Carnegie; cr. 1647; 14th Lord Rosehill and Inglismaldie (S) 1639. Born 3 November 1954. Son of 13th Earl; educated Eton College; University College, London (anthropology). Married Jacqueline Reid 1979 (1 son 3 daughters). *Career:* Landowner; Estate manager; Company director. *House of Lords:* First entered House of Lords 1994; Elected hereditary peer 1999–. Opposition Whip 1999–2002. Opposition Spokesperson for: Cabinet Office 2001–02, Treasury 2001–02, Work and Pensions 2001–02. Member, Select Committee on House of Lords' Offices 1997–99. *Special Interests:* Agriculture, Conservation, Heritage, Independent Television Commission. The Earl of Northesk, House of Lords, London, SW1A 0PW *Tel:* 020 7219 3597 *E-mail:* northeskdjm@parliament.uk.

NORTHFIELD, LORD   Labour

NORTHFIELD (Life Baron), (William) Donald Chapman; cr. 1975. Born 25 November 1923; educated Barnsley Grammar School; Emmanuel College, Cambridge (MA economics 1948, Senior Scholar). Cambridge City Councillor 1945–47; Chairman: HM Development Commissioners 1974–80, Telford Development Corporation 1975–87, Northfield Committee of Enquiry into Ownership and Occupancy of Agricultural land 1977–79. *Career:* G. Gibbon Fellow, Nuffield College, Oxford 1971–73; Special Adviser to ECC Commission on Environmental Policy 1981–85; Director, Wembley Stadium plc 1985–88; Chair, Consortium Developments Ltd 1986–92. *House of Commons:* MP (Labour) for Birmingham Northfield 1951–70. General Secretary, Fabian Society 1949–53; Formerly Hon. Secretary, Cambridge Trades Council and Labour Party. Vice-President, Federation of Economic Development Authorities. *Recreations:* Swimming, travel. Raised to the peerage as Baron Northfield, of Telford in the County of Shropshire 1975. The Lord Northfield, House of Lords, London, SW1A 0PW *Tel:* 020 7219 5353.

NORTHOVER, BARONESS   Liberal Democrat

NORTHOVER (Life Baroness), Lindsay Patricia Northover; cr. 2000. Born 21 August 1954. Daughter of Charles and Patricia Granshaw; educated Brighton and Hove High School; St Anne's College, Oxford (BA modern history 1976, MA); Bryn Mawr College, Pennsylvania University, USA (MA history and philosophy of science 1978, PhD 1981). Married John Northover 1988 (2 sons 1 daughter). *Trades Union:* Member AUT 1984–91. Former member Camden and Islington Family Practitioner Committee. *Career:* Research Fellow: University College London and St Mark's Hospital 1980–83, St Thomas's Medical School, London 1983–84; Lecturer, University College 1984–91; Historian of twentieth century medicine, Wellcome Institute, London 1984–91. Liberal Democrat Spokesperson for: Health 2001–02, International Development 2002–. Member Select Committee on Stem Cell Research 2001–02. Chair: SDP Health and Social Welfare Association 1987–88, Liberal Democrats' Parliamentary Candidates Association 1988–91, Women Liberal Democrats 1992–95. St Anne's College Exhibition 1973; Herbert Plumer Bursary for postgraduate study overseas 1976; English-speaking Union Fellowship 1976–77; Mrs Giles Whiting Fellowship in the Humanities 1979–80. Trustee, Bryn Mawr College Association, Great Britain. Contested Welwyn Hatfield 1983 and 1987 general elections; Contested Basildon in 1997 general election. *Publications:* Various academic publications. Raised to the peerage as Baroness Northover, of Cissbury in the County of West Sussex 2000. The Baroness Northover, House of Lords, London, SW1A 0PW *Tel:* 020 7219 8623 *E-mail:* northoverl@parliament.uk.

NORTON OF LOUTH, LORD   Conservative

NORTON OF LOUTH (Life Baron), Philip Norton; cr. 1998. Born 5 March 1951. Youngest son of late George E. Norton, and of Ena D. Norton; educated King Edward VI Grammar School, Louth; Sheffield University (BA political theory and institutions 1972, PhD 1997) (Nalgo Prize); University of Pennsylvania (MA political science 1975) (Thouron Scholar). Chairman, Standards Committee, Kingston-upon-Hull City Council 1999–2003. *Career:* Hull University: Politics lecturer 1977–82, Senior lecturer 1982–84, Reader 1984–86, Professor of Government 1986–, Director, Centre of Legislative Studies 1992–; Head of Department of Politics and International Studies 2002–. Member, Select Committee on European Union Sub-Committee E (Law and Institutions) 1998–2001; Chair Select Committee on the Constitution 2001–. Chair Conservative Academic Group 2000–; Executive Committee Conservative History Group 2003–. Council Member, Hansard Society 1997–, Director of Studies 2002–; Executive Committee Member: Study of Parliament Group 1981–93, Political Studies Association 1983–89; Member, Society and Politics Research Development Group, Economic and Social Research Council 1987–90; Associate Editor, *Political Studies* 1987–93; Governor, King Edward VI Grammar School, Louth 1988–, Warden 1990–93;

President: British Politics Group (USA) 1988–90, Politics Association 1993–; Co-chair, Research Committee of Legislative Specialists, International Political Science Association 1994–2003; Editor, *The Journal of Legislative Studies* 1995–; Chair, Commission to Strengthen Parliament 1999–2001; Vice-President, Political Studies Association 1999–. Trustee, History of Parliament Trust 1999–. FRSA 1995; ACSS 2001. *Publications:* Author or editor: *Dissension in the House of Commons 1945–74*, 1975; *Conservative Dissidents*, 1978; *Dissension in the House of Commons 1974–79*, 1980; *The Commons in Perspective*, 1981; *Conservatives and Conservatism*, (co-author) 1981; *The Constitution in Flux*, 1982; *Law and Order and British Politics*, 1984; *The British Polity*, 1984 (4th edition 2001); *Parliament in the 1980s*, 1985; *The Political Science of British Politics*, (joint editor) 1986; *Legislatures*, 1990; *Parliaments in Western Europe*, 1990; *New Directions in British Politics?*, 1991; *Parliamentary Questions*, (joint editor) 1993; *Back from Westminster*, (joint author) 1993; *Does Parliament Matter?*, 1993; *National Parliaments and the European Union*, 1996; *The New Parliaments of Central and Eastern Europe*, (joint editor) 1996; *The Conservative Party*, 1996; *Legislatures and Legislators*, 1998; *Parliaments and Governments in Western Europe*, 1998; *Parliaments and Pressure Groups in Western Europe*, 1998; *Parliaments in Asia*, 1999; *Parliaments and Citizens in Westen Europe*, 2002; *Politics UK*, (with others) 1990 (5th edition 2003). *Special Interests:* Constitutional Affairs, Parliamentary Reform, Legislatures, British Politics, American Politics. *Recreations:* Table-tennis, walking, writing. *Clubs:* Royal Overseas League, Royal Commonwealth Society. Raised to the peerage as Baron Norton of Louth, of Louth in the County of Lincolnshire 1998. Professor the Lord Norton of Louth, Department of Politics, University of Hull, HU6 7RX *Tel:* 01482 465863 *Fax:* 01482 466208 *E-mail:* nortonp@parliament.uk.

O

OAKESHOTT OF SEAGROVE BAY, LORD   Liberal Democrat

OAKESHOTT OF SEAGROVE BAY (Life Baron), Matthew Alan Oakeshott; cr. 2000. Born 10 January 1947. Son of Keith Robertson Oakeshott CMG and Eva Jill Oakeshott; educated Charterhouse School (Senior Foundation Scholar); University and Nuffield Colleges, Oxford (BA philosophy, politics and economics 1968, MA). Married Dr Philippa Poulton 1976 (2 sons 1 daughter). Former Oxford City Councillor, Vice-Chairman, Finance Committee. *Career:* ODI/Nuffield Fellow, Kenya Ministry of Finance and Economic Planning 1968–70; Special adviser to Roy Jenkins 1972–76; Director, Warburg Investment Management 1976–81; Manager, Courtaulds Pension Fund 1981–85; Founder Director, OLIM Ltd and Investment director, Value and Income Trust plc 1986–. Liberal Democrat Spokesperson for: Treasury 2001–, Pensions 2002–. Member Select Committee on: Economic Affairs 2001–, House of Lords' Offices Finance and Staff Sub-committee 2001–02; Member, Joint Committee on Reform of the House of Lords 2002–. Member: SDP National Committee 1981–82, National Economic Policy Committee 1981–85. Contested Horsham and Crawley (Labour) October 1974 and Cambridge (Alliance) 1983 general elections; Hon. Treasurer, Make Votes Count; Council Member, Centre for Reform. *Publications:* Chapter in *By-Elections in British Politics*, 1973. *Special Interests:* Economic Policy, Housing, Pensions, Overseas Development. *Recreations:* Music, elections, supporting Arsenal FC. Raised to the peerage as Baron Oakeshott of Seagrove Bay, of Seagrove Bay in the County of the Isle of Wight 2000. The Lord Oakeshott of Seagrove Bay, House of Lords, London, SW1A 0PW *Tel:* 020 7219 5353.

O'CATHAIN, BARONESS   Conservative

O'CATHAIN (Life Baroness), Detta O'Cathain; cr. 1991. Born 3 February 1938. Daughter of late Caoimhghin and Margaret O'Cathain; educated Laurel Hill, Limerick; University College, Dublin (BA economics, English and French 1961). Married William Ernest John Bishop 1968 (died 2001). *Career:* Assistant economist, Aer Lingus 1959–66; Group economist, Tarmac 1966–69; Economic adviser to Chairman, Rootes Motors/Chrysler 1969–72; Senior economist, Carrington Viyella 1972; Economic adviser, British Leyland 1973–74, Director, Market Planning 1974–76; Corporate planning executive, Unigate plc 1976–81; Head of strategic planning, Milk Marketing Board 1981–83, Director and General Manager 1984–85, Managing Director 1985–88;

Managing Director, Barbican Centre 1990–95; Non-executive director: Midland Bank plc 1984–93, Tesco plc 1985–2000, Sears plc 1987–94, British Airways plc 1993–, BET plc 1994–96, BNP/Paribas (UK) 1995–, Thistle Hotels plc 1996–2003, South East Water plc 1997–, Alldens plc 2000–03, William Baird plc 2000–02. Member, Public Service Select Committee 1996–97; Member, Select Committees on: Monetary Policy of the Bank of England/Economic Affairs 1998–, European Communities Sub Committee B (Energy, Industry and Transport) 1998–2002, European Union 1999–2001; Member Joint Committee on House of Lords Reform 2002–. Member, Council of Industrial Society 1986–92; Past President, Agricultural Section of the British Association for the Advancement of Science; Former Member: Design Council, Engineering Council; President, Chartered Institute of Marketing 1998–2001. OBE 1983; Commander: Royal Norwegian Order 1993, Order of the Lion of Finland 1994. Fellow: Royal Society of Arts 1986, Chartered Institute of Marketing 1987. Freeman, City of London. *Special Interests:* Arts, Agriculture, Industry, Commerce, Finance, Retail Industry, Disabled, Economic Policy. *Recreations:* Music, reading, swimming, walking, gardening. *Clubs:* Athenaeum. Raised to the peerage as Baroness O'Cathain, of The Barbican in the City of London 1991. The Baroness O'Cathain, OBE, Eglantine, Tower House Gardens, Arundel, West Sussex, BN18 9RU *Tel:* 01903 883 775 *Fax:* 01903 883 775; House of Lords, London, SW1A 0PW *Tel:* 020 7219 0662 *E-mail:* ocathaind@parliament.uk.

OLIVER OF AYLMERTON, LORD   Crossbencher

OLIVER OF AYLMERTON (Life Baron), Peter Raymond Oliver; cr. 1986. Born 7 March 1921. Son of late David Thomas Oliver, LLM, LLD; educated Leys School, Cambridge; Trinity Hall, Cambridge (Scholar). Married Mary Chichester 1945 (died 1985) (1 son 1 daughter); married Wendy Anne Lloyd Jones 1987. Military Service, 12th Battalion RTR 1941–45. *Career:* Called to the Bar, Lincoln's Inn 1948; QC 1965; Bencher, Lincoln's Inn 1973; Judge of the High Court 1974–80; Member, Restrictive Practices Court 1976–80; Chairman, Review Body on Chancery Division 1979–81; Lord Justice of Appeal 1980–86; Lord of Appeal in Ordinary 1986–92. Chairman, Sub-Committee E (Law and Institutions) of Select Committee on the European Communities 1989–91. Mentioned in Dispatches. Kt 1974; PC 1980. *Recreations:* Gardening, music. Raised to the peerage as Baron Oliver of Aylmerton, of Aylmerton in the County of Norfolk 1986. Rt Hon the Lord Oliver of Aylmerton, House of Lords, London, SW1A 0PW *Tel:* 020 7219 3202.

O'NEILL OF BENGARVE, BARONESS   Crossbencher

O'NEILL OF BENGARVE (Life Baroness), Onora Sylvia O'Neill; cr. 1999. Born 23 August 1941. Daughter of late Hon. Sir Con O'Neill, GCMG and Lady Garvey, neé Pritchard and widow of Sir Terence Garvey, KCMG; educated St Paul's Girls' School; Somerville College, Oxford (BA philosopy, psychology and physiology 1962, MA); Harvard University (PhD). Married Edward John Nell 1963 (2 sons) (divorced 1976). *Career:* Philosophy assistant, then associate professor, Barnard College, Columbia University 1970–77; Essex University: Philosophy lecturer 1977–78, Senior lecturer 1978–83, Reader 1983–87, Professor of philosophy 1987–92; Principal, Newnham College, Cambridge 1992–. Member Select Committee on Stem Cell Research –2002. Fellow, Wissenschaftskolleg, Berlin 1989–90, Academic Advisory Board 1996–; Foreign Hon. Member, American Academy of Arts and Sciences 1993; Foreign Hon. Member, Austrian Academy of Sciences, 2002; Foreign Member, American Philosophical Society 2003; Hon. Member, Royal Irish Academy 2003. Chairman, Nuffield Foundation 1998–. Five honorary degrees and fellowships. Isaac Newton Trust, Gates Cambridge Trust, Sir Ernest Cassel Education Trust. President, Aristotelian Society 1988–89; Member, Animal Procedures Committee 1990–94; Member, Nuffield Council on Bioethics 1991–98, Chair 1996–98; Member, Human Genetics Advisory Commission 1996–99, Chair 1998–99; President, Mind Association 2003–04. CBE 1995. FBA 1993; F Med Sci 2002. *Publications: Acting on Principle,* 1976, *Faces of Hunger,* 1986; *Constructions of Reason,* 1989, *Towards Justice and Virtue,* 1996; *Bounds of Justice,* 2000; *Autonomy and Trust in Bioethics,* 2002; *A Question of Trust,* 2002; Numerous articles on philosophy in learned journals. Raised to the peerage as Baroness O'Neill of Bengarve, of The Braid in the County of Antrim 1999. The Baroness O'Neill of Bengarve, CBE, FBA, Newnham College, Cambridge, CB3 9DF *Tel:* 01223 335821 *Fax:* 01223 359155 *E-mail:* 050/000@cus.cam.ac.uk.

ONSLOW, EARL OF   Conservative

ONSLOW (7th Earl of, UK), Michael William Coplestone Dillon Onslow; cr. 1801; Viscount Cranley; 10th Baron Onslow (GB) 1716; Baron Cranley (GB) 1776; 11th Bt of West Clandon (E) 1660. Born 28 February 1938. Son of 6th Earl; educated Eton College; Sorbonne. Married Robin Lindsay Bullard 1964 (1 son 2 daughters). *Career:* Farmer. *House of Lords:* First entered House of Lords 1971; Elected hereditary peer 1999–. Member Select Committee on Animals in Scientific Procedures 2001–02. *Clubs:* Beefsteak, White's. The Earl of Onslow, Temple Court, Clandon Park, Guildford, Surrey, GU4 7RQ.

OPPENHEIM-BARNES, BARONESS   Conservative

OPPENHEIM-BARNES (Life Baroness), Sally Oppenheim-Barnes; cr. 1989. Born 26 July 1930. Daughter of late Mark Viner; educated Sheffield High School; Lowther College, North Wales. Married Henry Oppenheim 1949 (died 1980) (1 son 2 daughters); married John Barnes 1984. *Career:* Non-executive Director, The Boots Co. plc 1981–93; Chair, National Consumer Council 1987–89; Director, Fleming High Income Trust plc 1989–97; Non-executive Director, HFC Bank plc 1990–98; Former Vice-President, South Wales and West Fire Liaison Panel. *House of Commons:* MP (Conservative) for Gloucester 1970–87; Member of the Shadow Cabinet 1975–79; Minister of State for Consumer Affairs 1979–82. Opposition Spokesperson for Prices and Consumer Protection 1974–79. Member, House of Lords' Offices Committee 2000–02. President, Conservative Club of Gloucester 1970. Former National Vice-President, National Mobile Homes Residents' Association; Vice-President, National Union of Townswomen's Guilds 1973–79; Former Vice-President, Western Centre of Public Health Inspectors; Former President, National Waterways Trust to 1990. PC 1979. *Special Interests:* Consumer Affairs. *Recreations:* Bridge, tennis. *Sportsclubs:* Vanderbilt Racquet Club. *Clubs:* House of Lords Bridge Club. Raised to the peerage as Baroness Oppenheim-Barnes, of Gloucester in the County of Gloucestershire 1989. Rt Hon the Baroness Oppenheim-Barnes, House of Lords, London, SW1A 0PW *Tel:* 020 7219 5353.

ORME, LORD   Labour

ORME (Life Baron), Stanley Orme; cr. 1997. Born 5 April 1923. Son of Sherwood Orme; educated Elementary school; Part-time technical; National Council of Labour Colleges; WEA. Married Irene Mary Harris 1951. *Trades Union:* Member, AEEU. Served in RAF 1942–47, Warrant Officer, Air Crew. Councillor, Sale Borough Council 1958–64. *Career:* Skilled engineer 1948–64. *House of Commons:* Contested Stockport South 1959; MP (Labour) for Salford West 1964–83 and for Salford East 1983–97; Minister of State: for Northern Ireland 1974–76, for Department of Health and Social Security April–September 1976; Minister for Social Security and Member of the Cabinet 1976–79. Principal Opposition Frontbench Spokesperson for: Health and Social Security 1979–80, Industry 1980–83, Energy 1983–87. Member: IPU, CPA. Chair, AEEU Parliamentary Group of Labour Members 1976–96; Chair, Parliamentary Labour Party 1987–92. Hon. President, The Lotteries Council. Hon. DSc, University of Salford 1985. PC 1974. *Recreations:* Walking, jazz, opera, reading American literature, supporting Manchester United Football Club and Lancashire County Cricket Club. Raised to the peerage as Baron Orme, of Salford in the County of Greater Manchester 1997. Rt Hon the Lord Orme, 8 Northwood Grove, Sale, Cheshire, M33 3DZ *Tel:* 0161–973 5341.

Visit the Vacher Dod Website . . .
www.DodOnline.co.uk

OUSELEY, LORD
Crossbencher

OUSELEY (Life Baron), Herman George Ouseley; cr 2001. Born 24 March 1945; educated William Penn School, South London; Catford College (Diploma in municipal administration). Married Margaret (1 son 1 daughter). Principal race relations adviser to Greater London Council 1981–84; Assistant Chief Executive London Borough of Lambeth 1984–86; Director of education and Chief Executive Inner London Education Authority 1986–90; Chief executive London Borough of Lambeth 1990–93. *Career:* Chair and chief executive Commission for Racial Equality 1993–2000; Managing director Different Realities Partnership Ltd 2000–. Eight honorary degrees. Policy Research Institute on Ageing and Ethnicity; PRESET Charitable Trust; Institute of Race Relations; Kick It Out Limited. Knighthood 1997. FCIPD (fellow, Chartered Institute of Personnel Development). *Publications: The System* 1981. Raised to the peerage as Baron Ouseley, of Peckham Rye in the London Borough of Southwark. The Lord Ouseley, House of Lords, London, SW1A 0PW *Tel:* 020 7219 5353.

OWEN, LORD
Crossbencher

OWEN (Life Baron), David Anthony Llewellyn Owen; cr. 1992. Born 2 July 1938. Son of late Dr John Owen, general practitioner and Alderman Molly Owen; educated Bradfield College; Sidney Sussex College, Cambridge (MA natural sciences, MB, BChir Cantab); St Thomas's Hospital, London 1956–59. Married Deborah Schabert 1968 (2 sons 1 daughter). *Career:* Various house appointments, St Thomas's Hospital 1962–64; Neurological and Psychiatric Registrar 1964–66; Research Fellow, Medical Unit 1966–68; Non-Executive Director: New Crane Publishing 1992–, Coats Viyella 1994–2001; Executive Chairman, Global Natural Energy plc 1995–; Director: Deborah Owen Ltd 1972–, Center for International Health and Cooperation 1995–, Abbott Laboratories plc 1996–; Chair New Europe 1999–; Non-executive Chairman, Europe-Steel Company 2000–; Chairman, Yukos International Services 2002–; Member, Supervisory Council of Mazeikin Nafta Oil Refinery, Lithuania 2002–; Director, Intelligent Energy 2003–. *House of Commons:* Contested (Labour) Torrington 1964 general election; MP (Labour) for: Plymouth Sutton 1966–74, Plymouth Devonport 1974–92 (Labour 1974–81, SDP 1981–92); PPS to Minister of Defence (Administration) 1966–68; Parliamentary Under-Secretary of State for Defence (Royal Navy) 1968–70; Parliamentary Under-Secretary of State, Department of Health and Social Security 1974, Minister of State 1974–76; Minister of State, Foreign Office 1976–77; Secretary of State for Foreign and Commonwealth Affairs 1977–79. Opposition Spokesperson for Defence 1970–72; Principal Opposition Spokesperson for Energy 1979–80. Chancellor, Liverpool University 1996–. Director, Center for International Health and Cooperation. One of the founders of the Social Democratic Party, Formally launched March 26 1981; Chairman, Parliamentary Committee 1981–82; Deputy Leader of the Party 1982–83, Leader 1983–87, Resigned over merger with Liberal Party; Re-elected SDP Leader 1988–92. Patron, Social Market Foundation; President, The Enabling Society. Three honorary fellowships. Member: Palme Commission on Disarmament and Security Issues 1980–89, Independent Commission on International Humanitarian Issues 1983–88; EU Co-Chairman, International Conference on former Yugoslavia 1992–95, Carnegie Commission on Preventing Deadly Conflict 1994–99; Eminent Persons Group on curbing illicit traffic in small arms and light weapons 1999–2001. PC 1976; CH 1994. Freeman, City of Plymouth 2000. *Publications: A Unified Health Service,* 1968; *The Politics of Defence,* 1972; *In Sickness and in Health,* 1976; *Human Rights,* 1978; *Face the Future,* 1981; *A Future that will Work,* 1984; *A United Kingdom,* 1986; *Personally Speaking* (to Kenneth Harris), 1987; *Our NHS,* 1988; *Time to Declare* (autobiography) 1991; *Seven Ages* (an anthology of poetry) 1992; *Balkan Odyssey,* 1995. *Special Interests:* International affairs (foreign and defence). *Recreations:* Sailing. Raised to the peerage as Baron Owen, of the City of Plymouth 1992. Rt Hon the Lord Owen, CH, House of Lords, London, SW1A 0PW *Tel:* 020 7787 2751 *Fax:* 01442 876 108; 78 Narrow Street, London, E14 8BP *Tel:* 020 7987 5441 *E-mail:* lordowen@nildram.co.uk.

OXBURGH, LORD   Crossbencher

OXBURGH (Life Baron), (Ernest) Ronald Oxburgh; cr. 1999. Born 2 November 1934. Son of Ernest Oxburgh and Violet Oxburgh (née Bugden); educated Liverpool Institute; Oxford University (BA natural sciences (geology) 1957, MA); Princeton University, USA (PhD geology 1960). Married Ursula Mary Brown 1958 (1 son 2 daughter). Chairman SETNET. *Career:* Oxford University: Departmental Demonstrator, 1960–61, Lecturer in Geology 1962–78, Fellow, St Edmund Hall 1964–78, Emeritus Fellow 1978; Visiting Professor: California Institute of Technology 1967–68 (Fairchild Fellow 1995–96), Stanford and Cornell Universities 1973–74; Cambridge University: Professor of Mineralogy and Petrology 1978–91, Head of Department of Earth Sciences 1980–88, Fellow of Trinity Hall 1978–82, President, Queens' College 1982–89, Professorial Fellow 1989–91; Chief Scientific Adviser, Ministry of Defence 1988–93; Rector, Imperial College of Science, Technology and Medicine 1993–2001. Member, Select Committees on: Science and Technology 1999–, Science and Technology Sub-Committee II (Science and Society) 1999–2000, Science and Technology Sub-Committee II (Aircraft Cabin Environment) 2000–01; Chair: Science and Technology Sub-Committee IIA (Human Genetic Databases) 2000–01, Science and Technology Committee 2001–; Member Science and Technology Sub-committee: I (Fighting Infection) 2002–, II (Innovations in Computer Processors/Microprocessing/Science and the Regional Development Agencies) 2002–. Member: Conseil National De La Science, France, Conseil D'Administration Ecole Polytechnique, France, University Grants Committee of Hong Kong, International Academic Advisory Council, Singapore. President, European Union of Geosciences 1985–87; Member, National Committee of Inquiry into Higher Education (Dearing Committee) 1996–97; Member of Geological and Scientific Academies and Societies in USA, Germany, Austria and Venezuela; President, Geological Society 1999–2001; Chairman, SETNET 2001–. Bigsby Medal, Geological Society 1979. Hon. Fellow: Trinity Hall, Cambridge 1982, University College, Oxford 1983, St Edmund Hall, Oxford 1986; Queens' College, Cambridge 1992; six honorary doctorates. Council Member, Winston Churchill Memorial Trust 1995–; Trustee, Natural History Museum 1993, Chairman of Trustees 1999–. Member, Parliamentary Office of Science and Technology (POST) 2000–. KBE 1992; Officier, Ordre des Palmes Académiques (France) 1995. FRS 1978, Hon FIMechE 1993, Hon FCGI 1996, Hon FREng 2000, Foreign Associate, US Academy of Sciences 2001. *Publications:* Has contributed to a number of geological, defence and scientific journals. *Special Interests:* Higher Education, Health, Energy. *Recreations:* Mountaineering, theatre, orienteering. *Sportsclubs:* Climbers, West Anglia Orienteering. *Clubs:* Athenaeum. Raised to the peerage as Baron Oxburgh, of Liverpool in the County of Merseyside 1999. The Lord Oxburgh, KBE, House of Lords, London, SW1A 0PW *Tel:* 020 7219 4341 *Fax:* 020 7219 5979 *E-mail:* oxburghe@parliament.uk.

OXFORD, LORD BISHOP OF   Non-affiliated

OXFORD (41st Bishop of), Richard Douglas Harries. Born 2 June 1936. Son of late Brigadier W. D. J. Harries, CBE; educated Wellington College; RMA, Sandhurst; Selwyn College, Cambridge (MA theology 1965); Cuddesdon College, Oxford. Married Josephine Bottomley, MB, BChir, DCH 1963 (1 son 1 daughter). Lieutenant, Royal Corps of Signals 1955–58. *Career:* Curate, Hampstead Parish Church 1963–69; Chaplain, Westfield College 1966–69; Lecturer, Wells Theological College 1969–72; Vicar, All Saints, Fulham 1972–81; Dean, King's College, London 1981–87; Bishop of Oxford 1987–; Took his seat in the House of Lords December 1993. *House of Lords:* Convener of Bench of Bishops 1998–. Member, Select Committee on House of Lords' Offices 1997–2001; Chair Select Committee on Stem Cell Research 2001–02. Member, Anglican Consultative Council 1994–2003; Consultant, Anglican Peace and Justice Network 1984–94. General Ordination examiner in Christian Ethics 1972–76; Director, Post Ordination Training, Kensington Jurisdiction 1973–79; Chairman, Southwark Ordination Course 1982–87; President, Johnson Society 1988–89. Two honorary doctorates; Hon. Fellow, Selwyn College Cambridge. Vice-Chair: Council for Christian Action 1979–87, Council for Arms Control 1982–87; Member, Home Office Advisory Committee for reform of sexual offences law 1981–85; Chair: Council of Christians and Jews 1992–2001, Board of Social Responsibility for the Church of England 1996–2001; Board Member, Christian Aid 1994–2000; Member, Royal Commission on the Reform of the House of Lords 1999–2000;

Visiting Professor, Liverpool Hope University College 2002; Nuffield Council on Bioethics. Fellow: King's College, London, Royal Society of Literature. *Publications: Prayers of Hope*, 1975; *Turning to Prayer*, 1978; *Prayers of Grief and Glory*, 1979; *Being a Christian*, 1981; *Should Christians Support Guerillas?* 1982; *The Authority of Divine Love*, 1983; *Praying Round the Clock*, 1983; *Prayer and the Pursuit of Happiness*, 1985; *Morning Has Broken*, 1985; *Christianity and War in a Nuclear Age*, 1986; *C. S. Lewis: the man and his God*, 1987; *Christ is Risen*, 1988; *Is There a Gospel for the Rich*, 1992; *Art and the Beauty of God*, 1993; *The Real God: A Response to Anthony Freeman*, 1994; *Questioning Belief*, 1995; *A Gallery of Reflections – The Nativity in Art*, 1995; *Two Cheers For Secularism*, (ed. with Sidney Brichto) 1998; *In The Gladness of Today*, 2000; Co-editor, *Christianity: Two Thousand Years*, 2001; *God outside the Box: Why spiritual people object to Christianity*, 2002; *After the End: Christianity and Judaism in the Shadow of the Holocaust*, 2003; Has edited and contributed to other Christian publications as well as articles in the press and periodicals. *Special Interests:* Overseas Aid and Development, Poverty, Housing, Business Ethics, Arts, Arms Control, Moral Issues. *Recreations:* Theatre, literature, sport. Rt Rev the Lord Bishop of Oxford, Diocesan Church House, North Hinksey, Oxford, OX2 0NB *Tel:* 01865 208222 *Fax:* 01865 790 470 *E-mail:* bishopoxon@oxford.anglican.org.

P

PALMER, LORD — Crossbencher

PALMER (4th Baron), Adrian Bailie Nottage Palmer; cr. 1933; 4th Bt of Grosvenor Crescent (UK) 1916. Born 8 October 1951. Son of Colonel Hon Sir Gordon Palmer KCVO; educated Eton College; Edinburgh University (MA farming practice 1979). Married Cornelia Dorothy Katharine Wadham 1977 (2 sons 1 daughter). *Trades Union:* Scottish National Farmers Union, Scottish Landowners' Federation, Historic Houses Association. *Career:* Apprentice Huntley and Palmers Ltd; Sales manager, Belgium and Luxembourg 1974–77; Scottish representative European Landowning Organisation 1977–86; Farmer. *House of Lords:* First entered House of Lords 1990; Elected hereditary peer 1999–. Member: Advisory Panel on Works of Art 1995–98, 2000–02, Refreshment Committee 1997–2000, 2003–, Select Committee on European Union, Sub-Committee D (Environment, Agriculture, Public Health and Consumer Protection) 2000–. Vice-chair, Historic Houses Association for Scotland 1993–94, Chair 1994–99; Member: Executive Council Historic Houses Association 1981–99, Council Scottish Landowners' Federation 1986–92; Secretary, Royal Caledonian Hunt 1989–; President: Palm Tree Silk Co (St Lucia), British Association of Biofuels and Oils. Chair, Country Sports Defence Trust 1994–. Member, Queen's Bodyguard for Scotland (The Royal Company of Archers) 1990–96. *Special Interests:* Agriculture, Environment, Heritage, Media. *Recreations:* Hunting, shooting, gardening. *Clubs:* New (Edinburgh), MCC, Pratt's. The Lord Palmer, Manderston, Duns, Berwickshire, TD11 3PP *Tel:* 01361 883450 *Fax:* 01361 882010 *E-mail:* palmer@manderston.co.uk.

PALUMBO, LORD — Conservative

PALUMBO (Life Baron), Peter Garth Palumbo; cr. 1991. Born 20 July 1935. Son of late Rudolph Palumbo and of Elsie Palumbo; educated Eton College; Worcester College, Oxford (MA law 1954). Married Denia Wigram 1959 (died 1986) (1 son 2 daughters); married Hayat Morowa 1986 (1 son 2 daughters). Chancellor, Portsmouth University 1992–. Governor, London School of Economics and Political Science 1976–94; Chairman: Tate Gallery Foundation 1986–87, Arts Council of Great Britain 1989–94, Serpentine Gallery 1994–; Member of Council, Royal Albert Hall 1995–99; Governor, The Royal Shakespeare Theatre 1995–2000; Member, The Whitgift School Committee 2002–. Hon. DLitt, Portsmouth University 1993. Trustee: Mies van der Rohe Archive 1977–, Tate Gallery 1978–85, Whitechapel Arts Gallery Foundation 1981–87; Trustee and Hon. Treasurer, Writers and Scholars Educational Trust 1984–99; Chairman, Painshill Park Trust Appeal 1986–96; Trustee: The Natural History Museum 1994–, The Design Museum 1995–. National Order of the Southern Cross (Brazil); Cranbrook Academy of Arts, Detroit, Michigan Patronage of the Arts Award 2002. Hon. FRIBA; Hon. FFB 1994; Hon. FIStructE 1994. Liveryman, Salters' Company. *Recreations:* Music, travel, gardening, reading. *Clubs:* White's, Pratt's, Athenaeum, Knickerbocker (New York), Garrick. Raised to the peerage as Baron Palumbo, of Walbrook in the City of London 1991. The Lord Palumbo, 2 Astell Street, London, SW3 3RU; Office:, Vestry House, Laurence Poutney Hill, London, EC4R 0EH *Tel:* 020 7626 9236.

PAREKH, LORD   Labour

PAREKH (Life Baron), Bhikhu Chhotalal Parekh; cr. 2000. Born 4 January 1935. Son of Chhotalal and Gajaraben Parekh; educated HDS High School, Amalsad 1943–50; Bombay University (BA economics 1954, MA political science 1956); London University (PhD the idea of equality in English political thought 1966). Married Pramila Dalal 1959 (3 sons). *Career:* Politics tutor, London School of Economics 1962–63; Politics assistant lecturer, Glasgow University 1963–64; Hull University: Politics lecturer, senior lecturer and reader 1964–82, Professor of Political Theory 1982–2001; Centennial Professor LSE 2001–; Professor and political philosophy, Westminster University 2001–. Vice-chancellor, University of Baroda 1981–84. Member Joint Select Committee on Human Rights 2001–. Founding Member and Past President, Research Committee on Political Philosophy of International Political Science Association. British Asian of the Year 1991; Gujarati of the year, 1994; BBC's Special Lifetime Achievement Award for Asians 1999. Six honorary doctorates. Trustee: Runnymede Trust 1986–, Gandhi Foundation 1988 (Vice-President 1996–), Anne Frank Educational Trust 1992–. Visiting Professor, University of British Columbia, Canada 1967–68; Visiting Professor: Concordia University 1974–75, McGill University 1976–77; Member, Rampton/Swann Committee of Inquiry into Educational Problems of Ethnic Minority Children 1978–82; Vice-Chancellor, University of Baroda 1981–84; Council Member, Policy Studies Institute 1985–90; Deputy Chairman, Commission for Racial Equality 1985–90; Vice-President, UK Council for Overseas Students Affairs 1989–; Council Member, Institute for Public Policy Research 1990–96; Visiting Professor: Harvard University 1996, Institute of Advanced Study, Vienna 1997, University of Pompeu Fabra, Barcelona 1997, University of Pennsylvania 1998; cole des Hautes tudes en Sciences Sociales, 2000; Chairman, Commission on Future of Multi-Ethnic Britain 1998–2001. FRSA 1988; President, Academy of the Learned Societies in Social Sciences (ALSSS) 1999. *Publications: Politics and Experience*, 1968; *Dissent and Disorder*, 1971; *The Morality of Politics*, 1972; *Knowledge and Belief in Politics*, 1973; *Bentham's Political Thought*, 1973; *Colour, Culture and Consciousness*, 1974; *Jeremy Bentham: ten critical essays*, 1974; *The Concept of Socialism*, 1975; *Hannah Arendt and the Search for a new Political Philosophy*, 1981; *Karl's Marx's Theory of Ideology*, 1982; *Contemporary Political Thinkers*, 1982; *Political Discourse*, 1986; *Gandhi's Political Philosophy*, 1989; *Colonialism, Tradition and Reform*, 1989; *Jeremy Bentham: critical assessments*, (4 volumes) 1993; *The Decolonisation of Imagination*, 1995; *Crisis and Change in Contemporary India*, 1995; *Gandhi*, 1997; *Rethinking Multiculturalism*, 2000; *The Future of Multi Ethnic Britain: The Parekh Report*, 2000 articles in various learned journals. *Special Interests:* Race relations, Higher education, Ethnic conflicts, Global justice, International trade. *Recreations:* Reading, music, walking. *Clubs:* Royal Society of Arts. Raised to the peerage as Baron Parekh, of Kingston upon Hull in the East Riding of Yorkshire 2000. Professor the Lord Parekh, 211 Victoria Avenue, Hull, HU5 3EF *Tel:* 01482 345530 *Fax:* 01482 345530 *Tel:* 020 7219 5353 *E-mail:* b.parekh@bigfoot.com.

PARK OF MONMOUTH, BARONESS   Conservative

PARK OF MONMOUTH (Life Baroness), Daphne Margaret Sybil Désirée Park; cr. 1990. Born 1 September 1921. Daughter of late John Alexander and Doreen Gwynneth Park; educated Rosa Bassett School, Streatham; Somerville College, Oxford (BA modern languages 1943); Newnham College, Cambridge (Certificate of Competent Knowledge Russian 1952). Single. Served WTS (FANY) 1943–48; Allied Commission, Austria 1946–48. Member, Sheffield Development Corporation Board 1989–92. *Career:* Entered Foreign Office 1948; Member, UK delegation to NATO 1952; Second Secretary, British Embassy, Moscow 1954–56; FO 1956–59; Consul and First Secretary, Leopoldville 1959–61; FO 1961–63; High Commission, Lusaka 1964–67;

FO 1967–69; Consul-General, Hanoi 1969–70; Hon. Research Fellow, University of Kent 1971–72; Chargé d'Affaires a.i. British Embassy, Ulan Bator, Mongolia April-June 1972; FCO 1973–79; Principal, Somerville College, Oxford 1980–89; Governor, BBC 1982–87; Member, British Library Board 1983–89; Chairman, Lord Chancellor's Advisory Committee on Legal Aid 1984–90; Pro-Vice Chancellor, University of Oxford 1985–89; Chairman, Royal Commission on the Historical Monuments of England 1989–94. Member: European Communities, Sub-Committee C: (Environment, Public Health and Education) 1994–97, (Common Foreign and Security Policy) 2000–, Select Committee on European Communities 2000–. Member, Royal Asiatic Society; Governor, Ditchley Foundation; Member, Forum UK 1994–96; President, Society for the Promotion of the Training of Women 1994–; Patron Action Congo. Hon. LLD: Bristol 1988, Mount Holyoke College 1993. Director, Zoo Development Trust 1989–90; Trustee: Jardine Educational Trust to 1998, Royal Armouries Development Trust 1991–92, Great Britain-Sasakawa Foundation 1994–2001, Patron 2001– Lucy Faithfull Travel Scholarship Fund. OBE 1960; CMG 1971. Fellow: Chatham House (RIIA), RSA. *Special Interests:* Higher Education, Foreign Affairs, Defence, Heritage, Northern Ireland, Africa. *Recreations:* Good talk, politics and difficult places. *Clubs:* Naval and Military, Commonwealth Trust, Special Forces, United Oxford and Cambridge University. Raised to the peerage as Baroness Park of Monmouth, of Broadway in the County of Hereford and Worcester 1990. The Baroness Park of Monmouth, CMG, OBE, House of Lords, London, SW1A 0PW *Tel:* 020 7219 5353.

PARKINSON, LORD — Conservative

PARKINSON (Life Baron), Cecil Edward Parkinson; cr. 1992. Born 1 September 1931. Son of Sydney Parkinson; educated Royal Grammar School, Lancaster; Emmanuel College, Cambridge (MA English and law 1955). Married Ann Mary Jarvis 1957 (3 daughters). *Career:* Chartered Accountant; Company director. *House of Commons:* MP (Conservative) for: Enfield West 1970–74, Hertfordshire South 1974–83, Hertsmere 1983–92; PPS to Minister for Aerospace and Shipping, Department of Trade and Industry 1972–74; Minister for Trade, Department of Trade 1979–81; Paymaster General 1981–83; Chancellor, Duchy of Lancaster 1982–83; Secretary of State for: Trade and Industry June-October 1983, Energy 1987–89, Transport 1989–90; Member, Shadow Cabinet 1997–98. Assistant Government Whip 1974; Opposition Whip 1974–79. Spokesperson for Trade 1976–79. Chairman, Conservative Party 1981–83 and 1997–98. Treasurer, The Wordsworth Trust. *Publications: Right at the Centre: An Autobiography*, 1992. *Recreations:* Reading, golf, skiing. *Clubs:* Beefsteak, Garrick, Pratt's, Hawks (Cambridge). Raised to the peerage as Baron Parkinson, of Carnforth in the County of Lancashire 1992. Rt Hon the Lord Parkinson, House of Lords, London, SW1A 0PW *Tel:* 020 7584 7977.

PARRY, LORD — Labour

PARRY (Life Baron), Gordon Samuel David Parry; cr. 1975. Born 30 November 1925. Son of late Rev. Thomas Lewis Parry; educated Trinity College, Carmarthen; Liverpool University (diploma advanced education). Married Glenys Catherine Incledon 1948 (1 daughter). *Trades Union:* Member, NUT 1945. Councillor, Neyland (Dyfed) Urban District Council 1948–65; DL, Dyfed 1993–. *Career:* Assistant teacher various schools 1945–52; Housemaster, County Secondary School, Haverfordwest 1952–62, 1963–67; Institute of Education, Liverpool University 1962–63; Warden, Pembrokeshire Teachers' Centre 1967–76; Milford Docks Co. chair 1984–91, president 1991–; Chairman; Milford Leisure Co. 1984–, Taylor Plan Services 1988–97; Director, Seacon 1990–97; Chairman, Clean World International 1991–; Director, Marriott UK 1997–98. Past and present president, chair numerous charities and organisations, especially in areas of physically and mentally handicapped and choirs. Hon. Fellow: James Cook University, Australia, Trinity College, Carmarthen, University of Glamorgan; Awarded Hon. Doctorate of Education, Swansea Institute of Higher Education 1992; Fellow, Pembrokeshire College 1996. Member: Welsh Independent TV Authority, Welsh Independent Broadcasting Authority, General Advisory Council, IBA, Welsh Development Agency, Welsh Arts Council, Schools Council for Wales; Chairman, The Wales Tourist Board; Member, British Tourist Authority 1978–84; Chairman, British Cleaning Council; Member: Board of British Rail, Western Region 1982–83, BBC Advisory Council and of its Council for Wales. Fellow: Tourism Society, Royal Society of Arts, British Institute of Cleaning Science, Hotel and Catering and Institutional Management Association; Hon. Fellow, Institute of Waste Management. Hon. Freedom: Niagara, New York, USA 1981; Dallas, Texas, USA 1982; Macon, Georgia, USA 1985; Myrtle Beach, North Carolina, USA 1985; Burgess (Hon. Freeman), Guild of Freemen of Haverford West, Pembrokeshire 1998. *Publications: A Legacy For Life*, 1996. *Special Interests:* Tourism, Wales, North American Matters, Australia. *Recreations:* Watching the Welsh Rugby XV win, travelling, reading and writing. *Sportsclubs:* Neyland Yacht Club, Neyland RFC. Raised to the peerage as Baron Parry, of Neyland in the County of Dyfed 1975. The Lord Parry, DL, House of Lords, London, SW1A 0PW *Tel:* 020 7219 3000; Willowmead, 52 Portlion, Llangwm, Pembrokeshire, Dyfed, SA62 4JT *Tel:* 01646 600667.

PATEL, LORD　　　　　　　　　　　　　　　　　　Crossbencher

PATEL (Life Baron), Naren Babubhai Patel; cr. 1999. Born 11 May 1938. Son of Babubhai and Lalita Patel; educated Government Secondary School, Dar Es Salaam, Tanzania; Harrow High School; St Andrews University (MB ChB 1964). Married Dr Helen Dally 1970 (twin sons 1 daughter). *Trades Union:* Member BMA. *Career:* Consultant Obstetrician, Ninewells Hospital, Dundee 1974–; Honorary Professor, Dundee University; Member, Armed Forces Pay Review Body. Member: Science and Technology Sub-Committee II (Aircraft Cabin Environment) 2000–02, Science and Technology Sub-Committee IIA (Human Genetic Databases) 2000–01, Science and Technology Sub-Committee: I (Fighting Infection) 2002–, II (Innovations in Computer Processors/Microprocessing) 2002; Chair Sub-Committee II (Science and the Regional Development Agencies) 2003–. President Elect, European Association of Obstetricians and Gynaecologists; Vice-President International Federation of Obstetrics and Gynaecology. President, Royal College of Obstetricians 1985–94; Chair, Academy of Medical Royal Colleges 1986–98; Council, General Medical Council 1998–; Chair, Specialist Training Authority of Medicine 1998–2001. Numerous honorary degrees. Chair, Clinical Standards Board of Scotland 1999–. Kt 1997. FMedSci; MB ChB; FRCOG; FRSE; MD(hc). *Publications:* On maternal/Foetal medicine, epidemiology, obstetrics, gynaecology, etc. *Special Interests:* Women's Health, Higher Education, Regulation of Medicine, Ethnic Minority Issues, Standards in Medicine. *Recreations:* Walking, golf, travel. Raised to the peerage as Baron Patel, of Dunkeld in Perth and Kinross 1999. The Lord Patel, House of Lords, London, SW1A 0PW *Tel:* 020 7219 8702 *E-mail:* npatel@sol.co.uk.

PATEL OF BLACKBURN, LORD　　　　　　　　　　　　　　Labour

PATEL OF BLACKBURN (Life Baron), Adam Hafejee Patel; cr. 2000. Born 7 June 1940. Son of late Hafejee Ismail Patel and of Aman Hafejee Patel; educated The Pioneer High School, Bharuch, Gujarat, India; MS Baroda University, India (Bachelor of Commerce). Married Ayesha 1964 (4 sons 4 daughters). *Career:* Retired Managing Director, clothing manufacturing company; Director: East Lancashire Training Enterprise Council, Enterprise plc. Member, CPA. Former President, Lancashire Council of Mosques; Vice-President, Blackburn Community Relations Council; Counsellor, Muslim Council of Britain. Honorary Fellowship: Boston Institute, Central Lancashire. *Special Interests:* Community and Social Work, Education, Race Relations, Economy and Regeneration. *Recreations:* Gardening, watching football and cricket. *Sportsclubs:* Blackburn Rovers Football Club. Raised to the peerage as Baron Patel of Blackburn, of Langho in the County of Lancashire 2000. The Lord Patel of Blackburn, House of Lords, London, SW1A 0PW *Tel:* 020 7219 8652.

DodOnline
An Electronic Directory without rival . . .

Peers' biographies and photographs available with daily updates *via* the internet

For a *free* trial, call Yasmin Mirza, Aby Farsoun or Michael Mand on 020 7630 7643

PATTEN, LORD

Conservative

PATTEN (Life Baron), John Haggitt Charles Patten; cr. 1997. Born 17 July 1945. Son of late Jack Patten; educated Wimbledon College; Sidney Sussex College, Cambridge (MA, PhD). Married Louise Alexandra Virginia Charlotte Rowe 1978 (1 daughter). Oxford City Councillor 1973–76. *Career:* Oxford University: University lecturer 1969–79, Fellow and tutor, Hertford College 1972–81, Supernumary Fellow, Hertford College 1981–94; Investment banker and company director 1995–. *House of Commons:* MP (Conservative) for Oxford 1979–83 and for Oxford West and Abingdon 1983–97; PPS to the Ministers of State at the Home Office 1980; Parliamentary Under-Secretary of State for: Northern Ireland 1981–83, Health 1983–85; Minister of State for: Housing, Urban Affairs and Construction, Department of Environment 1985–87, Home Office 1987–92; Secretary of State for Education 1992–94. Hon. Fellow, Harris Manchester College, Oxford. PC 1990. Liveryman, Drapers' Company. *Publications:* Co-editor *The Conservative Opportunity* 1976; *Things to Come: The Tories in the 21st Century*, 1995, and other volumes. *Recreations:* Talking with my wife and daughter. Raised to the peerage as Baron Patten, of Wincanton in the County of Somerset 1997. Rt Hon the Lord Patten, House of Lords, London, SW1A 0PW *Tel:* 020 7219 5353.

PAUL, LORD

Labour

PAUL (Life Baron), Swraj Paul; cr. 1996. Born 18 February 1931. Son of late Payare Paul and of Mongwati Paul; educated Foreman Christian College, Lahore; Punjab University (BSc physics, chemistry and maths 1949); Massachusetts Institute of Technology (BSc, MSc 1952, mechanical engineering). Married Aruna Vij 1956 (3 sons 1 daughter and 1 daughter deceased). Member, London Development Agency 2000–. *Career:* Partner in family firm in India, Apeejay Surrendra Group 1953; Came to the UK in 1966, establishing first business Natural Gas Tubes Ltd; Caparo Group Ltd formed in 1978; Chair: Caparo Group Ltd 1978–; Caparo Industries plc 1981–; Caparo Inc. USA 1988–. Chancellor, Wolverhampton University 1999–; Thames Valley University: Pro-Chancellor 1998–2000, Chancellor 2000–01. Member, Select Committees on: European Communities Sub-Committee B (Energy, Industry and Transport) 1997–2001, Monetary Policy of the Bank of England/Economic Affairs 1998–. Member, Parliamentarians for Global Action. President, BISPA (British Iron and Steel Producers Association) 1994–95; Vice-President, Engineering Employers Federation 1997–. Corporate Leadership Award, MIT 1987. Eleven honorary doctorates from England, Switzerland, Russia and USA. Founder and Chair, Ambika Paul Foundation; Piggy Bank Kids. Padma Bhushan (Government of India) 1983. Freeman, City of London 1998. *Publications: Indira Gandhi,* 1984; *Beyond Boundaries* (autobiography), 1998. *Sportsclubs:* Royal Calcutta Turf, Royal Calcutta Golf, Cricket of India (Bombay). *Clubs:* MCC, Royal Automobile. Raised to the peerage as Baron Paul, of Marylebone in the City of Westminster 1996. The Lord Paul, Caparo Group Ltd, Caparo House, 103 Baker Street, London, W1U 6LN *Tel:* 020 7486 1417.

PEARSON OF RANNOCH, LORD

Conservative

PEARSON OF RANNOCH (Life Baron), Malcolm Everard MacLaren Pearson; cr. 1990. Born 20 July 1942. Son of late Colonel John MacLaren Pearson; educated Eton College. Married Francesca Frua de Angeli 1965 (1 daughter) (divorced 1970); married Hon. Mary Charteris 1977 (2 daughters) (divorced 1995); married Caroline St Vincent Rose 1997. *Career:* Founded Pearson Webb Springbett (PWS) Group of reinsurance brokers 1964, currently Chairman. Member, House of Lords Select Committee on the European Communities and Sub-Committee on Social Affairs and the Environment 1992–96. Hon. President, RESCARE (The National Society for Mentally Handicapped People in Residential Care) 1994–; Co-founder, Global Britain; Hon President, Register of Chinese Herbal Medicine. Hon. LLD from CNAA 1992. Founded Rannoch Trust 1984. Member, Council for National Academic Awards 1983–93, Hon. Treasurer 1986–93.

Special Interests: European Union, Mental Handicap, Education, Scottish Highlands. *Recreations:* Stalking, fishing, golf. *Sportsclubs:* Swinley Forest Golf. *Clubs:* White's. Raised to the peerage as Baron Pearson of Rannoch, of Bridge of Gaur in the District of Perth and Kinross 1990. The Lord Pearson of Rannoch, House of Lords, London, SW1A 0PW; Office: PWS Holdings plc, 52 Minories, London, EC3N 1JJ *Tel:* 020 7480 6622.

PEEL, EARL   Conservative

PEEL (3rd Earl, UK), William James Robert Peel; cr. 1929. 4th Viscount Peel (UK) 1895; Viscount Clanfield (UK) 1929; 8th Bt of Drayton Manor (GB) 1800. Born 3 October 1947. Son of 2nd Earl; educated Ampleforth College; Tours University, France; Royal Agricultural College, Cirencester. Married Veronica Naomi Timpson 1973 (1 son 1 daughter) (divorced 1987); married Hon. Mrs. Charlotte Hambro, née Soames 1989 (1 daughter). DL, North Yorkshire 1998–. *House of Lords:* First entered House of Lords 1969; Elected hereditary peer 1999–. Former member, Yorkshire Dales National Parks Committee; Chair, North of England Grouse Research Project 1979–96; Member, The Moorland Association Executive Committee 1988–; President: Gun Trade Association, Yorkshire Wildlife Trust. President, The Game Conservancy; Council Member, Nature Conservancy Council 1989–95. Member, Council of the Duchy of Cornwall 1993–; Lord Warden of the Stannaries, Duchy of Cornwall 1994–; Vice-Chairman, Standing Committee on Country Sports. *Recreations:* Shooting, cricket, photography, ornithology. *Clubs:* White's. The Earl Peel, DL, Eelmire, Masham, Ripon, HG4 4PF *Tel:* 01465 688801 *Fax:* 01465 688802.

PENDRY, LORD   Labour

PENDRY (Life Baron), Thomas Pendry; cr 2001. Born 10 June 1934. Son of late Leonard E. Pendry; educated St Augustine's School, Ramsgate; Plater Hall, Oxford University. Married Moira Ann Smith 1966 (separated 1983) (1 son 1 daughter). *Trades Union:* Member AEEU. Councillor, Paddington Council 1962–65. *Career:* Steward, British Boxing Board of Control 1999–. *House of Commons:* Member for Stalybridge and Hyde 1970–2001; Under-Secretary of State Northern Ireland 1978–79. Opposition Whip 1971–74. Opposition Frontbench Spokesperson for: Northern Ireland 1979–82, Regional Affairs and Devolution 1982–92, National Heritage (Sport and Tourism) 1992–97. Member, Council of Europe and Western European Union 1973–75. Chair, Derby Labour Party 1966. Fellow, Industry and Parliament Trust; President, Football Foundation. Middleweight Colonial champion, Hong Kong 1957; Boxed for Oxford University 1957–59; President, Stalybridge Public Band. PC 2001. Freeman, Borough of Tameside (Lord Mottram of Longendale). *Special Interests:* Industrial Relations, Housing, Sport, Recreation, Finance, Social Security, Environment. *Recreations:* Watching all sport, meeting sportspersons. *Sportsclubs:* Lord's Taverners. *Clubs:* Wig and Pen, Vincent's; Lord's Taverners; MCC. Raised to the peerage as Baron Pendry, of Stalybridge in the County of Greater Manchester 2001. Rt Hon the Lord Pendry, House of Lords, London, SW1A 0PW *Tel:* 020 7219 4590 *Fax:* 020 7219 4419 *E-mail:* pendryt@parliament.uk.

PERRY OF SOUTHWARK, BARONESS   Conservative

PERRY OF SOUTHWARK (Life Baroness), Pauline Perry; cr. 1991. Born 15 October 1931. Daughter of late John and Elizabeth Welch; educated Wolverhampton Girls' High School; Girton College, Cambridge (BA moral sciences (philosophy) 1952, MA). Married George Perry 1952 (3 sons 1 daughter). *Career:* Secondary school history teacher, Staffordshire 1953–55; Philosophy lecturer: University of Manitoba, Canada 1956–59, University of Massachusetts, USA 1960–62; High school teacher, Andover, Massachusetts 1959–61; Part-time philosophy lecturer, Exeter University 1962–65; Part-time education lecturer, Oxford University 1966–70; HM Inspector, Department of Education and Science 1970–74; Staff Inspector, HM Inspectorate, responsible for: teacher training 1975–78 higher education 1978–81; Chief Inspector, HM Inspectorate, responsible for advice to Ministers on general higher education, research, LEA finance, teacher training and international relations 1981–86; Vice-Chancellor and Chief Executive, South Bank Polytechnic/University 1987–93; Chair, South Bank University Enterprises Ltd 1989–93; Member, Board of Directors, Greater London Enterprise 1990–91; Director, South Bank Arts Centre 1991–94; President, Lucy Cavendish College, Cambridge University 1994–2001; Member, Economic and Social Research Council 1989–93; Chair Church of England Review of the Crown Appointments Commission 1999–2001. Pro-Chancellor, Surrey University 2001–. Member: Select Committees on: Science and Technology 1992–97, Scrutiny of Delegated Powers 1993–97, Relations between Central and Local Government 1995–96, Joint Committee on Human Rights 2001–, Stem Cell Research 2001–02, Ecclesiastcal Committee 2002–, Religious Offences Committee 2002–. Member, Association of Conservative Peers 1991–, Executive Committee 2003–; President, Cambridge City Conservative Association 1998–. Member, IPU. British Council Committee on International Co-operation in Higher Education 1989–96 Chair, DTI Export Group for Education and Training 1993–98; Member: Overseas Projects Board, DTI 1993–98, British-Thai Business Group, Singapore-British Group, Korean Partnership, Korean Advisory Group, UK-Korean Forum for the Future, British-Israel Business Group, Indo-British Business Group. Rector's Warden, Southwark Cathedral 1990–94; Member of the Court, Bath University 1991–98; Member: British-Thai Business Group 1993–2000, Singapore-British Business Group 1993–98; Vice-President, City and Guilds of London Institute 1994–99; Member: Korea Trade Advisory Group 1995–2002, British-Israel Business Group 1995–98; Member, Board of Patrons of the Royal Society Appeal 1996–99; Chair, Friends of Southwark Cathedral 1996–2002; Governor (Board Member), English Speaking Union 1997–2003; Member: Indo-British Partnership 1997–99, UK-Korea Forum for the Future 1999–; Patron: British Youth Opera, Women's Engineering Society, Alzheimers Research Trust; Chair, Nuffield Council on Bio-Ethics Inquiry into the use of Animals in Scientific Experiments. Companion of the Chartered Management Institute. Thirteen honorary doctorates and fellowships. Trustee: Cambridge Foundation, Southwark Cathedral Millennium Project; Non-Executive Board Member, Addenbrooke's NHS Trust 1999–. Member: British Council's Committee on International Co-operation in Higher Education 1987–96, Economic and Social Research Council 1988–91; Academic Adviser, Home Office, Police Training Council 1990–92; Chair, DTI Committee for Education and Training Exports 1993–98; Member, Citizen's Charter Advisory Panel 1993–97; Chair, Charter Mark Judging Panel 1997–; Member Ecclesiastical Committee 2002–; President: Council for Independent Further Education, Westminster and City Branch of the Chartered Management Institute, Foundation for Higher Education. Hon. Fellow: College of Preceptors 1987, Royal Society of Arts 1988, Girton College, Cambridge 1995; City and Guilds London Institute 1999; Lucy Cavendish College, Cambridge 2001; Member, Institute of Directors; Companion, Institute of Management (now Chartered Management Institute). Freedom, City of London 1991. Liveryman, Worshipful Company of Bakers. *Publications:* Has published four books, chapters in ten other books and a wide variety of articles in educational journals and in the national press, and has participated in international seminars and study visits on education. *Special Interests:* Education, International Affairs. *Recreations:* Gardening, walking, listening to music, French countryside, food and literature. *Clubs:* Institute of Directors. Raised to the peerage as Baroness Perry of Southwark, of Charlbury in the County of Oxfordshire 1991. The Baroness Perry of Southwark, House of Lords, London, SW1A 0PW *Tel:* 020 7219 5474 *Fax:* 020 7738 2911 *Tel:* 020 7223 5039 *E-mail:* pp204@supanet.com.

PESTON, LORD   Labour

PESTON (Life Baron), Maurice Harry Peston; cr. 1987. Born 19 March 1931. Son of late Abraham and Yetta Peston; educated Belle Vue High School, Bradford; Hackney Downs School; London School of Economics (BSc economics); Princeton University, USA. Married Helen Conroy 1958 (2 sons 1 daughter). *Career:* Scientific and Senior Scientific Officer, Army Operations Research Group 1954–57, Assistant Lecturer, Lecturer, Reader in Economics, London School of Economics 1957–65; Economic Adviser, HM Treasury 1962–64; Professor of Economics, Queen Mary College, London University 1965–88, Emeritus Professor 1988–; Editor, Applied Economics 1972–; Special Adviser to Secretary of State for: Education and Science 1974–75, Prices 1976–79; Chairman: Pools Panel 1991–94, National Foundation for Education Research 1991–97, Office of Health Economics 1991–. Pro-Chancellor, Gyosei International College. Opposition Spokesman on: Energy 1987–97, Education and Science 1987–97, Treasury 1990–92, Trade and Industry 1992–97. Chair, Select Committees on: House of Lords Offices Refreshments Sub-Committee 1993–97, Monetary Policy of the Bank of England/Economic Affairs 1998–. Member, Council Royal Pharmaceutical Society of Great Britain 1986–96; Vice President, Speakability. Hon. DEd, University of East London 1984; Hon. Fellow: Portsmouth University 1987, Queen Mary and Westfield College 1992, London School of Economics 1995. Member, CNNA 1967–73, Chairman, Economics Board; Member, SSRC 1976–79, Chairman, Economics Board. Hon. Member, Royal Pharmaceutical Society of Great Britain 1996. *Publications: Elementary Matrices for Economics*, 1969; *Public Goods and the Public Sector*, 1972; *Theory of Macroeconomic Policy*, 1974; *Whatever Happened to Macroeconomics?*, 1980; *The British Economy*, 1982. Raised to the peerage as Baron Peston, of Mile End in Greater London 1987. The Lord Peston, House of Lords, London, SW1A 0PW *Tel:* 020 7219 3122 *E-mail:* pestonhh@parliament.uk.

PETERBOROUGH, LORD BISHOP OF   Non-affiliated

PETERBOROUGH (Bishop of), Ian Patrick Martyn Cundy. Born 23 April 1945. Son of (Henry) Martyn Cundy and Kathleen Ethel, née Hemmings; educated Monkton Combe School; Trinity College, Cambridge (BA mathematics and theology 1967, MA); Tyndale Hall, Bristol (General Ordination Exam 1969). Married Josephine Katherine Boyd 1969 (2 sons 1 daughter). Chair Peterborough South Bank Partnership 2001–2003. *Career:* Assistant curate, Christ Church, New Malden 1969–73; Lecturer and chaplain, Oak Hill College, Southgate 1973–77; Team rector, Mortlake and East Sheen 1978–83; Warden, Cranmer Hall, St John's College, Durham 1983–92; Bishop of Lewes, Diocese of Chichester 1992–96; Bishop of Peterborough 1996–; Took his seat in the House of Lords 2001. Trustee: Oakham School 1996–, Uppingham School 1996–, Archdeacon Johnson Almshouse Charity 1996–; President St. Johns College, Durham 1998–. *Publications: Ephesians–2 Thessalonians* (Bible Study Commentary), 1981; *Obeying Christ in a Changing World, Vol 2 The People of God* (Editor and Contributor), 1977. *Special Interests:* Education, Rural Affairs. *Recreations:* Music, walking, restoring clocks and vintage cars. *Clubs:* Farmers Club. Rt Rev the Lord Bishop of Peterborough, The Palace, Peterborough, Cambridgeshire, PE1 1YA *Tel:* 01733 562492 *Fax:* 01733 890077 *E-mail:* bishop@peterborough-diocese.org.uk.

PEYTON OF YEOVIL, LORD   Conservative

PEYTON OF YEOVIL (Life Baron), John Wynne William Peyton; cr. 1983. Born 13 February 1919. Son of late Ivor Eliot Peyton; educated Eton College; Trinity College, Oxford (MA law 1945). Married Diana Clinch 1947 (1 son 1 daughter and 1 son deceased) (divorced 1966); married Mrs Mary Cobbold, née Wyndham 1966. Served 1939–45 with 15/19 Hussars (POW Germany 1940–45). *Career:* Called to the Bar, Inner Temple June 1945; Chairman, Texas Instruments 1974–90; Non-Executive Chairman, British Alcan Aluminium 1987–91, President 1991–97. *House of Commons:* Contested (Conservative) Bristol Central 1950; MP (Conservative) for Yeovil 1951–1983; Parliamentary Secretary to Ministry of Power 1962–64; Minister of Transport June-October 1970; Minister of Transport Industries 1970–74. Treasurer, The Zoological Society of London 1984–91. Hon LittD (University of East Anglia) 2002. PC 1970. *Publications: Without Benefit of Laundry*, 1997; *Solly Zuckerman: A Scientist out of the Ordinary*, 2001. *Clubs:* Boodle's, Pratt's, Beefsteak. Raised to the peerage as Baron Peyton of Yeovil, of Yeovil in the County of Somerset 1983. Rt Hon the Lord Peyton of Yeovil, 6 Temple West Mews, West Square, London, SE11 4TJ *Tel:* 020 7582 3611; The Old Malt House, Hinton St George, Somerset, TA17 8SE *Tel:* 01460 73618.

PHILLIPS OF SUDBURY, LORD   Liberal Democrat

PHILLIPS OF SUDBURY (Life Baron), Andrew Wyndham Phillips; cr. 1998. Born 15 March 1939. Son of Alan Phillips and Dorothy, née Wyndham; educated Sudbury, Culford School, Uppingham School; Trinity Hall, Cambridge (BA economics and law 1962). Married Penelope Ann Bennett 1968 (1 son 2 daughters). *Trades Union:* Member Law Society. *Career:* Solicitor 1964; Established own practice, Bates, Wells & Braithwaite (London) 1970; Director of several commercial companies including Faraday Underwriting Limited; Chair, Gough Hotels; Freelance journalist and broadcaster: *Legal Eagle* on BBC Radio 2 Jimmy Young Show 1976–2001. Member, Joint Select Committee on Consolidation of Bills 2000–; Member, Select Committee on

House of Lords' Offices Administration and Works Sub-committee 2001–. Co-Founder and Chair, Legal Action Group 1971–6; Initiated: Lawyers in the Community Scheme 1987; Founder and President: Citizenship Foundation 1989–, Solicitors Pro Bono Group 1996–; Member: Charter 88 Committee from inception until 1994, National Lottery Charities Board 1994–96; President, British-Iranian Chamber of Commerce 2001–. Privacy International 'Winston' Parliamentarian of Year 2001. Trustee of: Scott Trust (owner of Guardian/Observer), 1991–2001, Gainsborough's House, Public Interest Research Centre, Phillips Fund. Contested: Harwich (Lab) 1970 general election, expelled as Lab candidate for North Norfolk 1973, Saffron Walden 1977 by-election (Lib) and 1979 general election (Lib), North East Essex 1979 European Parliament election (Lib), Gainsborough (Lib/All) 1983 general election. OBE 1996. *Publications: The Living Law, Charitable Status – A Practical Handbook* (5th edition), *Justice Beyond Reach*; Co-author: *Charity Investment – Law and Practice*. *Special Interests:* Voluntary Sector, Legal Services, Magistracy, Citizenship, Crime/Punishment, Libertarian Issues, Rural/Country Town Problems, Theatre/Arts, Tourism, Iran/Middle East, Heritage matters. *Recreations:* Theatre, local history (especially Suffolk), arts, architecture (especially parish churches), golf, walking, reading, family and friends. Raised to the peerage as Baron Phillips of Sudbury, of Sudbury in the County of Suffolk 1998. The Lord Phillips of Sudbury, OBE, House of Lords, London, SW1A 0PW *Tel:* 020 7219 8510 *E-mail:* a.phillips@bateswells.co.uk.

PHILLIPS OF WORTH MATRAVERS, LORD — Crossbencher

PHILLIPS OF WORTH MATRAVERS (Life Baron), Nicholas Addison Phillips; cr. 1999. Born 21 January 1938. Son of Michael Pennington Phillips and Dora Phillips, née Hassid; educated Bryanston School; King's College, Cambridge (BA law 1961, MA). Married Christylle Marie-Thérèse Rouffiac, née Doreau 1972 (2 daughters and 1 stepson 1 stepdaughter). Royal Navy national service commissioned RNVR 1956–58. *Career:* Called to the Bar, Middle Temple (Harmsworth Scholar) 1962; In practice at the Bar 1962–87; Junior Counsel to the Ministry of Defence and to Treasury in Admiralty matters 1973–78; QC 1978; Member, Panel of Wreck Commissioners 1979; Recorder 1982–87; Judge of the High Court of Justice (Queen's Bench Division) 1987–95; Chairman, Law Advisory Committee, British Council 1991–97; Chairman, Council of Legal Education 1992–97; Vice-President, British Maritime Law Association 1993–; Lord Justice of Appeal 1995–98; Chairman of the BSE Inquiry 1998–2000; Advisory Council of Institute of European and Comparative Law 1999–; Council of Management, British Institute of International and Comparative Law 1999–; Chairman Lord Chancellor's Advisory Committee on Public Records 2000–; Lord of Appeal in Ordinary 1999–2000; Master of the Rolls 2000–; Head of Civil Justice. Governor, Bryanston School 1975–, Chairman of Governors 1981–. Hon. LLD, Exeter 1998; Hon. Fellow of The Society for Advanced Legal Studies 1999; Visitor Nuffield College, Oxford 2000, Visitor University College, London 2000; Hon. Fellow King's College Cambridge 2003; Doctor of Civil Law City University, London 2003. Kt 1987; PC 1995. *Recreations:* Sea, mountains. *Clubs:* Brooks's. Raised to the peerage as Baron Phillips of Worth Matravers, of Belsize Park in the London Borough of Camden 1999. Rt Hon the Lord Phillips of Worth Matravers, Royal Courts of Justice, Strand, London, WC2A 2LL *E-mail:* mor@scgmor.demon.co.uk.

PIKE, BARONESS — Conservative

PIKE (Life Baroness), (Irene) Mervyn Pike; cr. 1974. Born 16 September 1918, Daughter of late Samuel Pike, and late Alice Goodhead; educated Hunmanby Hall, East Yorks; Reading University (BA). Served in WAAF 1941–46. *Career:* Managing Director, Clokie and Co. Ltd 1946–60; Director, Watts, Blake, Bearne 1964–89. *House of Commons:* Contested (Conservative): Pontefract (Yorkshire) 1951, Leek (Staffordshire) 1955 general elections; MP (Conservative) for Melton 1956–74; Assistant Postmaster-General 1959–63; Joint Parliamentary Under-Secretary of State, Home Office 1963–64. National Chairman, WRVS 1974–81. Chairman, Broadcasting Complaints Commission 1981–85. DBE 1981. *Recreations:* Gardening, reading, walking. Raised to the peerage as Baroness Pike, of Melton in the County of Leicestershire 1974. The Baroness Pike, DBE, Queen's House Nursing Home, Golf Course Road, Kelso, Roxburghshire, TD5 7NS.

PILKINGTON OF OXENFORD, LORD   Conservative

PILKINGTON OF OXENFORD (Life Baron), Peter Pilkington; cr. 1996. Born 5 September 1933. Son of late Frank and Doris Pilkington; educated Dame Allans School, Newcastle upon Tyne; Jesus College, Cambridge (MA history 1955). Married Helen Wilson 1966 (died 1997) (2 daughters). *Trades Union:* Member, National Association of Head Teachers. *Career:* Schoolmaster, Tanganyika 1955–57; Ordained 1959; Curate in Bakewell, Derbyshire 1959–62; Schoolmaster, Eton College 1962–75, Master in College 1965–75; Headmaster, The King's School, Canterbury 1975–86; High Master, St Paul's School 1986–92; Hon. Canon of Canterbury Cathedral 1975–90, currently Canon Emeritus; Member, Parole Board 1990–95; Chair, Broadcasting Complaints Commission 1992–96. Opposition Spokesperson on Education and Employment 1997–98. Co-opted Member European Union Sub-committee F (Social Affairs, Education and Home Affairs) 1997–2000; Member Joint Committee on Draft Communications Bill 2002. Member Ecclesiastical Committee 1997–. *Clubs:* Beefsteak, Garrick. Raised to the peerage as Baron Pilkington of Oxenford, of West Dowlish in the County of Somerset 1996. Rev Canon the Lord Pilkington of Oxenford, Oxenford House, Nr Ilminster, Somerset, TA19 OPP *Tel:* 01460 52813; House of Lords, London, SW1A 0PW *Tel:* 020 7219 3402.

PITKEATHLEY, BARONESS   Labour

PITKEATHLEY (Life Baroness), Jill Elizabeth Pitkeathley; cr. 1997. Born 4 January 1940. Daughter of Roland and May Bisson; educated Ladies' College, Guernsey; Bristol University (BA economics 1960). Married W. Pitkeathley 1961 (1 son 1 daughter) (divorced 1978). *Career:* Social Worker 1961–68; Voluntary Service Co-ordinator, West Berkshire Health Authority 1970–83; National Consumer Council 1983–86; Director, National Council for Carers 1986 until merger with Association of Carers 1988; Adviser to Griffith's Review of Community Care 1986–88; Chief Executive, Carers National Association 1988–98, Vice-President 2001–; Vice-President, Community Council for Berkshire 1990–98; President 1998–; Chair, New Opportunities Fund 1998–. *House of Lords:* Deputy Speaker 2002–; Deputy Chair of Committees 2002–. Member: Select Committee on Liaison 2000–, House of Lords' Offices Refreshment Sub-committee 2001–. Patron, Bracknell CVS; President: National Centre for Volunteering, National Institute for Social Work; Vice-President, Parkinson's Disease Society; Patron: Prostate Cancer Charity, Colon Cancer Concern. DL Bristol 2002, DL London Metropolitan 2002. Interim Chair, General Social Care Council. OBE 1993. Hon. RCGP. *Publications: When I Went Home*, 1978; *Mobilising Voluntary Resources*, 1984; *Supporting Volunteers*, 1985; *It's my duty, isn't it?*, 1989; *Age Gap Relationships*, 1996 (with David Emerson); *Only Child*, 1994 (with David Emerson). *Special Interests:* Health, Social Care, Voluntary Sector, Charities. *Recreations:* Gardening, grand-children, writing. Raised to the peerage as Baroness Pitkeathley, of Caversham in the Royal County of Berkshire 1997. The Baroness Pitkeathley, OBE, House of Lords, London, SW1A 0PW *Tel:* 020 7219 0358 *E-mail:* pitkeathleyj@parliament.uk.

PLANT OF HIGHFIELD, LORD   Labour

PLANT OF HIGHFIELD (Life Baron), Raymond Plant; cr. 1992. Born 19 March 1945. Son of late Stanley Plant and of Marjorie Plant; educated Havelock School, Grimsby; King's College, London (BA philosophy 1966); Hull University (PhD political philosophy 1971). Married Katherine Sylvia Dixon 1967 (3 sons). *Trades Union:* Member AUT. *Career:* Lecturer, then senior lecturer in philosophy, Manchester University 1967–79; Philosophy lecturer in several universities 1981–91; Professor of Politics, Southampton University 1979–94; Master, St Catherine's College, Oxford 1994–2000; Professor of: European Politics Southampton University 2000–02, Law and Philosophy King's College, London 2002–. Pro-Chancellor, Southampton University 1996–2000. Opposition Spokesperson for Home Affairs 1992–96. Member, Select Committee on Relations between Central and Local Government 1995–96; Member Sub-committee E European

Communities Committee 2000–. Chairman, Labour Party Commission on Electoral Systems 1991–93. President, National Council for Voluntary Organisations (NCVO) 1998–2002. Hon. DLitt: Hull University, London Guildhall; Fellow Cardiff University. Chair Hope Medical Trust, Southampton; Chair Centrepoint; Chair Southampton University Development Trust. FRSA 1992. *Publications:* A contributor to *The Times*, 1988–91; *Hegel*, 1974; *Community and Ideology*, 1974; *Political Philosophy and Social Welfare*, 1981; *Philosophy, Politics and Citizenship*, 1984; *Conservative Capitalism in Britain and the United States: a critical appraisal*, 1988; *Modern Political Thought*, 1991; *Politics, Theology and History*, 2001. *Recreations:* Music, opera, reading. *Clubs:* Athenaeum. Raised to the peerage as Baron Plant of Highfield, of Weelsby in the County of Humberside 1992. Professor the Lord Plant of Highfield, School of Law, King's College, Strand, London, WC2R 2CS *Tel:* 020 7836 5454 *Fax:* 020 7848 2465.

PLATT OF WRITTLE, BARONESS   Conservative

PLATT OF WRITTLE (Life Baroness), Beryl Catherine Platt; cr. 1981. Born 18 April 1923. Daughter of late Ernest and Dorothy Myatt; educated Westcliff High School for Girls; Girton College, Cambridge (BA mechanical sciences 1943, MA). Married Stewart Sydney Platt 1949 (died 2003) (1 son 1 daughter). Councillor, Chelmsford RDC 1959–73; Essex County Council 1965–85; Alderman 1969–74; Chair, Education Committee 1971–80; Vice-Chairman, County Council 1980–83; DL, County of Essex 1983. *Career:* Technical Assistant: Hawker Aircraft 1943–46, British European Airways 1946–49; Chairman, Equal Opportunities Commission 1983–88. First Chancellor, Middlesex University 1993–2000. Member Select Committees on: Murder and Life Imprisonment 1988–89, Science and Technology 1982–85, 1990–94, 1996–2001, Relations between Central and Local Government 1995–96, Science and Technology Sub-Committee II (Science and Society) 1999–2000, Sub-Committee II (Aircraft Cabin Environment) 2000–01, Stem Cell Research 2001–02. Member, Association of Conservative Peers. Member: European Communities Advisory Committee on Equal Opportunities for Women and Men 1983–88; UK Delegation to Nairobi for UN Decade for Women World Conference 1985. Member of court four universities since 1964; Member numerous organisations concerned with higher education, science, engineering, including: Foundation for Science and Technology 1989–, Member of Council 1991–97; Patron: Women into Science and Engineering 1995–, Women in Banking and Finance until 2000, and local charities. City and Guilds of London Insignia Award 1988. 21 honorary doctorates and fellowships. Trustee, Homerton College 1970–81. CBE 1978. Hon. FInst of Training and Development; Hon. Fellowship,: Royal Aeronautical Society 1994, Royal College of Preceptors 1986; Fellow, Fellowship of Engineering (FREng) (now Royal Academy of Engineering) 1987; European Engineer (EurIng) 1987; Hon. Fellow: Women's Engineering Society 1989, Smallpiece Trust 1989; Fellow, Institution of Gas Engineers 1990; Hon. Fellow: Institute of Civil Engineers 1991, Institute of Structural Engineers 1991, Institute of Mechanical Engineers; Companion: Institute of Energy, Institute of Personnel Development 1995. Freeman, City of London 1988. Liveryman, Worshipful Company of Engineers 1988, Assistant to the Court 1996–2002; 2002 Assistant Emeritus of the Court. *Special Interests:* Education, Women's Opportunities in Engineering, Local Government. *Recreations:* Reading, swimming for pleasure, cookery. *Clubs:* United Oxford and Cambridge University. Raised to the peerage as Baroness Platt of Writtle, of Writtle in the County of Essex 1981. The Baroness Platt of Writtle, CBE, DL, House of Lords, London, SW1A 0PW *Tel:* 020 7219 3188.

PLUMB, LORD   Conservative

PLUMB (Life Baron), (Charles) Henry Plumb; cr. 1987. Born 27 March 1925. Son of late Charles Plumb; educated King Edward VI School, Nuneaton. Married Marjorie Dorothy Dunn 194/ (1 son 2 daughters). DL, Warwick 1977. *Career:* Member, Council, NFU 1959, Vice-President 1964–65; Deputy President 1966–69, President 1970–79; Member, Duke of Northumberland's Committee of Enquiry, Foot and Mouth Disease 1967–68; President, Comité des Organisations Professionnelles Agricoles de la CEE (COPA) 1975–77; Chairman, British Agricultural Council 1975–79; Non-Executive Director, Lloyds Bank, United Biscuits, Fisons 1979–94; MEP (Conservative) for Cotswolds 1979–99: Chairman, EP Agricultural Committee 1979–82; Chairman (Conservative) EDG, EP 1982–87, 1994–99; President, European Parliament 1987–89; Co-President, EU-ACP Joint Assembly 1994–99; Chairman, Agricultural Mortgage Corporation 1994–95.

Chancellor, Coventry University. President, International Federation of Agricultural Producers 1979–82; Chairman: International Agricultural Training Programme 1987–2001, International Policy Council on Agriculture, Food and Trade 1987–, Hon President. Member Council, NFU 1959, Vice-President 1964–65, Deputy President 1966–69, President 1970–79; President, Royal Agricultural Society of England 1977; Deputy to HRH The Prince of Wales 1978. Hon. Fellow, Wye College 1995; Five honorary doctorates. Henry Plumb Trust. Kt 1973; Knight Commander's Cross of the Order of Merit, Federal Republic of Germany 1976; Ordén de Merito, Portugal 1987; Order of Merit, Luxembourg 1988; Grand Cross of the Order of Civil Merit, Spain 1989; Grand Order of the Phoenix, Greece 1997; Medal Mediterraneum, European Institute, Florence. Freeman, City of London. Court Member, Farmers' Company; Hon. Liveryman, Worshipful Company of Fruiterers. *Publications: The Plumb Line*, Greycoat Press, 2001. *Clubs:* St Stephen's Constitutional. Raised to the peerage as Baron Plumb, of Coleshill in the County of Warwickshire 1987. The Lord Plumb, DL, Maxstoke, Coleshill, Warwickshire, B46 2QJ *Tel:* 01675 463133 *Fax:* 01675 464156 *E-mail:* plumbh@parliament.uk.

PLUMMER OF ST MARYLEBONE, LORD — Conservative

PLUMMER OF ST MARYLEBONE (Life Baron), (Arthur) Desmond Herne Plummer; cr. 1981. Born 25 May 1914. Son of late Arthur Herne and Janet Plummer, née McCormick; educated Hurstpierpoint College; College of Estate Management. Married Pat Holloway 1941 (died 1998) (1 daughter). Served Royal Engineers 1938–46, field and staff. Councillor, St Marylebone Borough Council 1952–65, Mayor 1958–59; London County Council for St Marylebone 1960–65; Inner London Education Authority 1964–76; Greater London Council for: Cities of London and Westminster 1964–73, St Marylebone 1973–76; Leader of GLC Opposition 1966–67, 1973–74; Leader of Council 1967–73; JP 1958; DL, Greater London 1970. *Career:* Executive Committee British Section of International Union of Local Authorities 1967–74; Chairman, Horserace Betting Levy Board 1974–82; Chairman, National Stud 1975–82; Chairman, National Employers' Life Assurance Association 1983–88; Chairman, Portman Building Society 1983–90, President 1990–. Member, Association of Conservative Peers. President, Metropolitan Association of Building Societies 1983–89; Member Court, University of London 1967–77. Member: South Bank Theatre Board 1964–74, Standing Conference on South East Planning 1967–74, Transport Co-ordinating Council for London 1967–69, Local Authority Conditions of Service Advisory Board 1967–71; Chairman, Horserace Betting Levy Board 1974–82. TD 1950; Kt 1971; KStJ 1986. FRSA; FRICS; Hon. FASI. The Worshipful Company of Tin Plate Workers Alias Wireworkers of London. *Publications: Time For Change in Greater London*, 1958; *Report to London*, 1970. *Special Interests:* Greater London. *Recreations:* Swimming, horseracing. *Sportsclubs:* Otter Swimming Club. *Clubs:* Carlton, MCC, Royal Automobile. Raised to the peerage as Baron Plummer of St Marylebone, of the City of Westminster 1981. The Lord Plummer of St Marylebone, TD, DL, 4 The Lane, Marlborough Place, London, NW8 0PN *Tel:* 020 7935 4914 *Fax:* 020 7224 3735 *E-mail:* plumerne@clara.co.uk.

PONSONBY OF SHULBREDE, LORD — Labour

PONSONBY OF SHULBREDE (4th Baron), Frederick Matthew Thomas Ponsonby; cr. 1930; (Life) Baron Ponsonby of Roehampton 2000. Born 27 October 1958. Son of 3rd Baron; educated Holland Park Comprehensive School; University College, Cardiff (BSc physics 1980); Imperial College, London (MSc DIC petroleum engineering 1983). *Trades Union:* Member MSF. Councillor, London Borough of Wandsworth 1990–94. *House of Lords:* First entered House of Lords 1990. Opposition Spokesperson for Education 1992–97. Member, Select Committees on: European Communities Sub-Committee C 1997–98, Science and Technology 1998–99, Science and Technology Sub-Committee II (Science and Society) 1999, Constitution 2001. Delegate to: Council of Europe 1997–2001, Western European Union 1997–2001; OSCE 2001–. FIMM. Created a life peer as Baron Ponsonby of Roehampton, of Shulbrede in the County of West Sussex 2000. The Lord Ponsonby of Shulbrede, House of Lords, London, SW1A 0PW *Tel:* 020 7219 0071.

Visit the Vacher Dod Website . . . www.DodOnline.co.uk

PORTSMOUTH, LORD BISHOP OF   Non-affiliated

PORTSMOUTH (Bishop of), Kenneth William Stevenson. Born 9 November 1949. Son of Frederik and Margrete Stevenson; educated Edinburgh Academy; Edinburgh University (MA classics 1970); Southampton University (PhD theology 1975); Manchester University (DD for theological writings 1987). Married Sarah Glover 1970 (1 son 3 daughters). Governor, Portsmouth University 1996–2003. *Career:* Ordained Deacon 1973; Priest 1974–; Assistant Curate, Grantham with Manthorpe 1973–76; Part-time lecturer, Lincoln Theological College 1975–80; Lecturer, Boston 1976–80; Chaplain and lecturer, Manchester University 1980–86; Team vicar, Whitworth, Manchester 1980–82; Team rector, Whitworth, Manchester 1982–86; Visiting professor, University of Notre Dame, Indiana, USA 1983; Rector, Holy Trinity and St Mary's, Guildford 1986–95; Secretary, Anglo-Nordic Baltic Theological Conference, 1986–97 Member: Church of England Liturgical Commission 1986–96, Faith and Order Advisory Group 1991–96; Bishop of Portsmouth 1995–; Member, Church of England Doctrine Commission 1996–2003; Chair, Anglo-Nordic-Baltic Theological Conference 1997–; Took his seat in the House of Lords 1999; Vice-Chair, Church of England Porvoo Panel 2000–; Chairman, Church of England Board of Education and National Society 2003–; Member, Archbishops' Council 2003–. Member: House of Lords Offices Committee 2001–02, Religious Offences Committee 2002–. Fellow, Royal Historical Society 1990. *Publications:* include: *Nuptial Blessing*, 1982; *Eucharist and Offering*, 1986; *Jerusalem Revisited*, 1988; *The First Rites*, 1989; *Covenant of Grace Renewed*, 1994; Co-author *The Mystery of the Eucharist in the Anglican Tradition*, 1995; *The Mystery of Baptism in the Anglican Tradition*, 1998; *All the Company of Heaven*, 1998; *Abba, Father: Understanding and Using the Lord's Prayer*, 2000; *Do This: The Shape, Meaning and Style of the Eucharist*, 2002; Co-editor *Love's Redeeming Work: The Anglican Quest for Holiness*, 2001; Contributor to: *Theology, Scottish Journal of Theology, La Maison-Dieu* (international journal of the study of the church); Reviewer in: *Theology, Journal of Theological Studies; Church Times; Expository Times. Special Interests:* Education, Asylum Seekers. *Recreations:* Historical biographies, thrillers, walking, piano, chinese cooking, Denmark. *Clubs:* Royal Yacht Squadron 1995–; Royal Naval Club, Portsmouth 1995–; Farmers' Club 1999–; Nobody's Friends 2001–. Rt Rev the Lord Bishop of Portsmouth, Bishopgrove, 26 Osborn Road, Fareham, Hampshire, PO16 7DQ *Tel:* 01329 280247 *Fax:* 01329 231538 *E-mail:* bishports@clara.co.uk.

POWELL OF BAYSWATER, LORD   Crossbencher

POWELL OF BAYSWATER (Life Baron), Charles David Powell; cr. 2000. Born 6 June 1941. Son of Air Vice Marshal John Powell, OBE; educated King's School, Canterbury; New College, Oxford (BA modern history 1963). Married Carla Bonardi 1964 (2 sons). *Career:* Entered Diplomatic Service 1963; Third Secretary, Foreign Office 1963–65; Second Secretary, Helsinki 1965–67; Foreign and Commonwealth Office 1968–71; First Secretary and Private Secretary to HM Ambassador, Washington 1971–74; First Secretary, Bonn 1974–77; Foreign and Commonwealth Office 1977–80 (Counsellor 1979, Special Counsellor for Rhodesia negotiations 1979–80); Counsellor, Office of UK Permanent Representative to European Communities 1980–83; Private Secretary to Margaret Thatcher as Prime Minister 1983–90; Private Secretary to John Major as Prime Minister 1990–91; Director: Matheson and Company 1990–, Mandarian Oriental Hotel Group 1990–, Jardine Matheson Holdings and associated companies 1991–2000, National Westminster Bank 1991–2000, J Rothschild Name Company 1992–2003, Said Holdings 1993–2000, Arjo-Wiggins Appleton 1993–2000, Louis-Vuitton-Moet-Hennessy 1995–, British Mediterranean Airways 1997–; Caterpillar Inc 2001–, Textron Inc 2001–; YELL Group 2002–; International Advisory Board: Textron Corporation, Rolls Royce, GEMS, Barrick Gold, Hicks Muse, Magna Corporation, HCL Technologies; Chair: Phillips De Pury Luxembourg 2000–, LVMH (UK) 2000–, Sagitta Asset Management 2001–; Director, Schindler Holdings 2003–. Co-opted member, European Union Sub-committee C (Common Foreign and Security Policy) 2000–. President, China-Britain Business Council 1990–; Chair Singapore British Business Council 1994–2001; Vice-chair, Atlantic Partnership 2001–. Trustee, Aspen Institute, USA 1995–; Chair, Trustees Oxford University Business School 1997–; Trustee, British Museum 2001–. KCMG 1990; Public Service Star (Singapore) 2001. *Special Interests:* Foreign Affairs, Defence, Intelligence, Trade. *Recreations:* Walking. Raised to the peerage as Baron Powell of Bayswater, of Canterbury in the County of Kent 2000. The Lord Powell of Bayswater, KCMG, c/o Sagitta Asset Management, 4th Floor, Berkeley Square House, Berkeley Square, London, W1J 6BL.

PRASHAR, BARONESS   Crossbencher

PRASHAR (Life Baroness), Usha Kumari Prashar; cr. 1999. Born 29 June 1948. Daughter of late Naurhia Lal and Durga Devi Prashar; educated Duchess Gloucester School, Nairobi, Kenya; Wakefield Girls' High School, Yorkshire; Leeds University (BA political science 1970); Glasgow University (DipSocAdmin 1971). Married Vijay Kumar Sharma 1973. *Career:* Conciliation officer, Race Relations Board 1971–75; Director, Runnymede Trust 1976–84; Fellow, Policy Studies Institute 1984–86; Director, National Council of Voluntary Organisations 1986–91; Part-time Civil Service Commissioner 1991–96; Chairman, Parole Board of England and Wales 1997–2000; First Civil Service Commissioner 2000–. Chancellor, De Montfort University 2000–. Member, Joint Committee on Human Rights. Board Member, Salzburg Seminar. Patron: Sickle Cell Society 1986–, Hon. Vice-President, Council for Overseas Student Affairs 1986–; Governor, De Montfort University 1996–; Tara Arts 1999–; Wise Thoughts 2002–. Hon. Fellow, Goldsmith's College, London University; Six honorary doctorates. Trustee, Camelot Foundation 1995–2000; Management Board King's Fund 1997–2002; Trustee, Ethnic Minority Foundation 1997–2002; Chairman, National Literacy Trust 2000–; Trustee, BBC World Service Trust 2002–. Member: Arts Council of Great Britain 1979–81, 1994–97, Study Commission on the Family 1980–83, Social Security Advisory Committee 1980–83, Executive Committee, Child Poverty Action Group 1984–85, London Food Commission 1984–90, BBC Educational Broadcasting Council 1987–89, Solicitor's Complaints Bureau 1989–90, Royal Commission on Criminal Justice 1991–93, Lord Chancellor's Advisory Committee on Legal Education and Conduct 1991–97, Board of Energy Saving Trust 1992–98, Non-executive Director: Channel Four 1992–98, Unite 2000–, Chair Royal Commonwealth Society 2002–. CBE 1994. FRSA. *Publications:* Has contributed to several publications on health and race relations. *Special Interests:* Education, Criminal Justice, Human Rights, Race Relations. *Recreations:* Golf, music, art, reading. *Sportsclubs:* Foxhills Golf Club. *Clubs:* Reform, Royal Commonwealth Society. Raised to the peerage as Baroness Prashar, of Runnymede in the County of Surrey 1999. The Baroness Prashar, CBE, First Civil Service Commissioner, 35 Great Smith Street, London, SW1P 3BQ *Tel:* 020 7276 2601 *E-mail:* baroness.prashar@cabinet-office.x.gsi.gov.uk.

PRIOR, LORD   Conservative

PRIOR (Life Baron), James Michael Leathes Prior; cr. 1987. Born 11 October 1927. Son of late Charles Bolingbroke Leathes Prior, JP; educated Charterhouse; Pembroke College, Cambridge (BA estate management 1950). Married Jane Primrose Gifford, née Lywood 1954 (3 sons 1 daughter). Commissioned Service Royal Norfolk Regiment 1946; Served in India and Germany. *Career:* Farmer and land agent 1950; Chair: The General Electric Company plc 1984–98, Allders Ltd 1984–94; Director: United Biscuits plc 1984–94, J Sainsbury 1984–94, Barclays Bank 1985–90; Member: Tenneco Europe Ltd (Advisory Committee) to 1998, American International Group (Advisory Council); Chairman: East Anglia Radio plc 1992–95, African Cargo Handling Ltd 1998–2000; Deputy Chairman, MSI Cellular Investments BV 2000–; Ascot Underwriting Ltd; Palgrave Farming Co Ltd; South Pickenham Estate Co Ltd. *House of Commons:* MP (Conservative) for: Lowestoft 1959–83, Waveney 1983–87; PPS to the: President of the Board of Trade 1962–63, Minister of Power 1963–64, Leader of the Opposition 1965–70; Minister of Agriculture, Fisheries and Food 1970–72; Lord President and Leader of the House 1972–74; Secretary of State for: Employment 1979–81, Northern Ireland 1981–1984. Conservative Spokesperson for Employment 1974–79. Chancellor, Anglia Polytechnic University 1993–99. Chairman, Arab-British Chamber of Commerce 1996–. Vice-Chairman, Conservative Party 1965, Deputy Chairman 1972–74. Chairman, Royal Veterinary College 1990–99. Hon. Fellow, Pembroke College, Cambridge; Hon. Doctorate: Anglia Polytechnic University, Stafford University. Chair: Industry and Parliament Trust 1990–94, NAC Rural Housing Trust 1990–99, London Playing Fields Association 1998–2001; Chair, Special Trustees, Wishing Well Appeal (Great Ormond Street Children's Hospital). Chairman: Council for Industry and Higher Education 1985–92, Archbishops' Commission on Rural Areas. PC 1970. *Publications: A Balance of Power,* 1986. *Sportsclubs:* Izingari Cricket Club, Butterflies Cricket Club. *Clubs:* Garrick, MCC. Raised to the peerage as Baron Prior, of Brampton in the County of Suffolk 1987. Rt Hon the Lord Prior, House of Lords, London, SW1A 0PW *Tel:* 020 7219 5353.

PRYS-DAVIES, LORD   Labour

PRYS-DAVIES (Life Baron), Gwilym Prys-Davies; cr 1982. Born 8 December 1923. Son of late William Davies; educated Tywyn School, Gwynedd; University College of Wales, Aberystwyth (LLB 1949, LLM 1952). Married Llinos Evans 1951 (3 daughters). *Career:* Solicitor; Consultant and Partner, Morgan Bruce & Hardwickes, Cardiff and Pontypridd 1959–93; Chairman, Welsh Hospitals Board 1968–74; Special Adviser to Secretary of State for Wales 1974–78; Member, Economic and Social Committee, EEC 1978–82. Opposition Frontbench Spokesperson for: Health 1983–87, Welsh Office 1987–97, Northern Ireland 1982–93. Member, Select Committees on: Murder and Life Imprisonment 1988–89, Parochial Charities (Neighbourhood Trusts Bill and the Small Charities Bill) 1983–84, Relations between Central and Local Government 1995–96; Member: Joint Committee on Statutory Instruments 1993–99; Select Committee on Delegated Powers and Deregulation 1999–2002. Member, British-Irish Parliamentary Body 1990–97. President, University of Wales, Swansea 1997–2001. Four honorary university fellowships, one honorary doctorate. Raised to the peerage as Baron Prys-Davies, of Llanegryn in the County of Gwynedd 1982. The Lord Prys-Davies, Lluest, 78 Church Road, Tonteg, Pontypridd, Mid Glamorgan, CF38 1EN *Tel:* 01443 202462 *Tel:* Office: 01443 402233.

PUTTNAM, LORD   Labour

PUTTNAM (Life Baron), David Terence Puttnam; cr. 1997. Born 25 February 1941. Son of late Leonard and Marie Puttnam; educated Minchenden Grammar School, London; City and Guilds 1958–62. Married Patricia Jones 1961 (1 son 1 daughter). *Trades Union:* Hon. Member, BECTU. *Career:* Advertising 1958–68; Film production 1968–99; Producer of films including: *Bugsy Malone*, 1976 (four BAFTA Awards), *Midnight Express*, 1978 (two Academy Awards, three BAFTA Awards), *Chariots of Fire*, 1981 (four Academy Awards, three BAFTA Awards including awards for best film), *Local Hero*, 1982 (two BAFTA Awards); *The Killing Fields*, 1984 (three Academy Awards, seven nominations: eight BAFTA Awards including Best Film); *The Mission*, 1986 (Palme D'Or, Cannes, one Academy Award, seven nominations; three BAFTA Awards); *Memphis Belle*, 1990, as well as several others; Chair, Enigma Productions Ltd 1978–; Director: National Film Finance Corporation 1980–85, Anglia Television Group 1982–99; Chair and Chief Executive Officer, Columbia Pictures 1986–88; Village Roadshow plc 1988–99; Chair Spectrum Management Consultants 1998–. Chancellor, Sunderland University 1997–. Chair Joint Committee on Draft Communications Bill 2002. Fellow, World Economic Forum, Davos, Switzerland. Governor: American Film Institute 1986–88, National Film and Television School 1974–, Chairman 1988–96; Vice-President, BAFTA 1993–; Chairman, National Museum of Photography, Film and Television 1996–; Member, Court of Governors: The London School of Economics 1997–2002, The London Institute 1997–2002; Member: Academic Board Bristol University, Arts and Humanities Research Board, UK-China Forum 1999–; President, UNICEF UK 2002–. Michael Balcon Award for outstanding contribution to British Film Industry, BAFTA 1982; Benjamin Franklin Award, RSA 1996; The Crystal Award presented by The World Economic Forum 1997. 32 honorary doctorates and fellowships. Trustee: Sundance Institute 1985–90, Tate Gallery 1986–93, National Aids Trust 1988–, Landscape Foundation, Science Museum 1996–; Chairman: National Memorial Arboretum Trustees 1992–, Teaching Awards Trust 1998–, National Endowment for Science, Technology and Arts 1998–, General Teaching Council 1999–2002, BAFTA Trustees 2002–, UNICEF 2002. Chairman, Producers and Directors Section ACCT 1975–77; Visiting professor, Bristol University 1983–97; Governor, American Film Institute 1986–89; Chair, British Council TV and Video Advisory Panel 1987–97; Member: British Screen Advisory Council 1988–98, British Film Commission 1992–98, Arts Council Lottery Panel 1995–97; Visiting lecturer, London School of Economics 1997–; President, CPRE 1985–92, Vice-President 1997–; Vice-President, Royal Geographical Society 1997–99; Member, Government's Education Standards Task Force 1991–2001; Chairman, British Council Arts Advisory Committee 2002–. CBE 1983; Chevalier 1985; Officier de l'Ordre des Arts et des Lettres (France) 1992; Kt 1995. FRGS; FRSA; FRPS; FCGI; Fellow: Royal Society of Arts, Royal Geographical Society, The British Film Institute. *Publications:* Contributor *The Third Age of Broadcasting*, 1982; Co-author *Rural England*, 1988; *A Submission to the EC Think Tank on Audio-Visual Policy*, 1994; *The Creative Imagination* in 'What Needs to Change', 1996; *The Undeclared War*, 1997; *US Movies and Money*, 1998. *Recreations:* Reading, cinema, landscape gardening. *Clubs:* Chelsea Arts, MCC, Athenaeum. Raised to the peerage as Baron Puttnam, of Queensgate in the Royal Borough of Kensington and Chelsea 1997. The Lord Puttnam, CBE, House of Lords, London, SW1A 0PW *Tel:* 020 7219 3000 *E-mail:* puttnam@enigma.co.uk.

PYM, LORD   Conservative

PYM (Life Baron), Francis Leslie Pym; cr. 1987. Born 13 February 1922. Son of late Leslie Ruthven Pym, JP, MP; educated Eton College; Magdalene College, Cambridge (BA economics). Married Valerie Fortune, née Daglish 1949 (2 sons 2 daughters). Captain, 9th Lancers; Served in Africa and Italy, MC 1945. Councillor, Herefordshire County Council 1958–61; DL, Cambridgeshire 1973–. *Career:* Director, Christie Brockbank Shipton Ltd 1994–99; Chairman, Diamond Cable Communications 1995–99. *House of Commons:* Contested (Conservative) Rhondda West 1959 general election; MP (Conservative) for: Cambridgeshire 1961–83, Cambridgeshire South East 1983–87; PPS to the Chancellor of the Exchequer 1962; Secretary of State for Northern Ireland 1973–74; Secretary of State for Defence 1979–1981; Chancellor of the Duchy of Lancaster, Paymaster General and Leader of the House of Commons 1981; Lord President of the Council and Leader of the House of Commons 1981–82; Secretary of State for Foreign and Commonwealth Affairs 1982–83. Assistant Government Whip 1962–64; Opposition Whip 1964–67; Deputy Chief Opposition Whip 1967–70; Government Chief Whip 1970–73. Opposition Spokesperson for: Devolution and House of Commons Affairs 1974, Northern Ireland and Agriculture 1974, Agriculture, Fisheries and Food 1974–76, House of Commons Affairs and on Devolution 1976–78, Foreign and Commonwealth Affairs 1978–79. Member, Liverpool University Council 1949–53; President, Atlantic Treaty Association 1985–88; Chairman, English Speaking Union 1987–92. Hon. Fellow, Magdalene College, Cambridge 1979. Chairman, The St Andrew's (Ecumenical) Trust until 1998. MC 1945; PC 1970. *Publications: The Politics of Consent*, 1984; *Sentimental Journey: tracing an outline of family history*, 1998. *Special Interests:* Foreign Affairs, Defence, Rural Affairs, Parliamentary Affairs. *Clubs:* Buck's. Raised to the peerage as Baron Pym, of Sandy in the County of Bedfordshire 1987. Rt Hon the Lord Pym, MC, DL, Everton Park, Sandy, Bedfordshire, SG19 2DE.

Q

QUINTON, LORD   Conservative

QUINTON (Life Baron), Anthony Meredith Quinton; cr. 1983. Born 25 March 1925. Son of late Surgeon-Captain Richard Frith Quinton, RN; educated Stowe School; Christ Church, Oxford (BA, philosophy, politics and economics 1948, MA). Married Marcelle Wegier 1952 (1 son 1 daughter). Served RAF 1943–46; Flying Officer and Navigator. *Career:* Delegate, Oxford University Press 1970–76; Fellow: All Souls College, Oxford 1949–55, New College 1955–78, Winchester College 1970–85; President, Trinity College, Oxford 1978–87; Member, Arts Council 1979–81; Emeritus Fellow, New College, Oxford; Vice-Chair, Encyclopaedia Britannica Board of Editors 1980–95; Chair, British Library Board 1985–90. Governor, Stowe School 1963–84, Chairman of Governors 1969–75; President: Aristotelian Society 1975–76, Royal Institute of Philosophy 1990–; Chairman, Kennedy Memorial Foundation 1990–95; Vice-president, British Academy 1985–86. Hon DHum Lit, New York University USA; Hon DHum, Ball State University USA. Wolfson Foundation. Order of Leopold II (Belgium) 1984. British Academy (FBA) 1977. *Publications: Political Philosophy* (editor) 1967; *The Nature of Things*, 1973; *Utilitarian Ethics*, 1973, 1990; *The Politics of Imperfection*, 1978; *Francis Bacon*, 1980; *Thoughts and Thinkers*, 1982; *From Wodehouse to Wittgenstein*, 1998; *Hume*, 2000. *Special Interests:* Education, Arts, Media. *Recreations:* Nostalgic: re-reading books, watching old films. *Clubs:* Garrick, Beefsteak, Brooks's. Raised to the peerage as Baron Quinton, of Holywell in the City of Oxford and County of Oxfordshire 1983. The Lord Quinton, A11 Albany, Piccadilly, London, W1J 0AL *Tel:* 020 7287 8686.

QUIRK, LORD — Crossbencher

QUIRK (Life Baron), (Charles) Randolph Quirk; cr. 1994. Born 12 July 1920. Son of late Thomas and Amy Randolph Quirk; educated Douglas High School, Isle of Man; University College, London (BA English 1947, MA, PhD, DLitt); Yale University. Married Jean Williams 1946 (2 sons) (divorced 1979, she died 1995); married Gabriele Stein 1984. Served RAF 1940–45. *Career:* Lecturer in English, University College, London 1947–54; Commonwealth Fund Fellow, Yale University and University of Michigan 1951–52; Reader in English language and literature, Durham University 1954–58, Professor 1958–60 and at London University 1960–68; Quain Professor of English language and literature, University College, London 1968–81; Chairman, Committee of Enquiry in Speech Therapy Services 1969–72; Member of Senate, London University 1970–85; Governor, British Institute of Recorded Sound 1975–80; Member, BBC Archives Committee 1975–81; Vice-Chancellor, London University 1981–85; President, Institute of Linguistics 1982–86; Member, Board of British Council 1983–91; Chairman, Anglo-Spanish Foundation 1983–85; Chairman, British Library Advisory Committee 1984–97; Member, RADA Council 1985–; President, British Academy 1985–89; Trustee, City Technology Colleges 1986–98; President, College of Speech Therapists 1987–91; Trustee, Wolfson Foundation 1987–; Royal Commissioner, 1851 Exhibition 1987–95; President, North of England Educational Conference 1989. Member: Science and Technology Committee 1998–2003, Science and Technology Sub-Committee II (Science and Society) 1999–2000, Sub-Committee I (Complementary and Alternative Medicine) 2000–01, Sub-Committee I (Systematic Biology and Biodiversity) 2002. Member: Linguistic Society of America, Modern Language Association, Philological Society. Jubilee Medal, Institute of Linguistics 1973. Hon. LLD, DLitt, DSc. from universities in the United Kingdom, USA and Europe; Jubilee Medal, Institute of Linguistics 1973; Foreign Fellow, Royal Belgian Academy of Science 1975; Hon. Fellow: Imperial College 1985, Queen Mary College 1986, Goldsmiths' College 1987; Foreign Fellow, Royal Swedish Academy 1987; Member, Academia Europaea 1988; Hon. Fellow, King's College 1990; Foreign Fellow: Finnish Academy of Science 1991, American Academy of Arts and Sciences 1995. CBE 1975; Kt 1985. FBA 1975. *Publications:* Co-author of several works on the English Language, notably *A Comprehensive Grammar of the English Language*, 1985; Solely: *The Concessive Relation in Old English Poetry*, 1954; *Essays on the English Language – Medieval and Modern*, 1968; *The English Language and Images of Matter*, 1972; *The Linguist and the English Language*, 1974; *Style and Communication in the English Language*, 1984; *Words at Work – Lectures on Textual Structures*, 1986; *Grammatical and Lexical Variance in English*, 1995; Has contributed to conference proceedings and learned journals. *Special Interests:* Education, Public Communication, Health, Speech Pathology, Broadcasting, Media. *Clubs:* Athenaeum. Raised to the peerage as Baron Quirk, of Bloomsbury in the London Borough of Camden 1994. Professor the Lord Quirk, CBE, FBA, University College London, Gower Street, London, WC1E 6BT *Tel:* 020 7219 2226 *Fax:* 020 7916 2054.

R

RADICE, LORD — Labour

RADICE (Life Baron), Giles Heneage Radice; cr. 2001. Born 4 October 1936; educated Winchester College; Magdalen College, Oxford (BA history 1960). Married Lisanne Koch 1971. *Trades Union:* Member GMB. *Career:* Head of research department GMWU 1966–73. *House of Commons:* Contested Chippenham 1964 and 1966 general elections; MP (Labour) for Chester-le-Street by-election 1973–83 and for Durham North 1983–2001; PPS to Shirley Williams as Secretary of State for Education and Science 1978–1979. Opposition Front Bench Spokesman on: Foreign Affairs 1981, Employment 1982–83, Education 1983–87. Member Select Committee on European Union 2003–; Chair European Union Sub-committee A (Economic and Financial Affairs, Trade and External Relations) 2003–. Chair: British Association for Central and Eastern Europe 1997–, European Movement 1995–2001. PC 1999. *Publications: Democratic Socialism*, 1965;

Co-editor *More Power to People*, 1968; Co-author *Will Thorne*, 1974; *The Industrial Democrats*, 1978; Co-author *Socialists in the Recession: a Survey of European Socialism*, 1986; *Labour's Path to Power: the New Revisionism*, 1989; *Offshore – Britain and the European Idea*, 1992; *The New Germans*, 1995; Editor *What Needs to Change* 1996; *Friends and Rivals* 2002. *Special Interests:* Economic and European Affairs, Labour Party Policy Revision. *Recreations:* Reading, tennis, gardening. Raised to the peerage as Baron Radice, of Chester-le-Street in the County of Durham 2001. Rt Hon the Lord Radice, House of Lords, London, SW1A 0PW *Tel:* 020 7219 4194.

RAMSAY OF CARTVALE, BARONESS — Labour

RAMSAY OF CARTVALE (Life Baroness), Meta Ramsay; cr. 1996. Born 12 July 1936. Daughter of Alexander Ramsay and Sheila Ramsay (née Jackson); educated Battlefield Primary School; Hutchesons' Girls' Grammar School, Glasgow; Glasgow University (MA 1958, MEd 1961); Graduate Institute for International Affairs, Geneva 1967–68. Single. *Trades Union:* Member, GMB. Member, Lewisham Community Health Council 1992–94. *Career:* HM Diplomatic Service 1969–91; Foreign policy adviser to John Smith as Leader of the Labour Party 1992–94; Special Adviser to John Cunningham as Shadow Secretary of State for Trade and Industry 1994–95. *House of Lords:* Deputy Speaker 2002–. Government Whip (Baroness in Waiting) December 1997–2001. Government Spokesperson for: Culture, Media and Sport 1997–98, Health 1997–98, Scotland 1997–2001, Foreign Affairs and Europe 1998–2001. Member: Select Committee on European Union 1997, European Union Sub-committee F (Social Affairs, Education and Home Affairs) 1997. Member, British Delegation to the: Parliamentary Assembly of OSCE 1997, NATO Parliamentary Assembly 2003–. Member: Labour Party, Fabian Society, Co-operative Party, Labour Finance and Industry Group, Labour Movement in Europe. President, Scottish Union of Students 1959–60; Chair, Atlantic Council of the United Kingdom 1997; Member: RIIA, Institute for Jewish Policy Research, 300 Group; Chair, Board of Governors, Fairlawn Primary School, Forest Hill, South London until 1997. Hon. DLitt, Bradford University. Trustee, Smith Institute; Member: Advisory Council of Smith Memorial Trust, Advisory Council, Foreign Policy Centre. Honorary Visiting Research Fellow in Peace Studies, Bradford University; Member, Intelligence and Security Committee 1997. Commander of the Order of the White Rose of Finland 2002. FRSA. *Recreations:* Theatre, opera, ballet. *Clubs:* University Women's, Reform. Raised to the peerage as Baroness Ramsay of Cartvale, of Langside in the City of Glasgow 1996. The Baroness Ramsay of Cartvale, House of Lords, London, SW1A 0PW *Tel:* 020 7219 3145 *Fax:* 020 7219 5979.

RANDALL OF ST BUDEAUX, LORD — Labour

RANDALL OF ST BUDEAUX (Life Baron), Stuart Jeffrey Randall; cr. 1997. Born 22 June 1938. Son of late Charles Randall; educated University College of Wales, Cardiff. Married Gillian Michael 1963 (3 daughters). *Career:* Electrical fitter apprentice, HM Dockyard, Devonport 1953–58; Systems engineer: English Electric Computers, Radio Corporation of America, USA 1963–66; Project leader, Marconi Automation 1966–68; Consultant, Inter-Bank Research Organisation 1968–71; Manager: British Steel Corporation 1971–76, British Leyland 1976–80; Consultant, Nexos Office Systems 1980–82; Manager, Plessey Communications Systems Ltd 1982–83. *House of Commons:* Contested Worcestershire South October 1974 general election; Contested Midlands West 1979 European Parliament election; MP (Labour) for Hull West 1983–97; PPS to Roy Hattersley as Deputy Leader of the Labour Party and Shadow Chancellor of the Exchequer 1984–85. Opposition Spokesperson for: Agriculture 1985–87, Home Affairs 1987–92. Member, Select Committee on European Communities Sub-Committee A (Economic and Financial Affairs, Trade and External Relations) 1997–. *Special Interests:* Information Technology. *Recreations:* Sailing, walking, flying. Raised to the peerage as Baron Randall of St Budeaux, of St Budeaux in the County of Devon 1997. The Lord Randall of St Budeaux, House of Lords, London, SW1A 0PW *Tel:* 020 7219 5353.

RAWLINGS, BARONESS   Conservative

RAWLINGS (Life Baroness), Patricia Elizabeth Rawlings; cr. 1994. Born 27 January 1939. Daughter of late Louis Rawlings and of Mary Rawlings, née Boas de Winter; educated Oak Hall, Haslemere, Surrey; Le Manoir, Lausanne, Switzerland; Florence University; University College, London (BA English 1979); London School of Economics (Postgraduate diploma international relations 1983). Married Sir David Wolfson 1962 (created Baron Wolfson of Sunningdale, qv) (divorced 1967). *Career:* Director: California Dress Company 1969–82, Rheims and Laurent, French Fine Art Auctioneers 1969–71; Member, Peace through NATO Council 1985–88; Member, British Video Classification Council 1986–89; Special Adviser to Sir David Trippier, Minister for Inner Cities, Department of the Environment 1987–88; MEP (Conservative) for Essex South West 1989–94: Group Deputy Whip; Former Vice-President, Delegation for Relations with Albania, Bulgaria and Romania; Former Member, Delegation for Relations with USA; Board Member, British Association for Central and Eastern Europe 1994–. Opposition Whip 1997–98. Opposition Spokesman for: Culture, Media and Sport 1997–98, Foreign and Commonwealth Affairs December 1998–, International Development December 1998–. Member, House of Lords Offices Sub-Committee: Advisory Panel on Works of Art 2000–02. Governor, American University in Bulgaria. Member, Conservative Women's National Committee 1983–88. Member, LCC Children's Care Committee 1959–61; Member, British Red Cross Society 1964–, Chairman Appeals, London Branch (National Badge of Honour 1981), Hon. Vice-President 1988–; Director, English Chamber Orchestra and Music Society 1980–; Member, British Council 1997–; Council Member, NACF; Member: RIIA, IISS, Advisory Council, The Prince's Youth Business Trust; Chairman of Council, King's College, London; President, NCVO 2002. British Red Cross National Badge of Honour 1987. Hon. DLitt, University of Buckingham. Trustee, The Chevening Estate 2002; Patron, Afghan Mother and Child Health Care 2002. Contested (Conservative): Sheffield Central 1983, Doncaster Central 1987 general elections; Contested Essex West and Hertfordshire East 1994 European Parliament election. Order of the Rose (Silver), Bulgaria 1991; Grand Official, Order of the Southern Cross, Brazil 1997. *Special Interests:* International Affairs, Culture, Heritage, Broadcasting. *Recreations:* Music, art, architecture, gardening, travel, skiing, golf. *Sportsclubs:* Member Queen's, Royal West Norfolk Golf. *Clubs:* Honorary Secretary, Grillions. Raised to the peerage as Baroness Rawlings, of Burnham Westgate in the County of Norfolk 1994. The Baroness Rawlings, House of Lords, London, SW1A 0PW *Tel:* 020 7219 0664.

RAWLINSON OF EWELL, LORD   Conservative

RAWLINSON OF EWELL (Life Baron), Peter Anthony Grayson Rawlinson; cr. 1978. Born 26 June 1919. Son of late Lieutenant-Colonel A. R. Rawlinson, OBE; educated Downside; Christ's College, Cambridge (Exhibitioner 1938). Married Haidee Kavanagh 1940 (3 daughters) (marriage dissolved and annulled by Sacred Rota, Rome 1954); married Elaine Dominguez 1954 (2 sons 1 daughter). Irish Guards, Major, mentioned in despatches 1939–46. *Career:* Called to the Bar, Inner Temple 1946; Queen's Counsel 1959; Bencher, Inner Temple 1962; QC (NI) 1972; Treasurer 1984; Recorder, Salisbury 1960–62; Chairman of the Bar 1975–76; Leader, Western Circuit 1975–82; Recorder, Kingston-upon-Thames 1975–2002; President, Senate of Inns of Court and the Bar 1986–87. *House of Commons:* MP (Conservative) for Epsom and Ewell 1955–78; Solicitor General 1962–64; Attorney General 1970–74. Conservative Spokesman on Law 1967–70. Opposition Front Bench 1978–79, Member, Select Committee on Euthanasia 1995–. President, Senate of Inns of Court and the Bar 1986–87. Hon. Fellow, Christ's College, Cambridge 1981. Kt 1962; PC 1964. Hon. Member, Americans' Bar Association; Hon. Fellow, American College Trial Lawyers. *Publications:* War Poems and Poetry, 1943; *Public Duty and Personal Faith – the example of Thomas More*, 1978; *A Price Too High* (autobiography) 1989; *The Jesuit Factor*, 1990; *The Colombia Syndicate* (novel) 1991; *Hatred and Contempt* (novel) 1992; *His Brother's Keeper* (novel) 1993; *Indictment for Murder* (novel) 1994; *The Caverel Claim* (novel) 1998; *The Richmond Diary* (novel) 2001. *Recreations:* Painting. *Clubs:* White's, MCC, Royal Automobile (Vice-President). Raised to the peerage as Baron Rawlinson of Ewell, of Ewell in the County of Surrey 1978. Rt Hon the Lord Rawlinson of Ewell, QC, House of Lords, London, SW1A 0PW *Tel:* 020 7219 5353 *Fax:* 01747 871611.

RAYNE, LORD   Crossbencher

RAYNE (Life Baron), Max Rayne; cr. 1976. Born 8 February 1918. Son of late Phillip and Deborah Rayne; educated Central Foundation School, London; University College, London. Married Margaret Marco 1941 (1 son 2 daughters) (divorced 1960); married Lady Jane Vane-Tempest-Stewart 1965 (2 sons 2 daughters). Served RAF 1940–45. *Career:* Chair, London Merchant Securities 1960–2000, Life President 2000–; Deputy Chairman, British Lion Films 1967–72; Director, Housing Corporation (1974) Ltd 1974–78 Chair, Westpool Investment Trust 1980–2000; Deputy Chair, First Leisure Corporation plc 1984–92, Chair 1992–95, Non-executive Director 1995–99. Governor: St Thomas's Hospital 1962–74, Royal Ballet School 1966–79, Yehudi Menuhin School 1966–87, Malvern College 1966–, Centre for Environmental Studies 1967–73; Member: General Council, King Edward VII's Hospital Fund for London 1966–98, Council, St Thomas's Hospital Medical School 1965–82, Council of Governors, United Medical Schools of Guy's and St Thomas's Hospitals 1982–89; Hon. Vice-President, Jewish Care 1966–; Chairman, National Theatre Board 1971–88; Founder Patron, The Rayne Foundation 1962–; Vice-President, Yehudi Menuhin School 1987–; RADA Council 1973–; Founder Member, Motability 1979–96 (Life Vice-President 1996). Eight honorary university fellowships; honorary doctorate. Special Trustee, St Thomas's Hospital 1974–92; Chairman, London Festival Ballet Trust 1967–75. Kt 1969; Officier, Légion d'Honneur 1987; Chevalier 1973. Hon. Fellow: Royal College of Psychiatrists 1977, Royal College of Physicians 1992. Raised to the peerage as Baron Rayne, of Prince's Meadow in the County of Greater London 1976. The Lord Rayne, 33 Robert Adam Street, London, W1M 3HR *Tel:* 020 7935 3555.

RAZZALL, LORD   Liberal Democrat

RAZZALL (Life Baron), Edward Timothy Razzall; cr. 1997. Born 12 June 1943. Son of Leonard Humphrey Razzall and Muriel Razzall; educated St Paul's School; Open Scholar Worcester College, Oxford (BA jurisprudence 1965). Married Deirdre Bourke 1982 (1 son 1 daughter from previous marriage). Councillor, Mortlake Ward, London Borough of Richmond 1974–98; Deputy Leader, Richmond Council 1983–96. *Career:* Teaching Associate, North Western University, Chicago, USA 1965–66; Frere Cholmeley Bischoff, solicitors 1966–96, Partner 1973–96; Partner, Argonaut Associates 1996–; Director, Cala plc 1973–99; Chair, Abaco Investments plc 1974–90; Director, Star Mining Corporation NL 1993–. Liberal Democrat Spokesperson for Trade and Industry 1998–. Member, Joint Select Committee on Consolidation of Bills 1998–. Treasurer: Liberal Party 1986–87, Liberal Democrats 1987–2000; President, Association of Liberal Democrat Councillors 1990–95; Chair, Liberal Democrats General Election Campaign 1999–; Member Liberal Democrat Federal Executive Committee 1987–; Chair, Campaigns and Communications Committee 2000–. European Lawyer of the Year 1992. CBE 1993. *Clubs:* National Liberal, MCC. Raised to the peerage as Baron Razzall, of Mortlake in the London Borough of Richmond 1997. The Lord Razzall, CBE, House of Lords, London, SW1A 0PW *Tel:* 020 7976 1233 *E-mail:* Tim@Argonaut-Associates.net.

REA, LORD   Labour

REA (3rd Baron, UK), (John) Nicolas Rea; cr. 1937; 3rd Bt of Eskdale (UK) 1935. Born 6 June 1928. Son of late Hon. James Russell Rea; educated Dartington Hall School; Belmont Hill School, Massachusetts, USA; Dauntsey's School; Christ's College, Cambridge (MA natural sciences, MD 1951); University College Hospital, London (DObst, DCH, DPH 1954). Married Elizabeth Robinson 1951 (4 sons 2 daughters) (divorced 1991); married Judith Mary Powell 1991. *Trades Union:* Member, AMICUS. Acting Sergeant, Suffolk Regiment, National Service 1946–48. *Career:* Junior hospital posts 1954–57; Research fellow in paediatrics in Ibadan and Lagos, Nigeria 1962–65; Lecturer in social medicine, St Thomas' Hospital Medical School, London 1966–68; General practitioner, North London 1957–62, 1968–93. *House of Lords:* First entered House of Lords 1981; Elected hereditary peer 1999–. Opposition Spokesperson for Health and International

Development 1992–97. Member, Select Committee on: Science and Technology 1987–88, 1997–2002, Sub-Committee I (Complementary and Alternative Medicine) 2000, Sub-Committee IIA (Human Genetic Databases) 2000–02, Sub-Committee I (Systematic Biology and Biodiversity/Fighting Infection) 2002–. Member: IPU, CPA. Member: Healthlink Worldwide, Mary Ward Centre, Mother and Child Foundation, Caroline Walker Trust; Hon Secretary, National Heart Forum. Hon Degree, London Metropolitan University (formerly University of North London) 2002. MD, FRCGP. *Publications:* Papers in Medical Journals; Papers on epidemiology in various journals 1970–97. *Special Interests:* Health, Food and Nutrition, Third World, Arms Control, Human Rights. *Recreations:* Music (bassoon), outdoor activities. *Clubs:* Royal Society of Medicine. The Lord Rea, 11 Anson Road, London, N7 0RB *Tel:* 020 7607 0546 *Fax:* 020 7687 1219 *Tel:* Office: 020 7267 4411 *Fax:* 020 7687 1219 *E-mail:* reajn@parliament.uk.

REAY, LORD — Conservative

REAY (14th Lord, S), Hugh William Mackay; cr. 1628; 14th Bt of Far (NS) 1627; 7th Baron Mackay Van Ophemert (Netherlands) 1822. Born 19 July 1937. Son of 13th Lord; educated Eton College; Christ Church, Oxford (MA philosophy, politics and economics 1961). Married Hon. Annabel Therese Fraser 1964 (2 sons 1 daughter) (divorced 1978); married Hon. Victoria Isabella Warrender 1980 (2 daughters). *Career:* Member: European Parliament 1973–79, Council of Europe and WEU 1979–86. *House of Lords:* First entered House of Lords 1963; Joint Parliamentary Under-Secretary of State, Department of Trade and Industry 1991–92; An elected hereditary peer 1999–. Government Whip 1989–91. Spokesperson for Department of Environment, Home Office, Foreign and Commonwealth Office and Ministry of Defence and Welsh Office 1989–91. Member, European Select Committee 1993–97, 1997–99; Chairman, Select Committee on European Communities Sub-Committee D (Agriculture, Fisheries and Food) 1997–99. Chief of Clan Mackay. The Lord Reay, House of Lords, London, SW1A 0PW *Tel:* 020 7219 5459.

REDESDALE, LORD — Liberal Democrat

REDESDALE (6th Baron, UK), Rupert Bertram Mitford; cr. 1902; (Life) Baron Mitford 2000. Born 18 July 1967. Son of 5th Baron; educated Highgate School, London; Newcastle University (BA archaeology 1989). Married Helen Shipsey 1998 (1 son 1 daughter). *House of Lords:* First entered House of Lords 1991. Liberal Democrat Spokesperson for: Overseas Development 1994–99, Northern Ireland 1999, Tourism 2000, International Development 2000–01, Defence 2001–. Member: Select Committee on Science and Technology 1993–97, Sub-Committee II 1994–97, Advisory Panel on Works of Art 2003–. Member, Court of Newcastle University 1993–; Council Member, Institute of Advanced Motorists 1994–. *Special Interests:* Environment, Archaeology, Development. *Recreations:* Caving, climbing, skiing. Created a life peer as Baron Mitford, of Redesdale in the County of Northumberland 2000. The Lord Redesdale, 2 St Mark's Square, London, NW1 7TP *Tel:* 020 7722 1965; House of Lords, London, SW1A 0PW *Tel:* 020 7219 4343.

REES, LORD — Conservative

REES (Life Baron), Peter Wynford Innes Rees; cr. 1987. Born 9 December 1926. Son of late Major-General T. W. Rees, IA; educated Stowe School; Christ Church, Oxford (MA 1949). Married Mrs Anthea Wendell, née Hyslop 1969. Served with Scots Guards 1945–48. *Career:* Called to the Bar, Inner Temple 1953; QC 1969; Practised Oxford Circuit, Bencher, Inner Temple 1976; Former Chairman and Director of companies. *House of Commons:* Contested (Conservative): Abertillery 1964, 1965, Liverpool, West Derby 1966 general elections; MP (Conservative) for: Dover 1970–74, Dover and Deal 1974–83, Dover 1983–87; PPS to Solicitor General 1972–73; Minister of State, HM Treasury 1979–81; Minister for Trade 1981–83; Chief Secretary, HM Treasury 1983–85. Member Advisory Panel on Works of Art 2003–. Member: Court and Council of the Museum of Wales until 1997, Museums and Galleries Commission 1988–97. PC 1983. Liveryman, Clockmakers Company. *Clubs:* Boodle's, Beefsteak, White's, Pratt's. Raised to the peerage as Baron Rees, of Goytre in the County of Gwent 1987. Rt Hon the Lord Rees, QC, Goytre Hall, Nantyderry, Abergavenny, Gwent, NP7 9DL; 39 Headfort Place, London, SW1X 7DE.

REES-MOGG, LORD   Crossbencher

REES-MOGG (Life Baron), William Rees-Mogg; cr. 1988. Born 14 July 1928. Son of late Edmund Fletcher Rees-Mogg; educated Charterhouse; Balliol College, Oxford (BA history 1951, MA). Married Gillian Morris 1962 (2 sons 3 daughters). *Trades Union:* Institute of Journalists. RAF national service 1946–48. High Sheriff, Somerset 1978. *Career: Financial Times* 1952–60: Chief leader writer 1955–60, Assistant editor 1957–60; *Sunday Times* 1960–67: City editor 1960–61, Political and economic editor 1961–63, Deputy editor 1964–67; *The Times* 1967–81: Editor 1967–81, Member, Executive Board Times Newspapers 1968–81; Director, *The Times* Ltd 1978–81; Vice-Chairman, Board of Governors BBC 1981–86; Chairman and Proprietor, Pickering and Chatto (Publishers) Ltd 1983–; Chairman, Arts Council of Great Britain 1982–89; Chairman, Sidgwick and Jackson Ltd 1985–88; Director, M & G 1988–92; Chairman, Broadcasting Standards Council 1988–93; Chairman: American Trading Company Ltd 1992–, International Business Communications plc (now Informa plc) 1993–99, Fleet Street Publications Ltd 1995–; Director: General Electric Company 1981–97, J. Rothschild Investment Management Ltd 1987–96, St James's Place Capital plc 1990–96, EFG Private Bank and Trust Company 1993–, Private Financial Holdings Ltd 1995–, Value Realisation Trust plc 1996–99. Member Advisory Panel on Works of Art 2003–. Vice-Chairman, Conservative Party's National Advisory Committee on Political Education 1961–63. Contested (Conservative) Chester-le-Street, Co. Durham: 1956 by-election, 1959 general election; Visiting Fellow, Nuffield College, Oxford 1968–72. Kt 1981. *Publications: His Majesty Preserved*, 1954; *Sir Anthony Eden*, 1956; *The Reigning Error: the crisis of world inflation*, 1974; *An Humbler Heaven* 1977; *How to buy Rare Books*, 1985; Co-author: *Blood in the Streets*, 1987, *The Great Reckoning*, 1991; *Picnics on Vesuvius*, 1992; Co-author: *The Sovereign Individual*, 1997. *Recreations:* Collecting. *Clubs:* Garrick. Raised to the the peerage as Baron Rees-Mogg, of Hinton Blewitt in the County of Avon 1988. The Lord Rees-Mogg, 17 Pall Mall, London, SW1Y 5NB *Tel:* Office: 020 7242 2241.

RENDELL OF BABERGH, BARONESS   Labour

RENDELL OF BABERGH (Life Baroness), Ruth Barbara Rendell; cr. 1997. Born 17 February 1930. Daughter of Arthur and Ebba Grasemann. Married Donald Rendell 1950 (divorced 1975, re-married 1977) (died 1999) (1 son). *Trades Union:* Member Society of Authors. *Career:* Author and crime novelist 1964–. Member Select Committees on: Procedure, Refreshment 2003–. Arts Council National Book Award for Genre Fiction, 1981; *Sunday Times* Award for Literary Excellence, 1990; Crime Writers' Association Gold Dagger (4 times) and Diamond Dagger; Mystery Writers of America three Edgar Allan Poe Awards. Hon. DLitt: University of Bowling Green (Ohio), University of Essex, University of East Anglia; Hon. MLitt, University of East London. Member Ecclesiastical Committee 2002–. CBE 1996. FRSL. *Publications: From Doon with Death*, 1964; *To Fear a Painted Devil*, 1965; *Vanity Dies Hard*, 1966; *A New Lease of Death*, 1967; *Wolf to the Slaughter*, 1967; *The Secret House of Death*, 1968; *The Best Man to Die*, 1969; *A Guilty Thing Surprised*, 1970; *One Across Two Down*, 1971; *No More Dying Then*, 1972; *Some Die and Some Lie*, 1973; *The Face of Trespass*, 1974; *Shake Hands for Ever*, 1975; *A Demon in my View*, 1976; *A Judgement in Stone*, 1977; *A Sleeping Life*, 1978; *Make Death Love Me*, 1979; *The Lake of Darkness*, 1980; *Put on by Cunning*, 1981; *Master of the Moor*, 1982; *The Speaker of Mandarin*, 1983; *The Killing Doll*, 1984; *The Tree of Hands*, 1984; *An Unkindness of Ravens*, 1985; *Live Flesh*, 1986; *Heartstones*, 1987; *Talking to Strange Men*, 1987; (Editor) *A Warning to the Curious – The Ghost Stories of M. R. James*, 1987; *The Veiled One*, 1988; *The Bridesmaid*, 1989; *Ruth Rendell's Suffolk*, 1989; (with Colin Ward) *Undermining the Central Line*, 1989; *Going Wrong*, 1990; *Kissing the Gunner's Daughter*, 1992; *The Crocodile Bird*, 1993; *Simisola*, 1994; (Editor) *The Reason Why*, 1995; Short Stories: *The Fallen Curtain*, 1976; *Means of Evil*, 1979; *The Fever Tree*, 1982; *The New Girl Friend*, 1985; *Collected Short Stories*, 1987; *The Copper Peacock*, 1991; *Blood Lines*, 1995; *Road Rage*, 1997; *A Sight for Sore Eyes*, 1998; *Harm Done*, 1999; *Piranha to Scurfy*, 2000; *Adam and Eve and Pinch Me*, 2001; As Barbara Vine: *A Dark-Adapted Eye*, 1986; *A Fatal Inversion*, 1987; *The House of Stairs*, 1988; *Gallowglass*, 1990; *King Solomon's Carpet*, 1991; *Asta's Book*, 1993; *No Night is Too Long*, 1994; *The Brimstone Wedding*, 1996; *The Chimney Sweeper's Boy*, 1998; *Grasshopper*, 2001; *The Blood Doctor*, 2002. *Recreations:* Reading, walking, opera. *Clubs:* Groucho, Detection. Raised to the peerage as Baroness Rendell of Babergh, of Aldeburgh in the County of Suffolk 1997. The Baroness Rendell of Babergh, CBE, House of Lords, London, SW1A 0PW; 11 Maida Avenue, Little Venice, London, W2 1SR *E-mail:* ruth@ampelos.demon.co.uk.

RENFREW OF KAIMSTHORN, LORD | Conservative

RENFREW OF KAIMSTHORN (Life Baron), (Andrew) Colin Renfrew; cr. 1991. Born 25 July 1937. Son of late Archibald and Helena Renfrew; educated St Albans School; St John's College, Cambridge (Exhibitioner, BA archaeology and anthropology 1962, MA, PhD, ScD); British School of Archaeology, Athens. Married Jane Margaret Ewbank 1965 (2 sons 1 daughter). National Service with RAF 1956–58. National Art Collections Fund Committee. *Career:* Sheffield University: Lecturer in Prehistory and Archaeology 1965–70, Senior Lecturer 1970–72, Reader 1972; Professor of Archaeology, Southampton University 1972–81; Visiting Lecturer, University of California 1967; Has lectured on archaeology in numerous British and American Universities; Has excavated in Greece and the United Kingdom; Chairman, Hampshire Archaeological Committee 1974–81; Member: Ancient Monuments Board for England 1974–84, Royal Commission for Historical Monuments (England) 1977–87; Disney Professor of Archaeology, Cambridge University 1981–2004; A Vice-President, Royal Archaeological Institute 1982–85; Member: Historical Buildings and Monuments Commission for England 1984–86, Ancient Monuments Advisory Committee 1984–2001, UK National Commission for UNESCO 1984–86; Master, Jesus College, Cambridge 1986–97, Fellow 1986–; Director, McDonald Institute for Archaeological Research 1990–2004; A Trustee, British Museum 1991–2000. Member, House of Lords European Communities Select Committee, Sub-Committee A 1993–96; Chairman, Library and Computing Sub-Committee 1995–2003; Member: Select Committee on House of Lords' Offices 1995–2003, Administration and Works Sub-Committee 1995–2002, Finance and Staff Sub-Committee 1995–2002, House of Lords House Committee 2003–. Foreign Associate, National Academy of Sciences of the USA; Corresponding Member of the Austrian Academy of Sciences. Huxley Memorial Medal 1991; Fyssen Prize 1996. Hon. DLitt, Sheffield 1987; Hon. Doctorate, Athens 1991; Hon. DLitt, Southampton 1995. Antiquity Trust. Contested (Conservative) Sheffield Brightside 1968 by-election; Board Member, Parliamentary Office of Science and Technology (POST) 1997–98. FSA; Hon FSA (Scotland); FBA 1980; Hon FRSE 2001. Freeman, City of London. *Publications: The Emergence of Civilisation,* 1972; *The Explanation of Culture Change,* 1973 (editor); *Before Civilisation,* 1973; *British Prehistory, a New Outline,* 1974 (editor); *Investigations in Orkney,* 1979; *Problems in European Prehistory,* 1979; *An Island Polity,* 1982; *Approaches to Social Archaeology,* 1984; *The Prehistory of Orkney,* 1985; *The Archaeology of Cult,* 1985; *Archaeology and Language,* 1987; *The Cycladic Spirit,* 1991; *Loot, Legitimacy and Ownership: the Ethical Crisis in Archaeology,* 2000 Has also collaborated with other authors on archaeological subjects, as well as contributions to archaeological journals. *Special Interests:* National Heritage, Arts, Museums and Galleries, Education, Foreign Affairs. *Recreations:* Contemporary art. *Clubs:* Athenaeum, United Oxford and Cambridge University. Raised to the peerage as Baron Renfrew of Kaimsthorn, of Hurlet in the District of Renfrew 1991. Professor the Lord Renfrew of Kaimsthorn, FBA, FSA, McDonald Institute for Archaeological Research, Downing Street, Cambridge, CB2 3ER *Tel:* 01223 333521 *Tel:* 01223 369307 *Fax:* 01223 333536.

RENNARD, LORD | Liberal Democrat

RENNARD (Life Baron), Christopher John Rennard; cr. 1999. Born 8 July 1960. Son of late Cecil and Jean Rennard; educated Liverpool Blue Coat School; Liverpool University (BA politics and economics 1982). Married Ann McTegart 1989. *Trades Union:* Member, GMBATU. *Career:* Liberal Party agent, Liverpool, Mossley Hill 1982–84; Liberal Party regional agent, East Midlands 1984–88; Social and Liberal Democrats election co-ordinator 1988–89; Director of campaigns and elections, Liberal Democrats 1989–. Member: IPU, CPA. Member, Amnesty International. MBE 1989. *Publications: Winning Local Elections,* 1988; *The Campaign Manual,* 1995. *Recreations:* Cooking, wine, France. Raised to the peerage as Baron Rennard, of Wavertree in the County of Merseyside 1999. The Lord Rennard, MBE, Liberal Democrat Party, 4 Cowley Street, London, SW1P 3NB *Tel:* 020 7222 7999 *Fax:* 020 7233 3140 *E-mail:* chrisrennard@cix.co.uk.

Visit the Vacher Dod Website . . . **www.DodOnline.co.uk**

RENTON, LORD   Conservative

RENTON (Life Baron), David Lockhart-Mure Renton; cr. 1979. Born 12 August 1908. Son of late Dr Maurice Waugh Renton and Eszma Olivia Renton; educated Oundle; University College, Oxford (MA jurisprudence 1931, BCL). Married Claire Cicely Duncan 1947 (died 1986) (3 daughters). Commissioned in TA 1938; Major RA; Served 1939–45 (overseas 1942–45); TD. DL: Huntingdonshire 1962, Huntingdonshire and Peterborough 1964, Cambridgeshire 1974. *Career:* Called to the Bar, Lincoln's Inn 1933; QC 1954; Bencher of Lincoln's Inn 1962; Treasurer 1979; Recorder: Rochester 1963–68, Guildford 1968–71. *House of Commons:* MP for Huntingdonshire 1945–79 (National Liberal 1945–50, National Liberal and Conservative 1951–66, Conservative 1966–79); Parliamentary Secretary: Ministry of Fuel and Power December 1955–57, Ministry of Power 1957–58; Joint Parliamentary Under-Secretary of State, Home Office 1958–61; Minister of State 1961–62. Chairman, Conservative Transport 1953–55. *House of Lords:* Deputy Speaker 1982–88. President, Association of Conservative Peers 2003–. Delegate to Council of Europe 1951 and 1952. Patron, Huntingdon Conservative Association 1979–2001. President, Conservation Society 1971–72; Chair, MENCAP 1978–82, President 1982–88; President, Statute Law Society 1980–2000; Patron: National Law Library, Design and Manufacture for Disability, Greater London Association for the Disabled, Ravenswood Foundation, Royal British Legion, Huntingdonshire. Hon. Fellow, University College, Oxford 1990–. Royal Commission on the Constitution 1971–74; Chairman, Committee on Preparation of Legislation 1973–75; Vice-Chairman, Council of Legal Education 1968–73; President, National Council for Civil Protection 1980–91. PC 1962; KBE 1964; TD. *Publications:* Various Legal and Political Articles; Various Obituaries. *Special Interests:* Drafting of Legislation, Mental Handicap, Environment, Law and Order, Trade Union Law, Devolution, European Legislation, Armed Forces. *Recreations:* Gardening, cricket, listening to light opera. *Sportsclubs:* Vice-President, Huntingdonshire Cricket Club 1959–. *Clubs:* Carlton, Pratt's. Raised to the peerage as Baron Renton, of Huntingdon in the County of Cambridgeshire 1979. Rt Hon the Lord Renton, KBE, QC, TD, DL, 16 Old Buildings, Lincoln's Inn, London, WC2A 3TL *Tel:* 020 7242 8986; Moat House, Abbots Ripton, Huntingdon, Cambridgeshire, PE28 2PE *Tel:* 01487 773227.

RENTON OF MOUNT HARRY, LORD   Conservative

RENTON OF MOUNT HARRY (Life Baron), (Ronald) Timothy Renton; cr. 1997. Born 28 May 1932. Son of late R. K. D. Renton, CBE; educated Eton College (Kings Scholar); Magdalen College, Oxford (Roberts Gawen Scholar) (BA modern history 1953, MA). Married Alice Fergusson 1960 (2 sons 3 daughters). *Trades Union:* Member, APEX 1977–90. Member, Council of Sussex University 2000–. *Career:* C. Tennant Sons & Co. Ltd, Canada 1957–62; Managing Director, Tennant Trading Ltd 1964–71; Director: Silvermines Ltd 1966–84, ANZ Banking Group Ltd 1969–76, J. H. Vavasseur & Co. Ltd 1971–74; Director, Fleming Continental European Investment Trust 1992–, Chairman 1999–. *House of Commons:* Contested (Conservative) Sheffield Park 1970 general election; MP (Conservative) for Sussex Mid 1974–97; PPS: to Chief Secretary to the Treasury 1979–81, to Secretary of State for Trade January-May 1981, to Sir Geoffrey Howe as Chancellor of the Exchequer January-June 1983; Parliamentary Under-Secretary of State, Foreign and Commonwealth Office 1984–85; Minister of State: Foreign and Commonwealth Office 1985–87, Home Office 1987–89; Government Chief Whip 1989–90; Minister of State, Privy Council Office (Minister for the Arts) 1990–92. Government Chief Whip 1989–90. Member European Communities Committee Sub-Committee: A (Economic and Financial Affairs, Trade and External Relations) 1997–2001, D (Environment, Agriculture, Public Health and Consumer Protection) 2003–. President, Conservative Trade Unionists 1980–84. Chair Sussex Downs Conservative Board 1997–; President: Roedean School 1997–, Federation of Sussex Amenity Societies 2000–. Fellow, Industry and Parliament Trust. Member, Know How Fund Advisory Board 1992–99; Vice-Chair, British Council 1992–97, Board Member 1997–99; Chair Outsider Art Archive and Collection 1993–99. PC 1989. *Publications: The Dangerous Edge*, 1994; *Hostage to Fortune*, 1997; Articles published in journals and newspapers. *Special Interests:* Arts, Privatisation, Financial Institutions, Conservation. *Recreations:* Writing, mucking about in boats, arguing about opera, touring France on a bicycle. *Clubs:* Garrick, Grillions. Raised to the peerage as Baron Renton of Mount Harry, of Offham in the County of East Sussex 1997. Rt Hon the Lord Renton of Mount Harry, House of Lords, London, SW1A 0PW *Tel:* 020 7219 3308 *E-mail:* rentont@parliament.uk.

RENWICK OF CLIFTON, LORD

RENWICK OF CLIFTON (Life Baron), Robin William Renwick; cr. 1997. Born 13 December 1937. Son of the late Richard and Clarice Renwick; educated St Paul's School; Jesus College, Cambridge (MA history 1962); University of Paris (Sorbonne). Married Annie Colette Giudicelli 1965 (1 son 1 daughter). Army Service 1956–58. *Career:* Entered Foreign Service 1963; Dakar 1963–64; FO 1964–66; New Delhi 1966–70; Private Secretary to Minister of State, FCO 1970–72; First Secretary, Paris 1972–76; Counsellor, Cabinet Office 1976–78; Rhodesia Department, FCO 1978–80; Political Adviser to Governor of Rhodesia 1980; Head of Chancery, Washington 1981–84; Assistant Under-Secretary of State, FCO 1984–87; Ambassador to: South Africa 1987–91, USA 1991–95; Vice-chairman, Investment Banking, JP Morgan plc 2000–; Deputy Chair, Robert Fleming Holdings 1995–2000; Chair Fluor Ltd 1996–, Director: Compagnie Financiere Richemont AG 1995–, British Airways plc 1996–, Fluor Corporation 1997–, BHP Billiton plc 1997–, SAB Miller plc 1999–, Harmony Gold 1999–. Hon. Fellow, Jesus College 1992; Hon. DLitt: University of the Witwatersrand, South Africa 1990, College of William and Mary, USA 1993, Oglethorpe University 1995. Trustee: The Economist 1996–, The Hakluyt Foundation 2000–. Visiting Fellow, Center for International Affairs, Harvard University 1980–81. CMG 1980; KCMG 1988. FRSA. *Publications: Economic Sanctions*, 1981; *Fighting with Allies*, 1996; *Unconventional Diplomacy*, 1997. *Special Interests:* Defence, Foreign Affairs. *Recreations:* Tennis, trout fishing. *Clubs:* Brooks's, Hurlingham, Travellers'. Raised to the peerage as Baron Renwick of Clifton, of Chelsea in the Royal Borough of Kensington and Chelsea 1997. The Lord Renwick of Clifton, KCMG, J P Morgan plc, 10 Aldermanbury, London, EC2V 7RF *E-mail:* robin.renwick@jpmorgan.

RICHARD, LORD

RICHARD (Life Baron), Ivor Seward Richard; cr. 1990. Born 30 May 1932. Son of Seward Thomas Richard; educated St. Michael's School, Bryn, Llanelly; Cheltenham College; Pembroke College, Oxford (Wightwick Scholar, BA jurisprudence 1953). Married Geraldine Moore 1956 (1 son) (divorced 1962); married Alison Mary Imrie 1962 (1 son 1 daughter) (divorced); married Janet Jones 1989 (1 son). *Career:* Called to the Bar, Inner Temple 1955; Bencher 1985; Practised in London 1955–74; QC 1971; UK Permanent Representative to UN 1974–79; Member, EEC Commission 1981–85; Chairman, World Trade Centre Wales Ltd 1985–97. *House of Commons:* Contested (Labour) South Kensington general election 1959; MP (Labour) Barons Court 1964–74; PPS to Secretary of State for Defence 1966–67; Parliamentary Under-Secretary of State (Army) Ministry of Defence 1969–70. Opposition Spokesperson for Broadcasting, Posts and Telecommunications 1970–71; Deputy Spokesperson for Foreign Affairs 1971–74. *House of Lords:* Leader of the Opposition 1992–97; Lord Privy Seal and Leader of the House of Lords 1997–98. Opposition Spokesperson for: Home Office affairs 1990–92, The Civil Service 1992–97, European Affairs 1992–97, The Treasury and Economic Affairs 1992–93. Former Member, Select Committees on: House of Lords' Offices 1997–98, Finance and Staff Sub-Committee, Liaison, Privileges, Procedure, Selection; Member Select Committee on European Union Sub-committee E (Law and Institutions) 2001–02. Hon. Fellow, Pembroke College, Oxford 1981. Chairman, Welsh Independent Commission 2002–. PC 1993. *Publications:* Co-author *Europe or the Open Sea*, 1971; *We, the British*, 1983; Co-author *Unfinished Business – the Reform of the House of Lords*, 1999; as well as articles in political journals. *Recreations:* Music, talking. Raised to the peerage as Baron Richard, of Ammanford in the County of Dyfed 1990. Rt Hon the Lord Richard, QC, House of Lords, London, SW1A 0PW *Tel.* 020 7219 1495.

DodOnline
An Electronic Directory without rival . . .

Peers' biographies and photographs available with daily updates *via* the internet

For a *free* trial, call Yasmin Mirza, Aby Farsoun or Michael Mand on 020 7630 7643

RICHARDSON, LORD   Crossbencher

RICHARDSON (Life Baron), John Samuel Richardson; cr. 1979; 1st Bt of Eccleshall (UK) 1963. Born 16 June 1910. Son of late John Watson Richardson, solicitor, killed in action 1917; educated Charterhouse; Trinity College, Cambridge (BA medicine 1935); St Thomas's Hospital (MB, BChir 1935, MD, MRCP). Married Sybil Angela Stephanie Trist 1933 (2 daughters). RAMC, medical specialist – Major and Lieutenant-Colonel August 1939-November 1945. *Career:* Qualified 1935; Junior posts at St Thomas's Hospital until 1939; Deputy, Medical Unit at St Thomas's Hospital 1945–47, Physician 1947–75; Consulting physician for Metropolitan Police 1957–80; Consulting physician to army 1964–75; President, International Society for Internal Medicine 1966–70; Chairman, Joint Consultants Committee 1967–72; President: Royal Society of Medicine 1969–71, BMA 1970–71, GMC 1973–80. President, International Society for Internal Medicine. Gold Medal, BMA 1982. Hon. Fellow: King's College, London, Trinity College, Cambridge; Six honorary doctorates. Hon. Bencher, Gray's Inn. LVO 1943; Kt 1960; CStJ. FRCP; FRCPE; Hon. FRCPI; Hon. FRCS; Hon. FRCPSG; Hon. FRCPsych; Hon. FRPharm Soc. Member: Cutlers, Society of Apothecaries. *Publications: The Practice of Medicine,* 2nd ed. 1960; *Connective Tissue Disorders,* 1963. *Recreations:* Living in the country. Raised to the peerage as Baron Richardson, of Lee in the County of Devon 1979. The Lord Richardson, LVO, Windcutter, Lee, Nr Ilfracombe, Devon, EX34 8LW *Tel:* 01271 863198.

RICHARDSON OF CALOW, BARONESS   Crossbencher

RICHARDSON OF CALOW (Life Baroness), Kathleen Margaret Richardson; cr. 1998. Born 24 February 1938. Daughter of Francis William and Margaret Fountain; educated St Helena School, Chesterfield; Stockwell College; Wesley Deaconess College; Wesley House, Cambridge. Married Ian David Godfrey Richardson 1964 (3 daughters). Moderator of Churches Commission for Inter-faith Relations. *Career:* First Woman President of the Methodist Conference 1992–93; Moderator, Free Churches Council 1995–99; President, Churches Together In England 1995–99. Member: Animals in Scientific Procedures Committee 2001–02, Religious Offences 2002–. Three honorary doctorates. Citizen Organising Foundation. OBE 1994. *Special Interests:* Church Affairs, Inter Faith Relations. *Recreations:* Reading, needlework. Raised to the peerage as Baroness Richardson of Calow, of Calow in the County of Derbyshire 1998. Reverend the Baroness Richardson of Calow, OBE, House of Lords, London, SW1A 0PW *Tel:* 020 7219 0314 *E-mail:* richardsonk@parliament.uk.

RICHARDSON OF DUNTISBOURNE, LORD   Crossbencher

RICHARDSON OF DUNTISBOURNE (Life Baron), Gordon William Humphreys Richardson, cr. 1983. Born 25 November 1915. Son of late John Robert and Nellie Richardson; educated Nottingham High School; Gonville and Caius College, Cambridge (MA 1937, LLB 1938). Married Margaret Alison Sheppard 1941 (1 son 1 daughter). Commissioned South Notts Hussars Yeomanry 1939; Staff College, Camberley 1941; Served until 1946. HM Lieutenant, City of London 1974–83; DL, Gloucestershire 1983–. *Career:* Called to the Bar, Gray's Inn 1946; Member, Bar Council 1951–55; With Industrial & Commercial Finance Corporation 1955–57; Director, J. Henry Schroder & Co Ltd 1957, Deputy Chair 1960–62, Chairman 1962–72; Member, Company Law Amendment Committee 1959–62; Chair: Committee on Turnover Taxation 1963–64, Schroders Ltd 1966–73; Director, Bank of England 1967–83, Governor 1973–83; Chair, Schroders Incorporated 1968–73; Member, NEDC 1971–73, 1980–83; Chair, Industrial Development Advisory Board 1972–73; Director, Bank for International Settlements 1973–93, Vice-Chair 1985–88, 1991–93; Member, Morgan Stanley Advisory Board 1984–; Morgan Stanley International Incorporated 1986–95, International Advisory Board Chemical Bank, New York 1986–96; Vice-Chair, The Chase Manhattan Corporation International Advisory Council 1996–98, Chair Emeritus 1998–2000. High Steward, Westminster Cathedral 1985–89; Deputy High Steward, Cambridge University 1982–. Hon. LLD, Cambridge; Hon. Fellow: Gonville and Caius College, Cambridge, Wolfson College, Cambridge; Hon. DSc: City University, Aston University; Hon. DCL, University of East Anglia. Trustee, Pilgrim Trust, Chairman 1984–89. Hon. Bencher, Gray's Inn. MBE (Military) 1944; PC 1976; KG 1983. Freeman, City of London 1975. Liveryman, Mercers' Company. *Clubs:* Brooks's, Pratt's. Raised to the peerage as Baron Richardson of Duntisbourne, of Duntisbourne in the County of Gloucestershire 1983. Rt Hon the Lord Richardson of Duntisbourne, KG, MBE, TD, DL, 25 St Anselm's Place, London, W1K 5AF.

RIX, LORD   Crossbencher

RIX (Life Baron), Brian Norman Roger Rix; cr. 1992. Born 27 January 1924. Son of late Herbert and Fanny Rix; educated Bootham School, York. Married Elspet Gray, actress 1949 (2 sons 2 daughters). *Trades Union:* Life Member, British Actors' Equity Association. Served in RAF and as Bevin Boy. DL, Greater London 1987–88, 1997– (for life), Vice-Lord-Lieutenant, Greater London 1988–97. *Career:* Actor 1942–; Actor manager 1947–77 (mostly at the Whitehall Theatre and Garrick Theatre, London). Chancellor, University of East London. *House of Lords:* Concentrated on Bills, Regulations, Debates concerned with learning disability and disability generally. Co-opted Member, European Union Sub-committee F (Social Affairs, Education and Home Affairs) 1997–2000. Fellow, Hong Kong Association for Scientific Study of Mental Handicap. Chair, Friends of Normansfield 1973–; Secretary-General, MENCAP (Royal Society for Mentally Handicapped Children and Adults, now the Royal Mencap Society) 1980–87, Chair 1988–98, President 1998–; Founder and Governor, Mencap City Foundation 1984, Chair 1988–; Chair: Libertas Group of Charities 1988–, Mencap City Insurance Services (now MCIS Ltd) 1993–; Life Vice-President, Radio Society of Great Britain. Evian Health Award 1988; RNID Communicator of the Year Award 1990; *The Spectator* Campaigner of the Year Award 1999; Yorkshire Lifetime Achievement Award 1999; Lifetime Achievement UK Charity Awards 2001; Award for Public Service, British Neuroscience Association 2001. Eight honorary degrees and five fellowships. Chair, Family Charities Ethical Trust Advisory Panel 1994–2001. Member, Arts Council 1986–93; Chair: Drama Panel 1986–93, Monitoring Committee, Arts and Disabled People 1988–93, Independent Development Council for People with Mental Handicap 1981–86. CBE 1977; Kt 1986. Hon. FRSM, Hon. FRCPsch. *Publications: My Farce from My Elbow* (autobiography) 1975; *Farce about Face* (autobiography) 1989; *Tour de Farce* (history of theatre touring) 1992; *Life in the Farce Lane,* 1995 (history of farce); Editor and Contributor, *Gullible's Travails* 1996. *Special Interests:* Arts, Disability, Theatre, Voluntary Sector, Charities, Cricket. *Recreations:* Cricket, amateur radio, gardening. *Sportsclubs:* Yorkshire County Cricket. *Clubs:* Garrick, MCC, Lord's Taverners (Hon Member). Raised to the peerage as Baron Rix, of Whitehall in the City of Westminster and of Hornsea in Yorkshire 1992. The Lord Rix, CBE, DL, 8 Ellerton Road, Wimbledon Common, London, SW20 0EP *Tel:* 020 8879 7748 *Fax:* 020 8879 7748; House of Lords, London, SW1A 0PW *Tel:* 020 7219 0315.

ROBERTS OF CONWY, LORD   Conservative

ROBERTS OF CONWY (Life Baron), (Ieuan) Wyn Pritchard Roberts; cr. 1997. Born 10 July 1930. Son of late Rev. Evan Pritchard Roberts; educated Beaumaris County School; Harrow School; University College, Oxford (BA history 1952, MA). Married Enid Grace Williams 1956 (3 sons). Intelligence Corps 1948–49. *Career:* Sub-Editor, *Liverpool Daily Post* 1952–54; News Assistant, BBC 1954–57; Executive: TWW Ltd 1957–68, Harlech TV Ltd 1968–69. *House of Commons:* MP (Conservative) for Conwy 1970–97; PPS to Secretary of State for Wales 1970–74; Parliamentary Under-Secretary of State, Welsh Office 1979–87; Minister of State, Welsh Office 1987–94. Conservative Spokesperson for Welsh Affairs 1974–79. Opposition Spokesperson for: Welsh Affairs 1997–, Home Office 2002–. Life Member, CPA. President, Welsh Conservative Clubs 1991–2003. Member, Royal National Eisteddfod Gorsedd of Bards; President, University of Wales College of Medicine 1997–. Hon. Fellow, University Colleges of Wales, Bangor and Aberystwyth. Knighted 1990; PC 1991. *Special Interests:* Education, Health, Training, Tourism, Small Businesses, Transport, Economics, Conservation. *Recreations:* Fishing, walking. *Clubs:* Savile, Cardiff and County (Cardiff). Raised to the peerage as Baron Roberts of Conwy, of Talyfan in the County of Gwynedd 1997. Rt Hon the Lord Roberts of Conwy, House of Lords, London, SW1A 0PW *Tel:* 020 7219 2410 *E-mail:* robertsw@parliament.uk.

Visit the Vacher Dod Website . . .
www.DodOnline.co.uk

ROBERTSON OF PORT ELLEN, LORD   Crossbencher

ROBERTSON OF PORT ELLEN (Life Baron), George Islay MacNeill Robertson; cr. 1999. Born 12 April 1946. Son of the late George P. Robertson, police inspector, and late Marion Robertson; educated Dunoon Grammar School, Argyll; Dundee University (MA economics 1968). Married Sandra Wallace 1970 (2 sons 1 daughter). *Trades Union:* Member GMB 1965–. *Career:* Research assistant, Tayside Study, Economics Group 1968–69; Scottish organiser, GMWU 1969–78; Secretary-General, North Atlantic Treaty Organisation (NATO) 1999–. *House of Commons:* MP (Lab) for Hamilton from by-election May 1978–1997, and for Hamilton South from May 1, 1997–August 24, 1999; PPS to Secretary of State for Social Services February-May 1979; Shadow Secretary of State for Scotland 1993–97; Secretary of State for Defence 1997–99. Opposition Frontbench Spokesperson for: Scotland 1979–80, Defence 1980–81, Foreign and Commonwealth Affairs 1981–93, European and Community Affairs 1985–93. Chairman, Scottish Labour Party 1977–78. *House of Lords:* Secretary of State for Defence August-October 1999. Joint Vice-Chair, British-American Parliamentary Group 1996–99. Council, Royal Institute of International Affairs 1985–91; Joint President 2001–; Vice-President, Raleigh International 1984–; Chairman, Seatbelt Survivors Club; Governor, Ditchley Foundation 1990–; Council, British Executive Service Overseas 1991–97; Vice-Chairman, Westminster Foundation for Democracy 1992–94; Patron, Glasgow Islay Association. Seven honorary doctorates. Fellow, Industry and Parliament Trust; Trustee: 21st Century Trust, British American Project. Vice-Chairman, British Council 1985–94; Hon Reg Col, London-Scottish (Volunteers) 2000–; Elder Brother, Corporation of Trinity House, 2002–. Commander's Cross of the Order of Merit (Federal Republic of Germany) 1991; PC 1997; Grand Cross of Order of Star (Romania) 2000. FRSA 1999; Hon FRSE 2003. *Special Interests:* Foreign Affairs, Defence. *Recreations:* Photography, golf, reading. *Sportsclubs:* Hamilton Rugby; Islay Golf. *Clubs:* Army and Navy, Royal Commonwealth. Raised to the peerage as Baron Robertson of Port Ellen, of Islay in Argyll and Bute 1999. Rt Hon the Lord Robertson of Port Ellen, House of Lords, London, SW1A 0PW *Tel:* 020 7219 5353.

ROCHESTER, LORD BISHOP OF   Non-affiliated

ROCHESTER (106th Bishop of), Michael Nazir-Ali. Born 19 August 1949. Son of James and Patience Nazir-Ali; educated St Paul's School and St Patrick's College, Karachi; Karachi University (BA economics, sociology and Islamic history 1970); Fitzwilliam College and Ridley Hall, Cambridge (PGCTh 1972, MLitt 1976); St Edmund Hall, Oxford (BLitt 1974, MLitt 1981); Australian College of Theology, New South Wales (ThD 1985) with Centre for World Religions, Harvard 1983. Married Valerie Cree 1972 (2 sons). *Career:* Assistant: Christ Church, Cambridge 1970–72, St Ebbe's, Oxford 1972–74; Burney Lecturer in Islam, Cambridge 1973–74; Assistant curate, Holy Sepulchre Cambridge 1974–76; Tutorial supervisor in theology, Cambridge University 1974–76; Tutor, then senior tutor, Karachi Theological College 1976–81; Associate priest, Holy Trinity Cathedral, Karachi 1976–79; Priest-in-charge, St Andrew's, Akhtar Colony, Karachi 1979–81; Provost of Lahore Cathedral 1981–84; Bishop of Raiwind, Pakistan 1984–86; Assistant to Archbishop of Canterbury, Co-ordinator of studies and editor for the Lambeth Conference 1986–89; Director-in-residence, Oxford Centre for Mission Studies 1986–89; Member, Board of Christian Aid 1988–97; Secretary, Archbishop's Commission on Communion and Women in the Episcopate (Eames' Commission) 1988–98; General Secretary, Church Mission Society 1989–94; Member, Anglican-Roman Catholic International Commission 1991–; Member, Board of Mission of the General Synod of the Church of England 1991–2001; Chair, Church of England Mission Theology Advisory Group 1992–2001; Canon Theologian, Leicester Cathedral 1992–94; Bishop of Rochester 1994–; Visiting Professor, University of Greenwich 1996–; Took his seat in the House of Lords 1999; Chair, Trinity College, Bristol; Member, Archbishop's Council 2001; Chair, Working Party on Women and the Episcopate; Member House of Bishops: Theology Group 1996–, Standing Committee 2001–. World Council of Churches. Oxford Society Award for Graduate Studies 1972–73; Cambridge Burney Award 1974–75. Fellow, St Edmund Hall, Oxford 1998–; Two honorary doctorates. Chair of Trustees, Bishop's Fund for Mission (Education Enterprise); Trustee, Trinity College Bristol 1996–; Director, Christian Weekly Newspapers; Adviser to Layton Rahimtoola Trust 1999–; Director, Central Board of Finance of the Church of England;

Director, Diocesan Board of Finance, Rochester. Member, Human Fertilisation and Embryology Authority 1998–, Chairman, Ethics Committee 1998–. Fellow of St Edmund Hall, Oxford. *Publications: Islam: a Christian perspective*, 1983; *Frontiers in Muslim-Christian Encounter*, 1987; *Martyrs and Magistrates: toleration and trial in Islam*, 1989; *From Everywhere to Everywhere: a World-View of Christian Mission*, 1990; *Mission and Dialogue*, 1995; *The Mystery of Faith*, 1995; *Citizens and Exiles: Christian Faith in a plural world*, 1998; *Shapes of the Church to Come*, 2001; *Understanding my Muslim Neighbour*, 2002; Has edited various Lambeth Conference papers and reports as well as contributing articles for journals. *Special Interests:* Sufism, Middle Eastern History and Politics, Languages. *Recreations:* Cricket, hockey, reading fiction, humour and poetry, writing fiction and poetry, table-tennis, Persian poetry. *Sportsclubs:* Kent Brothers. *Clubs:* Nikaean. Rt Rev the Lord Bishop of Rochester, Bishopscourt, Rochester, Kent, ME1 1TS *Tel:* 01634 842721 *Fax:* 01634 831136 *E-mail:* bishops.secretary@rochester.anglican.org.

RODGER OF EARLSFERRY, LORD — Crossbencher

RODGER OF EARLSFERRY (Life Baron), Alan Ferguson Rodger; cr. 1992. Born 18 September 1944. Son of late Professor Thomas Ferguson Rodger and Jean Margaret Smith Chalmers; educated Kelvinside Academy, Glasgow; Glasgow University (MA 1964, LLB 1967); New College, Oxford (MA 1970, DPhil 1970, DCL 1989). *Career:* Junior research fellow, Balliol College, Oxford 1969–70; Fellow, New College, Oxford 1970–72 Member, Faculty of Advocates 1974, Clerk of Faculty 1976–79; QC (Scot) 1985; Advocate Depute 1985–88; Home Advocate Depute 1986–88; Maccabaean Lecturer, British Academy 1991; Solicitor-General for Scotland 1989–92; Lord Advocate 1992–95; Senator of the College of Justice 1995–96; President of the Court of Session and Lord Justice General of Scotland 1996–2001; Lord of Appeal in Ordinary 2001–. *House of Lords:* Lord Advocate 1992–95. Hon. Member, Society of Public Teachers of Law; Corresponding member, Bayerische Akademie der Wissenschaften. Three honorary doctorates. Member, Mental Welfare Commission for Scotland 1981–84; Hon. Bencher, Lincoln's Inn 1992; Honorary Fellow, Balliol College, Oxford 1999; Visitor, St Hugh's College, Oxford 2003–. PC 1992. FBA 1991; FRSE 1992. *Publications:* Author of several publications and articles on legal matters. *Recreations:* Walking. *Clubs:* Athenaeum. Raised to the peerage as Baron Rodger of Earlsferry, of Earlsferry in the District of North East Fife 1992. Rt Hon the Lord Rodger of Earlsferry, House of Lords, London, SW1A 0PW *Tel:* 020 7219 3135.

RODGERS OF QUARRY BANK, LORD — Liberal Democrat

RODGERS OF QUARRY BANK (Life Baron), William Thomas Rodgers; cr. 1992. Born 28 October 1928. Son of William and Gertrude Rodgers; educated Sudley Road Council School; Quarry Bank High School, Liverpool; Magdalen College, Oxford (BA modern history 1951). Married Silvia Szulman 1955 (3 daughters). National Service 1947–48. Borough Councillor, St Marylebone 1958–62. *Career:* General Secretary: The Fabian Society 1953–60, Publishing 1960–64, 1970–72; Director-General, Royal Institute of British Architects 1987–94; Chair, Advertising Standards Authority 1995–2000. *House of Commons:* Contested (Labour) Bristol West 1957 general election; MP (Labour) for Stockton-on-Tees 1962–74; Parliamentary Under-Secretary of State: Department of Economic Affairs 1964–67, Foreign Office 1967–68; Minister of State: Board of Trade 1968–69, Treasury 1969–70; Chair, Expenditure Committee on Trade and Industry 1971–74; MP (Labour) Teeside, Stockton 1974–81; Minister of State, Ministry of Defence 1974–76; Secretary of State for Transport 1976–79; Opposition (Shadow) Defence Secretary 1979–80; Elected to Shadow Cabinet (Labour) 1979 and 1980; MP (SDP) for Teesside, Stockton 1981–83; Contested: (SDP) Stockton North 1983, (SDP/Alliance) Milton Keynes 1987 general elections. Liberal Democrat Spokesperson for Home Office Affairs 1994–97. Member Select Committees on: House of Lords' Offices –2001, Liaison –2001, Privileges –2001, Procedure –2001, Selection –2001, House Committee 2003–. Leader, Liberal Democrat Peers 1998–2001. General Secretary, Fabian Society 1953–60; Joint founder, Social Democratic Party 1981, Vice-President 1982–87. PC 1975. Hon. FRIBA; Hon. FIStructE. *Publications:* Editor *Hugh Gaitskell 1906–1963*, 1964; Co-author *The People into Parliament*, 1966; *The Politics of Change*, 1982; Editor, *Government and Industry*, 1986; *Fourth Among Equals*, 2000. Raised to the peerage as Baron Rodgers of Quarry Bank, of Kentish Town in the London Borough of Camden 1992. Rt Hon the Lord Rodgers of Quarry Bank, 43 North Road, London, N6 4BE *Tel:* 020 8341 2434 *Fax:* 020 8347 7133.

ROGAN, LORD Crossbencher

ROGAN (Life Baron), Dennis Robert David Rogan; cr. 1999. Born 30 June 1942. Son of late Robert Henderson Rogan; educated The Wallace High School; Belfast Institute of Technology; The Open University (BA economics, politics 1976). Married Lorna Elizabeth Colgan 1968 (2 sons). Chairman, Lisburn Unit of Management Health Board 1984–85. *Career:* Moygashel Ltd 1960–69; William Ewart & Sons Ltd 1969–72; Lamont Holdings plc 1972–78; Managing Director Dennis Rogan Assoc 1978–; Chair Associated Processors Ltd 1985–; Director Belfast Gasworks Trust 1994; Chair Communications Ltd 1996–; Patron, The Somme Association 1999–; Deputy Chair Independent News and Media (NI) Ltd 2000–; Chair, DCL Group 2001–; Member, International Advisory Board, Independent News and Media 2001–; Director, Northern Ireland Police Fund 2001–; Chair, Events Management 2002–. *House of Lords:* Leader Ulster Unionist Party 2001–. Chair: Ulster Young Unionist Council 1968–69, South Belfast Constituency Association 1992–96; Ulster Unionist Party: Chair 1996–2001, Honorary secretary 2001–. *Special Interests:* Northern Ireland, Trade and Industry, Defence. *Recreations:* Rugby football, oriental carpets, gardening. *Clubs:* Ulster Reform, Belfast. Raised to the peerage as Baron Rogan, of Lower Iveagh in the County of Down 1999. The Lord Rogan, 31 Notting Hill, Malone Road, Belfast, BT9 5NS *Tel:* 028 9066 2468; House of Lords, London, SW1A 0PW.

ROGERS OF RIVERSIDE, LORD Labour

ROGERS OF RIVERSIDE (Life Baron), Richard George Rogers; cr. 1996. Born 23 July 1933. Son of Dada Geiringer and Nino Rogers; educated Architectural Association (AA Dip 1959); Yale University (MArch, Fulbright, Edward D. Stone and Yale Scholar 1961–62); RIBA. Married Su Brumwell 1961 (3 sons); married Ruth Elias 1973 (2 sons). *Career:* Team 4 1963–67; Richard & Su Rogers 1968–70; Piano + Rogers 1970–78; Visiting professor Yale University and University College, London 1978; Chair, Richard Rogers Architects Ltd 1978–; Gave the BBC Reith Lectures entitled 'Cities for a Small Planet' 1995; Masterplans for many city centres, including Shanghai, Berlin, Mallorca and London; Buildings designed include: Centre Georges Pompidou, Paris (with Renzo Piano); Lloyd's of London; European Court of Human Rights; Strasbourg; Kabuki-Cho Tower, Tokyo; Channel 4 headquarters, London; Millennium Dome, Greenwich, London; Law Courts, Bordeaux, France; Lloyd's Registry of Shipping, London; 88 Wood Street, London; Current projects include: Barajas Airport, Madrid; Terminal 5, Heathrow Airport, London; Law Courts, Antwerp, Belgium; Birmingham Library; Hesperia and Conference Centre, Barcelona, Spain; Bullring, Barcelona; Waterside, Paddington Basin, London; Advisor to the Mayor, Barcelona Urban Strategies Council; Greater London Authority: Mayor's Chief Advisor on Architecture and Urbanism Member of the Mayor of London's Advisory Cabinet. Member Barcelona Urban Strategy Council. Director, River Cafe; Member, United Nations Architects' Committee; Chairman, National Tenants Resource Centre; Patron, Society of Blaack Architects; Trustee, Medicins du Monde, UK Board; Membre de l'Acadamie d'Architecture 1983; Member RIBA Council and Policy Committees 1984–87; Honorary Member, Bund Deutscher Architekten 1989. International Union of Architects August Perret Prize for most outstanding international work (Centre Pompidon) 1975–78; Royal Gold Medal for Architecture 1985; American Academy and Institute of Arts and Letters, Arnold W Brunner Memorial Prize 1989; Friend of Barcelona 1997; Thomas Jefferson Memorial Foundation Medal in Architecture 1999; Japan Art Association Praemium Imperiale Award for Architecture 2000; Praemium Imperiale Architecture Laureate 2000. Five honorary degrees from British and Czech universities. Chair: Board of Trustees, Tate Gallery 1984–88, National Tenants Resource Centre 1991–, Architecture Foundation 1991–2001; Honorary Trustee MOMA. Vice-chair, Arts Council of England 1994–96; Chair, Urban Task Force 1997–99; United Nations World Commissions on 21st Century Urbanisations; Director River Cafe; Kt 1991; Chevalier l'Ordre National de la Légion d'Honneur (France) 1986; Officier de l'Ordre des Arts et des Lettres (France) 1995. Hon. Fellow: Royal Academy of Art, The Hague, American Institute of Architects, Tokyo Society of Architects and Building Engineers 1996; Fellow, Royal Society for the Arts 1996; Academician, International Academy of Architecture; Royal Academician, Royal Academy of London 1984. *Publications: Richard Rogers + Architects,* 1985; *A + U: Richard Rogers 1978–88,* 1988;

Architecture: A Modern View, 1990; (jointly) *A New London*, 1992; *Richard Rogers*, 1995; *Cities for a Small Planet*, 1997; *Towards an Urban Renaissance (Urban Task Force)*, 1999; *Richard Rogers, Complete Works*, Vol 1, 1999; *Paying for an Urban Renaissance*, 2000; Co-author *Cities for a Small Country*, 2000; *Richard Rogers, Complete Works, Vol 2*, 2001; *Delivering an Urban Renaissance*, 2002. *Special Interests:* Sustainable Built Environment, Arts. *Recreations:* Friends, food, art, architecture, travel. Raised to the peerage as Baron Rogers of Riverside, of Chelsea in the Royal Borough of Kensington and Chelsea 1996. The Lord Rogers of Riverside, Thames Wharf, Rainville Road, London, W6 9HA *Tel:* 020 7385 1235 *Fax:* 020 7385 8409 *Tel:* 020 7746 0411 *E-mail:* jo.m@richardrogers.co.uk.

ROLL OF IPSDEN, LORD   Crossbencher

ROLL OF IPSDEN (Life Baron), Eric Roll; cr. 1977. Born 1 December 1907. Son of late Mathias Roll, Banker; educated on the Continent; Birmingham University (BCom 1928, PhD economics 1930). Married Winifred Taylor 1934 (died 1998) (2 daughters). *Career:* Professor of economics, University College, Hull 1935–46; Entered Civil Service 1941; Under-Secretary, Treasury 1948; Deputy Head, UK delegation to NATO 1952; Under-Secretary, Ministry of Agriculture, Fisheries and Food 1953–57; Executive Director, International Sugar Council 1957–59; Economic Minister and Head of UK Treasury delegation Washington and UK Executive Director International Monetary Fund and World Bank 1963–64; Permanent Under-Secretary of State, Department of Economic Affairs 1964–66; Hon. Chairman, Book Development Council 1967–70; Director: Times Newspapers Ltd 1967–80, Bank of England 1968–77; Chairman (later Joint Chairman), S. G. Warburg & Co. Ltd 1974–86; Director, Times Newspapers Holdings Ltd 1980–83; President, S. G. Warburg Group plc 1986–95; Senior Adviser, UBS Warburg 1995–. Chancellor, Southampton University 1974–84. Member, Subcommittee A of Select Committee on European Community 1994–98; Member, Select Committees on: Economic Affairs, Formerly Monetary Policy of the Bank of England 1999–. Three honorary doctorates; Hon. Fellow, London School of Economics. CMG 1947; CB 1956; KCMG 1962; Grosses Goldene Ehrenzeichen Mit Stern (Austria) 1979; First Class Order of the Dannebrog (Denmark) 1981; Officer Légion d'Honneur (France) 1984; Order of the Sacred Treasure (First Class) (Japan) 1993; Grand Cross of the Order of Merit of the Republic of Italy 2000. Fellow, Royal Economic Society. *Publications: An Early Experiment in Industrial Organisation*, 1930; *Spotlight on Germany*, 1933; *About Money*, 1935; *Crowded Hours*, 1985; *A History of Economic Thought*, 1995 (fifth edition); *Where Did We Go Wrong?*, 1996; *Where Are We Going*, 2000. *Special Interests:* Economics, Finance. *Recreations:* Reading, music. *Clubs:* Brooks's. Raised to the peerage as Baron Roll of Ipsden, of Ipsden in the County of Oxfordshire 1977. The Lord Roll of Ipsden, KCMG, CB, UBS Warburg Ltd, 1 Finsbury Avenue, London, EC2M 2PP *Tel:* 020 7568 2477 *Fax:* 020 7568 0050 *E-mail:* lorderic.roll@ubsw.com.

ROOKER, LORD   Labour

ROOKER (Life Baron), Jeffrey William Rooker; cr. 2001. Born 5 June 1941; educated Aldridge Road Secondary Modern; Handsworth Technical School; Handsworth Technical College 1957–60; Aston University (BSc production engineering 1964); Warwick University (MA industrial relations 1972). Married Angela Edwards 1972 (died 2003). *Trades Union:* Member MSF. Member, Birmingham Education Committee 1972–74. *Career:* Apprentice toolmaker, Kings and Heath Engineering Company 1957–63; Production manager, Rola Celestion Ltd 1967–70; Lecturer, Lanchester Polytechnic, Coventry 1972–74. *House of Commons:* Member (Labour) for Birmingham Perry Barr February 1974–2001; PPS to the Government Law Officers 1974–77; Shadow Deputy Leader, House of Commons 1994–97; Minister of State and Deputy Minister, Ministry of Agriculture, Fisheries and Food (Minister for Food Safety) 1997–99; Minister of State, Department of Social Security 1999–2001. Opposition Frontbench Spokesperson for: Social Services 1979–80, Social Security 1980–83, Treasury and Economic Affairs 1983–84, Environment 1984–88, Community Care and Social Services 1990–92, Education 1992–93. *House of Lords:* Minister of State, Home Office 2001–02; Minister of State, Office of the Deputy Prime Minister 2002–: for Housing, Planning and Regeneration 2002–03, for Regeneration and Regional Development 2003–. Government Spokesperson for: Home Office 2001–02, Office of the Deputy Prime Minister 2002–. Member of Council, Institution of Production Engineers 1975–80. PC 1999. Raised to the peerage as Baron Rooker, of Perry Barr in the County of West Midlands 2001. Rt Hon the Lord Rooker, House of Lords, London, SW1A 0PW *Tel:* 020 7219 6469.

ROPER, LORD   Liberal Democrat

ROPER (Life Baron), John Francis Hodgess Roper; cr. 2000. Born 10 September 1935. Son of late Rev. Frederick Mabor Hodgess Roper, and of the late Ellen Frances Roper; educated William Hulme's Grammar School, Manchester; Reading School; Magdalen College, Oxford (BA philosophy, politics and economics 1959); University of Chicago (economics). Married Valerie Hope Edwards 1959 (1 daughter). Commissioned RNVR (National Service) 1954–56. *Career:* Harkness Fellow, Commonwealth Fund 1959–61; Manchester University 1961–70: Research fellow in economic statistics 1961; Assistant lecturer in economics 1962–64, lecturer 1964–70, faculty tutor 1968–70; Director: CWS 1969–74, Co-op Insurance Society 1973–74; RIIA: Editor *International Affairs* 1983–88, Head of International Security Programme 1985–88 and 1989–90, Head of WEU Institute for Security Studies, Paris 1990–95; Visiting Professor, College of Europe, Bruges 1997–2001. *House of Commons:* Contested (Labour) High Peak, Derbyshire 1964 general election; MP for Farnworth 1970–83 (Labour and Co-operative 1970–81, SDP 1981–83); PPS to Minister of State, Department of Industry 1978–79; Contested (SDP) Worsley 1983 general election. Opposition Spokesperson on Defence 1979–81. Liberal Democrat Chief Whip 2001–. Member: European Union Sub-committee C (Common Foreign and Security Policy) 2000–, Select Committee on: Procedure 2000–, House of Lords' Offices 2001–02, House of Lords' Offices Administration and Works Sub-committee 2001–, Liaison 2001–02. Council of Europe: Consultant 1965–6, Member, Consultative Assembly 1973–80, Chair, Committee on Culture and Education 1979–80; President, General Council, UNA 1972–78; Member, WEU Assembly 1973–80; Chair, Committee on Defence Questions and Armaments, WEU 1977–80. Hon. Treasurer, Fabian Society 1976–81; Chair: Labour Committee for Europe 1976–80. Vice-President, Manchester Statistical Society 1971–; Member, Council, Institute for Fiscal Studies 1975–90. Trustee, History of Parliament Trust 1974–84. *Publications: Towards Regional Co-operatives,* 1967; *The Teaching of Economics at University Level,* 1970; *The Future of British Defence Policy,* 1985; editor (with others) of publications on European Defence. *Clubs:* Oxford and Cambridge University. Raised to the peerage as Baron Roper, of Thorney Island in the City of Westminster 2000. The Lord Roper, House of Lords, London, SW1A 0PW *Tel:* 020 7219 8663.

ROSSLYN, EARL OF   Crossbencher

ROSSLYN (7th Earl of, UK), Peter St Clair-Erskine; cr. 1801; 7th Baron Loughborough (GB) 1795; 11th Bt of Alva (NS) 1666. Born 31 March 1958. Son of 6th Earl; educated Eton College; Bristol University (BA Hispanic and Latin American studies 1980). Married Helen Watters 1982 (2 sons 2 daughters). *Career:* Metropolitan Police 1980–94; Thames Valley Police 1994–2000; Commander, Metropolitan Police 2000–. *House of Lords:* First entered House of Lords 1979; Elected hereditary peer 1999–. Trustee, Dunimarle Museum. *Recreations:* Church music, piano, opera. *Clubs:* White's. The Earl of Rosslyn, House of Lords, London, SW1A 0PW *Tel:* 020 7219 5353.

ROTHERWICK, LORD   Conservative

ROTHERWICK (3rd Baron), (Herbert) Robin Cayzer; cr. 1939; 3rd Bt of Tylney (UK) 1924. Born 12 March 1954. Son of 2nd Baron; educated Harrow School; RMA, Sandhurst; Royal Agricultural College, Cirencester (Diploma in Agriculture 1982). Married Sara Jane McAlpine 1982 (2 sons 1 daughter) (divorced 1994); married Tania Jane Fox 2000 (1 son). Former Acting Captain, The Life Guards. *Career:* Aviation, Agriculture and Conservation. *House of Lords:* First entered House of Lords 1996; Elected hereditary peer 1999–. Opposition Whip 2001–; Council of Europe (COE) 2000–01; Western European Union 2000–01. Popular Flying Association: Member, Executive Committee 1997–2001, Vice-chairman 1999–2001; President, General Aviation Awareness Council. Industry and Parliamentary Trust. *Special Interests:* Defence, Aviation, Agriculture. *Recreations:* Flying, Conservation. *Clubs:* White's. The Lord Rotherwick, Cornbury Park, Charlbury, Oxford, OX7 3EH *E-mail:* rr@cpark.co.uk.

RUSSELL, EARL | Liberal Democrat

RUSSELL (5th Earl), Conrad Sebastian Robert Russell; cr. 1861; Viscount Amberley. Born 15 April 1937. Son of 3rd Earl, OM, FRS and of his third wife, Patricia Helen Spence; educated Eton College; Merton College, Oxford (BA history 1958, MA 1962). Married Elizabeth Sanders 1962 (died 2003) (2 sons). *Trades Union:* Member Association of University Teachers 1960–. *Career:* Bedford College, London University 1960–74: History lecturer 1960–74, Reader 1974–79; Professor of history, Yale University, USA 1979–84; Astor Professor of British history, University College, London 1984–89; Professor of history, King's College London 1990–2002; Fellow of the British Academy 1991–. *House of Lords:* First entered House of Lords 1988; Elected hereditary peer 1999–. Liberal Democrat Spokesperson for: Social Security 1990–2001, Work and Pensions 2001–. Member Joint Committee on Statutory Instruments 2003–. Highland Park/*Spectator*: Peer of the Year Award 1996. President of the Electoral Reform Society 1997–. FBA. *Publications: The Crisis of Parliaments: English History 1509–1660*, 1971; *Parliaments and English Politics 1621–1629*, 1979; *The Causes of the English Civil War*, 1990; *The Fall of the British Monarchies*, 1991; *An Intelligent Person's Guide to Liberalism*, 1999. Professor the Earl Russell, House of Lords, London, SW1A 0PW.

RUSSELL-JOHNSTON, LORD | Liberal Democrat

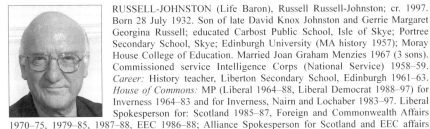

RUSSELL-JOHNSTON (Life Baron), Russell Russell-Johnston; cr. 1997. Born 28 July 1932. Son of late David Knox Johnston and Gerrie Margaret Georgina Russell; educated Carbost Public School, Isle of Skye; Portree Secondary School, Skye; Edinburgh University (MA history 1957); Moray House College of Education. Married Joan Graham Menzies 1967 (3 sons). Commissioned service Intelligence Corps (National Service) 1958–59. *Career:* History teacher, Liberton Secondary School, Edinburgh 1961–63. *House of Commons:* MP (Liberal 1964–88, Liberal Democrat 1988–97) for Inverness 1964–83 and for Inverness, Nairn and Lochaber 1983–97. Liberal Spokesperson for: Scotland 1985–87, Foreign and Commonwealth Affairs 1970–75, 1979–85, 1987–88; EEC 1986–88; Alliance Spokesperson for Scotland and EEC affairs 1987–88; SLD Spokesperson for Foreign and Commonwealth Affairs 1988–89; Liberal Democrat Spokesperson for: European Community Affairs 1988, Europe Affairs and East-West relations 1989–94, Central and Eastern Europe 1994–97. Member, European Parliament 1973–75, 1976–79. Member, WEU and Representative to Council of Europe 1984–86, 1987–; President: Council of Europe Liberal, Democratic and Reform Group 1994–99, Sub-Committee on Youth and Sport 1992–94; Vice-President: European Liberal, Democratic and Reform Parties 1990–92, Liberal International 1994–; President, Committee on Culture and Education 1995–99; WEU Defence Committee: Member 1984–86, 1987–; Vice Chairman: WEU Parliamentary and Public Relations Committee 1984–86, 2002–, WEU Liberal, Democratic and Reformers' Group; President, Parliamentary Assembly of the Council of Europe 1999–2002; COE, Hon. President Liberal Group 2002–. President, Edinburgh University Liberal Club 1956–57, Vice-President 1960–61; Member, Scottish Liberal Party Executive 1961–94; Research Assistant, Scottish Liberal Party 1963–64; Vice-Chair, Scottish Liberal Party 1965–70, Chair 1970–74, Leader 1974–88; President, Scottish Liberal Democrats 1988–94; Deputy Leader: SLD 1988–89, Liberal Democrats 1989–92. Former Member, Governing Body, Know How Fund for Poland; Former Vice-chair, Westminster Foundation for Democracy; Parliamentary Spokesman, Scottish National Federation for the Welfare of the Blind 1967–97; Parliamentary Representative, RNIB 1977–97; International Institute for Democracy: Chairman of Governing Board 2002–. Trustee, National Life Story Collection. Member, Royal Commission on Local Government in Scotland 1966–69. Knighted 1985; Grand Cross, Romania; Grand Cross, San Marino; Grand Cross, Austria; Order of Merit, Albania. *Publications: Highland Development*; *To Be A Liberal*; *Scottish Liberal Party Speeches*, (2 vols); *Humankind has no Nationality*, 1999; *Human Rights and Wrongs*, 2000; *Moral Politics*, 2001. *Special Interests:* Foreign Affairs, Commonwealth, European Union, East-West Relations, Scottish Affairs, Human Rights, Blind People, Light Rail Transport. *Recreations:* Reading, photography, shinty (Vice-Chief, Camanachd Association 1987–90). Raised to the peerage as Baron Russell-Johnston, of Minginish in Highland 1997. The Lord Russell-Johnston, House of Lords, London, SW1A 0PW *Tel:* 020 7219 5795 *Tel:* 020 7798 8005.

RYDER OF WENSUM, LORD Conservative

RYDER OF WENSUM (Life Baron), Richard Ryder; cr. 1997. Born 4 February 1949. Son of Stephen Ryder, DL, farmer; educated Radley College; Magdalene College, Cambridge (BA history 1971). Married Caroline Stephens MBE 1981 (1 daughter, 1 son deceased). *Career:* Former journalist; Director of family business in Suffolk; Political Secretary to Margaret Thatcher 1975–81; Chairman, Eastern Counties Radio 1997–2001; Vice-chairman BBC 2002–. *House of Commons:* Contested Gateshead East February and October 1974 general elections; MP (Conservative) for Norfolk Mid 1983–97; Former PPS to Financial Secretary to the Treasury; PPS to Foreign Secretary 1983–86; Parliamentary Secretary, Ministry of Agriculture, Fisheries and Food 1988–89; Economic Secretary, HM Treasury 1989–90; Paymaster-General July-November 1990. Government Whip 1986–88; Government Chief Whip 1990–95. Former Vice-Chairman, Eastern Region Council for Sport and Recreation. OBE 1981; PC 1990. Raised to the peerage as Baron Ryder of Wensum, of Wensum in the County of Norfolk 1997. Rt Hon the Lord Ryder of Wensum, OBE, House of Lords, London, SW1A 0PW *Tel:* 020 7219 5353.

S

SAATCHI, LORD Conservative

SAATCHI (Life Baron), Maurice Saatchi; cr. 1996. Born 21 June 1946. Son of Nathan and Daisy Saatchi; educated London School of Economics (BSc economics 1967). Married Josephine Hart 1984 (1 son 1 step-son). *Career:* Co-Founder, Saatchi & Saatchi 1970; Partner, M & C Saatchi Agency 1995–; Chairman Finsbury Foods Group plc 1995–. Opposition Spokesperson for: the Treasury 1999–, the Cabinet Office 2001–. Governor, London School of Economics; Director: Centre for Policy Studies, Museum of Garden History. *Publications: The Science of Politics*, 2001; *The War of Independence*, 1999; *Happiness Can't Buy Money*, 1999; *The Bad Samaritan*, 2000; *Poor People! Stop Paying Tax!*, 2001. Raised to the peerage as Baron Saatchi, of Staplefield in the County of West Sussex 1996. The Lord Saatchi, M & C Saatchi Ltd., 36 Golden Square, London, W1F 9EE *Tel:* 020 7543 4500 *E-mail:* maurices@mcsaatchi.com.

SAINSBURY OF PRESTON CANDOVER, LORD Conservative

SAINSBURY OF PRESTON CANDOVER (Life Baron), John Davan Sainsbury; cr. 1989. Born 2 November 1927. Son of late Lord Sainsbury (Life Peer); educated Stowe; Worcester College, Oxford (BA history). Married Anya Eltenton 1963 (2 sons 1 daughter). Served Life Guards 1945–48. *Career:* Joined J. Sainsbury 1950 in buying departments, Director 1958, Vice-Chairman 1967, Chairman and Chief Executive 1969–92, President 1992–; Director, Royal Opera House, Covent Garden 1969–85, Chairman 1987–91; Director, The Economist 1972–80; Joint Hon. Treasurer, European Movement 1972–75; Member of Council, British Retail Consortium 1975–79, President 1993–97; President's Committee CBI 1982–84. Governor, Royal Ballet School 1965–76, 1987–91; Director, Friends of the Nelson Mandela Children's Fund 1966–2000; Chairman, Council of Friends of Covent Garden 1969–81; Chairman, Royal Ballet Governors 1995–2003, Governor 1987–; Chairman, Benesh Institute of Choreology 1986–87; Member, Contemporary Arts Society 1958–, Hon. Secretary 1965–71, Vice-Chairman 1971–74, Vice-Patron 1984; Associate, Victoria and Albert Museum 1976–85; Member, National Committee for Electoral Reform 1976–85; President, Sparsholt College, Hampshire 1993–2000; Visitor, Ashmolean Museum 2003–. Awarded the Albert Medal, Royal Society of Arts 1989. Hon. Fellow, Worcester College, Oxford 1982; Hon. DSc Economics (London) 1985; Hon. DLitt, South Bank University 1992; Hon. LLD, Bristol University 1993; Hon. D.EconSc Cape Town 2000.

Director, Royal Opera House Trust 1974–84, 1987–97; Chairman, Trustees of Dulwich Picture Gallery 1994–2000; Trustee: National Gallery 1976–83, Westminster Abbey Trust 1977–83, Tate Gallery 1982–83, Rhodes Trust 1984–98. Kt 1980; Honorary Bencher, Inner Temple 1985; KG 1992. Fellow, Institute of Grocery Distribution 1973–; Hon. FRIBA 1993. *Special Interests:* Commerce, Arts. *Clubs:* Garrick, Beefsteak. Raised to the peerage as Baron Sainsbury of Preston Candover, of Preston Candover in the County of Hampshire 1989. The Lord Sainsbury of Preston Candover, KG, 33 Holborn, London, EC1N 2HT *Tel:* 020 7695 6663 *E-mail:* Offjds@tao.j-sainsbury.co.uk.

SAINSBURY OF TURVILLE, LORD — Labour

SAINSBURY OF TURVILLE (Life Baron), David John Sainsbury; cr 1997. Born 24 October 1940. Son of late Sir Robert Sainsbury; educated King's College, Cambridge (BA history and psychology 1963); Columbia University, New York (MBA 1971). Married Susan Carroll Reid 1973 (3 daughters). *Career:* Joined J. Sainsbury plc 1963: Finance Director 1973–90, Deputy Chairman 1988–92, Chairman and Chief Executive 1992–98. *House of Lords:* Parliamentary Under-Secretary of State, Department of Trade and Industry (Minister for Science and Innovation) 1998–. Government Spokesperson for Trade and Industry 1998–. Member, Committee of Review of the Post Office (Carter Committee) 1975–77; Member, Governing Body, London Business School 1985, Chairman 1991–98. Hon LLD, Cambridge University 1997. Trustee, Social Democratic Party 1982–90. Visiting Fellow, Nuffield College, Oxford 1987–95. *Publications: Government and Industry: a new partnership*, 1981; Co-author *Wealth Creation and Jobs*, 1987. Raised to the peerage as Baron Sainsbury of Turville, of Turville in the County of Buckinghamshire 1997. The Lord Sainsbury of Turville, House of Lords, London, SW1A 0PW *Tel:* 020 7215 5624 *Fax:* 020 7215 5410 *E-mail:* tlo.sainsbury@tlo.dti.gov.uk.

ST ALBANS, LORD BISHOP OF — Non-affiliated

ST ALBANS (Bishop of), Christopher William Herbert. Born 7 January 1944. Son of Walter Meredith Herbert and Hilda Lucy Dibben; educated Monmouth School; University of Wales, Lampeter (BA biblical studies and philosophy 1965); Bristol University (PGCE 1967); Wells Theological College 1967; Leicester University (MPhil 2002). Married Janet Elizabeth Turner 1968 (2 sons). *Career:* Assistant curate, Tupsley, Hereford 1967–71; Assistant master, Bishop's School, Hereford 1967–71; Diocese of Hereford: Adviser in religious education 1971–76, Director of education 1976–81; Vicar, St Thomas on The Bourne, Farnham, Surrey 1981–90; Archdeacon of Dorking 1990–95; Director of post ordination training, Diocese of Guildford 1984–90; Hon. Canon of Guildford 1990–95; Bishop of St Albans 1995–; Took his seat in the House of Lords 1999–. FRSA. *Publications: The New Creation*, 1971; *A Place to Dream*, 1976; *St Paul's: A Place to Dream*, 1981; *The Edge of Wonder*, 1981; *Listening to Children*, 1983; *On the Road*, 1984; *Be Thou My Vision*, 1985; *This Most Amazing Day*, 1986; *The Question of Jesus*, 1987; *Alive to God*, 1987; *Ways into Prayer*, 1987; *Help in your Bereavement*, 1988; *Prayers for Children*, 1993; *Pocket Prayers*, 1993; *The Prayer Garden*, 1994; *Words of Comfort*, 1994; *Pocket Prayers for Children*, 1999. *Special Interests:* Education, National Health Service (Hospital Chaplaincy). *Recreations:* Walking, cycling, gardening, reading, art history of fifteenth century northern Europe. Rt Rev the Lord Bishop of St Albans, Abbey Gate House, St Albans, Hertfordshire, AL3 4HD *Tel:* 01727 853305.

DodOnline
An Electronic Directory without rival ...

Peers' biographies and photographs available with daily updates *via* the internet

For a *free* trial, call Yasmin Mirza, Aby Farsoun or Michael Mand on 020 7630 7643

ST EDMUNDSBURY AND IPSWICH, LORD BISHOP OF   Non-affiliated

ST EDMUNDSBURY AND IPSWICH (Bishop of), (John Hubert) Richard Lewis. Born 10 December 1943. Son of the Ven John Wilfred and Mrs Mary Lewis; educated Radley College, Berkshire; King's College, London (Associate of King's College theology) 1966. Married Sara Patricia Hamilton 1968 (3 sons). *Career:* Curate, Hexham Abbey, Northumberland, Diocese of Newcastle 1967–70; Industrial Chaplain, Diocese of Newcastle 1970–77; Communications Officer, Diocese of Durham 1977–82; Agricultural Chaplain, Diocese of Hereford 1982–87; Archdeacon of Ludlow, Diocese of Hereford 1987–92; Bishop of Taunton, Diocese of Bath and Wells 1992–97; Bishop of St Edmundsbury and Ipswich 1997–. *Publications:* Co-editor, *The People, the Land and the Church,* 1987. *Special Interests:* Rural and Agricultural Issues, Economics and Small Business. *Recreations:* Brick laying, bumble bees. Rt Rev the Lord Bishop of St Edmundsbury and Ipswich, Bishop's House, 4 Park Road, Ipswich, Suffolk, IP1 3ST *Tel:* 01473 252829 *Fax:* 01473 232552 *E-mail:* bishop.richard@stedmundsbury.anglican.org.

ST JOHN OF BLETSO, LORD   Crossbencher

ST JOHN OF BLETSO (21st Baron, E), Anthony Tudor St John; cr. 1558; 18th Bt of Bletso (E) 1660. Born 16 May 1957. Son of 20th Baron, TD; educated Diocesan College, Cape Town; University of Cape Town (BSocSc 1977, BA law 1979, BProc law 1982); London University (LLM 1983). Married Dr Helen Jane Westlake 1994 (2 sons 2 daughters). *Career:* Solicitor; Attorney in South Africa 1983–85; Oil Analyst/Stockbroker, County Natwest 1985–88; Consultant to Merrill Lynch 1988–; Chairman, Eurotrust International 1993–; Managing Director, Globix 1997–2002; Non-executive Director, WMRC plc 2000–02. *House of Lords:* First entered House of Lords 1978; Elected hereditary peer 1999–. Member, Select Committee on European Communities/Union Sub-Committee A (Economic and Financial Affairs, Trade and External Relations) 1997–; Member, Library and Computers Sub-Committee 1998–2000. Chairman of Governing Board of Certification International. Trustee: TVE (Television for the Environment), TUSK, Citizens-on-Line, Life Neurological Trust. Extra Lord in Waiting to HM The Queen 1998–. *Special Interests:* Foreign Affairs, Finance, Legal Affairs, Sport, Southern Africa, IT. *Recreations:* Ski-ing, golf, tennis, bridge. *Sportsclubs:* Wisley Golf. *Clubs:* Hurlingham, Institute of Directors. The Lord St John of Bletso, House of Lords, London, SW1A 0PW *Tel:* 020 7219 3886 *E-mail:* asj@globix.com.

ST JOHN OF FAWSLEY, LORD   Conservative

ST JOHN OF FAWSLEY (Life Baron), Norman Anthony Francis St John-Stevas; cr. 1987. Born 18 May 1929. Son of late Stephen S. Stevas and late Kitty St John-O'Connor; educated Ratcliffe College, Leicester; Fitzwilliam College, Cambridge (MA Law 1950, Yorke Prize 1957) (President, Cambridge Union 1950); Christ Church, Oxford (BCL 1954); Yale University, USA (Blackstone and Harmsworth Scholar 1952). *Career:* Author and barrister; Called to the Bar, Middle Temple 1952; Tutored in jurisprudence: King's College, London, Christ Church and Merton, Oxford 1953–57; Political correspondent, *The Economist* 1959; Editor, *Dublin Review* 1961; Chairman, Royal Fine Arts Commission 1985–99; Master of Emmanuel College, Cambridge 1991–96. *House of Commons:* Contested (Conservative) Dagenham general election 1951; MP (Conservative) for Chelmsford 1964–87; Chancellor of the Duchy of Lancaster and Leader of the House of Commons 1979–1981. Conservative Spokesman on Education and the Arts 1975–79. Fellow, Yale Law School 1960. Fellow, Royal Society of Literature 1966. *Publications:* include *Obscenity and the Law,* 1956; *Walter Bagehot,* 1959; *Life, Death and the Law,* 1961; *The Right to Life,* 1963; *The Collected Works of Walter Bagehot,* in 15 volumes 1965–86; *The Agonising Choice,* 1971. *Clubs:* Garrick, White's, Pratt's. Raised to the peerage as Baron St John of Fawsley, of Preston Capes in the County of Northamptonshire 1987. Rt Hon the Lord St John of Fawsley, The Old Rectory, Preston Capes, Daventry, Northamptonshire, NN11 6TE.

SALISBURY, MARQUESS   Non-affiliated

SALISBURY (7th Marquess, GB), Robert Michael James Gascoyne-Cecil; cr. 1789; 13th Earl of Salisbury (E) 1605; 13th Viscount Cranborne (E) 1604; 13th Baron Cecil (E) 1603; (Life) Baron Gascoyne-Cecil 1999. Born 30 September 1946. Son of 6th Marquess of Salisbury, DL and Marjorie Olein, née Wyndham-Quin; educated Eton College; Christ Church, Oxford (BA 1968). Married Hannah Ann Stirling 1970 (2 sons 3 daughters). DL, Dorset 1987–. *House of Commons:* MP (Conservative) for Dorset South 1979–87. *House of Lords:* First entered House of Lords 1992; Parliamentary Under-Secretary of State for Defence, Ministry of Defence 1992–94; Lord Privy Seal and Leader of the House of Lords 1994–97; Member, Shadow Cabinet 1997–98; Leader of the Opposition 1997–98. Opposition Spokesperson on the Public Service 1997–98. Member Constitution Committee 2001–02. Summoned to the Upper House in his father's barony of Cecil, of Essendon in the County of Rutland, by a Writ in Acceleration 1992; Member Ecclesiastical Committee 2000–01. PC 1994. *Clubs:* White's, Pratt's, Beefsteak. Created a life peer as Baron Gascoyne-Cecil, of Essendon in the County of Rutland 1999. Most Hon the Marquess of Salisbury, PC, DL, The Manor House, Cranborne, Wimborne, Dorset, BH21 5PP.

SALISBURY, LORD BISHOP OF   Non-affiliated

SALISBURY (77th Bishop of), David Staffurth Stancliffe. Born 1 October 1942. Son of late Very Rev. Michael Staffurth Stancliffe; educated Westminster School; Trinity College, Oxford (BA literae humaniores 1965, MA 1969); Cuddesdon Theological College. Married Sarah Loveday Smith 1965 (1 son 2 daughters). *Career:* Assistant Curate, St Bartholomew's, Armley, Leeds 1967–70; Chaplain to Clifton College, Bristol 1970–77; Canon Residentiary of Portsmouth Cathedral, Diocesan Director of Ordinands and Lay Ministry Adviser 1977–82; Provost of Portsmouth 1982–93; Member, General Synod 1985–; Member, Liturgical Commission 1986, Chairman 1993–; Member, Cathedral's Fabric Commission 1991–2001; Bishop of Salisbury 1993–; Took his seat in the House of Lords 1998. President: Council of Marlborough College 1994–, Affirming Catholicism 1995–. DLitt, Portsmouth University 1993; Hon. Fellow: St Chad's College, Durham 2000; Fellow, Royal School of Church Music 2001; Hon Fellow, Trinity College, Oxford 2003. *Publications:* Editor, *Celebrating Common Prayer*, 1993; *The Pilgrim Prayerbook*, 2003; *God's Pattern*, 2003. *Special Interests:* Sudan; Heritage; International Trade; Rural Affairs. *Recreations:* Old music, Italy. Rt Rev the Lord Bishop of Salisbury, South Canonry, 71 The Close, Salisbury, Wiltshire, SP1 2ER *Tel:* 01722 334031 *E-mail:* dsarum@salisbury.anglican.org.

SALTOUN OF ABERNETHY, LADY   Crossbencher

SALTOUN OF ABERNETHY (Lady, 20th in line, S), Flora Marjory Fraser; cr. 1445. Born 18 October 1930. Daughter of 19th Lord, MC; educated St Mary's School, Wantage. Married Captain Alexander Ramsay of Mar, DL 1956 (died 2000) (3 daughters). *House of Lords:* First entered House of Lords 1979; Elected hereditary peer 1999–. Member: House of Lords Offices Sub-Committee: Advisory Panel on Works of Art 2000–02, Refreshment Committee 2003–. Cordon Bleu Diploma in Cookery 1950. Member, Standing Council of Scottish Chiefs; Chief of the Name of Fraser. *Special Interests:* Scottish Affairs, Defence. The Lady Saltoun of Abernethy, House of Lords, London, SW1A 0PW *Tel:* 020 7219 0313.

Visit the Vacher Dod Website . . .
www.DodOnline.co.uk

SANDBERG, LORD   Liberal Democrat

SANDBERG (Life Baron), Michael Graham Ruddock Sandberg; cr. 1997. Born 31 May 1927. Son of Gerald and Ethel Sandberg; educated St Edward's School, Oxford. Married Carmel Mary Donnelly 1954 (2 sons 2 daughters). 6th Lancers (Indian Army) and First King's Dragoon Guards 1945. *Career:* Joined Hong Kong and Shanghai Banking Corporation 1949, Chairman 1977–86. Member: European Union Sub-committee B (Energy, Industry and Transport) 1999–2000, Personal Bills Committee 2000–, Hybrid Instruments Committee 2003–. Commonwealth Party Association; British Council Associate Parliamentary Group; Inter-Parliamentary Union British Group. Member, Executive Council, Hong Kong 1978–86; Treasurer, University of Hong Kong 1977–86. Two honorary doctorates. Member: High Murlands Trust, Memorial Gates Trust, River Wey Trust, Graham Layton Trust; Patron Police Foundation. OBE 1977; CBE 1982; Kt 1986. FCIB; FRSA 1983. Freeman, City of London. Member of the Court, Clockmakers' Company. *Publications: The Sandberg Watch Collection,* 1998. *Special Interests:* Foreign Affairs, Hong Kong, Latin America. *Recreations:* Horse racing, bridge, cricket, horology. *Sportsclubs:* President, Surrey County Cricket Club 1988; Member HCCC. *Clubs:* Cavalry and Guards, Portland, White's, MCC. Raised to the peerage as Baron Sandberg, of Passfield in the County of Hampshire 1997. The Lord Sandberg, CBE, 11 St James's Square, London, SW1Y 4LB; House of Lords, London, SW1A 0PW *Tel:* 020 7219 3227 *E-mail:* lordsandberg@msandberg.com.

SANDERSON OF BOWDEN, LORD   Conservative

SANDERSON OF BOWDEN (Life Baron), (Charles) Russell Sanderson; cr. 1985. Born 30 April 1933. Son of late Charles Plummer Sanderson; educated St Mary's School, Melrose; Glenalmond College, Perthshire; Bradford Technical College; Scottish College of Textiles. Married Elizabeth Macaulay 1958 (1 son 2 daughters and 1 son deceased). Commissioned Royal Signals 1952. DL, Roxburgh, Ettrick and Lauderdale 1990–. *Career:* Partner, Charles P. Sanderson, Wool and Yarn Merchants 1958–87; Director: Johnston of Elgin 1980–87, Illingworth Morris 1982–87; Chairman: Edinburgh Financial Trust plc 1983–87, Shires Investment plc 1983–87; Director, Clydesdale Bank plc 1986–87, 1994–, Deputy Chairman 1996–99, Chairman 1999–2003; Chairman, Hawick Cashmere Co. 1991–; Director, Scottish Mortgage and Trust plc 1991–, Chairman 1993–2003; Director: Woolcombers plc 1992–95, Edinburgh Woollen Mills 1992–97, United Auctions Ltd 1992–99, Watson-Philip plc 1993–99, Morrison Construction 1995–2001. *House of Lords:* Minister of State, Scottish Office 1987–90. Vice-Chairman, Scottish Peers Association 1996, Chairman 1998–2000. President, Scottish Conservative and Unionist Association 1977–79; Vice-President, National Union of Conservative and Unionist Associations 1979–81; Chairman, National Union Executive Committee 1981–86; Chairman, Scottish Conservative Party 1990–93. Chairman, Eildon Housing Association 1976–82; Member, Scottish Council of Independent Schools 1984–87; Chairman, Council of Glenalmond College 1994–2000; Member of Court, Napier University, Edinburgh 1994–2001; Chairman, St Marys School, Melrose 1999–; President, Royal Highland Agricultural Society of Scotland 2002–03. Honorary Degree Glasgow University 2001; Napier University 2001. Kt 1981. Liveryman, The Worshipful Company of Framework Knitters; Assistant (Member of Court) 2000–; Under Warden, Framework Knitters Livery Co 2003–. *Special Interests:* Industry, Textile Industry, Small Businesses, Scottish Affairs, Housing, Transport. *Recreations:* Golf, fishing. *Sportsclubs:* Hon. Company of Edinburgh Golfers. *Clubs:* Caledonian. Raised to the peerage as Baron Sanderson of Bowden, of Melrose in the District of Ettrick and Lauderdale 1985. The Lord Sanderson of Bowden, DL, Becketts Field, Bowden, Melrose, Borders, TD6 0ST *Tel:* 01835 822736; Office: The Square, Bowden, Melrose, Borders, TD6 0ST *Tel:* 01835 822271 *Fax:* 01835 823272.

Visit the Vacher Dod Website . . .
www.DodOnline.co.uk

SANDWICH, EARL OF
Crossbencher

SANDWICH (11th Earl of, E), John Edward Hollister Montagu; cr. 1660; Viscount Hinchingbrooke and Baron Montagu. Born 11 April 1943. Son of Victor Montagu, 10th Earl, formerly Viscount Hinchingbrooke MP, who disclaimed the earldom and other honours for life in 1964; educated Eton College; Trinity College, Cambridge (MA history and modern language Tripos 1965); OU certificate in European studies 1973. Married (Susan) Caroline Hayman 1968 (2 sons 1 daughter). *Trades Union:* Former member NUJ. *Career:* Assistant editor, The Bodley Head 1966–68; Editor, India Tourism Development Corporation 1968–69; Christian Aid: Information Officer 1974–85, Research Officer 1985–86; Joint owner/administrator, Mapperton Estate, Dorset 1982–; Consultant, CARE Britain 1987–93; Editor, Save the Children 1990–92. *House of Lords:* First entered House of Lords 1995; Elected hereditary peer 1999–. Member, Standing Orders (Private Bills) Committee 2000–; Library and Computers Sub-Committee 2001–. Governor, Beaminster School, Dorset 1996–; Council, Anti-Slavery International 1997–; Vice-President, Worldaware 1997–2001; Board, Christian Aid 1999–; International Development Affairs Committee, Church House 1997–2001. Managing Trustee, St Francis School, Dorset 1987–92; TSW Telethon Trustee 1987–93; Trustee, Britain-Afghanistan Trust 1994–2001. President, Samuel Pepys Club. *Publications:* Author or Editor of: *The Book of the World*, 1971; *Prospects for Africa*, 1988; *Prospects for Africa's Children*, 1990; *Children at Crisis Point*, 1992; Co-editor *Hinch: A Celebration*, 1997. *Special Interests:* Overseas Aid and Development, International Affairs, National Heritage. *Recreations:* Walking, tennis, sailing, ski-ing. The Earl of Sandwich, House of Lords, London, SW1A 0PW *Tel:* 020 7219 3882.

SAVILLE OF NEWDIGATE, LORD
Crossbencher

SAVILLE OF NEWDIGATE (Life Baron), Mark Oliver Saville; cr. 1997. Born 20 March 1936. Son of Kenneth and Olivia Saville; educated Rye Grammar School; Brasenose College, Oxford (BA law 1959, BCL 1960). Married Jill Gray 1961 (2 sons). Second Lieutenant, Royal Sussex Regiment 1954–56. *Career:* Oxford University 1956–60, Vinerian Scholar 1960; Called to the Bar, Middle Temple 1962, Bencher 1983; QC 1975; Judge of the High Court, Queen's Bench Division 1985–93; Lord Justice of Appeal 1994–97; Lord of Appeal in Ordinary 1997–. Member, Joint Select Committee on Consolidation of Bills 1998–. Hon. LLD, Guildhall University 1997; Hon. Fellow, Brasenose College, Oxford 1998. Kt 1985; PC 1994. *Recreations:* Sailing, flying, gardening, computers. *Clubs:* Garrick. Raised to the peerage as Baron Saville of Newdigate, of Newdigate in the County of Surrey 1997. Rt Hon the Lord Saville of Newdigate, House of Lords, London, SW1A 0PW *Tel:* 020 7219 3202.

SAWYER, LORD
Labour

SAWYER (Life Baron), Lawrence Sawyer; cr. 1998. Born 12 May 1943; educated Dodmire School; Eastbourne School; Darlington Technical School. *Trades Union:* Member, UNISON. *Career:* Engineering apprentice, Robert Stephenson and Hawthorne 1958–63; Engineering inspector, Lockhead Brakes, Leamington Spa 1963–65; Engineering inspection and work study officer, Cummins Engines, Darlington 1965–71; NUPE Officer 1971–75, Northern Regional Officer 1975–81, Deputy General Secretary, NUPE/UNISON 1981–94; National Executive Member, Labour Party 1981–94; Chairman, Labour Party 1991–9?; General Secretary, The Labour Party 1994–98; Director: Investors in People UK 1998–, Reed Executive plc 1998–2001; Britannia Building Society 1999–; Visiting Professor, Cranfield Business School 1999–; Notting Hill Housing Association 1999–, Union Income Benefit Advisory Board 2000–, Royal Mail Partnership Board 2001, Reed Healthcare plc 2001–; Thompsons Solicitors Supervisory Board 2001–; Business consultant. Labour Party: Member, National Executive 1982–94, 1998–2001, Party Chair 1992; Chair, Labour Home Policy Committee 1994–98; General Secretary 1994–98. Member: Post Office Northern Advisory Board 1997–99, Nurses' and Midwives' Whitley Council 1997–99, NJIC for Manual Workers 1997–99. *Recreations:* Antiquarian book dealer and collector. *Clubs:* Royal Commonwealth Society, Royal Overseas League. Raised to the peerage as Baron Sawyer, of Darlington in the County of Durham 1998. The Lord Sawyer, House of Lords, London, SW1A 0PW *Tel:* 020 7219 8668.

SCANLON, LORD Labour

SCANLON (Life Baron), Hugh Parr Scanlon; cr. 1979. Born 26 October 1913. Son of late Hugh Scanlon; educated Stretford Elementary School; National Council of Labour Colleges (economics). Married Nora Markey 1943 (2 daughters). *Trades Union:* Divisional Organiser, AEU Manchester 1947–63, Member, Executive Council 1963–67; President, Amalgamated Union of Engineering Workers 1968–78; Member, TUC General Council 1968–78; President, European Metal Workers Federation 1974–78. Member, Science and Technology Committee. Hon. DCL, Kent University 1988. Member, British Gas Corporation 1976–82; Chairman, Engineering Industry Training Board 1975–82. *Recreations:* Golf, gardening. *Sportsclubs:* Member North Foreland Golf Club. Raised to the peerage as Baron Scanlon, of Davyhulme in the County of Greater Manchester 1979. The Lord Scanlon, 23 Seven Stones Drive, Broadstairs, Kent, CT10 1TW.

SCARMAN, LORD Crossbencher

SCARMAN (Life Baron), Leslie George Scarman; cr. 1977. Born 29 July 1911. Son of late George Charles Scarman, Lloyd's Underwriter; educated Radley College; Brasenose College, Oxford (BA mods and greats). Married Ruth Wright 1947 (1 adopted son). RAFVR 1940–45. *Career:* Called to the Bar, Middle Temple 1936; QC 1957; Judge of the High Court of Justice, Probate, Divorce and Admiralty Division 1961–72; Chairman, Law Commission 1965–72; Lord Justice of Appeal 1972–77; President, Senate of Inns of Court and Bar 1976–79; Lord of Appeal in Ordinary 1977–86. Chancellor, Warwick University 1977–89. Member, Charter 88. 12 honorary law doctorates from British and German universities. OBE (Mil) 1944; Order of Battle Merit (Russia) 1945; Kt 1961; PC 1972. *Publications: English Law: The New Dimension,* 1974. *Special Interests:* Law Reform, Constitutional Reform, Homeless, Human Rights, Education. *Recreations:* History, music, walking. *Clubs:* Royal Air Force, RAC, Garrick. Raised to the peerage as Baron Scarman, of Quatt in the county of Shropshire 1977. Rt Hon the Lord Scarman, OBE, House of Lords, London, SW1A 0PW *Tel:* 020 7219 3202.

SCOTLAND OF ASTHAL, BARONESS Labour

SCOTLAND OF ASTHAL (Life Baroness), Patricia Janet Scotland; cr. 1997. Born 19 August 1955; educated London University (LLB 1976). Married Richard Mawhinney 1985 (2 sons). *Career:* Called to the Bar, Middle Temple 1977, Bencher 1997; Barrister specialising in family law 1997–91; QC 1991; Assistant recorder 1994; Recorder 2000; Member, Antigua Bar and Commonwealth of Dominica. *House of Lords:* Parliamentary Under-Secretary of State, Foreign and Commonwealth Office 1999–2001; Parliamentary Secretary, Lord Chancellor's Department 2001–03; Minister of State (Criminal Justice System and Law Reform), Home Office 2003–. Government Spokesperson for: Foreign and Commonwealth Office 1999–2001, Law Officers' Department 2001–03, Women's Issues/Equal Agenda, Home Office 2003–. Former Member, Commission for Racial Equality; Member, Millennium Commission 1994–99; Alternate UK Government Representative European Convention 2002–. PC 2001. Honorary Fellow of Wolfson College, Cambridge and Cardiff University. Raised to the peerage as Baroness Scotland of Asthal, of Asthal in the County of Oxfordshire 1997. Rt Hon the Baroness Scotland of Asthal, QC, Home Office, 50 Queen Anne's Gate, London, SW1H 9AT *Tel:* 0870 000 1585 *Fax:* 020 7273 2065; House of Lords, London, SW1A 0PW *Tel:* 020 7219 5348 *E-mail:* baroness.scotland@homeoffice.gsi.gov.uk.

Visit the Vacher Dod Website . . .
www.DodOnline.co.uk

SCOTT OF FOSCOTE, LORD   Crossbencher

SCOTT OF FOSCOTE (Life Baron), Richard Rashleigh Folliott Scott; cr. 2000. Born 2 October 1934. Son of Lieutenant-Colonel C. W. F. Scott, 2/9th Gurkha Rifles and Katharine Scott; educated Michaelhouse College, Natal, South Africa; Cape Town University (BA 1954); Trinity College, Cambridge (BA, LLB 1957). Married Rima Elisa Ripoll 1959 (2 sons 2 daughters). *Career:* Called to the Bar, Inner Temple 1959, Bencher 1981; In practice, Chancery Bar 1960–83; QC 1975; Duchy and County Palatine of Lancaster: Attorney General 1980–83, Vice-Chancellor 1987–91; Chair of the Bar 1982–83; Judge of the High Court of Justice, Chancery Division 1983–91; Lord Justice of Appeal 1991–94; Inquiry into defence related exports to Iraq and related prosecutions 1992–96; Vice-Chancellor of the Supreme Court 1994–2000; Head of Civil Justice 1995–2000; Lord of Appeal in Ordinary 2000–. Member Select Committee on European Union 2001–; Chair European Union Sub-Committee E (Law and Institutions) 2001–. Two honorary doctorates; Hon. Member: American Bar Association 1983, Canadian Bar Association 1983. Kt 1983; PC 1991. *Publications:* Articles in legal journals. *Recreations:* Tennis, bridge, hunting (foxhounds and bloodhounds). *Sportsclubs:* Vanderbilt Racquet. *Clubs:* Hawks (Cambridge). Raised to the peerage as Baron Scott of Foscote, of Foscote in the County of Buckinghamshire 2000. Rt Hon the Lord Scott of Foscote, House of Lords, London, SW1A 0PW *Tel:* 020 7219 3117.

SCOTT OF NEEDHAM MARKET, BARONESS   Liberal Democrat

SCOTT OF NEEDHAM MARKET (Life Baroness), Rosalind Carol Scott; cr. 2000. Born 10 August 1957. Daughter of Kenneth Vincent and Carol Leadbeater; educated Whitby Grammar School; Kent School; University of East Anglia (BA European studies 1999). Divorced (1 son 1 daughter). Councillor: Mid Suffolk District Council 1991–94, Suffolk County Council 1993–, Vice-chair 1996–97, Vice-chair, Transport Committee, Local Government Association 1996–2002, Chair 2002–. Liberal Democrat Whip 2001–02; Deputy Chief Whip 2002. Liberal Democrat Spokesperson for: Transport, Local Government and the Regions 2001–02, Transport 2002–. Member, European Union Sub-committee B (Energy, Industry and Transport) 2000–02, Liaison Committee 2003–. IPU. Member: EU Committee of the Regions1998–2002, Council of European Municipalities and Regions, Congress of Local and Regional Authorities in Europe, North Sea Commission 1997–. Hon. President East Coast Sailing Trust; Patron: MacClean Wheelchair Trust, Pickerel Environment Project. *Special Interests:* Transport. *Recreations:* Walking, political biography. *Clubs:* Royal Commonwealth Society. Raised to the peerage as Baroness Scott of Needham Market, of Needham Market in the County of Suffolk 2000. The Baroness Scott of Needham Market, House of Lords, London, SW1A 0PW *Tel:* 020 7219 8660.

SECCOMBE, BARONESS   Conservative

SECCOMBE (Life Baroness), Joan Anna Dalziel Seccombe; cr. 1991. Born 3 May 1930. Daughter of late Robert John Owen, and of Olive Barlow Owen; educated St Martin's, Solihull. Married Henry Laurence Seccombe 1950 (2 sons). JP, Solihull 1968–2000, Chairman of Bench 1981–84; Councillor, West Midlands County Council 1977–81, Chairman, Trading Standards Committee 1979–81. Opposition Whip: Education, Northern Ireland 1997–2001; Opposition Deputy Chief Whip 2001–. Member, House of Lords Committees on: Offices 1992–94, 1998–2001, Broadcasting 1994–97, Personal Bills 1994–97; Member, Sub-Committees on: Administration and Works 1992–94, 2000–02, Finance and Staff 1994–97. Chairman: West Midlands Conservative Women's Committee 1975–78, Conservative Women's National Committee 1981–84, National Union of Conservative and Unionist Associations 1987–88, Vice-Chairman 1984–87, Member of Executive 1975–97; Chairman, Conservative Party Annual Conference, Blackpool 1987; Vice-chairman, Conservative Party with special responsibility for Women 1987–97. Vice-President, Institute of Trading Standards Administration 1992–; Governor, Nuffield Hospitals 1988–2001, Deputy Chairman 1993–2001.

Chairman, Trustees of Nuffield Hospitals Pension Scheme 1992–2001. Chairman, Lord Chancellor's Advisory Committee 1975–93; Member, Heart of England Tourist Board 1977–81, Chairman, Marketing Sub-committee 1979–81; Member, Women's National Commission 1984–90. DBE, 1984. *Special Interests:* Women's Issues, Family, Criminal Justice. *Recreations:* Golf, ski-ing, needlework. *Sportsclubs:* President, St Enedoc Golf Club 1992–. Raised to the peerage as Baroness Seccombe, of Kineton in the County of Warwickshire 1991. The Baroness Seccombe, DBE, House of Lords, London, SW1A 0PW *Tel:* 020 7219 4558 *Fax:* 020 7219 6069 *E-mail:* seccombej@parliament.uk.

SELBORNE, EARL OF   Conservative

SELBORNE (4th Earl of, UK), John Roundell Palmer; cr. 1882; Viscount Wolmer; 4th Baron Selborne (UK) 1872. Born 24 March 1940. Son of Captain Viscount Wolmer (died on active service 1942), son of 3rd Earl, PC, CH; educated Eton College; Christ Church, Oxford (BA history 1961, MA). Married Joanna Van Antwerp, née James 1969 (3 sons 1 daughter). DL, Hampshire 1982. *Career:* Member, Apple and Pear Development Council 1969–73; Chairman: Hops Marketing Board 1978–82, Agricultural and Food Research Council 1982–89; Chairman, Joint Nature Conservation Committee 1991–97; Member, NEDC Food Sector Group 1991–92; Member, Royal Commission on Environmental Pollution 1993–98; Director: Lloyds Bank Plc 1994–95, Lloyds TSB Group Plc 1995–. Chancellor, Southampton University 1996–. *House of Lords:* First entered House of Lords 1971; Elected hereditary peer 1999–. Chair, Sub-Committee D, European Communities Select Committee 1991–93, and 1999–; Member, Select Committee on Science and Technology 1992–97, Chair 1993–97; Co-opted Member, Select Committee on European Communities Sub-Committee (Environment, Public Health and Consumer Protection) 1998; Member, Select Committees on: Science and Technology Sub-Committee I (Non-Food Crops) 1999, European Union 1999–; Co-opted Member Science and Technology Sub-Committee I (Systematic Biology and Biodiversity) 2002; Member Joint Committee on House of Lords Reform 2002–. UNESCO, World Commission on the Ethics of Science and Technology. President: Royal Agricultural Society of England 1987–88, Royal Institute of Public Health and Hygiene 1991–97; Vice-President, Foundation for Science and Technology; President, Royal Geographical Society (with the Institute of British Geographers) 1997–2000. Five honorary doctorates. KBE 1987. FRS 1991. Master, Mercers' Company 1989. *Special Interests:* Science, Agriculture, Education, Conservation. *Clubs:* Travellers'. The Earl of Selborne, KBE, FRS, DL, Temple Manor, Selborne, Alton, Hampshire, GU34 3LR *Tel:* 01420 476 003 *Fax:* 01420 475 878 *Tel:* 020 7219 6171 *E-mail:* selbornejr@parliament.uk.

SELKIRK OF DOUGLAS, LORD   Conservative

SELKIRK OF DOUGLAS (Life Baron), James Alexander Douglas-Hamilton; cr. 1997. Born 31 July 1942. Son of 14th Duke of Hamilton and Brandon, KT, PC, GCVO, AFC, DL, and Lady Elizabeth Percy, OBE, DL, daughter of 8th Duke of Northumberland, KG, CBE, MVO; educated Eton College; Balliol College, Oxford (BA modern history 1964) (Oxford Boxing Blue 1961, President, Oxford University Conservation Association Winter 1963, President, Oxford Union Society Summer 1964); Edinburgh University (LLB Scots law 1967). Married Hon Susan Buchan 1974 (4 sons including twins). Officer 6/7th Btn, Cameronians TA 1961–66; Captain, 2nd Btn Lowland Volunteers, TAVR 1971–74; Hon. Air Commodore No 2 (City of Edinburgh), Maritime Headquarters Unit 1994; Hon. Air Commodore No 603 (City of Edinburgh) Squadron 2000. Councillor: Murrayfield-Cramond Ward 1972–74, Murrayfield District 1974. *Career:* Scots Advocate and Interim Procurator Fiscal Depute at Scottish Bar 1968–74; QC 1996. *House of Commons:* MP (Conservative) for Edinburgh West 1974–97; PPS to Malcolm Rifkind: as Minister of State, Foreign Office 1983–85, as Secretary of State for Scotland 1986–87; Parliamentary Under-Secretary of State, Scottish Office 1987–95: Minister for Home Affairs and Environment 1987–92, Minister for Education and Housing 1992–95; Minister of State for Health and Home Affairs 1995–97. Scottish Conservative Whip 1976–79; Government Whip 1979–81. President, Oxford University Conservative Association Winter 1963. Hon. President, Scottish Boxing Association 1975–98; President: Royal Commonweath Society in Scotland 1979–87, Scottish National Council, UN Association 1981–87. Honorary Air Commodore No 603 (City of Edinburgh) Squadron 2000. Trustee, Selkirk Charitable Trust. Disclaimed the Earldom of Selkirk, November 1994; Member, Royal Company of Archers, the Queen's Bodyguard for Scotland; Contested Edinburgh West 1997 general election; list MSP for Lothians region since May 6, 1999 and 2003 (contested the seat as Lord James Douglas-Hamilton); Scottish Parliament: Member, Parliamentary Bureau 1999–2001, Business Manager (Chief Whip of the Conservative Group) 1999–2001, Home Affairs spokesperson 2001–03, Education spokesperson 2003–. PC 1996. *Publications: Motive for a Mission: The Story Behind Hess's Flight to Britain*, 1971; *The Air Battle for Malta: The Diaries of a Fighter Pilot*, 1981; *Roof of the World: Man's First Flight over Everest*, 1983; *The Truth About Rudolph Hess*, 1993. *Special Interests:* Foreign Affairs, Defence, Scottish Affairs, Law Reform, Conservation, Arts, Housing, Health, Education, Local Government, Environment, Heritage. *Recreations:* Golf, boxing, forestry, debating, history. *Clubs:* Pratt's, New (Edinburgh). Raised to the peerage as Baron Selkirk of Douglas, of Cramond in the City of Edinburgh 1997. Rt Hon the Lord Selkirk of Douglas, House of Lords, London, SW1A 0PW *Tel:* 020 7219 2131.

SELSDON, LORD
Conservative

SELSDON (3rd Baron, UK), Malcolm McEacharn Mitchell-Thomson; cr. 1932; 4th Bt of Polmood (UK) 1900. Born 27 October 1937. Son of 2nd Baron, DSC; educated Winchester College. Married Patricia Anne Smith 1965 (1 son) (divorced); married Gabrielle Williams 1995. Royal Navy 1956–58, Sub-Lieutenant RNR. *Career:* Merchant banker, Midland Bank Group, Public Finance Adviser 1979–90; Delegate, Council of Europe and Western European Union 1972–78; Member, British Overseas Trade Board 1983–86; Chairman, Committee for Middle East Trade (COMET) 1979–86; Member, East European Trade Council 1983–87. *House of Lords:* First entered House of Lords 1963; Elected hereditary peer 1999–. President: British Exporters' Association 1992–98, Anglo Swiss Society 2001–. Chairman, Greater London and South East Council for Sport and Recreation 1977–83. *Special Interests:* Trade and Industry, Foreign Affairs, Defence, Economic Policy. *Recreations:* Ski-ing, sailing, tennis, lawn tennis, golf. *Sportsclubs:* Hon Secretary, House of Lords Yacht Club. *Clubs:* MCC. The Lord Selsdon, House of Lords, London, SW1A 0PW *Tel:* 020 7219 6668 *E-mail:* selsdonm@parliament.uk.

SEWEL, LORD
Labour

SEWEL (Life Baron), John Buttifant Sewel; cr. 1996. Born 15 January 1946. Son of late Leonard Sewel, and of Hilda Ivy Sewel; educated Hanson Boys' Grammar School, Bradford; Durham University (BA); University College of Wales, Swansea (MSc economics); Aberdeen University (PhD). Councillor, Aberdeen City Council 1974–84, Leader 1977–80. *Career:* Aberdeen University 1969–: successively research fellow, lecturer, senior lecturer, Dean, Faculty of Economic and Social Sciences 1989–94, Vice-principal and Dean, Faculty of Social Sciences and Law 1995–97, Professor and Vice-principal 1999–2001, Senior Vice-principal 2001–. *House of Lords:* Parliamentary Under-Secretary of State, Scottish Office (Minister for Agriculture, the Environment and Fisheries) 1997–99. Opposition Spokesperson for Scotland 1996–97. UK representative to NATO Parliamentary Assembly 1999–2002. President, Convention of Scottish Local Authorities 1982–84; Member: Accounts Commission for Scotland 1987–97, Scottish Constitutional Commission 1994–95. CBE 1984. *Publications:* Books and learned articles mainly on politics and development in Scotland. *Special Interests:* Scotland, Public Finance, Higher Education, Europe. *Recreations:* Hill walking, skiing. Raised to the peerage as Baron Sewel, of Gilcomstoun in the District of the City of Aberdeen 1996. The Lord Sewel, CBE, Birklands, Raemoir, Banchory, Kincardineshire, AB31 5QU *Tel:* 01330 844545.

Visit the Vacher Dod Website . . .
www.DodOnline.co.uk

SHARMAN, LORD   Liberal Democrat

SHARMAN (Life Baron), Colin Morven Sharman; cr. 1999. Born 19 February 1943. Son of Colonel Terence John Sharman; educated Bishops Wordsworth School, Salisbury, Wiltshire. Married Angela Timmins 1966 (1 son 1 daughter). *Career:* Qualified as a Chartered Accountant 1965; Peat Marwick Mitchell, later KPMG Peat Marwick, then KPMG 1966–99: Partner 1973, Senior Partner (National Marketing and Industry Groups) 1987–90, UK Senior Partner 1994–98, Chair, KPMG International 1998–99; Director: Youngs Brewery, Reed Elsevier, AEA Technology, B G International PLC; Chair: Le Gavroche Ltd, Aegis Group Plc. Liberal Democrat Spokesperson for Trade and Industry 2001–. Member, European Communities Committee Sub-Committee A (Economic and Financial Affairs, Trade and External Relations) 2000–. Member, Industry Society. Hon. Doctorate, Cranfield School of Management 1998. Companion, British Institute of Management; Member: Industrial Society, Advisory Board of the George Washington Institute for Management, Hon. Member, Securities Institute. OBE 1979. FCA; CIMgt. Freeman, City of London. Liveryman, Company of Gunmakers 1992. *Publications: Holding to Account* (Review of audit and accountability in central government); *Turning the Corner* (Report of Foresight Panel on Crime Prevention); Co-author *Living Culture. Recreations:* Shooting, sailing, opera, food and wine. *Sportsclubs:* Bembridge Sailing; Royal Yacht Squadron. *Clubs:* Flyfishers', Reform. Raised to the peerage as Baron Sharman, of Redlynch in the County of Wiltshire 1999. The Lord Sharman, OBE, KPMG, 8 Salisbury Square, London, EC4Y 8BB *E-mail:* lordsharman@kpmg.co.uk.

SHARP OF GUILDFORD, BARONESS   Liberal Democrat

SHARP OF GUILDFORD (Life Baroness), Margaret Lucy Sharp; cr. 1998. Born 21 November 1938. Daughter of Osmund Hailstone and Sydney Mary Ellen Hailstone; educated Tonbridge Girls' Grammar School; Newnham College, Cambridge (BA economics 1960). Married Thomas Sharp 1962. *Trades Union:* Member, Association of University Teachers. *Career:* Assistant principal, Board of Trade and Industry 1960–63; Lecturer, LSE 1964–72; Economic adviser, NEDO 1977–81; Sussex University: Research fellow 1981–84, Senior research fellow 1984–92, Director, ESRC Research Centre 1992–99, Visiting Fellow 2000–. Liberal Democrat Spokesperson for: Higher Education 2000, Education and Employment/Skills 2000–. Member, Select Committee on European Communities Sub Committee A (Economic and Financial Affairs, Trade and External Relations) 1998–2002. IPU. Founder Member: Social Democrat Party 1981, Liberal Democrats 1988; Member, Liberal Democrat Federal Policy Committee 1992–, Vice-Chair 1995–96, 1998–99; Liberal Democrat History Group; Centre for Reform. Local council member, Guildford High School; Save British Science: Executive committee member, 1988–97, Advisory Board 1997–; Editorial board member, *Political Quarterly* 1987–97; Member: Charter 88, Howard League; Britain in Europe. Trustee: Nancy Seear Trust, Age Concern Surrey. Contested Guildford: for SDP/Alliance 1983 and 1987, for Lib Dems 1992 and 1997 general elections. Fellow, Royal Economic Society. *Publications: The State, the Enterprise and the Individual,* 1974; Editor *Europe and the New Technologies,* 1985; Co-author *Managing Change in British Industry,* 1986; Co-editor *Strategies for New Technologies,* 1987; Co-author: *Technology and the Future of Europe,* 1992–; *Technology Policy in the European Union,* 1998; plus numerous articles, book chapters etc in learned journals on issues relating to science and technology policy. *Special Interests:* Economic Policy, Industrial Issues, Science and Technology, Education. *Recreations:* Reading, walking, theatre and concert going. Raised to the peerage as Baroness Sharp of Guildford, of Guildford in the County of Surrey 1998. The Baroness Sharp of Guildford, House of Lords, London, SW1A 0PW *Tel:* 020 7219 3121 *Fax:* 020 7219 5979 *E-mail:* sharpm@parliament.uk.

DodOnline
An Electronic Directory without rival . . .

Peers' biographies and photographs available with daily updates *via* the internet

For a *free* trial, call Yasmin Mirza, Aby Farsoun or Michael Mand on 020 7630 7643

SHARPLES, BARONESS   Conservative

SHARPLES (Life Baroness), Pamela Sharples; cr. 1973. Born 11 February 1923. Daughter of late Lieutenant-Commander K. W. Newall, RN (Retired); educated Southover Manor, Lewes; Florence. Married Major Richard C. Sharples, OBE, MC 1946 (later Sir Richard Sharples, Governor of Bermuda, assassinated 1973) (2 sons 2 daughters); married Patrick D. de Laszlo 1977 (died 1980); married Robert Douglas Swan 1983 (died 1995). WAAF 1941–46. *Career:* Director, TVS 1982–93; Former Publican. Member, Wessex Medical Trust 1997–2000. Member, Review Body on Armed Services Pay 1979–81. *Special Interests:* Small Businesses, Cheque-Book Journalism, Prisoners' Wives, Pet Quarantine. *Recreations:* Tennis, golf, walking, gardening, fishing. *Sportsclubs:* Royal Cape Golf, Rushmoor Golf. *Clubs:* Mid-Ocean Bermuda. Raised to the peerage as Baroness Sharples, of Chawton in the County of Hampshire 1973. The Baroness Sharples, Well Cottage, Higher Coombe, Shaftesbury, Dorset, SP7 9LR *Tel:* 01747 852971; 60 Westminster Gardens, London, SW1P 4JG *Tel:* 020 7821 1875.

SHAW OF NORTHSTEAD, LORD   Conservative

SHAW OF NORTHSTEAD (Life Baron), Michael Norman Shaw; cr. 1994. Born 9 October 1920. Son of late Norman Shaw, FCA; educated Sedbergh. Married Joan Mary Louise Mowat 1951 (3 sons). JP, Dewsbury 1953; DL, West Yorkshire 1977. *Career:* Chartered accountant; Member, UK Delegation to the European Parliament 1974–79. *House of Commons:* MP (Conservative) for: Brighouse and Spenborough 1960 by-election –1964, Scarborough and Whitby 1966–74, Scarborough 1974–92; PPS to: Minister of Labour 1962–63, Secretary of State for Trade and Industry 1970–72, Chancellor of the Duchy of Lancaster 1972–74. Co-opted Member, European Union Sub-committee A (Economic and Financial Affairs, Trade and External Relations) 1997–2000; Administration and Works 2002–. Member Association Conservative Peers. Kt 1982. ACA 1945; FCA 1952. *Recreations:* Golf, opera, music. *Clubs:* Carlton. Raised to the peerage as Baron Shaw of Northstead, of Liversedge in the County of West Yorkshire 1994. The Lord Shaw of Northstead, DL, Duxbury Hall, Liversedge, West Yorkshire, WF15 7NR *Tel:* 01924 402270; 603 Collingwood House, Dolphin Square, London, SW1V 3NF *Tel:* 020 7798 8499.

SHEFFIELD, LORD BISHOP OF   Non-affiliated

SHEFFIELD (Bishop of) John Nicholls. Born 16 July 1943. Son of late James Williams and Nellie Nicholls; educated Bacup and Rawtenstall Grammar School; King's College, London (theology 1966); St Boniface College, Warminster (theology 1967). Married Judith Dagnall 1969 (2 sons, 2 daughters). Council of the University of Sheffield. *Career:* Curate St Clements with St Cyprian, Salford 1967–69; All Saints and Martyrs, Manchester: Curate 1969–72, Vicar 1972–78; Director of pastoral studies, College of the Resurrection, Mirfield 1978–83; Canon Residentiary Manchester Cathedral 1983–90; Suffragan Bishop of Lancaster 1990–97; Bishop of Sheffield 1997–; Took his seat in the House of Lords 2003. Fellow University of Central Lancashire 1997. *Publications:* A Faith Worth Sharing and a Church Worth Joining. *Special Interests:* Monastic Life, the Orthodox Church. *Recreations:* Story-telling, singing, detective fiction, history, music. *Clubs:* Royal Overseas League. Rt Rev the Lord Bishop of Sheffield, Bishopscroft, Snaithing Lane, Sheffield S10 3LG *Tel:* 0114 230 2170 *Fax:* 0114 263 0110 *E-mail:* bishop.jack@bishopcroft.idps.co.uk.

Visit the Vacher Dod Website . . .
www.DodOnline.co.uk

SHELDON, LORD   Labour

SHELDON (Life Baron), Robert Edward Sheldon; cr 2001. Born 13 September 1923; educated Elementary; Grammar; Technical schools; London University (External graduate, Whitworth Scholar). Married Eileen Shamash 1945 (died 1969) (1 son 1 daughter); married Mary Shield 1971. *Trades Union:* Member T&G. *Career:* Qualified Engineer. *House of Commons:* Contested Manchester Withington 1959 general election; Member (Labour) for Ashton-under-Lyne 1964–2001; Minister of State: Department of Civil Service 1974, HM Treasury 1974–1975; Financial Secretary to HM Treasury 1975–79. Opposition Frontbench Spokesperson for Civil Service, Treasury Matters and Machinery of Government 1970–74; Deputy Opposition Frontbench Spokesperon for Treasury and Economic Affairs 1981–83. Member European Union Sub-committee A (Economic and Financial Affairs, Trade and External Relations) 2003–. Chair, Northwest Group Labour MPs 1970–74. Chair, Public Accounts Commission 1997–2001. PC 1977. *Special Interests:* Economy, Treasury. Raised to the peerage as Baron Sheldon, of Ashton-under-Lyne in the County of Greater Manchester 2001. Rt Hon the Lord Sheldon, House of Lords, London, SW1A 0PW *Tel:* 020 7219 6993 *E-mail:* sheldonr@parliament.uk.

SHEPPARD OF DIDGEMERE, LORD   Conservative

SHEPPARD OF DIDGEMERE (Life Baron), Allen John George Sheppard; cr. 1994. Born 25 December 1932. Son of late John and Lily Sheppard; educated Ilford County School; London School of Economics (BSc Econ business administration 1953). Married Peggy Jones 1959 (divorced 1980); married Mary Stewart 1980. *Career:* Ford Motor Company 1958–68; Rootes/Chrysler 1968–71; British Leyland 1971–75; Grand Metropolitan plc 1975–96: Group Managing Director 1982–86, Chief Executive 1986–93, Chair 1987–96; Chair: UBM Group 1981–85, Mallinson-Denny Group 1985–87; Director, Meyer International plc 1989–92, Deputy Chair 1992–94; Non-executive Director, Bowater plc 1994–95; Non-executive Chair: Bright Reasons Group plc 1995–96, Group Trust plc 1994–2001, McBride plc 1995–, Unipart Group 1996–; Non-executive Chair, GB Railways plc 1996–; Director, High-Point Rendel Group plc 1997–; Non-executive Chair, One Click HR plc 1999–; Director: Gladstone plc 1999–2001, Nyne plc 2000–, Transware plc 2001–03. Chancellor, Middlesex University 2000–. Member Select Committee on Economic Affairs 2003–. Member, Board of Management, Conservative Party 1993–98. Governor, London School of Economics 1989–; Deputy Chair, International Business Leaders' Forum 1990–96; Chair: Advisory Board, British-American Chamber of Commerce 1991–94, London First 1992–2002, President 2002–; Vice-President: United Response, Brewers and Licensed Retailers Association, Business in the Community, Blue Cross; Board Member: Central London Partnership, East London Business Alliance, London Business Board. Institute of Management Gold Medal 1993; Marketing Society International Hall of Fame Award 1994; British-American Chamber of Commerce Trans-Atlantic Business Award 1995. Six honorary doctorates; Three fellowships. Chair: Board of Trustees, Prince's Youth Business Trust 1990–94, Administrative Council, Prince of Wales' Trusts 1995–98; Trustee, Animal Health Trust. Part-time Member, British Rail Board 1985–90. Kt 1990; KCVO 1997. FCIM; FCMA; FCIS; ATII; FRSA. *Publications: Your Business Matters*, 1958; *Maximum Leadership*, 1995. *Recreations:* Gardens, reading, red setter dogs. *Clubs:* Athenaeum. Raised to the peerage as Baron Sheppard of Didgemere, of Roydon in the County of Essex 1994. The Lord Sheppard of Didgemere, KCVO, House of Lords, London, SW1A 0PW *E-mail:* lord_allen_sheppard@unipart.co.uk.

DodOnline
An Electronic Directory without rival ...

Peers' biographies and photographs available with daily updates *via* the internet

For a *free* trial, call Yasmin Mirza, Aby Farsoun or Michael Mand on 020 7630 7643

SHEPPARD OF LIVERPOOL, LORD — Labour

SHEPPARD OF LIVERPOOL (Life Baron), David Stuart Sheppard; cr. 1998. Born 6 March 1929. Son of late Stuart Morton Winter Sheppard and late Barbara Sheppard; educated Sherborne School; Trinity Hall, Cambridge (MA history 1953); Ridley Hall Theological College. Married Grace Isaac 1957 (1 daughter). 2nd Lieut, Royal Sussex Regiment, National Service 1947–49. *Career:* Assistant Curate, St Mary's, Islington 1955–57; Warden, Mayflower Family Centre, Canning Town 1957–69; Chairman, Evangelical Urban Training Project 1968–75; Bishop Suffragan of Woolwich 1969–75; Chairman, Martin Luther King Foundation 1970–75; Bishop of Liverpool 1975–97; Chairman, Merseyside Area Manpower Board, Manpower Services Commission 1976–83; First entered the House of Lords 1980; National President, Family Service Units 1987–97; Chairman: Central Religious Advisory Committee for BBC and IBA 1989–93, General Synod Board for Social Responsibility 1991–96, Churches' Enquiry in to Unemployment and the Failure of Work 1995–97. Seven honorary doctorates. Cricket: Cambridge University 1950–52, Captain 1952, Sussex 1947–62, Captain 1953, England (played 22 times) 1950–63, Captain 1954. Freeman, City of Liverpool 1995 (jointly with late Archbishop Derek Worlock). *Publications: Parson's Pitch,* 1964; *Built as a City,* 1974; *Bias to the Poor,* 1983; Co-author: *Better Together,* 1988, *Christ in the Wilderness,* 1990, *With Hope in our Hearts,* 1994, *Steps Along Hope Street,* 2002. *Special Interests:* Urban Policies, Race Relations, Unemployment, Future of Work, Youth Work. *Recreations:* Family, reading, music, painting, visiting gardens, following cricket. *Clubs:* MCC; Vice-president Lancashire County Cricket Club 1997–2003; President, Sussex County Cricket Club 2001–02. Raised to the peerage as Baron Sheppard of Liverpool, of West Kirby in the County of Merseyside 1998. Rt Rev the Lord Sheppard of Liverpool, Ambledown, 11 Melloncroft Drive, West Kirby, Merseyside, CH48 2JA.

SHREWSBURY AND WATERFORD, EARL OF — Conservative

SHREWSBURY (22nd Earl of, E), cr. 1442, AND WATERFORD (22nd Earl of, I), cr. 1446; Charles Henry John Benedict Crofton Chetwynd Chetwynd-Talbot; Earl Talbot and Viscount Ingestre (GB) 1784; Baron Talbot (GB) 1733. Born 18 December 1952. Son of 21st Earl; educated Harrow School. Married Deborah Hutchinson 1974 (2 sons 1 daughter). DL, Staffordshire 1994–. *Career:* Landowner and Farmer; Joint Deputy Chairman, Britannia Building Society 1987–92; Director, Richmount Enterprise Zone Trust 1988–94; Chairman, Firearms Consultative Committee 1994–99; President and National Executive Director, British Institute of Innkeeping 1996–98; Director: PMI Limited 1996–98, Banafix Limited 1996–98, Minibusplus 1997–2001. Chancellor, Wolverhampton University 1993–99. *House of Lords:* First entered House of Lords 1980; Elected hereditary peer 1999–. President, Building Societies Association 1993–97. Hon. LLD, Wolverhampton University 1994. Premier Earl on Rolls of both England and Ireland; Hereditary Lord High Steward of Ireland. Member: Worshipful Company of Weavers. *Special Interests:* Agriculture, Environment, Construction Industry, Property, West Midlands, Mineral Extraction. *Recreations:* Shooting, fishing. *Clubs:* Farmers'. The Earl of Shrewsbury and Waterford, DL, Wanfield Hall, Kingstone, Uttoxeter, Staffordshire, ST14 8QR *Tel:* 01889 500275 *Fax:* 01889 500275 *E-mail:* shrewsburyestate@aol.com.

SHUTT OF GREETLAND, LORD — Liberal Democrat

SHUTT OF GREETLAND (Life Baron), David Trevor Shutt; cr. 2000. Born 16 March 1942. Son of late Edward Angus Shutt and of Ruth Satterthwaite Shutt (née Berry); educated Pudsey Grammar School. Married Margaret Pemberton 1965 (2 sons 1 daughter). Mayor of Calderdale 1982–83 Member: Policy and Resources, Education, Town Planning and Environment Committees for several years, West Yorkshire Passenger Transport Authority 1987–90, Yorkshire Regional Assembly 1998–2000; Councillor, Calderdale MBC 1973–90, 1995–, Leader, Liberal Democrat Group 1979–82, 1995–2000. *Career:* Chartered accountant; Articled clerk: Smithson Blackburn and Company, Leeds 1959–66, Bousfield Waite and Company, Halifax 1967–70;

Partner, Bousfield Waite and Company, Halifax 1970–94, Consultant 1994–2001; Non-executive Director: Job Ownership Ltd 1978–85, Bradford Community Radio *Pennine Radio* 1984–89, Pluto Press Ltd 1985–86, New Society Ltd, *New Society* 1986–88, Statesman and Nation Publishing Company Ltd, *New Statesman* 1988–90, Gerald Duckworth and Co. Ltd 1990–95, Marcher Sound Ltd 1997–2000. Liberal Democrat Whip 2001–; Deputy Chief Whip 2002–. Liberal Democrat Spokesperson for: Northern Ireland 2001–, International Development 2001–. Member, House of Lords' Offices 2000–02; Co-opted member, European Union Sub-committee F (Social Affairs, Education and Home Affairs) 2000–01, Sub-committee B (Energy, Industry and Transport) 2001–; Member European Union Committee 2003–. Irish Peace Institute. The Brooksbank School, Elland, Governor, Chair 1979–2001; Former Board Member, DEMOS. Citoyen d'Honneur de la Ville de Riorges (France) 1983; Paul Harris Fellow 1999. Trustee: Joseph Rowntree Charitable Trust, The Irish Peace Institute, Joseph Rowntree Reform Trust Ltd; Treasurer, Institute for Citizenship Studies 1995–2001; Chair and founder, Calderdale Community Foundation 1990–99. Contested Sowerby and later Calder Valley (Lib/Lib.All) 1970, February 1974, 1979, 1983, 1987 and Pudsey (LibDem) 1992 general elections. OBE 1992. FCA. Freeman, Metropolitan Borough of Calderdale 2000. *Publications:* A couple of pamphlets. *Special Interests:* Member of the Society of Friends (Quakers). *Recreations:* Travel, Transport. Raised to the peerage as Baron Shutt of Greetland, of Greetland and Stainland in the County of West Yorkshire 2000. The Lord Shutt of Greetland, OBE, 197 Saddleworth Road, Greetland, Halifax, HX4 8LZ *Tel:* 01422 375276 *Fax:* 01422 310707; House of Lords, London, SW1A 0PW *Tel:* 020 7219 8624 *E-mail:* shutt@jrrt.org.uk.

SIMON, VISCOUNT   Labour

SIMON (3rd Viscount), Jan David Simon; cr. 1940. Born 20 July 1940. Son of 2nd Viscount, CMG; educated Westminster School; School of Navigation, Southampton University; Sydney Technical College. Married Mary Elizabeth Burns 1969 (1 daughter). *House of Lords:* First entered House of Lords 1993; Deputy Chairman of Committees 1998–; Deputy Speaker 1999–; Elected hereditary peer 1999–. Member, Select Committees on: Dangerous Dogs (Amendment) Bill 1995–96, London Local Authorities Bill 1998, Procedure 1999–2002. *Special Interests:* Disability, Motor Industry, Police, Road Safety, Science and Technology, Aviation. The Viscount Simon, House of Lords, London, SW1A 0PW *Tel:* 020 7219 6527 *E-mail:* simonj@parliament.uk.

SIMON OF GLAISDALE, LORD   Crossbencher

SIMON OF GLAISDALE (Life Baron), Jocelyn Edward Salis Simon; cr. 1971. Born 15 January 1911. Son of late Frank Cecil Simon; educated Gresham's School, Holt; Trinity Hall, Cambridge (BA English and law 1934). Married Gwendolen Helen Evans 1934 (died 1937); married Fay Elizabeth Leicester, née Pearson 1948 (3 sons). Served War World II; Commissioned Royal Tank Regiment 1939; Madagascar 1942 (despatches); Burma 1944. DL, North Yorkshire 1973–. *Career:* Called to the Bar, Middle Temple 1934; Bencher 1958; KC 1951; President, Probate, Divorce and Admiralty Division of High Court of Justice 1962–71; Lord of Appeal in Ordinary 1971–77. *House of Commons:* MP (Conservative) for Middlesbrough West 1951–62; Joint Parliamentary Under-Secretary, Home Office 1957–58; Financial Secretary, HM Treasury 1958–59; Solicitor-General 1959–62. Member, One-Nation Group. Chair, Joint Select Committee on Consolidation Bill 1973–76. Elder Brother, Trinity House. Two honorary doctorates; Honorary fellow Trinity Hall, Cambridge. Member, Royal Commission on Law relating to Mental Illness and Mental Deficiency 1954–57. Kt 1959; PC 1961. *Publications: Change is our Ally* (part), 1954; *The Church and the Law of Nullity of Marriage* (part), 1955. Raised to the peerage as Baron Simon of Glaisdale, of Glaisdale in the North Riding of the County of Yorkshire 1971. Rt Hon the Lord Simon of Glaisdale, DL, House of Lords, London, SW1A 0PW *Tel:* 020 7219 2229.

DodOnline
An Electronic Directory without rival . . .

Peers' biographies and photographs available with daily updates *via* the internet

For a *free* trial, call Yasmin Mirza, Aby Farsoun or Michael Mand on 020 7630 7643

SIMON OF HIGHBURY, LORD   Labour

SIMON OF HIGHBURY (Life Baron), David Alec Gwyn Simon; cr. 1997. Born 24 July 1939. Son of late Roger Simon; educated Christ's Hospital, Horsham; Gonville and Caius College, Cambridge (BA modern languages 1961, MA); INSEAD (MBA). Married Hanne Mohn 1964 (2 sons) (divorced 1987); married Sarah Roderick Smith 1992. *Career:* The British Petrolum Co plc 1961–97: Marketing co-ordinator, European Region 1975–80, Director, BP Oil UK and Chairman, National Benzole Company 1980–82, Managing Director, BP Oil International 1982–85, Managing Director 1986–95, Chief Operating Officer 1990–92, Deputy Chairman 1990–95, Chief Group Executive 1992–95, Chair 1995–97; Non-executive Director, Grand Metropolitan plc 1989–97; Member, Advisory Board, Deutsche Bank 1991–97; Non-executive Director, RTZ Corporation plc 1995–97; Member: International Advisory Council, Allianz AG Holding 1993–97, Court of Bank of England 1995–97; Advisory Director: Unilever 2000–, LEK 2000–, Morgan Stanley Europe 2000–, Suez Group 2001–; Member international advisory committee of Fitch global financial rating agency 2001–; Supervisory Board Member, Volkswagen AG 2002–. *House of Lords:* Minister of State, HM Treasury and Department of Trade and Industry (Minister for Trade and Competitiveness in Europe) 1997–99. Spokesperson for Department of Trade and Industry 1997–99. Hon. DSc Economics, Hull 1990; Hon. DU, North London 1995; Hon. DSc Economics, Bath 1997. Chair Cambridge Foundation 2001–; Herti Foundation, Hessen, Germany 2001–. Member: Sports Council 1988–92, 1994–95, President's Committee, CBI 1992–97, European Round Table 1993–97, Vice-Chair 1995–97, European Union Competitive Advisory Group 1995–97, International Council, INSEAD; Adviser, European Commission President 1999–2000. CBE 1991; Kt 1995; Commander Order of Leopold (Belgium) 2001. Liveryman: Tallow Chandlers, Carmen. *Recreations:* Golf, books, music. *Sportsclubs:* Highgate Golf, Royal West Norfolk Golf, Hunstanton Golf. *Clubs:* Brooks's, Athenaeum. Raised to the peerage as Baron Simon of Highbury, of Canonbury in the London Borough of Islington 1997. The Lord Simon of Highbury, CBE, House of Lords, London, SW1A 0PW *Tel:* 020 7219 5455.

SIMPSON OF DUNKELD, LORD   Labour

SIMPSON OF DUNKELD (Life Baron), George Simpson; cr. 1997. Born 2 July 1942. Son of late William and Elizabeth Simpson; educated Morgan Academy, Dundee; Dundee Institute of Technology. Married Eva Chalmers 1964 (1 son 1 daughter). *Career:* Senior accountant, Gas Industry, Scotland 1962–69; Central audit manager, British Leyland 1969–73; Financial controller, Leyland Bus and Truck Division 1973–76; Director of accounting, Leyland Cars 1976–78; Finance and systems director, Leyland Trucks 1978–80; Managing Director: Coventry Climax Ltd 1980–83, Freight Rover Ltd 1983–86; Chief Executive Officer, Leyland DAF 1986–88; Rover Group: Managing Director 1989–91, Chief Executive 1991–92, Chair 1991–94; Deputy Chief Executive, British Aerospace 1992–94, Director 1990–94; Chair, Ballast Nedam Construction Ltd 1992–94; Non-Executive Director: Pilkington plc 1992–99, Northern Venture Capital 1992–, Pro Share 1992–94; Chair, Arlington Securities 1993–94; Chief Executive, Lucas Industries plc 1994–96; Non-Executive Director, ICI plc 1995–2001; Chief Executive, General Electric Company plc (now Marconi plc) 1996–2001; Non-Executive Director: Nestlé SA 1999–, Alstom SA 1998–; Industrial Professor at Warwick University; Governor, London Business School; Board of Institute for Manufacturing; Non-Executive Director: Bank of Scotland 2000–01, Triumph Group Inc 2002–. Governor, Economic Forum; Member, European Round Table. Member, Executive Committee, Society of Motor Manufacturers and Traders 1986–, Vice-President 1986–95, President 1995–96. Hon. Degrees: Warwick University, Abertay University, Aston University. ACIS; FCCA; FIMI; FCIT. Liveryman, Worshipful Company of Coachmakers. *Special Interests:* Trade and Industry. *Recreations:* Golf, squash, watching rugby. *Sportsclubs:* Royal Birkdale, Gleneagles Golf, New Zealand Golf, Kenilworth Rugby Football, Pine Valley Golf, Blairgowrie Golf. *Clubs:* Royal Automobile Club. Raised to the peerage as Baron Simpson of Dunkeld, of Dunkeld in Perth and Kinross 1997. The Lord Simpson of Dunkeld, House of Lords, London, SW1A 0PW *Fax:* 01350 727198 *E-mail:* lordsimps@aol.com.

SKELMERSDALE, LORD — Conservative

SKELMERSDALE (7th Baron, UK), Roger Bootle-Wilbraham; cr. 1828. Born 2 April 1945. Son of Brigadier 6th Baron and late Ann Quilter; educated Eton College; Lord Wandsworth College, Odiham, Hampshire; Somerset Farm Institute; Hadlow College of Agriculture and Horticulture. Married Christine Joan Morgan 1972 (1 son 1 daughter). *Career:* Voluntary Service Overseas, Zambia 1969–71; Horticulturist; Managing director, Broadleigh Nurseries Ltd 1972–81, Director 1991–; Parliamentary affairs adviser 1992–96. *House of Lords:* First entered House of Lords 1973; Parliamentary Under-Secretary of State: Department of the Environment 1986–87, Department of Health and Social Security 1987–88, Department of Social Security 1988–89, Northern Ireland Office 1989–90; Deputy Chair of Committees 1991–94; Deputy Speaker 1994–; Elected hereditary peer 1999–. Government Whip 1981–86; Opposition Whip 2003–. Government Spokesperson 1981–86 at various times for: Environment, Transport, Foreign Affairs, Energy, Agriculture, Post Office. Member: European Union Sub-committee F (Environment) 1975–81, Co-opted Member, European Union Sub-committee B (Energy, Industry and Transport) 1997–2000, 2001–03; Member: Joint Committee on Statutory Instruments 1998–2003, Procedure Committee 1998–2000. Vice-chair, Co-En-Co (Council for Environmental Conservation) 1979–81; President, British Naturalists Association 1979–95; Governor, Castle School, Taunton 1992–96; Chair of Council, The Stroke Association 1993–; President, Somerset Opera 1980–. President, Somerset Trust for Nature Conservation 1980–; Trustee Hestercombe Gardens Trust 2001–. Fellow, Linnaen Society. Liveryman, Worshipful Company of Gardeners. *Special Interests:* Horticulture, Post Office, Energy, Environment, Privatised Utilities, Health. *Recreations:* Bridge, gardening, reading, walking. The Lord Skelmersdale, House of Lords, London, SW1A 0PW *Tel:* 020 7219 3224 *Fax:* 020 7630 0088 *E-mail:* skelmersdaler@parliament.uk.

SKIDELSKY, LORD — Crossbencher

SKIDELSKY (Life Baron), Robert Jacob Alexander Skidelsky; cr. 1991. Born 25 April 1939. Son of late Boris Skidelsky and Galia, née Sapelkin; educated Brighton College; Jesus College, Oxford (BA modern history 1961). Married Augusta Hope 1970 (2 sons 1 daughter). *Trades Union:* AUT. Member: Lord Chancellor's Advisory Council on Public Records 1987–92, School Examinations and Assessment Council 1992–93; Academic Council, Wilton Park 2002–. *Career:* Research Fellow, Nuffield College, Oxford 1965–68; Associate Professor, School of Advanced International Studies, Johns Hopkins University, Washington DC 1970–76; Head of the Department of History, Philosophy and European Studies, Polytechnic of North London 1976–78; Professor of International Studies, Warwick University 1978–90, Professor of Political Economy 1990–. Opposition Spokesman on: Culture, Media and Sport 1997–98, the Treasury 1998–99. Member, House of Lords Select Committees on: The European Communities 1991–94, Sustainable Development 1994–97. Member, Inter-Parliamentary Union. Chair: Social Market Foundation 1991–2001, Hands Off Reading Campaign 1994–97; Governor: Portsmouth University 1994–97, Brighton College 1998–, Moscow School of Political Studies 1999–. Wolfson Prize for History 1992; Duff Cooper Prize for Non-Fiction 2001; Lionel Gelber Prize for International Relations 2001; Council on Foreign Relations Prize 2002; James Tait Black Memorial Prize 2002. Hon. DLitt, University of Buckingham; Hon. Fellow, Jesus College, Oxford 1997. Chairman, Charleston Trust 1987–92; Trustee: Humanitas 1991, Manhattan Institute 1993–, The Hon. Dorothy Burns Will Trust 2000–, All Talents Foundation, Moscow 2002. Fellow: Royal Historical Society 1973, Royal Society of Literature 1978, British Academy 1994. Freeman, Knocksville, Tennessee, USA 1998. *Publications:* Include: *Politicians and the Slump*, 1967; *English Progressive Schools*, 1969; *Oswald Mosley*, 1975; *John Maynard Keynes*, Vol. 1, 1983, Vol. 2, 1992, Vol. 3, 2000; *The World After Communism*, 1995. *Special Interests:* Education, Economic Policy, Europe, Transition Economies, Hong Kong, Arts. *Recreations:* Opera, listening to music, tennis, table tennis, good conversation. *Clubs:* Grillion. Raised to the peerage as Baron Skidelsky, of Tilton in the County of East Sussex 1991. Professor the Lord Skidelsky, Tilton House, Firle, East Sussex, BN8 6LL *Tel:* 020 7219 8721 *E-mail:* skidelskyr@parliament.uk.

SLIM, VISCOUNT   Crossbencher

SLIM (2nd Viscount, UK), John Douglas Slim; cr. 1960. Born 20 July 1927. Son of Field Marshal 1st Viscount, KG, GCB, GCMG, GCVO, GBE, DSO, MC; educated Prince of Wales Royal Indian Military College, Dehra Dun. Married Elisabeth Spinney 1958 (2 sons 1 daughter). Served: Indian Army 6th Gurkha Rifles 1944, Argyll and Sutherland Highlanders 1948, Special Air Service 1952; Staff College Camberley 1961; Joint Services Staff College 1964; Retired Colonel from Army 1972. DL, Greater London 1988. *Career:* Chair, Peek plc 1976–91, Deputy Chair 1991–96, Consultant 1996–; Director, Trailfinders Ltd, and other companies. *House of Lords:* First entered House of Lords 1971; Elected hereditary peer 1999–. Member: Select Committee on House of Lords' Offices 1997–99, Committee of Selection 2001–, Defence Study Group. Parliamentary and Scientific Committee. Foundation for Aviation and Sustainable Tourism (New Delhi). President, Burma Star Association 1971–; Vice-President, Britain-Australia Society (former chairman); Vice-Chair, Arab-British Chamber of Commerce 1977–96; President SAS Association 2000–. OBE (Mil) 1973. Fellow, Royal Geographical Society 1983. Master, The Clothworkers' Company 1995–96. *Clubs:* White's, Special Forces. The Viscount Slim, OBE, DL, House of Lords, London, SW1A 0PW *Tel:* 020 7219 2122.

SLYNN OF HADLEY, LORD   Crossbencher

SLYNN OF HADLEY (Life Baron), Gordon Slynn; cr. 1992. Born 17 February 1930. Son of late John Slynn and of Edith Slynn; educated Sandbach School, Cheshire; Trinity College, Cambridge (Senior Scholar, MA, LLM 1956 honorary fellow 2001); Goldsmiths' College, London. Married Odile Marie Henriette Boutin 1962. Commissioned RAF 1951–54. *Career:* Called to the Bar, Gray's Inn 1956, Bencher 1970, Treasurer 1988; Junior Counsel, Ministry of Labour 1967–68; Junior Counsel to the Treasury (Common Law) 1968–74; Recorder of Hereford 1971; Recorder and Hon. Recorder of Hereford 1972–76; QC 1974; Leading Counsel to the Treasury 1974–76; Judge of the High Court of Justice, Queen's Bench Division 1976–81; President, Employment Appeal Tribunal 1978–81; Advocate-General of the Court of Justice of the European Communities 1981–88, Judge 1986–91; Visiting Professor in Law: Durham University 1981–88, Cornell University 1983, King's College, London 1985–90, 1995–, National University of India 1992–; Judge 1988–91; Lord of Appeal in Ordinary 1992–2002. Member, European Communities Select Committee 1992–97; Chairman: Sub-Committee E 1992–95, Select Committee on Public Service 1996–97. Chairman, Executive Council, International Law Association 1988–; Hon. Vice-President, Union Internationale des Avocats; President Fedération Internationale de Droit Européen 1990–92. Visitor, Mansfield College, Oxford; Prior of Priory of England and the Islands Order of St John. 19 honorary doctorates from UK, Australia, India, Argentina, USA; Five honorary fellowships. Deputy Chief Steward of Hereford 1977–78, Chief Steward 1978–. Kt 1976; PC 1992. FCIArb; FKC. Freeman, City of Hereford. Master, Broderers' Company 1994–95. *Publications:* Has contributed to *Halsbury's Laws of England* as well as lectures published in legal journals. *Clubs:* Beefsteak, Garrick, Whites. Raised to the peerage as Baron Slynn of Hadley, of Eggington in the County of Bedfordshire 1992. Rt Hon the Lord Slynn of Hadley, House of Lords, London, SW1A 0PW *Tel:* 020 7219 3110.

SMITH OF CLIFTON, LORD   Liberal Democrat

SMITH OF CLIFTON (Life Baron), Trevor Arthur Smith; cr. 1997. Born 14 June 1937. Son of late Arthur Smith, and of Vera Smith; educated Hounslow College; Chiswick Polytechnic; London School of Economics (BSc economics 1958). Married Brenda Eustace 1960 (divorced 1973) (2 sons); married Julia Bullock 1979 (1 daughter). Member, Tower Hamlets District Health Authority 1987–91; Non-executive Director, North Yorkshire Regional Health Authority 2000–02. *Career:* Schoolteacher, LCC 1958–59; Temporary assistant lecturer, Exeter University 1959–60; Research officer, Acton Society Trust 1960–62; Lecturer in politics, Hull University 1962–67; Visiting associate professor, California State University, Los Angeles 1969;

Queen Mary College, later Queen Mary and Westfield College, London: head of department 1972–85, dean of social studies 1979–82, pro-principal 1983–87, lecturer, senior lecturer, professor in political studies 1983–91, senior pro-principal 1987–89, senior vice-principal 1989–91; Director: Job Ownership Ltd 1978–85, New Society Ltd 1986–88; Member, Senate, London University 1987–91; Director, Statesman and Nation Publishing Company Ltd 1988–90, Chairman 1990; Director, Gerald Duckworth & Co 1990–95; Vice-chancellor, University of Ulster 1991–99; Hon. Professor 1991; Visiting Professor of Politics, York 1999–2003, Portsmouth Universities 2000–01. Liberal Democrat Spokesperson for Northern Ireland 2000–. Member, Science and Technology Sub-committee 1 (Complementary and Alternative Medicine) 1999–2000; Co-opted member, European Union Sub-committee E (Law and Institutions) 2000–; Chair Select Committee on Animals in Scientific Procedures 2000–02. British-Irish Interparliamentary Body 2000–. Member, Liberal Party Executive 1958–59. Governor: St John Cass and Redcoats School 1979–84, University of Haifa 1985–91; Chair, Political Studies Association of UK 1988–89, Vice-President 1989–91 and 1993–, President 1991–93; Vice-chair, Board of Governors, Princess Alexandra and Newnham College of Nursing and Midwifery 1990–91; Member, UK Socrates Council 1993–99, Chair 1996–99; Member: Administrative Board, International Association of Universities 1995–96, Editorial Board, Government and Opposition 1995–, Board, A Taste of Ulster 1996–99. Six honorary doctorates. Director, Joseph Rowntree Reform Trust Ltd 1975–, Chair 1987–99; Trustee: Acton Society Trust 1975–87, Employment Institute 1987–92; Institute of Citizenship 1991–2001; President, Belfast Civic Trust 1995–99; Chair, Hampden Trust 1999–2001; Joseph Rowntree Social Service Charitable Trust 1975–, Stroke Association 2002–. Kt 1996. FRHistS; CCIM (CBIM 1992); FICPD; FRSA; AcSS. *Publications:* Co-author: *Training Managers,* 1962, *Town Councillors,* 1964, *Direct Action and Democratic Politics,* 1972; *The Fixers,* 1996; *Town and County Hall,* 1966; *Anti-Politics: consensus and reform,* 1972; *The Politics of the Corporate Economy,* 1979; Various articles and papers, book reviews and broadcasts. *Special Interests:* Northern Ireland, Health, Transport (aircraft), Higher Education, Constitutional Reform. *Recreations:* Water colour painting. *Clubs:* Reform. Raised to the peerage as Baron Smith of Clifton, of Mountsandel in the County of Londonderry 1997. Professor the Lord Smith of Clifton, House of Lords, London, SW1A 0W *Tel:* 020 7219 5363 *Fax:* 020 7219 5979 *E-mail:* sirtas@jrrt.org.uk; smitht@parliament.uk.

SMITH OF GILMOREHILL, BARONESS   Labour

SMITH OF GILMOREHILL (Life Baroness), Elizabeth Margaret Smith; cr. 1995. Born 4 June 1940. Daughter of late Frederick William Moncrieff Bennett, and of late Elizabeth Waters Irvine Shanks; educated Hutchesons' Girls' Grammar School, Glasgow; Glasgow University (MA French and Russian 1962). Married John Smith 1967 (MP 1970–94, Leader of the Labour Party 1992–94) (died 1994) (3 daughters). DL, City of Edinburgh 1996. *Career:* Chairman, Lamda Development Board –2001; BP Advisory Board for Scotland; Non-executive director: Deutsche Bank, Scotland, City Inn Ltd. Chancellor, Birbeck College –2003. Opposition Spokeswoman on National Heritage (Tourism) 1996–97. Member, Labour Party Departmental Committee for Foreign Affairs. Executive Committee Member, IPU British Group –2002. Member: Britain-Russia Centre, British Association for Central and Eastern Europe. Member: British Heart Foundation –2000, English Speaking Union, Russo-British Chamber of Commerce, Centre for European Reform; President, Scottish Opera; Chairman, Edinburgh Festival Fringe; Board Member Edinburgh International Festival –1999; Council Member, Britain in Europe Campaign. Hon. LLD, University of Glasgow. Member: Mariinsky Theatre Trust, Future of Europe Trust, John Smith Memorial Trust, Know How Fund Advisory Board –2000; Trustee, Hakluyt Foundation –2001, 21st Century Trust. Member: Press Complaints Commission 1995–2001, BP Scottish Advisory Board. *Special Interests:* Arts, Russia, Former Soviet Union. Raised to the peerage as Baroness Smith of Gilmorehill, of Gilmorehill in the District of the City of Glasgow, 1995. The Baroness Smith of Gilmorehill, DL, House of Lords, London, SW1A 0PW *Tel:* 020 7219 5418.

Visit the Vacher Dod Website . . .
www.DodOnline.co.uk

SMITH OF LEIGH, LORD   Labour

SMITH OF LEIGH (Life Baron), Peter Richard Charles Smith; cr. 1999. Born 24 July 1945. Son of Ronald and Kathleen Smith; educated Bolton School; London School of Economics (BSc economics 1967); Garnett College, London University (CertEd(FE) 1969); Salford University (MSc Urban Studies 1983). Married Joy Lesley Booth 1968 (1 daughter). *Trades Union:* Member, NATFHE –2001. Wigan Metropolitan Borough Council: Councillor 1978–, Chairman, Finance Committee 1982–91, Leader of Council 1991–. *Career:* Lecturer: Walbrook College, London 1969–74, Manchester College of Art and Technology 1974–91, part-time 1991–2000. Member: Association of Metropolitan Authorities Policy Committee 1991–97, Local Government Association Policy and Strategy Committee 1997–2000; Vice-Chair, Special Interest Group for Municipal Authorities 1997–; Member, Improvement and Development Agency 1999–; Chair: North West Regional Assembly 1999–2000, Association of Greater Manchester Authorities 2000–; Manchester Airport plc: Board Director 1986–2001, Chair 1989–90; Board Director Manchester Airport Group 2001–. *Special Interests:* Local Government, Regionalism, Airport Policy, Health. *Recreations:* Gardening, sport, jazz. *Clubs:* Hindley Green Labour. Raised to the peerage as Baron Smith of Leigh, of Wigan in the County of Greater Manchester 1999. The Lord Smith of Leigh, Town Hall, Library Street, Wigan, WN1 1YN *Tel:* 01942 827001 *Fax:* 01942 827365; Mysevin, Old Hall Mill Lane, Atherton, Manchester, M46 0RG *Tel:* 01942 676127 *Fax:* 01942 676127 *E-mail:* leader@wiganmbc.gov.uk.

SNOWDON, EARL OF   Crossbencher

SNOWDON (1st Earl of, UK), Antony Charles Robert Armstrong-Jones; cr. 1961; Viscount Linley; (Life) Baron Armstrong-Jones 1999. Born 7 March 1930. Son of late Ronald Owen Lloyd Armstrong-Jones, MBE, QC, DL, and late Anne, Countess of Rosse; educated Eton College; Jesus College, Cambridge (architecture, 2 years, no degree). Married HRH The Princess Margaret, CI, GCVO 1960 (1 son 1 daughter) (divorced 1978); married Mrs Lucy Lindsay-Hogg 1978 (1 daughter). *Trades Union:* Member, NUJ. *Career:* Constable of Caernarfon Castle, Wales 1963–; Artistic adviser to the: *Sunday Times* and Sunday Times Publications Ltd 1962–90, *Daily Telegraph* Magazine 1990–95; Consultative adviser to the Design Council, London 1962–87; Editorial adviser to Design Magazine 1962–87; President for England, International Year for Disabled People 1981; Public appearances 1991; Television films: 'Don't Count the Candles' 1968 (2 Hollywood EMMY Awards); 'Love of a Kind' 1969; 'Born To Be Small' 1971 (Chicago Hugo Awards); 'Happy Being Happy' 1973; 'Mary Kingsley' 1975; 'Burke and Wills' 1975; 'Peter, Tina and Steve' 1977; 'Snowdon on Camera' (BAFTA nomination) 1981; Exhibitions: Photocall 1957, Assignments 1972, Serendipity 1989; Designer of: Snowdon Aviary for London Zoo 1965 (Listed Grade II* starred 1998), Mobile chair for disabled people (The Chairmobile) 1972; Retrospective Exhibition: National Portrait Gallery 2000, Edinburgh 2000, Vienna 2001, Yale 2001. *House of Lords:* First entered House of Lords 1961. President: Contemporary Art Society for Wales, Welsh Theatre Company; Member of Council, National Fund for Research into Crippling Diseases; Patron: National Youth Theatre 1962–87, Metropolitan Union of YMCAs, British Water Ski Federation, Welsh National Rowing Club, Physically Handicapped and Able Bodied, Circle of Guide Dog Owners; Started Snowdon award scheme for further education of disabled students 1981; Patron: Polio Plus 1988, British Disabled Water Ski Association; Provost, Royal College of Art. Hon. LLD: Bradford University 1989, Bath University 1989, Portsmouth University 1993. President, Civic Trust for Wales. Member, Prince of Wales Advisory Group on Disability. GCVO 1969. Senior Fellow, Royal College of Art 1986; Fellow: Manchester College of Art and Design; Chartered Society of Designers (London), Royal Photographic Society (London), Royal Society of Arts; FRSA, RDI. Liveryman, The Cloth Workers' Company. *Publications: Malta* (in collaboration with Sacheverell Sitwell) 1958; *London,* 1958; *Assignments,* 1972; *A View of Venice,* 1972; *Integrating the disabled –The Snowdon Report,* 1976; *Inchcape Review,* 1977; *Personal View,* 1979; *Private View* (in collaboration with John Russell and Bryan Robertson) 1965; *Pride of the Shires* (with John Oaksey) 1979; *Tasmania Essay,* 1981; *Sittings,* 1983; *Israel – A First View,* 1986; *My Wales* (with Viscount Tonypandy), 1986; *Stills,* 1987; *Personal Appearances,* 1992; *Wild Flowers,* 1995; *Snowdon On Stage,* 1996; *Wild Fruit,* 1997; *London Sight Unseen,* 1999; *Snowdon a retrospective,* 2000. *Special Interests:* Art and Design. *Recreations:* Photography. *Sportsclubs:* Leander (Henley-on-Thames), Hawks. *Clubs:* Buck's. Created a life peer as Baron Armstrong-Jones, of Nymans in the County of West Sussex 1999. The Earl of Snowdon, GCVO, 22 Launceston Place, London, W8 5RL.

SOULSBY OF SWAFFHAM PRIOR, LORD   Conservative

SOULSBY OF SWAFFHAM PRIOR (Life Baron), (Ernest Jackson) Lawson Soulsby; cr. 1990. Born 23 June 1926. Son of late William George Lawson Soulsby; educated Queen Elizabeth Grammar School, Penrith; Edinburgh University (MRCVS veterinary medicine 1948, DVSM 1949, PhD immunology 1952); Cambridge University (MA 1954). Married Margaret Macdonald 1950 (1 son 1 daughter); married Georgina Elizabeth Annette Williams 1962. *Career:* Veterinary officer, City of Edinburgh 1949–52; Lecturer in: clinical parasitology, Bristol University 1952–54, animal pathology, Cambridge University 1954–63; Professor of: parasitology, University of Pennsylvania 1964–78, animal pathology, Cambridge University 1978–93, Emeritus Professor 1993–; Ford Foundation Visiting Professor, University of Ibadan 1964; Member, EEC Advisory Committee on Veterinary Training 1981–86; Expert Adviser to several UN Agencies and overseas governments 1963–; Member, Veterinary Advisory Committee Horserace Betting Levy Board 1984, Chair 1985–98; Member, Agriculture and Food Research Council 1984–88; Chair, Animal Research Grants Board 1986–89; Member, Home Office Animal Procedures Committee 1987–95; Chair: Ethics Committee, British Veterinary Association 1994–, Companion Animal Welfare Council 1998–. Member: Sub-Committee F of European Communities 1990–92, Sub-Committee II, Select Committee for Science and Technology 1993–97, Select Committee for Science and Technology 1995–2000; Chairman, Science and Technology Sub-Committee I 1997–98; Member, Sub-Committee I 1999–; Chairman I 2002–. Advisory, General Parasitology, World Health Organisation, Geneva; Trustee, Windward Islands Research and Education Funds 1999–; Chair: 2001–. Member, Association of Conservative Peers. Council Member, Royal College of Veterinary Surgeons 1978–92, President 1984, Senior Vice-President 1985; Hon. Member, Parasitology Societies in Germany, Mexico, Argentina, UK and USA; Corresponding Member, Academie Royale de Médicine de Belgique; President, Pet Advisory Committee 1996–; Patron: Veterinary Benevolent Fund, Fund for the Replacement of Animals in Medical Research; President, Royal Society of Medicine 1998–2000; Wildlife Information Network. R. N. Chaudhury Gold Medal, Calcutta School of Tropical Medicine 1976; Behring-Bilharz Prize, Cairo 1977; Ludwig-Schunk Prize, Justus Liebig University, Germany 1979; Mussemmeir Medal, Humboldt University, Berlin 1991; Centaur Award 1999 (Brit. Vet. Assn). Six honorary degrees; Emeritus Fellow, Wolfson College, Cambridge 1993–. Member, Home Office Committee of Inquiry into *Hunting with Dogs* 2000–2001. FRCVS; Hon. Fellow, Royal Society of Medicine 1996; Fellow, Institute Medical Sciences 1998; Hon. Fellow, Institute of Biology 2002. Freeman, City of London. Member, Worshipful Company of Farriers. *Publications:* Include: *Textbook of Veterinary Clinical Parasitology*, 1965; *Biology of Parasites*, 1966; *Reaction of the Host to Parasitism*, 1968; *Immune Response to Parasitic Infections*, 1987; *Zoonoses*, 1998; As well as other works, articles in journals of parasitology, immunology and pathology. *Special Interests:* Higher Education, Environment, Agriculture, Animal Welfare, Foreign Affairs. *Recreations:* Gardening, travel. *Clubs:* Farmers', United Oxford and Cambridge University. Raised to the peerage as Baron Soulsby of Swaffham Prior, of Swaffham Prior in the County of Cambridgeshire 1990. The Lord Soulsby of Swaffham Prior, House of Lords, London, SW1A 0PW *Tel:* 020 7219 8500 *E-mail:* lordsoulsby@aol.com.

SOUTHWARK, LORD BISHOP OF   Non-affiliated

SOUTHWARK (9th Bishop of), Thomas Frederick Butler. Born 5 March 1940. Son of late Thomas and Elsie Butler; educated King Edward's Grammar School, Fiveways, Birmingham; Leeds University (BSc electronics 1961, MSc, PhD). Married Barbara Joan Clark 1964 (1 son 1 daughter). *Career:* College of the Resurrection, Mirfield 1962–64; Curate: St Augustine's, Wisbech 1964–66, St Saviour's, Folkestone 1966–68; Lecturer and Chaplain, University of Zambia 1968–73; Acting Dean of Holy Cross Cathedral, Lusaka, Zambia 1973; Chaplain to University of Kent at Canterbury 1973–80; Six Preacher, Canterbury Cathedral 1979–84; Archdeacon of Northolt 1980–85; Area Bishop of Willesden 1985–91; Bishop of Leicester 1991–98; Chairman: Board of Mission, General Synod of the Church of England 1995–2001, Board of Social Responsibility, General Synod of Church of England 2001–; Took his seat in the House of Lords 1996; Bishop of Southwark 1998–. Member, Select Committee on Science and Technology Sub-Committee on Digital Images as Evidence 1997–.

Hon. LLD: Leicester University, De Montfort University; Hon. DSc, Loughborough University. *Publications:* Co-author: *Just Mission, Just Spirituality in a World of Faiths. Special Interests:* Science, Technology, Education, Development. *Recreations:* Reading, mountain walking, marathon running. Rt Rev the Lord Bishop of Southwark, Bishop's House, 38 Tooting Bec Gardens, Streatham, London, SW16 1QZ *Tel:* 020 8769 3256 *Fax:* 020 8769 4126 *E-mail:* bishops.house@dswark.org.uk.

STALLARD, LORD — Labour

STALLARD (Life Baron), Albert William Stallard; cr. 1983. Born 5 November 1921. Son of late Frederick and Agnes Stallard, née Jupp; educated Low Waters School; Hamilton Academy. Married Julia Murphy 1944 (1 son 1 daughter). *Trades Union:* Member, AUEW (AUEW Order of Merit 1968). Councillor, St Pancras 1953–59, Alderman 1962–65; Councillor, Camden 1965–71, Alderman 1971–78. *Career:* Precision engineer 1937–65; Technical training officer 1965–70. *House of Commons:* MP (Labour) for: St Pancras North 1970–1974, St Pancras North division of Camden 1974–1983; PPS to: Minister of Agriculture 1974–75, Minister of Housing 1975–76. Assistant Government Whip 1976–78, Government Whip 1978–79. Vice-President, Camden Association for Mental Health; Chair and Member, Camden Town Disablement Advisory Committee 1951–. Formerly Member, Institution of Training Officers. *Special Interests:* Education, Social Services, Health, Housing, Northern Ireland, Cyprus. *Recreations:* Photography, chess, reading. Raised to the peerage as Baron Stallard, of St Pancras in the London Borough of Camden 1983. The Lord Stallard, Flat 2, 2 Belmont Street, Chalk Farm Road, London, NW1 8HH; House of Lords, London, SW1A 0PW *Tel:* 020 7219 3225.

STEEL OF AIKWOOD, LORD — Liberal Democrat

STEEL OF AIKWOOD (Life Baron), David Martin Scott Steel; cr. 1997. Born 31 March 1938. Son of the late Very Rev. Dr David Steel, Moderator of the General Assembly of the Church of Scotland 1974–75; educated Prince of Wales School, Nairobi; George Watson's College; Edinburgh University (MA 1960, LLB 1962). Married Judith MacGregor 1962 (2 sons 1 daughter). DL, Roxburgh, Ettrick and Lauderdale 1990. *Career:* President, Edinburgh University Students' Representative Council 1961; Broadcaster; Journalist; BBC Television interviewer in Scotland 1964–65; Rector, Edinburgh University 1982–85. *House of Commons:* Contested (Liberal) Roxburgh, Selkirk and Peebles 1965 by-election–83, and for Tweeddale, Ettrick and Lauderdale 1983–97 (as Liberal Democrat 1988–97); Sponsor, Abortion Act 1967. Liberal Chief Whip 1970–74. Liberal Democrat Convenor and Spokesperson for Foreign Affairs and Overseas Development 1989–94. *House of Lords:* Deputy Leader, Liberal Democrat Peers 1997–99. Deputy Leader, Liberal Democrat Peers 1997–99. President, Liberal International 1992–94. President, Edinburgh University Liberal Club 1960; Assistant Secretary, Scottish Liberal Party 1962–64; Leader, Liberal Party 1976–88; Joint Founder, Social and Liberal Democrats 1988. Past President, Anti-Apartheid Movement in GB; Chairman, Scottish Advisory Council of Shelter 1968–72; Vice-President, Countryside Alliance 1998–99. Queen's Lord High Commissioner to the General Assembly of the Church of Scotland 2003. Eight honorary doctorates. Visiting Fellow, Yale University 1987; MSP for Lothians Region 1999–2003 (stood as Sir David Steel); Presiding Officer of the Scottish Parliament May 1999–2003. PC 1977; KBE 1990; Commander's Cross of the Order of Merit (Germany) 1992. Freeman: Tweeddale 1987, Ettrick and Lauderdale 1989. *Publications: No Entry, A House Divided*; Editor *Partners in One Nation*; *David Steel's Border Country*; Co-author *Mary Stuart's Scotland*; *Against Goliath* (autobiography), 1989. *Special Interests:* International Democracy. *Recreations:* Angling, classic car rallying. *Clubs:* National Liberal, London. Raised to the Peerage as Baron Steel of Aikwood, of Ettrick Forest in The Scottish Borders 1997. Rt Hon the Lord Steel of Aikwood, KBE, DL, House of Lords, London, SW1A 0PW *Tel:* 020 7219 4433.

Visit the Vacher Dod Website . . . **www.DodOnline.co.uk**

STERLING OF PLAISTOW, LORD   Conservative

STERLING OF PLAISTOW (Life Baron), Jeffrey Maurice Sterling; cr. 1991. Born 27 December 1934. Son of late Harry and Alice Sterling; educated Reigate Grammar School; Preston Manor County School; Guildhall School of Music. Married Dorothy Ann Smith 1985 (1 daughter). Honorary Captain, Royal Naval Reserve 1991. *Career:* Paul Schweder and Co. (Stock Exchange) 1955–57; G. Eberstadt & Co. 1957–62; Financial Director, General Guarantee Corporation 1962–64; Managing Director, Gula Investments Ltd 1964–69; Chairman, Sterling Guarantee Trust plc 1969, merging with P & O 1985; Board Member, British Airways 1979–82; Chairman, The Peninsular and Oriental Steam Navigation Company 1983–; Special Adviser to: Secretary of State for Industry 1982–83, Secretary of State for Trade and Industry 1983–90; President, General Council of British Shipping 1990–91; President, European Community Shipowners' Associations 1992–94; Chairman, P&O Princess Cruises plc 2000–03. Chairman, Organisation Committee, World ORT Union 1969–73, Member: Executive 1966–, Technical Services 1974–; Vice-President, British ORT 1978–; Deputy Chairman and Hon. Treasurer, London Celebrations Committee, Queen's Silver Jubilee 1975–83; Chairman, Young Vic Company 1975–83; Chairman, Motability 1994–, Vice-Chairman 1977–94, Chairman of Executive 1977–; Chairman of Governors, Royal Ballet School 1983–99; Governor, Royal Ballet 1986–99; Elder Brother, Trinity House 1991. Interfaith Medallion 2003. Hon. D (Business Administration), Nottingham Trent University 1995; Hon. DCL, Durham University 1996. Kt 1985; CBE 1977; KStJ 1998; GCVO 2002. Hon. Fellow: Institute of Marine Engineers 1991, Institute of Chartered Shipbrokers 1992; Hon. Member, Royal Institute of Chartered Surveyors 1993; Fellow, Incorporated Society of Valuers and Auctioneers 1995; Hon. Fellow, Royal Institute of Naval Architects 1997. Freeman, City of London. *Special Interests:* Shipping, Economics, Disability, Arts, Music. *Recreations:* Music, swimming, tennis. *Clubs:* Carlton, Garrick, Hurlingham. Raised to the peerage as Baron Sterling of Plaistow, of Pall Mall in the City of Westminster 1991. The Lord Sterling of Plaistow, GCVO, CBE, The Peninsular and Oriental Steam Navigation Company, 79 Pall Mall, London, SW1Y 5EJ *Tel:* 020 7930 4343 *Fax:* 020 7930 8572.

STERN, BARONESS   Crossbencher

STERN (Life Baroness) Vivien Helen Stern; cr. 1999. Born 25 September 1941. Daughter of Frederick Stern and Renate Mills; educated Kent College, Pembury, Kent; Bristol University (BA English literature 1963, MLitt 1964, CertEd 1965). Married Professor Andrew Coyle CMG. *Career:* Lecturer in education 1970; Community Relations Commission 1970–77; Director, NACRO 1977–96; Visiting fellow, Nuffield College, Oxford 1984–91; Secretary-general, Penal Reform International 1989–; Senior research fellow, International Centre for Prison Studies, King's College London 1997–. Member: Select Committee on European Union 2000–, Select Committee on European Union Sub-committee F (Social Affairs, Education and Home Affairs). Member Advisory Council ILANUD (United Nations Latin American Institute for Crime Prevention and the Treatment of Offenders); Honorary Secretary-general Penal Reform International; Vice-president, Comité de Soutien, Français Incarcérés au Loin (FIL); Trustee, Milton S. Eisenhower Foundation, Washington; Board member of the Association for Prevention of Torture, Geneva 1993–2000. Patron: Clean Break, Rethink (formerly the National Schizophrenia Fellowship), Prisoners' Education Trust; President, New Bridge; Vice-president, RPS Rainer; Member, Law Advisory Committee of the British Council 1995–2000; Governance Advisory Committee of the British Council 2002–. Hon. LLD: Bristol 1990, Oxford Brookes 1996; Hon. Fellow, LSE 1996. Patron, Prisoners Education Trust. Member: Special Programmes Board, Manpower Services Commission 1980–82, Youth Training Board 1982–88, General Advisory Council, IBA 1982–87, Committee on the Prison Disciplinary System 1984–85, Advisory Council, PSI 1993–96. CBE 1992. *Publications: Bricks of Shame,* 1987; *Imprisoned by Our Prisons,* 1989; *Deprived of their Liberty, a report for Caribbean Rights,* 1990; *A Sin Against the Future: imprisonment in the world,* 1998; *Alternatives to Prison in Developing Countries,* 1999;* Editor *Sentenced to Die: The Problems of TB in Prisons in Eastern Europe and Central Asia,* 2000. *Special Interests:* Criminal Justice, Foreign Affairs, Human Rights, International Development, Penal Reform, Prisons. Raised to the peerage as Baroness Stern, of Vauxhall in the London Borough of Lambeth 1999. The Baroness Stern, CBE, House of Lords, London, SW1A 0PW *Tel:* 020 7219 3000 *E-mail:* icps@kcl.ac.uk.

STEVENS OF LUDGATE, LORD Conservative

STEVENS OF LUDGATE (Life Baron), David Robert Stevens; cr. 1987. Born 26 May 1936. Son of late A. Edwin Stevens, CBE and of Kathleen James; educated Stowe; Sidney Sussex College, Cambridge (BA economics 1959). Married Patricia Rose 1961 (1 son 1 daughter) (divorced 1971); married Mrs Melissa Sadoff, née Milicevic 1977 (died 1989); married Mrs Meriza Giori, née Dzienciolsky 1990. Second Lieutenant, Royal Artillery, National Service 1954–56. *Career:* Management Trainee, Elliot Automation 1959; Hill Samuel Securities 1959–68; Drayton Group 1968–74; Chairman: City and Foreign (Renamed in 1987 Alexander Proudfoot) 1976–95, Drayton Far East 1976–93, English and International 1976–89, Consolidated Venture 1979–93, Drayton Consolidated 1980–92, Drayton Japan 1980–88; Chairman and Chief Executive, MIM Britannia Ltd (formerly Montagu Investment Management Ltd) 1980–89, Chairman only 1989–93; Chairman, United Newspapers plc 1981–, United News and Media plc 1995–99, Director 1974–; Chairman, Express Newspapers plc 1985–99; Deputy Chairman, Britannia Arrow Holdings plc 1987–89; Chairman: Invesco MIM plc (formerly Britannia Arrow Holdings) 1989–92, Premier Asset Mangement 1997–2001, Express National Newspapers Limited 1998–99, The Personal Number Company 1998–2003. Helicopter Emergency Services (HEMS), Royal London Hospital 1988–97. Hon. Fellow, Sidney Sussex College, Cambridge. Chairman, EDC for Civil Engineering 1984–86. Grand Official Order of the Southern Cross (Brazil). Fellow: Sidney Sussex College, Cambridge, Royal College of Surgeons. *Recreations:* Gardening, golf. *Sportsclubs:* Sunningdale Golf, Swinley Forest Golf. *Clubs:* White's. Raised to the peerage as Baron Stevens of Ludgate, of Ludgate in the City of London 1987. The Lord Stevens of Ludgate, 22 Cheyne Gardens, London, SW3 5QT *E-mail:* stevensdavid@parliament.uk.

STEVENSON OF CODDENHAM, LORD Crossbencher

STEVENSON OF CODDENHAM (Life Baron), (Henry Dennistoun) Dennis Stevenson; cr. 1999. Born 19 July 1945. Son of late Alexander and Sylvia Stevenson (née Ingleby); educated Trinity College, Glenalmond; King's College, Cambridge (MA classics 1970). Married Charlotte Susan Vanneck 1972 (4 sons). Chairman, House of Lords Appointments Commission 2000–. *Career:* Chair, SRU Group of Companies 1972–96; Non-executive director, Manpower Inc 1988–; Chair: Sinfonia 21 1989–99, Pearson Plc 1996–, Halifax PLC 1999–, HBOS Plc 2001–. Chancellor London Institute 2000–. Chairman, National Association of Youth Clubs 1973–81; Governor: London School of Economics 1996–2002, London Business School 1996–2002; Director, Glyndebourne Productions 1998–; Chairman, Aldeburgh Productions 2000–. Chairman, Trustees, Tate Gallery 1988–98; Member, Tate Gallery Foundation 1998–2000. Chairman: Government Working Party on role of voluntary movements and youth in the environment 1971, Newton Aycliffe and Peterlee New Town Development Corporation 1971–80, Independent Advisory Committee on Pop Festivals 1972–76; Director, National Building Agency 1977–81; Adviser on Agricultural Marketing to the Minister of Agriculture 1979–83; Director, London Docklands Development Corporation 1981–88; Chairman, Intermediate Technology Development Group 1983–90; Member: Panel on Takeovers and Mergers 1992–2000, Board, British Council 1996–2003; Hon. Member, The Royal Society of Musicians of Great Britain 1998–. CBE 1981; Kt 1998. *Publications: Stevenson Commission Information and Communications Technology in UK Schools Report,* 1997. *Clubs:* Brooks's, MCC. Raised to the peerage as Baron Stevenson of Coddenham, of Coddenham in the County of Suffolk 1999. The Lord Stevenson of Coddenham, CBE, Little Tufton House, 3 Dean Trench Street, London, SW1P 3HB *E-mail:* dennis@maxima.demon.co.uk.

DodOnline
An Electronic Directory without rival …

Peers' biographies and photographs available with daily updates *via* the internet

For a *free* trial, call Yasmin Mirza, Aby Farsoun or Michael Mand on 020 7630 7643

STEWARTBY, LORD   Conservative

STEWARTBY (Life Baron), (Bernard Harold) Ian Halley Stewart; cr. 1992. Born 10 August 1935. Son of late Professor Harold Stewart of Stewartby, CBE, MD, DL, KStJ, FRSE; educated Haileybury; Jesus College, Cambridge (MA classics 1959, DLitt 1978). Married Hon. Deborah Charlotte, JP, daughter of 3rd Baron Tweedsmuir 1966 (1 son 2 daughters). Served RNVR 1954–56; Lieutenant-Commander RNR. *Career:* Brown Shipley & Co. Ltd 1960–83, Director 1971–83; Chairman, The Throgmorton Trust plc 1990–; Deputy Chairman, Standard Chartered plc 1993–; Director, Financial Services Authority 1993–97; Deputy Chairman: Amlin plc 1995–, Portman Building Society 1999–2002. *House of Commons:* Contested (Conservative) North Hammersmith 1970 general election; MP (Conservative) for: Hitchin 1974–83, Hertfordshire North 1983–92; PPS to Chancellor of the Exchequer 1979–83; Parliamentary Under-Secretary of State (Procurement) Ministry of Defence January-October 1983; Economic Secretary to the Treasury 1983–87; Minister of State: Armed Forces, MoD 1987–88, Northern Ireland Office 1988–89. Opposition Spokesperson for the Banking Bill 1978–79. Chairman, Bow Group Economic Standing Committee 1978–83. Director, British Numismatic Society 1965–75; Life Governor, Haileybury 1977; County Vice-President, St John's Ambulance Brigade for Hertfordshire 1978–; Numismatic Adviser, National Art Collections Fund 1989–. Royal Numismatic Society Medal 1996. Hon. Fellow, Jesus College, Cambridge 1994. Trustee: Sir Halley Stewart Trust 1978– (President 2002–), Parliamentary Pension Fund 2000–. Chairman: British Academy Committee for the Sylloge of Coins of the British Isles 1993–2003, Treasure Valuation Committee 1996–2001. RD 1972; PC 1989; Kt 1991; KStJ 1992. FSA (Council Member 1974–76); FBA 1981; FRSE 1986. *Publications: The Scottish Coinage,* 1955, 1967; *Scottish Mints,* 1971; Co-author: *Studies in Numismatic Method,* 1983, *Coinage in Tenth Century England,* 1989. *Special Interests:* Financial Markets, Tax, Charities, Foreign Affairs, Defence. *Recreations:* Archaeology, tennis, cricket. *Sportsclubs:* Lords and Commons Cricket Club; MCC. *Clubs:* New (Edinburgh), Beefsteak, MCC, Hawks (Cambridge), Royal Automobile. Raised to the peerage as Baron Stewartby, of Portmoak in the District of Perth and Kinross 1992. Rt Hon the Lord Stewartby, House of Lords, London, SW1A 0PW *Tel:* 020 7219 6418.

STEYN, LORD   Crossbencher

STEYN (Life Baron), Johan van Zyl Steyn; cr. 1995. Born 15 August 1932. Son of Van Zyl Steyn and Janet Steyn; educated Jan van Riebeeck School, Cape Town, South Africa; University of Stellenbosch, South Africa (BA law 1957, LLB law 1957); University College, Oxford (MA law 1957) Cape Province Rhodes Scholar 1955. Married Susan Lewis 1977 (2 sons and 2 daughters from previous marriage; 1 stepson and 1 stepdaughter). *Career:* Commenced practice at the South African Bar 1958; Senior Counsel of Supreme Court of South Africa 1970; English Bar 1973; QC 1979; Bencher, Lincoln's Inn 1985; Judge of the High Court, Queen's Bench Division 1985–91; Member Supreme Court Rule Committee 1985–89; Departmental Advisory Committee on Arbitration Law 1986–89, Chair 1990–94; Chair, Race Relations Committee of the Bar 1987–88; Presiding Judge, Northern Circuit 1989–91; President, British Insurance Law Association 1992–94; Lord Justice of Appeal 1992–95; Chair, Advisory Council, Centre for Commercial Law Studies, Queen Mary and Westfield College, London 1993–94; Chair, Lord Chancellor's Advisory Committee on Legal Aid and Conduct 1994–96; Lord of Appeal in Ordinary 1995–. Two honorary doctorates; Honorary fellow University College, Oxford. Kt 1985; PC 1992. Hon. Member: American Law Institute, Society of Legal Scholars 2002. Raised to the peerage as Baron Steyn, of Swafield in the County of Norfolk 1995. Rt Hon the Lord Steyn, House of Lords, London, SW1A 0PW *Tel:* 020 7219 0793.

Visit the Vacher Dod Website ...
www.DodOnline.co.uk

STODDART OF SWINDON, LORD — Independent Labour

STODDART OF SWINDON (Life Baron), David Leonard Stoddart; cr. 1983. Born 4 May 1926. Son of late Arthur L. Stoddart, Coal Miner; educated St Clement Danes and Henley Grammar Schools. Married 2nd Jennifer Percival-Alwyn 1961 (2 sons) (1 daughter by previous marriage). *Trades Union:* Trade Unions: EETPU (later AEEU, now AMICUS) 1953–, NALGO 1951–70. Councillor, Reading County Borough Council 1954–72; Leader of Labour Group on Council 1962–72; Leader of Council 1967–72; Served at various times as Chairman of Housing, Transport and Finance and General Purposes Committees and as a member of various Boards inc. Thames Valley Water Board and Police Authority. *Career:* British Railways; NHS; Power station clerical worker 1951–70. *House of Commons:* Contested (Labour) Newbury 1959, 1964 general elections; MP (Labour) for Swindon 1970–83; PPS to Minister for Housing and Construction 1974–75. Assistant Government Whip 1975–76; Government Whip 1976–77. Junior Opposition Spokesperson for Industry 1982–83. Opposition Whip 1983–88. Opposition Spokesperson for Energy 1983–88. Member, Court and Council of Reading University 1964–68; Treasurer, Anzac Group 1985–2002; Chairman: Campaign for an Independent Britain 1989–, Anti-Maastrich Alliance 1991–; Founder Member, Global Britain. Member, National Joint Council for the Electricity Supply Industry 1967–70. *Special Interests:* Commonwealth, Economic Policy, Energy, European Union, Housing, Industry, Local Government, Transport. *Clubs:* Phylis Court, Henley-on-Thames. Raised to the peerage as Baron Stoddart of Swindon, of Reading in the Royal County of Berkshire 1983. The Lord Stoddart of Swindon, 'Sintra', 37A Bath Road, Reading, Berkshire, RG1 6HL *Tel:* 0118–957 6726.

STOKES, LORD — Crossbencher

STOKES (Life Baron), Donald Gresham Stokes; cr. 1969. Born 22 March 1914. Son of late Harry Potts Stokes; educated Blundell's School; Harris Institute of Technology, Preston. Married Laura Elizabeth Courteney Lamb 1939 (died 1995) (1 son); married Patricia June Pascal 2000. Served War 1939–45, REME, Lieutenant-Colonel. DL, Lancs 1968. *Career:* Commenced student apprenticeship, Leyland Motors Ltd 1930; Re-joined Leyland as exports manager 1946, General sales and service manager 1950, Director 1954; Managing Director, The Leyland Motor Corporation 1963, Chairman 1967. Chairman and Chief Executive: British Leyland (UK) Ltd, British Leyland International and subsidiary companies 1968–75; President, British Leyland Limited 1975–79; Consultant to Leyland Vehicles Ltd 1979–81; Director, District Bank Limited 1964–69; President, Motor Industry Research Association 1966; Chairman, Electronics Committee of the NEDC 1966–68; Director, London Weekend Television Limited 1967–71; Deputy Chairman, Industrial Reorganisation Corporation 1969–71; Director, National Westminster Bank 1969–81; Member, CBI Council; President, EDC for the Motor Manufacturing Industry 1969–; Chairman, British Arabian Advisory Co. Ltd 1977–85; Chairman, Two Counties Radio Ltd 1979–84, 1990–, President 1994–; Director: GWR Group 1990–94, Opus Public Relations Ltd 1979–84, KBH Communications Ltd 1985–96; Chairman, Jack Barclay Ltd 1980–90; Director, Scottish and Universal Investments Ltd 1980–92; Chairman: Dovercourt Motor Co. Ltd 1980–90, Dutton-Forshaw Motor Group Ltd 1981–91, Beherman Auto-Transports NV (Belgium) 1982–89. President: SMMT Council 1961–2, Institution of Mechanical Engineers 1972, University of Manchester Institute of Science and Technology 1968–76. Four honorary doctorates. Chairman, Nuffield Trust for the Forces of the Crown 1971–96. TD 1945, Officier de l'Ordre de la Couronne (Belgium) 1964; Kt 1965; Commandeur de l'Ordre de Leopold II (Belgium) 1972. FREng; FIMechE; MSAE; FIMI; FCIT; FICE; FIRTE; Fellow, Institute of Road Transport Engineers 1968, President 1982. Liveryman, Worshipful Company of Carmen. *Recreations:* Sailing. *Sportsclubs:* Commodore, Royal Motor Yacht Club, Poole 1979–81. *Clubs:* Army and Navy, Royal Motor Yacht Club. Raised to the peerage as Baron Stokes, of Leyland in the County Palatine of Lancaster 1969. The Lord Stokes, Kt, TD, DL, Branksome Cliff, Westminster Road, Poole, Dorset, BH13 6JW *Tel:* 01202 763088.

Visit the Vacher Dod Website ... www.DodOnline.co.uk

STONE OF BLACKHEATH, LORD — Labour

STONE OF BLACKHEATH (Life Baron), Andrew Zelig Stone; cr. 1997. Born 7 September 1942. Son of Sydney and Louise Stone; educated Cardiff High School. Married Vivienne Wendy Lee 1973 (1 son 2 daughters). *Career:* Marks and Spencer plc 1966–: Personal Assistant to Chairman 1978–80, Director 1990–, Joint Managing Director 1994–2000; Director: Science Media Centre –2001, N Brown 2002–, Ted Baker Plc –2002. *House of Lords:* Departmental Liaison Peer to Baroness Jay (Leader) 1999–2001. Member, Refreshment Sub-Committee, House of Lords Offices Committee 2000–02. Governor Weizmann Institute of Science, Israel. Chairman, British Overseas Trade Board for Israel 1991–99. Two honorary degrees. Hon Vice-President Reform Synagogues of Great Britain; Council of The Royal Institution of Great Britain; Trustee Maimonedes Foundation (Muslims and Jews); Chair, Dipex (Direct Patient Experiences). Governor, Weizmann Institute Foundation 1993–; Patron, Interalia Institute of Arts and Science; Council Member, Arts and Business 1994–2001; President, British Overseas Trade Board for Israel 1995–2000; Member, National Advisory Committee for Creative and Cultural Education 1998–2000; Governor, Tel Aviv University 2001–. *Special Interests:* Middle East, Arts, Science, Conflict Resolution. *Recreations:* Reading, walking, thinking. Raised to the peerage as Baron Stone of Blackheath, of Blackheath in the London Borough of Greenwich 1997. The Lord Stone of Blackheath, House of Lords, London, SWIA 0W *Tel:* 020 7219 4556 *Fax:* 020 7219 5979 *E-mail:* stonea@parliament.uk.

STRABOLGI, LORD — Labour

STRABOLGI (11th Baron, E), David Montague de Burgh Kenworthy; cr. 1318. Born 1 November 1914. Son of Lieutenant-Commander Hon. Joseph Montague Kenworthy, RN, MP, later 10th Baron, and Doris Whitley, only child of Sir Frederick Whitley-Thomson MP; educated Gresham's School, Holt; Chelsea School of Art. Married Doreen Margaret Morgan 1961. Served BEF 1939–40; MEF 1940–45, Lieutenant-Colonel, RAOC. *Career:* Member, Parliamentary delegations to: Russia 1954, France 1981, 1983, 1985; Director, Bolton Building Society 1958–74, 1979–87, Deputy Chairman 1983–85, Chairman 1986–87; Member, British Section Franco-British Council 1981–98; President, Franco-British Society 1999. *House of Lords:* First entered House of Lords 1953; PPS to the Lord Shackleton, KG, Lord Privy Seal and the Leader of the House of Lords 1969–70; Deputy Speaker and Deputy Chairman of Committees 1986–2001; Extra Lord in Waiting to HM The Queen 1998–; Elected hereditary peer 1999–. Opposition Whip 1970–74; Captain of the Queen's Bodyguard of the Yeomen of the Guard and Deputy Chief Whip, House of Lords 1974–79. Opposition Frontbench Spokesman for the Arts 1979–85. Member: Select Committee for Privileges 1987–, Joint Committee (with Commons) on Consolidation Bills 1987–97, 1998–2001, Personal Bills Committee 1987–97, Ecclesiastical Committee 1991–97, 1997–2001, Select Committee on Procedure of the House 1993–97, 1998–2001. Officier de la Légion d'Honneur 1981. Freeman, City of London. *Special Interests:* Environment, National Heritage, France, Venice. *Recreations:* The arts. *Clubs:* Reform. The Lord Strabolgi, House of Lords, London, SW1A 0PW.

STRANGE, BARONESS — Crossbencher

STRANGE (Baroness, 16th in line, E), Jean Cherry Drummond of Megginch; cr. 1628. Born 17 December 1928. Daughter of 15th Baron and late Violet Margaret Florence Buchanan-Jardine; educated Oxenfoord Castle School; St Andrews University (MA 1951); Cambridge University. Married Captain Humphrey ap Evans, MC, 1952 who assumed the name of Drummond of Megginch by decree of the Lord Lyon, 1966 (3 sons 3 daughters). *House of Lords:* First entered House of Lords 1986; Elected hereditary peer 1999–. Member Refreshment Committee 2003–. Member, Executive Committee Association of Conservative Peers 1991–94; Moved to Crossbenches 1998. Member, Parliamentary Delegation, Bangladesh 1990; Delegate, Inter-Parliamentary Union Conference, Ottawa 1993; Member, Parliamentary Delegation: Bulgaria 1998, Isle of Man 1999, Kazakhstan 1999, Ukraine 2000; Member: IPU Executive Committee 1999–, CPA; Member, Parliamentary Delegation Malta 2001–. Chairman, Glencarse Junior Unionists 1947–52. President, War Widows Association of Great Britain 1990–;

Member: Age Concern, Scottish Peers Association. FSA (Scotland); Hon. FIMarE. *Publications: Love from Belinda*; *Lalage in Love*; *Creatures Great and Small*; *Love is For Ever*; *The Remarkable Life of Victoria Drummond – Marine Engineer*. *Special Interests:* Defence, Foreign Affairs, Children, Countryside, Arts. The Baroness Strange, Megginch Castle, Errol, Perthshire, PH2 7SW *Tel:* 01821 642222.

STRATHCLYDE, LORD — Conservative

STRATHCLYDE (2nd Baron), Thomas Galbraith; cr. 1955. Born 22 February 1960. Son of late Hon. Sir Thomas Galbraith, KBE, MP, eldest son of 1st Baron, PC; educated Wellington College; University of East Anglia 1978–82; University of Aix-en-Provence 1981. Married Jane Skinner 1992 (3 daughters). *Career:* Lloyd's Insurance Broker; Bain Clarkson Ltd 1982–88. *House of Lords:* First entered House of Lords 1985; Parliamentary Under-Secretary of State: Department of Employment (Minister for Tourism) 1989–90, Department of Environment July-Sept 1990, Scottish Office (Minister for Agriculture and Fisheries) 1990–92; Joint Parliamentary Under-Secretary of State, Department of Environment 1992–93; Joint Parliamentary Under-Secretary of State for Consumer Affairs and Small Firms, Department of Trade and Industry 1993–94, Minister of State January-July 1994; Member, Shadow Cabinet 1997–; Former Deputy Speaker; Former Deputy Chairman of Committees; Leader of the Opposition December 1998–; Elected hereditary peer 1999–. Government Whip 1988–89; Government Chief Whip 1994–97; Opposition Chief Whip 1997–98. Government Spokesperson for DTI, Treasury and Scotland 1988–89; Opposition Spokesperson for Constitutional Affairs December 1998–. Member: House of Lords' Offices, House of Lords' Offices Finance and Staff Sub-committee 2000–02, Select Committees on: Liaison, Privileges, Procedure. Peer of 2000, Channel 4 and *The House* Magazine 2000. Contested (Conservative) Merseyside East 1984 European Parliament election; Chairman, Commission on the Future Structure of the Scottish Conservative and Unionist Party 1997–98. PC 1995. Rt Hon the Lord Strathclyde, House of Lords, London, SW1A 0PW *Tel:* 020 7219 3236.

SUTHERLAND OF HOUNDWOOD, LORD — Crossbencher

SUTHERLAND OF HOUNDWOOD (Life Baron), Stewart Ross Sutherland; cr 2001. Born 25 February 1941. Son of late George and Ethel, née Masson, Sutherland; educated Woodside School, Aberdeen; Robert Gordon's College; Aberdeen University (MA philosophy 1963); Corpus Christi College, Cambridge (BA philosophy of religion 1965, MA). Married Sheena Robertson 1964 (2 daughters 1 son). Member, Council for Science and Technology 1993–2000; President, Royal Society of Edinburgh 2002–; Member: Council of British Academy 2002–, Council of Foundation for Science and Technology. *Career:* Assistant lecturer University College of North Wales, Bangor 1965–68; Lecturer, reader Stirling University 1968–77; King's College, London: Professor of history and philosophy of religion 1977–85, Titular professor 1985–94, Vice-principal 1981–85, Principal 1985–90; Inspector of Schools and founder Office for Standards in Education (OFSTED) 1992–94; Vice-chancellor London University 1990–94; Principal and Vice-chancellor Edinburgh University 1994–2002; Chair Committee on Appeal Court Procedure (Scotland) 1994–96; Non-executive Director, NHP 2001–; Member: Higher Education Funding Council for England 1995–2001, Hong Kong University Grants Committee 1995 ; Chair: Royal Commission on Long Term Care of the Elderly 1997–99, Quarry Products Association 2002–; Provost Gresham College 2002–; Member Board Courtauld Institute of Art 2002–; Chair English Care 2003–. Hon President Alzheimers and Dementia (Scotland) 2000–; Hon President Saltire Society 2002–. Several. Knighthood 1995; Order of the Thistle 2002. FBA 1992; FRSE 1995. Court of Assistants, Goldsmiths' Company 2000–. *Publications: Criminal Appeals and Alleged Miscarriages of Justice*, 1996; *With Respect to Old Age* (Royal Commission Report) 1999; Various books and academic articles. *Special Interests:* Education, Care of the Elderly, Research Policy. *Recreations:* Rough gardening, jazz, Tassie Medallions, theatre. *Clubs:* New Club. Raised to the peerage as Baron Sutherland of Houndwood, of Houndwood in the Scottish Borders 2001. The Lord Sutherland of Houndwood, House of Lords, London, SW1A 0PW *Tel:* 020 7219 5353 *Tel:* 018907 61200 *E-mail:* sutherlands@parliament.uk.

SWINFEN, LORD   Conservative

SWINFEN (3rd Baron, UK), Roger Mynors Swinfen Eady; cr. 1919. Born 14 December 1938. Son of 2nd Baron; educated Westminster School; RMA, Sandhurst. Married Patricia Anne Blackmore 1962 (1 son 3 daughters). Lieutenant, The Royal Scots (The Royal Regiment). JP, Kent 1983–85. *House of Lords:* First entered House of Lords 1977; Elected hereditary peer 1999–. Member: Select Committee on Greater Manchester Bill 1979, House of Lords European Communities Sub-Committee C 1990–94. President, South East Region British Sports Association for the Disabled; Patron: Disablement Income Group 1988–, 1 in 8 Group 1996, Labrador Rescue South East 1996; Hon. President, Britain Bangladesh Friendship Association. Honorary Research Fellow in the Centre for Online Health, University of Queensland 2001. Fellow, Industry and Parliament Trust 1983–; Swinfen Charitable Trust. Chairman, Parliamentary Working Party on Video Violence and Children 1982–85; Member, Direct Mail Services Standards Board 1983–97. Liveryman, Worshipfull Company of Drapers. *Publications:* Co-author *An Evaluation of the First Year's Experience with a Low-cost Telemedicine Link in Bangladesh,* 2001, *Store-and-Forward Teleneurology in Developing Countries,* 2001, *Experience with a Low-cost Telemedicine System in Three Developing Countries,* 2001. *Special Interests:* Disability, Telemedicine. *Recreations:* Gardening, painting, reading history. The Lord Swinfen, House of Lords, London, SW1A 0PW *Tel:* 020 7219 3500 *E-mail:* swinfenr@parliament.uk.

SYMONS OF VERNHAM DEAN, BARONESS   Labour

SYMONS OF VERNHAM DEAN (Life Baroness), Elizabeth Conway Symons; cr. 1996. Born 14 April 1951. Daughter of Ernest Vize Symons and Elizabeth Megan, neé Jenkins; educated Putney High School for Girls; Girton College, Cambridge (MA history 1974). Married Philip Bassett 2001 (1 son). *Career:* Research, Girton College, Cambridge 1972–74; Administration trainee, Department of the Environment 1974–77; Inland Revenue Staff Federation: Assistant secretary 1977–78, Deputy general secretary 1978–89; General secretary, Association of First Division Civil Servants 1989–97. *House of Lords:* Parliamentary Under-Secretary of State, Foreign and Commonwealth Office 1997–99; Minister of State for Defence Procurement, Ministry of Defence 1999–2001; Minister of State for International Trade and Investment, Foreign and Commonwealth Office and Department of Trade and Industry 2001–03; Deputy Leader of the Lords 2001–; Minister of State for Middle East, Foreign and Commonwealth Office 2003–. Government Spokesperson for: Foreign and Commonwealth Office 2001–, Trade and Industry 2001–. Member Select Committees on: House of Lords' Offices 2001–02, Procedure. Member Parliamentary Labour Party Parliamentary Committee 2001–. Former Member: General Council, TUC, Council, RIPA, Governor, Polytechnic of North London 1989–94; Member: Executive Council, Campaign for Freedom of Information 1989–97, Hansard Society Council 1992–97, Advisory Council, Civil Service College 1992–97; Governor, London Business School 1993–97; Member: Council, Industrial Society 1994–97, Council, Open University 1994–97. Hon. Associate, National Council of Women 1989; Member, Employment Appeal Tribunal 1995–97. PC 2001. FRSA. *Recreations:* Reading, gardening. Raised to the peerage as Baroness Symons of Vernham Dean, of Vernham Dean in the County of Hampshire 1996. Rt Hon the Baroness Symons of Vernham Dean, House of Lords, London, SW1A 0PW *Tel:* 020 7008 2090 *Fax:* 020 7008 3731 *E-mail:* ministersymons.action@fco.gov.uk.

DodOnline

An Electronic Directory without rival ...

Peers' biographies and photographs available with daily updates *via* the internet

For a *free* trial, call Yasmin Mirza, Aby Farsoun or Michael Mand on 020 7630 7643

T

TANLAW, LORD   Crossbencher

TANLAW (Life Baron), Simon Brooke Mackay; cr. 1971. Born 30 March 1934. Son of late 2nd Earl of Inchcape; educated Eton College; Trinity College, Cambridge (BA medieval history, archaeology and anthropology, MA). Married Joanna Susan Hirsch 1959 (1 son 2 daughters and 1 son deceased); married Rina Siew Yong 1976 (1 son 1 daughter). Served as 2nd Lieutenant, XII Royal Lancers, Malaya. *Career:* Worked in Inchcape Group of Companies India and Far East 1960–66, Managing Director 1967–71, Director 1971–92; Chairman and Managing Director, Fandstan Group of Companies 1973–; Member, Executive Committee of the Great Britain-China Centre 1981–88. Deputy Whip, Liberal Party 1971–83. Member, European Communities Committee Sub-Committee F (Energy Transport, Research and Technology) 1980–83. Chair, Building Committee, University College at Buckingham 1973–77, Council of Management 1973–2000; Member, Court of Governors, London School of Economics 1980–96; President, Sarawak Association 1973–75, 1997–99; Hon. Treasurer, Scottish Peers Association 1979–86. Hon. DUniversity, University of Buckingham 1983. Contested Galloway 1959, 1960 and 1964 general elections as Liberal candidate; Member, Lord Chancellor's Inner London Advisory Committee on Justices of the Peace 1972–83. Fellow, British Horological Institute. Member: Worshipful Company of Fishmongers, Worshipful Company of Clockmakers. *Publications:* In the *Horological Journal*: *The Case for a British Astro-Physical Masterclock, Spacetime and Horology GMT or UTC for the Millennium?*. *Special Interests:* Time, Space. *Recreations:* Fishing, horology. *Clubs:* White's, Oriental, Puffin's (Edinburgh). Raised to the peerage as Baron Tanlaw, of Tanlawhill in the County of Dumfries 1971. The Lord Tanlaw, 31 Brompton Square, London, SW3 2AE; Tanlawhill, Eskdalemuir, by Langholm, Dumfriesshire, DG13 0PQ *E-mail:* tanlaws@parliament.uk.

TAVERNE, LORD   Liberal Democrat

TAVERNE (Life Baron), Dick Taverne; cr. 1996. Born 18 October 1928. Son of late Dr N. J. M. Taverne and of Mrs L. V. Taverne; educated Charterhouse School; Balliol College, Oxford (First in Greats 1951). Married Janice Hennessey 1955 (2 daughters). *Career:* Called to the Bar, Middle Temple 1954; QC 1965; Director, Institute for Fiscal Studies 1970–79, Director-General 1979–81, Chairman 1981–83; Director, Axa Equity and Law 1972–, Chairman 1997–2001; Director, BOC Group 1975–95; Member, International Independent Review Body to review workings of the European Commission 1979; Chair, Public Policy Centre 1983–87; Director, PRIMA Europe Ltd 1987–, Chair 1991–93, President 1993–98; Chair, OLIM Investment Trust 1989–99; Deputy Chair: Central European Growth Fund 1994–2000, Industrial Finance Group 1995–2003. *House of Commons:* Contested Wandsworth, Putney (Labour) 1959 general election; MP (Labour) for Lincoln, March 1962-October 1972, resigned; Parliamentary Under-Secretary of State, Home Office 1966–68; Minister of State, HM Treasury 1968–69; Financial Secretary, HM Treasury 1969–70; MP (Democratic Labour) for Lincoln, March 1973-September 1974; Contested (SDP): Southwark, Peckham, October 1982, Dulwich 1983 general elections. Liberal Democrat Spokesperson for: Treasury Issues 1998–2001, Euro 2001–. Member, Select Committees on: Monetary Policy of the Bank of England 2000–, Animals in Scientific Procedures 2001–02, European Union Sub-committee A (Economic and Financial Affairs, Trade and External Relations) 2003–. Member: National Committee, Social Democratic Party 1981–87; Federal Policy Committee, Liberal Democrats 1989–90. Chairman: Council of Alcohol and Drug Abuse Prevention and Treatment Ltd, Advisory Board of Oxford Centre for the Environment, Ethics and Society, Sense About Science. *Publications: The Future of the Left: Lincoln and after*, 1974; *The Pension Time Bomb in Europe*, 1995; *Pensions in Europe*, 1997; *Qualified Majority Voting*, 1997; *Tax and the Euro*, 1999; *Can Europe Pay for its Pensions*, 2000. *Special Interests:* European Union, Pensions, Science and Technology, Crime and Drugs, Tax, Economic Policy. *Recreations:* Sailing. *Sportsclubs:* Cruising Association. Raised to the peerage as Baron Taverne, of Pimlico in the City of Westminster 1996. The Lord Taverne, QC, 60 Cambridge Street, London, SW1V 4QQ *Tel:* 020 7592 9684 *E-mail:* dick.taverne@lineone.net.

TAYLOR OF BLACKBURN, LORD   Labour

TAYLOR OF BLACKBURN (Life Baron), Thomas Taylor; cr. 1978. Born 10 June 1929. Son of James Taylor; educated Blakey Moor Elementary School. Married Kathleen Nurton 1950 (1 son). Councillor, Blackburn Council 1954–76, Leader of Council until 1976; JP, Blackburn 1960; Member North West Health Authority; DL, Lancashire 1994–. *Career:* Department of social administration Manchester University; Consultant: Initial Electronic Security Systems Ltd, BAE Systems plc 1994–; Adviser: Electronic Data Systems Ltd 1996–, Hammond Suddards Edge, Solicitors 1997–2002; Consultant Fleetwood Power Ltd 1998–2001; Adviser: AES Electric Ltd 1999–, Reality Group 1999–, United Utilities plc 2000–, Capgemini Ernst & Young UK Ltd 2001–; Non-executive Director AES Drax Ltd 2001–; President, Wrens Hotel Group. Deputy Pro-Chancellor, Lancaster University 1961–95. Member: Select Committee on Science and Technology 1987–92, House of Lords' Offices Committee 1993–97. Member, Labour North West Group. Member, CPA 1978–. Past President, Association of Education Committees; Member of Council, Lancaster University 1961–95; President, Free Church Council 1962–63; Chairman, Electricity Consumers Council for North West 1977–80; Member, Norweb Board; President, Association of Lancastrians in London 2001–; Patron/President of several voluntary organisations. Hon. LLD, Lancaster 1996. Patron, Lancashire Wildlife Trust. Past Chairman of several Government Committees of Enquiry. OBE 1969; CBE 1974. FRGS 1994; FICPD 1998. Freeman: Borough of Blackburn 1992, City of London 1999. *Publications: A New Partnership for our Schools,* 1977. *Special Interests:* Education, North West, Railways, Commonwealth, Energy, Local Government. *Recreations:* Gardening, radio, books, music. Raised to the peerage as Baron Taylor of Blackburn, of Blackburn in the County of Lancaster 1978. The Lord Taylor of Blackburn, CBE, DL, 9 Woodview, Cherry Tree, Blackburn, Lancashire, BB2 5LL *Tel:* 01254 209571 *Fax:* 01254 209571; House of Lords, London, SW1A 0PW *Tel:* 020 7219 5130 *Fax:* 020 7219 5979 *E-mail:* janetmrobinson@compuserve.com.

TAYLOR OF WARWICK, LORD   Conservative

TAYLOR OF WARWICK (Life Baron), John David Beckett Taylor; cr. 1996. Born 21 September 1952. Son of late Derief Taylor, Warwickshire professional cricketer, and Mrs Enid Taylor, nurse; educated Moseley Church of England School, Birmingham; Moseley Grammar School (Head Pupil); Keele University (BA law 1977); Gray's Inn, Inns of Court School of Law. Married Dr Katherine Taylor 1981 (1 son 2 daughters). *Trades Union:* Member, NUJ, Bar Council. Councillor, Solihull Borough Council 1986–91; Member: North West Thames Regional Health Authority 1992–93, Greater London Further Education Funding Council 1992–95; Vice-President, British Board of Film Classification 1998–; Member, Independent Football Commission 2002–03. *Career:* Barrister-at-Law, called Gray's Inn 1978; Television and radio presenter, writer and company director; Non-executive director, Mottram Holdings Plc; Chair Warwick Communications Ltd; Chairman, Westminster Executive Ltd. Chancellor Bournemouth University 2002–. *House of Lords:* Introduced the Criminal Evidence (Amendment) Bill which came into force March 1997 as the Criminal Evidence (Amendment) Act 1997. Member, Association of Conservative Peers. Member: CPU, IPU. Life Patron, West Indian Senior Citizens Association (WISCA); Patron: Parents Need Children Adoption Charity, Kidscape Charity; Executive Committee Member, Sickle Cell Anaemia Relief Charity; Member: Royal Television Society, Radio Academy; Vice-President, National Small Business Bureau; President, African Caribbean Westminster Business Initiative; Barker, Variety Club of Great Britain; Director, The Warwick Leadership Foundation Charity. Gray's Inn Advocacy Prize 1978. Honorary LLD Warwick University. Member, Industry and Parliament Trust. Contested (Conservative) Cheltenham 1992 general election; Member, Institute of Directors; Vice-President, British Board of Film Classification 1998–. City of London 1998. *Publications: The System on Trial* (BBC Publications) 1996. *Special Interests:* Law, Broadcasting, Film. *Recreations:* Singing, soccer and cricket, spending time with my family. *Sportsclubs:* Aston Villa Football Club; President, Ilford Town Football Club. Raised to the peerage as Baron Taylor of Warwick, of Warwick in the County of Warwickshire 1996. The Lord Taylor of Warwick, House of Lords, London, SW1A 0PW *Tel:* 020 7219 0665 *Fax:* 020 7219 5979 *E-mail:* taylorjdb@parliament.uk.

TEBBIT, LORD   Conservative

TEBBIT (Life Baron), Norman Beresford Tebbit; cr. 1992. Born 29 March 1931. Son of late Leonard Albert Tebbit; educated Edmonton County Grammar School. Married Margaret Elizabeth Daines 1956 (2 sons 1 daughter). *Trades Union:* Member, BALPA. RAF pilot, 1949–51, Commissioned; Served RAuxAF 604 Squadron 1952–55. *Career:* Journalist 1947–49; Publicist and publisher 1951–53; Airline pilot 1953–70; Assistant director of information, National Federation of Building Trades Employers 1975–79; Political commentator on Sky Television's Target programme 1989–98; Columnist: *Sun* newspaper 1995–97, *The Mail on Sunday* 1997–2001; Company Director: Sears Holdings plc 1987–99, British Telecom 1987–96, BET 1987–96, Spectator (1828) Ltd 1989–, Onix Ltd 1990–92. *House of Commons:* MP (Conservative) for: Epping 1970–74, Chingford 1974–92; PPS to Minister of State, Department of Employment 1972–73; Parliamentary Under-Secretary of State, Department of Trade 1979–81; Minister of State for Industry January-September 1981; Secretary of State for Employment 1981–83; Secretary of State for Trade and Industry and President of the Board of Trade 1983–85; Chancellor of the Duchy of Lancaster 1985–87. Held various offices in: YC organisation 1946–55, Hemel Hempstead Conservative Association 1960–67; Chairman, Conservative Party 1985–87. Chair: The Nuffield Ortholics Appeal, Nuffield Orthopaedic Appeal; Council Member and Past President of The Air League; Member Royal Aeronautical Society. Air Line Transport Pilots Licence; Flight Navigators Licence; Former office holder with BALPA (British Airline Pilots' Association). PC 1981; CH 1987. Freeman, City of London. Liveryman, Guild of Air Pilots and Air Navigators. *Publications: Upwardly Mobile*, 1988; *Unfinished Business*, 1991. *Recreations:* Gardening. *Clubs:* Royal Air Force, Beefsteak, The Other Club. Raised to the peerage as Baron Tebbit, of Chingford in the London Borough of Waltham Forest 1992. Rt Hon the Lord Tebbit, CH, House of Lords, London, SW1A 0PW *Tel:* 020 7219 6929.

TEMPLEMAN, LORD   Crossbencher

TEMPLEMAN (Life Baron), Sydney William Templeman; cr. 1982. Born 3 March 1920. Son of late Herbert William Templeman; educated Southall Grammar School; St John's College, Cambridge (BA history 1940, law 1947). Married Margaret Rowles 1946 (died 1988) (2 sons); married Mrs Sheila Edworthy 1996. Served Second World War 1939–45; Commissioned 4/1st Gurkha Rifles 1941; NW Frontier 1942; Arakan 1943; Imphal 1944 (despatches, Hon. Major); Burma 1945. *Career:* Called to the Bar, Middle Temple and Lincoln's Inn 1947; Member, Bar Council 1961–65; Attorney-General of the Duchy of Lancaster 1970–72; Judge of the High Court of Justice, Chancery Division 1972–78; President, Senate of the Inns of Court and the Bar 1974–76; Member, Royal Commission on Legal Services 1976–79; Lord Justice of Appeal 1978–82; Lord of Appeal in Ordinary 1982–94; Treasurer, Middle Temple 1987; Chair, Ecclesiastical Committee 1992–2001. Member: Chairman, Subcommittee law of European Union Committee 1984, Ecclesiastical Committee 1997–2002, Committee on Personal Bills. Hon. Fellow, St John's College, Cambridge 1982; Six honorary doctorates. MBE (Mil) 1946; Kt 1972; PC 1978. Raised to the peerage as Baron Templeman, of White Lackington in the County of Somerset 1982. Rt Hon the Lord Templeman, MBE, 'Mellowstone', 1 Rosebank Crescent, Exeter, Devon, EX4 6EJ *Tel:* 01392 275428.

TEMPLE-MORRIS, LORD   Labour

TEMPLE-MORRIS (Life Baron), Peter Temple-Morris; cr 2001. Born 12 February 1938. Son of late His Hon. Sir Owen Temple-Morris, QC; educated Malvern College; St. Catharine's College, Cambridge (BA law 1961, MA 1965). Married Tahere Alam 1964 (2 sons 2 daughters). *Career:* Barrister, Inner Temple 1962; Solicitor 1989–. *House of Commons:* Contested Newport 1964 and 1966, Norwood Lambeth 1970 general elections; Conservative Member for Leominster February 1974-October 1997, Independent Member October 1997-June 1998, Labour Member October 1998–2001; PPS to Norman Fowler as Minister of Transport 1979. Member Select Committee on Delegated Powers and Regulatory Reform 2003–. Executive British Branch of Inter-Parliamentary

Union: Member 1977–97, Chair 1982–85, Member, Parliamentary Delegation to United Nations 1980, 1984 (leader); Hon. Vice-President, United Nations Association 1987–; Founding Co-Chair, British-Irish Parliamentary Body 1990–97, Member 1997–; Vice-Chair, GB-Russia and Eastern Europe Centre 1993–98; Member, Executive, Commonwealth Parliamentary Association 1994–98 (vice-chairman 1996). Chair: Cambridge University Conservative Association 1961, Bow Group Standing Committee on Home Affairs 1975–80, Society of Conservative Lawyers, Executive Committee 1995–97. Member, Cambridge Afro-Asian Expedition 1961; Chair, Afghanistan Support Committee 1981–82; Member, Academic Council, Wilton Park (FCO) 1990–97. Honorary Citizen: New Orleans, Havana, Cuba; Hon. Member, National Party of Australia, Queensland. Fellow, Industry and Parliament Trust. Member, Advisory Council, British Institute of Persian Studies; Hon. President, British-Iranian Business Association; Chairman, British-Iranian Chamber of Commerce; Iran Society Council: Member 1968–80, President 1995–; Chevalier du Tastevin (Chat. de Vougeot) 1988–; Chair, Lords and Commons Solicitors Group 1992–97; Jurade De St Emilion 1999–. *Publications: Motoring Justice,* 1979, plus various articles on foreign affairs and Ireland. *Special Interests:* Foreign Affairs, Irish Affairs, European Union, Constitutional and Legal Affairs, Middle East and Iran. *Recreations:* Wine and food, travel, family relaxation. *Clubs:* Cardiff and County (Cardiff), Reform. Raised to the peerage as Baron Temple-Morris, of Llandaff in the County of South Glamorgan and of Leominister in the County of Herefordshire 2001. The Lord Temple-Morris, House of Lords, London, SW1A 0PW *Tel:* 020 7219 4181 *Fax:* 020 7219 6388 *E-mail:* templemorrisp@parliament.uk.

TENBY, VISCOUNT   Crossbencher

TENBY (3rd Viscount, UK), William Lloyd-George; cr. 1957. Born 7 November 1927. Son of 1st Viscount, PC, TD; educated Eastbourne College; St Catharine's College, Cambridge (Late Exhibitioner) (BA history 1949). Married Ursula Diana Ethel Medlicott 1955 (1 son 2 daughters). Former JP, Hampshire, North East Hampshire Bench, retired 1997; Member, Hampshire Police Authority 1985–94. *Career:* Editorial assistant, Herbert Jenkins Ltd 1951–54; Advertisement department, Associated Newspapers 1954–57; Group advertising manager, United Dominions Trust Ltd 1957–74; PR adviser to Chairman, Kleinwort Benson Ltd 1974–87; Consultant, Williams Lea Group 1985–93; Director, Ugland International plc 1993–95. *House of Lords:* First entered House of Lords 1983; Elected hereditary peer 1999–. Former Member: Finance and Building Sub-Committee, Committee on Procedure; Committee of Selection; Member, Refreshment Sub-Committee, House of Lords Offices Committee 2000–02. Member: Internal Lords Reform Committee 2001–02, Ad Hoc Committee on Smoking. Chairman Trustees, Byways Residential Home. *Special Interests:* Communications Industry, Magistracy, Railways, Environment. *Recreations:* Ornithology, music (choral singing), reading, countryside. The Viscount Tenby, The White House, Dippenhall Street, Crondall, Nr Farnham, Surrey, GU10 5PE *Tel:* 01252 850592 (Home) *Fax:* 01252 850913 (Home); House of Lords, London, SW1A 0PW *Tel:* 020 7219 5403 (Office).

THATCHER, BARONESS   Conservative

THATCHER (Life Baroness), Margaret Hilda Thatcher; cr. 1992. Born 13 October 1925. Daughter of late Alfred Roberts; educated Kesteven and Grantham High School; Somerville College, Oxford (MA, BSc natural science chemistry). Married Denis Thatcher, MBE, TD 1951 (created Sir Denis Thatcher, 1st Bt 1991, died 2003) (twin son and daughter). *Career:* Research chemist 1947–51; Called to the Bar, Lincoln's Inn 1954. *House of Commons:* Contested (Conservative) Dartford in 1950, 1951 general elections under her maiden name of Roberts; MP (Conservative) for Finchley 1959–92; Joint Parliamentary Secretary, Ministry of Pensions and National Insurance 1961–64; Shadow Minster of: Transport 1968–69, Education 1969–70; Secretary of State for Education and Science 1970–74; Leader of the Opposition 1975–79; Prime Minister, First Lord of the Treasury and Minister for the Civil Service 1979–90. Opposition Front Bench Spokesman on: Pensions and National Insurance 1964, Housing and Land 1965–66, The Treasury 1966–67; Chief Opposition Front Bench Spokesman on Power and Member of the Shadow Cabinet 1967; Opposition Treasury Spokesman 1974. Chancellor, Buckingham University 1992–98; Chancellor, College of William and Mary,

Williamsburg, Virginia 1993–2000. Leader of Conservative and Unionist Party 1975–90. Hon. Doctorates: Louisiana State University 1993, Mendeleyev University, Moscow 1993. Hon. Bencher 1975; Elected Honorary Master of the Bench of Gray's Inn 1983; Hon. President, The Bruges Group 1991–. PC 1970; OM 1990; LG 1995; Presidential Medal of Freedom (USA) 1991; Order of Good Hope (South Africa) 1991; Order of the White Lion (First Class) (Czech Republic) 1999. FRS 1983. Freedom, London Borough of Barnet 1980; Hon. Freedom: Falkland Islands 1983, City of London 1989; Freeman, City of Westminster 1991. Hon. Freeman, Worshipful Company of Grocers 1980. *Publications: The Downing Street Years,* 1993; *The Path to Power,* 1995; *Collected Speeches,* 1998; *Statecraft,* 2002. *Recreations:* Music, reading. *Clubs:* Carlton. Raised to the peerage as Baroness Thatcher, of Kesteven in the County of Lincolnshire 1992. Rt Hon the Baroness Thatcher, LG, OM, House of Lords, London, SW1A 0PW *Tel:* 020 7219 4545.

THOMAS OF GRESFORD, LORD — Liberal Democrat

THOMAS OF GRESFORD (Life Baron), (Donald) Martin Thomas; cr. 1996. Born 13 March 1937. Son of late Hywel Thomas and of Olwen Thomas; educated Grove Park Grammar School, Wrexham; Peterhouse, Cambridge (MA classics, LLB law). Married Nan Thomas, née Kerr 1961 (died 2000) (3 sons 1 daughter). *Career:* Solicitor, Wrexham 1961–66; Lecturer in law 1966–68; QC 1979; Called to the Bar, Gray's Inn 1967, Bencher 1989; Barrister, Wales and Chester Circuit 1968–; Deputy Circuit Judge 1974–76; Recorder of the Crown Court 1976–2002; Deputy High Court Judge 1985–. Liberal Democrat Spokesman on Welsh Affairs. Member Joint Committee on Statutory Instruments 1999–2002. Vice-Chair, Welsh Liberal Party 1967–69, Chair 1969–74; President: Wrexham Liberal Association 1975–, Welsh Liberal Party 1977, 1978, 1979, Welsh Liberal Democrats 1993, Vice-President 1991–93. Chair, Marcher Sound 1991–2000, Vice-Chair 1983–91; President, London Welsh Chorale 2000–. President, Gresford Memorial Trust 1993–. Contested (Liberal): West Flintshire 1964, 1966, 1970, Wrexham February and October 1974, 1979, 1983, 1987; Member, Criminal Injury Compensation Board 1985–93. OBE 1982. *Special Interests:* Hong Kong, China, Criminal Justice, Wales. *Recreations:* Rugby football, rowing, golf, fishing, cooking, harp, piano, bagpipes, singing. *Sportsclubs:* Wrexham Rugby; Rex Rowing; Commons and Lords Rugby Football. *Clubs:* Reform, Western (Glasgow). Raised to the peerage as Baron Thomas of Gresford, of Gresford in the County Borough of Wrexham 1996. The Lord Thomas of Gresford, OBE, QC, Glasfryn, Gresford, Wrexham, LL12 8RG *Tel:* 01978 852205 *Fax:* 01978 855081 *Tel:* 020 7219 5453 *E-mail:* thomasm@parliament.uk.

THOMAS OF GWYDIR, LORD — Conservative

THOMAS OF GWYDIR (Life Baron), Peter John Mitchell Thomas; cr. 1987. Born 31 July 1920. Son of late David Thomas, Solicitor; educated Epworth College, Rhyl; Jesus College, Oxford (BA law 1946, MA). Married Frances Elizabeth Tessa Dean 1947 (died 1985), (2 sons 2 daughters). War Service in RAF (POW Germany 1941–45). *Career:* Called to the Bar, Middle Temple 1947; QC 1965; Master of the Bench 1971, Emeritus 1991; Deputy Chairman, Cheshire Quarter Sessions 1966–70; Denbighshire Quarter Sessions 1968–70; Recorder of Crown Courts 1974–88; An Arbitrator, International Chamber of Commerce Courts of Arbitration, Paris 1974–88. *House of Commons:* MP (Conservative) for: Conway 1951–66, Hendon South 1970–87; PPS to Solicitor-General 1954–59; Parliamentary Secretary, Ministry of Labour and National Service 1959–61; Parliamentary Under-Secretary of State, Foreign Office 1961–63; Minister of State for Foreign Affairs 1963–64; Secretary of State for Wales and Member of the Cabinet June 1970–74. Opposition Frontbench Spokesman on Foreign Affairs and Law 1964–66. Chairman, Conservative Party 1970–72; President, National Union of Conservative and Unionist Association 1974–76; National President, Conservative Friends of Israel 1984–91. Fellow, Jesus College, Oxford 2001. PC 1964. *Special Interests:* Foreign Affairs. *Clubs:* Carlton. Raised to the peerage as Baron Thomas of Gwydir, of Llanrwst in the County of Gwynedd 1987. Rt Hon the Lord Thomas of Gwydir, QC, 37 Chester Way, London, SE11 4UR *Tel:* 020 7735 6047; Millicent Cottage, Elstead, Surrey, GU8 6HD *Tel:* 01252 702052.

THOMAS OF MACCLESFIELD, LORD   Labour

THOMAS OF MACCLESFIELD (Life Baron), Terence James Thomas; cr. 1997. Born 19 October 1937. Son of late William Emrys Thomas, and of Mildred Evelyn Thomas; educated Queen Elizabeth Grammar School, Carmarthen; School of Management, Bath University (postgraduate diploma 1973); INSEAD (AMP) 1987. Married Lynda Stevens 1963 (3 sons). *Career:* National Provincial Bank (later National Westminster) 1962–71; Market research manager, later national sales manager, The Joint Credit Card Company 1971–73; Marketing manager, The Co-operative Bank plc 1973–77, Assistant general manager, later Joint general manager 1977–83, General manager, customer services 1984–87, Executive director 1984–88, Managing director 1988–97; Visiting professor, Stirling University 1988–91; Various company directorships including: Unity Trust Bank plc 1983–95, Co-operative Commercial Ltd 1985–87, Co-operative City Investments Ltd 1988–90, Vector Investments Ltd 1992–95 (Chairman), Stanley Leisure Organisation plc 1994–98, Venture Technic (Cheshire) Ltd (Chairman), FI Group Shareholders Trust (Chairman); Rathbone CI 1997–98; Capita Group 1997–98; Chairman, North West Development Agency 1998–2002. Member, Select Committees on: European Affairs, Monetary Policy of the Bank of England 1998–99. President, International Co-operative Banking Association (ICBA) 1988–95; Lords' Member, Parliamentary Broadcasting Unit 2000–. Chief Examiner, Chartered Institute of Bankers 1983–85; Trustee, Board of UNICEF 1998; President, Society for Co-operative Studies; Fellow and Member, General Council of the Institute of Bankers; Member: British Invisibles European Committee (Bank of England appointment), The Parliamentary Renewable and Sustainable Energy Group (PRASEG), Court of Governors, UMIST 1996–; Patron, Northern Friends of ARMS (Multiple Sclerosis Therapy Centre); Appeal Chairman, City of Manchester and District Macmillan Nurse Appeal. Mancunian of the Year 1998. Hon. DLitt, University of Salford 1996; Hon. Dr Business Administration, Manchester Metropolitan University 1998; Hon. Degree Business Management, Manchester Federal School of Business and Management. Patron: Macclesfield Museums Trust, Red Rose Community Forest, Youth Charter for Sport, Art and Culture, West Lancs Disability Helpline. CBE 1997. FCIB; CIMgt; MCIM. *Special Interests:* England's North East. Raised to the peerage as Baron Thomas of Macclesfield, of Prestbury in the County of Cheshire 1997. The Lord Thomas of Macclesfield, CBE, House of Lords, London, SW1A 0PW *Tel:* 020 7219 1201.

THOMAS OF SWYNNERTON, LORD   Crossbencher

THOMAS OF SWYNNERTON (Life Baron), Hugh Swynnerton Thomas; cr. 1981. Born 21 October 1931. Son of late Hugh Whitelegge Thomas, CMG and of Margery Swynnerton; educated Sherborne School; Queens' College, Cambridge (BA history 1953) Sorbonne, Paris. Married Hon Vanessa Jebb 1961 (2 sons 1 daughter). *Career:* Professor of history, Reading University 1966–76; Chairman, Centre for Policy Studies 1979–90; King Juan Carlos I Professor of Spanish Civilisation, New York University 1995–96; Professor, University Professors' Programme, Boston University, USA 1996–. Somerset Maugham Prize 1962; Arts Council Prize for History 1980. Trustee, Fundación Medinaceli. Grand Cross of the Order of Isabel la Católica (Spain); Order of the Aztec Eagle (Mexico). *Publications: The Spanish Civil War*, 1961, 1976; *The Suez Affair*, 1967; *Cuba or The Pursuit of Freedom*, 1971; *John Strachey*, 1973; *Goya and the Third of May*, 1973; *An Unfinished History of the World*, 1979; *Havannah!*, 1984; *Armed Truce*, 1986; *Ever Closer Union: Britain's Destiny in Europe*, 1991; *The Conquest of Mexico*, 1993; *The Slave Trade*, 1997; *The Future of Europe*, 1997; *Who's Who of the Conquistadors*, 2000. *Clubs:* Athenaeum, Beefsteak. Raised to the peerage as Baron Thomas of Swynnerton, of Notting Hill in Greater London 1981. The Lord Thomas of Swynnerton, 29 Ladbroke Grove, London, W11 3BB *Tel:* 020 7727 2288.

Visit the Vacher Dod Website . . .
www.DodOnline.co.uk

THOMAS OF WALLISWOOD, BARONESS   Liberal Democrat

THOMAS OF WALLISWOOD (Life Baroness), Susan Petronella Thomas; cr. 1994. Born 20 December 1935. Daughter of John Arrow, and of Mrs Ebba Fordham; educated Cranborne Chase; Lady Margaret Hall, Oxford University (BA history 1967). Married David Churchill Thomas CMG 1958 (separated) (1 son 2 daughters). Councillor, Surrey County Council 1985–97, Vice-Chair 1993–96, Chair 1996–97; Chair, Highways and Transport Committee 1993–96; Surrey County Representative, Association of County Councils 1993–97; Member, East Surrey Community Health Council 1989–92; Non-executive Director, East Surrey Hospital and Community Healthcare Trust 1992–96; DL, Surrey 1996; Member, Surrey Probation Committee 1997–2001, Surrey Probation Board 2001–. *Career:* National Economic Development Office 1971–74; Chief Executive, British Clothing Industries, Council for Europe 1974–78. *House of Lords:* Deputy Chair of Committees 2002–; Deputy Speaker 2002–. Liberal Democrat Spokesperson for: Transport 1994–2001, Women's Issues 2001–. Member Select Committee of European Union Sub-Committee E (Law and Institutions). Member, IPU. Has served on many Liberal and Liberal Democrat policy committees; Former President, Women Liberal Democrats; Member, Liberal International 1999–. School Governor 1985–94. Contested (Liberal Alliance) Mole Valley in 1983, 1987 general elections; Contested (Liberal Democrat) Surrey 1994 European Parliament election. OBE 1989. *Recreations:* Gardening, reading, ballet, theatre, travel. Raised to the peerage as Baroness Thomas of Walliswood, of Dorking in the County of Surrey 1994. The Baroness Thomas of Walliswood, OBE, DL, House of Lords, London, SW1A 0PW *Tel:* 020 7219 3599.

THOMSON OF MONIFIETH, LORD   Liberal Democrat

THOMSON OF MONIFIETH (Life Baron), George Morgan Thomson; cr. 1977. Born 16 January 1921. Son of late James Thomson, of Dundee; educated Grove Academy, Broughty Ferry. Married Grace Jenkins 1948 (2 daughters). *Trades Union:* Member, NUJ. RAF 1941–46. DL, Kent 1992–98; Chair, Honours Scrutiny Committee. *Career:* Journalist and Editor of "Forward" 1946–56; Joint Chair, Council for Education in the Commonwealth 1960–64; Chair, David Davies Institute of International Affairs 1971–77; UK Commissioner for Regional Policy to EEC Brussels 1973–77; Chair: British Council European Movement 1977–79, Advertising Standards Authority 1977–80; First Crown Estate Commissioner 1977–80; Chair, Independent Broadcasting Authority 1981–88; Deputy Chair, Woolwich Building Society 1988–91; Member, Committee on Standards in Public Life 1994–97. *House of Commons:* Contested (Labour) Glasgow Hillhead Division 1950; MP (Labour) Dundee East 1952–72; Minister of State, Foreign Office 1964–66; Chancellor of the Duchy of Lancaster 1966–67; Secretary of State for Commonwealth Affairs 1967–68; Minister without Portfolio 1968-October 1969; Chancellor of the Duchy of Lancaster and Deputy Foreign Secretary 1969–70; Shadow Defence Minister 1970–72. Spokesperson for Colonial Affairs 1957–64. Chancellor, Heriot-Watt University 1977–91. Liberal Democrat Party Spokesperson for: Broadcasting and Foreign Affairs 1989–97, Media 2001. Chair Select Committee on Broadcasting 1993–97; Member Select Committee on European Union Sub-committee E (Law and Institutions) 2001–. Chairman, Labour Committee for Europe 1972–73. Chair: Franco-British Council 1977–80, Centre European Agricultural Institute 1978–82; European Television and Film Forum 1989–91. Five honorary doctorates. Trustee, Thomson Foundation 1978–; Trustee, Leeds Castle Foundation 1978–, Chair 1994–2001; Pilgrim Trustee 1977–97; President, History of Advertising Trust 1985–99. Lords' Member, Parliamentary Broadcasting Unit 1993–. PC 1966; KT 1981. FRS Edinburgh; Fellow of the Royal Television Society. Freeman: Monifieth 1967, Dundee 1973. *Recreations:* Swimming. Raised to the peerage as Baron Thomson of Monifieth, of Monifieth in the District of the City of Dundee 1977. Rt Hon the Lord Thomson of Monifieth, KT, House of Lords, London, SW1A 0PW *Tel:* 020 7219 6718.

Visit the Vacher Dod Website . . . **www.DodOnline.co.uk**

THORNTON, BARONESS   Labour

THORNTON (Life Baroness), (Dorothea) Glenys Thornton; cr. 1998. Born 16 October 1952. Daughter of Peter and Jean Thornton, of Bradford, West Yorkshire; educated Thornton Secondary School, Bradford; London School of Economics (BSc economics 1976). Married John Carr 1977 (1 son 1 daughter). *Trades Union:* Member, GMB. Member, Court of Governors London School of Economics; Director, IDEA; Chair, Coalition of Social Enterprise. *Career:* National Co-ordinator, Gingerbread 1977–79; CAB area officer 1979–81; General Secretary, Fabian Society 1993–96; Public affairs adviser, CWS 1981–93; Chairman, Pall Mall Consult. Member: European Union Sub-committee C (Environment, Public Health and Consumer Protection) 1999–2000, Special Joint Committee on Local Government Legislation on Elected Mayors 1999; Member, European Union Sub-committee D (Environment, Agriculture, Public Health and Consumer Protection) 2000. Chair, The Greater London Labour Party 1986–91; Member, The Co-operative Party. Chair, Makespace Trust. RSA. *Special Interests:* Children, London, Media, Social Enterprise. *Recreations:* Canoeing, hill-walking, *Star Trek*. Raised to the peerage as Baroness Thornton, of Manningham in the County of West Yorkshire 1998. The Baroness Thornton, House of Lords, London, SW1A 0PW *Tel:* 020 7219 8502 *E-mail:* thorntong@parliament.uk.

TOMBS, LORD   Crossbencher

TOMBS (Life Baron), Francis Leonard Tombs; cr. 1990. Born 17 May 1924. Son of late Joseph and Jane Tombs; educated Elmore Green School, Walsall; Birmingham College of Technology (HNC electrical engineering 1943); London University (BSc economics 1963). Married Marjorie Evans 1949 (3 daughters). *Career:* GEC 1939–45; Birmingham Corporation 1946–47; British Electricity Authority, Midlands, then Central Electricity Authority, Merseyside and North Wales 1948–57; General Manager, GEC, Erith 1958–67; Director and General Manager, James Howden and Co., Glasgow 1967–68; Successively director of engineering, Deputy Chair and Chair, South of Scotland Electricity Board 1969–77; Chair: The Electricity Council 1977–80, The Weir Group 1981–83, Turner and Newall 1982–89; Director: N M Rothschild & Sons Ltd 1981–94; Shell UK 1983–94; Chair, Rolls-Royce plc 1985–92, Director 1982–92. Chancellor, Strathclyde University 1991–98. Member, Science and Technology Committee 1992–94, 1997–2000; Chair, Sustainable Development Committee 1994–95; Chair, Sub-committee II (Management of Nuclear Waste) 1998–99; Member: Science and Technology Sub-committee II (Science and Society) 1999–2000, Delegated Powers and Deregulation Committee 2000–. Chairman, The Molecule Theatre of Science 1985–92, President 1992–94. 14 honorary doctorates from British and Polish universities. Chair, Brooklands Museum Trust 1994–2001. Kt 1978. FREng 1977; Hon. FIChemE 1985; Hon. FICE 1986; Hon. FIProdE 1986; Hon. FIMechE 1989; Hon. FIEE 1991; Hon. FRAeS 1995; Hon. FRSE 1996. City of London. Liveryman, Goldsmiths' Company 1981–, Prime Warden 1994–95. *Special Interests:* Science, Technology, Engineering. *Recreations:* Golf, music. Raised to the peerage as Baron Tombs, of Brailes in the County of Warwickshire 1990. The Lord Tombs, House of Lords, London, SW1A 0PW; Honington Lodge, Honington, Shipston-on-Stour, Warwickshire, CV36 5AA *Tel:* 01608 661437.

TOMLINSON, LORD   Labour

TOMLINSON (Life Baron), John Edward Tomlinson; cr. 1998. Born 1 August 1939. Son of Frederick and Doris Tomlinson; educated Westminster City School; Co-operative College, Loughborough (diploma in political, economic and social studies 1961); Brunel University (health services management 1974–76); Warwick University (MA industrial relations 1982). Married 1st (divorced); married Paulette Fuller 1998. *Trades Union:* Member, TGWU. *Career:* Senior lecturer in industrial relations and management, Solihull College of Technology 1979–84; Head of research for AUEW 1968–70; MEP for Birmingham West 1984–99: Socialist Group Spokesman on: Budgetary Control Committee 1984–99. *House of Commons:* MP (Lab) for Meriden 1974–79;

PPS to Harold Wilson as Prime Minister 1975–76; Parliamentary Under-Secretary of State, Foreign and Commonwealth Office 1976–79; Parliamentary Secretary, Ministry of Overseas Development 1977–79. Member: European Union Select Committee 1998–2002, European Union Sub-committee A (Economic and Financial Affairs, Trade and External Relations) 1998–2002, Chair 2000–01, House of Lords' Offices 2001–02. House of Lords Representative on Convention on Future of Europe 2002–03. Vice-President, The Hansard Society; President, British Fluoridation Society. Trustee, Industry and Parliament Trust; Chairman of Trustees. Alternate National Parliamentary Representative European Convention 2002–. *Special Interests:* Finance, Europe, International Development, Foreign Policy. *Recreations:* Walking, reading, sport. *Clubs:* West Bromwich Labour. Raised to the peerage as Baron Tomlinson, of Walsall in the County of West Midlands 1998. The Lord Tomlinson, House of Lords, London, SW1A 0PW *Tel:* 020 7219 3770.

TOPE, LORD   Liberal Democrat

TOPE (Life Baron), Graham Norman Tope; cr. 1994. Born 30 November 1943. Son of late Leslie Tope; educated Whitgift School, South Croydon. Married Margaret East 1972 (2 sons). London Scottish TA 1962–64. London Borough of Sutton: Councillor 1974–, Leader of the Liberal (later Liberal Democrat) Group 1974–99, Leader of Opposition 1984–86, Leader of the Council 1986–99; Cabinet member 1999–; Member, Greater London Authority 2000–: Leader, Liberal Democrat Group, Member Environment Committee; Public Services Committee; Member, Metropolitan Police Authority 2000–, Chair: Finance, Planning and Best Value Committee, 2000–02, Finance Committee 2002–; Mayor of London Advisory Cabinet 2000–. *Career:* Company secretary and insurance manager 1965–72; Deputy General Secretary, Voluntary Action Camden 1975–90; Chair, Community Investors Ltd 1995–98. *House of Commons:* MP (Liberal) Sutton and Cheam December 1972-February 1974; Contested (Liberal) Sutton and Cheam February and October 1974 general elections. Spokesperson for The Environment and Northern Ireland 1973–74. Assistant Whip 1998–2000. Liberal Democrat Spokesperson for Education 1994–2000. Member, Relations between Central and Local Government Committee 1995–96. EU Committee of the Regions: Member 1994–, Vice-Chair, UK Delegation 1996–, Bureau Member 1996–; President (Leader), ELDR (Liberal) Group 1998–2002; Member, Council of Europe, Congress of Local and Regional Authorities in Europe 1996–; President, Committee of the Regions Constitutional Affairs and European Governance Commission 2002–. Vice-Chair, National League of Young Liberals 1971–73, President 1973–75; Member, Liberal Party National Council 1970–76; Executive Committee of London Liberal Party 1981–84; President, London Liberal Democrats 1991–2000. Member, London Boroughs Association Policy and Finance Committee 1986–95, Chair 1994–95; Member, Association of London Goverment Leaders' Committee 1995–2000; Deputy Leader of Opposition, Association of Metropolitan Authorities 1995–97; Member, London Fire and Civil Defence Authority 1995–97; Vice-President, Local Government Association 1997–; Vice-Chair, Association of London Government 1997–2000. CBE 1991. Freeman, City of London 1998. Member, Needle Makers Company. *Publications:* Co-author of *Liberals and the Community*, 1974. *Special Interests:* Local Government, Europe, London, Police, Environment. Raised to the peerage as Baron Tope, of Sutton in the London Borough of Sutton 1994. The Lord Tope, CBE, 88 The Gallop, Sutton, Surrey, SM2 5SA *Tel:* 020 8770 7269 *Fax:* 020 8642 8595; Greater London Authority, City Hall, London, SE1 2AA *Tel:* 020 7983 4413 *Fax:* 020 7983 4344 *E-mail:* graham.tope@london.gov.uk.

TORDOFF, LORD   Liberal Democrat

TORDOFF (Life Baron), Geoffrey Johnson Tordoff; cr. 1981. Born 11 October 1928. Son of late Stanley Acomb Tordoff; educated Manchester Grammar School; Manchester University. Married Mary Patricia Swarbrick 1953 (2 sons 3 daughters). *Career:* Shell 1950–83: Marketing executive, Shell Chemicals, Public affairs manager (Chemicals), Shell UK; Hon. President, British Youth Council 1986–92; Chair, Middle East Committee, Refugee Council 1990–94; Member, Press Complaints Commission 1995–2002. *House of Lords:* Principal Deputy Chairman of Committees 1994–2001; Deputy Speaker 1994–; Chairman of Committees 2001–02; Deputy Chair of Committees 2002–. Deputy Whip 1983–84; Chief Whip 1984–88; Liberal Democrat Chief Whip 1988–94. Liberal Democrat Transport Spokesperson 1988–94. Chair, European Communities/Union 1994–2001;

Member, House of Lords' Offices 1997–2002, Chair 2001–02; Chair: Administration and Works Sub-Committee 2001–02, Finance and Staff Sub-Committee 2001–02, Hybrid Instruments 2001–02, Liaison 2001–02, Personal Bills 2001–02, Privileges 2001–02, Procedures 2001–02, Selection 2001–02, Standing Orders (Private Bills) 2001–02; Member Advisory Panel on Works of Art 2003–. Chairman: Liberal Party Assembly Committee 1974–76, Liberal Party 1976–79, Liberal Party Campaigns and Elections Committee 1980–82; President, Liberal Party 1983–84. Contested (Liberal): Northwich 1964, Knutsford 1966, 1970 general elections. *Special Interests:* Foreign Affairs, Europe. *Clubs:* National Liberal. Raised to the peerage as Baron Tordoff, of Knutsford in the County of Cheshire 1981. The Lord Tordoff, House of Lords, London, SW1A 0PW *Tel:* 020 7219 6613 *E-mail:* tordoffg@parliament.uk.

TREFGARNE, LORD   Conservative

TREFGARNE (2nd Baron, UK), David Garro Trefgarne; cr. 1947. Born 31 March 1941. Son of 1st Baron; educated Haileybury, Hertford; Princeton University, USA. Married Rosalie Lane 1968 (2 sons 1 daughter). *Career:* Non-executive Director, Siebe plc 1991–98; Chair, Engineering and Marine Training Authority (now SEMTA) 1994–. *House of Lords:* First entered House of Lords 1962; Parliamentary Under-Secretary of State: Department of Trade 1980–81, Foreign and Commonwealth Office 1981–82, Department of Health and Social Security 1982–83, for the Armed Forces June 1983–85; Minister of State: for Defence Support 1985–86, for Defence Procurement 1986–89, Department of Trade and Industry (Minister for Trade) 1989–90; Elected hereditary peer 1999–. Opposition Whip 1977–1979; Government Whip 1979–80. Member: Procedure Committee 2000–, Privileges Committee 2002–. Treasurer, Association of Conservative Peers 1997–2000, Chairman 2000–. President: Mechanical and Metal Trades Confederation (METCOM) 1990–, Governor, Guildford School of Acting 1992–2001; Life Governor and Member of Council, Haileybury 1993–2001; Hon. President, British Association of Aviation Consultants 1993–; Vice-chair, Army Cadet Force 1993–2001; Director, Arab-British Chamber of Commerce, 2000–; Hon President, Popular Flying Association 1992–. Royal Aero Club Bronze Medal 1963. Member, Mary Rose Trust –2001; Chairman, Brooklands Museum Trust 2001–. PC 1989. *Special Interests:* Aviation. *Recreations:* Photography. *Clubs:* White's. Rt Hon the Lord Trefgarne, House of Lords, London, SW1A 0PW *Tel:* 020 7219 5450.

TROTMAN, LORD   Crossbencher

TROTMAN (Life Baron), Alexander James Trotman; cr. 1999. Born 22 July 1933. Son of late Charles and Agnes Trotman; educated Boroughmuir School, Edinburgh; Michigan State University, USA (MBA 1972). Married Valerie Anne Edgar 1963. Flying Officer Navigator, Royal Air Force 1951–55. *Career:* Ford 1955–98: Various positions Ford of Britain 1955–67; Director, Car Product Planning, Ford Europe 1967–69; Positions in Car Product Planning and Sales Planning Departments, Ford US 1969–75; Chief Car Planning Manager, Ford Motor Co 1975–79; Vice-President, European Truck Operations 1979–83; President: Ford Asia Pacific 1983–84, Ford of Europe 1984–88; Executive Vice-President, North American Automotive Operations 1989–93; President, Ford Automotive Group 1993; Chairman and Chief Executive Officer, Ford Motor Company 1993–98; Director: IBM Corporation 1995–, New York Stock Exchange 1996–2002, ICI UK 1997–, chair 2002–. Hon. Doctorate, University of Edinburgh. Trustee, Shakespeare Globe Trust. Kt 1996. *Clubs:* Royal Air Force. Raised to the peerage as Baron Trotman, of Osmotherley in the County of North Yorkshire 1999. The Lord Trotman, Kt, House of Lords, London, SW1A 0PW.

DodOnline
An Electronic Directory without rival . . .

Peers' biographies and photographs available with daily updates *via* the internet

For a *free* trial, call Yasmin Mirza, Aby Farsoun or Michael Mand on 020 7630 7643

TRUMPINGTON, BARONESS — Conservative

TRUMPINGTON (Life Baroness), Jean Alys Barker; cr. 1980. Born 23 October 1922. Daughter of Major Arthur Edward Campbell-Harris and Doris Marie Robson; educated privately in England and France. Married William Alan Barker 1954 (died 1988) (1 son). Landgirl to David Lloyd George 1939–41; Naval intelligence, Bletchley Park 1941–45. Cambridge City Councillor 1963–73, Hon. City Councillor (Cambridge) 1975; Mayor of Cambridge 1971–72, Deputy Mayor 1972–73; Cambridgeshire County Councillor 1973–75; JP, Cambridgeshire 1972–75; South Westminster 1975–82. *Career:* European Central Inland Transport Organization (in London and Paris) 1946–49; Secretary to Viscount Hinchingbrooke, MP 1949–52; Copywriter in advertising agency, New York City 1952–54; Member: Board of visitors HM Prison, Pentonville 1975–81, Mental Health Review Tribunal 1975–1981; General Commissioner of Taxes 1975–83; United Kingdom representative to the United Nations Status of Women Commission 1979–81. *House of Lords:* Parliamentary Under-Secretary of State for Health and Social Security 1985–87; Parliamentary Secretary, Ministry of Agriculture, Fisheries and Food 1987–89; Minister of State 1989–92. Government Whip 1983–1985, 1992–97. Government Spokesperson for: Foreign Commonwealth Office 1983–85, Home Office 1983–85, Office of Public Service 1996–97, Department of National Heritage. Member House of Lords' Offices Advisory Panel on Works of Art 2001–. Vice-president, International League for the Protection of Horses 1990–99. Chair, Cambridge City Conservative Association 1969–71. Member, Airline Users Committee 1973–80, Deputy Chair 1977, Chair 1979–80; President, Association of Heads of Independent Schools 1980–90; Steward, Folkestone Racecourse 1980–92. Hon. Fellow, Lucy Cavendish College, Cambridge 1980. Member, Council and Executive Committee of the Animal Health Trust 1981–87. Extra Baroness in Waiting to HM The Queen 1998–. PC 1992. Hon. Fellow, Royal College of Pathologists; Hon. Associate, Royal College of Veterinary Surgeons 1994; Hon. Member, British Veterinary Association. *Recreations:* Antiques, bridge, cookery, needlepoint, racing. *Clubs:* Grillions, Farmers'. Raised to the peerage as Baroness Trumpington, of Sandwich in the County of Kent 1980. Rt Hon the Baroness Trumpington, House of Lords, London, SW1A 0PW *Tel:* 020 7219 6255.

TRURO, LORD BISHOP OF — Non-affiliated

TRURO (Bishop of), (William) Bill Ind. Born 26 March 1942; educated Duke of York's School, Dover; Leeds University (BA history 1964); College of the Resurrection, Mirfield. Married Frances Isobel Bramald 1967 (3 sons). *Career:* Deacon 1966; Priest 1967; Curate of: Feltham 1966–71, Northolt St Mary 1971–73; Team vicar of Basingstoke 1974–87: Vice-Principal, Aston Training Scheme; Director of Ordinands, Winchester Diocese 1982–87; Member, Doctrine Commission; Hon Canon of Winchester 1984–87; Suffragan Bishop of Grantham 1987–97; Bishop of Truro 1997–; Entered House of Lords 2002. *Recreations:* Cricket, bird-watching. *Clubs:* Farmers. Rt Rev the Lord Bishop of Truro, Lis Escop, Truro, Cornwall, TR3 6QQ *Tel:* 01872 862657 *Fax:* 01872 862037 *E-mail:* bishop@truro-anglican.org.

TUGENDHAT, LORD — Conservative

TUGENDHAT (Life Baron), Christopher Samuel Tugendhat; cr. 1993. Born 23 February 1937. Son of late Dr Georg Tugendhat and Mrs Malré Tugendhat; educated Ampleforth College; Gonville and Caius College, Cambridge (BA history 1960, MA). Married Julia Dobson 1967 (2 sons). Army national service 1955–57; Second Lieutenant, Essex Regiment 1956–57. *Career:* Journalist with *The Financial Times* 1960–70; Director: Sunningdale Oils 1971–76, Phillips Petroleum International (UK) Ltd 1972–76, EEC Commission: Member 1977–85, Vice-President 1981–85; Director: National Westminster Bank 1985–91, The BOC Group 1985–96; Chair, Civil Aviation Authority 1986–91; Director, Commercial Union Assurance 1988–91; Deputy Chairman, National Westminster Bank 1990–91; Director: LWT (Holdings) plc 1991–94, Chair: Abbey National plc 1991–2002, Blue Circle Industries plc 1996–2001; Non-executive: Eurotunnel plc 1991–2003;

Director, Rio Tinto plc 1997–, Chairman Lehman Brothers, Europe 2002–. *House of Commons:* MP (Conservative): Cities of London and Westminster 1970–74, City of London and Westminster South 1974–76. Deputy Spokesperson for: Employment 1975, Foreign Affairs 1975–76. Chancellor, Bath University 1998–. Chair, The Royal Institute for International Affairs (Chatham House) 1986–95; Governor, Council of Ditchley Foundation 1986–; Chair European Policy Forum 1997. Hon. LLD, Bath University 1998; Hon. DLitt, UMIST 2002. Kt 1990. Freeman, City of London. *Publications: Oil: the biggest business*, 1968; *The Multinationals*, 1971; *Making Sense of Europe*, 1986; Co-author *Options for British Foreign Policy in the 1990s*, 1988. *Recreations:* Family, reading, conversation. *Clubs:* Athenaeum, Anglo-Belgian. Raised to the peerage as Baron Tugendhat, of Widdington in the County of Essex 1993. The Lord Tugendhat, 35 Westbourne Park Road, London, W2 5QD *E-mail:* cstug@lehman.com.

TURNBERG, LORD   Labour

TURNBERG (Life Baron), Leslie Arnold Turnberg; cr. 2000. Born 22 March 1934. Son of Hyman and Dora Turnberg; educated Stand Grammar School, Whitefield; Manchester University (MB, ChB 1957, MD 1966). Married Edna Barme 1968 (1 son 1 daughter). *Career:* Junior medical posts: Manchester Jewish Hospital, Northern Hospital, Ancoats Hospital, Manchester Royal Infirmary 1957–61 and 1964–66; Registrar, UCH 1961–64; Lecturer, Royal Free Hospital 1967; Research Fellow, University of Texas South-Western Medical School, Dallas, Texas 1968; Manchester University: Lecturer, then Senior Lecturer 1968–73, Professor of Medicine 1973–97; Dean, Faculty of Medicine 1986–89, President, Royal College of Physicians 1992–97; Chair: Conference of Medical Royal Colleges 1994–96, Specialist Training Authority 1996–98, Public Health Laboratory Service Board 1997–2002, Health Quality Service 1999–; Scientific Adviser, Association of Medical Research Charities 1997–. Co-opted Member, Select Committee on Science and Technology Sub-Committee IIA (Human Genetic Databases) 2000–; Member, Select Committee on: Science and Technology 2001, Science and Technology Sub-Committee I (Systematic Biology and Biodiversity/ Fighting Infection) 2002–. Member, Labour Friends of Israel. Member: Salford Health Authority 1974–81 and 1990–92, North West Regional Health Authority 1986–89; Member of Council, Royal College of Physicians 1989–92, President 1992–97; President: Medical Council on Alcoholism 1997–2002, Medical Protection Society 1997–, British Society of Gastroenterology 1999–2000; Vice-president, Academy of Medical Sciences 1998–2003. Hon DSc: Salford 1996, Manchester 1998, Imperial College, London 2000. Kt 1994. MRCP 1961; FRCP 1973; FRCPE 1993; FRCP(I) 1993; Hon. Fellow: Academy of Medicine, Singapore 1994, College of Medicine, South Africa 1994; FRCPSGlas 1994; FCPPak 1994; Hong Kong Coll of Physns 1995; FRAustCP 1995; FRCS 1996; FRCOphth 1996; FRCObsGyna 1996; FRCPsych 1997; Malaysia Coll of Med 1997; FMedSci 1998. *Publications:* Author of publications on intestinal research and clinical gastroenterology. *Special Interests:* Health Service, Medical Education, Research. *Recreations:* Reading, antiquarian books, Chinese ceramics, walking. Raised to the peerage as Baron Turnberg, of Cheadle in the County of Cheshire 2000. The Lord Turnberg, 17 Maresfield Gardens, London, NW3 5SN *E-mail:* laturnberg@onetel.net.uk.

TURNER OF CAMDEN, BARONESS   Labour

TURNER OF CAMDEN (Life Baroness), Muriel Turner; cr. 1985. Born 18 September 1927. Daughter of Edward Price. Married Wing-Commander Reginald Turner, MC, DFC 1955 (died 1995). *Trades Union:* Assistant General Secretary, Association of Scientific, Technical and Managerial Staffs 1970–87; Member, TUC General Council 1980–87. Council Member OPAS (Pension Advisory Service) 1989–. *House of Lords:* Deputy Chairman of Committees 1997–; Deputy Speaker 2002–. Opposition Spokesman on: Social Security 1987–96, Employment 1987–96. Former Member, European Select Committee (Consumer Affairs); Co-opted Member, Select Committee on European Communities Sub-Committee F (Social Affairs, Education and Home Affairs) 1997–; Member, Select Committee on House of Lords' Offices 1997–98. Council Member, Save The Children Fund 1991–98. Hon. LLD, Leicester University 1991. Member: Equal Opportunities Commission 1982–88, Occupational Pensions Board 1977–93; Chair, PIA Ombudsman Council 1994–97. *Special Interests:* Employment, Social Security, Pensions. *Recreations:* Reading, music. *Clubs:* RAF. Raised to the peerage as Baroness Turner of Camden, of Camden in Greater London 1985. The Baroness Turner of Camden, 87 Canfield Gardens, London, NW6 3EA *Tel:* 020 7624 3561.

U

UDDIN, BARONESS   Labour

 UDDIN (Life Baroness), Pola Manzila Uddin; cr. 1998. Born 17 July 1959. Born 1959. Daughter of Mr and Mrs Khan; educated Plashet School for Girls, Newham; Polytechnic of North London (Diploma in Social Work 1990). Married Komar Uddin 1976 (4 sons 1 daughter). Councillor, London Borough of Tower Hamlets 1990–98, Deputy Leader of Council 1994–96. *Career:* Youth and community worker; Senior social services officer; Local government adviser; Management consultant. European Select Committee. Patron for: Summer University, Bethnal Green and Victoria Housing Association, Social Action for Health, City University Council, Oxford Brookes University, Womens Aid, Black Womens Health Project. *Special Interests:* Education, Health, Children, Local Government, Equal Opportunities, Disability, Foreign and Commonwealth Affairs, Women and Race. *Recreations:* Family, community work. Raised to the peerage as Baroness Uddin, of Bethnal Green in the London Borough of Tower Hamlets 1998. The Baroness Uddin, House of Lords, London, SW1A 0PW *Tel:* 020 7219 8506 *E-mail:* uddinm@parliament.uk.

ULLSWATER, VISCOUNT   Conservative

ULLSWATER (2nd Viscount, UK), Nicholas James Christopher Lowther; cr. 1921; PC 1994. Born 9 January 1942. Son of late Lieutenant John Arthur Lowther, MVO, RNVR, grandson of 1st Viscount, PC, GCB; educated Eton College; Trinity College, Cambridge (BA agriculture 1963, MA). Married Susan Weatherby 1967 (2 sons 2 daughters). Captain, Royal Wessex Yeomanry, Retired. JP 1971–88; Councillor King's Lynn and West Norfolk Borough Council 2003–. *Career:* Chairman, Wincanton Races Co. Ltd 1986–93; Private Secretary and Comptroller to HRH The Princess Margaret, Countess of Snowdon 1998 2002. *House of Lords:* First entered House of Lords 1963; Parliamentary Under-Secretary of State, Department of Employment 1990–93; Minister of State, Department of the Environment (Minister for Construction and Planning) 1994–95; Re-elected to Lords 2003. Government Whip 1989–90; Captain of the Honourable Corps of the Gentlemen-at-Arms (Government Chief Whip) 1993–94. Member, Select Committee on House of Lords' Offices 1997–99. Chairman, Wiltshire Association of Boys Clubs 1966–74, Vice-President 1975–. PC 1994 LVO 2002. *Recreations:* Racing, golf. *Clubs:* Jockey (Newmarket), Pratt's. Rt Hon the Viscount Ullswater, LVO, The Old Rectory, Docking, King's Lynn, Norfolk, PE31 8LJ *Tel:* 01485 518822 *Fax:* 01485 518844 *E-mail:* ullswatern@parliament.uk.

V

VARLEY, LORD   Labour

 VARLEY (Life Baron), Eric Graham Varley; cr. 1990. Born 11 August 1932. Son of late Frank Varley; educated Chesterfield Technical College; Ruskin College, Oxford; Sheffield University (extra mural studies). Married Marjorie Turner 1955 (1 son). *Trades Union:* Branch Secretary, NUM 1955–64, Member, Area Executive Committee, Derbyshire 1956–64. DL, Derbyshire 1989. *Career:* Craftsman in mining industry 1947–64; Chairman and Chief Executive, Coalite Group 1984–89; Regional Director, Lloyds Bank plc 1987–91; Director: Cuthelco Ltd 1989–99, Laxgate Ltd 1991–92; Member, Thyssen (UK) Ltd Advisory Board 1991–98. *House of Commons:* MP (Labour) for Chesterfield 1964–84; PPS to Harold Wilson as Prime Minister 1968–69; Minister of State, Ministry of Technology 1969–70; Secretary of State for: Energy 1974–75, Industry 1975–79. Assistant Government Whip 1967–68. Principal Opposition Spokesman on Employment 1979–83. Former Member: House of Lords European Communities Select Committee, Sub-committee A. Chairman, Trade Union Group of Labour MPs 1971–74; Treasurer, Labour Party 1981–83. Vice President, Ashgate Hospital Chesterfield. Visiting Fellow, Nuffield College 1981–83. PC, 1974. *Recreations:* Reading, gardening, music, sport. Raised to the peerage as Baron Varley, of Chesterfield in the County of Derbyshire 1990. Rt Hon the Lord Varley, DL, House of Lords, London, SW1A 0PW *Tel:* 020 7219 3406.

VINCENT OF COLESHILL, LORD   Crossbencher

VINCENT OF COLESHILL (Life Baron), Richard Frederick Vincent; cr. 1996. Born 23 August 1931. Son of late Frederick Vincent and Frances Elizabeth (née Coleshill); educated Aldenham School; Royal Military College of Science. Married Jean Stewart 1955 (1 son 1 daughter and 1 son deceased). Commissioned, Royal Artillery, National Service 1951, Germany 1951–55, Gunnery Staff 1959; Radar Research Establishment, Malvern 1960–61; BAOR 1962, Technical Staff Training 1963–64; Staff College 1965; Commonwealth Brigade, Malaysia 1966–68; Ministry of Defence 1968–70; Commanded 12th Light Air Defence Regiment, Germany, UK and Northern Ireland 1970–72; Instructor, Staff College 1972–73; Greenlands Staff College, Henley 1974; Military Director of Studies, Royal Military College of Science 1974–75; Commanded 19th Airportable Brigade 1975–77; Royal College of Defence Studies 1978; Deputy Military Secretary 1979–80; Commandant, Royal Military College of Science 1980–83; Colonel Commandant, REME 1981–87; Hon. Colonel 100 (Yeomanry) Field Regiment RA (TA) 1982–91; Master General of the Ordnance, Ministry of Defence 1983–87; Colonel Commandant, RA 1983–2000; Hon. Colonel 12th Air Defence Regiment 1987–91; Vice-Chief, Defence Staff 1987–91; Chief 1991–92; Chair, Military Committee, NATO 1993–96; Master Gunner, St James's Park 1996–2000. *Career:* Director: Vickers Defence Systems 1996–2002, Royal Artillery Museums Ltd; Chairman: Imperial College of Science, Technology and Medicine 1996–, Hunting Defence Ltd 1996–, Hunting Engineering Ltd 1998–2001, Hunting – BRAE 1998–, INSYS Ltd 2001–. Chancellor, Cranfield University 1998–. Member, The Pilgrims. Past and present member, president, chair numerous organisations, especially those concerned with military, education and sport, including: Vice-President, Defence Manufacturers Association 1996–2000, President 2000–; Chair, Imperial College of Science, Technology and Medicine 1996–; President, Old Aldenhamian Society 1999–2003. Hon. DSc, Cranfield 1985; Fellow, Imperial College of Science, Technology and Medicine 1996; Hon. Fellow, City and Guilds of London Institute. Patron, INSPIRE Foundation; Visiting Fellow, Australian College of Defence and Strategic Studies 1995–99; Member, Commission on Britain and Europe (Royal Institute of International Affairs) 1996–98; Adviser to Secretary of State on The Strategic Defence Review 1997–98. DSO 1972; KCB 1984; GBE 1990; Jordanian Order of Military Merit 1992; Commander, US Legion of Merit 1993. FRAeS 1990; FIMechE 1990; FIC 1996; Fellow, City and Guilds of London Institute. Freeman, City of London 1992. Member, The Guild of Freemen of the City of London; Freeman, Worshipful Company of Wheelwrights 1997. *Publications:* Has contributed to military journals and publications. *Clubs:* Army and Navy, Royal Scots, Grillions. Raised to the peerage as Baron Vincent of Coleshill, of Shrivenham in the County of Oxfordshire 1996. Field Marshal The Lord Vincent of Coleshill, GBE, KCB, DSO, c/o Midland Bank, The Commons, High Street, Shaftesbury, Dorset, SP7 8JX.

VINSON, LORD   Conservative

VINSON (Life Baron), Nigel Vinson; cr. 1985. Born 27 January 1931. Son of late Ronald Vinson, farmer; educated Nautical College, Pangbourne. Married Yvonne Collin 1972 (3 daughters). Lieutenant, Queen's Royal Regiment 1948–50. DL, Northumberland 1990. *Career:* Founder, Plastic Coatings Ltd 1952; Director, Sugar Board 1968–75; Member: Crafts Advisory Committee 1971–77, Design Council 1973–80; Director, British Airports Authority 1973–; Co-Founder, Centre for Policy Studies 1974–80; Member: CBI Grand Council 1975–, President's Committee 1979–83; Deputy Chairman, CBI Smaller Firms Council 1979–84; Chairman, The Rural Development Commission 1980–90; Director, Barclays Bank UK 1982–87; Member, Industry Year Steering Committee, Royal Society of Arts, Chairman 1985; Deputy Chairman, Electra Investment Trust 1990–98. Member, Select Committees on: Pollution 1997–98, Monetary Policy of the Bank of England/Economic Affairs 1998–. Hon. Director, Queen's Silver Jubilee Appeal 1976–78; Member, Northumbrian National Parks and Countryside Committee 1977–87; Member, Foundation of Science and Technology 1991–96. Queen's Award to Industry 1971. Member, Regional Committee, National Trust 1977–84; Chair, Trustees of Institute of Economic Affairs 1988–95, Vice-President 1995–; Trustee, St George's House, Windsor 1990–96; Chair North East Civic Trust 1996–2001. LVO 1979. CBIM; FRSA. *Publications: Personal Pensions for All. Special Interests:* Small Businesses, De-Regulation, Tax, Pensions. *Recreations:* Objets d'art, farming, horses. *Clubs:* Boodle's, Pratt's. Raised to the peerage as Baron Vinson, of Roddam Dene in the County of Northumberland 1985. The Lord Vinson, LVO, DL, 34 Kynance Mews, London, SW7 4QR *Tel:* 01668 217230.

VIVIAN, LORD | Conservative

VIVIAN (6th Baron), Nicholas Crespigny Laurence Vivian; cr. 1841; 6th Bt of Truro (UK) 1828. Born 11 December 1935. Son of 5th Baron; educated Eton College; Madrid University (foreigners' certificate in Spanish literature, history and culture). Married Catherine Joyce Hope 1960 (1 son 1 daughter) (divorced 1972); married Carol Martineau 1972 (2 daughters). Commissioned 3rd Carabiniers (Prince of Wales's Dragoon Guards) 1955; Royal Scots Dragoon Guards (Carabiniers and Greys) 1971; Commanded independent squadron, Royal Scots Dragoon Guards 1973; Principal Staff Officer to Commander British Contingent, UNFICYP 1975–76; Lieutenant Colonel, Commanding Officer, 16th/5th The Queen's Royal Lancers 1976–79; MoD Defence Intelligence Staff 1979–81; Colonel, General Staff Officer, Future Anti-Armour Study, MoD 1982–84; Chief of Staff and Deputy Commander, Land Forces, Cyprus 1984–87; Brigadier; Commander, British Communication Zone (North West Europe, Netherlands, Belgium and North West France) 1987–90; Retired in rank of Brigadier 1990. *House of Lords:* First entered House of Lords 1991; Elected hereditary peer 1999–. Opposition Whip 2001–. Opposition Spokesperson for Defence 2001–. Member, Joint Committee on Statutory Instruments 1997–2001. Deputy Chair, Association of Conservative Peers 1999–2001. Member, RUSI, IPU, CPA. Commissioner, Royal Hospital, Chelsea 1994–2000. Special Trustee: Westminster and Roehampton Hospitals, Chelsea and Westminster Hospital 1995–2001; Commissioner Royal Hospital 1994–2000. *Special Interests:* Defence, United Nations, Drug Abuse, Terrorism, Cyprus, Cornwall. *Recreations:* Travel. *Clubs:* White's, Cavalry and Guards. The Lord Vivian, House of Lords, London, SW1A 0PW *Tel:* 020 7219 5488.

W

WADDINGTON, LORD | Conservative

WADDINGTON (Life Baron), David Charles Waddington; cr. 1990. Born 2 August 1929. Son of late Charles Waddington, JP; educated Sedbergh School; Hertford College, Oxford (MA law 1950). Married Gillian Rosemary Green 1958 (3 sons 2 daughters). Second Lieutenant, 12th Royal Lancers 1951–53; Captain, Duke of Lancaster's Yeomanry 1953–60. DL, Lancashire 1991–. *Career:* Called to Bar, Gray's Inn 1951; QC 1971; Bencher 1985; Recorder of the Crown Court 1972; Governor and Commander-in-Chief, Bermuda 1992–97. *House of Commons:* Contested (Conservative): Farnworth 1955, Nelson and Colne 1964, Heywood and Royton 1966 general elections; MP (Conservative) for: Nelson and Colne 1968–74, Clitheroe 1979–83, Ribble Valley 1983–90; Parliamentary Under-Secretary of State, Department of Employment 1981–83; Minister of State, Home Office 1983–87; Secretary of State for the Home Department 1989–90. Government Whip 1979–81; Government Chief Whip 1987–89. *House of Lords:* Lord Privy Seal and Leader of the House of Lords 1990–92. Member, Select Committees on: Parliamentary Privilege (Joint Committee) 1997–98, Delegated Powers and Deregulation 1999–2002, Procedure 2000–. President, Oxford University Conservative Association 1950; Chairman, Clitheroe Constituency Young Conservatives 1953. Honorary Fellow, Hertford College, Oxford. President: Hertford Society 1997–, East Lancashire Scout Council 1997–, President, OSPA (Overseas Service Pensioners Association) 1998–; Vice-Chair, Bermuda Society 1999–. PC 1987; GCVO 1994. *Special Interests:* Legal Affairs, Textile Industry, Lancashire. *Recreations:* Sailing. *Clubs:* Buck's. Raised to the peerage as Baron Waddington, of Read in the County of Lancashire 1990. Rt Hon the Lord Waddington, GCVO, DL, QC, House of Lords, London, SW1A 0PW *Tel:* 020 7219 6448 *Fax:* 020 7820 9338; Stable House, Sabden, Nr Clitheroe, Lancashire, BB7 9HP *Tel:* 01282 771070 *Fax:* 01282 774407 *E-mail:* waddingtond@parliament.uk.

Visit the Vacher Dod Website . . . **www.DodOnline.co.uk**

WADE OF CHORLTON, LORD   Conservative

WADE OF CHORLTON (Life Baron), (William) Oulton Wade; cr. 1990. Born 24 December 1932. Son of late Samuel Norman Wade, farmer, and late Joan Ferris Wade (née Wild); educated Birkenhead School; Queen's University, Belfast (agriculture). Married Gillian Margaret Leete 1959 (1 son 1 daughter). JP, Cheshire 1965; Councillor, Cheshire County Council 1973–77. *Career:* Farmer and Cheesemaster; Chair, Cheese Export Council 1982–84; Member, Food From Britain Export Council 1984–88; Chair: William Wild and Son (Mollington) Ltd; Director: Murray Vernon Holdings Ltd, Murray Vernon Limited, Cartmel PR Limited, Chair, NIMTECH; President, Campus Ventures Ltd; Chair: Risingstars Growth Fund Ltd, Stirling Energy Systems Ltd, Midas Capital Partner Ltd. Member, European Committee D 1997–2000; Former Member: Science and Technology Committee Biotechnology Sub-Committee 1993, Committee on Relationship between Central and Local Government 1995–96; Member: Science and Technology Sub-Committee II (Aircraft Cabin Environment) 2000–01, Science and Technology Select Committee (Genetic Data Bases) 2000–01, Science and Technology Sub-committee II (Science and the Regional Development Agencies) 2003–; Chairman Science and Technology Sub Committee II (Chips for Everything Opportunties in Micro Processors) 2002. UK Representative to The International Business Advisory Council (IBAC) of UNIDO. Chairman, North West Area Conservative Association 1976–81; Member, National Union Executive Committee 1975–90; Joint Hon. Treasurer, Conservative Party 1982–90. President: CHPA. Chairman Cheshire Historic Churches Trust 1993–. Chairman, Rural Economy Group. Kt 1982. Freeman, City of London 1980. Member, Worshipful Company of Farmers. *Special Interests:* Food Industry, Agriculture, Industry, Transport, Planning, Technology. *Recreations:* Shooting, reading, farming. *Clubs:* The City (Chester), St James Manchester. Raised to the peerage as Baron Wade of Chorlton, of Chester in the County of Cheshire 1990. The Lord Wade of Chorlton, House of Lords, London, SW1A 0PW *Tel:* 020 7219 5499.

WAKEHAM, LORD   Conservative

WAKEHAM (Life Baron), John Wakeham; cr. 1992. Born 22 June 1932. Son of late Major Walter John Wakeham; educated Charterhouse. Married Anne Roberta Bailey 1965 (died 1984) (2 sons); married Alison Ward, MBE 1985 (1 son). Army national service 1955–57, commissioned Royal Artillery. JP, Inner London 1972; DL, Hampshire 1997. *Career:* Non-Executive Director: Azurix Corporation 1991–2001, Enron Corporation 1994–2002; N. M. Rothschild & Sons 1995–2002, Bristol and West plc 1997–2002; Chair: Genner Holdings 1994–, Kalon 1995–2001, Vosper Thornycroft 1995–2002 (Deputy Chairman 2002–03), Press Complaints Commission 1995–2002, British Horseracing Board 1996–98; Non-executive Director, Rothschilds Continuation Holdings AG (Switzerland) 1999–2002; Michael Page International plc 2001–2002. *House of Commons:* Contested (Conservative): Coventry East 1966, Putney 1970 general elections; MP (Conservative) for: Maldon 1974–83, South Colchester and Maldon 1983–92; Parliamentary Under-Secretary of State, Department of Industry 1981–82; Minister of State, HM Treasury 1982–83; Lord Privy Seal and Leader of the House of Commons 1987–88; Lord President of the Council and Leader of the House of Commons 1988–89; Secretary of State for Energy 1989–92; Given additional responsibility for co-ordinating the development and presentation of Government policies 1990–92. Assistant Government Whip 1979–81; Government Whip 1981; Government Chief Whip 1983–87. Chancellor, Brunel University 1997–. *House of Lords:* Lord Privy Seal and Leader of the House of Lords 1992–94. Chairman, Carlton Club 1992–98. Member, Governing Body, Charterhouse 1986–; Governor, Sutton's Hospital, Charterhouse 1992–; Governor, St Swithun's School 1994–; President: GamCare 1997–2003, Brendoncare Foundation 1998–, Printers' Charitable Corporation 1998; Chairman: Alexandra Rose Day 1998–, Cothill House 1998–. Hon. PhD, Anglia Polytechnic University 1992; Hon. DUniv, Brunel University 1998. Trustee: HMS Warrior 1860 1997–, and Committee of Management, RNLI 1995–. Chairman, Royal Commission on the Reform of the House of Lords 1999. PC 1983. FCA. *Recreations:* Sailing, farming, racing, reading. *Clubs:* Buck's, Carlton, St Stephen's Constitutional, Garrick, Royal Yacht Squadron (Cowes). Raised to the peerage as Baron Wakeham, of Maldon in the County of Essex 1992. Rt Hon the Lord Wakeham, DL, House of Lords, London, SW1A 0PW *Tel:* 020 7219 3162.

WALDEGRAVE OF NORTH HILL, LORD — Conservative

WALDEGRAVE OF NORTH HILL (Life Baron), William Arthur Waldegrave; cr. 1999. Born 15 August 1946. Son of 12th Earl Waldegrave, KG, GCVO, TD, DL and Mary Hermione Grenfell; educated Eton College; Corpus Christi College, Oxford (Open Scholar, BA literae humaniores 1969) (President of Union); Harvard University (Kennedy Scholar) 1969–70. Married Caroline Burrows OBE 1977 (1 son 3 daughters). JP, Inner London Juvenile Court 1975–79; Chairman, National Museum of Science and Industry 2002–. *Career:* Fellow, All Souls, Oxford 1971–86, 1999–; Member: Central Policy Review Staff, Cabinet Office 1971–73, Political Staff at 10 Downing Street 1973–74; Leader of Opposition's Office 1974–75; With GEC Ltd 1975–81; Non-executive Director: Bristol and West plc (formerly Bristol and West Building Society) 1997–, Bank of Ireland UK Holdings plc, Finsbury Life Sciences Investment Trust plc, Waldegrave Farms Ltd, Henry Sotheran Ltd; Dresdner Kleinwort Wasserstein 1998–2003: Managing Director, Investment Banking, UBS, Vice-chairman and managing director, Investment Banking 2003–. *House of Commons:* MP (Conservative) for Bristol West 1979–97; Parliamentary Under-Secretary of State at: Department of Education and Science 1981–83, Department of Environment 1983–85; Minister of State for: Department of the Environment 1985–86, Environment Countryside and Planning 1986–87, Housing and Planning 1987–88, Foreign and Commonwealth Office 1988–90; Secretary of State for Health 1990–92; Chancellor of the Duchy of Lancaster and Minister for Public Service and Science 1992–94; Minister of Agriculture, Fisheries and Food 1994–95; Chief Secretary to HM Treasury 1995–97. Royal Society of Chemistry Parliamentary Award 2001. Hon. Fellow, Corpus Christi College, Oxford. Trustee: Rhodes Trust 1992–, Chairman, 2002– Beit Memorial Fellowships. Chair National Museum of Science and Industry 2002–. PC 1990. Liveryman, The Merchant Taylors' Company. *Publications: The Binding of Leviathan*, 1978; Various pamplets. *Sportsclubs:* Eton Vikings. *Clubs:* Whites, Beefsteak, Pratt's, Clifton (Bristol). Raised to the peerage as Baron Waldegrave of North Hill, of Chewton Mendip in the County of Somerset 1999. Rt Hon the Lord Waldegrave of North Hill, 66 Palace Gardens Terrace, London, W8 4RR.

WALKER OF DONCASTER, LORD — Labour

WALKER OF DONCASTER (Life Baron), Harold Walker; cr. 1997. Born 12 July 1927. Son of late Harold Walker; educated Audenshaw Council School, Manchester; Manchester College of Technology; NCLC. Married Barbara Hague 1956 (died 1981) (1 daughter); married Mary Griffin 1984. *Trades Union:* Chair of stewards and convener, AEU 1949–51, 1962–64. Served Fleet Air Arm 1946–48. DL, South Yorkshire 1997–. *Career:* Toolmaker; Industrial administrator; Political and trade union lecturer/tutor. *House of Commons:* MP (Labour) for Doncaster 1964–83 and for Doncaster Central 1983–97; Parliamentary Under-Secretary of State, Department of Employment and Productivity 1968–70; Parliamentary Under-Secretary of State for Employment 1974–76; Minister of State for Employment 1976–79; Chairman, Ways and Means and Deputy Speaker 1983–92. Assistant Government Whip April 1967–68. Opposition Spokesperson for Employment 1970–74, 1979–83. Member, Joint Select Committee on Statutory Instruments 1998–2000. Member: IPU 1964–, CPA 1964–. President: St John's Hospice Appeal, Doncaster Multiple Sclerosis, Doncaster Mencap. Institute of Safety and Health, Lifetime Achievement Award. President, Doncaster Cancer Detection Trust. PC 1979; Knighted 1992. Freeman, Doncaster 1998. *Special Interests:* Industrial Relations, Health and Safety at Work, Manpower Policy. *Recreations:* Gardening, reading. *Clubs:* Wimbledon Village Club, Doncaster Trades and Labour Club, Doncaster Catholic Club, Westminster Recreational Club, Clay Lane Club (Doncaster), Balby Bridge Club (Doncaster). Raised to the peerage as Baron Walker of Doncaster, of Audenshaw in the County of Greater Manchester 1997. Rt Hon the Lord Walker of Doncaster, DL, House of Lords, London, SW1A 0PW *Tel:* 020 7219 5353.

Visit the Vacher Dod Website . . .
www.DodOnline.co.uk

WALKER OF GESTINGTHORPE, LORD   Crossbencher

WALKER OF GESTINGTHORPE (Life Baron), Robert Walker; cr. 2002. Born 17 March 1938. Son of late Ronald Robert Antony Walker and late Mary Helen Walker, née Welsh; educated Downside School; Trinity College, Cambridge (BA classics and law 1959). Married Suzanne Diana Leggi 1962 (3 daughters 1 son). *Career:* Barrister, Lincoln's Inn 1960; Queen's Counsel 1982; High Court Judge, Chancery Division 1994–97; Lord Justice of Appeal 1997–2002; Lord of Appeal in Ordinary 2002–. KB 1994; PC 1997. *Publications:* Articles in legal periodicals. *Recreations:* Walking, gardening. Raised to the peerage as Baron Walker of Gestingthorpe, of Gestingthorpe in the County of Essex 2002. Rt Hon the Lord Walker of Gestingthorpe, Law Lords Corridor, House of Lords, London, SW1A 0PW *Tel:* 020 7219 5353.

WALKER OF WORCESTER, LORD   Conservative

WALKER OF WORCESTER (Life Baron), Peter Edward Walker; cr. 1992. Born 25 March 1932. Son of late Sydney Walker; educated Latymer Upper School. Married Tessa Pout 1969 (3 sons 2 daughters). *Career:* Non-Executive Director: Smith New Court 1990–95, British Gas plc 1990–96, Tate & Lyle 1990–2001, Chair: English Partnerships 1992–98, Cornhill Insurance plc 1992–2002; Non-Executive Director, Liffe 1995–; Chair, Kleinwort Benson Group plc 1996–98; Vice-Chair: Dresdner Kleinwort Benson 1998–2001, Dresdner Kleinwort Wasserstein 2001–; Chair, Allianz Cornhill Insurance plc 2003–. *House of Commons:* Contested (Conservative) Dartford 1955, 1959 general elections; MP (Conservative) for Worcester 1961–92; PPS to Selwyn Lloyd, MP 1963–64; Minister of Housing and Local Government June-October 1970; Secretary of State for: The Environment 1970–72, Trade and Industry 1972–74; Minister of Agriculture, Fisheries and Food 1979–83; Secretary of State for: Energy 1983–87, Wales 1987–90. Opposition Frontbench Spokesperson for: Finance and Economics 1964–66, Transport 1966–68, Local Government, Housing and Land 1968–70; Opposition Spokesperson for: Trade, Industry and Consumer Affairs February-June 1974, Defence 1974–75. Member, National Executive Committee of Conservative Party 1956–62; National Chairman, Young Conservatives 1968–70. Two honorary LLBs. MBE 1960; PC 1970; Commander's Cross of the Order of Merit (Germany) 1994; Chilean Order of Bernardo O'Higgins, Degree Gran Oficial 1995; Grand Officer of the Order of May of the Argentine Republic 2002. Freeman, City of Worcester 2003. *Publications: The Ascent of Britain,* 1977; *Trust the People,* 1987; *Staying Power,* 1991. *Sportsclubs:* Worcestershire County Cricket. *Clubs:* Carlton. Raised to the peerage as Baron Walker of Worcester, of Abbots Morton in the County of Hereford and Worcester 1992. Rt Hon the Lord Walker of Worcester, MBE, Abbots Morton Manor, Gooms Hill, Abbots Morton, Worcester, WR7 4LT.

WALLACE OF COSLANY, LORD   Labour

WALLACE OF COSLANY (Life Baron), George Douglas Wallace; cr. 1974. Born 18 April 1906. Son of late George Wallace; educated Cheltenham Central School. Married Vera Randall 1932 (1 son 1 daughter). *Trades Union:* Member, TGWU. Sergeant, RAF 1941–45. Councillor: Chislehurst, Sidcup UDC 1937–45, Kent County Council 1952–57. *House of Commons:* MP (Labour) for: Chislehurst 1945–50, Norwich North 1964–74; Contested (Labour): Chislehurst 1951, 1955, Norwich South 1959 general elections; PPS to: Lord President of Council 1964–66, Secretary of State for Commonwealth Affairs 1966–67, Minister of State, Housing and Local Government 1967–68. Assistant Government Whip 1947–50. Member, UK delegation to IPU Conference, Stockholm 1949; Delegate to: CPA Conference, Ottawa 1966, IPU Conference, Delhi 1969. Government Whip 1977–79; Opposition Whip 1979–84. Opposition Spokesperson for Health, Social Security 1983–84. President, Radio Society of Gt Britain 1977; Formerly President, London Society of Recreational Gardeners; President, League of Friends, Queen Mary's Hospital, Sidcup 1980–. Commissioner, Commonwealth War Graves Commission 1970–86. *Recreations:* Amateur radio, gardening. *Sportsclubs:* President, Norwich City London Supporters. Raised to the peerage as Baron Wallace of Coslany, of Coslany in the City of Norwich 1974. The Lord Wallace of Coslany, 44 Shuttle Close, Sidcup, Kent, DA15 8EP *Tel:* 020 8300 3634; House of Lords, London, SW1A 0PW *Tel:* 020 7219 5408.

WALLACE OF SALTAIRE, LORD   Liberal Democrat

WALLACE OF SALTAIRE (Life Baron), William John Lawrence Wallace; cr. 1995. Born 12 March 1941. Son of late William Edward Wallace and late Mary Agnes Tricks; educated Westminster Abbey Choir School; St Edward's School, Oxford; King's College, Cambridge (BA history 1962); Cornell University, USA (PhD government 1968); Nuffield College, Oxford (MA 1965). Married Helen Sarah Rushworth 1968 (1 son 1 daughter). *Career:* Lecturer in government, Manchester University 1967–77; Director of studies, Royal Institute of International Affairs 1978–90; Walter F. Hallstein Fellow, St Antony's College, Oxford 1990–95; London School of Economics 1995–; international relations reader 1995–99; Professor 1999–. Liberal Democrat Spokesperson for: Defence 1997–2001, Foreign and Commonwealth Affairs 1998–. Member Select Committee on European Union 1997–2000, 2001–02; Chair European Union Sub-committee F (Social Affairs, Education and Home Affairs) 1997–2000; Member Select Committee on European Union Sub-committee C (Common Foreign and Security Policy) 2001–02. Doctorate hc, Université Libre de Bruxelles 1992. Member Ecclesiastical Committee 1997–. Chevalier, Ordre pour le Mérite (France) 1995. *Publications: The Foreign Policy Process in Britain,* 1977; *The Transformation of Europe,* 1990; *The Dynamics of European Integration,* 1990; *Regional Integration – The West European Experience,* 1994; *Policy-making in the European Union,* with Helen Wallace 1996, 2000. *Special Interests:* Foreign Affairs, Defence, Europe, Constitutional Affairs. *Recreations:* Swimming, walking, gardening. *Sportsclubs:* Saltaire Tennis Club. Raised to the peerage as Baron Wallace of Saltaire, of Shipley in the County of West Yorkshire 1995. The Lord Wallace of Saltaire, House of Lords, London, SW1A 0PW *Tel:* 020 7219 3125.

WALMSLEY, BARONESS   Liberal Democrat

WALMSLEY (Life Baroness), Joan Margaret Walmsley; cr. 2000. Born 12 April 1943. Daughter of Leo and Monica Watson; educated Notre Dame High School, Liverpool; Liverpool University (BSc biology 1966); Manchester Polytechnic (PGCE 1979). Married John Caro Richardson 1966 (divorced 1980); married Christopher Walmsley 1986 (died 1995) (1 son 1 daughter 1 stepson 2 stepdaughters). *Career:* Cytologist, Christie Hospital, Manchester 1965–67; Teacher, Buxton College, Derbyshire 1979–86; Public relations consultant 1987–. Liberal Democrat Spokesperson for: Early Years Education, Education and Skills 2001–03, Home Office 2003–. Member, Science and Technology Committee 2000–; Chair Science and Technology Sub-Committee I (Systematic Biology and Biodiversity) 2002; Member Science and Technology Sub-Committee I (Fighting Infection) 2002–. Member, Liberal Democrats Federal Executive; President, Women Liberal Democrats. Patron: Family Planning Association, Helena Kennedy Trust; Ambassador for NSPCC. Trustee, Medical Cannabis Research Foundation. Contested (Liberal Democrat) Leeds South and Morley 1992 and Congleton 1997 general elections. *Publications:* Chaired Report entitled *What on Earth? The threats to the Science Underpinning Conservation* 2002. *Special Interests:* Child Protection. *Recreations:* Music, theatre, gardening, good company. Raised to the peerage as Baroness Walmsley, of West Derby in the County of Merseyside 2000. The Baroness Walmsley, House of Lords, London, SW1A 0PW *Tel:* 020 7219 6047 *E-mail:* walmsleyj@parliament.uk.

WALPOLE, LORD   Crossbencher

WALPOLE (10th Baron, GB), (Robert) Robin Horatio Walpole; cr 1723; 8th Baron Walpole of Wolterton (GB) 1756. Born 8 December 1938. Son of 9th Baron, TD; educated Eton College; King's College, Cambridge (MA natural sciences, DipAgric 1961). Married Judith Schofield 1962 (divorced 1979) (2 sons 2 daughters); married Laurel Celia Ball 1980 (2 sons 1 daughter). Councillor, Norfolk County Council 1970–81; Variously Chair: Highways, Library and Recreation, Planning and Transportation, Norfolk Joint Museums Committees; JP, Norfolk 1972. *House of Lords:* First entered House of Lords 1989; Elected hereditary peer 1999–. Member, European Communities Committee: Agriculture Sub-committee 1991–94, Environment Sub-committee

1995–97, Select Committee on European Communities 1997–2000; Co-opted member, European Union Sub-committee D (Environment, Agriculture, Public Health and Consumer Protection) 2000–. Chair: Area Museums Service for South East England 1976–79, Norwich School of Art 1977–87, Textile Conservation Centre 1981–88, President 1988; Member: CPRE, RSPB. Hon. Fellow, St Mary's University College, Strawberry Hill 1997. Chair, East Anglian Tourist Board 1982–88. Liveryman, Carpenter's Company. *Special Interests:* Agriculture, Arts, Tourism, Conservation. The Lord Walpole, Mannington Hall, Norwich, Norfolk, NR11 7BB *Tel:* 01263 587763; House of Lords, London, SW1A 0PW *Tel:* 020 7219 3173 *E-mail:* walpolerh@parliament.uk.

WALTON OF DETCHANT, LORD — Crossbencher

WALTON OF DETCHANT (Life Baron), John Nicholas Walton; cr. 1989. Born 16 September 1922. Son of late Herbert and Eleanor Walton; educated Alderman Wraith Grammar School, Spennymoor, Co. Durham; Medical School, King's College, Newcastle upon Tyne (Durham University) (MB BS MD 1945 DSc MA Oxon). Married Mary Elizabeth Harrison 1946 (1 son 2 daughters). *Trades Union:* Member BMA. Service in RAMC 1947–49; Colonel (late RAMC) and Officer Commanding 1 (N) General Hospital (TA) 1963–66; Hon. Colonel 1968–73. *Career:* Nuffield Foundation Fellow in Neurology, Massachusetts General Hospital, Boston USA 1953–54; King's College Travelling Fellow in Medicine, National Hospital, London 1954–55; First assistant in neurology, King's College and Royal Infirmary, Newcastle 1956–58; Consultant neurologist, Newcastle General Hospital 1958–83; Lecturer in neurology, Newcastle University 1966–68; Director, Muscular Dystrophy Group Research Laboratories, Newcastle General Hospital 1965–83; Professor of neurology, Newcastle University 1968–83; Dean of medicine, Newcastle University 1971–81; Warden, Green College, Oxford 1983–89. Member, Select Committees on: Science and Technology 1992–96, 1997–2001; Chairman, Medical Ethics 1993–94; Science and Technology Sub-Committee IIA (Human Genetic Databases) 2000–01. Chair, Muscular Dystrophy Group of Great Britain and Northern Ireland 1971–95, now Life President; Member: General Medical Council 1971–79, President 1982–89; Medical Research Council 1974–78; President: British Medical Association 1980–82, Royal Society of Medicine 1984–86, Association of British Neurologists 1987–88; First Vice-President, World Federation of Neurology 1987–89, President 1989–97. 11 honorary degrees from British, Italian and Thai universities. TD 1962; Kt 1979. FRCP; Hon. FRCPEd; Hon. FRCPC; Hon. FRCPsych; Hon. FRCPath; Hon. FRCPCH; FMedSci; Hon. Fellow, Institute of Education, London. Hon. Freeman, Newcastle upon Tyne 1980; Freeman, City of London 1981. *Publications:* Several medical titles including: *Essentials of Neurology*, 1961; *Brain's Disease of the Nervous System*, eds 7, 8, 9, 10, 1993; *Disorders of Voluntary Muscle*, eds 1–6 1964–93; *Oxford Companion to Medicine*, 1988, 1993; *The Spice of Life* (autobiography), 1993; as well as numerous chapters in books and articles in scientific journals. *Special Interests:* Medicine, Health, Science, Education. *Recreations:* Golf, cricket, reading, music, opera. *Sportsclubs:* President, Bamburgh Castle Golf Club. *Clubs:* Athenaeum, United Oxford and Cambridge University, Royal Society of Medicine, MCC. Raised to the peerage as Baron Walton of Detchant, of Detchant in the County of Northumberland 1989. The Lord Walton of Detchant, TD, The Old Piggery, Detchant, Belford, Norhumberland, NE70 7PF *Tel:* 01668 213374 *Fax:* 01668 213012 *E-mail:* waldetch@aol.com.

WARNER, LORD — Crossbencher

WARNER (Life Baron), Norman Reginald Warner; cr. 1998. Born 8 September 1940. Son of Albert and Laura Warner; educated Dulwich College; University of California, Berkeley (MPH) (Harkness Fellowship 1971–73). Married Anne Lesley Lawrence 1961 (1 son 1 daughter) (divorced 1981); married Suzanne Elizabeth Reeve 1990 (1 son). Chairman, City and East London FHSA 1991–94. *Career:* Joined Ministry of Health 1959; Assistant private secretary: to Minister of Health 1967–68, to Secretary of State for Social Services 1968–69; Executive Councils Division, Department of Health and Social Security 1969–71; NHS Reorganisation, DHSS 1973–74; Principal private secretary to Secretary of State for Social Services 1974–76; Supplementary Benefits Division 1976–78; Management Services, DHSS 1979–81; Regional controller, Wales and South

Western Region, DHSS 1981–83; Gwilym Gibbon Fellow, Nuffield College, Oxford 1983–84; Under-Secretary, Supplementary Benefits Division, DHSS 1984–85; Director of Social Services, Kent County Council 1985–91; Managing Director, Warner Consultancy and Training Services Ltd 1991–97; Senior policy adviser to the Home Secretary 1997–; Chairman: Youth Justice Board for England and Wales 1998–, London Sports Board 2003–. *House of Lords:* Parliamentary Under-Secretary of State, Department of Health 2003–. Member, Carers National Association 1991–94; Member, Royal Philanthropic Society 1991–, Chairman 1993–98; Chair: Expert Panel for UK Harkness Fellowships 1994–97, Residential Forum, in Association with National Institute for Social Work 1994–97; National Council for Voluntary Organisations 2001–. Trustee: Leonard Cheshire Foundation 1994–96, MacIntyre Care 1994–97. Chairman, National Inquiry into Selection, Development and Management of Staff in Children's Homes 1991–92; Member, Local Government Commission 1995–96. Harkness Fellow, USA 1971–72; Gwilym Gibbon Fellow, Nuffield College, Oxford 1984. *Publications:* Editor, *Commissioning Community Alternatives in European Social and Health Care*, 1993; several articles in specialised journals. *Special Interests:* Law and Order, Children, Social and Health Care. *Recreations:* Reading, cinema, theatre, exercise, travel. *Sportsclubs:* Surrey Cricket Club. Raised to the peerage as Baron Warner, of Brockley in the London Borough of Lewisham 1998. The Lord Warner, House of Lords, London, SW1A 0HA *Tel:* 020 7219 8651.

WARNOCK, BARONESS   Crossbencher

WARNOCK (Life Baroness), Helen Mary Warnock; cr. 1985. Born 14 April 1924. Daughter of late Archibald Edward Wilson; educated St Swithun's, Winchester; Lady Margaret Hall, Oxford (MA literae humariores 1948, BPhil). Married Sir Geoffrey James Warnock 1949 (died 1995) (2 sons 3 daughters). Archbishop of Canterbury's Medical Ethics Board. *Career:* Fellow and tutor in philosophy, St Hugh's College, Oxford 1952–66, Headmistress, Oxford High School 1966–72; Chairman, Committee of Inquiry into Special Education 1974–78; Member: Royal Commission on Environmental Pollution 1979–84, IBA 1972–1983; Chairman: Committee of Inquiry on Human Fertilisation and Embryology 1982–84, Home Office Committee on Animal Experimentation 1984–89; Mistress, Girton College, Cambridge 1985–91; Gifford Lecturer, Glasgow University 1991–92; Visiting Professor, Gresham College 2000–01. Member, Select Committees on: Medical Ethics 1993–94, Dangerous Dogs 1996, Animals in Scientific Procedures 2001–02, Procedures 2003–. President, British Dyslexia Association. Albert Medalist, Royal Society of Arts 1998. 13 honorary degrees from UK and Australia; 6 honorary university fellowships. Trustee, National Primary Trust; Chairman Planning Aid Trust. Research Fellow, St Hugh's College, Oxford 1972–84; Hon. Bencher, Gray's Inn. DBE 1984. Fellow, College of Teachers (formerly College of Preceptors); Hon. FRCM; Hon. Fellow: Royal Society of Physicians, Scotland, British Academy 2000, Royal College of Physicians 2002. *Publications:* Author of books on ethics and education and philosophy of mind. *Special Interests:* Education, Broadcasting, Medicine, Environment. *Recreations:* Music, gardening. Raised to the peerage as Baroness Warnock, of Weeke in the City of Winchester 1985. The Baroness Warnock, DBE, 60 Church Street, Great Bedwyn, Marlborough, Wiltshire, SN8 3PF *Tel:* 01672 870 214 *Tel:* 020 7219 8619.

WARWICK OF UNDERCLIFFE, BARONESS   Labour

WARWICK OF UNDERCLIFFE (Life Baroness), Diana Warwick; cr. 1999. Born 16 July 1945. Daughter of Jack and Olive Warwick; educated St Joseph's College, Bradford; Bedford College, London University (BA 1967). Married Sean Bowes Young 1969. Member: Board, British Council 1985–95, Employment Appeal Tribunal 1987–99, Executive and Council, Industrial Society 1987–, Commonwealth Institute 1988–95, Nolan/Neill Committee on Standards in Public Life 1994–99, OST Technology Foresight Steering Group 1997–. *Career:* Technical assistant to general secretary, NUT 1969–72; Assistant secretary, Civil and Public Services Association 1972–83; General secretary, Association of University Teachers 1983–92; Chief Executive: Westminster Foundation for Democracy 1992–95, Universities UK (previously Committee of Vice-Chancellors and Principals/Universities UK) 1995–; Non-executive director: Lattice plc 2000–02, Universities Superannuation Scheme Ltd 2001–. Member, Select Committee on: Science and Technology 1999–,

Sub-Committee II (Aircraft Cabin Environment) 2000–01, Stem Cell Research 2001–02, Sub-Committee II (Innovations in Computer Processors) 2001–02, Sub-Committee I (Fighting Infection) 2002–, Advisory Panel on Works of Art 2003–. Member: RIIA, IPU, CPA, British American Parliamentary Group. Chair, Voluntary Service Overseas 1994–. Two honorary degrees. Trustee: Royal Anniversary Trust 1991–93, St Catherine's Foundation, Windsor 1996–, International Students House 2000–. Member: TUC General Council 1989–92, Council, Duke of Edinburgh's Seventh Commonwealth Study Conference 1991. FRSA 1984. *Recreations:* Theatre, opera, looking at pictures. Raised to the peerage as Baroness Warwick of Undercliffe, of Undercliffe in the County of West Yorkshire 1999. The Baroness Warwick of Undercliffe, Universities UK, Woburn House, 20 Tavistock Square, London, WC1H 9HQ *Tel:* 020 7419 5402 *Fax:* 020 7380 0137 *E-mail:* diana.warwick@universities.ac.uk.

WATSON OF INVERGOWRIE, LORD — Labour

WATSON OF INVERGOWRIE (Life Baron), Michael Goodall Watson; cr. 1997. Born 1 May 1949. Son of late Clarke and late Senga Watson; educated Dundee High School; Heriot-Watt University, Edinburgh (BA economics and industrial relations 1974). Married Lorraine Therese McManus 1986 (Divorced). *Trades Union:* Member, Amicus (formerly MSF) 1975–. *Career:* Development Officer, Workers Educational Association East Midlands District 1974–77; MSF: Full-time official 1977–89, Industrial officer 1977–79, Regional officer based in Glasgow 1979–89; Director, PS Communication Consultants Ltd, Edinburgh 1997–99. *House of Commons:* MP (Labour) for Glasgow Central 1989–97. Member, Select Committee on European Communities Sub-Committee F (Social Policy) 1997–98. Member, Parliamentary Labour Party: Education and Employment Group, Foreign Affairs Group, Overseas Development Group. Member, Labour Party Scottish Executive Committee 1987–90. Hon. LLD, University of Abertay Dundee 1998. MSP for Glasgow Cathcart constituency since May 6, 1999 (contested the seat as Mike Watson); Scottish Parliament Committees: Convener, Finance Committee 1999–2001; Member, Social Inclusion, Housing and Voluntary Sector Committee 1999–2001; Minister for Tourism, Culture and Sport in the Scottish Executive 2001–03. Visiting Research Fellow, Department of Government, Strathclyde University 1993–. *Publications: Rags to Riches: The Official History of Dundee United FC*, 1985; *The Tannadice Encyclopedia*, 1997; *Year Zero: An Inside View of the Scottish Parliament*, 2001. *Special Interests:* The Financing of Devolution, Social Inclusion Policy, Overseas Aid and Development. *Recreations:* Supporting Dundee United FC, running, reading, especially political biographies. Raised to the peerage as Baron Watson of Invergowrie, of Invergowrie in Perth and Kinross 1997. The Lord Watson of Invergowrie, MSP, House of Lords, London, SW1A 0PW *Tel:* 020 7219 8731 *E-mail:* watsonm@parliament.uk.

WATSON OF RICHMOND, LORD — Liberal Democrat

WATSON OF RICHMOND (Life Baron), Alan John Watson; cr. 1999. Born 3 February 1941. Son of Rev. John William Watson and Edna Mary (née Peters); educated Diocesan College, Cape Town, South Africa; Kingswood School, Bath; Jesus College, Cambridge (Open Scholar in history 1959, State Scholar 1959, MA 1963) (Vice-President, Cambridge Union). Married Karen Lederer 1965 (2 sons). *Career:* Research assistant, Cambridge University 1962–64; BBC 1965–68: General trainee 1965–66, Reporter, BBC TV, The Money Programme 1966–68; Chief public affairs commentator, London Weekend Television 1969–70; Presenter, Panorama, BBC TV 1971–74; Presenter, The Money Programme 1974–75; Head of TV, radio, audio-visual division, EEC, and Editor, European Community Newsreel service to Lomé Convention Countries 1975–79; Director, Charles Barker City Ltd 1980–85, Chief Executive 1980–83; Deputy chair, Sterling Public Relations 1985–86; Chair: City and Corporate Counsel Ltd 1987–94, Threadneedle Publishing Group 1987–94, Corporate Vision Ltd 1989–98, Corporate Television Networks 1992–; Member, Y&R Partnership Board; Chairman: Burson-Marsteller UK 1994–, Burson-Marsteller Europe 1996–, The Cola Cola Company European Advisory Board. Liberal Democrat Spokesperson for Foreign and Commonwealth Affairs (Europe) 2000–01, 2002–. Member, Select Committee on European Union, Sub-Committee C (Common Foreign and Security Policy) 2000–. Chairman, British-German Association 1992–2000;

Vice-Chairman, The European Movement 1995–2001; Chairman, English Speaking Union 2000–; President, British-German Association 2000–; Member, High Level EU-Romania Group 2000–02; Chairman: UK Steering Committee of The Koenigswinter Conference, The Joint Commonwealth Societies Council. President, Cambridge University Liberal Club 1961–; Chair, Liberal Party Parliamentary Association 1982–84; Member, Liberal Party National Executive 1982–86; President, Liberal Party 1984–85. Chairman of Governors, Westminster College, Oxford 1988–94; Chairman, Royal Television Society 1990–91; President, Heathrow Association for Control of Aircraft Noise 1992–95; Prince of Wales Business Leaders Forum 1996–. Grand Prix Euro Diaporama for European TV coverage 1974; Jean Mannet Prize. Hon. Doctorate: St Lawrence University, St Petersburg University. Chair The Father Thames Trust 1999–; Trustee and Patron, Richmond Museum 2002–; Patron, Richmond Society 2002–. Contested Richmond, Surrey (Liberal) 1974 and 1979, Richmond and Barnes (Liberal/Aliance) 1983 and 1987 general elections Member, Executive Board UNICEF 1985–92; Presenter: BBC 1 1990, Channel 4 1992, You and 92, Documentary Series *The Germans*; Visiting Fellow, Louvanium International Business Centre, Brussels 1990–95; Visiting Erasmus Professor in European studies, Louvain University 1990; Hon. Professor, German Studies, Birmingham University 1997–; Member of Council British Studies Centre, Humboldt University, Berlin; Chair, Chemistry Appeal Advisory Board, Cambridge; Visiting Fellow, Oriel College, Oxford. CBE 1985; Order of Merit (Germany) 1995; Grand Cross Order of Merit (Germany) 2001. FRSA; FIPR; FIVCA; FRTS. *Publications: Europe at risk*, 1972; *The Germans: who are they now?*, 1992; *Thatcher and Kohl: old rivalries revisited*, 1996. *Special Interests:* European History, South Africa. *Recreations:* Boating, wines, foreign travel, art. *Clubs:* Brooks's, Royal Automobile, Kennel, House of Lords Yacht. Raised to the peerage as Baron Watson of Richmond, of Richmond in the London Borough of Richmond upon Thames 1999. The Lord Watson of Richmond, CBE, Cholmondeley House, 3 Cholmondeley Walk, Richmond upon Thames, Surrey, TW9 1NS; Somerset Lodge, Nunney, Somerset, BA11 4NP *E-mail:* alan_watson@uk.bm.com.

WAVERLEY, VISCOUNT   Crossbencher

WAVERLEY (3rd Viscount, UK), John Desmond Forbes Anderson; cr. 1952. Born 31 October 1949. Son of 2nd Viscount; educated Malvern College. Married HE Dr Ursula Barrow 1994 (1 son). *Career:* Adviser: The CCC Group, Currie and Brown. *House of Lords:* First entered House of Lords 1993; Elected hereditary peer 1999–. Joint Chairman, Nigeria British Consultative Process 2002–. Member, Royal Institute of International Affairs. Grand Cross Order of San Carlos, Colombia 1998; Jubilee Medal, Kazakhstan 2002. Companion, Institute of Export. *Publications: Trade Preferences, Parliaments and the Fate of the Lomé Convention*, 1996. *Special Interests:* International Relations, Commonwealth, Conflict Resolution, Overseas Aid and Development, Export.
Recreations: Golf, scuba diving, walking, travel. *Sportsclubs:* Rye Golf. The Viscount Waverley, House of Lords, London, SW1A 0PW *Tel:* 020 7219 3174 *E-mail:* waverley@int-affairs.com.

WEATHERILL, LORD   Crossbencher

WEATHERILL (Life Baron), (Bruce) Bernard Weatherill; cr. 1992. Born 25 November 1920. Son of late Bernard Weatherill and Gertrude Weatherill (née Creak); educated Malvern College. Married Lyn Eatwell 1949 (2 sons 1 daughter). Commissioned 1940 in 4/7 Royal Dragoon Guards; Transferred to 19th King George V's Own Lancers (Indian Army) 1941–46; Served Burma and North-West Europe. DL, Kent 1992. *Career.* Employed in family business of Bernard Weatherill Ltd, Tailors, of Savile Row, London, W1 1946–70, President of the Company 1992. *House of Commons:* MP (Conservative) for Croydon North East 1964–83, and as an Independent 1983–92; Chairman of Ways and Means and Deputy Speaker 1979–83; Speaker 1983–92. Opposition Whip 1967–70; Government Whip 1970–73; Deputy Chief Whip 1973–74; Opposition Deputy Chief Whip 1974–79. *House of Lords:* Alternate Convenor of the Crossbench Peers 1993–95, Convenor 1995–99. Member: Constitution Committee 2000–02, Ecclesiastical Committee 2000–02, Joint Committee on House of Lords Reform 2002–. Vice-President Intra-Parliamentary Union; Commonwealth Parliamentary Association President 1983–92, Vice-president 1992–. Chair, Commonwealth Speakers and Presiding Officers 1986–88; High Bailiff of Westminster Abbey and Searcher of the Sanctuary 1989–99;

Chair, Industry and Churches Forum; President: The Institute for Citizenship, Kent County Scout Association; Patron, president, vice-president numerous charities in fields of disability, animal welfare, young people. Four honorary doctorates. Chair, Industry and Parliamentary Trust 1993–2002, International Association of Business and Parliamentary Trusts 1995–; Trustee: The Prince's Trust, Prince's Youth Business Trust; Hon Recorder, Royal Commonwealth Ex-services League 2001. Vice-Chancellor, Order of St John of Jerusalem 1983–2000; Hon. Bencher of Lincoln's Inn 1988–. PC 1980; KStJ 1992; Hilal-i-Pakistan 1993. Freeman: City of London 1949, Borough of Croydon 1983. Member: Gold and Silver Wyre Drawers, Merchant Taylors, Blacksmiths. *Publications: Acorns To Oaks*, (a policy for small businesses) 1967. *Special Interests:* Parliamentary Reform, Constitution. *Recreations:* Tennis, golf. *Sportsclubs:* President: Lucifer Golfing Society 1992, Tandridge Golf, West Hill Golf 2003–. *Clubs:* Cavalry and Guards, Reform. Raised to the peerage as Baron Weatherill, of North East Croydon in the London Borough of Croydon 1992. Rt Hon the Lord Weatherill, DL, Emmetts House, Ide Hill, Kent, TN14 6BA; House of Lords, London, SW1A 0PW *Tel:* 020 7219 2224 *Fax:* 020 7219 5979.

WEDDERBURN OF CHARLTON, LORD   Labour

WEDDERBURN OF CHARLTON (Life Baron), Kenneth William Wedderburn; cr. 1977. Born 13 April 1927. Son of late Herbert J. Wedderburn; educated Aske's Hatcham Boys School; Whitgift School, Croydon; Queens' College, Cambridge (MA law 1948, LLB 1949). Married Nina Salaman 1951 (1 son 2 daughters) (divorced 1962); married Mrs Dorothy Cole 1962 (divorced 1969); married Frances Knight 1969 (1 son). *Trades Union:* Member, Association of University Teachers. Served RAF 1949–51. *Career:* Fellow of Clare College, Cambridge and University Lecturer in Law 1952–64; Called to the Bar, Middle Temple 1953; Cassel Professor of Commercial Law, London University (London School of Economics) 1964–92, Emeritus Professor 1992–; Visiting Professor, Harvard Law School 1969–70; General Editor, Modern Law Review 1971–88; QC 1990. Deputy Opposition Front Bench Spokesman on Employment 1980–92. Co-opted Member, Select Committee on European Communities Sub-Committee E (Law and Institutions) 1997–. Editorial Board, International Labour Law Reports 1975–. Chairman, London and Provincial Theatre Councils 1973–93; Hon. President, Industrial Law Society 1997–; Staff Panel Member, Civil Service Arbitration Tribunal 1975–. George Long Prize for Jurisprudence 1948; Chancellor's Medal for English Law 1949. Hon. Dottore Giur, University Pavia; Hon. Dottore Econ, University Siena; Hon. Doctor of Laws, University of Stockholm; Hon. Fellow: Clare College, Cambridge 1997–, London School of Economics 1999–. Chairman, TUC Independent Review Committee 1976–. FBA 1980. *Publications: Employment Rights in Britain and Europe*, 1991; *Labour Law and Freedom*, 1995; *The Worker and The Law*, 1965, 1972, 1986; *Clerk and Linsell on Torts* (Ass. Ed.) 1961–2000; *I Diritti del Lavoro*, 1998. *Special Interests:* Industrial Relations, Employment Law, Company Law, Education. *Recreations:* Charlton Athletic Football Club. Raised to the peerage as Baron Wedderburn of Charlton, of Highgate in the County of Greater London 1977. Professor the Lord Wedderburn of Charlton, QC, 29 Woodside Avenue, Highgate, London, N6 4SP *Tel:* 020 8444 8472 *Fax:* 020 8444 8472; Chambers: 1 Verulam Buildings, Gray's Inn, London, WC1R 5LQ *Tel:* 020 7269 0300.

WEIDENFELD, LORD   Crossbencher

WEIDENFELD (Life Baron), (Arthur) George Weidenfeld; cr. 1976. Born 13 September 1919. Son of late Max Weidenfeld; educated Piaristen Gymnasium, Vienna; Vienna University (Diplomatic Academy, Vienna). Married Jane Sieff 1952 (1 daughter); married Mrs Barbara Connolly 1956 (divorced 1961, she died 1996); married Mrs Sandra Meyer 1966 (divorced 1976); married Annabelle Whitestone 1992. *Career:* BBC Monitoring Service 1939–42; News commentator, BBC Empire and North American Service 1942–46; Columnist, *News Chronicle* 1943–44; Political adviser and chief of cabinet to President Weizmann of Israel 1949–50; Chairman, Weidenfeld and Nicolson Ltd, Publishers; Chairman, Cheyne Capital Management Limited. SDP Spokesperson for Foreign Affairs, the Arts, Broadcasting 1983–90. Chairman, Board of Governors, Ben Gurion University of the Negev, Beer-Sheva, Israel; Governor: Weizmann Institute of Science, Tel Aviv University, Jerusalem Foundation; Board Member, English National Opera 1988–98;

Member, South Bank Board; Vice-President, Oxford University Development Programme; Board Member, Diplomatic Academy, Vienna 1997–; Consultant, Bertelsmann Foundation; Trustee, Quandt Stiftung, Bad Homburg; Advisory Body, Telegraph Group Ltd; Vice-chairman, EU-Israel Forum. Charlemagne Medal for European Media (Germany 2000). Hon. PhD, Ben Gurion University of the Negev 1984; Hon. MA, Oxon 1992; Hon. Fellow: St Peter's College, Oxford 1992, St Anne's College, Oxford 1993; Hon. Senator (Ehrensenator), Bonn University 1996; Magister, Diplomatic College, Vienna University 1999; Hon. DLitt, University of Exeter 2001. Trustee Emeritus, Aspen Foundation; Former Trustee, National Portrait Gallery; British Museum Development Trust. Kt 1969; Chevalier de l'Ordre National de la Légion d'Honneur; Golden Knight's Cross with Star of the Austrian Order of Merit; Knight Commander's Cross (Badge and Star) of the Order of Merit of Germany 1991; Cross of Honour First Class for Arts and Science of Austria 2002; Decoration of Honour in Gold for Services to the County of Vienna 2003. City of London; City of San Francisco; Jerusalem. *Publications:* The *Goebbels Experiment*, 1943; *Remembering My Good Friends*, 1994. *Special Interests:* International Affairs, especially Europe, Middle East and Transatlantic Relations, The Arts and Media. *Recreations:* Travel, opera. *Clubs:* Garrick. Raised to the peerage as Baron Weidenfeld, of Chelsea in the County of Greater London 1976. The Lord Weidenfeld, Orion House, 5 Upper St Martin's Lane, London, WC2H 9EA *Tel:* 020 7520 4411 *Fax:* 020 7379 1604 *E-mail:* agw@orionbooks.co.uk.

WHADDON, LORD   Labour

WHADDON (Life Baron), (John) Derek Page; cr. 1978. Born 14 August 1927. Son of late John Page; educated St Bedes College, Manchester; London External BSc sociology. Married Catherine Audrey Halls 1948 (died 1979) (1 son 1 daughter); married Mrs Angela Rixon 1981. Councillor Lymm District Council 1954. *Career:* Sales manager, Carnegies of Welwyn 1960–62; Director, Cambridge Chemical Co Ltd 1962–95; Member, East Anglia Economic Planning Council until 1980; Director, Microautomatics Ltd 1981–87; Member, Lloyd's 1981–94; Former Member, COSIRA Board; Director, Rindalbourne Ltd 1983–89; Chair: Daltrade plc 1984–, Skorimpex-Rind Ltd 1985–, Britpol Ltd 1989–90, Crag Group Ltd 1996–2001. *House of Commons:* MP (Labour) for King's Lynn 1964–70. Former Member, Select Committee on Science and Technology. Patron, International Piano Festival, Warsaw. Golden Insignia of Order of Merit (Poland) 1989. Fellow Cambridge Philosophical Society. *Special Interests:* Eastern Europe. *Recreations:* Private pilot. *Clubs:* Reform. Raised to the peerage as Baron Whaddon, of Whaddon in the County of Cambridgeshire 1978. The Lord Whaddon, The Old Vicarage, Whaddon, Royston, Hertfordshire *Tel:* 01223 207209.

WHITAKER, BARONESS   · Labour

WHITAKER (Life Baroness), Janet Alison Whitaker; cr. 1999. Born 1936. Daughter of Alan Harrison Stewart and Ella, née Saunders; educated Nottingham High School for Girls; Girton College, Cambridge (BA English 1957); Bryn Mawr College, USA (MA English 1959); Harvard University, USA (Radcliffe Fellow 1960). Married Ben Whitaker CBE 1964 (2 sons 1 daughter). *Trades Union:* Member, FDA. Member: Employment Tribunal 1995–2000; Immigration Complaints Audit Committee 1998–99; Non-executive Director, Tavistock and Portman NHS Trust 1997–2001; Chair, Working Men's College for Men and Women 1998–2001; Advisory Council, Transparency International (UK) 2001–; Deputy chair ITC 2001–; Camden Racial Enquiry Council Deputy Chair and Chair 1996–99. *Career:* André Deutsch (Publishers) 1961–66; Health and Safety Executive 1974–88; Department of Education and Employment 1988–96; Citizens' Charter Chartermark Assessor 1996; Consultant: Commission for Racial Equality 1995–96, Commonwealth Secretariat 1996, Committee of Reference, Friends Provident Group 2000–. *House of Lords:* International Development Liaison Peer. Select Committee on the European Union Sub-Committee F (Education, Employment and Home Affairs) 1999–2002; Joint Human Rights Committee 2001–; Joint Committee on the draft Corruption Bill 2003–. Member: Race and Community, Women; Vice-chair, Civil Liberty, International Development. Member: IPU, CPA. Member/Associate: Fabian Society 1964–, British Humanist Association 1965–, Society of Labour Lawyers 1983–, Commonwealth Magistrates and Judges Association 1997–, Population Concern 1998–, Opportunity International 2002–. Trustee: Runnymede Trust 1997–2001, Patron 2001–, SOS Sahel 1997–, One World Trust 1999–. FRSA. *Special Interests:* International Development, Race Relations. *Recreations:* Travel, walking, art, music, reading. *Clubs:* Reform. Raised to the peerage as Baroness Whitaker, of Beeston in the County of Nottinghamshire 1999. The Baroness Whitaker, House of Lords, London, SW1A 0PW *Tel:* 020 7219 8524.

WHITTY, LORD   Labour

WHITTY (Life Baron), (John Lawrence) Larry Whitty; cr. 1996. Born 15 June 1943. Son of late Frederick James and Kathleen May Whitty; educated Latymer Upper School; St John's College, Cambridge (BA economics 1965). Married Tanya Margaret Gibson 1969 (divorced 1986) (2 sons); married Angela Forrester 1993. *Trades Union:* Member, GMB. *Career:* Hawker Siddeley Aviation 1960–62; Ministry of Aviation and Ministry of Technology 1965–70; Trades Union Congress 1970–73; General, Municipal, Boilermakers and Allied Trade Union 1973–85; The Labour Party: General Secretary 1985–94, European Co-ordinator 1994–97. *House of Lords:* Parliamentary Under-Secretary of State, Department of the Environment, Transport and the Regions (Minister for Roads and Road Safety) 1998–2001; Parliamentary Under-Secretary, Department for Environment, Food and Rural Affairs 2001–: Minister for: Food, Farming and Waterways 2001–02, Farming, Food and Sustainable Energy 2002–. Government Whip 1997–98. Government Spokesperson for: European Affairs, International Development, Foreign and Commonwealth Affairs, Education and Employment 1997–98, Environment, Transport and the Regions –2001, Environment, Food and Rural Affairs 2001–. Member, Fabian Society. Member, Friends of the Earth. *Recreations:* Theatre, cinema, swimming. Raised to the peerage as Baron Whitty, of Camberwell in the London Borough of Southwark 1996. The Lord Whitty, House of Lords, London, SW1A 0PW *Tel:* 020 7219 3118; Department for Environment, Food and Rural Affairs, Nobel House, 17 Smith Square, London, SW1P 3TR *E-mail:* pus.lords@defra.gsi.gov.uk.

WIGODER, LORD   Liberal Democrat

WIGODER (Life Baron), Basil Thomas Wigoder; cr. 1974. Born 12 February 1921. Son of late Dr Philip Wigoder; educated Manchester Grammar School; Oriel College, Oxford (MA law 1946) (President, Oxford Union 1946). Married Yoland Levinson 1948 (3 sons 1 daughter). Royal Artillery 1942–45. *Career:* Called to the Bar, Grays Inn 1946; QC 1966; General Council of the Bar 1970–74; Recorder of the Crown Court 1972–84; Master of the Bench, Gray's Inn 1972; Chair, Health Services Board 1977–80; Member, Council on Tribunals 1980; Chair, BUPA 1981–92; Treasurer, Gray's Inn 1989. Liberal Chief Whip 1976–85. Liberal Party Spokesman for Home Affairs and Law 1983–88. Former Member: Consolidation Bills Joint Committee, Delegated Powers Scrutiny Committee, Member: European Union Sub-Committee E (Law and Institutions) 1997–2000, Joint Committee on Parliamentary Privilege 1997–, Committee for Privileges Sub-committee on Lords' Interests 2001–, Select Committee on Delegated Powers and Regulatory Reform 2001–. Chairman, Liberal Party Executive 1963–65. *Special Interests:* Home Office Affairs, Health Service. *Recreations:* Cricket. *Clubs:* National Liberal, MCC. Raised to the peerage as Baron Wigoder, of Cheetham in the City of Manchester 1974. The Lord Wigoder, QC, House of Lords, London, SW1A 0PW *Tel:* 020 7219 3115.

WILCOX, BARONESS   Conservative

WILCOX (Life Baroness), Judith Ann Wilcox; cr. 1996. Born 31 October 1940. Daughter of John and Elsie Freeman; educated St Dunstan's Abbey, Devon; St Mary's Convent, Wantage; Plymouth University. Married Keith Davenport 1961 (divorced 1986) (1 son), married Sir Malcom George Wilcox CBE 1986 (died 1986). *Career:* Management of family business in Devon 1969–79; Founder/Financial Director, Capstan Fisheries Ltd, Devon 1979–84; Founder/Chair, Channel Foods Ltd, Cornwall 1984–89; President Directeur-General, Pecheries de la Morinie, Boulogne-sur-Mer, France 1989–91; Chair, National Consumer Council 1990–96; Chair, Morinie et Cie, Boulogne-sur-Mere, France 1991–94; Board Member, Automobile Association 1991–; Member (non-executive), Inland Revenue Board 1992–95; Member, Prime Minister's Advisory Panel to Citizen's Charter Unit 1992–97; Commissioner, Local Government Commission 1992–95; Chair, Citizen's Charter Complaints Task Force 1993–95; Board Member, Port of London Authority 1993–2000,

Vice-chair 2000–; Director: Cadbury Schweppes plc 1997–, Carpetright plc 1997–, Elexon Ltd 2000–. Opposition Whip 2002–. Opposition Spokesperson for the Treasury 2003–. Member: European Union Sub-committee D (Environment, Public Health and Consumer Protection) 1997–2000, Ecclesiastical Committee 1997–, Science and Technology Sub-committee II (Science and Society) 1999–2000, Science and Technology Committee 2000–02, Science and Technology Sub-committee IIA (Human Genetic Databases) 2000–; Chair, Science and Technology Sub-committee II (Aircraft Cabin Environment) 2000; Member: Liaison Committee 2000–, Science and Technology Sub-committee I (Fighting Infection) 2002–, Science and Technology Sub-committee II (Innovation in Computer Processors/Microprocessing) 2002–. Member: Council of Institute of Directors 1991–98, General Advisory Council of the BBC 1996, Lord Chancellor's Review of the Court of Appeal 1996–97, Tax Law Review Committee 1996–, Governing Body of Institute of Food Research 1996–; President: National Federation of Consumer Groups 1996–, Institute of Trading Standards Administration (ITSA) 1996–; Chair, London Diocesan Advisory Committee 2000–. Member Ecclesiastical Committee 2002–. FIMgt; FRSA. Freeman, City of London. Hon. Member, Fishmongers' Company 1998. *Special Interests:* Fishing Industry, Mariculture, Consumer Affairs, Environment. *Recreations:* Sailing, birdwatching, flyfishing, calligraphy. *Sportsclubs:* St Mawes Sailing. Raised to the peerage as Baroness Wilcox, of Plymouth in the County of Devon 1996. The Baroness Wilcox, 17 Great College Street, London, SW1P 3RX *E-mail:* wilcoxj@parliament.uk.

WILKINS, BARONESS   Labour

WILKINS (Life Baroness), Rosalie Catherine Wilkins; cr. 1999. Born 6 May 1946. Daughter of late Eric Frederick and Marjorie Phyllis Elizabeth Wilkins; educated Dr Challoner's Grammar School, Amersham; St Helen's School, Northwood, Middlesex; Manchester University (BA government and sociology 1969). Single. *Trades Union:* Former member BECTU. Member: Central Health Services Council 1974–76, BBC General Advisory Council 1976–78, Prince of Wales' Advisory Group on Disability 1982–90. *Career:* PA to director, Central Council for the Disabled 1971–74; Information officer, MIND (National Association for Mental Health) 1974–78; Researcher/Presenter, The Link Programme (magazine programme for disabled people), ATV Network/Central Television 1975–88; Freelance video and documentary producer 1988–96; Information officer, National Centre for Independent Living 1997–99. Member Select Committee on: Hybrid Instruments 2000–, House of Lords' Offices Library and Computers Sub-committee 2001–. Patron: Artsline, No Solo (not alone), League of Friends, Amersham and Chesham Hospitals. The Snowdon Award 1983. Vice-chair HAFAD (Hammersmith and Fulham Action for Disability). *Publications:* Contributing Author to *Able Lives – Women's Experience of Paralysis*, 1989. *Special Interests:* Disability. *Recreations:* Friends, gardening, theatre, genealogy. Raised to the peerage as Baroness Wilkins, of Chesham Bois in the County of Buckinghamshire 1999. The Baroness Wilkins, House of Lords, London, SW1A 0PW *Tel:* 020 7381 1227 *Fax:* 020 7381 1227 *E-mail:* wilkinsrc@parliament.uk.

WILLIAMS OF CROSBY, BARONESS   Liberal Democrat

WILLIAMS OF CROSBY (Life Baroness), Shirley Vivian Teresa Brittain Williams; cr. 1993. Born 27 July 1930. Daughter of late Professor Sir George Catlin, and late Mrs Catlin (Vera Brittain); educated Schools in Great Britain and the United States; Somerville College, Oxford (Scholar, BA philosophy, politics and economics 1951, MA); Columbia University, New York (Fulbright Scholarship). Married Professor Sir Bernard Arthur Owen Williams FBA 1955 (1 daughter) (divorced 1974); married Professor Richard Elliott Neustadt 1987 (1 stepson deceased, 1 stepdaughter). *Trades Union:* Member, NUGMW 1960–. *Career:* Journalist: *Daily Mirror* 1952–54, *Financial Times* 1954–58; General Secretary, Fabian Society 1960–64; Fellow, Institute of Politics, Harvard University 1979–80, Acting Director 1987–88; Professor of Elective Politics, John F. Kennedy School of Government, Harvard University 1988–2000, Professor Emeritus 2000–; Lectureships: Pick Lecturer, Chicago University, Godkin Lecturer, Harvard University, Janeway Lecturer, Princeton University, Regents Lecturer, University of California at Berkeley, Rede Lecturer, Darwin Lecturer, Cambridge University, Dainton Lecturer, British Library, Gresham Lecturer, Corporation of London; Associate: Center for European Studies, Harvard, Belfer Center for Science and International Affairs. *House of Commons:* Contested: (Labour) Harwich 1954, 1955, Southampton Test 1959, (SDP) Crosby

1981, 1983, (SDP/Alliance) Cambridge 1987 general elections; MP: (Labour) Hitchin 1964–74, Hertford and Stevenage 1974–79, (SDP) Crosby 1981–83; PPS to Minister of Health 1964–66; Parliamentary Secretary, Ministry of Labour 1966–67; Minister of State: Department of Education and Science 1967–69, Home Office 1969–70; Secretary of State for: Prices and Consumer Protection 1974–76, Education and Science 1976–79; Paymaster General 1976–79. Opposition Spokesperson for: Social Services 1970–71, Home Affairs 1971–73, Prices and Consumer Protection 1973–74. Liberal Democrat Spokesperson for Foreign and Commonwealth Affairs 1998–2001. Member Select Committees on: European Communities 1997–99, European Communities Sub-Committee A (Economic and Financial Affairs, Trade and External Relations) 1997–99, House of Lords' Offices 2001–, Liaison 2001–, Privileges 2001–, Procedure 2001–, Selection 2001–, House of Lords' Offices Finance and Staff Sub-committee 2001–02. Deputy Leader, Liberal Democrat peers 1999–2001, Leader 2001–. International Advisory Committee Member, Council on Foreign Relations, USA; President, British-Russian Society and East-West Centre; Board Member, Moscow School of Political Studies; Co-Chair, Anglo-Dutch Society 1998–2001; Board Member, European Movement; Council Member, Britain in Europe; Board Member: International Crisis Group, Brussels 1998–2001, Overseers of John F Kennedy School of Government, Harvard University 2001–. Joined the Labour Party 1946; General Secretary, Fabian Society 1960–64, Chairman 1980–81; Member, Labour Party National Executive Committee 1970–81; Co-founder, Social Democratic Party 1981, President 1982–88. Director, Turing Institute, Glasgow 1985–90; Board Member, Rand Corporation, Europe 1993–; Governor, Ditchley Foundation 1994–; Director, Nuclear Threat Initiative 2002–. Silver Medal, Royal Society of Arts. Hon. Fellow: Somerville College, Oxford 1970, Newnham College, Cambridge 1977; Eleven honorary doctorates from British, European and US universities. Trustee: Century Foundation, New York 1976–, IPPR, London. Visiting Fellow, Nuffield College, Oxford 1967–75; Member, Advisory Committee on Business Appointments 1999–2001. PC 1974; Grand Cross (second class), Federal Republic of Germany. *Publications: Shirley Williams in Conversation* BBC TV series 1979; *Jobs for the 1980s*; *Youth Without Work*, 1981; *Politics is for People*, 1981; Co-author *Unemployment and Growth in the Western Economies*, 1984; *A Job to Live*, 1985; *Snakes and Ladders – A Political Diary*, BBC radio series 1996; *Women in the House*, BBC Radio Four, 1998; Chapter on Human Rights in Europe in *Human Rights Policy: What Works?*, 2000; *Making Globalisation Good* in *The Moral Responsibility of the Rich to the Poor*, (OUP) 2003; *God and Caesar* (Continuum) 2003; Numerous newspaper articles and broadcasts. *Special Interests:* Globalisation, Human Rights, Internal Affairs. *Recreations:* Music, hill-walking, poetry. *Clubs:* The Other Club. Raised to the peerage as Baroness Williams of Crosby, of Stevenage in the County of Hertfordshire 1993. Rt Hon the Baroness Williams of Crosby, House of Lords, London, SW1A 0PW *Tel:* 020 7219 5850.

WILLIAMS OF ELVEL, LORD   Labour

WILLIAMS OF ELVEL (Life Baron), Charles Cuthbert Powell Williams; cr. 1985. Born 9 February 1933. Son of late Dr N. P. Williams, DD, Lady Margaret Professor of Divinity at Oxford, and Mrs Muriel de Lérisson Williams, née Cazenove; educated Westminster; Christ Church, Oxford (BA literae humaniores 1955, MA); London School of Economics (economics). Married Jane Gillian Portal 1975 (1 stepson). National Service 1955–57, Subaltern KRRC (60th Rifles) HQ Battalion (Winchester) and Derna (Libya). *Career:* British Petroleum Co. Ltd 1958–64; Bank of London and Montreal 1964–66; Eurofinance SA Paris 1966–70; Baring Bros & Co. Ltd 1970–77, Managing Director 1971–77; Chairman, Price Commission 1977–79;
Managing Director: Henry Ansbacher & Co. Ltd 1979–82, Henry Ansbacher Holdings 1982–85; Director, Mirror Group Newspapers plc 1985–92. Opposition Spokesperson for: Trade and Industry 1987–92, Defence 1990–97, the Environment 1992–97. Member Select Committee on: European Union 1999–2002, European Union Sub-committee C (Common Foreign and Security Policy). Deputy Leader of the Opposition in the House of Lords 1989–92. Chair, Academy of St Martin-in-the-Fields 1988–90; President, Campaign for the Protection of Rural Wales 1989–95, Immediate Past President and Vice-President 1995–, President, CPRW Radnor Branch 1995–; Vice-President, Federation of Economic Development Authorities. A Busby Trustee, Westminster School 1989–99. Member Ecclesiastical Committee 1997–. CBE 1980. *Publications: The Last Great Frenchman: a life of General de Gaulle*, 1993; *Bradman: an Australian Hero*, 1996; *Adenauer: the Father of the New Germany*, 2000. *Special Interests:* Banking, Finance, Environment. *Recreations:* Cricket, music. *Sportsclubs:* MCC. *Clubs:* MCC, Reform. Raised to the peerage as Baron Williams of Elvel, of Llansantffraed in Elvel in the County of Powys 1985. The Lord Williams of Elvel, CBE, House of Lords, London, SW1A 0PW *Tel:* 020 7581 1783 *Tel:* Wales: 01597 823235 *E-mail:* williamscc@parliament.uk.

WILLIAMS OF MOSTYN, LORD   Labour

WILLIAMS OF MOSTYN (Life Baron), Gareth Wyn Williams; cr. 1992. Born 5 February 1941. Son of late Albert and Selina Williams; educated Rhyl Grammar School; Queens' College, Cambridge (Open Scholar history, LLM 1962, MA 1964). Married Pauline Clarke 1962 (divorced) (1 son 2 daughters); married Veena Maya Russell 1994 (1 daughter). *Career:* Called to the Bar, Gray's Inn 1965; QC 1978; A Recorder of the Crown Court 1978–97; Deputy High Court Judge 1986–97; Member, Bar Council 1986–92; Leader of the Wales and Chester Circuit 1987–89; Bar Council: Vice-Chair 1991–92, Chair 1992–93; Fellow, University College of Wales, Aberystwyth 1993–; President, Welsh College of Music and Drama 1993–; Hon. Professor, School of Sociology and Social Policy, University College of North Wales 1994; Visiting Professor, City University, London 1994–95; Fellow, University College of Wales, Bangor 1996. Pro-Chancellor, University of Wales 1994–. *House of Lords:* Parliamentary Under-Secretary of State, Home Office (Minister for Constitutional Issues) 1997–98; Minister of State, Home Office (Minister for Prisons and Probation) 1998–99; Deputy Leader of the House of Lords 1998–2001; Attorney-General 1999–2001; Leader of the House of Lords 2001–. Opposition Spokesperson for: Legal Affairs 1992–97, Northern Ireland 1993–97, Wales 1995–96; Government Spokesperson for: Northern Ireland 2001–, Cabinet Office 2003–. Member Select Committees on: House of Lords' Offices, House of Lords' Offices Finance and Staff Sub-committee 2001–02, Liaison 2001–, Privileges, Procedures. President: Commonwealth and Ethnic Bar Association 1993–97, Prisoners' Rights 1993–97, Welsh College of Music and Drama 1993–. Trustee: NSPCC 1993–97, Council of Justice 1993–97. PC 1999. Hon. Fellow, Institute of Advanced Legal Studies 1997–. *Special Interests:* Law, Foreign Affairs, Europe. Raised to the peerage as Baron Williams of Mostyn, of Great Tew in the County of Oxfordshire 1992. Rt Hon the Lord Williams of Mostyn, QC, House of Lords, London, SW1A 0PW *Tel:* 020 7219 3201 *Fax:* 020 7219 3051 *E-mail:* psgwilliams@cabinet-office.x.gsi.gov.uk.

WILLIAMSON OF HORTON, LORD   Crossbencher

WILLIAMSON OF HORTON (Life Baron), David Francis Williamson; cr. 1999. Born 8 May 1934. Son of late Samuel and Marie Williamson; educated Tonbridge School; Exeter College, Oxford (BA literae humaniores 1956, MA). Married Patricia Margaret Smith 1961 (2 sons). Second Lieutenant, Royal Signals 1956–58. Chairman Somerset Strategic Partnership. *Career:* Joined Ministry of Agriculture, Fisheries and Food 1958; Private Secretary to Permanent Secretary and to successive Parliamentary Secretaries 1960–62; HM Diplomatic Service as First Secretary (Agriculture and Food) Geneva, for Kennedy Round Trade Negotiations 1965–67; Principal Private Secretary to successive Ministers of Agriculture, Fisheries and Food 1967–70; Head of Milk and Milk Products Division, Marketing Policy Division and Food Policy Division 1970–74; Under-Secretary, General Agricultural Policy Group 1974–76, EEC Group 1976–77; Deputy Director-General, Agriculture, European Commission 1977–83; Deputy Secretary, Cabinet Office 1983–87; Secretary-General, Commission of the European Communities 1987–97; Visiting Professor, Bath University 1997–2001; Non-Executive Director, Whitbread plc 1998–. Member, Science and Technology Sub-committee I (Non-Food Crops) 1999–2000; Member: European Union Sub-committee C (Common Foreign and Security Policy) 1999–, European Union Select Committee 2000–. President, University Association for Contemporary European Studies; Co-chair, Europe 21; Member, Wessex Regional Committee, National Trust. Trustee, Thomson Foundation. CB 1984; Knight Commander's Cross of the Order of Merit (Germany) 1991; GCMG 1998; Commander Grand Cross of the Royal Order of the Polar Star (Sweden) 1998; Commander Légion d'Honneur (France) 1999. Raised to the peerage as Baron Williamson of Horton, of Horton in the County of Somerset 1999. The Lord Williamson of Horton, GCMG, CB, Thatchcroft, Broadway, Ilminster, Somerset, TA19 9QZ *Tel:* 01460 55832; House of Lords, London, SW1A 0PW *Tel:* 020 7219 3583.

Visit the Vacher Dod Website . . . **www.DodOnline.co.uk**

WILLOUGHBY DE BROKE, LORD   Conservative

WILLOUGHBY DE BROKE (21st Baron, E), (Leopold) David Verney; cr. 1491. Born 14 September 1938. Son of 20th Baron, MC, AFC; educated Le Rosey, Switzerland; New College, Oxford. Married Petra Aird 1965 (divorced 1989) (3 sons). DL, Warwickshire 1999–. *Career:* Chair: St Martin's Magazines 1992–, SM Theatre Ltd 1992–; President, Heart of England Tourist Board. *House of Lords:* First entered House of Lords 1986; Elected hereditary peer 1999–. Member: European Union Select Committee 1997–2000, European Union Sub-committee D (Environment, Agriculture, Public Health and Consumer Protection) 1997–2001. Vice-President, Conservatives Against a Federal Europe (CAFE) 1997–. Patron, Warwickshire Association of Boys' Clubs 1990–; Governor, Royal Shakespeare Theatre 1992–; President, CPRE Warwickshire 2002–. FRSA; FRGS. *Special Interests:* Hong Kong, Tibet, Europe. *Sportsclubs:* All England Lawn Tennis. The Lord Willoughby de Broke, DL, Ditchford Farm, Moreton in Marsh, Gloucestershire, GL56 9RD *Tel:* 01608 661990 *E-mail:* willoughbyl@parliament.uk.

WILSON OF TILLYORN, LORD   Crossbencher

WILSON OF TILLYORN (Life Baron), David Clive Wilson; cr. 1992. Born 14 February 1935. Son of late Rev. William Skinner Wilson and late Enid Wilson; educated Trinity College, Glenalmond; Keble College, Oxford (Scholar, MA history); London University (PhD 1973). Married Natasha Alexander 1967 (2 sons). National Service, The Black Watch 1953–55. *Career:* Entered Foreign Service 1958; Served Vientiane, Laos 1959–60; Language student, Hong Kong 1960–62; First Secretary, Peking Embassy 1963–65; FCO 1965–68; Resigned 1968; Editor, China Quarterly 1968–74; Visiting Scholar, Columbia University, New York 1972; Rejoined Diplomatic Service 1974; Cabinet Office 1974–77; Political Adviser, Hong Kong 1977–81; FCO: Head of Southern European Department 1981–84, Assistant Under-Secretary of State 1984–87; Governor and Commander-in-Chief, Hong Kong 1987–92; Chair: Scottish Hydro Electric plc (now Scottish and Southern Energy plc) 1993–2000), of Council, Glenalmond College 2000–; Trustees National Museums of Scotland 2002–; Master Peterhouse, Cambridge 2002–. Chancellor, Aberdeen University 1997–. Chair, Revised Red Deer Act (Scotland) Select Committee 1996; Co-opted Member, European Union Sub-committee B (Energy, Industry and Transport) 2000–02. President, Bhutan Society of the UK; Member: Oxford University Expedition to Somaliland 1957, British Mount Kongur Expedition (North West China) 1981; President: Hong Kong Society, Hong Kong Association; Vice-President, Royal Scottish Geographical Society; Member, Royal Society for Asian Affairs; Registrar, Order of Saint Michael and Saint George 2001–. Four honorary doctorates. Member, Hopetoun House Preservation Trust 1993–98; Trustee, Scotland's Churches Trust 1999–2002; Trustee, Museums of Scotland 1999–; Carnegie Trust for the Universities of Scotland 2000–. Member, Board of British Council 1993–2002; Chair, Scottish Committee of the British Council 1993–2002; Member of Council, CBI Scotland 1993–2000; Vice-chair Scottish Peers Association 1998–2000, Chair 2000–02; Member: Prime Minister's Advisory Committee on Public Appointments 2000–, Council, Royal Society of Edinburgh 2000–. CMG 1985; KCMG 1987; KStJ 1987; GCMG 1991; KT 2000. FRSE. *Special Interests:* Hong Kong, East and South-East Asia, Scottish Affairs, Education. *Recreations:* Mountaineering, reading, theatre. *Clubs:* Alpine, New (Edinburgh); Royal Northern and University (Aberdeen). Raised to the peerage as Baron Wilson of Tillyorn, of Finzean in the District of Kincardine and Deeside and of Fanling in Hong Kong 1992. The Lord Wilson of Tillyorn, KT, GCMG, House of Lords, London, SW1A 0PW *Tel:* 020 7219 3161; The Master's Lodge, Peterhouse, Cambridge, CB2 1QY *Tel:* 01223 766271 *Fax:* 01223 330862 *E-mail:* master@pet.cam.ac.uk.

DodOnline
An Electronic Directory without rival . . .

Peers' biographies and photographs available with daily updates *via* the internet

For a *free* trial, call Yasmin Mirza, Aby Farsoun or Michael Mand on 020 7630 7643

WILSON OF DINTON, LORD — Crossbencher

WILSON OF DINTON (Life Baron), Richard Thomas James Wilson; cr. 2002. Born 11 October 1942; educated Radley College; Clare College, Cambridge (BA 1964, LLB 1965). Married Caroline Margaret Lee 1972. *Career:* Called to Bar, Middle Temple 1965; Assistant principal, Board of Trade 1966–71; Principal, Cabinet Office 1971–73; Department of Energy 1974–86: Principal establishment and finance officer 1983–86; Seconded to Cabinet Office 1986–90: Head, economic secretariat 1987–90; Deputy secretary, Industry, HM Treasury 1990–92; Permanent secretary, Department of the Environment 1992–94; Permanent Under-secretary, Home Office 1994–98; Cabinet Secretary and Head, Home Civil Service 1998–2002; Master of Emmanuel College, Cambridge University 2002–. CB 1991, KCB 1997, GCB 2001. *Recreations:* Home, garden. Raised to the peerage as Baron Wilson of Dinton, of Dinton in the County of Buckinghamshire 2002. The Lord Wilson of Dinton, GCB, House of Lords, London, SW1A 0PW.

WINCHESTER, LORD BISHOP OF — Non-affiliated

WINCHESTER (96th Bishop of), Michael Charles Scott-Joynt. Born 15 March 1943. Son of The Revd A. G. and Mrs D. B. M. Scott-Joynt; educated Bradfield College; King's College, Cambridge (BA classics and theology 1965); Cuddesdon Theological College. Married Louise White 1965 (2 sons 1 daughter). *Career:* Deacon 1967; Priest 1968; Curate, Cuddesdon 1967–70; Tutor, Cuddesdon College 1967–71, Chaplain 1971–72; Team Vicar, Newbury 1972–75; Priest-in-charge: Caversfield 1975–79, Bicester 1975–79, Bucknell 1976–79; Rural Dean of Bicester and Islip 1976–81; Rector, Bicester Area Team Ministry 1979–81; Canon Residentiary of St Albans 1982–87; Director, Ordinands and In-Service Training, Diocese of St Albans 1982–87; Suffragan Bishop of Stafford 1987–95; Bishop of Winchester 1995–; Prelate of the Most Noble Order of the Garter 1995–; Took his seat in the House of Lords 1996. *Special Interests:* Education, Local Government, Poverty, Welfare, Marriage, Uganda, Rwanda, Burundi, Congo, Burma, Gender Issues. Rt Rev the Lord Bishop of Winchester, Wolvesey, Winchester, Hampshire, SO23 9ND *Tel:* 01962 854050 *Fax:* 01962 842376 *E-mail:* michael.scott-joynt@dial.pipex.com.

WINDLESHAM, LORD — Conservative

WINDLESHAM (3rd Baron, UK), David James George Hennessy; cr. 1937; (Life) Baron Hennessy 1999; 3rd Bt of Winchester (UK) 1927. Born 28 January 1932. Son of 2nd Baron; educated Ampleforth College; Trinity College, Oxford (MA law 1954); Brasenose College, Oxford (DLitt legal history 1995). Married Prudence Glynn 1965 (died 1986) (1 son 1 daughter). Councillor, Westminster City Council 1958–62. *Career:* ATV Network: Managing Director 1974–81, Joint Managing Director 1974, Chairman 1981; Trustee, British Museum 1981–96, Chairman 1986–96; Chairman, The Parole Board 1982–88; Member, Museums and Galleries Commission 1984–86; Director, W. H. Smith Group plc 1986–95; Principal, Brasenose College, Oxford 1989–2002; Weinberg/Goldman, Sachs Visiting Professor, 1997, and Visiting Professor of Public and International Affairs, Princeton University, 2002–. *House of Lords:* First entered House of Lords 1962; Minister of State, Home Office 1970–72; Minister of State for Northern Ireland 1972–73; Lord Privy Seal and Leader of the House of Lords 1973–74; Leader of the Opposition 1974. Member, Select Committee on Murder and Life Imprisonment 1988–89. Chairman, Bow Group 1959–60, 1962–63. Vice-President, Royal Television Society 1977–82; Joint Deputy Chair, Queen's Silver Jubilee Appeal 1977; President, Victim Support 1992–01; Chair, Oxford Society 1985–88. Hon. Fellow: Trinity College, Oxford 1982; Brasenose College 2002; Hon. LLD, London 2002. Deputy Chair, Royal Jubilee Trust 1977–80; Chair, Oxford Preservation Trust 1979–89; Trustee: The Royal Collection 1993–2000, Community Service Volunteers 1981–2000. Visiting Fellow, All Souls College, Oxford 1986; Hon. Bencher, Inner Temple 1999. PC 1973; CVO 1981; Commendatore, Order of Merit of the Italian Republic 2003. *Publications: Communication and Political Power*, 1966; *Politics in Practice*, 1975; *Broadcasting in a Free Society*, 1980; *Responses to Crime*, Vol 1, 1987, Vol 2, 1993, Vol 3, 1996, Vol 4, 2001; *Politics, Punishment, and Populism*, 1998; Co-author *The Windlesham/Rampton Report on Death on the Rock*, 1989. *Clubs:* Brooks's. Created a life peer as Baron Hennessy, of Windlesham in the County of Surrey 1999. Rt Hon the Lord Windlesham, CVO, House of Lords, London, SW1A 0PW *Tel:* 020 7219 8674.

WINSTON, LORD   Labour

WINSTON (Life Baron), Robert Maurice Lipson Winston; cr. 1995. Born 15 July 1940. Son of late Laurence Winston, and of Ruth Winston-Fox, MBE; educated St Paul's School; London Hospital Medical College, London University (MB, BS 1964). Married Lira Helen Feigenbaum 1973 (2 sons 1 daughter). *Career:* Wellcome Research Senior Lecturer, Institute of Obstetrics and Gynaecology 1974–78; Has held other posts in the United Kingdom, Belgium and USA; Consultant Obstetrician and Gynaecologist: Hammersmith Hospital 1978–; Presenter, *Your Life in their Hands*, BBC TV 1979–87; Past Dean, Institute of Obstetrics and Gynaecology, RPMS, London; Past Chairman, British Fertility Society; Professor of Fertility Studies, Institute of Obstetrics and Gynaecology, Royal Postgraduate Medical School, London University 1987–97; Imperial College, London; Presenter: *Making Babies*, BBC TV 1995, *The Human Body*, BBC TV 1998, *Secret Life of Twins*, BBC TV 1999; *The Superhuman*, BBC TV 2000; *Child of our Time* BBC TV 2000–02. Chancellor, Sheffield Hallam University 2001–. Member, Select Committee on: Science and Technology 1996–, Chair 1998–2001, Innovation Exploitation Barrier 1997; Sub-Committee II (Cannabis) 1998; II Antibiotic Resistance 1999–2000; Member: Science and Technology Sub-Committee I (Non-food Crops) 1999; Science and Technology Sub-Committee II (Science and Society) 1999–2000, Science and Technology Sub-Committee II (Aircraft Cabin Environment) 2000–, Science and Technology Sub-Committee IIA (Human Genetic Databases) 2000–; Chair Science and Technology Sub-Committee I (Science in Schools) 2000–01. Member: Council of Imperial Cancer Research Fund; Board of Lyric Theatre, Hammersmith. Cedric Carter Medal, Clinical Genetics Society 1993; Victor Bonney Triennial Prize, Royal College of Surgeons of England 1993; Gold Medal, Royal Society for Promotion of Health 1998; Michael Faraday Gold Medal, The Royal Society 1999. Hon. Fellow, Queen Mary Westfield College; Five honorary doctorates. Member, Parliamentary Office of Science and Technology (POST) 1998–; Commisioner, UK Pavilion Expo 2001. MRCS; LRCP; FRCOG 1983; FRCP; FRSA; FMedSci. *Publications: Reversibility of Sterilization*, 1978; Co-author *Tubal Infertility*, 1981; *Infertility, a Sympathetic Approach*, 1987; *The IVF Revolution*, 1999; *The Superhuman*, 2000; *Human Instinct*, 2002; As well as over 250 papers in scientific journals on human and experimental reproduction. *Special Interests:* Health, Science and Technology, Education, Arts. *Recreations:* Theatre, broadcasting, music, wine. *Clubs:* Athenaeum; MCC. Raised to the peerage as Baron Winston, of Hammersmith in the London Borough of Hammersmith and Fulham 1995. Professor the Lord Winston, 11 Denman Drive, London, NW11 6RE *Tel:* 020 8455 7475 *E-mail:* rwinston@globalnet.co.uk.

WOLFSON, LORD   Conservative

WOLFSON (Life Baron), Leonard Gordon Wolfson; cr. 1985; 2nd Bt of St Marylebone (UK) 1991. Born 11 November 1927. Son of late Sir Isaac Wolfson, 1st Bt, and late Lady Edith Wolfson; educated King's School, Worcester. Married Ruth Sterling 1949 (4 daughters) (divorced 1991); married Mrs Estelle Jackson 1991 (1 step son, 1 step daughter). *Career:* Founder Trustee, Wolfson Foundation 1955–; Chairman: Wolfson Foundation 1972–, Burberry's Ltd 1978–96; Great Universal Stores: Director 1952–96, Managing Director 1962–81, Chairman 1981–96. President, Jewish Welfare Board 1972–82. Hon. Phd, Tel Aviv 1971; Hon. DCL, Oxon 1972; 14 honorary doctorates from British and Israeli universities; Honorary fellowships of five Oxbridge colleges, including Wolfson College, Oxford and Wolfson College, Cambridge and six other honorary university fellowships. Trustee, Imperial War Museum 1988–94. Kt 1977. Hon. FRCP 1977; Hon. FBA 1986; Hon. FRCS 1988; Hon. Member, Royal College of Surgeons, Edinburgh 1997; Hon. Fellow, Royal College of Engineering 1997. *Recreations:* History, economics. Raised to the peerage as Baron Wolfson, of Marylebone in the City of Westminster 1985. The Lord Wolfson, House of Lords, London, SW1A 0PW *Tel:* 020 7219 5353.

Visit the Vacher Dod Website . . . **www.DodOnline.co.uk**

WOLFSON OF SUNNINGDALE, LORD   Conservative

WOLFSON OF SUNNINGDALE (Life Baron), David Wolfson; cr. 1991. Born 9 November 1935. Son of late Charles and Hylda Wolfson; educated Clifton College; Trinity College, Cambridge (MA economics and law 1956); Stanford University, California, USA (MBA 1959). Married Patricia Rawlings 1962 (created Baroness Rawlings, *qv*) (divorced 1967); married Susan Davis 1967 (2 sons 1 daughter). *Career:* Director, Great Universal Stores 1973–78, 1993–2000, Chairman 1996–2000; Secretary to Shadow Cabinet 1978–79; Chief of Staff, Political Office, 10 Downing Street 1979–85; Chairman: Alexon Group plc 1982–86, Next plc 1990–98, William Baird 2002–03; Non-executive director: Fibernet 2001–, Chairman 2002–, Compco 1995–. Hon. Fellow, Hughes Hall, Cambridge 1989. Kt 1984. Hon. FRCR; Hon. FRCOG. *Special Interests:* Health. *Recreations:* Golf, bridge. *Sportsclubs:* Sunningdale Golf, Woburn Golf, Trevose Golf. *Clubs:* Portland. Raised to the peerage as Baron Wolfson of Sunningdale, of Trevose in the County of Cornwall 1991. The Lord Wolfson of Sunningdale, Kt, House of Lords, London, SW1A 0PW *Tel:* 020 7636 0604.

WOOLF, LORD   Crossbencher

WOOLF (Life Baron), Harry Kenneth Woolf; cr. 1992. Born 2 May 1933. Son of late Alexander and Leah Woolf; educated Fettes College, Edinburgh; University College, London (LLB 1954). Married Marguerite Sassoon 1961 (3 sons). Commissioned (National Service) 15/19th Royal Hussars 1954; Seconded to Army Legal Services 1954; Captain 1955. *Career:* Called to Bar, Inner Temple 1954, Bencher 1976; Started practice at Bar 1956; Recorder of the Crown Court 1972–79; Junior Counsel, Inland Revenue 1973–74; First Treasury Junior Counsel (Common Law) 1974–79; Judge of the High Court of Justice, Queen's Bench Division 1979–86; Presiding Judge, South Eastern Circuit 1981–84; Member, Senate, Inns of Court and Bar 1981–85; Member, Board of Management, Institute of Advanced Legal Studies 1985–93; Chair, Lord Chancellor's Advisory Committee on Legal Education 1986–90; Lord Justice of Appeal 1986–92; Chair, Board of Management, Institute of Advanced Legal Studies 1986–93; Held inquiry into prison disturbances 1990, part II with Judge Tumim, report 1991; Lord of Appeal in Ordinary 1992–96; Held inquiry into Access to Justice 1994–96 (interim report 1995, final report and rules 1996); Master of the Rolls 1996–2000; Chair, Advisory Committee on Public Records 1996; Visitor: University College, London 1996–2000, Nuffield College, Oxford 1996–2000; Downing College, Cambridge 2000–; Lord Chief Justice of England and Wales 2000–. Pro Chancellor, London University 1994–2002. President: Association of Law Teachers 1985–89, South West London Magistrates Association 1987–92, Central Council of Jewish Social Services 1989–99; Mogen Dovid Adom 1995–; Governor, Oxford Centre of Hebrew Studies 1990–93 (Emeritus). Fellow: University College, London 1981, British Academy 2000; Twelve honorary doctorates; Hon. Fellow, Leeds Municipal University. Chairman: Butler Trust 1992–96, President 1996–, St Mary's Hospital Special Trustees 1993–97. Kt 1979; PC 1986. FBA. Honorary Liveryman of the Drapers' Company. *Publications: Protection of the public: A New Challenge* (Hamlyn lecture) 1990; Co-author: *Zamir and Woolf: The Declaratory Judgement* 2nd edition, 1993, *De Smith, Woolf and Jowell,* 5th edition 1995, *Principles of Judicial Review. Clubs:* Garrick, Royal Automobile. Raised to the peerage as Baron Woolf, of Barnes in the London Borough of Richmond 1992. Rt Hon the Lord Woolf, Royal Courts of Justice, Strand, WC2A 2LL.

WOOLMER OF LEEDS, LORD   Labour

WOOLMER OF LEEDS (Life Baron), Kenneth John Woolmer; cr. 1999. Born 25 April 1940. Son of late Joseph Woolmer; educated Kettering Grammar School; Leeds University (BA economics 1961). Married Janice Chambers 1961 (3 sons). *Trades Union:* Member, AUT. Councillor, Leeds County Borough Council 1970–74, Deputy Leader 1972–74; Councillor, Leeds Metropolitan District Council 1973–78; Councillor, West Yorkshire Metropolitan County Council 1973–80, Deputy Leader 1973–75, Leader 1975–77, Leader of the Opposition 1977–79; Chairman, Planning and Transportation Committee of Association of Metropolitan Authorities 1974–77; Chair, Regional Energy Forum, Yorkshire Forward 2001–. *Career:* Research

Fellow, University of the West Indies 1961–62; Teacher, Friern Road Secondary Modern School, London 1963; Lecturer: Leeds University (economics) 1963–66, University of Ahmadu Bello, Nigeria 1966–68, Leeds University 1968–79; Principal, Halton Gill Associates 1979–96; Leeds University Business School: Director of MBA Programmes 1991–97, Dean of External Relations 1997, Dean of Business School 1997–2000; Partner: Hilton Gill Associates 1998–, Anderson McGraw 2001–; Non-executive Director: Thornfield Development Ltd 1999–2002, Courtcom Ltd 2001–, Thornfield Properties plc 2002–. *House of Commons:* MP (Labour) for Batley and Morley 1979–83; Contested Batley and Spen (Labour) 1983 and 1987 general elections. Frontbench Opposition Spokesperson for: Trade, Aviation, Shipping, Film Industry 1981–82, Prices and Consumer Protection 1982. Chairman, PLP Finance and Economic Committee 1980–81, Vice-Chairman 1981–82. *House of Lords:* Chair, Yorkshire and Humber Regional Peers Group 2002–. Member Select Committee on European Union Sub-committee B (Energy, Industry and Transport) 1999–, Chairman 2002–; Member European Union Committee 2002–. Director, Leeds United AFC 1991–96. Former Parliamentary Adviser, Inland Revenue Staff Federation. *Recreations:* Football, cricket. *Sportsclubs:* Leeds United AFC supporter, Yorkshire CCC supporter. Raised to the peerage as Baron Woolmer of Leeds, of Leeds in the County of West Yorkshire 1999. The Lord Woolmer of Leeds, 8 Ancaster Crescent, Leeds, LS16 5HS *E-mail:* woolmerk@parliament.uk.

WORCESTER, LORD BISHOP OF   Non-affiliated

WORCESTER (Bishop of), Peter Stephen Maurice Selby. Born 7 December 1941. Son of Frank and Maria Selby; educated Merchant Taylors' School; St John's College, Oxford (BA classics 1964, MA psychology and philosophy 1967); Episcopal Divinity School, Cambridge, Massachusetts, USA (BD theology 1966); King's College, London (PhD theology 1975). Married Janice Margery Lowe 1968 (1 son 2 daughters). Chair, Standards and Ethics Committee, Worcestershire County Council 2000–. *Career:* Assistant Curate, Queensbury 1966–69; Assistant Director of Training, Southwark Diocese 1969–73; Assistant Curate, Limpsfield with Titsey 1969–77; Vice-Principal, Southwark Ordination Course 1970–72; Assistant Missioner, Southwark Diocese 1973–77; Canon Missioner, Newcastle 1977–84; Bishop of Kingston upon Thames (Diocese of Southwark) 1984–92; William Leech Professorial Fellow in Applied Christian Theology, Durham University 1992–97; Bishop of Worcester 1997–; Entered House of Lords 2002. Various diocesan trusts. *Publications: Look for the Living*, SCM 1976; *Liberating God*, SPCK 1982; *Rescue*, SPCK 1995; *Belonging*, SPCK 1991; *Grace and Mortgage*, DLT 1997. *Recreations:* Music. Rt Rev Dr the Lord Bishop of Worcester, The Bishop's House, Hartlebury Castle, Kidderminster, Worcestershire, DY11 7XX *Tel:* 01299 250214 *Fax:* 01299 250027 *E-mail:* bishop.peter@cofe-worcester.org.uk.

WRIGHT OF RICHMOND, LORD   Crossbencher

WRIGHT OF RICHMOND (Life Baron), Patrick Richard Henry Wright; cr. 1994. Born 28 June 1931. Son of late Herbert and Rachel Wright; educated Marlborough College; Merton College, Oxford (BA literae humaniores 1955). Married Virginia Anne Gaffney 1958 (2 sons 1 daughter). Served Royal Artillery 1950–51. *Career:* Entered Diplomatic Service 1955; Middle East Centre for Arabic Studies 1956–57; Third Secretary, Beirut Embassy 1958–60; Private Secretary and later First Secretary, Washington DC Embassy 1960–65; Private Secretary to Permanent Under-Secretary, Foreign Office 1965–67; First Secretary and Head of Chancery, Cairo Embassy 1967–70; Deputy Political Resident, Bahrain 1971–72; Head of Middle East Department, FCO 1972–74; Private Secretary (Overseas Affairs) to Prime Minister 1974–77; Ambassador to: Luxembourg 1977–79, Syria 1979–81; Deputy Under-Secretary of State, FCO 1982–84; Ambassador to Saudi Arabia 1984–86; Permanent Under-Secretary of State and Head of the Diplomatic Service 1986–91; Director: Barclays Bank plc 1991–96, British Petroleum Co. (now BP Amoco) 1991–2001, De La Rue 1991–2000, Unilever 1991–99, BAA 1992–98; Member, Security Commission 1993–2002. Member European Union Sub-Committee F (Social Affairs, Education and Home Affairs) 2001–. Member, Council of Royal Institute of International Affairs 1992–99, Chairman 1995–99; Member of Council: Atlantic College 1993–2000, Royal College of Music 1991–2001; Governor: Ditchley Foundation 1986–, Wellington College 1991–2001; Registrar, OStJ 1991–95, Director of Overseas Relations 1995–97. Hon. Fellow, Merton

College, Oxford 1987. Trustee, Home-Start International 1998–. CMG 1978; KCMG 1984; GCMG 1989; KStJ 1990. FRCM 1994. *Special Interests:* Foreign Affairs, Commonwealth. *Recreations:* Music, philately, travel. *Clubs:* Oxford and Cambridge. Raised to the peerage as Baron Wright of Richmond, of Richmond upon Thames in the London Borough of Richmond upon Thames 1994. The Lord Wright of Richmond, GCMG, House of Lords, London, SW1A 0PW *Tel:* 020 7219 5353.

Y

YORK, LORD ARCHBISHOP OF   Non-affiliated

YORK (96th Archbishop of), David Michael Hope. Born 14 April 1940. Son of late Jack and Florence Hope; educated Queen Elizabeth Grammar School, Wakefield; Nottingham University (BA theology 1962); St Stephen's House; Linacre College, Oxford (DPhil 1965). *Career:* Curate, St John, Tuebrook, Liverpool 1965–67, 1968–70; Chaplain, Church of the Resurrection, Bucharest 1967–68; Vicar, St Andrew, Orford, Warrington 1970–74; Principal, St Stephen's House, Oxford 1974–82; Vicar, All Saints, Margaret Street, London W1 1982–85; Diocesan Bishop of Wakefield 1985–91; Took his seat in the House of Lords 1990; Prelate of the Most Excellent Order of the British Empire 1991–95; Bishop of London 1991–95; Archbishop of York 1995–. Hon. LLD CNAA; Hon. DD, Nottingham University. PC 1991; KCVO 1995. *Publications: The Leonine Sacramentary*, *The Living Gospel*, *Friendship with God*. *Special Interests:* Eastern Europe, Inner Cities, Africa. *Recreations:* Music, fell walking, photography. *Clubs:* Athenaeum. Most Rev and Rt Hon the Lord Archbishop of York, KCVO, Bishopthorpe, York, North Yorkshire, YO23 2GE *Tel:* 01904 707021 *E-mail:* office@bishopthorpe.u_net.com.

YOUNG OF GRAFFHAM, LORD   Conservative

YOUNG OF GRAFFHAM (Life Baron), David Ivor Young; cr. 1984. Born 27 February 1932. Son of late Joseph Young; educated Christ's College, Finchley; University College, London (LLB 1954). Married Lita Marianne Shaw 1956 (2 daughters). DL, West Sussex 1999–. *Career:* Solicitor 1956; Executive, Great Universal Stores 1956–61; Chair: Eldonwall Ltd 1961–75, Manufacturers Hanover Property Services Ltd 1974–84; Industrial Adviser/Special Adviser, Department of Industry 1979–82; Chair, Manpower Services Commission 1982–84; Executive Chair, Cable and Wireless plc 1990–95; Director, Salomon Inc 1990–94; Chair, Young Associates Ltd 1996–; Currently Chair of several companies, including: Autohit plc 2000–, Neoscorp Ltd 1997–2001; Pixology Ltd 1997–, Newhaven Management Services, Indigo Vision plc 2001–02, British Israel Chamber of Trade, International Telecommunications clearing Corp 2001–, European Advisory Board of Convergys Corporation 2001–; Director, Business for Sterling. *House of Lords:* Cabinet Minister without Portfolio 1984–85; Secretary of State for: Employment 1985–87, Trade and Industry 1987–89; Advisor on tax simplification to Michael Howard as Shadow Chancellor 2001–. Member: Science and Technology Committee 2003–, Science and Technology Sub-committee II (Science and the Regional Development Agencies) 2003–. Deputy Chairman, Conservative Party 1989–90. President, Institute of Directors 1993–, Chair of Council, University College, London 1995–; Chair: Chichester Festival Theatre Ltd, West Sussex Economic Forum. PC 1984. *Publications: The Enterprise Years*, 1990. *Recreations:* Fishing, photography, music, book collecting, golf. *Clubs:* Savile. Raised to the peerage as Baron Young of Graffham, of Graffham in the County of West Sussex 1984. Rt Hon the Lord Young of Graffham, DL, Young Associates Ltd, Harcourt House, 19 Cavendish Square, London, W1G 0PL *Tel:* 020 7447 8800 *E-mail:* young@youngassoc.com.

YOUNG OF OLD SCONE, BARONESS   Labour

YOUNG OF OLD SCONE (Life Baroness), Barbara Scott Young; cr. 1997. Born 8 April 1948. Daughter of late George Young and of late Mary Young; educated Perth Academy; Edinburgh University (MA classics 1970); Strathclyde University (DipSocSci 1971); DipHSM 1974. *Career:* Sector administrator, Glasgow Health Board 1973–78; Director of planning and development, St Thomas' Health District 1978–79; District general administrator, Kensington and Chelsea and Westminster Area Health Authority 1979–82; District administrator, Haringey Health Authority (HA) 1982–85; District general manager: Paddington and North Kensington HA 1985–88, Parkside HA 1988–91; Chief executive, Royal Society for the Protection of Birds 1991–98; Chair, English Nature 1998–2000; Vice-chair, BBC 1998–2000; Non-executive Director, Anglian Water 1998–2000; Chief executive, Environment Agency 2000–. Member, Select Committee on European Communities Sub-Committee D (Agriculture, Fisheries and Food) 1998–2000. Member: Committee, King's Fund Institute 1986–90, Delegacy, St Mary's Hospital Medical School 1991–94, World Council, Birdlife International 1994–98, Vice President 1999–; Vice-President: Flora and Fauna International 1998–, Plantlife 2000–, RSPB 2000–. Eight honorary doctorates. Trustee: National Council for Voluntary Organisations 1994–98, Institute for Public Policy Research 2000–; President, Beds, Cambs, Northants and Peterborough Wildlife Trust 2001–. Member, BBC General Advisory Council 1985–88; President, Institute of Health Services Management 1987–88; Patron, Institute of Ecological and Environment Management 1993– Member: Committee of Secretary of State for the Environment's Going for Green Initiative 1994–96, UK Round Table on Sustainability 1995–2000, Commission on the Future of the Voluntary Sector 1995–97, Committee on the Public Understanding of Science 1996–97. *Special Interests:* Environment, Abortion Law Reform, Assisted Dying, Broadcasting. *Recreations:* Cinema, gardening. Raised to the peerage as Baroness Young of Old Scone, of Old Scone in Perth and Kinross 1997. The Baroness Young of Old Scone, House of Lords, London, SW1A 0PW *E-mail:* youngb@parliament.uk.

Visit the Vacher Dod Website . . .

www.DodOnline.co.uk

Political information updated daily

The Queen's Speech	House of Commons
Today's Business	House of Lords
This Week's Business	Scottish Parliament
Progress of Government Bills	National Assembly for Wales
Select Committees	Northern Ireland Assembly
Government and Opposition	Greater London Authority
Stop Press News	European Union

Check changes daily as they happen

Peers' Special Interests

Abortion Law Reform
Young of Old Scone, B.

Administration of Justice
Ackner, L.

Adoption
Gibson of Market Rasen, B.

Africa
Chalker of Wallasey, B.
Park of Monmouth, B.
York, Abp.

Ageing
Barker, B.

Agriculture
Brookeborough, V.
Callaghan of Cardiff, L.
Carlile of Berriew, L.
Carter, L.
Cavendish of Furness, L.
Christopher, L.
Corbett of Castle Vale, L.
Courtown, E.
Deedes, L.
Dixon-Smith, L.
Geraint, L.
Home, E.
Hooson, L.
Howe, E.
Hughes of Woodside, L.
Inglewood, L.
Keith of Castleacre, L.
Kilclooney, L.
Kimball, L.
Livsey of Talgarth, L.
MacGregor of Pulham Market,
   L.
Mackie of Benshie, L.
Mallalieu, B.
Mar, C.
Monro of Langholm, L.
Montrose, D.
Northbourne, L.
Northbrook, L.
Northesk, E.
O'Cathain, B.
Palmer, L.
Rotherwick, L.
Selborne, E.
Shrewsbury and Waterford, E.
Soulsby of Swaffham Prior, L.

Wade of Chorlton, L.
Walpole, L.

Airport Policy
Morris of Manchester, L.
Smith of Leigh, L.

Alcohol and Drug Addiction
Falkland, V.

Alcoholism
Mancroft, L.

**Alternative Dispute
   Resolutions**
Ackner, L.

Alternative Energy
Corbett of Castle Vale, L.

American Politics
Norton of Louth, L.

Amnesty International
Gilbert, L.

Anglo-American Relations
Acton, L.
Blatch, B.

Animal Welfare
Allenby of Megiddo, V.
Corbett of Castle Vale, L.
Fookes, B.
Gale, B.
Soulsby of Swaffham Prior, L.

Anti Smoking
Gale, B.

Anti-Apartheid Work
Hughes of Woodside, L.

Archaeology
Redesdale, L.

Architecture
Lloyd-Webber, L.

Arctic: Greenland
Brightman, L.

Armed Forces
Renton, L.

Arms Control
Oxford, Bp.
Rea, L.

Army
Glentoran, L.

Art
Lloyd-Webber, L.
Luke, L.
Snowdon, E.

Arts
Alexander of Weedon, L.
Andrews, B.
Armstrong of Ilminster, L.
Attenborough, L.
Blackstone, B.
Cameron of Lochbroom, L.
Carlile of Berriew, L.
Colwyn, L.
Crickhowell, L.
Davies of Oldham, L.
Donoughue, L.
Eatwell, L.
Feldman, L.
Gibson, L.
Hamwee, B.
Healey, L.
Hoyle, L.
Inglewood, L.
James of Holland Park, B.
Jellicoe, E.
Jenkins of Putney, L.
Macfarlane of Bearsden, L.
McIntosh of Hudnall, B.
Maclennan of Rogart, L.
Moser, L.
O'Cathain, B.
Oxford, Bp.
Quinton, L.
Renfrew of Kaimsthorn, L.
Renton of Mount Harry, L.
Rix, L.
Rogers of Riverside, L.
Sainsbury of Preston
   Candover, L.
Selkirk of Douglas, L.
Skidelsky, L.
Smith of Gilmorehill, B.
Sterling of Plaistow, L.
Stone of Blackheath, L.
Strange, B.
Walpole, L.

Weidenfeld, L.
Winston, L.

Arts Sponsorship
Dean of Thornton-le-Fylde, B.

Assisted Dying
Young of Old Scone, B.

Asylum Seekers
Portsmouth, Bp.

Australia
Parry, L.

Aviation
Brougham and Vaux, L.
Glenarthur, L.
MacKenzie of Culkein, L.
Monro of Langholm, L.
Rotherwick, L.
Simon, L.
Trefgarne, L.

Banking
Williams of Elvel, L.

Blind People
Russell-Johnston, L.

Breast Cancer
Falkender, B.

British Film Industry
Falkender, B.

British Politics
Norton of Louth, L.

British-Irish Relations
Hylton, L.

Broadcasting
Brigstocke, B.
Colwyn, L.
Crickhowell, L.
Eames, L.
Gordon of Strathblane, L.
Griffiths of Fforestfach, L.
Holme of Cheltenham, L.
Howe of Idlicote, B.
James of Holland Park, B.
Jay of Paddington, B.
Lipsey, L.
McNally, L.
Manchester, Bp.

Quirk, L.
Rawlings, B.
Taylor of Warwick, L.
Warnock, B.
Young of Old Scone, B.

Burma
Winchester, Bp.

Burundi
Winchester, Bp.

Business
Hollick, L.

Business Ethics
Oxford, Bp.

Cane Sugar
Clark of Kempston, L.

Care of the Elderly
Sutherland of Houndwood, L.

**Central and Eastern
  Europe**
Carlile of Berriew, L.

Charities
Arran, E.
Goudie, B.
Pitkeathley, B.
Rix, L.
Stewartby, L.

Cheque-Book Journalism
Sharples, B.

Children
Blood, B.
Canterbury, Abp.
Corbett of Castle Vale, L.
David, B.
Gale, B.
Golding, B.
Goudie, B.
Hardie, L.
Harrison, L.
Knight of Collingtree, B.
Massey of Darwen, B.
Murray of Epping Forest, L.
Strange, B.
Thornton, B.
Uddin, B.
Walmsley, B.
Warner, L.

China
Cobbold, L.
Geddes, L.
Marlesford, L.
Thomas of Gresford, L.

Church Affairs
Luke, L.
Moore of Wolvercote, L.
Richardson of Calow, B.

Citizenship
Alton of Liverpool, L.
Phillips of Sudbury, L.

City
Alexander of Weedon, L.
Cuckney, L.
Grabiner, L.
Northbrook, L.

Civil Liberties
Barker, B.
Clinton-Davis, L.
Corbett of Castle Vale, L.
Dubs, L.
Morgan, L.

Co-operative Movement
Fyfe of Fairfield, L.
Morris of Manchester, L.

Coal Industry
Dormand of Easington, L.
Mason of Barnsley, L.

Commerce
Nicol, B.
O'Cathain, B.
Sainsbury of Preston
  Candover, L.

**Commercial and Company
  Law**
Grabiner, L.
Wedderburn of Charlton, L.

Commonwealth
Blaker, L.
Janner of Braunstone, L.
Moore of Wolvercote, L.
Russell-Johnston, L.
Stoddart of Swindon, L.
Taylor of Blackburn, L.
Waverley, V.
Wright of Richmond, L.

Communications Industry
Tenby, V.

Community and Social Work
Carter, L.
Eames, L.
Patel of Blackburn, L.

Community Participation
Chan, L.
Howells of St Davids, B.

Comparative Law
Goff of Chieveley, L.

Complementary Medicine
Baldwin of Bewdley, E.
Colwyn, L.

Conflict Resolution
Ahmed, L.
Hylton, L.
Stone of Blackheath, L.
Waverley, V.

Congo
Winchester, Bp.

Conservation
Archer of Sandwell, L.
Gilbert, L.
Hardy of Wath, L.
Marlesford, L.
Nicol, B.
Northesk, E.
Renton of Mount Harry, L.
Roberts of Conwy, L.
Selborne, E.
Selkirk of Douglas, L.
Walpole, L.

Constitutional Affairs
Campbell of Alloway, L.
Carnegy of Lour, B.
Dean of Harptree, L.
Forsyth of Drumlean, L.
Gordon of Strathblane, L.
Gould of Potternewton, B.
Hogg of Cumbernauld, L.
Hollick, L.
Holme of Cheltenham, L.
Hooson, L.
Irvine of Lairg, L.
Lester of Herne Hill, L.
Maclennan of Rogart, L.

Mayhew of Twysden, L.
Michie of Gallanach, B.
Molyneaux of Killead, L.
Morgan, L.
Norton of Louth, L.
Scarman, L.
Smith of Clifton, L.
Temple-Morris, L.
Wallace of Saltaire, L.
Weatherill, L.

Construction Industry
Feldman, L.
Howie of Troon, L.
Shrewsbury and Waterford, E.

Consumer Affairs
Campbell of Croy, L.
Graham of Edmonton, L.
Janner of Braunstone, L.
Joffe, L.
Oppenheim-Barnes, B.
Wilcox, B.

Cornwall
Vivian, L.

Council
Lea of Crondall, L.

Council of Europe and Western European Union
Knight of Collingtree, B.

Country Houses
Crathorne, L.

Countryside
Carnegy of Lour, B.
Chorley, L.
Haskins, L.
Kingsdown, L.
MacGregor of Pulham Market, L.
Strange, B.

Cricket
Rix, L.

Crime and Criminal Justice
Bach, L.
Hilton of Eggardon, B.
Imbert, L.
James of Holland Park, B.
Mayhew of Twysden, L.
Phillips of Sudbury, L.

Prashar, B.
Seccombe, B.
Stern, B.
Taverne, L.
Thomas of Gresford, L.

Crofting
Michie of Gallanach, B.

Culture
Rawlings, B.

Current Affairs
Evans of Watford, L.

Cycling
Colwyn, L.

Cyprus
Stallard, L.
Vivian, L.

De-Regulation
Vinson, L.

Defence
Allenby of Megiddo, V.
Ashdown of Norton-sub-Hamdon, L.
Astor of Hever, L.
Attlee, E.
Blaker, L.
Field MarshalBramall, L.
Brookeborough, V.
Campbell of Croy, L.
Chalfont, L.
Craig of Radley, L.
Erroll, E.
Fookes, B.
Gilbert, L.
Glenarthur, L.
GeneralGuthrie of Craigiebank, L.
Hardy of Wath, L.
Healey, L.
Hill-Norton, L.
Hooson, L.
Inge, L.
Judd, L.
Luke, L.
MacKenzie of Culkein, L.
Maginnis of Drumglass, L.
Mason of Barnsley, L.
Mayhew of Twysden, L.
Monro of Langholm, L.
Moore of Wolvercote, L.

Murton of Lindisfarne, L.
Park of Monmouth, B.
Powell of Bayswater, L.
Pym, L.
Renwick of Clifton, L.
Robertson of Port Ellen, L.
Rogan, L.
Rotherwick, L.
Saltoun of Abernethy, Ly.
Selkirk of Douglas, L.
Selsdon, L.
Stewartby, L.
Strange, B.
Vivian, L.
Wallace of Saltaire, L.

**Democratic and
    Constitutional Reform**
Livsey of Talgarth, L.

Development
Brett, L.
Desai, L.
Falkland, V.
Joffe, L.
Redesdale, L.
Southwark, Bp.

Devolution
Gale, B.
Geraint, L.
Hunt of Kings Heath, L.
Mar and Kellie, E.
Renton, L.

Dialogue of Civilisation
Ahmed, L.

Disability
Addington, L.
Ashley of Stoke, L.
Attenborough, L.
Carter, L.
Corbett of Castle Vale, L.
Darcy de Knayth, B.
Gould of Potternewton, B.
Jenkin of Roding, L.
McColl of Dulwich, L.
Masham of Ilton, B.
Morris of Manchester, L.
Murray of Epping Forest, L.
Newton of Braintree, L.
O'Cathain, B.
Rix, L.
Simon, L.
Sterling of Plaistow, L.

Swinfen, L.
Uddin, B.
Wilkins, B.

Disadvantaged
Ashley of Stoke, L.
Northbourne, L.

Disarmament
Jenkins of Putney, L.

Drafting of Legislation
Renton, L.

Drug and Alcohol Issues
Brooke of Alverthorpe, L.
Cavendish of Furness, L.
Mancroft, L.
Masham of Ilton, B.
Vivian, L.

Dyslexia
Laird, L.

East and South-East Asia
Wilson of Tillyorn, L.

East-West Relations
Russell-Johnston, L.

Eastern Europe
Whaddon, L.
York, Abp.

Ecological Economics
Beaumont of Whitley, L.

Economic Affairs
Brett, L.
Bruce of Donington, L.
Christopher, L.
Coe, L.
Crickhowell, L.
Croham, L.
Cuckney, L.
Currie of Marylebone, L.
Davies of Oldham, L.
Desai, L.
Eatwell, L.
Forsyth of Drumlean, L.
Fyfe of Fairfield, L.
Gilbert, L.
Grenfell, L.
Griffiths of Fforestfach, L.
Harris of High Cross, L.
Hollick, L.

Howell of Guildford, L.
Jenkin of Roding, L.
Lamont of Lerwick, L.
MacGregor of Pulham Market,
    L.
Marsh, L.
Oakeshott of Seagrove Bay, L.
O'Cathain, B.
Patel of Blackburn, L.
Radice, L.
Roberts of Conwy, L.
Roll of Ipsden, L.
Selsdon, L.
Sharp of Guildford, B.
Sheldon, L.
Skidelsky, L.
Sterling of Plaistow, L.
St Edmundsbury and Ipswich,
    Bp.
Stoddart of Swindon, L.
Taverne, L.

Education
Addington, L.
Ahmed, L.
Andrews, B.
Attenborough, L.
Baker of Dorking, L.
Baldwin of Bewdley, E.
Billingham, B.
Blackstone, B.
Blake, L.
Blatch, B.
Bramall, L.
Briggs, L.
Brigstocke, B.
Campbell-Savours, L.
Carlisle of Bucklow, L.
Carnegy of Lour, B.
Cavendish of Furness, L.
Chilver, L.
Coe, L.
Cox, B.
Cumberlege, B.
David, B.
Davies of Coity, L.
Davies of Oldham, L.
Dearing, L.
Desai, L.
Dormand of Easington, L.
Elton, L.
Evans of Watford, L.
Griffiths of Fforestfach, L.
Hayman, B.
Hollis of Heigham, B.
Howe of Idlicote, B.

Jellicoe, E.
Judd, L.
Kilpatrick of Kincraig, L.
King of West Bromwich, L.
Levy, L.
Lewis of Newnham, L.
Linklater of Butterstone, B.
Lockwood, B.
Lucas of Crudwell and
    Dingwall, L.
Macaulay of Bragar, L.
McFarlane of Llandaff, B.
MacGregor of Pulham Market,
    L.
McIntosh of Hudnall, B.
Maddock, B.
Massey of Darwen, B.
Merlyn-Rees, L.
Michie of Gallanach, B.
Morgan, L.
Morgan of Huyton, B.
Moser, L.
Northbourne, L.
Patel of Blackburn, L.
Pearson of Rannoch, L.
Perry of Southwark, B.
Peterborough, Bp.
Platt of Writtle, B.
Portsmouth, Bp.
Prashar, B.
Quinton, L.
Quirk, L.
Renfrew of Kaimsthorn, L.
Roberts of Conwy, L.
St Albans, Bp.
Scarman, L.
Selborne, E.
Selkirk of Douglas, L.
Sharp of Guildford, B.
Skidelsky, L.
Southwark, Bp.
Stallard, L.
Sutherland of Houndwood, L.
Taylor of Blackburn, L.
Uddin, B.
Walton of Detchant, L.
Warnock, B.
Wedderburn of Charlton, L.
Wilson of Tillyorn, L.
Winchester, Bp.
Winston, L.

Electoral Affairs
Blake, L.
Gould of Potternewton, B.
Lipsey, L.

Employment
Brooke of Alverthorpe, L.
Davies of Oldham, L.
Evans of Parkside, L.
Hoyle, L.
Turner of Camden, B.

Employment Law
Janner of Braunstone, L.
Wedderburn of Charlton, L.

Energy
Cooke of Islandreagh, L.
Croham, L.
Evans of Parkside, L.
Gardner of Parkes, B.
Geddes, L.
Hardy of Wath, L.
Howell of Guildford, L.
Jenkin of Roding, L.
Lindsay, E.
Lofthouse of Pontefract, L.
Mar and Kellie, E.
Naseby, L.
Nicol, B.
Oxburgh, L.
Skelmersdale, L.
Stoddart of Swindon, L.
Taylor of Blackburn, L.

**Engagement of the Christian
    faith with contemporary
    culture**
Liverpool, Bp.

Engineering
Attlee, E.
Tombs, L.

England's North East
Thomas of Macclesfield, L.

Environment
Alton of Liverpool, L.
Baldwin of Bewdley, E.
Barber of Tewkesbury, L.
Beaumont of Whitley, L.
Berkeley, L.
Bradshaw, L.
Bridgeman, V.
Campbell of Croy, L.
Cavendish of Furness, L.
Chilver, L.
Chorley, L.
Clinton-Davis, L.
Coe, L.

Corbett of Castle Vale, L.
Courtown, E.
Crickhowell, L.
David, B.
Dixon-Smith, L.
Erroll, E.
Flowers, L.
Forsyth of Drumlean, L.
Gale, B.
Gibson, L.
Glentoran, L.
Graham of Edmonton, L.
Hanham, B.
Hereford, Bp.
Hilton of Eggardon, B.
Holme of Cheltenham, L.
Howe of Idlicote, B.
Hunt of Chesterton, L.
Hunt of Kings Heath, L.
Inglewood, L.
Jellicoe, E.
Judd, L.
Lewis of Newnham, L.
Lindsay, E.
London, Bp.
Maddock, B.
Mallalieu, B.
Mar, C.
Miller of Chilthorne Domer,
    B.
Nicol, B.
Palmer, L.
Pendry, L.
Redesdale, L.
Renton, L.
Selkirk of Douglas, L.
Shrewsbury and Waterford, E.
Skelmersdale, L.
Soulsby of Swaffham Prior, L.
Strabolgi, L.
Tenby, V.
Tope, L.
Warnock, B.
Wilcox, B.
Williams of Elvel, L.
Young of Old Scone, B.

Equal Opportunities
Crawley, B.
Fookes, B.
Gibson of Market Rasen, B.
Howe of Idlicote, B.
Lester of Herne Hill, L.
Lockwood, B.
Uddin, B.
Weidenfeld, L.

Ethics
Habgood, L.

Ethnic conflicts
Parekh, L.

Ethnic Minority Issues
Patel, L.

Europe
Biffen, L.
Billingham, B.
Bowness, L.
Bruce of Donington, L.
Campbell of Alloway, L.
Carnegy of Lour, B.
Chalker of Wallasey, B.
Cobbold, L.
Crawley, B.
Flather, B.
Gallacher, L.
Goudie, B.
Grenfell, L.
Harris of High Cross, L.
Haskins, L.
Hooper, B.
Hooson, L.
Hylton, L.
Inglewood, L.
Kilclooney, L.
Lamont of Lerwick, L.
Lester of Herne Hill, L.
Ludford, B.
Maclennan of Rogart, L.
Michie of Gallanach, B.
Montrose, D.
Morgan, L.
Newby, L.
Pearson of Rannoch, L.
Renton, L.
Russell-Johnston, L.
Sewel, L.
Skidelsky, L.
Stoddart of Swindon, L.
Taverne, L.
Temple-Morris, L.
Tomlinson, L.
Tope, L.
Tordoff, L.
Wallace of Saltaire, L.
Watson of Richmond, L.
Williams of Mostyn, L.
Willoughby de Broke, L.

Exports
Falkender, B.

Naseby, L.
Waverley, V.

Family
Blood, B.
Northbourne, L.
Seccombe, B.

Far East
Marsh, L.

Farming
Barber of Tewkesbury, L.
Callaghan of Cardiff, L.
Michie of Gallanach, B.

Film Industry
Dormand of Easington, L.
Falkland, V.
Taylor of Warwick, L.

Finance
Bruce of Donington, L.
Christopher, L.
Clark of Kempston, L.
Croham, L.
Donoughue, L.
Higgins, L.
Howe, E.
Jenkin of Roding, L.
Joffe, L.
Kimball, L.
Lipsey, L.
Lucas of Crudwell and
    Dingwall, L.
Marsh, L.
O'Cathain, B.
Pendry, L.
Renton of Mount Harry, L.
Roll of Ipsden, L.
St John of Bletso, L.
Stewartby, L.
Tomlinson, L.
Williams of Elvel, L.

Fishing Industry
Hughes of Woodside, L.
Wilcox, B.

Food
Haskins, L.
Lindsay, E.
Mar, C.
Rea, L.
Wade of Chorlton, L.

Football
Carter, L.

Foreign Affairs
Arran, E.
Ashdown of Norton-sub-
    Hamdon, L.
Blackstone, B.
Blake, L.
Blaker, L.
Field MarshalBramall, L.
Campbell of Croy, L.
Cavendish of Furness, L.
Chalfont, L.
Clinton-Davis, L.
Coe, L.
Elles, B.
Gilbert, L.
Glenarthur, L.
Grocott, L.
Hardy of Wath, L.
Healey, L.
Holme of Cheltenham, L.
Home, E.
Howell of Guildford, L.
Jellicoe, E.
Judd, L.
Lamont of Lerwick, L.
McNally, L.
Moore of Wolvercote, L.
Morgan, L.
Moynihan, L.
Northbrook, L.
Park of Monmouth, B.
Powell of Bayswater, L.
Pym, L.
Renfrew of Kaimsthorn, L.
Renwick of Clifton, L.
Robertson of Port Ellen, L.
Russell-Johnston, L.
St John of Bletso, L.
Sandberg, L.
Selkirk of Douglas, L.
Selsdon, L.
Soulsby of Swaffham Prior, L.
Stern, B.
Stewartby, L.
Strange, B.
Temple-Morris, L.
Thomas of Gwydir, L.
Tomlinson, L.
Tordoff, L.
Uddin, B.
Wallace of Saltaire, L.
Williams of Mostyn, L.
Wright of Richmond, L.

Forestry
Barber of Tewkesbury, L.
Cavendish of Furness, L.
McColl of Dulwich, L.
Nicol, B.

Former Soviet Union
Hylton, L.
Smith of Gilmorehill, B.

France
Astor of Hever, L.
Strabolgi, L.

Franz Josef Land
Brightman, L.

Freemasonry
Burnham, L.

Future of Work
Sheppard of Liverpool, L.

Gaelic language
Michie of Gallanach, B.

Gambling
Golding, B.

Gender Issues
Winchester, Bp.

Global justice
Parekh, L.

Globalisation
Williams of Crosby, B.

Golf
Bell, L.

Government – Civil Service Issues
Hunt of Chesterton, L.

Greyhound Welfare
Lipsey, L.

Gypsies
Avebury, L.

Health
Ashley of Stoke, L.
Barker, B.
Billingham, B.
Bridgeman, V.

Brigstocke, B.
Brookeborough, V.
Carter, L.
Coe, L.
Colwyn, L.
Cox, B.
Dean of Harptree, L.
Ewing of Kirkford, L.
Falkender, B.
Fearn, L.
Fookes, B.
Forsyth of Drumlean, L.
Gardner of Parkes, B.
Glenarthur, L.
Hanham, B.
Hayman, B.
Hollis of Heigham, B.
Hoyle, L.
Jay of Paddington, B.
Jenkin of Roding, L.
Kilpatrick of Kincraig, L.
Knight of Collingtree, B.
McColl of Dulwich, L.
McFarlane of Llandaff, B.
MacKenzie of Culkein, L.
Masham of Ilton, B.
Massey of Darwen, B.
Michie of Gallanach, B.
Miller of Hendon, B.
Morgan of Huyton, B.
Newton of Braintree, L.
Noakes, B.
Oxburgh, L.
Pitkeathley, B.
Quirk, L.
Rea, L.
Roberts of Conwy, L.
Selkirk of Douglas, L.
Skelmersdale, L.
Smith of Clifton, L.
Smith of Leigh, L.
Stallard, L.
Uddin, B.
Walton of Detchant, L.
Winston, L.
Wolfson of Sunningdale, L.

Health and Safety at Work
Gibson of Market Rasen, B.
Walker of Doncaster, L.

Health Service
Carnegy of Lour, B.
Cumberlege, B.
Davies of Coity, L.
Dubs, L.

Golding, B.
Grocott, L.
Hughes of Woodside, L.
McColl of Dulwich, L.
Mar, C.
Naseby, L.
Turnberg, L.
Wigoder, L.

Heritage
Chorley, L.
Gibson, L.
Hollis of Heigham, B.
Luke, L.
Monro of Langholm, L.
Montagu of Beaulieu, L.
Northesk, E.
Palmer, L.
Park of Monmouth, B.
Phillips of Sudbury, L.
Rawlings, B.
Renfrew of Kaimsthorn, L.
Salisbury, Bp.
Sandwich, E.
Selkirk of Douglas, L.
Strabolgi, L.

Higher Education
Flowers, L.
Grabiner, L.
Howie of Troon, L.
McColl of Dulwich, L.
Oxburgh, L.
Parekh, L.
Park of Monmouth, B.
Patel, L.
Sewel, L.
Smith of Clifton, L.
Soulsby of Swaffham Prior, L.

Historic Buildings
Cobbold, L.

History
Baker of Dorking, L.

Home Affairs
Anelay of St Johns, B.
Bridgeman, V.
Carlile of Berriew, L.
Corbett of Castle Vale, L.
David, B.
Deedes, L.
Hardy of Wath, L.
Irvine of Lairg, L.
Mackenzie of Framwellgate, L.

Mallalieu, B.
Wigoder, L.

Home Rule for Scotland
Michie of Gallanach, B.

Homeless
Murray of Epping Forest, L.
Scarman, L.

Hong Kong
Bramall, L.
Geddes, L.
Marlesford, L.
Sandberg, L.
Skidelsky, L.
Thomas of Gresford, L.
Willoughby de Broke, L.
Wilson of Tillyorn, L.

Horse Racing
Lipsey, L.
Noakes, B.

Horticulture
Northbourne, L.
Skelmersdale, L.

Hospital Chaplaincy
St Albans, Bp.

Housing
Alton of Liverpool, L.
Best, L.
Clark of Kempston, L.
Dean of Thornton-le-Fylde, B.
Dixon, L.
Filkin, L.
Fisher of Rednal, B.
Fookes, B.
Gardner of Parkes, B.
Hamwee, B.
Hylton, L.
Jenkin of Roding, L.
Lofthouse of Pontefract, L.
MacGregor of Pulham Market,
    L.
Maddock, B.
Merlyn-Rees, L.
Oakeshott of Seagrove Bay, L.
Oxford, Bp.
Pendry, L.
Sanderson of Bowden, L.
Selkirk of Douglas, L.
Stallard, L.
Stoddart of Swindon, L.

Human Rights
Ackner, L.
Ahmed, L.
Alton of Liverpool, L.
Archer of Sandwell, L.
Ashley of Stoke, L.
Avebury, L.
Brett, L.
Carlisle of Bucklow, L.
Cox, B.
Dubs, L.
Faulkner of Worcester, L.
Goodhart, L.
Hylton, L.
Janner of Braunstone, L.
Joffe, L.
Lester of Herne Hill, L.
Lofthouse of Pontefract, L.
McCluskey, L.
Mason of Barnsley, L.
Prashar, B.
Rea, L.
Russell-Johnston, L.
Scarman, L.
Stern, B.
Williams of Crosby, B.

Humanitarian Aid
Cox, B.

ICT
Erroll, E.

Immigration
Ahmed, L.
Dubs, L.
Geddes, L.
Hoyle, L.

Import Substitution
Feldman, L.

**Independence of the
    Judiciary**
Ackner, L.

**Independent Television
    Commission**
Northesk, E.

India
Janner of Braunstone, L.

Industrial Democracy
Campbell-Savours, L.

Industrial Relations
Campbell of Alloway, L.
Clarke of Hampstead, L.
Davies of Coity, L.
Evans of Parkside, L.
Evans of Watford, L.
Gibson of Market Rasen, B.
Hoyle, L.
Janner of Braunstone, L.
Lofthouse of Pontefract, L.
McCarthy, L.
Pendry, L.
Walker of Doncaster, L.
Wedderburn of Charlton, L.

Industrial Training
Lockwood, B.

Industry
Ashdown of Norton-sub-
    Hamdon, L.
Bruce of Donington, L.
Cavendish of Furness, L.
Chilver, L.
Christopher, L.
Clark of Kempston, L.
Dean of Thornton-le-Fylde, B.
Feldman, L.
Geddes, L.
Hanson, L.
Holme of Cheltenham, L.
Home, E.
Jenkin of Roding, L.
Knight of Collingtree, B.
Lockwood, B.
MacGregor of Pulham Market,
    L.
Marsh, L.
O'Cathain, B.
Sanderson of Bowden, L.
Sharp of Guildford, B.
Stoddart of Swindon, L.
Wade of Chorlton, L.

Information Technology
Baker of Dorking, L.
Mitchell, L.
Randall of St Budeaux, L.
St John of Bletso, L.

Informational Aspects
Hunt of Chesterton, L.

Inner Cities
Alton of Liverpool, L.
Hooper, B.

Knights, L.
Moynihan, L.
York, Abp.

Insurance
Clark of Kempston, L.

Intelligence
Powell of Bayswater, L.

Inter Faith Relations
erendRichardson of Calow, B.

Internal Affairs
Williams of Crosby, B.

International Affairs
Hooson, L.
Islwyn, L.
Owen, L.
Perry of Southwark, B.
Rawlings, B.
Sandwich, E.
Steel of Aikwood, L.
Weidenfeld, L.

International Development
Andrews, B.
Massey of Darwen, B.
Stern, B.
Tomlinson, L.
Whitaker, B.

International Finance
Howell of Guildford, L.

International Relations
GeneralGuthrie of
    Craigiebank, L.
Waverley, V.

International Trade
Clinton-Davis, L.
Parekh, L.
Salisbury, Bp.

**Investigative Political and
    Social Work**
Campbell-Savours, L.

Iran/Middle East
Phillips of Sudbury, L.

Ireland
Dubs, L.
Goudie, B.
Temple-Morris, L.

Irish Politics
Kilclooney, L.

Jewish Causes
Janner of Braunstone, L.

Justice and Home Affairs
Ludford, B.
Hanham, B.

Juvenile Justice
Elton, L.

**Kashmiri Right of Self
    Determination**
Ahmed, L.

Labour Issues
Brett, L.

**Labour Party Policy
    Revision**
Radice, L.

Lancashire
Waddington, L.

Land Reform
MacKenzie of Culkein, L.

Landscape Industry
Courtown, E.

Language and Culture
Geraint, L.

Languages
Rochester, Bp.

Latin America
Hooper, B.
Sandberg, L.

Law
Ackner, L.
Alexander of Weedon, L.
Archer of Sandwell, L.
Buscombe, B.
Cameron of Lochbroom, L.
Carlile of Berriew, L.
Carlisle of Bucklow, L.
Clinton-Davis, L.
Donaldson of Lymington, L.
Grabiner, L.
Hooson, L.
Howe of Idlicote, B.

Inglewood, L.
Irvine of Lairg, L.
Lester of Herne Hill, L.
Mackenzie of Framwellgate,
    L.
Mallalieu, B.
Phillips of Sudbury, L.
St John of Bletso, L.
Scarman, L.
Selkirk of Douglas, L.
Taylor of Warwick, L.
Waddington, L.
Williams of Mostyn, L.

Law and Order
Buscombe, B.
Knights, L.
Miller of Hendon, B.
Renton, L.
Warner, L.

**Legislative Drafting in Plain
    English**
Brightman, L.

Legislatures
Norton of Louth, L.

Leisure
Fearn, L.
McNally, L.

Libertarian Issues
Lucas of Crudwell and
    Dingwall, L.
Phillips of Sudbury, L.

Licensed Trade
Evans of Parkside, L.

Light Rail Transport
Russell-Johnston, L.

Literature
James of Holland Park, B.

Local Government
Bach, L.
Blatch, B.
Bowness, L.
Bridgeman, V.
Cameron of Lochbroom, L.
Carnegy of Lour, B.
Cumberlege, B.
Dormand of Easington, L.
Fearn, L.

Fisher of Rednal, B.
Forsyth of Drumlean, L.
Graham of Edmonton, L.
Hamwee, B.
Hanham, B.
Hogg of Cumbernauld, L.
Hollis of Heigham, B.
Inglewood, L.
King of West Bromwich, L.
Knights, L.
Lofthouse of Pontefract, L.
Ludford, B.
Macaulay of Bragar, L.
Maddock, B.
Molyneaux of Killead, L.
Platt of Writtle, B.
Selkirk of Douglas, L.
Smith of Leigh, L.
Stoddart of Swindon, L.
Taylor of Blackburn, L.
Tope, L.
Uddin, B.
Winchester, Bp.

Local Issues
Cavendish of Furness, L.

London
Bowness, L.
Hamwee, B.
London, Bp.
Plummer of St Marylebone, L.
Thornton, B.
Tope, L.

Low Pay
Blood, B.

Machinery of Government
Grocott, L.
Lipsey, L.

Magistracy
Phillips of Sudbury, L.
Tenby, V.

Manpower Policy
Walker of Doncaster, L.

Manufacturing
Cooke of Islandreagh, L.
Corbett of Castle Vale, L.
Evans of Parkside, L.
Jones, L.

Mariculture
Wilcox, B.

Marine Industry
Greenway, L.

Maritime Affairs
Cooke of Islandreagh, L.
Dixon, L.
Glentoran, L.
MacKenzie of Culkein, L.

Maritime Safety
Donaldson of Lymington, L.

Marketing
Naseby, L.

Marriage
Winchester, Bp.

Media
Arran, E.
Cumberlege, B.
Currie of Marylebone, L.
Dean of Thornton-le-Fylde, B.
Deedes, L.
Gibson, L.
Grocott, L.
Hamwee, B.
Hollis of Heigham, B.
Inglewood, L.
Jay of Paddington, B.
Jenkins of Putney, L.
Lester of Herne Hill, L.
Palmer, L.
Quinton, L.
Quirk, L.
Thornton, B.

Medical Drugs
Ashley of Stoke, L.

Medical Education
Turnberg, L.

Medical Ethics
Finlay of Llandaff, B.

Medical Profession
Carlile of Berriew, L.

Medical Research Ethics
Carnegy of Lour, B.

Medicine
Baldwin of Bewdley, E.
Habgood, L.
McColl of Dulwich, L.

Walton of Detchant, L.
Warnock, B.

Mental Handicap
Forsyth of Drumlean, L.
Pearson of Rannoch, L.
Renton, L.

Mental Health
Acton, L.
Alderdice, L.
Carlile of Berriew, L.
McCluskey, L.
Molyneaux of Killead, L.

Middle East
Canterbury, Abp.
Hylton, L.
Janner of Braunstone, L.
Levy, L.
Rochester, Bp.
Stone of Blackheath, L.
Temple-Morris, L.
Weidenfeld, L.

Migration
Judd, L.

Military History
Luke, L.

Mineral Extraction
Shrewsbury and Waterford, E.

Minorities Rights
Ahmed, L.

Monastic Life
Sheffield, Bp.

Moral Issues
Oxford, Bp.

**Mother and Child Health in
    North India**
Chan, L.

Motor Industry
Brougham and Vaux, L.
Corbett of Castle Vale, L.
Islwyn, L.
Montagu of Beaulieu, L.
Simon, L.

Motorcycle Industry
Falkland, V.

Motoring
Luke, L.

Motorsport Industry
Astor of Hever, L.

Museums and Galleries
Armstrong of Ilminster, L.
Brigstocke, B.
Montagu of Beaulieu, L.
Renfrew of Kaimsthorn, L.

Music
Bell, L.
Sterling of Plaistow, L.

Mutuality
Fyfe of Fairfield, L.

National Lottery
Naseby, L.

New Technology
Ashdown of Norton-sub-
   Hamdon, L.

North American Matters
Parry, L.

North West
Taylor of Blackburn, L.

Northern Ireland
Alderdice, L.
Alton of Liverpool, L.
Archer of Sandwell, L.
Brookeborough, V.
Eames, L.
Glentoran, L.
Harris of Richmond, B.
Hylton, L.
Mason of Barnsley, L.
Mayhew of Twysden, L.
Park of Monmouth, B.
Rogan, L.
Smith of Clifton, L.
Stallard, L.

Nuclear Disarmament
Jenkins of Putney, L.

Nursing
Cox, B.
MacKenzie of Culkein, L.

Oil
Howell of Guildford, L.

Open Spaces
Clark of Windermere, L.

Orthodox Church
Sheffield, Bp.

**Overseas Aid and
   Development**
Attlee, E.
Chalker of Wallasey, B.
Clarke of Hampstead, L.
Deedes, L.
Hughes of Woodside, L.
Jay of Paddington, B.
Moynihan, L.
Oakeshott of Seagrove Bay,
   L.
Oxford, Bp.
Sandwich, E.
Watson of Invergowrie, L.
Waverley, V.

Parliamentary Affairs
Pym, L.

Parliamentary Procedure
Naseby, L.

Parliamentary Reform
Norton of Louth, L.
Weatherill, L.

Peace Building
Hylton, L.

Penal Affairs and Policy
Acton, L.
Carlisle of Bucklow, L.
Christopher, L.
Dubs, L.
Fookes, B.
Glenarthur, L.
Howe, E.
Hylton, L.
Judd, L.
Linklater of Butterstone, B.
Masham of Ilton, B.
Merlyn-Rees, L.
Stern, B.

Pensions
Christopher, L.
Dean of Thornton-le-Fylde,
   B.
Grabiner, L.

Newton of Braintree, L.
Oakeshott of Seagrove Bay, L.
Taverne, L.
Turner of Camden, B.
Vinson, L.

Pesticides
Mar, C.

Pet Quarantine
Sharples, B.

Planning
Bradshaw, L.
Gardner of Parkes, B.
Hamwee, B.
Jenkin of Roding, L.
Wade of Chorlton, L.

Police
Bradshaw, L.
Corbett of Castle Vale, L.
Harris of Richmond, B.
Imbert, L.
Knights, L.
Mackenzie of Framwellgate,
   L.
Simon, L.
Tope, L.

Policy Development
Filkin, L.

Policy Implementation
Ashton of Upholland, B.
Filkin, L.

Pollution
Mason of Barnsley, L.

Population and Development
Gould of Potternewton, B.

Post Office
Dearing, L.
Skelmersdale, L.

Poverty
Ashley of Stoke, L.
Barker, B.
Beaumont of Whitley, L.
Oxford, Bp.
Winchester, Bp.

Press
Corbett of Castle Vale, L.

Prison Reform
Addington, L.
McIntosh of Hudnall, B.

Prisoners' Wives
Sharples, B.

Prisons
Ackner, L.
Avebury, L.
Hylton, L.
Mar and Kellie, E.
Stern, B.

Privatisation
Forsyth of Drumlean, L.
Renton of Mount Harry, L.

Privatised Utilities
Skelmersdale, L.

Pro Life
Alton of Liverpool, L.

Probation
Mar and Kellie, E.

Professional Engineers
Howie of Troon, L.

Professional Self-Regulation
Kilpatrick of Kincraig, L.

Property
Courtown, E.
Shrewsbury and Waterford, E.

Psephology
Lipsey, L.

**Psychoanalysis and Political
    Conflict Resolution**
Alderdice, L.

Public Communication
Quirk, L.

Public Finance
Noakes, B.
Sewel, L.

Public Health
McIntosh of Hudnall, B.

Public Service
Armstrong of Ilminster, L.
Noakes, B.

Public Transport
Hogg of Cumbernauld, L.

Race Relations
Ahmed, L.
Chan, L.
Deedes, L.
Dubs, L.
Flather, B.
Gould of Potternewton, B.
Hilton of Eggardon, B.
Judd, L.
Parekh, L.
Patel of Blackburn, L.
Prashar, B.
Sheppard of Liverpool, L.
Whitaker, B.

Racing
Golding, B.

Railways
Taylor of Blackburn, L.
Tenby, V.

Recreation
Monro of Langholm, L.
Pendry, L.

Refugees
Alton of Liverpool, L.
Judd, L.
Moynihan, L.

Regeneration
Best, L.

Regional Policy
Dearing, L.
Dormand of Easington, L.
Elliott of Morpeth, L.
Goudie, B.
Inglewood, L.
Kilclooney, L.
Morris of Manchester, L.
Newby, L.
Smith of Leigh, L.

Regulation
Currie of Marylebone, L.

Regulation of Medicine
Patel, L.

**Relations with Muslim
    countries**
Ahmed, L.

Research
Sutherland of Houndwood, L.
Turnberg, L.

**Restrictive Trade Practices
    and Monopolies**
Campbell of Alloway, L.

Retail Industry
Feldman, L.
McNally, L.
O'Cathain, B.

River Thames
Luke, L.

Road Safety
Brougham and Vaux, L.
Simon, L.

Road Transport
Islwyn, L.
Montagu of Beaulieu, L.

Rural Affairs
Carter, L.
Geraint, L.
Inglewood, L.
Maclennan of Rogart, L.
Mancroft, L.
Montrose, D.
Noakes, B.
Peterborough, Bp.
Phillips of Sudbury, L.
Pym, L.
St Edmundsbury and Ipswich,
    Bp.
Salisbury, Bp.

Russia
Smith of Gilmorehill, B.

Rwanda
Winchester, Bp.

Science and Technology
Andrews, B.
Erroll, E.
Flowers, L.
Habgood, L.
Haskel, L.
Hunt of Chesterton, L.
Jenkin of Roding, L.
Morris of Manchester, L.
Selborne, E.
Sharp of Guildford, B.

Simon, L.
Southwark, Bp.
Stone of Blackheath, L.
Taverne, L.
Tombs, L.
Walton of Detchant, L.
Winston, L.

Scottish Affairs
Carnegy of Lour, B.
Erroll, E.
Glenarthur, L.
Goudie, B.
Home, E.
Mar and Kellie, E.
Monro of Langholm, L.
Russell-Johnston, L.
Saltoun of Abernethy, Ly.
Sanderson of Bowden, L.
Selkirk of Douglas, L.
Sewel, L.
Wilson of Tillyorn, L.

Scottish Highlands
Pearson of Rannoch, L.

Scottish Law
Macaulay of Bragar, L.

Sexual Health
Gould of Potternewton, B.

Shipping
Geddes, L.
Greenway, L.
Sterling of Plaistow, L.

Ships and Shipbuilding
Dixon, L.

Small Businesses
Harrison, L.
King of West Bromwich, L.
Miller of Hendon, B.
Mitchell, L.
Roberts of Conwy, L.
Sanderson of Bowden, L.
Sharples, B.
Vinson, L.

Social and Health Care
Pitkeathley, B.
Warner, L.

Social Enterprise
Thornton, B.

Social Inclusion Policy
Watson of Invergowrie, L.

Social Policy
Best, L.
Blackstone, B.
Briggs, L.
Eames, L.
Griffiths of Fforestfach, L.
Harris of High Cross, L.
Mar and Kellie, E.
Moser, L.

Social Security
Anelay of St Johns, B.
Dean of Harptree, L.
Higgins, L.
Knight of Collingtree, B.
Mar, C.
Newton of Braintree, L.
Pendry, L.
Turner of Camden, B.

Social Services
Barker, B.
Bridgeman, V.
Dixon, L.
Emerton, B.
Ewing of Kirkford, L.
Levy, L.
Newton of Braintree, L.
Stallard, L.

South Africa
Watson of Richmond, L.

South East Asia
Geddes, L.
Naseby, L.

Southern Africa
Acton, L.
Filkin, L.
St John of Bletso, L.

Space
Tanlaw, L.

Speech Pathology
Quirk, L.

Spitsbergen
Brightman, L.

Sport
Addington, L.
Arran, E.

Bach, L.
Billingham, B.
Colwyn, L.
Donoughue, L.
Faulkner of Worcester, L.
Feldman, L.
Glentoran, L.
Higgins, L.
Islwyn, L.
Macaulay of Bragar, L.
Massey of Darwen, B.
Monro of Langholm, L.
Moynihan, L.
Pendry, L.
St John of Bletso, L.

Sri Lanka
Naseby, L.

Standards in Medicine
Patel, L.

Steel
Islwyn, L.

Street Children
Miller of Chilthorne Domer,
  B.

Sudan
Salisbury, Bp.

Sufism
Rochester, Bp.

**Sustainable Built
  Environment**
Rogers of Riverside, L.

Tax
Newton of Braintree, L.
Stewartby, L.
Taverne, L.
Vinson, L.

Technology
Jenkin of Roding, L.
Southwark, Bp.
Tombs, L.
Wade of Chorlton, L.

Telecommunications
Dean of Thornton-le-Fylde, B.

Telemedicine
Swinfen, L.

Terrorism and Internal Security
Maginnis of Drumglass, L.
Vivian, L.

Textile Industry
Sanderson of Bowden, L.
Waddington, L.

Theatre
Macaulay of Bragar, L.
McCarthy, L.
Phillips of Sudbury, L.
Rix, L.

Third Age
Howe of Idlicote, B.

Third World
Archer of Sandwell, L.
Geraint, L.
Judd, L.
Rea, L.

Tibet
Willoughby de Broke, L.

Time
Tanlaw, L.

Tourism
Blaker, L.
Brookeborough, V.
Dormand of Easington, L.
Fearn, L.
Feldman, L.
Geddes, L.
Gordon of Strathblane, L.
Harrison, L.
Luke, L.
McNally, L.
Montagu of Beaulieu, L.
Parry, L.
Phillips of Sudbury, L.
Roberts of Conwy, L.
Walpole, L.

Trade
Chalker of Wallasey, B.
Hoyle, L.
Powell of Bayswater, L.

Trade and Industry
Buscombe, B.
Clark of Kempston, L.
Eatwell, L.

Haskel, L.
Lucas of Crudwell and
    Dingwall, L.
McNally, L.
Moynihan, L.
Noakes, B.
Rogan, L.
Selsdon, L.
Simpson of Dunkeld, L.

Trade Unions
Dixon, L.
Golding, B.
Jenkins of Putney, L.
Renton, L.

Training
Davies of Oldham, L.
Lockwood, B.
Roberts of Conwy, L.

Transition Economies
Skidelsky, L.

Transport
Attlee, E.
Berkeley, L.
Brabazon of Tara, L.
Bradshaw, L.
Brooke of Alverthorpe, L.
Brougham and Vaux, L.
Chalker of Wallasey, B.
Clinton-Davis, L.
Davies of Oldham, L.
Dixon, L.
Dixon-Smith, L.
Evans of Parkside, L.
Falkland, V.
Faulkner of Worcester, L.
Fearn, L.
Fyfe of Fairfield, L.
Gardner of Parkes, B.
Geddes, L.
Gilbert, L.
Hereford, Bp.
Higgins, L.
Hollick, L.
Hughes of Woodside, L.
Hunt of Kings Heath, L.
Laird, L.
Lindsay, E.
Mar and Kellie, E.
Roberts of Conwy, L.
Sanderson of Bowden, L.
Scott of Needham Market, B.
Stoddart of Swindon, L.
Wade of Chorlton, L.

Transport (aircraft)
Smith of Clifton, L.

Travel
Evans of Watford, L.

Treasury
Sheldon, L.

UFOs
Hill-Norton, L.

Uganda
Winchester, Bp.

Ulster Scots Activity
Laird, L.

Underdeveloped Countries
Attenborough, L.

Unemployment
Sheppard of Liverpool, L.

United Nations
Carlile of Berriew, L.
Vivian, L.

Urban Policies
Crickhowell, L.
Sheppard of Liverpool, L.

Urban Regeneration
Liverpool, Bp.

USA Affairs
Bach, L.

Value of the family to social cohesion
Liverpool, Bp.

Venice
Strabolgi, L.

Visual and Performing Arts
Crathorne, L.
Freyberg, L.

Voluntary Sector
Chalker of Wallasey, B.
Coe, L.
Emerton, B.
Evans of Watford, L.
Levy, L.
Liverpool, Bp.

Phillips of Sudbury, L.
Pitkeathley, B.
Rix, L.

Wales
Carlile of Berriew, L.
Gale, B.
Geraint, L.
Hooson, L.
Livsey of Talgarth, L.
Parry, L.
Thomas of Gresford, L.

Welfare
Winchester, Bp.

West Africa
Filkin, L.

West Country
Courtown, E.

West Midlands
Shrewsbury and Waterford, E.

Wildlife
Hardy of Wath, L.

Women and Race
Uddin, B.

Women's Careers
Finlay of Llandaff, B.

Women's Equality
Gould of Potternewton, B.

Women's Health
Patel, L.

Women's Issues
Blood, B.
Dean of Thornton-le-Fylde, B.
Gale, B.
Gibson of Market Rasen, B.
Miller of Hendon, B.
Morgan of Huyton, B.
Seccombe, B.

Women's Opportunities in Engineering
Platt of Writtle, B.

Women's Rights
Crawley, B.

Working Class Issues
Blood, B.

World Government
Archer of Sandwell, L.

Young Under-privileged
Listowel, E.

Youth Affairs
Ashdown of Norton-sub-Hamdon, L.
Linklater of Butterstone, B.

Youth Work
Sheppard of Liverpool, L.

Visit the Vacher Dod Website . . .

www.DodOnline.co.uk

Political information updated daily

The Queen's Speech	House of Commons
Today's Business	House of Lords
This Week's Business	Scottish Parliament
Progress of Government Bills	National Assembly for Wales
Select Committees	Northern Ireland Assembly
Government and Opposition	Greater London Authority
Stop Press News	European Union

Check changes daily as they happen

Hereditary Peer members

Those who have also received life peerages are given in bold. Peers of Ireland are marked*, with their British honours in parenthesis.
There are two hereditary office holders, Duke of Norfolk (Earl Marshal), and Marquess of Cholmondeley (Lord Great Chamberlain)

Lord Aberdare
Lord Acton (LP **Baron Acton of Bridgnorth** 2000)
Lord Addington
Viscount Allenby of Megiddo
Lord Ampthill
Earl of Arran* (Baron Sudley)
Lord Astor of Hever
Viscount Astor
Earl Attlee
Lord Avebury
Earl Baldwin of Bewdley
Lord Belstead (LP **Baron Ganzoni** 1999)
Lord Berkeley (LP **Baron Gueterbock** 2000)
Viscount Bledisloe
Lord Brabazon of Tara
Viscount Bridgeman
Lord Bridges
Viscount Brookeborough
Lord Brougham and Vaux
Lord Burnham
Earl of Caithness
Lord Carrington (LP **Baron Carington of Upton** 1999)
Viscount Chandos (LP **Baron Lyttelton of Aldershot** 2000)
Marquess of Cholmondeley
Lord Chorley
Lord Cobbold
Viscount Colville of Culross
Lord Colwyn
Earl of Courtown* (Baron Saltersford)
Viscount Craigavon
Lord Crathorne
Earl of Crawford and Balcarres (LP **Baron Balniel** 1974)
Baroness Darcy de Knayth
Lord Denham
Earl of Dundee
Lord Elton
Earl of Erroll
Viscount of Falkland
Earl Ferrers
Lord Freyberg
Lord Geddes
Lord Glenarthur
Lord Glentoran
Viscount Goschen

Lord Greenway
Lord Grenfell (LP **Baron Grenfell of Kilvey** 2000)
Lord Henley* (Baron Northington)
Earl of Home
Earl Howe
Lord Hylton
Lord Inglewood
Earl Jellicoe (LP **Baron Jellicoe of Southampton** 1999)
Earl of Lindsay
Earl of Listowel* (Baron Hare)
Earl of Liverpool
Lord Lucas of Crudwell and Dingwall
Lord Luke
Lord Lyell
Lord Mancroft
Countess of Mar
Earl of Mar and Kellie
  (LP **Baron Erskine of Alloa Tower** 2000)
Lord Methuen
Lord Monson
Lord Montagu of Beaulieu
Duke of Montrose
Lord Moran
Lord Mowbray and Stourton
Lord Moynihan
Duke of Norfolk
Lord Northbourne
Lord Northbrook
Earl of Northesk
Earl of Onslow
Lord Palmer
Earl Peel
Lord Ponsonby of Shulbrede (LP **Baron Ponsonby of Roehampton** 2000)
Lord Rea
Lord Reay
Lord Redesdale (LP **Baron Mitford** 2000)
Earl of Rosslyn
Lord Rotherwick
Earl Russell
Lord St John of Bletso
Marquess of Salisbury (LP **Baron Gascoyne-Cecil** 1999)
Lady Saltoun of Abernethy
Earl of Sandwich
Earl of Selborne

Lord Selsdon	Lord Swinfen
Earl of Shrewsbury and Waterford	Viscount Tenby
Viscount Simon	Lord Trefgarne
Lord Skelmersdale	Viscount Ullswater
Viscount Slim	Lord Vivian
Earl of Snowdon (LP **Baron Armstrong-Jones** 1999)	Lord Walpole
	Viscount Waverley
Lord Strabolgi	Lord Willoughby de Broke
Baroness Strange	Lord Windlesham (LP **Baron Hennessy** 1999)
Lord Strathclyde	

Hereditary Peers' Election Results 27/28 October 1999

At the elections held on 27/28 October 1999 for 15 hereditary peers ready to serve as Deputy Speakers and other office holders, in accordance with the provisions of the House of Lords Bill and Standing Order 9(2)(ii), the candidates received the following number of votes:

Candidate	Votes	Place			
C. Mar	570	1st	L. Colwyn	488	9th
L. Strabolgi	558	2nd	V. Oxfuird	482	10th
L. Elton	558	3rd	L. Reay	471	11th
L. Lyell	547	4th	L. Geddes	461	12th
L. Skelmersdale	544	5th	V. Simon	453	13th
L. Aberdare	530	6th	L. Methuen	421	14th
L. Brougham and Vaux	525	7th	L. Ampthill	418	15th
V. Falkland	519	8th			

3/4 November 1999

At the elections held on 3/4 November 1999 for 75 hereditary peers elected by the hereditary peers in their party or group, in accordance with the provisions of the House of Lords Bill and Standing Order 9(2)(i), the candidates received the following number of votes:

CONSERVATIVE PEERS

Candidate	Votes	Place			
E. Ferrers	190	1st	E. Selborne	125	22nd
L. Strathclyde	174	2nd	V. Bridgeman	125	23rd
L. Trefgarne	173	3rd	L. Luke	124	24th
L. Denham	169	4th	E. Lindsay	116	25th
L. Mancroft	168	5th	L. Lucas of Crudwell and Dingwall	115	26th
E. Howe	165	6th	L. Montagu of Beaulieu	113	27th
L. Brabazon of Tara	165	7th	E. Home	113	28th
E. Caithness	161	8th	L. Glentoran	104	29th
L. Henley	160	9th	E. Onslow	99	30th
L. Glenarthur	157	10th	L. Crathorne	97	31st
L. Astor of Hever	151	11th	L. Willoughby de Broke	96	32nd
V. Astor	146	12th	L. Inglewood	95	33rd
E. Courtown	143	13th	L. Northbrook	95	34th
E. Peel	142	14th	L. Swinfen	95	35th
L. Moynihan	137	15th	E. Shrewsbury	95	36th
E. Attlee	135	16th	L. Selsdon	94	37th
V. Goschen	132	17th	E. Liverpool	93	38th
D. Montrose	127	18th	E. Arran	90	39th
L. Burnham	127	19th	E. Dundee	90	40th
L. Vivian	126	20th	L. Mowbray and Stourton	88	41st
E. Northesk	126	21st	L. Rotherwick	88	42nd

CROSSBENCH PEERS

Candidate	Votes	Place
B. Darcy de Knathy	85	1st
L. Freyberg	82	2nd
L. St John of Bletso	81	3rd
L. Northbourne	78	4th
E. Sandwich	78	5th
V. Allenby of Megiddo	75	6th
V. Tenby	74	7th
L. Palmer	72	8th
V. Slim	72	9th
V. Bledisloe	70	10th
L. Monson	70	11th
V. Brookeborough	68	12th
L. Bridges	68	13th
Lady Saltoun of Abernethy	64	14th
L. Hylton	64	15th
E. Baldwin of Bewdley	63	16th
E. Carnarvon	58	17th
E. Listowel	58	18th
L. Moran	57	19th
B. Strange	53	20th
E. Erroll	52	21st
L. Walpole	52	22nd
V. Craigavon	51	23rd
B. Wharton*	48	24th
V. Colville of Culross	47	25th
V. Waverley	47	26th
L. Greenway	47	27th
E. Rosslyn	45	28th
L. Cobbold*	43	29th

* Lord Cobbold replaced the late Baroness Wharton

LABOUR PEERS

Candidate	Votes	Place
L. Milner of Leeds	8	1st
L. Rea	7	2nd

LIBERAL DEMOCRAT PEERS

Candidate	Votes	Place
E. Russell	17	1st
L. Avebury	13	2nd
L. Addington	10	3rd

Lords of Appeal
†*Lord of Appeal in Ordinary (working law lords)*

†Lord Bingham of Cornhill
  (Senior Lord of Appeal in Ordinary)
Lord Browne-Wilkinson
Lord Cameron of Lochbroom
Lord Clyde
Lord Hardie
†Lord Hobhouse of Woodborough
†Lord Hoffmann
†Lord Hope of Craighead
†Lord Hutton
Lord Irvine of Lairg
Lord Lloyd of Berwick
Lord McCluskey

Lord Mackay of Drumadoon
†Lord Millett
Lord Mustill
†Lord Nicholls of Birkenhead
Lord Phillips of Worth Matravers
  (Master of the Rolls)
†Lord Rodger of Earlsferry
†Lord Saville of Newdigate
†Lord Scott of Foscote
Lord Slynn of Hadley
†Lord Steyn
†Lord Walker of Gestingthorpe
Lord Woolf *(Lord Chief Justice)*

Note: Lords of Appeal who, having attained the age of 75, are no longer eligible to hear appeals, are excluded from this list.

Visit the Vacher Dod Website . . .
www.DodOnline.co.uk

Bishops

By ancient usage the two Anglican archbishops and the bishops of London, Durham and Winchester automatically have seats in the House of Lords. Since the mid-nineteenth century the number of bishops in the House (known as lords spiritual as opposed to lords temporal) has been limited to 26. The remaining diocesan bishops qualify for membership according to seniority, the longest serving bishop outside the Lords succeeding to a vacancy among the lords spiritual.

ARCHBISHOPS (2) AND DIOCESAN BISHOPS (3) EX OFFICIO

Most Rev. Rowan Williams	Canterbury
Most Rev. David Michael Hope	York
Rt Rev. Richard John Carew Chartres	London
Rt Rev. Tom Wright	Durham
Rt Rev. Michael Charles Scott-Joynt	Winchester

BISHOPS IN ORDER OF SENIORITY (21)

		Elected
Rt Rev. Richard Douglas Harries	Oxford	1987
Rt Rev. John Keith Oliver	Hereford	1990
Rt Rev. Thomas Frederick Butler	Southwark	1991
Rt Rev. Nigel Simeon McCulloch	Wakefield	1992
Rt Rev. David Staffurth Stancliffe	Salisbury	1993
Rt Rev. David Edward Bentley	Gloucester	1993
Rt Rev. Michael James Nazir-Ali	Rochester	1994
Rt Rev. John Warren Gladwin	Guildford	1994
Rt Rev. Kenneth William Stevenson	Portsmouth	1995
Rt Rev. Jonathan Sansbury Bailey	Derby	1995
Rt Rev. Christopher William Herbert	St Albans	1995
Rt Rev. Ian Patrick Martyn Cundy	Peterborough	1996
Rt Rev. Peter Robert Foster	Chester	1996
Rt Rev. Richard Lewis	St Edmundsbury and Ipswich	1997
Rt Rev. William Ind	Truro	1997
Rt Rev. Peter Stephen Maurice Selby	Worcester	1997
Rt Rev. Martin Wharton	Newcastle	1997
Rt Rev. John Nicholls	Sheffield	1997
Rt Rev. Colin Bennetts	Coventry	1998
Rt Rev. James Jones	Liverpool	1998
Rt Rev. Timothy Stevens	Leicester	1999

Women members

Women were first admitted into the House of Lords by the Life Peerage Act, 1958. Women peers by succession (indicated with an asterisk) were not admitted into the Upper House until 1963. All four were elected by their fellow hereditary peers.

Baroness Amos   1997
Baroness Andrews   2000
Baroness Anelay of St Johns   1996
Baroness Ashton of Upholland   1999
Baroness Barker   1999
Baroness Billingham   2000
Baroness Blackstone   1987
Baroness Blatch   1987
Baroness Blood   1999
Baroness Boothroyd   2001
Baroness Brigstocke   1990
Baroness Buscombe   1998
Baroness Byford   1996

Baroness Carnegy of Lour   1982
Baroness Chalker of Wallasey   1992
Baroness Cohen of Pimlico   2000
Baroness Cox   1983
Baroness Crawley   1998
Baroness Cumberlege   1990
Baroness Darcy de Knayth*   1332
Baroness David   1978
Baroness Dean of Thornton-le-Fylde   1993
Baroness Delacourt-Smith of Alteryn   1974
Baroness Dunn   1990
Baroness Eccles of Moulton   1990
Baroness Elles   1972

Baroness Emerton   1997
Baroness Falkender   1974
Baroness Farrington of Ribbleton   1994
Baroness Finlay of Llandaff   2001
Baroness Fisher of Rednal   1974
Baroness Flather   1990
Baroness Fookes   1997
Baroness Gale   1999
Baroness Gardner of Parkes   1981
Baroness Gibson of Market Rasen   2000
Baroness Golding   2001
Baroness Goudie   1998
Baroness Gould of Potternewton   1993
Baroness Greenfield   2001
Baroness Greengross   2000
Baroness Hamwee   1991
Baroness Hanham   1999
Baroness Harris of Richmond   1999
Baroness Hayman   1996
Baroness Hilton of Eggardon   1991
Baroness Hogg   1995
Baroness Hollis of Heigham   1990
Baroness Hooper   1985
Baroness Howarth of Breckland   2001
Baroness Howe of Idlecote   2001
Baroness Howells of St Davids   1999
Baroness Hylton-Foster   1965
Baroness James of Holland Park   1991
Baroness Jay of Paddington   1992
Baroness Jeger   1979
Baroness Kennedy of The Shaws   1997
Baroness Knight of Collingtree   1997
Baroness Linklater of Butterstone   1997
Baroness Lloyd of Highbury   1996
Baroness Lockwood   1978
Baroness Ludford   1997
Baroness McFarlane of Llandaff   1979
Baroness McIntosh of Hudnall   1999
Baroness Maddock   1997
Baroness Mallalieu   1991
Countess of Mar*   1114/1404
Baroness Masham of Ilton   1970
Baroness Massey of Darwen   1999
Baroness Michie of Gallanach   2001

Baroness Miller of Chilthorne Domer   1998
Baroness Miller of Hendon   1993
Baroness Morgan of Huyton   2001
Baroness Nicholson of Winterbourne   1997
Baroness Nicol   1982
Baroness Noakes   2000
Baroness Northover   2000
Baroness O'Cathain   1991
Baroness O'Neill of Bengarve   1999
Baroness Oppenheim-Barnes   1989
Baroness Park of Monmouth   1990
Baroness Perry of Southwark   1991
Baroness Pike   1974
Baroness Pitkeathley   1997
Baroness Platt of Writtle   1981
Baroness Prashar   1999
Baroness Ramsay of Cartvale   1996
Baroness Rawlings   1994
Baroness Rendell of Babergh   1997
Baroness Richardson of Calow   1998
Lady Saltoun of Abernethy*   1445
Baroness Scotland of Asthal   1997
Baroness Scott of Needham Market   2000
Baroness Seccombe   1991
Baroness Sharp of Guildford   1998
Baroness Sharples   1973
Baroness Smith of Gilmorehill   1995
Baroness Stern   1999
Baroness Strange*   1628
Baroness Symons of Vernham Dean   1996
Baroness Thatcher   1992
Baroness Thomas of Walliswood   1994
Baroness Thornton   1998
Baroness Trumpington   1980
Baroness Turner of Camden   1985
Baroness Uddin   1998
Baroness Walmsley   2000
Baroness Warnock   1985
Baroness Warwick of Undercliffe   1999
Baroness Whitaker   1999
Baroness Wilcox   1996
Baroness Wilkins   1999
Baroness Williams of Crosby   1993
Baroness Young of Old Scone   1997

Peers who are members of other assemblies

Lord Alderdice	Northern Ireland Assembly
Lord Elis-Thomas	National Assembly for Wales
Baroness Hamwee	Greater London Assembly
Lord Harris of Haringey	Greater London Assembly
Lord Inglewood	European Parliament
Lord Kilclooney	Northern Ireland Assembly
Baroness Ludford	European Parliament
Baroness Nicholson of Winterbourne	European Parliament
Lord Selkirk of Douglas	Scottish Parliament
Lord Tope	Greater London Assembly
Lord Watson of Invergowrie	Scottish Parliament

New members 2003

Viscount Ullswater	27 March
Bishop of Durham	1 May
Bishop of Coventry	1 June
Baron Boyce	16 June
Baron Cullen of Whitekirk	17 June
Bishop of Liverpool	1 July
Bishop of Leicester	1 September

Deaths 2003

Viscount of Oxfuird (Hereditary Peer) died 3 January
Lord Jenkins of Hillhead (Life Baron) died 5 January
Lord Dacre of Glanton (Life Baron) died 26 January
Lord Younger of Leckie (Life Baron and Hereditary Peer) died 26 January
Lord Wilberforce (Life Baron) died 15 February
Lord Boardman (Life Baron) died 10 March
Lord Gladwin of Clee (Life Baron) died 10 April
Lord Ryder of Eaton Hastings (Life Baron) died 12 May
Lord Stodart of Leaston (Life Baron) died 31 May
Lord Butterworth (Life Baron) died 19 June
Lord Shawcross (Life Baron) died 10 July
Lord Perry of Walton (Life Baron) died 17 July
Lord Milner of Leeds (Hereditary Peer) died 20 August

DodOnline

An Electronic Directory without rival . . .

Peers' biographies and photographs available with daily updates *via* the internet

For a *free* trial, call Yasmin Mirza, Aby Farsoun or Michael Mand on 020 7630 7643

Speaker and Deputies

Lord Chancellor

(*ex officio* Speaker)

The Lord Chancellor presides over the deliberations of the House, except when it is in Committee.

Lord Chancellor: Lord Falconer of Thoroton.

Deputy Speakers

Several Lords are appointed to act as Speaker of the House of Lords in the absence of the Lord Chancellor. Deputy Chairmen may also act as Speaker. In the event of none of these Lords being present, the House may appoint its own Speaker.

Viscount Allenby of Megiddo
Lord Ampthill
Lord Boston of Faversham
Lord Brabazon of Tara
Lord Brougham and Vaux
Lord Burnham
Lord Carter
Lord Cope of Berkeley
Baroness Cox
Lord Dean of Harptree
Lord Elton
Baroness Fookes
Lord Geddes
Baroness Gould of Potternewton
Lord Grenfell
Lord Grocott
Lord Haskel
Lord Hogg of Cumbernauld
Baroness Hooper
Baroness Lockwood
Lord Lyell
Countess of Mar
Lord Murton of Lindisfarne
Baroness Pitkeathley
Baroness Ramsay of Cartvale
Viscount Simon
Lord Skelmersdale
Baroness Thomas of Walliswood
Lord Tordoff
Baroness Turner of Camden

Chairman and deputy chairmen

At the beginning of every session, or whenever a vacancy occurs, Lords are appointed by the House to fill the offices of Chairman and Principal Deputy Chairman of Committees. The Chairman takes the Chair in all Committees of the Whole House and is also chairman ex-officio of all committees of the House unless the House otherwise directs. In addition to his duties in the House, he exercises a general supervision and control over Provisional Order Confirmation Bills, Private Bills and Hybrid Instruments. He is also the first of the Deputy Speakers, appointed by Commission. The Principal Deputy Chairman of Committees, in addition to assisting the Chairman in his duties, is appointed to act as Chairman of the European Union Committee. Other Deputy Chairmen may also take the Chair in Committees of the Whole House.

Chairman of Committees:
    Lord Brabazon of Tara
Principal Deputy Chairman of Committees:
    Lord Grenfell
Panel of Deputy Chairmen:
Viscount Allenby of Megiddo
Lord Ampthill
Lord Boston of Faversham
Lord Brougham and Vaux
Lord Burnham
Lord Carter
Lord Cope of Berkeley
Baroness Cox
Lord Dean of Harptree
Lord Elton
Baroness Fookes
Lord Geddes
Baroness Gould of Potternewton
Lord Grocott
Lord Haskel
Lord Hogg of Cumbernauld
Baroness Hooper
Baroness Lockwood
Lord Lyell
Countess of Mar
Lord Murton of Lindisfarne
Baroness Pitkeathley
Baroness Ramsay of Cartvale
Viscount Simon
Lord Skelmersdale
Baroness Thomas of Walliswood
Lord Tordoff
Baroness Turner of Camden

Select Committees

Consolidation Bills: Joint Committee

The function of this Committee is to consider Consolidation Bills and report them with or without amendment to the House. These Bills fall into five categories:

(a) Consolidation Bills, whether public or private, which are limited to re-enacting existing law;

(b) Statute Law Revision Bills, which are limited to repeal of obsolete, spent, unnecessary or superseded enactments;

(c) Bills presented under the Consolidation of Enactments (Procedure) Act 1949, which include corrections and minor improvements to the existing law;

(d) Bills to consolidate any enactments with amendments to give effect to recommendations made by the Law Commissions;

(e) Bills prepared by the Law Commissions to promote the reform of the Statute Law by the repeal of enactments which are no longer of practical utility.

The committee consists of 24 members, 12 from each House, appointed on the recommendation of the Lord Chancellor and the Speaker respectively. The Committee appoints its own chair.

Chairman: Lord Hobhouse of Woodborough
Lords' Members: Lord Acton, Lord Brightman, Lord Campbell of Alloway, Lord Christopher, Viscount Colville of Culross, Earl of Dundee, Baroness Fookes, Lord Janner of Braunstone, Baroness Mallalieu, Lord Phillips of Sudbury, Lord Razzall
Clerk: Tom Mohan

Constitution Committee

Examines constitutional implications of all public bills; reviews operation of the constitution

Chairman: Lord Norton of Louth
Members: Lord Acton, Lord Elton, Lord Fellowes, Baroness Gould of Potternewton, Lord Holme of Cheltenham, Baroness Howells of St Davids, Lord Jauncey of Tullichettle, Lord Lang of Monkton, Lord MacGregor of Pulham Market, Earl of Mar and Kellie, Lord Morgan
Clerk: Thomas Elias

Delegated Powers and Regulatory Reform Committee

Reports whether the provisions of any bill inappropriately delegate legislative powers or whether they subject the exercise of legislative power to an inappropriate degree of parliamentary scrutiny; reports on documents laid before Parliament under section 3(3) of the Deregulation and Contracting Out Act 1994 and on draft orders laid under section 1(4) of that Act; reports on documents laid before Parliament under section 1(1) of the Regulatory Reform Act 2001 and on draft orders laid under section 6(1) of that Act; and performs, in respect of such documents and orders, and subordinate provisions laid under section 4 of the Regulatory Reform Act 2001, the functions performed in respect of other instruments by the Joint Committee on Statutory Instruments.

Chairman: Lord Dahrendorf
Members: Lord Brooke of Sutton Mandeville, Baroness Carnegy of Lour, Lord Desai, Lord Harrison, Lord Mayhew of Twysden, Lord Temple-Morris, Lord Tombs, Lord Wigoder
Clerk: Christine Salmon
Counsel: Allan Roberts

Economic Affairs Committee

Chairman: Lord Peston
Members: Lord Barnett, Lord Burns, Lord Elder, Baroness Hogg, Lord Newby, Lord Oakeshott of Seagrove Bay, Baroness O'Cathain, Lord Paul, Lord Roll of Ipsden, Lord Sheppard of Didgemere, Lord Vinson
Clerk: Susan Michell

European Union Committee

Chairman: Lord Grenfell
Members: Baroness Billingham, Lord Brennan, Lord Cavendish of Furness, Lord Dubs, Lord Hannay of Chiswick, Baroness Harris of Richmond, Lord Jopling, Lord Lamont of Lerwick, Baroness Maddock, Lord Neill of Bladen, Baroness Park of Monmouth, Lord Radice, Lord Scott of Foscote, Earl of Selborne, Lord Shutt of Greetland, Baroness Stern, Lord Williamson of Horton, Lord Woolmer of Leeds
Clerk: Simon Burton
Legal Adviser: Dr Christopher Kerse

Sub-committee A
Economic and Financial Affairs, Trade and External Relations
Chairman: Lord Radice
Members: Lord Armstrong of Ilminster*, Lord Geddes*, Lord Hannay of Chiswick, Lord Jones*, Lord Lamont of Lerwick, Lord Lea of Crondall*, Lord Marlesford*, Lord Sharman*, Lord St John of Bletso*, Lord Sheldon*, Lord Taverne*
Clerk: Dr Richard McLean

Sub-committee B
Energy, Industry and Transport
Chairman: Lord Woolmer of Leeds
Members: Lord Cavendish of Furness, Lord Chadlington*, Baroness Cohen of Pimlico*, Lord Cooke of Islandreagh*, Lord Faulkner of Worcester*, Lord Fearn*, Lord Howie of Troon*, Lord Shutt of Greetland, Lord Skelmersdale*
Clerk: Patrick Wogan

Sub-committee C
Common Foreign and Security Policy
Chairman: Lord Jopling
Members: Lord Bowness*, Lord Harrison*, Baroness Hilton of Eggardon*, Lord Inge*, Lord Maclennan of Rogart*, Lord Morris of Aberavon*, Baroness Park of Monmouth, Lord Powell of Bayswater*, Lord Watson of Richmond*, Lord Williams of Elvel*, Lord Williamson of Horton
Clerk: Audrey Nelson

Sub-committee D
Environment, Agriculture, Public Health and Consumer Protection
Chairman: Earl of Selborne
Members: Baroness Billingham, Lord Carter*, Lord Crickhowell*, Lord Fyfe of Fairfield*, Lord Haskins, Lord Lewis of Newnham*, Lord Livsey of Talgarth*, Baroness Maddock, Countess of Mar*, Lord Palmer*, Lord Renton of Mount Harry*, Lord Walpole*
Clerk: Thomas Radice

Sub-committee E
Law and Institutions
Chairman: Lord Scott of Foscote
Members: Lord Brennan, Lord Fraser of Carmyllie*, Lord Grabiner*, Lord Henley*, Lord Lester of Herne Hill*, Lord Mayhew of Twysden*, Lord Neill of Bladen, Lord Plant of Highfield*, Baroness Thomas of Walliswood*, Lord Thomson of Monifieth*
Clerk: Nicholas Besly
Legal Adviser: Dr Christopher Kerse

Sub-committee F
Social Affairs, Education and Home Affairs
Chairman: Baroness Harris of Richmond
Members: Lord Corbett of Castle Vale*, Lord Dubs, Baroness Gibson of Market Rasen*, Lord Greaves*, Baroness Greengross*, Lord Griffiths of Fforestfach*, Lord King of West Bromwich*, Baroness Knight of Collingtree*, Baroness Stern, Lord Wright of Richmond*
Clerk: Anthony Rawsthorne

*Co-opted members, ie not members of the main committee

House Committee

Chairman: Lord Brabazon of Tara
Members: Lord Barnett, Lord Burlison, Lord Craig of Radley, Lord Hunt of Wirral, Lord Lloyd of Berwick, Lord Renfrew of Kaimsthorn, Lord Rodgers of Quarry Bank, Lord Strathclyde, Baroness Williams of Crosby, Lord Williams of Mostyn, with the Clerk of the Parliaments and the Gentleman Usher of the Black Rod
Clerk: Christopher Johnson

Administration and Works Committee

Chairman: Lord Brabazon of Tara
Members: Lord Cope of Berkeley, Lord Craig of Radley, Baroness Darcy de Knath, Lord Evans of Parkside, Lord Grocott, Bishop of Guildford, Lord Kirkham, Baroness McFarlane of Llandaff, Baroness Massey of Darwen, Lord Phillips of Sudbury, Lord Roper, Lord Shaw of Northstead, with the Clerk of the Parliaments and the Gentleman Usher of the Black Rod
Clerk: Christopher Johnson

Works of Art Committee

Chairman: Baroness Hilton of Eggardon
Members: Lord Cobbold, Lord Eames, Lord Gavron, Lord Luke, Lord Redesdale, Lord Rees, Lord Rees-Mogg, Lord Tordoff, Baroness Trumpington, Baroness Warwick of Undercliffe, with the Clerk of the Parliaments
Clerk: Christopher Johnson

Information Committee

Chairman: Lord Baker of Dorking
Members: Lord Avebury, Lord Burnham, Earl of Erroll, Baroness Gale, Baroness Gardner of Parkes, Baroness Goudie, Lord Hobhouse of Woodborough, Lord Lucas, Lord Methuen, Lord Mitchell, Earl of Sandwich, Baroness Wilkins, with the Clerk of the Parliaments
Clerk: Rebecca Neal

Refreshment Committee

Chairman: Lord Colwyn
Members: Lord Ahmed, Lord Burnham, Viscount of Falkland, Lord Geddes, Lord Grocott, Baroness Harris of Richmond, Lord Palmer, Baroness Pitkeathley, Baroness Rendell of Babergh, Lady Saltoun of Abernethy, Baroness Strange, with the Clerk of the Parliaments
Clerk: Edward Ollard

House of Lords Reform: Joint Committee

Chairman: Jack Cunningham MP
Members: Lord Archer of Sandwell, Viscount Bledisloe, Lord Brooke of Alverthorpe, Lord Carter, Lord Forsyth of Drumlean, Baroness Gibson of Market Rasen, Lord Goodhart, Lord Howe of Aberavon, Lord Oakeshott of Seagrove Bay, Baroness O'Cathain, Earl of Selborne, Lord Weatherill
Clerk: David Beamish

Human Rights: Joint Committee

This Joint Committee of six members from each House considers matters relating to human rights in the United Kingdom (but excluding consideration of individual cases), and has functions relating to remedial orders under the Human Rights Act 1998

Chair: Jean Corston MP
Members: Lord Bowness, Lord Lester of Herne Hill, Lord Parekh, Baroness Perry of Southwark, Baroness Prashar, Baroness Whitaker
Clerk (Lords): Thomas Elias
Legal Adviser: Professor David Feldman

Hybrid Instruments Committee

The function of the Committee is to consider Hybrid Instruments against which Petitions have been presented and to recommend to the House what action should be taken in each case.

Chairman: Lord Brabazon of Tara
Members: Lord Campbell of Alloway, Viscount Craigavon, Baroness Fookes, Lord King of West Bromwich, Lord Luke, Lord Sandberg, Baroness Wilkins
Clerk: Tom Mohan

Liaison Committee

The duties of this Committee are to advise the House on the resources required for select committee work and to allocate resources between select committees; to review the select committee work of the House; to consider requests for *ad hoc* committees and report to the House with recommendations; to ensure effective coordination between the two Houses; and to consider the availability of Lords to serve on committees.

Chairman: Lord Brabazon of Tara
Members: Lord Clinton-Davis, Viscount Colville of Culross, Lord Craig of Radley, Lord Kimball, Baroness Pitkeathley, Baroness Scott of Needham Market, Lord Strathclyde, Baroness Wilcox, Baroness Williams of Crosby, Lord Williams of Mostyn
Clerk: Rhodri Walters

Personal Bills Committee

The duties of the Committee are to examine Petitions for Personal Bills and the provisions of such Bills and consider whether the objects of the Bill are proper to be enacted by a Personal Bill; and if so, to see whether the provisions of the Bill are proper for carrying its purposes into effect, and to make any amendments, either of substance or drafting to the draft Bill for this purpose.

Chairman: Lord Brabazon of Tara
Members: Lord Faulkner of Worcester, Baroness Knight of Collingtree, Lord Templeman, Baroness Thomas of Walliswood
Clerk: Tom Mohan

Privileges, Committee for

The House refers to this Committee questions regarding its privileges and claims of peerage and of precedence. In any claim of peerage, the Committee may not sit unless four Lords of Appeal are present. In certain circumstances claims to Irish Peerages are also referred to the Committee.

Chairman: Lord Brabazon of Tara
Members: Lord Allen of Abbeydale, Lord Cope of Berkeley, Lord Craig of Radley, Lord Graham of Edmonton, Lord Grocott, Lord Mackay of Clashfern, Lord Marsh, Lord Mayhew of Twysden, Lord Merlyn-Rees, Lord Strabolgi, Lord Strathclyde, Lord Trefgarne, Lord Wigoder, Baroness Williams of Crosby, Lord Williams of Mostyn, together with any four Lords of Appeal
Clerk: David Beamish
Clerk (Peerage Claims): Brendan Keith

Sub-committee on Lords' Interests

The Sub-committee oversees the operation of the register of Lords' interests and investigates alleged breaches of the code of conduct.

Chairman: Lord Browne-Wilkinson
Members: Earl Ferrers, Lord Marsh, Baroness Nicol, Lord Wigoder
Clerk to the Sub-Committee and Registrar of Lords' Interests: Brendan Keith

Procedure Committee

Chairman: Lord Brabazon of Tara
Members: Lord Alderdice, Baroness Blatch, Lord Brookeborough, Earl of Caithness, Lord Chalfont, Lord Cope of Berkeley, Lord Craig of Radley, Lord Crickhowell, Lord Denham, Lord Donaldson of Lymington, Lord Geddes, Lord Gladwin of Clee, Lord Goodhart, Baroness Goudie, Lord Grenfell, Lord Grocott, Lord Haskel, Lord Irvine of Lairg, Lord Judd, Baroness Rendell of Babergh, Lord Roper, Lord Strathclyde, Baroness Symons of Vernham Dean, Lord Trefgarne, Lord Waddington, Baroness Warnock, Baroness Williams of Crosby, Lord Williams of Mostyn, with the Clerk of the Parliaments
Clerk: David Beamish

Religious Offences Committee

Chairman: Viscount Colville of Culross
Members: Lord Avebury, Lord Bhatia, Lord Clarke of Hampstead, Lord Grabiner, Lord Griffiths of Fforestfach, Earl of Mar and Kellie, Baroness Massey of Darwen, Baroness Perry of Southwark, Bishop of Portsmouth, Baroness Richardson of Calow, Baroness Wilcox
Clerk: Ian Mackley

Science and Technology Committee

Chairman: Lord Oxburgh
Members: Baroness Finlay of Llandaff, Lord Lewis of Newnham, Lord McColl of Dulwich, Lord Methuen, Lord Mitchell, Lord Patel, Lord Soulsby of Swaffham Prior, Lord Turnberg, Lord Wade of Chorlton, Baroness Walmsley, Baroness Warwick of Undercliffe, Lord Winston, Lord Young of Graffham
Clerk: Mary Robertson

Sub-committee I (Fighting Infection)
Chairman: Lord Soulsby of Swaffham Prior
Members: Baroness Emerton, Baroness Finlay of Llandaff, Lord Haskel, Lord Lewis of Newnham,

Lord McColl of Dulwich, Lord Oxburgh, Lord Patel, Lord Rea, Lord Turnberg, Baroness Walmsley, Baroness Warwick of Undercliffe
Clerk: Rebecca Neal

Sub-committee II (Science and the Regional Development Agencies)
Chairman: Lord Patel
Members: Baroness Finlay of Llandaff, Lord Freeman, Lord Lewis of Newnham, Lord Methuen, Lord Mitchell, Lord Oxburgh, Lord Thomas of Macclesfield, Lord Turnberg, Lord Wade of Chorlton, Lord Winston, Lord Young of Graffham
Clerk: Roger Morgan

Selection, Committee of

The main function of the Committee is to select Lords to form each Select Committee of the House, and the Lords members of Joint Committees. It also selects and proposes to the House the panel of Lords to act as Deputy Chairmen of Committees for each session.

Chairman: Lord Brabazon of Tara
Members: Lord Cope of Berkeley, Lord Craig of Radley, Lord Dubs, Lord Grocott, Lord Roper, Viscount Slim, Lord Strathclyde, Lord Trefgarne, Baroness Williams of Crosby, Lord Williams of Mostyn
Clerk: Christopher Johnson

Standing Orders (Private Bills) Committee

The function of this Committee is to consider cases referred to it on a report from the Examiners of Petitions for Private Bills, who certify whether in the case of a particular Private Bill the Standing Orders have, or have not, been complied with and report the circumstances in cases where they have not. The Committee then considers whether, in such cases, the Standing Orders ought, or ought not, to be dispensed with and, if so, on what conditions.

The parties either appear in person or are represented by their parliamentary agents. Counsel are not heard.

Chairman: Lord Brabazon of Tara
Members: Lord Brett, Lord Brougham and Vaux, Baroness Gould of Potternewton, Lord Greaves, Lord Luke, Lord Naseby, Earl of Sandwich
Clerk: Tom Mohan

Statutory Instruments: Joint Committee

This Joint Committee of seven members from each House scrutinises nearly all Statutory Instruments to ensure they comply with relevant requirements.

Chairman: David Tredinnick MP
Lords' Members: Lord Brougham and Vaux, Lord Greenway, Lord Hardy of Wath, Lord Lea of Crondall, Lord Mancroft, Earl Russell, Lord Skelmersdale
Clerk (Lords): Anna Murphy

Other Committees

House of Lords Collection Trust

The Trust is a registered charity whose aim (in brief) is to establish a collection of works of art, books etc. which will enhance public awareness and understanding of the British political system past and present, placing particular emphasis on the role of the House of Lords and its members.

Trustees
Lord Brabazon of Tara *(Chair)*, Baroness Hilton of Eggardon, Lord Williams of Mostyn, The Clerk of the Parliaments, The Clerk of the Records
Secretary: Christopher Johnson

Lords' Members of British–Irish Inter-parliamentary Body

Lord Alderdice (Associate Member), Lord Brooke of Sutton Mandeville, Lord Dubs, Lord Glentoran, Lord Smith of Clifton, Lord Temple-Morris
British Clerk to the Body: Alda Barry

Lords Members of International Assemblies

United Kingdom delegation to the NATO Parliamentary Assembly

Representatives
Lord Gladwin of Clee
Lord Jopling

Secretary: Shona McGlashan

Parliamentary Assembly of the Council of Europe and the Assembly of Western European Union

Representatives	*Substitutes*
Lord Judd	Baroness Billingham
Baroness Knight of Collingtree	Lord Burlison
Lord Russell-Johnston	Baroness Hooper
	Lord Kilclooney
	Lord Tomlinson

Secretary: James Rhys

Parliamentary Assembly of the Organisation for Security and Co-operation in Europe

Representative	*Substitute*
Baroness Hilton of Eggardon	Lord Ponsonby of Shulbrede
Earl of Northesk	

Secretary: James Rhys

Ecclesiastical Committee: Joint Committee

Lords' Members
Lord Brightman, Lord Campbell of Alloway, Lord Elton, Lord Hardy of Wath, Lord Judd, Lord Laming *(Chair)*, Lord Lloyd of Berwick, Baroness Massey of Darwen, Lord Newby, Baroness Perry of Southwark, Lord Pilkington of Oxenford, Baroness Rendell of Babergh, Lord Wallace of Saltaire, Baroness Wilcox, Lord Williams of Elvel
Secretary: Rhodri Walters

Parliamentary Broadcasting Unit Ltd

Lords' Members
Lord Burnham, Lord Paul, Lord Thomson of Monifieth, Lord Brabazon of Tara

Principal Officers and Officials

Lord Chancellor: Rt Hon Lord Falconer QC
Clerk of the Crown in Chancery: Sir Hayden Phillips KCB

Chairman of Committees

Chairman of Committees: Lord Brabazon of Tara
Principal Deputy Chairman of Committees: Lord Grenfell
Counsel to the Chairman of Committees: Dr Christopher Kerse CB, Allan Roberts,
   David Saunders CB

Department of Clerk of the Parliaments

Clerk of the Parliaments: Paul Hayter LVO
Clerk Assistant and Clerk of Legislation: Michael Pownall
Reading Clerk and Clerk of the Journals: David Beamish
Principal Table Clerk of the Judicial Office, and Registrar of Lords' Interests: Brendan Keith
Clerk of the Journals: David Beamish
Clerk of Committees and Clerk of the Overseas Office: Rhodri Walters DPhil
Principal Finance Officer: Ed Ollard
Head of Human Resources: Dr Philippa Tudor
Clerk of Public Bills: Tom Mohan
Clerk of Private Bills: Tom Mohan
Clerks of Select Committees: Simon Burton, Mary Robertson
Examiners of Petitions for Private Bills: Frank Cranmer, Tom Mohan
Taxing Officer (Private Bills): Tom Mohan
Clerk of the Records: Stephen Ellison
Assistant Clerks of the Records: David Prior, Caroline Shenton DPhil, Frances Grey
Accountant: Andrew Underwood
Librarian: David Jones
Deputy Librarian: Dr Peter Davis
Head of Research Services: Dr Isolde Victory
Director of Public Information: Mary Morgan
Staff Adviser: John Rankine
Internal Auditor: Paul Thompson
Director of Parliamentary Estates: Henry Webber
Editor of the Official Report: Jackie Bradshaw
Deputy Editor: Simon Nicholls

Department of Gentleman Usher of the Black Rod

Gentleman Usher and Serjeant at Arms: Lt Gen Sir Michael Willcocks KCB
Yeoman Usher and Deputy Serjeant at Arms: Brigadier Hedley Duncan MBE
Administration Officer: Brigadier Alastair Clark
Staff Superintendent: Major Mike Charlesworth BEM

Refreshment Department

Superintendent: Timothy Lamming
Banqueting Manager: Rupert Ellwood

Visit the Vacher Dod Website . . .
www.DodOnline.co.uk

All-Party Groups

Subject Groups

All-Party groups are unofficial, and have a membership from both Houses. The groups tend to change frequently according to the Members' interests and with the topicality of the various subjects.

Abuse Investigations

Chair: Claire Curtis-Thomas   *Lab*
Vice-chairs:
  Tim Boswell   *Con*
  Earl Howe   *Con*
Secretary: Diana Organ   *Lab*
Treasurer: Rev Martyn Smyth   *UUP*

Contact: Alex Hampton, 8 Ivanhoe Road, Blundellsands, Merseyside L23 3AH
Tel: 0151-924 2920

Adoption

Chairs:
  Dari Taylor   *Lab*
  Julian Brazier   *Con*
  Mark Oaten   *Lib Dem*
Secretary:
  Baroness Gibson of Market Rasen   *Lab*
Treasurer: Earl Howe   *Con*

Contact: Liv O'Hanlon, 16 Albert Square, London SW8 1BS Tel: 020 7582 9932

Advertising

Chair: Austin Mitchell   *Lab*
Vice-chairs:
  Graham Brady   *Con*
  Nigel Evans   *Con*
  Jane Griffiths   *Lab*
Secretary: Lord McNally   *Lib Dem*

Contact: Jim Rothwell, The Advertising Association, Abford House, 15 Wilton Road, London SW1V 1NJ Tel: 020 7828 2771

Aerospace

Chair: David Borrow   *Lab*
Vice-chairs:
  Gerald Howarth   *Con*
  David Chidgey   *Lib Dem*
Secretary: Mark Tami   *Lab*

Contact: Edward Cox, The Air League, Broadway House, Tothill Street, London SW1H 9NS Tel: 020 7222 8463

Ageing and Older People

Chairs:
  Eddie O'Hara   *Lab*
  Nigel Waterson   *Con*

Vice-chairs:
  Paul Burstow   *Lib Dem*
  Nick Gibb   *Con*
  Linda Gilroy   *Lab*
  Lord Lane of Horsell   *Con*
  Baroness Barker   *Lib Dem*
  Lord Rix   *Crossbencher*
  Baroness Greengross   *Crossbencher*
Secretary: Linda Perham   *Lab*
Treasurer: Roy Beggs   *UUP*

Contact: Katie Ghose, Age Concern England, Astral House, 1268 London Road, London SW16 4ER Tel: 020 8765 7509

AIDS

Chair: Neil Gerrard   *Lab*
Vice-chairs:
  Baroness Masham of Ilton   *Crossbench*
  Francis Maude   *Con*
  Dr Jenny Tonge   *Lab*
  David Borrow   *Lab*
  Lord Fowler of
    Sutton Coldfield   *Con*
Treasurer: Laura Moffatt   *Lab*

Contact: Ms Edwige-Aimee Fortier, c/o Neil Gerrard MP, House of Commons, London SW1A 0AA Tel: 020 7219 6916

Airport for the South East

Chair: Francis Maude   *Con*
Vice-chairs:
  John McDonnell   *Lab*
  Dr Vincent Cable   *Lib Dem*
Secretary: Mark Prisk   *Con*

Contact: Mark Prisk MP, House of Commons, London SW1A 0AA
Tel: 020 7219 8246

Alcohol Misuse

Chair: Ross Cranston   *Lab*
Vice-chairs:
  Marion Roe   *Con*
  Viscount of Falkland   *Lib Dem*

Contact: Geethika Jayatilaka, Director of Policy and Public Affairs, Alcohol Concern, Waterbridge House, 32-36 Loman Street, London SE1 0EE Tel: 020 7928 7377

Aluminium Industry

Chair: Denis Murphy	Lab
Vice-chairs:	
John Cummings	Lab
Alan Beith	Lib Dem
Secretary: Brian Jenkins	Lab
Treasurer: Tim Boswell	Con

Contact: Dr David Harris, Aluminium Federation Ltd, Broadway House, Calthorpe Road, Five Ways, Birmingham B15 1TN Tel: 0121-456 1103

Animal Welfare

Chair: Ian Cawsey	Lab
Vice-chairs:	
Dr Nick Palmer	Lab
Tony Banks	Lab
Secretaries:	
Norman Baker	Lib Dem
Lord Soulsby of Swaffham Prior	Con
Baroness Gale	Lab
Treasurer: Tim Loughton	Con

Contact: Claire Robinson, RSPCA, Wilberforce Way, Oakhurst Business Park, Southwater, West Sussex RH12 1HG Tel: 0870 7540 106

Anti-Semitism, Council against

President:	
Lord Merlyn-Rees	Lab
Vice-Presidents:	
Lord Campbell of Croy	Con
Lord Archer of Sandwell	Lab
Chair: Lord Hunt of Wirral	Con
Vice-chair: James Clappison	Con
Secretary: Lord Janner of Braunstone	Lab
Treasurer: Andrew Dismore	Lab

Contact: Edward Lewin, c/o Lord Janner of Braunstone, House of Lords, London SW1A 0PW Tel: 020 7222 2863

Archaelogical

Chair: Lord Renfrew of Kaimsthorn	Con
Secretary: Lord Redesdale	Lib Dem
Treasurer: Tim Loughton	Con

Contact: Lord Redesdale, House of Lords, London SW1A 0PW. Tel: 020 7219 4342

Architecture and Planning

Honorary Chair: Lord Foster of Thames Bank	Crossbench
Chairs:	
Lord Rogers of Riverside	Lab
Debra Shipley	Lab
Vice-chairs:	
John Gummer	Con
Alan Howarth	Lab
Lord King of Bridgwater	Con
David Wright	Lab

Secretary: Christine Russell	Lab
Treasurer: Lord Palmer	Crossbench

Contact: Stephen Harding, Royal Institute of British Architects, 66 Portland Place, London W1B 1AD Tel: 020 7307 3728

Areas of Outstanding Natural Beauty

Chair: Martin Caton	Lab
Vice-chairs:	
Cheryl Gillan	Con
Matthew Green	Lib Dem
Secretary: Gwyn Prosser	Lab
Treasurer: Sir George Young	Con

Contact: Martin Caton MP, House of Commons, London SW1A 0AA Tel: 020 7219 5111

Arts and Heritage

Chair: Sir Patrick Cormack	Con
Vice-chair: Tam Dalyell	Lab
Secretary: Lord Crathorne	Con
Treasurer: Baroness Noakes	Con

Contact: Lord Crathorne, House of Lords, London SW1A 0PW Tel: 020 7219 5224

Asthma

Chair: Andrew George	Lib Dem
Vice-chairs:	
Dr Howard Stoate	Lab
Viscount Simon	Lab
David Amess	Con

Contact: Louisa Stevens, National Asthma Campaign, Providence House, Providence Place, London N1 0NT Tel: 020 7704 5817

Astronomy and Space Environment Group (APASEG)

Chair: Lord Tanlaw	Crossbench
Vice-chairs:	
Viscount Simon	Lab
Lembit Öpik	Lib Dem

Contact: Professor David Cope, Parliamentary Office of Science and Technology, 7 Millbank, London SW1A 3JA Tel: 020 7219 2848

Autism

Chair: Liz Blackman	Lab
Vice-chairs:	
Stephen Hesford	Lab
Tim Loughton	Con
Lord Clement Jones	Lib Dem
Secretary: Lord Astor of Hever	Con
Treasurer: Brian Cotter	Lib Dem

Contact: Senay Camgoz, National Autistic Society, 393 City Road, London EC1V 1NG Tel: 020 7903 3769

Aviation

Chair: David Marshall — *Lab*
Vice-chairs:
Alan Keen — *Lab*
Anne McIntosh — *Con*
Secretary: David Wilshire — *Con*

Contact: David Marshall MP, House of
Commons, London SW1A 0AA
Tel: 020 7219 5134

Friends of the Bahá'is

Chair: Lembit Öpik — *Lib Dem*
Vice-chairs:
Peter Bottomley — *Con*
Lord Avebury — *Lib Dem*
Ian Stewart — *Lab*
Secretary: David Lepper — *Lab*
Treasurer: Peter Luff — *Con*

Contact: Daniel Wheatley, Bahá'i Community
of the United Kingdom, 27 Rutland Gate,
London SW7 1PD Tel: 020 7590 8786

Back Care

Chair: Paul Burstow — *Lib Dem*
Vice-chair: Janet Dean — *Lab*
Secretary: Christopher Chope — *Con*
Treasurer: Rev Martin Smyth — *UUP*

Contact: Pamela Dow, AS Biss & Co,
100 Rochester Row, London SW1P 1JP
Tel: 020 7219 1196

Bar

Chair: Ross Cranston — *Lab*
Vice-chairs:
Edward Garnier — *Con*
David Lammy — *Lab*
Secretary: Tony Baldry — *Con*
Treasurer: Lord Goodhart — *Lib Dem*

Contact: Elizabeth Jackman, Weber Shandwick,
Fox Court, 14 Gray's Inn Road, London
WC1X 8WS Tel: 020 7067 0304

BBC

Chair: John Grogan — *Lab*
Vice-chairs:
Lembit Öpik — *Lib Dem*
David Ruffley — *Con*
Lord Gordon of Strathblane — *Lab*
Secretary: Anne Begg — *Lab*
Treasurer: Adrian Flook — *Con*

Contact: Anne Begg MP, House of Commons,
London SW1A 0AA Tel: 020 7219 2140

Beer

Chair: John Grogan — *Lab*
Vice-chairs:
Jane Griffiths — *Lab*
Nigel Evans — *Con*
Nigel Jones — *Lib Dem*

Treasurers:
Bill Olner — *Lab*
Nick Hawkins — *Con*
Contact: Robert Humphreys, Pentre Farm,
Pentre, Bucknall, Shropshire SY7 0BU
Tel: 01547 520724

Betting and Gaming

Chairs:
George Howarth — *Lab*
Baroness Golding — *Lab*
Vice-chairs:
James Paice — *Con*
Lord Lipsey — *Lab*
Secretary: Lord Donoughue — *Lab*
Treasurer: Viscount Falkland — *Lib Dem*

Contact: George Howarth MP, House of
Commons, London SW1A 0AA
Tel: 020 7219 6902

Boxing

Chair: James Wray — *Lab*
Vice-chairs:
Kenneth Clarke — *Con*
Ian Stewart — *Lab*
Secretary: David Heathcoat-Amory — *Con*
Treasurer: Ronnie Campbell — *Lab*

Contact: James Wray MP, House of Commons,
London SW1A 0AA Tel: 020 7219 4606

Brain Injury

Chair: Bob Russell — *Lib Dem*
Vice-chair: David Cairns — *Lab*
Secretary: John Hayes — *Con*

Contact: Graham Nickson, Headway – The
Brain Injury Association, 2 Tavistock Place,
London WC1H 9RA Tel: 020 7841 0240

Breast Cancer

Chairs:
Alice Mahon — *Lab*
Marion Roe — *Con*
Patsy Calton — *Lib Dem*
Secretary: Anne Campbell — *Lab*

Contact: Vicki Nash, Breakthrough Breast
Cancer, 6th Floor, Kingsway House,
103 Kingsway, London WC2D 6QX
Tel: 020 7557 6635

British Council

Chair: Derek Wyatt — *Lab*
Vice-chair: Patsy Calton — *Lib Dem*
Secretary: Valerie Davey — *Lab*
Treasurer: Iain Luke — *Lab*

Contact: Brionie Huish, The British Council,
10 Spring Gardens, London SW1A 2BN
Tel: 020 7389 4608

Building Societies and Financial Mutuals

Chair: Adrian Bailey	*Lab*

Vice-chairs:

John Butterfill	*Con*
Kelvin Hopkins	*Lab*
Baroness Maddock	*Lib Dem*
Howard Flight	*Con*
Lord Naseby	*Con*
Secretary: Peter Pike	*Lab*
Treasurer: Bill O'Brien	*Lab*

Contact: Christine Stewart-Munro, Managing Director, CSM Parliamentary Consultants, 17 Dartmouth Street, London SW1H 9BL Tel: 020 7222 9559

Built Environment

Joint chairs:

Tom Cox	*Lab*
Sir Sydney Chapman	*Con*
Vice-chair: Lord Davies of Coity	*Lab*
Secretary: David Chidgey	*Lib Dem*
Treasurer: Lord Gregson	*Lab*

Contact: Douglas Smith, 19 Douglas Street, London SW1P 4PA Tel: 020 7828 0828

Business Services

Chair: Fabian Hamilton	*Lab*
Treasurer: Tim Boswell	*Con*

Contact: Val Hiscock, Business Services Association, Suite 66, Warnford Court, 29 Throgmorton Street, London EC2N 2AT Tel: 020 7786 6302

Cable, Satellite and Digital

Chair: Bill Olner	*Lab*

Vice-chairs:

John Austin	*Lab*
Michael Fabricant	*Con*
Secretary: Dr Robert Spink	*Con*
Treasurer: Andy King	*Lab*

Contact: Samantha Filmer-Cox, Naldred Cottages, 65 Borde Hill Lane, Ardingly, West Sussex RH16 1XR Tel: 01444 415629

Cafod

(Catholic aid and development agency)

Chair: John Battle	*Lab*

Vice-chairs:

Baroness Williams of Crosby	*Lib Dem*
Edward Leigh	*Con*
Secretary: Paul Goggins	*Lab*

Treasurer:

Lord Alton of Liverpool	*Crossbench*

Contact: Paul Goggins MP, House of Commons, London SW1A 0AA Tel: 0161-499 7900

Camping and Traveller Management

Chairs:

Julia Drown	*Lab*
Philip Hammond	*Con*
Secretary: Barbara Follett	*Lab*
Treasurer: Andrew Mackay	*Con*

Contact: Philip Hammond, House of Commons, London SW1A 0AA Tel: 020 7219 4055

Cancer

Chair: Dr Ian Gibson	*Lab*

Vice-chairs:

Julie Kirkbride	*Con*
Sandra Gidley	*Lib Dem*
Dr Richard Taylor	*Ind KHHC*

Contact: Catriona Moore, Policy and Public Affairs Officer, Cancer BACUP, 3 Bath Place, Rivington Street, London EC2A 3JR Tel: 020 7920 7220

Cast Metal

Chair: Tom Watson	*Lab*
Vice-chair: Tony Baldry	*Con*
Secretary: Adrian Bailey	*Lab*

Contact: Adrian Bailey MP, House of Commons, London SW1A 0AA Tel: 020 7219 6060

Charitable Giving

Chair: Sue Doughty	*Lib Dem*

Vice-chairs:

Paul Goggins	*Lab*
Tim Boswell	*Con*

Contact: Peter Gilheany, The Giving Campaign, 6th Floor, Haymarket House, 1a Oxenden Street, London SW1Y 4EE Tel: 020 7930 2636

Charities and the Voluntary Sector

Chair: Tom Levitt	*Lab*

Vice-chairs:

Adrian Sanders	*Lib Dem*
David Drew	*Lab*
Derek Conway	*Con*

Secretaries:

Lord Rix	*Crossbench*
John Burnett	*Lib Dem*
Treasurer: Robert Walter	*Con*

Contact: Pete Moorey, National Council for Voluntary Organisations, Regent's Wharf, 8 All Saints Street, London N1 9RL Tel: 020 7520 6161

Chemical Industry

Chair: Dr Ashok Kumar	*Lab*

Vice-chairs:

Richard Page	*Con*
Dr Vincent Cable	*Lib Dem*

Secretaries:

Michael Connarty	*Lab*
Baroness Hooper	*Con*

Treasurer: Dari Taylor   *Lab*

Contact: Gillian Buzzard, Government and EU Relations Manager, Chemical Industries Association, Kings Building, Smith Square, London SW1P 3JJ Tel: 020 7963 6772

Child Abduction

Chair: Bill Olner	*Lab*

Vice-chairs:

Sir John Stanley	*Con*
Helen Clark	*Lab*

Secretary: Tony Colman   *Lab*
Treasurer: Rev Martyn Smyth   *UUP*

Contact: Denise Carter, Reunite, PO Box 24875, London E1 6FR Tel: 020 7375 3441

Childcare

Chair: Caroline Flint	*Lab*

Vice-chairs:

Julie Kirkbride	*Con*
Paul Keetch	*Lib Dem*

Contact: Stephen Burke, The Daycare Trust, 21 St George's Road, London SE1 6ES Tel: 020 7840 3350

Child Migrants

Chair: Vernon Coaker	*Lab*

Vice-chairs:

Henry Bellingham	*Con*
Candy Atherton	*Lab*

Secretary: Jonathan Shaw   *Lab*
Treasurer: Malcolm Savidge   *Lab*

Contact: Jonathan Shaw MP, House of Commons, London SW1A 0AA Tel: 020 7219 6919

Children

Chairs:

Baroness Massey of Darwen	*Lab*
Hilton Dawson	*Lab*

Vice-chairs:

Baroness David	*Lab*
Baroness Walmsley	*Lib Dem*
Matthew Green	*Lib Dem*
Andrew Lansley	*Con*

Secretaries:

Baroness Goudie	*Lab*
Baroness Howarth of Breckland	*Crossbench*

Treasurer: Earl of Listowel   *Crossbench*

Contact: Lisa Payne, National Children's Bureau, 8 Wakley Street, London EC1V 7QE Tel: 020 7843 6013

Children and Young People in Care

Chair: Hilton Dawson	*Lab*
Vice-chair: Jonathan Shaw	*Lab*
Secretary: Tony McWalter	*Lab*
Treasurer: Earl of Listowel	*Crossbencher*

Contact: Yvonne Wood, The Who Cares Trust, Kemp House, 152-160 City Road, London EC1V 2NP Tel: 020 7251 3117

Children in Wales

Chair: Julie Morgan	*Lab*

Vice-chairs:

Simon Thomas	*PC*
Roger Williams	*Lib Dem*
Lord Roberts of Conwy	*Con*

Secretaries:

Win Griffiths	*Lab*
Dr Hywel Francis	*Lab*

Treasurer: Betty Williams   *Lab*

Contact: Julie Morgan MP, House of Commons, London SW1A 0AA Tel: 020 7219 6960

Chinese in Britain

Chair: Andrew Dismore	*Lab*

Vice-chairs:

Keith Vaz	*Lab*
Karen Buck	*Lab*

Secretary: Mark Field   *Con*
Treasurer: Paul Marsden   *Lib Dem*

Contact: Andrew Dismore MP, House of Commons, London SW1A 0AA Tel: 020 7219 4026

Chocolate and Confectionery Industry

Chair: Claire Ward	*Lab*

Vice-chairs:

Michael Fabricant	*Con*
Bill Wiggin	*Con*

Secretary: Baroness Golding   *Lab*
Treasurer: Lord Faulkner of Worcester   *Lab*

Contact: Pippa Cracknell, c/o Claire Ward MP, House of Commons, London SW1A 0AA Tel: 020 7219 4910

Choir

Chair: Jonathan Sayeed	*Con*

Vice-chairs:

Cheryl Gillan	*Con*
Dari Taylor	*Lab*
Baroness Walmsley	*Lib Dem*

Treasurer: Lord Shutt of Greetland   *Lib Dem*

Contact: Jane Jacomb-Hood, Choir Secretary, The Parliament Choir, PO Box 16, Aldeburgh, Suffolk IP15 5HE Tel: 01728 452392

Christians and Jews

Chair: Sir Sydney Chapman   *Con*
Vice-chair: Baroness
    Richardson of Calow   *Crossbencher*
Secretary: Kerry Pollard   *Lab*
Treasurer: Dr Evan Harris   *Lib Dem*

Contact: Sir Sydney Chapman MP, House of
Commons, London SW1A 0AA
Tel: 020 7219 4542

Christian Fellowship

Chair: Alistair Burt   *Con*
Vice-chairs:
    Jeffrey Donaldson   *UUP*
    Lord Elton   *Con*
    Andy Reed   *Lab*
Secretary: David Drew   *Lab*
Treasurer: Steve Webb   *Lib Dem*

Contact: Laura Durbin, c/o Alistair Burt MP,
House of Commons, London SW1A 0AA
Tel: 020 7219 8132

Cider

Chair: Paul Keetch   *Lib Dem*
Secretary: Shona McIsaac   *Lab*
Treasurer: Robert Syms   *Con*

Contact: Paul Keetch MP, House of Commons,
London SW1A 0AA Tel: 020 7219 2419

Cleaning and Hygiene Industry

Chair: Ben Chapman   *Lab*
Vice-chairs:
    Peter Atkinson   *Con*
    Edward Davey   *Lib Dem*
Secretary/Treasurer: David Crausby   *Lab*

Contact: Tim Rowbottom, c/o Ben Chapman
MP, House of Commons, London SW1A 0AA
Tel: 020 7219 1143

Clothing, Textiles and Footwear

Chair: Judy Mallaber   *Lab*
Vice-chairs:
    Sir Nicholas Winterton   *Con*
    Andy Reed   *Lab*
    Rev Martin Smyth   *UUP*
Secretary: Kali Mountford   *Lab*
Treasurer: Michael Moore   *Lib Dem*

Contact: Judy Mallaber MP, House of
Commons, London SW1A 0AA
Tel: 020 7219 3428

Coalfield Communities

Chair: Michael Clapham   *Lab*
Vice-chairs:
    Bill Etherington   *Lab*
    Bill Cash   *Con*
    Alan Beith   *Lib Dem*
    Ann Clwyd   *Lab*

Secretaries:
    John Grogan   *Lab*
    Jon Trickett   *Lab*
Treasurer: Denis Murphy   *Lab*

Contact: John Grogan MP, House of Commons,
London SW1A 0AA Tel: 020 7219 4403

Commercial Radio

Chair: Chris Smith   *Lab*
Vice-chairs:
    Chris Bryant   *Lab*
    Lord Gordon of Strathblane   *Lab*
    Malcolm Moss   *Con*
Secretary: George Osborne   *Con*
Treasurer: Lord Thomson
    of Monifieth   *Lib Dem*

Contact: Laura Batchelor, Finsbury Group,
52-58 Tabernacle Street, London EC2A 4NJ
Tel: 020 7251 3801

Community Health Councils

Chair: Patrick Hall   *Lab*
Vice-chair: Peter Bottomley   *Con*
Secretary: Linda Perham   *Lab*

Contact: Linda Perham MP, House of
Commons, London SW1A 0AA
Tel: 020 7219 5853

Compassion in Dying

Chair: James Plaskitt   *Lab*
Secretary: Dr Jenny Tonge   *Lib Dem*

Contact: Keith Reed, Voluntary Euthanasia
Society, 13 Prince of Wales Terrace,
London W8 5PG Tel: 020 7937 7781

Connecting Communities

Chair: Kevin Barron   *Lab*
Vice-chairs:
    Baroness Flather   *Con*
    Sandra Gidley   *Lib Dem*
Secretary: Tony Baldry   *Con*
Treasurer: John Battle   *Lab*

Contact: Kevin Barron MP, House of
Commons, London SW1A 0AA
Tel: 020 7219 6306

Conservation and Wildlife

Chair: David Kidney   *Lab*
Vice-chairs:
    Helen Clark   *Lab*
    Peter Bottomley   *Con*
    Lord Brooke of Sutton
        Mandeville   *Con*
Secretary: Jane Griffiths

Contact: Maggie Paun, c/o Helen Clark MP,
House of Commons, London SW1A 0AA
Tel: 020 7219 6062

Constitution and Citizenship

Chair: Dr Tony Wright — Lab
Vice-chairs:
  Lembit Öpik — Lib Dem
  Baroness Gould of Potternewton — Lab
Secretary: David Kidney — Lab
Treasurer: Lord Phillips of Sudbury — Lib Dem

Contact: Dr Tony Wright MP, House of Commons, London SW1A 0AA
Tel: 020 7219 5029

Construction

(Construction industry)
Chair: Tom Cox — Lab
Vice-chairs:
  Sir Sydney Chapman — Con
  Ian Davidson — Lab
Secretary: Bill Olner — Lab
Treasurer: Andy King — Lab

Contact: Adrian Barrick, Building Magazine, 2 Harbour Exchange Square, London E14 9GE
Tel: 020 7560 4141

Consumer Affairs and Trading Standards

Chair: Austin Mitchell — Lab
Vice-chairs:
  Lord Borrie — Lab
  Lord Ezra — Lib Dem
  Sir Teddy Taylor — Con
  Baroness Wilcox — Con
  Norman Baker — Lib Dem
Secretaries:
  Michael Jabez Foster — Lab
  Jim Murphy — Lab

Contact: Paul Allen, Trading Standards Institute, 19 Cranedown, Lewes, East Sussex BN7 3NA Tel: 01273 475877

Corporate Social Responsibility

Chair and Treasurer:
  Baroness Greengross — Crossbench
Vice-chairs:
  David Drew — Lab
  Michael Moore — Lib Dem
  Ian Taylor — Con
  Lord Holme of Cheltenham — Lib Dem
  Lord Sheppard of Didgemere — Con
  Lord Stone of Blackheath — Lab
Secretary: Linda Perham — Lab

Contact: Mark McLaren, Business in the Community, Communications Department, 137 Shepherdess Walk, London N1 7RQ
Tel: 020 7564 8677

Council of Christians and Jews

Chair: Sir Sydney Chapman — Con
Vice-chair:
  Baroness Richardson of Calow — Crossbench
Secretary: Kerry Pollard — Lab
Treasurer: Dr Evan Harris — Lib Dem

Contact: Sir Sydney Chapman MP, House of Commons, London SW1A 0AA
Tel: 020 7219 4542

Cricket

Chair: Lord Hoyle of Warrington — Lab
Vice-chairs:
  Cheryl Gillan — Con
  Andrew Miller — Lab
Secretary: Sir Alan Haselhurst — Con
Treasurer: Colin Breed — Lib Dem

Contact: Sir Alan Haselhurst MP, House of Commons, London SW1A 0AA
Tel: 020 7219 5214

Cricket Club

Vice-President:
  Lord King of Bridgwater — Con
Secretaries:
  Alan Keen — Lab
  Henry Bellingham — Con
Treasurer: Crispin Blunt — Con

Contact: Henry Bellingham MP, House of Commons, London SW1A 0AA
Tel: 020 7219 8484

Cycling

Chair: Jane Griffiths — Lab
Vice-chairs:
  Austin Mitchell — Lab
  Andrew Robathan — Con
  David Rendel — Lib Dem
Secretary: Lord Berkeley — Lab
Treasurer:
  Viscount Craigavon — Crossbench

Contact: Oliver Hatch, 31 Arodene Road, London SW2 2BQ Tel: 020 8671 7561

Deep Vein Thrombosis Awareness

Chair: John Smith — Lab
Vice-chairs:
  Baroness Gardner of Parkes — Con
  Bob Spink — Con
Secretary: David Kidney — Lab
Treasurer:
  Baroness O'Cathain — Con

Contact: David Kidney MP, House of Commons, London SW1A 0AA
Tel: 020 7219 6472

Design and Innovation

Chairs:

Lord Freyberg	*Crossbench*
Barry Sheerman	*Lab*
David Curry	*Con*

Vice-chairs:

Lawrie Quinn	*Lab*
Debra Shipley	*Lab*

Secretary: Gareth Thomas   *Lab*
Treasurer: Bill O'Brien   *Lab*

Contact: Francesca Templeman, Networking for Industry, 7th Floor, 1 Great Cumberland Place, London W1H 7AL Tel: 020 7723 1157

Diabetes

Chair: Adrian Sanders   *Lib Dem*
Vice-chairs:

Cheryl Gillan	*Con*
Anne McIntosh	*Con*

Secretary: David Stewart   *Lab*

Contact: Claire Francis, Public Affairs Officer, Diabetes UK, 10 Queen Anne Street, London W1G 9LH Tel: 020 7424 1120

Dignity at Work

Chair: Baroness Gibson
  of Market Rasen   *Lab*
Vice-chairs:

John Bercow	*Con*
Lady Hermon	*UUP*

Secretary: Valerie Davey   *Lab*

Contact: Valerie Davey MP, House of Commons, London SW1A 0AA Tel: 020 7219 3576

Disability

Chairs:

Lord Ashley of Stoke	*Lab*
John Hayes	*Con*

Vice-chairs:

Rev Martin Smyth	*UUP*
Paul Burstow	*Lib Dem*

Secretary: Dr Roger Berry   *Lab*

Contact: Juliet Tunney, Royal Association for Disability and Rehabilitation, 12 City Forum, 250 City Road, London EC1V 8AF Tel: 020 7566 0126 (extn 200)

Domestic Violence

Chair: Margaret Moran   *Lab*
Vice-chairs:

Debra Shipley	*Lab*
Marion Roe	*Con*

Secretary: Sandra Gidley   *Lib Dem*
Treasurer: Vera Baird   *Lab*

Contact: Nicola Harwin, Women's Aid Federation of England, PO Box 391, Bristol BS99 7WS Tel: 0117-983 7120

Drugs Misuse

Chair: Dr Brian Iddon   *Lab*
Vice-chairs:

Paul Flynn	*Lab*
Laura Moffatt	*Lab*
Lord Mancroft	*Con*
David Cameron	*Con*
Dr Evan Harris	*Lib Dem*

Secretary:
  Baroness Masham of Ilton   *Crossbench*
Treasurer: Lord Rea   *Lab*

Contact: Natasha Vromen, Communications Officer, Drug Scope, 32-36 Loman Street, London SE1 0EE Tel: 020 7922 8609

Earth Sciences

Chair: Jane Griffiths   *Lab*
Vice-chair: Gillian Shephard   *Con*
Treasurer: Lord Oxburgh   *Crossbench*

Contact: Professor Allan Rogers, Room 2/17 Norman Shaw North, Victoria Embankment, London SW1A 2JF Tel: 020 7219 2147

E-Democracy

Chair: Margaret Moran   *Lab*
Vice-chair: Sir George Young   *Con*
Secretary: Richard Allan   *Lib Dem*
Treasurer: Brian White   *Lab*

Contact: Margaret Moran MP, House of Commons, London SW1A 0AA Tel: 020 7219 5049

Education, Pluralism in

Chair: Kerry Pollard   *Lab*
Vice-chair: Phil Willis   *Lib Dem*
Secretary: Nick Palmer   *Lab*

Contact: Sylvie Sklan, Laburnum House, Little Birch, Hereford HR2 8AT Tel: 01981 540239

Electoral Reform

Chair: Richard Burden   *Lab*
Vice-chairs:

Baroness Maddock	*Lib Dem*
Baroness Gould of Potternewton	*Lab*
Austin Mitchell	*Lab*

Secretaries:

Andrew Stunell	*Lib Dem*
Hugh Bayley	*Lab*

Treasurer: Lorna Fitzsimons   *Lab*

Contact: Peter Moorey, Electoral Reform Society, 6 Chancel Stree, London SE1 0UU Tel: 020 7928 1622

Endangered Species

Chair: John Mann   *Lab*
Secretary: Bill Wiggin   *Con*

Contact: John Mann MP, House of Commons, London SW1A 0AA Tel: 020 7219 8130

Endometriosis

Chair: Anne Begg — *Lab*
Vice-chair: Annette Brooke — *Lib Dem*
Secretary: John McDonnell — *Lab*
Treasurer: Jim Dobbin — *Lab*

Contact: John McDonnell MP, Constituency Office, Pump Lane, Hayes, Middlesex UB3 3NB Tel: 020 8569 0010

Energy Studies

Chair: Paddy Tipping — *Lab*
Deputy-chairs:
  John Battle — *Lab*
  Robert Key — *Con*
  Lord Skelmersdale — *Con*
  Andrew Stunell — *Lib Dem*
  Dr Ashok Kumar — *Lab*
Secretaries:
  Michael Clapham — *Lab*
  Sir Michael Spicer — *Con*
Treasurers:
  Lord Fraser of Carmyllie — *Con*
  Denis Murphy — *Lab*

Contact: Christine Stewart-Munro, Managing Director, CSM Parliamentary Consultants, 17 Dartmouth Street, London SW1H 9BL Tel: 020 7222 9559

Engineering

Chair: Bill Olner — *Lab*
Vice-chairs:
  David Crausby — *Lab*
  Lord Methuen — *Lib Dem*
  Richard Page — *Con*
Secretary: Brian Cotter — *Lib Dem*
Treasurer: Lord Haskel — *Lab*

Contact: Jennifer Lindley, 29 Great Peter Street, London SW1P 3LW Tel: 020 7227 0500

English Language Teaching

Chair: David Lepper — *Lab*
Vice-chairs:
  Baroness Anelay of St Johns — *Con*
  Bob Russell — *Lib Dem*
Secretary: Lawrie Quinn — *Lab*
Treasurer: Anne Campbell — *Lab*

Contact: Tony Millns, Association of Recognised English Language Services, 56 Buckingham Gate, London SW1E 6AG Tel: 020 7802 9200

Environment

Chair: Norman Baker — *Lib Dem*
Vice-chairs:
  Joan Walley — *Lab*

David Chaytor — *Lab*
John Horam — *Con*
Baroness Young of Old Scone — *Lab*
Helen Jackson — *Lab*
Simon Thomas — *PlC*

Contact: Adrian Wilkes, 45 Weymouth Street, London W1N 3LD Tel: 020 7935 1689

Epilepsy

Chair: Baroness Gould of Potternewton — *Lab*
Vice-chairs:
  Cheryl Gillan — *Con*
  Norman Lamb — *Lib Dem*
  Lord Smith of Leigh — *Lab*
Secretary: Patsy Calton — *Lib Dem*
Treasurer: John Battle — *Lab*

Contact: Sharon Harvey, General Secretary, Joint Epilepsy Council, PO Box 186, Leeds LS20 8WY Tel: 01943 871852

European Secure Vehicle Alliance

(Reduction of vehicle crime and fraud in the UK and Europe)
Chair: Lord Brougham and Vaux — *Con*
Vice-chairs:
  Steve McCabe — *Lab*
  Paul Goodman — *Con*

Contact: Vivian Nicholas, Executive Director, European Secure Vehicle Alliance, 104 The Fairway, Burnham, Slough SL1 8DY Tel: 01628 661887

European Union Enlargement

Chair: Lord Dubs — *Lab*
Vice-chairs:
  Lord Howells of St Davids — *Lab*
  David Curry — *Con*
Secretaries:
  Baroness Gould of Potternewton — *Lab*
  Calum Macdonald — *Lab*
Treasurer: Mark Oaten — *Lab*

Contact: Baroness Gould of Potternewton, House of Lords, London SW1A 0PW Tel: 020 7219 3138

Export

Chairs:
  Ken Purchase — *Lab*
  Nigel Evans — *Con*
Vice-chair: Viscount Waverley — *Crossbench*

Contact: Douglas Smith, 19 Douglas Street, London SW1P 4PA Tel: 020 7828 0828

Eye Health and Visual Impairment

Chair: David Heath   *Lib Dem*
Vice-chairs:
  Baroness Knight of Collingtree   *Con*
  Jonathan Shaw   *Lab*
Secretary: David Amess   *Con*
Treasurer: Andy Burnham   *Lab*

Contact: Beth Elgood, College of Optometrists, 42 Craven Street, London WC2N 5NG Tel: 020 7839 6000

Fairs and Showgrounds

Co-chairs:
  David Wilshire   *Con*
  Lindsay Hoyle   *Lab*
Vice-chairs:
  Marion Roe   *Con*
  Bill Olner   *Lab*
Secretary: Dr Stephen Ladyman   *Lab*
Treasurer: James Wray   *Lab*

Contact: Keith Miller, Showmen's Guild of Great Britain, Guild House, 41 Clarence Street, Staines, Middlesex TW18 4SY Tel: 01784 461805

Far East Prisoners of War and Internees

Chair: Andrew Dismore   *Lab*
Vice-chair: Roger Gale   *Con*
Secretary: Kelvin Hopkins   *Lab*
Treasurer: Peter Bottomley   *Con*

Contact: Andrew Dismore MP, House of Commons, London SW1A 0AA Tel: 020 7219 4026

Fibromyalgia

Chair: Countess of Mar   *Crossbench*
Vice-chairs:
  Baroness Gibson of Market Rasen   *Lab*
  Oliver Letwin   *Con*
  Martin Salter   *Lab*
Secretary: Jane Griffiths   *Lab*
Treasurer: Liz Blackman   *Lab*

Contact: Jane Griffiths MP, House of Commons, London SW1A 0AA Tel: 020 7219 4197

Film Industry

Chair: Claire Ward   *Lab*
Vice-chairs:
  Michael Fabricant   *Con*
  Lord Faulkner of Worcester   *Lab*
Treasurer: Lord Corbett
  of Castle Vale   *Lab*

Contact: Claire Ward MP, House of Commons, London SW1A 0AA Tel: 020 7219 4910

Financial Markets and Services

Chair: Nigel Beard   *Lab*
Vice-chair: Tim Loughton   *Con*
Secretary: David Ruffley   *Con*

Contact: Patricia Duncan, Futures and Options Association, 4th Floor, 150 Minories, London EC3N 1LS Tel: 020 7426 7258

Fire Safety

Chairs:
  Michael Clapham   *Lab*
  David Amess   *Con*
Vice-chair: Lord Brookman   *Lab*
Secretary: Bob Russell   *Lib Dem*
Treasurer: Jim Knight   *Lab*

Contact: Douglas Smith, 19 Douglas Street, London SW1P 4PA Tel: 020 7828 0828

Fireworks

Chair: Shona McIsaac   *Lab*
Vice-chairs:
  Sir Teddy Taylor   *Con*
  Annette Brooke   *Lib Dem*
  Linda Gilroy   *Lab*
Secretary: Christine Russell   *Lab*
Treasurer: Barry Gardiner   *Lab*

Contact: Christine Russell MP, House of Commons, London SW1A 0AA. Tel: 020 7219 6398

Fisheries

Chair: Austin Mitchell   *Lab*
Vice-chairs:
  Anthony Steen   *Con*
  Andrew George   *Lib Dem*
  Alex Salmond   *SNP*
Secretary: Frank Doran   *Lab*
Treasurer: Bob Blizzard   *Lab*

Contact: Frank Doran MP, House of Commons, London SW1A 0AA Tel: 020 7219 3481

Flood Prevention

Chair: Michael John Foster   *Lab*
Vice-chairs:
  Andrew Lansley   *Con*
  Dr Richard Taylor   *Ind*
  Norman Baker   *Lib Dem*
Secretary: John Grogan   *Lab*

Contact: Daniel Guthrie, Luther Pendragon, Priory Court, Pilgrim Street, London EC4V 6DR Tel: 020 7618 9100

Fluoridation

(Prevention of)
Chair: James Wray   *Lab*
Vice-chairs:
  Brian Donohoe   *Lab*
  Earl Baldwin of Bewdley   *Crossbencher*

Secretary: Bill Etherington   *Lab*

Contact: Bill Etherington MP, House of Commons, London SW1A 0AA Tel: 020 7219 4603/0191

Food and Health Forum

Chair: Lord Rea   *Lab*
Vice-chairs:
  Dr Ian Gibson   *Lab*
  Tony Baldry   *Con*
  Baroness Gibson of Market Rasen   *Lab*
Secretary:
  Earl Baldwin of Bewdley   *Crossbench*
Treasurer: Rev Martin Smyth   *UUP*

Contact: Helen Donoghue, Central Lobby Consultants, 1 Millbank, London SW1P 3JZ Tel: 020 7222 1265

Football

Chair: Alan Keen   *Lab*
Vice-chairs:
  John Greenway   *Con*
  Claire Ward   *Lab*
  Bob Russell   *Lib Dem*
Secretary: Peter Pike   *Lab*
Treasurer: Clive Betts   *Lab*

Contact: Alan Keen MP, House of Commons, London SW1A 0AA Tel: 020 7219 2819

Football Club

Chair: Gerry Sutcliffe   *Lab*
Vice-chair: Alan Keen   *Lab*
Secretary: Ian Stewart   *Lab*
Treasurer: Clive Betts   *Lab*

Contact: Ian Stewart MP, House of Commons, London SW1A 0AA Tel: 020 7219 6175

Forestry

Chair: Paddy Tipping   *Lab*
Vice-chair: Lawrie Quinn   *Lab*
Secretary: Peter Atkinson   *Con*
Treasurer: Baroness Sharples   *Con*

Contact: Peter Wilson, Forestry Industries Development Council, 53 George Street, Edinburgh EH2 2HT Tel: 0131-220 9290

FRAME (Fund for the Replacement of Animals in Medical Experiments)

Chair: Dr Nick Palmer   *Lab*
Vice-chairs:
  John Butterfill   *Con*
  Bill Etherington   *Lab*
Secretary: Fabian Hamilton   *Lab*
Treasurer: Norman Baker   *Lib Dem*

Contact: Gerard Duvé, c/o FRAME, Evergreen Cottage, The Green, Ripley, Surrey GU3 6AJ Tel: 01483 224650

Free Trade

Chair: John Baron   *Con*
Vice-chair: Hugh Bayley   *Lab*
Secretary: Colin Challen   *Lab*
Treasurer: Robert Walter   *Con*

Contact: Colin Challen MP, House of Commons, London SW1A 0AA Tel: 020 7219 8260

Friends of Islam

Chair: Christine McCafferty   *Lab*
Vice-chairs:
  Khalid Mahmood   *Lab*
  Gary Streeter   *Con*
  Simon Hughes   *Lib Dem*
Secretary: Gareth Thomas   *Lab*
Treasurer: Oona King   *Lab*

Contact: Ahmed Suleiman, 50 Brook Mews, London W1K 4ED Tel: 07785 730409

Fruit Industry

Chair: Lord Mayhew of Twysden   *Con*
Vice-chair: Lord Mackie of Benshie   *Lib Dem*
Secretary: Hugh Robertson   *Con*
Treasurer: Dr Stephen Ladyman   *Lab*

Contact: Carole Quinlan, Marden Fruit Show Society, Bradbourne House, East Malling, West Malling, Kent ME19 6DZ Tel: 01732 874564

Funerals and Bereavement

Chair: Bill Olner   *Lab*
Vice-chair: Rev Martin Smyth   *UUP*
Secretary: Jim Cunningham   *Lab*
Treasurer: Janet Dean   *Lab*

Contact: James Pawsey, Chilton House, Chilton, Warwickshire CV7 9HT Tel: 02476 612922

Further Education and Lifelong Learning

Chairs:
  Dennis Turner   *Lab*
  David Chaytor   *Lab*
Vice-chairs:
  Alistair Burt   *Con*
  Lord Dormand of Easington   *Lab*
  Phil Willis   *Lib Dem*
Secretary: Khalid Mahmood   *Lab*
Treasurer: Kelvin Hopkins   *Lab*

Contact: Christopher Walden, Parliamentary Officer, Association of Colleges, 5th Floor, Centre Point, 103 New Oxford Street, London WC1A 1RG Tel: 020 7827 4600

Future of Europe

Chair: Gordon Marsden   *Lab*
Vice-chairs:
  Lord Tomlinson   *Lab*
  Lord Biffen   *Con*
Contact: Oliver Pauley, c/o Gordon Marsden
MP, House of Commons, London SW1A 0AA
Tel: 020 7219 1262

Gardening and Horticulture

Chair: Lord Walker of Doncaster   *Lab*
Vice-chairs:
  Bob Russell   *Lib Dem*
  Marion Roe   *Con*
Secretary: Brian Donohoe   *Lab*
Contact: Mark Glover, Chelgate Ltd, 1 Tanner
Street, London SE1 3LE Tel: 020 7939 7997

Gas Safety

Chair: Jon Trickett   *Lab*
Vice-chairs:
  Andrew Hunter   *Con*
  Tom Brake   *Lib Dem*
  Dr Bob Spink   *Con*
Secretary: David Lepper   *Lab*
Treasurer: Bill O'Brien   *Lab*
Contact: Jon Trickett MP, House of Commons,
London SW1A 0AA Tel: 020 7219 5074

Global Security and Non-Proliferation

Convener: Malcolm Savidge   *Lab*
Vice-Conveners:
  David Davis   *Con*
  Menzies Campbell   *Lib Dem*
  Austin Mitchell   *Lab*
Secretary: Mike Gapes   *Lab*
Contact: Malcolm Savidge MP, House of
Commons, London SW1A 0AA
Tel: 020 7219 3570

Globe UK

(sustainable development)
Chair: Joan Ruddock   *Lab*
Vice-chairs:
  Peter Bottomley   *Con*
  Tom Brake   *Lib Dem*
  Sue Doughty   *Lib Dem*
  David Drew   *Lab*
  Alan Simpson   *Lab*
  Simon Thomas   *PlC*
  Gregory Barker   *Con*
Secretary: David Chaytor   *Lab*
Treasurer: Malcolm Bruce   *Lib Dem*
Contact: Shelaine Weller, Room LG6,
Norman Shaw North, London SW1A 2JF
Tel: 020 7219 2260

Golf

Joint Captains:
  Humfrey Malins   *Con*
  John McFall   *Lab*
Vice-Captain: Lord Davies of Oldham   *Lab*
Secretary: Jonathan Sayeed   *Con*
Contact: Rupert Ellwood, Banqueting Manager,
House of Lords, London SW1A 0PW
Tel: 020 7219 3356

Great Lakes Region and Genocide Prevention

Chair: Oona King   *Lab*
Vice-chairs:
  Andrew Robathan   *Con*
  Ann McKechin   *Lab*
Secretaries:
  Julia Drown   *Lab*
  Dr Jenny Tonge   *Lib Dem*
Treasurer: Eric Joyce   *Lab*
Contact: Ben Shepherd, c/o Oona King MP,
House of Commons, London SW1A 0AA
Tel: 020 7219 1165

Greyhound

Chair; Dennis Turner   *Lab*
Vice-chairs:
  Richard Page   *Con*
  Lord Evans of Parkside   *Lab*
Secretary: Neil Gerrard   *Lab*
Treasurer: Baroness Golding   *Lab*
Contact: Peter Wilson, c/o Lindsay Hoyle MP,
House of Commons, London SW1A 0AA
Tel: 020 7219 3515

Guide Association

Chair: Chris McCafferty   *Lab*
Vice-chairs:
  David Amess   *Con*
  Diana Organ   *Lab*
Secretary: Stephen Pound   *Lab*
Treasurer: Tim Boswell   *Con*
Contact: Paul Werb, The Guide Association,
17–19 Buckingham Palace Road,
London SW1W 0PT Tel: 020 7834 6242

Gun Crime

Chair: Diane Abbott   *Lab*
Vice-chairs:
  Baroness Anelay of St Johns   *Con*
  Stephen McCabe   *Lab*
  Simon Hughes   *Lib Dem*
Secretary: Tony Lloyd   *Lab*
Contact: Laurence Meehan, Saferworld,
46 Grosvenor Gardens, London SW1W OE8
Tel: 020 7881 9289

Haemophilia

Chair: Michael Connarty	*Lab*
Vice-chair: Robert Syms	*Con*
Secretary/Treasurer: Paddy Tipping	*Lab*
Honorary President:	
Lord Morris of Manchester	*Lab*

Contact: Sue Rocks, Haemophilia Society, Chesterfield House, 385 Euston Road, London NW1 3AU Tel: 020 7380 0600

Headache Disorders

Chair: Phil Hope	*Lab*
Vice-chair: Stephen O'Brien	*Con*
Secretary: Jane Griffiths	*Lab*
Treasurer: David Heath	*Lib Dem*

Contact: Ann Turner, Migraine Action Association, Unit 6, Oakley Hay Lodge Business Park, Great Folds Road, Great Oakley, Northamptonshire NN18 9AS Tel: 01536 461333

Health

Chairs:	
Dr Howard Stoate	*Lab*
Baroness Cumberlege	*Con*
Baroness Masham of Ilton	*Crossbench*
Secretary: Patrick Hall	*Lab*
Treasurer: David Drew	*Lab*

Contact: Andrew Bonser, Networking for Industry, 7th Floor, 1 Great Cumberland Place, London W1H 7AZ Tel: 020 7723 8947

Heart Disease

Chair: Chris Ruane	*Lab*
Vice-chairs:	
Tony Baldry	*Con*
Nigel Jones	*Lib Dem*
Secretary: Lord Elder	*Lab*
Treasurer: Baroness Gardner of Parkes	*Con*

Contact: Maura Gillespie, British Heart Foundation, 14 Fitzhardinge Street, London W1H 6DH Tel: 020 7487 7158

Heavily Indebted Poor Countries

Chair: Julia Drown	*Lab*
Vice-chairs:	
Peter Bottomley	*Con*
Stephen O'Brien	*Con*
Secretaries:	
Andy Reed	*Lab*
Steve Webb	*Lib Dem*
Treasurer: Vernon Coaker	*Lab*

Contact: Ms Zuleikha Salim-Said, c/o Julia Drown MP, House of Commons, London SW1A 0AA Tel: 020 7219 1429

Homelessness and Housing Need

Chairs:	
David Curry	*Con*
Andrew Love	*Lab*
Vice-chairs:	
Peter Pike	*Lab*
Peter Bottomley	*Con*
Adrian Sanders	*Lib Dem*
Secretary: Baroness Maddock	*Lib Dem*
Treasurer: Baroness Thornton	*Lab*

Contact: Robina Rafferty, CHAS, 209 Old Marylebone Road, London NW1 5QT Tel: 020 7723 7273

Hospice

Chair: Marion Roe	*Con*
Vice-chairs:	
Fabian Hamilton	*Lab*
Sir Teddy Taylor	*Con*
Secretaries:	
Edward Davey	*Lib Dem*
Tony Colman	*Lab*

Contact: Marion Roe MP, House of Commons, London SW1A 0AA Tel: 020 7219 3528

Housing and Planning

Chairs:	
David Drew	*Lab*
Tony Baldry	*Con*
Vice-chair/	
Secretary: Matthew Green	*Lib Dem*

Contact: Feyi Rodway, Campaign Support Officer, Council for the Protection of Rural England, 128 Southwark Street, London SE1 0SW Tel: 020 7981 2800

Housing Co-operatives

Chair: David Drew	*Lab*
Vice-chair: Adrian Sanders	*Lib Dem*
Secretary: David Lepper	*Lab*

Contact: David Rogers, CDS Co-operatives, 3 Marshalsea Road, London SE1 1EP Tel: 020 7397 5711

Humanist

Chair: Lord Hughes of Woodside	*Lab*
Vice-chairs:	
Viscount Falkland	*Lib Dem*
Baroness Flather	*Con*
Kelvin Hopkins	*Lab*
Secretary: Lord Dormand of Easington	*Lab*

Contact: Lord Dormand of Easington, House of Lords, London SW1A 0PW Tel: 020 7219 5419

Human Rights

Chair: Ann Clwyd — Lab
Vice-chairs:
Lord Avebury — Lib Dem
Jeremy Corbyn — Lab
Robert Walter — Con
Secretary: Julie Morgan — Lab
Treasurer: Mark Oaten — Lib Dem

Contact: Ann Clwyd MP, House of Commons, London SW1A 0AA Tel: 020 7219 6609

Infertility

Chairs:
Kevin Barron — Lab
Lord Patel — Crossbench
Vice-chairs:
Andrew Lansley — Con
Diana Organ — Lab
Secretary: Paul Marsden — Lib Dem
Treasurer: Bob Russell — Lib Dem

Contact: Kevin Barron MP, House of Commons, London SW1A 0AA Tel: 020 7219 6306

Information Technology (PITCOM)

Chair: John McWilliam — Lab
Vice-chairs:
Ian Taylor — Con
Andrew Miller — Lab
Secretary: Roger Gale — Con
Treasurer: Brian White — Lab

Contact: Frank Richardson, 22 Gloucester Mews, London W1H 8BA Tel: 020 7487 4872

Insurance and Financial Services

Chair: John Greenway — Con
Vice-chairs:
Baroness Turner of Camden — Lab
Nick Hawkins — Con
Dr Vincent Cable — Lib Dem
Secretaries:
Jim Cousins — Lab
John Butterfill — Con

Contact: David Worsfold, Post Magazine, 39 Earlham Street, London WC2H 9LT Tel: 020 7306 7002

Integrated and Complementary Healthcare

Presidents:
Lord Colwyn — Con
Earl Baldwin of Bewdley — Crossbench
Chairs:
Jean Corston — Lab
David Tredinnick — Con

Secretary: Alan Simpson — Lab
Contact: David Tredinnick MP, 5/19 Norman Shaw North, Victoria Embankment, London SW1A 2HZ Tel: 020 7219 4474

Integrated Education in Northern Ireland

Chair: Lord Dubs — Lab
Vice-chairs:
Sir Brian Mawhinney — Con
Lembit Öpik — Lib Dem
Secretary: Baroness Blood — CB
Treasurers:
Lord Donoughue — Lab
Crispin Blunt — Con

Contact: Lord Dubs, House of Lords, London SW1A 0PW Tel: 020 7219 3590

Intellectual Property Protection

Chair: Janet Anderson — Lab
Vice-chair: Peter Luff — Con
Secretary: Dr Vincent Cable — Lib Dem
Treasurer: Brian White — Lab

Contact: Sophie Sheehan, Luther Pendragon, Priory Court, Pilgrim Street, London EC4V 6DR Tel: 020 7618 9100

Intelligent Energy

Chair: David Chaytor — Lab
Vice-chair: John Horam — Con
Secretary: Sue Doughty — Lib Dem
Treasurer: Simon Thomas — PlC

Contact: David Chaytor MP, House of Commons, London SW1A 0AA Tel: 020 7219 6625

Internet

Chair: Derek Wyatt — Lab
Vice-chairs:
Michael Fabricant — Con
Richard Allan — Lib Dem
Secretary: Dr Nick Palmer — Lab
Treasurer: Brian White — Lab

Contact: Dr Nick Palmer MP, House of Commons, London SW1A 0AA Tel: 020 7219 3000

Irish in Britain

Chair: Kevin McNamara — Lab
Vice-chairs:
Simon Hughes — Lib Dem
Michael Mates — Con
Margaret Moran — Lab
Secretary/Treasurer: John McDonnell — Lab

Contact: John McDonnell MP, House of Commons, London SW1A 0AA Tel: 020 8569 0160

Jazz Appreciation

Chairs:

Michael Connarty	*Lab*
Lord Colwyn	*Con*
Secretary: Kelvin Hopkins	*Lab*
Treasurer: Lord Dormand of Easington	*Lab*

Contact: Chris Hodgkins, Jazz Services Ltd, First Floor, 132 Southwark Street, London SE1 0SW Tel: 020 7928 9089

Kidney

(As health issue)

Chairs:

Dr Evan Harris	*Lib Dem*
Peter Pike	*Lab*
John Randall	*Con*

Secretaries:

Rev Martin Smyth	*UUP*
Paul Marsden	*Lab*

Treasurers:

Linda Gilroy	*Lab*
Lindsay Hoyle	*Lab*

Contact: Timothy Statham, National Kidney Federation, 56 Sapcote Road, Burbage, Leicestershire LE10 2AU Tel: 01455 619128

Landmine Eradication

Chair: Frank Cook	*Lab*
Vice-chair: Lord Jopling	*Con*
Secretary: Jenny Tonge	*Lib Dem*
Treasurer: Brian White	*Lab*

Contact: Richard Lloyd, Landmine Action, 1st Floor, 89 Albert Embankment, London SE1 7TP Tel: 020 7820 0222

Learning Disabilities

Chairs:

Tom Clarke	*Lab*
Lord Rix	*Crossbench*

Vice-chairs:

Peter Bottomley	*Con*
Huw Edwards	*Lab*
Mike Hancock	*Lib Dem*
Secretary: Viscount Tenby	*Crossbench*
Treasurer: Baroness Wilkins	*Lab*

Contact: Anthony Noun, Mencap, 123 Golden Lane, London EC1Y 0RT Tel: 020 7696 5568

Leisure

Chair: Barry Gardiner	*Lab*

Vice-chairs:

Nick Hawkins	*Con*
Nigel Jones	*Lib Dem*
Secretary: Gareth R Thomas	*Lab*

Contact: Toby Greene, c/o Barry Gardiner MP, House of Commons, London SW1A 0AA Tel: 020 7219 2104

Libraries and Information Management

Chair: Linda Perham	*Lab*

Vice-chairs:

Lord Tope	*Lib Dem*
Peter Bottomley	*Con*
Secretary: Christine Russell	*Lab*
Treasurer: Bill O'Brien	*Lab*

Contact: Pamela Dow, AS Biss & Co, 100 Rochester Row, London SW1P 1JP Tel: 020 7312 6717

Lighting

(Industry and technology)

Chairs:

Phil Hope	*Lab*
Tony Baldry	*Con*

Secretaries:

Joan Walley	*Lab*
Edward Davey	*Lib Dem*

Contact: Phil Hope MP, House of Commons, London SW1A 0AA Tel: 020 7219 2549

Local Government Councillors

Chair: John Cummings	*Lab*
Vice-chair: Sir Teddy Taylor	*Con*
Secretary: Denis Murphy	*Lab*
Treasurer: Bob Russell	*Lib Dem*

Contact: Councillor Grahame Morris, c/o John Cummings MP, Seaton Holme, Hall Walks, Easington Village, Peterlee, County Durham SR8 3BS Tel: 0191-527 3773

Local Hospitals

Chair: Peter Viggers	*Con*
Vice-chair: Dr Richard Taylor	*Ind KHHC*
Secretary: Andrew George	*Lib Dem*

Contact: Peter Viggers MP, House of Commons, London SW1A 0AA Tel: 020 7219 5081

Lupus (Systemic Lupus Erythematosus)

Chair: Janet Dean	*Lab*

Vice-chairs:

Dr Evan Harris	*Lib Dem*
Robert Walter	*Con*
Secretary: James Paice	*Con*
Treasurer: Dennis Turner	*Lab*

Contact: Carol McGirr, c/o Janet Dean MP, House of Commons, London SW1A 0AA Tel: 020 7219 6320

Management

Chair: Tony Colman	*Lab*
Deputy-chair: Lord Haskel	*Lab*
Vice-presidents:	
Dr Vincent Cable	*Lib Dem*
Archie Norman	*Con*

Contact: Petra Cook, Head of Policy, Institute of Management, 2 Savoy Court, Strand, London WC2R 0EZ Tel: 020 7421 2708

Management Consultancy

Chair: Mark Todd	*Lab*
Vice-chairs:	
Brian White	*Lab*
Baroness Buscombe	*Con*

Contact: Alix Billam, Management Consultancies Association, 49 Whitehall, London SW1A 2BX Tel: 020 7321 3990

Manchester 2002 Commonwealth Games

Chair: Tony Lloyd	*Lab*
Vice-chairs:	
Nicholas Winterton	*Con*
Paul Goggins	*Lab*
Secretary: Andrew Stunell	*Lib Dem*
Treasurer: Nick Hawkins	*Con*

Contact: Tony Lloyd MP, House of Commons, London SW1A 0AA Tel: 020 7219 3488

Manufacturing Industry

Chairs:	
Barry Sheerman	*Lab*
Brian Cotter	*Lib Dem*
Lord Paul	*Lab*
Vice-chairs:	
Peter Pike	*Lab*
Richard Page	*Con*
Mark Tami	*Lab*
Secretary: Bill O'Brien	*Lab*
Treasurer: Liz Blackman	*Lab*

Contact: Andrew Bonser, Networking for Industry, Irwin House, 118 Southwark Street, London SE1 0SN Tel: 020 7202 9415

Maritime

Chair: Peter Bottomley	*Con*
Vice-chairs:	
Jonathan Sayeed	*Con*
Lord Greenway	*Crossbench*
Secretaries:	
Stephen Hesford	*Lab*
Lord Geddes	*Con*
Treasurer: Tim Loughton	*Con*

Contact: Commander Michael Ranken, 44 Castelnau Mansions, Castelnau, Barnes, London SW13 9QU Tel: 020 8748 4103

Markets Industry

Chairs:	
Dennis Turner	*Lab*
Lord Wade of Chorlton	*Con*
Vice-chairs:	
Liz Blackman	*Lab*
Ann Coffey	*Lab*
Peter Bottomley	*Con*
David Chidgey	*Lib Dem*
Colin Pickthall	*Lab*
Secretary: Lord Graham of Edmonton	*Lab*

Contact: Lord Graham of Edmonton, House of Lords, London SW1A 0PW Tel: 020 7219 6704

Maternity

Chair: Julia Drown	*Lab*
Vice-chairs:	
Baroness Cumberlege	*Con*
Lord Patel of Blackburn	*Crossbench*
Secretary: Sandra Gidley	*Lib Dem*
Treasurer: Earl of Listowel	*Crossbench*

Contact: Catherine Eden, Parliamentary Officer, National Childbirth Trust, Alexandra House, Oldham Terrace, London W3 6NH Tel: 0870 770326

ME (Myalgic Encephalomyelitis)

Chair: Anthony D Wright	*Lab*
Vice-chairs:	
Paul Burstow	*Lib Dem*
Rev Martin Smyth	*UUP*
Secretary: Stephen McCabe	*Lab*
Treasurer: David Amess	*Con*

Contact: Anthony D Wright MP, 21 Euston Road, Great Yarmouth, Norfolk NR30 1DZ Tel: 01493 332291

Media

Chair: Austin Mitchell	*Lab*
Vice-chairs:	
Derek Wyatt	*Lab*
Lord Taylor of Warwick	*Con*
Lord Lipsey	*Lab*
Secretaries:	
John Greenway	*Con*
Roger Gale	*Con*
Hon Treasurer: Peter Bottomley	*Con*

Contact: Christopher Whitehouse, Third Floor, 9 Old Queen Street, London SW1H 9JA Tel: 020 7222 4179

Men's Health

Chair: Dr Howard Stoate	*Lab*
Vice-chairs:	
Peter Bottomley	*Con*
Sandra Gidley	*Lib Dem*
Linda Perham	*Lab*

Contact: Colin Penning, The Men's Health Forum, Tavistock House, Tavistock Square, London WC1H 9HR Tel: 020 7388 4449

Mental Health

Chairs:

Dr Lynne Jones	*Lab*
Virginia Bottomley	*Con*
Sandra Gidley	*Lib Dem*
Secretary: Lord Alderdice	*Lib Dem*

Contact: Agnes Wheatcroft, Royal College of Psychiatrists, 17 Belgrave Square, London SW1X 8PG Tel: 020 7235 2351

Methodist

Chair: Donald Anderson	*Lab*
Vice-chair: Colin Breed	*Lib Dem*
Secretary: David Wilshire	*Con*
Treasurer: David Burnside	*UUP*

Contact: David Wilshire MP, House of Commons, London SW1A 0AA Tel: 020 7219 3534

Microfinance/Microcredit

Chair: Annette Brooke	*Lib Dem*
Secretary: John Barrett	*Lib Dem*
Treasurer: Robert Syms	*Con*

Contact: Ms Peta Cubberley, c/o Annette Brooke MP, House of Commons, London SW1A 0AA Tel: 020 7219 8193

Middle Way

(In relation to hunting and other field sports)

Chairs:

Baroness Golding	*Lab*
Peter Luff	*Con*
Lembit Öpik	*Lib Dem*
Vice-chair: Alan Beith	*Lib Dem*

Secretaries:

Lord Carlile of Berriew	*Lib Dem*
Kate Hoey	*Lab*
Treasurer: Baroness Sharples	*Con*

Contact: James Barrington, c/o Lembit Öpik MP, House of Commons, London SW1A 0AA Tel: 020 7219 1144

Minerals

Chairs:

Tom Levitt	*Lab*
Stephen O'Brien	*Con*
Vice-chair: Earl of Shrewsbury	*Con*
Treasurer: Bill O'Brien	*Lab*
Secretary: Bill Olner	*Lab*

Contact: Joe Phelan, Hill & Knowlton, 35 Red Lion Square, London WC1R 4SG Tel: 020 7413 3124

Mobile Communications

Chair: Phil Willis	*Lib Dem*

Vice-chairs:

Derek Wyatt	*Lab*
Mark Oaten	*Lib Dem*
Peter Bottomley	*Con*
Secretary: Paul Truswell	*Lab*
Treasurer: Brian White	*Lab*

Contact: Phil Willis MP, House of Commons, London SW1A 0AA Tel: 020 7219 3846

Motor

(Motor and motorsport industries)

Chair: Richard Burden	*Lab*

Vice-chairs:

Michael Jack	*Con*
Lord Corbett of Castle Vale	*Lab*

Secretaries:

Fabian Hamilton	*Lab*
Lord Astor of Hever	*Con*
Treasurer: Bill Olner	*Lab*

Contact: Keith Lewis, Society of Motor Manufacturers and Traders Ltd, Forbes House, Halkin Street, London SW1X 7DS Tel: 020 7344 1635

Motorcycling

Chair: Lembit Öpik	*Lib Dem*

Vice-chairs:

Lord Jopling	*Con*
Stephen Pound	*Lab*
Secretary: Viscount of Falkland	*Lib Dem*
Treasurer: David Chidgey	*Lib Dem*

Contact: Jenny Luckman, Motorcycle Industry Association Ltd, Starley House, Eaton Road, Coventry CV1 2FH Tel: 0870 330 7806

Motor Neurone Disease

Chair: Mark Todd	*Lab*

Vice-chairs:

Dr Vincent Cable	*Lib Dem*
Nick Gibb	*Con*
Treasurer: Baroness Noakes	*Con*

Contact: Alison Morris, Campaigns Manager, Motor Neurone Disease Association, PO Box 246, Northampton NN1 2PR Tel: 01604 250505

MS (Multiple Sclerosis)

Chair: Gordon Prentice	*Lab*

Vice-chairs:

Paul Burstow	*Lib Dem*
James Gray	*Con*
Secretary: Lord Corbett of Castle Vale	*Lab*

Contact: Rachel Duke, MS Society, 372 Edgware Road, London NW2 6ND Tel: 020 8438 0827

Muscular Dystrophy

Chair: Kevin Brennan   *Lab*
Vice-chair: Dr Hywel Francis   *Lab*

Contact: Nathan Yeowell, 2/4 Norman Shaw
North, Victoria Embankment,
London SW1A 2HZ
Tel: 020 7219 3572

Music

Chair: Siobhain McDonagh   *Lab*
Vice-chairs:
    Nigel Evans   *Con*
    Tom Harris   *Lab*
    Sandra Gidley   *Lib Dem*
Secretary: Janet Anderson   *Lab*
Treasurer: Rosemary McKenna   *Lab*
Vice-Treasurer: Tom Watson   *Lab*

Contact: Siobhain McDonagh MP, House of
Commons, London SW1A 0AA
Tel: 020 7219 4522

Myodil

Chair: Joan Humble   *Lab*
Vice-chairs:
    David Kidney   *Lab*
    Steve Webb   *Lib Dem*
Secretary: Tim Collins   *Con*

Contact: Tim Collins MP, Constituency Office,
112 Highgate, Kendal, Cumbria LA9 4HE
Tel: 01539 721010

National Parks

Chair: Jackie Lawrence   *Lab*
Vice-chairs:
    Patrick McLoughlin   *Con*
    Roger Williams   *Lib Dem*
    Lord Clark of Windermere   *Lab*
Secretary: Lawrie Quinn   *Lab*
Treasurer: Colin Pickthall   *Lab*

Contact: Mrs Jackie Lawrence MP, House of
Commons, London SW1A 0AA
Tel: 020 7219 3510

New Europe

(Promotion UK's simultaneous membership of
EU and non-membership of Euro)
Chair: Frank Field   *Lab*
Vice-chairs:
    John Burnett   *Lib Dem*
    Lord Prior   *Con*
Secretary: Ian Davidson   *Lab*

Contact: Ian Davidson MP, House of
Commons, London SW1A 0AA
Tel: 020 7219 3610

Non-Profit Making Members' Clubs

Chair: Dennis Turner   *Lab*
Vice-chairs:
    David Chidgey   *Lib Dem*
    David Clelland   *Lab*
    Greg Knight   *Con*
Secretary: Lord Brooks of Tremorfa   *Lab*
Treasurer: David Clelland   *Lab*

Contact: Maxine Murphy, Parliamentary
Liaison Officer, Committee of Registered Club
Associations, 253-254 Upper Street,
London N1 1RY Tel: 020 7288 8020

Nuclear Energy

Chair: Bill Tynan   *Lab*
Vice-chairs:
    Lord Christopher   *Lab*
    Lord Jenkin of Roding   *Con*
    Lord McNally   *Lib Dem*
Secretary: David Drew   *Lab*
Treasurer: Jimmy Hood   *Lab*

Contact: Miranda Kirschel, Nuclear Industry
Association, First Floor, Whitehall House,
41 Whitehall, London SW1A 2BY
Tel: 020 7766 6641

Obesity

Chairs:
    Dr Howard Stoate   *Lab*
    Vernon Coaker   *Lab*
Vice-chair: Michael Fabricant   *Con*

Contact: Helen Johnson, c/o National Obesity
Forum, PO Box 6625, Nottingham NG2 5PA
Tel: 0115 01438 840981

Occupational Pensions

Chair: John Butterfill   *Con*
Vice-chairs:
    Eric Illsley   *Lab*
    Nick Gibb   *Con*
Secretary: Jim Cousins   *Lab*
Treasurer: Peter Pike   *Lab*

Contact: David Robertson, Association of
Consulting Actuaries, No 1 Wardrobe Place,
London EC4V 5AG Tel: 020 7248 3163

Occupational Safety and Health

Chair: Michael Clapham   *Lab*
Vice-chairs:
    Mike Hancock   *Lib Dem*
    Harold Best   *Lab*
Secretary: Nigel Evans   *Con*
Hon President: Lord Hunt of Wirral   *Con*

Contact: Michael Clapham MP, House of
Commons, London SW1A 0AA
Tel: 020 7219 2907

Offshore Oil and Gas Industry

Chair: Bob Blizzard	*Lab*
Vice-chairs:	
Lord Fraser of Carmyllie	*Con*
Sir Robert Smith	*Lib Dem*
Angus Robertson	*SNP*
Secretary: Michael Connarty	*Lab*
Treasurer: Frank Doran	*Lab*

Contact: Bob Blizzard MP, House of Commons, London SW1A 0AA Tel: 01502 514913

Olympics

Chair: Barry Gardiner	*Lab*
Vice-chairs:	
Richard Ottaway	*Con*
Bob Russell	*Lib Dem*
Lord Glentoran	*Con*
Secretary: Jon Cruddas	*Lab*
Treasurer: Andy Reed	*Lab*

Contact: Lucy Webster, London Development Agency, Devon House, 58-60 St Katherine's Way, London E1W 1JX Tel: 020 7954 4766

Opera

Chair: John Greenway	*Con*
Vice-chairs:	
Kelvin Hopkins	*Lab*
Andrew Love	*Lab*
Secretary: John Horam	*Con*
Treasurer: Dari Taylor	*Lab*

Contact: John Greenway MP, House of Commons, London SW1A 0AA
Tel: 020 7219 5483

Organophosphates

Chair: Paul Tyler	*Lib Dem*
Vice-chairs:	
Countess of Mar	*Crossbench*
Ian Liddell-Grainger	*Con*
Dr Ian Gibson	*Lab*
Elfyn Llwyd	*PC*
Roy Beggs	*UUP*

Contact: Seth Williams, c/o Paul Tyler MP, Room 303, Portcullis House, Bridge Street, London SW1A 2LW Tel: 020 7219 6355

Osteoporosis

Chairs:	
John Austin	*Lab*
Baroness Cumberlege	*Con*
Vice-chairs:	
Sandra Gidley	*Lib Dem*
Christine Russell	*Lab*
Secretary: Julia Drown	*Lab*

Contact: Linda Edwards, National Osteoporosis Society, Camerton, Bath BA2 0PJ
Tel: 01761 471771

Overseas Development

Chair: Tony Worthington	*Lab*
Vice-chairs:	
Tony Baldry	*Con*
John Battle	*Lab*
Secretaries:	
Peter Luff	*Con*
Peter Pike	*Lab*
Treasurer: Dr Jenny Tonge	*Lib Dem*

Contact: Adrian Hewitt, Deputy Director, Overseas Development Institute, 111 Westminster Bridge Road, London SE1 7JD Tel: 020 7922 0300

Panjabis in Britain

Chair: John McDonnell	*Lab*
Vice-chairs:	
John Randall	*Con*
Lord Avebury	*Lib Dem*
Secretary: Martin Salter	*Lab*
Treasurer: Rob Marris	*Lab*

Contact: John McDonnell MP, House of Commons, London SW1A 0AA
Tel: 020 7219 6908

Paper Related Industries

Chair: Jonathan Shaw	*Lab*
Vice-chairs:	
Peter Pike	*Lab*
James Paice	*Con*
Andrew Stunell	*Lib Dem*
Secretary: Derek Wyatt	*Lab*

Contact: Kathy Bradley, Confederation of Paper Industries, Paper Makers House, Rivenhall Road, Swindon, Wiltshire SN5 7BN
Tel: 01793 889605

Parents and Families

Chair: Lord Northbourne	*Crossbench*
Vice-chair: Phil Hope	*Lab*
Secretary:	
Baroness Sharp of Guildford	*Lib Dem*
Treasurer: Peter Bottomley	*Con*

Contact: Anne Page, National Family and Parenting Institute, 430 Highgate Studios, 53-79 Highgate Road, London NW5 1TL
Tel: 020 7424 3460

Park Home Owners

(Permanently parked caravan homes)

Chair: Hilton Dawson	*Lab*
Vice-chairs:	
Baroness Maddock	*Lib Dem*
Roger Gale	*Con*
David Taylor	*Lab*
John Butterfill	*Con*
Secretary: Lord Graham of Edmonton	*Lab*

Contact: Lord Graham of Edmonton, House of Lords, London SW1A 0PW Tel: 020 7219 6704

Parliamentarians for Global Action

Chair: Tony Worthington	*Lab*
Vice-chairs:	
Michael Fallon	*Con*
Menzies Campbell	*Lib Dem*
Secretary: Joan Walley	*Lab*
Treasurer: Meg Munn	*Lab*

Contact: Tony Worthington MP, House of
Commons, London SW1A 0AA
Tel: 020 7219 3507

Parliamentary Reform

Chair: Anne Campbell	*Lab*
Vice-chair: Andrew Tyrie	*Con*
Secretary: Richard Allan	*Lib Dem*

Contact: Clare Ettinghausen, Hansard Society,
London School of Economics, 9 Kingsway,
London WC2B 6XF Tel: 020 7955 7459

Penal Affairs

Chair: Lord Corbett of Castle Vale	*Lab*
Vice-chairs:	
Vera Baird	*Lab*
Lord Carlisle of Bucklow	*Con*
Baroness Stern	*Crossbench*
Secretary: Mike Hancock	*Lib Dem*

Contact: Geoff Dobson, Prison Reform Trust,
15 Northburgh Street, London EC1V 0JR
Tel: 020 7251 5070

Personal Social Services

Chair: Joan Humble	*Lab*
Vice-chairs:	
Paul Burstow	*Lib Dem*
Rev Martin Smyth	*UUP*
Bill O'Brien	*Lab*
Secretary: Stephen McCabe	*Lab*
Treasurer: Hilton Dawson	*Lab*

Contact: Richard Clough, Chief Executive,
Social Care Association, Thornton House,
Hook Road, Surbiton, Surrey KT6 5AN
Tel: 020 8397 1411

Pharmaceutical Industry

Chair: Kevin Barron	*Lab*
Vice-chair: Virginia Bottomley	*Con*

Contact: Kevin Barron MP, House of
Commons, London SW1A 0AA
Tel: 020 7219 6306

Pharmacy

Chair: Dr Howard Stoate	*Lab*
Vice-chairs:	
Dr Jenny Tonge	*Lib Dem*
Lord Newton of Braintree	*Con*

Secretary: Mark Todd	*Lab*
Treasurer: David Heath	*Lib Dem*

Contact: Simon Whale, Managing Partner,
Luther Pendragon, Priory Court, Pilgrim Street,
London EC4V 6DR Tel: 020 7618 9100

Photography

Chair: Austin Mitchell	*Lab*
Vice-chairs:	
David Wilshire	*Con*
Viscount Allenby of Megiddo	*CB*
Baroness Hilton of Eggardon	*Lab*
Rev Martin Smyth	*UUP*
Secretaries:	
Lord Crathorne	*Con*
Peter Bottomley	*Con*

Contact: Austin Mitchell MP, Room 542,
Portcullis House, Bridge Street,
London SW1A 2LW
Tel: 020 7219 4559

Police

Chair: Dr Vincent Cable	*Lib Dem*
Vice-chairs:	
Helen Clark	*Lab*
Lady Sylvia Hermon	*UUP*
Tony Baldry	*Con*
Secretary: Stephen Hesford	*Lab*

Contact: Andrew Reeves, c/o Dr Vincent Cable
MP, House of Commons, London SW1A 0AA
Tel: 020 7219 5746

Political Art

Chair: Hugo Swire	*Con*
Vice-chair: Tony Banks	*Lab*
Secretary: John Burnett	*Lib Dem*

Contact: Bendor Grosvenor, c/o Tony Banks
MP, Room 605, Portcullis House, Bridge Street,
London SW1A 2LW
Tel: 020 7219 3522

Population, Development and Reproductive Health

Chair: Christine McCafferty	*Lab*
Vice-chairs:	
Viscount Craigavon	*Crossbench*
Richard Ottaway	*Con*
Secretaries:	
Martyn Jones	*Lab*
Baroness Flather	*Con*
Treasurer: Tony Worthington	*Lab*

Contact: Ann Mette Kjaerby, c/o Christine
McCafferty MP, Room 563, Portcullis House,
Bridge Street, London SW1A 2LW
Tel: 020 7219 2492

Ports and Merchant Navy

Chair: Gwyn Prosser — *Lab*
Vice-chair: Ivan Henderson — *Lab*
Deputy Vice-chair: John Gummer — *Con*
Secretary: Dr Doug Naysmith — *Lab*
Treasurer: Mike Hancock — *Lib Dem*

Contact: Doug Naysmith MP, House of Commons, London SW1A 0AA
Tel: 020 7219 4187

Poverty

Chair: Ernie Ross — *Lab*
Vice-chairs:
Andrew Selous — *Con*
Steve Webb — *Lib Dem*
Treasurer: David Drew — *Lab*

Contact: Ruth Bush, UK Coalition Against Poverty, c/o Church Action on Poverty, London Diocesan House, 36 Causton Street, London SW1P 4AU Tel: 020 7932 1266

Primary Care and Public Health

Chairs:
Baroness Eccles of Moulton — *Con*
Dr Howard Stoate — *Lab*
Sandra Gidley — *Lib Dem*
Secretary: Stephen Hesford — *Lab*
Treasurer: Laura Moffat — *Lab*

Contact: Stephen Hesford MP, House of Commons, London SW1A 0AA
Tel: 020 7219 6227

Printing Industry

Chair: Gerry Sutcliffe — *Lab*
Vice-chair: John Bercow — *Con*
Secretary: Bob Russell — *Lib Dem*
Treasurer: Lord Evans of Watford — *Lab*

Contact: Gerry Sutcliffe MP, House of Commons, London SW1A 0AA Tel: 020 7219 6483

Private Equity and Venture Capital

Chair: Andy Burnham — *Lab*
Secretary: Mark Field — *Con*

Contact: Mark Fox, British Venture Capital Association, Tower 3, 3 Clements Inn, London WC2A 2AZ Tel: 020 7025 2950

Pro-Choice

(In relation to abortion)
Chair: Baroness Gould of Potternewton — *Lab*
Vice-chairs:
Crispin Blunt — *Con*
Dr Jenny Tonge — *Lib Dem*
Secretary: Gareth R Thomas — *Lab*
Treasurer: Viscount Craigavon — *Crossbench*

Contact: Clare Norden, Voice for Choice, 2-12 Pentonville Road, London N1 9FP
Tel: 020 7837 4792

Pro-Life

(In relation to abortion, euthanasia and research on the human embryo)
Chair: Jim Dobbin — *Lab*
Vice-chairs:
Ann Winterton — *Con*
Lord Stallard — *Lab*
Baroness Masham of Ilton — *Crossbench*
Ann Widdecombe — *Con*
Hon secretaries:
Joe Benton — *Lab*
Kerry Pollard — *Lab*
Hon Treasurers:
Rev Martin Smyth — *UUP*
Lord Alton of Liverpool — *Crossbench*

Contact: Martin Foley, c/o Jim Dobbin MP, House of Commons, London SW1A 0AA
Tel: 020 7219 4530

Public Service Broadcasting

Chair: Fiona Mactaggart — *Lab*
Vice-chairs:
David Cameron — *Con*
Chris Bryant — *Lab*
Lembit Öpik — *Lib Dem*
Secretary: Tom Harris — *Lab*
Treasurer:
Lord Gordon of Strathblane — *Lab*

Contact: Tim Gledhill, ITV Network Centre, 200 Grays Inn Road, London WC1X 8HF
Tel: 020 7843 8203

Pulmonary Hypertension

Chair: Dr Vincent Cable — *Lib Dem*
Vice-chair:
Lord Thomas of Gresford — *Lib Dem*
Secretary:
Jon Owen Jones — *Lab*

Contact: Nick Ainger MP, House of Commons, London SW1A 0AA
Tel: 020 7219 2241

Race and Community

Chair: Diane Abbott — *Lab*
Vice-chairs;
Peter Bottomley — *Con*
Simon Hughes — *Lib Dem*
Baroness Howells of
St Davids — *Lab*
Marsha Singh — *Lab*
Secretary: Harry Cohen — *Lab*
Treasurer: Keith Vaz — *Lab*

Contact: Harry Cohen MP, House of Commons, London SW1A 0AA
Tel: 020 7219 6376

Racing and Bloodstock

Chairs:

Richard Page	Con
Jeff Ennis	Lab

Vice-chairs:

Peter Atkinson	Con
David Rendel	Lib Dem

Secretary: Lord Donoughue — Lab
Treasurer: Baroness Golding — Lab

Contact: David Oliver, Hill and Knowlton, 35 Red Lion Square, London WC1R 4SG
Tel: 020 7413 3048

Rail

Chairs:

Nick Hawkins	Con
Lawrie Quinn	Lab

Vice-chairs:

Michael Moore	Lib Dem
Jane Griffiths	Lab
Chris Grayling	Con

Secretary: Lord Berkeley — Lab
Treasurer: Lord Faulkner of Worcester — Lab

Contact: Lord Berkeley, Rail Freight Group, 17 Queen Anne's Gate, London SW1
Tel: 020 7233 3177

Refugees

Chair: Neil Gerrard — Lab
Vice-chairs:

Earl Russell	Lib Dem
Karen Buck	Lab
Peter Bottomley	Con

Contact: Imran Hussain, Parliamentary Officer, The Refugee Council, 3 Bondway, London SW8 1SJ Tel: 020 7820 3046

Regeneration

Chair: Joan Walley — Lab
Vice-chairs:

Bob Russell	Lib Dem
Janet Anderson	Lab
Tim Loughton	Con
Baroness Blood	Crossbench

Treasurer: Dr Howard Stoate — Lab

Contact: Sophie Livingstone, Groundwork UK, 85-87 Cornwall Street, Birmingham B3 3BY
Tel: 0121-236 8565

Renewable and Sustainable Energy (PRASEG)

Chair: Dr Alan Whitehead — Lab
Vice-chairs:

Andrew Robathan	Con
Sue Doughty	Lib Dem
Dr Desmond Turner	Lab
Simon Thomas	PC
Lord Corbett of Castle Vale	Lab

Secretary: Tony Colman	Lab
Treasurer: Andrew Stunell	Lib Dem

Contact: Catherine Pearce, Co-ordinator, PRASEG, 145 Fourth Floor, 35/37 Grosvenor Gardens, London SW1W 0BS
Tel: 020 7233 5887

Retail Industry

Chair: Barbara Follett — Lab
Vice-chairs:

Brian Cotter	Lib Dem
Nigel Evans	Con
Rev Martin Smyth	UUP
Lord Graham of Edmonton	Lab

Secretary:

Baroness Thornton	Lab

Contact: Russell Hamblin-Boone, British Retail Consortium, 5 Grafton Street, London W1X 4EG Tel: 020 7647 1594

Rheumatoid Arthritis

Chair: David Amess — Con
Vice-chairs:

Dr Bob Spink	Con
Paul Flynn	Lab

Secretary: Stephen Hesford — Lab
Treasurer: Andy King — Lab

Contact: Stephen Hesford MP, House of Commons, London SW1A 0AA
Tel: 020 7219 6227

Road Passenger Transport

Joint-chairs:

Sir Sydney Chapman	Con
Peter Pike	Lab

Treasurer: Lord Hogg of Cumbernauld — Lab

Contact: Ling Tang, Confederation of Passenger Transport, Imperial House, 15-10 Kingsway, London WC2B 6UN
Tel: 020 7240 3131

Road Safety

Chairs:

Patrick McLoughlin	Lab
Alice Mahon	Con
Tom Brake	Lib Dem

Contact: Cathy Keeler, BRAKE, PO Box 548, Huddersfield HD1 2XZ Tel: 01484 559909

Road Traffic Victims

Chair: Andrew Miller — Lab
Vice-chairs:

Bob Russell	Lib Dem
Peter Bottomley	Con

Contact: Brigitte Chaudhry, National Secretary, RoadPeace, PO Box 2579, London NW10 3PW
Tel: 020 8964 1800

Roma Affairs

Chair: Paul Stinchcombe   *Lab*
Vice-chairs:
    Andrew George   *Lib Dem*
    Iain Coleman   *Lab*
Contact: Paul Stinchcombe MP, House of
Commons, London SW1A 0AA
Tel: 020 7219 4066

Royal Marines

Chairs:
    Michael Fabricant   *Con*
    Syd Rapson   *Lab*
Vice-chairs:
    John Burnett   *Lib Dem*
    Peter Pike   *Lab*
    Claire Ward   *Lab*
Treasurer: John Wilkinson   *Con*
Contact: Michael Fabricant MP, Room 4/27,
Norman Shaw North, Victoria Embankment,
London SW1A 2JF Tel: 020 7219 5022

Rugby League

Chair: Lord Lofthouse of Pontefract   *Lab*
Vice-chairs:
    James Clappison   *Con*
    Lindsay Hoyle   *Lab*
Secretary: David Hinchliffe   *Lab*
Treasurer: Andy Burnham   *Lab*
Contact: David Hinchliffe MP, House of
Commons, London SW1A 0AA
Tel: 020 7219 4447

Rugby Union

Chair: Derek Wyatt   *Lab*
Vice-chairs:
    Sir Brian Mawhinney   *Con*
    Andrew George   *Lib Dem*
Secretary: Tony Cunningham   *Lab*
Treasurer: Nick Hawkins   *Con*
Contact: Tony Cunningham MP, House of
Commons, London SW1A 0AA
Tel: 020 7219 8344

Rugby Union Football Club

Chairs:
    Ian Davidson   *Lab*
    Sir Michael Lord   *Con*
Secretary: Huw Edwards   *Lab*
Treasurer: Nick Hawkins   *Con*
Contact: Huw Edwards MP, House of Commons,
London SW1A 0AA Tel: 020 7219 3489

Scientific Committee

Chair: Richard Page   *Con*
Vice-chairs:
    Dr Doug Naysmith   *Lab*
    Lord Hunt of Wirral   *Con*

Secretaries:
    Dr Desmond Turner   *Lab*
    Rev Martin Smyth   *UUP*
Treasurer: Dr Brian Iddon   *Lab*
Contact: Dr Alan Whitehouse, 3 Birdcage
Walk, London SW1H 9JJ Tel: 020 7222 7085

Scotch Whisky

Chair: Irene Adams   *Lab*
Vice-chairs:
    Earl of Lindsay   *Con*
    Angus Robertson   *SNP*
    Alan Reid   *Lib Dem*
Secretary: Brian Donohoe   *Lab*
Treasurer: John McFall   *Lab*
Contact: Ruth Brown, c/o Brian Donohoe MP,
House of Commons, London SW1A 0AA
Tel: 01294 276844

Scottish Football

Chair: Jim Sheridan   *Lab*
Vice-chairs:
    Iain Luke   *Lab*
    Anne Picking   *Lab*
    Angus Robertson   *SNP*
Secretary: John Lyons   *Lab*
Treasurer: John Robertson   *Lab*
Contact: Jim Sheridan MP, House of Commons,
London SW1A 0AA Tel: 020 7219 8314

Scout Association

Chairs:
    David Amess   *Con*
    Stephen Pound   *Lab*
Secretary: Bob Russell   *Lib Dem*
Contact: Bob Russell MP, House of Commons,
London SW1A 0AA Tel: 020 7219 5150

Sewers and Sewerage

Chair: Andy King   *Lab*
Vice-chairs:
    Bob Spink   *Con*
    Colin Pickthall   *Lab*
Contact: Andy King MP, Room 305,
Norman Shaw North, Victoria Embankment,
London SW1A 2HZ Tel: 020 7219 6229

Sex Equality

Chair: Julie Morgan   *Lab*
Vice-chairs:
    Peter Bottomley   *Con*
    Patsy Calton   *Lib Dem*
    Vera Baird   *Lab*
Secretary:
    Baroness Gould of Potternewton   *Lab*
Contact: Clare Cozens, Equal Opportunities
Commission, 36 Broadway,
London SW1H 0BH Tel: 020 7960 7415

Shipbuilding and Ship Repair

Chair: Stephen Hepburn   *Lab*
Vice-chairs:
   John Burnett   *Lib Dem*
   John Robertson   *Lab*
Secretary: Ian Davidson   *Lab*

Contact: Ian Davidson MP, House of
Commons, London SW1A 0AA
Tel: 020 7219 3610

Shooting and Conservation

Chair: Dr Jack Cunningham   *Lab*
Joint Vice-chairs:
   James Paice   *Con*
   John Thurso   *Lib Dem*
Joint Secretaries:
   Lord Astor of Hever   *Con*
   Dr Stephen Ladyman   *Lab*
Joint Treasurers:
   Martyn Jones   *Lab*
   Lord Woolmer of Leeds   *Lab*

Contact: Christopher Graffius, British
Association of Shooting and Conservation,
Marford Mill, Rossett, Wrexham LL12 0HL
Tel: 01244 573 045

Skin

(As health issue)
Chair: Bruce George   *Lab*
Vice-chairs:
   Frank Cook   *Lab*
   Baroness Masham of Ilton   *Crossbench*
   Cheryl Gillan   *Con*
Secretary: Candy Atherton   *Lab*
Treasurer: Lord Henley   *Con*

Contact: Natalie de Lima, Portcullis Research,
26 Cadogan Square, London SW1X 0JP
Tel: 020 7591 4833

Small Business

Chair: Kerry Pollard   *Lab*
Vice-chairs:
   Brian Cotter   *Lib Dem*
   David Ruffley   *Con*
Secretary: Andrew Love   *Lab*
Treasurer: Mark Prisk   *Con*

Contact: Alan Cleverly, Curzon House,
Church Road, Windlesham, Surrey GU20 6BH
Tel: 01276 452010

Smoking and Health

Chair: David Taylor   *Lab*
Vice-chairs:
   Michael Fabricant   *Con*
   Lord Clement-Jones   *Lib Dem*

Secretaries:
   John Robertson   *Lab*
   Lord Faulkner of Worcester   *Lab*
Treasurer: Bob Russell   *Lib Dem*

Contact: Daniel Crimes, Room 213 Portcullis
House, Bridge Street, London SW1A 2LW
Tel: 020 7219 2237

Social Development in Europe

Chair: Earl of Dundee   *Con*
Vice-chairs:
   Tom Cox   *Lab*
   Mike Hancock   *Lib Dem*
   Tony Lloyd   *Lab*
   Lord Taylor of Blackburn   *Lab*
   Lord Biffen   *Con*
Secretary: Baroness Cox   *Con*

Contact: Earl of Dundee, House of Lords,
London SW1A 0PW Tel: 020 7219 6781

Social Science and Policy

Chair: Alan Simpson   *Lab*
Vice-chair: Virginia Bottomley   *Con*

Contact: Ms Brenda Grant, Vista Conferences,
Collingham House, 10–12 Gladstone Road,
London SW19 1QT Tel: 020 8542 8233

Socially Responsible Investment

Chair: Tony Colman   *Lab*
Vice-chairs:
   Peter Bottomley   *Con*
   Dr Vincent Cable   *Lib Dem*
Secretary: Gareth R Thomas   *Lab*

Contact: Helen Harrison, UK Social Investment
Forum, Unit 203, Hatton Square Business
Centre, 16 Baldwins Gardens, London
EC1N 2RJ Tel: 020 7405 0040

Solvent Abuse

Chair: David Amess   *Con*
Vice-chair: Bill Cash   *Con*
Secretary: Andrew Love   *Lab*

Contact: Andrew Love MP, House of
Commons, London SW1A 0AA
Tel: 020 7219 6377

Space

Chair: John McWilliam   *Lab*
Vice-chairs:
   Richard Page   *Con*
   Bill Olner   *Lab*
Hon Secretaries:
   Lord Selsdon   *Con*
   Ian Taylor   *Con*
Hon Treasurer: Nigel Evans   *Con*

Contact: Frank Richardson, 22 Gloucester Place
Mews, London W1H 8BA Tel: 020 7487 4872

Sports

Chair: Lord Pendry — Lab
Vice-chairs:
Nick Hawkins — Con
Alan Keen — Lab
Baroness Billingham — Lab
Lord Addington — Lib Dem
Secretary: Andy Reed — Lab

Contact: John Zerafa, Sport England, 16 Upper Woburn Place, London WC1H 0QP
Tel: 020 7273 1729

State Boarding Schools

Chair: Norman Lamb — Lib Dem
Secretary: Richard Bacon — Con

Contact: Norman Lamb MP, House of Commons, London SW1A 0AA Tel: 020 7219 8480

Steel

Chair: Helen Jackson — Lab
Vice-chairs:
Tony Baldry — Con
Roger Williams — Lib Dem
Adam Price — PC
Lord Brookman — Lab
Secretary: Dr Hywel Francis — Lab
Treasurer: Ian Cawsey — Lab

Contact: Dr Hywel Francis MP, House of Commons, London SW1A 0AA
Tel: 020 7219 8121

Street Children

Chairs:
Edward Leigh — Con
Win Griffiths — Lab
Baroness Miller of
Chilthorne Domer — Lib Dem

Contact: Wilfred Wong, Room LG6, Norman Shaw North, Victoria Embankment, London SW1A 2HZ Tel: 020 7219 5129

Stroke

Chair: Jim Cunningham — Lab
Vice-chairs:
Andrew Lansley — Con
Lord Rodgers of Quarry Bank — Lib Dem
Secretary: Harry Barnes — Lab
Treasurer: Judy Mallaber — Lab

Contact: Harry Barnes MP, House of Commons, London SW1A 0AA Tel: 020 7219 4521/5013

Sub Post Offices

Chair: Frank Field — Lab
Vice-chair: Sir Archy Kirkwood — Lib Dem
Secretary: Oliver Letwin — Con

Contact: Oliver Letwin MP, House of Commons, London SW1A 0AA Tel: 01308 456 891

Sustainable Waste

Chairs:
Bill O'Brien — Lab
Roy Beggs — UUP
Peter Bottomley — Con
Dr Alan Whitehead — Lab
Sue Doughty — Lib Dem
Vice-chair: Helen Clark — Lab
Secretary: Barry Sheerman — Lab
Treasurer: Malcolm Bruce — Lib Dem

Contact: Mark Dempsey, Project Manager, Networking for Industry, 7th Floor, 1 Great Cumberland Place, London W1H 7AL
Tel: 020 7723 5562

Telecommunications

Chair: John Robertson — Lab
Vice-chairs:
Nigel Jones — Lib Dem
Sir George Young — Con
Secretary: Parmjit Dhanda — Lab

Contact: Helen Newton, c/o John Robertson MP, Room 1/28 Norman Shaw North, London SW1A 2JF
Tel: 020 7219 6964

Tennis Club

Chairman/Captain: Sir Michael Spicer — Con
Vice-chair: Andrew Miller — Lab
Secretary: Michael Jabez Foster — Lab
Treasurer: Phil Hope — Lab
President: Tony Blair

Contact: Sir Michael Spicer MP, House of Commons, London SW1A 0AA
Tel: 020 7219 6250

Thalidomide

Chair: Roger Berry — Lab
Vice-chair and Secretary:
Jonathan Djanogly — Con

Contact: Jonathan Djanogly MP, 1 Parliament Street, London SW1A 2NE
Tel: 020 7219 2367

Theatre

Chair: Ann Keen — Lab
Vice-chairs:
Peter Luff — Con
Christine Russell — Lab
Nick Hawkins — Con
Michael Mates — Con
Lord McCarthy — Lab

Contact: Peter Finch, Performers' Alliance, 44 Hazel Road, London NW10
Tel: 020 8969 9941

Tourism

Chair: Lord Pendry — *Lab*
Vice-chairs:
Virginia Bottomley	*Con*
Lawrie Quinn	*Lab*
John Thurso	*Lib Dem*

Secretary: Janet Anderson — *Lab*

Contact: Craig Beaumont, VisitBritain, Thames Tower, Black's Road, London W6 9EL Tel: 020 8563 3297

Town and Country

Chairs:
David Taylor	*Lab*
Sue Doughty	*Lib Dem*
Virginia Bottomley	*Con*

Secretary: David Kidney — *Lab*
Treasurer: Mark Francois — *Con*

Contact: Belinda Darwall Smith, LLM Communications, Bugle House, 21a Noel Street, London W1F 8GR Tel: 020 7437 1122

Town Centre Management Issues

Chair: David Lepper — *Lab*
Vice-chairs:
Lord Jenkin of Roding	*Con*
Helen Southworth	*Lab*
David Chidgey	*Lib Dem*

Secretary: Rosemary McKenna — *Lab*
Treasurer: Patrick Hall — *Lab*

Contact: David Lepper MP, John Saunders House, 179 Preston Road, Brighton BN1 6AG Tel: 01273 551532

Transport Forum

Chairs:
Peter Pike	*Lab*
David Chidgey	*Lib Dem*

Treasurer: Clive Efford — *Lab*

Contact: Douglas Smith, Parliamentary Monitoring Services, 19 Douglas Street, London SW1P 4PA Tel: 020 7828 0828

Transport Infrastructure and Trans European Networks

Chair: Anne McIntosh — *Con*
Vice-chairs:
Ivan Henderson	*Lab*
Bob Russell	*Lib Dem*

Joint secretaries:
Bill Wiggin	*Con*
Kelvin Hopkins	*Lab*

Treasurer: Anthony D Wright — *Lab*

Contact: Anne McIntosh MP, House of Commons, London SW1A 0AA Tel: 020 7219 3541

Transport Safety

Chairs:
Peter Bottomley	*Con*
David Kidney	*Lab*

Vice-chairs:
Barry Sheerman	*Lab*
Baroness Thomas of Walliswood	*Lib Dem*

Contact: Robert Gifford, PACTS, St Thomas' Hospital, Lambeth Palace Road, London SE1 7EH Tel: 020 7922 8112

Traveller Law Reform

Chair: Kevin McNamara — *Lab*
Vice-chairs:
David Atkinson	*Con*
Julie Morgan	*Lab*
Bob Russell	*Lib Dem*

Secretary: Lord Avebury — *Lib Dem*
Treasurer: John Battle — *Lab*

Contact: Andrew Ryder, Flat A, 25 Clarence Road, London N22 8PG Tel: 07946 847571

Underground Space (Tunnels)

Chair: Lawrie Quinn — *Lab*
Vice-chair: Peter Viggers — *Con*
Secretary: Claire Curtis-Thomas — *Lab*
Treasurer: Lindsay Hoyle — *Lab*

Contact: Claire Curtis-Thomas MP, Room 5/24, Norman Shaw North, Victoria Embankment, London SW1A 2HZ Tel: 020 7219 2739

United Nations

Chair: Tony Colman — *Lab*
Vice-chairs:
Mike Gapes	*Lab*
Peter Luff	*Con*
David Heath	*Lib Dem*

Secretary: Meg Munn — *Lab*
Treasurer: Hugh Robertson — *Con*

Contact: Tony Colman MP, House of Commons, London SW1A 0AA Tel: 020 7219 6639

University

Chairs:
Baroness Maddock	*Lib Dem*
Baroness Lockwood	*Lab*
Baroness Perry of Southwark	*Con*

Vice-chairs:
Barry Sheerman	*Lab*
David Rendel	*Lib Dem*
Tim Boswell	*Con*

Secretary: Dr Doug Naysmith — *Lab*
Treasurer: John Grogan — *Lab*

Contact: Glynthea Modood, 101 Kingsdown Parade, Bristol BS6 5UJ Tel: 0117-923 2938

Voice

(Charity for people with learning disabilities
who have been abused)

Chair: Fiona Mactaggart	*Lab*
Vice-chairs:	
Julia Drown	*Lab*
Tom Levitt	*Lab*
Lord Laming	*Crossbench*
Meg Munn	*Lab*
Sue Doughty	*Lib Dem*
Peter Bottomley	*Con*

Contact: Katherine Stone, Voice UK,
The College Business Centre, Uttoxeter New
Road, Derby DE22 3WZ Tel: 01332 202555

War Crimes

President: Lord Merlyn-Rees	*Lab*
Vice-President: Lord Campbell of Croy	*Con*
Chair: Baroness Golding	*Lab*
Vice-chairs:	
Lord Hunt of Wirral	*Con*
Lord Carlile of Berriew	*Lib Dem*
Lembit Öpik	*Lib Dem*
Lord Campbell of Croy	*Con*
Sir Brian Mawhinney	*Con*
Andrew Dismore	*Lab*
Lord Archer of Sandwell	*Lab*
Secretary: Lord Janner of Braunstone	*Lab*
Treasurer: Andrew Dismore	*Lab*

Contact: Mitchell Coen, c/o Lord Janner,
House of Lords, London SW1A 0PW
Tel: 020 7222 2863 or 020 7976 8443

War Graves and Battlefield Heritage

Chair: Lord Faulkner of Worcester	*Lab*
Vice-chairs:	
Nigel Dodds	*DUP*
Lord Burnham	*Con*
Lord Roper	*Lib Dem*
Dr Rudi Vis	*Lab*
Treasurer: Jeffrey Donaldson	*UUP*

Contact: Peter Barton, 8 Egbert Road,
Faversham, Kent ME13 8SJ Tel: 01795 533035

Warm Homes

Chair: Alan Simpson	*Lab*
Vice-chairs:	
Sir Sidney Chapman	*Con*
Andrew Stunell	*Lib Dem*
Secretary: Debra Shipley	*Lab*
Treasurer: Dr Brian Iddon	*Lab*

Contact: Jenny Saunders, c/o NEA,
St Andrew's House, 90-92 Pilgrim Street,
Newcastle upon Tyne NE1 6SG
Tel: 0191-261 5677

Water

Chair: Candy Atherton	*Lab*
Vice-chairs:	
Peter Bottomley	*Con*
Linda Gilroy	*Lab*
Baroness Hilton of Eggardon	*Lab*
Secretary: Dr Phyllis Starkey	*Lab*
Treasurer:	
Dr Desmond Turner	*Lab*

Contact: Alex Pykett, c/o Candy Atherton MP,
House of Commons, London SW1A 0AA
Tel: 020 7219 1207

Waterways

Chair: Bill O'Brien	*Lab*
Vice-chair: Lembit Öpik	*Lib Dem*
Secretary: Dominic Grieve	*Con*
Treasurer: Candy Atherton	*Lab*

Contact: Penny Barber, 67 Chawn Park Drive,
Stourbridge DY9 0UQ
Tel: 07976 591727

Weight Watchers

Chair: Bruce George	*Lab*
Vice-chairs:	
Baroness Fookes	*Con*
Bob Russell	*Lib Dem*

Contact: Natalie Whatford, c/o Bruce George
MP, House of Commons, London SW1A 0AA
Tel: 020 7219 4049

West Coast Main Line

Chairs:	
Eric Martlew	*Lab*
Sir Nicholas Winterton	*Con*
Vice-chair: Bill Olner	*Lab*
Secretary:	
Lord Taylor of Blackburn	*Lab*
Treasurer: Andrew Stunell	*Lib Dem*

Contact: Tony Page, GJW/WSW, Fox Court,
14 Gray's Inn Road, London WC1X 8WS
Tel: 07970 139878

Wine

Chairs:	
Geoffrey Clifton-Brown	*Con*
Barry Gardiner	*Lab*
Secretary:	
Ian Liddell-Grainger	*Con*
Treasurer: John Thurso	*Lib Dem*

Contact: Quentin Rappoport, Wine and Spirit
Association, Five Kings House, 1 Queen Street
Place, London EC4R 1XX
Tel: 020 7248 5377

World Government

Chair: Dr Gavin Strang	Lab
Vice-chairs:	
Dr Nick Palmer	Lab
Malcolm Savidge	Lab
Secretary: Dr Jenny Tonge	Lib Dem
Treasurer: David Atkinson	Con

Contact: Simon Burall, One World Trust,
House of Commons, London SW1A 2JF
Tel: 020 7219 3825

Yacht Club, House of Commons

Chair: Dr Des Turner	Lab
Vice-chair: Jonathan Sayeed	Con
Secretary: Martyn Jones	Lab
Treasurer: Sir Robert Smith	Lib Dem

Contact: Dr Des Turner MP, House of
Commons, London SW1A 0AA
Tel: 020 7219 3417

Youth Affairs

Chair/Secretary: Claire Ward	Lab
Vice-chairs:	
Charles Hendry	Con
Matthew Green	Lib Dem
Treasurer: Phil Hope	Lab

Contact: Rebecca Leete, National Council for
Voluntary Youth Services, 2 Plough Yard,
Shoreditch High Street, London EC2A 3LP
Tel: 020 7422 8638

Youth Hostelling

Chair: Chris Smith	Lab
Vice-chairs:	
Patrick McLoughlin	Con
Paul Tyler	Lib Dem
Michael Connarty	Lab
Roy Beggs	UUP
John Mann	Lab

Contact: Hannah Curzon, Youth Hostels
Association (England and Wales),
PO Box 6028, Matlock, Derbyshire DE4 3XB
Tel: 01629 592779

DodOnline

An Electronic Directory without rival . . .

MPs' biographies and photographs available with daily updates *via* the internet

For a *free* trial, call Yasmin Mirza, Aby Farsoun or Michael Mand on 020 7630 7643

Country Groups

Most All-Party Country Groups are formed under the auspices of the Commonwealth Parliamentary Association or the Inter-Parliamentary Union. These organisations have a UK branch, CPA and IPU, which contains affiliated groups of members interested in a particular country.

Afghanistan

Chair: Tony Cunningham — *Lab*
Vice-chairs:
Lord Plumb — *Con*
Baroness Udin — *Lab*
Joan Ruddock — *Lab*
Secretary: Paul Burstow — *Lib Dem*
Treasurer: Khalid Mahmood — *Lab*

Contact: David Harris, c/o Tony Cunningham MP, House of Commons, London SW1A 0AA
Tel: 020 7219 8344

Africa

Chair: Hugh Bayley — *Lab*
Vice-chairs:
Lord Lea of Crondall — *Lab*
David Chidgey — *Lib Dem*
Laurence Robertson — *Con*
Secretary: Oona King — *Lab*
Treasurer:
Lord Holme of Cheltenham — *Lib Dem*

Contact: Laura Holmes, c/o Hugh Bayley MP, House of Commons, London SW1A 0AA
Tel: 020 7219 6824

Albania

Chair: John Austin — *Lab*
Vice-chair: Lord Biffen — *Con*
Secretary: Paul Keetch — *Lib Dem*

Contact: John Austin MP, House of Commons, London SW1A 0AA Tel: 020 7219 5195

America

(USA)
Joint Presidents:
Lord Irvine of Lairg — *Lab*
Michael Martin — *Speaker*
Vice-Presidents:
Baroness Boothroyd — *Crossbench*
Lord Callaghan of Cardiff — *Lab*
Lord Carrington — *Con*
Robin Cook — *Lab*
Iain Duncan Smith — *Con*
William Hague — *Con*
Lord Howe of Aberavon — *Con*
Lord Hurd of Westwell — *Con*
Lord Jopling — *Con*
Charles Kennedy — *Lib Dem*
Lord Mackay of Clashfern — *Con*
Lord Owen — *Crossbench*
Lord Pym — *Con*
Jack Straw — *Lab*
Baroness Thatcher — *Con*
Lord Weatherill — *Crossbench*
Chair: Tony Blair — *Lab*
Vice-Chairs:
Paul Murphy — *Lab*
Michael Howard — *Con*
Hon Secretary: Alan Williams — *Lab*
Hon Treasurers:
Brian Donohoe — *Lab*
Peter Viggers — *Con*

Contact: Lady Auriol Moate, Westminster House, 7 Millbank, London SW1P 3JA
Tel: 020 7219 6209

Angola

Chair: Hilton Dawson — *Lab*
Vice-chairs:
Andrew Robathan — *Con*
Lord Joffe — *CB*
Secretary: Earl of Listowel — *Crossbench*
Treasurer: Tony Colman — *Lab*

Contact: Liz Horn, Africa Programme Co-ordinator, Royal Institute of International Affairs, 10 St James's Square, London SW1Y 4LE Tel: 020 7957 5718

Argentina

Chair: Tom Cox — *Lab*
Vice-chairs:
Baroness Hooper — *Con*
David Cairns — *Lab*
Secretary: Lord Faulkner of Worcester — *Lab*
Treasurer: Lord McNally — *Lib Dem*

Contact: Tom Cox MP, House of Commons, London SW1A 0AA Tel: 020 7219 5034

Armenia

Chair: Baroness Cox — *Con*
Vice-chairs:
Lord Avebury — *Lib Dem*
Lord Biffen — *Con*
Terry Davis — *Lab*
Secretary: Jane Griffiths — *Lab*

Contact: Odette Bazil, Upper Haik, Hammersley Lane, Penn, Buckinghamshire HP13 7BY Tel: 01494 816757

Australia and New Zealand (ANZAC)

President: Lord Morris of Manchester	*Lab*
Chair: David Marshall	*Lab*
Vice-chairs:	
Lord Ashley of Stoke	*Lab*
Michael Howard	*Con*
Secretaries:	
Terry Davis	*Lab*
Andrew Rosindell	*Con*
Treasurer: Lord Evans of Parkside	*Lab*

Contact: David Marshall MP, House of Commons, London SW1A 0AA
Tel: 020 7219 5134

Austria

Chair: Nicholas Winterton	*Con*
Vice-chairs:	
Tom Cox	*Lab*
Owen Paterson	*Con*
Angus Robertson	*SNP*
Secretaries:	
Viscount Craigavon	*Crossbench*
John Mann	*Lab*
Treasurer: Lord Methuen	*Lib Dem*

Contact: The Viscount Craigavon,
54 Westminster Mansions, 1 Little Smith Street,
London SW1P 3DQ Tel: 020 7222 1949

Azerbaijan

Chair: Bruce George	*Lab*
Vice-chairs:	
Dari Taylor	*Lab*
Lord Fraser of Carmyllie	*Con*
Secretary/Treasurer: Robert Wareing	*Lab*

Contact: Natalie Whatford, c/o Bruce George
MP, House of Commons, London SW1A 0AA
Tel: 020 7219 4049

Bahrain

Chair: Dr Ashok Kumar	*Lab*
Deputy chair: David Wilshire	*Con*
Vice-chairs:	
Nigel Evans	*Con*
Nigel Jones	*Lib Dem*
Secretary: Ken Purchase	*Lab*
Treasurer: Baroness Uddin	*Lab*

Contact: Ken Purchase MP, House of
Commons, London SW1A 0AA
Tel: 020 7219 3602

Bangladesh

Chair: Kerry Pollard	*Lab*
Vice-chairs:	
Baroness Uddin	*Lab*
John Wilkinson	*Con*
Secretary: Ernie Ross	*Lab*

Treasurer: Simon Hughes	*Lib Dem*

Contact: Ernie Ross MP, Room 275, Portcullis
House, Bridge Street, London SW1A 2LW
Tel: 020 7219 3480

Belarus

Chair: Terry Davis	*Lab*
Vice-chair: David Atkinson	*Con*
Secretary: Lord Ponsonby of Shulbrede	*Lab*

Contact: Lord Ponsonby of Shulbrede, House of
Lords, London SW1A 0PW Tel: 020 7219 0071

Belgium

Chair: Terry Davis	*Lab*
Vice-chair: Lord Grenfell	*Lab*
Vice-chair and	
Secretary: Baroness Hooper	*Con*
Treasurer: Lord Tomlinson	*Con*

Contact: Baroness Hooper, House of Lords,
London SW1A 0PW Tel: 020 7219 5489

Bermuda

Chair: Ian Davidson	*Lab*
Vice-chairs:	
Lord Ashley of Stoke	*Lab*
Nick Hawkins	*Con*
Lord Tope	*Lib Dem*
Secretary: Andy Reed	*Lab*
Treasurers:	
David Crausby	*Lab*
Andrew Rosindell	*Con*

Contact: Andy Reed MP, House of Commons,
London SW1A 0AA Tel: 020 7219 3529

Bosnia

Chair: Sir Patrick Cormack	*Con*
Vice-chairs:	
Nigel Jones	*Lib Dem*
Kate Hoey	*Lab*
Secretary: Calum MacDonald	*Lab*
Treasurer: John Austin	*Lab*

Contact: Sir Patrick Cormack MP, House of
Commons, London SW1A 0AA
Tel: 020 7219 5514

Botswana

Chair: Nigel Jones	*Lib Dem*
Vice-chairs:	
Bob Spink	*Con*
Malcolm Moss	*Con*
Win Griffiths	*Lab*
David Chidgey	*Lib Dem*
Secretary Derek Wyatt	*Lab*

Contact: Nigel Jones MP, House of Commons,
London SW1A 0AA Tel: 020 7219 4415

Brazil

Chair: Bob Blizzard — *Lab*
Vice-chairs:
 Rev Martin Smyth — *UUP*
 Tony Baldry — *Con*
Treasurer:
 Baroness Gibson of Market Rasen — *Lab*
Secretary: Lawrie Quinn — *Lab*

Contact: Bob Blizzard MP, House of Commons, London SW1A 0AA
Tel: 01502 514913

Bulgaria

Chair: Kevin Barron — *Lab*
Vice-chair: John Randall — *Con*
Secretary: Nigel Jones — *Lib Dem*
Treasurer: Lord Biffen — *Con*

Contact: Kevin Barron MP, House of Commons, London SW1A 0AA Tel: 020 7219 6306

Burma

Chair: Vera Baird — *Lab*
Vice-chair: Dr John Pugh — *Lib Dem*
Secretary: Iain Luke — *Lib Dem*
Treasurer:
 Lord Faulkner of Worcester — *Lib Dem*

Contact: Iain Luke MP, House of Commons, London SW1A 0AA Tel: 01382 466702

Canada

Chair: David Marshall — *Lab*
Vice-chair: Marion Roe — *Con*
Secretary: Colin Pickthall — *Lab*
Treasurer: Rev Martin Smyth — *UUP*

Contact: David Marshall MP, House of Commons, London SW1A 0AA
Tel: 020 7219 5134

Caribbean

Chair: Diane Abbott — *Lab*
Vice-chair: Lord Faulkner of Worcester — *Lab*
Secretary: Anthony Steen — *Con*
Treasurer: Michael Mates — *Con*

Contact: Anthony Steen MP, House of Commons, London SW1A 0AA
Tel: 020 7219 5045

Cayman Islands

Chair: Lord Davies of Coity — *Lab*
Vice-chair: Nigel Evans — *Con*
Secretary: Graham Brady — *Con*
Treasurer: Lindsay Hoyle — *Lab*

Contact: Jennifer Dilbert, Cayman Islands Government Office, 6 Arlington Street, London SW1A 1RE Tel: 020 7491 7772

Central Asia

Chair: Jim Cousins — *Lab*
Vice-chairs:
 Viscount Waverley — *Crossbench*
 David Chaytor — *Lab*
Secretary: John Randall — *Con*
Treasurer: Robert Wareing — *Lab*

Contact: Jim Cousins MP, House of Commons, London SW1A 0AA
Tel: 020 7219 4204

Chile

Chair: John Wilkinson — *Con*
Vice-chairs:
 Baroness Hooper — *Con*
 Tony Lloyd — *Lab*
Secretary and Treasurer:
 Gerald Howarth — *Con*

Contact: John Wilkinson MP, House of Commons, London SW1A 0AA
Tel: 020 7219 5165

China

Chair: Ben Chapman — *Lab*
Vice-chairs:
 Tony Baldry — *Con*
 Ian Stewart — *Lab*
 Brian Cotter — *Lib Dem*
Secretary/Treasurer: Gordon Prentice — *Lab*

Contact: Ben Chapman MP, House of Commons, London SW1A 0AA
Tel: 020 7219 1143

Colombia

Chair: Richard Allan — *Lib Dem*
Vice-chairs:
 Tony Lloyd — *Lab*
 Baroness Hooper — *Con*
Secretary and Treasurer:
 John Wilkinson — *Con*

Contact: John Wilkinson MP, House of Commons, London SW1A 0AA
Tel: 020 7219 5165

Croatia

Chair: Tom Cox — *Lab*
Vice-chairs:
 Earl of Dundee — *Con*
 Sir Patrick Cormack — *Con*
 Mike Hancock — *Lib Dem*
 Lord Biffen — *Con*
 Lord Gladwin of Clee — *Lab*
Secretary: Lord Grenfell — *Lab*

Contact: Earl of Dundee, House of Lords, London SW1A 0PW Tel: 020 7219 6781

Cuba

Chair: Dr Ian Gibson — *Lab*
Vice-chairs:
Richard Allan — *Lib Dem*
Nigel Evans — *Con*
Secretary: Jeremy Corbyn — *Lab*

Contact: Philippa Coughlan, c/o Nick Palmer MP, Room 254, Portcullis House, Bridge Street, London SW1A 2LW
Tel: 020 7219 2397

Cyprus

Chair: Tox Cox — *Lab*
Vice-chair: Nigel Waterson — *Con*
Secretary: Edward O'Hara — *Lab*
Treasurer: Roger Gale — *Con*

Contact: Tom Cox MP, House of Commons, London SW1A 0AA Tel: 020 7219 5034

Czech and Slovak

Chair: John Cummings — *Lab*
Vice-chairs:
Earl of Liverpool — *Con*
Lord Dubs — *Lab*
Nigel Jones — *Lib Dem*
Secretary/Treasurer: John Austin — *Lab*

Contact: John Austin MP, House of Commons, London SW1A 0AA Tel: 020 7219 5195

Denmark

Chair: Sir Nicholas Winterton — *Con*
Vice-chairs:
Terry Davis — *Lab*
Roy Beggs — *UUP*
Anne McIntosh — *Con*
Treasurers:
Lord Faulkner of Worcester — *Lab*
Ann Winterton — *Con*
Andrew Rosindell — *Con*
Secretaries:
Viscount Craigavon — *Crossbench*
Dr Nick Palmer — *Lab*

Contact: Viscount Craigavon, 54 Westminster Mansions, 1 Little Smith Street, London SW1P 3DQ
Tel: 020 7222 1949

Egypt

Chair: Jim Cousins — *Lab*
Vice-chair: Nigel Evans — *Con*
Secretary: Ken Purchase — *Lab*
Treasurer: Graham Brady — *Con*

Contact: Ken Purchase MP, House of Commons, London SW1A 0AA
Tel: 020 7219 3602

Estonia

Chair: Gordon Marsden — *Lab*
Vice-chairs:
Lembit Öpik — *Lib Dem*
John Wilkinson — *Con*
Christine Russell — *Lab*
Treasurer: John Randall — *Con*

Contact: Oliver Pauley, c/o Gordon Marsden MP, House of Commons, London SW1A 0AA
Tel: 020 7219 1262

Ethiopia

Chair: John Austin — *Lab*
Vice-chairs:
Tom Cox — *Lab*
Colin Breed — *Lib Dem*
Secretary: Laurence Robertson — *Con*
Treasurer: John McDonnell — *Lab*

Contact: John Austin MP, House of Commons, London SW1A 0AA Tel: 020 7219 5195

Euro–Arab Co-operation

Chairs:
John Austin — *Lab*
David Atkinson — *Con*
Secretary: Christine Russell — *Lab*
Treasurer: Nigel Jones — *Lib Dem*

Contact: John Austin MP, House of Commons, London SW1A 0AA Tel: 020 7219 5195

Falkland Islands

Chair: Nicholas Winterton — *Con*
Vice-chair: John Austin — *Lab*
Secretary: Andrew Rosindell — *Con*
Treasurer: Lord Shutt of Greetland — *Lib Dem*

Contact: Sukey Cameron, Falkland Islands Government Representative, Falkland House, 14 Broadway, London SW1H 0BH
Tel: 020 7222 2742

Finland

Chair: Sir Patrick Cormack — *Con*
Vice-chairs:
Brian White — *Lab*
Baroness Ramsay of Cartvale — *Lab*
Lord Hardy of Wath — *Lab*
Ann Winterton — *Con*
Secretaries:
Viscount Craigavon — *Crossbench*
Robert Syms — *Con*
Treasurers:
Rachel Squire — *Lab*
Simon Hughes — *Lib Dem*

Contact: Viscount Craigavon, 54 Westminster Mansions, Little Smith Street, London SW1P 3DQ Tel: 020 7222 1949

France

Chair: Joyce Quin	*Lab*

Vice-chairs:

Quentin Davies	*Con*
Lord Randall of St Budeaux	*Lab*

Secretaries:

Lord Grenfell	*Lab*
Tom Brake	*Lib Dem*
Treasurer: Lord Astor of Hever	*Con*

Contact: Evie Soames, Weber Shandwick GJW, 14 Gray's Inn Road, London WC1X 8WS Tel: 020 7067 0328

Germany

Chairs:

Quentin Davies	*Con*
Donald Anderson	*Lab*
Vice-chair: Ian Davidson	*Lab*
Secretary: Mark Field	*Con*

Contact: Mark Field MP, House of Commons, London SW1A 0AA Tel: 020 7219 8160

Gibraltar

Chair: Lindsay Hoyle	*Lab*

Vice-chairs:

David Crausby	*Lab*
Tim Loughton	*Con*
Simon Hughes	*Lib Dem*
Secretary: Eleanor Laing	*Con*
Treasurer: Colin Breed	*Lib Dem*

Contact: Lindsay Hoyle MP, House of Commons, London SW1A 0AA Tel: 020 7219 3515

Greece

Chair: Eddie O'Hara	*Lab*

Vice-chairs:

Nigel Waterson	*Con*
Andrew Dismore	*Lab*
Secretary: Tom Cox	*Lab*
Treasurer: Baroness Golding	*Lab*

Contact: Eddie O'Hara MP, House of Commons, London SW1A 0AA Tel: 020 7219 4538

Hungary

Chair: Tom Cox	*Lab*
Vice-chair: David Amess	*Con*
Secretary: John Austin	*Lab*
Treasurer: Tim Boswell	*Con*

Contact: John Austin MP, House of Commons, London SW1A 0AA Tel: 020 7219 5195

Iceland

Chair: Austin Mitchell	*Lab*

Vice-chairs:

John Wilkinson	*Con*
Alan Beith	*Lib Dem*

Secretary: Viscount Craigavon	*Crossbench*
Treasurer: Rachel Squire	*Lab*

Contact: Viscount Craigavon, 54 Westminster Mansions, 1 Little Smith Street, London SW1P 3DQ Tel: 020 7222 1949

India

President: Lord Janner of Braunstone	*Lab*

Deputy President:

Lord Weatherill	*Crossbench*
Chair: Piara Khabra	*Lab*

Vice-chairs:

Lord Corbett of Castle Vale	*Lab*
Baroness Flather	*Con*
Peter Luff	*Con*
Lord Dholakia	*Lib Dem*
Secretary: Dr Ashok Kumar	*Lab*
Membership Secretary: Barry Gardiner	*Lab*
Treasurer: Rev Martyn Smyth	*UUP*

Contact: Dr Ashok Kumar MP, House of Commons, London SW1A 0AA Tel: 020 7219 4460

Indonesia

Chair: Win Griffiths	*Lab*
Vice-chair: Lord Avebury	*Lib Dem*
Secretary: Ann Winterton	*Con*
Treasurer: Lord Reay	*Lab*

Contact: Win Griffiths MP, House of Commons, London SW1A 0AA Tel: 020 7219 6538

Iran

Chair: Lord Temple-Morris	*Lab*

Vice-chairs:

David Atkinson	*Con*
Tam Dalyell	*Lab*
Robert Jackson	*Con*
Lord Kilclooney	*UUP*
Baroness Nicholson of Winterbourne	*Lib Dem*

Secretaries:

Jim Cousins	*Lab*
Lord Phillips of Sudbury	*Lib Dem*
Treasurer: Tony Baldry	*Con*

Contact: Lord Temple-Morris, House of Lords, London SW1A 0PW Tel: 020 7219 4181

Iraq

Chair: Ann Clwyd	*Lab*

Vice-chairs:

Andrew Robathan	*Con*
John Burnett	*Lib Dem*
Secretary: Jim Knight	*Lab*
Treasurer: Huw Irranca-Davies	*Lab*

Contact: Jim Knight MP, House of Commons, London SW1A 0AA Tel: 020 7219 8466

Iraqi Kurdistan

Chair: Tom Clarke	*Lab*
Vice-chairs:	
Dr Jenny Tonge	*Lib Dem*
Baroness Cox	*Con*
Jeremy Corbyn	*Lab*
Secretary: Michael Weir	*SNP*
Treasurer: Michael Connarty	*Lab*

Contact: Lesley-Anne Robertson,
c/o Mike Weir MP, House of Commons,
London SW1A 0AA Tel: 020 7498 3485

Israel

Chair: Lord Hogg of Cumbernauld	*Lab*
Vice-chairs:	
Lord Stevens of Ludgate	*Con*
Lord Janner of Braunstone	*Lab*
Baroness Miller of Hendon	*Con*
Louise Ellman	*Lab*
Lord Turnberg	*Lab*
Lord Clarke of Hampstead	*Lab*
Baroness Blatch	*Con*
Lord Evans of Watford	*Lab*
Secretary: Linda Perham	*Lab*
Treasurer: Dr Evan Harris	*Lib Dem*
President: Lord Weidenfeld	*Crossbencher*
Vice-Presidents:	
Gillian Shephard	*Con*
James Purnell	*Lab*

Contact: Edward Lewin, c/o Lord Janner of
Brunstone, House of Lords,
London SW1A 0PW Tel: 020 7976 8443

Italy

Chair: Roger Casale	*Lab*
Vice-chairs:	
Quentin Davies	*Con*
John Burnett	*Lib Dem*
Secretary: Rachel Squire	*Lab*

Contact: Michael Nathanson, Radcliffes Le
Brasseur, 5 Great College Street,
London SW1P 3SJ Tel: 020 7222 7040

Japan

Chair: Roger Godsiff	*Lab*
Vice-chairs:	
Sir John Stanley	*Con*
Peter Viggers	*Con*
David Marshall	*Lab*
Secretaries:	
Ian Davidson	*Lab*
Jane Griffiths	*Lab*
Treasurer: Robert Walter	*Con*

Contact: Ian Hughes, Assistant to Roger
Godsiff MP, Room 409, 1 Parliament Street,
London SW1A 2NE Tel: 020 7219 5191

Kashmir

Chair: Roger Godsiff	*Lab*
Vice-chairs:	
Lord Avebury	*Lib Dem*
Baroness Knight of Collingtree	*Con*
Secretary: Lorna Fitzsimons	*Lab*
Treasurer: Marsha Singh	*Lab*

Contact: Ian Hughes, Assistant to Roger
Godsiff MP, Room 409, 1 Parliament Street,
London SW1A 2NE Tel: 020 7219 5191

Kazakhstan

Chair: Viscount Waverley	*Crossbench*
Vice-chairs:	
Linda Gilroy	*Lab*
Bob Spink	*Con*
Lord Kilclooney	*UUP*
Secretary: John Mann	*Lab*

Contact: Viscount Waverley, PO Box 29160,
London SW1P 3WE Tel: 020 7219 3000

Kenya

Chair: Tom Cox	*Lab*
Vice-chair: William Cash	*Con*
Secretary: John McDonnell	*Lab*
Treasurer: Nigel Jones	*Lib Dem*

Contact: Tom Cox MP, House of Commons,
London SW1A 0AA Tel: 020 7219 5034

Korea

(South Korea/Republic of Korea)

Chair: Sir John Stanley	*Con*
Vice-chair: Rachel Squire	*Lab*
Secretary: Edward Garnier	*Con*
Treasurer: William O'Brien	*Lab*

Contact: Sir John Stanley MP, House of
Commons, London SW1A 0AA
Tel: 020 7219 5977

Kosova

Chairs:	
John Austin	*Lab*
Baroness Ludford	*Lib Dem*
Vice-chair: Lord Biffen	*Con*

Contact: John Austin MP, House of Commons,
London SW1A 0AA Tel: 020 7219 5195

Kuwait

Chair: Mohammad Sarwar	*Lab*
Vice-chairs:	
Cheryl Gillan	*Con*
Khalid Mahmood	*Lab*
Secretary: Alistair Carmichael	*Lib Dem*
Treasurer: Baroness Uddin	*Lab*

Contact: Maria Holt, c/o Mohammad Sarwar
MP, Room 572, Portcullis House, Bridge Street,
London SW1A 2LW Tel: 020 7219 0547

Latin America

Chair: Tam Dalyell	*Lab*
Vice-chair: John Wilkinson	*Con*
Secretary: Mark Simmonds	*Con*
Treasurer: Bob Blizzard	*Lab*

Contact: John Wilkinson MP, House of Commons, London SW1A 0AA
Tel: 020 7219 5165

Lebanon

Chair: Andrew Love	*Lab*
Vice-chairs:	
Hugo Swire	*Con*
Christine Russell	*Lab*
Secretary: John Austin	*Lab*
Treasurer: Iain Luke	*Lab*

Contact: John Austin MP, House of Commons, London SW1A 0AA Tel: 020 7219 5195

Lithuania

Co-chairs:	
Paul Keetch	*Lib Dem*
Roger Berry	*Lab*
Lord Bowness	*Con*
Secretary: Lord Janner of Braunstone	*Lab*
Treasurer: Lord Faulkner of Worcester	*Lab*

Contact: Paul Keetch MP, House of Commons, London SW1A 0AA Tel: 020 7219 2419

Macedonia

Chair: Alice Mahon	*Lab*
Vice-chairs:	
Robert Wareing	*Lab*
Andrew Tyrie	*Con*
Secretary: John Randall	*Con*
Treasurer: Lord Lea of Crondall	*Lab*

Contact: John Randall MP, House of Commons, London SW1A 0AA Tel: 020 7219 3400

Isle of Man

Chair and Secretary: John Wilkinson	*Con*
Vice-chair and Treasurer: John Austin	*Lab*
Vice-chairs:	
Nick Hawkins	*Con*
Lord Kilclooney	*Crossbencher*
Lord Shutt of Greetland	*Lib Dem*
Secretary: Andrew Rosindell	*Con*

Contact: John Wilkinson MP, House of Commons, London SW1A 0AA
Tel: 020 7219 5165

Latvia

Chair and Secretary:	
John Wilkinson	*Con*
Vice-chairs:	
Bruce George	*Lab*
Terry Davis	*Lab*
Treasurer: Gordon Marsden	*Lab*

Contact: John Wilkinson MP, House of Commons, London SW1A 0AA
Tel: 020 7219 5165

Malta

Chair: Harry Barnes	*Lab*
Vice-chair: Lord Kilclooney	*UUP*
Secretary: Nick Hawkins	*Con*
Treasurer: Baroness Golding	*Lab*

Contact: Nick Hawkins MP, House of Commons, London SW1A 0AA
Tel: 020 7219 6329

Mongolia

Chair: Peter Pike	*Lab*
Vice-chair: Jane Griffiths	*Lab*
Secretary: Peter Luff	*Con*
Treasurer: Baroness Trumpington	*Con*

Contact: Peter Pike MP, House of Commons, London SW1A 0AA Tel: 020 7219 3514/6488

Morocco

Chair: Derek Conway	*Con*
Vice-chairs:	
Lord Janner of Braunstone	*Lab*
Lindsay Hoyle	*Lab*
Secretary: Rev Martin Smyth	*UUP*
Treasurer: Andrew Mitchell	*Con*

Contact: Derek Conway MP, House of Commons, London SW1A 0AA
Tel: 020 7219 8305

Nepal

Chair: Sir John Stanley	*Con*
Vice-chairs:	
Tom Cox	*Lab*
John Wilkinson	*Con*
Tam Dalyell	*Lab*
Secretary: Dr Julian Lewis	*Con*
Treasurer: Bill O'Brien	*Lab*

Contact: Sir John Stanley MP, House of Commons, London SW1A 0AA
Tel: 020 7219 5977

Netherlands

Chair: Dr Stephen Ladyman	*Lab*
Vice-chairs:	
Donald Anderson	*Lab*
Quentin Davies	*Con*
Mike Gapes	*Lab*
Menzies Campbell	*Lib Dem*
Secretary: Lord Temple-Morris	*Lab*
Treasurers:	
Edward Garnier	*Con*
Dr Rudi Vis	*Lab*

Contact: Lord Temple-Morris, House of Lords, London SW1A 0PW Tel: 020 7219 4181

Northern Cyprus

Chair: Lord Kilclooney	UUP
Vice-chairs:	
Lord Butterworth	Con
Roy Beggs	UUP
Treasurer: Nicholas Winterton	Con

Contact: Lady Butterworth, 727 Nell Gwynn House, Sloane Avenue, London SW3 3AX Tel: 020 7581 4838

Norway

Chair: Donald Anderson	Lab
Vice-chairs:	
Alan Beith	Lib Dem
Lord Elton	Con
Viscount Craigavon	Crossbench
Secretary: Lord Faulkner of Worcester	Lab

Contact: Lord Faulkner of Worcester, House of Lords, London SW1A 0PW Tel: 020 7219 8503

Oman

Chair: Alan Duncan	Con
Vice-chair: Kate Hoey	Lab
Secretary: Lindsay Hoyle	Lab
Treasurer: Hugo Swire	Con

Contact: Alan Duncan MP, House of Commons, London SW1A 0AA Tel: 020 7219 5204

Overseas Territories

(Bermuda, British Virgin Islands, Cayman Islands, Falkland Islands, Gibraltar, Montserrat, St Helena, Turks and Caicos Islands)

Chair: John Austin	Lab
Vice-chairs:	
Lord Beaumont of Whitley	Green
Baroness Hooper	Con
Secretary/Treasurer: Jimmy Hood	Lab

Contact: Jimmy Hood MP, House of Commons, London SW1A 0AA Tel: 020 7219 4585

Pakistan

Chair: Tom Cox	Lab
Vice-chairs:	
John Wilkinson	Con
Mohammad Sarwar	Lab
Secretary: Peter Pike	Lab
Treasurer: Jonathan Sayeed	Con

Contact: Peter Pike MP, House of Commons, London SW1A 0AA Tel: 020 7219 3514

Palestine

Chair: Richard Burden	Lab
Vice-chairs:	
Colin Breed	Lib Dem
Patrick Mercer	Con
Secretary: Dr Brian Iddon	Lab

Treasurer: Christine Russell	Lab

Contact: Richard Burden MP, House of Commons, London SW1A 0AA Tel: 020 7219 5002

Philippines

Chair: Michael Connarty	Lab
Vice-chairs:	
John Wilkinson	Con
Duke of Montrose	Con
Secretary: Stephen Pound	Lab
Treasurer: James Purnell	Lab

Contact: Michael Connarty MP, House of Commons, London SW1A 0AA Tel: 020 7219 2487

Poland

Chair: Wayne David	Lab
Vice-chairs:	
Eric Pickles	Con
Lord MacLennan of Rogart	Lib Dem
Secretary: Dr Alan Whitehead	Lab
Treasurer: John Mann	Lab

Contact: Wayne David MP, House of Commons, London SW1A 0AA Tel: 020 7219 8152

Qatar

Chair: Robert Jackson	Con
Vice-chair: Mark Fisher	Lab
Secretary: Lord Redesdale	Lib Dem
Treasurer: John Austin	Lab

Contact: Lord Redesdale, House of Lords, London SW1A 0PW Tel: 020 7219 4342

Romania

Chair and Secretary: Peter Pike	Lab
Vice-chair and Secretary:	
Mark Hendrick	Lab
Vice-chairs:	
David Heath	Lib Dem
Lord Biffen	Con
Treasurer: Mike Hancock	Lib Dem

Contact: Peter Pike MP, House of Commons, London SW1A 0AA Tel: 020 7219 3514

Russia

Chair: Tony Lloyd	Lab
Vice-chairs:	
Baroness Smith of Gilemorehill	Lab
David Atkinson	Con
Mike Hancock	Lib Dem
Secretary: Robert Wareing	Lab
Treasurer: Gregory Barker	Con

Contact: Robert Wareing MP, House of Commons, London SW1A 0AA Tel: 020 7219 3482

St Helena

Chair: Bob Russell   *Lib Dem*
Vice-chair: John Cummings   *Lab*
Secretary: Ann Winterton   *Con*
Treasurer: Lord Beaumont of Whitley   *Green*

Contact: Bob Russell MP, House of Commons, London SW1A 0AA Tel: 020 7219 5150

Saudi Arabia

Chair: Lawrie Quinn   *Lab*
Vice-chairs:
    Charles Hendry   *Con*
    Norman Lamb   *Lib Dem*
Secretary: Derek Wyatt   *Lab*
Treasurer: Tony Clarke   *Lab*

Contact: Lawrie Quinn MP, Room 218, Portcullis House, Bridge Street, London SW1A 2LW Tel: 020 7219 4170

Senegal and Guinea

Chair: David Chidgey   *Lib Dem*
Vice-chair: David Borrow   *Lab*
Secretary: Bob Spink   *Con*

Contact: David Chidgey MP, House of Commons, London SW1A 0AA Tel: 020 7219 4298

Serbia and Montenegro

Chair: Alice Mahon   *Lab*
Vice-chair: Robert Wareing   *Lab*
Secretary: John Randall   *Con*
Treasurer: Paul Keetch   *Lib Dem*

Contact: John Randall MP, House of Commons, London SW1A 0AA Tel: 020 7219 3400

Singapore

Chair: James Paice   *Con*
Vice-chairs:
    Ann Keen   *Lab*
    Lord Naseby   *Con*
Treasurer: Richard Ottaway   *Con*
Secretary: Nigel Waterson   *Con*

Contact: James Paice MP, House of Commons, London SW1A 0AA Tel: 020 7219 4101

Slovenia

Chair: John Austin   *Lab*
Vice-chair: Lord Biffen   *Con*
Secretary: Nigel Jones   *Lib Dem*

Contact: John Austin MP, House of Commons, London SW1A 0AA Tel: 020 7219 5195

South Africa

Chair: Helen Jackson   *Lab*
Vice-chairs:
    Donald Anderson   *Lab*

Simon Hughes   *Lib Dem*
John McFall   *Lab*
Anthony Steen   *Con*
Elfyn Llwyd   *PC*
Lord St John of Bletso   *Crossbench*
Secretary: Anne McIntosh   *Con*
Treasurer: Lord Astor of Hever   *Con*

Contact: Anne McIntosh MP, House of Commons, London SW1A 0AA
Tel: 020 7219 3541

Southern Africa

(South Africa, Mozambique, Namibia and other Southern African countries)

Chair: Peter Pike   *Lab*
Vice-chairs:
    Lord Judd   *Lab*
    Baroness Flather   *Con*
    David Wilshire   *Con*
    Lord Janner of Braunstone   *Lab*
Secretary: Win Griffiths   *Lab*
Treasurer: Rev Martin Smyth   *UUP*

Contact: Peter Pike MP, House of Commons, London SW1A 0AA
Tel: 020 7219 3514

South Korea see Korea

South Pacific

(Cook Islands, Fiji, Kiribati, Nauru, Pitcairn Islands, Solomon Islands, Tonga, Tuvala and Vanuatu, Western Samoa)

Chair: David Marshall   *Lab*
Vice-chairs:
    Sir Nicholas Winterton   *Con*
    Sir Paul Beresford   *Con*
Secretary: Lord Evans of Parkside   *Lab*

Contact: David Marshall MP, House of Commons, London SW1A 0AA
Tel: 020 7219 5134

Spain

Chair: Peter Mandelson   *Lab*
Vice-chairs:
    Donald Anderson   *Lab*
    Robert Jackson   *Con*
    Margaret Moran   *Lab*
    Lord Kilclooney   *UUP*
Secretary: John Butterfill   *Con*
Treasurers:
    Baroness Golding   *Lab*
    Lord Temple-Morris   *Lab*

Contact: Lord Temple-Morris, House of Lords, London SW1A 0PW
Tel: 020 7219 4181

Sri Lanka

Joint-chairs:
Barry Gardiner	*Lab*
Lord Naseby	*Con*

Vice-chairs:
Sir Nicholas Winterton	*Con*
Graham Allen	*Lab*

Secretary: Andrew Love   *Lab*
Treasurer: Edward Davey   *Lib Dem*

Contact: Andrew Love MP, House of Commons, London SW1A 0AA
Tel: 020 7219 6377

Sudan

Chair: Hilton Dawson   *Lab*
Vice-chair: Dr Jenny Tonge   *Lib Dem*
Secretary: Baroness Cox   *Con*
Treasurer: Earl of Sandwich   *Crossbench*

Contact: Colin Robertson, Office of Hilton Dawson MP, House of Commons,
London SW1A 0AA Tel: 020 7219 4207

Sweden

Chair: Alan Beith   *Lib Dem*
Vice-chairs:
Sir Nicholas Winterton	*Con*
Terry Davis	*Lab*
Martin Linton	*Lab*

Secretaries:
Viscount Craigavon	*Crossbench*
John Mann	*Lab*

Treasurers:
Kelvin Hopkins	*Lab*
Angela Watkinson	*Con*
Lord Faulkner of Worcester	*Lab*

Contact: Viscount Craigavon, 54 Westminster Mansions, 1 Little Smith Street,
London SW1P 3DQ Tel: 020 7222 1949

Switzerland

Chair: Tom Levitt   *Lab*
Vice-chairs:
Caroline Spelman	*Con*
Lord Lea of Crondall	*Lab*

Secretary: Lord Astor of Hever   *Con*
Treasurer: Huw Edwards   *Lab*

Contact: Tom Levitt MP, House of Commons, London SW1A 0AA Tel: 020 7219 4189

Syria

Chair: John Austin   *Lab*
Vice-chairs:
Robert Jackson	*Con*
Iain Luke	*Lab*
Lord Phillips of Sudbury	*Lib Dem*

Secretary: Neil Gerrard   *Lab*

Treasurer: Christine Russell   *Lab*

Contact: John Austin MP, House of Commons, London SW1A 0AA
Tel: 020 7219 5195

Taiwan

Chair: Tom Cox   *Lab*
Vice-chairs:
Sir Nicholas Winterton	*Con*
Lord Faulkner of Worcester	*Lab*

Secretary: Rev Martin Smyth   *UUP*
Treasurer: Ann Winterton   *Con*

Contact: Tox Cox MP, House of Commons, London SW1A 0AA
Tel: 020 7219 5034

Tanzania

Chair: Stephen O'Brien   *Con*
Vice-chairs:
William Cash	*Con*
Hugh Bayley	*Lab*

Secretary: David Borrow   *Lab*
Treasurer: Valerie Davey   *Lab*

Contact: Stephen O'Brien MP, House of Commons, London SW1A 0AA
Tel: 020 7219 4996

Tibet

Chair: John Wilkinson   *Con*
Vice-chairs:
Lord Willoughby de Broke	*Con*
Lord Avebury	*Lib Dem*
Norman Baker	*Lib Dem*

Treasurer: Harry Cohen   *Lab*

Contact: Lady Philippa Carrick, 116 Hallowell Road, Northwood, Middlesex HA6 1DU
Tel: 020 7272 1414

Trinidad and Tobago

Chairs:
George Foulkes	*Lab*
Nick Hawkins	*Con*

Secretary: John Austin   *Lab*
Treasurer: David Marshall   *Lab*

Contact: John Austin MP, House of Commons, London SW1A 0AA
Tel: 020 7219 5195

Tunisia

Chair: Mark Fisher   *Lab*
Vice-chair: Roger Gale   *Con*
Secretary: Lord McNally   *Lib Dem*
Treasurer: Lord Tope   *Lib Dem*

Contact: Lord McNally, 30 Cunningham Avenue, St Albans, Hertfordshire AL1 1JL
Tel: 01727 760689

Turkey

Chair: Frank Cook   *Lab*
Vice-chairs:
  Andy King   *Lab*
  Andrew Dismore   *Lab*
Secretary: Robert Walter   *Con*

Contact: Tony Baldry MP, House of Commons,
London SW1A 0AA Tel: 020 7219 4476

Uganda

Chair: William Cash   *Con*
Vice-chairs:
  Stephen O'Brien   *Con*
  Andrew Reed   *Lab*
Secretary: Andy Reed   *Lab*

Contact: William Cash MP, House of Commons,
London SW1A 0AA Tel: 020 7219 6330

Ukraine

Chair: Ann Clwyd   *Lab*
Vice-chairs:
  Lord Howe of Aberavon   *Con*
  John Wilkinson   *Con*
Secretary: Tom Cox   *Lab*
Treasurer: Robert Wareing   *Lab*

Contact: Tom Cox MP, House of Commons,
London SW1A 0AA Tel: 020 7219 5034

Venezuela

Chair: Derek Conway   *Con*
Vice-chairs:
  Tony Lloyd   *Lab*
  Baroness Hooper   *Con*
Secretary: Andrew Mitchell   *Con*
Treasurer: Joe Benton   *Lab*

Contact: Derek Conway MP, House of
Commons, London SW1A 0AA
Tel: 020 7219 8305

Vietnam

Chair: Chris Mullin   *Lab*
Vice-chair: Peter Kilfoyle   *Lab*
Secretary: Ben Chapman   *Lab*

Contact: Ben Chapman MP, House of
Commons, London SW1A 0AA
Tel: 020 7219 1143

Yemen

Chair: Keith Vaz   *Lab*
Vice-chairs:
  Alan Duncan   *Con*
  Lord Lea of Crondall   *Lab*
Secretary: Richard Burden   *Lab*
Treasurers:
  Roy Beggs   *UUP*
  John Cummings   *Lab*

Contact: Keith Vaz MP, House of Commons,
London SW1A 0AA
Tel: 020 7219 4605

Zimbabwe

Chair: Derek Wyatt   *Lab*
Vice-chairs:
  Caroline Spelman   *Con*
  Lord Blake   *Con*
Secretary: John Barrett   *Lib Dem*
Treasurer: Frank Field   *Lab*

Contact: Derek Wyatt MP, House of Commons,
London SW1A 0AA
Tel: 020 7219 5807

DodOnline
An Electronic Directory without rival ...

MPs' biographies and photographs available with daily updates *via* the internet

For a *free* trial, call Yasmin Mirza, Aby Farsoun or Michael Mand on 020 7630 7643

Parliamentary Terms and Procedures

Terms relate to the House of Commons unless otherwise specified.
For further details see *Handbook of House of Commons Procedure* by Paul Evans (Vacher Dod Publishing 2003). References in bold italics have entries of their own.

accounting officer: the person (usually the permanent secretary of a government department) responsible for accounting to Parliament, in respect of each of the *Estimates* (or part of such Estimate), for the resources voted by Parliament for the public service.

adjournment motion: although technically a motion moved for the purpose of bringing to a conclusion a sitting of the House or a committee, when it is rarely debated, such a motion is often used as a procedural device for enabling a debate to take place without having to come to a conclusion in terms.

adjournment debate: a debate on an *adjournment motion* (see also *daily adjournment*).

affirmation: see *oath*.

allocation of time motion: see *guillotine*.

allotted days: the days allotted to debate a *bill* under a *programme order* or a *guillotine*, also the 20 days allotted each session as *opposition days*.

ambit: the description of the scope of expenditure covered by a Request for Resource (see also *appropriation* and *Estimates*).

amendment: a proposal to change the terms of a motion or to alter a *bill*.

annunciator: the television screens situated around the House and its precincts on which details of the current proceedings and future business of the House are shown.

appropriation: the allocation of money by Parliament to specified purposes. The Resource Accounts are the *Comptroller & Auditor General*'s audited accounts showing that money has been spent in accordance with Parliament's instructions embodied in the Appropriation Act (see also *Consolidated Fund* and *Estimates*).

back bench: the back benches are the places where Members who are not government Ministers or official opposition *shadows* sit in the Chamber, hence *back bencher*, the term used to describe a Member who holds no official position in government or in his or her party and who is therefore not bound by the convention of collective responsibility: such a Member may more formally be referred to as a private Member, though strictly speaking, this term applies to any Member not in receipt of a ministerial salary.

ballot: the term is used in the House to refer to the draw for *private Members' bills*. There is also provision for secret ballots in the House's proceedings relating to the election of its Speaker.

Bar of the House: the line across the floor of the Chamber which marks its formal threshold: the Bar is also marked by a rail (now invariably retracted) to which, in former times, *strangers* might be summoned to address the House or to be arraigned before it.

bill: a proposal for legislation formally presented to either House of Parliament.

Black Rod: the Gentleman Usher of the Black Rod, a member of the royal household, the broad equivalent in the Lords of the *Serjeant at Arms*, sent to summon the Commons to the Lords at the opening and closing of *sessions*.

board of management: the executive body of the permanent service of the House.

book entry: an entry in the *Votes and Proceedings* which records as a procedural event something which occurred without any actual proceedings taking place on the floor of the House.

breach of privilege: an abuse of one of the privileges of the House or an attempt to impede or frustrate the House or one of its Members in the exercise of one of its privileges.

budget resolutions: the series of financial resolutions, passed by the House at the conclusion of the debate on the *budget statement*, on which the *Finance Bill* is founded.

budget statement: the annual statement made by the Chancellor of the Exchequer (usually in March) setting out the government's tax and spending plans and proposals for their reconciliation for the forthcoming financial year: at the end of the debate on the budget, the *budget resolutions* are passed and the *Finance Bill* is introduced.

business motion: a motion proposing to regulate the time available to the House for consideration of a specified item of business at a specified sitting (see *ten o'clock motions*).

business question: the question addressed each Thursday to the *Leader of the House* under the urgent question procedure in reply to which the main items of business to be taken on each sitting day for the next week or so are announced.

by-election: an election in a single constituency to fill a vacancy caused by the death or *disqualification*, etc. of a Member.

C&AG: see *Comptroller & Auditor General*.

Cabinet: the inner circle of the government to which the Minister in charge of each government department belongs (and certain other Ministers), presided over by the *Prime Minister*.

casting vote: where any *division* (either in the House or in *standing committee*) results in a tie, it is decided on the vote of the occupant of the Chair, which is given in accordance with precedent.

Central Lobby: the main public area of the Palace of Westminster, equidistant from the two Houses of Parliament, where members of the public are received by Members.

Chairman of Ways and Means: the first deputy Speaker, with particular responsibilities for *private business* and *committees of the whole House* and sittings in Westminster Hall.

Chairmen's Panel: the body of Members appointed by the *Speaker* from among whom he chooses the chairmen of each *standing committee*.

Chief Whip: the senior *Whip* in each party: the government chief whip attends meetings of the Cabinet.

Chiltern Hundreds: the steward or bailiff of the three Chiltern Hundreds is the mythical 'office of profit under the Crown' to which Members are appointed when wishing to resign their seats by disqualifying themselves from membership of the House (see *disqualification*): the Stewardship of the Manor of Northstead is also used for this purpose.

Clandestine Outlawries Bill: the bill presented *proforma* on the first day of each session.

Clerk Assistant: the second *Clerk at the Table*, and first deputy to the *Clerk of the House*.

Clerks at the Table: the senior clerks in the Clerk of the House's Department who sit at the *Table* of the House.

Clerk of Bills: the Principal Clerk with particular responsibility for public and private bills.

Clerk of Legislation: the Principal Clerk in charge of the *Legislation Service* of the House.

Clerk of the House: the principal permanent officer of the House and also the *accounting officer* for the House of Commons Votes and Chief Executive of the House's permanent service.

closure: a procedural device for bringing a debate to a conclusion.

code of conduct: the code adopted by the House to guide Members on questions relating to the interpretation of its resolutions in respect of the declarations in the *Register of Members' Interests*, the rule against paid advocacy, the deposit of copies of contracts of employment and other matters relating to financial relationships with outside persons and bodies.

command paper: a government publication (more often than not a *White Paper*) presented to Parliament by 'command of Her Majesty'.

Commissioner for Standards: the officer of the House appointed to supervise the *Register of Members' Interests*, to advise Members on the interpretation of the *code of conduct* and to assist the *Committee on Standards and Privileges* in its work.

committal: the act of sending a *bill* to a committee of one kind or another after it has received a *second reading*.

committee: see *committee of the whole House, joint committee, select committee, standing committee*.

Committee of Selection: the committee which appoints Members to *standing committees* and proposes Members to the *departmental select committees* and the *domestic committees*.

Committee on Standards and Privileges: the select committee which investigates allegations of *breaches of privilege, contempts* and, with the assistance of the *Commissioner for Standards*, matters relating to the *code of conduct*, in particular complaints about Members in relation to outside financial interests and related matters.

committee of the whole House: the House forms itself into a committee of all its Members when it decides to take the committee stage of a *bill* in the whole House.

Comptroller & Auditor General: the officer of the House responsible for the running of the National Audit Office and for assisting the *Public Accounts Committee* in their scrutiny of public expenditure.

consideration: the more formal title for the *report stage* of a bill.

Consolidated Fund: the general fund into which almost all government receipts (in the form of taxes, duties, etc.) are paid (under section 10 of the Exchequer and Audit Act 1866) and out of which almost all government expenditure is met: Parliament passes the regular *Consolidated Fund Bills* which appropriate to the government service out of the Fund the total sums voted for particular purposes by way of the *Estimates*.

consolidation bill: a *bill* which consolidates much of the existing law on a particular subject into one convenient statute: because such bills do not (except within strict and very narrow limits) change the law, they are subject to special procedures distinct from the general procedures applying to public bills.

contempt: disobedience to, or defiance of, an order of the House, or some other insult to the House or its dignity or a *breach of privilege*.

crown prerogative: essentially, prerogative actions are those which the executive may take without the sanction of Parliament: they include *prorogation* and *dissolution* of Parliament, the grant of honours, the declaration of war and, in some circumstances, the making of treaties with foreign governments.

CWH: see *committee of the whole House*.

daily adjournment: the half-hour debate at the end of each day's sitting in the House at which a *back bench* Member has the opportunity to raise a matter with a Minister.

delegated legislation: legislation made by Ministers under powers granted to them in Acts of Parliament, usually by means of *statutory instrument*.

departmental select committees: the select committees established to oversee the work of government departments.

Deputy Chairmen: the First and Second Deputy Chairmen of Ways and Means, who with the *Chairman of Ways and Means* share with the *Speaker* the duties of presiding over the House.

despatch box: the two despatch boxes are situated at either side of the *Table*, at the far end from the Speaker's Chair, and serve as lecterns for those leading debate (or answering questions) from the government and official opposition front benches.

dilatory motion: a motion for the adjournment of debate or for the adjournment of the House or a standing committee moved for the purpose of superseding the business in hand.

Director of Broadcasting Services: the officer of the House responsible for day to day oversight of the broadcasting of its proceedings.

disqualification: there are a large number of offices the holding of which disqualify a person from sitting as a Member of the House of Commons. Broadly speaking, these fall within the general disqualifying category of 'offices of profit under the Crown', though the holders of ministerial office (up to a maximum of 95) are exempt (see also *Chiltern Hundreds*). There is also a general disqualification for civil servants, police officers, members of the armed forces, some judges and members of non-Commonwealth overseas legislatures. So too, in general terms, are persons ineligible to vote in a general election, for example Peers entitled to sit in the House of Lords, aliens, minors (though for this purpose the age of majority remains 21 not 18), sentenced prisoners and persons detained under the Mental Health Act 1983. So too are bankrupts, under the Insolvency Act 1986. Members may also be disqualified after an election for breach of electoral law.

dissolution: on the advice of the Prime Minister, the Queen may at any time dissolve Parliament, thereby initiating a general election.

division: the means by which the House or one of its committees ascertains the number of Members for and against a proposition before it when the Chair's opinion as to which side is in the majority on a *Question* is challenged. A division on a question which might otherwise take place after the moment of interruption may, in certain circumstances, be automatically deferred under the terms of the temporary standing order adopted by the House of Commons in 2001. Deferred divisions are then taken by collecting voting papers from members on the following Wednesday afternoon.

division bell area: the area from within which it is deemed to be possible to reach the *division lobbies* within the period from the ringing of the *division bells* to the closing of the lobby doors during a *division*.

division bells: the bells, situated in the House and its precincts and outbuildings, and elsewhere (such as government offices, pubs and restaurants and the private homes of Members) within the *division bell area*, which are rung to summon Members to vote in a *division*. Their function has been largely superseded off the premises by pagers, activated by the *Whips* offices.

division lobbies: the lobbies running down either side of the Chamber through which Members must pass to register their votes in a *division*.

domestic committees: the *select committees* concerned with the running of the House.

dropped order: when, for instance, the *Member in charge* of a bill does not name a new day for it to be set down for one of its stages after a stage has been completed or adjourned on any day, the order for that stage becomes a dropped order and the bill enters a sort of procedural limbo where it remains unless the Member in charge revives it (which he or she can do by means of a *book entry*).

dummy bill: when a *bill* is presented to the House by a Member he or she hands to the *Clerk at the Table* a folded card on which the short and long titles of the bill and the names of any supporters (up to a maximum of 12, including the *Member in charge*) are written, together with other details. These dummy bills are prepared by the *Public Bill Office*. Usually the bill is properly printed and published shortly afterwards, but in the case of *private Members' bills*, they sometimes never have an existence beyond this dummy form.

early day motions: expressions of opinion by Members on almost any subject which are published in the form of motions printed in the *Notice Paper* part of the *Vote Bundle*, to which other Members may add their names to indicate support.

Ecclesiastical Committee: the statutory committee of Members of both Houses which considers Church of England *Measures*.

Editor: the officer of the House in charge of the publication of the *Official Report* of debates in the Chamber and in standing committees (aka *Hansard*).

EDM: see *early day motions*.

effective orders: that part of the *Order Paper* which includes the items of business actually to be taken at a sitting, so called to distinguish it from the *remaining orders*.

Erskine May: Erskine May's *Treatise on the Law, Privileges, Proceedings and Usage of Parliament*, first published by the then *Clerk of the House*, Thomas Erskine May in 1844, and revised by his successors ever since: it is acknowledged as the authoritative text book on the law and practice of both Houses of Parliament: the latest edition is the 22nd, edited by Limon and McKay (Butterworths, London, 1997).

Estimates: the form in which the government presents, for approval by the Commons, its requests for the resources needed to cover recurring public expenditure.

Estimates days: the three days in each session set aside for consideration of the Estimates, in practice used for debate on one or more select committee reports chosen by the *Liaison Committee*.

Examiner of Petitions: the officer of the House with responsibility for examining certain matters relating to private bills and hybrid bills for compliance with the standing orders relating to *private business*; there is an equivalent officer in the House of Lords who joins in this examination.

exempted business: business which, under standing orders or under a specific order of the House, may be carried on after the *moment of interruption*.

Father of the House: see *Senior Member*.

Finance Bill: the annual bill, founded upon the *budget resolutions*, which embodies the government's statutory power to levy most taxes and duties, and which may include other provisions relating to taxes management.

financial privilege: the right to approve proposals for taxation or for government expenditure which the Commons asserts as its exclusive privilege, not shared with the Lords.

financial resolutions: the collective term for *money resolutions*, *ways and means resolutions*, and *supply resolutions*.

first reading: the formal first stage of a *bill*'s progress, which occurs without debate or vote after it has been introduced to the House.

forthwith: where, under standing orders, a Question is to be decided forthwith, that is usually indicated by an italicised rubric on the *Order Paper*. It means that there can be no debate on the Question, and that as soon as it is moved the Chair must immediately put it to the House or committee for decision: although there can be no debate on such a Question, there may be a *division*. Many Questions which are put forthwith are also *exempted business*.

front bench: the front benches are where Ministers and their official opposition *shadows* sit in the Chamber, hence *front bencher* or *front bench spokesman* (the government front bench is also known as the *Treasury Bench*).

guillotine: an order of the House which limits the time available to debate any stage or stages of a bill, now largely superseded by *programme orders*.

Hansard: the colloquial name for the *Official Report*, the publications containing the accurate and full (though not strictly verbatim as often claimed) reports of what is said and done in the debates of the House and its *standing committees*.

health service commissioners: the officer of the House who acts as the ombudsman for the NHS who also holds the office of *PCA* and who reports to the Public Administration Committee select committee: there are separate commissioners for England, Wales and Scotland.

House of Commons Commission: the executive body of Members responsible for the running of the House.

instruction: after *committal* of a bill, the House may give an instruction to any committee to which it is committed to do certain things that the committee might not otherwise be empowered to do.

Joint Committee on Human Rights: a joint committee charged with examining matters relating to human rights in the UK.

joint committees: committees which include Members of both Houses.

Journal Office: the office of the Clerk's Department responsible, among other duties, for the preparation of the *Votes and Proceedings*, the oversight of *Public Petitions*, and the preparation of the *Journals* of the House. It is also the office where papers are formally laid before the House by Ministers and others.

Journals: the *Votes and Proceedings* are consolidated into the Journals on a sessional basis and these form the authoritative record of the decisions of the House.

law commissions: the law commissions for England and Wales and for Scotland prepare proposals for reform of the law and also for its rationalisation by means of *consolidation bills* and statute law repeal bills.

Leader of the House: the Cabinet Minister with this title is charged with special responsibility for the management of the House and its business, but is distinct from the *usual channels*. He or she is a member, *ex officio*, of the *House of Commons Commission*. He or she also has responsibility for the cabinet committees dealing with the management of the government's legislative programme. His or her name will frequently appear on motions relating to the business of the House, and he or she will initiate government proposals for the reform of its procedures. His or her most public role is the period of questioning which, each Thursday, follows the *business question*. In recent sessions, he or she has also chaired the *Modernisation Committee*.

leader of the opposition: the person elected leader of the second largest party in the House is the leader of the official opposition. He or she receives official recognition in this role in the receipt of a ministerial salary and appointment to the Privy Council. The leader of the opposition has certain well-entrenched conventional rights to initiate certain kinds of business, in particular to demand, and to expect in most circumstances to receive, an opportunity to move a motion of no confidence in the government. He also has certain rights under standing orders (see *official opposition*).

leave: there are a number of types of proceeding which may only be done *by leave of the House* (or a committee). These include to speak more than once to a Question other than in committee, to withdraw a motion before the House or a committee and to move certain types of motion. Generally leave must be unanimous, that is, any single objection from any Member in the House or in a committee means that leave is thereby denied.

Legislation Service: The section of the Department of the *Clerk of the House* comprising the *Public Bill Office*, the Private Bill Office and the delegated legislation office.

Liaison Committee: the select committee consisting mainly of chairmen of other select committees, which under standing orders has certain powers and duties in relation to the proceedings of the House, as well as a more informal role exercising oversight of the work, and as an advocate of the interests, of select committees in general. It also has a power to examine the Prime Minister on matters of public policy.

lobby correspondents: certain representatives of the various news media who have the authority of the *Serjeant at Arms* to enter the *Members' Lobby* when the House is sitting and who enjoy certain other privileges of access to areas of the Palace otherwise closed to persons apart from Members and permanent staff. They also subscribe to a code of conduct relating to the disclosure of the sources of their information (hence the expression 'on lobby terms').

Lords Amendments: the amendments proposed by the Lords to a *bill* which has been passed by the Commons.

Lords Commissioners: the Peers appointed by the Queen to deliver her *proclamation* proroguing Parliament and her *royal assent* to Acts agreed just before *prorogation*.

Loyal Address: the motion moved in reply to the *Queen's Speech* on which the debate on the Queen's Speech takes place.

Mace: the symbol of the Crown's authority in Parliament, which is displayed on the *Table* whenever the House is in session.

maiden speech: the first speech delivered by a Member after he or she is first elected to the House. By convention it includes a tribute to his or her predecessor, an encomium to his or her constituency, and avoids controversy (though this latter tradition shows signs of dying out). Also, by tradition, it is heard without interruption from other Members.

main committee corridor: the corridor on the first floor of the Palace, accessed *via* the upper and lower waiting halls, off which the standing committee rooms and the majority of select committee rooms are situated.

manuscript amendment: an amendment of which no *notice* has been given, which is presented to the Chair during debate in manuscript or typescript form, and only selected in very rare circumstances.

Measure: a legislative proposal of the General Synod of the Church of England.

Member in charge: the Member in charge of a bill is the one who introduces it to the House, and he or she has certain prerogatives in relation to that bill. In the case of a government bill, any Minister (including a *Whip*) may exercise the rights of the Member in charge.

Members' lobby: the area immediately outside the Chamber generally reserved to Members and *lobby correspondents* and staff of the House when the House is sitting.

Minister: a member of the government, usually entitled to receive a ministerial salary and bound by the convention of collective responsibility for decisions of government. For procedural purposes, the members of the government (including *Whips*) are each regarded as being able to act on behalf of any other Minister.

Modernisation Committee: the Select Committee on the Modernisation of the House of Commons, chaired by the Leader of the House, appointed to bring forward proposals for the modernisation of the procedures and practices of the House.

moment of interruption: the time set by standing orders at which the main business of a day's sitting normally ends after which business may only be taken if it is *exempted business* or unopposed business.

money bill: a bill which is concerned exclusively with raising or spending public money and which, under the terms of the *Parliament Acts*, cannot be amended by the Lords.

money resolution: a *resolution* of the House, agreed on a motion which may only be moved by a *Minister*, authorising the provisions of a *bill* which entail novel forms of public expenditure.

naming: a Member who persistently defies the authority of the Chair in the House may be *named* by the Chair, which immediately causes a motion to be moved to suspend the Member from the service of the House.

National Audit Office: the office under the direction of the *Comptroller & Auditor General* which audits the expenditure of government departments.

Northstead, Manor of: see *Chiltern Hundreds*.

notice: where it is a requirement of standing orders or the rules of the House that a motion requires notice, it means that such a motion cannot be moved unless it appears on the *Order Paper*. In most circumstances, the latest time for giving notice of a motion to appear on a Paper for the next sitting day is the rising of the House on the previous day. Standing orders in certain circumstances have more stringent requirements of notice: for example, a motion to refer a bill to a second reading committee requires at least ten days' notice; a motion in the name of the *Committee of Selection* to nominate Members to certain select committees must appear at least once on the *remaining orders* before it can be put on the *effective orders*. While there is no formal requirement for notice of amendments to bills in committee or on report, the Chair will generally not select *manuscript amendments* or *starred amendments* for debate. Written notice is required of oral and written *PQ*s except *PNQ*s. Notice is required of presentation of bills and there are rather complicated rules relating to notice of a motion for leave to bring in a *ten minute rule bill*. Notices generally appear on one or other of the *Notice Papers*, or otherwise on the *remaining orders*.

Notice Paper: the blue pages of the *Vote Bundle* include the Notice Papers for notices of questions, notices of motions for future days, notices of *early day motions* and notices of amendments to bills.

oath: on their election at a general election or a *by-election*, each Member is required to take the parliamentary oath or to make the required affirmation before taking his or her seat. Witnesses before a committee of the House may also be required to take an oath before giving evidence, though this requirement is generally only imposed on witnesses before a private bill committee.

office costs allowance: the element of expenses paid to Members to cover the costs of maintaining and staffing their personal offices.

official opposition: the party with the second largest number of Members in the House is the official opposition, a status which gains it certain privileges by long standing convention (such as the right of its official spokesmen and spokeswomen to sit on the *front bench* and to address the House from the *despatch box*) as well as certain rights under the standing orders (to initiate debate on the majority of *opposition days*) and by statute (such as for certain of its officers to receive ministerial salaries).

Official Report: see *Hansard*.

ombudsman: see *Parliamentary Commissioner for Administration*.

opposition days: the 20 days each session set aside under standing orders on which the opposition parties have the right to choose the business for debate.

oral question: see *PQ*.

order: when the House agrees a motion that something should happen (such as a bill being set down for a second reading or for consideration) it becomes an order of the House. Other examples of orders might be the outcome of a *business motion* or *allocation of time motion* (see also *resolution*). The word is also commonly used in a parliamentary context to connote procedural regularity (as in the expression 'in order') or to correct parliamentary behaviour (as in the Chair's call of 'Order, order', which is also used as a form of oral procedural 'punctuation').

Order Paper: the paper, published each sitting day (except the first day of a *session*), which lists the business of the House and for any sitting in Westminster Hall for that day, as well as *parliamentary questions*/(PQs) for oral or written answer to be asked that day, PQs for written answer that day which have not previously appeared in print, and certain other items such as notices of *written statements* committee notices, *remaining orders* and lists of future business.

other business: business of the House which is neither *private business* nor public business, when there is no *Question* before the House for decision, principally covering question time and ministerial statements.

Outlawries Bill: see *Clandestine Outlawries Bill*.

PAC: see *Public Accounts Committee*.

Parliament Acts: the Parliament Act 1911 as amended and supplemented by the Parliament Act 1949 restrict the powers of the Lords to amend *money bills* or delay other *bills* agreed by the Commons.

Parliamentary Commissioner for Administration: the officer of the House appointed under statute to investigate complaints of maladministration in the public service, commonly known as the ombudsman. His work is overseen by the Public Administration Committee and also *health service commissioners*).

Parliamentary Commissioner for Standards: see *Commissioner for Standards*.

parliamentary question: a question addressed (generally) to a Minister for answer orally on the floor of the House at question time, or in a *grand committee*, or at a *sitting in Westminster Hall* or in writing in *Hansard*.

periodic adjournment: the formal name for one of the House's recesses.

PCA: see *Parliamentary Commissioner for Administration*.

PNQ: see *urgent question*.

PQ: see *parliamentary question*.

point of order: properly, a request by a Member to the Chair for elucidation of, or a ruling on, a question of procedure, but not infrequently misused by Members who do not have the floor of the House or of a committee to interrupt proceedings for other purposes.

prayers: each sitting of the House begins with prayers, conducted by the *Speaker's Chaplain*. The term is also used colloquially to describe a motion to annul a *statutory instrument* subject to negative resolution procedure and to designate the final paragraph of a *public petition*.

prerogative: see *Crown prerogative*.

press gallery: the gallery of the Chamber above and behind the Speaker's Chair reserved to accredited representatives of the various news media, also used more generally to describe the large area outside and behind this gallery given over to the use of journalists etc. and also to describe collectively the accredited members of the press gallery (see also *lobby correspondents*).

previous question: a procedural device for superseding debate, now generally disregarded in favour of the *closure*.

Prince of Wales's consent: see *Queen's consent*.

private bill: a bill to confer upon individuals, or more commonly corporate bodies of one kind or another, powers in excess of the general law.

private business: the business of the House for the most part relating directly or indirectly to *private bills*.

private Member's bill: a *bill* introduced to the House by a Member who is not a *Minister*.

private notice question: the former name for what is now called an *urgent question*.

privilege: a privilege enjoyed by the House collectively or its Members individually in excess or contradiction to the general law which enables it or them to fulfil the functions and duties of the House.

Privy Counsellor: a Member of the Queen's Privy Council, the body of senior royal advisers which in former times was something equivalent to the *Cabinet*, membership of which is now conferred automatically upon Cabinet Ministers and also upon certain senior judges; it is also by convention granted to the leaders of parties of any size in the Commons and is occasionally conferred as a mark of honour upon senior back benchers. The Council retains certain judicial functions and residual executive functions. Membership, once conferred, is for life, unless withdrawn.

Procedure Committee: a *select committee* of the House appointed to consider proposals for the reform of its procedures

proclamation: the Queen issues proclamations for the *prorogation, dissolution* and summoning Parliament, on the advice of the Prime Minister.

programme: an order made by the House after agreement through the *usual channels* after a *bill*'s *second reading* to *timetable* the subsequent proceedings on that bill.

prorogation: the end of a *session*.

Public Accounts Commission: the board of the *National Audit Office*.

Public Accounts Committee: the *select committee* of the House with particular responsibility for ensuring propriety, efficiency, economy and effectiveness in the spending of public money.

Public Bill Office: the office within the *Legislation Service* of the *Clerk of the House*'s department with particular responsibility for the management of legislation and for clerking the *standing committees* of the House.

public gallery: the gallery of the Chamber in which *strangers* may sit to observe its proceedings; there is also an area designated for the same purpose in each committee room and at *sittings in Westminster Hall*.

public petition: a petition to the House for redress of a grievance or other relief.

Queen's consent: where the legislation proposed in a *bill* touches upon the prerogatives or private interests of the Crown, her consent is required for the bill to proceed: this may be required to be given either before the *second reading* or *third reading* (or, conceivably, before *first reading*), depending on the nature of the interest and the extent to which it is fundamental to the bill's purposes. Consent must be obtained from the Queen by a Minister and must be signified at the appropriate time by a *Privy Counsellor*. The Prince of Wales's consent may also be required, as the heir to the throne, before certain bills may be debated at certain stages.

Queen's recommendation: only the government can propose increases in public expenditure and the recommendation of the 'Crown' is therefore required for a motion which proposes to increase or widen the scope of public expenditure: such a motion can therefore be moved only by a Minister; where a motion of this nature is to be moved in the House the words 'Queen's recommendation signified' appear by its title on the *Order Paper*.

Queen's Speech: the speech read by the Queen from her throne on the first day of each session setting out, among other matters, details of the government's proposed legislative programme.

question: see *parliamentary question*.

Question: in procedural jargon, the matter before the House or a committee awaiting decision at any time.

question time: the period set aside for *PQs* to be asked and answered orally on the floor of the House.

quorum: the quorum of the House is 40 but only for divisions; the quorum of a *standing committee* (except a European standing committee) is one-third of its members, with fractions rounded up; the quorum of an European standing committee is 3 of its appointed members, not including the chairman; the quorums of *select committees* is one-third of their membership or three, whichever is the greater, unless otherwise set out in the standing orders or their orders of appointment.

reasoned amendment: an amendment proposed to the motion to give a *bill* a *second reading* or *third reading*.

recess: strictly speaking, the period when the House is prorogued; now used to refer to the House's holiday adjournments.

Register of Members' Interests: the register, published annually, in which Members record their outside financial interests and the receipt of gifts, free travel , etc.; it is updated regularly and made available to the public in updated form on application to the *Registrar of Members' Interests*.

Registrar of Members' Interests: the officer of the House responsible for the maintenance of the *Register of Members' Interests* and for giving advice (along with the *Commissioner for Standards*) about declarations made in it; a member of the Speaker's Office.

remaining orders: the list of forthcoming government business published with the *Order Paper* each day.

remedial order: a form of delegated legislation which remedies an incompatibility between UK law and the European Convention on Human Rights.

report stage: the stage of a *bill*'s progress between its being reported from committee and its *third reading*, at which further detailed amendments may be made.

resolution: when a motion is agreed by the House, it becomes a resolution (unless it is an *order*).

resource accounts: the audited accounts of *voted expenditure* authorised by the *Estimates*.

return: an answer or response to an address from the House.

royal assent: the Queen's assent to a *bill* agreed to by both Houses of Parliament is the final act which makes that bill an Act of Parliament.

royal recommendation: see *Queen's recommendation.*

seconder: no seconder is required for a motion to be proposed to the House or a committee, but by tradition the motion for the *Loyal Address* is seconded.

second reading: the first stage at which a *bill* is debated and voted upon.

select committees: committees established by the House to inquire into particular matters or subject areas and to report back their findings and recommendations.

Senior Member: the Member of the House who has the longest *continuous* period of service in the House, also known as the *Father of the House*; on a *select committee* the senior Member on that committee (the one with the longest total service in the House) has the duty to name the time of its first meeting.

Serjeant at Arms: the officer of the House responsible for security, housekeeping functions and the maintenance and repair of the physical infrastructure of the buildings.

session: the period between the state opening of Parliament and its prorogation or dissolution, generally a year running from November to November, but often altered by the timing of general elections.

sessional orders: the traditional orders passed on the first day of a *session*, also any *order* made by the House which is explicitly framed to have effect for a session (for example, those specifying the dates during a session for private Members' bill Fridays and non-sitting Fridays).

shadow: broadly speaking, the official opposition appoints or elects Members of its party to 'shadow' each government Minister, that is, to take particular responsibility for presenting in and out of Parliament the policies of the opposition for the areas which are that *Minister*'s responsibility, hence 'Shadow Home Secretary' etc (also called *front bench spokesmen or spokeswomen*).

shuffle: the process by which the *PQ*s for oral answer are randomly sorted to determine which Members' questions will be printed on the *Order Paper* on any given day, and in what order.

sitting: a single meeting of the House or one of its committees.

sittings in Westminster Hall: the 'parallel chamber' of the House of Commons which meets in the Grand Committee Room off Westminster Hall.

Speaker: the impartial presiding officer of the House.

Speaker's Chaplain: the personal chaplain to the Speaker, whose main public duty is the leading of *prayers* at the beginning of each *sitting* of the House, but who may also choose to offer a more general pastoral service to Members and staff of the House.

Speaker's Counsel: the officers of the House who head its legal services office, including those lawyers providing legal advice to the Speaker and to certain of the committees of the House.

standing committee: a committee to which the House delegates the task of debating certain matters such as *bills*, *delegated legislation*, proposals for European legislation, etc.

standing orders: the rules formulated by the House to regulate its own proceedings.

starred amendment: an amendment to a bill which has not appeared on a notice paper on a day before the sitting at which it is to be considered; as a rule, the Chair will not select such an amendment for debate (see also *notice*).

state opening: the occasion on the first day of each *session* on which the Queen usually attends in the House of Lords to deliver the *Queen's Speech*.

statutory instruments: the form in which most *delegated legislation* is made.

strangers: the traditional appellation for anyone who is not a Member, officer or official of the House, hence *Strangers' Gallery* etc.

Strangers' Gallery: the more traditional name for the *public gallery*.

supplementary question: an oral question asked as a separate but supplementary question to one which has appeared on the *Order Paper* and has been asked during *question time*; it should be within the scope of that main question to be in order; the Member asking the main question has the prerogative right in general to ask the first supplementary; the *Speaker* then chooses other Members to ask further supplementaries.

supply days: the old name for what now are called *opposition days*.

supply resolution: one of the *resolutions* upon which the *Consolidated Fund* bills are founded.

Table: the Table of the House, situated between the government and opposition *front benches*, in front of the Speaker's Chair; in former times this was the place where motions, questions, reports etc. were delivered into the possession of the House *via* the Clerks, hence 'tabled' or 'laid upon the Table'; nowadays most such things are done in the *Table Office*, *Journal Office* or *Public Bill Office*.

Table Office: the office, situated outside the Chamber behind the Speaker's Chair, in which *PQ*s and *EDM*s are tabled; it also deals with all matters relating to the business on the floor of the House other than legislation: it may also be regarded as the first port of call for any Member seeking procedural advice. The office on the principal floor is the *Lower* Table Office, there is also an *Upper* Table Office on the third floor above the Chamber.

ten minute rule bill: a *bill* introduced where the Member seeking the *leave* of the House to introduce the bill, and a Member who opposes granting it, may each make a short speech before the House comes to a decision on whether to allow the bill to proceed.

ten o'clock motion: a motion, moved by a Minister, to suspend the operation of the *moment of interruption* which now occurs at ten o'clock only on a Monday.

Test Roll: the Test Roll must be signed by each Member after he or she has taken the oath or affirmed after being elected to the House.

third reading: the final stage of a whole *bill*'s passage through the House, though Lords Amendments to the bill may subsequently be considered.

timetable: In essence, a timetable for a bill fixes the points at which various stages of its consideration will be completed: at present the House generally uses *programmes* orders to timetable a proceedings on government bills at the outset of their progress, varying and supplementing their terms at later stages.

tomorrow: the day usually named by the government for a bill to be put down for its next stage: in fact this means only that it will be placed on the *remaining orders* and will wait there until the government decides that it is to go on the *effective orders* for a particular day.

upper committee corridor: the corridor above the *main committee corridor* on which select committee rooms 17 to 21 are situated.

Upper Waiting Hall: the lobby area off the *main committee corridor*.

urgent question: an oral parliamentary question asked without published *notice* relating to an urgent and important matter.

usual channels: the colloquial name for the discussions which take place between the *Whips*.

Voted expenditure: the House's agreement to an *Estimate* represents the detailed *appropriation* of public money to the public service by Parliament.

Votes and Proceedings: the daily minute of the House's proceedings.

Vote Bundle: the papers published each day on which the House sits, including among other things the *Order Paper*, the *remaining orders*, the *Votes and Proceedings*, and the *notice papers*.

Vote Office: the distribution centre for all parliamentary papers.

ways and means resolution: a *resolution* authorising a charge upon the people, that is, for the most part, taxes and duties: the *Finance Bill* is founded upon ways and means resolutions.

Westminster Hall: the oldest remaining part of the Palace of Westminster, now used solely as a public area and for occasional ceremonial purposes (see also *sittings in Westminster Hall*.)

Whips: the officers of each party in the House with particular responsibilities for party management and organisation of the business of the House and its committees.

White Paper: a *command paper* embodying some statement of government policy, often including proposals for legislation.

writ: the issue of a writ is the formal process for initiating a by-election.

written statement: a vehicle which may be used by a *minister* to inform the House on various types of matter relating to his or her responsibilities; they are announced on the *Order Paper* and published in *Hansard*.

Political Parties

Labour Party

16 Old Queen Street, London SW1H 9HP
Tel: 08705 900 200   Fax: 020 7802 1234
Website: www.labour.org.uk

Chair: Diana Holland; *Vice-Chair:* Mary Turner; *Leader:* Rt Hon Tony Blair MP; *Deputy Leader:* Rt Hon John Prescott MP; *General Secretary:* David Triesman; *Treasurer:* Jimmy Elsby

National Executive Committee 2002–03

Treasurer: Jimmy Elsby; *Youth Representative* Blair McDougall; *Ex-officio:* Rt Hon Tony Blair MP; Rt Hon John Prescott MP; David Triesman; Gary Titley MEP

Division I – Trade Unions
John Gibbins (AMICUS-AEEU); Cath Speight (AMICUS-AEEU); Mike Griffiths – Graphical, Paper, Media Union (GPMU); John Hannett – Union of Shop, Distributive and Allied Workers (USDAW); Mick Cash –   Rail, Maritime and Transport Union (RMT); John Keggie – Communication Workers Union (CWU); Diana Holland – Transport and General Workers Union (TGWU); Maggie Jones – UNISON; Steve Pickering – General Municipal, Boilermakers Union (GMB); Nancy Coull – UNISON; Mary Turner – General Municipal, Boilermakers Union (GMB); Margaret Wall (AMICUS-MSF)

Division II – Socialist Societies
Dianne Hayter

Division III – Constituency Labour Parties
Ann Black, Shahid Malik, Tony Robinson, Christine Shawcroft, Mark Seddon, Ruth Turner

Division IV – Local Government
Sir Jeremy Beecham, Sally Powell

Division V – Parliamentary Labour Party/European Parliamentary Labour Party
Michael Cashman MEP, Helen Jackson MP, Dennis Skinner MP

Division VI – Government
Rt Hon Helen Liddell MP; Rt Hon Ian McCartney MP; Rt Hon John Reid MP

Parliamentary Office – House of Commons

Secretary: Alan Haworth (Tel: 020 7219 4266); *Administrator:* Vacant (Tel: 020 7219 4552); *Senior Committee Officer:* Catherine Jackson (Tel: 020 7219 5278); *Committee Officers:* David Arnold (Tel: 020 7219 5953); Tim Nuthall (Tel: 020 7219 5277)

Co-operative Party

77 Weston Street, London SE1 3SD
Tel: 020 7357 0230   Fax: 020 7407 4476
E-mail: p.hunt@co-op-party.org.uk   Website: www.co-op-party.org.uk

Chair: Gareth R Thomas MP; *Vice-Chair:* Jeanette Timmins; *Chair of Parliamentary Group:* Linda Gilroy MP; *National Secretary:* Peter Hunt
The Co-operative Party is not affiliated to the Labour Party at national level, but its candidates stand as joint candidates of both parties and are badged 'Labour/Co-operative'. There are 30 Labour/Co-operative MPs in Westminster, eight MSPs in Scotland and five AMs in Wales.

Visit the Vacher Dod Website . . . **www.DodOnline.co.uk**

Conservative and Unionist Party

32 Smith Square, London SW1P 3HH
Tel: 020 7222 9000   Fax: 020 7222 1135
Websites: www.conservatives.com

Chairman: Theresa May MP; *Deputy Chairmen:* Rt Hon Gillian Shephard MP, Raymond Monbiot CBE; *Vice-Chairmen:* Angela Browning MP, Kay Coleman OBE, Roger Gale MP, Trish Morris OBE, Robert Syms MP, Shailesh Vara; *Party Treasurer:* Sir Stanley Kalms; *Director of Field Operations and Deputy Chief Executive:* Stephen Gilbert; *Director of Strategic Communications:* Paul Baverstock; *Head of Media:* Nick Wood; *Director of Policy:* Dr Greg Clark; *Director of Operations and Conferences:* Stephen Phillips; *Director of Development and Candidates:* Christina Dykes; *Director of Treasurers:* Victoria Borwick; *Director of IT:* Anne Nunan; *Director of Finance:* Chris Hutton

Leader's Office
Leader of the Opposition: Rt Hon Iain Duncan Smith MP; *Parliamentary Private Secretaries:* Alistair Burt MP, Owen Paterson MP; *Chief of Staff:* Barry Legg; *Head of the Leader's Office:* Vanessa Gearson; *Private Secretary:* Christine Watson; *Head of Planning and Tours:* Annabelle Eyre; *Diary Secretary:* Paula Malone

Liberal Democrats

4 Cowley Street, London SW1P 3NB
Tel: 020 7222 7999   Fax: 020 7799 2170
E-mail: info@libdems.org.uk   Website: www.libdems.org.uk

Leader: Rt Hon Charles Kennedy MP; *President:* Lord Dholakia OBE; *Vice-Presidents:* Dawn Davidson (England), Lembit Öpik MP (Wales), Tavish Scott MSP (Scotland); *Chief Executive:* Hugh Rickard CBE; *Director of Campaigns and Elections:* Lord Rennard MBE; *Director of Policy:* Dr Richard Grayson; *Head of Policy Unit:* Christian Moon; *Senior Policy Officer:* Helen Belcher; *Director of Marketing, Fundraising and Members' Services:* David Loxton; *Head of Membership Services:* David Allworthy; *Director of Press and Broadcasting:* Robin Banerji; *Deputy Director of Press and Broadcasting:* Greg Simpson; *Conference and Events Organiser:* Penny McCormack; *Financial Controller:* Nigel Bliss; *Head of International Office:* Karla Hatrick; *Editor of Liberal Democrat News:* Deirdre Razzall

Federal Executive

President: Lord Dholakia OBE; *Vice-Presidents:* Dawn Davidson (England), Lembit Öpik MP (Wales), Tavish Scott MSP (Scotland); *Leader:* Rt Hon Charles Kennedy MP; *MPs:* Patsy Calton MP, Mark Oaten MP; *MEP:* Diana Wallis MEP; *Chief Whip:* Andrew Stunell OBE MP (non-voting); *Peer:* Lord Razzall CBE; *Treasurer:* Reg Clark (non-voting); *Councillors:* Cllr Stan Collins, Cllr Brian Hall; *State representatives:* Paul Farthing (England), Rob Humphreys (Wales), Derek Young (Scotland); *Directly elected:* Sharon Bowles, Ramesh Dewan, Gareth Epps, James Graham, Tony Greaves, Rosalyn Harper, Elizabeth Johnson, Susan Kramer, Gordon Lishman, Chris Maines, Donnachadh McCarthy, Candy Piercy, Martin Tod, Joan Walmsley, Ian Walton; *Staff Representative:* Mark Pack (non-voting)

Federal Policy Committee

Leader: Rt Hon Charles Kennedy MP; *MPs:* Edward Davey MP, John Thurso MP, Prof Steven Webb MP, Roger Williams MP; *MEPs:* Baroness Ludford MEP; *Peer:* Baroness Sharp of Guildford; *President:* Lord Dholakia OBE; *Councillors:* Cllr Stan Collins, Cllr Brian Hall, Cllr Rabi Martins; *English representative:* Geoff Payne; *Scottish representative:* Keith Raffan MSP or Gurudeo Saluja; *Welsh representative:* Peter Price; *Directly elected:* Lord Alderdice MLA, David Boyle, Theodore Butt-Philip, Jonathan Calder, Ruth Coleman, Chris Gurney, Jeremy Hargreaves, Jo Hayes, Roger Heape, Margaret Leach, Dai Liyanage, Brian Niblett, Sarah Teather, Serena Tierney, John Vincent, Alex Wilcock

Federal Conference Committee

President: Lord Dholakia OBE; *Chief Whip:* Andrew Stunell OBE MP; *English representative:* Jane Smithard; *Scottish representative:* Karen Freel; *Welsh representative:* Mark Soady; *Directly elected:* Qassim Afzal, Jon Ball, Baroness Barker, Sarah Boad, Duncan Brack, Dee Doocey, Gareth Epps, Arnie Gibbons, Susan Heinrich, Ruth Polling, Harriet Smith, Andrew Wiseman; *Chief Executive:* Hugh Rickard (non-voting); *Staff representative:* Sarah Morris; *Federal Executive representatives:* Elizabeth Johnson, Ian Walton; *Federal Policy Committee representative:* Geoff Payne, Vacant

Parliamentary Office – House of Commons

Secretary: Ben Williams Tel: 020 7219 5654; *Deputy Secretary:* Maria Menezes
Tel: 020 7219 1415   Fax: 020 7219 5894
E-mails: libdemcommons@cix.co.uk; menezesm@parliament.uk

Ulster Unionist Party (UUP)

Cunningham House, 429 Holywood Road, Belfast BT4 2LN
Tel: 028 9076 5500   Fax: 028 9076 9419
E-mail: uup@uup.org   Website: www.uup.org

Patron: Rt Hon Lord Molyneaux of Killead KBE; *Party Leader:* Rt Hon David Trimble MP; *Chief Whip:* Roy Beggs MP

Ulster Unionist Council
President: Rev W Martin Smyth MP; *Leader:* Rt Hon David Trimble MP; *Chair of the Executive Committee:* James Cooper LLB; *Vice-Chair of the Executive Committee:* Donn McConnell OBE; *Vice-Presidents:* Jeffrey Donaldson MP, Sir Reg Empey OBE, Lord Maginnis of Drumglass, Jim Nicholson MEP; *Hon Treasurer:* Jack Allen OBE; *Assistant Hon Treasurer:* Mrs May Steele MBE JP; *Hon Secretaries:* Cllr Jim Rodgers, Mrs Arlene Foster LLB; Lord Rogan of Lower Iveagh; Dermot Nesbitt; *Chief Executive:* Alastair Patterson

Scottish National Party (SNP)

107 McDonald Road, Edinburgh EH7 4NW
Tel: 0131-525 8900   Fax: 0131-525 8901
E-mail: snp.hq@snp.org   Website: www.snp.org

National Convener: John Swinney MSP
President: Winnie Ewing
Senior Vice-Convener: Roseanna Cunningham MSP
Chief Executive: Peter Murrell
Europe: Ian Hudghton MEP and Professor Sir Neil MacCormick MEP
Westminster Parliamentary Group Leader: Alex Salmond MP

Plaid Cymru – The Party of Wales (PlC)

Tŷ Gwynfor, 18 Park Grove, Cardiff CF10 3BN
Tel: 029 2064 6000   Fax: 029 2064 6001
E-mail: post@plaidcymru.org   Website: www.plaidcymru2001.com

President: Ieuan Wyn Jones AM; *Vice-President:* Dafydd Iwan *Chair:* John Dixon; *Treasurer:* Jeff Canning; *Chief Executive:* Dafydd Trystan, *Press Officer:* Meleri Evans

Social Democratic and Labour Party (SDLP)

Northern Ireland
121 Ormeau Road, Belfast BT7 1SH
Tel: 028 9024 7700   Fax: 028 9023 6699
E-mail: sdlp@indigo.ie   Website: www.sdlp.ie

Leader: Mark Durkan; *Deputy Leader:* Brid Rodgers; *Chief Whip:* Eddie McGrady MP; *Chairperson:* Alex Attwood; *Vice-Chairperson:* Mary McKeown; *Treasurer:* Berna McIvor; *International Secretary:* Margaret Ritchie; *General Secretary:* Gerry Cosgrove

Democratic Unionist Party (DUP)

91 Dundela Avenue, Belfast BT4 3BU
Tel: 028 9047 1155   Fax: 028 9047 1797
E-mail: info@dup.org.uk   Websites: www.dup.org.uk   www.dup2win.com

Leader: Rev Dr Ian Paisley MP MEP; *Deputy Leader:* Ald Peter Robinson MP; *Chair:* Cllr Maurice Morrow; *Vice-Chair:* Ald William McCrea; *Vice-Chair:* Ald Iris Robinson MP; *Party Secretary:* Nigel Dodds OBE MP; *Treasurer:* Ald Gregory Campbell MP; *Chief Executive:* Allan Ewart

Sinn Fein (SF)

44 Parnell Square, Dublin 1
Tel: +353 1 8726932/8726100   Fax +353 1 8733441/8783595
E-mail: sfadmin@eircom.net   Website: www.sinnfein.ie

President: Gerry Adams MP; *Press Officer:* Mark Joyce

Green Party

1A Waterlow Road, London N19 5NJ
Tel: 020 7272 4474   Fax: 020 7272 6653
E-mail: office@greenparty.org.uk   Website: www.greenparty.org.uk

Green Party National Executive:
Chair: Andrew Cornwell (020 7272 4474) E-mail: chair@greenparty.org.uk
External Communications Co-ordinator: Spencer Fitz-Gibbon (0161-225 4863)
E-mail: media@greenpartynw.org

Press Office – England and Wales Green Party:
020 7561 0282   E-mail: press@greenparty.org.uk

Press Office – Wales Green Party/Plaid Werdd Cymru: Matthew Wootton
01443 836594   E-mail: media@walesgreenparty.org.uk

Representatives:
House of Lords: Lord Beaumont of Whitley (020 7219 3000 messages)

UK Greens MEPs:
Caroline Lucas MEP (SE England) E-mail: clucas@europarl.eu.int
Jean Lambert MEP (London) E-mail: jelambert@europarl.eu.int
Press officer: Benjamin Duncan (020 7407 6280 or 0776 997 0691)
E-mail: press@greenmeps.org.uk
Assistants: 020 7233 4007 (London) 00 32 2 284 71 53 (Brussels)

DodOnline

An Electronic Directory without rival ...

MPs' biographies and photographs available with daily updates *via* the internet

For a *free* trial, call Yasmin Mirza, Aby Farsoun or Michael Mand on 020 7630 7643

Parliamentary Press Gallery

The Parliamentary Lobby Journalists are those journalists authorised to work in Parliament. There are about 120 British and Irish journalists who are allowed access to the Members' Lobby of the House of Commons. A further 50 or so foreign correspondents also have access to the Lobby. Members of the Lobby are marked with an asterisk

Tel 020 7219 4700; for individual desk numbers prefix 020 7219 in most cases.

Chairman	Chris Moncrieff 4282 (PA)
Vice-Chairman	Brian Shallcross 6729 (Capital Radio)
Secretary	Greg Hurst 5284 (The Times)
Treasurer	Rodney Foster 020 7973 6029 (BBC)
Administrator	Elizabeth Johnson 4395
	E-mail: press.gallery@virgin.net
Attendants	5371
Lobby Journalists' Chairman	Jon Smith 4282 (PA)
Secretary	Paul Linford 4389 (The Journal, Newcastle)
Treasurer	Nigel Morris 4392 (Independent)
Press Bar	4284
Press Dining Room	6406

National Daily Newspapers

DAILY EXPRESS
*Patrick O'Flynn (Political editor) 6764/3389
*Alison Little 3387
*Kirsty Walker 6149
Administrator: Jackie Murray 020 7925 2708

DAILY MAIL
*David Hughes (Political editor) 3679
*Michael Clark 6140
*Paul Eastham 3683
Quentin Letts 020 7233 2413
*Rebecca Paveley 0616
*Graeme Wilson 6561
Administrator: Gill Watmough 6894

DAILY TELEGRAPH
*George Jones (Political editor) 5719
*Benedict Brogan 3688
*Toby Helm 3687
Frank Johnson 4927
Michael Kallenbach 6890
*Andrew Sparrow 3689
Rachel Sylvester 4960
Administrator: Henrietta Courtauld 3685

EVENING STANDARD
*Charles Reiss (Political editor) 5718
*Patrick Hennessy 0052
*Ben Leapman 4680
*Joe Murphy 4281
Anne McElvoy 020 7938 6000

FINANCIAL TIMES
*James Blitz (Political editor) 4380
*Chris Adams 6892
*Jean Eaglesham
*Krishna Guha 6142
*Cathy Newman 6893

GUARDIAN
*Michael White (Political editor) 6143
*David Hencke 6769
Simon Hoggart 6738
*Anne Perkins 6891
*Nick Watt 6831
Administrator: Elizabeth Watson

INDEPENDENT
*Andy Grice (Political editor) 4665
*Don Macintyre 6580
*Nigel Morris 4392
Ben Russell 4392
*Paul Waugh 4392
*Marie Woolf 2037

THE MIRROR
*James Hardy (Political editor) 4377
*Oonagh Blackman 3639
*Paul Routledge 4583
*Bob Roberts 4359
*Paul Gilfeather 6733

THE STAR
6743

THE SUN
*Trevor Kavanagh (Political editor) 6144
*Nic Cecil 4683
*George Pascoe-Watson 3337
*David Wooding 0140

THE TIMES
*Phil Webster (Political editor) 5241
*Peter Riddell 4751
Tom Baldwin 3009
*Rosemary Bennett 6543
*David Charter 4751
*Greg Hurst 6543
*Melissa Kite 5284
Administrator: Maggie Ronald 5241

National Sunday Newspapers

INDEPENDENT ON SUNDAY
*Andy McSmith 5285
*Jo Dillon 2058
*Steve Richards

MAIL ON SUNDAY
*Simon Walters 4730
*Jonathan Oliver 4386

NEWS OF THE WORLD
*Ian Kirby (Political editor) 6768
*Keith Gladdis 3386

OBSERVER
*Kamal Ahmed (Political editor) 3380
*Gaby Hinsliff 6687
*Andrew Rawnsley

SCOTLAND ON SUNDAY
*Brian Brady 6763

SUNDAY BUSINESS
*Allistair Heath 6560

SUNDAY EXPRESS
*Julia Hartley-Brewer (Political editor) 5596
*Tim Shipman 5596

SUNDAY HERALD
*Jim Cuisick 0156

SUNDAY MERCURY
*Gerri Peev 2908/2035

SUNDAY MIRROR
*Chris MacLaughlin 4377

SUNDAY PEOPLE
*Nigel Nelson (Political editor) 4583

SUNDAY TELEGRAPH
*Colin Brown 6116
*Francis Elliot 0615
*Matthew D'Ancona 020 7538 7301

SUNDAY TIMES
*Eben Black 5397
*David Cracknell 5397
*Jonathan Carr-Brown 5397

Regional Press

ABERDEEN PRESS AND JOURNAL
*David Perry 4390

BIRMINGHAM MAIL
*Shaun Connolly 4277

BIRMINGHAM POST
*Jon Walker 3765

CENTRAL PRESS

Bristol Evening Post
Oldham Evening Chronicle
HTV West
*Rob Merrick 5287

Brighton Argus
Cambridgeshire Evening News
Worcester Evening News
Yorkshire Evening Press
*James Slack 3385

Carlisle News and Star
Hartlepool Mail
NW Evening Mail
Shields Gazette
Sunderland Echo
*Ian Drury 6539

Liverpool Daily Post
Northern Echo
Tariq Tahir 020 7930 3247

Western Daily Press
Big Issue (South West)
Local Government Chronicle
*Matthew George 3673

DAILY RECORD
*Ian Smith 3336
*Dave King 3336

EAST ANGLIAN DAILY TIMES
*Graham Dines 4700

EASTERN DAILY PRESS
*Chris Fisher 3384
*Ian Collins 3339

EDINBURGH EVENING NEWS
NEWCASTLE EVENING CHRONICLE
LANCASHIRE EVENING TELEGRAPH
*Bill Jacobs 4391

HERALD (GLASGOW)
*Catherine McLeod 6722
*Mike Settle 0156
*Deborah Summers 6147

LIVERPOOL ECHO
*Ian Hernon 4396

MANCHESTER EVENING NEWS
*Ian Craig 6672

MIDDLESBROUGH EVENING GAZETTE
*William Doult 4388

NEWCASTLE JOURNAL
*Paul Linford 4389

NORTHCLIFFE NEWSPAPERS
*Michael Litchfield
David Macaulay
Zoe Hughes 4691

SCOTSMAN
*Fraser Nelson 4682
*Jason Beattie 6740
*Alison Hardie 4370

SOUTH WALES ECHO
SOUTH WALES ARGUS
*David Rose 3383

WESTERN MAIL
*Kirsty Buchanan (Political editor) 4382

WESTERN MORNING NEWS
*Jason Groves 6742

WOLVERHAMPTON EXPRESS & STAR
*John Hipwood 3381
*Anne Alexander 1307

YORKSHIRE EVENING POST
SHEFFIELD STAR
LANCASHIRE EVENING POST
*Hugh Lawrence 6766

YORKSHIRE POST
*Brendan Carlin 3674

Magazines

THE ECONOMIST
*Adam Raphael 020 7830 7047

NEW STATESMAN
*John Kampfner 020 7592 3625

SPECTATOR
*Peter Oborne 07768 446163

TRIBUNE
*Mark Seddon 4700

Irish Newspapers and Media

BELFAST TELEGRAPH
Brian Walker 6725

INDEPENDENT NEWSPAPERS
(IRELAND) LTD
*Bernard Purcell (London editor) 020 7828 4070

IRISH PRESS
*Aiden Hennigan 4700

IRISH TIMES
*Frank Millar 4700

RTE – IRISH BROADCASTING
*Brian O'Connell 4700

Agencies

AFX NEWS
*Frank Prenesti 6146

BLOOMBERG NEWS
*James Kirkup 020 7222 5241
*Reed Landberg

GALLERY NEWS
*Robert Gibson 2908/2035
*Gerri Peev 2908

MARKET NEWS
*David Robinson 0618
*Christoper Davidson

NEWSPOINT
*Peter Bell
Julia Moseley
*Mike Steele 4278
*Jason Williams

PRESS ASSOCIATION (PA NEWS)
*Jon Smith 4299
Amanda Brown 4299/4282
*Joe Churcher 4282
*Gavin Cordon 4299
Pippa Crerar 4282

*John Deane 4282
Trevor Mason 4299/4282
Chris Meade 4299/4282
Jane Merrick 4299/4282
*Chris Moncrieff 4282
Vivienne Morgan 4282
*Andrew Woodcock 4282

REUTERS
*Michael Peacock 5389/5389
*Katherine Baldwin 5389
*Dominic Evans 4389

**ROBINSON'S PARLIAMENTARY
NEWS AGENCY**
*Julian Robinson 4283
*Mike Peters 4283

Broadcasting

ANGLIA TV
*Emma Hutchinson 020 7222 3927

BBC
4 Millbank 020 7973 6000
Political Correspondents
020 7973 6050/6044/6010
*Andrew Marr
(Political Editor – 020 7973 6001)
*Jonathan Beale
*Reeta Chakrabarti
Joanne Coburn
*Jon Devitt (World Service)
*Guto Harri
*Martha Kearney (Newsnight 020 7973 6072)
*Shaun Ley
*Mark Mardell
*John Pienaar
*Carolyn Quinn
*Paul Rowley
*Norman Smith
*Laura Trevelyan
*Carole Walker

Regional Political Editors
Bob Ledwidge (Editor 020 7973 6170)
Mary Askew (North East 07860 336769)
Patrick Burns (West Midlands 0121-432 8308)
Jon Craig (South East 020 7973 6167)
Paul Cannon (West 0117-974 6766)
Jim Hancock (North West 0161-244 3119)
John Hess (East Midlands 07801 317273)
Deborah McGurran (East 03744 679244)
Bruce Parker (South 023 8037 4204)
Chris Rogers (South West 01752 234331)
Len Tingle (North)

National Regional Correspondents
*David Cornock (Wales 020 7973 6245)
*David Porter (Scotland 020 7973 6187)
*John Stevenson (Wales) 020 7973 6243
Stephen Walker (N Ireland)

Parliamentary Correspondents
Sean Curran
Mark Darcy
Susan Hulme
Robert Orchard
David Willby
Press Gallery 020 7973 6243
Nick Assinder (BBC On Line) 07710 615255
Nyta Mann ((BBC On Line)
Sue Plimmer Clarke 07979 602065
Sh'lair Teimourian

CAPITAL RADIO NETWORK
*Brian Shallcross 6729/6728

CENTRAL TV
*Peter Hayes 020 7233 0203
*Simon Mares 020 7976 0412
Simon Garrett

GM-TV
*Suzanna Norton 3678
*David Mills (Sunday Programme)
*Sue Jamieson

GRAMPIAN TV
*Michael Crow 6724

GRANADA TV
*Rishi Bhattacharya 020 7233 2020

HTV – WALES
*Jo Kiernan 4278

HTV WEST
*Bob Constantine
*Rob Merrick 5287

INDEPENDENT RADIO NEWS (IRN)
*Gordon Campbell (Scotland) 3338
*Peter Murphy 020 7799 2360
*Peter Russell 020 7799 2360

INDEPENDENT TELEVISION NEWS (ITN)
4 Millbank 020 7430 4900
Newsdesk (Gray's Inn Road 020 7430 4551
Press Gallery 3334/4387
*Nick Robinson (Political Editor)
Emma Hoskyns (News Editor)
Anne Lingley
*John Ray
*Angus Walker
*Libby Wiener

Channel 4 News
*Elinor Goodman (Political Editor) 3334/4387
*Gary Gibbon
*Oliver King

Channel 5 News
*Andrew Bell 020 7430 4100

ISRAEL RADIO
*Jerry Lewis 0452

LONDON NEWS NETWORK
*Simon Harris
*David Lockwood 020 7233 2020

LONDON NEWS RADIO
*Mark Demery 4700

LONDON WEEKEND TV (LWT)
*Matthew Drury 4700
Alaina MacDonald 4700

MERIDIAN TV
*Kevin Harrison
*Phil Hornby 6729

RTE – IRISH BROADCASTING
*Brian O'Connell 4700

SCOTTISH TV
*Rae Stewart 6724
*Michael Crow 6724
*Bernard Ponsonby 6724

SKY TV NEWS
Newsdesk 020 7705 3232
*Adam Boulton (Political editor) 020 7705 5500
*Jon Craig
Peter Lowe
*Glen Oglaza
Clare Parry
*Jenny Percival
*Peter Spencer

TYNE TEES TV
*Gerry Foley 6739

ULSTER TV
*Ken Reid 5381

WELSH FOURTH CHANNEL – S4C
*Beth Kilfoil 4700
*Vaughan Roderick 4700

WEST COUNTRY TV
*Neil Bradford 020 7976 3399

YORKSHIRE TV
*David Harrison 6720

DodOnline
An Electronic Directory without rival . . .

MPs' biographies and photographs available with daily updates *via* the internet

For a *free* trial, call Yasmin Mirza, Aby Farsoun or Michael Mand on 020 7630 7643

Parliamentary Agents

Parliamentary Agents provide general information on Parliament to both individuals and firms, fully reporting on progress of Bills. There are two types of Agent, those registered to propose and oppose bills on behalf of their clients and those who only oppose Bills.

The Register of authorised Parliamentary Agents is kept in the Private Bills Office of the House of Commons. Generally associated with the legal profession, Agents carry out their duties under the rules, originally laid down by the Speaker in 1837, of both the Houses of Parliament.

One or more of the Partners of the firms listed below are authorised to practise as Parliamentary Agents.

Bircham Dyson Bell
50 Broadway, London SW1H 0BL
Tel: 020 7227 7000   Fax: 020 7233 1351
E-mail: ppl@bdb-law.co.uk
Partners: Ian McCulloch, Paul Thompson,
Nicholas Brown, Robert Owen, David Mundy,
Jonathan Bracken

Lewin Gregory & Co
1 The Sanctuary, London SW1P 3JT
Tel: 020 7222 5381   Fax: 020 7222 4646
E-mail: enquiries@1thesanctuary.com
Partners: Joe Durkin, Monica Peto, Stephen
Collings, Patrick Cronin, Graham Fountain,
Philip Sergeant

Rees & Freres
1 The Sanctuary, London SW1P 3JT
Tel: 020 7222 5381   Fax: 020 7222 4646
E-mail: enquiries@1thesanctuary.com
Partners: Joe Durkin, Monica Peto,
Stephen Collings, Peter Beesley, Patrick Cronin,
Michael Fletcher, Graham Fountain,
Ziggy Reisman, Nicholas Richens,
Peter Robinson, Philip Sergeant, Keith Wallace

Sharpe Pritchard
Elizabeth House, Fulwood Place,
London WC1V 6HG
Tel: 020 7405 4600   Fax: 020 7222 1451
E-mail: parliamentary@sharpepritchard.co.uk
Paliamentary Agents: Alastair Lewis,
Michael Pritchard (Consultant)

Vizard Oldham Brooke Blain
42 Bedford Row, London WC1R 4JL
Tel: 020 7663 2222   Fax: 020 7663 2226
E-mail: ron.perry@vizold.co.uk
Partner: Ron Perry

Winckworth Sherwood
35 Great Peter Street, London SW1P 3LR
Tel: 020 7593 5000   Fax: 020 7593 5199
E-mail: amhgorlov@winckworths.co.uk
Parliamentary Agents (Partners): Alison Gorlov,
Paul Irving, Stephen Wiggs,
(Consultant) Chris Vine

DodOnline

An Electronic Directory without rival . . .

MPs' biographies and photographs available with daily updates *via* the internet

For a *free* trial, call Yasmin Mirza, Aby Farsoun or Michael Mand on 020 7630 7643

HISTORICAL INFORMATION

Parliaments of the 20th and 21st centuries

Assembled	Dissolved	Length	Ministries	Took Office
Victoria		yrs. m. d.		
Dec. 3, 1900	Jan. 8, 1906	5 1 5	⎰ Salisbury (C)	Dec. 6, 1900
			⎱ Balfour (C)	July 12, 1902
Edward VII				
Feb. 13, 1906	Jan. 10, 1910	3 10 28	⎰ C. Bannerman (L)	Dec. 5, 1905
			⎱ Asquith (L)	April 5, 1908
Feb. 15, 1910	Nov. 28, 1910	9 13	Asquith (L)	Feb. 15, 1910
George V				
Jan. 31, 1911	Nov. 25, 1918	7 9 25	⎰ Asquith (L)	May 25, 1915
Feb. 4, 1919	Oct. 25, 1922	3 8 21	⎰ Lloyd George (L)	Dec. 6, 1916
			⎱ Coalition	
Nov. 20, 1922	Nov. 16, 1923	11 27	A. Bonar Law (C)	Oct. 23, 1922
Jan. 8, 1924	Oct. 9, 1924	9 1	J. R. MacDonald (Lab.)	Jan. 22, 1924
Dec. 2, 1924	May 10, 1929	4 5 8	S. Baldwin (C)	Nov. 4, 1924
June 25, 1929	Oct. 7, 1931	2 3 12	J. R. MacDonald (Lab.)	June 5, 1929
			⎰ J. R. MacDonald	Aug. 24, 1931
Nov. 3, 1931	Oct. 25, 1935	3 11 22	⎰ (Nat. Govt.)	
			⎱ S. Baldwin	
Nov. 26, 1935			S. Baldwin	June 7, 1935
			(Nat. Govt.)	
Edward VIII			N. Chamberlain	May 28, 1937
			(Nat. Govt.)	
George VI	June 15, 1945	9 6 20	W. Churchill	May 10, 1940
			(Nat. Govt.)	
Aug. 1, 1945	Feb. 3, 1950	4 6 2	C. R. Attlee (Lab.)	July 26, 1945
Mar. 1, 1950	Oct. 5, 1951	1 7 4	C. R. Attlee (Lab.)	Feb. 25, 1950
Oct. 31, 1951	May 6, 1955	3 6 6	⎰ W. Churchill (C)	Oct. 26, 1951
			⎱ A. Eden (C)	
Elizabeth II			A. Eden (C)	Apr. 6, 1955
June 7, 1955	Sept. 18, 1959	4 3 11	⎰ H. Macmillan (C)	Jan. 10, 1957
			⎱ H. Macmillan (C)	Oct. 9, 1959
Oct. 20, 1959	Sept. 25, 1964	4 11 5	A. Douglas-Home (C)	Oct. 9, 1963
Oct. 27, 1964	Mar. 10, 1966	1 4 11	⎰ H. Wilson (Lab.)	Oct. 16, 1964
Apr. 18, 1966	May 29, 1970	4 1 11	⎱ H. Wilson (Lab.)	Apr. 1, 1966
June 29, 1970	Feb. 8, 1974	3 7 10	E. R. G. Heath (C)	June 19, 1970
Mar. 6, 1974	Sept. 20, 1974	6 14	H. Wilson (Lab.)	Mar. 4, 1974
			(Minority Govt.)	
Oct. 22, 1974	April 7, 1979	4 5 15	⎰ H. Wilson (Lab.)	Oct. 11, 1974
			⎱ J. Callaghan (Lab.)	Apr. 5, 1976
May 9, 1979	May 13, 1983	4 0 4	Mrs M. Thatcher (C)	May 3, 1979
June 15, 1983	May 18, 1987	3 11 3	Mrs M. Thatcher (C)	June 9, 1983
June 17, 1987	Mar. 16, 1992	4 8 28	⎰ Mrs M. Thatcher (C)	June 11, 1987
			⎱ J. Major (C)	Nov. 28, 1990
April 27, 1992	April 8, 1997	4 11 19	J. Major (C)	April 10, 1992
May 7, 1997	May 14, 2001	4 0 7	T. Blair (Lab.)	May 1, 1997
June 20, 2001			T. Blair (Lab.)	June 7, 2001

Size of the House of Commons since 1801

With the Union of Great Britain and Ireland in 1801 the number of members of Parliament of the United Kingdom was fixed at 658. This number was adhered to by the Reform Act, 1832. In 1885 the total was increased to 670, and by the Act of 1918 to 707. With the creation of the Irish Free State in 1922, the Irish representation was reduced to 13 members from Ulster, making the membership of the House of Commons 615. In 1945, owing to the division of large Constituencies, the number was increased by 25 to 640. Under the Act of 1948 the number was decreased to 625. Under the Orders passed in 1954 and 1955 the number was increased to 630. As the result of redistribution and boundary changes, the total number of MPs elected at the 1979 General Election was 635. The House of Commons (Redistribution of Seats) Act 1979 and the Boundary Commission reports of 1983 resulted in an increase of 15 seats after the 1983 Election. The size of the House of Commons up until the 1992 General Election was 650 members. At the 1992 Election, 651 Members were elected, an extra seat having been created for Milton Keynes. Reports from the Boundary Commission caused an increase to 659 at the 1997 Election.

General Election Majorities since the Reform Act

(NB *In certain cases, such as the election of 1910, the Government party had a working arrangement with other parties, which ensured them a majority in the House*)

1832	Lib	300	1923	Con	No majority
1835	Lib	108	1924	Con	223
1837	Lib	40	1929	Lab	No majority
1841	Con	78	1931	Nat Govt	493
1847	Lib	2	1935	Nat Govt	249
1852	Con	8	1945	Lab	146
1857	Lib	92	1950	Lab	5
1859	Lib	40	1951	Con	17
1865	Lib	62	1955	Con	58
1868	Lib	106	1959	Con	100
1874	Con	52	1964	Lab	4
1880	Lib	176	1966	Lab	96
1885	Lib	No majority	1970	Con	30
1886	Unionist	120	1974	(Feb) Lab	No majority
1892	Lib	No majority	1974	(Oct) Lab	3
1895	Unionist	152	(3 over all parties, 42 over Cons)		
1900	Unionist	135	1979	Con	43
1906	Lib	130	1983	Con	144
1910	(Jan) Lib	No majority	1987	Con	101
1910	(Dec) Lib	No majority	1992	Con	21
1918	Coalition	249	1997	Lab	177
1922	Con	75	2001	Lab	165

Long Parliaments

The longest lived Parliaments in English history have been the Elizabethan Parliament of 1572–83, the Long Parliament of 1640–53, and the Cavalier Parliament of 1661–79. The First World War Parliament met on 31st January, 1911, and was dissolved on 25 November 1918. That of the Second met 26 November 1935, and was dissolved 15 June 1945.

Prime Ministers since 1721

1721–42	Sir Robert Walpole (Whig)
1742–43	Spencer Compton (Whig)
1743–54	Henry Pelham (Whig)
1754–56	Duke of Newcastle (Whig)
1756–57	Duke of Devonshire (Whig)
1757–62	Duke of Newcastle (Whig)
1762–63	Earl of Bute (Tory)
1763–65	George Grenville (Whig)
1765–66	Marquess of Rockingham (Whig)
1766–67	William Pitt (the Elder) (Whig)
1767–70	Duke of Grafton (Whig)
1770–82	Lord North (Tory)
1782	Marquess of Rockingham (Whig)
1782–83	Earl of Shelburne (Whig)
1783	Duke of Portland (Coalition)
1783–1801	William Pitt (the Younger) (Tory)
1801–04	Henry Addington (Tory)
1804–06	William Pitt (the Younger) (Tory)
1806–07	Lord Grenville (Whig)
1807–09	Duke of Portland (Tory)
1809–12	Spencer Perceval (Tory)
1812–27	Earl of Liverpool (Tory)
1827	George Canning (Tory)
1827–28	Viscount Goderich (Tory)
1828–30	Duke of Wellington (Tory)
1830–34	Earl Grey (Whig)
1834	Viscount Melbourne (Whig)
1834–35	Sir Robert Peel (Tory)
1835–41	Viscount Melbourne (Whig)
1841–46	Sir Robert Peel (Tory)
1846–52	Lord John Russell (Whig)
1852	Earl of Derby (Con)
1852–55	Earl of Aberdeen (Coalition)
1855–58	Viscount Palmerston (Lib)
1858–59	Earl of Derby (Con)
1859–65	Viscount Palmerston (Lib)
1865–66	Earl Russell (Lib)
1866–68	Earl of Derby (Con)
1868	Benjamin Disraeli (Con)
1868–74	William Gladstone (Lib)
1874–80	Benjamin Disraeli (Con)
1880–85	William Gladstone (Lib)
1885–86	Marquess of Salisbury (Con)
1886	William Gladstone (Lib)
1886–92	Marquess of Salisbury (Con)
1892–94	William Gladstone (Lib)
1894–95	Earl of Rosebery (Lib)
1895–1902	Marquess of Salisbury (Con)
1902–05	Arthur Balfour (Con)
1905–08	Sir Henry Campbell-Bannerman (Lib)
1908–16	Herbert Asquith (Lib)
1916–22	David Lloyd George (Coalition)
1922–23	Andrew Bonar Law (Con)
1923–24	Stanley Baldwin (Con)
1924	Ramsay MacDonald (Lab)
1924–29	Stanley Baldwin (Con)
1929–35	Ramsay MacDonald (Lab)
1935–37	Stanley Baldwin (Nat Govt)
1937–40	Neville Chamberlain (Nat Govt)
1940–45	Winston Churchill (Coalition)
1945–51	Clement Attlee (Lab)
1951–55	Winston Churchill (Con)
1955–57	Sir Anthony Eden (Con)
1957–63	Harold Macmillan (Con)
1963–64	Sir Alec Douglas-Home (Con)
1964–70	Harold Wilson (Lab)
1970–74	Edward Heath (Con)
1974–76	Harold Wilson (Lab)
1976–79	James Callaghan (Lab)
1979–90	Margaret Thatcher (Con)
1990–97	John Major (Con)
1997–	Tony Blair (Lab)

Visit the Vacher Dod Website . . .
www.DodOnline.co.uk

Essential Political Information from Vacher Dod Publishing

Dod's Parliamentary Companion
Published since 1832. Parliament's leading annual reference book
Biographies of MPs and Peers

Dod's Scotland, Wales and Northern Ireland Companion
First edition 2003
Biographies; election results; structure and functions; constituency profiles

Dod's European Companion
Biographies of MEPs, European Commissioners and EU civil servants

Dod's Civil Service Companion
Biographies of over 2,500 civil servants

www.DodOnline.co.uk
A comprehensive, live political database on the web

Dod's Constituency Guide
In-depth profiles of every constituency in the UK

Vacher's Parliamentary Companion
Parliament's foremost quarterly contact directory

Vacher's Civil Service Companion
The definitive civil service contact companion

Handbook of House of Commons Procedure
Revised 4th edition. Clear, jargon-free and accessible. An essential reference
work for those who need to know the procedures of the House of Commons

The Challenge for Parliament
Report of the Hansard Society Commission. Sets out a vision of how
a reformed Parliament might work

To order call our Hotline now on 020 7630 7619

Vacher Dod Publishing
1 Douglas Street, London, SW1P 4PA
Tel: 020 7630 7619   Fax: 020 7233 7266
Email: subscriptions@vacherdod.co.uk
Website: www.DodOnline.co.uk

DEPARTMENTS OF STATE AND GOVERNMENT OFFICES

PERMANENT SECRETARIES

Office of the Deputy Prime Minister

Mavis McDonald CB

Private Secretary
Andrew Vaughan

020 7944 8965   Fax: 020 7944 8966
E-mail: andrew.vaughan@odpm.gsi.gov.uk

Cabinet Office

Secretary of the Cabinet and Head of the Home Civil Service
Sir Andrew Turnbull KCB CVO

Private Secretary
Sue Pither

020 7270 0101   Fax: 020 7270 0208
E-mail: psaturnbull@cabinet-office.x.gsi.gov.uk

Security and Intelligence Co-ordinator and Permanent Secretary to the Cabinet Office
Sir David Omand KCB

Principal Private Secretary
Sebastian Madden

020 7276 0191   Fax: 020 7276 0169
E-mail: sebastian.madden@cabinet-office.x.gsi.gov.uk

Constitutional Affairs

Sir Hayden Phillips GCB

Private Secretary
Nicola Webster

020 7210 8395
E-mail: nicola.webster@dca.gsi.gov.uk

Second Permanent Secretary and Chief Executive, Operations
Ian Magee CB

Personal Assistant
Maureen Sullivan

020 7210 2177   Fax: 020 7210 1734
E-mail: maureen.sullivan@dca.gsi.gov.uk

Culture, Media and Sport

Sue Street

Private Secretary
Eleanor Street

020 7211 6256   Fax: 020 7211 6259
E-mail: eleanor.street@culture.gsi.gov.uk

Defence

Sir Kevin Tebbit KCB CMG

Private Secretary
Dominic Wilson

020 7218 2839
E-mail: pus-pa@mod.gsi.gov.uk

Second Permanent Secretary
Ian Andrews CBE

Private Secretary
Paul Wyatt

020 7218 7115
E-mail: 2ndpus.ps@modho.gsi.gov.uk

Education and Skills

David Normington CB

Private Secretary
Paul Price · 020 7925 6937 · Fax: 020 7925 6599
E-mail: paul.price@dfes.gsi.gov.uk

Environment, Food and Rural Affairs

Sir Brian Bender KCB

Private Secretary
Suzie Daykin · 020 7238 5446 · Fax: 020 7238 6118
E-mail: perm.secretary@defra.gsi.gov.uk

Foreign and Commonwealth Office

Permanent Secretary and Head of HM Diplomatic Service
Sir Michael Jay KCMG

Private Secretary
Menna Rawlings · 020 7008 2142
E-mail: pspus@fco.gov.uk

Health

Permanent Secretary and Chief Executive NHS
Sir Nigel Crisp KCB

Private Secretary
Matthew Hamilton · 020 7210 5579 · Fax: 020 7210 5409
E-mail: matthew.hamilton@doh.gsi.gov.uk

Home Office

John Gieve CB

Private Secretary
Diana Luchford · 020 7273 2199 · Fax: 020 7273 2972
E-mail: diana.luchford@homeoffice.gsi.gov.uk

Commissioner for Correctional Services and Permanent Secretary for Human Resources
Martin Narey

Private Secretary
Debbie Drew · 020 7217 6720 · Fax: 020 7217 6961
E-mail: martin.narey@homeoffice.gsi.gov.uk

Permanent Secretary for Crime, Policy, Counter-Terrorism and Delivery
Leigh Lewis CB

Private Secretary
David Rasmussen · 020 7273 3601
E-mail: david.rasmussen@homeoffice.gsi.gov.uk

International Development

Suma Chakrabarti

Private Secretary
Charlie Whetham · 020 7023 0514 · Fax: 020 7023 0732
E-mail: c-whetham@dfid.gov.uk

National Assembly for Wales
Sir Jon Shortridge KCB
Private Secretary
Keith Moses   029 2082 3289
                                     E-mail: keith.moses@wales.gsi.gov.uk

Work and Pensions
Sir Richard Mottram KCB
Private Secretary
Judith Tunstall   020 7238 0702
                                     E-mail: judith.tunstall@dwp.gsi.gov.uk

Northern Ireland Office
Sir Joseph Pilling KCB
Private Secretary
Ruth Sloan   020 7210 6456 (London)   Fax: 020 7210 0256
                                     028 9052 8121 (Belfast)   Fax: 028 9052 2918
                                     E-mail: ruth.sloan@nio.x.gsi.gov.uk

Northern Ireland Executive
Head of Northern Ireland Civil Service and Secretary to the Executive
Nigel Hamilton
Private Secretary
Bernie Rooney   028 9037 8132
                                     E-mail: bernie.rooney@ofmdfmni.gov.uk

Second Permanent Secretary
Will Haire
Private Secretary
Angela Dullaghan   028 9037 8132
                                     E-mail: angela.dullaghan@ofmdfmni.gov.uk

Scottish Executive
John Elvidge
Private Secretary
Ian Davidson   0131-244 4026   Fax: 0131-244 2756
                                     E-mail: prmperm.sec@scotland.gsi.gov.uk

Trade and Industry
Sir Robin Young KCB
Private Secretary
Tom Ridge   020 7215 5536
                                     E-mail: mpst.young@dti.gsi.gov.uk

Transport
David Rowlands CB
Private Secretary
Jessica Bowles   020 7944 4388/3017   Fax: 020 7944 4389
                                     E-mail: jessica.bowles@dft.gsi.gov.uk

Treasury
Gus O'Donnell CB
Private Secretary
Ciaran Martin   020 7270 4360   Fax: 020 7270 4834
                                     E-mail: ciaran.martin@hm-treasury.gsi.gov.uk

DEPARTMENTS OF STATE

Prime Minister's Office

10 Downing Street, London SW1A 2AA
Tel: 020 7270 3000
Websites: www.number-10.gov.uk
www.pm.gov.uk

Prime Minister: Rt Hon Tony Blair MP
Chief of Staff: Jonathan Powell
Director of Communications and Strategy:
   Alastair Campbell
Director of Government Relations:
   Baroness Morgan of Huyton
Principal Private Secretary and Head of Policy
   Directorate: Jeremy Heywood CB
Adviser on EU Affairs and Head of the European
   Secretariat: Sir Stephen Wall KCMG LVO
Adviser on Foreign Policy and Head of the
   Overseas and Defence Secretariat:
   Sir Nigel Sheinwald KCMG
Parliamentary Private Secretary:
   David Hanson MP
Policy Directorate: Andrew Adonis (Head of
   Policy), Simon Virley, Geoffrey Norris,
   Matthew Elson, Carey Oppenheim,
   Derek Scott, Ed Richards, Patrick Diamond,
   Sarah Hunter, Simon Stevens, Justin Russell,
   Martin Hurst, Clare Sumner,
   Alasdair McGowan
Foreign Policy: Matthew Rycroft,
   David Hallam, Liz Lloyd, Roger Liddle
Secretary for Appointments:
   William Chapman
Executive Secretary: Jay Jayasundara
Political Secretary: Pat McFadden
Director of Events and Visits: Fiona Millar
Personal Assistant to Prime Minister:
   Katie Kay (Diary)
Parliamentary Clerk: Nicholas Howard
Communications and Strategy
Prime Minister's Official Spokesman (PMOS):
   Godric Smith and Tom Kelly
Chief Press Officer: Anne Shevas
Press Officers: Martin Sheehan, Daniel Pruce,
   Hilary Coffman, Emily Hands, Ben Wilson,
   John Shield
Strategic Communications Unit:
   Peter Hyman
Research and Information Unit:
   Phil Bassett
Corporate Communications: Vacant
Direct Communications Unit: Jan Taylor

Office of the Deputy Prime Minister – ODPM

26 Whitehall, London SW1A 2WH
Switchboard Tel: 020 7944 4400
GTN: 3533 4400
E-mail: [firstname.surname]@odpm.gsi.gov.uk
Website: www.odpm.gov.uk

Ashdown House, 123 Victoria Street,
London SW1E 6DE

Eland House, Bressenden Place,
London SW1E 5DU

Portland House, Stag Place, London SW1E 5LP

Bridge House, 1 Walnut Tree Close, Guildford,
Surrey GU1 4GA

City House, New Station Street, Leeds LS1 4US

Great Minister House, 76 Marsham Street,
London SW1P 4DR

Hempstead House, 2 Felden Hill,
Hemel Hempstead, Hertfordshire HP2 4XN

77 Paradise Circus, Queensway, Birmingham,
West Midlands B1 2DT

2 Rivergate, Temple Quay, Bristol BS1 6ED

Riverwalk House, 157-161 Millbank,
London SW1P 4RR

Sunley Tower, Piccadilly Plaza,
Manchester M1 4BE

The Belgrave Centre, Stanley Place,
Talbot Street, Nottingham NG1 5GG

Westbrook, Milton Road, Cambridge,
Cambridgeshire CB4 1YG

Wellbar House, Gallowgate,
Newcastle upon Tyne NE1 4TD

Thriving, inclusive and sustainable communities
in all regions. Work with the full range of
government departments and policies to raise the
levels of social inclusion, neighbourhood
renewal and regional prosperity. Provide for
effective devolved decision making within a
framework of national targets and policies.
Deliver effective programmes to help raise the
quality of life for all in urban areas and other
communities.

Private Offices

26 Whitehall
Deputy Prime Minister and First Secretary of
   State: Rt Hon John Prescott MP
Parliamentary Private Secretary:
   David Watts MP

Special Advisers: Joan Hammell, Ian McKenzie,
  Paul Hackett
Special Advisers' Numbers: 020 7944 8615
  Fax: 020 7944 8618
Principal Private Secretary: David Prout
  020 7944 8604 Fax: 020 7944 8621
  E-mail: john.prescott@odpm.gsi.gov.uk
Private Secretaries: Ciara Mulligan
  020 7944 8611, Clare Buckee 020 7944 8608,
  Christopher Parr 020 7944 8607
Assistant Private Secretary: Tracey Temple
  (Diary) 020 7944 8605, Aine Sheeham (Visits)
  020 7944 8606

Minister of State for Local and Regional
  Government: Rt Hon Nick Raynsford MP
Parliamentary Private Secretary:
  Linda Gilroy MP
Private Secretary: Sarah Sturrock
  020 7944 4344 Fax: 020 7944 4539
  E-mail: nick.raynsford@odpm.gsi.gov.uk
Assistant Private Secretary: Anna Wojtowicz
  020 7944 4345

Minister of State for Regeneration and Regional
  Development: Rt Hon Lord Rooker
Parliamentary Private Secretary:
  Ivan Henderson MP 020 7219 3434
Private Secretary: Julia Penton 020 7944 4487
  Fax: 020 7944 4489
Assistant Private Secretaries:
  Jenny Mainland 020 7944 4488,
  Paul Smith 020 7944 4551
Diary Secretary: Claire Hoskins 020 7944 4486
  E-mail: jeff.rooker@odpm.gsi.gov.uk

Minister of State for Housing and Planning:
  Rt Hon Keith Hill MP
Parliamentary Private Secretary:
  Terry Rooney MP
Private Secretary: Mark Livesey 020 7944 8951
  Fax: 020 7944 8953
  E-mail: keith.hill@odpm.gsi.gov.uk
Assistant Private Secretaries: Arthur Young
  020 7944 8959, Uzma Ahmed 020 7944 8958,
  Thomas Lovesey (Diary) 020 7944 8952

Parliamentary Under-Secretary of State:
  Yvette Cooper MP
Private Secretary: Sam Wilkinson 020 7944 4537
  Fax: 020 7944 4538
  E-mail: yvette.cooper@odpm.gsi.gov.uk
Assistant Private Secretaries: Katherine White
  020 7944 4536, Matthew Wells 020 7944 4533
Diary Secretary: Fiona Rodrigo 020 7944 4534

Parliamentary Under-Secretary of State:
  Phil Hope MP
Private Secretary: Karen Abbott
  020 7944 4334 Fax: 020 7944 4339

Assistant Private Secretaries: Katie Jones
  020 7944 4335, Andrew Darvill
  020 7944 4346
Diary Secretary: Dionne Campbell 020 7944 5897
  E-mail: phil.hope@odpm.gsi.gov.uk

Spokespeople in the House of Lords:
Lord Rooker, Lord Evans of Temple Guiting

Permanent Secretary: Mavis McDonald CB
Private Secretary: Andrew Vaughan
  020 7944 8965 Fax: 020 7944 8966
Deputy Private Secretary: Angela Kerr
  020 7944 8962
Parliamentary Clerk: Selvin Brown
  020 7944 8967 Fax: 020 7944 8995

DIRECTORATE OF COMMUNICATION
26 Whitehall
Director of Communication: Derek Plews
  E-mail: derek.plews@odpm.gsi.gov.uk
Head of Operations: Jane Groom

CORPORATE STRATEGY AND RESOURCES DIRECTORATE
Director: Peter Unwin
Divisional Managers
Corporate Business and Delivery:
  Stuart Hoggan
Finance Accounting Services: Alan Beard
International and Central Policy:
  Shona Dunn

Analysis and Research
Deputy Director: Vacant
Divisional Managers
Central Economics and Policy:
  Michael Kell
Housing Data and Statistics: Bruce Oelman
Planning and Land Use Statistics:
  Mick Johnston
Research Analysis and Evaluation:
  Waqar Ahmad

Corporate Services
Deputy Director: Mike Acheson
Divisional Managers
Human Resources: Janet Fortune
Information Management: David A Smith
Infrastructure Services: Simon Barnes

Finance
Deputy Director: Andrew Lean
Divisional Managers
Budget and Data Management:
  Amanda McFeeters
Finance and Advice and Administration:
  Chris Smith
Internal Audit Services: Steve Simmonds

HOUSING, HOMELESSNESS, URBAN POLICY AND PLANNING GROUP
Eland House
Director-General: Genie Turton CB
Director, Housing Directorate: Neil McDonald

Equality and Diversity Unit
Unit Manager: Shelagh Prosser

Housing Directorate
Director: Neil McDonald
Divisional Managers
Affordable Housing: Vacant
Community Housing Task Force: Hilary Bartle
Housing Associations and Private Finance:
    Richard Horsman
Housing Care and Support: Bert Provan
Housing Management: Dawn Eastmead
Housing Private Sector: Phil Carey
Decent Homes Finance and Co-ordination:
    Anne Kirkham
Local Authority Housing: Wendy Jarvis

Homelessness Directorate
Ashdown House
Director: Terrie Alafat
Divisional Managers
Performance Monitoring and Finance:
    Gordon Campbell
Bed and Breakfast Unit: Ashley Horsey
Homelessness: Neil O'Connor
Rough Sleeping Policy and Services: Ian Brady
Strategic Policy, Communications and
    Secretariat: Charlie Chappell

Planning Directorate
Eland House
Director: Brian Hackland
Deputy Director: Mike Ash
Divisional Managers
Planning Policy: Vacant
Minerals and Waste Planning: Lester Hicks
Planning Development Control Policy:
    John Stambollouian
Plans, International Compensation and
    Assessment: Lisette Simcock
PINS Review Task Force: Alan Gray
Planning Central Casework: Joan Bailey
Planning, Legislation and Implementation:
    Bob Ledscombe

LEGAL GROUP
Eland House
Director-General and Legal Adviser:
    David Hogg CB
E-mail: david.hogg@odpm-dft.gsi.gov.uk

Legal Directorate
Director: Sandra Unerman

Divisional Managers
Constitutional and Regional Development:
    Donatella Phillips
Employment and Commercial: Fred Croft
Housing and Land: John Wright
Legislative Unit: David Ingham
Local Government (Finance):
    Pamela Conlon
Local Government (General):
    Judith-Anne MacKenzie
Planning: Gloria Hedley-Dent CBE

LOCAL AND REGIONAL GOVERNMENT GROUP
Eland House
Director-General: Neil Kingham

Civil Resilience Directorate
Director: Alun Evans
Divisional Managers
To be appointed

Fire, Health and Safety Directorate
Director: Clive Norris
Divisional Managers
Building Decontamination:
    Christopher Bowden
Built Environment: Paul Everall
Fire Policy: Diana Khan
Fire Research: Dr David Peace
Fire Service Modernisation Team:
    Dave Lawrence
HM Fire Service Inspectorate, Chief Inspector:
    Sir Graham Meldrum
Negotiation Support: Su Bonfanti

Local Government Directorate of Practice
Director: John Haward
Divisional Managers
Local Government Capacity and Modernisation:
    Geoff Tierney
Local Government Intervention:
    Robert Whittaker
Local Government Regional Teams:
    Rita Petty

LOCAL GOVERNMENT FINANCE DIRECTORATE
Director: Bob Linnard
Divisional Managers
Modernisation and Grant Distribution:
    Robert Davies
Taxation, Valuation and General:
    Andrew Morrison
Statistics, Payments and IT: Meg Green
Capital Finance and Accountancy Advice:
    Pam Williams
Local Government Pensions: Terry Crossley

Local Government Performance Unit
Director: Phillip Ward
Divisional Managers
Local Government Legislation: Kevin Lloyd
Local Government Public Service Agreements:
  Richard Gibson
Local Government Quality and Performance:
  Richard Footitt

REGIONAL POLICY UNIT AND LOCAL GOVERNANCE
Director: Richard Allan
Divisional Manager, Regional Assemblies:
  Ian Scotter
Democracy and Local Government: Paul Rowsell
Regional Economic Performance: Philip Cox

NEIGHBOURHOOD RENEWAL UNIT
Eland House
Director-General: Joe Montgomery

Neighbourhood Renewal Operations Directorate
Director: Alan Riddell
Divisional Managers
Neighbourhood Renewal Implementation:
  Jon Bright
Neighbourhood Renewal Policy: Graham Duncan
Neighbourhood Renewal Research: Raj Patel

Neighbourhood Renewal Strategy Directorate
Director: Lindsay Bell
Divisional Managers
Communications: Sarah Clifford
Neighbourhood Renewal Delivery: Vacant
Whitehall Advice and Co-ordination:
  Martin Joseph

REGIONAL CO-ORDINATION UNIT – RCU
Riverwalk House, 157-161 Millbank,
London SW1P 4RR
Tel: 020 7217 3595   Fax: 020 7217 3590
GTN: 217 3595
E-mail:
rcusecretariatenquiries@go-regions.gsi.gov.uk
Website: www.rcu.gov.uk
Director-General: Rob Smith
Director: Andrew Campbell
Divisional Managers
Strategy: Nick Dexter
Corporate Communications: Ian Jones
Business Development: Teresa Vokes
Resilience and Civil Contingencies: Richard Bruce

Government Offices for the Regions

GO – North East
Regional Director: Jonathan Blackie

GO – Yorkshire and Humber
Regional Director: Felicity Everiss

GO – West Midlands
Regional Director: Graham Garbutt

GO – East
Regional Director: Caroline Bowdler

GO – London
Regional Director: Elizabeth Meek

GO – North West
Regional Director: Keith Barnes

GO – East Midlands
Regional Director: Jane Todd

GO – South East
Regional Director: Paul Martin

GO – South West
Regional Director: Jane Henderson

NB: See Government Offices for the Regions' entry for full details

SOCIAL EXCLUSION UNIT – SEU
Eland House
Director: Claire Tyler
Divisional Managers
Business Development/Impact and Trends:
  Vanessa Scarborough, Sally Burlington
Children in Care: Cath Shaw
Implementation External Relations: Jos Joures
Transport and Social Exclusion: Marcus Bell
Mental Health: Ruth Stainer

SUSTAINABLE COMMUNITIES DELIVERY UNIT
Director-General: Vacant

Sustainable Communities Directorate
Director: Andrew Wells
Divisional Managers
Growth Areas and House Supply:
  Henry Cleary
Market Renewal: Duncan Campbell
PSA 5 Delivery Plan: Michelle Banks

Urban Policy Directorate
Director: David Lunts
Divisional Managers
ERDF and State Aid: Mitesk Dhanak
Land and Property: Martin Leigh-Pollitt
Livability and Sustainable Communities:
  Peter Matthew
Regional and Agency Sponsorship:
  David Liston-Jones
Thames Gateway Strategic Executive:
  John Sienkiewicz

Executive Agencies: Fire Service College (FSC); Ordnance Survey; Planning Inspectorate (PINS); Queen Elizabeth II Conference Centre; The Rent Service (TRS)

Cabinet Office

Ministers' Offices, 70 Whitehall,
London SW1A 2AS
Switchboard Tel: 020 7276 3000
020 7276 1234   GTN: 270 1234
E-mail:
[firstname.surname]@cabinet-office.x.gsi.gov.uk
Website: www.cabinet-office.gov.uk

- supports the Prime Minister in leading the Government
- supports the Government in transacting its business
- helps deliver key public service priorities
- leads the reform programme for public services
- co-ordinates security, intelligence and civil contingency matters and protects the UK against disruptive challenges.

Minister for the Cabinet Office and Chancellor of the Duchy of Lancaster:
Douglas Alexander MP
Parliamentary Private Secretary:
Lawrie Quinn MP 020 7219 4170
Private Secretary: Georgia Hutchinson
020 7276 0652
E-mail: psdouglasalexander@
cabinet-office.x.gsi.gov.uk
Assistant Private Secretaries: Harriet Canabeare
020 7276 0656, Clare Blomeley 020 7276 0654,
Stephanie Tuffe 020 7276 0653
Diary Secretary: Sarah Harvey 020 7276 0656

Duchy of Lancaster Office
1 Lancaster Place, Strand, London WC2E 7ED
Tel: 020 7836 8277   Fax: 020 7836 3098
Chief Executive and Clerk of the Council:
Paul Clarke
Secretary for Appointments:
Lindsay M Addison

Administrative and Civil Service support services are based at the Cabinet Office for:
Rt Hon Peter Hain MP as Leader of the House of Commons
Phil Woolas MP as Deputy Leader of the House of Commons
Rt Hon Lord Williams of Mostyn QC as Leader of the House of Lords and Lord President of the Council
Rt Hon Ian McCartney as Minister without Portfolio
Prof David King ScD FRS as Chief Scientific Adviser to the Government

Spokesman in the House of Lords:
Lord Bassam of Brighton

Private Offices
Secretary of the Cabinet and Head of the Home Civil Service:
Sir Andrew Turnbull KCB CVO
70 Whitehall, London SW1A 2AS
Tel: 020 7270 0101   Fax: 020 7270 0208
GTN: 270 0101
Principal Private Secretary: Ian Fletcher
Private Secretary: Sue Pither
Assistant Private Secretaries: Karen Chong,
Lynne Sheasgreen, Amanda Fraser
E-mail: psaturnbull@cabinet-office.x.gsi.gov.uk
Parliamentary Clerk:
Pauline Reece 020 7276 0508
Fax: 020 7276 0514

Security and Intelligence Co-ordinator and Permanent Secretary to the Cabinet Office:
Sir David Omand KCB
Principal Private Secretary: Sebastian Madden
020 7276 0191
E-mail:
sebastian.madden@cabinet-office.x.gsi.gov.uk
Private Secretary: Lisa Harlow 020 7276 0169
Diary Secretary: Shelley Williams-Walker
020 7276 0178 Fax: 020 7276 0128

ECONOMIC AND DOMESTIC SECRETARIAT
Tel: 020 7270 0240
Head: Paul Britton CB
Deputy Head: Robin Fellgett

DEFENCE AND OVERSEAS AFFAIRS SECRETARIAT
Prime Minister's Foreign Policy Adviser and Head of Secretariat:
Sir David Manning KCMG
Deputy Head: Desmond Brown

EUROPEAN SECRETARIAT
Prime Minister's European Policy Adviser and Head of Secretariat:
Sir Stephen Wall KCMG LVO
Deputy Head: Katrina Williams

CEREMONIAL SECRETARIAT
Great Smith Street, London SW1P 2BQ
Tel: 020 7276 2728
Honours Nomination Unit: Tel: 020 7276 2775
E-mail: ceremonial@cabinet-office.x.gsi.gov.uk
Websites:
www.cabinet-office.gov.uk/ceremonial
www.number-10.gov.uk (Honours List)
Ceremonial Officer: Gay Catto

CIVIL CONTINGENCIES SECRETARIAT – CCS

10 Great George Street, London SW1P 3AE
Tel: 020 7276 5056
E-mail: ccs-support@cabinet-office.x.gsi.gov.uk
Head: Susan Scholefield CMG
Private Secretary: Vacant 020 7276 6299
    Fax: 020 7276 5628
Assistant Private Secretary: Natalie Keyte
    (Diary) 020 7276 0433
Deputy Head: Dr John Fuller

OFFICE OF THE COMMISSIONER FOR PUBLIC APPOINTMENTS – OCPA

The Commissioner for Public Appointments is responsible for monitoring, regulating, reporting and advising on ministerial appointments to public bodies. The Commissioner publishes a Code of Practice and an Annual Report. The Commissioner can investigate complaints about the way in which appointments were made or applicants treated.
3rd Floor, 35 Great Smith Street,
London SW1P 3BQ
Tel: 020 7276 2625 Fax: 020 7276 2633
E-mail: ocpa@gtnet.gov.uk
Website: www.ocpa.gov.uk/
Commissioner for Public Appointments:
    Dame Rennie Fritchie DBE
*Secretary to the Commissioner and Head of
    OCPA Office:* Jim Barron
Policy Adviser to the Commissioner:
    Alistair Howie

OFFICE OF THE CIVIL SERVICE COMMISSIONERS – OCSC

The independent Civil Service Commissioners are the custodians of the rules for selection on merit by fair and open competition; they publish a Recruitment Code and audit departments and agencies' performance against it. When senior posts are opened to people from outside the Service the Commissioners normally chair the recruitment process. The Commissioners also act as an independent appeals body under the Civil Service Code.
3rd Floor, 35 Great Smith Street,
London SW1P 3BQ
Tel: 020 7276 2615 Fax: 020 7276 2606
E-mail: ocsc@cabinet-office.x.gsi.gov.uk
Website: www.cabinet-office.gov.uk/ocsc/
First Commissioner:
    Baroness Usha Prashar CBE
Commissioners (part-time): David Bell, Peter
    Bounds, James Boyle, Ms Bronwyn Curtis,
    Ms Sheila Forbes CBE, Dame Rennie
    Fritchie DBE, Prof Edward Gallagher CBE,

Hamish Hamill CB, Gerard Lemos CMG,
Alaistair MacDonald CB, Geoffrey
Maddrell, Geraldine Peacock CBE,
Dr Maggie Semple OBE
*Secretary to the Commissioners and Head of
    OCSC Office:* Jim Barron
Tel: 020 7276 2604
E-mail: jim.barron@cabinet-office.x.gsi.gov.uk

REGULATORY IMPACT UNIT – RIU

The Regulatory Impact Unit works with other government departments, agencies and regulators to help ensure that regulations are fair and effective and help reduce bureaucracy and red tape. The Unit also works with and supports the Better Regulation Task Force.
22 Whitehall, London SW1A 2WH
Tel: 020 7276 2193 Fax: 020 7276 2136
E-mail: regulation@cabinet-office.x.gsi.gov.uk
Website: www.cabinet-office.gov.uk/regulation
Director: Simon Virley
Deputy Directors: Mark Courtney, Jeanie
    Cruickshank*, Shelley Grey, Karen Hill,
    Kate Jennings, Dr Philip Rushbrook
*Based at 2 Little Smith Street,
London SW1P 3DH

THE PRIME MINISTER'S DELIVERY UNIT – PMDU

The Prime Minister's Delivery Unit was established in June 2001 to monitor progress on and strengthen the Government's capacity to deliver its key priorities across education, health, crime and transport. The Unit reports to the Prime Minister through the Head of the Civil Service and Minister for the Cabinet Office. Following the Spending Review 2002, the role of the Delivery Unit has widened to include the other main domestic service delivery departments. The Unit's work is carried out by a team of staff with experience of delivery, drawn from the public and private sectors.
1 Horse Guards Road, London SW1A 2HG
Tel: 020 7270 5857 Fax: 020 7270 5789
E-mail: pmdu@cabinet-office.x.gsi.gov.uk
Website: www.cabinet-office.gov.uk/pmdu
Prime Minister's Chief Adviser on Delivery:
    Prof Michael Barber
Deputy Directors: William Jordan, Peter Thomas

OFFICE OF THE E-ENVOY – OeE

The Office of the e-Envoy is part of the Prime Minister's Delivery and Reform team based in the Cabinet Office. The primary focus of the Office of the e-Envoy is to improve the delivery of public services and achieve long term cost

savings by joining-up online government services around the needs of customers. The e-Envoy is responsible for ensuring that all government services are available electronically by 2005 with key services achieving high levels of use. The Office continues to ensure that the country, its citizens and its businesses derive maximum benefit from the knowledge economy. It works to meet the Prime Minister's target for internet access for all who want it by 2005 and supports work across government to develop the UK as a world leader for electronic business. At the Department for Trade and Industry Patricia Hewitt MP, Secretary of State, is the e-Minister with overall responsibility for the government's e-agenda, and Stephen Timms MP, Minister of State for e-Commerce and Competitiveness, takes the day-to-day lead on e-commerce issues. In the Cabinet office Douglas Alexander MP is responsible for e-transformation.
Stockley House, 130 Wilton Road, Victoria, London SW1V 1LQ
Tel: 020 7276 3300 Fax: 020 7276 3290
E-mail: info@e-envoy.gsi.gov.uk
Website: www.e-envoy.gov.uk
e-Envoy: Andrew Pinder

REFORM STRATEGY GROUP

The Reform Strategy Group is tasked with: defining the overall reform strategy; co-ordinating the work of the other Delivery and Reform Units; ensuring departments have rigorous change programmes; supporting the Civil Service Management Board; communicating the reform message throughout the civil service; co-ordinating work on a Civil Service Bill. The Reform Strategy Group is leading the work to develop 'Performance Partnerships' with Departments. The objectives of these Partnerships are: to ensure that Departments have clarity of purpose and priorities, matched by a Departmental Change Programme which urgently and effectively improves its capacity to fulfil the agreed purpose and priorities; to improve co-ordination within the wider centre, ie Delivery and Reform Team, No 10 Directorate and HM Treasury; to strengthen the partnerships available to Departments on performance improvement, including their relationship with the combined centre of Government, so all partners inform the assessment of priorities, improve the efficiency of partnership working and openly evaluate progress.
Ripley Court, 26 Whitehall, London SW1A 2WH
Enquiries: 020 7276 1738 GTN: 276 1738
Fax: 020 7276 1670
Director: Paul Kirby
Deputy Director: Jo Thorne

STRATEGY UNIT – SU

The Strategy Unit (SU) was created in June 2002 as the result of a merger between the Performance and Innovation Unit (PIU) the Prime Minister's Forward Strategy Unit (PMFSU) and part of the Centre for Management and Policy Studies (CMPS). The SU carries out long-term strategic reviews and policy analysis which can take several forms: long-term strategic reviews of major areas of policy; studies of cross-cutting policy issues; strategic audit; and working with departments to promote strategic thinking and improve policy making across Whitehall. The Unit reports directly to the Prime Minister through the Cabinet Secretary. Since 1998, when the PIU was set up, the Unit has undertaken work on a wide range of policy areas, including: e-commerce; rural policy; modernising central Government; the future of the Post Office; recovery of criminal assets; adoption; e-government; trade policy; global health; resource productivity; workforce development; voluntary sector regulation; childcare; waste; and sport. To date, the Unit has published 27 reports as well as discussion papers and analytical pieces.
Admiralty Arch, The Mall, London SW1A 2WH
Tel: 020 7276 1881 Fax: 020 7276 1407
E-mail: strategy@cabinet-office.x.gsi.gov.uk
Website: www.strategy.gov.uk
Director: Geoff Mulgan
Deputy Directors: Jamie Rentoul, Stephen Aldridge, Patricia Greer, Catriona Laing
Government Chief Social Researcher: Sue Duncan

THE PRIME MINISTER'S OFFICE OF PUBLIC SERVICES REFORM – OPSR

The reform and modernisation of the public services is the Government's top priority. To strengthen the Government's ability to deliver the change in public services, the Prime Minister established the Office of Public Services Reform based in the Cabinet Office. OPSR will focus on reform of public services (eg the health service, schools, local policing, local government), taking responsibility for work on: communicating the principles and values of public service reform and customer focus; models for improving public service delivery; pay and recruitment problems in the public sector; developing systems for managing cross-cutting issues affecting service delivery; devising improved methods of public service management that reduce the impact of regulation on front line services.

22 Whitehall, London SW1A 2WH
Tel: 020 7276 3600 Fax: 020 7276 3530
E-mail: opsr@cabinet-office.x.gsi.gov.uk
Website: www.pm.gov.uk/opsr
*Prime Minister's Chief Adviser on Public
Services Reform:* Dr Wendy Thomson

Charter Mark Team
Tel: 020 7276 1755 Fax: 020 7276 1704
GTN: 276 1755
Website: www.chartermark.gov.uk
Head of Team: Roy Stephenson 020 7276 1741
E-mail:
roy.stephenson@cabinet-office.x.gsi.gov.uk

Charter Mark Programme
Quality Networks
Public Servant of the Year Award
Head of Policy: Jane Jones 020 7276 1746
Fax: 020 7276 1704 GTN: 276 1746
E-mail: jane.jones@cabinet-office.x.gsi.gov.uk

**CORPORATE DEVELOPMENT GROUP –
CDG**
CDG spearheads work on identifying and
bringing in more talent, developing and
rewarding it better, and raising the capability of
HR management throughout Whitehall. CDG
includes the Civil Service College Directorate
which is based in Sunningdale, Berkshire.
Admiralty Arch, The Mall, London SW1P 3AE
Tel: 020 7276 1566
Websites: www.civil-service.gov.uk
www.cmps.gov.uk
Director-General: Alice Perkins CB
Directors: John Barker CB, Ewart Wooldridge,
  Richard Kornicki, Tim Kemp,
  Richard Furlong

**GOVERNMENT INFORMATION AND
COMMUNICATION SERVICES – GICS**
GNN is the regional arm of the Government
Information and Communication Service (GICS)
and serves all the English Regions, Scotland and
Wales. Formerly the regional network of COI
Communications GNN moved to GICS in the
Cabinet Office in April 2002. The GNN acts as a
regional arm of press offices of Government
Departments in Whitehall and elsewhere and
supports Government Offices for the Regions in
their co-ordination and policy delivery pro-
grammes.
10 Great George Street, London SW1P 3AE
Enquiries: 020 7276 0014 Fax: 020 7276 5628
Website: www.gics.gov.uk
Director-General: Mike Granatt CB
Private Secretary: Mike Winter 020 7276 6299
  Fax: 020 7276 5628

Assistant Private Secretary: Natalie Keyte
  020 7276 0433
*Deputy Head of GICS (Corporate and HR
  Strategy):* Sue Jenkins 020 7276 5090
Director of GICS Development Centre:
  Tim Dunmore 020 7276 2700
Director of Operations: Lyn Salisbury
  020 7276 5089
*Director of Counter Terrorism Communications
  Strategy:* Brian Butler 020 7276 5047
Head of Government News Network (GNN):
  Rob Haslam 020 7276 5166
  E-mail: rob.haslam@gnn.gsi.gov.uk
  GNN Website: www.gnn.gov.uk

Emergency Services
Tel: 0117-945 6972
Out of office hours the emergency call out number
is 020 8938 3560
E-mail: bristol@gnn.gsi.gov.uk
Regional Director GNN South West:
  Peter Whitbread

Social Diversity
Tel: 0121-626 2018/2786
E-mail: birmingham@gnn.gsi.gov.uk
Contacts: Andrew Myatt, Sophia Everitt

Education
Tel: 0121-626 2017
E-mail: birmingham@gnn.gsi.gov.uk
Regional Director GNN West Midlands:
  Brent Garner

Media Training
GNN offers media training tailored to individual
needs. Contact your local GNN office

Government News Distribution Service – NDS
Hercules House, Hercules Road,
London SE1 7DU
Tel: 020 7261 8527
E-mail: nds@gnn.gsi.gov.uk
Government News Network – News Distribution
Service (NDS) is the partner of choice for
government news targeting and distribution.
NDS distributes press releases for the main
Whitehall government departments and for a
wide range of non-departmental public bodies
and agencies to a variety of audiences, to the
highest quality standards, and using the most
cost-effective methods.
Head of News NDS: Hugh Brown MBE

GNN Regional Offices
East – Cambridge
Eastbrook, Shaftesbury Road, Cambridge CB2 2DF
Tel: 01223 372799   Fax: 01223 372870
E-mail: cambridge@gnn.gsi.gov.uk
Director: Mary Basham

North East – Newcastle
Wellbar House, Gallowgate,
Newcastle upon Tyne NE1 4TB
Tel: 0191-202 3601   GTN: 5227
Fax: 0191-261 8571
E-mail: newcastle@gnn.gsi.gov.uk
Director: Chris Child

North West – Manchester
Sunley Tower, Piccadilly Plaza,
Manchester M1 4BD
Tel: 0161-952 4501   GTN: 4301
Fax: 0161-228 0025
E-mail: manchester@gnn.gsi.gov.uk
Director: Eileen Jones

Scotland – Edinburgh
1 Melville Crescent, Edinburgh EH3 7HW
Tel: 0131-244 9062   GTN: 7188
Fax: 0131-244 9063
E-mail: scotland@gnn.gsi.gov.uk
Senior Information Officers: Val Morgan,
    Paul Burgess

Yorkshire and the Humber – Leeds
City House, New Station Street, Leeds LS1 4JG
Tel: 0113-283 6590   GTN: 5173
Fax: 0113-283 6586
E-mail: leeds@gnn.gsi.gov.uk
Director: Wendy Miller

West Midlands – Birmingham
Five Ways House, Islington Row Middleway,
Edgbaston, Birmingham B15 1SL
Tel: 0121-626 2028   GTN: 6161
Fax: 0121-626 2041
E-mail: birmingham@gnn.gsi.gov.uk
Director: Brent Garner

East Midlands – Nottingham
Belgrave Centre, Talbot Street,
Nottingham NG1 5GG
Tel: 0115-971 2781   Fax: 0115-971 2791
E-mail: nottingham@gnn.gsi.gov.uk
Director: Peter Smith

London
Hercules House, Hercules Road,
London SE1 7DU
Tel: 020 7261 8762   Fax: 020 7928 6974/7082
E-mail: london@gnn.gsi.gov.uk
Director: Virginia Burdon

South East – Guildford
Bridge House, 1 Walnut Tree Close, Guildford,
Surrey GU1 4GA
Tel: 01483 882877   Fax: 01483 882255
E-mail: southeast@gnn.gsi.gov.uk
Director: James Peacock

South West – Bristol
Bristol Office:
2nd Floor, 2 Rivergate, Bristol BS1 6EL
Tel: 0117-900 3550   GTN: 1361
Fax: 0117-922 1768
E-mail: bristol@gnn.gsi.gov.uk
Plymouth Office:
Mast House, Shepherd Wharf, 24 Sutton Road,
Plymouth PL4 0HJ
Tel: 01752 635053   Fax: 01752 672892
E-mail: plymouth@gnn.gsi.gov.uk
Director: Peter Whitbread

Wales – Cardiff
Cathays Park, Cardiff CF10 3NQ
Tel: 029 2082 1531   Fax: 029 9208 2301
E-mail: wales@gnn.gsi.gov.uk
Press Officer: Joanna Nurse

**MANAGING DIRECTOR AND
ACCOUNTING OFFICER**
70 Whitehall, London SW1A 2AS
Managing Director and Accounting Officer:
    Colin Balmer
E-mail:
colin.balmer@cabinet-office.x.gsi.gov.uk
Principal Finance Officer: Vacant
Director, Human Resources: Claudette Francis
Deputy Director, Business Development:
    John Sweetman
Deputy Director, Infrastructure: Eric Hepburn
Deputy Director, Histories and Records:
    Tessa Stirling
Head of Internal Audit: Peter Norris

**HER MAJESTY'S STATIONERY OFFICE
– HMSO**
Tel: 01603 621000
Website: HMSOnline at www.hmso.gov.uk
HMSO delivers a wide range of services to the
public, information industry and government
relating to access and reuse of government
information protected by Crown copyright.
HMSO manages and sets standards for the use of
information produced within government
through the Information Fair Trader Scheme
which links to policy on access to public sector
information. HMSO also oversees the printing
and publication of UK legislation and related
materials and advises government departments
on all aspects of official publishing.
St Clements House, 2-16 Colegate,
Norwich NR3 1BQ
Tel: 01603 723012   Fax: 01603 723018
Controller and Queen's Printer: Carol Tullo
Admiralty Arch, The Mall, London SW1A 2WH
Tel: 020 7276 2660   Fax: 020 7276 2661
E-mail: carol.tullo@cabinet-office.x.gsi.gov.uk

COMMUNICATION GROUP

Advises on presentation of departmental policy and activity. Handles media and public relations activities other than recruitment publicity and advertising.

70 Whitehall, London SW1A 2AS
Tel: 020 7276 0432/1272/1191
Fax: 020 7276 0618
Director of Communication: Léonie Austin
E-mail:
leonie.austin@cabinet-office.x.gsi.gov.uk
Head of News: John Bretherton
Head of Corporate Communications:
   Graham Hooper
Head of Strategic Communication and Planning:
   Vacant

CENTRAL SPONSOR FOR INFORMATION ASSURANCE – CSIA

Stockley House, 130 Wilton Road,
London SW1V 1LQ
Tel: 020 7276 3267
E-mail: csia@cabinet-office.x.gsi.gov.uk
The CSIA was established as a new unit of the Cabinet Office on 1st April 2003. The CSIA works with partners in both the public and private sectors, as well as its international counterparts, to help safeguard the nation's IT and telecommunications services.

Information Assurance (IA) is the confidence that information systems will protect the information they carry, and will function as they need to, when they need to, under the control of legitimate users. The CSIA will provide a central focus for information assurance initiatives. It will promote the understanding that is essential for government and business alike to maintain a reliable, secure and resilient national information infrastructure.

The CSIA works with a number of government departments involved in the protection of the nation's information infrastructure (the electronic systems vital for government, business, finance, telecommunications, utilities and emergency services and others). These include NISCC (National Infrastructure Security Co-ordination Centre), NHTCU (National Hi-tech Crime Unit), Home Office, DTI, CESG and the Cabinet Office Security Policy Division.
Director: Steve Marsh

Executive Agencies: Government Car and Despatch Agency (GCDA); Central Office of Information (COI) (is not part of the Cabinet Office but reports to Cabinet Office Ministers)

Department for Constitutional Affairs – DCA

Selborne House, 54 Victoria Street,
London SW1E 6QW
Tel: 020 7210 8500   Fax: 020 7210 0647
GTN: 210 8500
E-mails: general.queries@dca.gsi.gov.uk
[firstname.surname]@dca.gsi.gov.uk
Court Service: cust.serv.cs@qtnet.gov.uk
Website: www.dca.gov.uk

The Secretary of State for Constitutional Affairs is responsible for promoting general reforms in the civil law and for the procedure of the civil courts. He has ministerial responsibility for magistrates' courts which are administered locally. He is responsible for advising the Crown on the appointment of Masters and Registrars of the High Court and District and County Court Registrars and Magistrates other than in the Duchy of Lancaster. He is responsible for ensuring that letters patent and other formal documents are passed in the proper form under the Great Seal of the Realm, of which he is the custodian. The work in connection with this is carried out in the Office of the Clerk of the Crown in Chancery. Similar work on Warrants and Charters is prepared under the Lesser Seal. He is also responsible for a number of constitutional policy matters, including Royal, church and hereditary matters and policy on fundamental marriage law, same sex issues, and trans-sexual people.

The Secretary of State is the Privy Counsellor primarily concerned with the affairs of the Crown Dependencies of Guernsey, Jersey and the Isle of Man and is the channel of communication between the insular authorities and the Crown and the UK Government. The oversight of a wide programme of Government civil legislation and reform in such fields as human rights, freedom of information, data protection, family law, property law, defamation, legal aid and House of Lords Reform. Also responsibility for the Electoral Commission, policy on electoral law, referendums and party funding.

Secretary of State for Constitutional Affairs and
   Lord Chancellor: Rt Hon Lord Falconer QC
Parliamentary Private Secretaries:
   Laura Moffatt MP, Geraint Davies MP
Special Expert Adviser: Garry Hart
   020 7210 8590 Fax 020 7210 0647
Principal Private Secretary: Sarah Albon
   020 7210 8380 Fax 020 7210 4711
E-mail: sarah.albon@dca.gsi.gov.uk

Private Secretaries: Amrita Dhaliwal,
Nicola Follis
Assistant Private Secretary: Scott Taylor
Diary Secretary: Daniel Flury 020 7210 8380
Fax 020 7219 4711
Parliamentary Under-Secretary of State:
David Lammy MP
Private Secretary: Paul Zimmermann
020 7210 0701 Fax 020 7210 8869
E-mail: paul.zimmermann@dca.gsi.gov.uk
Assistant Private Secretary: Clair Smith
020 7210 8678
Diary Secretary: Alexandra Bearn
020 7210 0703
Parliamentary Under-Secretary of State:
Christopher Leslie MP
Private Secretary: Grant Morris 020 7210 8683
Fax 020 7210 8620
E-mail: grant.morris@dca.gsi.gov.uk
Assistant Private Secretary: Nancy Hey
Diary Secretary: Christopher Joslin
Parliamentary Under-Secretary of State:
Lord Filkin CBE
Private Secretary: David Liddemore
020 7210 8562 Fax 020 7210 8620
E-mail: david.liddemore@dca.gsi.gov.uk
Assistant Private Secretary: Nicola Westmore
Diary Secretary: Pam Goodwin 020 7210 8708

Scotland Office
Secretary of State for Scotland:
Rt Hon Alistair Darling MP
Parliamentary Under-Secretary of State:
Anne McGuire MP
See Scotland Office entry for full details

Wales Office
Secretary of State for Wales:
Rt Hon Peter Hain MP
Parliamentary Under-Secretary of State:
Don Touhig MP
See Wales Office for full details
Parliamentary Clerk: Ann Nixon 020 7210 8386
Fax: 020 7210 8627

Spokespeople in the House of Lords:
Lord Falconer of Thoroton, Baroness
Scotland of Asthal, Lord Bassam of Brighton

Change Programme
The Department for Constitutional Affairs is in
the process of undergoing a total reorganisation.
The change agenda will result in the largest
transformation in thirty years (since the Depart-
ment was created out of the old Lord
Chancellor's Office and more recently the Lord
Chancellor's Department) of how DCA is

organised and how it works. It is not just about
structural change, or just about change at the top.
It will affect everyone in the Department in the
months ahead because it is, fundamentally, about
cultural change – transforming how we work,
and how we behave, so that we can transform
how we deliver services to our customers.
The aim is to change the culture of the whole
Department. The change programme is about
putting better service delivery at the centre of all
that we do in this Department, its agencies, its
non-departmental public bodies and its
associated offices.
A new Corporate Board was appointed in
January 2003.

Permanent Secretary: Sir Hayden Phillips GCB
Private Secretary: Nicola Webster 020 7210 8395
E-mail: nicola.webster@dca.gsi.gov.uk
Second Permanent Secretary and Chief
Executive, Operations: Ian Magee CB
Personal Assistant: Maureen Sullivan
020 7210 2177
E-mail: maureen.sullivan@dca.gsi.gov.uk
Assistant PA and Diary Secretary: Iwa Chan
020 7210 1734

Crown Office
House of Lords
Tel: 020 7219 4687   Fax: 020 7219 2957
Clerk of the Crown in Chancery:
Sir Hayden Phillips KCB
Clerk of the Chamber: Ian Denyer

Lord Chancellor's Ecclesiastical Office
Ecclesiastical Patronage, 10 Downing Street,
London SW1 2AA
020 7930 4433
Secretary for Ecclesiastical Patronage:
Nick Wheeler

Clients and Policy Group
Selborne House
Tel: 020 7210 8719
Director-General, Policy:
Dr Jonathan Spencer CB
Directors
Civil Justice and Legal Services Directorate:
David Nooney
Case Preparation Project: Nick Smedley
Public and Private Rights Directorate:
Amanda Finlay CBE
Criminal Justice Division: Kay Birch
Constitution Directorate: Andrew McDonald
Heads of Division
Public Legal Services: Derek Hill
Civil Justice: John Tanner

Privacy and Data Sharing: Judith Simpson
Constitutional Policy: Rick Evans
Civil Law Development: Andrew Frazer
Administrative Justice: Lee Hughes
Human Rights: Mark de Pulford
Family Policy 1 (Families and Adults):
    Rosemary Pratt, Susan Johnson
Family Policy 2 (Children and Families):
    Sally Field
Criminal Justice Legislation Division:
    Dr Colin Myerscough
Support and Research Unit: David Watts
Asylum Policy and Programme Delivery:
    Mary Shaw

Legal and Judicial Services Group
Selborne House
Tel: 020 7210 8928
Director-General: John Lyon CB
Directors: David Nooney,
    Elizabeth Grimsey LVO
Heads of Division: David Staff, John Powell,
    Alistair Shaw, Ray Sams, Helen Baker,
    Maggie Pigott, Judith Killick

Legal and International Group
Southside, 105 Victoria Street,
London SW1E 6QT
Tel: 020 7210 0712   Fax 020 7210 0748
E-mail: cleitao@dca.gsi.gov.uk

Director-General: Paul Jenkins
Michael Collon, Alasdair Wallace, Peter Fish,
    Richard Heaton, Claire Johnston

Corporate Diversity Unit
Responsible for ensuring a strategic approach to
the delivery of the equality and diversity agenda
across the Department's business; co-ordinating
the Department's interests in anti-discrimination
legislation and compliance with legislative
requirements; monitoring progress against the
Equality and Diversity Action Plan; providing
support to the Diversity Steering Group, senior
management and Ministers; and co-ordinating
support to the Corporate Board Diversity
Champions and the Corporate Staff Networks.

Head of Corporate Diversity: Ms V Hodgson
    020 7210 8852

Finance Group – CSG
Director-General: Simon Ball 020 7210 2801
Director of Finance: Peter Lovell 020 7210 1992
Principal Finance Officer: Alan Cogbill
Head of Finance Division: Alan Pay

The COMPASS Team
Corporate Management Planning and
Strategic Services
Secretary to the LCD Corporate Board and
    Head of Division: Steve Humphreys

Corporate Board Secretariat
Head of Secretariat: Rob Moore
Heads of Divisions:
Strategy and Delivery: Jeremy Gould
Public Private Partnership Unit: Stan Coats

Communications Group
Press enquiries (24 hours): 020 7210 8512
Fax: 020 7210 8633
Press Office E-mail:
press.office@dca.gsi.gov.uk

Director of Communications:
    Allan Percival LVO
E-mail: apercival@dca.gsi.gov.uk
Head of External Communications:
    Mike Wicksteed
E-mail: mike.wicksteed@dca.gsi.gov.uk
Chief Press Officer: Peter Farr
E-mail: peter.farr@dca.gsi.gov.uk
Head of Corporate Communications:
    Gillian Haizelden
E-mail: gillian.haizelden@dca.gsi.gov.uk

Departmental Correspondence Unit
Iain Walters
E-mail: iain.walters@dca.gsi.gov.uk

CHANGE MANAGEMENT IN PROGRESS
Change Directorate
Southside
Chief Executive: Ian Magee CB
Change Director: Bernadette Kenny
Members of the Change Team:
Head of Change Team: Rick Evans
Change Agenda Co-ordinator: Ian Baugh
Change Projects Resource: Amanda Jones
Change Co-ordinators: Eddie Coleman,
    Juliette Dodd, Joan Watson
Change Consultant: Justine Brewood
Directors:
Finance: Simon Ball
Criminal Courts Development: Kevin Sadler
Human Resources: Helen Dudley

e-Delivery Group
Director of Information and Communications
    Technologies and e-Delivery Group:
    Annette Vernon 020 7210 2050
E-mail: annette.vernon@dca.gsi.gov.uk

NORTHERN IRELAND COURT SERVICE
Windsor House, Bedford Street,
Belfast BT2 7LT
028 9032 8594 Fax 028 9043 9110

*Director General
Head of Department, Principal Accounting
Officer, and Accountant General of the Supreme
Court of Judicature of Northern Ireland,
maintenance of Courts' Charter, customer
service and communications

Operations
Director

Policy and Legislation
Director

Corporate Services
Director

Executive Agencies: Court Service; HM Land Registry; National Archives; Public Guardianship Office

Department for Culture, Media and Sport – DCMS

2–4 Cockspur Street, London SW1Y 5DH
Tel: 020 7211 6200   Fax: 020 7211 6032
GTN: 211 6000/211 6200
E-mails: enquiries@culture.gov.uk
[firstname.surname]@culture.gsi.gov.uk
E-mail enquiries:
Art: arts@culture.gov.uk
Broadcasting: broadcasting@culture.gov.uk
Creative Industries: ciu@culture.gov.uk
Film: film@culture.gov.uk
Media: media@culture.gov.uk
Music: music@culture.gov.uk
Website: www.culture.gov.uk

Personnel and Central Services Division
020 7211 2031

Government Art Collection, Queen's Yard,
179a Tottenham Court Road, London W1P 0BE
020 7580 9120
E-mail: gac@culture.gov.uk

Responsible for Government policies on arts and libraries, broadcasting and the press; sports, including the safety of sports grounds; tourism and heritage; film policy; the export licensing of antiques; the National Lottery; volunteering and charities; museums and galleries; Commonwealth Games.

Secretary of State for Culture, Media and Sport:
   Rt Hon Tessa Jowell MP
Parliamentary Private Secretary:
   Gordon Marsden MP
Special Advisers: Bill Bush 020 7211 6010
   E-mail: bill.bush@culture.gsi.gov.uk
Private Secretary to the Special Adviser:
   Elvan Faik 020 7211 6010 Fax: 020 7211 6485
Principal Private Secretary: Hugh Ind 020 7211
   6243 Fax: 020 7211 6249
   E-mail: hugh.ind@culture.gsi.gov.uk
Private Secretaries: Alex Towers 020 7211
   6975, Andrew Scattergood 020 7211 6257,
   Helen McNamara 020 7211 6238, Tina
   Sawyer 020 7211 6306

Diary Secretary: Sheila Chatrath 020 7211 6241
Assistant Diary Secretary: Graham Brown
   020 7211 6242 Fax: 020 7211 6249
Minister of State (Minister for Sport):
   Rt Hon Richard Caborn MP
Parliamentary Private Secretary:
   Ben Chapman MP
Private Secretary: Graeme Cornell 020 7211 6246
   Fax: 020 7211 6546
   E-mail: graeme.cornell@culture.gsi.gov.uk
Assistant Private Secretary: Martin Niblett
   020 7211 6247
Diary Secretary: Leonie Phillips 020 7211 6233
Minister of State (Minister for the Arts):
   Rt Hon Estelle Morris MP
Parliamentary Private Secretary: Howard Stoate
   MP 020 7219 4619 Fax: 020 7219 5728
Private Secretary: David McLaren 020 7211 6252
   Fax: 020 7211 6309
   E-mail: david.mclaren@culture.gsi.gov.uk
Assistant Private Secretary: Mark Balcar
   020 7211 6421
Diary Secretary: Lucy Blackburn 020 7211 6285
*Parliamentary Under-Secretary of State
   (Minister for Media and Heritage):*
   Rt Hon Lord McIntosh of Haringey
Private Secretary: Gareth Maybury
   020 7211 6303
   E-mail: gareth.maybury@culture.gsi.gov.uk
Assistant Private Secretary: Suzanne Bullock
   020 7211 6305
Assistant Private Secretary (Diary):
   Alistair MacDonald 020 7211 6304
   Fax: 020 7211 6546

Parliamentary Unit
Head of Unit: Harvey Vasey 020 7211 6288
Parliamentary Manager: Andrew Calnan
   020 7211 6320
Parliamentary Officer: Russell Gould
   020 7211 6289 Fax: 020 7211 6294
Private Office Support Team:
Correspondence Manager: Faye McDonald
   020 7211 6302 Fax: 020 7211 6249

Spokesman in the House of Lords:
Lord Davies of Oldham

Permanent Secretary: Sue Street
   E-mail: sue.street@culture.gov.uk
Private Secretary: Eleanor Street 020 7211 6256
   Fax: 020 7211 6259
   E-mail: eleanor.street@culture.gsi.gov.uk

Corporate Services Group
*Deputy Permanent Secretary and Group
   Director:* Nicholas Kroll CB
Director of Finance: Keith Smith

Head of Personnel and Central Services Division: Paul Heron
Head of Accounts: Kathy Hosker
Head of Internal Audit: Michael Kirk
Head of Public Appointments and Honours Unit: Janet Evans
Head of Golden Jubilee: Helen Bayne CVO
Head of Analytical Services: Vanessa Brand

Creative Industries, Broadcasting and Gambling and Lottery Directorate – CIBG

Director: Andrew Ramsay
Head of Gaming Board for Great Britain: Tom Kavanagh CBE*
Head of Creative Industries Division: Michael Seeney
Head of Broadcasting: Jon Zeff
Head of Gambling and National Lottery Licensing: Elliot Grant
Head of National Lottery Distribution and Communities Division: Simon Broadley
*Based at Berkshire House, 168-173 High Holborn, London WC1V 7AA

Arts and Culture Directorate

Director: Alex Stewart
Head of Architecture and Historic Environment: Clare Pillman
Head of Cultural Property Unit: Hillary Bauer
Head of Museums and Libraries Sponsorship Unit: Richard Hartman
Head of Arts Division: Alan Davey
Head of Museums Policy and Digital Access: Bryony Lodge
Director, Government Art Collection: Penny Johnson

Strategy and Communications Directorate

Director: Siobhan Kenny
Head of Policy, Innovation and Delivery Unit: Vacant
Head of Education and Social Policy: Philip Clapp
Head of News: Paddy Feeny
Head of Publicity and Communications: Graham Newsom

Sport Directorate

Director: Alec McGivan
Head of Sports Division: Robert Raine
Olympic Games Unit: Dave Bawden

Tourism, Libraries and Communities Directorate

Director: Brian Leonard
Head of Libraries and Communities Division: Mark Ferrero
Head of Tourism Division: Harry Reeves

Legal Adviser
Isabel Letwin
Tel: 020 7211 2230 Fax 020 7211 2170

Deputy Legal Advisers
Nick Beach, Peter De Val

Executive Agency: Royal Parks

Ministry of Defence – MoD

Old War Office Building, Whitehall,
London SW1A 2EU
Main switchboard 020 7218 9000
Fax: 020 7218 6538   GTN: 3218 89000
E-mail: public@ministers.mod.uk
Website: www.mod.uk

Metropole Building, Northumberland Avenue,
London WC2N 5BP

Northumberland House, Northumberland
Avenue, London WC2N 5BP

St Giles Court, 1-13 St Giles High Street,
London WC2H 8LD

St Georges Court, 14 New Oxford Street,
London WC1A 1EJ

Responsible for the control, administration, equipment and support of the armed forces.

Old War Office Building
Secretary of State for Defence:
    Rt Hon Geoffrey Hoon MP
Parliamentary Private Secretary:
    Liz Blackman MP
Team Parliamentary Private Secretary:
    Syd Rapson MP
Special Advisers: Richard Taylor 020 7218 2911,
    Michael Dugher 020 7218 1964
Principal Private Secretary: Peter Watkins
    020 7218 2112 Fax: 020 7218 7140
Assistant Private Secretaries: Peter Davies,
    Commander Martyn Williams RN,
    Danielle Latham, Deborah Lowe
Minister of State for the Armed Forces:
    Rt Hon Adam Ingram MP
Parliamentary Private Secretary:
    Alan Campbell MP
Private Secretary: Geoff Dean 020 7218 6385
    Fax: 020 7218 6542
Military Assistant:
    Lieutenant Colonel Mark Van der Lande
Assistant Private Secretaries: Paula Hothersall,
    Beryl MacMaster
*Parliamentary Under-Secretary of State
    (Minister for Defence Procurement):*
    Lord Bach
Private Secretary: Ben Palmer 020 7218 6621
    Fax: 020 7218 6625

Assistant Private Secretaries: Lee McCauley,
Kevin Pollard, Ms Ravi Bansal
E-mail: mindp@dpa.mod.uk
*Parliamentary Under-Secretary of State
(Minister for Veterans):* Ivor Caplin MP
Private Secretary: Alex Cruttwell 020 7218 2452
Fax: 020 7218 7610
Military Assistant:
Lieutenant Commander Nigel Amphlett RN
Assistant Private Secretaries:
Lorraine Robertson 020 7218 2216,
Sarah Duffin

Parliamentary Clerk: Patricia Parkin
020 7218 1991
Parliamentary Branch: 020 7218 6169

Spokespeople in the House of Lords:
Lord Bach, Baroness Crawley

Senior Officials
Permanent Secretary:
Sir Kevin Tebbit KCB CMG
Private Secretary: Dominic Wilson
020 7218 2839
Second Permanent Secretary: Ian Andrews CBE
Private Secretary: Paul Wyatt 020 7218 7115
Chief of the Defence Staff: General Sir Michael
Walker GCB CMG CBE ADC Gen
Chief of the Naval Staff and First Sea Lord:
Admiral Sir Alan West KCB DSC
Chief of the General Staff: General Sir Mike
Jackson KCB CBE DSO SDC Gen
Chief of the Air Staff: Air Marshal Sir Graham
Stirrup KCB AFC FRAeS FRIMgt RAF
Vice-Chief of the Defence Staff:
Air Chief Marshal Sir Anthony Bagnall KCB
OBE FRAeS RAF*
Chief of Defence Procurement:
Vice-Admiral Sir Peter Spencer KCB ADC†
Chief Scientific Adviser:
Prof Sir Robert Keith O'Nions FRS
Chief of Defence Logistics: Air Chief Marshal
Sir Malcolm Pledger KCB OBE AFC BSc
FRAeS RAF

* Also the Joint Manager of the Central Top
Level Budget of the Ministry of Defence
† Also the Chief Executive of the Defence
Procurement Agency, a Top Level Budget of the
Ministry of Defence

Senior Central Staff
Old War Office Building
Chief of Defence Intelligence:
Air Marshal Joseph French CBE FRAeS RAF

Metropole Building
Deputy Chief of the Defence Staff (Commitments):
Lieutenant General Robert Fry CBE

Policy Director: Simon Webb CBE
Science and Technology Director:
Graham Jordan
*Director-General of Corporate
Communications:* Martin Howard

Northumberland House
*Deputy Chief of the Defence Staff (Equipment
Capability):* Lieutenant General Robert
Fulton RM
Finance Director: Colin Balmer CB

St Giles Court
Deputy Chief of the Defence Staff (Personnel):
Lieutenant General Anthony Palmer CBE
Personnel Director: Richard Hatfield CBE
Surgeon-General:
Lieutenant General Kevin O'Donoghue

St Georges Court
Head of Defence Export Services: Alan Garwood

MoD Top Level Budget Holders
Most MoD activity is managed through eleven
Top Level Budget (TLB) Holders. The Permanent Secretary grants each TLB Holder extensive
delegated powers over his/her resources

Central TLB
Second Permanent Under-Secretary of State:
Ian Andrews CBE
Vice-Chief of the Defence Staff:
Air Chief Marshal Sir Anthony Bagnall KCB
OBE FRAeS RAF

Operational TLBs
Commander-in-Chief Fleet:
Admiral Sir Jonathan Band KCB
HMS Warrior, Northwood, Middlesex HA6 3HP
Tel: 01923 826161

Commander-in-Chief Land Command: General
Sir Timothy Granville-Chapman KCB CBE
Erskine Barracks, Wilton, Salisbury,
Wiltshire SP2 0AG
Tel: 01722 336222

General Officer Commanding (Northern Ireland):
Lieutenant General Philip Trousdell CB
Headquarters Northern Ireland, BFPO 825
Tel: 00892 665111

*Commander in Chief Headquarters Strike
Command:* Air Chief Marshal Sir John Day
KCB OBE ADC RAF
RAF High Wycombe,
Buckinghamshire HP14 4UE
Tel: 01494 461461

Chief of Joint Operations:
Lieutenant General John Reith CB CBE
Permanent Joint Headquarters (UK), JHQ,
Northwood, Middlesex HA6 3TJ
Tel: 01923 826161

Military Manpower TLBs

The three TLB Holders are primarily responsible for personnel issues affecting their individual Services

Principal Personnel Officers

Second Sea Lord and Commander-in-Chief Naval Home Command: Vice-Admiral Sir Peter Spencer KCB ADC
Victory Building, HM Naval Base,
Portsmouth PO1 3LS
Tel: 02392 722351

Adjutant General:
Lieutenant General Sir Alistair Irwin KCB CBE
Trenchard Lines, Upavon, Pewsey,
Wiltshire SN9 6BE
Tel: 01980 615000

Air Member for Personnel and Commander-in-Chief Personnel and Training Command:
Air Marshal Sir Christopher Coville KCB FCIPD FRAeS RAF
RAF Innsworth, Gloucester GL3 1EZ
Tel: 01452 712612

Equipment Procurement TLB

Chief of Defence Procurement and Chief Executive Defence Procurement Agency:
Vice-Admiral Sir Peter Spencer KCB ADC
MoD Abbey Wood, Maple No 1, PO Box 702, Bristol BS34 8JH
Tel: 0117-969 1166

Logistic Support TLB

Chief of Defence Logistics: Air Chief Marshal Sir Malcolm Pledger KCB OBE AFC BSc FRAeS RAF
Room 259, Old War Office, London SW1A 2EU
Tel: 020 7218 9000

Executive Agencies: Armed Forces Personnel Administration Agency (AFPAA); Army Base Repair Organisation (ABRO); Army Personnel Centre (APC); Army Training and Recruiting Agency (ATRA); British Forces Post Office (BFPO); Defence Analytical Services Agency (DASA); Defence Aviation Repair Agency (DARA); Defence Bills Agency (DBA); Defence Communication Services Agency (DCSA); Defence Dental Agency (DDA); Defence Estates (DE); Defence Geographic and Imagery Intelligence Agency (DGIA); Defence Housing Executive (DHE); Defence Intelligence and Security Centre (DISC); Defence Medical Training Organisation (DMTO); Defence Procurement Agency (DPA); Defence Science and Technology Laboratory (DSTL); Defence Secondary Care Agency (DSCA); Defence Storage and Distribution Agency (DSDA); Defence Transport and Movements Agency (DTMA); Defence Vetting Agency (DVA); Disposal Services Agency (DSA); Duke of York's Royal Military School (DYRMS); Medical Supplies Agency (MSA); Met Office; Ministry of Defence Police Agency (MDP); Naval Manning Agency (NMA); Naval Recruiting and Training Agency (NRTA); Pay and Personnel Agency (PPA); Queen Victoria School (QVS); RAF Personnel Management Agency (RAFPMA); RAF Training Group Defence Agency (RAF TGDA); Service Children's Education (SCE); United Kingdom Hydrographic Office (UKHO); Veterans Agency (VA); Warship Support Agency (WSA)

Department for Education and Skills – DfES

Sanctuary Buildings, Great Smith Street,
London SW1P 3BT

Caxton House, Tothill Street,
London SW1H 9NA

Castle View House, East Lane,
Runcorn WA7 2GJ

Moorfoot, Sheffield S1 4PQ

Mowden Hall, Staindrop Road,
Darlington DL3 9BG

Main Switchboard: 0870 0012345
Press Office: 020 7925 6789
Fax: 01928 794248
Public Enquiry Unit: 0870 000 2288
GTN: 3060 5000
E-mails: info@dfes.gov.uk
dfes.ministers@dfes.gsi.gov.uk
[firstname.surname]@dfes.gsi.gov.uk
Website: www.dfes.gov.uk

The Department for Education and Skills aims to help build a competitive economy and inclusive society by: creating opportunities for everyone to develop their learning. Realising potential in people to make the most of themselves. Achieving excellence in standards of education and levels of skills. The Department's objectives are to give children an excellent start in education so that they have a better foundation for future learning, enable all young people to develop and equip themselves with the skills, knowledge and personal qualities needed for life and work. Encourage and enable adults to learn, improve their skills and enrich their lives.

Secretary of State for Education and Skills:
Rt Hon Charles Clarke MP
Parliamentary Private Secretary:
Steve McCabe MP

Team Parliamentary Private Secretary:
Meg Munn MP
Special Advisers: Lisa Tremble 020 7925 6874,
Robert Hill 020 7925 6530 Fax: 020 7925 6536
Principal Private Secretary: Chris Wormald
020 7925 5829 Fax: 020 7925 6995
E-mail: sec-of-state.ps@dfes.gsi.gov.uk
Deputy Principal Private Secretary:
Jenny Loosley
Private Secretaries: Jane Whitfield,
Alison Ismail 020 7925 5829
Diary Secretary:
Hannah Pawlby 020 7925 5313
E-mail: sec-of-state-diary.ps@dfes.gsi.gov.uk

Minister of State for Children:
Rt Hon Margaret Hodge MBE MP
Parliamentary Private Secretary:
Michael John Foster MP 020 7219 6379
Private Secretary: Claire Carroll 020 7925 6951
Fax: 020 7925 5011
E-mail: hodge.ps@dfes.gsi.gov.uk
Assistant Private Secretaries: Gill Cholerton
020 7925 6950, Nicola Sams 020 7925 6242
Diary Manager: Natalie Perera 020 7925 6952
E-mail: hodge.ps-diary@dfes.gsi.gov.uk

Minister of State for School Standards:
David Miliband MP
Parliamentary Private Secretary:
Ian Cawsey MP
Private Secretary: Nick Carson
020 7925 6254/6255 Fax: 020 7925 6996
E-mail: miliband.ps@dfes.gsi.gov.uk
Assistant Private Secretaries: Suzanne Robinson
020 7925 6256, Paul Shand 020 7925 6259
Diary Manager: Dunstan Hadley 020 7925 6287
E-mail: miliband.ps-diary@dfes.gsi.gov.uk

*Minister of State for Lifelong Learning, Further
and Higher Education:* Alan Johnson MP
Parliamentary Private Secretary:
Bob Laxton MP
Private Secretary: Jo Ware 020 7925 3707
Fax: 020 7925 5011
E-mail: johnson.ps@dfes.gsi.gov.uk

*Parliamentary Under-Secretary of State for Sure
Start (also DWP):* Baroness Ashton of
Upholland
Private Secretary: Luke O'Shea
020 7925 6391/6389 Fax: 020 7925 6688
E-mail: ashton.ps@dfes.gsi.gov.uk
Assistant Private Secretaries: Joanne Hill
020 7925 6388/6389, Andrew Hudson
020 7925 6390
Diary Manager: Christopher Juliff
020 7925 6612
E-mail: ashton.ps-diary@dfes.gsi.gov.uk

*Parliamentary Under-Secretary of State for
Skills and Vocational Education:*
Ivan Lewis MP
Private Secretary: Jo Bewley
020 7925 5870/6340 Fax: 020 7925 5151
E-mail: lewis.ps@dfes.gsi.gov.uk
Assistant Private Secretary: Chris Burton
020 7925 5874
Diary Manager: Cathy Hare 020 7925 5873
E-mail: lewis-diary.ps@dfes.gsi.gov.uk

*Parliamentary Under-Secretary of State for
Schools:* Stephen Twigg MP
Private Secretary: Kathryn McManus
020 7925 6341/6343 Fax: 020 7925 6994
E-mail: twigg.ps@dfes.gsi.gov.uk
Assistant Private Secretary: Natalie Proctor
020 7925 6344
Diary Manager: Charles Deighton-Fox
020 7925 6342
E-mail: twigg-diary.ps@dfes.gsi.gov.uk
Assistant Diary Manager: Mizanur Chaudhury
020 7925 6343

Parliamentary Clerk: Jonathan Duff
020 7925 5927 Fax: 020 7925 6992
E-mail: jonathan.duff@dfes.gsi.gov.uk

Spokesperson in the House of Lords:
Baroness Ashton of Upholland

Permanent Secretary: David Normington CB
Secretary: Paul Price 020 7925 6937
Fax: 020 7925 6599
Head of Strategy and Innovation Unit:
Anne Jackson 020 7925 5939

**STRATEGY AND COMMUNICATIONS
DIRECTORATE – SCD**
Director: Michael Stevenson
Head of Press Office: Trevor Cook
Head of News: DJ Collins
Divisional Managers
Corporate Communications: Yasmin Diamond
Publicity: John Ross
Regions, Delivery Support and Regeneration:
Mohammad Haroon

SCHOOLS DIRECTORATE
Director-General: Peter Housden
Divisional Managers
Strategy and Performance:
Christina Bienkowska
London Challenge Programme: Jon Coles
School Communications Unit : Richard Graham

Secondary Education Group
Director: Peter Wanless
Divisional Managers

School Diversity: Susanna Todd
Academies Division: Neil Flint
School Improvement and Excellence:
  Barnaby Shaw
London Challenge Programme: Jon Coles

Standards and Effectiveness Unit
Director: David Hopkins
Director, Innovation Unit: Mike Gibbons
Divisional Managers
Pupil Standards: Andrew McCully
Leadership and Teacher Development:
  Richard Harrison
Transforming Standards Advisers: David Woods
School Performance and Accountability:
  Nick Baxter

**Resources, Infrastructure and Governance
Group**
Director: Stephen Crowne
Divisional Managers
*School Admissions, Organisation and
  Governance:* Caroline Macready
School and LEA Funding: Andrew Wye
Schools Capital and Buildings: Sally Brooks
Schools Building and Design Unit:
  Mukund Patel

School Workforce Unit
Director: Stephen Kershaw
Deputy Directors: Stuart Edwards, Stephen
  Hillier, Graham Holley, David Russell,
  Richard Blows, Robert Woods

Primary Education and e-Learning Group
Director: Helen Williams
Divisional Managers
Curriculum: Mela Watts
ICT in Schools: Doug Brown
PE and School Sport and Club Links Project:
  Matthew Conway*

*Joint Department for Education and Skills and
Department for Culture, Media and Sport

**CHILDREN AND FAMILIES (Interim
Structure)**
Interim Director-General: Peter Makeham CB
Transition Manager: Jeanette Pugh

Sure Start Unit*
Director: Naomi Eisenstadt
Divisional Managers
Strategy: Tamara Finkelstein
Quality and Standards: Alan Cranston
Programme Delivery Central: Jackie Doughty
Infrastructure: Nick Tooze

Connexions Service National Unit
Chief Executive: Anne Weinstock

Divisional Managers
Strategy and Communications: Dr Jeanette Pugh
Operational Policy: Gordon McKenzie
Delivery and Quality: Steve Jackson
Activities for Young People and Volunteers:
  Jane Haywood

Children and Families Group
Acting Director: Sheila Scales
Schools Plus: Michael Phipps
Ethnic Minority Achievement Project:
  Annabel Burns
Special Educational Needs: Ann Gross
Improving Behaviour and Attendance:
  Alex Sevier, Ian Whitehouse
Pupil Support and Independent Schools:
  Penny Jones

Children and Young People's Unit*
Director: Althea Efunshile
Deputy Director, National Policy: Sue Lewis
Divisional Managers
Local Partnerships: Kathy Bundred
Resources and Planning: Vacant

*Cross Government Units

Children's Group
Head of Children's Group: Janice Shersby
Divisional Managers
Children in Need 1: Vacant
Children in Need 2: Janet Grauberg
Placement, Permanence and Children's Trust:
  David Holmes

Public and Private Rights
Director: Amanda Finlay
Divisional Managers
Children and Families: Bruce Clark
Public Law: Sally Field

Teenage Pregnancy Unit
Head of Unit: Cathy Hamlyn

Family and Policy Unit
Divisional Manager: Vacant

Strategy and Policy
Interim Director: Tom Jeffery
Divisional Manager, Green Paper:
  Ravi Gurumurthy
Change and Bill Team Manager: Vacant

YOUTH DIRECTORATE
Director-General: Peter Shaw
Divisional Managers
Strategy and Funding: John Temple*
e-Learning Strategy Unit: Diana Laurillard

*Supports both Lifelong Learning Directorate
and Youth Directorate

Qualifications and Young People
Director: Rob Hull
Divisional Managers
Qualifications for Work: Sara Marshall
School and College Qualifications:
   Celia Johnson
Young People Learner Support: Trevor Fellowes
Young People's Policy: Alan Davies
Examinations System: Jane Benham
Youth Co-ordination: Carol Hunter
Review of Post-Qualifications Admissions to
   HE: Linda Dale

Joint International Unit
(Links with DWP)
Director: Clive Tucker
Divisional Managers
European Union: Vacant
European Social Fund: Jane Evans
International Relations: Marie Niven

**LIFELONG LEARNING DIRECTORATE –
LLD**
Director-General: Janice Shiner
Divisional Managers:
Strategy and Funding: John Temple*
Offenders Learning and Skills Unit: Alan Clarke

*Supports both Lifelong Learning Directorate
and Youth Directorate

Adult Basic Skills Strategy Unit
Director: Susan Pember
Deputy Directors
Planning and Delivery: Mark Dawe
Standards and Achievement: Barry Brooks

Adult Learning Group
Director: Stephen Marston
Divisional Managers
Access to Learning for Adults: Tim Down
Lifelong Learning and Technologies:
   Margaret Bennett
Skills for Employment: Simon Perryman
Workplace Learning: Hugh Tollyfield
ILA Project: Vacant
ITB Review: Jane Mark-Lawson

Student Finance Group
HE Adviser and Acting Director:
   Nick Sanders CB
Divisional Managers
Student Finance Policy: Peter Swift
Student Finance Delivery: Ian Morrison (acting)
Student Finance Modernisation: Noreen Graham
Delivery and Strategy Overview, HE Programme
   Manager: Chris Barnham
HE Bill Team: Lesley Longstone

**Higher Education Strategy and
Implementation Group**
Acting Director: Michael Hipkins
Divisional Managers
Foundation Degrees, Employability and
   Progression Division: Steve Geary
Quality and Participation: Paul Cohen
Funding and Research: Rachel Green
Access and Modernisation: Martin Williams

Learning Delivery and Standards Group
Moorfoot
Director: Peter Lauener
Divisional Managers
FE Strategy: Peter Mucklow
Learning and Skills Partnerships Unit:
   James Turner
Provider Plus: Eric Galvin
Financial and Management Systems Review of
   the LSC: Linda Dale

Standards Unit
Director for Teaching and Learning:
   Jane Williams
Divisional Managers
Workforce Development: Heidi Adcock
Teaching and Learning and Success for All
   Programme Management: David Taylor

**CORPORATE SERVICES AND
DEVELOPMENT DIRECTORATE**
Director-General: Susan Thomas
Divisional Managers
Leadership and Personnel: Graham Archer
Change: Anne-Marie Lawlor
Learning Academy: Mike Daly
Information Services: Colin Moore
Commercial Services: Paul Neill
Equality and Diversity Unit: Jan Stockwell
e-Delivery: Katie Driver

LEGAL ADVISERS' OFFICE
Legal Adviser: Jonathan Jones
Divisional Managers
Lifelong Learning and School Workforce:
   Dudley Aries
Special Needs and Curriculum: Nic Ash
Governance and Finance: Patrick Kilgarriff
Effectiveness and Admissions: Francis Clarke
Equality, Establishment and EC: Carole Davies
Higher Education and Student Support:
   Carola Geist-Divver

**FINANCE AND ANALYTICAL SERVICES
DIRECTORATE – FASD**
Acting Director-General: Ruth Thompson
Divisional Managers
Internal Audit: Suzanne Orr
Programme and Project Management Unit:
   Ray Hinchcliffe

Finance
Director: Ruth Thompson
Divisional Managers
Finance Strategy: Peter Houten
Corporate Planning and Performance:
  Marion Maddox
Financial Accounting: Peter Connor CBE

Analytical Services
Director: Paul Johnson
Divisional Managers
Schools 1: Audrey Brown
Schools 2: Richard Bartholomew
Youth: Tony Moody, John Elliott, Phil Emmott
Higher Education: Karen Hancock
Adults: Dr Bob Butcher
Central Economics and International:
  John Elliott, Steve Leman
Qualifications, Pupil Assessment and IT:
  Malcolm Britton

Department for Environment, Food and Rural Affairs – Defra

Nobel House, 17 Smith Square,
London SW1P 3JR
Tel: 020 7238 3000   Defra Helpline: 08459
335577   Fax: 020 7238 6591
E-mails: helpline@defra.gsi.gov.uk
[firstname.surname]@defra.gsi.gov.uk
Website: www.defra.gov.uk

Ergon House, Horseferry Road,
London SW1P 2AL
Tel: 020 7238 3000   Fax: 020 7238 6591

London Page Street: 1A Page Street,
London SW1P 4PQ
Tel: 020 7904 6000

Woburn Place: 19-29 Woburn Place,
London WC1H 0LU
Tel: 020 7273 3000

East Block, Whitehall Place, London SW1A 2HH
Tel: 020 7270 6000   Fax: 020 7270 8125

9 Millbank, c/c Nobel House, 17 Smith Square,
London SW1P 3JR

Ashdown House, 123 Victoria Street,
London SW1E 6DE
Tel: 020 7944 3000

Romney House, Tufton Street, London SW1P 3RA
Tel: 020 7944 3000

Cromwell House, Dean Stanley Street,
London SW1P 3JH
Tel: 020 7238 6000

Eastbury House, 30-34 Albert Embankment,
London SE1 7TL
Tel: 020 7238 6000

Foss House, 1-2 Peasholme Green, Kings Pool,
York YO1 7PX
Tel: 01904 641000   Fax: 01904 455222

Curwen Road, Workington, Cumbria CA14 2DD
Tel: 01900 702222

Temple Quay House, Houlton Street,
Bristol BS1 6EB
Tel: 0117-372 8000

Government Buildings, Epsom Road, Guildford,
Surrey GU1 2LD
Tel: 01483 568121

White House Lane, Hungtingdon Road,
Cambridge CB3 0LE
Tel: 01223 277151

Defra works to enhance the quality of life through promoting: a better environment; thriving rural economies and communities; diversity and abundance of wildlife resources; a countryside for all to enjoy; and sustainable and diverse farming and food industries that work together to meet the needs of the consumers.

Secretary of State for Environment, Food and
  Rural Affairs: Rt Hon Margaret Beckett MP
Parliamentary Private Secretary:
  Mark Hendrick MP
Team Parliamentary Private Secretary:
  Nick Palmer MP
Special Advisers: Sheila Watson 020 7238 5378
  Fax: 020 7238 5514, Nicci Collins
  020 7238 5378 Fax: 020 7238 5514
Principal Private Secretary: Gavin Ross
  020 7238 5339 Fax: 020 7238 5727
E-mail: secretaryofstate@defra.gsi.gov.uk
Private Secretaries: Marian Janner 020 7238
  6200, Robin Healey 020 7238 5342,
  Janice Kerr 020 7238 5500

Minister of State (Minister for Environment and
  Agri-Environment): Elliot Morley MP
Parliamentary Private Secretary:
  Tony Cunningham MP
Private Secretary: Bradley Bates 020 7238 6034
  Fax: 020 7238 5976
E-mail: mos.environment@defra.gsi.gov.uk

Minister of State (Minister for Rural Affairs and
  Local Environmental Quality):
  Rt Hon Alun Michael MP
Parliamentary Private Secretary:
  Peter Bradley MP
Private Secretaries: Tim Higginson
  020 7238 5379 Fax: 020 7238 5867,
  Rory Wallace 020 7238 6603
E-mail: mos.ruralaffairs@defra.gsi.gov.uk
Assistant Private Secretaries: Louise Parry
  020 7238 5393, Lewis Mortimer 020 7238 1148

*Parliamentary Under-Secretary of State
(Commons) (Minister for Nature
Conservation and Fisheries):*
Ben Bradshaw MP
Private Secretary: Kath Cameron 020 7238 5764
Fax: 020 7238 5996
E-mail: pus.commons@defra.gsi.gov.uk
Assistant Private Secretary: Belinda Gordon
020 7238 5497 Fax: 020 7238 5996

*Parliamentary Under-Secretary of State (Lords)
(Farming, Food and Sustainable Energy):*
Lord Whitty
Senior Private Secretary: Charlotte Middleton
020 7238 5386 Fax: 020 7238 1100
Private Secretary: Emily Garner 020 7238 5385
Fax: 020 7238 1180
E-mail: pus.lords@defra.gsi.gov.uk
Assistant Private Secretaries: Fiona Tranter
020 7238 5790, Maroona Chughtai
020 7238 5387

Parliamentary Clerk: Deirdre Kennedy
020 7238 5455 Fax:020 7238 6241
Parliamentary Branch: 020 7238 5456

**Spokespeople in the House of Lords: Lord
Whitty, Baroness Farrington of Ribbleton**

Permanent Secretary: Sir Brian Bender KCB
Private Secretary: Suzie Daykin 020 7238 5446
Fax: 020 7238 6118
Assistant Private Secretary: Alison Thomas
020 7238 5454

FOOD, FARMING AND FISHERIES
DIRECTORATE-GENERAL
Director-General: Andrew Lebrecht

EU and International Policy
Director: David Hunter
Heads of Division: David Dawson, Tom Eddy

Sustainable Agriculture and Livestock
Products Directorate
Director: Sonia Phippard
Heads of Division: Nigel Atkinson,
Ivor Llewelyn, Dr Mike Segal, Andrew Slade

Food Industry and Crops Directorate
Director: John Robbs
Heads of Division: Judy Allfrey,
Nicholas Denton, Heather Hamilton,
Dr Stephen Hunter, David Jones,
Andrew Kuyk, Callton Young

Fisheries Directorate
Fisheries Director: Stephen Wentworth CB
Heads of Division: Peter Boyling,
Richard Cowan, Barry Edwards, Chris Ryder
Chief Inspector, Sea Fisheries Inspectorate:
Vacant

Economics and Statistics Directorate
Director: David Thompson
Heads of Division: Rachel Chandler,
Simon Harding, Peter Helm, Peter Muriel,
Stuart Platt, John Watson

LAND USE AND RURAL AFFAIRS
DIRECTORATE GENERAL
Director-General: Anna Walker CB

Land Management and Rural Development
Directorate
Director: Jane Brown
Heads of Division: Ray Anderson, Peter Cleasby,
Martin Nesbit, Marcus Nisbet, John Osmond,
Andrew Perrins, Ann Tarran, Alan Taylor

Rural Economies and Communities
Directorate
Director: Paul Elliott
Heads of Division: Christopher Braun, David
Coleman, Graham Cory, Christopher Dunabin

Wildlife, Countryside, Land Use and Better
Regulation
Director: Brian Harding
Heads of Division: Terry Bird, Martin Brasher,
Martin Capstick, Susan Carter, Peter Costigan,
Lindsay Harris, Sheila McCabe, Alan Taylor

ANIMAL HEALTH AND WELFARE
DIRECTORATE GENERAL
Chief Veterinary Officer and Director-General:
Jim Scudamore
Deputy Chief Veterinary Officer:
Dr Richard Cawthorne
Heads of Division: Nigel Gibbens, Fred Landeg,
Ruth Lysons, David Pritchard,
Alick Simmons, Peter Soul
Dave Bench (reports direct to CVO)

Animal Health and Welfare Directorate
Director: Neil Thornton
Heads of Division: Simon Hewitt,
Malcolm Hunt, George Noble, Jill Wordley

TSE Directorate
Director: Peter Nash
Heads of Division: Mandy Bailey, Sue Eades,
Francis Marlow, Catherine Boyle

ENVIRONMENT DIRECTORATE-
GENERAL
Director-General: Bill Stow CB

Environment Quality and Waste Directorate
Director: Lindsay Cornish
Heads of Division: John Burns, Sue Ellis,
Bob Ryder, Martin Williams

Climate, Energy and Environmental Risk Directorate
Director: Henry Derwent
Heads of Division: Colin Church, Jeremy Eppel, Sarah Hendry, Duncan Prior, Richard Wood

Environmental Protection Strategy Directorate
Director: Robert Lowson
Heads of Division: Stephen Claughton, John Custance, Bob Davies, Scott Ghagan, Roy Hathaway, Bronwen Jones, Helen Marquard

Water and Land Directorate
Director: John Ballard CB
Heads of Division: Rodney Anderson, Prof Jenie Colbourne, Daniel Instone, John Roberts

SOLICITOR AND LEGAL SERVICES DIRECTORATE GENERAL
Solicitor and Director-General Legal Services: Donald Macrae
Directors: Stephen Parker, Francis Nash
Heads of Division: Charles Allen, Chris Burke, John Comber, Ian Corbett, Jeremy Cowper, Gisela Davis, Peter Davis, Brian Dickinson, Nigel Lefton, Alistair McGlone, Mayur Patel, Jonathon Robinson, Anne Sachs, Sue Spence, Anne Werbicki
Chief Investigation Officer: Jan Panting

SCIENCE DIRECTORATE
Chief Scientific Adviser and Head of Directorate: Prof Howard Dalton FRS
Deputy Chief Scientific Adviser: Dr Miles Parker
Heads of Division: Dr Tony Burne, Dr Nick Coulson, Dr John Sherlock

OPERATIONS AND SERVICE DELIVERY DIRECTORATE GENERAL
Director-General: Mark Addison

State Veterinary Services
State Veterinary Service Director: Martin Atkinson
Heads of Veterinary Services
(West): John Cross
Block 3 Government Buildings, Burghill Road, Westbury on Trym, Bristol BS10 6NJ
Tel: 0117-959 1000
(North): Robert Paul
Windsor House, Cornwall Road, Harrogate, North Yorkshire HG1 2PW
Tel: 01423 530678
(East): Gareth Jones
Government Buildings, Coley Park, Reading, Berkshire RG1 6DT
Tel: 0118-958 1222

(Scotland): Derick McIntosh
Animal Health Regional Office, Grayfield House, Bankhead Avenue, Edinburgh EH11 4AE
Tel: 0131-244 48273
Assistant Chief Veterinary Officers
*(Scotland):*Charles Milne
Pentland House, 47 Robbs Loan, Edinburgh EH14 1TW
Tel: 0131-244 46275
(Wales): Tony Edwards
National Assembly for Wales, Agriculture Department, Cathays Park, Cardiff CF1 3NQ
Tel: 029 2082 5111
Head of Veterinary Resource Team: Betty Phillip
Head of Service Delivery: Richard Drummond
Operational Planning: Ann Waters

Corporate Services Directorate
Director: Richard Allen
Heads of Division: Wendy Cartwright, Teresa Newell, Tony Nickson, Caroline Smith

Communications Directorate
Director of Communications: Lucian Hudson
Head of News: Martyn Smith
Head Corporate Communications: Kelly Freeman

e-business Directorate
Director: David Rossington
Director of IT: Shaun Soper
Heads of division: Peter Barber, David Brown, Alan Hill, David Myers

Delivery Strategy Team
Head: George Trevelyan

Review of Science based Agencies
Head: Lindsay Cornish

Service Delivery Development Programme
Head: Jim Smellie

Rural Development Service – RDS
Head of RDS: John Adams
Business Process Director: Jeff Robinson
Head of Technical Advice: Alan Hooper

RDS Regional Managers
East England
Block B, Government Buildings, Brooklands Avenue, Cambridge CB2 2DR
01223 455968 Fax 01223 455652
Martin Edwards

East Midlands Region
Block 7, Government Buildings, Chalfont Drive, Nottingham NG8 3SN
0115-929 1191 Fax 0115-929 4886
Sue Buckenham

South East Region
Block A, Government Buildings, Coley Park,
Reading, Berkshire RG1 6DT
0118-958 1222 Fax 0118-939 2399
Nick Beard

North East Region
Kenton Bar, Newcastle upon Tyne NE5 3EW
0191-286 3377
Fiona Gough

North West Region
Electra Way, Crewe Business Park,
Crewe CW1 6GJ
01270 754000 Fax 01270 669494
Tony Percival

South West Region
Block 3, Government Buildings, Burghill Road,
Westbury-on-Trym, Bristol BS10 6NJ
0117-959 1000 Fax 0117-950 5392
David Sisson

West Midlands Region
Government Buildings, Whittington Road,
Worcester WR5 2LQ
01905 763355
Carol Deakins

Yorkshire and the Humber
Government Buildings, Otley Road,
Lawnswood, Leeds LS16 5QT
0113-230 3964
Mike Silverwood

POLICY AND CORPORATE STRATEGY UNIT

Policy making, co-ordinating Defra's Change Management and Modernising Government programme and risk management. Co-ordinating Defra's relationship with the Government Offices for the Regions.
Cromwell House
Director and Secretary to the Management Board: Francesca Okosi 020 7238 1682
Policy and Corporate Strategy Deputy Director: Chris DeGrouchy 020 7238 1677

GOVERNMENT OFFICES FOR THE REGIONS

Defra Rural Directors
GO – East
Jane Rabagliati

GO – East Midlands
Graham Norbury

GO – North East
John Bainton

GO – North West
Neil Cumberlidge

GO – South East
Alison Parker

GO – South West
Tim Render

GO – West Midlands
Brin Davies

GO – Yorkshire and the Humber
Gordon Kingston

NB: See Government Offices for the Regions entry for full details

FINANCE, PLANNING AND RESOURCES DIRECTORATE

Finance Director: Andrew Burchell
Deputy Director: Ian Grattidge
Heads of Division: Roger Atkinson, David Fisher, Julie Flint, David Littler, David Rabey, Richard Wilkinson

Executive Agencies: Central Science Laboratory (CSL); Centre for Environment, Fisheries and Aquaculture Science (CEFAS); Pesticides Safety Directorate (PSD); Rural Payments Agency (RPA); Veterinary Laboratories Agency (VLA); Veterinary Medicines Directorate (VMD)

Foreign and Commonwealth Office – FCO

King Charles Street, Whitehall,
London SW1A 2AH
Tel: 020 7008 1500 (FCO Enquiries)
GTN: 7008 1500
Tel: 020 7270 3000 (Switchboard)
GTN: 270 3000
E-mail: [firstname.surname]@fco.gov.uk
Website: www.fco.gov.uk
Telegraphic address: Prodrome, London
Telex: 297711 (a/b PRDRME G)

3 Carlton Gardens, London SW1Y 5AA
Tel: 020 7008 1500

Cromwell House, Dean Stanley Street,
London SW1P 3JG
Tel: 020 7276 7676

Downing Street West, London SW1A 2AL
Tel: 020 7008 1500

Downing Street East, London SW1A 2AL
Tel: 020 7008 1500

Old Admiralty Building, London SW1A 2PA
Tel: 020 7008 1500   Fax: 020 7008 0302

Vauxhall Cross, 85 Albert Embankment,
London SE1 7TP
Tel: 020 7008 4440

94 Victoria Street, London SW1E 5JL
Tel: 020 7917 7000

Apollo House, 36 Wellesley Road, Croydon,
Surrey CR9 3RR
Tel: 020 8686 5622

Hanslope Park, Hanslope, Milton Keynes,
Buckinghamshire MK19 7BH
Tel: 01908 510444

British Trade International, Kingsgate House,
66-74 Victoria Street, London SW1E 6SW
Tel: 020 7215 5000

The Foreign and Commonwealth Office provides, through its staff in the UK and through its diplomatic missions abroad, the means of communication between the British Government and other governments and international governmental organisations on all matters falling within the field of international relations. It is responsible for alerting the British Government to the implications of developments overseas; for promoting British interests overseas; for protecting British citizens abroad; for explaining British policies to, and cultivating relationships with, governments overseas; for the discharge of British responsibilities to the overseas territories; for entry clearance (through UKvisas, with the Home Office) and for promoting British business overseas (jointly with the Department of Trade and Industry through British Trade International).

Secretary of State for Foreign and
  Commonwealth Affairs (Foreign Secretary):
  Rt Hon Jack Straw MP
Parliamentary Private Secretary:
  Colin Pickthall MP
Team Parliamentary Private Secretary:
  Roger Casale MP
Special Advisers: Ed Owen 020 7008 2117,
  Dr Michael Williams 020 7008 2112
  Fax: 020 7008 2336
Principal Private Secretary: Geoffrey Adams
  CMG 020 7008 2059 Fax: 020 7008 2144
Private Secretaries: Jonathan Sinclair
  020 7008 2061, Kara Owen 020 7008 2070
Diary Secretary: Kate Hemmings 020 7008 2079
Minister of State for Europe:
  Dr Denis MacShane MP
Parliamentary Private Secretary:
  Phyllis Starkey MP
Private Secretary: Peter Boxer 020 7008 8294
  Fax: 020 7008 8036
  E-mail: peter.boxer@fco.gov.uk

Assistant Private Secretary: Sian Price
  020 7008 8032
Diary Secretary: Jan Abbott 020 7008 8031
Minister of State for the Middle East:
  Rt Hon Baroness Symons of Vernham Dean
Parliamentary Private Secretary:
  Mark Todd MP
Private Secretary: Nick Allan 020 7008 2090
  Fax: 020 7008 3731
  E-mail: nick.allan@fco.gov.uk
Assistant Private Secretaries: Jennifer Townson
  020 7008 2091, Tracey McLelland
  020 7008 2092
Diary Secretary: Sally Kilvington
  020 7008 2093

Minister of State for Trade and Foreign Affairs
  (also DTI): Mike O'Brien MP
Parliamentary Private Secretary: Eric Joyce MP
Private Secretary: Peter Elder 020 7008 2126
  Fax: 020 7008 3539
  E-mail: peter.elder@fco.gov.uk
Assistant Private Secretaries: Alison Keeling
  020 7008 2128, Bradley Jones 020 7008 2127
Diary Secretary: Sarah Latham 020 7008 2126

Parliamentary Under-Secretary of State:
  Bill Rammell MP
Private Secretary: David Whineray
Assistant Private Secretary: Lisa Glover
  020 7008 3362
Diary Secretary: Louise Whitley

Parliamentary Under-Secretary of State:
  Chris Mullin MP
Private Secretary: Tom Fletcher 020 7008 2173
Assistant Private Secretaries: Kay Stokoe
  020 7008 2172, Nicky Wilbrey 020 7008 3363
Diary Secretary: Vaishali Patel 020 7008 2520

Parliamentary Clerk: Jeremy Hill 020 7008 4005
  Fax: 020 7008 2746
  E-mail: jeremy.hill@fco.gov.uk

***Spokespeople in the House of Lords:* Baroness Symons of Vernham Dean, Baroness Crawley**

Permanent Secretary and Head of HM
  Diplomatic Service: Sir Michael Jay KCMG
Private Secretary: Menna Rawlings
  020 7008 2142
  E-mail: pspus@fco.gov.uk
Assistant Private Secretaries: Martin Duffy,
  Andrea McGlone
Diary Secretary: Adam Duke 020 7008 2150
  E-mail: ps.pus.action@fco.gov.uk
Chief Executive, British Trade International:
  Sir Stephen Brown KCVO
Private Secretary: Simon Cooper 020 7215 4300

Directors-General
Peter Collecott CMG (Corporate Affairs)
John Sawyers CMG (Political)
Kim Darroch CMG (EU Policy)
William Ehrman CMG (Defence/Intelligence)
Graham Fry CMG LVO (Economic)

Directors
James Bevan (Africa)
Robert Culshaw MVO (Americas Overseas
    Territories)
Edward Oakden CMG (International Security)
Linda Duffield CVO (Wider Europe)
Dominick Chilcott (Mediterranean, Europe
    Bilateral Resources)
Paul Sizeland (Consular Services)
Stephen Sage (Chief Executive FCO Services)
Philippa Drew (Global Issues)
Edwin Chaplin OBE (Middle East and North
    Africa)
Simon Fraser (Strategy and Innovation)
Nigel Cox (Asia Pacific)
Tom Phillips CMG (South Asia)
Alan Charlton CMG (Personnel)
Dickie Stagg CMG (Information)
Simon Gass CMG CVO (Finance)

SPECIAL REPRESENTATIVES
Alan Goulty CMG (UK Special Representative
    for Sudan)
Tom Phillips CMG (UK Special Representative
    for Afghanistan)
Lord David Hannay GCMG (UK Special
    Representative for Cyprus)
Sir Brian Fall KCMG (UK Special
    Representative for Georgia)

HEADS OF DEPARTMENT
Afghanistan Unit: Jan Thompson
Africa (Equatorial): Tim Hitchens
Africa (Southern): Dr Andrew Pocock
Aviation, Maritime and Energy: Andrew Levi
British Trade International – see Department of
    Trade and Industry for full details
China Hong Kong: Denis Keefe
Commonwealth Co-ordination: Asif Ahmad
Consular Directorate
Consular Assistance Group: Richard Morris
Consular Crisis Group: Ralph Publicover
Passports and Documentary Services:
    David Clegg MVO
Consular Service Quality Group: Tim Flear MVO
Consular Resources Group: David Popplestone
Counter-Proliferation Department: Tim Dowse
Counter Terrorism Policy: Rob Macaire
Diplomatic Service Families Association:
    Emilie Salveson (Chair)

Directorate for Strategy and Innovation:
    Simon Fraser
Drugs and International Crime: Lesley Pallet
Eastern: Simon Butt
Eastern Adriatic: Karen Pierce LVO
Economic Policy: Creon Butler
e-media: Moray Angus
Environment Policy: Valerie Caton
Estate Strategy: Julian Metcalfe
European Union (External):
    Tim Barrow LVO MBE
Common Foreign and Security Policy Team:
    James Morrison
EU Northern Europe and International Team:
    Andrew Key
EU Enlargement and Wider Europe Team:
    Charles Garrett
European Union (Internal): David Frost
European Union – Mediterranean: Rob Fenn
    (Eastern), Wendy Wyver (Western)
FCO Association: David Burns CMG
    (Chairman)
Financial Compliance: David Major
Human Rights Policy: Jon Benjamin
Internal Audit (FCO/DFID): Jon Hews
IT Strategy Unit: Nick Westcott
Latin America and Caribbean: John Dew
Legal Advisers: Michael Wood CMG
Middle East: Charles Gray
National Audit Office: Martin Daynes
Near East and North Africa:
    Nicholas Archer
North America: Nicholas Armour
North East Asia and Pacific: Simon Smith
*Organisation for Security and Co-operation in
    Europe:* Peter January
Overseas Territories: Alan Huckle
Parliamentary Relations and Devolution:
    Matthew Hamlyn
Press Office: John Williams
Prism Programme: Fiona Moore
Procurement Policy: Michael Gower
Protocol: Charles de Chassiron LVO
Public Diplomacy Policy: Carole Sweeney
    (acting)
Records and Historical: Heather Yasamee
Research Analysts: Simon Buckle
Resource Accounting: Iain Morgan
Resource Budgeting: Tristan Price
Science and Technology:
    Fiona Clouder Richards
Security Policy: Paul Johnston
Security Strategy: Peter Millett
South Asia: Stephen Smith
South-East Asia: Michael Reilly
Sudan Unit: Dr Alastair McPhail

Trade Union Side (Diplomatic Service Whitley Council): Stephen Watson (Chair)
UK Visas (Joint FCO/HO Unit):
  Robin Barnett
United Nations: Stephen Pattison
Whitehall Liaison Department:
  Matthew Kidd

FCO Services
Client Services: James Clark
Supply Chain Service Delivery Group:
  Rod Peters
Promotions and Events Service Delivery Group:
  John Elgie
Finance Group: Kerry Simmonds
Human Resource Group:
  Elaine Kennedy
People and Best Practice Service Delivery Group: Dr Vanessa Davies
Facilities Service Delivery Group:
  Michael Blake
ICT Service Delivery Group:
  Patrick Cullen

Personnel Directorate
Interchange: Debbie Clare
Local Staff Management: Vacant
Medical and Welfare: Andrew George
Performance, Assessment and Development:
  Gerry Reffo
Personnel Management: Simon Pease
Personnel Policy: Judith Slater
Personnel Services: David Powell
Prosper: Ivor Rawlinson
Recruitment: Alison Cookson-Hall
Training: Richard Tauwhare

Executive Agency: Wilton Park

British Trade International – BTI

(A joint FCO and DTI organisation)

Kingsgate House, 66-74 Victoria Street,
London SW1E 6SW
Tel: 020 7215 5444/5
Websites: www.tradepartners.gov.uk;
www.invest.uk.com

British Trade International (BTI) is the Government's organisation set up to support Britain's trade and investment effort. BTI's two operating arms are Trade Partners UK, which helps UK companies trading overseas, and Invest UK, which promotes the whole of the UK as an inward investment location.

See – Department of Trade and Industry for full details

Department of Health – DH

Richmond House, 79 Whitehall,
London SW1A 2NL
Tel: 020 7210 3000
Fax: 020 7210 5523
E-mail: [firstname.surname]@doh.gov.uk
Website: www.doh.gov.uk

Skipton House, 80 London Road,
London SE1 6LH
Tel: 020 7972 2000

Wellington House, 133–155 Waterloo Road,
London SE1 8UG
Tel: 020 7972 2000

Quarry House, Quarry Hill, Leeds LS2 7UE
Tel: 0113-254 5000

Hannibal House, Elephant and Castle,
London SE1 6TQ
Tel: 020 7972 8000

Market Towers, 1 Nine Elms Lane,
London SW8 5NQ
Tel: 020 7273 3000

Eileen House, 80–94 Newington Causeway,
London SE1 6EF
Tel: 020 7972 2000

Government Office London
5th Floor, Riverwalk House, 157-161 Millbank,
London SW1P 4RR
020 7217 3328 Fax: 020 7217 3464

Government Offices for the East Midlands
The Belgrave Centre, Stanley Place,
Talbot Street, Nottingham NG1 5GG
0115-971 9971 Fax: 0115-971 2404

Government Office North East
9th Floor, Wellbar House, Gallowgate,
Newcastle upon Tyne NE1 4TD
0191-201 3300 Fax: 0191-201 3998

Government Offices North West
18th Floor, Sunley Tower, Piccadilly Plaza,
Manchester M1 4BE
0161-952 4000 Fax: 0161-952 4099

Government Offices South East
Bridge House, 1 Walnut Tree House, Guildford,
Surrey GU1 4GA
01438 882255 Fax: 01438 882259

Government Offices for the South West
2 Rivergate, Temple Quay, Bristol BS1 6ED
0117-900 1700 Fax: 0117-900 1900

Government Offices West Midlands
77 Paradise Circus, Queensway,
Birmingham B1 2DT
0121-212 5050 Fax: 0121-212 1010

Government Offices for Yorkshire and the Humber
6th Floor West Wing, PO Box 213, City House,
New Station Street, Leeds LS1 4US
0113-280 0600 Fax: 0113-233 8301

Social Services Regional Offices

Social Services Inspectorate
40 Berkeley Square, Clifton, Bristol BS8 1HP
0117-941 6500

2nd Floor, St James's Place, Castle Quay,
Castle Boulevard, Nottingham NG7 1FW
0115-959 7500

Ladywood House, 45/46 Stephenson Street,
Birmingham B2 4DH
0121-606 4360

Tyne Bridge Tower, Church Street, Gateshead,
Tyne and Wear NE8 2DU
0191-490 3400

West Point, 501 Chester Road, Old Trafford,
Manchester M16 9HU
0161-876 2400

National Cancer Services
St Thomas's Hospital, Lambeth Palace Road,
London SE1 7EH
020 7928 9292

NHS Purchases and Supplies Agency
Foxbridge Way, Normanton,
West Yorkshire WF6 1TL
01924 328700

80 Lightfoot Street, Chester CH2 3AD
01244 586700

Millennium House, 30 Junction Road,
Sheffield S11 8XB
0114-267 6004

Premier House, 60 Caversham Road, Reading,
Berkshire RG1 7EB
0118-980 8600

Blenheim House, West Avenue, Dunscombe
Street, Leeds LS1 4 PL
0113-295 2000

The Department of Health's is responsible for: supporting activity at national level to protect, promote and improve the nation's health; securing the provision of comprehensive, high quality care for all those who need it, regardless of their ability to pay or where they live or their age; securing responsive social care for those who lack the support they need.

Secretary of State for Health:
Rt Hon Dr John Reid MP
Parliamentary Private Secretary: Mike Hall MP
Special Advisers: Prof Paul Corrigan 020 7210
5942, Richard Olszewski 020 7210 5942,
Steve Bates 020 7210 5945

Principal Private Secretary: Dominic Hardy
020 7210 5158 Fax: 020 7210 5410
E-mail: dominic.hardy@doh.gsi.gov.uk
Private Secretaries: Sammy Sinclair
020 7210 5798, Alastair Finney 020 7210 5157,
Suzanne Rowe 020 7210 5607, Nicola Hewer
020 7210 5540
Assistant Private Secretary: Suzanne Rowe
020 7210 5607
Diary Secretary: Jessie Keuneman
020 7210 5320 Fax: 020 7210 5410

Minister of State for Health:
Rt Hon John Hutton MP
Parliamentary Private Secretary:
Claire Ward MP
Private Secretary: Tony Sampson
020 7210 5105 Fax: 020 7210 5823
E-mail: tony.sampson@doh.gsi.gov.uk
Assistant Private Secretaries: Katy Holloway
020 7210 5109 Fax: 020 7210 5823,
Andrew Larter 020 7210 5106,
Graeme Wilson 020 7210 5103
Diary Secretary: Lyn Saunders

Minister of State: Rosie Winterton MP
Parliamentary Private Secretary:
Jim Knight MP
Private Secretary: Alastair Finney 020 7210 5325
Fax: 020 7210 5548
E-mail: alastair.finney@doh.gsi.gov.uk
Assistant Private Secretaries: Katie Cusick
020 7210 5328, Sophie Rees 020 7210 5643
Diary Secretary: Kiran Kapoor 020 7210 5644

Parliamentary Under-Secretary of State (Lords):
Lord Warner
Acting Private Secretary: Catherine Davies
020 7210 5826 Fax: 020 7210 5066
E-mail: catherine.e.davies@doh.gsi.gov.uk
Assistant Private Secretaries: Andrew Black
020 7210 5333, Matthew Harpur
020 7210 5457
Diary Secretary: Annette Craze 020 7210 5425

*Parliamentary Under-Secretary of State for
Public Health:* Melanie Johnson MP
Private Secretary: Emily Stott 020 7210 5114
Fax: 020 7210 5534
E-mail: emily.stott@doh.gsi.gov.uk
Assistant Private Secretaries: John Stewart
020 7210 5119, Robert Finch 020 7210 5113,
Jacky Buchan 020 7210 5233
Diary Secretary: James Holton (temp)
020 7210 5115

*Parliamentary Under-Secretary of State for
Health:* Dr Stephen Ladyman MP
Private Secretary: Wendy Brown 020 7210 5325
Fax: 020 7210 5616
E-mail: wendy.brown@doh.gsi.gov.uk

Assistant Private Secretaries: Yvette Gyampoh 020 7210 5041, Helen Shaw 020 7210 5549
Diary Secretary: Ivanne Waring 020 7210 5451
Parliamentary Clerk: Neil Townley
020 7210 5808 Fax: 020 7210 5814
E-mail: neil.townley@doh.gsi.gov.uk
Ministerial Correspondence: 020 7210 5197

Spokesperson in the House of Lords:
Baroness Andrews

Permanent Secretary and Chief Executive NHS:
Sir Nigel Crisp KCB
Head of Private Office: David McNeil
020 7210 5801
E-mail: david.mcneil@doh.gsi.gov.uk
Acting Private Secretary: Matthew Hamilton
020 7210 5579 Fax: 020 7210 5409
E-mail: matthew.hamilton@doh.gsi.gov.uk
Assistant Private Secretary: Errol Lawrence
020 7210 5579

Chief Medical Officer
Prof Sir Liam Donaldson
Private Secretary: Rachel Dickson
020 7210 5150 Fax 020 7210 5407

Deputy Chief Medical Officers
Vacant (Public Health)
Second Deputy Chief Medical Officer (Specialist Health Services): Prof Aidan Halligan*
0116-295 2004
Director of National Cancer Services:
Prof Michael Richards MA MD FRCP
(Based at St Thomas's Hospital)
*Co-located in London and Leicester

CHIEF NURSING OFFICER'S DIRECTORATE
Chief Nursing Officer and Director of Nursing:
Sarah Mullally
Assistant Chief Nursing Officer:
Kate Billingham
Division Head: Flora Goldhill

Corporate Development Team
Head of Team: Peter Allanson

Allied Health Professions
Branch Head: Kay East

Health Care Scientists
Branch Head: Sue Hill

Mental Health Legislation
Branch Head: Adrian Sieff

Mental Health Services and Policy
Branch Heads: Anne Richardson

National Institute for Mental Health in England (NIMHE)
Head of NIMHE and Chief Executive:
Anthony Sheehan

Nursing and Midwifery Policy
Branch Head/Assistant Chief Nursing Officer:
David Moore

Patient and Public Involvement
Branch Head: David Mowat

Disability Policy Branch
Joint Heads: Ian Berry and Sue White
Principal Medical Officer: Dr Jeffrey Graham

COMMUNICATIONS DIRECTORATE
Richmond House, Skipton House and Quarry House
020 7210 5440   Fax: 020 7210 5134
Director of Communications: Sian Jarvis
E-mail: sian.jarvis@doh.gsi.gov.uk

Corporate Development Team
Team Leader: Susan Miller
Deputy Directors
Strategic Communications: John Worne
Marketing Communications Group:
Wyn Roberts
Media Centre: Jon Hibbs

DIRECTORATE FOR CHILDREN, OLDER PEOPLE AND SOCIAL CARE SERVICES
Richmond House, Wellington House, Eileen House
Acting Chief Inspector: Averil Nottage
Deputy Chief Inspector, SSI: Averil Nottage
Deputy Director and Head of Policy:
Giles Denham
Director of the Change Agent Team:
Richard Humphries (Secondee)

Social Care Modernisation
Branch Head: Jonathan Stopes-Roe

CHILDREN'S TASKFORCE

Children
Branch Head: Janice Shersby

Social Care Policy – Children in Need 2
Branch Head: Janet Grauberg

Clinical Director's Office
National Clinical Director for Children:
Prof Albert Anysley-Green

Children's National Service Framework
Project Manager – Children's NSF:
Claire Phillips

Corporate Development Team
Head of Team: Anthea Smith

Social Care Policy – Adoption and Permanence
Branch Head: Mike Lauerman

Children: Child Health and Maternity
Branch Head: Jonathan Stopes-Roe

Social Care Policy – Children in Need 1
Branch Head: Vacant

OLDER PEOPLE TASKFORCE

Older People Taskforce
Branch Head: Craig Muir

Social Care Policy – Community Care
Branch Head: Richard Campbell

Social Care – Quality and Standards
Branch Head: Helen Robinson

Public Sector Relocation Project
Project Leader: Adrian McNeil

National Director for Older People's Services
Branch Head: Prof Ian Philp (Secondee)

HEALTH AND SOCIAL CARE JOINT UNIT
Head of Unit: Helen Robinson

Social Services Inspection – SSI
East Midlands: Glen Mason
North East: John Fraser
North West: Vacant
South East: Lynda Hoare
Yorkshire and the Humber: Jonathan Phillips
London: Mike Rourke
Information and Methodology: Paul Brearley
West Midlands: John Cypher
Eastern: Jenny Owen
South Western: Steve Pitt
Joint Review Group: John Bolton (Consultant)
Social Care Quality Programme Co-ordinator: Vacant

DIRECTORATE OF CORPORATE AFFAIRS
Quarry House, Richmond House, Skipton House, Wellington House
Director, Corporate Affairs: Hugh Taylor CB
E-mail: hugh.taylor@doh.gsi.gov.uk
Group Heads
Corporate Change: Vacant
Equality Strategy: Elisabeth Al-Khalifa
Information Services: Dr Andrew Holt
Medicines, Pharmacy and Industry:
    Dr Felicity Harvey

Career Management Group: John Middleton
Chief Pharmaceutical Officer: Dr Jim Smith
Deputy Chief Pharmacist: Jeanette Howe
Head of Corporate Development Team:
    Olga Senior
Head of Business Planning: Paul Stocks

STRATEGY UNIT
Director: Prof Chris Ham
Deputy Director, Policy and Planning: Ivan Ellul

Customer Service Centre
Division Head: Linda Percival

British Pharmacopoeia
Secretary and Acting Scientific Director:
    Dr Gerard Lee

Change Management and Development
Branch Head: Mark Collyer

Employee Relations Support Communication
Branch Head: Simon Fuchs

Employee Reward
Branch Head: Sue Fathers

Strategic Human Resources
Branch Head: Phillipa Parr

Equality Strategy Group
Branch Heads: Barry Mussenden, Lydia Yee

Estates and Commercial
Head of Accommodation Office Services:
    Mike Rainsford

IT Services
Branch Head: Chris Horsey

Information Technology Services
Branch Head: Sue Lake

Information Management
Branch Head: Linda Wishart

Financial Management
Branch Head: Judith Dainty

CLINICAL AND COST EFFECTIVENESS – MPI GROUP
Branch Head: Alan Angilley
Senior Medical Officer: Dr Peter Clappison
Special Projects Adviser: Charles Dobson

Industry Branch
Branch Head: Shaun Gallagher

Pharmacy and Prescriptions
Branch Head: Kevin Guinness

Pricing and Supply
Branch Head: Mike Brownlee

POLICY AND PLANNING

Legislation
Branch Head: Richard Carter

PCT's Systems and Partnership
Branch Head: Chris Dowse

Performance Development Unit
Branch Head: Giles Wilmore

Performance Development Unit
Head: Jane Colman

Planning and Programme Unit
Branch Head: Julie Taylor

NHS Foundation Trusts
Branch Head: Clare Moriarty

FINANCE AND INVESTMENT DIRECTORATE
Quarry House, Richmond House, Eileen House
Director of Finance: Richard Douglas
E-mail: richard.douglas@doh.gsi.gov.uk
Director of NHS Counter-Fraud Services:
   Jim Gee

Corporate Development Team
Head of Team: Liz Eccles

Accounting
Branch Head: Jeff Tomlinson

Cash, Administration Costs and Financial Effectiveness
Branch Head: Peter Kendall

Capital Team
Acting Branch Head: John Guest

Financial Management
Branch Head: Alastair MacLellan

Internal Audit
Branch Head: Bill Burleigh

Private Finance and Investment
Branch Head: Peter Coates CBE

NHS Revenue Resource Allocation
Branch Head: Carl Vincent

Resource Planning and Acquisition
Acting Branch Head: Martin Campbell

NHS MODERNISATION AGENCY
Director of the Modernisation Agency:
   David Fillingham
E-mail: david.fillingham@doh.gsi.gov.uk
Head of National Primary Care Development
   Programme: Dr John Oldham
Directors
NHS Collaborative: Sarbjit Purewal (Associate)

NHS Leadership Centre: Penny Humphris
Changing Workforce Programme:
   Judy Hargadon

Corporate Development Team
Head of Human Resources: Caroline Corrigan

Service Improvement
Division Head: Michael Scott

Analyst Team
Branch Head: Mike Davidge (Consultant)

Critical Care Team
Branch Head: Dr Valerie Day

Idea Project
Branch Head: Ben Gowland (Consultant)

Redesign Team
Branch Head: Prof Helen Bevan (Secondee)

Visit Team
Branch Head: Nick Patten (Consultant)

National Primary Care Development Team
Branch Head: Dr Ian Rutter

Changing Workforce
Programme: Anne Hackett

National Clinical Government Support Team
Deputy Head: Steve O'Neill

National Institute for Mental Health in England
Chief Executive: Antony Sheehan

Valuing People Support Team
Branch Head: Rob Greig

DIRECTORATE OF ACCESS AND CHOICE
Director: Margaret Edwards

Corporate Development Team and Projects
Head of Operations: Dr Steven Lowden

Access Delivery
Acting Branch Head: Mark Svenson

Capacity and Choice
Division Head: Bob Ricketts

Primary Care Services
Branch Head: Rob Webster

Emergency Care Strategy
Branch Head: Mark Davies

NHS Direct National Programme
Branch Head: Paul Jenkins

Diagnostic Services
Branch Head: Keith Smith

Effective Care and Booking
Branch Head: Liz Fleck

Programme Officer
Branch Head: Amanda Phillips

NHS HUMAN RESOURCES DIRECTORATE – HRD
Quarry House, Richmond House
Director of Human Resources: Andrew Foster
Deputy Directors of Human Resources:
Martin Staniforth, David Amos
Deputy Director of Human Resources and Head of Learning and Personnel Development:
Prof Maggie Pearson
Corporate Development Team
Head of Team: Richard Mundon

Health Regulatory Bodies
Branch Head: Martin Sturges

Learning and Personal Development Post Qualification and Professional Development
Acting Branch Head: Paul Loveland

Corporate Affairs and Partnership Unit
Branch Head: John Ennis

Access to Learning and Initial Qualifications
Branch Head: Helen Fields

Quality Assurance – Education Team
Branch Head: Sandy Goulding

Policy Development
Deputy Director, Human Resources:
Martin Staniforth

NHS Pay
Branch Head: Ben Dyson

Policy Delivery
Deputy Director of HRD and Head of Policy Division: David Amos

Employment Policy
Branch Head: Debbie Mellor OBE

Strategic Medical Workforce Issues
Senior Medical Officer: Dr Julia Moore
(Secondee)

Workforce Development
Branch Head: Tim Sands

PUBLIC HEALTH AND CLINICAL QUALITY DIRECTORATE
Richmond House, Skipton House
Director of Public Health and Clinical Quality Directorate/Chief Medical Officer:
Prof Sir Liam Donaldson

Deputy Chief Medical Officer – Public Health:
Vacant
Head of Clinical Quality, Ethics and Genetics:
Ann Stephenson
Head of Public Health Division:
Prof Donald Nutbeam

Corporate Development Team
Acting Head of Team: John Bywater

CLINICAL QUALITY, ETHICS AND GENETICS DIVISION
Clinical Ethics and Human Tissue
Branch Head: Nick Dean

Genetics, Embryology and Assisted Conception
Branch Head: Liz Woodeson

Inquiries and Distinction Awards
Branch Head: Janet Walden

Controls Assurance Team
Acting Branch Head: Bob May

Clinical Quality
Branch Head: Patience Wilson

PUBLIC HEALTH DIVISION
International Branch
Branch Head: Nick Boyd

NHS Plus/Healthy Workplace Team
Head of NHS Plus: Dr Kit Harling

Environment and Health
Chief Scientist and Divisional Director, Environment and Health: Dr David Harper

Communicable Disease
Branch Head: Dr Graham Bickler

Sexual Health and Substance Misuse
Branch Head: Cathy Hamlyn

Public Health Development and Health Inequalities Unit
Branch Head: Dr Sunjai Gupta

Cardiovascular Disease and Cancer Prevention
Branch Head: Imogen Sharp

Public Health Development
Branch Head: Fiona Sim

RESEARCH, ANALYSIS AND INFORMATION DIRECTORATE
Richmond House, Skipton House
Director, Research, Analysis and Information Directorate: Prof Sir John Pattison
Assistant Director, Research and Development:
Peter Greenaway

Chief Economic Adviser: Prof Barry McCormick
Head of Information Policy Unit: Dr Peter Drury
Director of Statistics: Dr John Fox

Corporate Development Team
Head of Team: Anne Kauder

Advisers

Economics – Leeds
Branch Head: Nick York

Operational Research – Leeds
Branch Head: Dr Geoff Royston

Health Service Economics for London
Branch Head: Richard Murray

Operational Research – London
Branch Head: Andre Hare

RESEARCH AND DEVELOPMENT
Strategy and Corporate Affairs
Branch Head: Anne Kauder

Policy Research and Development
Division Head: Prof Gillian Parker

National Health Service Research Policy
Branch Head: Marc Taylor
Scientific Manager: Dr John Stephenson

INFORMATION POLICY UNIT
Primary Care IT
Branch Head: Simon Old

Information Governance
Branch Head: Phil Walker

Implementation Review
Branch Head: Mark Freeman

Management Information
Branch Head: Dr Pam Westley

STATISTICS
Policy and Dissemination, Population and Lifestyles
Acting Head of Division: Patsy Bailey

Dental, Optical, Pharmacy and Prescriptions
Chief Statistician: Jim Stokoe

Public Health, Diseases, Hospital Care and Quality
Chief Statistician: Richard Willmer

Statistics – Social Care, Population Groups and Surveys
Acting Head of Division: Anne Custance
Statistician: Roger Staton

Workforce and General Practice
Branch Head: Dr Andy Sutherland

SPECIALIST HEALTH SERVICES DIRECTORATE
Richmond House, Wellington House, Quarry House
Deputy Chief Medical Officer:
  Prof Aidan Halligan
Chief Dental Officer: Prof Raman Bedi
Senior Dental Officer: Chris Audrey
Taskforce Manager for Coronary Heart Disease and Cancer: Heather Gwynn
Head of Planning and Performance:
  Simon Reeve
Director of Prison Health: John Boyington
Website: www.doh.gov.uk/prisonhealth
Head of Specialist Services: David Hewlett

Corporate Development Team
Head of Team: Andy Cobb
Organisational Development Facilitator:
  Marion Furr

National Health Service Cancer Services
Branch Head: Stephen Waring
Director of National Cancer Services:
  Prof Michael Richards MA MD FRCP
(Based at St Thomas's Hospital)

Department of Health Cardiac Services
Acting Branch Head: Gavin Larner

Evidence
Branch Head: Dr Jennie Carpenter

Prison Health Care – Clinical Services
Branch Head: Dr Savas Hadjipavlou

Prison Health Care – Public Health
Branch Head: Dr Mary Piper

Dental and Optical
Branch Head: Almas Mithani

Diabetes, Renal and Transplants NSF Co-ordination
Branch Head: Dr Gillian Chapman

PERFORMANCE ANALYSIS
Branch Head: Dr Simon Peck

HM INSPECTOR OF ANATOMY
HM Inspector of Anatomy:
  Dr Jeremy Metters CB

SHARED SERVICES UNIT
Chief Executive/Programme Director:
  Phillip Hewitson

OFFICE OF THE SOLICITORS (DWP)
New Court
Solicitor: Marilynne Morgan CB
E-mail: m.a.morgan@dwp.gsi.gov.uk

Health and Personal Social Services Matters (other than National Health Service Superannuation)
Director of Legal Services: Greer Kerrigan
E-mail: greer.kerrigan@dwp.gsi.gov.uk
Assistant Directors: Gillian Aitken, Peter Bridges, Paula Cohen, Sue Edwards, Anita James, Naomi Mallick, Lynn Mear, Ronald Powell, Rachel Sandby-Thomas, Mary Trefgarne, Sandra Walker, Mark Wilson

Executive Agencies: Medical Devices Agency (MDA); Medicines and Health-Care Products Regulatory Agency (MHRA); NHS Estates (NHSE); NHS Pensions Agency (NHSPA); NHS Purchasing and Supply Agency (NHSPASA)

Home Office

50 Queen Anne's Gate, London SW1H 9AT
Main switchboard: 0870 000 1585
Fax: 020 7273 2065   GTN: 273 4000
Telex: 24986
E-mails:
public.enquiries@homeoffice.gsi.gov.uk;
[firstname.surname]@homeoffice.gsi.gov.uk
Website: www.homeoffice.gov.uk

Allington Towers, 19 Allington Street, London SW1E 5EB

Apollo House, Wellesley Road, Croydon, Surrey CR9 3RR

11 Carteret Street, London SW1H 9DC

Clive House, Petty France, London SW1H 9HT

Horseferry House, Dean Ryde Street, London SW1P 2AW

Grenadier House, 99-105 Horseferry Road, London SW1P 2DD

Litherland House, Litherland Road, Bootle, Merseyside L20 3QE

Lunar House, 40 Wellesley Road, Croydon, Surrey CR9 2BY

Portland House, London SW1E 5LP

To reduce crime and the fear of crime. To reduce organised and international crime and to combat terrorism and other threats to national security. To ensure the effective delivery of justice. To deliver effective custodial and community sentences to reduce reoffending and protect the public. To reduce availability and abuse of dangerous drugs. To regulate entry to and settlement in the United Kingdom effectively in the interests of sustainable growth and social inclusion. To support strong and active communities in which people of all races and backgrounds are valued and participate on equal terms.

Secretary of State for the Home Department (Home Secretary): Rt Hon David Blunkett MP
Parliamentary Private Secretary:
Andy Burnham MP
Special Advisers: Nick Pearce, Katharine Raymond, Matthew Seward, Huw Evans
Special Advisers' Numbers: 020 7273 2713/2852
Fax: 020 7273 2972
Principal Private Secretary: Jonathan Sedgwick
020 7273 4647 Fax: 020 7273 3965
E-mail:
jonathan.sedgwick@homeoffice.gsi.gov.uk
Private Secretaries: Gareth Redmond
020 7273 2091, Rebecca Razavi
020 7273 2096, Lizzy Gummer 020 7273 2275, Kevin O'Connor 020 7273 3585, Nichola Thomas 020 7273 2095
Senior Personal Secretary: Tricia Jones
020 7273 4410
Diary Secretary: Karen Hall 020 7273 2559

Minister of State (Crime Reduction, Policing and Community Safety): Hazel Blears MP
Parliamentary Private Secretary:
Dari Taylor MP
Private Secretary: Richard Austin 020 7273 2769
Fax: 020 7273 4606
E-mail: richard.austin@homeoffice.gsi.gov.uk
Assistant Private Secretary: Sunil Parekh
020 7273 2369
Diary Manager: Paul Daly 020 7273 2615

Minister of State (Criminal Justice System and Law Reform): Rt Hon Baroness Scotland of Asthal QC
Parliamentary Private Secretary:
Shona McIsaac MP
Private Secretary: Tom Walker 020 7273 2741
Fax: 020 7273 3094
E-mail: tom.walker@homeoffice.gsi.gov.uk
Assistant Private Secretaries: Alastair Noble
020 7273 4625, Sarah Getgood 020 7273 2524, Louisa Chichester 020 7273 3437
Diary Manager: Korena Butler 020 7273 2572

Minister of State (Citizenship, Immigration and Counter Terrorism): Beverley Hughes MP
Parliamentary Private Secretary:
Barry Gardiner MP
Private Secretary: Neil Roberts 020 7273 2742
Fax: 020 7273 2043
E-mail:
neilprivoff.roberts@homeoffice.gsi.gov.uk
Assistant Private Secretaries: Steve Eggett
020 7273 3191, Natasha Yusuf
020 7273 3200, Sara Kvanstom
020 7273 4689, Lee Ong 020 7273 3546
Diary Manager: Helen O'Shea 020 7273 2117

Parliamentary Under-Secretary of State (Tackling Drugs, Reducing Organised and International Crime): Caroline Flint MP
Private Secretary: Peter Grime 020 7273 2750
Fax: 020 7273 3381
E-mail: peter.grime@homeoffice.gsi.gov.uk
Assistant Private Secretaries: Nadine Walsh 020 7273 2585, Owain Jones 020 7273 2843
Diary Manager: Mark Bibby 020 7273 4621

Parliamentary Under-Secretary of State (Correctional Services and Reducing Re-offending): Paul Goggins MP
Private Secretary: Tony Lord 020 7273 3458
Fax: 020 7273 4090
E-mail: tony.lord@homeoffice.gsi.gov.uk
Assistant Private Secretaries: James Lowe 020 7273 2576, Andrew Latimore 020 7273 2833
Diary Manager: Sarah Wilson 020 7273 2429

Parliamentary Under-Secretary of State (Race Equality, Community Policy and Civil Renewal): Fiona Mactaggart MP
Private Secretary: Kishor Mistry 020 7273 2500
Fax: 020 7273 2565
E-mail: kishor.mistry@homeoffice.gsi.gov.uk
Assistant Private Secretaries: Kate Campbell 020 7273 2219, Chioma Obi 020 7273 2408, Kris Macnaughton 020 7273 4658
Diary Manager: Lorraine Cavill 020 7273 4358

Parliamentary Under-Secretary of State (Information Technology in the Criminal Justice System): Vacant
Private Secretary: Vacant 020 7273 8146
Fax: 020 7273 2539
E-mail: asma.samuel@homeoffice.gsi.gov.uk
Assistant Private Secretary: Frances Elliot 020 7273 8140
E-mail: frances.elliot@homeoffice.gsi.gov.uk

Parliamentary Clerk: Tony Strutt 020 7273 3591
Fax: 020 7273 3429

Spokespeople in the House of Lords: Baroness Scotland of Asthal, Lord Filkin, Lord Bassam of Brighton

Permanent Secretary: John Gieve CB
Private Secretary: Diana Luchford 020 7273 2199
Fax: 020 7273 2972
E-mail: diana.luchford@homeoffice.gsi.gov.uk
Commissioner for the Correctional Services and Permanent Secretary of Human Resources: Martin Narey
Private Secretary: Debbie Drew 020 7217 6720
Fax: 020 7217 6961
E-mail: martin.narey@homeoffice.gsi.gov.uk

Permanent Secretary for Crime, Policy, Counter-Terrorism and Delivery: Leigh Lewis CB
Private Secretary: David Rasmussen 020 7273 3601
E-mail: david.rasmussen@homeoffice.gsi.gov.uk

LEGAL ADVISERS
Senior Legal Adviser: David Seymour
Chief Medical Officer (at Department of Health and Social Security): Prof Sir Liam Donaldson QHP
Deputy Legal Advisers: David Noble, Clive Osborne
Director-General Resource and Performance: Margaret Aldred

DIRECTORATES

COMMUNICATIONS DIRECTORATE – CD
Director of Communications: Julia Simpson
Assistant Director and Head of Direct Communications Unit: Geoff Sampher
Customer Communications Manager: Julia Speight
Deputy Director and Head of News (Press Office): Terry Norman
Deputy Director of Communications and Head of Marketing and Strategic Communications: Anne Nash
Deputy Heads: Alison Cogger, Steve Park
Head of Information Services Unit: Peter Griffiths
Head of Internal Communications: Vacant

CORPORATE DEVELOPMENT AND SERVICES DIRECTORATE
Director: Charles Everett
Heads of Unit:
Agreement and Service Delivery: Mike Fitzpatrick
Building and Estate Management: Tony Edwards
Business Support and Communications Unit: Vacant
Commercial and Procurement Unit: Vacant
Home Office Pay and Pensions Service: Tony Fitzpatrick
Information Management Unit: Peter Lowe
Programme Project Management Support Service: Carol Anderson
Records Management: Richard Thompson

CORRECTIONAL SERVICES
Commissioner for Correctional Services: Martin Narey

Directors
*Finance, Contracts and Competition and
    Performance Monitoring:* John Steel
Correctional and Rehabilitation:
    Christine Stewart
Directors-General
Public Sector Prisons: Phil Wheatley
National Probation: Eithne Wallis
Heads of Units
Adult Offenders and Rehabilitation:
    Louise Dominian
Contracting Out and Competitions: David Kent
Correctional Services Standards Unit:
    Henry Tam
Juvenile Offenders Unit: Simon Hickson
Management of Private Sector Prisons: Vacant
Mental Health Unit: Elizabeth Moody,
    Fiona Spencer (job share)
Parole Board: Christine Glen
Sentencing Policy: Vacant
Strategy and Finance: Peter Brook

CRIMINAL JUSTICE GROUP – CJG

Directors-General:
Criminal Justice: Moira Wallace OBE
Criminal Justice IT: Jo Wright
Directors
Criminal Justice Systems Performance:
    Jane Furniss
Criminal Law and Policy: Mark Ormerod
Head, Active Community Unit: Helen Edwards
Animals Inspectorate (Scientific Procedures)
Chief Inspector: Dr Jon Richmond
Heads of Unit
Criminal Justice System IT: Mark Gladwyn
Race and Equality Unit: Bruce Gill
Strategic Support Group: Richard Jenkins
Animals, Procedures and Coroners Unit:
    Trevor Cobley
Community Cohesion Unit: Susan Hadland
Entitlement Cards Unit: Stephen Harrison
Crime, Law and Policy Unit: Deborah Grice
Independent Monitoring Board: Peter Curwen
Justice, Victims and Witnesses Unit:
    Catherine Lee
Local Performance and Delivery Unit:
    Anne-Marie Field
Resource Planning and Communications:
    Clive Manning
Criminal Justice System Confidence Unit:
    William Arnold
Criminal Procedures and Evidence Unit:
    Ian Chisholm
Criminal Justice System Race Unit:
    David Reardon
Regions and Renewal Unit: Betty Moxon

IMMIGRATION AND NATIONALITY DIRECTORATE – IND

Director-General: Bill Jeffrey
Deputy Directors-General
Operations: Robin Halward
Policy: Martin Donnelly
Asylum Support and Casework: Ken Sutton
Finance, Planning and Performance:
    David Stephens
Directors
Appeals Group: Mary Bowden
Asylum and Appeals Policy Directorate:
    Richard Westlake
Asylum Casework – Croydon: Chris Hudson
Asylum Group: Terry Neal
*Business Information Systems and Technology
    Directorate:* Stephen Calvard
Change and Reform Strategy: Mark Tonzer
Detention Services Directorate: Clem Norman
Finance: Tony Arber
General Group: Bill Brandon
Human Resources Directorate: Steven Barnett
Human Resources Services: Ros McCool
Immigration and Nationality Policy Directorate:
    Brian Caffrey
International Policy Directorate: Jenny Rumble
*Immigration Service – Border Control
    Operations:* David Roberts
*Immigration Service Enforcement and
    Removals:* Colin Allars
*Immigration Service – London Operations and
    Enforcement:* Don Ingham
Immigration Service – Regional Operations:
    Stacey Thornton
Intelligence: David Wilson
International Delivery: Nick Baird
Joint Delivery Programme: Dee Bourke
Learning and Development and IND College:
    Jonathan Potts
Major Projects: Brodie Clark
Managed Migration (acting): Alan Underwood
National Asylum Support Service:
    Freda Chaloner
Research, Development and Statistics:
    Peter Ward
Social Policy: Jonathan Duke-Evans
Zones of Protection: Edward Bannerman

CRIME REDUCTION AND COMMUNITY SAFETY GROUP – CRCSG
(Merging of PCRG and OCDIG)

*Permanent Secretary for Crime, Policy,
    Counter-Terrorism and Delivery:*
    Leigh Lewis CB
Director-General: Stephen Boys-Smith CB

Directors
Crime Reduction Centre: Steve Trimmins
Drugs Strategy: Sue Killen
Police Standards: Kevin Bond
Policing Policy: Stephen Rimmer
Policing and Crime Reduction: Jim Daniell
Assistant Director, Crime Reduction Delivery:
Peter Edwards

Heads of Units
Police Leadership and Powers: Paul Pugh
Policy Personnel Unit: Jeremy Crump
Police Resources Unit: Andy Ford
Science Policy Unit: Dr Anthony Whitehead
Performance and Strategic Management Unit:
Martin Parker
Management Support Unit: Fenella Tayler
Police Performance Delivery Unit:
Teresa Burnhams

Criminal Records and Security:
Charles Goldie
Public Order and Crime Issues Unit:
Michael Gillespie
Police Scientific and Development Branch:
Brian Coleman
Street Crime Action Team: Clare Checksfield

Drugs Legislation and Enforcement Unit:
Vic Hogg
Intelligence and Security Liaison Unit: Vacant
Terrorism and Protection Unit: Vacant
*Chemical, Biological, Radiological and Nuclear
Unit:* Vacant
Financial Crime Team: Peter Vallance

Policing and Organised Crime Team:
Stephen Webb
Judicial Co-operation Unit: Clive Welsh
*Strategy, Co-ordination and Planning Drugs
Unit:* Judy Youell
European and International Unit:
Lesley Pallett

PERFORMANCE AND FINANCE DIRECTORATE – PFD
Director of Performance and Finance:
William Nye
Heads of Unit
Performance and Finance Support:
Alison Barnett
Accounting and Finance Unit:
Paul De-Rivaz
Audit and Assurance: Tim Hurdle
Performance Delivery Unit: Vacant
Strategic Policy: Ben Jupp
Special Conference Centre: Betty Sandars
Corporate Change Team: Phillip Colligan

RESEARCH, DEVELOPMENT AND STATISTICS DIRECTORATE – RDSD
Director: Prof Paul Wiles
Assistant Directors
Crime and Policing Group: Carole Willis
Immigration and Community Group: Peter Ward
*International, Drugs, Economics and Resource
Analysis Group:* David Pyle
Programme Directors
Analysing Crime: Jon Simmons
Offending and Crime Justice Group:
Dr Carole Hedderman
Communication and Development Group:
Christine Lehman
Corporate Management Unit: Vacant

INSPECTORATES
50 Queen Anne's Gate, London SW1H 9AT

HM Inspectorate of Prisons
Tel: 020 7273 2554   Fax: 020 7273 3702
Website: www.hmprisonservice.gov.uk/prisons
HM Chief Inspector of Prisons:
Anne Owers CBE
HM Deputy Chief Inspector of Prisons:
Colin Allen

HM Inspectorate of Probation
Tel: 020 7273 2320   Fax: 020 7273 2131
Website:
www.homeoffice.gov.uk/cpg/hmiprobhome.htm
Chief Inspector: Prof Rod Morgan
Assistant Chief Inspector: John Hutchings
Acting Deputy Chief Inspector:
Frances Flaxington

HM Inspectorate of Constabulary
Tel: 020 7273 6084   Fax: 020 7273 3379
Website:
www.homeoffice.gov.uk/hmic/hmic.htm
HM Chief Inspector: Sir Keith Povey QPM
Assistant Inspectors: Tim Hollis, Peter Todd,
Mike Franklin
Heads of Unit: Stephen Wells, Debbie Keane,
Barry Coker

Chief Medical Officer:
Prof Sir Liam Donaldson (also DoH)
Legal Adviser: David Seymour
Deputy Legal Advisers: David Noble,
Clive Osborne
Assistant Legal Advisers: Steve Bramley, Steve
Braviner Roman, Harry Carter CBE, Richard
Clayton, Rowena Collins Rice, Kevin Norris,
Jim O'Meara, Caroline Price, Sally Weston

Executive Agencies: Criminal Records Bureau
(CRB); Forensic Science Service (FSS); HM
Prison Service; UK Passport Service (UKPS)

Department for International Development – DFID

1 Palace Street, London SW1E 5HE
Tel: 020 7023 0000   Fax: 020 7023 0019
GTN: 3535 70000

Abercrombie House, Eaglesham Road,
East Kilbride, Glasgow G75 8EA
Tel: 01355 844000   Fax: 01355 844099
GTN: 7243 4000
Public Enquiry Point: 0845 3004100
E-mails: enquiry@dfid.gov.uk;
[initial-surname]@dfid.gov.uk
Website: www.dfid.gov.uk

Responsible for managing Britain's bilateral and multilateral development programme with the aim of eliminating poverty and promoting sustainable development.

Secretary of State for International Development: Rt Hon Baroness Amos
Parliamentary Private Secretary:
Tom Levitt MP
Special Adviser: Alexander Evans
020 7023 0508
Principal Private Secretary: Anna Bewes
020 7023 0419 Fax 020 7023 0634
E-mail: privatesecretary@dfid.gov.uk
Private Secretaries: Cicely Warren
020 7023 0409, Vanessa Head 020 7023 0418
Diary Secretary: Lynn Foord-Divers
020 7023 0410 Fax 020 7023 0634

Minister of State for International Development:
Hilary Benn MP
Parliamentary Private Secretary:
Ashok Kumar MP
Private Secretary: Alison Cochrane
020 7023 0008
E-mail: psminister@dfid.gov.uk
Assistant Private Secretary: Joanne Simpson
020 7023 0757
Diary Secretary: Vacant 020 7023 0150

Parliamentary Under-Secretary of State:
Gareth R Thomas MP
Private Secretary: Elizabeth Peri 020 7023 0621
Fax 020 7023 0831
E-mail: pspuss@dfid.gov.uk
Assistant Private Secretary: Will Guest
020 7023 0182 Fax: 020 7023 0831
Personal Assistant and Diary Secretary:
Louisa Roberts 020 7023 0511

Head of Parliamentary Unit and Assistant Private Secretary: Peter Gordon
020 7023 0559
E-mail: p-gordon@dfid.gov.uk

Spokespeople in the House of Lords: Baroness Crawley, Baroness Whittaker (Liaison Peer)

Permanent Secretary: Suma Chakrabarti
Private Secretary: Charlie Whetham
020 7023 0514 Fax: 020 7023 0732
E-mail: c-whetham@dfid.gov.uk

REGIONAL PROGRAMMES DIVISION
Director-General: Nicola Brewer CMG

AFRICA DIVISION
Director: Graham Stegmann

Africa Great Lakes and Horn Department
Head of Department: Tim Craddock

Africa Policy Department
Head of Department: Graham Teskey

Central and Southern Africa Department
Deputy Director, Africa Division:
Anthony Smith

East Africa Department
Head of Department: David Batt

West Africa Department
Head of Department: Brian Thomson

DFID Ghana (Accra)
Head of Office: John Winter

DFID Kenya (Nairobi)
Head of Office: Matthew Wyatt

DFID Malawi (Lilongwe)
Head of Office: Roger Wilson

DFID Mozambique (Maputo)
Head of Office: Eamon Cassidy

DFID Nigeria (Abuja)
Head of Office: William Kingsmill

DFID Southern Africa (Pretoria)
Head of Office: Sam Sharpe

DFID Tanzania (Dar es Salaam)
Head of Office: Caroline Sergeant

DFID Uganda (Kampala)
Head of Office: Mike Hammond

DFID Zambia (Lusaka)
Head of Office: Helen Mealins

DFID Zimbabwe (Harare)
Head of Office: Gill Wright

ASIA AND PACIFIC DIVISION
Director: Martin Dinham CBE

Asia Directorate
Deputy Director, Asia and Pacific Division:
Marcus Manuel
Head of Asia Regional Policy: John Gordon

Eastern Asia and Pacific Department
Head of Department: Margaret Vowles

Western Asia Department
Head of Department: Chris Austin

DFID Bangladesh (Dhaka)
Head of Office: Paul Ackroyd

DFID Cambodia (Phnom Penh)
Head of Office: Dr Daniel Arghiros

DFID India (New Delhi)
Head of Office: Charlotte Seymour Smith

DFID Indonesia (Jakarta)
Head of Office: Vacant

DFID Nepal (Kathmandu)
Head of Office: David Wood

DFID South East Asia (Bangkok)
Head of Office: Mark Mallalieu

DFID Sri Lanka (Colombo)
Head of Office: Penny Thorpe

DFID Vietnam (Hanoi)
Head of Office: Alan Johnson

EUROPE, MIDDLE EAST AND AMERICAS DIVISION
Director: Carolyn Miller

Europe, Middle East and Americas Policy Department
Head of Department: Brenda Killen

Europe and Central Asia Department
Head of Department: Jessica Irvine

Latin America Department
Head of Department: Richard Teuten

Middle East and North Africa Department
Head of Department: Alistair Fernie

Overseas Territories Department
Head of Department: Clive Warren

UK Delegation to the European Bank for Reconstruction and Development (EBRD)
UK Representative: Simon Ray

DFID Caribbean (Barbados)
Head of Office: Joanne Alston

DFID Bolivia (La Paz)
Head of Office: Sam Bickersteth

DFID Brazil (Brasilia)
Head of Office: Vacant

DFID Central Nicaragua (Managua)
Head of Office: Georgia Taylor

DFID Guyana (Georgetown)
Head of Office: Gregory Briffa

DFID Honduras (Tequcigalpa)
Head of Office: Vic Heard

DFID Jamaica (Kingston)
Head of Office: Elizabeth Carrière

DFID Peru (Lima)
Head of Office: Mark Lewis

DFID Russia (Moscow)
Head of Office: Simon Bland

DFID Ukraine (Kiev)
Head of Office: Doug Houston

POLICY AND INTERNATIONAL DIVISION
Director-General: Masood Ahmed

POLICY DIVISION
Director: Sharon White
Deputy Directors: Marshall Elliott,
Susanna Moorehead, Dr Michael Schultz

OFFICE OF THE CHIEF ADVISERS
Chief Economist: Prof Adrian Wood
Head of Economics Profession: John Burton
Head of Enterprise Profession: David Stanton
Chief Statistician and Head of Statistics Profession: Roger Edmunds
Chief Social Development Adviser:
Dr Andrew Norton
Chief Governance Adviser: Sue Unsworth
Chief Human Development Adviser:
Dr Julian Lob-Levyt
Head of Education Profession: Marshall Elliott
Chief Environment Adviser: Steve Bass
Head of Engineering Profession:
Martin Sergeant
Head of Livelihoods Profession: Jim Harvey

INTERNATIONAL DIVISION
Director: Peter Grant

Conflict and Humanitarian Affairs
Head of Department: Michael Mosselmans

European Union
Head of Department: Nick Dyer

International Financial Institutions
Head of Department: Margaret Cund

International Trade
Head of Department: Dianna Melrose

United Nations and Commonwealth
Head of Department: Tony Williams

International Division Advisory Team
Head of Department: Rachel Turner

MISSIONS AND DELEGATIONS
UK Representation at the UN Agencies for Food and Agriculture (Rome)
UK Permanent Representative: Anthony Beattie

UK Delegation to UNESCO (Paris)
UK Permanent Delegate: David Leslie Stanton

CORPORATE PERFORMANCE AND KNOWLEDGE SHARING DIVISION
Director-General: Mark Lowcock

FINANCE AND CORPORATE PERFORMANCE DIVISION
Director: Richard Calvert
Heads of Department
Finance: Kevin Sparkhall
Accounts: Mike Smithson
Internal Audit: Mike Noronha
Performance and Effectiveness: Sue Wardell
Procurement: Stephen Chard

HUMAN RESOURCES DIVISION
Director: Dave Fish
Heads of Department
Human Resources Operations: John Anning
Human Resources Policy: Ian McKendry
Overseas Pensions: Peter Brough

INFORMATION, KNOWLEDGE AND COMMUNICATIONS DIVISION
Director: Owen Barder

Information and Civil Society Department
Head of Department: Mike Green

Information Systems and Services Department
Head of Department: David Gillett

Evaluation Department
Head of Department: Dr Colin Kirk

Private Sector Infrastructure/CDC Department
Head of Unit: Gavin McGillivray

Law Officers' Department

Attorney General's Chambers,
9 Buckingham Gate, London SW1E 6JP
Tel: 020 7271 2400   Fax: 020 7271 2432
E-mails: lslo@gtnet.gov.uk
[firstname.surname]@lslo.x.gsi.gov.uk
Website: www.lslo.gov.uk

Overall responsibility for the work of the Treasury Solicitor's Department, the Crown Prosecution Service, the Serious Fraud Office and the Legal Secretariat to the Law Officers.

The Attorney General is the Government's principal legal adviser; deals with questions of law arising on Bills, and with issues of legal policy; is concerned with all major international and domestic litigation involving the Government; and has specific responsibilities for the enforcement of the criminal law.

The Director of Public Prosecution for Northern Ireland is also responsible to the Attorney General, who is also Attorney General for Northern Ireland.

Attorney General:
Rt Hon The Lord Goldsmith QC

Solicitor General:
Rt Hon Harriet Harman QC MP

Parliamentary Private Secretary to the Law Officers: Vacant

Private Secretary to the Law Officers:
Carolyn Bartlett 020 7271 2405
Fax 020 7271 2432

Parliamentary Clerk and Assistant Private Secretary to the Attorney General:
Vacant 020 7271 2406

Assistant Private Secretary to the Solicitor General: Karen Appleby 020 7271 2457

Legal Secretary to the Law Officers:
David Brummell 020 7271 2401

Executive Agency: Treasury Solicitor's Department

Office of the Leader of the House of Commons

2 Carlton Gardens, London SW1Y 5AA
Tel: 020 7210 1025   Fax: 020 7210 1075
E-mail: [firstname.surname]@
CommonsLeader.x.gsi.gov.uk
Website: www.CommonsLeader.gov.uk

Leader of the House of Commons
Tel: 020 7210 1025   Fax: 020 7210 1075
E-mail:
Leader@CommonsLeader.x.gsi.gov.uk

The leader of the House of Commons is responsible for supervising the government's legislative programme and upholding the rights and privileges of the House.

Leader of the House of Commons and Lord Privy Seal: Rt Hon Peter Hain MP
Parliamentary Private Secretary:
Martin Linton MP 020 7219 4619
Special Advisers: Phil Taylor 020 7210 1081, Greg Power 020 7210 1084
Personal Secretary to the Advisers:
Michal Sasiadek 020 7210 1082
E-mail:
michal.sasiadek@commonsleader.x.gsi.gov.uk
Principal Private Secretary and Head of Private Office: Glynne Jones
Private Secretary and Deputy Head of Private Office: Stephen Hillcoat 020 7210 1025
Fax: 020 7210 1075
House of Commons: 020 7219 4040
Fax: 020 7219 6845
Diary Secretary: Jon Williams
020 7210 1025

Deputy Leader of the House of Commons:
  Phil Woolas MP
E-mail: deputy@commonsleader.x.gsi.gov.uk
Private Secretary: Frances Slee 020 7210 1022
E-mail:
  frances.slee@commonsleader.x.gsi.gov.uk
Diary Manager: Howie Taylor 020 7210 1021

Leader of the House of Lords and Lord President of the Council

2 Carlton Gardens, London SW1Y 5AA
Tel: 020 7210 1033   Fax: 020 7210 1071
GTN: 210 1033
E-mail: [firstname.surname]@pco.x.gsi.gov.uk
Website: www.privy-council.gov.uk

Leader of the House of Lords and Lord President
  of the Council:
  Rt Hon Lord Williams of Mostyn QC
Parliamentary Private Secretary: Vacant
Special Adviser: Matthew Seward
  020 7276 1960
E-mail:
  matthew.seward@cabinet-office.x.gsi.gov.uk
Principal Private Secretary: Chris Jacobs
  020 7276 0501 Fax: 020 7276 0491
Private Secretary: Nicki Daniels 020 7276 1297
Assistant Private Secretary: Donna Smith
  020 7276 0504
Deputy Leader of the House of Lords:
  Rt Hon Baroness Symons of Vernham Dean
Private Secretary: Nick Allan 020 7008 2090
  Fax: 020 7008 3731
E-mail: nick-allan@fco.gov.uk

Lord Chancellor – see Department for Constitutional Affairs

Minister without Portfolio and Labour Party Chair

Cabinet Office, 70 Whitehall, London SW1A 2AS
Tel: 020 7276 0636   Fax: 020 7276 1088
Website: www.cabinet-office.gov.uk

Minister without Portfolio and Labour Party
  Chair: Rt Hon Ian McCartney MP
Parliamentary Private Secretary:
  Neil Turner MP
Special Advisers: Martin O'Donovan,
  Patrick Loughran

Private Secretary: Christian D'Cunha
  020 7276 0636
Diary Secretary: Charlotte Lewsey
  020 7276 1091

Northern Ireland Office – NIO

11 Millbank, Whitehall, London SW1 4PN
Tel: 020 7210 3000   Fax: 020 7210 0246
E-mails: privateofficelondon@nio.x.gsi.gov.uk
press.nio@nics.gov.uk
[firstname.surname]@nio.x.gsi.gov.uk
Website: www.nio.gov.uk

Castle Buildings, Stormont, Belfast BT4 3SG
Tel: 028 9052 0700   Fax: 028 9052 8195
E-mail: privateoffice.belfast@nio.x.gsi.gov.uk

Stormont House, Stormont Estate,
Belfast BT4 3SH

Massey House, Stormont Estate,
Belfast BT4 3SX

Security restrictions

Northern Ireland matters not devolved to the
Assembly: policing, security policy, prisons,
criminal justice, victims, rights and equality and
political development. Is jointly responsible with
the Irish Government for the British Irish
Intergovernmental Conference. Represents
Northern Ireland's interest in the UK Cabinet.

Following the suspension of the devolution of
the 14 October 2002, the eleven departments
previously led by the Northern Ireland Executive
are now the responsibility of the Secretary of
State for Northern Ireland.

Secretary of State for Northern Ireland:
  Rt Hon Paul Murphy MP
Parliamentary Private Secretary:
  Gareth Thomas MP (Clwyd West)
Special Adviser: Owen Smith 020 7210 6487
Principal Private Secretary: David Brooker
  E-mail: david.brooker@nio.x.gsi.gov.uk
Private Secretaries: Kate Udy, Richard Lemon
  (London): 020 7210 6462 Fax: 020 7210 0246
  (Belfast): 028 9052 8111 Fax: 028 9052 8201
Minister of State: Rt Hon John Spellar MP
Parliamentary Private Secretary:
  Tom Harris MP
Private Secretary: John Ball
  (London): 020 7210 6488 Fax: 020 7210 6449
  (Belfast): 028 9052 8349 Fax: 028 9052 8202
  E-mail: john.ball@nio.x.gsi.gov.uk
Assistant Private Secretary: Norah Donnelly
  028 9052 8129

Minister of State: Jane Kennedy MP
Parliamentary Private Secretary:
   Huw Irranca-Davies MP
Private Secretary: Doreen McClintock
E-mail: doreen.mcclintock@nio.x.gsi.gov.uk
(London): 020 7210 6498 Fax: 020 7210 6449
(Belfast): 028 9052 8133 Fax: 028 9052 8202
*Parliamentary Under-Secretary of State:
   Ian Pearson MP
Private Secretary: Emma Croot
(London): 020 7210 6489 Fax: 020 7210 6449
(Belfast): 028 9052 2779 Fax: 028 9052 2822
*Parliamentary Under-Secretary of State:
   Angela Smith MP
Private Secretary: Teresa Hewitt
(London): 020 7210 6489 Fax: 020 7210 6449
(Belfast): 028 9052 2779 Fax: 028 9052 2822
*NB: Two newly appointed Parliamentary
Under-Secretaries of State due to the suspension
of the devolved government in Northern Ireland.
Parliamentary Clerk: Noel Marsden
   020 7210 6551 Fax: 020 7210 6550

Spokespeople in the House of Lords:
Lord Williams of Mostyn,
Baroness Farrington of Ribbleton

Permanent Secretary: Sir Joseph Pilling KCB
Private Secretary: Ruth Sloan
(London): 020 7210 6456 Fax: 020 7210 0256
(Belfast): 028 9052 8121 Fax: 028 9052 2918

Executive Agencies: Compensation Agency
(CA); Forensic Science Northern Ireland
(FSNI); Northern Ireland Prison Service (NIPS)

Parliamentary Counsel Office

36 Whitehall, London SW1A 2AY
Tel: 020 7210 6611   Fax: 020 7210 6632/0950
GTN: 210 6611
E-mails: lhowes@cabinet-office.x.gsi.gov.uk
[firstname.surname]@cabinet-office.x.gsi.gov.uk
Website: www.parliamentary-counsel.gov.uk

Parliamentary Counsel draft all Government Bills
except commonform ones and those relating
exclusively to Scotland. They also advise on all
aspects of Parliamentary procedure in connection
with such Bills and draft Government
amendments to them as well as any motions
(including financial resolutions) necessary to
secure their introduction into, and passage
through, Parliament. The First Parliamentary
Counsel is the legal adviser on constitutional
matters to the Prime Minister, the Cabinet Office
and the Treasury. This covers issues such as the
machinery of government, elections, the monarchy and the appointment of Ministers.

First Parliamentary Counsel
Geoffrey Bowman CB
Private Secretary: Peter Moore MBE
   020 7210 6629
Assistant Private Secretary: John Healy
   020 7210 6619 Fax 020 7210 0963
E-mail: john.healy@cabinet-office.x.gsi.gov.uk
Diary/PA: Linda Howes 020 7210 6644

Parliamentary Counsel
**Sir Edward Caldwell KCB QC, Helen
   Caldwell, David Cook, Philip Davies CB,
   Elizabeth Gardiner, Daniel Greenberg, Adrian
   Hogarth, Catherine Johnston CB, Peter
   Knowles CB*, Stephen Laws CB, Robert
   Parker CB, David Saunders CB*, Geoffrey
   Sellers CB, John Sellers, Euan Sutherland CB

Deputy Parliamentary Counsel
Robin Dormer, Gregor Kowalski,
   Léonie McLaughlin, Douglas Ramsay,
   Hayley Rogers, David Sewell, Edward Stell,
   Beverley Waplington

Research Counsel
Charles Carey

*Counsel at Inland Revenue
**Counsel at Law Commission

Privy Council Office – PCO

2 Carlton Gardens, London SW1Y 5AA
Tel: 020 7210 1033   Fax: 020 7210 1071
GTN: 210 1033
E-mail: [firstname.surname]@pco.x.gsi.gov.uk
Website: www.privy-council.org.uk

Office of the Lord President of the Council
Tel: 020 7210 1025   Fax: 020 7210 1075
E-mail: president@pco.x.gsi.gov.uk

Responsible for numerous formalities and
appointments relating to Crown and government
business.

*Lord President of the Council and Leader of the
   House of Lords:*
   Rt Hon Lord Williams of Mostyn QC
Parliamentary Private Secretary: Vacant
Special Adviser: Matthew Seward 020 7276 1960
E-mail: matthew.seward@pco.x.gsi.gov.uk
Principal Private Secretary: Chris Jacobs
   020 7276 0501 Fax: 020 7276 0491
Private Secretary: Nicki Daniels 020 7276 1297
Assistant Private Secretary: Donna Smith
   020 7276 0504
Diary Secretary: Jacqueline Kugler
   020 7276 0503
Support Officer: Sima Patel 020 7276 0502

Officials
E-mail: secretariat@pco.x.gsi.gov.uk
Website: www.pco.gov.uk
Clerk of the Council (Permanent Head of the
Privy Council Office):
Alex Galloway 020 7210 1033
Fax: 020 7210 1071
E-mail: alex.galloway@pco.x.gsi.gov.uk

Clerks
Deputy Clerk of the Council and Director of
Corporate Services:
Graham Donald 020 7210 1047
Fax: 020 7210 1072
E-mail: graham.donald@pco.x.gsi.gov.uk
Senior Clerk of the Council: Meriel McCullagh
020 7210 1044 Fax: 020 7210 1072
E-mail: meriel.mccullagh@pco.x.gsi.gov.uk
Deputy Director of Corporate Services:
Ceri King 020 7210 1050 Fax: 020 7210 1078
E-mail: ceri.king@pco.x.gsi.gov.uk
HR Manager: Vanessa Pountney-Chadhia
020 7210 1043
E-mail: vanessa.pountney@pco.x.gsi.gov.uk

Secretariat
Office Manager: Jackie Lindsay 020 7210 1030
E-mail: jackie.lindsay@pco.x.gsi.gov.uk

Judicial Committee of the Privy Council
Downing Street, London SW1A 2AJ
Tel: 020 7276 0485   Fax: 020 7276 0460
E-mail: judicial.committee@pco.x.gsi.gov.uk

Court of final appeal for those Commonwealth
countries which have retained the appeal to Her
Majesty in Council or, in the case of Republics,
to the Judicial Committee, and for devolution
issues within the United Kingdom.

Registrar: John Watherston 020 7276 0487
Fax: 020 7276 0460
E-mail: judicial.committee@jcpc.x.gsi.gov.uk

Clerks
Chief Clerk: Frank Hart 020 7276 0486
E-mail: frank.hart@pco.x.gsi.gov.uk
Second Clerk: Susan Condon 020 7276 0483
Fax: 020 7276 1071
E-mail: susan.condon@jcpc.x.gsi.gov.uk

Scotland Office

Ministerial Offices
Dover House, Whitehall, London SW1A 2AU
Tel: 020 7270 6754   Fax: 020 7270 6811/6812
E-mails: scottishsecretary@scotland.gsi.gov.uk
[firstname.surname]@scotland.gsi.gov.uk
Website: www.scottishsecretary.gov.uk

Finance and Administration
1 Melville Crescent, Edinburgh EH3 7HW
Tel: 0131-244 9010   Fax: 0131-244 9059
GTN: 7188 9010
Economy and Industry Division
Home and Social Division
1st Floor, Meridian Court, Glasgow G2 6AT
Tel: 0141-248 2855   Fax: 0141-242 5994

The role of the Secretary of State and the
Scotland Office is to represent Scottish interests
in matters that are reserved to the United
Kingdom Parliament and promote the devolution
settlement for Scotland. In particular, pay grant to
the Scottish Consolidated Fund and manage other
financial transactions; Exercise certain residual
functions in reserved matters (for example, the
conduct and funding of elections and the making
of private legislation at Westminster). Reserved
Matters include: The Constitution, Foreign
Affairs, Defence, International Development, the
Civil Service, financial and economic matters,
national Security, Immigration and nationality,
misuse of drugs, Trade and Industry, Various
aspects of energy regulation (e.g. electricity; coal,
oil and gas; nuclear energy); Various aspects of
transport; Social security, Employment, abortion,
genetics, surrogacy, medicines, broadcasting,
equal opportunities.

Secretary of State for Scotland:
Rt Hon Alistair Darling MP
Parliamentary Private Secretary:
David Stewart MP
Special Adviser: Iain Gray 0131-244 9027
E-mail: iain.gray@scotland.gsi.gov.uk
Principal Private Secretary: Jayne Colquhoun
020 7270 6740 Fax: 020 7270 6815
0131-244 9023 Fax: 0131-244 9028 (Edinburgh)
E-mail: ps/secretaryofstate@scotland.gsi.gov.uk
Private Secretaries: Elaine Hood 0131-244 9022
(Edinburgh), Eileen Roberts 020 7270 6735

Parliamentary Under-Secretary of State:
Anne McGuire MP
Private Secretary: Chloe Squires 020 7270 6806
Fax: 020 7270 6703
0131-244 9031 Fax: 0131-244 9028 (Edinburgh)
0141-242 5973 Fax: 0141-242 5967 (Glasgow)
E-mail: ps/pusofs@scotland.gsi.gov.uk
Personal Secretaries: Jeannie Nicholls
020 7270 6741, Elaine Gilmour 0141-242 5853
Parliamentary Clerk: Ian Stage 020 7270 6727
Fax: 020 7270 6834
E-mail: parlyclerk@scotland.gsi.gov.uk

Spokesperson in the House of Lords:
Lord Evans of Temple Guiting

Scotland Office Management

Head of Office: David Crawley
020 7270 6742/6769 Fax: 020 7270 6703
Heads of Division
  Parliamentary and Constitutional –
  Dover House:
  Vacant 020 7270 6800 Fax: 020 7270 6812
  Home and Social – Meridian Court: Gerald
  McHugh 0141-242 5446 Fax: 0141-242 5992
  Economy and Industry – Meridian Court:
  Ian Hooper 0141-242 5965 Fax: 0141-242 5992
  Finance and Administration – Melville Crescent:
  Norman Kernohan 0131-244 9001
  Fax: 0131-244 9028

Information Division

London: 020 7270 6828, Edinburgh:
  0131-244 9052
0131-244 9040 (Outside office hours)
Website: www.scottishsecretary.gov.uk
Principal Private Secretary to the Secretary of
  State and Head of Information Division:
  Jayne Colquhoun 020 7270 6740
  Fax: 020 7270 6815
E-mail: jayne.colquhoun@scotland.gsi.gov.uk
Chief Press Officer: Elaine Ravenscroft
  0131-244 9053 Fax: 0131-244 9051
E-mail: elaine.ravenscroft@scotland.gsi.gov.uk
Information Officers
Christine Cumming 0131-244 9052
E-mail: christine.cumming@scotland.gsi.gov.uk
Michael Duncan 020 7270 6875
E-mail: michael.duncan@scotland.gsi.gov.uk

Office of the Solicitor to the Advocate General

Victoria Quay, Edinburgh EH6 6QQ
0131-244 1635 Fax: 0131-244 1640
Solicitor (Edinburgh): Hugh Macdiarmid
  0131-244 1634
Head of Division A: Ian Harvie 0131-244 1631
  Fax: 0131-244 1640
Head of Division B: Allan Williams
  0131-244 1637 Fax: 0131-244 1650

OFFICE OF THE ADVOCATE GENERAL FOR SCOTLAND

Advocate General for Scotland:
  Dr Lynda Clark QC MP
Private Secretary: Gary Whyte 020 7270 6720
  Fax: 020 7270 6813
E-mail: ps/advocategeneral@scotland.gsi.gov.uk
0131-244 9033 Fax: 0131-244 9034 (Edinburgh)
Assistant Private Secretary: Kevin Tyson
  020 7270 6713
0131-244 9034 (Edinburgh)
E-mail: kevin.tyson@scotland.gsi.gov.uk

Department of Trade and Industry – DTI

1 Victoria Street, London SW1H 0ET
Tel: 020 7215 5000   Fax: 020 7215 0105
Minicom: 020 7215 6740   GTN: 215 5000
E-mail: [firstname.surname]@dti.gsi.gov.uk
Website: www.dti.gov.uk
151 Buckingham Palace Road,
London SW1W 9SS
10 Victoria Street, London SW1H 0NN
Kingsgate House, 66-74 Victoria Street,
London SW1E 6SW
Website: www.tradepartners.gov.uk
4 Abbey Street, London SW1P 2HT

Responsibilities include industrial sponsorship, trade policy, inward investment, export promotion, energy policy, science and technology, consumer and investor protection, corporate government, industrial relations, company law, support for small and medium-sized industries, e-commerce and the information society.

DTI incorporates the Office of Science and Technology, whose aim is to develop and co-ordinate, transdepartmentally, Government policy on science, engineering and technology. The Head of OST is also the Chief Scientific Adviser to the Government, with direct access to the Prime Minister.

Secretary of State for Trade and Industry,
  Minister for Women and e-Minister in
  Cabinet: Rt Hon Patricia Hewitt MP
Parliamentary Private Secretary: Oona King MP
Equalities Parliamentary Private Secretary:
  Jackie Lawrence MP
Team Parliamentary Private Secretary:
  Andrew Miller MP
Special Advisers: Jim Godfrey 020 7215 6620,
  Roger Sharp 020 7215 6480, Kitty Ussher 020
  7215 6176, Deborah Lincoln 020 7215 3971
Special Advisers Private Secretary:
  Nicola Harrison 020 7215 0005
Correspondence Manager to Special Advisers:
  Barbara Williams 020 7215 6629
Assistant Private Secretary to Special Advisers:
  Saleh Ahmed 020 7215 5204
Principal Private Secretary: Erica Zimmer
  020 7215 5621 Fax: 020 7215 5468
E-mail: mpst.hewitt@dti.gsi.gov.uk
Private Secretaries: Angela Piearce
  020 7215 5622, Sarah Hodgetts 020 7215 5623
Assistant Private Secretary: Susannah Johnson
  020 7215 5233
Diary Secretary: Victoria Fletcher 020 7215 5422
Senior Correspondence Manager:
  Margaret Housden 020 7215 6272

Minister of State (Energy, e-Commerce and Postal Services): Stephen Timms MP
Parliamentary Private Secretary: Ian Stewart MP
Private Secretary: Mike Warnes 020 7215 5144
Fax: 020 7215 5551
E-mail: mpst.timms@dti.gsi.gov.uk
Assistant Private Secretaries: Colin Cushway 020 7215 5146, Nicola Barber 020 7215 5229
Diary Secretary: Danny Mason 020 7215 6274

Minister of State for International Trade and Investment (also FCO): Mike O'Brien MP
Parliamentary Private Secretary: Eric Joyce MP
Private Secretary: Pete Elder 020 7008 2129
E-mail: mpst.o'brien@dti.gsi.gov.uk
Assistant Private Secretaries: Alison Keeling 020 7008 2128, Bradley Jones 020 7008 2127

Minister of State (Industry and the Regions and Deputy Minister for Women and Equality): Jacqui Smith MP
Parliamentary Private Secretary: Andy Love MP
Private Secretary: Giles Smith 020 7215 6202
Fax: 020 7215 6908
E-mail: mpst.smith@dti.gsi.gov.uk
Assistant Private Secretary: Justine Jeffrey 020 7215 2875
Diary Secretary: Craig Greenaway 020 7215 6196

Parliamentary Under-Secretary of State (Science and Innovation): Lord Sainsbury of Turville
Private Secretary: Charlotte DuBern 020 7215 5624 Fax: 020 7215 5410
E-mail: mpst.sainsbury@dti.gsi.gov.uk
Assistant Private Secretaries: Joanne Aldridge (Parliamentary Business) 020 7215 6864, Sandra Desir 020 7215 6374
Diary Secretary: David Simmonds 020 7215 5286

Parliamentary Under-Secretary of State (Employment Relations, Competition and Consumers): Gerry Sutcliffe MP
Private Secretary: Sam Myers 020 7215 5568
Fax: 020 7215 5560
E-mail: mpst.sutcliffe@dti.gsi.gov.uk
Assistant Private Secretary: Ross Hunter 020 7215 0476
Diary Secretary: Jason Goddard 020 7215 5519

Parliamentary Under-Secretary of State (Small Business and Enterprise): Nigel Griffiths MP
Private Secretary: Louise Robson 020 7215 5503 Fax: 020 7215 5675
E-mail: mpst.griffiths@dti.gsi.gov.uk
Assistant Private Secretaries: Celia Romain 020 7215 5578, Emily Wiltshear 020 7215 6799
Diary Secretary: Jackie Cameron 020 7215 5502

Parliamentary Clerk: Tim Williams 020 7215 6630
E-mail: tim.williams@dti.gsi.gov.uk
Deputy Parliamentary Clerk: Tracey Churchyard 020 7215 6658
Parliamentary Branch: 020 7215 6630
Fax: 020 7799 1531
Correspondence Manager: Bill Rose 020 7215 2855 Fax: 020 7215 6908

Spokespeople in the House of Lords:
Lord Sainsbury of Turville, Lord McIntosh of Haringey, Baroness Scotland of Asthal, Baroness Farrington of Ribbleton

British Trade International Board Chair: Mike O'Brien MP
British Trade International Group Chief Executive: Sir Stephen Brown KCVO
Permanent Secretary: Sir Robin Young KCB
Private Secretary: Tom Ridge 020 7215 5536
E-mail: mpst.young@dti.gsi.gov.uk

Chief Scientific Adviser to the Government and Head of Office of Science and Technology: Prof David King ScD FRS
Director-General, Research Councils: Dr John Taylor OBE

STRATEGY UNIT
Directory Strategy Unit: Geoff Dart
Chief Economic Adviser: Vicky Pryce
Directors:
Strategic Planning: Caroline Normand
Economic Analysis: Ken Warwick
Performance and Evaluation: Andrew Rees
Statistical Analysis: Glenn Everett

INNOVATION GROUP
Director-General: David Hughes
Chief Executive and Patent Office Comptroller General: Alison Brimelow
Senior Economic Adviser: John Barber
British National Space Centre
Director-General, BNSC and Director, Space: Dr Colin Hicks
Deputy Director-General, BNSC, Technology/Industrial Policy: David Leadbeater
Director, BNSC Space Applications and Programmes: Paula Freedman
Directors
Business Planning and Strategy: Peter Burke
Facilitating Innovation: John Rhodes
Technical Innovation and Sustainable Development: Vacant
Director and Chief Executive, National Weights and Measures: Jeffrey Llewellyn
Standards and Technical Regulations: David Reed

BUSINESS GROUP

Director-General: Mark Gibson
Directors
Change Management Team: Amanda Brooks
Business Relations 1: John Alty
Business Relations 2: David Hendon
Industry Economics and Statistics Directorate:
　Christopher Moir
Business Relations Postal Services:
　Mark Higson
Business Support: David Saunders
Deputy Director-General, Regions:
　Katharine Elliott
Chief Executive, Small Business Service (SBS):
　Martin Wynn-Griffith
*Chief Executive, Radiocommunications Agency
(RA):* Rolande Anderson

Business Relations – BR

Director, Business Relations 1: John Alty
Director, Business Relations 2: David Hendon
Director, Business Relations Postal Services:
　Mark Higson
Directors:
BR Strategic Management: Sheila Morris
Policy, Business Relations: Rosa Wilkinson
Relationship Management and the Regions:
　Martin Berry
Aerospace and Defence Industries Technology:
　David Way
Automotive Unit: Sarah Chambers
Bioscience: Monica Darnbrough
Construction: Elizabeth Whatmore
Consumer Goods and Services: Jane Swift
Chemicals: David Jennings
Joint DTI/Defra Environment Markets Unit:
　Duncan Prior
Marine: Chris North
Materials and Engineering: Simon Edmonds
Post Office Network: Nigel Leese
Postal Service: Rupert Huxter
Industry Economics and Statistics Directorate:
　Christopher Moir
Business Support: David Saunders

Regions

Deputy Director-General: Katherine Elliott
Directors;
RDA Sponsorship and Finance: Tony Medawar
Regional Policy: Peter Bunn
Regional European Funds and Devolution:
　John Neve
Regional Assistance: Andrew Steele
Social Enterprise Unit: Barbara Phillips

Small Business Service

An Executive Agency of the DTI
Chief Executive: Martin Wyn-Griffith

Deputy Chief Executive: Stephen Lyle Smythe
Channel Management: Howard Capelin
Business Services: Ken Poulter
Finance Director: Peter Bentley
Director, Strategy and Planning: Mandy Mayer

SERVICES GROUP

Director-General: Dr Catherine Bell CB
Director, Internal Audit: Helen Taylor
Director, Finance and Resource Management:
　David Evans
Directors
Finance: Peter Mason
Resource Accounting and Budgeting:
　Curtis Juman
*Business Planning and Procurement
Management:* Adam Jackson

*Director, Human Resources and Change
　Management:* Susan Haird
Directors
Change and Knowledge Management: Tim Soane
HR-Operations: Rosemary Heyhoe
HR Strategy and Terms of Employment:
　Christine Hewitt, Jan Dixon
Staff Personnel Operations: Rosemary Heyhoe
People Deployment and Development:
　Howard Ewing

Director, Export Control and Non-Proliferation:
　Mike O'Shea
Director, Export Control Organisation:
　Glyn Williams

*Director, Information Management and
　Workplace Services:* Yvonne Gallagher
Directors
e-Strategy and Major Projects: Andrew Matthew
Information and Policy: Liz Maclachlan
*Chair, Advisory Conciliation and Arbitration
　Service:* Rita Donaghy
Chief Executive, Companies House:
　Claire Clancy
*Inspector-General and Chief Executive,
　Insolvency Service:* Desmond Flynn
Chief Executive, Employment Tribunal Service:
　Roger Heathcote
*Secretary and Chief Executive, Central
　Arbitration Committee:* Graeme Charles

ENERGY GROUP

Director-General: Joan MacNaughton CB
Head of Licensing and Consents Unit:
　Jim Campbell
Director, Licensing Exploration Department:
　Simon Toole
*Director, Electricity Consents and Agency
　Project Management:* Nigel Peace

Head of Nuclear Coal Liabilities Unit:
Derek Davis
Director, Liabilities Management Unit:
Alan Edwards
Director, Legislation Team: Stephen Spivey
Director, Nuclear Business Relations:
Ian Gregory
Director, Coal Health Claims: Ann Taylor
Head of Energy Innovation and Business Unit:
Claire Durkin
Director, Energy Industries Business Unit and Oil and Gas Industry Development:
Iain Todd
Director, Nuclear Safety and Security:
Patrick Robinson
Director, Engineering Inspectorate:
Peter Fenwick
Director, International Nuclear Policy and Programmes: Ian Downing
Director, Civil Nuclear Policy and Programme:
Michael Buckland-Smith
Head of Energy Markets Unit: Neil Hirst
Director, Domestic and European Energy:
Liz Baker
Director, International and Infrastructure:
Ann Eggington
Director, Social Issues and Information:
Graham White
Head, British Energy Team: Paul McIntyre
Director, British Energy:
Graham Turnock
Head, Energy Strategy Unit : Rob Wright
Director, Strategic Issues: David Hayes
Director, Strategy Development (Research and Analysis): Adrian Gault
Director, Energy Management Support Unit (MSU: John Hobday

FAIR MARKETS GROUP
Director-General: Stephen Haddrill
Joint Directors, Strategy Fair Markets:
Jenny Eastabrook, Elizabeth Hodkinson
Director, Consumer and Competition Policy:
Jonathan Rees
Directors
Research, Analysis and Evidence Database:
David Miner
Strategy and Delivery: Katherine Wright
Economic Regulation and Reform:
Thoss Shearer
Europe and International: Tony Sims
Specific Market Interventions: Pat Sellers
Consumer Credit: Adrian Walker-Smith
Cross-Market Intervention: Fiona Price
Consumer Advice and Information:
Barbara Habberjam

Europe and World Trade
Directors
World Trade: Edmund Hosker
Europe: Jo Durning

Directors
International Trade Policy: Tim Abraham
EC Trade Policy: Elaine Drage
Market Access: David Andrews
EU Economic Reform: Hugh Savill
Future of Europe: Anthony Murphy
International Economics: Peter Dodd
State Aid: Vacant
Chief Executive, SITPRO: David Wakeford

Employment Relations
Director, Employment Relations: Janice Munday
Directors
Employment Market Analysis and Research:
Grant Fitzner
European Strategy and Labour Market Flexibility: Jane Whewell
Participation and Skills: Julie Carney
Selected Employment Rights:
Ros McCarthy-Ward
Dispute Resolutions: Sarah Rhodes
Secretary to the Low Pay Commission:
Kate Harre

Corporate Law and Governance
Director, Corporate Law and Governance:
Bernadette Kelly
Company Law: Robert Burns
Financial Reporting Policy: John Grewe
Accountancy Adviser: Andrew Watchman
Review of Non-Executive Directors:
Anne Willcocks
Policy and Resources: Roger Watson
Investigations and Inspector of Companies:
Grahame Harp

LEGAL SERVICES GROUP
The Solicitor and Director-General, Legal Services: Anthony Inglese
Directors:
Legal Services A: Tessa Dunstan
Legal Services B: Alex Brett-Holt
Legal Services C: Deborah Collins
Legal Services D: Scott Milligan
Legal Services E: Philip Bovey

WOMEN AND EQUALITY UNIT
Gender Equality; Kingsmill Review Team; Public Service Delivery Strategy and External Relations, Policy Adviser for EU/International Unit – Commonwealth; ESPC; Returns; Equality co-ordination Team

Director, Women and Equality Unit: Angela Mason
Deputy Directors
Equality Co-ordination: Kate Allan
Gender Equality and Social Justice:
 Liz Chennells
Productivity and Diversity:
 Hilary Samson-Barry

Women's National Commission
Chair: Margaret Prosser
Director: Janet Veitch

Office of Science and Technology
1 Victoria Street, London SW1H 0ET
020 7215 5000
Website: www.ost.gov.uk
Chief Scientific Adviser, Head of Office of
Science and Technology:
 Prof Sir David King ScD FRS
Directors:
Transdepartmental Science and Teaching:
 Jeremy Clayton
International Science and Technology:
 Rachel Jenkinson
LINK: Alan Wooton
Foresight: Dr Claire Craig
Science in Government: Judy Britton
Director-General, Research Councils:
 Dr John Taylor OBE FRS FEng
Science and Engineering Base:
 Dr Chris Henshall
Exploitation: Dr Stephanie DeSouza
Finance, Policy and Corporate Affairs:
 Stephen Speed
Research Councils: Dr Francis Saunders

Executive Agencies: Companies House (CH);
Employment Tribunals Service (ETS); Insol-
vency Service (INSS); National Weights and
Measures Laboratory (NWML); Patent Office
(PATS); Radiocommunications Agency (RA);
Small Business Service (SBS)

British Trade International
(A joint FCO and DTI organisation)

Kingsgate House, 66-74 Victoria Street,
London SW1E 6SW
Tel: 020 7215 5444/5
Websites: www.tradepartners.gov.uk;
www.invest.uk.com

British Trade International (BTI) is the Government's organisation set up to support Britain's
trade and investment effort. BTI's two operating
arms are Trade Partners UK, which helps UK
companies trading overseas, and Invest UK,
which promotes the whole of the UK as an
inward investment location.

Responsibility for British Trade International:
 Mike O'Brien MP
British Trade International Group Chief
Executive: Sir Stephen Brown KCVO
Private Secretary: Simon Cooper
Personal Secretary: Maggie Tresadern
Diary Secretary: Leena Patel
Deputy Group Chief Executive and Director,
Corporate Services: Ian Jones
Personal Assistant: Joyce Levy
Director, Human Resources and Finance:
 Bronwen Northmore

Strategy and Communications Group
Group Director: John Reynolds
Personal Assistant: Maureen Brindle
Director, e-Business and Knowledge
Management: Ian McKenzie
Director, e-Services to Business: Clive Stitt
Director, Change Management and Internal
Communications: John Doddrell
Director, Change Management:
 Peter McDermott
Ministerial and Parliamentary Support Unit:
 Steve Loach

INVEST UK – INUK
Chief Executive: William Pedder
Personal Assistant: Diana Gallimore
Director, Operations: Steve O'Leary OBE
Director, International: Martin Uden
Director, Marketing: Peter McDermott

International Trade Development Group
Group Director: David Warren
Personal Assistant: Rita Davis
Director, English Regions: Elizabeth Duthie
Director, Middle East and Africa:
 Bill Henderson LVO
Director, Asia Pacific: Tim Holmes
Director, Europe: Malcolm Scott
Director, The Americas: Kenneth Timmins

International Sectors Group – ISG
Group Director: Dr Peter Tibber
Personal Assistant: Christina Waller
Director, Infrastructure Projects:
 Dr Graeme Reid
Director, Services Industries and Consumer
Goods: Martin Raven
Director, Technology and Sectoral Partnership:
 Tim Torlot
Director, International Business Schemes:
 Ken White*
Director, International Oil and Gas Business and
Engineering: Brian Gallagher*

*Based at Tay House, 300 Bath Street,
Glasgow G2 4DX

REGIONAL INTERNATIONAL TRADE OFFICES – TRADE PARTNERS UK

International Trade Directors

East of England Region
East England Development Agency
Director: Robert Driver

East Midlands Region
East Midlands Development Agency
Director: Peter Hogarth

North East Region
One Northeast Development Agency
Director: John Williams

North West Region
Northwest Development Agency
Director: Vicki Treadell

London International
Director: David Train

South West Region
South West England Development Agency
Director: Neil Blakeman

West Midlands Region
Advantage West Midlands
Director: Doug Mahoney

Yorkshire and the Humber
Yorkshire Forward
Director: Mark Robson

NB: See Regional Development Agencies entry for full details

Export Credits Guarantee Department – ECGD

PO Box 2200, 2 Exchange Tower, Harbour Exchange Square, London E14 9GS
Tel: 020 7512 7000   Fax: 020 7512 7649   Telex: 290350 ECGD HQ G
E-mails: public.enquiries@ecgd.gov.uk
[initialsurname]@ecgd.gov.uk
Website: www.ecgd.gov.uk

To assist the export of UK capital and project-related goods by providing exporters with insurance against the commercial and political risks of not being paid by their buyers. ECGD also guarantees the repayment of bank loans to overseas borrowers which finance the purchase of UK goods and services and insures UK investors against the political risks of not receiving earnings from their overseas investments. ECGD reinsurance is available for private sector insurers who cover the export of UK goods sold on credit terms of less than two years.

Ministers
Secretary of State for Trade and Industry:
  Rt Hon Patricia Hewitt MP
Minister of State for International Trade,
  Investment and Foreign Affairs:
  Mike O'Brien MP

Chief Executive: Vivian Brown 020 7512 7004
  Fax: 020 7512 7146
  E-mail: vbrown@ecgd.gov.uk

BUSINESS GROUP – BG
John Weiss 020 7512 7376 Fax: 020 7512 7400
E-mail: jweiss@ecgd.gov.uk
Directors
Business Division 1: Gordon Welsh
  020 7512 7656 Fax: 020 7512 7312
Business Division 2: Roger Gotts 020 7512 7621
  Fax: 020 7512 7797
Divisional Manager, Metals, Mining and
  Process Engineering:
  Peter Crabb 020 7512 7557
Business Division 3: Mike Pentecost
  020 7512 7088 Fax: 020 7512 7692
Business Division 4: Customer Relationship
  Management: Vacant

PORTFOLIO AND ASSET MANAGEMENT GROUP – PAMG
Group Director: Victor Lunn-Rockcliffe
  020 7512 7008 Fax: 020 7512 7400
E-mail: vlunnroc@ecgd.gov.uk
Directors
Guarantee Management Division: Anthony
  Faulkner 020 7512 7729 Fax: 020 7512 7283
International Debt and Development Division:
  Eric Walsby 020 7512 7728
  Fax: 020 7512 7697
Recovery Division: Ross Lethbridge 020 7512
  7729, 029 2032 8529 Fax: 020 7512 7691
Portfolio Management Division: Yoav Tamir
  020 7512 7061 Fax: 020 7512 7312

RISK MANAGEMENT GROUP – RMG
Group Director: Tom Jaffray 020 7512 7731
  Fax: 020 7512 7400
E-mail: tom.jaffray@ecgd.gov.uk
Directors
Capital and Pricing Division: Jimmy Croall
  020 7512 7251 Fax: 020 7512 7758
Operational Research and Portfolio Risk
  Analysis: Ruth Kaufman 020 7512 7380
  Fax: 020 7512 7263
Country Risk and Economics Division and Chief
  Economist: Paul Radford 020 7512 7667
  Fax: 020 7512 7337

STRATEGY AND COMMUNICATIONS DIRECTORATE – SCD

Director: John Ormerod   020 7512 7405
Fax: 020 7512 7021
E-mail: john.ormerod@ecgd.gov.uk
Managers
Public Affairs: Rodney Watson 020 7512 7319
Business Strategy: David Wyatt 020 7512 7426
International Relations: Robin Mayer
  020 7512 7519
Business Principles Unit: David Allwood
  020 7512 7323

FINANCE DIVISION – FD

Finance Director: Ian Dickson 020 7512 7812
Fax: 020 7512 7400
E-mail: idickson@ecgd.gov.uk
Directors
Financial Controller: Tony Read*
  029 2032 8501
Internal Audit: Graham Cassell 020 7512 7225
Fax: 020 7512 7758
Information Systems: Linda Woods
  020 7512 7123 Fax: 020 7512 7356
Financial Structures Manager: Tony Cattell*
  029 2032 8503

*Based at Lamborne House, Lamborne
  Crescent, Llanishen, Cardiff CF14

GENERAL COUNSEL'S OFFICE – GCO

General Counsel: Nicholas Ridley
  020 7512 7845 Fax: 020 7512 7052
E-mail: nridley@ecgd.gov.uk
Legal Advisers: Michael Allen 020 7512 7073,
  Victoria Bui 020 7512 7849, Maria Carvajal-
  Navia 020 7512 7855, Richard Drummond
  020 7512 7863 Fax: 020 7512 4056,
  Mark Looi 020 7512 7858 Fax: 020 7512
  4087, Arthur O'Loan 020 7512 7854,
  Charles Redfearn 020 7512 7177
  Fax: 020 7512 4114, Beatrice Russ
  020 7512 7862

CENTRAL SERVICES DIVISION – CSD

*Director of Central Services Division and
  Principal Establishment Officer:* Steve
  Dodgson 020 7512 7013 Fax: 020 7512 7903
E-mail: sdodgson@ecgd.gov.uk
Managers
Personnel and Pay: Sue Johnson 020 7512 7046
  Fax: 020 7512 7903
Personnel Policy and Development: Tom Malby
  020 7512 7175 Fax: 020 7512 7056
Facilities Management and Purchasing Branch:
  Simon Richardson 020 7512 7171
  Fax: 020 7512 7903

ECGD ADVISORY COUNCIL

Chair: Liz Airey
Council Members: John Armitt, John Elkington,
  Prof Jonathan Kydd, David McLachlan,
  Prof Kate Phylaktis, Martin Roberts, Anthony
  Shepherd, Dr Raj Thamotheram, Sir Stephen
  Brown KCVO (Chief Executive, British Trade
  International)

Department for Transport – DfT

Great Minster House, 76 Marsham Street,
London SW1P 4DR
Switchboard Tel: 020 7944 8300
GTN: 3533 8300
E-mail: [firstname.surname]@dft.gsi.gov.uk
Website: www.dft.gov.uk

Ashdown House, 123 Victoria Street,
London SW1E 6DE

Berkeley House, Croydon Street,
Bristol BS5 0DA

The Eastgate Office Centre, Eastgate Road,
Bristol BS5 6XX

Longview Road, Morriston, Swansea SA6 7JL

Romney House, 43 Marsham Street,
London SW1P 3HW

Stanley House, 56 Talbot Street,
Nottingham NG1 5GU

Spring Place, 105 Commercial Road,
Southampton SO15 1EG

The Department's aim is *transport that works for
everyone.*
To that end, it works in partnership with others
to:
– tackle congestion;
– improve accessibility;
– reduce casualties;
– respect the environment; and
– support the economy.

Secretary of State for Transport:
  Rt Hon Alistair Darling MP
Parliamentary Private Secretaries:
  Ann Coffey MP, David Stewart MP
Special Advisers: Andrew Maugham, Tom
  Restrick 020 7944 4531 Fax: 020 7944 4329
E-mail: special.advisers@dft.gsi.gov.uk
Principal Private Secretary: Andrew Campbell
  020 7944 4394 Fax: 020 7944 4399
E-mail: alistair.darling@dft.gsi.gov.uk
Minister of State for Transport:
  Dr Kim Howells MP

Parliamentary Private Secretary:
David Borrow MP
Private Secretary: Deborah Heenan
020 7944 4483 Fax: 020 7944 4492
E-mail: kim.howells@dft.gsi.gov.uk
Parliamentary Under-Secretary of State for Transport: David Jamieson, MP
Private Secretary: Kirstin Blagden
020 7944 3084 Fax: 020 7944 4592
E-mail: david.jamieson@dft.gsi.gov.uk
Parliamentary Under-Secretary of State for Transport: Tony McNulty MP
Private Secretary: Philip Graham 020 7944 8695
Fax: 020 7944 4309
E-mail: tony.mcnulty@dft.gsi.gov.uk
Parliamentary Clerk: Paul Davies
020 7944 4472 Fax: 020 7944 4466
E-mail: parliamentary@dft.gsi.gov.uk
Ministerial Support: Helen Kelly 020 7944 4473
Fax: 020 7944 4309

Spokespeople in the House of Lords:
Lord Davies of Oldham,
Lord Bassam of Brighton

Permanent Secretary: David Rowlands CB
Private Secretary: Jessica Bowles
020 7944 4388/3017 Fax: 020 7944 4389
E-mail: jessica.bowles@dft.gsi.gov.uk

DRIVER, VEHICLE AND OPERATOR GROUP

Director-General: Stephen Hickey
Director: John Plowman
Divisional Managers:
Driver, Vehicle and Operator Secretariat:
Richard Verge
Driver, Vehicle and Operator Resource Division:
Jeff Belt
Licensing, Roadworthiness and Insurance Division: Richard Jones
Chief Executives
Driving Standards Agency: Gary Austin
Driver and Vehicle Licensing Agency:
Clive Bennett
Vehicle Certification Agency: Derek Harvey
Vehicle and Operator Services Agency:
Maurice Newey

BUSINESS DELIVERY SERVICES

Director of Business Delivery Services:
Hazel Parker-Brown
Divisional Managers:
Equality and Diversity: Phillipa Barber
Human Resources: Christine Bennett
IT Services: Ray Long
Procurement and Estates: Mike Acheson

RAILWAYS, AVIATION LOGISTICS, MARITIME SECURITY GROUP
Director-General: Vacant

Aviation Directorate
Director: Roy Griffins CB
Divisional Managers:
Aviation Environmental: Graham Pendlebury
Airports Policy: Michael Fawcett
Civil Aviation: Jonathan Sharrock
Economics, Aviation, Maritime and International: Michael Mann
International Aviation Negotiations: Tony Baker
Multilateral: Mike Smethers
UK Representative at the ICAO: Douglas Evans

LOGISTICS AND MARITIME TRANSPORT DIRECTORATE
Director: Brian Wadsworth
Divisional Managers:
Defence and Civil Contingency Planning:
John Parkinson
Ports: Stephen Reeves
Permanent Representative International Maritime Organisation: Thomas Allan
Road Freight Operations Policy:
Beth-Ann Bostock
Radioactive Materials Transport: Clive Young
Shipping Policy 1: David Rowe
Shipping Policy 2: Frank Wall
Coastal and Marine Development Unit:
Penny Brooke
Transport Statistics:
Freight: Antonia Roberts
Freight Logistics: Martin Jones

RAIL DIRECTORATE
Director: Mark Lambirth
Divisional Managers:
Passenger and Freight Services: Ian McBrayne
Railways Economics and Modelling:
Tracey Waltho
Railways Major Projects: Andrew Murray
Railways International Safety and Economic Regulation: John Aspinall
Network Rail: Alison Munro
Rail Delivery, Strategy and Communications:
Phil West

Transport Security Division
Director of Transport Security:
Niki Tompkinson
Deputy Director: John Grubb

Air Accidents Investigation
Chief Inspector: Ken Smart
Deputy Chief Inspector: David King

Marine Accidents Investigation
Chief Inspector: Stephen Meyer
Deputy Chief Inspector: Simon Harwood

Rail Accidents Investigation Branch
Principal Inspector: Carolyn Griffiths

Maritime and Coastguard Agency
Chief Executive: Captain Stephen Bligh
Directors:
Directorate of Quality and Standards:
  Alan Cubbin
Directorate of Operations: John Astbury

Major Projects Directorate
Director: Mike Fuhr

People and Skills Programme
Director: Vivien Bodnar

ROADS, REGIONAL AND LOCAL TRANSPORT GROUP
Director-General: Robert Deveraux

Integrated and Local Transport Directorate
Director: Alan Davis
Divisional Managers:
Buses and Taxis: Jane Anderson, Sandra Webber
Charging and Local Transport: Patricia Hayes
Economics, Local Transport and General:
  Mike Walsh
Local Transport Policy: Michael Faulkner
Traffic Management: Mike Talbot
Transport Statistics (Personal Travel):
  Hillary Hillier

REGIONAL TRANSPORT DIRECTORATE
Director: Bronwyn Hill
Divisional Manager:
London Underground: Peter Thomas
Multi-Modal Studies: Phillip Mills
Regional Transport Policy: Ian Jordan
Regional Transport London and South:
  Nick Bisson
Regional Transport North, Midlands and East:
  Alice Baker

ROADS AND VEHICLES DIRECTORATE
Director: Dennis Roberts
Divisional Managers:
Roads Policy: Sarah Thomson
Road Safety: Sandy Bishop
Road Safety Chief Medical Officer: Tim Carter
Transport Statistics – Roads: Alan Oliver
Vehicle Standards and Engineering:
  Malcolm Fendick
Lorry Road User Charging: David Lamberti

Transport Environment and Taxation:
  Leslie Packer
Transport Technology and Telematics:
  Eric Simpson

STRATEGY, FINANCE AND DELIVERY GROUP
Director-General: Willy Rickett

TRANSPORT ANALYSIS AND ECONOMICS DIRECTORATE
Director: Chris Riley
Divisional Managers:
In House Policy Consultancy: Sarah Thomson
Science and Technology Policy: Alan Apling
Transport Analysis and Review:
  Nigel Campbell
Integrated Transport Economics and Appraisal:
  Tom Worsley
Transport Research Unit: Gillian Smith

TRANSPORT FINANCE DIRECTORATE
Director of Transport Finance: Ken Beeton
Deputy Director: Peter McCarthy
Divisional Managers:
Finance Strategy: Tim Wellburn
Financial Management: Vacant
Financial Accounting: Vacant
Finance Corporate: Vacant

TRANSPORT STRATEGY AND DELIVERY DIRECTORATE
Director: David McMillan
Divisional Managers:
Europe: John Stevens
Strategy and Review: Paul Collins
Planning and Performance: Ewan West
Board Secretariat: Edward Neve

TRANSPORT TECHNOLOGY DIRECTORATE
Director: Edward Neve
Divisional Managers:
Transport Direct Team: Nick Illsley
Transport and Work Act Orders:
  Peter Saunders

COMMUNICATION DIRECTORATE
Director of Communication: Charles Skinner
Head of News: Simon Wren
*Head of Marketing and Corporate
  Communications:* David Murphy
Stakeholder Relations: Nick Court

MOBILITY AND INCLUSION UNIT
Manager, Mobility and Inclusion Unit: Ann Frye

LEGAL SERVICES DIRECTORATE
Director: Christopher Muttukumaru
Divisional Managers:
Aviation: Alan Jones
Driving and Road Safety: Stephen Rock
Highways: Hussein Kaya
Railways Operations and International:
Elizabeth Walsh
Railways: Robert Caune
Road Vehicles: David Jordan
Employment and Corporate Services:
Karen Booth

Executive Agencies: Driver and Vehicle Licensing Agency (DVLA); Driving Standards Agency (DSA); Highways Agency; Maritime and Coastguard Agency (MCA); Vehicle Certification Agency (VCA); Vehicle Inspectorate (VI)

HM Treasury – HMT

Treasury Chambers, 1 Horse Guards Road, London SW1A 2HQ
Tel: 020 7270 5000   Fax: 020 7270 5653
GTN: 270 5000
E-mail:
[firstname.surname]@hm-treasury.gsi.gov.uk
Website: www.hmt.gov.uk

To raise the rate of sustainable growth, and achieve rising prosperity, through creating economic and employment opportunities for all.

Maintaining a stable macroeconomic framework with low inflation; Maintaining sound public finances in accordance with the Code for Fiscal Stability; Improving the quality and the cost effectiveness of public services; Increasing the productivity of the economy; Expanding economic and employment opportunities for all; Promoting a fair and efficient tax and benefit system with incentives to work, save and invest; Achieving a high standard of regularity, propriety and accountability in public finance; Securing an innovative, fair dealing, competitive and efficient market in financial services, while striking the right balance with regulation in the public interest; Promoting UK economic prospects by pursuing increased productivity and efficiency in the EU, international financial stability and increased global prosperity, including especially protecting the most vulnerable.

The Prime Minister, First Lord of the Treasury:
Rt Hon Tony Blair MP
Chancellor of the Exchequer:
Rt Hon Gordon Brown MP
Parliamentary Private Secretary: Ann Keen MP

Chief Economic Adviser to the Treasury:
Ed Balls 020 7270 4941
Special Advisers: Ian Austin, Sue Nye,
Spencer Livermore 020 7270 5027
Principal Private Secretary: Mark Bowman
020 7270 5678 Fax: 020 7270 4580
E-mail: privateoffice@hm-treasury.gsi.gov.uk
Private Secretaries: Beth Russell (speech
writer), William Price
Assistant Private Secretaries: Lindsey Whyte,
Alex Skinner
Diary Manager: Leeanne Johnston
020 7270 5011

Council of Economic Advisers: Stewart Wood,
Maeve Sherlock, Shriti Vadera, Chris Wales,
Paul Gregg

Chief Secretary to the Treasury:
Rt Hon Paul Boateng MP
Parliamentary Private Secretary:
Helen Southworth MP
Special Adviser: Nicola Murphy 020 7270 1823
Fax: 020 7270 4836
Private Secretary: Dan Rosenfield
020 7270 4339 Fax: 020 7451 7600
E-mail:
dan.rosenfield@hm-treasury.gsi.gov.uk
Assistant Private Secretaries: Graham Floater
020 7270 5086, Richard Clarke
020 7270 5654
Diary Secretary: Les Smith 020 7270 5088

Paymaster General:
Rt Hon Dawn Primarolo MP
Parliamentary Private Secretary:
Tom Watson MP
Private Secretary: Andy Gordon 020 7270 4349
Fax: 020 7270 5131
E-mail: actioninf.pmg@hm-treasury.gsi.gov.uk
Assistant Private Secretaries: Adam Skinner
020 7270 5126 Fax: 020 7270 5131,
Vincent Contini (Diary) 020 7270 5128

Financial Secretary: Ruth Kelly MP
Parliamentary Private Secretary:
James Purnell MP
Private Secretary: Rob Gregory 020 7270 4340
Fax: 020 7270 5419
E-mail: robert.gregory@hm-treasury.gsi.gov.uk
Assistant Private Secretary: Matt Holmes
Diary Secretary: Sudesh Krishnan

Economic Secretary: John Healey MP
Private Secretary: Sam Woods 020 7270 4340
Fax: 020 7270 5179
E-mail: sam.woods@hm-treasury.gsi.gov.uk
Assistant Private Secretary: James Fraser
020 7270 5104
Diary Secretary: Mark Fox 020 7270 5103

Lords Commissioners: John Heppell MP,
Nick Ainger MP, Jim Fitzpatrick MP,
Jim Murphy MP, Derek Twigg MP,
Joan Ryan MP
Assistant Whips: Fraser Kemp MP,
Gillian Merron MP, Charlotte Atkins MP,
Vernon Coaker MP, Paul Clark MP,
Margaret Moran MP, Bridget Prentice MP

Parliamentary Clerk: David S Martin
020 7270 5005 Fax: 020 7270 4325

Spokesperson in the House of Lords:
Lord McIntosh of Haringey

Directorate Management
Permanent Secretary: Gus O'Donnell CB
Private Secretary: Ciaran Martin 020 7270 4360
Fax: 020 7270 4834
E-mail: ciaran.martin@hm-treasury.gsi.gov.uk

DIRECTORATES
Macroeconomic Policy and International
Finance – MPIF
Managing Director: Jon Cunliffe CB
Directors: Simon Brooks, Stephen Pickford,
Sue Owen, Melanie Dawes

Budget and Public Finances – BPF
Managing Director: Prof Nicholas Stern
Directors: Nicholas Holgate, Ivan Rogers

Finance Regulation and Industry – FRI
Managing Director: James Sassoon
Directors: Phil Wynn Owen, John Kingman

Public Services – PS
Managing Director: Nick Macpherson
Directors: Jonathan Stephens, Lucy De Groot,
Joe Grice, Anita Charlesworth

Financial Management, Reporting and Audit
– FMRA
Managing Director:
Prof Sir Andrew Likierman†
Director: Brian Glicksman*

*combined director and head of standing team
†head of cross-directorate standing team

Corporate Services and Development – CSD
Managing Director: Hilary Douglas CB

Executive Agency: UK Debt Management
Office (DMO)

OFFICE OF GOVERNMENT COMMERCE
Trevelyan House, 26-30 Great Peter Street,
London SW1P 2BY
Tel: 020 7271 2601   Fax: 020 7271 2733

OGC Service Desk: 0845 333 4999
E-mails: servicedesk@ogc.gov.uk
servicedesk@ogc.gsi.gov.uk
Website: www.ogc.gov.uk
Chief Executive: Peter Gershon CBE
Private Secretary: Alex Pritchard 020 7211 1377
Fax: 020 7211 1361
Deputy Chief Executive: John Oughton
Private Secretary: Sally Herrtage 020 7271 1385

Executive Agency: OGCbuying.solutions

Wales Office

Gwydyr House, Whitehall, London SW1A 2ER
Tel: 020 7270 0549/0583   Fax: 020 7270 0568
GTN: 270 0583
E-mails: [firstname.surname]@wales.gsi.gov.uk
wales.office@wales.gsi.gov.uk
Website: www.walesoffice.gov.uk

National Assembly for Wales, Cardiff Bay,
Cardiff CF99 1NA
Switchboard: 029 2082 5111
Wales Office: Tel: 029 2089 8778
Fax: 029 2089 8138
Website: www.wales.gov.uk

The Secretary of State is Wales' voice in the
Cabinet and in Parliament. His job is to make
sure the interests of Wales are fully considered
when Government policy is developed at
Westminster. And he is the key Government
Minister responsible for working with the
National Assembly administration in Cardiff.

Secretary of State for Wales:
Rt Hon Peter Hain MP
Parliamentary Private Secretary:
Chris Ruane MP
Special Adviser: Andrew Bold 029 2089 8549
E-mail: andrew.bold@wales.gsi.gov.uk
Principal Private Secretary: Simon Morris
020 7270 0550 Fax: 020 7270 0568
E-mail: simon.morris@wales.gsi.gov.uk
Private Secretary: Cherie Jones 020 7270 0538
E-mail: cherie.jones2@wales.gsi.gov.uk
Press Secretary and Director of News: Alan
Cummins 020 7270 0565 Fax: 020 7270 0578
Diary Secretary: Natalie Thomas 020 7270 0543
Parliamentary Under-Secretary of State:
Don Touhig MP
Private Secretary: Anna Rushall 020 7270 0569
Fax: 020 7270 0548
E-mail: anna.rushall@wales.gsi.gov.uk
Assistant Private Secretary: Kathryn Gray
020 7270 0546
Parliamentary Clerk: Michael Williams
020 7270 0544/0584

Spokesperson in the House of Lords:
Lord Evans of Temple Guiting
Head of Office: Alison Jackson 020 7270 0549

Information Division
Director of News and Press Secretary to the
Secretary of State: Alan Cummins
020 7270 0565

Finance and Administration
Head of Finance: John Kilner 020 7270 0557

Policy Group 1
Head of Group: Andrew Nicholas
020 7270 0585
Responsibility for Economic Affairs

Policy Group 2
Head of Group: Anne Morrice 020 7270 0587
Responsibility for Social Affairs

Policy Group 3
Head of Group: David Webb 029 2089 8513
Responsibility for Local Government, Transport
and Home Affairs

Legal Adviser's Office
Legal Advisers: Cedric Longville
029 2089 8484, Roger Bonehill 029 2089 8568

Department for Work and Pensions – DWP

Richmond House, 79 Whitehall,
London SW1A 2NS
Tel: 020 7238 0800
E-mail: ministers@dwp.gsi.gov.uk
Website: www.dwp.gov.uk

Adelphi, 1–11 John Adam Street,
London WC2N 6HT
Tel: 020 7962 8000

Central Office DSS,
Newcastle upon Tyne NE98 1YX
Tel: 0191-213 5000

New Court, 48 Carey Street, London WC2A 2LS
Tel: 020 7962 8000

Jobcentre Plus, Caxton House, Tothill Street,
London SW1H 9NA
Tel: 020 7273 3000   Fax: 020 7273 6143
Website: jobcentreplus.gov.uk

The Pension Service, Room 4C21,
Quarry House, Quarry Hill, Leeds LS2 7UA
Helpline: 0113-232 4143   Tel: 0113-232 4393
E-mail: pensiondirectorsoffice@dwp.gsi.gov.uk
Website: www.thepensionservice.gov.uk

Durham House, Washington,
Tyne and Wear NE38 7SD

Longbenton, Newcastle upon Tyne NE98 1YX
Moorfoot, Sheffield S1 4PQ

Government Buildings, Norcross Lane,
Norcross, Blackpool, Lancashire FY5 3TA

Peel Park, Brunel Way, Blackpool,
Lancashire FY4 5ES

Porterbrook House, 7 Pear Street,
Sheffield S11 8JF

Cavendish House, Newmarket Street, Skipton,
North Yorkshire BD23 2JQ

Tavis House, Tavistock Square,
London WC1H 9NB

Wellington House, 133-135 Waterloo Road,
London SE1 8UG

Helping people of working age without a job into
work and employers to fill their vacancies.
Providing financial support to people unable to
support themselves through back to work
programmes. Supporting families with the cost of
raising children. Promoting financial security in
retirement. Payment of social security benefits
and administration of the Social Fund. Administration of the Child Support System. Reciprocal
social security arrangements with other countries.

Secretary of State for Work and Pensions:
Rt Hon Andrew Smith MP
Parliamentary Private Secretary:
Ivan Henderson MP
Special Advisers: Chris Norton, Tom Clark
Principal Private Secretary: Susan Park
020 7238 0654 Fax: 020 7238 0661
E-mail: sos@dwp.gsi.gov.uk
Private Secretaries: Liz Wood 020 7238 0659,
Kate Kelly 020 7238 0656,
Charlotte Wightwick 020 7238 0655,
Frances Thompson 020 7238 0657
Diary Secretary: Kiran Teli 020 7238 0658

Minister of State for Work: Des Browne MP
Parliamentary Private Secretary:
Kali Mountford MP
Private Secretary: Caroline Crowther
020 7238 0738 Fax: 020 7238 0608
E-mail: mos-w-ps@dwp.gsi.gov.uk
Assistant Private Secretaries: Elenor Filer
020 7238 0726, David Pearce 020 7238 0735
Diary Manager: Marika Fawcett 020 7238 0741
E-mail: mos.w.diary@dwp.gsi.gov.uk

Minister of State for Pensions:
Malcolm Wicks MP
Parliamentary Private Secretary:
David Cairns MP
Private Secretary: Denise Whitehead
020 7238 0671 Fax: 020 7238 0675
E-mail: mos-p@dwp.gsi.gov.uk

Assistant Private Secretaries:
Robert Sanguinazzi, Sean Scarle,
Dulcie Reynolds (Diary)

Parliamentary Under-Secretary of State
(Minister for Children and the Family):
Rt Hon Baroness Hollis of Heigham
Private Secretary: Mary Curran 020 7238 0678
Fax: 020 7238 0682
E-mail: psl@dwp.gsi.gov.uk
Assistant Private Secretaries: Toni Clark
020 7238 0679, Judith Darcy 020 7238 0680,
Sibel Numan
Diary Secretary: Brian Gahagan 020 7238 0681

Parliamentary Under-Secretary of State
(Minister for Disabled People):
Maria Eagle MP
Private Secretary: Emma Davis 020 7238 0684
Fax: 020 7238 0687
E-mail: pscme@dwp.gsi.gov.uk
Assistant Private Secretary: Colin Willis
Diary Manager: Jay Seera 020 7238 0897

Parliamentary Under-Secretary of State (Work):
Chris Pond MP
Private Secretary: Fiona Walshe 020 7238 0690
Fax: 020 7238 0845
E-mail: pscmw@dwp.gsi.gov.uk
Assistant Private Secretaries: Christopher Raitt,
Robin Gordon-Farleigh
Diary Secretary: Alan Trevor

Parliamentary Under-Secretary of State
(DfES/DWP):
Baroness Ashton of Upholland
Private Secretary: Luke O'Shea 020 7925 6391
Fax: 020 7925 6688
E-mail: ashton.ps@dfes.gsi.gov.uk
Parliamentary Clerk: Tim Elms 020 7238 0715

Spokespeople in the House of Lords:
Baroness Hollis of Heigham, Baroness
Andrews

Permanent Secretary:
Sir Richard Mottram KCB
E-mail: richard.mottram@dwp.gsi.gov.uk
Private Secretary: Judith Tunstall
020 7238 0702
E-mail: judith.tunstall@dwp.gsi.gov.uk

INFORMATION AND ANALYSIS
DIRECTORATE – IAD
Adelphi
Director: Nick Dyson 020 7962 8611

COMMUNICATIONS DIRECTORATE
Director of Communications: Simon MacDowall
020 7238 0742

OFFICE OF CHIEF MEDICAL ADVISER,
MEDICAL POLICY AND CORPORATE
MEDICAL GROUP
Adelphi
Chief Medical Adviser and Medical Director:
Prof Mansel Aylward CB

Principal Medical Adviser – Working Age
(Incapacity Benefits, Sickness Certification,
Vocational Rehabilitation)
Dr Philip Sawney

Disability and Carer Benefits: Disability Living
Allowance, Attendance Allowance, Disability
Living Allowance Advisory Board.
Medical Policy Managers: Dr Mark Allerton,
Dr Anne Braidwood, Dr Pamela Ford,
Dr Moira Henderson, Dr Susan Reed,
Dr Roger Thomas, Dr Peter Wright

EU of Medical Advisers in Social Security
(UEMASS).
Medical Policy Manager:
Dr Paul Stidolph

LAW AND SPECIAL POLICY GROUP
New Court
Solicitor: Marilynne Morgan CB
E-mail: m.a.morgan@dwp.gsi.gov.uk

SOL A
Director of Legal Services: John Catlin
Assistant Directors of Legal Services
SOL A1: Naomi Mallick
SOL A2: Anne McGaughrin
SOL A3: Stephen Cooper
SOL A4: Peter Milledge
SOL B: Cathy Cooper
SOL Prosecutions: Sue Edwards
Commercial Branch: Ronald Powell
SOL Litigation: Anita James

PROJECT MANAGEMENT
Project Director: Gordon Hextall CB
Director, Digital Infrastructure:
Andrew Stott

WORKING AGE AND CHILDREN GROUP
Adelphi
Group Director: Ursula Brennan
Directors
Work and Welfare:
Michael Richardson
Fraud, Planning and Presentation:
Rod Clark
National Employment Panel: Cay Stratton
Children and Housing: Mark Neale

PENSIONS AND DISABILITY DIRECTORATE

Adelphi
Managing Director: Paul Gray CB
Directors
Pensions Strategy and Client Programme:
  Hilary Reynolds
Private Pensions 1: Janet Hill
Private Pensions 2: Charles Ramsden
Disability and Carers: Don Brereton CB
Disability and Carers (Blackpool): John Sumner

CORPORATE AND SHARED SERVICES GROUP

Quarry House and Durham House
Group Director and Principal Finance Officer:
  John Codling 0113-232 4229
Directors
Financial Services: Phil Robinson
Financial Management: Mick Davison
Commercial and Estate: David Smith
Corporate Management Information: David Kirk
Internal Audit Manager: Christopher Turner

PROGRAMME AND SYSTEMS DELIVERY GROUP

Adelphi
Group Director: Robert Westcott
  020 7712 2373
Directors
Programme Governance: Sandra Newton
Planning and Finance: Keith Palmer
External Supply: Peter Crahan

HUMAN RESOURCES GROUP

Adelphi
Group Director: Kevin White CB
  020 7712 2566
Diversity Director: Dr Barbara Burford

Executive Agencies: Appeals Service (AS); Child Support Agency (CSA); Jobcentre Plus; The Pension Service

---

DodOnline

An Electronic Directory without rival . . .

Civil Servants' biographies and photographs available with daily updates
via the internet

For a *free* trial, call Yasmin Mirza, Aby Farsoun or Michael Mand on 020 7630 7643

GOVERNMENT OFFICES FOR THE REGIONS

The Government Offices for the Regions (GOs) influence or control more than £7 billion of government expenditure annually on behalf of ten government departments in areas such as sustainable development, neighbourhood renewal, social inclusion, regeneration, competitiveness, fighting crime, European funding, public health, employment, training, business support and rural affairs.

They also handle land use planning, road scheme decisions, local transport priorities and statutory casework. GOs have a sponsorship role for the Regional Development Agencies (RDAs). GOs also co-ordinate planning for civil contingencies in their regions.

REGIONAL CO-ORDINATION UNIT
Riverwalk House, 157-161 Millbank,
London SW1P 4RR
020 7217 3595 Fax 020 7217 3590
E-mails:
rcusecretariatenquiries@go-regions.gsi.gov.uk
[firstinitialsurname].rcu@go-regions.gsi.gov.uk
Website: www.rcu.gov.uk

Set up in 2000, the Regional Co-ordination Unit has the following key tasks: to act as a corporate centre for the Government Offices; to make Government Offices more representative of Government as a whole; to feed the experiences of Government Offices into Whitehall policy making; and to rationalise Area-Based Initiatives, completing a fundamental initial review in October 2002.

Both the Regional Co-ordination Unit and the Government Offices are part of the Office of the Deputy Prime Minister.

Director-General: Rob Smith
Director: Andrew Campbell
Divisional Managers:
Corporate Communications: Ian Jones
Strategy: Nick Dexter
Business Development: Teresa Vokes
Resilience and Civil Contingencies:
  Richard Bruce

GO – EAST
Eastbrook, Shaftesbury Road,
Cambridge CB2 2DF
01223 372500 Fax 01223 372501
E-mails:
customerservices.go-east@go-regions.gsi.gov.uk
[initialsurname].go-east@go-regions.gsi.gov.uk
Website: www.go-east.gov.uk

Regional Director: Caroline Bowdler
Directors, Business Development Group
Corporate Strategy and Development:
  Hilary Cooper

Business and Europe: Martin Oldham
Corporate Services and Resilience Planning:
  Clive Whitworth
Directors, Environment Group
Planning and Transport: John Dowie
Sustainable Development and Rural Affairs:
  Jane Rabagliati
Directors, Social Inclusion Group
Learning and Local Government:
  John Street
Community Safety and Regeneration:
  Sue Howl

GO – EAST MIDLANDS
The Belgrave Centre, Stanley Place,
Talbot Street, Nottingham NG1 5GG
Switchboard: 0115-971 9971
Fax 0115-971 2404
E-mail: enquiries.goem@go-regions.gov.uk
Website: www.go-em.gov.uk

Regional Director: Jane Todd
Directors:
Derbyshire and Leicestershire: Industry,
  Education and Skills : Roger Poole
Lincolnshire and Rutland: European and Rural
  Affairs: Graham Norbury
Northamptonshire and Nottinghamshire:
  Regional Infrastructure and Community
  Affairs: Mike Jackson
Crime Reduction: Steve Brookes
Corporate Affairs: Robert Smith
Deputy Directors:
Derbyshire and Leicestershire: Jan Sensier
Northamptonshire and Nottinghamshire:
  Rowena Limb
Regional Resilience: John Perkins
Co-located – Department of Health
Regional Director, Public Health:
  Prof Lindsey Davies
Deputy Director, Public Health:
  Nick Salfield

GO – LONDON

Riverwalk House, 157–161 Millbank,
London SW1P 4RR
020 7217 3111 Fax 020 7217 3450
E-mails: enquiries-london.gol@go-regions.gov.uk
[initialsurname].gol@go.regions.gsi.gov.uk
Website: www.go-london.gov.uk

Regional Director: Elizabeth Meek
Head of Division, GOL Central Unit:
  Marion Kerr
Head of Division, North and West: Liz Walton
Head of Division, Thames Gateway:
  Corinne Lyons
Head of Division, South and Central:
  Richard Wragg
Head of Division, GLA, Business and Europe:
  Jonathan Tillson
Head of Division, Planning: Andrew Melville
Head of Division, London Resilience Team:
  Zyg Kowalczyk
Head of Division, Corporate Change
  Management: Pauline Clarke
Head of Division, Crime and Drugs: Ellie Roy

GO – NORTH EAST

Wellbar House, Gallowgate,
Newcastle upon Tyne NE1 4TD
0191-201 3300 Fax 0191-202 3998
E-mail:
general.enquiries.gone@go-regions.gsi.gov.uk
Website: www.go-ne.gov.uk

Regional Director: Jonathan Blackie
Director, Regional Group: Jim Darlington
Director, Regional Intelligence and Emergency
  Planning: Bryan Rees
Director, Corporate Services: Lynda Keith
Director, Business Group: David Slater
Director, Europe: John Rundle
Director, Environment Group: John Bainton
Director, Built Environment: Diana Pearce
Director, Public Health Group: Dr Bill Kirkup
Director, Communities Group: Alan Brown
Director, Neighbourhood Renewal and Crime
  Reduction: Fiona Young
Director, Children and Young People:
  Patrick Chapman

GO – NORTH WEST

Sunley Tower, Piccadilly Plaza,
Manchester M1 4BE
0161-952 4000 Fax 0161-952 4099
E-mail:
[initialsurname].gonw@go-regions.gsi.gov.uk
Website: www.go-nw.gov.uk

Cunard Building, Pier Head, Liverpool L3 1QB
0151-224 6300 Fax 0151-224 6470

Regional Director: Keith Barnes
Director, Corporate Services: David Hopewell
Director, Communities: Peter Styche
Director, Competitiveness and Infrastructure:
  Dr David Higham
Director, European Programmes, North West
  (excluding Merseyside): Jo Lappin
Director, Education, Social Inclusion and
  Connexions: Nigel Burke
Director, Home Office Group: David Smith
Director, European Programmes, Merseyside:
  John Flamson
Deputy Director, European Programmes,
  Merseyside: Chris Musson
Director, Neighbourhood Renewal: Brian Holmes
Director, Environment and Rural:
  Neil Cumberlidge
Director, Public Health: John Ashton
Head, Ministerial Business: Julie Crawford

GO – SOUTH EAST

Bridge House, 1 Walnut Tree Close, Guildford,
Surrey GU1 4GA
01483 882255 Fax 01483 882259
E-mail: [initialsurname].gose@go-regions.gov.uk
Website: www.go-se.gov.uk

Regional Director: Paul Martin
Director, Planning and Innovation, Hants/IoW:
  Colin Byrne
Director, Education, Skills and Business, Thames
  Valley: Dr Julian Lomas
Director, Defra, Europe, Sustainability, DCMS:
  Alison Parker
Director, Regeneration, Housing and
  Communities, Kent: Mark Bilsborough
Director, Transport, Surrey/E Sussex/W Sussex:
  David Cooper (temporary)
Director, Finance and Corporate Management:
  Peter Craggs
Director, Home Office: Hugh Marriage
Regional Director for Public Health:
  Dr Mike Gill

GO – SOUTH WEST

Bristol: 2 Rivergate, Temple Quay,
Bristol BS1 6ED
0117-900 1700 Fax 0117-900 1900
E-mails: contactus@go-regions.gsi.gov.uk
[initialsurname].gosw@go-regions.gsi.gov.uk
Website: www.gosw.gov.uk

Plymouth: Mast House, Shepherds Wharf,
24 Sutton Road, Plymouth PL4 0HJ
01752 635000 Fax 01752 227647
E-mail: goswdc@eurobell.co.uk

Truro: Castle House, Pydar Street, Truro TR1 2UD
01872 264500 Fax 01872 264503

Regional Director: Jane Henderson
*Director, Local Government, Housing and
  Planning:* Vacant
Director, Regional Policies and Enterprise:
  Liz Carter
Director, Transport and European Programmes:
  Richard Bayly
Director, Corporate Services: Malcolm Davey
*Director, Community Safety and Emergency
  Planning:* Paul Rowlandson
*Director, Sustainability, Intelligence and Rural
  Affairs:* Tim Render
*Director, Young People, Regeneration and
  Communities:* Peter Cloke
*Department of Health Regional Director for
  Public Health:* Dr Gabriel Scally

GO – WEST MIDLANDS
77 Paradise Circus Queensway,
Birmingham B1 2DT
0121-212 5050 Fax 0121-212 1010
GTN: 6177 5050
E-mail:
[initialsurname].gowm@go-regions.gsi.gov.uk
Website: www.go-wm.gov.uk

Regional Director: Graham Garbutt
Director, National Focus Division:
  Margaret Geary
*Director, Regional Strategy and Europe
  Division:* Chris Marsh
Director, Corporate Services Division:
  Jack Markiewizc
*Department of Health Regional Director for
  Public Health Division:* Prof Rod Griffiths
Director, South Eastern Division: Chris Beesley
Director, Western Division: Brin Davies
Director, Northern Division: Philippa Holland
Director, Special Projects: James Bradley

GO – YORKSHIRE AND THE HUMBER
PO Box 213, City House, New Station Street,
Leeds LS1 4US
0113-280 0600 Fax 0113-233 8301
E-mail:
[initialsurname].goyh@go-regions.gsi.gov.uk
Website: www.goyh.gov.uk

Regional Director: Felicity Everiss
Director, Europe and Secretariat:
  Alison Biddulph
Director, Regional Affairs: John Jarvis
Director, People and Communities:
  Isobel Mills
*Director, Neighbourhood Renewal and
  Communities:* Carol Cooper-Smith
Director, Competitiveness and Sustainability:
  Margaret Jackson
Director, Rural: Gordon Kingston
Director, Objective 1: Sylvia Yates
Director, Community Safety: Greg Dyche
Regional Director for Public Health:
  Paul Johnstone
*Director, Resilience Planning and Corporate
  Services:* Nick Best

DodOnline
An Electronic Directory without rival . . .
Civil Servants' biographies and photographs available with daily updates
via the internet

For a *free* trial, call Yasmin Mirza, Aby Farsoun or Michael Mand on 020 7630 7643

REGIONAL DEVELOPMENT AGENCIES

Regional Development Agencies in the eight English regions outside London began work on 1 April 1999. They are the lead bodies at the regional level for co-ordinating inward investment, raising people's skills, improving competitiveness of business and social and physical regeneration.

ADVANTAGE WEST MIDLANDS
3 Priestley Wharf, Holt Street,
Birmingham B7 4BN
0121-380 3500   Fax: 0121-380 3501
E-mail: name@advantagewm.co.uk
Website: www.advantagewm.co.uk
Chairman: Nick Paul
Vice-Chair: Cllr Sue Davis CBE
Board Members: Richard A Barnes, Prof Kumar
   Bhattacharyya CBE, Dr Tony Harris OBE,
   Dr Ahmed Hassam, Cllr Richard Hyde,
   Isabella Moore, Norman Price, Tony Sealey,
   Cllr David Sparks, Cllr Paul Tilsley MBE,
   Brian Woods-Scawen
Chief Executive: John Edwards
Executive Directors: Michael Laverty (Finance
   and Strategy), Mary Harpley (Inward
   Investment and Marketing), Karen Yeomans
   (Development and Partnerships), David Blake
   (acting) (Business Growth)
Head of Marketing and Public Relations:
   Mike Goodall
Public Relations Manager: Neil Skitt
   0121-503 3251

**EAST ENGLAND DEVELOPMENT
AGENCY – EEDA**
The Business Centre, Station Road, Histon,
Cambridge CB4 9LQ
0845 456920   Fax: 01223 713940
E-mail: knowledge@eeda.org.uk
Website: www.eeda.org.uk
Chairman: Vincent Watts (Richard Ellis from
   December 2003)
Deputy Chairmen: Neville Reyner, Sal Brinton
Board Members: Roger Ali, Ruth Bagnall,
   Stephen Castle, Marco Cereste, Greg Grant,
   George Keiffer, Leo Murray, Chris Paveley,
   Richard Powell, Bryony Rudkin,
   Yasmin Shariff, Marie Skinner
Chief Executive: Bill Samuel
Executive Directors: Brian Hayes (Organisation
   and Development), Alex Mackay (Sustainable
   Development), Stephen Holton (Enterprise
   and Innovation)
Director of Communications: Rachel Bosworth
Head of Policy: Philip Amison
Communications Manager (Press Office):
   Vivienne Oxley

**EAST MIDLANDS DEVELOPMENT
AGENCY – EMDA**
Apex Court, City Link, Nottingham,
East Midlands NG2 4LA
0115-988 8300   Fax: 0115-853 3666
E-mail: info@emd.org.uk
Website: www.emda.org.uk
Chairman: Derek Mapp
Board Members: Kashmir Bilgan, Jane Bradford
   CBE, Bryan Carr, Cllr Graham Chapman,
   Samantha Gemmell, Neville Jackson,
   Jonathan McLeod, Dame Patricia Morgan-
   Webb DBE, Rita Patel, Peter Ramsden,
   Andrew Scarborough, Dr Ron Whittaker,
   Ross Wilmott, Valerie Owyer
Chief Executive: Martin Briggs
Executive Directors: Sue Kirby (Economic
   Development), Jeff Moore (Corporate
   Services and Investment), David Wallace
   (Strategy and Communications), Ian Lodder
   (Partnerships), Abby Johnson Brennan
   (International Development), Alison Simpson
   (Sustainable Communities)
Head of Marketing and Communications:
   Louise O'Reilly 0115-988 8540

**NORTHWEST DEVELOPMENT AGENCY
– NWDA**
PO Box 37, Renaissance House,
Warrington WA1 1XB
01925 400100   Fax: 01925 400400
E-mails:information@nwda.co.uk
[firstname.surname]@nwda.co.uk
Website: www.nwda.co.uk
Chair: Bryan Gray MBE, DL
Board Members: Leslie Neville Chamberlain
   CBE, John Dunning CBE JP, Sir Martin Harris
   CBE DL, Clive Jeanes OBE, Robert Johnston,
   Cllr Dr Pauleen Lane, Cllr Richard Leese
   CBE, Alan Manning, Dennis Mendoros OBE,
   Cllr Marie Rimmer, Anil Ruia OBE,
   Brenda Smith, Dr Maureen Williams
Chief Executive: Steven Broomhead
Executive Directors: Peter Mearns (Marketing),
   Peter White (Strategy), John Burrows
   (Business Development), Geoff Parker
   (Finance), Baron Isherwood (Regeneration),
   Steve Ashcroft (Corporate Services)
Head of Public Relations: Emma Degg

ONE NORTHEAST

Stella House, Goldcrest Way, Newburn
Riverside, Newcastle Upon Tyne NE15 8NY
0191-229 6200   Fax: 0191-229 6201
E-mail:
[firstname.surname]@onenortheast.co.uk
Website: www.onenortheast.co.uk
Chairman: Dr John Bridge (Margaret Fay from
December 2003)
Deputy Chairman: Vacant
Board Members: Alistair Arkley, Tim Cantle
Jones, Barbara Dennis, Prof Christopher
Edwards, Jackie Fisher, Chey Garland,
Geoffrey Hodgson, Cllr Phillip Hughes,
Richard Maudsley, Jane Nolan, Kevin Rowan,
Christine Smith, Keith Taylor,
Cllr David Walsh
Chief Executive: Alan Clarke
Executive Directors: Brian Ham (Strategy and
External Affairs), Neil Mundy (Integration),
Mark Henderson (Operations), Malcolm Page
(Finance)

SOUTH EAST ENGLAND DEVELOPMENT AGENCY – SEEDA

Cross Lanes, Guildford, Surrey GU1 1YA
01483 484200   Fax: 01483 484247
E-mail: info@seeda.co.uk
Website: www.seeda.co.uk
Chairman: James Brathwaite CBE
Board Members: Ken Bodfish OBE,
Prof Sir Clive Booth, Elizabeth Brighouse,
Barry Camfield, Poul Christensen CBE,
Robert Douglas, Sarah Hohler, Keith House,
Janis Kong OBE, Mary McAnally, Terry
Mills, John Peel, Dr Peter Read CBE FRCP,
Ken Thornber CBE
Chief Executive: Anthony Dunnett
Executive Directors: Jeff Alexander (Business
and International), Charlotte Dixon
(Economic Inclusion and Sustainability),
Paul Hudson (Development and
Infrastructure), Marianne Neville-Rolfe CB
(Strategy and Corporate Services),
Prof John Parsonage (Learning and Skills)
Head of Communications: Debbie Catt
Press Office: 01483 484230

SOUTH WEST OF ENGLAND DEVELOPMENT AGENCY – South West RDA

Sterling House, Dix's Field, Exeter,
Devon EX1 1QA
01392 214747   Fax: 01392 214848
E-mail: enquiries@southwestrda.org.uk
Website: www.southwestrda.org.uk
Chair: Juliet Williams
Deputy Chairman: Jeremy Pope OBE
Board Members: Doris Ansari, Nicholas
Buckland, Peter Chalke, Nigel Costley, Helen
Holland, Brian Kemp, Michael Leece, Robin
Nicoll, Jonathon Porritt CBE, Judith
Reynolds, Colin Skellet, Harry Studholme,
Prof Eric Thomas
Chief Executive: Geoffrey Wilkinson
Executive Directors: Caroline Bull (Enterprise
and Innovation), Colin Molton (Operations
and Development), Suzanne Bond (Strategy
and Communications), Nick Lewis (Corporate
Services)
Head of Press and Communications: James Harper

YORKSHIRE FORWARD

2 Victoria House, Victoria Place, Leeds LS11 5AE
0113-394 9600   Fax: 0113-243 1088
E-mail:
[firstname.surname]@yorkshire-forward.com
Website: www.yorkshire-forward.com
Chairman: Sir Graham Hall (Terry Hodgkinson
from December 2003)
Deputy Chairman: Richard Gregory
Board Members: John Ashcroft, Muriel Barker,
Eileen Bosomworth, Jeanne Coburn,
Brian Greenwood, Lord Haskins,
Stephen Houghton, Paul Jagger, Julie Kenny,
Chris King, Adeeba Malik, John Napier,
Kath Pinnock
Chief Executive: Martin Havenhand
Executive Directors: Susan Johnson (Business),
Don Stewart (People), Heather Hancock
(Environment), Tom Riordan (Strategy and
Policy), Trevor Shaw (Finance)
Head of Communications: Theresa Lindsay
0113-394 9707
Senior Media Relations Officer: Keith Crane
0113-394 9710

Visit the Vacher Dod Website . . .
www.DodOnline.co.uk

NON-MINISTERIAL DEPARTMENTS

Non-Ministerial Departments are headed by office-holders, boards or Commissioners with specific statutory responsibilities

Assets Recovery Agency – ARA

c/o PO Box 39992, London EC4M 7XQ
Tel: 020 7025 5700
Website: www.assetsrecovery.gov.uk

The Assets Recovery Agency was set up under the Proceeds of Crime Act 2002 and became operational in February 2003. The Agency uses powers to recover assets through criminal confiscation, civil recovery and taxation so as to reduce crime. The Agency also supports law enforcement agencies engaged in asset recovery, through the provision of advice and accredited training.

Director: Jane Earl

Charity Commission

Harmsworth House, 13-15 Bouverie Street, London EC4Y 8DP
Tel: 0870 333 0123   Fax: 020 7674 2310
E-mails:
feedback@charitycommission.gsi.gov.uk
[firstname.surname]@
charitycommission.gsi.gov.uk
Website: www.charitycommission.gov.uk

Liverpool Office:
2nd Floor, 20 Kings Parade, Queens Dock, Liverpool L3 4DQ
0870 333 0123 Fax 0151-703 1555

Taunton Office:
Woodfield House, Tangier, Taunton, Somerset TA1 4BL
0870 333 0123 Fax 01823 345003

Responsible for the registration and regulation of registered charities in England and Wales.

Chief Commissioners: John Stoker
Legal Commissioner: Vacant
Non-Executive Commissioners: David Taylor,
    David Unwin QC, Geraldine Peacock CBE
Director of Operations: Simon Gillespie
Director of Resources: Bill Richardson
Director of Policy and Strategy: Rosie Chapman
Director of Legal Services: Kenneth Dibble
Head of Communications (London):
    Antony Robbins
Head of Regulatory Framework: Ceinwen Thorne
Head of Financial Regulation: Jon Thorne
*Head of Compliance and Enforcement
    (Taunton):* Paul Fredericks
Head Customer Service (Taunton): Mary Cridge

Commissioners for the Reduction of the National Debt – CRND

UK Debt Management Office, Eastcheap Court, 11 Philpot Lane, London EC3M 8UD
Tel: 020 7862 6500   Fax: 020 7862 6509
E-mail: crnd@dmo.gsi.gov.uk
Websites: www.crnd.gov.uk   www.dmo.gov.uk

The Commissioners retain some of their orginal responsibilities for the reduction of the National Debt but their principal function is managing the investment portfolios of certain public funds (including the National Insurance Fund Investment Accounts, the National Lottery Distribution Fund and the Court Funds Investment Account).

Chief Executive: Robert Stheeman
*Deputy Chief Executive and Comptroller-
    General to CRND:* Jo Whelan
Assistant Comptroller to CRND: Alex Lawrie
Head of Operations and Resources: Jim Juffs
See Public Works Loan Board and UK Debt Management Office

Crown Estate

16 Carlton House Terrace, London SW1Y 5AH
Tel: 020 7210 4377   Fax: 020 7930 8187
E-mail: pr@crownestate.co.uk
Website: www.crownestate.co.uk

The Crown Estate is a landed estate including over 120,000 hectares (300,000 acres) of agricultural land in England, Scotland and Wales, substantial blocks of urban property and almost half the foreshore, together with the sea bed out to the twelve mile territorial limit. The Crown Estate is part of the hereditary possessions of the Sovereign "in right of the Crown", managed under the provisions of The Crown Estate Act 1961 by The Crown Estate Commissioners who have a duty to maintain and enhance the capital value of The Crown Estate and the income obtained from it. The net surplus is paid to the Exchequer and amounted to £163.3 million for the year ending 31 March 2002.

Chairman and First Commissioner:
    Ian Grant CBE
Chief Executive and Second Commissioner:
    Roger Bright
Director of Urban Estates: Tony Bickmore

Divisional Heads:
Communications: Irene Belcher
Corporate Planning and Human Resources:
    Martin Gravestock
Finance and Information Systems: John Lelliott
Valuation: Roland Spence
Internal Audit: John Ford
Legal Services, Legal Adviser and Head of Legal Services: David Harris
Marine Estates: Frank Parrish
Rural Estates: Chris Bourchier
Central London Estate: Elspeth Miller
Regent Street Strategy and Development:
    David Shaw
Regent Street Estate Development:
    Alan Meakin
Regional Estates: Mal Dillon
Residential Estate: Giles Clarke
Special Projects: Liam Colgan
Windsor Estate: Deputy Ranger: Philip Everett

Crown Prosecution Service – CPS
Headquarters, 50 Ludgate Hill,
London EC4M 7EX
Tel: 020 7796 8000   Fax: 020 7796 8650
E-mails: enquiries@cps.gov.uk
[firstname.surname]@cps.gsi.gov.uk
Website: www.cps.gov.uk

Responsible for the independent review and conduct of criminal proceedings instituted by police forces in England and Wales (with the exception of cases conducted by the Serious Fraud Office and certain minor offences).

Director of Public Prosecutions:
    Sir David Calvert-Smith, QC
Chief Executive: Richard Foster
Directors
Information Technology: Claire Hamson
Casework: Chris Newell
Finance: John Graham
Human Resources: Angela O'Connor
Policy: Garry Patten
Business Development: Peter Lewis
Head of Communications: Sue Cunningham
Head of Management Audit Services:
    Bob Capstick
Head of Equality and Diversity Unit:
    Dr Rohan Collier

HM Customs and Excise – C&E
New King's Beam House, 22 Upper Ground,
London SE1 9PJ
Tel: 020 7620 1313   Fax: 020 7865 5048
E-mail: [firstname.surname@hmce.gsi.gov.uk
Website: www.hmce.gov.uk

Collects and administers taxes and duties mainly on consumer expenditure (indirect taxation), including Value Added Tax (VAT), excise duties on hydrocarbon oils, tobacco products, alcoholic drinks, betting and gaming and Insurance Premium Tax and Air Passenger Duty and the Landfill Tax. It also collects customs duties and agricultural levies on behalf of the EU.

Customs' other main responsibility is the enforcement of import prohibitions and restrictions on drugs, firearms, indecent material and endangered species.

Minister responsible:
Economic Secretary: John Healey MP

Acting Chairman: Mike Eland
Private Secretary: Kerrie Spendiff
Commissioners of the Board:
Director-General, Business Services and Taxes:
    Vacant
Director-General, Law Enforcement:
    Terry Byrne CB
Directors
Regional Business Services:
    Ray McAfee CBE
Logistics and Finance: Michael Hanson
Intelligence: Mike Norgrove
The Solicitor: David Pickup CB
Information and e-Services:
    David Garlick
Communications – Press and Publicity:
    Peter Rose

Regional Business Services
Regional Heads:
South England – Southampton
Hugh Burnard 023 8079 7162
    Fax: 023 8079 7018
Central England – Birmingham
Doug Tweddle 0121-697 4234
    Fax: 0121-697 4240
North England – Leeds
Arthur Durrant 0113-389 4397
    Fax: 0113-389 4482
London
Mike Hill 020 8929 2800
Scotland – Edinburgh
Ian Mackay 0131-469 7275
    Fax: 0131-469 7340
Northern Ireland – Belfast
Jim McLean 028 9056 2601
    Fax: 028 9056 2970
Wales – Cardiff
Kathy Barnes 029 2038 6030
    Fax: 029 2038 6033

Office of Fair Trading – OFT

Fleetbank House, 2–6 Salisbury Square,
London EC4Y 8JX
Tel: 020 7211 8000   Fax: 020 7211 8800
E-mails: enquiries@oft.gov.uk
[firstname.surname]@oft.gov.uk
Website: www.oft.gov.uk

To promote and safeguard the economic interests of consumers. It administers a wide range of competition and consumer protection legislation, and the Board has a duty to keep under review the market place for goods and services in the UK with a view to identifying practices or behaviour that may adversely affect consumers' interests and either taking direct remedial action (through, for example, references to the Competition Commission or revocation of Consumer Credit licences) or making recommendations to Ministers for legislative change. The Board also has a statutory duty to publish advice and information for consumers.

- has responsibility to keep all commercial activities under review, to identify behaviour that adversely affects the consumer or damages competition;
- has the power to take regulatory enforcement action to protect the interests of consumers;
- has the power among other things, to make references to the Competition Commission and impose penalties on companies.

Chairman: Prof John Vickers
Executive Director: Penny Boys
Directors:
Consumer Regulation Enforcement:
    Caroline Banks
Competition Enforcement: Chris Mayock
Legal: Pat Edwards
Markets and Policy Initiatives: Jonathan May
Communications: Mike Ricketts
Resources and Services: David Fisher

Food Standards Agency

Aviation House, 125 Kingsway, Holborn,
London WC2B 6NH
Tel: 020 7276 8000   Fax: 020 7276 8627
E-mail: helpline@foodstandards.gsi.gov.uk
Website: www.food.gov.uk

Responsible for all aspects of food safety and standards throughout the UK.

Chairman: Prof Sir John Krebs
Acting Deputy Chair: Ann Hemingway
Chief Executive: Dr Jon Bell
Deputy Chief Executive: Pat Stewart

Executive Agency: Meat Hygiene Service

Forestry Commission

Silvan House, 231 Corstorphine Road,
Edinburgh EH12 7AT
Tel: 0131-334 0303   Fax: 0131-334 3047
GTN: 7135 0303
E-mails: enquiries@forestry.gsi.gov.uk
[firstname.surname]@forestry.gsi.gov.uk
Website: www.forestry.gov.uk

The Forestry Commission is the Government Department responsible for forestry policy in Great Britain. It reports directly to forestry Ministers to whom it is responsible for advice on forestry policy and for the implementation of that policy. It manages nearly 1 million hectares of public forests throughout Great Britain. The Secretary of State for Environment, Food and Rural Affairs has responsibility for forestry in England, Scottish Ministers have responsibility for forestry in Scotland, and the National Assembly for Wales has responsibility for forestry in Wales. For matters affecting forestry in Britain as a whole, all three have equal responsibility but the Secretary of State for Environment, Food and Rural Affairs takes the lead.

The mission of the Forestry Commission is to protect and expand Britain's forests and woodlands and increase their value to society and the environment.

Chairman: Rt Hon Lord Clark of Windermere
Director-General and Deputy Chairman:
    David Bills CBE
Board of Commissioners: David Bills CBE,
    Dr Bob McIntosh, Simon Hewitt
Non-Executive Commissioners: Rt Hon Lord
    Clark of Windermere, Anthony Bosanquet,
    Tony Cooper, Dr Victoria Edwards, Martin
    Gale, John James OBE, Andrew Raven,
    Gareth Wardell CBE
Secretary to the Commissioners: Frank Strang
Director-General's Office
Head of Director-General's Office: Frank Strang
Commissioners's Branch: Stephen Bennett
Communications: Colin Morton
Head of Internal Audit: Liz Holmes
Director of Personnel Development:
    Jim Anderson
Head of Business Services: Alan Mitchell
Head of Forestry Group: Tim Rollinson
Head of Country Services: Roger Herbert
Country Directors
England: Paul Hill-Tout
E-mail: paul.hill-tout@forestry.gsi.gov.uk
Great Eastern House, Tenison Road,
    Cambridge CB1 2DU
01223 314546 Fax: 01223 460699

Scotland (Edinburgh): Dr Bob McIntosh
0113-334 0303
Wales: Simon Hewitt
Victoria Terrace, Aberystwyth,
Ceredigion SY23 2DQ
01970 625866 Fax: 01970 626177

Executive Agencies: Forest Enterprise, Forest Research

Inland Revenue – IR

Somerset House, Strand, London WC2R 1LB
Tel: 020 7438 6622
E-mail: [firstname.surname]@ir.gsi.gov.uk
Website: www.inlandrevenue.gov.uk

Collects income tax, corporation tax, capital gains tax, stamp duty, inheritance tax, petroleum revenue, National Insurance Contributions and administers Child Benefit, Working Tax Credits, Children's Tax Credits, Disabled Person's Tax Credits, collection of Student Loans and enforces compliance with National Minimum Wage. Advises the Chancellor of the Exchequer on tax policy. The Department's Valuation Office is an Executive Agency responsible for valuing property for tax purposes.

Minister responsible:
Paymaster General:
   Rt Hon Dawn Primarolo MP

The Board
Chairman: Sir Nicholas Montagu KCB
Deputy Chairmen: Ann Chant CB,
   Dave Hartnett CB
Director-General Corporate Services:
   Helen Ghosh
Chief Executive Valuation Office Agency (VOA):
   Michael Johns CB
Solicitor of Inland Revenue: Philip Ridd
Head Office Directors
Analysis and Research: Prof David Ulph
Business Services: John Yard CBE
Business Tax: Mary Hay
Capital and Savings: Gabs Makhlouf
Central Finance: John Gant CB
Cross Cutting Policy: John Middleton
Human Resources: Stephen Banyard
Information Resources: Gwenda Sippings
International: Vacant
Marketing and Communications: Ian Schoolar
National Services: Steve Heminsley
Revenue Policy: People and Planning:
   Neil Munro CBE
Personal Tax: Tony Orhnial
Quality Public Services Team: Steve Johnson
Receivable Management Service: Gordon Smith

Local Services: Marjorie Williams
Strategy and Planning: Simon Norris
Study of Personal Tax: Brian Mace
Tax Law Rewrite: Robin Martin
Revenue Policy: Strategy and Co-ordination:
   Peter Michael CBE

Large Business Office
22 Kingsway, London, WC2B 6NR
Director: Stephen Jones

Special Compliance Office
Angel Court, 199 Borough High Street,
London SE1 1HZ
020 7234 3840 Fax: 020 7234 3730
Director: John Middleton

Tax Credit Office
Inland Revenue, 2nd Floor West, St Mary's House, St Mary's Street, Preston PR1 4AT
01772 235557 Fax: 01772 235553
Director: Jim Harra

NICO – National Insurance Contribution Office
Benton Park View, Longbenton,
Newcastle upon Tyne NE98 1ZZ
0191-225 5778 Fax: 0191-225 9753
Director: Steve McGrath

Regional Directors
Northern England: Richard Cooke
Concept House, 5 Young Street,
Sheffield S1 4LF
0114-296 9779 Fax: 0114-296 9669

Central England: Ed McKeegan
Churchgate, New Road, Peterborough PE1 1TD
01733 754321 Fax: 01733 755003

Southern England: Tony Sleeman
Lynx House, 1 Northern Road, Cosham,
Portsmouth PO6 3AY

London: Geoff Lunn
New Court, 48 Carey Street, London WC2A 2JE
020 7324 1229 Fax: 020 7324 1076

Scotland: David Hinstridge
Clarendon House, 114-116 George Street,
Edinburgh EH2 4LH
0131 473 4100 Fax: 0131-473 9118

Wales: Keith Cartwright
Phase II Building, Tŷ Glas, Llanishen,
Cardiff CF14 5TS
029 2032 6600 Fax: 029 2075 5730

Northern Ireland: Naomi Ferguson
Dorchester House, 52-58 Great Victoria Street,
Belfast BT2 7QE
028 9050 5050 Fax: 028 9050 5058

Executive Agency: Valuation Office

Public Works Loan Board – PWLB

UK Debt Management Office, Eastcheap Court,
11 Philpot Lane, London EC3M 8UD
Tel: 020 7862 6610   Fax: 020 7862 6509
E-mail: pwlb@dmo.gsi.gov.uk
Websites: www.pwlb.gov.uk
www.dmo.gov.uk

The Public Works Loan Board lends to local
authorities for capital purposes.

Chairman of PWLB: Anthony Loehnis CMG
Deputy Chairman of PWLB: John Parkes CBE
Secretary to PWLB: Hamish Watson
Assistant Secretary to PWLB: Mark Frankel

See Commissioners for the Reduction of the
National Debt and UK Debt Management Office

Serious Fraud Office – SFO

Elm House, 10-16 Elm Street,
London WC1X 0BJ
Tel: 020 7239 7272   Fax: 020 7837 1689
E-mails: public.enquiries@sfo.gsi.gov.uk
[firstname.surname]@sfo.gsi.gov.uk
Website: www.sfo.gov.uk

The Serious Fraud Office is responsible in
England, Wales and Northern Ireland for the
investigation and prosecution of cases involving
serious and complex fraud.

Director: Robert Wardle
Assistant Directors: Roddy Gillanders,
   Tricia Howse, Peter Kiernan, Philip Lewis,
   Stephen Low
Head of Corporate Services: Dave Partridge
Non-Executive Director: Myra Kinghorn

For the organisations below – see Regulators

**Ofgem – Office of Gas and Electricity
Markets**

**OFREG – Office of the Regulation of
Electricity and Gas**

Ofsted – Office for Standards in Education

Oftel – Office of Telecommunications

Ofwat – Office of Water Services

**ORR – Office of the Rail and International
Rail Regulator**

Postcomm – The Postal Services Commission

DodOnline

An Electronic Directory without rival ...

Civil Servants' biographies and photographs available with daily updates
via the internet

For a *free* trial, call Yasmin Mirza, Aby Farsoun or Michael Mand on 020 7630 7643

EXECUTIVE AGENCIES

ABRO

Monxton Road, Andover, Hampshire SP11 8HT
Tel: 01264 383295   Fax: 01264 383200
Website: www.abro.mod.uk/

Provides an equipment repair and refurbishment service for the armed services.

Chief Executive: Mike Hayle
Finance Director: Stuart Ash
Commercial Director: Geoff Thompson
Sales and Marketing Director:
   Graeme Rumbol
Operations Director: David Mather
Department: Ministry of Defence
Launched: 1/4/93
Trading Fund Status: 1/4/2002

Appeals Service – AS

5th Floor, Fox Court, 14 Grays Inn Road,
London WC1X 8HN
Tel: 020 7712 2600   Fax: 020 7712 2650
Website: www. appeals-service.gov.uk

Chief Executive: Vacant
Finance Director: Alex Maddocks
National Operational Director: Norman Egan
Department: Department for Work and
   Pensions
Launched: 3/4/00

Armed Forces Personnel Administration Agency – AFPAA

Building 182, RAF Innsworth,
Gloucester GL3 1HW
Tel: 01452 712612 ext 7081
Fax: 01452 510874

To support the Armed Forces through the accurate payment of military personnel and the provision of quality personnel information services on a harmonised basis.

Acting Chief Executive:
   Commodore Trevor Spires RN
Director Strategy, Requirements and
   Programmes: Air Commodore Brian Jerstice
Agency Secretary: Peter Northen
Director Operations:
   Group Captain Iain Harvey
Joint Personnel Administration:
   Air Commodore David Tonks
Department: Ministry of Defence
Launched: 1/4/97

Army Personnel Centre – APC

Kentigern House, 65 Brown Street,
Glasgow G2 8EX
Tel: 0141-224 2832   Fax: 0141-224 3555
Website: www.army.mod.uk/servingsoldier

Task is to man the army and manage the careers of army personnel.

Military Secretary/Chief Executive:
   Major General Peter Grant Peterkin CB OBE
Deputy Military Secretary:
   Brigadier Tony Faith OBE
Deputy Chief Executive/Secretary: Greg Miller
Department: Ministry of Defence
Launched: 2/12/96

Army Training and Recruiting Agency – ATRA

Trenchard Lines, Upavon, Pewsey,
Wiltshire SN9 6BE
Tel: 01980 618009   Fax: 01980 615305
E-mail: hqatra@gtnet.gov.uk
Website: www.atra.mod.uk

Provides manpower trained in the individual skills required to sustain the army's military effectiveness.

Chief Executive:
   Major General David Leakey CBE
Deputy Chief Executive: David Dick
Chief of Staff: Colonel David Eccles OBE
Head of Strategy: Colonel Paul Lane
Head of Operations and Plans:
   Colonel John Ibbotson
Head of Resources, Programmes and Finance:
   Rory Riordon
Integrated Project Team Leader: Michael Horrell
Head of Management Information Systems:
   Colonel Tim Wilton MBE
Head of Personnel: Phil Allen
Head of Commercial Branch ATRA/AG:
   Jeremy Richards
Department: Ministry of Defence
Launched: 1/4/97

British Forces Post Office – BFPO

Inglis Barracks, Mill Hill, London NW7 1PX
Tel: 020 8818 6315   Fax: 020 8818 6309
E-mail: bfpo@compuserve.com
Website: www.bfpo.org
Customer care unit: 08457 697978

Provides postal and courier services.

Chief Executive: Brigadier Peter Maggs CBE
Deputy Chief Executive/Head of Policy and
　Strategy: Colonel Don Kent
Head of Postal and Courier
　Services/Operations: Colonel Charles Hillyer
Head of Finance and Corporate Affairs:
　Andrew Carine
Department: Ministry of Defence
Launched: 1/7/92 as DPCSA
Re-launched: 1/7/99 as BFPO

Central Science Laboratory – CSL
Sand Hutton, York YO41 1LZ
Tel: 01904 462000　Fax: 01904 462111
E-mails: science@csl.gov.uk
[firstname.surname]@csl.gov.uk
Website: www.csl.gov.uk

Provides a wide range of scientific services including:
– plant health
– the authenticity, chemical and microbiological safety and nutritional value of the food supply
– pesticide safety, including monitoring of residues in food
– veterinary drug residues
– proficiency testing schemes
– the control of pests and diseases of growing and stored crops
– the impact of food production on the environment and the consumer
– alternative crops and biotechnology
– animal health and welfare, and
– conservation and wildlife management.

Chief Executive: Prof Michael Roberts
Science Director (Agriculture and
　Environment): Prof Tony Hardy
Science Director (Food): Prof John Gilbert
Commercial Director: Dr Robert Bolton
Finance and Procurement Director: Richard Shaw
Corporate Services Director: Dr Helen Crews
Department: Department for Environment,
　Food and Rural Affairs
Launched: 1/4/92

Centre for Environment, Fisheries and Aquaculture Science – CEFAS
Lowestoft Laboratory, Pakefield Road,
Lowestoft, Suffolk NR33 0HT
Tel: 01502 562244　Fax: 01502 513865
E-mail: marketing@cefas.co.uk
Website: www.cefas.co.uk

Provides scientific research, assessment and advice in fisheries management, environmental protection, and fish health, hygiene and aquaculture.

Chief Executive: Dr Peter Greig-Smith
Deputy to the Chief Executive and Chief
　Fisheries Science Adviser to DEFRA:
　Dr Joe W Horwood
Department: Department for Environment,
　Food and Rural Affairs
Launched: 1/4/97

Child Support Agency – CSA
Room BP6201, Longbenton,
Newcastle upon Tyne NE98 1YX
Tel: 0191-225 7743
Fax: 0191-225 3461
E-mails:
csa-chief-execs-office@dwp.gsi.gov.uk
[firstname.surname]@dwp.gsi.gov.uk
Website: www.gov.dwp.uk/csa

Assesses, collects and, where necessary, enforces child support maintenance.

Chief Executive: Doug Smith
Deputy Chief Executive: Mike Isaac
Child Support Reform Programme Director:
　Vince Gaskell
Director of Finance: Jim Edgar
Director of Customer Relations:
　Elaine Fox
Department: Department for Work and
　Pensions
Launched: 5/4/93

COI Communications
Hercules Road, London SE1 7DU
Tel: 020 7928 2345　Fax: 020 7928 5037
E-mail:
[firstname.surname]@coi.gsi.gov.uk
Website: www.coi.gov.uk

Provides consultancy, procurement and project management services to central government for marketing and publicity. The Chief Executive is the Government's chief adviser on marketing communications.

Chief Executive: Alan Bishop
Deputy Chief Executive and Marketing
　Communications Director: Peter Buchanan
Directors
　Finance: Graham Beasant
　Films, Radio Events: Sally Whetton
　Client Services, Publications and Digital
　Media: Ian Hamilton
　Human Resources: Emma Lochhead
Department: Cabinet Office
Launched: 5/4/90

Companies House

Crown Way, Cardiff CF14 3UZ
Tel: 0870 3333636   Fax: 029 2038 0900
E-mail: enquiries@companieshouse.gov.uk
Website: www.companieshouse.gov.uk

Registers companies and collects statutory documents and returns and makes information available to the public.

*Chief Executive and Registrar of Companies for
England and Wales:* Claire Clancy
Director of Operations: Jeanne Spinks
Director of Information Technology:
Mark Pacey
Director of Finance: Jack Mansfield
Director of Policy and Planning:
Helen Thewlis

London Information Centre
Companies House
21 Bloomsbury Street, London WC1B 3XD
0870 3333636 Fax 029 2038 0900

Companies House
37 Castle Terrace, Edinburgh EH1 2EB
0131-535 5855 Fax 0131-535 5879
Registrar of Companies for Scotland:
Jim Henderson

**Department: Department of Trade and
Industry**
Launched: 3/10/88

Compensation Agency

Royston House, 34 Upper Queen Street,
Belfast BT1 6FD
Tel: 028 9024 9944   Fax: 028 9024 6956
E-mail: comp-agency@nics.gov.uk
Website: www.compensationni.gov.uk

Administers the criminal injuries and criminal damage compensation schemes and pays compensation under the Terrorism Act 2000.

Chief Executive: Anne McCleary
Head of Operations: Frank Branningan
Department: Northern Ireland Office
Launched: 1/4/92

Court Service

Southside, 105 Victoria Street,
London SW1E 6QT
Tel: 020 7210 2266   Fax: 020 7210 1797
E-mail: cust.ser.cs@gtnet.gov.uk
Website: www.courtservice.gov.uk

Provides administrative support to the Court of Appeal, High Court, Crown Court, County courts and some tribunals in England and Wales.

Chief Executive: Peter Handcock
Director of Field Services: Kevin Pogson
**Department: Department for Constitutional
Affairs**
Launched: 3/4/95

Criminal Records Bureau – CRB

PO Box 110, Liverpool L3 6ZZ
Information Line: 0870 90 90 811
Websites: www.crb.gov.uk
www.disclosure.gov.uk

The Criminal Records Bureau (CRB) has been set up to help organisations make safer recruitment decisions. Providing wider access to criminal record information the CRB helps employers in the public, private and voluntary sectors identify candidates who may be unsuitable for certain work, especially that involving contact with children and other vulnerable members of society. It is a sister organisation to the UK Passport Service and, although it functions as a separate business, together they fall within the Passport and Records Agency (PRA).

Chief Executive: Bernard Herdan*
Director: John O'Brien
Resource Director: Edward James
Development Director: Julian Trill
*Globe House, London
Department: Home Office
Launched: 1/3/02

Defence Analytical Services Agency –
DASA

Ministry of Defence, St Georges Court,
2-12 Bloomsbury Way, London WC1A 2SH
Tel: 020 7305 2192   Fax: 020 7305 2196
E-mail: info@dasa.mod.uk
Website: www.dasa.mod.uk

Publishes national statistics on defence (available on website). Provides statistics on a wide range of defence activity for use within MoD, and forecasting, advice and research to support the Department's policy, financial, and personnel planning.

Chief Executive: Colin Youngson
Director (Personnel Statistics and Planning):
Janet Dougharty
Director (Information Services and Logistics):
Glen Watson
Head of Corporate Business Management:
Jim Blackburn
Department: Ministry of Defence
Launched: 1/7/92

Defence Aviation Repair Agency – DARA

St Athan, Barry, Vale of Glamorgan CF62 4WA
Tel: 01446 798439   Fax: 01446 798892
Website: www.dara.mod.uk

DARA provides deep repair, maintenance, modification and overhaul of aircraft and aerosystems for the UK armed forces and commercial customers.

The agency also provides aircraft storage services, marine gas turbine engine repair and overhaul, and complementary support services for the logistics supply chain and UK armed forces operations.

Chief Executive: Steve Hill, OBE
Commercial Director and Deputy Chief Executive: Ron Jones
Finance Director: Andy Akerman
Company Secretary: Bernard Galton
Chief Operating Officer: John Reilly
Department: Ministry of Defence
Launched: 1/4/99

Defence Bills Agency – DBA

Ministry of Defence, Mersey House, Drury Lane, Liverpool L2 7PX
Tel: 0151-242 2225   Fax: 0151-242 2470
E-mail: heocorp@dba.mod.uk
Website: www.defencebills.gov.uk

Provides bill payment, debt collection and associated management information services for MoD.

Chief Executive: Norman Swanney
Department: Ministry of Defence
Launched: 1/1/96

Defence Communication Services Agency – DCSA

Basil Hill Site, Corsham, Wiltshire SN13 9NR
Tel: 01225 814785   Fax: 01225 814966
Website: www.mod.uk/dlo/dcsa

Manages world-wide communications and delivery of information systems solutions to Defence.

Chief Executive:
    Rear Admiral Rees G J Ward CB
Director Operations:
    Air Commodore Andy Warnes
Director Resources: Nigel Jarvis
Department: Ministry of Defence
Launched: 1/4/98
Joined Defence Logistics Organisation 1/4/00

Defence Dental Agency – DDA

Ministry of Defence, RAF Halton, Aylesbury, Buckinghamshire HP22 5PG
Tel: 01296 623535 ext 6103
Fax 01296 624497
E-mail: dda@hqdda.demon.co.uk

Provides dental treatment to service personnel, entitled dependants and other entitled civilians.

Chief Executive: Major General John Gamon
Director Clinical Services (Director Naval Dental Services): Air Commodore John Reid
Director Resources (Director Army Dental Services): Brigadier Stuart Poole
Director Policy and Plans and Chief of Staff (Director Naval Dental Services): Surgeon Commodore Geoff Myers
Head of Finance and Secretariat: Brian Mathiew
Department: Ministry of Defence
Launched: 1/3/96

Defence Estates – DE

Blakemore Drive, Sutton Coldfield, West Midlands B75 7RL
Tel: 0121-311 2140   Fax: 0121-311 2100
E-mails: de_hq@dial.pipex.com
[firstname.surname]@de.mod.uk
Website: www.defence-estates.mod.uk

Chief Executive:
    Vice-Admiral Peter A Dunt
Operations Director: David Olney
Finance Director: Mike Martindale
Commercial Director: Mike Pengelly
Personnel Director: Elaine Northen
Estates Director: Allan Baillie
Projects and Quality Director: Howard Lawrence
Programming Director: Nick Kurth
Agency Secretary: Hugh Kernohan
Department: Ministry of Defence
Launched as Defence Estate Organisation: 18/3/97
Re-launched as Defence Estates: 29/3/99

Defence Geographic and Imagery Intelligence Agency – DGIA

Watson Building, Elmwood Avenue, Feltham, Middlesex TW13 7AH
Tel: 020 8818 2422   Fax: 020 8818 2246

Chief Executive: Air Commodore Martin Hallam
Director Plans and Systems and Deputy Chief Executive: Colonel Jim Mitchell
Commander Geographic Engineer Group: Colonel Angus Cross

Officer Commanding Joint Air Reconnaissance Intelligence Centre:
Group Captain David Walker
Director Defence Geographic Centre:
Stuart Haynes
Finance Director: Lucille Hurley
Director International: Pete Jones MBE
Non-Executive Director: Richard Garner
Department: Ministry of Defence
Launched: 1/04/00

Defence Housing Executive – DHE

St Christopher House, Southwark Street,
London SE1 0TD
Tel: 020 7305 2035   Fax: 020 7305 3041

Provides a housing service to Service families across mainland UK, including allocation, maintenance and construction.

Chief Executive: John Wilson
Director Housing:
Brigadier Chrisotpher Lunn CBE
Director Plans, Programmes and Services Liaison: Air Commodore Kevin Pellatt
Director Finance and Secretariat:
Roger Mansell
Department: Ministry of Defence
Launched: 1/4/99

Defence Intelligence and Security Centre – DISC

Chicksands, Shefford, Bedfordshire SG17 5PR
Tel: 01462 752181   Fax: 01462 752291
E-mail: adjtdiscsu-capt@disc.mod.uk

To train authorised personnel in the intelligence, security and information support disciplines while maintaining an operational capability; to provide advice on the formulation of concepts, policy and doctrine across the spectrum of intelligence and security issues.

Chief Executive: Brigadier Peter Everson OBE
Chief of Staff/Deputy Chief Executive:
Group Captain John Gimblett
Department: Ministry of Defence
Launched: 1/10/96

Defence Medical Education and Training Agency – DMETA

Mackenzie Block, Fort Blockhouse, Gosport,
Hampshire PO12 2AB
Tel: 023 9276 5284   Fax: 023 9276 5501

Educates and trains defence medical service personnel to meet the operational requirements of the Commanders in Chief.

Chief Executive:
Rear Admiral Peter Kidner CEng FRAeS
Ministry of Defence
Launched: 1/4/03

Defence Procurement Agency – DPA

Abbey Wood, Bristol BS34 8JH
Tel: 0117-913 0000   Fax: 0117-913 0900
Website: www.mod.uk/dpa

Procures new equipment for the Armed Forces in response to approved requirements and provides other procurement related services to its customers in and beyond the Ministry of Defence.

Chief of Defence Procurement and Chief Executive: Sir Peter Spencer KCB ADC
Deputy Chief Executive: David Gould

Executive Directors
Executive Director 1: Ian Fauset CB
Executive Director 2:
Major General Peter Gilchrist
Executive Director 3:
Air Vice Marshal D N Williams
Executive Director 4:
Rear Admiral Nigel Guild
Executive Director 5: Stan Porter
Executive Director 6: David Noble
Department: Ministry of Defence
Launched: 1/4/99

Defence Science and Technology Laboratory – dstl

Ively Road, Farnborough,
Hampshire GU14 0LX
Tel: 01252 455000   Fax: 01252 455464
E-mail: centralenquiries@dstl.gov.uk
Website: www.dstl.gov.uk

Provides defence research and specialist technical services to the Ministry of Defence.

Dstl Main Board:
Chief Executive: Martin Earwicker
Deputy Chief Executive and Director Programmes and Operations: Nick Helbren
Science Director: Richard Scott
Technology Director: Mike Jenden
Systems Director: Peter Starkey
Human Resources and Communications Director: Dick Eade
Technical Director: Andrew Baird
Finance Director: Mark Hone
Non-Executive Directors:
Major General Peter Gilchrist, Roger Platt
Department: Ministry of Defence

Defence Storage and Distribution Agency – DSDA

Ploughley Road, Lower Arncott, Bicester,
Oxfordshire OX25 2LD
Tel: 01869 256804   Fax: 01869 256860
E-mail: css@dsda.org.uk
Website: www.dsda.org.uk

Store, maintains and distributes stock to the three armed services, other government departments, MoD administrative and training units and other authorities including NATO allies, Commonwealth and foreign governments, defence contractors and other agencies.

Chief Executive: Peter Foxton, CBE
Director Business Management: Paul Clasper
Director Plans: Group Captain Bill Mahon
Director Operations:
    Colonel Philip Naylor, OBE
Department: Ministry of Defence
Launched: 1/4/99

Defence Transport and Movements Agency – DTMA

Headquarters Defence Logistics Organisation (Andover), Monxton Road, Andover,
Hampshire SP11 8HT
Tel: 01264 383766   Fax: 01264 382881

Provides defence and other authorised users with agreed transport and movements services to meet their world-wide requirements in peace, crisis and war.

Chief Executive: Brigadier Chris M Stein CBE
Department: Ministry of Defence
Launched: 1/4/99

Defence Vetting Agency – DVA

Imphal Barracks, Fulford Road, York YO10 4AS
Tel: 01904 662444   Fax: 01904 665820
Help Desks: 01904 662644/662541
E-mail: ce@dva.mod.uk
Website: www.dva.mod.uk

Grants and maintains security clearances for armed forces personnel, MoD staff, defence industry employees and undertakes investigation work for other government departments.

Chief Executive: Michael Wilson
Deputy Chief Executive and Head of Corporate Services: Clive Hodgeon
Head of Primary Clearance Division:
    Michael Salkeld
Head of Developed Clearance Division:
    Mark Wraight
Head of Field Investigation Force: Vacant
Department: Ministry of Defence
Launched: 1/4/97

Disposal Services Agency – DSA

St George's Court, 2-12 Bloomsbury Way,
London WC1A 2SH
Tel/Fax: 020 7305 3172
E-mail: disposalservices@dial.pipex.com
Website: www.disposalservices.agency.mod.uk

Sells surplus MoD equipment and stockholdings and surplus equipment on behalf of the public sector as a whole.

Chief Executive: Sym Taylor, CBE
Deputy Chief Executive and Director Customer Services: Colin MacPhee
Department: Ministry of Defence
Relaunched: 1/12/00

Driver and Vehicle Licensing Agency – DVLA

Longview Road, Morriston, Swansea SA6 7JL
Tel: 01792 782341   Fax: 01792 782793
E-mail: press.dvla@gtnet.gov.uk
Website: www.dvla.gov.uk

Principal responsibilities are the registration and licensing of drivers in Great Britain and the registration and licensing of vehicles, together with the collection and enforcement of vehicle excise duty in the UK.

Chief Executive: Clive Bennett
Director of Central Operations: Richard Ley
Director of External and Corporate Services:
    Trevor Horton
Director of Finance: Ieuan Griffiths
Director of Human Resources: Avril Beynon
Director of Local Operations: David Hancock
Director of Development: Graham Pritchard
Director of Service Excellence: Tony Connell
Department: Department for Transport
Launched: 2/4/90

Driving Standards Agency – DSA

Stanley House, 56 Talbot Street,
Nottingham NG1 5GU
Tel: 0115-901 2500   Fax: 0115-901 2940
E-mail: customer.services@dsa.gsi.gov.uk
Website: www.dsa.gov.uk

Driver testing for cars, motorcycles, lorries and buses and supervision of car and lorry driving instructors and approved training bodies for motorcyclists in Great Britain.

Chief Executive: Gary Austin
Finance Director: Kathy Gillatt
Operations Director: Brian Gilhooley
IT Director: Gordon Court
Chief Driving Examiner: Robin Cummins

Commercial Director: Christine Morris
Registrar of Approved Driving Instructors:
 Bob Jarvis
Policy Director: Paul Butler
Department: Department for Transport
Launched: 2/4/90

Duke of York's Royal Military School – DYRMS

Dover, Kent CT15 5EQ
Tel: 01304 245024   Fax: 01304 245019
E-mail: headmaster@doyrms.com

Provides boarding school secondary education for the children of serving and retired service personnel.

Headmaster and Chief Executive:
 John Cummings
Deputy Headmasters: Alan Bisby, Terry Porter
Director of Studies: John English
Bursar: Lieutenant Colonel Roger Say
Department: Ministry of Defence
Launched: 1/4/92

Employment Tribunals Service – ETS

Head Office: 7th Floor, 19-29 Woburn Place,
London WC1H 0LU
Tel: 0845 7959 775   Fax: 020 7273 8670
Websites: www.ets.gov.uk
www.employmentappeals.gov.uk

Provides administrative support to the Employment Tribunals and to the Employment Appeal Tribunal (EAT).

Chief Executive: Dr Roger Heathcote
Operations Directors, Employment Tribunals:
Richard Leyland (London and South East),
 Valerie Taylor (Midlands and West),
 Ken Hollingworth
(Scotland and North)
Registrar EAT: Pauline Donleavy
Director of Finance: Lorna Windmill
Director of Human Resources: Gerard Oates
*Director of Information and Communication
 Technology:* Jeremy Ilic
Director of Estates: Alastair Scott
*Head of Secretariat and Secretary of the
 Employment Tribunals (England and Wales):*
 Lynn Adams
**Department: Department of Trade and
Industry**
Launched: 1/4/97

Fire Service College – FSC

Moreton-in-Marsh, Gloucestershire GL56 0RH
Tel: 01608 650831   Fax: 01608 651788
E-mail: enquiries@fireservicecollege.ac.uk
Website: www.fireservicecollege.ac.uk

Provides a wide range of specialist fire related and management and finance training for UK fire officers. It also provides training for commerce and industry, and for students from overseas fire brigades.

Chief Executive: Robin Currie
E-mail: rcurrie@fireservicecollege.ac.uk
**Department: Office of the Deputy Prime
 Minister**
Launched: 1/4/92

Forensic Science Northern Ireland – FSNI

151 Belfast Road, Carrickfergus,
Co Antrim BT38 8PL
Tel: 028 9036 1888   Fax: 028 9036 1900
E-mail: forensic.science@fsni.gov.uk
Website: www.fsni.gov.uk

Provides scientific support in the investigation of crime and expert evidence to the courts in Northern Ireland.

Chief Executive: Dr Richard Adams
Department: Northern Ireland Office
Launched: 1/9/95

Forensic Science Service – FSS

Priory House, Gooch Street North,
Birmingham B5 6QQ
Tel: 0121-607 6800   Fax: 0121-666 7327
Website: www.forensic.gov.uk

Provides scientific support in the investigation of crime and expert evidence to the courts.

Chief Executive: Dr David Werrett
Business Development Director: Trevor Howitt
Chief Operating Officer: Mike Loveland
Chief Scientist: Dr Bob Bramley
Service Delivery Director: Peter Twitchett
Communications Director: Alan Matthews
Customer Relations Director: Phil Jones
Finance Director: Rod Anthony
Information Systems Director: Colin Bradley

Corporate Office
109 Lambeth Road, London SE1 7LP
020 7840 2952   Fax 020 7840 2950
Department: Home Office
Launched: 1/4/91

Forest Enterprise Scotland

231 Corstorphine Road, Edinburgh EH12 7AT
Tel: 0131-334 0303   Fax: 0131-314 6170
E-mail: carol.finlayson@forestry.gsi.gov.uk
Website: www.forestry.gov.uk

Manages the national forest.

Chief Executive: Dr Bob McIntosh (acting)
Mechanical Engineering Services (Stirling):
  Craig Heaney 01786 435600
  Fax 01786 435601
Heads of Divisions:
  Forest Planning: Peter Weston
  Forest Operations: Ian Forshaw
  Estate Management: Peter Ranken
  Corporate Services: Keith Gliddon
  Environment and Communications:
    Alan Stevenson
Chief Executives:
  Forest Enterprise England: Geoff Hatfield
    0117-906 6001 Fax 0117-931 2859
  Forest Enterprise Wales: Bob Farmer
    01970 612367 Fax 01970 625282
Directors:
  Forest Enterprise Scotland (North):
    Hugh Insley 01463 232811
    Fax 01463 243846
  Forest Enterprise Scotland (South):
    Mike Lofthouse 01387 272440
    Fax 01387 251491
**Department: An agency of the Forestry
Commission**
Launched: 1/4/96

Forest Research
Northern Research Station, Roslin,
Midlothian EH25 9SY
Tel: 0131-445 2176   Fax: 0131-445 5124
E-mail: research.info@forestry.gsi.gov.uk
Website: www.forestry.gov.uk/forest_research

Provides research, development, surveys and
technical services to the forest industry.

Chief Executive: Jim Lynch
Alice Holt Lodge, Wrecclesham,
Farnham, Surrey GU10 4LH
01420 22255 Fax 01420 23653
**Department: An agency of the Forestry
Commission**
Launched: 1/4/97

Government Car and Despatch Agency – GCDA
46 Ponton Road, London SW8 5AX
Tel: 020 7217 3821   Fax: 020 7217 3875
E-mail: info@gcda.gsi.gov.uk
Website: www.gcda.gov.uk

Provides secure transport and mail services to
central government.

Chief Executive: Nick Matheson
Operations Director: Jerry Doyle
Department: Cabinet Office
Launched: 1/4/97

Highways Agency
Romney House, 43 Marsham Street,
London, SW1P 3HW
Tel: Information Line: 08457 504030
Switchboard: 08459 556575
E-mails: ha_info@highways.gsi.gov.uk
[firstname.surname]@highways.gsi.gov.uk
Website: www.highways.gov.uk

Responsible for maintaining, operating and improving England's motorways and trunk roads.

Chief Executive (acting): Dr Stephen Hickey
Director, Network Strategy: Hilary Chipping
Director, Operations: David York
Director, Safety Standards and Research:
  Ginny Clarke
Director, Finance Services: Mel Quinn
Director, Human Resource Services:
  Steve Williams
Director, Procurement: Steve Rowsell
Director, Corporate: Richard Thorndike
Department: Department for Transport
Launched 1/4/94

Insolvency Service
PO Box 203, 21 Bloomsbury Street,
London WC1B 3QW
Tel: 020 7637 1110   Fax: 020 7636 4709
Website: www.insolvency.gov.uk

Administers and investigates the affairs of
bankrupts and companies in compulsory liquidation, deals with the disqualification of directors
in all corporate failures, regulates insolvency
practitioners and their professional bodies, provides banking and investment services for
bankruptcy and liquidation estates, and advises
ministers on insolvency policy issues.

The Insolvency Service also has responsibility
in Scotland for disqualifications, insolvency
practitioner regulation and certain aspects of
corporate insolvency policy.

Inspector General and Chief Executive:
  Desmond Flynn
Deputy Inspector Generals: Les Cramp,
  Graham Horne
Director Policy and Enterprise Issues:
  Alistair Kennard
Director of Policy: Eamon Murphy
Director of Enforcement: Tony Wilkin
*Director of Finance, Planning and Corporate
  Resources:* Lesley Beech
Director of Human Resources: Terry Hart
Director of Banking: Jim Curtois
**Department: Department of Trade and
Industry**
Launched: 21/3/90

Jobcentre Plus

Caxton House, Tothill Street,
London SW1H 9NA
Tel: 020 7273 3000   Fax: 020 7273 6143
E-mail:
[firstname.surname]@jobcentreplus.gov.uk
Website: www.jobcentreplus.gov.uk
Steel City House, West Street, Sheffield S1 2GQ
Tel: 0870 001 0171   Fax: 0114-259 5003

The aim of Jobcentre Plus is to help more people
into work and employers to fill their vacancies,
and to provide people of working age with the
help and support to which they are entitled. The
service will cover the whole of England,
Scotland and Wales by 2006. The service is
supported by a small head office and by district
and regional offices based on local authorities
and Government Offices respectively.

Acting Chief Executive: Clare Dodgson
Board Members:
Acting Chief Operating Officer: Alan Brown
Director, Performance and Product
  Management: Mark Fisher
Project Director: Jeremy Groombridge
Director, Business Design: Stephen Hewitt
Director, Modernisation and Strategy:
  Stephen Holt OBE
Director, Employer Services: Mark Grimshaw
Finance Director: Peter Ward
Director, Human Resources: Jane Saint
Non-Executive Directors: Sarah Anderson,
  David Coles
Field Directors
London: Lesley Strathie
Scotland: Alan Brown
South East: Roger Lasko
South West: Diana Ross
North West: Terry Moran
East Midlands: Mel Groves CBE
North East: Val Gibson
East: Nicola Bastin
Wales: Sheelagh Keyse
West Midlands: Rosemary Thew
Yorkshire and the Humber: Vince Robinson
**Department: Department for Work and
  Pensions**
Launched: 1/4/02

HM Land Registry

Lincoln's Inn Fields, London WC2A 3PH
Tel: 020 7917 8888   Fax: 020 7955 0110
E-mail: hmlr@landreg.gov.uk
Website: www.landregistry.gov.uk

Maintains and develops a unified and reliable
system of land registration in England and Wales.

Land Registry Directing Board
  Chief Land Registrar and Chief Executive:
    Peter Collis
  Deputy Chief Executive: Ted Beardsall
  Director of Legal Services: Joe Timothy
  Director of Operations: Andy Howarth
Non-executive Directors: Jan Smith, Alison
  Porter
**Department: Lord Chancellor's Department
Launched: 2/7/90**

Maritime and Coastguard Agency – MCA

Spring Place, 105 Commercial Road,
Southampton SO15 1EG
Tel: 023 8032 9100   Fax: 023 8032 9298
E-mail: infoline@mcga.gov.uk
Website: www.mcga.gov.uk

The MCA's role is to prevent loss of life at sea
and at the coast, to continuously improve maritime safety, and to protect the marine environment. The agency's main functions are the
provision of HM Coastguard Services including
the 24 hour maritime search and rescue capacity,
and surveys of UK ships and inspections of
foreign ships visiting UK ports.

Chief Executive: Maurice Storey CB;
  Captain Stephen Bligh from October 2003
Director of Operations and Chief Coastguard:
  John Astbury
Director of Quality and Standards:
  Alan Cubbin
Director of Finance: Neil Goodall
Director of Human Resources: Alison Thorne
**Department: Department for Transport
Launched: 1/4/98**

Meat Hygiene Service

Kings Pool, Peasholme Green, York YO1 7PR
Tel: 01904 455500   Fax: 01904 455502
E-mail: enquire@foodstandards.gsi.gov.uk
Website:
www.food.gov.uk/enforcement/mhservice

Veterinary supervision and meat inspection in
licensed fresh meat premises.

Chief Executive: Chris Lawson
Director of Operations: Mike Greaves
Veterinary and Technical Director:
  Jane Downes
Acting Director of Finance: Mike McEvoy
Director of Human Resources:
  Monica Redmond
Director of IT: Jenny Sergeant

Regional Directors:
Acting Regional Director North: Penny Howarth
Regional Director Central: Paul Thomas
Regional Director South and West:
Robin Harback
Acting Regional Director Wales: Adrian Thorne
Regional Director Scotland: Spencer Dawson
Project Director (Organisational Change):
Ivor Pumfrey
Department: An Executive Agency of the Food Standards Agency
Launched: 1/4/95

Medical Supplies Agency – MSA

Drummond Barracks, Ludgershall, Andover,
Hampshire SP11 9RU
Tel: 01264 798502   Fax: 01264 798476
E-mail: postmaster@msa.mod.uk

Provides medical, dental and veterinary materiel, blood and blood products, trained personnel and technical and logistic support to the armed forces.

Chief Executive: Peter Jones
Director Management Services: Felicity Belsey
Department: Ministry of Defence
Launched: 1/3/96

Medicines and Health-Care Products Regulatory Agency – MHRA

Market Towers, 1 Nine Elms Lane,
London SW8 5NQ
Tel: 020 7273 0000   Fax: 020 7273 0353
E-mail: info@mca.gsi.gov.uk
Website: www.mca.gov.uk

Chief Executive: Alasdair Breckenridge
Directors:
Licensing: Dr Ian Hudson
Post-Licensing: Dr June Raine
Inspection and Enforcement: Dr Gordon Munro
Devices: Dr David Jefferys
Department: Department of Health
Launched: 1/4/03

Met Office

London Road, Bracknell, Berkshire RG12 2SZ
Tel: 0845 300 0300   Fax: 0845 300 1300
E-mails: customercentre@metoffice.com
[firstname.surname]@metoffice.com
Website: www.metoffice.com

Responsible for provision of meteorological services to the armed forces and civil aviation, shipping, emergency services, media, commerce, industry and the public, and for undertaking research related to meteorology and climate.

Chief Executive: Peter Ewins CB
Chief Scientist: John F B Mitchell
Company Secretary: Martin Sands
Finance Director: Philip Mabe
Operations Director: Roger Hunt
Special Projects: Colin Flood
Business Director: Steve Noyes
International Director: Dr Jim Caughey
Director Numerical Weather Prediction:
Dr Alan Dickinson
Director Climate Research: Dr David Griggs
Chief Information Officer: John Ponting
Director Relocation Programme: Alan Douglas
Department: Ministry of Defence
Launched: 2/4/90

Ministry of Defence Police Agency – MDP

Wethersfield, Braintree, Essex CM7 4AZ
Tel: 01371 854000   Fax: 01371 854060

Responsible for the prevention, detection and investigation of crime within the MoD and Crown Estate.

Chief Executive/Chief Constable: Lloyd Clarke
Deputy Chief Constable: David Ray
Agency Secretary and Director of Finance and Administration: Paul Crowther
Assistant Chief Constable (Personnel and Training): Anthony McDermott
Assistant Chief Constable (Operations):
Gerry McAuley
Assistant Chief Constable Operations (Support):
John Bligh
Department: Ministry of Defence
Launched: 1/4/96

National Archives

Ruskin Avenue, Kew, Richmond,
Surrey TW9 4DU
Tel: 020 8876 3444   Fax: 020 8878 8905
E-mail: enquiry@nationalarchives.gov.uk
Website: www.nationalarchives.gov.uk

National Archives brings together the Public Record Office and the Historical Manuscripts Commissioner. It houses the national archives of England and Wales and the UK, that is, records created by the actions of central government and the courts of law. Its responsibilities include ensuring the selection of records which should be permanently preserved, their preservation and their accessibility to the public. It also provides information about private archives throughout the UK and overseas, relating to all aspects of British history.

Keeper of Public Records, Historical
  Manuscripts Keeper and Chief Executive:
  Sarah Tyacke, CB
Director of Public Services:
  Dr Elizabeth Hallam-Smith
Director of Government and Archival Services:
  Dr David Thomas
Director of Corporate Services: Wilma Jones
Department: Lord Chancellor's Department
Launched: 1/4/92

National Savings and Investments – NS&I

375 Kensington High Street, London W14 8SD
Tel: 020 7348 9200
E-mail: [firstname.surname]@nsandi.com
Website: www.nsandi.com

Government backed savings provider.

Chief Executive: Alan Cook
Commercial Director: Gill Cattanach
Finance Director: Trevor Bayley
Partnerships and Operations Director:
  Steve Owen
National Savings and Investments is a
  Government Department and an Executive
  Agency of the Chancellor of the Exchequer
Launched: 1/7/96

National Weights and Measures Laboratory – NWML

Stanton Avenue, Teddington, Middlesex TW11 0JZ
Tel: 020 8943 7272   Fax: 020 8943 7270
E-mail: info@nwml.gov.uk
Website: www.nwml.gov.uk

Administers weights and measures legislation; regulation and certification of measuring equipment in use for trade; EU Directives on measuring instruments; equipment testing, calibration and training services.

Chief Executive: Jeff Llewellyn
Department: Department of Trade and
  Industry
Launched: 18/4/89

Naval Manning Agency – NMA

Victory Building, HM Naval Base, Portsmouth, Hampshire PO1 3LS
Tel: 023 9272 7400   Fax: 023 9272 7413

Ensures that sufficient naval manpower is available in trained strength and effectively deployed at all times.

Chief Executive: Rear Admiral Mark Kerr
Department: Ministry of Defence
Launched: 1/7/96

Naval Recruiting and Training Agency – NRTA

Room 039, Victory Building, HM Naval Base, Portsmouth, Hampshire PO1 3LS
Tel: 023 9272 7600   Fax: 023 9272 7613

Primarily involved in providing and maintaining a pool of suitably trained manpower for deployment in the Naval Service.

Chief Executive: Rear Admiral Peter Davies CBE
Deputy Chief Executive:
  Commodore Mike Potter ADC RN
Director Naval Recruiting:
  Commodore Gerry Thwaites RN
Director Naval Reserves:
  Captain Chris Massie-Taylor OBE RN
Director Naval Training and Education:
  Captain John Rees RN
Estates Project Director: Captain Ian Jenkins RN
Training Projects Director:
  Captain Peter Marley RN
Commercial Director: Peter Clark
Finance Director: David Allen
Department: Ministry of Defence
Launched: 1/4/95

NHS Estates – NHSE

Department of Health, 1 Trevelyan Square, Boar Lane, Leeds LS1 6AE
Tel: 0113-254 7000   Fax: 0113-254 7299
E-mail: nhs.estates@doh.gov.uk
Website: www.nhsestates.gov.uk

Provides expertise and advice on all aspects of estates and facilities management in the National Health Service.

Chief Executive: Peter Wearmouth
Executive Finance Director: Tim Straughan
Director of Policy: Jane Riley
Director of Property: Terry Murphy
Department: Department of Health
Launched: 1/4/91

NHS Pensions Agency – NHSPA

Hesketh House, 200–220 Broadway, Fleetwood, Lancashire FY7 8LG
Tel: 01253 774774   Fax: 01253 774592
E-mail: pat.corless@doh.gsi.gov.uk
Website: www.nhspa.gov.uk

Administers the NHS Occupational Pension Scheme.

Chief Executive: Pat Corless
Scheme Policy Director: Ian McHenry
Resource and Development Director: Allison Beal
Information Systems Director: Bill McCallum
Department: Department of Health
Launched: 20/11/92

NHS Purchasing and Supply Agency – NHSPASA

Premier House, 60 Caversham Road,
Reading RG1 7EB
Tel: 0118-980 8600   Fax: 0118-980 8650
Website: www.pasa.doh.gov.uk

80 Lightfoot Street, Chester CH2 3AD

Foxbridge Way, Normanton,
West Yorkshire WF6 1TL

Chief Executive: Duncan Eaton
Director of Finance and IT: Richard Chantler
Director of Corporate Development: Chris Uden
Associate Directors of Purchasing: Neil Argyle,
  Marcus Brindle, John Cooper, Andrew Rudd
Department: Department of Health
Launched: 1/4/00

Northern Ireland Prison Service – NIPS

Dundonald House, Upper Newtownards Road,
Belfast BT4 3SU
Tel: 028 9052 2922   Fax: 028 9052 5100
Tel: Press Office: 028 9052 5354/5139
E-mail: info@niprisonservice.gov.uk
Website: www.niprisonservice.gov.uk

Provides prison services in Northern Ireland.

Director-General: Peter Russell
Department: Northern Ireland Office
Launched: 3/4/95

Office for National Statistics – ONS

1 Drummond Gate, London SW1V 2QQ
Tel: 020 7533 5888   Fax 01633 652747
E-mails: info@ons.gov.uk
[firstname.surname]@ons.gov.uk
Website: www.statistics.gov.uk

ONS provides government at all levels with a statistical service to support the formulation and monitoring of economic and social policies, informs Parliament and the citizen about the state of the nation and performance of government; and registers key life events.

Chief Executive: Len Cook
Directors:
  Surveys and Administrative Sources:
  Karen Dunnell
  Sources Transformation: Mike Pepper
  Macroeconomics and Labour: Colin Mowl
  Methodology: Vacant
  Economic and Social Reporting: John Pullinger
  Organisational Development and Resources:
  Peter Walton
Principal Establishment Officer: Susan Young
Head of Communication: Helena Rafalowska

Parliamentary Clerks: Robert Smith,
  Alex Elton-Wall
Department: The Office for National Statistics is a separate Government Department which reports directly to the Chancellor of the Exchequer
Launched: 1/4/96

OGCbuying.solutions

Royal Liver Building, Pier Head, Liverpool L3 1PE
Tel: 0151-227 4262   Fax: 0151-227 3315
Customer Care: 0870 268 2222
E-mail: marketing@ogcbs.gsi.gov.uk
Website: www.ogcbuyingsolutions.gov.uk

Trevelyan House, Great Peter Street,
London SW1P 2BY
Tel: 020 7271 2910

Rosebery Court, St Andrews Business Park,
Norwich NR7 0HS
Tel: 01603 704601 Fax: 01603 704747

OGCbuying.solutions provides a professional procurement service to government, public sector organisations and their private sector contractors.

Chief Executive: Hugh Barrett
Deputy Chief Executive: Dr Clare Poulter
Director of Human and Financial Resources:
  David Murray
Director of Commercial Services: Stephen Heard
Department: Office of Government Commerce, HM Treasury
Launched: 1/04/01

Ordnance Survey

Romsey Road, Southampton,
Hampshire SO16 4GU
Tel: 023 8079 2000   Fax: 023 8079 2452
E-mail: enquiries@ordsvy.gov.uk
Website: www.ordnancesurvey.co.uk

Carries out official topographic surveying and mapping of Great Britain and produces a wide range of maps and computer data products for Government, business, administrative, educational and leisure use.

Director-General and Chief Executive Officer:
  Vanessa Lawrence
Director of Data Collection and Management:
  Neil Ackroyd
Director of Programmes and Products:
  Steve Erskine
Director of Sales and Marketing Development:
  James Brayshaw
Director of Human Resources and Corporate Services: Jan Hutchinson

Director of Strategy: Duncan Shiell
Chief Technology Officer: Ed Parsons
Chief Press Officer: Scott Sinclair
Department: Office of the Deputy Prime Minister
Launched: 1/5/90

Patent Office

Concept House, Cardiff Road, Newport NP10 8QQ
Tel: 01633 814000   Fax: 01633 814444
E-mail: enquiries@patent.gov.uk
Website: www.patent.gov.uk

Grants patents and trade marks, registers designs, and formulates policy on intellectual property.

Chief Executive: Alison Brimelow
Director Patents: Ron Marchant
Director Trade Marks and Designs:
  Peter Lawrence
Director Intellectual Property Policy:
  Graham Jenkins
Director of IT and Corporate Services:
  Caren Fullerton
Director of Finance: Kevin Woodrow
Director Intellectual Property and Innovation:
  Anthony Murphy
Department: Department of Trade and Industry
Launched: 1/3/90

Pay and Personnel Agency – PPA

Ministry of Defence, Warminster Road,
Bath BA1 5AA
Tel: 01225 828105   Fax: 01225 828728

Provides payroll, pensions, expenses management and personnel information services for civil service staff in the Ministry of Defence, and other government customers on repayment.

Chief Executive: David Ball
Deputy Chief Executive: David Wealthall
Director Corporate Services:
  Christopher Edwards
Director Payments: Eddie Taylor
Director Pensions Customer Services: Tim Taylor
Department: Ministry of Defence
Launched: 1/2/96

The Pension Service

Room 4C21, Quarry House, Quarry Hill,
Leeds LS2 7UA
Helpline: 0113-232 4143   Fax: 0113-232 4393
E-mails: pensiondirectorsoffice@dwp.gsi.gov.uk
[firstname.surname]@dwp.gsi.gov.uk
Website: www.thepensionservice.gov.uk

The Pension Service has been set up to improve the present payment service that pensioners receive and for planning for retirement, no matter how far off it might be.

Chief Executive: Alexis Cleveland
Chief Operating Officer: Charlie MacKinnon
Director of Change: George McCorkell
Director, Business Performance: Phil Bartlett
Director, Customer Services and Human Resources: Indi Seehra
Director of Finance: Simon Furse
Operations Directors
East Midlands and East: Bernie Keay
London: Vacant
North East, Yorkshire and the Humber:
  John Myers
North West: Lee Brown
South East: Barry Cox
South West: Graham Carter
West Midlands: Jenni Ord
Scotland: Archie Roy
Wales: Viv Hopkins
Department: Department for Work and Pensions
Launched: 1/04/02

Pesticides Safety Directorate – PSD

Mallard House, Kings Pool, 3 Peasholme Green,
York YO1 7PX
Tel: 01904 640500   Fax: 01904 455733
E-mail: information@psd.defra.gsi.gov.uk
Website: www.pesticides.gov.uk

Controls the sale, supply and use of pesticides.

Chief Executive: Dr Kerr Wilson
Director (Policy): Dr Sue Popple
Director of Finance, IT and Corporate Services:
  Kathryn Dyson
Director (Approvals): Richard Davis
Department: Department for Environment, Food and Rural Affairs
Launched: 1/4/93

Planning Inspectorate – PINS

Temple Quay House, 2 The Square,
Temple Quay, Bristol BS1 6PN
Tel: 0117-372 6372
E-mail: enquiries@pins.gsi.gov.uk
Website: www.planning-inspectorate.gov.uk

Cathays Park, Cardiff CF1 3NQ
Tel: 029 2082 5007

Appeals and other casework under planning, housing, environment, highways, transport and works legislation. Also provision of inspectors to hold local inquiries into objections to local authority plans, and administration of the Lord Chancellor's Panel of Independent Inspectors.

Chief Executive: Katrine Sporle
Deputy Chief Executive: David Hanchet
Directors:
  Highways, Rights of Way: Brian Dodd
  Rights of Way: 0117-372 8895
  Highways: 0117-372 8905/8907
  Enforcement Casework: Alan Langton
All National Assembly for Wales Appeals and
  Casework: Alan Langton (Cardiff Office)
  029 2082 5007
Structure and Local Plans: Brian Dodd
Planning Appeals Administration and
  E-business Strategy: Graham Saunders
Finance and Management Services:
  Roger Pritchard
Department: Office of the Deputy Prime
  Minister
Launched: 1/4/92

HM Prison Service

Cleland House, Page Street, London SW1P 4LN
Tel: 020 7217 6000   Fax 020 7217 6403
Website: www.hmprisonservice.gov.uk

Provides prison services in England and Wales.

Management Board
Director-General: Phil Wheatley
Deputy Director-General: Peter Atherton
Director of Operations: Michael Spurr
Director of Prison Health Policy:
  John Boyington*
Director of Finance and Procurement:
  Ann Beasley
Director of High Security Prisons:
  Peter Atherton
Director of Resettlement: Peter Wrench
Director of Corporate Affairs: Derek Howard
Director of Personnel: Gareth Hadley
Non-Executive Directors of the Strategy Board
  for Correctional Services:
  Sir Duncan Nichol CBE, Patrick Carter,
  Richard Rosser
*Co-located at DoH, Wellington House

AREA MANAGERS

East Midlands (North)
Training Unit, HMP Ranby, Retford,
Nottingham DN22 8FD
01777 869904
Area Manager: Steve Wagstaff

East Midlands (South)
2 St John Street, Leicester LE1 3BE
0116-242 1032
Area Manager: Bob Perry

Eastern
HMP/YOI Norwich, Knox Road, Norwich,
Norfolk NR1 4LU
01603 708828
Area Manager: Vacant

London
Cleland House
020 7217 2893
Area Manager: Bill Duff

North East
3rd Floor, Eagle Star House, Regent Centre,
Gosforth, Newcastle upon Tyne NE3 3TW
0191-255 3925
Area Manager: Mitch Egan

North West
Stirling House, Ackhurst Business Park,
Foxhole Road, Chorley, Lancashire PR7 1NY
01257 275 458
Area Manager: Ian Lockwood

**South East 1 (Thames Valley, Hampshire and
Isle of Wight)**
The Old Wardens House, 21 Brierton Road,
Aylesbury, Buckinghamshire HP20 1EN
01296 390667
Area Manager: Sarah Payne

South East 2 (Kent, Surrey and Sussex)
80 Sir Evelyn Road, Rochester, Kent ME1 3LU
01634 817694
Area Manager: Adrian Smith

South West
1 Tortworth Road, Leyhill, Wotton Under Edge,
Gloucestershire GL12 8BQ
01454 264053
Area Manager: Jerry Petherick

Wales
102 Maryport Street, Usk, Gwent NP15 1AH
01291 674820
Area Manager: John May

West Midlands
PO Box 458, HMP Shrewsbury, The Dana,
Shrewsbury, Shropshire SY1 2WB
01743 280048
Area Manager: Bryan Payling

Yorkshire and Humberside
c/o HMYOI Wetherby, York Road, Near
Wetherby, West Yorkshire LS22 5NG
01937 544217
Area Manager: Peter Earnshaw

High Security Prisons
Cleland House
020 7217 2888
Operational Manager: Peter Atherton

Female Estate
Units 1&2, Faraday Court, First Avenue,
Centrum 100 Business Park,
Burton Upon Trent DE14 2WX
01283 524525
Managers: Niall Clifford, Hazel Banks

Juvenile Estate
Area Office: c/o The Prison Service College,
Aberford Road, Wakefield,
West Yorkshire WF1 4DE
Operational Manager: David Waplington
01924 434107

Department: Home Office
Launched: 1/4/93

Public Guardianship Office

Archway Tower, 2 Junction Road,
London N19 5SZ
General Enquiries: 0845 330 2900
Text Phone: T020 7664 7755
DX Number: 141150 Archway 2
Fax: 020 7664 7705
E-mail: custserv@guardianship.gov.uk
Website: www.guardianship.gov.uk

Promoting the financial and social well-being of
people with a mental incapacity.

Chief Executive: David Lye
Department: Lord Chancellor's Department
Launched: 1/4/01

Queen Elizabeth II Conference Centre

Broad Sanctuary, London SW1P 3EE
Tel: 020 7222 5000   Fax: 020 7798 4200
E-mail: info@qeiicc.co.uk
Website: www.qeiicc.co.uk

Provides conference and banqueting facilities for
government and commercial use on a national
and international scale.

Chief Executive: John McCarthy
Finance Director: Bob Jackson
Commercial Director: Steve Norcliffe
Operations Director: Geoff Booth
Department: Office of the Deputy Prime
Minister
Launched: 6/7/86

Queen Victoria School – QVS

Dunblane, Perthshire FK15 0JY
Tel: 0131-310 2901   Fax: 0131-310 2926
E-mail: headmaster@qvs.org.uk
Website: www.qvs.org.uk

Provides secondary boarding education for the
children of Scottish service personnel and those
serving in Scotland.

Headmaster and Chief Executive:
Brian Raine
Deputy Head: Colin Philson
Assistant Head: Lyn Smith
Department: Ministry of Defence
Launched: 1/4/92

Radiocommunications Agency – RA

Wyndham House, 189 Marsh Wall,
London E14 9SX
Tel: 020 7211 0211
Fax: 020 7211 0507
E-mail: library@ra.gsi.gov.uk
Website: www.radio.gov.uk

Responsible for the management of the civil
radio spectrum in the UK. It also represents UK
radio interests internationally.

Chief Executive: Rolande Anderson
Spectrum and International Policy Director:
Mike Goddard
Spectrum Services Director:
Hazel Canter
Customer Services Director:
Barry Maxwell
Corporate Services and Facilities Director:
David Smith
Department: Department of Trade and
Industry
Launched: 2/4/90

RAF Personnel Management Agency – RAFPMA

RAF Innsworth, Gloucester GL3 1EZ
Tel: 01452 712612 Ext 7849
Fax: 01452 510805
Website: www.raf.mod.uk/ptc/pma

Provides personnel to meet the RAF's worldwide manpower commitments and manages
individuals' careers.

Air Secretary and Chief Executive:
Air Vice-Marshal Ian Stewart CB AFC
Director of Personnel Management Agency
(Officers and Non-Commissioned Aircrew):
Air Commodore Peter Hilling
Director of Personnel Management Agency
(Ground Trades and Support):
Air Commodore Peter Whalley
Personnel Management Agency Air Secretary 1:
Air Commodore (Retd) Malcolm Fuller
Department: Ministry of Defence
Launched: 2/2/97

RAF Training Group Defence Agency – RAFTGDA

Royal Air Force Innsworth, Gloucester,
Gloucestershire GL3 1EZ
Tel: 01452 712612 Ext 5368
Fax: 01452 510850
E-mail: mail@tgda.gov.uk
Website: www.tgda.gov.uk

Responsible for the recruitment and selection of all Royal Air Force personnel and for RAF non-operational training.

Chief Executive: Air Vice-Marshal David Walker
Air Commodore Flying Training:
    Air Commodore John Cliffe
Air Commodore Ground Training:
    Air Commodore Peter Dye
Department: Ministry of Defence
Launched: 1/4/94

The Rent Service – TRS

5 Welbeck Street, London W1G 9YQ
Tel: 020 7023 6000   Fax: 020 7023 6222
Website: www.therentservice.gov.uk

Chief Executive: Charlotte Copeland
Finance Director: Joanne Lang
Operational Policy Director: Rebecca Lawrence
Director of Human Resources:
    Mark Merka-Richards
Director of Quality: Alan Corcoran
Regional Director, North: Michael Derbyshire
Regional Director, South and Midlands:
    Nigel Bravery
Regional Director, London and Eastern:
    Helen Bratten
Department: Office of the Deputy Prime Minister
Launched: 1/10/99

Royal Mint

Llantrisant, Pontyclun CF72 8YT
Tel: 01443 222111   Fax: 01443 623148
E-mail: victoria.francis@royalmint.gov.uk
Website: www.royalmint.com

The manufacture and distribution of UK and overseas coins, commemorative medals and seals.

Chief Executive: Gerald Sheehan
Acting Director of Finance: Huw Edwards
Director of Sales: Keith Cottrell
Director of Collector Coin: Alan Wallace
Director of Circulating Coin Production:
    Mick Slater
Director of Human Resources: Allan E Pearce
Department: The Royal Mint is a Government Department which reports to the Chancellor of the Exchequer
Launched: 1/4/90

Royal Parks

The Old Police House, Hyde Park,
London W2 2UH
Tel: 020 7298 2000   Fax: 020 7298 2005
E-mail: hq@royalparks.gsi.gov.uk
Website: www.royalparks.gov.uk

Manages and polices the Royal Parks in London – St James's Park, Green Park, Hyde Park, Kensington Gardens, Regent's Park, Primrose Hill, Greenwich Park, Richmond Park and Bushy Park. It also manages and polices a number of other open spaces in London.

Chief Executive: William Weston MVO
Deputy Chief Executive and Director of Parks:
    Michael Fitt OBE
Acting Chief Officer, Royal Parks Constabulary:
    Superintendent Derek Pollock
Department: Department for Culture, Media and Sport
Launched: 1/4/93

Rural Payments Agency – RPA

Kings House, 33 Kings Road, Reading,
Berkshire RG1 3BU
Tel: 0118-958 3626   Fax: 0118-959 7736
E-mail: enquiries@rpa.gsi.gov.uk
Website: www.rpa.gov.uk

It is the single paying agency responsible for Common Agricultural Policy (CAP) schemes in England and certain schemes throughout the UK.

Chief Executive: Johnston McNeill
Department: Department for Environment, Food and Rural Affairs

Service Children's Education – SCE

BFPO 40
Tel: 00 49 2161 908 + Ext 2372
Fax 00 49 2161 908 + Ext 2396
E-mail: sce.hq@bfgnet.de

Provides an education service for the dependent children of service personnel and UK based civilian support staff residing overseas.

Chief Executive Officer:
    David Wadsworth
Deputy Chief Executive: Mike Smith
Assistant Chief Executive (Operations):
    Paul S Niedzwiedzki
Assistant Chief Executive (Corporate Affairs):
    Les Berriman
Assistant Chief Executive (Schools Effectiveness): Judith Morris
Department: Ministry of Defence
Launched: 1/4/96

Small Business Service – SBS

Kingsgate House, 66-74 Victoria Street,
London SW1E 6SW
Tel: 0114-259 7788   Fax: 0114-259 7330
E-mail: enquiries@sbs.gsi.gov.uk
Website: www. sbs.gov.uk
St Mary's House, c/o Moorfoot, Sheffield S1 4PQ

Chief Executive: Martin Wyn Griffith
Deputy Chief Executives: Stephen Lyle Smythe,
Dan Bernard
**Department: Department of Trade and
Industry
Launched: 1/4/00**

Treasury Solicitor's Department – TSOL

The Treasury Solicitor, Queen Anne's Chambers,
28 Broadway, London SW1H 9JS
Tel: 020 7210 3000   Fax: 020 7222 6006
E-mails:
thetreasurysolicitor@treasury-solicitor.gsi.gov.uk
[initialsurname]@treasury-solicitor.gsi.gov.uk
Website: www.treasury-solicitor.gov.uk

Provides litigation and advisory services to
government departments and other publicly
funded bodies in England and Wales. Also
administers estates of people who die intestate
with no known kin.

HM Procurator-General and Treasury Solicitor:
Juliet Wheldon CB QC
Cabinet Office and Central Advisory Division:
Rosemary Jeffreys (Legal Adviser),
Chris House, Susanna McGibbon
Department of Culture, Media and Sport:
Isabel Letwin (Legal Adviser), Nicolas Beach,
Peter de Val, Colin Gregory,
Gillian Richmond
Department for Education and Skills:
Jonathan Jones (Legal Adviser),
Dudley Aires, Nic Ash, Francis Clarke,
Carol Davis, Patrick Kilgarriff
Employment and Commercial Contracts Group:
Simon Harker (Legal Adviser), Peter Bennett,
Hugh Giles
*Legal Secretariat to the Cabinet Office and
European Division:* Mike Thomas (Legal
Adviser), John Collins, Arnold Ridout
Litigation Division: David Pearson (Head of
Division), Robert Aitken, Diana Babar,
Adam Chapman, Lee John-Charles, Vivienne
Collett, Philip Kent, Anthony Lawton, Barrie
McKay, Peter Messer, Roland Philips CB,
John Sandford, Martin Truran,
Peter Whitehurst

Ministry of Defence:* Martin Hemming CB
(Legal Adviser), Humphrey Morrison,
Linday Nicoll, Vivien Rose, Robert Miller
Treasury Advisory:* Mark Blythe CB (Legal
Adviser), James Braggins, Phinella
Henderson, Sue Cochrane, Charles Raikes,
Andrew Stewart
Administrators: Mike Fuhr OBE, Alison
Schofield, Doug Walters (GLS Secretariat)

*Co-located with the Department

UK Passport Service – UKPS

Globe House, 89 Eccleston Square,
London SW1V 1PN
Information Line: 0870 521 0410
Website: www.passport.gov.uk

The UK Passport Service (UKPS) is responsible
for issuing passports to British nationals living in
the UK. The UKPS falls within the Passport and
Records Agency (PRA). Globe House is the
UKPS London Headquarters with seven passport
offices in Belfast, Glasgow, Liverpool, London,
Newport, Peterborough and Durham.

Chief Executive: Bernard Herdan
Operations Director: Kevin Sheehan
Directors (PRA Board Members):
Bernard Herdan
Human Resources: Ruth Pearson
Finance: Alistair Cook
Systems: John Davies
**Department: Home Office
Launched: 2/4/91**

United Kingdom Debt Management Office – DMO

Eastcheap Court, 11 Philpot Lane,
London EC3M 8UD
Tel: 020 7862 6500   Fax: 020 7862 6509
E-mail: firstname.surname@dmo.gsi.gov.uk
Website: www.dmo.gov.uk

Responsible for carrying out the Government's
debt management policy of minimising its
financing costs over the long term, taking
account of risk, and for managing the aggregate
cash needs of the Exchequer in the most cost-
effective way. Since July 2002, the functions of
the Public Works Loan Board (managing
Government lending to local authorities) and the
Commissioners for the Reduction of the National
Debt (managing certain public sector funds)
have also been integrated into the DMO (as part
of a reorganisation designed to deliver improved
management of the central government balance
sheet, and to develop the PWLB and CRND
services to public sector clients.)

Chief Executive: Robert Stheeman
Executive PA: Pam Henness
Deputy Chief Executive: Jo Whelan
Head of Operations and Resources: Jim Juffs
Press Officer: Steve Whiting
Department: HM Treasury
Launched: 1/4/98

United Kingdom Hydrographic Office – UKHO

Admiralty Way, Taunton, Somerset TA1 2DN
Tel: 01823 337900   Fax: 01823 284077
E-mail: helpdesk@ukho.gov.uk
Website: www.ukho.gov.uk

Produces navigational charts and publications for the Royal Navy and commercial shipping worldwide.

Chief Executive and National Hydrographer:
    Dr Wyn Williams
Deputy Chief Executive and Director of
    Operations: Vic Jenkins
Director of Finance: Barrie Bussey
Director of Marketing and Supply: Bob Moss
Director of Corporate Development:
    Steve Parnell
Department: Ministry of Defence
Launched: 6/4/90
Trading Fund status

Valuation Office Agency

New Court, Carey Street, London WC2A 2JE
Tel: 020 7506 1700   Fax: 020 7506 1998
E-mail: custserv.voa@gtnet.gov.uk
Website: www.voa.gov.uk

Provides land and buildings valuation service to government departments, other public bodies and a number of local authorities throughout Great Britain.

Ministers: Chancellor of the Exchequer,
    Paymaster General
Commissioner of the Board and Chief Executive:
    Michael Johns CB
Deputy Chief Executive and Director of Local
    Taxation: John Ebdon CB
Director of District Valuer Services:
    John Wilkinson
Director of Business Resources:
    Anne Wheatcroft
Director Finance, Technology and Planning:
    John Keelty
Director of Corporate Communications:
    Angela McKenna
Director of Modernisation: Paul Sanderson
Chief Valuer, Scotland: Allan Ainslie

Chief Valuer, Wales: Peter Clement
The Valuation Office is an Executive Agency of the Chancellor Exchequer within the Inland Revenue
Launched: 30/9/91

Vehicle and Operator Services Agency

Berkeley House, Croydon Street,
Bristol BS5 0DA
Tel: 0117-954 3200   Fax: 0117-954 3212
E-mails: enquiries@vosa.gov.uk
Website: www.vosa.gov.uk

Checks vehicles and drivers at the roadside and other enforcement checks, supervises MOT testing and carries out annual testing of vehicles.

Chief Executive: Maurice Newey
Head of Traffic Area Network: Ann Godfrey
Product Strategy and Policy Director:
    Hugh Edwards
Operations Director: Bob Tatchell
Process Director: Jeff Belt
Human Resources Director: Martin Jones
Operator Compliance Director: John Bannister
Operator Licensing Director: Bill Buckley
Department: Department for Transport
Launched: 1/4/03

Vehicle Certification Agency – VCA

1 The Eastgate Office Centre, Eastgate Road,
Bristol BS5 6XX
Tel: 0117-951 5151   Fax: 0117-952 4103
E-mail: enquiries@vca.gov.uk
Website: www.vca.gov.uk

Tests and certificates vehicles and their components to UK and international standards.

Chief Executive: Derek Harvey
Department: Department for Transport
Launched: 2/4/90

Veterans Agency

Norcross, Blackpool, Lancashire FY5 3WP
Freephone: 0800 169 2277   Textphone: 0800 169 3458   Fax: 01253 330561
E-mail: help@veteransagency.mod.uk
Website: www.veteransagency.mod.uk

Responsible for the assessment and payment of war pensions, the War Pensions Welfare Offices and the Ilford Park Polish Home in Devon.

Chief Executive: Alan Burnham
Medical Director: Dr Paul Kitchen
Head of IPPH and Welfare: Sue Turner
Department: Ministry of Defence
Launched: 1/4/94
Former War Pensions Agency

Veterinary Laboratories Agency – VLA

Woodham Lane, New Haw, Addlestone,
Surrey KT15 3NB
Tel: 01932 341111   Fax: 01932 347046
E-mail: enquiries@vla.defra.gsi.gov.uk
Website: www.defra.gov.uk/corporate/vla

Provides specialist veterinary advice to DEFRA based on disease surveillance, laboratory services and research and development. It also offers these services to other government departments and the private sector.

Chief Executive: Prof Steve Edwards
Research Director: Prof John Morris
Director of Surveillance and Laboratory
  Services: Roger Hancock
Department: Department for Environment,
  Food and Rural Affairs
Launched: 1/10/95

Veterinary Medicines Directorate – VMD

Woodham Lane, New Haw, Addlestone, Surrey KT15 3LS
Tel: 01932 336911   Fax: 01932 336618
E-mail: postmaster@vmd.defra.gsi.gov.uk
Website: www.vmd.gov.uk

Assesses applications for veterinary medicines, issues authorisations and monitors suspected adverse reactions and the presence of residues of veterinary medicines in animals and animal products. Advises Ministers on policy for veterinary medicines.

Director and Chief Executive: Steve Dean
Director of Licensing: David Mackay
Director of Policy: John FitzGerald
Director of Corporate Business: Chris Bean
Department: Department for Environment,
  Food and Rural Affairs
Launched: 2/4/90

Warship Support Agency

Main Office: Birch 1c, No 3131, MoD Abbey Wood, Bristol BS34 8JH
Tel: 0117-913 5792   Fax: 0117-913 2958
E-mail: wsacecoord@wsa.dlo.mod.uk
Website: www.mod.uk/wsa/index.html

Provision of support to the Royal Navy's ships and submarines worldwide.

Director-General Equipment Support (Sea) and
  Chief Executive: John Coles
Deputy Chief Executive:
  Rear Admiral Jonathon Reeve
Executive Directors
Director Finance and Communications:
  John Clayton
Director Operations Equipment:
  Fred Edwards
Director Operations Platforms:
  Mike Frowde
Director Support Chain/DWOps:
  Commodore Peter Horsted
Director Commercial: Trevor Strong
Director Naval Base Clyde:
  Commodore John Borley
Flag Officer Scotland, Northern England and
  Northern Ireland:
  Rear Admiral Nicholas Harris
Naval Base Commander Devonport:
  Commodore Andrew Mathews ADC
Naval Base Commander Portsmouth:
  Commodore Amjad Hussain ADC
Chief Strategic Systems Executive:
  Commodore Ian Rankin
Submarine Integrated Project Team Leader:
  Commodore Howard Mathers
Department: Ministry of Defence
Launched: 2/4/2001 with merger of Ships
  Support Agency and Naval Bases and
  Supply Agency

Wilton Park

Wiston House, Steyning, Sussex BN44 3DZ
Tel: 01903 815020   Fax: 01903 815931
E-mail: wilton@pavilion.co.uk
Website: www.wiltonpark.org.uk

Arranges and runs conferences on international affairs for politicians, officials, academics and others from around the world. Also hosts conferences for public and private sector customers.

Chief Executive: Colin Jennings
Director, Wilton Park Conferences:
  Dr Richard Latter
Department: Foreign and Commonwealth
  Office
Launched: 1/9/91

Visit the Vacher Dod Website . . .
www.DodOnline.co.uk

OMBUDSMEN AND COMPLAINT-HANDLING BODIES

Ombudsmen deal with complaints about the public or private sector bodies within their jurisdiction. Their services are free.

The majority of Ombudsman schemes are set up by statute. Others are voluntary, non-statutory schemes set up on the initiative of the service sectors concerned. In most schemes there are individual Ombudsmen.

All Ombudsmen schemes, other than the European Ombudsman, are recognised members of the British and Irish Ombudsman Association. To be recognised they have to meet four key criteria: Independence from the organisations the Ombudsman has the power to investigate; effectiveness; fairness and public accountability.

A number of complaint-handling bodies are also listed. They are Associate members of the Association.

British and Irish Ombudsman Association
24 Paget Gardens, Chislehurst, Kent BR7 5RX
Tel/Fax: 020 8467 7455
E-mail: bioa@btinternet.com
Website: www.bioa.org.uk

Secretary: Gordon Adams, OBE

Adjudicator's Office
Haymarket House, 28 Haymarket,
London SW1Y 4SP
Tel: 020 7930 2292   Fax 020 7930 2298
E-mail: adjudicators@gtnet.gov.uk
Website: www.adjudicatorsoffice.gov.uk

The Adjudicator investigates complaints from people and businesses about the Inland Revenue (including the Valuation Office Agency), Customs and Excise, the Public Guardianship Office and the Insolvency Service.

The Adjudicator: Dame Barbara Mills DBE QC
Head of Office: Charlie Gordon

Assembly Ombudsman and Commissioner for Complaints – Northern Ireland
Progressive House, 33 Wellington Place,
Belfast BT1 6HN
Tel: 028 9023 3821   Fax: 028 9023 4912
Information: 0800 343424
E-mail: ombudsman@ni-ombudsman.org.uk
Website: www.ni-ombudsman.org.uk

Investigates complaints from those who think they have been unfairly treated by a government department or other public body in Northern Ireland. Included are matters relating to the Code of Practice on Access to Government Information, duties in relation to Health Services and matters in the Public Service.

Ombudsman: Tom Frawley
Deputy Ombudsman: John MacQuarrie

Broadcasting Standards Commission
7 The Sanctuary, London SW1P 3JS
Tel: 020 7808 1000   Fax: 020 7233 0397
E-mail: bsc@bsc.org.uk
Website: www.bsc.org.uk

Statutory body for standards and fairness in broadcasting.

Chairman: Lord Dubs of Battersea
Deputy Chair: Lady Suzanne Warner
Commissioners: David Boulton, Uday Dholakia, Geoff Elliott, Strachan Heppell, CB, Rev Rose Hudson-Wilkin, Sally O'Sullivan, Maggie Redfern, Rev Richard Holloway, Kath Worrall
Director: Paul Bolt
Deputy Director: Norman McLean
Communications Director: Donia Tahbaz
Research Director:
   Andrea Millwood Hargrave

Commission for Local Administration In England
(Local Government Ombudsman)
Millbank Tower, Millbank, London SW1P 4QP
Tel: 020 7217 4620
Adviceline: 0845 602 1983
Fax: 020 7217 4621
E-mail: enquiries.london@lgo.org.uk
Website: www.lgo.org.uk

Chairman of the Commission and Local Government Ombudsman for London Boroughs north of the River Thames (including Richmond, excluding Harrow and Tower Hamlets), Essex, Kent, Surrey, Suffolk, East and West Sussex, Hertfordshire, Buckinghamshire, Berkshire and Coventry City: Tony Redmond
Secretary to the Commission: Nigel Karney

*Vice-Chairman and Local Government
Ombudsman for London Borough of Tower
Hamlets, Birmingham City, Cheshire,
Derbyshire, Nottinghamshire, Lincolnshire
and the North of England (except the Cities of
York and Lancaster):* Patricia Thomas
Beverley House, 17 Shipton Road,
York YO30 5FZ
01904 380200 Fax 01904 380269
E-mail: enquiries.york@lgo.org.uk

*Local Government Ombudsman for London
Boroughs south of the River Thames (except
Richmond) plus Harrow, the Cities of York and
Lancaster and the rest of England not
included in the areas of Mr Redmond and
Mrs Thomas:* Jerry White
The Oaks No 2, Westwood Way, Westwood
Business Park, Coventry CV4 8JB
024 7682 0000 Fax 024 7682 0001
E-mail: enquiries.coventry@lgo.org.uk

Commissioner for Local Administration in Scotland
See Scottish Public Services Ombudsman

Commission for Local Administration in Wales
Derwen House, Court Road,
Bridgend, CF31 1BN
Tel: 01656 661325   Fax: 01656 673279
E-mail: enquiries@ombudsman-wales.org
Website: www.ombudsman-wales.org

Local Commissioner (Ombudsman):
    Elwyn Moseley
Secretary to the Commission: David Bowen
Parliamentary Commissioner (ex officio):
    Ann Abraham

Complaints Adjudicator for Companies House
PO Box 2, Fakenham, Norfolk NR21 0RJ
(Written enquiries only)
Website: www.companieshouse.gov.uk

Adjudicator: William Thomas

Complaints Commissioner to the General Council of the Bar
Northumberland House, 303-306 High Holborn,
London WC1V 7JZ
Tel: 020 7440 4000   Fax: 020 7440 4001
E-mail: laycommissioner@barcouncil.org.uk
Website: www.barcouncil.org.uk

Complaints Commissioner:
    Michael Scott CB CBE DSO

European Ombudsman
1 avenue du Président Robert Schuman, BP 403,
67001 Strasbourg Cedex, France
Tel: 00 33 3 88 17 23 13   Fax: 00 33 3 88 17 90 62
E-mail: euro-ombudsman@europarl.eu.int
Website: www.euro-ombudsman.eu.int

The European Ombudsman is empowered to
receive complaints from any citizen of the
European Union concerning instances of
maladministration in the activities of the EU
institutions or bodies.

Ombudsman: Prof Nikiforos Diamandouros

Financial Ombudsman Service
South Quay Plaza, 183 Marsh Wall,
London E14 9SR
Tel: 020 7964 1000   Fax: 020 7964 1001
E-mail: enquiries@financial-ombudsman.org.uk
Website: www.financial-ombudsman.org.uk

The Financial Ombudsman Service was set up
under the Financial Services and Markets Act
2000 to provide consumers with a free,
independent service for resolving disputes with
financial firms. The Ombudsman service can
consider most personal finance disputes – from
insurance and banking services to pensions and
investments.

Chief Ombudsman: Walter Merricks
Principal Ombudsmen: David Thomas,
    Tony Boorman, Jane Whittles
Operations Director: Roy Hewlett
Head of Communications: David Cresswell

Now part of the Financial Ombudsman Service:
Banking Ombudsman; Building Societies
Ombudsman; Insurance Ombudsman; Investment Ombudsman; Personal Investment Authority Ombudsman.

Financial Services Ombudsman Scheme for the Isle of Man
Government Buildings, Lord Street, Douglas,
Isle of Man IM1 1LE
Tel: 01624 686500   Fax: 01624 686504
E-mail: ombudsman@iomoft.gov.im
Website: www.gov.im/oft/ombudsman

Chief Adjudicator: Peter Crellin

Gibraltar Ombudsman
Office of the Ombudsman, 10 Governor's Lane,
Gibraltar
Tel: 00 350 46001   Fax: 00 350 46002
E-mail: ombuds@gibnet.gi
Website: www.ombudsman.org.gi

Ombudsman: Mario M Hook

Health Service Ombudsman for England

Millbank Tower, Millbank, London SW1P 4QP
Tel: 0845 015 4033   Fax: 020 7217 4000
E-mail: ohsc.enquiries@ombudsman.gsi.gov.uk
Text telephone: 020 7217 4066
Website: www.ombudsman.org.uk

The Health Service Ombudsman considers complaints from members of the public about the NHS which have not been dealt with to the satisfaction of the complainant by the body concerned.

She is completely independent of the NHS and government. The Ombudsman also considers complaints about failures to provide information.

Health Service Ombudsman: Ann Abraham
Deputy Health Service Commissioner: Vacant

Health Service Ombudsman for Wales

5th Floor, Capital Tower, Greyfriars Road,
Cardiff CF10 3AG
Tel: 0845 601 0987   Fax: 029 2022 6909
E-mail: whsc.enquiries@ombudsman.gsi.gov.uk
Website: www.ombudsman.org.uk

The Health Service Ombudsman considers complaints from members of the public about the NHS, which have not been dealt with to the satisfaction of the complainant by the body concerned. She is completely independent of the NHS and government. The Ombudsman also considers complaints about failures to provide information.

Health Service Ombudsman: Ann Abraham
Investigations Manager: Stan Drummond

Independent Case Examiner

PO Box 155, Chester CH99 9SA
Tel: 0151-801 8800   Fax: 0151-801 8801
Minicom: 0151-801 8888
Local call rate number: 0845 606 0777
E-mail: ice@ukgov.demon.co.uk
Website: www.ind-case-exam.org.uk
PO Box 1245, Belfast BT2 7DF

Independent Case Examiner: Jodi Berg
Case Director: Phil Latus

Independent Complaints Reviewer – ICR

New Premier House, 150 Southampton Row,
London WC1B 5AL
Tel: 020 7278 6251   Fax: 020 7278 9675
DX35744 Bloomsbury
E-mail: icr@icrev.demon.co.uk
Website: www.icrev.demon.co.uk/icrbook.htm

The ICR investigates complaints about HM Land Registry, the Charity Commission, the Public Record Office and the Housing Corporation.

Independent Complaints Reviewer: Jodi Berg

Independent Housing Ombudsman Scheme

Norman House, 105–109 Strand,
London WC2R 0AA
Tel: 020 7836 3630   Fax: 020 7836 3900
Lo-call Tel: 0845 7125973
Minicom: 020 7240 6776
E-mail: ombudsman@ihos.org.uk
Website: www.ihos.org.uk

IHO deals with complaints against social landlords registered with the Housing Corporation, and other landlords who have volunteered to join the scheme. IHO is also managing a pilot scheme (Tenancy Deposit Scheme) to resolve disputes about rent deposits in the private sector.

Chair: Gill Lewis
Ombudsman: Dr Michael Biles
General Manager and Company Secretary:
  Wilma Jarvie

Lay Observer for Northern Ireland

4th Floor, Brookmount Buildings, 42 Fountain Street, Belfast BT1 5EE
Tel: 028 9024 5028   Fax: 028 9025 1944

The Lay Observer is an independent non-legal person appointed to monitor the nature of complaints against solicitors made to the Law Society and to report on the manner in which the Law Society handles them.

The Lay Observer: Prof Vincent Mageean, OBE

Office for the Supervision of Solicitors – OSS

Victoria Court, 8 Dormer Place, Leamington Spa, Warwickshire CV32 5AE
Tel: 01926 820082   Fax: 01926 431435
Helpline: 0845 608 6565
Website: www.lawsociety.org.uk

Director: Stuart Bushell

Office of the Legal Services Ombudsman

3rd Floor, Sunlight House, Quay Street,
Manchester M3 3JZ
Local call rate: 0845 601 0794
Tel: 0161-839 7262   Fax: 0161-832 5446
E-mail: lso@olso.gsi.gov.uk
Website: www.olso.org

Ombudsman: Ms Zahida Manzoor CBE

Office of the Parliamentary Commissioner for Administration

Millbank Tower, Millbank, London SW1P 4QP
Tel: 0845 015 4033   Fax: 020 7217 4000
E-mail: opca.enquiries@ombudsman.gsi.gov.uk
Website: www.ombudsman.org.uk

The Parliamentary Commissioner for Administration (the Parliamentary Ombudsman) is independent of Government and is an officer of Parliament. She investigates complaints, referred to her by MPs from members of the public, about maladministration by, or on behalf of, government departments and certain non-departmental public bodies. She also investigates complaints referred by MPs alleging that access to official information has been wrongly refused under the Code of Practice on Access to Government Information 1994.

Parliamentary Commissioner for
Administration: Ann Abraham
Deputy Parliamentary Commissioner for
Administration: Alan Watson

Office of the Subsidence Adviser

PO Box 314, Saxilby, Lincoln LN1 2ZD
Tel: 01522 820215   Fax: 01522 820215
E-mail: admin@subsidenceadviser.org.uk
Website: www.subsidenceadviser.org.uk

Subsidence Adviser: Malcolm Webb

Office of the Telecommunications Ombudsman – Otelo

Wilderspool Park, Greenhall's Avenue,
Warrington WA4 6HL
Tel: 08450 501614   Fax: 08450 501615
E-mail: enquiries@otelo.org.uk
Website: www.otelo.org.uk

Ombudsman: Mrs Elizabeth France CBE
Company Secretary: Richard Brown
Director of Operations: Dr Richard Sills

Ombudsman for Estate Agents

Beckett House, 4 Bridge Street, Salisbury,
Wiltshire SP1 2LX
Tel: 01722 333306   Fax: 01722 332296
E-mail: admin@oea.co.uk
Website: www.oea.co.uk

Ombudsman: Stephen Carr-Smith

Pensions Ombudsman

11 Belgrave Road, London SW1V 1RB
Tel: 020 7834 9144   Fax: 020 7821 0065
E-mail: enquiries@pensions-ombudsman.org.uk
Website: www.pensions-ombudsman.org.uk

The Pensions Ombudsman investigates and decides complaints and disputes about the way that pensions schemes are run. Complaints about the sales and marketing of pension schemes are dealt with by the Financial Ombudsman Service. The Pensions Ombudsman's role and powers have been decided by Parliament. The appointment of the Ombudsman is made by the Secretary of State for Work and Pensions. The Ombudsman is completely independent and acts as an impartial adjudicator. The Pensions Ombudsman's decision is final and binding on all the parties to the complaint or dispute. It can be enforced in the Courts. A decision can only be changed by appealing to the appropriate court on a point of law. Only the Ombudsman has power to make the final and binding decision.

Ombudsman: David Laverick

Police Complaints Authority – PCA

10 Great George Street, London SW1P 3AE
Tel: 020 7273 6450   Fax: 020 7273 6401
E-mail: info@pca.gov.uk
Website: www.pca.gov.uk

Chairman: Sir Alistair Graham
Deputy Chairman: Ian Bynoe
Deputy Chairman: Wendy Towers

Police Ombudsman for Northern Ireland

New Cathedral Buildings, St Anne's Square,
11 Church Street, Belfast BT1 1PG
Tel: 028 9082 8600
E-mail: info@policeombudsman.org
Website: www.policeombudsman.org

The Office of the Police Ombudsman for Northern Ireland provides an independent and impartial system for the investigation of complaints against police officers. The Office was established under the Police (Northern Ireland) Act 1998 to provide this system for the public and the police. It deals with complaints about how police officers behave when on duty. Complaints may involve allegations of criminal behaviour by a police officer or allegations that a police officer has broken the police code of conduct. The Police Ombudsman may also investigate a matter – even if no complaint has been received – if she has reason to believe it is in the public interest to do so. The Office also monitors trends and patterns in police complaints.

Ombudsman: Nuala O'Loan

Prisons and Probation Ombudsman for England and Wales

Ashley House, 2 Monck Street,
London SW1P 2BQ
Tel: 020 7035 2876   Fax: 020 7035 2860
E-mails: info@ppo.gsi.gov.uk
mail@ppo.gsi.gov.uk
Website: www.ppo.gov.uk

Considers complaints from prisoners and those subject to probation supervision who have failed to obtain satisfaction from the internal complaints systems.

Ombudsman: Stephen Shaw

Scottish Legal Services Ombudsman

17 Waterloo Place, Edinburgh EH1 3DL
Tel: 0131-556 9123   Fax: 0131-556 9292
E-mail: ombudsman@slso.org.uk
Website: www.slso.org.uk

Ombudsman: Mrs Linda Costelloe Baker

Scottish Parliamentary Commissioner for Administration

See Scottish Public Services Ombudsman

Scottish Public Services Ombudsman

23 Walker Street, Edinburgh, EH3 7HX
Tel: 0870 011 5378   Fax: 0870 011 5379
E-mail: enquiries@scottishombudsman.org.uk
Website: www.scottishombudsman.org.uk

The Scottish Public Services Ombudsman considers complaints from members of the public about Scottish Government Departments, Councils, Housing Associations, other public bodies and the NHS. She is completely independent.

Ombudsman: Prof Alice Brown
Deputy Ombudsmen: Eric Drake, Carolyn Hirst, Lewis Shand Smith

Waterways Ombudsman

PO Box 406, Haywards Heath, West Sussex
RH17 5GF
Tel/Fax: 01273 832624

Investigates and resolves complaints of maladministration against British Waterways.

Ombudsman: Stephen Edell

Welsh Administration Ombudsman

5th Floor, Capital Tower, Greyfriars Road,
Cardiff CF10 3AG
Tel: 0845 601 0987   Fax: 029 2022 6909
E-mail: wao.enquiries@ombudsman.gsi.gov.uk
Website: www.ombudsman.org.uk

The Welsh Administration Ombudsman investigates complaints about injustice resulting from maladministration by the National Assembly for Wales or certain public bodies involved in devolved Welsh affairs. She can also look at complaints that individuals have been refused information to which they are entitled under the Code of Practice on Public Access to Information adopted by the National Assembly.

Welsh Administration Ombudsman:
    Ann Abraham
Investigations Manager: Stan Drummond

DodOnline

An Electrical Directory without rival ...

Civil Servants' biographies and photographs available with daily updates
via the internet

For a *free* trial, call Yasmin Mirza, Aby Farsoun or Michael Mand on 020 7630 7643

REGULATORY BODIES

Advertising Standards Authority – ASA

2 Torrington Place, London WC1E 7HW
Tel: 020 7580 5555   Fax: 020 7631 3051
E-mail: enquiries@asa.org.uk
Website: www.asa.org.uk

The ASA is the independent, self-regulatory body for non-broadcast advertisements in the UK. It administers the British Code of Advertising, Sales Promotion and Direct Marketing to ensure that marketing communications are legal, decent, honest and truthful.

Chairman: Lord Borrie QC
Director-General: Christopher Graham
Council Members: Jean Coussins, Christine Farnish, Sunil Gadhia, Mike Ironside, David Lipsey, David McNair, Lizzie Marsden, Susan Murray, Dan O'Donoghue, Martyn Percy, Pauline Thomas, Donald Trelford

Consumers' Association – CA

2 Marylebone Road, London NW1 4DF
Tel: 020 7770 7000
E-mail: public_affairs@which.co.uk
Website: www.which.net/

Consumers' Association, publishers of Which? magazines and books, are a not-for-profit organisation and has been researching and campaigning on behalf of consumers since they were founded in 1957. With over 700,000 members, they are the largest consumer organisation in Europe.

Chairman: Brian Yates
Chief Executive: Dame Sheila McKechnie

Financial Services Authority – FSA

25 The North Colonnade, Canary Wharf,
London E14 5HS
Tel: 020 7066 1000
Consumer Helpline: 0845 606 1234
(including Central Register authorisation queries)
Website: www.fsa.gov.uk

On 1 December 2001 the FSA assumed its full powers and responsibilities under the Financial Services and Markets Act 2000. The FSA is now the single statutory regulator responsible for regulating deposit taking, insurance and investment business. New responsibilities for tackling market abuse, promoting public understanding of the financial system and reducing financial crime have now come under the FSA remit.

Chairman: Callum McCarthy
Deputy Chairman: Stewart Boyd QC
Board Members: Moira Black CBE, Tom de Swaan, Michael Foot CBE MD FSA, Kyra Hazou, Deirdre Hutton CBE, Sir Andrew Large, Gillian Nott OBE, Christopher Rodrigues, Dr Shamit Saggar, Carol Sergeant MD FSA, Stephen Thieke, Clive Wilkinson
Chief Executive: John Tiner

General Consumer Council for Northern Ireland – GCCNI

Elizabeth House, 116 Holywood Road,
Belfast BT4 1NY
Tel: 028 9067 2488   Fax: 028 9065 7701
E-mail: info@gccni.org.uk
Websites: www.gccni.org.uk;
www.consumerline.org

The GCCNI is a statutory body whose aims are to promote and safeguard the interests of all consumers in Northern Ireland. The Council campaigns on behalf of consumers for the best possible standards of service and protection; undertakes research and data collection; gives advice, information and issues publications. It deals with individual complaints about passenger transport, coal, natural gas and electricity.

Set up by Government, the Council is funded by the Department of Enterprise, Trade and Investment.

Chair: Stephen Costello MBE
Deputy Chairman: Bill Osborne
Chief Executive: Eleanor Gill

Heathrow Airport Consultative Committee – HACC

Visitor Centre, Heathrow Airport,
Middlesex UB3 5AP
Tel: 020 8745 7589   Fax: 020 8745 0580
E-mail: hacc@hacc.org.uk
Website: www.lhr-acc.org

The HACC provides an effective forum for discussion of all matters concerning the development or operation of the airport which have an impact on its users and people living and working in affected areas and the economy of the region.

Chairman: Sam Jones CBE DL
Technical Adviser:
   Maurice Hudson DiptTS MRAeS FLIT FIHT
Secretary: Carole Havercroft

National Consumer Council – NCC
20 Grosvenor Gardens, London SW1W 0DH
Tel: 020 7730 3469   Fax: 020 7730 0191
E-mails: info@ncc.org.uk   press@ncc.org.uk
Website: www.ncc.org.uk

The National Consumer Council is an independent consumer expert, championing the consumer interest to bring about change for the benefit of all consumers. Issues of disadvantage are at the heart of its work, as often the most vulnerable people find it hardest to be heard. It is a Non-Departmental Public Body funded mostly by the Department of Trade and Industry.

Chair: Deirdre Hutton CBE
Chief Executive: Ed Mayo
Head of External Affairs: Diane Gaston

Northern Ireland Authority for Energy Regulation – NIAER – OFREG
Brookmount Buildings, 42 Fountain Street,
Belfast BT1 5EE
Tel: 028 9031 1575   Fax: 028 9031 1740
E-mail: ofreg@nics.gov.uk
Website: ofreg.nics.gov.uk/

The Energy (Northern Ireland) Order 2003 established the Northern Ireland Authority for Energy Regulation (the Authority) on 1 April 2003. Most of the functions of the Directors General for Electricity Supply and Gas for Northern Ireland transferred to the Authority which has responsibility for promoting competition in the generation and supply of electricity; promoting the development of the natural industry, and regulating certain electricity and gas prices. The Authority will continue to use the popular name Ofreg for its day to day working arrangements.

Chief Executive, Ofreg/Chairman, NIAER:
  Douglas McIldoon
Deputy Chief Executive: Dermot MacCann

OFCOM – the Office of Communications
Riverside House, 2A Southwark Bridge Road,
London, SE1 9HA
Switchboard: 020 7981 3000
Fax: 020 7981 3333
E-mails: webmaster@ofcom.org.uk
[firstname.surname]@ofcom.org.uk
Website: www.ofcom.org.uk

Ofcom (the Office of Communications) will be the UK's new media and communications regulator when it launches at the end of 2003.

An independent regulatory body, Ofcom will enact the provisions laid down in the Communications Act intended to ensure that commercial television and radio, telecommunications networks and wireless and satellite services operate, compete and develop in the greater public interest. In addition, Ofcom will have limited powers over BBC television and radio and will advise the Secretary of State on proposed newspaper mergers.

The organisation will also inherit the powers and statutory duties of the five existing regulators it will replace – the Broadcasting Standards Commission, the Independent Television Commission, Oftel, the Radio Authority and the Radiocommunications Agency.

Chairman: Lord Currie of Marylebone
Deputy Chairman: Richard Hooper
Chief Executive: Stephen Carter

Board Members
Executive Members
Kip Meek
Ed Richards
Non-Executive Members
Millie Banerjee
David Edmonds, CBE
Ian Hargreaves
Sara Nathan

Ofcom Senior Staff
Policy – Strategy and Market Developments
*Senior Partner, Strategy and Market
  Developments:* Ed Richards
Partner, Strategy Development: Robin Foster
Strategy Adviser: Alan Bell

Policy – Competition and Content
Senior Partner, Competition and Content:
  Kip Meek

Partners
Policy Development: Tim Suter
Competition and Investigations:
  Sean Williams
Competition and Strategic Resources:
  Philip Rutnam

Operations
Operations Director: Vic Brashko
Partner, Licensing: Hazel Canter

External Relations
Director: Tony Stoller
Communications Director:
  Matt Peacock
Director, Office of the Chief Executive:
  Dominic Morris

Content Board

The Ofcom Content Board is a sub-committee of the main Board responsible for championing the interests of audiences. It serves in an advisory capacity as Ofcom's primary forum for the regulation of television and radio quality and standards.

The Content Board has thirteen members, appointed by the Ofcom Board. The majority of content Board members are part-time and drawn from diverse backgrounds across the UK, including both lay members and members with extensive broadcasting experience. Four are appointed to represent the interests and opinions of those living in Scotland, Wales, Northern Ireland and the English Regions.

Chairman: Richard Hooper
Deputy Chair: Sara Nathan

Members
Sue Balsom – (Wales)
Floella Benjamin OBE
Kevin Carey
Jonathan Edwards CBE – (English Regions)
Pam Giddy
Rosemary Kelly – (Northern Ireland)
Matthew MacIver – (Scotland)
Kip Meek
Adam Singer
Tim Suter
Kath Worrall

Available websites for further details:
Broadcasting Standards Commission:
www.bsc.org.uk
Department for Culture, Media and Sport:
www.culture.gov.uk
Department of Trade and Industry:
www.dti.gsi.gov.uk
Independent Television Commission:
www.itc.org.uk
Ofcom (Office of Communications):
www.ofcom.org.uk
Oftel (Office of Telecommunications):
www.oftel.gov.uk
Radio Authority: www.radioauthority.org.uk
Radiocommunications Agency:
www.radio.gov.uk

N.B. Ofcom will not be vested with its statutory powers until the end of the year.

Office for Standards in Education – Ofsted

Alexandra House, 33 Kingsway,
London WC2B 6SE
Tel: 020 7421 6800   Fax 020 7421 6707

E-mails: geninfo@ofsted.gov.uk
[initialsurname]@ofsted.gov.uk
Website: www.ofsted.gov.uk

A non-ministerial government department responsible for inspecting and reporting on standards in schools, initial teacher training, local educational authorities, all 16-19 education, and regulation of children's daycare (eg childminders, nurseries, creches and after-school clubs).

HM Chief Inspector: David Bell
Director of Inspection: David Taylor
Director of Early Years: Maurice Smith
Director of Strategy and Resources:
    Robert Green
Head of Research, Analysis and International:
    Timothy Key
Head of School Improvement:
    Kath Cross
Head of Secondary: Mike Raleigh
Head of Primary: Roger Shippam
Head of Post Compulsory:
    David Singleton
Head of Contracts: Ceridwen Clarke
Head of Teacher Education: Cliff Gould
Head of Personnel Management:
    Andrew White
*Head of Subjects and Quality Assurance
    Division:* Miriam Rosen
Head of Information Technology:
    Peter Duffy
Head of Communications and Strategy:
    Lorraine Chapman
Head of Inspection Quality (Schools):
    Peter Matthews OBE
Head of Curriculum Advice and Inspection:
    Brian McCafferty
Head of LEA 1 (LEA Inspection):
    Sheila Brown
Head of Finance: Peter Jolly
Head of Corporate Management: Roger Knight
Head of Early Years Policy: Denise Hevey
Head of Early Years Operations:
    Dorian Bradley
Heads of Early Years Regional Divisions:
East Anglia: David Gane
East Midlands: Toni Smith
London: Clive Bramley
North-East: Nancy Palmer
North-West: Bryan Roberts
South-East: Marion Witton
South-West: Elspeth Davis
West Midlands: Heather Mytton-Sanneh

Office of Gas and Electricity Markets – Ofgem

9 Millbank, London SW1P 3GE
Tel: 020 7901 7000   Fax: 020 7901 7066
E-mail: [firstname.surname]@ofgem.gov.uk
Website: www.ofgem.gov.uk

Ofgem is governed by a board of executive and non-executive members, known as the Gas and Electricity Markets Authority.

Executive

Chairman, Gas and Electricity Markets Authority: Sir John Mogg
Managing Director, Competition and Trading Arrangements: Dr Boaz Moselle
Managing Director, Customers and Supply: John Neilson
Managing Director, Regulation and Financial Affairs: David Gray
Chief Executive: To be appointed
Chief Operating Officer: Roy Field

Non-Executive Members of the Authority

John Belcher, Richard Farrant, Margaret Ford, James Strachan, Sir Keith Stuart, Prof Leonard Waverman, Dr Robin Bidwell

Office of Telecommunications – Oftel

50 Ludgate Hill, London EC4M 7JJ
Tel: 020 7634 8700   Fax: 020 7634 8943
E-mails: infocent@oftel.gov.uk
[firstname.surname]@oftel.gov.uk
Website: www.oftel.gov.uk

The independent regulator of the UK telecommunications industry. Aims to deliver the best deal for UK telecommunications customers in terms of quality, choice and value for money through a competitive telecoms market. Oftel is one the five communications regulators that will form the new communications regulator Ofcom.

Director-General: David Edmonds CBE
Director of Operations: Peter Waller
Director of Regulatory Policy: Philip Rutnam
Director of Compliance: Christopher Kenny
Director of Technology: Peter Walker
Director of Strategy and Forecasting: Alan Bell
Director of Business Support: David Smith
Director of Communications: Duncan Stroud

Office of the Rail Regulator and International Rail Regulator – ORR

1 Waterhouse Square, 138–142 Holborn, London EC1N 2TQ
Tel: 020 7282 2000   Fax: 020 7282 2040
E-mail: rail.library@orr.gsi.gov.uk
Website: www.rail-reg.gov.uk

The Office of the Rail Regulator was established in 1993. In Britain's railways, the Rail Regulator is responsible for regulation of the monopoly and dominant elements of the rail industry, especially the infrastructure owner. He sets the contractual and financial framework within which the infrastructure owner works to maintain, renew and expand the network. His job is to ensure that its income – a combination of private finance and public subsidy set by the Regulator – is spent on the right things at the right times. He also approves agreements governing the terms and conditions by which train operators gain access to the track and infrastructure, and licenses all operators.

Rail Regulator: Tom Winsor
Director of Strategy, Planning, Communications and Resources: Keith Webb
Chief Rail Adviser: Michael Beswick
Director of Access, Competition and Licensing: Steve Gooding
Chief Economist, Director of Finance and Economics: Tim Martin
Head of Information: Ian Cooke
Senior Press Officer: David Davies

Office of Water Services – Ofwat

Centre City Tower, 7 Hill Street, Birmingham B5 4UA
Tel: 0121-625 1300   Fax: 0121-625 1400
E-mails: enquiries@ofwat.gsi.gov.uk
[firstname.surname]@ofwat.gsi.gov.uk
Website: www.ofwat.gov.uk

Responsible for regulating the water and sewerage industry in England and Wales, protecting customers, facilitating competition and promoting economy and efficiency.

Director-General: Philip Fletcher
Directors
Costs and Performance, and Chief Engineer: Dr Bill Emery
Competition and Consumer Affairs: Tony Smith
Operations: Roger Dunshea
Regulatory Finance: Keith Mason
Legal Services: Huw Brooker
Publications and Parliamentary Affairs: Ingrid Olsen
Head of Consumer Representation Division: Roy Wardle

Postal Services Commission – Postcomm

Hercules House, 6 Hercules Road,
London SE1 7DB
Tel: 020 7593 2100   Fax: 020 7593 2142
E-mail: info@psc.gov.uk
Website: www.postcomm.gov.uk

Postcomm is an independent regulator. It was created by the Postal Services Act 2000 to further the interests of users of postal services. Its main tasks are to: seek to ensure the provision of a universal postal service at a uniform tariff, promote effective competition in postal services, license The Royal Mail Group, control prices and its quality of service, license other companies wishing to enter the market, advise Government on developments in the Post Office network.

Chairman: Graham Corbett CBE
Chief Executive: Martin Stanley
Director, Competition: Nick Fincham
Director, Regulation: Roger Louth
Director, Customers and Operators: Debbie Gillatt
Director, Network: Jeanette Darrell
Director, Legal Adviser: William Sprigge
Director, Operations: Nancy Holloway

Postwatch

28-30 Grosvenor Gardens, London SW1W 0TT
Tel: 020 7259 1200
Customer Helpline: 08456 013 265
Fax: 020 7730 3044
E-mail: info@postwatch.co.uk
Website: www.postwatch.co.uk

Postwatch, the consumer watchdog for postal services, was created by parliament. It is an independent organisation, not attached to the Royal Mail Group or part of the government. Postwatch was set up to ensure that Royal Mail, post offices, Parcelforce and any other licensed operator provide the best service possible to their customers.

Chairman: Peter Carr
Chief Executive: Gregor McGregor

Press Complaints Commission – PCC

1 Salisbury Square, London EC4Y 8JB
Tel: 020 7353 1248
Fax: 020 7353 8355
Helpline: 020 7353 3732
Scottish Helpline: 0131-220 6652
Welsh Helpline: 029 2039 5570

Emergencies only:
24-hour Press Office: 07669 195539
24-hour Advice Line: 07659 152656
E-mail: pcc@pcc.org.uk
Website: www.pcc.org.uk

Chairman:
   Sir Christopher Meyer KCMG
Director: Guy Black

Scottish Consumer Council – SCC

Royal Exchange House, 100 Queen Street,
Glasgow G1 3DN
Tel: 0141-226 5261   Fax: 0141-221 0731
E-mail: scc@scotconsumer.org.uk
Website: www.scotconsumer.org.uk

The Scottish Consumer Council was set up by government in 1975 to promote the interests of Scottish consumers, with particular regard to those people who experience disadvantage in society.

Chairman: Graeme Millar BSc
Director: Martyn Evans

Strategic Rail Authority – SRA

55 Victoria Street, London SW1H 0EU
Tel: 020 7654 6000   Fax: 020 7654 6010
E-mails: info@sra.gov.uk
[firstname.surname]@sra.gov.uk
Website: www.sra.gov.uk

Specifies the rail services delivered by franchised train operating companies, and the upgrades required to rail infrastructure in Great Britain. Provides strategic leadership and public funding to the rail industry (passenger and freight), and has responsibility for consumer protection issues.

Chairman and Chief Executive:
   Richard Bowker
Secretary to the Board: Peter Trewin
Chief Operating Officer: Nicola Shaw
Managing Directors:
Operations: Nick Newton
Finance and Commercial:
   Doug Sutherland
Strategic Planning: Jim Steer
Executive Directors:
Communications: Ceri Evans
Corporate Affairs: Chris Austin
Technical: David Wabosa
Freight: Jonathan Riley (acting)
General Legal Counsel: Tim Reardon

Trading Standards Institute – TSI

4/5 Hadleigh Business Centre, 351
London Road, Hadleigh, Essex SS7 2BT
Tel: 0870 872 9000   Fax: 0870 872 9025
E-mail: institute@tsi.org.uk
Trading Standards Central Website Link:
www.tradingstandards.gov.uk

Its purpose is to promote excellence and enhance the professionalism of members in support of informing consumers and encouraging traders about fair and honest trading.

President: Baroness Wilcox of Plymouth
Chairman: Bryn Aldridge
Vice-Chairman: Ian Warwick
Chief Executive: Ron Gainsford
Hon Secretary: Chris Armstrong
Hon Treasury: John Evans
Director of Training: Katherine McDiarmid
Editor in Chief: Tony Northcott
Chairman of Executive Board: Mike Drewry
Chairman of Board of Directors itsa Ltd:
  Ian Warwick

Welsh Consumer Council – WCC

5th Floor, Longcross Court, 47 Newport Road,
Cardiff CF24 0WL
Tel: 029 2025 5454   Fax: 029 2025 5464
E-mail: info@wales-consumer.org.uk
Websites: www.wales-consumer.org.uk
www.consumereducation.org.uk

The WCC is the national consumer body for Wales. It works to represent the interests of domestic buyers and users of goods and services in Wales. The Council carries out research on behalf of consumers. It uses publications, conferences, lobbying, television, radio, the press and all other appropriate means to highlight and represent the needs and interests of consumers in Wales to industry, government and local authorities.

Chair: Vivienne Sugar
Vice-Chairman: Vacant

DodOnline

An Electronic Directory without rival . . .

Civil Servants' biographies and photographs available with daily updates
via the internet

For a *free* trial, call Yasmin Mirza, Aby Farsoun or Michael Mand on 020 7630 7643

POLITICAL AND PARLIAMENTARY ORGANISATIONS

Armed Forces Parliamentary Scheme
13 Cowley Street, London SW1P 3LZ
Tel: 020 7222 0480   Fax: 020 7222 7783

Provides MPs with work experience in the armed services at major or equivalent level based on attachments for 22 days a year, at least six of which are continuous. After a year MPs are eligible for further experience at Lieutenant Colonel or equivalent level for an additional 18 days.

Chair: Sir Neil Thorne OBE TD DL

Auditor General for Wales
3-4 Park Place, Cardiff CF10 3DP
Tel: 029 2067 8545   Fax: 029 2067 8501
Website: www.agw.wales.gov.uk

Auditor General for Wales: Sir John Bourn KCB
Head of Press Office: Mark Strathdene
Directors: Ian Summers, Mike Usher,
    Gillian Body, Frank Grogan, Janice Lawler
Private Secretary: Helen Kirkby

CBI
Centre Point, 103 New Oxford Street,
London WC1A 1DU
Tel: 020 7395 8123   Fax: 020 7395 8009
E-mail: anthony.thompson@cbi.org.uk
sarah.singleton@cbi.org.uk
Website: www.cbi.org.uk

Independent non party-political body financed entirely by industry and commerce. It exists primarily to ensure that Governments of all political complexions understand the intentions, needs and problems of British business. It is the acknowledged spokesman for business and is consulted as such by Governments.

President: Sir John Egan
Director-General: Digby Jones
Deputy Director-General: John Cridland
Parliamentary Affairs: Anthony Thompson

Commonwealth Parliamentary Association
(United Kingdom Branch)
Westminster Hall, Houses of Parliament,
London SW1A 0AA
Tel: 020 7219 5373   Fax: 020 7233 1202
E-mail: cpa@parliament.uk

Chairman of the Executive Committee:
    Tom Cox MP
Joint Hon Treasurer: Sir Patrick Cormack MP
Secretary: Andrew Pearson

Electoral Commission
Trevelyan House, 30 Great Peter Street,
London SW1P 2HW
Tel: 020 7271 0500   Fax: 020 7271 0505
E-mail: info@electoral.commission.org.uk
Website: www.electoralcommission.org.uk

Northern Ireland Office, 55-59 Adelaide Street,
Belfast BT2 8FE
Tel: 028 9072 6008   Fax: 028 9072 6066

Wales Office, 1-6 St Andrews Place,
Cardiff CF10 3BE
Tel: 029 2034 6801   Fax: 029 2034 6805

Scotland Office, 28 Thistle Street,
Edinburgh EH2 1EN
Tel: 0131-225 0201   Fax: 0131-225 0205

Registration of political parties; reporting of donations to political parties; monitoring election campaign spending; reviewing electoral law and practice; voter education and awareness of electoral systems; local government boundaries.

Commissioners:
Chair: Sam Younger
Pamela Gordon, Glyn Mathias,
    Sir Neil McIntosh CBE, Karamjit Singh CBE,
    Professor Graham Zellick

Electoral Office for Northern Ireland
St Anne's House, 15 Church Street,
Belfast BT1 1ER
Tel: 028 9033 9955   Fax: 028 9033 0661
E-mail: [firstname.surname]@eoni.gov.uk

Chief Electoral Officer: Denis Stanley

Electoral Reform Society
6 Chancel Street, Blackfriars, London SE1 0UU
Tel: 020 7928 1622   Fax: 020 7401 7789
E-mail: ers@reform.demon.co.uk
Website: www.electoral-reform.org.uk

The Society promotes the modernisation of our democracy, principally through improvements in voting systems for all levels of government. It also provides information services on electoral issues. The Society has two subsidiaries:

– Electoral Reform Ballot Services (ERBS: 020 8365 8909) which conducts and advises on ballots and market research
– Electoral Reform International Services (ERIS: 020 7620 3794) which provides electoral assistance in Africa, Asia, Latin America and eastern Europe.

President: Prof the Earl Russell FBA
Chair: Keith Best
Vice-Chair: Dr Nina Fishman
Treasurer: Dr Crispin Allard
Chief Executive and Company Secretary:
  Dr Ken Ritchie
Managing Director, ERBS: Owen Thomas
Executive Director, ERIS: Simon Osborn

Hansard Society for Parliamentary Government

London School of Economics, 9 Kingsway, London WC2B 6XF
Tel: 020 7955 7459   Fax: 020 7955 7492
E-mail: hansard@hansard.lse.ac.uk
Website: www.hansardsociety.org.uk

The Hansard Society promotes effective parliamentary democracy. Supported by Mr Speaker, Party leaders, MPs and Peers, the Society's activities range from mock elections in schools to research, on-line debates, study days and publications. Its programmes cover e-democracy, the modernisation of Parliament and citizenship education.

President: Rt Hon Michael Martin MP
Vice-Presidents: Rt Hon Tony Blair MP,
  Rt Hon Iain Duncan Smith MP,
  Rt Hon Charles Kennedy MP,
Chairman:
  Rt Hon Lord Holme of Cheltenham CBE
Vice-Chairs: Austin Mitchell MP,
  Rt Hon Gillian Shephard MP,
  Rt Hon Sir George Young MP,
  Lord Tomlinson
Hon Treasurer: Wilf Weeks
Director: Clare Ettinghausen
Director, E-democracy Programme:
  Mark Rickard
Director, Citizenship Education Programme:
  Raji Hunjan
Communications Manager:
  Virginia Gibbons

Industry and Parliament Trust

1 Buckingham Place, London SW1E 6HR
020 7630 3700 Fax 020 7630 3701
E-mail: admin@ipt.org.uk
Website: www.ipt.org.uk

The Trust, an independent educational charity, was established in 1977 to make a positive contribution towards improving understanding between the world of industry including finance and commerce and Members and Officers of both Houses of Parliament and MEPs – of all parties.
The Trust is non-partisan, non-profit making and is not a parliamentary lobby.

Presidents: Rt Hon Lord Irvine of Lairg, QC (The
  Lord Chancellor), Rt Hon Michael Martin MP
  (Speaker of the House of Commons)
Vice-President: Rt Hon Lord Weatherill, DL
Chairman of Trustees: Lord Tomlinson
Chairman of the Executive Committee:
  Jim Meredith (Managing Director, Shanks
  Group plc)
Acting Chief Executive: Peter Sharp

Inter-Parliamentary Union
British Group

Palace of Westminster, London SW1A 0AA
Tel: 020 7219 3011/2/3   Fax: 020 7222 1213
E-mail: bgipu@parliament.uk

Chair: John Austin MP
Vice-Chairs: Ann Clwyd MP, John Wilkinson MP
Treasurer: Derek Conway MP

National Audit Office

157–197 Buckingham Palace Road, Victoria, London SW1W 9SP
Tel: 020 7798 7000 Press: 020 7798 7400
Fax: 020 7828 3774
E-mail: enquiries@nao.gsi.gov.uk
Website: www.nao.gov.uk

The Office has total financial and operational independence from the government and its head, the Comptroller and Auditor-General, is an officer of the House of Commons.
The NAO provides independent information, advice and assurance to Parliament on all aspects of the financial operations of government departments and many other bodies receiving public funds.

Comptroller and Auditor-General:
  Sir John Bourn, KCB
Deputy Comptroller and Auditor-General:
  Tim Burr
Assistant Auditors-General: Jeremy Colman,
  Wendy Kenway-Smith, Michael Whitehouse,
  Caroline Mawhood, Martin Sinclair,
  Jim Rickleton
Director of Communications: Gabrielle Cohen
Head of Press Office: Mark Andrews
Parliamentary Relations Officer: Steve Luxford

Police Service Parliamentary Scheme

13 Cowley Street, London SW1P 3LZ
Tel: 020 8501 1673   Fax: 020 8500 6854

Provides MPs with work experience with the police for 22 days a year of which a minimum of six are on the beat with police constables.

Chair: Sir Neil Thorne OBE TD DL

Trades Union Congress

Congress House, Great Russell Street,
London WC1B 3LS
Tel: 020 7636 4030   Fax: 020 7636 0632
E-mail: info@tuc.org.uk
Website: www.tuc.org.uk

The Trades Union Congress is a voluntary association of independent unions. It consists of 69 unions representing 6.7 million workers. Its governing body is the annual Congress consisting of 767 delegates. Between Congresses, a General Council of 56 members meets seven times a year. The main job of the TUC is to campaign for trade union aims and values. It prepares common policies on matters of importance to people at work and has representatives on a number of public bodies. It maintains close links with trade union movements overseas and runs a substantial education service for union officers on issues such as employment law. There is also an extensive regional network.

President: Nigel de Gruchy
General Secretary: Brendan Barber
Deputy-General Secretary: Frances O'Grady
Assistant General Secretary: Kay Carberry
Head, Economic and Social Affairs Department:
    David Coats
Head, Organisation and Services Department:
    Tom Wilson
*Head, Equality and Employment Rights
    Department:* Sarah Veale
Head, Europe and International Dept:
    Tom Jenkins
Head, Management Services Department:
    Mike Jones
*Head, Campaigns and Communications
    Department:* Nigel Stanley
Parliamentary Officer: Isobel Larkin

Whitehall and Industry Group

22 Queen Anne's Gate, London SW1H 9AA
Tel: 020 7222 1166   Fax: 020 7222 1167
E-mail: info@wig.co.uk
Website: www.wig.co.uk

The Whitehall & Industry Group, established in 1984, is an independent, not-for-profit organisation which works to improve communication and understanding between government and the private sector through exchange of people, ideas, information and best practice.

It works in close co-operation with all major government departments and agencies, with local government and with companies, encouraging and organising a wide variety of interchange activity. This ranges from information, awareness raising and networking events, attachments and secondments (both short and longer term) to workshops and leadership development programmes.

Chief Executive: Sally Cartello

Visit the Vacher Dod Website . . .
www.DodOnline.co.uk

PRIVY COUNSELLORS

Privy Counsellors historically advised the monarch. The title is now largely honorary; it is given automatically to all cabinet members and the Speaker, the archbishops of Canterbury and York and the Bishop of London and to holders of certain judicial appointments. Leaders of the main political parties are conventionally nominated. Other members from the UK and Commonwealth are appointed on the prime minister's recommendation.

The appointment is for life, unless withdrawn, and holders are addressed as 'Right Honourable' (Rt Hon).

HRH The Duke of Edinburgh		James Bolger	1991
HRH The Prince of Wales		Albert Booth	1976
Lord Aberdare	1974	Baroness Boothroyd	1992
Lord Ackner	1980	Hon Robert Boscawen	1992
Earl of Airlie	1984	Virginia Bottomley	1992
Sir William Aldous	1995	Colin Boyd	2000
Ezekiel Alebua	1988	Sir Rhodes Boyson	1987
Michael Alison	1981	Keith Bradley	2001
Baroness Amos	2003	Sir Nicholas Brathwaite	1991
Lord Ampthill	1995	Lord Bridge of Harwich	1975
Michael Ancram	1996	Lord Brightman	1979
Donald Anderson	2000	Lord Brittan of Spennithorne	1981
Douglas Anthony	1971	Sir Henry Brooke	1996
James Arbuthnot	1998	Lord Brooke of Sutton Mandeville	1988
Lord Archer of Sandwell	1977	Gordon Brown	1996
Dame Mary Arden	2000	Nicholas Brown	1997
Hilary Armstrong	1999	Sir Simon Brown	1992
Sir John Arnold	1979	Sir Stephen Brown	1983
Hon Owen Arthur	1995	*Lord Browne-Wilkinson	1983
Lord Ashdown of Norton-sub-Hamdon	1989	Sir Adam Butler	1984
Lord Ashley of Stoke	1979	Dame Elizabeth Butler-Sloss	1988
Sir Robert Atkins	1995	Sir Richard Buxton	1997
Sir Robin Auld	1995	Stephen Byers	1998
Lord Baker of Dorking	1984	Richard Caborn	1999
Sir Thomas Baker	2002	Earl of Caithness	1990
Lord Barber	1963	Lord Callaghan of Cardiff	1964
Lord Barnett	1975	Lord Cameron of Lochbroom	1984
Kevin Barron	2001	Lord Camoys	1997
John Battle	2002	Menzies Campbell	1999
Margaret Beckett	1993	Sir William Campbell	1999
Alan Beith	1992	Lord Campbell of Croy	1970
Sir Roy Beldam	1989	Archbishop of Canterbury	2002
Lord Belstead	1983	Lord Carey of Clifton	1991
Tony Benn	1964	Lord Carlisle of Bucklow	1979
Lord Biffen	1979	Sir Robert Carnwath	2002
*Lord Bingham of Cornhill	1986	Lord Carr of Hadley	1963
William Birch	1992	Lord Carrington	1959
Sir Gordon Bisson	1987	Sir Robert Carswell	1993
Baroness Blackstone	2001	Lord Carter	1997
Tony Blair	1994	Sir Maurice Casey	1986
Lord Blaker	1983	Sir John Chadwick	1997
†Peter Blanchard	1998	Lord Chalfont	1964
Baroness Blatch	1993	Baroness Chalker of Wallasey	1987
David Blunkett	1997	Sir Julius Chan	1981
Paul Boateng	1999	Sir Christopher Chataway	1970

Lord Clark of Windermere	1997
Helen Clark	1990
Lord Clark of Kempston	1990
Sir Anthony Clarke	1998
Charles Clarke	2001
Kenneth Clarke	1984
Thomas Clarke	1997
Lord Clinton-Davis	1998
Lord Clyde	1996
Lord Cockfield	1982
Fraser Colman	1986
Sir John Compton	1983
John Concannon	1978
Robin Cook	1996
Lord Cooke of Thorndon	1977
Lord Cope of Berkeley	1988
Sir Frederick Corfield	1970
Jean Corston	2003
Hon Lady Cosgrove	2003
Lord Coulsfield	2000
Sir Zelman Cowen	1981
Sir Percy Cradock	1993
Earl of Crawford and Balcarres	1972
Hon Wyatt Creech	1999
Lord Crickhowell	1979
Sir David Croom-Johnson	1984
Hon Lord Cullen of Whitekirk	1997
Jack Cunningham	1993
David Curry	1996
Alistair Darling	1997
Denzil Davies	1978
Ron Davies	1997
David Davis	1997
Terence Davis	1999
Sir Ronald Davison	1978
Lord Dean of Harptree	1991
Baroness Dean of Thornton-le-Fylde	1998
Lord Deedes	1962
Lord Denham	1981
John Denham	2000
Duke of Devonshire	1964
Lord Diamond	1965
Lord Dixon	1996
Frank Dobson	1997
Lord Donaldson of Lymington	1979
Stephen Dorrell	1994
Sir William Douglas	1977
Sir Edward Du Cann	1964
Iain Duncan Smith	2001
Sir Robin Dunn	1980
Sir John Dyson	2001
Paul East	1998
Lord Eden of Winton	1972
Timothy Eggar	1995
†Sir Thomas Eichelbaum	1989
†Hon Dame Sian Elias	1999

Sir Peter Emery	1993
Manuel Esquivel	1986
*Sir Anthony Evans	1992
Sir Edward Eveleigh	1977
Lord Falconer of Thoroton	2003
*Sir Donald Farquharson	1989
Lord Fellowes	1990
Earl Ferrers	1982
Frank Field	1997
†Sir Vincent Floissac	1992
Michael Foot	1974
Lord Forsyth of Drumlean	1995
Eric Forth	1997
Derek Foster	1993
George Foulkes	2002
Lord Fowler	1979
Sir Michael Fox	1981
Malcolm Fraser	1976
Lord Fraser of Carmyllie	1989
John Freeman	1966
Lord Freeman	1993
Reginald Freeson	1976
Lord Garel-Jones	1992
†Thomas Gault	1992
Bruce George	2000
Sir Edward George	1999
Telford Georges	1986
Sir Harry Gibbs	1972
Sir Peter Gibson	1993
Sir Ralph Gibson	1985
Lord Gilbert	1978
Lord Gill	2002
Lord Gilmour of Craigmillar	1973
Lord Glenamara	1964
Sir Iain Glidewell	1985
*Lord Goff of Chieveley	1982
Lord Goldsmith	2002
Sir Alastair Goodlad	1992
Earl of Gowrie	1984
Lord Graham of Edmonton	1998
Hon Sir Douglas Graham	1998
Lord Gray of Contin	1982
Lord Griffiths	1980
Lord Grocott	2002
John Gummer	1985
Lord Habgood	1983
William Hague	1995
Peter Hain	2001
Dame Brenda Hale	1999
Sir Archibald Hamilton	1991
Lord Hamilton	2002
Sir Jeremy Hanley	1994
Lord Hardie	1997
Sir Michael Hardie Boys	1989
Harriet Harman	1997
Walter Harrison	1997

Sir Alan Haselhurst	1999	Lord Kelvedon	1980
Lord Hattersley	1975	Sir Peter Kenilorea	1979
Lord Hayhoe	1985	Charles Kennedy	1999
Baroness Hayman	2000	Jane Kennedy	2003
Lord Healey	1964	Sir Paul Kennedy	1992
Sir Edward Heath	1955	Lord King of Bridgwater	1979
David Heathcoat-Amory	1996	Lord Kingsdown	1987
Sir Denis Henry	1993	Lord Kingsland	1994
†John Henry	1996	Neil Kinnock	1983
Lord Heseltine	1979	Lord Kirkwood	2000
Sir William Heseltine	1986	Gregory Knight	1995
Lord Hesketh	1991	Lord Lamont of Lerwick	1986
Patricia Hewitt	2001	Lord Lane	1975
Lord Higgins	1979	Lord Lang of Monkton	1990
Keith Hill	2003	David Lange	1984
Sir David Hirst	1992	Kamuta Latasi	1996
*Lord Hobhouse of Woodborough	1993	Sir David Latham	2000
Margaret Hodge	2003	Sir Toaripi Lauti	1979
*Lord Hoffmann	1992	Sir John Laws	1999
Hon Douglas Hogg	1992	Lord Lawson of Blaby	1981
Baroness Hollis of Heigham	1999	Sir Frederick Lawton	1972
Lord Holme of Cheltenham	2000	Sir Andrew Leggatt	1990
Geoffrey Hoon	1999	Rt Revd Graham Leonard	1981
*Lord Hope of Craighead	1989	Oliver Letwin	2002
Sir Peter Hordern	1993	Helen Liddell	1998
Michael Howard	1990	Peter Lilley	1990
Alan Howarth	2000	Lord Lloyd of Berwick	1984
Lord Howe of Aberavon	1972	Sir Peter Lloyd	1994
Lord Howell of Guildford	1979	Bishop of London	1995
Lord Hunt of Wirral	1980	Sir Andrew Longmore	2001
Jonathan Hunt	1989	Allan Louisy	1981
Lord Hurd of Westwall	1982	Lord Luce	1986
*Sir Michael Hutchison	1995	Sir Nicholas Lyell	1990
*Lord Hutton	1988	Dickson Mabon	1977
John Hutton	2001	McAvoy, Thomas	2003
Hubert Ingraham	1993	Ian McCartney	1999
Adam Ingram	1999	Sir Liam McCollum	1997
*Lord Irvine of Lairg	1997	Jack McConnell	2001
John Michael Jack	1997	*Sir Anthony McCowan	1989
Sir Robin Janvrin	1998	*Sir John MacDermott	1987
Lord Jauncey of Tullichettle	1988	Lord Macdonald of Tradeston	1999
Baroness Jay of Paddington	1998	Lord Macfadyen	2002
Earl Jellicoe	1963	Lord MacGregor of Pulham Market	1985
Lord Jenkin of Roding	1973	Lord McIntosh of Haringey	2002
Alan Johnson	2003	Duncan MacIntyre	1980
Sir Geoffrey Johnson Smith	1996	*Lord Mackay of Clashfern	1979
Lord Jones	1999	Lord Mackay of Drumadoon	1996
Lord Jopling	1979	Andrew Mackay	1998
Tessa Jowell	1998	†Ian McKay	1992
Sir Igor Judge	1996	Donald McKinnon	1992
Sir Anerood Jugnauth	1987	David Maclean	1995
Gerald Kaufman	1978	Lord MacLean	2001
Sir John Kay	2000	Henry McLeish	2000
Sir David Keene	2000	Lord Maclennan of Rogart	1997
†Sir Kenneth Keith	1998	†Sir Duncan McMullin	1980
Sir Basil Kelly	1984	John Major	1987

Sir Jonathan Mance	1999	Turlough O'Donnell	1979
Peter Mandelson	1998	Francis O'Flynn	1987
Sir Charles Mantell	1997	Sir Angus Ogilvy	1997
Ratu Sir Kamisese Mara	1973	Lord Oliver of Aylmerton	1980
Lord Marnoch	2001	Baroness Oppenheim-Barnes	1979
Lord Marsh	1966	Lord Orme	1974
Michael Martin	2000	Lord Osborne	2001
Lord Mason of Barnsley	1968	*Sir Philip Otton	1995
Hon Francis Maude	1992	Lord Owen	1976
Sir Brian Mawhinney	1994	Bikenibeu Paeniu	1991
Sir Anthony May	1998	Sir Michael Palliser	1983
Theresa May	2003	Sir Geoffrey Palmer	1986
Lord Mayhew of Twysden	1986	Sir Jonathan Parker	2000
Michael Meacher	1997	Sir Roger Parker	1983
Sir Robert Megarry	1978	Lord Parkinson	1981
David Mellor	1990	Chris Patten	1989
Lord Merlyn-Rees	1974	Lord Patten	1990
Alun Michael	1998	Percival Patterson	1993
Alan Milburn	1998	Sir Geoffrey Pattie	1987
Bruce Millan	1975	Lord Pendry	2000
*Lord Millett	1994	Lord Penrose	2001
Lord Milligan	2000	Winston Peters	1998
Sir James Mitchell	1985	Lord Peyton of Yeovil	1970
Lord Molyneaux of Killead	1983	Lord Phillips of Worth Matravers	1995
Lord Monro of Langholm	1995	Sir Malcolm Pill	1995
Lord Moore of Lower Marsh	1986	Sir Lynden Pindling	1976
Lord Moore of Wolvercote	1977	Michael Portillo	1992
Michael Moore	1990	Sir Mark Potter	1996
Rhodri Morgan	2000	John Prescott	1994
Lord Morris of Manchester	1979	George Price	1982
Charles Morris	1978	Dawn Primarolo	2002
Estelle Morris	1999	Lord Prior	1970
Lord Morris of Aberavon	1970	Lord Prosser	2000
Sir Robert Morritt	1994	Sir Tomasi Puapua	1982
Marjorie Mowlam	1997	Sir Francis Purchas	1982
Roland Moyle	1978	Lord Pym	1970
Sir John Mummery	1996	Joyce Quin	1998
Paul Murphy	1999	Lord Radice	1999
Sir Donald Murray	1989	Sir Timothy Raison	1982
Hon Lord Murray	1974	James Ramsden	1963
Lord Murray of Epping Forest	1976	Lord Rawlinson of Ewell	1964
Lord Murton of Lindisfarne	1976	Nick Raynsford	2001
*Lord Mustill	1985	John Redwood	1993
Sir Patrick Nairne	1982	Lord Rees	1983
Sir Rabbie Namaliu	1989	John Reid	1998
Lord Naseby	1994	Lord Renton	1962
Sir Richard Needham	1994	Lord Renton of Mount Harry	1989
Sir Brian Neill	1985	Lord Richard	1993
Lord Newton of Braintree	1988	†Sir Ivor Richardson	1978
*Lord Nicholls of Birkenhead	1995	Lord Richardson of Duntisbourne	1976
Sir Michael Nicholson	1995	Sir Malcolm Rifkind	1986
*Lord Nolan	1991	Sir Bernard Rix	2000
Sir John Nott	1979	Lord Roberts of Conwy	1991
*Sir Martin Nourse	1985	Lord Robertson of Port Ellen	1997
Gordon Oakes	1979	*Sir John Roch	1993
Sir Patrick O'Connor	1980	Lord Rodger of Earlsferry	1992

Lord Rodgers of Quarry Bank	1975	Ann Taylor	1997
Lord Rooker	1999	Lord Tebbit	1981
Sir Christopher Rose	1992	Lord Templeman	1978
*Hon Lord Ross	1985	Baroness Thatcher	1970
Dame Angela Rumbold	1991	Lord Thomas of Gwydir	1964
Lord Ryder of Wensum	1990	†Edmund Thomas	1996
Sir Timothy Sainsbury	1992	*Sir Swinton Thomas	1994
Lord St John of Fawsley	1979	Lord Thomson of Monifieth	1966
Marquess of Salisbury	1994	Jeremy Thorpe	1967
Erskine Sandiford	1989	Sir Mathew Thorpe	1995
*Lord Saville of Newdigate	1994	†Andrew Tipping	1998
Lord Scarman	1973	Robert Tizard	1986
Sir Konrad Schiemann	1995	Lord Trefgarne	1989
Baroness Scotland of Asthal	2001	David Trimble	1997
Sir Nicholas Scott	1989	Baroness Trumpington	1992
*Lord Scott of Foscote	1991	Sir Simon Tuckey	1998
Edward Seaga	1981	Viscount Ullswater	1994
Sir Stephen Sedley	1999	Hon Simon Upton	1999
Lord Selkirk of Douglas	1996	Lord Varley	1974
Hon Hugh Shearer	1969	Lord Waddington	1987
Lord Sheldon	1977	*Sir John Waite	1993
Gillian Shephard	1992	Lord Wakeham	1983
Jennifer Shipley	1998	Lord Waldegrave of North Hill	1990
Clare Short	1997	Lord Walker of Doncaster	1979
Kennedy Simmonds	1984	Lord Walker of Worcester	1970
Lord Simon of Glaisdale	1961	Sir Robert Walker	1997
Ian Sinclair	1977	Jim Wallace	2000
*Sir Christopher Slade	1982	Sir Mark Waller	1996
*Lord Slynn of Hadley	1992	Sir Alan Ward	1995
Andrew Smith	1997	Sir Tasker Watkins	1980
Chris Smith	1997	Lord Weatherill	1980
Dame Janet Smith DBE	2002	Sir John Wheeler	1993
Jacqui Smith	2003	Ann Widdecombe	1997
Sir Michael Somare	1977	Dafydd Wigley	1997
John Spellar	2001	Alan Williams	1977
Sir John Stanley	1984	Baroness Williams of Crosby	1974
*Sir Christopher Staughton	1988	Lord Williams of Mostyn	1999
Lord Steel of Aikwood	1977	Brian Wilson	2003
Sir Ninian Stephen	1979	Lord Windlesham	1973
Lord Stewartby	1989	Paias Winti	1987
*Lord Steyn	1992	Reginald Withers	1977
Gavin Strang	1997	*Sir Owen Woodhouse	1974
Lord Strathclyde	1995	Lord Woolf	1986
Jack Straw	1997	Hon Lord Wylie	1970
*Sir Murray Stuart-Smith	1988	Archbishop of York	1991
Lord Sutherland	2000	Lord Young of Graffham	1984
Baroness Symons of Vernham Dean	2001	Sir George Young	1993
Sir Brian Talboys	1977	†Edward Zacca	1992

* Members of the Judicial Committee
† Commonwealth members of the Judicial Committee

DEVOLVED PARLIAMENT AND ASSEMBLIES

Dod's Scotland, Wales and Northern Ireland Companion 2003

FIRST EDITION

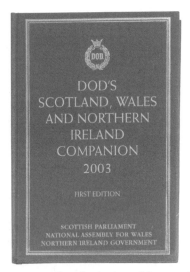

Dod's Scotland, Wales and Northern Ireland Companion 2003 provides unrivalled biographical information on all individuals within the Scottish Parliament, National Assembly for Wales and the Northern Ireland Government.

With in-depth biographies, latest election results and detailed information about each parliament or assembly and the role they play within the UK political scene, this companion will quickly become indispensable.

Dod's Scotland, Wales and Northern Ireland Companion 2003 includes the results from the May 2003 elections held in Wales and Scotland.

A comprehensive review of the results includes details of how the results affect each party structure, the share of the vote, seats by percentage majority, share of the vote by region and the geographical whereabouts of the constituencies.

To order call our Hotline now on 020 7630 7619

Vacher Dod Publishing
1 Douglas Street, London SW1P 4PA
Tel: 020 7630 7619   Fax: 020 7233 7266
Email: subscriptions@vacherdod.co.uk
Website: www.DodonLine.co.uk

SCOTTISH PARLIAMENT

George IV Bridge, Edinburgh EH99 1SP
0131-348 5000   Fax 0131-348 5601   *General Enquiries:* 0845 278 1999
Textphone: 0131-348 5415
Public Information: E-mail: sp.info@scottish.parliament.uk
Presiding Officer: E-mail: presiding.officer@scottish.parliament.uk
Website: www.scottish.parliament.uk

E-mails:
sp.media@scottish.parliament.uk (Media enquiries)
education.service@scottish.parliament.uk
chamber.office@scottish.parliament.uk (Debating chamber)
committee.office@scottish.parliament.uk
petitions@scottish.parliament.uk
webmaster@scottish.parliament.uk

First election 6 May 1999
1 July 1999 Official Opening by HM The Queen
Elections are held every four years. The 2003 election was held on 1 May 2003

Electoral system

Elections are conducted using a method combining the traditional first past the post system and a form of proportional representation called the Additional Member System. Each voter casts two votes. One vote is for one of 73 constituency members, based on the Westminster parliament constituencies. The second goes towards the election of 56 regional members, seven for each of the eight regions formerly used in the European Parliament elections. These seats ensure that each party's representation in the Parliament reflects its overall share of the vote.

Boundary Commission for Scotland Review 2002

At present, the average Scottish seat represents only 55,000 electors, compared with around 70,000 voters in England. Westminster retains reserved power over the Boundary Commission and, at present, any reduction in Scottish Westminster seats would lead to an automatic reduction in the number of seats at Holyrood. In the next few years, there is likely to be growing demand inside Scotland for the current law to be changed to allow the Scottish Parliament to decide its own level of representation.

The Boundary Commission published its provisional recommendations for the redrawing of Scottish seats on 7 February 2002. The Commission recognised that operating strictly under English quota rules would produce a theoretical cut of 15 in the number of Scottish seats. However, it opted for a reduction of 13 seats from the present 72 to 59.

Beyond a statutory obligation to maintain the Orkney and Shetland seat, the Commission felt that the Western Isles (Na h-Eileanan An-Iar) should be given a single constituency, because the islands were detached from the mainland and already governed by a Western Isles Council. The Highland Council area was left with three seats.

The city of Glasgow will provisionally lose three of its ten seats, renaming the constituencies Central, East, North, North East, North West, South and South West. The number of Edinburgh city seats will be cut from six to five: North East, North West, South, South East and West. In the North East of Scotland, Dundee would keep its two seats under the proposals, but Aberdeen would lose one of its three seats (Aberdeen Central).

Outside the major cities, Hamilton North and Bellshill might disappear. Dunfermline East is also set to disappear. In Ayrshire, the constituency of Carrick, Cumnock and Doon Valley is likely to be dismembered.

In Central Scotland, Falkirk East will disappear into the expanded Livingston and Linlithgow constituencies, leaving the town of Falkirk with only one seat. In Mid Scotland and Fife, Tayside North is likely to disappear into an expanded Angus and a new Perth and Atholl constituency. In the West of Scotland, Clydebank and Milngavie will be dismembered with Milngavie joining Bearsden while Clydebank goes in with West Dunbartonshire. Meanwhile, the two Paisley seats and Renfrewshire West will be merged into two constituencies.

The County of Dumfriesshire will move into an enormous new seat of Peebles, Clydesdale and Annandale, while the town of Dumfries will be linked with Kirkcudbrightshire and Wigtownshire, taking territory from Tory-held Galloway and Upper Nithsdale to form Dumfries and Galloway. Berwickshire, Roxburgh and Selkirk will be the only remaining Liberal Democrat seat in the region.

Despite the publication of the Boundary Commission's provisional recommendations, the proposals will not be finalised until December 2006, meaning that the 2003 Scottish parliamentary elections was, and the next Westminster election in Scotland will be, fought on the basis of the existing constituencies.

Powers and responsibilities

The Parliament has administrative and legislative powers relating to Scotland in the following areas:

agriculture	law and order
economic development	local government
education	social work
environment	transport
health	

It can vary the basic rate of income tax in Scotland by 3p in the £.

Westminster retains responsibility for:

defence	national finance and economics
employment	social security
international relations	

The interests of Scotland in the United Kingdom Government are represented by the Secretary of State for Scotland and the Westminster Parliament allocates a budget to the Scottish Parliament.

Operation/procedures

The First Minister is elected by Members and appoints Ministers from among Members to be responsible for specific areas of policy. The First Minister, Ministers and the Law Officers, the Lord Advocate and the Solicitor General for Scotland (who do not have to be Members), make up the Scottish Executive. The Cabinet consists of all these except the Solicitor General.

The Parliament appoints a Presiding Officer and deputies from among its members, to oversee debates and advise on procedure in a similar role to the Speaker of the House of Commons.

Committees made up of members of the Parliament consider various policy areas in detail.

Parliament sits for 30 to 33 weeks a year, fitting in with school holidays, and works normal business hours.

DodOnline

An Electronic Directory without rival...

MSPs' biographies and photographs available with daily updates *via* the internet

For a *free* trial, call Yasmin Mirza, Aby Farsoun or Michael Mand on 020 7630 7643

Cabinet

(Labour/Liberal Democrat Partnership)

First Minister	Rt Hon **Jack McConnell** MSP (Labour)
Deputy First Minister and Minister for Enterprise and Lifelong Learning	Rt Hon **Jim Wallace** QC MSP (Lib Dem)
Minister for Justice	**Cathy Jamieson** MSP (Lab/Co-op)
Minister for Health and Community Care	**Malcolm Chisholm** MSP (Labour)
Minister for Education and Young People	**Peter Peacock** MSP (Labour)
Minister for Finance and Public Services	**Andy Kerr** MSP (Labour)
Minister for Environment and Rural Development	**Ross Finnie** MSP (Lib Dem)
Minister for Communities	**Margaret Curran** MSP (Labour)
Minister for Parliamentary Business	**Patricia Ferguson** MSP (Labour)
Minister for Tourism, Culture and Sport	**Frank McAveety** MSP (Labour)
Minister for Transport	**Nicol Stephen** MSP (Lib Dem)

Law Officer

Lord Advocate	Rt Hon **Colin Boyd** QC
Deputy (Solicitor-General for Scotland) (not a member of the Cabinet)	**Elish Angiolini** QC

Deputy Ministers

Justice	**Hugh Henry** MSP (Labour)
Education and Young People	**Euan Robson** MSP (Lib Dem)
Enterprise and Lifelong Learning	**Lewis Macdonald** MSP (Labour)
Environment and Rural Development	**Allan Wilson** MSP (Labour)
Finance, Public Services and Parliamentary Business	**Tavish Scott** MSP (Lib Dem)
Health and Community Care	**Tom McCabe** MSP (Labour)
Communities	**Mary Mulligan** MSP (Labour)

Visit the Vacher Dod Website . . .
www.DodOnline.co.uk

Ministerial Responsibilities and Staff

The First Minister

St Andrew's House, Regent Road, Edinburgh EH1 3DG
Tel: 0131-556 8400   Fax: 0131-244 6915
E-mail: scottish.ministers@scotland.gsi.gov.uk

First Minister   Rt Hon **Jack McConnell** MSP – Labour

Head of the Scottish Executive. With the Deputy First Minister, responsible for the development, implementation and presentation of SE policies

Special Advisers	Mike Donnelly	0131-244 1812
	Jeane Freeman	0131-244 1813
	Rachel McEwen	0131-244 1813
	Peter Hastie	0131-244 4094
	Andy Rowe	0131-244 2527
	Adrian Colwell	0131-244 2250
	Douglas Campbell	0131-244 5190
Principal Private Secretary	Derek Feeley	0131-244 5218
Private Secretaries	Karen Watson	0131-244 5215
	Jennifer Smith	0131-244 5214
	Lorraine Kay	0131-244 5216
	Andrew Brown	0131-244 2016

Enterprise and Lifelong Learning

Meridian Court, 5 Cadogan Street, Glasgow G2 6AT
Tel: 0131-556 8400

Deputy First Minister and Minister for Enterprise and Lifelong Learning
Rt Hon **Jim Wallace** QC MSP – Lib Dem

With the FM, responsible for the development, implementation and presentation of SE policies. As Enterprise Minister responsible for economy, business and industry, including Scottish Enterprise, Highlands and Islands Enterprise, European Structural Funds, trade and inward investment, energy (including renewable energy), further and higher education, lifelong learning and training and science

Special Adviser	Matthew Clarke	
Private Secretary	Kirsty McNeil	0131-244 5227

Deputy Minister for Enterprise and Lifelong Learning
Lewis Macdonald MSP – Labour

Private Secretary	Victoria Beattie	0141-242 5757

Justice

St Andrew's House, Regent Road, Edinburgh EH1 3DG
Tel: 0131-556 8400

Minister for Justice   **Cathy Jamieson** MSP – Lab/Co-op

Responsible for criminal Justice, youth justice, victims support, criminal justice social work, police, prisons and sentencing policy, courts, law reform including civil law and fire services

Private Secretary	Dr P S Curtis	0131-244 7716

Deputy Minister for Justice   **Hugh Henry** MSP – Labour

Private Secretary	Amanda Callaghan	0131-244 4579

Health and Community Care

St Andrew's House, Regent Road, Edinburgh EH1 3DG
Tel: 0131-556 8400

Minister for Health and Community Care   **Malcolm Chisholm** MSP – Labour

Responsible for the NHS, community care, health service reform, health improvement, health promotion, allied healthcare services, acute, primary and mental health services, addiction services, pharmaceutical services, performance, quality and improvement framework and food safety

Private Secretary   Linda Fenocchi   0131-244 4017

Deputy Minister for Health and Community Care
Tom McCabe MSP – Labour

Private Secretary   David Keenan   0131-348 5830

Education and Young People

Victoria Quay, Edinburgh EH6 6QQ
Tel: 0131-556 8400

Minister for Education and Young People   **Peter Peacock** MSP – Labour

Responsible for school education, nurseries and childcare, Gaelic, children's services, social work, HMIE, HMSWI and SQA

Private Secretary   David Stewart   0131-244 7716

Deputy Minister for Education and Young People   **Euan Robson** MSP – Lib Dem

Private Secretary   Kirsty McKenna   0131-244 1469

Finance and Public Services

Victoria Quay, Edinburgh EH6 6QQ
Tel: 0131-556 8400

Minister for Finance and Public Services   **Andy Kerr** MSP – Labour

Responsible for the Scottish Budget, public service delivery, modernising government including civil service reform, local government, cities and community planning

Private Secretary   Lindsay Blakemore   0131-244 1558

Deputy Minister for Finance and Public Services
Tavish Scott MSP – Lib Dem

Private Secretary   Philip Lamont   0131-244 0228

Environment and Rural Development

Pentland House, 47 Robbs Loan, Edinburgh EH14 1TY
Tel: 0131-556 8400

Minister for Environment and Rural Development   **Ross Finnie** MSP – Lib Dem

Responsible for environment and natural heritage, land reform, water, sustainable development, agriculture, fisheries, rural development including aquaculture and forestry

Private Secretary   James How   0131-244 4456

Deputy Minister for Environment and Rural Development
Allan Wilson MSP – Labour

Private Secretary   Nikki Tonge   0131-244 4426

Communities

Victoria Quay, Edinburgh EH6 6QQ
Tel: 0131-556 8400

Minister for Communities   **Margaret Curran** MSP – Labour

Responsible for anti-social behaviour, poverty, housing and area regeneration, the land use planning system and building standards, equality issues, voluntary sector, religious and faith organisations and charity law

| Private Secretary | Richard Lyall | 0131-244 7818 |

Deputy Minister for Communities   **Mary Mulligan** MSP – Labour

| Private Secretary | Pat Allan | 0131-244 5539 |

Parliamentary Business

George IV Bridge, Edinburgh EH99 1SP
Tel: 0131-348 5000

Minister for Parliamentary Business   **Patricia Ferguson** MSP – Labour

Responsible for Parliamentary affairs and the management of Executive business in the Parliament

| Private Secretary | Ian Campbell | 0131-348 5593 |

Deputy Minister for Parliamentary Business   **Tavish Scott** MSP – Lib Dem

| Private Secretary | James Johnston |

Tourism, Culture and Sport

Victoria Quay, Edinburgh EH6 6QQ
Tel: 0131-556 8400

Minister for Tourism, Culture and Sport   **Frank McAveety** MSP – Labour

Responsible for tourism, culture and the arts, sport, built heritage, architecture, Historic Scotland and lottery funding

| Private Secretary | Alasdair Creraral | 0131-244 0627 |

Transport

Meridian Court, 5 Cadogan Street, Glasgow G2 6AT
Tel: 0131-556 8400

Minister for Transport   **Nicol Stephen** MSP – Lib Dem

Responsible for transport policy and delivery, public transport, road, rail services, lifeline air and ferry services

| Private Secretary | Lesley Clinkscales | 0131-244 7005 |

Law Officers

Crown Office, 25 Chambers Street, Edinburgh EH1 1LA
Tel: 0131-226 2626   Website: www.crownoffice.gov.uk

Lord Advocate   Rt Hon **Colin Boyd** QC

| Private Secretary | Kirsten Davidson | 0131-247 2875 |

E-mail: ps/lordadvocate@scotland.gsi.gov.uk

Solicitor-General for Scotland   **Elish Angiolini** QC

| Private Secretary | Robbie Kent | 0131-247 2690 |

E-mail: ps/solicitorgeneral@scotland.gsi.gov.uk

Opposition Spokespeople and Whips

SNP (Scottish Shadow Cabinet)

Shadow First Minister	**John Swinney**
Deputy Leader of the Scottish National Party and Shadow Minister for Environment and Rural Affairs	**Roseanna Cunningham**
Shadow Minister for Justice	**Nicola Sturgeon**
Shadow Minister for Enterprise and the Economy	**Jim Mather**
Shadow Minister for Education and Lifelong Learning	**Fiona Hyslop**
Shadow Minister for Tourism, Transport and Telecommunications	**Kenny MacAskill**
Shadow Minister for Health and Social Justice	**Shona Robison**
Shadow Minister for Finance and Public Services	**Fergus Ewing**
Business Manager and Chief Whip	**Bruce Crawford**
Convener of the SNP Scottish Parliamentary Group meetings of the Shadow Cabinet	**Alasdair Morgan**

Deputy Spokespeople

Deputy Spokesperson for Justice	**Michael Matheson**
Deputy Spokesperson for Education and Lifelong Learning	**Brian Adam**
Deputy Spokesperson for Health and Social Justice	**Stewart Stevenson**
Deputy Spokesperson for Health and Social Justice	**Sandra White**
Deputy Business Manager and Whip	**Linda Fabiani**
Deputy Spokesperson for Environment and Rural Affairs	**Richard Lochhead**

Scottish Conservatives

Leader of the Scottish Conservative Party	**David McLetchie**
Deputy Leader of the Scottish Conservative Party and Spokesperson for Justice and Home Affairs	**Annabel Goldie**
Spokesperson for Education	**Lord James Douglas-Hamilton**
Spokesperson for Finance and Local Government	**Brian Monteith**
Spokesperson for Health	**David Davidson**
Spokesperson for Communities	**Mary Scanlon**
Spokesperson for Environment and Rural Development	**Alex Johnstone**

Spokesperson for Agriculture and Forestry	**Alex Fergusson**
Spokesperson for Fisheries	**Ted Brocklebank**
Business Manager and Chief Whip	**Bill Aitken**
Spokesperson for Constitutional Affairs and Europe	**Phil Gallie**
Spokesperson for IT, Telecommunications and Transport	**David Mundell**
Spokesperson for Tourism, Culture and Sport	**Jamie McGrigor**

Deputy Spokespeople

Deputy Spokesperson for Justice and Home Affairs	**Margaret Mitchell**
Deputy Spokesperson for Health and Community Care	**Nanette Milne**

Scottish Liberal Democrats

Spokesperson for Education and Young People	**Robert Brown**
Spokesperson for Communities, Culture and Sport	**Donald Gorrie**
Scottish Parliamentary Business Manager and Chief Whip	**George Lyon**
Spokesperson for Gaelic Language	**John Farquhar Munro**
Spokesperson for Equal Opportunities	**Mike Pringle**
Spokesperson for Finance	**Jeremy Purvis**
Spokesperson for Environment and Rural Development, Convener of the Parliamentary Party	**Nora Radcliffe**
Spokesperson for European Affairs in the Scottish Parliament	**Keith Raffan**
Spokesperson for Health	**Mike Rumbles**
Spokesperson for Transport and Local Government	**Iain Smith**
Spokesperson for Justice	**Margaret Smith**
Spokesperson for Enterprise, Lifelong Learning and Tourism	**Jamie Stone**

Scottish Green Party

Leader of the Green Group in the Scottish Parliament and Spokesperson for Education and Young People	**Robin Harper**
Spokesperson for Enterprise and Lifelong Learning	**Shiona Baird**
Spokesperson for Transport, Tourism, Culture and Sport	**Chris Ballance**
Spokesperson for Finance, Public Services and Parliamentary Business	**Mark Ballard**
Spokesperson for Justice and Communities	**Patrick Harvie**
Spokesperson for Environment and Rural Development	**Mark Ruskell**

Scottish Socialist Party

Convener of the Scottish Socialist Party and Spokesperson for Finance, Public Services and Communities	**Tommy Sheridan**
Spokesperson for Health and Community Care	**Carolyn Leckie**
Spokesperson for Environment and Transport	**Rosie Kane**
Spokesperson for Justice, Tourism, Culture and Sport	**Colin Fox**
Spokesperson for Education and Young People	**Rosemary Byrne**
Spokesperson for Enterprise and Lifelong Learning	**Frances Curran**

Members (MSPs)

State of the Parties (August 2003)

	Constituency MSPs	Regional MSPs	Total MSPs
Scottish Labour Party	46*	4	50
(includes Scottish Labour/Co-operative Party)			
Scottish National Party	8†	18	26
Scottish Conservative and Unionist Party	3	15*	18
Scottish Liberal Democrats	13	4	17
Scottish Green Party	0	7	7
Scottish Socialist Party	0	6	6
Independent	1	1	2
MSP for Falkirk West	1	0	1
Scottish Senior Citizens Unity Party	0	1	1
Presiding Officer	1	0	1
	73	**56**	**129**

*Includes a deputy Presiding Officer who can participate and vote fully in the Parliament when not in the Chair.
†Excludes the Presiding Officer who has no party allegiance while in post.

DodOnline

An Electronic Directory without rival ...

MSPs' biographies and photographs available with daily updates *via* the internet

For a *free* trial, call Yasmin Mirza, Aby Farsoun or Michael Mand on 020 7630 7643

MSPS' Directory

Lab	Labour Party
SNP	Scottish National Party
Con	Conservative
Lib Dem	Liberal Democrats
Green	Green Party
SSP	Scottish Socialist Party
MSPFW	MSP for Falkirk West
Ind	Independent
SSCUP	Scottish Senior Citizens Unity Party
Pres Off	Presiding Officer

ADAM, Brian   SNP   **Aberdeen North**
SNP Deputy Spokesperson for Education and Lifelong Learning
Member Parliamentary Committee: Enterprise and Culture
Tel: 0131-348 5692   Fax: 0131-348 5953   E-mail: brian.adam.msp@scottish.parliament.uk
Constituency: 70 Rosemount Place, Aberdeen AB25 2XJ
Tel: 01224 623150   Fax: 01224 623160

AITKEN, Bill   Con   **Glasgow**
Scottish Conservative Chief Whip and Business Manager
Tel: 0131-348 5642   Fax: 0131-348 5655   E-mail: bill.aitken.msp@scottish.parliament.uk
Constituency: 570 Mosspark Boulevard, Glasgow G52 1SD
Tel: 0141-810 5743   Fax: 0141-810 5897

ALEXANDER, Wendy   Lab   **Paisley North**
Member Parliamentary Committees:
    Education
    Finance
Tel: 0131-348 5827   E-mail: wendy.alexander.msp@scottish.parliament.uk
Constituency: Mile End Mill, Abbey Mill Business Centre, Paisley PA1 1JS
Tel: 0141-561 5800   Fax: 0141-561 5900

BAILLIE, Jackie   Lab   **Dumbarton**
Member Parliamentary Committees:
    Justice 2
    Public Petitions
Tel: 0131-348 5905   Fax: 0131-348 5986   E-mail: jackie.baillie.msp@scottish.parliament.uk
Constituency: Dumbarton Constituency Office, 125 College Street, Dumbarton G82 1NH
Tel: 01389 734214   Fax: 01389 761498

BAIRD, Shiona   Green   **North East Scotland**
Green Spokesperson for Enterprise and Lifelong Learning
Member Parliamentary Committee: Equal Opportunities
E-mail: shiona.baird.msp@scottish.parliament.uk

BAKER, Richard   Lab   **North East Scotland**
Member Parliamentary Committees:
    Enterprise and Culture
    Procedures
Tel: 0131-348 5916   E-mail: richard.baker.msp@scottish.parliament.uk
Constituency: 1 Clifton Road, Aberdeen AB24 4RZ
Tel: 01224 488100   Fax: 01224 276919

BALLANCE, Chris   Green   **South of Scotland**
Green Spokesperson for Transport, Tourism, Culture and Sport
Member Parliamentary Committee: Enterprise and Culture
E-mail: chris.ballance.msp@scottish.parliament.uk

BALLARD, Mark   Green   **Lothian**
Green Spokesperson for Finance, Public Services and Parliamentary Business
Member Parliamentary Committee: Procedures
E-mail: mark.ballard.msp@scottish.parliament.uk

BARRIE, Scott   Lab   **Dunfermline West**
Member Parliamentary Committee: Justice 2
Tel: 0131-348 5849   Fax: 0131-348 5987   E-mail: scott.barrie.msp@scottish.parliament.uk
Constituency: Music Hall Lane, Dunfermline KY12 7NG
Tel: 01383 731884   Fax: 01383 731835

BOYACK, Sarah   Lab   **Edinburgh Central**
Convener Parliamentary Committee: Environment and Rural Development
Member Parliamentary Committee: The Conveners Group
Tel: 0131-348 5751   Fax: 0131-348 0785   E-mail: sarah.boyack.msp@scottish.parliament.uk
Constituency: 15a Stafford Street, Edinburgh EH3 7BU
Tel: 0131-476 2539   Fax: 0131-467 3574

BRANKIN, Rhona   Lab/Co-op   **Midlothian**
Member Parliamentary Committees:
   Audit
   Education
Tel: 0131-348 5838   Fax: 0131-348 5988
E-mail: rhona.brankin.msp@scottish.parliament.uk
Constituency: PO Box 11, 95 High Street, Dalkeith EH22 1AX
Tel: 0131-654 1585   Fax: 0131-654 1586

BROCKLEBANK, Ted   Con   **Mid Scotland and Fife**
Scottish Conservative Spokesperson for Fisheries
Member Parliamentary Committee: Finance
E-mail: ebrocklebank@aol.com
Constituency: 6 Alexandra Place, St Andrews KY16 9XD
Tel: 01334 653297   Fax: 01334 653670

BROWN, Robert   Lib Dem   **Glasgow**
Member, Scottish Parliamentary Corporate Body; Scottish Liberal Democrat Spokesperson for Education and Young People
Convener Parliamentary Committee: Education
Member Parliamentary Committee: The Conveners Group
Tel: 0131-348 5792   Fax: 0131-348 5807
E-mail: robert.brown.msp@scottish.parliament.uk
Constituency: Olympic House, Suite 1, 2nd Floor, 142 Queen Street, Glasgow G1 3BU
Tel: 0141-243 2421   Fax: 0141-243 2451

BUTLER, Bill   Lab   **Glasgow Anniesland**
Member Parliamentary Committees:
   Justice 1
   Standards
Tel: 0131-348 5771   E-mail: bill.butler.msp@scottish.parliament.uk
Constituency: 129 Dalsetter Avenue, Glasgow G15 8SZ
Tel: 0141-944 9441   Fax: 0141-944 9442

BYRNE, Rosemary   SSP   **South of Scotland**
SSP Spokesperson for Education and Young People
Member Parliamentary Committee: Education
E-mail: rosemary.byrne.msp@scottish.parliament.uk

CANAVAN, Dennis   MSPFW   **Falkirk West**
Member Parliamentary Committee: European and External Relations
Tel: 0131-348 5629   Fax: 0131-348 5941
E-mail: dennis.canavan.msp@scottish.parliament.uk

Constituency: 37 Church Walk, Denny, Stirlingshire FK6 6DF
Tel: 01324 825922   Fax: 01324 823972

CHISHOLM, Malcolm   Lab   **Edinburgh North and Leith**
Minister for Health and Community Care
Tel: 0131-348 5908   E-mail: malcolm.chisholm.msp@scottish.parliament.uk

Constituency: 86-88 Brunswick Street, Edinburgh EH7 5HU
Tel: 0131-558 8358   Fax: 0131-557 6781

CRAIGIE, Cathie   Lab   **Cumbernauld and Kilsyth**
Member Parliamentary Committees:
  Communities
  Procedures
Tel: 0131-348 5756   Fax: 0131-348 5977
E-mail: cathie.craigie.msp@scottish.parliament.uk

Constituency: 6 Market Square, Kilsyth G65 0AZ
Tel: 01236 825372   Fax: 01236 820556

CRAWFORD, Bruce   SNP   **Mid Scotland and Fife**
SNP Business Manager and Chief Whip
Member Parliamentary Committee: Procedures
E-mail: bruce.crawford.msp@scottish.parliament.uk

Constituency: SNP Constituency Office, Langgarth Lodge House, St Ninians Road, Viewforth, Stirling FK8 2HE
Tel: 01786 471899   Fax: 01786 471853

CUNNINGHAM, Roseanna   SNP   **Perth**
Shadow Minister for Environment and Rural Affairs; Deputy Leader, SNP
Member Parliamentary Committee: Environment and Rural Development
Tel: 0131-348 5696   Fax: 0131-348 5952   E-mail: roseanna.cunningham.msp@scottish.parliament.uk

Constituency: 51 York Place, Perth PH2 8EH
Tel: 01738 444002   Fax: 01738 444602

CURRAN, Frances   SSP   **West of Scotland**
SSP Spokesperson for Enterprise and Lifelong Learning
Member Parliamentary Committee: Equal Opportunities

CURRAN, Margaret   Lab   **Glasgow Baillieston**
Minister for Communities
Tel: 0131-348 5842   Fax: 0131-348 5984
E-mail: margaret.curran.msp@scottish.parliament.uk

Constituency: Westwood Business Centre, 69 Aberdalgie Road, Easterhouse, Glasgow G34 9HJ
Tel: 0141-771 4844   Fax: 0141-771 4877

DAVIDSON, David   Con   **North East Scotland**
Scottish Conservative Spokesperson for Health and Community Care
Member Parliamentary Committee: Health
Tel: 0131-348 5653   Fax: 0131-348 5934
E-mail: david.davidson.msp@scottish.parliament.uk

Constituency: 8 Robert Street, Stowehaven AB39 2DW
Tel: 01569 762785   Fax: 01569 767177

DEACON, Susan   Lab   **Edinburgh East and Musselburgh**
Member Parliamentary Committees:
  Audit
  Enterprise and Culture
Tel: 0131-348 5753   Fax: 0131-348 9162   E-mail: susan.deacon.msp@scottish.parliament.uk

Constituency: 54 Portobello High Street, Edinburgh EH15 1DA
Tel: 0131-669 6446   Fax: 0131-669 9162

DOUGLAS-HAMILTON, Rt Hon Lord James   Con   **Lothian**
Scottish Conservative Spokesperson for Education
Deputy Convener Parliamentary Committee: Education
Tel: 0131-348 5660   Fax: 0131-348 5936
E-mail: james.douglas-hamilton.msp@scottish.parliament.uk

Constituency: 67 Northumberland Street, Edinburgh EH3 6JG
Tel: 0131-557 5158   Fax: 0131-557 6682

EADIE, Helen   Lab/Co-op   **Dunfermline East**
Member Parliamentary Committees:
  Health
  Public Petitions
Tel: 0131-348 5749   E-mail: helen.eadie.msp@scottish.parliament.uk

Constituency: 25 Church Street, Inverkeithing, Fife KY11 1LG
Tel: 01383 412856   Fax: 01383 412855

EWING, Fergus   SNP   **Inverness East, Nairn and Lochaber**
Shadow Minister for Finance and Public Services
Deputy Convener Parliamentary Committee: Finance
Tel: 0131-348 5732   Fax: 0131-348 5737   E-mail: fergus.ewing.msp@scottish.parliament.uk

Constituency: Highland Rail House, Station Square, Inverness IV1 1LE
Tel: 01463 713004   Fax: 01463 710194

EWING, Margaret   SNP   **Moray**
Member Parliamentary Committee: European and External Relations
Tel: 0131-348 5705   Fax: 0131-348 5857   E-mail: margaret.ewing.msp@scottish.parliament.uk

Constituency: 9 Wards Road, Elgin, Moray IV30 1NL
Tel: 01343 551111   Fax: 01343 556355

FABIANI, Linda   SNP   **Central Scotland**
SNP Deputy Business Manager and Whip
Member Parliamentary Committee: Public Petitions
E-mail: linda.fabiani.msp@scottish.parliament.uk

Constituency: Dalziel Workspace, Mason Street, Motherwell ML1 1YE
Tel: 01698 265925   Fax: 01698 269033

FERGUSON, Patricia   Lab   **Glasgow Maryhill**
Minister for Parliamentary Business
Tel: 0131-348 5311   E-mail: patricia.ferguson.msp@scottish.parliament.uk

Constituency: 154 Raeberry Street, Maryhill, Glasgow G20 6EA
Tel: 0141-946 1300   Fax: 0141-946 1412

FERGUSSON, Alex   Con   **Galloway and Upper Nithsdale**
Scottish Conservative Spokesperson for Agriculture and Forestry
Member Parliamentary Committee: Standards
Tel: 0131-348 5636   Fax: 0131-348 5932   E-mail: alex.fergusson.msp@scottish.parliament.uk

Constituency: 41a Castle Street, Dumfries DG1 1DU
Tel: 01387 256719   Fax: 01387 257039

FINNIE, Ross Lib Dem   **West of Scotland**
Minister for Environment and Rural Development
Tel: 0131-348 5783   E-mail: ross.finnie.msp@scottish.parliament.uk
Constituency: 9 Duff Street, Greenock PA15 1DB
Tel: 01475 805020   Fax: 01475 805021

FOX, Colin SSP   **Lothian**
SSP Spokesperson for Justice, Tourism, Culture and Sport
Member Parliamentary Committee: Justice 2
E-mail: colin.zillah@virgin.net
Constituency: 17-23 Calton Road, Edinburgh EH8 6DG
Tel: 0131 557 0426

FRASER, Murdo Con   **Mid Scotland and Fife**
Scottish Conservative Spokesperson for Enterprise and Lifelong Learning
Member Parliamentary Committee: Enterprise and Culture
Tel: 0131-348 5646   Fax: 0131-348 5933   E-mail: murdo.fraser.msp@scottish.parliament.uk
Constituency: North Tayside Conservative Association, 34 Lower Mill Street, Blairgowrie,
Perthshire PH10 6AQ
Tel: 01250 874782   Fax: 01250 876770

GALLIE, Phil Con   **South of Scotland**
Scottish Conservative Spokesperson for Constitutional Affairs and Europe
Member Parliamentary Committee: European and External Relations
Tel: 0131-348 5665   Fax: 0131-348 5938   E-mail: phil.gallie.msp@scottish.parliament.uk
Constituency: 1 Wellington Square, Ayr KA7 1EN
Tel: 01292 283439   Fax: 01292 280480

GIBSON, Rob SNP   **Highlands and Islands**
Member Parliamentary Committee: Environment and Rural Development
E-mail: robgibson@sol.co.uk

GILLON, Karen Lab   **Clydesdale**
Deputy Convener Parliamentary Committee: Procedures
Member Parliamentary Committee: Environment and Rural Development
Tel: 0131-348 5823   Fax: 0131-348 5992   E-mail: karen.gillon.msp@scottish.parliament.uk
Constituency: 11 Wellgate, Lanark ML11 9DS
Tel: 01555 660526   Fax: 01555 660528

GLEN, Marlyn Lab   **North East Scotland**
Member Parliamentary Committees:
  Equal Opportunities
  Justice 1

GODMAN, Trish Lab   **West Renfrewshire**
Deputy Presiding Officer
Member Parliamentary Committee: European and External Relations
Tel: 0131-348 5837   Fax: 0131-348 5991   E-mail: trish.godman.msp@scottish.parliament.uk
Constituency: Suite A, 16 Bridgewater Place, Bridgewater Shopping Centre, Erskine PA8 7AA
Tel: 0141-812 8246   Fax: 0141-812 5953

GOLDIE, Annabel Con   **West of Scotland**
Deputy Leader, Scottish Conservative Party; Scottish Conservative Spokesperson for Justice and
Home Affairs
Convener Parliamentary Committee: Justice 2
Member Parliamentary Committee: The Conveners Group
Tel: 0131-348 5662   Fax: 0131-348 5937   E-mail: annabel.goldie.msp@scottish.parliament.uk
Constituency: Upper Floor, 10 Shuttle Street, Paisley PA1 1YD
Tel: 0141 887 6161   Fax: 0141 889 0223

GORRIE, Donald, OBE   Lib Dem   **Central Scotland**
Scottish Liberal Democrat Spokesperson for Communities, Culture and Sport
Deputy Convener Parliamentary Committee: Communities
Member Parliamentary Committee: Standards
Tel: 0131-348 5795   Fax: 0131-348 5963   E-mail: donald.gorrie.msp@scottish.parliament.uk
Constituency: St Leonard's House, 110-112 Hamilton Road, Motherwell ML1 3DG
Tel: 01698 264955   Fax: 01698 263416

GRAHAME, Christine   SNP   **South of Scotland**
Convener Parliamentary Committee: Health
Member Parliamentary Committee: The Conveners Group
Tel: 0131-348 5729   Fax: 0131-348 5954   E-mail: christine.grahame.msp@scottish.parliament.uk
Constituency: 69 Bank Street, Galashiels TD1 1EL
Tel: 01896 759575   Fax: 01896 759579

HARPER, Robin   Green   **Lothian**
Leader of the Green Group in the Scottish Parliament and Spokesperson for Education and Young People
Member Parliamentary Committee: Audit
Tel: 0131-348 5926   Fax: 0131-348 5972   E-mail: robin.harper.msp@scottish.parliament.uk
Constituency: 62 Candlemaker Row, Edinburgh EH1 2QE
Tel: 0131-478 7895   Fax: 0131-478 7891

HARVIE, Patrick   Green   **Glasgow**
Green Spokesperson for Justice and Communities
Member Parliamentary Committee: Communities
Tel: 0131-348 6365   E-mail: patrick.harvie@ntlworld.com
Constituency: 47 Parnie Street, Glasgow G1 5LU
Tel: 0141-553 2070

HENRY, Hugh   Lab   **Paisley South**
Deputy Minister for Justice
Tel: 0131-348 5929   Fax: 0131-348 5991   E-mail: hugh.henry.msp@scottish.parliament.uk
Constituency: Anchor House, Blackhall Lane, Paisley PA1 1TA
Tel: 0141-848 7361   Fax: 0141-848 7384

HOME ROBERTSON, John   Lab   **East Lothian**
Member Parliamentary Committee: European and External Relations
Tel: 0131-348 5839   E-mail: john.home.robertson.msp@scottish.parliament.uk
Constituency: Town House, High Street, Dunbar, East Lothian EH42 1ER
Tel: 01368 863679   Fax: 01368 863679

HUGHES, Janis   Lab   **Glasgow Rutherglen**
Deputy Convener Parliamentary Committee: Health
Tel: 0131-348 5820   Fax: 0131-348 5992   E-mail: janis.hughes.msp@scottish.parliament.uk
Constituency: 51 Stonelaw Road, Glasgow G73 3TN
Tel: 0141-647 0707   Fax: 0141-647 0102

HYSLOP, Fiona   SNP   **Lothian**
Shadow Minister for Education and Lifelong Learning
Member Parliamentary Committee: Education
Tel: 0131-348 5920   Fax: 0131-348 5735   E-mail: fiona.hyslop.msp@scottish.parliament.uk
Constituency: 107 McDonald Road, Edinburgh EH7 4NW
Tel: 0131-525 8900

INGRAM, Adam   SNP   **South of Scotland**
Member Parliamentary Committee: Education
Tel: 0131-348 5720   Fax: 0131-348 5735   E-mail: adam.ingram.msp@scottish.parliament.uk
Constituency: 45 Dalblair Road, Ayr KA7 1UF
Tel: 01292 290611   Fax: 01292 290629

JACKSON, Gordon   Lab   **Glasgow Govan**
Deputy Convener Parliamentary Committee: Subordinate Legislation
Member Parliamentary Committee: European and External Relations
Tel: 0131-348 5898   E-mail: gordon.jackson.msp@scottish.parliament.uk
Constituency: 247 Paisley Road West, Glasgow G51 1NE
Tel: 0141-427 7047   Fax: 0141-427 9374

JACKSON, Dr Sylvia   Lab   **Stirling**
Convener Parliamentary Committee: Subordinate Legislation
Member Parliamentary Committees:
   Local Government and Transport
   The Conveners Group
Tel: 0131-348 5742   E-mail: sylvia.jackson.msp@scottish.parliament.uk
Constituency: 22 Viewfield Street, Stirling FK8 1UA
Tel: 01786 446515   Fax: 01786 446513

JAMIESON, Cathy   Lab/Co-op   **Carrick, Cumnock and Doon Valley**
Minister for Justice
Tel: 0131-348 5777   Fax: 0131-348 5582   E-mail: cathy.jamieson.msp@scottish.parliament.uk
Constituency: Skerrington House, Glaisnock Road, Cumnock KA18 3BU
Tel: 0845 458 1800   Fax: 0845 458 1801

JAMIESON, Margaret   Lab   **Kilmarnock and Loudoun**
Member Parliamentary Committee: Audit
Tel: 0131-348 5775   Fax: 0131-348 5778
E-mail: margaret.jamieson.msp@scottish.parliament.uk
Constituency: Parliamentary Advice Centre, 32 Grange Street, Kilmarnock KA1 2DD
Tel: 01563 520267   Fax: 01563 539439

JOHNSTONE, Alex   Con   **North East Scotland**
Scottish Conservative Spokesperson for Environment and Rural Development
Member Parliamentary Committee: Environment and Rural Development
Tel: 0131-348 5649   Fax: 0131-348 5656
E-mail: alexander.johnstone.msp@scottish.parliament.uk
Constituency: 265a High Street, Arbroath, Angus DD11 1EE
Tel: 01241 430467   Fax: 01241 430476

KANE, Rosie   SSP   **Glasgow**
SSP Spokesperson for Environment and Transport
Member Parliamentary Committee: Local Government and Transport

KERR, Andy   Lab   **East Kilbride**
Minister for Finance and Public Services
Tel: 0131-348 5903   Fax: 0131-348 5986   E-mail: andy.kerr.msp@scottish.parliament.uk
Constituency: Civic Centre, Andrew Street, East Kilbride G74 1AB
Tel: 01355 806223   Fax: 01355 806343

LAMONT, Johann   Lab/Co-op   **Glasgow Pollok**
Convener Parliamentary Committee: Communities
Member Parliamentary Committee: The Conveners Group
Tel: 0131-348 5847   Fax: 0131-348 5987   E-mail: johann.lamont.msp@scottish.parliament.uk
Constituency: 3 Kilmuir Drive, Arden, Glasgow G46 8BW
Tel: 0141-621 1213   Fax: 0141-621 0606

LECKIE, Carolyn   SSP   **Central Scotland**
SSP Spokesperson for Health and Community Care
Member Parliamentary Committee: Public Petitions

LIVINGSTONE, Marilyn   Lab/Co-op   **Kirkcaldy**
Member Parliamentary Committee: Equal Opportunities
Tel: 0131-348 5744   Fax: 0131-348 5973
E-mail: marilyn.livingstone.msp@scottish.parliament.uk

Constituency: Suite D, Carlyle House, Carlyle Road, Kirkcaldy KY1 1DB
Tel: 01592 564114   Fax: 01592 561085

LOCHHEAD, Richard   SNP   **North East Scotland**
SNP Deputy Spokesperson for Environment and Rural Affairs
Convener Parliamentary Committee: European and External Relations
Member Parliamentary Committee: The Conveners Group
Tel: 0131-348 5713   Fax: 0131-348 5737   E-mail: richard.lochhead.msp@scottish.parliament.uk

Constituency: 70 Rosemount Place, Aberdeen AB25 2XJ
Tel: 01224 623150   Fax: 01224 623160

LYON, George   Lib Dem   **Argyll and Bute**
Liberal Democrat Chief Whip and Parliamentary Business Manager
Member Parliamentary Committee: Audit
Tel: 0131-348 5787   Fax: 0131-348 5807   E-mail: george.lyon.msp@scottish.parliament.uk

Constituency: First Floor, 7 Castle Street, Rothesay, Isle of Bute PA20 9HA
Tel: 01700 500222   Fax: 01700 502704

MacASKILL, Kenny   SNP   **Lothian**
Shadow Minister for Tourism, Transport and Telecommunications
Deputy Convener Parliamentary Committee: Audit
E-mail: kenny.macaskill.msp@scottish.parliament.uk

Constituency: 107 McDonald Road, Edinburgh EH7 4NW
Tel: 0131-525 8916   Fax: 0131-525 8935

McAVEETY, Frank   Lab/Co-op   **Glasgow Shettleston**
Minister for Tourism
E-mail: frank.mcaveety.msp@scottish.parliament.uk

Constituency: 1346 Shettleston Road, Glasgow G32 9AT
Tel: 0141-764 0175   Fax: 0141-764 0876

McCABE, Tom   Lab   **Hamilton South**
Deputy Minister for Health and Community Care
Tel: 0131-348 5830   Fax: 0131-348 5152   E-mail: tom.mccabe.msp@scottish.parliament.uk

Constituency: 23 Beckford Street, Hamilton ML3 0BT
Tel: 01698 454018   Fax: 01698 454222

McCONNELL, Jack   Lab   **Motherwell and Wishaw**
First Minister; Leader Scottish Labour Party
Tel: 0131-348 5590   Fax: 0131-348 5562   E-mail: jack.mcconnell.msp@scottish.parliament.uk

Constituency: 265 Main Street, Wishaw ML2 7NE
Tel: 01698 303040   Fax: 01698 303060

MacDONALD, Lewis   Lab   **Aberdeen Central**
Deputy Minister for Enterprise and Lifelong Learning
Tel: 0131-348 5915   E-mail: lewis.macdonald.msp@scottish.parliament.uk

Constituency: 1 Clifton Road, Aberdeen AB24 4RZ
Tel: 01224 488100   Fax: 01224 276919

MacDONALD, Margo   Ind   **Lothian**
Tel: 0131-348 5715   Fax: 0131-348 6271   E-mail: margo.macdonald.msp@scottish.parliament.uk

Constituency: 12 Torphichen Street, Edinburgh EH3 8JQ
Tel: 0131-525 8916   Fax: 0131-525 8935

McFEE, Bruce   SNP   **West of Scotland**
Member Parliamentary Committee: Local Government and Transport

McGRIGOR, Jamie   Con   **Highlands and Islands**
Scottish Conservative Spokesperson for Tourism, Culture and Sport
Member Parliamentary Committee: Procedures
Tel: 0131-348 5648   Fax: 0131-348 5656   E-mail: jamie.mcgrigor.msp@scottish.parliament.uk
Constituency: 61 Chalmers Street, Ardrishaig, Argyll PA30 8DX
Tel: 01546 606586   Fax: 01546 605387

MACINTOSH, Kenneth   Lab   **Eastwood**
Deputy Convener Parliamentary Committee: Standards
Member Parliamentary Committee: Education
Tel: 0131-348 5897   E-mail: kenneth.macintosh.msp@scottish.parliament.uk
Constituency: 1st Floor, 238 Ayr Road, Newton Mearns, East Renfrewshire G77 6AA
Tel: 0141-577 0100   Fax: 0141-616 3613

MACLEAN, Kate   Lab   **Dundee West**
Member Parliamentary Committees:
   Finance
   Health
Tel: 0131-348 5897   Fax: 0131-348 5983   E-mail: kate.maclean.msp@scottish.parliament.uk
Constituency: 57 Blackscroft, Dundee DD4 6AT
Tel: 01382 466700   Fax: 01382 466719

McLETCHIE, David   Con   **Edinburgh Pentlands**
Leader, Scottish Conservative MSPs
Tel: 0131-348 5659   Fax: 0131-348 5935
E-mail: david.mcletchie.msp@scottish.parliament.uk
Constituency: 67 Northumberland Street, Edinburgh EH3 6JG
Tel: 0131-557 5158   Fax: 0131-557 6682

McMAHON, Michael   Lab   **Hamilton North and Bellshill**
Convener Parliamentary Committee: Public Petitions
Member Parliamentary Committees:
   Local Government and Transport
   The Conveners Group
Tel: 0131-348 5828   E-mail: michael.mcmahon.msp@scottish.parliament.uk
Constituency: 188 Main Street, Bellshill, Lanarkshire ML4 1AE
Tel: 01698 304501   Fax: 01698 300223

MACMILLAN, Maureen   Lab   **Highlands and Islands**
Member Parliamentary Committees:
   Communities
   Environment and Rural Development
Tel: 0131-348 5762   Fax: 0131-348 5767
E-mail: maureen.macmillan.msp@scottish.parliament.uk
Constituency: Highlands and Islands Labour MSPs' Office, PO Box 5717, Dingwall IV15 9WB
Tel: 01349 867650   Fax: 01349 867762

McNEIL, Duncan   Lab   **Greenock and Inverclyde**
Member, Scottish Parliamentary Corporate Body
Member Parliamentary Committee: Health
Tel: 0131-348 5912   Fax: 0131-348 5960
E-mail: duncan.mcneil.msp@scottish.parliament.uk
Constituency: Parliamentary Advice Office, 20 Union Street, Greenock, Inverclyde PA16 8JL
Tel: 01475 791820   Fax: 01475 791821

McNEILL, Pauline Lab   **Glasgow Kelvin**
Convener Parliamentary Committee: Justice 1
Member Parliamentary Committee: The Conveners Group
E-mail: pauline.mcneill.msp@scottish.parliament.uk
Constituency: 1274 Argyle Street, Glasgow G3 8AA
Tel: 0141-589 7120

McNULTY, Des Lab   **Clydebank and Milngavie**
Convener Parliamentary Committee: Finance
Member Parliamentary Committee: The Conveners Group
Tel: 0131-348 5918   Fax: 0131-348 5978   E-mail: des.mcnulty.msp@scottish.parliament.uk
Constituency: Clydebank Central Library, Dumbarton Road, Clydebank G81 1XH
Tel: 0141-952 7711   Fax: 0141-952 7711

MARTIN, Campbell SNP   **West of Scotland**
Member Parliamentary Committees:
  Communities
  Equal Opportunities
E-mail: campbell@campbellmartin.com
Constituency: 3 Stanley Drive, Ardrossan, Ayrshire KA22 8NX
Tel: 01294 601488   Fax: 01294 603666

MARTIN, Paul Lab   **Glasgow Springburn**
Member Parliamentary Committee: Local Government and Transport
Tel: 0131-348 5845   Fax: 0131-348 5984   E-mail: paul.martin.msp@scottish.parliament.uk
Constituency: Millburn Centre, 221 Millburn Street, Glasgow G21 2HL
Tel: 0141-564 1364/1365   Fax: 0141-564 1112

MARWICK, Tricia SNP   **Mid Scotland and Fife**
Convener Parliamentary Committee: Standards
Member Parliamentary Committee: The Conveners Group
E-mail: tricia.marwick.msp@scottish.parliament.uk
Constituency: 10 Commercial Street, Markinch KY7 6DE
Tel: 01592 750500   Fax: 01592 750624

MATHER, Jim SNP   **Highlands and Islands**
Shadow Minister for Enterprise and the Economy
Member Parliamentary Committee: Finance
E-mail: jim.mather@btinternet.com
Constituency: 31 Combie Street, Oban, Argyll PA34 5HE
Tel: 01631 571359

MATHESON, Michael SNP   **Central Scotland**
SNP Deputy Spokesperson for Justice
Member Parliamentary Committee: Justice 1
Tel: 0131-348 5672   Fax: 0131-348 5954   E-mail: michael.matheson.msp@scottish.parliament.uk
Constituency: Dalziel Workspace, Mason Street, Motherwell ML1 1YE
Tel: 01324 849670   Fax: 01324 849671

MAXWELL, Stewart SNP   **West of Scotland**
Deputy Convener Parliamentary Committee: Justice 1
Member Parliamentary Committee: Subordinate Legislation
E-mail: stewartmaxwell@snp.org

MAY, Christine Lab/Co-op   **Central Fife**
Member Parliamentary Committees:
  Enterprise and Culture
  Subordinate Legislation
E-mail: christine.may.msp@scottish.parliament.uk

MILNE, Nanette   Con   **North East Scotland**
Scottish Conservative Deputy Spokesperson for Health and Community Care
Member Parliamentary Committee: Equal Opportunities
E-mail: GCUA@gcua.fsnet.co.uk

Constituency: 7 Northern Road, Kintore, Aberdeenshire AB51 0YL
Tel: 01467 633062   Fax: 01467 633074

MITCHELL, Margaret   Con   **Central Scotland**
Scottish Conservative Deputy Spokesperson for Justice and Home Affairs
Member Parliamentary Committee: Justice 1

Constituency: Huntly Lodge, Fairfield Place, Bothwell G71 8RP
Tel: 01698 854400   Fax: 01698 852963

MONTEITH, Brian   Con   **Mid Scotland and Fife**
Scottish Conservative Spokesperson for Finance and Local Government
Convener Parliamentary Committee: Audit
Member Parliamentary Committee: The Conveners Group
Tel: 0131-348 5644   Fax: 0131-348 5933
E-mail: brian.monteith.msp@scottish.parliament.uk

Constituency: 6 Gladstone Place, Stirling FK8 2NN
Tel: 01786 461200   Fax: 01786 473799

MORGAN, Alasdair   SNP   **South of Scotland**
Convener, SNP Scottish Parliamentary Group
Convener Parliamentary Committee: Enterprise and Culture
Member Parliamentary Committee: The Conveners Group
Tel: 0131-348 5728   Fax: 0131-348 5735
E-mail: alasdair.morgan.msp@scottish.parliament.uk

Constituency: 40a High Street, Dalbeattie, Kirkcudbrightshire DG5 4AA
Tel: 01556 611956   Fax: 01556 613240

MORRISON, Alasdair   Lab   **Western Isles (Eilean Siar)**
Member Parliamentary Committee: Environment and Rural Development
Tel: 0131-348 5760   E-mail: alasdair.morrison.msp@scottish.parliament.uk

Constituency: 4 South Beach Street, Stornoway, Isle of Lewis HS1 2XY
Tel: 01851 704684   Fax: 01851 703048

MULDOON, Bristow   Lab   **Livingston**
Convener Parliamentary Committee: Local Government and Transport
Member Parliamentary Committee: The Conveners Group
Tel: 0131-348 5759   Fax: 0131-348 5971   E-mail: bristow.muldoon.msp@scottish.parliament.uk

Constituency: 4 Newyearfield Farm, Hawk Brae, Ladywell West, Livingston EH54 6TW
Tel: 01506 497961   Fax: 01506 497962

MULLIGAN, Mary   Lab   **Linlithgow**
Deputy Minister for Communities
Tel: 0131-348 5779   Fax: 0131-348 5967   E-mail: mary.mulligan.msp@scottish.parliament.uk

Constituency: 62 Hopetoun Street, Bathgate, West Lothian EH48 4PD
Tel: 01506 636555   Fax: 01506 636555

MUNDELL, David   Con   **South of Scotland**
Scottish Conservative Spokesperson for Transport, Telecommunications and IT
Member Parliamentary Committee: Local Government and Transport
Tel: 0131-348 5635   Fax: 0131-348 5932
E-mail: david.mundell.msp@scottish.parliament.uk

Constituency: 41A Castle Street, Dumfries DG1 1DU
Tel: 01387 256719   Fax: 01387 257039

MUNRO, John Farquhar   Lib Dem   **Ross, Skye and Inverness West**
Scottish Liberal Democrat Spokesperson for the Gaelic Language
Member Parliamentary Committee: Public Petitions
Tel: 0131-348 5793   E-mail: john.munro.msp@scottish.parliament.uk

Constituency: 1A Montague Row, Inverness IV3 5DX
Tel: 01463 714377   Fax: 01463 714380

MURRAY, Dr Elaine   Lab   **Dumfries**
Member Parliamentary Committees:
  Education
  Finance
Tel: 0131-348 5826   Fax: 0131-348 5778   E-mail: elaine.murray.msp@scottish.parliament.uk

Constituency: 5 Friars Vennel, Dumfries DG1 2RQ
Tel: 01387 279205   Fax: 01387 279206

NEIL, Alex   SNP   **Central Scotland**
Member Parliamentary Committee: Standards
E-mail: alex.neil.msp@scottish.parliament.uk

Constituency: Dalziel Workspace, Mason Street, Motherwell ML1 1YE
Tel: 01698 269238   Fax: 01698 269033

OLDFATHER, Irene   Lab   **Cunninghame South**
Deputy Convener Parliamentary Committee: European and External Relations
Tel: 0131-348 5768   Fax: 0131-348 5778
E-mail: irene.oldfather.msp@scottish.parliament.uk

Constituency: Sovereign House, Academy Road, Irvine, Ayrshire KA12 8RL
Tel: 01294 313078   Fax: 01294 313605

PEACOCK, Peter   Lab   **Highlands and Islands**
Minister for Education and Young People
Tel: 0131-348 5766   E-mail: peter.peacock.msp@scottish.parliament.uk

Constituency: Highlands and Islands Labour MSPs' Office, PO Box 5717, Dingwall,
Ross-shire IV15 9WB
Tel: 01349 867650   Fax: 01349 867762

PEATTIE, Cathy   Lab   **Falkirk East**
Convener Parliamentary Committee: Equal Opportunities
Member Parliamentary Committee: The Conveners Group
Tel: 0131-348 5746   Fax: 0131-348 5750
E-mail: cathy.peattie.msp@scottish.parliament.uk

Constituency: 5 Kerse Road, Grangemouth FK3 8HQ
Tel: 01324 666026   Fax: 01324 473951

PRINGLE, Mike   Lib Dem   **Edinburgh South**
Scottish Liberal Democrat Spokesperson for Equal Opportunities
Member Parliamentary Committees:
  Justice 2
  Subordinate Legislation
E-mail: migpringle@aol.com

Constituency: 26 Morningside Park, Edinburgh EH10 5HB

PURVIS, Jeremy   Lib Dem   **Tweeddale, Ettrick and Lauderdale**
Scottish Liberal Democrat Spokesperson for Finance
Member Parliamentary Committee: Finance
E-mail: jeremy@jeremypurvis.com

Constituency: Lower Westwood, Westwood Gardens, Galashiels TD1 1RD
Tel: 01896 759759   Fax: 01896 759799

RADCLIFFE, Nora   Lib Dem   **Gordon**
Convener, Scottish Liberal Democrat Parliamentary Party; Scottish Liberal Democrat Spokesperson for Environment and Rural Development
Member Parliamentary Committee: Environment and Rural Development
Tel: 0131-348 5804   Fax: 0131-348 5964
E-mail: nora.radcliffe.msp@scottish.parliament.uk
Constituency: 67 High Street, Inverurie AB51 3QJ
Tel: 01467 672220   Fax: 01467 625267

RAFFAN, Keith   Lib Dem   **Mid Scotland and Fife**
Scottish Liberal Democrat Spokesperson for European Affairs in the Scottish Parliament
Deputy Convener Parliamentary Committee: Equal Opportunities
Member Parliamentary Committee: European and External Relations
Tel: 0131-348 5800   Fax: 0131-348 5964   E-mail: keith.raffan.msp@scottish.parliament.uk
Constituency: 15-19 North Port, Perth PH1 5LU
Tel: 01738 566100   Fax: 01738 566101

REID, George   PO   **Ochil**
Presiding Officer
Tel: 0131-348 5911   Fax: 0131-348 5996   E-mail: george.reid.msp@scottish.parliament.uk
Constituency: Langgarth Lodge House, St Ninians Road, Stirling FK8 2HE
Tel: 01786 472470

ROBISON, Shona   SNP   **Dundee East**
Shadow Minister for Health and Social Justice
Member Parliamentary Committee: Health
Tel: 0131-348 5707   Fax: 0131-348 5949
E-mail: shona.robison.msp@scottish.parliament.uk
Constituency: 8 Old Glamis Road, Dundee DD3 8HP
Tel: 01382 623200   Fax: 01382 903205

ROBSON, Euan   Lib Dem   **Roxburgh and Berwickshire**
Deputy Minister for Education and Young People
Tel: 0131-348 5806   Fax: 0131-348 5963   E-mail: euan.robson.msp@scottish.parliament.uk
Constituency: 56 Horsemarket, Kelso, Roxburghshire TD5 7AE
Tel: 01573 228635   Fax: 01573 228636

RUMBLES, Mike   Lib Dem   **West Aberdeenshire and Kincardine**
Scottish Liberal Democrat Spokesperson for Health
Member Parliamentary Committee: Health
Tel: 0131-348 5798   Fax: 0131-348 5964   E-mail: mike.rumbles.msp@scottish.parliament.uk
Constituency: 6 Dee Street, Banchory, Aberdeenshire AB31 5ST
Tel: 01330 820268   Fax: 01330 820106

RUSKELL, Mark   Green   **Mid Scotland and Fife**
Green Spokesperson for Environment and Rural Development
Tel: 0131-348 6368   E-mail: ruskell@gn.apc.org
Constituency: 2 Mine Road, Bridge of Allan, Stirling FK9 4DT
Tel: 0131-478 7896

SCANLON, Mary   Con   **Highlands and Islands**
Scottish Conservative Spokesperson for Communities
Member Parliamentary Committee: Communities
Tel: 0131-348 5650   Fax: 0131-348 5656
E-mail: mary.scanlon.msp@scottish.parliament.uk
Constituency: 37 Ardconnel Terrace, Inverness IV2 3AE
Tel: 01463 241004   Fax: 01463 237497

SCOTT, Eleanor Green   **Highlands and Islands**
Green Spokesperson for Health and Community Care
Deputy Convener Parliamentary Committee: Environment and Rural Development
E-mail: eleanorsco@aol.com

SCOTT, John Con   **Ayr**
Member, Scottish Parliamentary Corporate Body
Deputy Convener Parliamentary Committee: Public Petitions
Tel: 0131-348 5664   Fax: 0131-348 5617   E-mail: john.scott.msp@scottish.parliament.uk
Constituency: 1 Wellington Square, Ayr KA7 1EN
Tel: 01292 286251   Fax: 01292 280480

SCOTT, Tavish Lib Dem   **Shetland**
Deputy Minister for Finance and Public Services
Tel: 0131-348 5815   Fax: 0131-348 5807   E-mail: tavish.scott.msp@scottish.parliament.uk
Constituency: Albert Building, Lerwick, Shetland ZE1 0LL
Tel: 01595 690044   Fax: 01595 690055

SHERIDAN, Tommy SSP   **Glasgow**
Convener, SSP; SSP Spokesperson for Finance, Public Services and Communities
Tel: 0131-348 5631   Fax: 0131-348 5948
E-mail: tommy.sheridan.msp@scottish.parliament.uk
Constituency: 73 Robertson Street, Glasgow G2 8QD
Tel: 0141-221 7719   Fax: 0141-221 7715

SMITH, Elaine Lab   **Coatbridge and Chryston**
Member Parliamentary Committees:
   Communities
   Equal Opportunities
Tel: 0131-348 5824   Fax: 0131-348 5834
E-mail: elaine.smith.msp@scottish.parliament.uk
Constituency: Unit 65, Fountain Business Centre, Ellis Street, Coatbridge ML5 3AA
Tel: 01236 449122   Fax: 01236 449137

SMITH, Iain Lib Dem   **North East Fife**
Scottish Liberal Democrat Spokesperson for Transport and Local Government
Convener Parliamentary Committee: Procedures
Member Parliamentary Committees:
   Local Government and Transport
   The Conveners Group
Tel: 0131-348 5817   Fax: 0131-348 5962   E-mail: iain.smith.msp@scottish.parliament.uk
Constituency: 16 Millgate, Cupar, Fife KY15 5EG
Tel: 01334 656361   Fax: 01334 654045

SMITH, Margaret Lib Dem   **Edinburgh West**
Scottish Liberal Democrat Spokesperson for Justice
Member Parliamentary Committee: Justice 1
Tel: 0131-348 5785   Fax: 0131-348 5965
E-mail: margaret.smith.msp@scottish.parliament.uk
Constituency: West Edinburgh Liberal Democrats, 11 Drum Brae Avenue, Edinburgh EH12 8TE
Tel: 0131-339 0339   Fax: 0131-476 7101

STEPHEN, Nicol Lib Dem   **Aberdeen South**
Minister for Transport
Tel: 0131-348 5347   E-mail: nicol.stephen.msp@scottish.parliament.uk
Constituency: 173 Crown Street, Aberdeen AB11 6JA
Tel: 01224 252728   Fax: 01224 590926

STEVENSON, Stewart   SNP   **Banff and Buchan**
SNP Deputy Spokesperson for Health and Social Justice
Member Parliamentary Committee: Communities
E-mail: msp@stewartstevenson.net
Constituency: 17 Maiden Street, Peterhead, Aberdeenshire AB42 1EE
Tel: 01779 470444   Fax: 01779 474460

STONE, Jamie   Lib Dem   **Caithness, Sutherland and Easter Ross**
Scottish Liberal Democrat Spokesperson for Enterprise, Lifelong Learning and Tourism
Member Parliamentary Committee: Enterprise and Culture
Tel: 0131-348 5789   Fax: 0131-348 5807
E-mail: jamie.stone.msp@scottish.parliament.uk
Constituency: 26 Tower Street, Tain IV19 1DY
Tel: 01862 892726   Fax: 01862 893698

STURGEON, Nicola   SNP   **Glasgow**
Shadow Minister for Justice
Member Parliamentary Committee: Justice 2
Tel: 0131-348 5695   Fax: 0131-348 5949
E-mail: nicola.sturgeon.msp@scottish.parliament.uk
Constituency: SNP Office, 7th Floor, Telfer House, 74 Miller Street, Glasgow G1 1DT
Tel: 0141-204 1775   Fax: 0141-204 1776

SWINBURNE, John   **Central Scotland**
Member Parliamentary Committee: Finance
E-mail: john.swinburne.msp@scottish.parliament.uk
Constituency: The Scottish Senior Citizens Unity Party, PO Box 26420, East Kilbride G75 8XS

SWINNEY, John   SNP   **North Tayside**
Shadow First Minister and Opposition Leader; National Convener, SNP
Tel: 0131-348 5717   Fax: 0131-348 5946   E-mail: john.swinney.msp@scottish.parliament.uk
Constituency: 35 Perth Street, Blairgowrie PH10 6DL
Tel: 01250 876576   Fax: 01250 876991

TOSH, Murray   Con   **West of Scotland**
Deputy Presiding Officer
Member Parliamentary Committee: Subordinate Legislation
Tel: 0131-348 5637   Fax: 0131-348 5932
E-mail: murray.tosh.msp@scottish.parliament.uk

TURNER, Dr Jean   Ind   **Strathkelvin and Bearsden**
Member Parliamentary Committee: Health
E-mail: jean.turner.msp@scottish.parliament.uk

WALLACE, Rt Hon Jim, QC   Lib Dem   **Orkney**
Leader, Scottish Liberal Democrats; Deputy First Minister and Minister for Enterprise
Tel: 0131-348 5815   E-mail: jim.wallace.msp@scottish.parliament.uk
Constituency: 31 Broad Street, Kirkwall, Orkney KW15 2DH
Tel: 01856 876541   Fax: 01856 876162

WATSON, Mike   Lab   **Glasgow Cathcart**
Deputy Convener Parliamentary Committee: Enterprise and Culture
Member Parliamentary Committee: Public Petitions
Tel: 0131-348 5840   Fax: 0131-348 5904
E-mail: mike.watson.msp@scottish.parliament.uk
Constituency: Somerville Drive, Mount Florida, Glasgow G42 9BA
Tel: 0141-636 6121   Fax: 0141-636 6121

WELSH, Andrew   SNP   **Angus**
Member, Scottish Parliamentary Corporate Body
Deputy Convener Parliamentary Committee: Local Government and Transport
Tel: 0131-348 5690   Fax: 0131-348 5954   E-mail: andrew.welsh.msp@scottish.parliament.uk
Constituency: 31 Market Place, Arbroath, Angus DD11 1HR
Tel: 01241 439369   Fax: 01241 871561

WHITE, Sandra   SNP   **Glasgow**
SNP Deputy Spokesperson for Health and Social Justice
Member Parliamentary Committee: Public Petitions
Tel: 0131-348 5688   Fax: 0131-348 5953   E-mail: sandra.white.msp@scottish.parliament.uk
Constituency: Telfer House, 74 Miller Street, Glasgow G1 1DT
Tel: 0141-204 1767   Fax: 0141-204 1781

WHITEFIELD, Karen   Lab   **Airdrie and Shotts**
Deputy Convener Parliamentary Committee: Justice 2
Member Parliamentary Committee: Standards
Tel: 0131-348 5833   Fax: 0131-348 5993   E-mail: karen.whitefield.msp@scottish.parliament.uk
Constituency: 135 Station Road, Shotts, North Lanarkshire ML7 4BJ
Tel: 01501 822200   Fax: 01501 823650

WILSON, Allan   Lab   **Cunninghame North**
Deputy Minister for Environment and Rural Development
E-mail: allan.wilson.msp@scottish.parliament.uk
Constituency: 55 Hamilton Street, Saltcoats KA21 5DX
Tel: 01294 605040

Constituencies

			Majority
Aberdeen Central	Lewis Macdonald	Lab	1,242
Aberdeen North	Brian Adam	SNP	457
Aberdeen South	Nicol Stephen	LibDem	8,016
Airdrie and Shotts	Karen Whitefield	Lab	8,977
Angus	Andrew Welsh	SNP	6,687
Argyll and Bute	George Lyon	LibDem	4,196
Ayr	John Scott	Con	1,890
Banff and Buchan	Stewart Stevenson	SNP	8,364
Caithness, Sutherland and Easter Ross	Jamie Stone	LibDem	2,092
Carrick, Cumnock and Doon Valley	Cathy Jamieson	Lab/Co-op	7,454
Central Fife	Christine May	Lab/Co-op	2,762
Clydebank and Milngavie	Des McNulty	Lab	4,534
Clydesdale	Karen Gillon	Lab	6,671
Coatbridge and Chryston	Elaine Smith	Lab	8,571
Cumbernauld and Kilsyth	Cathie Craigie	Lab	520
Cunninghame North	Allan Wilson	Lab	3,390
Cunninghame South	Irene Oldfather	Lab	6,083
Dumbarton	Jackie Baillie	Lab	6,612
Dumfries	Elaine Murray	Lab	1,096
Dundee East	Shona Robison	SNP	70
Dundee West	Kate Maclean	Lab	1,066
Dunfermline East	Helen Eadie	Lab/Co-op	7,290
Dunfermline West	Scott Barrie	Lab	4,080
East Kilbride	Andy Kerr	Lab	5,281
East Lothian	John Home Robertson	Lab	8,175
Eastwood	Kenneth Macintosh	Lab	3,702

Edinburgh Central	Sarah Boyack	Lab	2,666
Edinburgh East and Musselburgh	Susan Deacon	Lab	6,158
Edinburgh North and Leith	Malcolm Chisholm	Lab	5,014
Edinburgh Pentlands	David McLetchie	Con	2,111
Edinburgh South	Mike Pringle	LibDem	158
Edinburgh West	Margaret Smith	LibDem	5,914
Falkirk East	Cathy Peattie	Lab	6,659
Falkirk West	Dennis Canavan	MPFW	10,000
Galloway and Upper Nithsdale	Alex Fergusson	Con	99
Glasgow Anniesland	Bill Butler	Lab	6,253
Glasgow Baillieston	Margaret Curran	Lab	6,178
Glasgow Cathcart	Mike Watson	Lab	5,112
Glasgow Govan	Gordon Jackson	Lab	1,235
Glasgow Kelvin	Pauline McNeill	Lab	3,289
Glasgow Maryhill	Patricia Ferguson	Lab	5,368
Glasgow Pollok	Johann Lamont	Lab/Co-op	3,341
Glasgow Rutherglen	Janis Hughes	Lab	6,303
Glasgow Shettleston	Frank McAveety	Lab/Co-op	6,347
Glasgow Springburn	Paul Martin	Lab	8,007
Gordon	Nora Radcliffe	LibDem	4,071
Greenock and Inverclyde	Duncan McNeil	Lab	3,009
Hamilton North and Bellshill	Michael McMahon	Lab	7,905
Hamilton South	Tom McCabe	Lab	4,824
Inverness East, Nairn and Lochaber	Fergus Ewing	SNP	1,046
Kilmarnock and Loudoun	Margaret Jamieson	Lab	1,240
Kirkcaldy	Marilyn Livingstone	Lab/Co-op	4,824
Linlithgow	Mary Mulligan	Lab	1,970
Livingston	Bristow Muldoon	Lab	3,670
Midlothian	Rhona Brankin	Lab/Co-op	5,542
Moray	Margaret Ewing	SNP	5,312
Motherwell and Wishaw	Jack McConnell	Lab	9,259
North East Fife	Iain Smith	LibDem	5,055
North Tayside	John Swinney	SNP	4,503
Ochil	George Reid	Pres Off	296
Orkney	Jim Wallace	LibDem	1,755
Paisley North	Wendy Alexander	Lab	4,310
Paisley South	Hugh Henry	Lab	2,453
Perth	Roseanna Cunningham	SNP	727
Ross, Skye and Inverness West	John Farquhar Munro	LibDem	6,848
Roxburgh and Berwickshire	Euan Robson	LibDem	2,490
Shetland	Tavish Scott	LibDem	2,260
Stirling	Sylvia Jackson	Lab	2,880
Strathkelvin and Bearsden	Dr Jean Turner	Ind	438
Tweeddale, Ettrick and Lauderdale	Jeremy Purvis	LibDem	538
West Aberdeenshire and Kincardine	Mike Rumbles	LibDem	5,399
West Renfrewshire	Trish Godman	Lab	2,492
Western Isles (Eilean Siar)	Alasdair Morrison	Lab	720

Visit the Vacher Dod Website . . .
www.DodOnline.co.uk

Regions

Central Scotland	Linda Fabiani	SNP
Central Scotland	Donald Gorrie	LibDem
Central Scotland	Michael Matheson	SNP
Central Scotland	Alex Neil	SNP
Central Scotland	Margaret Mitchell	Con
Central Scotland	Carolyn Leckie	SSP
Central Scotland	John Swinburne	SCUP
Glasgow	Bill Aitken	Con
Glasgow	Robert Brown	LibDem
Glasgow	Tommy Sheridan	SSP
Glasgow	Nicola Sturgeon	SNP
Glasgow	Sandra White	SNP
Glasgow	Patrick Harvie	Green
Glasgow	Rosie Kane	SSP
Highlands and Islands	Jamie McGrigor	Con
Highlands and Islands	Maureen Macmillan	Lab
Highlands and Islands	Peter Peacock	Lab
Highlands and Islands	Mary Scanlon	Con
Highlands and Islands	Rob Gibson	SNP
Highlands and Islands	Eleanor Scott	Green
Highlands and Islands	Jim Mather	SNP
Lothian	Lord James Douglas-Hamilton	Con
Lothian	Robin Harper	Green
Lothian	Fiona Hyslop	SNP
Lothian	Kenny MacAskill	SNP
Lothian	Margo MacDonald	Independent
Lothian	Mark Ballard	Green
Lothian	Colin Fox	SSP
Mid Scotland and Fife	Bruce Crawford	SNP
Mid Scotland and Fife	Tricia Marwick	SNP
Mid Scotland and Fife	Brian Monteith	Con
Mid Scotland and Fife	Keith Raffan	LibDem
Mid Scotland and Fife	Murdo Fraser	Con
Mid Scotland and Fife	Mark Ruskell	Green
Mid Scotland and Fife	Ted Brocklebank	Con
North East Scotland	David Davidson	Con
North East Scotland	Alex Johnstone	Con
North East Scotland	Richard Lochhead	SNP
North East Scotland	Shiona Baird	Green
North East Scotland	Nanette Milne	Con
North East Scotland	Richard Baker	Lab
North East Scotland	Marlyn Glen	Lab
South of Scotland	Phil Gallie	Con
South of Scotland	Christine Grahame	SNP
South of Scotland	Adam Ingram	SNP
South of Scotland	Alasdair Morgan	SNP
South of Scotland	David Mundell	Con
South of Scotland	Chris Ballance	Green
South of Scotland	Rosemary Byrne	SSP
West of Scotland	Ross Finnie	LibDem
West of Scotland	Annabel Goldie	Con
West of Scotland	Murray Tosh	Con
West of Scotland	Bruce McFee	SNP
West of Scotland	Campbell Martin	SNP
West of Scotland	Stewart Maxwell	SNP
West of Scotland	Frances Curran	SSP

Women Members

ALEXANDER, Wendy
BAILLIE, Jackie
BAIRD, Shiona
BOYACK, Sarah
BRANKIN, Rhona
BYRNE, Rosemary
CRAIGIE, Cathie
CUNNINGHAM, Roseanna
CURRAN, Frances
CURRAN, Margaret
DEACON, Susan
EADIE, Helen
EWING, Margaret
FABIANI, Linda
FERGUSON, Patricia
GILLON, Karen
GLEN, Marlyn
GODMAN, Trish
GOLDIE, Annabel
GRAHAME, Christine
HUGHES, Janis
HYSLOP, Fiona
JACKSON, Sylvia
JAMIESON, Cathy
JAMIESON, Margaret
KANE, Rosie

LAMONT, Johann
LECKIE, Carolyn
LIVINGSTONE, Marilyn
MacDONALD, Margo
MACLEAN, Kate
MACMILLAN, Maureen
McNEILL, Pauline
MARWICK, Tricia
MAY, Christine
MILNE, Nanette
MITCHELL, Margaret
MULLIGAN, Mary
MURRAY, Elaine
OLDFATHER, Irene
PEATTIE, Cathy
RADCLIFFE, Nora
ROBISON, Shona
SCANLON, Mary
SCOTT, Eleanor
SMITH, Elaine
SMITH, Margaret
STURGEON, Nicola
TURNER, Jean
WHITE, Sandra
WHITEFIELD, Karen

Parliamentary Committees

The Conveners Group

Sarah Boyack, Robert Brown, Annabel Goldie, Christine Grahame, Sylvia Jackson, Johann Lamont, Richard Lochhead, Michael McMahon, Pauline McNeill, Des McNulty, Tricia Marwick, Brian Monteith, Alasdair Morgan, Bristow Muldoon, Cathy Peattie, Iain Smith
Note: The Convenors Group is the new title of the informal group previously known as the Convenors' Liaison Group. It comprises the converners of the mandatory and subject committees of the Parliament

Mandatory and Subject Committees

Audit

Convener: Brian Monteith
Deputy Convener: Kenny MacAskill
Rhona Brankin, Susan Deacon, Robin Harper, Margaret Jamieson, George Lyon
Clerk to the Committee: Shelagh McKinlay
(0131-348 5215)

Senior Assistant Clerk: Joanna Hardy
Assistant Clerk: Sean Wixted
Remit: The remit of the Audit Committee is to consider and report on:
(a) any accounts laid before the Parliament;
(b) any report laid before or made to the Parliament by the Auditor General for Scotland; and
(c) any other document laid before the Parliament concerning financial control, accounting and auditing in relation to public expenditure.
Website: www.scottish.parliament.uk/ official_report/cttee/aud.htm

Communities

Convener: Johann Lamont
Deputy Convener: Donald Gorrie
Cathie Craigie, Patrick Harvie, Maureen Macmillan, Campbell Martin, Mary Scanlon, Elaine Smith, Stewart Stevenson
Remit: To consider and report on matters relating to anti-social behaviour, housing and regeneration, poverty, voluntary sector issues, charity

law and religious and faith organisations and matters relating to the land use planning system and building standards and such other matters as fall within the responsibility of the Minister for Communities.

Education

Convener: Robert Brown
Deputy Convener: Lord James Douglas-Hamilton
Wendy Alexander, Rhona Brankin, Rosemary Byrne, Fiona Hyslop, Adam Ingram, Kenneth Macintosh, Elaine Murray
Remit: To consider and report on matters relating to school and pre-school education and social work and such other matters relating to young people as fall within the responsibility of the Minister for Education and Young People.

Enterprise and Culture

Convener: Alasdair Morgan
Deputy Convener: Mike Watson
Brian Adam, Richard Baker, Chris Ballance, Susan Deacon, Murdo Fraser, Christine May, Jamie Stone
Remit: To consider and report on matters relating to the Scottish economy, business and industry, energy, training, further and higher educationm, lifelong learning and such other matters as fall within the responsibility of the Minister for Enterprise and Lifelong Learning; and matters relating to tourism, culture and sport and such other matters as fall within the responsibility of the Minister for Tourism, Culture and Sport.

Environment and Rural Development

Convener: Sarah Boyack
Deputy Convener: Eleanor Scott
Roseanna Cunningham, Rob Gibson, Karen Gillon, Alex Johnstone, Maureen Macmillan, Alasdair Morrison, Nora Radcliffe
Remit: To consider and report on matters relating to transport and rural development, environment and natural heritage, agriculture and fisheries and such other matters as fall within the responsibility of the Minister for Environment and Rural Development.

Equal Opportunities

Convener: Cathy Peattie
Deputy Convener: Keith Raffan
Shiona Baird, Frances Curran, Marlyn Glen, Marilyn Livingstone, Campbell Martin, Nanette Milne, Elaine Smith

Clerk to the Committee: James Johnston (0131-348 5211)
Senior Assistant Clerk: Richard Walsh
Assistant Clerk: Roy McMahon
Remit: The remit of the Equal Opportunities Committee is to consider and report on matters relating to equal opportunities and upon the observance of equal opportunities within the Parliament.
Website: www.scottish.parliament.uk/ official_report/cttee/equal.htm

European and External Relations

Convener: Richard Lochhead
Deputy Convener: Irene Oldfather
Dennis Canavan, Margaret Ewing, Phil Gallie, John Home Robertson, Gordon Jackson, Alasdair Morrison, Keith Raffan
Remit: The remit of the European and External Relations Committee is to consider and report on:
(a) proposals for European Communities legislation;
(b) the implementation of European Communities legislation;
(c) any European Communities or European Union issue;
(d) the development and implementation of the Scottish Administration's links with countries and territories outside Scotland, the European Communities (and their institutions) and other international organisations; and
(e) co-ordination of the international activities of the Scottish Administration.

Finance

Convener: Des McNulty
Deputy Convener: Fergus Ewing
Wendy Alexander, Ted Brocklebank, Kate Maclean, Jim Mather, Elaine Murray, Jeremy Purvis, John Swinburne
Clerk to the Committee: David McGill (0131-348 5215)
Senior Assistant Clerk: Terry Shevlin
Assistant Clerk: Gerry McInally
Remit: The remit of the Finance Committee is to consider and report on:
(a) any report or other document laid before the Parliament by members of the Scottish Executive containing proposals for, or budgets of, public expenditure or proposals for the making of a tax-varying resolution, taking into account any report of recommendations

concerning such documents made to them by any other committee with power to consider such documents or any part of them;

(b) any report made by a committee setting out proposals concerning public expenditure;

(c) Budget Bills; and

(d) any other matter relating to or affecting the expenditure of the Scottish Administration or other expenditure payable out of the Scottish Consolidated Fund.

Website: www.scottish.parliament.uk/ official_report/cttee/finance.htm

Health

Convener: Christine Grahame
Deputy Convener: Janis Hughes
David Davidson, Helen Eadie, Kate Maclean, Duncan McNeil, Shona Robison, Mike Rumbles, Jean Turner
Remit: To consider and report on matters relating relating to the health policy and the National Health Service in Scotland and such other matters as fall within the responsibility of the Minister of Health and Community Care.

Justice 1

Convener: Pauline McNeill
Deputy Convener: Stewart Maxwell
Bill Butler, Marlyn Glen, Michael Matheson, Margaret Mitchell, Margaret Smith
Clerk to the Committee: Alison Taylor (0131-348 5195)
Senior Assistant Clerk: Claire Menzies
Assistant Clerk: Jenny Goldsmith
Remit: To consider and report on matters relating to the administration of civil and criminal justice, the reform of the civil and criminal law and such other matters as fall within the responsibility of the Minister for Justice, and the functions of the Lord Advocate other than as head of the systems of criminal prosecution and investigations of deaths in Scotland.
Website: www.scottish.parliament.uk/ official_report/cttee/just1.htm

Justice 2

Convener: Annabel Goldie
Deputy Convener: Karen Whitefield
Jackie Baillie, Scott Barrie, Colin Fox, Mike Pringle, Nicola Sturgeon
Clerk to the Committee: Gillian Baxendine (0131-348 5054)
Senior Assistant Clerk: Irene Fleming
Assistant Clerk: Richard Hough

Remit: To consider and report on matters relating to the administration of civil and criminal justice, the reform of the civil and criminal law and such other matters as fall within the responsibility of the Minister for Justice, and the functions of the Lord Advocate other than as head of the systems of criminal prosecution and investigations of deaths in Scotland.
Website: www.scottish.parliament.uk/ official_report/cttee/just2.htm

Local Government and Transport

Convener: Bristow Muldoon
Deputy Convener: Andrew Welsh
Sylvia Jackson, Rosie Kane, Bruce McFee, Michael McMahon, Paul Martin, David Mundell, Iain Smith
Remit: To consider and report on matters relating to local government (including local government finance), cities and community planning and such other matters (excluding finance other than local government finance) which fall within the responsibility of the Minister for Finance and Public Services; and matters relating to transport which fall within the responsibility of the Minister for Transport.

Procedures

Convener: Iain Smith
Deputy Convener: Karen Gillon
Richard Baker, Mark Ballard, Cathie Craigie, Bruce Crawford, Jamie McGrigor
Clerk to the Committee: John Patterson (0131-348 5175)
Senior Assistant Clerk: Mark MacPherson
Assistant Clerk: Lewis McNaughton
Remit: The remit of the Procedures Committee is to consider and report on the practice and procedures of the Scottish Parliament in relation to its business.
Website: www.scottish.parliament.uk/ official_report/cttee/proced.htm

Public Petitions

Convener: Michael McMahon
Deputy Convener: John Scott
Jackie Baillie, Helen Eadie, Linda Fabiani, Carolyn Leckie, John Farquhar Munro, Mike Watson, Sandra White
Clerk to the Committee: Steve Farrell (0131-348 5186)
Website: www.scottish.parliament.uk/ official_report/cttee/petit.htm

Standards

Convener: Tricia Marwick
Deputy Convener: Kenneth Macintosh
Bill Butler, Alex Fergusson, Donald Gorrie, Alex Neil, Karen Whitefield
Clerk to the Committee: Samantha Jones (0131-348 5239)
Senior Assistant Clerk: Sarah Robertson
Remit: The remit of the Standard Comittee is to consider and report on:

(a) whether a member's conduct is in accordance with these Rules and any Code of Conduct for members, matters relating to members' interests, and any other matters relating to the conduct of members in carrying out their Parliamentary duties; and
(b) the adoption, amendment and application of any Code of Conduct for members.

Website: www.scottish.parliament.uk/ official_report/cttee/stan.htm

Subordinate Legislation

Convener: Sylvia Jackson
Deputy Convener: Gordon Jackson
Stewart Maxwell, Christine May, Mike Pringle, Murray Tosh
Clerk to the Committee: Alasdair Rankin (0131-348 5212)
Senior Assistant Clerk: Steve Farrell
Assistant Clerk: Alistair Fleming
Assistant Clerk: Joanne Clinton
Remit: The remit of the Subordinate Legislation Committee is to consider and report on:

(a) (i) subordinate legislation which is laid before the Parliament
(ii) any Scottish Statutory Instrument not laid before the Parliament but classified as general according to its subject matter, and, in particular, to determine whether the attention of the Parliament should be drawn to any of the matters referred to in Rule 10.3.1;
(b) proposed powers to make subordinate legislation in particular Bills or other proposed legislation;
(c) general questions relating to powers to make subordinate legislation; and
(d) whether any proposed delegated powers in particular Bills or other legislation should be expressed as a power to make subordinate legislation.

Website: www.scottish.parliament.uk/ official_report/cttee/subord.htm

Principal Officers and Officials

Office of the Presiding Officer

Presiding Officer

George Reid MSP
Tel: 0131-348 5302   Fax: 0131-348 5301
E-mail: presiding.officer@scottish.parliament.uk

Deputy Presiding Officers

Trish Godman MSP (Lab)
Murray Tosh MSP (Con)

Scottish Parliamentary Corporate Body

(responsible for administration)

Robert Brown MSP (Lib Dem)
Duncan McNeil MSP (Lab)

Andrew Welsh MSP (SNP)
John Scott MSP (Con)

Parliamentary Bureau

(responsible for all-party business programme and forward planning)

George Reid
(Presiding Officer)
Bill Aitken MSP (Con)
Mark Ballard MSP (Green)

Patricia Ferguson MSP (Lab)
Fiona Hyslop MSP (SNP)
Tavish Scott MSP (Lib Dem)
Carolyn Leckie MSP (SSP)

Senior Management Team

Clerk/Chief Executive	**Paul Grice**
Director of Legal Services	**Ann Nelson**
Director of Clerking and Reporting Services	**Vacant**
Director of Facilities and Technology	**Stewart Gilfillan**
Director of Resources	**Vacant**
Director of Communications and Information	**Carol Dean**
Holyrood Project Director	**Sarah Davidson**
Head of Chamber Office	**Ken Hughes**
Head of Committee Office	**Elizabeth Watson**
Editor of the Official Report	**Henrietta Hales**
Head of Research and Information Group	**Janet Seaton**
Head of Business Information Technology	**Alan Balharrie**
Head of Personnel	**Ian Macnicol**
Head of Corporate Services	**Derek Croll**
Head of Implementation	**Bill Thomson**

Scottish Executive

Website: www.scotland.gov.uk

The Scottish Executive (civil service) consists of several main departments:

Development Department; Education Department; Enterprise, Transport and Lifelong Learning Department; Environment and Rural Affairs Department; Financial and Central Services Department; Health Department; Justice Department* – together with Corporate Services.

Includes Scottish Courts Group

Scottish Executive Senior Management

Office of the Permanent Secretary
(St Andrew's House)
Permanent Secretary: John Elvidge
Private Secretary: Ian Davidson
Tel: 0131-244 4026 *Fax:* 0131-244 2756

Development Department
(Victoria Quay)
Head: Nicola Munro
Private Secretary: Mark Rae *Tel:* 0131-244 0760
Fax: 0131-244 0785

Housing and Area Regeneration Group
Head of Group: Mike Neilson
Tel: 0131-244 0769

Planning and Building Standards Group
Chief Planner: Jim Mackinnon
Tel: 0131-244 0771

Inquiry Reporters Unit
Based in Greenside Lane,
Edinburgh EH1 3AG
Chief Reporter: Jim McCulloch
Tel: 0131-244 5641

Social Justice Group
Head of Group: Mark Batho
Tel: 0131-244 7414

Education Department
(Victoria Quay)
Head: Michael Ewart
Private Secretary: Steven Szymoszowskyj
Tel: 0131-244 1484 *Fax:* 0131-244 1479

Schools Group
Head of Group: Philip Rycroft
Private Secretary: Janet Leavy
Tel: 0131-244 7107

Social Work Services – Inspectorate
Chief Inspector: Angus Skinner
Private Secretary: Moira Hughes
Tel: 0131-244 3680

Children and Young People's Group
Head of Group: Colin MacLean
Private Secretaries: Irene Szmoszowskyj, Fiona Brown *Tel:* 0131-244 0835

Tourism, Culture and Sport
Head of Group: John Mason
Private Secretary: Marie Wilson
Tel: 0131-244 1466

Enterprise, Transport and Lifelong Learning Department

(Meridian Court)
Head: Eddie Frizzell CB
Private Secretary: Debbie Sheldon
Tel: 0141-242 5704 Fax: 0141-242 5477

Enterprise and Industrial Affairs
Head of Group: Graeme Dickson

Lifelong Learning Group
Head of Group: Ed Weeple

Transport Group
Head of Group: John Martin Tel: 0131-244 0628

Environment and Rural Affairs Department

(Pentland House)
Head: John Graham
Private Secretary: David Brown
Tel: 0131-244 6022 Fax: 0131-244 6116

Agricultural and Biological Research Group
Head of Group: Dr Andrew Rushworth
Tel: 0131-244 6043

Food and Agriculture Group
Head of Group: David F Middleton
Tel: 0131-244 6296

Fisheries and Rural Development Group
Head of Group: Dr Paul Brady
Tel: 0131-244 6035

Environment Group
Head of Group: Mike Foulis Tel: 0131-244 0780

Health Department

(St Andrew's House)
Head of Department and Chief Executive:
Trevor Jones
Personal Assistant to Chief Executive:
Trisha Hanlon Tel: 0131-244 2790

Professional Staff
Chief Medical Officer: Dr Mac Armstrong
Deputy Chief Medical Officers:
Dr Andrew Fraser, Dr Aileen Keel
Chief Dental Officer: Ray Watkins
Chief Pharmacist: Bill Scott

Chief Scientist Office
Chief Scientist: Professor Roland Jung

Directorate of Service Policy and Planning
Director: Ian Gordon Tel: 0131-244 1727

Human Resources Directorate
Director: Mark Butler Tel: 0131-244 2036

Directorate of Finance and Performance Management
Director: John Aldridge Tel: 0131-244 3464

Directorate of Nursing
Chief Nursing Officer: Anne Jarvie CBE
Tel: 0131-244 2314

Directorate of Health Improvement
Director: Pam Whittle Tel: 0131-244 1826

Justice Department

(St Andrew's House)
Head: Jim Gallagher
Private Secretary: Scott Rogerson
Tel: 0131-244 2791 Fax: 0131-244 2121

Police and Community Safety
Head of Group: Colin Baxter
Tel: 0131-244 2127 Fax: 0131-244 2121

Criminal Justice Group
Head of Group: Micheline Brannan
Tel: 0131-244 2131 Fax: 0131-244 2121

Civil and International Group
Head of Group: Valerie MacNiven
Tel: 0131-244 8491 Fax: 0131-244 8325

Judicial Appointments and Finance Division
Head of Division: David Stewart
Tel: 0131-221 6801 Fax: 0131-221 6895

Corporate Services

(Saughton House)
Head: Agnes Robson
Private Secretary: Carolyn Murdoch
Tel: 0131-244 3939 Fax: 0131-244 3095

Human Resources Division
Head: Sally Carruthers
Private Secretary: Evelyn McKenna
Tel: 0131-244 3877

Corporate Learning Services
Head: Clive Matthew

Facilities and Estates Services
Head: Paul Rhodes
Private Secretary: June Duncan
Tel: 0131-244 4262 Fax: 0131-244 4229

Communication and Information Services Division
Director of IT: Paul Gray
Private Secretary: Moreen White
Tel: 0131-244 5732 Fax: 0131-244 8102

Finance and Central Services Department

(St Andrew's House)
Head: Vacant
Private Secretary: Scott Sutherland
Tel: 0131-244 5598

Finance Group
Principal Finance Officer: John Aldridge
Tel: 0131-244 7286

Local Government Group
Head of Group: Christie Smith
Tel: 0131-244 7762

External Relations Group
Head of Group: George Calder
Tel: 00 322 282 8331

Analytical Services Group
Chief Economic Adviser: Dr Andrew Goudie
Tel: 0131-244 2788

Media and Communications Group
(St Andrew's House)
Provision of advice to Ministers and Scottish Executive Departments on public presentation and policy.
Head of News: Andrew Baird
Tel: 0131-244 2661
Head of New Media and Presentation: Roger Williams *Tel:* 0131-244 2706

Legal and Parliamentary Services

(Chambers Street)
Legal and Parliamentary Services brings together four central commands in support of central Ministers, in particular the Law Officers and the Ministers for Parliamentary Business. It is the repository of the Executive's expertise on legal and constitutional issues.
Head: Robert Gordon CB (also Chief Executive of the Crown Office)
Private Secretary: Douglas Blair
Tel: 0131-247 3476 *Fax:* 0131-225 7473

Constitution and Parliamentary Secretariat
(St Andrew's House)
Tel: 0131-244 0357
Head: Michael Lugton

Office of the Solicitor to the Scottish Executive
(Victoria Quay)
Tel: 0131-244 0495
Solicitor: Richard Henderson
Deputy Solicitors: Patrick Layden, Lynda Towers

Office of the Scottish Parliamentary Counsel
(Victoria Quay)
Tel: 0131-244 1663
First Scottish Parliamentary Counsel:
 John McCluskie, QC
Counsel: Gregor Clark, Colin Wilson, Madelaine Mackenzie

Legal Secretariat to the Lord Advocate
(Chambers Street)
Tel: 0131-247 2665
Legal Secretary: Stuart Foubister

Crown Office and Procurator Fiscal Service

25 Chambers Street, Edinburgh EH1 1LA
Tel: 0131-226 2626   Fax: 0131-226 6910
E-mail: co.isunit@dial.pipex.com
Website: www.crownoffice.gov.uk

The Crown Office is the prosecuting authority in Scotland and is also responsible for investigating sudden deaths. It is a government department within the Scottish Executive.

Ministers
Lord Advocate: Rt Hon Colin Boyd QC
Solicitor-General for Scotland:
Elish Angiolini QC

Crown Office
Chief Executive: Robert Gordon CB
Crown Agent: Norman McFayden CBE
Deputy Crown Agent: William Gilchrist
Crown Counsel
Tel: 0131-226 2626
Robert Anthony
Murdo MacLeod
Dorothy Bain
Andrew MacMillan
John Beckett
Geoff Mitchell
Frank Gallagher
Frank Mulholland
Angela Grahame
Sean Murphy
Hugh Irwin
Norman Ritchie
Johanna Johnston
Keith Stewart
Brian McConnachie
Mark Stewart
Alan Mackay
Alan Turnbull
Alan Mackenzie

Procurator Fiscal Service
Argyll and Clyde: John Miller
Tel: 0141-887 5225
Ayrshire: Janet Cameron
Tel: 01563 536211
Central: Geraldine Watt *Tel:* 01786 462021
Dumfries and Galloway: David Howdle
Tel: 01387 263034
Fife: Cameron Ritchie *Tel:* 01592 268661

Glasgow and Strathkelvin: Len Higson
Tel: 0141-429 5566
Grampian: John Watt *Tel:* 01224 585111
Highlands and Islands: Graeme Napier
Tel: 01463 224858
Lanarkshire: James Brisbane *Tel:* 01698 284000
Lothians and Borders: Douglas Brown
Tel: 0131-226 4962
Tayside: Barry Heywood *Tel:* 01382 227535

Scottish Executive Agencies

Communities Scotland
Thistle House, 91 Haymarket Terrace,
Edinburgh EH12 5HE
Tel: 0131-313 0044   Fax: 0131-313 2680
E-mail: millarb@communitiesscotland.gov.uk
Website: www.communitiesscotland.gov.uk

Works on behalf of Ministers to promote social
justice and tackle exclusion through the delivery
of sustainable community regeneration; regulates and inspects all registered social landlords
and the housing, homeless and factoring
functions of local authorities; invests in housing
by managing Scotland's development funding
programme and advising Scottish Ministers on
housing investment.

Chief Executive: Bob Millar
Directors:
  Regeneration: Heather Koronka
  Investment and Performance:
  Angiolina Foster
  Regulation and Inspection: Vacant
  Business East: Martyn Rendle
  Business North: Richard Burn
  Business West: Ewan Johnston
Scottish Executive Development Department
Launched: 1/11/01

Fisheries Research Services – FRS
Marine Laboratory, PO Box 101,
375 Victoria Road, Aberdeen AB11 9DB
Tel: 01224 876544   Fax: 01224 295511
E-mail: heaths@marlab.ac.uk
Website: www.frs scotland.gov.uk

Provides expert scientific and technical advice
and information on marine and freshwater
fisheries, on aquaculture, and on the protection
of the aquatic environment and its wildlife.

Chief Executive and Director: Prof Robin Cook
*Deputy Director, FRS and Director, Aquaculture
  and Aquatic Animal Health:* Dr Ron Stagg
Director of Corporate Affairs: Gary Craig

Aquatic Environment Programme:
  Dr Colin Moffat
Fisheries Management: Nick Bailey
Freshwater Laboratory: Dr Malcolm Beveridge
Marine Ecosystems: Dr Bill Turrell
**Scottish Executive Environment and Rural
Affairs Department**
Launched: 1/4/97

Her Majesty's Inspectorate of Education – HMIE
T1 Saughton House, Broomhouse Drive,
Edinburgh EH11 3XD
Tel: 0131-244 0649/0650
E-mails: david.pearcy@hmie.gov.uk;
enquiries@hmie.gov.uk

Promotes improvements in standards, quality
and attainment in Scottish education through
first-hand, independent evaluation.

HM Senior Chief Inspector: Graham Donaldson
Headquarters Division: Ann McVie
HM Chief Inspectors:
  Primary Directorate: Frank Crawford
  *Pres-School/Independent/Care and Welfare
  Directorate:* Gill Robinson
  *Secondary/Special Educational Needs
  Directorate:* Bill Maxwell
  *Further Education/Teacher Education
  Directorate:* Wray Bodys
  *Education Authorities/Community Learning
  and Development Directorate:* Ian Gamble
Scottish Executive Education Department
Launched: 1/4/01

Historic Scotland
Longmore House, Salisbury Place,
Edinburgh EH9 1SH
Tel: 0131-668 8600   Fax: 0131-668 8699
Website: www.historic-scotland.gov.uk

Protects and promotes public understanding and
enjoyment of Scotland's ancient monuments and
archaeological sites and landscapes, historic
buildings, parks, gardens and designed landscapes.

Director and Chief Executive: Graeme Munro
Directors: Sheenagh Adams, Ingval Maxwell,
Owen Kelly, Brian O'Neil, Laura Petrie
Chief Inspector of Historic Buildings:
Richard Emerson
Chief Inspector of Ancient Monuments:
David Breeze
Scottish Executive Education Department
Launched: 1/4/91

National Archives of Scotland – NAS
HM General Register House,
Edinburgh EH1 3YY
Tel: 0131-535 1314   Fax: 0131-535 1360
E-mail: enquiries@nas.gov.uk
Website: www.nas.gov.uk

To select, preserve and make available the national archives of Scotland; to promote the growth and maintenance of proper archive provision throughout Scotland.

Keeper: George MacKenzie
Deputy Keepers: Dave Brownlee,
Peter Anderson
Scottish Executive
Launched: 1/4/93

Registers of Scotland – ROS
Meadowbank House, 153 London Road,
Edinburgh EH8 7AU
Tel: 0131-659 6111 Ext 3293
Fax: 0131-459 1221
E-mail: keeper@ros.gov.uk
Website: www.ros.gov.uk

Maintains registers of land etc. in Scotland.

Chief Executive: Alan Ramage
Deputy Keeper: Alistair Rennie
Managing Director: Frank Manson
Director of Legal Services: Ian Davis
Scottish Executive Justice Department
Launched: 6/4/90

Scottish Agricultural Science Agency – SASA
82 Craigs Road, East Craigs,
Edinburgh EH12 8NJ
Tel: 0131-244 8890   Fax: 0131-244 8940
E-mail: info@sasa.gsi.gov.uk
Website: www.sasa.gov.uk

Provides Government, primarily the Scottish Executive, with expert scientific information and advice on agricultural and horticultural crops and aspects of the environment.

Director: Dr Robert Hay
Deputy Director: Simon Cooper
Head of Administration: Shelagh Quinn
Scottish Executive Environment and Rural Affairs Department
Launched: 1/4/92

Scottish Court Service
Hayweight House, 23 Lauriston Street,
Edinburgh EH3 9DQ
Tel: 0131-229 9200   Fax: 0131-221 6895
E-mail: enquiries@scotcourts.gov.uk
Website: www.scotcourts.gov.uk

Responsible for the provision and maintenance of Court Houses, and for ensuring the supply of trained staff and of administrative and organisational services, to support the judiciary, in the Supreme and Sheriff Courts in Scotland.

Chief Executive: John Ewing
Deputy Chief Executive and Director of Change: Ian Scott
Director, Operations, Policy and Planning: Cliff Binning
Director, Finance and Information Technology: Nicola Bennett
Director of Personnel and Development: Alan Swift
Director, Property and Services: Gillian Jewel
Scottish Executive Justice Department
Launched: 3/4/95

Scottish Fisheries Protection Agency – SFPA
Pentland House, 47 Robb's Loan,
Edinburgh EH14 1TY
Tel: 0131-244 6059   Fax: 0131-244 6086
E-mail: paul.duvivier@scotland.gsi.gov.uk
Website: www.scotland.gov.uk

Enforces UK, EU and international fisheries law and regulations in Scottish waters and ports.

Chief Executive: Paul Du Vivier
Director of Corporate Strategy and Resources: John Roddin
Director, Operations: Robert Walker
Marine Superintendent: Captain Alan Brown
Scottish Executive Environment and Rural Affairs Department
Launched: 12/4/91

Scottish Prison Service – SPS
Calton House, 5 Redheughs Rigg,
Edinburgh EH12 9HW
Tel: 0131-244 8745   Fax: 0131-244 8774
Website: www.sps.gov.uk

Provides prison services in Scotland.

Chief Executive: Tony Cameron
Operations Director (North and East):
  Peter Withers
Operations Director (South and West):
  Mike Duffy
Deputy Director of Operations: John Bywalec
Director of Human Resources: Barbara Allison
Director of Rehabilitation and Care:
  Alec Spencer
Director of Strategy and Business Performance:
  Ken Thomson
Director of Finance and Business Services:
  Willie Pretswell
Scottish Executive Justice Department
Launched: 1/4/93

Scottish Public Pensions Agency – SPPA
7 Tweedside Park, Tweedbank,
Galashiels, TD1 3TE
Tel: Teachers Scheme Helpline: 01896 893000
Tel: NHS Scheme Helpline: 01896 893100
Fax: 01896 893260
E-mail: sppa@scotland.gsi.gov.uk

Responsible for the pension arrangements of
employees of the NHS and teaching service and
for the regulation of other Scottish public
pension schemes.

Chief Executive: Ralph Garden
Policy Director: Gavin Mowat
Director of Operations: Gordon Taylor
Director of Development: John Nelson
Finance Manager: David Weir
HR Manager: Sally Paterson
**Scottish Executive Finance and Central Services
Department**
Launched: 1/4/93

**Student Awards Agency for Scotland –
SAAS**
Gyleview House, 3 Redheughs Rigg,
Edinburgh EH12 9HH
Tel: 0131-476 8212   Fax: 0131-244 5887
E-mail: saas.geu@scotland.gsi.gov.uk
Website: www.saas.gov.uk

Administers student awards and other related
services for Scottish domiciled students in full-
time higher education throughout the United
Kingdom.

Chief Executive: David Stephen
Customer Services Manager: Audrey Heatlie
**Scottish Executive Enterprise, Transport and
Lifelong Learning Department**
Launched: 5/4/94

Political Parties
Scottish Labour Party
John Smith House, 145 West Regent Street,
Glasgow G2 4RE
Tel: 0141-572 6900 *Fax:* 0141-572 2566
E-mail: scotland@new.labour.org.uk
Website: www.scottishlabour.org.uk

Leader of Labour in the Scottish Parliament:
Rt Hon Jack McConnell MSP
Deputy Leader: Cathy Jamieson MSP
General Secretary: Lesley Quinn
Head of Press: Colin Edgar *Tel:* 0141-572 6909
Leader of the Labour Party:
Rt Hon Tony Blair MP

Scottish National Party
107 McDonald Road, Edinburgh EH7 4NW
Tel: 0131-525 8900 *Fax:* 0131-525 8901
E-mail: snp.hq@snp.org
Website: www.snp.org

National Convener: John Swinney MSP
President: Dr Winnie Ewing
Senior Vice-Convener:
Roseanna Cunningham MSP
Chief Executive: Peter Murrell

Europe: Ian Hudghton MEP and Professor Sir
Neil MacCormick MEP
Westminster Parliamentary Group Leader:
Alex Salmond MP

Scottish Parliament:
Scottish Parliamentary Group Convener:
Alasdair Morgan MSP
Tel: 0131-348 5000

Scottish Conservative and Unionist Party
83 Princes Street, Edinburgh EH2 2ER
Tel: 0131-247 6890
Fax: 0131-247 6891
E-mail: central.office@scottishtories.org.uk
Website: www.scottishtories.org.uk

Chairman: David W Mitchell CBE
Leader: David McLetchie MSP

Scottish Parliament:
Tel: 0131-348 5000
Fax: 0131-348 5628
Press Officer: Ramsay Jones

Scottish Liberal Democrats

4 Clifton Terrace, Edinburgh EH12 5DR
Tel: 0131-337 2314 *Fax:* 0131-337 3566
E-mail: scotlibdem@cix.co.uk
Website: www.scotlibdems.org.uk

Leader: Rt Hon Jim Wallace QC MSP
Deputy Leader: Michael Moore MP
President: Malcolm Bruce MP
Chief of Staff: Dr Derek Barrie
Office Manager: Tiffany Treharne
Events Officer: Fraser Grieve
Membership Officer: James Spence
Campaign Officer: Peter Barrett
Head of Research: Matthew Clark
Tel: 0131-348 5818
Chief Press Officer: Neil Mackinnon
Tel: 0131-348 5810
Policy Officer: Emma Granville
Tel: 0131-348 5813

Westminster Spokespeople:
Scottish Affairs: John Thurso MP
Deputies:
Alistair Carmichael MP (Energy Review)
Alan Reid MP (Fisheries Policies)
John Barrett MP (Cross-Border Transport)

Europe Spokesperson:
Elspeth Attwooll MEP

Scottish Green Party

PO Box 14080, Edinburgh EH10 6YG
Tel: 0131-478 7896
E-mail: info@scottishgreens.org.uk
Website: www.scottishgreens.org.uk

Principal Spokesperson: Robin Harper MSP

Council Convener: Eleanor Scott MSP
Executive Convener: Gavin Corbett

Scottish Parliament:
Tel: 0131-348 5927 *Fax:* 0131-348 5972
E-mail:
robin.harper.msp@scottish.parliament.uk
Policy Support Officer and Press Officer:
Dr Steve Burgess
Administrative Support Officer:
Alison Johnstone

Scottish Socialist Party

73 Robertson Street, Glasgow G2 8QD
Tel: 0141-221 7714 *Fax:* 0141-221 7715
E-mail: ssp.glasgow@btconnect.com
Website: www.scottishsocialistparty.org

Convener and Leader:
Tommy Sheridan MSP
West of Scotland Convener: Richie Venton
Press Officer: Hugh Kerr *Tel:* 0131-348 5632

Scottish Parliament:
Tel: 0131-348 5632 *Fax:* 0131-348 5948
E-mail:
thomas.sheridan.msp@scottish.parliament.uk

MSP for Falkirk West

Constituency Office, 37 Church Walk, Denny,
Stirlingshire FK6 6DF
Tel. 01324 825922 *Fax:* 01324 823972

Dennis Canavan MSP

Scottish Parliament:
0131-348 5630
E-mail:
dennis.canavan.msp@scottish.parliament.uk

Parliamentary Assistant: Maureen Conner
0131-348 5630
Constituency Secretary: Anne Thomson
01324 825922

DodOnline

An Electronic Directory without rival . . .

MSPs' biographies and photographs available with daily updates *via* the internet

For a *free* trial, call Yasmin Mirza, Aby Farsoun or Michael Mand on 020 7630 7643

NATIONAL ASSEMBLY FOR WALES

Cynulliad Cenedlaethol Cymru

Cardiff Bay, Cardiff CF99 1NA
029 2082 5111 Cathays Park
E-mail: assembly.info@wales.gsi.gov.uk   Website: www.wales.gov.uk

First election 6 May 1999
26 May 1999 Official Opening by HM The Queen

Elections are held every four years. The 2003 election was held on 1 May 2003

Electoral System

Elections are conducted using a method combining the traditional first past the post system and a form of proportional representation called the Additional Member System. Each voter casts two votes. One vote is for one of 40 constituency members, based on the Westminster parliament constituencies. The second goes towards the election of 20 regional members, four for each of the five regions used in the European Parliament elections. These seats ensure that each party's representation in the Assembly reflects its overall share of the vote.

The Assembly operates a three-day week conducted during normal business hours.

Powers and Responsibilities

The Assembly decides on its priorities and allocates funds in the following policy areas as they apply to Wales:

agriculture	industry
ancient monuments and historic buildings	local government
culture	social services
economic development	sport and leisure
education and training	tourism
environment	town and country planning
health	transport and roads
highways	Welsh language
housing	

The Assembly does not have powers to enact primary legislation.

The following areas remain the responsibility of Westminster:

broadcasting policy	labour market policy
competition policy	macro-economic policy
defence	National Lottery
fiscal and common markets policy	police service
fire service	prisons
foreign affairs	social security benefits
justice system	taxation

The Secretary of State for Wales represents the interests of Wales in the Cabinet of the UK Government.

Composition

The Assembly has 60 members elected by universal suffrage.

The members elected the First Secretary, who appointed Assembly Secretaries to be responsible for particular policy areas. The title Secretary was changed to Minister in late 2000. The First Minister and the Assembly Ministers make up the Cabinet, which is responsible to the Assembly.

Welsh Assembly Government

Cabinet

First Minister	Rt Hon **Rhodri Morgan** AM
Minister for Finance, Local Government and Public Services	**Sue Essex** AM
Minister for Assembly Business	**Karen Sinclair** AM
Minister for Social Justice and Regeneration	**Edwina Hart** AM MBE
Minister for Health and Social Services	**Jane Hutt** AM
Minister for Economic Development and Transport	**Andrew Davies** AM
Minister for Education and Lifelong Learning	**Jane Davidson** AM
Minister for Culture, Sport and Welsh Language	**Alun Pugh** AM
Minister for Environment, Planning and Countryside	**Carwyn Jones** AM
Minister for Culture, Welsh Language and Sport	**Alun Pugh** AM

Deputy Ministers

Economic Development and Transport	**Brian Gibbons** AM
Health and Social Services	**John Griffiths** AM
Social Justice and Regeneration	**Huw Lewis** AM

Ministerial Responsibilities and Staff

First Minister

Cardiff Bay, Cardiff CF99 1NA
Tel: Main Switchboard: 029 2082 5111 (Cathays Park)

First Minister   Rt Hon **Rhodri Morgan** AM – Labour

Exercise of functions by the Assembly Cabinet. Policy development and co-ordination of policy. The relationships with the rest of the United Kingdom, Europe and Wales Abroad. The maintenance of Open Government. Staffing/Civil Service

Special Advisers	Mark Drakeford	029 2089 8798
	Rachel Jones	029 2089 8193
	Paul Griffiths	029 2089 8488
Principal Private Secretary	Lawrence Conway	029 2089 8765
	E-mail: lawrence.conway@wales.gsi.gov.uk	

Finance, Local Government and Public Services

Cardiff Bay, Cardiff CF99 1NA
Tel: Main Switchboard: 029 2082 5111 (Cathays Park)

Minister for Finance, Local Government and Public Services
Sue Essex AM – Labour

Budgeting and managing the finances of the Government. The development of the strategic approach to the delivery of public services. Local Government

Private Secretary	Caron Wenrees	029 2089 8773

Assembly Business

Cardiff Bay, Cardiff CF99 1NA
Tel: Main Switchboard: 029 2082 5111 (Cathays Park)

Minister for Assembly Business   **Karen Sinclair** AM – Labour
Managing the business of the Government in the Assembly. Acting as Chief Whip to the Government's supporters in the Assembly

Private Secretary	Helen Sinclair	029 2089 8304

Social Justice and Regeneration

Cardiff Bay, Cardiff CF99 1NA
Tel: Main Switchboard: 029 2082 5111 (Cathays Park)

Minister for Social Justice and Regeneration   **Edwina Hart** AM – Labour
The Government's programme for regenerating the communities of Wales in particular those suffering the greatest disadvantage: including Community First, Anti-Poverty initiatives, the Social Economy, the Voluntary Sector, Community Safety and relations with the Police, the Fire Service, Drug and alcohol abuse, Youth Justice, Housing. Equality

Deputy Minister for Communities   **Huw Lewis** AM – Lab/Co-op
Mr Lewis assists Edwina Hart as Deputy Minister with responsibility for communities

Private Secretary	Leon Rees	029 2089 8386

Health and Social Services

Cardiff Bay, Cardiff CF99 1NA
Tel: Main Switchboard: 029 2082 5111 (Cathays Park)

Minister for Health and Social Services   **Jane Hutt** AM – Labour
Health and NHS Wales. Social Services and social care. Food safety

Special Adviser	Mark Drakeford	029 2089 8798
	E-mail: mark.drakeford@wales.gov.uk	
Private Secretary	Margaret Davies	029 2089 8783
	E-mail: psjanehutt@wales.gsi.gov.uk	

Deputy Minister for Health   **John Griffiths** AM – Lab/Co-op
Mr Griffiths works alongside Jane Hutt as Deputy Minister with responsibility for older people

Private secretary	Suzanne Willis	029 2089 8303

Economic Development and Transport

Cardiff Bay, Cardiff CF99 1NA
Tel: Main Switchboard: 029 2082 5111 (Cathays Park)

Minister for Ecoomic Development and Transport   **Andrew Davies** AM – Labour
Innovation and enterprise. Industrial policy and business support. Inward investment, promotion of indigenous companies and regional development. Transport. Energy. Tourism. Strategic co-ordinating responsibility for ICT. Structural Funds

Special Adviser	Rachel Jones	
Private Secretary	Angela Williams	029 2089 8772

Deputy Minister for Transport   Dr **Brian Gibbons** AM – Labour
Dr Gibbons assists Andrew Davies as Deputy Minister with specific responsibility for transport

Private Secretary	Suzanne Brooks	029 2089 8938

Education and Lifelong Learning

Cardiff Bay, Cardiff CF99 1NA
Tel: Main Switchboard: 029 2082 5111 (Cathays Park)

Minister for Education and Lifelong Learning   **Jane Davidson** AM – Labour
Schools. Further Education and Skills development. Higher education. Youth Service

Special Adviser	Rachel Jones	029 2089 8773
Private Secretary	Craig Stephenson	029 2089 8768

Environment, Planning and Countryside

Cardiff Bay, Cardiff CF99 1NA
Tel: Main Switchboard: 029 2082 5111 (Cathays Park)

Minister for Environment, Planning and Rural Countryside
Carwyn Jones AM – Labour
The environment and sustainable development. Town and country planning. Countryside and conservation issues. Agriculture and rural development including forestry and food production

Private Secretary	Helen Childs	029 2089 8767

Culture, Welsh Language and Sport

Cardiff Bay, Cardiff CF99 1NA
Tel: Main Switchboard: 029 2082 5111 (Cathays Park)

Minister for Culture, Welsh Language and Sport   **Alun Pugh** AM – Labour
Arts. Libraries and Museums. Sport and recreation. The languages of Wales. CADW

Private Secretary	Catherine Cody	029 2089 8769

Opposition Spokespeople and Whips

Plaid Cymru (Welsh Shadow Cabinet)

Shadow First Minister	**Ieuan Wyn Jones**
Shadow Minister for Assembly Business	**Jocelyn Davies**
Shadow Minister for Economic Development and Transport	**Elin Jones**
Shadow Minister for Environment, Planning and Countryside	**Rhodri Glyn Thomas**
Shadow Minister for Education	**Helen Mary Jones**
Shadow Minister for Health and Social Services	**David Lloyd**
Shadow Minister for Finance	**Alun Ffred Jones**
Shadow Minister for Local Government and Public Services	**Janet Ryder**
Shadow Minister for Social Justice and Regeneration	**Leanne Wood**
Shadow Minister for Culture, Welsh Language and Sport	**Owen John Thomas**
Plaid Cymru Chief Whip	**Janet Davies**

Welsh Conservatives

Leader of Conservative Group in the National Assembly	**Nick Bourne**
Spokesman for Economic Development and Transport	**Alun Cairns**
Spokesman for Education and Lifelong Learning	**David Davies**
Spokesman for Local Government, Environment and Planning	**Glyn Davies**
Spokesman for the Welsh Language and Culture	**Lisa Francis**
Spokesman for Social Justice and Chief Whip	**William Graham**
Spokesman for Finance	**Mark Isherwood**
Spokesman for Sport	**Laura Anne Jones**
Spokesman for Health, Social Services and Assembly Business	**Jonathan Morgan**
Spokesman for Farming and Rural Development	**Brynle Williams**

Welsh Liberal Democrats

Leader of Liberal Democrat Group in the National Assembly	**Mike German**
Spokesperson for Economic Development, Finance and Transport	**Jennifer Randerson**
Spokesperson for Local Government, Health and Social Care and Business Manager	**Kirsty Williams**
Spokesperson for Education and Social Justice	**Peter Black**
Spokesperson for Environment, Planning and Countryside	**Mick Bates**
Spokesperson for Culture, Welsh Language and Sport	**Eleanor Burnham**

Members (AMs)

State of the Parties (August 2003)

	First past post	Top up	Total seats
Labour	30	0	30
Plaid Cymru	4*	7	11
Conservative	1	10	11
Liberal Democrat	3	3	6
John Marek Independent Party	1†	0	1
Presiding Officer	1	0	1
			60 seats

*Excludes the Presiding Officer who has no party allegiance while in post.
†Deputy Presiding Officer who can participate and vote fully in the Assembly when not in the Chair.

Visit the Vacher Dod Website . . . **www.DodOnline.co.uk**

AMs' Directory

Lab	Labour Party
PlC	Plaid Cymru
Con	Conservative
Lib Dem	Liberal Democrats
Lab/Co-op	Labour/Co-operative
JMIP	John Marek Independent Party
Pres Off	Presiding Officer

ANDREWS, Leighton   Lab   **Rhondda**
Member Assembly Committees:
   Audit
   Culture, Welsh Language and Sport
   Education and Lifelong Learning
   South East Wales
Tel: 029 2089 8298
Constituency: 5 Cemetery Road, Porth, Rhondda CF39 0LG
Tel: 01443 685261

BARRETT, Lorraine   Lab/Co-op   **Cardiff South and Penarth**
Chair Assembly Committee: South East Wales
Member Assembly Committees:
   Culture, Welsh Language and Sport
   Equality of Opportunity
   House
   Local Government and Public Services
Tel: 029 2089 8376   Fax: 029 2089 8377   E-mail: lorraine.barrett@wales.gov.uk

BATES, Mick   Lib Dem   **Montgomeryshire**
Liberal Democrat Spokesperson for Environment, Planning and Countryside
Member Assembly Committees:
   Audit
   Environment, Planning and Countryside
   Mid Wales
Tel: 029 2089 8340   Fax: 029 2089 8341   E-mail: mick.bates@wales.gov.uk
Constituency: 3 Park Street, Newtown, Powys SY16 1EE
Tel: 01686 625527   Fax: 01686 628891

BLACK, Peter   Lib Dem   **South Wales West**
Liberal Democrat Spokesperson for Education and Social Justice
Chair Assembly Committees:
   Education and Lifelong Learning
   South West Wales
Member Assembly Committees:
   House
   Social Justice and Regeneration
   South East Wales
Tel: 029 2089 8361   Fax: 029 2089 8362   E-mail: peter.black@wales.gov.uk
Constituency: First Floor, 70 Mansel Street, Swansea SA1 5TN
Tel: 01792 536353, Minicom 01792 536354   Fax: 01792 536354

BOURNE, Nicholas   Con   **Mid and West Wales**
Leader, Welsh Conservative Party
Member Assembly Committees:
   European and External Affairs
   Mid Wales
   South West Wales
Tel: 029 2089 8349   Fax: 029 2089 8350   E-mail: nicholas.bourne@wales.gov.uk
Constituency: 4a Lion Yard, Brecon, Powys LD3 7BA
Tel: 01874 624796   Fax: 01874 623208

BURNHAM, Eleanor   Lib Dem   **North Wales**
Liberal Democrat Spokesperson for Culture, Sport and the Welsh Language
Member Assembly Committees:
  Culture, Welsh Language and Sport
  Legislation
  North Wales
Tel: 029 2089 8343   Fax: 029 2089 8344

Constituency: The Office, At the Rear of Kenmar, Chester Road, Rossett LL12 0DL
Tel: 01244 571918   Fax: 01244 570694

BUTLER, Rosemary   Lab   **Newport West**
Chair Assembly Committee: Culture, Welsh Language and Sport
Member Assembly Committees:
  European and External Affairs
  Legislation
  South East Wales
Tel: 029 2082 8528   Fax: 029 2089 8527   E-mail: rosemary.butler@wales.gov.uk

Constituency: Suite 21, 2 Chepstow Road, Newport NP19 8EA
Tel: 01633 222523   Fax: 01633 221981

CAIRNS, Alun   Con   **South Wales West**
Conservative Spokesperson for Economic Development and Transport
Member Assembly Committees:
  Audit
  Economic Development and Transport
  South East Wales
  South West Wales
Tel: 029 2089 8331   Fax: 029 2089 8332   E-mail: alun.cairns@wales.gov.uk

Constituency: 43a St James Crescent, Uplands, Swansea SA1 5QA
Tel: 01792 480860   Fax: 01792 470008

CHAPMAN, Christine   Lab/Co-op   **Cynon Valley**
Member Assembly Committees:
  Economic Development and Transport
  European and External Affairs
  Legislation
  South East Wales
Tel: 029 2089 8364   Fax: 029 2089 8365   E-mail: christine.chapman@wales.gov.uk

Constituency: Cynon Valley Assembly Office, 28a Oxford Street, Mountain Ash CF45 3EU
Tel: 01443 478098   Fax: 01443 478311

CUTHBERT, Jeff   Lab   **Caerphilly**
Member Assembly Committees:
  Education and Lifelong Learning
  Legislation
  South East Wales
  Standards of Conduct
Tel: 029 2089 8079   E-mail: jeff.cuthbert@wales.gov.uk

DAVIDSON, Jane   Lab   **Pontypridd**
Minister for Education and Lifelong Learning
Minister Assembly Committee: Education and Lifelong Learning
Member Assembly Committee: South East Wales
Tel: 029 2089 8174   Fax: 029 2089 8543   E-mail: jane.davidson@wales.gov.uk

Constituency: Interlink , Maritime Offices, Woodland Terrace, Maes y Coed,
Pontypridd CF37 1DZ
Tel: 01443 406400   Fax: 01443 406402

DAVIES, Andrew Lab   **Swansea West**
Minister for Economic Development and Transport
Minister Assembly Committee: Economic Development and Transport
Member Assembly Committee: South West Wales
Tel: 029 2089 8249   Fax: 029 2089 8189   E-mail: andrew.davies@wales.gov.uk

Constituency: 42 High Street, Swansea SA1 1LT
Tel: 01792 460836   Fax: 01792 460806

DAVIES, David Con   **Monmouth**
Conservative Spokesperson for Education and Lifelong Learning
Member Assembly Committees:
　Education and Lifelong Learning
　Equality of Opportunity
　South East Wales
　Standards of Conduct
Tel: 029 2089 8325   Fax: 029 2089 8326   E-mail: david.davies@wales.gov.uk

Constituency: Monmouth Conservative Association, 16 Maryport Street, Usk,
Monmouthshire NP5 1AB
Tel: 01291 672780   Fax: 01291 672737

DAVIES, Glyn Con   **Mid and West Wales**
Conservative Spokesperson for Local Government, Environment and Planning
Chair Assembly Committee: Legislation
Member Assembly Committees:
　Environment, Planning and Countryside
　Local Government and Public Services
　Mid Wales
　South West Wales
Tel: 029 2089 8337   Fax: 029 2089 8338   E-mail: glyn.davies@wales.gov.uk

Constituency: 20 High Street, Welshpool, Powys SY21 7JP
Tel: 01938 552315   Fax: 01938 552315

DAVIES, Janet PlC   **South Wales West**
PlC Chief Whip
Chair Assembly Committee: Audit
Member Assembly Committees:
　Economic Development and Transport
　House
　South East Wales
　South West Wales
Tel: 029 2089 8289   Fax: 029 2089 8290   E-mail: janet.davies@wales.gov.uk

Constituency: 6 Gaylard Buildings, Court Road, Bridgend CF31 1BD
Tel: 01656 646085   Fax: 01656 649419

DAVIES, Jocelyn PlC   **South Wales East**
Shadow Minister for Assembly Business
Member Assembly Committees:
　Audit
　Health and Social Services
　South East Wales
　Standards of Conduct
Tel: 029 2089 8259   Fax: 029 2089 8260   E-mail: jocelyn.davies@wales.gov.uk

Constituency: 10 High Street, Newport, Gwent NP20 1FQ
Tel: 01633 220022   Fax: 01633 220603

DUNWOODY-KNEAFSEY, Tamsin Lab   **Preseli Pembrokeshire**
Member Assembly Committees:
  Environment, Planning and Countryside
  Local Government and Public Services
  South West Wales
  Standards of Conduct
Tel: 029 2089 8614

ELIS-THOMAS, Lord Dafydd   PO   **Meirionnydd Nant Conwy**
Presiding Officer
Member Assembly Committees:
  House
  Mid Wales
  North Wales
Tel: 029 2089 8911   Fax: 029 2089 8117
E-mail: dafydd.elis-thomas@wales.gov.uk

Constituency: Ty Glyndwr, Heol Glyndwr, Dolgellan, Gwynedd LL40 1BD
Tel: 01341 422661   Fax: 01341 423990

ESSEX, Sue   Lab   **Cardiff North**
Minister for Finance, Local Government and Public Services
Minister Assembly Committee: Local Government and Public Services
Member Assembly Committee: South East Wales
Tel: 029 2089 8391   Fax: 029 2089 8129   E-mail: sue.essex@wales.gov.uk

Constituency: 29 Lon-Y-Dail, Rhiwbina, Cardiff CF14 6DZ
Tel: 029 2089 8391   Fax: 029 2089 8393

FRANCIS, Lisa   Con   **Mid and West Wales**
Conservative Spokesperson for the Welsh Language and Culture
Chair Assembly Committee: Mid Wales
Member Assembly Committees:
  Culture, Welsh Language and Sport
  Economic Development and Transport
  Equality of Opportunity
  South West Wales
Tel: 029 2089 8286

GERMAN, Michael, OBE   Lib Dem   **South Wales East**
Assembly Leader, Liberal Democrats
Member Assembly Committees:
  European and External Affairs
  South East Wales
Tel: 029 2089 8741   Fax: 029 2089 8354   E-mail: michael.german@wales.gov.uk

Constituency: 101a The Highway, New Inn, Pontypool, Torfaen NP4 0PN
Tel: 01495 740358   Fax: 01495 740357

GIBBONS, Brian   Lab   **Aberavon**
Deputy Minister for Transport
Member Assembly Committees:
  Economic Development and Transport
  South West Wales
Tel: 029 2089 8382   Fax: 029 2089 8383   E-mail: brian.gibbons@wales.gov.uk

Constituency: Eagle House, 2 Talbot Road, Port Talbot SA13 1DH
Tel: 01639 870779   Fax: 01639 870779

GRAHAM, William   Con   **South Wales East**
Conservative Spokesperson for Social Justice
Member Assembly Committees:
  House
  Social Justice and Regeneration
  South East Wales
Tel: 029 2089 8346   Fax: 029 2089 8347   E-mail: william.graham@wales.gov.uk

Constituency: 19a East Street, Newport NP20 4BR
Tel: 01633 250455   Fax: 01633 222694

GREGORY, Janice   Lab   **Ogmore**
Chair Assembly Committee: Social Justice and Regeneration
Member Assembly Committees:
  House
  South East Wales
Tel: 029 2089 8373   Fax: 029 2089 8375   E-mail: janice.gregory@wales.gov.uk

Constituency: 44a Penybont Road, Pencoed, Bridgend CF35 5RA
Tel: 01656 860034   Fax: 01656 860189

GRIFFITHS, John   Lab/Co-op   **Newport East**
Deputy Minister for Health
Member Assembly Committees:
  Equality of Opportunity
  Health and Social Services
  South East Wales
Tel: 029 2089 8307   Fax: 029 2089 8308   E-mail: john.griffiths@wales.gov.uk

Constituency: Suite 21, 2 and 4 Chepstow Road , Newport NP19 8FA
Tel: 01633 222302

GWYTHER, Christine   Lab   **Carmarthen West and South Pembrokeshire**
Chair Assembly Committee: Economic Development and Transport
Member Assembly Committees:
  Audit
  European and External Affairs
  South West Wales
Tel: 029 2089 8534   Fax: 029 2089 8302   E-mail: christine.gwyther@wales.gov.uk

Constituency: 17 Morley Street, Carmarthen SA31 1RB
Tel: 01297 238306   Fax: 01267 220555

HART, Edwina, MBE   Lab   **Gower**
Minister for Social Justice and Regeneration
Minister Assembly Committee: Social Justice and Regeneration
Member Assembly Committee: South West Wales
Tel: 029 2089 8186   Fax: 029 2089 8187   E-mail: edwina.hart@wales.gov.uk

Constituency: 26 Pontarddulais Road, Gorseinon, Swansea SA4 4FE
Tel: 01792 895481   Fax: 01792 895646

HUTT, Jane   Lab   **Vale of Glamorgan**
Minister for Health and Social Services
Minister Assembly Committee: Health and Social Services
Member Assembly Committee: South East Wales
Tel: 029 2089 8783   Fax: 029 2089 8129   E-mail: jane.hutt@wales.gov.uk

Constituency: 115 High Street, Barry CF62 7DT
Tel: 01446 740981   Fax: 01446 741172

ISHERWOOD, Mark   Con   **North Wales**
Conservative Spokesperson for Finance
Member Assembly Committees:
  Audit
  Education and Lifelong Learning
  North Wales
  Social Justice and Regeneration
Tel: 029 2089 8322   E-mail: mark.isherwood@wales.gov.uk

Constituency: Delyn Conservative Association, 5 Halkyn Street, Holywell,
Flintshire CH8 7TX
Tel: 01352 710232   Fax: 01352 714074

JAMES, Irene   Lab   **Islwyn**
Member Assembly Committees:
  Education and Lifelong Learning
  Environment, Planning and Countryside
  Legislation
  South East Wales
Tel: 029 2089 8529   E-mail: irene.james@wales.gov.uk

JONES, Alun Ffred   PlC   **Caernarfon**
Shadow Minister for Finance
Chair Assembly Committee: Environment, Planning and Countryside
Member Assembly Committee: North Wales
Tel: 029 2089 8265

JONES, Ann   Lab   **Vale of Clwyd**
Chair Assembly Committee: Local Government and Public Services
Member Assembly Committees:
  Health and Social Services
  North Wales
Tel: 029 2089 8388   Fax: 029 2089 8390
E-mail: ann.jones@wales.gov.uk

Constituency: 47 Kinmel Street, Rhyl, Denbighshire LL18 IAG
Tel: 01745 332813   Fax: 01745 369038

JONES, Carwyn   Lab   **Bridgend**
Minister for Environment, Planning and Countryside
Minister Assembly Committee: Environment, Planning and Countryside
Member Assembly Committee: South East Wales
Tel: 029 2089 8301   E-mail: carwyn.jones@wales.gov.uk

Constituency: 12 Queen Street, Bridgend CF31 1HX
Tel: 01656 664320   Fax: 01656 669349

JONES, Denise Idris   Lab   **Conwy**
Member Assembly Committees:
  Audit
  Culture, Welsh Language and Sport
  Education and Lifelong Learning
  North Wales
Tel: 029 2089 8381   Fax: 029 2089 8371
E-mail: denise.idris-jones@wales.gov.uk

Constituency: 23 Augusta Street, Llandudno LL30 2AD
Tel: 01492 873064   Fax: 01492 879828

JONES, Elin   PlC   **Ceredigion**
Shadow Minister for Economic Development and Transport
Member Assembly Committees:
  Culture, Welsh Language and Sport
  Economic Development and Transport
  Legislation
  Mid Wales
Tel: 029 2089 8262   Fax: 029 2089 2863   E-mail: elin.jones@cymru.gov.uk
Constituency: 8 Stryd y Dwr, Aberaeron, Ceredigion SA46 0DG
Tel: 01545 571688   Fax: 01545 571567

JONES, Helen Mary   PlC   **Mid and West Wales**
Shadow Minister for Education and Lifelong Learning
Member Assembly Committees:
  Education and Lifelong Learning
  Equality of Opportunity
  Mid Wales
  South West Wales
Tel: 029 2089 8274   Fax: 029 2089 8275   E-mail: helen-mary.jones@wales.gov.uk
Constituency: 11 John Street, Llanelli, Carmarthen SA15 1UH
Tel: 01554 774393   Fax: 01554 759174

JONES, Ieuan Wyn   PlC   **Ynys Môn**
Shadow First Minister
Member Assembly Committees:
  European and External Affairs
  North Wales
Tel: 029 2089 8268   Fax: 029 2089 8269   E-mail: ieuan.wynjones@wales.gov.uk
Constituency: 45 Bridge Street, Llangefni, Ynys Môn LL77 7PN
Tel: 01248 723599   Fax: 01248 722868

JONES, Laura Anne   Con   **South Wales East**
Conservative Spokesperson for Sport
Member Assembly Committees:
  Culture, Welsh Language and Sport
  Legislation
  Local Government and Public Services
  South East Wales
Tel: 029 2089 8271   Fax: 029 2089 8272

LAW, Peter   Lab/Co-op   **Blaenau Gwent**
Member Assembly Committees:
  Local Government and Public Services
  South East Wales
Tel: 029 2089 8531   Fax: 029 2089 8532   E-mail: peter.law@wales.gov.uk
Constituency: 1 Bethcar Street, Ebbw Vale, Blaenau Gwent NP23 6HH
Tel: 01495 304569   Fax: 01495 306908

LEWIS, Huw   Lab/Co-op   **Merthyr Tydfil and Rhymney**
Deputy Minister for Communities
Member Assembly Committees:
  Equality of Opportunity
  Social Justice and Regeneration
  South East Wales
Tel: 029 2089 8385   Fax: 029 2089 8387   E-mail: huw.lewis@wales.gov.uk
Constituency: Venture Wales Building, Merthyr Industrial Park, Pontmorlais,
Merthyr Tydfil CF48 4DR
Tel: 01443 692299   Fax: 01443 691847

LLOYD, Dr David   PlC   **South Wales West**
Shadow Minister for Health and Social Care
Member Assembly Committees:
   Health and Social Services
   Legislation
   Local Government and Public Services
   South East Wales
   South West Wales
Tel: 029 2089 8283   Fax: 029 2089 8284   E-mail: dai.lloyd@wales.gov.uk

Constituency: 39 St James Crescent, Uplands, Swansea SA1 6DR
Tel: 01792 646430   Fax: 01792 477170

LLOYD, Val   Lab   **Swansea East**
Member Assembly Committees:
   Audit
   Health and Social Services
   South West Wales
Tel: 029 2089 8316   E-mail: val.lloyd@swansea.gov.uk

Constituency: 42 High Street, Swansea SA1 1LT
Tel: 01792 480555   Fax: 01792 477146

MAREK, Dr John   **Wrexham**
Deputy Presiding Officer
Chair Assembly Committee: House
Member Assembly Committee: North Wales
Tel: 029 2089 8313   Fax: 029 2089 8117   E-mail: john.marek@wales.gov.uk

Constituency: 67 Regent Street, Wrexham LL11 1PG
Tel: 01978 364334   Fax: 01978 314085

MELDING, David   Con   **South Wales Central**
Chair Assembly Committee: Health and Social Services
Member Assembly Committee: South East Wales
Tel: 029 2089 8328   Fax: 029 2089 8329   E-mail: david.melding@wales.gov.uk

Constituency: 55a Holton Road, Barry CF63 4HU
Tel: 01446 733516   Fax: 01446 733516

MEWIES, Sandy   Lab   **Delyn**
Chair Assembly Committee: European and External Affairs
Member Assembly Committees:
   North Wales
   Social Justice and Regeneration
   Standards of Conduct
Tel: 029 2089 8280   Fax: 029 2089 8281

Constituency: 5 Village Court, Wrexham LL11 2PX

MORGAN, Jonathan   Con   **South Wales Central**
Conservative Spokesperson for Health, Social Services and Assembly Business
Member Assembly Committees:
   European and External Affairs
   Health and Social Services
   South East Wales
Tel: 029 2089 8334   Fax: 029 2089 8335
E-mail: jonathan.morgan@wales.gov.uk

Constituency: 1st Floor, 5 Penlline Road, Whitchurch, Cardiff CF14 2AA
Tel: 029 2061 7474   Fax: 029 2061 7474

MORGAN, Rt Hon Rhodri Lab   **Cardiff West**
First Minister
Member Assembly Committees:
  European and External Affairs
  South East Wales
Tel: 029 2089 8134   Fax: 029 2089 8198
E-mail: rhodri.morgan@wales.gsi.gov.uk

Constituency: Transport House, 1 Cathedral Road, Cardiff CF11 9SD
Tel: 029 2022 3207   Fax: 029 2023 0422

NEAGLE, Lynne Lab   **Torfaen**
Member Assembly Committees:
  Economic Development and Transport
  South East Wales
  Standards of Conduct
Tel: 029 2089 8367   Fax: 029 2089 8387   E-mail: lynne.neagle@wales.gov.uk

Constituency: 35A Commercial Street, Pontypool, Torfaen NP4 6JQ
Tel: 01495 740022   Fax: 01495 740316

PUGH, Alun Lab   **Clwyd West**
Minister for Culture, Welsh Language and Sport
Minister Assembly Committee: Culture, Welsh Language and Sport
Member Assembly Committee: North Wales
Tel: 029 2089 8370   Fax: 029 2089 8371   E-mail: alun.pugh@wales.gov.uk

Constituency: Copthorne House, The Broadway, Abergele LL22 7DD
Tel: 01745 825855   Fax: 01745 827709

RANDERSON, Jenny Lib Dem   **Cardiff Central**
Liberal Democrat Spokesperson for Economic Development, Finance and Transport
Member Assembly Committees:
  Economic Development and Transport
  Equality of Opportunity
  South East Wales
Tel: 029 2089 8355   Fax: 029 2089 8356
E-mail: jenny.randerson@wales.gov.uk

Constituency: 133 City Road, Roath, Cardiff CF24 3BQ
Fax: 029 2047 1168

RYDER, Janet PlC   **North Wales**
Shadow Minister for Local Government and Public Services
Chair Assembly Committee: North Wales
Member Assembly Committees:
  Local Government and Public Services
  Social Justice and Regeneration
Tel: 029 2089 8250   Fax: 029 2089 8251   E-mail: janet.ryder@wales.gov.uk

Constituency: Plaid Cymru The Party of Wales, Wrexham Office, 20 Chester Street,
Wrexham LL13 8BG
Tel: 01978 313909   Fax: 01978 310651

SARGEANT, Carl Lab   **Alyn and Deeside**
Member Assembly Committees:
  Audit
  Environment, Planning and Countryside
  North Wales
Tel: 029 2089 8292   E-mail: carl.sargeant@wales.gov.uk

SINCLAIR, Karen Lab   **Clwyd South**
Minister for Assembly Business
Member Assembly Committees:
  House
  North Wales
Tel: 029 2089 8304   Fax: 029 2089 8305   E-mail: karen.sinclair@wales.gov.uk

Constituency: 6 Oak Mews, Oak Street, Llangollen, Denbighshire LL20 8RP
Tel: 01978 869105   Fax: 01978 869464

THOMAS, Catherine Lab   **Llanelli**
Member Assembly Committees:
  Environment, Planning and Countryside
  Equality of Opportunity
  Legislation
  Social Justice and Regeneration
  South West Wales
Tel: 029 2089 8321

THOMAS, Gwenda Lab   **Neath**
Chair Assembly Committee: Equality of Opportunity
Member Assembly Committees:
  Health and Social Services
  South West Wales
  Standards of Conduct
Tel: 029 2089 8379   Fax: 029 2089 8380   E-mail: gwenda.thomas@wales.gov.uk

Constituency: 7 High Street , Pontardawe, Swansea SA8 4HU
Tel: 01792 869993   Fax: 01792 869994

THOMAS, Owen John PlC   **South Wales Central**
Shadow Minister for Culture, Sport and the Welsh Language
Member Assembly Committees:
  Culture, Welsh Language and Sport
  Education and Lifelong Learning
  South East Wales
  Standards of Conduct
Tel: 029 2089 8295   Fax: 029 2089 8296   E-mail: owen-john.thomas@wales.gov.uk

Constituency: Ty'r Cymru, 11 Gordon Road, Cardiff CF2 3AJ
Tel: 029 2045 0614   Fax: 029 2045 0616

THOMAS, Rhodri Glyn PlC   **Carmarthen East and Dinefwr**
Shadow Minister for Environment, Planning and Countryside
Member Assembly Committees:
  Environment, Planning and Countryside
  European and External Affairs
  South West Wales
Tel: 029 2089 8277   Fax: 029 2089 8278   E-mail: rhodri.thomas@wales.gov.uk

Constituency: 37 Wind Street, Ammanford, Carmarthenshire SA18 3DN
Tel: 01269 597677   Fax: 01269 591334

WILLIAMS, Brynle Con   **North Wales**
Conservative Spokesperson for Farming and Rural Development
Member Assembly Committees:
  Environment, Planning and Countryside
  North Wales
  Standards of Conduct
Tel: 029 2089 8394

Constituency: 3 Llewelyn Road, Colwyn Bay, Conwy LL29 7AP

WILLIAMS, Kirsty   Lib Dem   **Brecon and Radnorshire**
Liberal Democrat Spokesperson for Local Government, Health and Social Care
Chair Assembly Committee: Standards of Conduct
Member Assembly Committees:
    Health and Social Services
    Local Government and Public Services
    Mid Wales
Tel: 029 2089 8358   Fax: 029 2089 8359   E-mail: kirsty.williams@wales.gov.uk
Constituency: 99 The Struet, Brecon, Powys LD3 7LS
Tel: 01874 620181   Fax: 01874 620182

WOOD, Leanne   PlC   **South Wales Central**
Shadow Minister for Social Justice and Regeneration
Member Assembly Committees:
    Equality of Opportunity
    Social Justice and Regeneration
    South East Wales
Tel: 029 2089 8256   E-mail: leanne.wood@wales.gov.uk

Constituencies

Constituency	Member	Party	Votes
Aberavon	Brian Gibbons	Lab	7,813
Alyn and Deeside	Carl Sargeant	Lab	3,503
Blaenau Gwent	Peter Law	Lab/Co-op	11,736
Brecon and Radnorshire	Kirsty Williams	Lib Dem	5,308
Bridgend	Carwyn Jones	Lab	2,421
Caernarfon	Alun Ffred Jones	PlC	5,905
Caerphilly	Jeff Cuthbert	Lab	4,974
Cardiff Central	Jenny Randerson	Lib Dem	7,156
Cardiff North	Sue Essex	Lab	540
Cardiff South and Penarth	Lorraine Barrett	Lab/Co-op	4,114
Cardiff West	Rt Hon Rhodri Morgan	Lab	6,837
Carmarthen East and Dinefwr	Rhodri Glyn Thomas	PlC	4,614
Carmarthen West and South Pembrokeshire	Christine Gwyther	Lab	515
Ceredigion	Elin Jones	PlC	4,618
Clwyd South	Karen Sinclair	Lab	2,891
Clwyd West	Alun Pugh	Lab	436
Conwy	Denise Idris Jones	Lab	72
Cynon Valley	Christine Chapman	Lab/Co-op	7,117
Delyn	Sandy Mewies	Lab	1,624
Gower	Edwina Hart	Lab	5,688
Islwyn	Irene James	Lab	7,320
Llanelli	Catherine Thomas	Lab	21
Meirionnydd Nant Conwy	Lord Elis-Thomas	Pres Off	5,826
Merthyr Tydfil and Rhymney	Huw Lewis	Lab/Co-op	8,160
Monmouth	David Davies	Con	8,510
Montgomeryshire	Mick Bates	Lib Dem	2,297
Neath	Gwenda Thomas	Lab	4,946
Newport East	John Griffiths	Lab/Co-op	3,484
Newport West	Rosemary Butler	Lab	3,752
Ogmore	Janice Gregory	Lab	6,504
Pontypridd	Jane Davidson	Lab	6,920
Preseli Pembrokeshire	Tamsin Dunwoody-Kneafsey	Lab	1,326
Rhondda	Leighton Andrews	Lab	7,954
Swansea East	Val Lloyd	Lab	3,997

Swansea West	Andrew Davies	Lab	2,562
Torfaen	Lynne Neagle	Lab	6,954
Vale of Clwyd	Ann Jones	Lab	2,769
Vale of Glamorgan	Jane Hutt	Lab	2,653
Wrexham	Dr John Marek	JMIP	973
Ynys Môn	Ieuan Wyn Jones	PlC	2,255

Regions

Mid and West Wales	Nicholas Bourne	Con
Mid and West Wales	Lisa Francis	Con
Mid and West Wales	Helen Mary Jones	PlC
Mid and West Wales	Glyn Davies	Con
North Wales	Eleanor Burnham	LibDem
North Wales	Janet Ryder	PlC
North Wales	Mark Isherwood	Con
North Wales	Brynle Williams	Con
South Wales Central	Owen John Thomas	PlC
South Wales Central	Leanne Wood	PlC
South Wales Central	Jonathan Morgan	Con
South Wales Central	David Melding	Con
South Wales East	Jocelyn Davies	PlC
South Wales East	Michael German	LibDem
South Wales East	William Graham	Con
South Wales East	Laura Anne Jones	Con
South Wales West	Janet Davies	PlC
South Wales West	Dr David Lloyd	PlC
South Wales West	Alun Cairns	Con
South Wales West	Peter Black	LibDem

Women Members

BARRETT, Lorraine	JONES, Ann
BURNHAM, Eleanor	JONES, Denise Idris
BUTLER, Rosemary	JONES, Elin
CHAPMAN, Christine	JONES, Helen Mary
DAVIDSON, Jane	JONES, Laura Anne
DAVIES, Janet	LLOYD, Val
DAVIES, Jocelyn	MEWIES, Sandy
DUNWOODY-KNEAFSEY, Tamsin	NEAGLE, Lynne
ESSEX, Sue	RANDERSON, Jenny
FRANCIS, Lisa	RYDER, Janet
GREGORY, Janice	SINCLAIR, Karen
GWYTHER, Christine	THOMAS, Catherine
HART, Edwina	THOMAS, Gwenda
HUTT, Jane	WILLIAMS, Kirsty
JAMES, Irene	WOOD, Leanne

DodOnline
An Electronic Directory without rival...

AMs' biographies and photographs available with daily updates *via* the internet

For a *free* trial, call Yasmin Mirza, Aby Farsoun or Michael Mand on 020 7630 7643

Committees

Subject Committees

Members are elected onto various subject committees in proportion to their party's representation in the Assembly.

Culture, Welsh Language and Sport

Chair: Rosemary Butler
Minister: Alun Pugh
Leighton Andrews, Lorraine Barrett, Eleanor Burnham, Lisa Francis, Denise Idris Jones, Elin Jones, Laura Anne Jones, Owen John Thomas
Clerk: Julia Annand (029 2089 8238)
Acting Deputy Clerk: Gareth Woodhead (029 2089 8153)
Committee Support: Charles Woods (029 2089 8020)

Economic Development and Transport

Chair: Christine Gwyther
Minister: Andrew Davies
Alun Cairns, Christine Chapman, Janet Davies, Lisa Francis, Brian Gibbons, Elin Jones, Lynne Neagle, Jenny Randerson
Clerk: John Grimes (029 2089 8225)
Deputy Clerk: Sian Wilkins (029 2089 8224)
Committee Support: Paul Davies (029 2089 8229)

Education and Lifelong Learning

Chair: Peter Black
Minister: Jane Davidson
Leighton Andrews, Jeff Cuthbert, David Davies, Mark Isherwood, Irene James, Denise Idris Jones, Helen Mary Jones, Owen John Thomas
Clerk: Chris Reading (029 2089 8164)
Deputy Clerk: Holly Pembridge (029 2089 8019)
Committee Support: Ruth Hatton (029 2089 8618)
E-mail: education.comm@wales.gsi.gov.uk

Environment, Planning and Countryside

Chair: Alun Ffred Jones
Minister: Carwyn Jones
Mick Bates, Glyn Davies, Tamsin Dunwoody-Kneafsey, Irene James, Carl Sargeant, Catherine Thomas, Rhodri Glyn Thomas, Brynle Williams

Clerk: Siwan Davies (029 2089 8501)
Deputy Clerk: Vaughan Watkin (029 2089 8146)
Committee Support: Silvia Ricondo (029 2089 8018)

Health and Social Services

Chair: David Melding
Minister: Jane Hutt
Jocelyn Davies, John Griffiths, Ann Jones, David Rhys Lloyd, Val Lloyd, Jonathan Morgan, Gwenda Thomas, Kirsty Williams
Clerk: Jane Westlake (029 2089 8149)
Deputy Clerk: Claire Morris (029 2089 8148)
Committee Support: Catherine Lewis (029 2089 8505)
E-mail:
health-socserv.comm@wales.gsi.gov.uk

Local Government and Public Services

Chair: Ann Jones
Minister: Sue Essex
Lorraine Barrett, Glyn Davies, Tamsin Dunwoody-Kneafsey, Laura Anne Jones, Peter Law, David Rhys Lloyd, Janet Ryder, Kirsty Williams
Clerk: Adrian Crompton (029 2089 8264)
Deputy Clerk: Liz Wilkinson (029 2089 8151)
Committee Support: Ruth Hughes (029 2089 8617)

Social Justice and Regeneration

Chair: Janice Gregory
Minister: Edwina Hart
Peter Black, William Graham, Mark Isherwood, Huw Lewis, Sandy Mewies, Janet Ryder, Catherine Thomas, Leanne Wood
Clerk: Roger Chaffey (029 2089 8409)
Deputy Clerk: Claire Griffiths (029 2089 8034)
Committee Support: Dan Collier (029 2089 8506)

Standing Committees

Audit

Chair: Janet Davies
Leighton Andrews, Mick Bates, Alun Cairns, Jocelyn Davies, Christine Gwyther, Mark Isherwood, Denise Idris Jones, Val Lloyd, Carl Sargeant
Clerk: Claire Bennett (029 2089 8155)
Deputy Clerk: Lara Date (029 2089 8026)
Committee Support: Nichola Coleman (029 2089 8025)
E-mail: audit.comm@wales.gsi.gov.uk

Equality of Opportunity

Chair: Gwenda Thomas
Lorraine Barrett, David Davies, Lisa Francis, John Griffiths, Helen Mary Jones, Huw Lewis, Jenny Randerson, Catherine Thomas, Leanne Wood
Clerk: Claire Bennett (029 2089 8155)
Deputy Clerk: Lara Date (029 2089 8026)
Committee Support: Nichola Coleman (029 2089 8025)
E-mail: equality.comm@wales.gsi.gov.uk

European and External Affairs

Chair: Sandy Mewies
Nicholas Bourne, Rosemary Butler, Christine Chapman, Michael German, Christine Gwyther, Ieuan Wyn Jones, Jonathan Morgan, Rhodri Morgan, Rhodri Glyn Thomas
Clerk: Claire Bennett (029 2089 8155)
Deputy Clerk: Lara Date (029 2089 8026)
Committee Support: Nichola Coleman (029 2089 8025)

House

Chair: John Marek
Lorraine Barrett, Peter Black, Janet Davies, Dafydd Elis Thomas, William Graham, Janice Gregory, Karen Sinclair
Clerk to the Assembly: Paul Silk
Clerk to the Committee: Dianne Bevan
Director of Assembly Communications: Gwen Parry
Director of Corporate Services: John Bowley
Counsel to Assembly Committees: Peter Jones
Head of Fees Office: Wayne Cowley
House Committee Secretariat: Nerys Evans
House Committee Secretariat: Sara Lloyd

Remit: The Assembly has delegated responsibility for matters relating to services for Members to the House Committee including:
– services, facilities and accommodation;
– Members' allowances; and
– related matters that support the operation of the Assembly.
It is the only committee to which the Assembly has delegated executive powers.
The National Assembly's Standing Order 36 provides full details of the Committee's remit.
Membership of the Committee reflects, as far as possible, the balance of the political groups in the Assembly.

Legislation

Chair: Glyn Davies
Eleanor Burnham, Rosemary Butler, Christine Chapman, Jeff Cuthbert, Irene James, Elin Jones, Laura Anne Jones, David Rhys Lloyd, Catherine Thomas
Clerk: Olga Lewis
Deputy Clerk: Simon Thwaite
E-mail: legislation.comm@wales.gsi.gov.uk

Standards of Conduct

Chair: Kirsty Williams
Jeff Cuthbert, David Davies, Jocelyn Davies, Tamsin Dunwoody-Kneafsey, Sandy Mewies, Lynne Neagle, Gwenda Thomas, Owen John Thomas, Brynle Williams,

Regional Committees

The four regional committees are made up from members for the relevant constituencies and regions and represent the interests of those areas.

The role of the four regional committees is to advise the Assembly on:
• matters affecting the regions
• the effect of Assembly policies in those regions
• the work of public bodies in the regions.
Regional Committees will form a crucial link between the Assembly and local communities.

Mid Wales

Ceredigion and Powys and the area of Gwynedd comprising the former district of Merionydd
Chair: Lisa Francis
Mick Bates, Nicholas Bourne, Glyn Davies, Dafydd Elis-Thomas, Elin Jones, Helen Mary Jones, Kirsty Williams
Clerk: Adrian Crompton
Deputy Clerk: Liz Wilkinson
E-mail: mwales.regcomm@wales.gsi.gov.uk

North Wales

Conwy, Denbighshire, Flintshire, Isle of Anglesey, Wrexham and the area of Gwynedd made up of the former districts of Arfon and Dwyfor

Chair: Janet Ryder

Eleanor Burnham, Dafydd Elis-Thomas, Mark Isherwood, Alun Ffred Jones, Ann Jones, Denise Idris Jones, Ieuan Wyn Jones, John Marek, Sandy Mewies, Alun Pugh, Carl Sargeant, Karen Sinclair, Brynle Williams

Clerk: Siwan Davies

Deputy Clerk: Vaughan Watkin

E-mail: nwales.regcomm@wales.gsi.gov.uk

South East Wales

Blaenau Gwent, Bridgend, Caerphilly, Cardiff, Merthyr Tydfil, Monmouthshire, Newport, Rhondda Cynon Taff, Torfaen, Vale of Glamorgan

Chair: Lorraine Barrett

Leighton Andrews, Peter Black, Rosemary Butler, Alun Cairns, Christine Chapman, Jeff Cuthbert, Jane Davidson, David Davies, Janet Davies, Jocelyn Davies, Sue Essex, Michael German, William Graham, Janice Gregory, John Griffiths, Jane Hutt, Irene James, Carwyn Jones, Laura Anne Jones, Peter Law, Huw Lewis, David Rhys Lloyd, David Melding, Jonathan Morgan, Rhodri Morgan, Lynne Neagle, Jenny Randerson, Owen John Thomas, Leanne Wood

Clerk: Roger Chaffey

Deputy Clerk: Claire Griffiths

E-mail: sewales@wales.gsi.gov.uk

South West Wales

Carmarthenshire, Neath, Port Talbot, Pembrokeshire, Swansea

Chair: Peter Black

Nicholas Bourne, Alun Cairns, Andrew Davies, Glyn Davies, Janet Davies, Tamsin Dunwoody-Kneafsey, Lisa Francis, Brian Gibbons, Christine Gwyther, Edwina Hart, Helen Mary Jones, David Rhys Lloyd, Val Lloyd, Catherine Thomas, Gwenda Thomas, Rhodri Glyn Thomas

Clerk: Jane Westlake

Deputy Clerk: Claire Morris (029 2089 8148)

E-mail: swwales.regcomm@wales.gsi.gov.uk

Principal Officers and Officials

Presiding Office

Presiding Officer
Private Secretary: Adrian Green

Lord **Dafydd Elis-Thomas** AM
Tel: 029 2089 8766   Fax: 029 2089 8117

Deputy Presiding Officer
Private Secretary: Catherine Morris

Dr **John Marek** AM
Tel: 029 2089 8029

Clerk to the Assembly
Deputy Clerk
Legal Adviser

Paul Silk
Dianne Bevan
David Lambert

Presiding Office Heads

Communication Service
Chamber Services
Committee Secretariat
Members' Research Service
Corporate Services

Gwen Parry
Andrew George
Marie Knox
Karin Phillips
John Bowley

Civil Service (Welsh Assembly Government)

Office of the Permanent Secretary
(Cathays Park)
Permanent Secretary: Sir Jon Shortridge KCB

Economic Affairs, Transport, Planning and the Environment

Senior director: Derek Jones *Tel:* 029 2082 3325

Economic Development Department
Head of department: David Pritchard
Tel: 029 2082 6646

Agriculture Department
Head of department: Gareth Jones
Tel: 029 2082 1656

Transport, Planning and Environment Group
Head of group: Martin Evans
Tel: 029 2082 5727

Strategy and Communications Directorate
Director: Huw Brodie *Tel:* 029 2082 3114

Social Policy and Local Government Affairs

Senior director: George Craig
Tel: 029 2082 3695

NHS Directorate
Head: Ann Lloyd *Tel:* 029 2082 1182

Health Protection and Improvement Directorate
Director and Chief Medical Officer:
Dr Ruth Hall *Tel:* 029 2082 3911

Nursing
Chief Nursing Officer: Rosemary Kennedy
Tel: 029 2082 3469

Social Care Group
Director: Helen Thomas *Tel:* 029 2082 3060

Local Government and Housing Group
Director: Adam Peat *Tel:* 029 2082 5565

Training and Education Department
Head of Department: Richard Davies
Tel: 029 2082 3207

Counsel General

Counsel General: Winston Roddick
Tel: 029 2082 6962
Legal adviser to Legislation Committee:
John Turnbull
Assistant counsels general: Jeffrey Godfrey,
Mark Partridge, Angela Parkes

Cabinet Executive
Director: Vacant

Personnel and Accommodation Services Group
Senior Director: George Craig
Tel: 029 2082 3695

Finance Group
Principal finance officer: David Richards
Tel: 029 2082 5220

Research and Development Group
Head: Barbara Wilson *Tel:* 029 2082 5706

Non-ministerial Department

Estyn: Her Majesty's Inspectorate for Education and Training in Wales
Anchor Court, Keen Road, Cardiff CF24 5JW
Tel: 029 2044 6446   Fax: 029 2044 6448
E-mail: enquiries@estyn.gsi.gov.uk
Website: www.estyn.gov.uk

Responsible for standards and quality in education and training in Wales through independent inspection and advice.

HM Chief Inspector of Education and Training in Wales: Susan Lewis
Head of Inspection Division – Early Years Education, Schools and the Work of LEAs:
Hilary Anthony
Head of Inspection Division – Post-16 Education and Training: Elizabeth Kidd
Head of Policy, Planning and Corporate Services: Shan Howells

Visit the Vacher Dod Website . . .

www.DodOnline.co.uk

Executive Agencies

Cadw/Welsh Historic Monuments

Crown Buildings, Cathays Park,
Cardiff CF10 3NQ
Tel: 029 2050 0200   Fax: 029 2082 6375
E-mail: lorraine.griffiths@wales.gsi.gov.uk
Website: www.cadw.wales.gov.uk

Maintains and preserves the built heritage of
Wales and presents those monuments in the care
of the National Assembly for Wales to the public.

Chief Executive: Thomas Cassidy
Head of Policy and Administration: Jean Booker
Chief Architect: Douglas Hogg
Chief Inspector: Richard Avent
Head of Presentation: Andrew Hood
Head of Corporate Services: Jeffrey Jenkins
**Welsh Assembly Government Environment
Department**
Launched 2/4/91

Welsh European Funding Office

Cwm Cynon Business Park, Mountain Ash,
Rhondda, Cynon Taf CF45 4ER
Tel: 01443 471100   Fax: 01443 471120
E-mail: enquiries-wefo@wales.gsi.gov.uk
Website: www.wefo.wales.gov.uk

Manages all aspects of European Structural Fund
Programmes in Wales and the Local
Regeneration Fund.

Chief Executive: John Clarke
Welsh Assembly Government
Launched 1/4/00

Political Parties

Welsh Labour

LLAFUR CYMRU
Transport House, 1 Cathedral Road,
Cardiff CF11 9HA
029 2087 7700 *Fax:* 029 2022 1153
E-mail: wales@new.labour.org.uk
Websites: www.welshlabour.org.uk
www.llafurcymru.org.uk

National Assembly Labour Party Leader:
Rt Hon Rhodri Morgan AM
General-Secretary: Jessica Morden
Press Officer: Jackie Aplin

Assembly Office: 029 2089 8398

Plaid Cymru

THE PARTY OF WALES
Tŷ Gwynfor, 18 Park Grove, Cardiff CF10 3BN
029 2064 6000 *Fax:* 020 2064 6001
E-mail: post@plaidcymru.org
Website: www.plaidcymru.org

President: Ieuan Wyn Jones AM
Vice-President: Dafydd Iwan
Chief Executive: Dafydd Trystan

Assembly Office: 029 2089 8710
Press Officer: Emyr Williams 029 2089 8401
E-mail: emyr.williams@wales.gov.uk

Welsh Conservative Party

PLAID GEIDWADOL CYMRU
Conservative Central Office Wales
4 Penlline Road, Whitchurch, Cardiff CF14 2XS
029 2061 6031 *Fax:* 029 2061 0544
E-mail: ccowales@tory.org
Website: www.welshconservatives.com

Director: Leigh Jeffes
Deputy Director: Sue Gillett

Assembly Office:
029 2089 8351 *Fax:* 029 2089 8350

Welsh Liberal Democrats

**DEMOCRATIAID RHYDDFRYDOL
CYMRU**
Bay View House, 102 Bute Street,
Cardiff CF10 5AD
029 2031 3400 *Fax:* 029 2031 3401
E-mail: enquiries@welshlibdems.org.uk
Websites: www.welshlibdems.org.uk
www.demrhyddcymru.org.uk

Chief Executive: Chris Lines
Administrator: Helen Ceri Jones
Campaigns Officer: John Ault
Policy Officer: Rob Roffe

NORTHERN IRELAND ASSEMBLY

Parliament Buildings
Belfast BT4 3XX
028 9052 1333 Fax 028 9052 1961
E-mail: info.office@niassembly.gov.uk
Website: www.niassembly.gov.uk

First election 25 June 1998

Suspension

The Northern Ireland Assembly was suspended with effect from midnight on Tuesday 14 October 2002 and was dissolved on 28 April 2003. The government of Northern Ireland has reverted to Westminster.

2003 Northern Ireland Assembly election postponed

The British Government announced in May 2003 that the elections to the Northern Ireland Assembly had been postponed, at least until the autumn.

The Northern Ireland Assembly Elections Act 2003, which received Royal Assent on 20 March 2003, had previously postponed the elections due on 1 May to 29 May. Unfortunately, lack of progress in multi-party talks aimed at the restoration of the devolved institutions in Northern Ireland has led to further postponement.

Background

From 1921, Northern Ireland was governed by a devolved parliament under the terms of the Government of Ireland Act 1920 which provided for separate parliaments in the north and south of Ireland. In 1972, the Government at Westminster prorogued the Northern Ireland Parliament and introduced a system of direct rule. Various political initiatives attempted to restore some form of devolved government at different times. Eventually multi-party talks under the chairmanship of former US Senator George Mitchell, which began in June 1996, led to the publication on 10 April 1998 of what has become known as the 'Good Friday' or Belfast Agreement.

The Belfast Agreement

The governments of the United Kingdom and Ireland, together with a number of the political parties in Northern Ireland, agreed to support a three stranded approach to resolving the historical differences which had provided the context for political instability in Northern Ireland. The three strands provided for arrangements within Northern Ireland; within Ireland north and south; and within the British Isles as a whole. The Agreement was endorsed by referenda in both parts of Ireland on 22 May 1998.

The Assembly under Devolution

Under Strand One of the Agreement, a new democratic institution was created within Northern Ireland. Elections to this body of 108 members were held on 25 June 1998 and the new Northern Ireland Assembly held its first meeting at Castle Buildings, Stormont on 1 July 1998.

Certain powers were first devolved to the Northern Ireland Assembly on 2 December 1999, but returned to the UK Parliament on 14 October 2002 as a result of suspension.

Under devolution, the Assembly is responsible for all *transferred* matters, which are all public services not *reserved* or *excepted* in the Northern Ireland Act 1998. The Secretary of State retains responsibility for these matters. *Excepted* matters may never be devolved and include taxation, foreign affairs and defence. *Reserved* matters, such as policing, prisons, criminal justice and security policy, may be devolved. The Secretary of State may initiate legislation to change a *transferred* matter to a *reserved* one, or vice-versa, but the cross-community support of the Assembly is necessary for legislation to be made.

The devolved government of Northern Ireland consists of ten departments, with each department shadowed by a departmental committee to scrutinise the policy of the department and play a role in the initiation and development of legislation. Ten ministers and chairpersons, deputy chairpersons and members for the ten departmental committees were initially appointed on 29 November 1999.

Electoral System

The 1998 election was conducted using a Single Transferable Vote (STV) system. Each of Northern Ireland's 18 Westminster parliamentary constituencies elected 6 members by STV. The STV system in use requires electors to vote for at least one candidate, and then to declare their preferences for as many or as few of the other candidates as they wish. Preferences are declared numerically, with '1' being written alongside the voter's first preference candidate, '2' alongside the second choice and so on. To be elected a candidate must receive a minimum number of votes – the 'quota' determined by a set formula. The formula is calculated by dividing the total number of valid voting papers cast by the number of seats to be filled plus one.

North/South Co-operation

On 2 December 1999, the day power was devolved to the Assembly, the following became fully functioning institutions:
North/South Ministerial Council
and its six implementation bodies:
Waterways Ireland
Food Safety Promotion Board
Trade and Business Development Board
Special European Union Programmes Body
Foyle, Carlingford and Irish Lights Commission
North/South Language Body

British/Irish Co-operation

British-Irish Council
To promote the harmonious and mutually beneficial development of the totality of relationships among the people of these islands.
British-Irish Inter-Governmental Conference
Will replace the Anglo-Irish Inter-Governmental Conference established under the 1985 Anglo-Irish Agreement.

Northern Ireland Departments

Due to the suspension of the Northern Ireland Assembly, the Secretary of State for Northern Ireland has taken over the role previously held by the First Minister and Deputy First Minister. Ministers from the Northern Ireland Office have extended their portfolios to include the departments previously run by Northern Ireland executive ministers.

DodOnline
An Electronic Directory without rival ...

MLAs' biographies and photographs available with daily updates
via the internet

For a *free* trial, call Yasmin Mirza, Aby Farsoun or Michael Mand on 020 7630 7643

Ministerial Responsibilities and Staff
Secretary of State for Northern Ireland

Castle Buildings, Stormont, Belfast BT4 3SG
Tel: 028 9052 0700   Fax: 028 9052 8195
E-mail: privateoffice.belfast@nio.x.gsi.gov.uk

Secretary of State for Northern Ireland   Rt Hon **Paul Murphy** MP

Parliamentary Private Secretary	Gareth Thomas MP
Special Adviser	Owen Smith
Principal Private Secretary	David Brooker
	E-mail: david.brooker@nio.x.gsi.gov.uk
Private Secretaries	Kate Udy
	Richard Lemon 028 9052 8111

Agriculture and Rural Development

Dundonald House, Upper Newtownards Road, Belfast BT4 3SB
Tel: 028 9052 0100
E-mail: libraryi@dardni.gov.uk

Permanent Secretary   Pat Toal

Minister of Agriculture and Rural Development   **Ian Pearson** MP

Food, farming and environmental policy; agri-food development; science; veterinary matters; science service; rural development; forestry; sea fisheries, rivers

Private Secretary   Philip Gilmore   028 9052 4159

Culture, Arts and Leisure

Interpoint, 3rd Floor, 20-24 York Street, Belfast BT15 1AQ
Tel: 028 9025 8825
E-mail: dcal@dcalni.gov.uk

Permanent Secretary   Dr Aideen McGinley OBE

Minister of Culture, Arts and Leisure   **Angela Smith** MP

Arts and culture; sport and leisure; libraries; museums; Armagh Observatory and Planetarium; Ulster Historical Foundation; inland waterways; inland fisheries; Ordnance Survey; Public Record Office; language diversity; lottery matters; diversity 21; Northern Ireland Events Company; visitor amenities; creative industries

Private Secretary   Julie Childs   028 9025 8807

Education

Rathgael House, Balloo Road, Bangor BT19 7PR
Tel: 028 9127 9279
E-mail: private.office@deni.gov.uk

Permanent Secretary   Gerry McGinn

Minister of Education   **Jane Kennedy** MP

Schools' funding and administration; special education; school effectiveness; school planning and provision; Schools' Inspectorate; pre-school education; Youth Service; teachers (numbers and remuneration); Education and Library Board appointments

Private Secretary   Fiona Barnes   028 9127 9303

Employment and Learning

Adelaide House, 39/49 Adelaide Street, Belfast BT2 8FD
Tel: 028 9025 7777
E-mail: del@nics.gov.uk
Permanent Secretary   Alan Shannon

Minister for Employment and Learning   **Jane Kennedy** MP

Higher education; further education; vocational training; employment services; employment law and labour relations; student support and postgraduate awards; training grants

Private Secretary   Fiona Neupert   028 9025 7791
                                       E-mail: delprivateoffice@nics.gov.uk

Enterprise, Trade and Investment

Netherleigh House, Massey Avenue, Belfast BT4 2JP
Tel: 028 9052 9900
E-mail: private.office@detini.gov.uk
Permanent Secretary   Bruce Robinson

Minister for Enterprise, Trade and Investment   **Ian Pearson** MP

Economic development policy; industry (Invest Northern Ireland); tourism (NITB); Health and Safety Executive; Employment Medical Advisory Service; company regulation; consumer affairs; energy policy; Minerals and Petroleum Unit (including Geological Survey); NICO; company training grant schemes (Company Development Programme and Explorers)

Private Secretary   Michael Harris   028 9052 9452
                                       E-mail: michael.harris@detini.gov.uk

Environment

Clarence Court, 10-18 Adelaide Street, Belfast BT2 8GB
Tel: 028 9054 0540
E-mail: private.office@doeni.gov.uk
Permanent Secretary   Stephen Peover

Minister of the Environment   **Angela Smith** MP

Planning control; environment and heritage; protection of the countryside; waste management; pollution control; wildlife protection; local government; sustainable development; mineral resources (planning aspects); Driver and Vehicle Testing Agency; Road Safety and Vehicle Standards Division; Driver and Vehicle Licensing Agency; Transport Licensing and Enforcement

Private Secretary (acting)   Julian Smyth   028 9054 1166
                                       E-mail: julian.smyth@doeni.gov.uk

Finance and Personnel

Craigantlet Buildings, Stoney Road, Belfast BT4 3SX
Tel: 028 9052 9140
E-mail: private.office@dfpni.gov.uk
Permanent Secretary   Pat Carvill

Minister of Finance and Personnel   Dr **Ian Pearson** MP

Central Finance Group; Central Personnel Group, IT and corporate services; accommodation and Construction Division; legal services; Business Development Service; Central Procurement Directorate; Land Registers of NI; NI Statistics and Research Agency; Rate Collection Agency; Valuation and Lands Agency; Office of Law Reform

Private Secretary   Veronica Holland   028 9052 9140
                                       E-mail: private.office@dfpni.gov.uk

Health, Social Services and Public Safety

Castle Buildings, Stormont Estate, Belfast BT4 3SQ
Tel: 028 9052 0643
E-mail: aq@dhsspsni.gov.uk
Permanent Secretary   Clive Gowdy

Minister of Health, Social Services and Public Safety   **Angela Smith** MP
Health; social services; public health and safety; health promotion; Fire Authority
Private Secretary   Sharon Lindsay   028 9052 0642

Regional Development

Clarence Court, 10-18 Adelaide Street, Belfast BT2 8GB
Tel: 028 9054 1186
E-mail: private.office@drdni.gov.uk
Permanent Secretary   Stephen Quinn

Minister for Regional Development   **John Spellar** MP
Transport regional planning; regional transportation strategy; roads; rail; ports and airports; water
Private Secretary (Acting)   Stewart Matthews   028 9054 0105

Social Development

7th Floor, Churchill House, Victoria Square, Belfast BT1 4SD
Tel: 028 9056 9216
E-mail: minister@dsdni.gov.uk
Permanent Secretary   John Hunter

Minister for Social Development   **John Spellar** MP
Housing policy; Northern Ireland Housing Executive; voluntary activity; urban regeneration; community sector; Laganside Corporation; Rent Assessment Panel; Housing Benefit Review Boards; Social Security Agency; Child Support Agency; Lands Division; The Appeals Service; Office of Social Fund Commissioner; social legislation; North West Development Office; Regional Development Office
Private Secretary   Beverley Bigger   028 9056 9216

Members (MLAs) 1998-2003

State of the Parties (October 2002)

UUP	Ulster Unionist Party	26 seats
SDLP‡	Social Democratic and Labour Party	24 seats
DUP†	Democratic Unionist Party	22 seats
SF	Sinn Féin	18 seats
APNI	Alliance Party of Northern Ireland	*6 seats
NIUP	Northern Ireland Unionist Party	3 seats
UUAP	United Unionist Assembly Party	3 seats
PUP	Progressive Unionist Party	2 seats
NIWC	Women's Coalition	2 seats
UKUP	UK Unionist Party	1 seat
Ind Unionist	Independent Unionist	1 seat
		108 seats

18 Constituencies
6 Members per constituency
108 Members

*Includes the Speaker
†Roger Hutchinson, formerly an Independent Unionist, joined the DUP on 1 April 2002
‡Includes Annie Courtney who left the SDLP in March 2003 following deselection in Foyle

MLAs' Directory

ADAMS, Gerry SF   **Belfast West**
President, Sinn Féin Party
Tel: 028 9052 1144   Fax: 028 9052 1474
Constituency: Sinn Féin, 51-55 Falls Road, Belfast BT12 4PD
Tel: 028 9022 3000   Fax: 028 9022 0045

ADAMSON, Dr Ian, OBE UUP   **Belfast East**
Tel: 028 9052 1529   Fax: 028 9052 1760   E-mail: ian@ianadamson.co.uk
Constituency: 4a Belmont Road, Belfast BT4 2AN
Tel: 028 9065 8217   Fax: 028 9047 1161

AGNEW, Fraser UUAP   **Belfast North**
Tel: 028 9052 1033   Fax: 028 9052 1032
Constituency: 212 Shore Road, Belfast BT15 3QB
Tel: 028 9059 3333   Fax: 028 9059 3303

ALDERDICE, Lord All   **Belfast East**
Speaker of the Northern Ireland Assembly
Tel: 028 9052 1130   Fax: 028 9052 1959   E-mail: alderdice@parliament.uk
Constituency: 442a Newtownards Road, Belfast BT4 1HJ
Tel: 028 9073 8703   Fax: 028 9022 5276

ARMITAGE, Pauline Ind Unionist   **East Londonderry**
Tel: 028 9052 1912   Fax: 028 9052 1764
Constituency: 12 Dunmore Street, Coleraine, Co Londonderry BT52 1EL
Tel: 028 7032 7294   Fax: 028 7032 7474

ARMSTRONG, Billy UUP   **Mid Ulster**
Tel: 028 9052 0305   Fax: 028 9052 0302
E-mail: billy.armstrong@niassembly.gov.uk
Constituency: Prospect House, Coagh Road, Dungannon, Stewartstown, Co Tyrone BT71 5JH
Tel: 028 8773 8641   Fax: 028 8773 8844

ATTWOOD, Alex SDLP   **Belfast West**
SDLP Spokesperson for Policing
Tel: 028 9052 0375   Fax: 028 9052 0377
Constituency: 60 Andersontown Road, Belfast BT11 9AN
Tel: 028 9080 7808   Fax: 028 9080 7370

BEGGS, Roy Jnr UUP   **East Antrim**
Tel: 028 9052 1546   Fax: 028 9052 1556   E-mail: roy.beggs@niassembly.gov.uk
Constituency: East Antrim UUP Advice Centre, 32c North Street, Carrickfergus,
Co Antrim BT38 7AQ
Tel: 028 9336 2995   Fax: 028 9336 8048

BELL, Billy UUP   **Lagan Valley**
Tel: 028 9052 1344   Fax: 028 9052 1756   E-mail: billybell@niassembly.gov.uk
Constituency: 2 Sackville Street, Lisburn, Co Antrim BT27 4AB
Tel: 028 9262 9171   Fax: 028 9260 5672

BELL, Eileen All   **North Down**
Alliance Spokesperson for Education; Higher and Further Education; Training and Employment;
Equality and Community Relations
Tel: 028 9052 0352   Fax: 028 9052 1654   E-mail: eileen.bell@niassembly.gov.uk

BERRY, Paul   DUP   **Newry and Armagh**
DUP Spokesperson for Heath, Social Services and Public Safety
Tel: 028 9052 1191   Fax: 028 3884 1668

Constituency: 78 Market Street, Tandragee, Co Armagh BT62 2BP
Tel: 028 3884 1668   Fax: 028 3884 9166

BIRNIE, Dr Esmond   UUP   **Belfast South**
UUP Assembly Spokesperson for Employment and Learning
Tel: 028 9052 0304   Fax: 028 9052 1560   E-mail: esmond.birnie@niassembly.gov.uk

Constituency: 117 Cregragh Road, Belfast BT6 0LA
Tel: 028 9087 3794

BOYD, Norman   NIUP   **South Antrim**
Tel: 028 9052 1733   Fax: 028 9052 1754   E-mail: norman.boyd@niassembly.gov.uk

Constituency: 38 Main Street, Ballyclare, Co Antrim BT39 9AA
Tel: 028 9334 9132   Fax: 028 9334 9128

BRADLEY, PJ   SDLP   **South Down**
SDLP Spokesperson for Agriculture
Tel: 028 9052 0344   Fax: 028 9052 0342   E-mail: pj.bradley@niassembly.gov.uk

Constituency: 2 East Street, Warrenpoint, Co Down BT34 3JE
Tel: 028 4177 2228   Fax: 028 4177 2229

BYRNE, Joe   SDLP   **West Tyrone**
SDLP Spokesperson for Regional Development
Tel: 028 9052 0326   Fax: 028 9052 0327   E-mail: j.byrne@dnet.co.uk

Constituency: 9b Dromore Road, Omagh, Co Tyrone BT78 1QZ
Tel: 028 8225 0060   Fax: 028 8225 0065

CAMPBELL, Gregory   DUP   **East Londonderry**
Tel: 028 9052 1106   Fax: 028 9052 1839

Constituency: 25 Bushmills Road, Coleraine, Co Londonderry BT52 2BP
Tel: 028 7032 7327   Fax: 028 7032 7328

CARRICK, Mervyn   DUP   **Upper Bann**
DUP Spokesperson for Higher and Further Education, Training and Development
Tel: 028 9052 1193   Fax: 028 9052 1834

Constituency: 15A Mandeville Street, Portadown, Co Armagh BT62 3PB
Tel: 028 3833 5965   Fax: 028 3833 5977

CARSON, Joan   UUP   **Fermanagh and South Tyrone**
Tel: 028 9052 1557   Fax: 028 9052 1766
E-mail: joan.carson@niassembly.gov.uk

Constituency: Drumgold House, 115 Moy Road, Dungannon, Co Tyrone BT71 7DX
Tel: 01868 784285   Fax: 01868 784285

CLOSE, Séamus, OBE   All   **Lagan Valley**
Alliance Spokesperson for Finance and Personnel; Social Development
Tel: 028 9052 0353   Fax: 028 9052 1650

Constituency: 123 Moira Road, Lisburn, Co Antrim BT28 1RJ
Tel: 028 9267 0639   Fax: 028 9266 6803

CLYDE, Wilson   DUP   **South Antrim**
Tel: 028 9052 1111   Fax: 028 9052 1822

Constituency: 69 Church Street, Antrim, Co Antrim BT41 4BA
Tel: 028 9446 2280   Fax: 028 9446 9011

COBAIN, Fred   UUP   **Belfast North**
UUP Spokesperson for Social Development
Tel: 028 9052 1358   Fax: 028 9052 1854   E-mail: fred.cobain@niassembly.gov.uk
Constituency: 23a York Road, Belfast BT15 3GU
Tel: 028 9059 4801   Fax: 028 9059 4802

COULTER, Rev Robert   UUP   **North Antrim**
UUP Assembly Spokesperson for Health, Social Services and Public Safety
Tel: 028 9052 1246   Fax: 028 9052 1741
Constituency: 30a Ballymoney Street, Ballymena, Co Antrim BT43 6AL
Tel: 028 2564 2262   Fax: 028 2564 2264

COURTNEY, Annie   Ind   **Foyle**
Tel: 028 9052 0375   Fax: 028 9052 1329
Constituency: 2a Spencer House, Spencer Road, Derry City, Co Derry BT47 6AA
Tel: 028 7131 3831   Fax: 028 7128 0221

COYLE, Michael   SDLP   **East Londonderry**
SDLP Spokesperson for the Environment

DALLAT, John   SDLP   **East Londonderry**
SDLP Spokesperson for Employment and Learning
Tel: 028 9052 0347   Fax: 028 9052 0345   E-mail: johndallat@demon.co.uk
Constituency: 11 Bridge Street, Kilrea, Co Derry BT51 5RR
Tel: 028 2554 1880   Fax: 028 2554 1798

DAVIS, Ivan   UUP   **Lagan Valley**
UUP Senior Deputy Whip
Tel: 028 9052 1029   Fax: 028 9052 1027   E-mail: ivan.davis@niassembly.gov.uk
Constituency: 29 Roseville Park, Lisburn, Co Antrim BT27 4XT
Tel: 028 9267 8164   Fax: 028 9266 7699

DE BRUN, Bairbre   SF   **Belfast West**
Tel: 028 9052 1675   Fax: 028 9052 1673   E-mail: sinnfein@iol.ie
Constituency: Sinn Féin, 51-55 Falls Road, Belfast BT12 4PD
Tel: 028 9023 0227   Fax: 028 9050 8331

DODDS, Nigel, OBE   DUP   **Belfast North**
DUP Chief Whip
Tel: 028 9052 1101   Fax: 028 9052 1750   E-mail: nigel.dodds@niassembly.gov.uk
Constituency: 210 Shore Road, Belfast BT15 3QB
Tel: 028 9077 4774   Fax: 028 9077 7685

DOHERTY, Pat   SF   **West Tyrone**
SF Spokesperson for Enterprise, Trade and Investment; Agriculture and Rural Development
Tel: 028 9052 0323   Fax: 028 9052 1722
Constituency: 12b Bridge Street, Strabane, Co Tyrone BT82 9AE
Tel: 028 7188 6464   Fax: 028 7188 6466

DOUGLAS, Boyd   UUAP   **East Londonderry**
Tel: 028 9052 1141   Fax: 028 9052 1465   E-mail: boyd.douglas@tibus.com
Constituency: 90 Main Street, Limavady, Co Londonderry BT49 0EP
Tel: 028 7776 3380   Fax: 028 7776 3380

DURKAN, Mark   SDLP   **Foyle**
Leader, SDLP
Tel: 028 9052 1691   Fax: 028 9052 1688   E-mail: m.durkan@sdlp.ie
Constituency: 7B Messines Terrace, Racecourse Road, Derry BT48 7QZ
Tel: 028 7136 0700   Fax: 028 7136 0808

EMPEY, Sir Reg   UUP   **Belfast East**
Tel: 028 9052 1335   Fax: 028 9052 1761
Constituency: 4a Belmont Road, Belfast BT4 2AN
Tel: 028 9065 8217   Fax: 028 9047 1161

ERVINE, David   PUP   **Belfast East**
Leader, Progressive Unionist Party
Tel: 028 9052 1143   Fax: 028 9052 1468   E-mail: david.ervine@niassembly.gov.uk
Constituency: 229 Newtownards Road, Belfast BT4 1AG
Tel: 028 9022 5040   Fax: 028 9022 5041

FARREN, Dr Sean   SDLP   **North Antrim**
Tel: 028 9052 1708   Fax: 028 9052 1706   E-mail: sean.farren.co@niassembly.gov.uk
Constituency: Bryan House, Bryan Street, Ballymena BT43 6YA
Tel: 028 7083 3042/2563 8765   Fax: 028 7083 4152/2563 8725

FEE, John   SDLP   **Newry and Armagh**
SDLP Spokesperson for the Bill of Rights
Tel: 028 9052 0378   Fax: 028 9052 0381   E-mail: johnfee@dial.pipex.com
Constituency: 2 Bridge Street, Newry, Co Down BT35 8AE
Tel: 028 3025 2999   Fax: 028 3026 7828

FORD, David   All   **South Antrim**
Leader, Alliance Party; Alliance Spokesperson on Agricultural and Rural Development, Environment
Tel: 028 9052 1052   Fax: 028 9052 1053   E-mail: david.ford@niassembly.gov.uk
Constituency: 9 Carnmoney Road, Glengormley, Co Antrim BT36 6HL
Tel: 028 9084 0930   Fax: 028 9083 7774

FOSTER, Sam, CBE   UUP   **Fermanagh and South Tyrone**
Tel: 028 9052 1355   Fax: 028 9052 1856
Constituency: 1 Regal Pass, Enniskillen, Co Fermanagh BT74 7NT
Tel: 028 6632 2028

GALLAGHER, Tommy   SDLP   **Fermanagh and South Tyrone**
SDLP Spokesperson for Education
Tel: 028 9052 1702   Fax: 028 9052 1701   E-mail: t.gallagher@sdlp.ie
Constituency: 39 Darling Street, Enniskillen, Co Fermanagh BT74 7DP
Tel: 028 6634 2848   Fax: 028 6634 2838

GIBSON, Oliver   DUP   **West Tyrone**
DUP Spokesperson on Finance and Personnel
Tel: 028 9052 1102   Fax: 028 9052 1811   E-mail: ogibson@saqnet.co.uk
Constituency: 12 Main Street, Beragh, Omagh, Co Tyrone BT70 0SY
Tel: 028 8275 7000   Fax: 028 8075 7024

GILDERNEW, Michelle   SF   **Fermanagh and South Tyrone**
SF Spokesperson for Employment and Learning
Tel: 028 9052 1627   Fax: 028 9052 1625

GORMAN, Sir John, CVO CBE   UUP   **North Down**
Tel: 028 9052 0306   Fax: 028 9052 1543
Constituency: 77a High Street, Bangor, Co Down BT20 5DB
Tel: 028 9147 0300   Fax: 028 9147 0301

HAMILTON, Thomas   UUP   **Strangford**
Tel: 028 9052 0307   Fax: 028 9052 1017
Constituency: 6 William Street, Newtonards, Belfast, Co Down BT23
Tel: 028 9181 4123

HANNA, Carmel SDLP **Belfast South**
Tel: 028 9052 0369 Fax: 028 9052 0367 E-mail: carmel.hanna@niassembly.gov.uk
Constituency: 17 Elmwood Mews, Belfast BT9 6BD
Tel: 028 9068 3535 Fax: 028 9068 3503

HAUGHEY, Denis SDLP **Mid Ulster**
Junior Minister
Tel: 028 9052 1684 Fax: 028 9052 1685 E-mail: d.haughey@sdlp.ie
Constituency: 54a William Street, Cookstown, Co Tyrone BT80 8NB
Tel: 028 8676 3349 Fax: 028 8676 9187

HAY, William DUP **Foyle**
DUP Spokesperson for Regional Development
Tel: 028 9052 1107 Fax: 028 9052 1815
Constituency: 9 Ebrington Terrace, Waterside, Londonderry BT47 1JS
Tel: 028 7134 6271 Fax: 028 7132 9550

HENDRON, Dr Joe SDLP **Belfast West**
SDLP Spokesperson for Social Services
Tel: 028 9052 1681 Fax: 028 9052 1679
Constituency: 60 Springfield Road, Belfast BT12 7AH
Tel: 028 9023 6278 Fax: 028 9023 3033

HILDITCH, David DUP **East Antrim**
DUP Spokesperson for Culture, Arts and Leisure; Higher and Further Education, Training and Development
Tel: 028 9052 1115 Fax: 028 9052 1842 E-mail: david.hilditch@niassembly.gov.uk
Constituency: 22 High Street, Carrickfergus, Co Antrim BT38 7AA
Tel: 028 9332 9980 Fax: 028 9332 9979

HUSSEY, Derek UUP **West Tyrone**
Tel: 028 9052 1247 Fax: 028 9052 1741
Constituency: 48 Main Street, Castlederg, Co Tyrone BT81 7AT
Tel: 028 8167 9299 Fax: 028 8167 9298

HUTCHINSON, Billy PUP **Belfast North**
Tel: 028 9052 1299 Fax: 028 9052 1311
Constituency: 135 Shore Road, Belfast BT15 3PN
Tel: 028 9077 2307 Fax: 028 9077 0060

HUTCHINSON, Roger DUP **East Antrim**
Tel: 028 9052 1743 Fax: 028 9052 1752 E-mail: roger.hutchinson@niassembly.gov.uk
Constituency: 38a Point Street, Larne, Co Antrim BT40 1HU
Tel: 028 2827 9369 Fax: 028 2827 3035

KANE, Gardiner DUP **North Antrim**
DUP Spokesperson for Agriculture and Rural Development; Finance and Personnel
Tel: 028 9052 1108 Fax: 028 9052 1817 E-mail: gakbtoy@mailcity.com
Constituency: 4 Linenhall Street, Ballymoney BT53 6DP
Tel: 028 2766 7888 Fax: 028 2766 7999

KELLY, Gerry SF **Belfast North**
SF Spokesperson for Policing and Prisoners; Social Development
Tel: 028 9052 0359 Fax: 028 9052 0357

KELLY, John SF **Mid Ulster**
SF Spokesperson for Culture, Arts and Leisure; Health, Social Services and Public Safety
Tel: 028 9052 1633 Fax: 028 9052 1631

KENNEDY, Danny   UUP   **Newry and Armagh**
UUP Assembly Spokesperson for Education
Tel: 028 9052 1336   Fax: 028 9052 1757   E-mail: danny.kennedy@niassembly.gov.uk
Constituency: 3 Mallview Terrace, Armagh, Co Armagh BT61 9AN
Tel: 028 3751 1651   Fax: 028 3751 1771

KILCLOONEY, Rt Hon the Lord (John David Taylor)   UUP   **Strangford**
Tel: 028 9052 1803   Fax: 028 9052 1581
Constituency: Strangford Unionist Office, 6 William Street, Newtownards BT23 4AE
Tel: 028 9181 4123   Fax: 028 9181 4123

LESLIE, James   UUP   **North Antrim**
UUP Junior Minister
Tel: 028 9052 1850   Fax: 028 9052 1536   E-mail: james.leslie@niassembly.gov.uk
Constituency: 30a Ballymoney Street, Ballymena, Co Antrim BT43 6AL
Tel: 028 2564 2262   Fax: 028 2564 2264

LEWSLEY, Patricia   SDLP   **Lagan Valley**
SDLP Spokesperson for Children and Equality; Review of Public Administration
Tel: 028 9052 0331   Fax: 028 9052 0332   E-mail: patricia.lewsley@niassembly.gov.uk
Constituency: 21B Railway Street, Lisburn BT28 1XG
Tel: 028 9029 0846

McCARTHY, Kieran   All   **Strangford**
Alliance Party Chief Whip; Alliance Spokesperson for Culture, Arts and Leisure; Health and Social
Services
Tel: 028 9052 0351   Fax: 028 9052 1651
Constituency: 7 Main Street, Kircubbin, Co Down BT22 2SS
Tel: 028 4273 8221   Fax: 028 9173 9023

McCARTNEY, Robert, QC   UKUP   **North Down**
Leader, United Kingdom Unionist Party
Tel: 028 9052 1068   Fax: 028 9052 1845   E-mail: info@robertmccartney.org

McCLARTY, David   UUP   **East Londonderry**
Deputy Whip
Tel: 028 9052 0310   Fax: 028 9052 0309   E-mail: david.mcclarty@niassembly.gov.uk
Constituency: 12 Dunmore Street, Coleraine, Co Londonderry BT52 1EL
Tel: 028 7032 7294   Fax: 028 7032 7474

McCLELLAND, Donovan   SDLP   **South Antrim**
Deputy Speaker
Tel: 028 9052 1693   Fax: 028 9052 1694   E-mail: d.mcclelland@sdlp.ie
Constituency: 13a Massereene, Antrim, Co Antrim BT41 4DB
Tel: 028 9446 4615   Fax: 028 9446 1794

McCREA, Rev William   DUP   **Mid Ulster**
DUP Spokesperson for the Environment and the Elderly
Tel: 028 9052 1249   Fax: 028 9052 1748   E-mail: william.mccrea@niassembly.gov.uk
Constituency: 10 Highfield Road, Magherafelt, Co Londonderry BT45 5JD
Tel: 028 7963 2664   Fax: 028 7930 0701

McDONNELL, Dr Alasdair   SDLP   **Belfast South**
SDLP Spokesperson for Enterprise, Trade and Investment
Tel: 028 9052 0329   Fax: 028 9052 1724   E-mail: alasdair.mcdonnell@niassembly.gov.uk
Constituency: 150 Ormeau Road, Belfast BT7 2EB
Tel: 028 9024 2474   Fax: 028 9043 9935

McELDUFF, Barry   SF   West Tyrone
SF Spokesperson for Employment and Learning; Europe
Tel: 028 9052 1624   Fax: 028 9052 1622

McFARLAND, Alan   UUP   **North Down**
Tel: 028 9052 1528   Fax: 028 9052 1768   E-mail: alan.mcfarland@niassembly.gov.uk
Constituency: 77A High Street, Bangor, Co Down BT20 5DB
Tel: 028 9147 0300   Fax: 028 9147 0301

McGIMPSEY, Michael   UUP   **Belfast South**
Tel: 028 9052 1361   Fax: 028 9052 1852   E-mail: michael.mcgimpsey@niassembly.gov.uk
Constituency: Unit 2, 127-145 Sandy Row, Belfast BT12 5ET
Tel: 028 9024 5801   Fax: 028 9024 5801

McGRADY, Eddie   SDLP   **South Down**
Chief Whip, Social Democratic and Labour Party; SDLP Spokesperson for Public Administration
Tel: 028 9052 1287   Fax: 028 9052 1545   E-mail: e.mcgrady@sdlp.ie
Constituency: 30/32 Saul Street, Downpatrick, Co Down BT30 6NQ
Tel: 028 4461 2882   Fax: 028 4461 9574

McGUINNESS, Martin   SF   Mid Ulster
Tel: 028 9052 0362   Fax: 028 9052 0360
Constituency: 32 Burn Road, Cookstown, Co Tyrone BT80 8DN
Tel: 028 8676 5850   Fax: 028 8676 6734

McHUGH, Gerry   SF   **Fermanagh and South Tyrone**
SF Spokesperson for Agriculture and Rural Development; Education
Tel: 028 9052 1621   Fax: 028 9052 1619

McLAUGHLIN, Mitchel   SF   **Foyle**
Chairman, Sinn Féin Party; SF Spokesperson for Education; Europe; Criminal Justice
Tel: 028 9052 1603   Fax: 028 9052 1601
Constituency: Sinn Féin Foyle Constituency Office, Ráth Mór Centre, Bligh's Lane, Creggan, Co Derry BT48 0LZ

McMENAMIN, Eugene   SDLP   **West Tyrone**
SDLP Spokesperson for Culture, Arts and Leisure (with Tourism)
Tel: 028 9052 0324   Fax: 028 9052 1354   E-mail: eugene.mcmenamin@niassembly.gov.uk
Constituency: 33A Abercorn Square, Strabane, Co Tyrone BT82 8AQ
Tel: 028 7188 6633   Fax: 028 7188 6233

McNAMEE, Pat   SF   **Newry and Armagh**
SF Spokesperson for Regional Development; Human Rights and Equality
Tel: 028 9052 0355   Fax: 028 9052 0356
Constituency: 38 Irish Street, Armagh City
Tel: 028 3751 1797   Fax: 028 3751 8493

McWILLIAMS, Prof Monica   NIWC   Belfast South
Tel: 028 9052 1462   Fax: 028 9052 1461   E-mail: mmcwilliams@niassembly.gov.uk
Constituency: 50 University Street, Belfast BT7 1HB
Tel: 028 9023 3100   Fax: 028 9024 0021

MAGINNESS, Alban   SDLP   **Belfast North**
SDLP Spokesperson for Justice
Tel: 028 9052 1705   Fax: 028 9052 1703   E-mail: a.maginness@sdlp.ie
Constituency: 228 Antrim Road, Belfast BT15 2AN
Tel: 028 9022 0520   Fax: 028 9022 0522

MALLON, Séamus SDLP **Newry and Armagh**
Tel: 028 9052 1319 Fax: 028 9052 1329
Constituency: 2 Bridge Street, Newry, Co Down BT35 8AE
Tel: 028 3026 7933 Fax: 028 3026 7828

MASKEY, Alex SF **Belfast West**
SF Spokesperson for Finance and Personnel
Tel: 028 9052 1224 Fax: 028 9052 1341

MOLLOY, Francie SF **Mid Ulster**
SF Spokesperson for Finance and Personnel; Environment
Tel: 028 9052 0364 Fax: 028 9052 0365
Constituency: 7-9 The Square, Coalisland, Co Tyrone BT71 4LN
Tel: 028 8774 8689 Fax: 028 8774 6903

MORRICE, Jane NIWC **North Down**
Deputy Speaker
Tel: 028 9052 1463 Fax: 028 9052 1461 E-mail: jane.morrice@niassembly.gov.uk
Constituency: NIWC North Down, 108 Dufferin Avenue, Bangor, Co Down BT20 3AY
Tel: 028 9147 0739 Fax: 028 9147 0738

MORROW, Maurice DUP **Fermanagh and South Tyrone**
Chief Whip, Democratic Unionist Party
Tel: 028 9052 1296 Fax: 028 9052 1295
Constituency: 62b Scotch Street, Dungannon, Co Tyrone BT70 1BJ
Tel: 028 8775 2799 Fax: 028 8775 2799

MURPHY, Conor SF **Newry and Armagh**
SF Spokesperson for Public Accounts; Assembly Group Leader
Tel: 028 9052 1630 Fax: 028 9052 1628
Constituency: Main Street, Camlough, Newry, Co Down BT35
Tel: 028 3083 9470 Fax: 028 3083 9423

MURPHY, Mick SF **South Down**
SF Spokesperson for Culture, Arts and Leisure; Standards and Privileges
Tel: 028 9052 1618 Fax: 028 9052 1616
Constituency: 17 Circular Road, Castlewellan Co Down

NEESON, Sean All **East Antrim**
Alliance Spokesperson for Enterprise, Trade and Investment; Regional Development; European;
Political Development
Tel: 028 9052 1139 Fax: 028 9052 1313
E-mail: marjorie.hawkins@niassembly.gov.uk
Constituency: 18 North Street, Carrickfergus, Co Antrim BT38 7A
Tel: 028 9335 0286 Fax: 028 9335 0286

NELIS, Mary SF **Foyle**
SF Spokesperson for Environment; Social Development
Tel: 028 9052 0322 Fax: 028 9052 1721 E-mail: mary.nelis@niassembly.gov.uk
Constituency: 21a Glenbrook Terrace, Derry BT48 0DY
Tel: 028 7137 7551 Fax: 028 7137 7319

NESBITT, Dermot UUP **South Down**
Tel: 028 9052 1444 Fax: 028 9052 1419
Constituency: 19 Causeway Road, Newcastle, Co Down BT33 0DL
Tel: 028 4372 4400 Fax: 028 4372 5116

O'CONNOR, Danny SDLP   **East Antrim**
SDLP Spokesperson for Social Development
Tel: 028 9052 0372   Fax: 028 9052 0374   E-mail: d.oconnor@sdlp.ie
Constituency: 55c Main Street, Larne, Co Antrim BT40 1JE
Tel: 028 2827 0033   Fax: 028 2827 0077

O'HAGAN, Dr Dara SF   **Upper Bann**
SF Spokesperson for Enterprise, Trade and Investment; Energy
Tel: 028 9052 1671   Fax: 028 9052 1672   E-mail: dara.ohagan@niassembly.gov.uk
Constituency: 77 North Street, Lurgan, Co Armagh BT67 9AH
Tel: 028 3834 9675   Fax: 028 3832 2610

O NEILL, Eamonn SDLP   **South Down**
SDLP Spokesperson for Housing
Tel: 028 9052 0461   Fax: 028 9052 1015   E-mail: eoneill@sdlp.ie
Constituency: 60 Main Street, Castlewellan, Co Down BT31 9DJ
Tel: 028 4377 8833   Fax: 028 4477 8844

PAISLEY, Rev Ian DUP   **North Antrim**
Leader (co-founder), Democratic Unionist Party; DUP Spokesperson for Agriculture and Rural Development
Tel: 028 9052 1140   Fax: 028 9052 1289
Constituency: 142a Main Street, Bushmills, Co Antrim BT57 8QE
Tel: 028 2073 1303

PAISLEY, Ian Jnr DUP   **North Antrim**
DUP Spokesperson for Justice, Prisons and Policing
Tel: 028 9052 1248   Fax: 028 9052 1746   E-mail: ipj@dup.co.uk
Constituency: 46 Hill Street, Ballymena, Co Antrim BT43 6BH
Tel: 028 9045 8900   Fax: 028 9262 2212

POOTS, Edwin DUP   **Lagan Valley**
DUP Spokesperson for the Environment
Tel: 028 9052 1114   Fax: 028 9052 1824
Constituency: 46 Bachelors Walk, Lisburn, Co Antrim BT28 1XM
Tel: 028 9260 3003   Fax: 028 9262 7994

RAMSEY, Sue SF   **Belfast West**
SF Spokesperson for Children and Young People; Health, Social Services and Public Safety; SF Chief Whip
Tel: 028 9052 1615   Fax: 028 9052 1613

ROBINSON, Iris DUP   **Strangford**
Whip, Democratic Unionist Party; DUP Spokesperson for Health, Social Services and Public Safety
Tel: 028 9052 1103   Fax: 028 9052 1813   E-mail: iris.robinson@ukgateway.net
Constituency: 2B James Street, Newtownards, Co Down BT23 4DY
Tel: 028 9182 7701   Fax: 028 9182 7703

ROBINSON, Ken UUP   **East Antrim**
Tel: 028 9052 1881   Fax: 028 9052 1925   E-mail: kenrobinson@niassembly.gov.uk
Constituency: 32C North Street, Carrickfergus, Co Antrim BT38 7AQ
Tel: 028 9085 2914   Fax: 028 9085 2914

ROBINSON, Mark DUP   **Belfast South**
Tel: 028 9052 1129   Fax: 028 9052 1829   E-mail: mark.robinson@niassembly.gov.uk
Constituency: South Belfast DUP Advice Centre, 215a Lisburn Road, Belfast BT9 7EG
Tel: 028 9022 5969   Fax: 028 9022 5905

ROBINSON, Peter   DUP   **Belfast East**
Deputy Leader, Democratic Unionist Party
Tel: 028 9052 1728   Fax: 028 9052 1337

Constituency: Strandtown Hall, 96 Belmont Avenue, Belfast BT4 3DE
Tel: 028 9047 3111   Fax: 028 9047 1797

ROCHE, Patrick   NIUP   **Lagan Valley**
Tel: 028 9052 1994/9052 1901   Fax: 028 9052 1848   E-mail: patrick.roche@niassembly.gov.uk

Constituency: 56a Bachelors Walk, Lisburn, Co Antrim BT28 1XN
Tel: 028 9267 4100   Fax: 028 9267 4100

RODGERS, Bríd   SDLP   **Upper Bann**
Deputy Leader, SDLP
Tel: 028 9052 1319

Constituency: 41 North Street, Lurgan, Co Armagh BT67 9AG
Tel: 028 3832 2140   Fax: 028 3831 6996

SAVAGE, George   UUP   **Upper Bann**
Deputy Whip; UUP Assembly Spokesperson for Agriculture and Rural Development
Tel: 028 9052 0314   Fax: 028 9052 0313

Constituency: 147 Dunmore Road, Donacloney, Craigavon BT66 7NR
Tel: 028 3882 0402   Fax: 028 3888 1448

SHANNON, Jim   DUP   **Strangford**
DUP Spokesperson for Culture, Arts and Leisure
Tel: 028 9052 1128   Fax: 028 9052 1828

Constituency: 34A Francis Street, Newtownards, Co Down BT23 7ND
Tel: 028 9182 7990   Fax: 028 9182 7991

SHIPLEY DALTON, Duncan   UUP   **South Antrim**
UUP Spokesperson for Home Affairs (Legislation)
Tel: 028 9052 0517   Fax: 028 9052 0315   E-mail: duncan.sd@niassembly.gov.uk

Constituency: 19A Fountain Street, Antrim, Co Antrim BT41 4BB
Tel: 028 9446 0776

TIERNEY, John   SDLP   **Foyle**
SDLP Whip
Tel: 028 9052 1319   Fax: 028 9052 1329   E-mail: john.tierney.co@niassembly.gov.uk

Constituency: 5 Bayview Terrace, Derry BT48 7EE
Tel: 028 7136 2631   Fax: 028 7136 2632

TRIMBLE, Rt Hon David   UUP   **Upper Bann**
Leader, Ulster Unionist Party
Tel: 028 9052 1013   Fax: 028 9052 1963   E-mail: ps.ministers@ofmdfmni.gov.uk

Constituency: 2 Queen Street, Lurgan BT66 8BQ
Tel: 028 3832 8088   Fax: 028 3832 2343

WATSON, Dennis   UUAP   **Upper Bann**
Tel: 028 9052 1148   Fax: 028 9052 1465

Constituency: 10 Windsor Avenue, Lurgan BT67 9BG
Tel: 028 3834 1111   Fax: 028 3834 6123

WEIR, Peter   DUP   **North Down**
DUP Spokesperson for Finance and Personnel
Tel: 028 9052 0320   Fax: 028 9052 0319

Constituency: 77a High Street, Bangor, Co Down BT20 4PH
Tel: 028 9147 0300   Fax: 028 9147 0301

WELLS, Jim   DUP   **South Down**
Assistant Secretary, Democratic Unionist Party
Tel: 028 9052 1110   Fax: 028 9052 1820

Constituency: 2 Belfast Road, Ballynahinch, Co Down BT24 8BD
Tel: 028 9756 4200

WILSON, Cedric   NIUP   **Strangford**
Leader, Northern Ireland Unionist Party
Tel: 028 9052 1293   Fax: 028 9052 1294   E-mail: cedric.wilson@niassembly.gov.uk

Constituency: 26 Ann Street, Newtownards, Co Down BT23 7AB
Tel: 028 9181 0484   Fax: 028 9182 0952

WILSON, Jim   UUP   **South Antrim**
Deputy Speaker; Chief Whip, Ulster Unionist Party, Assembly Party
Tel: 028 9052 1292   Fax: 028 9052 1291   E-mail: jim.wilson@niassembly.co.uk

Constituency: 3a Rashee Road, Ballyclare, Co Antrim BT39 9HJ
Tel: 028 9332 4461   Fax: 028 9332 4462

WILSON, Sammy   DUP   **Belfast East**
DUP Spokesperson for Education; Social Development
Tel: 028 9052 1192   Fax: 028 9052 1834

Constituency: 13 Castlereagh Road, Belfast BT5 5FB
Tel: 028 9045 9500   Fax: 028 9045 9400

Constituencies

Belfast East	Sir Reg Empey	UUP
Belfast East	Dr Ian Adamson	UUP
Belfast East	David Ervine	PUP
Belfast East	Sammy Wilson	DUP
Belfast East	Lord Alderdice	Speaker
Belfast East	Peter Robinson	DUP
Belfast North	Nigel Dodds	DUP
Belfast North	Alban Maginness	SDLP
Belfast North	Fred Cobain	UUP
Belfast North	Fraser Agnew	UUAP
Belfast North	Billy Hutchinson	PUP
Belfast North	Gerry Kelly	SF
Belfast South	Dr Esmond Birnie	UUP
Belfast South	Carmel Hanna	SDLP
Belfast South	Dr Alasdair McDonnell	SDLP
Belfast South	Michael McGimpsey	UUP
Belfast South	Monica McWilliams	NIWC
Belfast South	Mark Robinson	IDUP
Belfast West	Alex Attwood	SDLP
Belfast West	Bairbre De Brún	SF
Belfast West	Dr Joe Hendron	SDLP
Belfast West	Sue Ramsey	SF
Belfast West	Gerry Adams	SF
Belfast West	Alex Maskey	SF
East Antrim	Roy Beggs Jnr	UUP
East Antrim	Ken Robinson	UUP
East Antrim	Danny O'Connor	SDLP
East Antrim	David Hilditch	DUP
East Antrim	Roger Hutchinson	DUP
East Antrim	Sean Neeson	APNI
East Londonderry	Michael Coyle	SDLP

East Londonderry	Boyd Douglas	UUAP
East Londonderry	David McClarty	UUP
East Londonderry	John Dallat	SDLP
East Londonderry	Pauline Armitage	Ind Unionist
East Londonderry	Gregory Campbell	DUP
Fermanagh and South Tyrone	Sam Foster	UUP
Fermanagh and South Tyrone	Michelle Gildernew	SF
Fermanagh and South Tyrone	Joan Carson	UUP
Fermanagh and South Tyrone	Tommy Gallagher	SDLP
Fermanagh and South Tyrone	Gerry McHugh	SF
Fermanagh and South Tyrone	Maurice Morrow	DUP
Foyle	Mark Durkan	SDLP
Foyle	Mary Nelis	SF
Foyle	William Hay	DUP
Foyle	Mitchel McLaughlin	SF
Foyle	John Tierney	SDLP
Foyle	Annie Courtney	SDLP Ind
Lagan Valley	Séamus Close	APNI
Lagan Valley	Ivan Davis	UUP
Lagan Valley	Patrick Roche	NIUP
Lagan Valley	Billy Bell	UUP
Lagan Valley	Patricia Lewsley	SDLP
Lagan Valley	Edwin Poots	DUP
Mid Ulster	Rev William McCrea	DUP
Mid Ulster	Francie Molloy	SF
Mid Ulster	Denis Haughey	SDLP
Mid Ulster	Billy Armstrong	UUP
Mid Ulster	John Kelly	SF
Mid Ulster	Martin McGuinness	SF
Newry and Armagh	Danny Kennedy	UUP
Newry and Armagh	Pat McNamee	SF
Newry and Armagh	Paul Berry	DUP
Newry and Armagh	John Fee	SDLP
Newry and Armagh	Connor Murphy	SF
Newry and Armagh	Séamus Mallon	SDLP
North Antrim	James Leslie	UUP
North Antrim	Ian Paisley Jnr	DUP
North Antrim	Rev Robert Coulter	UUP
North Antrim	Dr Sean Farren	SDLP
North Antrim	Gardiner Kane	DUP
North Antrim	Rev Ian Paisley	DUP
North Down	Sir John Gorman	UUP
North Down	Alan McFarland	UUP
North Down	Peter Weir	DUP
North Down	Jane Morrice	NIWC
North Down	Eileen Bell	APNI
North Down	Robert McCartney	UKUP
South Antrim	Norman Boyd	NIUP
South Antrim	David Ford	APNI
South Antrim	Jim Wilson	UUP
South Antrim	Wilson Clyde	DUP
South Antrim	Duncan Shipley-Dalton	UUP
South Antrim	Donovan McClelland	SDLP
South Down	PJ Bradley	SDLP
South Down	Eamonn ONeill	SDLP
South Down	Jim Wells	DUP
South Down	Mick Murphy	SF
South Down	Dermot Nesbitt	UUP

South Down	Eddie McGrady	SDLP
Strangford	Jim Shannon	DUP
Strangford	Cedric Wilson	NIUP
Strangford	Thomas Hamilton	UUP
Strangford	Kieran McCarthy	APNI
Strangford	Iris Robinson	DUP
Strangford	Lord Kilclooney	UUP
Upper Bann	Mervyn Carrick	DUP
Upper Bann	Bríd Rodgers	SDLP
Upper Bann	George Savage	UUP
Upper Bann	Dr Dara O'Hagan	SF
Upper Bann	Dennis Watson	UUAP
Upper Bann	David Trimble	UUP
West Tyrone	Eugene McMenamin	SDLP
West Tyrone	Joe Byrne	SDLP
West Tyrone	Pat Doherty	SF
West Tyrone	Derek Hussey	UUP
West Tyrone	Oliver Gibson	DUP
West Tyrone	Barry McElduff	SF

Women Members

ARMITAGE Pauline	McWILLIAMS Monica
BELL Eileen	MORRICE Jane
CARSON Joan	NELIS Mary
COURTNEY Annie	O'HAGAN Dr Dara
DE BRÚN Bairbre	RAMSEY Sue
GILDERNEW Michelle	ROBINSON Iris
HANNA Carmel	RODGERS Bríd
LEWSLEY Patricia	

Principal Officers and Officials

The Speaker: The Lord Alderdice, FRCPI, FRCPsych
Deputy Speakers: Donovan McClelland, Jane Morrice, Jim Wilson

Assembly Commission

The Assembly Commission is the body corporate of the Northern Ireland Assembly and has the responsibility to provide the Assembly, or ensure that the Assembly is provided, with the property, staff and services required for the Assembly to carry out its work.

Members (6):
Chairman: The Speaker
Eileen Bell, Rev Robert Coulter, John Fee, Dr Dara O'Hagan, Jim Wells
Clerk to the Commission: Tony Logue
Tel: 028 9052 1930   Fax: 028 9052 1699
E-mail: officeoftheassemblycommission@niassembly.gov.uk

The Speaker's Office

Speaker: The Lord Alderdice
Private Secretary: Georgina Campbell
Tel: 028 9052 1130   Fax: 028 9052 1959
E-mail: speaker@niassembly.gov.uk
Speaker's Adviser: Richard Good
Speaker's Counsel: Nicolas Hanna QC

Principal Officers

Clerk to the Assembly	**Arthur Moir**
Deputy Clerk	**Joe Reynolds**
Deputy Chief Executive	**Tom Evans**
Clerk Assistant	**Nuala Dunwoody**
Editor of Debates	**Simon Burrowes**
Keeper of the House	**Agnes Peacocke**
Director of Research and Information	**Allan Black**
Director of Legal Services	**Clare McGivern**
Director of Finance	**Fiona Hamill**
Director of Personnel	**Evan Hobson**
Principal Clerk of Bills	**Martin Wilson**
Principal Clerk of Business	**Alan Rogers**
Principal Clerks of Committees	**Debbie Pritchard**
	Alan Patterson
	John Torney
Examiner of Statutory Rules	**Gordon Nabney**
Comptroller and Auditor General	**John Dowdall**
Assembly Ombudsman	**Tom Frawley**

Civil Service

Head of Northern Ireland Civil Service and Secretary to the Executive
Nigel Hamilton
Stormont Castle, Stormont, Belfast BT4 3TT
Tel: 028 9037 8132
Private secretary: Bernie Rooney
Second Permanent Secretary
Will Haire
Tel: 028 9037 8132
Private secretary: Angela Dullaghan

Permanent Secretaries

Office of the First and Deputy First Minister
Nigel Hamilton
Will Haire

Agriculture and Rural Development
Peter Small CB

Culture, Arts and Leisure
Dr Aideen McGinley OBE

Education
Gerry McGinn

Enterprise, Trade and Investment
Bruce Robinson

Environment
Stephen Peover

Finance and Personnel
Pat Carvill

Health, Social Services and Public Safety
Clive Gowdy

Employment and Learning
Alan Shannon

Regional Development
Stephen Quinn

Social Development
John Hunter

DodOnline

An Electronic Directory without rival . . .

MLAs' biographies and photographs available with daily updates
via the internet

For a *free* trial, call Yasmin Mirza, Aby Farsoun or Michael Mand on 020 7630 7643

Executive Agencies

Business Development Service – BDS

Craigantlet Buildings, Stoney Road,
Belfast BT4 3SX
Tel: 028 9052 0444   Fax: 028 9052 7447
E-mail: bds@nics.gov.uk
Website: www.nics.gov.uk/bds/

Provides business support services to Northern Ireland departments, their executive agencies and the wider public sector.

Acting Chief Executive: Derek Orr
Northern Ireland Executive Department: Finance and Personnel
Launched: 1/10/96

Driver and Vehicle Licensing Northern Ireland – DVLNI

County Hall, Castlerock Road, Coleraine,
County Londonderry BT51 3HS
Tel: 028 7034 1249   Fax: 028 7034 1424
E-mail: dvlni@doeni.gov.uk
Website: www.doeni.gov.uk/dvlni

The Agency is responsible for licensing drivers (including taxi drivers) and road freight and passenger transport operators and also for the registration and licensing of vehicles and the collection and enforcement of Vehicle Excise Duty in Northern Ireland.

Chief Executive: Brendan Magee
Director of Development: Trevor Evans
Director of Vehicle Licensing:
    Ann McCabe
Director of Finance: Lucia O'Connor
Director of Corporate Services:
    Seamus McClean
Director of IT: Bernie Cosgrove
Director of Road Transport and Driver Licensing: Colin Campbell
Northern Ireland Executive Department: Environment
Launched: 2/8/93

Driver and Vehicle Testing Agency – DVTA

Balmoral Road, Belfast BT12 6QL
Tel: 028 9068 1831   Fax: 028 9066 5520
E-mail: dvta@nics.gov.uk
Website: www.doeni.gov.uk/dvta

Tests drivers and vehicles in Northern Ireland.

Chief Executive: Stanley Duncan
Director of Operations: Trevor Hassin

Director of Human Resources:
    Marianne Fleming
Director of Technical Policy and Legislation:
    Alastair Peoples
Director of Corporate Policy: Vacant
Director of Finance: Colin Berry
Director of Customer Service:
    John Crosby
Northern Ireland Executive Department: Environment
Launched: 1/4/92

Environment and Heritage Service – EHSNI

Commonwealth House, 35 Castle Street,
Belfast BT1 1GU
Tel: 028 9025 1477   Fax: 028 9054 6660
E-mail: ca@doeni.gov.uk
Website: www.ehsni.gov.uk

Protects and conserves the natural and built environment and promotes its appreciation for the benefit of present and future generations.

Chief Executive: Richard Rogers
Director of Natural Heritage:
    Dr John Faulkner
Director of Environmental Protection:
    Dr Roy Ramsay
Director of Built Heritage: Michael Coulter
Director of Corporate Affairs: Vacant
Northern Ireland Executive Department: Environment
Launched: 1/4/96

Forest Service

Dundonald House, Upper Newtownards Road,
Belfast BT4 3SB
Tel: 028 9052 4480   Fax: 028 9052 4570
E-mail: customer.forestservice@dardni.gov.uk
Website: www.forestserviceni.gov.uk

Sustainable management of Northern Ireland forests and the development of afforestation.

Chief Executive: Malcolm Beatty
Director, Operations: John Joe O'Boyle
Director, Policy and Standards:
    Pat Hunter Blair
Director, Corporate Services:
    Crawford McCully
Northern Ireland Executive Department: Agriculture and Rural Development
Launched: 1/4/98

Health Estates

Stoney Road, Dundonald, Belfast BT16 1US
Tel: 028 9052 0025   Fax: 028 9052 3900
E-mail: health.estates@dhsspsni.gov.uk
Website: www.dhsspsni.gov.uk/hea/index.html

Provides professional advice, guidance and support on estate matters at strategic and operational levels to the various bodies charged with responsibility for the Health and Social Services estate in Northern Ireland.

Chief Executive: Ronnie Browne
Northern Ireland Executive Department: Health, Social Services and Public Safety
Launched: 2/10/95

Invest Northern Ireland

64 Chichester Street, Belfast BT1 4JX
Tel: 028 9023 9090   Fax: 028 9049 0490
E-mail: info@investni.com
Website: www.investni.com

Encourages economic development, innovation and business success in Northern Ireland, increasing opportunity for all in a renewed culture of enterprise.

Chairman: Professor Fabian Monds
Chief Executive: Leslie Morrison
Managing Directors:
   Innovation and Capability Development: Tracy Meharg
   Entrepreneurship and Enterprise: Professor Terri Scott
   Business International: Leslie Ross
   Corporate Services: Chris Buckland
Northern Ireland Executive Department: Enterprise, Trade and Investment
Launched: 3/4/02

Land Registers of Northern Ireland – LRNI

Lincoln Building, 27–45 Great Victoria Street, Belfast BT2 7SL
Tel: 028 9025 1515   Fax: 028 9025 1550
E-mail: customer.information@lrni.gov.uk
Website: www.lrni.gov.uk

Maintains and develops a unified and reliable system of land registration in Northern Ireland.

Chief Executive and Registrar of Titles: Patricia Montgomery
Northern Ireland Executive Department: Finance and Personnel
Launched: 1/4/96

Northern Ireland Child Support Agency

Great Northern Tower, 17 Great Victoria Street, Belfast BT2 7AD
Tel: 028 9089 6666   Fax: 028 9089 6850
E-mail: belfast-customer-service@dwp.gsi.gov.uk
Website: www.dsdni.gov.uk/csa/introduction.asp

Assesses, collects and enforces child maintenance in Northern Ireland.

Chief Executive: Gerry Keenan
Northern Ireland Executive Department: Social Development
Launched: 5/4/93

Northern Ireland Statistics and Research Agency – NISRA

McAuley House, 2–14 Castle Street, Belfast BT1 1SA
Tel: 028 9034 8100   Fax: 028 9034 8106
E-mail: info@dfpni.gov.uk
Website: www.nisra.gov.uk

Produces statistics and social research to meet the needs of the public service at local, UK and European level, academic research and the wider community; and undertakes the registration of births, marriages, adoptions and deaths; and produces summary statistics relating to these events, as well as annual population estimates.

Registrar General and Acting Chief Executive: Dr Norman Caven
Senior Principal Statisticians: Dr John Mallon
Dr Kevin Sweeney
Dr Liz McWhirter
Dr James Gillan
Robert Beatty
Northern Ireland Executive Department: Finance and Personnel
Launched: 1/4/96

Ordnance Survey Mapping Northern Ireland – OSNI

Colby House, Stranmillis Court, Belfast BT9 5BJ
Tel: 028 9025 5755   Fax: 028 9025 5700
E-mail: osni@nics.gov.uk
Website: www.osni.gov.uk

The official survey and cartographic organisation for Northern Ireland.

Chief Executive: Michael Cory
Northern Ireland Executive Department: Culture, Arts and Leisure
Launched: 1/4/92

Planning Service

Headquarters, Clarence Court, 10-18 Adelaide Street, Belfast BT2 8GB
Tel: 028 9054 0540   Fax: 028 9054 0665
E-mail: planning.service.hq@nics.gov.uk
Website:
www.doeni.gov.uk/planning/index.htm

Implements the Government's policies and strategy for town and country planning in Northern Ireland.

Acting Chief Executive: John McConnell
Director of Corporate Services:
  Ian Maye
Director of Area Plans and Policy:
  Pat Quinn
Director of Operations: Pat McBride
Professional Services Manager:
  Anne Garvey
Northern Ireland Executive Department: Environment
Launched: 1/4/96

Public Record Office of Northern Ireland – PRONI

66 Balmoral Avenue, Belfast BT9 6NY
Tel: 028 9025 1318   Fax: 028 9025 5999
E-mail: proni@dcalni.gov.uk
Website: www.proni.gov.uk

Identifies and preserves Northern Ireland's archival heritage and ensures public access to that heritage which fully meets Open Government and Freedom of Information standards.

Chief Executive: Dr Gerry Slater
Northern Ireland Executive Department: Culture, Arts and Leisure
Launched: 3/4/95

Rate Collection Agency – RCA

Oxford House, 49–55 Chichester Street, Belfast BT1 4HH
Tel: 028 9025 2252   Fax: 028 9025 2113
E-mail: rca@dfpni.gov.uk
Website: www.dfpni.gov.uk/rca/

Collects rates and administers the Housing Benefit Scheme for owner-occupiers.

Chief Executive: Arthur Scott
Northern Ireland Executive Department: Finance and Personnel
Launched: 1/4/91

Rivers Agency

Hydebank, 4 Hospital Road, Belfast BT8 8JP
Tel: 028 9025 3355   Fax: 028 9025 3455
E-mail: rivers@dardni.gov.uk

Management of flood and sea defences and watercourse maintenance and protection in Northern Ireland.

Chief Executive: John Hagan
Northern Ireland Executive Department: Agriculture and Rural Development
Launched: 1/10/96

Roads Service

Clarence Court, 10–18 Adelaide Street, Belfast BT2 8GB
Tel: 028 9054 0540   Fax: 028 9054 0024
E-mail: roads@drdni.gov.uk
Website: www.roadsni.gov.uk

Responsible for the public road network in Northern Ireland.

Chief Executive: Malcolm McKibbin
Director of Corporate Services: Jim Carlisle
Director of Network Services: David Orr
Director of Finance: John McNeill
Director of Engineering: Geoff Allister
Northern Ireland Executive Department: Regional Development
Launched: 1/4/96

Social Security Agency – SSA

Churchill House, Victoria Square, Belfast BT1 4SS
Tel: 028 9056 9100   Fax: 028 9056 9178
E-mail: ssa@nics.gov.uk
Website: http://ssani.gov.uk

Delivers a wide range of social security benefits and services. It also provides processing services for the Jobcentre Plus in Great Britain.

Chief Executive: Chris Thompson
Director of Operations: Barney McGahan
Director of Benefit Security: David McCurry
Director of Business Development:
  Tommy O'Reilly
Director of Customer Services: Anne Flanagan
Director of Finance: Heather Cousins
Director of Personnel: Tommy O'Reilly
Director of Medical Support Services:
  Dr Terry Dixon
Non-Executive Director: Andrew Smith
Northern Ireland Executive Department: Social Development
Launched: 1/7/91

Valuation and Lands Agency – VLA

Queen's Court, 56–66 Upper Queen Street,
Belfast BT1 6FD
Tel: 028 9025 0700   Fax: 028 9054 3750
E-mail: anne.kennedy@dfpni.gov.uk
Website: vla.nics.gov.uk

Responsible for maintenance of the Valuation
List for rating purposes in Northern Ireland and,
periodically, the preparation of a new Valuation
List; provision of a valuation, estate management
and property data service to the public sector,
promoting a proactive approach to estate
management through its Central Advisory Unit.

Chief Executive and Commissioner of
Valuation: Nigel Woods
Assistant Commissioner Rating: Brian McClure
(on secondment)
Assistant Commissioner Operations:
David Rainey
Acting Assistant Commissioner Corporate
Services: Alan Brontë
Northern Ireland Executive Department:
Finance and Personnel
Launched: 1/4/93

Water Service

Northland House, 3–5 Frederick Street,
Belfast BT1 2NR
Tel: 028 9024 4711   Fax: 028 9035 4888
E-mail: water.service@nics.gov.uk
Website: www.waterni.gov.uk

Provides water and sewerage services in
Northern Ireland.

Chief Executive: Vacant
Director of Corporate Services: Robin Mussen
Director of Operations: John Kelly
Director of Development: Trevor Haslett
Director of Finance: David Carson
Director of Customer Services:
William Duddy
Technical Director: Harry Thompson
Northern Ireland Executive Department:
Regional Development
Launched: 1/4/96

Political Parties

Ulster Unionist Party

Cunningham House, 429 Holywood Road,
Belfast BT4 2LN
028 9076 5500 *Fax:* 028 9076 9419
E-mail: uup@uup.org
Website: www.uup.org

Leader: Rt Hon David Trimble MP
Chief Executive: Alastair Patterson
Press Officer: Alex Benjamin 028 9076 5510
Fax: 028 9076 9419
Policy Unit: 028 9076 5511
Press Officer: Alex Benjamin
Tel: 028 9076 5510
Assembly:
028 9052 1327/1328 Fax: 028 9052 1395
Administration Office: 028 9052 1327

Social Democratic and Labour Party

121 Ormeau Road, Belfast BT7 1SH
028 9024 7700 *Fax:* 028 9023 6699
E-mail: sdlp@indigo.ie
Website: www.sdlp.ie

Leader: Mark Durkan
Deputy Leader: Bríd Rodgers
General Secretary: Gerry Cosgrove
International Secretary: Margaret Richie
Press Officer: Gail McGreevy
Tel: 028 9052 1837
Assembly:
Catherine Matthews
Room 272
028 9052 1319/1649 *Fax:* 028 9052 1329

Democratic Unionist Party

91 Dundela Avenue, Belfast BT4 3BU
028 9047 1155 *Fax:* 028 9047 1797
E-mail: info@dup.org.uk
Websites: www.dup.org.uk; www.dup2win.com

Leader: Rev Ian Paisley MP MEP
Deputy Leader: Peter Robinson MP
Assembly:
Room 207
028 9052 1322/1323 Fax: 028 9052 1289
Chief Executive: Allan Ewart
Director of Communications: Timothy Johnston
Tel: 07710 132098

Sinn Féin

44 Parnell Square, Dublin 1
+353 1 8726932/8726100
Fax: +353 1 8733441/8783595
E-mail: sfadmin@eircom.net
Website: www.sinnfein.ie

President: Gerry Adams MP
Vice-Presidents: Pat Doherty MP, Joe Cahill
Press Officer: Dawn Doyle
+353 1 872 2609
E-mail: sfpress@eircom.net
Assembly:
028 9052 1470/1472 *Fax:* 028 9052 1474

Alliance

88 University Street, Belfast BT7 1HE
028 9032 4274 *Fax:* 028 9033 3147
E-mail: alliance@allianceparty.org
Website: www.allianceparty.org

Chair: Jayne Dunlop
Leader: David Ford
Hon Treasurer: Stewart Dickson, Mervyn Jones
General Secretary: Stephen Farry
Press Officer: Steven Alexander
028 9052 1849 *Mobile:* 07768 151972
Assembly:
028 9052 1314 *Fax:* 028 9052 1313
Assistant to Chief Whip: Marjorie Hawkins
028 9052 1052 *Fax:* 028 9052 1053
E-mail: alliance.party@niassembly.gov.uk

Northern Ireland Unionist Party

Room 358, Parliament Buildings, Stormont,
Belfast BT4 3XX
028 9052 1533/1901 *Fax:* 028 9052 1845

Leader: Cedric Wilson
028 9052 1294 Fax: 028 9052 1293
E-mail: cedric.wilson@niassemby.gov.uk
Website: www.niup.org
Party Whip: Norman Boyd
028 9052 1733 *Fax:* 028 9052 1754
E-mail: norman.boyd@niassembly.gov.uk
Deputy Leader: Patrick Roche
028 9052 1994 Fax: 028 9052 1848
E-mail: patrick.roche@niassembly.gov.uk

United Unionist Assembly Party

Room 259, Parliament Buildings, Stormont,
Belfast BT4 3XX
Party Leader: Denis Watson
Assembly:
028 9052 1464/1466 Fax: 028 9052 1465

Progressive Unionist Party

182 Shankill Road, Belfast BT13 2BH
028 9032 6233 *Fax:* 028 9024 9602
Leader: David Ervine
Deputy Leader: David Rose
President: Hugh Smyth OBE
E-mail: david.ervine@niassembly.gov.uk
Billy Hutchinson, MLA
Assembly:
028 9052 1469 *Fax:* 028 9052 1468

Northern Ireland Women's Coalition

50 University Street, Belfast BT7 1HB
028 9023 3100 *Fax:* 028 9024 0021
E-mail: info@niwc.org
Website: www.niwc.org
Monica McWilliams
Jane Morrice
Assembly:
028 9052 1463 *Fax:* 028 9052 1461
Constituency Office:
028 9023 3100 *Fax:* 028 9024 0021

UK Unionist Party

Leader: Robert McCartney QC
Chairman: Nelson Wharton
Secretary: Joan Dealey
Treasurer: Anne Moore
Special Adviser: Tom Sheridan
Assembly:
Room 214
028 9052 1482 *Fax:* 028 9052 1483
E-mail: info@ukup.org
Website: www.ukup.org

Visit the Vacher Dod Website . . .
www.DodOnline.co.uk

EUROPEAN UNION

History

In 1957 France, Germany and Italy joined Belgium, the Netherlands and Luxembourg in setting up the European Economic Community (EEC) and the European Atomic Energy Agency (EAEC) through the Treaties of Rome. The United Kingdom joined this founding group together with Ireland and Denmark in 1973. The European Community continued to expand, in both membership and the policy areas coming within its competence. In 1981 Greece became the tenth member state followed by Spain and Portugal in 1986. In 1990 the unification of Germany automatically brought the former East German territory within the Community. In 1995 the European Community became the European Union, and was further enlarged with the accession of Austria, Finland and Sweden. In March 1998 accession discussions were launched with Cyprus, Poland, Hungary, the Czech Republic, Slovenia and Estonia. A further six countries opened accession talks to join the European Union in February 2000: Bulgaria, Latvia, Lithuania, Malta, Romania and Slovakia. Turkey is also now accepted as a candidate for membership of the European Union. In December 2002 the European Council invited Cyprus, the Czech Republic, Estonia, Hungary, Latvia, Lithuania, Malta, Poland, Slovakia and Slovenia to accede to the EU on 1 May 2004.

The European Union is managed by five institutions:

Council of the European Union

Rue de la Loi 170, 1048 Brussels, Belgium
Tel: 00 32 2 285 6111 *Fax:* 00 32 2 285 7381
E-mail: public.relations@consilium.eu.int *Website:* ue.eu.int

The 15-member Council of the European Union is the only institution which directly represents the member governments. For major decisions the foreign ministers are usually present – at other times the appropriate ministers according to the subject before the Council. The presidency rotates every six months. From 1 January 2002 the six-monthly presidency rotates in the following order: Spain, Denmark, Greece, Italy, Ireland.

European Commission

Rue de la Loi 200, 1049 Brussels, Belgium
Tel: 00 32 2 299 1111
E-mail: forename.surname@cec.eu.int *Website:* europa.eu.int/comm

UK Commissioners: Rt Hon Neil Kinnock, Rt Hon Chris Patten

The European Commission's main powers are those of supervision, initiative and implementation. It proposes Union policies and legislation, supervises the day-to-day running of Union policies and is the 'guardian' of the Treaties and can initiate action against member states which do not comply with Union rules. It also has wide powers of its own in certain sectors such as coal and steel and competition.

Representation of the European Commission in the UK:

London Office: 8 Storey's Gate, London SW1P 3AT
Tel: 020 7973 1992 *Fax:* 020 7973 1900
Website: www.cec.org.uk

Regional Offices
Windsor House, 9-15 Bedford Street, Belfast BT2 7EG
Tel: 028 9024 0708 *Fax:* 028 9024 8241

2 Caspian Point, Caspian Way, Cardiff CF10 4QQ
Tel: 029 2089 5020 *Fax:* 029 2089 5035

9 Alva Street, Edinburgh EH2 4PH
Tel: 0131-225 2058 *Fax:* 0131-226 4105

European Parliament

The European Parliament exercises democratic control over the running of the European Union. Its 626 MEPs are elected every five years with the most recent election for the 1999–2004 Parliament having taken place in June 1999. The Parliament meets and debates in public, with plenary sessions taking place in Strasbourg for on average one week in each month except for August. In addition there are mini sessions in Brussels to facilitate contacts with the Commission and the Council. The major working unit of the European Parliament is the specialised committee where much of the legislative scrutiny takes place. The Parliament has 17 permanent committees. As well as legislative powers, the Parliament also has powers relating to the budget, to the conclusion of international agreements and general supervisory powers.

United Kingdom Information Office:
2 Queen Anne's Gate, London SW1H 9AA
Tel: 020 7227 4300 *Fax:* 020 7227 4302
E-mail: eplondon@europarl.eu.int *Website:* www.europarl.org.uk

Scotland: The Tun, 4 Jackson's Entry, Holyrood Road, Edinburgh EH8 8PJ
Tel: 0131-557 7866 *Fax:* 0131-557 4977
E-mail: epedinburgh@europarl.eu.int
Website: www.europarl.org.uk/office/scotlandofficemain.htm

PARTY MEMBERSHIP OF UK MEPs

Conservative	36
Labour	28
Liberal Democrat	11
UK Independence Party	3
Green Party	2
Scottish National Party	2
Plaid Cymru	2
Democratic Unionist Party (DUP)	1
Social Democratic and Labour (SDLP)	1
Ulster Unionist Party (UUP)	1
Total	**87**

UK MEPs

England	71
Scotland	8
Wales	5
Northern Ireland	3
Total	**87**

UK MEPs' DIRECTORY

Adam, Gordon   **PES**   **Lab**   **North East**
Member Agriculture and Rural Development Committee
Member Foot and Mouth Temporary Committee
Substitute Industry, External Trade, Research and Energy Committee
Substitute Fisheries Committee
Chair EU-Lithuania Joint Parliamentary Committee Delegation
Member Ukraine, Belarus and Moldova Delegation

7 Palmersville, Great Lime Road, Forest Hall, Newcastle upon Tyne NE12 9HN
Tel: 0191 280 2929   Fax: 0191 256 6067
E-mail: gadammep@aol.com

Atkins, Robert   **EPP-ED**   **Con**   **North West**
Member Industry, External Trade, Research and Energy Committee
Substitute Employment and Social Affairs Committee
Member South Africa Delegation

Manor House, Lancaster Road, Garstang Lancashire PR3 1JA
Tel: 01995 602225   Fax: 01995 605690   E-mail: ratsmep@aol.com
Website: www.sir-robertatkins.org

Attwooll, Elspeth   **ELDR**   **LD**   **Scotland**
Member Employment and Social Affairs Committee
Member Fisheries Committee
Substitute Agriculture and Rural Development Committee
Member Canada Delegation
Suite 1, 2nd Floor, Olympic House, 142 Queen Street, Glasgow G1 3BU
Tel: 0141 243 2421   Fax: 0141 243 2451   E-mail: info@scotlibdem.fsnet.co.uk

Balfe, Richard   **EPP-ED**   **Con**   **London**
Member Petitions Committee
Substitute Economic and Monetary Affairs Committee
Substitute Development and Co-operation Committee
Member ACP-EU Joint Assembly
28 Honeyden Road, Sidcup DA14 5LX
Tel: 020 8302 1405   Fax: 020 8302 1427   E-mail: rbalfe@honeyden.fsnet.co.uk
Website: www.poptel.org.uk/richard.balfe

Beazley, Christopher   **EPP-ED**   **Con**   **Eastern**
Member Culture, Youth, Education, Media and Sport Committee
Substitute Employment and Social Affairs Committee
Chair EU-Estonia Joint Parliamentary Committee Delegation
Hertford and Stortford Conservative Association, 4a Swains Mill, Crane Mead, Ware,
Hertfordshire SG12 9PY
Tel: 01920 462182   Fax: 01920 485805

Bethell, Lord   **EPP-ED**   **Con**   **London**
Member Citizens' Freedoms and Rights, Justice and Home Affairs Committee
Substitute Foreign Affairs, Human Rights, Common Security and Defence Policy Committee
Vice-chair Russia Delegation
Substitute EU-Poland Joint Parliamentary Committee Delegation
Manor Farm House, Brill, Buckinghamshire HP18 9SL
Tel: 01844 238446   Fax: 01844 237821

Booth, Graham   **EDD**   **UKIP**   **South West**
Substitute Regional Policy, Transport and Tourism Committee
UKIP, 31 West Street, Wilton, Wiltshire SP2 0DL
Tel: 01722 744814   Fax: 01722 744325

Bowe, David   **PES**   **Lab**   **Yorkshire and the Humber**
Member Environment, Public Health and Consumer Policy Committee
Substitute Industry, External Trade, Research and Energy Committee
Member China Delegation
2 Blenheim Terrace, Leeds LS2 9JG
Tel: 0113 245 8993   Fax: 0113 244 2782   E-mail: mail@davidbowe.demon.co.uk

Bowis, John   **EPP-ED**   **Con**   **London**
Member Environment, Public Health and Consumer Policy Committee
Member Development and Co-operation Committee
Vice-chair Kazakhstan, Kyrgyzstan, Uzbekistan, Tajikistan, Turkmenistan and Mongolia Delegation
Member ACP-EU Joint Assembly
PO Box 262, New Malden, Surrey KT3 4WJ
Tel: 020 8949 2555   Fax: 020 8395 7463   E-mail: johnbowis@aol.com

Bradbourn, Philip   **EPP-ED**   **Con**   **West Midlands**
Member Regional Policy, Transport and Tourism Committee
Substitute Budgets Committee
Substitute Legal Affairs and Internal Market Committee
Member Canada Delegation
Substitute EU-Malta Joint Parliamentary Committee Delegation
66-68 Hagley Road, Birmingham B16 8PF
Tel: 0845 606 0239   Fax: 0121 456 5989   Website: www.torymeps.com

Bushill-Matthews, Philip   **EPP-ED**   **Con**   **West Midlands**
Member Employment and Social Affairs Committee
Substitute Environment, Public Health and Consumer Policy Committee
Member Mashreq and Gulf States Delegation
Manor House, Harbury, Leamington Spa, Warwickshire CV33 9HX
Tel: 01926 612476   Fax: 01926 613168   E-mail: bushillm@aol.com
Website: www.torymeps.com

Callanan, Martin   **EPP-ED**   **Con**   **North East**
Member Environment, Public Health and Consumer Policy Committee
Substitute Foot and Mouth Temporary Committee
Member Kazakhstan, Kyrgyzstan, Uzbekistan, Tajikistan, Turkmenistan and Mongolia Delegation
Member ACP-EU Joint Assembly
22 Osborne Road, Jesmond, Newcastle upon Tyne NE2 2AD
Tel: 0191 240 2600   Fax: 0191 240 2612

Cashman, Michael   **PES**   **Lab**   **West Midlands**
Member Citizens' Freedoms and Rights, Justice and Home Affairs Committee
Member Petitions Committee
Substitute Foreign Affairs, Human Rights, Common Security and Defence Policy Committee
Member EU-Bulgaria Joint Parliamentary Committee Delegation
West Midlands Labour European Office, AEEU House, 1 George Street, West Bromwich B70 6NT
Tel: 0121 569 1923   Fax: 0121 569 1935   E-mail: jheenan@michael-cashman-mep.org.uk

Chichester, Giles   **EPP-ED**   **Con**   **South West**
Member Industry, External Trade, Research and Energy Committee
Substitute Employment and Social Affairs Committee
Member Australia and New Zealand Delegation
Constituency Office, 48 Queen Street, Exeter, Devon EX4 3SR
Tel: 01392 491815   Fax: 01392 491588   E-mail: gileschichestermep@eclipse.co.uk
Website: www.gileschichestermep.org.uk

Clegg, Nicholas   **ELDR**   **LD**   **East Midlands**
Member Industry, External Trade, Research and Energy Committee
Member Foot and Mouth Temporary Committee
Substitute Regional Policy, Transport and Tourism Committee
Member Maghreb and Arab Maghreb Union Delegation
17-21 High Street, Ruddington, Nottinghamshire NG11 6DT
Tel: 0115 846 0661   Fax: 0115 846 1796   E-mail: ld_eastmidland@cix.co.uk

Corbett, Richard   **PES**   **Lab**   **Yorkshire and the Humber**
Member Constitutional Affairs Committee
Substitute Economic and Monetary Affairs Committee
Member ASEAN, South-east Asia and Republic of Korea Delegation
2 Blenheim Terrace, Leeds LS2 9JG
Tel: 0113 245 8978   Fax: 0113 245 8992   E-mail: richard@corbett-euro.demon.co.uk
Website: www.corbett-euro.demon.co.uk

Corrie, John   **EPP-ED**   **Con**   **West Midlands**
Member Development and Co-operation Committee
Substitute Budgets Committee
Vice-chair ACP-EU Joint Assembly
Park of Tongland, Kirkcudbright DG6 4NE

Davies, Chris   **ELDR**   **LD**   **North West**
Member Environment, Public Health and Consumer Policy Committee
Substitute Petitions Committee
Member EU-Cyprus Joint Parliamentary Committee Delegation
87A Castle Street, Edgeley, Stockport, Lancashire SK3 9AR
Tel: 0161 477 7070   Fax: 0161 477 7007   E-mail: chrisdaviesmep@cix.co.uk

Deva, Nirj   **EPP-ED**   **Con**   **South East**
Member Development and Co-operation Committee
Substitute Regional Policy, Transport and Tourism Committee
Member ASEAN, South-east Asia and Republic of Korea Delegation

169B Kennington Road, London SE11 6SF
Tel: 020 7642 8880   Fax: 020 7642 8879   E-mail: nirjdevamep@hotmail.com

Dover, Densmore   **EPP-ED**   **Con**   **North West**
Member Budgets Committee
Substitute Regional Policy, Transport and Tourism Committee
Vice-chair EU-Malta Joint Parliamentary Committee Delegation

30 Countess Way, Euxton, Chorley, Lancashire PR7 6PT
Tel: 01257 273183

Duff, Andrew   **ELDR**   **LD**   **Eastern**
Member Constitutional Affairs Committee
Substitute Foreign Affairs, Human Rights, Common Security and Defence Policy Committee
Vice-chair EU-Turkey Joint Parliamentary Committee Delegation

Orwell House, Cowley Road, Cambridge CB4 0PP
Tel: 01223 566700   Fax: 01223 566698   E-mail: mep@andrewduffmep.org
Website: www.andrewduffmep.org

Elles, James   **EPP-ED**   **Con**   **South East**
Member Budgets Committee
Substitute Foreign Affairs, Human Rights, Common Security and Defence Policy Committee
Substitute Budgetary Control Committee
Member EU-Cyprus Joint Parliamentary Committee Delegation

Beaconsfield Constituency Conservative Association, Disraeli House, 12 Aylesbury End,
Beaconsfield, Buckinghamshire HP9 1LW
Tel: 01494 673 745   Fax: 01494 670 428

Evans, Jill   **Green-EFA**   **PC**   **Wales**
Vice-chair Women's Rights and Equal Opportunities Committee
Member Employment and Social Affairs Committee
Substitute Environment, Public Health and Consumer Policy Committee
Member EU-Lithuania Joint Parliamentary Committee Delegation
Substitute EU-Estonia Joint Parliamentary Committee Delegation

3 Hill Street, Haverfordwest SA61 1QQ
Tel: 01437 779042   Fax: 01437 779048

Evans, Jonathan   **EPP-ED**   **Con**   **Wales**
Member Economic and Monetary Affairs Committee
Substitute Foreign Affairs, Human Rights, Common Security and Defence Policy Committee
Substitute Foot and Mouth Temporary Committee
Member Japan Delegation
Substitute EU-Czech Republic Joint Parliamentary Committee Delegation

4 Penlline Road, Whitchurch, Cardiff CF4 2XS
Tel: 029 2061 6031   Fax: 029 2061 3539   E-mail: jonathan@jonathanevans.co.uk

Evans, Robert   **PES**   **Lab**   **London**
Vice-chair Citizens' Freedoms and Rights, Justice and Home Affairs Committee
Substitute Environment, Public Health and Consumer Policy Committee
Substitute Development and Co-operation Committee
Member South Asia and SAARC Delegation
Substitute EU-Romania Joint Parliamentary Committee Delegation

101 High Street, Feltham, Middlesex TW13 4HG
Tel: 020 8890 1818   Fax: 020 8890 1628   E-mail: robertevansmep@btclick.com
Website: www.robertevansmep.net

Farage, Nigel   **EDD**   **UKIP**   **South East**
Member Fisheries Committee
Member EU-Malta Joint Parliamentary Committee Delegation

The Old Grain Store, Church Lane, Lyminster, West Sussex BN17 7QJ
Tel: 01903 885573   Fax: 01903 885574   E-mail: ukip.se@ukip.org

Ford, Glyn   **PES**   **Lab**   **South West**
Member Foreign Affairs, Human Rights, Common Security and Defence Policy Committee
Member Petitions Committee
Substitute Industry, External Trade, Research and Energy Committee
Member Kazakhstan, Kyrgyzstan, Uzbekistan, Tajikistan, Turkmenistan and Mongolia Delegation
Member Japan Delegation

Southwest Labour Party, 1 Newfoundland Court, Newfoundland Street, Bristol BS2 9AP
Tel: 0117 924 6399   Fax: 0117 924 8599   E-mail: penny_richardson@new.labour.org.uk
Website: www.glynford.com

Foster, Jacqueline   **EPP-ED**   **Con**   **North West**
Member Regional Policy, Transport and Tourism Committee
Substitute Industry, External Trade, Research and Energy Committee
Member ACP-EU Joint Assembly

ASP 08E264, European Parliament, Rue Wiertz, 1047 Brussels, Belgium
Tel: 00 32 2 284 79 57   Fax: 00 32 2 284 99 57   E-mail: jfoster@europarl.eu.int

Gill, Neena   **PES**   **Lab**   **West Midlands**
Member Budgets Committee
Substitute Industry, External Trade, Research and Energy Committee
Vice-chair South Asia and SAARC Delegation

West Midlands Labour European Office, AEEU House, 1 George Street, West Bromwich B70 6NT
Tel: 0121 569 1921   Fax: 0121 569 1935   E-mail: jacquis@neena-gill-mep.new.labour.org.uk

Goodwill, Robert   **EPP-ED**   **Con**   **Yorkshire and the Humber**
Member Environment, Public Health and Consumer Policy Committee
Member Women's Rights and Equal Opportunities Committee
Member Ukraine, Belarus and Moldova Delegation

Southwood Farm, Terrington, York YO6 6QB
Tel: 01653 648459   Fax: 01653 648225   E-mail: r.goodwill@farmline.com

Hannan, Daniel   **EPP-ED**   **Con**   **South East**
Member Constitutional Affairs Committee
Substitute Development and Co-operation Committee
Member Central America and Mexico Delegation
Substitute EU-Slovenia Joint Parliamentary Committee Delegation

Conservative Central Office, 32 Smith Square, London SW1P 3HH
Tel: 020 7984 8238   Fax: 020 7984 8207   E-mail: office@hannan.co.uk
Website: www.hannan.co.uk

Harbour, Malcolm   **EPP-ED**   **Con**   **West Midlands**
Member Legal Affairs and Internal Market Committee
Substitute Industry, External Trade, Research and Energy Committee
Member Japan Delegation

Manor Cottage, Manor Road, Solihull, West Midlands B91 2BL
Tel: 0121 711 3158   Fax: 0121 711 3159   E-mail: manor_cottage@compuserve.com

Heaton-Harris, Christopher   **EPP-ED**   **Con**   **East Midlands**
Member Budgetary Control Committee
Substitute Budgets Committee

Blaby Conservative Association, 35 Lutterworth Road, Blaby, Leicester LE8 4DW
Tel: 0845 234 0059   Fax: 0116 278 6664   Website: www.heatonharris.org.uk

Helmer, Roger   **EPP-ED**   **Con**   **East Midlands**
Member Employment and Social Affairs Committee
Substitute Industry, External Trade, Research and Energy Committee
Substitute Regional Policy, Transport and Tourism Committee
Member ASEAN, South-east Asia and Republic of Korea Delegation
Substitute EU-Slovak Republic Joint Parliamentary Committee Delegation

Blaby Conservative Association, 35 Lutterworth Road, Blaby, Leicester LE8 4DW
Tel: 0116 277 9992   Fax: 0116 278 6664   Website: www.rogerhelmer.com

Honeyball, Mary   **PES**   **Lab**   **London**
Member Economic and Monetary Affairs Committee
Member Women's Rights and Equal Opportunities Committee
Substitute Environment, Public Health and Consumer Policy Committee
Member EU-Cyprus Joint Parliamentary Committee Delegation
Substitute EU-Malta Joint Parliamentary Committee Delegation

Labour European Office, 16 Charles Square, London N1 6HP
Tel: 020 7490 4904   Fax: 020 7490 2143

Howitt, Richard   **PES**   **Lab**   **Eastern**
Member Development and Co-operation Committee
Member Foreign Affairs, Human Rights, Common Security and Defence Policy Committee
Substitute Employment and Social Affairs Committee
Member ACP-EU Joint Assembly

Labour European Office, Labour Hall, Collingwood Road, Witham, Essex CM8 2EE
Tel: 01376 501700   Fax: 01376 501900
E-mail: richard.howitt@geo2.poptel.org.uk

Hudghton, Ian   **Green-EFA**   **SNP**   **Scotland**
Member Budgets Committee
Member Fisheries Committee
Substitute Agriculture and Rural Development Committee
Member EEA Joint Parliamentary Committee Delegation

8 Old Glamis Road, Dundee DD3 8HP
Tel: 01382 623200   Fax: 01382 903 205   E-mail: ihmep.ne@snp.org

Hughes, Stephen   **PES**   **Lab**   **North East**
Member Employment and Social Affairs Committee
Substitute Budgets Committee
Member Russia Delegation

North East European Constituency Office, Room 4/38, County Hall, Durham DH1 5UR
Tel: 0191 384 9371   Fax: 0191 384 6100   E-mail: alma@mep.u-net.com
Website: www.daltonet.com/stephenhughesmep

Huhne, Chris   **ELDR**   **LD**   **South East**
Member Economic and Monetary Affairs Committee
Substitute Budgets Committee
Member ASEAN, South-east Asia and Republic of Korea Delegation
Substitute EU-Slovak Republic Joint Parliamentary Committee Delegation

Liberal Democrat Office European Parliament, 2 Queen Anne's Gate, London SW1H 9AA
Tel: 020 7227 4319   Fax: 020 7233 3959
E-mail: chuhneoffice@cix.co.uk

Hume, John   **PES**   **SDLP**   **Northern Ireland**
Member Regional Policy, Transport and Tourism Committee
Substitute Agriculture and Rural Development Committee

5 Bayview Terrace, Derry BT48 7EE, Northern Ireland
Tel: 028 7126 5340   Fax: 028 7136 3423

Inglewood, Lord   **EPP-ED**   **Con**   **North West**
Member Legal Affairs and Internal Market Committee
Member Constitutional Affairs Committee
Vice-chair China Delegation

Hutton-in-the-Forest, Penrith, Cumbria CA11 9TH
Tel: 017684 84500   Fax: 017684 84571

Jackson, Caroline   **EPP-ED**   **Con**   **South West**
Chair Environment, Public Health and Consumer Policy Committee
Substitute Women's Rights and Equal Opportunities Committee

European Office, 14 Bath Road, Swindon, Wiltshire SN1 4BA
Tel: 01793 422663   Fax: 01793 422664
E-mail: cj@carolinejackson.demon.co.uk
Website: www.carolinejacksonmep.org.uk

Khanbhai, Bashir   **EPP-ED**   **Con**   **Eastern**
Member Industry, External Trade, Research and Energy Committee
Substitute Development and Co-operation Committee
Member Transcaucasian Republics: Armenia, Azerbaijan and Georgia Delegation
Member ACP-EU Joint Assembly

57 Peninsula Cottage, Staitheway Road, Wroxham, Norfolk NR12 8RN
Tel: 001603 781480   Website: www.bashirkhanbhai.co.uk

Kinnock, Glenys   **PES**   **Lab**   **Wales**
Member Development and Co-operation Committee
Substitute Citizens' Freedoms and Rights, Justice and Home Affairs Committee
Chair ACP-EU Joint Assembly

Labour European Office, 16 Sachville Avenue, The Heath, Cardiff CF14 3NY
Tel: 029 2061 8337   Fax: 029 2061 8226
E-mail: gkinnock@europe-wales.new.labour.org.uk

Kirkhope, Timothy   **EPP-ED**   **Con**   **Yorkshire and the Humber**
Member Citizens' Freedoms and Rights, Justice and Home Affairs Committee
Substitute Constitutional Affairs Committee
Vice-chair EEA Joint Parliamentary Committee Delegation

7 Dewar Close, Collingham, Wetherby, North Yorkshire LS22 5JR
Tel: 01937 574649   Fax: 01937 574651   E-mail: timothy@leedsne.demon.co.uk
Website: www.kirkhope.org.uk

Lambert, Jean   **Green-EFA** **Green**   **London**
Member Employment and Social Affairs Committee
Member Petitions Committee
Substitute Citizens' Freedoms and Rights, Justice and Home Affairs Committee
Member EU-Malta Joint Parliamentary Committee Delegation

Suite 58, The Hop Exchange, 24 Southwark Street, London SE1 1TY
Tel: 020 7407 62 69   Fax: 020 7234 01 83   E-mail: jeanlambert@greenmeps.org.uk
Website: www.greenparty.org.uk

Lucas, Caroline   **Green-EFA** **Green**   **South East**
Vice-chair Foot and Mouth Temporary Committee
Member Industry, External Trade, Research and Energy Committee
Substitute Environment, Public Health and Consumer Policy Committee
Member ACP-EU Joint Assembly

Suite 58, Hop Exchange, 24 Southwark Street, London SE1 1TY
Tel: 020 7407 6281   Fax: 020 7734 0183   E-mail: carolinelucas@greenmeps.org.uk
Website: www.carolinelucasmep.org.uk

Ludford, Baroness   **ELDR**   **LD**   **London**
Member Citizens' Freedoms and Rights, Justice and Home Affairs Committee
Substitute Foreign Affairs, Human Rights, Common Security and Defence Policy Committee
Vice-chair South-east Europe Delegation
Substitute EU-Cyprus Joint Parliamentary Committee Delegation

36 St Peter's Street, London N1 8JT
Tel: 020 7288 2526   Fax: 020 7288 2581   E-mail: sludfordmep@europarl.eu.int
Website: www.sarahludfordmep.org.uk

Lynne, Liz   **ELDR**   **LD**   **West Midlands**
Member Employment and Social Affairs Committee
Substitute Foreign Affairs, Human Rights, Common Security and Defence Policy Committee
Member South Asia and SAARC Delegation

55 Ely Street, Stratford upon Avon, Warwickshire CV37 6LN
Tel: 01789 266354   Fax: 01789 268848

McAvan, Linda   **PES**   **Lab**   **Yorkshire and the Humber**
Member Foreign Affairs, Human Rights, Common Security and Defence Policy Committee
Substitute Regional Policy, Transport and Tourism Committee

Labour Constituency Office, 79 High Street, Wath upon Dearne, South Yorkshire S63 7QB
Tel: 01709 875665   Fax: 01709 874207   E-mail: lindamcavan@lindamcavanmep.org.uk

McCarthy, Arlene   **PES**   **Lab**   **North West**
Member Legal Affairs and Internal Market Committee
Substitute Regional Policy, Transport and Tourism Committee
Member ACP-EU Joint Assembly

3-5 St John Street, Manchester M3 4DN
Tel: 0161 831 9848   Fax: 0161 831 9849   E-mail: arlene.mccarthy@easynet.co.uk

MacCormick, Neil   **Green-EFA**   **SNP**   **Scotland**
Member Legal Affairs and Internal Market Committee
Substitute Constitutional Affairs Committee
Member EU-Romania Joint Parliamentary Committee Delegation

Scottish National Party, 107 McDonald Road, Edinburgh EH7 4NW
Tel: 0131 525 8918   Fax: 0131 525 8933   E-mail: nmaccmep@snp.sol.co.uk

McMillan-Scott, Edward   **EPP-ED**   **Con**   **Yorkshire and the Humber**
Member Budgets Committee
Substitute Foreign Affairs, Human Rights, Common Security and Defence Policy Committee
Member EU-Poland Joint Parliamentary Committee Delegation
Substitute EEA Joint Parliamentary Committee Delegation

1 Ash St, York YO26 4UR
Fax: 020 7222 2501

McNally, Eryl   **PES**   **Lab**   **Eastern**
Member Industry, External Trade, Research and Energy Committee
Substitute Women's Rights and Equal Opportunities Committee
Member South America and MERCOSUR Delegation

European Office, 270 St Albans Road, Watford, Hertfordshire WD24 6PE
Tel: 01923-242102   Fax: 01923-242063   Website: www.erylmcnallymep.org.uk

Martin, David   **PES**   **Lab**   **Scotland**
Member Economic and Monetary Affairs Committee
Substitute Constitutional Affairs Committee
Member Canada Delegation

PO Box 27030, Edinburgh EH10 7YP
Tel: 0131 654 1606   Fax: 0131 654 1607   E-mail: david.martin@ccis.org.uk

Miller, Bill   **PES**   **Lab**   **Scotland**
Vice-chair Legal Affairs and Internal Market Committee
Substitute Regional Policy, Transport and Tourism Committee
Member EU-Latvia Joint Parliamentary Committee Delegation

John Smith House, 145-65 West Regent Street, Glasgow G2 4 RZ
Tel: 0141 221 3024   Fax: 0141 221 4912   E-mail: bmillermep@aol.com

Moraes, Claude   **PES**   **Lab**   **London**
Member Employment and Social Affairs Committee
Substitute Citizens' Freedoms and Rights, Justice and Home Affairs Committee
Vice-chair South Africa Delegation

Labour European Office, 16 Charles Square, London N1 6HP
Tel: 020 7253 9615   Fax: 020 7253 9614
E-mail: cmoraes@europarl.fsnet.co.uk

Morgan, Eluned   **PES**   **Lab**   **Wales**
Member Budgetary Control Committee
Substitute Environment, Public Health and Consumer Policy Committee
Member Mashreq and Gulf States Delegation

Labour European Office, 16 Sachville Avenue, The Heath, Cardiff CF14 3NY
Tel: 029 2061 8337   Fax: 029 2061 8226
E-mail: emorgan@europe-wales.new.labour.org.uk
Website: www.poptel.org.uk/eluned.morgan.mep

Murphy, Simon   **PES**   **Lab**   **West Midlands**
Member Budgets Committee
Substitute Legal Affairs and Internal Market Committee
Member EU-Slovak Republic Joint Parliamentary Committee Delegation

West Midlands Labour European Office, Terry Duffy House, Thomas Street,
West Bromwich B70 6NT
Tel: 0121 569 1920   Fax: 0121 569 1935   E-mail: tony-caroll@new.labour.org.uk

Newton Dunn, Bill   **ELDR**   **LD**   **East Midlands**
Member Citizens' Freedoms and Rights, Justice and Home Affairs Committee
Substitute Industry, External Trade, Research and Energy Committee
Member Russia Delegation
Member Transcaucasian Republics: Armenia, Azerbaijan and Georgia Delegation
Member Palestinian Legislative Council Delegation

10 Church Lane, Navenby, Lincoln LN5 0EG
Tel: 01552 810812   Fax: 01552 810812   Website: www.newton-dunn.com

Nicholson, Jim   **EPP-ED**   **UUP**   **Northern Ireland**
Member Regional Policy, Transport and Tourism Committee
Substitute Agriculture and Rural Development Committee
Substitute Fisheries Committee
Substitute Foot and Mouth Temporary Committee
Chair USA Delegation

European Office, 3 Glengall Street, Belfast BT12 5AE
Tel: 028 9043 9431   Fax: 028 9024 6738   E-mail: j_nicholson@uup.org

Nicholson of Winterbourne, Baroness ELDR   **LD**   **South East**
Vice-chair Foreign Affairs, Human Rights, Common Security and Defence Policy Committee
Substitute Agriculture and Rural Development Committee
Member Mashreq and Gulf States Delegation
Substitute EU-Romania Joint Parliamentary Committee Delegation

House of Lords, London SW1A 0PW
Tel: 020 7219 3000

O'Toole, Mo   **PES**   **Lab**   **North East**
Member Culture, Youth, Education, Media and Sport Committee
Substitute Economic and Monetary Affairs Committee
Member EU-Poland Joint Parliamentary Committee Delegation

7 Palmersville, Great Lime Road, Forest Hall, Newcastle upon Tyne NE12 9HN
Tel: 0191 256 6066   Fax: 0191 256 6067   E-mail: botoolemep@aol.com

Paisley, Ian   **NA**   **DUP**   **Northern Ireland**
Member Development and Co-operation Committee
Substitute Economic and Monetary Affairs Committee
Member EU-Estonia Joint Parliamentary Committee Delegation

256 Ravenhill Road, Belfast BT6 8GF
Tel: 028 9045 4255   Fax: 028 9045 7783   E-mail: ianrkpaisley@btinternet.com

Parish, Neil   **EPP-ED**   **Con**   **South West**
Member Agriculture and Rural Development Committee
Member Foot and Mouth Temporary Committee
Substitute Environment, Public Health and Consumer Policy Committee
Substitute Fisheries Committee
Member Israel Delegation

16 Northgate, Bridgwater, Somerset TA6 3EU
Tel: 01278 423110   Fax: 01278 431034

Perry, Roy   **EPP-ED**   **Con**   **South East**
Vice-chair Petitions Committee
Member Culture, Youth, Education, Media and Sport Committee
Member Palestinian Legislative Council Delegation

Tarrants Farmhouse, Maurys Lane, Romsey, Hampshire SO51 6DA
Tel: 01794 322472   Fax: 01794 323498   E-mail: royperry@europe.com
Website: www.royperry.org

Provan, James   **EPP-ED**   **Con**   **South East**
Member Employment and Social Affairs Committee
Member Women's Rights and Equal Opportunities Committee
Member EU-Slovenia Joint Parliamentary Committee Delegation

Middle Lodge, Barns Green, near Horsham, West Sussex RH13 7NL
Tel: 01403 733700   Fax: 01403 733588   E-mail: jamesprovanmep@jamesprovan.com
Website: www.jamesprovan.com

Purvis, John   **EPP-ED**   **Con**   **Scotland**
Vice-chair Economic and Monetary Affairs Committee
Member Industry, External Trade, Research and Energy Committee
Member Mashreq and Gulf States Delegation
Substitute EU-Bulgaria Joint Parliamentary Committee Delegation

Gilmerton, St Andrews KY16 8NB
Tel: 01334 475830   Fax: 01334 477754   E-mail: purvisco@compuserve.com
Website: www.scottishtorymeps.org.uk

Read, Mel   **PES**   **Lab**   **East Midlands**
Member Industry, External Trade, Research and Energy Committee
Substitute Legal Affairs and Internal Market Committee
Member USA Delegation

East Midlands Labour MEPs - Regional Centre, 23 Barratt Lane, Attenborough,
Nottingham NG9 6AD
Tel: 0115 922 0624   Fax: 0115 922 0621
E-mail: readm@labmeps-emids.fsnet.co.uk
Website: www.labmeps-emids.fsnet.co.uk

Simpson, Brian   **PES**   **Lab**   **North West**
Member Regional Policy, Transport and Tourism Committee
Substitute Environment, Public Health and Consumer Policy Committee
Member Switzerland, Iceland and Norway Delegation
Substitute EU-Poland Joint Parliamentary Committee Delegation

Cheshire East European Office, Gilbert Wakefield House, 67 Bewsey Street, Warrington, Greater Lancashire WA2 7JQ
Tel: 01925 654074   Fax: 01925 654077   E-mail: briansimpson@lab.u-net.com

Skinner, Peter   **PES**   **Lab**   **South East**
Member Economic and Monetary Affairs Committee
Substitute Employment and Social Affairs Committee
Member USA Delegation

99 Kent Road, Dartford, Kent DA1 2AJ
Tel: 01634 409222   Fax: 01634 409333

Stevenson, Struan   **EPP-ED**   **Con**   **Scotland**
Chair Fisheries Committee
Substitute Agriculture and Rural Development Committee
Member China Delegation

Scottish Conservative and Unionist Central Office, 83 Princes Street, Edinburgh EH2 2ER
Tel: 0131 247 6890   Fax: 0131 247 6891
E-mail: struanmep@aol.com

Stihler, Catherine   **PES**   **Lab**   **Scotland**
Member Environment, Public Health and Consumer Policy Committee
Member Fisheries Committee
Substitute Foot and Mouth Temporary Committee
Member EU-Hungary Joint Parliamentary Committee Delegation

Constituency Office, Music Hall Lane, Dunfermline KY12 7NG
Tel: 01383 731 890   Fax: 01383 731 835

Stockton, Earl of   **EPP-ED**   **Con**   **South West**
Member Petitions Committee
Substitute Foreign Affairs, Human Rights, Common Security and Defence Policy Committee
Substitute Citizens' Freedoms and Rights, Justice and Home Affairs Committee
Member South Asia and SAARC Delegation

South West Region European Office, Glenthorne House, 131 Coronation Road, Redlands, Bristol BS3 1RE
Tel: 0117 953 7200   Fax: 0117 953 7261
E-mail: alexanderstockton@tory.org

Sturdy, Robert   **EPP-ED**   **Con**   **Eastern**
Member Agriculture and Rural Development Committee
Member Foot and Mouth Temporary Committee
Substitute Environment, Public Health and Consumer Policy Committee
Chair Australia and New Zealand Delegation

153 St Neots Road, Hardwick, Cambridge CB3 7QJ
Tel: 01954 211790   Fax: 01954 211786   E-mail: rsturdy@tory.org

Sumberg, David   **EPP-ED**   **Con**   **North West**
Member Foreign Affairs, Human Rights, Common Security and Defence Policy Committee
Substitute Employment and Social Affairs Committee
Member USA Delegation

Northwest Regional Office, 9 Montford Enterprise Centre, Wynford Square, Salford, Greater Manchester M5 2SN
Tel: 0161 745 7880   Fax: 0161 737 1980

Tannock, Charles   EPP-ED   Con   **London**
Member Foreign Affairs, Human Rights, Common Security and Defence Policy Committee
Substitute Economic and Monetary Affairs Committee
Substitute Environment, Public Health and Consumer Policy Committee
Member EU-Slovak Republic Joint Parliamentary Committee Delegation
Member Ukraine, Belarus and Moldova Delegation
Substitute EU-Estonia Joint Parliamentary Committee Delegation
Conservative Central Office, 32 Smith Square, London SW1P 3HH
Tel: 020 7984 8235/8231   Fax: 020 7984 8292

Titford, Jeffrey   EDD   UKIP   **Eastern**
Member Budgetary Control Committee
Member Foot and Mouth Temporary Committee
Substitute Agriculture and Rural Development Committee
Suites 1 and 2, Rochester House, 145 New London Road, Chelmsford, Essex CM2 0QT
Tel: 01245 266466/251651   Fax: 01245 252071   E-mail: ukipeast@globalnet.co.uk
Website: www.ukip.org/htm/eastern_region.html

Titley, Gary   PES   Lab   **North West**
Member Industry, External Trade, Research and Energy Committee
Substitute Foreign Affairs, Human Rights, Common Security and Defence Policy Committee
Substitute EU-Lithuania Joint Parliamentary Committee Delegation
Member EEA Joint Parliamentary Committee Delegation
Substitute EU-Slovenia Joint Parliamentary Committee Delegation
European Office, 16 Spring Lane, Radcliffe, Manchester M26 2TQ
Tel: 0161 724 4008   Fax: 0161 724 4009   E-mail: contact@gary-titley-mep.new.labour.org.uk
Website: www.garytitley.com

Van Orden, Geoffrey   EPP-ED   Con   **Eastern**
Vice-chair Foreign Affairs, Human Rights, Common Security and Defence Policy Committee
Substitute Regional Policy, Transport and Tourism Committee
Member EU-Turkey Joint Parliamentary Committee Delegation
Substitute EU-Hungary Joint Parliamentary Committee Delegation
Conservative Regional Office, 88 Rectory Lane, Chelmsford, Essex CM1 1RF
Tel: 01245 345188   Fax: 01245 269757

Villiers, Theresa   EPP-ED   Con   **London**
Member Economic and Monetary Affairs Committee
Substitute Legal Affairs and Internal Market Committee
Member EU-Cyprus Joint Parliamentary Committee Delegation
Conservative Central Office, 32 Smith Square, London SW1P 3HH
Tel: 020 7984 8227   Fax: 020 7984 8292   E-mail: tvilliers@conservatives.org.uk

Wallis, Diana   ELDR   LD   **Yorkshire and the Humber**
Member Legal Affairs and Internal Market Committee
Substitute Regional Policy, Transport and Tourism Committee
Vice-chair Switzerland, Iceland and Norway Delegation
Member EEA Joint Parliamentary Committee Delegation
Land of Green Ginger, Hull HU1 2EA
Tel: 01482 609943   Fax: 01482 609951   E-mail: dianawallismep@cix.co.uk
Website: www.dianawallismep.org.uk

Watson, Graham   ELDR   LD   **South West**
Substitute Citizens' Freedoms and Rights, Justice and Home Affairs Committee
Bagehot's Foundry, Beard's Yard, Bow Street, Langport, Somerset TA10 9PS
Tel: 01458 259176/252265   Fax: 01458 259174/253174   E-mail: euro_office@cix.co.uk
Website: www.grahamwatsonmep.org

Watts, Mark   **PES**   **Lab**   **South East**
Member Regional Policy, Transport and Tourism Committee
Substitute Employment and Social Affairs Committee
Vice-chair EU-Malta Joint Parliamentary Committee Delegation

European Office, 29 Park Road, Sittingbourne, Kent ME10 1DR
Tel: 01795 477880   Fax: 01795 437224   E-mail: mfwatts1@aol.com

Whitehead, Phillip   **PES**   **Lab**   **East Midlands**
Member Environment, Public Health and Consumer Policy Committee
Member Foot and Mouth Temporary Committee
Substitute Culture, Youth, Education, Media and Sport Committee
Member EU-Czech Republic Joint Parliamentary Committee Delegation

East Midlands Labour MEPs Regional Centre, 23 Barratt Lane, Attenborough,
Nottingham NG9 6AD
Tel: 0115 922 0624   Fax: 0115 922 0621   E-mail: whiteheadp@labmeps-emids.fsnet.co.uk
Website: www.labmeps-emids.fsnet.co.uk

Wyn, Eurig   **Green-EFA** **PC**   **Wales**
Member Culture, Youth, Education, Media and Sport Committee
Member Petitions Committee
Member Foot and Mouth Temporary Committee
Substitute Agriculture and Rural Development Committee
Member EU-Czech Republic Joint Parliamentary Committee Delegation

70 High Street, Bangor, Gwynedd LL57 1NR
Tel: 01248 352306

Wynn, Terence   **PES**   **Lab**   **North West**
Chair Budgets Committee
Substitute Budgetary Control Committee
Member Australia and New Zealand Delegation

Lakeside, Alexandra Park, Prescot Road, St Helens, Lancashire WA10 3TT
Tel: 01744 451609   Fax: 01744 29832   Website: www.terrywynn.com

Court of Justice of the European Communities

Palais de la Cour de Justice, 2925 Luxembourg
Tel: 00 352 43031 *Fax:* 00 352 4303 2600 (Press and Information)
Website: www.curia.eu.int

The Court of Justice of the European Communities and the Court of First Instance rule on questions of Union law, and whether actions by the Commission, the Council of Ministers, member governments and other bodies are compatible with the Treaties.

European Court of Auditors

12 Rue Alcide de Gasperi, 1615 Luxembourg
Tel: 00 352 4398 45410 *Fax:* 00 352 4398 46430
E-mail: firstname.surname@eca.eu.int *Website:* www.eca.eu.int

The European Court of Auditors examines all revenue and expenditure accounts of the Union. There are 15 members, one per member state (25 from 1 May 2004).

Economic and Social Committee

Rue Ravenstein 2, 1000 Brussels, Belgium
Tel: 00 32 2 546 90 11 *Fax:* 00 32 2 513 48 93
E-mail: info@esc.eu.int *Website:* www.esc.eu.int

An advisory body of the EU established by the Rome Treaties. It is consulted by the Commission and the Council and may deliver opinions on its own initiative. It has 222 members from the 15 member states, which will expand on 1 May 2004 to 350 members, including 24 from the UK.

Committee of the Regions

Rue Montoyer 92-102, 1000 Brussels, Belgium
Tel: 00 32 2 282 22 11 *Fax:* 00 32 2 282 23 25
Website: www.cor.eu.int

A consultative assembly of representatives of regional and local authorities such as mayors, county councillors and regional presidents. It began working in 1994. There are 222 members (350 from 1 May 2004) and the same number of alternative members, of which 24 members and 24 alternate members are from the UK.

European Central Bank

Postfach 160319, 60066 Frankfurt-am-Main, Germany
Tel: 00 49 69 13 440 *Fax:* 00 49 69 13 44 6000 *Website:* www.ecb.int

The bank, together with the European Union national central banks, comprises the European System of Central Banks (ESCB). The national central banks of the member states which do not participate in the euro are members of the ESCB with special status: they do not take part in the decision-making on the single monetary policy for the euro and the implementation of such decisions.

European Investment Bank

100 Boulevard Konrad Adenauer, 2950 Luxembourg
Tel: 00 352 43791 *Fax:* 00 352 43 79 31 89
E-mail: info@eib.org *Website:* www.eib.org

The EU's financing institution, providing long-term loans for capital investment.

London Office: 68 Pall Mall, London SW1Y 5ES
Tel: 020 7343 1200 *Fax:* 020 7930 9929

Dodonline

An Electronic Directory without rival...

MEPs' biographies and photographs available with daily updates
via the internet

For a *free* trial, call Yasmin Mirza, Aby Farsoun or Michael Mand on 020 7630 7643

Website Directory

Members of Parliament

Diane Abbott: www.hackney-labour.org.uk
Nick Ainger: www.nickainger.labour.co.uk
Douglas Alexander: www.douglasalexander.labour.co.uk
Richard Allan: www.sheffieldhallam.co.uk
Graham Allen: www.grahamallen.labour.co.uk
Michael Ancram: www.devizesconservatives.org.uk
James Arbuthnot: www.nehants-conservatives.org.uk
Hilary Armstrong: www.hilaryarmstrong.com
John Austin: www.john-austin-mp.org.uk
Norman Baker: www.normanbaker.org.uk
John Barrett: www.johnbarrettmp.com; www.edinburghwestlibdems.org.uk
Kevin Barron: www.rothervalley.org.uk; www.rothervalley.org.uk
John Battle: www.johnbattle-mp.org.uk
Hugh Bayley: www.hughbayley.labour.co.uk
Nigel Beard: www.mymp.org.uk/nigelbeard
Anne Begg: www.annebegg.co.uk
Stuart Bell: www.stuartbellmp.org
Andrew Bennett: www.poptel.org.uk/andrew.bennett/index.html
John Bercow: www.buckinghamconservative.co.uk
Dr Roger Berry: www.digitalbristol.org/members/rberry
Harold Best: www.haroldbest.co.uk
Clive Betts: www.integer.org.uk/labour
Tony Blair: www.number-10.gov.uk; www.sedgefieldlabour.org.uk
Hazel Blears: www.hazelblearsmp.org.uk
Bob Blizzard: bobblizzardmp.co.uk
David Blunkett: www.integer.org.uk/labour
Crispin Blunt: www.crispinbluntmp.com
Timothy Boswell: www.site.yahoo.com/daventryconservatives; www.daventryconservatives.org
Keith Bradley: www.mcr-withington-clp.new.labour.org.uk
Peter Bradley: www.peterbradley.org.uk
Ben Bradshaw: www.benbradshaw.co.uk; www.exeter-labour.org.uk
Graham Brady: www.traffordconservatives.org.uk; www.traffordconservatives.org.uk
Tom Brake: www.tombrake.co.uk
Julian Brazier: www.julianbrazier.co.uk
Colin Breed: www.forsiteuk.com/ColinBreed
Kevin Brennan: www.cardiffwestlabour.fsnet.co.uk
Annette Brooke: www.middorsetlib-dems.org.uk
Russell Brown: www.russellbrown.labour.co.uk
Malcolm Bruce: www.scotlibdems.org.uk/lp/gordon
Chris Bryant: www.chrisbryantmp.co.uk
Richard Burden: www.richardburden.com

Paul Burstow: www.burstowmp.org.uk
Alistair Burt: www.alistair-burt.co.uk
Dr Vincent Cable: www.vincentcable.com
Richard Caborn: www.integer.org.uk/labour
David Cameron: www.davidcameronmp.com
Alan Campbell: www.alancampbellmp.co.uk
Anne Campbell: www.annecampbell.org.uk
Menzies Campbell: www.scotlibdems.org.uk/lp/nefife/campbemp.htm
Ivor Caplin: www.ivorcaplinmp.com; www.labourparty.brighton.co.uk
Alistair Carmichael: www.scotlibdems.org.uk/lp/slps.htm
Roger Casale: www.rogercasale.labour.co.uk
William Cash: www.europeanfoundation.org/ef/billcash.htm
Ben Chapman: www.ben-chapman.org; www.wirral-south.co.uk
Sydney Chapman: www.barnetconservatives.co.uk/chapman.htm
David Chidgey: www.eastleighlibdems.org.uk
Michael Clapham: www.michael-clapham-mp.new.labour.org.uk
James Clappison: www.tory-herts.org
Paul Clark: www.paulclark.labour.co.uk
Charles Clarke: www.norwich-labour-mps.org.uk; www.norwich-labour-mps.org.uk
Tony Clarke: www.tonyclarke.org.uk
Geoffrey Clifton-Brown: www.cliftonbrown.co.uk; www.cotswoldconservative.co.uk
Vernon Coaker: www.vernon-coaker-mp.co.uk
Harry Cohen: www.harrycohen.labour.co.uk
Tim Collins: www.timcollins.co.uk
Michael Connarty: www.mconnartymp.org.uk
Robin Cook: www.robincook.org.uk
Jeremy Corbyn: www.northislington.freeserve.co.uk
Brian Cotter: www.briancotter.org
David Curry: www.davidcurry.co.uk/default.htm
Edward Davey: www.edwarddavey.co.uk
Valerie Davey: www.labourbriswest.demon.co.uk
Geraint Davies: www.geraintdaviesmp.org.uk; www.geraintdaviesmp.org.uk
David Davis: www.modernconservatives.com
Hilton Dawson: www.hiltondawson.fsnet.co.uk
John Denham: www.southampton-labour.org.uk
Jonathan Djanogly: www.jonathandjangoly.com
Frank Doran: www.frankdoran.org.uk
Stephen Dorrell: www.stephendorrell.org.uk
Sue Doughty: www.suedoughty.org
David Drew: www.daviddrew.ik.org
Alan Duncan: www.alanduncan.org.uk
Peter Duncan: www.peterduncan.org.uk
Gwyneth Dunwoody: www.gwynethdunwoody.co.uk
Angela Eagle: www.angelaeagle.labour.co.uk
Nigel Evans: www.nigelmp.com
Annabelle Ewing: www.annabelle-ewing.org

Michael Fabricant: www.michael.fabricant.mp.co.uk

Michael Fallon: www.sevenoaksconsassoc.freeserve.co.uk; www.sevenoaksconsassoc.freeserve.co.uk

Howard Flight: www.the-flight-site.org/

Caroline Flint: www.carolineflint.co.uk

Adrian Flook: www.TauntonTories.org.uk

Paul Flynn: www.paulflynnmp.co.uk

Barbara Follett: www.barbara-follett.org.uk

Don Foster: www.donfoster.co.uk

Michael Jabez Foster: www.1066.net/mp

Michael John Foster: www.michaelfoster.co.uk

George Foulkes: www.georgefoulkesmp.co.uk

Roger Gale: www.rogergale.co.uk

Mike Gapes: www.mikegapes.org.uk

Andrew George: www.andrewgeorge.org.uk

Neil Gerrard: www.neilgerrard.co.uk

Dr Ian Gibson: www.norwich-labour-mps.org.uk

Sandra Gidley: www.sandragidley.org

Linda Gilroy: www.lindagilroy.org.uk

Paul Goodman: www.wycombe.tory.org.uk

James Gray: www.jamesgray.org

Christopher Grayling: www.chrisgrayling.net

Damian Green: www.hardyhouse.freeserve.co.uk

Matthew Green: www.mathewgreen.org.uk

John Greenway: www.ryedaleconservatives.org.uk

Dominic Grieve: www.beaconsfield-conservatives.org.uk

Jane Griffiths: www.janestheone.com

Nigel Griffiths: www.nigelgriffiths.co.uk

Win Griffiths: www.wingriffithsmp.co.uk

John Grogan: www.johngrogan.co.uk

Peter Hain: www.peterhain.org

David Hamilton: www.davidhamilton.labour.co.uk

Fabian Hamilton: www.leedsne.co.uk

Mike Hancock: www.mikehancock.co.uk

Harriet Harman: www.harrietharman.labour.co.uk

Tom Harris: www.tomharrismp.com

Nick Harvey: www.nickharveymp.com

Sir Alan Haselhurst: www.siralanhaselhurst.net

Oliver Heald: www.oliverhealdmp.com

David Heath: www.davidheath.co.uk

David Heathcoat-Amory: wellsconservatives.org.uk

Charles Hendry: www.wealden.uk.com

John Heppell: www.john-heppell.new.labour.org.uk

Stephen Hesford: www.merseyworld.com/wwlp; www.poptel.org.uk/cfl/usr/w-wirral/

Patricia Hewitt: www.patriciahewitt.labour.co.uk

Keith Hill: www.keithhill.labour.co.uk

Mark Hoban: www.markhoban.com
Douglas Hogg: www.conservatism.org.uk/sleaford
Paul Holmes: www.paulholmes.org.uk; www.members.aol.com/liberaldems
Jimmy Hood: www.jimmyhood.labour.co.uk
Phil Hope: www.philhope.org.uk
Michael Howard: www.political.co.uk/howard
Kevin Hughes: www.doncasternorth.co.uk
Simon Hughes: www.simonhughes.org.uk
Dr Brian Iddon: www.brianiddonmp.org.uk
Eric Illsley: www.ericillsley.co.uk
Michael Jack: www.michaeljack.fylde-web.co.uk
Helen Jackson: www.integer.org.uk/labour
Robert Jackson: www.wantagecca.demon.co.uk
David Jamieson: www.davidjamieson.co.uk
Bernard Jenkin: www.bernardjenkinmp.com; www.northessex.tory.org.uk
Alan Johnson: www.alanjohnson.org
Melanie Johnson: www.welwyn-hatfield-labour02.fsnet.co.uk
Dr Lynne Jones: www.lynnejones.org.uk
Nigel Jones: www.nigeljones.org.uk
Alan Keen: www.alankeenmp.org
Ann Keen: www.annkeen.org.uk
Paul Keetch: www.paulkeetch.co.uk
Charles Kennedy: www.charleskennedy.org.uk
Robert Key: www.robertkey.com; www.salisburyconservatives.org
David Kidney: www.davidkidney.labour.co.uk; www.staffordlab.freeserve.co.uk
Oona King: www.oonaking.org.uk
Archy Kirkwood: www.archykirkwood.co.uk
Greg Knight: www.eyorksconservatives.com
Dr Stephen Ladyman: www.souththanetlp.freeserve.co.uk
Eleanor Laing: www.efca.org.uk
Jacqui Lait: www.jacquilaitmp.com
Norman Lamb: www.normanlamb.org
David Lammy: www.davidlammy.co.uk
Andrew Lansley: www.andrewlansley.co.uk
David Laws: www.davidlaws.org.uk
Bob Laxton: www.boblaxton.org.uk
Mark Lazarowicz: www.marklazarowicz.labour.co.uk
David Lepper: www.labourparty.brighton.co.uk
Tom Levitt: www.tomlevitt.org.uk
Dr Julian Lewis: www.julianlewis.net
Helen Liddell: www.helenliddellmp.co.uk
David Lidington: www.aylesbury.tory.org.uk; www.aylesbury.tory.org.uk
Peter Lilley: www.peterlilley.co.uk
Martin Linton: www.battersea.labour.co.uk
Tim Loughton: www.timloughton.com
Andrew Love: www.valleymedia.co.uk/AndyLove

Ian Lucas: www.ianlucas.co.uk

Peter Luff: www.peterluff.co.uk

Iain Luke: www.dundeeeastlabour.org.uk

John Lyons: www.johnlyons-mp.com

Siobhain McDonagh: www.siobhainmcdonagh.org.uk

John McDonnell: www.john-mcdonnell.net

Eddie McGrady: www.eddiemcgrady.com

Shona McIsaac: www.shona-mp.com

Andrew Mackay: www.andrewmackaymp.com; www.bracknellconservatives.com

Ann McKechin: www.annmckechinmp.net

Rosemary McKenna: www.rosemarymckenna.labour.co.uk

Kevin McNamara: www.kevinmcnamara.co.uk

Humfrey Malins: www.wcca.org.uk

Peter Mandelson: www.petermandelson.com

John Mann: www.johnmannmp.co.uk

John Maples: freespace.virgin.net/stratford.tory

Paul Marsden: www.paulmarsdenmp.com; www.paulmarsdenmp.com

Eric Martlew: www.geocities.com/CapitolHill/Senate/3524

Francis Maude: www.francismaude.com

Theresa May: www.tmay.co.uk

Alan Meale: www.alanmeale.co.uk

Andrew Miller: www.andrew-miller-mp.co.uk

Austin Mitchell: www.austinmitchell.org

Laura Moffatt: www.lauramoffattmp.co.uk

Chris Mole: www.ipswich-labour.org.uk

Michael Moore: www.michaelmoore.org.uk

Margaret Moran: www.margaretmoran.org

Julie Morgan: www.cardiffnorthclp.btinternet.co.uk

Malcolm Moss: www.malcmoss.easynet.co.uk

Meg Munn: www.megmunnmp.org.uk

Jim Murphy: www.jimmurphymp.com

Dan Norris: freespace.virgin.net/norris.wansdyke

Edward O'Hara: www.knowsleysouth.labour.co.uk

Lembit Öpik: www.montgomery.libdems.org

George Osborne: www.georgeosborne.co.uk; www.tattonconservatives.org.uk

Richard Ottaway: richardottaway.com

Richard Page: www.tory-herts.org

Jim Paice: www.jimpaice.com

Dr Nick Palmer: www.broxtowelabour.org

Ian Pearson: www.ianpearson.org.uk

Linda Perham: www.lindaperham.labour.co.uk

Eric Pickles: www.ericpickles.com; www.tory.org/home/bocaweb

James Plaskitt: www.jamesplaskitt.com; www.poptel.org.uk/warwickshire—labour/our—mp.htm

Michael Portillo: www.michaelportillo.co.uk; www.kcca.org.uk

Stephen Pound: www.stevepound.org.uk

Gordon Prentice: www.gordonprenticemp.com

Dawn Primarolo: www.dawnprimarolo.labour.co.uk

Mark Prisk: www.markprisk.com

Lawrie Quinn: www.lawrie-quinn.org.uk

Andy Reed: www.andyreedmp.org.uk

Alan Reid: www.argyllandbute-libdems.org.uk

Dr John Reid: www.johnreidmp.co.uk

David Rendel: www.davidrendel.org.uk

Angus Robertson: www.moraymp.org; www.moraymp.org

John Robertson: www.johnrobertsonmp.co.uk

Marion Roe: www.tory-herts.org

Andrew Rosindell: www.andrew.rosindell.com

Ernie Ross: www.sol.co.uk/e/ernross

Joan Ruddock: www.joanruddock.org.uk

David Ruffley: www.davidruffleymp.com

Bob Russell: www.bob-russell.co.uk

Martin Salter: www.martinsalter.com

Mohammad Sarwar: www.sarwar.org.uk

Phil Sawford: www.philsawford.labour.co.uk

Brian Sedgemore: www.hackney-labour.org.uk

Alan Simpson: www.alansimpsonmp.co.uk

Andrew Smith: www.andrewsmithmp.org.uk

Angela Smith: www.angelasmithmp.org

Chris Smith: www.islington.org.uk/labour

Robert Smith: www.scotlibdems.org.uk/lp/waberkin/smithmp.htm

Clive Soley: homepages.poptel.org.uk/lp.org.ruskin/soley

Caroline Spelman: www.carolinespelman.com

Richard Spring: www.richardspringmp.com

Dr Phyllis Starkey: www.phyllisstarkey.labour.co.uk

Gerry Steinberg: www.pcrrn.co.uk/steinberg/index.htm; www.gerry-steinberg.org.uk

David Stewart: www.davidstewartmp.co.uk

Gavin Strang: www.gavinstrangmp.co.uk

Gary Streeter: www.garystreeter.co.uk

Andrew Stunell: www.stunell.co.uk

Gerry Sutcliffe: www.gerrysutcliffe.labour.co.uk

Desmond Swayne: desmondswaynemp.com

Hugo Swire: www.hugoswiremp.org.uk; www.eastdevonconservatives.org.uk

Robert Syms: www.tory.org/home/poole

Mark Tami: www.marktamimp.org.uk

Ian Taylor: www.political.co.uk/iantaylor

Matthew Taylor: www.matthewtaylor.info

Stephen Timms: www.stephentimmsmp.org.uk

Mark Todd: www.marktodd.fsnet.co.uk

Dr Jenny Tonge: www.jennytonge.org.uk

Andrew Turner: www.islandmp.com

Dennis Turner: www.dfid.gov.uk

Dr Des Turner: www.desturnermp.co.uk; www.desturnermp.co.uk

Derek Twigg: www.derektwigg.org.uk/; www.haltonlabourparty.org.uk
Stephen Twigg: www.stephentwigg.com
Paul Tyler: www.paultyler.libdems.org
Bill Tynan: www.billtynan.labour.co.uk
Peter Viggers: www.peterviggers.co.uk
Robert Walter: www.robertwaltermp.com; www.northdorsetconservatives.org.uk
Claire Ward: www.watford-labour.com
Nigel Waterson: www.eastbourneconservatives.com
Angela Watkinson: www.conservatives.com
Prof Steve Webb: www.stevewebb.org.uk
Mike Weir: www.angussnp.org; www.angussnp.org
Brian White: www.brianwhite.org.uk
Dr Alan Whitehead: www.alan-whitehead.org.uk; www.southampton-labour.org.uk
Malcolm Wicks: www.malcolmwicks.labour.co.uk
Ann Widdecombe: www.annwiddecombemp.com
David Willetts: www.davidwilletts.com
Roger Williams: www.rogerwilliams.org.uk; www.rogerwilliams.org.uk
Phil Willis: www.philwillis.org.uk
Peter Wishart: www.petewishart.com
Mike Wood: www.mikewood.org.uk
Shaun Woodward: www.shaunwoodward.com
Tony Worthington: www.tonyworthington.labour.co.uk
Dr Tony Wayland Wright: www.cannock-online.co.uk/tonywright
Derek Wyatt: www.derekwyatt.labour.co.uk
Sir George Young: www.sirgeorgeyoung.org.uk
Richard Younger-Ross: www.teignbridgelibdems.com

Parliaments and Assemblies

Houses of Parliament: www.parliament.uk
Scottish Parliament: www.scotland.gov.uk
National Assembly for Wales: www.swyddfa.cymru.gov.uk/dangoseg.html
Northern Ireland Assembly: www.niassembly.gov.uk
Greater London Authority: www.london.gov.uk

Political Parties and Groupings

Alliance: www.allianceparty.org
Conservative Party: www.conservatives.com
Co-operative Party: www.co-op-party.org.uk
Crossbench Peers: www.crossbenchpeers.org.uk
Democratic Unionist Party: www.dup.org.uk
Labour Party: www.labour.org.uk
Liberal Democrats: www.libdems.org.uk
Northern Ireland Unionist Party: www.niup.org
Northern Ireland Women's Coalition: www.niwc.org
Plaid Cymru: www.plaidcymru.org

Scottish Green Party: www.scottishgreens.org.uk
Scottish Labour Party: www.scottishlabour.org.uk
Scottish Liberal Democrats: www.scotlibdems.org.uk
Scottish National Party: www.snp.org
Scottish Socialist Party: www.scottishsocialistparty.org
Sinn Fein: www.sinnfein.ie
Social Democratic and Labour Party: www.sdlp.ie
UK Unionist Party: www.ukup.org
Ulster Unionist Party: www.uup.org
Welsh Labour Party: www.waleslabourparty.org.uk
Welsh Conservative Party: www.welshconservatives.com
Welsh Liberal Democrats: www.welshlibdems.org.uk

Government Departments

British Trade International: www.tradepartners.gov.uk; www.invest.uk.com
Cabinet Office: www.cabinet-office.gov.uk
    Chartermark: www.chartermark.gov.uk
    Government Information and Communication Services: www.gics.gov.uk
    HMSO: www.hmso.gov.uk
    Office of the Civil Service Commissioners: www.civilservicecommissioners.gov.uk
    Office of the Commissioner for Public Appointments: www.ocpa.gov.uk
    Office of the e-Envoy: www.e-envoy.gov.uk
    Prime Minister's Office of Public Services Reform: www.pm.gov.uk/opsr
    Strategy Unit, Cabinet Office: www.strategy.gov.uk
Department for Constitutional Affairs: www.dca.gov.uk
    Crown Office: www.crownoffice-gov.uk
Department for Culture, Media and Sport: www.culture.gov.uk
    Cultureonline: www.cultureonline.gov.uk
Ministry of Defence: www.mod.uk
Department for Education and Skills: www.dfes.gov.uk
    Connexions National Unit: www.connexions.gov.uk
    Standards and Effectiveness Unit: www.standards.dfes.gov.uk
Department for Environment, Food and Rural Affairs: www.defra.gov.uk
Export Credits Guarantee Department: www.ecgd.gov.uk
Foreign and Commonwealth Office: www.fco.gov.uk
    FCO Association: www.fco-association.co.uk
Government News Network: www.gnn.gov.uk
Department of Health: www.doh.gov.uk
    National Cancer Services: www.guysandstthomas.nhs.uk
Home Office: www.homeoffice.gov.uk
Department for International Development: www.dfid.gov.uk
Law Officers: www.lslo.gov.uk
Leader of the House of Lords: www.cabinet-office.gov.uk
Minister without Portfolio: www.cabinet-office.gov.uk
Northern Ireland Office: www.nio.gov.uk
Office of the Deputy Prime Minister: www.odpm.gov.uk

Parliamentary Counsel Office: www.parliamentary-counsel.gov.uk
Paymaster General: www.opg.gov.uk
Performance and Innovation Unit: www.piu.gov.uk
Prime Minister's Office: www.number-10.gov.uk; www.pm.gov.uk
Privy Council Office: www.privy-council.org.uk
   Council Secretariat: www.pco.goc.uk
Regional Co-ordination Unit: www.rcu.gov.uk
Scotland Office: www.scottishsecretary.gov.uk
Social Exclusion Unit: www.socialexclusionunit.gov.uk
Department of Trade and Industry: www.dti.gov.uk
   Office of Science and Technology: www.ost.gov.uk
Department for Transport: www.dft.gov.uk
HM Treasury: www.hmt.gov.uk
   Office of Government Commerce: www.ogc.gov.uk
   Trade Partners UK: www.tradepartners.gov.uk
Treasury Solicitors: www.treasury-solicitor.gov.uk
Wales Office: www.walesoffice.gov.uk
Department for Work and Pensions: www.dfwp.gov.uk

Government Offices for the Regions

Go-East: www.go-east.gov.uk
Go-East Midlands: www.go-em.gov.uk
Go-London: www.go-london.gov.uk
Go-North East: www.go-ne.gov.uk
Go-North West: www.go-nw.gov.uk
Go-South East: www.go-se.gov.uk
Go-South West: www.gosw.gov.uk
Go-West Midlands: www.go-wm.gov.uk
Go-Yorkshire and the Humber: www.goyh.gov.uk
Regional Co-ordination Unit: www.rcu.gov.uk

Regional Development Agencies

Advantage West Midlands: www.advantagewm.co.uk
East England Development Agency: www.eeda.org.uk
East Midlands Development Agency: www.emda.org.uk
Northwest Development Agency: www.nwda.co.uk
One Northeast Development Agency: www.onenortheast.co.uk
South East England Development Agency: www.seeda.co.uk
South West England Development Agency: www.southwestrda.org.uk
Yorkshire Forward: www.yorkshire-forward.com

Non-Ministerial Departments

Assets Recovery Agency: www.homeoffice.gov.uk/index.htm
Charity Commission: www.charitycommission.gov.uk

Commissioners for the Reduction of the National Debt:
www.crnd.gov.uk/index—crnd.htm; www.dmo.gov.uk

Crown Estate: www.crownestate.co.uk

Crown Prosecution Service: www.cps.gov.uk

HM Customs and Excise: www.hmce.gov.uk

Food Standards Agency: www.food.gov.uk

Forestry Commission: www.forestry.gov.uk

Inland Revenue: www.inlandrevenue.gov.uk

Office of Fair Trading: www.oft.gov.uk

Public Works Loan Board: www.pwlb.gov.uk; www.dmo.gov.uk

Serious Fraud Office: www.sfo.gov.uk

Executive Agencies

Appeals Service: www.appeals-service.gov.uk

Army Base Repair Organisation: www.abro.mod.uk

Army Training and Recruiting Agency: www.atra.mod.uk

Business Development Service: www.nics.gov.uk/bds

Cadw/Welsh Historic Monuments: www.cadw.wales.gov.uk

Central Office of Information: www.coi.gov.uk

Central Science Laboratory: www.csl.gov.uk

Centre for Environment, Fisheries and Aquaculture Science: www.cefas.co.uk

Child Support Agency: www.csa.gov.uk

Communities Scotland: www.communitiesscotland.gov.uk

Companies House: www.companieshouse.gov.uk

Compensation Agency: www.nics.gov.uk/ca

Court Service: www.courtservice.gov.uk

Criminal Records Bureau: www.disclosure.gov.uk

Defence Analytical Services Agency: www.dasa.mod.uk

Defence Aviation Repair Agency: www.dara.mod.uk

Defence Bills Agency: www.defencebills.gov.uk

Defence Communication Services Agency: www.dei.mod.uk

Defence Estates: www.defence-estates.mod.uk

Defence Procurement Agency: www.mod.uk/dpa

Defence Science and Technology Laboratory: www.dstl.gov.uk

Defence Secondary Care Agency: www.open.gov.uk/dsca

Defence Storage and Distribution Agency – DSDA: www.dsda.org.uk

Defence Vetting Agency – DVA: www.dva.mod.uk

Disposal Services Agency: www.disposalservices.agency.mod.uk

Driver and Vehicle Licensing Agency: www.dvla.gov.uk

Driver and Vehicle Licensing Northern Ireland: www.dvlni.gov.uk

Driver and Vehicle Testing Agency: www.doeni.gov.uk/dvta

Driving Standards Agency: www.driving-tests.co.uk

Employment Tribunal Service: www.ets.gov.uk

Environment and Heritage Service: www.ehsni.gov.uk

Estyn: www.estyn.gov.uk

Fire Service College: www.fireservicecollege.ac.uk

Fisheries Research Services: www.marlab.ac.uk
Forensic Science Northern Ireland: www.fsni.gov.uk
Forensic Science Service: www.forensic.gov.uk
Forest Enterprise: www.forestry.gov.uk
Forest Research: www.forestry.gov.uk/forest—research
Forest Service: www.forestserviceni.gov.uk
Government Car and Despatch Agency: www.gcda.gov.uk
Health Estates: www.dhsspsni.gov.uk/hpss/hea
Highways Agency: www.highways.gov.uk
Historic Scotland: www.historic-scotland.gov.uk
Insolvency Service: www.insolvency.gov.uk
Invest Northern Ireland: www.investin.com
Jobcentre Plus: www.jobcentreplus.gov.uk
Land Registers of Northern Ireland: www.lrni.gov.uk
HM Land Registry: www.landregistry.gov.uk
Her Majesty's Inspectorate of Education: www.scotland.gov.uk/hmie
Maritime and Coastguard Agency: www.mcga.gov.uk
Meat Hygiene Service: www.food.gov.uk
Medical Devices Agency: www.medical-devices.gov.uk
Medicines Control Agency: www.mca.gov.uk
Met Office: www.metoffice.com
National Archives: www.nationalarchives.gov.uk
National Archives of Scotland: www.nas.gov.uk
National Savings and Investments: www.nsandi.com
National Weights and Measures Laboratory: www.nwml.gov.uk
NHS Estates: www.nhsestates.gov.uk
NHS Pensions Agency: www.nhspa.gov.uk
NHS Purchasing and Supply Agency: www.pasa.doh.gov.uk
Northern Ireland Child Support Agency: www.dsdni.gov.uk/csa/introduction.asp
Northern Ireland Prison Service: www.niprisonservice.gov.uk
Northern Ireland Statistics and Research Agency: www.nisra.gov.uk
Office for National Statistics: www.statistics.gov.uk
OGCbuying.solutions: www.ogcbuyingsolutions.gov.uk
Ordnance Survey: www.ordnancesurvey.co.uk
Ordnance Survey Mapping of Northern Ireland: www.osni.gov.uk
Patent Office: www.patent.gov.uk
Pension Service: www.thepensionservice.gov.uk
Pesticides Safety Direcorate: www.pesticides.gov.uk
Planning Inspectorate: www.planning-inspectorate.gov.uk
Planning Service: www.doeni.gov.uk/planning
HM Prison Service: www.hmprisonservice.gov.uk
Public Guardianship Office: www.guardianship.gov.uk
Public Record Office of Northern Ireland: www.proni.gov.uk
Queen Elizabeth II Conference Centre: www.qeiicc.co.uk
Queen Victoria School: www.qvs.org.uk
Radiocommunications Agency: www.radio.gov.uk

RAF Personnel Management Agency: www.raf.mod.uk/ptc/pma
RAF Training Group Defence Agency: www.tgda.gov.uk
Rate Collection Agency: www.dfpni.gov.uk/rca
Registers of Scotland: www.ros.gov.uk
Rivers Agency: www.dardni.gov.uk
Roads Service: www.drdni.gov.uk/roads
Royal Mint: www.royalmint.com
Royal Parks: www.royalparks.gov.uk
Rural Payments Agency: www.rpa.gov.uk
Scottish Agricultural Science Agency: www.sasa.gov.uk
Scottish Court Service: www.scotcourts.gov.uk
Scottish Fisheries Protection Agency: www.scotland.gov.uk/who.agencies—sfpa.asp
Scottish Prison Service: www.sps.gov.uk
Scottish Public Pensions Agency: www.scotland.gov.uk/sppa
Small Business Service: www.sbs.gov.uk
Social Security Agency: www.ssani.gov.uk
Student Awards Agency for Scotland: www.saas.gov.uk
Treasury Solicitor's Department: www.treasury-solicitor.gov.uk
UK Passport Service: www.passport.gov.uk
United Kingdom Debt Management Office: www.dmo.gov.uk
United Kingdom Hydrographic Office: www.ukho.gov.uk
Valuation and Lands Agency: www.vla.nics.gov.uk
Valuation Office: www.voa.gov.uk
Vehicle Certification Agency: www.vca.gov.uk
Vehicle Inspectorate: www.via.gov.uk
Veterans Agency: www.veteransagency.mod.uk
Veterinary Laboratories Agency: www.defra.gov.uk/vla
Veterinary Medicines Directorate: www.vmd.gov.uk
Water Service: www.waterni.gov.uk
Warship Support Agency: www.mod.uk/wsa/index.html
Welsh European Funding Office: www.wefo.wales.gov.uk
Wilton Park: www.wiltonpark.org.uk

Ombudsmen and Complaint-Handling Bodies

Adjudicator's Office: www.adjudicatorsoffice.gov.uk
Assembly Ombudsman and Commissioner for Complaints: www.ni-ombudsman.org.uk
British and Irish Ombudsman Association: www.bioa.org.uk
Broadcasting Standards Commission. www.bsc.org.uk
Commission for Local Administration in England: www.lgo.org.uk
Commissioner for Local Administration in Scotland: www.ombudslgscot.org.uk
Commissioner for Local Administration in Wales: www.ombudsman-wales.org
Complaints Adjudicator for Companies House: www.companieshouse.gov.uk
Complaints Commissioner to the General Council of the Bar: www.barcouncil.org.uk
European Ombudsman: www.euro-ombudsman.eu.int
Financial Ombudsman Service: www.financial-ombudsman.org.uk
Financial Services Ombudsman Scheme for the Isle of Man: www.gov.im/oft

Funeral Ombudsman Scheme: www.funeralombudsman.org.uk
Gibraltar Ombudsman: www.ombudsman.org.gi
Health Service Ombudsman for England: www.ombudsman.org.uk
Health Services Ombudsman for Scotland: www.ombudsman.org.uk
Health Services Ombudsman for Wales: www.ombudsman.org.uk
Independent Case Examiner: www.ind-case-exam.org.uk
Independent Complaints Reviewer: www.icrev.demon.co.uk/icrbook.htm
Independent Housing Ombudsman Scheme: www.ihos.org.uk
Local Government Ombudsman: www.lgo.org.uk
Local Government Ombudsman, Scotland: www.ombudslgscot.org.uk
Local Government Ombudsman, Wales: www.ombudsman-wales.org
Office of the Legal Services Ombudsman: www.olso.org
Office for the Supervision of Solicitors: www.oss.lawsociety.org.uk
Office of the Parliamentary Commissioner: www.ombudsman.org.uk
Office of the Subsidence Adviser: www.subsidenceadviser.org.uk
Ombudsman for Estate Agents: www.oea.co.uk
Pensions Ombudsman: www.pensions-ombudsman.org.uk
Police Complaints Authority: www.pca.gov.uk
Police Ombudsman for Northern Ireland: www.policeombudsman.org
Prisons and Probation Ombudsman: www.ppo.gov.uk
Scottish Legal Services Ombudsman: www.slso.org.uk
Scottish Parliamentary Commissioner for Administration: www.ombudsman.org.uk
Scottish Public Services Ombudsman: www.ombudsmanscotland.org.uk
Welsh Administration Ombudsman: www.ombudsman.org.uk

Regulatory Bodies

Advertising Standards Authority: www.asa.org.uk
Consumers' Association: www.which.net/
Financial Services Authority: www.fsa.gov.uk
General Consumer Council for Northern Ireland: www.consumerline.org
Heathrow Airport Consultative Committee: www.lhr-acc.org
National Consumer Council: www.ncc.org.uk
Office for Standards in Education: www.ofsted.gov.uk
Office for the Regulation of Electricity and Gas: www.ofreg.nics.gov.uk/
Office of Communications: www.ofcom.gov.uk
Office of Gas and Electricity Markets: www.ofgem.gov.uk
Office of Telecommunications: www.oftel.gov.uk
Office of the Rail Regulator and International Rail Regulator: www.rail-reg.gov.uk
Office of Water Services: www.ofwat.gov.uk
Postal Services Commission: www.postcomm.gov.uk
Postwatch: www.postwatch.co.uk
Press Complaints Commission: www.pcc.org.uk
Scottish Consumer Council: www.scotconsumer.org.uk
Strategic Rail Authority: www.sra.gov.uk
Trading Standards Institute: www.tradingstandards.gov.uk
Welsh Consumer Council: www.wales-consumer.org.uk; www.consumereducation.org.uk

Political and Parliamentary Organisations

Boundary Commission for England: www.statistics.gov.uk/pbc
Committee on Standards in Public Life: www.public-standards.gov.uk
Confederation of British Industry: www.cbi.org.uk
Electoral Commission: www.electoralcommission.org.uk
Electoral Reform Society: www.electoral-reform.org.uk
Hansard Society for Parliamentary Government: www.hansardsociety.org.uk
Inter-Parliamentary Union: www.ipn.org/english/home.htm
National Audit Office: www.nao.gov.uk
Parliamentary Counsel Office: www.parliamentary-counsel.gov.uk
Registrar of Political Parties: www.party-register.gov.uk
Study of Parliament Group: www.spg.org.uk
Trades Union Congress: www.tuc.org.uk
Whyte's Northern Ireland Election Results Site: www.ark.ac.uk/election
Working for an MP: www.adaptwestminster.co.uk

European Union

European Council: www.ue.eu.int
European Commission: www.europa.eu.int/comm/index—en.htm
UK Representation: www.cec.org.uk
Eurostat: www.europa.eu.int/comm/eurostat
Publications Office: www.eur-op.eu.int
Secretariat-General: www.europa.eu.int/comm/dgs/secretariat—general
European Parliament: www.europarl.eu.int
Court of Justice of the EC: www.curia.eu.int
European Court of Auditors: www.eca.eu.int
Committee of the Regions: www.cor.eu.int
Economic and Social Committee: www.esc.eu.int

Member State Parliaments

Austria: www.parlament.gv.at
Belgium: www.dekamer.be
Denmark: www.folketinget.dk
Finland: www.eduskunta.fi
France: www.assemblee-nat.fr
Germany: www.bundesregierung.de
Greece: www.parliament.gr
Ireland: www.irlgov.ie
Italy: www.parlamento.it
Luxembourg: www.chd.lu
Netherlands: www.parlement.nl
Portugal: www.parlamento.pt
Spain: www.congreso.es
Sweden: www.riksdagen.se
UK: www.parliament.uk

Other European Organisations

Council of Europe: www.coe.int
European Bank for Reconstruction and Development: www.ebrd.com
European Free Trade Association: www.efta.int
Nordic Council: www.norden.org
Western European Union: www.weu.int

Think Tanks

Adam Smith Institute: www.adamsmith.org.uk
Atlantic Partnership: www.atlanticpartnership.com
Bow Group: www.bowgroup.org
Britain in Europe: www.britainineurope.org
Bruges Group: www.brugesgroup.com
Business for Sterling: www.no-euro.com
Centre for Advancement of Women in Politics: www.qub.ac.uk/cawp
Campaign for Conservative Democracy: www.copov.org.uk
Catalyst Forum: www.catalyst-trust.co.uk
Centre for the Analysis of Social Exclusion: www.sticerd.lse.ac.uk/case
Centre for Defence and International Security Studies: www.cdiss.org
Centre for Economic Performance, LSE: www.cep.lse.ac.uk
Centre for Economic Policy Research: www.cepr.org.uk
Centre for Economic and Social Inclusion: www.cesi.org.uk
Centre for European Migration and Ethnic Studies: www.cemes.org
Centre for European Policy Studies: www.ceps.be
Centre for European Reform: www.cer.org.uk
Centre for Policy on Ageing: www.cpa.org.uk
Centre for Policy Studies: www.cps.org.uk
Centre for Reform: www.cfr.org.uk
Centre for the Study of Financial Innovation: www.csfi.org.uk
Charter 88: www.charter88.org.uk
Charter Movement: www.tory-charter.org.uk
Child Poverty Action Group: www.cpag.org.uk
Christian Socialist Movement: www.christiansocialist.org.uk
Civitas (The Institute for the Study of Civil Society): www.civitas.org.uk
Confederation of British Industry: www.cbi.org.uk
Conservative Christian Fellowship: www.ccfwebsite.com
Conservative Monday Club: www.conservativeuk.com
Conservatives Against a Federal Europe: www.cafe.org.uk
Conservative Way Forward: www.conwayfor.org
Constitution Unit: www.ucl.ac.uk/constitution-unit
Democratic Dialogue: www.democraticdialogue.org
Demos: www.demos.co.uk
Electoral Reform Society: www.electoral-reform.org.uk
European Foundation: www.europeanfoundation.org
European Movement: www.euromove.org.uk

European Policy Centre: www.theepc.be

Fabian Society: www.fabian-society.org.uk

Fawcett Society: www.fawcettsociety.org.uk

Federal Trust for Education and Research: www.fedtrust.co.uk

Foreign Policy Centre: www.fpc.org.uk

Global Britain: www.globalbritain.org

Hansard Society: www.hansardsociety.org.uk

Industrial Relations Research Unit: www.users.wbs.warwick.ac.uk/irru

Institute of Directors: www.iod.com

Institute of Economic Affairs: www.iea.org.uk

Institute of Employment Rights: www.ier.org.uk

Institute for Employment Studies: www.employment-studies.co.uk

Institute for Fiscal Studies: www.ifs.org.uk

Institute of Ideas: www.instituteofideas.com

Institute for Jewish Policy Research: www.jpr.org.uk

Institute for Public Policy Research: www.ippr.org.uk

Institute of Race Relations: www.irr.org.uk

Institute of Welsh Affairs: www.iwa.org.uk

International Institute for Strategic Studies: www.iiss.org

International Labour Organization: www.ilo.org

Joseph Rowntree Foundation: www.jrf.org.uk

Kings Fund: www.kingsfund.org.uk

Libertarian Alliance: www.libertarian.co.uk

Liberty: www.liberty-human-rights.org.uk

Localis: www.localis.org.uk

Margaret Thatcher Foundation: www.margaretthatcher.org

National Centre for Social Research: www.natcen.ac.uk

National Foundation for Educational Research: www.nfer.ac.uk

National Institute of Economic and Social Research (NIESR): www.niesr.ac.uk

New Economics Foundation: www.neweconomics.org

New Europe: www.new-europe.co.uk

New Health Network: www.newhealthnetwork.co.uk

New Local Government Network: www.nlgn.org.uk

New Policy Institute: www.npi.org.uk

Nexus: www.netnexus.org

Organisation for Economic Co-operation and Development: www.oecd.org

Overseas Development Institute: www.odi.org.uk

Policybrief. www.policybrief.org

Policy Studies Institute: www.psi.org.uk

Politeia: www.politeia.co.uk

Public Management Foundation: www.pmfoundation.org.uk

Regulatory Policy Institute: www.rpieurope.org

Royal Institute of International Affairs: www.riia.org

Royal United Services Institute for Defence Studies: www.rusi.org

Runnymede Trust: www.runnymedetrust.org

Science and Technology Policy Research: www.susx.ac.uk/spru

Scottish Council for Development and Industry: www.scdi.org.uk
Scottish Council Foundation: www.scottishpolicynet.org.uk
Social Affairs Unit: www.socialaffairsunit.org.uk
Socialist Educational Association: www.socialisteducation.org.uk
Socialist Health Association: www.sochealth.co.uk
Social Market Foundation: www.smf.co.uk
Society for Individual Freedom: www.individualist.org.uk
SustainAbility: www.sustainability.com
Tory Reform Group: www.trg.org.uk
TUC: www.tuc.org.uk
Work Foundation: www.theworkfoundation.com

Trades Unions

Accord (HBOS Group Staff Union): www.iuhs.org
ACM (Association for College Management): www.acm.uk.com
AEEU (Amalgamated Engineering and Electrical Union (Amicus)): www.aeeu.org.uk
AEP (Association of Educational Psychologists): www.aep.org.uk
AFA (Association of Flight Attendants): www.afalhr.org.uk
ALGUS (Alliance and Leicester Group Union of Staff): www.algus.org.uk
AMO (Association of Magisterial Officers): www.amo-online.org.uk
ANGU (Abbey National Group Union): www.angu.org.uk
ASLEF (Associated Society of Locomotive Engineers and Firemen):
www.aslef.org.uk
ATL (Association of Teachers and Lecturers): www.askatl.org.uk
AUT (Association of University Teachers): www.aut.org.uk
BACM-TEAM (British Association of Colliery Management – Technical, Energy and
Administrative Management): www.bacmteam.org.uk
BALPA (British Air Line Pilots Association): www.balpa.org.uk
BDA (British Dietetic Association): www.bda.uk.com
BECTU (Broadcasting, Entertainment, Cinematograph and Theatre Union):
www.bectu.org.uk
BFAWU (Bakers, Food and Allied Workers Union): www.bfawu.org
BOS (British Orthoptic Society): www.orthoptics.org.uk
BSU (Britannia Staff Union): www.britanniasu.org.uk
CATU (Ceramic and Allied Trades Union): www.catu.org.uk
CDNA (Community and District Nursing Association): www.cdna.tvu.ac.uk
Connect (Professionals in Communications Union): www.connectuk.org
CSP (Chartered Society of Physiotherapy): www.csp.org.uk
CWU (Communication Workers Union): www.cwu.org
CYWU (Community and Youth Workers' Union): www.cywu.org.uk
EIS (Educational Institute of Scotland): www.eis.org.uk
EQUITY (Actors Union): www.equity.org.uk
FBU (Fire Brigades Union): www.fbu.org.uk
FDA (Senior Public Servants Union): www.fda.org.uk
GMB (General Union): www.gmb.org.uk
GPMU (Graphical, Paper and Media Union): www.gpmu.org.uk

HCSA (Hospital Consultants and Specialists Association): www.hcsa.com
ISTC (Iron and Steel Workers Union): www.istc-tu.org
KFAT (National Union of Knitwear, Footwear and Apparel Trades): www.kfat.org.uk
MSF (Skilled Workers and Professionals Union): www.msf.org.uk
MU (Musicians' Union): www.musiciansunion.org.uk
Napo (Family Court and Probation Staff Union): www.napo.org.uk
NAEIAC (National Association of Educational Inspectors, Advisers and Consultants): www.naeiac.co.uk
NATFHE (University and College Lecturers' Union): www.natfhe.org.uk
NASUWT (National Association of Schoolmasters Union of Women Teachers): www.teachersunion.org.uk
NUJ (National Union of Journalists): www.nuj.org.uk
NGSU (Nationwide Group Staff Union): www.ngsu.org.uk
NUMAST (National Union of Marine, Aviation and Shipping Transport Officers): www.numast.org
NUT (National Union of Teachers): www.teachers.org.uk
PCS (Public and Commercial Services Union): www.pcs.org.uk
PFA (Professional Footballers Association): www.givemefootball.com
POA (Prison Officers Association): www.poauk.org.uk
Prospect General Union (formed from merged EMA and IPMS): www.prospect.org.uk
RMT (Rail, Maritime and Transport Workers Union): www.rmt.org.uk
SCP (Society of Chiropodists and Podiatrists): www.podiatrists-chiropodists.co.uk/
SoR (Society of Radiographers): www.sor.org
T&G (Transport and General Workers' Union): www.tgwu.org.uk
TSSA (Transport Salaried Staffs' Association): www.tssa.org.uk
UCAC (Undeb Cenedlaethol Athrawon Cymru (Welsh Education Workers Union)): www.Athrawon.com
UCATT (Union of Construction, Allied Trades and Technicians): www.ucatt.org.uk
UNIFI (Financial Sector Workers Union): www.unifi.org.uk
USDAW (Union of Shop, Distributive and Allied Workers): www.usdaw.org.uk
UNISON (General Union): www.unison.org.uk

National Newspapers

Daily Express: www.express.co.uk
Daily Mail: www.dailymail.co.uk
Daily Mirror: www.mirror.co.uk
The Daily Telegraph: www.telegraph.co.uk
Financial Times: www.ft.com
The Guardian: www.guardian.co.uk
The Independent: www.independent.co.uk
The Sun: www.the-sun.co.uk
The Times: www.thetimes.co.uk
The Independent on Sunday: www.independent.co.uk
The Mail on Sunday: www.mailonsunday.co.uk
News of the World: www.thenewsoftheworld.co.uk
The Observer: www.observer.co.uk

The Sunday Express: www.express.co.uk
Sunday Mirror: www.sundaymirror.co.uk
Sunday People: www.people.co.uk
The Sunday Telegraph: www.telegraph.co.uk
The Sunday Times: www.sunday-times.co.uk

Public Corporations

Bank of England: www.bankofengland.co.uk
British Broadcasting Corporation: www.bbc.co.uk
British Nuclear Fuels: www.bnfl.com
British Waterways Board: www.britishwaterways.co.uk
Channel Four Television Corporation: www.channel4.com
Civil Aviation Authority: www.caa.co.uk
Covent Garden Market Authority: www.cgma.gov.uk
Independent Television Commission: www.itc.org.uk
Radio Authority: www.radioauthority.org.uk
Royal Mail Group: www.royalmailgroup.com
Welsh Fourth Channel: www.s4c.co.uk

UK GOVERNMENT REPRESENTATIVES/ OVERSEAS REPRESENTATIVES IN UK

Vacher's Parliamentary Companion

Published continuously since 1832 and updated quarterly

Published quarterly, *Vacher's Parliamentary Companion* covers the UK and European political scene, with constantly updated information on:

- House of Commons
- House of Lords
- Government Departments
- Scottish Parliament
- National Assembly for Wales
- Northern Ireland Assembly
- European Union – 200-page coverage will keep you abreast of moves and appointments in the EU

To order call our Hotline now on 020 7630 7619

Vacher Dod Publishing
1 Douglas Street, London, SW1P 4PA
Tel: 020 7630 7619   Fax: 020 7233 7266
Email: subscriptions@vacherdod.co.uk
Website: www.DodOnline.co.uk

British Embassies and High Commissions

Afghanistan
(Post currently vacant)

Albania
British Embassy, Rruga, Skenderbej 12, Tirana
Tel: 00 355 42 34973   Fax: 00 355 42 47697
Ambassador: HE Richard Jones

Algeria
British Embassy, 6 Avenue Souidani
Bondjemaa, BP08 Alger-Gare 1600
Tel: 00 213 21 23 00 68
Fax: 00 213 21 23 00 67
Ambassador: HE Graham Hand

Andorra – see Spain

Angola
British Embassy, Rua Diogo Caõ, 4
(Caixa Postal 1244), Luanda
Tel: 00 244 2 334582   Fax: 00 244 2 333331
E-mail: postmaster.luanda@fco.gov.uk
Ambassador: HE John Thompson
(Non-resident: São Tomé)

Antigua and Barbuda
British High Commission, PO Box 483,
Price Waterhouse Centre, 11 Old Parham Road,
St John's
Tel: 00 1 268 462 0008/463 0010
Fax: 00 1 268 562 2124
E-mail: britishh@candw.ag
High Commissioner: HE John White
(Resides in Barbados)
Resident High Commissioner:
HE Mrs S Murphy

Argentina
British Embassy, Dr Luis Agote 2142, C1425
EOF Buenos Aires
Tel: 00 54 11 4576 2222
Fax: 00 54 11 4803 1731
E-mail: askinformation.baires@fco.gov.uk
Website: www.britain.org.ar
Ambassador:
HE Sir Robin Christopher KBE CMG

Armenia
British Embassy, 28 Charents Street, Yerevan
Tel: 00 374 1 543 822   Fax: 00 374 1 543 820
E-mail: britemb@arminco.com
Website: www.britemb.am
Ambassador: HE Thorda Abbott-Watt

Australia
British High Commission, Commonwealth
Avenue, Yarralumla, Canberra, ACT 2600
Tel: 00 61 2 6270 6666   Fax: 00 61 2 6273 3236

E-mail: bhc.canberra@uk.emb.gov.au
Website: www.britaus.net
High Commissioner:
HE Rt Hon Sir Alastair Goodlad KCMG

Austria
British Embassy, Jaurèsgasse 12, 1030 Vienna
Tel: 00 43 1 716130   Fax: 00 43 1 71613 2999
E-mail: britem@netway.at
Website: www.britishembassy.at
Ambassador: HE John Macgregor CVO

Azerbaijan
British Embassy, 2 Izmir Street, Baku 370065
Tel: 00 99 412 975188   Fax: 00 99 412 922739
E-mail: office@britemb.baku.az
Website: www.britishembassy.az
Ambassador: HE Andrew Tucker; Dr Laurie
Bristow from December 2003

Bahamas
British High Commission, Ansbacher House
(3rd Floor), East Street,
PO Box N7516, Nassau
Tel: 00 1 242 325 7471   Fax: 00 1 242 323 3871
High Commissioner: HE Roderick Gemmell

Bahrain
British Embassy, 21 Government Avenue,
Manama 306, PO Box 114
Tel: 00 973 534404   Fax: 00 973 536109
E-mail: britemb@batelco.com.bh
Website: www.ukembassy.gov.bh
Ambassador and Consul-General:
HE Robin Lamb

Bangladesh
British High Commission, United Nations
Road, Baridhara, Dhaka 1212
Tel: 00 880 2 8822705
Fax: 00 880 2 8823 437
E-mail: dhaka.press@fco.gov.uk
Website: www.ukinbangladesh.org
High Commissioner: HE David Carter CVO

Barbados
British High Commission, Lower Collymore
Rock (PO Box 676), Bridgetown
Tel: 00 1 246 430 7800
Fax: 00 1 246 430 7851
E-mail: britishhc@sunbeach.net
Website: www.britishhc.org
High Commissioner: HE John White
(Non-resident: St Lucia, Grenada, St Kitts &
Nevis, Commonwealth of Dominica, St Vincent
& the Grenadines, Antigua & Barbuda)

Belarus
British Embassy, 37 Karl Marx Street, 220030
Minsk
Tel: 00 375 172 105920
Fax: 00 375 172 292306
E-mail: britinfo@nsy.by
Ambassador: HE Brian Bennett

Belgium
British Embassy, Rue d'Arlon 85,
1040 Brussels
Tel: 00 32 2 287 62 11
Fax: 00 32 2 287 63 55
E-mail:
brussels.visa.section@brussels.mail.fco.gov.uk
Website: www.british-embassy.be
Ambassador: HE Gavin Hewitt CMG

Belize
British High Commission, PO Box 91
Belmopan, or BFPO 12
Tel: 00 501 8 22146/7   Fax: 00 501 8 22761
E-mail: brithicom@btl.net
High Commissioner: HE Philip Priestley CBE

Benin – see Nigeria

Bolivia
British Embassy, Avenida Arce 2732
(Casilla 697), La Paz
Tel: 00 591 2 2433424
Fax: 00 591 2 2431073
E-mail: ppa@mail.megalink.com
Website: www.britishembassy.gov.uk/bolivia
Ambassador: HE Bill Sinton

Bosnia and Herzegovina
8 Tina Ujevica, Sarajevo
Tel: 00 387 33 444429
Fax: 00 387 33 666131
E-mail: britem@bih.net.ba
Website: www.britishembassy.ba
Ambassador: HE Ian Cliff OBE

Botswana
British High Commission, Private Bag 0023,
Gaborone
Tel: 00 267 3 52841/2/3   Fax: 00 267 356105
E-mail: bhc@botsnet.bw
High Commissioner: HE David Merry CMG

Brazil
British Embassy, Setor de Embaixadas Sul,
Quadra 801, Lote 8 CjK Avenida das Nações,
70408-900 Brasilia-DF
Tel: 00 55 61 225 2710
Fax: 00 55 61 225 1777
E-mail: britemb@terra.com.br
Website: www.reinounido.org.br
Ambassador: HE Sir Roger Bone KCMG

Brunei
British High Commission, PO Box 2197,
Bandar Seri Begawan 8674
Tel: 00 673 2 222231   Fax: 00 673 2 234315
E-mail: brithc@brunet.bn
Website: www.britain-brunei.org
High Commissioner: HE Andrew Caie

Bulgaria
British Embassy, 9 Moskovska Street, Sofia
Tel: 00 359 2 933 9222   Fax: 00 359 2 933 9219
E-mail: britembinfo@mail.orbitel.bg
Website: www.british-embassy.bg
Ambassador: HE Ian Soutar

Burkina Faso – see Ivory Coast

Burma
British Embassy, 80 Strand Road (PO Box
No 638), Rangoon
Tel: 00 95 1 295300   Fax: 00 95 1 289566
Ambassador: HE Vicky Bowman

Burundi – see Rwanda

Cambodia
British Embassy, 29 Street 75, Phnom Penh
Tel: 00 855 23 427124   Fax: 00 855 23 427125
E-mail: britemb@bigpond.com.kh
Ambassador: HE Stephen Bridges

Cameroon
British High Commission, Avenue Winston
Churchill, BP 547, Yaoundé
Tel: 00 237 222 05 45   Fax: 00 237 222 01 48
E-mail: bhc@yaounde.mail.fco.gov.uk
Website: www.britcam.org
High Commissioner: HE Richard Wildash
(Non-resident: Chad, Central African Republic,
Equatorial Guinea, Gabon)

Canada
British High Commission, 80 Elgin Street,
Ottawa K1P 5K7
Tel: 00 1 613 237 1530   Fax: 00 1 613 237 7980
E-mail: bhc@ottawa.mail.fco.gov.uk
Website: www.britainincanada.org
High Commissioner:
HE David Reddaway CMG MBE

Cape Verde – see Senegal

Central African Republic – see Cameroon

Chad – see Cameroon

Chile
British Embassy, Av El Bosque Norte 0125,
Las Condes, Santiago
Tel: 00 56 2 370 4100   Fax: 00 56 2 335 5988
E-mail: chancery.santiago@fco.gov.uk
Website: www.britemb.cl
Ambassador: HE Richard Wilkinson CVO

China

British Embassy, 11 Guang Hua Lu, Jian Guo Men Wai, Beijing 100 600
Tel: 00 86 10 6532 1961
Fax: 00 86 10 6532 1937
E-mail:
commercialmail@peking.mail.fco.gov.uk
Website: www.britishembassy.org.cn
Ambassador: HE Christopher Hum CMG

Hong Kong

British Consulate General, No 1 Supreme Court Road, Central, Hong Kong (PO Box 528)
Tel: 00 852 2901 3000   Fax: 00 852 2901 3066
E-mail: political@britishconsulate.org.hk
Website: www.britishconsulate.org.hk
Consul-General: Sir James Hodge KCVO CMG

Colombia

British Embassy, Edificio Ing Barings, Carrera 9 No 76-49 Piso 9, Bogotá
Tel: 00 57 1 317 6690   Fax: 00 57 1 317 6298
E-mail: britain@cable.net.co
Website: www.britain.gov.co
Ambassador: HE Tom Duggin

Comoros – see Madagascar

Congo, Democratic Republic of

British Embassy, 83 Avenue du Roi Baudouin, Kinshasa
Tel: 00 243 88 46102
E-mail: ambrit@ic.cd
Ambassador: HE James Atkinson
(Non-resident: Congo Republic)

Congo, Republic of – see Congo, Democratic Republic

Costa Rica

British Embassy, Apartado 815, Edificio Centro Colon, (11th Floor), San José 1007
Tel: 00 506 258 20 25   Fax: 00 506 233 99 38
E-mail: britemb@racsa.co.cr
Ambassador and Consul-General:
HE Georgina Butler

Cote d'Ivoire – see Ivory Coast

Croatia

British Embassy, Vlaska, 121, 3rd Floor, PO Box 454, 10001 Zagreb
Tel: 00 385 1 455 5310   Fax: 00 385 1 455 1685
E-mail: british.embassyzagreb@fco.gov.uk
Ambassador: HE Nicholas Jarrold

Cuba

British Embassy, Calle 34 No. 702/4 entre 7ma Avenida 17, Miramar, Havana
Tel: 00 53 7 204 1771   Fax: 00 53 7 204 8104
E-mail: embrit@ceniai.inf.cu
Ambassador: HE Paul Hare LVO

Cyprus

British High Commission, Alexander Pallis Street (PO Box 21978), Nicosia or BFPO 567
Tel: 00 357 2 861100   Fax: 00 357 2 861125
E-mail: infobhc@cylink.com.cy
Website: www.britain.org.cy
High Commissioner: HE Mr Lyn Parker

Czech Republic

British Embassy, Thunovská 14, 118 00 Prague 1
Tel: 00 420 2 5740 2111
Fax: 00 420 2 5740 2296
E-mail: info@britain.cz
Website: www.britain.cz
Ambassador: HE Anne Pringle

Denmark

British Embassy, Kastelsvej 36/38/40, DK-2100 Copenhagen Ø
Tel: 00 45 35 44 52 00   Fax: 00 45 35 44 52 93
E-mail: info@britishembassy.dk
Website: www.britishembassy.dk
Ambassador: HE Philip Astley LVO

Djibouti – see Ethiopia

Dominica – see Barbados

Dominican Republic

British Embassy, Edificio Corominas Pepin, Ave 27 de Febrero No 233, Santo Domingo
Tel: 00 1 809 472 7111   Fax: 00 1 809 472 7574
E-mail: brit.emb.sadom@codetel.net.do
Ambassador: HE Andrew Ashcroft
(Non-resident: Haiti)

East Timor

British Embassy, Pantai Kelapa, Avenida de Portugal, Dili
Tel: 00 61 417 841 046
E-mail: dili.fco@gtnet.gov.uk
Ambassador: HE Hamish Daniel;
Tina Redshaw from December 2003

Ecuador

British Embassy, Citiplaza Building, Naciones Unidas Avenue and República de El Salvador, 14th Floor, Quito
Tel: 00 593 2 970 800   Fax: 00 593 2 970 811
E-mail: britembq@impsat.net.ec
Website: www.britembquito.org.ec
Ambassador: HE Richard Lewington

Egypt

British Embassy, 7 Ahmed Ragheb Street, Garden City, Cairo
Tel: 00 20 2 794 0852   Fax: 00 20 2 794 0859
E-mail: chancery.cairocl@fco.gov.uk
Website: www.britishembassy.org.eg
Ambassador: HE Sir Derek Plumbly

El Salvador
British Embassy, Edifio Inter-Inversiones,
Paseo General Escalón 4828, PO Box 1591,
San Salvador
Tel: 00 503 263 6527   Fax: 00 503 263 6516
E-mail: britemb.sansalv@fco.gov.uk
Ambassador and Consul-General:
HE Richard Austen MBE

Equatorial Guinea – see Cameroon

Eritrea – see Ethiopia

Estonia
British Embassy, Wismari 6, Tallinn 10136
Tel: 00 372 667 4700   Fax: 00 372 667 4755
E-mail: information@britishembassy.ee
Website: www.britishembassy.ee
Ambassador: HE Sarah Squire;
Nigel Haywood from November 2003

Ethiopia
British Embassy, Fikre Mariam Abatechan
Street, Addis Ababa
Tel: 00 251 161 2354   Fax: 00 251 161 0588
Postal address: PO Box 858
E-mail: britishembassy.addisababa@fco.gov.uk
Ambassador: HE Myles Wickstead
(Non-resident: Eritrea and Djibouti)

Fiji Islands
British High Commission, Victoria House,
47 Gladstone Road, Suva (PO Box 1355)
Tel: 00 679 311033   Fax: 00 679 301406
E-mail: ukinfo@bhc.org.fj
Website: www.ukinthepacific.bhc.org.fj
High Commissioner: HE Charles Mochan
(Non-resident: Nauru, Tuvalu and Kiribati)
HE Christopher Haslam – Deputy Head of
Mission and Consul, and non-resident
Ambassador to Micronesia, Marshall Islands,
Palau and Deputy High Commissioner to
Kiribati, Nauru and Tuvalu

Finland
British Embassy, Itainen Puistotie 17, 00140
Helsinki
Tel: 00 358 9 2286 5100
Fax: 00 358 9 2286 5284
E-mail: info@ukembassy.fi
Website: www.ukembassy.fi
Ambassador: HE Matthew Kirk

France
British Embassy, 35 rue du Faubourg St
Honoré, 75383 Paris Cedex 08
Tel: 00 33 1 44 51 31 00
Fax: 00 33 1 44 51 32 88
Website: www.amb-grandebretagne.fr
Ambassador: HE Sir John Holmes

Gabon – see Cameroon

Gambia, The
British High Commission, 48 Atlantic Road,
Fajara (PO Box 507), Banjul
Tel: 00 220 4 95133   Fax: 00 220 4 96134
E-mail: bhcbanjul@commet.gm
High Commissioner: HE Eric Jenkinson

Georgia
British Embassy, Metechi Palace Hotel,
380003 Tbilisi
Tel: 00 995 32 955 497   Fax: 00 995 32 001 065
E-mail: britishembassy@caucasus.net
Website: www.britishembassy.org.ge
Ambassador: HE Deborah Barnes Jones

Germany
British Embassy, Wilhelmstrasse 70,
10117 Berlin
Tel: 00 49 30 204570   Fax: 00 49 30 20457 574
Website: www.britischebotschaft.de
Ambassador: HE Peter Torry

Ghana
British High Commission, Osu Link, off Gamel
Abdul Nasser Avenue (PO Box 296), Accra
Tel: 00 233 21 221665   Fax: 00 233 21
7010655
E-mail: high.commission.accra@fco.gov.uk
Website:
www.britishhighcommission.gov.uk/ghana
High Commissioner: HE Dr Roderick Pullen
(Non-resident: Togo)

Greece
British Embassy, 1 Ploutarchou Street,
106 75 Athens
Tel: 00 30 1 727 2600   Fax: 00 30 1 727 2743
E-mail: information.athens@fco.gov.uk
Website: www.british-embassy.gr
Ambassador: HE David Madden CMG

Grenada
British High Commission, Netherlands
Building, Grand Anse, St George's
Tel: 00 1 473 440 3222   Fax: 00 1 473 440 4939
E-mail: bhcgrenada@caribsurf.com
High Commissioner: HE John White
(Resides in Barbados)
Resident Acting High Commissioner:
David Miller

Guatemala
British Embassy, Avenida La Reforma 16-00,
Zona 10, Edificio Torre Internacional, Nivel 11,
Guatemala City
Tel: 00 502 367 5425/29   Fax: 00 502 367 5430
E-mail: embassy@intelnett.com
Ambassador: HE Richard Lavers

Guinea – see Senegal

Guinea-Bissau – see Senegal

Guyana
British High Commission, 44 Main Street
(PO Box 10849), Georgetown
Tel: 00 592 22 65881   Fax: 00 592 22 53555
E-mail: bhcguyana@solutions2000.net
High Commissioner: HE Stephen Hiscock
(Non-resident: Suriname)

Haiti – see Dominican Republic

Holy See
British Embassy, 91 Via dei Condotti,
I-00187 Rome
Tel: 00 39 6 699 23561   Fax: 00 39 6 6994 0684
Ambassador: HE Kathryn Colvin

Honduras
British Embassy, Edificio Financiero Banexpo,
3er Piso, Boulevard San Juan Bosco, Colonia
Payaqui, PO Box 290, Tegucigalpa
Tel: 00 504 232 0612   Fax: 00 504 232 5480
E-mail: british.embassy.tegucipalpa@fco.gov.uk
Ambassador and Consul-General:
HE Kay Coombs

Hungary
British Embassy, Harmincad Utca 6,
Budapest 1051
Tel: 00 36 1 266 2888   Fax: 00 36 1 266 0907
E-mail: info@britemb.hu
Website: www.britishembassy.hu
Ambassador: HE John Nichols

Iceland
British Embassy, Laufasvegur 31,
101 Reykjavík
(Postal address: PO Box 460, 121 Reykjavík)
Tel: 00 354 550 5100   Fax: 00 354 550 5105
E-mail: britemb@centrum.is
Ambassador and Consul-General:
HE John Culver LVO

India
British High Commission, Chanakyapuri, New
Delhi 110021
Tel: 00 91 11 687 2161   Fax: 00 91 11 687 2882
E-mail:bhcndpa@w3c.com
Website: www.ukindia.com
High Commissioner: HE Sir Robertson Young
KCMG; Michael Arthur CMG from October
2003

Indonesia
British Embassy, Jalan M H Thamrin 75,
Jakarta 10310
Tel: 00 62 21 315 6264   Fax: 00 62 21 392 6263
Website: www.britain-in-indonesia.or.id
Ambassador: HE Richard Gozney CMG

Iran
British Embassy, 143 Ferdowsi Avenue, Tehran
11344, (PO Box No 11365-4474)
Tel: 00 98 21 675011   Fax: 00 98 21 6708021
E-mail: britemb@neda.net
Ambassador: HE Richard Dalton

Iraq – No representation

Ireland
British Embassy, 29 Merrion Road, Ballsbridge,
Dublin 4
Tel: 00 353 1 205 3700   Fax: 00 353 1 205 3885
E-mail: publicaffairs.dubli@fco.gov.uk
Website: www.britishembassy.ie
Ambassador: HE Sir Ivor Roberts KCMG

Israel
British Embassy, 192 Hayarkon Street,
Tel Aviv 63405
Tel: 00 972 3 7251222   Fax: 00 972 3 524 3313
E-mail: webmaster.telaviv@fco.gov.uk
Website: www.britemb.org.il
Ambassador: HE Simon McDonald

Italy
British Embassy, Via XX Settembre 80a,
00187 Rome
Tel: 00 39 6 4220 0001   Fax: 00 39 6 487 3324
E-mail: info@rome.mail.fco.gov.uk
Ambassador: HE Sir John Shepherd KCVO
CMG (Non-resident: San Marino)

Ivory Coast
British Embassy, 3rd Floor, Immeuble "Les
Harmonies", Angle Boulevard Carde et Avenue
Dr Jamot, Plateau, Abidjan
Postal address: 01 BP 2581, Abidjan 01
Tel: 00 225 2030 0800   Fax: 00 225 2030 0834
E-mail: britemb.a@aviso.ci
Website: www.britaincdi.com
Ambassador and Consul-General: HE Jean-
François Gordon (Non-resident: Burkina Faso,
Niger and Liberia)

Jamaica
British High Commission, PO Box 575,
Trafalgar Road, Kingston 10
Tel: 00 1 876 510 0700   Fax: 00 1 876 510 0737
E-mail: bhckingston@cwjamaica.com
High Commissioner: HE Peter Mathers

Japan
British Embassy, No 1 Ichiban-cho, Chiyoda-
ku, Tokyo 102-8381
Tel: 00 81 3 5211 1100   Fax: 00 81 3 5275 3164
E-mail: embassy.tokyo@fco.gov.uk
Website: www.uknow.or.jp
Ambassador:
HE Sir Stephen Gommersall KCMG

Jerusalem
British Consulate-General, 19 Nashashibi
Street, Sheikh Jarrah Quarter, PO Box 19690,
East Jerusalem 97200
Tel: 00 972 2 541 4100
Fax: 00 972 2 532 5629
E-mail: britain@palnet.com
Consul General: Geoffrey Adams

Jordan
British Embassy, (PO Box 87) Abdoun,
Amman 11118
Tel: 00 962 6 5923100
Fax: 00 962 6 5923759
E-mail: info@britain.org.jo
Ambassador: HE Christopher Prentice

Kazakhstan
British Embassy, Ul Furmanova 173, Almaty
Tel: 00 7 3272 506191
Fax: 00 7 3272 506260
E-mail: british-embassy@nursat.kz
Ambassador: HE James Sharp
(Non-resident: Kyrgyzstan)

Kenya
British High Commission, Upper Hill Road,
Nairobi, PO Box 30465
Tel: 00 254 2 714699   Fax: 00 254 2 719082
E-mail: bhcinfo@iconnect.co.ke
Website: www.britain.or.ke
High Commissioner: HE Edward Clay

Kiribati – see Fiji Islands

Korea, Democratic People's Republic
British Embassy, Munsu Dong District,
Pyongyang
Tel: 00 850 2 381 7980
Fax: 00 850 2 381 7985
Ambassador: HE David Slinn OBE

Korea, Republic (South)
British Embassy, 4 Chung-Dong, Chung-Ku,
Seoul 100-120
Tel: 00 82 2 3210 5500
Fax: 00 82 2 725 1738
E-mail: bembassy@britain.or.kr
Website: www.britishembassy.or.kr
Ambassador: HE Charles Humfrey CMG;
Warwick Morris from November 2003

Kuwait
British Embassy, Arabian Gulf Street, Postal
address: PO Box 2 Safat, 13001 Safat
Tel: 00 965 240 3334   Fax: 00 965 242 6799
E-mail: general@britishembassy-kuwait.org
Website: www.britishembassy-kuwait.org
Ambassador: HE Christopher Wilton

Kyrghyzstan – see Kazakhstan

Laos
British Embassy, PO Box 6626, Vientiane
Tel: 00 856 21 413606
Fax: 00 856 21 413607
Ambassador: HE Lloyd Barnaby Smith CMG
(Resides in Thailand)

Latvia
British Embassy, 5 J Alunana Street,
Riga LV 1010
Tel: 00 371 774 4700   Fax: 00 371 777 4707
E-mail: british.embassy@apollo.lv
Website: www.britain.lv
Ambassador: HE Andrew Tesoriere

Lebanon
British Embassy, East Beirut: 8th Street, Rabieh
Tel: 00 961 4 417007   Fax: 00 961 4 402032
E-mail: britemb@cyberia.net.lb
Website: www.britishembassy.org.lb
Ambassador: HE Richard Kinchen MVO

Lesotho
British High Commission, PO Box Ms 521,
Maseru 100
Tel: 00 266 22313961   Fax: 00 266 22310120
E-mail: hcmaseru@lesoff.co.za
Website: www.bhc.org.ls
High Commissioner: HE Francis Martin

Liberia – see Ivory Coast

Libya
British Embassy, Sharia Uahran 1,
PO Box 4206, Tripoli
Tel: 00 218 21 334 3630
Fax: 00 218 334 3634
E-mail: belibya@hotmail.com
Website: www.britain-in-libya.org
Ambassador: HE Anthony Layden

Liechtenstein – see Switzerland

Lithuania
British Embassy, 2 Antakalnio, 2055 Vilnius
Tel: 00 370 2 22 20 70
Fax: 00 370 2 72 75 79
E-mail: be-vilnius@britain.lt
Website: www.britain.lt
Ambassador: HE Jeremy Hill

Luxembourg
British Embassy, 14 Boulevard Roosevelt,
2450 Luxembourg
Tel: 00 352 22 98 64   Fax: 00 352 22 98 67
E-mail: britemb@pt.lu
Website: britishembassy.gov.uk.luxembourg
Ambassador and Consul-General:
HE Gordon Wetherell

Macedonia
British Embassy, Dimitrija Chupovski 26
(4th Floor), Skopje 1000
Tel: 00 389 91 116 772   Fax: 00 389 91 117 005
E-mail: beskopje@mt.net.mk
Website: www.britishembassy.org.uk
Ambassador: HE George Edgar

Madagascar
British Embassy, Lot II 1 164 TER, Alarobia-
Amboniloa, BP 167, Antananarivo 101
Tel: 00 261 20 2249378 Fax: 00 261 20 2249381
E-mail: ukembant@simicro.mg
Ambassador: HE Brian Donaldson
(Non-resident: Comoros)

Malawi
British High Commission, PO Box 30042,
Lilongwe 3
Tel: 00 265 772 400   Fax: 00 265 772 657
E-mail: bhclilongwe@fco.gov.uk
High Commissioner: HE Norman Ling

Malaysia
British High Commission, 185 Jalan Ampang,
50450 Kuala Lumpur, or
PO Box 11030, 50732 Kuala Lumpur
Tel: 00 60 3 2170 2200   Fax: 00 60 3 2170 2370
E-mail: press.kualalumpur@fco.gov.uk
Website: www.britain.org.my
High Commissioner: HE Bruce Cleghorn CMG

Maldives – see Sri Lanka

Mali
BP2069, Bamako
Tel: 00 223 23 34 12   Fax: 00 223 34 12
E-mail: info@britembmali.org
Ambassador: HE Graeme Loten
(Resident in Senegal)

Malta
British High Commission, PO Box 506,
7 St Anne Street, Floriana
Tel: 00 356 233134   Fax: 00 356 242001
E-mail: bhc@vol.net.mt
Website: www.britain.com.mt
High Commissioner: HE Vincent Fean

Marshall Islands – see Fiji Islands
Ambassador: HE Charles Mochan
(Resident in Fiji)

Mauritania – see Morocco

Mauritius
British High Commission, Les Cascades
Building, Edith Cavell Street, Port Louis,
PO Box 1063
Tel: 00 230 202 9400   Fax: 00 230 202 9408
E-mail: bhc@intnet.mu
High Commissioner: HE David Snoxell

Mexico
British Embassy, Rio Lerma 71,
Col Cuauhtémoc, 06500 Mexico City
Tel: 00 52 55 5242 8500
Fax: 00 52 55 5242 8517
E-mail: ukinmex@att.net.mx
Website: www.embajadabritanica.com.mx
Ambassador: HE Denise Holt

Micronesia – see Fiji Islands

Moldova
British Embassy, ASITO Building Office 320,
57/1 Banulescu-Bodoni Street, Chisinau 2005
Tel: 00 3732 238 991   Fax: 00 3732 238 992
Ambassador: HE Bernard Whiteside MBE

Monaco
British Consulate, 33 Boulevard Princesse
Charlotte, BP 265, MC 98005 Monaco CEDEX
Tel: 00 377 93 50 99 66
Fax 00 377 97 70 72 00
Consul-General: Ian Davies
(Resident in Marseilles)

Mongolia
British Embassy, 30 Enkh Taivny Gudamzh
(PO Box 703), Ulaanbaatar 13
Tel: 00 976 11 458133   Fax: 00 976 11 458036
E-mail: britemb@magicnet.mn
Ambassador and Consul-General:
HE Philip Rouse

Morocco
British Embassy, 17 Boulevard de la Tour
Hassan (BP 45), Rabat
Tel: 00 212 37 72 96 96
Fax: 00 212 37 70 45 31
E-mail: consular.rabat@fco.gov.uk
Website: www.britain.org.ma
Ambassador: HE Haydon Warren-Gash
(Non-resident: Mauritania)

Mozambique
British High Commission, Av Vladimir I Lenine
310, Caixa Postal 55, Maputo
Tel: 00 258 1 420111   Fax: 00 258 1 421666
E-mail: bhc@virconn.com
High Commissioner: HE Robert Dewar;
Howard Parkinson from December 2003

Myanmar – see Burma

Namibia
British High Commission, 116 Robert Mugabe
Avenue, PO Box 22202, Windhoek 9000
Tel: 00 264 61 274800
Fax: 00 264 61 228895
E-mail: bhc@mweb.com.na
High Commissioner: HE Alasdair MacDermott

Nauru – see Fiji Islands

Nepal
British Embassy, Lainchaur Kathmandu
(PO Box 106)
Tel: 00 977 1 410583   Fax: 00 977 1 411789
E-mail: britemb@wlink.com.np
Website: www.britain.gov.np
Ambassador: HE Keith Bloomfield

Netherlands
British Embassy, Lange Voorhout 10, 2514 ED,
The Hague
Tel: 00 31 70 427 0427   Fax: 00 31 70 427 0345
Website: www.britain.nl
Ambassador: HE Colin Budd CMG

New Zealand
British High Commission, 44 Hill Street,
Wellington 1
Tel: 00 64 4 924 2888   Fax: 00 64 4 473 4982
E-mail: ppa.mailbox@fco.gov.uk
Website: www.britain.org.nz
High Commissioner: HE Richard Fell
(Non-resident: Samoa)
(Also Governor of Pitcairn, Henderson, Ducie
& Oeno Islands)

Nicaragua
British Embassy, Plaza Churchill, Reparto "Los
Robles", Managua, Apartado A-169, Managua
Tel: 00 505 2 780014   Fax: 00 505 2 784085
E-mail: britemb@ibw.com.ni
Ambassador and Consul-General:
HE Timothy Brownhill

Niger – see Ivory Coast

Nigeria
British High Commission, Shehu Shangari Way
(North), Maitama, Abuja
Tel: 00 234 9 413 2010   Fax: 00 234 9 413 3552
E-mail: consular.@abuja@fco.gov.uk
High Commissioner: HE Philip Thomas CMG
(Non-resident: Benin)

Norway
British Embassy, Thomas Heftyesgate 8,
0244 Oslo
Tel: 00 47 23 13 27 00   Fax: 00 47 23 13 27 41
E-mail: britem@online.no
Website: www.britain.no
Ambassador: HE Mariot Leslie

Oman
British Embassy, PO Box 300, Muscat,
Postal Code 113
Tel: 00 968 693077   Fax: 00 968 693087
E-mail: enquiries.muscat@fco.gov.uk
Website: www.uk.gov.om
Ambassador: HE Stuart Laing

Pakistan
British High Commission, Diplomatic Enclave,
Ramna 5, PO Box 1122, Islamabad
Tel: 00 92 51 2822131
Fax: 00 92 51 2823439
E-mail: bhcmedia@isb.comsats.net.pk
Website: britainonline.org.pk
High Commissioner:
HE Mark Lyall Grant CMG

Palau – see Fiji Islands
Ambassador: HE Christopher Haslam
(Resident in Fiji)

Panama
British Embassy, Torre Swiss Bank, Calle 53
(Apartado 889) Zona 1, Panama City
Tel: 00 507 269 0866   Fax: 00 507 223 0730
E-mail: britemb@cwpanama.net
Ambassador and Consul-General:
HE Jim Malcolm

Papua New Guinea
British High Commission, PO Box 212,
Waigani NCD 131
Tel: 00 675 3251643
Fax: 00 675 3253547
E-mail: bhcpng@datec.com.pg
High Commissioner: HE Simon Scadden;
David Gordon-Macleod from November 2003

Paraguay
British Embassy, Avenida Boggiani 5848, C/R
16 Boqueron, Asunción
Tel: 00 595 21 612611   Fax: 00 595 21 605007
E-mail: brembasu@rieder.net.py
Ambassador and Consul-General:
HE Anthony Cantor

Peru
British Embassy, Torre Parque Mar (Piso 22),
Avenida Jose Larco 1301, Miraflores, Lima
Tel: 00 51 1 617 3000
Fax: 00 51 1 617 3100
E-mail: britemb@terra.com.pe
Website: www.britemb.org.pe
Ambassador: HE Roger Hart CMG

Philippines
British Embassy, Floors 15–17 LV Locsin
Building, 6752 Ayala Avenue, Cor Makati
Avenue, 1226 Makati, (PO Box 2927 MCPO),
Manila
Tel: 00 63 2 816 7116
Fax: 00 63 2 819 7206
E-mail: uk@info.com.ph
Website:
www.britishembassy.gov.uk/philippines
Ambassador: HE Paul Dimond

Poland

British Embassy, Aleje Roz No 1, 00-556
Warsaw
Tel: 00 48 22 6281001   Fax: 00 48 22 621 7161
E-mail: britemb@it.com.pl
Website: www.britishembassy.pl
Ambassador: HE Hon Michael Pakenham

Portugal

British Embassy, Rua de São Bernardo 33,
1249-082 Lisbon
Tel: 00 351 21 392 4000
Fax: 00 351 21 392 4185
E-mail: ppa@lisbon.mail.fco.gov.uk
Website: www.uk-embassy.pt
Ambassador: HE Glynne Evans PhD CMG DBE

Qatar

British Embassy, PO Box 3, Doha
Tel: 00 974 4421991   Fax: 00 974 4438692
E-mail: bembcomm@qatar.net.qa
Ambassador: HE David MacLennan

Romania

British Embassy, 24 Strada Jules Michelet,
70154 Bucharest
Tel: 00 40 1 201 7200   Fax: 00 40 1 201 7317
E-mail: press@bucharest.mail.fco.gov.uk
Website: www.britain.ro
Ambassador: HE Quinton Quayle

Russian Federation

British Embassy, Smolenskaya Naberezhnaya
14, Moscow 121099
Tel: 00 7 095 956 7200   Fax: 00 7 095 956 7201
E-mail: moscow@britishembassy.ru
Website: www.britemb.msk.ru
Ambassador: HE Sir Roderic Lyne KBE CMG

Rwanda

British Embassy, Parcelle No 1131, Boulevard
de l'Umuganda, Kacyira-Sud, BP 576, Kigali
Tel: 00 250 85771   Fax: 00 250 82044
E-mail: ppao@rwanda1.com
Website: www.britishembassykigali.org.rw
Ambassador: HE Sue Hogwood MBE
(Non-resident: Burundi)

St Christopher and Nevis

British High Commission, PO Box 483,
Price Waterhouse Centre, 11 Old Parham Road,
St John's, Antigua
Tel: 00 1 268 462 0008
Fax: 00 1 268 462 2806
E-mail: britishh@candw.ag
High Commissioner: HE John White (Resident
in Barbados)
Resident Acting High Commissioner:
HE Sandra Murphy

St Lucia

British High Commission, NIS Waterfront
Building, 2nd Floor (PO Box 227), Castries
Tel: 00 1 758 45 22484
Fax: 00 1 758 45 31543
E-mail: britishhc@candw.lc
High Commissioner: HE John White
(Resident in Barbados)
Resident Acting High Commissioner:
HE Peter Hughes

St Vincent and the Grenadines

British High Commission, Granby Street
(PO Box 132), Kingstown
Tel: 00 1 784 457 1701
Fax: 00 1 784 456 2750
E-mail: bhcsvg@caribsurf.com
High Commissioner: HE John White
(Resident in Barbados)
Resident Acting High Commissioner:
HE Brian Robertson

Samoa – see New Zealand

San Marino – see Italy

São Tomé & Príncipe – see Angola

Saudi Arabia

British Embassy, PO Box 94351, Riyadh 11693
Tel: 00 966 1 488 0077
Fax: 00 966 1 488 2373
E-mail: information.riyadh@fco.gov.uk
Website: www.ukm.org.sa
Ambassador:
HE Sherard Cowper-Coles CMG, LVO

Senegal

British Embassy, 20 Rue du Docteur Guillet
(BP 6025), Dakar
Tel: 00 221 823 7392   Fax: 00 221 823 2766
E-mail: britemb@telecomplus.sn
Ambassador: HE Alan Burner
(Non-resident: Cape Verde, Guinea-Bissau,
Mali, Guinea)

Serbia and Montenegro

British Embassy, Resavska 46, 11000 Belgrade
Tel: 00 381 11 645055
Fax: 00 381 11 659651
E-mail: britemb@eunet.yu
Ambassador: HE David Gowan

Seychelles

British High Commission, Oliaji Trade Centre,
PO Box 161, Victoria, Mahé
Tel: 00 248 225225   Fax: 00 248 225127
E-mail: bhcsey@seychelles.net
Website: www.bhcvictoria.sc
High Commissioner: HE Fraser Wilson

Sierra Leone
British High Commission, Spur Road, Freetown
Tel: 00 232 22 232961
Fax: 00 232 22 228169
E-mail: bhc@sierratel.sl
High Commissioner: HE Dr John Mitchiner

Singapore
British High Commission, Tanglin Road,
Singapore 247919
Tel: 00 65 6424 4200   Fax: 00 65 6424 4218
E-mail: commercial.singapore@fco.gov.uk
Website: www.britain.org.sg

Slovakia
British Embassy, Panska 16, 811 01 Bratislava
Tel: 00 421 2 5441 9632
Fax: 00 421 2 5441 0002
E-mail: bebra@internet.sk
Website: www.britemb.sk
Ambassador: HE Ric Todd

Slovenia
British Embassy, 4th Floor, Trg Republike 3,
61000 Ljubljana
Tel: 00 386 1 200 3910
Fax: 00 386 1 425 0174
E-mail: info@british-embassy.si
Website: www.british-embassy.si
Ambassador: HE Hugh Mortimer LVO

Solomon Islands
British High Commission, Telekom House,
Mendana Avenue, Honiara
Postal address: PO Box 676
Tel: 00 677 21705   Fax: 00 677 21549
E-mail: bhc@solomon.com.sb
High Commissioner: HE Brian Baldwin

Somalia – No representation

South Africa
British High Commission, 255 Hill Street,
Arcadia 0002, Pretoria 0002
Tel: 00 27 12 4831200
Fax: 00 27 12 4831302
E-mail: media.pretoria@fco.gov.uk
Website: www.britain.org.za
High Commissioner: HE Ann Grant

Spain
British Embassy, Calle de Fernando el Santo
16, 28010 Madrid
Tel: 00 34 91 700 82 00
Fax: 00 34 91 700 83 09
E-mail: webmaster@ukinspain.com
Website: www.ukinspain.com
Ambassador: HE Stephen Wright
(Non-resident: Andorra)

Sri Lanka
British High Commission, 190 Galle Road,
Kollupitiya (PO Box 1433), Colombo 3
Tel: 00 94 1 437336   Fax: 00 94 1 430308
E-mail: bhc@eureka.lk
High Commissioner: HE Stephen Evans
(Non-resident: Maldives)

Sudan
British Embassy, off Sharia Al Baladia,
Khartoum East, (PO Box No 801)
Tel: 00 249 11 777105
Fax: 00 249 11 776457
E-mail: information.khartoum@fco.gov.uk
Ambassador: HE William Patey

Suriname – see Guyana

Swaziland
British High Commission, 2nd Floor, Lilunga
House, Gilfillan Street, Mbabane
Postal address: Private Bag, Mbabane
Tel: 00 268 404 2582   Fax: 00 268 404 2585
E-mail: mbabane@fco.gov.uk
High Commissioner: HE David Reader

Sweden
British Embassy, Skarpögatan 6–8, Box 27819,
115 93 Stockholm
Tel: 00 46 8 671 3000
Fax: 00 46 8 662 9989
E-mail: britishembassy@telia.com
Website: www.britishembassy.com
Ambassador: HE John Grant CMG

Switzerland
British Embassy, Thunstrasse 50, 3005 Berne
Tel: 00 41 31 359 77 00
Fax: 00 41 31 359 77 01
E-mail: info@britain-in-switzerland.ch
Website:
www.britain-in-switzerland.ch/index2.htm
Ambassador: HE Basil Eastwood
(Non-resident: Liechtenstein);
Simon Featherstone from March 2004

Syria
British Embassy, Kotob Building, 11
Mohammad Kurd Ali Street,
Malki, PO Box 37, Damascus
Tel: 00 963 11 373 9241
Fax: 00 963 11 373 1600
Ambassador: HE Henry Hogger

Tajikistan
British Embassy, 43 Lutfiy Street, Dushanbe
Tel: 00 99 2372 242221
Fax: 00 99 2372 241477
Ambassador: Michael Smith

Tanzania
British High Commission, 78 Haile Selassie,
Dar es Salaam
Postal address: PO Box 9200, Dar es Salaam
Tel: 00 255 22 211 0101
Fax: 00 225 22 211 0102
E-mail: bhc.dar@dar.mail.fco.gov.uk
High Commissioner: HE Richard Clarke

Thailand
British Embassy, Wireless Road, Bangkok 10330
Tel: 00 66 2 305 8333   Fax: 00 66 2 255 8619
E-mail: info.bankok@fco.gov.uk
Website: www.britishemb.or.th
Ambassador: HE David Fall
(Non-resident: Laos)

Togo – see Ghana

Tonga
British High Commission, PO Box 56,
Nuku'alofa
Tel: 00 676 24285   Fax: 00 676 24109
E-mail: britcomt@kalianet.to
*High Commissioner and Consul for American
Samoa:* HE Paul Nessling

Trinidad and Tobago
British High Commission, 19 St Clair Avenue,
St Clair, Port of Spain
Tel: 00 1 868 622 2748   Fax: 00 1 868 622 4555
E-mail: csbhc@opus.co.tt
High Commissioner: HE Peter Harborne

Tunisia
British Embassy, 5 Place de la Victoire,
Tunis 1000
Tel: 00 2167 1 341 444   Fax: 00 2167 1 354 877
E-mail: british.emb@planet.tn
Website: www.britishembassy.gov.uk/tunisia
Ambassador and Consul-General:
HE Robin Kealy

Turkey
British Embassy, Sehit Ersan Caddesi 46/A,
Cankaya, Ankara
Tel: 00 90 312 455 3344
Fax: 00 90 312 455 3353
E-mail: britembinf@turk.net
Website: www.britishembassy.org.tr
Ambassador: HE Peter Westmacott CMG LVO

Turkmenistan
British Embassy, 3rd Floor, Office Building,
Ak Altin Hotel, Ashgabat
Tel: 00 993 12 363462
Fax: 00 993 12 363465
E-mail: beasb@online.tm
Website: www.britishembassytm.org.uk
Ambassador: HE Paul Brummell

Tuvalu – see Fiji Islands

Uganda
British High Commission, 10/12 Parliament
Avenue, PO Box 7070, Kampala
Tel: 00 256 41 257054   Fax: 00 256 41 257304
E-mail: bhcinfo@starcom.co.ug
Website: www.britain.or.ug
High Commissioner: HE Adam Wood

Ukraine
British Embassy, 252025 Kiev Desyatinna 9
Tel: 00 380 44 462 0011
Fax: 00 380 44 462 0013
E-mail: ukembinf@sovam.com
Website: www.britemb-ukraine.net
Ambassador: HE Robert Brinkley

United Arab Emirates
British Embassy, PO Box 248, Abu Dhabi
Tel: 00 971 2 6326600
Fax: 00 971 2 6345968
E-mail: information.abudhabi@fco.gov.uk
Website: www.britain.uae.org
British Embassy, PO Box 65, Dubai
Tel: 00 971 4397 1070   Fax:00 971 4397 2153
Ambassador: HE Richard Makepeace

United States of America
British Embassy, 3100 Massachusetts Avenue
NW, Washington DC 20008
Tel: 00 1 202 588 6500   Fax: 00 1 202 588 7870
E-mail: ppa@washington.mail.fco.gov.uk
Website: www.britainusa.com/embassy
Ambassador: HE Sir David Manning

Uruguay
British Embassy, Calle Marco Bruto 1073,
11300 Montevideo, PO Box 16024
Tel: 00 598 2 622 3630   Fax: 00 598 2 622 7815
E-mail: bemonte@internet.com.uy
Website: www.britishembassy.org.uy
Ambassador: HE John Everard

Uzbekistan
British Embassy, Ul.Gulyamova 67,
Tashkent 700000
Tel: 00 998 71 120 6451
Fax: 00 998 71 120 6549
E-mail: brit@emb.uz
Ambassador: HE Craig Murray

Vanuatu
British High Commission, KPMG House,
Rue Pasteur, Port Vila, Vanuatu, PO Box 567
Tel: 00 678 23100   Fax: 00 678 23651
E-mail: bhcvila@vanuatu.com.vu
High Commissioner: HE Michael Hill

Vatican City – see Holy See

Venezuela
British Embassy, Edificio Torre Las Mercedes
(Piso 3), Avenida La Estancia, Chuao, Caracas
1061, (Postal address: Embajada Britanica,
Apartado 1246 Caracas 1010-A)
Tel: 00 58 21 2 993 41 11
Fax: 00 58 21 2 993 99 89
E-mail: britishembassy@internet.ve
Website: www.britain.org.ve
Ambassador: HE Donald Lamont

Vietnam
British Embassy, Central Building,
31 Hai Ba Trung, Hanoi
Tel: 00 84 4 8252510   Fax: 00 84 4 8265762
E-mail: behanoi@fpt.vn
Website: www.uk-vietnam.org
Ambassador: HE Robert Gordon

Yemen
British Embassy, 129 Haddah Road, Sana'a,
Postal address: PO Box 1287
Tel: 00 967 1 264081   Fax: 00 967 1 263059
Ambassador and Consul-General:
HE Frances Guy

Zaire – see Democratic Republic of Congo

Zambia
British High Commission, 5210 Independence
Avenue (PO Box 50050), Lusaka
Tel: 00 260 1 251133
Fax: 00 260 1 253798
E-mail: brithc@zamnet.zm
High Commissioner: HE Tim David

Zimbabwe
British High Commission, Corner House,
Samora Machel Avenue/ Leopold Takawaira
Street (PO Box 4490), Harare
Tel: 00 263 4 772990
Fax: 00 263 4 774617
E-mail: british.info@fco.gov.uk
Website: www.britainzw.org
High Commissioner:
HE Brian Donnelly CMG

Missions and Delegations

**United Kingdom Permanent Representation
to the European Union**
Avenue d'Auderghem 10, 1040 Brussels,
Belgium
Tel: 00 32 2 287 82 11
Fax: 00 32 2 287 83 98
UK Permanent Representative:
HE John Grant CMG

**United Kingdom Delegation to the North
Atlantic Treaty Organisation**
NATO, Autoroute Bruxelles – Zavbentem,
Evere, 1110 Brussels, Belgium
Tel: 00 32 2 707 72 11
Fax: 00 32 2 707 75 96
E-mail: ukdelnato@csi.com
*UK Permanent Representative on the North
Atlantic Council:* HE Peter Ricketts

**United Kingdom Delegation to the Western
European Union**
Rue de la Régence 4, Room 301, 1000 Brussels,
Belgium
Tel: 00 32 2 287 63 36
Fax: 00 32 2 502 49 84
UK Permanent Representative:
HE David Richmond

**United Kingdom Permanent Representation
to the Conference on Disarmament**
37-39 Rue de Vermont, 1211 Geneva 20,
Switzerland
Tel: 00 41 22 918 23 00
Fax: 00 41 22 918 23 44
E-mail: disarm.uk@ties.itu.int
UK Permanent Representative:
HE David Broucher

**United Kingdom Mission to the Office of the
United Nations and other International
Organisations at Geneva**
37-39 Rue de Vermont, 1211 Geneva 20,
Switzerland
Tel: 00 41 22 918 23 00
Fax: 00 41 22 918 23 33
E-mail: mission.uk@ties.itu.int
UK Permanent Representative:
HE Simon Fuller CMG

**United Kingdom Delegation to the United
Nations Educational, Scientific and Cultural
Organisation (UNESCO)**
1 Rue Miollis, 75732 Paris, Cedex 15, France
Tel: 00 33 1 45 68 27 84
Fax: 00 33 1 47 83 27 77
UK Permanent Representative:
HE David Stanton

United Kingdom Mission to the United Nations
1 Dag Hammarskjold Plaza, 28th Floor, 885 Second Avenue, New York, NY 10017, USA
Tel: 00 1 212 745 9250
Fax: 00 1 212 745 9316
UK Permanent Representative to the UN and UK Representative on the Security Council:
HE Sir Emyr Jones Parry

United Kingdom Delegation to the Organisation for Economic Co-operation and Development
19 Rue de Franqueville, 75116 Paris, France
Tel: 0 33 1 45 24 98 28
Fax: 0 33 1 45 24 98 37
UK Permanent Representative:
HE Christopher Crabbie CMG;
David Lyscom from January 2004

United Kingdom Delegation to the Council of Europe
18 rue Gottfried, 67000 Strasbourg, France
Tel: 00 33 3 88 35 00 78 Fax: 00 33 3 88 36 74 39
UK Permanent Representative to the Council of Europe: HE Stephen Howarth

United Kingdom Delegation to the Organisation for Security and Co-operation in Europe (OSCE) in Vienna
Jaurèsgasse 12, 1030 Vienna, Austria
Tel: 00 43 1 716130   Fax: 00 43 1 71613 3900
Head of UK Delegation:
HE John de Fonblanque CMG

United Kingdom Missions to the United Nations in Vienna
Jaurèsgasse 12, 1030 Vienna, Austria
Tel: 00 43 1 716130   Fax: 00 43 1 71613 4900
UK Permanent Representative: HE Peter Jenkins

Visit the Vacher Dod Website . . .

www.DodOnline.co.uk

Political information updated daily

The Queen's Speech
Today's Business
This Week's Business
Progress of Government Bills
Select Committees
Government and Opposition
Stop Press News

House of Commons
House of Lords
Scottish Parliament
National Assembly for Wales
Northern Ireland Assembly
Greater London Authority
European Union

Check changes daily as they happen

London Embassies and High Commissions

Afghanistan
Embassy of the Islamic State of Afghanistan, 31 Prince's Gate, London SW7 1QQ
Tel: 020 7589 8891   Fax: 020 7581 3452
Ambassador: HE Ahmad Wali Masoud

Albania
Embassy of the Republic of Albania, 2nd Floor, 24 Buckingham Gate, London SW1E 6LB
Tel: 020 7828 8897   Fax: 020 7828 8869
Ambassador: HE Kastriot Robo

Algeria
Embassy of Algeria, 54 Holland Park, London W11 3RS
Tel: 020 7221 7800   Fax: 020 7221 0448
Ambassador: HE Ahmed Attaf

Andorra
Delegation of Andorra, 63 Westover Road, London SW18 2RF
Tel: 020 8874 4806   Fax: 020 8874 4806
Ambassador: HE Albert Pintat

Angola
Embassy of the Republic of Angola, 22 Dorset Street, London W1U 6QY
Tel: 020 7299 9850   Fax: 020 7486 9397
E-mail: embassyangola@cwcom.net
Ambassador: HE Antonio DaCosta Fernandes

Antigua and Barbuda
High Commission for Antigua and Barbuda, 15 Thayer Street, London W1M 5LD
Tel: 020 7486 7073   Fax: 020 7486 9970
E-mail: ronald@antiguahc.sonnet.co.uk
High Commissioner:
HE Sir Ronald Sanders KCN CMG

Argentina
Embassy of the Argentine Republic, 65 Brook Street, London W1Y 1YE
Tel: 020 7318 1300   Fax: 020 7318 1301
Website: www.argentine-embassy-uk.org
Ambassador: HE Vicente Berasategui

Armenia
Embassy of the Republic of Armenia, 25A Cheniston Gardens, London W8 6TG
Tel: 020 7938 5435   Fax: 020 7938 2595
Ambassador: HE Vahe Gabrielyan

Australia
Australian High Commission, Australia House, Strand, London WC2B 4LA
Tel: 020 7379 4334   Fax: 020 7240 5333
Website: www.australia.org.uk
High Commissioner: HE Michael L'Estrange

Austria
Austrian Embassy, 18 Belgrave Mews West, London SW1X 8HU
Tel: 020 7235 3731   Fax: 020 7344 0292
E-mail: embassy@austria.org.uk
Website: www.austria.org.uk
Ambassador: HE Dr Alexander Christiani

Azerbaijan
Embassy of the Azerbaijan Republic, 4 Kensington Court, London W8 5DL
Tel: 020 7938 3412   Fax: 020 7937 1783
E-mail: sefir@btinternet.com
Website: www.president.az
Ambassador: HE Rafael Ibrahimov

Bahamas
High Commission for the Commonwealth of the Bahamas, 10 Chesterfield Street, London W1X 8AH
Tel: 020 7408 4488   Fax: 020 7499 9937
E-mail: bahamas.hicom.lon@cableinet.co.uk
High Commissioner:
HE Basil O'Brien CMG

Bahrain
Embassy of the State of Bahrain, 98 Gloucester Road, London SW7 4AU
Tel: 020 7370 5132/3   Fax: 020 7370 7773
Ambassador:
HE Shaikh Khalid bin Ahmed Al Khalifa

Bangladesh
High Commission for the People's Republic of Bangladesh, 28 Queen's Gate, London SW7 5JA
Tel: 020 7584 0081   Fax: 020 7225 2130
Website:
www.bangladeshhighcommission.co.uk
High Commissioner: HE Sheikh Razzak Ali

Barbados
Barbados High Commission, 1 Great Russell Street, London WC1B 3JY
Tel: 020 7631 4975   Fax: 020 7323 6872
E-mail: barcomuk@dial.pipex.com
High Commissioner:
HE Peter Patrick Simmons

Belarus
Embassy of the Republic of Belarus, 6 Kensington Court, London W8 5DL
Tel: 020 7937 3288   Fax: 020 7361 0005
E-mail: uk@belembassy.org
Website: www.belemb.freeserve.co.uk
Ambassador: HE Alyaksei Mazhukhov

Belgium
Belgian Embassy, 103–105 Eaton Square,
London SW1W 9AB
Tel: 020 7470 3700   Fax: 020 7259 6213
E-mail: info@belgium-embassy.co.uk
Website: www.belgium-embassy.co.uk
Ambassador: HE Baron Thierry de Gruben

Belize
Belize High Commission, 22 Harcourt House,
19 Cavendish Square, London W1M 9AD
Tel: 020 7499 9728   Fax: 020 7491 4139
E-mail: bzhc-lon@btconnect.com
High Commissioner: HE Alexis Rosado

Benin
No London Embassy
Embassy of the Republic of Benin,
87 Avenue Victor Hugo, 75116 Paris, France
Tel: 00 33 1 45 00 98 82
Fax: 00 33 1 45 01 82 02
E-mail: ambassade-benin@gofornet.com
Website: www.ambassade-benin.org
Ambassador: Vacant (Resident in Paris)
Chargé d'Affaires: Antoine Dimon Afouda
Honorary Consulate: Lawrence Landau,
Dolphin House, 16 The Broadway, Stanmore,
Middlesex HA7 4DW
Tel: 020 8954 8800   Fax: 020 8954 8844

Bolivia
Bolivian Embassy, 106 Eaton Square,
London SW1W 9AD
Tel: 020 7235 4248/2557
Fax: 020 7235 1286
E-mail: info@embassyofbolivia.co.uk
Website: www.embassyofbolivia.co.uk
Ambassador: Vacant
Chargé d'Affaires: Roberto Calzadilla

Bosnia and Herzegovina
Embassy of the Republic of Bosnia and
Herzegovina, 4th Floor, Morley House,
320 Regent Street, London W1R 5AB
Tel: 020 7255 3758   Fax: 020 7255 3760
Ambassador: HE Elvira Begovic

Botswana
Botswana High Commission, 6 Stratford Place,
London W1C 1AY
Tel: 020 7499 0031   Fax: 020 7495 8595
High Commissioner: HE Roy Blackbeard

Brazil
Brazilian Embassy, 32 Green Street,
London W1Y 4AT
Tel: 020 7499 0877   Fax: 020 7493 5105
Website: www.brazil.org.uk
Ambassador: José Mauricio Bustani

Brunei
Brunei Darussalam High Commission,
19–20 Belgrave Square, London SW1X 8PG
Tel: 020 7581 0521   Fax: 020 7235 9717
High Commissioner: HE Pengiran Haji Yunus

Bulgaria
Embassy of the Republic of Bulgaria,
186–188 Queen's Gate, London SW7 5HL
Tel: 020 7584 9400/9433   Fax: 020 7584 4948
Ambassador: HE Valentin Dobrev

Burkina Faso
No London Embassy
Embassy of the Republic of Burkina Faso,
16 Place Guy d'Arezzo 16, 1060 Brussels,
Belgium
Tel: 00 32 2 345 99 12
Fax: 00 32 2 345 06 12
E-mail: ambassade.burkina@skynet.be
Ambassador: HE Kadré Désiré Ouedraogo
(Resident in Brussels)

Burma
19A Charles Street, Berkeley Square,
London W1X 8ER
Tel: 020 7499 8841   Fax: 020 7629 4169
Website: www.myanmar.com
Ambassador: HE Dr Kyaw Win

Burundi
No London Embassy
Embassy of the Republic of Burundi, 46 Square
Marie-Louise, 1000 Brussels, Belgium
Tel: 00 32 2 230 45 48
Fax: 00 32 2 230 78 83
Ambassador: HE Ferdinand Nyabenda

Cameroon
High Commission of the Republic of
Cameroon, 84 Holland Park, London W11 3SB
Tel: 020 7727 0771   Fax: 020 7792 9353
High Commissioner: HE Samuel Libock Mbei

Canada
Canadian High Commission, Macdonald House,
1 Grosvenor Square, London W1X 0AB
Tel: 020 7258 6600   Fax: 020 7258 6333
Website: www.canada.org.uk
High Commissioner: HE Mel Cappe

Cape Verde
No London Embassy
Embassy of the Republic of Cape Verde,
Burgemeester Patijnlaan 1930, 2585 CB,
The Hague, Netherlands
Tel: 00 31 70 355 36 51
Fax: 00 31 70 355 35 68
Ambassador: Vacant (Resident in The Hague)

Central African Republic
No London Embassy
Embassy of the Central African Republic,
30 rue des Perchamp, 75016 Paris, France
Tel: 00 33 1 42 24 42 56
Ambassador: Vacant (Resident in Paris)

Chad
No London Embassy
Embassy of the Republic of Chad, Boulevard
Lambermont 52, 1030 Brussels, Belgium
Tel: 00 32 2 215 19 75
Ambassador: HE Aberahim Yacoub Ndiaye
(Resident in Brussels)

Chile
Embassy of Chile, 12 Devonshire Street,
London W1N 2DS
Tel: 020 7580 6392   Fax: 020 7436 5204
E-mail: echileuk@echileuk.demon.uk
Ambassador: HE Mariano Fernandez

China
Embassy of the People's Republic of China,
49–51 Portland Place, London W1N 4JL
Tel: 020 7299 4049
Website: www.chinese-embassy.org.uk
Ambassador: HE Zha Peixin

Colombia
Colombian Embassy, Flat 3A, 3 Hans Crescent,
London SW1X 0LN
Tel: 020 7589 9177/5037   Fax: 020 7581 1829
E-mail: colombia@colombia.demon.co.uk
Ambassador: HE Alfonso Lopez

Congo, Democratic Republic of
Embassy of the Democratic Republic of Congo,
38 Holne Chase, London N2 0QQ
Tel: 020 8458 0254   Fax: 020 8458 0254
Chargé d'Affaires: Henri N'Swana

Congo, Republic of
No London Embassy
Embassy of the Republic of Congo,
37 bis Rue Paul Valery, 75116 Paris, France
Tel: 00 33 1 45 00 60 57
Ambassador: HE Henri Marie Joseph
Lopes(Resident in Paris)
Honorary Consul: Louis Muzzu,
4 Wendle Court, 131–137 Wandsworth Road,
London SW8 2LH
Tel: 020 7622 0419   Fax: 020 7622 0371

Costa Rica
Costa Rican Embassy, Flat 1, 14 Lancaster
Gate, London W2 3LH
Tel: 020 7706 8844   Fax: 020 7706 8655
E-mail: info@embcrlon.demon.co.uk
Website: www.embcrlon.demon.co.uk
Ambassador: HE Rodolfo Gutiérrez

Cote d'Ivoire – see Ivory Coast

Croatia
Embassy of the Republic of Croatia,
21 Conway Street, London W1P 5HL
Tel: 020 7387 2022
Fax: 020 7387 0310
E-mail: info-press@croatianembassy.co.uk
Ambassador: HE Josip Paro

Cuba
Embassy of the Republic of Cuba,
167 High Holborn, London WC1V 6PA
Tel: 020 7240 2488   Fax: 020 7836 2602
E-mail: embacuba.ind@virgin.net
Ambassador: HE Jose Fernandez de Cossio

Cyprus
Cyprus High Commission, 93 Park Street,
London W1K 7ET
Tel: 020 7499 8272   Fax: 020 7491 0691
E-mail: presscounsellor@chclondon.com
High Commissioner:
HE Mrs Myrna Y Kleopas

Czech Republic
Embassy of the Czech Republic, 26–30
Kensington Palace Gardens, London W8 4QY
Tel: 020 7243 1115   Fax: 020 7727 9654
E-mail: london@embassy.mzv.cz
Website: www.czech.org.uk
Ambassador: HE Štefan Füle

Denmark
Royal Danish Embassy, 55 Sloane Street,
London SW1X 9SR
Tel: 020 7333 0200
Fax: 020 7333 0270
E-mail: lonamb@um.dk
Website: www.denmark.org.uk
Ambassador: HE Tom Risdahl Jensen

Djibouti
No London Embassy
Embassy of the Republic of Djibouti,
26 Rue Emile Mènier, 75116 Paris, France
Tel: 00 33 1 47 27 49 22
Ambassador: HE Mohamed Goumaneh Guirreh
(Resident in Paris)

Dominica
Office of the High Commissioner for the
Commonwealth of Dominica,
1 Collingham Gardens, London SW5 0HW
Tel: 020 7370 5194/5
Fax: 020 7373 8743
E-mail: highcommision@dominica.co.uk
Website: www.dominica.co.uk
Acting High Commissioner: Brian Bellevue

Dominican Republic

Embassy of the Dominican Republic,
139 Inverness Terrace, London W2 6JF
Tel: 020 7727 6285   Fax: 020 7727 3693
E-mail:
general@embajadadom-london.demon.co.uk
Website: www.serex.gov.do
Ambassador: HE Rafael Ludovino Fernández

Eastern Caribbean States

see St Christopher and Nevis; St Lucia;
St Vincent and the Grenadines

Ecuador

Embassy of Ecuador, Flat 3B, 3 Hans Crescent,
London SW1X 0LS
Tel: 020 7584 2648/8084   Fax: 020 7823 9701
Ambassador Vacant
Chargé d'Affaires: Ricardo Falconi-Puig

Egypt

Embassy of the Arab Republic of Egypt,
26 South Street, London W1Y 6DD
Tel: 020 7499 3304/2401
Fax: 020 7491 1542
Website: www.egypt-embassy.org.uk
Ambassador: HE Adel El Gazzar

El Salvador

Embassy of El Salvador, Tennyson House,
159 Great Portland Street, London W1N 5FD
Tel: 020 7436 8282   Fax: 020 7436 8181
E-mail: consulsalvadoruk@compuserve.com
Ambassador: HE Eduardo Vilanova

Equatorial Guinea

No London Embassy
Embassy of the Republic of Equatorial Guinea,
29 boulevard de Courcelles, 75008 Paris,
France
Tel: 00 33 1 56 88 10 48
Fax: 00 33 1 56 88 54 58
Ambassador: Vacant
Chargé d'Affaires: Moises Mba Sima Nchama

Eritrea

Embassy of the State of Eritrea,
96 White Lion Street, London N1 9PF
Tel: 020 7713 0096   Fax: 020 7713 0161
Ambassador: HE Negassi Ghebrezghi

Estonia

Embassy of the Republic of Estonia,
16 Hyde Park Gate, London SW7 5DG
Tel: 020 7589 7690/3428
Fax: 020 7589 3430
E-mail: tvaravas@estonia.gov.uk
Website: www.estonia.gov.uk
Ambassador: HE Dr Kaja Tael

Ethiopia

Embassy of the Federal Democratic Republic of
Ethiopia, 17 Prince's Gate, London SW7 1PZ
Tel: 020 7589 7212/5
Fax: 020 7584 7054
Website: www.ethioembassy.org.uk
Ambassador: HE Fisseha Adugna

Fiji

High Commission of the Republic of Fiji,
34 Hyde Park Gate, London SW7 5DN
Tel: 020 7584 3661   Fax: 020 7584 2838
E-mail: fijirepuk@compuserve.com
High Commissioner: HE Emitai Boladuadua

Finland

Embassy of Finland, 38 Chesham Place,
London SW1X 8HW
Tel: 020 7838 6200   Fax: 020 7235 3680
Website: www.finemb.org.uk
Ambassador: HE Pertti Salolainen

France

French Embassy, 58 Knightsbridge,
London SW1X 7JT
Tel: 020 7073 1000   Fax: 020 7073 1004
E-mail: presse.londres-amba@diplomatie.fr
Website: www.ambafrance-uk.org
Ambassador: HE Gerard Errera

Gabon

Embassy of the Republic of Gabon,
27 Elvaston Place, London SW7 5NL
Tel: 020 7823 9986   Fax: 020 7584 0047
Ambassador: HE Alain Mensah-Zoguelet

Gambia, The

The Gambia High Commission,
57 Kensington Court, London W8 5DG
Tel: 020 7937 6316/7/8
Fax: 020 7937 9095
High Commissioner: HE Gibril Seman Joof

Georgia

Embassy of Georgia, 4 Russell Gardens,
London W14 8EZ
Tel: 020 7603 7799   Fax: 020 7603 6682
E-mail: geoemb@dircon.co.uk
Website: www.embassyofgeorgia.org.uk
Ambassador: HE Teimuraz Mamatsashvili

Germany

Embassy of the Federal Republic of Germany,
23 Belgrave Square, London SW1X 8PZ
Tel: 020 7824 1300   Fax: 020 7824 1435
E-mail: mail@german-embassy.org.uk
Website: www.german-embassy.org.uk
Ambassador: HE Thomas Matussek
E-mail: geoemb@dircon.co.uk

Ghana
Office of the High Commissioner for Ghana,
13 Belgrave Square, London SW1X 8PN
Tel: 020 7235 4142
Fax: 020 7245 9552
E-mail: enquiries@ghana-com.co.uk
Website: www.ghana-com.co.uk
High Commissioner: HE Isaac Osei

Greece
Embassy of Greece, 1A Holland Park,
London W11 3TP
Tel: 020 7229 3850   Fax: 020 7229 7221
E-mail: pressoffice@greekembassy.org.uk
Website: www.greekembassy.org.uk
Ambassador: HE Alexandros Sandis

Grenada
High Commission for Grenada, 8 Queen Street,
London W1X 7PH
Tel: 020 7290 2275   Fax: 020 7409 1031
E-mail:
grenada@high-commission.freeserve.co.uk
High Commissioner: HE Ruth Rouse

Guatemala
Embassy of Guatemala, 13 Fawcett Street,
London SW10 9HN
Tel: 020 7351 3042   Fax: 020 7376 5708
Ambassador: HE Alberto Sandoval

Guinea
Embassy of the Republic of Guinea, Churchill
House, Brent Street, London NW4 4DJ
Tel: 020 8457 2902   Fax: 020 8457 2603
Ambassador Ibrahima Haïdara Chérif
(Resident in Paris)

Guinea-Bissau
No London Embassy
Embassy of the Republic of Guinea-Bissau,
94 rue St Lazare, Paris 9, France
Tel: 00 33 1 45 26 18 51
Ambassador: Vacant

Guyana
High Commission for Guyana, 3 Palace Court,
Bayswater Road, London W2 4LP
Tel: 020 7229 7684-8   Fax: 020 7727 9809
High Commissioner:
HE Laleshwar K N Singh

Holy See
Apostolic Nunciature, 54 Parkside,
London SW19 5NF
Tel: 020 8946 1410/7971
Fax: 020 8947 2494
E-mail: nuntius@globalnet.co.uk
Apostolic Nuncio: HE Archbishop Pablo Puente

Honduras
Embassy of Honduras, 115 Gloucester Place,
London W1H 3PJ
Tel: 020 7486 4880   Fax: 020 7486 4550
E-mail: hondurasuk@lineone.net
Ambassador: HE Hernan Antonio Bermudez

Hungary
Embassy of the Republic of Hungary,
35 Eaton Place, London SW1X 8BY
Tel: 020 7235 5218   Fax: 020 7823 1348
Website: www.huemblon.org.uk/front.htm
Ambassador: HE Bela Szombati

Iceland
Embassy of Iceland, 2 Hans Street,
London SW1X 0JE
Tel: 020 7259 3999   Fax: 020 7245 9649
E-mail: icemb.london@utn.stjr.is
Website: www.iceland.org.uk
Ambassador: HE Sverrir Haukur Gunnlaugsson

India
Office of the High Commissioner for India,
India House, Aldwych, London WC2B 4NA
Tel: 020 7836 8484   Fax: 020 7836 4331
E-mail: hom@highcom.fsnet.co.uk
Website: www.hcilondon.org
High Commissioner: HE Ranendra Sen

Indonesia
Embassy of the Republic of Indonesia,
38 Grosvenor Square, London W1X 9AD
Tel: 020 7499 7661   Fax: 020 7491 4993
E-mail: kbri@indolondon.freeserve.co.uk
Website: www.indonesianembassy.org.uk
Ambassador: Vacant
Chargé d'Affaires: Nicholas Tandi Dammen

Iran
Embassy of the Islamic Republic of Iran,
16 Prince's Gate, London SW7 1PT
Tel: 020 7225 3000   Fax: 020 7589 4440
E-mail: info@iran-embassy.org.uk
Website: www.iran-embassy.org.uk
Ambassador: HE Morteza Sarmadi

Iraq
Diplomatic Relations broken February 1991
Iraqi Interests Section: Embassy of the
Hashemite Kingdom of Jordan,
21 Queen's Gate, London SW7 5JG
Tel: 020 7584 7141   Fax: 020 7584 7716
Minister/Head of Iraqi Interests Section:
Dr Mudhafer Amin

Ireland
Irish Embassy, 17 Grosvenor Place, London
SW1X 7HR
Tel: 020 7235 2171   Fax: 020 7245 6961
Ambassador: HE Daithi O Ceallaigh

Israel
Embassy of Israel, 2 Palace Green,
London W8 4QB
Tel: 020 7957 9500   Fax: 020 7957 9555
E-mail: info@israel-embassy.org.uk
Website: www.israel-embassy.org.uk
Ambassador: HE Zvi M Shtauber

Italy
Italian Embassy, 14 Three Kings Yard,
Davies Street, London W1Y 2EH
Tel: 020 7312 2200   Fax: 020 7312 2230
E-mail: emblondon@embitaly.org.uk
Website: www.embitaly.org.uk
Ambassador: HE Luigi Amaduzzi

Ivory Coast
Embassy of the Republic of Côte d'Ivoire,
2 Upper Belgrave Street, London SW1X 8BJ
Tel: 020 7235 6991   Fax: 020 7259 5320
Ambassador: HE Youssoufou Bamba

Jamaica
Jamaican High Commission,
1–2 Prince Consort Road, London SW7 2BZ
Tel: 020 7823 9911   Fax: 020 7589 5154
E-mail: jamhigh@jhcuk.com
Website: www.jhcuk.com
High Commissioner: HE Maxine Roberts

Japan
Embassy of Japan, 101–104 Piccadilly,
London W1V 9FN
Tel: 020 7465 6500   Fax: 020 7491 9348
E-mail: info@embjapan.org.uk
Website: www.embjapan.org.uk
Ambassador: HE Masaki Orita

Jordan
Embassy of the Hashemite Kingdom of Jordan,
6 Upper Phillimore Gardens, London W8 7HB
Tel: 020 7937 3685
Fax: 020 7937 8795
E-mail: lonemb@dircon.co.uk
Website: www.jordanembassyuk.gov.jo
Ambassador: HE Timoor Ghazi Daghistani

Kazakhstan
Embassy of the Republic of Kazakhstan,
33 Thurloe Square, London SW7 2DS
Tel: 020 7581 4646   Fax: 020 7584 8481
Ambassador: Erlan Idrissov

Kenya
Kenya High Commission, 45 Portland Place,
London W1N 4AS
Tel: 020 7636 2371/5
Fax: 020 7323 6717
High Commissioner: HE Mrs Nancy Kirui

Kiribati
Kiribati High Commission, c/o Office of the
President, PO Box 68, Bairiki, Tarawa, Kiribati
Acting High Commissioner: David Yeeting
(Resident in Tarawa, Kiribati)

Korea, Democratic People's Republic (North)
Chargé d'Affaires: Ri Si Hong

Korea, Republic (South)
Embassy of the Republic of Korea,
60 Buckingham Gate, London SW1E 6AJ
Tel: 020 7227 5500
Fax: 020 7227 5503
Website: www.mofat.go.kr/uk.htm
Ambassador: HE Lee Tae-sik

Kuwait
Embassy of the State of Kuwait, 2 Albert Gate,
London SW1X 7JU
Tel: 020 7590 3400   Fax: 020 7823 1712
E-mail: kuwait@dircon.co.uk
Website: www.kuwaitinfo.org.uk
Ambassador:
HE Khaled A A S Al Duwaisan GCVO

Kyrgyzstan
Embassy of the Kyrgyz Republic, Ascot House,
119 Crawford Street, London W1H 1AF
Tel: 020 7935 1462   Fax: 020 7935 7449
E-mail: embassy@kyrgyz-embassy.org.uk
Ambassador: Vacant
Chargé d'Affaires: Kanat Tursunkulov

Laos
No London Embassy
Embassy of the Lao People's Democratic
Republic, 74 Avenue Raymond-Poincaré,
75116 Paris, France
Tel: 00 33 1 45 53 02 98
Fax: 00 33 1 47 27 57 89
Ambassador: Soutsakhone Pathammavong
(Resident in Paris)

Latvia
Embassy of the Republic of Latvia,
45 Nottingham Place, London W1M 3FE
Tel: 020 7312 0040   Fax: 020 7312 0042
E-mail: latemb@dircon.co.uk
Ambassador: HE Janis Dripe

Lebanon
Lebanese Embassy, 21 Kensington Palace
Gardens, London W8 4QM
Tel: 020 7229 7265
Fax: 020 7243 1699
E-mail: emb.leb@btinternet.com
Ambassador: HE Jihad Mortada

Lesotho
High Commission for the Kingdom of Lesotho,
7 Chesham Place, London SW1 8HN
Tel: 020 7235 5686   Fax: 020 7235 5023
E-mail:
lesotholondonhighcom@compuserve.com
High Commissioner:
HE Miss Lebohang Ramohlanka

Liberia
Embassy of the Republic of Liberia,
2 Pembridge Place, London W2 4XB
Tel: 020 7221 1036
Ambassador: Vacant
Chargé d'Affaires:
Jeff Gongoer Dowana, Senior

Libya
Libyan People's Bureau, 61-62 Ennismore
Gardens, London SW7 1NH
Tel: 020 7589 6120   Fax: 020 7589 6087
Ambassador:
HE Mohamed Abu Al Qassim Azwai

Lithuania
Embassy of the Republic of Lithuania,
84 Gloucester Place, London W1V 6AU
Tel: 020 7486 6401   Fax: 020 7486 6403
E-mail: lralon@globalnet.co.uk
Ambassador: HE Aurimas Taurantas

Luxembourg
Embassy of Luxembourg, 27 Wilton Crescent,
London SW1X 8SD
Tel: 020 7235 6961   Fax: 020 7235 9734
Ambassador: HE Jean-Louis Wolzfeld

Macedonia
Embassy of the Republic of Macedonia,
25 James Street, London W1U 1DU
Tel: 020 7935 2823   Fax: 020 7935 3842
E-mail: mkuk@btinternet.com
Ambassador: HE Stevo Crvenkovski

Madagascar
No London Embassy
Embassy of the Republic of Madagascar,
4 Avenue Raphael, 75016 Paris, France
Tel: 00 33 1 45 04 62 11
Fax: 00 33 1 40 72 75 28
Ambassador: Vacant (Resident in Paris)
Chargé d'Affaires: Maxime Eloi Dovo

Malawi
High Commission for the Republic of Malawi,
33 Grosvenor Street, London W1X 0DE
Tel: 020 7491 4172/7   Fax: 020 7491 9916
High Commissioner:
HE Mr Bright Mcbin Msaka

Malaysia
Malaysian High Commission,
45 Belgrave Square, London SW1X 8QT
Tel: 020 7235 8033   Fax: 020 7235 5161
E-mail: mwlondon@btinternet.com
High Commissioner:
HE Dato Haji Salim Hashim

Maldives
High Commission of the Republic of Maldives,
22 Nottingham Place, London W1M 3FB
Tel: 020 7224 2135   Fax: 020 7224 2157
E-mail: maldives.high.commission@virgin.net
Acting High Commissioner: HE Adam Hassan

Mali
No London Embassy
Embassy of the Republic of Mali, Avenue
Moliére 487, 1050 Brussels, Belgium
Tel: 00 32 2 345 74 32
Fax: 00 32 2 344 57 00
Ambassador: HE Ahmed Mohamed AG
Hamani (Resident in Brussels)

Malta
Malta High Commission, Malta House,
36–38 Piccadilly, London W1P 0PQ
Tel: 020 7292 4800   Fax: 020 7734 1831
High Commissioner:
HE Dr George Bonello Dupuis

Mauritania
Embassy of the Islamic Republic of Mauritania,
8 Carlos Place, London W1K 3AS
Tel: 020 7478 9323   Fax: 020 7478 9339
Ambassador: HE Dr Diaganna Youssouf

Mauritius
Mauritius High Commission,
32/33 Elvaston Place, London SW7 5NW
Tel: 020 7225 3331   Fax: 020 7225 1135
High Commissioner:
HE Mohunlall Goburdhun

Mexico
Embassy of Mexico, 42 Hertford Street,
London W1Y 7TF
Tel: 020 7499 8586   Fax: 020 7495 4035
Website: www.demon.co.uk/mexuk
Ambassador: HE Alma Rosa Moreno Razo

Moldova
No London Embassy
Embassy of the Republic of Moldova,
Rue de Tenbosch 54, 1050 Brussels, Belgium
Tel: 00 32 2 732 93 00
Fax: 00 32 2 732 96 60
Ambassador: Vacant (Resident in Brussels)
Chargé d'affaires: Alexei Cracan

Mongolia
Embassy of Mongolia, 7 Kensington Court,
London W8 5DL
Tel: 020 7937 0150
E-mail: embmong@aol.com
Ambassador: HE Dalrain Davaasambuu

Morocco
Embassy of the Kingdom of Morocco,
49 Queen's Gate Gardens, London SW7 5NE
Tel: 020 7581 5001/4   Fax: 020 7225 3862
Ambassador: HE Mohammed Belmahi

Mozambique
High Commission of the Republic of
Mozambique, 21 Fitzroy Square,
London W1P 5HJ
Tel: 020 7383 3800   Fax: 020 7383 3801
E-mail: mozalon@compuserve.com
High Commissioner: HE António Gumende

Myanmar – see Burma

Namibia
High Commission of the Republic of Namibia,
6 Chandos Street, London W1M 0LQ
Tel: 020 7636 6244   Fax: 020 7637 5694
E-mail: namibia.hicom@btconnect.com
High Commissioner: HE Monica Nashandi

Nauru
No London High Commission
Honorary Consulate: Romshed Courtyard,
Under River, Nr Sevenoaks, Kent TN15 0SD
Tel: 01732 746061   Fax: 01732 454136
Honorary Consul: Martin Weston
E-mail: nauru@weald.co.uk

Nepal
Royal Nepalese Embassy, 12A Kensington
Palace Gardens, London W8 4QU
Tel: 020 7229 1594   Fax: 020 7792 9861
Website: www.nepembassy.org.uk
Ambassador: Vacant
Chargé d'Affaires: Prabal S.J.B.Rana CVO

Netherlands
Royal Netherlands Embassy,
38 Hyde Park Gate, London SW7 5DP
Tel: 020 7590 3200   Fax: 020 7225 0947
E-mail: london@netherlands-embassy.org.uk
Website: www.netherlands-embassy.org.uk
Ambassador: HE Count Jan d'Ansembourg

New Zealand
New Zealand High Commission, New Zealand
House, Haymarket, London SW1Y 4TQ
Tel: 020 7930 8422   Fax: 020 7839 4580
Website: www.nzembassy.com
High Commissioner: HE Russell Marshall

Nicaragua
Embassy of Nicaragua, Suite 12, Vicarage
House, 58–60 Kensington Church Street,
London W8 4DP
Tel: 020 7938 2373   Fax: 020 7937 0952
E-mail: emb.ofnicaragua@virgin.net
Website: freespace.virgin.net/embofnicaragua
Ambassador: HE Juan B Sacasa

Niger
No London Embassy
Embassy of the Republic of Niger,
154 Rue de Longchamp, 75116 Paris, France
Tel: 00 33 1 45 04 80 60
Ambassador: HE Madame Mariama Hima
(Resident in Paris)

Nigeria
High Commission for the Federal Republic of
Nigeria, Nigeria House, 9 Northumberland
Avenue, London WC2N 5BX
Tel: 020 7839 1244   Fax: 020 7839 8746
Website: www.nigeriahouseuk.com
High Commissioner: HE Dr Christopher Kolade

Norway
Royal Norwegian Embassy,
25 Belgrave Square, London SW1X 8QD
Tel: 020 7591 5500   Fax: 020 7245 6993
E-mail: presse.london@mfa.no
Website: www.norway.org.uk
Ambassador: HE Tarald Osnes Brautaset

Oman
Embassy of the Sultanate of Oman,
167 Queen's Gate, London SW7 5HE
Tel: 020 7225 0001   Fax: 020 7584 6435
Ambassador: HE Hussain Ali Abdullatif

Pakistan
High Commission for the Islamic Republic of
Pakistan, 35–36 Lowndes Square,
London SW1X 9JN
Tel: 020 7664 9200   Fax: 020 7664 9224
E-mail:
informationdivision@highcommission-uk.gov.pk
Website: www.pakmission-uk.gov.pk
High Commissioner: HE Madiha Lodhi

Panama
Embassy of the Republic of Panama,
40 Hertford Street, London W1Y 7TG
Tel: 020 7493 4646   Fax: 020 7493 4333
Ambassador: HE Ariadne E Singares Robinson

Papua New Guinea
Papua New Guinea High Commission,
3rd Floor, 14 Waterloo Place, London SW1R 4AR
Tel: 020 7930 0922/7   Fax: 020 7930 0828
High Commissioner: HE Jean Kekedo

Paraguay
Embassy of Paraguay, 344 High Street
Kensington, London W14 8NS
Tel: 020 7610 4180   Fax: 020 7937 5687
E-mail: embapar@londresdy.freeserve.co.uk
Ambassador: Vacant
Chargé d'Affaires: Cristina Acosta

Peru
Embassy of Peru, 52 Sloane Street,
London SW1X 9SP
Tel: 020 7235 1917/2545   Fax: 020 7235 4463
E-mail: postmaster@peruembassy-uk.com
Website: www.peruembassy-uk.com
Ambassador: HE Armando Lecaros de Cossio

Philippines
Embassy of the Republic of the Philippines,
9A Palace Green, London W8 4QE
Tel: 020 7937 1600   Fax: 020 7937 2925
E-mail: embassy@philemb.demon.co.uk
Ambassador: HE César B Bautista

Poland
Embassy of the Republic of Poland,
47 Portland Place, London W1N 3AG
Tel: 0870 774 2700   Fax: 020 7323 4018
E-mail: polishembassy@polishembassy.org.uk
Website: www.poland-embassy.org.uk
Ambassador: HE Dr Stanislaw Komorowski

Portugal
Portuguese Embassy, 11 Belgrave Square,
London SW1X 8PP
Tel: 020 7235 5331   Fax: 020 7245 1287
Website: www.portembassy.gla.ac.uk
Ambassador: HE José Gregório Faria

Qatar
Embassy of the State of Qatar,
1 South Audley Street, London W1Y 5DQ
Tel: 020 7493 2200   Fax: 020 7493 2661
Ambassador:
HE Nasser bin Hamad M Al-Khalifa

Romania
Embassy of Romania, 4 Palace Green,
London W8 4QD
Tel: 020 7937 9666   Fax: 020 7937 8069
E-mail: romania@roemb.demon.co.uk
Website: www.embassyhomepage.com/romania
Ambassador: HE Dan Ghibernea

Russia
Embassy of the Russian Federation,
13 Kensington Palace Gardens, London W8 4QX
Tel: 020 7229 3628/2666/6412
Fax: 020 7727 8625
Ambassador: HE Grigory B Karasin

Rwanda
Embassy of the Republic of Rwanda,
Uganda House, 58–59 Trafalgar Square,
London WC2N 5DX
Tel: 020 7930 2570
Fax: 020 7930 2572
E-mail: ambrwanda@compuserve.com
Ambassador: HE Rosemary Museminali

St Christopher and Nevis
High Commission for St Christopher and Nevis,
10 Kensington Court, London W8 5DL
Tel: 020 7460 6500   Fax: 020 7460 6505
E-mail: sknhighcomm@aol.com
High Commissioner: HE James Williams

St Lucia
High Commission for St Lucia,
1 Collingham Gardens, London SW5 0HW
Tel: 020 7370 7123   Fax: 020 7370 1905
High Commissioner:
HE Emmanuel Cotter MBE

St Vincent and the Grenadines
High Commission for St Vincent and the
Grenadines, 10 Kensington Court,
London W8 5DL
Tel: 020 7565 2874
E-mail: highcommission.svg.uk@cwcom.net
High Commissioner: HE Cenio Lewis

Samoa
No London High Commission
Embassy of the Independent State of Samoa,
Avenue Franklin D Roosevelt 123,
1050 Brussels, Belgium
Tel: 00 32 2 660 84 54
Fax: 00 32 2 675 03 36
High Commissioner:
HE Mr Tau'ili'ili U'ili Meredith
(Resident in Brussels)

San Marino
No London Embassy
Embassy of the Republic of San Marino,
15 Largo Olgiata Isola 16D, 00123 Rome,
Italy
Tel: 020 7299 9850   Fax: 020 7486 9397

São Tomé and Príncipé
No London embassy
Embassy of the Democratic Republic of São
Tomé and Principé, Square Montgomery,
175 Avenue de Tervuren, 1150 Brussels,
Belgium
Tel: 00 32 2 734 89 66
Fax: 00 32 2 734 88 15
Chargé d'Affaires: Armindo do Brito Fernandes
(Resident in Brussels)

Saudi Arabia
Royal Embassy of Saudi Arabia,
30 Charles Street, London W1X 7PM
Tel: 020 7917 3000
Website: www.saudiembassy.org.uk
Ambassador: HRH Prince Turki Al-Faisal

Senegal
Embassy of the Republic of Senegal,
39 Marloes Road, London W8 6LA
Tel: 020 7937 7237   Fax: 020 7938 2546
Ambassador: HE El Hadj Amadou Niang

Serbia and Montenegro
Embassy of Serbia and Montenegro,
28 Belgrave Square, London SW1X 8BT
Tel: 020 7370 6105   Fax: 020 7370 3838
Ambassador: HE Dr Vladeta Jankovic

Seychelles
High Commission for Seychelles, Box 4PE,
2nd Floor, Eros House, 111 Baker Street,
London W1M 1FE
Tel: 020 7224 1660   Fax: 020 7487 5756
High Commissioner: HE Bertrand Rassool

Sierra Leone
Sierra Leone High Commission, Oxford Circus
House, 245 Oxford Street, London W1R 1LF
Tel: 020 7287 9884   Fax: 020 7734 3822
E-mail: info@slhn-uk.org.uk
Website: www.slhc-uk.org.uk
High Commissioner: HE Sulaiman Tejan-Jalloh

Singapore
High Commission for the Republic of
Singapore, 9 Wilton Crescent,
London SW1X 8RW
Tel: 020 7235 8315   Fax: 020 7245 5874
E-mail: shclondon@singcomm.demon.co.uk
Website: www.sg/mfa/london
High Commissioner:
HE Michael Eng Cheng Teo

Slovakia
Embassy of the Slovak Republic,
25 Kensington Palace Gardens, London W8 4QY
Tel: 020 7243 0803   Fax: 020 7727 5824
E-mail: mail@slovakembassy.co.uk
Website: www.slovakembassy.co.uk
Ambassador: HE Frantisek Dlhopolcek

Slovenia
Embassy of the Republic of Slovenia,
10 Little College Street, London SW1P 3SH
Tel: 020 7222 5400   Fax: 020 7222 5277
E-mail: vlo@mzz-dkp.gov.si
Website: www.embassy-slovenia.org.uk
Ambassador: HE Marjan Senjur

Solomon Islands
No London High Commission
Embassy of the Solomon Islands, Avenue
Edouard Lacombert, 1040 Brussels, Belgium
Tel: 00 32 2 732 70 85
Fax: 00 32 2 732 68 85
High Commissioner: HE Robert Sisilo
(Resident in Brussels)

Somalia
No representation

South Africa
High Commission of the Republic of South
Africa, South Africa House, Trafalgar Square,
London WC2N 5DP
Tel: 020 7451 7299   Fax: 020 7451 7284
E-mail: general@southafricahouse.com
Website: southafricahouse.com
High Commissioner: HE Dr Lindiwe Mabuza

Spain
Spanish Embassy, 39 Chesham Place,
London SW1X 8SB
Tel: 020 7235 5555/6/7
Fax: 020 7235 9905
Ambassador: HE The Marqués de Tamarón

Sri Lanka
High Commission for the Democratic Socialist
Republic of Sri Lanka, 13 Hyde Park Gardens,
London W2 2LU
Tel: 020 7262 1841/7   Fax: 020 7262 7970
E-mail: mail@slhc.globalnet.co.uk
Website: www.slhclondon.org
High Commissioner: HE Faiz Mustafa

Sudan
Embassy of the Republic of Sudan,
3 Cleveland Row, London SW1A 1DD
Tel: 020 7839 8080   Fax: 020 7839 7560
E-mail: zb24@pipex.com
Ambassador: HE Dr Hassan Abdin

Suriname
No London Embassy
Embassy of the Republic of Suriname,
2 Alexander Gogelweg, The Hague 2517JH,
The Netherlands
Tel: 00 31 70 3650 844
Ambassador: Vacant
Chargé d'Affaires: Nell J Stadwijk-Kappel

Swaziland
Kingdom of Swaziland High Commission,
20 Buckingham Gate, London SW1E 6LB
Tel: 020 7630 6611   Fax: 020 7630 6564
High Commissioner:
HE Rev Percy Sipho Mngomezulu

Sweden
Embassy of Sweden, 11 Montagu Place,
London W1H 2AL
Tel: 020 7917 6400
Fax: 020 7724 4174
E-mail: embassy@swednet.net
Website: www.swedish-embassy.org.uk
Ambassador: HE Mats Bergquist CMG

Switzerland
Embassy of Switzerland, 16/18 Montagu Place,
London W1H 2BQ
Tel: 020 7616 6000   Fax: 020 7724 7001
E-mail: vertretung@lon.rep.admin.ch
Website: www.swissembassy.org.uk
Ambassador: HE Bruno Spinner

Syria
Embassy of the Syrian Arab Republic,
8 Belgrave Square, London SW1X 8PH
Tel: 020 7245 9012   Fax: 020 7235 4621
Ambassador: HE Mouafak Nassar

Tajikistan
No London Embassy
Honorary Consulate: 33 Ovington Square,
London SW3 1LJ
Tel: 020 7584 5111

Tanzania
High Commission for the United Republic of
Tanzania, 43 Hertford Street,
London W1Y 8DB
Tel: 020 7499 8951/4   Fax: 020 7491 9321
E-mail: balozi@tanzania-online.gov.uk
High Commissioner:
HE Hassan Omar Gumbo Kibelloh

Thailand
Royal Thai Embassy, 29–30 Queen's Gate,
London SW7 5JP
Tel: 020 7589 2944   Fax: 020 7823 9695
Ambassador: HE Vikrom Koompirochana

Togo
No London Embassy
Embassy of the Republic of Togo,
8 rue Alfred-Roll, 75017 Paris, France
Tel: 00 33 1 43 80 12 13
Fax: 00 33 1 43 80 90 71
Ambassador: Vacant (Resident in Paris)

Tonga
Tonga High Commission, 36 Molyneux Street,
London W1H 6AB
Tel: 020 7724 5828   Fax: 020 7723 9074
E-mail: fetu@btinternet.com
High Commissioner:
HE Colonel Fetu'utolu Tupou

Trinidad and Tobago
Office of the High Commissioner for the
Republic of Trinidad and Tobago,
42 Belgrave Square, London SW1X 8NT
Tel: 020 7245 9351   Fax: 020 7823 1065
E-mail: tthc.info@virgin.net
Acting High Commissioner:
HE Sandra McIntyre-Trotman

Tunisia
Tunisian Embassy, 29 Prince's Gate,
London SW7 1QG
Tel: 020 7584 8117   Fax: 020 7225 2884
Ambassador: HE Khemaies Jhinaoui

Turkey
Turkish Embassy, 43 Belgrave Square,
London SW1X 8PA
Tel: 020 7393 0202   Fax: 020 7393 0066
E-mail: turkish.emb@btclick.com
Website: www.turkishembassy-london.com
Ambassador: HE Akin Alptuna

Turkmenistan
Embassy of Turkmenistan, St George's House,
14-17 Wells Street, London W1P 3FP
Tel: 020 7255 1071   Fax: 020 7323 9184
Ambassador: HE Yazmurad Seryaev

Tuvalu
No London High Commission
Honorary Consulate: Tuvalu House,
230 Worple Road, London SW20 8RH
Tel: 020 8879 0985

Uganda
Uganda High Commission, Uganda House,
58/59 Trafalgar Square, London WC2N 5DX
Tel: 020 7839 5783   Fax: 020 7839 8925
High Commissioner: Vacant
Acting High Commissioner:
Elizabeth Kanyogonya

Ukraine
Embassy of Ukraine, 60 Holland Park,
London W11 3SJ
Tel: 020 7727 6312   Fax: 020 7792 1708
Ambassador: Ihor Mittiukov

United Arab Emirates
Embassy of the United Arab Emirates,
30 Princes Gate, London SW7 1PT
Tel: 020 7581 1281   Fax: 020 7581 9616
E-mail: embinfo@cocoon.co.uk
Ambassador: HE Easa Sakh Al Gurg CBE

United States of America
American Embassy, 24 Grosvenor Square,
London W1A 1AE
Tel: 020 7499 9000
Website: www.usembassy.org.uk
Ambassador: HE William S Farish

Uruguay
Embassy of the Oriental Republic of Uruguay,
2nd Floor, 140 Brompton Road,
London SW3 1HY
Tel: 020 7589 8835   Fax: 020 7581 9585
E-mail: emb@urubri.demon.co.uk
Ambassador: HE Miguel J Berthet

Uzbekistan
Embassy of the Republic of Uzbekistan,
41 Holland Park, London W11 2RP
Tel: 020 7229 7679   Fax: 020 7229 7029
Website: www.uzbekistanembassy.uk.net
Ambassador: HE Tukhtapulat Riskiev

Vanuatu
No London High Commission
c/o Department for Foreign Affairs, Port Vila,
Vanuatu
High Commissioner: Vacant
(Residence in Vanuatu)

Venezuela
Venezuelan Embassy, 1 Cromwell Road,
London SW7 2HR
Tel: 020 7584 4206/7   Fax: 020 7589 8887
E-mail: venezlon@venezlon.demon.co.uk
Website: www.venezlon.demon.co.uk
Ambassador: HE Alfredo Toro Hardy

Vietnam
Embassy of the Socialist Republic of Vietnam,
12–14 Victoria Road, London W8 5RD
Tel: 020 7937 1912   Fax: 020 7937 6108
E-mail: vp@dsqvnlondon.demon.co.uk
Ambassador: HE Vuong Thua Phong

Western Samoa – see Samoa

Yemen
Embassy of the Republic of Yemen,
57 Cromwell Road, London SW7 2ED
Tel: 020 7584 6607   Fax: 020 7589 3350
Website: users.pgen.net/embassy/yemen.htm
Ambassador:
HE Dr Mutahar Abdullah Al-Saeede

Zaïre – see Democratic Republic of Congo

Zambia
High Commission for the Republic of Zambia,
2 Palace Gate, London W8 5NG
Tel: 020 7589 6655   Fax: 020 7581 1353
Acting High Commissioner: Anderson Chibwa

Zimbabwe
High Commission for the Republic of
Zimbabwe, Zimbabwe House, 429 Strand,
London WC2R 0SA
Tel: 020 7836 7755   Fax: 020 7379 1167
E-mail: zimlondon@callnetuk.com
Website: www.zimbabwelink.com
High Commissioner:
HE Mr Simbarashe S Mumbengegwi

Visit the Vacher Dod Website . . .
www.DodOnline.co.uk

HM Lord-Lieutenants

ENGLAND

Bedfordshire	Samuel Charles Whitbread
Berkshire	Philip Lavallin Wroughton
Bristol	James Napier Tidmarsh MBE
Buckinghamshire	Sir Nigel Mobbs
Cambridgeshire	Hugh Duberly
Cheshire	William Arthur Bromley-Davenport
Cornwall	Lady Mary Holborow
Cumbria	James Cropper
Derbyshire	John Knollys Bather
Devon	Eric Dancer CBE
Dorset	Captain Michael Fulford-Dobson CVO RN
Durham	Sir Paul Nicholson
East Riding of Yorkshire	Richard Marriott TD
East Sussex	Phyllida Stewart-Roberts OBE
Essex	Lord Petre
Gloucestershire	Henry William George Elwes
Greater London	Lord Imbert QPM
Greater Manchester	Sir John Timmins KCVO OBE TD
Hampshire	Mary Fagan
Herefordshire	Sir Thomas Dunne KCVO
Hertfordshire	Simon Alexander Bowes Lyon
Isle of Wight	Christopher Donald Jack Bland
Kent	Allan Willett CMG
Lancashire	Lord Shuttleworth
Leicestershire	Lady Gretton
Lincolnshire	Bridget Cracroft-Eley
Merseyside	Alan William Waterworth
Norfolk	Sir Timothy Colman KG
Northamptonshire	Lady Juliet Margaret Townsend LVO
Northumberland	Sir John Riddell Bt CVO
North Yorkshire	Lord Crathorne
Nottinghamshire	Sir Andrew George Buchanan Bt
Oxfordshire	Hugo Brunner
Rutland	Dr Laurence Howard
Shropshire	Algernon Heber-Percy
Somerset	Lady Gass
South Yorkshire	Earl of Scarbrough
Staffordshire	James Appleton Hawley TD
Suffolk	Lord Tollemache
Surrey	Sarah Goad
Tyne and Wear	Nigel Sherlock
Warwickshire	Martin Dunne
West Midlands	Robert Richard Taylor OBE
West Sussex	Hugh Wyatt
West Yorkshire	John Lyles CBE
Wiltshire	Lieutenant-General Sir Maurice Johnston KCB OBE
Worcestershire	Michael Brinton

SCOTLAND

The Lord Provosts for the time being of the four City Districts (Aberdeen, Dundee, Edinburgh and Glasgow) are Lord-Lieutenants of those districts ex-officio

Aberdeen City	Lord Provost *ex officio* John Reynolds
Aberdeenshire (Grampian Region)	Angus Farquharson OBE
Angus (Tayside Region)	Georgiana Osborne
Argyll and Bute (Strathclyde Region)	Kenneth Alasdair MacKinnon RD WS
Ayrshire and Arran (Strathclyde Region)	Major Richard Henderson TD
Banffshire (Grampian Region)	Clare Russell
Berwickshire (Borders Region)	Major Alexander Trotter
Caithness (Highland Region)	Major Graham Dunnett TD
Clackmannan (Central Region)	Sheena Cruickshank
Dumfries (Dumfries and Galloway Region)	Captain Ronald Charles Cunningham-Jardine
Dunbartonshire (Strathclyde Region)	Brigadier Donald David Graeme Hardie TD
Dundee	Lord Provost *ex officio* John Letford
East Lothian (Lothian Region)	Garth Morrison CBE
Edinburgh	Lord Provost *ex officio* Lesley Hinds
Fife	Margaret Dean
Glasgow	Lord Provost *ex officio* Elizabeth Cameron
Inverness (Highland Region)	Donald Cameron of Lochiel (the Younger)
Kincardineshire (Grampian Region)	John Smart
Lanarkshire (Strathclyde Region)	Gilbert Cox
Midlothian (Lothian Region)	Patrick Prenter
Moray (Grampian Region)	Air Vice-Marshal George Arthur Chesworth CB OBE DFC
Nairn (Highland Region)	Ewen Brodie
Orkney	George Robert Marwick
Perth and Kinross (Tayside Region)	Sir David Montgomery Bt
Renfrewshire (Strathclyde Region)	Cameron Holdsworth Parker OBE
Ross and Cromarty (Highland Region)	Captain Roderick William Kenneth Stirling of Fairburn TD
Roxburgh, Ettrick and Lauderdale (Borders Region)	Dr June Paterson-Brown CBE
Shetland	John Hamilton Scott
Stewartry of Kirkcudbright (Dumfries and Galloway Region)	Lieutenant-General Sir Norman Arthur KCB
Stirling and Falkirk (Central Region)	Colonel James Stirling of Garden CBE TD
Sutherland (Highland Region)	Major-General David Houston CBE
Tweeddale (Borders Region)	Captain David Younger
Western Isles	Alexander Matheson OBE
West Lothian (Lothian Region)	Isobel Brydie MBE
Wigtown (Dumfries and Galloway Region)	Major Edward Orr Ewing

WALES

Clwyd	Trefor Jones CBE
Dyfed	Lord Morris of Aberavon
Gwent	Simon Boyle
Gwynedd	Professor Eric Sunderland OBE
Mid Glamorgan	Kathrin Thomas
Powys	Hon Shän Legge-Bourke LVO
South Glamorgan	Captain Norman Lloyd-Edwards RD RNR (retired)
West Glamorgan	Robert Cameron Hastie CBE RD

NORTHERN IRELAND

Antrim	Lord O'Neill TD
Armagh	Earl of Caledon
Belfast	Lady Carswell OBE
Down	William Joseph Hall
Fermanagh	Earl of Erne
Londonderry	Denis Desmond CBE
Londonderry City	Dr Donal A J Keegan OBE
Tyrone	Duke of Abercorn KG

Association of Lord-Lieutenants

Chairman	Lord Kingsdown KG
Secretary	Andrew Mackersie
	(House of Lords, London SW1P 3JY)

Crown Dependencies

The Isle of Man, Jersey and Guernsey are dependencies of the Crown, which is represented by a Lieutenant-Governor. They are internally self-governing, but defence and international affairs, including foreign representation are the responsibility of the UK government.

Isle of Man

Lieutenant-Governor: HE Air Marshal Ian David MacFadyen CB OBE
The President of Tynwald: Hon Noel Q Cringle
Speaker of the House of Keys: Hon J Anthony Brown SHK
Chief Minister: Hon Richard K Corkill

Population: 76,315
Area: 227 square miles
Capital: Douglas

Clerk of Tynwald: M Cornwell-Kelly LLB

Legislative Buildings, Douglas,
Isle of Man IM1 3PW

01624 685500 Fax 01624 685504
Tynwald (www.tynwald.org.im)
Government offices: 01624 685685
Isle of Man Government (www.gov.im)

Jersey

Lieutenant-Governor: HE Air Chief Marshal Sir John Cheshire KBE CB
The Bailiff (President of the States Assembly and the Royal Court): Sir Philip Bailhache

Population: 87,186
Area: 45 square miles
Capital: St Helier

The Bailiff's Chambers,
Royal Court House, St Helier,
Jersey, JE1 1BA, Channel Islands

01534 502100 Fax 01534 502199

Michael de la Haye
Greffier (Clerk) of the States, States Greffe
Morier House, Halkett Place, St Helier,
Jersey JE1 1DD, Channel Islands

01534 502013 Fax 01534 502098
E-mail: m.delahaye@gov.je

Guernsey

Lieutenant-Governor: HE Lieutenant General Sir John Foley KCB OBE MC
The Bailiff Sir de Vic Carey

Population: 60,000 approx
Area: 24 square miles
Capital: St Peter Port

Alderney, Sark, Herm, Jethou, Brecqhou and Lihou are included in the Bailiwick.

The Bailiff's Chambers,
The Royal Court House,
Guernsey GY1 2PB, Channel Islands

01481 726161

British Overseas Territories
Governors and Commanders-in-Chief

Anguilla	Peter Johnstone *(Governor)*
Bermuda	Sir John Vereker KCB *(Governor and Commander-in-Chief)*
British Antarctic Territory	Alan Huckle *(Commissioner)* (Non-resident)
British Indian Ocean Territory	Alan Huckle *(Commissioner)* (Non-resident)
British Virgin Islands	Tom Macan *(Governor)*
Cayman Islands	Bruce Dinwiddy *(Governor)*
Falkland Islands	Howard Pearce *(Governor)*
Gibraltar	Francis Jefferies *(Governor and Commander-in-Chief)*
Montserrat	HE Anthony Longrigg CMG *(Governor)*
Pitcairn, Henderson, Ducie and Oeno Islands	Richard Fell CVO *(Governor)* (Non-resident) see New Zealand – British Embassies and High Commissions Overseas section
St Helena and Dependencies	David Hollamby *(Governor and Commander-in-Chief)*
South Georgia and South Sandwich Islands	Howard Pearce *(Commissioner)* (Resident in Stanley)
Turks and Caicos Islands	Jim Poston *(Governor)*

Visit the Vacher Dod Website . . .
www.DodOnline.co.uk

The Commonwealth

Of the 54 member countries of the Commonwealth, Queen Elizabeth II is Head of State of 16 (including the United Kingdom), 33 are republics, and 5 are monarchies with other sovereigns. The Queen remains symbolically Head of the Commonwealth.

Governors-General

In the overseas realms of which she is Queen, Her Majesty is represented by a Governor-General

Antigua and Barbuda	HE Sir James Carlisle KCMG *Prime Minister:* Hon Lester B Bird
Australia	HE Rt Reverend Dr Peter Hollingworth *Prime Minister:* Hon John Howard MP
Bahamas	HE Dame Ivy Dumont *Prime Minister:* Hon Perry Christie
Barbados	HE Sir Clifford Husbands GCMG *Prime Minister:* Rt Hon Owen Arthur
Belize	HE Sir Colville Norbert Young Sr KCMG *Prime Minister:* Hon Said Musa
Canada	HE Hon Adrienne Clarkson CE CMM CD *Prime Minister:* Rt Hon Jean Chrétien
Grenada	HE Sir Charles Daniel Williams GCMG QC *Prime Minister:* Hon Dr Keith Mitchell
Jamaica	HE Sir Howard Felix Cooke ON GCMG GCVO CD *Prime Minister:* Rt Hon P J Patterson QC
New Zealand	HE Dame Silvia Cartwright PCNZM DBE *Prime Minister:* Rt Hon Helen Clark
Papua New Guinea	HE Sir Sailas Atopare GCMG KStJ *Prime Minister:* Hon Sir Michael Somare
Solomon Islands	HE Rev John Ini Lapli GCMG *Prime Minister:* Hon Sir Allan Kemakeza
*St Christopher and Nevis	HE Sir Cuthbert M Sebastian GCMG OBE *Prime Minister:* Hon Dr Denzil Douglas
*St Lucia	HE Dame Calliopa Pearlette Louisy GCMG *Prime Minister:* Dr Hon Kenny D Anthony
*St Vincent and The Grenadines	HE Dr Frederick Ballantyne *Prime Minister:* Rt Hon Dr Ralph Gonsalves
Tuvalu	HE Rt Hon Sir Tomasi Puapua KBE *Prime Minister:* Saufatu Sopoanga

*Eastern Caribbean States

Republics and other Commonwealth Monarchies
Heads of State and Heads of Government

Bangladesh	*Head of State:* HE Prof Iajuddin Ahmed *Head of Government:* Hon Begum Khaleda Zia
Botswana	*President and Head of Government:* HE Festus G Mogae
Brunei	*Sultan and Head of Government:* HM Sultan Haji Hassanal Bolkiah, Sultan and Yang Di-Pertuan Negara Brunei Darussalam
Cameroon	*President and Head of Government:* HE Paul Biya
Cyprus	*President and Head of Government:* HE Tassos Papadopoulos
Dominica	*President and Head of State:* HE Vernon Shaw *Prime Minister and Head of Government:* Hon Pierre Charles
†Fiji Islands	*President:* HE Ratu Josefa Iloilo *Prime Minister:* Laisenia Qarase
The Gambia	*President and Head of Government:* HE Alhaji Yahya A J J Jammeh

Ghana	*President and Head of Government:* HE John A Kufuor
Guyana	*President and Head of Government:* HE Bharrat Jagdeo
India	*President and Head of State:* HE Dr A P J Abdul Kalam
	Prime Minister and Head of Government: Hon Atal Bihari Vajpayee
Kenya	*President and Head of Government:* HE Mwai Kibaki
Kiribati	*President and Head of Government:* HE Teburoro Tito
Lesotho	*Head of State:* HM King Letsie III
	Prime Minister and Head of Government: Hon Bethuel Pakalitha Mosisili
Malawi	*President and Head of Government:* HE Bakili Muluzi
Malaysia	*Head of State:* HM Tuanka Syed Sirajuddin Syed Putra Jamalullail *(King of Malaysia)*
	Prime Minister and Head of Government: Hon Datuk Seri Dr Mahathir Mohamad
Maldives	*President and Head of Government:* HE Maumoon Abdul Gayoom GCMG
Malta	*President and Head of State:* HE Professor Guido de Marco
	Prime Minister and Head of Government: Hon Dr Edward Fenech Adami
Mauritius	*President and Head of State:* HE Karl Auguste Offmann
	Prime Minister and Head of Government: Rt Hon Sir Anerood Jugnauth
Mozambique	*President and Head of State:* HE Joaquim A Chissano
Namibia	*President and Head of Government:* HE Dr Sam Nujoma
Nauru	*President and Head of Government:* HE Ludwig Scotty
Nigeria	*President and Head of State:* HE Chief Olusegun Obasanjo
†Pakistan	*President and Head of State:* HE General Pervaiz Musharraf
	Prime Minister and Head of Government: Mir Zafarullah Khan Jamali
Samoa	*Head of State:* HH Malietoa Tanumafili II GCMG CBE
	Prime Minister and Head of Government: Hon Tuilaepa Sailele Malielegaoi
Seychelles	*President and Head of Government:* HE France Albert René
Sierra Leone	*President:* HE Alhaji Dr Ahmed Tejan Kabbah
Singapore	*President and Head of State:* HE S R Nathan
	Prime Minister and Head of Government: Hon Goh Chok Tong
South Africa	*President and Head of Government:* HE Thabo Mbeki
Sri Lanka	*President and Head of Government:* HE Chandrika Bandaranaike Kumaratunga
Swaziland	*Head of State:* HM King Mswati III
	Prime Minister and Head of Government: Hon Dr Barnabas Dlamini
Tanzania	*President and Head of Government:* HE Benjamin William Mkapa
Tonga	*Head of State:* HM King Taufa'ahau Tupou IV GCMG
	Prime Minister and Head of Government: HRH Prince 'Ulukalala Lavaka Ata
Trinidad and Tobago	*President and Head of State:* HE Prof George Maxwell Richards
	Prime Minister and Head of Government: Hon Patrick Manning
Uganda	*President and Head of Government:* HE Yoweri Museveni
Vanuatu	*President and Head of State:* HE Fr John Bani
	Prime Minister and Head of Government: Hon Nipake Edward Nalapei
Western Samoa	– See Samoa
Zambia	*President and Head of Government:* HE Levy Patrick Mwanawasa
Zimbabwe	*President and Head of Government:* HE Robert Mugabe MP

†Currently suspended from the Councils of the Commonwealth.

Visit the Vacher Dod Website . . .
www.DodOnline.co.uk

Royal Households

HER MAJESTY'S HOUSEHOLD
Buckingham Palace, London SW1A 1AA   Tel: 020 7930 4832

Private Secretary to HM The Queen: Rt Hon Sir Robin Janvrin KCVO KCB

HRH THE PRINCE PHILIP, DUKE OF
EDINBURGH
Buckingham Palace, London SW1A 1AA
Tel: 020 7930 4832

Private Secretary:
Brigadier Miles Hunt-Davis CVO CBE

HRH THE PRINCE OF WALES
St James's Palace, London SW1A 1BS
Tel: 020 7930 4832

Private Secretary and Treasurer:
Sir Michael Peat KCVO

HRH THE DUKE OF YORK
Buckingham Palace, London SW1A 1AA
Tel: 020 7930 4832

Private Secretary and Treasurer:
Alastair Watson

TRH THE EARL AND COUNTESS OF
WESSEX
Bagshot Park, Bagshot, Surrey GU19 5PJ
Tel: 01276 707042

Private Secretary: Brigadier John Smedley

HRH THE PRINCESS ROYAL
Buckingham Palace, London SW1A 1AA
Tel: 020 7930 4832

Private Secretary:
Captain Nick Wright LVO RN

HRH PRINCESS ALICE, DUCHESS OF
GLOUCESTER AND TRH THE DUKE AND
DUCHESS OF GLOUCESTER
Kensington Palace, London W8 4PU
Tel: 020 7937 6374

Private Secretary, Comptroller and Equerry:
Major Nicholas Barne LVO

HRH THE DUKE OF KENT
St James's Palace, London SW1A 1BQ
Tel: 020 7930 4872

Private Secretary:
Nicolas Adamson Esq LVO OBE

HRH THE DUCHESS OF KENT
Wren House, Palace Green, London W8 4PY
Tel: 020 7937 2730

Secretary: Virginia Uttley

TRH PRINCE AND PRINCESS MICHAEL
OF KENT
Kensington Palace, London W8 4PU
Tel: 020 7938 3519

Private Secretary: Nicholas Chance Esq

HRH PRINCESS ALEXANDRA, THE
HONOURABLE LADY OGILVY
Buckingham Palace, London SW1A 1AA
Tel: 020 7024 4270

Private Secretary:
Lieutenant Colonel Richard Macfarlane

Forms of Address

Formal modes of address become less formal every year but there are occasions when a person may want to address someone with strict formality. The first form of address given is that which should always be used on the envelope, the second is the formal salutation and conclusion and the third is the less formal salutation and conclusion. Each is detailed respectively as (1), (2) and (3).

The following points should be noted:–

1. The honorific prefix 'The Right Honourable' is not now generally used for Peers other than Privy Counsellors.

2. The courtesy titles Honourable, Lady and Lord to which sons and daughters of Peers (depending on the rank of their father) are not prefixed by the definite article. These are the practices adopted by the Earl Marshal's Office and that of the Lord Chamberlain of the Household and consequently have been followed here.

3. In the formal mode of address the conclusion '. . . Obedient Servant' has been used. This is a matter of choice as it can be 'humble and obedient servant' or simply 'I am, Sir (my Lord or whatever) Yours faithfully'.

4. In all appropriate cases the use of the masculine can be interpreted as including the feminine.

AMBASSADOR—(1) His Excellency Mr., Dr., etc. as appropriate, (Esquire is never used), Ambassador of the Italian Republic, (the name of the Country in full i.e. not The Italian Ambassador). (2) Your Excellency, conclude I am Your Excellency's Obedient Servant. (3) Dear Mr Ambassador, conclude Yours sincerely. A list of Ambassadors is given towards the end of the book. In conversation an Ambassador is addressed as 'Your Excellency', but once is sufficient, thereafter 'Sir' is normal.

AMBASSADOR'S WIFE—(1) As an ordinary married woman. She is not 'Your Excellency' nor 'Ambassadress'.

ARCHBISHOP—(1) The Most Rev. The Lord Archbishop of York. Or, The Most Rev. John Smith, Lord Archbishop of York. (2) Your Grace or My Lord Archbishop, conclude I am My Lord Grace's Obedient Servant. (3) Dear Archbishop, conclude Yours sincerely. Note: The Archbishops of Canterbury and York are Privy Counsellors and are therefore addressed as The Most Reverend and Right Honourable.

BARON—(1) The Lord Barton. (2) My Lord, conclude I am, My Lord, Your Obedient Servant. (3) Dear Lord Barton, conclude Yours sincerely.

BARONESS IN HER OWN RIGHT OR BARON'S WIFE —(1) The Lady Barton or, in the case of Baronesses in their own right, most prefer to be styled The Baroness Barton (see biographies of Members of the House of Lords). (2) Dear Madam, conclude Yours faithfully. (3) Dear Lady Barton or Dear Baroness Barton, conclude Yours sincerely.

BARONETS—(1) Sir John Smith, Bt. (the abbreviation Bart. is not much used today but is not incorrect). (2) Dear Sir, conclude Yours faithfully. (3) Dear Sir John, conclude Yours sincerely.

BISHOP—(1) The Right Reverend The Lord Bishop of Buxton. Or, The Right Reverend John Smith, Lord Bishop of Buxton. (2) My Lord Bishop, conclude I am, My Lord, Your Obedient Servant. (3) Dear Lord Bishop, Dear Bishop or Dear Bishop of Buxton, conclude Yours sincerely. Note: Bishops suffragan are addressed by courtesy in the same way as diocesan bishops.

COUNTESS—(1) The Countess of Poole. (2) Dear Madam, conclude Yours faithfully. (3) Dear Lady Poole, conclude Yours sincerely.

DAME—(1) Dame Mary Smith, followed by appropriate post-nominal letters (e.g. D.B.E.). (2) Dear Madam, conclude Yours faithfully. (3) Dear Dame Mary, conclude Yours sincerely.

DUCHESS—(1) Her Grace The Duchess of Avon. (2) Your Grace, conclude I am, Your Grace's Obedient Servant. (3) Dear Duchess of Avon, conclude Yours sincerely.

DUKE—(1) His Grace The Duke of Avon. (2) Your Grace, or My Lord Duke, conclude I am, Your Grace's Obedient Servant. (3) Dear Duke of Avon, conclude Yours sincerely.

EARL—(1) The Earl of Hethe. (2) My Lord, conclude I am my Lord Your Obedient Servant. (3) Dear Lord Hethe, conclude Yours sincerely.

GOVERNORS GENERAL, GOVERNORS AND LIEUTENANT GOVERNORS—As for Ambassadors but followed by description of office, such as Governor General and Commander-in-Chief of New Zealand. (3) Dear Governor General, Governor or Lieutenant-Governor, conclude Yours sincerely. The Lieutenant-Governors of Guernsey, Jersey and the Isle of Man enjoy this style. The Governor General of Canada has the style 'The Right Honourable' for life and a Lieutenant-Governor of a Canadian Province is 'His Honour' for life.

JUDGE (LORD JUSTICE OF APPEAL)—(1) The Right Honourable Sir John Smith, as he is invariably a Privy Counsellor and a Knight, or the Right Honourable Lord Justice Smith. (2) My Lord, conclude I am My Lord, Your Obedient Servant. (3) Dear Sir John, conclude Yours sincerely.

JUDGE (JUSTICE OF THE HIGH COURT)—(1) The Honourable Sir John Smith, as he is invariably a Knight, or The Honourable Mr Justice Smith. (2) and (3) as for a Lord Justice of Appeal.

JUDGE (CIRCUIT JUDGE)—(1) His Honour Judge Smith. (2) Your Honour, conclude I have the honour to be Your Honour's Obedient Servant. (3) Dear Sir (or Judge Smith), conclude Yours sincerely.

JUDGE (WOMEN JUDGES)—(1) The Right Honourable Dame Ann Smith, D.B.E. (if a Lord of Appeal), The Honourable Dame Anne Smith, D.B.E. (if a High Court Judge). (2) and (3) as for a male Judge with suitable gender changes.

KNIGHT—(1) Sir John Smith, if a Knight Bachelor there is no post-nominal addition in this respect (Kt., K. Bach., or K.T. is quite wrong) but if a Knight or Knight Grand Cross or Grand Commander of an Order of Chivalry the appropriate post-nominal letters should be added. A Knight may be so addressed when his knighthood is announced, there is now no need to wait for the accolade to have been conferred. (2) Dear Sir, conclude Yours faithfully. (3) Dear Sir John, conclude Yours sincerely.

LORD LIEUTENANT—(1) The normal form of address, followed by, for courtesy, H.M.'s Lord Lieutenant for the County of Newshire. (2) My Lord Lieutenant, conclude I have the honour to be my Lord Lieutenant, Your Obedient Servant. (3) Dear Lord (Sir John or Mr. as appropriate), conclude Yours sincerely.

LORD OF SESSION IN SCOTLAND—(1) The Honourable (or Right Honourable if a Privy Counsellor), Lord Glentie. (2) My Lord, conclude I have the honour to be My Lord, Your Obedient Servant. (3) Dear Lord Glentie, conclude Yours sincerely. Note: The wife of a Lord of Session is styled as the wife of a Baron but her children have no courtesy titles. The Lord Justice General or Lord Justice Clerk is usually so addressed in correspondence, rather than by his juridical title.

MEMBER OF NATIONAL ASSEMBLY FOR WALES—Address according to rank with the addition of the letters AM after the name.

MEMBER OF NORTHERN IRELAND ASSEMBLY—Address according to rank with the addition of the letters MLA after the name.

MEMBER OF PARLIAMENT—(1) Address according to rank with the addition of the letters M.P. after the name. Privy Counsellors have the prefix 'The Right Honourable'. Letters to Ministers may start Dear Minister.

MEMBER OF SCOTTISH PARLIAMENT—Address according to rank with the addition of the letters MSP after the name.

PRIME MINISTER—The Prime Minister has the prefix 'The Right Honourable', as a Member of the Privy Council and the letters M.P. after the name, as a Member of Parliament. Letters to the Prime Minister may start Dear Prime Minister.

PRINCE—(1) H.R.H. The Prince Henry of Wales or, if a Duke, H.R.H. The Duke of Kent; the children of the Sovereign use the definite article before Prince (e.g. The Prince Edward). (2) Your Royal Highness or Sir, conclude I have the honour to be Your Royal Highness's Obedient Servant. In conversation address as Your Royal Highness but once is sufficient, thereafter Sir is normal.

PRINCESS—(1) H.R.H. Princess Beatrice of York, or, if the wife of a Royal Duke, H.R.H. The Duchess of Kent; a daughter of the Sovereign uses the definite article before Princess (e.g. The Princess Margaret, Countess of Snowdon). (2) Your Royal Highness or Madam, conclude I have the honour to be Your Royal Highness's Obedient Servant. In conversation address as Your Royal Highness but once is sufficient, thereafter Ma'am (pronounced so as to rhyme with lamb) is normal.

PRIVY COUNSELLOR—(1) The Right Honourable prefixes the name and style except in respect of Marquesses and Dukes when the letters P.C. are placed after the name. The letters follow those indicating membership of Orders of Chivalry. (2) Address according to rank. (See also Member of Parliament).

QUEEN—(1) Her Majesty the Queen, although letters are usually addressed to The Private Secretary to Her Majesty the Queen. (2) Your Majesty or 'May it please your Majesty', conclude I have the honour to be Your Majesty's Obedient Subject. (3) Madam, conclude With my humble duty to Your Majesty. In conversation address as Your Majesty at first thereafter as Ma'am (see Princess).

Recommended Reading

Bagehot, W. *The English Constitution*, Introduction by R. H. S. Crossman, London, Fontana, 1963

Biffen, John. *Inside the House of Commons*, Grafton, 1989

Bradshaw, K. A., and Pring, D. A. M. *Parliament and Congress*, Quartet Books, Revised Edition, 1981

Butler, D. and Kavanagh, D. *The British General Election of 1997*, London, Macmillan, 1997

Cook, Sir Robert. *The Palace of Westminster*, Burton Skira, 1987

de Smith, S. A. *Constitutional and Administrative Law*, Penguin, 8th edition, 1998

Dod's European Companion 2003, Vacher Dod Publishing

Dod's Scotland, Wales and Northern Ireland Companion 2003, Vacher Dod Publishing

Drewry, G. (ed.) *The New Select Committees*, Oxford, 2nd edition, 1989

Englefield, D. J. T. (Ed.) *Workings of Westminster*, Dartmouth, 1991

Evans, Paul. *Handbook of House of Commons Procedure*, Vacher Dod Publishing, 4th edition, 2003

Fell, Sir Bryan and Mackenzie, K. R. *The Houses of Parliament: A guide to the Palace of Westminster*, Editor: D. L. Natzler. London, HMSO, 15th edition, 1994

Franklin, Mark and Norton, Philip (eds.). *Parliamentary Questions*, Oxford, 1993

Garrett, John, *Westminster—Does Parliament Work?* Gollancz, 1992

Giddings, Philip and Drewry, Gavin (eds.), *Westminster and Europe*, Macmillan 1995

Griffith, J. A. G. *Parliamentary Scrutiny of Government Bills*, London, Allen & Unwin, 1974

Griffith J. A. G. and Ryle M. T., *Parliament*, Sweet and Maxwell, 1989

Hansard Society. *The Challange for Parliament: Making Government Accountable*, Vacher Dod Publishing, 2001

Joint Committee on Parliamentary Privilege, Session 1998–99 Report, House of Lords Paper 43-I, House of Commons Paper 214-I

Jones, Christopher. *The Great Palace: the Story of Parliament*, London, BBC Books, 1983

Judge, D. (ed.). *The Politics of Parliamentary Reform*, Heinemann, 1983

Liaison Committee. First Report, Session 1999–2000, *Shifting the Balance: Select Committees and the Executive*, House of Commons Paper 300; Second Report, Session 1999–2000, *Independence or Control?*, HC 748; First Report, Session 2000–01, *Shifting the Balance: Unfinished Business*, HC 321-I

May, Sir T. Erskine. *Parliamentary Practice*, 22nd edn. ed. Limon and McKay. London, Butterworth, 1997

Miers, D. and Page, A., *Legislation*, Sweet and Maxwell, 2nd edition 1990

Norton, Philip, *Legislatures*, Oxford, 1990

Radice, L., Vallance, E. and Willis, V. *Member of Parliament*, London, Macmillan, 1987

Report of the Royal Commission on Reform of the House of Lords, *A House for the Future*, January 2000, Cm 4534

Riddell, P. *Parliament Under Pressure*, London, Gollancz, 1997

Rush, Michael (ed), *Parliament and Pressure Groups*, Oxford, 1990

Rush, Michael, *Parliamentary Government in Britain*, Pitman, 1981

Ryle, M. and Richards, P. *The Commons Under Scrutiny*, Routledge, 1988

Ryle, M and Griffith, J. *Parliament*, Sweet and Maxwell, 1989

Shell, Donald. *The House of Lords*, Harvester Wheatsheaf, 2nd edition, 1992

Shell, Donald and Beamish, David (eds.). *The House of Lords at Work*, Oxford, 1993

Silk, Paul and Walters, Rhodri. *How Parliament Works*, Longman, fourth edition, 1998

Parliamentary Papers (including Hansard and the Votes and Proceedings) are available from the Parliamentary Bookshop, or from the Stationery Office. Various fact sheets are also available from the Public Information Offices of both Houses (see Index)

Abbreviations

ABRO	Army Base Repair Organisation	AERE	Atomic Energy Research Establishment (Harwell)
AC	Companion of the Order of Australia	AEU	Amalgamated Engineering Union
ACA	Associate, Institute of Chartered Accountants	AFC	Air Force Cross
		AFFOR	All Faiths for One Race
ACAF	Advisory Committee on Animal Feedstuffs	AFHQ	Allied Force Headquarters
		AFP	Accounts, Finance and Purchasing
ACAS	Advisory, Conciliation and Arbitration Service	AFPAA	Armed Forces Personnel Administration Agency
ACBE	Advisory Committee on Business and the Environment	AFPRB	Armed Forces' Pay Review Body
		Agric	Agricultural; Agriculture
ACC	Anglican Consultative Council; Association of County Councils	AHED	Architecture and Historic Environment Division
ACCA	Association of Chartered Certified Accountants	ai	ad interim
		AIB	Associate, Institute of Bankers
ACCAC	Qualifications, Curriculum and Assessment Authority for Wales	AIF	Australian Imperial Forces
		AIM	Alternative Investment Market
ACDA	Advisory Committee on Distinction Awards	AM	Assembly Member (National Assembly for Wales)
ACDP	Advisory Committee on Dangerous Pathogens	AMS	Additional Member System; Army Medical Services; Assistant Military Secretary
ACDS	Assistant Chief of Defence Staff		
ACE	Action for Community Employment; Allied Command Europe	ANAF	Arab Non-Arab Friendship
		ANZAC	Australia and New Zealand All-Party Committee
ACF	Army Cadet Force	AOC	Air Office Commanding
ACMSF	Advisory Committee on the Microbiological Safety of Food	APA	Audit Policy and Advice
		APACS	Association for Payment Clearing Services
ACNFP	Advisory Committee on Novel Foods and Processes	APC	Animal Procedures Committee; Army Personnel Centre
ACOPS	Advisory Committee on Protection of the Sea	APEX	Association of Professional, Executive, Clerical and Computer Staff
ACP	African/Caribbean/Pacific		
ACPO	Association of Chief Police Officers	APNI	Alliance Party of Northern Ireland
		APRC	Apple and Pear Research Council
ACRE	Advisory Committee on Releases into the Environment	ARA	Associate, Royal Academy
		ARCM	Associate, Royal College of Music
ACSSI	Advisory Committee on Sites on Special Scientific Interest	ARCS	Associate, Royal College of Science
ACTT	Association of Cinematograph, Television and Allied Technicians	ARICS	Professional Associate, Royal Institution of Chartered Surveyors
ADC	Aide-de-camp	ARINI	Agricultural Research Institute of Northern Ireland
ADHAC	Agricultural Dwelling House Advisory Committees		
AE	Air Efficiency Award	ARSAC	Administration of Radioactive Substances Advisory Committee
AEC	Agriculture Executive Council; Atomic Energy Commission	AS	Accommodation and Security; Appeals Service
AEEU	Amalgamated Engineering and Electrical Union	ASA	Advertising Standards Authority
		ASEAN	Association of South East Asian Nations
AEF	Amalgamated Union of Engineering and Foundry Workers	ASLEF	Associated Society of Locomotive Engineers and Firemen
AERC	Alcohol Education and Research Council		

ASTMS	Association of Scientific, Technical and Management Staffs (now part of MSF, *qv*)
ATII	Associate Member, Incorporated Institute of Taxation
ATRA	Army Training and Recruiting Agency
ATSA	Army Technical Support Agency
AUA	Association of University Administrators
AUC	Air Transport Users Council
AUEW	Amalgamated Union of Engineering Workers
AWB	Agricultural Wages Board for Northern Ireland
B&B	Bed and Breakfast
BA	Bachelor of Arts; Benefits Agency
BAA	British Airports Authority
BACC	Broadcast Advertising Clearance Centre
BACEE	British Association for Central and Eastern Europe
BAFTA	British Academy of Film and Television Arts
BARB	Broadcasters Audience Research Board
BBA	British Board of Agrément
BBC	British Broadcasting Corporation
BBSRC	Biotechnology and Biological Sciences Research Council
BCCI	Bank of Credit and Commerce International
BCE	Boundary Commission for England
BChir	Bachelor of Surgery
BCL	Bachelor of Civil Law
BCom	Bachelor of Commerce
BCU	Business Consultancy Unit
BD	Bachelor of Divinity
Bde	Brigadier
BDS	Business Development Service
BECTa	British Educational Communications and Technology Agency
BECTU	Broadcasting, Entertainment, Cinematograph and Theatre Union
BEd	Bachelor of Education
BEF	British Equestrian Federation; British Expeditionary Force
BEM	British Empire Medal
BFB	Budget and Public Finance
BFI	British Film Institute
BFPO	British Forces Post Office
BIC	British-Irish Council
BIG	Welsh Language Board
BIGC	British-Irish Governmental Conference

BLESMA	British Limbless Ex-Servicemen's Association
BLitt	Bachelor of Literature
BMA	British Medical Association
BMH	British Military Hospital
BMus	Bachelor of Music
BNAF	British North Africa Force
BNIF	British Nuclear Industry Forum
BNSC	British National Space Centre
BPD	Broadcasting Policy Division
BR	British Rail; Building Regulations
BRB	British Railways Board
BRC	British Retail Consortium
BRE	Building Research Establishment
BSc	Bachelor of Science
BSC	Broadcasting Standards Commission; British Society of Cinematographers
BSD	Business Support Division
BSE	Bovine Spongiform Encephalopathy
BSI	British Standards Institution
BSkyB	British Sky Broadcasting
Bt	Baronet
BT	British Telecommunication Plc
BTA	British Tourist Authority
BTI	British Trade International
BUD	Budget Co-ordination
BUPA	British United Provident Association
BWI	British West Indies
C	Conservative
C&E	HM Customs and Excise
C-in-C	Commander-in-Chief
CA	Central Accountancy; Contributions Agency
CAA	Civil Aviation Authority
CABE	Commission for Architecture and the Built Environment
CAC	Central Arbitration Committee
CAFCASS	Children and Family Court Advisory Service
CAFOD	Catholic Aid Fund for Overseas Development
Cantab	Cantabrigiensis (of Cambridge)
CAO	Chief Adjudication Officer
CAP	Common Agricultural Policy
Capt	Captain
CAS	Central Adjudication Services; Chief of the Air Staff
CAT	Competition Appeal Tribunal
CB	Companion of the Order of the Bath; Chemical and Biotechnology
CBC	County Borough Council
CBE	Commander of the Order of the British Empire

CBI	Confederation of British Industry	CFIT	Commission for Integrated Transport
CBIM	Companion, British Institute of Management	CGG	Commonwealth Games Group
CC	City Council; County Council; Cricket Club	CGMA	Covent Garden Market Authority
		CGS	Chief of the General Staff
CCC	Civil Contingencies Committees	CH	Companion of Honour
CCE	Consumer Communications for England	ChB	Bachelor of Surgery
		CHC	Community Health Council
CCEA	Northern Ireland Council for the Curriculum, Examinations and Assessment	CHD	Coronary Heart Disease
		Chev	Chevalier
		CHI	Commission for Health Improvement
CCETSW	Central Council for Educational and Training in Social Work (UK)	ChM	Master of Surgery
		CHRP	Council for Regulation of Healthcare
CCF	Combined Cadet Force	CI	Imperial Order of the Crown of India; Channel Islands
CCLRC	Council for the Central Laboratory of the Research Councils		
CCRC	Criminal Cases Review Commission	CIBG	Creative Industries, Broadcasting and Gambling Group
CCS	Civil Contingencies Secretariat	CICA	Criminal Injuries Compensation Authority
CCMS	Centre for Coastal and Marine Science; Council for Catholic Maintained Schools	CICAP	Criminal Injuries Compensation Appeals Panel
		CID	Criminal Investigation Department; Creative Industries Division
CCTA	Central Computer and Telecommunications Agency		
		CIE	Companion of the Order of the Indian Empire
CCW	Countryside Council for Wales		
CD	Canadian Forces Decoration	CIMA	Chartered Institute of Management Accountants
CDA	Co-operative Development Agency		
CDC	Commonwealth Development Corporation	CIPFA	Chartered Institute of Public Finance and Accountancy
CDF	Community Development Foundation	CIS	Institute of Chartered Secretaries and Administrators
CDG	Corporate Development Group	CITB	Construction Industry Training Board
CDipAF	Certified Diploma in Accounting and Finance		
		CITBNI	Construction Industry Training Board (Northern Ireland)
CDL	Chief of Defence Logistics		
CDP	Chief of Defence Procurement	CITES	Convention on International Trade in Endangered Species
Cdr	Commander		
Cdre	Commodore	CITU	Central IT Unit
CDS	Chief of the Defence Staff	CIU	Club and Institute Union
CEA	Central Economic Advice	CJC	Civil Justice Court
CEE	Communauté Economique Européenne	CJS	Criminal Justice System
		CLA	Country Landowners' Association
CEFAS	Centre for Environment, Fisheries and Aquaculture Science	CLP	Constituency Labour Party
		CMG	Companion of the Order of St Michael and St George
CEG	Consumers in Europe Group		
CEGB	Central Electricity Generating Board	CML	Council of Mortgage Lenders
		CMPS	Centre for Management and Policy Studies
CEH	Centre for Ecology and Hydrology		
CEng	Chartered Engineer	CMS	Church Mission Society
CEO	Chief Executive Officer	CNAA	Council for National Academic Awards
CEP	Country Economic and Policy		
CertEd	Certificate of Education	CND	Campaign for Nuclear Disarmament
CFB	Communications for Business		
CFE	Centre of Financial Expertise	CNN	Turner Broadcasting
CFF	National Funding Formula	CNT	Commission for the New Towns

CO	Crown Office; Commanding Officer	CSIA	Central Sponsor for Information Assurance
COHSE	Confederation of Health Service Employees (see Unison)	CSL	Central Science Laboratory
COI	Central Office of Information	CSR	Corporate Strategy and Resources Directorate
Col Sergt	Colour Sergeant		
COMARE	Committee on Medical Aspects of Radiation in the Environment	CST	Council for Science and Technology
Comdr	Commander	CStJ	Commander, Most Venerable Order of the Hospital of St. John of Jerusalem
Comdt	Commandant		
Con	Conservative		
COPUS	Committee on the Public Understanding of Science	CTBI	Churches Together in Britain and Ireland
CORE	Central Operational Research and Economics	CVCP	Committee of Vice-Chancellors and Principals of the Universities of the UK
COS	Chief of Staff		
COSHEP	Committee of Scottish Higher Education Principals	CVHAT	Castle Vale Housing Trust
		CVO	Commander of the Royal Victorian Order
COSLA	Convention of Scottish Local Authorities		
		CVS	Council for Voluntary Service
CPA	Commonwealth Parliamentary Association	CWP	Community Work Programme
		CWS	Co-operative Wholesale Society
CPAS	Church Pastoral Aid Society	CWU	Communication Workers Union
CPC	Conservative Political Centre	DA	Directing Staff
CPG	Criminal Policy Group	DAB	Digital Audio Broadcast
CPP	Committee on Products and Processes for Use in Public Water Supply	DANI	Department of Agriculture for Northern Ireland
		DARA	Defence Aviation Repair Agency
CPRE	Council for the Protection of Rural England	DARD	Department of Agriculture and Rural Development
CPS	Crown Prosecution Service	DART	Development of Accountancy Resources
cr	Created		
CRB	Criminal Records Bureau	DASA	Defence Analytical Services Agency
CRCA	Commercial Radio Companies Association		
		DBA	Defence Bills Agency
CRE	Commission for Racial Equality; Competition, Regulation and Energy Markets	DBC	Deaf Broadcasting Council
		DBE	Dame Commander of the Order of the British Empire
CRP	Constitutional Reform Policy	DBI	Data Broadcasting International
CRP(EC)	Incorporation of the European Convention of Human Rights	DC	District Council
		DCA	Department for Constitutional Affairs
CRP(FOI)	Freedom of Information		
CRP(HL)	House of Lords Reform	DCB	Dame Commander of the Order of the Bath
CS	Construction Service		
CSA	Child Support Agency; Chief Scientific Adviser	DCDS	Deputy Chief of Defence Staff
		DCL	Doctor of Civil Law
CSAC	Chief Scientific Adviser Committee	DCM	Distinguished Conduct Medal
CSC	Civil Service College	DCMG	Dame Commander of the Order of St Michael and St George
CSCE	Conference on Security and Co-operation in Europe		
		DCMS	Department for Culture, Media and Sport
CSCI	Commission for Social Care Inspection		
		DCP	Development Control Policy
CSD	Corporate Services and Development	DCR	Devolved Countries and Regions
		DCS	Deer Commission for Scotland
CSG	Corporate Services Group	DCSA	Defence Communication Services Agency
CSI	Committee on the Intelligence Services; Companion of the Order of the Star of India		
		DCTA	Defence Clothing and Textiles Agency

DCVO	Dame Commander of the Royal Victorian Order	DOS	Dental and Optical Services Branch
DD	Doctor of Divinity	DP	Devolution Policy
DDA	Defence Dental Agency	DPA	Defence Procurement Agency
DDI	Defence, Diplomacy and Intelligence	DPH	Diploma in Public Health
		DPhil	Doctor of Philosophy
DDRB	Review Body on Doctors' and Dentists' Remuneration	DPM	Deputy Prime Minister
		DPTAC	Disabled Persons Transport Advisory Committee
DDX	Debt, Development and Export Finance	DRC	Disability Rights Commission
		DRM	Debt and Reserves Management Unit
DE	Defence Estates		
DEFRA	Department of the Environment, Food and Rural Affairs	DSA	Disposal Sales Agency; Driving Standards Agency
DENI	Department of Education for Northern Ireland	DSC	Distinguished Service Cross
		DSc	Doctor of Science
DERA	Defence Evaluation and Research Agency	DSCA	Defence Secondary Care Agency
		DSDA	Defence Storage and Distribution Agency
DETI	Department of Enterprise, Trade and Industry		
		DSO	Distinguished Service Order
DFC	Distinguished Flying Cross	DST	Defence Science and Technology
DfES	Department for Education and Skills	DStJ	Dame of Grace/Dame of Justice, Most Venerable Order of the Hospital of St. John of Jerusalem
DFID	Department for International Development		
		DSTJ	Dame of Grace/or Dame of Justice, Order of the Hospital of St John of Jerusalem
DFM	Distinguished Flying Medal		
DfT	Department for Transport		
DFWP	Department for Work and Pensions	Dstl	Defence Science and Technology Laboratory
DG	Director-General; Directors Group		
DGIA	Defence Geographic and Imagery Intelligence Agency	DTLR	Department for Transport, Local Government and the Regions
DH	Department of Health	DTMA	Defence Transport and Movements Agency
DHE	Defence Housing Executive		
DHSS	Department of Health and Social Security	DU	Doctor of the University
		DUP	Democratic Unionist Party
DIEL	Advisory Committee on Telecommunications for Disabled and Elderly People	DVA	Defence Vetting Agency
		DVLA	Driver and Vehicle Licensing Agency
DipAgriSci	Diploma in Agricultural Science	DVLNI	Driver and Vehicle Licensing Northern Ireland
DipEd	Diploma in Education		
DipObst	Diploma in Obstetrics	DVO	Driver Vehicle and Operator (Group)
DISC	Defence Intelligence and Security Centre		
		DVTA	Driver and Vehicle Testing Agency
DL	Deputy Lieutenant	DYRMS	The Duke of York's Royal Military School
DLAAB	Disability Living Allowance Advisory Board		
		E	England
DLG	Democracy and Local Government	EA	Economic Affairs; Economic Assessment; Environment Agency; Executive Agency
DLI	Durham Light Infantry		
DLO	Defence Logistics Organisation		
DMO	UK Debt Management Office	EA(N)	Energy Policy
DMS	Diploma in Management Studies	EA(PC)	Productivity and Competitiveness
DMTO	Defence Medical Training Organisation	EA(WW)	Welfare to Work
		EAGA	Expert Advisory Group on Aids
DOC	Directorate of Communication	EAP	Energy Advisory Panel
DoH	Department of Health	EAT	Employment Appeal Tribunal
DOP	Defence and Overseas Policy	EC	European Community
DOP(E)	European Issues	ECA	Economic Commission for Africa (UN)
DOP(E)(T)	European Trade Issues		

ECAC	European Civil Aviation Conference
ECCs	Electricity Consumers' Committees
ECE	Economic Commission for Europe (UN)
ECGD	Export Credits Guarantee Department
ECHR	European Convention of Human Rights
ECITB	Engineering Construction Industry Training Board
ECLAC	Economic Commission for Latin America and the Caribbean (UN)
Econ	Economics
EDC	Economic Development Committee
EDG	European Democratic Group
EEC	European Economic Community
EEDA	East England Development Agency
EEF	Engineering Employers' Federation
EER	European Economic Reform
EETPU	Electrical, Electronic Telecommunications and Plumbing Union
EFA	Exchequer Funds and Accounts
EFS	European Financial Services
EGMU	Economist Group Management Unit
EH	English Heritage
EHS	Environment and Heritage Service
EHSNI	Environment and Heritage Service Northern Ireland
EID	Engineering Industries Directorate
ELLID	Employment, Lifelong Learning and International Directorate
EMDA	East Midlands Development Agency
EMU	European Monetary Union
ENB	English National Board for Nursing, Midwifery and Health Visiting
ENP	Energy Group
ENT	Enterprise Issues
ENV	The Environment
EOC	Equal Opportunities Commission
EP	English Partnerships; European Parliament
EPSRC	Engineering and Physical Sciences Research Council
EPU	European Preparations Unit
ERD	Emergency Reserve Decoration (Army)
ERDF	European Regional Development Fund
ERDP	England Rural Development Programme
ES	Employment Service

ESCAP	Economic and Social Commission for Asia and the Pacific (UN)
ESCWA	Economic and Social Commission for Western Asia (UN)
ESPU	Education and Social Policy Unit
ESRC	Economic and Social Research Council
ETC	Education, Training and Culture
ETS	Employment Tribunals Service
ETT	Environmental Tax
EU	European Union
EUBI	EU Budgetary Issues
EUCS	EU Co-ordination and Strategy
EUF	EU Finances
EUIT	EU and International Taxation
EUMD	EU Monetary Developments
FANY	First Aid Nursing Yeomanry
FAO	Food and Agriculture Organization of the UN
FAS	Funding Agency for Schools
FASD	Financial Accounting Services Division
FAWC	Farm Animal Welfare Council
FBA	Fellow, British Academy
FBIM	Fellow, British Institute of Management
FC	Football Club
FCC	Federal Conference Committee (Lib Dem)
FCCA	Fellow, Chartered Association of Certified Accountants
FCIM	Fellow, Chartered Institute of Marketing
FCIT	Fellow, Chartered Institute of Transport
FCO	Foreign and Commonwealth Office
FDA	Association of First Division Civil Servants
FE	Further Education
FEC	Federal Executive Committee (Lib Dem)
FEDA	Federation of Economic Development Authorities
FEFC	Further Education Funding Council
FEFCW	Further Education Funding Council for Wales
FFB	Food from Britain
FHCIMA	Fellow, Hotel, Catering and Institutional Management Association
FICE	Fellow, Institution of Civil Engineers
FICO	Financial Intermediaries and Claims Office
FIEE	Fellow, Institution of Electrical Engineers

FILA	Fellow, Institute of Landscape Architects	FSAA	Fellow, Society of Incorporated Accountants and Auditors
FIMechE	Fellow, Institution of Mechanical Engineers	FSB	Federation of Small Businesses
FIMgt	Fellow, Institute of Management	FSC	Fire Service College
FIMI	Fellow, Institute of the Motor Industry	FSM	Financial Stability and Markets
		FSNI	Forensic Science Northern Ireland
FIMT	Fellow, Institute of the Motor Trade	FSR	Financial Services Regulation
FInstM	Fellow, Institute of Marketing	FSS	Forensic Science Service
FInstPS	Fellow, Institute of Purchasing and Supply	FTE	Full Time Equivalents
		GAC	Government Art Collection
FIQA	Fellow, Institute of Quality Assurance	GAIC	Genetics and Insurance Committee
		GATT	General Agreement on Tariffs and Trade
FIRTE	Fellow, Institute of Road Transport Engineers	GB	Great Britain
		GBCC	Great Britain-China Centre
FKC	Fellow, King's College, London	GBE	Knight or Dame Grand Cross of the Order of the British Empire
FLA	Football Licensing Authority		
FMD	Foot and Mouth Disease	GBGB	Gaming Board for Great Britain
FMP	Fiscal and Macroeconomic Policy	GC	George Cross
FMRA	Financial Management Reporting and Audit	GCB	Knight or Dame Grand Cross of the Order of the Bath
FOI	Freedom of Information	GCC	Gas Consumers Council
FPC	Family Practitioner Committee; Federal Policy Committee (Lib Dem)	GCCNI	General Consumer Council for Northern Ireland
		GCDA	Government Car and Despatch Agency
FPD	Fire Policy Division		
FRAM	Fellow, Royal Academy of Music	GCHQ	Government Communication Headquarters
FRAME	Fund for the Replacement of Animals in Medical Experiments	GCIE	Knight Grand Commander, Order of the Indian Empire
FRCA	Farming and Rural Conservation Agency	GCIT	General Commissioners of Income Tax
FRCOG	Fellow, Royal College of Obstetricians and Gynaecologists	GCMG	Knight or Dame Grand Cross of the Order of St Michael and St George
FRCP	Fellow, Royal College of Physicians, London	GCSI	Knight Grand Commander, Order of the Star of India
FRCS	Fellow, Royal College of Surgeons of England	GCTS	General Teaching Council for Scotland
FRCVS	Fellow, Royal College of Veterinary Surgeons	GCVO	Knight or Dame Grand Cross of the Royal Victorian Order
FRD	Fire Research Division		
FREng	Fellow, Royal Academy (formerly Fellowship) of Engineering	GDC	General Dental Council
		GEB	Group Executive Board
FRGS	Fellow, Royal Geographical Society	GECC	Gas and Electricity Consumer Council
FRI	Financial Regulation and Industry		
FRIBA	Fellow, Royal Institute of British Architects	GEP	General Expenditure Policy
		GES	General Expenditure Statistics
FRPS	Fellow, Royal Photographic Society	GEST	Grant for Education, Support and Training
FRS	Fellow, The Royal Society; Fisheries Research Services	GICS	Government Information and Communication Service
FRSA	Fellow, Royal Society of Arts		
FRSE	Fellow, The Royal Society of Edinburgh	GIFNFC	Government Industry Forum on Non-Food Uses of Crops
FRSS	Fellow of the Royal Statistical Society	GL	Local Government
		GL(L)	London
FSA	Fellow, Society of Antiquaries; Financial Services Authority	GLA	Greater London Assembly; Greater London Authority

GLC	Greater London Council	HHEW	Heads of Higher Education Institutions in Wales
GM	Genetic Modification		
GMB	General Municipal Boilermakers Union	HIE	Highlands and Islands Enterprise
		HL	Home and Legal
GMBATU	General, Municipal, Boilermakers and Allied Trades Union (see GMB)	HLI	Highland Light Infantry
		HM	His (or Her) Majesty (Majesty's)
		HMC	Historical Manuscripts Commission
GMF	Genetically Modified Foods		
GMP	General Medical Practitioner	HMCI	Her Majesty's Chief Inspector
GMS	General Medical Services	HMFSI	HM Fire Service Inspectorate
GMTV	Good Morning TV	HMI	HM Inspectorate
GMW	General Municipal Boilermakers and Allied Trades Union	HMOs	Housing Management Organisation
		HMS	His (or Her) Majesty's Ship
GMWU	General Municipal Workers' Union	HMT	Her Majesty's Treasury
GNLL	Gambling and National Lottery Licensing Division	HO	Home Office
		Hon	Honorary; Honourable
GNN	Government News Network	HPS	Housing Private Sector
GOC	General Officer Commanding	HPSS	Distinction and Meritorious Service Awards Committee
GOL	Government Office for London		
GOs	Government Offices for the Regions	HQ	Headquarters
		HR	Human Resources
GP	General Practitioner	HRA	Housing Revenue Account
GPA	Government Purchasing Agency	HRDO	Human Resources Division ODPM
GPDST	Girls' Public Day School Trust	HRH	His (or Her) Royal Highness
GPI	Global Policy and Institutions	HRI	Hannah Research Institute; Horticultural Research International
GPMU	Graphical, Paper, Media Union		
GPO	General Post Office		
Green	Green Party	HRP	Historic Royal Palace
gsi	Government Security Intranet	HRSG	HR Strategy Group
GSO	General Staff Officer	HS	Health and Safety; Home and Social Affairs
GSO1	General Staff Officer 1		
GTAC	Gene Therapy Advisory Committee	HS(D)	Drug Misuse
GTN	Government Telephone Network	HS(H)	Health Strategy
HAC	Honourable Artillery Company	HS(W)	Women's Issues
HACC	Heathrow Airport Consultative Committee	HSC	Health and Safety Commission
		HSE	Health and Safety Executive
HAPF	Housing Association and Private Finance	HSENI	Health and Safety Executive for Northern Ireland
HAT	Housing Action Trusts	HSH	His (or Her) Serene Highness
HAZ	Health Action Zones	HSU	Housing Support Unit
HBLB	Horserace Betting Levy Board	HSW	Health and Safety at Work
HDC	Horticultural Development Council	HTV	Harlech Television
HDS	Housing Data and Statistics	HU	Housing and Urban
HDU	Housing Delivery Unit	HVS	Head of Veterinary Services
HE	His (Her) Excellency; Higher Education	I	Ireland
		IA	Indian Army
HEA	Health Education Authority	IAEA	International Atomic Energy Agency (UN)
HEFCE	Higher Education Funding Council for England		
		IAR	Information Asset Register
HEFCW	Higher Education Funding Council for Wales	IAS	Internal Audit Services
		IB	Intervention Board
HEO	Higher Executive Officer	IBA	Independent Broadcasting Authority
HFEA	Human Fertilisation and Embryology Authority		
		ICE	Independent Case Examiner
HFS	Home Financial Services	ICR	Independent Complaints Reviewer
HGC	Human Genetics Commission	ICS	Indian Civil Service; Investors Compensation Scheme
HGCA	Home-Grown Cereals Authority		

ICSTIS	Independent Committee for the Supervision of Standards of Telephone Information Services	IRTU	Industrial Research and Technology Unit
ICT	Information and Communications Technology	IS	Information Systems
		ISA	Individual Savings Account
IDB	Industrial Development Board	ISC	Independent Schools Council
IDBNI	Industrial Development Board for Northern Ireland	ISIS	Independent Schools Information Service
IDC	Imperial Defence College	ISO	Imperial Service Order
IDS	InterDespatch Service	IT	Information Technology
IFAD	International Fund for Agricultural Development (UN)	ITC	Independent Television Commission
IFC	International Finance Corporation (UN)	ITD	Information Technology Directorate
IFI	International Fund for Ireland	ITFC	Independent Television Facilities Centre
IFS	International Financial Services; Institute for Fiscal Studies	ITN	Independent Television News
IHO	Independent Housing Ombudsman Scheme	ITSA	Information Technology Services Agency
IIAC	Industrial Injuries Advisory Council	ITU	International Telecommunication Union (UN)
IIP UK	Investors in People UK	ITV	Independent Television Network
ILO	International Labour Office (or Organization)	IUA	International Underwriting Association
ILT	Institute of Logistics and Transport	IVF	*In Vitro* Fertilisation
IM	Institute of Management	IWAAC	Inland Waterways Amenity Advisory Council
IMD	Indepenent Media Division	IWM	Imperial War Museum
IMF	International Monetary Fund (UN)	JARIC	Joint Air Reconnaissance Intelligence Centre
IMO	International Maritime Organization (UN)	JCC	Joint Consultative Committee with the Liberal Democrat Party
IMPACT	Contractorisation of Medical Services Project	JECU	Joint Entry Clearance Unit
IMRO	Investment Management Regulatory Organisation	JIC	Joint Intelligence Committee
		JNCC	Joint Nature Conservation Committee
IN	Northern Ireland	JP	Justice of the Peace
Ind	Independent	JSB	Judicial Studies Board
Inf	Infantry	JSD	Doctor of Juristic Science
INSEAD	Institut Européen d'Administration des Affaires	KAR	King's African Rifles
		KBE	Knight Commander of the Order of the British Empire
INSTRAW	International Research and Training Institute for the Advancement of Women (UN)	KCB	Knight Commander of the Order of the Bath
INTERPOL	International Criminal Police Organization	KCIE	Knight Commander of the Order of the Indian Empire
IOCA	Interception of Communications Act	KCMG	Knight Commander of the Order of St Michael and St George
IOD	Institute of Directors	KCSI	Knight Commander of the Order of the Star of India
IOM	Isle of Man		
IPP	Import Parity Price	KCVO	Knight Commander of the Royal Victorian Order
IPPP	Import Parity Price Panel		
IPT	Integrated Project Team	KG	Knight of the Order of the Garter
IPU	Inter-Parliamentary Union	KHHC	Kidderminster Hospital and Health Concern
IR	Inland Revenue		
IRN	Independent Radio News	KM	Knight of Malta
IRS	Independent Review Service for The Social Fund	KP	Knight, Order of St Patrick
		KRRC	King's Royal Rifle Corps

KStJ	Knight of the Most Venerable Order of the Hospital of St John of Jerusalem
KT	Knight of the Order of the Thistle
Kt	Knight Bachelor; knighted
Lab	Labour
Lab Co-op	Labour Co-operative
LACOTS	Local Authorities Co-ordinating Body on Food and Trading Standards
LAH	Local Authority Housing
LAM	London Assembly Member
LAO	Lord of Appeal in Ordinary
LAPADA	London and Provincial Dealers' Association
LCC	London County Council (Later GLC)
LCD	Lord Chancellor's Department; Libraries and Communities Division
LDA	London Development Agency
LDS	Licentiate in Dental Surgery
LEA	Local Education Authority
LEDU	Local Enterprise Development Unit
LEG	Legislation
LG	Lady Companion, Order of the Garter; Local Government
LGA	Local Government Association
LGBC	Local Government Boundary Commission for Scotland
LGBW	Local Government Boundary Commission for Wales
LGCE	Local Government Boundary Commission for England
LGCM	Local Government Capacity and Modernisation
LGD	Local Government Directorate
LGL	Local Government Legislation
LGM	Local Government Modernisation
LGO	London Regional Office; Local Government Office
LGP	Local Government Pensions
LGPSA	Local Government Public Service Agreements
LGPU	Local Government Performance Unit
LGQ	Local Government Quality and Performance
LGSM&D	Licentiate, Guildhall School of Music and Drama
LHS	Local Management of Schools
Lib Dem	Liberal Democrat
LIBiol	Licentiate, Institute of Biology
LiP	Investment in people Project Team
LISA	Logistic Information Systems Agency
LLB	Bachelor of Laws

LLD	Doctor of Laws
LLM	Master of Laws
LMCNI	Livestock and Meat Commission for Northern Ireland
LMP	Labour Market Policy
LNN	London News Network
LPC	Low Pay Commission
LPD	Land and Property Division
LRA	Labour Relations Agency
LRAM	Licentiate, Royal Academy of Music
LRCP	Licentiate, Royal College of Physicians, London
LRGG	Local and Regional Government Group
LRNI	Land Registers of Northern Ireland
LRT	London Regional Transport
LSC	Learning and Skills Council
LSE	London School of Economics
LT	London Transport
LTS	Lands Tribunal for Scotland; Learning and Teaching Scotland
LVO	Lieutenant of the Royal Victorian Order
LWT	London Weekend Television
MA	Master of Arts
MACC	Marshall and Commemoration Commission
MAGNI	National Museums and Galleries of Northern Ireland
MB	Bachelor of Medicine
MBA	Master of Business Administration
MBC	Metropolitan Borough Council
MBE	Member of the Order of the British Empire
MC	Military Cross; Meridian Court
MCA	Committee on the Safety of Medicines; Maritime and Coastguard Agency; Medicines Control Agency
MCTC	Military Corrective Training Centre
MD	Doctor of Medicine
mda	Museum Documentation Association
MDA	Medical Devices Agency
MDC	Metropolitan District Council; Milk Development Council
MDP	Ministry of Defence Police Agency
ME	Myalgic Encephalomyelitis
MEd	Master of Education
MELF	Middle East Land Forces
MEP	Member of the European Parliament
MFCM	Member, Faculty of Community Medicine
MHC	Mental Health Commission for Northern Ireland

MHS	Meat Hygiene Service	NAS	National Academy of Sciences; National Archives of Scotland
MI5	Military Intelligence Section 5		
MI6	Military Intelligence Section 6	NATFHE	National Association of Teachers in Further and Higher Education
MIBiol	Member, Institute of Biology		
MICE	Member, Institution of Civil Engineers	NATO	North Atlantic Treaty Organization
		NATS	National Air Traffic Services
MIMechE	Member, Institution of Mechanical Engineers	NBA	National Blood Authority
		NBSA	Naval Bases and Supply Agency
MIMinE	Member, Institution of Mining Engineers	NCB	National Coal Board
		NCC	National Consumer Council
MISC	Miscellaneous	NCSC	National Care Standards Commission
MIU	Mobility and Inclusion Unit		
MLA	Member of Legislative Assembly (Northern Ireland Assembly)	NCSL	National College for School Leadership
MLC	Meat and Livestock Commission	NCVQ	National Council for Vocational Qualifications
MM	Military Medal		
MN	Merchant Navy	NDPB	Non-Departmental Public Body
MNN	Media News Network	NDS	Government News Distribution Service
MO	Medical Officer; Military Operations		
		NEC	National Executive Committee
MoD	Ministry of Defence	NECC	National Electricity Consumers' Council
MP	Member of Parliament		
MPA	Metropolitan Police Authority	NEDC	National Economic Development Council
MPC	Medical Practices Committee		
MPDA	Museums Policy and Digital Access Division	NELC	National Employers' Liaison Committee
MPH	Master of Public Health	NERC	Natural Environment Research Council; National Research Development Corporation
MPhil	Master of Philosophy		
MPIF	Macroeconomic Policy and International Finance		
		NESTA	National Endowment for Science, Technology and the Arts
MRC	Medical Research Council		
MRCGP	Member, Royal College of General Practitioners	NFER	National Foundation for Educational Research
MRI	Moredun Research Institute	NFU	National Farmers' Union
MS	Master of Surgery	NGO	Non-governmental Organisation
MSA	Medical Supplies Agency	NHBC	National House-Building Council
MSAE	Member, Society of Automotive Engineers (USA)	NHM	Natural History Museum
		NHMF	National Heritage Memorial Fund
MSc	Master of Science	NHS	National Health Service
MSC	Manpower Services Commission	NHSE	NHSEstates
MSDA	Military Survey Defence Agency	NHSIT	NHS Information Technology
MSF	Manufacturing Science Finance Union	NHS LIFT	NHS Local Improvement Finance Trust
MSIM	Museum of London	NHSPA	NHS Pensions Agency
MSP	Member of Scottish Parliament	NHSPASA	NHS Purchasing and Supply Agency
MSPFW	MSP for Falkirk West		
MVO	Member of the Royal Victorian Order	NHSSS	NHS Superannuation Scheme (Scotland)
MWP	Minerals and Waste Planning	NI	Northern Ireland; National Insurance
NA	National Academician (USA)		
NAC	National Agriculture Centre	NIACT	Northern Ireland Advisory Committee on Telecommunications
NALGO	National and Local Government Officers' Association (see Unison)		
		NIAO	Northern Ireland Audit Office
NAO	National Audit Office	NIBSC	National Institute for Biological Standards and Control; National Biological Standards Board (UK)
NAPRB	Review Body for Nursing Staff, Midwives, Health Visitors and Professions Allied to Medicine		

NICCE	Northern Ireland Consumer Committee for Electricity
NICO	National Insurance Contributions Office; Northern Ireland Company Overseas
NICPMDE	Northern Ireland Council for Postgraduate Medical and Dental Education
NICS	Northern Ireland Civil Service
NIEC	Northern Ireland Economic Council
NIFHA	Northern Ireland Fishery Harbour Authority
NIH	North Irish Horse
NIHEC	Northern Ireland Higher Education Council
NIHRC	Northern Ireland Human Rights Commission
NILGOSC	Northern Ireland Local Government Officers' Superannuation Committee
NILO	National Investment and Loans Office
NIO	Northern Ireland Office
NIPS	Northern Ireland Prison Service
NISRA	Northern Ireland Statistics and Research Agency
NITB	Northern Ireland Tourist Board
NIUP	Northern Ireland Unionist Party
NIWC	Northern Ireland Women's Coalition
NJC	National Joint Council
NLB	Northern Lighthouse Board
NLCB	National Lottery Charities Board
NLIS	National Land Information Service
NLP	Natural Law Party
NLS	National Library of Scotland
NLW	National Library of Wales
NMA	Naval Manning Agency
NMGM	National Museums and Galleries on Merseyside
NMGW	National Museums and Galleries of Wales
NMM	National Maritime Museum
NMRS	National Monuments Record of Scotland
NMS	National Museums of Scotland
NMSI	National Museum of Science and Industry
NOF	New Opportunities Fund
NPG	National Portrait Gallery
NRA	National Rifle Association; National Rivers Authority
NRD	Neighbourhood Renewal Division
NRI	Neighbourhood Renewal Implementation
NRP	Neighbourhood Renewal Programme
NRPB	National Radiological Protection Board
NRR	Neighbourhood Renewal Research
NRTA	Naval Recruiting and Training Agency
NRU	Neighbourhood Renewal Unit
NS	National Savings; Nova Scotia
ns&I	National Savings and Investments
NSCAG	National Specialised Commissioning Advisory Group
NSMC	North-South Ministerial Council
NTL	NTL Group Ltd
NUJ	National Union of Journalists
NUM	National Union of Mineworkers
NUPE	National Union of Public Employees (see Unison)
NUR	National Union of Railwaymen
NUT	National Union of Teachers
NVALA	National Viewers' and Listeners' Association
NVQ	National Vocational Qualification
NWA	Northwest Development Agency
NWDA	North West Development Agency
NWML	National Weights and Measures Laboratory
NY	New York
OAU	Organisation for African Unity
OBE	Officer of the Order of the British Empire
OC	Officer Commanding; Officer, Order of Canada
OCPA	Office of the Commissioner for Public Appointments
OCSC	Office of the Civil Service Commissioners
ODI	Overseas Development Institute
ODPM	Office of the Deputy Prime Minister
OECD	Organisation for Economic Co-Operation and Development
OeE	Office of the e-Envoy
OFCOM	Office of Communications
Ofgem	Office of Gas and Electricity Markets
OFREG	Office for the Regulation of Electricity and Gas
OFSTED	Office for Standards in Education
OFT	Office of Fair Trading
OFTEL	Office of Telecommunications
OFWAT	Office of Water Services
OGC	Office of Government Commerce
OGD	Other Government Departments
OHMCI W	HM Chief Inspector of Schools, Wales
OIRR	Office of the International Rail Regulator
OIS	Office Information Systems

OISC	Office of the Immigration Services Commissioner	PC	Privy Counsellor; Productivity and Competitiveness; Plaid Cymru
OLA	Other Lords of Appeal	PCA	Police Complaints Authority
O & M	organisation and method	PCC	Press Complaints Commission
OM	Order of Merit	PCID	Plans, Compensation and International Division
OME	Office of Manpower Economics		
ONS	Office for National Statistics	PCSD	Personnel and Central Services Division
OP	Organo Phosphate Group		
OPA	Oil and Pipelines Agency	PE	Procurement Executive
OPRA	Occupational Pensions Regulatory Authority	PEP	Public Enterprise Partnerships
		PERM	Permanent Secretary
OPRAF	Office of Passenger Rail Franchising	PES	Public Expenditure Survey
		PFI	Private Finance Initiative
OPS	Office of Public Service	PGCE	Post Graduate Certificate of Education
OPSR	Office of Public Service Reform		
ORR	Office of the Rail Regulator	PH	Pentland House
OS	Ordnance Survey	PHAB	Physically Handicapped and Able-bodied
OSCE	Organisation on Security and Co-operation in Europe		
		PhD	Doctor of Philosophy
OSNI	Ordnance Survey of Northern Ireland	PHGD	Planning, Housing and Growth Division
OSS	Office for the Supervision of Solicitors	PHLS	Public Health Laboratory Service Board
OSSW	Office of the Secretary of State for Wales	PHQ	Parliament Headquarters
		PHSI	Plant Health and Seeds Inspectorate
		PIA	Personal Investment Authority
OST	Office of Science and Technology	PIDU	Policy Innovation and Delivery Unit
OStJ	Officer of the Most Venerable Order of the Hospital of St John of Jerusalem		
		PINS	Planning Inspectorate
		PITCOM	Parliamentary Information Technology Committee
OTC	Officers' Training Corps		
Otelo	Office of the Telecommunications Ombudsman	PITO	Police Information Technology Organisation
OTs	Overseas Territories	PIU	Performance and Innovations Unit
OU	Open University; Oxford University	PlC	Plaid Cymru
		plc	Public Limited Company
PA	Personal Assistant	PLP	Parliamentary Labour Party
PAC	Public Accounts Committee	PLR	Public Lending Right and the Public Lending Right Advisory Committee; Registrar of Public Lending Right
PACE	Property Advisers to the Civil Estate		
PACNI	Planning Appeals Commission (Northern Ireland)		
		PM	Personnel Management; Prime Minister
PACTS	Parliamentary Advisory Council for Transport Safety		
		PMB	Private Member's Bill
PAG	Property Advisory Group	PMDU	Prime Minister's Delivery Unit
PAM	Professions Allied to Medicine	PMF	Performance Monitoring and Finance
PANI	Northern Ireland Policing Board		
PAO	Prince Albert's Own	PMFSU	Prime Minister's Forward Strategy Unit
PASEG	Parliamentary Astronomy and Space Environment Group		
		PMG	Post Master General
PATS	Pensions Appeal Tribunal for Scotland	PMOS	Prime Minister's Official Spokesman
PAU	Public Appointments Unit	PMPA	Public Management and Policy Association
PBC	Parliamentary Boundary Commission for England		
		PMS	Personal Medical Services
PBNI	Probation Board for Northern Ireland	PO	Post Office
		POEU	Post Office Engineering Union

POST	Parliamentary Office of Science and Technology	QCCAC	Qualifications, Curriculum and Assessment Authority for Wales
POUNC	Post Office Users' National Council	QFL	Queen's Speeches and Future Legislation
PoW	Prisoner of War	QMG	Quartermaster General
PPA	Pay and Personnel Agency	QPM	Queen's Police Medal
PPARC	Particle Physics and Astronomy Research Council	QSO	Queen's Service Order (New Zealand)
PPB	Professional and Policy Branch	QUB	Queen's University, Belfast
PPD	Planning Policy Division	qv	quod vide (which see)
PPE	Philosophy, Politics and Economics	QVS	Queen Victoria School
PPP	Public Private Partnerships	R&D	Research and Development
PPRS	Pharmaceutical Price Regulatory Scheme	RA	Radiocommunications Agency; Royal Academician; Royal Regiment of Artillery
PPS	Parliamentary Private Secretary; Political Planning Services; Principal Private Secretary	RAB	Renewables Advisory Board
		RAC	Royal Agricultural College; Royal Automobile Club
PQs	Parliamentary Questions	RACC	Radio Advertising Clearance Centre
PR	Proportional Representation; Public Relations	RACS	Royal Arsenal Co-operative Society
PRA	Passport and Records Agency	RAE	Research Analysis and Evaluation
PRASEG	Parliamentary Renewable and Sustainable Energy Group	RAF	Royal Air Force
PRO	Public Record Office	RAFPMA	RAF Personnel Management Agency
PROD	Productivity	RAFSEE	RAF Signals Engineering Establishment
PRODS	Public Requests Orders for Disposal (of Land)	RAF TGDA	RAF Training Group Defence Agency
PRONI	Public Record Office of Northern Ireland	RAFVR	Royal Air Force Volunteer Reserve
PS	Public Services	RAJAR	Radio Joint Audience Research
PSA	Public Services Agreement	RAMC	Royal Army Medical Corps
psc	Graduate of Staff College	RAP	Rent Assessment Panel
PSD	Pesticides Safety Directorate	RAPC	Royal Army Pay Corps
PSDA	Public Services Delivery Analysis	RAPS	Rent Assessment Panels
PSF	Public Sector Finances	RARO	Regular Army Reserve of Officers
PSI	Policy Studies Institute	RASC	Royal Army Service Corps
PSO	Personnel Staff Officer	RAuxAF	Royal Auxiliary Air Force
PSP	Public Service Pension	RBGE	Royal Botanic Gardens Edinburgh
PSPP	Public Services Productivity Panel Unit	RBGK	Royal Botanic Gardens Kew
		RC	Roman Catholic
PSPSU	Productivity Services Panel Support Unit	RCA	Rate Collection Agency
		RCAC	Royal Canadian Armoured Corps
PSSF	Personal Social Services Finance	RCAHMS	Royal Commission on the Ancient and Historical Monuments of Scotland
PSV	Public Service Vehicle		
PSX	Public Services and Public Expenditure	RCAHMW	Royal Commission on the Ancient and Historical Monuments of Wales
PTEs	Passenger Transport Executive		
PTO	Public Trust Office	RCDS	Royal College of Defence Studies
PUP	Progressive Unionist Party	RCEP	Royal Commission on Environmental Pollution
PUS	Parliamentary Under-Secretary; Permanent Under-Secretary		
		RCT	Royal Corps of Transport
PWO	Prince of Wales's Own	RCU	Regional Co-Ordination Unit
QAA	Quality Assurance Agency for Higher Education	RCVS	Royal College of Veterinary Surgeons
QC	Queen's Counsel		
QCA	Qualifications and Curriculum Authority		

RD	Royal Naval and Royal Marine Forces Reserve Decoration	RTS	Royal Television Society
RDA	Regional Development Agency	RUCC	Rail Users' Consultative Committee
RDC	Rural Development Commission; Rural District Council	RUR	Royal Ulster Regiment
		RUSI	Royal United Services Institute
RE	Royal Engineers	RYS	Royal Yacht Squadron
REME	Royal Electrical and Mechanical Engineers	S	Scotland
		S4C	Welsh Fourth Channel
Retd LAO	Retired Lord of Appeal in Ordinary	SA	South Africa; South Australia
		SAAS	Student Awards Agency for Scotland
Rev	Reverend		
RFC	Royal Flying Corps; Rugby Football Club	SAC	Scottish Arts Council
		SACOT	Scottish Advisory Committee on Telecommunications
RGD	Revenue Grant Distribution		
RGN	Registered General Nurse	SAH	St Andrews House
RGS	Royal Geographical Society	SASA	Scottish Agricultural Science Agency
RHG	Royal Horse Guards		
RHT	Registered Homes Tribunal	SBAC	Society of British Aerospace Companies
RHV	Royal Health Visitor		
RI	Rhode Island	SBS	Small Business Service
RICS	Royal Institution of Chartered Surveyors	SCAA	School Curriculum and Assessment Authority
RIDP	Regional Industrial Development Board	SCARAB	Steering Committee on Resource Accounts and Budgeting
RIIA	Royal Institute of International Affairs	SCCRC	Scottish Criminal Cases Review Commission
RIU	Regulatory Impact Unit	SCE	Service Children's Education
RLC	Royal Logistics Corps	SCESB	Scottish Conveyancing and Executry Services Board
RMC	Royal Military College (now RMA)		
		SCRA	Scottish Children's Reporter Administration
RMN	Registered Mental Nurse		
RMT	Rail, Maritime and Transport Union	SCRI	Scottish Crop Research Institute
		SCS	Senior Civil Servant
RN	Royal Navy	SDA	Scottish Development Agency
RNIB	Royal National Institute for the Blind	SDLP	Social Democratic and Labour Party
RNLI	Royal National Lifeboat Institution	SDP	Social Democratic Party
RNR	Royal Navy Reserve	SECS	Scottish Executive Corporate Services
RNVR	Royal Naval Volunteer Reserve		
ROSA	Rent Office Service Agreements	SEDD	Scottish Executive Development Department
RPA	Rural Payments Agency		
RPC	Rail Passengers Committee	SEED	Scottish Executive Education Department
RPMS	Royal Postgraduate Medical School		
RPTS	Residential Property Tribunal Service	SEEDA	South East England Development Agency
RPU	Regional Policy Unit	SEELLD	Scottish Executive Enterprise and Lifelong Learning Department
RRI	Rowett Research Institute		
RROs	Regulatory Reforms	SEF	Scottish Executive Finance
RSC	Royal Society of Chemistry; Royal Shakespeare Company	SEHD	Scottish Executive Health Department
RSCG	Regional Specialised Commissioning Group	SEJD	Scottish Executive Justice Department
RSG	Revenue Support Grant	SEN	Special Educational Needs
RSLs	Registered Social Landlords	SENT	Special Education Needs Tribunal
RSO	Resident Surgical Officer	SEO	Society of Education Officers
Rt Hon	The Right Honourable	SEPA	Scottish Environment Protection Agency
Rt Rev	The Right Reverend		

SERAD	Scottish Executive Rural Affairs Department	SRA	Strategic Rail Authority
SERC	Science and Engineering Research Council	SRB	Single Regeneration Budget
		SRC	Science Research Council; Students' Representative Council
SERO	South East Regional Office	SRN	State Registered Nurse
SES	Scottish Executive Secretariat	SRO	Supplementary Reserve of Officers
SEU	Social Exclusion Unit	SS	Saints
SF	Sinn Féin	SSA	Ships Support Agency; Social Security Agency; Standard Spending Assessment
SFC	Scottish Further Education Funding Council		
SFEFC	Scottish Further Education Funding Council	SSAC	Social Security Advisory Committee
SFO	Serious Fraud Office	SSAFA	Soldiers', Sailors' and Airmen's Families Association
SFPA	Scottish Fisheries Protection Agency		
		SSC	Solicitor before Supreme Court (Scotland)
SH	Saughton House		
SHAC	London Housing Aid Centre	SSCUP	Scottish Senior Citizens Unity Party
SHAEF	Supreme Headquarters, Allied Expeditionary Force		
		SSEB	South of Scotland Electricity Board
SHAPE	Supreme Headquarters, Allied Powers, Europe	SSG	Small Systems Group
		SSP	Scottish Socialist Party
SHEFC	Scottish Higher Education Funding Council	SSRA	Shadow Strategic Rail Authority
		SSRB	Review Body on Senior Salaries
SHERT	Scottish Hospital Endowments Research Trust	SSRC	Social Science Research Council
		SSSI	Sites of Special Scientific Interest
SIs	Statutory Instruments	STRB	School Teachers' Review Body
SIS	Secret Intelligence Service	STSS	Scottish Teachers' Superannuation Scheme
SITPRO	Simpler Trade Procedures Board		
SLAB	Scottish Legal Aid Board	STV	Single Transferable Vote
SLC	Student Loans Company	SU	Strategy Unit
SLD	Scottish Liberal Democrats; Social and Liberal Democrats	SVQ	Scottish Vocational Qualification
		SWRDA	South West England Development Agency
SMAG	Spectrum Management Advisory Group		
		SWRO	South West Regional Office
SMG	Scottish Media Group	T&AF	Territorial and Auxiliary Forces
SMMT	Society of Motor Manufacturers and Traders Ltd	TA	Tax Administration; Territorial Army
SNH	Scottish Natural Heritage	TARO	Territorial Army Reserve of Officers
SNP	Scottish National Party		
SOGAT	Society of Graphical and Allied Trades	TASS	Technical Administrative and Supervisory Section of MSF (qv)
SOLACE	Society of Local Authority Chief Executives	TAVRA	Territorial Auxiliary and Volunteer Reserve Association
SP	Scottish Parliament	TBA	The Buying Agency
SPARTA	Sports and Recreational Association of the ODPM and DfT	TD	Territorial Efficiency Decoration
		TEA	Training and Employment Agency
		TEC	Technician Education Council; Training and Enterprise Council
SPAs	Special Advisers		
SPCB	Scottish Parliament Corporate Body	TEF	Treasury Economic Forecast
		TfL	Transport for London
SPICE	Scottish Parliament Information Centre	TGO	Timber Growers' Association
		TGWU	Transport and General Workers Union
SPPA	Scottish Public Pensions Agency		
SPS	Scottish Prison Service	THHAT	Tower Hamlets Housing Action Trust
SPUC	Society for the Protection of the Unborn Child		
		TI	Tax Issues
SQA	Scottish Qualifications Authority	TIA	Treasury Internal Audit

TL	Team Leader
TLB	Top Level Budget
TMB	Treasury Management Board
TOA	Treasury Office of Accounts
TOTE	Horserace Totalisator Board
TP	Tax Policy
TRS	The Rent Service
TSEs	Transmissible Spungiform Encephalopathies
TSRB	Top Salaries Review Body
TTA	Teacher Training Agency
TU	Trade Union
TUC	Trades Union Congress
TUPE	Transfer of Undertakings (Protection of Employment Regulation)
TUS	Trade Union Side
TV	Television
UC	University College
UCATT	Union of Construction, Allied Trades and Technicians
UCH	University College Hospital (London)
UCL	University College London
UDC	Urban Development Corporation; Urban District Council
UDUP	Ulster Democratic Unionist Party
UEMASS	European Union of Medical Advisers in Social Security
UFI	University for Industry
UGC	University Grants Committee
UK	United Kingdom
UKAEA	United Kingdom Atomic Energy Authority
UKHO	United Kingdom Hydrographic Office
UKIP	United Kingdom Independence Party
UKPS	UK Passport Service
UK Sport	United Kingdom Sports Council
UKU	United Kingdom Unionist
UKUP	United Kingdom Unionist Party
UKXIRA	UK Xenotransplantation Interim Regulatory Authority
ULTRA	Unrelated Live Transplant Regulatory Authority
UMIST	University of Manchester Institute of Science and Technology
UN	United Nations
UNCTAD	United Nations Conference on Trade and Development
UNDCP	United Nations International Drug Control Programme
UNDP	United Nations Development Programme
UNEP	United Nations Environment Programme

UNESCO	United Nations Educational, Scientific and Cultural Organization
UNFICYP	United Nations Force in Cyprus
UNFPA	United Nations Population Fund
UNHCR	United Nations High Commissioner for Refugees
UNICEF	United Nations Children's Fund
UNICRI	United Nations Inter-Regional Crime and Justice Research Institute
UNIDIR	United Nations Institute for Disarmament Research
UNIDO	United Nations Industrial Development Organization
UNISON	(an amalgamation of COHSE, NALGO and NUPE)
UNITAR	United Nations Institute for Training and Research
UNOG	United Nations Office at Geneva
UNRISD	United Nations Research Institute for Social Development
UNRWA	United Nations Relief and Works Agency for Palestine Refugees in the Near East
UNU	United Nations University
UPU	Universal Postal Union (UN)
URA	Urban Regeneration Agency
US	United States
USA	United States of America
USDAW	Union of Shop Distributive and Allied Workers
USEL	Ulster Supported Employment Ltd
UTV	Ulster Television
UUAP	United Unionist Assembly Party
UUP	Ulster Unionist Party
UUUC	United Ulster Unionist Coalition
VAM	Victoria and Albert Museum
VAT	Value Added Tax
VC	Victoria Cross
VCA	Vehicle Certification Agency
VCDS	Vice Chief of the Defence Staff
VI	Vehicle Inspectorate
VIP	Very Important Person/People
VLA	Valuation and Lands Agency; Veterinary Laboratories Agency
VLV	Voice of the Listener and Viewer
VMD	Veterinary Medicines Directorate
VOA	Valuation Office Agency
VPC	Veterinary Products Committee
VQ	Victoria Quay
VR	Volunteer Reserve
VRD	Royal Naval Volunteer Reserve Officers' Decoration
VS	Voluntary Sector
VSO	Voluntary Services Overseas
WAAF	Women's Auxiliary Air Force

WACT	Welsh Advisory Committee on Telecommunications	WLB	Welsh Language Board
WDA	Welsh Development Agency	WLGA	Welsh Local Government Association
WEA	Workers' Educational Association	WMO	World Meteorological Organization (UN)
WEU	Western European Union		
WFD	Westminster Foundation for Democracy	WNC	Women's National Commission
		WPA	War Pensions Agency
WFP	World Food Programme (UN)	WPC	War Pensions Committee
WGA	Whole of Government Accounts	WS	Writer to the Signet
WHC	Welsh Medical Committee	WTB	Wales Tourist Board
WHO	World Health Organization (UN)	WTO	World Tourism Organization (UN); World Trade Organization
WIPA	Work Incentives, Poverty Analysis		
WIPO	World Intellectual Property Organization (UN)	WW	Welfare to Work
		www	World Wide Web
WIR	Workforce, Innovation and Reward	YC	Young Conservative
		YJB	Youth Justice Board for England and Wales
WIT	White Paper Implementation Team		

Visit the Vacher Dod Website . . .

www.DodOnline.co.uk

Political information updated daily

The Queen's Speech	House of Commons
Today's Business	House of Lords
This Week's Business	Scottish Parliament
Progress of Government Bills	National Assembly for Wales
Select Committees	Northern Ireland Assembly
Government and Opposition	Greater London Authority
Stop Press News	European Union

Check changes daily as they happen

dodonline.co.uk

The UK's leading political website from Vacher Dod Publishing . . .

DodOnline is the premier service designed for those at the forefront of their fields with a need for accurate and updated political knowledge. Simple to use, with thousands of contacts at your fingertips, as well as a mass of supporting information – and the ability to interactively tailor the service to your needs.

- Full biographies with photographs
- Fully printable and searchable
- Comprehensive contact database
- Export names and addresses for mail merge
- Personal notepad and search facility
- Constituency profiles
- General election and by-election results
- Events as they happen

Extensive coverage of: Westminster, Scotland, Wales, Northern Ireland, European Union and the GLA.

Call Yasmin Mirza, Aby Farsoun or Michael Mand now on 020 7630 7643 for a instant free trial

Vacher Dod Publishing
1 Douglas Street, London, SW1P 4PA
Tel: 020 7630 7619
Fax: 020 7233 7266
E-mail: subscriptions@vacherdod.co.uk
Website: www.DodOnline.co.uk

GOVERNMENT RELATIONS DIRECTORY

INDEX BY SPECIALIST ACTIVITIES

Local Government Planning

Bircham Dyson Bell
Citigate Public Affairs
Keene Public Affairs
Politics International
Portcullis Research
Waterfront Partnership

Media

Politics International
Portcullis Research
Waterfront Partnership

Mergers and Acquisitions

Bircham Dyson Bell
Citigate Public Affairs
Politics International
Portcullis Research

Monitoring, News and Information

Bircham Dyson Bell
Keene Public Affairs
Politics International
Portcullis Research
Waterfront Partnership

Policy Research and Analysis

Bircham Dyson Bell
Citigate Public Affairs
Keene Public Affairs
Politics International
Portcullis Research
Waterfront Partnership

Political Advocacy

Bircham Dyson Bell
Citigate Public Affairs
Keene Public Affairs
Politics International
Portcullis Research
Waterfront Partnership

Presentation Skills

Bircham Dyson Bell
Keene Public Affairs
Politics International
Portcullis Research
Waterfront Partnership

Pressure Groups

Keene Public Affairs
Politics International
Portcullis Research
Waterfront Partnership

Public Policy Analysis

Bircham Dyson Bell
Citigate Public Affairs
Keene Public Affairs
Politics International
Portcullis Research
Waterfront Partnership

Regulation

Bircham Dyson Bell
Keene Public Affairs
Politics International
Waterfront Partnership

Speech Writing

Bircham Dyson Bell
Keene Public Affairs
Politics International
Waterfront Partnership

Strategy

Bircham Dyson Bell
Citigate Public Affairs
Keene Public Affairs
Politics International
Waterfront Partnership

PARLIAMENTARY CONSULTANTS

BIRCHAM DYSON BELL

Bircham Dyson Bell

UK OFFICES
50 Broadway, Westminster, London SW1H 0BL
Tel: +44 (0)20 7227 7000 **Fax:** +44 (0)20 7233 1351
Temple Court, Cathedral Road, Cardiff CF11 9HA
Tel: +44 (0)29 2078 6574 **Fax:** +44 (0)29 2078 6573
1-3 St Colme Street, Edinburgh EH3 6AA
Tel: +44 (0)131 220 8294 **Fax:** +44 (0)131 220 8394
EUROPEAN OFFICE
Rond Point Schuman 6, Box 5, 1040 Brussels, Belgium
Tel: +32 (0)2 234 63 06 **Fax:** +32 (0)2 234 79 11
E-mail: ppl@bdb-law.co.uk
Website: www.bdb-law.co.uk
Established: 1834
No. UK partners: 42
We provide cost-effective, professional advice and support on all aspects of the governmental, policy-making, legislative and regulatory processes of the United Kingdom and the European Union.
Our services include: constitutional and procedural advice; policy research and analysis; legislative drafting.

KEY SPECIALIST ACTIVITIES
Constitutional and Procedural Advice
Crisis Management
Legislative Drafting
Policy Research and Analysis
Presentation Skills

Citigate Public Affairs
The Strategic Public Policy Advisers

26 Grosvenor Gardens, London SW1W 0GT
Tel: +44 (0)20 7838 4800 **Fax:** +44 (0)20 7838 4801
E-mail: info@citigatepa.co.uk **Website:** www.citigatepa.com
Senior Staff: Warwick Smith, Managing Director; Simon Nayyar, Thierry Lebeaux, Executive Directors
Parent Company: Incepta Group plc
Professional Associations: APPC, PRCA
In an ever-changing and increasingly complex political and regulatory environment, businesses cannot ignore their relationship with government or the threats and opportunities posed by official decisions or new legislation.
Citigate Public Affairs ensures that clients are fully aware of public policy developments and decisions taken by governments and official bodies at all levels – from local councils to the United Nations. We help our clients put that information into context, and assess its relevance for their corporate objectives: identifying opportunities and threats. We help our clients ensure that governments and official agencies understand them and their contribution to society and the economy. And we help our clients put their case to governments and their agencies.
Our consultants are researchers, analysts, counsellors, and lobbyists. During the last year, Citigate Public Affairs has helped over 100 clients understand and influence what is happening at all levels of government: from local authorities, through national governments and their agencies and the European Union institutions, through to international bodies such as the World Health Organisation.

KEY SPECIALIST ACTIVITIES
Campaign Management
Coalition Building
Competition and Regulation Issues
Corporate Positioning
European Institutions
Mergers and Acquisitions
Monitoring and Intelligence
Policy Research and Analysis
Political Advocacy
Regulation
Strategic Advice

appc association of professional political consultants

KEENE PUBLIC AFFAIRS CONSULTANTS LTD

KEENE

Victory House,
99-101 Regent Street, London W1B 4EZ
Tel: 020 7287 0652   **Fax:** 020 7494 0493
E-mail: kpac@keenepa.co.uk
Website: www.keenepa.co.uk
Established: 1986
No. UK consultants: 8
Parent Company: Independent, with associate companies in Europe and North America
Established in 1986 as an independent consultancy, we specialise in government relations and public relations in the UK and Europe. Through our London office and our European associate, we offer a professional, cost-effective service based on a thorough analysis of our clients' needs.
Our services include: Monitoring, research and strategic advice; Assistance in contact-making and campaigning; Government marketing; Public and media relations; Crisis communications and media training; Speech writing; Event and conference organisation.

KEY INDUSTRY SECTORS

Aviation and Transport

Energy and Utilities

Environment Regulations

Healthcare

Representational – Governments, Industry and Trade Associations

POLITICS INTERNATIONAL

Politics International

Greencoat House, Francis Street, London SW1P 1DH
Tel: 020 7592 3800   **Fax:** 020 7630 7283
E-mail: pi@politicsint.co.uk   **Website:** www.politicsint.com
Senior Staff: Andrew Dunlop, Managing Director;
David Massingham, Director
Established: 1991
Professional Associations: APPC
Politics International provides the full range of political and strategic communications services, from campaigning and contact management through to procurement support and strategic advice. Our staff have extensive and first hand experience of working with the political and governmental institutions in a wide range of policy areas. Our Westminster team is strengthened by a countrywide network of highly experienced consultants and associate companies in Brussels, Edinburgh and Berlin.
Clients benefit from our rigorously ethical approach, in-depth understanding of their businesses and priorities, and acute awareness of the commercial implications of political and public policy decisions. Our track record speaks for itself.

KEY SPECIALIST AREAS

Strategic Advice and Intelligence

National and Local Campaigns

Project and Bid Support

Message Development and Delivery

Crisis Management and Political PR

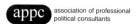 **appc** association of professional political consultants

Vacher Dod Publishing
Government Relations Directory

Are you a Political Consultant or Leading Company?
Ensure your listing is included

Call Yasmin Mirza, Aby Farsoun or Michael Mand
on 020 7630 7643

PORTCULLIS PUBLIC AFFAIRS

26 Cadogan Square,
London SW1X 0JP
Tel: 020 7591 4830
Fax: 020 7591 4831
E-mail: info@portcullispublicaffairs.com
Website: www.portcullispublicaffairs.com
Contact: Berkeley Greenwood
Sound business decisions spring from solid advice, backed by the best intelligence.
Our clients benefit from:
• Understanding and informing public policy-making, thus influencing policy outcomes
• Delivery of commercial and organisational objectives through well-targeted, high quality campaigns, backed by clear strategy and strong implementation skills
• Willingness to gain a detailed grasp of clients' businesses
• Work of the highest ethical standard. Our services help to protect and enhance corporate reputation, which is amongst our clients' most valuable assets
We advise corporates, Government institutions, trade associations and charities, utilising a full spread of Government relations services, including monitoring, research, audit and advocacy. We specialise in dealing with highly regulated sectors and lobby a broad range of governmental and regulatory bodies across the UK and EU.

WATERFRONT PARTNERSHIP

THE **WATERFRONT** *PARTNERSHIP*

130-132 Tooley Street,
London SE1 2TU
Tel: 020 7787 1200
Fax: 020 7787 1201
E-mail: partnership@thewaterfront.co.uk
Website: www.thewaterfront.co.uk
Senior Staff: Nicholas Finney OBE, Managing Director;
Stephen Bramall, Deputy Managing Director;
Mark Walker, Public Affairs Director;
Arthur Leathley, Communications Director
Professional Associations: APPC
The Waterfront Partnership is a public affairs, strategic and media consultancy giving advice on Westminster, Whitehall and the European institutions. Waterfront has a highly developed specialism in transport, incorporating local government, fiscal, environmental and regulatory policy issues. The Waterfront Partnership's staff advise a wide variety of corporate and public sector clients. The Waterfront Partnership is a member of the Association of Professional Political Consultants.

KEY SPECIALIST AREAS
Transport/Aviation incorporating:
Industrial Relations
Media
Local Government
Environment
Planning
Regulation

appc association of professional political consultants

Visit the Vacher Dod Website . . .
www.DodOnline.co.uk

TRADE ASSOCIATIONS AND PUBLIC AFFAIRS DEPARTMENTS

ADVERTISERS

ISBA

44 Hertford Street,
London W1J 7AE
Tel: 020 7499 7502
Fax: 020 7629 5355
E-mail: iant@isba.org.uk
Website: www.isba.org.uk
Senior Staff: Malcolm Earnshaw, Director General;
Dr Ian Twinn, Director of Public Affairs
ISBA is the authoritative source on all advertising matters from the
advertiser's perspective. The economic contribution of our members
makes us a crucial reference point for you on advertising and
commercial communication issues.

The Voice of British Advertisers

DIRECTOR OF PUBLIC AFFAIRS
Dr Ian Twinn   020 7499 7502

ANIMAL WELFARE

ANIMAL DEFENDERS INTERNATIONAL

261 Goldhawk Road, London W12 9PE
Tel: 020 8846 9777   **Fax:** 020 8846 9712
E-mail: campaigns@animaldefenders.org.uk
Website: www.animaldefenders.org.uk
Senior Staff: Jan Creamer, Chief Executive
Established: 1990
Educates, creates awareness, and promotes interest in the cause of
justice and the suppression of all forms of cruelty to animals; to
alleviate suffering, to conserve and protect animals and the
environment.
Initiatives include a campaign against the use of animals in circuses
and to bring permanent circus quarters under regulation such as the
Zoo Licensing Act.

CHIEF EXECUTIVE
Jan Creamer   020 8846 9777

NATIONAL ANTI-VIVISECTION SOCIETY

261 Goldhawk Road, London W12 9PE
Tel: 020 8846 9777   **Fax:** 020 8846 9712
E-mail: campaigns@navs.org.uk
Website: www.navs.org.uk
Senior Staff: Jan Creamer, Chief Executive
Established: 1875
Provides scientific reports, briefing papers, video and photos from
investigations of animals in experiments.
Currently campaigning on excessive secrecy of animal research
licensing process.
We also fund sophisticated non-animal techniques; projects include
cataracts, drugs, cot deaths, safety testing, tissue engineering,
hepatitis B, infertility, cancer, vascular disease and a database for
schools offering alternatives to the use of animals in teaching.

CHIEF EXECUTIVE
Jan Creamer   020 8846 9777

BUSINESS REPRESENTATION

INSTITUTE OF DIRECTORS

116 Pall Mall,
London SW1Y 5ED
Tel: 020 7451 3280
Fax: 020 7839 2337
E-mail: policy-unit@iod.com
Website: www.iod.com
Senior Staff: Ruth Lea, Head of the Policy Unit
The Institute of Directors is a non-political business organisation, with around 55,000 members. It helps directors to carry out their leadership responsibilities in creating wealth for the benefit of business and society. The IoD represents members' interests to government and opinion formers, in the areas of small business policy, corporate governance, employment, education and training, taxation, economic policy, environment and regulation.

HEAD OF THE POLICY UNIT	
Ruth Lea	020 7451 3291
POLICY UNIT MANAGER	
Lisa Tilsed	020 7451 3280
DIRECTOR OF PUBLIC AFFAIRS	
David Marshall	020 7451 3263

CONSTRUCTION

NHBC

Buildmark House, Chiltern Avenue,
Amersham, Buckinghamshire HP6 5AP
Tel: 01494 735262   **Fax:** 01494 735365
E-mail: ahoward@nhbc.co.uk
Website: www.nhbc.co.uk
Senior Staff: Andrew Howard, Head of Corporate Communications
Established: 1936
NHBC is the standard setting body and leading warranty and insurance provider for new homes and provides risk management services to the house-building and wider construction industry.
We were established over 65 years ago as a non-profit distributing company. Our primary purpose is to help raise the standards in the new house-building industry and provide consumer protection for new home buyers.
Approximately 18,000 builders are registered with NHBC and nearly 1.6 million home owners benefit from the 10 year Buildmark cover. Independent of government, NHBC's governing council represents all those interested in improving the standards of new home construction.

HEAD OF CORPORATE COMMUNICATIONS	
Andrew Howard	01494 735262

Vacher Dod Publishing
Government Relations Directory

Are you a Political Consultant or Leading Company?
Ensure your listing is included

Call Yasmin Mirza, Aby Farsoun or Michael Mand
on 020 7630 7643

DISTRIBUTION SERVICES

ROYAL MAIL GROUP plc

Group Communications,
148 Old Street,
London EC1V 9HQ
Tel: 020 7250 2888
Website: www.royalmail.com
Senior Staff: Mick Fisher, Head of Westminster Affairs;
Steve Newsome, Head of European Affairs.
Royal Mail Group plc is the parent company for the well known
brands of Royal Mail, Post Office® and Parcelforce Worldwide,
which provide distribution services in the UK and internationally.

HEAD OF WESTMINSTER AFFAIRS	
Mick Fisher	020 7250 2446

HEAD OF EUROPEAN AFFAIRS	
Steve Newsome	00 322 280 28 20

ENERGY

Scottish Power plc

1 Atlantic Quay, Glasgow G2 8SP
Tel: 0141-636 4563
Fax: 0141-636 4566
E-mail: jamie.maxton@scottishpower.com
Website: www.scottishpower.com
Senior Staff: Jamie Maxton, Government Affairs Manager
Established: 1991
ScottishPower is a leading international energy company serving
over 5,000,000 customers in both the UK and USA. ScottishPower is
committed to investing for growth. We continuously invest in every
aspect of our services. We invest in the communities we serve, in
learning and in protecting the environment.

GOVERNMENT AFFAIRS MANAGER	
Jamie Maxton	0141-636 4563

GROUP DIRECTOR CORPORATE COMMUNICATIONS	
Dominic Fry	0141-636 4561

TELECOMMUNICATIONS

BT

BT Public Affairs, PPA5D,
BT Centre, 81 Newgate Street,
London EC1A 7AJ
Tel: 020 7356 5392
Fax: 020 7356 5610
E-mail: suzanne.masterton@bt.com
Website: www.bt.com
Senior Staff: Suzanne Masterton, Public Affairs Manager
For advice on enquiries from constituents, and for guidance on
national and international telecommunications policy issues, please
contact Suzanne Masterton.
If you have an enquiry about your own home or business lines,
including new orders, please call the Parliamentary Helpline on 0800
200 789 (Monday – Friday 8am – 5pm).

PUBLIC AFFAIRS MANAGER	
Suzanne Masterton	020 7356 5392

Visit the Vacher Dod Website . . .
www.DodOnline.co.uk

Index